⁂ MINDTAP

MindTap empowers students.
Personalized content in an easy-to-use interface
helps you achieve better grades.

The new **MindTap Mobile App** allows for learning anytime, anywhere with flashcards, quizzes and notifications.

The **MindTap Reader** lets you highlight and take notes online, right within the pages, and easily reference them later.

nelson.com/mindtap

NELSON

FIFTH CANADIAN EDITION

PSYCHOLOGY
THEMES AND VARIATIONS

FIFTH CANADIAN EDITION

PSYCHOLOGY
THEMES AND VARIATIONS

WAYNE WEITEN
UNIVERSITY OF NEVADA, LAS VEGAS

DOUG McCANN
YORK UNIVERSITY

WITH CONTRIBUTIONS FROM
MARK HOLDER
UNIVERSITY OF BRITISH COLUMBIA

NELSON

NELSON

Psychology: Themes and Variations,
Fifth Canadian Edition

by Wayne Weiten and Doug McCann

VP, Product Solutions, K–20:
Claudine O'Donnell

Publisher, Digital and Print Content:
Lenore Taylor-Atkins

Marketing Managers:
Ann Byford and Claire Varley

Content Manager:
Suzanne Simpson Millar

Photo and Permissions Researcher:
Jessie Coffey

Production Project Manager:
Jaime Smith

Production Service:
MPS Limited

Copy Editor:
Valerie Adams

Proofreader:
MPS Limited

Indexer:
MPS Limited

Design Director:
Ken Phipps

Higher Education Design PM:
Pamela Johnston

Interior Design:
Jennifer Stimson

Cover Design:
Courtney Hellam

Cover Image:
NASA/Col. Chris Hadfield

Compositor:
MPS Limited

Library and Archives Canada Cataloguing in Publication Data

Weiten, Wayne, 1950-, author
Psychology: themes & variations / Wayne Weiten, University of Nevada, Las Vegas, Doug McCann, York University; with contributions from Mark Holder, University of British Columbia.—Fifth Canadian edition.

Includes bibliographical references and index.
Issued in print and electronic formats.
ISBN 978-0-17-672127-5 (hardcover).—ISBN 978-0-17-685381-5 (PDF)

1. Psychology—Textbooks.
2. Textbooks. I. McCann, Douglas, 1951-, author II. Holder, Mark D., author III. Title.

BF121.W44 2018 150
C2017-906742-7
C2017-906743-5

ISBN-13: 978-0-17-672127-5
ISBN-10: 0-17-672127-4

For Nancy, Harry,
Jackie, Lucy, and Tuck—D. M.

Beth and T.J.,
this one is for you—W. W.

WAYNE WEITEN is a graduate of Bradley University and received his Ph.D. in social psychology from the University of Illinois, Chicago in 1981. He has taught at the College of DuPage and Santa Clara University, and currently teaches at the University of Nevada, Las Vegas. He has received distinguished teaching awards from Division Two of the American Psychological Association (APA) and from the College of DuPage. He is a Fellow of Divisions 1, 2, and 8 of the American Psychological Association and a Fellow of the Midwestern Psychological Association. In 1991, he helped chair the APA National Conference on Enhancing the Quality of Undergraduate Education in Psychology. He is a former President of the Society for the Teaching of Psychology and the Rocky Mountain Psychological Association. In 2006, one of the five national teaching awards given annually by the Society for the Teaching of Psychology was named in his honour. Weiten has conducted research on a wide range of topics, including educational measurement, jury decision making, attribution theory, pressure as a form of stress, and the technology of textbooks. He is also the co-author of *Psychology Applied to Modern Life: Adjustment in the 21st Century* (with Dana S. Dunn and Elizabeth Yost Hammer, Cengage, 2015, 11th ed.). Weiten has created an educational CD-ROM titled *PsykTrek: A Multimedia Introduction to Psychology,* and he recently co-authored a chapter on the Introductory Psychology course for *The Oxford Handbook of Psychology Education* (Weiten & Houska, 2015).

DOUG McCANN received his B.A. from the University of Waterloo and his M.A. and Ph.D. from the University of Western Ontario. Following completion of his Ph.D., he did a post-doctoral fellowship at Ohio State University. He has been a member of the Psychology Department at York University since 1983. At York he has taught at the graduate level in the Clinical, Developmental, and Social/Personality programs and at the undergraduate level. His current teaching interests focus on Introductory Psychology, Social Psychology, and the Psychology of Depression. He has won a variety of teaching awards while at York University and has served in several administrative positions there, most recently as Director of the Graduate Program in Psychology at York University. His research interests focus on social cognition, information processing models of depression, mindfulness meditation, and the effects of childhood trauma on emotional processing. He would be delighted to receive comments about this textbook—just email him at dmccann@yorku.ca.

BRIEF CONTENTS

CHAPTER 1

The Evolution of Psychology

© Rebecca Atkins, York University

CHAPTER 2

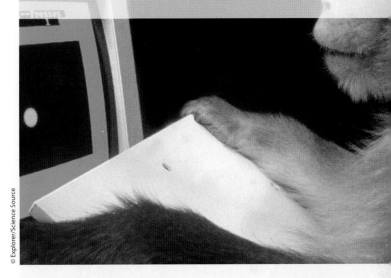

The Research Enterprise in Psychology

© Explorer/Science Source

CHAPTER 3

The Biological Bases of Behaviour

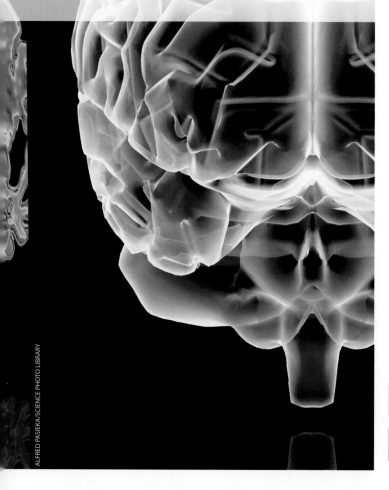

ALFRED PASIEKA/SCIENCE PHOTO LIBRARY

CHAPTER 4

Sensation and Perception

© Ocean/Corbis

CHAPTER 5

Variations in Consciousness

CHAPTER 6

Learning

Rob Melnychuk/Photodisc/Getty Images

CHAPTER 7

Human Memory

© Debbie Steel, Trent University

CHAPTER 8

Language and Thought

© PictureNet/Corbis

CHAPTER 9

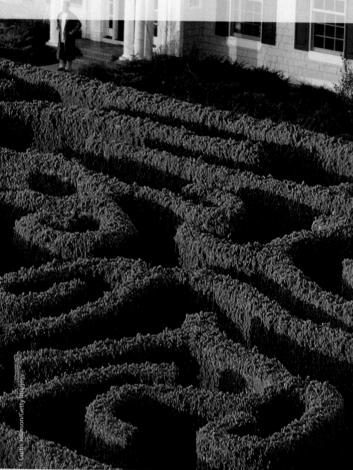

Intelligence and Psychological Testing

CHAPTER 10

Motivation and Emotion

© Buzz Pictures/Alamy Stock Photo

CHAPTER 11

Human Development across the Life Span

© Masterfile RF

CHAPTER 12

Personality: Theory, Research, and Assessment

© Three Images/Lifesize/Getty Images

CHAPTER 13

Social Behaviour

Flashpop/Iconica/Getty Images

CHAPTER 14

PERSONAL APPLICATION

Stress, Coping, and Health

© Pete Saloutos/CORBIS

CRITICAL THINKING APPLICATION

CHAPTER 15

Psychological Disorders

Nick Dolding/Stone/Getty Images

CHAPTER 16

Treatment of Psychological Disorders

© Radius/SuperStock

WELCOME TO *PSYCHOLOGY: THEMES AND VARIATIONS*

Welcome to the fifth Canadian edition of *Psychology: Themes and Variations*. Not only has this book been extensively updated and revised, but we have managed to do all of this while producing a text that is considerably shorter than our previous editions. A good textbook must evolve with the field of inquiry it covers, as well as new directions in higher education. We have updated and revised this edition of the text extensively to reflect recent changes and findings in the field. We have included references to almost 1000 new articles and scholarly works. We have also shortened the text. The last decade has seen a pronounced trend toward greater brevity in textbooks in psychology, as well as many other fields. This trend is not limited to undergraduate texts, as we have also witnessed it in the medical textbooks that we often consult on topics such as neuroscience, sleep, pediatrics, and psychiatry. We have revised our text not only to reflect recent changes in psychology, but have done so with a Canadian context in mind. As just one example, we have included new data, research, and discussion reflecting the experiences of Indigenous Canadians, including, but not limited to, the residential school system in Canada.

In writing this text we have several objectives in mind. If we had to sum up in a single sentence what we hope will distinguish this text, the sentence would be this: We have set out to create a *paradox* instead of a *compromise*.

An introductory psychology text must satisfy two disparate audiences: professors and students. Because of the tension between the divergent needs and preferences of these audiences, textbook authors usually indicate that they have attempted to strike a compromise between being theoretical versus practical, comprehensive versus comprehensible, research oriented versus applied, rigorous versus accessible, and so forth. However, we believe that many of these dichotomies are false. As Kurt Lewin once remarked, "What could be more practical than a good theory?" Similarly, is rigorous really the opposite of accessible? Not in our courses in psychology. We maintain that many of the antagonistic goals that we strive for in our textbooks only *seem* incompatible and that we may not need to make compromises as often as we assume.

In our view, a good introductory textbook is a paradox in that it integrates characteristics and goals that appear contradictory. With this in mind, we have endeavoured to write a text that is paradoxical in three ways. First, in surveying psychology's broad range of content, we have tried to show that our interests are characterized by diversity *and* unity. Second, we have emphasized both research *and* application and how they work in harmony. Finally, we have aspired to write a book that is challenging to think about *and* easy to learn from. Let's take a closer look at these goals.

Goals

1. *To show both the unity and the diversity of psychology's subject matter.* Students entering an introductory psychology course are often unaware of the immense diversity of subjects studied by psychologists. We find this diversity to be part of psychology's charm, and throughout the book we highlight the enormous range of questions and issues addressed by psychology. Of course, psychology's diversity proves disconcerting for some students, who see little continuity between such disparate areas of research as physiology, motivation, cognition, and abnormal behaviour. Indeed, in this era of specialization, even some psychologists express concern about the fragmentation of the field.

However, we believe there is considerable overlap among the subfields of psychology and that we should emphasize their common core by accenting the connections and similarities among them. Consequently, we portray psychology as an integrated whole rather than as a mosaic of loosely related parts. A principal goal of this text, then, is to highlight the unity in psychology's intellectual heritage (the *themes*), as well as the diversity of psychology's interests and uses (the *variations*).

2. *To illuminate the process of research and its intimate link to application.* For us, a research-oriented book is not one that bulges with summaries of many studies but one that enhances students' appreciation of the logic and excitement of empirical inquiry. We want students to appreciate the strengths of the empirical approach and to see scientific psychology as a creative effort to solve intriguing behavioural puzzles. For this reason, the text emphasizes not only *what* psychologists know (and don't know) but *how* they attempt to find out. It examines methods in some detail and encourages students to adopt the skeptical attitude of a scientist and to think critically about claims regarding behaviour.

Learning the virtues of research should not mean that students cannot also satisfy their desire for concrete, personally useful information about the challenges of everyday life. Most researchers believe that psychology has a great deal to offer those outside the field and that psychologists should share the practical implications of their work. In this text, practical insights are carefully qualified and closely tied to data, so that students can see the interdependence of research and application. We find that students come to appreciate the science of psychology more when they see that worthwhile practical applications are derived from careful research and sound theory.

3. *To make the textbook challenging to think about and easy to learn from.* Perhaps most of all, we have sought to create a *book of ideas* rather than a compendium of studies. We consistently emphasize concepts and theories over facts, and focus on major issues and tough questions that cut across the subfields of psychology (e.g., the extent to which behaviour is governed by nature, nurture, and their interaction), as opposed to parochial debates (e.g., the merits of averaging versus adding in impression formation). Challenging students to think also means urging them to confront the complexity and ambiguity of psychological knowledge. Hence, the text doesn't skirt around grey areas, unresolved questions, and theoretical controversies. Instead, it encourages readers to contemplate open-ended questions, to examine their assumptions about behaviour, and to apply psychological concepts to their own lives. Our goal is not simply to describe psychology but to stimulate students' intellectual growth.

However, students can grapple with "the big issues and tough questions" only if they first master the basic concepts and principles of psychology—ideally, with as little struggle as possible. In our writing, we never forget that a textbook is a tool for teaching. Accordingly, we have taken great care to ensure that the book's content, organization, writing, illustrations, and pedagogical aids work in harmony to facilitate instruction and learning.

Admittedly, these goals are ambitious. If you're skeptical, you have every right to be. Let us explain how we have tried to realize these objectives.

Special Features

The book contains a variety of unusual features, each contributing in its own way to the book's paradoxical nature. These special elements include unifying themes, Personal Application sections, Critical Thinking Application sections, a didactic illustration program, an integrated running glossary, Concept Checks, Key Learning Goals, and Concept Charts.

Unifying Themes

Chapter 1 introduces seven key ideas that serve as unifying themes throughout the text. The themes serve several purposes. First, they provide threads of continuity across chapters that help students see the connections among various areas of research in psychology. Second, as the themes evolve over the course of the book, they provide a forum for a relatively sophisticated discussion of enduring issues in psychology, thus helping to make this a "book of ideas." Third, the themes focus a spotlight on a number of basic insights about psychology and its subject matter that should leave lasting impressions on your students.

In selecting the themes, the question we asked ourselves (and other instructors) was "What do we really want students to remember five years from now?" The resulting themes are grouped into two sets.

THEMES RELATED TO PSYCHOLOGY AS A FIELD OF STUDY

Theme 1: Psychology is empirical. This theme is used to enhance the student's appreciation of psychology's scientific nature and to demonstrate the advantages of empiricism over uncritical common sense and speculation. We also use this theme to encourage the reader to adopt a scientist's skeptical attitude and to engage in more critical thinking about information of all kinds.

Theme 2: Psychology is theoretically diverse. Students are often confused by psychology's theoretical pluralism and view it as a weakness. We don't downplay or apologize for the field's theoretical diversity, because we believe that it is one of psychology's greatest strengths. Throughout the book, we provide concrete examples of how clashing theories have stimulated productive research, how converging on a question from several perspectives can yield increased understanding, and how competing theories are sometimes reconciled in the end.

Theme 3: Psychology evolves in a sociohistorical context. This theme emphasizes that psychology is embedded in the ebb and flow of everyday life. The text shows how the spirit of the times has often shaped psychology's evolution and how progress in psychology leaves its mark on our society.

THEMES RELATED TO PSYCHOLOGY'S SUBJECT MATTER

Theme 4: Behaviour is determined by multiple causes. Throughout the book, we emphasize, and repeatedly illustrate, that behavioural processes are complex and that multifactorial causation is the rule. This theme is used to discourage simplistic, single-cause thinking and to encourage more critical reasoning.

Theme 5: Behaviour is shaped by cultural heritage. This theme is intended to enhance students' appreciation of how cultural factors moderate psychological processes and how the viewpoint of one's own culture can distort one's interpretation of the behaviour of people from other cultures. The discussions that elaborate on this theme do not simply celebrate diversity. They strike a careful balance—one that accurately reflects the research in this area—highlighting both cultural variations *and* similarities in behaviour.

Theme 6: Heredity and environment jointly influence behaviour. Repeatedly discussing this theme permits us to air out the nature versus nurture issue in all of its complexity. Over a series of chapters, students gradually learn how biology shapes behaviour, how experience shapes behaviour, and how scientists estimate the relative importance of each. Along the way, students will gain an in-depth appreciation of what it means when we say that heredity and environment interact.

Theme 7: People's experience of the world is highly subjective. All of us tend to forget the extent to which people view the world through their own personal lenses. This theme is used to explain the principles that underlie the subjectivity of human experience, to clarify its implications, and to repeatedly remind the readers that their view of the world is not the only legitimate view.

After introducing all seven themes in Chapter 1, we discuss different sets of themes in each chapter as they are relevant to the subject matter. The connections between a chapter's content and the unifying themes are highlighted in a standard section near the end of the chapter, "Putting It in Perspective," in which we reflect on the "lessons to be learned" from the chapter. We have not tried to make every chapter illustrate a certain number of themes. Rather, the themes were allowed to emerge naturally, and we found that two to five surfaced in any given chapter. The chart on the next page shows which themes are highlighted in each chapter. Colour-coded icons at the beginning of each "Putting It in Perspective" section indicate the specific themes featured in each chapter.

Personal Applications

To reinforce the pragmatic implications of theory and research stressed throughout the text, each chapter closes with a Personal Application section that highlights the practical side of psychology. Personal Applications devote two to three *pages* of text (rather than the usual box) to a single issue that should be of special interest to many of your students. Although most of the Personal Application sections have a "how to" character, they continue to review studies and summarize data in much the same way as the main body of each chapter. Thus, they portray research and application not as incompatible polarities but as two sides of the same coin. Many of the Personal Applications—such as those on finding and reading journal articles, understanding art and illusion, and improving stress management—provide topical coverage unusual for an introductory text.

Critical Thinking Applications

A great deal of unusual coverage can also be found in the Critical Thinking Applications that follow the Personal Applications. These applications are based on the assumption that critical thinking skills can be taught. They do not simply review research controversies, as is typically the case in other introductory texts. Instead, they introduce and model a host of critical thinking *skills*, such as looking for contradictory evidence or alternative explanations; recognizing anecdotal evidence, circular reasoning, hindsight bias, reification, weak analogies, and false dichotomies; evaluating arguments systematically; and working with cumulative and conjunctive probabilities.

The specific skills discussed in the Critical Thinking Applications are listed in the accompanying table (page xxviii), where they are organized into five categories using a taxonomy developed by Halpern (2004). In each chapter, some of these skills are applied to topics and issues related to the chapter's content. For instance, in the chapter that covers drug abuse (Chapter 5), the concept of alcoholism is used to highlight the immense power of definitions and to illustrate how circular reasoning can seem so seductive. Skills that are particularly important may surface in more than one chapter, so students see them applied in a variety of contexts. For example, in Chapter 7, students learn how hindsight bias can contaminate memory, and in Chapter 12 they see how hindsight can distort analyses of personality. Repeated practice across chapters should help students spontaneously recognize the relevance of specific critical thinking skills when they encounter certain types of information.

UNIFYING THEMES HIGHLIGHTED IN EACH CHAPTER

Chapter	THEME						
	1 Empiricism	2 Theoretical Diversity	3 Sociohistorical Context	4 Multifactorial Causation	5 Cultural Heritage	6 Heredity and Environment	7 Subjectivity of Experience
1. The Evolution of Psychology	●	●	●	●	●	●	●
2. The Research Enterprise in Psychology	●						●
3. The Biological Bases of Behaviour	●			●		●	
4. Sensation and Perception		●			●		●
5. Variations in Consciousness		●	●	●	●		●
6. Learning			●			●	
7. Human Memory		●		●			●
8. Language and Thought	●				●	●	●
9. Intelligence and Psychological Testing			●		●	●	
10. Motivation and Emotion		●	●	●	●	●	
11. Human Development across the Life Span		●	●	●	●	●	
12. Personality: Theory, Research, and Assessment		●	●		●		
13. Social Behaviour	●				●		●
14. Stress, Coping, and Health				●			●
15. Psychological Disorders			●	●	●	●	
16. Treatment of Psychological Disorders		●			●		

TAXONOMY OF SKILLS COVERED IN THE CRITICAL THINKING APPLICATIONS

Verbal Reasoning Skills

Understanding the way definitions shape how people think about issues	Chapter 5
Identifying the source of definitions	Chapter 5
Avoiding the nominal fallacy in working with definitions and labels	Chapter 5
Understanding the way language can influence thought	Chapter 8
Recognizing semantic slanting	Chapter 8
Recognizing name-calling and anticipatory name-calling	Chapter 8
Recognizing and avoiding reification	Chapter 9

Argument/Persuasion Analysis Skills

Understanding the elements of an argument	Chapter 10
Recognizing and avoiding common fallacies, such as irrelevant reasons, circular reasoning, slippery slope reasoning, weak analogies, and false dichotomies	Chapters 10 and 11
Evaluating arguments systematically	Chapter 10
Recognizing and avoiding appeals to ignorance	Chapter 9
Understanding how Pavlovian conditioning can be used to manipulate emotions	Chapter 6
Developing the ability to detect conditioning procedures used in the media	Chapter 6
Recognizing social influence strategies	Chapter 13
Judging the credibility of an information source	Chapter 13

Skills in Thinking as Hypothesis Testing

Looking for alternative explanations for findings and events	Chapters 1, 9, and 11
Looking for contradictory evidence	Chapters 1, 3, and 9
Recognizing the limitations of anecdotal evidence	Chapters 2 and 15
Understanding the need to seek disconfirming evidence	Chapter 7
Understanding the limitations of correlational evidence	Chapters 11 and 14
Understanding the limitations of statistical significance	Chapter 14
Recognizing situations in which placebo effects might occur	Chapter 16

Skills in Working with Likelihood and Uncertainty

Utilizing base rates in making predictions and evaluating probabilities	Chapter 14
Understanding cumulative probabilities	Chapter 15
Understanding conjunctive probabilities	Chapter 15
Understanding the limitations of the representativeness heuristic	Chapter 15
Understanding the limitations of the availability heuristic	Chapter 15
Recognizing situations in which regression toward the mean may occur	Chapter 16
Understanding the limits of extrapolation	Chapter 3

Decision-Making and Problem-Solving Skills

Using evidence-based decision making	Chapter 2
Recognizing the bias in hindsight analysis	Chapters 7 and 12
Seeking information to reduce uncertainty	Chapter 14
Making risk–benefit assessments	Chapter 14
Generating and evaluating alternative courses of action	Chapter 14
Recognizing overconfidence in human cognition	Chapter 7
Understanding the limitations and fallibility of human memory	Chapter 7
Understanding how contrast effects can influence judgments and decisions	Chapter 4
Recognizing when extreme comparitors are being used	Chapter 4

Reality Checks

Each chapter includes three or four Reality Checks, which address common misconceptions related to psychology and provide direct refutations of the misinformation. These Reality Checks are sprinkled throughout the chapters, appearing adjacent to the relevant material. Examples of misconceptions that are dispelled include the myth that B. F. Skinner raised his daughter in a Skinner box, which led to her becoming severely disturbed (Chapter 1); the notion that people use only 10 percent of their brains (Chapter 3); the assumption that people who are colour blind see the world in black and white (Chapter 4); and the idea that it is dangerous to awaken someone who is sleepwalking (Chapter 5).

Most of the misconceptions covered in these Reality Checks were addressed in previous editions, but not always with direct refutations. In other words, accurate information was provided on the issues, but usually without explicitly stating the misconception and providing a rebuttal. Why the change in strategy? The impetus was a fascinating article in *Teaching of Psychology* by Patricia Kowalski and Annette Taylor (2009). This article summarized evidence that students typically come into introductory psychology with a variety of misconceptions and that, for the most part, they tend to leave the course with their misconceptions intact. To see if this problem could be ameliorated, they tested the impact of direct refutations on students' misconceptions in the introductory course. Their data suggested that explicit repudiations of erroneous ideas reduce students' misconceptions more effectively than the simple provision of correct information. With that evidence in mind, we decided to craft this feature that explicitly confronts and disputes common fallacies that range from oversimplified to profoundly inaccurate. Because the Reality Checks mostly supplement the normal coverage in the text, they have been kept concise.

Featured Studies

Each chapter is accompanied in our online content by at least one Featured Study that provides a relatively detailed but clear summary of a particular piece of research. Each Featured Study is presented in the conventional purpose–method–results–discussion format seen in journal articles, followed by a comment in which we discuss why the study is featured (to illustrate a specific method, raise ethical issues, and so forth). By showing research methods in action, we hope to improve students' understanding of how research is done while also giving them a painless introduction to the basic format of journal articles. Additionally, the Featured Studies show how complicated research can be, so students can better appreciate why scientists may disagree about the meaning of a study. The Featured Studies are fully incorporated into the flow of discourse in the text and are *not* presented as optional boxes.

In selecting the Featured Studies, we assembled a mixture of classic and recent studies that illustrate a wide variety of methods. To make them enticing, we tilted our selections in favour of those that students find interesting. So, readers will encounter explorations of the effects of day-dreaming or mind wandering in class on university students' understanding of lectures and their performance on exams, the effects of fear on sexual attraction, bullying in Canadian schoolyards, the brain and mental time travel, the relationship between depression and heart disease, studies of infant babbling, and studies of suicide rates among Canada's Indigenous youth.

A Didactic Illustration Program

When we outlined our plans for the fifth Canadian edition of the text, we wanted every aspect of the illustration program to have a genuine didactic purpose. We were intimately involved in planning every detail of the illustration program. We have endeavoured to create a program of figures, diagrams, photos, and tables that work hand in hand with the prose to strengthen and clarify the main points in the text.

The most obvious results of this didactic approach to illustration are the eight Illustrated Overviews that combine tabular information, photos, diagrams, and sketches to provide well-organized and exciting overviews of key ideas in the areas of methods, sensation and perception, learning, personality theory, psychopathology, and psychotherapy.

We hope you will also notice the subtleties of the illustration program. For instance, diagrams of important concepts (conditioning, synaptic transmission, experimental design, and so forth) are often repeated in the end-of-chapter Concept Charts and in several other chapters (with variations) to highlight connections among research areas and to enhance students' mastery of key ideas.

Numerous easy-to-understand graphs of research results underscore psychology's foundation in research, and photos and diagrams often bolster each other (e.g., see the treatment of classical conditioning in Chapter 6). Colour is used carefully as an additional organizational device, and visual schematics are used to simplify hard-to-visualize concepts (e.g., see Figure 9.15 on page 334, which explains reaction range for intelligence). All of these efforts were made in the service of one master: the desire to make this an inviting book that is easy to learn from.

Integrated Running Glossary

An introductory text should place great emphasis on acquainting students with psychology's technical language—not for the sake of jargon, but because a great many of the key terms are also cornerstone concepts (e.g., *independent variable*, *reliability*, and *cognitive dissonance*). This text handles terminology with a running glossary embedded in the prose itself. The terms are set off in **blue boldface italics**, and the definitions follow in **blue, boldface** type. This approach retains the two advantages of a conventional running glossary: vocabulary items are made salient and their definitions are readily accessible. However, the approach does so without interrupting the flow of discourse, while eliminating redundancy between text matter and marginal entries.

Concept Checks

To help students assess their mastery of important ideas, Concept Checks are sprinkled throughout the book. In keeping with the goal of making this a book of ideas, the Concept Checks challenge students to apply ideas instead of testing rote memory. For example, in Chapter 6 the reader is asked to analyze realistic examples of conditioning and identify conditioned stimuli and responses, reinforcers, and schedules of reinforcement.

Many of the Concept Checks require the reader to put together ideas introduced in different sections of the chapter. For instance, in Chapter 4, students are asked to identify parallels between vision and hearing. Some of the Concept Checks are quite challenging, but students find them engaging and they report that the answers (available in Appendix A) are often illuminating.

Key Learning Goals

To help students organize, assimilate, and remember important ideas, each major section of every chapter begins with a succinct set of Key Learning Goals. The Key Learning Goals are found adjacent to the main headings that begin each major section. The Key Learning Goals are thought-provoking learning objectives that should help students focus on the key issues in each section.

Concept Charts for Study and Review

This fifth Canadian edition for the text has incorporated summaries—Concept Charts—directly into the end of each chapter. In previous editions, these Concept Charts had been separate booklets for student study. Designed to help students organize and master the main ideas contained in each chapter, Concept Charts provide a detailed visual map of the key ideas found in the main body of that chapter.

Seeing how it all fits together should help students better understand each chapter. You can use these charts to preview chapters, to get a handle on how key ideas fit together, to double-check your mastery of the chapters, and to memorize the crucial principles in chapters. We have tested these out with our own students and they tell us that they are a very valuable tool in preparing for course exams.

Content

The text is divided into 16 chapters. The chapters are not grouped into sections or parts, primarily because such groupings can limit your options if you want to reorganize the order of topics. The chapters are written in a way that facilitates organizational flexibility, as we assume that some chapters might be omitted or presented in a different order.

The topical coverage in the text is relatively conventional, but there are some subtle departures from the norm. For instance, Chapter 1 presents a relatively "meaty" discussion of the evolution of ideas in psychology. This coverage of history lays the foundation for many of the crucial ideas emphasized in subsequent chapters. The historical perspective is also our way of reaching out to the students who find that psychology just isn't what they expected it to be. If we want students to contemplate the mysteries of behaviour, we must begin by clearing up the biggest mysteries of them all: "Where did these rats, statistics, synapses, and JNDs come from, what could they possibly have in common, and why doesn't this course bear any resemblance to what I anticipated?" We use history as a vehicle to explain how psychology evolved into its modern form and why misconceptions about its nature are so common.

We also devote an entire chapter (Chapter 2) to the scientific enterprise—not just the mechanics of research methods but the logic behind them. We believe that an appreciation of the nature of empirical evidence can contribute greatly to improving students' critical thinking skills. Ten years from now, many of the "facts" reported in this book will have changed, but an understanding of the methods of science will remain invaluable. An introductory psychology course, by itself, isn't going to make a student think like a scientist, but we can't think of a better place to start the process. Essential statistical concepts are introduced in Chapter 2, but no effort is made to teach actual calculations.

Changes in the Fifth Canadian Edition

The text length has been significantly reduced. We have managed to do this while at the same time adding new material and topics and updating our existing text with new examples, findings, and explanations. As we have noted, students now have Concept Charts for review at the end of each chapter.

The following is a partial list of specific chapter changes that highlights some of the new key and updated topics and examples that have been included in the fifth Canadian edition.

CHAPTER 1: THE EVOLUTION OF PSYCHOLOGY

- Revised introduction.
- Revised section on the history of psychology.
- Revised discussion of the value of text highlighting in the coverage of study skills.
- Updated statistics on CPA membership and increasing enrollment in psychology courses.
- New Featured Study by McGill researchers on how children's psychopathologies influence how they respond to their peers.
- Updated statistics on Canada's diversity.
- New section and figures with statistics on where graduates of Canadian university graduate studies (MA, PHD) find jobs, and what types of jobs they find.

CHAPTER 2: THE RESEARCH ENTERPRISE IN PSYCHOLOGY

- New research study used to illustrate the five steps in a scientific investigation.
- New research study used to illustrate experimental research.
- Revised discussion and new research illustration of placebo effects.
- New research, statistics, and figure on the criminal victimization of Indigenous peoples in Canada used to illustrate survey research methods.
- New example of naturalistic observation focuses on how larger plate sizes lead to increased eating at real-world buffets.
- Another new example of naturalistic observation profiles a study of how depression affects everyday social behaviour.
- New example of case-study research evaluating anxiety and depressive disorders as risk factors for dementia.
- New discussion of how clinicians sometimes publish individual case histories to share insights regarding effective treatment.
- Added discussion of how manipulating two or more variables in an experiment can permit the detection of interactions between variables.
- Revised and updated discussion of ethics, including new material related to the complicity of psychologists and the American Psychological Association in developing interrogation techniques for the U.S. military to use at Guantanamo Bay, and a photo and brief discussion of Omar Khadr as a child imprisoned there.
- Updated discussion on animal research ethics.
- Updated discussion and illustration in Personal Application of how to use PSYCHINFO in research.
- Revised Concept Chart included.

CHAPTER 3: THE BIOLOGICAL BASES OF BEHAVIOUR

- New introduction.
- Updated discussion of Western University's Adrian Owen and his work on those suffering from locked-in syndrome, and detecting signs of awareness in patients who have suffered traumatic brain injury.
- Revised discussion of glial cells.
- Updated and significantly revised discussion of how neurons function.
- Revised discussion of neurotransmitters.
- Revised discussion of oxytocin.
- New section that discusses new tool in genetic research—CRISPR, which enables scientists to edit genes.
- Updated and discussion of epigenetics.
- Revised Concept Chart included.

CHAPTER 4: SENSATION AND PERCEPTION

- Revised discussion of synesthesia—theory, research, and examples.
- Revised discussion of information processing in the visual cortex.
- Revised discussion of cultural effects in depth/distance processing.
- New coverage of auditory localization.
- New figure illustrating what and where visual pathways included.
- New Canadian chronic pain statistics included.
- Updated discussion on pain perception.
- New statistics on migraine sufferers in Canada.
- New Featured Study focused on social support and pain perception in seniors.
- Updated discussion on endorphins.

CHAPTER 5: VARIATIONS IN CONSCIOUSNESS

- Updated discussion of the sleep crisis in North America.
- New statistics on sleep problems in Canada.
- Revised discussion on mind wandering, including the neuroscience of mind wandering.
- Two new Featured Studies by Canadian researchers dealing with mind wandering by university students and links to grades and course performance.

- Updated discussion on circadian rhythms.
- Revised discussion on sleep deprivation, and the connections between sleep disturbance and Alzheimer's disease.
- Revised and updated discussion on sleep problems and health and sleep problems and decision making.
- Updated discussion of sleep disturbance and childhood deficits.
- Revised discussion of sleep disorders.
- Updated discussion on hypnosis, and individual differences in responses to hypnotic induction.
- New Canadian statistics on alcohol and drug abuse, and on impaired driving offences in Canada.
- Reference made to legalization of marijuana in Canada.
- New statistics added concerning drug use by Canadian students.
- New discussion of increase in opioid use and overdose deaths from fentanyl and carfentanil.

CHAPTER 6: LEARNING

- Updated discussion of learning theory and superstitions, including new cultural examples.
- New coverage of studies of evaluative conditioning.
- New discussion of theoretical issues related to evaluative conditioning.
- New discussion of how the renewal effect in classical conditioning makes it difficult to extinguish troublesome phobias.
- New coverage of the renewal effect in operant conditioning and the context-dependent nature of operant extinction.
- Updated research on Little Albert.
- Updated material on the Canadian Department of Justice's guidelines for and restrictions on the use of physical punishment on children.
- Updated discussion on the negative effects of physical punishment on children.
- New Featured Study on social learning across psychological distance.
- New figure and discussion regarding the effects of media violence on children's aggression.
- Updated discussion on the effects of playing violent video games.
- Second new Featured Study on learning that deals with electrophysiological correlates of observational learning in children.
- New illustrations of the use of classical conditioning in advertising.

CHAPTER 7: HUMAN MEMORY

- Updated discussion of divided attention, cell phone use and its effects, and laws in Canada regarding distracted driving penalties.
- Updated and expanded discussion of working memory and hereditary and situational influences.
- Updated discussion and illustrations of flashbulb memories.
- Updated discussion on hypnosis and memory.
- New discussion of the reconsolidation effect in memory.
- Updated discussion and research on the declarative/nondeclarative memory distinction.
- New discussion of autobiographical memory.
- Updated discussion on prospective memory.
- Updated discussion on test-enhanced memory.
- New research showing that the misinformation effect can distort basic factual knowledge as well as personal memories.
- New findings on test-enhanced learning.
- Expanded discussion of the eyewitness post-identification feedback effect.
- New data on how often faulty eyewitness testimony contributes to wrongful convictions.

CHAPTER 8: LANGUAGE AND THOUGHT

- Updated statistics on bilingualism in Canada.
- New discussion on the effects of bilingualism on social skills development in infants.
- New discussion of "crib bilingualism."
- Updated research on interactionist theories of language.
- New theory and research concerning critical periods.
- Updated research on functional fixedness and mental sets.
- Revised discussion on culture and problem solving.
- New discussion on rationality and decision making.
- New discussion and research added on choice and decision making.
- New Critical Thinking Application on pitfalls in reasoning about decisions.
- New coverage of framing effects.

CHAPTER 9: INTELLIGENCE AND PSYCHOLOGICAL TESTING

- Revised chapter introduction.
- Reorganized, resequenced discussion of structural characteristics of intelligence.

- New section on broadening the concept of intelligence.
- New discussion of the development of and justification for distinct Canadian and American IQ test norms.
- Significant revision of the section discussing the history of IQ testing.
- New Featured Study examining the nature of IQ from the high-profile lab of Adrian Owen of Western University.
- Expanded discussion of hierarchical models of intelligence.
- Replaced previous discussion of IQ tests with new and elaborate discussion of WAIS (4th edition).
- Updated discussion and illustration of relation between IQ and mortality.
- Updated discussion of emotional intelligence.
- Updated discussion of research on the heritability estimates of IQ.

CHAPTER 10: MOTIVATION AND EMOTION

- New discussion of affiliation motivation and evolutionary analyses of motivation.
- Revised discussion of hormones and hunger.
- Updated research on contextual factors affecting eating/obesity.
- New discussion on stress and eating.
- New statistics on obesity in Canada.
- New material on obesity and health problems.
- Extensive revision and updating of section on excessive eating and exercise.
- New Canadian statistics on lack of exercise, with a focus on Canadian children.
- New research and discussion on set-point theory.
- New material on gender differences in sexual response.
- New statistics on hate crimes based on sexual orientation in Canada.
- New statistics on marriage in Canada.
- New statistics on self-reported sexual orientation in Canada.
- New Featured Study on affiliation motivation, ostracism, and factors associated with an ostracism experience that can reduce the negative effects of that experience.
- New second Featured Study on detecting lies told by children.
- New research on the connection between the amygdala and fear.
- New discussion of the classic Dutton and Aron study examining the two-factor theory of emotions.

- Updated research on the connection between money and happiness.
- Updated research on marriage and happiness.

CHAPTER 11: HUMAN DEVELOPMENT ACROSS THE LIFE SPAN

- Revised chapter introduction.
- Updated statistics regarding fetal alcohol syndrome in Canada.
- Updated research on fetal development and maternal nutrition.
- Updated research on fetal development and maternal stress.
- Revised discussion of fetal origins of adult disease.
- Updated statistics on breastfeeding in Canada.
- Revised discussion on day-care and attachment.
- Updated statistics on day-care use in Canada.
- Revised discussion of evaluating Piaget's contribution.
- Revised discussion of physiological changes in adolescence with updated research.
- Revised and updated discussion of the teen brain.
- Updated discussion, new research, and new figure regarding stability of personality in adulthood.
- Updated discussion of adjusting to marriage, and new statistics regarding marriage and divorce in Canada.
- New statistics on marriage and household responsibilities over time.
- Updated statistics on life expectancy in Canada.
- Discussion on the new Canadian doctor-assisted suicide law and its implications for end-of-life planning for the elderly.
- New statistics and figure on aging and health.
- Updated discussion and new statistics on aging and neural changes.
- New statistics and figure concerning aging and mental speed.
- New section on death and dying.
- New discussion on attitudes about death and dying.
- New coverage of the work of Kübler-Ross on reactions to bereavement.
- New discussion of cultural variations in dealing with bereavement.
- New coverage of various patterns of grieving.
- Revised and updated discussion on gender differences.
- New coverage of disparities in Vygotsky's and Piaget's theories of cognitive development.
- New discussion of the importance of private speech in Vygotsky's theory.

CHAPTER 12: PERSONALITY: THEORY, RESEARCH, AND ASSESSMENT

- Revised chapter introduction.
- Revised and updated (with new research) discussion of the five-factor model of personality.
- New discussion on the Dark Triad, the Dark Tetrad, and personality and evil.
- Revised discussion of Jung's analytical psychology.
- Revised discussion of Adler's theory.
- Revised and updated discussion of behavioural genetics and personality with new research.
- Revised and updated discussion of the evolutionary approach to personality.
- Revised and updated discussion of projective tests.

CHAPTER 13: SOCIAL BEHAVIOUR

- New Featured Study.
- Updated statistics on prejudice and hate crimes in Canada.
- New discussion on the experiences of Indigenous Canadians, including the residential school system and criminal victimization rates.
- Expanded discussion on the attractiveness stereotype and its relations to job success.
- New discussion of how Weiner's model of attribution can shed light on people's explanations for poverty.
- New discussion of defensive attribution.
- New research on attractiveness and the Big Five personality traits.
- New research on face perception.
- New research linking skin colour with perceptions of negativity.
- New research and findings on attachment anxiety and problems in intimate relationships.
- New findings on Facebook usage and loneliness.
- New discussion of how online matching sites have changed the landscape of dating and mating.
- New research showing a lower percentage of marital breakups in relationships formed online as opposed to offline.
- New discussion of why women's waist-to-hip ratio is an aspect of physical attractiveness that transcends culture.
- New research examining whether evolutionary hypotheses regarding gender differences in mating preferences hold up in speed-dating situations.
- New evolutionary research on how menstrual cycles influence women's mating preferences and strategies.

- New evolutionary research on how men use conspicuous consumption to signal wealth and success to potential mating partners.
- Updated discussion on attitudes and their attributes.
- New research linking implicit attitudes to real world behaviour.
- New section on the power of the situation and new critique of the Stanford Prison experiment.
- New research on Milgram's obedience paradigm.

CHAPTER 14: STRESS, COPING, AND HEALTH

- New discussion of and reference made to the community trauma and stress experienced and the potential for an increase in post-traumatic stress disorder as a result of the Fort McMurray wildfires.
- New statistics concerning the stress levels of Canadian college and university students.
- New discussion of stress-busting activities promoted by Canadian universities.
- New statistics on stress levels experienced by Canadians in their day-to-day living.
- Revised discussion on stress and change.
- New research on stress and heart disease.
- New discussion on the impact of stress on neurogenesis.
- New discussion on stress-induced shopping.
- New discussion on Internet addiction.
- New research and statistics on post-traumatic stress disorder and first-responders in Canada.
- New research and statistics on stress and hypertension in Canada.
- New findings on the association between social isolation and health.
- New research on the surprising benefits of weak social ties.
- New Featured Study.
- New discussion on social support and therapy animals.
- New statistics on post-traumatic stress disorder and how it relates to suicide in the Canadian military.
- New statistics on health problems in Canada.
- New statistics on alcohol and nicotine abuse.
- New findings on the effect of natural disasters on mental and physical health.
- New coverage of Internet addiction and well-being.
- New research on anger and heart attacks.
- New discussion of social class and health.
- New discussion of the relationship between social class and health.

- New research on how one's stress mindset affects one's response to stress.
- New evidence linking moderate levels of adversity to future resilience.

CHAPTER 15: PSYCHOLOGICAL DISORDERS

- Revised discussion of the DSM-5 and a new discussion of the distinction between categorical and dimensional systems of classification of disorders as reflected in the DSM-5.
- Expanded discussion of how the stigma of mental illness is a source of stress and an impediment to treatment.
- New discussion of the exponential growth of the DSM system and its tendency to medicalize everyday problems.
- New statistics on the incidence of psychological disorders in Canada and the cost to Canadian society.
- Updated discussion of Roméo Dallaire's continuing struggles with post-traumatic stress disorder.
- New Canadian statistics on suicide rates over time.
- New statistics on the incidence of suicide in the Canadian military.
- Updated discussion of some of the controversy surrounding the changes introduced in the DSM-5.
- New statistics on demographic differences in suicide in Canada.
- New Featured Study.
- Revised and updated discussion of psychopathy.
- Revised discussion concerning the history of the subtyping of schizophrenia.
- Revised discussion concerning the etiology of autism spectrum disorder.
- Updated discussion concerning the mental health needs of Canada's First Nations people and how they are addressed in Canada's new mental health strategy with reference to traditional healing practices.
- Updated material concerning mindfulness-based cognitive-behavioural therapy.
- New mention of peer influence and history of child abuse as etiological factors in eating disorders.
- New research on the importance of early life stress in increasing the risk for a wide variety of adult-onset disorders many years later.
- New research on genetic and neurobiological overlap among depression, bipolar disorder, schizophrenia, and autism.

CHAPTER 16: TREATMENT OF PSYCHOLOGICAL DISORDERS

- Updated discussion on Psy.D. programs in Canada.
- New Featured Study.
- New findings on the importance of empathy and unconditional positive regard to therapeutic climate.
- New graphic on improvement in therapy over time.
- New coverage of common factors as an explanation for the effects of therapy.
- New discussion of empirical effort to partition the variance in therapeutic outcomes to quantify the influence of common factors.
- New data on prescription trends for antianxiety, antipsychotic, antidepressant, and mood-stabilizing drugs.
- New findings on ECT, including relapse rates, availability, and use.
- New research on ethnic matching between therapist and client.
- Discussion on how therapy can be delivered via the Internet.

Instructor Resources

The **Nelson Education Teaching Advantage (NETA)** program delivers research-based instructor resources that promote student engagement and higher-order thinking to enable the success of Canadian students and educators. Visit Nelson Education's **Inspired Instruction** website at www.nelson.com/inspired/ to find out more about NETA.

The following instructor resources have been created for *Psychology: Themes and Variations*, Fifth Canadian Edition. Access these ultimate tools for customizing lectures and presentations at www.nelson.com/instructor.

NETA Test Bank, Volumes 1 and 2

This resource was written by Kimberly Robinson, Saint Mary's University. Careful attention has been paid to ensuring questions reflect the material in this fifth Canadian edition, while matching the outstanding U.S. original in scope, effectiveness, and accuracy. The questions are closely tied to learning goals, and to the key terms and key people found in the text. The items follow Bloom's Taxonomy and are categorized as remember and higher order. In Volume 1, each chapter includes more than 200 multiple-choice questions written according to NETA guidelines for effective construction and development of higher-order questions. Also included are an average of five essay questions, accompanied by suggested answers. In Volume 2, each chapter includes more than 100 questions per chapter, offering more varied test materials and ensuring that students are challenged by fresh items.

The NETA Test Banks are available in a new, cloud-based platform. **Nelson Testing Powered by Cognero®** is a secure online testing system that allows instructors to author, edit, and manage test bank content from anywhere Internet access is available. No special installations or downloads are needed, and the desktop-inspired interface, with its drop-down menus and familiar, intuitive tools, allows instructors to create and manage tests with ease. Multiple test versions can be created in an instant, and content can be imported or exported into other systems. Tests can be delivered from a learning management system, the classroom, or wherever an instructor chooses. Nelson Testing Powered by Cognero for *Psychology: Themes and Variations,* Fifth Canadian Edition, can be accessed through www.nelson.com/instructor.

Case-Based Test Bank, Volume 3

A third, case-based question bank is available for use with *Psychology: Themes and Variations*, Fifth Canadian Edition. Developed by Bruce H. Tsuji, Chelsie Smith, Vasileia Karasaava, and Vichheka Oeur of Carleton University, these case-based multiple-choice questions can be offered in open-book test format for online and face-to-face courses. There are over 550 questions based on 86 cases, with an average of five cases and 35 questions per chapter.

NETA PowerPoint

Microsoft® PowerPoint® lecture slides for every chapter have been created by Dax Urbszat, University of Toronto. There is an average of 30 slides per chapter, many featuring key figures, tables, and photographs from *Psychology: Themes and Variations*. Notes are provided for many slides, allowing for additional information or sidebars to engage students in discussion. NETA principles of clear design and engaging content have been incorporated throughout, making it simple for instructors to customize the deck for their courses.

Image Library

This resource consists of digital copies of figures, short tables, and photographs used in the book. Instructors may use these jpegs to customize the NETA PowerPoint or create their own PowerPoint presentations. An Image Library Key describes the images and lists the codes under which the jpegs are saved. Codes normally reflect the chapter number (e.g., C01 for Chapter 1), the figure or photo number (e.g., F15 for Figure 15), and the page in the textbook. C01-F15-pg26 corresponds to Figure 1-15 on page 26.

NETA Instructor Guide

This resource has been specifically designed for you to use with *Psychology: Themes and Variations*. It presents chapter-by-chapter suggestions for lecture and discussion topics, demonstrations and activities that can be done during class sessions, suggested readings for each chapter, and handout or transparency masters to supplement lectures or demonstrations/activities.

Media Guide

The Media Guide includes a list of video cases selected to accompany *Psychology: Themes and Variations,* correlated with the chapter(s) they are most suitable. Compiled by Carolyn Ensley, Wilfrid Laurier University, this guide includes episode titles, descriptions, running time, and URLs.

Resource Integration Guide

This document organizes all the ancillary resources for *Psychology: Themes and Variations* under each major heading within every chapter. It's an indispensable tool for planning and coordinating resources for lectures and assignments.

MindTap

Offering personalized paths of dynamic assignments and applications, **MindTap** is a digital learning solution that turns cookie-cutter into cutting-edge, apathy into engagement, and memorizers into higher-level thinkers. MindTap enables students to analyze and apply chapter concepts within relevant assignments, and allows instructors to measure skills and promote better outcomes with ease. A fully online learning solution, MindTap combines all student learning tools—readings, multimedia, activities, and assessments—into a single Learning Path that guides the student through the curriculum. Instructors personalize the experience by customizing the presentation of these learning tools to their students, even seamlessly introducing their own content into the Learning Path.

ACKNOWLEDGMENTS
FOR THE FIFTH CANADIAN EDITION

Working on this fifth Canadian edition of *Psychology: Themes and Variations* has proven to be a pleasure. Creating a text such as this is a complicated challenge, and I am indebted to a group of dedicated professionals at Nelson Education Ltd. for all the assistance they provided.

Suzanne Simpson Millar, developmental editor, was a constant source of innovative ideas and guidance, and was invaluable to this project. Working with her was a pleasure. Valerie Adams was a superb copy editor whose expertise was much appreciated. I would like to thank Lenore Taylor-Atkins, Publisher, at Nelson. Lenore has been with the text from its first Canadian edition and her expertise shows in each. Thanks to Ann Byford, who initiated this revision as marketing manager. Ann has provided not only her expertise, but also her friendship. Thanks also to Jessie Coffey, permissions editor and photo researcher. She has an uncanny ability to track anything down.

A host of psychologists deserve thanks for the contributions they made to this revision. First, thanks so much to Mark Holder who authored the revisions for Chapter 3. Dr. Holder earned his Ph.D. at the University of California at Berkeley and is now Associate Professor of Psychology at the University of British Columbia, Okanagan. Mark was initially a reviewer for the text, but his suggestions were so inspired that we asked him to revise Chapter 3. We are grateful that he said yes.

Thanks also to Vic Catano of Saint Mary's University for his work on the appendix on industrial and organizational psychology; Diane Halpern for her work on the Critical Thinking Applications; and Susan Koger and Britain Scott for crafting a compelling online appendix on sustainability.

I would also like to thank the many reviewers and chapter consultants who provided insightful and constructive critiques of various portions of the manuscript:

R. Nicholas Carleton, University of Regina
Stephanie Denison, University of Waterloo
Mark Holder, University of British Columbia
Rick Mehta, Acadia University
Trudith Ohki, MacEwan University

Alissa Pencer, Dalhousie University
Tara Perrot, Dalhousie University
Lisa Sinclair, University of Winnipeg

In working on the fifth Canadian edition, I was fortunate to be surrounded by a world-class group of colleagues at York University who were more than willing to talk to me about issues in psychology and to give generously of their time and expertise. They include Gordon Flett, Chris Green, Alex Rutherford, Hiroshi Ono, Thomas Teo, Maxine Wintre, the late Ann-Marie Wall, Henny Westra, Frances Wilkinson, Janice Johnson, Laurence Harris, Doug Crawford, Regina Schuller, Myriam Mongrain, and Richard Lalonde. Thanks too to Chris Cornell, Dave Grohl, Glenn Gould, and a host of others who supplied the background while I worked.

During the time the book was in preparation, I was fortunate to have the support and enthusiasm of a small group who made the task easy and enjoyable. Thanks to Jackie Chan and Lucy Lui for allowing me to try out language and ideas while we played serious ball. They were particularly helpful with regard to the comparative psychology sections. Thanks to David for continuing to pull out all the stops in helping us all out; I hope the picture is enough. Thanks to Harry for his editing and Sensei Waith for his continued support and encouragement, to Dr. Zindel Segal of CAMH for introducing me to mindfulness meditation, and to Dr. Paul Ritvo for continuing as my mindfulness coach. Thanks also to Harry whose editing skills and insights are unrivaled.

In the end, as always, it comes down to the ineffable Nancy. Nothing is possible without her. Thanks for getting it started, for sharing, and for keeping the motivation for research and writing going when it seemed to stop. Her enthusiasm for the project through each edition has never wavered. Given that she is the most generous and intelligent person I know, I depended on her good counsel and advice whenever a problem came up: her knowledge of pedagogy and of human nature never failed to inspire.

Doug McCann

© Rebecca Atkins, York University

CHAPTER 1

The Evolution of Psychology

Themes in this Chapter

Empiricism

Theoretical Diversity

Sociohistorical Context

Multifactorial Causation

Cultural Heritage

Heredity & Environment

Subjectivity

As you begin your course in introductory psychology and start reading this textbook, you may be wondering, "What is psychology?" Your initial answer to this question is likely to bear little resemblance to the picture of psychology that will emerge as you work your way through this book. Many students initially associate psychology with the study of psychological disorders or abnormal psychology. While abnormal psychology is an important component, psychology is about much more than that.

It's also about how people are able to perceive colour, how hunger is regulated by the brain, whether chimpanzees can use language to communicate, why it is so hard to diet and lose weight, why we procrastinate on getting our essays and studying done, what causes bullying and aggression and how you can protect yourself, and a multitude of other topics. We are confident that you will come away from your study of this text with a new appreciation for the subject matter of psychology and what it can do for you.

Psychology as a scientific discipline has something for everyone. It addresses basic issues such as how we see, how the brain forms and stores memories, and what is the nature of consciousness. In addition, psychologists do research on issues that affect our individual lives and society at large. For example, one topic that has been the subject of intensive research in Canada and elsewhere is the topic of violence and peer aggression in children and young adults. Motivated by high-profile bullying cases such as those of Reena Virk, Dawn-Marie Wesley, Jamie Hubley, Todd Loik, Amanda Todd, and the more recent cyberbullying case of Rehtaeh Parsons, Canadian researchers Debra Pepler and Wendy Craig got together with their colleagues and established *PREVNet*. PREVNet (http://www.prevnet.ca) is a network of researchers and organizations focused on ending bullying in Canada. This group is at the forefront of bullying research and prevention.

While psychology is practical, addressing both basic and applied issues, it is more than that—it is a way of thinking. Beyond its practical value, psychology is worth studying because it provides a powerful way of thinking. All of us make judgments every day about why people do the things they do. For example, we might think that chronic two-pack-a-day smokers are weak willed, irrational, or just not smart enough to understand that the odds are stacked against them. Or we might believe they are in the grip of an addiction that simply overpowers them. How do we decide which of these judgments—if any—is right?

Psychologists are committed to investigating questions about human behaviour in a scientific way. This means that they seek to formulate precise questions about behaviour and then test possible answers through systematic observation. This commitment to testing ideas means that psychology provides a means of building knowledge that is relatively accurate and dependable. It also provides a basis for assessing the assertions we hear every day about behaviour, from friends and family, as well as in the popular media. Although most people probably don't think about it much, psychology is in the news all the time—in newspapers and magazines, on TV and radio, and on the Internet. Unfortunately, this coverage is often distorted or grossly oversimplified, so that misinformation is commonplace. Thus, many "truisms" about behaviour come to be widely believed, when they really are misconceptions or myths. A small sampling of some popular myths related to psychology is shown in Table 1.1. This list of common misconceptions comes from an excellent book entitled *50 Great Myths of Popular Psychology* (Lilienfeld et al., 2010). In the pages to come we'll touch upon a host of misconceptions about psychology and provide more accurate, science-based information on these matters. For example, in Chapter 3 you will learn that the idea that people only use 10 percent of their brains is not correct. Research suggests that the best way to dispel

Table 1.1

Popular Myths Related to Psychology

MYTH	RELEVANT CHAPTER
Most people use only 10% of their brain power.	Chapter 3
Playing Mozart's music to infants boosts their intelligence.	Chapter 3
Hypnosis is a unique "trance" state that differs in kind from wakefulness.	Chapter 5
Hypnosis is useful for retrieving memories of forgotten events.	Chapter 7
The polygraph ("lie detector") test is an accurate means of detecting dishonesty.	Chapter 10
Opposites attract: We are most romantically attracted to people who differ from us.	Chapter 13
People with schizophrenia have multiple personalities.	Chapter 15
A large portion of criminals successfully use the insanity defence.	Chapter 14

Source: Based on Lilienfeld, S.O., Lynn, S. J., Ruscio ,J., & Beyerstein, B. L. (2010). *50 great myths of popular psychology: Shattering widespread misconceptions about human behavior*. Malden, MA: Wiley-Blackwell./© 2017 Cengage Learning.

Photo by Jean Catuffe/Getty Images

Photo by Christopher Morris/Corbis via Getty Images

Modern psychology ranges widely in its investigations, looking at divergent topics such as work, sleep, stress, trauma, and brain function. It covers situations in which you work as a member of a group, such as an Olympic gold medal-winning hockey team, and situations in which individual motivation is key, such as 16-year-old Penny Oleksiak's gold-medal-winning swim in the women's 100 metre freestyle event at the 2016 Olympics. As you progress through this book, you will see that the range and diversity of psychology's subject matter are enormous.

students' misconceptions is to confront these beliefs head-on and provide a direct refutation (Kowalski & Taylor, 2009). Hence, throughout this book you will find a feature called Reality Checks that will highlight common fallacies and counter them with more accurate, realistic information. The Reality Check features will be found adjacent to relevant material, supplementing the normal text by explicitly attacking naïve, fallacious beliefs. We also highlight the science of psychology through Featured Studies in each chapter. The Featured Studies are part of our online content; they will be identified throughout the book with a link so you can access a more detailed and critical analysis of a particularly relevant research study.

We begin by taking a journey into psychology's past—a pictorial overview of the highlights of psychology's history can be found on pages 16–17. We then turn to considering psychology as it is today, a sprawling, multifaceted science and profession (Brock, 2006). To help keep psychology's diversity in perspective, the chapter concludes with a discussion of seven unifying themes that will serve as connecting threads in the chapters to come. Finally, in the chapter's Personal Application, we'll review research that gives insights on how to be an effective student, and in the Critical Thinking Application, we'll discuss how critical thinking skills can be enhanced.

From Speculation to Science: How Psychology Developed

Psychology's story is one of people working toward a better understanding of themselves. As the discipline has evolved, its focus, methods, and explanatory models have changed. Let's look at how psychology has developed from philosophical speculations about the mind into a modern research-based science.

The term *psychology* comes from two Greek words, *psyche*, meaning the soul, and *logos*, referring to the study of a subject. These two Greek roots were first put together to define a topic of study in the 16th century, when *psyche* was used to refer to the soul, spirit, or mind, as distinguished from the body (Boring, 1966). Not until the early 18th century did the term *psychology* gain more than rare usage among

scholars. By that time it had acquired its literal meaning, "the study of the mind."

Of course, people have always wondered about the mysteries of the mind. In that sense, psychology is as old as the human race. But it was only about 140 years ago that psychology emerged as a scientific discipline.

Scholars interested in the history of psychology often point to developments in philosophy and physiology as influencing the course of early psychology (Green & Groff, 2003; Pickren & Rutherford, 2010). Ancient Greek philosophers such as Socrates (469–399 B.C.E.), Plato (427–347 B.C.E.), and Aristotle (385–322 B.C.E.) considered and debated issues of relevance to psychology, including such subjects as the

Key Learning Goals

▶ Summarize Wundt's contributions to psychology, and describe the chief tenets of structuralism and functionalism.

▶ Articulate Freud's principal ideas and why they inspired controversy.

▶ Trace the development of behaviourism, and assess Watson's impact on the evolution of psychology.

▶ Summarize Skinner's key insights, and explain the emergence of humanism and its underlying philosophy.

Wilhelm Wundt
1832–1920

"Physiology informs us about those life phenomena that we perceive by our external senses. In psychology, the person looks upon himself as from within and tries to explain the interrelations of those processes that this internal observation discloses."

separation of mind and body and whether knowledge is inborn (nativism) or gained through experience (empiricism) (Hothersall, 1995).

As ideas in philosophy concerning the nature of mind and behaviour continued to develop, other disciplines, such as the study of experimental physiology and medicine, left their own marks on the later development of psychology. Physiologists and physicians such as Robert Whyte (1714–1766), Franz Gall (1758–1828), Paul Broca (1824–1880), and Johannes Müller (1801–1858) showed that important insights could be gained into the workings of the body and brain through the application of systematic, empirical methods. One of Müller's students, Hermann von Helmholtz (1821–1894), began one of the first experimental examinations in psychology of human reaction time.

Although all of this work was important to the eventual form of psychology, many date the emergence of psychology as a distinct discipline to the work of Wilhelm Wundt (1832–1920).

A New Science Is Born

As just discussed, psychology's intellectual parents were the disciplines of philosophy and physiology. By the 1870s, a small number of scholars in both fields were actively exploring questions about the mind. How are bodily sensations turned into a mental awareness of the outside world? Are people's perceptions of the world accurate reflections of reality? How do mind and body interact? The philosophers and physiologists who were interested in the mind

viewed such questions as fascinating issues within their respective fields. It was a German professor, Wilhelm Wundt, who eventually changed this view. Wundt mounted a campaign to make psychology an independent discipline rather than a stepchild of philosophy or physiology. Wundt's pioneering work had an enormous impact on the development of psychology (Wong, 2009).

In 1879 Wundt succeeded in establishing the first formal laboratory for research in psychology at the University of Leipzig. In recognition of this landmark event, historians have christened 1879 as psychology's "date of birth." Soon after, in 1881, Wundt established the first journal devoted to publishing research on psychology. All in all, Wundt's campaign was so successful that today he is widely characterized as the founder of psychology (Benjamin, 2014).

Wundt's conception of psychology dominated the field for two decades and was influential for several more. Borrowing from his training in physiology, Wundt (1874) declared that the new psychology should be a science modelled after fields such as physics and chemistry. What was the subject matter of the new science? According to Wundt, it was consciousness—the awareness of immediate experience. Thus, psychology became the scientific study of conscious experience. This orientation kept psychology focused squarely on the mind. But it demanded that the methods used to investigate the mind be as scientific as those of chemists or physicists.

Many outstanding scholars came to Leipzig to study under Wundt and then fanned out around the world, establishing laboratories that formed the basis for the new science of psychology. The growth of this new field was particularly rapid in North America, where some 23 new psychological research labs sprang up between 1883 and 1893 at the universities shown in Figure 1.1 (Benjamin, 2014). Although psychology was born in Germany, it blossomed into adolescence in North America.

The Battle of the "Schools" Begins: Structuralism versus Functionalism

Competing schools of thought exist in most scientific disciplines. Sometimes the disagreements among these schools are sharp. Such diversity in thought is natural and often stimulates enlightening debate. In psychology, the first two major schools of thought, structuralism and functionalism, were entangled in the first great intellectual battles in the field (Wertheimer, 2012).

The establishment of the first research laboratory in psychology by Wilhelm Wundt (far right) marked the birth of psychology as a modern science.

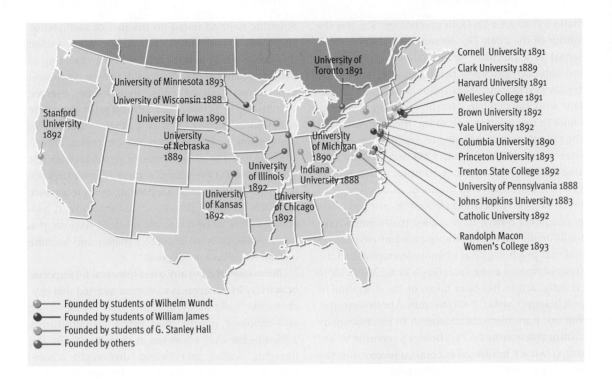

Figure 1.1
Early research laboratories in North America. This map highlights the location and year of founding of the first 24 psychological research labs established in North American colleges and universities. As the colour coding shows, a great many of these labs were founded by the students of Wilhelm Wundt, G. Stanley Hall, and William James.

Source: Based on Benjamin, 2000.

University of Toronto 1891
University of Minnesota 1893
University of Wisconsin 1888
University of Iowa 1890
Stanford University 1892
University of Nebraska 1889
University of Illinois 1892
University of Michigan 1890
Indiana University 1888
University of Kansas 1892
University of Chicago 1892

Cornell University 1891
Clark University 1889
Harvard University 1891
Wellesley College 1891
Brown University 1892
Yale University 1892
Columbia University 1890
Princeton University 1893
Trenton State College 1892
University of Pennsylvania 1888
Johns Hopkins University 1883
Catholic University 1892
Randolph Macon Women's College 1893

- ── Founded by students of Wilhelm Wundt
- ── Founded by students of William James
- ── Founded by students of G. Stanley Hall
- ── Founded by others

Structuralism emerged through the leadership of Edward Titchener, an Englishman who emigrated to the United States in 1892. After training in Wundt's lab, he taught for decades at Cornell University. *Structuralism* was based on the notion that the task of psychology is to analyze consciousness into its basic elements and investigate how these elements are related. Just as physicists were studying how matter is made up of basic particles, the structuralists wanted to identify the fundamental components of conscious experience, such as sensations, feelings, and images.

Although the structuralists explored many questions, most of their work concerned sensation and perception in vision, hearing, and touch. To examine the contents of consciousness, the structuralists depended on the method of introspection, or the careful, systematic self-observation of one's own conscious experience. As practised by the structuralists, *introspection* required training to make the subject—the person being studied—more objective and more aware. Once trained, participants were typically exposed to auditory tones and visual stimuli, and then they were asked to analyze and describe the quality, intensity, and clarity of what they experienced.

The functionalists were heavily influenced by William James (1842–1910), a brilliant American scholar, who took a different view of psychology's task. *Functionalism* was based on the belief that psychology should investigate the function or purpose of consciousness, rather than its structure. James argued that the structuralists' approach missed the real nature of conscious experience. Consciousness, he argued, consists of a continuous flow of thoughts. In analyzing consciousness into its "elements," the structuralists were looking at static points in that flow. James wanted to understand the flow itself, which he called the *stream of consciousness*. Today, people take this metaphorical description of mental life for granted, but at the time it was a revolutionary insight. James went on to make many important contributions to psychology, including a theory of emotion that remains influential today (Laird & Lacasse, 2014; see Chapter 9). His landmark book, *Principles of Psychology* (1890), became standard reading for generations of psychologists. It is perhaps the most influential text in the history of psychology (Weiten & Wight, 1992).

Whereas structuralists naturally gravitated to the lab, the functionalists were more interested in how people adapt their behaviour to the demands of the real world around them. Instead of focusing on sensation and perception, the functionalists began to investigate mental testing, patterns of development in children, the effectiveness of educational practices, and behavioural differences between the sexes. These new topics may have played a role in attracting the first women into the field of psychology, some of whom played critical roles in the developing science of psychology. Margaret Floy Washburn was the first woman in the United

From Weiten. Cengage Advantage Books: Psychology, 9E. © 2013 South-Western, a part of Cengage, Inc. Reproduced by permission. www.cengage.com/permissions

**William James
1842–1910**

"It is just this free water of consciousness that psychologists resolutely overlook."

The Evolution of Psychology

States to receive a Ph.D. in psychology. She was the author of the book *The Animal Mind* (1908), which served as a precursor to behaviourism, a theoretical approach discussed below. Another pioneering female psychologist, Leta Hollingworth, did important work on children's intelligence and was influential in debunking some of the theories current at the time that were proposed to explain why women were "inferior" to men. Mary Whiton Calkins, who studied with William James, went on to become the first woman to serve as president of the American Psychological Association (APA). Feminist psychologists, among others, have argued that women have traditionally been underrepresented in psychology and that psychology has often underemphasized the study of women and gender (Eagly et al., 2012). More recently, action has been taken in the discipline of psychology (Cynkar, 2007) to address both concerns. You can learn more about women in psychology by visiting the website for Psychology's Feminist Voices (http://www.feministvoices.com/), a project directed by psychologist Alexandra Rutherford.

The impassioned advocates of structuralism and functionalism saw themselves as fighting for high stakes: the definition and future direction of the new science of psychology. Their war of ideas continued energetically for many years. Who won? Most historians give the edge to functionalism. Both schools of thought gradually faded away. But the practical orientation of functionalism fostered the development of two important descendants—behaviourism and applied psychology (Green, 2009). We will discuss both momentarily.

Watson Alters Psychology's Course as Behaviourism Makes Its Debut

The debate between structuralism and functionalism was only the prelude to other fundamental controversies in psychology. In the early 1900s, another major school of thought appeared that dramatically altered the course of psychology (Todd & Morris, 1994). Founded by John B. Watson (1878–1958), *behaviourism* is a theoretical orientation based on the premise that scientific psychology should study only observable behaviour. It is important to understand what a radical change this definition represents. Watson (1913, 1919) was proposing that psychologists abandon the study of consciousness altogether and focus exclusively on behaviours that they could observe directly. In essence, he was redefining what scientific psychology should be about.

Why did Watson argue for such a fundamental shift in direction? Because to him, the power of the scientific method rested on the idea of verifiability. In principle, scientific claims can always be verified (or disproved) by anyone who is able and willing to make the required observations. However, this power depends on studying things that can be observed objectively. Otherwise, the advantage of using the scientific approach—replacing vague speculation and personal opinion with reliable, exact knowledge—is lost. For Watson, mental processes were not a proper subject for scientific study because they are ultimately private events. After all, no one can see or touch another's thoughts. Consequently, if psychology were to be a science, it would have to give up consciousness as its subject matter and become instead the *science of behaviour*.

Behaviour refers to any overt (observable) response or activity by an organism. Watson asserted that psychologists could study anything that people do or say—shopping, playing chess, eating, complimenting a friend—but they could not study scientifically the thoughts, wishes, and feelings that might accompany these observable behaviours. Influenced by Ivan Pavlov's discovery of the conditioned reflex (discussed in Chapter 6), the behaviourists eventually came to view psychology's mission as an attempt to relate overt behaviours ("responses") to observable events in the environment ("stimuli").

Watson's radical reorientation of psychology did not end with his redefinition of its subject matter. He also staked out a rather extreme position on one of psychology's oldest and most fundamental questions: the issue of nature versus nurture. This age-old debate is concerned with whether behaviour is determined mainly by genetic inheritance ("nature") or by environment and experience ("nurture"). To oversimplify, the question is this: Is a great concert pianist or a master criminal born, or made? Watson argued that each is made, not born. In other words, he downplayed the importance of heredity, maintaining that behaviour is governed primarily by the environment. Indeed, he boldly claimed:

Give me a dozen healthy infants, well-formed, and my own specified world to bring them up in and I'll guarantee to take any one at random and train him to become any type of specialist I might select—doctor, lawyer, artist, merchant-chief, and yes, even beggar-man and thief, regardless of his talents, penchants, tendencies, abilities, vocations and race of his ancestors. I am going beyond my facts and I admit it, but so have the advocates of the contrary and they have been doing it for many thousands of years. (Watson, 1924, p. 82)

John B. Watson
1878–1958

"The time seems to have come when psychology must discard all references to consciousness."

For obvious reasons, Watson's tongue-in-cheek challenge was never put to a test. Although this widely cited quotation overstated and oversimplified Watson's views on the nature–nurture issue (Todd & Morris, 1992), his writings contributed to the strong environmental slant that became associated with behaviourism (Horowitz, 1992).

Although Watson's views shaped the evolution of psychology for many decades, he ended up watching the field's progress from the sidelines. Because of a heavily publicized divorce scandal in 1920, Watson was forced to resign from Johns Hopkins University (Buckley, 1994). Bitterly disappointed, he left academia at the age of 42, never to return. Psychology's loss proved to be the business world's gain, as Watson went on to become an innovative, successful advertising executive (Brewer, 1991; King, Woody, & Viney, 2013). The advertising industry was just emerging as a national force in the 1920s, and Watson quickly became one of its most prominent practitioners.

He pioneered fear appeals, testimonials, selling the "prestige" of products, and the promotion of style over substance, all of which remain basic principles in modern marketing (Buckley, 1982). Moreover, "through an enormous output of books, magazine articles, and radio broadcasts he was able to establish himself as the public spokesman for the profession of psychology and an expert on subjects ranging from childrearing to economics. In effect, Watson became the first 'pop' psychologist" (Buckley, 1982, p. 217). So, ironically, Watson became the public face of the discipline that had banished him from its mainstream.

concept check 1.1

Understanding the Implications of Major Theories: Wundt, James, and Watson

Check your understanding of the implications of some of the major theories reviewed in this chapter by indicating who is likely to have made each of the statements quoted below. Choose from the following theorists: (a) Wilhelm Wundt, (b) William James, and (c) John B. Watson. You'll find the answers in Appendix A at the back of the book.

_____ **1.** "Our conclusion is that we have no real evidence of the inheritance of traits. I would feel perfectly confident in the ultimately favourable outcome of careful upbringing of a healthy, well-formed baby born of a long line of crooks, murderers and thieves, and prostitutes."

_____ **2.** "The book which I present to the public is an attempt to mark out a new domain of science. ... The new discipline rests upon anatomical and physiological foundations. ... The experimental treatment of psychological problems must be pronounced from every point of view to be in its first beginnings."

_____ **3.** "Consciousness, then, does not appear to itself chopped up in bits. Such words as 'chain' or 'train' do not describe it fitly. ... It is nothing jointed; it flows. A 'river' or 'stream' is the metaphor by which it is most naturally described."

Freud Brings the Unconscious into the Picture

Sigmund Freud (1856–1939) was an Austrian physician whose theories made him one of the most influential—and controversial—intellectual figures of the 20th century. Freud's (1900, 1933) approach to psychology grew out of his efforts to treat mental disorders. In his medical practice, Freud treated people troubled by psychological problems such as irrational fears, obsessions, and anxieties with an innovative procedure he called *psychoanalysis* (described in detail in Chapter 15). Decades of experience probing into his patients' lives provided much of the inspiration for Freud's theory.

His work with patients and his own self-exploration persuaded Freud of the existence of what he called the *unconscious*. According to Freud, the **unconscious contains thoughts, memories, and desires that are well below the surface of conscious awareness but that nonetheless exert great influence on behaviour.** Freud based his concept of the unconscious on a variety of observations. For instance, he noticed that seemingly meaningless slips of the tongue (such as "I decided to take a summer school curse") often appeared to reveal a person's true feelings. He also noted that his patients' dreams often seemed to express important feelings they were unaware of. Knitting these and other observations together, Freud eventually concluded that psychological disturbances are largely caused by personal conflicts existing at an unconscious level. More generally, his *psychoanalytic theory* **attempts to explain personality, motivation, and mental disorders by focusing on unconscious determinants of behaviour.**

Freud's concept of the unconscious was not entirely new (Lothane, 2006). However, it was a major departure from the prevailing belief that

© 2017 Cengage Learning

**Sigmund Freud
1856–1939**

"The unconscious is the true psychical reality; in its innermost nature it is as much unknown to us as the reality of the external world."

The Evolution of Psychology

A portrait taken at the famous Clark University psychology conference, September 1909. Pictured are (seated, left to right) Sigmund Freud, G. Stanley Hall, and Carl Jung, and (standing) three of Freud's students and associates: Abraham Brill, Ernest Jones, and Sandor Ferenczi.

B. F. Skinner 1904–1990

"I submit that what we call the behaviour of the human organism is no more free than its digestion."

people are fully aware of the forces affecting their behaviour. In arguing that behaviour is governed by unconscious forces, Freud made the disconcerting suggestion that people are not masters of their own minds. Other aspects of Freud's theory also stirred up debate. For instance, he proposed that behaviour is greatly influenced by how people cope with their sexual urges. At a time when people were far less comfortable discussing sexual issues than they are today, even scientists were offended and scandalized by Freud's emphasis on sex. Small wonder, then, that Freud was soon engulfed in controversy.

In spite of its controversial nature, Freud's theory gradually won acceptance, attracting prominent followers such as Carl Jung and Alfred Adler. Important public recognition from psychology came in 1909, when Freud was invited to give a series of lectures at Clark University in Massachusetts. By the 1920s psychoanalytic theory was widely known around the world. Although psychoanalytic theory continued to generate heated debate, it survived to become an influential theoretical perspective (Luborsky, O'Reilly-Landry, & Arlow, 2011). Today, many psychoanalytic concepts have filtered into the mainstream of psychology (Eagle, 2013; Westen, Gabbard, & Ortigo, 2008).

Skinner Questions Free Will as Behaviourism Flourishes

The advocates of behaviourism and psychoanalysis tangled frequently during the 1920s, 1930s, and 1940s. As psychoanalytic thought slowly gained a foothold within psychology, many psychologists softened their stance on the acceptability of studying internal mental events. However, this movement toward the consideration of internal states was dramatically reversed in the 1950s by a Harvard psychologist named B. F. Skinner (1904–1990).

Skinner did not deny the existence of internal mental events. However, he insisted that they could not be studied scientifically. Moreover, he maintained, there was no need to study them. According to Skinner, if the stimulus of food is followed by the response of eating, we can fully describe what is happening without making any guesses about whether the animal is experiencing hunger. Like Watson, Skinner also emphasized how environmental factors mould behaviour.

The fundamental principle of behaviour documented by Skinner is deceptively simple: Organisms tend to repeat responses that lead to positive outcomes, and they tend not to repeat responses that lead to neutral or negative outcomes. Despite its simplicity, this principle turns out to be quite powerful. Working with laboratory rats and pigeons in a small chamber called a Skinner box (see Chapter 6), Skinner showed that he could exert remarkable control over the behaviour of animals by manipulating the outcomes of their responses. He was even able to train animals to perform unnatural behaviours. For example, he once trained some pigeons to play a respectable version of table tennis. They pecked a ball back and forth on a ping-pong table.

B. F. Skinner created considerable controversy when he asserted that free will is an illusion.

reality check

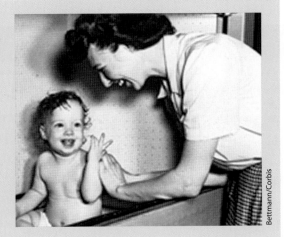

Bettmann/Corbis

Skinner's followers eventually showed that the principles uncovered in their animal research could be applied to complex human behaviours as well. Behavioural principles are now widely used in factories, schools, prisons, mental hospitals, and a variety of other settings.

Skinner's ideas had repercussions that went far beyond the debate among psychologists about what they should study. Skinner spelled out the full implications of his findings in his book *Beyond Freedom and Dignity* (1971). There he asserted that all behaviour is fully governed by external stimuli. In other words, your behaviour is determined in predictable ways by lawful principles, just as the flight of an arrow is governed by the laws of physics. Thus, if you believe that your actions are the result of conscious decisions, you're wrong. According to Skinner, we are all controlled by our environment, not by ourselves. In short, Skinner arrived at the conclusion that free will is an illusion.

As you can readily imagine, such a disconcerting view of human nature was not universally acclaimed. Like Freud, Skinner was the target of harsh criticism. Much of this criticism stemmed from misinterpretations of his ideas reported in the popular press (Rutherford, 2000). For example, his analysis of free will was often misconstrued as an attack on the concept of a free society—which it was not. Somehow, a myth also emerged that Skinner raised his daughter in a version of a Skinner box and that this experience led her to be severely disturbed later in life. Despite the misinformation and controversy, however, behaviourism flourished as the dominant school of thought in psychology during the 1950s and 1960s (Gilgen, 1982).

The Humanists Revolt

By the 1950s, behaviourism and psychoanalytic theory had become the most influential schools of thought in psychology. However, many psychologists found these theoretical orientations unappealing. The principal charge hurled at both schools was that they were "dehumanizing." Psychoanalytic theory was attacked for its belief that behaviour is dominated by primitive, sexual urges. Behaviourism was criticized for its preoccupation with the study of simple animal behaviour. Both theories were criticized because they suggested that people are not masters of their own destinies. Above all, many people argued, both schools of thought failed to recognize the unique qualities of *human* behaviour.

Beginning in the 1950s, the diverse opposition to behaviourism and psychoanalytic theory blended into a loose alliance that eventually became a new school of thought called "humanism" (Bühler & Allen, 1972). In psychology, *humanism* **is a theoretical orientation that emphasizes the unique qualities of humans, especially their freedom and their potential for personal growth.** Some of the key differences between the humanistic, psychoanalytic, and behavioural viewpoints are summarized in Figure 1.2, which compares six influential contemporary theoretical perspectives in psychology.

Humanists take an *optimistic* view of human nature. They maintain that people are not pawns of either their animal heritage or environmental circumstances. Furthermore, they say, because humans are fundamentally different from other animals,

Figure 1.2

Contemporary theoretical perspectives in psychology. The theoretical approaches outlined in this table remain influential in modern psychology. As you can see, each theoretical perspective has its own take on what psychology should study.

© 2017 Cengage Learning

PERSPECTIVE AND ITS INFLUENTIAL PERIOD	PRINCIPAL CONTRIBUTORS	SUBJECT MATTER	BASIC PREMISE
Behavioural (1913–present) 	John B. Watson Ivan Pavlov B. F. Skinner	Effects of environment on the overt behaviour of humans and animals	Only observable events (stimulus–response relations) can be studied scientifically.
Psychoanalytic (1900–present) 	Sigmund Freud Carl Jung Alfred Adler	Unconscious determinants of behaviour	Unconscious motives and experiences in early childhood govern personality and mental disorders.
Humanistic (1950s–present) 	Carl Rogers Abraham Maslow	Unique aspects of human experience	Humans are free, rational beings with the potential for personal growth, and they are fundamentally different from animals.
Cognitive (1950s–present) 	Jean Piaget Noam Chomsky Herbert Simon	Thoughts; mental processes	Human behaviour cannot be fully understood without examining how people acquire, store, and process information.
Behavioural Neuroscience (1950s–present) 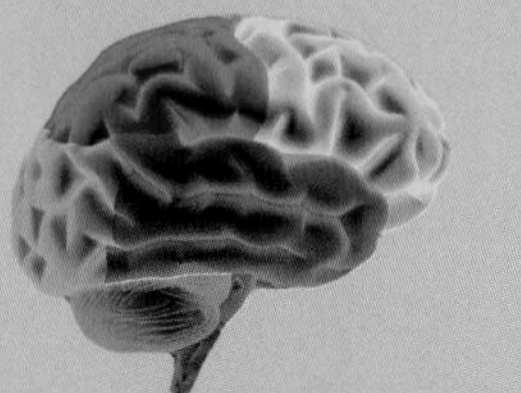	James Olds Roger Sperry David Hubel Torsten Wiesel	Physiological, genetic, and neural bases of behaviour in humans and animals	An organism's functioning can be explained in terms of the brain structures and biochemical processes that underlie behaviour.
Evolutionary (1980s–present) 	David Buss Martin Daly Margo Wilson Leda Cosmides John Tooby	Evolutionary bases of behaviour in humans and animals	Behaviour patterns have evolved to solve adaptive problems; natural selection favours behaviours that enhance reproductive success.

research on animals has little relevance to the understanding of human behaviour. The most prominent architects of the humanistic movement have been Carl Rogers (1902–1987) and Abraham Maslow (1908–1970). Rogers (1951) argued that human behaviour is governed primarily by each individual's sense of self, or "self-concept"—which animals presumably lack. Both he and Maslow (1954) maintained that to fully understand people's behaviour, psychologists must take into account the fundamental human drive toward personal growth. They asserted that people have a basic need to continue to evolve as human beings and to fulfill their potential. In fact, the humanists argued that many psychological disturbances are the result of thwarting these uniquely human needs.

Fragmentation and dissent have reduced the influence of humanism in recent decades, although some advocates are predicting a renaissance for the humanistic movement (Taylor, 1999). To date, the humanists' greatest contribution to psychology

has probably been their innovative treatments for psychological problems and disorders. More generally, the humanists have argued eloquently for a different picture of human nature than those implied by psychoanalysis and behaviourism (Wertz, 1998). To date, humanists' greatest contribution to psychology has probably been their innovative treatments for psychological problems and disorders. Notably, Carl Rogers pioneered a new approach to psychotherapy—known as *person-centred therapy*—that remains extremely influential today (Kirschenbaum & Jourdan, 2005).

Psychology in Canada

The first experimental laboratory in the British Empire was established by James Mark Baldwin at the University of Toronto in 1891 (Green, 2004; Hoff, 1992). The first psychology course offered at a Canadian university was likely at Dalhousie in 1838 (Wright & Myers, 1982). According to Wright and Myers (1982), the teaching of psychology at universities in Canada became more common in the 1850s, beginning then at McGill University in Montreal and the University of Toronto. Much of the rest of the country followed soon after. Psychology in Canada is distinct from psychology in the United States in several respects (Brock, 2013), including the nature of the impact of Canadian cultural diversity on the directions taken in research and theory in the area of cultural psychology (Bhatt, Tonks, & Berry, 2013).

The Canadian Psychological Association (CPA) was formed in 1939. The CPA is Canada's largest organization for psychology and has 7116 members and affiliates (CPA, 2016), over half of whom are women. In the past, women and their history have been underrepresented in psychology (Gul et al., 2013) and in science in general, but recently this pattern has begun to change (Wright, 1992). The last few years have seen tremendous growth in the number of students studying full-time at Canadian universities. Students studying psychology comprise one of the areas showing the greatest increase since 2000 (AUCC, 2011). The past few decades have seen a tremendous growth in the number of women studying at universities. Women now make up the majority of undergraduate and M.A. students at Canadian universities and more women from the ages of 25 to 34 have completed university degrees than men of the same age group, a reversal of the statistics of 20 years before (Turcotte, 2011).

Canadian psychologists have been at the forefront of research and theory in many areas of psychology. Few psychologists anywhere have made a more

© 2017 Cengage Learning

Carl Rogers 1902–1987

"It seems to me that at bottom each person is asking, 'Who am I, really? How can I get in touch with this real self, underlying all my surface behaviour? How can I become myself?'"

....

concept **check** 1.2

Understanding the Implications of Major Theories: Freud, Skinner, and Rogers

Check your understanding of the implications of some of the major theories reviewed in this chapter by indicating who is likely to have made each of the statements quoted below. Choose from the following: (a) Sigmund Freud, (b) B. F. Skinner, and (c) Carl Rogers. You'll find the answers in Appendix A at the back of the book.

_____ **1.** "In the traditional view, a person is free. ... He can therefore be held responsible for what he does and justly punished if he offends. That view, together with its associated practices, must be re-examined when a scientific analysis reveals unsuspected controlling relations between behaviour and environment."

_____ **2.** "He that has eyes to see and ears to hear may convince himself that no mortal can keep a secret. If the lips are silent, he chatters with his fingertips; betrayal oozes out of him at every pore. And thus the task of making conscious the most hidden recesses of the mind is one which it is quite possible to accomplish."

_____ **3.** "I do not have a Pollyanna view of human nature. ... Yet one of the most refreshing and invigorating parts of my experience is to work with [my clients] and to discover the strongly positive directional tendencies which exist in them, as in all of us, at the deepest levels."

Figure 1.3
Women pioneers in Canadian psychology.

These three female psychologists represent just some of the different forms of significant contributions that women have made to psychology in Canada.

Sources: Bretherton, I., & Main, M. (2000). Mary Dinsmore Salter Ainsworth (1913–1999). *American Psychologist,* 55, 1148–1149 [Ainsworth]; Wright, M. J. (1993). Women groundbreakers in Canadian psychology: World War II and its aftermath. *Canadian Psychology,* 33, 14–26 [Wright]; Simon Fraser University document retrieved March 15, 2005, from http://www.sfu.ca/~dkimura/dkhome.htm, and profiles retrieved March 15, 2005, from Science.ca, http://www.science.ca/scientists/scientistprofile.php?pID=10 and the Society for Academic Freedom and Scholarship, http://www.safs.ca/academic.html [Kimura].

Mary Salter Ainsworth

Mary Salter Ainsworth (1913–1999) was one of the most important figures in developmental psychology in the last century. Although born in Ohio, she moved to Toronto at the age of four and earned her Ph.D. from the University of Toronto. She lectured at the University of Toronto and then joined the Canadian Women's Army Corps, where she attained the rank of major. After the war, Ainsworth returned to teaching at the University of Toronto. She married another student of that university and went with him to London, England, while he completed his studies. There she worked with John Bowlby, who was interested in attachment. She later went on to a position at Johns Hopkins University and made important contributions to attachment theory and the study of developmental psychology. She retired in 1984 from the University of Virginia.

Mary Wright

Mary Wright was a professor of psychology at the University of Western Ontario, retiring in 1980. She was a developmental psychologist who made important contributions to educational psychology and developmental training at the University of Western Ontario, establishing a laboratory preschool there that now bears her name. Wright served during World War II in the Canadian Children's Service in charge of training child-care workers. She is a historian of academic psychology in Canada (Wright & Myers, 1982), she served as president of the Ontario Psychological Association (OPA: 1951–1952), and she was the first female president of the Canadian Psychological Association (CPA: 1968–1969). She has received numerous honorary degrees and awards, including two Distinguished Contribution Awards from the OPA and the CPA Gold Medal Award for Distinguished Lifetime Contribution to Canadian Psychology.

Doreen Kimura

Doreen Kimura was a professor of psychology at the University of Western Ontario for 31 years. She received her undergraduate and graduate training at McGill University. Kimura has made significant and sustained contributions to the study of the brain, including neuromotor mechanisms in human communication and sex differences in cognition. She is also active in the area of promoting academic freedom; she was the founding president (1992–1993) of the Society for Academic Freedom and Scholarship and remains active in that organization. She is a fellow of the Royal Society of Canada and was honoured in 1985 by the Canadian Psychological Association with its Donald O. Hebb Award for Distinguished Contributions to Psychology as a Science.

---

important contribution to psychology than Brenda Milner of McGill University. Among other things, she is well known for her pioneering work with the patient known as H.M. (Corkin, 2013), she has made crucial contributions to our understanding of memory, and she was one of the founders of neuropsychology in Canada. Now in her 90s, she continues to teach, do research, and publish in the area of neuropsychology (e.g., Banks, Feindel, Milner, & Jones-Gotman, 2016; Milner & Klein, 2016). We discuss some of her contributions in Chapters 3 and 7. Three other women who have made significant contributions to psychology in Canada are profiled in Figure 1.3.

Psychology Comes of Age as a Profession

As you know, psychology is not all pure science. It has a highly practical side. Many psychologists provide a variety of professional services to the public and address issues emerging from important social issues. The first applied arm of psychology to achieve any prominence was clinical psychology. As practised today, *clinical psychology* is the branch of psychology concerned with the diagnosis and treatment of psychological problems and disorders. In the early days, however, the emphasis was almost exclusively on psychological testing and adjustment problems in schoolchildren, and clinicians were a small minority in a field devoted primarily to research (Goldenberg, 1983).

reality check

Misconception

Psychologists have always been involved in the treatment of mental illness.

Reality

In the first six decades of its existence as an independent discipline, psychology had virtually no role in the diagnosis and treatment of mental illness, which was thoroughly dominated by psychiatry. Psychologists were mostly academics and researchers. It was only during World War II and its aftermath that psychology was drawn into the field of mental health.

Key Learning Goals

▶ Discuss how historical events contributed to the emergence of psychology as a profession.

▶ Describe two trends emerging in the 1950s–1960s that represented a return to psychology's intellectual roots.

▶ Explain why Western psychology has shown an increased interest in cultural variables in recent decades.

▶ Discuss the emergence and basic ideas of evolutionary psychology and positive psychology.

That picture changed with dramatic swiftness during and after World War II, in the 1940s and 1950s (Cautin, Freedheim, & DeLeon, 2013; Nathan, 2009). Because of the war, many academic psychologists were pressed into service as clinicians. They were needed to screen military recruits and to treat soldiers suffering from trauma. Many of these psychologists (often to their surprise) found the clinical work to be challenging and rewarding, and a substantial portion continued to do clinical work after the war. In the United States, government funding for clinical training increased significantly. Approximately 40 000 U.S. veterans, many with severe psychological scars, returned to seek post-war treatment in Veterans Administration (VA) hospitals; with the demand for clinicians far greater than the supply, the government stepped in to finance many new training programs in clinical psychology (Routh, 2013). Within a few years, about half of the new Ph.D.s in psychology were specializing in clinical psychology. In Canada, World War II also provided an opportunity for the Canadian Psychological Association to validate clinical psychology as an important applied discipline (Granger, 2006). Training models for clinical psychologists in Canada have remained relatively homogenous across all of Canada, with all accredited programs having to meet the high training standards set by the CPA (Dobson, 2016).

Since the 1950s, the professionalization of psychology has spread into additional areas of psychology. Today the broad umbrella of applied psychology covers a variety of professional specialties, including school psychology, industrial/organizational psychology, and counselling psychology (Benjamin & Baker, 2004).

In Canada, clinical psychologists are licensed and governed by the various provincial and territorial psychology colleges and boards of examiners. The websites of these organizations contain information about practice, standards, and relevant legislation. In some circumstances, these organizations may be responsible for disciplinary action toward a psychologist. For an example, visit the College of Psychologists of British Columbia's website at http://www.collegeofpsychologists.bc.ca for some details regarding practice in British Columbia.

Cognition and Neuroscience in Psychology

While applied psychology has blossomed in recent decades, research has continued to evolve. Ironically, two of the relatively recent trends in research hark back more than a century to psychology's beginning, when psychologists were principally interested in consciousness and physiology. Today, psychologists are showing renewed interest in consciousness (now called *cognition*) and the physiological bases of behaviour manifested primarily in a focus on neuroscience.

Cognition **refers to the mental processes involved in acquiring knowledge.** In other words, cognition involves thinking or conscious experience. For many decades, the dominance of behaviourism discouraged investigation of "unobservable" mental processes, and most psychologists showed little interest in cognition (Mandler, 2002). During the 1950s and 1960s, however, research on cognition slowly began to change (Miller, 2003). The research of Swiss psychologist Jean Piaget (1954) focused increased attention on the study of children's cognitive development, while the work of Noam Chomsky (1957) elicited new interest in the psychological underpinnings of language. Around the same time, Herbert Simon and his colleagues (Newell, Shaw, & Simon, 1958) began influential, groundbreaking research on problem solving that eventually led to a Nobel Prize for Simon (in 1978). These advances along with many others (e.g., Benjafeld, 2008; Kelly, 1955) sparked a surge of interest in cognitive processes.

Since then, cognitive theorists have argued that psychology must study internal mental events to fully understand behaviour (Gardner, 1985; Hyman et al., 2012; Neisser, 1967). Advocates of the *cognitive perspective* point out that people's manipulations of mental images surely influence how they behave. Consequently, focusing exclusively on overt behaviour yields an incomplete picture of why individuals behave as they do. Equally important, psychologists investigating decision

FEATURED STUDY

Youth's responses to peer provocation: Links to symptoms.

Description
This study by Melanie Dirks, a clinical psychologist at McGill University, and her associates examines how children's symptoms of anxiety and depression affect how they respond to being targeted aggressively by their peers.

Investigators
Dirks, M. A., Treat, T. A., & Weersing, V. R. (2014). *Journal of Psychopathology and Behavioural Assessment, 36,* 339–349.

Figure 1.4

The relative prominence of four major schools of thought in psychology. To estimate the relative productivity and influence of various theoretical orientations in recent decades, Joseph Spear (2007) conducted a keyword search of the psychological research literature indexed in PsycINFO to estimate the percentage of articles relevant to each school of thought. Obviously, his approach is just one of many ways one might gauge the prominence of various theoretical orientations in psychology. Nonetheless, the data are thought provoking. His findings suggest that the cognitive perspective surpassed the behavioural perspective in its influence on research sometime around 1975 and that it has continued as the leading perspective since then. As you can see, his data also demonstrate that the neuroscience perspective has grown steadily in influence since the 1950s.

Source: Adapted from Spear, J. H. (2007). Prominent schools or other active specialties? A fresh look as some trends in psychology. *Review of General Psychology*, 11, 363–380. Copyright © 2007 by the American Psychological Association.

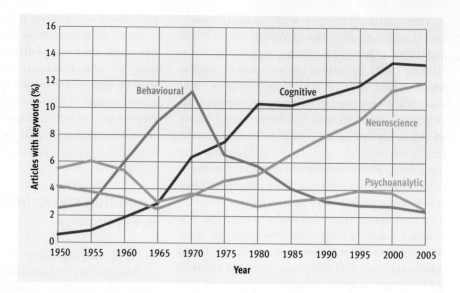

Donald Hebb's pioneering ideas highlighted the importance of physiological and neuropsychological perspectives.

making, reasoning, and problem solving have shown that methods can be devised to study cognitive processes scientifically. Although the methods are different from those used in psychology's early days, modern research on the inner workings of the mind has put the psyche back in psychology. In fact, many observers maintain that along with neuroscience, the cognitive perspective has become the dominant perspective in contemporary psychology—and some interesting data support this assertion, as can be seen in Figure 1.4, which plots the research productivity of four theoretical perspectives since 1950. As you can see, since 1975 the cognitive and neuroscience perspectives have generated more published articles than the once-dominant behavioural and psychoanalytic perspectives (Spear, 2007).

The 1950s and 1960s also saw many discoveries that highlighted the interrelations among mind, body, and behaviour (Thompson & Zola, 2003). In this work, research on the brain and its connection to behaviour plays a pre-eminent role. For example, Canadian psychologist James Olds (1956) demonstrated that electrical stimulation of the brain could evoke emotional responses such as pleasure and rage in animals. Other work, which eventually earned a Nobel Prize for Roger Sperry (in 1981), showed that the right and left halves of the brain are specialized to handle different types of mental tasks (Gazzaniga, Bogen, & Sperry, 1965). The 1960s also brought the publication of David Hubel and Torsten Wiesel's (1962, 1963) Nobel Prize–winning work on how visual signals are processed in the brain.

These and other findings stimulated an increase in research on the biological, and especially the neurobiological, bases of behaviour. Advocates of the behavioural neuroscience perspective maintain that much of our behaviour can be explained in terms of structures of and processes in the brain. For example, early research by Wilder Penfield, Director of the Montreal Neurological Institute, showed that it was possible to map out the parts of the brain associated with speech, memory, and sensory and motor activities (e.g., Milner, 1977). Another very important figure in this area was Donald Hebb (Jusczyk & Klein, 1980). He was a professor of psychology at McGill University in Montreal whose pioneering ideas are credited with highlighting the importance of physiological and neuropsychological perspectives and as having paved the way for the recent cognitive and neuroscience revolutions in psychology (Klein, 1999).

Hebb's emphasis on the importance of the brain in behaviour provided an important counterweight to that time's dominance of the behaviourist models. He argued that the locus of behaviour should be sought in the brain. One of the pivotal concepts he introduced was the cell assembly. Hebb suggested that repeated stimulation leads to the development of cell assemblies. These cell assemblies resemble cognitive units that together or in concert with other cell assemblies facilitate behaviour. Recent research in neuroscience continues to provide support for these ideas (Ghassemzadeh, Posner, & Rothbart, 2013; Palm et al., 2014; Shapiro, 2015). Hebb's ideas suggested how neural networks might work and be organized. He proposed that the key to understanding this was activity at the neuronal level. According to many, his innovative ideas set the stage for contemporary developments in cognition and neuroscience and underscored the importance of the neuropsychological approach to understanding behaviour (Posner & Rothbart, 2004; Wikelgren, 1999).

Interest in the neuroscience approach to psychology has increased dramatically in the past few years and is pervasive across all areas of psychology, including developmental, clinical, personality, and social psychology (e.g., Amodio & Ratner, 2013; Hajcak, 2016; Zaki & Ochsner, 2012). It has even spawned its own concern with ethics in neuroscience—*neuroethics* (Clausen & Levy, 2015; Gazzaniga, 2005; Illes & Sahakian, 2011).

A Focus on Culture and Diversity

Throughout psychology's history, most researchers have worked under the assumption that they were seeking to identify general principles of behaviour that would be applicable to all of humanity (Smith, Spillane, & Annus, 2006). In reality, however, psychology has largely been a Western (North American and European) enterprise with a rather provincial slant (Hall, 2014; Norenzayan & Heine, 2005). Traditionally, Western psychologists have paid scant attention to how well their theories and research might apply to non-Western cultures, to ethnic minorities in Western societies, or even to women as compared to men.

However, in recent decades Western psychologists have begun to recognize that their neglect of cultural variables has diminished the value of their work. They are now devoting increased attention to culture as a determinant of behaviour. What brought about this shift? The new interest in culture appears mainly attributable to two recent trends: (1) Advances in communication, travel, and international trade have "shrunk" the world and increased global interdependence, bringing more and more North Americans and Europeans into contact with people from non-Western cultures; and (2) the ethnic makeup of the Western world has become an increasingly diverse multicultural mosaic (Brislin, 2000; Hermans & Kempen, 1998; Mays et al., 1996; Valsiner, 2012). This increasing focus on diversity and its implications for behaviour are key in a country such as Canada.

There is no question that Canada is becoming more diverse. A recent study by Statistics Canada gives a snapshot of Canada's incredible diversity (Statistics Canada, 2011). For example, Canada's foreign-born residents make up over 20 percent of the total population—6 775 800 people—which is one of the highest proportions in developed countries.

The most common origin of these immigrants is Asia (including the Middle East). There was also a increase in immigration from Africa, the Caribbean, and South America. In addition, 6 264 800 of our citizens (19.1 percent of our population) self-identify as representing a visible minority. Over 200 ethnic origins were reported in the survey. These trends and other factors led to a dramatic surge in research on cultural factors that began in the 1980s and continues today.

Today, more and more Western psychologists are broadening their horizons and incorporating cultural factors into their theories and research (e.g., Heine, 2015). These psychologists are striving to study previously underrepresented groups of subjects to test the generality of earlier findings and to catalogue both the differences and similarities among cultural groups. They are working to increase knowledge of how culture is transmitted through socialization practices, how culture colours one's view of the world, and how people cope with cultural change, and they are trying to enhance understanding of how cultural groups are affected by prejudice, discrimination, and racism. In all of these efforts, they are striving to understand the unique experiences of culturally diverse people *from the point of view of those people*. These efforts to ask new questions, study new groups, and apply new perspectives promise to enrich the discipline of psychology in the 21st century (Fowers & Davidov, 2006; Lehman, Chiu, & Schaller, 2004; Matsumoto, 2003; Sue, 2003).

Psychology Adapts: The Emergence of Evolutionary Psychology

A relatively recent development in psychology has been the emergence of evolutionary psychology, a theoretical perspective that is likely to be influential in the years to come (Ketelaar, 2015; Shackelford & Liddle, 2014). Evolutionary psychologists assert that the patterns of behaviour seen in a species are products of evolution in the same way that anatomical characteristics are. *Evolutionary psychology* **examines behavioural processes in terms of their adaptive value for members of a species over the course of many generations.** The basic premise of evolutionary psychology is that natural selection favours behaviours that enhance organisms' reproductive success—that is, passing on genes to the next generation. Thus, if a species is highly aggressive, evolutionary psychologists argue that it's because

An Illustrated Overview of Psychology's History

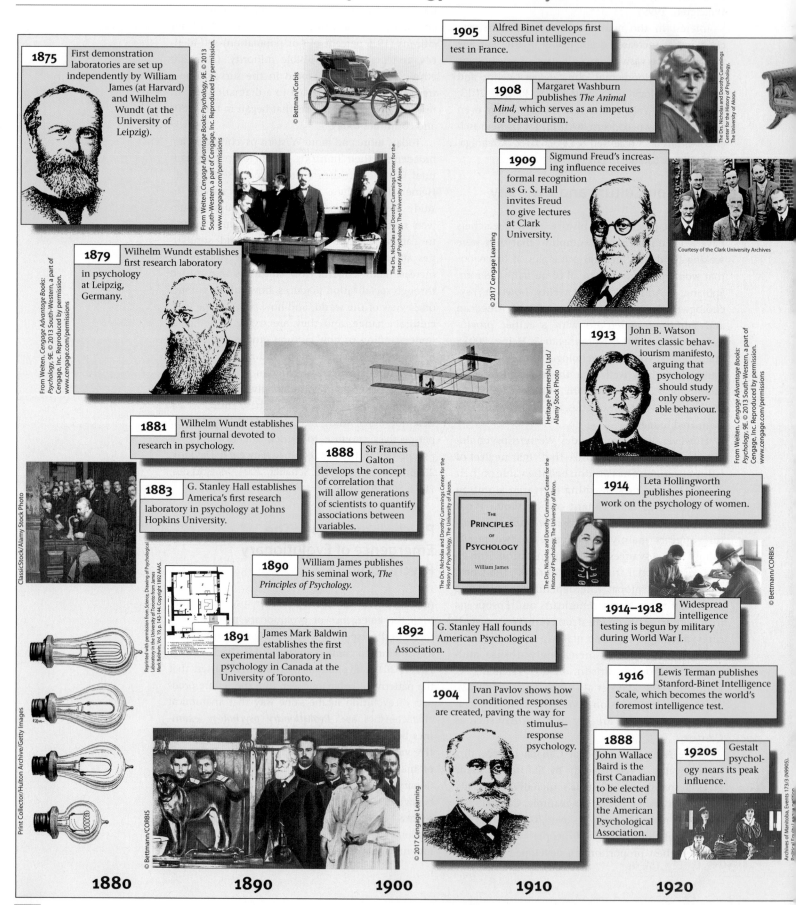

1875 First demonstration laboratories are set up independently by William James (at Harvard) and Wilhelm Wundt (at the University of Leipzig).

1879 Wilhelm Wundt establishes first research laboratory in psychology at Leipzig, Germany.

1881 Wilhelm Wundt establishes first journal devoted to research in psychology.

1883 G. Stanley Hall establishes America's first research laboratory in psychology at Johns Hopkins University.

1890 William James publishes his seminal work, *The Principles of Psychology.*

1891 James Mark Baldwin establishes the first experimental laboratory in psychology in Canada at the University of Toronto.

1888 Sir Francis Galton develops the concept of correlation that will allow generations of scientists to quantify associations between variables.

1892 G. Stanley Hall founds American Psychological Association.

1904 Ivan Pavlov shows how conditioned responses are created, paving the way for stimulus–response psychology.

1888 John Wallace Baird is the first Canadian to be elected president of the American Psychological Association.

1905 Alfred Binet develops first successful intelligence test in France.

1908 Margaret Washburn publishes *The Animal Mind,* which serves as an impetus for behaviourism.

1909 Sigmund Freud's increasing influence receives formal recognition as G. S. Hall invites Freud to give lectures at Clark University.

1913 John B. Watson writes classic behaviourism manifesto, arguing that psychology should study only observable behaviour.

1914 Leta Hollingworth publishes pioneering work on the psychology of women.

1914–1918 Widespread intelligence testing is begun by military during World War I.

1916 Lewis Terman publishes Stanford-Binet Intelligence Scale, which becomes the world's foremost intelligence test.

1920s Gestalt psychology nears its peak influence.

THE PRINCIPLES OF PSYCHOLOGY

William James

1880   1890   1900   1910   1920

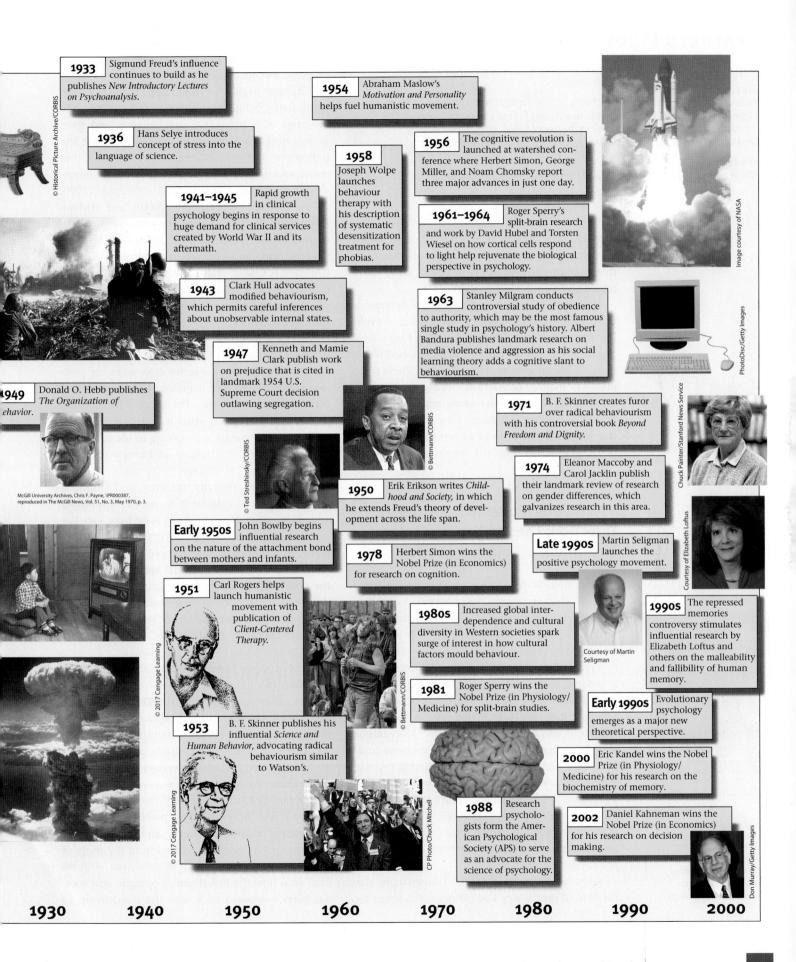

1933 Sigmund Freud's influence continues to build as he publishes *New Introductory Lectures on Psychoanalysis.*

© Historical Picture Archive/CORBIS

1936 Hans Selye introduces concept of stress into the language of science.

1941–1945 Rapid growth in clinical psychology begins in response to huge demand for clinical services created by World War II and its aftermath.

1943 Clark Hull advocates modified behaviourism, which permits careful inferences about unobservable internal states.

1947 Kenneth and Mamie Clark publish work on prejudice that is cited in landmark 1954 U.S. Supreme Court decision outlawing segregation.

1949 Donald O. Hebb publishes *The Organization of Behavior.*

McGill University Archives, Chris F. Payne, \PR000387, reproduced in The McGill News, Vol. 51, No. 3, May 1970, p. 3.

Early 1950s John Bowlby begins influential research on the nature of the attachment bond between mothers and infants.

1951 Carl Rogers helps launch humanistic movement with publication of *Client-Centered Therapy.*

© 2017 Cengage Learning

1953 B. F. Skinner publishes his influential *Science and Human Behavior,* advocating radical behaviourism similar to Watson's.

© 2017 Cengage Learning

1954 Abraham Maslow's *Motivation and Personality* helps fuel humanistic movement.

1958 Joseph Wolpe launches behaviour therapy with his description of systematic desensitization treatment for phobias.

1950 Erik Erikson writes *Childhood and Society,* in which he extends Freud's theory of development across the life span.

© Ted Streshinsky/CORBIS

© Bettmann/CORBIS

1956 The cognitive revolution is launched at watershed conference where Herbert Simon, George Miller, and Noam Chomsky report three major advances in just one day.

1961–1964 Roger Sperry's split-brain research and work by David Hubel and Torsten Wiesel on how cortical cells respond to light help rejuvenate the biological perspective in psychology.

1963 Stanley Milgram conducts controversial study of obedience to authority, which may be the most famous single study in psychology's history. Albert Bandura publishes landmark research on media violence and aggression as his social learning theory adds a cognitive slant to behaviourism.

1971 B. F. Skinner creates furor over radical behaviourism with his controversial book *Beyond Freedom and Dignity.*

1974 Eleanor Maccoby and Carol Jacklin publish their landmark review of research on gender differences, which galvanizes research in this area.

1978 Herbert Simon wins the Nobel Prize (in Economics) for research on cognition.

1980s Increased global interdependence and cultural diversity in Western societies spark surge of interest in how cultural factors mould behaviour.

© Bettmann/CORBIS

1981 Roger Sperry wins the Nobel Prize (in Physiology/Medicine) for split-brain studies.

1988 Research psychologists form the American Psychological Society (APS) to serve as an advocate for the science of psychology.

CP Photo/Chuck Mitchell

Image courtesy of NASA

PhotoDisc/Getty Images

Chuck Painter/Stanford News Service

Courtesy of Elizabeth Loftus

Late 1990s Martin Seligman launches the positive psychology movement.

Courtesy of Martin Seligman

1990s The repressed memories controversy stimulates influential research by Elizabeth Loftus and others on the malleability and fallibility of human memory.

Early 1990s Evolutionary psychology emerges as a major new theoretical perspective.

2000 Eric Kandel wins the Nobel Prize (in Physiology/Medicine) for his research on the biochemistry of memory.

2002 Daniel Kahneman wins the Nobel Prize (in Economics) for his research on decision making.

Don Murray/Getty Images

1930   1940   1950   1960   1970   1980   1990   2000

FEATURED STUDY

Social dialect and men's voice pitch influence women's mate preferences.

Description
Research has demonstrated the effects of specific features of a man's voice on women's judgments of his heritable health and fitness as a mate. This research conducted at McMaster University in the area of evolutionary psychology examines the effects of social dialect and voice pitch on women's judgments.

Investigator
O'Connor, et al. (2014). *Evolution and Human Behavior, 35*, 368–375.

aggressiveness confers a survival or reproductive advantage for members of that species. Hence, genes that promote aggressiveness are more likely to be passed on to the next generation.

Evolutionary psychology began to emerge in the middle to late 1980s. A growing band of evolutionary psychologists (Buss, 1985, 1989; Cosmides & Tooby, 1989; Daly & Wilson, 1985) published widely cited studies on a broad range of topics. These topics included mating preferences, jealousy, aggression, sexual behaviour, decision making, and development. By the mid-1990s, it became clear that psychology was witnessing the birth of its first major new theoretical perspective since the cognitive revolution in the 1950s and 1960s.

Psychology Moves in a Positive Direction: The Positive Psychology Movement

Shortly after Martin Seligman was elected president of the American Psychological Association in 1997, he experienced a profound insight that he characterized as an "epiphany." This pivotal insight came from an unusual source—Seligman's five-year-old daughter, Nikki. She scolded her over-achieving, task-oriented father for being "grumpy" far too often. Provoked by his daughter's criticism, Seligman suddenly realized that his approach to life *was* overly and unnecessarily negative. More important, he recognized that the same assessment could be made of the field of psychology—that it, too, was excessively and needlessly negative in its approach (Seligman, 2003; Seligman, Parks, & Steen, 2006; Seligman, Rashid, & Parks, 2006). This revelation inspired Seligman to launch a new initiative within psychology that came to be known as the *positive psychology movement.*

Seligman went on to argue convincingly that the field of psychology had historically devoted too

Courtesy of Martin Seligman

Martin Seligman

Martin Seligman of the University of Pennsylvania is one of the founders of the *positive psychology movement* in psychology.

much attention to pathology, weakness, and damage, and ways to heal suffering. He acknowledged that this approach had yielded valuable insights and progress. But he argued that it also resulted in an unfortunate neglect of the forces that make life worth living. Seligman convened a series of informal meetings with influential psychologists and then more formal conferences to gradually outline the philosophy and goals of positive psychology. Other major architects of the positive psychology movement have included Mihaly Csikszentmihalyi (1990, 2000), Christopher Peterson (2000), and Barbara Fredrickson (2002). Emphasizing some of the same themes as humanism, positive psychology seeks to shift the field's focus away from negative experiences (Downey & Chang, 2014). Thus, *positive psychology uses theory and research to better understand the positive, adaptive, creative, and fulfilling aspects of human existence.*

The emerging field of positive psychology has three areas of interest (Seligman, 2003). The first is the study of *positive subjective experiences,* or positive emotions, such as happiness, love, gratitude, contentment, and hope. The second focus is on *positive individual traits*—that is, personal strengths and virtues. Theorists are working to identify, classify, and analyze the origins of human strengths and virtues, such as courage, perseverance, nurturance, tolerance, creativity, integrity, and kindness. The third area of interest is in *positive institutions and communities*. Here the focus is on how societies can foster civil discourse, strong families, healthy work environments, and supportive neighbourhood communities. As we will see in Chapter 16, the positive psychology movement has also led to the development of interventions and exercises designed to promote well-being (e.g., Mongrain & Anselmo-Matthews, 2012).

Our review of psychology's past has shown the field's evolution (an Illustrated Overview of Psychology's History can be found on pages 16–17). We have seen psychology develop from philosophical speculation into a rigorous science committed to research. We have seen how a highly visible professional arm involved in mental health services emerged from this science. We have seen how psychology's focus on physiology is rooted in its 19th-century origins. We have seen how and why psychologists began conducting research on lower animals. We have seen how psychology has evolved from the study of mind and body to the study of behaviour. And we have seen how the investigation of mind and body has been welcomed back into the mainstream of modern psychology. We have seen how various theoretical schools have defined the scope and mission of psychology in different ways. We have seen how psychology's interests have expanded and become increasingly diverse. Above all else, we have seen that psychology is a growing, evolving intellectual enterprise.

Psychology's history is already rich, but its story has barely begun. The century or so that has elapsed since Wilhelm Wundt put psychology on a scientific footing is only an eye-blink of time in human history. What has been discovered during those years, and what remains unknown, is the subject of the rest of this book.

Psychology Today: Vigorous and Diversified

We began this chapter with an informal description of what psychology is about. Now that you have a feel for how psychology has developed, you can better appreciate a definition that does justice to the field's modern diversity: *Psychology* is the science that studies behaviour and the physiological and cognitive processes that underlie it, and it is the profession that applies the accumulated knowledge of this science to practical problems.

Psychology's vigorous presence in modern society is also demonstrated by the great variety of settings in which psychologists work. Psychologists were once found almost exclusively in the halls of academia. Today, however, colleges and universities are the primary work setting for less than one-third of North American psychologists. The remaining two-thirds work in hospitals, clinics, police departments, research institutes, government agencies, business and industry, schools, nursing homes, counselling centres, and private practice. A recent survey by the Canadian Psychological Association of almost 4500 masters (M.A.) and doctoral (Ph.D.) graduates (Canadian Psychological Association, 2016; Votta-Bleeker, Tiessen, & Murdoch, 2016) illustrates the variety of work settings for those

holding graduate degrees in psychology in Canada (see Table 1.2). Over one-third of the respondents were working in independent practice, with the next largest group working in academia. Hospital/health care and school/education were the next largest settings. Table 1.2 also provides details regarding the types of duties assumed by graduates in those work settings, with treatment, assessment, education, research, and administration accounting for the largest proportions of the work activities.

Clearly, contemporary psychology is a multifaceted field, a fact that is especially apparent when we consider the many areas of specialization within psychology today. Let's look at the current areas of specialization in both the science and the profession of psychology.

Research Areas in Psychology

Although most psychologists receive broad training that provides them with knowledge about many areas of psychology, they usually specialize when it comes to doing research. Such specialization is necessary because the subject matter of psychology has become so vast over the years. Today it is virtually impossible for anyone to stay abreast of the new research in all specialties. Specialization is also necessary because specific skills and training are required to do research in some areas.

The nine research areas in modern psychology are (1) developmental psychology, (2) social psychology, (3) experimental psychology, (4) behavioural neuroscience/biological psychology, (5) cognitive psychology, (6) personality, (7) psychometrics, (8) educational psychology, and (9) health psychology. Figure 1.5 describes these areas briefly and shows the percentage of research psychologists in the APA who identify each area as their primary interest. As you can see, social psychology and developmental psychology have become especially active areas of research.

Key Learning Goals

▶ Discuss the growth of psychology, and identify the most common work settings for contemporary psychologists.

▶ List and describe the major research areas and professional specialties in psychology.

reality check

Misconception
Psychology is the study of the mind.

Reality
When the term was coined in the 16th century, *psychology* did refer to the study of the mind, but the term's original meaning is much too narrow today. Since the 19th century, scientific psychology has focused heavily on physiological processes, and the 20th century brought a new focus on overt behaviour. Modern psychology encompasses the study of behaviour and the mental and physiological processes that regulate behaviour.

Table 1.2

Work Settings for Those Holding Graduate Degrees in Psychology in Canada

This table presents the current or recent work settings reported by those with masters or doctoral degrees in psychology responding to a 2015 survey developed by the Canadian Psychological Association.

WORK SETTINGS*	PERCENTAGE (%)	TOTAL NUMBER
Academia	26.9	1212
Independent practice—solo	23.6	1062
Independent practice—group	12.2	549
Hospital/health care	25.1	1130
School/education	13.7	616
Government	7.3	330
Private sector	5.6	254
Research	5.5	249
Corrections	2.4	108
Military	0.7	34
Community	3.7	169
Not-for-profit/non-governmental organization	5.5	247
Other	4.7	211

WORK ACTIVITIES AND TOTAL TIME	PERCENTAGE (%)
Treatment	22.6
Assessment	15.4
Education/teaching	11.6
Research	10.9
Management/administration	10.2
Consultation	7.8
Other activities	7.3
Supervision	5.7
Development or design	3.5
Program evaluation	3.0
Public policy	2.0

*Total exceeds 100% due to option to select multiple responses.

Source: Votta-Bleeker, E., Tiessen, M., & Murdoch, M. (2016). A snapshot of Canada's psychology graduates: Initial analysis of the 2015 Psychology Graduates Survey. *Canadian Psychology*, 57, 172–180. http://dx.doi.org/10.1037/cap0000059. Copyright © 2016 by the American Psychological Association.

Professional Specialties in Psychology

Applied psychology consists of four clearly identified areas of specialization: (1) clinical psychology, (2) counselling psychology, (3) educational and school psychology, and (4) industrial and organizational psychology. Descriptions of these specialties can be found in Figure 1.5, along with the percentage of professional psychologists in the APA who are working in each area. As the graphic indicates, clinical psychology is the most prominent and widely practised professional specialty in the field.

The data in Figures 1.5 and 1.6 are based on APA members' reports of their single, principal area of specialization. However, many psychologists work on both research and application. Some academic psychologists work as consultants, therapists, and counsellors on a part-time basis. Similarly, some applied psychologists conduct basic research on issues related to their specialty. For example, many clinical psychologists are involved in research on the nature and causes of abnormal behaviour.

Some people are confused about the difference between clinical psychology and psychiatry. The confusion is understandable, as both clinical psychologists and psychiatrists are involved in analyzing and treating psychological disorders. Although some overlap exists between the two professions, the training and educational requirements for the

AREA	FOCUS OF RESEARCH
Developmental psychology	Looks at human development across the life span. Developmental psychology once focused primarily on child development, but today devotes a great deal of research to adolescence, adulthood, and old age.
Social psychology	Focuses on interpersonal behaviour and the role of social forces in governing behaviour. Typical topics include attitude formation, attitude change, prejudice, conformity, attraction, aggression, intimate relationships, and behaviour in groups.
Educational psychology	Studies how people learn and the best ways to teach them. Examines curriculum design, teacher training, achievement testing, student motivation, classroom diversity, and other aspects of the educational process.
Health psychology	Focuses on how psychological factors relate to the promotion and maintenance of physical health and the causation, prevention, and treatment of illness.
Behavioural neuroscience	Examines the influence of genetic factors on behaviour and the role of the nervous system, endocrine system, bodily chemicals, and especially the brain in the regulation of behaviour.
Experimental psychology	Encompasses the traditional core of topics that psychology focused on heavily in its first half-century as a science: sensation, perception, learning, conditioning, motivation, and emotion. The name *experimental psychology* is somewhat misleading, as this is not the only area in which experiments are done. Psychologists working in all the areas listed here conduct experiments.
Cognitive psychology	Focuses on "higher" mental processes, such as memory, reasoning, information processing, language, problem solving, decision making, and creativity.
Psychometrics	Is concerned with the measurement of behaviour and capacities, usually through the development of psychological tests. Psychometrics is involved with the design of tests to assess personality, intelligence, and a wide range of abilities. It is also concerned with the development of new techniques for statistical analysis.
Personality	Is interested in describing and understanding individuals' consistency in behaviour, which represents their personality. This area of interest is also concerned with the factors that shape personality and with personality assessment.

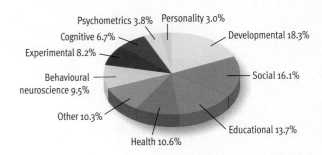

Figure 1.5

Major research areas in contemporary psychology. Most research psychologists specialize in one of the nine broad areas described here. The figures in the pie chart reflect the percentage of academic and research psychologists belonging to the APA who identify each area as their primary interest.

Source: Based on data published by the American Psychological Association/© 2017 Cengage Learning.

reality check

Misconception

Psychology and psychiatry are largely the same.

Reality

Psychiatry is a branch of medicine that has always focused almost exclusively on the treatment of mental disorders. Psychology is an academic field that is vastly broader in scope, focusing on learning, perception, human development, memory, intelligence, and social behaviour, although it does have a clinical arm concerned with mental disorders. Psychologists and psychiatrists get very different kinds of training, earn different degrees, and tend to have different approaches to the treatment of mental illness (see Chapter 16).

two are quite different. Clinical psychologists go to graduate school to earn a doctoral degree in order to enjoy full status in their profession. Psychiatrists go to medical school for their postgraduate education, where they receive general training in medicine and earn an M.D. degree. They then specialize by completing residency training in psychiatry at a hospital. Clinical psychologists and psychiatrists also differ in the way they tend to approach the treatment of mental disorders, as we will see in Chapter 16. To summarize, *psychiatry* is a branch of medicine concerned with the diagnosis and treatment of psychological problems and disorders. In contrast, clinical psychology takes a nonmedical approach to such problems.

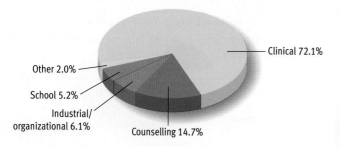

Other 2.0%

School 5.2%

Industrial/
organizational 6.1%

Counselling 14.7%

Clinical 72.1%

Figure 1.6
Principal professional specialties in contemporary psychology.
Most psychologists who deliver professional services to the public specialize in one of the four areas described here. The figures in the pie chart reflect the percentage of APA members delivering professional services who identify each area as their chief specialty.

Source: Source: Based on data published by the American Psychological Association/ © 2017 Cengage Learning.

SPECIALTY	FOCUS OF PROFESSIONAL PRACTICE
Clinical psychology	Clinical psychologists are concerned with the evaluation, diagnosis, and treatment of individuals with psychological disorders, as well as treatment of less severe behavioural and emotional problems. Principal activities include interviewing clients, psychological testing, and providing group or individual psychotherapy.
Counselling psychology	Counselling psychology overlaps with clinical psychology in that specialists in both areas engage in similar activities—interviewing, testing, and providing therapy. However, counselling psychologists usually work with a somewhat different clientele, providing assistance to people struggling with everyday problems of moderate severity. Thus, they often specialize in family, marital, or career counselling.
Educational and school psychology	Educational psychologists work to improve curriculum design, achievement testing, teacher training, and other aspects of the educational process. School psychologists usually work in elementary or secondary schools, where they test and counsel children having difficulties in school and aid parents and teachers in solving school-related problems.
Industrial and organizational psychology	Psychologists in this area perform a wide variety of tasks in the world of business and industry. These tasks include running human resources departments, working to improve staff morale and attitudes, striving to increase job satisfaction and productivity, examining organizational structures and procedures, and making recommendations for improvements.

Putting It in Perspective: Seven Key Themes

Key Learning Goals

▶ Understand the text's three unifying themes relating to psychology as a field of study.

▶ Understand the text's four unifying themes relating to psychology's subject matter.

In this book we will try to help you make your way through the vast scientific literature that has grown up in psychology. In the pages ahead, you will be introduced to many areas of research and a multitude of ideas, concepts, and principles. Fortunately, ideas are not all created equal: Some are far more important than others. In this section, we will highlight seven fundamental themes that will reappear in a number of variations as we move from one area of psychology to another in this text. You have already met some of these key ideas in our review of psychology's past and present. Now we will isolate them and highlight their significance. In the remainder of the book, these ideas serve as organizing themes to provide threads of continuity across chapters and to help you see the connections among the various areas of research in psychology.

In studying psychology, you are learning about both behaviour and the scientific discipline that investigates it. Accordingly, our seven themes come in two sets. The first set consists of statements highlighting crucial aspects of psychology as a way of thinking and as a field of study. The second set consists of broad generalizations about psychology's subject matter: behaviour and the cognitive and physiological processes that underlie it.

Themes Related to Psychology as a Field of Study

Looking at psychology as a field of study, we see three crucial ideas: (1) psychology is empirical, (2) psychology is theoretically diverse, and (3) psychology evolves in a sociohistorical context. Let's look at each of these ideas in more detail.

Theme 1: Psychology Is Empirical

Everyone tries to understand behaviour. Most of us have our own personal answers to questions such as why some people are hard workers, why some are overweight, and why others stay in demeaning relationships. If all of us are amateur psychologists, what makes scientific psychology different? The critical difference is that psychology is empirical. This aspect of psychology is fundamental, and virtually every page of this book reflects it.

What do we mean by empirical? *Empiricism* is the premise that knowledge should be acquired through observation. This premise is crucial to the scientific method that psychology embraced in the late 19th century. To say that psychology is empirical means that its conclusions are based on direct observation rather than on reasoning, speculation, traditional beliefs, or common sense. The empirical approach requires a certain attitude—a healthy brand of skepticism. Empiricism is a tough taskmaster. It demands data and documentation. Psychologists' commitment to empiricism means that they must learn to think critically about generalizations concerning behaviour.

Theme 2: Psychology Is Theoretically Diverse

Although psychology is based on observation, a string of unrelated observations would not be terribly enlightening. Psychologists do not set out to just collect isolated facts; they seek to explain and understand what they observe. To achieve these goals they must construct theories. A *theory* is a system of interrelated ideas used to explain a set of observations. In other words, a theory links apparently unrelated observations and tries to explain them.

Our review of psychology's past should have made one thing abundantly clear: Psychology is marked by theoretical diversity. Why do we have so many competing points of view? One reason is that no single theory can adequately explain everything that is known about behaviour. Sometimes different theories focus on different aspects of behaviour—that is, different collections of observations. Sometimes there is simply more than one way to look at something. Contemporary psychologists increasingly recognize that theoretical diversity is a strength rather than a weakness.

Theme 3: Psychology Evolves in a Sociohistorical Context

Science is often seen as an "ivory tower" undertaking, isolated from the ebb and flow of everyday life. In reality, however, psychology and other sciences do not exist in a cultural vacuum. Interconnections exist between what happens in psychology and

what happens in society at large (Altman, 1990; Braginsky, 1985; Danziger, 1990). Trends, issues, and values in society influence psychology's evolution. Similarly, progress in psychology affects trends, issues, and values in society. To put it briefly, psychology develops in a *sociohistorical* (social and historical) context.

Psychology's past is filled with examples of how social trends have left their imprint on psychology. For example, Sigmund Freud's groundbreaking ideas emerged out of a specific sociohistorical context. Cultural values in Freud's era encouraged the suppression of sexuality. As a result, people tended to feel guilty about their sexual urges to a much greater extent than is common today. This situation clearly contributed to Freud's emphasis on unconscious sexual conflicts. As another example, consider how World War II sparked the rapid growth of psychology as a profession.

If we reverse our viewpoint, we can see that psychology has in turn left its mark on society. Consider, for instance, the pervasive role of mental testing in modern society. Your own career success may depend in part on how well you weave your way through a complex maze of intelligence and achievement tests made possible (to the regret of some) by research in psychology. As another example of psychology's impact on society, consider the influence that various theorists have had on parenting styles. Trends in child-rearing practices have been shaped by the ideas of John B. Watson, Sigmund Freud, B. F. Skinner, and Carl Rogers—not to mention a host of other psychologists yet to be discussed. In short, society and psychology influence each other in complex ways. In the chapters to come, we will frequently have occasion to notice this dynamic relationship.

Social trends and values have shaped the evolution of psychology and progress in psychology has left its mark on everyday life in our society. For example, standardized psychological tests are pervasive in our educational system, where they exert great influence over students' lives.

The Evolution of Psychology

Themes Related to Psychology's Subject Matter

Looking at psychology's subject matter, we see four additional crucial ideas: (4) behaviour is determined by multiple causes, (5) behaviour is shaped by cultural heritage, (6) heredity and environment jointly influence behaviour, and (7) people's experience of the world is highly subjective.

Theme 4: Behaviour Is Determined by Multiple Causes

As psychology has matured, it has provided more and more information about the forces that govern behaviour. This growing knowledge has led to a deeper appreciation of a simple but important fact: Behaviour is exceedingly complex, and most aspects of behaviour are determined by multiple causes.

Although the complexity of behaviour may seem self-evident, people usually think in terms of single causes. Thus, they offer explanations such as "Andrea flunked out of school because she is lazy." Or they assert that "teenage pregnancies are increasing because of all the sex in the media." Single-cause explanations are sometimes accurate as far as they go, but they usually are incomplete. In general, psychologists find that behaviour is governed by a complex network of interacting factors, an idea referred to as the *multifactorial causation of behaviour*.

As you proceed through this book, you will learn that complexity of causation is the rule rather than the exception. If we expect to understand behaviour, we usually have to take into account multiple determinants.

Theme 5: Behaviour Is Shaped by Cultural Heritage

Among the multiple determinants of human behaviour, cultural factors are particularly prominent. Just as psychology evolves in a sociohistorical context, so, too, do individuals. People's cultural backgrounds exert considerable influence over their behaviour. What is culture? It's the human-made part of the environment. More specifically, **culture refers to the widely shared customs, beliefs, values, norms, institutions, and other products of a community that are transmitted socially across generations.**

Culture is a broad construct, encompassing everything from a society's legal system to its assumptions about family roles, from its dietary habits to its political ideals, from its technology to its attitudes about time, from its modes of dress to its spiritual beliefs, and from its art and music to its unspoken rules about sexual liaisons. We tend to think of culture as belonging to entire societies or broad ethnic groups within societies—which it does—but the concept can also be applied to small groups (a tiny Aboriginal tribe in Australia, for example) and to non-ethnic groups (LGBTQ culture, for instance).

Although the influence of culture is everywhere, generalizations about cultural groups must always be tempered by the realization that great diversity also exists within any society or ethnic group. Caveats aside, if we hope to achieve a sound understanding of human behaviour, we need to consider cultural determinants (Heine & Buchtel, 2009; Oyserman & Lee, 2008; Sue et al., 2009).

Theme 6: Heredity and Environment Jointly Influence Behaviour

Are individuals who they are—athletic or artistic, quick-tempered or calm, shy or outgoing, energetic or laid-back—because of their genetic inheritance or because of their upbringing? This question about the importance of nature versus nurture, or heredity versus environment, has been asked in one form or another since ancient times. Historically, the nature-versus-nurture question was framed as an all-or-none proposition. In other words, theorists argued that personal traits and abilities are governed either entirely by heredity or entirely by environment. John B. Watson, for instance, asserted that personality and ability depend almost exclusively on an individual's environment. In contrast, Sir Francis Galton, a pioneer in mental testing, maintained that personality and ability depend almost entirely on genetic inheritance.

Today, most psychologists agree that heredity and environment are both important. A century of research has shown that genetics and experience jointly influence an individual's intelligence, temperament, personality, and susceptibility to many psychological disorders (Manuck & McCaffery, 2014; Rutter, 2012). If we ask whether individuals are born or made, psychology's answer is "Both." This does not mean that nature versus nurture is a dead issue. Lively debate about the relative influence of genetics and experience continues unabated. Furthermore, psychologists are actively seeking to understand the complex ways in which genetic inheritance and experience interact to mould behaviour.

Theme 7: People's Experience of the World Is Highly Subjective

Even elementary perception—for example, of sights and sounds—is not a passive process. People actively process incoming stimulation, selectively focusing on some aspects of that stimulation while ignoring others. Moreover, they impose organization on the stimuli that they pay attention to. These tendencies combine to make perception personalized and subjective.

The subjectivity of perception was demonstrated nicely in a classic study by Hastorf and Cantril (1954). They showed students at Princeton and Dartmouth universities a film of a recent football game between the two schools. The students were told to watch for rules infractions. Both groups saw the same film, but the Princeton students "saw" the Dartmouth players engage in twice as many infractions as the Dartmouth students "saw." The investigators concluded that the game "actually was many different games and that each version of the events that transpired was just as 'real' to a particular person as other versions were to other people" (Hastorf & Cantril, 1954). In this study, the subjects' perceptions were swayed by their motives. It shows how people sometimes see what they *want* to see. Other studies reveal that people also tend to see what they expect to see (e.g., Kelley, 1950).

Human subjectivity is precisely what the scientific method is designed to counteract. In using the scientific approach, psychologists strive to make their observations as objective as possible. In some respects, overcoming subjectivity is what science is all about. Left to their own subjective experience, people might still believe that the earth is flat and that the sun revolves around it. Thus, psychologists are committed to the scientific approach because they believe it is the most reliable route to accurate knowledge.

Now that you have been introduced to the text's organizing themes, let's turn to an example of how psychological research can be applied to the challenges of everyday life. In our first Personal Application, we'll focus on a subject that should be highly relevant to you: how to be a successful student. In the Critical Thinking Application that follows it, we discuss the nature and importance of critical thinking skills.

How can you critically evaluate these claims? If your first thought was that you need more information, good for you, because you are already showing an aptitude for critical thinking. Some additional information about gender differences in cognitive abilities is presented in Chapter 11 of this text. You also need to develop the habit of asking good questions, such as "Are there alternative explanations for these results? Are there contradictory data?" Let's briefly consider each of these questions.

Are there alternative explanations for gender differences in spatial skills? Well, there certainly are other explanations for males' superiority on most spatial tasks. For example, one could attribute this finding to the

concept check 1.3

Understanding the Seven Key Themes

Check your understanding of the seven key themes introduced in the chapter by matching the vignettes with the themes they exemplify. You'll find the answers in Appendix A.

Themes

_____ **1.** Psychology is empirical.

_____ **2.** Psychology is theoretically diverse.

_____ **3.** Psychology evolves in a sociohistorical context.

_____ **4.** Behaviour is determined by multiple causes.

_____ **5.** Behaviour is shaped by cultural heritage.

_____ **6.** Heredity and environment jointly influence behaviour.

_____ **7.** People's experience of the world is highly subjective.

Vignettes

_____ **a.** Several or more theoretical models of emotion have contributed to our overall understanding of the dynamics of emotion.

_____ **b.** According to the stress-vulnerability model, some people are at greater risk for developing certain psychological disorders for genetic reasons. Whether these people actually develop the disorders depends on how much stress they experience in their work, families, or other areas of their lives.

_____ **c.** Physical health and illness seem to be influenced by a complex constellation of psychological, biological, and social system variables.

_____ **d.** One of the difficulties in investigating the effects of drugs on consciousness is that individuals tend to have different experiences with a given drug because of their different expectations.

gender-typed activities that males are encouraged to engage in more than females, such as playing with building blocks, Lego sets, Lincoln Logs, and various types of construction sets, as well as a host of spatially oriented video games. These gender-typed activities appear to provide boys with more practice than girls on most types of spatial tasks (Voyer, Nolan, & Voyer, 2000), and experience with spatial activities appears to enhance spatial skills (Lizarraga & Ganuza, 2003). For example, one study conducted by researchers at the University of Toronto found that just ten hours of playing an action video game could produce substantial gains in spatial ability and significantly reduce gender differences in spatial attention and mental rotation ability (Feng, Spence, & Pratt, 2007). If we can explain gender differences in spatial abilities in terms of disparities in the everyday activities of contemporary males and females, we may have no need to appeal to natural selection.

Are there data that run counter to the evolutionary explanation for modern gender differences in spatial skills? Again,

Improving Academic Performance

Today, many students enter college and university with poor study skills and habits—and it's not entirely their fault. The educational system generally provides minimal instruction on good study techniques. In this first Application, we will try to remedy this situation to some extent by reviewing some insights that psychology offers on how to improve academic performance. We will discuss how to promote better study habits, how to enhance reading efforts, how to get more out of lectures, and how to improve test-taking strategies. You may also want to jump ahead and read the Personal Application for Chapter 7, which focuses on how to improve everyday memory.

Developing Sound Study Habits

Effective study is crucial to success in college and university. Although you may run into a few classmates who boast about getting good grades without studying, you can be sure that if they perform well on exams, they do study. Students who claim otherwise simply want to be viewed as extremely bright rather than as studious.

Learning can be immensely gratifying, but studying usually involves hard work. The first step toward effective study habits is to face up to this reality. You don't have to feel guilty if you don't look forward to studying. Most students don't. Once you accept the premise that studying doesn't come naturally, it should be apparent that you need to set up an organized program to promote adequate study. According to Siebert (1995), such a program should include the following considerations:

1. Set up a schedule for studying. If you wait until the urge to study strikes you, you may still be waiting when the exam rolls around.

Thus, it is important to allocate definite times to studying. Review your various time obligations (work, chores, and so on) and figure out in advance when you can study. When allotting certain times to studying, keep in mind that you need to be wide awake and alert. Be realistic about how long you can study at one time before you wear down from fatigue. Allow time for study breaks—they can revive sagging concentration.

It's important to write down your study schedule. A written schedule serves as a reminder and increases your commitment to following it. This approach to scheduling should help you avoid cramming for exams at the last minute. Cramming is an ineffective study strategy for most students (Underwood, 1961; Zechmeister & Nyberg, 1982). It will strain your memorization capabilities, it can tax your energy level, and it may stoke the fires of test anxiety.

In planning your weekly schedule, try to avoid the tendency to put off working on major tasks such as term papers and reports. Time-management experts such as Alan Lakein (1996) point out that many people tend to tackle simple, routine tasks first, saving larger tasks for later when they supposedly will have more time. This common tendency leads many individuals to repeatedly delay working on major assignments until it's too late to do a good job. A good way to avoid this trap is to break major assignments down into smaller component tasks that can be scheduled individually.

2. Find a place to study where you can concentrate. Where you study is also important. The key is to find a place where distractions are likely to be minimal. Most people cannot study effectively while the TV or stereo is on or while other people are talking. Don't depend on willpower to carry you through such distractions. It's much easier to plan ahead and avoid the distractions altogether. In fact, you would be wise to set up one or two specific places to be used solely for study (Hettich, 1998).

3. Reward your studying. One reason that it is so difficult to be motivated to study regularly is that the payoffs often lie in the distant future. The ultimate reward, a degree, may be years away. Even short-term rewards, such as an A in the course, may be weeks or months away. To combat this problem, it helps to give yourself immediate, tangible rewards for studying, such as a snack, TV show, or phone call to a friend. Thus, you should set realistic study goals for yourself and then reward yourself when you meet them. The systematic manipulation of rewards involves harnessing the principles of *behaviour modification* described by B. F. Skinner and other behavioural psychologists. These principles are covered in the Chapter 6 Personal Application.

Improving Your Reading

Much of your study time is spent reading and absorbing information. The keys to improving reading comprehension are to preview reading assignments section by section, work hard to actively process the meaning of the information, strive to

Some locations are far more conducive to successful studying than others.

identify the key ideas of each paragraph, and carefully review these key ideas after each section. Modern textbooks often contain a variety of learning aids that you can use to improve your reading. If a book provides a chapter outline or learning objectives, don't ignore them. These advance organizers can encourage deeper processing and enhance your encoding of information (Marsh & Butler, 2013). In other words, they can help you recognize the important points in the chapter. *Graphic organizers* (such as the Concept Charts available at the end of each chapter) can also enhance understanding of text material (Nist & Holschuh, 2000). A lot of effort and thought go into formulating these and other textbook learning aids. It is wise to take advantage of them.

Another important issue related to textbook reading is whether and how to mark up one's reading assignments. Many students deceive themselves into thinking that they are studying by running a marker through a few sentences here and there in their text. If they do so without thoughtful selectivity, they are simply turning a textbook into a colouring book. This situation probably explains why a recent review of the evidence on highlighting reported that it appears to have limited value (Dunlosky et al., 2013). That said, the review also noted that the value of highlighting probably depends on the skill with which it is executed. Consistent with this conclusion, other experts have asserted that highlighting textbook material is a useful strategy—if students are reasonably effective in focusing on the main ideas in the material and if they subsequently review what they have highlighted (Caverly, Orlando, & Mullen, 2000; Hayati & Shariatifar, 2009).

In theory, when executed effectively, highlighting should foster active reading, improve reading comprehension, and reduce the amount of material that one has to review later (Van Blerkom, 2012). The key to effective text marking is to identify (and highlight) only the main ideas, key supporting details, and technical terms (Daiek & Anter, 2004). Most textbooks are carefully crafted such that every paragraph has a purpose for being there. Try to find the sentence or two that best captures the purpose of each paragraph. Text marking is a delicate balancing act. If you highlight too little of the content, you are not identifying enough of the key ideas. But if you highlight too much of the content, you probably are not engaging in active reading and you are not going to succeed in making the important information stand out (Dunlosky et al., 2013). Overmarking appears to undermine the utility of highlighting more than undermarking.

Getting More Out of Lectures

Although lectures are sometimes boring and tedious, it is a simple fact that poor class attendance is associated with poor grades. For example, in one study, Lindgren (1969) found that absences from class were much more common among "unsuccessful" students (grade average C– or below) than among "successful" students (grade average B or above), as shown in Figure 1.7. Even when you have an instructor who delivers hard-to-follow lectures, it is still important to go to class. If nothing else, you can get a feel for how the instructor thinks, which can help you anticipate the content of exams and respond in the manner expected by your professor.

Fortunately, most lectures are reasonably coherent. Studies indicate that attentive note-taking is associated with enhanced learning and performance in university classes (Titsworth & Kiewra, 2004; Williams & Eggert, 2002). However, research also shows that many students' lecture notes are surprisingly incomplete, with the average student often recording less than 40 percent of the crucial ideas in a lecture (Armbruster, 2000). Thus, the key to getting more out of lectures is to stay motivated, stay attentive, and expend the effort to make your notes as complete as possible. Books on study skills (Longman & Atkinson, 2002; Sotiriou, 2002) offer a number of suggestions on how to take good-quality lecture notes, some of which are summarized here:

- Extracting information from lectures requires *active listening*. Focus your full attention on the speaker. Try to anticipate what's coming and search for deeper meanings.
- When course material is especially complex, it is a good idea to prepare for the lecture by *reading ahead* on the scheduled subject in your text. Then you have less brand-new information to digest.
- You are not supposed to be a human tape recorder. Insofar as possible, try to

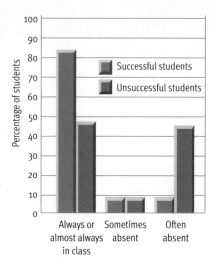

Figure 1.7
Attendance and grades. When Lindgren (1969) compared the class attendance of successful students (B average or above) and unsuccessful students (C– average or below), he found a clear association between poor attendance and poor grades.

Source: Copyright © 1969 by Henry Clay Lindgren. Adapted by permission of H.C. Lindgren.

write down the lecturer's thoughts *in your own words*. Doing so forces you to organize the ideas in a way that makes sense to you. In taking notes, pay attention to clues about what is most important. These clues may range from subtle hints, such as an instructor repeating a point, to not-so-subtle hints, such as an instructor saying, "You'll run into this again."

- *Asking questions* during lectures can be helpful. Doing so keeps you actively involved in the lecture and allows you to clarify points that you may have misunderstood. Many students are more bashful about asking questions than they should be. They don't realize that most professors welcome questions.

In summary, sound study skills and habits are crucial to academic success. Intelligence alone won't do the job (although it certainly helps). Good academic skills do not develop overnight. They are acquired gradually, so be patient with yourself. Fortunately, tasks such as reading textbooks, writing papers, and taking tests get easier with practice. Ultimately, we think you'll find that the rewards—knowledge, a sense of accomplishment, and progress toward a degree—are worth the effort.

Developing Critical Thinking Skills: An Introduction

Key Learning Goal

▶ Explain the nature of critical thinking, and evaluate evolutionary explanations for gender differences in spatial abilities.

If you ask any group of professors, parents, employers, or politicians, "What is the most important outcome of an education?" the most popular answer is likely to be "the development of the ability to think critically." *Critical thinking* is the use of cognitive skills and strategies that increase the probability of a desirable outcome. Such outcomes would include good career choices, effective decisions in the workplace, wise investments, and so forth. In the long run, critical thinkers should have more desirable outcomes than people who are not skilled in critical thinking (Halpern, 1998, 2003). Critical thinking is purposeful, reasoned, goal-directed thinking that involves solving problems, formulating inferences, working with probabilities, and making carefully thought-out decisions. Here are some of the skills exhibited by critical thinkers:

- They understand and use the principles of scientific investigation. (How can the effectiveness of punishment as a disciplinary procedure be determined?)
- They apply the rules of formal and informal logic. (If most people disapprove of sex sites on the Internet, why are these sites so popular?)
- They carefully evaluate the quality of information. (Can I trust the claims made by this politician?)
- They analyze arguments for the soundness of the conclusions. (Does the rise in drug use mean that a stricter drug policy is needed?)

The topic of thinking has a long history in psychology, dating back to Wilhelm Wundt in the 19th century. Modern cognitive psychologists have found that a useful model of critical thinking has at least two components: (1) knowledge of the skills of critical thinking—the *cognitive component,* and (2) the attitude or disposition of a critical thinker—the *emotional or affective component.* Both are needed for effective critical thinking.

The Skills and Attitudes of Critical Thinking

Instruction in critical thinking is based on two assumptions: (1) a set of skills or strategies exists that students can learn to recognize and apply in appropriate contexts; (2) if the skills are applied appropriately, students will become more effective thinkers (Halpern, 2007). Critical thinking skills that would be useful in any context might include understanding how reasons and evidence support or refute conclusions; distinguishing among facts, opinions, and reasoned judgments; using principles of likelihood and uncertainty when thinking about probabilistic events; generating multiple solutions to problems and working systematically toward a desired goal; and understanding how causation is determined. This list provides some typical examples of what is meant by the term *critical thinking skills.* Because these skills are useful in a wide variety of contexts, they are sometimes called *trans-contextual skills.*

It is of little use to know the skills of critical thinking if you are unwilling to exert the hard mental work to use them or if you have a sloppy or careless attitude toward thinking. A critical thinker is willing to plan, flexible in thinking, persistent, able to admit mistakes and make corrections, and mindful of the thinking process. The use of the word *critical* represents the notion of a critique or evaluation of thinking processes and outcomes. It is not meant to be negative (as in a "critical person") but rather to convey that critical thinkers are vigilant about their thinking (Riggio & Halpern, 2006).

The Need to Teach Critical Thinking

Decades of research on instruction in critical thinking have shown that the skills and attitudes of critical thinking need to be deliberately and consciously taught, because they often do not develop by themselves with standard instruction in a content area (Nisbett, 1993). For this reason, each chapter in this text ends with a Critical Thinking Application. The material presented in each of these Critical Thinking Applications relates to the chapter topics, but the focus is on how to think about a particular issue, line of research, or controversy. Because the emphasis is on the thinking process, you may be asked to consider conflicting interpretations of data, judge the credibility of information sources, or generate your own testable hypotheses. The specific critical thinking skills highlighted in each lesson are summarized in a table so that they are easily identified. Some of the skills will show up in multiple chapters because the goal is to help you spontaneously select the appropriate critical thinking skills when you encounter new information. Repeated practice with selected skills across chapters should help you to develop this ability.

An Example

As explained in the main body of the chapter, *evolutionary psychology* is emerging as an influential school of thought. To show you how critical thinking skills can be applied to psychological issues, let's examine the evolutionary explanation of gender differences in spatial talents and then use some critical thinking strategies to evaluate this explanation.

On the average, males tend to perform slightly better than females on most visual-spatial tasks, especially tasks involving mental rotation of images and navigation in space (Halpern, 2000; Silverman & Choi,

Figure 1.8

An example of a spatial task involving mental rotation. Spatial reasoning tasks can be divided into a variety of subtypes. Studies indicate that males perform slightly better than females on most, but not all, spatial tasks. The tasks on which males are superior often involve mentally rotating objects, such as in the problem shown here. In this problem, the person has to figure out which object on the right (A through E) could be a rotation of the object at the left.

Source: Stafford, R. E. (1962). Identical Blocks, Form AA. University Park: Pennsylvania State University, Office of Student Affairs.

2005; see Figure 1.8). Irwin Silverman and his colleagues maintain that these gender differences originated in human evolution as a result of the sex-based division of labour in ancient hunting-and-gathering societies (Silverman & Phillips, 1998; Silverman et al., 2000). According to this analysis, males' superiority in mental rotation and navigation developed because the chore of *hunting* was largely assigned to men over the course of human history, and these skills would have facilitated success on hunting trips (by helping men to traverse long distances, aim projectiles at prey, and so forth) and thus been favoured by natural selection. In contrast, women in ancient societies generally had responsibility for *gathering* food rather than hunting it. This was an efficient division of labour because women spent much of their adult lives pregnant, nursing, or caring for the young and, therefore, could not travel long distances. Hence, Silverman and Eals (1992) hypothesized that females ought to be superior to males on spatial skills that would have facilitated gathering, such as memory for locations, which is exactly what they found in a series of four studies. Thus, evolutionary psychologists explain gender differences in spatial ability—like other aspects of human behaviour—in terms of how such abilities evolved to meet the adaptive pressures faced by our ancestors. See Table 1.3.

Table 1.3

Critical Thinking Skills Discussed in This Application

SKILL	
Looking for alternative explanations for findings and events	In evaluating explanations, the critical thinker explores whether there are other explanations that could also account for the findings or events under scrutiny.
Looking for contradictory evidence	In evaluating the evidence presented on an issue, the critical thinker attempts to look for contradictory evidence that may have been left out of the debate.

the answer is yes. Some scholars who have studied hunting-and-gathering societies suggest that women often travelled long distances to gather food and that women were often involved in hunting (Adler, 1993). In addition, women wove baskets and clothing and worked on other tasks that required spatial thinking (Halpern, 1997). Moreover—think about it—men on long hunting trips obviously needed to develop a good memory for locations or they might never have returned home. So, there is room for some argument about exactly what kinds of adaptive pressures males and females faced in ancient hunting-and-gathering societies.

Thus, you can see how considering alternative explanations and contradictory evidence weakens the evolutionary explanation of gender differences in spatial abilities. The questions we raised about alternative explanations and contradictory data are two generic critical thinking questions that can be asked in a wide variety of contexts. The answers to these questions do *not* prove that evolutionary psychologists are wrong in their explanation of gender differences in visual-spatial skills, but they do *weaken* the evolutionary explanation. In thinking critically about psychological issues, you will see that it makes more sense to talk about the *relative strength of an argument,* as opposed to whether an argument is right or wrong, because we will be dealing with complex issues that rarely lend themselves to being correct or incorrect.

PSYCHOLOGY'S EARLY HISTORY

A new science is born

- Philosophy and physiology are psychology's intellectual parents.
- Psychology's founder was Wilhelm Wundt, who set up the first research lab in 1879 in Germany.
- Wundt argued that psychology should be the scientific study of consciousness.

The battle of the schools begins

- Advocates of *structuralism* argued that psychology should use introspection to analyze consciousness into its basic elements.
- Advocates of *functionalism*, such as William James, argued that psychology should investigate the purposes (or functions) of consciousness.
- Functionalism had a more lasting impact on psychology because it fostered the emergence of behaviourism and applied psychology.

Freud focuses on unconscious forces

- Sigmund Freud's views were controversial but gradually became influential.
- *Psychoanalytic theory* emphasizes unconscious determinants of behaviour and the importance of sexuality.
- According to Freud, the *unconscious* consists of thoughts that one is not aware of but that still influence one's behaviour.

Behaviourism debuts

- *Behaviourism*, founded by John B. Watson, asserted that psychology should study only observable behaviour.

- Behaviourism gradually took hold, and psychology became the scientific study of *behaviour* (instead of *consciousness*).
- Behaviourists stressed the importance of environment over heredity, and pioneered animal research.

Behaviourism flourishes with the work of Skinner

- Boosted by the research of B. F. Skinner, behaviourism reached its peak of influence in the 1950s.
- Like Waston, Skinner emphasized animal rresearch, a strict focus on observable behaviour, and the importance of the environment.
- Skinner generated controversy by arguing that free will is an illusion.

The humanists revolt

- Finding both behaviourism and psychoanalysis unappealing, advocates of *humanism*, such as Carl Rogers and Abraham Maslow, began to gain influence in the 1950s.
- Humanists emphasize the unique qualities of human behaviour and the irrelevance of animal research.
- Humanists take an optimistic view of human nature, stressing humans' freedom and potential for growth.

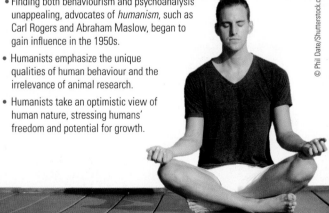

PSYCHOLOGY'S MODERN HISTORY

Psychology becomes a profession

- Professional psychological services to the public were rare in first half of the 20th century.
- However, stimulated by the demands of World War II, *clinical psychology* grew rapidly as a profession, starting in the 1950s.
- Today, psychology includes many professional specialties, such as school psychology, industrial/organizational psychology, and counselling psychology.

Cognition and Neuroscience resurface

- In its early days, psychology emphasized the study of consciousness and physiology, but these topics languished as behaviourism grew dominant.
- During the 1950s and 1960s, advances in research on mental and physiological processes led to renewed interest in cognition and the biological bases of behaviour.

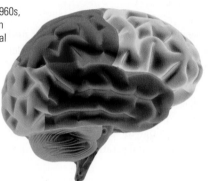

Interest in cultural factors grows

- In the 1980s, Western psychologists developed an increased interest in how culture influences behaviour.
- This trend was stimulated by the increased cultural diversity in Western societies and by growing global interdependence.

Evolutionary psychology gains prominence

- In the 1990s, *evolutionary psychology* emerged as a major new theoretical perspective.
- Evolutionary psychology's premise is that behaviour patterns in a species are the product of evolution, just like anatomical characteristics.
- Evolutionary psychologists argue that *natural selection* favours behaviours that enhance an organism's reproductive success.

Psychology moves in a positive direction

- Arguing that psychology had historically focused too much on pathology and suffering, Martin Seligman launched the *positive psychology* movement in the late 1990s.
- Positive psychology uses theory and research to understand the adaptive, creative, and fulfilling aspects of human experience.

PSYCHOLOGY TODAY

Psychology is the science that studies behaviour and the physiological and cognitive processes that underlie behaviour, and it is the profession that applies this science to practical problems.

Professional specialties

- Clinical psychology
- Counselling psychology
- School psychology
- Industrial/organizational psychology

Research specialties

- Developmental psychology
- Social psychology
- Experimental psychology
- Behavioural neuroscience
- Cognitive psychology
- Personality
- Psychometrics
- Educational psychology
- Health psychology

© iStockphoto.com/Franckreporter

APPLICATIONS

- To foster sound study habits, you should devise a written study schedule, find a place to study where you can concentrate, and use active reading techniques to select the most important ideas from the material you read.
- Good note taking depends on active listening techniques and recording ideas in your own words.
- Critical thinking is the use of cognitive skills and strategies that increase the probability of a desirable outcome.

KEY THEMES

Themes related to psychology as a field of study

Psychology is empirical—it is based on objective observations made through research.

Psychology is theoretically diverse—a variety of perspectives are needed to fully understand behaviour.

Psychology evolves in a sociohistorical context—dense connections exist between what happens in psychology and what happens in society.

Themes related to psychology's subject matter

Behaviour is determined by multiple causes—complex causation is the rule, and single-cause explanations are usually incomplete.

Behaviour is shaped by cultural heritage—cultural factors exert influence over most aspects of behaviour.

Heredity and environment jointly influence behaviour—nature and nurture interactively shape most behavioural traits.

People's experience of the world is highly subjective—people tend to see what they expect to see and what they want to see.

CHAPTER 2

© Explorer/Science Source

The Research Enterprise in Psychology

Themes in this Chapter

Empiricism   Subjectivity

Q uestions, questions, questions—everyone has questions about behaviour. Investigating these questions is what psychology is all about. Some of these questions pop up in everyday life. Many a parent, for example, has wondered whether violent video games could have a harmful effect on their children's behaviour. Other questions explored by psychologists might not occur to most people. For example, you may never have wondered what effects your sleeping habits or IQ could have on your life expectancy or whether the colour of the clothes you wear affects both your own behaviour and the impressions others have of you. Canadian Olympic team members, for example, typically wear red uniforms. While wearing a uniform that symbolizes your country will result in a feeling of pride and a commitment to give your best effort, is it possible that the colour red may have other effects, both on the wearers' own behaviour and on the perceptions that others have of them? We do know that as social observers, we use a wide variety of cues in generating inferences and perceptions of individual people and of groups (Hamilton et al., 2015). Is the colour of our clothing one of these cues? Of course, now that you've been exposed to these questions, you may be curious about the answers!

In the course of this book, you'll find out what psychologists have learned about the questions asked above. Right now we want to call your attention to the most basic question of all—namely, how should we go about investigating questions like these? How do we find answers that are accurate and trustworthy? As noted in Chapter 1, psychology is empirical. Psychologists are committed to addressing questions about behaviour through formal, systematic observation. This commitment to the empirical method is what makes psychology a scientific endeavour. Many people may have beliefs about the effects of playing violent video games based on personal opinion, a feeling of aversion toward violence, a generally permissive attitude toward children's games, anecdotal reports from parents, or other sources. As scientists, however, psychologists withhold judgment on questions like these until they have objective evidence based on valid, reproducible studies.

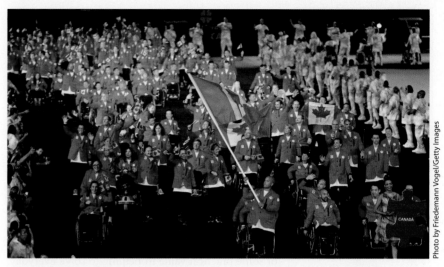

As the 2016 Canadian Olympic team proudly enters into the stadium in Brazil, are other competitors' perceptions of them affected by the colour of their clothing? Does the colour of their clothing affect their own psychological functioning? Research suggests that in some circumstances, including competition, colour can affect performance and perception.

Photo by Friedemann Vogel/Getty Images

In their scientific studies psychologists rely on a large toolkit of research methods because different kinds of questions call for different strategies of investigation. In this chapter, you'll learn about some of the principal methods used by psychologists in their research.

We'll begin our introduction to the research enterprise in psychology by examining the scientific approach to the study of behaviour. From there we'll move to the specific research methods that psychologists use most frequently. Although scientific methods have stood the test of time, individual scientists are human and fallible. For this reason we'll conclude our discussion with a look at some common flaws in research. This section alone can make you a more skilled evaluator of claims that are said to be based on psychological studies. Then, in the Personal Application, you'll learn how to find and read journal articles that report on research. Finally, in the Critical Thinking Application, we'll examine the perils of a type of evidence people are exposed to all the time—anecdotal evidence.

The Scientific Approach to Behaviour

Goals of the Scientific Enterprise

Psychologists and other scientists share three sets of interrelated goals: measurement and description, understanding and prediction, and application and control.

1. *Measurement and description.* Science's commitment to observation requires that an investigator figure out a way to measure the phenomenon under study. For example, if you were interested in the effects of different situations on emotion, you would first have to develop some means of measuring

Key Learning Goals

▶ Describe the goals of the scientific enterprise, and clarify the relationships among theory, hypotheses, and research.

▶ Identify the steps in a scientific investigation, and list the advantages of the scientific approach.

emotions. Thus, the first goal of psychology is to develop measurement techniques that make it possible to describe behaviour clearly and precisely.

2. *Understanding and prediction.* A higher-level goal of science is understanding. Scientists believe that they understand events when they can explain the reasons for the occurrence of the events. To evaluate their understanding, scientists make and test predictions called *hypotheses.* A *hypothesis* is a tentative statement about the relationship between two or more variables. *Variables* are any measurable conditions, events, characteristics, or behaviours that are controlled or observed in a study.

3. *Application and control.* Ultimately, many scientists hope that the information they gather will be of some practical value in helping to solve everyday problems. Once people understand a phenomenon, they often can exert more control over it. Today, the profession of psychology attempts to apply research findings to practical problems in schools, businesses, factories, and mental hospitals. For example, a clinical psychologist might use what we know about typical, everyday emotions to assist individuals suffering from emotional disorders.

How do theories help scientists to achieve their goals? As noted in Chapter 1, psychologists do not set out just to collect isolated facts about relationships between variables. To build toward a better understanding of behaviour, they construct theories. A *theory* is a system of interrelated ideas used to explain a set of observations. By integrating apparently unrelated facts and principles into a coherent whole, theories permit psychologists to make the leap from the *description* of behaviour to the *understanding* of behaviour. Moreover, the enhanced understanding afforded by theories guides future research by generating new predictions and suggesting new lines of inquiry (Higgins, 2004).

A scientific theory must be testable, as the cornerstone of science is its commitment to putting ideas to an empirical test. There is a crucial interplay between theory and research in science. The hypotheses generated through theories are then tested in empirical research. Research allows scientists to provide support for theories and/or to suggest that the theory needs refinement. Publication in scientific journals and presentation of research at academic conferences allow others to evaluate the reliability of the findings by conducting replications of that research. Before scientific articles are published in academic journals, they go through a rigorous evaluation by experts in the field—this is referred to as *peer review.* According to Jennings (2015), peer review and replication are the essential features of error control in science. In the peer review process, scientific articles submitted for publication are reviewed and evaluated by journal editors and other experts in the field. Evaluations obtained through peer review are the primary determinants of whether or not the article will be published.

Recently, there has been discussion regarding the need for increased attention to the reproducibility of findings in psychology (Fiedler & Schwarz, 2016; Franco et al., 2016; Gilbert et al., 2016; Maxwell et al., 2015) and concern over the difficulty in replicating some important research findings (Open Science Collaboration, 2015). These recent concerns are referred to as the "replication" or "reproducibility crisis" (American Psychological Association, 2015). These concerns have led to calls for an increased focus on cumulative findings (Open Science Collaboration, 2015). Increasingly, scientific journals and organizations in psychology are underscoring the importance of this in the publication of research findings and in developing a set of best research practices to be used in conducting research (e.g., Finkel et al., 2015; Funder, 2014; Funder et al., 2014; SPSP Board of Directors, 2016;).

Steps in a Scientific Investigation

Curiosity about a question provides the point of departure for any kind of investigation, scientific or otherwise. Scientific investigations, however, are *systematic.* They follow an orderly pattern described here and illustrated in Figure 2.1. Let's look at how this standard series of steps was followed in a study of the implications of colour on psychological functioning conducted by Elliot, Greitemeyer, and Pazda (2012). The objective of the research was to determine if female participants at a university would choose to wear red clothing when anticipating an interaction with an attractive male student.

Step 1: Formulate a Testable Hypothesis

The first step in a scientific investigation is to translate a theory or an intuitive idea into a testable hypothesis. Although there has long been an extensive popular literature on how colours affect behaviour, this literature has mostly been based on speculation rather than sound empirical research. However, Andrew Elliot and Markus Maier (2012, 2014) have formulated a theory of how colour might influence behaviour. According to their theory, colours can have automatic, unconscious effects on behaviour. The theory asserts that these effects are probably rooted in two basic sources. First, people

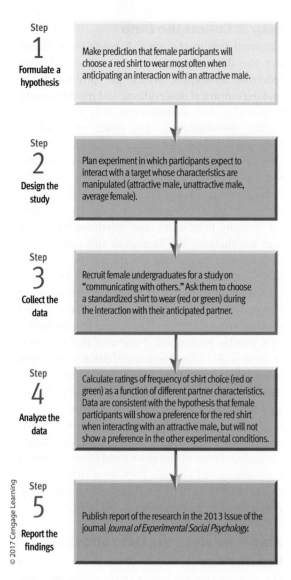

Step 1
Formulate a hypothesis

Make prediction that female participants will choose a red shirt to wear most often when anticipating an interaction with an attractive male.

Step 2
Design the study

Plan experiment in which participants expect to interact with a target whose characteristics are manipulated (attractive male, unattractive male, average female).

Step 3
Collect the data

Recruit female undergraduates for a study on "communicating with others." Ask them to choose a standardized shirt to wear (red or green) during the interaction with their anticipated partner.

Step 4
Analyze the data

Calculate ratings of frequency of shirt choice (red or green) as a function of different partner characteristics. Data are consistent with the hypothesis that female participants will show a preference for the red shirt when interacting with an attractive male, but will not show a preference in the other experimental conditions.

Step 5
Report the findings

Publish report of the research in the 2013 Issue of the journal *Journal of Experimental Social Psychology*.

© 2017 Cengage Learning

Figure 2.1
Flowchart of steps in a scientific investigation. As illustrated in the study by Elliot et al. (2013), a scientific investigation consists of a sequence of carefully planned steps, beginning with the formulation of a testable hypothesis and ending with the publication of the study, if its results are worthy of examination by other researchers.

learn associations based on certain colours being paired repeatedly with certain experiences. For instance, red ink is usually used to mark students' errors, and red lights and red signs are often used to warn of danger. Second, over the course of human evolution, certain colours may have had adaptive significance for survival or reproduction. For example, blood and fire, which often appear red, both can signal danger.

In their first study of the behavioural effects of colour, Elliot et al. (2007) theorized that red is associated with the danger of failure in achievement settings. Consistent with their theory, they found that subjects exposed to a red cover on an IQ test scored significantly lower on the test than those exposed to green or white covers. Although red has negative effects in achievement contexts, the researchers believed that it may have positive effects in sexual contexts for both males and females. They noted a host of ways in which the colour red is associated with romance (red hearts on Valentine's day), lust (red-light districts), and sexual liaisons (the redness of aroused sexual organs). Among other things, they have found that when females wear red clothing this leads men to view women as more sexually desirable (Elliot & Niesta, 2008). They continued this line of reasoning, combining it with research showing that individuals often use subtle, nonverbal means to engage in sexual signalling, hypothesizing *that female participants would be more likely to choose a red shirt over other shirt colours to wear when they anticipated meeting with an attractive male student* (Elliott et al., 2013).

To be testable, scientific hypotheses must be formulated precisely, and the variables under study must be clearly defined. Researchers achieve these clear formulations by providing operational definitions of the relevant variables. An *operational definition* describes the actions or operations that will be used to measure or control a variable. Operational definitions—which may be quite different from dictionary definitions—establish precisely what is meant by each variable in the context of a study.

To illustrate, let's see how Elliot et al. (2013) operationalized their variables. The manipulation of the attractiveness of the target student female participants anticipated meeting was executed by providing them with descriptions of their anticipated partner, descriptions suggesting that the target was an attractive male (e.g., tall, clear skin, athletic, high grades in school), an unattractive male (e.g., short, unclear skin, out of shape, and a poor student), or an average female (e.g., average height and skin, with an average body and school grades). Participants were then told that in the meeting with the target, they would have to wear a *standardized* shirt, and were given the chance to choose between the pictures of a red and a green shirt. The shirts were only differed in colour; two identical pictures were coloured through Adobe Photoshop. Although this sounds simple enough, they had to equate the pictures in terms of characteristics such as in brightness and saturation, so that only the colour was different. In the specific study that we will look at (Elliot et al., 2013), they measured sexual signalling by examining the frequency of each colour choice when participants expected an attractive male, an unattractive male, or an average female.

Step 2: Select the Research Method and Design the Study

The second step in a scientific investigation is to figure out how to put the hypothesis to an empirical test. The research method chosen depends to a large degree on the nature of the question under study. The various methods—experiments, case studies, surveys, naturalistic observation, and so forth—each have advantages and disadvantages. The researcher has to consider the pros and cons, and then select the strategy that appears to be the most appropriate and practical. In this case, Elliot and his colleagues decided that their question called for an experiment, which involves manipulating one variable to see if it has an impact on another variable (we will describe the experimental method in more detail later in the chapter). Actually, they chose to conduct a series of two experiments to evaluate their hypothesis. We will mostly focus on Study One in their series.

Once researchers have chosen a general method, they must make detailed plans for executing their study. Thus, Elliot and his colleagues had to decide how many people they needed to recruit for each experiment and where they would get their participants. *Participants* are the persons or animals whose behaviour is systematically observed in a study. For their series of studies, the researchers chose to use undergraduate students. Their sample size in the series of studies ranged from 75 to 147. The sample in Study One consisted of 147 female undergraduates whose mean age was 22.36 years. Participation was restricted to heterosexual/bisexual students who were not colour-blind. The pictures of the shirts they were to choose from were identical pictures of long-sleeved shirts, except the shirts were presented in different colours.

Step 3: Collect the Data

The third step in the research enterprise is to collect the data. Researchers use a variety of *data collection techniques*, which are procedures for making empirical observations and measurements. Commonly used techniques include direct observation, questionnaires, interviews, psychological tests, physiological recordings, and examination of archival records (see Table 2.1). The data collection techniques used in a study depend largely on what is being investigated. For example, questionnaires are well suited for studying attitudes, psychological tests for studying personality, and physiological recordings for studying the biological and neural bases of behaviour. Depending on the nature and complexity of the study, data collection can often take months or even longer. In this case, the volunteer participants came to a lab where they were informed that the experiment involved having a conversation with another participant. They were told that each of them would complete a questionnaire describing themselves and that the answers would be given to their interaction partner. After completing their own questionnaire, they received the answers given by their partner and they were told their partner would be receiving their answers. Those answers contained the manipulation of the gender and attractiveness of their anticipated partner. They were then asked to choose which of the two standardized shirts they would prefer to wear during the interaction.

Step 4: Analyze the Data and Draw Conclusions

The observations made in a study are usually converted into numbers, which constitute the raw data of the study. Researchers use statistics to analyze their data and to decide whether their hypotheses have

Table 2.1

Key Data Collection Techniques in Psychology

TECHNIQUE	DESCRIPTION
Direct observation	Observers are trained to watch and record behaviour as objectively and precisely as possible. They may use some instrumentation, such as a stopwatch or video recorder.
Questionnaire	Participants are administered a series of written questions designed to obtain information about attitudes, opinions, and specific aspects of their behaviour.
Interview	A face-to-face dialogue is conducted to obtain information about specific aspects of a subject's behaviour.
Psychological test	Participants are administered a standardized measure to obtain a sample of their behaviour. Tests are usually used to assess mental abilities or personality traits.
Physiological/neural recording	An instrument is used to monitor and record a specific physiological process in a subject. Examples include measures of blood pressure, heart rate, muscle tension, and brain activity.
Examination of archival records	The researcher analyzes existing institutional records (the archives), such as census, economic, medical, legal, educational, and business records.

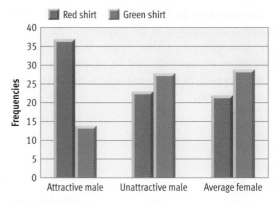

Figure 2.2
Frequencies of shirt colour choice by expected interaction condition.

Source: Andrew J. Elliot, Tobias Greitemeyer, Adam D. Pazda. 2013. Women's use of red clothing as a sexual signal in intersexual interaction. *Journal of Experimental Psychology*, 48: 599–602 (Figure 2).

been supported. Thus, statistics play an essential role in the scientific enterprise. Based on their statistical analyses, the researchers concluded that their data supported their hypothesis. The data for frequency of colour choice are shown in Figure 2.2. As you can see, participants choose the red shirt significantly more often only when anticipating an interaction with an attractive male. The findings of this experiment were consistent with the results of the other experiment in the series, leading the authors to suggest that the women in the study may have used red to communicate a romantic interest in the attractive male participant or at least a willingness to interact with him.

Step 5: Report the Findings

The publication of research results is a fundamental aspect of the scientific enterprise (Roberts, Brown, & Smith-Boydston, 2003). Scientific progress can be achieved only if researchers share their findings with one another and with the general public. Therefore, the final step in a scientific investigation is to write up a concise summary of the study and its findings. Typically, researchers prepare a report that is delivered at a scientific meeting and submitted to a journal for publication. **A *journal* is a periodical that publishes technical and scholarly material, usually in a narrowly defined area of inquiry.** The series of studies by Elliot and his colleagues (2013) was published in the *Journal of Experimental Social Psychology*, a top journal in the field.

The process of publishing scientific studies allows other experts to evaluate and critique new research findings. When articles are submitted to scientific journals, they go through a demanding peer review process. Experts thoroughly scrutinize each submission. They carefully evaluate each study's methods, statistical analyses, and conclusions, as well as its contribution to knowledge and theory. The peer

review process is so demanding that many top journals reject over 90 percent of submitted articles! The purpose of this process is to ensure that journals publish reliable findings based on high-quality research. The peer review process is a major strength of the scientific approach because it greatly reduces the likelihood of publishing erroneous findings.

As a final note on the effects of wearing the colour red, research suggests that in some contexts—and, notably, for some sports—teams and individual competitors wearing red may have a performance advantage over those wearing other colours (Elliot & Maier, 2014). While this certainly does not explain the success of Canadian athletes in the Olympics, it does suggest that wearing red may do more for athletes than simply signalling their country of origin.

Advantages of the Scientific Approach

Science is certainly not the only method that can be used to draw conclusions about behaviour. Everyone uses logic, casual observation, and good old-fashioned common sense. Because the scientific method often requires painstaking effort, it seems reasonable to ask what advantages make it worth the trouble.

Basically, the scientific approach offers two major advantages. The first is its clarity and precision. Commonsense notions about behaviour tend to be vague and ambiguous. The scientific approach requires that people specify *exactly* what they are talking about when they formulate hypotheses. This clarity and precision enhances communication about important ideas.

The second and perhaps greatest advantage offered by the scientific approach is its relative intolerance of error. Scientists are trained to be skeptical. They subject their ideas to empirical tests. They also scrutinize one another's findings with a critical eye. Peer review of articles submitted for publication and replication of results by other researchers provides self-correcting mechanisms. Scientists demand objective data and thorough documentation before they accept ideas. When the findings of two studies conflict, the scientist tries to figure out why, usually by conducting additional research.

All of this is not to say that science has an exclusive copyright on truth. However, the scientific approach does tend to yield more accurate and dependable information than casual analyses and armchair speculation do. Knowledge of scientific data can thus provide a useful benchmark against which to judge claims and information from other kinds of sources.

Now that we have had an overview of how the scientific enterprise works, we can focus on how specific research methods are used. *Research methods* consist of various approaches to the observation, measurement, manipulation, and control of variables in empirical studies. In other words, they are general strategies for conducting studies. No single research method is ideal for all purposes and situations. Much of the ingenuity in research involves selecting and tailoring the method to the question at hand. The next two sections of this chapter discuss the two basic types of methods used in psychology: *experimental research methods* and *descriptive/correlational research methods*.

Looking for Causes: Experimental Research

Key Learning Goals

▶ Describe the experimental method, independent and dependent variables, and experimental and control groups.

▶ Explain how experiments can vary in design, and evaluate the major advantages and disadvantages of the experimental method.

Does misery love company? The expression "misery loves company" is a common saying that many of us accept without question. How many of us go further and inquire about whether or not there is any evidence for this statement. This question intrigued social psychologist Stanley Schachter, so he decided to put it to a scientific test. He examined this question in one of the classic studies in social psychology (Schachters, 1959). When people feel anxious, he wondered, do they want to be left alone, or do they prefer to have others around? Schachter's review of relevant theories suggested that in times of anxiety people would want others around to help them sort out their feelings. Thus, his hypothesis was that increases in anxiety would cause increases in the desire to be with others, which psychologists call the *need for affiliation*. To test this hypothesis, Schachter (1959) designed a clever experiment.

The *experiment* is a research method in which the investigator manipulates a variable under carefully controlled conditions and observes whether any changes occur in a second variable as a result. The experiment is a relatively powerful procedure that allows researchers to detect cause-and-effect relationships. Psychologists depend on this method more than any other. To see how an experiment is designed, let's use Schachter's study as an example.

Independent and Dependent Variables

The purpose of an experiment is to find out whether changes in one variable (let's call it X) cause changes in another variable (let's call it Y). To put it more concisely, we want to find out how X affects Y. In this formulation, we refer to X as the independent variable and to Y as the dependent variable.

An *independent variable* is a condition or event that an experimenter varies in order to see its impact on another variable. The independent variable is the variable that the experimenter controls or manipulates. It is hypothesized to have some effect on the dependent variable. The experiment is conducted to verify this effect. The *dependent variable* is the variable that is thought to be affected by manipulation of the independent variable. In psychology studies, the dependent variable is usually a measurement of some aspect of the participants' behaviour. The independent variable is called *independent* because it is free to be varied by the experimenter. The dependent variable is called *dependent* because it is thought to depend (at least in part) on manipulations of the independent variable.

In Schachter's experiment, the independent variable was the participants' anxiety level. He manipulated anxiety level in a clever way. Participants assembled in his lab were told by a "Dr. Zilstein" that they would be participating in a study on the physiological effects of electric shock. They were further informed that during the experiment they would receive a series of electric shocks from an intimidating-looking apparatus while their pulse and blood pressure were being monitored. Half of the participants were warned that the shocks would be very painful. They made up the high-anxiety group. The other half of the participants (the low-anxiety group) were told that the shocks would be mild and painless. In reality, there was no plan to shock anyone at any time. These orientation procedures were simply intended to evoke different levels of anxiety. After the orientation, the experimenter indicated that there would be a delay while he prepared the shock apparatus for use. The participants were asked whether they would prefer to wait alone or in the company of others. The participants' desire to be with others was the dependent variable.

Experimental and Control Groups

In an experiment the investigator typically assembles two groups of subjects who are treated differently with regard to the independent variable. These two groups are referred to as the *experimental group* and the *control group*. The *experimental group* consists of the subjects who receive some special treatment in regard to the independent variable. The *control group* consists of similar subjects who do not receive the special treatment given to the experimental group.

In the Schachter study, those in the high-anxiety condition constituted the experimental group. They received a special treatment designed to create an unusually high level of anxiety. The participants in the low-anxiety condition constituted the control group. They were not exposed to the special anxiety-arousing procedure. It is crucial that the experimental and control groups in a study be very similar, except for the different treatment that they receive in regard to the independent variable. This stipulation brings us to the logic that underlies the experimental method. If the two groups are alike in all respects except for the variation created by the manipulation of the independent variable, then any differences between the two groups on the dependent variable must be due to the manipulation of the independent variable. In this way researchers isolate the effect of the independent variable on the dependent variable. Schachter, for example, isolated the impact of anxiety on the need for affiliation. As predicted, he found that increased anxiety led to increased affiliation. As Figure 2.3 indicates, the percentage of participants in the high-anxiety group who wanted to wait with others was roughly twice that of the low-anxiety group.

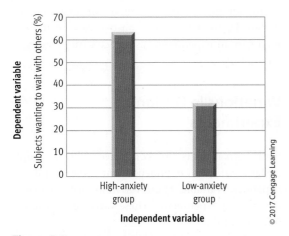

Figure 2.3
Results of Schachter's study of affiliation. The percentage of people wanting to wait with others was higher in the high-anxiety (experimental) group than in the low-anxiety (control) group, consistent with Schachter's hypothesis that anxiety would increase the desire for affiliation. The graphic portrayal of these results allows us to see at a glance the effects of the experimental manipulation on the dependent variable.

© 2017 Cengage Learning

Extraneous Variables

As we have seen, the logic of the experimental method rests on the assumption that the experimental and control groups are alike except for their treatment in regard to the independent variable. Any other differences between the two groups can cloud the situation and make it difficult to draw conclusions about how the independent variable affects the dependent variable.

In practical terms, of course, it is impossible to ensure that two groups of participants are exactly alike in every respect. The experimental and control groups have to be alike only on dimensions that are relevant to the dependent variable. Thus, Schachter did not need to worry about whether his two groups were similar in hair colour, height, or interest in ballet. Obviously, these variables weren't likely to influence the dependent variable of affiliation behaviour.

Instead, experimenters concentrate on making sure that the experimental and control groups are alike on a limited number of variables that could have a bearing on the results of the study. These variables are called extraneous, secondary, or nuisance variables. *Extraneous variables* are any variables other than the independent variable that seem likely to influence the dependent variable in a specific study.

In Schachter's study, one extraneous variable could have been the participants' tendency to be sociable. Why? Because subjects' sociability could affect their desire to be with others (the dependent variable). If the participants in one group had happened to be more sociable (on the average) than those in the other group, the variables of anxiety and sociability would have been confounded. A *confounding of variables* occurs when two variables are linked in a way that makes it difficult to sort out their specific effects. When an extraneous variable is confounded with an independent variable, a researcher cannot tell which is having what effect on the dependent variable. Unanticipated confoundings of variables have wrecked innumerable experiments. That is why so much care, planning, and forethought must go into designing an experiment. A key quality that separates a talented experimenter from a mediocre one is the ability to foresee troublesome extraneous variables and control them to avoid confoundings.

Experimenters use a variety of safeguards to control for extraneous variables. For instance, participants are usually assigned to the experimental and control groups randomly. *Random assignment* of participants occurs when all participants have an equal chance of being assigned to any group or condition in the study. When experimenters distribute participants into groups through some random procedure, they can be reasonably confident that the groups will be similar in most ways. Thus, by using random assignment Schachter could be confident that the participants in the experimental and control groups did not differ in their overall level of sociability.

To summarize the essentials of experimental design, Figure 2.4 provides an overview of the elements in an experiment, using Schachter's study as an example.

Variations in Designing Experiments

Some experiments are conducted with a simple design, with just one independent variable and one dependent variable. Many variations are possible in conducting experiments. These variations warrant a brief mention.

First, it is sometimes advantageous to use only one group of participants who serve as their own control group. The effects of the independent variable are evaluated by exposing this single group to two different conditions—an experimental condition and a control condition. For example, imagine that you wanted to study the effects of loud music

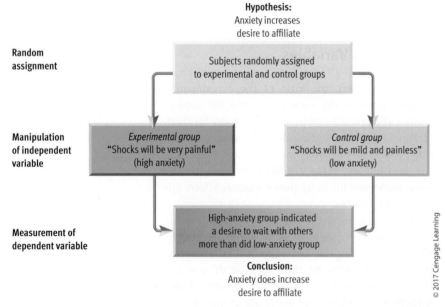

Random assignment

Manipulation of independent variable

Measurement of dependent variable

Hypothesis:
Anxiety increases desire to affiliate

Subjects randomly assigned to experimental and control groups

Experimental group
"Shocks will be very painful" (high anxiety)

Control group
"Shocks will be mild and painless" (low anxiety)

High-anxiety group indicated a desire to wait with others more than did low-anxiety group

Conclusion:
Anxiety does increase desire to affiliate

© 2017 Cengage Learning

Figure 2.4
The basic elements of an experiment. As illustrated by the Schachter study, the logic of experimental design rests on treating the experimental and control groups exactly alike (to control for extraneous variables) except for the manipulation of the independent variable. In this way, the experimenter attempts to isolate the effects of the independent variable on the dependent variable.

on typing performance. You could have a group of participants work on a typing task while loud music was played (experimental condition) and in the absence of music (control condition). This approach would ensure that the participants in the experimental and control conditions would be alike on any extraneous variables involving their personal characteristics, such as motivation or typing skill. After all, the same people would be studied in both conditions. When participants serve as their own control group, the experiment is said to use a *within-subjects design* because comparisons are made within the same group of subjects or participants. In contrast, when two or more independent groups of participants are exposed to a manipulation of an independent variable, the experiment is said to use a *between-subjects design* because comparisons are made between two different groups of subjects or participants. Although within-subjects designs are not used as frequently as between-subjects designs, they are advantageous for certain types of investigations (Curran & Bauer, 2011). They also require fewer participants and they ensure that the experimental and control groups are equivalent (Davis & Bremner, 2006).

It is also possible to manipulate more than one independent variable or measure more than one dependent variable in a single experiment. For example, in another study of typing performance, you could vary both room temperature and the presence of distracting music as independent variables (see Figure 2.5), while measuring two aspects of typing performance (speed and accuracy) as dependent variables. The main advantage of manipulating two or three independent variables is that this approach permits the experimenter to see whether two variables interact (Smith, 2014). An interaction means that the effect of one variable depends on the effect of another. For instance, if we found that distracting music impaired typing performance only when room temperature was high, we would be detecting an interaction.

Advantages and Disadvantages of Experimental Research

The experiment is a powerful research method. Its principal advantage is that it permits conclusions about cause-and-effect relationships between variables. Researchers are able to draw these conclusions about causation because the precise control available in the experiment allows them to isolate the relationship between the independent variable and the dependent variable, while neutralizing the effects of extraneous variables. No other research method

Figure 2.5

Manipulation of two independent variables in an experiment. As this example shows, when two independent variables are manipulated in a single experiment, the researcher has to compare four groups of participants (or conditions) instead of the usual two. The main advantage of this procedure is that it allows an experimenter to see whether two variables interact.

can duplicate this strength of the experiment. This advantage is why psychologists usually prefer to use the experimental method whenever possible.

For all its power, however, the experiment has limitations. One problem is that experiments are often artificial. Because experiments require great control over proceedings, researchers must often construct simple, contrived situations to test their hypotheses experimentally. When experiments are highly artificial, doubts arise about the applicability of findings to everyday behaviour outside the experimental laboratory. One way to address this limitation is to conduct a *field experiment*. Field experiments are research studies that use settings that are very much like real life; in fact, the research may occur in the context of everyday life and events. In conducting field experiments, the researcher may sacrifice some control over extraneous variables for greater *generalizability*. Some researchers believe that the results of field experiments are more generalizable or applicable to everyday life than are the typically more artificial lab experiments, and some have suggested that the use of field experimentation is on the rise (Shadish & Cooke, 2009). Not all researchers see the artificiality of the typical lab experiment as a serious limitation (Mook, 1983). The best strategy might be to use both approaches in your research program. One excellent example of a field experiment was conducted by two researchers at the University of British Columbia (Dutton & Aron, 1974). This field experiment was designed to examine hypotheses derived from Schachter's (1964) seminal theory of emotions (discussed more fully in Chapter 10). The study by Dutton and Aron is our Featured Study in this chapter.

Another disadvantage is that the experimental method can't be used to explore some research questions. Psychologists are frequently interested in the effects of factors that cannot be manipulated as independent variables because of ethical concerns or practical realities. In some cases, manipulations of variables are difficult or impossible. For example, you might want to know whether being brought up in an urban as opposed to a rural area affects people's values. An experiment would require you to

FEATURED STUDY

Some evidence for heightened sexual attraction under conditions of high anxiety.

Description
This field research examines predictions derived from Stanley Schachter's theory of emotion. This theory states that salient contextual cues can be used to provide labels for our physiological arousal in such a way that the cues determine the emotion we perceive we are feeling.

Investigators
Dutton, D., & Aron, A. P. (1974). *Journal of Personality and Social Psychology, 30*, 510–517.

randomly assign similar families to live in urban and rural areas, which obviously is impossible to do. To explore this question, you would have to use descriptive/correlational research methods, which we turn to next.

Looking for Links: Descriptive/Correlational Research

Key Learning Goals

▶ Explain the role of naturalistic observation, case studies, and surveys in psychological research.

▶ Evaluate the major advantages and disadvantages of descriptive/correlational research.

In some situations, psychologists cannot exert experimental control over the variables they want to study, for either ethical or practical reasons. For example, if you were interested in the effects of nutritious and non-nutritious maternal diets on the health of babies, you would never try to get some expectant mothers to follow poor nutritional habits. In such situations, investigators must rely on *descriptive/correlational research methods*. These methods include naturalistic observation, case studies, and surveys. What distinguishes these methods is that the researcher cannot manipulate the variables under study. This lack of control means that these methods cannot be used to demonstrate cause-and-effect relationships between variables. *Descriptive/correlational methods permit investigators to only describe patterns of behaviour and discover links or associations between variables.* That is not to suggest that associations are unimportant. You'll see in this section that information on associations between variables can be extremely valuable in our efforts to understand behaviour.

Naturalistic Observation

Is eating behaviour influenced by the size of the plates and bowls that people use? How do depressive disorders influence individuals' social behaviour? These are just a couple examples of the kinds of questions that have been explored through naturalistic observation in recent studies (Baddeley et al., 2013;

Wansink & van Ittersum, 2013). In *naturalistic observation* a researcher engages in careful observation of behaviour without intervening directly with the subjects. This type of research is called *naturalistic* because behaviour is allowed to unfold naturally (without interference) in its natural environment—that is, the setting in which it would normally occur. Of course, researchers have to make careful plans to ensure systematic, consistent observations (Heyman et al., 2014). Let's look at an example.

One recent study investigated whether plate size influenced the amount of food consumed at all-you-can-eat buffets. Laboratory studies have shown

Caroline von Tuempling/Getty Images

Wansink and van Ittersum (2013) used naturalistic observation to replicate laboratory findings on how plate size affects the amount eaten. Consistent with laboratory research, they found that real-world diners at buffet restaurants consumed more food when given larger plates.

that people eat more when they are served on larger plates. Wansink and van Ittersum (2013) wanted to determine whether similar findings would be observed in real buffet restaurants where patrons could choose between two plate sizes when they served themselves. At four buffets the eating behaviour of 43 unsuspecting diners was monitored by carefully trained observers who estimated consumption and waste. Consistent with previous research, diners who chose the larger plate served themselves 52 percent more food than those who used the smaller plate. Those using the larger plates ended up consuming 41 percent more food and wasted 135 percent more than those using the smaller plates. These findings provide further support for the hypothesis that larger dinnerware leads to increased food consumption.

The major strength of naturalistic observation is that it allows researchers to study behaviour under conditions that are less artificial than in experiments. Another plus is that engaging in naturalistic observation can be a good starting point when little is known about the behavior under study. And, unlike case studies and surveys, naturalistic observation can be used to study animal behaviour. Many landmark studies of animal behaviour, such as Jane Goodall's (1986, 1990) work on the social and family life of chimpanzees, have depended on naturalistic observation. More recent examples of naturalistic observation with animals include studies of communication in Australian sea lions (Pitcher, Harcourt, & Charrier, 2012), parental favouritism in Eastern bluebirds (Barrios-Miller & Siefferman, 2013), and tool use in capuchin monkeys and chimpanzees (la Cour et al., 2014).

Jane Goodall is known internationally for her pioneering work with chimpanzees in Gombe Stream National Park in Tanzania. Her study of the social interactions of the chimpanzees over the past five decades demonstrates the power of observational techniques in research.

A major problem with this method is that researchers often have trouble making their observations unobtrusively so they don't affect their participants' behaviour. *Reactivity* **occurs when a participant's behaviour is altered by the presence of the observer.** Even animals may exhibit reactivity if observational efforts are readily apparent (Iredale, Nevill, & Lutz, 2010). Another disadvantage is that it often is difficult to translate naturalistic observations into numerical data that permit precise statistical analyses.

Case Studies

Another descriptive research method that has been used profitably in psychology is the *case study*. **A *case study* is an in-depth investigation of an individual participant or group of participants.** Case studies are particularly well suited for investigating certain phenomena, such as psychological disorders and neuropsychological issues. For example, Brenda Milner of McGill University made important contributions to our knowledge about the importance of the temporal lobes of the brain in memory and the existence of multiple memory systems in the brain by using this method. Case studies such as Milner's work with the patient H.M. have given us great insight into the brain and its connection to behaviour (Scoville & Milner, 1957). Henry Molaison (H.M.) began experiencing seizures as a young child and these seizures escalated to such an extent that surgeon Henry Scoville decided upon an "experimental operation" in which portions of Molaison's hippocampus and some surrounding tissue were removed (Fancher & Rutherford, 2012). While his epileptic seizures were significantly reduced, Molaison suffered memory problems—in particular, an inability to form new memories (Dittrich, 2016). Through systematic study of Henry Molaison and other patients, Milner (Milner, Corkin & Teuber, 1968) and other neuropsychologists were able to learn a great deal about the brain and its connection to memory (Corkin, 2013). For example, from her work with Molaison, Milner was able to show that we possess multiple memory systems, each with its own characteristics, uses, and limitations (Squire & Wixted, 2011).

Clinical psychologists, who diagnose and treat psychological problems, often do case studies of their clients. When clinicians assemble a case study for diagnostic purposes, they generally are not conducting empirical research. Case study research may involve investigators analyzing a collection of case studies to look for patterns that permit general conclusions. For example, one recent study (Arcelus et al., 2009) evaluated the efficacy of a treatment called interpersonal psychotherapy (IPT) for people

Henry Molaison, known for years as the patient H.M., was one of the most important figures in research on the brain and memory systems. He was the subject of many investigations by Brenda Milner of McGill University and her colleagues.

Henry Molaison, aged 60, at MIT in 1986. Photograph by Jenni Ogden, author of *Trouble in Mind: Stories from a Neuropsychologist's Casebook.*

Case studies are used in both clinical work and research. When used in research, investigators look for threads of continuity across a series of case studies.

suffering from bulimia (an eating disorder marked by out-of-control overeating followed by self-induced vomiting, fasting, and excessive exercise). Careful case assessments were made of 59 bulimic patients before, during, and after the 16-session course of IPT treatment. The results demonstrated that IPT can be an effective treatment for bulimic disorders. Although case study research typically involves looking for common threads in a series of cases, descriptions of individual case studies are sometimes published when they are particularly interesting or valuable to other clinicians.

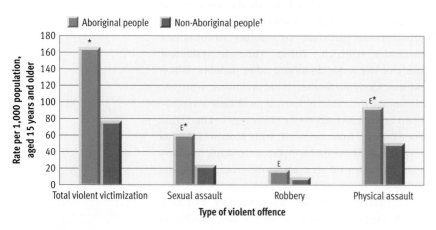

E use with caution

* significantly different from reference category (p < 0.05)

† reference category

Figure 2.6

Violent victimization incidents. Violence, including spousal violence, reported by Canadians, by Aboriginal people and non-Aboriginal people, and type of violent offence, provinces and territories, 2014.

Source: From Jillian Boyce, 2015. "Victimization of Aboriginal people in Canada, 2014," *Juristat*, 36 (1): Chart 1. Ottawa: Statistics Canada, http://www.statcan.gc.ca/pub/85-002-x/2016001/article/14631-eng.htm

Case studies can also provide compelling, real-life illustrations that bolster a hypothesis or theory. However, the main problem with case studies is that they can be highly subjective. Information from several sources must be knit together in an impressionistic way. In this process, clinicians and researchers may focus selectively on information that fits with their expectations, which usually reflect their theoretical slant. Thus, it is relatively easy for investigators to see what they expect to see in case study research.

Surveys

One research method that many of us are frequently exposed to is the survey. In a *survey*, **researchers use questionnaires or interviews to gather information about specific aspects of participants' behaviour.** Large companies may survey the buying habits of specific segments of the buying public. Political parties often do extensive polling before they call an election or propose specific legislation. Surveys may also be used to gather information on important social issues that may have legal and public policy implications, such as the study examining the criminal victimization of Aboriginal people in Canada (Boyce, 2016). The data used in this study were obtained through the General Social Survey (GSS; Statistics Canada, 2015), a telephone survey administered by Statistics Canada of Canadians' experiences with crime victimization. Of the many trends revealed in the survey, few are more striking than the statistics indicating the higher frequency of criminal victimization of Canada's Aboriginal people as compared to non-Aboriginal Canadians. For example, the data presented in Figure 2.6 clearly reveals that Aboriginal Canadians are significantly more likely to be the victims of violent crimes than are non-Aboriginal Canadians.

Surveys are often used to obtain information on aspects of behaviour that are difficult to observe directly. Surveys also make it relatively easy to collect data on attitudes and opinions from large samples of participants. Survey methods are widely used in psychological research (Krosnick, Lavrakas, & Kim, 2014). However, potential participants' tendency to cooperate with surveys appears to have declined noticeably in recent decades (Tourangeau, 2004). The growing resentment of intrusive telemarketing and heightened concerns about privacy and identity theft seem to be the culprits underlying the reduced response rates for research surveys. The major weakness of surveys is that they depend on *self-report data.* As we'll discuss later, intentional deception, wishful thinking, memory lapses, and poorly worded questions can distort participants' verbal reports about their behaviour (Krosnick, 1999).

Advantages and Disadvantages of Descriptive/Correlational Research

Descriptive/correlational research methods have advantages and disadvantages, which are compared with the strengths and weaknesses of experimental research in the Illustrated Overview of research methods on pages 48–49. As a whole, the foremost advantage of correlational methods is that they give researchers a way to explore questions they could not examine with experimental procedures. For example, after-the-fact analyses would be the only ethical way to investigate the possible link between poor maternal nutrition and birth defects in humans. In a similar vein, if researchers hope to learn how urban versus rural upbringing relates to people's values, they have to depend on descriptive methods, since they can't control where subjects grow up. Thus, *descriptive research broadens the scope of phenomena that psychologists are able to study.*

Unfortunately, descriptive methods have one significant disadvantage: Investigators cannot control events to isolate cause and effect. *Consequently, descriptive/correlational research cannot demonstrate conclusively that correlated variables are causally related.* Consider for instance, the correlation between plate size and food consumption observed in the study by Wansink and van Ittersum (2013). The correlational data from this specific study do not permit us to conclude that larger plates *caused* people to consume more food. Other factors might play a role in this association. For example, it could be that hungrier people grabbed larger plates, and their increased eating could be caused by their greater hunger. To draw causal conclusions about the relationship

between larger plates and increased eating would require experiments on this issue—which have been conducted, and which do suggest that there is a causal link between bigger plates and greater eating. You may be wondering: If we already had experimental data linking plate size to consumption, why conduct the naturalistic observation study? The value of the naturalistic observation study lies in its demonstration that laboratory findings generalize to the real world. As you can see, the various research methods each make different types of contributions to our understanding of behaviour.

··

concept check 2.2

Matching Research Methods to Questions

Check your understanding of the uses and strengths of various research methods by figuring out which method would be optimal for investigating the following questions about behavioural processes. Choose from the following methods: (a) experiment, (b) naturalistic observation, (c) case study, and (d) survey. Indicate your choice (by letter) next to each question. You'll find the answers in Appendix A at the back of the book.

_____ **1.** Are people's attitudes about nuclear disarmament related to their social class or education?

_____ **2.** Do people who suffer from anxiety disorders share similar early childhood experiences?

_____ **3.** Do troops of baboons display territoriality—that is, do they mark off an area as their own and defend it from intrusion by other baboons?

_____ **4.** Can the presence of food-related cues (e.g., delicious-looking desserts in advertisements) cause an increase in the amount of food that people eat?

Looking for Conclusions: Statistics and Research

Whether researchers use experimental or correlational methods, they need some way to make sense of their data. *Statistics* **is the use of mathematics to organize, summarize, and interpret numerical data.** Statistical analyses permit researchers to draw conclusions based on their observations. Many students find statistics intimidating, but statistics are an integral part of modern life. Although you may not realize it, you are bombarded with statistics nearly every day. When you read about economists'

projections for inflation, when you check a baseball player's batting average, when you see the popularity ratings of television shows, you are dealing with statistics.

In this section, we will examine a few basic statistical concepts that will help you understand the research discussed throughout this book. For the most part, we won't concern ourselves with the details of statistical *computations*.

Key Learning Goals

▶ Describe the three measures of central tendency and the measures of variability.

▶ Distinguish between positive and negative correlations, and discuss correlation in relation to prediction and causation.

The Research Enterprise in Psychology

Descriptive Statistics

Descriptive statistics are used to organize and summarize data. They provide an overview of numerical data. Key descriptive statistics include measures of central tendency, measures of variability, and the coefficient of correlation. Let's take a brief look at each of these.

Central Tendency

In summarizing numerical data, researchers often want to know what constitutes a typical or average score. To answer this question, they use three measures of central tendency: the median, the mean, and the mode. The *median* is the score that falls exactly in the centre of a distribution of scores. Half of the scores fall above the median and half fall below it. The *mean* is the arithmetic average of the scores in a distribution. It is obtained by adding up all the scores and dividing by the total number of scores. Finally, the *mode* is the most frequent score in a distribution.

In general, the mean is the most useful measure of central tendency because additional statistical manipulations can be performed on it that are not possible with the median or mode. However, the mean is sensitive to extreme scores in a distribution, which can sometimes make the mean misleading. To illustrate, imagine that you're interviewing for a sales position at a company. Unbeknownst to you, the company's five salespeople earned the following incomes in the previous year: $20 000, $20 000, $25 000, $35 000, and $200 000. You ask how much the typical salesperson earns in a year. The sales director proudly announces that her five salespeople earned a *mean* income of $60 000 last year (the calculations are shown in Figure 2.7). However, before you order that expensive new sports car, you had better

inquire about the *median* and *modal* income for the sales staff. In this case, one extreme score ($200 000) has inflated the mean, making it unrepresentative of the sales staff's earnings. In this instance, the median ($25 000) and the mode ($20 000) both provide better estimates of what you are likely to earn.

Variability

In describing a set of data, it is often useful to have some estimate of the variability among the scores. *Variability* refers to how much the scores in a data set vary from each other and from the mean. Just as there are several measures of central tendency, there are also different measures of variability. One of the most useful measures of variability is the *standard deviation*. The *standard deviation* is an index of the amount of variability in a set of data. It gives you a measure of how the scores in your sample cluster around the average. When variability is great, the standard deviation will be relatively large. When variability is low, the standard deviation will be smaller. This relationship is apparent if you examine the two sets of data in Figure 2.8. The mean is the same for both sets of scores, but variability clearly is greater in set B than in set A. This greater variability yields a higher standard deviation for set B than for set A. Estimates of variability play a crucial role when researchers use statistics to decide whether the results of their studies support their hypotheses.

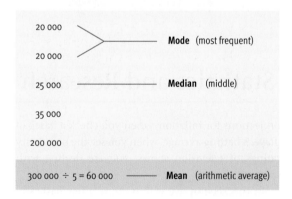

Speed (kilometres per hour)	
Set A Perfection Boulevard	Set B Wild Street
35	21
34	37
33	50
37	28
38	42
40	37
36	39
33	25
34	23
30	48
35 — Mean — 35	
2.87 — Standard deviation — 10.39	

Figure 2.8
Variability and the standard deviation. Although these two sets of data produce the same mean, or average, an observer on Wild Street would see much more variability in the speeds of individual cars than an observer on Perfection Boulevard would. As you can see, the standard deviation for set B is higher than that for set A because of the greater variability in set B.

Source: From Weiten. *Cengage Advantage Books: Psychology*, 9E. © 2013 South-Western, a part of Cengage, Inc. Reproduced by permission. www.cengage.com/permissions

20 000
20 000   **Mode** (most frequent)

25 000   **Median** (middle)

35 000

200 000

300 000 ÷ 5 = 60 000 ——— **Mean** (arithmetic average)

Figure 2.7
Measures of central tendency. The three measures of central tendency usually converge, but that is not always the case, as these data illustrate. Which measure is most useful depends on the nature of the data. Generally, the mean is the best index of central tendency, but in this instance the median is more informative.

The standard deviation is also useful in understanding another important concept in psychology and statistics, the *normal curve or normal distribution*. The **normal distribution** is a symmetrical, bell-shaped curve that represents the pattern in which many human characteristics are dispersed in the population. A great many physical qualities (e.g., height, nose length, and running speed) and psychological traits (intelligence, spatial reasoning ability, introversion) are distributed in a manner that closely resembles this bell-shaped curve. When a trait is normally distributed, most scores fall near the centre of the distribution (the mean), and the number of scores gradually declines as one moves away from the centre in either direction. The normal distribution is *not* a law of nature. It's a mathematical function, or theoretical curve, that approximates the way nature seems to operate.

The normal distribution is the bedrock of the scoring system for most psychological tests, such as intelligence quotient (IQ) tests. As we discuss in Chapter 9, psychological tests are *relative measures*; they assess how people score on a trait in comparison to other people. The normal distribution gives us a precise way to measure how people stack up in comparison to each other. The scores under the normal curve are dispersed in a fixed pattern, with the standard deviation serving as the unit of measurement, as shown in Figure 2.9. About 68 percent of the scores in the distribution fall within plus or minus 1 standard deviation of the mean, while 95 percent of the scores fall within plus or minus 2 standard deviations of the mean. Given this fixed pattern, if you know the mean and standard deviation of a normally distributed trait, you can tell where any score falls in the distribution for the trait.

Test scores such as those derived from IQ tests that place examinees in the normal distribution can always be converted to percentile scores, which are a little easier to interpret. A *percentile score* indicates the percentage of people who score at or below a particular score. For example, if you score at the 60th percentile on an IQ test, 60 percent of the people who take the test score the same or below you, while the remaining 40 percent score above you. There are tables available that permit us to convert any standard deviation placement in a normal distribution into a precise percentile score. Figure 2.9 gives some percentile conversions for the normal curve. Of course, not all distributions are normal and special statistical operations may be necessary when the distributions depart significantly from normality.

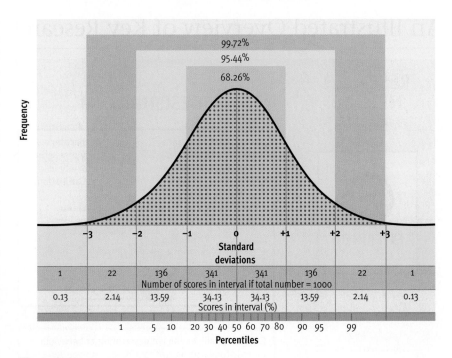

Figure 2.9

The normal distribution. Many characteristics are distributed in a pattern represented by this bell-shaped curve (each dot represents a case). The horizontal axis shows how far above or below the mean a score is (measured in plus or minus standard deviations). The vertical axis shows the number of cases obtaining each score. In a normal distribution, most cases fall near the centre of the distribution, so that 68.26 percent of the cases fall within plus or minus 1 standard deviation of the mean. The number of cases gradually declines as one moves away from the mean in either direction, so that only 13.59 percent of the cases fall between 1 and 2 standard deviations above or below the mean, and even fewer cases (2.14 percent) fall between 2 and 3 standard deviations above or below the mean.

The next statistic we consider is the correlation coefficient. Correlational analyses can be very useful in answering a wide variety of research questions.

Correlation

A *correlation* exists when two variables are related to each other. Investigators often want to quantify the strength of an association between two variables, such as between class attendance and course grade, or between cigarette smoking and physical disease. In this effort, they depend extensively on a useful descriptive statistic: the correlation coefficient. *The correlation coefficient* is a numerical index of the degree of relationship between two variables. A correlation coefficient indicates (1) the direction (positive or negative) of the relationship and (2) how strongly the two variables are related.

Positive versus Negative Correlation. A positive *correlation* indicates that two variables co-vary in the *same* direction. This means that high scores on variable X are associated with high scores on variable Y and that low scores on variable X are associated with low scores on variable Y. For example, there

The Research Enterprise in Psychology

An Illustrated Overview of Key Research Methods in Psychology

RESEARCH METHOD	DESCRIPTION	EXAMPLE APPLIED TO RESEARCH ON AGGRESSION

EXPERIMENT

Manipulation of an independent variable under carefully controlled conditions to see whether any changes occur in a dependent variable.

Example: Schachter's (1959) study of whether increased anxiety leads to increased affiliation.

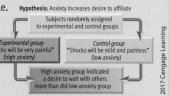

Hypothesis: Anxiety increases desire to affiliate

Random assignment — Subjects randomly assigned to experimental and control groups

Manipulation of independent variable — Experimental group "Shocks will be very painful" (high anxiety) | Control group "Shocks will be mild and painless" (low anxiety)

Measurement of dependent variable — High-anxiety group indicated a desire to wait with others more than did low-anxiety group

Conclusion: Anxiety does increase desire to affiliate

© 2017 Cengage Learning

Youngsters are randomly assigned to watch a violent or nonviolent film (manipulation of the independent variable), and some aspect of aggression (the dependent variable) is measured in a laboratory situation.

© T.M.O.Pictures/Alamy; (TV screen) © Andre Blais/Shutterstock

---

NATURALISTIC OBSERVATION

Careful, usually prolonged observation of behaviour in its natural setting, without direct intervention.

Example: The Ramirez-Esparza et al. (2007) study comparing sociability in Mexican and American samples, using an electronically activated recorder (EAR).

Caroline von Tuempling/Getty Images

Youngsters' spontaneous acts of aggression during recreational activities on their playground are recorded unobtrusively by a team of carefully trained observers.

© Laurence Mouton/Getty Images

CASE STUDIES

© Alain SHRODER/Getty Images

In-depth investigation of a single individual using direct interview, direct observation, review of records, interviews of those close to the person, and other data sources.

Example: The Isometsa et al. (1995) study of all known suicide cases in Finland for an entire year.

Detailed case histories are worked up for youngsters referred to counselling because of excessive aggressive behaviour in school. The children are interviewed, as are their parents and teachers.

MBI / Alamy Stock Photo

SURVEYS

Use of questionnaires or interviews to gather information about specific aspects of participants' behaviour, attitudes, and beliefs.

Example: The Stamatakis et al. (2009) study of sedentary behaviour, which related hours per day devoted to TV viewing to social class and physical health.

© Gabe Palmer/Alamy

A large sample of youngsters are given a questionnaire describing hypothetical scenarios that might be expected to trigger aggressive behaviour and are asked about how they think they would respond in the situations.

© David Grossman/Alamy

ADVANTAGES

DISADVANTAGES

Precise control over variables can eliminate alternative explanations for findings.

Researchers are able to draw conclusions about cause-and-effect relationships between variables.

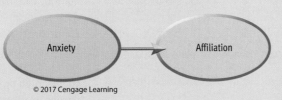

© 2017 Cengage Learning

Confounding of variables must be avoided.

Contrived laboratory situations are often artificial, making it risky to generalize findings to the real world.

Ethical concerns and practical realities preclude experiments on many important questions.

Artificiality that can be a problem in laboratory studies is minimized.

It can be good place to start when little is known about the phenomena under study.

Unlike other descriptive/correlational methods, it can be used to study animal as well as human behaviour.

© DAVID GRAY/Reuters/Corbis

It can be difficult to remain unobtrusive; even animal behaviour may be altererd by the observation process.

Researchers are unable to draw causal conclusions.

Observational data are often difficult to quantify for statistical analyses.

Case studies are well suited for study of psychological disorders and therapeutic practices.

Individual cases can provide compelling illustrations to support or undermine a theory.

© Alain SHRODER/Getty Images

Subjectivity makes it easy to see what one expects to see based on one's theoretical slant.

Researchers are unable to draw causal conclusions.

Clinical samples are often unrepresentative and suffer from sampling bias.

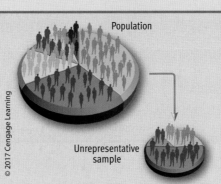

Population

Data collection can be relatively easy, saving time and money.

Researchers can gather data on difficult-to-observe aspects of behaviour.

Questionnaires are well suited for gathering data on attitudes, values, and beliefs from large samples.

© 2017 Cengage Learning

Unrepresentative sample

Self-report data are often unreliable, due to intentional deception, social desirability bias, response sets, memory lapses, and poor wording of questions.

Researchers are unable to draw causal conclusions.

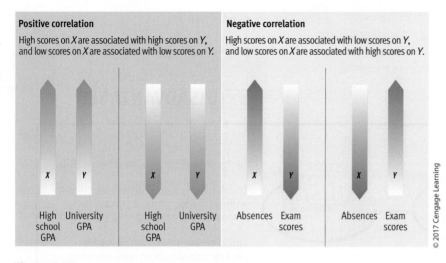

Positive correlation

High scores on *X* are associated with high scores on *Y*, and low scores on *X* are associated with low scores on *Y*.

Negative correlation

High scores on *X* are associated with low scores on *Y*, and low scores on *X* are associated with high scores on *Y*.

| High school GPA (X) | University GPA (Y) | High school GPA (X) | University GPA (Y) | Absences (X) | Exam scores (Y) | Absences (X) | Exam scores (Y) |

© 2017 Cengage Learning

Figure 2.10
Positive and negative correlation. Notice that the terms *positive* and *negative* refer to the direction of the relationship between two variables, not to its strength. Variables are positively correlated if they tend to increase and decrease together and are negatively correlated if one tends to increase when the other decreases.

is a positive correlation between high school grade point average (GPA) and subsequent university GPA. That is, people who do well in high school tend to do well in university, and those who perform poorly in high school tend to perform poorly in university (see Figure 2.10).

In contrast, a *negative* correlation indicates that two variables co-vary in the *opposite* direction. This means that people who score high on variable *X* tend to score low on variable *Y*, whereas those who score low on *X* tend to score high on *Y*. For example, in most university courses, there is a negative correlation between how frequently students are absent and how well they perform on exams. Students who have a high number of absences tend to get low exam scores, while students who have a low number of absences tend to earn higher exam scores (see Figure 2.10).

If a correlation is negative, a minus sign (−) is always placed in front of the coefficient. If a correlation is positive, a plus sign (+) may be placed in front of the coefficient, or the coefficient may be shown with no sign. Thus, if there's no sign, the correlation is positive.

Strength of the Correlation. Whereas the positive or negative sign indicates the direction of an association, the *size of the coefficient* indicates the *strength* of an association between two variables. The coefficient can vary between 0 and +1.00 (if positive) or between 0 and −1.00 (if negative). A coefficient near zero indicates no relationship between the variables; that is, high or low scores on variable *X* show no consistent relationship to high or low scores on variable *Y*. A coefficient of +1.00 or −1.00 indicates a perfect, one-to-one correspondence between the two variables. Most correlations fall between these extremes.

The closer the correlation to either −1.00 or +1.00, the stronger the relationship (see Figure 2.11). Thus, a correlation of 0.90 represents a stronger tendency for variables to be associated than a correlation of 0.40 does. Likewise, a correlation of −0.75 represents a stronger relationship than a correlation of −0.45. Keep in mind that the *strength* of a correlation depends only on the size of the coefficient. The positive or negative sign simply indicates the direction of the relationship. Therefore, a correlation of −0.60 reflects a stronger relationship than a correlation of +0.30.

Correlation and Prediction. You may recall that one of the key goals of scientific research is accurate *prediction*. A close link exists between the magnitude of a correlation and the power it gives scientists to make predictions. *As a correlation increases in strength (gets closer to either −1.00 or +1.00), the ability to*

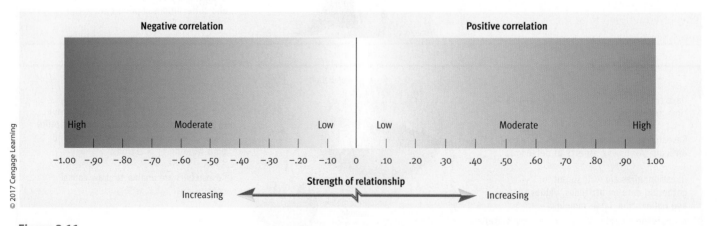

© 2017 Cengage Learning

Figure 2.11
Interpreting correlation coefficients. The magnitude of a correlation coefficient indicates the strength of the relationship between two variables. The sign (plus or minus) indicates whether the correlation is positive or negative. The closer the coefficient comes to +1.00 or −1.00, the stronger the relationship between the variables.

predict one variable based on knowledge of the other variable increases.

To illustrate, consider the various subtests of the *Graduate Record Exam* (GRE). The GRE is a standardized test developed by the Educational Testing Service (http://www.ets.org) that you may be asked to take if you apply for graduate study in psychology at most Canadian universities. Many psychology departments in Canada require students' scores on this test as part of the application package. The GRE has several subtests that examine specific abilities such as verbal, analytical, and quantitative reasoning (GRE, 2008). Researchers have been interested in examining various aspects of the GRE tests. For example, Sternberg and Williams (1997) showed that students' scores on the quantitative and analytical subtests correlated 0.47. This correlation shows that the two abilities as measured by the GRE are moderately positively correlated. Because of this, you should be able to predict with modest accuracy how well students do on one test from scores on the other. If the correlation was much higher, say 0.90, you would be able to predict one from the other with much higher accuracy. In contrast, if the correlation was 0.20, one test's prediction of the other would be much less meaningful.

Correlation and Causation. Although a high correlation allows us to predict one variable from another, it does not tell us whether a cause-and-effect relationship exists between the two variables. The problem is that variables can be highly correlated even though they are not causally related. For example, there is a substantial positive correlation between the size of young children's feet and the size of their vocabulary. That is, larger feet are associated with a larger vocabulary. Obviously, increases in foot size do not *cause* increases in vocabulary size. Nor do increases in vocabulary size cause increases in foot size. Instead, both are caused by a third variable, often referred to as the third-variable problem

(Bordens & Abbott, 2002). In this case, a third variable that might explain the correlation between the size of children's feet and vocabulary size is age. As children increase in age, both their vocabulary and their feet increase in size. The other two variables, while correlated, do not cause each other.

reality check

Misconception

A strong correlation between variables suggests that one of those variables causes the other.

Reality

The magnitude of a correlation is not a useful guide to the likelihood of causation. Two variables could be highly correlated, but both could be caused by a third variable. In contrast, a relatively low correlation might reflect a genuine, but weak causal effect.

When we find that variables *X* and *Y* are correlated, we can safely conclude only that *X* and *Y* are related. We do not know *how X* and *Y* are related. We do not know whether *X* causes *Y* or *Y* causes *X* or whether both are caused by a third variable. For example, survey studies have found a positive correlation between smoking and the risk of experiencing a major depressive disorder (Breslau, Kilbey, & Andreski, 1991, 1993). Although it's clear that there is an association between smoking and depression, it's hard to tell what's causing what. The investigators acknowledge that they don't know whether smoking makes people more vulnerable to depression or whether depression increases the tendency to smoke. Moreover, they note that they can't rule out the possibility that both are caused by a third variable (*Z*). Perhaps anxiety and neuroticism increase the likelihood of both taking up smoking and becoming depressed. The plausible causal relationships in this case are diagrammed in Figure 2.12, which illustrates

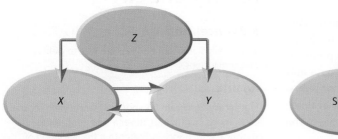
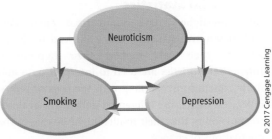

© 2017 Cengage Learning

Figure 2.12
Three possible causal relationships between correlated variables. If variables *X* and *Y* are correlated, does *X* cause *Y*, does *Y* cause *X*, or does some hidden third variable, *Z*, account for the changes in both *X* and *Y*? As the relationship between smoking and depression illustrates, a correlation alone does not provide the answer. We will encounter this problem of interpreting the meaning of correlations frequently in this text.

the "third variable problem" in interpreting correlations. This is a common problem in research, and you'll see this type of diagram again when we discuss other correlations. Thus, it is important to remember that *correlation is not equivalent to causation.*

Inferential Statistics

After researchers have summarized their data with descriptive statistics, they still need to decide whether their data support their hypotheses. *Inferential statistics* are used to interpret data and draw conclusions. Working with the laws of probability, researchers use inferential statistics to evaluate the possibility that their results might be due to the fluctuations of chance.

To illustrate this process, envision a hypothetical experiment. A computerized tutoring program (the independent variable) is designed to increase Grade 6 students' reading achievement (the dependent

variable). Our hypothesis is that program participants (the experimental group) will score higher than nonparticipants (the control group) on a standardized reading test given near the end of the school year. Let's assume that we compare 60 participants in each group. We obtain the following results, reported in terms of participants' grade-level scores for reading:

CONTROL GROUP		EXPERIMENTAL GROUP
6.3	Mean	6.8
1.4	Standard deviation	2.4

We hypothesized that the training program would produce higher reading scores in the experimental group than in the control group. Sure enough, that is indeed the case. However, we have to ask ourselves a critical question: Is this observed difference between the two groups large enough to support our hypothesis? That is, do the higher scores in the experimental group reflect the effect of the training program? Or could a difference of this size have occurred by chance? If our results could easily have occurred by chance, they don't provide meaningful support for our hypothesis.

When statistical calculations indicate that research results are not likely to be due to chance, the results are said to be *statistically significant*. You will probably hear your psychology professor use this phrase quite frequently. In discussing research, it is routine to note that "statistically significant differences were found." In statistics, the word *significant* has a precise and special meaning. *Statistical significance* is said to exist when the probability that the observed findings are due to chance is very low. "Very low" is usually defined as fewer than 5 chances in 100, which is referred to as the 0.05 level of significance.

Notice that in this special usage, *significant* does not mean "important," or even "interesting." Statistically significant findings may or may not be theoretically significant or practically significant. They simply are research results that are unlikely to be due to chance.

You don't need to be concerned here with the details of how statistical significance is calculated. However, it is worth noting that a key consideration is the amount of variability in the data. That is why the standard deviation, which measures variability, is such an important statistic. When the necessary computations are made for our hypothetical experiment, the difference between the two groups does *not* turn out to be statistically significant. Thus, our results would not be adequate to demonstrate that our tutoring program leads to improved reading achievement. Psychologists have to do this kind of statistical analysis as part of virtually every study. Thus, inferential statistics are an integral element in the research enterprise.

Statistics even provide you with a way of combining the results of several experiments that have examined the same issues. *Meta-analysis combines the statistical results of many studies of the same question yielding an estimate of the size and consistency of a variable's effects* (e.g., Fitzgerald & Price, 2015; Pool, Brosch, Delplanque & Sanders, 2016). For example, as a clinical psychologist you may be aware of several studies that have examined the effects of different therapies for the treatment of depression and you are wondering about their relative effectiveness. Through the use of meta-analysis, you can generate conclusions regarding the size of the therapeutic effects (Cuipers, van Straten, & van Oppen, 2008). Meta-analysis can also be used to help make sense of conflicting research results. Meta-analysis allows researchers to test the generalizability of findings and the strength of a variable's effect across people, places, times, and variations in procedure in a relatively precise and objective way (Schmidt, 2013; Valentine, 2012).

Looking for Flaws: Evaluating Research

Scientific research is a more reliable source of information than casual observation or popular belief. However, it would be wrong to conclude that all published research is free of errors. Scientists are fallible human beings, and flawed studies do make their way into the body of scientific literature. That is one of the reasons that scientists often try to replicate studies.

Replication is the repetition of a study to see whether the earlier results are duplicated. The replication process helps science identify and purge erroneous findings. Of course, the replication process sometimes leads to contradictory results. You'll see some examples in later chapters. Inconsistent findings on a research question can be frustrating and confusing for students. However, some inconsistency in results is to be expected, given science's commitment to replication. This raises the question of how students and research consumers can make sense of inconsistent results. One of the strengths of the empirical approach is that scientists work to reconcile or explain conflicting results.

As you will see, scientific advances often emerge out of efforts to double-check perplexing findings or to explain contradictory research results. Thus, like all sources of information, scientific studies need to be examined with a critical eye. This section describes a number of common methodological problems that often spoil studies. Being aware of these pitfalls will make you more skilled in evaluating research.

Sampling Bias

A *sample* is the collection of participants selected for observation in an empirical study. In contrast, the *population* is the much larger collection of animals or people (from which the sample is drawn) that researchers want to generalize about (see Figure 2.13). For example, when political pollsters attempt to predict elections, all of the voters in a jurisdiction represent the population, and the voters who are actually surveyed constitute the sample. If a researcher were interested in the ability of six-year-old children to form concepts, those six-year-olds actually studied would be the sample and all similar six-year-old children (perhaps those in modern, Western cultures) would be the population.

Empirical research always involves making statistical inferences about a population based on a sample. The strategy of observing a limited sample in order to generalize about a much larger population rests on the assumption that the sample is reasonably *representative* of the population. A sample is representative if its composition is similar to the composition of the population. *Sampling bias* exists

Key Learning Goals

▶ Describe placebo effects, the nature of distortions in self-report data, and sampling bias.

▶ Recognize the common flaws in the design and execution of research.

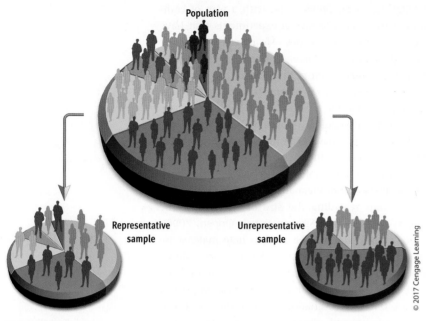

Population

Representative sample

Unrepresentative sample

© 2017 Cengage Learning

Figure 2.13
The relationship between the population and the sample. The process of drawing inferences about a population based on a sample works only if the sample is reasonably representative of the population. A sample is representative if its demographic makeup is similar to that of the population, as shown on the left. If some groups in the population are overrepresented or underrepresented in the sample, as shown on the right, inferences about the population may be skewed or inaccurate.

when a sample is not representative of the population from which it was drawn. When a sample is not representative, generalizations about the population may be inaccurate. For instance, if a political pollster were to survey only people in posh shopping areas frequented by the wealthy, the pollster's generalizations about the voting public as a whole would be off the mark.

As we discussed in Chapter 1, North American psychologists have historically tended to undersample ethnic minorities and people from non-Western

© Winston Davidian/iStockphoto.com

Before accepting the results of a survey poll, one should know something about how the poll was conducted. A polling could, for instance, contain sampling bias. Opinions collected solely from middle-class people but generalized to the voting public as a whole would be an example of such bias.

cultures. In fact, some critics have referred to the typical participant as being drawn almost entirely from WEIRD societies (Henrich, Heine, & Norenzayan, 2010; Suedfeld, 2016). The letters in WEIRD refer to Western, Educated, Industrialized, Rich, and Democratic. This has led to a healthy debate about whether it is appropriate to generalize from these types of participants, and whether any conclusions drawn in studies employing WEIRD participants can be used to draw more general claims about "human nature" (e.g., Arnett, 2008; Asttuti & Bloch, 2010; Baumard & Sperber, 2010; Chaio & Cheon, 2010; Danks & Rose, 2010; Fernald, 2010; Gachter, 2010).

Placebo Effects

In medical research, a placebo is a substance that resembles a drug but has no actual pharmacological effect. In studies that assess the effectiveness of medications, placebos are given to some participants to control for the effects of a problematic extraneous variable: subjects' expectations. Placebos are used because researchers know that participants' expectations can influence their feelings, reactions, and behaviour (Benedetti, 2009). Thus, *placebo effects* occur when participants' expectations lead them to experience some change even though they receive empty, fake, or ineffectual treatment. In studies of new medications, inert placebos often produce surprisingly large beneficial effects (Agid et al., 2013). The power of people's expectations has been demonstrated in studies in which hospitalized subjects are given genuine painkillers covertly (morphine is slipped into their IV without their knowledge). With expectations of pain relief not aroused (due to the hidden drug administration), analgesic medications are typically found to be much less effective than they are under normal circumstances (Benedetti, 2013). This finding suggests that the benefits of genuine drugs are amplified considerably by expectations.

In a similar vein, psychologists have found that participants' expectations can be powerful determinants of their perceptions and behaviour when they are under the microscope in an empirical study (Boot et al., 2013). For example, placebo effects have been seen in lab experiments on the effects of alcohol. In these studies, some of the participants are led to believe that they are drinking alcoholic beverages when in reality the drinks only appear to contain alcohol. Many of the subjects show effects of intoxication even though they haven't really consumed any alcohol (Assefi & Garry, 2003). If you know someone who shows signs of intoxication as soon as

When lab subjects are given "alcoholic beverages" that do not really contain alcohol, many of them show signs of intoxication, illustrating the power of placebo effects.

he or she starts drinking, before alcohol intake can have taken effect physiologically, you have seen placebo effects in action.

Placebo effects are typically attributable to people's expectations (Colagiuri & Boakes, 2010; Oken, 2008). However, recent studies have demonstrated that mere expectations themselves can have actual physiological effects. For example, studies of placebos given to subjects to reduce pain suggest that the placebos actually alter activity in brain circuits that are known to suppress pain (Benedetti, 2013; Wager, Scott, & Zubieta, 2007). Research has also shown that placebo effects can be observed even when conscious expectations are not observed (Jensen et al., 2012).

Researchers should guard against placebo effects whenever participants are likely to have expectations that a treatment will affect them in a certain way. The possible role of placebo effects can be assessed by including a fake version of the experimental treatment (a placebo condition) in a study.

reality check

Misconception
Placebo effects tend to be weak effects.

Reality
Not necessarily. In recent years scientists have developed new respect for the power of the placebo. The strength of placebo effects can vary considerably, depending on the condition treated, the plausibility of the placebo, and a variety of other factors. However, a careful review of the evidence concluded that placebo effects often are powerful effects, frequently approaching the strength of the treatment effects to which they are compared (Wampold, Imel, & Minami, 2007; Wampold et al., 2005).

Distortions in Self-Report Data

Research psychologists often work with *self-report data*, consisting of participants' verbal accounts of their behaviour. This is the case whenever questionnaires, interviews, or personality inventories are used to measure variables. Self-report methods can be quite useful, taking advantage of the fact that people have a unique opportunity to observe themselves full-time (Baldwin, 2000). However, self-reports can be plagued by several kinds of distortion.

One of the most problematic of these distortions is the *social desirability bias*, which is a tendency to give socially approved answers to questions about oneself. Participants who are influenced by this bias work overtime trying to create a favourable impression (Holtgraves, 2004). For example, many survey respondents will report that they voted in an election or gave to a charity when, in fact, it is possible to determine that they did not (Granberg & Holmberg, 1991). Respondents influenced by social desirability bias also tend to report that they are healthier, happier, and less prejudiced than other types of evidence would suggest.

Other problems can also produce distortions in self-report data (Krosnick, 1999; Schuman & Kalton, 1985), including response sets. A *response set* is a tendency to respond to questions in a particular way that is unrelated to the content of the questions. For example, some people tend to agree with nearly everything on a questionnaire (Krosnick & Fabrigar, 1998).

Yet another source of concern is the halo effect (Nisbett & Wilson, 1977). The halo effect occurs when one's overall evaluation of a person, object, or institution spills over to influence more specific ratings. For example, a supervisor's global assessment of an employee's merit might sway specific ratings of the employee's dependability, initiative, communication, knowledge, and so forth. The crux of the problem is that a rater is unable to judge specific evaluative dimensions independently. Obviously, distortions like these can produce inaccurate results. Although researchers have devised ways to neutralize these problems—such as carefully pretesting survey instruments—we should be cautious in drawing conclusions from self-report data (Schaeffer, 2000).

Experimenter Bias

As scientists, psychologists try to conduct their studies in an objective, unbiased way so that their own views will not influence the results. However, objectivity is

Mahzarin Banaji

Harvard psychologist Mahzarin Banaji, along with Anthony Greenwald of the University of Washington, developed the *Implicit Association Test* (IAT), one of the most widely used of the new implicit measures. This approach is often used in research on prejudice and research on self-concept. You can take (anonymously) an implicit test of your own unconscious levels of prejudice about age, gender, race, self-esteem, and other things by visiting the IAT website at https://implicit.harvard.edu.

Robert Rosenthal

"Quite unconsciously, a psychologist interacts in subtle ways with the people he is studying so that he may get the response he expects to get."

a *goal* that scientists strive for, not an accomplished fact that can be taken for granted (MacCoun, 1998). In reality, most researchers have an emotional investment in the outcome of their research. Often they are testing hypotheses that they have developed themselves and that they would like to see supported by the data. It is understandable, then, that *experimenter bias* is a possible source of error in research.

Experimenter bias occurs when a researcher's expectations or preferences about the outcome of a study influence the results obtained. Experimenter bias can slip through to influence studies in many subtle ways. One problem is that researchers, like others, sometimes *see what they want to see*. For instance, when experimenters make apparently honest mistakes in recording participants' responses, the mistakes tend to be heavily slanted in favour of supporting the hypothesis (O'Leary, Kent, & Kanowitz, 1975).

Research by Robert Rosenthal (1976) suggests that experimenter bias may lead researchers to unintentionally influence the behaviour of their participants. In one study, Rosenthal and Fode (1963) recruited undergraduate psychology students to serve as the "experimenters." The students were told that they would be collecting data for a study of how participants rated the success of people portrayed in photographs. In a pilot study, photos were selected that generated (on the average) neutral ratings on a scale extending from –10 (extreme failure) to +10 (extreme success). Rosenthal and Fode then manipulated the expectancies of their experimenters. Half of them were told that, based on pilot data, they

would probably obtain average ratings of –5. The other half were led to expect average ratings of +5. The experimenters were forbidden to converse with their participants except for reading some standardized instructions. Even though the photographs were exactly the same for both groups, the experimenters who *expected* positive ratings *obtained* significantly higher ratings than those who expected negative ratings.

How could the experimenters have swayed the participants' ratings? According to Rosenthal, the experimenters may have unintentionally influenced their participants by sending subtle nonverbal signals as the experiment progressed. Without realizing it, they may have smiled, nodded, or sent other positive cues when participants made ratings that were in line with the experimenters' expectations. Thus, experimenter bias may influence both researchers' observations and their participants' behaviour (Rosenthal, 1994, 2002).

The problems associated with experimenter bias can be neutralized by using a double-blind procedure. The **double-blind procedure** is a research strategy in which neither participants nor experimenters know which participants are in the experimental or control groups. It's not particularly unusual for participants to be "blind" about their treatment condition. However, the double-blind procedure keeps the experimenter in the dark as well. Of course, a member of the research team who isn't directly involved with participants keeps track of who is in which group.

Looking at Ethics: Do the Ends Justify the Means?

Key Learning Goals

- ▶ What are the arguments against using deception in research?
- ▶ What are the ethical guidelines that researchers must adhere to, and where do they come from?
- ▶ Are there any special ethical guidelines for research with animals?

Think back to Stanley Schachter's (1959) study on anxiety and affiliation. Imagine how you would have felt if you had been one of the participants in Schachter's high-anxiety group. You show up at a research lab, expecting to participate in a harmless experiment. The room you are sent to is full of unusual electronic equipment. An official-looking man in a lab coat announces that this equipment will be used to give you a series of painful electric shocks. His statement that the shocks will leave "no permanent tissue damage" is hardly reassuring. Surely, you think, there must be a mistake. All of a sudden, your venture into research has turned into a nightmare! Your stomach knots up in anxiety. The researcher explains that there will be a delay while he prepares his apparatus. He asks you to fill out a short questionnaire about whether you would prefer

to wait alone or with others. Still reeling in dismay at the prospect of being shocked, you fill out the questionnaire. He takes it and then announces that you won't be shocked after all. It was all a hoax! Feelings of relief wash over you, but they're mixed with feelings of anger. You feel as though the experimenter has just made a fool out of you. You're embarrassed and resentful.

Should researchers be allowed to play with your feelings in this way? Should they be permitted to deceive participants in such a manner? Is this the cost that must be paid to advance scientific knowledge? As these questions indicate, the research enterprise sometimes presents scientists with difficult ethical dilemmas (Fried, 2012). These dilemmas reflect concern about the possibility for inflicting harm on subjects. In psychological research, the major ethical dilemmas centre on the use of deception and the use of animals.

Some issues in ethics are easy. For example, psychologists should not participate in torture (Malin, 2012). Ethical problems not only plague some researchers, but can also impact major professional organizations. After reports that the American Psychological Association was "complicit" in the U.S. Department of Defense and Central Intelligence Agency's extreme interrogation program at Guantanamo Bay detention camp run by the U.S. military in Cuba (Hoffman et al., 2015; Risen, 2015; *The Economist*, 2015), it amended its ethical principles (APA, 2016a) and affirmed its opposition to such practices. According to the APA's position on ethics and interrogation, "Any direct or indirect participation in any act of torture or other forms of cruel, inhuman, or degrading treatment or punishment by psychologists is strictly prohibited. There are no exceptions" (APA, 2016b). Specifically mentioned in the APA's statement are interrogation/torture techniques such as waterboarding, sexual humiliation, stress positions, and exploitation of phobias. These and other interrogation techniques have had serious long-term effects on detainees at Guantanamo Bay and other similar facilities (Apuzzo, Fink, & Risen, 2016).

Another part of the ethical considerations for psychologists concerns how they handle their research findings. Researchers should tell the truth and present their findings accurately (Cooper, 2013). Although it is rare, there have been some recent high-profile cases of fraud/academic misconduct in the conducting and reporting of research in psychology (Gross, 2016). For example, Professor Marc Hauser resigned his position from Harvard's Psychology Department in 2011 after internal and external investigations found him responsible for several instances of "scientific misconduct" (*Harvard Magazine*, 2012). It was alleged that he showed a pattern of "fabricating and falsifying data" (Gross, 2012).

Other questions pose issues that are not so easy to resolve. Critics argue against the use of deception on several grounds (Baumrind, 1985; Kelman, 1982; Ortmann & Hertwig, 1997). First, they assert that deception is only a nice word for lying, which they see as inherently immoral. Second, they argue that by deceiving unsuspecting participants, psychologists may undermine many individuals' trust in others. Third, they point out that many deceptive studies produce distress for participants who were not forewarned about that possibility. Specifically, participants may experience great stress during a study or be made to feel foolish when the true nature of a study is explained. Those who defend the use

Included among the detainees at Guantanamo Bay was Canadian citizen Omar Khadr (Shephard, 2008). Khadr was imprisoned shortly after 9/11 when he was just 15 years of age and was held at Guantanamo Bay until he was transferred to a Canadian prison in 2012 (CBC, 2015). Khadr has since been released (Ackerman, 2015). The Canadian government offered an apology to Khadr and paid him a settlement of $10.5 million in 2017. The Supreme Court of Canada had ruled earlier that the participation of Canadian officials in interrogations at Guantanamo Bay had violated Canadian standards concerning the treatment of youth (Fife, 2017).

of deception in research maintain that many important issues could not be investigated if experimenters were not permitted to sometimes mislead participants (Bröder, 1998).

While ethical abuses are the exceptions, they can often be very serious. In the *Tuskegee Syphilis Study* carried out in the United States from 1932 to 1972, a group of black men who had contracted syphilis were enrolled in the study but were never told that they had the disease, and the doctors conducting the study never treated them for it. In the 1940s and 1950s, Canadian First Nations children and adults were used as unwitting participants in nutritional experiments (Mosby, 2013; Weber, 2013). Among other things, milk rations were cut in half, some participants were denied important vitamins, and some dental care services were delayed (Livingstone, 2013). All of this occurred without participants' consent. Also consider the secret CIA-funded experiments carried out at the Allan Memorial Institute in Montreal in the 1950s and 1960s. The abuses inflicted on the unsuspecting patients were horrifying, such as being left in drug-induced comas for days at a time. Patients were not informed about the nature of the research, and it was typically carried out without their consent. This set of experiments was thankfully exposed in the 1970s.

Finally, consider the ethics of a study in which a researcher intentionally induces total paralysis in himself by means of the poison *curare* in order to

The Research Enterprise in Psychology

Michelle Shephard/Toronto Star via Getty Images

examine whether or not thinking was just a form of speech. Because of his paralysis he required a respirator to live and he could not speak. Even though he could not speak, it turned out that he could still think (Oppenheim & Dell, 2010; Smith et al., 1947). He concluded that thinking was not just a form of speech.

While there may be no easy answers to questions concerning deception in psychological research, it is clear that psychologists and their professional associations must be very serious about protecting the rights of clients and research participants.

The Question of Animal Research

Another major ethics controversy concerns the use of animals in research. Every effort must be made to minimize the discomfort felt by animals and to ensure that they will not be used unless there is a strong expectation that the results will benefit both humans and animals. Additional guidelines regarding the treatment of animals have been developed by the Canadian Council on Animal Care (see http://www.ccac.ca). This national organization is responsible for setting guidelines for the care and use of animals in research.

Psychologists use animals as research subjects for several reasons. Sometimes they simply want to know more about the behaviour of a specific type of animal (e.g., Arden et al., 2016; Engle & Zentall, 2016;

Roberts & Macpherson, 2016). In other instances, they want to identify general laws of behaviour that apply to both humans and animals. Finally, in some cases psychologists use animals because they can expose them to treatments that clearly would be unacceptable with human participants. For example, most of the research on the relationship between deficient maternal nutrition during pregnancy and the incidence of birth defects has been done with animals.

It's this third reason for using animals that has generated most of the controversy. Many people maintain that it is wrong to subject animals to harm or pain for research purposes. Essentially, they argue that animals are entitled to the same rights as humans (J. Johnson, 2013; Ryder, 2006). They assert that researchers violate these rights by subjecting animals to unnecessary cruelty in many trivial studies (Bowd & Shapiro, 1993; Hollands, 1989). They also argue that most animal studies are a waste of time because the results may not even apply to humans (Millstone, 1989; Norton, 2005).

Only 7–8 percent of all psychological studies involve animals (mostly rodents and birds). Relatively few of these studies require subjecting the animals to painful or harmful manipulations (American Psychological Association, 1984). Psychologists who defend animal research point to the major advances attributable to psychological research on animals, which many people are unaware of (Baldwin, 1993; Bennett, 2012). Among them are advances in the treatment of mental disorders, neuromuscular disorders, strokes, brain injuries, visual defects, headaches, memory defects, high blood pressure, and problems with pain (Carroll & Overmier, 2001; Domjan & Purdy, 1995).

The manner in which animals can ethically be used for research is a highly charged controversy. Seeking a balanced solution to this issue, Bateson (2011) suggests that the ethical acceptability of specific animal studies should be judged by assessing the studies along three independent dimensions: (1) the extent of anticipated animal suffering, (2) the importance of the research problem addressed, and (3) the likelihood of beneficial discoveries. Psychologists are becoming increasingly sensitive to questions about animal research. Although they continue to use animals in research, strict regulations have been imposed that control nearly every detail of how laboratory animals must be treated (Akins & Panicker, 2012). Most Canadian universities have published guidelines concerning the use and treatment of animals in research. As an example, you can see the guidelines used at the University of Alberta at http://www.reo.ualberta.ca/Animal-Research-Ethics.aspx.

© Brandon Laufenberg/iStockphoto.com

The use of rats and other animals in scientific research is now a major ethical issue. Researchers claim that experiments on animals often yield results and knowledge beneficial to humankind. Opponents maintain that humans have no right to subject animals to harm for research purposes. What is your view?

Ethical Guidelines for Research in Psychology in Canada

In Chapter 1, we introduced you to the major organization for psychology in Canada, the Canadian Psychological Association (CPA). Like its more senior counterpart in the United States, the American Psychological Association (APA), the CPA has spent a great deal of effort developing ethical guidelines to inform psychological research. Both organizations are continually evaluating and updating their ethical guidelines (e.g., American Psychological Association, 2016b; Canadian Psychological Association, 2016), as are the federal and provincial agencies in Canada that fund scientific research (Panel on Research Ethics, 2015). Ethical questions are often quite complex and the answers to such dilemmas aren't easy. While the CPA's statements on ethics are quite detailed (the interested reader is referred to the Canadian Code of Ethics for Psychologists: http://www.cpa.ca/aboutcpa/committees/ethics/codeofethics), we will refer to the four principles underlying the CPA's ethical guidelines. The general principles and their relative ranking of importance are illustrated in Table 2.2.

The CPA ethical principles deal with how people with whom the psychologist comes into contact should be treated. All such persons should be treated with dignity and the psychologist should ensure that their value is not dependent upon culture, race, nationality, or other such factors. Psychologists have a responsibility to protect the rights, privacy, personal liberty, and self-determination of others. Psychologists are also expected to be especially vigilant to provide safeguards to protect the vulnerable (e.g., children) and to ensure in all cases that freedom of consent is assured. Psychologists should take all available measures to ensure that their activities will benefit (or at least, do no harm to) those with whom they interact in a professional capacity. Psychologists should emphasize integrity in their relationships with their clients, students, and research participants. Finally, psychologists must recognize that psychology

Table 2.2

Ethics in Research

Key principles of the Canadian Psychological Association's *Code of Ethics for Psychologists* are presented here. These principles are designed to ensure the welfare of both human and animal participants:

- Principle I: Respect for the Dignity of Persons.
- Principle II: Responsible Caring.
- Principle III: Integrity in Relationships.
- Principle IV: Responsibility to Society.

Source: Canadian Psychological Association (2000), *Code of Ethics for Psychologists* (3rd ed.). Retrieved March 6, 2014, from http://www.cpa.ca/aboutcpa/committees/ethics/codeofethics. Reprinted with permission of the Canadian Psychological Association.

has a responsibility to society to increase knowledge and promote the welfare of all human beings.

In Canadian universities, great care is taken in the application of high ethical standards to research conducted by their members. Before students participate in university-sponsored research, that research must be approved at a variety of levels. Most psychology departments have their own research ethics boards or committees to approve research. It is also typical that the research has to be approved by a committee at the university level consisting of members from various academic departments and groups. Finally, most university research conducted in Canada is funded by the federal government, by the Social Sciences and Humanities Research Council, the National Sciences and Engineering Research Council, and/or the Canadian Institutes of Health Research. These three federal funding agencies, known collectively as the Tri-Council, have formulated their own set of ethical standards (O'Neill, 2011) that must be adhered to for any research to be eligible for funding (see http://www.pre.ethics.gc.ca).

While many of these decisions are not easy, such as on the use of animals in research, psychologists hope that ethical guidelines such as those described here will promote responsible and ethical treatment of all clients and research participants.

Putting It in Perspective: Themes 1 and 7

Two of our seven unifying themes have emerged strongly in this chapter. First, the entire chapter is a testimonial to the idea that psychology is empirical. Second, the discussion of methodological flaws in research provides numerous examples of how people's experience of the world can be highly subjective. Let's examine each of these points in more detail.

As explained in Chapter 1, the empirical approach entails testing ideas, basing conclusions on systematic observation, and relying on a healthy brand of skepticism. All of those features of the empirical approach have been apparent in our review of the research enterprise in psychology. As you have seen, psychologists test their ideas by formulating clear hypotheses that involve predictions about

Key Learning Goal

▶ Identify the two unifying themes highlighted in this chapter.

Finding and Reading Journal Articles

This Personal Application is intended to help you cope with the information explosion in psychology. It assumes that there may come a time when you need to examine original psychological research. Perhaps it will be in your role as a student (working on a term paper, for instance), in another role (parent, teacher, nurse, administrator), or merely out of curiosity. In any case, this Personal Application explains the nature of technical journals and discusses how to find and read articles in them.

The Nature of Technical Journals

As you will recall from earlier in the chapter, a *journal* is a periodical that publishes technical and scholarly material, usually in a narrowly defined area of inquiry. Scholars in most fields—whether economics, chemistry, education, or psychology—publish the bulk of their work in these journals. Journal articles represent the core of intellectual activity in any academic discipline.

In general, journal articles are written for other professionals in the field. Hence, authors assume that their readers are other interested economists or chemists or psychologists. Because journal articles are written in the special language unique to a particular discipline, they are often difficult for nonprofessionals to understand. You will be learning a great deal of psychology's special language in this course, which will improve your ability to understand articles in psychology journals.

In psychology, most journal articles are reports that describe original empirical studies. These reports permit researchers to disseminate their findings to the scientific

The various types of research studies conducted by psychologists are published in professional journals, such as those shown here.

community. Another common type of article is the review article. *Review articles* summarize and reconcile the findings of a large number of studies on a specific issue. Some psychology journals also publish comments or critiques of previously published research, book reviews, theoretical treatises, and descriptions of methodological innovations.

Finding Journal Articles

Reports of psychological research are commonly mentioned in newspapers and on the Internet. These summaries can be helpful to readers, but they often embrace the most sensational conclusions that might be drawn from the research. They also tend to include many oversimplifications and factual errors. Thus, if a study mentioned in the press is of interest to you, you may want to track down the original article to ensure that you get accurate information.

Most discussions of research in the popular press do not mention where you can locate the original technical article. However, there is a way to find out. A computerized database called PsycINFO makes it possible to locate journal articles by specific researchers or scholarly work on specific topics. This huge online database, which is updated constantly, contains brief summaries, or abstracts, of journal articles, books, and chapters in edited books, reporting, reviewing, or theorizing about psychological research. Over 2500 journals are checked regularly to select items for inclusion. The abstracts are concise—about 75 to 175 words. They briefly describe the hypotheses, methods, results, and conclusions of the studies. Each abstract should allow you to determine whether an article is relevant to your interests. If it is, you should be able to find the article in your library (or to order it) because a complete bibliographic reference is provided. The PsycINFO database can be accessed online through most academic libraries or directly via the Internet. Although news accounts of research rarely mention where a study was published, they often mention the name of the researcher. If you have this information, the easiest way to find a specific article is to search PsycINFO for materials published by that researcher. For example, let's say you read a magazine article about the study we discussed earlier in the chapter that found that men were more sexually attracted to women who wore the colour red. Let's assume that the news report mentioned the name of Andrew Elliot as the lead author and indicated that the article was published in 2013. To track down the original article, you would search for journal articles published by Andrew Elliot in 2013. If you conducted this search, you would turn up a list of 27 articles, and the relevant article, titled "Women's use of red clothing as a sexual signal in intersexual interaction" (Elliot, Greitemeyer, & Pazda, 2013), would be obvious. Figure 2.14 shows what you would see if you clicked to obtain the abstract and citation for this article. As you can see, the abstract shows that the original report was published in the

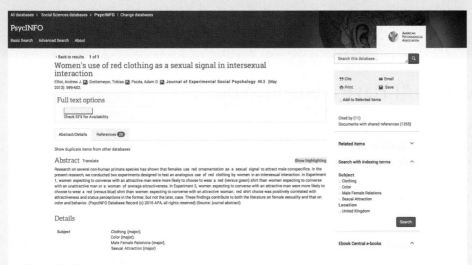

Figure 2.14

Example of a PsycINFO abstract. This information is what you would see if you chose to view the abstract of the relevant item by Elliot et al. (2013). It is a typical abstract from the online PsycINFO database. Each abstract in PsycINFO provides a summary of a specific journal article, book, or chapter in an edited book, and complete bibliographical information.

May issue of the *Journal of Experimental Social Psychology*. Armed with this information, you could obtain the article easily.

You can also search PsycINFO for research literature on particular topics, such as achievement motivation, aggressive behaviour, alcoholism, appetite disorders, or artistic ability. These computerized literature searches can be much more powerful, precise, and thorough than traditional, manual searches in a library. PsycINFO can sift through a few million articles in a matter of seconds to identify all the articles on a subject, such as alcoholism. Obviously, there is no way you can match this efficiency stumbling around in the stacks at your library. Moreover, the computer allows you to pair up topics to swiftly narrow your search to exactly those issues that interest you. For example, if you were preparing a term paper on whether marijuana affects memory, you could quickly identify all the articles dealing with marijuana and memory, which would be invaluable.

Reading Journal Articles

Once you find the journal articles that you want to examine, you need to know how to decipher them. You can process the information in such articles more efficiently if you understand how they are organized. Depending on your needs and purpose, you may want to simply skim through some of the sections. Journal articles follow a fairly standard organization, which includes the following sections and features.

Abstract Most journals print a concise summary at the beginning of each article. This abstract allows readers scanning the journal to quickly decide whether articles are relevant to their interests.

Introduction The introduction presents an overview of the problem studied in the research. It mentions relevant theories and quickly reviews previous research that bears on the problem, usually citing shortcomings in previous research that necessitate the present study. This review of the current state of knowledge on the topic usually progresses to a specific and precise statement regarding the hypotheses under investigation.

Method The method section provides a thorough description of the research methods used in the study. Information is provided on the participants used, the procedures followed, and the data collection techniques employed. This description is made detailed enough to permit another researcher to attempt to replicate the study.

Results The data obtained in the study are reported in the results section. This section often creates problems for novice readers because it includes complex statistical analyses, figures, tables, and graphs. This section does *not* include any inferences based on the data, as such conclusions are supposed to follow in the next section. Instead, it simply contains a concise summary of the raw data and the statistical analyses.

Discussion In the discussion section, you will find the conclusions drawn by the author(s). In contrast to the results section, which is a straightforward summary of empirical observations, the discussion section allows for interpretation and evaluation of the data. Implications for theory and factual knowledge in the discipline are discussed. Conclusions are usually qualified carefully, and any limitations in the study may be acknowledged. This section may also include suggestions for future research on the issue.

References At the end of each article, you will find a list of bibliographical references for any studies cited. This list permits you to examine firsthand other relevant studies mentioned in the article. The references list is often a rich source of leads about other articles that are germane to the topic that you are looking into.

The Perils of Anecdotal Evidence: "I Have a Friend Who . . ."

Key Learning Goal

▶ Recognize anecdotal evidence and understand why it is unreliable.

Here's a tough problem. Suppose you are the judge in a family law court. As you look over the cases that will come before you today, you see that one divorcing couple has managed to settle almost all of the important decisions with minimal conflict—such as who gets the house, who gets the car and the dog, and who pays which bills. However, there is one crucial issue left: Each parent wants custody of the children, and because they could not reach an agreement on their own, the case is now in your court. You will need the wisdom of the legendary King Solomon for this decision. How can you determine what is in the best interests of the children?

Child custody decisions have major consequences for all of the parties involved. As you review the case records, you see that both parents are loving and competent, so there are no obvious reasons for selecting one parent over the other as the primary caretaker. In considering various alternatives, you mull over the possibility of awarding *joint custody,* an arrangement in which the children spend half of their time with each parent, instead of the more usual arrangement where one parent has primary custody and the other has visitation rights. Joint custody seems to have some obvious benefits, but you are not sure how well these arrangements actually work. Will the children feel more attached to both parents if the parents share custody equally? Or will the children feel hassled by always moving around, perhaps spending half of the week at one parent's home and half at the other parent's home? Can parents who are already feuding over child custody issues make these complicated arrangements work? Or is joint custody just too disruptive to everyone's life? You really don't know the answer to any of these vexing questions.

One of the lawyers involved in the case knows that you are thinking about the possibility of joint custody. She also understands that you want more information about how well joint custody tends to work before you render a decision. To help you make up your mind, she tells you about a divorced couple that has had a joint custody arrangement for many years and offers to have them appear in court to describe their experiences "firsthand." They and their children can answer any questions you might have about the pros and cons of joint custody. They should be in the best position to know how well joint custody works because they are living it. Sounds like a reasonable plan. What do you think?

Hopefully, you said, "No, No, No!" What's wrong with asking someone who's been there how well joint custody works? The crux of the problem is that the evidence a single family brings to the question of joint custody is *anecdotal evidence,* **which consists of personal stories about specific incidents and experiences.** Anecdotal evidence can be very seductive. For example, one study found that psychology majors' choices of future courses to enroll in were influenced more by a couple of students' brief anecdotes than by extensive statistics on many other students' ratings of the courses from the previous term (Borgida & Nisbett, 1977). The power of anecdotes was also apparent in a more recent study that explored how to persuade people to take a personal health risk (for hepatitis B infection) more seriously. The researchers found that anecdotal accounts had more persuasive impact than sound factual and statistical evidence (de Wit, Das, & Vet, 2008). Anecdotes readily sway people because they often are concrete, vivid, and memorable. Indeed, people tend to be influenced by anecdotal information even when they are explicitly forewarned that the information is *not* representative (Hamill, Wilson, & Nisbett, 1980). Many politicians are keenly aware of the power of anecdotes and they frequently rely on a single vivid story rather than solid data to sway voters' views. However, anecdotal evidence is fundamentally flawed (Ruscio, 2002; Stanovich, 2004). See Table 2.3.

What, exactly, is wrong with anecdotal evidence? First, in the language of research designs, the anecdotal experiences of one family resemble a single *case study*. The story they tell about their experiences with joint custody may be quite interesting, but their experiences—good or bad—cannot be used to generalize to other couples. Why not? Because they are only one family, and they may be unusual in some way that affects how well they manage joint custody. To draw general conclusions based on the case study approach, you need a systematic series of case studies, so you can look for threads of consistency. A single family is a sample size of one, which surely is not large enough to derive broad principles that would apply to other families.

Second, anecdotal evidence is similar to *self-report data,* which can be distorted for a variety of reasons, such as people's tendency

Table 2.3

Critical Thinking Skills Discussed in This Application

SKILL	DESCRIPTION
Recognizing the limitations of anecdotal evidence	The critical thinker is wary of anecdotal evidence, which consists of personal stories used to support one's assertions.
	Anecdotal evidence tends to be unrepresentative, inaccurate, and unreliable.
Using evidence-based decision making	The critical thinker understands the need to seek sound evidence to guide decisions in everyday life.

An abundance of anecdotal reports suggest that an association exists between the full moon and strange, erratic behaviour. These reports often sound compelling, but as the text explains, anecdotal evidence is flawed in many ways. When researchers have examined the issue systematically, they have consistently found no association between lunar phases and the incidence of psychiatric emergencies, domestic violence, suicide, and so forth (Biermann et al., 2005; Chudler, 2007; Dowling, 2005; Kung & Mrazek, 2005; Lilienfeld & Arkowitz, 2009; McLay, Daylo, & Hammer, 2006).

to give socially approved information about themselves (the *social desirability bias*).

Anecdotes are often inaccurate and riddled with embellishments. We will see in Chapter 7 that memories of personal experiences are far more malleable and far less reliable than widely assumed (Brown et al., 2012; Loftus, 2005; Schacter, 2016).

Can you think of any other reasons for being wary of anecdotal evidence? After reading the chapter, perhaps you thought about the possibility of *sampling bias*. Do you think that the lawyer will pick a couple at random from all those who have been awarded joint custody? It seems highly unlikely. One reason people love to work with anecdotal evidence is that it is so readily manipulated; they can usually find an anecdote or two to support their position, whether or not these anecdotes are representative of most people's experiences.

If the testimony of one family cannot be used in making this critical custody decision, what sort of evidence should you be looking for? One goal of effective critical thinking is to make decisions based on solid evidence. This process is called *evidence-based decision making*. The importance of evidence-based decision making is pervasive in psychology (e.g., American Psychological Association, 2006; Falzon et al., 2010; Kazdin, 2011). In this case, you would need to consider the overall experiences of a large sample of families who have tried joint custody arrangements. In general, across many different families, did the children in joint custody develop well? Was there a disproportionately high rate of emotional problems or other signs of stress for the children or the parents? Was the percentage of families who returned to court at a later date to change their joint custody arrangements higher than for other types of custody arrangements? You can probably think of additional information that you would want to collect regarding the outcomes of various custody arrangements.

In examining research reports, many people recognize the need to evaluate the evidence by looking for the types of flaws described in the main body of the chapter (sampling bias, experimenter bias, and so forth). Curiously, though, many of the same people then fail to apply the same principles of good evidence to their personal decisions in everyday life. The tendency to rely on the anecdotal experiences of a small number of people is sometimes called the *"I have a friend who" syndrome*, because no matter what the topic is, it seems that someone will provide a personal story about a friend as evidence for his or her particular point of view. In short, when you hear people support their assertions with personal stories, a little skepticism is in order.

relationships between variables and use a variety of research methods to collect data so they can see whether their predictions are supported. They carefully analyze their results and publish them in academic journals. Collectively, these procedures represent the essence of the empirical approach.

The subjectivity of personal experience became apparent in the discussion of methodological problems, especially placebo effects and experimenter bias. When participants report beneficial effects from a fake treatment (the placebo), it's because they expected to see these effects. As pointed out in Chapter 1, psychologists and other scientists are not immune to the effects of subjective experience. Although they are trained to be objective, even scientists may see what they expect to see or what they want to see. This is one reason that the empirical approach emphasizes precise measurement and a skeptical attitude. The highly subjective nature of experience is exactly what the empirical approach attempts to neutralize.

The publication of empirical studies allows us to apply a critical eye to the research enterprise. However, you cannot critically analyze studies unless you know where and how to find them. In the upcoming Personal Application, we will discuss where studies are published, how to find studies on specific topics, and how to read research reports. In the subsequent Critical Thinking Application, we'll analyze the shortcomings of anecdotal evidence, which should help you to appreciate the value of empirical evidence.

The Research Enterprise in Psychology

THE SCIENTIFIC APPROACH

Goals

- Measurement and description
- Understanding and prediction
- Application and control

Steps in an investigation

1. Formulate a testable hypothesis.
2. Select the method and design the study.
3. Collect the data.
4. Analyze the data and draw conclusions.
5. Report the findings.

Advantages

- Clarity and precision yield better communication.
- Intolerance of error yields more reliable data.

EXPERIMENTAL RESEARCH

Elements

Independent variable (IV): Condition or event manipulated by the experimenter

Dependent variable (DV): Aspect of behaviour thought to be affected by the independent variable

Experimental group: Participants, or subjects, who receive special treatment

Control group: Similar subjects who do not receive the treatment given to the experimental group

Extraneous variables: Factors besides the IV that might affect the DV; hence, they need to be controlled

Variations

- Can have one group of subjects serve as their own control group
- Can manipulate more than one independent variable in a study

Advantages and disadvantages

- Permits conclusions about cause-and-effect relationships
- Manipulations and control often make experiments artificial
- Practical realities and ethical concerns make it impossible to conduct experiments on many issues

Hypothesis:
Anxiety increases desire to affiliate

Random assignment

Subjects randomly assigned to experimental and control groups

Manipulation of independent variable

Experimental group
"Shocks will be very painful"
(high anxiety)

Control group
"Shocks will be mild and painless"
(low anxiety)

Measurement of dependent variable

High-anxiety group indicated a desire to wait with others more than did low-anxiety group

Conclusion:
Anxiety does increase desire to affiliate

© 2017 Cengage Learning

DESCRIPTIVE/CORRELATIONAL RESEARCH

Correlation

Correlation exists when two variables are related to each other.

Types: *Positive* (variables covary in the same direction) or *negative* (variables co-vary in the opposite direction)

Correlation coefficient: Numerical index of degree of relationship between two variables

Strength: The closer the correlation to either −1.00 or +1.00, the stronger the relationship.

Prediction: The stronger the correlation, the better one can predict.

Causation: Correlation is not equivalent to causation.

Examples of specific correlational/ descriptive methods

Naturalistic observation: Careful, systematic observation, but no intervention with subjects

Case study: In-depth investigation of a single participant, typically involving data from many sources

Survey: Questionnaires and interviews are used to gather information about specific aspects of participants' behaviour

Advantages and disadvantages

- Broadens the scope of the phenomena that psychologists can study (can explore issues that could not be examined with experimental methods)
- Cannot demonstrate that two variables are causally related

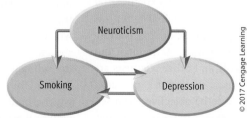

© 2017 Cengage Learning

COMMON FLAWS IN RESEARCH

Sampling bias

Exists when a sample is not representative of the population

Placebo effects

Occur when participants' expectations lead them to experience some change, even though they receive empty or fake treatment

Distortions in self-report data

Result from problems, such as social desirability bias and halo effects, that happen when participants give verbal accounts of their behaviour

Experimenter bias

Occurs when a researcher's expectations or preferences about the outcome of a study influence the results obtained

ETHICAL ISSUES

The question of deception

Q: Should researchers be permitted to mislead participants?

Yes
- Otherwise, important issues could not be investigated.
- Empirical evidence suggests that deception is not harmful to subjects.

No
- Deception is inherently immoral and may undermine participants' trust in others.
- Deceptive studies often create stress for subjects.

© 2005 Foundation for Biomedical Research

The question of animal research

Q: Should researchers be permitted to subject animals to harmful or painful procedures?

Yes
- Otherwise, important issues could not be investigated.
- Relatively little animal research involves pain or harm.

No
- Animals are entitled to the same rights as humans.
- Animal studies are often trivial or may not apply to humans.

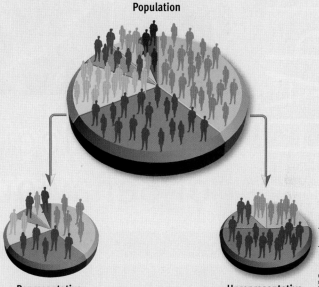

Population

Representative sample

Unrepresentative sample

© 2017 Cengage Learning

APPLICATIONS

- Most original research in psychology is published in journal articles.

- PsycINFO is a computerized database that contains brief summaries of newly published journal articles, books, and chapters in edited books.

- Anecdotes tend to influence people because they are often concrete, vivid, and memorable.

- However, anecdotal evidence is based on the equivalent of a single case study; there are no safeguards to reduce distortions in self-report data; and many anecdotes are inaccurate, second-hand reports.

© Wayne Weiten

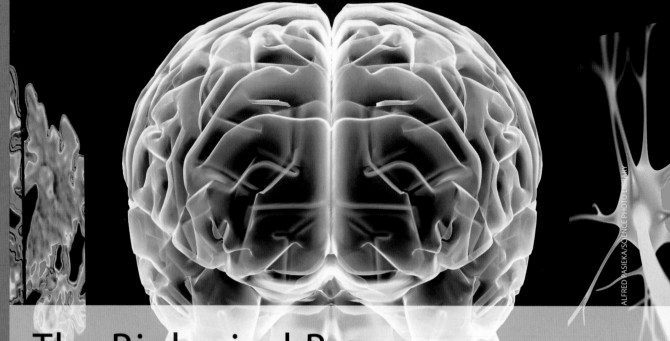

CHAPTER 3

ALFRED PASIEKA/SCIENCE PHOTO LIBRARY

The Biological Bases of Behaviour

Themes in this Chapter

Empiricism

Multifactorial Causation

Heredity & Environment

An adolescent is sitting at the kitchen table having lunch with his favourite uncle. He gets up from the table and goes behind the uncle to retrieve a knife from the drawer. Without warning, he attempts to slice open his uncle's neck. He actually doesn't want to hurt his uncle; he is only trying to prove that this is not really his uncle but a robot posing as his uncle. By exposing the wires, the adolescent figures that he can expose the robot as an imposter. This is not a B-grade horror movie. This is an example of a brain disorder called Capgras delusion. Capgras delusion is a disorder where a person recognizes the external characteristics (e.g., the voice, face, and actions) of someone they know (e.g., a friend, family member, or romantic partner). However, the person does not recognize the internal characteristics of the person they know (e.g., their personality) and do not feel the expected emotional connection with that person (Hirstein, 2010).

A central job of the brain is to make sense of one's experience. If one experiences the familiar external characteristics of the person, but this is not accompanied by the normal emotions, how does the brain make sense of this? For people with Capgras delusion, they think the person is an imposter and they conclude that this person is either a robot, an actor, or an alien who looks and acts like the familiar person, but is not actually the person they know.

The consequences of Capgras delusion can be quite tragic, as in the case of the adolescent who tried to cut his uncle's neck. Or the 74-year-old wife who believed her husband was really an actor pretending to be her husband so she locked him out of the bedroom and asked for a gun to protect herself (Passer & Warnock, 1991). However, the results are not always so negative. There was a housewife with Capgras delusion who thought her husband was actually an imposter. However, she did not want to complain because she thought the "imposter" performed better in bed than her actual husband.

Capgras delusion isn't limited to thinking that people are imposters. People with this disorder may think that their pet has been replaced with an imposter as well. Though it was originally thought that this delusion was purely psychiatric, it is now considered a neurological disorder resulting from lesions or degeneration in the amygdala (a part of the brain that connects emotions to what we see) and the fusiform gyrus (a part of the brain involved in perceiving faces; Pearn & Gardner-Thorpe, 2002). However, damage to these areas does not always result in Capgras delusion. Sometimes damage to these regions results in Coltard's syndrome which is when the affected person believes him- or herself to be dead!

One of the most rapidly developing areas of research is the study of the relationships between the brain and behaviour (Cacioppo et al., 2008; Poldrack & Wagner, 2008). You may have already heard about the work of neuroscientists, such as McMaster University's Sandra Witelson, Dalhousie University's John Connolly, and Western University's Adrian Owen.

Sandra Witelson is well known for her research and for having one of the most extensive collections of preserved human brains. She studied one of the world's most famous brains—that of Albert Einstein. The tale of how Einstein's brain got to Witelson is fascinating in itself and has been the subject of numerous articles and Carolyn Abraham's (2002) book *Possessing Genius*. Einstein died in April 1955 from a ruptured aneurysm for which he had previously refused surgery. His brain was removed by Tom Harvey, a hospital pathologist, and injected with formalin to preserve it.

Over the years, Harvey donated small pieces of Einstein's brain for analysis, although he was waiting for the right person who could conduct a scientific examination of the brain. Eventually, Harvey read about the scientific work of Sandra Witelson and offered her the brain. He drove across the border in 1996 with Einstein's brain in the trunk of his car and delivered it to her.

Witelson examined and measured the pieces of the brain and examined photos originally taken of the brain. She compared Einstein's brain with other "control" brains she had in her laboratory. Witelson found that Einstein's brain seemed highly similar overall to most other brains; it was about the same size and weight (Witelson, Kigar, & Harvey, 1999). But there were important exceptions, including a wider parietal region (toward the top and back of the brain) and a distinct Sylvian fissure (a fissure or groove separating the frontal lobe from the temporal lobe). Witelson speculated that these differences made sense in light of Einstein's intellect and approach to science: "Visuospatial cognition, mathematical thought, and imagery of movement are strongly dependent on this region. Einstein's exceptional intellect in these cognitive domains and his self-described mode of scientific thinking may be related to the atypical anatomy in his inferior parietal lobules" (Witelson et al., 1999, p. 2152). Work on Einstein's brain continues, suggesting, among other things, that his primary motor and somatosensory areas were distinctive (Falk, 2009). Scientists continue to try to link these differences to Einstein's abilities and aptitudes.

The Biological Bases of Behaviour

Professor Adrian Owen is a neuroscientist at Western University. He conducts research and developed techniques to detect awareness in patients after they have suffered traumatic brain injury.

© SWS Photography

In this chapter we will consider the brain and the techniques used to investigate it. One method examines the electrical activity of the brain through EEG recordings. A more recent method examines the brain and its processes with functional magnetic resonance imaging (fMRI). Both methods have been used to examine and evaluate patients thought to be in a vegetative state.

Adrian Owen (Owen, 2017; Naci & Owen, 2013; Young et al., 2013) of Western University used an fMRI to assess Scott Routley, who was thought to be in a chronic vegetative state after suffering a head injury in a car accident (Lunau, 2013). In spite of what they were told by his doctors, his parents believed that their son was responsive and conscious and that he was capable of communicating despite his paralysis. All they needed was for someone to unlock his abilities. Using fMRI technology, Owen demonstrated that Scott was cognitively intact. Scott was able to activate different parts of his brain to answer yes-or-no questions, and this showed up on fMRI scans. He was even able to inform Owen that he was not in any physical pain despite his injuries. Scott's mother and father were not surprised—it was just that now somebody else believed them.

Though not all of the research findings you will read about in this chapter are as dramatic as these three examples, they have the potential for unlocking some of the mysteries of the brain and improving the lives of people suffering from various disorders.

The Anatomy of the Nervous System

Key Learning Goals

▶ Identify the various parts of the neuron and the main functions of the glia cells.

▶ Describe the neural impulse, and explain how neurons communicate at chemical synapses.

▶ Discuss some of the functions of acetylcholine, the monoamine neurotransmitters, GABA, and endorphins.

Housed in your skull is about 1300–1400 grams (almost three pounds) of electrified "jelly" that is the most wondrous of objects. The brain consists of two types of cells: *neurons* and *glia*. Much of the efforts of scientists have focused on understanding neurons. **Neurons are individual cells in the nervous system that receive, integrate, and transmit information.** The term "information" is used here and by neuroscientists to convey that the activity of neurons is meaningful as it relates to an organism's behaviour. Before we consider neurons and their activity in detail, let us first consider the sometimes neglected glial cells.

Glial Cells

Glia **are cells found throughout the nervous system and they provide various types of support for neurons.** Glia (from the Greek word meaning "glue") tend to be much smaller than neurons. It was once thought that glia outnumbered neurons by as much as ten to one, but research suggests that the human brain consists of roughly equal numbers of neurons and glial cells (Azevedo et al., 2009).

The importance of glial cells is hinted at by a study of Albert Einstein's brain. Einstein's brain, or at least a small part of it, was available to scientists with captivating ideas. Marion Diamond and her research team had one such idea (Diamond et al., 1985). They wondered about the relation between neurons and glial cells in Einstein's brain. What they found was surprising; the ratio of glial cells to neurons in the left parietal lobe of Einstein's brain was actually higher than the ratio for the average person. What was different about Einstein's brain was that he may have had relatively more glial cells. Though Diamond's work has been criticized for, among other things, the age and appropriateness of the comparison brains, perhaps it was the supporting cells, the glial cells, that contributed to Einstein's genius, and not simply the neurons.

There are many different types of glial cells and they have a wide range of critical functions. For example, some act like parents, providing nutrition, healing, protection, and physical support for the neurons. Some act like cleaners, removing debris from the brain. Some act like a miniature Pac Man from a video game, devouring dead and damaged cells.

Glial cells provide protection to the brain in three ways. First, they produce *cerebral spinal fluid*, **which cushions the brain during an impact.** Second, they form the *blood-brain barrier*, which prevents foreign material, including some viruses and drugs, from entering the brain. Third, they contribute to the immune system of the brain.

Glial cells have a host of additional functions that are critical to the neurons' health and survival. The glial cells provide the neurons with nutrients and energy from the blood. Glial cells provide structure for the neurons, holding them in place and forming scar tissue if the brain is injured. Glia also play a complicated role in the development of the nervous system in the human embryo. Glial cells may play an important role in memory formation (Bains & Oliet, 2007). As we will learn when we discuss neurons, glial cells also insulate the neurons, allowing them to process information faster and with less energy.

Traditionally, it was thought that the "glamorous" work in the nervous system—the transmission and integration of informational signals—was the exclusive province of the neurons. However, research has changed this view by suggesting that glia may also send and receive chemical signals (Deitmer & Rose, 2010; Fields, 2011). Some types of glia can detect neural impulses and send signals to other glial cells, some of which can feed signals back to neurons. Surprised by this discovery, neuroscientists are now trying to determine how this signalling system interfaces with the neural communication system. One view is that glia *modulate* the signalling of neurons, dampening or amplifying synaptic activity (Halassa & Haydon, 2010). Another view is that glial cells' shield synapses from the "chatter" of surrounding neuronal activity, thus enhancing the signal-to-noise ratio in the nervous system (Nedergaard & Verkhratsky, 2012). These alternate viewpoints are not necessarily incompatible, and much remains to be learned.

reality check

Misconception

Neurons are responsible for all the information processing in the nervous system.

Reality

Until recently, it was thought that the transmission and integration of informational signals was the exclusive role of the neurons. However, newer research has demonstrated that glial cells also play an important role in information processing.

Research shows that glial cells play a role in a variety of major disorders. For example, dysfunction in glial cells may contribute to the cognitive impairment seen in schizophrenic disorders (Mitterauer, 2011) and to some forms of depressive disorders (Jellinger, 2013). Additionally, the gradual deterioration of glia might contribute to Alzheimer's disease (Olabarria et al., 2010). Glial cells have also been implicated in the experience of chronic pain (Ji, Berta, & Nedergaard, 2013).

Although glia may contribute to information processing in the nervous system, the bulk of this crucial work is handled by the neurons. Thus, to understand the nervous system, we need to examine the process of neural activity in some detail.

Neurons

The most recent and careful calculations estimate that there are roughly *86 billion* neurons in the human brain (Azevedo et al., 2009). Don't try and count them yourself. If you counted them nonstop at the rate of one per second, you'd be counting for more than 3000 years! And, remember, most neurons have synaptic connections to many other neurons, so there may be *100 trillion* synapses in a human brain! A *synapse* **is a junction where information is transmitted from one neuron to the next.**

A vast majority of neurons communicate only with other neurons. However, a small minority receive signals from outside the nervous system (from sensory organs) or carry messages from the nervous system to the muscles that move the body.

A highly simplified drawing of a "typical" neuron is shown in Figure 3.1. Actually, neurons come in

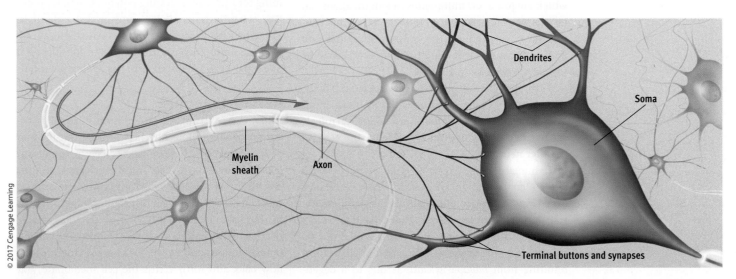

© 2017 Cengage Learning

Figure 3.1
Structure of the neuron. Neurons are the communication links of the nervous system. This diagram highlights the key parts of a neuron, including specialized receptor areas (dendrites), the cell body (soma), the axon fibre along which impulses are transmitted, and the terminal buttons, which release chemical messengers that carry signals to other neurons. Neurons vary considerably in size and shape and are usually densely interconnected.

such a tremendous variety of types and shapes that no single drawing can adequately represent them. Trying to draw the "typical" neuron is like trying to draw the "typical" tree. Though neurons differ in shape and size, they share five common structural properties. First, all neurons have a barrier, like a skin, that separates the inside of the cell from the outside. This barrier, called the *cell membrane*, has small channels or gates that allow, or prevent, molecules from entering or leaving the cell. This will become important when we discuss resting and action potentials of neurons.

Second, each neuron has a *cell body*, also called a *soma*, which contains the nucleus and acts like a tiny factory where proteins and neurotransmitters (or at least the building blocks of neurotransmitters) are manufactured. (The word *soma* comes from the Greek word meaning *body*.) The cell body is where information from thousands of other cells is gathered and sorted out.

Third, all cells have *dendrites*, which gather much of the incoming information from other cells. Dendrites are the structures that branch out from the cell body. (*Dendrite* is a Greek word for *tree*.) Their main purpose is to increase the surface area of the neuron so that chemicals, released from thousands of other cells, can influence the activity of the neuron that the dendrites belong to.

Fourth, in addition to the many dendrites that branch out from the cell body, each neuron has a single main extension called the *axon*. The *axon* is a long, thin fibre that transmits signals away from the soma to other neurons or to muscles or glands. The axon's main role is to conduct a brief electrical charge away from the cell body. Unlike dendrites, which are just a few millimetres in length, axons can be relatively long. For example, some axons that control movement connect the brain to the spinal cord and can be a metre in length. Some axons may be several metres long in a giraffe.

Fifth, though only one axon leaves each cell body, this axon can branch and each branch ends in an *axon terminal*. Axon *terminals* are where chemicals are released by the neuron to influence the activity of other neurons.

In humans, many axons are wrapped in cells with a high concentration of a white, fatty substance called *myelin*. The *myelin sheath* is insulating material, derived from specialized glial cells. If an axon's myelin sheath deteriorates, its signals may not be transmitted effectively. The loss of muscle control resulting from *multiple sclerosis* is due to a degeneration of myelin sheaths (Joffe, 2009). Multiple sclerosis is a disease where the immune system malfunctions and attacks the glial cells that insulate the neurons in the brain and spinal cord. The result of these attacks can be extreme fatigue and problems in vision (e.g., blurred or double vision) and movement (e.g., muscle stiffness, speech and coordination difficulties, and paralysis). It is interesting to note that a single change, the peeling back of the myelin from the axon, can result in a large number of symptoms.

When the myelin sheath is intact it helps to stabilize the axon structure and the patterns of connectivity in the neural network (Fields, 2014). It contributes two big advantages. First, it speeds up the transmission of signals that move along axons (Zorumski, Isenberg, & Mennerick, 2009). You have probably already experienced the results of this increased speed. For example, when you stub your toe you get an almost-instant feeling of a sharp pain followed a second or two later by a dull ache. The quickly processed pain is a message carried from your toe to your brain via myelinated axons (the fast ones). The dull pain is delayed because it is carried to the brain via unmyelinated axons. The second benefit of the myelin sheath is that it is very efficient. Each cell maintains an electric charge across its membrane. In fact, roughly half the energy used by the brain is to maintain this charge. Cells whose axons are wrapped in a myelin sheath only have to maintain this charge at small gaps in the myelin along the length of the axon. This charge is one of the four basic activities of the cell, which we consider next.

The Function of Neurons: Information Transmission

The activity of neurons can be understood by examining four processes: resting potential, action potential, synaptic transmission, and graded potentials. Though these processes are intertwined and all are working simultaneously, it is helpful to consider each one separately. We'll start with the resting potential.

Resting Potential

When the cell is at rest, there is an unequal distribution of some molecules between the outside and inside of the cell. These molecules have an important feature; they have gained or lost an electron so they possess an electrical charge. This type of molecule is called an *ion*. The uneven distribution of ions results in the inside of the cell having an electrical charge relative to the outside. Positively charged sodium and potassium ions and negatively charged chloride ions flow back and forth across the cell membrane, but they do not cross at the same rate. The difference in flow rates leads to a slightly higher concentration of negatively charged ions inside the cell. The resulting voltage means that the neuron at rest is a tiny battery, a store of potential energy. The *resting potential of a neuron is its stable, negative charge when the cell is inactive.* As shown in Figure 3.2 this charge is about −70 millivolts, roughly one-twentieth of the voltage of a flashlight battery.

To create and maintain the resting potential, two ions are critical: potassium (K+) and sodium (Cl−). There are small openings in the cell membrane, called gates or channels, which allow potassium to move more easily in and out of the cell. There are channels for sodium (Na+) as well, but they are usually closed. To create the resting potential there is an exchange system that pumps three sodium ions out of the cell for every two potassium cells it pumps in. This exchange system is known as the *sodium-potassium pump.* It is responsible for keeping more sodium ions just outside the cell membrane. Because sodium ions are positively charged, the greater concentration of sodium just outside of the cell membrane means that the inside of the cell has a relatively negative charge—this is critical for maintaining the resting potential.

We call this first process the *resting potential* for two reasons. First, the resting potential is maintained when the cell is relatively at rest. Second, the uneven distribution of ions represents a potential energy stored in the cell. You might think of this like a dam across a river. The dam contains potential energy such that if small channels are opened in the dam, the built-up water pressure will result in the release of energy as the water rushes through the channels.

How important is the resting potential? Well, half the energy the brain uses is used to create and maintain the resting potential. Without the resting potential, the brain would not allow us to think, feel, learn, or move. This is because the second process, the *action potential,* requires the resting potential.

Action Potential

When a neuron is stimulated by the activity of other cells there can be a complete, rapid, and brief reversal of the electrical potential across that neuron's membrane. During this reversal, the inside of the cell may go from its resting potential of −70 millivolts to +30 millivolts. This reversal in polarity allows for an electric charge to race down the axon. This charge is called the *action potential,* **which is a very brief shift in a neuron's electrical charge that travels along an axon.** After the action potential, the cell must use the sodium-potassium pump to restore the resting potential.

Like the resting potential, the stars of the show for the action potential are the ions and ion channels. When the cell is sufficiently stimulated, sodium

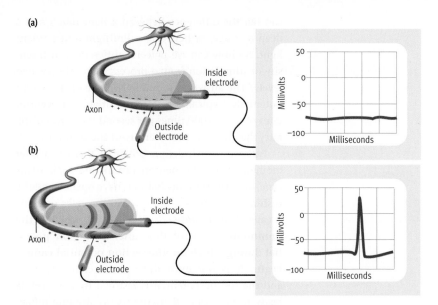

Figure 3.2
The neural impulse. The electrochemical properties of the neuron allow it to transmit signals. The electric charge of a neuron can be measured with a pair of electrodes connected to an oscilloscope, as Hodgkin and Huxley (1952) showed with a squid axon. Because of its exceptionally thick axons, the squid has frequently been used by scientists studying the neural impulse. (a) At rest, the neuron's voltage hovers around 70 millivolts. (b) When a neuron is stimulated, a brief jump occurs in the neuron's voltage, resulting in a spike on the oscilloscope recording of the neuron's electrical activity. This change in voltage, called an action potential, travels along the axon like a spark travelling along a trail of gunpowder.

channels from a small section of the membrane open. This allows for the sodium ions near this channel, which have been built up on the outside of the cell membrane, to rush into the cell. This in turn causes the next section of the membrane to open its sodium channels. This process continues so that the opening of the channels allows for the electrical charge to race down the length of the axon until it reaches the end of the axon.

The action potential process is somewhat like fans in a huge stadium performing the wave. A column of fans stands up while raising their arms. As they sit down, the fans next to them stand up and raise their arms, and so on. The fans here are like small portions of the membrane. The "wave" that their action creates is like the electrical charge racing down the axon.

Once this process starts, no additional energy or input is required. Once started, the full action potential completes its journey to the cell's end, the axon terminals. This has been referred to as the *all-or-none law* because either the cell fires or it does not. It's kind of like being pregnant in that either you are or you are not; no one is partially pregnant and there are, with few exceptions, no partial action potentials.

The all-or-none law poses a riddle: How can we detect degrees of stimulation if the only information the brain receives is an on or off pulse? Clearly, we can tell the difference between a light touch and a deep massage, or between a dim light and a bright light. So how can we perceive differences in intensity of stimulation from a process that only has two levels? The answer is found in the rate of the action potentials. Typically, action potentials can occur at rates of up to 1000 times per second. The greater the rate, the greater is the intensity of the stimulus.

Following each action potential there is a brief moment when the neuron cannot fire again. This time, after the sodium channels have opened and the rushing in of the sodium reverses the cell's polarity, is called the *absolute refractory period*, which is the minimum length of time after an action potential during which another action potential cannot begin. It is not until the sodium channels close and the resting potential is restored that the cell is ready to fire again. If there was no absolute refractory period, the action potential would continue bouncing up and down the axon like the steel ball in a game of pinball.

A limiting factor in the speed of the action potential is the size of the axon. Axons with a larger diameter have less resistance, so the speed of the action potential can be increased. Based on this fact alone, a simple way to increase the speed of action potentials, and therefore the speed of the brain's processing, would be to have bigger axons. However, if your billions of neurons were all larger, your head would also have to be larger. This would pose a greater problem than simply not having your hat fit you anymore. There may be structural problems supporting an enlarged head, and giving birth to a child with an enormous head would be unwelcome.

Many neurons have developed an elegant solution to the need for faster action potentials without a substantial increase in the size of the neurons. Some neurons are insulated. Glial cells provide this insulation by wrapping themselves around the axons of many neurons through *myelination*. This process produces the *myelin sheath*, the insulating material derived from the glial cells that encase some axons of neurons. There are small gaps in the myelination that leave the axon exposed. These gaps are key to two important benefits of myelination. First, the resting potential only needs to be maintained at these gaps. This has the important benefit of saving energy. Remember, maintaining the resting potential uses a lot of energy. By only requiring the resting potential at the gaps in the myelin, significant energy is saved. Second, during an action potential, the rapid reversal of polarity only occurs at these gaps. This allows the action potential to "leap frog" down the axon up to 30 times faster than down an unmyelinated axon.

To understand these two benefits of myelination more clearly, let's return to our example of fans performing the wave at a large stadium. Imagine that not every column of fans must jump up and raise their hands after the person next to them does the same. Instead, if fans from only every tenth column participate in the wave, there will be a clear energy savings as 90 percent of the fans can remain seated. Furthermore, the wave can skip over nine columns at a time, allowing for the speed of the wave to be substantially increased.

The action potential allows for the communication of information from one area of a neuron, typically from the dendrites and cell body, to another area, typically the terminal buttons. Action potentials occur *within* one cell and are *electrical* in nature. Communication *between* two or more cells is largely *chemical* in nature and involves synaptic transmission.

Synaptic Transmission

The primary way that neurons communicate with other neurons is called *synaptic transmission*. Understanding synaptic transmission is critical for psychologists because it is directly linked to everything we care about. Your inclination to take risks, your feelings of depression, your memory of your first kiss, your use of recreational drugs, your learning how to drive a car, and your basic personality are all tied to synaptic transmission.

Basically, each neuron makes a chemical and stores it in the terminal buttons. When a neuron is sufficiently stimulated, an action potential causes the chemical to be released into very tiny gaps between the neuron and adjacent neurons. These gaps are referred to as *synaptic clefts*. This chemical that is released can cling to specialized areas of these adjacent neurons and stimulate them. If this stimulation, combined with the stimulation from chemicals released from hundreds of other cells, is sufficient, these adjacent neurons may have their own action potential.

To understand synaptic transmission in detail, let's consider how one neuron can affect just one other adjacent neuron. The first neuron is called the *presynaptic neuron* because it occurs before the *synapse*, which is the tiny gap that separates neurons (see Figure 3.3 for an illustration of the synapse and positioning of the synaptic cleft). The adjacent neuron is called the *postsynaptic neuron* because it occurs after the synapse. Synaptic transmission can be organized into eight steps:

1. *Synthesis*. Chemicals, or at least parts of them, are made in the cell body of each neuron. These chemicals, known as *neurotransmitters*, transmit information from one neuron to another. There are

many different types of chemicals that serve as neurotransmitters and they are made, in part, from the food we eat.

2. *Transportation and storage.* When molecules of the neurotransmitter are made, they are transported from the cell body to the axon terminal where they are stored. They are stored in small bead-like containers called *synaptic vesicles.*

3. *Release.* When an action potential in the neuron reaches the axon terminal, the synaptic vesicles melt into the cell membrane, causing the release of the neurotransmitter into the synapse (Schwarz, 2008). Because this part of the membrane is before the synapse, it is called the *presynaptic membrane.*

4. *Binding.* The released molecules of neurotransmitter float across the gap and some bind with the membrane of the cell after the synapse. The molecules bind to specialized proteins called *receptors.* These receptors allow the molecules to influence whether this next cell, the postsynaptic cell, will have its own action potential. A specific neurotransmitter can bind only to receptor sites that its molecular structure will fit into, much like a key must fit a lock.

5. *Deactivation.* One type of neurotransmitter (we will talk about the importance of this neurotransmitter, acetylcholine, shortly) can be destroyed by an enzyme in the synapse. This prevents the neurotransmitter from having a never-ending influence on the postsynaptic cell.

6. *Autoreceptor activation.* Some neurotransmitters bind to receptors on the same neuron that released it. This type of receptor is called an autoreceptor. Autoreceptors only respond to neurotransmitters that have been released by the same neuron on which it is situated. Binding on these presynaptic receptors can regulate Steps 1 and 3. For example, this binding can decrease the synthesis and release of the neurotransmitter.

7. *Reuptake.* Leftover and excess neurotransmitter molecules can be brought back in to the presynaptic region of the cell. This is one of the original recycling mechanisms. By taking the extra molecules out of the synapse, this can stop the effect of the neurotransmitter on the postsynaptic cell and reduce the amount of neurotransmitter that the presynaptic cell must make.

8. *Degradation.* Given that you are continually synthesizing neurotransmitters (Step 1) and recycling used neurotransmitters (Step 7), there needs to be a mechanism to ensure that you don't end up with too much. Enzymes in the presynaptic region break down excess neurotransmitter molecules, which are then eliminated.

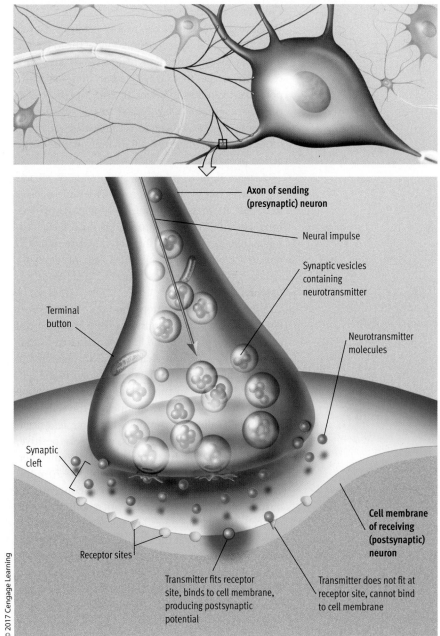

© 2017 Cengage Learning

Axon of sending (presynaptic) neuron

Neural impulse

Synaptic vesicles containing neurotransmitter

Neurotransmitter molecules

Terminal button

Cell membrane of receiving (postsynaptic) neuron

Synaptic cleft

Receptor sites

Transmitter fits receptor site, binds to cell membrane, producing postsynaptic potential

Transmitter does not fit at receptor site, cannot bind to cell membrane

Figure 3.3
The synapse. When a neural impulse reaches an axon's terminal buttons, it triggers the release of chemical messengers called neurotransmitters. The neurotransmitter molecules diffuse across the synaptic cleft and bind to receptor sites on the postsynaptic neuron. A specific neurotransmitter can bind only to receptor sites that its molecular structure will fit into, much like a key must fit a lock.

The first four steps of synaptic transmission share a common purpose; they all increase the influence of the presynaptic cell on the postsynaptic cell. The last four steps share a common purpose as well; they are all involved in stopping the presynaptic cell from continuing to influence the postsynaptic cell. It would be pretty useless to have a light switch with only one position. For example, imagine that once you turned your bedroom light on, it stayed on forever even when you wanted to sleep. We need to both turn on and off our lights. Similarly, the influence of a presynaptic cell on a postsynaptic cell can be turned on (Steps 1–4) and turned off (Steps 5–8).

The Biological Bases of Behaviour

Graded Potentials

We have covered three (i.e., resting potential, action potential, and synaptic transmission) of the four basic processes in the activity of neurons. The final process is the trigger that takes a neuron from its resting potential to an action potential. This trigger is called the *graded potential* (*potential* because it involves an electrical change, and *graded* because there are many different levels, unlike the "all or none" nature of the action potential).

A neuron may receive a symphony of signals from *thousands* of other neurons. The same neuron may pass its messages along to thousands of neurons as well. Thus, a neuron must do a great deal more than simply relay the individual messages it receives. It must *integrate* signals arriving at many synapses before it "decides" whether to fire an action potential.

When neurotransmitters bind to the receptors (Step 4 of synaptic transmission) this causes the cell membrane to change. The important change is that small holes, called ion channels, in the membrane open and allow for ions to move in or out of the cell. Changes in these ion channels are of two types. One type of change is that the channels in the cell membrane open, allowing the cell to become less negative. For example, sodium ions, which are positive, enter the cell through sodium channels. Remember, the resting potential is negative (about -70 millivolts) in part because sodium has been concentrated outside of the cell. Therefore, when sodium enters the cell, the cell becomes less negative. The second type of change is that the channels in the membrane open, allowing the cell to become more negative. For example, potassium ions, which are also positive, may leave the cell through potassium channels. When potassium ions leave the cell, the cell becomes more negative.

If the cell becomes more negative, called *hyperpolarization*, an action potential will not occur. However, if the cell becomes sufficiently more positive, called *depolarization*, an action potential may occur. What do we mean by "sufficiently more positive"? The resting potential is -70 millivolts, but if the cumulative effects of the changes in the cell membrane change this electrical differential to about -50 millivolts, then this triggers the action potential.

Remember, each neuron is influenced by thousands of synapses. Activity at some synapses causes the postsynaptic membrane to become more negative. These changes are called *inhibitory postsynaptic potentials*, as they inhibit or decrease the chance of an action potential. Some synapses cause the postsynaptic membrane to become less negative. These changes are called *excitatory postsynaptic potentials*, as they increase the chance of an action potential. Thus, the state of the neuron is a weighted balance between excitatory and inhibitory influences (Byrne, 2008).

Whether the thousands of excitatory and inhibitory postsynaptic potentials result in an action potential depends on whether the -50 millivolt threshold is reached. Graded potentials act as if they are in a shouting match. Some synapses are yelling at the cell to fire, and others are yelling for the cell to not fire. In a shouting match, when two people are standing close together, their voices can be added together, so you are more likely to hear them. Similarly, graded potentials that occur close together in space (i.e., close together on the cell membrane) can be added together. This process of combining excitatory and inhibitory inputs at different, but very close, branches of a dendrite is called *spatial summation*.

In a shouting match, if the same person shouts repeatedly very close together in time, the individual shouts can be added together (i.e., you are more likely to hear that person). Similarly, graded potentials from the same synapse that occur close together in time can be added together. This process of combining excitatory and inhibitory inputs that arrive at the dendrites in rapid succession is called *temporal summation*. For each fraction of a second, the cell calculates the overall impact of graded potentials through spatial and temporal summation. If the result at any moment is that the cell reaches the firing threshold, an action potential occurs.

Summary of the Activity of Neurons

The four main processes of cells work together. A neuron is constantly receiving input from thousands of other cells. This input is the result of synaptic transmission. In particular, neurotransmitter molecules bind to the postsynaptic receptors. This binding causes the cell's membrane to become more negative (i.e., inhibitory postsynaptic potentials hyperpolarize the membrane) or more positive (i.e., excitatory postsynaptic potentials cause the cell to depolarize). The effects of the synaptic binding, therefore, cause graded potentials. If the combined effect of the graded potentials causes the cell membrane to reach a threshold of about -50 millivolts, then an action potential occurs. This action potential consists of an electrical pulse rocketing down the length of the neuron. When the action potential reaches the end of the axon, a neurotransmitter is released so that this neuron can cause graded potentials in subsequent neurons. Following the action potential, the cell needs to regain its resting potential before it is ready for another action potential and the whole activity can reoccur.

Neuronal activity involves four main processes. The first process is the creation and maintenance of a *resting potential*. The resting potential is the −70 milli-volt charge, with the inside of the cell being negative relative to the outside. This potential is the result of the uneven distribution of ions. This uneven distri-bution is partially the result of an exchange system, the sodium potassium pump, which concentrates sodium outside of the membrane.

The second process is the *action potential*. The action potential is the electrical pulse that travels down the axon. It results from sodium channels opening up to allow sodium to rush into the cell. The action potential briefly reverses the charge across the membrane, changing it from negative to posi-tive. Some axons are myelinated, which means they are insulated and protected by specialized glial cells. Myelination results in two advantages: (1) increased speed of the action potential, and (2) energy savings, as the restoration and maintenance of the resting potential, which takes energy, only has to occur in the gaps in the myelin.

The third process is *synaptic transmission*. This transmission allows for neurons to influence other neurons through the release of chemicals. These chemicals, called *neurotransmitters*, are synthesized in the cell body, stored in the axon terminals, and released into the synapse. There are four mecha-nisms to stop synaptic transmission: (1) autore-ception, in which a neurotransmitter binds to the neuron that released it, causing the activity of the neurotransmitter to be decreased; (2) deactivation, in which the neurotransmitter is rendered useless by enzymes in the synapse; (3) reuptake, when the neurotransmitter is taken back into the cell that just released it; and (4) degradation, in which the neu-rotransmitter is broken down in the cell and then eliminated.

The fourth process is the *graded potential*. This is the trigger that starts the action potential. The release of neurotransmitters from neighbouring cells into the synapses can increase (excitatory postsyn-aptic potentials) or decrease (inhibitory postsynaptic potentials) the chance of a neuron having an action potential. The effect of each excitatory and inhibi-tory postsynaptic potential is summed up across small distances of the cell membrane (spatial sum-mation) and across small amounts of time (temporal summation). If the net result of the graded potentials is to change the resting potential from −70 millivolts to about −50 millivolts then an action potential takes place.

These four processes are orchestrated into a continual dynamic action. A single neuron might fire hundreds of times each second. Therefore, the summing of the graded potentials, causing the action potential, resulting in the release of neurotrans-mitter, and the restoration of the resting potential are all completed very quickly.

As Rita Carter (1998) pointed out in *Mapping the Mind*, "The firing of a single neuron is not enough to create the twitch of an eyelid in sleep, let alone a conscious impression. . . . Millions of neurons must fire in unison to produce the most trifling thought" (p. 19). Most neurons are interlinked in complex chains, pathways, circuits, and networks. Our per-ceptions, thoughts, and actions depend on *patterns* of neural activity in elaborate neural networks. These networks consist of interconnected neurons that fre-quently fire together or sequentially to perform cer-tain functions (Song et al., 2005). The links in these networks are fluid, as new synaptic connections may be made while some old connections wither away (Hua & Smith, 2004).

Normal development is characterized more by the *elimination of old synapses* than the *creation of new synapses*. Your nervous system forms more synapses than needed and then gradually eliminates the less-active synapses. For example, the number of syn-apses in the human visual cortex peaks when we are about one year old and then declines, as diagrammed in Figure 3.4 (Huttenlocher, 1994). This elimination

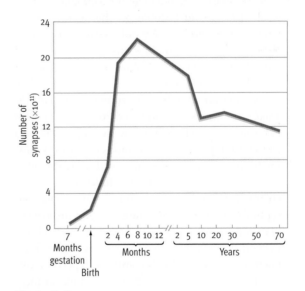

Figure 3.4
Synaptic pruning. This graph summarizes data on the estimated number of synapses in the human visual cortex as a function of age (Huttenlocher, 1994). As you can see, the number of syn-apses in this brain region peaks around age one and then mostly declines over the course of the life span. This decline reflects the process of *synaptic pruning*, which involves the gradual elimina-tion of less active synapses.

Source: Data based on Huttenlocher, P. R. (1994). Synaptogenesis in human cere-bral cortex. In G. Dawson & K. W. Fischer (Eds.), *Human behavior and the developing brain*. New York: Guilford Press. Graphic adapted from Kolb, B., & Whishaw, I. Q. (2001). An introduction to brain and behavior. New York: Worth Publishers. / From Weiten. *Cengage Advantage Books: Psychology*, 9E. © 2013 South-Western, a part of Cengage, Inc. Reproduced by permission. www.cengage.com/permissions

of less-active synapses is called *synaptic pruning*, and it is a key process in the formation of the neural networks that are crucial to communication in the nervous system (Tapia & Lichtman, 2008).

The linking of neurons to form networks was the focus of the work of McGill University's Donald Hebb. Hebb's influential text *The Organization of Behavior* (Hebb, 1949) described his analysis of the neural basis of behaviour and highlighted his view that understanding the brain and its processes was fundamental to understanding behaviour. He realized that individual neurons do not influence behaviour but that they are linked in complex networks he called *cell assemblies*. He formulated the *Hebbian learning rule*, which specified how cell assemblies might be created and work. In his well-known neurophysiological postulate, he claimed that when a neuron stimulates another neuron repeatedly, this produces changes in the synapse between them. How big a deal is this? Well, this is actually the basis for learning.

Hebb's ideas concerning cellular communication led to work by other scientists on long-term potentiation. *Long-term potentiation* refers to a long-lasting increase in neural excitability in synapses along a specific neural pathway. Repeated synaptic activity leads to a strengthening of the synapse. Work by Kandel and his colleagues (Carew et al., 1984; Kandel, 2006) on the neurochemical basis of this process, not only served to support Hebb's initial conceptualizations, but it also earned Kandel the 2000 Nobel Prize in Physiology or Medicine (Kandel, 2006).

As Rita Carter (1998) pointed out in *Mapping the Mind,* "The firing of a single neuron is not enough to create the twitch of an eyelid in sleep, let alone a conscious impression. . . . Millions of neurons must fire in unison to produce the most trifling thought" (p. 19). Most neurons are interlinked in complex chains, pathways, circuits, and networks. Our perceptions, thoughts, and actions depend on *patterns* of neural activity in elaborate neural networks. These networks consist of interconnected neurons that frequently fire together or sequentially to perform certain functions (Song et al., 2005). The links in these networks are fluid, as new synaptic connections may be made while some old connections wither away (Hua & Smith, 2004).

Although Hebb could not specify the exact changes in the synapses that result from neurons forming assemblies (Posner & Rothbart, 2004), he did speculate about their metabolic nature. His ideas are often referred to as the *Hebb Synapse* and continue to guide research today (Hinton, 2003; Milner,

concept check 3.1

Understanding Nervous System Hardware Using Metaphors

A useful way to learn about the structures and functions of parts of the nervous system is through metaphors. Check your understanding of the basic components of the nervous system by matching the metaphorical descriptions below with the correct terms in the following list: (a) glia, (b) neuron, (c) soma, (d) dendrite, (e) axon, (f) myelin, (g) terminal button, and (h) synapse. You'll find the answers in Appendix A.

_____ **1.** Like a tree. Also, each branch is a telephone wire that carries incoming messages to you.

_____ **2.** Like the insulation that covers electrical wires.

_____ **3.** Like a silicon chip in a computer that receives and transmits information between input and output devices as well as between other chips.

_____ **4.** Like an electrical cable that carries information.

_____ **5.** Like the maintenance personnel who keep things clean and in working order so that the operations of the enterprise can proceed.

_____ **6.** Like the nozzle at the end of a hose, from which water is squirted.

_____ **7.** Like a railroad junction, where two trains may meet.

2003; Sejnowski, 2003). Hebb's 1949 text set the stage for a focus on neurophysiology and has been listed as number four of the 100 most influential publications in cognitive science (Tees, 2003). Remarkably, over 50 years after its publication, it was reissued (Hebb, 2002) and continues to serve as an important resource in neuroscience.

Neurotransmitters and Behaviour

As we have seen, neurotransmitters are molecules that are released from the presynaptic region to allow one neuron to influence the firing rate of another neuron.

Thus, neurotransmitters are like chemical couriers that allow for the communication of information between neurons. *Neurotransmitters* are fundamental to behaviour, playing a key role in everything from muscle movements to moods and mental health.

Neurotransmitters share four common properties:

1. They are synthesized in the neuron.
2. They are stored in the synaptic terminals.
3. They are released when the neuron has an action potential.
4. They are deactivated or removed from the synapse when they have completed their task.

Scientists do not know how many neurotransmitters are in your brain. There may be hundreds. Perhaps you wish you had taken this course in 1921 when there was only one known neurotransmitter to learn about. Otto Loewi identified the first neurotransmitter. Based on two dreams he had, Loewi conducted an innovative experiment. He placed a frog's heart in fluid and stimulated it with electricity. After the stimulation, the frog's heart rate decreased. Then he took the fluid and put it on another frog's heart and he observed the same decrease. Loewi inferred that a chemical was released from the nerves of the first heart. This chemical ended up in the fluid and slowed the rate of the second heart when it was bathed in it. He called this chemical *acetylcholine.*

Neurotransmitters have only one of two effects when they are released into the synapse. They either increase the chance of the postsynaptic cell firing (i.e., they produce excitatory postsynaptic potentials) or they decrease the chance of the postsynaptic cell firing (i.e., they produce inhibitory postsynaptic potentials). The same neurotransmitter can be excitatory or inhibitory. It depends on the receptor they bind to.

If neurotransmitters only have two effects, why are there so many? The variety and specificity of neurotransmitters reduces cross-talk between densely packed neurons, making the nervous system's communication more precise. Though much to your relief you are not expected to know the names and functions of all neurotransmitters, there are a few that are particularly interesting and important to psychologists. You can begin to appreciate the importance of neurotransmitters by reviewing the following six: acetylcholine, dopamine, norepinephrine, serotonin, GABA, and endorphins (see Table 3.1).

Acetylcholine

Acetylcholine (ACh) is present throughout the nervous system. It is the only transmitter between motor neurons and voluntary muscles. Every move you make—typing, walking, talking, breathing—requires that ACh is released to your muscles by motor neurons (Kandel & Siegelbaum, 2013). ACh also appears to contribute to attention, arousal, and memory.

An inadequate supply of ACh in certain areas of the brain is associated with the memory losses seen in Alzheimer's disease (Mesulam, 2013). Although

Table 3.1

Common Neurotransmitters and Some of Their Relations to Behaviour

NEUROTRANSMITTER	CHARACTERISTICS AND RELATIONS TO BEHAVIOUR	DISORDERS ASSOCIATED WITH DYSREGULATION
Acetylcholine (ACh)	Released by motor neurons controlling skeletal muscles Contributes to the regulation of attention, arousal, and memory Some ACh receptors stimulated by nicotine	Alzheimer's disease
Dopamine (DA)	Contributes to control of voluntary movement Cocaine and amphetamines elevate activity at DA synapses Dopamine circuits in medial forebrain bundle characterized as "reward pathway"	Parkinsonism Schizophrenic disorders Addictive disorders
Norepinephrine (NE)	Contributes to modulation of mood and arousal Cocaine and amphetamines elevate activity at NE synapses	Depressive disorders
Serotonin	Involved in regulation of sleep and wakefulness, eating, aggression Prozac and similar antidepressant drugs affect serotonin circuits	Depressive disorders Obsessive-compulsive disorders Eating disorders
GABA	Serves as widely distributed inhibitory transmitter, contributing to regulation of anxiety and sleep/arousal Valium and similar antianxiety drugs work at GABA synapses	Anxiety disorders
Endorphins	Resemble opiate drugs in structure and effects Play role in pain relief and response to stress Contribute to regulation of eating behaviour	

© 2017 Cengage Learning

ACh depletion does *not* appear to be the crucial causal factor underlying Alzheimer's disease, the drug treatments currently available, which can produce slight improvements in cognitive functioning, work by increasing ACh activity (Weiner, 2014).

The activity of ACh (and other neurotransmitters) may be influenced by other chemicals in the brain. For example, if you smoke tobacco, some of your ACh synapses will be stimulated by the nicotine that arrives in your brain because at these synapses, the nicotine acts like ACh. It binds to receptor sites for ACh, causing postsynaptic potentials (PSPs). In technical language, nicotine is an ACh agonist. **An *agonist* is a chemical that mimics the action of a neurotransmitter.**

Not all chemicals that fool synaptic receptors are agonists. Some chemicals bind to receptors but fail to produce a PSP (the key slides into the lock, but it doesn't work). They temporarily *block* the action of the natural transmitter by occupying its receptor sites, rendering them unusable. Thus, they act as antagonists. **An *antagonist* is a chemical that opposes the action of a neurotransmitter.** For example, the drug curare is an ACh antagonist. It blocks action at the same ACh synapses that are fooled by nicotine. As a result, muscles are unable to move. Some South American indigenous peoples use a form of curare on arrows. If they wound an animal, the curare blocks the synapses from nerve to muscle, paralyzing the animal.

If more ACh is released in the synapse, muscle spasms or temporary paralysis could occur. This is how the venom of a black widow spider works. If less ACh is released, paralysis, including paralysis of the respiratory system, can occur. Botox treatments decrease ACh, causing facial muscles to relax so that there are fewer wrinkles. Low levels of ACh in the brain are linked to difficulties with the learning and memory impairments found in people with the most common form of dementia, Alzheimer's disease. Some approaches to help people with Alzheimer's focus on increasing ACh activity through drugs (Neugroschl et al., 2005).

Monoamines

The *monoamines* are a category of neurotransmitters that includes dopamine, norepinephrine, and serotonin. Monoamines regulate many aspects of everyday behaviour. Dopamine (DA) is one of the most fascinating neurotransmitters as it plays a role in pleasure and rewards, as well as movement, learning, and attention. More dopamine is released when you engage in rewarding activities such as eating when you are hungry, drinking when you are thirsty, and sex almost anytime. Recreational and abused drugs, such as cocaine and amphetamines, are rewarding and addictive because they increase dopamine activity (Paczynski & Gold, 2011; Schmidt, Vassoler, & Pierce, 2011) (see Chapter 5). Furthermore, dysregulation of dopamine appears to be the chief factor underlying drug craving and addiction (Wise, 2013). The destruction of cells that produce dopamine can have devastating effects. For example, Parkinson's disease results from the degeneration of a dopamine-producing area of the brain, resulting in tremors, muscular rigidity, and reduced control over voluntary movements (Marsh & Margolis, 2009).

Like other neurotransmitters, norepinephrine (NE) has many different functions—and it has different roles as well. In the brain, NE has the role of a neurotransmitter, and in the body NE acts as a hormone. NE is synthesized from dopamine and it affects arousal and alertness. For example, watching a horror film may increase your NE levels so that when you go to bed you cannot sleep as you are too aroused and hear every little sound in your house. People with attention deficit disorder (ADD) may be prescribed drugs such as Ritalin (methylphenidate) and Dexedrine (dextroamphetamine), which increase NE and DA levels. These drugs are used to increase activity of brain regions responsible for attention.

Serotonin helps regulate mood, eating, arousal, and sleeping (McGinty & Szymusiak, 2011). About 80 percent of serotonin in your body is concentrated in your digestive tract and helps food move

Photo by Mark Wilson/Getty Images

The late world heavyweight boxing champion Muhammad Ali suffered from Parkinson's disease, as does Canadian actor Michael J. Fox. Parkinson's disease is caused by the decline in the synthesis of the neurotransmitter dopamine. The reduction in dopamine synthesis occurs because of the deterioration of a structure located in the midbrain. Fox's (2002) autobiography *Lucky Man: A Memoir* details the effects the disease has had on him and his family.

through your system, including down your throat (swallowing) and along your intestines. Serotonin is also linked to aggressive behaviour in animals (higher levels are associated with lower aggression), and some preliminary evidence relates serotonin activity to aggression in humans (Duke et al., 2013; Wallner & Machatschke, 2009). Serotonin seems to play a role in depression. A common treatment for depression is to take drugs that increase the activity of serotonin by impeding the reuptake of serotonin (i.e., preventing Step 6 of the eight steps of synaptic transmission). Antidepressants such as Prozac (fluoxetine), Celexa (citalopram), and Paxil (parotetine) all increase serotonin activity. However, despite that these drugs are the most established therapy for depression, some meta-analyses (studies of already published groups of studies) suggest that these antidepressants may have no, or very little effect on depression, particularly for those with mild or moderate depression (Fournier et al., 2010; Jakubovski et al., 2015).

GABA

Gamma-aminobutyric acid (GABA) seems to produce only *inhibitory* postsynaptic potentials. Most neurotransmitters, such as ACh and NE, produce both excitatory or inhibitory potentials, depending on the synaptic receptors they bind to. To appreciate the importance of GABA, imagine that there were only excitatory neurotransmitters. The excitation of one cell would lead to the excitation of another. Because neurons are so well interconnected, soon whole populations of cells would be firing together unchecked. In fact, this is what happens during epileptic seizures. Fortunately, GABA inhibits neuronal activity and puts a check on this uncontrolled behaviour.

GABA receptors are widely distributed in the brain and may be present at 40 percent of all synapses. GABA is involved in the regulation of anxiety in humans, and disturbances in GABA circuits may contribute to some types of anxiety disorders (Long et al., 2013; Rosso et al., 2014). GABA circuits also appear to contribute to the modulation of sleep and arousal (Luppi, Clement, & Fort, 2013; Nguyen et al., 2013).

Endorphins

After a horseback-riding accident, Candace Pert, a graduate student in neuroscience, received frequent shots of morphine, a painkilling drug derived from the opium plant. She wondered why morphine works. A few years later, she and Solomon Snyder rocked the scientific world by showing that morphine exerts its effects by binding to specialized receptors in the brain (Pert & Snyder, 1973).

Why does the brain have receptors for morphine, a powerful, addictive opiate drug? It occurred to Pert and others that the nervous system must produce its own, endogenous (natural internal) morphine-like substances. Investigators called these as-yet undiscovered substances *endorphins—internally produced chemicals that resemble opiates in structure and effects.* Soon, a number of endogenous opioids were identified (Hughes et al., 1975). Endorphins and their receptors are widely distributed throughout our bodies and they decrease pain (Millecamps et al., 2013), as we will discuss in Chapter 4. Endogenous opioids also contribute to eating behaviour and the body's response to stress (Adam & Epel, 2007).

In addition to their painkilling effects, opiate drugs such as morphine and heroin produce highly pleasurable feelings. These feelings explain why heroin is so widely abused. The body's natural endorphins may also be capable of producing feelings of pleasure as well. This capacity might explain why joggers sometimes experience a "runner's high" (Boecker et al., 2008; Harte, Eifert, & Smith, 1995; Scheef et al., 2012).

Solomon Snyder

"Brain research of the past decade, especially the study of neurotransmitters, has proceeded at a furious pace, achieving progress equal in scope to all the accomplishments of the preceding 50 years—and the pace of discovery continues to accelerate."

Candace Pert

"When human beings engage in various activities, it seems that neurojuices are released that are associated with either pain or pleasure."

concept **check** 3.2

Linking Brain Chemistry to Behaviour

Check your understanding of the relationships between brain chemistry and behaviour by indicating which neurotransmitter has been linked to the phenomena listed below. Choose your answers from the following list: (a) acetylcholine, (b) norepinephrine, (c) dopamine, (d) serotonin, (e) endorphins. Indicate your choice (by letter) in the spaces on the left. You'll find the answers in Appendix A.

_____ **1.** A transmitter involved in the regulation of sleep, eating, and aggression.

_____ **2.** The two monoamines that have been linked to depression.

_____ **3.** Chemicals that resemble opiate drugs in structure and that are involved in pain relief.

_____ **4.** A neurotransmitter for which abnormal levels have been implicated in schizophrenia.

_____ **5.** The only neurotransmitter between motor neurons and voluntary muscles.

Long-distance runners sometimes report experiencing a "runner's high." Recent research suggests that the release of endorphins probably underlies this experience.

Organization of the Nervous System

Key Learning Goal

▶ Distinguish between the central nervous system and the peripheral nervous system.

Communication in the nervous system is fundamental to behaviour. So far we have examined how information is communicated within and between cells. Next, we examine the organization of the nervous system as a whole.

You may have heard that we use only 10 percent of our brains. This tidbit of folk wisdom is utter nonsense (McBurney, 1996). If 90 percent of the human brain consisted of unused excess baggage, localized brain damage would not be a problem much of the time. In reality, damage in even very small brain regions usually has severe, disruptive effects (Zillmer, Spiers, & Culbertson, 2008). Furthermore, brain-imaging research shows that even simple mental operations depend on activity spread across many areas in the brain. Even during sleep, the brain is highly active.

reality check

Misconception

People use only about 10 percent of their brains.

Reality

The 10 percent myth appeals to people because it suggests that they have a huge reservoir of untapped potential. Hucksters selling self-improvement programs often talk about the 10 percent myth because it makes their claims and promises seem more realistic ("Unleash your potential!").

Multitudes of neurons must work together to keep information flowing effectively. To understand how the nervous system is organized to accomplish this task, researchers divide it into two main parts: the peripheral nervous system and the central nervous system. Figure 3.5 illustrates these two divisions.

The Peripheral Nervous System

The first and most important division separates the central nervous system (the brain and spinal cord) from the peripheral nervous system (see Figure 3.6). **The *peripheral nervous system* is made up of all the nerves that lie outside the brain and spinal cord. Nerves are bundles of neuron fibres (axons) that are routed together in the peripheral nervous system.** The peripheral nervous system is the part that extends outside the central nervous system. The peripheral nervous system can be subdivided into the *somatic nervous system* and the *autonomic nervous system*.

The Somatic Nervous System

The somatic nervous system lets you feel the world and move around in it. **The *somatic nervous system* is made up of nerves that connect to voluntary skeletal muscles and to sensory receptors.** These nerves are like cables that carry information from receptors in the skin, muscles, and joints to the central

Figure 3.5
Organization of the human nervous system.
This overview of the human nervous system shows the relationships of its various parts and systems. The brain is traditionally divided into three regions: the hindbrain, the midbrain, and the forebrain. The reticular formation runs through both the midbrain and the hindbrain on its way up and down the brainstem. These and other parts of the brain are discussed in detail later in the chapter. The peripheral nervous system is made up of the somatic nervous system, which controls voluntary muscles and sensory receptors, and the autonomic nervous system, which controls the involuntary activities of smooth muscles, blood vessels, and glands.

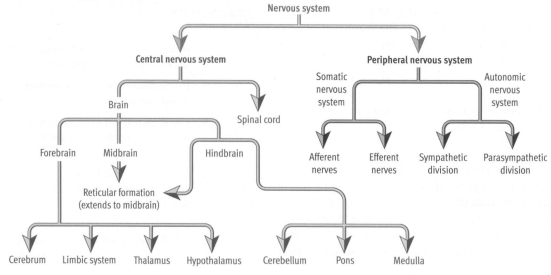

© 2017 Cengage Learning

nervous system and carry commands from the central nervous system to the muscles. These functions require two types of nerve fibres. *Afferent nerve fibres are axons that carry information inward to the central nervous system from the periphery of the body. Efferent nerve fibres are axons that carry information outward from the central nervous system to the periphery of the body.* Each nerve contains many axons of each type. Thus, somatic nerves are "two-way streets" with incoming (afferent) and outgoing (efferent) lanes.

The Autonomic Nervous System

The *autonomic nervous system (ANS)* is made up of nerves that connect to the heart, blood vessels, smooth muscles, and glands. The autonomic nervous system controls automatic, involuntary, visceral functions that people don't normally think about, such as heart rate, digestion, and perspiration (Powley, 2008; see Figure 3.7).

The autonomic nervous system mediates much of the physiological arousal that occurs when people experience emotions. For example, imagine that you're arriving home alone one night when you notice that your front door is open and a window is broken. You suspect that your home has been broken into and your heart rate and breathing speed up. As you cautiously go inside, your blood pressure increases, you get goosebumps, and your palms sweat. These difficult-to-control reactions are aspects of autonomic arousal. Walter Cannon (1932), one of the first psychologists to study this reaction, called it the *fight-or-flight response.* Cannon carefully monitored these responses in animals and concluded that organisms generally respond to danger by preparing physically for attacking (fight) or fleeing (flight) the threat. According to McGill University's Hans Selye (1974), prolonged autonomic arousal can eventually contribute to the development of physical diseases.

The autonomic nervous system has two subdivisions: the sympathetic and parasympathetic divisions (see Figure 3.7). The *sympathetic division is the branch of the autonomic nervous system that mobilizes the body's resources for emergencies.* It creates the fight-or-flight response. Activation of the sympathetic division slows digestive processes and shunts blood toward the periphery (to the muscles) to prepare for physical activity. Key sympathetic nerves send signals to the adrenal glands, triggering the release of hormones that ready the body for exertion. In contrast, the *parasympathetic division is the branch of the autonomic nervous system that conserves bodily resources.* This system can be thought of as the "rest and digest" system. It activates processes that allow the body to save and store energy. For example, actions by parasympathetic nerves slow heart rate, reduce blood pressure, and promote digestion.

Rather than memorizing all the changes in the body that accompany the activation of the sympathetic and parasympathetic nervous systems, we suggest you link them to real events in your life. For example, during an interview for a job you really want, you may find that your breathing and heart rate have quickened. Or if you are nervous when you are delivering an important speech, your mouth may be quite dry and you will sweat. The changes in your body associated with these two examples indicate that your sympathetic nervous system is activated. Historically, this information was used in Asia as the basis for a low-tech lie detector (Bartol & Bartol, 2015). When people were suspected of a crime, they were given dry uncooked rice to swallow. If they were guilty, they would feel threatened, thus activating their sympathetic nervous system. Activation of this system inhibits saliva production and the resulting dry mouth would make it difficult to swallow the rice, indicating guilt.

Instead of being threatened and alert, imagine that you are relaxing after a large meal. Your heart and breathing rates are slow. Or if you are receiving a massage, you may drool on the pillow and your pupils would be small. In these examples, your parasympathetic system is activated. This knowledge is used by photographers. "Red-eye" in photos can be reduced by decreasing the size of the pupil. To do this, you need the model to be relaxed. In other words, you need to activate the model's parasympathetic nervous system by making him or her feel rested and nonthreatened (Bartol & Bartol, 2015).

Sex involves both systems. Initial arousal in males and females requires activation of the parasympathetic nervous system. This may be helped by soft music, dim lighting, and a massage. However, prior to orgasm, there is a switch from the parasympathetic to the sympathetic nervous system. Sexual climaxing is controlled by activation of the sympathetic nervous system (Bartol & Bartol, 2015).

The biathlon, where athletes furiously cross-country ski and then intermittently must calm their bodies to shoot targets with a rifle, is a competition requiring mastery over the autonomic nervous system. During the ski portion of the race, the sympathetic nervous system is maximally stimulated, where the blood is shunted to the muscles, the heart rate soars, and breathing is rapid. During the shooting portion, the parasympathetic system

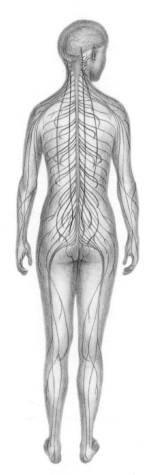

Figure 3.6
The central and peripheral nervous systems. The central nervous system consists of the brain and the spinal cord. The peripheral nervous system consists of the remaining nerves that fan out throughout the body. The peripheral nervous system is divided into the somatic nervous system (shown in blue) and the autonomic nervous system (shown in green).

Source: From Weiten. *Cengage Advantage Books: Psychology*, 9E. © 2013 South-Western, a part of Cengage, Inc. Reproduced by permission. www.cengage.com/permissions

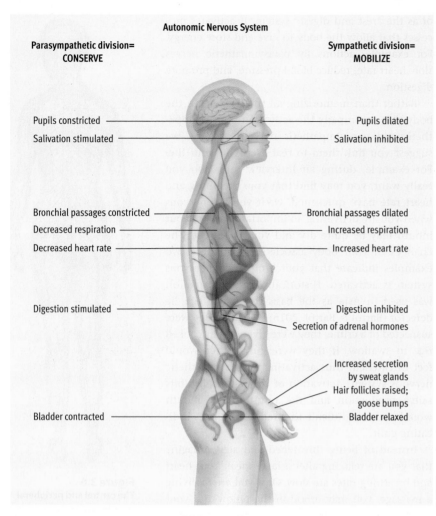

Autonomic Nervous System

Parasympathetic division=
CONSERVE

Sympathetic division=
MOBILIZE

Pupils constricted — Pupils dilated

Salivation stimulated — Salivation inhibited

Bronchial passages constricted — Bronchial passages dilated

Decreased respiration — Increased respiration

Decreased heart rate — Increased heart rate

Digestion stimulated — Digestion inhibited

Secretion of adrenal hormones

Increased secretion by sweat glands

Hair follicles raised; goose bumps

Bladder contracted — Bladder relaxed

Figure 3.7
The autonomic nervous system. The ANS is comprised of the nerves that connect to the heart, blood vessels, smooth muscles, and glands. The ANS is divided into the sympathetic division, which mobilizes bodily resources in times of need, and the parasympathetic division, which conserves bodily resources. Some of the key functions controlled by each division of the ANS are summarized in this diagram.

must be quickly stimulated to lower the heart and breathing rates (Bartol & Bartol, 2015).

The Central Nervous System

The central nervous system consists of portion of the nervous system that lies within the skull and spinal column (see Figure 3.6). Thus, the *central nervous system (CNS)* consists of the brain and the spinal cord. It is protected by enclosing sheaths called the *meninges* (hence, *meningitis*, the name for the disease in which the meninges become inflamed). In addition, the central nervous system is bathed in its own special nutritive "soup," the cerebrospinal fluid. The *cerebrospinal fluid (CSF)* nourishes the brain and provides a protective cushion for it. The hollow cavities in the brain that are filled with CSF are called ventricles (see Figure 3.8).

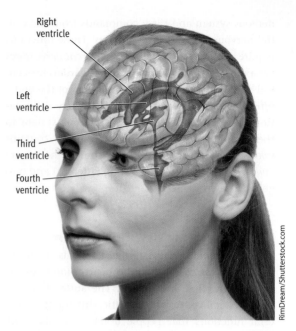

Right ventricle

Left ventricle

Third ventricle

Fourth ventricle

Figure 3.8
The ventricles of the brain. Cerebrospinal fluid (CSF) circulates around the brain and the spinal cord. The hollow cavities in the brain filled with CSF are called *ventricles*. The four ventricles in the human brain are depicted here.

Source: From Weiten. *Cengage Advantage Books: Psychology*, 9E. © 2013 South-Western, a part of Cengage, Inc. Reproduced by permission. www.cengage.com/permissions

The Spinal Cord

The *spinal cord* connects the brain to the rest of the body through the peripheral nervous system. Although the spinal cord looks like a cable from which the somatic nerves branch, it is part of the central nervous system. Your spinal cord runs from the base of your brain to just below your waist. It houses bundles of axons that carry the brain's commands to peripheral nerves so we can move, and it relays sensations from the periphery of the body to the brain. Many forms of paralysis result from spinal cord damage, which shows the critical role the spinal cord plays in transmitting signals from the brain to the neurons that allow our muscles to move.

The Brain

The crowning glory of the central nervous system is, of course, the *brain*. Anatomically, the brain is the part of the central nervous system that fills the upper portion of the skull. Although it weighs only about 1.5 kilograms and could be held in one hand, the brain contains billions of interacting cells that integrate information from inside and outside the body, coordinate the body's actions, and enable human beings to talk, think, remember, plan, create, and dream. Because of its central importance for behaviour, the brain is the subject of the next three sections of this chapter.

Looking Inside the Brain: Research Methods

Investigators who conduct research on the brain or other parts of the nervous system are called *neuroscientists*. Often, brain research involves collaboration by neuroscientists from several disciplines, including anatomy, physiology, biology, pharmacology, neurology, neurosurgery, psychiatry, and psychology.

To discover how parts of the brain are related to behaviour, neuroscientists are faced with a formidable task (Mukamel & Fried, 2012; Tong & Pratte, 2012). Mapping brain *functions* requires a working brain. Thus, special methods are needed to discover relationships between brain activity and behaviour.

One method involves examining changes in behaviour that accompany brain damage resulting from tumours, strokes, head injuries, and other misfortunes. This research approach, as we discussed in Chapter 2, is referred to as the *case study method*. One of the most famous case studies of an individual suffering from brain damage was conducted by Brenda Milner. Along with Donald Hebb and Wilder Penfield, Milner was one of the pioneers in neuroscience research in Canada. Milner was a Ph.D. student of Donald Hebb's at McGill University. The patient she studied is referred to as "H.M." H.M. was very significant in the development of our knowledge of the brain and its connections to behaviour, in particular to our understanding of the brain and memory. His brain has been referred to as "the brain that changed everything" (Dittrich, 2010).

Doing research with patients with brain damage has its limitations. Subjects are not plentiful, and neuroscientists can't control the location or severity of patients' brain damage. Furthermore, variations in patients' histories create a host of extraneous variables that make it difficult to isolate cause-and-effect relationships between brain damage and behaviour. The experimental methods that we discuss next help overcome these limitations.

Neuroscientists sometimes observe what happens when specific brain structures in animals are purposely disabled. *Lesioning* **involves destroying a piece of the brain.** It is typically done by inserting an electrode into a brain structure and passing a high frequency electric current through it to burn the tissue and disable the structure. Lesioning can also be accomplished with chemicals or with knife cuts. Another valuable technique involves *electrical stimulation of the brain (ESB)*, **where a weak electric current is sent into a brain structure to stimulate (activate) it.** The current is delivered through an implanted electrode, but a different type of current is used than with electrical lesioning. ESB does not exactly duplicate normal electrical signals in the brain. However, it is usually similar enough to activate the brain structures in which the electrodes are lodged (Desmurget et al., 2013). Obviously, these techniques are very invasive and are usually limited to animal research, although these approaches are sometimes used on humans in the context of brain surgery required for medical purposes.

In recent decades, the invention of new brain-imaging devices has led to dramatic advances in scientists' ability to look inside the human brain. For example, the *CT (computerized tomography) scan* is a computer-enhanced X-ray of brain structure. X-rays are taken from many angles, and the computer combines these images to create vivid pictures of cross sections of the brain, as illustrated in the horizontal slices shown in Figure 3.9. However, these pictures are two dimensional. The more recently developed *MRI (magnetic resonance imaging) scan* uses magnetic fields, radio waves, and computerized enhancement to map out brain structures with more detail than a CT scan, and they are three dimensional (Wilde et al., 2014) (see Figure 3.10). Using CT and MRI scans, researchers have discovered abnormalities in brain structures in people suffering from specific types of mental illness including schizophrenia (Shenton & Kubicki, 2009) (see Chapter 14).

Though valuable, CT and MRI scans are limited because they only give a snapshot of the structure of the brain at a single point in time. They do not show the active functioning of the brain. The *electroencephalograph (EEG)* **is a device that monitors the electrical activity of the brain over time to**

Wilder Penfield and Brenda Milner, pioneers in neuroscience in Canada.

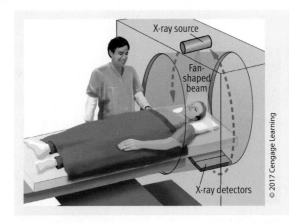

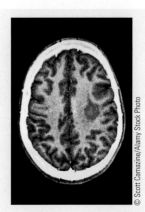

Figure 3.9
CT technology. CT scans are used to examine aspects of brain structure. They provide computer enhanced X-rays of horizontal slices of the brain. (a) An X-ray beam and X-ray detector rotate around the patient's head, taking multiple X-rays of a horizontal slice of the patient's brain. (b) A computer combines X-rays to create an image of a horizontal slice of the brain. This scan shows a tumour (in blue) on the right.

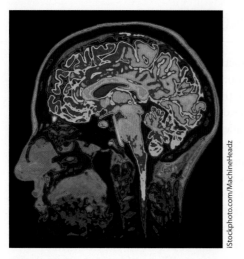
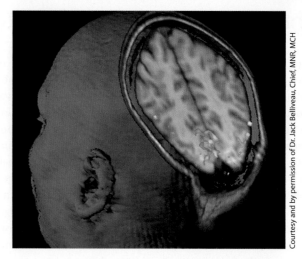

Figure 3.10

MRI scans. (a) MRI scans can be used to produce remarkably high-resolution pictures of brain structure. A vertical view of a brain from the left side is shown here. (b) Like PET scans, functional MRIs can monitor chemical activity in the brain. This image shows regions of the brain that were activated by a flashing light.

show the functioning of the brain (see Figure 3.11). EEGs use small electrodes attached to the scalp to measure electric potentials (primarily graded potentials) occurring in thousands of brain cells. EEGs have been critical in identifying stages of sleep and consciousness (Rosler, 2005). Researchers have used EEG recordings to investigate how meditation affects brain activity (Lagopoulos et al., 2009).

Another brain imaging technique that shows the functioning of the brain is *PET (positron emission tomography) scans* (Staley & Krystal, 2009). PET scans use radioactive markers to map chemical activity in the brain over time. PET scans can provide colour-coded maps indicating which areas of the brain are

active when people clench their fist, sing, or contemplate the mysteries of the universe (see Figure 3.12). To pinpoint the brain areas that handle various mental tasks, neuroscientists are increasingly using *functional magnetic resonance imaging (fMRI)*, which consists of new variations of MRI technology that monitor blood flow and oxygen consumption in the brain to identify areas of high activity (Small & Heeger, 2013). This technology is similar to PET scans in that it can map actual *activity* in the brain over time, but it does so with vastly greater precision (Wilde et al., 2014). For example, using fMRI scans, researchers have identified patterns of brain activity associated with specific creative-thinking

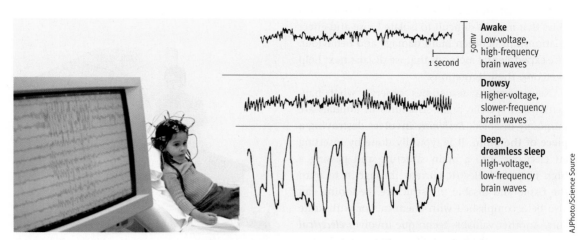

Figure 3.11

The electroencephalograph. Recording electrodes attached to the surface of the scalp permit the EEG to record electrical activity in the cortex over time. The EEG provides output in the form of line tracings called brain waves. Brain waves vary in frequency (cycles per second) and amplitude (measured in voltage). Various states of consciousness are associated with different brain waves. Characteristic EEG patterns for alert wakefulness, drowsiness, and deep, dreamless sleep are shown here. The use of the EEG in research is discussed in more detail in Chapter 5.

tasks (Abraham et al., 2014); the contemplation of complex decisions related to gambling (Hinvest et al., 2014); and reactions to pictures of alcoholic beverages (Dager et al., 2014). Adrian Owen and his colleagues (Owen et al., 2006) asked their "locked-in" patient to imagine doing routine activities such as playing tennis or moving around her home. They showed that their patient's brain was indistinguishable on these tasks from those of healthy volunteers and indicating conscious awareness in the patient.

Transcranial Magnetic Stimulation

Transcranial magnetic stimulation (TMS) is a technique that permits scientists to temporarily enhance or depress activity in a specific area of the brain. In TMS, a magnetic coil mounted on a small paddle is held over a specific area of a subject's head (see Figure 3.13). The coil creates a magnetic field that penetrates to a depth of 2 centimetres (Sack & Linden, 2003). By varying the timing and duration of the magnetic pulses, a researcher can either increase or decrease the excitability of neurons in the local tissue (George et al., 2007; Sandrini & Manenti, 2009). This technology allows scientists to create "virtual lesions" in humans for short periods of time, using a painless, noninvasive method (Siebner et al., 2009). Moreover, this approach circumvents the host of uncontrolled variables that plague the study of natural lesions in humans who have experienced brain damage (Rafal, 2001).

TMS has been used to explore whether specific areas of the brain are involved in visual–spatial processing (McKeefry, Burton, & Moreland, 2010), short-term memory (Silvantro & Cattaneo, 2010), and language (Manenti et al., 2010).

The chief limitation of TMS is that it cannot be used to study areas deep within the brain. Still, its potential as a research tool is enormous (Sparing, Hesse, & Fink, 2010). Moreover, scientists are studying whether it might have potential as a therapeutic treatment for eating disorders (Van den Eynde et al., 2010), anxiety disorders (Kuo et al., 2014; Zwanger et al., 2009), depression (Fitzgerald, 2009), and schizophrenia (Matheson et al., 2010), as well as a way of enhancing cognitive performance in healthy individuals (Luber & Lisanby, 2014).

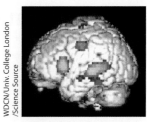

WDCN/Univ. College London /Science Source

Figure 3.12
PET scans. PET scans are used to map brain activity rather than brain structure. They provide colour-coded maps that show levels of activity in different areas of the brain over time. The PET scan shown here pinpointed two areas of high activity (indicated by the red and green colours) when a research participant worked on a verbal short-term memory task.

FEATURED STUDY

Remembering the past and imagining the future: Common and distinct neural substrates during event construction and elaboration.

Description
The researchers use fMRI technology to test the hypothesis that remembering the past and simulating the future draw upon similar types of neural processes.

Investigators
Addis, S. Wong, A., & Schachter, D. (2007). *Neuropsychologia, 45,* 1363–1377.

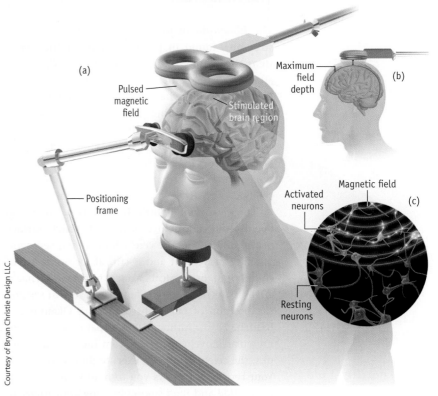

Courtesy of Bryan Christie Design LLC.

(a) Pulsed magnetic field
Positioning frame
Stimulated brain region
Maximum field depth
(b)
Activated neurons
Magnetic field
(c)
Resting neurons

Figure 3.13
Transcranial magnetic stimulation. In TMS, (a) magnetic pulses are delivered to an area of the brain from a magnet mounted on a small paddle. (b) The magnetic field penetrates to a depth of only 2 centimetres. This technique can be used to either increase or decrease the excitability of the affected neurons. (c) The inset at the bottom right depicts neurons near the surface of the brain being temporarily activated by TMS.

Courtesy of Donna Rose Addis

Donna Rose Addis, a graduate of the University of Toronto, along with her colleagues Daniel Schacter and Alana Wong, has made important contributions to our understanding of the neural bases of memory. These neuroscientists co-authored our Featured Study.

The Brain and Behaviour

Now that we have reviewed selected neuroscience techniques, let's examine what researchers have discovered about the functions of various parts of the brain.

The brain can be divided into three major regions: the hindbrain, the midbrain, and the forebrain. The principal structures found in each of these regions are listed in the organizational chart of the nervous system in Figure 3.5 (page 80). You can see where these regions are located in the brain by looking at Figure 3.14. They can be found easily in relation to the *brainstem*. The brainstem looks like its name—it appears to be a stem from which the rest of the brain "flowers," like a head of cauliflower. At its lower end, it is attached to the spinal cord. At its higher end, it lies deep within the brain.

We'll begin at the brain's lower end. As we proceed upward, notice how the functions of brain structures go from the regulation of basic bodily processes to the control of "higher" mental processes.

The Hindbrain

The *hindbrain* includes the cerebellum and two structures found in the lower part of the brainstem: the medulla and the pons. The *medulla*, which attaches to the spinal cord, is in charge of largely unconscious but vital functions, including circulating blood, breathing, maintaining muscle tone, and regulating reflexes such as sneezing, coughing, and salivating. The *pons* (literally "bridge") includes a bridge of fibres that connects the brainstem with the cerebellum. The pons also contains several clusters of cell bodies involved with sleep and arousal.

The *cerebellum* ("little brain") is a large and deeply folded structure next to the back surface of the brainstem. The cerebellum is involved coordinating movement and is critical for our sense of equilibrium, or physical balance (Lisberger & Thach, 2013). Parts of the cerebellum play a role in sensing the position of our limbs (Bhanpuri, Okamura, & Bastian, 2013). Although the actual commands for muscular movements come from higher brain centres, the cerebellum helps execute these commands. Your cerebellum allows you to hold your hand out to the side and then smoothly bring your finger to a stop on your nose. This exercise is a roadside test for drunk driving because the cerebellum is one of the structures first affected by alcohol. Damage to the cerebellum disrupts fine motor skills, including those involved in writing, typing, or playing a musical instrument. Brain circuits running from the cerebellum to the prefrontal cortex appear to be involved in higher-order functions, including attention, planning, and visual perception (Dum & Strick, 2009).

The Midbrain

The *midbrain* is the segment of the brainstem located between the hindbrain and the forebrain. The midbrain contains a region that integrates sensory processes, including vision and hearing (Stein, Wallace, & Stanford, 2000). An important system of dopamine-releasing neurons that projects into various higher brain centres originates in the midbrain. Among other things, this dopamine system is involved in the performance of voluntary movements. The decline in dopamine synthesis that causes Parkinson's disease is due to degeneration of a structure located in the midbrain (Marsh & Margolis, 2009).

Running through both the hindbrain and the midbrain is the *reticular formation* (see Figure 3.14). Situated at the central core of the brainstem, the reticular formation helps with the modulation of muscle reflexes, breathing, and pain perception (Saper, 2000). It is best known for its role in the regulation of sleep and arousal. Activity in the ascending fibres of the reticular formation contributes to arousal (Jones & Benca, 2013 ; McGinty & Szymusiak, 2011).

The Forebrain

The *forebrain* is the largest and most complex region of the brain, encompassing a variety of structures, including the thalamus, hypothalamus, limbic system, and cerebrum (see Figure 3.14 again). The thalamus, hypothalamus, and limbic system form the core of the forebrain. All three structures are located near the top of the brainstem. Above them is the *cerebrum*—the seat of complex thought. The wrinkled surface of the cerebrum is the *cerebral cortex*—the outer layer of the brain, which looks like a cauliflower.

The Thalamus: A Relay Station
The *thalamus* is a structure in the forebrain through which all sensory information (except smell) must pass to get to the cerebral cortex (Sherman, 2009). The thalamus is made up of clusters of cell bodies, or somas. Each cluster is concerned with relaying sensory information to a particular part of the cortex.

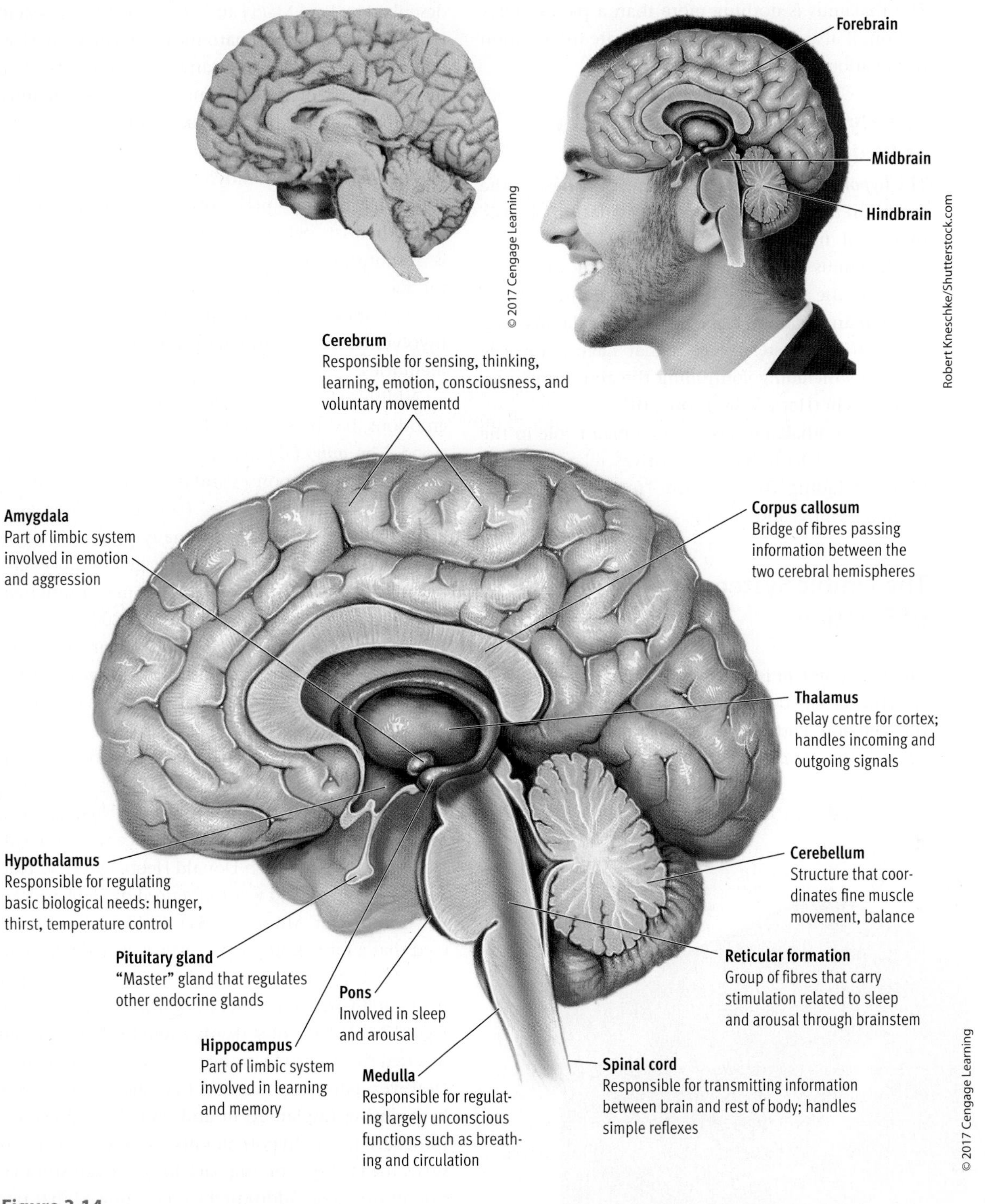

Forebrain

Midbrain

Hindbrain

© 2017 Cengage Learning

Robert Kneschke/Shutterstock.com

Cerebrum
Responsible for sensing, thinking, learning, emotion, consciousness, and voluntary movementd

Amygdala
Part of limbic system involved in emotion and aggression

Corpus callosum
Bridge of fibres passing information between the two cerebral hemispheres

Thalamus
Relay centre for cortex; handles incoming and outgoing signals

Hypothalamus
Responsible for regulating basic biological needs: hunger, thirst, temperature control

Cerebellum
Structure that coordinates fine muscle movement, balance

Pituitary gland
"Master" gland that regulates other endocrine glands

Pons
Involved in sleep and arousal

Reticular formation
Group of fibres that carry stimulation related to sleep and arousal through brainstem

Hippocampus
Part of limbic system involved in learning and memory

Medulla
Responsible for regulating largely unconscious functions such as breathing and circulation

Spinal cord
Responsible for transmitting information between brain and rest of body; handles simple reflexes

© 2017 Cengage Learning

Figure 3.14
Structures and areas in the human brain. (Top left) This illustration of a human brain shows many of the structures discussed in this chapter. (Top right) The brain is divided into three major areas: the hindbrain, midbrain, and forebrain. In humans, the forebrain has become so large that it makes the other two divisions look trivial. However, the hindbrain and midbrain aren't trivial; they control such vital functions as breathing, waking, and maintaining balance. (Bottom) This cross-section of the brain highlights key structures and some of their principal functions. As you read about the functions of a brain structure, such as the corpus callosum, you may find it helpful to refer back to this figure.

The thalamus is nothing more than a passive relay station. It also appears to help integrate information from various senses.

The Hypothalamus: A Regulator of Biological Needs

The *hypothalamus* is a structure near the base of the forebrain that is involved in the regulation of basic biological needs. The hypothalamus lies beneath the thalamus (*hypo* means *under*, making the hypothalamus the area under the thalamus). Although no larger than a kidney bean, the hypothalamus contains various clusters of cells that have many key functions including controlling the autonomic nervous system (Horn & Swanson, 2013).

The hypothalamus also plays a major role in the regulation of basic biological drives related to survival, including the so-called "four Fs": fighting, fleeing, feeding, and mating.

The Limbic System: The Centre of Emotion

The *limbic system* is a loosely connected network of structures located roughly along the border between the cerebral cortex and deeper subcortical areas (hence, the term *limbic*, which means *edge*). First

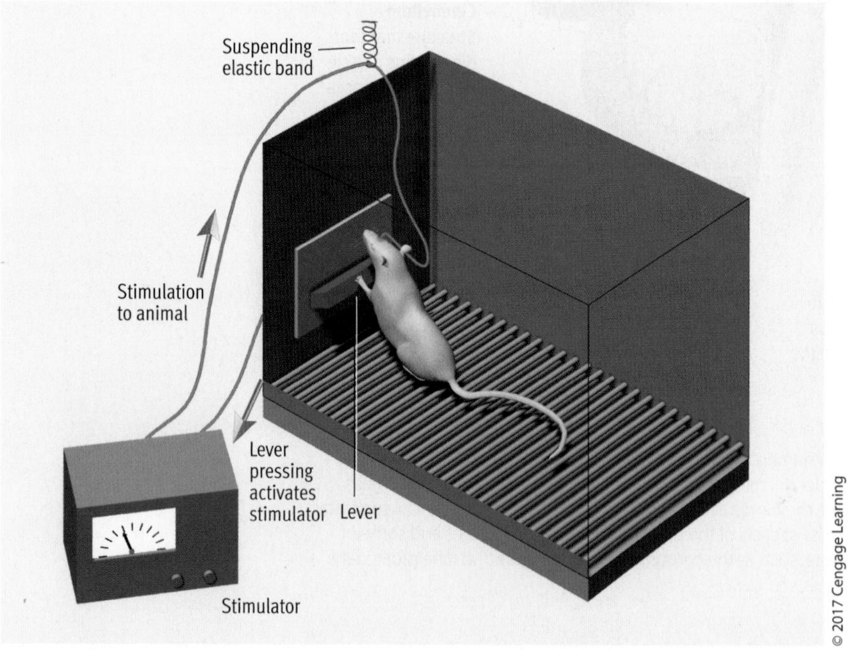

Figure 3.15
Electrical stimulation of the brain (ESB) of a rat. Olds and Milner (1954) were using an apparatus like that depicted here when they discovered self-stimulation centres, or "pleasure centres," in the brain of a rat. In this setup, the rat's lever pressing produces brief electrical stimulation in a specific brain region where an electrode has been implanted.

described by Paul MacLean (1954), the limbic system is *not* a well-defined anatomical system with clear boundaries. Broadly speaking, the limbic system includes parts of the thalamus and hypothalamus, the hippocampus, the amygdala, and other nearby structures.

The *hippocampus* and adjacent structures play a role in memory processes (Eichenbaum, 2013). Some theorists believe that the hippocampal region is responsible for the *consolidation* of memories for factual information and perhaps other types of memories (Albouy et al., 2013). Consolidation involves the conversion of information into durable memories.

Additionally, the limbic system is involved in emotions, but how it does this is not yet well understood. The *amygdala* may play a central role in the learning of fear responses and the processing of other basic emotional responses (LeDoux & Damasio, 2013; Phelps, 2006). Traditionally it was thought that the amygdala was mostly engaged in processing negative emotions and events. William Cunningham (Cunningham, Bavel, & Johnsen, 2008), at the University of Toronto, and other researchers (e.g., Murray, 2007) questioned this thinking because their work suggests that the amygdala processes both positive and negative stimuli.

The limbic system also appears to contain "pleasure centres"—parts of the brain that are involved in pleasure. This intriguing possibility first surfaced with research by James Olds, who came to McGill University to work with Donald Hebb. Olds had read Hebb's 1949 text and was influenced by Hebb's ideas. Olds and Peter Milner (1954) accidentally discovered that a rat would press a lever repeatedly to send brief bursts of electrical stimulation to a specific spot in its brain where an electrode was implanted (see Figure 3.15). They mistakenly thought that they had inserted the electrode in the rat's reticular formation. However, later they learned that the electrode was bent during implantation and ended up elsewhere (probably in the hypothalamus). Much to their surprise, the rat kept coming back for more self-stimulation in this area. Additional studies showed that rats and monkeys would press a lever *thousands of times per hour,* until they sometimes collapsed from exhaustion, to stimulate certain brain sites. Apparently, the animals really liked the stimulation.

Where are the pleasure centres located in the brain? Many of them have been located in the limbic system (Olds & Fobes, 1981). The heaviest concentration appears to be where the *medial forebrain bundle* (a bundle of axons) passes through the hypothalamus. The medial forebrain bundle is rich in dopamine-releasing neurons. The rewarding effects of ESB may be largely mediated by the activation of these dopamine circuits (Koob, Everitt, & Robbins, 2008). The pleasurable effects of opiates and stimulant drugs (cocaine and amphetamines) likely also depend on excitation of this dopamine system (Schmidt, Vassoler, & Pierce, 2011). The so-called pleasure centres in the brain may not be anatomical centres so much as neural circuits releasing dopamine.

The Cerebrum: The Centre of Complex Thought

The *cerebrum* is the largest and most complex part of the human brain. It is responsible for the most complex mental activities, including learning, remembering, thinking, and consciousness. **The *cerebral cortex* is the convoluted outer layer of the cerebrum.** The cortex is folded and bent, so that its large surface area—about 1400 cm²—can be packed into the limited volume of the skull (Hubel & Wiesel, 1979).

The cerebrum is divided into two halves called hemispheres. Hence, **the *cerebral hemispheres* are the right and left halves of the cerebrum** (see Figure 3.16). The hemispheres are separated in the centre of the brain by a longitudinal fissure (a split or crevice) that runs from the front to the back of the brain. This fissure descends to a thick band of fibres called the *corpus callosum* (also shown in Figure 3.16). **The *corpus callosum* is the structure that connects the two cerebral hemispheres.** We'll discuss the functional specialization of the cerebral hemispheres in the next section of this chapter. Each cerebral hemisphere is divided into four parts called *lobes*. To some extent, each of these lobes is dedicated to specific purposes. The location of these lobes can be seen in Figure 3.17.

The *occipital lobe,* at the back of the head, includes the cortical area, where most visual signals are sent and visual processing is begun.

The *parietal lobe* is in front of the occipital lobe. It includes the area that registers the sense of touch, called the *primary somatosensory cortex.* Various sections of this area receive signals from different regions of the body. When ESB is delivered in these parietal lobe areas, people report physical sensations—as if someone actually touched them on the arm or cheek, for example. The parietal lobe is involved in integrating visual input and monitoring the body's position in space. York University neuroscientist Doug Crawford has examined the role of the parietal cortex in helping us reach for and grasp objects. He suggests that the parietal cortex mediates the visual control of reaching (Crawford, Medendorp, & Marotta, 2004).

The *temporal lobe* (meaning *near the temples*) lies below the parietal lobe. Near its top, the temporal lobe contains an area devoted to auditory processing, called the *primary auditory cortex.* As we will see in the next section, damage to an area in the temporal lobe on the left side of the brain can impair the comprehension of speech and language.

In the front of the brain, just behind your forehead, is the *frontal lobe,* the largest lobe in the human brain. It contains the principal areas that control the movement of muscles, the *primary motor cortex.* ESB applied to these areas can cause muscle contractions. The amount of motor cortex allocated to the control of a body part depends not on the part's size but on the diversity and precision of its movements. Thus, more of the cortex is given to parts we have fine control over, such as fingers, lips, and the tongue. Less of the cortex is devoted to larger parts that make crude movements, such as the thighs and shoulders (see Figure 3.18).

Just in front of the primary visual cortex is where "mirror neurons" were first discovered accidentally in the mid-1990s. Italian researchers were recording activity in individual neurons as monkeys reached for various objects (Gallese et al., 1996). One researcher happened to reach out and pick up one of the designated objects, and much to his amazement, the monkey's neuron fired—just as it did when the monkey picked up the object itself. The researchers went on to find many such neurons in the frontal lobe, which they named mirror neurons. ***Mirror neurons* are neurons that are activated by performing an action or by seeing another animal perform the same action.**

Researchers have used fMRI scans to demonstrate that humans also have mirror neurons in both the frontal and parietal lobes (Iacoboni &

Corpus callosum

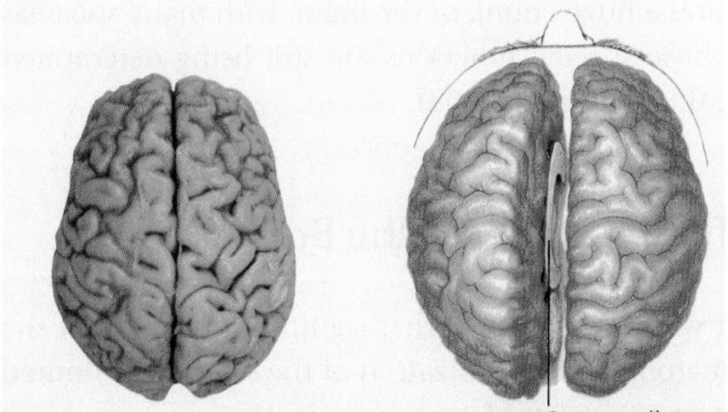

© 2017 Cengage Learning

Figure 3.16
The cerebral hemispheres and the corpus callosum. (Left) As this photo shows, the longitudinal fissure running down the middle of the brain (viewed from above) separates the left and right halves of the cerebral cortex. (Right) In this drawing, the cerebral hemispheres have been "pulled apart" to reveal the corpus callosum. This band of fibres is the communication bridge between the right and left halves of the human brain.

The Biological Bases of Behaviour

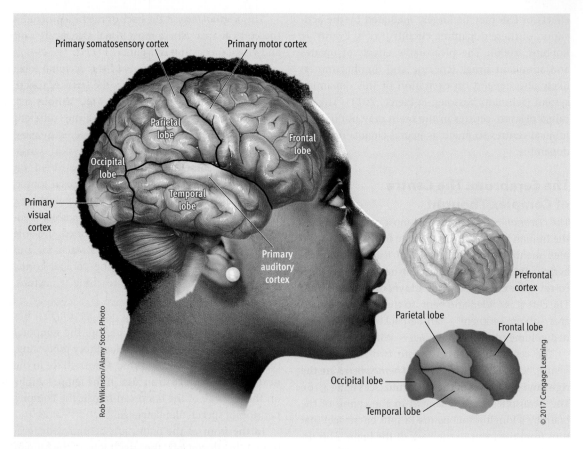

Figure 3.17
The cerebral cortex in humans. The cerebral cortex is divided into right and left halves, called *cerebral hemispheres*. This diagram provides a view of the right hemisphere. Each cerebral hemisphere can be divided into four lobes (highlighted in the bottom inset): the occipital, parietal, temporal, and frontal lobes. Each lobe has areas that handle particular functions, such as visual processing. The functions of the prefrontal cortex are something of a mystery, but they appear to include working memory and relational reasoning.

Dapretto, 2006; Rizzolatti & Craighero, 2004). Mirror neurons appear to provide a new model for understanding complex social cognition at a neural level. Mirror neurons may play a fundamental role in the acquisition of new motor skills (Buccino & Riggio, 2006); the imitation of others, which is crucial to much of human development (Iacoboni, 2012); and the understanding of others' intentions and the ability to feel empathy for others (Baird, Scheffer, & Wilson, 2011). Thus, the accidental discovery of mirror neurons may have a dramatic impact on brain-behaviour research in the future.

The portion of the frontal lobe to the front of the motor cortex is called the *prefrontal cortex* (see the inset in Figure 3.17). This area is disproportionately large in humans, accounting for about one-third of the cerebral cortex (Huey, Krueger, & Grafman, 2006). Its apparent contribution to certain types of decision making and key aspects of self-control (Gläscher et al., 2012) suggests that the prefrontal cortex houses some sort of "executive control system," which is thought to organize and direct thought processes (Beer, Shimamura, & Knight, 2004). Much remains to be learned, however, as the prefrontal cortex constitutes a huge chunk of the brain, with many subareas whose specific functions are still being determined (Miller & Wallis, 2008).

The Plasticity of the Brain

It was once believed that significant changes in the anatomy and organization of the brain were limited to early periods of development. However, according to University of Lethbridge behavioural neuroscientist Bryan Kolb (Kolb & Gibb, 2007), research has gradually demonstrated that the anatomical structure and functional organization of the brain are more malleable than previously assumed (Bryck & Fisher, 2012; Kolb, Gibb, & Robinson, 2003; Pascual-Leone, 2009). Neuroscientists call this *brain plasticity*, which is "the brain's ability to change structure and function" (Kolb & Whishaw, 1998, p. 85). Kolb suggested that experience stimulates brain plasticity, including changes in dendritic length, synapse formation, and altered metabolic activity.

Conclusions about brain plasticity in general are based on at least three research findings. *First, experience can sculpt features of brain structure.* For example, neuroimaging studies report that people who practise a juggling routine for three months show structural changes in brain areas known to process visual and motor tasks (Draganski et al., 2004). Similarly, three months of intense preparation for the Law School Admission Test produced structural changes in brain areas crucial to reasoning (Mackey, Whitaker, & Bunge, 2012). Additionally, British taxi drivers who pass extremely demanding exams on the complex streets of London show structural changes in the hippocampal areas, but these changes are not observed in those who fail the exams (Woollett & Maguire, 2011).

Second, damage to incoming sensory pathways or the destruction of brain tissue can lead to neural reorganization. For example, when scientists amputated the third finger in an owl monkey, the part of its cortex that formerly responded to the third finger gradually became responsive to the second and fourth fingers (Kaas, 2000). Similarly, in some blind people, areas in the occipital lobe that normally process visual information are "recruited" to help process verbal input (Amedi et al., 2004).

Third, the adult brain can generate new neurons (Gage, 2002). Historically, it was believed that *neurogenesis—the formation of new neurons*—did not occur in **adult humans.** It was thought that no new brain neurons were formed after infancy (Gross, 2000). However, research has found that adult humans and monkeys can form new neurons in the olfactory bulb and the hippocampus (DiCicco-Bloom & Falluel-Morel, 2009), and now that neuroscientists know where to look, neurogenesis has been found in the brains of all vertebrate species studied (Kozorovitskiy & Gould, 2008). Neurogenesis taking place in the dentate gyrus of the hippocampus appears to be particularly important (Drew, Fusi, & Hen, 2013). The new neurons generated here migrate to the cortex where they sprout axons and form new synapses with existing neurons, becoming fully integrated into the brain's communication networks. Neuroscientists are now focusing on the functional significance of neurogenesis. Accumulating evidence suggests that neurogenesis may play an important role in learning and memory (Benarroch, 2013; Koehl & Abrous, 2011) (see Chapter 7). Much remains to be learned about neurogenesis, but many theorists believe that it is a key factor in the brain's plasticity (Kohman & Rhodes, 2013).

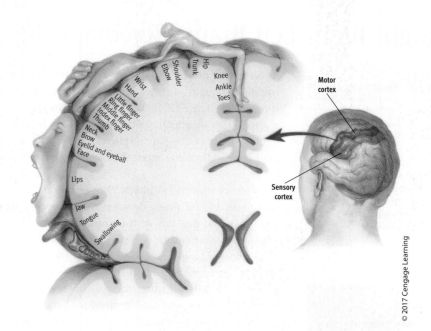

© 2017 Cengage Learning

Figure 3.18

The primary motor cortex. This diagram shows the amount of motor cortex devoted to the control of various muscles and limbs. The anatomical features in the drawing are distorted because their size is proportional to the amount of cortex devoted to their control. As you can see, more of the cortex is allocated to muscle groups that must make relatively precise movements.

The demonstration of brain plasticity has stimulated new applied research. For example, studies have explored the effects of increased exercise in protecting and enhancing brain functioning (Kramer & Erickson, 2007), and the potential benefits of the harvesting and transplantation of stem cells (Abbott, 2004; Gage, 2002; Kitner, 2002). Stem cells are "unspecialized" cells that renew themselves through cell division and, under special circumstances, can be "induced" to become cells suitable for other specialized purposes, such as the beating cells of the heart (Stem Cell Basics, 2007) and neurons. Some researchers are exploring whether stem cells can be transplanted into diseased or damaged brains to relieve symptoms and dysfunction. Work in Canada is guided by the Government of Canada's updated *Guidelines for Human Pluripotent Stem Cell Research* (*Updated Guidelines*, 2010).

In sum, research suggests that the brain is not "hard-wired" the way a computer is. It appears that the neural wiring of the brain is flexible and constantly evolving. That said, this plasticity is not unlimited. Rehabilitation efforts with people who have suffered severe brain damage clearly demonstrate limits to the extent to which the brain can rewire itself (Zillmer, Spiers, & Culbertson, 2008). Furthermore, the brain's plasticity declines with age (Rains, 2002); younger brains are more flexible than older brains. Still, the neural circuits of the brain show substantial plasticity, which helps organisms adapt to their environments.

Right Brain/Left Brain: Cerebral Laterality

Michael Gazzaniga

"Nothing can possibly replace a singular memory of mine: that of the moment when I discovered that case W. J. could no longer verbally describe (from his left hemisphere) stimuli presented to his freshly disconnected right hemisphere."

Roger Sperry

"Both the left and right hemispheres of the brain have been found to have their own specialized forms of intellect."

As we noted previously, the cerebrum—the seat of complex thought—consists of two separate hemispheres (see Figure 3.16 on page 89). Fascinating research has identified specialized abilities of the right and left cerebral hemispheres. Some theorists have gone so far as to suggest that we really have two brains in one!

Hints of this hemispheric specialization have been available for many decades, based on people who have had one side of their brain damaged. In 1861, the left hemisphere was implicated in the production of language by Paul Broca, a French surgeon. Broca treated a patient who had been unable to speak for 30 years. After the patient died, Broca conducted an autopsy and showed that the probable cause of his speech deficit was a localized lesion on the left side of the frontal lobe. Since then, many similar cases have shown that this area of the brain—known as *Broca's area*—is important in the *production* of speech (see Figure 3.19). In 1874, another area, in the temporal lobe of the left hemisphere, was identified as being a major language centre. Damage in *Wernicke's area* (also shown in Figure 3.19) usually leads to problems with the *comprehension* of language.

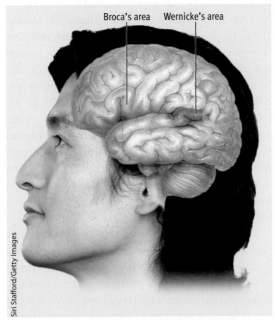

Figure 3.19

Language processing in the brain. This view of the left hemisphere highlights the location of two centres for language processing in the brain: Broca's area, which is involved in speech production, and Wernicke's area, which is involved in language comprehension.

Evidence that the left hemisphere usually processes language led scientists to characterize it as the "dominant" hemisphere. Because thoughts are usually coded in language, the left hemisphere was given the lion's share of credit for handling the "higher" mental processes, such as reasoning, remembering, planning, and problem solving. Meanwhile, the right hemisphere was viewed as the "nondominant," or "lesser," hemisphere, lacking any special functions or abilities.

This characterization of the left and right hemispheres as major and minor partners in the brain's work began to change in the 1960s. It started with landmark research by Roger Sperry, Michael Gazzaniga, and their colleagues, who studied "split-brain" patients: individuals whose cerebral hemispheres had been surgically disconnected (Gazzaniga, 1970; Gazzaniga, Bogen, & Sperry, 1965; Levy, Trevarthen, & Sperry, 1972; Sperry, 1982). In 1981, Sperry received a Nobel Prize in Physiology or Medicine for this work.

Bisecting the Brain: Split-Brain Research

In *split-brain surgery*, the bundle of fibres that connects the cerebral hemispheres (the corpus callosum) is cut to reduce the severity of epileptic seizures. It is a radical procedure that is chosen only in exceptional cases that have not responded to other treatments (Wolford, Miller, & Gazzaniga, 2004). But the surgery provides scientists with an unusual opportunity to study people who have had their brain literally split in two (Lassonde & Quimet, 2010).

To appreciate the logic of split-brain research, you need to understand how sensory and motor information is routed to and from the two hemispheres. *Each hemisphere's primary connections are to the opposite side of the body.* For example, the left hemisphere controls, and communicates with, the right hand, right arm, right leg, right eyebrow, and so on, whereas the right hemisphere controls, and communicates with, the left side of the body.

Vision and hearing are more complex. Both eyes deliver information to both hemispheres, but this input is still separated. Stimuli in the right half of the *visual field* are registered by receptors on the left side of each eye, which send signals to the left hemisphere. Stimuli in the left half of the visual field are transmitted by both eyes to the right hemisphere (see Figure 3.20). Auditory inputs to each ear also go to both hemispheres. However, connections to the opposite hemisphere are stronger and more immediate. As a result, sounds presented exclusively to the right ear (through headphones) are registered in the left hemisphere first, while sounds presented to the left ear are registered more quickly in the right hemisphere.

We typically don't notice this asymmetric, "crisscrossed" organization because the two hemispheres are in close communication with each other. Information received by one hemisphere is readily shared with the other via the corpus callosum. However, when the two hemispheres are surgically disconnected, the functional specialization of the brain becomes apparent.

In their classic study of split-brain patients, Gazzaniga, Bogen, and Sperry (1965) presented visual stimuli such as pictures, symbols, and words in a single visual field (the left or the right), so that the stimuli would be sent to only one hemisphere. The stimuli were projected onto a screen in front of the patients, who stared at a fixation point (a spot) in the centre of the screen (see Figure 3.21). The images were flashed to the right or the left of the fixation point for only a fraction of a second. Thus, the patients did not have a chance to move their eyes, and the stimuli were glimpsed in only one visual field.

When pictures were flashed in the right visual field and thus sent to the left hemisphere, the split-brain patients could name and describe the objects depicted (such as a cup or spoon). However, the patients could *not* name and describe the same objects when they were flashed in the left visual field and sent to the right hemisphere. These findings supported the notion that language is housed in the left hemisphere.

Although the split-brain patients' right hemispheres were not able to speak up for themselves, further tests revealed that the right hemispheres *were* processing the information presented. If patients were asked to *point to a picture* of an object that had been flashed to their left visual field, they were able to do so. Furthermore, the right hemisphere (which controls the left hand) turned out to be *superior* to the left hemisphere (right hand) in assembling little puzzles and copying drawings, even though the subjects were right-handed. These findings provided the first compelling demonstration that the right hemisphere has its own special talents. Subsequent studies of additional split-brain patients showed the right hemisphere was better than the left on a variety of visual–spatial tasks,

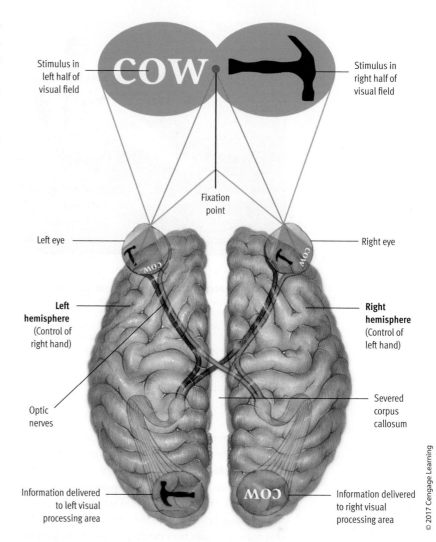

© 2017 Cengage Learning

Figure 3.20

Visual input in the split brain. If a participant stares at a fixation point, the point divides the subject's visual field into right and left halves. Input from the right visual field (a picture of a hammer in this example) strikes the left side of each eye and is transmitted to the left hemisphere. Input from the left visual field strikes the right side of each eye and is transmitted to the right hemisphere. Normally, the hemispheres share the information from the two halves of the visual field, but in split-brain patients, the corpus callosum is severed and the two hemispheres cannot communicate. Hence, the experimenter can present a visual stimulus to just one hemisphere at a time.

including discriminating colours, arranging blocks, and recognizing faces.

Hemispheric Specialization in the Intact Brain

In terms of research, the problem with the split-brain operation is that it creates an abnormal situation. The surgery is done only with people who suffer from prolonged, severe cases of epilepsy. These people may have a somewhat atypical brain organization even before the operation as well, as they

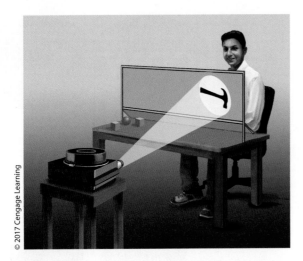

Figure 3.21
Experimental apparatus in split-brain research. On the left is a special slide projector that can present images very briefly, before the subject's eyes can move and thus change the visual field. Images are projected on one side of the screen to present stimuli to just one hemisphere. The portion of the apparatus beneath the screen is constructed to prevent participants from seeing objects that they may be asked to handle with their right or left hand, another procedure that can be used to send information to just one hemisphere.

typically have an extended history of medication to help with their epilepsy. Furthermore, there are very few split-brain patients; only ten split-brain patients have been studied intensively (Gazzaniga, 2008). Thus, theorists wondered whether it was safe to generalize broadly from the split-brain studies. For this reason, researchers developed methods to study cerebral specialization in the intact brain (Lassonde & Quimet, 2010).

One method involves looking at left-right imbalances in visual or auditory processing, called *perceptual asymmetries*. As we just discussed, it is possible to present visual stimuli to just one visual field at a time. In normal individuals, the input sent to one hemisphere is quickly shared with the other. However, subtle differences in the "abilities" of the two hemispheres can be detected by precisely measuring how fast and accurately people can recognize different types of stimuli. For instance, when *verbal* stimuli are presented to the right visual field (and thus sent to the *left hemisphere* first), they are identified more quickly and more accurately than when they are presented to the left visual field (and sent to the right hemisphere first). The faster reactions in the left hemisphere presumably occur because it can recognize verbal stimuli on its own, while the right hemisphere has to take extra time to "consult" the left hemisphere. In contrast, the *right hemisphere* is faster than the left on *visual–spatial*

tasks, such as locating a dot or recognizing a face (Bradshaw, 1989).

Researchers have used a variety of other approaches to explore hemispheric specialization in normal people. For example, brain-imaging studies reveal different patterns of activation for each hemisphere when participants work on specific cognitive tasks. For the most part, their findings have converged nicely with the results of the split-brain studies (Hervé et al., 2013). Overall, the data suggest that the two hemispheres *are* specialized, with each handling certain types of cognitive tasks better than the other (Corballis, 2003; Gazzaniga, 2005; Machado et al., 2013). *The left hemisphere is usually better at tasks involving verbal processing, such as language, speech, reading, and writing. The right hemisphere exhibits superiority on many tasks involving nonverbal processing, such as most spatial, musical, and visual recognition tasks and tasks involving the perception of emotions.*

Research on hemispheric specialization has been increasingly conducted with modern brain-imaging technology, especially fMRI scans (Friston, 2003; Pizzagalli, Shackman, & Davidson, 2003). These scans can provide a more direct and precise view of hemispheric activation on various types of tasks than can the study of perceptual asymmetries. For the most part, this new approach has painted a picture that is consistent with previous findings but more nuanced and detailed. While imaging research has provided new insights into the workings of the brain, it is also clear that other techniques, such as presenting different information to the two ears, as used by University of New Brunswick researcher Daniel Voyer (Voyer, Bowes, & Soraggi, 2009) and his colleagues, are key tools in our attempt to understand laterality effects in the brain.

Although brain-imaging research has provided additional support for the notion that areas in the right and left hemisphere are specialized to handle certain cognitive functions, this research has also provided evidence that the two sides of the brain are constantly collaborating. Newer brain-imaging methods reveal a great deal of highly dynamic interhemispheric communication and coordination (Doron, Bassett, & Gazzaniga, 2012). Interestingly, a study of Albert Einstein's brain suggests that the quality of this communication may be critical (Men et al., 2013). Using newly published photos of Einstein's brain (originally taken after his death in 1955) and an innovative method to quantify the nerve fibres in the corpus callosum, research suggests that Einstein's brilliance may have been partly due to an exceptional degree of connectivity between his hemispheres.

Imagine that you are a neuropsychologist and are asked to diagnose the cases described below. You need to identify the probable cause(s) of the disorders in terms of nervous system malfunctions. Based on the information in this chapter, indicate the probable location of any brain damage or the probable disturbance of neurotransmitter activity. The answers can be found at the back of the book in Appendix A.

Case 1. Miriam is exhibiting language deficits. In particular, she does not seem to comprehend the meaning of words.

_____

_____

Case 2. Camille displays tremors and muscular rigidity and is diagnosed as having Parkinson's disease.

_____

_____

Case 3. Ricardo, a 28-year-old computer executive, has gradually seen his strength and motor coordination deteriorate badly. He is diagnosed as having multiple sclerosis.

_____

_____

Case 4. Wendy is highly irrational, has poor contact with reality, and reports hallucinations. She is given a diagnosis of schizophrenic disorder.

_____

_____

The Endocrine System: Another Way to Communicate

The major way the brain communicates with the rest of the body is through the nervous system. However, the body has a second communication system that is also important to behaviour. The *endocrine system* consists of glands that secrete hormones into the bloodstream that help control bodily functioning. The messengers in this communication network are called hormones. *Hormones* are the chemicals released by the endocrine glands. Hormones are like neurotransmitters in the nervous system in that they are stored for subsequent release as chemical messengers, and once released, they bind to special receptors on target cells. In fact, some chemical substances do double duty, functioning as hormones when they're released in the endocrine system and as neurotransmitters in the nervous system (norepinephrine, for example). However, there are important differences between hormones and neurotransmitters. Neurotransmitters generally communicate across very short distances with lightning speed (measured in milliseconds) along very specific pathways, whereas hormonal messages often travel to distant cells at a much slower speed (measured in seconds and minutes) and tend to be less specific, as they can act on many target cells throughout the body.

The major endocrine glands are shown in Figure 3.22. Hormones tend to be released several times per day in brief bursts or pulses that last only a few minutes. The levels of many hormones increase and decrease in a rhythmic pattern throughout the day.

Much of the endocrine system is controlled by the nervous system through the *hypothalamus* (Gore, 2008). This structure at the base of the forebrain has intimate connections with the pea-sized *pituitary gland*. The *pituitary gland* releases a variety of hormones that are distributed throughout the body, stimulating activity in other endocrine glands. In this sense, the pituitary is the "master gland" of the endocrine system, although the hypothalamus is the real power behind the throne. The intermeshing of the nervous system and the endocrine system can be seen in the fight-or-flight response described earlier. In times of stress, the hypothalamus sends signals along two pathways—through the autonomic nervous system and through the pituitary gland—to the adrenal glands (Clow, 2001). In response, the adrenal glands secrete hormones that radiate throughout the body, preparing it to cope with an emergency.

Oxytocin is a hormone released by the pituitary gland, which regulates reproductive behaviours.

Key Learning Goal

▶ Identify the key components of the endocrine system, and describe ways in which hormones regulate behaviour.

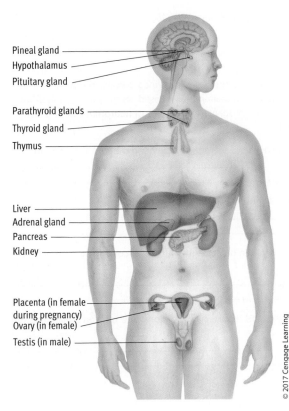

Pineal gland
Hypothalamus
Pituitary gland

Parathyroid glands
Thyroid gland
Thymus

Liver
Adrenal gland
Pancreas
Kidney

Placenta (in female during pregnancy)
Ovary (in female)
Testis (in male)

© 2017 Cengage Learning

Figure 3.22

The endocrine system. This graphic depicts most of the major endocrine glands. The endocrine glands release hormones into the bloodstream. These chemicals regulate a variety of physical functions and affect many aspects of behaviour.

oxytocin spray, males who were in committed relationships kept more distance between themselves and an attractive female than did those who inhaled a placebo spray.

Oxytocin may facilitate the development of a sense of security, feelings of safety, and a highly tuned sensitivity to and empathy for others (Carter, 2014). Oxytocin fosters feelings of extraversion, openness, and warmth, which promote social bonding between people (Cardoso, Ellenbogen, & Linnen, 2012). Oxytocin may enhance fathers' engagement with their infant children (Weisman, Zagoory-Sharon, & Feldman, 2014), increase empathy for others' suffering (Shamay-Tsoory et al., 2013), and promote sharing of one's emotions (Lane et al., 2013).

Oxytocin may increase trust in humans. In one study, research participants who inhaled an oxytocin spray trusted others more with their money than those in a control condition (Kosfeld et al., 2005). Other studies have also found a link between oxytocin and trusting behaviour (Merolla et al., 2013). However, in some situations, this increased trust could backfire, because oxytocin can decrease subjects' ability to detect deception by others (Israel, Hart, & Winter, 2013).

Hormones also influence human physiological development. For example, the pituitary releases *gonadotropin hormones*, which affect the *gonads*, or sexual glands. These hormones direct the formation of the external sexual organs in the developing fetus (Gorski, 2000). Thus, your sexual identity as a male or female was shaped during prenatal development by hormones. Around puberty, increased levels of sexual hormones determine secondary sexual characteristics, such as male facial hair and female breasts (Susman, Dorn, & Schiefelbein, 2003).

These developmental effects of hormones illustrate how genetic programming has a hand in behaviour. The hormonal actions that shaped your sex and aroused your interest in sexuality were preprogrammed over a decade earlier by your genetic inheritance.

Oxytocin triggers contractions when a woman gives birth and stimulates the mammary glands to release milk for breastfeeding (Donaldson & Young, 2008). Oxytocin also has far-reaching effects on complex social behaviour (e.g., Barraza, McCullough, & Zak, 2011; Carter, 2014; Kis et al., 2013; Zak, 2012). For example, oxytocin fosters adult–adult pair-bonding in many mammals (Lim & Young, 2006). Consistent with this finding, oxytocin may promote relationship fidelity in men (Scheele et al., 2012). After inhaling an

Heredity and Behaviour: Is It All in the Genes?

Most people realize that physical characteristics such as height, hair colour, blood type, and eye colour are largely shaped by heredity. But what about psychological characteristics, such as intelligence, moodiness, impulsiveness, and shyness? To what extent are people's behavioural qualities moulded by their genes? These questions are the central focus of *behavioural genetics*—an interdisciplinary field that studies the influence of genetic factors on behavioural traits.

Basic Principles of Genetics

Every cell in your body contains enduring messages from your mother's and father's genetic code. These messages are found on the *chromosomes* that lie within the nucleus of each cell.

Chromosomes and Genes

Chromosomes are threadlike strands of DNA (deoxyribonucleic acid) molecules that carry genetic information (see Figure 3.23). With the exception of sex cells (sperm and eggs), every cell in humans contains 46 chromosomes. These chromosomes operate in 23 pairs, with one chromosome of each pair being contributed by each parent. Each chromosome in turn contains thousands of biochemical messengers called *genes*. *Genes* **are DNA segments that serve as the key functional units in hereditary transmission.**

If all offspring are formed by a union of the parents' sex cells, why aren't family members identical clones? The reason is that a single pair of parents can produce children with an extraordinary variety of combinations of chromosomes. Each parent's 23 chromosome pairs can be scrambled in over 8 million (2^{23}) different ways, yielding roughly 70 trillion (2^{46}) possible configurations when sperm and egg unite. In fact, when complexities such as *mutations* (changes in the genetic code) or *crossing over* during sex-cell formation (an interchange of material between chromosomes), the total number of combinations is even higher. Thus, genetic transmission is a complicated process.

Although different combinations of genes explain why family members aren't all alike, family members do tend to resemble one another because they share more of the same genes than do nonmembers. Traditionally, researchers have assumed that the genetic overlap for identical twins is 100 percent, whereas parents and their children, and full siblings including fraternal twins, share 50 percent of their genes. More-distant relatives share less genetic overlap, as outlined in Figure 3.24. However, when the actual overlap was carefully assessed, researchers found that the genetic overlap was overestimated (Bruder et al., 2008). For example, identical twins actually share substantially less than 100 percent of their genes, and parents and their children, and full siblings share less than 50 percent.

Like chromosomes, genes operate in pairs, with one gene of each pair coming from each parent. In the simplest scenario, a single pair of genes determines a trait. However, most human characteristics appear to be *polygenic traits*, **or characteristics that are influenced by more than one pair of genes.** For example, three to five gene pairs are thought to interactively determine skin colour. Complex physical abilities, such as motor coordination, may be influenced by interactions among a great many pairs of genes. Most psychological characteristics that appear to be affected by heredity seem to involve complex polygenic inheritance (Plomin, DeFries et al., 2013).

Genotype versus Phenotype

It might seem that two parents with the same manifest trait, such as detached earlobes, should always produce offspring with that trait. However, that isn't always the case. For instance, two parents with detached earlobes can produce a child with attached earlobes. This happens because there are unexpressed recessive genes in the family's gene pool—in this case, genes for attached earlobes.

This point brings us to the distinction between genotype and phenotype. *Genotype* **refers to a person's genetic makeup.** *Phenotype* **refers to the ways in which a person's genotype is manifested in observable characteristics.** Different genotypes (such as two genes for detached earlobes as opposed to one gene for detached and one for attached) can yield the same phenotype (detached earlobes). Genotype is determined at conception and is fixed forever. In contrast, phenotypic characteristics (hair colour, for instance) may change over time. They may also be modified by environmental factors.

Genotypes translate into phenotypic characteristics in a variety of ways. Not all gene pairs operate according to the principles of dominance. In some instances, when paired genes are different, they produce a blend, an "averaged-out" phenotype. In other cases, paired genes that are different strike another type of compromise, and both characteristics show up phenotypically. In the case of type AB blood, for example, one gene is for type A and the other is for type B.

Investigating Hereditary Influence: Research Methods

How do scientists disentangle the effects of genetics and experience to determine how heredity affects human behaviour? Researchers have designed special methods to assess the impact of heredity. Three of the most important methods are family studies, twin studies, and adoption studies.

Family Studies

In *family studies*, **researchers assess hereditary influence by examining blood relatives to assess how much they resemble one another on a specific trait.** If heredity affects the trait under scrutiny, phenotypic similarity should be higher among relatives. Furthermore, there should be more similarity among relatives who share more genes. For instance, siblings should exhibit more similarity than cousins.

Family studies are used in psychology to estimate the risk of a relative developing a mental health disorder based on whether other family members suffer with this disorder. For example, numerous family studies have assessed the contribution of heredity to the development of schizophrenic disorders. These

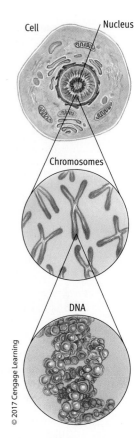

Cell Nucleus

Chromosomes

DNA

© 2017 Cengage Learning

Figure 3.23
Genetic material. This series of enlargements shows the main components of genetic material. (Top) In the nucleus of every cell are chromosomes, which carry the information needed to construct new human beings. (Centre) Chromosomes are threadlike strands of DNA that carry thousands of genes, the functional units of hereditary transmission. (Bottom) DNA is a double spiral chain of molecules that can copy itself to reproduce.

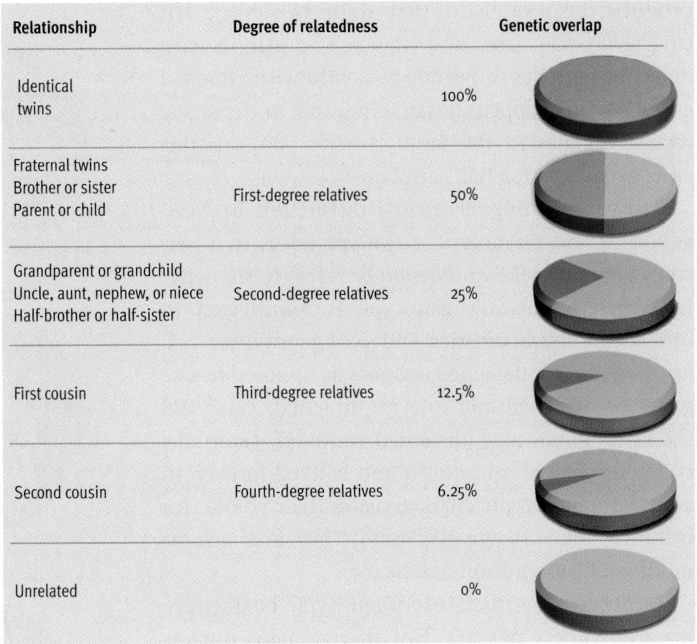

Relationship	Degree of relatedness	Genetic overlap	
Identical twins		100%	
Fraternal twins Brother or sister Parent or child	First-degree relatives	50%	
Grandparent or grandchild Uncle, aunt, nephew, or niece Half-brother or half-sister	Second-degree relatives	25%	
First cousin	Third-degree relatives	12.5%	
Second cousin	Fourth-degree relatives	6.25%	
Unrelated		0%	

© 2017 Cengage Learning

Figure 3.24

Genetic relatedness. Research on the genetic bases of behaviour takes advantage of the different degrees of genetic relatedness between various types of relatives. If heredity influences a trait, relatives who share more genes should be more similar with regard to that trait than are more distant relatives, who share fewer genes. Comparisons involving various degrees of biological relationships will come up frequently in later chapters.

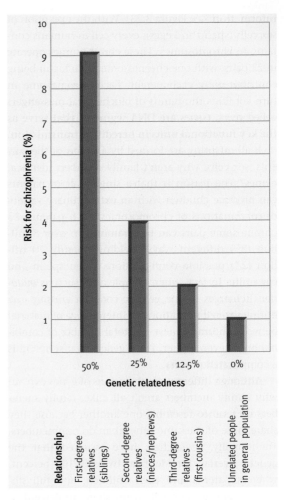

Figure 3.25

Family studies of risk for schizophrenic disorders. First-degree relatives of schizophrenic patients have an elevated risk of developing schizophrenia (Gottesman, 1991). For instance, the risk for siblings of schizophrenic patients is about 9 percent instead of the baseline 1 percent for unrelated people. Second- and third-degree relatives have progressively smaller elevations in risk for this disorder. Although these patterns of risk do not prove that schizophrenia is partly inherited, they are consistent with this hypothesis.

Source: From Weiten. *Cengage Advantage Books: Psychology*, 9E. © 2013 South-Western, a part of Cengage, Inc. Reproduced by permission. www.cengage.com/permissions

disorders strike approximately 1 percent of the population, yet as Figure 3.25 reveals, 9 percent of the siblings of schizophrenic patients exhibit schizophrenia themselves (Gottesman, 1991). Thus, the risk for first-degree relatives of schizophrenic patients is nine times higher than normal. This risk is greater than that observed for more distantly related relatives, such as nieces and nephews (4 percent), who, in turn, are at greater risk than second cousins (2 percent). This pattern of results is consistent with the hypothesis that genetic inheritance influences the development of schizophrenic disorders (Kirov & Owen, 2009).

Family studies can indicate whether a trait runs in families. However, this correlation does not provide conclusive evidence that the trait is influenced by heredity because family members not only share more genes but they generally share more similar environments. For example, closer relatives are more likely to live together than more distant relatives. Thus, genetic similarity and environmental similarity *both* tend to be greater for closer relatives. Either of these confounded variables could be responsible when greater phenotypic similarity is found in closer relatives. Family studies can offer useful insights about the possible impact of heredity, but they cannot provide definitive evidence.

Twin Studies

Twin studies provide stronger evidence about the possible role of genetic factors. In *twin studies*, researchers assess hereditary influence by comparing the resemblance of identical twins and fraternal twins with respect to a trait. The logic of twin studies hinges on the genetic relatedness of identical and fraternal twins (see Figure 3.26). *Identical (monozygotic) twins* emerge from one zygote that splits for unknown reasons. Thus, they have a very similar genotype; though not the 100 percent genetic relatedness that is commonly reported. *Fraternal (dizygotic) twins* result when two eggs are fertilized simultaneously by different sperm cells, forming two separate zygotes. Fraternal twins are only as genetically similar as siblings born to the same parents at different times. Their genetic relatedness is roughly half that of identical twins.

Fraternal twins provide a useful comparison to identical twins because in both cases the twins usually grow up in the same home, at the same time, exposed to the same configuration of relatives, neighbours, peers, teachers, events, and so forth. Thus, both kinds of twins normally develop under similar environmental conditions. However, identical twins share more genetic kinship than fraternal twins. Consequently, if sets of identical twins tend to exhibit more similarity of a trait than sets of fraternal twins do, this suggests that this greater similarity may be due to heredity rather than environment.

Twin studies have assessed the impact of heredity on a variety of traits (e.g., Laceulle et al., 2013). Some representative results are summarized in Figure 3.27. The higher correlations found for identical twins indicate that they tend to be more similar to each other than fraternal twins on measures of general intelligence (McGue et al., 1993) and measures of specific personality traits, such as extraversion (Plomin et al., 2008). These results support the notion that intelligence and personality are influenced to some degree by genetic makeup.

Adoption Studies

Adoption studies assess hereditary influence by examining the resemblance between adopted children and both their biological and their adoptive parents. If adopted children resemble their biological parents in a trait, even though they were not raised by them, this suggests that genetic factors may influence that trait. In contrast, if adopted children resemble their adoptive parents, even though they inherited no genes from them, environmental factors probably influence the trait.

In recent years, adoption studies have contributed to science's understanding of the influence of genetics and the environment on intelligence. The research shows modest similarity between adopted children and their biological parents, as indicated by an average correlation of 0.22 (Grigorenko, 2000). Interestingly, adopted children resemble their adoptive parents to a very similar degree (an average correlation of about 0.20). These findings suggest that both heredity and environment have an influence on intelligence.

However, we need to "adopt" a critical eye when we review the results of studies that use family, twin, and adoption methods. A main limitation of these methods is that they can't clearly separate genes from the environment. For example, identical twins typically look very similar. As a result, people and society typically treat them similarly (parents may even dress them the same). Additionally, because identical

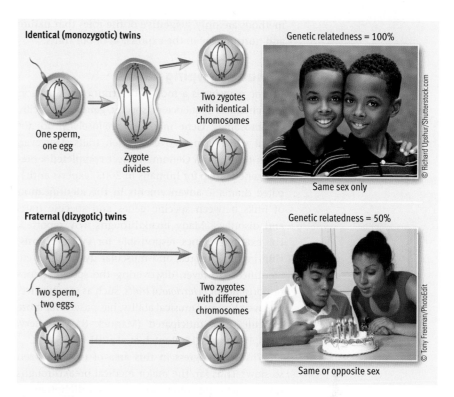

Figure 3.26

Identical versus fraternal twins. Identical (monozygotic) twins emerge from one zygote that splits, so their genetic relatedness is 100 percent. Fraternal (dizygotic) twins emerge from two separate zygotes, so their genetic relatedness is only 50 percent.

Source: From KALAT. *Introduction to Psychology*, 4E. © 1996 South-Western, a part of Cengage, Inc. Reproduced by permission. www.cengage.com/permissions

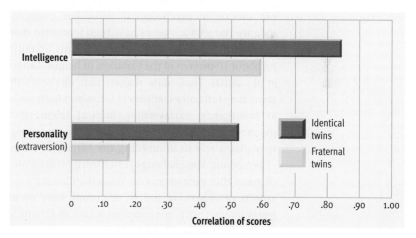

Figure 3.27

Twin studies of intelligence and personality. Identical twins tend to be more similar than fraternal twins (as reflected in higher correlations) with regard to intelligence and specific personality traits, such as extraversion. These findings suggest that intelligence and personality are influenced by heredity.

Sources: Intelligence data from McGue et al., 1993; extraversion data based on Loehlin, 1992.

twins do not share 100 percent of their genetics, differences may be the result of the environment, or the nonoverlapping genetics. For these, and many other reasons, identical twins share very similar genetics *and* environments. This confounding of genetics and environments means that results based on these

The Biological Bases of Behaviour

methods are only suggestive of the roles that nature and nurture play in the expression of our traits.

Genetic Mapping

Genetic mapping is a tool to determine the location and chemical sequence of specific genes on specific chromosomes. Gene maps, by themselves, do not reveal which genes govern which traits. However, when the Human Genome Project completed a precise genetic map for humans in 2003, experts anticipated dramatic advancements in the identification of links between specific genes and specific traits and disorders. Many breakthroughs *were* reported. For example, genes responsible for cystic fibrosis, Huntington's chorea, and muscular dystrophy were identified. However, discovering the specific genes responsible for *behavioural traits*, such as intelligence, extraversion, and musical ability, has proven far more difficult than anticipated (Manuck & McCaffery, 2014; Plomin, 2013; Roofeh et al., 2013).

Why has progress in this area of research been so slow? Thus far, the major medical breakthroughs from genetic mapping have involved dichotomous traits (you either do or do not have the trait, such as muscular dystrophy) governed by a single gene pair. However, almost all behavioural traits (e.g., intelligence, extraversion, and musical ability) appear to be *polygenic*, which means they are shaped by many genes rather than a single gene. These problems are not unique to psychological traits. For example, roughly 180 relevant genes have been identified that influence height, but collectively they only account for about 10 percent of the variation in height (Lango et al., 2010). These data suggest that *thousands* of genes may influence complex abilities and traits such as intelligence, extraversion, musical talent, and psychological disorders. However, genetic mapping may play a role in unravelling the hereditary bases of behaviour. The challenge is to identify collections of genes that each exert very modest influence over aspects of behaviour and to determine how these genes interact with environmental factors (Manuck & McCaffery, 2014; Plomin, 2013).

The Cutting Edge: CRISPR

Advancements in science may be revolutionized by a new tool to edit genes. This tool has the almost-impossible-to-remember description "clustered regularly interspaced short palindromic repeats" (CRSPR; Cong et al., 2013; Dow et al., 2015). CRSPR is a natural part of our immune systems. CRSPR store a small section of harmful viruses in order to recognize them next time you are attacked. When CRSPR recognize an invading virus, they can precisely snip the DNA of the virus so that it can't replicate.

So why are CRSPR so groundbreaking? Scientists can use them to modify the genomes of animals (Cyranoski, 2016). Though the tools to modify genomes have been around for decades, CRSPR have many advantages, including they are much more precise, faster, and cheaper. Additionally, they can be used on any animal, including humans. As a result, the hope is that genetic modification may soon be available to help with many diseases including cystic fibrosis, Alzheimer's, and Huntington's. But a cautionary note is needed. Genetic manipulation has profound implications. Potentially this tool can be used for treating genetic disorders, but it could also be used for developing designer offspring.

The Interplay of Heredity and Environment

We began this section by asking: Is it all in the genes? When it comes to behavioural traits, the answer clearly is no. According to Robert Plomin (1993, 2004), a leading behavioural genetics researcher, research repeatedly shows that heredity and experience jointly influence most behaviours. Moreover, their effects are interactive—genetics and experience play off each other (Gottesman & Hanson, 2005; Rutter, 2006, 2007; Rutter & Silberg, 2002).

For example, consider the development of schizophrenic disorders. Although the evidence indicates that genetic factors influence the development of schizophrenia, it does *not* appear that anyone directly inherits the disorder itself. Rather, people appear to inherit a certain degree of *vulnerability* to the disorder (McDonald & Murphy, 2003). Whether this vulnerability is converted into an actual disorder depends on each person's experiences. As we will discuss in Chapter 15, some stressful experiences seem to evoke the disorder in people who are more vulnerable to it. Thus, as Danielle Dick and Richard Rose (2002) wrote in a major review of behavioural genetics research, "We inherit dispositions, not destinies."

Epigenetics: The Interplay of Heredity and Environment

Scientists repeatedly find that heredity and experience *jointly* influence most aspects of behaviour. Moreover, their effects are interactive—they play off each other (Asbury & Plomin, 2014; Rutter, 2012). Research in the emerging field of *epigenetics* has emphasized that genetic and environmental factors are inextricably intertwined. **Epigenetics is the study of heritable changes in gene expression that do not involve modifications to the DNA sequence.** Specific effects of genes can be dampened or silenced by chemical events at the cellular level, leading to alterations in traits, health, and behaviour (Tsankova et al., 2007). These chemical events can be stimulated by environmental events, such as poor nurturing or nutrition during infancy, or early exposure to stress (Kofink et al., 2013). What has surprised scientists is that these *epigenetic marks* that influence gene expression can be passed on to successive generations (Bohacek et al., 2013). Epigenetic changes may contribute to many psychological disorders, including drug addiction, schizophrenia, and bipolar disorder (Dempster et al., 2011; Nestler, 2014). The finding that genes are influenced by environmental influence has a number of far-reaching implications. Among other things, it means that efforts to quantify the respective influences of heredity and environment—informative though they may be—are ultimately artificial.

The Evolutionary Bases of Behaviour

To complete our look at the biological bases of behaviour, we need to discuss how evolutionary forces have shaped many aspects of human and animal behaviour. *Evolutionary psychology* is a major new theoretical perspective that analyzes behavioural processes in terms of their adaptive significance.

Darwin's Insights

Charles Darwin, the legendary British naturalist, was *not* the first person to describe the process of evolution. Long before Darwin, other biologists who had studied the earth's fossil record noted that species appeared to have undergone gradual changes over the course of a great many generations. What Darwin (1859) contributed in his landmark book, *On the Origin of Species*, was a creative, new explanation for *how and why* evolutionary changes unfold over time. He identified *natural selection* as the mechanism that orchestrates the process of evolution (Dewsbury, 2009).

Darwin set out to explain how characteristics of a species might change over generations and why these changes tended to be adaptive. In other words, he wanted to shed light on why organisms tend to have characteristics that are advantageous. For example, how did giraffes acquire their long necks that allow them to reach high into acacia trees to secure their main source of food? Darwin's explanation for the seemingly purposive nature of evolution centred on four crucial insights.

First, he noted that organisms vary in endless ways, such as size, speed, strength, aspects of appearance, visual abilities, hearing capacities, digestive processes, and cell structure. Second, he noted that many of these characteristics are heritable—that is, they tend to be passed down from one generation to the next. Although genes and chromosomes had not yet been discovered, the concept of heredity was well established. Third, borrowing from the work of Thomas Malthus, he noted that organisms tend to produce more offspring than local resources (e.g., food and living space availability) could support. As a population increases and resources dwindle, the competition for limited resources intensifies. Thus, it occurred to Darwin—and this was his grand insight—that variations in hereditary traits might affect organisms' ability to obtain the resources necessary for survival and reproduction. Fourth, building on this insight, Darwin argued that if a specific heritable trait contributes to an organism's survival or reproductive success, organisms with that trait should produce more offspring than those without the trait (or those with less of the trait), and the prevalence of that trait should gradually increase over generations resulting in evolutionary change.

Although evolution is widely characterized as a matter of "survival of the fittest," Darwin recognized from the beginning that survival is important only insofar as it relates to reproductive success. In evolutionary theory, *fitness refers to the reproductive success (number of descendants) of an individual organism relative to the average reproductive success in the population. Variations in reproductive success are what really fuel evolutionary change.* But survival is crucial because organisms typically need to mature and thrive before they can reproduce. So, Darwin theorized that traits might contribute to evolution in two ways:

Key Learning Goals

▶ Understand the key insights that represent the essence of Darwin's theory of evolution.

▶ Describe subsequent refinements to evolutionary theory, and give some examples of animal behaviour that represent adaptations.

© Jupiterimages

Ch. Darwin

Charles Darwin

"Can we doubt (remembering that many more individuals are born than can possibly survive) that individuals having any advantage, however slight, over others, would have the best chance of surviving and procreating their kind? . . . This preservation of favourable variations and the rejection of injurious variations, I call Natural Selection."

In evolutionary theory, fitness is a matter of reproductive success—the number of offspring produced by an organism.

by providing either a survival advantage or a reproductive advantage. For example, a turtle's shell has great protective value *that* provides a survival advantage. In contrast, a firefly's emission of light is a courtship *overture* that provides a reproductive advantage.

To summarize, the principle of *natural selection* posits that heritable characteristics that provide a *survival* or reproductive advantage are more likely than alternative characteristics to be passed on to subsequent generations and thus come to be "selected" over time. Please note that the process of natural selection works on *populations* rather than *organisms*. Evolution occurs when the gene pool in a population changes gradually because of *selection* pressures. Although there are occasional exceptions, this process tends to be extremely gradual—it generally takes thousands to millions of generations for one trait to be selected over another.

The fight-or-flight response discussed earlier in the chapter (see page 81) is an example of a behaviour that provides a survival advantage. Variations in survival advantage, along with variations in reproductive fitness, determine evolutionary change.

Darwin's theory has two important, far-reaching implications (Buss, 2009). First, the awe-inspiring diversity of life is the result of an unplanned, natural process rather than divine creation. Second, humans are not unique and that they share a common ancestry with other species. Although these implications would prove highly controversial, Darwin's theory eventually gained considerable acceptance because it provided a compelling explanation for how the characteristics of various species gradually changed over many generations and for the functional, adaptive direction of these changes.

Later Refinements to Evolutionary Theory

Although Darwin's evolutionary theory quickly gained supporters, it remained controversial for decades. One legitimate objection was that the theory did not adequately explain the details of the inheritance process. This shortcoming was successfully addressed in 1937 by Theodore Dobzhansky, who united Darwin's theory with modern genetics.

Contemporary models of evolution recognize that natural selection operates on the gene pool of a population. *Adaptations* are the key product of this process. An *adaptation* is an inherited characteristic that has increased in a population (through natural selection) because it increased the probability of survival or reproduction during the time it emerged. Because of the slow, gradual nature of evolution, adaptations sometimes linger in a population even after they no longer provide a survival or reproductive advantage (Durrant & Ellis, 2013). For example, humans typically prefer the taste of fatty foods. This preference was adaptive in an era of hunting and gathering when calories were scarce. However, in our modern world, calories are typically abundant, and this taste preference for fats leads many people to consume too much fat, resulting in obesity, heart disease, and other health problems. Thus, the preference for fatty foods is now a liability for humans.

Behaviours as Adaptive Traits

In addition to the evolution of *physical characteristics* in animals, Darwin recognized that natural selection was applicable to *behavioural traits* (Durrant & Ellis, 2013). Modern evolutionary psychology recognizes that a species' typical patterns of behaviour often reflect evolutionary solutions to adaptive problems.

Consider, for instance, rats' caution when they encounter new foods. Rats eat a wide variety of foods, but this variety can be risky because foods can contain toxins. When rats encounter unfamiliar foods, they consume only small amounts and they won't eat two new foods together. If the consumption of a new food is followed by illness, they avoid that food in the future (Logue, 1991). These precautions allow rats to learn what makes them sick, while reducing the likelihood of consuming a lethal amount of something poisonous. These patterns of eating are highly adaptive solutions to the food selection problems faced by rats.

Many behavioural adaptations improve organisms' chances of reproductive success. Consider, for instance, the wide variety of species in which females actively choose which male to mate with. In many such species, females demand material goods and services from males in return for copulation opportunities. For example, in one type of moth, males must spend hours extracting sodium from mud puddles, which they then transfer to prospective mates, who use it to supply their larvae with an important nutritional element (Smedley & Eisner, 1996). In the black-tipped hangingfly, females insist on a nuptial gift of food before they mate. They reject suitors bringing unpalatable food, and they tie the length of subsequent copulation to the size of the nuptial gift (Thornhill, 1976).

The behaviour that helps the grasshopper hide from predators is a product of evolution, just like the physical characteristics that help it to blend in with its surroundings.

Putting It in Perspective: Themes 1, 4, and 6

Key Learning Goal

▶ Identify the three unifying themes that were highlighted in this chapter.

Three of our seven themes are illustrated in this chapter: (1) heredity and environment jointly influence behaviour, (2) behaviour is determined by multiple causes, and (3) psychology is empirical. Let's examine each of these points.

In Chapter 1, it was emphasized that heredity and environment jointly shape behaviour. However, you may have been a little perplexed at first about how your genes could be responsible for your sarcastic wit or your interest in art. Experts do not expect to find genes for sarcasm or artistic interest. But genes can play a role in your behaviour *indirectly* by moulding the physiological machine that you work with. Thus, your genes can influence your physiological makeup, which in turn influences your personality, temperament, intelligence, interests, and other traits. However, genetic factors do not operate in a vacuum. Genes exert their effects in an environmental context.

Throughout the chapter it was illustrated that behaviour is determined by multiple causes. For example, schizophrenia may be a function of (1) abnormalities in neurotransmitter activity (especially dopamine), (2) structural abnormalities in the brain identified with CT and MRI scans, and (3) genetic vulnerability to the illness. These findings do not contradict one another. Rather, they demonstrate that many biological factors are involved in the development of schizophrenia.

The empirical nature of psychology was illustrated in discussions of the specialized research methods used to study the physiological bases of behaviour. As you know, the empirical approach depends on precise observation. Throughout this chapter, you've seen innovative methods developed to observe and measure elusive phenomena such as electrical activity in the brain, neural impulses, brain function, cerebral specialization, and the impact of heredity on behaviour. Empirical methods are the lifeblood of the scientific enterprise. When researchers develop better methods, this usually facilitates major advances in our scientific knowledge. That is why brain-imaging techniques and CRSPR hold such exciting promise.

The importance of empiricism will also be apparent in the upcoming Personal Application and Critical Thinking Application. In both, you'll see the importance of distinguishing between scientific findings and conjecture based on those findings.

Evaluating the Concept of "Two Minds in One"

Do people have two minds that think differently located in a single brain? Do some people depend on one side of the brain more than the other? Is the right side of the brain neglected? These questions are too complex to resolve with a simple "true" or "false," but in this Application we'll take a closer look at the issues involved in these questions about cerebral specialization. You'll learn that some of these ideas are plausible, but in many cases the hype has outstripped the evidence.

Cerebral Specialization and Cognitive Processes

There is now an extensive literature on the specialized abilities of the right and left hemispheres. These findings have led to extensive theorizing about how the right and left brains might be related to cognitive processes. Three of the more intriguing ideas include the following:

1. *The two hemispheres are specialized to process different types of cognitive tasks* (Corballis, 1991; Ornstein, 1977). Research findings have been widely interpreted as showing that the left hemisphere handles language, speech, writing, math, and logic, while the right hemisphere handles spatial problems, music, art, fantasy, and creativity. These conclusions have attracted a great deal of public interest and media attention. For example, Figure 3.28 shows a *Newsweek* artist's depiction of how the brain divides its work.

2. *The two hemispheres have different modes of thinking* (Davis & Dean, 2005). According to this notion, the differences between the hemispheres in dealing with verbal and nonverbal materials are due to more basic differences in *how* each hemisphere processes information. Theory holds that the reason the left hemisphere handles verbal material well is that it is analytic, abstract, rational, logical, and linear. In contrast, the right hemisphere is thought to be better equipped to handle spatial and musical material because it is synthetic, concrete, nonrational, intuitive, and holistic.

3. *People vary in their reliance on one hemisphere as opposed to the other* (Bakan, 1971; Pinker, 2005). Allegedly, some people are "left-brained." Their greater dependence on their left hemisphere supposedly makes them analytical, rational, and logical. Other people are "right-brained." Their greater use of their right hemisphere supposedly makes them intuitive, holistic, and irrational. Being right-brained or left-brained is thought to explain many personal characteristics, such as whether an individual likes to read, is good with maps, or enjoys music. This notion of "brainedness" has even been used to explain occupational choice. Supposedly, right-brained people are more likely to become artists or musicians, while left-brained people are more likely to become writers or scientists.

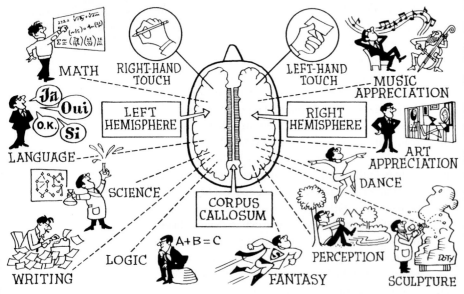

HOW THE BRAIN DIVIDES ITS WORK

Figure 3.28
Popular conceptions of hemispheric specialization. As this *Newsweek* diagram illustrates, depictions of hemispheric specialization in the popular press have often been oversimplified.

Source: Cartoon courtesy of Roy Doty.

reality check

Misconception

People are either left-brained or right-brained, and this disparity can predict their abilities and interests.

Reality

Pop psychology books with little scientific basis routinely discuss how being right-brained or left-brained ought to relate to personal talents and occupational choice. There is just one small problem. There are no studies that support these views.

Complexities and Qualifications

The three ideas just outlined have clearly captured the imagination of the general public. However, the research on cerebral specialization is complex, and these ideas need to be qualified carefully. Let's examine the three ideas.

1. There is ample evidence that the right and left hemispheres are specialized to handle different types of cognitive tasks, *but only to a degree* (Corballis, 2003; Hervé et al., 2013). While at the University of Western Ontario, Doreen Kimura (1973) compared the abilities of the right and left hemispheres to quickly recognize letters, words, faces, and melodies in a series of perceptual asymmetry studies. She found that the superiority of one hemisphere over the other was usually quite modest, as you can see in Figure 3.29. Most tasks probably engage both hemispheres, albeit to different degrees.

Furthermore, people differ in the amount of cerebral specialization they display (Springer & Deutsch, 1998). Some people show little specialization—their hemispheres seem to have equal abilities on various types of tasks. For example, experienced musicians display less cerebral specialization than nonmusicians (Gibson, Folley, & Park, 2009; Patston et al., 2007). The similarity between the hemispheres of musicians may develop because musicians often use both hands independently to play their instruments. If this explanation is accurate, it would provide another example of how experience can shape brain organization. Other people show a reversal of the usual specialization, so that verbal processing might be housed in the right hemisphere. These unusual patterns are especially common among left-handed people (Josse & Tzourio-Mazoyer, 2004).

2. There is little direct evidence to suggest that each hemisphere has its own mode of thinking, or *cognitive style* (Corballis, 2007). This notion is plausible, but the evidence is inconsistent and more research is needed (Reuter-Lorenz & Miller, 1998). One key problem with this idea is that aspects of cognitive style are difficult to define and measure (Brownell & Gardner, 1981). For instance, there is debate about the meaning of analytic versus synthetic thinking, or linear versus holistic thinking.

3. The assertion that some people are left-brained while others are right-brained is not grounded in science. Recent brain-imaging research has not shown that some people consistently display more activation of one hemisphere than the other (Nielsen et al., 2013). Contrary to popular belief, researchers do not have convincing data linking "brainedness" to musical ability, occupational choice, personality, or the like (Knecht et al., 2001).

Theories linking cerebral specialization to cognitive processes are highly speculative. There's nothing wrong with theoretical speculation. Unfortunately, the tentative, conjectural nature of these ideas about cerebral specialization has become lost in the popular descriptions of research on the right and left hemispheres (Coren, 1992). Commenting on this popularization, Hooper and Teresi (1986) wrote: "A widespread cult of the right brain ensued, and the duplex house that Sperry built grew into the Kmart of brain science. Today our hairdresser lectures us about the Two Hemispheres of the Brain" (p. 223). It is unrealistic to expect that the hemispheric divisions in the brain will provide a biological explanation for every dichotomy or polarity in modes of thinking.

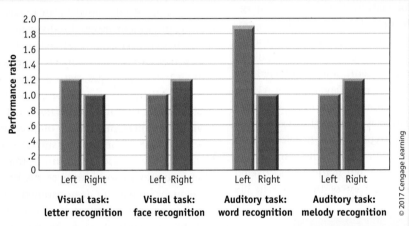

© 2017 Cengage Learning

Figure 3.29
Relative superiority of one brain hemisphere over the other in studies of perceptual asymmetry. These performance ratios from a study by Doreen Kimura (1973) show the degree to which one hemisphere was "superior" to the other on each type of task in normal participants. For example, the right hemisphere was 20 percent better than the left hemisphere in quickly recognizing melodic patterns (ratio: 1.2 to 1). Most differences in the performance of the two hemispheres are quite small.

Building Better Brains: The Perils of Extrapolation

Discoveries in neuroscience have led to the development of programs to help parents and educators optimize infants' and children's brain development. Unfortunately, as we saw in our discussion of research on hemispheric specialization, the hype in the media has greatly outstripped the realities of what scientists have learned in the laboratory (Chance, 2001).

This focus on the brain led many child-care advocates and educational reformers to use research in neuroscience as the rationale for the policies they sought to promote, as a host of books on "brain-based learning" were published (see Jensen, 2000; Sousa, 2000; Sprenger, 2001). The people advocating these ideas likely have good intentions, but the neuroscience rationale is weak. The result? An enlightening case study in the perils of overextrapolation.

The Key Findings on Neural Development

Education and child-care reformers who have used brain science as the basis for their campaigns have focused on two key findings: the discovery of critical periods in neural development and the demonstration that rats raised in "enriched environments" have more synapses than rats raised in "impoverished environments." Let's look at each of these findings.

A *critical period* is a limited time span in an organism's development when it is optimal for certain capacities to emerge because the organism is especially responsive to certain experiences. Ground-breaking research on critical periods in neural development was conducted by Torsten Wiesel and David Hubel (1963, 1965). They showed that if an eye of a newborn kitten is sutured shut early in its development (typically the first four to six weeks), the kitten will become permanently blind in that eye, but if the eye is covered for the same amount of time later in life (after four months) blindness does not result. Such studies show that certain types of visual input are necessary during a critical period of development or else neural pathways between the eye and brain will not form properly. Basically, inactive synapses from the closed eye are displaced by the active synapses from the open eye. Critical periods have been found for other aspects of neural development and in other species, but a great deal remains to be learned.

Pioneering work on environment and brain development was conducted by Mark Rosenzweig and his colleagues (1961, 1962). They compared rats raised in an impoverished environment (housed individually in small, barren cages) with rats raised in an enriched environment (housed in groups of 10 to 12 in larger cages, with a variety of objects available for exploration), as shown in Figure 3.30. The rats raised in the enriched environment performed better on problem-solving tasks than the impoverished rats and had a slightly heavier brain and a thicker cerebral cortex in some areas of the brain. Subsequent research demonstrated that enriched environments resulted in heavier and thicker cortical areas because they had denser dendritic branching, more synaptic contacts, and richer neural networks (Greenough, 1975; Greenough & Volkmar, 1973). More recently, scientists have learned that enriched environments also promote the newly discovered process of *neurogenesis* in the brain (Nithianantharajah & Hannan, 2006). Based on findings from this type of research, some child-care reformers argued that human infants need to be brought up in enriched environments during the critical period before age three, to promote synapse formation and to optimize the development of their emerging neural circuits. However, researchers have raised many doubts about whether this research can serve as a meaningful guide for decisions about parenting practices, day-care programs, educational policies, and welfare reform (Goswami, 2006; Thompson & Nelson, 2001).

Figure 3.30
Enriched environments in the study of rats' neural development. Rosenzweig and his colleagues (1961, 1962) raised rats in an impoverished environment or an enriched environment. Although the enriched conditions provided more stimulating environments than laboratory rats normally experience, these enriched conditions were not more stimulating than rats' natural habitats. Thus, the "enriched" condition may reveal more about the importance of normal stimulation than about the benefits of extra stimulation (Gopnik, Meltzoff, & Kuhl, 1999).

The Risks of Overextrapolation

Extrapolation in science occurs when the implications of research findings are extended beyond the original observations and findings. Extrapolation is a normal and valuable process when the extrapolations are conservative, plausible projections drawn from directly relevant data. Extrapolations can lose their value when they are wild leaps of speculation based on loosely related data. The extrapolations made regarding the educational implications of critical periods and environmental effects on synapse formation are highly conjectural *overextrapolations*. The studies that highlighted the possible importance of early experience in animals all used extreme conditions to make their comparisons, such as depriving an animal of all visual input or raising it in stark isolation. The so-called enriched environments probably resemble more normal conditions in the real world, whereas the standard laboratory environment may reflect extreme environmental deprivation (Gould, 2004). Based on the research, it seems plausible to speculate that children probably need normal stimulation to experience normal brain development. However, concluding that adding *more* stimulation to a normal environment will be beneficial to brain development is not warranted based on the research (Shatz, 1992). See Table 3.2.

The ease with which people fall into the trap of overextrapolating was demonstrated when child advocates recommended that infants should listen to classical music to enhance their brain development. This recommendation was based on two studies that showed that university students performed slightly better on spatial reasoning tasks for about 10–15 minutes after listening to a brief Mozart recording (Rauscher, Shaw, & Ky, 1993, 1995). However, the findings from these two studies, dubbed the "Mozart effect," have proven difficult to replicate, as shown in studies by researchers from the University of Toronto (Thompson, Schellenberg, & Husain, 2001) and others (Gray & Della Sala, 2007; McKelvie & Low, 2002; Steele, 2003). The pertinent point here is that when the recommendations were made, there was no research on how classical music affects *infants*, no research relating classical music to *brain development*, and no research on anyone showing *lasting effects*. Nonetheless, many people were quick to extrapolate the shaky findings on the Mozart effect to infants' brain development.

reality check

Misconception

Exposing infants and children to classical music can enhance their brain development and boost their intelligence.

Reality

If only it were that easy! The so-called Mozart effect has garnered a great deal of publicity, but the actual findings are utterly unimpressive. A recent meta-analysis of nearly 40 studies concluded that "there is little support for the Mozart effect" (Pietschnig, Voracek, & Formann, 2010). The typical dependent variable in these studies is a simple spatial task (paper folding and cutting) that won't get anyone through college. When small, short-term positive effects are observed, they appear to be due to the fact that music can be arousing, not to any durable change in the architecture of the brain.

Ironically, there is much better evidence linking *musical training* to enhanced cognitive performance. Studies have found a thought-provoking association between measures of intelligence and the extent of individuals' exposure to music lessons (Moreno et al., 2011; Schellenberg, 2006, 2011). Of course, if you think critically about this correlation, it might only mean that brighter youngsters are more likely to take music lessons. That caveat aside, musical training has been associated with structural changes in the brain (James et al., 2014; Rodrigues, Loureiro, & Caramelli, 2010). The cortical changes produced by musical training may slow age-related cognitive decline later in life (Hanna-Pladdy & MacKay, 2011; Oechslin et al., 2013).

As discussed in Chapter 1, thinking critically about issues often involves asking questions such as: What is missing from this debate? Is there any contradictory evidence? In this case, there is contradictory evidence that is worthy of consideration. The basis for advocating infant educational programs is the belief that the brain is malleable during the hypothesized critical period of birth to age three but not at later ages. However, recent work on brain plasticity discussed in this chapter suggests that the brain remains somewhat malleable throughout life, responding to stimulation into old age. Thus, advocates for the aged could just as readily argue for new educational initiatives for the elderly to help them maximize their potential. Indeed, recent years have seen a surge of interest in designing cognitive training programs for older adults that might slow age-related cognitive decline (Bamidis et al., 2014; Rebok et al., 2014). Another problem is the implicit assumption that greater synaptic density is better. However, infant animals and humans begin life with an overabundance of synaptic connections, and learning involves selective *pruning* of inactive synapses (Huttenlocher, 2002; Rakic, Bourgeois, & Goldman-Rakic, 1994). Thus, in the realm of synapses, more may *not* be better.

In conclusion, there are many valid reasons for increasing educational programs for infants, but research in neuroscience does not provide a clear rationale for specific infant care policies (Bruer, 2002). One problem in evaluating these proposals is that few people want to argue against high-quality child-care or education. But modern societies need to allocate their limited resources to programs with proven effectiveness; even intuitively appealing ideas need to be subjected to critical scrutiny.

Table 3.2

Critical Thinking Skills Discussed in This Application

SKILL	DESCRIPTION
Understanding the limits	The critical thinker appreciates that extrapolations are based on certain assumptions, vary in plausibility, and ultimately involve speculation.
Looking for contradictory evidence	In evaluating the evidence presented on an issue, the critical thinker attempts to look for contradictory evidence that may have been left out of the debate.

COMMUNICATION IN THE NERVOUS SYSTEM

Key parts of the neuron

Soma: Cell body

Dendrites: Branching structures that receive signals from other cells

Axon: Fibre that carries signals away from soma to other cells

Myelin sheath: Insulating material that encases some axons

Terminal buttons: Small knobs (at ends of axons) that release neurotransmitters at synapses

Glia

Glia are cells that provide support for neurons and contribute to signalling in the nervous system.

The neural impulse

Resting potential: Neuron's stable, negative charge when inactive

Action potential: Voltage spike that travels along an axon

Absolute regractory period: Brief time after an action potential, before another action potential can begin

All-or-none law: A neuron either fires or doesn't fire

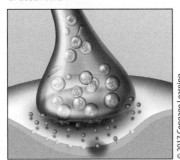

Synaptic transmission

Synthesis, transportation, and storage of neurotransmitters in synaptic vesicles

↓

Release of neurotransmitters into synaptic cleft

↓

Binding of neurotransmitters at receptor sites leads to *excitatory* and *inhibitory* PSPs. Some neurotransmitters bind to receptors on the same neuron that released them. This is called *autoreceptor activation*.

↓

Inactivation or removal (drifting away) of neurotransmitters

Reuptake of neurotransmitters by presynaptic neuron

© 2017 Cengage Learning

Neurotransmitters and behaviour

Acetylcholine: Released by neurons that control skeletal muscles

Serotonin: Involved in the regulation of sleep and arousal, and aggression; abnormal levels linked to depression

Dopamine: Abnormal levels linked to schizophrenia; dopamine circuits activated by cocaine and amphetamines

Norepinephrine: Abnormal levels linked to depression; norepinephrine circuits can be activated by cocaine and amphetamines

GABA: Inhibitory transmitter that contributes to regulation of anxiety

Endorphins: Opiate-like chemicals involved in modulation of pain

© 2017 Cengage Learning

ORGANIZATION OF THE NERVOUS SYSTEM

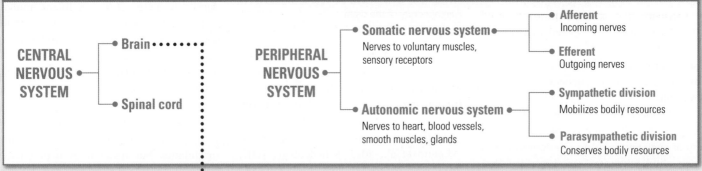

CENTRAL NERVOUS SYSTEM
- Brain
- Spinal cord

PERIPHERAL NERVOUS SYSTEM
- **Somatic nervous system**
  Nerves to voluntary muscles, sensory receptors
  - **Afferent** Incoming nerves
  - **Efferent** Outgoing nerves
- **Autonomic nervous system**
  Nerves to heart, blood vessels, smooth muscles, glands
  - **Sympathetic division** Mobilizes bodily resources
  - **Parasympathetic division** Conserves bodily resources

BRAIN AND BEHAVIOUR

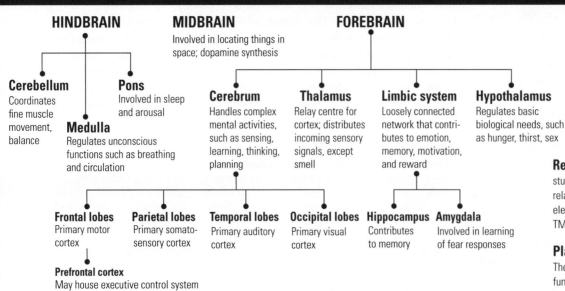

HINDBRAIN

MIDBRAIN
Involved in locating things in space; dopamine synthesis

FOREBRAIN

Cerebellum
Coordinates fine muscle movement, balance

Pons
Involved in sleep and arousal

Medulla
Regulates unconscious functions such as breathing and circulation

Cerebrum
Handles complex mental activities, such as sensing, learning, thinking, planning

Thalamus
Relay centre for cortex; distributes incoming sensory signals, except smell

Limbic system
Loosely connected network that contributes to emotion, memory, motivation, and reward

Hypothalamus
Regulates basic biological needs, such as hunger, thirst, sex

Frontal lobes
Primary motor cortex

Prefrontal cortex
May house executive control system crucial to planning and organization

Parietal lobes
Primary somato-sensory cortex

Temporal lobes
Primary auditory cortex

Occipital lobes
Primary visual cortex

Hippocampus
Contributes to memory

Amygdala
Involved in learning of fear responses

Research methods for studying brain-behaviour relations include lesioning; electrical stimulation; and CT, TMS, MRI, PET, and fMRI scans.

Plasticity of the brain
The anatomical structure and functional organization of the brain is somewhat malleable.

© 2017 Cengage Learning

RIGHT BRAIN / LEFT BRAIN

Methods for study of lateralization

Split brain surgery: Bundle of fibres (corpus callosum) that connects two hemispheres is severed.

Perceptual asymmetries: Left-right imbalances in speed of processing are studied in normal subjects.

Left hemisphere

Usually handles verbal processing, including language, speech, reading, writing

Right hemisphere

Usually handles nonverbal processing, including spatial and musical processing, and visual recognition tasks

HEREDITY AND BEHAVIOUR

Basic concepts

- *Chromosomes* are threadlike strands of DNA that carry information.
- *Genes* are DNA segments that are the key functional units in hereditary transmission.
- Closer relatives share greater genetic overlap.
- Most behavioural traits appear to involve *polygenic inheritance*.

Research methods

Family studies assess trait resemblance among blood relatives.

Twin studies compare trait resemblance of identical and fraternal twins.

Adoption studies compare adopted children to their adoptive parents and to their biological parents.

Genetic mapping facilitates efforts to link specific genes to specific traits.

CRISPRs are a natural part of our immune system. They can be used to modify genomes.

Interactions

- Research indicates that most behavioural qualities are influenced jointly by heredity and environment, which play off of each other in complex interactions.
- New work in *epigenetics* has further demonstrated that genetic and environmental factors are deeply intertwined.

ENDOCRINE SYSTEM

- System consists of *glands* that secrete *hormones* into the bloodstream in a pulsatile fashion.
- Governed by the hypothalamus and pituitary gland, the endocrine system regulates our response to stress.
- Recent research suggests that the hormone *oxytocin* fosters bonding, and influences social behaviour.

EVOLUTIONARY BASES OF BEHAVIOUR

Darwin's insights

- Organisms vary in endless ways.
- Some traits are heritable.
- Variations in hereditary traits might affect organisms' survival and reproductive success.
- Heritable traits that provide a survival or reproductive advantage will become more prevalent over generations (natural selection will change the gene pool of the population).

Key concepts

Fitness refers to the reproductive success of an organism relative to the population.

Adaptations are inherited characteristics sculpted through natural selection because they helped solve a problem of survival or reproduction when they emerged.

Behaviours as adaptive traits

- Species' typical patterns of behaviour often reflect evolutionary solutions to adaptive problems.
- For example, behavioural strategies that help organisms avoid predators have obvious adaptive value.
- Many behavioural adaptations improve organisms' chances of reproductive success.

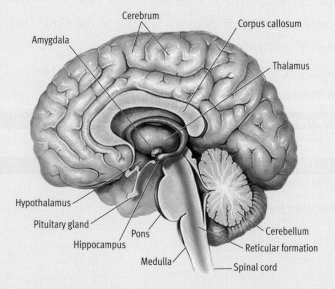

Cerebrum

Corpus callosum

Amygdala

Thalamus

Hypothalamus

Pituitary gland

Pons

Hippocampus

Cerebellum

Reticular formation

Medulla

Spinal cord

APPLICATIONS

- It is widely believed that the cerebral hemispheres are specialized to handle specific cognitive tasks, that people are right- or left-brained, and that each hemisphere has its own cognitive style.
- However, task specialization is a matter of degree, evidence does not support the idea that people are right- or left-brained, and the data on hemispheres' cognitive style are inconclusive.
- Efforts to use brain science to justify various education initiatives have shown that people often overextrapolate the implications of research findings.

CHAPTER 4

Sensation and Perception

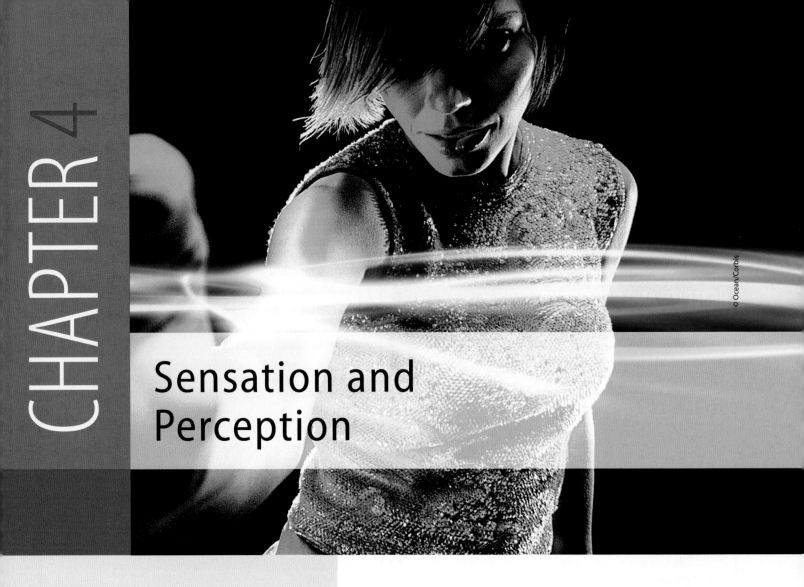

© Ocean/Corbis

Themes in this Chapter

Theoretical
Diversity

Cultural
Heritage

Subjectivity of
Experience

Sensation and perception are sometimes viewed only as topics in basic science, topics that may have little connection to our everyday lives. As you will learn in your study of this chapter, research in sensation and perception is very relevant to our experiences in our everyday life. In fact, sensation and perception are critical to our experiences; they connect us to the physical world. *Sensation* **is the stimulation of sense organs. Perception is the selection, organization, and interpretation of sensory input.** Sensation involves the absorption of energy, such as light or sound waves, by sensory organs, such as the ears and eyes. Perception involves organizing and translating sensory input into something meaningful, such as your best friend's face or other environmental stimuli.

For most of us, these processes operate smoothly and effortlessly, allowing us to experience and make our way around the world in quite ordinary ways. For some, however, the experience is not at all ordinary. For some individuals, those who experience *synesthesia*, a sensory experience in one domain is accompanied by a sensory experience in another domain (Gregersen et al., 2013). For example, seeing the colour "red" when you hear the word "train." Generally, *synesthesia* **is a condition in which perceptual or cognitive activities (e.g., listening to music, reading) trigger exceptional experiences (e.g., of colour, taste)** (Simner, Mayo, & Spiller, 2009, p. 1246). Synesthesia can take many forms (Marks, 2014; Rouw & Scholte, 2016). Consider the experiences of a 45-year-old Canadian man reported in a recent case study (Schwiezer et al., 2013). When the man hears high-pitched brass instruments—particularly in music from James Bond movies—he has the experience of "riding the music" and seeing the colour blue. Words written in specific colours lead to him having strong feelings of disgust. He experiences *emotional synesthesia*, a condition in which "specific stimuli are consistently and involuntarily associated with emotional responses" (Schweizer et al., 2013, p. 509).

In synesthesia, experiences from different senses become paired (Cytowic, 2002; Cytowic & Eagleman, 2009). Grapheme-colour synesthesia refers to a condition in which words, letters, or digits are associated reliably with specific colours (Witthoft & Winawer, 2013). The philosopher Ludwig Wittgenstein was a famous synesthete (i.e., one who experiences synesthesia), for whom the vowel *e* was experienced as yellow. Physicist Richard Feynman was famous not only for the quality of his work in physics (he won the Nobel Prize in Physics in 1965), but also for being a synesthete. He reported that he "saw his formulae in color and wondered what they looked like to his students" (Ward, 2013, p. 51). Other common forms include taste-touch synesthesia (when tastes lead to specific feelings), word-taste synesthesia (when words or names lead to taste sensations), and sound-colour synesthesia (when sounds/musical notes lead to colour sensations). You can learn more about synesthesia at the Canadian Synesthesia Association (http://synesthesiacanada.com).

You may be wondering what leads to this condition. Is there something different about the brains of people with synesthesia as compared to those of us who do not have these enriched experiences? While much research remains to be done, the results of recent research do suggest that the brains of synesthetes are different, perhaps reflecting hyperconnectivity between parts of the brain associated with different sensory experiences (Dovern et al., 2012) and that those with synesthesia may experience some cognitive benefits derived from the experience (Ward, 2013). For example, there is research suggesting that synesthesia and absolute/perfect pitch are associated genetically (Gregersen et al., 2013). Synesthesia points to the sophisticated and complex nature of our sensory processes and perceptual experiences, and the intimate link between sensation, perception, and the brain.

We'll begin our discussion of sensation and perception by examining some general concepts that are relevant to all of the senses. Next, we'll examine individual senses, in each case beginning with the sensory aspects and working our way through to the perceptual aspects. The chapter's Personal Application explores how principles of visual perception come into play in art and illusion. The Critical Thinking Application discusses how perceptual contrasts can be manipulated in persuasive efforts.

Physicist and Nobel Laureate Richard Feynman of the California Institute of Technology was one of the individuals who experienced synesthesia, or the pairing of sensory experiences from different sensory modalities.

Psychophysics: Basic Concepts and Issues

As you may recall from Chapter 1, the first experimental psychologists were interested mainly in sensation and perception. They called their area of interest *psychophysics*—**the study of how physical stimuli are translated into psychological experience.** A particularly important contributor to psychophysics was Gustav Fechner, who published a seminal work on the subject in 1860. Fechner was a German scientist working at the University of Leipzig, where Wilhelm Wundt later founded the first formal laboratory and journal devoted to psychological research. Even though these ideas were first generated over a century ago, interest in these fundamental issues continues today (Dai & Micheyl, 2012; Rouder & Morey, 2009).

Thresholds: Looking for Limits

Sensation begins with a *stimulus*, any detectable input from the environment. What counts as detectable, though, depends on who or what is doing the detecting. For instance, you might not be able to detect a weak odour that is readily apparent to your dog. Thus, Fechner wanted to know: For any given sense, what is the weakest detectable stimulus? For example, what is the minimum amount of light needed for a person to see that there is light?

Implicit in Fechner's question is a concept central to psychophysics: the threshold. A *threshold* is a dividing point between energy levels that do and do not have a detectable effect. For example, hardware stores sell a gadget with a photocell that automatically turns a lamp on when a room gets dark. The level of light intensity at which the gadget clicks on is its threshold.

An *absolute threshold* for a specific type of sensory input is the minimum amount of stimulation that an organism can detect. Absolute thresholds define the boundaries of an organism's sensory capabilities. Fechner and his contemporaries used a variety of methods to determine humans' absolute threshold for detecting light. They discovered that absolute thresholds are anything but absolute. When lights of varying intensity are flashed at a subject, there is no single stimulus intensity at which the subject jumps from no detection to completely accurate detection. Instead, as stimulus intensity increases, subjects' probability of responding to stimuli *gradually* increases, as shown in red in Figure 4.1. Thus, researchers had to arbitrarily define the absolute threshold as the stimulus intensity *detected 50 percent of the time*.

Using this definition, investigators found that under ideal conditions, human abilities to detect weak stimuli were greater than previously thought. Some concrete examples of the absolute thresholds for various senses can be seen in Table 4.1. For example, on a clear, dark night, in the absence of other distracting lights, you could see the light of a candle burning 50 kilometres in the distance! Of course, we're talking about ideal conditions—you would have to go out to the middle of nowhere to find the darkness required to put this assertion to a suitable test.

Fechner was also interested in people's sensitivity to differences between stimuli. A *just noticeable difference (JND)* is the smallest difference in the amount of stimulation that a specific sense can detect. JNDs are close cousins of absolute thresholds. In fact, an absolute threshold is simply the just noticeable difference from nothing (no stimulus input). JNDs vary by sense, and the smallest

Gustav Fechner

"The method of just noticeable differences consists in determining how much the weights have to differ so that they can just be discriminated."

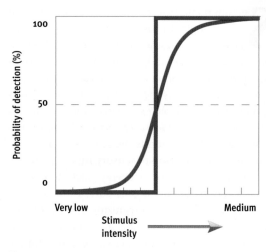

Figure 4.1

The absolute threshold. If absolute thresholds were truly absolute, then the probability of detecting a stimulus at threshold intensity would jump from 0 to 100 percent, as graphed here in blue. In reality, the chances of detecting a stimulus increase gradually with stimulus intensity, as shown in red. Accordingly, an "absolute" threshold is defined as the intensity level at which the probability of detection is 50 percent.

Source: From Weiten. *Cengage Advantage Books: Psychology*, 9E. © 2013 South-Western, a part of Cengage, Inc. Reproduced by permission. www.cengage.com/permissions

detectable difference is a fairly stable proportion of the size of the original stimulus.

This principle was first demonstrated by Fechner's brother-in-law, Ernst Weber, and came to be known as Weber's law. *Weber's law* states that the size of a just noticeable difference is a constant proportion of the size of the initial stimulus. This constant proportion is called the *Weber fraction*. Weber's law applies not only to weight perception but to all of the senses. Different fractions apply to different types of sensory input. For example, the Weber fraction for lifting weights is approximately 1/30. This means that you should be just able to detect the difference between a 300 gram weight and a 310 gram weight (i.e., the JND for 300 grams is 10 grams).

Table 4.1

Examples of Absolute Thresholds

SENSE	ABSOLUTE THRESHOLD
Vision	A candle flame seen at 50 kilometres on a dark clear night
Hearing	The tick of a watch under quiet conditions at 6 metres
Taste	Five millilitres of sugar in 7.5 litres of water
Smell	One drop of perfume diffused into the entire volume of a six-room apartment
Touch	The wing of a fly falling on your cheek from a distance of 1 centimetre

Source: Galanter, E. (1962). Contemporary psychophysics. In R. Brown (Ed.), *New directions in psychology*. New York: Holt, Rinehart & Winston. © 1962 Eugene Galanter. Reprinted by permission.

Signal-Detection Theory

The fact that perceptions can't be measured on absolute scales applies not only to sensory scaling but to sensory thresholds as well. *Signal-detection theory* proposes that the detection of stimuli involves decision processes as well as sensory processes, which are both influenced by a variety of factors besides stimulus intensity (Egan, 1975; Szakma & Hancock, 2013). Signal-detection theory replaces Fechner's sharp threshold with the concept of "detectability." Detectability is measured in terms of probability and depends on decision-making processes as well as sensory processes.

Imagine that you are monitoring a radar screen, looking for signs of possible enemy aircraft. Your mission is to detect signals that represent approaching airplanes as quickly and as accurately as possible. In this situation, there are four possible outcomes, which are outlined in Figure 4.2: *hits* (detecting signals when they are present), *misses* (failing to detect signals when they are present), *false alarms* (detecting signals when they are not present), and *correct rejections* (not detecting signals when they are absent). Given these possibilities, signal-detection theory attempts to account for the influence of decision-making processes on stimulus detection. In detecting weak signals on the radar screen, you will often have to decide whether a faint signal represents an airplane or whether you're just imagining that it does. Your responses will depend in part on the *criterion* you set for how sure you must feel before you react. Setting this criterion involves higher mental processes rather than raw sensation and depends on your expectations and on the consequences of missing a signal or of reporting a false alarm.

Perception without Awareness

The concepts of thresholds and detectability lie at the core of an interesting debate: Can sensory stimuli that fall beneath the threshold of awareness still influence behaviour? This issue centres on the concept of *subliminal perception*—the registration of sensory input without conscious awareness (*limen* is another term for *threshold*, so *subliminal* means "below threshold"). This question might be just another technical issue in the normally staid world of psychophysics, except that subliminal perception has become tied up in highly charged controversies relating to money, sex, religion, and rock music.

The controversy began in 1957 when an executive named James Vicary placed hidden messages such as "Eat popcorn" in a film showing at a theatre in New Jersey. The messages were superimposed on

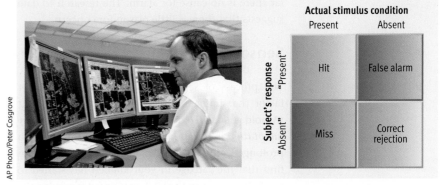

Figure 4.2

Possible outcomes in signal-detection theory. This diagram shows the four outcomes that are possible in attempting to detect the presence of weak signals. The criterion you set for how confident you want to feel before reporting a signal will affect your responding. For example, if you require high confidence before reporting a signal, you will minimize false alarms but you'll be more likely to miss some signals.

Source: From Weiten. *Cengage Advantage Books: Psychology,* 9E. © 2013 South-Western, a part of Cengage, Inc. Reproduced by permission. www.cengage.com/permissions

only a few frames of the film, so that they flashed by quickly and imperceptibly. Nonetheless, Vicary claimed in the press that popcorn sales increased by 58 percent, and a public outcry ensued (McConnell, Cutler, & McNeil, 1958; Merikle, 2000).

Can your sexual urges be manipulated by messages hidden under music? Can advertisers influence your product preferences with subliminal stimuli? Research on subliminal perception was sporadic in the 1960s and 1970s because scientists initially dismissed the entire idea as preposterous. However, empirical studies have begun to accumulate since the 1980s, and quite a number of these studies have found support for the existence of subliminal effects (Era, Candidi, & Aglioti, 2015; Gibson & Zielaskowski, 2013; Posten, Ockenfels, & Mussweller, 2014), showing that perception without awareness can take place (Abrams, Klinger, & Greenwald, 2002).

So, should we be worried about the threat of subliminal persuasion? The effects of subliminal stimuli turn out to be nearly as subliminal as the stimuli themselves. Subliminal stimulation generally produces weak effects that typically disappear in a short time (De Houwer, Hendrickx, & Baeyens, 1997; Kihlstrom, Barnhardt, & Tataryn, 1992). These effects can be detected only by very precise measurement under carefully controlled laboratory conditions in which subjects are asked to focus their undivided attention on visual or auditory materials that contain the subliminal stimuli. Although these effects are theoretically interesting, they appear unlikely to have much practical importance (Merikle, 2000). For example, there is no evidence that subliminal CDs that promise self-help cures or language learning actually work (Greenwald, Spangenberg, Pratkanis, & Eskenzi, 1991). More research on the manipulative potential of subliminal persuasion is needed, but so far there is no cause for alarm. The research to date suggests that there is little reason for concern.

Sensory Adaptation

The process of sensory adaptation is yet another factor that influences registration of sensory input (Arnold et al., 2016; Rosenbaum et al., 2015). *Sensory adaptation is a gradual decline in sensitivity due to prolonged stimulation.* For example, let's say you find that the garbage in your kitchen has started to smell. If you stay in the kitchen without removing the garbage, the stench will soon start to fade. In reality, the stimulus intensity of the odour is stable, but with continued exposure, your *sensitivity* to it decreases.

Sensory adaptation is an automatic, built-in process that keeps people tuned in to the *changes* rather than the *constants* in their sensory input. It allows people to ignore the obvious and focus on changes in their environment that may signal threats to safety. Thus, as its name suggests, sensory adaptation probably is a behavioural adaptation that has been sculpted by natural selection (McBurney, 2010). Sensory adaptation also shows once again that there is no one-to-one correspondence between sensory input and sensory experience.

The general points we've reviewed so far begin to suggest the complexity of the relationships between the world outside and people's perceived experience of it. As we review each of the principal sensory systems in detail, we'll see repeatedly that people's experience of the world depends on both the physical stimuli they encounter and their active processing of stimulus inputs. We begin our exploration of the senses with vision—the sense that most people think of as nearly synonymous with a direct perception of reality. The case is actually quite different, as you'll see.

Our Sense of Sight: The Visual System

Key Learning Goals

▶ Identify the three properties of light, and describe the role of key eye structures in the retina.

▶ Trace the routing of signals from the eye to the brain, and explain the brain's role in visual processing.

▶ Distinguish two types of colour mixing and compare the trichromatic and opponent process theories of colour vision.

Humans are visual animals. People rely heavily on their sense of sight, and they virtually equate it with what is trustworthy. Although it is taken for granted, you'll see that the human visual system is amazingly complex. Furthermore, as in all sensory domains, what people "sense" and what they "perceive" may be quite different.

The Stimulus: Light

For people to see, there must be light. *Light* is a form of electromagnetic radiation that travels as a wave, moving, naturally enough, at the speed of light. As Figure 4.3(a) shows, light waves vary in *amplitude* (height) and in *wavelength* (the distance between peaks). Amplitude affects mainly the perception of brightness, while wavelength affects mainly the perception of colour. The lights that humans normally see are mixtures of several wavelengths. Hence, light can also vary in its *purity* (how varied the mix is). Purity influences perception of the saturation, or richness, of colours. Saturation is difficult to describe, but if you glance at Figure 4.4, you'll find it clearly illustrated. Of course, most objects do not emit light; they reflect it (the sun, lamps, and fireflies being some exceptions).

What most people call *light* includes only the wavelengths that humans can see. But as Figure 4.3(c) shows, the visible spectrum is only a slim portion of the total range of wavelengths. Vision is a filter that permits people to sense but a fraction of the real world. Other animals have different capabilities and so live in a quite different visual world. For example, many insects can see shorter wavelengths than humans can see, in the *ultraviolet* spectrum, whereas many fish and reptiles can see longer wavelengths, in the *infrared* spectrum. Although the sense of sight depends on light waves, for people to *see*, incoming visual input must be converted into neural impulses that are sent to the brain. Let's investigate how this transformation is accomplished.

The Eye: A Living Optical Instrument

The eyes serve two main purposes: They channel light to the neural tissue that receives it, called the *retina*, and they house that tissue. The structure of the eye is shown in Figure 4.5. Each eye is a living optical instrument that creates an image of the visual world on the light-sensitive retina lining its inside back surface.

Light enters the eye through a transparent "window" at the front, the *cornea*. The cornea and the crystalline *lens*, located behind it, form an upside-down image of objects on the retina. It might seem disturbing that the image is upside down, but the brain knows the rule for relating positions on the retina to the corresponding positions in the world.

The lens is the transparent eye structure that focuses the light rays falling on the retina. The lens is made up of relatively soft tissue, capable of adjustments that facilitate a process called *accommodation.* Accommodation occurs when the curvature of the lens adjusts to alter visual focus. When you

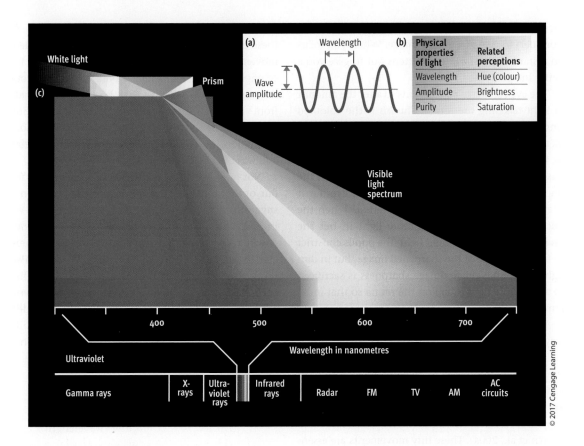

(a)

| Wavelength |
| Wave amplitude |

(b)

Physical properties of light	Related perceptions
Wavelength	Hue (colour)
Amplitude	Brightness
Purity	Saturation

White light

Prism

(c)

Visible light spectrum

400   500   600   700

Wavelength in nanometres

Ultraviolet

| Gamma rays | X-rays | Ultra-violet rays | Infrared rays | Radar | FM | TV | AM | AC circuits |

© 2017 Cengage Learning

Figure 4.3
Light, the physical stimulus for vision. (a) Light waves vary in amplitude and wavelength. (b) Within the spectrum of visible light, amplitude (corresponding to physical intensity) affects mainly the experience of brightness. Wavelength affects mainly the experience of colour, and purity is the key determinant of saturation. (c) If white light (such as sunlight) passes through a prism, the prism separates the light into its component wavelengths, creating a rainbow of colours. However, visible light is only the narrow band of wavelengths to which human eyes happen to be sensitive.

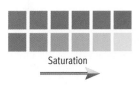

Saturation

Figure 4.4
Saturation. Variations in saturation are difficult to describe, but you can see examples for two colours here.

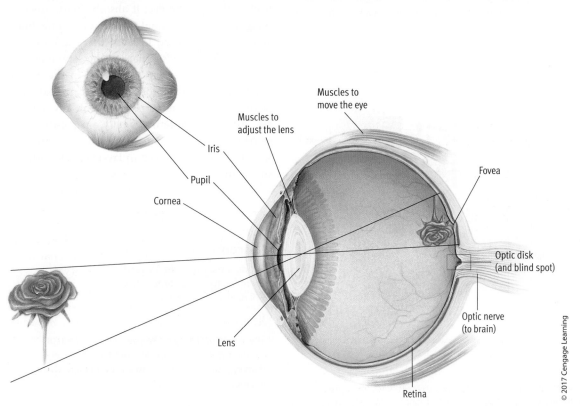

Iris

Muscles to adjust the lens

Muscles to move the eye

Pupil

Cornea

Fovea

Optic disk (and blind spot)

Optic nerve (to brain)

Lens

Retina

© 2017 Cengage Learning

Figure 4.5
The human eye. Light passes through the cornea, pupil, and lens and falls on the light-sensitive surface of the retina, where images of objects are reflected upside down. The lens adjusts its curvature to focus the images falling on the retina. The iris and pupil regulate the amount of light passing into the rear chamber of the eye.

focus on a close object, the lens of your eye gets fatter (rounder) to give you a clear image. When you focus on distant objects, the lens flattens out to give you a better image of the objects.

The eye can make adjustments to alter the amount of light reaching the retina. The *iris* is the coloured ring of muscle surrounding the *pupil*, or black centre of the eye. **The *pupil* is the opening in the centre of the iris that helps regulate the amount of light passing into the rear chamber of the eye.** When the pupil constricts, it lets less light into the eye but it sharpens the image falling on the retina. When the pupil dilates (opens), it lets more light in but the image is less sharp. In bright light, the pupils constrict to take advantage of the sharpened image. But in dim light, the pupils dilate; image sharpness is sacrificed to allow more light to fall on the retina so that more remains visible.

The eye itself is constantly in motion, moving in ways that are typically imperceptible to us. When we are looking at something, our eyes are scanning the visual environment and making brief fixations at various parts of the stimuli. **These eye movements are referred to as *saccades*.** Saccades have been the subject of research interest for many years (e.g., M. R. Brown et al., 2004). These tiny movements are essential to good vision; if there is even a small reduction in these voluntary eye movements, our vision degrades

(Martinez-Conde, 2006). In fact, if there were none of these eye movements, if you were able to stop these movements while looking at your sleeping dog, for example, your visual system would adapt, and your dog, or any other static scene, would "simply fade from view" (Martinez-Conde & Macknik, 2007, p. 56). This would be the ultimate disappearing act. Sensory adaptation is a characteristic of our sensory systems and was discussed on page 114 of this chapter.

Not only are these eye movements necessary for our optimal visual experience, but there is even a suggestion that they may give away more than we intend. One form of saccade may give away your covert gaze even when you are looking somewhere else (Martinez-Conde & Macknik, 2007; see also Engbert & Kliegl, 2003). Thus, it is possible that they can provide details concerning what you are focusing on, perhaps even "revealing hidden thoughts and desires" (Martinez-Conde & Macknik, 2011, p. 50). Given this possibility, it is likely that research in the area will continue for some time.

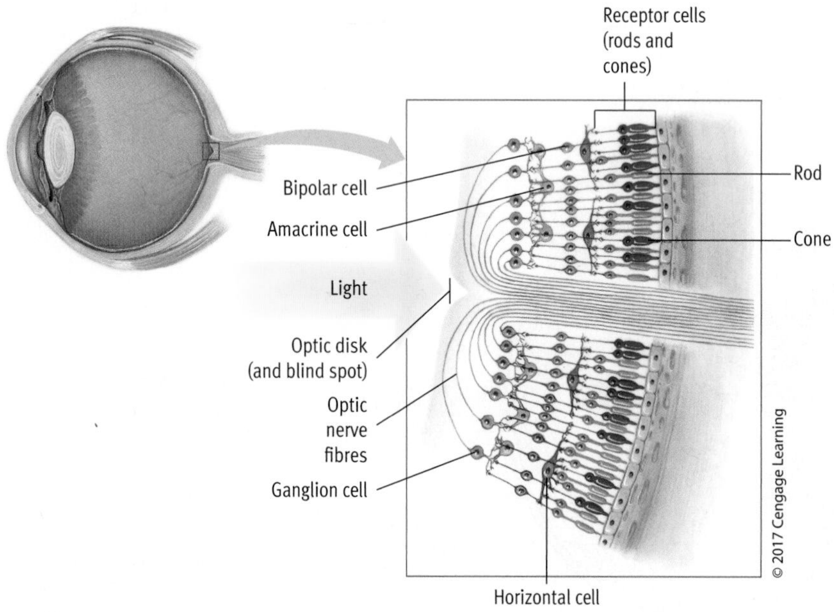

The Retina: The Brain's Envoy in the Eye

The *retina* is the neural tissue lining the inside back surface of the eye; it absorbs light, processes images, and sends visual information to the brain. You may be surprised to learn that the retina *processes* images. But it's a piece of the central nervous system that happens to be located in the eyeball. Much as the spinal cord is a complicated extension of the brain, the retina is the brain's envoy in the eye. Although the retina is only a paper-thin sheet of neural tissue, it contains a complex network of specialized cells arranged in layers (Baker, 2013), as shown in Figure 4.6.

Bipolar cell
Amacrine cell
Light
Optic disk (and blind spot)
Optic nerve fibres
Ganglion cell
Horizontal cell
Receptor cells (rods and cones)
Rod
Cone

© 2017 Cengage Learning

Figure 4.6
The retina. The close-up shows the several layers of cells in the retina. The cells closest to the back of the eye (the rods and cones) are the receptor cells that actually detect light. The intervening layers of cells receive signals from the rods and cones and form circuits that begin the process of analyzing incoming information. The visual signals eventually converge into *ganglion cells*, whose axons form the optic fibres that make up the optic nerve. These optic fibres all head toward the "hole" in the retina where the optic nerve leaves the eye—the point known as the *optic disk* (which corresponds to the blind spot).

reality check

Misconception
Sitting too close to the TV/reading in the dark/spending too much time in front of a computer screen will damage your vision.

Reality
These activities may make your eyes feel tired or strained, but there is no evidence that they can damage your eyes or lead to any permanent changes in vision.

The axons that run from the retina to the brain converge at the *optic disk*, a place in the retina where the optic nerve fibres exit the eye (Hoffman et al., 2007). Because there are no photoreceptors there, you cannot see the part of an image that falls on the optic disk. It is therefore known as the *blind spot*. You may not be aware that you have a blind spot in each eye, as each normally compensates for the blind spot of the other.

Visual Receptors: Rods and Cones

The retina contains millions of receptor cells that are sensitive to light. Surprisingly, these receptors are located in the innermost layer of the retina. Hence, light must pass through several layers of cells before it gets to the receptors that actually detect it. Interestingly, only about 10 percent of the light arriving at the cornea reaches these receptors (Leibovic, 1990). The retina contains two types of receptors, *rods* and *cones*. Their names are based on their shapes, as rods are elongated and cones are stubbier. Rods outnumber cones by a huge margin, as humans have 100 million to 125 million rods, but only around 6 million cones (Meister & Tesner-Lavigne, 2013).

Cones are specialized visual receptors that play a key role in daylight vision and colour vision. The cones handle most of our daytime vision because bright lights dazzle the rods. The special sensitivities of cones also allow them to play a major role in the perception of colour. However, cones do not respond well to dim light, which is why you don't see colour very well in low illumination. Nonetheless, cones provide better *visual acuity*—that is, sharpness and precise detail—than rods. Cones are concentrated most heavily in the centre of the retina and quickly fall off in density toward its periphery. The fovea is a tiny spot in the centre of the retina that contains only cones; visual acuity is greatest at this spot. When you want to see something sharply, you usually move your eyes to centre the object in the fovea.

Rods are specialized visual receptors that play a key role in night vision and peripheral vision. Rods handle night vision because they are more sensitive than cones to dim light (Kefalov, 2010). They handle the lion's share of peripheral vision because they greatly outnumber cones in the periphery of the retina. The density of the rods is greatest just outside the fovea and gradually decreases toward the periphery of the retina. Because of the distribution of rods, when you want to see a faintly illuminated object in the dark, it's best to look slightly above or below the place where the object should be. Averting your gaze this way moves the image from the cone-filled fovea, which requires more light, to the rod-dominated area just outside the fovea, which requires less light. This trick of averted vision is well known to astronomers, who use it to study dim objects viewed through the eyepiece of a telescope.

Information Processing in the Retina

In processing visual input, the retina transforms a pattern of light falling onto it into a very different representation of the visual scene. Light striking the retina's receptors (rods and cones) triggers the firing of neural signals that pass into the intricate network of cells in the retina. Thus, signals move from receptors to bipolar cells to ganglion cells, which in turn send impulses along the optic nerve—a collection of axons that connect the eye with the brain (refer back to Figure 4.6). These axons, which depart the eye through the optic disk, carry visual information, encoded as a stream of neural impulses, to the brain. A great deal of complex information processing goes on in the retina itself before visual signals are sent to the brain. Ultimately, the information from over 100 million rods and cones converges to travel along "only" 1 million axons in the optic nerve. This means that the bipolar and ganglion cells in the intermediate layers of the retina integrate and compress signals from many receptors.

The collection of rod and cone receptors that funnel signals to a particular visual cell in the retina (or ultimately in the brain) make up that cell's *receptive field*. Thus, the *receptive field* of a visual cell is the retinal area that, when stimulated, affects the firing of that cell. Receptive fields in the retina come in a variety of shapes and sizes. Particularly common are circular fields with a centre-surround arrangement (Levitt, 2010). In these receptive fields, light falling in the centre has the opposite effect of light falling in the surrounding area. For example, the rate of firing of a visual cell might be increased by light in the centre of its receptive field and decreased by light in the surrounding area.

concept check 4.1

Understanding Sensory Processes in the Retina

Check your understanding of sensory receptors in the retina by completing the following exercises. Consult Appendix A for the answers.

The receptors for vision are rods and cones in the retina. These two types of receptors have many important differences, which are compared systematically in the chart below. Fill in the missing information to finish the chart.

Dimension	Rods	Cones
Physical shape	_____	_____
Number in the retina	_____	_____
Area of the retina in which they are dominant receptor	_____	_____
Critical to colour vision	_____	_____
Critical to peripheral vision	_____	_____
Sensitivity to dim light	_____	_____

Vision and the Brain

Light falls on the eye, but you see with your brain. Although the retina does an unusual amount of information processing for a sensory organ, visual input is meaningless until it is processed in the brain.

Visual Pathways to the Brain

How does visual information get to the brain? Axons leaving the back of each eye form the optic nerves, which travel to the *optic chiasm*—the point at which the optic nerves from the inside half of each eye cross over and then project to the opposite half of the brain. This arrangement ensures that signals from both eyes go to both hemispheres of the brain. Thus, as Figure 4.7 shows, axons from the left half of each retina carry signals to the left side of the brain, and axons from the right half of each retina carry information to the right side of the brain.

After reaching the optic chiasm, the optic nerve fibres diverge along two pathways. The main pathway projects into the thalamus, the brain's major relay station. Here, about 90 percent of the axons from the retinas synapse in the (LGN) *lateral geniculate nucleus* (Baker, 2013). Visual signals are processed in the LGN and then distributed to areas in the occipital lobe that make up the *primary visual cortex* (see Figure 4.7). The second visual pathway leaving the optic chiasm branches off to an area

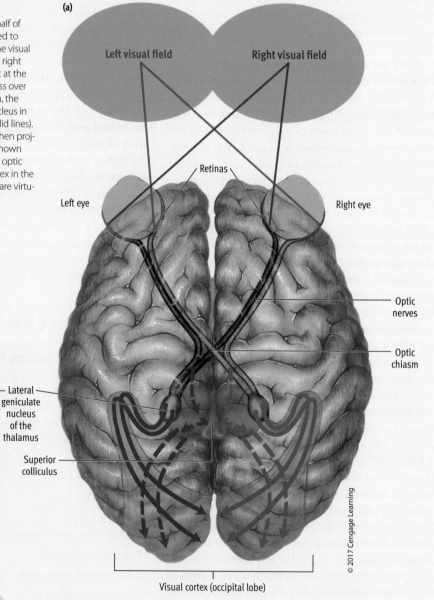

Figure 4.7
Visual pathways through the brain. (a) Input from the right half of the visual field strikes the left side of each retina and is transmitted to the left hemisphere (shown in blue). Input from the left half of the visual field strikes the right side of each retina and is transmitted to the right hemisphere (shown in red). The nerve fibres from each eye meet at the optic chiasm, where fibres from the inside half of each retina cross over to the opposite side of the brain. After reaching the optic chiasm, the major visual pathway projects through the lateral geniculate nucleus in the thalamus and onto the primary visual cortex (shown with solid lines). A second pathway detours through the superior colliculus and then projects through the thalamus and onto the primary visual cortex (shown with dotted lines). (b) This inset shows a vertical view of how the optic pathways project through the thalamus and onto the visual cortex in the back of the brain (the two pathways mapped out in diagram (a) are virtually indistinguishable from this angle).

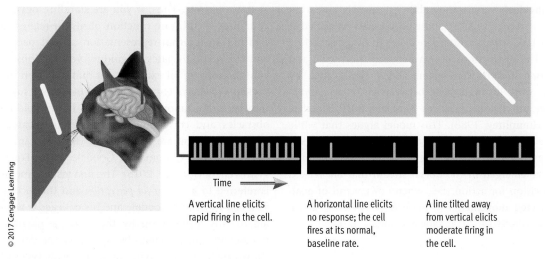

A vertical line elicits rapid firing in the cell.

A horizontal line elicits no response; the cell fires at its normal, baseline rate.

A line tilted away from vertical elicits moderate firing in the cell.

Figure 4.8
Hubel and Wiesel's procedure for studying the activity of neurons in the visual cortex. As the cat is shown various stimuli, a microelectrode records the firing of a neuron in the cat's visual cortex. The figure shows the electrical responses of a visual cell apparently "programmed" to respond to lines oriented vertically.

© 2017 Cengage Learning

Figure 4.9
The *what* and *where* pathways from the primary visual cortex. Cortical processing of visual input is begun in the primary visual cortex. From there, signals are shuttled onward to a variety of other areas in the cortex along a number of pathways. Two prominent pathways are highlighted here. The dorsal stream, or *where pathway*, which processes information about motion and depth, moves on to areas of the parietal lobe. The ventral stream, or *what pathway*, which processes information about colour and form, moves on to areas of the temporal lobe.

© 2017 Cengage Learning

in the midbrain called the *superior colliculus* before travelling through the thalamus and on to the occipital lobe. The principal function of the second pathway appears to be the coordination of visual input with other sensory input (Casanova et al., 2001; Stein & Meredith, 1993).

Information Processing in the Visual Cortex

Visual input ultimately arrives in the primary visual cortex located in the occipital lobe. Research that won a Nobel Prize for Canadian David Hubel and Swedish neurophysiologist Torsten Wiesel (1962, 1963) demonstrated that cells in the visual cortex respond to very specific types of stimuli. Some are sensitive to lines, some respond to edges, and some only react to more complicated stimuli. Some respond best to a line of the correct width, oriented at the correct angle, and located in the correct position in its receptive field (see Figure 4.8).

The key point here is that the cells in the visual cortex seem to be highly specialized. They have been characterized as *feature detectors*, neurons that respond selectively to very specific features of more complex stimuli. Ultimately, most visual stimuli could be represented by combinations of lines, such as those registered by these feature detectors. Some theorists believe that feature detectors are registering the basic building blocks of visual perception and that the brain somehow assembles the blocks into a coherent picture of complex stimuli (Maguire, Weisstein, & Klymenko, 1990). After visual input is processed in the primary visual cortex, it is often routed

to other cortical areas for additional processing. These signals travel through two streams that have sometimes been characterized as the *what* and *where* pathways (see Figure 4.9). The *ventral stream* processes the details of *what* objects are out there (the perception of form and colour), while the dorsal stream processes *where* the objects are (the perception of motion and depth) (Connor et al., 2009).

As signals move farther along in the visual processing system, neurons become even more specialized and the stimuli that activate them become more and more complex. For example, researchers have identified cells in the temporal lobe (along the *what* pathway) of monkeys and humans that are especially sensitive to pictures of faces (Kanwisher & Yovel, 2009). These neurons respond even to pictures that merely suggest the form of a face (Cox, Meyers, & Sinha, 2004).

The discovery of neurons that respond to facial stimuli raises an obvious question: Why does the cortex have face detectors? Theorists are far from sure, but one line of thinking is that the ability to quickly perceive and recognize faces—such as those of friends or foes—probably has had adaptive significance over the course of evolution (Chai, 2015; Sugita, 2009). Thus, natural selection may have wired the brains of some species to quickly respond to faces. Although this hypothesis seems plausible, a recent study raised questions about whether the face detector areas in the brain are devoted exclusively to facial recognition (McGugin et al., 2012). The study found that people with expertise on automobiles have cells in these areas that are especially sensitive to images of cars. Another interesting finding in this area of research is that

David Hubel

"One can now begin to grasp the significance of the great number of cells in the visual cortex. Each cell seems to have its own specific duties."

Image by Dwayne Drown, Dwayne Brown Studios, Inc.

Mel Goodale is internationally known for his work in the area of vision and neuroscience. He holds the Canada Research Chair in Visual Neuroscience in the departments of Psychology and Physiology at the University of Western Ontario. In 1999, he was awarded the D. O. Hebb Award by the Canadian Society for Brain, Behaviour, and Cognitive Science and was made a Fellow of the Royal Society of Canada in 2001.

individuals vary in their ability to quickly and accurately recognize faces. Some people are very skilled at the task, whereas others are deficient (Rhodes, 2013).

The distinctions drawn between the *ventral* and *dorsal streams* were given added significance by the work distinguishing between vision for *perception* and vision for *action* (Goodale, 2010; Goodale & Humphrey, 1988). This model argues that while the ventral stream is associated with our perception of the world (i.e., what), visuomotor modules have emerged in the dorsal stream that are related to vision for action (i.e., where) or control of goal-directed movements (Briscoe & Schwenkler, 2015; Goodale, 2013, 2014; Yabe & Goodale, 2017).

Vision for Perception and Vision for Action

James, Goodale, and Humphrey (2001) distinguish between two functions that vision serves. The first is to create an internal representation or model of the external world. This function is the subject of most of the research that we have discussed so far in this chapter. If you think about some of the things you might do as a result of being able to see the external world, it might give you a hint as to the nature of the second function that Goodale and Humphrey emphasized. The second function is not concerned with perceiving objects per se but with the related process of controlling your actions that are directed

at those objects. Thus, if you are standing next to your best friend, one function of vision relates to creating an internal representation of that person and the second relates to guiding your actions in your attempt to, for example, pat him or her on the back as a means of congratulation. This second function includes, among other things, both avoiding obstacles and correcting for changes in location in the target you are reaching for (Buckingham & Goodale, 2013; Chapman & Goodale, 2010; Foley, Whitwell, & Goodale, 2015). The first visual process is referred to as *vision for perception* and the second as *vision for action*. Goodale and his colleagues were led to this formulation by the work of previous researchers and through observation of the deficits shown by individuals who suffered specific types of brain damage, such as that experienced by an individual referred to as "DF" (Goodale, 2014; Goodale & Milner, 1992, 2004; Milner & Goodale, 2013; Whitwell et al., 2013).

DF had suffered a tragic accident. She was young, well educated, and fluent in several languages. She was living at the time in Milan, Italy, with her partner, Carlo. One day while taking a shower, she was overcome by carbon monoxide fumes—the water was heated by a propane heater. As a result of the carbon monoxide poisoning, she suffered brain damage. DF had difficulty with her vision—with seeing things and making sense out of them. Her visual problems were quite remarkable. She could see the surface detail of objects and their colour, but she could not use their form or contours to identify them. For example, although she could see grids of lines projected onto a screen, she could not tell whether they were vertical or horizontal: "[DF] has never regained a full and integrated experience of the visual world. The world she sees still lacks shape and form. [DF] is unable to identify objects on the basis of their form alone" (Goodale & Milner, 2004, p. 9). DF was unable to copy simple drawings but could draw them from memory (see Figure 4.10); these drawings show that her problems resulted from difficulties in perceptual organization, not in a "failure of the visual input to invoke the stored representation of the objects" (Goodale & Humphrey, 2001, p. 319). Her inability to recognize common objects is known as *agnosia*.

DF's neurological deficits were highly selective. For example, her motor abilities were intact. While testing DF one day, Goodale and Milner were struck by her ability to grasp a pencil they had placed in front of her, while she was not able to identify it. They wondered how she could perform all of the motor acts dependent on vision that enabled her to grasp the object, while still being unable to identify

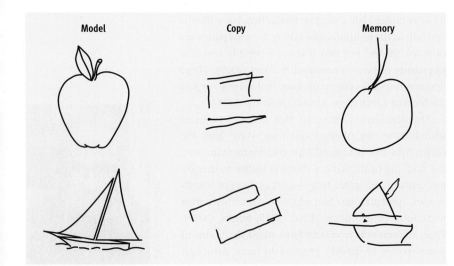

Model	Copy	Memory

Figure 4.10

Samples of drawings made by DF. The left column shows examples of line drawings that were shown to DF, the right column shows some of DF's drawings of the objects from memory, and the middle column shows examples of DF's copies of the line drawings shown in the left column.

Source: Republished with permission of John Wiley & Sons, Inc., from *Blackwell handbook of perception*, E. Bruce Goldstein, Glyn Humphreys, Margaret Shiffrar, and William Yost. Copyright © 2001 Blackwell Publishing Ltd. Permission conveyed through Copyright Clearance Center, Inc.

it. She had to be using some kind of vision. They went on to test DF's abilities systematically in the laboratory. Drawing on earlier work by Ungerleider and Mishkin (1982) and his own work (Goodale & Westwood, 2004) and that of others, Goodale suggested that these two types of vision follow different pathways in the brain. The two pathways—sometimes referred to as the *where* and *what* pathways, respectively—are a *dorsal stream* for the visual control of action and a *ventral stream* for perception of the external world. Research examining this distinction and its connection to the brain is one of the most active research areas in vision (e.g., Crawford, Medendorp, & Marotta, 2004; Wood & Goodale, 2010).

Viewing the World in Colour

So far, we've considered only how the visual system deals with light and dark. Let's journey now into the world of colour. Colour adds not only spectacle but information to perceptions of the world. The ability to identify objects against a complex background is enhanced by the addition of colour (Tanaka, Weiskopf, & Williams, 2001). Thus, some theorists have suggested that the development of colour vision has important evolutionary significance (Jacobi, 2015) and that colour vision evolved in humans and monkeys because it improved their abilities to find food through foraging, to spot prey, and to quickly recognize predators (Spence et al., 2006). Although the purpose of colour vision remains elusive, scientists have learned a great deal about the mechanisms underlying the perception of colour.

The Stimulus for Colour

As noted earlier, the lights people see are mixtures of different wavelengths. Perceived colour is primarily a function of the dominant wavelength in these mixtures. Although wavelength wields the greatest influence, the perception of colour depends on complex blends of all three properties of light.

People can perceive many different colours. Indeed, experts estimate that humans can discriminate between millions of colours (Webster, 2010), with females showing slightly better colour discrimination than males (Abramov et al., 2012). Most of these diverse variations are the result of mixing a few basic colours. There are two kinds of colour mixture: subtractive and additive. *Subtractive colour mixing works by removing some wavelengths of light, leaving less light than was originally there.* You probably became familiar with subtractive mixing as a child when you mixed yellow and blue paints to make green. Paints yield subtractive mixing because pigments absorb most wavelengths, selectively reflecting back specific wavelengths that give rise to particular colours. Subtractive colour mixing can also be demonstrated by stacking colour filters. If you look through a sandwich of yellow and blue cellophane filters, they will block out certain wavelengths. The middle wavelengths that are left will look green.

Additive colour mixing works by superimposing lights, putting more light in the mixture than exists in any one light by itself. If you shine red, green, and blue spotlights on a white surface, you'll have an additive mixture. As Figure 4.11 shows, additive and subtractive mixtures of the

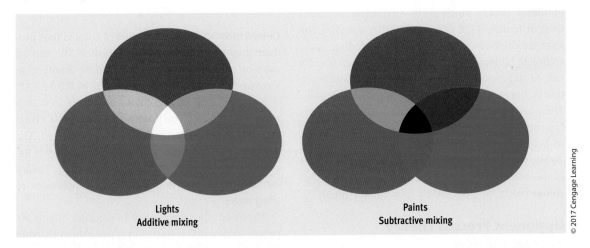

Lights
Additive mixing

Paints
Subtractive mixing

© 2017 Cengage Learning

Figure 4.11
Additive versus subtractive colour mixing. Lights mix additively because all of the wavelengths contained in each light reach the eye. If red, blue, and green lights are projected onto a white screen, they produce the colours shown on the left, with white at the intersection of all three lights. If paints of the same three colours were combined in the same way, the subtractive mixture would produce the colours shown on the right, with black at the intersection of all three colours.

Sensation and Perception

same colours produce different results. Human processes of colour perception parallel additive mixing much more closely than subtractive mixing, as you'll see in the following discussion of theories of colour vision.

Trichromatic Theory of Colour Vision

The *trichromatic theory* of colour vision (*tri* for *three*, *chroma* for *colour*) was first stated by Thomas Young and modified later by Hermann von Helmholtz (1852). **The *trichromatic theory* of colour vision holds that the human eye has three types of receptors with differing sensitivities to different light wavelengths.** Helmholtz theorized that the eye contains specialized receptors sensitive to the specific wavelengths associated with red, green, and blue. According to this model, people can see all of the colours of the rainbow because the eye does its own "colour mixing" by varying the ratio of neural activity among these three types of receptors.

The impetus for the trichromatic theory was the demonstration that a light of any colour can be matched by the additive mixture of three *primary colours*. Any three colours that are appropriately spaced out in the visible spectrum can serve as primary colours, although red, green, and blue are usually used. Does it sound implausible that three colours should be adequate for creating all other colours? If so, consider that this is exactly what happens on your colour TV screen and computer monitor (Stockman, 2010).

Most of the known facts about colour-blindness also meshed well with trichromatic theory. *Colour-blindness* encompasses a variety of deficiencies in the ability to distinguish among colours. Colour-blindness occurs much more frequently in males than in females (Tait & Carroll, 2010). Actually, the term *colour-blindness* is somewhat misleading, since complete blindness to differences in colours is quite rare. Most people who are colour-blind are *dichromats*; that is, they make do with only two colour channels. There are three types of dichromats, and each type is insensitive to one of the primary colours—red, green, or blue—although the latter is rare (Reid & Usrey, 2008). The three deficiencies seen among dichromats support the notion that there are three channels for colour vision, as proposed by trichromatic theory.

Opponent Process Theory of Colour Vision

Although trichromatic theory explained some facets of colour vision well, it ran aground in other areas. Consider complementary afterimages, for instance.

Complementary colours are pairs of colours that produce grey tones when mixed together. The various pairs of complementary colours can be arranged in a *colour circle*, such as the one shown in Figure 4.12. If you stare at a strong colour and then look at a white background, you'll see an *afterimage*—a visual image that persists after a stimulus is removed. The colour of the afterimage will be the *complement* of the colour you originally stared at. Trichromatic theory cannot account for the appearance of complementary afterimages.

Here's another peculiarity to consider. If you ask people to describe colours but restrict them to using three names, they run into difficulty. For example, using only red, green, and blue, they simply don't feel comfortable describing yellow as "reddish green." However, if you let them have just one more

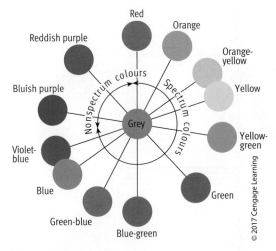

Figure 4.12
The colour circle and complementary colours. Colours opposite each other on this colour circle are complements, or "opposites." Additively, mixing complementary colours produces gray. Opponent process principles help to explain this effect, as well as the other peculiarities of complementary colours noted in the text.

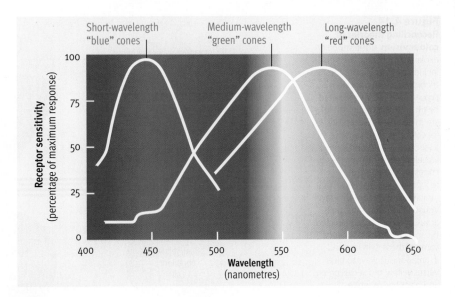

Figure 4.13
Three types of cones. Research has identified three types of cones that show varied sensitivity to different wavelengths of light. As the graph shows, these three types of cones correspond only roughly to the red, green, and blue receptors predicted by trichromatic theory, so it is more accurate to refer to them as cones sensitive to short, medium, and long wavelengths.

Source: Wald, G., and Brown, P.K. (1965). Human color vision and color blindness. *Symposium Cold Spring Harbor Laboratory of Quantitative Biology*, 30, 345–359 (p. 351). Copyright © 1965. Reprinted by permission of the author.

name, they usually choose yellow; they can then describe any colour quite well (Gordon & Abramov, 2001). If colours are reduced to three channels, why are four colour names required to describe the full range of possible colours?

In an effort to answer questions such as these, Ewald Hering proposed the *opponent process theory* in 1878. The *opponent process* theory of colour vision holds that colour perception depends on receptors that make antagonistic responses to three pairs of colours. The three pairs of opponent colours posited by Hering were red versus green, yellow versus blue, and black versus white. The antagonistic processes in this theory provide plausible explanations for complementary afterimages and the need for four names (red, green, blue, and yellow) to describe colours. Opponent process theory also explains some aspects of colour-blindness. For instance, it can explain why dichromats typically find it hard to distinguish either green from red or yellow from blue.

Reconciling Theories of Colour Vision

Advocates of trichromatic theory and opponent process theory argued about the relative merits of their models for almost a century. Most researchers assumed that one theory must be wrong and the other must be right. In recent decades, however, it has become clear that *it takes both theories to explain colour vision*. Eventually, a physiological basis for both theories was found. Research that earned George

Wald a Nobel Prize (Wald, 1964) demonstrated that *the eye has three types of cones*, with each type being most sensitive to a different band of wavelengths, as shown in Figure 4.13 (Gegenfurtner, 2010; Wald, 1964). The three types of cones represent the three different colour receptors predicted by trichromatic theory.

Researchers also discovered a biological basis for opponent processes. They found cells in the retina, the LGN, and the visual cortex *that respond in opposite ways to red versus green and blue versus yellow* (Purves, 2009; Zrenner et al., 1990). For example, there are ganglion cells in the retina that are excited by green and inhibited by red. Other ganglion cells in the retina work in just the opposite way, as predicted in opponent process theory.

In summary, the perception of colour appears to involve sequential stages of information processing (Gegenfurtner, 2010; Hurvich, 1981). The receptors that do the first stage of processing (the cones) seem to follow the principles outlined in trichromatic theory. In later stages of processing, at least some cells in the retina, the LGN, and the visual cortex seem to follow the principles outlined in opponent process theory (see Figure 4.14). As you can see, vigorous theoretical debate about colour vision produced a solution that went beyond the contributions of either theory alone.

Sensation and Perception

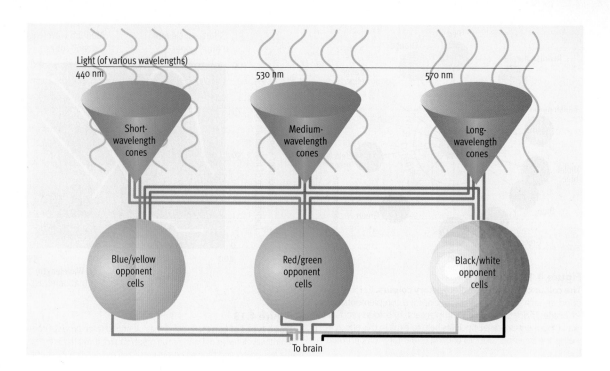

Figure 4.14

Reconciling theories of colour vision. Contemporary explanations of colour vision include aspects of both the trichromatic and opponent process theories. As predicted by trichromatic theory, there are three types of receptors for colour—cones sensitive to short, medium, and long wavelengths. However, these cones are organized into receptive fields that excite or inhibit the firing of higher-level visual cells in the retina, thalamus, and cortex. As predicted by opponent process theory, some of these cells respond in antagonistic ways to blue versus yellow, red versus green, and black versus white.

The Visual System: Perceptual Processes

Perceiving Forms, Patterns, and Objects

The drawing in Figure 4.15 is a poster for a circus act involving a trained seal. Take a good look at it. What do you see?

No doubt you see a seal balancing a ball on its nose and a trainer holding a fish and a whip. But suppose you had been told that the drawing is actually a poster for a costume ball. Would you have perceived it differently?

If you focus on the idea of a costume ball (stay with it a minute if you still see the seal and trainer), you will probably see a costumed man and woman in Figure 4.15. She's handing him a hat, and he has a sword in his right hand. This tricky little sketch was made ambiguous quite intentionally. It's a *reversible figure*, a drawing that is compatible with two interpretations that can shift back and forth. Another classic reversible figure is shown in Figure 4.16. What do you see? A rabbit or a duck? It all depends on how you look at the drawing.

The key point is simply this: The same visual input can result in radically different perceptions. No one-to-one correspondence exists between sensory input and what you perceive. This is a principal reason that people's experience of the world is subjective. Perception involves much more than passively receiving signals from the outside world. It involves the interpretation of sensory input. To some extent, this interpretive process can be influenced by manipulating people's expectations. For example,

information given to you about the drawing of the "circus act involving a trained seal" created a *perceptual set*—a readiness to perceive a stimulus in a particular way. A perceptual set creates a certain slant in how someone interprets sensory input.

© 2017 Cengage Learning

Figure 4.15

A poster for a trained seal act. Or is it? The picture is an ambiguous figure, which can be interpreted as either of two scenes, as explained in the text.

Form perception also depends on the selection of sensory input—that is, what people focus their attention on (Chun & Wolfe, 2001). A visual scene may include many objects and forms. Some of them may capture viewers' attention while others may not. In fact, while much of what we have discussed so far is about what and how we see, sometimes it is even more interesting to consider what we fail to see and under what conditions we fail to see it. This fact has been demonstrated in dramatic fashion in studies of change blindness and inattentional blindness (Jensen et al., 2011). *Change blindness* involves the failure to notice a seemingly obvious change in a visual display. For example, experimental participants may fail to notice that a central actor in the scene is in fact a different person from the actor playing the character in an earlier scene (Resnick, 2002). *Inattentional blindness* involves the failure to see unexpected visible objects or events in a visual display (Chabris & Simons, 2010; Jensen, 2016; Levin et al., 2015). This occurs even for experts performing a familiar task in their domain of expertise (Drew, Vo, & Wolfe, 2013). In what has become one of the most famous experiments in psychology in the past two decades (Simons & Chabris, 1999), participants watched a video of a group of people in white shirts passing a basketball that was laid over another video of people in black shirts passing a basketball (the two videos were partially transparent). The observers were instructed to focus on one of the two teams and press a key whenever that team passed the ball. Thirty seconds into the task, a woman carrying an umbrella clearly walked through the scene for four seconds. You might guess that this bizarre development would be noticed by virtually all of the observers, but 44 percent of the participants failed to see the woman. Moreover, when someone in a gorilla suit strolled through the same scene, even more subjects (73 percent) missed the unexpected event.

The idea that we see much less of the world than we think we do surprises many people, but an auditory parallel exists that people take for granted (Mack, 2003). Think of how often you have had someone clearly say something to you, but you did not hear a word of what was said because you were "not listening." Inattentional blindness is essentially the same thing in the visual domain.

An understanding of how people perceive forms and objects also requires knowledge of how people *organize* their visual inputs. Several influential approaches to this issue emphasize *feature analysis*.

Feature Analysis: Assembling Forms

The information received by your eyes would do you little good if you couldn't recognize objects and forms—ranging from words on a page to mice in your cellar and friends in the distance. According to some theories, perceptions of form and pattern entail *feature analysis* (Lindsay & Norman, 1977; Maguire et al., 1990). *Feature analysis* is the process of detecting specific elements in visual input and assembling them into a more complex form. In other words, you start with the components of a form, such as lines, edges, and corners, and build them into perceptions of squares, triangles, stop signs, bicycles, ice cream cones, and telephones. An application of this model of form perception is diagrammed in Figure 4.17.

Feature analysis assumes that form perception involves *bottom-up processing*, a progression from individual elements to the whole (see Figure 4.18). The plausibility of this model was bolstered greatly when Hubel and Wiesel (1962) showed that cells in the visual cortex operate as highly specialized feature

Figure 4.16
Another ambiguous figure. What animal do you see here? As the text explains, two very different perceptions are possible. This ambiguous figure was devised around 1900 by Joseph Jastrow, a prominent psychologist at the turn of the 20th century (Block & Yuker, 1992).

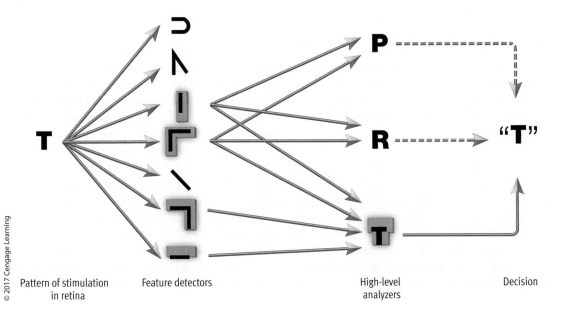

Pattern of stimulation in retina — Feature detectors — High-level analyzers — Decision

© 2017 Cengage Learning

Figure 4.17
Feature analysis in form perception. One vigorously debated theory of form perception is that the brain has cells that respond to specific aspects or features of stimuli, such as lines and angles. Neurons functioning as higher-level analyzers then respond to input from these "feature detectors." The more input each analyzer receives, the more active it becomes. Finally, other neurons weigh signals from these analyzers and make a "decision" about the stimulus. In this way, perception of a form is arrived at by assembling elements from the bottom up.

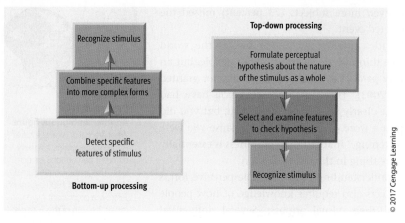

Figure 4.18

Bottom-up versus top-down processing. As explained in these diagrams, bottom-up processing progresses from individual elements to whole elements, whereas top-down processing progresses from the whole to the individual elements.

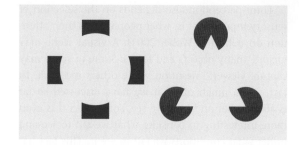

Figure 4.19

Subjective contours. Our perception of the triangle on the right and the circle on the left results from subjective contours that are not really there. The effect is so powerful, the triangle and circle appear lighter than the background, which they are not. To demonstrate the illusory nature of these contours for yourself, cover the red circles that mark off the triangle. You'll see that the triangle disappears.

Source: From Weiten. *Cengage Advantage Books: Psychology,* 9E. © 2013 South-Western, a part of Cengage, Inc. Reproduced by permission. www.cengage.com/permissions

detectors. Indeed, their findings strongly suggested that at least some aspects of form perception involve feature analysis.

Can feature analysis provide a complete account of how people perceive forms? Clearly not. A crucial problem for the theory is that form perception often does not involve bottom-up processing. A distinction can be drawn between bottom-up and top-down processing (e.g., Wu et al., 2015). There is ample evidence that perceptions of form frequently involve *top-down processing,* a progression from the whole to the elements (see Figure 4.18). For example, there is evidence that people can perceive a word before its individual letters, a phenomenon that has to reflect top-down processing (Johnston & McClelland, 1974). If readers depended exclusively on bottom-up processing, they would have to analyze the features of letters in words to recognize them and then assemble the letters into words. This would be a terribly time-consuming task and would slow down reading speed to a snail's pace.

Subjective contours are another phenomenon traditionally attributed to top-down processing, although that view is changing. The phenomenon of *subjective contours* is the perception of contours where none actually exist. Consider, for instance, the triangle shown in Figure 4.19. We see the contours of the triangle easily, even though no physical edges or lines are present. It is hard to envision how feature detectors could detect edges that are not really there, so most theorists have argued that bottom-up models of form perception are unlikely to account for subjective contours. Until recently, the prevailing view was that subjective contours depend on viewing stimulus configurations as wholes and then filling in the blanks (Rock, 1986). However, researchers have demonstrated that feature detectors *do* respond to the edges in subjective contours (Peterhans & von der

Heydt, 1991). At present, neural theories of subjective contours that emphasize bottom-up processing or both types of processing are under investigation, with promising results (Gunn et al., 2000; Lesher, 1995). In sum, it appears that both top-down and bottom-up processing have their niches in form perception.

Looking at the Whole Picture: Gestalt Principles

Top-down processing is clearly at work in the principles of form perception described by the Gestalt psychologists. *Gestalt psychology* was an influential school of thought that emerged out of Germany during the first half of the 20th century. (*Gestalt* is a German word for "form" or "shape.") Gestalt psychologists repeatedly demonstrated that the whole can be greater than the sum of its parts. Although no longer an active theoretical orientation in psychology, it continues to influence the study of perception (Banks & Krajicek, 1991; Frank et al., 2010; Hecht et al., 2016) and other areas of psychology (Asch, 1946).

A simple example of this principle is the *phi phenomenon,* first described by Max Wertheimer in 1912. The *phi phenomenon* is the illusion of movement created by presenting visual stimuli in rapid succession. You encounter examples of the phi phenomenon nearly every day. For example, movies and TV consist of separate still pictures projected rapidly one after the other. You see smooth motion, but in reality the "moving" objects merely take slightly different positions in successive frames. Viewed as a whole, a movie has a property (motion) that isn't evident in any of its parts (the individual frames). The Gestalt psychologists formulated a series of principles that describe how the visual system organizes a scene into discrete forms (Schirillo, 2010). Let's examine some of these principles.

Max Wertheimer

"The fundamental 'formula' of Gestalt theory might be expressed in this way: There are wholes, the behaviour of which is not determined by that of their individual elements."

Figure and Ground. Take a look at Figure 4.20. Do you see the figure as two silhouetted faces against a white background, or as a white vase against a black background? This reversible figure illustrates the Gestalt principle of *figure and ground*. Dividing visual displays into figure and ground is a fundamental way in which people organize visual perceptions (Baylis & Driver, 1995; Hecht et al., 2016). The *figure* is the thing being looked at, and the *ground* is the background against which it stands. Figures seem to have more substance and shape, appear closer to the viewer, and seem to stand out in front of the ground. More often than not, your visual field may contain many figures sharing a background. The following Gestalt principles relate to how these elements are grouped into higher-order figures (Palmer, 2003).

Proximity. Things that are close to one another seem to belong together. The black dots in the upper left panel of Figure 4.21(a) could be grouped into vertical columns or horizontal rows. However, people tend to perceive rows because of the effect of proximity (the dots are closer together horizontally).

Closure. People often group elements to create a sense of *closure*, or completeness. Thus, you may "complete" figures that actually have gaps in them. This principle is demonstrated in the upper right panel of Figure 4.21(b).

Similarity. People also tend to group stimuli that are similar. This principle is apparent in Figure 4.21(c), where viewers group elements of similar lightness into the number 2.

Simplicity. The Gestaltists' most general principle was the law of *Pragnanz*, which translates from German as "good form." The idea is that people tend to group elements that combine to form a good figure. This principle is somewhat vague in that it's often difficult to spell out what makes a figure "good" (Biederman, Hilton, & Hummel, 1991). Some theorists maintain that goodness is largely a matter of simplicity, asserting that people tend to organize forms in the simplest way possible (see Figure 4.21(d)). But the concept of simplicity is also plagued by ambiguity (Donderi, 2006).

Continuity. The principle of continuity reflects people's tendency to follow in whatever direction they've been led. Thus, people tend to connect points that result in straight or gently curved lines that create "smooth" paths, as shown in Figure 4.21(e).

Formulating Perceptual Hypotheses

The Gestalt principles provide some indications of how people organize visual input. However, scientists are still one step away from understanding how these organized perceptions result in a representation of the real world. Understanding the problem requires distinguishing between two kinds of stimuli: distal and proximal (Hochberg, 1988). *Distal stimuli* are stimuli that lie in the distance (i.e., in the world outside the body). In vision, these are the objects that you're looking at. They are "distant" in that your eyes don't touch them. What your eyes do "touch" are the images formed by patterns of light falling on your retinas. These images are the *proximal stimuli*, the stimulus energies that impinge directly on sensory receptors. The distinction is important, because there are great differences between the objects you perceive and the stimulus energies that represent them.

In visual perception, the proximal stimuli are distorted, two-dimensional versions of their actual, three-dimensional counterparts. For example, consider the distal stimulus of a square such as the one in Figure 4.22. If the square is lying on a desk in front of you, it is actually projecting a trapezoid

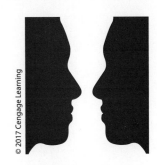

Figure 4.20
The principle of figure and ground. Whether you see two faces or a vase depends on which part of this drawing you see as figure and which as background. Although this reversible drawing allows you to switch back and forth between two ways of organizing your perception, you can't perceive the drawing in both ways at once.

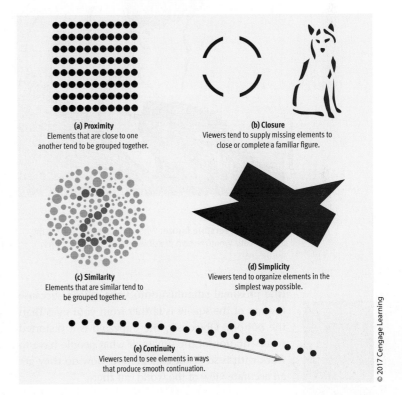

Figure 4.21
Gestalt principles of perceptual organization. Gestalt principles help explain some of the factors that influence form perception. (a) **Proximity**: These dots might well be organized in vertical columns rather than horizontal rows, but because of proximity (the dots are closer together horizontally), they tend to be perceived in rows. (b) **Closure:** Even though the figures are incomplete, you fill in the blanks and see a circle and a dog. (c) **Similarity**: Because of similarity of colour, you see dots organized into the number 2 instead of a random array. If you did not group similar elements, you wouldn't see the number 2 here. (d) **Simplicity:** You could view this as a complicated 11-sided figure, but given the preference for simplicity, you are more likely to see it as an overlapping rectangle and triangle. (e) **Continuity:** You tend to group these dots in a way that produces a smooth path rather than an abrupt shift in direction.

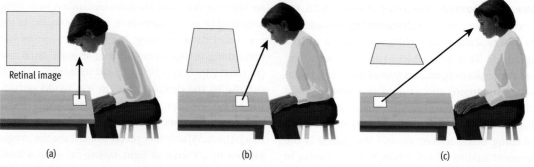

(a)   (b)   (c)

Retinal image

Figure 4.22

Distal and proximal stimuli. Proximal stimuli are often distorted, shifting representations of distal stimuli in the real world. If you look directly down at a small, square piece of paper on a desk (a), the distal stimulus (the paper) and the proximal stimulus (the image projected on your retina) will both be square. But as you move the paper away on the desktop, as shown in (b) and (c), the square distal stimulus projects an increasingly trapezoidal image on your retina, making the proximal stimulus more and more distorted. Nevertheless, you continue to perceive a square.

Source: From Weiten. *Cengage Advantage Books: Psychology*, 9E. © 2013 South-Western, a part of Cengage, Inc. Reproduced by permission. www.cengage.com/permissions

© 2017 Cengage Learning

Figure 4.23

A famous reversible figure. What do you see? Consult the text to learn what the two possible interpretations of this figure are.

One explanation is that people bridge the gap between distal and proximal stimuli by constantly making and testing *hypotheses* about what's out there in the real world (Gregory, 1973). Thus, a *perceptual hypothesis* is an inference about which distal stimuli could be responsible for the proximal stimuli sensed. In effect, people make educated guesses about what form could be responsible for a pattern of sensory stimulation. The square in Figure 4.22 may project a trapezoidal image on your retinas, but your perceptual system "guesses" correctly that it's a square—and that's what you see.

Let's look at another ambiguous drawing to further demonstrate the process of making a perceptual hypothesis. Figure 4.23 is a famous reversible figure, first published as a cartoon in a humour magazine. Perhaps you see a drawing of a young woman looking back over her right shoulder. Alternatively, you might see an old woman with her chin down on her chest. The ambiguity exists because there isn't enough information to force your perceptual system to accept only one of these hypotheses. Incidentally, studies show that people who are led to *expect* the young woman or the old woman generally see the one they expect (Leeper, 1935). This is another example of how perceptual sets influence what people see.

Psychologists have used a variety of reversible figures to study how people formulate perceptual hypotheses. Another example can be seen in Figure 4.24, which shows the *Necker cube*. The shaded surface can appear as either the front or the rear of the transparent cube. If you look at the cube for a while, your perception will alternate between these possibilities.

The *context* in which something appears often guides people's perceptual hypotheses (Bravo, 2010). To illustrate, take a look at Figure 4.25. What do you

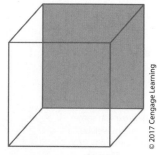

© 2017 Cengage Learning

Figure 4.24

The Necker cube. The tinted surface of this reversible figure can become either the front or the back of the cube.

(the proximal stimulus) onto your retinas, because the top of the square is farther from your eyes than the bottom. Obviously, the trapezoid is a distorted representation of the square. If what people have to work with is so distorted a picture, how do they get an accurate view of the world out there?

THE CHT

© 2017 Cengage Learning

Figure 4.25

Context effects. The context in which a stimulus is seen can affect your perceptual hypotheses.

see? You probably saw the words "THE CAT." But look again; the middle characters in both words are identical. You identified an "H" in the first word and an "A" in the second because of the surrounding letters, which created an expectation—another example of top-down processing in visual perception. The power of expectations explains why typographocal errors like those in this sentence often pass unoberved (Lachman, 1996).

Perceiving Depth or Distance

More often than not, forms and figures are objects in space. Spatial considerations add a third dimension to visual perception. *Depth perception involves interpretation of visual cues that indicate how near or far away objects are.* To make judgments of distance, people rely on quite a variety of clues, which can be classified into two types: binocular and monocular (Hochberg, 1988; Proffitt & Caudek, 2003).

Binocular Cues

Because the eyes are set apart, each eye has a slightly different view of the world. *Binocular depth cues are clues about distance based on the differing views of the two eyes.* The new 3-D movies take advantage of this fact. Two cameras are used to record slightly different images of the same scene. The special polarized glasses that viewers wear separate the images for each eye. The brain then supplies the "depth" and you perceive a three-dimensional scene.

The principal binocular depth cue is *retinal disparity*, which refers to the fact that objects project images to slightly different locations on the right and left retinas, so the right and left eyes see slightly different views of the object. The closer an object gets, the greater the disparity between the images seen by each eye. Thus, retinal disparity increases as objects come closer, providing information about distance. Another binocular cue is *convergence*, which involves sensing the eyes converging toward each other as they focus on closer objects.

Monocular Cues

Monocular depth cues are clues about distance based on the image in either eye alone. There are two kinds of monocular cues to depth. One kind is the result of active use of the eye in viewing the world. For example, if you cover one eye and move your head from side to side, closer objects appear to move more than distant objects. In a similar vein,

you may notice when driving along a highway that nearby objects (e.g., fence posts along the road) appear to move by more rapidly than objects that are farther away (such as trees in the distance). Thus, you get cues about depth from *motion parallax*, which involves images of objects at different distances moving across the retina at different rates. The study of motion parallax was one of the earliest areas of study in depth perception; it was first suggested as a depth cue over 300 years ago (Ono & Wade, 2005).

The other kind of monocular cues are *pictorial depth cues*—clues about distance that can be given in a flat picture. There are many pictorial cues to depth, which is why some paintings and photographs seem so realistic that you feel you can climb right into them. Six prominent pictorial depth cues are described and illustrated in Figure 4.26. *Linear perspective* is a depth cue reflecting the fact that lines converge in the distance. Because the details are too small to see when they are far away, *texture gradients* can provide information about depth. If an object comes between you and another object, it must be closer to you, a cue called *interposition*. *Relative size* is a cue because closer objects appear larger. *Height in plane* reflects the fact that distant objects appear higher in a picture. Finally, the familiar effects of shadowing make *light and shadow* useful in judging distance. Research also suggests that application of pictorial depth cues to pictures varies to some degree across cultures (Berry et al., 1992; Hudson, 1960).

Some cultural differences appear to exist in the ability to take advantage of pictorial depth cues in two-dimensional drawings. These differences were first investigated by Hudson (1960, 1967), who presented pictures such as the one in Figure 4.27 to various cultural groups in South Africa. Hudson's approach was based on the assumption that subjects who indicate that the hunter is trying to spear the elephant instead of the antelope don't understand the depth cues (interposition, relative size, height in plane) in the picture, which place the elephant in the distance. Hudson found that participants from a rural South African tribe (the Bantu), who had little exposure at that time to pictures and photos, frequently misinterpreted the depth cues in his pictures. Similar difficulties with depth cues in pictures have been documented for other cultural groups who have little experience with two-dimensional representations of three-dimensional space (Berry et al., 1992; Phillips, 2011). Thus, the application of pictorial depth cues to pictures varies to some degree across cultures.

Linear perspective: Parallel lines that run away from the viewer seem to get closer together.

kwest/Shutterstock.com

Texture gradient: As distance increases, a texture gradually becomes denser and less distinct.

© Christopher Talbot Frank

Interposition: The shapes of near objects overlap or mask those of more distant ones.

© Deborah Davis/PhotoEdit

Relative size: If separate objects are expected to be of the same size, the larger ones are seen as closer.

© Deborah Davis/PhotoEdit

Height in plane: Near objects are low in the visual field; more distant ones are higher up.

Nataliya Hora/Shutterstock.com

Light and shadow: Patterns of light and dark suggest shadows that can create an impression of three-dimensional forms.

U.S. Department of Energy

Figure 4.26
Pictorial cues to depth. Six pictorial depth cues are explained and illustrated here. Although one cue stands out in each photo, in most visual scenes several pictorial cues are present. Try looking at the light-and-shadow picture upside down. The change in shadowing reverses what you see.

© 2017 Cengage Learning

Figure 4.27
Testing understanding of pictorial depth cues. In his cross-cultural research, Hudson (1960) asked subjects to indicate whether the hunter is trying to spear the antelope or the elephant. He found cultural disparities in subjects' ability to make effective use of the pictorial depth cues, which place the elephant in the distance and make it an unlikely target.

Source: Adapted by permission from an illustration by Ilil Arbel in Deregowski, J. B. (1972, November). Pictorial perception and culture. *Scientific American, 227*(5), p. 83. Copyright © 1972 by Scientific American, Inc. All rights reserved.

Recent research has shown that estimates of distance can be skewed by people's motivational states. (Cole, Balcetis, & Zhang, 2013). Studies suggest that people see desirable objects as closer to them than less desirable objects. For example, Balcetis and Dunning (2010) found that participants who are very thirsty estimate that a bottle of water sitting across a room is closer to them than do participants who are not thirsty. In another study, subjects were asked to estimate the distance between them and a $100 bill that they had a chance to win or a $100 bill that they knew belonged to the experimenter. Once again, the more desirable object (the $100 bill that could be won) was perceived to be closer than the less desirable object. Thus, like other perceptual experiences, judgments of distance can be highly subjective.

Perceptual Constancies in Vision

When a person approaches you from a distance, his or her image on your retinas gradually changes in size. Do you perceive that the person is growing right before your eyes? Of course not. Your perceptual system constantly makes allowances for this variation in visual input. The task of the perceptual system is to provide an accurate rendition of distal stimuli based on distorted, ever-changing proximal stimuli. In doing so, it relies in part on perceptual constancies. A *perceptual constancy* is a tendency to experience a stable perception in the face of continually changing sensory input. Among other things, people tend to view objects as having a stable size, shape, brightness, hue, and texture (Goldstein, 2010).

The Power of Misleading Cues: Visual Illusions

In general, perceptual constancies, depth cues, and principles of visual organization (such as the Gestalt laws) help people perceive the world accurately. Sometimes, however, perceptions are based on inappropriate assumptions, and *visual illusions* can result. An *visual illusion* involves an apparently inexplicable discrepancy between the appearance of a visual stimulus and its physical reality.

One famous visual illusion is the Müller-Lyer illusion, shown in Figure 4.28. The two vertical lines in this figure are equally long, but they certainly don't look that way. Why not? Several mechanisms probably play a role (Deregowski, 2015; Gregory, 1978). The drawing on the left looks like the outside of a building, thrust toward the viewer, while the one on the right looks like an inside corner, thrust away (see Figure 4.29). The vertical line in the left-hand drawing therefore seems closer. If two lines cast equally long retinal images but one seems closer, the closer one is assumed to be shorter. Thus, the Müller-Lyer illusion may result from a combination of size constancy processes and misperception of depth.

The geometric illusions shown in Figure 4.30 also demonstrate that visual stimuli can be highly deceptive. The *Ponzo illusion*, which is shown at the top left of this figure, appears to result from the same factors at work in the Müller-Lyer illusion (Coren & Girgus, 1978). The upper and lower horizontal lines are the same length, but the upper one appears to be longer. This illusion probably occurs because the converging lines convey linear perspective, a key depth cue suggesting that the upper line lies farther away. Figure 4.31 shows a drawing by Stanford University psychologist Roger Shepard (1990) that creates a similar illusion. The second monster appears much larger than the first, even though they are really identical in size.

Adelbert Ames designed a striking illusion that makes use of misperception of distance. It's called, appropriately enough, the *Ames room*. It's a specially

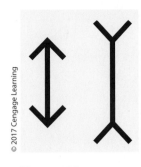

Figure 4.28
The Müller-Lyer illusion. Go ahead, measure them: The two vertical lines are of equal length.

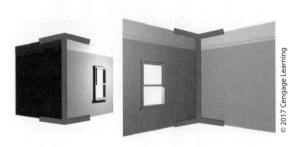

Figure 4.29
Explaining the Müller-Lyer illusion. The drawing on the left seems to be closer, since it looks like an outside corner, thrust toward you, whereas the drawing on the right looks like an inside corner thrust away from you. Given retinal images of the same length, you assume that the "closer" line is shorter.

Figure 4.30
Four geometric illusions. Ponzo: The horizontal lines are the same length. **Poggendorff**: The two diagonal segments lie on the same straight line. **Upside-down T**: The vertical and horizontal lines are the same length. **Zollner**: The long diagonals are all parallel (try covering up some of the short diagonal lines if you don't believe it).

Figure 4.31

A monster of an illusion. The principles underlying the Ponzo illusion also explain the striking illusion seen here, in which two identical monsters appear to be quite different in size.

Source: Image: "Monster Illusion" from the book MIND SIGHTS: Original Visual Illusions, and Other Anomalies, With a Commentary on the Play of Mind in Perception and Art by Roger N. Shepard. Copyright © 1990 by Roger N. Shepard. Used by permission of Henry Holt and Company. All rights reserved.

A puzzling perceptual illusion common in everyday life is the moon illusion: The moon looks larger when at the horizon than when overhead.

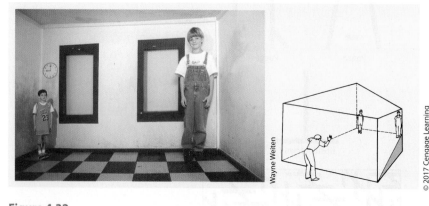

Figure 4.32

The Ames room. The diagram to the right shows the room as it is actually constructed. However, the viewer assumes that the room is rectangular, and the image cast on the retina is consistent with this hypothesis. Because of this reasonable perceptual hypothesis, the normal perceptual adjustments made to preserve size constancy lead to the illusions described in the text. For example, naïve viewers "conclude" that one boy is much larger than the other, when in fact he is merely closer.

contrived room built with a trapezoidal rear wall and a sloping floor and ceiling with the size of some objects adjusted to produce the illusion of the objects appearing on the same plane. When viewed from the correct point, as in the photo in Figure 4.32, it looks like an ordinary rectangular room. But in reality, the left corner is much taller and much farther from the viewer than the right corner, as the diagram in this figure shows. Hence, bizarre illusions unfold in the Ames room. People standing in the right corner appear to be giants, while those standing in the left corner appear to be very small. Even more disconcerting, a person who walks across the room from right to left appears to shrink before your eyes! The Ames room creates these misperceptions by toying with the perfectly reasonable assumption that the room is vertically and horizontally rectangular.

Yet another well-known visual illusion is the *moon illusion*. The full moon appears to be as much as 50 percent smaller when overhead than when looming on the horizon (Ross & Plug, 2002). As with many of the other illusions we have discussed, the moon illusion seems to result mainly from size constancy effects, coupled with the misperception of distance (Kaufman et al., 2007).

Cross-cultural studies have uncovered some interesting differences among cultural groups in their propensity to see certain illusions (Bremer et al., 2016; Masuda, 2010; Yoon et al., 2014). For example, Segall, Campbell, and Herskovits (1966) found that people from Western cultures are more susceptible to the Müller-Lyer illusion than are people from some non-Western cultures. The most plausible explanation is that in the West, we live in a "carpentered world" dominated by straight lines, right angles, and rectangular rooms, buildings, and furniture. Thus, our experience prepares us to readily view the Müller-Lyer figures as inside and outside corners of buildings, inferences that help foster the illusion (Segall et al., 1990).

What do visual illusions reveal about visual perception? They drive home the point that people go through life formulating perceptual hypotheses about what lies out there in the real world. And like ambiguous figures, illusions clearly demonstrate that human perceptions are not simple reflections of objective reality. Once again, we see that perception of the world is subjective. These insights do not apply to visual perception only. We will encounter these lessons again as we examine other sensory systems, such as hearing.

Unlike people in Western nations, the Zulus live in a culture where straight lines and right angles are scarce. Thus, they are not affected by such phenomena as the Müller-Lyer illusion nearly as much as are people raised in environments that abound with rectangular structures.

concept **check** 4.2

Figure 4.26 describes and illustrates six pictorial depth cues, most of which are apparent in the adjacent photo. Check your understanding of depth perception by trying to spot the depth cues in the picture. In the list below, check off the depth cues seen in the photo. The answers can be found in Appendix A.

_____ **1.** Interposition

_____ **2.** Height in plane

_____ **3.** Texture gradient

_____ **4.** Relative size

_____ **5.** Light and shadow

_____ **6.** Linear perspective

Our Sense of Hearing: The Auditory System

Like vision, the auditory (hearing) system provides input about the world "out there," but not until incoming information is processed by the brain. A distal stimulus—a screech of tires, someone laughing, the hum of the refrigerator—produces a proximal stimulus in the form of sound waves reaching the ears. The perceptual system must somehow transform this stimulation into the psychological experience of hearing. We'll begin our discussion of hearing by looking at the stimulus for auditory experience: sound.

The Stimulus: Sound

Sound waves are vibrations of molecules, which means that they must travel through some physical medium, such as air. They move at a fraction of the speed of light. Sound waves are usually generated by vibrating objects, such as a guitar string, a loudspeaker cone, or your vocal cords. However, sound waves can also be generated by forcing air past a chamber (as in a pipe organ), or by suddenly releasing a burst of air (as when you clap).

Key Learning Goals

▶ Identify the three properties of sound and summarize information on human hearing capacities.

▶ Describe how sensory processing occurs in the ear, compare the place and frequency theories of pitch perception, and discuss factors in auditory localization.

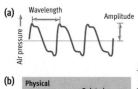

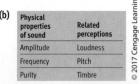

Physical properties of sound	Related perceptions
Amplitude	Loudness
Frequency	Pitch
Purity	Timbre

© 2017 Cengage Learning

Figure 4.33
Sound, the physical stimulus for hearing. (a) Like light, sound travels in waves—in this case, waves of air pressure. A smooth curve would represent a pure tone, such as that produced by a tuning fork. Most sounds, however, are complex. For example, the wave shown here is for middle C played on a piano. The sound wave for the same note played on a violin would have the same wavelength (or frequency) as this one, but the "wrinkles" in the wave would be different, corresponding to the differences in timbre between the two sounds. (b) The table shows the main relationships between objective aspects of sound and subjective perceptions.

Like light waves, sound waves are characterized by their amplitude, their *wavelength*, and their *purity* (see Figure 4.33). The physical properties of amplitude, wavelength, and purity affect mainly the perceived (psychological) qualities of loudness, pitch, and timbre, respectively. However, the physical properties of sound interact in complex ways to produce perceptions of these sound qualities (Hirsh & Watson, 1996).

Human Hearing Capacities

Wavelengths of sound are described in terms of their *frequency,* which is measured in cycles per second, or *hertz (Hz).* For the most part, higher frequencies are perceived as having higher pitch. That is, if you strike the key for high C on a piano, it will produce higher-frequency sound waves than the key for low C. Although the perception of pitch depends mainly on frequency, the amplitude of the sound waves also influences it.

Just as the visible spectrum is only a portion of the total spectrum of light, so, too, what people can hear is only a portion of the available range of sounds. Humans can hear sounds ranging from a low of 20 Hz up to a high of about 20 000 Hz. Sounds at either end of this range are harder to hear, and sensitivity to high-frequency tones declines as adults grow older (Dubno, 2010). Other organisms have different capabilities. Low-frequency sounds under 10 Hz are audible to homing pigeons, for example. At the other extreme, bats and porpoises can hear frequencies well above 20 000 Hz.

In general, the greater the amplitude of sound waves, the louder the sound perceived. Whereas frequency is measured in hertz, amplitude is measured in *decibels (dB).* The relationship between decibels (which measure a physical property of sound) and loudness (a psychological quality) is very complex. A rough rule of thumb is that perceived loudness doubles about every 6–10 decibels (Florentine & Heinz, 2010).

Very loud sounds can have negative effects on the quality of your hearing. Even brief exposure to sounds over 120 decibels can be painful and may cause damage to your auditory system. In recent years, there has been great concern about hearing loss in young people using personal listening devices who play their music too loudly (Punch, Elfenbein, & James, 2011). Portable music players can easily deliver over 100 decibels through headphones. One study found significant hearing impairment in 14 percent of the young people sampled (Peng, Tao, & Huang, 2007). Unfortunately, adolescents tend not to worry much about the risk of hearing loss (Vogel et al., 2008). However, it is a serious problem that is likely to lead to a great deal of preventable hearing loss given the increased popularity of portable music players (Muchnik et al., 2012). Statistics Canada (2013) reports that almost 90 percent of Canadians 15 to 24 years of age listen to their downloaded music on a regular basis. Health Canada has outlined a series of recommendations that people should follow in order to minimize potential damage when listening to personal portable music devices. These include lowering the volume, reducing background noise, and limiting the time that you use the devices (Health Canada, 2010).

As shown in Figure 4.34, the absolute thresholds for the weakest sounds people can hear differ for sounds of various frequencies. The human ear is most sensitive to sounds at frequencies near 2000 Hz. That is, these frequencies yield the lowest absolute thresholds. To summarize, amplitude is the principal determinant of loudness, but loudness ultimately depends on an interaction between amplitude and frequency.

People are also sensitive to variations in the purity of sounds. The purest sound is one that has only a single frequency of vibration, such as that produced by a tuning fork. Most everyday sounds are complex mixtures of many frequencies. The purity or complexity of a sound influences how *timbre* is perceived. To understand timbre, think of a note with precisely the same loudness and pitch played on a French horn and then on a violin. The difference you perceive in the sounds is a difference in timbre.

Sensory Processing in the Ear

Like your eyes, your ears channel energy to the neural tissue that receives it. Figure 4.35 shows that the human ear can be divided into three sections: the external ear, the middle ear, and the inner ear. Sound is conducted differently in each section. The external ear depends on the *vibration of air molecules.* The middle ear depends on the *vibration of movable bones.* And the inner ear depends on *waves in a fluid,* which are finally converted into a stream of neural signals sent to the brain (Hackney, 2010; Kaas, O'Brien, & Hackett, 2013).

The *external ear* consists mainly of the *pinna,* a sound-collecting cone. When you cup your hand behind your ear to try to hear better, you are augmenting that cone. Many animals have large external ears that they can aim directly toward a sound source. However, humans can adjust their aim only crudely, by turning their heads. Sound waves collected by the pinna are funnelled along the auditory canal toward the *eardrum,* a taut membrane that vibrates in response.

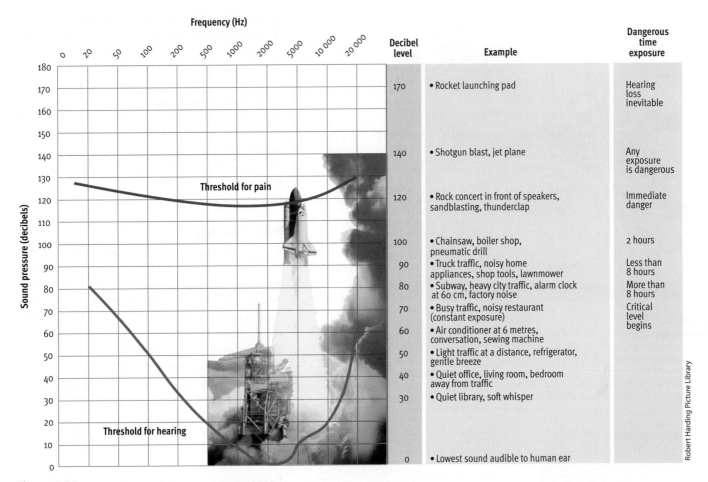

Figure 4.34

Sound pressure and auditory experience. The threshold for human hearing (graphed in green) is a function of both sound pressure (decibel level) and frequency. Human hearing is keenest for sounds at a frequency of about 2000 Hz; at other frequencies, higher decibel levels are needed to produce sounds people can detect. On the other hand, the human threshold for pain (graphed in red) is almost purely a function of decibel level. Some common sounds corresponding to various decibel levels are listed to the right of the graph, together with the amount of time at which exposure to higher levels becomes dangerous.

Source: Decibel level examples from Atkinson, R.L., Atkinson, R.C., Smith, E.F., and Hilgard, E.R. (1987). *Introduction to psychology.* San Diego: Harcourt. Reprinted by permission of Wadsworth Publishing.

In the *middle ear,* the vibrations of the eardrum are transmitted inward by a mechanical chain made up of the three tiniest bones in your body (the hammer, anvil, and stirrup), known collectively as the *ossicles.* The ossicles form a three-stage lever system that converts relatively large movements with little force into smaller motions with greater force. The ossicles serve to amplify tiny changes in air pressure.

The *inner ear* consists largely of the *cochlea,* a fluid-filled, coiled tunnel that contains the receptors for hearing. The term *cochlea* comes from the Greek word for a spiral-shelled snail, which this chamber resembles (see Figure 4.36). Sound enters the cochlea through the *oval window,* which is vibrated by the ossicles. The ear's neural tissue, analogous to the retina in the eye, lies within the cochlea. This tissue sits on the basilar membrane that divides the cochlea into upper and lower

chambers. The *basilar membrane,* which runs the length of the spiralled cochlea, holds the auditory receptors. The auditory receptors are called *hair cells* because of the tiny bundles of hairs that protrude from them. Waves in the fluid of the inner ear stimulate the hair cells. Like the rods and cones in the eye, the hair cells convert this physical stimulation into neural impulses that are sent to the brain (Hackett & Kaas, 2009).

These signals are routed through the thalamus to the auditory cortex, which is located mostly in the temporal lobes of the brain. Studies demonstrate that the auditory cortex has specialized cells—similar to the feature detectors found in the visual cortex—that have special sensitivity to certain features of sound (Pickles, 1988). Evidence also suggests that the parallel processing of input seen in the visual system also occurs in the auditory pathways (Rouiller, 1997).

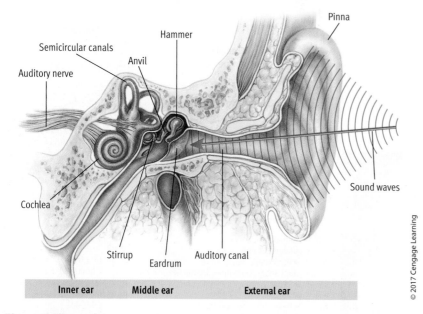

Figure 4.35
The human ear. Converting sound pressure into information processed by the nervous system involves a complex relay of stimuli. Waves of air pressure create vibrations in the eardrum, which in turn cause oscillations in the tiny bones in the inner ear (the hammer, anvil, and stirrup). As they are relayed from one bone to the next, the oscillations are magnified and then transformed into pressure waves moving through a liquid medium in the cochlea. These waves cause the basilar membrane to oscillate, stimulating the hair cells that are the actual auditory receptors (see Figure 4.36).

© 2017 Cengage Learning

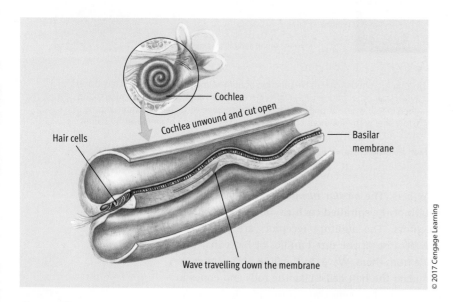

Figure 4.36
The basilar membrane. This graphic shows how the cochlea might look if it were unwound and cut open to reveal the basilar membrane, which is covered with thousands of hair cells (the auditory receptors). Pressure waves in the fluid filling the cochlea cause oscillations to travel in waves down the basilar membrane, stimulating the hair cells to fire. Although the entire membrane vibrates, as predicted by frequency theory, the point along the membrane where the wave peaks depends on the frequency of the sound stimulus, as suggested by place theory.

© 2017 Cengage Learning

Auditory Perception: Theories of Hearing

Theories of hearing need to account for how sound waves are physiologically translated into the perceptions of pitch, loudness, and timbre. To date, most of

the theorizing about hearing has focused on the perception of pitch, which is reasonably well understood. Researchers' understanding of loudness and timbre perception is primitive by comparison. Hence, we'll limit our coverage to theories of pitch perception.

Two theories have dominated the debate on pitch perception: *place theory* and *frequency theory*. You'll be able to follow the development of these theories more easily if you can imagine the spiralled cochlea unravelled, so that the basilar membrane becomes a long, thin sheet, lined with about 25 000 individual hair cells (see Figure 4.36).

Place Theory

Long ago, Hermann von Helmholtz (1863) proposed that specific sound frequencies vibrate specific portions of the basilar membrane, producing distinct pitches, just as plucking specific strings on a harp produces sounds of varied pitch. This model, called *place theory*, **holds that perception of pitch corresponds to the vibration of different portions, or places, along the basilar membrane.** Place theory assumes that hair cells at various locations respond independently and that different sets of hair cells are vibrated by different sound frequencies. The brain then detects the frequency of a tone according to which area along the basilar membrane is most active.

Frequency Theory

Other theorists in the 19th century proposed an alternative theory of pitch perception, called *frequency theory* (Rutherford, 1886). *Frequency theory* **holds that perception of pitch corresponds to the rate, or frequency, at which the entire basilar membrane vibrates.** This theory views the basilar membrane as more like a drumhead than a harp. According to frequency theory, the whole membrane vibrates in unison in response to sounds. However, a particular sound frequency, say 3000 Hz, causes the basilar membrane to vibrate at a corresponding rate of 3000 times per second. The brain detects the frequency of a tone by the rate at which the auditory nerve fibres fire.

Reconciling Place and Frequency Theories

The competition between these two theories is similar to the dispute between the trichromatic and opponent process theories of colour vision. In the end, both theories of pitch perception proved to have some flaws, but both turned out to be valid in part. Place theory was basically on the mark except for one detail. The hair cells along the basilar membrane are not independent. They vibrate together, as suggested by frequency theory. The pattern of vibration is a travelling wave that moves along the basilar membrane. Place theory is correct, however, in that the wave peaks at a particular place, depending on the frequency of the sound wave. In sum, the current thinking is that pitch perception depends on both place and frequency coding of vibrations along the basilar membrane (Moore, 2010; Yost, 2010). Although much remains to be learned, once again we find that theories that were pitted against each other for decades are complementary rather than contradictory.

Auditory Localization: Perceiving Sources of Sound

You're driving down a street when suddenly you hear a siren wailing in the distance. As the wail grows louder, you glance around, cocking your ear to the sound. Where is it coming from? Behind you? In front of you? From one side? This example illustrates a common perceptual task called *auditory localization*—locating the source of a sound in space. The process of recognizing where a sound is coming from is analogous to recognizing depth or distance in vision. Both processes involve spatial aspects of sensory input. The fact that human ears are set *apart* contributes to auditory localization, just as the separation of the eyes contributes to depth perception.

Many features of sounds can contribute to auditory localization, but two cues are particularly important: the intensity (loudness) and the timing of sounds arriving at each ear (Yost, 2000). For example, a sound source to one side of the head produces a greater intensity at the ear nearer to the sound. This difference is due partly to the loss of sound intensity with extra distance. Another factor at work is the "shadow," or partial sound barrier, cast by the head itself (see Figure 4.37). The intensity difference between the two ears is greatest when the sound source is well to one side. The human

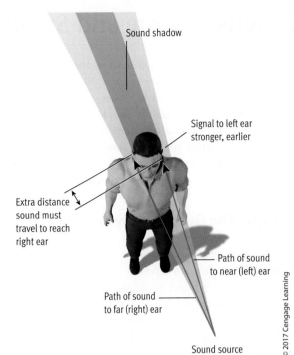

Figure 4.37
Cues in auditory localization. A sound coming from the left reaches the left ear sooner than the right. When the sound reaches the right ear, it is also less intense because it has travelled a greater distance and because it is in the sound shadow produced by the listener's head. These cues are used to localize the sources of sound in space.

perceptual system uses this difference as a clue in localizing sounds. Furthermore, because the path to the farther ear is longer, a sound takes longer to reach that ear. This fact means that sounds can be localized by comparing the timing of their arrival at each ear. Such comparison of the timing of sounds is remarkably sensitive. Evidence suggests that people depend primarily on timing differences to localize low-frequency sounds, and on intensity differences to localize high-frequency sounds (Yost, 2013).

Hermann von Helmholtz

"The psychic activities, by which we arrive at the judgment that a certain object of a certain character exists before us at a certain place, are generally not conscious activities but unconscious ones…. It may be permissible to designate the psychic acts of ordinary perception as unconscious inferences."

concept **check** 4.3

Comparing Vision and Hearing

Check your understanding of both vision and audition by comparing key aspects of sensation and perception in these senses. The dimensions of comparison are listed in the first column below. The second column lists the answers for the sense of vision. Fill in the answers for the sense of hearing in the third column. The answers can be found in Appendix A near the back of the book.

Dimension	Vision	Hearing
1. Stimulus	*Light waves*	_____
2. Elements of stimulus and related perceptions	*Wavelength/hue amplitude/ brightness purity/saturation*	_____
3. Receptors	*Rods and cones*	_____
4. Location of receptors	*Retina*	_____
5. Main location of processing in brain	*Occipital lobe/visual cortex*	_____
6. Spatial aspect of perception	*Depth perception*	_____

Our Chemical Senses: Taste and Smell

Psychologists have devoted most of their attention to the visual and auditory systems. Although less is known about the chemical senses, taste and smell also play a critical role in people's experience of the world. Let's take a brief look at what psychologists have learned about the *gustatory system*—the sensory system for taste—and its close cousin, the *olfactory system*—the sensory system for smell.

Taste: The Gustatory System

True wine lovers go through an elaborate series of steps when they are served a good bottle of wine. Typically, they begin by drinking a little water to cleanse their palate. Then they sniff the cork from the wine bottle, swirl a small amount of the wine around in a glass, and sniff the odour emerging from the glass. Finally, they take a sip of the wine, rolling it around in the mouth for a short time before swallowing it. At last they are ready to confer their approval or disapproval. Is all this activity really a meaningful way to put the wine to a sensitive test? Or is it just a harmless ritual passed on through tradition? You'll find out in this section.

The physical stimuli for the sense of taste are chemical substances that are soluble (dissolvable in water). The gustatory receptors are clusters of taste cells found in the *taste buds* that line the trenches around tiny bumps on the tongue (see Figure 4.38). When these cells absorb chemicals dissolved in saliva, they trigger neural impulses that are routed through the thalamus to the cortex. Interestingly, taste cells have a short life, spanning only about ten days, and they are constantly being replaced (Cowart, 2005). New cells are born at the edge of the taste bud and migrate inward to die at the centre.

It's generally agreed that there are four *primary tastes:* sweet, sour, bitter, and salty (Buck, 2000). However, scientists are suggesting we add a fifth primary taste called *umami*, which is a Japanese word for the savoury taste of glutamate found in foods like meats and cheeses (DuBois, 2010; Singh, Hummel, Gerber, & Landis, 2015). The case of umami as a fifth basic taste has been strengthened by recent evidence that umami substances activate specific receptors on the tongue (Di Lorenzo & Rosen, 2010). Sensitivity to the primary tastes is distributed somewhat unevenly across the tongue, but the variations in sensitivity are quite small and highly complicated (Bartoshuk, 1993b; see Figure 4.38). Perceptions of taste quality appear to depend on complex *patterns* of neural activity initiated by taste receptors (Erickson, Di

Linda Bartoshuk

"Good and bad are so intimately associated with taste and smell that we have special words for the experiences (e.g., repugnant, foul). The immediacy of the pleasure makes it seem absolute and thus inborn. This turns out to be true for taste but not for smell."

Courtesy of Linda Bartoshuk

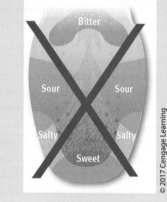
Lorenzo, & Woodbury, 1994). Taste signals are routed through the thalamus and onto the *insular cortex* in the frontal lobe, where the initial cortical processing takes place (Di Lorenzo & Rosen, 2010).

Some basic taste preferences appear to be innate and to be automatically regulated by physiological mechanisms, but taste preferences are largely learned and heavily influenced by social processes (Rozin, 1990). This extensive social influence contributes greatly to the striking ethnic and cultural disparities found in taste preferences (Kittler & Sucher, 2008). Foods that are a source of disgust in Western cultures—such as worms, fish eyes, and blood—may be delicacies in other cultures (see Figure 4.39).

Research by Linda Bartoshuk and others reveals that people vary considerably in their sensitivity to certain tastes (Bartoshuk, 1993a; Rawal et al., 2013). People characterized as *nontasters*, as determined by their insensitivity to PTC (phenythiocarbamide), or its close relative PROP (propylthiouracil), tend to have about one-quarter as many taste buds per square centimetre as people at the other end

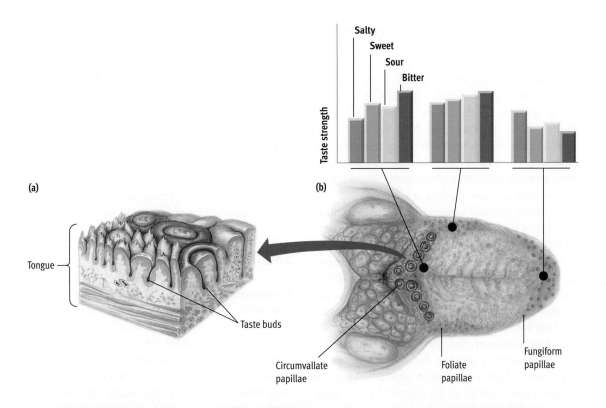

Salty
Sweet
Sour
Bitter

Taste strength

(a)

(b)

Tongue

Taste buds

Circumvallate
papillae

Foliate
papillae

Fungiform
papillae

Figure 4.38
The tongue and taste. (a) Taste buds line the trenches around tiny bumps on the tongue called *papillae*. There are three types of papillae, which are distributed on the tongue as shown in (b). The taste buds found in each type of papillae show slightly different sensitivities to the four basic tastes, as mapped out in the graph at the top. Thus, sensitivity to the primary tastes varies across the tongue, but these variations are small, and all four primary tastes can be detected wherever there are taste receptors. (Data adapted from Bartoshuk, 1993a)

Source: Adapted from Bartoshuk, L. M. (1993). Genetic and pathological taste variation: What can we learn from animal models and human disease? In D. Chadwick, J. Marsh, & J. Goode (Eds.), *The molecular basis of smell and taste transduction* (pp. 251–267). New York: Wiley. / © 2017 Cengage Learning

GordonImages/Thinkstock

Grubs. For most North Americans, the thought of eating a worm would be totally unthinkable. For the Asmat of New Guinea, however, a favourite delicacy is the plump, white, 5-cm larva or beetle grub.

© Guy Mary-Rousseliere/Catholic Mission, Northwest Territories, Canada

Fish eyes. For some Inuit children, raw fish eyes are like candy. Here you see a young girl using the Inuit's all-purpose knife to gouge out the eye of an already-filleted Arctic fish.

Daniele Pellegrini/Photo Researchers, Inc.

Blood. Several tribes in East Africa supplement their diet with fresh blood that is sometimes mixed with milk. They obtain the blood by puncturing a cow's jugular vein with a sharp arrow. The blood—milk drink provides a rich source of protein and iron.

Figure 4.39
Culture and taste preferences. Taste preferences are largely learned, and they vary dramatically from one society to the next, as these examples demonstrate.

of the spectrum, who are called *supertasters* (Miller & Reedy, 1990; Pickering, Jain, & Bezawada, 2013). Supertasters also have specialized taste receptors that are not found in nontasters (Bufe et al., 2005). In North America, roughly 25 percent of people are nontasters, another 25 percent are supertasters, and the remaining 50 percent fall between these extremes and are characterized as *medium tasters* (Di Lorenzo & Youngentob, 2003). Supertasters and nontasters respond similarly to many foods, but supertasters are much more sensitive to certain sweet and bitter

substances (Prescott, 2010). These variations in sensitivity mean that when two people taste the same food they will not necessarily have the same sensory experience. In regard to taste, different people live in somewhat different sensory worlds (Breslin, 2010).

These differences in taste sensitivity influence people's eating habits in ways that can have important repercussions for their physical health. For example, supertasters, who experience taste with far greater intensity than average, are less likely to be fond of sweets (Yeomans et al., 2007) and tend to consume fewer high-fat foods, both of which are likely to reduce their risk for cardiovascular disease (Duffy, Lucchina, & Bartoshuk, 2004). Supertasters also tend to react more negatively to alcohol and smoking, which reduces their likelihood of developing drinking problems or nicotine addiction (Duffy, Peterson, & Bartoshuk, 2004; Snedecor et al., 2006). The main health disadvantage identified for supertasters thus far is that they respond more negatively to many vegetables, which seems to hold down their vegetable intake (Basson et al., 2005; Dinehart et al., 2006). Overall, however, supertasters tend to have better health habits than nontasters, thanks to their strong reactions to certain tastes (Duffy, 2004).

Women are somewhat more likely to be supertasters than men (Bartoshuk, Duffy, & Miller, 1994). Some psychologists speculate that the gender gap in this trait may have evolutionary significance. Over the course of evolution, women have generally been more involved than men in feeding children. Increased reactivity to sweet and bitter tastes would have been adaptive in that it would have made women more sensitive to the relatively scarce high-caloric foods (which often taste sweet) needed for survival and to the toxic substances (which often taste bitter) that hunters and gatherers needed to avoid.

When you eat, you are constantly mixing food and saliva and moving it about in your mouth, so the stimulus is constantly changing. However, if you place a flavoured substance in a single spot on your tongue, the taste will fade until it vanishes (Krakauer & Dallenbach, 1937). This fading effect is an example of *sensory adaptation*—a gradual decline in sensitivity to prolonged stimulation. Sensory adaptation is not unique to taste. This phenomenon occurs in other senses, as well. In the taste system, sensory adaptation can leave aftereffects. For example, adaptation to a sour solution makes water taste sweet, whereas adaptation to a sweet solution makes water taste bitter.

So far, we've been discussing taste, but what we are really interested in is the *perception of flavour*. Flavour is a combination of taste, smell, and the tactile sensation of food in one's mouth. Odours make a surprisingly great contribution to the perception of flavour (Di Lorenzo & Youngentob, 2013). Although taste and smell are distinct sensory systems, they interact extensively. The ability to identify flavours declines noticeably when odour cues are absent. You might have noticed this interaction when you ate a favourite meal while enduring a severe head cold. The food probably tasted bland, because your stuffy nose impaired your sense of smell.

Now that we've explored the dynamics of taste, we can return to our question about the value of the wine-tasting ritual. This elaborate ritual is indeed an authentic way to put wine to a sensitive test. The aftereffects associated with sensory adaptation make it wise to cleanse one's palate before tasting the wine. Sniffing the cork and sniffing the wine in the glass are important because odour is a major determinant of flavour. Swirling the wine in the glass helps release the wine's odour. And rolling the wine around in your mouth is especially critical, because it distributes the wine over the full diversity of taste cells. It also forces the wine's odour up into the nasal passages. Thus, each action in this age-old ritual makes a meaningful contribution to the tasting.

Smell: The Olfactory System

Humans are usually characterized as being relatively insensitive to smell; often the only thing we can say about an odour is whether it is pleasant or not (Yeshurun & Sobel, 2010). In this regard humans are often compared unfavourably to dogs, which are renowned for their ability to track a faint odour over long distances. Are humans really inferior in the sensory domain of smell? Let's examine the facts.

The olfactory system, the sensory system for smell, resembles the sense of taste in many ways. The physical stimuli are chemical substances—volatile ones that can evaporate and be carried in the air. These chemical stimuli are dissolved in fluid—specifically, the mucus in the nose. The receptors for smell are olfactory cilia, hair-like structures located in the upper portion of the nasal passages (see Figure 4.40). They resemble taste cells in that they have a short life and are constantly being replaced (Buck & Bargmann, 2013). Olfactory receptors have axons that synapse with cells in the olfactory bulb and then are routed directly to the olfactory cortex in the temporal lobe and other areas in the cortex (Scott, 2008). This arrangement is unique. Smell is the only sensory system that is not routed through the thalamus before it projects onto the cortex.

Odours cannot be classified as neatly as tastes, since efforts to identify primary odours have proven unsatisfactory (Doty, 1991). Humans have about 350 different types of olfactory receptors (Buck, 2004). Most olfactory receptors respond to a wide range of odours. Specific odours trigger responses in different *combinations* of receptors (Doty, 2010a). Like the other senses, the sense of smell shows sensory adaptation. The perceived strength of an odour usually fades to less than half its original strength within about four minutes (Cain, 1988).

Humans can distinguish among about 10 000 different odours (Axel, 1995). However, when people are asked to identify the sources of specific odours (such as

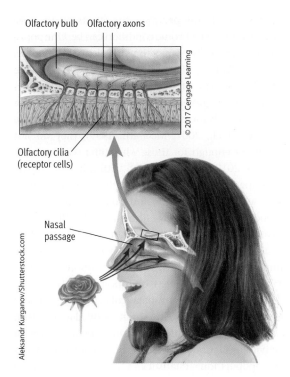

Olfactory bulb   Olfactory axons

Olfactory cilia
(receptor cells)

Nasal
passage

Figure 4.40
The olfactory system.

smoke or soap), their performance is rather mediocre. For some unknown reason, people have a hard time attaching names to odours (Cowart & Rawson, 2001).

The sense of smell is also involved as an important mechanism of communication for some animals. **Pheromones are chemical messages, typically** imperceptible, that can be sent by one organism and received by another member of the same species. As originally defined by Karlson & Luscher (1959), they were considered to be species-specific, composed of a single chemical, and had specific effects on the organisms that received them. In the literature they are often linked to sexual activity and physical attraction in many species (Kohl et al., 2003). Their relevance to human activity is still debated (e.g., Doty, 2010b, 2010c; Simard, 2014).

So, then, how *do* human olfactory capacities compare to other species? We do have notably fewer olfactory receptors than many other animals (Wolfe et al., 2006). Evolutionary processes have helped to shape our perceptual systems (Hoffman, 2016; Pazzoglia, 2015) and our relative paucity of olfactory receptors may reflect evolutionary trends that gradually allocated more and more of the brain to colour vision (Gilad et al., 2004). However, recent studies have found that humans and monkeys, when compared to other mammals, have a better sense of smell than previously thought (Laska, Seibt, & Weber, 2000; Shepherd, 2004). For example, one innovative study (Porter et al., 2007) that asked humans to get on their hands and knees to track the scent of chocolate oil that had been dribbled through a field, found that the subjects performed quite well and that their patterns of tracking mimicked those of dogs. Gordon Shepherd (2004) offers several possible explanations for our surprising olfactory capabilities, including the fact that "humans smell with bigger and better brains" (p. 0574).

Our Sense of Touch: Sensory Systems in the Skin

If there is any sense that people trust almost as much as sight, it is the sense of touch. Yet, like all the senses, touch involves converting the sensation of physical stimuli into a psychological experience, and as such, it can be influenced by a variety of psychological factors (e.g., McCabe et al., 2008)—and it can be fooled.

The physical stimuli for touch are mechanical, thermal, and chemical energy that impinge on the skin. These stimuli can produce perceptions of tactile stimulation (the pressure of touch against the skin), warmth, cold, and pain. The human skin is saturated with at least six types of sensory receptors. To some degree, these different types of receptors are specialized for different functions, such as the registration of pressure, heat, cold, and so forth. However, these distinctions are not as clear as researchers had originally expected (Sinclair, 1981).

Feeling Pressure

If you've been to a mosquito-infested picnic, you'll appreciate the need to quickly know where tactile stimulation is coming from. The sense of touch is set up to meet this need for tactile localization with admirable precision and efficiency. Cells in the nervous system that respond to touch are sensitive to specific patches of skin. These skin patches, which vary considerably in size, are the functional equivalents of *receptive fields* in vision. Like visual receptive fields, they often involve a centre-surround arrangement (see Figure 4.41). Thus, stimuli falling in the centre produce the opposite effect of stimuli falling in the surrounding area (Kandel & Jessell, 1991). If a stimulus is applied continuously to a specific spot on the skin, the perception of pressure gradually fades. Hence, sensory adaptation occurs

Key Learning Goal

▶ Describe the stimulus and receptors for touch, and explain what is known about pain perception.

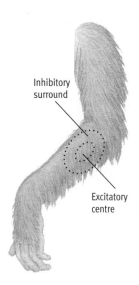

Figure 4.41
Receptive field for touch. A receptive field for touch is an area on the skin surface that, when stimulated, affects the firing of a cell that responds to pressure on the skin. Shown here is a centre-surround receptive field for a cell in the thalamus of a monkey.

Inhibitory surround

Excitatory centre

in the perception of touch, as it does in other sensory systems.

The nerve fibres that carry incoming information about tactile stimulation are routed through the spinal cord to the brainstem. There, the fibres from each side of the body cross over, mostly to the opposite side of the brain. The tactile pathway then projects through the thalamus and onto the *somatosensory cortex* in the brain's parietal lobe. Some cells in the somatosensory cortex function like the *feature detectors* discovered in vision (Gardner & Kandel, 2000). They respond to specific features of touch, such as a movement across the skin in a particular direction.

Feeling Pain

As unpleasant as pain is, the sensation of pain is crucial to survival. Pain is a marvellous warning system. It tells people when they should stop shovelling snow, or it lets them know that they have a pinched nerve that requires treatment (Jensen & Turk, 2014). However, chronic pain is a frustrating, demoralizing affliction (Ehde, Dillworth, & Turner, 2014; Page et al., 2013) that affects millions of people and is a major factor in lost productivity (Gatchel & Maddrey, 2004; Turk, 1994). For example, all you have to do is to talk with any of your friends who suffer recurrent migraines to

get a sense of how pervasive the effects of this very painful and often chronic condition can be. One population-based study of migraine prevalence by Statistics Canada (Ramage-Morin & Gilmour, 2014) revealed that 8.3 percent of Canadians (2.7 million people) have been diagnosed with migraines. Although some treatment advances have been made in this area (DaSilva et al., 2007; McGrath, 1999), they do not come fast enough for those who suffer (Gladstone & Cooper, 2010). People afflicted with migraines report suffering from depression and other negative effects such as sleep disturbance, and trouble with work and school (Ramage-Morin & Gilmour, 2014). While some treatments are physiological, Canada Research Chair Patrick McGrath and his colleagues also emphasize the importance of psychological interventions (Huguet, McGrath, Stinson, Tougas, & Doucette, 2014).

According to recent data collected by Statistics Canada (Gilmour, 2015), limitations due to pain, especially chronic pain, are the most frequent type of activity limitation reported in the Canadian working-age population (Statistics Canada, 2001), with 6 million Canadians reporting that they suffer from chronic pain (Gilmour, 2015). It has been estimated that chronic pain costs the Canadian economy more than $10 billion annually because of medical expenses, lost income, and lost productivity (Jackson, 2007). Pain can be problematic across the life span (Molton & Terrill, 2014; Palermo, Valrie, & Karlson, 2014). Thus, there are pressing practical reasons for psychologists' keen interest in the perception of pain, particularly chronic pain (e.g., Katz, Rosenbloom, & Fashler, 2016).

Pathways to the Brain

The receptors for pain are mostly free nerve endings in the skin. Pain messages are transmitted to the brain via two types of pathways that pass through different areas in the thalamus (Cholewiak & Cholewiak, 2010). One is a *fast pathway* that registers localized pain and relays it to the cortex in a fraction of a second. This is the system that hits you with sharp pain when you first cut your finger. The second system uses a *slow pathway* that lags a second or two behind the fast system. This pathway (which also carries information about temperature) conveys the less localized, longer-lasting, aching or burning pain that comes after the initial injury. The slow pathway depends on thin, unmyelinated neurons called *C fibres*, whereas the fast pathway is mediated by thicker, myelinated neurons called *A-delta fibres* (see Figure 4.42). Pain signals may be sent to many areas in the cortex, as well as to subcortical centres associated with emotion (such as the hypothalamus and amygdala), depending in part on the nature of the pain (Hung & Mantyh, 2001).

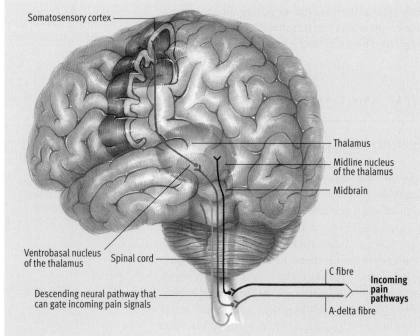

Somatosensory cortex

Thalamus
Midline nucleus of the thalamus
Midbrain

Ventrobasal nucleus of the thalamus
Spinal cord

Descending neural pathway that can gate incoming pain signals

C fibre
Incoming pain pathways
A-delta fibre

© 2017 Cengage Learning

Figure 4.42
Pathways for pain signals. Pain signals are sent inward from receptors to the brain along the two ascending pathways depicted here in red and black. The fast pathway, shown in red, and the slow pathway, shown in black, depend on different types of nerve fibres and are routed through different parts of the thalamus. The gate-control mechanism hypothesized by Melzack and Wall (1965) apparently depends on signals in a descending pathway (shown in green) that originates in an area of the midbrain.

Puzzles in Pain Perception

As with other perceptions, pain is not an automatic result of certain types of stimulation. The perception of pain can be influenced greatly by expectations, personality, mood, and other factors involving higher mental processes (Rollman, 1992; Stalling, 1992; Turk & Okifuji, 2003). The subjective nature of pain is illustrated by placebo effects. As we saw in Chapter 2, many people suffering from pain report relief when given a placebo—an inert "sugar pill" that is presented to them as if it were a painkilling drug (Benedetti, 2008; Stewart-Williams, 2004). Evidence regarding the subjective quality of pain has come from studies that have found ethnic and cultural differences in the pain associated with childbirth (Jordan, 1983) and the experience of chronic pain (Bates, Edwards, & Anderson, 1993). According to Melzack and Wall (1982), culture does not affect the process of pain perception so much as the willingness to tolerate certain types of pain, a conclusion echoed by Zatzick and Dimsdale (1990).

Several recent studies have also highlighted how contextual factors influence the experience of pain. For example, one recent study found that the experience of pain was reduced when female participants looked at a picture of their boyfriend or held their boyfriend's hand (Master et al., 2009). In a similar vein, another study found that looking at pleasant pictures reduced subjects' pain responses, while looking at unpleasant pictures led to stronger pain reactions (Roy et al., 2009). And a study by Gray and Wegner (2008) demonstrated that pain responses increase when participants believe that the pain was inflicted upon them intentionally, rather than accidentally.

The psychological element in pain perception becomes clear when something distracts your attention from pain and the hurting temporarily disappears. For example, imagine that you've just hit your thumb with a hammer and it's throbbing with pain. Suddenly, your child cries out that there's a fire in the laundry room. As you race to deal with this emergency, you forget all about the pain in your thumb. Of course, psychological factors also can work in the reverse. As pain researcher Joel Katz and his colleagues (Asmundson & Katz, 2009; Bilanovic et al., 2013; Page et al., 2013) have shown, as the number of concerns and intrusive thoughts that patients experience about an upcoming surgery increases, so does the amount of pain medication they request after surgery, even if the amount of actual pain is controlled (Katz, Buis, & Cohen, 2008). Theories of pain clearly must include some explanation of such psychological effects on pain perception (Katz & Fashler, 2015; Katz & Seltzer, 2009), as well as accounting for the effects of psychological interventions on the experience of pain (Flor, 2014; Jensen & Patterson, 2014; McCracken &

FEATURED STUDY

Experiencing pain in the presence of others: A structured experimental investigation of older adults.

Description
This study by Gallant and Hadjistravropoulos examines the effects of social support on the experience of pain by the elderly.

Investigators
Gallant, N., & Hadjistavropoulos, T. (2017). *Journal of Pain, 18*(4), 456–467.

Vowles, 2014). These types of psychological factors in the experience of pain are explored in our Featured Study for this chapter by University of Regina scientists Natasha Gallant and Thomas Hadjistravropoulos (Gallant & Hadjistravropoulos, 2017).

If being told about a fire leads you to forget about your painful thumb, then tissue damage that sends pain impulses on their way to the brain doesn't necessarily result in the experience of pain. Cognitive and emotional processes that unfold in higher brain centres can somehow block pain signals coming from peripheral receptors. Thus, any useful explanation of pain perception must be able to answer a critical question: How does the central nervous system block incoming pain signals?

In an influential effort to answer this question, McGill University psychologists Ronald Melzack and Patrick Wall (1965) devised the gate-control theory of pain. *Gate-control theory* holds that **incoming pain sensations must pass through a "gate" in the spinal cord that can be closed, thus blocking ascending pain signals.** The gate in this model is not an anatomical structure but a pattern of neural activity that inhibits incoming pain signals. Melzack and Wall suggested that this imaginary gate can be closed by signals from peripheral receptors or by signals from the brain. They theorized that the latter mechanism can help explain how factors such as attention and expectations can shut off pain signals. The measurement of pain is an important issue in this area and according to University of Regina psychologist Thomas Hadjistavropoulos (2016) and others (Lichtner et al., 2016), pain in certain populations (such as the very young and the elderly) with communication limitations can be particularly difficult to assess (Hadjistavropoulos, 2016).

Melzack, winner of the American Psychological Association Grawemeyer Award (APA, 2010), has continued his research on pain and is well known for his development of the *McGill Pain Questionnaire*, which is one of the most important tools for research on pain (Melzack, 1975). Most recently, along with York University pain researcher Joel Katz (Katz & Fashler,

concept **check** 4.4

Comparing Taste, Smell, and Touch

Check your understanding of taste, smell, and touch by comparing these sensory systems on the dimensions listed in the first column below. A few answers are supplied; see whether you can fill in the rest. The answers can be found in Appendix A.

Dimension	Taste	Smell	Touch
1. Stimulus	_____	_____	_____
2. Receptors	_____	_____	*Many (at least 6) types*
3. Location of receptors	_____	_____	_____
4. Basic elements of perception	*Sweet, sour, salty, bitter*	_____	_____

2015), Melzack has examined the puzzle of phantom-limb pain, in which patients continue to "feel" the missing limb, including pain in the nonexistent limb (Melzack & Katz, 2004). Melzack's (2001) neuromatrix theory of pain suggests that pain is a multidimensional phenomenon, produced by many influences.

As a whole, research suggests that the concept of a gating mechanism for pain has merit (Craig & Rollman, 1999). However, relatively little support has been found for the neural circuitry originally hypothesized by Melzack and Wall in the 1960s. Other neural mechanisms, discovered after gate-control theory was proposed, appear to be implicated in the experience of pain.

One of these discoveries was the identification of endorphins. As discussed in Chapter 3, endorphins are the body's own natural morphine-like painkillers, which are widely distributed in the central nervous system (Millecamps et al., 2013). For example, placebo effects in the treatment of pain often (but not always) depend on the action of endorphins (Eippert et al., 2009). One study showed that endorphins play a key role when distractions temporarily reduce the experience of pain (Sprenger et al., 2012). In this study, the pain-relieving effects of a distraction were reduced by 40 percent when subjects were given a drug that temporarily blocks the activity of endorphins. The other discovery involved the identification of a descending neural pathway that mediates the suppression of pain (Basbaum & Jessell, 2013). This pathway appears to originate in an area of the midbrain (see Figure 4.42). Neural activity in this pathway is probably initiated by endorphins. The circuits in this pathway inhibit the activity of neurons that would normally transmit incoming pain impulses to the brain.

Research also suggests that certain types of glial cells may contribute to the regulation of pain (Millecamps et al., 2013). At least two types of glia in the spinal cord appear to play an important role in the experience of chronic pain (Milligan & Watkins, 2009). The discovery that glia play a role in the human pain system may eventually open up new avenues for treating chronic pain.

Our Other Senses

Preview Question

▶ Identify and distinguish between the functions of the kinesthetic and vestibular systems.

We have discussed the dynamics of sensation and perception in five sensory domains—vision, hearing, taste, smell, and touch. Since it is widely known that humans have five senses, that should wrap up our coverage, right? Wrong! People have still other sensory systems: the kinesthetic system (which monitors positions of the body) and the vestibular system (sense of balance).

The Kinesthetic System

The *kinesthetic system* monitors the positions of the various parts of the body. To some extent, you know where your limbs are because you commanded the muscles that put them there. Nonetheless, the kinesthetic system allows you to double-check these locations. Where are the receptors for your kinesthetic sense? Some reside in the joints, indicating how much they are bending. Others reside within the muscles, registering their tautness, or extension. Most kinesthetic stimulation is transmitted to the brain along the same pathway as tactile stimulation. However, the two types of information are kept separate (Vierck, 1978).

The Vestibular System

When you're jolting along in a bus, the world outside the bus window doesn't seem to jump about as your head bounces up and down. Yet a movie taken with a camera fastened to the bus would show a

Misconception

Humans have just five senses: sight, hearing, taste, smell, and touch.

Reality

In addition to these five senses, humans have other sensory systems. For example, the *kinesthetic system* monitors the positions of the various parts of the body through receptors in the muscles and joints. And the *vestibular system*, which relies on fluid movements in the semicircular canals in the inner ear, provides our sense of balance, or equilibrium.

bouncing world. How are you and the camera different? Unlike the camera, you are equipped with a *vestibular system*, which responds to gravity and keeps you informed of your body's location in space. The vestibular system provides the sense of balance, or equilibrium, compensating for changes in the body's position.

The vestibular system shares space in the inner ear with the auditory system. The *semicircular canals* (consult Figure 4.35 on page 136 once again) make up the largest part of the vestibular system. They look like three

inner tubes joined at the base. Any rotational motion of the head is uniquely represented by a combination of fluid flows in the semicircular canals (Kelly, 1991). These shifts in fluid are detected by hair cells similar to those found along the basilar membrane in the cochlea (Goldberg & Hudspeth, 2000). Your perceptual system integrates the vestibular input about your body's position with information from other senses. After all, you can see where you are and you know where you've instructed your muscles to take you.

This integration of sensory input raises a point that merits emphasis as we close our tour of the human sensory systems. Although we have discussed the various sensory domains separately, it's important to remember that all of the senses send signals to the same brain, where the information is pooled. We have already encountered examples of sensory integration. For example, it's at work when the sight and smell of food influence taste. *Sensory integration is the norm in perceptual experience.* For instance, when you sit around a campfire, you *see* it blazing, you *hear* it crackling, you *smell* it burning, and you feel the *touch* of its warmth. If you cook something over it, you may even *taste* it. Thus, perception involves building a unified model of the world out of integrated input from all of the senses.

Putting It in Perspective: Themes 2, 5, and 7

In this chapter, three of our unifying themes stand out in sharp relief. Let's discuss the value of theoretical diversity first. Contradictory theories about behaviour can be disconcerting and frustrating for theorists, researchers, teachers, and students alike. Yet this chapter provides two dramatic demonstrations of how theoretical diversity can lead to progress in the long run. For decades, the trichromatic and opponent process theories of colour vision and the place and frequency theories of pitch perception were viewed as fundamentally incompatible. As you know, in each case, the evidence eventually revealed that both theories were needed to fully explain the sensory processes that each sought to explain individually. If it hadn't been for these theoretical debates, current understanding of colour vision and pitch perception might be far more primitive, as the understanding of timbre still is.

Our coverage of sensation and perception should also have enhanced your appreciation of why human experience of the world is highly subjective. As ambiguous figures and visual illusions clearly show, there is no one-to-one correspondence between sensory input and perceived experience of the world. Perception is an active process in which people organize and interpret the information received by the

senses. These interpretations are shaped by a host of factors, including the environmental context and perceptual sets. Small wonder, then, that people often perceive the same event in very different ways.

Finally, this chapter provided numerous examples of how cultural factors can shape behaviour—in an area of research where one might expect to find little cultural influence. Most people are not surprised to learn that there are cultural differences in attitudes, values, social behaviour, and development. But perception is widely viewed as a basic, universal process that should be invariant across cultures. In most respects it is, as the similarities among cultural groups in perception far outweigh the differences. Nonetheless, culture has been shown to have a variety of effects on our perceptual experiences. For example, in this chapter we discussed cultural variations in depth perception, susceptibility to illusions, taste preferences, and pain tolerance. Thus, even a fundamental, heavily physiological process such as perception can be modified to some degree by one's cultural background.

The following Personal Application demonstrates the subjectivity of perception once again. It focuses on how painters have learned to use the principles of visual perception to achieve a variety of artistic goals.

Key Learning Goal

▶ Identify the three unifying themes that were highlighted in this chapter.

An Illustrated Overview of Five Major Senses

SENSE	STIMULUS	ELEMENTS OF THE STIMULUS

The Visual System: SIGHT

Light is electromagnetic radiation that travels in waves. Humans can register only a slim portion of the total range of wavelengths, from 400 to 700 nanometres.

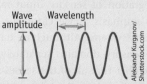

Wave amplitude — Wavelength

Aleksandr Kurganov/Shutterstock.com

© houfaard malan/IStock-photo.com

Light waves vary in *amplitude*, *wavelength*, and *purity*, which influence perceptions as shown below.

Physical properties	Related perceptions
Wavelength	Hue (colour)
Amplitude	Brightness
Purity	Saturation

The Auditory System: HEARING

Sound waves are vibrations of molecules, which means that they must travel through some physical medium, such as air. Humans can hear wavelengths between 20 and 20 000 Hz.

Andreas Gradin/Shutterstock.com

Wavelength — Amplitude

© 2017 Cengage Learning

Sound waves vary in *amplitude*, *wavelength*, and *purity*, which influence perceptions, as shown below.

Physical properties	Related perceptions
Amplitude	Loudness
Frequency	Pitch
Purity	Timbre

The Gustatory System: TASTE

The stimuli for taste generally are chemical substances that are soluble (dissolvable in water). These stimuli are dissolved in the mouth's saliva.

AAGAMIA/Getty Images

It is generally, but not universally, agreed that there are four primary tastes: *sweet*, *sour*, *bitter*, and *salty*.

Many researchers have recently added *umami* to the list of primary tastes. *Umami* is a Japanese word for the savoury taste of glutamates.

The Olfactory System: SMELL

Peter Cade/Iconica/Getty Images

The stimuli are volatile chemical substances that can evaporate and be carried in the air. These chemical stimuli are dissolved in the mucus of the nose.

Efforts to identify primary odours have proven unsatisfactory. If primary odours exist, there must be a great many of them.

The Tactile System: TOUCH

Yanik Chauvin/Shutterstock.com

The stimuli are mechanical, thermal, and chemical energy that impinge on the skin.

Receptors in the skin can register *pressure*, *warmth*, *cold*, and *pain*.

NATURE AND LOCATION OF RECEPTORS

The *retina*, which is neural tissue lining the inside back surface of the eye, contains millions of receptor cells called *rods* and *cones*. Rods play a key role in night and peripheral vision; cones play a key role in daylight and colour vision.

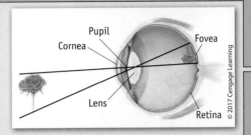

© 2017 Cengage Learning

The receptors for hearing are tiny *hair cells* that line the *basilar membrane* that runs the length of the *cochlea*, a fluid-filled, coiled tunnel in the inner ear.

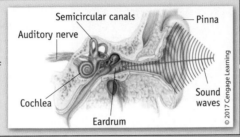

© 2017 Cengage Learning

The gustatory receptors are clusters of *taste cells* found in the *taste buds* that line the trenches around tiny bumps in the tongue. Taste cells have a short life span (about 10 days) and are constantly being replaced.

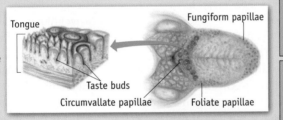

Adapted from Bartoshuk, L. M. (1993). Genetic and pathological taste variation: What can we learn from animal models and human disease? In D. Chadwick, J. Marsh, & J. Goode (Eds.), *The molecular basis of smell and taste transduction* (pp. 251–267). New York: Wiley. / © 2017 Cengage Learning

The receptors for smell are *olfactory cilia*, hairlike structures in the upper portion of the nasal passages. Like taste cells, they have a short lifespan (about 30–60 days) and are constantly being replaced.

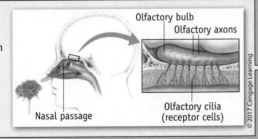

© 2017 Cengage Learning

The human skin is saturated with at least six types of sensory receptors. The four types shown here respond to pressure, whereas *free nerve endings* in the skin respond to pain, warmth, and cold.

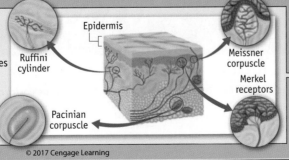

© 2017 Cengage Learning

BRAIN PATHWAYS IN INITIAL PROCESSING

Neural impulses are routed through the *LGN* in the *thalamus* and then distributed to the *primary visual cortex* at the back of the *occipital lobe*.

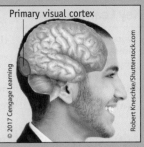

Robert Kneschke/Shutterstock.com

© 2017 Cengage Learning

Neural impulses are routed through the *thalamus* and then sent to the *primary auditory cortex*, which is mostly located in the *temporal lobe*.

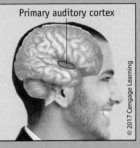

© 2017 Cengage Learning

Neural impulses are routed through the *thalamus* and on to the *insular cortex* in the frontal lobe.

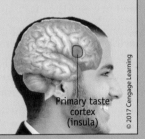

© 2017 Cengage Learning

Neural impulses are routed through the *olfactory bulb* and then sent directly to the *olfactory cortex* in the *temporal lobe* and other cortical areas. Smell is the only sensory input not routed through the thalamus.

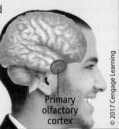

© 2017 Cengage Learning

Neural impulses are routed through the *brainstem* and *thalamus* and on to the *somatosensory cortex* in the *parietal lobe*.

© 2017 Cengage Learning

Sensation and Perception

Appreciating Art and Illusion

Key Learning Goal

▶ Discuss how artists have used various principles of visual perception.

Answer the following multiple-choice question.

Artistic works such as paintings:

___ **(a)** render an accurate picture of reality.

___ **(b)** create an illusion of reality.

___ **(c)** provide an interpretation of reality.

___ **(d)** make us think about the nature of reality.

___ **(e)** do all of the above.

The answer to this question is (e), "all of the above." Historically, artists have had many and varied purposes, including each of those listed in the question (Goldstein, 2001). To realize their goals, artists have had to use a number of principles of perception—sometimes quite deliberately, and sometimes not. Here we'll use the example of painting to explore the role of perceptual principles in art and illusion.

The goal of most early painters was to produce a believable picture of reality. This goal immediately created a problem familiar to most of us who have attempted to draw realistic pictures: The real world is three-dimensional, but a canvas or a sheet of paper is flat. Paradoxically, then, painters who set out to recreate reality had to do so by creating an illusion of three-dimensional reality.

Prior to the Renaissance, these efforts to create a convincing illusion of reality were awkward by modern standards. Why? Because artists did not understand how to use depth cues. This fact is apparent in Figure 4.43, a religious scene painted around 1300. The painting clearly lacks a sense of depth. The people seem paper-thin. They have no real position in space.

Although earlier artists made some use of depth cues, Renaissance artists manipulated the full range of pictorial depth cues, especially linear perspective (Solso, 1994).

Scala/Art Resource, NY

Figure 4.43
Master of the Arrest of Christ (detail, central part) by S. Francesco, Assisi, Italy (circa 1300). Notice how the absence of depth cues makes the painting seem flat and unrealistic.

Figure 4.44 dramatizes the resulting transition in art. This scene, painted by Italian Renaissance artists Gentile and Giovanni Bellini, seems much more realistic and lifelike than the painting in Figure 4.43 because it uses a number of pictorial depth

cues. Notice how the buildings on the sides converge to make use of linear perspective. Additionally, distant objects are smaller than nearby ones, an application of relative size. This painting also uses height in relation to plane, as well as interposition. By taking advantage of pictorial depth cues, an artist can enhance a painting's illusion of reality.

In the centuries since the Renaissance, painters have adopted a number of viewpoints about the portrayal of reality. For instance, the French Impressionists of the 19th century did not want to re-create the photographic "reality" of a scene. They set out to interpret a viewer's fleeting perception or impression of reality. To accomplish this end, they worked with colour in unprecedented ways.

Consider, for instance, the work of Georges Seurat, a French artist who used a technique called *pointillism*. Seurat carefully studied what scientists knew about the composition of colour in the 1880s, and then applied this knowledge in a calculated, laboratory-like manner. Indeed, critics in his era dubbed him the "little chemist." Seurat constructed his paintings out of tiny dots

Scala/Art Resource, NY

Figure 4.44
A painting by the Italian Renaissance artists Gentile and Giovanni Bellini (circa 1480). In this painting a number of depth cues—including linear perspective, relative size, height in plane, and interposition—enhance the illusion of three-dimensional reality.

Figure 4.45
Georges Seurat's *Sunday Afternoon on the Island of La Grande Jatte* (without artist's border) (1884–1886). Seurat used thousands of tiny dots of colour and the principles of colour mixing; the eye and brain combine the points into the colours the viewer actually sees.

Source: Georges Seurat, French, 1859–1891, *Sunday Afternoon on the Island of La Grande Jatte* oil on canvas, 1884–1886, 207.6 X 308 cm, Helen Birch Bartlett Memorial Collection, 1926.224, © 1990 The Art Institute of Chicago. All rights reserved.

Figure 4.46
Salvador Dali's *Mae West's Face which May Be Used as a Surrealist Apartment* (1934–1935).
This painting can be viewed as a room or as the face of the legendary actress.

of pure, intense colours. He used additive colour mixing, a departure from the norm in painting, which usually depends on subtractive mixing of pigments. A famous result of Seurat's "scientific" approach to painting was *Sunday Afternoon on the Island of La Grande Jatte* (see Figure 4.45). As the work of Seurat illustrates, modernist painters were moving away from attempts to re-create the world as it is literally seen.

So too, were the Surrealists, who toyed with reality in a different way. Influenced by Sigmund Freud's writings on the unconscious, the Surrealists explored the world of dreams and fantasy. Specific elements in their paintings are often depicted realistically, but the strange combination of elements yields a disconcerting irrationality reminiscent of dreams. A prominent example of this style is Salvador Dali's *Mae West's Face which May be Used as a Surrealist Apartment*, shown in Figure 4.46. Notice that

this is a reversible figure that can be seen as a face or a room. Dali often used reversible figures to enhance the ambiguity of his surreal visions.

Perhaps no one has been more creative in manipulating perceptual ambiguity than M. C. Escher, a modern Dutch artist. Escher closely followed the work of the Gestalt psychologists, and he readily acknowledged his debt to psychology as a source of inspiration (Teuber, 1974). *Waterfall*, a 1961 lithograph by Escher, is a perplexing drawing that appears to defy the law of gravity (see Figure 4.47). The puzzling problem here is that a level channel of water terminates in a waterfall that "falls" into the same channel two levels "below." You have to look carefully to realize that this structure could not exist in the real world. Escher's goal, which he achieved admirably, was to challenge viewers to think long and hard about the remarkable process of perception.

Figure 4.47
Escher's lithograph *Waterfall* (1961). Escher's clever manipulation of depth cues deceives the brain into seeing water flow uphill.

Recognizing Contrast Effects: It's All Relative

You're sitting at home one night, when the phone rings. It's Simone, an acquaintance from school who needs help with a recreational program for youngsters that she runs for the local park district. She tries to persuade you to volunteer four hours of your time every Friday night throughout the school year to supervise the volleyball program. The thought of giving up your Friday nights and adding this sizable obligation to your already busy schedule makes you cringe with horror. You politely explain to Simone that you can't possibly afford to give up that much time and you won't be able to help her. She accepts your rebuff graciously, but the next night she calls again. This time she wants to know whether you would be willing to supervise volleyball every third Friday. You still feel like it's a big obligation that you really don't want to take on, but the new request seems much more reasonable than the original one. So, with a sigh of resignation, you agree to Simone's request.

What's wrong with this picture? Well, there's nothing wrong with volunteering your time for a good cause, but you just succumbed to a social influence strategy called the *door-in-the-face technique*. The *door-in-the-face technique* involves making a large request that is likely to be turned down as a way to increase the chance that people will agree to a smaller request later (see Figure 4.48). The name for this strategy is derived from the expectation that the initial request will be quickly rejected (hence, the door is slammed in the requester's face). Although they may not be familiar with the strategy's name, many people use this manipulative tactic. For example, a husband who wants to coax his frugal wife into agreeing to buy a $25 000 sports car might begin by proposing that they purchase a $44 000 sports car. By the time the wife talks her husband out of the $44 000 car, the $25 000 price tag may look quite reasonable to her—which is what the husband wanted all along.

Research has demonstrated that the door-in-the-face technique is a highly effective persuasive strategy (Cialdini, 2001, 2007; Pansu, Lima, & Fointait, 2016). One of the reasons it works so well is that it depends on a simple and pervasive perceptual principle. In the domain of perceptual experience, *everything is relative*. This relativity means that people are easily swayed by *contrast effects*. For example, lighting a match or a small candle in a dark room will produce a burst of light that seems quite bright, but if you light the same match or candle in a well-lit room, you may not even detect the additional illumination. The relativity of perception is apparent in the painting by Josef Albers shown in Figure 4.49. The two Xs are exactly the same colour, but the X in the top half looks yellow, whereas the X in the bottom half looks brown. These varied perceptions occur because of contrast effects—the two Xs are contrasted against different background colours.

The same principles of relativity and contrast that operate when we are making judgments about the intensity or colour of visual stimuli also affect the way we make judgments in a wide variety of domains. For example, a 185-cm basketball player, who is really quite tall, can look downright small when surrounded by teammates who are all over 200 cm. And a salary of $40 000 per year for your first full-time job may seem like a princely sum, until a close friend gets an offer of $75 000 per year. The assertion that everything is relative raises the issue of relative to what? *Comparitors* are people, objects, events, and other standards used as a baseline for comparison in making judgments. It is fairly easy to manipulate many types of judgments by selecting *extreme* comparitors that may be unrepresentative.

Figure 4.48
The door-in-the-face technique. The door-in-the-face technique is a frequently used compliance strategy in which you begin with a large request and work down to the smaller request you are really after. It depends in part on contrast effects.

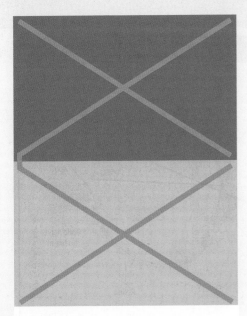

Figure 4.49
Contrast effects in visual perception. This composition by Joseph Albers shows how one colour can be perceived differently when contrasted against different backgrounds. The top X looks yellow and the bottom X looks brown, but they're really the same colour.

Source: Albers, Joseph. *Interaction of color.* Copyright © 1963 and reprinted by permission of the publisher, Yale University Press.

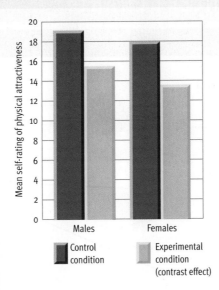

Figure 4.50
Contrast effects in judgments of physical attractiveness. Participants rated their own physical attractiveness under two conditions. In the experimental condition, the ratings occurred after subjects were exposed to a series of photos depicting very attractive models. The resulting contrast effects led to lower self-ratings in this condition. (Data based on Thornton & Moore, 1993)

The influence of extreme comparitors was demonstrated in a couple of interesting studies of judgments of physical attractiveness. In one study, undergraduate males were asked to rate the attractiveness of an average-looking female (who was described as a potential date for another male in the dorm) presented in a photo either just before or just after the participants watched a TV show dominated by strikingly beautiful women (Kenrick & Gutierres, 1980). The female was viewed as less attractive when the ratings were obtained just after the men had seen gorgeous women cavorting on TV as opposed to when they hadn't. In another investigation (Thornton & Moore, 1993), both male and female participants rated *themselves* as less attractive after being exposed to many pictures of extremely attractive models (see Figure 4.50). Thus, contrast effects can influence important social judgments that are likely to affect how people feel about themselves and others.

Anyone who understands how easily judgments can be manipulated by a careful choice of comparitors could influence your thinking. For example, a politician who is caught in some illegal or immoral act could sway public opinion by bringing to mind (perhaps subtly) the fact that many other politicians have committed acts that were much worse. When considered against a backdrop of more extreme comparitors, the politician's transgression will probably seem less offensive. A defence lawyer could use a similar strategy in an attempt to obtain a lighter sentence for a client by comparing the client's offence to much more serious crimes. And a realtor who wants to sell you an expensive house that will require huge mortgage payments will be quick to mention other homeowners who have taken on even larger mortgages.

In summary, critical thinking is facilitated by conscious awareness of the way comparitors can influence, and perhaps distort, a wide range of judgments. In particular, it pays to be vigilant about the possibility that others may manipulate contrast effects in their persuasive efforts. One way to reduce the influence of contrast effects is to consciously consider comparitors that are both worse and better than the event you are judging, as a way of balancing the effects of the two extremes. See Table 4.2.

Table 4.2

Critical Thinking Skills Discussed in This Application

SKILL	DESCRIPTION
Understanding how contrast effects can influence judgments and decisions	The critical thinker appreciates how striking contrasts can be manipulated to influence many types of judgments.
Recognizing when extreme comparitors are being used	The critical thinker is on the lookout for extreme comparitors that distort judgments.

© 2017 Cengage Learning

THE VISUAL SYSTEM

Light waves

vary in		which affect perceptions of
Amplitude	▶	Brightness
Wavelength	▶	Colour (hue)
Purity	▶	Saturation

Light is registered by receptors in the eye

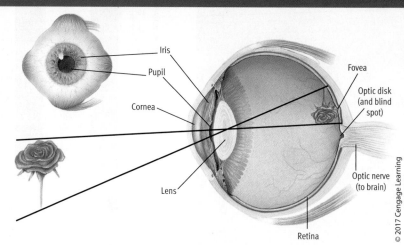
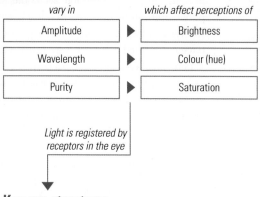

Iris
Pupil
Cornea
Lens
Fovea
Optic disk (and blind spot)
Optic nerve (to brain)
Retina

© 2017 Cengage Learning

Key eye structures

include:

Lens, which focuses light rays falling on the retina

Pupil, which regulates the amount of light passing to the rear of the eye

Retina, which is the neural tissue lining the inside back surface of the eye

Optic disk, which is a hole in the retina that corresponds to the blind spot

Fovea, which is a tiny spot in the centre of the retina where visual acuity is greatest

In the retina

Visual receptors

consist of *rods* and *cones*, which are organized into *receptive fields*.

Rods play a key role in night and peripheral vision and greatly outnumber cones.

Cones play a key role in day and colour vision and provide greater acuity than rods.

Receptive fields are collections of rods and cones that funnel signals to specific visual cells in the retina or the brain.

Visual signals are sent onward to the brain

Visual pathways and processing

Main visual pathway projects through the thalamus, where signals are processed and distributed to the occipital lobe.

Second visual pathway handles coordination of visual input with other sensory input.

Primary visual cortex in the *occipital lobe* handles initial processing of visual input.

Feature detectors are neurons that respond selectively to specific features of complex stimuli.

After processing in the primary visual cortex, visual input is routed to other cortical areas along the *where pathway* (dorsal stream) and the *what pathway* (ventral stream).

Colour perception

Subtractive colour mixing works by removing some wavelengths of light, leaving less light.

Additive colour mixing works by putting more light in the mixture than any one light.

Trichromatic theory holds that the eye has three groups of receptors sensitive to wavelengths associated with red, green, and blue.

Opponent process theory holds that receptors make antagonistic responses to three pairs of colours.

Conclusion: The evidence suggests that both theories are necessary to explain colour perception.

Form perception

• The same visual input can result in very different perceptions.

• Form perception is selective, as the phenomenon of *inattentional blindness* demonstrates.

• Some aspects of form perception depend on *feature analysis*, which involves detecting specific elements and assembling them into complex forms.

• *Gestalt principles*—such as *figure and ground, proximity, closure, similarity, simplicity,* and *continuity*—help explain how scenes are organized into discrete forms.

• Form perception often involves *perceptual hypotheses*, which are inferences about the forms that could be responsible for the stimuli sensed.

Depth perception

Binocular cues are clues about distance based on the differing views of the two eyes.

Retinal disparity, for example, refers to the fact that the right and left eyes see slightly different views of objects. The closer the object gets, the greater the disparity.

Monocular cues are clues about distance based on the image in either eye alone.

Pictorial cues are monocular cues that can be given in a flat picture, such as *linear perspective, texture gradients, relative size, height in plane, interposition,* and *light and shadow.*

Visual illusions

• *A visual illusion* is a discrepancy between the appearance of a visual stimulus and its physical reality.

• Illusions—such as the *Müller-Lyer illusion*, the *Ponzo illusion*, and the *moon illusion*—show that perceptual hypotheses can be wrong and that perception is not a simple reflection of objective reality.

THE AUDITORY SYSTEM

Sound waves

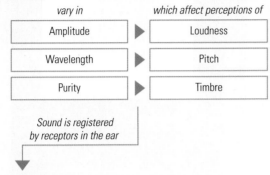

vary in	which affect perceptions of
Amplitude	▶ Loudness
Wavelength	▶ Pitch
Purity	▶ Timbre

Sound is registered by receptors in the ear

Key ear structures

include:

Pinna, which is the external ear's sound-collecting cone

Eardrum, which is a taut membrane (at the end of the auditory canal) that vibrates in response to sound waves

Ossicles, which are three tiny bones in the middle ear that convert the eardrum's vibrations

Cochlea, which is the fluid-filled, coiled tunnel that houses the inner ear's neural tissue

Basilar membrane, which holds the hair cells that serve as auditory receptors

Pitch perception

Place theory: Perception of pitch depends on the portion of the basilar membrane vibrated.

Frequency theory: Perception of pitch depends on the basilar membrane's rate of vibration.

Conclusion: Evidence suggests that both theories are needed to explain pitch perception.

Auditory localization

- *Auditory localization* consists of locating where a sound is coming from in space.
- Two key cues are differences in the *intensity* (loudness) and the *timing* of sounds arriving at each ear.

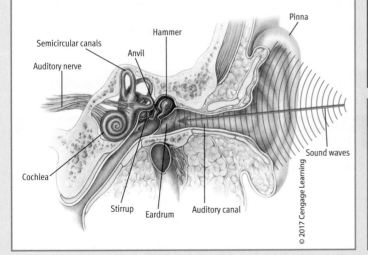

Semicircular canals
Auditory nerve
Hammer
Anvil
Pinna
Cochlea
Stirrup
Eardrum
Auditory canal
Sound waves

© 2017 Cengage Learning

OTHER SENSES

Taste

- Taste cells absorb chemicals in saliva and trigger neural impulses routed through the thalamus.
- Taste buds are sensitive to four basic tastes: sweet, sour, bitter, and salty. Umami may be a fifth basic taste.
- Sensitivity to these tastes is distributed somewhat unevenly across the tongue, but the variations are small.
- Supertasters have more taste buds and are more sensitive than others to certain sweet and bitter substances.
- Roughly 25 percent of people are supertasters, another 25 percent are nontasters, and the remaining 50 percent fall in between.
- Women are more likely to be supertasters than are men.
- Nontasters tend to be more susceptible to the lure of sweets, high-fat foods, alcohol, and smoking, which means their consumption habits tend to be less healthy than those of supertasters.

Smell

- Olfactory cilia absorb chemicals in the nose and trigger neural impulses.
- Olfactory receptors have a short life and are constantly being replaced.
- Smell is the only sensory system that is not routed through the thalamus.
- Most olfactory receptors respond to more than one odour.
- Humans can distinguish a great many odours.
- When compared with other mammals, humans may have a better sense of smell than previously thought.

AAGAMIA/Getty Images

Touch

- Sensory receptors in the skin respond to pressure, temperature, and pain.
- Pain signals travel along a *fast pathway* that registers localized pain and a *slow pathway* that carries less localized pain sensations.
- Cultural variations in the experience of pain show the subjective nature of pain perception.
- *Gate-control theory* holds that incoming pain signals can be blocked in the spinal cord.
- Endorphins and a descending neural pathway appear responsible for this suppression of pain.
- Recent studies indicate that glial cells contribute to the modulation of chronic pain.

APPLICATIONS

- Painters routinely use pictorial depth cues to make their scenes more lifelike.
- The Surrealists toyed with reality, and Escher tried to stimulate thinking about perception.
- The study of perception highlights the relativity of experience, which can be manipulated through contrast effects.
- Critical thinking is enhanced by awareness of how extreme comparators can distort judgments.

CHAPTER 5

Variations in Consciousness

Themes in this Chapter

Theoretical Diversity

Sociohistorical Context

Multifactorial Causation

Cultural Heritage

Subjectivity of Experience

© Shaun R. George Fotografx/Getty Images

Sleep and conversation seem to be interconnected. While only some people seem to talk in their sleep (referred to as *somniloquy*), it seems as if everyone likes to talk about their sleep. Or, to be more accurate, most people like to talk about their lack of sleep. Getting enough sleep is a problem for many. Recent national surveys found that 67 percent of Canadians want more and better sleep (Pelley, 2016), and that up to 40 percent of Canadians may experience some type of sleep disorder in their lifetime (CBC, 2015). No wonder sleep is such a common topic. To ask someone, anyone, how they slept last night seems to be an open invitation for complaint. Canadians' lack of sleep has been linked to a variety of factors (Statistics Canada, 2014), many of which we discuss in this chapter. It is worth noting that our lack of sleep is more than just a temporary inconvenience. In fact, the Centers for Disease Control has stated that North Americans' lack of sleep has reached a stage where it is a public health epidemic, linked to traffic crashes, psychological and physical disorders, industrial disasters, and significantly reduced well-being. We seem to be in the midst of a sleep crisis (Savage, 2013).

For those of us who are lucky enough to sleep well most of the time, sleep becomes part of our conversation and consciousness only after those occasional nights when we do not sleep well. For others, though, sleep, lack of sleep, and sleep disorders and disturbances can be much more significant. For these individuals, lack of sleep is not just an occasional inconvenience—it can alter one's life, or even end it.

Ontario resident Ken Parks always had difficulty with sleep and had a history of sleepwalking. One night in 1987, while asleep, he drove almost 40 kilometres to where his wife's parents lived. There, while still asleep, he proceeded to assault them both and ultimately kill his mother-in-law. Did he intend to do it? By all reports, he had a comfortable relationship with his in-laws. All he really remembered of that night was lying in bed alone watching *Saturday Night Live* and then later stumbling into a police station shouting, "Oh my god. I think I just killed two people" (Callwood, 1990, p. 7). Even more startling to some than the murder itself was the fact that he was ultimately acquitted of the crime. He was examined by experts and it was decided that the crime had most likely been committed while he was sleepwalking (Broughton et al., 1994; Callwood, 1990).

Of course, we all know that most of us do not have the kinds of experiences that Ken Parks had. But why do we sleep and what does it do for us, anyway? You may not know that sleep has many important functions for us in addition to allowing us to work more effectively and to be in a better mood the next day. In fact, without sleep animals die. We do not function well without sleep at school or at work, for example. Many Canadian workplace injuries have been linked directly to sleep problems (King, McLeod, & Koehoorn, 2010). Students who continually stay up late at night cramming often do less well than students who do not pull all-nighters (Thatcher, 2008). Sleep has been shown to play an important role in helping us remember things (Verweij, Onuki, Van Sommers, & Van der Werf, 2016; Walker & Stickgold, 2006). Sleep deprivation has been linked to a variety of negative outcomes, and we discuss some of these later in this chapter.

Recent reports by Statistics Canada give us a hint about some of the factors that seem to be associated with sleeplessness (Hurst, 2014). Men tend to get less sleep than women, and increases in stress and working full-time are associated with getting less sleep. Those with higher incomes sleep less, and married adults sleep less than unmarried adults. Finally, and this will not come as a surprise if you have any children of your own, Canadians with children get

Sleep deprivation is an increasing problem in contemporary society. The negative effects of sleep deprivation are varied but are significant enough that some schools in Canada start classes later so that students can get more sleep.

Ken Parks, pictured here, was acquitted of the murder of his mother-in-law partially based on a history of sleepwalking.

Globe & Mail—Erik Christensen

Chris Ryan/OJO Images/Getty Images

Variations in Consciousness

less sleep than those without children, and the more children you have, the less sleep you get. Given that one in seven Canadians reports sleep difficulties (Tjepkema, 2005), it should come as no surprise that sleep research is an extremely active research area in the psychology of consciousness.

It may seem a little surprising that we are discussing the topic of sleep in a chapter devoted to consciousness: When we are sleeping, aren't we unconscious—don't our brains shut off and rest during sleep? As you will see later in the chapter, our brains are anything but inactive during sleep. But it is true that the topic of consciousness includes more than just the scientific examination of sleep, both in its typical and atypical forms. It also includes an examination of our typical everyday awareness of things that are going on around us and inside us, as well as altered states of consciousness such as meditation, hypnosis, and drug- and alcohol-induced conditions. Consciousness and attention are quite dynamic (Besner et al., 2016), and we tend to drift in and out of specific states throughout the day. In this chapter, we will consider these various states of consciousness. But first, let's consider the nature of our consciousness in general.

The Nature of Consciousness

Consciousness is the awareness of internal and external stimuli. As you read this sentence, it becomes part of your consciousness. But as you read the last sentence, you were probably not aware of the weight of the textbook in your hands until you got to this section of this sentence. We even seem to maintain some degree of awareness when we are asleep, and sometimes even when we are under anesthesia for surgery.

The contents of consciousness are continually changing. Rarely does consciousness come to a standstill. It moves, it flows, it fluctuates, it wanders (Wegner, 1997). Recognizing that consciousness is in constant flux, William James (1902) long ago named this flow the *stream of consciousness*. If you recorded your thoughts, you would find an endless flow of ideas that zigzag in all directions. As you will soon learn, even when you are asleep your consciousness moves through a series of transitions. Constant shifting and changing seem to be part of the essential nature of consciousness.

The interest of psychologists in the study of consciousness seems obvious: Psychologists are interested in understanding human behaviour and, after all, isn't our behaviour the result of conscious thought? While there is no question that conscious thoughts cause behaviour (Baumeister, Mascicampo, & Vohs, 2011), it appears that this is not the whole story. Psychologists are also interested in unconscious influences on behaviour (Bargh & Morsella, 2008; Cona & Treccani, 2016) and the suggestion that "almost every human behaviour comes from a mixture of conscious and unconscious processing" (Baumeister et al., 2011, p. 331).

Variations in Awareness and Control

While attention and consciousness are clearly closely related, they are not identical, and as Koch and Tsuchiya (2006) have argued, you can have either one without the other. While some of what enters our consciousness seems intentional and designed to further specific goals or motivations—for example, your tendency to listen carefully to what your professor has to say in class, especially as the exam draws closer—at other times our thoughts and minds seem to wander (McVay & Kane, 2010; Seli, Risko, Smilek, & Schacter, 2016). No matter how hard you try to listen to your professor, sometimes your mind may wander to other topics (Wammes et al., 2016a, 2016b). *Mind wandering* refers to people's experience of task-unrelated thoughts, thoughts that are not related to what they are intentionally trying to do at a given moment. Mind wandering is something we have all had experience with; it is estimated that people spend 15 to 50 percent of their time mind wandering (Smallwood & Schooler, 2006). Recent research in this area has focused on uncovering the processes and structures of the brain that are implicated in mind wandering (e.g., Fox et al., 2015; Gruberger, Ben-Simon, Lekovitz, & Zangen, 2011; Mitter, Hawkins, Boekel, & Forstmann, 2016); these include the *default mode network* and the *frontoparietal network*, among others. There are clear costs to mind wandering, you still have to answer questions on the lecture content, even though you are not paying attention to the professor. But are there any benefits of mind wandering? A number of lines of research are exploring the potential benefits of mind wandering. These include the fact that mind wandering has the potential to facilitate future planning, to produce novel and creative thoughts, to enable one to capture the meaning in one's own personal experiences, and to relieve boredom (Smallwod & Schooler, 2015). The two Featured Studies in this chapter, which were conducted at the University of Waterloo, explore the frequency, nature, and effects on grades of students' mind wandering in university lectures.

Table 5.1

EEG Patterns Associated with States of Consciousness

EEG PATTERN	FREQUENCY (CPS)	TYPICAL STATES OF CONSCIOUSNESS
Beta (β)	13–24	Normal waking thought, alert problem solving
Alpha (α)	8–12	Deep relaxation, blank mind, meditation
Theta (θ)	4–7	Light sleep
Delta (Δ)	Less than 4	Deep sleep

© 2017 Cengage Learning

FEATURED STUDY

Mind wandering during lectures I: Changes in rates across an entire semester.

Description
The researchers use a novel technique to assess and chart across lecture sessions the mind wandering of their students.

Investigators
Wammes, J. D., Boucher, P. O., Seli, P., Cheyne, J. A., & Smilek, D. (2016). *Scholarship of Teaching and Learning in Psychology, 2*(1), 13–32.

FEATURED STUDY

Mind wandering during lectures II: Relation to academic performance.

Description
In this research, the authors examine the relations between mind wandering in class and academic grades.

Investigators
Wammes, J. D., Seli, P., Cheyne, J. A., Boucher, P. O., & Smilek, D. (2016). *Scholarship of Teaching and Learning in Psychology, 2*(1), 33–48.

Consciousness and Brain Activity

Consciousness does not arise from any distinct structure in the brain but rather from activity in distributed networks of neural pathways (Kinsbourne, 1997; Postle, 2016; Singer, 2007). Scientists are increasingly using brain-imaging methods to explore the link between brain activity and levels of consciousness (Koch, Massimini, Boly, & Tonini, 2015; Owen, 2013; Wager, Hernandez, & Lindquist, 2009). But historically, the most commonly used indicator of variations in consciousness has been the EEG, which records activity from broad swaths of the cortex. The *electroencephalograph (EEG)* is a device that monitors the electrical activity of the brain over time by means of recording electrodes attached to the surface of the scalp. Ultimately, the EEG summarizes the rhythm of cortical activity in the brain in terms of line tracings

called *brain waves*. These brain-wave tracings vary in *amplitude* (height) and *frequency* (cycles per second, abbreviated *cps*). You can see what brain waves look like if you glance ahead to Figure 5.4 on page 161. Human brain-wave activity is usually divided into four principal bands, based on the frequency of the brain waves. These bands, named after letters in the Greek alphabet, are *beta* (13–24 cps), *alpha* (8–12 cps), *theta* (4–7 cps), and *delta* (under 4 cps).

Different patterns of EEG activity are associated with different states of consciousness, as summarized in Table 5.1. For instance, when you are alertly engaged in problem solving, beta waves tend to dominate. When you are relaxed and resting, alpha waves increase. When you slip into deep, dreamless sleep, delta waves become more prevalent. Although these correlations are far from perfect, changes in EEG activity are closely related to variations in consciousness (Wallace & Fisher, 1999).

As we discussed in Chapter 2, measures of association such as correlations between mental states and brain waves don't allow you to make firm statements regarding causation. We do not know based on such measures whether changes in mental states cause brain wave changes or vice versa. Also, it could be that some third factor, such as signals coming from a subcortical structure of the brain, is causing both (see Figure 5.1).

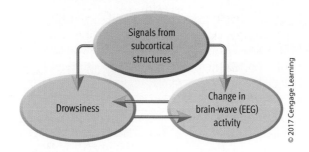

© 2017 Cengage Learning

Figure 5.1
The correlation between mental states and electrical activity in the brain. As discussed in Chapter 2, correlations alone do not establish causation. For example, there are strong correlations between drowsiness and a particular pattern of cortical activity, as reflected by EEG brain waves. But does drowsiness cause a change in cortical activity, or do changes in cortical activity cause drowsiness? Or does some third variable account for the changes in both?

Biological Rhythms and Sleep

Key Learning Goals

▶ Summarize what is known about human biological clocks and their relationship to sleep.

▶ Explain how getting out of sync with one's circadian rhythms can have effects on sleep.

According to University of Ottawa psychologist Joseph De Koninck (De Koninck, 2012; Razavi, Matwin, Amini, & De Koninck, 2014), the past three decades have increasingly demonstrated the critical impact that sleep has on many of the important processes and tasks that we engage in every day (De Koninck, 1997). This work has also indicated the important links between sleep quality and the body's natural rhythm. Variations in consciousness are shaped in part by biological rhythms. Rhythms pervade the world around us. The daily alternation of light and darkness, the annual pattern of the seasons, and the phases of the moon all reflect this rhythmic quality of repeating cycles. Humans, many other animals, and even plants, display biological rhythms that are tied to these planetary rhythms (Foster, 2004). *Biological rhythms* are periodic fluctuations in physiological functioning. The existence of these rhythms means that organisms have internal "biological clocks" that somehow monitor the passage of time.

The Role of Circadian Rhythms

Circadian rhythms are the 24-hour biological cycles found in humans and many other species. In humans, circadian rhythms are particularly influential in the regulation of sleep (Moore, 2006). However, daily cycles also produce rhythmic variations in blood pressure, urine production, hormonal secretions, and other physical functions (see Figure 5.2), as well as alertness, short-term memory, and other aspects of cognitive performance (Refinetti, 2006; Van Dongen & Dinges, 2005).

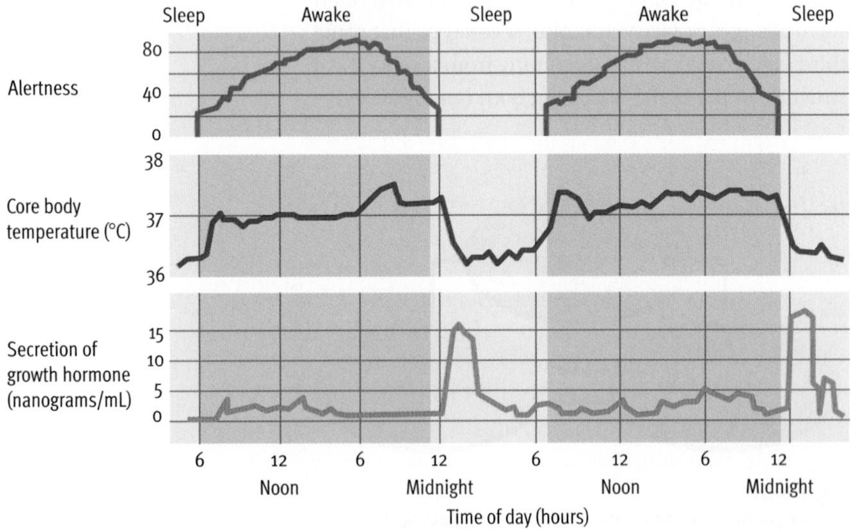

Research indicates that people generally fall asleep as their body temperature begins to drop and awake as it begins to rise once again (Szymusiak, 2009). Researchers have concluded that circadian rhythms can leave individuals physiologically primed to fall asleep most easily at a particular time of day (Richardson, 1993). This optimal time varies from person to person, depending on their schedules. Finding your ideal bedtime may help promote better-quality sleep during the night (Akerstedt et al., 1997). People often characterize themselves as a "night person" or a "morning person." These preferences reflect individual variations in circadian rhythms (Minkel & Dinges, 2009).

Researchers have worked out many of the details regarding how the day–night cycle resets biological clocks. When exposed to light, some receptors in the retina send direct inputs to a small structure in the hypothalamus called the *suprachiasmatic nucleus (SCN)* (Weaver & Reppert, 2008). According to Simon Fraser University sleep researcher Ralph Mistlberger and his colleague Mary Harrington (Harrington & Mistlberger, 2000), the SCN sends signals to the nearby *pineal gland*, whose secretion of the hormone *melatonin* plays a key role in adjusting biological clocks (Norman, 2009).

Ignoring Circadian Rhythms

What happens when you ignore your biological clock and go to sleep at an unusual time? Typically, the quality of your sleep suffers and research shows clearly that proper sleep plays an important role in promoting good physical and psychological health (Irwin, 2015). Getting out of sync with your circadian rhythms also causes jet lag. When you fly across several time zones, your biological clock keeps time as usual, even though official clock time changes. You then go to sleep at the "wrong" time and are likely to experience difficulty falling asleep and poor-quality sleep. This inferior sleep, which can continue to occur for several days, can make you feel fatigued, sluggish, and irritable during the daytime (Sletten & Arendt, 2012).

People differ in how quickly they can reset their biological clocks to compensate for jet lag, and the speed of readjustment depends on the direction

Figure 5.2
Examples of circadian rhythms. These graphs show how alertness, core body temperature, and the secretion of growth hormone typically fluctuate in a 24-hour rhythm. Note how alertness tends to diminish with declining body temperature.

Source: "Circadian rhythms graph" from the book *WIDE AWAKE AT 3 AM* by Richard M. Coleman. Copyright © 1986 by Richard M. Coleman. Reprinted by permission of Henry Holt and Company, LLC.

travelled. Generally, it's easier to fly westward and lengthen your day than it is to fly eastward and shorten it (Sletten & Arendt, 2012). This east-west disparity in jet lag is sizable enough to have an impact on the performance of sports teams. Studies have found that teams flying westward perform significantly better than teams flying eastward in professional baseball (Recht, Lew, & Schwartz, 1995) (see Figure 5.3) and college football (Worthen & Wade, 1999). A rough rule of thumb for jet lag is that the readjustment process takes about a day for each time zone crossed when flying eastward and about two-thirds of a day per time zone when flying westward (Monk, 2006). With advancing age, individuals take longer to realign their circadian rhythms (Bliwise, 2011).

Of course, you don't have to hop on a jet to get out of sync with your biological clock. For many of us, going to work means something other than a standard 9 to 5 job. Data collected by Statistics Canada indicates that 12 percent of Canadian workers are subjected to rotating shifts, while 6 percent and 2.3 percent work regular evening and night shifts (Demers, Wond, & McLeod, 2010). The rotating and late-night work shifts endured by many nurses, firefighters, and industrial workers also play havoc with biological rhythms. Shift rotation tends to have far more detrimental effects than jet lag (Monk, 2000). People suffering from jet lag get their circadian rhythms realigned within a matter of days, but workers on night or in rotating shifts are constantly at odds with local time cues and normal rhythms. Studies show that such workers get less total sleep and poorer-quality sleep (Akerstedt & Kecklund, 2012). These work schedules can have a negative impact on employees' productivity at work, social relations, and mental health (Drake & Wright, 2011; Waage et al., 2009). Studies have also linked rotating shifts to a higher incidence of many physical diseases, including cancer, diabetes, ulcers, high blood pressure, and heart disease (Kriegsfeld & Nelson, 2009; Vyas et al., 2012). University of British Columbia psychologist Stanley Coren (1996a) suggests that the sleep lost when the clock is set ahead in the spring shift to Daylight Saving Time is associated with an increase in traffic accidents during the week after the switch.

Realigning Circadian Rhythms

As scientists have come to appreciate the importance of circadian rhythms, they have begun to look for new ways to help people harness their daily rhythms. A promising line of research has focused on giving people small doses of the hormone melatonin, which

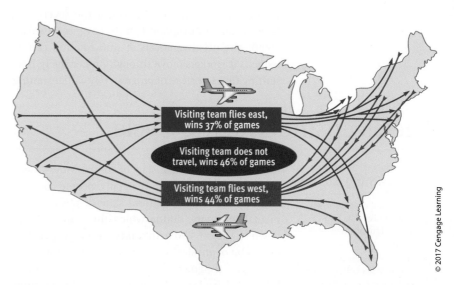

Figure 5.3

Effects of direction travelled on the performance of professional baseball teams. To gain some insight into the determinants of jet lag, Recht, Lew, and Schwartz (1995) analyzed the performance of visiting teams in major league baseball over a three-year period. In baseball, visiting teams usually play three or four games in each destination city, so there are plenty of games in which the visiting team has not travelled the day before. These games, which served as a baseline for comparison, were won by the visiting team 46 percent of the time. Consistent with the observation that flying west creates less jet lag than flying east, visiting teams that flew westward the day (or night) before performed only slightly worse, winning 44 percent of the time. In contrast, visiting teams that flew eastward the day before won only 37 percent of their games, presumably because flying east and shortening one's day creates greater jet lag.

Source: Adapted from Kalat, J.W. (2001). *Biological psychology*. Belmont, CA: Wadsworth. Reprinted by permission.

appears to regulate the human biological clock. The evidence from a number of studies suggests that melatonin *can* reduce the effects of jet lag by helping travellers resynchronize their biological clocks, but the research results are inconsistent (Arendt & Skene, 2005; Monk, 2006). One reason for the inconsistent findings is that when melatonin is used to ameliorate jet lag, the timing of the dose is crucial; because calculating the optimal timing is rather complicated, it is easy to get it wrong (Arendt, 2009). It is also important to note that pediatricians emphasize caution when parents are considering using melatonin supplements to regulate the bedtime of their children. This practice has increased in recent years (Eastwood, 2013).

Researchers have also tried carefully timed exposure to bright light as a treatment to realign the circadian rhythms of rotating shift workers in industrial settings. Positive effects have been seen in some studies (Lowden, Akerstedt, & Wibom, 2004). This treatment can accelerate workers' adaptation to a new sleep–wake schedule, leading to improvements in sleep quality and alertness during work hours. However, the effects of bright-light administration have been modest and somewhat inconsistent (Rogers & Dinges, 2002), and it isn't a realistic option in many work settings. Another strategy to help rotating shift workers involves carefully planning their rotation schedules to reduce the severity of their circadian disruption (Smith, Fogg, & Eastman, 2009). The negative effects of shift rotation can be reduced if workers move through progressively later starting times (instead of progressively earlier starting times) and if they have longer periods between shift changes (Kostreva, McNelis, & Clemens, 2002). Although enlightened scheduling practices can help, the unfortunate reality is that most people find rotating shift work very difficult (Arendt, 2010).

The Sleep and Waking Cycle

▶ Describe the nightly sleep cycle, and explain how age and culture influences sleep.

▶ Describe evidence on the effects of sleep deprivation and the health ramifications of sleep loss.

▶ Identify the symptoms of insomnia, narcolepsy, sleep apnea, somnambulism, and REM sleep behaviour disorder.

Although it is a familiar state of consciousness, sleep is widely misunderstood. Generally, people consider sleep to be a single, uniform state of physical and mental inactivity, during which the brain is "shut down" (Dement, 2003). In reality, sleepers experience quite a bit of physical and mental activity throughout the night (Peigneux, Urbain, & Schmidtz, 2012). Scientists have learned a great deal about sleep since the landmark discovery of REM sleep in the 1950s.

The advances in psychology's understanding of sleep are the result of hard work by researchers who have spent countless nighttime hours watching other people sleep. This work is done in sleep laboratories, where volunteer subjects come to spend the night. Sleep labs have one or more "bedrooms" in which the subjects retire, usually after being hooked up to a variety of physiological recording devices. In addition to an EEG, the other two crucial devices are an *electromyograph (EMG)*, which records muscular activity and tension, and an *electrooculograph (EOG)*, which records eye movements (Carskadon & Rechtschaffen, 2005; Collop, 2006). Typically, other instruments are also used to monitor heart rate, breathing, pulse rate, and body temperature. The researchers observe the sleeping subject through a window (or with a video camera) from an adjacent room, where they also monitor their elaborate physiological recording equipment. For most people, it takes just one night to adapt to the strange bedroom and the recording devices and

Researchers in a sleep laboratory can observe subjects while using elaborate equipment to record physiological changes during sleep. This kind of research has disclosed that sleep is a complex series of physical and mental states.

return to their normal mode of sleeping (Carskadon & Dement, 1994, Pace-Schott, 2009; Rosenthal, 2006).

Cycling through the Stages of Sleep

Not only does sleep occur in a context of daily rhythms, but subtler rhythms are evident within the experience of sleep itself. During sleep, people cycle through a series of five stages. Let's take a look at what researchers have learned about the changes that occur during each of these stages (Carskadon & Dement, 2005).

Stages 1–4

Although it may take only a few minutes, the onset of sleep is gradual and there is no obvious transition point between wakefulness and sleep (Rechtschaffen, 1994). The length of time it takes people to fall asleep varies considerably. It depends on quite an array of factors, including how long it has been since the person has slept, where the person is in his or her circadian cycle, the amount of noise or light in the sleep environment, and the person's age, desire to fall asleep, boredom level, recent caffeine or drug intake, and stress level, among other things (Broughton, 1994). In any event, stage 1 is a brief transitional stage of light sleep that usually lasts only a few (1–7) minutes. Breathing and heart rate slow as muscle tension and body temperature decline. The alpha waves that probably dominated EEG activity just before falling asleep give way to lower-frequency EEG activity in which theta waves are prominent (see Figure 5.4). *Hypnic jerks*, those brief muscular contractions that occur as people fall asleep, generally occur during stage 1 drowsiness (Broughton, 1994).

As the sleeper descends through stages 2, 3, and 4 of the cycle, respiration rate, heart rate, muscle tension, and body temperature continue to decline. During stage 2, which typically lasts about 10–25 minutes, brief bursts of higher-frequency brain waves, called *sleep spindles*, appear against a background of mixed EEG activity (refer again to Figure 5.4). Gradually, brain waves become higher in amplitude and slower in frequency, as the body moves into a deeper form of sleep, called *slow-wave sleep*. *Slow-wave sleep (SWS)* consists of sleep stages 3 and 4, during which high-amplitude, low-frequency delta waves become prominent in EEG recordings. Typically, individuals reach slow-wave sleep in about half an hour and stay there for roughly 30 minutes. Then the cycle reverses itself and the sleeper gradually moves back upward through the lighter stages. That's when things start to get especially interesting.

REM Sleep

When sleepers reach what should be stage 1 once again, they usually go into the fifth stage of sleep, which is most widely known as *REM sleep*. As we have seen, REM is an abbreviation for the *rapid eye movements* prominent during this stage of sleep. In a sleep lab, researchers use an electrooculograph to monitor these lateral (side-to-side) movements that occur beneath the sleeping person's closed eyelids. However, they can be seen with the naked eye if you closely watch someone in the REM stage of sleep (little ripples move back and forth across the person's closed eyelids).

REM sleep was discovered accidentally in the 1950s in Nathaniel Kleitman's lab at the University of Chicago (Aserinsky & Kleitman, 1953; Dement, 2005). The term *REM sleep* was coined by grad student William Dement, who went on to become one of the world's foremost sleep researchers. The REM stage tends to be a "deep" stage of sleep in the conventional sense that people are relatively hard to awaken from it (although arousal thresholds vary during REM). The REM stage is also marked by irregular breathing and pulse rate. Muscle tone is extremely relaxed—so much so that bodily movements are minimal and the sleeper is virtually paralyzed. *Although REM is a relatively deep stage of sleep, EEG activity is dominated by high-frequency beta waves that resemble those observed when people are alert and awake* (see Figure 5.4 again).

This paradox is probably related to the association between REM sleep and dreaming. When researchers systematically awaken subjects from various stages of sleep to ask whether they were dreaming, dream reports are notably more likely during the REM stage (McCarley, 1994). Although decades of research have revealed that some dreaming occurs in the non-REM stages, dreaming is more frequent, vivid, memorable, emotional, dramatic, and rich in characters during REM sleep (Nielsen, 2011; Pace-Schott, 2011).

Carlyle Smith, a psychology professor at Trent University, is a prominent sleep researcher who has been active in examining the relationships between brain functioning in sleep and memory (Smith, 1996, 2003). His research suggests that brain activity during sleep is central to consolidation of information acquired during the day. While sleep

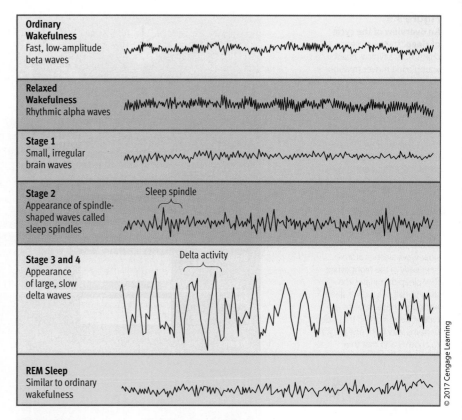

Figure 5.4

EEG patterns in sleep and wakefulness. Characteristic brain waves vary, depending on one's state of consciousness. Generally, as people move from an awake state through deeper stages of sleep, their brain waves decrease in frequency (cycles per second) and increase in amplitude (height). However, brain waves during REM sleep resemble "wide-awake" brain waves.

Source: Adapted from Nevid, J. S. (2012). *Essentials of psychology: Concepts and applications.* Belmont, CA: Wadsworth. Reprinted by permission.

is important for learning, it may be that different types of sleep are important for different types of learning.

To summarize, *REM sleep* is a relatively deep stage of sleep marked by rapid eye movements; high-frequency, low-amplitude brain waves; and vivid dreaming. It is such a special stage of sleep that the other four stages are often characterized simply as *non-REM sleep*. *Non-REM (NREM) sleep* consists of sleep stages 1 through 4, which are marked by an absence of rapid eye movements, relatively little dreaming, and varied EEG activity.

Repeating the Cycle

During the course of a night, people usually repeat the sleep cycle about four times. As the night wears on, the cycle changes gradually. The first REM period is relatively short, lasting only a few minutes. Subsequent REM periods get progressively longer, peaking at around 40–60 minutes in length. Additionally, NREM intervals tend to get shorter, and descents into NREM stages usually become

William Dement

"Sleep deprivation is a major epidemic in our society. . . . Americans spend so much time and energy chasing the American dream, that they don't have much time left for actual dreaming."

Figure 5.5

An overview of the cycle of sleep. The white line charts how a typical, healthy, young adult moves through the various stages of sleep during the course of a night. This diagram also shows how dreams and rapid eye movements tend to coincide with REM sleep, whereas posture changes occur between REM periods (because the body is nearly paralyzed during REM sleep). Notice how the person cycles into REM four times, as descents into NREM sleep become shallower and REM periods become longer. Thus, slow-wave sleep is prominent early in the night, while REM sleep dominates the second half of a night's sleep. Although these patterns are typical, keep in mind that sleep patterns vary from one person to another and that they change with age.

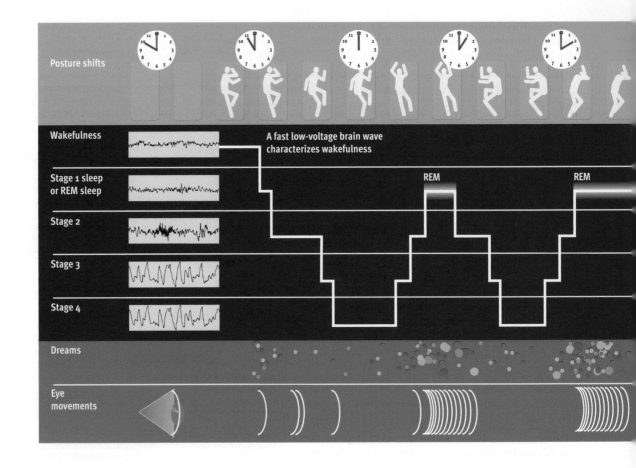

REM sleep is not unique to humans. Nearly all mammals and birds exhibit REM sleep. The only known exceptions among warm-blooded vertebrates are dolphins and some whales (Morrison, 2003). Dolphins are particularly interesting, as they sleep while swimming, resting one hemisphere of the brain while the other hemisphere remains alert.

more shallow. These trends can be seen in Figure 5.5, which provides an overview of a typical night's sleep cycle. These trends mean that most slow-wave sleep occurs early in the sleep cycle and that REM sleep tends to pile up in the second half of the sleep cycle. Summing across the entire cycle, young adults typically spend about 15–20 percent of their sleep time in slow-wave sleep and another 20–25 percent in REM sleep (Rama, Cho, & Kushida, 2006). What we have described thus far is the big picture—the typical structure of sleep averaged over many people. However, recent research by Tucker, Dinges, and Van Dongen (2007) has shown that the "architecture" of sleep—how quickly one falls asleep, how long one sleeps, how one cycles through the various stage—does differ across people.

Age Trends in Sleep

There seems to be a clear relationship between age and our sleep patterns. In a survey conducted by Statistics Canada in 2010, Canadians between the ages of 15 and 24 reported the greatest sleep time. Those between 35 and 44 reported the least sleep (Vanier Institute for the Family, 2013). This group was characterized by "time stress" due to balancing work and family roles.

Age alters the sleep cycle. What we have described so far as the sleep cycle is the typical pattern for young adults. Children, however, display different patterns (Bootzin et al., 2001; Roffwarg, Muzio, & Dement, 1966). The sleep cycle of babies immediately after birth is quite simple: There are only two sleep types: REM and non-REM sleep (Dement, 1999). Newborns will sleep six to eight times in a 24-hour period, often exceeding a total of 16 hours of sleep. Fortunately for parents, during the first several months, much of this sleep begins to be consolidated into one particularly long nighttime sleep period (Huber & Tononi, 2009). Interestingly, infants spend much more of their sleep time in the REM stage than adults do. In the first few months, REM accounts for about 50 percent of babies' sleep, as compared to 20 percent of adults' sleep.

During the remainder of the first year, the REM portion of infants' sleep declines to roughly 30 percent (Ohayon et al., 2004). The REM portion of sleep continues to decrease gradually until it levels off at about 20 percent (see Figure 5.6). During adulthood, gradual age-related changes in sleep continue. Although the proportion of REM sleep remains fairly stable (Bliwise, 2005), the percentage of slow-wave sleep declines dramatically and the percentage of time spent in stage 1 increases slightly, with these trends stronger in men than in women (Bliwise, 2005).

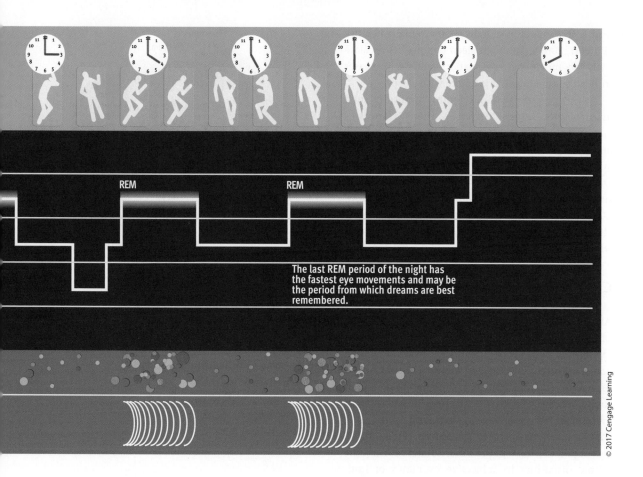

The last REM period of the night has the fastest eye movements and may be the period from which dreams are best remembered.

© 2017 Cengage Learning

These shifts toward lighter sleep *may* contribute to the increased frequency of nighttime awakening seen among the elderly. As Figure 5.6 shows, the average amount of total sleep time also declines with advancing age.

Until recently, it was assumed that this decline in sleep time was due to older people having more difficulty initiating sleep or remaining asleep. In other words, it was attributed to a decrease in their ability to sleep effectively. However, a recent, carefully controlled laboratory study that allowed for extended sleep opportunities found that older adults (aged 60–80) showed significantly less sleepiness during the day than younger adults (aged 18–30), even though the older group chose to sleep an average of 1.5 hours less per day (Klerman & Dijk, 2008). The authors conclude that the elderly *may* simply need less sleep than younger adults. Consistent with this line of thinking, another recent study yielded the surprising finding that older adults tolerate sleep deprivation with less impairment than younger adults (Duffy et al., 2009). Older people do have more difficulty adapting to circadian phase shifts, such as those produced by jet lag or rotating work shifts (Monk, 2005), but excessive daytime sleepiness does not increase with age (Young, 2004). The bottom line is that growing older, by itself, does not appear to

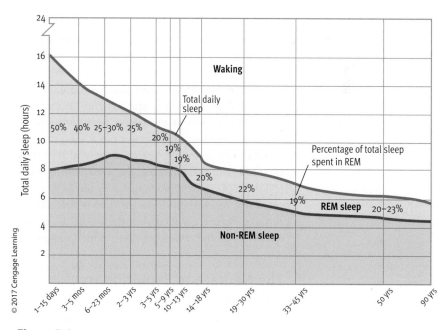

Figure 5.6

Changes in sleep patterns over the life span. Both the total amount of sleep per night and the portion of sleep that is REM sleep change with age. Sleep patterns change most dramatically during infancy, with total sleep time and amount of REM sleep declining sharply in the first two years of life. After a noticeable drop in the average amount of sleep in adolescence, sleep patterns remain relatively stable, although total sleep and slow-wave sleep continue to decline gradually with age.

Source: Adapted from an updated revision of a figure in Roffwarg, H.P., Muzio, J.N., and Dement, W.C. (1996). Ontogenetic development of human sleep-dream cycle. *Science*, 152, 604–609. Copyright © by the American Association for the Advancement of Science. Adapted and revised by permission of the authors.

lead to poor sleep if elderly people remain healthy (Vitiello, 2009). Although sleep complaints escalate with age, much of this escalation is due to increases in health problems that interfere with sleep.

As we age, our risk of developing conditions such as Alzheimer's disease increases. There is an association between Alzheimer's and sleep disturbance, and these sleep problems may show up before other symptoms of Alzheimer's. This association has led Dalhousie University professor Benjamin Rusak and his colleagues (Sterniczuk, Theo, Rusak, & Rockwood, 2013) to suggest that sleep-disturbance assessments should be included in the screening of individuals thought to be at risk for developing the disease.

Culture and Sleep

Although age clearly affects the nature and structure of sleep itself, the psychological and physiological experience of sleep does not appear to vary much across cultures. For example, a cross-cultural survey of ten divergent countries (Soldatos et al., 2005) found relatively modest differences in the average amount of time that people sleep, and in the time that it takes for them to fall asleep. That said, a recent poll of people in the United States found some ethnic disparities in subjective estimates of individuals' sleep quality (National Sleep Foundation, 2010). In this poll, whites (20 percent) and African Americans (18 percent) were more likely to report that they "rarely" or "never" enjoyed a good night's sleep than were either Hispanics (14 percent) or Asians (9 percent).

Napping practices also vary along cultural lines. In many societies, shops close and activities are curtailed in the afternoon to permit people to enjoy a one- to two-hour midday nap. These "siesta cultures" are found mostly in tropical regions of the world (Webb & Dinges, 1989). There, this practice is adaptive in that it allows people to avoid working during the hottest part of the day. As a rule, the siesta tradition is not found in cultures where it conflicts with the emphasis on productivity and the philosophy that "time is money."

The Neural and Evolutionary Bases of Sleep

The rhythm of sleep and waking appears to be regulated by subcortical structures that lie deep within the brain. One brain structure that is important to sleep and wakefulness is the *reticular formation* in the core of the brainstem (Garcia-Rill, 2009; Steriade, 2005). The *ascending reticular activating system (ARAS)* consists of the afferent fibres running through the reticular

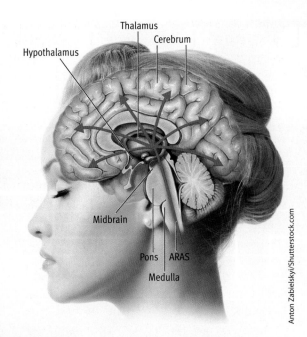

Figure 5.7
The ascending reticular activating system (ARAS). A number of brain areas and structures interact to regulate sleep and waking, including all of those highlighted in this graphic. Particularly important is the ARAS (represented by the green arrows), which conveys neural stimulation to many areas of the cortex.

© 2017 Cengage Learning.

formation that influence physiological arousal. As you can see in Figure 5.7, the ARAS projects diffusely into many areas of the cortex. When these ascending fibres are cut in the brainstem of a cat, the result is continuous sleep (Moruzzi, 1964). Electrical stimulation along the same pathways produces arousal and alertness.

Many other brain structures are also involved in the regulation of sleeping and waking (Marks, 2006). For example, activity in the *pons* and adjacent areas in the *midbrain* seems to be critical to the generation of REM sleep (Siegel, 2005). Recent research has focused on the importance of various areas in the *hypothalamus* for the regulation of sleep and wakefulness (Fuller & Lu, 2009). Specific areas in the medulla, thalamus, and basal forebrain have also been noted in the control of sleep and a variety of neurotransmitters are involved (see Figure 5.7). Thus, the ebb and flow of sleep and waking is regulated through activity in a *constellation* of interacting brain centres (Pace-Schott, Hobson, & Stickgold, 2008).

What is the evolutionary significance of sleep? The fact that sleep is seen in a highly diverse range of organisms and that it appears to have evolved independently in birds and mammals suggests that it has considerable adaptive value. But theorists disagree about how exactly sleep is adaptive. One hypothesis is that sleep evolved to conserve organisms' energy. For example, in humans energy consumption by the brain is reduced by about 30 percent during sleep (Siegel, 2009). An alternative hypothesis is that the inactivity of sleep is adaptive because it reduces exposure to predators and the consumption of precious resources. A third hypothesis is that sleep is adaptive because it helps animals restore bodily resources depleted by waking activities. But what, exactly, sleep restores is not readily apparent (Frank, 2006; Huber & Tononi, 2009). Overall, the evidence seems strongest for the energy and conservation hypotheses, but there is room for extensive debate about the evolutionary bases of sleep (Siegel, 2009; Zepelin et al., 2005).

Doing Without: Sleep Deprivation

Scientific research on sleep deprivation presents something of a paradox. On the one hand, some studies suggest that sleep deprivation is not as detrimental as most people subjectively feel it to be. On the other hand, evidence suggests that sleep deprivation may be a major social problem, undermining efficiency at work and contributing to countless accidents.

Research has mostly focused on partial sleep deprivation, or sleep restriction, which occurs when people make do with substantially less sleep than normal over a period of time. Many sleep experts believe that much of North American society suffers from chronic sleep deprivation (Walsh, Dement, & Dinges, 2011). It appears that more and more people are trying to squeeze additional waking hours out of their days as they attempt to juggle conflicting work, family, household, and school responsibilities. The epidemic of sleep deprivation does not appear to be limited to North America; a recent study showed that inadequate sleep is a global problem (Stranges et al., 2012).

How serious are the effects of partial sleep deprivation? The emerging consensus is that sleep restriction has far more negative effects than most people assume. Studies indicate that sleep restriction can impair individuals' attention, reaction time, motor coordination, and decision making and may also have negative effects on endocrine and immune system functioning (Banks & Dinges, 2011). Children who are sleep deprived show deficits in emotional regulation, attention, and memory, among other things (Vriend, Davison, Rusak, & Corkim, 2015; Vriend, Davidson, Corkum, Rusak, & Chalmers, 2013). Sleep deprivation has also been blamed for a large proportion of transportation accidents and mishaps in the workplace (Walsh et al., 2011). For example, research suggests that drowsy driving increases accident risk eightfold

and is a contributing factor in about 20 percent of motor vehicle accidents (Philip, Sagaspe, & Taillard, 2011). Unfortunately, research shows that sleep-deprived individuals are not particularly good at predicting if and when they will fall asleep (Kaplan, Itoi, & Dement, 2007). Thus, tired drivers often fail to pull off the road when they should.

reality check

Misconception
The effects of partial sleep deprivation generally are modest and insignificant.

Reality
The basis for this belief is that the most obvious effect of sleep deprivation is increased sleepiness, which sounds pretty harmless. However, sleep deprivation impairs attention, motor coordination, decision making, and memory and increases the likelihood of many kinds of accidents. Moreover, sleep loss is associated with increased vulnerability to a variety of serious diseases and elevated mortality.

Darren Mower/Getty Images

Many traffic accidents occur because drivers get drowsy or fall asleep at the wheel. Although the effects of sleep deprivation seem innocuous, sleep loss can be deadly.

The unique quality of REM sleep led researchers to look into the effects of a special type of partial sleep deprivation—selective deprivation. In a number of laboratory studies, participants were awakened over a period of nights whenever they began to go into the REM stage. These subjects usually got a decent amount of sleep in non-REM stages, but they were selectively deprived of REM sleep.

What are the effects of REM deprivation? The evidence indicates that it has little impact on daytime functioning and task performance, but it does have some interesting effects on subjects' patterns of sleeping (Bonnet, 2005). As the nights go by in REM deprivation studies, it becomes necessary to awaken the participants more and more often to deprive them of their REM sleep, because they spontaneously shift into REM more and more frequently. Whereas most subjects normally go into REM about four times a night, REM-deprived participants start slipping into REM every time the researchers turn around. Furthermore, when a REM-deprivation experiment comes to an end and participants are allowed to sleep without interruption, they experience a "rebound effect." That is, they spend extra time in REM periods for one to three nights to make up for their REM deprivation (Achermann & Borbely, 2011).

Similar results have been observed when subjects have been selectively deprived of slow-wave sleep (Achermann & Borbely, 2011). What do theorists make of these spontaneous pursuits of REM and slow-wave sleep? They conclude that people must have specific needs for REM and slow-wave sleep—and rather strong needs, at that.

Why do we need REM and slow-wave sleep? Some influential studies suggest that REM and slow-wave sleep contribute to firming up learning that takes place during the day—a process called memory consolidation. Efforts to explore this hypothesis have led to some interesting findings. For example, in one study, participants were given training on a perceptual-motor task and then retested 12 hours later. Those who slept during the 12-hour interval showed substantial improvement in performance that was not apparent in participants who did not sleep (Walker et al., 2002). A growing number of similar studies have shown that sleep seems to enhance subjects' memory of specific learning activities that occurred during the day (Nguyen, Tucker, et al., 2013; Payne et al., 2012; Stickgold & Walker, 2013). These studies have found sleep-enhanced recall on a wide range of very different types of memory tasks. The theoretical meaning of these findings is still being debated, but the most widely accepted explanations centre on how time spent in specific stages of sleep may stabilize or solidify memories formed during the day (Stickgold & Wamsley, 2011). In addition, recent theorizing on the issue suggests that sleep may also contribute to assimilating new memories into existing networks of knowledge (Stickgold, 2013; Walker, 2012).

Further underscoring the importance of REM sleep, some studies even suggest that REM may promote creative insights related to previous learning (Stickgold & Walker, 2004). In one study, participants worked on a challenging task requiring creativity before and after an opportunity to take a nap or enjoy quiet rest (Cai et al., 2009). The naps were monitored physiologically, and subjects were divided into those who experienced REM during their nap and those who did not. The REM-sleep group showed dramatic increases in creative performance after the nap that were not seen in the group without REM or the group that engaged in quiet rest.

Another study found that sleep improved performance on a complicated decision-making task that resembled casino gambling (Pace-Schott et al., 2012). The participants who played the game following sleep (rather than a day of waking activities) made more advantageous draws and showed a better understanding of the game. The researchers attributed the sleep-enhanced performance to subjects' opportunity to experience REM sleep. Yet another study found that sleep led to superior performance on difficult verbal insight problems (Sio, Monaghan, & Ormerod, 2013). These studies suggest that the beneficial effects of sleep may not be limited to enhancing memory; sleep may also improve learning and problem solving. Obviously, this conclusion has important implications for students who want to maximize their academic success. Consistent with this conclusion, studies have found modest correlations between sleep duration and measures of academic performance (Dewald et al., 2010). As you might guess, students who sleep less tend to get lower grades. Moreover, a recent study of high school students found that sacrificing sleep in order to fit in additional study can actually backfire, resulting in lower performance on tests, quizzes, and homework (Gillen-O'Neel, Huynh, & Fuligni, 2013).

....

concept **check** 5.1

Comparing REM and NREM Sleep

A table here could have provided you with a systematic comparison of REM sleep and NREM sleep, but that would have deprived you of the opportunity to check your understanding of these sleep phases by creating your own table. Fill in each of the blanks below with a word or phrase highlighting the differences between REM and NREM sleep with regard to the various characteristics specified. You can find the answers near the back of the book in Appendix A.

Characteristic	REM Sleep	NREM Sleep
1. Type of EEG activity	_____	_____
2. Eye movements	_____	_____
3. Dreaming	_____	_____
4. Depth (difficulty in awakening)	_____	_____
5. Percentage of total sleep (in adults)	_____	_____
6. Increases or decreases (as a percentage of sleep) during childhood	_____	_____
7. Timing in sleep cycle (dominates early or late)	_____	_____

Sleep Loss and Health

In recent years, researchers have begun to investigate the notion that sleep deprivation might have serious health consequences. Accumulating evidence suggests that sleep loss can affect physiological processes in ways that may undermine physical health. For example, sleep restriction appears to trigger hormonal changes that increase hunger (Shlisky et al., 2012). One study found that just one night of sleep deprivation increased the caloric value of food purchased the next morning by 9 percent (Chapman et al., 2013). Consistent with these findings, studies have found a link between short sleep duration and increased obesity, which is a risk factor for a variety of health problems (Knutson, 2012). Researchers have also found that sleep loss leads to impaired immune system functioning (Motivala & Irwin, 2007) and increased inflammatory responses (Patel et al., 2009), which are likely to heighten vulnerability to a variety of diseases. Thus, it is not surprising that studies have uncovered links between short sleep duration and an increased risk of diabetes, hypertension, and coronary disease (Grandner et al., 2012, 2014).

These findings have motivated researchers to explore the correlation between habitual sleep time and overall mortality. The results of this research have provided a bit of a surprise. As expected, people who consistently sleep less than seven hours exhibit an elevated mortality risk, but so do those who routinely sleep more than eight hours. In fact, mortality rates are especially high among those who sleep more than ten hours (see Figure 5.8) (Grandner et al., 2010; Kakizaki et al., 2013). Researchers are now scrambling to figure out why long sleep duration is correlated with elevated mortality. It could be that prolonged sleep is a "marker" for other problems, such as depression or a sedentary lifestyle, that have negative effects on health (Patel et al., 2006). Bear in mind, also, that the studies linking typical sleep duration to mortality have depended on participants' self-report estimates of how long they normally sleep, and these subjective reports may be inaccurate (Bianchi et al., 2013). In any event, the relationship between sleep duration and health is an emerging area of research that will probably yield some interesting findings in the years to come.

Problems in the Night: Sleep Disorders

Not everyone is able to consistently enjoy the luxury of a good night's sleep (Gradisar, Gardner, & Dohnt, 2011). According to the American Sleep Disorders

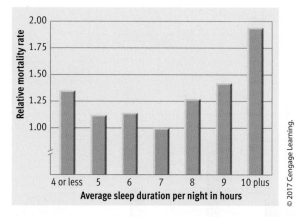

Figure 5.8

Mortality rates as a function of typical sleep duration. In a study of over 100 000 subjects followed for ten years, Tamakoshi et al. (2004) estimated mortality rates in relation to typical sleep duration. The lowest mortality rate was found among those who slept seven hours, so that figure was arbitrarily set to 1.00 and the mortality rates for other sleep lengths were calculated relative to that baseline. The rates shown here are averaged for males and females. As you can see, higher mortality rates are associated with both shorter sleep durations and longer sleep durations. Mortality rates were especially elevated among those who reported that they slept ten or more hours per night. (Data from Tamakoshi et al., 2004)

Association's *International Classification of Sleep Disorders: Diagnostic and Coding Manual*, there are 78 different types of sleep disorders (Dement, 1999). While we will not be able to discuss them all, in this section we will briefly discuss what is currently known about a variety of relatively common or well-known sleep disorders.

Insomnia

Insomnia is the most common sleep disorder. Insomnia refers to chronic problems in getting adequate sleep that result in daytime fatigue and impaired functioning. It occurs in three basic patterns: (1) difficulty in falling asleep initially, (2) difficulty in remaining asleep, and (3) persistent early-morning awakening. Insomnia may sound like a minor problem to those who haven't struggled with it, but it can be a very unpleasant ailment. Moreover, insomnia is associated with reduced productivity; increased absenteeism at work; an elevated risk for accidents, anxiety, and depression; and notable increases in quite a variety of serious health problems, as shown in Figure 5.9 (Kucharczyk, Morgan, & Hall, 2012; Sivertsen et al., 2014).

How common is insomnia? Nearly everyone suffers occasional sleep difficulties because of stress, disruptions of biological rhythms, or other temporary circumstances. Fortunately, these problems clear up spontaneously for most people. However, studies suggest that about 10 percent of adults suffer

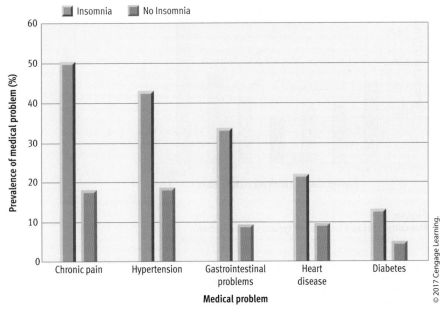

Figure 5.9

Insomnia and medical conditions. Insomnia is associated with quite a variety of medical problems. As you can see in this graph, people with insomnia (blue bars) are more likely to suffer from a number of serious medical conditions than people without insomnia (green bars). The causal relations underlying these findings are under investigation. (Based on data from Lichstein et al., 2011)

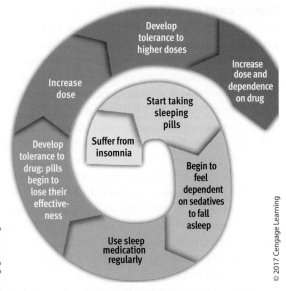

Figure 5.10

The vicious circle of dependence on sleeping pills. Because of the body's ability to develop tolerance to drugs, using sedatives routinely to "cure" insomnia can lead to a vicious circle of escalating dependency as larger and larger doses of the sedative are needed to produce the same effect.

Heath Ledger, the Australian star of movies such as *Brokeback Mountain* and *The Dark Knight*, suffered from insomnia. Just before his untimely death in 2008 from a possible accidental overdose of, among other things, sleep medications, he reported that he had been sleeping less than two hours a night (Graham, 2008).

from chronic, serious problems with insomnia, and another 20–30 percent report intermittent symptoms of insomnia (Morgan, 2012). The prevalence of insomnia increases with age and is about 50 percent more common in women than in men (Partinen & Hublin, 2011).

A large portion of people suffering from insomnia do not pursue professional treatment. Many of them probably depend on over-the-counter sleep aids, which have questionable value (Mahowald & Schenck, 2005). The most common approach in the medical treatment of insomnia is the prescription of two classes of drugs: benzodiazepine sedatives (such as Dalmane, Halcion, and Restoril), which were originally developed to relieve anxiety, and newer non-benzodiazepine sedatives (such as Ambien, Sonata, and Lunesta), which were designed primarily for sleep problems (Mendelson, 2011). Both types of sedative medications are fairly effective in helping people fall asleep more quickly, and they reduce nighttime awakenings and increase total sleep (Walsh & Roth, 2011).

Nonetheless, sedatives can be a problematic long-range solution for insomnia, for a number of reasons. It is possible to overdose on sleeping pills (especially in conjunction with alcohol use), and they have some potential for abuse. Sedatives also have carryover effects that can make people drowsy and sluggish the next day (Walsh & Roth, 2011). Moreover,

with continued use, sedatives gradually become less effective, so people need to increase their dose, creating a vicious circle of escalating dependency (Lader, 2002) (see Figure 5.10). Another problem is that when people abruptly discontinue their sleep medication, they can experience unpleasant withdrawal symptoms (Lee-Chiong & Sateia, 2006). Fortunately, the newer nonbenzodiazepine sedatives have reduced (but not eliminated) some of the problems associated with earlier generations of sleeping pills (Mendelson, 2011).

The potential risks of sleep medications have been put in sharp focus by studies that report dramatic increases in mortality among those who use sleeping pills. One study of electronic medical records compared 10 529 patients who had received sedative prescriptions against 23 676 matched control cases from the same database (Kripke, Langer, & Kline, 2012). In just 2.5 years, 6.1 percent of the sedative users died, whereas the death rate among non-users was only 1.2 percent. Thus, sleep medications were associated with a fivefold increase in mortality in a relatively short time frame! Another study, using a database of more than 104 000 medical records, yielded similar results (Weich et al., 2014). Patients who were prescribed benzodiazepine sedatives exhibited an almost fourfold elevation in mortality over a period of 7.5 years. Although many physicians assert that the problems associated with sleeping pills have been exaggerated (Walsh & Roth, 2011), these surprising findings on mortality rates raise new questions about the safety of sleep medications.

There are alternatives to sleep medications. Quite a variety of effective therapeutic interventions for insomnia have been developed, including relaxation training, sleep hygiene education, and cognitive-behavioural therapy, but they tend to be underutilized (Morin, 2011).

Other Sleep Problems

Although insomnia is the most common difficulty associated with sleep, people are plagued by many other types of sleep problems, as well. Let's briefly look at the symptoms, causes, and prevalence of five additional sleep problems.

Narcolepsy is a disease marked by sudden and irresistible onsets of sleep during normal waking periods. A person suffering from narcolepsy goes directly from wakefulness into REM sleep, usually for a short period (10–20 minutes). This is a potentially dangerous condition because some victims fall asleep instantly, even while walking across a room or driving a car. Narcolepsy is relatively uncommon; it is seen in only about 0.05 percent of the population (Partinen & Hublin, 2011). Impairment in the regulation of REM sleep is the main cause of narcolepsy (Siegel, 2011). This impairment appears to be due to the loss of orexin neurons in the hypothalamus (Sakurai, 2013). Some individuals show a genetic predisposition to the disease. Stimulant drugs have been used to treat this condition with modest success (Guilleminault & Cao, 2011). But as you will see in our upcoming discussion of drugs, stimulants carry many problems of their own.

Sleep apnea involves frequent, reflexive gasping for air that awakens a person and disrupts sleep. Some victims are awakened from their sleep hundreds of times a night. Apnea occurs when a person literally stops breathing for a minimum of ten seconds. This disorder, which is usually accompanied by loud snoring, is seen in about 8 percent of adults, and its prevalence is increasing (Cao, Guilleminault, & Kushida, 2011). A higher incidence is seen among males, older adults, postmenopausal women, obese people, and those with a genetic predisposition to the disease (Redline, 2011; Sanders & Givelber, 2006). As you might expect, sleep apnea can have a disruptive effect on sleep, leading to excessive daytime sleepiness. Sleep apnea is a more serious disorder than widely appreciated because it increases vulnerability to cardiovascular diseases and more than doubles one's overall mortality risk (Kendzerska et al., 2014; Lee, Lee, et al., 2013). Apnea is also associated with declines in attention, memory, and other aspects of cognitive functioning (Weaver & George, 2011). Apnea may be treated with lifestyle modifications (weight loss, reduced alcohol intake, improved sleep hygiene); drug therapy; special masks and oral devices that improve airflow; and upper airway and craniofacial surgery (Phillips & Kryger, 2011).

Night terrors (also called "sleep terrors") are abrupt awakenings from NREM sleep, accompanied by intense autonomic arousal and feelings of panic. Night terrors, which can produce remarkable accelerations of heart rate, usually occur during stage 4 sleep early in the night (Nielsen & Zadra, 2000). Victims typically let out a piercing cry, bolt upright, and then stare into space. They do not usually recall a coherent dream, although they may remember a simple, frightening image. The panic normally fades quickly, and a return to sleep is fairly easy. Night terrors occur in adults, but they are more common in children. Approximately 6 percent of children experience these night terrors (Buysse et al., 1993). Night terrors are not indicative of an emotional disturbance. Treatment may not be necessary, as night terrors are often a temporary problem.

Somnambulism, or sleepwalking, occurs when a person arises and wanders about while remaining asleep. About 15 percent of children exhibit sleepwalking (Cartwright, 2006). According to a recent study (Petit et al., 2015), the peak age for sleep terrors is one-and-a-half years of age, while for sleepwalking it is ten years of age. A survey of a representative sample of more than 19 000 adults found that 3.6 percent of adults reported a sleepwalking episode in the last year (Ohayon et al., 2012). A study of 100 individuals who sought treatment for their somnambulism (and presumably had relatively severe cases) found that 23 percent had daily episodes of sleepwalking, and 43 percent had weekly episodes (Lopez et al., 2013). Sleepwalking tends to occur during the first three hours of sleep, when individuals are in slow-wave sleep (see Figure 5.11) (Zadra & Pilon, 2012). Episodes can last from a minute or two up to 30 minutes. Sleepwalkers may awaken during their journey, or they may return to bed without any recollection of their excursion. The causes of this unusual disorder are unknown, although it appears to have a genetic predisposition, and episodes are associated with prior sleep deprivation and increased stress (Lopez et al., 2013). Also, episodes may be more likely in people who use nonbenzodiazepine sedatives, especially Ambien (Gunn & Gunn, 2006). During sleepwalking episodes, some people engage in inappropriate aggressive or sexual behaviour. Accidents and injuries are common during sleepwalking, including

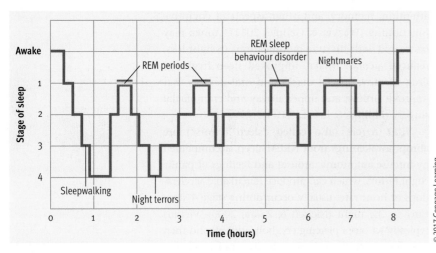

Figure 5.11
Sleep problems and the cycle of sleep. Different sleep problems tend to occur at different points in the sleep cycle. Whereas sleepwalking tends to occur during slow-wave sleep, disturbances due to REM-sleep behaviour disorder obviously occur during REM periods. Routine nightmares are also associated with the heightened dream activity of REM sleep.

© 2017 Cengage Learning

life-threatening incidents (Zadra & Pilon, 2012). A history of injuries is often what finally motivates people to seek treatment for their somnambulism. For example, the sleepwalkers who sought treatment in the Lopez et al. (2013) study included an individual who had jumped out a third-story window and another who had fallen down a flight of stairs.

reality **check**

Misconception

Sleepwalkers are acting out their dreams and it is dangerous to awaken them.

Reality

Sleepwalking does not occur in conjunction with dreams. It is not rare for sleepwalkers to hurt themselves. Hence, it's best to waken people (gently) from a sleepwalking episode. Waking them is much safer than letting them wander about.

REM sleep behaviour disorder (RBD) **is marked by potentially troublesome dream enactments during REM periods.** People who exhibit this syndrome may talk, yell, gesture, flail about, or leap out of bed during their REM dreams. When questioned, many report they were being chased or attacked in their dreams. Their dream enactments can get surprisingly violent, and they often hurt themselves or their bed partners (Mahowald & Schenck, 2005). RBD occurs mostly in men, who typically begin experiencing this problem in their 50s or 60s. As noted earlier, people in REM sleep normally are virtually paralyzed, which prevents dream enactments. The cause of RBD appears to be deterioration in the brainstem structures that are normally responsible for immobilization during REM periods (Chen et al., 2013). A majority of people who suffer from RBD eventually go on to develop neurodegenerative disorders, especially Parkinson's disease (Mahowald & Schenck, 2005). The RBD symptoms may precede the emergence of Parkinson's disease by as much as ten years.

Nightmares **are anxiety-arousing dreams that lead to awakening, usually from REM sleep** (see Figure 5.11). Typically, a person who awakens from a nightmare recalls a vivid dream and may have difficulty getting back to sleep. Nightmares tend to occur during REM sleep, as you might expect (Augedal et al., 2013). There is evidence that nightmares are associated with measures of an individual's well-being. Significant stress in one's life is associated with increased frequency and intensity of nightmares (Nielsen & Levin, 2009).

Although about 5 percent of adults have occasional trouble with nightmares, these frightening episodes are mainly a problem among children (Schredl, 2009). Between 10 and 50 percent of children experience nightmares on a regular basis (Schredl, 2010). Most children have periodic nightmares, but persistent nightmares may reflect an emotional disturbance. If a child's nightmares are frequent and unpleasant, counselling may prove helpful. But most children outgrow the problem on their own.

The World of Dreams

For the most part, dreams are not taken very seriously in Western societies. Paradoxically, though, Robert Van de Castle (1994) points out that dreams have sometimes changed the world. For example, Van de Castle describes how René Descartes's philosophy of dualism, Frederick Banting's discovery of insulin, Elias Howe's refinement of the sewing machine, Mohandas Gandhi's strategy of nonviolent protest,

and Lyndon Johnson's withdrawal from the 1968 U.S. presidential race were all inspired by dreams. He also explains how Mary Shelley's *Frankenstein* and Robert Louis Stevenson's *The Strange Case of Dr. Jekyll and Mr. Hyde* emerged out of their dream experiences. In his wide-ranging discussion, Van de Castle also relates how the Surrealist painter Salvador Dali characterized his works as "dream photographs," and how legendary filmmakers Ingmar Bergman, Orson Welles, and Federico Fellini all drew on their dreams in making their films. Thus, Van de Castle concludes that "dreams have had a dramatic influence on almost every important aspect of our culture and history" (p. 10).

The Contents of Dreams

What do people dream about? Overall, dreams are not as exciting as advertised. Perhaps dreams are seen as exotic because people are more likely to remember their more bizarre nighttime dramas (De Koninck, 2000). After analyzing the contents of more than 10 000 dreams, Calvin Hall (1966) concluded that most dreams are relatively mundane. They tend to unfold in familiar settings with a cast of characters dominated by family, friends, and colleagues (Zadra & Domhoff, 2011). We *are* more tolerant of logical discrepancies and implausible scenarios in our dreams than our waking thought (Kahn, 2007), but in our dreams we generally move through coherent, sensible, realistic virtual worlds (Nielsen & Stenstrom, 2005). The one nearly universal element of dreams is a coherent sense of self—we almost always experience dreams from a first-person perspective (Valli & Revonsuo, 2009).

In one large study, sleep researchers from the University of Montreal, Trent University, and the University of Alberta administered the *Typical Dreams Questionnaire* to over 1000 first-year Canadian university students. The dream themes and their frequency as reported by those students are shown in Table 5.2.

Certain themes tend to be more common than others in dreams (see Table 5.2). While college students often dream quite a bit about sex, aggression, and misfortune, they also dream about negative and potentially traumatic events. However the notion

Table 5.2

Common Themes in Dreams

Studies of dream content find that certain themes are particularly common. The data shown here are from a study of 1181 college students in Canada (Nielsen et al., 2003). This list shows the 25 dreams most frequently reported by the students. Total prevalence refers to the percentage of students reporting each dream. © Cengage Learning 2013.

RANK	DREAM CONTENT	TOTAL PREVALENCE (%)
1	Chased or pursued, not physically injured	81.5
2	Sexual experiences	76.5
3	Falling	73.8
4	School, teachers, studying	67.1
5	Arriving too late (e.g., missing a train)	59.5
6	Being on the verge of falling	57.7
7	A person now alive as dead	54.1
8	Trying again and again to do something	53.5
9	Flying or soaring through the air	48.3
10	Vividly sensing . . . a presence in the room	48.3
11	Failing an examination	45.0
12	Physically attacked (beaten, stabbed, raped)	42.4
13	Being frozen with fright	40.7
14	A person now dead as alive	38.4
15	Being a child again	36.7
16	Being killed	34.5
17	Swimming	34.3
18	Insects or spiders	33.8
19	Being nude	32.6
20	Being inappropriately dressed	32.5
21	Discovering a new room at home	32.3
22	Losing control of a vehicle	32.0
23	Eating delicious foods	30.7
24	Being half awake and paralyzed in bed	27.2
25	Finding money	25.7

Source: Nielsen, T. A., Zadra, A. L., Simard, V., Saucier, S., Stenstrom, P., Smith, C., & Kuiken, D. (2003). The typical dreams of Canadian university students. *Dreaming*, 13(4), 211–235 [Table 2.1, page 217]. Copyright © 2003 American Psychological Association. Reprinted with permission.

reality check

Misconception

If you fall from a height in a dream, you'd better wake up on the plunge downward, because if you hit the bottom, the shock to your system could be so great that you could die in your sleep.

Reality

Think about this one for a moment. *If* it were a genuine problem, who would have reported it? You can be sure that no one has ever testified to experiencing a fatal dream. This myth presumably exists because many people do awaken during the downward plunge, thinking that they've averted a close call. In reality, people do have dreams about their own death—and live to tell about them.

that a traumatic dream could be fatal, is just not true. According to Hall (1966), dreams tend to centre on classic sources of internal conflict, such as the conflict between taking chances and playing it safe. Hall was struck by how rarely people dream about public affairs and current events. Typically, dreams are self-centred; people dream mostly about themselves.

Links between Dreams and Waking Life

Although dreams seem to belong in a world of their own, what people dream about is affected by what is going on in their lives (Walmsley & Stickgold, 2009).

If you're struggling with financial problems, worried about an upcoming exam, or sexually attracted to a classmate, these themes may very well show up in your dreams. As Domhoff (2001) puts it, "dream content in general is continuous with waking conceptions and emotional preoccupations" (p. 13). Freud noticed long ago that the contents of waking life often tended to spill into dreams; he labelled this spillover the *day residue*. Thus, it seems as if there is significant continuity between our waking and dreaming states of consciousness (Lee, 2015).

On occasion, the content of dreams can also be affected by stimuli experienced while one is dreaming (De Koninck, 2000). For example, William Dement sprayed water on one hand of sleeping subjects while they were in the REM stage (Dement & Wolpert, 1958). Subjects who weren't awakened by the water were awakened by the experimenter a short time later and asked what they had been dreaming about. Dement found that 42 percent of the subjects had incorporated the water into their dreams. They said that they had dreamt that they were in rainfalls, floods, baths, swimming pools, and the like. Some people report that they occasionally experience the same sort of phenomenon at home when the sound of their alarm clock fails to awaken them. The alarm is incorporated into their dream as a loud engine or a siren, for instance. As with day residue, the incorporation of external stimuli into dreams shows that people's dream world is not entirely separate from their real world.

Sometimes people may realize they are dreaming while still in the dream state (Laberge, 2009; Stumbrys & Daniel, 2010; Voss et al., 2009). These are often referred to as "lucid dreams" (Denis & Poerio, 2017; Gackenbach & Sheikh, 1991; Zink & Pietrowsky, 2015). *Lucid dreams* **are dreams in which people can think clearly about the circumstances of waking life and the fact that they are dreaming, yet they remain asleep in the midst of a vivid dream.** In some of these dreams, the dreamer may be able to exert some control over the dream. According to members of the Dream and Nightmare Laboratory established at Montreal's Sacré-Coeur Hospital in 1991 (*Lucid Dreaming*, 2005), it has been suggested that lucid dreaming might be useful in the treatment of nightmares. To be useful, however, the therapist must be able to somehow control or influence the onset of the lucid dreams. Thus, one of the issues here is the induction of lucid dreaming for therapeutic use.

Culture and Dreams

Striking cross-cultural variations occur in beliefs about the nature of dreams and the importance attributed to them (Lohman, 2007). In modern Western society, people typically make a distinction between the "real" world they experience while awake and the "imaginary" world they experience while dreaming. Some people realize that events in the real world can affect their dreams, but few believe that events in their dreams hold any significance for their waking life. Although a small minority of individuals take their dreams seriously, in Western cultures, dreams are largely written off as insignificant, meaningless meanderings of the unconscious (Tart, 1988).

In many non-Western cultures, however, dreams are viewed as important sources of information about oneself, about the future, or about the spiritual world (Kracke, 1991). Although no culture confuses dreams with waking reality, many view events in dreams as another type of reality that may be just as important as, or perhaps even more important than, events experienced while awake. Among the Inuit who live in the far north of Canada, *angakoks* or shamans often had the power to travel and visit hidden places that other people were unable to visit. They made these visits through their trances and dreams. Dreams clearly played an important part in the Inuit culture (Houston, 2008). Dreams continue to play a large role in contemporary Canadian Aboriginal culture in, for example, works such as the *Rez Sisters* by Canadian Cree playwright, author, and musician Tomson Highway (1988).

In regard to dream content, both similarities and differences occur across cultures in the types of dreams that people report (Domhoff, 2005b; H. Hunt, 1989). Some basic dream themes appear to be nearly universal (falling, being pursued, having sex). However, the contents of dreams vary somewhat from one culture to another because people in different societies deal with different worlds while awake. For example, in a 1950 study of the Siriono, a hunting-and-gathering people of the Amazon who were almost always hungry and spent most of their time in a grim search for food, *half* of the reported dreams focused on hunting, gathering, and eating food (D'Andrade, 1961).

Theories of Dreaming

Many theories have been proposed to explain why people dream (Barrett, 2011; Voss, 2011). Sigmund Freud (1900), who analyzed clients' dreams in therapy, believed that the principal purpose of dreams is *wish fulfillment*. He thought that people fulfill ungratified needs from waking hours through wishful thinking in dreams. For example, someone who is sexually frustrated might have highly erotic dreams, while an unsuccessful person might dream

National Library of Medicine

Sigmund Freud

"[Dreams are] the royal road to the unconscious."

about great accomplishments. Although these examples involve blatant wishful thinking, Freud asserted that the wish-fulfilling quality of many dreams may not be readily apparent because the unconscious attempts to censor and disguise the true meaning of dreams. Freud distinguished between the manifest and latent content of dreams. The *manifest content* consists of the plot of a dream at the surface level. The *latent content* refers to the hidden or disguised meaning of the events in the plot. Freud felt that deciphering the latent content of a dream was a complex matter that requires intimate knowledge of the dreamer's current issues and childhood conflicts.

Other theorists, such as Rosalind Cartwright (1977; Cartwright & Lamberg, 1992), have proposed that dreams provide an opportunity to work through everyday problems. According to her *cognitive, problem-solving view*, there is considerable continuity between waking and sleeping thought. Proponents of this view believe that dreams allow people to engage in creative thinking about problems because dreams are not restrained by logic or realism. Consistent with this view, Cartwright (1991) has found that women going through divorce frequently dream about divorce-related problems. Cartwright's analysis is thought-provoking, but critics point out that just because people dream about problems from their waking life doesn't mean they are dreaming up solutions (Blagrove, 1992, 1996). Nonetheless, research showing that sleep can enhance learning (Walker & Stickgold, 2004) adds new credibility to the problem-solving view of dreams (Cartwright, 2004).

J. Allan Hobson and Robert McCarley argue that dreams are simply the by-product of bursts of activity emanating from subcortical areas in the brain (Hobson, 2002; Hobson & McCarley, 1977; Hobson, Pace-Schott, & Stickgold, 2000). Their *activation-synthesis model* and its more recent revisions (Hobson, 2007; Hobson et al., 2000) propose that dreams are side effects of the neural activation that produces "wide-awake" brain waves during REM sleep. According to this model, neurons firing periodically in lower brain centres send random signals to the cortex (the seat of complex thought). The cortex supposedly synthesizes (constructs) a dream to make sense out of these signals. The activation-synthesis model does *not* assume that dreams are meaningless. As Hobson (1988) puts it, "Dreams are as meaningful as they can be under the adverse working conditions of the brain in REM sleep" (p. 214). In contrast to the theories of Freud and Cartwright, this theory obviously downplays the role of emotional factors as determinants of dreams. Like other theories of dreams, the activation-synthesis model has its share of critics. They point out that the model cannot accommodate the fact that dreaming occurs outside of REM sleep and that the contents of dreams are considerably more meaningful than the model would predict (Domhoff, 2005a; Foulkes, 1996).

These approaches, summarized in Figure 5.12, are only three of a host of theories about the functions of dreams. All of these theories are based more on conjecture than solid evidence, and none of them has been tested adequately. In part, this is because the private, subjective nature of dreams makes it difficult to put the theories to an empirical test. Thus, the purpose of dreaming remains a mystery.

Courtesy of Rosalind Cartwright

Rosalind Cartwright

"One function of dreams may be to restore our sense of competence. . . . It is also probable that in times of stress, dreams have more work to do in resolving our problems and are thus more salient and memorable."

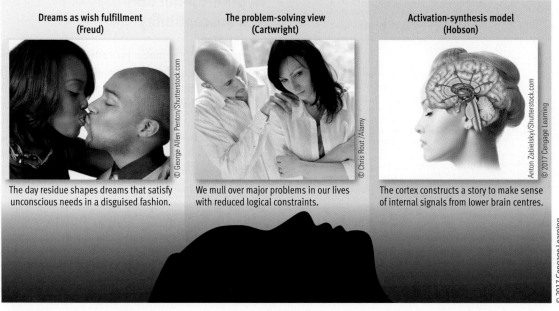

Dreams as wish fulfillment (Freud)

The day residue shapes dreams that satisfy unconscious needs in a disguised fashion.

The problem-solving view (Cartwright)

We mull over major problems in our lives with reduced logical constraints.

Activation-synthesis model (Hobson)

The cortex constructs a story to make sense of internal signals from lower brain centres.

Figure 5.12

Three theories of dreaming. Dreams can be explained in a variety of ways. Freud stressed the wish-fulfilling function of dreams. Cartwright emphasizes the problem-solving function of dreams. Hobson and McCarley assert that dreams are merely a by-product of periodic neural activation. All three theories are speculative and have their critics.

Hypnosis: Altered Consciousness or Role Playing?

Key Learning Goals

▶ Discuss hypnotic susceptibility, and list some prominent effects of hypnosis.

▶ Compare the role-playing and altered-state theory of hypnosis.

Hypnosis has a long and checkered history (Schmit, 2010). The recent history of hypnosis begins with a flamboyant 18th-century Austrian physician by the name of Franz Anton Mesmer. Working in Paris, Mesmer claimed to cure people of illnesses through an elaborate routine involving a "laying on of hands." Mesmer had some complicated theories about how he had harnessed "animal magnetism." However, we know today that he had simply stumbled onto the power of suggestion (Green, Laurence, & Lynne, 2014). It was rumoured that the French government offered him a princely amount of money to disclose how he effected his cures. He refused, probably because he didn't really know. Eventually he was dismissed as a charlatan and run out of town by the local authorities. Although officially discredited,

Mesmer inspired followers—practitioners of "mesmerism"—who continued to ply their trade. To this day, our language preserves the memory of Franz Mesmer: When we are under the spell of an event or a story, we are "mesmerized."

Eventually, a Scottish physician, James Braid, became interested in the trancelike state that could be induced by the mesmerists. It was Braid who popularized the term *hypnotism* in 1843, borrowing it from the Greek word for *sleep*. Braid thought that hypnotism could be used to produce anesthesia for surgeries. However, just as hypnosis was catching on as a general anesthetic, more powerful and reliable chemical anesthetics were discovered, and interest in hypnotism dwindled.

Since then, hypnotism has led a curious dual existence. On the one hand, it has been the subject of numerous scientific studies and discussions (Barabasz & Barabasz, 2015; Sanchez-Armass, 2015). Furthermore, it has enjoyed considerable use as a clinical tool by physicians, dentists, and psychologists for over a century and has empirically supported value in the treatment of a variety of psychological and physical maladies (Green et al., 2014; Lynn et al., 2000). On the other hand, however, an assortment of entertainers and quacks have continued in the less respectable tradition of mesmerism, using hypnotism for parlour tricks and chicanery. It is little wonder, then, that many myths about hypnosis have come to be widely accepted (see Figure 5.13). In this section, we'll work on clearing up some of the confusion surrounding hypnosis.

Hypnotic Induction and Susceptibility

Hypnosis is a systematic procedure that typically produces a heightened state of suggestibility. It may also lead to passive relaxation, narrowed attention, and enhanced fantasy. If only in popular films, virtually everyone has seen a *hypnotic induction* enacted with a swinging pendulum. Actually, many techniques can be used for inducing hypnosis (Gibbons & Lynn, 2010). Usually, the hypnotist will suggest to the subject that he or she is relaxing. Repetitively and softly, subjects are told that they are getting tired, drowsy, or sleepy. Often, the hypnotist vividly describes bodily sensations that should be occurring. Subjects are told that their arms are going limp, their feet are getting warm, their eyelids are getting heavy. Gradually, most subjects succumb

Hypnosis: Myth and Reality	
If you think . . .	**The reality is . . .**
Relaxation is an important feature of hypnosis.	It's not. Hypnosis has been induced during vigorous exercise.
It's mostly just compliance.	Many highly motivated subjects fail to experience hypnosis.
It's a matter of willful faking.	Physiological responses indicate that hypnotized subjects generally are not lying.
It has something to do with a sleeplike state.	It does not. Hypnotized subjects are fully awake.
Responding to hypnosis is like responding to a placebo.	Placebo responsiveness and hypnotizability are not correlated.
People who are hypnotized lose control of themselves.	Subjects are perfectly capable of saying no or terminating hypnosis.
Hypnosis can enable people to "relive" the past.	Age-regressed adults behave like adults play-acting as children.
When hypnotized, people can remember more accurately.	Hypnosis may actually muddle the distinction between memory and fantasy and may artificially inflate confidence.
Hypnotized people do not remember what happened during the session.	Posthypnotic amnesia does not occur spontaneously.
Hypnosis can enable people to perform otherwise impossible feats of strength, endurance, learning, and sensory acuity.	Performance following hypnotic suggestions for increased muscle strength, learning, and sensory acuity does not exceed what can be accomplished by motivated subjects outside hypnosis.

Figure 5.13

Misconceptions regarding hypnosis. Mistaken ideas about the nature of hypnosis are common. Some widely believed myths about hypnosis are summarized here along with more accurate information on each point, based on an article by Michael Nash (2001), a prominent hypnosis researcher. Many of these myths and realities are discussed in more detail in the text.

Source: Adapted from Nash, M.R. (2001, July). The truth and the hype of hypnosis. *Scientific American, 285*, 36–43. Copyright © 2001 by Scientific American, Inc.

and become hypnotized. People differ in how well they respond to hypnotic induction. About 10–20 percent of people don't respond well at all. At the other end of the continuum, about 15 percent of people are exceptionally good hypnotic subjects (Barnier, Cox, & McConkey, 2014). Many interesting effects can be produced in people who are susceptible to hypnosis. Some of the more prominent hypnotic phenomena include:

1. *Anesthesia.* Drugs are more reliable, but hypnosis can be surprisingly effective in the treatment of both acute and chronic pain (Boly et al., 2007; Jensen & Patterson, 2014). Although the practice is not widespread, some physicians, dentists, and psychologists use hypnosis as a treatment for problems with pain, especially chronic pain.

2. *Sensory distortions and hallucinations.* Hypnotized subjects may be led to experience auditory or visual hallucinations (Spiegel, 2003b). They may hear sounds or see things that are not there, or fail to hear or see stimuli that are present (Spiegel et al., 1985). Subjects may also have their sensations distorted so that something sweet tastes sour or an unpleasant odour smells fragrant.

3. *Disinhibition.* Hypnosis can sometimes reduce inhibitions that would normally prevent subjects from acting in ways they would see as immoral or unacceptable. In experiments, hypnotized subjects have been induced to throw what they believed to be nitric acid into the face of a research assistant. Similarly, stage hypnotists are sometimes successful in getting people to disrobe in public. This disinhibition effect may occur simply because hypnotized people feel that they cannot be held responsible for actions taken while hypnotized.

4. *Posthypnotic suggestions and amnesia.* Suggestions made during hypnosis may influence a participant's later behaviour (Cox & Bryant, 2008). The most common posthypnotic suggestion is the creation of posthypnotic amnesia. That is, subjects who are told that they will remember nothing that happened while they were hypnotized do indeed usually remember nothing.

Theories of Hypnosis

Although a number of theories have been developed to explain hypnosis, it is still not well understood. One popular view is that hypnotic effects occur because participants are put into a special, altered state of consciousness, called a *hypnotic trance* (Christensen, 2005). Although hypnotized subjects may feel as though they are in an altered state, they do not seem to show reliable alterations in brain activity that are unique to hypnosis (Burgess, 2007;

Lynn et al., 2007). The failure to find any special physiological changes associated with hypnosis has led some theorists to conclude that hypnosis is a normal state of consciousness that is simply characterized by dramatic role playing.

Social-Cognitive Theory of Hypnosis: Hypnosis as Role Playing

Theodore Barber (1979) and Carleton University's Nicholas Spanos (1986; Spanos & Coe, 1992) have been the leading advocates of the view that hypnosis produces a normal mental state in which suggestible people act out the role of a hypnotic subject and behave as they think hypnotized people are supposed to. According to this notion, hypnosis is not the result of a person being in a "trance" but rather results from normal everyday processes including an individual's expectations and attitudes. Thus, it is subjects' role expectations that produce hypnotic effects, rather than a special trancelike state of consciousness.

Two lines of evidence support the role-playing view. First, many of the seemingly amazing effects of hypnosis have been duplicated by nonhypnotized participants or have been shown to be exaggerated (Kirsch, 1997; Kirsch, Mazzoni, & Montgomery, 2007). For example, anecdotal reports that hypnosis can enhance memory have not stood up well to empirical testing. Although hypnosis may occasionally facilitate recall in some people, experimental studies have tended to find that hypnotized participants make more memory errors than nonhypnotized participants, even though they often feel more confident about their recollections (McConkey, 1992; Scoboria et al., 2002). These findings suggest that no special state of consciousness is required to explain hypnotic feats.

Biomedical Research Foundation

Theodore Barber

"Thousands of books, movies, and professional articles have woven the concept of 'hypnotic trance' into the common knowledge. And yet there is almost no scientific support for it."

reality check

Misconception

Under hypnosis, people can perform feats that they could never perform otherwise.

Reality

Stage hypnotists make their living by getting people to do things that appear out of the ordinary. For example, much has been made of the fact that hypnotized subjects can be used as "human planks," lying down between two chairs so stiffly that people can walk right over them without them falling between the chairs. However, it turns out that nonhypnotized subjects can match this feat. Research suggests that all the phenomena produced in hypnosis can also be produced by suggestion without hypnosis.

The second line of evidence involves demonstrations that hypnotized participants are often acting out a role. For example, Martin Orne (1951) regressed hypnotized subjects back to their sixth birthday and asked them to describe it. They responded with detailed descriptions that appeared to represent great feats of hypnosis-enhanced memory. However, instead of accepting this information at face value, Orne compared it with information that he had obtained from the subjects' parents. It turned out that many of the participants' memories were inaccurate and invented! Many other studies have also found that age-regressed subjects' recall of the distant past tends to be more fanciful than factual (Green, 1999; Perry, Kusel, & Perry, 1988). Thus, the role-playing explanation of hypnosis suggests that situational factors lead some subjects to act out a certain role in a highly cooperative manner (Lynn, Kirsch, & Hallquist, 2008; Wagstaff et al., 2010).

Hypnosis as an Altered State of Consciousness

Despite the doubts raised by role-playing explanations, many prominent theorists still maintain that hypnotic effects are attributable to a special, altered state of consciousness (Beahrs, 1983; Fromm, 1979, 1992; Hilgard, 1986; Spiegel, 1995, 2003b; Woody & Sadler, 2008). These theorists argue that it is doubtful that role playing can explain all hypnotic phenomena. For instance, they assert that even the most cooperative subjects are unlikely to endure surgery without a drug anesthetic just to please their physician and live up to their expected role. They also cite studies in which hypnotized participants have continued to display hypnotic responses when they thought they were alone and not being observed (Perugini et al., 1998). If hypnotized participants were merely acting, they would drop the act when alone.

The most impressive research undermining the role-playing view has come from recent brain-imaging studies, which suggest that hypnotized participants experience changes in brain activity that appear consistent with their reports of hypnosis-induced hallucinations (Spiegel, 2003b) or pain suppression (Hofbauer et al., 2001).

The most influential explanation of hypnosis as an altered state of awareness has been offered by Ernest Hilgard (1986, 1992). According to Hilgard, hypnosis creates a *dissociation* in consciousness. **Dissociation is a splitting off of mental processes into two separate, simultaneous streams of awareness.** In other words, Hilgard theorizes that hypnosis splits consciousness into two streams. One stream is in communication with the hypnotist and the external world, while the other is a difficult-to-detect "hidden observer." Hilgard believes that many hypnotic effects are a product of this divided consciousness. For instance, he suggests that a hypnotized subject might appear to be unresponsive to pain because the pain isn't registered in the portion of consciousness that communicates with other people.

One appealing aspect of Hilgard's theory is that *divided consciousness* is a common, normal experience. For example, people will often drive a car a great distance, responding to traffic signals and other cars, with no recollection of having consciously done so. In such cases, consciousness is clearly divided between driving and the person's thoughts about other matters. Interestingly, this common experience has long been known as *highway hypnosis*. In this condition, there is even an "amnesia" for the component of consciousness that drove the car, similar to posthypnotic amnesia.

A resolution to the debate about whether hypnosis involves an altered state of consciousness does not appear imminent. The issue continues to generate insightful research that enhances our understanding of hypnosis, but the results remain equivocal and open to varied interpretations (Accardi et al., 2013; Mazzoni et al., 2013).

Courtesy of Ernest R. Hilgard

Ernest Hilgard

"Many psychologists argue that the hypnotic trance is a mirage. It would be unfortunate if this skeptical view were to gain such popularity that the benefits of hypnosis are denied to the numbers of those who could be helped."

Meditation: Pure Consciousness or Relaxation?

Key Learning Goals

▶ Explain the nature of meditation, and describe the two main types of meditation.

▶ Assess the evidence of the long-term benefits of meditation.

Recent years have seen growing interest in the ancient discipline of meditation (Davidson & Kaszniak, 2015; Garland et al., 2015; Karremans et al., 2017; Lutz et al., 2015). **Meditation refers to a family of practices that train attention to heighten awareness and bring mental processes under greater voluntary control.** There are many approaches to meditation. In North America, the most widely practised approaches are those associated with yoga, Zen, and transcendental

meditation (TM). All three of these approaches are rooted in Eastern religions (Hinduism, Buddhism, and Taoism). However, meditation has been practised throughout history as an element of all religious and spiritual traditions, including Judaism and Christianity (Walsh & Shapiro, 2006). Moreover, the practice of meditation can be largely divorced from religious beliefs. In fact, most North Americans who meditate have only vague ideas regarding its religious significance. Of interest to psychology is the fact that meditation involves a deliberate effort to alter consciousness.

Approaches to meditation can be classified into two main styles that reflect how attention is directed: *focused attention* or *open monitoring* (Cahn & Polich, 2006; Manna et al., 2010). In focused attention approaches, attention is concentrated on a specific object, image, sound, or bodily sensation (such as breathing). The intent in narrowing attention is to clear the mind of its clutter. In open monitoring approaches, attention is directed to the contents of one's moment-to-moment experience in a nonjudgmental and nonreactive way. The intent in expanding attention is to become a detached observer of the flow of one's own sensations, thoughts, and feelings. Both approaches seek to achieve a "higher" form of consciousness than people normally experience. The meditative disciplines that have received the most research attention are TM and mindfulness meditation. Mindfulness meditation is an open monitoring approach with roots in Zen Buddhism, whereas TM is primarily a focused attention approach with roots in Hinduism. As we discuss in Chapter 16, mindfulness meditation has been integrated with cognitive-behavioural therapy (CBT) to produce a particularly effective form of psychotherapy used in the treatment of many disorders, including depression and anxiety and obsessive-compulsive disorders among others (Dimidjian & Segal, 2015; Harrington & Dunne, 2015; Segal, Williams et al., 2007).

What happens when an experienced meditator goes into the meditative state? One intriguing finding is that alpha waves and theta waves become more prominent in EEG recordings (Cahn & Polich, 2006; Logopoulos et al., 2009). Many studies also find that subjects' heart rate, skin conductance, respiration rate, oxygen consumption, and carbon dioxide elimination decline (Dillbeck & Orme-Johnson, 1987; Fenwick, 1987; Travis, 2001). Taken together, these changes suggest that meditation leads to a potentially beneficial physiological state characterized by suppression of bodily arousal. However, some researchers have argued that a variety of systematic relaxation training procedures can produce similar results (Holmes, 1987; Shapiro, 1984). But mere relaxation hardly seems like an adequate explanation for the transcendent experiences reported by many meditators.

To shed new light on this lingering question, some researchers have begun to use new brain-imaging technologies in an effort to identify the neural circuits that are affected by meditation (Tang, Holzel, & Posner, 2015). In general, the results of research employing brain-imaging techniques such as PET and fMRI scans are extremely complicated, in part because different approaches to meditation appear to produce different patterns of change in brain activity, but the changes observed seem unlikely to be due to simple relaxation effects (Lutz, Dunne, & Davidson, 2007).

Long-Term Benefits

What about the long-term benefits that have been claimed for meditation? Research suggests that meditation may have some value in reducing the effects of stress (Grossman, 2004; Salmon et al., 2004). In particular, regular meditation is associated with lower levels of some "stress hormones" (Infante et al., 2001) and enhanced immune response (Davidson et al., 2003a). Research also suggests that meditation can improve mental health (Davis & Hayes, 2012) while reducing anxiety and drug abuse (Alexander et al., 1994). Other studies report that meditation may have beneficial effects on blood pressure (Barnes, Treiber, & Davis, 2001), reduced rumination (Chambers et al., 2008), working memory and focus (Jha et al., 2013; Moore & Malinowski, 2009), self-esteem (Emavardhana & Tori, 1997), cognitive flexibility and relationship satisfaction (Barnes et al., 2007; Siegel, 2007), mood and one's sense of control (Easterlin & Cardena, 1999), happiness (W. P. Smith, Compton, & West, 1995), cardiovascular health (Walton et al., 2004), patterns of sleep (Pattanshetty et al., 2010), and overall physical health and well-being (Reibel et al., 2001). In addition, health-care professionals such as psychologists and other therapists who do mindfulness meditation have shown increases in empathy, compassion, and counselling skills (Schure et al., 2008; Shapiro et al., 2007; Wang, 2006). One study even reported that regular meditation led to increased creativity and intelligence in a sample of high school students (So & Orme-Johnson, 2001). Finally, although more difficult to measure, some theorists assert that meditation can enhance human potential by improving focus, heightening awareness, building emotional resilience, and fostering moral maturity (Walsh & Shapiro, 2006).

A number of recent experiments have demonstrated that meditation can increase the tolerance of pain (Zeidan et al., 2015), which could have important implications for the management of a variety of health problems (Grant & Rainville, 2009; Grant et al., 2010; Zeidan et al., 2010). Grant and Rainville (2009) compared the pain sensitivity of 13 experienced Zen meditators and 13 comparable nonmeditators. Carefully controlled pain was administered by applying a heating plate to participants' calves.

The meditators were able to handle considerably more pain than the nonmeditators. Moreover, a follow-up study suggested that the meditators' greater pain tolerance was associated with increased thickness in brain regions that register pain (Grant et al., 2010). In other words, it appeared that meditation experience had produced enduring alterations in brain structure that were responsible for meditators' increased pain tolerance. Other recent studies have also reported evidence that suggests that meditation may have the potential to modify brain structure and process (Creswall et al., 2016; Gladding, 2013; Hölzel et al., 2011). For instance, Luders et al. (2009) examined experienced meditators and found that they had significantly more grey matter (than control subjects) in several regions of the brain. Clearly, a great deal of additional research is needed, but these are impressive, thought-provoking findings that would seem to undermine the idea that meditation is nothing more than relaxation.

Altering Consciousness with Drugs

Key Learning Goals

▶ Identify the major types of abused drugs and their main effects.

▶ Understand why drug effects vary, how drugs affect the brain, and drug dependence.

▶ Summarize evidence of the major health risks associated with drug abuse.

Like hypnosis and meditation, drugs are commonly used in deliberate efforts to alter consciousness. In this section, we focus on the use of drugs for nonmedical purposes, commonly referred to as "drug abuse" or "recreational drug use." Drug abuse takes many forms and reaches into every corner of modern society (Bielski, 2013). For example, the Chief Public Health Officer for Canada released a report that highlights the high rates of alcohol abuse and its effects in Canada (Taylor, 2016). He notes that almost 80 percent of the Canadian population drank in the preceding year and over 3 million drinkers drank at rates to put them at risk for immediate harm, with over 4 million drinking enough to be at risk for long-term health problems such as liver cirrhosis and some types of cancer. He also notes that in the preceding year that almost 3000 children were born with fetal alcohol syndrome. We know from reports prepared by the Centre for Addiction and Mental Health that unhealthy drinking is not restricted to Canada (Rehm et al., 2015). For example, people in Eastern Europe and sub-Saharan Africa drink alcohol at the most unhealthy levels (Shield et al., 2013). In addition, college and university students are showing increasing abuse of controlled stimulants to help with their studies—to help them cram for midterms and finals (Bradshaw, 2013).

The personal, social, and economic costs of drug abuse can be enormous. While there has been a decline in the number of impaired driving charges in Canada over the past few years, with 201 incidents per 100 000 drivers in 2015, the number of impaired driving incidents involving drug-impaired driving is on the rise (Statistics Canada, 2015). The latter is of particular concern given the impending legalization of marijuana use promised by Justin Trudeau when he was elected prime minster in 2015 (Liberal Party of Canada, 2017). In spite of extraordinary efforts by governments and health organizations to reduce drug abuse, it seems reasonable to conclude that widespread recreational drug use is here to stay for the foreseeable future.

Recreational drug use involves personal, moral, political, and legal issues that are not matters for science to resolve. However, the more knowledgeable you are about drugs, the more informed your decisions and opinions about them will be. Accordingly, this section describes the types of drugs that are most commonly used for recreational purposes and summarizes their effects on consciousness, behaviour, and health.

Principal Abused Drugs and Their Effects

The drugs that people use recreationally are *psychoactive*. **Psychoactive drugs** are chemical substances that modify mental, emotional, or behavioural functioning. Not all psychoactive drugs produce effects that lead to recreational use. Generally, people prefer drugs that elevate their mood or produce other pleasurable alterations in consciousness.

A recent survey by Health Canada (Health Canada, 2014) identified the prevalence and use of various drugs (see Table 5.3). For example, while 78 percent of those surveyed indicated that they drank alcohol over

Table 5.3

Overview of Alcohol and Illicit Drug Use by Canadians

	CAS 2004 (sample size 13 909) %	CADUMS 2008 (sample size 16 672) %	CADUMS 2009 (sample size 13 082) %	CADUMS 2010 (sample size 13 615) %	CADUMS 2011 (sample size 10 076) %	CADUMS 2012 (sample size 11 090) %
Cannabis Use						
Cannabis—lifetime	44.5	43.9	42.4	41.5	39.4^	41.5
Cannabis—past-year	14.1	11.4*	10.6**	10.7(*)	9.1^¥	10.2†
Cannabis—average age of initiation for youth	15.6 years	15.5 years	15.6 years	15.7 years	15.6 years	16.1 years#
Other Illicit Drug Use in Past Year						
Cocaine/Crack	1.9	1.6	1.2Q	0.7(*)	0.9Q^	1.1Q
Speed	0.8	1.1Q	0.4Q	0.5Q	0.5Q	s
Hallucinogens (excluding salvia)	0.7	n/a	0.7Q	0.9	0.6Q	0.9Q
Hallucinogens (including salvia)	–	–	0.9Q±	1.1	0.9Q	1.1Q
Ecstasy	1.1	1.4	0.9Q	0.7	0.7Q	0.6Q
Salvia	–	–	s	0.3Q	s	s
Methamphetamine/Crystal meth	0.2	s	s	s	s	s
Any 6 drugs[a] (hallucinogens excl. salvia)	14.5	–	11.0**	11.0(*)	9.4^¥	10.6†
Any 5 drugs[b] (hallucinogens excl. salvia)	3.0	–	2.0	1.8(*)	1.7^	2.0†
Any 6 drugs[a] (hallucinogens incl. salvia)	–	12.1	11.1	11.1	9.4¥	10.6
Any 5 drugs[b] (hallucinogens incl. salvia)	–	3.9	2.1¥	2.0	1.9	2.0
Drug Related Harms in Past Year						
Any drug harm to self—among users of any drug	17.5	21.7	–	17.0	17.6	16.6
Any drug harm to self— among total population	2.8	2.7	–	2.1	1.8^	2.0Q
Alcohol Use						
Lifetime use	92.8	90.2*	88.6**	88.9(*)	89.7^	91.0
Past 12 month use	79.3	77.3	76.5**	77.0	78.0	78.4
Average age of initiation for youth 15 to 24 years	15.6 years	15.6 years	15.9 years	15.9 years	16.0 years	16.2 years†
2011 Low-Risk Drinking Guidelines (LRDG)—Past 12 Months						
Exceeds LRDG chronic	14.3	15.0	14.5	14.5	14.4	14.4
Exceeds LRDG acute	10.2	10.9	11.7	10.5	10.1	9.9
Exceeds LRDG chronic—among drinkers	18.0	19.8	19.1	19.1	18.7	18.6
Exceeds LRDG acute— among drinkers	12.9	14.3	15.5	13.8	13.1	12.8

* Indicates that the difference between 2008 and 2004 is statistically significant.

**Indicates that the difference between 2009 and 2004 is statistically significant.

(*)Indicates that the difference between 2010 and 2004 is statistically significant.

^Indicates that the difference between 2011 and 2004 is statistically significant.

†Indicates that the difference between 2012 and 2004 is statistically significant.

±Indicates that the difference between 2008 and 2009 is statistically significant.

¥There are no statistically significant differences between 2010 and 2009 in this table.

¥Indicates that the difference between 2011 and 2010 is statistically significant.

#Indicates that the difference between 2012 and 2011 is statistically significant.

s Estimate suppressed due to high sampling variability.

Q Estimate qualified due to high sampling variability; interpret with caution.

⁻No comparable estimates.

n/a In 2008, the list of substances under hallucinogens included salvia and "magic mushrooms"; as a result the estimate is not comparable to 2004, 2009–2012.

[a] Cannabis, cocaine/crack, speed, ecstasy, hallucinogens, heroin.

[b] Cocaine/crack, speed, ecstasy, hallucinogens, heroin.

Source: © All rights reserved. *Canadian Alcohol and Drug Use Monitoring Survey - 2012.* Health Canada, 2014. Adapted and reproduced with permission from the Minister of Health, 2017.

Variations in Consciousness

the past year, only 10 percent indicated they had used cannabis. Of those surveyed and who drank alcohol in the past year, 18 percent exceeded guidelines to be considered low-risk drinkers. High-risk drinking is more characteristic of men than women: 15.9 percent of women and 21.2 percent of men were considered to be high-risk drinkers. As we know, of course, alcohol abuse is not without it risks, both for the drinker and for those around him or her. This fact is highlighted in the survey by the finding that 16.6 percent of the respondents reported having been harmed in some way. Harm in this survey is characterized by harm to physical health, relationships, finances, work or school, legal problems, learning difficulties, and problems with housing. A detailed study of drug use by Ontario students has revealed a significant increase between the years 2013 to 2015 in the use of two types of drugs, ecstasy and nonmedical use of ADHD (attention-deficit hyperactivity disorder) drugs such as Ritalin, Adderall, and Concerta (Boak, Hamilton, Adlaf, & Mann, 2015).

The principal types of recreational drugs are described in Table 5.4. The table lists representative drugs in each of six categories. It also summarizes their medical uses, their effects on consciousness,

and their common side effects (based on Levinthal, 2014; Ruiz & Strain, 2011). The six categories of psychoactive drugs that we will focus on are narcotics, sedatives, stimulants, hallucinogens, cannabis, and alcohol. We will also discuss one specific drug that is not listed in the table (because it does not fit into traditional drug categories) but that cannot be ignored in light of its escalating popularity: MDMA, better known as "ecstasy."

Narcotics, or *opiates*, **are drugs derived from opium that are capable of relieving pain.** The main drugs in this category are heroin and morphine, although less potent opiates such as codeine, Demerol, and methadone are also abused. According to the Canadian Medical Association (2015a), there are a few emerging problems in this category, including abuse of oxycodone and, more recently, fentanyl and carfentanil. Oxycodone's (trade name: OxyContin) time-release format was supposed to make it an effective analgesic with less potential for abuse than the other opiates (Cicero, Inciardi, & Munoz, 2005). But people quickly learned that they could grind it up and gain a powerful high. This has led to a new epidemic of serious drug abuse (Tunnell, 2005). According to figures

Table 5.4

Psychoactive Drugs: Methods of Ingestion, Medical Uses, and Effects

DRUGS	PRINCIPAL MEDICAL USES	DESIRED EFFECTS	POTENTIAL SHORT-TERM SIDE EFFECTS
Narcotics (opiates) Morphine Heroin Oxycodone	Pain relief	Euphoria, relaxation, anxiety, reduction, pain relief	Lethargy, drowsiness, nausea, impaired coordination, impaired mental functioning, constipation
Sedatives Barbiturates (e.g., Seconal) Nonbarbiturates (e.g., Qaalude)	Sleeping pill, anticonvulsant	Euphoria, relaxation, anxiety reduction, reduced inhibitions	Lethargy, drowsiness, severely impaired coordination, impaired mental functioning, emotional swings, dejection
Stimulants Amphetamines Cocaine	Treatment of hyperactivity and narcolepsy, local anesthetic (cocaine only)	Elation, excitement, increased alertness, increased energy, reduced fatigue	Increased blood pressure and heart rate, increased talkativeness, restlessness, irritability, insomnia, reduced appetite, increased sweating and urination, anxiety, paranoia, increased aggressiveness, panic
Hallucinogens LSD Mescaline Psilocybin	None	Increased sensory awareness, euphoria, altered perceptions, hallucinations, insightful experiences	Dilated pupils, nausea, emotional swings, paranoia, jumbled thought processes, impaired judgment, anxiety, panic reaction
Cannabis Marijuana Hashish THC	Treatment of glaucoma and chemotherapy-induced nausea and vomiting; other uses under study	Mild euphoria, relaxation, altered perceptions, enhanced awareness	Elevated heart rate, bloodshot eyes, dry mouth, reduced short-term memory, sluggish motor coordination, sluggish mental functioning, anxiety
Alcohol	none	Mild euphoria, relaxation, anxiety reduction, reduced inhibitions	Severely impaired coordination, impaired mental functioning, increased urination, emotional swings, depression, quarrelsomeness, hangover

released by the Government of Canada, prescription drug abuse is a growing problem. For example, in 2012, 410 000 Canadians admitted to abusing prescription drugs including stimulants, benzodiazapines, and opioids (Government of Canada, 2016).

Even more serious than oxycodone is the danger posed by the use of fentanyl and its analogue carfentanil. Fentanyl is taken by itself or added to other drugs such as heroin or cocaine. Carfentanil is over 100 times more potent than fentanyl and was originally designed to be used to sedate large animals such as elephants. The rising number of overdose deaths related to these drugs has been called the worst drug-safety crisis in Canadian history (Canadian Press, 2017; Ireland, 2016). The opiate drugs can produce an overwhelming sense of euphoria or well-being. This euphoric effect has a relaxing "Who cares?" quality that makes the high an attractive escape from reality. Common side effects include lethargy, nausea, and impaired mental and motor functioning.

Sedatives are sleep-inducing drugs that tend to decrease central nervous system (CNS) activation and behavioural activity. Historically, the most widely abused sedatives have been the *barbiturates*. But in recent decades stricter controls have reduced their availability and people have turned to the *benzodiazepine* sedatives—which, fortunately, have notably less appeal as a drug of abuse. People abusing sedatives, or "downers," generally consume larger doses than are prescribed for medical purposes. The desired effect is a euphoria similar to that produced by drinking large amounts of alcohol. Feelings of tension or dejection are replaced by a relaxed, pleasant state of intoxication, accompanied by loosened inhibitions.

Stimulants are drugs that tend to increase central nervous system activation and behavioural activity. Stimulants range from mild, widely available drugs such as caffeine and nicotine, to stronger, carefully regulated ones such as cocaine. We will focus on cocaine and amphetamines. Cocaine is a natural substance that comes from the coca shrub. In contrast, amphetamines are synthesized in a pharmaceutical laboratory. Cocaine and amphetamines have fairly similar effects, except that cocaine produces a briefer high. Stimulants produce a euphoria very different from that created by narcotics or sedatives. They produce a buoyant, elated, energetic "I can conquer the world!" feeling accompanied by increased alertness. In recent years, cocaine and amphetamines have become available in much more potent (and dangerous) forms than

before. "Freebasing" is a chemical treatment used to extract nearly pure cocaine from ordinary street cocaine. "Crack" is the most widely distributed by-product of this process, consisting of chips of pure cocaine that are usually smoked. Amphetamines are increasingly sold as a crystalline powder, called "crank," that can be snorted or injected intravenously. Drug dealers are also beginning to market a smokable form of methamphetamine called "ice" or "crystal meth." In Canada, 605 of the drug labs that were raided by the RCMP in 2005 were involved in the production of crystal meth (Dark Crystal, 2005). Side effects of stimulants vary with dosage and potency but may include restlessness, anxiety, paranoia, and insomnia.

Hallucinogens are a diverse group of drugs that have powerful effects on mental and emotional functioning, marked most prominently by distortions in sensory and perceptual experience. The principal hallucinogens are LSD (lysergic acid diethylamide), mescaline, and psilocybin. These drugs have similar effects, although they vary in potency. Hallucinogens produce euphoria, increased sensory awareness, and a distorted sense of time. In some users, they lead to profound, dreamlike, "mystical" feelings that are difficult to describe. The latter effect is why they have been used in religious ceremonies for centuries in some cultures and why they were adopted by members of the counterculture in the 1960s.

In the fall of 1960 a group of academics centred at Harvard University began a psychedelic research project focused on the use of LSD for personal growth and development. This group included Timothy Leary, a Harvard professor, personality, and clinical psychologist (e.g., Devonis, 2012; Leary, 1957); Huston Smith, a professor of philosophy at the Massachusetts Institute of Technology; Richard Alpert, another Harvard psychology professor (who later changed his name to Ram Dass); and Dr. Andrew Weil, who is well known now as an advocate of holistic medicine (Greenfield, 2006; Higgs, 2006; Lattin, 2010). Leary, the best known of the group, began his experiences with psilocybin, popularizing it and LSD as routes to enlightenment to the counterculture in the 1960s and as a possible tool for use in psychotherapy. He declared that people should "turn on, tune in, and drop out." He was eventually dismissed by Harvard University and was labelled by U.S. President Nixon as the "most dangerous man in America" (Mansnerus, 1996). Interestingly, research on the potential therapeutic uses of psychedelics has a Canadian connection, as it was used for such purposes both in Saskatchewan (Dyck, 2008) and Ontario (Rice & Harris, 1993).

Cannabis is the hemp plant from which marijuana, hashish, and THC are derived. Marijuana is a mixture of dried leaves, flowers, stems, and seeds taken from the plant. Hashish comes from the plant's resin. Smoking is the usual route of ingestion for both marijuana and hashish. THC, the active chemical ingredient in cannabis, can be synthesized for research purposes (e.g., to give to animals, who can't very well smoke marijuana). When smoked, cannabis has an immediate impact that may last several hours. The desired effects of the drug are a mild, relaxed euphoria and enhanced sensory awareness. Unintended effects may include anxiety, sluggish mental functioning, and impaired memory. According to the World Health Organization (2014), Canada has one of the highest levels of use of cannabis among youth, ranking second only to France. Canadian youth who regularly use cannabis suggest several reasons for using it, including fitting in with friends, its ready availability, and its positive effects on coping with stress (McKiernan & Fleming, 2017).

Alcohol encompasses a variety of beverages containing ethyl alcohol, such as beers, wines, and distilled spirits. The concentration of ethyl alcohol varies from about 4 percent in most beers to 40 percent in 80-proof liquor—and occasionally more in higher-proof liquors. When people drink heavily, the central effect is a relaxed euphoria that temporarily boosts self-esteem, as problems seem to melt away and inhibitions diminish. Common side effects include impairments in mental and motor functioning, mood swings, and quarrelsomeness. Alcohol is the most widely used recreational drug in our society. Because alcohol is legal, many people use it casually without even thinking of it as a drug.

While alcohol abuse occurs across ages, heavy drinking and binge drinking on Canadian university campuses is of particular concern (Tamburri, 2012). Heavy drinking on campus is not just a Canadian concern, it occurs across North America in colleges and universities. Researchers from the Harvard School of Public Health (Wechsler, 2002) surveyed nearly 11 000 undergraduates at 119 schools and found that over 80 percent of students drank, with 49 percent of the men and 41 percent of the women reporting that they engage in binge drinking with the intention of getting drunk. A follow-up study several years later found that these rates remained high (Nelson et al., 2009). In the Harvard study, 29 percent of the students who did *not* binge drink reported that they had been insulted or humiliated by a drunken student, 19 percent had experienced a serious argument, 9 percent had been hit

Overindulging in alcohol is particularly widespread among college and university students.

or assaulted, and 19.5 percent had been the target of unwanted sexual advances. Another problem is that the brain is still maturing during adolescence, making it particularly vulnerable to the negative effects of alcohol. Recent studies have found that binge drinking may impair neural functioning in the adolescent brain (Lehsdahl et al., 2013; Lopez-Caneda et al., 2014).

MDMA ("ecstasy," "molly") is a compound drug related to both amphetamines and hallucinogens, especially mescaline. MDMA was originally formulated in 1912 but was not widely used in North America until the 1990s, when it became popular in the context of raves and dance clubs. MDMA produces a short-lived high that typically lasts a few hours or more. Users report that they feel warm, friendly, euphoric, sensual, insightful, and empathetic, but alert and energetic. Problematic side effects include increased blood pressure, muscle tension, sweating, blurred vision, insomnia, and transient anxiety. Possible long-term negative effects, among others, include sleep and memory problems, high blood pressure, and liver problems (Canadian Centre on Substance Abuse, 2016).

Factors Influencing Drug Effects

The drug effects summarized in Table 5.4 (see page 180) are the *typical* ones. Drug effects can vary from person to person and even for the same person in different situations. The frequency of use and quantity consumed often play a role. Phenomena such as "binge drinking" are of particular concern. According to a recent report by Canada's Chief Office of Medical Health (2015), while it is uncommon in lower grades, by the time Canadian children reach Grades 10–12, almost half report having engaged in binge-drinking in the previous year. The impact of any drug depends in part on the

Table 5.5

Psychoactive Drugs: Tolerance, Dependence, Potential for Fatal Overdose, and Health Risks

DRUGS	TOLERANCE	RISK OF PHYSICAL DEPENDENCE	RISK OF PSYCHOLOGICAL DEPENDENCE	FATAL OVERDOSE POTENTIAL	HEALTH RISKS
Narcotics (opiates)	Rapid	High	High	High	Infectious diseases, accidents, immune suppression, overdose
Sedatives	Rapid	High	High	High	Accidents
Stimulants	Rapid	Moderate	High	Moderate to high	Sleep problems, malnutrition, nasal damage, hypertension, respiratory disease, stroke, liver disease, heart attack, overdose
Hallucinogens	Gradual	None	Very low	Very low	Accidents, acute pain
Cannabis	Gradual	None	Low to moderate	Very low	Accidents, lung cancer, respiratory disease, pulmonary disease, increased vulnerability to psychosis, cognitive deficits
Alcohol	Gradual	Moderate	Moderate	Low to high	Accidents, liver disease, malnutrition, brain damage, neurological disorders, heart disease, stroke, hypertension, ulcers, cancer, birth defects, overdose

© 2017 Cengage Learning

user's age, mood, motivation, personality, previous experience with the drug, body weight, and physiology. The dose and potency of a drug, the method of administration, and the setting in which a drug is taken also influence its effects. Our theme of *multifactorial causation* clearly applies to the effects of drugs.

So, too, does our theme emphasizing the *subjectivity of experience*. Expectations are potentially powerful factors that can influence the user's perceptions of a drug's effects. You may recall from our discussion of placebo effects in Chapter 2 that some people who are misled to *think* that they are drinking alcohol actually show signs of intoxication (Assefi & Garry, 2003). If people *expect* a drug to make them feel giddy, serene, or profound, their expectation may contribute to the feelings they experience.

A drug's effects can also change as the person's body develops a tolerance for the chemical as a result of continued use. *Tolerance* refers to a progressive decrease in a person's responsiveness to a drug. Tolerance usually leads people to consume larger and larger doses of a drug to attain the effects they desire. Most drugs produce tolerance effects, but some do so more rapidly than others. For example, tolerance to alcohol usually builds slowly, while tolerance to heroin increases much more quickly. Table 5.5 indicates whether various categories of drugs tend to produce tolerance rapidly or gradually.

Mechanisms of Drug Action

Most drugs have effects that reverberate throughout the body. A great deal of recent research on addiction has focused on uncovering its neural basis (Everitt

& Robbins, 2016). Psychoactive drugs work primarily by altering neurotransmitter activity in the brain. As we discussed in Chapter 3, neurotransmitters are chemicals that transmit information between neurons at junctions called *synapses*.

The actions of amphetamines and cocaine illustrate how drugs have selective, multiple effects on neurotransmitter activity (see Figure 5.14). Amphetamines exert their main effects on two of the monoamine

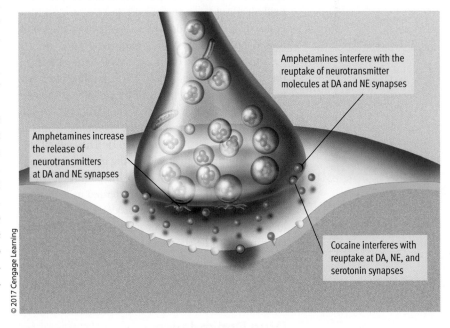

Amphetamines interfere with the reuptake of neurotransmitter molecules at DA and NE synapses

Amphetamines increase the release of neurotransmitters at DA and NE synapses

Cocaine interferes with reuptake at DA, NE, and serotonin synapses

© 2017 Cengage Learning

Figure 5.14
Stimulant drugs and neurotransmitter activity. Like other psychoactive drugs, amphetamines and cocaine alter neurotransmitter activity at specific synapses. Amphetamines primarily increase the release of dopamine (DA) and norepinephrine (NE) and secondarily inhibit the reuptake of these neurotransmitters. Cocaine slows the reuptake process at DA, NE, and serotonin synapses. The psychological and behavioural effects of the drugs have largely been attributed to their impact on dopamine circuits.

neurotransmitters: norepinephrine (NE) and dopamine (DA). Indeed, the name *amphetamines* reflects the kinship between these drugs and the *monoamines*. Amphetamines mainly increase the release of DA and NE by presynaptic neurons. They also interfere with the reuptake of DA and NE from synaptic clefts (Koob & Le Moal, 2006). These actions serve to increase the levels of dopamine and norepinephrine at the affected synapses. Cocaine shares some of these actions, which is why cocaine and amphetamines produce similar stimulant effects. Cocaine mainly blocks reuptake at DA, NE, and serotonin synapses. For both amphetamines and cocaine, elevated activity in certain *dopamine circuits* is believed to be crucial to the drugs' pleasurable, rewarding effects (Volkow et al., 2004).

The discovery of endorphins (the body's internally produced opiate-like chemicals) has led to new insights about the actions of opiate drugs (see Chapter 3). These drugs apparently bind to specific subtypes of endorphin receptors, and their actions at these receptor sites indirectly elevate activity in the dopamine pathways that modulate reward (Cami & Farre, 2003). In the 1990s, scientists discovered two types of receptors in the brain for THC, the active chemical ingredient in marijuana, which are called *cannabinoid receptors* (Stephens, 1999). Soon after, they found two internally produced chemicals similar to THC—christened *endocannabinoids*—that activate these receptors and thereby influence activity at GABA and glutamate synapses (Julien et al., 2008). It appears that THC from marijuana "hijacks" the brain's cannabinoid receptors (Piomelli, 2004), eventually leading to an increased release of endorphins and activation of the dopamine circuits associated with reward (Solinas et al., 2003, 2006).

Although specific drugs exert their initial effects in the brain on a wide variety of neurotransmitter systems, many theorists believe that virtually all abused drugs eventually increase activity in a particular neural pathway, called the *mesolimbic dopamine pathway* (Schmidt, Vassoler, & Pierce, 2011). This neural circuit, which runs from an area in the midbrain through the *nucleus accumbens* and on to the prefrontal cortex (see Figure 5.15), has been characterized as a "reward pathway" (Pierce & Kumaresan, 2006). Large and rapid increases in the release of dopamine along this pathway are thought to be the neural basis of the reinforcing effects of most abused drugs (Knapp & Kornetsky, 2009; Volkow & Koob, 2012).

Drug Dependence

People can become either physically or psychologically dependent on a drug. Physical dependence is a common problem with narcotics, sedatives, alcohol,

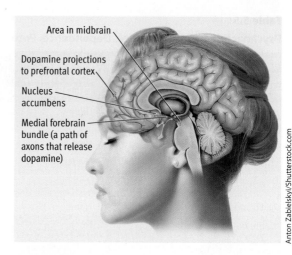

Area in midbrain

Dopamine projections to prefrontal cortex

Nucleus accumbens

Medial forebrain bundle (a path of axons that release dopamine)

Anton Zabielskyi/Shutterstock.com

Figure 5.15

The "reward pathway" in the brain. The neural circuits shown here in blue make up the *mesolimbic dopamine pathway*. Axons in this pathway run from an area in the midbrain through the medial forebrain bundle to the *nucleus accumbens* and on to the prefrontal cortex. Recreational drugs affect a variety of neurotransmitter systems, but theorists believe that heightened dopamine activity in this pathway—especially the portion running from the midbrain to the nucleus accumbens—is responsible for the reinforcing effects of most abused drugs.

Source: Adapted from Kalat, J.W. (2001). *Biological psychology*. Belmont, CA: Wadsworth. Reprinted by permission. / © 2017 Cengage Learning.

and stimulants. *Physical dependence* exists when a person must continue to take a drug to avoid withdrawal illness. The symptoms of withdrawal illness depend on the specific drug. Withdrawal from heroin, barbiturates, and alcohol can produce fever, chills, tremors, convulsions, vomiting, cramps, diarrhea, and severe aches and pains. Withdrawal from stimulants can lead to a more subtle syndrome, marked by fatigue, apathy, irritability, depression, and feelings of disorientation.

McMaster University psychologist Shepard Siegel has found that some of the withdrawal symptoms experienced by addicts are conditioned responses that are elicited by stimuli that have been paired with the drug in the past (McDonald & Siegel, 2004; Siegel, 2002). According to McDonald and Siegel, "Cues accompanying the drug effect function as conditional stimuli (CSs), and the direct drug effect constitutes the unconditional stimulus (US)" (p. 3). This means when addicts are presented with cues typically associated with drug injections in the past, they may experience withdrawal symptoms. Thus, if an addict always injects in a particular room, entering the room itself may produce withdrawal symptoms. You will learn more about the process of classical conditioning and about conditioned responses in Chapter 6. In general, classical conditioning is a type of learning in which a stimulus has acquired the capacity to evoke a response that was originally evoked by another stimulus. According to Siegel and Ramos (2002), conditioning is implicated in dependency in many ways. For example, the situational cues present in the situation in which a drug is typically injected may contribute to the individual's increased tolerance of the drug. This has been termed the "situational specificity of tolerance" (Siegel, 1976). Siegel has applied similar conditioning analyses to account for some cases of overdose (Siegel, 2016). According to Seigel, typical cues associated with drug use serve to elicit responses in the user that can help reduce the effects of the drug. If the drug is administered in a new context containing different cues, then the users "do not make the preparatory conditional responses that mediate chronic tolerance, and thus are not sufficiently tolerant to the drug to survive" (p. 378), and an overdose may ensue.

Psychological dependence exists when a person must continue to take a drug to satisfy intense mental and emotional craving for the drug. Psychological dependence is more subtle than physical dependence, but the need it creates can be powerful. Cocaine, for instance, can produce an overwhelming psychological need for continued use. Psychological dependence is possible with all recreational drugs, although it seems rare for hallucinogens.

Both types of dependence are established gradually with repeated use of a drug. It was originally assumed that only physical dependence has a physiological basis, but theorists now believe that both types of dependence reflect alterations in synaptic transmission (Di Chiara, 1999; Self, 1997). Dysregulation in the mesolimbic dopamine pathway appears to be the chief factor underlying drug craving and addiction (Nestler & Malenka, 2004). Drugs vary in their potential for creating either physical or psychological dependence. Table 5.5 provides estimates of the risk of each kind of dependence for the six categories of recreational drugs covered in our discussion.

Drugs and Health

It is clear that drugs, especially their abuse, can be very harmful. While there are several ways to assess and categorize the harmful effects of drugs (e.g., Nutt, King, Saulsbury, & Blakemore, 2007), there is consensus that recreational drug use can negatively affect by triggering an overdose, by producing various types of physiological damage (direct effects),

and by causing health-impairing behaviour (indirect effects).

Overdose

Any drug can be fatal if a person takes enough of it, but some drugs are much more dangerous than others. Table 5.5 shows estimates of the risk of accidentally consuming a lethal overdose of each listed drug. Drugs that are CNS depressants—sedatives, narcotics, and alcohol—carry the greatest risk of overdose. It's important to remember that these drugs are synergistic with each other, so many overdoses involve lethal *combinations* of CNS depressants. What happens when a person overdoses on these drugs? The respiratory system usually grinds to a halt, producing coma, brain damage, and death within a brief period.

Fatal overdoses with CNS stimulants usually involve a heart attack, stroke, or cortical seizure. Deaths due to overdoses of stimulant drugs used to be relatively infrequent, but cocaine overdoses have increased sharply as more people have experimented with freebasing, smoking crack, and other more dangerous modes of ingestion (Repetto & Gold, 2005).

Direct Effects

In some cases, drugs cause tissue damage directly. For example, snorting cocaine can damage nasal membranes. Cocaine can also alter cardiovascular functioning in ways that increase the risk of heart attack and stroke, and crack smoking is associated with a host of respiratory problems (Paczynski & Gold, 2011).

Actors Cory Monteith and Philip Seymour Hoffman both died of drug overdoses. Both had attended drug rehab programs and Hoffman had been sober for 23 years before developing a heroin problem (CBC News, 2013, 2014).

Photo by Brian To/FilmMagic/Getty Images

Photo by Frazer harrison/Getty Images

Variations in Consciousness

Long-term, excessive alcohol consumption is associated with an elevated risk for a wide range of serious health problems, including liver damage, ulcers, hypertension, stroke, heart disease, neurological disorders, and some types of cancer (Hernandez-Avila & Kranzler, 2011; Lee, McNeely, & Gourevitch, 2011). One recent study of alcohol-dependent individuals found a twofold increase in mortality among males, and more than a fourfold elevation in mortality among females (John et al., 2013). Another study (Stahre et al., 2014) estimated that one in ten deaths among working age (20–64) adults in North America is attributable to excessive drinking!

The health risks of marijuana have generated considerable debate in recent years. Although many people have come to view marijuana as a relatively harmless drug, many experts assert that the risks of cannabis use have been underestimated (Volkow et al., 2014). The available evidence suggests that chronic marijuana use increases the risk of respiratory and pulmonary disease (Budney, Vandrey, & Fearer, 2011). Some studies have found a link between long-term marijuana use and the risk of lung cancer, although the data are surprisingly inconsistent (Aldington et al., 2008; Callaghan, Allebeck, & Sidorchuk, 2013). Finally, a rash of recent studies have reported an unexpected link between cannabis use and severe, psychotic disorders, including schizophrenia (Burns, 2013; Greiner et al., 2013). Obviously, the vast majority of marijuana users do not develop psychoses, but it appears that cannabis can trigger psychotic illness in individuals who have a genetic vulnerability to such disorders (Parakh & Basu, 2013). A number of studies have found an association between chronic, heavy marijuana use and measurable impairments in attention, learning, and memory that show up when users are not high (Hanson et al., 2010; Thames, Arbid, & Sayegh, 2014). The results of one such study (Solowij et al., 2002) are shown in Figure 5.16. However, these cognitive deficits may disappear after three to four weeks of marijuana abstinence (Schreiner & Dunn, 2012). Clearly, marijuana is not harmless, although some widely publicized dangers have been exaggerated by the popular press. For instance, contrary to popular reports, it appears that cannabis does not produce meaningful reductions in immune system responding (Hall & Degenhardt, 2009) or any significant effects on male smokers' fertility or sexual functioning (Grinspoon, Bakalar, & Russo, 2005).

Indirect Effects

The negative effects of drugs on physical health are often indirect results of the drugs' impact on attitudes, intentions, and behaviour. For instance,

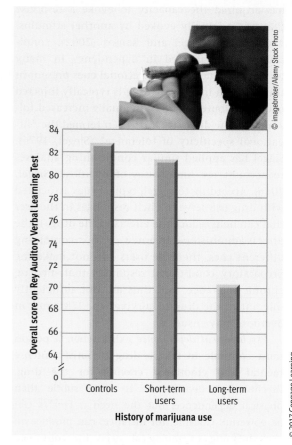

Figure 5.16

Chronic cannabis use and cognitive performance. Solowij and associates (2002) administered a battery of neuropsychological tests to 51 long-term cannabis users who had smoked marijuana regularly for an average of 24 years, 51 short-term cannabis users who had smoked marijuana regularly for an average of 10 years, and 33 control subjects who had little or no history of cannabis use. The cannabis users were required to abstain from smoking marijuana for a minimum of 12 hours prior to their testing. The study found evidence suggestive of subtle cognitive impairments among the long-term cannabis users on many of the tests. The graph depicts the results observed for overall performance on the Rey Auditory Verbal Learning Test, which measures several aspects of memory functioning.

people using stimulants tend not to eat or sleep properly. Sedatives increase the risk of accidental injuries because they severely impair motor coordination. People who abuse downers often trip down stairs, fall off stools, and suffer other mishaps. Tara MacDonald of Queen's University, in a series of studies, has found that alcohol can affect students' intentions to engage in risky sexual behaviour, including unprotected sex (Ebel-Lam, MacDonald, Zanna, & Fong, 2009; Klein, Geaghan, & MacDonald, 2007; MacDonald, Fong, et al., 2000; MacDonald & Hynie, 2008). For example, intoxicated students who were sexually aroused reported more favourable intentions toward having unprotected sex.

According to University of Waterloo researchers (G. MacDonald, Zanna, & Holmes, 2000), alcohol can also play a causal role in relationship conflict, a result that mirrors some of the harm results reported in the *Canadian Abuse Survey*. That survey also suggested that physical abuse was frequently associated with alcohol intoxication. Of course, not everyone who becomes intoxicated becomes violent. According to McGill psychologist Robert Pihl and his colleagues (Pihl, Assaad, & Hoaken, 2003), certain types of people are more at risk for intoxicated aggression than are other types of people (Assaad et al., 2006).

Many drugs impair driving ability, increasing the risk of automobile accidents. Alcohol, for instance, may contribute to roughly 40 percent of all automobile deaths (Hingson & Sleet, 2006). Although cannabis impairs driving less than alcohol intoxication does, marijuana use within three hours of driving appears to roughly double one's risk of an accident (Asbridge, Hayden, & Cartwright, 2012). Intravenous drug users risk contracting infectious diseases that can be spread by unsterilized needles. For example, acquired immune deficiency syndrome (AIDS) has been transmitted at an alarming rate through the population of intravenous drug users (Epstein, Phillips, & Preston, 2011).

The major health risks of various recreational drugs are listed in the fifth column of Table 5.5 (see page 183). As you can see, alcohol appears to have the most diverse negative effects on physical health. The irony, of course, is that alcohol is the only recreational drug listed that has a long history of being legal.

Putting It in Perspective: Themes 2, 3, 4, 5, and 7

This chapter highlights five of our unifying themes. First, we can see how psychology evolves in a sociohistorical context. Psychology began as the science of consciousness in the 19th century, but consciousness proved difficult to study empirically. Research on consciousness dwindled after John B. Watson and others redefined psychology as the science of behaviour. However, in the 1960s, people began to turn inward, showing a new interest in altering consciousness through drug use, meditation, hypnosis, and biofeedback. Psychologists responded to these social trends by beginning to study variations in consciousness in earnest. This renewed interest in consciousness shows how social forces can have an impact on psychology's evolution.

A second theme that predominates in this chapter is the idea that people's experience of the world is highly subjective. We encountered this theme at the start of the chapter when we mentioned the difficulty that people have describing their states of consciousness. The subjective nature of consciousness was apparent elsewhere in the chapter, as well. For instance, we found that the alterations of consciousness produced by drugs depend significantly on personal expectations.

Third, we saw once again how culture moulds some aspects of behaviour. Although the basic physiological process of sleep appears largely invariant from one society to another, culture influences certain aspects of sleep habits and has a dramatic impact on whether people remember their dreams and how they interpret and feel about their dreams.

Fourth, we learned once again that behaviour is governed by multifactor causation. For example, we discussed how the effects of jet lag, sleep deprivation, and psychoactive drugs depend on a number of interacting factors. Likewise, we saw that insomnia is rooted in a constellation of factors.

Finally, the chapter illustrates psychology's theoretical diversity. We discussed conflicting theories about dreams, hypnosis, and meditation. For the most part, we did not see these opposing theories converging toward reconciliation, as we did in the areas of sensation and perception. However, it's important to emphasize that rival theories do not always merge neatly into tidy models of behaviour. Many theoretical controversies go on indefinitely. This fact does not negate the value of theoretical diversity. While it's always nice to resolve a theoretical debate, the debate itself can advance knowledge by stimulating and guiding empirical research.

Indeed, our upcoming Personal Application demonstrates that theoretical debates need not be resolved in order to advance knowledge. Many theoretical controversies and enduring mysteries remain in the study of sleep and dreams. Nonetheless, researchers have accumulated a great deal of practical information on these topics, which we'll discuss in the next few pages.

Key Learning Goal

▶ Identify the five unifying themes highlighted in the chapter.

Addressing Practical Questions about Sleep and Dreams

Key Learning Goal

▶ Summarize the evidence of various practical questions about sleep and dreams.

Common Questions about Sleep

How much sleep do people need? The average amount of daily sleep for young adults is 7.5 hours. However, there is considerable variability in how long people sleep. Based on a synthesis of data from many studies, Webb (1992b) estimates that sleep time is normally distributed. Sleep needs vary some from person to person. That said, many sleep experts believe that most people would function more effectively if they increased their amount of sleep (Banks & Dinges, 2011). Bear in mind also, that research suggests that people who sleep seven to eight hours per night have the lowest mortality rates (Kakizaki et al., 2013).

Can short naps be refreshing? Some naps are beneficial and some are not. The effectiveness of napping varies from person to person. Also, the benefits of any specific nap depend on the time of day and the amount of sleep one has had recently (Dinges, 1993). On the negative side, naps are not very *efficient* ways to sleep because you're often just getting into the deeper stages of sleep when your nap time is up. Naps tend to be more beneficial when they are rich in slow-wave sleep or REM sleep (Mednick & Drummond, 2009). Another potential problem is that overly long naps or naps that occur too close to bedtime can disrupt nighttime sleep (Thorpy & Yager, 2001).

Nonetheless, many highly productive people (including Thomas Edison, Winston Churchill, and John F. Kennedy) have made effective use of naps. Naps can enhance subsequent alertness and task performance and reduce sleepiness (Ficca et al., 2010). Evidence also suggests that naps can improve learning and memory—even more so than loading up on caffeine (Mednick et al., 2008). In conclusion, naps can be refreshing for most people, and they can pay off in the long run if they don't interfere with nighttime sleep.

What is the significance of snoring? Snoring is a common phenomenon seen in roughly 30–40 percent of adults (Li & Hoffstein, 2011). Snoring increases after age 35, occurs in men more than women, and is more frequent among people who are overweight (Kryger, 1993; Stoohs et al., 1998). Many factors, including colds, allergies, smoking, and some drugs, can contribute to snoring, mainly by forcing people to breathe through their mouths while sleeping. Some people who snore loudly disrupt their own sleep as well as that of their bed partners. It can be difficult to prevent snoring in some people, whereas others are able to reduce their snoring by simply losing weight or by sleeping on their side instead of their back (Lugaresi et al., 1994). Snoring may seem like a trivial problem, but it is associated with sleep apnea and cardiovascular disease, and it may have considerably more medical significance than most people realize (Dement & Vaughn, 1999; Olson & Park, 2006).

What can be done to avoid sleep problems? There are many ways to improve your chances of getting satisfactory sleep. Most of them involve developing sensible daytime habits that won't interfere with sleep (see Epstein & Mardon, 2007; Stevenson, 2014). For example, if you've been having trouble sleeping at night, it's wise to avoid daytime naps so that you will be tired when bedtime arrives. Some people find that daytime exercise helps them fall asleep more readily at bedtime (Flausino et al., 2012). Of course, the exercise should be part of a regular regimen that doesn't leave one sore or aching.

It's also a good idea to minimize consumption of stimulants such as caffeine or nicotine. Because coffee and cigarettes aren't prescription drugs, people don't appreciate how much the stimulants they contain can heighten physical arousal. Many foods (such as chocolate) and beverages (such as cola drinks) contain more caffeine than people realize. Also, bear in mind that ill-advised eating habits can interfere with sleep. Try to avoid going to bed hungry, uncomfortably stuffed, or soon after eating foods that disagree with you.

What can be done about insomnia? First, don't panic if you run into a little trouble sleeping. An overreaction to sleep problems can begin a vicious circle of escalating problems, like that depicted in Figure 5.17. If you jump to the conclusion that you are becoming an insomniac, you may approach sleep with anxiety that will aggravate the problem. The harder you work at falling asleep, the less success you're likely to have. As noted earlier, temporary sleep problems are common and generally clear up on their own.

It's often a good idea to simply launch yourself into a pleasant daydream. This normal

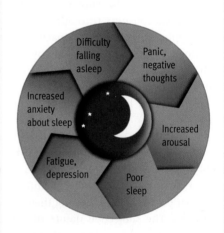

Figure 5.17
The vicious circle of anxiety and sleep difficulty. Anxiety about sleep difficulties leads to poorer sleep, which increases anxiety further, which in turn leads to even greater difficulties in sleeping.

Source: From Weiten. *Cengage Advantage Books: Psychology,* 9E. © 2013 South-Western, a part of Cengage, Inc. Reproduced by permission. www.cengage.com/permissions

© TopFoto/The Image Works

People typically get very upset when they have difficulty falling asleep. Unfortunately, the emotional distress tends to make it even harder for people to get to sleep.

presleep process can take your mind off your difficulties. Whatever you think about, try to avoid ruminating about the current stresses and problems in your life. Research has shown that the tendency to ruminate is one of the key factors contributing to insomnia (Gehrman, Findley, & Perlis, 2012). Anything that relaxes you—whether it's music, meditation, prayer, a warm bath, or a systematic relaxation procedure—can aid you in falling asleep.

Evidence also suggests that melatonin can help you fall asleep without all the issues and risks associated with sleeping pills (Buysse, 2011). Many people consume alcohol near bedtime for its sedative effects. The evidence related to this strategy is a mixed bag (Ebrahim et al., 2013). On the one hand, alcohol does tend to help people fall asleep more quickly and stay asleep more effectively for the first half of the night. On the other hand, alcohol disrupts sleep in the second half of the night and decreases the

time spent in REM sleep in a dose-related manner. Given the accumulating findings on the importance of REM sleep, alcohol's REM-suppressing effects are certainly cause for concern.

Common Questions about Dreams

Does everyone dream? Yes. Some people just don't *remember* their dreams. However, when these people are brought into a sleep lab and awakened from REM sleep, they report having been dreaming—much to their surprise. Scientists have studied a small number of people who have sustained brain damage in the area of the pons that has wiped out their REM sleep, but even these people report dreams (Klosch & Kraft, 2005).

Why don't some people remember their dreams? The evaporation of dreams appears to be quite normal. Most dreams are lost forever

unless people wake up during or just after a dream. Even then, dream recall fades quickly (Nir & Tononi, 2010). Most of the time, people who *do* recall dreams upon waking are remembering either their *last* dream from their final REM period or a dream that awakened them earlier in the night. Hobson's (1989) educated guess is that people probably forget 95–99 percent of their dreams. This forgetting is natural and is not due to repression. People who never remember their dreams probably have a sleep pattern that puts too much time between their last REM/dream period and awakening, so even their last dream is forgotten.

Do dreams require interpretation? Most theorists would say yes, but interpretation may not be as difficult as generally assumed. People have long believed that dreams are symbolic and that it is necessary to interpret the symbols to understand the meaning of dreams. We saw earlier in the chapter that Freud, for instance, believed that dreams have a hidden ("latent") content that represent their true meaning. Thus, a Freudian therapist might equate sexual intercourse with such dream events as walking into a tunnel or riding a horse.

Freudian theorists assert that dream interpretation is a complicated task requiring considerable knowledge of symbolism. However, many dream theorists argue that symbolism in dreams is less deceptive and mysterious than Freud thought (Faraday, 1974; Foulkes, 1985). Calvin Hall (1979) makes the point that dreams require some interpretation simply because they are more visual than verbal. That is, pictures need to be translated into ideas. According to Hall, dream symbolism is highly personal and the dreamer may be the person best equipped to decipher a dream. Thus, it is not unreasonable for you to try to interpret your own dreams. Unfortunately, you'll never know whether you're "correct," because there is no definitive way to judge the validity of different dream interpretations.

Is Alcoholism a Disease? The Power of Definitions

Key Learning Goal

▶ Recognize the influence of definitions, and understand the nominal fallacy.

Alcoholism is a major problem in most—perhaps all—societies. It destroys countless lives and tears families apart. With roughly 17 million problem drinkers in the United States (National Institute on Alcohol Abuse and Alcoholism, 2013), it seems likely that alcoholism has touched the lives of a majority of Americans. In Canada, according to figures compiled by Statistics Canada (2016), almost a quarter of Canadian adult males and 10 percent of Canadian females reported engaging in heavy drinking (five drinks or more on a single occasion).

In almost every discussion about alcoholism, someone will ask, "Is alcoholism a disease?" If alcoholism is a disease, it is a strange one because the alcoholic is the most direct cause of his or her own sickness. If alcoholism is not a disease, what else might it be? Over the course of history, alcoholism has been categorized under many labels—from a personal weakness to a crime, a sin, a mental disorder, and a physical illness (Meyer, 1996). Each of these definitions carries important personal, social, political, and economic implications.

Consider, for instance, the consequences of characterizing alcoholism as a disease. If that is the case, alcoholics should be treated like diabetics, heart patients, or victims of other physical illnesses. That is, they should be viewed with sympathy and should be given appropriate medical and therapeutic interventions to foster recovery from their illness. These treatments should be covered by medical insurance and delivered by health-care professionals. Just as important, if alcoholism is defined as a disease, it should lose much of its stigma. After all, we don't blame people with diabetes or heart disease for their illnesses. Yes, alcoholics admittedly contribute to their own disease (by drinking too much), but so do many victims of diabetes and heart disease who eat all the wrong foods, fail to control their weight, and so forth (McLellan et al., 2000). And, as is the case with many physical illnesses, one can inherit a genetic vulnerability to alcoholism (Nguyen et al., 2011), so it is difficult to argue that alcoholism is caused solely by one's behaviour.

Alternatively, if alcoholism is defined as a personal failure or a moral weakness, alcoholics are less likely to be viewed with sympathy and compassion. They might be admonished to quit drinking, put in prison, or punished in some other way. These responses to their alcoholism would be administered primarily by the legal system, rather than the health-care system, because medical interventions are not designed to remedy moral failings. Obviously, the interventions that would be available would not be covered by health insurance, which would have enormous financial repercussions (for both health-care providers and alcoholics).

The key point here is that definitions lie at the centre of many complex debates. People tend to think of definitions as insignificant, arbitrary sets of words found buried in the obscurity of thick dictionaries compiled by ivory tower intellectuals. Much of this characterization may be accurate, but definitions are not insignificant. They are vested with enormous power to shape how people think about important issues. An endless array of issues boil down to matters of definition. For example, the next time you hear people arguing over whether a particular movie is pornographic, whether the death penalty is cruel and unusual punishment, or whether spanking is child abuse, you'll find it helps to focus the debate on clarifying the definitions of the crucial concepts.

The Power to Make Definitions

So, how can we resolve the debate about whether alcoholism is a disease? Scientists generally try to resolve their debates by conducting research. You may have noticed already that "we need more research on this issue" is a frequent refrain in this text. Is more research the answer in this case? For once, the answer is "no." There is no conclusive way to determine whether alcoholism is a disease. It is not as though there is a "right" answer to this question that we can discover through more and better research.

The question of whether alcoholism is a disease is a matter of definition: Does alcoholism fit the currently accepted definition of what constitutes a disease? If you consult medical texts or dictionaries, you will find that disease is typically defined as an impairment in the normal functioning of an organism that alters its vital functions. Given that alcoholism clearly impairs people's normal functioning and disrupts a variety of vital functions, it seems reasonable to characterize it as a disease. Moreover, like other diseases, it causes increased mortality due to acute incidents, such as automobile accidents (see Figure 5.18 for U.S. statistics on alcohol and acute causes of death), and due to its contribution to various chronic diseases (see Figure 5.19 for U.S. statistics on alcohol and illness). Thus, the disease model has been the dominant view of alcoholism in North America since the middle of the 20th century (Meyer, 1996). This view has only been strengthened by recent evidence that addiction to alcohol (and other drugs) is the result of dysregulation in key neural circuits in the brain (Koob, 2012). Still, some critics express vigorous doubts about the wisdom of defining alcoholism as a disease (Peele, 1989, 2000; Satel & Lilienfeld, 2013). They raise a question that comes up frequently in arguments about definitions: Who should have the power to make the definition? In this case, the power lies in the hands of the medical community, which seems sensible, given that disease is a medical concept. But some critics argue that the medical community has a strong bias in favour of defining conditions as diseases because doing so creates new markets and fuels economic growth for the health industry (Nikelly, 1994). Framing alcoholism as a brain disease has also elevated the prestige of addiction research and helped well-intentioned researchers to coax more funding out of government agencies (Satel & Lilienfeld, 2013). Thus, debate about whether alcoholism is a disease seems likely to continue for the indefinite future.

To summarize, definitions generally do not emerge out of research. They are typically

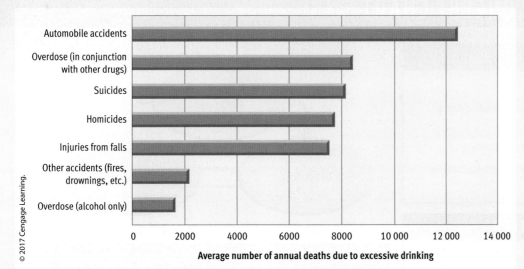

Figure 5.18
Alcohol and acute causes of death. This graph shows estimates of the average number of annual deaths from acute causes that are attributable to excessive drinking. The death toll for alcohol-related accidents, overdoses, suicides, and homicides is staggering. (Based on data from Stahre et al., 2014)

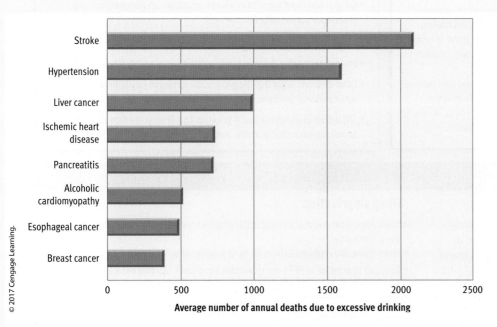

Figure 5.19
Alcohol and chronic diseases. Although the death toll for alcohol-induced chronic diseases is not as staggering as that attributed to acute causes, excessive drinking contributes to quite a variety of chronic diseases that lead to elevated mortality risk. (Based on data from Stahre et al., 2014)

Definitions, Labels, and Circular Reasoning

One additional point about definitions is worth discussing. Perhaps because definitions are imbued with so much power, people have an interesting tendency to incorrectly use them as explanations for the phenomena they describe. This logical error, which equates *naming* something with *explaining* it, is sometimes called the *nominal fallacy*. Names and labels that are used as explanations often sound quite reasonable at first. But definitions do not really have any explanatory value; they simply specify what certain terms mean. Consider an example. Let's say your friend, Frank, has a severe drinking problem. You are sitting around with some other friends discussing why Frank drinks so much. Rest assured, at least one of these friends will assert that "Frank drinks too much because he is an alcoholic." This is circular reasoning, which is just as useless as explaining that Frank is an alcoholic because he drinks too much.

The diagnostic labels that are used in the classification of mental disorders— labels such as schizophrenia and autism—also seem to invite this type of circular reasoning. For example, people often say things like "That person is delusional because she is schizophrenic" or "He is afraid of small, enclosed places because he is claustrophobic." These statements may sound plausible, but they are no more logical or insightful than saying "She is a redhead because she has red hair." The logical fallacy of mistaking a label for an explanation will get us as far in our understanding as a dog gets in chasing its own tail. See Table 5.6.

crafted by experts or authorities in a specific field who try to reach a consensus about how to best define a particular concept. Thus, in analyzing the validity of a definition, you need to look not only at the definition itself but at where it came from. Who decided what the definition should be? Does the source of the definition seem legitimate? Did the authorities who formulated the definition have any biases that should be considered?

Table 5.6

Critical Thinking Skills Discussed in This Application

SKILL	DESCRIPTION
Understanding the way definitions shape how people think about issues	The critical thinker appreciates the enormous power of definitions and the need to clarify definitions in efforts to resolve disagreements.
Identifying the source of definitions	The critical thinker recognizes the need to determine who has the power to make specific definitions and to evaluate their credibility.
Avoiding the nominal fallacy in working with definitions and labels	The critical thinker understands that labels do not have explanatory value.

 191

CONSCIOUSNESS

The nature of consciousness

- **Consciousness** is awareness of internal and external stimuli, including awareness of a self and your thoughts.

- Consciousness involves varied levels of awareness or alertness.

- Variations in consciousness are associated with variations in brain activity, as measured by an EEG.

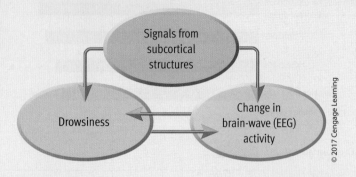

BIOLOGICAL RHYTHMS AND SLEEP

- **Biological rhythms** are periodic fluctuations in physiological functions tied to planetary rhythms.
- **Circadian rhythms** are 24-hour cycles that are influential in the regulation of sleep.
- Internal biological clocks are reset by exposure to light, which stimulates the SCN in the hypothalamus.

- The poor sleep associated with jet lag and rotating work shifts is due to being out of sync with circadian rhythms.
- Melatonin and well-planned rotation schedules can reduce the effects of circadian rhythm disruption.

THE WORLD OF DREAMS

The nature of dreams

- Dreams are less exotic than widely assumed.

- Dreams can be affected by external stimuli and events in one's life.

- Cultural variations are seen in dream content, dream interpretation, and the importance attributed to dreams.

Theories of dreaming

- Freud asserted that the chief purpose of dreams is wish fulfillment.

- Other theorists argue that dreams provide an opportunity to think creatively about personal problems.

- The activation-synthesis model proposes that dreams are side effects of the neural activation that produces waking-like brain waves during REM sleep.

SLEEP

The architecture of sleep

- **Non-REM sleep** (stages 1–4) is marked by an absence of rapid eye movements, relatively little dreaming, and varied EEG activity.
- **REM sleep** is a deep stage of sleep marked by rapid eye movements, high-frequency brain waves, and dreaming.
- During the course of sleep, REM periods gradually get longer and non-REM periods get shorter and shallower.
- The architecture of sleep varies somewhat from one person to the next.

Age, culture, and sleep

- Time spent in REM sleep declines from 50 percent among newborns to about 20 percent among adults.
- Total sleep time declines with advancing age.
- Cultural variations in sleep patterns appear to be small.
- Napping practices vary along cultural lines, and siesta cultures are found in tropical regions.

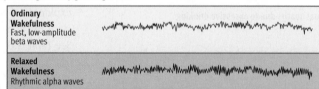

Ordinary Wakefulness
Fast, low-amplitude beta waves

Relaxed Wakefulness
Rhythmic alpha waves

Stage 1
Small, irregular brain waves

Stage 2
Appearance of spindle-shaped waves called sleep spindles

Stage 3 and 4
Appearance of large, slow delta waves

REM Sleep
Similar to ordinary wakefulness

Sleep deprivation

- Sleep experts believe that much of North American society suffers from chronic sleep deprivation.
- Sleep deprivation appears to have far more negative effects than most people assume.
- Selective deprivation of REM and slow-wave sleep leads to increased attempts to shift into these stages of sleep and increased time in these stages after sleep deprivation ends.

- REM and slow-wave sleep may help with memory consolidation.
- Short sleep duration is associated with a variety of health problems, but both short and long sleepers exhibit elevated mortality rates.

Sleep disorders

Insomnia: Chronic problems in getting adequate sleep

Narcolepsy: Marked by sudden, irresistible onsets of sleep during normal waking hours

Nightmares: Anxiety-arousing dreams that lead to awakening, usually from REM sleep.

Night terrors (also called "sleep terrors"): Abrupt awakenings from NREM sleep, accompanied by intense autonomic arousal and feelings of panic

Sleep apnea: Frequent reflexive gasping for air that disrupts sleep

Somnambulism (sleepwalking): Wandering around while remaining asleep

REM sleep behaviour disorder (RBD): Potentially troublesome, even violent, dream enactments during REM periods

HYPNOSIS

Hypnotic induction and phenomena

- *Hypnosis* is a procedure that produces a heightened state of suggestibility.
- People vary in their susceptibility to hypnosis.
- Hypnosis can produce a variety of effects, including anesthesia, sensory distortions, disinhibition, and posthypnotic amnesia.

Theories of hypnosis

- According to some theorists, hypnosis produces a normal state of consciousness in which people act out the role of a hypnotized subject.
- The *role-playing view* is supported by evidence that hypnotic feats can be duplicated by non-hypnotized subjects and that hypnotic subjects are often acting out a role.
- According to Ernest Hilgard, hypnosis produces an altered state of awareness characterized by dissociation.
- The *altered-state view* is supported by evidence that divided consciousness is a common experience, as illustrated by highway hypnosis.

MEDITATION

Types and effects

- Meditation refers to a family of practices that train attention to heighten awareness and bring mental processes under greater voluntary control.
  - Two main styles: *focused attention* and *open monitoring*.
  - Effective meditation leads to a beneficial physiological state that may be accompanied by changes in brain activity.
  - Meditation may produce alterations in brain structure.

© Dean Mitchell/Shutterstock.com

ALTERING CONSCIOUSNESS WITH DRUGS

Principal abused drugs

Narcotics: Drugs derived from opium, such as heroin

Sedatives: Sleep-inducing drugs that decrease CNS activation, such as barbiturates

Stimulants: Drugs that increase CNS activation, such as cocaine and amphetamines

Hallucinogens: Drugs that produce sensory distortions and diverse mental and emotional effects, such as LSD and mescaline

Cannabis: Hemp plant from which marijuana, hashish, and THC are derived

Alcohol: Includes a variety of beverages that contain ethyl alcohol

Factors influencing drug effects

- Drug effects depend on users' age, mood, personality, weight, and expectations.
- Drug effects also depend on the potency of the drug, the method of administration, and the user's tolerance.
- *Tolerance* refers to a progressive decrease in a person's responsiveness to a drug as a result of continued use.

© 2017 Cengage Learning

Mechanisms of drug action

- Psychoactive drugs exert their effects by selectively altering neurotransmitter activity.
- Increased activation in the *mesolimbic dopamine pathway* may be responsible for the reinforcing effects of many drugs.

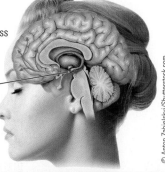

Mesolimbic dopamine pathway

© Anton Zabielskyi/Shutterstock.com

Risks associated with drug abuse

- *Physical dependence* exists when drug use must be continued to avoid withdrawal illness.
- *Psychological dependence* exists when drug use must be continued to satisfy craving for the drug.
- Many drugs, especially CNS depressants, can produce a lethal overdose.
- Many drugs cause deleterious health effects by producing direct tissue damage.
- The negative effects of drugs on physical health are often due to indirect behavioural effects.

APPLICATIONS

- Naps can prove helpful, but their effects vary; snoring has more medical significance than most people realize.
- Individuals troubled by insomnia should avoid panic, pursue relaxation, and try distracting themselves.
- Everyone dreams, but some people don't remember their dreams. Freud distinguished between the manifest and latent content of dreams.
- In evaluating the validity of a definition, one should look not only at the definition but also at where it came from.

© Photographee.eu/Shutterstock.com

CHAPTER 6

Rob Melnychuk/Photodisc/Getty Images

Learning

Themes in this Chapter

Sociohistorical
Context

Heredity &
Environment

- In 1953, a Japanese researcher observed a young macaque (a type of monkey) on the island of Koshima washing a sweet potato in a stream before eating it. No one had ever seen a macaque do this before. Soon, other members of the monkey's troop were showing the same behaviour. Several generations later, macaques on Koshima still wash their potatoes before eating them (De Waal, 2001).
- Barn swallows in Minnesota built nests inside a Home Depot warehouse store, safe from the weather and from predators. So how do they get in and out to bring food to their chicks when the doors are closed? They flutter near the motion sensors that operate the doors until they open.
- A firefighter in Georgia routinely braves life-threatening situations to rescue people in distress. Yet the firefighter is paralyzed with fear whenever he sees someone dressed as a clown. He has been terrified of clowns ever since he was in Grade 3 (Ryckeley, 2005).
- Canadian freestyle skier Rosalind (Roz) Groenewoud (Olympic silver medalist in 2014, World Champion in 2011, and X Games Champion in 2012) listens to the same song before each of her competitions ("The Game Needs Me" by Dyme Def) and always wears the same shade of bright red lipstick. Freestyle skier Mikael Kingsbury (a silver medalist in the 2014 Olympics) wears the same T-shirt under his clothes for each competition, and legendary tennis champion Serena Williams wears the same pair of socks for an entire tournament and always brings her shower sandals to the tennis court.

What connects superstitious Olympic and professional athletes or a clown-phobic firefighter to potato-washing monkeys and door-opening swallows? What do all of these scenarios have in common? At first glance, very little. The answer is *learning*. To a psychologist, **learning is any relatively durable change in behaviour or knowledge that is due to experience.** Macaques aren't born with the habit of washing their sweet potatoes, nor do swallows begin life knowing how to operate motion sensors. Elite athletes adopt their superstitious rituals because they seemed to be related to their success. The firefighter in Georgia wasn't born with a fear of clowns, since he only began to be frightened of them when he was in Grade 3. In short, all these behaviours are the product of experience—that is, they represent learning. When most people think of learning, they imagine someone reading a textbook, studying for an exam, or taking lessons to learn how

Although Tennis Champion Serena Williams is the most accomplished tennis champion in history, she engages in a series of superstitious behaviours during each tennis tournament; just in case.

Leonard Zhukovsky/Shutterstock.com

to snowboard. Although these do involve learning, they represent only the tip of the iceberg in psychologists' eyes.

Superstitions are often the result of obtaining a reward after engaging in some behaviour, even if the behaviour and reward are not really linked. For example, Boston Bruins hockey legend Phil Esposito was known for always wearing a black turtleneck under his hockey jersey. It all began before one game when he put on a turtleneck because he was suffering from a cold. That night he scored three goals, a hat trick, and so wore a turtleneck under his uniform every game until he retired.

JAVIER SORIANO/AFP/Getty Images

Photo by Jag Gundu/Getty Images

Canadian Olympians Roz Groenewoud and Mikael Kingsbury are just two examples of elite athletes who engage in superstitious behaviour before competitions.

As we will discuss later in the chapter, superstitions have been the subject of scientific learning research and are an example of what psychologists are referring to when they use the term *learning*—in this case, a type of learning known as *operant conditioning*.

Learning is a key topic in psychology. When you think about it, it would be hard to name a lasting change in behaviour that is *not* the result of experience. That's why learning is one of the most fundamental concepts in all of psychology. As the examples in this section show, learning is not an exclusively human process. Learning is pervasive in the animal world as well, a fact that won't amaze anyone who's ever owned a dog or seen a trained seal in action. Another insight, however, is even more startling: *The principles that explain learned responses in animals explain much of human learning, too.* Thus, the same mechanisms that explain how barn swallows learn to operate an automated door can account for a professional athlete's bizarre superstitions. In fact, many of the most fascinating discoveries in the study of learning originated in studies of animals.

In this chapter, you'll see how fruitful the research into learning has been and how wide-ranging its applications are. We'll focus most of our attention on a specific kind of learning: conditioning. *Conditioning* **involves learning connections between events that occur in an organism's environment** (wearing a black turtleneck and scoring three goals in a hockey game is one example). In researching conditioning, psychologists study learning at a fundamental level. This strategy has paid off with insights that have laid the foundation for the study of more complex forms of learning, such as learning by observation (the kind of learning that may account for the Koshima macaques picking up one monkey's habit of washing her sweet potatoes). In the Personal Application, you'll see how you can harness the principles of conditioning to improve your self-control. The Critical Thinking Application shows how conditioning procedures can be used to manipulate emotions.

Classical Conditioning

Key Learning Goals

▶ Describe Pavlov's demonstration of classical conditioning and the key elements in this form of learning.

▶ Clarify how classical conditioning can shape emotions, physiological responses, and attitudes.

▶ Describe acquisition, extinction, and spontaneous recovery in classical conditioning.

▶ Explain what happens in generalization, discrimination, and higher-order conditioning.

Do you go weak in the knees at the thought of standing on the roof of a tall building? Does your heart race when you imagine encountering a harmless garter snake? If so, you can understand, at least to some degree, what it's like to have a phobia. *Phobias* **are irrational fears of specific objects or situations.** Mild phobias are common. Over the years, students in our classes have described their phobic responses to a diverse array of stimuli, including bridges, elevators, tunnels, heights, dogs, cats, bugs, snakes, professors, doctors, strangers, thunderstorms, and germs. If you have a phobia, you may have wondered how you managed to acquire such a foolish fear. Chances are, it was through classical conditioning (Field & Purkis, 2012). *Classical conditioning* **is a type of learning in which a stimulus acquires the capacity to evoke a response that was originally evoked by another stimulus.** The process was first described in 1903 by Ivan Pavlov, and it was originally called *Pavlovian conditioning* in tribute to him. This learning process was characterized as "classical" conditioning decades later (starting in the 1940s) to distinguish it from other types of conditioning that attracted research interest around that time (Clark, 2004).

Pavlov's Demonstration: "Psychic Reflexes"

Ivan Pavlov was a prominent Russian physiologist who did the Nobel Prize winning research on digestion. Pavlov was one of those who was responsible for turning psychology from research focusing on subjective accounts of experience, *introspection*, to a more objective, rigorous, scientific approach. His work showed how stimuli in the external world controlled our actions and behaviour (Pickren &

Surrounded by his research staff, the great Russian physiologist Ivan Pavlov (white beard) demonstrates his famous classical conditioning experiment with dogs.

Rutherford, 2010). He de-emphasized the mind, and mentalistic accounts of behaviour, and showed how learning was under the influence of experience and that "associations could be built up in consciousness" (Pickren & Rutherford, 2010, p. 59).

Pavlov was studying the role of saliva in the digestive processes of dogs when he stumbled onto what he called "psychic reflexes" (Pavlov, 1906). Like many great discoveries, Pavlov's was partly accidental, although he had the insight to recognize its significance. His subjects were dogs restrained in harnesses in an experimental chamber (see Figure 6.1). Their saliva was collected by means of a surgically implanted tube in the salivary gland. Pavlov would present meat powder to a dog and then collect the resulting saliva. As his research progressed, he noticed that dogs accustomed to the procedure would start salivating *before* the meat powder was presented. For instance, they would salivate in response to a clicking sound made by the device that was used to present the meat powder.

Intrigued by this unexpected finding, Pavlov decided to investigate further. To clarify what was happening, he paired the presentation of the meat powder with various stimuli that would stand out in the laboratory situation. For instance, in some experiments, he used a simple auditory stimulus—the presentation of a tone. After the tone and the meat powder had been presented together a number of times, the tone was presented alone. What happened? The dogs responded by salivating to the sound of the tone alone.

What was so significant about a dog salivating when a tone was presented? The key is that the tone started out as a *neutral* stimulus. That is, it did not originally produce the response of salivation. However, Pavlov managed to change that by pairing the tone with a stimulus (meat powder) that did produce the salivation response. Through this process, the tone acquired the capacity to trigger the response of salivation.

What Pavlov had demonstrated was how learned associations—which were viewed as the basic building blocks of the entire learning process—were formed by events in an organism's environment. Based on this insight, he built a broad theory of learning that attempted to explain aspects of emotion, temperament, neuroses, and language (Windholz, 1997).

Terminology and Procedures

A special vocabulary is associated with classical conditioning. It often looks intimidating to the

Time & Life Pictures/Getty Images

Ivan Pavlov

"Next time there's a revolution, get up earlier!"

uninitiated, but it's really not all that mysterious. The bond Pavlov noted between the meat powder and salivation was a natural, unlearned association. It did not have to be created through conditioning. It is therefore called an *unconditioned* association. Thus, the ***unconditioned stimulus (UCS)*** is a stimulus that evokes an unconditioned response without previous conditioning. The ***unconditioned response (UCR)*** is an unlearned reaction to an unconditioned stimulus that occurs without previous conditioning.

Figure 6.1
Classical conditioning apparatus. An experimental arrangement similar to the one depicted here (taken from Yerkes & Morgulis, 1909) has typically been used in demonstrations of classical conditioning, although Pavlov's original setup (see inset) was quite a bit simpler. The dog is restrained in a harness. A tone is used as the conditioned stimulus (CS) and the presentation of meat powder is used as the unconditioned stimulus (UCS). The tube inserted into the dog's salivary gland allows precise measurement of its salivation response. The pen and rotating drum of paper on the left are used to maintain a continuous record of salivary flow. (Inset) The less elaborate setup that Pavlov originally used to collect saliva on each trial is shown here (Goodwin, 1991).

Sources: Adapted from Yerkes, R.M., and Morgulis, S. (1909). The method of Pavlov in animal psychology, *Psychological Bulletin*, 6, 257–273. American Psychological Association. Inset: From Goodwin, C.J., Misportraying Pavlov's apparatus, 1991. *American Journal of Psychology*, 104 (1): 135–141. © 1991 by the Board of Trustees of the University of Illinois.

In contrast, the link between the tone and salivation was established through conditioning. It is therefore called a *conditioned* association. Thus, the *conditioned stimulus (CS)* is a previously neutral stimulus that has, through conditioning, acquired the capacity to evoke a conditioned response. The *conditioned response (CR)* is a learned reaction to a conditioned stimulus that occurs because of previous conditioning. Ironically, the names for the four key elements in classical conditioning (the UCS, UCR, CS, and CR) are the by-product of a poor translation of Pavlov's writing into English. Pavlov actually used the words condition*al* and uncondition*al* to refer to these concepts (Todes, 1997).

To avoid possible confusion, it is worth noting that the unconditioned response and conditioned response often consist of the same behaviour, although there may be subtle differences between them. In Pavlov's initial demonstration, the UCR and CR were both salivation. When evoked by the

UCS (meat powder), salivation was an unconditioned response. When evoked by the CS (the tone), salivation was a conditioned response. The procedures involved in classical conditioning are outlined in Figure 6.2.

Pavlov's "psychic reflex" came to be called the *conditioned reflex*. Classically conditioned responses have traditionally been characterized as reflexes and are said to be *elicited* (drawn forth) because most of them are relatively automatic or involuntary. However, research in recent decades has demonstrated that classical conditioning is involved in a wider range of human and animal behaviour than previously appreciated, including some types of nonreflexive responding (Allan, 1998). Finally, a *trial* in classical conditioning consists of any presentation of a stimulus or pair of stimuli. Psychologists are interested in how many trials are required to establish a particular conditioned bond. The number needed to form an association varies considerably. Although classical conditioning generally proceeds gradually, it *can* occur quite rapidly, sometimes in just one pairing of the CS and UCS.

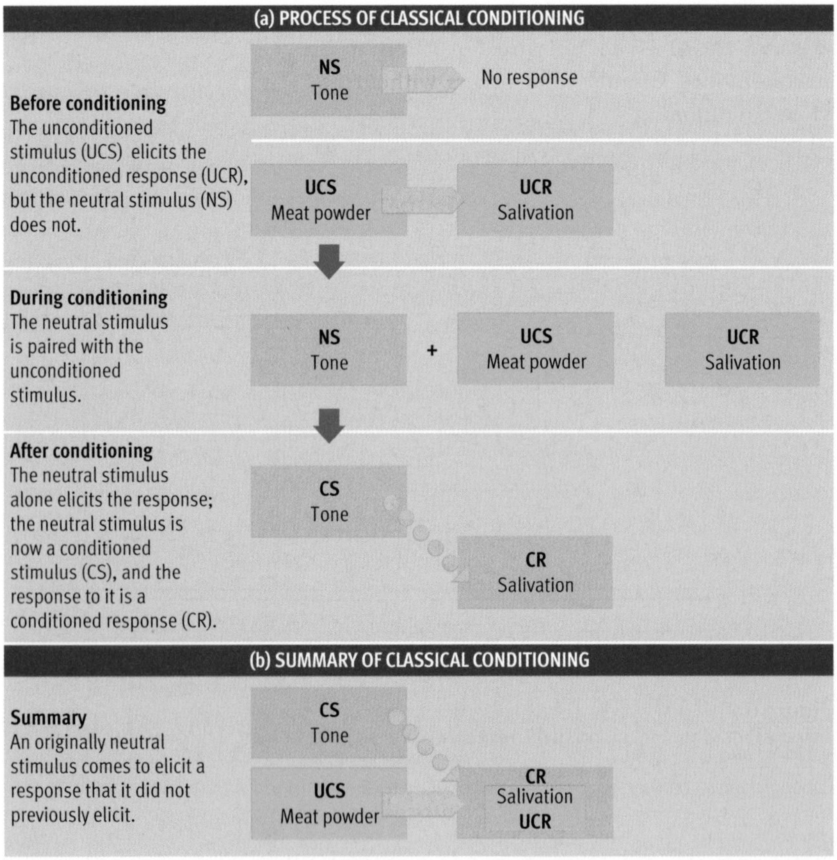

Classical Conditioning in Everyday Life

In laboratory experiments on classical conditioning, researchers have generally worked with extremely simple responses. Besides salivation, frequently studied favourites include eyelid closure, knee jerks, the flexing of various limbs, and fear responses. The study of such simple responses has proven both practical and productive. However, these responses do not even begin to convey the rich diversity of everyday behaviours regulated by classical conditioning. Let's look at some examples of classical conditioning taken from everyday life.

Conditioned Fear and Anxiety

Classical conditioning often plays a key role in shaping emotional responses such as fears. Phobias are a good example of such responses. Case studies of patients suffering from phobias suggest that many irrational fears can be traced back to experiences that involve classical conditioning (Antony & McCabe, 2003; Fields & Prukis, 2012). It's easy to imagine how such conditioning can occur outside of the lab. For example, one of our students troubled by a severe bridge phobia was able to pinpoint childhood conditioning experiences as the source of her phobia (see Figure 6.3). Whenever her family

(a) PROCESS OF CLASSICAL CONDITIONING

Before conditioning
The unconditioned stimulus (UCS) elicits the unconditioned response (UCR), but the neutral stimulus (NS) does not.

NS Tone → No response

UCS Meat powder → UCR Salivation

During conditioning
The neutral stimulus is paired with the unconditioned stimulus.

NS Tone + UCS Meat powder → UCR Salivation

After conditioning
The neutral stimulus alone elicits the response; the neutral stimulus is now a conditioned stimulus (CS), and the response to it is a conditioned response (CR).

CS Tone

CR Salivation

(b) SUMMARY OF CLASSICAL CONDITIONING

Summary
An originally neutral stimulus comes to elicit a response that it did not previously elicit.

CS Tone

UCS Meat powder

CR Salivation
UCR

© 2017 Cengage Learning

Figure 6.2
The sequence of events in classical conditioning. (a) Moving downward, this series of three panels outlines the sequence of events in classical conditioning, using Pavlov's original demonstration as an example. (b) As we encounter other examples of classical conditioning throughout the book, we will see many diagrams like the one in this panel, which will provide snapshots of specific instances of classical conditioning.

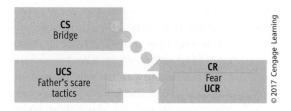

© 2017 Cengage Learning

Figure 6.3

Classical conditioning of a fear response. Many emotional responses that would otherwise be puzzling can be explained by classical conditioning. In the case of one woman's bridge phobia, the fear originally elicited by her father's scare tactics became a conditioned response to the stimulus of bridges.

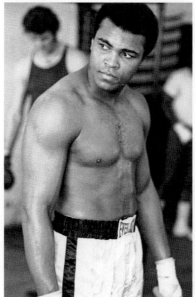

Many professional athletes have to deal with fear of one of the necessities of their occupation—flying. Legendary boxer Muhammad Ali and Pittsburgh Steeler James Harrison are two athletes with a fear of flying.

drove to visit her grandmother, they had to cross a rickety, old bridge in the countryside. Her father, in a misguided attempt at humour, would stop short of the bridge and carry on about the great danger. The young girl was terrified by her father's joke. Hence, the bridge became a conditioned stimulus eliciting great fear. The fear then spilled over to *all* bridges and 40 years later she was still troubled by this phobia.

Everyday fear responses that are less severe than phobias may also be products of classical conditioning. For instance, if you cringe when you hear the sound of a dentist's drill, this response is a result of classical conditioning. In this case, pain has been paired with the sound of the drill, which became a CS eliciting your cringe. That is *not* to say that traumatic experiences associated with stimuli *automatically* lead to conditioned fears or phobias. Whether fear conditioning takes place depends on many factors (Oehlberg & Mineka, 2011). Conditioned fears are less likely to develop when events seem escapable and controllable, and when people have a history of nontraumatic encounters in similar situations (e.g., with dentists). People who are relatively low in anxiety probably acquire conditioned fears less readily than those who are highly anxious.

Evaluative Conditioning of Attitudes

Pavlovian conditioning can also influence people's attitudes. In recent decades, researchers have shown great interest in a subtype of classical conditioning called *evaluative conditioning*. **Evaluative conditioning refers to changes in the liking of a stimulus that result from pairing that stimulus with other positive or negative stimuli.** In other words, evaluative conditioning involves the acquisition of likes and dislikes, or preferences, through classical conditioning (De Houwer, 2011). Typically, a neutral stimulus is paired with unconditioned stimuli that trigger positive reactions so that the neutral stimulus becomes a conditioned stimulus that elicits similar positive reactions. For example, in one study, funny cartoons paired with two types of energy drinks increased participants' liking of the drinks (Strick et al., 2009). Another study showed that pairing pictures of high-calorie snacks with images of adverse health effects (obesity and cardiovascular disease) fostered more negative attitudes about the unhealthy snacks, and subsequently led subjects to choose fruit over highly caloric snacks (Hollands, Prestwich, & Marteau, 2011). Other studies have found that evaluative conditioning can be used to reduce prejudicial attitudes toward the homeless (Balas & Sweklej, 2013); to foster more favourable attitudes about recycling (Geng et al., 2013); and to create more negative attitudes toward beer drinking (Houben, Schoenmakers, & Wiers, 2010).

Advertising campaigns routinely try to take advantage of evaluative conditioning (see the Personal Application at the end of this chapter). Advertisers often pair their products with UCSs that elicit pleasant emotions (Till & Priluck, 2000). The most common strategy is to present a product in association with an attractive person or enjoyable surroundings (see Figure 6.4). Advertisers hope that these pairings will make their products conditioned stimuli that evoke good feelings. For example, automobile manufacturers like to show their sports-utility vehicles in beautiful outdoor scenes that evoke pleasant feelings and nostalgic thoughts of

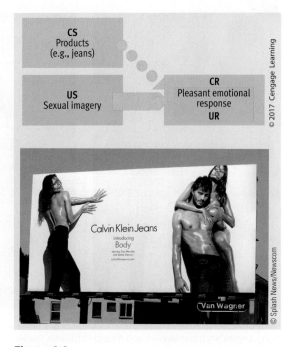

Figure 6.4

Classical conditioning in advertising. Many advertisers attempt to make their products conditioned stimuli that elicit pleasant emotional responses by pairing their products with attractive or popular people or sexual imagery.

past vacations. Puppies and cute children are also popular stimuli used in advertisements designed to promote positive associations with their product. Politicians know this, too, and they often have pictures taken with popular people and with babies, perhaps in an attempt to boost their own popularity. This practice is great news for Olympic athletes who often have trouble making ends meet. Athletes such as Canadian Olympic medalists Alex Bilodeau and Joannie Rochette have obtained lucrative endorsement deals after their success at the Olympics.

Conditioning and Drug Effects

As we discussed in Chapter 5, *drug tolerance* involves a gradual decline in responsiveness to a drug with repeated use, so that larger and larger doses are required to attain the user's customary effect. Most theories assert that drug tolerance is largely attributable to physiological changes in the user. However, research by Shepard Siegel (2005, 2016) demonstrates that classical conditioning also contributes to drug tolerance—sometimes in unexpected ways.

Stimuli that are consistently paired with the administration of drugs can acquire the capacity to elicit conditioned responses in both humans and laboratory animals. There is a special wrinkle, however, when drug administration serves as a UCS.

In many instances, the conditioned responses are physiological reactions that are just the *opposite* of the normal effects of the drugs (Siegel et al., 2000). These opponent responses, which have been seen as the result of conditioning with narcotics, stimulants, and alcohol, are called *compensatory CRs* because they partially compensate for some drug effects. These compensatory CRs help to maintain homeostasis (internal balance) in physiological processes. They are adaptive in the short term, as they counterbalance some of the potentially dangerous effects of various drugs.

What role do these compensatory CRs play in drug tolerance? Most drug users have routines that lead to the consistent pairing of drug administration and certain stimuli, such as syringes, cocaine bottles, and specific settings and rituals. Even the drug administration process itself can become a CS associated with drug effects (Weise-Kelly & Siegel, 2001). According to Siegel (2005), these environmental cues eventually begin to elicit compensatory CRs that partially cancel out some of the anticipated effects of abused drugs. As these compensatory CRs strengthen, they neutralize more and more of a drug's pleasurable effects, producing a gradual decline in the user's responsiveness to the drug (in other words, tolerance).

Things can go awry, however, when drug users depart from their normal drug routines. If drugs are taken in new ways or in new settings, the usual compensatory CRs may not occur. With their counterbalancing effects eliminated, the drugs may have a much stronger impact than usual, thus increasing the risk of an overdose (Siegel, 2001). This model may explain why heroin addicts seem more prone to overdose when they shoot up in unfamiliar settings. Another problem is that when people try to quit drugs, exposure to drug-related cues—in the absence of actual drug administration—may trigger compensatory CRs that increase drug cravings and fuel drug addiction and relapse (McDonald & Siegel, 2004). Thus, complicated conditioning processes appear to play a role in drug tolerance, drug craving, and drug overdoses, which need to be factored into the treatment of drug addiction (Siegel & Ramos, 2002).

The contextual cues (in the park, by the swings) may themselves come to elicit (conditioned) compensatory responses that contribute to the development of tolerance for the drug. "When the drug is administered repeatedly in the context of the usual pre-drug cues, these cues elicit a CCR that attenuates the drug effect. As the drug is administered more and more often, and the CCR grows in strength, the attenuation of the drug effect becomes more pronounced" (Siegel, 2002, p. 4). In addition, when the drug user is in the company of the cues associated with drug use but is not administering the drug itself, withdrawal symptoms may be produced (McDonald & Siegel, 2004).

Basic Processes in Classical Conditioning

Classical conditioning is often portrayed as a mechanical process that inevitably leads to a certain result. This view reflects the fact that most conditioned responses are reflexive and difficult to control—Pavlov's dogs would have been hard-pressed to withhold their salivation. Similarly, most people with phobias have great difficulty suppressing their fear. However, this vision of classical conditioning as an "irresistible force" is misleading because it fails to consider the many factors involved in classical conditioning (Urcelay & Miller, 2014). In this section, we'll look at basic processes in classical conditioning to expand on the rich complexity of this form of learning.

Acquisition: Forming New Responses

We have already discussed *acquisition* without attaching a formal name to the process. *Acquisition refers to the initial stage of learning something.* Pavlov theorized that the acquisition of a conditioned response depends on *stimulus contiguity.* Stimuli are contiguous if they occur together in time and space.

Stimulus contiguity is important, but learning theorists now realize that contiguity alone doesn't automatically produce conditioning (Miller & Grace, 2003). People are bombarded daily by countless stimuli that could be perceived as being paired, yet only some of these pairings produce classical conditioning.

If conditioning does not occur to all of the stimuli present in a situation, what determines its occurrence? Evidence suggests that stimuli that are novel, unusual, or especially intense have more potential to become CSs than routine stimuli, probably because they are *salient*, that is, they are more likely to stand out among other stimuli (Miller & Grace, 2013).

Extinction: Weakening Conditioned Responses

Fortunately, a newly formed stimulus–response bond does not necessarily last indefinitely. If it did,

concept check 6.1

Identifying Elements in Classical Conditioning

Check your understanding of classical conditioning by trying to identify the unconditioned stimulus (UCS), unconditioned response (UCR), conditioned stimulus (CS), and conditioned response (CR) in each of the examples below. Fill in the diagram next to each example. You'll find the answers in Appendix A near the back of the book.

_____ **1.** Sam is three years old. One night, his parents build a roaring fire in the family room fireplace. The fire spits out a large ember that hits Sam in the arm, giving him a nasty burn that hurts a great deal for several hours. A week later, when Sam's parents light another fire in the fireplace, Sam becomes upset and fearful, crying and running from the room.

_____ **2.** Melanie is driving to work on a rainy highway when she notices that the brake lights of all of the cars just ahead of her have come on. She hits her brakes but watches in horror as her car glides into a four-car pileup. She's badly shaken up in the accident. A month later, she's driving in the rain again and notices that she tenses up every time she sees brake lights come on ahead of her.

_____ **3.** At the age of 24, Tyrone has developed an allergy to cats. When he's in the same room with a cat for more than 30 minutes, he starts wheezing. After a few such allergic reactions, he starts wheezing as soon as he sees a cat in a room.

learning would be inflexible, and organisms would have difficulty adapting to new situations. Instead, the right circumstances produce *extinction*, **the gradual weakening and disappearance of a conditioned response tendency.**

What leads to extinction in classical conditioning? The consistent presentation of the conditioned stimulus *alone*, without the unconditioned stimulus. For example, when Pavlov consistently presented *only* the tone to a previously conditioned dog, the tone gradually lost its capacity to elicit the response of salivation. Such a sequence of events is depicted in the yellow portion of Figure 6.5, which graphs the amount of salivation by a dog over a series of conditioning trials. Note how the salivation response declines during extinction.

How long does it take to extinguish a conditioned response? That depends on many factors, but particularly the strength of the conditioned bond when

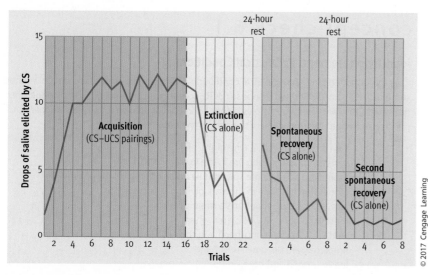

Figure 6.5

Acquisition, extinction, and spontaneous recovery. During acquisition, the strength of the dog's conditioned response (measured by the amount of salivation) increases rapidly and then levels off near its maximum. During extinction, the CR declines erratically until it's extinguished. After a "rest" period in which the dog is not exposed to the CS, a spontaneous recovery occurs, and the CS once again elicits a (weakened) CR. Repeated presentations of the CS alone re-extinguish the CR, but after another "rest" interval, a weaker spontaneous recovery occurs.

extinction begins. Some conditioned responses extinguish quickly, while others are difficult to weaken.

Spontaneous Recovery: Resurrecting Responses

Some conditioned responses display the ultimate in tenacity by "reappearing from the dead" after having been extinguished. Learning theorists use the term *spontaneous recovery* to describe such a resurrection from the graveyard of conditioned associations. *Spontaneous recovery* **is the reappearance of an extinguished response after a period of nonexposure to the conditioned stimulus.**

Pavlov (1927) observed this phenomenon in some of his pioneering studies. He fully extinguished a dog's CR of salivation to a tone and then returned the dog to its home cage for a "rest interval" (a period of nonexposure to the CS). On a subsequent day, when the dog was brought back to the experimental chamber for retesting, the tone was sounded and the salivation response reappeared. Although it had returned, the rejuvenated response was weak. The salivation was less than when the response was at its peak strength. If Pavlov consistently presented the CS by itself again, the response re-extinguished quickly. However, in some of the dogs, the response made still another spontaneous recovery (typically even weaker than the first) after they had spent another period in their cages (see Figure 6.5 once again).

More recent studies have uncovered a related phenomenon called the ***renewal effect***—if a response is extinguished in a different environment than it was acquired, the extinguished response will reappear if the animal is returned to the original environment where acquisition took place. This phenomenon, along with the evidence on spontaneous recovery, suggests that extinction somehow *suppresses* a conditioned response rather than *erasing* a learned association (Bouton, Todd, Vurbic, & Winterbauer, 2011). In other words, extinction does not appear to lead to unlearning (Bouton & Woods, 2009). The theoretical meanings of spontaneous recovery and the renewal effect are complex and the subject of some debate. However, their practical significance is quite simple: Even if you manage to rid yourself of an unwanted conditioned response (such as cringing when you hear a dental drill), there is an excellent chance that it may make a surprise reappearance later. Unfortunately, this insight also applies to behaviour therapies that are used to extinguish troublesome phobias. Although patients are prone to relapse after these treatments, new research on extinction has yielded new techniques designed to reduce the likelihood of relapse (Laborda, McConnell, & Miller, 2011).

Stimulus Generalization and the Mysterious Case of Little Albert

After conditioning has occurred, organisms often show a tendency to respond not only to the exact CS used but also to other, similar stimuli. For example, Pavlov's dogs might have salivated in response to a different-sounding tone, or you might cringe at the sound of a jeweller's as well as a dentist's drill. These are examples of stimulus generalization. *Stimulus generalization* **occurs when an organism that has learned a response to a specific stimulus responds in the same way to new stimuli that are similar to the original stimulus.** Generalization is adaptive, given that organisms rarely encounter the exact same stimulus more than once (Thomas, 1992). Stimulus generalization is also commonplace. We have already discussed a real-life example: the woman who acquired a bridge phobia during her childhood because her father scared her whenever they went over a particular old bridge. The original CS for her fear was that specific bridge, but her fear was ultimately *generalized* to all bridges.

The likelihood and amount of generalization to a new stimulus depend on the similarity between the new stimulus and the original CS (Balsam, 1988). The basic law governing generalization is this: *The more* similar new stimuli are to the original CS, the greater the generalization. This principle can be quantified in graphs called *generalization gradients,* such as those shown in Figure 6.6. These generalization gradients map out how a dog conditioned to salivate to a tone of 1200 hertz might respond to other tones. As you can see, the strength of the generalization response declines as the similarity between the new stimuli and the original CS decreases.

The process of generalization can have important implications. For example, it appears to contribute to the development of *panic disorder,* which involves recurrent, overwhelming anxiety attacks that occur suddenly and unexpectedly (see Chapter 15). Recent research suggests that panic patients have a tendency to overgeneralize—that is, to have broader generalization gradients than control subjects—when exposed to stimuli that trigger anxiety (Lissek et al., 2010). Thus, conditioned fear to a stimulus environment where panic occurs (e.g., a specific shopping mall) readily generalizes to similar stimulus situations (all shopping malls), fuelling the growth of patients' panic disorder.

John B. Watson, the founder of behaviourism (see Chapter 1), conducted an influential early study of generalization. Watson and a colleague, Rosalie Rayner, examined the generalization of conditioned fear in an 11-month-old boy, known in the annals of psychology as "Little Albert." Like many babies, Albert was initially unafraid of a live white rat. Then Watson and Rayner (1920) paired the presentation of the rat with a loud, startling sound (made by striking a steel gong with a hammer). Albert *did* show fear in response to the loud noise. After seven pairings of the rat and the gong, the rat was established as a CS eliciting a fear response (see Figure 6.7).

Five days later, Watson and Rayner exposed the youngster to other stimuli that resembled the rat in being white and furry. They found that Albert's fear response generalized to a variety of stimuli, including a rabbit, a dog, a fur coat, a Santa Claus mask, and Watson's hair.

What happened to Little Albert? Did he grow up with a phobia of Santa Claus? There was endless speculation for decades because no one had any idea who Albert was or what happened to him. He was taken from the hospital where Watson and Rayner conducted their study before they got around to extinguishing the conditioned fears that they had created. Watson and Rayner were roundly criticized in later years for failing to ensure that Albert experienced no lasting ill effects. Their failure to do so clearly was remiss by today's much stricter code of research ethics, but normal for the time.

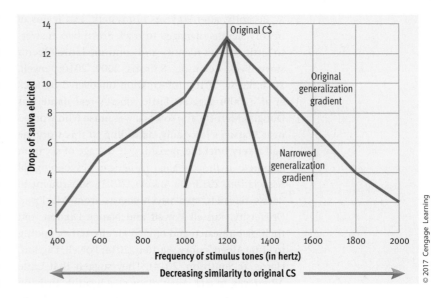

Figure 6.6
Generalization gradients. In a study of stimulus generalization, an organism is typically conditioned to respond to a specific CS, such as a 1200-hertz tone, and then is tested with similar stimuli, such as other tones between 400 and 2000 hertz. Graphs of the organism's responding are called *generalization gradients.* The graphs normally show, as depicted here, that generalization declines as the similarity between the original CS and the new stimuli decreases. When an organism gradually learns *to discriminate* between a CS and similar stimuli, the generalization gradient tends to narrow around the original CS.

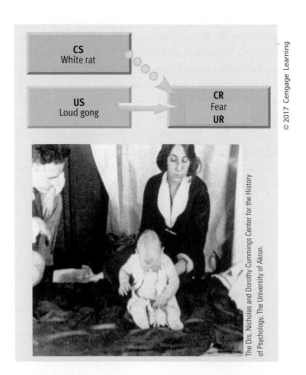

Figure 6.7
The conditioning of Little Albert. The diagram shows how Little Albert's fear response to a white rat was established. Albert's fear response to other white, furry objects illustrates generalization. In the photo, made from a 1919 film, John B. Watson's collaborator, Rosalie Rayner, is shown with Little Albert before he was conditioned to fear the rat.

Recently, after 90 years of mystery, two teams of history sleuths managed to track down two answers to Little Albert's identity and continue Little Albert's story (Beck, Levinson, & Irons, 2009, 2010; Powell, 2010; Reese, 2010). Information uncovered by Beck et al. (2009) suggests Little Albert's real name was Douglas Merritte, the son of a wet nurse who worked near Watson's lab. Sadly, according to this story, he had a very brief life, perishing at the age of six from acquired hydrocephalus (American Psychological Association, 2013; De Angelis, 2012). Subsequent to Beck's research, two psychologists from MacEwan University, Russell Powell and Nancy Digdon, did their own research and offered an alternative ending to Little Albert's story (Bartlett, 2014; Powell, Digdon, Harris, & Smithson, 2014). They suggest that Little Albert was, in fact, Albert Barger—a healthy, thriving baby. Albert Barger lived to 85 years of age and died in 2007.

While we may never know Little Albert's real identity, it is clear that one of psychology's most legendary studies continues to fascinate us.

Stimulus Discrimination

Stimulus discrimination is just the opposite of stimulus generalization. *Stimulus discrimination* **occurs when an organism that has learned a response to a specific stimulus does not respond in the same way to new stimuli that are similar to the original stimulus.** Like generalization, discrimination is adaptive in that an animal's survival may hinge on its being able to distinguish friend from foe, or edible from poisonous food (Thomas, 1992). Organisms can gradually learn to discriminate between an original CS and similar stimuli if they have adequate experience with both. For instance, let's say your pet dog runs around, excitedly wagging its tail, whenever it hears your car pull into the driveway. Initially it will probably respond to *all* cars that pull into the driveway (stimulus generalization). However, if there is anything distinctive about the sound of your car, your dog may gradually respond with excitement to only your car and not to other cars (stimulus discrimination).

The development of stimulus discrimination usually requires that the original CS (your car) continues to be paired with the UCS (your arrival) while similar stimuli (the other cars) not be paired with the UCS. As with generalization, a basic law governs discrimination: *The less similar new stimuli are to the original CS, the greater the likelihood (and ease) of discrimination.* Conversely, if a new stimulus is quite similar to the original CS, discrimination will be relatively difficult to learn. What happens to a generalization gradient when an organism learns a discrimination? The generalization gradient gradually narrows around the original CS, which means that the organism is generalizing to a smaller and smaller range of similar stimuli (see Figure 6.6 again).

Higher-Order Conditioning

Imagine that you were to conduct the following experiment. First, you condition a dog to salivate in response to the sound of a tone by pairing the tone with meat powder. Once the tone is firmly established as a CS, you pair the tone with a new stimulus—let's say a red light, for 15 trials. You then present the red light alone, without the tone. Will the dog salivate in response to the red light?

The answer is "yes." Even though the red light has never been paired with the meat powder, it will acquire the capacity to elicit salivation by virtue of being paired with the tone (see Figure 6.8). This is a demonstration of *higher-order conditioning*, in which a conditioned stimulus functions as if it were an unconditioned stimulus. Higher-order conditioning shows that classical conditioning does not

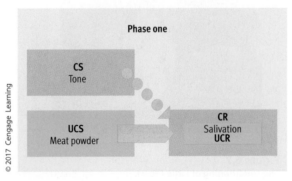
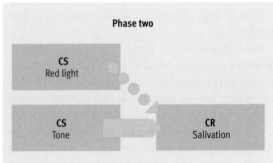

Figure 6.8

Higher-order conditioning. Higher-order conditioning involves a two-phase process. In the first phase, a neutral stimulus (such as a tone) is paired with an unconditioned stimulus (such as meat powder) until it becomes a conditioned stimulus that elicits the response originally evoked by the UCS (such as salivation). In the second phase, another neutral stimulus (such as a red light) is paired with the previously established CS, so that it also acquires the capacity to elicit the response originally evoked by the UCS.

depend on the presence of a genuine, natural UCS. An already established CS will do just fine. In higher-order conditioning, new conditioned responses are built on the foundation of already established conditioned responses. For example, using Pavlov's original method, once conditioning has occurred and the tone reliably elicits the salivation, the tone itself can then be paired with another stimulus such as a light. After subsequent conditioning trials, the light itself then will serve to elicit the salivation. Many human conditioned responses are the product of higher-order conditioning (Rescorla, 1980). The phenomenon of higher-order conditioning greatly extends the reach of classical conditioning.

Cognition and Classical Conditioning

The cognitive element in conditioning was absent from Pavlov's original theorizing and much of the classic work that followed. However, not all theorists believe that cognitions did not play a role. Cognitions, specifically expectations, played an especially prominent in research conducted by Robert Rescorla (1978, 1980; Rescorla & Wagner, 1972). Rescorla asserts that environmental stimuli serve as signals and that some stimuli are better, or more dependable, signals than others. Hence, he has manipulated *signal relations* in classical conditioning—that is, CS–UCS relations that influence whether a CS is a good signal. A "good" signal is one that allows accurate prediction of the UCS. In effect, the classical conditioning procedure might have set up expectations that food would follow the simple auditory stimuli, the tone.

In essence, Rescorla manipulates the *predictive value* of a conditioned stimulus. How does he do so? He varies the proportion of trials in which the CS and UCS are paired. Consider the following example. A tone and shock are paired 20 times for one group of rats. Otherwise, these rats are never shocked. For these rats, the CS (tone) and UCS (shock) are paired in 100 percent of the experimental trials. Another group of rats also receive 20 pairings of the tone and shock. However, the rats in this group are also exposed to the shock on 20 other trials when the tone does *not* precede it. For this group, the CS and UCS are paired in only 50 percent of the trials. Which group would be more likely to expect a shock following the tone? The two groups of rats have had an equal number of CS–UCS pairings, but the CS is a better signal or predictor of shock for the 100 percent CS–UCS group than for the 50 percent CS–UCS group.

What did Rescorla find when he tested the two groups of rats for conditioned fear? He found that the CS elicits a much stronger response in the 100 percent CS–UCS group than in the 50 percent CS–UCS group. Given that the two groups have received an equal number of CS–UCS pairings, this difference must be due to the greater predictive power of the CS for the 100 percent group. In essence, the rats were responding to probabilities, the probability that the shock would or would not follow from the tone. The expectation that the tone signals the shock is greater for the 100 percent CS UCS group. Numerous studies of signal relations have shown that the predictive value of a CS is an influential factor governing classical conditioning (Rescorla, 1978). Through his work he introduced a cognitive element—predictions/expectations—into the models of learning. We will see later in the chapter that cognition was also used by another behaviourist, in this case, Edward Tolman, in interpreting the mechanisms responsible for another type of conditioning—operant conditioning.

Evolutionary and Biological Effects on Conditioning

Learning theorists have traditionally assumed that the fundamental laws of conditioning have great generality—that they apply to a wide range of species. Most psychologists assumed that associations could be conditioned between any stimulus that an organism could register and any response that it could make. However, findings in recent decades have demonstrated that there are limits to the generality of conditioning principles—limits imposed by an organism's biological/evolutionary heritage. For example, consider the work on *taste aversion* and research on *preparedness and phobia*.

Conditioned Taste Aversion: The "Sauce Béarnaise Syndrome"

A number of years ago, a prominent psychologist, Martin Seligman, dined out with his wife and enjoyed a steak with sauce béarnaise. About six hours afterward, he developed a wicked case of stomach flu and endured severe nausea. Subsequently, when he ordered sauce béarnaise, he was chagrined to discover that its aroma alone nearly made him throw up.

Seligman's experience was not unique. Many people develop aversions to food that has been followed by nausea from illness, alcohol intoxication, or food poisoning (Rosenblum, 2009). However, Seligman was puzzled by what he called his "sauce béarnaise syndrome" (Seligman & Hager, 1972). On the one hand, it appeared to be the straightforward result of classical conditioning. A neutral stimulus (the sauce) had been paired with an unconditioned

University of Pennsylvania

Robert Rescorla

"Pavlovian conditioning is a sophisticated and sensible mechanism by which organisms represent the world.... I encourage students to think of animals as behaving like little statisticians.... They really are very finely attuned to small changes in the likelihood of events."

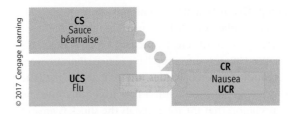

Figure 6.9

Conditioned taste aversion. Taste aversions can be established through classical conditioning, as in the "sauce béarnaise syndrome." However, as the text explains, taste aversions can be acquired in ways that seem to violate basic principles of classical conditioning.

Figure 6.10

Garcia and Koelling's research on conditioned taste aversion. In a landmark series of studies, Garcia and Koelling (1966) demonstrated that some stimulus–response associations are much easier to condition than others. Their apparatus is depicted here. Rats drink saccharin-flavoured water out of the tube on the right. When they make contact with the tube, they may trigger a bright light and buzzer, or a brief electric shock, or radiation exposure that will make them nauseated. This setup allowed Garcia and Koelling to pair various types of stimuli, as discussed in the text.

stimulus (the flu), which caused an unconditioned response (the nausea). Hence, the béarnaise sauce became a conditioned stimulus eliciting nausea (see Figure 6.9).

On the other hand, Seligman recognized that his aversion to béarnaise sauce seemed to violate certain basic principles of conditioning. First, the lengthy delay of six hours between the CS (the sauce) and the UCS (the flu) should have prevented conditioning from occurring. In laboratory studies, a delay of more than *30 seconds* between the CS and UCS makes it difficult to establish a conditioned response, yet this conditioning occurred in just one pairing. Second, why was it that *only* the béarnaise sauce became a CS eliciting nausea? Why not other stimuli that were present in the restaurant? Shouldn't plates, knives, tablecloths, or his wife, for example, also trigger Seligman's nausea?

The riddle of Seligman's sauce béarnaise syndrome was solved by John Garcia (1989) and his colleagues. They conducted a series of studies on *conditioned taste aversion* (Garcia, Clarke, & Hankins, 1973; Garcia & Koelling, 1966; Garcia & Rusiniak, 1980). In these studies, they manipulated the kinds of stimuli preceding the onset of nausea and other noxious experiences in rats, using radiation to artificially induce the nausea (see Figure 6.10). They found that when taste cues were followed by nausea, rats quickly acquired conditioned taste aversions. However, when taste cues were followed by other types of noxious stimuli (such as shock), rats did *not* develop conditioned taste aversions. Furthermore, visual and auditory stimuli followed by nausea also failed to produce conditioned aversions. In short, Garcia and his co-workers found that it was almost impossible to create certain associations, whereas taste–nausea associations (and odour–nausea associations) were almost impossible to prevent.

What is the theoretical significance of this unique readiness to make connections between taste and nausea? Garcia argues that it is a by-product

of the evolutionary history of mammals. Animals that consume poisonous foods and survive must learn not to repeat their mistakes. Natural selection will favour organisms that quickly learn what *not* to eat. Thus, evolution may have biologically programmed some organisms to learn certain types of associations more easily than others. Interest in the antecedents of, processes involved in, and consequences of taste-aversion continue today (e.g., Vidal & Chamizo, 2009).

Preparedness and Phobias

According to Martin Seligman, evolution has also programmed organisms to acquire certain fears more readily than others because of a phenomenon he calls *preparedness*. *Preparedness* involves a species-specific predisposition to be conditioned in certain ways and not others. Seligman (1971) believes that preparedness can explain why certain phobias are vastly more common than others. People tend to develop phobias to snakes, spiders, heights, and darkness relatively easily. However, even after painful experiences with hammers, knives, hot stoves, and electrical outlets, phobic fears of these objects are infrequent. What characteristics do common phobic objects share? Most were once genuine threats to our ancestors. Consequently, a fear response to such objects has survival value for our species. According to Seligman, evolutionary forces gradually programmed humans to acquire conditioned fears of these objects easily and rapidly.

John Garcia

"Taste aversions do not fit comfortably within the present framework of classical or instrumental conditioning: These aversions selectively seek flavors to the exclusion of other stimuli. Interstimulus intervals are a thousandfold too long."

People tend to develop phobias to snakes very easily but to electrical outlets rarely, even though the latter are just as dangerous. Preparedness theory can explain this paradox.

Lab simulations of phobic conditioning have provided some support for the concept of preparedness (Mineka & Öhman, 2002). For example, slides of phobic stimuli (snakes, spiders) for which we seem to show a preparedness and slides of neutral stimuli (flowers, mushrooms) or modern fear-relevant stimuli (guns, knives) have been paired with shock. Consistent with the concept of preparedness, physiological monitoring of the participants indicates that the prepared phobic stimuli tend to produce more rapid conditioning, stronger fear responses, and greater resistance to extinction. Arne Öhman and Susan Mineka (2001) have elaborated on the theory of preparedness, outlining the key elements of what they call an *evolved module for fear learning*. They assert that this evolved module is (1) preferentially activated by stimuli related to survival threats in evolutionary history, (2) automatically activated by these stimuli, (3) relatively resistant to conscious efforts to suppress the resulting fears, and (4) dependent on neural circuitry running through the amygdala.

Operant Conditioning

Even Pavlov recognized that classical conditioning is not the only form of conditioning. Classical conditioning best explains reflexive responding that is largely controlled by stimuli that *precede* the response. However, humans and other animals make a great many responses that don't fit this description. Consider the response that you are engaging in right now: studying. It is definitely not a reflex (life might be easier if it were). The stimuli that govern it (exams and grades) do not precede it. Instead, your studying is mainly influenced by stimulus events that *follow* the response—specifically, its *consequences*.

In the 1930s, this kind of learning was christened *operant conditioning* by B. F. Skinner. The term was derived from his belief that in this type of responding, an organism "operates" on the environment instead of simply reacting to stimuli. Learning occurs because responses come to be influenced by the outcomes that follow them. Thus, *operant conditioning* is a form of learning in which responses come to be controlled by their consequences. Learning theorists originally distinguished between classical and operant conditioning on the grounds that the former regulated reflexive, involuntary responses, whereas the latter governed voluntary responses. This distinction holds up much of the time, but it is not absolute.

Thorndike's Law of Effect

Another name for operant conditioning is *instrumental learning*, a term introduced earlier by Edward L. Thorndike (1913). Thorndike wanted to emphasize that this kind of responding is often *instrumental* in obtaining some desired outcome. His pioneering work provided the foundation for many of the ideas proposed later by Skinner (Chance, 1999). Thorndike began studying animal learning around the turn of

B. F. Skinner

"Operant conditioning shapes behaviour as a sculptor shapes a lump of clay."

the last century. Setting out to determine whether animals could think, he conducted some classic studies of problem solving in cats. In these studies, a hungry cat was placed in a small cage or "puzzle box" with food available just outside. The cat could escape to obtain the food by performing a specific response, such as pulling a wire or depressing a lever (see Figure 6.11). After each escape, the cat was rewarded with a small amount of food and then returned to the cage for another trial. Thorndike monitored how long it took the cat to get out of the box over a series of trials. If the cat could think, Thorndike reasoned, there would be a sudden drop in the time required to escape when the cat recognized the solution to the problem.

Instead of a sudden drop, Thorndike observed a gradual, uneven decline in the time it took cats to escape from his puzzle boxes (see the graph in Figure 6.11). The decline in solution time showed that the cats *were learning*. But the gradual nature of this decline suggested that this learning did *not* depend on thinking and understanding. Instead, Thorndike attributed this learning to a principle he called the *law of effect*. **According to the *law of effect*, if a response in the presence of a stimulus leads to satisfying effects, the association between the stimulus and the response is strengthened.** Thorndike viewed instrumental learning as a mechanical process in which successful responses are gradually "stamped in" by their favourable effects. His law of effect became the cornerstone of Skinner's theory of operant conditioning, although Skinner used different terminology.

Skinner's Demonstration: It's All a Matter of Consequences

Like Pavlov, Skinner (1953, 1969, 1984) conducted some deceptively simple research that became enormously influential (Lattal, 1992; Ledoux, 2012). Ironically, he got off to an inauspicious start. His first book, *The Behavior of Organisms* (1938), sold only 80 copies in its first four years in print. Nonetheless, he went on to become, in the words of historian Albert Gilgen (1982), "without question the most famous American psychologist in the world" (p. 97). He was a very recognizable face to North Americans and wrote popular as well as scientific articles (Rutherford, 2005). He was an inveterate inventor, applying his scientific knowledge and ingenuity to many problems. One of his most (in)famous inventions was the so-called *Baby Box* (named a *Baby Tender*, or later the *Air Crib* by Skinner himself) (Rutherford, 2005). It was an enclosed temperature- and humidity-controlled crib that Skinner designed for his daughter Deborah after his wife asked him for some assistance in improving ways to bring up a baby. He had hoped to modernize child-rearing and

reality **check**

Skinner designed the Air Crib to assist in raising his daughter Deborah. He hoped to modernize the raising of children.

Misconception

B. F. Skinner raised his daughter, Deborah, in a Skinner box, contributing to her becoming severely disturbed later in life, which led to her suicide.

Reality

Skinner did design an innovative crib called a "baby tender" for Deborah, which was featured in *Ladies' Home Journal* (Skinner, 1945; see the photo above). But it was not analogous to a Skinner box, was not used for experiments, and apparently was quite comfortable. Deborah grew up normally, was very close to her father, has not suffered from psychological problems as an adult, and is alive and well, working as an artist (Buzan, 2004).

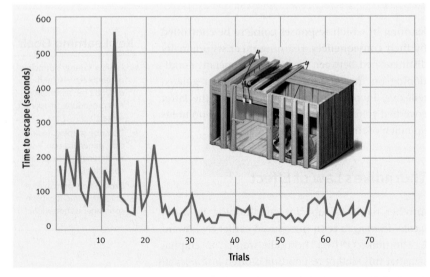

Figure 6.11

The learning curve of one of Thorndike's cats. The inset shows one of Thorndike's puzzle boxes. The cat had to perform three separate acts to escape the box, including depressing the pedal on the right. The learning curve shows how the cat's escape time declined gradually over a number of trials.

to improve things for everyone—babies and parents included. His attempts to popularize this idea to the masses were less than successful.

The fundamental principle of operant conditioning is uncommonly simple and was anticipated by Thorndike's law of effect. *Skinner demonstrated that organisms tend to repeat those responses that are followed by favourable consequences.* This fundamental principle is embodied in Skinner's concept of reinforcement. *Reinforcement* occurs when an event following a response increases an organism's tendency to make that response. In other words, a response is strengthened because it leads to rewarding consequences (see Figure 6.12).

The principle of reinforcement may be simple, but it is immensely powerful. Skinner and his followers have shown that much of everyday behaviour is regulated by reinforcement. For example, you put money in a pop vending machine and you get a pop back as a result. The principle of reinforcement clearly governs complex aspects of human behaviour.

It is important to note, however, that reinforcement is defined *after the fact*, in terms of its effect on behaviour, strengthening a response. Something that is reinforcing for an organism may not be reinforcing later (Catania, 1992). Similarly, something that is reinforcing for one person may not be reinforcing for another. To know whether an event is reinforcing, researchers must make it contingent on a response and observe whether the rate of this response increases.

Terminology and Procedures

Like Pavlov, Skinner created a prototype experimental procedure that has been repeated (with variations) thousands of times. In his research, Skinner typically used pigeons or rats. They made ideal participants for his research where the focus was on observable behaviour. In the typical procedure, a rat or a pigeon is placed in an *operant chamber* that has come to be better known as a "Skinner box." An *operant chamber*, or *Skinner box*, is a small enclosure in which an animal can make a specific response that is recorded while the consequences of the response are systematically controlled. In the boxes designed for rats, the main response made available is pressing a small lever mounted on one side wall (see Figure 6.13). In the boxes made for pigeons, the designated response is pecking a small disk mounted on a side wall. Because operant responses tend to be voluntary, they are said to be *emitted* rather than *elicited*. To *emit* means to send forth.

The Skinner box permits the experimenter to control the reinforcement contingencies that are in

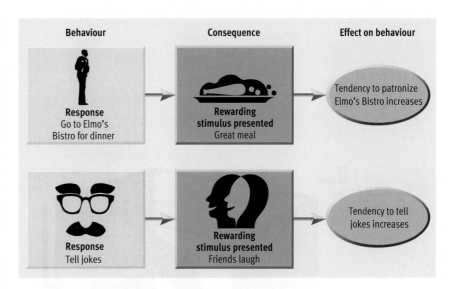

Figure 6.12

Reinforcement in operant conditioning. According to Skinner, reinforcement occurs when a response is followed by rewarding consequences and the organism's tendency to make the response increases. The two examples diagrammed here illustrate the basic premise of operant conditioning—that voluntary behaviour is controlled by its consequences. These examples involve positive reinforcement (for a comparison of positive and negative reinforcement, see Figure 6.17 on page 216).

source: From Weiten. *Cengage Advantage Books: Psychology,* 9E. © 2013 South-Western, a part of Cengage, Inc. Reproduced by permission. www.cengage.com/permissions

effect for the animal. *Reinforcement contingencies* are the circumstances or rules that determine whether responses lead to the presentation of reinforcers. Typically, the experimenter manipulates whether positive consequences occur when the animal makes the designated response. The main positive consequence is usually delivery of a small bit of food into a food cup mounted in the chamber. Because the animals are deprived of food for a while prior to the experimental session, their hunger virtually ensures that the food serves as a reinforcer.

The key dependent variable in most research on operant conditioning is the subjects' *response rate* over time. An animal's rate of lever pressing or disk pecking in the Skinner box is monitored continuously by a device known as a cumulative recorder (see Figure 6.13). The *cumulative recorder* creates a graphic record of responding and reinforcement in a Skinner box as a function of time. The recorder works by means of a roll of paper that moves at a steady rate underneath a movable pen. When there is no responding, the pen stays still and draws a straight horizontal line, reflecting the passage of time. Whenever the designated response occurs, however, the pen moves upward a notch. The pen's movements produce a graphic summary of the animal's responding over time. The pen also makes slash marks to record the delivery of each reinforcer.

The results of operant-conditioning studies are usually portrayed in graphs. In these graphs, the horizontal axis is used to mark the passage of time,

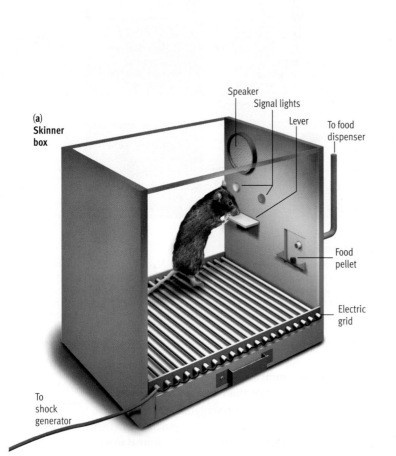

(a)
Skinner box

Speaker
Signal lights
Lever
To food dispenser
Food pellet
Electric grid
To shock generator

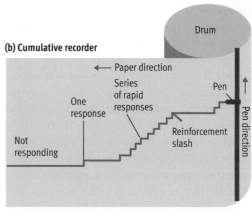

(b) Cumulative recorder

Drum
Paper direction
Series of rapid responses
One response
Pen
Not responding
Reinforcement slash
Pen direction

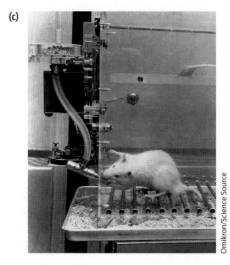

(c)

Omikron/Science Source

Figure 6.13
Skinner box and cumulative recorder. (a) This diagram highlights some of the key features of an operant chamber, or Skinner box. In this apparatus designed for rats, the response under study is lever pressing. Food pellets, which may serve as reinforcers, are delivered into the food cup on the right. The speaker and light permit manipulations of visual and auditory stimuli, and the electric grid gives the experimenter control over aversive consequences (shock) in the box. (b) A cumulative recorder connected to the box keeps a continuous record of responses and reinforcements. A small segment of a cumulative record is shown here. The entire process is automatic as the paper moves with the passage of time; each lever press moves the pen up a step, and each reinforcement is marked with a slash. (c) This photo shows the real thing—a rat being conditioned in a Skinner box. Note the food dispenser on the left, which was omitted from the diagram.

© 2017 Cengage Learning

while the vertical axis is used to plot the accumulation of responses, as shown in Figure 6.14. In interpreting these graphs, the key consideration is the *slope* of the line that represents the record of responding. *A rapid response rate produces a steep slope, whereas a slow response rate produces a shallow slope.* Because the response record is cumulative, the line never goes down. It can only go up as more responses are made or flatten out if the response rate slows to zero. The magnifications shown in Figure 6.14 show how slope and response rate are related.

Operant theorists make a distinction between unlearned, or primary, reinforcers as opposed to conditioned, or secondary, reinforcers. *Primary reinforcers* are events that are inherently reinforcing because they satisfy biological needs. A given species has a limited number of primary reinforcers because they are closely tied to physiological needs. In humans, primary reinforcers include food, water, warmth, sex, and perhaps affection expressed through hugging and close bodily contact. *Secondary*, or *conditioned, reinforcers* are events that acquire reinforcing qualities by being associated with primary reinforcers. The events that function as secondary reinforcers vary among members of a species because they depend on learning. Examples of common secondary reinforcers in humans include money, good grades, attention, flattery, praise, and applause. Similarly, people *learn* to find stylish clothes, sports cars, fine jewellery, and exotic vacations reinforcing.

Basic Processes in Operant Conditioning

Although the principle of reinforcement is strikingly simple, many other processes involved in operant conditioning make this form of learning just as complex as classical conditioning. In fact, some of the *same* processes are involved in both types of conditioning. In this section, we'll discuss how the processes of acquisition, extinction, generalization, and discrimination occur in operant conditioning.

Acquisition and Shaping

As in classical conditioning, *acquisition* in operant conditioning refers to the initial stage of learning some new pattern of responding. However, the procedures used to establish a tendency to emit an operant response are different from those used to create the typical conditioned response. Operant responses are usually established through a gradual process called *shaping*, **which consists of the reinforcement of closer and closer approximations of a desired response.**

Shaping is necessary when an organism does not, on its own, emit the desired response. One of our colleagues used shaping to help her housetrain her new puppy. Because the dog, named Meisje, was small and quiet, our colleague had difficulty in determining when the puppy needed to go outside. She thought that she would train the puppy to ring a bell but, of course, puppies do not naturally ring bells. So she began to shape the puppy by rewarding him as he came progressively closer to the bell, finally reinforcing Meisje's behaviour only when he rang the bell with his nose. Of course, ultimately he was rewarded for bell ringing with a trip outside and a congratulatory "Good boy" on successful completion of his very important task. He now can communicate his needs to her easily. Our colleague reports a couple of other interesting effects. When she leaves town, she can readily find someone to dog-sit her puppy because no matter where he stays, she brings along the bell and he can let the caretaker know when he needs to go outside. Curiously, however, at home, she finds herself frequently getting up and running to the back door whenever she hears any bell—she suspects the puppy may be ringing the bell just to see her run to the back door.

Shaping was an important component of Skinner's research. For example, when a rat is first placed in a Skinner box, it may not press the lever at all. In this case, an experimenter begins shaping by releasing food pellets whenever the rat moves toward the lever. As this response becomes more frequent, the experimenter starts requiring a closer approximation of the desired response, possibly releasing food

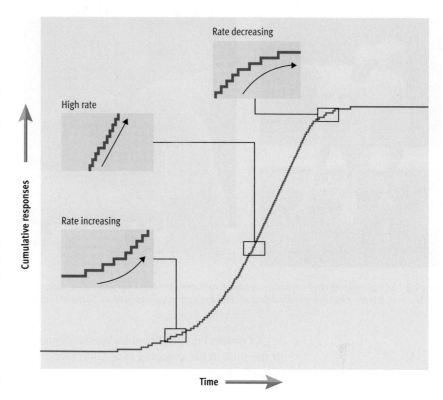

Figure 6.14

A graphic portrayal of operant responding. The results of operant conditioning are often summarized in a graph of cumulative responses over time. The insets magnify small segments of the curve to show how an increasing response rate yields a progressively steeper slope (bottom); a high, steady response rate yields a steep, stable slope (middle); and a decreasing response rate yields a progressively flatter slope (top).

source: From Weiten. *Cengage Advantage Books: Psychology*, 9E. © 2013 South-Western, a part of Cengage, Inc. Reproduced by permission. www.cengage.com/permissions

only when the rat actually touches the lever. As reinforcement increases the rat's tendency to touch the lever, the rat will spontaneously press the lever on occasion, finally providing the experimenter with an opportunity to reinforce the designated response. These reinforcements will gradually increase the rate of lever pressing.

The mechanism of shaping is the key to training animals to perform impressive tricks. When you go to a zoo, circus, or marine park and see bears riding bicycles, monkeys playing the piano, and whales leaping through hoops, you are witnessing the results of shaping. To demonstrate the power of shaping techniques, Skinner once trained some pigeons so that they appeared to play Ping-Pong. They would run about on opposite ends of a Ping-Pong table and peck the ball back and forth. Keller and Marian Breland, a couple of psychologists influenced by Skinner, went into the business of training animals for advertising and entertainment purposes. One of their better-known feats was shaping "Priscilla, the Fastidious Pig" to turn on a radio, eat at a kitchen table, put dirty clothes in a hamper, run a vacuum, and then "go shopping" with a shopping

Shaping—an operant technique in which an organism is rewarded for closer and closer approximations of the desired response—is used in teaching both animals and humans. It is the main means of training animals to perform unnatural tricks. Some of Breland and Breland's (1961) famous subjects are shown above.

cart. Of course, Priscilla picked the sponsor's product off the shelf in her shopping expedition (Breland & Breland, 1961).

Extinction

In operant conditioning, *extinction* refers to the gradual weakening and disappearance of a response tendency because the response is no longer followed by a reinforcer. Extinction begins in operant conditioning whenever previously available reinforcement is stopped. In laboratory studies with rats, this usually means that the experimenter stops delivering food when the rat presses the lever. When the extinction process is begun, a brief surge often occurs in the rat's responding, followed by a gradual decline in response rate until it approaches zero.

A key issue in operant conditioning is how much *resistance to extinction* an organism will display when reinforcement is halted. **Resistance to extinction occurs when an organism continues to make a response after delivery of the reinforcer has been terminated.** The greater the resistance to extinction, the longer the responding will continue. Thus, if a researcher stops giving reinforcement for lever pressing and the response tapers off slowly, the response shows high resistance to extinction. However, if the response tapers off quickly, it shows relatively little resistance to extinction.

Resistance to extinction may sound like a matter of purely theoretical interest, but it's actually quite practical. People often want to strengthen a response in such a way that it will be relatively resistant to extinction. For instance, most parents want to see their child's studying response survive even if the child hits a rocky stretch when studying doesn't lead to reinforcement (good grades). In a similar fashion,

a casino wants to see patrons continue to gamble even if they encounter a lengthy losing streak.

Another complexity relating to extinction is that the *renewal effect* (Bustamante, Uengoer, & Lachnit, 2016) seen in classical conditioning is also seen in operant conditioning. Bouton and colleagues (2011) tested for a renewal effect by modifying two Skinner boxes to create very different contexts. The two chambers had different scents, different floors (even versus uneven), and different walls and ceilings (painted with dots versus stripes). They found that if acquisition of lever-pressing occurred in one context and subsequent extinction in another context, responding recovered when the rats were returned to the original context or placed in a new, neutral context. *In other words, it appears that the result of extinction is that organisms learn not to make a specific response in a specific context, as opposed to any and all contexts* (Bouton & Todd, 2014). The context-dependent nature of extinction may help explain why maladaptive responses that are successfully extinguished in behaviour therapists' offices can reappear in other contexts.

Stimulus Control: Generalization and Discrimination

Operant responding is ultimately controlled by its consequences, as organisms learn response–outcome (R–O) associations (Colwill, 1993). However, stimuli that *precede* a response can also exert considerable influence over operant behaviour. When a response is consistently followed by a reinforcer in the presence of a particular stimulus, that stimulus comes to serve as a "signal," indicating that the response is likely to lead to a reinforcer. Once an organism learns the signal, it tends to respond accordingly (Honig &

Table 6.1

Comparison of Basic Processes in Classical and Operant Conditioning

PROCESS AND DEFINITION	DESCRIPTION IN CLASSICAL CONDITIONING	DESCRIPTION IN OPERANT CONDITIONING
Acquisition: The initial stage of learning	CS and UCS are paired, gradually resulting in CR.	Responding gradually increases because of reinforcement, possibly through shaping.
Extinction: The gradual weakening and disappearance of a conditioned response tendency	CS is presented alone until it no longer elicits CR.	Responding gradually slows and stops after reinforcement is terminated.
Stimulus generalization: An organism's responding to stimuli other than the original stimulus used in conditioning	CR is elicited by new stimulus that resembles original CS.	Responding increases in the presence of new stimulus that resembles discriminative stimulus.
Stimulus discrimination: An organism's response to stimuli that are similar to the original stimulus used in conditioning	CR is not elicited by new stimulus that resembles original CS.	Responding does not increase in the lack of presence of new stimulus that resembles the original discriminative stimulus.

© 2017 Cengage Learning

Alsop, 1992). For example, a pigeon's disk pecking may be reinforced only when a small light behind the disk is lit. When the light is out, pecking does not lead to the reward. Pigeons quickly learn to peck the disk only when it is lit. The light that signals the availability of reinforcement is called a *discriminative stimulus. Discriminative stimuli* are cues that influence operant behaviour by indicating the probable consequences (reinforcement or nonreinforcement) of a response.

Discriminative stimuli play a key role in the regulation of operant behaviour. For example, birds learn that hunting for worms is likely to be reinforced after a rain. Human social behaviour is also regulated extensively by discriminative stimuli. Consider the behaviour of asking someone for a date. Many people emit this response only cautiously, after receiving many signals (such as eye contact, smiles, encouraging conversational exchanges) that reinforcement (a favourable answer) is fairly likely.

Reactions to a discriminative stimulus are governed by the processes of *stimulus generalization* and *stimulus discrimination*, just like reactions to a CS in classical conditioning. For instance, envision a cat that comes running into the kitchen whenever it hears the sound of a can opener because that sound has become a discriminative stimulus signalling a good chance of its getting fed. If the cat also responded to the sound of a new kitchen appliance (e.g., a blender), this response would represent *generalization*—responding to a new stimulus as if it were the original. *Discrimination* would occur if the cat learned to respond only to the can opener and not to the blender.

As you have learned in this section, the processes of acquisition, extinction, generalization, and discrimination in operant conditioning parallel these same processes in classical conditioning. Table 6.1 compares these processes in the two kinds of conditioning.

Reinforcement and Superstitious Behaviour

Reinforcement, of course, is key to the development of the kinds of superstitious behaviours exhibited by elite athletes (Domotor, Ruiz-Barquin & Szabo, 2016; Hori, Numata, & Nakajima, 2014; Todd, 2003) and others as described in the introduction to this chapter. In the case of superstitious behaviours, the reinforcement is most likely accidental—for example, a hat trick when one just happens to be wearing a black turtleneck underneath one's hockey uniform. Skinner himself was fascinated by the development of superstitious behaviour and even designed an experiment in 1948 to chart its development in pigeons (Skinner, 1948b). Pigeons were placed in an experimental cage into which Skinner introduced a reinforcer (food), which according to Skinner had *"no reference whatsoever to the bird's behavior"* (p. 168). Skinner observed that the birds would tend to repeat whatever behaviour they had been engaged in when the food was presented, behaviour that was, in a sense, accidentally reinforced. Among the "superstitious" behaviours he engendered were a bird who turned counterclockwise about the cage, a bird who repeatedly thrust its head into one of the upper corners of the cage, and a third who developed an unusual "tossing" motion with its head, as if it was "placing its head beneath an invisible bar and lifting it repeatedly" (p. 168). It is not so far, perhaps, from head tossing to the wearing of black turtlenecks when playing hockey, or red lipstick when freestyle skiing.

Skinner himself observed that the behaviour of his pigeons was no different from the behaviour of a bowler who twists and turns his or her body after releasing the ball. The bowler's behaviour, like the head tossing of the pigeon, has no real impact on the probability of receiving a reward, be it food or a strike. But, the behaviour continues. Skinner's theory that noncontingent reinforcement is the basis for superstitious behaviour held sway for many years, although some have argued that not all research consistently replicated his findings (Staddon & Simmelhag, 1971). Nonetheless, interest in superstitious behaviour continues (Domotor et al., 2016; Sheehana et al., 2012), with some contemporary research ascribing it to normal cognitive biases and errors that promote irrational reasoning rather than solely to the unpredictable vagaries of operant conditioning (Pronin et al., 2006; Risen, 2016).

Schedules of Reinforcement

In operant conditioning, a favourable outcome is much more likely to strengthen a response if the outcome follows immediately (Powell, Honey, & Symbaluk, 2017). If a delay occurs between a response and the positive outcome, the response may not be strengthened. Furthermore, studies show that the longer the delay between the designated response and the delivery of the reinforcer, the more slowly conditioning proceeds (McDevitt & Williams, 2001).

Organisms make innumerable responses that do not lead to favourable consequences. It would be nice if people were reinforced every time they took an exam, watched a movie, hit a golf shot, asked for a date, or made a sales call. However, in the real world, most responses are reinforced only some of the time. How does this fact affect the potency of reinforcers? To find out, operant psychologists have devoted an enormous amount of attention to how *intermittent schedules of reinforcement* influence operant behaviour (Ferster & Skinner, 1957; Skinner, 1938, 1953).

A *schedule of reinforcement* determines which occurrences of a specific response result in the presentation of a reinforcer. The simplest pattern is continuous reinforcement. *Continuous reinforcement* occurs when every instance of a designated response is reinforced. In the laboratory, experimenters often use continuous reinforcement to shape and establish a new response before moving on to more realistic schedules involving intermittent reinforcement. *Intermittent, or partial, reinforcement* occurs when a designated response is reinforced only some of the time.

Which do you suppose leads to longer-lasting effects—being reinforced every time you emit a response, or being reinforced only some of the time? Studies show that, given an equal number of reinforcements, *intermittent* reinforcement makes a response more resistant to extinction than continuous reinforcement does (Falls, 1998; Schwartz & Robbins, 1995). In other words, organisms continue responding longer after removal of reinforcers when a response has been reinforced only *some* of the time. In fact, schedules of reinforcement that provide only sporadic delivery of reinforcers can yield great resistance to extinction. This finding explains why behaviours that are reinforced only occasionally—such as youngsters' temper tantrums—can be very durable and difficult to eliminate.

reality check

Misconception

The best way to ensure that a desired behaviour will persist is to reward the behaviour every time it occurs.

Reality

This statement certainly sounds logical, but research clearly shows that continuous reinforcement generates less resistance to extinction than intermittent reinforcement. If you want a response to remain strong in the absence of reinforcement, you should reinforce the response intermittently so that the organism becomes accustomed to some degree of nonreinforcement.

Reinforcement schedules come in many varieties, but four particular types of intermittent schedules have attracted the most interest (Miller & Grace, 2013). These schedules are described here along with examples drawn from the laboratory and everyday life (see Figure 6.15 for additional examples).

Ratio schedules require the organism to make the designated response a certain number of times to gain each reinforcer. With a *fixed-ratio (FR) schedule*, the reinforcer is given after a fixed number of nonreinforced responses. *Examples:* (1) A rat is reinforced for every tenth lever press. (2) A salesperson receives a bonus for every fourth set of encyclopedias sold. With a *variable-ratio (VR) schedule*, the reinforcer is given after a variable number of nonreinforced responses. The number of nonreinforced responses varies around a predetermined average. *Examples:* (1) A rat is reinforced for every tenth lever press on the average. The exact number of responses required for reinforcement varies from one time to the next. (2) A slot machine in a casino pays off once every six tries on the average. The number of nonwinning responses between payoffs varies greatly from one time to the next.

Interval schedules require a time period to pass between the presentation of reinforcers. With a *fixed-interval (FI) schedule*, the reinforcer is given for the first response that occurs after a fixed time interval has elapsed. *Examples:* (1) A rat is reinforced for the first lever press after a two-minute interval has elapsed and then must wait two minutes before being able to earn the next reinforcement. (2) A man washing his clothes periodically checks to see whether each load is finished. The reward (clean clothes) is available only after a fixed time interval (corresponding to how long the washer takes to complete a cycle) has elapsed, and checking responses during the interval is not reinforced. With a *variable-interval (VI) schedule*, the reinforcer is given for the first response after a variable time interval has elapsed. The interval length varies around a predetermined average. *Examples:* (1) A rat is reinforced for the first lever press after a one-minute interval has elapsed, but the following intervals are three minutes, two minutes, four minutes, and so on—with an average length of two minutes. (2) A person repeatedly dials a busy phone number (getting through is the reinforcer).

More than 50 years of research has yielded an enormous volume of data on how these schedules of reinforcement are related to patterns of responding (Williams, 1988; Zeiler, 1977). Some of the more prominent findings are summarized in Figure 6.16, which depicts typical response patterns generated by each schedule. For example, with fixed-interval schedules, a pause in responding usually occurs after each reinforcer is delivered, and then responding gradually increases to a rapid rate at the end of the interval. This pattern of behaviour yields a "scalloped" response curve. In general, ratio schedules tend to produce more rapid responding than interval schedules. Why? Because faster responding leads to reinforcement sooner when a ratio schedule is in effect. Variable schedules tend to generate steadier response rates and greater resistance to extinction than their fixed counterparts.

Most of the research on reinforcement schedules was conducted on rats and pigeons in Skinner boxes. However, the available evidence suggests that humans react to schedules of reinforcement in much the same way as animals (de Villers, 1977; Perone, Galizio, & Baron, 1988). For example, when animals are placed on ratio schedules, shifting to a higher ratio (i.e., requiring more responses per reinforcement) tends to generate faster responding. Managers of factories who pay on a piecework basis (a fixed-ratio schedule) have seen the same reaction in humans. Shifting to a higher ratio (more pieces for the same pay) usually stimulates harder work and greater productivity (although workers often complain).

Figure 6.15
Reinforcement schedules in everyday life. Complex human behaviours are regulated by schedules of reinforcement. Piecework in factories is reinforced on a fixed-ratio schedule. Playing slot machines is based on variable-ratio reinforcement. Watching the clock at work is rewarded on a fixed-interval basis (the arrival of quitting time is the reinforcer). Surfers waiting for a big wave are rewarded on a variable-interval basis.

© 2017 Cengage Learning

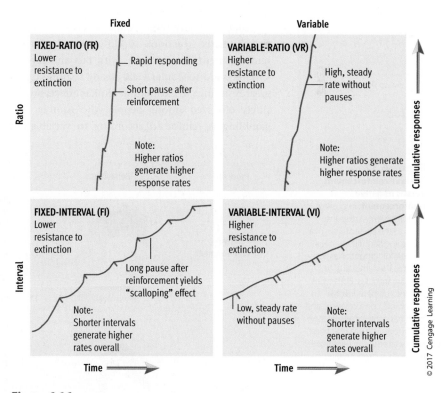

Figure 6.16
Schedules of reinforcement and patterns of response. Each type of reinforcement schedule tends to generate a characteristic pattern of responding. In general, ratio schedules tend to produce more rapid responding than interval schedules (note the steep slopes of the FR and VR curves). In comparison to fixed schedules, variable schedules tend to yield steadier responding (note the smoother lines for the VR and VI schedules on the right) and greater resistance to extinction.

There are many other parallels between animals' and humans' reactions to different schedules of reinforcement. For instance, with rats and pigeons, variable-ratio schedules yield steady responding and great resistance to extinction. Similar effects are routinely observed among people who gamble. Most gambling is reinforced according to variable-ratio schedules, which tend to produce rapid, steady responding and great resistance to extinction—exactly what casino operators want.

Positive Reinforcement versus Negative Reinforcement

According to Skinner, reinforcement can take two forms, which he called *positive reinforcement* and *negative reinforcement*. **Positive reinforcement** occurs when a response is strengthened because it is followed by the presentation of a rewarding stimulus. Thus far, for purposes of simplicity, our examples of reinforcement have involved positive reinforcement. Good grades, tasty meals, paycheques, scholarships, promotions, nice clothes, nifty cars, attention, and flattery are all positive reinforcers.

In contrast, **negative reinforcement** occurs when a response is strengthened because it is followed by the removal of an aversive (unpleasant) stimulus. Don't let the word *negative* confuse you. Negative reinforcement *is* reinforcement. As with all reinforcement, it involves a favourable outcome that *strengthens* a response tendency. However, this strengthening takes place because a response leads to the *removal of an aversive stimulus* rather than the arrival of a pleasant stimulus (see Figure 6.17).

In laboratory studies, negative reinforcement is usually accomplished as follows. While a rat is in a Skinner box, a moderate electric shock is delivered to the animal through the floor of the box. When the rat presses the lever, the shock is turned off for a period of time. Thus, lever pressing leads to removal of an aversive stimulus (shock). Although this sequence of

Figure 6.17
Positive reinforcement versus negative reinforcement. In positive reinforcement, a response leads to the presentation of a rewarding stimulus. In negative reinforcement, a response leads to the removal of an aversive stimulus. Both types of reinforcement involve favourable consequences and both have the same effect on behaviour: The organism's tendency to emit the reinforced response is strengthened.

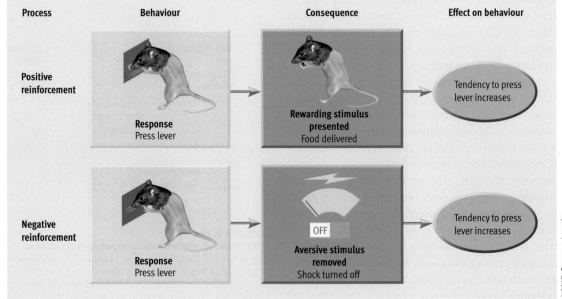

Process	Behaviour	Consequence	Effect on behaviour
Positive reinforcement	**Response** Press lever	**Rewarding stimulus presented** Food delivered	Tendency to press lever increases
Negative reinforcement	**Response** Press lever	OFF **Aversive stimulus removed** Shock turned off	Tendency to press lever increases

© 2017 Cengage Learning

events is different from those for positive reinforcement, it reliably strengthens the rat's lever-pressing response.

Everyday human behaviour is regulated extensively by negative reinforcement. Consider a handful of examples. You rush home in the winter to get out of the cold. You clean house to get rid of a disgusting mess. You give in to your child's begging to halt the whining. You take medication to get rid of pain or discomfort. You give in to a roommate or spouse to bring an unpleasant argument to an end. Negative reinforcement plays a key role in both *escape* and *avoidance learning.*

The roots of avoidance lie in escape learning. In *escape learning*, an organism acquires a response that decreases or ends some aversive stimulation. Psychologists often study escape learning in the laboratory with rats that are conditioned in a *shuttle box.* The shuttle box has two compartments connected by a doorway, which can be opened and closed by the experimenter, as depicted in Figure 6.18(a). In a typical study, an animal is placed in one compartment and an electric current in the floor of that chamber is turned on, with the doorway open. The animal learns to escape the shock by running to the other compartment. This escape response leads to the removal of an aversive stimulus (shock), so it is strengthened through negative reinforcement.

Escape learning often leads to avoidance learning. In *avoidance learning*, an organism acquires a response that prevents some aversive stimulation from occurring. In laboratory studies of avoidance learning, the experimenter simply gives the animal a signal that a shock is forthcoming. The typical signal is a light that goes on a few seconds prior to the shock. At first, the rat runs only when shocked (escape learning). Gradually, however, the animal learns to run to the safe compartment as soon as the light comes on, demonstrating avoidance learning.

Avoidance learning presents an interesting example of how classical conditioning and operant conditioning can work together to regulate behaviour (Levis, 1989; Mowrer, 1947). In avoidance learning, the warning light that goes on before the shock becomes a CS (through classical conditioning), eliciting reflexive, conditioned fear in the animal. However, the response of fleeing to the other side of the box is operant behaviour. This response is strengthened through *negative reinforcement* because it reduces the animal's conditioned fear (see Figure 6.18). Thus, in avoidance learning, a fear response is acquired through classical conditioning and an avoidance response is maintained by operant conditioning.

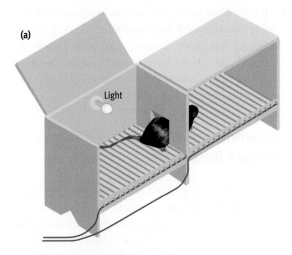

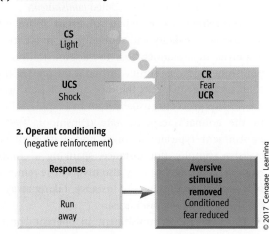

Figure 6.18
Escape and avoidance learning. (a) Escape and avoidance learning are often studied with a shuttle box like that shown here. Warning signals, shock, and the animal's ability to flee from one compartment to another can be controlled by the experimenter. (b) Avoidance begins because classical conditioning creates a conditioned fear that is elicited by the warning signal (panel 1). Avoidance continues because it is maintained by operant conditioning (panel 2). Specifically, the avoidance response is strengthened through negative reinforcement, since it leads to removal of the conditioned fear.

The principles of avoidance learning shed some light on why phobias are so resistant to extinction (Levis, 1989). Suppose you have a phobia of elevators. Chances are, you acquired your phobia through classical conditioning. At some point in your past, elevators became paired with a frightening event. Now whenever you need to use an elevator, you experience conditioned fear. If your phobia is severe, you probably take the stairs instead. Taking the stairs is an avoidance response that should lead to consistent negative reinforcement by relieving your conditioned fear. Thus, it's hard to get rid of phobias for two reasons. First, responses that allow you to avoid a phobic stimulus earn negative reinforcement each time they are made—so the avoidance behaviour is strengthened and continues. Second, these avoidance responses prevent any opportunity to extinguish the phobic conditioned response because you're never exposed to the conditioned stimulus (in this case, riding in an elevator).

Punishment: Consequences That Weaken Responses

Reinforcement is defined in terms of its consequences. It *increases* an organism's tendency to make a certain response. Are there also consequences that *decrease* an organism's tendency to make a particular response? Yes. In Skinner's model of operant behaviour, such consequences are called *punishment*.

Punishment occurs when an event following a response weakens the tendency to make that response. In a Skinner box, the administration of punishment is very simple. When a rat presses the lever or a pigeon pecks the disk, it receives a brief shock. This procedure usually leads to a rapid decline in the animal's response rate (Dinsmoor, 1998). Punishment typically involves presentation of an aversive stimulus (for instance, spanking a child). However, punishment may also involve the removal of a rewarding stimulus (for instance, taking away a child's TV-watching privileges).

The concept of punishment in operant conditioning is confusing to many students on two counts. First, they often confuse it with negative reinforcement, which is entirely different. Negative reinforcement involves the *removal* of an aversive stimulus,

thereby *strengthening* a response. Punishment, on the other hand, involves the *presentation* of an aversive stimulus, thereby *weakening* a response. Thus, punishment and negative reinforcement are opposite procedures that yield opposite effects on behaviour (see Figure 6.19).

The second source of confusion involves the tendency to equate punishment with *disciplinary procedures* used by parents, teachers, and other authority figures. In the operant model, punishment occurs any time that undesirable consequences weaken a response tendency. Defined in this way, the concept of punishment goes far beyond things like parents spanking children and teachers handing out detentions. For example, if you wear a new outfit and your classmates make fun of it, your behaviour will

Figure 6.19
Comparison of negative reinforcement and punishment. Although punishment can occur when a response leads to the removal of a rewarding stimulus (negative punishment), it more typically involves the presentation of an aversive stimulus (positive punishment). Students often confuse positive punishment with negative reinforcement because they associate both with aversive stimuli. However, as this diagram shows, punishment and negative reinforcement represent opposite procedures that have opposite effects on behaviour.

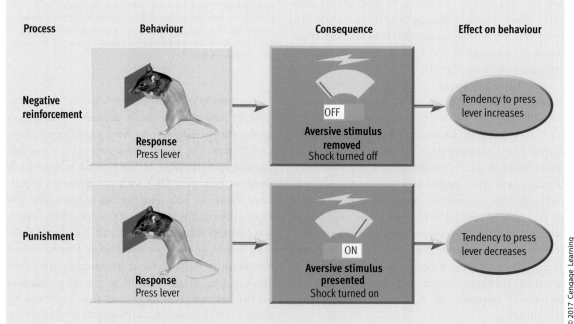

© 2017 Cengage Learning

have been punished and your tendency to emit this response (wear the same clothing) will probably decline. Similarly, if you go to a restaurant and have a horrible meal, your response will have been punished, and your tendency to go to that restaurant will probably decline. Although punishment in operant conditioning encompasses far more than disciplinary acts, it is used frequently for disciplinary purposes. In light of this reality, it is worth looking at the research on punishment as a disciplinary measure.

Side Effects of Physical Punishment

About three-quarters of parents report that they sometimes spank their children (Straus & Stewart, 1999), but quite a bit of controversy exists about the wisdom of using physical punishment. Some parents use punishments such as spanking as a way of disciplining and socializing their children. Other parents disagree that such physical means are appropriate. For example, Alisa Watkinson of Saskatchewan felt so strongly that physical punishment should not be used with children that she went to the Supreme Court of Canada to legally challenge its use (Supreme Court, 2004). The Supreme Court, in a vote of six to three, ruled to uphold Section 43 of the Canadian Criminal Code. The Court ruled that "reasonable corrective force" can be used, but only for children between the ages of 2 and 12. It further ruled that it was not acceptable to use objects in hitting the child, and that the child should not be hit about the head. Although the Supreme Court of Canada in its ruling provided increased protection through the law for children, its impact may not be as far reaching as intended. A national survey commissioned by a metropolitan Public Health Commission found that of those who believed that parents had the right to punish their children, few were aware of the limitations regarding punishment contained in the ruling (Public Health Toronto, 2006). Nonetheless, the Department of Justice in Canada is very clear about the nature of physical means that are acceptable and the conditions under which they may be applied. For example, they specify that the use of force is appropriate only to help a child learn; the parent, caregiver, or teacher must be correcting behaviour at the time; and that force should not be used in anger (Department of Justice, 2016).

How frequently are Canadian children spanked? It's often hard to obtain good data, but in a survey of Ontario adults (MacMillan et al., 1999), 20 percent reported they had never been slapped or spanked, 41 percent reported "rarely," 33 percent reported "sometimes," and 5.5 percent reported that they had often been slapped or spanked. But it seems as if a majority of Canadians surveyed recently believe

that parents do not discipline their children under the age of 18 enough, and almost half believe that spanking children would be of benefit to the child (Pearce, 2012). Significant organizations such as the Canadian Paediatric Society and the Public Health Agency of Canada oppose the use of spanking, and almost three dozen countries across the world, including Sweden, Finland, Norway, and Austria, have outlawed the practice (CBC News, 2009).

Although punishment in operant conditioning encompasses far more than disciplinary acts, it is used frequently for disciplinary purposes. In light of this situation, it is worth looking at the research on punishment as a disciplinary measure. Controversy exists about the wisdom of using *physical* punishment. The main concern is that spanking and other forms of corporal punishment may produce many unintended and undesirable side effects. Studies generally find that corporal punishment is associated with elevated aggression, delinquency, and behavioural problems in youngsters (Gershoff, 2002). In the long term, physical punishment is also associated with slowed cognitive development, increases in criminal behaviour, and a wide range of mental health problems (Durrant & Ensom, 2012; Straus, Douglas, & Medeiros, 2014). Some critics have pointed out that the evidence linking spanking to negative effects is correlational, and correlation is no assurance of causation (Kazdin & Benjet, 2003). Perhaps spanking causes children to be more aggressive, but it's also plausible that aggressive children cause their parents to rely more on physical punishment (see Figure 6.20).

Although this critique has merit, evidence on the negative effects of corporal punishment has continued to pile up (Gershoff et al., 2012; Smith, 2012).

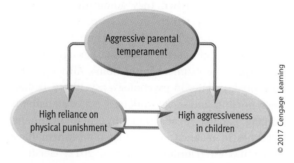

Figure 6.20
The correlation between physical punishment and aggressiveness. As we have discussed earlier, a correlation does not establish causation. It seems plausible that extensive reliance on physical punishment causes children to be more aggressive, as many experts suspect. However, it is also possible that highly aggressive children cause their parents to depend heavily on physical punishment. Or perhaps parents with an aggressive, hostile temperament pass on genes for aggressiveness to their children, who then also prefer to rely on heavy use of physical punishment.

Although physical punishment is frequently administered to suppress aggressive behaviour, in the long run it actually is associated with an increase in aggressive behaviour.

Recognizing Outcomes in Operant Conditioning

Check your understanding of the various types of consequences that can occur in operant conditioning by indicating whether the examples below involve positive reinforcement (PR), negative reinforcement (NR), punishment (P), or extinction (E). The answers can be found in Appendix A.

_____ **1.** Antonio gets a speeding ticket and is fined.

_____ **2.** Diane's supervisor compliments her on her hard work.

_____ **3.** Audrey lets her dog out so she won't have to listen to its whimpering.

_____ **4.** Richard shoots up heroin to ward off tremors and chills associated with heroin withdrawal.

_____ **5.** Sharma constantly complains about minor aches and pains to obtain sympathy from colleagues at work. Three co-workers who share an office with her decide to ignore her complaints instead of responding with sympathy.

Many of the newer studies have statistically controlled for children's initial level of aggression and other confounding variables, which strengthens the case for a causal link between spanking and negative outcomes (Durrant & Ensom, 2012). In spite of all the evidence of its negative effects, physical punishment continues to be widely used by parents (Lee, Grogan-Kaylor, & Berger, 2014; MacKenzie et al., 2013). Ironically, research suggests that corporal punishment is not very effective in ensuring children's obedience (Gershoff, 2013). For example, one recent study (Holden, Williamson, & Holland, 2014) based on audio recordings of family interactions (as opposed to self-report data) found that when children were spanked, 73 percent of the time they misbehaved again within ten minutes! This study also revealed that parents who use physical punishment do not use it as a last resort when other techniques have failed; that they mostly spank their children for mundane, trivial offences; and that the parents are often angry when they administer spankings. These findings, which probably provide a more accurate snapshot of parental disciplinary practices than self-report data do, paint a rather ugly portrait of corporal punishment in the home. Although professional societies in psychology, psychiatry, pediatrics, nursing, and social work have issued statements urging parents to abandon physical punishment, declines in reliance on corporal punishment have been modest (Durrant & Ensom, 2012; Gershoff, 2013).

Cognitive Processes in Conditioning: Latent Learning and Cognitive Maps

Historically there has often been a tension between behaviourism and cognitive theory (Shanks, 2010). Pavlov, Skinner, and their followers traditionally viewed conditioning as a mechanical process in which stimulus–response associations are stamped in by experience. Learning theorists asserted that if creatures such as flatworms can be conditioned, conditioning can't depend on higher mental processes. Although this viewpoint did not go entirely unchallenged (e.g., Tolman, 1922, 1932, 1938), mainstream theories of conditioning did not allocate a major role to cognitive processes.

The first major "renegade" to chip away at the conventional view of learning was Edward C. Tolman (1932, 1938), an American psychologist who was something of a gadfly for the behaviourist movement in the 1930s and 1940s. His ideas were ahead of their time, and mostly attracted rebuttals and criticism from the influential learning theorists of his era (Hilgard, 1987). In the long run, however, Tolman's ideas prevailed, as models of conditioning were eventually forced to incorporate cognitive factors. In recent decades, research findings have led theorists to shift toward more cognitive explanations of conditioning. Let's review some of these findings and the theories that highlighted the potential role of cognition.

Tolman and his colleagues conducted a series of studies that posed some difficult questions for the prevailing views of conditioning. In one landmark study (Tolman & Honzik, 1930), three groups of food-deprived rats learned to run a complex maze over a series of once-a-day trials (see Figure 6.21(a)). The rats in Group A received a food reward (positive reinforcement) when they got to the end of the maze each day. Because of this reinforcement, their performance in running the maze gradually improved over the course of 17 days (see Figure 6.21(b)). The rats in Group B did not receive any food reward. Lacking reinforcement, this group showed only modest improvement in performance. Group C was the critical group; they did not get any reward for their first 10 trials in the maze, but they were rewarded from the 11th trial onward. The rats in this group showed little improvement in performance over the first 10 trials (just like Group B). But once reinforcement began on the 11th trial, they showed sharp improvement on subsequent trials (see Figure 6.21(b)). In fact, their performance was even a little better than that of the Group A rats, who had been rewarded after every trial.

Tolman concluded that the rats in Group C had been learning about the maze all along, just as much as the rats in group A, but they had no motivation to demonstrate this learning until a reward was introduced. Tolman called this phenomenon *latent learning*—learning that is not apparent from behaviour when it first occurs. *Why did these findings present a challenge for the prevailing view of learning?* First, they suggested that learning can take place in the absence of reinforcement—at a time when learned responses were thought to be stamped in by reinforcement. Second, they suggested that the rats who displayed latent learning had formed a *cognitive map* of the maze (a mental representation of the spatial layout) at a time when cognitive processes were thought to be irrelevant to understanding conditioning even in humans.

Evolutionary and Biological Effects on Conditioning

One biological constraint on learning is *instinctive drift*. **Instinctive drift** occurs when an animal's innate response tendencies interfere with conditioning processes. Instinctive drift was first described by the Brelands, the operant psychologists who went into the business of training animals for commercial purposes (Breland & Breland, 1966). The Brelands were students of Skinner (Hall & Halliday, 1998). They have described many amusing examples of their "failures" to control behaviour through conditioning. For instance, they once were training some raccoons to deposit coins into a piggy bank. They were successful in shaping the raccoons to pick up a coin and put it into a small box, using food as the reinforcer. However, when they gave the raccoons a couple of coins, an unexpected problem arose: The raccoons wouldn't give the coins up, in spite of the reinforcers available for depositing the coins. "Now the raccoon really had problems. . . . Not only would he not let go of the coins, but he spent seconds, even minutes, rubbing them together (in a most miserly fashion)" (Breland & Breland, 1961, p. 682).

What had happened to disrupt the conditioning program? Apparently, associating the coins with food had brought out the raccoons' innate food-washing

Edward Tolman developed one of the first major cognitive theories of learning.

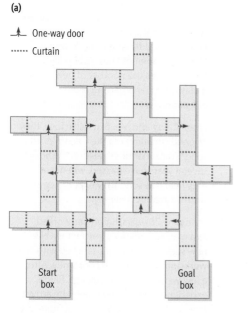

(a)

🔺 One-way door

..... Curtain

Start box   Goal box

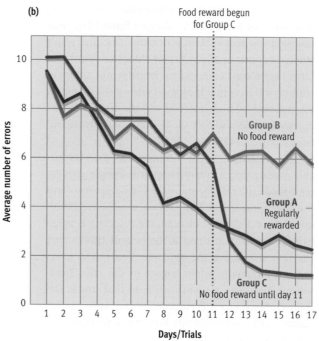

(b)

Food reward begun for Group C

Average number of errors

Group B
No food reward

Group A
Regularly rewarded

Group C
No food reward until day 11

Days/Trials

Figure 6.21
Latent learning. (a) In the study by Tolman and Honzik (1930), rats learned to run the complicated maze shown here. (b) The results obtained by Tolman and Honzik (1930) are summarized in this graph. The rats in Group C showed a sudden improvement in performance when a food reward was introduced on Trial 11. Tolman concluded that the rats in this group were learning about the maze all along, but that their learning remained "latent" until reinforcement was made available.

Source: Adapted from Tolman, E., C., & Honzik, C. H. (1930). Introduction and removal of reward and maze performance in rats. *University of California Publications in Psychology*, 3, 257-275. / © 2017 Cengage Learning

behaviour. Raccoons often rub things together to clean them. The Brelands report that they have run into this sort of instinct-related interference on many occasions with a wide variety of species.

Evolutionary Perspectives on Learning

Clearly, several lines of research suggest that there are species-specific biological constraints on learning. So, what is the current thinking on the idea that the laws of learning are *universal* across various species? The predominant view among learning theorists seems to be that the basic mechanisms of learning are *similar* across species but that these mechanisms have sometimes been modified in the course of evolution as species have adapted to the specialized demands of their environments (Shettleworth, 1998). According to this view, learning is a very general process because the biological bases of learning and the basic problems confronted by various organisms are much the same across species. For example, developing the ability to recognize stimuli that signal important events (e.g., lurking predators) is probably adaptive for virtually any organism. However, given that different organisms confront different adaptive problems to survive and reproduce, it makes sense that learning has evolved along somewhat different paths in different species (Hollis, 1997; Sherry, 1992).

Response–Outcome Relations and Reinforcement

Studies of response–outcome relations and reinforcement also highlight the role of cognitive processes in conditioning. Imagine that on the night before an important exam, you study hard while repeatedly playing a Rage Against the Machine song—for example, their cover of Bob Dylan's "Maggie's Farm." The next morning you earn an A on your exam. Does this result strengthen your tendency to play "Maggie's Farm" and other Rage songs before exams? Probably not. Chances are, you will recognize the logical relationship between the response of studying hard and the reinforcement of a good grade, and only the response of studying will be strengthened (Killeen, 1981).

Thus, reinforcement is *not* automatic when favourable consequences follow a response. People actively reason out the relationships between responses and the outcomes that follow. When a response is followed by a desirable outcome, the response is more likely to be strengthened if the person thinks that the response *caused* the outcome. You might guess that only humans would engage in this causal reasoning. However, evidence suggests that under the right circumstances, even pigeons can learn to recognize causal relationships between responses and outcomes (Killeen, 1981).

In sum, modern, reformulated models of conditioning view it as a matter of detecting the *contingencies* among environmental events (Matute & Miller, 1998). According to these theories, organisms actively try to figure out what leads to what (the contingencies) in the world around them. Stimuli are viewed as signals that help organisms minimize their aversive experiences and maximize their pleasant experiences. The new, cognitively oriented theories of conditioning are quite a departure from older theories that depicted conditioning as a mindless, mechanical process. We can also see this new emphasis on cognitive processes in our next subject, observational learning.

concept check 6.4

Distinguishing between Classical Conditioning and Operant Conditioning

Check your understanding of the usual differences between classical conditioning and operant conditioning by indicating the type of conditioning process involved in each of the following examples. In the space on the left, place a C if the example involves classical conditioning, an O if it involves operant conditioning, or a B if it involves both. The answers can be found in Appendix A.

_____ 1. Whenever Midori takes her dog out for a walk, she wears the same old blue windbreaker. Eventually, she notices that her dog becomes excited whenever she puts on this windbreaker.

_____ 2. The Creatures are a successful rock band with three hit albums to their credit. They begin their world tour featuring many new, unreleased songs, all of which draw silence from their concert fans. The same fans cheer wildly when the Creatures play any of their old hits. Gradually, the band reduces the number of new songs it plays and starts playing more of the old standbys.

_____ 3. When Cindy and Mel first fell in love, they listened constantly to the Creatures' hit song "Transatlantic Obsession." Although several years have passed, whenever they hear this song they experience a warm, romantic feeling.

_____ 4. For nearly 20 years, Ralph has worked as a machinist in the same factory. His new supervisor is never satisfied with his work and criticizes him constantly. After a few weeks of heavy criticism, Ralph experiences anxiety whenever he arrives at work. He starts calling in sick more and more frequently to evade this anxiety.

Observational Learning

Can classical and operant conditioning account for all learning? Absolutely not. Consider how people learn a fairly basic skill such as driving a car. They do not hop naïvely into an automobile and start emitting random responses until one leads to favourable consequences. On the contrary, most people learning to drive know exactly where to place the key and how to get started. How are these responses acquired? Through *observation*. Most new drivers have years of experience observing others drive, and they put those observations to work. Learning through observation accounts for a great deal of learning in both animals and humans. There is also evidence that learning by observation leads to different types of learning and construing information than does learning through one's own actions. This is the focus of our first Featured Study in this chapter.

FEATURED STUDY

Social learning across psychological distance.

Description
The researchers compare direct learning with observation learning in terms of their effects on whether or not participants learn at a concrete or on a more abstract level.

Investigators
Kalkstein, D. A., Kleiman, T., Wakslak, C. J., Liberman, N., & Trope, Y. (2016). *Journal of Personality and Social Psychology, 110*(1), 1–20.

Observational learning occurs when an organism's responding is influenced by the observation of others, who are called models. This process has been investigated extensively by Albert Bandura (1977, 1986), who is viewed as one of psychology's greatest living theorists. Bandura's theory and research on observational learning is one of the pivotal contributions to the psychology of learning in the past few decades. Interestingly, Bandura, who was born in Alberta and did his undergraduate studies at the University of British Columbia, began his career in psychology almost by chance (Evans, 1989). He commuted to classes with friends who were early risers so he found himself with morning class periods to fill. One of the courses available was in psychology and the rest, as they say, is history. Bandura's insights on the mediating role of modelling or observational

learning came from his analysis of the differences between animal and human learning. The literature on human conditioning suggested to him at the time that for humans "representation of the connection between action and consequence is an important determinant of whether or not a change will occur" (Evans, 1980, p. 161). While this might seem obvious to us now, it was not an insight that was compatible with the prevailing orientation of learning theory at the time.

Bandura does not see observational learning as entirely separate from classical and operant conditioning. Instead, he asserts that it greatly extends the reach of these conditioning processes. Although previous conditioning theorists emphasized the organism's direct experience, Bandura has demonstrated that both classical and operant conditioning can take place vicariously through observational learning.

Essentially, observational learning involves being conditioned indirectly by virtue of observing another's conditioning (see Figure 6.22). To illustrate, suppose you observe a friend behaving assertively with a car salesperson. You see your friend's assertive behaviour reinforced by the exceptionally good buy she gets on the car. Your own tendency to behave assertively with salespeople might well be strengthened as a result. Notice that the reinforcement is experienced by your friend, not you. The good buy should strengthen your friend's tendency to bargain assertively, but your tendency to do so may also be strengthened indirectly.

Albert Bandura

"Most human behavior is learned by observation through modeling."

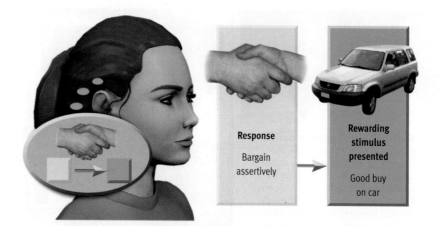

Response

Bargain assertively

Rewarding stimulus presented

Good buy on car

Figure 6.22
Observational learning. In observational learning, an observer attends to and stores a mental representation of a model's behaviour (e.g., assertive bargaining) and its consequences (e.g., a good buy on a car). If the observer sees the modelled response lead to a favourable outcome, the observer's tendency to emit the modelled response will be strengthened.

Basic Processes

Bandura has identified four key processes that are crucial in observational learning. The first two—attention and retention—highlight the importance of the type of cognition he was referring to in the quote on the left in this type of learning:

- *Attention.* To learn through observation, you must pay attention to another person's behaviour and its consequences.
- *Retention.* You may not have occasion to use an observed response for weeks, months, or even years. Hence, you must store in your memory a mental representation of what you have witnessed.
- *Reproduction.* Enacting a modelled response depends on your ability to reproduce the response by converting your stored mental images into overt behaviour. This may not be easy for some responses. For example, most people cannot execute a breathtaking windmill dunk after watching Steve Nash do it in a basketball game.
- *Motivation.* Finally, you are unlikely to reproduce an observed response unless you are motivated to do so. Your motivation depends on whether you encounter a situation in which you believe that the response is likely to pay off for you.

Observational learning has proven especially valuable in explaining complex human behaviours, but animals can also learn through observation. A simple example is the thieving behaviour of the English titmouse, a small bird renowned for its early-morning raids on its human neighbours. The titmouse has learned how to open cardboard caps on bottles of milk delivered to the porches of many homes in England. Having opened the bottle, the titmouse skims the cream from the top of the milk. This clever learned behaviour has been passed down from one generation of titmouse to the next through observational learning.

Bandura points out that people have many learned responses that they may or may not perform, depending on the situation. Thus, he distinguishes between the *acquisition* of a learned response and the *performance* of that response. He maintains that reinforcement affects which responses are actually performed more than which responses are acquired. People emit those responses that they think are likely to be reinforced. Thus, like Skinner, Bandura asserts that reinforcement is a critical determinant of behaviour. However, Bandura maintains that reinforcement influences performance *rather than* learning per se.

Observational Learning and the Media Violence Controversy

It is the power of observational learning that makes television such an influential determinant of behaviour. Canadians seem to be spending a large amount of their free time in front of a screen. Recent research suggests that the typical adult Canadian spends an average of 30 hours a week in front of the TV and almost as long online. For 18-to 24-year-old Canadians, the balance seems to be tipped to online activities; they report spending almost twice as much time online as in front of the TV (Oliveira, 2013). For example, sitting in front of the screen, a computer screen or TV, for long periods is linked to obesity in Canadians (Shields & Tremblay, 2008). Thirty-one percent of Canadian kids, ages 5 to 17, are overweight or obese (Crowe, 2012). According to the Canadian Paediatric Society (2017), parents' concerns about how much screen time their children engage in and how to control it are common matters discussed with pediatricians. Canadian children watch excessive amounts of TV, and such TV watching may have negative effects on academic performance and health. The Canadian Paediatric Society (2017) is particularly concerned about very young children engaging in excessive screen time. They do not recommend screen time for children under two years of age and suggest that screen time for children ages two to five years be limited to under one hour per day.

Observational learning occurs in both humans and animals. For example, the English titmouse has learned how to break into containers to swipe cream from its human neighbours and this behaviour has been passed across generations through observational learning. In a similar vein, children acquire a diverse array of responses from role models.

Children are very impressionable, and extensive evidence indicates that they pick up many responses from viewing models on TV (Huston et al., 1992). Social critics have expressed concern about the amount of violence on television ever since TV became popular in the 1950s. In the 1960s, Bandura and his colleagues conducted landmark research on the issue that remains widely cited and influential. Along with his colleague and first graduate student Richard Walters (later a professor at the University of Waterloo), Bandura was an early advocate of the application of learning principles to explain aggression in children (Bandura & Walters, 1959, 1963). Young children are especially impressionable, and extensive evidence indicates that they pick up many responses—including aggressive behaviours—from viewing models on TV (Huston & Wright, 1982; Liebert & Sprafkin, 1988).

Bandura conducted a series of classic experiments on aggression often referred to as the "Bobo doll" experiments (Bandura, 1965; Bandura, Ross, & Ross, 1961, 1963a). In these and other studies, Bandura showed that children would imitate aggressive behaviour directed toward a Bobo doll (a large, inflatable toy clown) by an adult model. Children who saw the model rewarded were more likely than children who saw the model punished for the aggression to aggress (i.e., performance) themselves toward the Bobo doll when left alone with it. However, all of the children behaved aggressively (i.e., acquisition) if they were offered a reward for imitating the model's behaviour. This early research by Bandura suggested a connection between children watching violence on television and their own aggressiveness. Because of the significance of Bandura's modelling research, the Bobo doll has achieved a type of stardom on its own. Bandura states that when he visits and lectures at other universities, the hosts often place Bobo dolls close to the stage and that people frequently bring him Bobo dolls to autograph (Evans, 1989).

Decades of research since Bandura's pioneering work have indicated that media violence fosters increased aggression (Bushman & Huesmann, 2012; Gentile & Bushman, 2012). The short-term effects of media violence have been investigated in hundreds of experimental studies, which consistently demonstrate that exposure to violent content in TV shows, movies, and video games increases the likelihood of physical aggression, verbal aggression, aggressive thoughts, and aggressive emotions in both children and adults (Anderson et al., 2010; Warburton, 2014).

Photo courtesy of Albert Bandura

The Bobo doll was employed in Bandura's well-known research on observational learning and aggression. You can see clearly in the second and third rows how the children model the behaviour of the adult model, displayed in the first row.

A particular source of concern in recent research has been the finding that exposure to media violence appears to desensitize people to the effects of aggression in the real world (Crawford, 2012; Krahe et al., 2011). Desensitization means that people show muted reactions to real violence. For example, one study showed that subjects who had played violent video games for a mere 20 minutes showed smaller physiological reactions to video recordings of real-life aggression (prison fights and such) than did those who played nonviolent games (Carnagey, Anderson, & Bushman, 2007). Another study found that playing violent video games changed participants' perceptions of aggression in everyday life, as they rated specific acts of aggressive behaviour as being less aggressive than control subjects did (Greitemeyer, 2014).

Yet another study suggested that the "numbing" effect of media violence makes people less sensitive to the suffering of others and less likely to help others in need (Bushman & Anderson, 2009). In this study, participants who had just played a violent or nonviolent video game overheard a staged fight (just outside the door of the lab) in which one person was injured. The aggressive actor clearly had left the scene, so there was no perceived danger to the participants. Researchers monitored how long it took subjects to come out into the hall to offer help to the groaning victim. Participants who had just played a violent video game took much longer to help (average 73 seconds) than those who had just played a nonviolent game (16 seconds). Thus, it appears that media violence can desensitize individuals to acts of aggression.

The real-world and long-term effects of media violence have been investigated through correlational research. The findings of these studies show that the more violence children watch on TV, the more aggressive they tend to be at home and at school (Krahe, 2013). Of course, critics point out that this correlation could reflect a variety of causal relationships (Ferguson & Savage, 2012). Perhaps high aggressiveness in children causes an increased interest in media violence (see Figure 6.23). However, a growing number of studies have controlled for initial levels of subjects' aggressiveness and still found that a diet of media violence promotes increased aggression (Bushman & Huesmann, 2014).

Critics have also argued that the effects of media violence on aggression are relatively weak effects (Elson & Ferguson, 2014; Ferguson, 2013). This assertion is accurate, but exactly what one would

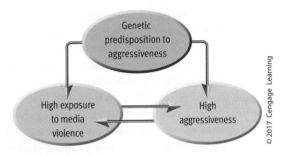

Figure 6.23
The correlation between exposure to media violence and aggression. The more violence children watch on TV, the more aggressive they tend to be, but this correlation could reflect a variety of underlying causal relationships. Although watching violent shows probably causes increased aggressiveness, it is also possible that aggressive children are drawn to violent shows. Or perhaps a third variable (such as a genetic predisposition to aggressiveness) leads to both a preference for violent shows and high aggressiveness.

expect. Like other aspects of complex human behaviour, aggression is surely influenced by a host of factors, such as genetic predispositions, parental modelling, and peer influences. Exposure to media violence is just one actor on a crowded stage. That said, the researchers who are concerned about the effects of media violence worry that even weak effects may have far-reaching repercussions (Cade & Gates, 2017; Wells, 2016). They point out that TV shows, movies, and video games reach millions upon millions of people (Bushman & Anderson, 2001). Suppose that 25 million people watch an extremely violent movie. Even if only one in 1000 viewers become a little more prone to aggression, that is 25 000 people who are a bit more likely to wreak havoc in someone's life.

As an aside, it is worth noting that the research findings on the effects of video games are not all bad. Studies have found that a number of benefits can be derived from playing video games, including the much-maligned first-person shooter games that are extremely violent (Granic, Lobel, & Engels, 2014). The cognitive benefits of gaming include improvements in attention allocation, visual-spatial processing, and problem solving. Video games can also demonstrate the rewards of persistence in the face of setbacks. And the advent of games that unfold in virtual communities can have some payoffs in terms of enhancing social skills.

In any event, the heated debate about media violence shows that observational learning plays an important role in regulating behaviour. It represents a third major type of learning that builds on the first two types (classical conditioning and operant conditioning). These three basic types of learning are summarized and compared in the Illustrated Overview on pages 228–229.

Observational Learning and the Brain: Mirror Neurons

To date, a variety of explanations have been offered to account for observational learning and modelling that often depend on principles and processes related to learning theory. More recent research has suggested the relevance of a specific type of neuron—the mirror neuron—in imitation, observational learning, and other facets of social cognition (e.g., Schilbach et al., 2008; Sinigaglia & Rizzolatti, 2015; Von Hofsten & Rosander, 2015).

Research into the nature and role of mirror neurons began almost by accident. *Mirror neurons* **are neurons that are activated by performing an action or by seeing another monkey or person perform the same action.** A team of neuroscientists at the University of Parma in Italy led by Giacomo Rizzolatti was recording the activity of individual neurons in the brains of two macaque monkeys (Rizzolatti et al., 1996; Rizzolatti & Sinigaglia, 2008) as the monkeys performed a series of reaching and grasping movements with their hands. As the monkeys performed the actions, the researchers were able to record brain activity. In an important discovery, the researchers found that some of these same neurons also became activated when the animals observed one of the experimenters performing similar actions, at a point when the monkeys themselves were not engaged in the action. It was quite accidental; a member of the research team happened to reach out and pick up one of the objects the monkeys had been working with.

In interpreting the activity in these mirror neurons, Rizzolatti and his colleagues highlighted the view that "mirror neurons are neurons that internally represent an action" (1996, p. 137). Further research by Rizzolatti and others confirmed that similar mirror neurons exist in humans. In human subjects, it is difficult to record from individual neurons, but researchers have used fMRI scans to demonstrate that humans also have mirror neuron circuits, which have been found in both the frontal lobe and the parietal lobe (Iacoboni & Dapretto, 2006; Rizzolatti & Craighero, 2004). The operation of mirror neurons and related structures and processes of the brain may underlie imitation and observational learning (Society for Neuroscience, 2008). It has also been suggested that mirror neurons may underlie our ability to understand others, to understand what is going on in the minds of others, making "inter-subjectivity" possible, thus setting the stage for our social behaviour (Iacoboni, 2009). They may be responsible for our ability to empathize with others. They are part of our evolution because they confer these advantages on us (Iacoboni, 2009). In fact, we may even have evolved to observe and imitate other people (van Gog et al., 2009). New thinking in the area suggests a parallel between impairment in their operation and some of the symptoms of autism; in the future they may provide a key to understanding this disorder (Rizzolatti, Fabbri-Destro, & Cattaneo, 2009). Research in the area is ongoing. The next time you wince in sympathy when Sidney Crosby takes a brutal hit or smile when you see a group of people across the street laugh at what one of the group says, perhaps you are a witness to the effects of activity in your mirror neurons!

Neuroscientists are understandably very excited by the identification of mirror neurons and by a consideration of their possible effects (Keysers & Perrett, 2004; Lago-Rodriguez, et al., 2013; Ramachandran & Oberman, 2006; van der Gaag, Minderaa, & Keysers, 2007). Some have even suggested that the mirror neuron will be as important to psychology as the discovery of DNA has been for biology (Miller, 2005). We will have to wait to see if this prediction is realized. It is possible that, in the future, research on mirror neurons may even provide an explanation for why viewing TV violence produces increased aggression on the part of the viewer. But it seems clear that the accidental discovery of mirror neurons may have a dramatic impact on brain-behaviour research in the years to come. Recent research on observational learning has explored other connections between the brain and learning. This is the focus of our second Featured Study in this chapter.

FEATURED STUDY

Electrophysiological correlates of observational learning in children.

Description
The researchers use an event related potential approach (FRN) to explore some of the neurophysiological mechanisms underlying specific types of observational learning in children.

Investigators
Buritica, J. M. R., Eppinger, B., Schuck, N. W., Heekeren, H. R., & Li, S. C. (2016). *Developmental Science, 19*(5), 699–709.

An Illustrated Overview of Three Types of Learning

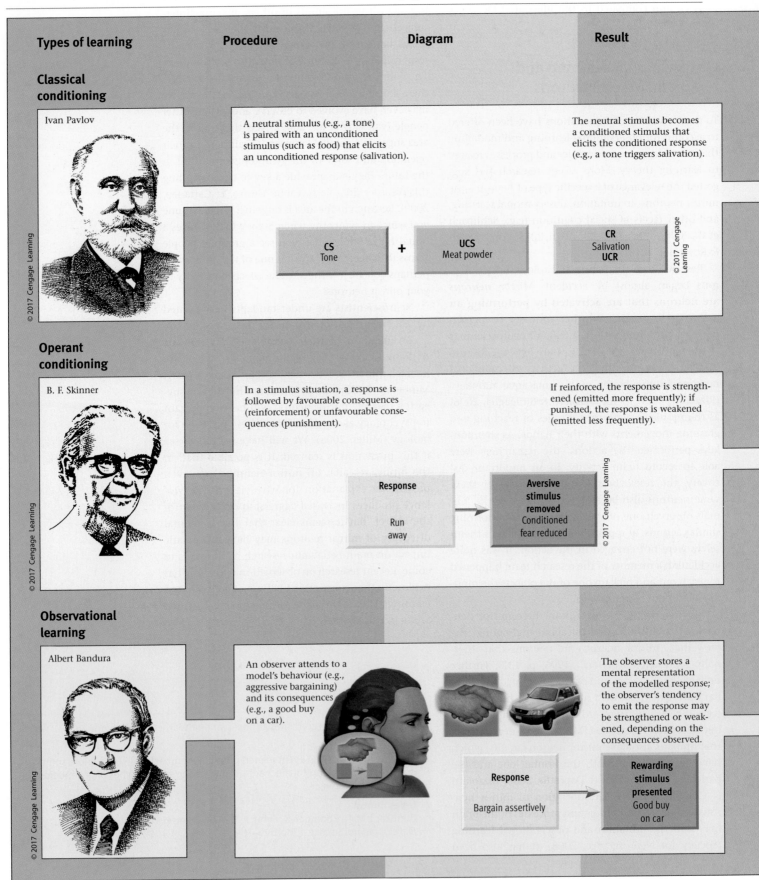

Types of learning	Procedure	Diagram	Result

Classical conditioning

Ivan Pavlov

A neutral stimulus (e.g., a tone) is paired with an unconditioned stimulus (such as food) that elicits an unconditioned response (salivation).

CS Tone + UCS Meat powder → CR Salivation UCR

The neutral stimulus becomes a conditioned stimulus that elicits the conditioned response (e.g., a tone triggers salivation).

© 2017 Cengage Learning

Operant conditioning

B. F. Skinner

In a stimulus situation, a response is followed by favourable consequences (reinforcement) or unfavourable consequences (punishment).

Response — Run away → Aversive stimulus removed — Conditioned fear reduced

If reinforced, the response is strengthened (emitted more frequently); if punished, the response is weakened (emitted less frequently).

© 2017 Cengage Learning

Observational learning

Albert Bandura

An observer attends to a model's behaviour (e.g., aggressive bargaining) and its consequences (e.g., a good buy on a car).

Response — Bargain assertively → Rewarding stimulus presented — Good buy on car

The observer stores a mental representation of the modelled response; the observer's tendency to emit the response may be strengthened or weakened, depending on the consequences observed.

© 2017 Cengage Learning

Typical kinds of responses	**Examples in animals**	**Examples in humans**

Dogs learn to salivate to the sound of a tone that has been paired with meat powder.

© Bettman/CORBIS

Political candidates draw on the power of classical conditioning when they associate with popular celebrities who elicit positive feelings among many voters.

Source: Photo by Adam Scotti. Photo provided by the Office of the Prime Minister. © Her Majesty the Queen in Right of Canada, 2017. / Photo par Adam Scotti. Photo fournie par le Bureau du Premier ministre. © Sa Majesté la Reine du Chef du Canada, 2017.

Mostly (but not always) involuntary reflexes and visceral responses

Trained animals perform remarkable feats because they have been reinforced for gradually learning closer and closer approximations of responses they do not normally emit.

Casino patrons tend to exhibit high, steady rates of gambling, as most games of chance involve complex variable-ratio schedules of reinforcement.

© Jon Feingersh/Getty Images

Mostly (but not always) voluntary, spontaneous responses

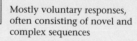

AP Photo/The Herald-Palladium, Don Campbell

A young boy performs a response that he has acquired through observational learning.

An English titmouse learns to break into milk bottles by observing the thievery of other titmice.

Mostly voluntary responses, often consisting of novel and complex sequences

Roger Wilmshurst/Alamy Stock Photo

© Ole Graf/Corbis

Putting It in Perspective: Themes 3 and 6

Two of our seven unifying themes stand out in this chapter. First, you can see how nature and nurture interactively govern behaviour. Second, looking at psychology in its sociohistorical context, you can see how progress in psychology spills over to affect trends and values in society at large. Let's examine each of these points in more detail.

In regard to nature versus nurture, research on learning clearly demonstrates the enormous power of the environment in shaping behaviour. Pavlov's model of classical conditioning shows how experiences can account for everyday fears and other emotional responses. Skinner's model of operant conditioning shows how reinforcement and punishment can mould everything from a child's bedtime whimpering to an adult's restaurant preferences. Indeed, many learning theorists once believed that *all* aspects of behaviour could be explained in terms of environmental determinants. In recent decades, however, evidence on instinctive drift, conditioned taste aversion, and preparedness has shown that there are biological constraints on conditioning.

Thus, even in explanations of learning—an area once dominated by nurture theories—we see once again that heredity and environment jointly influence behaviour.

The history of research on conditioning also shows how progress in psychology can seep into every corner of society. For example, the behaviourists' ideas about reinforcement and punishment have influenced patterns of discipline in our society. Research on operant conditioning has also affected management styles in the business world, leading to an increased emphasis on positive reinforcement. In the educational arena, the concept of individualized, programmed learning is a spinoff from behavioural research. The fact that the principles of conditioning are routinely applied in homes, businesses, schools, and factories clearly shows that psychology is not an ivory tower endeavour.

In the upcoming Personal Application, you will see how you can apply the principles of conditioning to improve your self-control, as we discuss the techniques of behaviour modification.

Achieving Self-Control through Behaviour Modification

Key Learning Goals

- Describe how to specify your target behaviour and gather baseline data for a self-modification program.
- Discuss how to design and execute a self-modification program.

Behaviour modification **is a systematic approach to changing behaviour through the application of the principles of conditioning.** Advocates of behaviour modification assume that behaviour is a product of learning, conditioning, and environmental control. They further assume that *what is learned can be unlearned.* Thus, they set out to "recondition" people to produce more desirable patterns of behaviour.

The technology of behaviour modification has been applied with great success in schools, businesses, hospitals, factories, child-care facilities, prisons, and mental health centres (Kazdin, 1982, 2001; Mittenberger, 2012). Moreover, behaviour modification techniques have proven particularly valuable in efforts to improve self-control. Our discussion will borrow liberally from an excellent book on self-modification by David Watson and Roland Tharp (2014). We will discuss five steps in the process of self-modification, which are outlined in Figure 6.24.

Specifying Your Target Behaviour

The first step in a self-modification program is to specify the target behaviour(s) that you want to change. Behaviour modification can be applied only to a clearly defined, overt response, yet many people have difficulty pinpointing the behaviour they hope to alter. They tend to describe their problems in terms of unobservable personality *traits* rather than overt *behaviours*. For example, asked what behaviour he would like to change, a man might say, "I'm too irritable." That may be true, but it is of little help in designing a self-modification program. To use a behavioural approach, vague

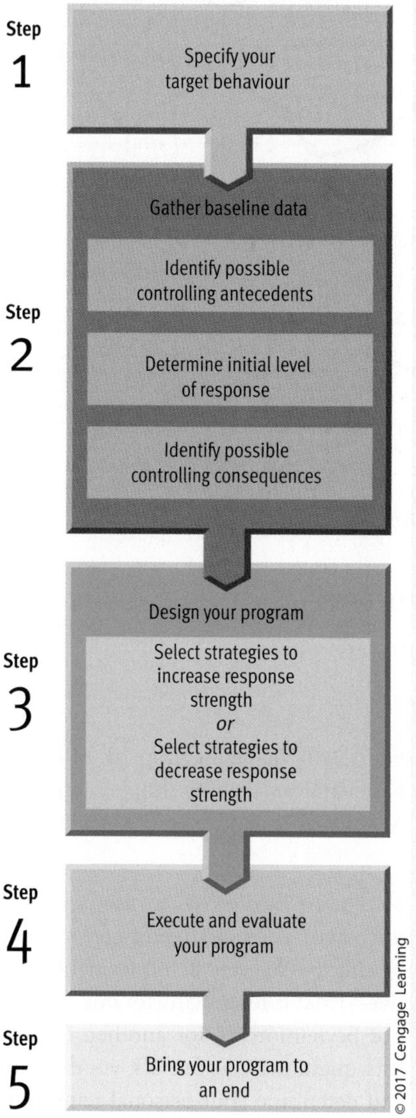

Figure 6.24
Steps in a self-modification program. This flow chart provides an overview of the five steps necessary to execute a self-modification program.

statements about traits need to be translated into precise descriptions of specific target behaviours.

To identify target responses, you need to ponder past behaviour or closely observe future behaviour and list specific *examples* of responses that lead to the trait description. For instance, the man who regards himself as "too irritable" might identify two overly frequent responses, such as arguing with his wife and snapping at his children. These are specific behaviours for which he could design a self-modification program.

Gathering Baseline Data

The second step in behaviour modification is to gather baseline data. You need to systematically observe your target behaviour for a period of time (usually a week or two) before you work out the details of your program. In gathering your baseline data, you need to monitor three things.

First, you need to determine the initial response level of your target behaviour. After all, you can't tell whether your program is working effectively unless you have a baseline for comparison. In most cases, you would simply keep track of how often the target response occurs in a certain time interval. Thus, you might count the daily frequency of snapping at your children, smoking cigarettes, or biting your fingernails. If studying is your target behaviour, you will probably monitor hours of study. If you want to modify your eating, you will probably keep track of how many calories you consume. Whatever the unit of measurement, *it is crucial to gather accurate data.* You should keep permanent written records, and it is usually best to portray these records graphically (see Figure 6.25).

Second, you need to monitor the antecedents of your target behaviour. ***Antecedents*** **are events that typically precede the target response.** Often these events play a major role in evoking your target behaviour. For example, if your target is overeating, you might discover that the bulk of your overeating occurs late in the evening while you watch TV. If you can pinpoint this kind of antecedent–response connection, you may be able to design your program to circumvent or break the link.

Third, you need to monitor the typical consequences of your target behaviour. Try to identify the reinforcers that are maintaining an undesirable target behaviour or the

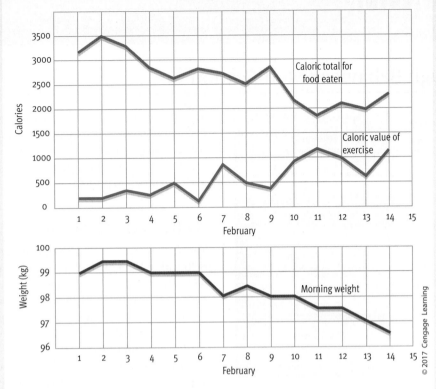

Figure 6.25

Example of record-keeping in a self-modification program. Graphic records are ideal for tracking progress in behaviour modification efforts. The records shown here illustrate what people would be likely to track in a behaviour modification program for weight loss.

1. What will be the rewards of achieving your goal?
2. What kind of praise do you like to receive, from yourself and others?
3. What kinds of things do you like to have?
4. What are your major interests?
5. What are your hobbies?
6. What people do you like to be with?
7. What do you like to do with those people?
8. What do you do for fun?
9. What do you do to relax?
10. What do you do to get away from it all?
11. What makes you feel good?
12. What would be a nice present to receive?
13. What kind of things are important to you?
14. What would you buy if you had an extra $20? $50? $100?
15. On what do you spend your money each week?
16. What behaviours do you perform every day? (Don't overlook the obvious or commonplace.)
17. Are there any behaviours you usually perform instead of the target behaviour?
18. What would you hate to lose?
19. Of the things you do every day, which would you hate to give up?
20. What are your favourite daydreams and fantasies?

Figure 6.26

Selecting a reinforcer. Finding a good reinforcer to use in a behaviour modification program can require a lot of thought. The questions listed here can help people identify their personal reinforcers.

Source: Adapted from Watson, D. L., & Tharp, R. G. (1997). Self-directed behavior: Self-modification for personal adjustment. Belmont, CA: Wadsworth. / © 2017 Cengage Learning

unfavourable outcomes that are suppressing a desirable target behaviour. In trying to identify reinforcers, remember that avoidance behaviour is usually maintained by negative reinforcement. That is, the payoff for avoidance is usually the removal of something aversive, such as anxiety or a threat to self-esteem. You should also take into account the fact that a response may not be reinforced every time, as most behaviour is maintained by intermittent reinforcement.

Designing Your Program

Once you have selected a target behaviour and gathered adequate baseline data, it is time to plan your intervention program. Generally speaking, your program will be designed either to increase or to decrease the frequency of a target response.

Increasing Response Strength Efforts to increase the frequency of a target response depend largely on the use of positive reinforcement. In other words, you reward yourself for behaving properly. Although the basic strategy is quite simple, doing it skillfully involves a number of considerations.

Selecting a Reinforcer. To use positive reinforcement, you need to find a reward that will be effective for you. Reinforcement is subjective—what is reinforcing for one person may not be reinforcing for another. Figure 6.26 lists questions you can ask yourself to help you determine your personal reinforcers. Be sure to be realistic and choose a reinforcer that is really available to you.

You don't have to come up with spectacular new reinforcers that you've never experienced before. *You can use reinforcers that you are already getting.* However, you have to restructure the contingencies so that you get them only if you behave appropriately. For example, if you normally buy two DVDs per week, you might make these purchases contingent on studying a certain number of hours during the week. Making yourself earn rewards that you used to take for granted is often a useful strategy in a self-modification program.

Arranging the Contingencies. Once you have chosen your reinforcer, you have to set up reinforcement contingencies. These contingencies will describe the exact behavioural goals that must be met and the reinforcement that may then be awarded. For example, in a program to increase exercise, you might make spending $50 on clothes (the reinforcer) contingent on having jogged 25 kilometres during the week (the target behaviour).

Try to set behavioural goals that are both challenging and realistic. You want your goals to be challenging so that they lead to improvement in your behaviour. However, setting unrealistically high goals—a common mistake in self-modification—often leads to unnecessary discouragement.

Decreasing Response Strength Let's turn now to the challenge of reducing the frequency of an undesirable response. You can go about this task in a number of ways. Your principal options include reinforcement, control of antecedents, and punishment.

Reinforcement. Reinforcers can be used in an indirect way to decrease the frequency of a response. This may sound paradoxical, since you have learned that reinforcement strengthens a response. The trick lies in how you define the target behaviour. For example, in the case of overeating, you might define your target behaviour as eating more than 1600 calories a day (an excess response that you want to decrease) or eating fewer than 1600 calories a day (a deficit response that you want to increase). You can choose the latter definition and reinforce yourself whenever you eat fewer than 1600 calories in a day. Thus, you can reinforce yourself for not emitting a response, or for emitting it less, and thereby decrease a response through reinforcement.

Control of Antecedents. A worthwhile strategy for decreasing the occurrence of an undesirable response may be to identify its antecedents and avoid exposure to them. This strategy is especially useful when you are trying to decrease the frequency of a consummatory response, such as smoking or eating. In the case of overeating, for instance, the easiest way to resist temptation is to avoid having to face it. Thus, you might stay away from enticing restaurants, minimize time spent in your kitchen, shop for groceries just after eating (when willpower is higher), and avoid purchasing favourite foods. Control of antecedents can also be helpful in a program to increase studying. The key often lies in *where* you study. You can reduce excessive socializing by studying somewhere devoid of people. Similarly, you can reduce loafing by studying someplace where there is no TV, stereo, or phone to distract you.

Punishment. The strategy of decreasing unwanted behaviour by punishing yourself for that behaviour is an obvious option that people tend to overuse. The biggest problem with punishment in a self-modification effort is that it is difficult to follow through and punish yourself. Nonetheless, there may be situations in which your manipulations of reinforcers need to be bolstered by the threat of punishment.

If you're going to use punishment, keep two guidelines in mind. First, do not use punishment alone. Use it in conjunction with positive reinforcement. If you set up a program in which you can earn only negative consequences, you probably won't stick to it. Second, use a relatively mild punishment so that you will actually be able to administer it to yourself. Nurnberger and Zimmerman (1970) developed a creative method of self-punishment. They had subjects write out a cheque to an organization they hated (e.g., the campaign of a political candidate whom they despised). The cheque was held by a third party who mailed it if subjects failed to meet their behavioural goals. Such a punishment is relatively harmless, but it can serve as a strong source of motivation.

Donna Day/The Image Bank/Getty Images

Overeating is just one of the many types of maladaptive behaviour that can be changed with a self-modification program.

Executing Your Program

Once you have designed your program, the next step is to put it to work by enforcing the contingencies that you have carefully planned. During this period, you need to continue to accurately record the frequency of your target behaviour so you can evaluate your progress. The success of your program depends on your not "cheating." The most common form of cheating is to reward yourself when you have not actually earned it.

Ending Your Program

Generally, when you design your program, you should spell out the conditions under which you will bring it to an end. Doing so involves setting terminal goals such as reaching a certain weight, studying with a certain regularity, or going without cigarettes for a certain length of time. Often, it is a good idea to phase out your program by planning a gradual reduction in the frequency or potency of your reinforcement for appropriate behaviour.

Manipulating Emotions: Pavlov and Persuasion

With all due respect to the great Ivan Pavlov, when we focus on his demonstration that dogs can be trained to slobber in response to a tone, it is easy to lose sight of the importance of classical conditioning. At first glance, most people do not see a relationship between Pavlov's slobbering dogs and anything that they are even remotely interested in. However, in the main body of the chapter, we saw that classical conditioning actually contributes to the regulation of many important aspects of behaviour, including fears, phobias, and other emotional reactions; immune function and other physiological processes; food preferences; and even sexual arousal. In this Application, you will learn that classical conditioning is routinely used to manipulate emotions in persuasive efforts. If you watch TV, you have been subjected to Pavlovian techniques. An understanding of these techniques can help you recognize when your emotions are being manipulated by advertisers, politicians, and the media.

Perhaps the most interesting aspect of classically conditioned emotional responses is that people often are unaware of the origin of these responses, or even that they feel the way they do. Consistent with this observation, research by Jim Olson of the University of Western Ontario has shown that attitudes can be shaped through classical conditioning without participants' conscious awareness (Olson & Fazio, 2001; Walther, Nagengast, & Trasselli, 2005). The key to the process is simply to manipulate the automatic, subconscious associations that people make in response to various stimuli. Let's look at how this manipulation is done in advertising, business negotiations, and the world of politics.

Classical Conditioning in Advertising

The art of manipulating people's associations has been perfected by the advertising industry, leading Till and Priluck (2000) to comment, "Conditioning of attitudes towards products and brands has become generally accepted and has developed into a unique research stream" (p. 57). Advertisers consistently endeavour to pair the products they are peddling with stimuli that seem likely to elicit positive emotional responses (Schachtman et al., 2011). An extensive variety of stimuli are used for this purpose. Products are paired with well-liked celebrity spokespersons; depictions of warm, loving families; beautiful pastoral scenery; cute, cuddly pets; enchanting, rosy-cheeked children; upbeat, pleasant music; and opulent surroundings that reek of wealth. Advertisers also like to pair their products with exciting events, such as the Stanley Cup Hockey Finals, and cherished symbols, such as the Canadian flag and the Olympic rings insignia. But, above all else, advertisers like to link their products with sexual imagery and extremely attractive models—especially, glamorous, alluring women (Reichert, 2003; Reichert & Lambiase, 2003).

Advertisers mostly seek to associate their products with stimuli that evoke pleasurable feelings of a general sort, but in some cases they try to create more specific associations. For example, vehicles such as four-wheel drive trucks, sold mainly to men, are frequently paired with tough-looking men in rugged settings to create an association between the vehicle and masculinity. In contrast, vehicles that are mainly marketed to women are paired with images that evoke feelings of femininity. In a similar vein, manufacturers of designer jeans typically seek to forge associations between their products and things that are young, urban, and hip. Advertisers marketing expensive automobiles or platinum credit cards pair their products with symbols of affluence, luxury, and privilege, such as mansions, butlers, and dazzling jewellery.

Classical Conditioning in Business Negotiations

In the world of business interactions, two standard practices are designed to get customers to make an association between one's business and pleasurable feelings. The first is to take customers out to dinner at fine restaurants. The provision of delicious food and fine wine in a luxurious environment is a powerful unconditioned stimulus that reliably elicits pleasant feelings that are likely to be associated with one's host. The second practice is the strategy of entertaining customers at major events, such as concerts and hockey games. Over the last decade, many sports arenas have been largely rebuilt with vastly more "luxury skyboxes" to accommodate this business tactic. One of us has a friend who uses his Toronto Blue Jays season tickets solely for entertaining business clients. He maintains that the cost of the tickets is more than offset by the increased business this practice brings him. This practice pairs the host with both pleasant feelings and the excitement of a big event.

It is worth noting that these strategies take advantage of other processes besides classical conditioning. They also make use of the *reciprocity norm*—the social rule that one should pay back in kind what one receives from others (Cialdini, 2001). Thus, wining and dining clients creates a sense of obligation that they should reciprocate their hosts' generosity—presumably in their business dealings.

Classical Conditioning in the World of Politics

Like advertisers, candidates running for election need to influence the attitudes of many people quickly, subtly, and effectively—and they depend on classical conditioning to help them do so. For example, have you noticed how politicians show up at an endless variety of pleasant public events (such as the opening of a new mall) that often have nothing to do with their public service? When a sports team wins some sort of championship, local politicians are drawn like flies to the subsequent celebrations. Past prime ministers have made a practice of calling the Grey Cup winners. It is noteworthy that they do this during the postgame celebrations when many Canadians are watching the festivities on TV, ensuring the prime minister maximum coverage. They want to pair themselves with these positive events, so that they are associated with pleasant emotions.

Election campaign ads use the same techniques as commercial ads. Candidates are paired with popular celebrities, wholesome families, children, pleasant music, and symbols of patriotism. In the 2015 federal election, we saw many photos of Justin Trudeau with babies, pandas, and many other positive stimuli.

Cognizant of the power of classical conditioning, politicians also exercise great care to ensure that they are not paired with people or events that might trigger negative feelings.

The ultimate political perversion of the principles of classical conditioning probably occurred in Nazi Germany. The Nazis used many propaganda techniques to create prejudice toward Jews and members of other targeted groups (such as the Roma). One such strategy was the repeated pairing of disgusting, repulsive images with stereotypical pictures of Jews. For example, the Nazis would show alternating pictures of rats or roaches crawling over filthy garbage and stereotypical Jewish faces, so that the two images would become associated in the minds of the viewers. Thus, the German population was conditioned to have negative emotional reactions to Jews and to associate them with vermin subject to extermination. The Nazis reasoned that if people would not hesitate to exterminate rats and roaches, then why not human beings associated with these vermin?

Becoming More Aware of Classical Conditioning Processes

How effective are the efforts to manipulate people's emotions through Pavlovian conditioning? It's hard to say. In the real world, these strategies are always used in combination with other persuasive tactics, which creates multiple confounds that make it difficult to assess the impact of the Pavlovian techniques (Walther, Nagengast, & Trasselli, 2005). Laboratory research can eliminate these confounds, but surprisingly little research on these strategies has been published, and virtually all of it has dealt with advertising. The advertising studies suggest that classical conditioning can be effective and leave enduring imprints on consumers' attitudes (Schachtman et al., 2011), but a great deal of additional research is needed. Given the monumental sums that advertisers spend using these techniques, it seems reasonable to speculate that individual companies have data on their specific practices to demonstrate their efficacy, but these data are not made available to the public.

What can you do to reduce the extent to which your emotions are manipulated through Pavlovian procedures? Well, you could turn off your radio and TV, close up your magazines, stop your newspaper, disconnect your modem, and withdraw into a media-resistant shell, but that hardly seems practical

Political candidates are very savvy about the potential power of classical conditioning. For example, they like to be seen with celebrities, children, and animals, all of which elicit positive feelings among many voters.

Source: Photo by Adam Scotti. Photo provided by the Office of the Prime Minister. © Her Majesty the Queen in Right of Canada, 2017. / Photo par Adam Scotti. Photo fournie par le Bureau du Premier ministre. © Sa Majeste la Reine du Chef du Canada, 2017.

for most people. Realistically, the best defence is to make a conscious effort to become more aware of the pervasive attempts to condition your emotions and attitudes. Some research on persuasion suggests that *to be forewarned is to be forearmed* (Pfau et al., 1990). In other words, if you know how media sources try to manipulate you, you should be more resistant to their strategies. See Table 6.2.

Table 6.2

Critical Thinking Skills Discussed in This Application

SKILL	DESCRIPTION
Understanding how Pavlovian conditioning can be used to manipulate emotions	The critical thinker understands how stimuli can be paired together to create automatic associations of which people may not be aware.
Developing the ability to detect conditioning procedures used in the media	The critical thinker can recognize Pavlovian conditioning tactics in commercial and political advertisements.

CLASSICAL CONDITIONING

Description

- *Classical conditioning* is a type of learning in which a stimulus acquires the capacity to evoke a response originally evoked by another stimulus.
- Classical conditioning was pioneered by Ivan Pavlov, who conditioned dogs to salivate when a tone was presented.
- Classical conditioning mainly regulates involuntary, reflexive responses.
- Examples include emotional responses (such as fears) and physiological responses (such as immunosuppression and sexual arousal).

Terminology and procedures

- Responses controlled through classical conditioning are said to be *elicited*.
- Classical conditioning begins with an *unconditioned stimulus (UCS)* that elicits an *unconditioned response (UCR)*.
- Then a neutral stimulus is paired with the UCS until it becomes a *conditioned stimulus (CS)* that elicits a *conditioned response (CR)*.

Basic processes

- *Acquisition* occurs when a CS and UCS are paired, gradually resulting in a CR.

Acquisition
is the formation of a conditioned response tendency.

- *Extinction* occurs when a CS is repeatedly presented alone until it no longer elicits a CR.
- *Spontaneous recovery* is the reappearance of an extinguished response after a period of non-exposure to the CS.

Extinction
is the gradual weakening of a conditioned response tendency.

- *Generalization* occurs when a CR is elicited by a new stimulus that resembles the original CS, as in Watson and Rayner's study of Little Albert.

Generalization
occurs when an organism responds to new stimuli besides the original stimulus.

- *Discrimination* occurs when a CR is not elicited by a new stimulus that resembles the original CS.

Discrimination
occurs when an organism does not respond to other stimuli that resemble the original stimulus.

- *Higher-order conditioning* occurs when a CS functions as if it were a US.

OPERANT CONDITIONING

Description

- *Operant conditioning* is a type of learning in which responses come to be controlled by their consequences.
- Operant conditioning was pioneered by B. F. Skinner, who showed that rats and pigeons tend to repeat responses that are followed by favourable outcomes.
- Operant conditioning mainly regulates voluntary, spontaneous responses.
- Examples include studying, going to work, telling jokes, asking someone out, gambling.

Terminology and procedures

- *Reinforcement* occurs when an event following a response increases an organism's tendency to make that response.
- Responses controlled through operant conditioning are said to be *emitted*.
- Demonstrations of operant conditioning typically occur in a *Skinner box*, where an animal's reinforcement is controlled.
- The key dependent variable is the animal's *response rate*, as monitored by a *cumulative recorder*, with results portrayed in graphs.

Basic processes

- *Acquisition* occurs when a response gradually increases due to contingent reinforcement.
- Acquisition may involve *shaping*—the reinforcement of closer and closer approximations of the desired response.

- *Extinction* occurs when responding gradually slows and stops after reinforcement is terminated.

- *Generalization* occurs when responding increases in the presence of a stimulus that resembles the original discriminative stimulus.

- *Discrimination* occurs when responding does not increase in the presence of a stimulus that resembles the original discriminative stimulus.

- *Primary reinforcers* are inherently reinforcing, whereas *secondary reinforcers* develop through learning.

Schedules of reinforcement

- *Intermittent reinforcement* occurs when a response is reinforced only some of the time.

- In *ratio schedules*, the reinforcer is given after a fixed (FR) or variable (VR) number of nonreinforced responses.

- In *interval schedules*, the reinforcer is given for the first response that occurs after a fixed (FI) or variable (VI) time interval has elapsed.

- Ratio schedules (FR and VR) tend to yield higher response rates, whereas variable schedules (VR and VI) tend to yield more resistance to extinction.

Distinctions among operant outcomes

- *Positive reinforcement* occurs when a response is followed by the presentation of a rewarding stimulus.

- *Negative reinforcement* occurs when a response is followed by the removal of an aversive stimulus.

- Negative reinforcement plays a key role in *escape learning* and *avoidance learning*.

- *Punishment* occurs when an event following a response weakens the tendency to make that response.

- When used as a disciplinary procedure, physical punishment is associated with a variety of negative outcomes.

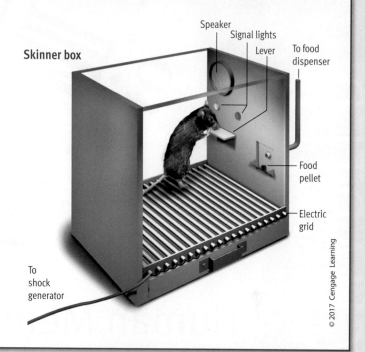

Skinner box

Speaker
Signal lights
Lever
To food dispenser
Food pellet
Electric grid
To shock generator

© 2017 Cengage Learning

NEW DIRECTIONS IN THE STUDY OF CONDITIONING

Recognizing biological constraints on learning

- John Garcia found that it is almost impossible to create some associations, whereas conditioned taste aversions are readily acquired in spite of long CS-UCS delays, which he attributed to evolutionary influences.

© Don Farrall/Digital Vision/Getty Images

- *Preparedness* appears to explain why people acquire phobias to ancient sources of threat much more readily than to modern sources of threat.

Recognizing cognitive processes in conditioning

- Tolman's studies suggested that learning can take place in the absence of reinforcement.

- Robert Rescorla showed that the predictive value of a CS influences the process of classical conditioning.

- When a response is followed by a desirable outcome, the response is more likely to be strengthened if it appears to have caused the favourable outcome.

- Noncontingent reinforcement, cognitive biases, and irrational reasoning appear to contribute to superstitious behaviour.

- Modern theories hold that conditioning is a matter of detecting the contingencies that govern events.

OBSERVATIONAL LEARNING

- *Observational learning* occurs when an organism's responding is influenced by the observation of others, called *models*.

- Observational learning was pioneered by Albert Bandura, who showed that conditioning does not have to be a product of direct experience.

- Both classical and operant conditioning can take place through observational learning.

- Observational learning depends on the processes of attention, retention, reproduction, and motivation.

- In research on the effects of media violence, both experimental and correlational studies suggest that violent media contribute to increased aggression among children and adults.

APPLICATIONS

- Behaviour modification techniques can be used to increase self-control; if you are trying to increase the strength of a response, you'll depend on positive reinforcement.

- A number of strategies can be used to decrease the strength of a response, including reinforcement, control of antecedents, and punishment.

- Evaluative conditioning can be used to manipulate people's emotional responses, making it a very useful tool for advertisers.

CHAPTER 7

Human Memory

Themes in this Chapter

Theoretical
Diversity

Multifactorial
Causation

Subjectivity of
Experience

Have you ever thought about the possibility of travelling through time? If you are like most people, you have likely imagined how useful it might be in some situations. Time travel would allow you to accomplish more—for example, to take those extra classes that you are so interested in, allowing you to complete your degree sooner than is ordinarily possible. The concept of time travel is fascinating and has been the subject of many books and movies. Can you remember any books you have read or movies you have seen in the past couple of years in which time travel plays an important role? Of course, there are many well-known novels, including Charles Dickens's *A Christmas Carol* (1843), H. G. Wells's *The Time Machine* (1895), Robert Heinlein's *All You Zombies* (1959), Kurt Vonnegut's *Slaughterhouse-Five* (1969), Douglas Adams's *The Restaurant at the End of the Universe* (1980), and Michael Crichton's *Timeline* (1999). By the way, there was another famous book published in 1999 that involved time travel. If you are like most others of your age (any age really, both of us are fans), you have probably read the book or seen the movie of the same name that was released in 2004. Do you remember the name of the book now? As a hint, we can tell you that the author was J. K. Rowling. *Harry Potter and the Prisoner of Azkaban* is the answer. That was too easy! Let's test your Harry Potter trivia knowledge again. Do you remember the name of the object that allowed Hermione to time travel? (If not, you can find the answer at the end of this section.) This might be more difficult—take a moment. If you can't answer right away, it might seem that you almost know, that the answer is, well, on the tip of your tongue. Memory is a fascinating topic and process. While you are trying to remember, reflect a little on how you might describe to someone else how you are able to remember such things or, perhaps, why you cannot. These processes, including remembering, forgetting, the tip-of-the-tongue phenomenon, and much more, constitute the subject matter of this chapter on human memory.

Our memory is something that helps define who we are, our sense of self (Prebble et al., 2013), and it is intimately tied to our ability to function effectively and efficiently in the immediate moment in both social (Hirst & Echterhoff, 2012) and nonsocial contexts. In order to get to school on time, you have to remember where you left your room keys so you can lock the door before you leave. The importance of memory in our ability to orient ourselves in the present is clear. So, what does memory have to do with time travel?

Time travel itself, while clearly fascinating, isn't as rare as you might think; in fact, most of us can do it and if you think carefully about it, it shouldn't surprise you to know that such time travel is intimately linked with the nature of our cognition and memory systems (Ainslie, 2007; Schacter & Addis, 2007a, 2007b). It is the nature of our cognitive and memory processes that allows us all to travel through time (Devitt & Addis, 2016; Michaelin, 2016; Schacter, Addis, & Szpunar, 2017; Tulving, 2005). We can go backward to remember specific events that happened to us, such as attending a screening of *The Prisoner of Azkaban* and the people with whom we attended the movie. Other memories are not tied to us personally, but may relate more to general knowledge, such as what the word *prisoner* means or what kind of animal a *hippogriff* is.

These two kinds of memory—memory for general information and memory for personal events—were labelled *semantic* and *episodic* memory, respectively, by psychologist Endel Tulving (1972). Tulving's well-known patient referred to as K.C. gives a dramatic example of the distinction between these types of memories (Rosenbaum et al., 2005). K.C. suffered serious brain damage in 1981 after a motorcycle accident. But you might never realize it if you restricted yourself to asking him questions such as "Who wrote *The Time Machine*?" After the accident, K.C.'s semantic memory for facts was unimpaired. He was not distinguishable from anyone else and frequently outperformed "normal" undergraduates at the University of Toronto, where Tulving conducted his work, on various cognitive/perceptual tasks. What is impaired, however, is his episodic memory: No matter how hard he tries, he cannot remember anything that has ever happened *to him* (Tulving, 2001). He depends on a personal digital assistant to remind him to eat. K.C. admits that without the device "I would get hungry but wouldn't remember to eat. I wouldn't know what time to go for lunch" (Branswell & Hall, 2007, p. A6).

K.C. has been important in terms of our understanding of memory (Rosenbaum et al., 2005). Research with K.C. has contributed to, among other things, our knowledge about the distinction between semantic and episodic memory, the distinction between implicit and explicit memory, and new learning in amnesia (Kwan et al., 2012; Rosenbaum et al., 2005; Rosenbaum, Murphy, & Rich, 2011).

In this chapter we focus on the nature of our memory systems. As the preceding discussion suggests, memory involves more than taking information in and storing it in some mental compartment. In fact, psychologists probing the workings of memory have had to grapple with three enduring questions:

1. How does information get *into* memory?
2. How is information *maintained* in memory?
3. How is information pulled *back out* of memory?

These three questions correspond to the three key processes involved in memory: *encoding* (getting information in), *storage* (maintaining it), and *retrieval* (getting it out).

***Encoding* involves forming a memory code.** For example, when you form a memory code for a word, you might emphasize how it looks, how it sounds, or what it means. Encoding usually requires attention. ***Storage* involves maintaining encoded information in memory over time.** Psychologists have focused much of their memory research on trying to identify just what factors help or hinder memory storage.

Information storage isn't enough to guarantee that you'll remember something. You need to be able to get information out of storage. ***Retrieval* involves recovering information from memory stores.** Research issues concerned with retrieval include the study of how people search memory and why some retrieval strategies are more effective than others.

Most of this chapter is devoted to an examination of memory encoding, storage, and retrieval. As you'll see, these basic processes help explain the ultimate puzzle in the study of memory: why people forget. Just as memory involves more than storage, forgetting involves more than "losing" something from the memory store. Forgetting may be due to deficiencies in any of the three key processes in memory—encoding, storage, or retrieval. After our discussion of forgetting, we will take a brief look at the physiological bases of memory. Finally, we will discuss the theoretical controversy about whether there are separate memory systems for different types of information. The chapter's Personal Application provides some practical advice on how to improve your memory. The Critical Thinking Application discusses some reasons why memory is less reliable than people assume it to be.

We began this introductory section discussing the concept of time travel. It is of interest to psychologists not only because it seems to be tied up with our memory system, but also because it has been suggested that the ability to imagine oneself in the future gives us an adaptive advantage in terms of our flexibility in dealing with novel situations (Quoidbach, Wood, & Hanenne, 2009; Suddendorf & Corballis, 2007). It has also been found that specific types of future mental time travel may help increase our happiness and reduce our stress (Quoidbach et al., 2009). Oh yes, we almost *forgot*: Hermione used a *Time Turner* in order to be able to attend more classes than she had time for. The use of the *Time Turner* also allowed for the rescue of Sirius Black and Buckbeak (a hippogriff).

Encoding: Getting Information into Memory

Key Learning Goals

▶ Clarify the role of attention and depth of processing in memory.

▶ Explain how elaboration, visual imagery, and motivation to remember can enrich encoding.

Have you ever been introduced to someone and then realized only 30 seconds into your interaction that you had already forgotten his or her name? More often than not, this familiar kind of forgetting results from a failure to form a memory code for the name. When you're introduced to people, you're often busy sizing them up and thinking about what you're going to say. With your attention diverted in this way, names go in one ear and out the other. Sometimes the information just doesn't seem important, so you devote very little or no attention to it. For example, can you remember the first name of either author of this book? While we are a little disappointed that you can't, we are not surprised. You don't remember them because they aren't encoded for storage into memory. This common problem illustrates that active encoding is a crucial process in memory. In this section, we discuss the role of attention in encoding, various types of encoding, and the ways to enrich this process.

The Role of Attention

You generally need to pay attention to information if you intend to remember it (Lachter, Forster, & Ruthruff, 2004; Mulligan, 1998). For example, if you sit through a class lecture but pay little attention to it, you're unlikely to remember much of what the professor had to say. **Attention involves focusing awareness on a narrowed range of stimuli or events.** Selective attention is critical to everyday functioning. If your attention were distributed equally among all stimulus inputs, life would be utter chaos. You need to screen out most of the potential stimulation around you in order to read a book, converse with a friend, or even carry on a coherent train of thought.

Attention is often likened to a *filter* that screens out most potential stimuli while allowing a select few to pass through into conscious awareness. However, a great deal of debate has been devoted to *where* the filter is located in the information-processing system. The key issue in this debate is whether stimuli are screened out *early*, during sensory input, or *late*, after the brain has processed the meaning or significance of the input (see Figure 7.1).

Evidence on the "cocktail party phenomenon" suggests the latter. For example, imagine a young woman named Tamara at a crowded party where many conversations are taking place. Tamara is paying attention to her conversation with a friend and filtering out the other conversations. However, if someone in another conversation mentions her name, Tamara may notice it, even though she has been ignoring that conversation. In experimental simulations of this situation, about 35 percent of participants report hearing their own name (Wood & Cowan, 1995). If selection is early, how can these people register input they've been blocking out? This cocktail party phenomenon suggests that attention involves *late* selection, based on the *meaning* of input.

Which view is supported by the weight of scientific evidence—early selection or late selection? Studies have found ample evidence for *both* as well as for intermediate selection (Cowan, 1988; Treisman 2009). These findings have led some theorists to conclude that the location of the attention filter may be flexible rather than fixed (Shiffrin, 1988).

The importance of attention to memory is apparent when participants are asked to focus their attention on two or more inputs simultaneously. Studies indicate that when participants are forced to divide their attention between memory encoding and some other task, large reductions in memory performance are seen (Craik, 2001). Actually, the negative effects of divided attention are not limited to memory. Divided attention can have a negative impact on the performance of quite a variety of tasks, especially when the tasks are complex or unfamiliar (Pashler, Johnston, & Ruthruff, 2001).

Although people tend to think that they can multitask with no deterioration in performance, research suggests that the human brain can effectively handle only one attention-consuming task at a time (Lien, Ruthruff, & Johnston, 2006). When people multitask, they are really switching their attention back and forth among tasks, rather than processing them simultaneously. That may be fine in many circumstances, but the cost of divided attention does have profound implications for the advisability

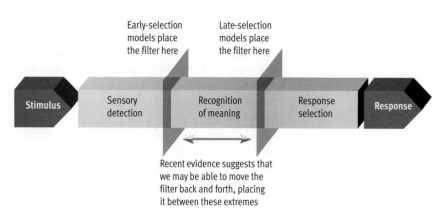

Figure 7.1

Models of selective attention. Early-selection models propose that input is filtered before meaning is processed. Late-selection models hold that filtering occurs after the processing of meaning. There is evidence to support early, late, and intermediate selection, suggesting that the location of the attentional filter may not be fixed. (Based on data from MacMillan et al., 1997)

Source: From Weiten. *Cengage Advantage Books: Psychology*, 9E. © 2013 South-Western, a part of Cengage, Inc. Reproduced by permission. www.cengage.com/permissions

of driving while conversing on a cell phone, for example. Carefully controlled research clearly demonstrates that cell phone conversations undermine people's driving performance, even when hands-free phones are used (Chen & Yan, 2013; Strayer, Drews, & Crouch, 2006). Most jurisdictions have banned the use of any device that might lead to distracted driving. Distracted driving convictions in Canada are typically accompanied by significant fines and demerit points (CBC News, 2014).

One study shed light on why cell phone conversations are more distracting to drivers than conversations with passengers. The research showed that passengers adapt their conversation to the demands of the traffic and can provide assistance to the driver (Drews, Pasupathi, & Strayer, 2008). In other words, when passengers see that traffic is heavy or that the driving task has become complicated, they reduce the rate and complexity of their communication and try to help the driver navigate through the situation. As distracting as cell phone conversations are, research indicates that texting while driving is substantially more dangerous (Drews et al., 2009). There is some variability in how well people can juggle multiple tasks. Unfortunately, those who report that they engage in more multitasking tend to be those who are least able to juggle multiple tasks (Sanbonmatsu et al., 2013).

Levels of Processing

Attention is critical to the encoding of memories. But not all attention is created equal. You can attend to things in different ways, focusing on different aspects of the stimulus input. According to some theorists, differences in *how* people attend to information are the main factors influencing

People think they can do several things simultaneously, but in reality they are switching their attention back and forth among various tasks.

how much they remember. Fergus Craik and Robert Lockhart (1972), both at the University of Toronto, proposed an important model in this area. In their formulation, they argue that different rates of forgetting occur because some methods of encoding create more durable memory codes than others.

Craik and Lockhart propose that incoming information can be processed at different levels. For instance, they maintain that in dealing with verbal information, people engage in three progressively deeper levels of processing: structural, phonemic, and semantic encoding (see Figure 7.2). *Structural encoding* is relatively shallow processing that emphasizes the physical structure of the stimulus. For example, if words are flashed on a screen, structural encoding registers such matters as how they were printed (capital letters, lowercase, and so on) or the length of the words (how many letters). Further analysis may result in *phonemic encoding*, which emphasizes what a word sounds like. Phonemic encoding involves naming or saying (perhaps silently) the words. Finally, *semantic encoding* emphasizes the meaning of verbal input; it involves thinking about the objects and actions the words represent. **Levels-of-processing theory** proposes that deeper levels of processing result in longer-lasting memory codes.

In one experimental test of levels-of-processing theory, Craik and Tulving (1975) compared the durability of structural, phonemic, and semantic encoding. They directed subjects' attention to

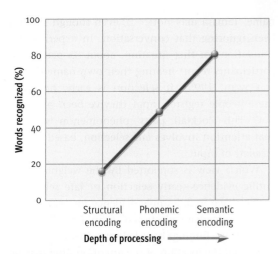

Figure 7.3
Retention at three levels of processing. In accordance with levels-of-processing theory, Craik and Tulving (1975) found that structural, phonemic, and semantic encoding, which involve progressively deeper levels of processing, led to progressively better retention. (Data from Craik & Tulving, 1975)

particular aspects of briefly presented stimulus words by asking them questions about various characteristics of the words (see Figure 7.2). The questions were designed to engage the subjects in different levels of processing. The key hypothesis was that retention of the stimulus words would increase as subjects moved from structural to phonemic to semantic encoding. After responding to 60 words, the subjects received an unexpected test of their memory for the words. As predicted, the subjects' recall was low after structural encoding, notably better after phonemic encoding, and highest after semantic encoding (see Figure 7.3). While the theory is not without its critics, the hypothesis that deeper processing leads to enhanced memory has been replicated in many studies (Craik, 2002; Lockhart & Craik, 1990). Levels-of-processing theory has been enormously influential; it has shown that memory involves more than just storage and has inspired a great deal of research on how processing considerations affect memory (Arkes, 2016; Nunoi & Yoshikawa, 2016; Roediger, Gallo, & Geraci, 2002).

Enriching Encoding

Structural, phonemic, and semantic encoding do not exhaust the options when it comes to forming memory codes. There are other dimensions to encoding, dimensions that can enrich the encoding process and thereby improve memory (Nairne,

Level of processing	Type of encoding	Example of questions used to elicit appropriate encoding
Shallow processing	*Structural encoding:* emphasizes the physical structure of the stimulus	Is the word written in capital letters?
Intermediate processing	*Phonemic encoding:* emphasizes what a word sounds like	Does the word rhyme with weight?
Deep processing	*Semantic encoding:* emphasizes the meaning of verbal input	Would the word fit in the sentence: "He met a _____ on the street"?

Depth of processing

© 2017 Cengage Learning

Figure 7.2
Levels-of-processing theory. According to Craik (2002), Craik and Lockhart (1972), and Lockhart and Craik (1990), structural, phonemic, and semantic encoding—which can be elicited by questions such as those shown on the right—involve progressively deeper levels of processing, which should result in more durable memories.

Pandeirada, & Thompson, 2008): elaboration, visual imagery, and self-referent coding.

Elaboration

Semantic encoding can often be enhanced through a process called *elaboration*. *Elaboration* is linking a stimulus to other information at the time of encoding. For example, let's say you read that phobias are often caused by classical conditioning, and you apply this idea to your own fear of spiders. In doing so, you are engaging in elaboration. The additional associations created by elaboration usually help people to remember information. Differences in elaboration can help explain why different approaches to semantic processing result in varied amounts of retention (Craik & Tulving, 1975).

Visual Imagery

Imagery—the creation of visual images to represent the words to be remembered—can also be used to enrich encoding. Of course, some words are easier to create images for than others. If you were asked to remember the word *juggler*, you could readily form an image of someone juggling balls. However, if you were asked to remember the word *truth*, you would probably have more difficulty forming a suitable image. The difference is that *juggler* refers to a concrete object, whereas *truth* refers to an abstract concept. Allan Paivio (1969, 2007) points out that it is easier to form images of concrete objects than of abstract concepts. He believes that this ease of image formation affects memory.

The beneficial effect of imagery on memory was demonstrated in a study by Paivio, Smythe, and Yuille (1968). They asked subjects to learn a list of 16 pairs of words. They manipulated whether the words were concrete, high-imagery words, or abstract, low-imagery words. In terms of imagery potential, the list contained four types of pairings: high–high (*juggler–dress*), high–low (*letter–effort*), low–high (*duty–hotel*), and low–low (*quality–necessity*). Figure 7.4 shows the recall for each type of pairing. The impact of imagery is quite evident. The best recall was of high–high pairings, and the worst recall was of low–low pairings, showing that high-imagery words are easier to remember than low-imagery words. Similar results were observed in another study that controlled for additional confounding factors (Paivio, Khan, & Begg, 2000).

According to Paivio (1986), imagery facilitates memory because it provides a second kind of memory code, and two codes are better than one. His

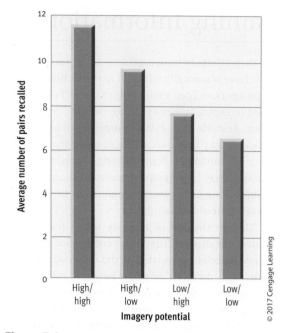

Figure 7.4
The effect of visual imagery on retention. Participants given pairs of words to remember showed better recall for high-imagery pairings than for low-imagery pairings, demonstrating that visual imagery can enrich encoding. (Data from Paivio, Smythe, & Yuille, 1968)

dual-coding theory holds that memory is enhanced by forming semantic and visual codes, since either can lead to recall. Although some aspects of dual-coding theory have been questioned, it's clear that the use of mental imagery can enhance memory in many situations (Marschark, 1992; McCauley, Eskes, & Moscovitch, 1996).

Self-Referent Encoding

Making material personally relevant can also enrich encoding (Hamami, Serbun, & Gutchess, 2011). *Self-referent encoding* involves deciding how or whether information is personally relevant. This approach to encoding was compared to structural, phonemic, and semantic encoding in a study by Rogers, Kuiper, and Kirker (1977). Like Craik and Tulving (1975), these researchers manipulated encoding by asking their subjects certain kinds of questions. To induce self-referent encoding, subjects were asked to decide whether adjectives flashed on a screen applied to them personally. The results showed that self-referent encoding led to improved recall of the adjectives. Self-referent encoding appears to enhance recall by promoting additional elaboration and better organization of information (Symons & Johnson, 1997).

Storage: Maintaining Information in Memory

Key Learning Goals

▶ Describe the sensory store in memory, and discuss the durability and capacity of short-term memory.

▶ Describe Baddeley's model of working memory, and discuss research on working memory capacity.

▶ Evaluate the permanence of long-term memory, and discuss how knowledge is represented in memory.

In their efforts to understand memory storage, theorists have historically related it to the technologies of their age (Roediger, 1980). One of the earliest models used to explain memory storage was the wax tablet. Both Aristotle and Plato compared memory to a block of wax that differed in size and hardness for various individuals. Remembering, according to this analogy, was like stamping an impression into the wax. As long as the image remained in the wax, the memory would remain intact.

Modern theories of memory reflect the technological advances of the 20th century. For example, many theories formulated at the dawn of the computer age drew an analogy between information storage by computers and information storage in human memory (Atkinson & Shiffrin, 1968, 1971; Broadbent, 1958; Waugh & Norman, 1965). The main contribution of these *information-processing theories* was to subdivide memory into three separate memory stores (Estes, 1999; Pashler & Carrier, 1996). The names for these stores and their exact characteristics varied some from one theory to the next. For purposes of simplicity, we'll organize our discussion around the model devised by Richard Atkinson and Richard Shiffrin, which proved to be the most influential of the information-processing theories (e.g., Lehman & Malmberg, 2013). According to their model, incoming information passes through two temporary storage buffers—the sensory store and short-term store—before it is transferred into a long-term store (see Figure 7.5). Like the wax tablet before it, the information-processing model of memory is a metaphor; the three memory stores are not viewed as anatomical structures in the brain, but rather as functionally distinct types of memory.

Sensory Memory

The *sensory memory* preserves information in its original sensory form for a brief time, usually only a fraction of a second. Sensory memory allows the sensation of a visual pattern, sound, or touch to linger for a brief moment after the sensory stimulation is over. In the case of vision, people really perceive an *afterimage* rather than the actual stimulus. You can demonstrate the existence of afterimages for yourself by rapidly moving a lighted sparkler or flashlight in circles in the dark. If you move a sparkler fast enough, you should see a complete circle even though the light source is only a single point. The sensory memory preserves the sensory image long enough for you to perceive a continuous circle rather than separate points of light.

The brief preservation of sensations in sensory memory gives you additional time to try to recognize stimuli. However, you'd better take advantage of sensory storage immediately because it doesn't last long. This fact was demonstrated in a classic experiment by George Sperling (1960). His subjects saw three rows of letters flashed on a screen for just 1/20 of a second. A tone following the exposure signalled which row of letters the subject should report to the experimenter (see Figure 7.6). Subjects were fairly accurate when the signal occurred immediately. However, their accuracy steadily declined as the delay of the tone increased to one second. Why? Because the memory trace in the visual sensory store decays in about 1/4 of a second. Memory traces in

Figure 7.5
The Atkinson and Shiffrin model of memory storage. Atkinson and Shiffrin (1971) proposed that memory is made up of three information stores. *Sensory memory* can hold a large amount of information just long enough (a fraction of a second) for a small portion of it to be selected for longer storage. *Short-term memory* has a limited capacity, and unless aided by rehearsal, its storage duration is brief. *Long-term memory* can store an apparently unlimited amount of information for indeterminate periods.

Sensory memory · Short-term memory · Long-term memory · Rehearsal · Storage · Sensory input · Attention · Retrieval

© 2017 Cengage Learning

Wayne Weiten

Because the image of the sparkler persists briefly in sensory memory, when the sparkler is moved fast enough, the blending of afterimages causes people to see a continuous stream of light instead of a succession of individual points.

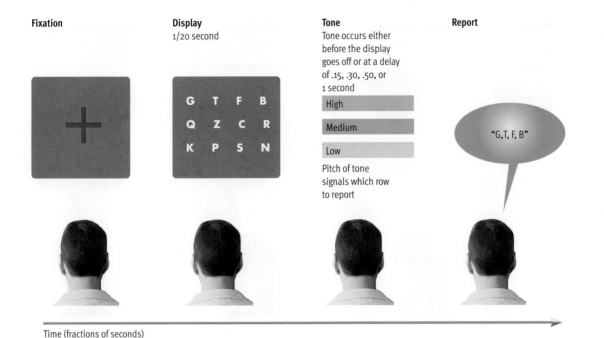

Fixation

Display
1/20 second

G	T	F	B
Q	Z	C	R
K	P	S	N

Tone
Tone occurs either before the display goes off or at a delay of .15, .30, .50, or 1 second

High

Medium

Low

Pitch of tone signals which row to report

Report

"G, T, F, B"

Time (fractions of seconds)

Figure 7.6
Sperling's (1960) study of sensory memory. After the participants had fixated on the cross, the letters were flashed on the screen just long enough to create a visual afterimage. High, medium, and low tones signalled which row of letters to report. Because subjects had to rely on the afterimage to report the letters, Sperling was able to measure how rapidly the afterimage disappeared by varying the delay between the display and the signal to report.

the auditory sensory store also appear to last less than a second (Massaro & Loftus, 1996). While very brief, these sensory memories are clearly important affecting, among other things, the richness of our visual perception, the accuracy of our construal of our world, and the decisions we make (Vandenbrouke et al., 2014; Vlassova & Pearson, 2013).

Short-Term Memory

Short-term memory (STM) is a limited-capacity store that can maintain unrehearsed information for up to about 20 seconds. In contrast, information stored in long-term memory may last weeks, months, or years. However, there is a way that you can maintain information in your short-term store indefinitely. How? Primarily, by engaging in *rehearsal*—the process of repetitively verbalizing or thinking about the information. Cognitive psychologists often distinguish between *maintenance* rehearsal and more *elaborative* rehearsal or processing (e.g., Craik & Lockhart, 1972). In using maintenance rehearsal you are simply maintaining the information in consciousness, while in more elaborative processing, you are increasing the probability that you will retain the information in the future (Brown & Craik, 2000) by, for example, focusing on the meaning of the words in the list you are trying to remember.

Durability of Storage

Without rehearsal, information in short-term memory is lost in less than 20 seconds (Nairne, 2003; Wickens, 1999). This rapid loss was demonstrated

in a study by Peterson and Peterson (1959). They measured how long undergraduates could remember three consonants if they couldn't rehearse them. To prevent rehearsal, the Petersons required the students to count backward by threes from the time the consonants were presented until they saw a light that signalled the recall test (see Figure 7.7). Their results showed that subjects' recall accuracy was pretty dismal (about 10 percent) after only 15 seconds. Other approaches to the issue have suggested that the typical duration of STM storage may even be shorter (Baddeley, 1986). Theorists originally believed that the loss of information from short-term memory was due purely to time-related *decay* of memory traces, but follow-up research showed that *interference* from competing material also contributes (Nairne & Neath, 2013; Oberauer & Lewandowsky, 2014).

Capacity of Storage

Short-term memory is also limited in the number of items it can hold. The small capacity of STM was pointed out by George Miller (1956) in a famous paper called "The Magical Number Seven, Plus or Minus Two: Some Limits on Our Capacity for Processing Information." Miller noticed that people could recall only about seven items in tasks that required them to remember unfamiliar material. The common thread in these tasks, Miller argued, was that they required the use of STM. The limited capacity of STM constrains people's ability to perform tasks in which they need to mentally juggle various pieces of information (Baddeley & Hitch, 1974).

Figure 7.7
Peterson and Peterson's (1959) study of short-term memory. After a warning light was flashed, the participants were given three consonants to remember. The researchers prevented rehearsal by giving the subjects a three-digit number at the same time and telling them to count backward by three from that number until given the signal to recall the letters. By varying the amount of time between stimulus presentation and recall, Peterson and Peterson (1959) were able to measure how quickly information is lost from short-term memory.

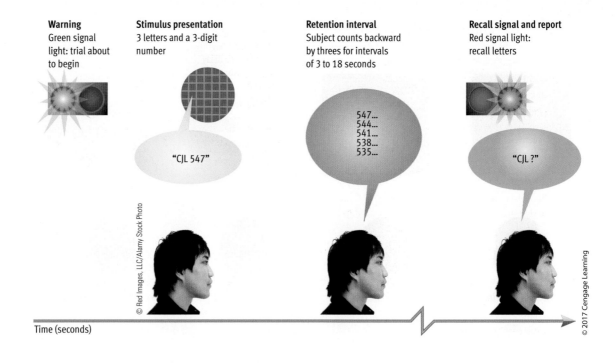

George Miller

"The Magical Number Seven, Plus or Minus Two."

reality check

Misconception

The capacity of short-term memory is seven plus or minus two.

Reality

Calling this assertion a misconception is a little harsh, as it has been the conventional wisdom since the 1950s and there is room for argument on the matter. However, in the last decade or so, researchers using more sophisticated methods have been chipping away at this maxim. The consensus among memory experts has shifted toward the belief that the capacity of STM is four plus or minus one.

The capacity of short-term memory may even be less than widely assumed. Nelson Cowan (2005, 2010) cites evidence indicating that the capacity of STM might be even lower—*four* plus or minus *one*. The consensus on the capacity of STM seems to be moving toward this smaller estimate (Lustig et al., 2009). According to Cowan, the capacity of STM has historically been overestimated because researchers have often failed to take steps to prevent covert rehearsal or *chunking* by participants.

It has long been known that you can increase the capacity of your short-term memory by combining stimuli into larger, possibly higher-order units, called *chunks* (Simon, 1974). A *chunk is a group of familiar stimuli stored as a single unit.* You can demonstrate the effect of chunking by asking someone to recall a sequence of 12 letters grouped in the following way:

NF - BCT - VC - BCIB - M

As you read the letters aloud, pause at the hyphens. Your subject will probably attempt to remember each letter separately because there are no obvious groups or chunks. But a string of 12 letters is too long for STM, so errors are likely. Now present the same string of letters to another person, but place the pauses in the following locations:

NFB - CTV - CBC - IBM

The letters now form four familiar chunks that should occupy only four slots in STM, resulting in successful recall (Bower & Springston, 1970).

To successfully chunk the letters C B C a subject must first recognize these letters as a familiar unit. This familiarity has to be stored somewhere in long-term memory. Hence, in this case, information was transferred from long-term into short-term memory. This is not unusual. People routinely draw information out of their long-term memory banks to evaluate and understand information that they are working with in short-term memory.

Individuals who are experts in specific areas have been shown to process information related to that expertise differently than nonexperts. This was demonstrated by William Chase and the 1978 Nobel Prize winner Herbert Simon, when they studied how expert and novice chess players remembered the positions of chess pieces on a chessboard after having a chance to look at the board for only a few seconds

(Chase & Simon, 1973). Chase and Simon (1973) suggested that the experts "chunked" the information differently and more effectively. But this advantage holds only when the chess pieces appear in meaningful and familiar patterns. In this case, the expert's advantage lies in the ability to "encode the position into larger perceptual chunks, each consisting of a familiar subconfiguration of pieces" (p. 80).

Short-Term Memory as "Working Memory"

Research eventually suggested that short-term memory involves more than a simple rehearsal buffer, as originally envisioned. To make sense of such findings, Alan Baddeley (1986, 1989, 1992) proposed a more complex, modularized model of short-term memory that characterizes it as "working memory." According to Baddeley (2003), *working memory* is a **limited capacity storage system that temporarily maintains and stores information by providing an interface between perception, memory, and action.** Since its introduction, the concept of "working memory" has proven invaluable in our attempts to understand human behaviour and experience (e.g., Baddeley, 2012; Bae & Flombaum, 2013; Camos, 2015; Rose et al., 2012; Sims et al., 2012). While the term was first used by Miller, Galanter, and Pribaum (1960), it is Baddeley's model that has been most influential.

Baddeley's model of working memory consists of four components (see Figure 7.8). The first component is the *phonological loop* that represented all of STM in earlier models. This component is at work when you use recitation to temporarily remember a phone number. Baddeley (2003; Repovš & Baddeley, 2006) believes that the phonological loop evolved to facilitate the acquisition of language. The second component in working memory is a *visuospatial sketchpad* that permits people to temporarily hold and manipulate visual images. This element is at work when you try to mentally rearrange the furniture in your bedroom or map out a complicated route that you need to follow to travel somewhere.

The third component is a *central executive* system. It controls the deployment of attention, switching the focus of attention and dividing attention as needed (e.g., dividing your attention between a message you are trying to text to your friend during a lecture and what your professor told the class about next week's exam, "What was that? Which chapters are on next week's exam?"). The central executive also coordinates the actions of the other modules. The fourth component is the *episodic buffer*, a temporary, limited-capacity store that allows the various

components of working memory to integrate information and that serves as an interface between working memory and long-term memory. The two key characteristics that originally defined short-term memory—limited capacity and storage duration—are still present in the concept of working memory, but Baddeley's model accounts for evidence that STM handles a greater variety of functions than previously thought.

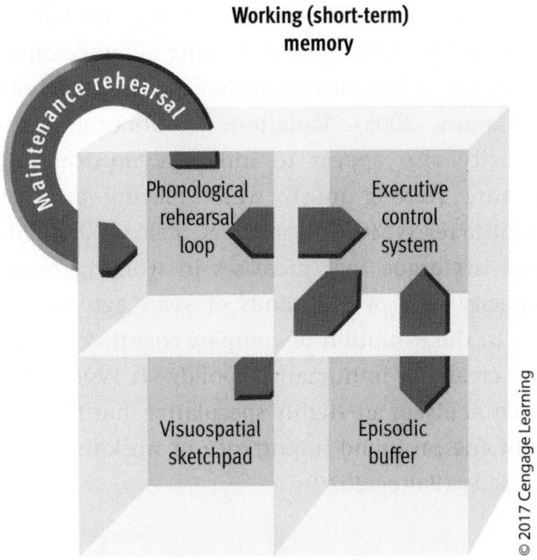

Baddeley's model of working memory has generated an enormous volume of research (Courtney, 2004; Theeuwes, Belopolsky, & Olivers, 2009). For example, one line of research has shown that people vary in how well they can juggle information in their working memory while fending off distractions (Engle, 2001). *Working memory capacity (WMC)* refers to one's ability to hold and manipulate information in conscious attention. Working memory capacity is a stable personal trait (Unsworth et al., 2005) that appears to be influenced to a considerable degree by heredity (Kremen et al., 2007). That said, working memory capacity can be temporarily reduced by situational factors, such as pressure to perform or rumination (Curci et al., 2013; Gimmig et al., 2006). Interestingly, people with greater working memory capacity tend to be especially flexible and effective in their allocation of working memory (Rummel & Boywitt, 2014). In other words, high-WMC individuals tend to let their mind wander from the task at hand more than low-WMC individuals when the attentional demands of the task are modest—presumably because they can afford to do so—but they also are better at staying focused when they need to do so.

Variations in working memory capacity correlate positively with measures of high-level cognitive abilities, such as reading comprehension, complex reasoning, and even intelligence (Logie, 2011;

Working (short-term) memory

Maintenance rehearsal

Phonological rehearsal loop

Executive control system

Visuospatial sketchpad

Episodic buffer

© 2017 Cengage Learning

Figure 7.8
Short-term memory as working memory. This diagram depicts the revised model of the short-term store proposed by Alan Baddeley. According to Baddeley (2001), working memory includes four components: a phonological rehearsal loop, a visuospatial sketchpad, an executive control system, and an episodic buffer.

Unsworth et al., 2014). This finding has led some theorists to conclude that working memory capacity is critical to complex cognition (Lepine, Barrouillet, & Camos, 2005). Variations in working memory capacity also appear to influence musical ability because reading music while playing an instrument taxes WMC (Hambrick & Meinz, 2013). Some theorists argue that increases in working memory capacity tens of thousands of years ago were crucial to the evolution of complex cognitive processes and creativity in humans (Coolidge & Wynn, 2009). Their analyses are highly speculative, but they highlight the profound importance of working memory capacity (Balter, 2010).

Long-Term Memory

Long-term memory (LTM) **is an unlimited capacity store that can hold information over lengthy periods of time.** Unlike sensory and short-term memory, which have very brief storage durations, LTM can store information indefinitely. In fact, one point of view is that all information stored in long-term memory is stored there *permanently*. According to this view, forgetting occurs only because people sometimes cannot *retrieve* needed information from LTM.

The notion that LTM storage may be permanent is certainly intriguing. A couple of interesting lines of research have seemed to provide compelling evidence of permanent storage. However, each line of research turns out to be less compelling than it appears at first glance. The first line of research consisted of some landmark studies conducted by neuroscientist Wilder Penfield at McGill University. He reported triggering long-lost memories through electrical stimulation of the brain (ESB) during brain surgeries (Penfield & Perot, 1963). When Penfield used ESB to map brain function in patients undergoing surgery for epilepsy, he found that stimulation of the temporal lobe sometimes elicited vivid descriptions of events long past. Patients would describe events that apparently came from their childhood—such as "being in a lumberyard" or "watching Mom make a phone call"—as if they were there once again. Penfield and others inferred that these descriptions were exact playbacks of long-lost memories unearthed by electrical stimulation of the brain.

The existence of *flashbulb memories* is one piece of evidence that has been cited to support the notion that long-term memory storage may be permanent. At first glance, *flashbulb memories*, **which are thought to be unusually vivid and detailed recollections of momentous events**, provide striking examples of seemingly permanent storage (Brown & Kulik, 1977). Many adults, for instance, can remember exactly where they were, what they were doing, and how they felt when they learned of the death of a favourite celebrity such as musicians Prince or David Bowie, both in 2016, or traumatic events such as the 2001 terrorist attacks that took place in New York City and Washington, DC, on September 11, 2001. Although flashbulb memories have mostly been studied in relation to negative events, people also report flashbulb memories of positive events (Kraha & Boals, 2014). For example, Tinti and colleagues (2014) studied flashbulb memories in Italian citizens after Italy won the World Cup in 2006.

Does the evidence on flashbulb memories provide adequate support for the idea that long-term memory storage is permanent? No, research eventually showed that flashbulb memories are perhaps neither as accurate nor as special as once believed (Hirst & Phelps, 2016; Hirst et al., 2009; Schmolck, Buffalo, & Squire, 2000). Like other memories, they become less detailed and complete with time and are often inaccurate (Talarico & Rubin, 2009). Research suggests that it is not extraordinary accuracy or longevity that distinguish flashbulb memories. Rather, what makes them special is that people subjectively feel that these memories are exceptionally vivid, that they have exceptional confidence (albeit misplaced) in their memories' accuracy, and that more emotional intensity is attached to these recollections (Talarico & Rubin, 2003, 2007). So, perhaps flashbulb memories are "special," but not in the way originally envisioned.

Returning to the question at hand, the research findings on flashbulb memories conflict with the hypothesis that memory storage is permanent. Although the possibility cannot be ruled out completely, there is still no convincing evidence that memories are stored away permanently and that forgetting is all a matter of retrieval failure (Payne & Blackwell, 1998; Schacter, 1996).

How Is Knowledge Represented and Organized in Memory?

Over the years, memory researchers have wrestled endlessly with another major question relating to memory storage: How is knowledge represented and organized in memory? In other words, what forms do our mental representations of information take? Most theorists seem to agree that our mental representations probably take a variety of forms, depending on the nature of the material that needs to be tucked away in memory. Most of the theorizing to date has focused on how factual information may

Flashbulb memories are vivid and detailed recollections of momentous events. For example, many people will long remember exactly where they were and how they felt when they learned about the terrorist attacks on the World Trade Center.

Dan Howell/Shutterstock.com

concept **check** 7.1

Comparing the Memory Stores

Check your understanding of the three memory stores by filling in the blanks in the table below. The answers can be found near the back of the book in Appendix A.

Feature	Sensory memory	Short-term memory	Long-term memory
Main encoding format	*copy of input*		*Largely semantic*
Storage capacity	*Limited*		
Storage duration		*up to 20 seconds*	

be represented in memory. In this section, we'll look at a small sample of the organizational structures that have been proposed for semantic information.

Clustering and Conceptual Hierarchies

People spontaneously organize information into categories for storage in memory. This reality was apparent in a study by Bousfield (1953), who asked subjects to memorize a list of 60 words. Although presented in a scrambled order, each of the words in the list fits into one of four categories: animals, men's names, vegetables, or professions. Bousfield showed that subjects recalling this list engage in *clustering*—the tendency to remember similar or related items in groups. Even though the words were not presented in organized groups, participants tended to remember them in bunches that belonged in the same category. Thus, when applicable, factual information is routinely organized into simple categories.

Factual information is routinely represented in categories, and when possible, this information is organized into conceptual hierarchies. A *conceptual hierarchy* is a multilevel classification system based on common properties among items. A conceptual hierarchy that a person might construct for minerals can be found in Figure 7.9. According to Gordon Bower (1970), organizing information into a conceptual hierarchy can improve recall dramatically.

Schemas

Imagine that you've just visited your psychology professor's office, which is shown in the photo on page 250. Take a brief look at the photo and then cover it up. Now pretend that you want to describe your professor's office to a friend. Write down what you saw in the picture of the office.

After you finish, compare your description with the picture. Chances are, your description will include elements—books or filing cabinets, for instance—that were *not* in the office. This common phenomenon demonstrates how *schemas* can influence memory.

A *schema* is an organized cluster of knowledge about a particular object or event abstracted from previous experience with the object or event. For example, university students have schemas for what professors' offices are like. When Brewer and Treyens (1981) tested the recall of 30 subjects who had briefly visited the office shown in the photo on page 250, most subjects recalled the desks and chairs, but few recalled the wine bottle or the picnic basket, which aren't part of a typical office schema. Moreover, nine subjects in the Brewer and Treyens study falsely recalled that the office contained books. Perhaps you made the same mistake.

These results and other studies (Tuckey & Brewer, 2003) suggest that *people are more likely to remember things that are consistent with their schemas than things that are not.* Although this principle seems applicable much of the time, the inverse is also true: *People*

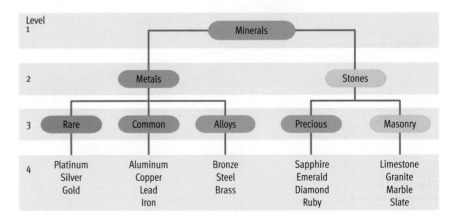

Figure 7.9

Conceptual hierarchies and long-term memory. Some types of information can be organized into a multilevel hierarchy of concepts, like the one shown here, which was studied by Bower and others (1969). They found that subjects remember more information when they organize it into a conceptual hierarchy.

Source: Reprinted from *Cognitive psychology, 1*(1), Gordon H. Bower, Organizational factors in memory, pp. 18–46. Copyright © 1970, with permission from Elsevier.

The professor's office is shown in this photo. Follow the instructions in the text to learn how Brewer and Treyens (1981) used it in a study of memory.

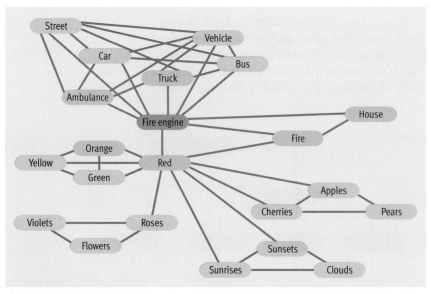

Figure 7.10

A semantic network. Much of the organization of long-term memory depends on networks of associations among concepts. In this highly simplified depiction of a fragment of a semantic network, the shorter the line linking any two concepts, the stronger the association between them. The colouration of the concept boxes represents activation of the concepts. This is how the network might look just after a person hears the words *fire engine*.

Source: Adapted from Collins, A.M., and Loftus, E.F. (1975). A spreading activation theory of semantic processing. *Psychological Review*, 82, 407–428. Copyright © by the American Psychological Association.

sometimes exhibit better recall of things that violate their schema-based expectations (Koriat, Goldsmith, & Pansky, 2000; Neuschatz et al., 2002). Information that really clashes with a schema may attract extra attention and deeper processing and thus become more memorable. For instance, if you saw a slot machine in a professor's office, you would probably remember it. In either case, it's apparent that information stored in memory is often organized around schemas (Brewer, 2000).

Semantic Networks

Of course, not all information fits neatly into conceptual hierarchies or schemas. Much knowledge seems to be organized into less systematic frameworks, called *semantic networks* (Collins & Loftus, 1975). A *semantic network* consists of nodes representing concepts, joined together by pathways that link related concepts. A small semantic network is shown in Figure 7.10. The ovals are the nodes, and the words inside the ovals are the interlinked concepts. The lines connecting the nodes are the pathways. A more detailed figure would label the pathways to show how the concepts are related to one another. However, in this instance, the relationships should be fairly clear. The length of each pathway represents the degree of association between two concepts. Shorter pathways imply stronger associations.

Semantic networks have proven useful in explaining why thinking about one word (such as *butter*) can make a closely related word (such as *bread*) easier to remember (Meyer & Schvaneveldt, 1976). According to Collins and Loftus (1975), when people think about a word, their thoughts naturally go to related words. These theorists call this process *spreading activation* within a semantic network. They assume that activation spreads out along the pathways of the semantic network surrounding the word. They also theorize that the strength of this activation decreases as it travels outward, much as ripples decrease in size as they radiate outward from a rock tossed into a pond. Consider again the semantic network shown in Figure 7.10. If subjects see the word *red*, words that are closely linked to it (such as *orange*) should be easier to recall than words that have longer links (such as *sunrises*).

Connectionist Networks and Parallel Distributed Processing (PDP) Models

Instead of taking their cue from how computers process information, *connectionist models* of memory take their inspiration from how neural networks appear to handle information. The human brain appears to depend extensively on *parallel distributed* processing—that is, simultaneous processing of the same information that is spread across networks of neurons. Based on this insight and basic findings about how neurons operate, *connectionist, or parallel distributed processing (PDP), models* assume that cognitive processes depend on patterns of activation in highly interconnected computational networks that resemble neural networks (McClelland, 2000; McClelland & Rogers, 2003; McClelland & Rumelhart, 1985; Smolensky, 1995).

A PDP system consists of a large network of interconnected computing units, or *nodes*, that operate much like neurons. These nodes may be inactive or they may send either excitatory or inhibitory signals to other units. Like an individual neuron, a specific node's level of activation reflects the weighted balance of excitatory and inhibitory inputs from many other units. Given this framework, *PDP models assert that specific memories correspond to particular patterns of activation in these networks* (McClelland, 1992). Connectionist networks bear some superficial resemblance to semantic networks, but there is a crucial difference. In semantic networks, specific nodes represent specific concepts or pieces of knowledge. In connectionist networks, a piece of knowledge is represented by a particular *pattern* of activation across an entire network. Thus, the information lies in the strengths of the *connections*, which is why the PDP approach is called *connectionism.*

Retrieval: Getting Information Out of Memory

Entering information into long-term memory is a worthy goal, but an insufficient one if you can't get the information back out again when you need it. Some theorists maintain that understanding retrieval is the key to understanding human memory (Roediger, 2000). Understanding retrieval may also be important to success in your studies. When you study for your exams, you are attempting to encode the information in such a way that it is stored in your long-term memory so that it will be there when you need it. As most of us know, however, we don't get all of the questions correct. What does this indicate? Tulving distinguished between the *availability* and *accessibility* of information in memory (Tulving & Pearlstone, 1966). You might not be able to answer a particular question because the information is unavailable (no longer present in the memory system) or because it is not accessible (present in the system but not accessible to you at the moment). The information may not be accessible because the cues you are using in your attempt to answer the question are not effective.

Using Cues to Aid Retrieval

The *tip-of-the-tongue phenomenon*—the temporary inability to remember something you know, accompanied by a feeling that it's just out of reach—is a common experience that is typically triggered by a name that one can't quite recall. Most people experience this temporary frustration about once a week, although its occurrence increases with age (Salthouse & Mandell, 2013; Schwartz & Metcalfe, 2014). However, the exact mechanisms underlying this failure are the subject of debate. A number of explanations have been proposed for this phenomenon and it continues to be the target of research interest (A.S. Brown, 2012a; Cleary & Claxton, 2015; Schwartz & Cleary, 2016).

Fortunately, memories can often be jogged with *retrieval cues*—stimuli that help gain access to memories. This was apparent when Roger Brown and David McNeill (1966) studied the tip-of-the-tongue phenomenon. They gave subjects definitions of obscure words and asked them to come up with the words. Brown and McNeill found that subjects groping for obscure words were correct in guessing the first letter of the missing word 57 percent of the time. This figure far exceeds chance and shows that partial recollections are often headed in the right direction.

Reinstating the Context of an Event

Let's test your memory: What did you have for breakfast two days ago? If you can't immediately answer, you might begin by imagining yourself sitting at the breakfast table. Trying to recall an event by putting yourself back into the context in which it occurred involves working with *context cues* to aid retrieval (Tulving & Thompson, 1973).

Context cues often facilitate the retrieval of information (Hanczakowski, Zawadzka, & Coote, 2014). Most people have experienced the effects of context cues on many occasions. For instance, when people return after a number of years to a

Key Learning Goals

▶ Explain the tip-of-the-tongue phenomenon, and understand how context cues can influence retrieval.

▶ Summarize research on the reconstructive nature of memory, and apply the concept of source monitoring to everyday memory errors.

place where they used to live, they typically are flooded with long-forgotten memories. Or consider how often you have gone from one room to another to get something (scissors, perhaps), only to discover that you can't remember what you were after. However, when you return to the first room (the original context), you suddenly recall what it was ("Of course, the scissors!"). These examples illustrate the potentially powerful effects of context cues on memory.

The value of reinstating the context of an event may account for how hypnosis *occasionally* stimulates eyewitness recall in legal investigations (Meyer, 1992). The hypnotist usually attempts to reinstate the context of the event by telling the witness to imagine being at the scene of the crime once again. Although it is widely believed by the general public that hypnosis can help people remember things that they would not normally

reality check

Misconception

Hypnosis can be used to retrieve memories of forgotten events.

Reality

Advocates of hypnosis have claimed that it can enhance recall for over a century, but the empirical evidence is quite clear. Hypnosis does not improve memory retrieval. Quite to the contrary, hypnotized subjects are more likely than others to get things wrong—and feel overconfident about their memories.

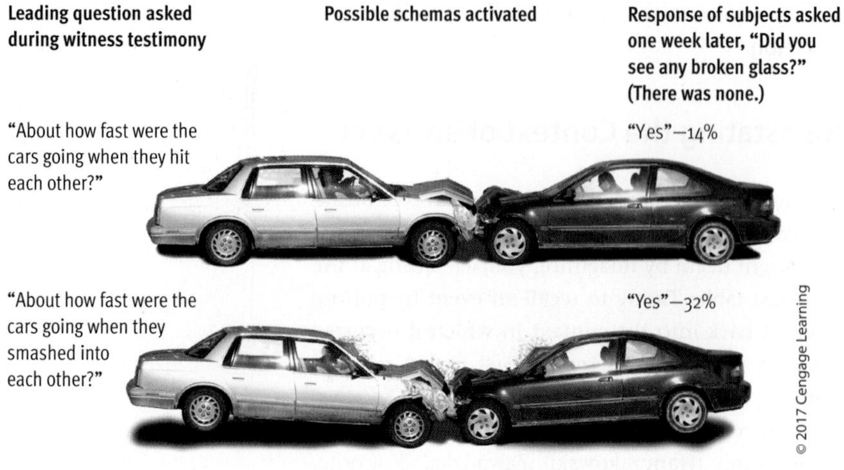

recall (Simons & Chabris, 2011), extensive research has failed to demonstrate that hypnosis can reliably enhance retrieval (Mazzoni, Heap, & Scoboria, 2010). Quite to the contrary, research suggests that hypnosis often increases individuals' tendency to report *incorrect* information (Mazzoni, Laurence, & Heap, 2014).

Reconstructing Memories

One recent survey on people's notions about memory found that 63 percent believe that when you retrieve information from long-term memory, you're able to pull up a "mental videotape" that provides an exact replay of the past (Simons & Chabris, 2011). However, countless studies have demonstrated that this is an inaccurate view of memory. This was shown many years ago by Sir Frederick Bartlett (1932), a prominent psychologist at Cambridge University. His work highlighted the reconstructive nature of memory. In reality, all memories are *reconstructions* of the past that may be distorted and may include details that did not actually occur (Gallo & Wheeler, 2013; Schacter & Loftus, 2013).

Research by Elizabeth Loftus (1979, 1992, 2005) and others on the *misinformation effect* has shown that reconstructive distortions show up frequently in eyewitness testimony. The *misinformation effect* occurs when participants' recall of an event they witnessed is altered by introducing misleading post-event information. For example, in one study, Loftus and Palmer (1974) showed participants a videotape of an automobile accident. Participants were then "grilled" as if they were providing eyewitness testimony, and biasing information was introduced. Some subjects were asked, "How fast were the cars going when they *hit* each other?" Other subjects were asked, "How fast were the cars going when they *smashed into* each other?" A week later, participants' recall of the accident was tested. They were asked whether they remembered seeing any broken glass in the accident (there was none). Subjects who had earlier been asked about the cars *smashing into* each other were more likely to "recall" broken glass. Why would they add this detail to their reconstructions of the accident? Probably because broken glass is consistent with their schemas for cars *smashing* together (see Figure 7.11). The misinformation effect, which has been replicated in countless studies (Frenda, Nichols, & Loftus, 2011), is a remarkably reliable phenomenon that "challenged prevailing views about the validity of memory" (Zaragoza, Belli, &

Leading question asked during witness testimony	Possible schemas activated	Response of subjects asked one week later, "Did you see any broken glass?" (There was none.)
"About how fast were the cars going when they hit each other?"		"Yes"—14%
"About how fast were the cars going when they smashed into each other?"		"Yes"—32%

© 2017 Cengage Learning

Figure 7.11

The misinformation effect. In an experiment by Loftus and Palmer (1974), participants who were asked leading questions in which cars were described as *hitting* or *smashing* each other were prone to recall the same accident differently one week later, demonstrating the reconstructive nature of memory.

Payment, 2007, p. 37). Indeed, the effect is so difficult to escape that even subjects who have been forewarned can be swayed by post-event misinformation (Chrobak & Zaragoza, 2013).

Studies have demonstrated that the influence of misinformation is not limited to memories of events that one has personally experienced or witnessed; it can also distort one's knowledge of basic facts (Bottoms, Eslick, & Marsh, 2010). For example, most people know that the Pacific is the largest ocean on Earth and that Thomas Edison invented the light bulb. These are facts that most people have encountered repeatedly. They should be stable memories that ought to be resistant to change. But, consider what happened when Fazio and colleagues (2013) had participants read short fictional stories that contradicted these facts by casually mentioning that the Atlantic was the largest ocean and that Benjamin Franklin invented the light bulb. Although the participants had shown correct knowledge of these and other well-known facts two weeks earlier, when they took a test of general knowledge after reading misleading stories, about 20 percent got basic facts wrong—such as indicating that Franklin invented the light bulb—even though they were explicitly warned that the fictional stories might contain factual errors. Thus, in a portion of subjects, a single, brief exposure to misinformation disrupted basic factual knowledge. Sorry to say, these findings suggest that just reading about this study might distort your own future recall of these simple facts.

Other research on the reconstructive nature of memory has demonstrated that the simple act of retelling a story can introduce inaccuracies into memory (Marsh, 2007). When people retell a story, they may streamline it, embellish the facts, exaggerate their role, and so forth. In such retellings, people may be aware that they are being a little loose with the facts (Marsh & Tversky, 2004). However,

what is interesting is that their intentional distortions can reshape their subsequent recollections of the same events. Somehow, the "real" story and the storyteller's "spin" on it begin to blend imperceptibly. So, even routine retellings of events can contribute to the malleability of memory.

Source Monitoring

The misinformation effect appears to be due, *in part*, to the unreliability of *source monitoring*—the **process of making inferences about the origins of memories**. Marcia Johnson and her colleagues (Johnson, 1996, 2006; Johnson et al., 2012) maintain that source monitoring is a crucial facet of memory retrieval that contributes to many of the mistakes that people make in reconstructing their experiences. According to Johnson, memories are not tagged with labels that specify their sources. Thus, when people pull up specific memory records, they have to make decisions *at the time of retrieval* about where the memories came from (e.g., "Did I read that in the *New York Times* or *the Peterborough Examiner*"?). Much of the time, these decisions are so easy and automatic that people make them without being consciously aware of the source-monitoring process. In other instances, however, they may consciously struggle to pinpoint the source of a memory. **A *source-monitoring error* occurs when a memory derived from one source is misattributed to another source.** For example, you might attribute something that your roommate said to your psychology professor, or something you heard from Dr. David Suzuki on *The Nature of Things* to your psychology textbook. Inaccurate memories that reflect source-monitoring errors can seem quite compelling (Kuhlmann & Bayen, 2016). People often feel quite confident about the authenticity of their assertions even though the recollections really are inaccurate (Lampinen, Neuschatz, & Payne, 1999).

Source-monitoring errors appear to be commonplace and may shed light on many interesting memory phenomena. For instance, in studies of eyewitness suggestibility, some subjects have gone so far as to insist that they "remember" seeing something that was only verbally suggested to them. Most theories have a hard time explaining how people can have memories of events that they never actually saw or experienced. But this paradox doesn't seem all that perplexing when it is explained as a source-monitoring error (Lindsay et al., 2004).

Elizabeth Loftus

"One reason most of us, as jurors, place so much faith in eyewitness testimony is that we are unaware of how many factors influence its accuracy."

Marcia K. Johnson

"Our long-term goal is to develop ways of determining which aspects of mental experience create one's sense of a personal past and one's conviction (accurate or not) that memories, knowledge, beliefs, attitudes, and feelings are tied to reality in a veridical fashion."

reality check

Misconception

Memory is like a mental videotape that can provide faithful reproductions of past events.

Reality

Countless studies in recent decades have demonstrated that memories are incomplete, distorted, fuzzy reconstructions of past events. The adjectives that best describe memory are not *exact* or *accurate*, but rather *fragile*, *fallible*, and *malleable*.

Forgetting: When Memory Lapses

Wellcome Library, London

Hermann Ebbinghaus

"Left to itself every mental content gradually loses its capacity for being revived. … Facts crammed at examination time soon vanish."

Forgetting gets "bad press" that it may not deserve. People tend to view forgetting as a failure, weakness, or deficiency in cognitive processing. Although forgetting important information *can* be extremely frustrating, some memory theorists argue that forgetting is actually adaptive. How so? Imagine how cluttered your memory would be if you never forgot anything (Storm, 2011). According to Daniel Schacter (1999), we need to forget information that is no longer relevant, such as out-of-date phone numbers, discarded passwords, lines that were memorized for a play in Grade 10, and where you kept your important papers three apartments ago. Forgetting can reduce competition among memories that can cause confusion.

Although forgetting may be adaptive in the long run, the fundamental question of memory research remains: Why do people forget information that they would like to remember? There isn't one simple answer to this question. Research has shown that forgetting can be caused by defects in encoding, storage, retrieval, or some combination of these processes.

How Quickly We Forget: Ebbinghaus's Forgetting Curve

The first person to conduct scientific studies of forgetting was Hermann Ebbinghaus. He published a series of insightful memory studies way back in 1885. Ebbinghaus studied only one subject—himself.

To give himself lots of new material to memorize, he invented *nonsense syllables*—consonant-vowel-consonant arrangements that do not correspond to words (such as BAF, XOF, VIR, and MEQ). He wanted to work with meaningless materials that would be uncontaminated by his previous learning.

Ebbinghaus was a remarkably dedicated researcher. For instance, in one study he went through over 14 000 practice repetitions, as he tirelessly memorized 420 lists of nonsense syllables (Slamecka, 1985). He tested his memory of these lists after various time intervals. Figure 7.12 shows what he found. This diagram, called a *forgetting curve*, **graphs retention and forgetting over time.** Ebbinghaus's forgetting curve shows a precipitous drop in retention during the first few hours after the nonsense syllables were memorized. Thus, he concluded that most forgetting occurs very rapidly after learning something.

That's a depressing conclusion. What is the point of memorizing information if you're going to forget it all right away? Fortunately, subsequent research showed that Ebbinghaus's forgetting curve was unusually steep (Postman, 1985). Forgetting isn't usually quite as swift or as extensive as Ebbinghaus thought. One problem was that he was working with such meaningless material. When subjects memorize more meaningful material, such as prose or poetry, forgetting curves aren't nearly as steep. Studies of how well people recall their high school classmates suggest that forgetting curves for autobiographical information are much shallower (Bahrick, 2000). Also, different methods of measuring forgetting yield varied estimates of how quickly people forget. This variation underscores the importance of the methods used to measure forgetting, the matter we turn to next.

Measures of Forgetting

To study forgetting empirically, psychologists need to be able to measure it precisely. Measures of forgetting inevitably measure retention as well. **Retention** refers **to the proportion of material retained (remembered).** In studies of forgetting, the results may be reported in terms of the amount forgotten or the amount retained. In these studies, the *retention interval* is the length of time between the presentation of materials to be remembered and the measurement of forgetting. The three principal methods used to measure forgetting are recall, recognition, and relearning (Lockhart, 1992).

Who is the current premier of Manitoba? What movie won the Academy Award for best picture last year? These questions involve recall measures of

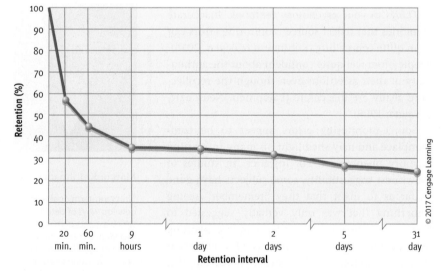

© 2017 Cengage Learning

Figure 7.12
Ebbinghaus's forgetting curve for nonsense syllables. From his experiments on himself, Ebbinghaus (1885) concluded that forgetting is extremely rapid immediately after the original learning and then levels off. Although this generalization remains true, subsequent research has shown that forgetting curves for nonsense syllables are unusually steep. (Data from Ebbinghaus, 1885)

retention. A recall measure of retention requires subjects to reproduce information on their own without any cues. If you were to take a recall test on a list of 25 words you had memorized, you would simply be told to write down on a blank sheet of paper as many of the words as you could remember.

In contrast, in a recognition test you might be shown a list of 100 words and asked to choose the 25 words that you had memorized. A *recognition measure of retention* requires subjects to select previously learned information from an array of options. Subjects not only have cues to work with, they have the answers right in front of them. In educational testing, essay questions and fill-in-the-blank questions are recall measures of retention. Multiple-choice, true–false, and matching questions are recognition measures.

If you're like most students, you probably prefer multiple-choice tests over essay tests. This preference is understandable, because evidence shows that recognition measures tend to yield higher scores than recall measures of memory for the same information (Lockhart, 2000). This reality was demonstrated many decades ago by Luh (1922), who measured subjects' retention of nonsense syllables with both a recognition test and a recall test. As Figure 7.13 shows, subjects' performance on the recognition measure was far superior to their performance on the recall measure. There are two ways of looking at this disparity between recall and recognition tests. One view is that recognition tests are especially *sensitive* measures of retention. The other view is that recognition tests are excessively *easy* measures of retention.

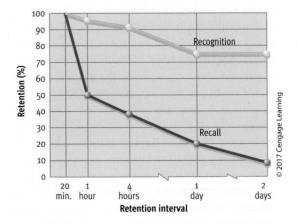

Figure 7.13
Recognition versus recall in the measurement of retention. Luh (1922) had participants memorize lists of nonsense syllables and then measured their retention with either a recognition test or a recall test at various intervals up to two days. As you can see, the forgetting curve for the recall test was quite steep, whereas the recognition test yielded much higher estimates of subjects' retention. (Data from Luh, 1922)

Actually, there is no guarantee that a recognition test will be easier than a recall test. This tends to be the case, but the difficulty of a recognition test can vary greatly, depending on the number, similarity, and plausibility of the options provided as possible answers. To illustrate, see whether you know the answer to the following multiple-choice question:

The capital of Nunavut is
a. *Umingmaktok*
b. *Rankin Inlet*
c. *Igloolik*
d. *Iqaluit*

Many students who aren't from Nunavut find this a fairly difficult question. The answer is Iqaluit. Now take a look at the next question:

The capital of Nunavut is
a. *London*
b. *New York City*
c. *Tokyo*
d. *Iqaluit*

Virtually anyone can answer this question because the incorrect options are readily dismissed. Although this illustration is a bit extreme, it shows that two recognition measures of the same information can be dramatically different in difficulty.

The third method of measuring forgetting is relearning. A *relearning* measure of retention requires a subject to memorize information a second time to determine how much time or how many practice trials are saved by having learned it before. Subjects' *savings scores* provide an estimate of their retention. Relearning measures can detect retention that is overlooked by recognition tests (Crowder & Greene, 2000).

Why We Forget?

Measuring forgetting is only the first step in the long journey toward explaining why forgetting occurs. In this section, we explore the possible causes of forgetting, looking at factors that may affect encoding, storage, and retrieval processes.

Ineffective Encoding

A great deal of forgetting may only *appear* to be forgetting. The information in question may never have been inserted into memory in the first place. Since you can't really forget something you never learned, this phenomenon is sometimes called *pseudoforgetting*. People usually assume that they know what a penny looks like, but most have actually failed to encode this information. If presented with a picture of a real quarter and some realistic fakes, however, most people would have difficulty picking out the real quarter. This is a good example of pseudoforgetting: Pseudoforgetting is usually due to *lack of attention*. Although we handle them every day, most of us do not really look at coins closely.

Even when memory codes *are* formed for new information, subsequent forgetting may be the result of ineffective or inappropriate encoding (Brown & Craik, 2000). The research on levels of processing shows that some approaches to encoding lead to more forgetting than others (Craik & Tulving, 1975). For example, if you're distracted while you read your textbooks, you may be doing little more than saying the words to yourself. This is *phonemic encoding*, which is inferior to *semantic encoding* for retention of verbal material. When you can't remember the information that you've read, your forgetting may be due to ineffective encoding.

Decay

Instead of focusing on encoding, decay theory attributes forgetting to the impermanence of memory storage. *Decay theory* **proposes that forgetting occurs because memory traces fade with time.** The implicit assumption is that decay occurs in the physiological mechanisms responsible for memories. According to decay theory, the mere passage of time produces forgetting. This notion meshes nicely with common sense views of forgetting.

As we saw earlier, decay *does* appear to contribute to the loss of information from the sensory and short-term memory stores. However, the critical task for theories of forgetting is to explain the loss of information from long-term memory. Researchers have *not* been successful in providing clear demonstrations that decay causes long-term memory forgetting (Roediger, Weinstein, & Agarwal, 2010). Not all theorists have abandoned the concept of decay, however. Based on complicated evidence relating to the neurological and molecular bases of memory, Hardt, Nader, and Nadel (2013) argue that decay processes contribute to the selective removal of some memories. They believe that decay weakens the neurobiological substrate of selected memories, and that this process unfolds primarily during sleep. It remains to be seen if this new theory will gain traction.

For many decades, the key problem for decay theory has been researchers' inability to validate its cornerstone prediction that the principal cause and strongest correlate of forgetting should be the passage of time. In studies of long-term memory, researchers have repeatedly found that the passage of time is not nearly as influential as *what happens* during the time interval. Research has shown that forgetting depends not on the amount of time that has passed since learning, but on the amount, complexity, and type of information that subjects have had to absorb *during* that period of time. The negative impact of competing information on retention is called *interference*, which we turn to next.

Interference

Interference theory **proposes that people forget information because of competition from other material.** Although demonstrations of decay in long-term memory have remained elusive, hundreds of studies have shown that interference influences forgetting (Anderson & Neely, 1996; Bjork, 1992; Bower, 2000; Jonker, Seli, & MaLeod, 2016). In many of these studies, researchers have controlled interference by varying the *similarity* between the original material given to subjects (the test material) and the material studied in the intervening period. Interference is assumed to be greatest when intervening material is most similar to the test material. Decreasing the similarity should reduce interference and cause less forgetting. This is exactly what McGeoch and McDonald (1931) found in an influential study. They had subjects memorize test material that consisted of a list of two-syllable adjectives. They varied the similarity of intervening learning by having subjects then memorize one of five lists. In order of decreasing similarity to the test material, they were synonyms of the test words, antonyms of the test words, unrelated adjectives, nonsense syllables, and numbers. Later, subjects' recall of the test material was measured.

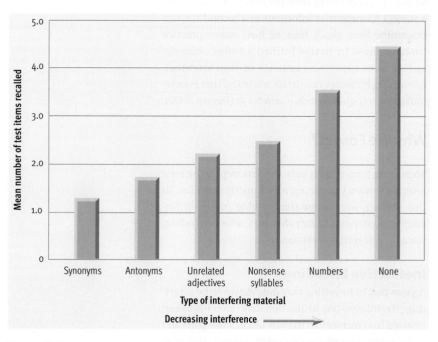

Figure 7.14

Effects of interference. According to interference theory, more interference from competing information should produce more forgetting. McGeoch and McDonald (1931) controlled the amount of interference with a learning task by varying the similarity of an intervening task. The results were consistent with interference theory. The amount of interference is greatest at the left of the graph, as is the amount of forgetting. As interference decreases (moving to the right on the graph), retention improves. (Data from McGeoch & McDonald, 1931)

Source: From Weiten. *Cengage Advantage Books: Psychology*, 9E. © 2013 South-Western, a part of Cengage, Inc. Reproduced by permission. www.cengage.com/permissions

Figure 7.14 shows that as the similarity of the intervening material decreased, the amount of forgetting also decreased—because of reduced interference.

There are two kinds of interference: *retroactive* interference and *proactive* interference (Jacoby, Hessels, & Bopp, 2001). **Retroactive interference occurs when new information impairs the retention of previously learned information.** Retroactive interference occurs between the original learning and the retest on that learning, during the retention interval (see Figure 7.15). For example, the interference manipulated by McGeoch and McDonald (1931) was retroactive interference. In contrast, *proactive interference* occurs when previously learned information interferes with the retention of new information. Proactive interference is rooted in learning that comes *before* exposure to the test material.

Retrieval Failure

People often remember things that they were unable to recall at an earlier time. This phenomenon may be obvious only during struggles with the tip-of-the-tongue phenomenon, but it happens frequently. In fact, a great deal of forgetting may be due to breakdowns in the process of retrieval.

Why does an effort to retrieve something fail on one occasion and succeed on another? That's a tough question. As we suggested earlier in our discussion of context- and state-dependent encoding, one theory is that retrieval failures may be more likely when a mismatch occurs between retrieval cues and the encoding of the information you're searching for. According to Tulving and Thomson (1973), a good retrieval cue is consistent with the original encoding of the information to be recalled. For example, if the sound of a word—its phonemic quality—was emphasized during encoding, an effective retrieval cue should emphasize the sound of the word. If the meaning of the word was emphasized during encoding, semantic cues should be best.

A general statement of the principle at work here was formulated by Tulving and Thomson.

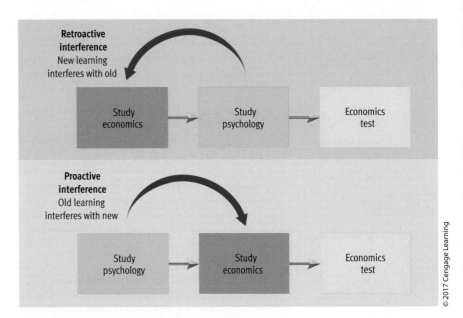

© 2017 Cengage Learning

Figure 7.15

Retroactive and proactive interference. Retroactive interference occurs when learning produces a "backward" effect, reducing recall of previously learned material. Proactive interference occurs when learning produces a "forward" effect, reducing recall of subsequently learned material. For example, if you were to prepare for an economics test and then study psychology, the interference from the psychology study would be retroactive interference. However, if you studied psychology first and then economics, the interference from the psychology study would be proactive interference. (Data fro Luh, 1922)

The *encoding specificity principle* states that the value of a retrieval cue depends on how well it corresponds to the memory code (Tulving & Thomson, 1973). This principle provides one explanation for the inconsistent success of retrieval efforts.

Motivated Forgetting

Many years ago, Sigmund Freud (1901) came up with an entirely different explanation for retrieval failures. As we noted in Chapter 1, Freud asserted that people often keep embarrassing, unpleasant, or painful memories buried in their unconscious. For example, a person who was deeply wounded by perceived slights at a childhood birthday party might suppress all recollection of that party. In his therapeutic work with patients, Freud recovered many such buried memories. He theorized that the memories were there all along, but their retrieval was blocked by unconscious avoidance tendencies.

The tendency to forget things one doesn't want to think about is called *motivated forgetting*, or to use Freud's terminology, *repression*. In Freudian theory, **repression refers to keeping distressing thoughts and feelings buried in the unconscious** (see Chapter 12). Although it is difficult to demonstrate the operation of repression in laboratory studies (Holmes, 1990), a number of experiments suggest that people don't remember anxiety-laden material as readily as emotionally neutral material, just as Freud proposed

(Guenther, 1988; Reisner, 1998). Thus, when you forget unpleasant things such as a dental appointment, a promise to help a friend move, or a term paper deadline, motivated forgetting *may* be at work.

....

concept check 7.2

Figuring Out Forgetting

Check your understanding of why people forget by identifying the probable causes of forgetting in each of the following scenarios. Choose from (a) motivated forgetting (repression), (b) decay, (c) ineffective encoding, (d) proactive interference, (e) retroactive interference, or (f) retrieval failure. You will find the answers in Appendix A.

1. Ellen can't recall the reasons for the Charlottetown Accord because she was daydreaming when it was discussed in her political science class.

2. Rufus hates his job at Taco Heaven and is always forgetting when he is scheduled to work.

3. Ray's new assistant in the shipping department is named John Cocker. Ray keeps calling him "Joe," mixing him up with the rock singer Joe Cocker.

4. Tania studied history on Sunday morning and sociology on Sunday evening. It's Monday, and she's struggling with her history test because she keeps mixing up prominent historians with influential sociologists

The Repressed Memories Controversy

Although the concept of repression has been around for a century, interest in this phenomenon has surged in recent years, thanks to a spate of prominent reports involving the return of individuals' long-lost memories of sexual abuse and other traumas during childhood. The media have been flooded with reports of adults accusing their parents, teachers, and neighbours of horrific child abuse decades earlier, based on previously repressed memories of these travesties. For the most part, these parents, teachers, and neighbours have denied the allegations. Many of them have seemed genuinely baffled by the accusations, which have torn some previously happy families apart (Gudjonsson, 2001; McHugh et al., 2004). In an effort to make sense of the charges, some accused parents have argued that their children's recollections are false memories created inadvertently by well-intentioned therapists through the power

of suggestion. This is a critical issue since we know that false memories and confessions can have great impact and can be very persuasive in legal contexts (Gorman, 2013; Kassin, 2012).

The controversy surrounding recovered memories of abuse is complex and difficult to sort out (Patihis et al., 2013). The crux of the problem is that child abuse usually takes place behind closed doors. In the absence of corroborative evidence, there is no way to reliably distinguish genuine recovered memories from false ones. A handful of recovered memory incidents have been substantiated by independent witnesses or belated admissions of guilt by the accused (Brewin, 2003, 2007; Bull, 1999; Shobe & Schooler, 2001). But in the vast majority of cases, the allegations of abuse have been vehemently denied, and independent corroboration has not been available. The issues surrounding maltreatment and memory are of great importance and have been the subject of a great deal of research (Goodman, Quas, & Ogle, 2009). What do psychologists and psychiatrists have to say about the authenticity of repressed memories? They are sharply divided on the issue.

Support for Recovered Memories

Many psychologists and psychiatrists, especially clinicians involved in the treatment of psychological disorders, largely accept recovered memories of abuse at face value (Banyard & Williams, 1999; Briere & Conte, 1993; Legault & Laurence, 2007; Skinner, 2001; Terr, 1994; Whitfield, 1995). They assert that sexual abuse in childhood is far more widespread than most people realize. For example, one large-scale Canadian survey (MacMillan et al., 1997), using a random sample of 9953 residents of Ontario, found that 12.8 percent of the females and 4.3 percent of the males reported that they had been victims of sexual abuse during childhood (see Figure 7.16).

Some psychologists and psychiatrists further assert that there is ample evidence that it is common for people to bury traumatic incidents in their unconscious (Brewin, 2012; DePrince et al., 2012). For instance, in one widely cited study, L. M. Williams (1994) followed up on 129 female children who had been brought to a hospital emergency room for treatment of sexual abuse. When interviewed approximately 17 years later about a variety of things, including their history of sexual abuse, 38 percent of the women failed to report the original incident, which Williams largely attributed to amnesia for the incident. In a study of psychiatric patients hospitalized for post-traumatic or dissociative disorders (see Chapter 15), one-third of those who reported childhood sexual abuse said that they experienced complete amnesia for the abuse at some point in their lives (Chu

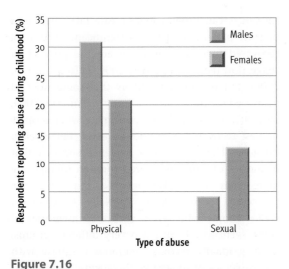

Figure 7.16

Estimates of the prevalence of childhood physical and sexual abuse. In one of the better efforts to estimate the prevalence of child abuse, MacMillan and her colleagues (1997) questioned a random sample of almost 10 000 adults living in Ontario about whether they were abused during childhood. As you can see, males were more likely to have experienced physical abuse and females were more likely to have suffered from sexual abuse. The data support the assertion that millions of people have been victimized by childhood sexual abuse, which is far from rare. (Based on data from MacMillan et al., 1997)

et al., 1999). According to Freyd (1996, 2001; Freyd, DePrince, & Gleaves, 2007), sexual abuse by a parent evokes coping efforts that attempt to block awareness of the abuse because that awareness would interfere with normal attachment processes. The clinicians who accept the authenticity of recovered memories of abuse attribute the recent upsurge in recovered memories to therapists' and clients' increased sensitivity to an issue that people used to be reluctant to discuss.

Skepticism Regarding Recovered Memories

In contrast, beginning in the 1990s, many other psychologists, especially memory researchers, have expressed skepticism about the recent upsurge of recovered memories of abuse (Kihlstrom, 2004; Loftus, 1998, 2003; Lynn & Nash, 1994; McNally, 2003, 2007; Takarangi et al., 2008). They point out that the women in the Williams (1994) study may have failed to report their earlier sexual abuse for a variety of reasons besides amnesia, including embarrassment, poor rapport with the interviewer, normal forgetfulness, or a conscious preference not to revisit painful experiences from the past (Loftus, Garry, & Feldman, 1998; Pope & Hudson, 1998). Many memory researchers are also skeptical about retrospective self-reports of amnesia—such as those seen in the Chu et al. (1999) study—because self-assessments of personal memory are often distorted

and because it is difficult to distinguish between a period when a memory was not *accessed* versus a period when a memory was not *available* due to repression (Belli et al., 1998; Schooler, 1999).

The skeptics do *not* say that people are lying about their previously repressed memories. Rather, they maintain that some suggestible people wrestling with emotional problems have been convinced by persuasive therapists that their emotional problems must be the result of abuse that occurred years before. Critics blame a minority of therapists who presumably have good intentions but who operate under the dubious assumption that virtually all psychological problems are attributable to childhood sexual abuse (Lindsay & Read, 1994; Spanos, 1994). Using hypnosis, dream interpretation, and leading questions, they supposedly prod and probe patients until they inadvertently create the memories of abuse that they are searching for (Lynn et al., 2003; Thayer & Lynn, 2006).

Psychologists who doubt the authenticity of repressed memories support their analysis by pointing to discredited cases of recovered memories (Brown, Goldstein, & Bjorklund, 2000). For example, with the help of a church counsellor, one woman recovered memories of how her minister father had repeatedly raped her, gotten her pregnant, and then aborted the pregnancy with a coat hanger; however, subsequent evidence revealed that the woman was still a virgin and that her father had had a vasectomy years before (Loftus, 1997; Testa, 1996). The skeptics also point to published case histories that clearly involved suggestive questioning and to cases in which patients have recanted recovered memories of sexual abuse after realizing that these memories were implanted by their therapists (Goldstein & Farmer, 1993; Loftus, 1994; Shobe & Schooler, 2001).

Those who question the accuracy of repressed memories also point to findings on the misinformation effect, research on source-monitoring errors, and other studies that demonstrate the relative ease of creating "memories" of events that never happened (Laney & Loftus, 2005; Lindsay et al., 2004; Loftus & Cahill, 2007; Strange, Clifasefi, & Garry, 2007). For example, working with college students, Ira Hyman and his colleagues have managed to implant recollections of fairly substantial events (such as spilling a punch bowl at a wedding, being in a grocery store when the fire sprinkler system went off, being hospitalized for an earache) in about 25 percent of their subjects, just by asking them to elaborate on events supposedly reported by their parents (Hyman, Husband, & Billings, 1995; Hyman & Kleinknecht, 1999).

In a similar vein, building on earlier work by James Deese (1959), Roediger and McDermott (1995, 2000) have devised a simple laboratory paradigm involving

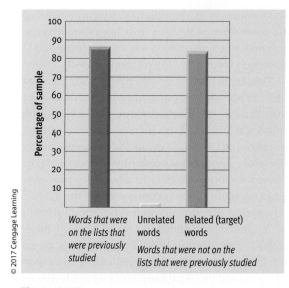

Figure 7.17

The prevalence of false memories observed by Roediger and McDermott (1995). The graph shown here summarizes the recognition test results in Study 1 conducted by Roediger and McDermott (1995). Participants correctly identified words that had been on the lists that they had studied 86 percent of the time and misidentified unrelated words that had not been on the lists only 2 percent of the time, indicating that they were paying careful attention to the task. Nonetheless, they mistakenly reported that they "remembered" related target words that were *not* on the lists 84 percent of the time—a remarkably high prevalence of false memories. (Data from Roediger & McDermott, 1995)

the learning of word lists that is remarkably reliable in producing memory illusions. In this procedure, now known as the *Deese-Roediger-McDermott (DRM) paradigm*, a series of lists of 15 words are presented to participants. They are asked to recall the words immediately after each list is presented and are given a recognition measure of their retention at the end of the session. The trick is that each list consists of a set of words (such as *bed, rest, awake, tired*) that are strongly associated with another target word that is not on the list (in this case, *sleep*). When subjects *recall* the words on each list, they remember the nonpresented target word over 50 percent of the time, and when they are given the final *recognition* test, they typically indicate that about 80 percent of the nonstudied target words were presented in the lists (see Figure 7.17). Using the DRM paradigm, false memories can be created reliably in normal, healthy participants in a matter of minutes, with no pressure or misleading information. Thus, this line of research provides a dramatic demonstration of how easy it is to get people to remember that they saw something they really didn't see (McDermott, 2007; Neuschatz et al., 2007).

Conclusions

So, what can we conclude about the recovered memories controversy? It seems pretty clear that

therapists can unknowingly create false memories in their patients and that a significant portion of recovered memories of abuse are the product of suggestion (Follette & Davis, 2009; Loftus & Davis, 2006). But it also seems likely that some cases of recovered memories are authentic (Colangelo, 2009; Ost, 2013). It is difficult to estimate what proportion of recovered memories of abuse fall in each category. That said, some evidence suggests that memories of abuse recovered through therapy are more likely to be false memories than are those recovered spontaneously (McNally & Geraerts, 2009). People who report recovered memories of abuse seem to fall into two very different groups. Some gradually recover memories of abuse with the assistance of suggestive therapeutic techniques, whereas others suddenly and unexpectedly recover memories of abuse when they encounter a relevant retrieval cue (such as returning to the scene of the abuse). A study that sought to corroborate reports of abuse from both groups found a much higher corroboration rate among those who recovered their memories spontaneously (37 percent) as opposed to those who recovered their memories in therapy (0 percent) (Geraerts, 2012).

The recovered memories controversy continues to generate heated debate (Patihis et al., 2014). One upside is that the debate has inspired a tremendous amount of research that has greatly increased our understanding of just how fragile, fallible, malleable, and subjective human memory can be (Gallo & Lampinen, 2016). Indeed, the implicit dichotomy underlying the repressed memories debate—that some memories are true, whereas others are false—is misleading and oversimplified. Research demonstrates that all human memories are imperfect reconstructions of the past that are subject to many types of distortion.

Seven Sins of Memory: How Memory Goes Wrong

Our discussion of memory thus far has highlighted several important points. Memory is key to understanding who we are and what we do. For most of us in our everyday lives our memory serves us just fine. It enables us to get through the day without major mishap, to be where we are supposed to be at the right time, to get the things done we need to get done, to know the names of the people who are most important to us, and to remember when the next psychology test will be held. In fact, memory is typically so effective that we rarely think about it. When we do reflect on it, it is often because it has failed us—it has let us down. Memory doesn't fail us only because we simply forget; sometimes our memories for events are distorted and biased.

Do any of the following failures sound familiar? You don't remember where you left your keys. You show up to class on Monday sure that it was your psychology professor who told you this week's test was postponed when it was actually your sociology professor. You can't stop thinking about what your best friend said to you last night when you had a fight, and so on. We may forget things, our recollections may be distorted, or our memory for past events might haunt us like some unwelcome visitor we cannot get rid of. People have many misconceptions about memory (Kassam et al., 2009) with regard to its strengths and its weaknesses. Memory failures strike us all. Former U.S. vice-presidential candidate Sarah Palin was taking no chances with memory failure when giving speeches and interviews during the 2008 U.S. presidential election campaign and afterward: She wrote memory cues on her palms. One well-known picture for which she was mocked shows her palm with memory prompts for three key issues—energy, tax, and lifting American spirit (Christmas, 2010).

Daniel Schacter (2001) of Harvard University, recently given an American Psychological Association Award for his Distinguished Scientific Contributions (American Psychological Association, 2012), has collated and summarized the ways that memory fails us in what he refers to as the *seven sins of memory*. These seven sins are important not only because they affect us in our daily life, but also because knowing more about them gives us insight into how memory works and perhaps give us some insight into ways to help those with disorders such as Alzheimer's disease (Schacter & Dodson, 2001).

The first three memory sins, *transience*, *absentmindedness*, and *blocking*, according to Schacter, are sins of omission in which we cannot bring the memory to mind. *Transience* is the simple weakening of a memory over time. This is what we tend to think of most often when we think about memory failure. *Absentmindedness* refers to a memory failure that is often due to a failure to pay attention because we are perhaps preoccupied with other things. Examples might be losing your keys, misplacing your flash drive, or—like cellist Yo Yo Ma—leaving your $2.5 million cello in the trunk of a New York City taxi (it was later returned to him) (Murray, 2003). *Blocking* is an often temporary problem that occurs when we fail to retrieve an item of information such as someone's name when we meet them. Of course, this is similar to what we have referred to as the tip-of-the-tongue phenomenon (see page 251).

The next four sins, *misattribution*, *suggestibility*, *bias*, and *persistence*, are sins of commission. Sins of commission are memory problems where some type of memory is present, but the memory is either "incorrect or unwanted" (Schacter, 2001, p. 5). In *misattribution*, we assign a memory to the wrong source, as in the earlier example about whether the psychology professor or the sociology professor delayed the exam (see our discussion of source monitoring on page 253). In the sin of *suggestibility* our memory is distorted because of, for example, misleading questions (see the discussion of the misinformation effect on page 252). The sin of *bias* refers to inaccuracy due to the effect of our current knowledge on our reconstruction of the past. According to Schacter, we often edit or rewrite our previous experiences: "The result can be a skewed rendering of a specific incident, or even of an extended period in our lives, which says more about how we feel *now* than about what happened *then*" (Schacter, 2001, p. 5). For example, if currently you are having trouble with your romantic partner, your memory for past events in the relationship may be disproportionately negative (Murray, 2003). The final sin, *persistence*, involves unwanted memories or recollections that you cannot forget—memories that haunt you. While we all have experience with seemingly automatic, unwanted memories and thoughts, in the extreme they can be associated with depression and post-traumatic stress disorder (see Chapter 15).

While these memory sins or failures are clearly problematic and cause discomfort and embarrassment to us, does this mean that it is accurate to call our memory system a failed system? Not at all. As we suggested at the beginning of this section, most of the time, it serves us extremely well. Even though Schacter is well known for his analysis of memory sins, he comes to the same conclusion: "I suggest that the seven sins are by-products of otherwise adaptive features of memory, a price we pay for processes and functions that serve us well in many respects" (Schacter, 2001, p. 184). Each of the seven sins has an adaptive upside. For example, the forgetting that occurs over time (*transience*) allows us to reduce the accessibility of or to discard information that is no longer relevant, such as the date of your first test in psychology (so that you can concentrate on your next test!). The reality of the seven sins of memory doesn't mean that there aren't ways to improve it. You can read more about techniques to improve your memory in the Personal Application section at the end of this chapter (see page 271).

Daniel Schacter of Harvard University is a memory researcher and neuroscientist. Among other things, he is well known for his cataloging of the seven sins of memory.

In Search of the Memory Trace: The Physiology of Memory

Key Learning Goals

▶ Distinguish between two types of amnesia, and identify the anatomical structures implicated in memory.

▶ Describe evidence on neural circuits and memory, and evidence on neurogenesis and memory.

Eric Kandel was awarded the Nobel Prize for Medicine/Physiology in 2000 for his work on the neural basis of memory.

For decades, neuroscientists have ventured forth in search of the physiological basis for memory, often referred to as the "memory trace." On several occasions scientists have been excited by new leads, only to be led down blind alleys. For example, as we noted earlier, Montreal neurosurgeon Wilder Penfield's work with electrical stimulation of the brain during surgery suggested that the cortex houses exact tape recordings of past experiences (Penfield & Perot, 1963). At the time, scientists believed that this was a major advance. Ultimately, it was not.

Similarly, James McConnell rocked the world of science when he reported that he had chemically transferred a specific memory from one flatworm to another. McConnell (1962) created a conditioned reflex (contraction in response to light) in flatworms and then transferred RNA (a basic molecular constituent of all living cells) from trained worms to untrained worms. The untrained worms showed evidence of "remembering" the conditioned reflex. McConnell boldly speculated that in the future, chemists might be able to formulate pills containing the information for Physics 201 or History 101! Unfortunately, the RNA transfer studies proved difficult to replicate (Rilling, 1996). Today, more than five decades after McConnell's "breakthrough," we are still a long way from breaking the chemical code for memory.

Investigators continue to explore a variety of leads about the physiological and neural bases for memory, using a variety of classic and more recent techniques (Rissman & Wagner, 2012). In light of past failures, these lines of research should probably be viewed with guarded optimism. But we'll look at some of the more promising approaches.

The Neural Circuitry of Memory

One line of research suggests that memory formation results in *alterations in synaptic transmission* at specific sites. According to this view, specific memories depend on biochemical changes that occur at specific synapses. Like McConnell, Eric Kandel (2001) and his colleagues have studied conditioned reflexes in a simple organism—the aplysia, a sea slug, commonly referred to as the sea hare. In research that earned a Nobel Prize for Kandel, they showed that reflex learning in the sea slug produces changes in the strength of specific synaptic connections by enhancing the availability and release of neurotransmitters at these synapses (Bailey & Kandel, 2009; Kennedy, Hawkins, & Kandel, 1992).

The aplysia is an ideal animal to examine if you are interested in the neuronal basis of behaviour. It has only 20 000 neurons as compared to our 100 billion, and its neurons are large enough to see and identify with only the naked eye (Kandel, 2008). The aplysia is distinguished by a reflex it uses to protect its external gill by withdrawing it. This reflex action is referred to as the GSWR (gill and siphon withdrawal reflex). The slug typically draws water over its gill by using its siphon. The gill is withdrawn if there is a threat or noxious stimulus. By applying a noxious stimulus to the slug's tail—a mild electrical shock—Kandel and his colleagues were able to elicit the reflex.

Once the animal is "sensitized," according to Kandel (2008), it has exhibited *implicit memory*, it has learned it is afraid—it has learned fear. (We discuss implicit and explicit memory on page 266.) Kandel found that if the shock producing the reflex was then applied to the siphon, the slug withdrew its gills more quickly than before and exhibited the reflex more quickly than unsensitized animals. Repetition was found to produce long-term memory in the aplysia. A durable memory had been produced through changes in synaptic connections (Hawkins, Lalevic, Clark, & Kandel, 1989). Kandel then went on to uncover the neurochemistry of the implicit memory or learning. Kandel believes that durable changes in synaptic transmission may be the neural building blocks of more complex memories as well (Kandel, 2006, 2008). He was convinced that the biology of the mind was one of the most critical topics in science (Kandel, 2000a, 2000b). Kandel details his thinking and research in his very readable autobiography *In Search of Memory: The Emergence of a New Science of Mind* (Kandel, 2006).

Richard F. Thompson (1989, 1992, 2013) and his colleagues have shown that specific memories may depend on *localized neural circuits* in the brain. In other words, memories may create unique, reusable pathways in the brain along which signals flow. Thompson has traced the pathway that accounts for a rabbit's memory of a conditioned eye-blink response. The key link in this circuit is a microscopic spot in the *cerebellum*, a structure in the hindbrain (see Figure 7.18).

Evidence on *long-term potentiation* also supports the idea that memory traces consist of specific neural circuits. **Long-term potentiation (LTP) is a long-lasting increase in neural excitability at synapses along a specific neural pathway.** Researchers produce LTP artificially by sending a

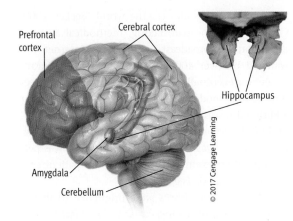

Figure 7.18
The hippocampus and memory. The hippocampus and adjacent areas in the brain are thought to play an especially central role in memory. The hippocampus appears to be responsible for the initial consolidation of memories, which are then stored in diverse and widely distributed areas of the cortex.

burst of high-frequency electrical stimulation along a neural pathway, but theorists suspect that natural events produce the same sort of potentiated neural circuit when a memory is formed (Abraham, 2006; Lynch, 2004; Sweatt, 2009). LTP appears to involve changes in both presynaptic (sending) and postsynaptic (receiving) neurons in neural circuits in the hippocampus (Bi & Poo, 2001). The evidence on LTP has inspired promising work on the development of drugs that might enhance memory in humans (Lynch & Gall, 2006). Of course, research in this area confirms the ideas proposed by McGill psychologist Donald Hebb (1949; reviewed in Chapters 1 and 3), who developed the *Hebbian learning rule* laying out the effects of neurons repeatedly stimulating other neurons (Sejnowski & Tesauro, 1989).

More recent research suggests that the process of *neurogenesis*—the formation of new neurons—may contribute to the sculpting of neural circuits that underlie memory (Koehl & Abrous, 2011). As we noted in Chapter 3, scientists have discovered that new brain cells are formed constantly in the *dentate gyrus* of the *hippocampus* (Drew, Fusi, & Hen, 2013; Leuner & Gould, 2010). Animal studies show that manipulations that suppress neurogenesis lead to memory impairments on many types of learning tasks, and conditions that increase neurogenesis are associated with enhanced learning on many tasks (Leuner, Gould, & Shors, 2006). According to Becker and Wojtowicz (2007), newly formed neurons are initially more excitable than mature neurons, so they may be more readily recruited into new neural circuits corresponding to memories. Moreover, neurogenesis provides the brain with a supply of neurons

that vary in age and these variations may somehow allow the brain to "time-stamp" some memories. The theorizing about how neurogenesis contributes to memory encoding is highly speculative (Jessberger, Aimone, & Gage, 2009), but research on neurogenesis is an exciting new line of investigation.

The Anatomy of Memory

Cases of *organic amnesia*—extensive memory loss due to head injury—are another source of clues about the physiological bases of memory (Mayes, 1992). There are two basic types of amnesia: retrograde and anterograde (see Figure 7.19). *Retrograde amnesia* involves the loss of memories for events that occurred prior to the onset of amnesia. For example, a 25-year-old gymnast who sustains a head trauma might find the prior three years, or seven years, or her entire lifetime erased. *Anterograde amnesia* involves the loss of memories for events that occur after the onset of amnesia. For instance, after her accident, the injured gymnast might suffer impaired ability to remember people she meets, where she has parked her car, and so on.

The study of anterograde amnesia has proven to be an especially rich source of information about the brain and memory. One well-known case that we referred to in Chapters 1 and 3, that of a man referred to as H.M., has been followed by McGill's Brenda Milner and her colleagues since 1953 (Casey, 2016; Corkin, 1984; Milner, Corkin, & Teuber, 1968; Scoville & Milner, 1957).

H.M. had a relatively normal childhood until, on his 16th birthday, he suffered his first of many grand mal seizures (Schaffhausen, 2007). By 1953 he was having as many as 11 epileptic seizures a

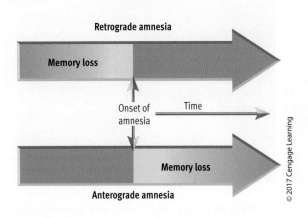

Figure 7.19
Retrograde versus anterograde amnesia. In retrograde amnesia, memory for events that occurred prior to the onset of amnesia is lost. In anterograde amnesia, memory for events that occur subsequent to the onset of amnesia suffers.

Montreal Neurological Institute

Brenda Milner

"Some effects of temporal lobe lesions in man are hard to reconcile with any unitary-process theory of memory."

McGill researcher Brenda Milner was a co-winner of the 2005 Gairdner Award, along with Endel Tulving of the University of Toronto. The Gairdner Award is a prestigious international bio-medical award.

week and he needed some type of intervention. He had surgery to relieve debilitating epileptic seizures in 1953. Unfortunately, the surgery inadvertently wiped out most of his ability to form long-term memories. H.M.'s short-term memory remained fine, but he had no recollection of anything that happened after 1953 (other than about the most recent 20–30 seconds of his life). He didn't recognize the doctors treating him and he couldn't remember routes to and from places. He could read a magazine story over and over, thinking he was reading it for the first time each time. He couldn't remember what he did the previous day, let alone what he had done decades earlier. He couldn't even recognize current photos of himself, despite having looked in the mirror every day, as aging had changed his appearance considerably. Although he could not form new long-term memories, H.M.'s intelligence remained intact. He could care for himself (around his own home), carry on complicated conversations, and solve crossword puzzles. H.M.'s misfortune provided a golden opportunity for memory researchers.

In the decades after his surgery, over 100 researchers have studied various aspects of his memory performance, leading to several major discoveries about the nature of memory (Maugh, 2008). As one scientist put it in commenting on H.M., "More was learned about memory by research with just one patient than was learned in the previous 100 years of research on memory" (Miller, 2009). After his death, H.M.'s brain was donated to a lab at the University of California, San Diego. It was subjected to extensive brain imaging and then one year after his death his brain was cut into thousands of thin slices for further

study by scientists all over the world (Becker, 2009; Carey, 2009). The painstaking, methodical 53-hour dissection was broadcast live over the Internet and watched by over 400 000 people. The meticulous dissection eventually led to the creation of a three-dimensional model of H.M.'s brain that should foster additional research (Annese et al., 2014). Named H. M. in order to protect his privacy while he was alive, his real name was Henry Molaison, and he was perhaps the most examined and important patient ever in neuroscience (LaFee, 2009).

H.M.'s memory losses were originally attributed to the removal of his *hippocampus* (see Figure 7.18), although theorists now understand that other nearby structures that were removed also contributed to H.M.'s dramatic memory deficits (Delis & Lucas, 1996). Based on decades of additional research, scientists now believe that the entire *hippocampal region* and the adjacent areas in the cortex are critical for many types of long-term memory (Zola & Squire, 2000). Many scientists now refer to this broader memory complex as the *medial temporal lobe memory system* (Shrager & Squire, 2009). Given its apparent role in long-term memory, it's interesting to note that the hippocampal region is one of the first areas of the brain to sustain significant damage in the course of Alzheimer's disease, which produces severe memory impairment in many people, typically after age 65 (Shrager & Squire, 2009; see Chapter 11).

Do these findings mean that memories are stored in the hippocampal region and adjacent areas? Probably not. Many theorists believe that the hippocampal region plays a key role in the *consolidation* of memories (Alvarez & Squire, 1994; Dudai, 2004; Gluck & Myers, 1997). *Consolidation* is a hypothetical

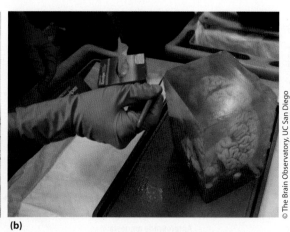

(a)   **(b)**   **(c)**

To protect his privacy, H.M. was identified only by his initials for over 50 years. After his death it was revealed that his name was Henry Molaison. He is shown as a young man in (a). His death triggered a complex, multifaceted team effort, orchestrated by Suzanne Corkin of the Massachusetts Institute of Technology, to preserve, image, and dissect the brain of the most important research subject in the history of neuroscience. His brain is shown in a mould of gelatin in (b). The challenge of slicing Molaison's brain into razor-thin sections for preservation and digital imaging was allocated to Jacob Annese of the University of California, San Diego, who spent years preparing for the delicate task. Annese is shown looking at a mounted slide of a brain slice in (c). The digital atlas of Molaison's brain will reveal the exact boundaries of his surgical lesions. This information will permit scientists to analyze the precise relations between his brain damage and 50 years of data on his memory performance.

Photograph of H.M. by Suzanne Corkin. Copyright © Suzanne Corkin, used courtesy of Suzanne Corkin and used by permission of The Wylie Agency LLC.

© The Brain Observatory, UC San Diego

© The Brain Observatory, UC San Diego

process involving the gradual conversion of information into durable memory codes stored in long-term memory. According to this view, memories are consolidated in the hippocampal region and then stored in diverse and widely distributed areas of the cortex (Eichenbaum, 2004; Markowitsch, 2000). This setup allows new memories to become independent of the hippocampal region and to gradually be integrated with other memories already stored in various areas of the cortex (Frankland & Bontempi, 2005). Interestingly, more recent research suggests that much of the consolidation process may unfold while people sleep (Rascmany, Conway, & Demeter, 2010; Stickgold & Walker, 2005).

Even after consolidation, however, memories may be subject to modification, primarily when they are reactivated. Studies suggest that when consolidated memories are retrieved, the reactivated memories are temporarily returned to an unstable state, from which they must be restabilized through a process called *reconsolidation* (Hardt, Einarsson, & Nader, 2010). During reconsolidation, depending on what happens, the memories may be weakened, strengthened, or updated to take into account more recent information (Schwabe, Nader, & Pruessner, 2014). This dynamic flexibility is thought to make long-term memory more adaptive than it would be if memories were etched in concrete, but it is important to note that the updating process can introduce distortions (St. Jacques & Schacter, 2013). Hence, even the neural architecture of long-term memory seems to be inherently reconstructive.

As you can see, a variety of biochemical processes, neural circuits, and anatomical structures have been implicated as playing a role in memory. Looking for the physiological basis for memory is only slightly less daunting than looking for the physiological basis for thought itself.

Systems and Types of Memory

Some theorists believe that evidence on the physiology of memory is confusing because investigators are unwittingly probing into several distinct memory systems that have different physiological bases. A number of research findings inspired this view, foremost among them being the discovery of *implicit memory*. Let's look at this perplexing phenomenon.

Implicit versus Explicit Memory

As noted earlier, patients with anterograde amnesia often appear to have no ability to form long-term memories. If they're shown a list of words and subsequently given a test of retention, their performance is miserable. However, different findings emerge when "implicit" techniques are used to measure their memory indirectly. For instance, they might be asked to work on a word recognition or completion task that is not presented as a measure of retention. In this task, they are shown fragments of words (e.g., _ss_ss_ for *assassin*) and are asked to complete the fragments with the first appropriate word that comes to mind. The series of word fragments includes ones that correspond to words on a list they saw earlier. In this situation, the amnesiac subjects respond with words that were on the list just as frequently as normal subjects who also saw the initial list (Schacter, Chiu, & Ochsner, 1993). Thus, the amnesiacs *do* remember words from the list. However, when asked, they don't even remember having been shown the list.

One of the issues that has been raised in this literature concerns the durability of our implicit memories. In fact, research has suggested that they are quite durable (Maylor, 1998), in their effects, often lasting much longer than our explicit memories for such events (Mitchell & Brown, 1988; Sloman et al., 1988). Thus, our implicit memory for events can continue to affect our behaviour long after our explicit/conscious memory for the events that created them has deteriorated (Tulving, Schacter, & Stark, 1982). But, how long is long in this context? Could our implicit memories continue to have effects even decades later? This question was examined in our Featured Study by David Mitchell.

FEATURED STUDY

Nonconscious priming after 17 years: Invulnerable implicit memory?

Description
In this research, the author examines the durability of implicit memory.

Investigator
Mitchell, D. (2006). *Psychological Science, 17*(11), 925–929.

The demonstration of long-term retention in amnesiacs who previously appeared to have no long-term memory shocked memory experts when it was first reported by Warrington and Weiskrantz (1970).

However, this surprising finding has been replicated in many subsequent studies. This phenomenon has come to be known as *implicit memory*. **Implicit memory is apparent when retention is exhibited on a task that does not require intentional remembering.** Implicit memory is contrasted with *explicit memory*, **which involves intentional recollection of previous experiences.** According to Kandel (2008), three characteristics serve to distinguish implicit and explicit memory. First, they differ in the types of knowledge stored—mostly perceptual and motor skills in implicit memory and facts and events in explicit memory. Implicit memories though are not restricted to perceptual or procedural memories. Second, the primary sites in the brain where storage takes place differ—reflex pathways; the cerebellum for implicit memory and the hippocampus and temporal lobe for explicit memory. Third, there are differences in the recall strategies used in accessing or using the information; they are conscious and deliberate for explicit memory but unconscious or unintentional for implicit memories. While we may intentionally try to remember the name of our psychology professor (explicit memory), our use of implicit memories is not the result of conscious retrieval. Thus, we may not be able to remember the name when asked by a friend. But our implicit memory can still affect us. But how can we assess whether such implicit memories actually exist? The effects of implicit memories are commonly inferred from their effects on tasks such as the word completion task referred to earlier (e.g., _ss_ss__ for *assassin*).

Is implicit memory peculiar to people suffering from amnesia? No. When normal subjects are exposed to material and their retention of it is measured indirectly, they, too, show implicit memory (Schacter, 1987, 1989). To draw a parallel with everyday life, implicit memory is simply incidental, unintentional remembering (Mandler, 1989). People frequently remember things that they didn't deliberately store in memory. For example, you might recall the colour of a jacket that your professor wore yesterday. Likewise, people remember things without deliberate retrieval efforts. For instance, you might be telling someone about a restaurant, which somehow reminds you of an unrelated story about a mutual friend.

Research has uncovered many interesting differences between implicit and explicit memory (May, Hasher, & Fong, 2005; Reder, Park, & Kieffaber, 2009; Roediger, 1990; Smith et al., 2014; Tulving & Schacter, 1990). Explicit memory is conscious, is accessed directly, and can best be assessed with recall or recognition measures of retention. Implicit memory is unconscious, must be accessed indirectly, and can best be assessed with variations on relearning (savings) measures of retention. Implicit memory is largely unaffected by amnesia, age, the administration of certain drugs (such as alcohol), the length of the retention interval, and manipulations of interference. In contrast, explicit memory is affected very much by all of these factors.

Some theorists think these differences are found because implicit and explicit memory rely on *different cognitive processes* in encoding and retrieval (Graf & Gallie, 1992; Jacoby, 1988; Roediger, 1990). However, many other theorists argue that the differences exist because implicit and explicit memory are handled by *independent memory systems* (Schacter, 1992, 1994; Squire, 1994). These independent systems are referred to as *declarative* and *procedural memory*.

Declarative versus Nondeclarative Memory

Many theorists have suggested that people have separate memory systems for different kinds of information (see Figure 7.20). The most basic division of memory into distinct systems contrasts *declarative*

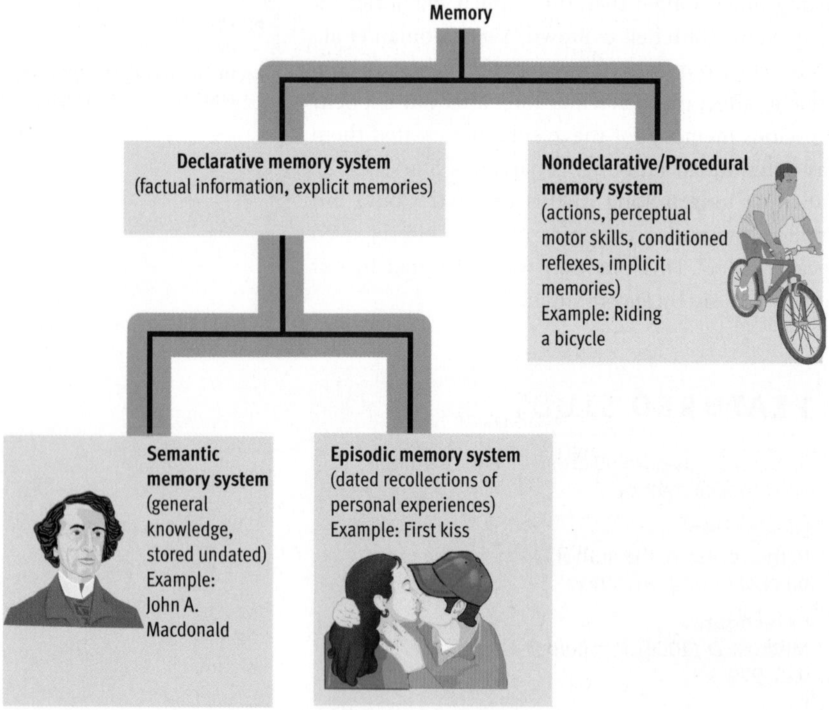

Memory

Declarative memory system
(factual information, explicit memories)

Nondeclarative/Procedural memory system
(actions, perceptual motor skills, conditioned reflexes, implicit memories)
Example: Riding a bicycle

Semantic memory system
(general knowledge, stored undated)
Example: John A. Macdonald

Episodic memory system
(dated recollections of personal experiences)
Example: First kiss

Figure 7.20
Theories of independent memory systems. There is some evidence that different types of information are stored in separate memory systems, which may have distinct physiological bases. The diagram shown here, which blends the ideas of several theorists, is an adaptation of Larry Squire's (1987) scheme. Note that implicit and explicit memory are not memory systems. They are observed behavioural phenomena that appear to be handled by different hypothetical memory systems (the procedural and declarative memory systems), which cannot be observed directly.

memory with *nondeclarative* or *procedural memory* (Squire 2004, 2009; Winograd, 1975). The *declarative memory* system handles factual information. It contains recollections of words, definitions, names, dates, faces, events, concepts, and ideas. The *nondeclarative or procedural memory* system houses memory for actions, skills, operations, and conditioned responses. It contains *procedural* memories of how to execute such actions as riding a bike, typing, and tying one's shoes. To illustrate the distinction, if you know the rules of tennis (the number of games in a set, scoring, and such), this factual information is stored in declarative memory. If you remember how to hit a serve and swing through a backhand, these perceptual-motor skills are stored in procedural memory. The nondeclarative system also includes the memory base for conditioned reactions based on previous learning, such as a person's tensing up in response to the sound of a dental drill.

Support for the distinction between declarative and nondeclarative memory comes from evidence that the two systems seem to operate somewhat differently (Johnson, 2013; Squire, Knowlton, & Musen, 1993). For example, the recall of factual information generally depends on conscious, effortful processes, whereas memory for conditioned reflexes is largely automatic, and memories for skills often require little effort and attention (Johnson, 2003). People execute perceptual-motor tasks—such as playing the piano or typing—with little conscious awareness of what they're doing. In fact, performance on such tasks sometimes deteriorates if people think too much about what they're doing. Another disparity is that the memory for skills—such as typing and bike riding—doesn't decline much over long retention intervals, whereas declarative memory is more vulnerable to forgetting.

The notion that declarative and procedural memories are separate is supported by certain patterns of memory loss seen in amnesiacs. In many cases, declarative memory is severely impaired, while procedural memory is left largely intact (Mulligan & Besken, 2013). For example, H.M., the victim of amnesia discussed earlier, was able to learn and remember new motor skills, even though he couldn't remember what he looked like as he aged. The sparing of procedural memory in H.M. provided crucial evidence for the distinction between declarative and nondeclarative memory. The finding also suggested that different brain structures may be involved in the two types of memory. Indeed, decades of research have led to progress toward identifying the neural bases for declarative versus nondeclarative memory (Eichenbaum, 2013).

Photo by Cameron Spencer/Getty Images

Research suggests that memory for perceptual-motor skills, such as the skilled manoeuvres that make two-time Olympic gold medalist (in 2010 and 2014) and Quebec native Alexandre Bilodeau the world's best male freestyle skier, are stored in the procedural (nondeclarative) memory system. In contrast, memory for factual information, such as the rules of freestyle skiing, are thought to be stored in the declarative memory system.

Semantic versus Episodic Memory

As we discussed at the beginning of the chapter, Endel Tulving (1986, 2002; Tulving & Szpunar, 2009) has further subdivided declarative memory into episodic and semantic memory (see Figure 7.20). Both contain factual information, but episodic memory contains *personal facts* and semantic memory contains *general facts* (Mayes & Roberts, 2001; Tulving, 2001). The *episodic memory system* is made up of chronological, or temporally dated, recollections of personal experiences. Episodic memory is a record of things you've done, seen, and heard—it serves to associate the stimuli you have experienced with the personal context in which you were exposed to them (Yim, Denni, & Sloutsky, 2013). It includes information about *when* you did these things, saw them, or heard them. It contains recollections about being in a school play, visiting the Parliament buildings in Ottawa, seeing the Pixies in concert, or going to see the long-awaited final episode of the *Harry Potter* film series as part of a field trip with your school classmates.

While most of us frequently have trouble remembering specific events in our past and wish we had a better memory, what do you think it would be like to be able to remember almost everything that has ever happened to you and to have these memories unintentionally intrude on what you are trying to do now? This is the case for a woman named "AJ" who was born in 1965. Her episodic memory is so powerful that it "dominates" her waking life (Parker, Cahill, & McGaugh, 2006). According to her own account, it's a burden:

> *My memory has ruled my life…. There is no effort to it…. I want to know why I remember everything…. It's like a running movie that never stops…. I'll be talking to someone and seeing something else…. Like we're sitting here talking and I'm talking to you and in my head I'm thinking about something that happened to me in December 1982, it was a Friday, I started to work at G's (a store)…. When I hear a date, I see it, the day, the month, the year…. I see it as I saw it that day…. it's a burden. (Parker et al., 2006, p. 35)*

AJ seems to be able to accurately remember almost everything that happened to her, especially since she was 14 years old. What a great thing to have this memory of her experiences, right? This superior autobiographical memory did not help her in school; she was a mediocre student. It also did not help her in her career; she has spent the past few years in a series of temporary jobs. She has suffered from several psychological disorders because of her unrelenting memory. Her autobiographical memory was so unique that the psychologists who did research on her memory gave it a new term: *hyperthymestic syndrome* (Parker et al., 2006). While she was known as "AJ" in the scientific community for years, because of the publication of her autobiography (Price, 2008), we now know that her real name is Jill Price.

While AJ's experiences are very unusual, for most of us our episodic memory is critical. Episodic memory is important to us in terms of keeping a record of our personal experiences. It is important to us in other ways too. For example, it affords us the opportunity for time travel (Tulving, 2002). In travelling through time, we use our episodic memories to simulate what might happen in the future, we "project ourselves into the future based on what we remember from the past" (Schacter & Addis, 2007c, p. 27). One of the deficits that accompanies memory loss when we age is the fact that we tend to remember the past and imagine what might happen to us in the future in "less episodic detail" (Schacter, Gaesser, & Addis, 2013).

The *semantic memory* system contains general knowledge that is not tied to the time when the information was learned. Semantic memory contains information such as Christmas is December 25, dogs have four legs, and Saskatoon is located in Saskatchewan. You probably don't remember when you learned these facts (McNamara, 2013). Information like this is usually stored undated. The distinction between episodic and semantic memory can be better appreciated by drawing an analogy to books: Episodic memory is like an autobiography, while semantic memory is like an encyclopedia.

Some studies suggest that episodic and semantic memory may have distinct neural bases (Moscovitch, Cabeza, Winocur, & Nadel, 2016; Schacter, Wagner, & Buckner, 2000; Tulving, 2002). For instance, some amnesiacs forget mostly personal facts, while their recall of general facts is largely unaffected (Szpunar & McDermott, 2009). Also consistent with this distinction is the case of patient K.C., to whom we referred earlier. K.C. retained much of his general knowledge of the world after suffering head trauma in an accident but was unable to remember any personally experienced events (Rosenbaum et al., 2005). However, debate continues about the neural substrates of episodic and semantic memory (Barba et al., 1998; Wiggs, Weisberg, & Martin, 1999).

Some of our specific memories represent a combination of episodic and semantic memories (Conway & Williams, 2008), and these *autobiographical memories* have been the subject of a great deal of research activity (Holland & Kensinger, 2010; Koppel & Rubin, 2016; Willoughby, Desrosher, Levine, & Rovet, 2012). According to Conway and Williams (2008), autobiographical memories are constructive in nature, and represent an act of remembering where episodic and semantic long-term memories are "brought together in an act of remembering where they form a specific memory" (p. 893) about your life. They enable us to know who we are now, who we were in the past, and who we might yet become.

Prospective versus Retrospective Memory

A 1984 paper with a clever title, "Remembering to Do Things: A Forgotten Topic" (Harris, 1984), introduced yet another distinction between types of memory: *prospective memory* versus *retrospective memory* (see Figure 7.21). *Prospective memory* involves remembering to perform actions in the future. Examples of prospective memory tasks include remembering to walk the dog, to call someone, to grab the tickets for the big game, and to turn off your lawn sprinkler. In contrast, *retrospective memory* involves remembering events from the past or previously learned information. Retrospective memory is at work when you try to recall who won the Stanley Cup last year,

Dan Tuffs/Getty Images

Jill Price suffered from a memory disorder referred to as hyperthymestic syndrome, which caused her to be haunted by her episodic memories.

Courtesy of Endel Tulving

Endel Tulving

"Memory systems constitute the major subdivisions of the overall organization of the memory complex. … An operating component of a system consists of a neural substrate and its behavioral or cognitive correlates."

University of Toronto researcher Endel Tulving was co-winner of the 2005 Gairdner Award, along with Brenda Milner of McGill University.

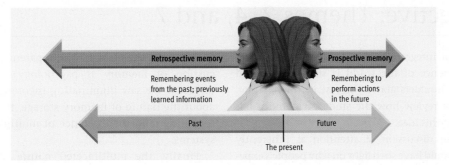

Figure 7.21
Retrospective versus prospective memory. Most memory research has explored the dynamics of *retrospective memory*, which focuses on recollections from the past. However, *prospective memory*, which requires people to remember to perform actions in the future, also plays an important role in everyday life.

when you reminisce about your high school days, or when you try to recall what your professor said in a lecture last week. A key difference between retrospective and prospective memory is that in the latter no one prompts the individual to remember the intended action. Thus, one needs to *remember to remember* (Smith, 2016). However, experiments demonstrate that it is easy to *forget to remember*, especially when one is confronted by interruptions and distractions. Although our examples of prospective memory involve relatively trivial tasks, failures of prospective memory can potentially have serious consequences. Dismukes (2012) discusses what can happen when prospective memory goes awry in the workplace. For example, it appears that several airline disasters have been attributable to pilots forgetting to complete intended actions. In a similar vein,

medical errors that lead to negative consequences for hospital patients often involve lapses in following through on intentions. Research indicates that sleep deprivation tends to increase prospective memory failures, which may contribute to major mistakes in aviation, medicine, and other work areas where safety is of paramount importance (Grundgeiger, Bayen, & Horn, 2014).

People vary considerably in their ability to successfully carry out prospective memory tasks. Individuals who appear deficient in prospective memory are often characterized as "absentminded." Research suggests that older adults are somewhat more vulnerable to problems with prospective memory than younger people are, although the findings are complicated and not entirely consistent (Niedźwieńska & Barzykowski, 2012).

concept **check** 7.3

Recognizing Various Types of Memory

Check your understanding of the various types of memory discussed in this chapter by matching the definitions below with the following: (a) declarative memory, (b) episodic memory, (c) explicit memory, (d) implicit memory, (e) long-term memory, (f) procedural memory, (g) prospective memory, (h) retrospective memory, (i) semantic memory, (j) sensory memory, and (k) short-term memory. The answers can be found in Appendix A.

_____ **1.** Memory for factual information.

_____ **2.** An unlimited capacity store that can hold information over lengthy periods of time.

_____ **3.** The preservation of information in its original sensory form for a brief time, usually only a fraction of a second.

_____ **4.** Type of memory apparent when retention is exhibited on a task that does not require intentional remembering.

_____ **5.** Chronological, or temporally dated, recollections of personal experiences.

_____ **6.** The repository of memories for actions, skills, operations, and conditioned responses.

_____ **7.** General knowledge that is not tied to the time when the information was learned.

_____ **8.** Remembering to perform future actions.

_____ **9.** A limited-capacity store that can maintain unrehearsed information for about 20 seconds.

Putting It in Perspective: Themes 2, 4, and 7

One of our integrative themes—the idea that people's experience of the world is subjective—stood head and shoulders above the rest in this chapter. Let's briefly review how the study of memory has illuminated this idea.

First, our discussion of attention as inherently selective should have shed light on why people's experience of the world is subjective. To a great degree, what you see in the world around you depends on where you focus your attention. This is one of the main reasons that two people can be exposed to the "same" events and walk away with entirely different perceptions. Second, the reconstructive nature of memory should further explain people's tendency to view the world with a subjective slant. When you observe an event, you don't store an exact copy of the event in your memory. Instead, you store a rough, "bare bones" approximation of the event that may be reshaped as time goes by.

A second theme that was apparent in our discussion of memory is psychology's theoretical diversity. We saw illuminating theoretical debates about the nature of memory storage, the causes of forgetting, and the existence of multiple memory systems.

Finally, the multifaceted nature of memory demonstrated once again that behaviour is governed by multiple causes. For instance, your memory of a specific event may be influenced by your attention to it, your level of processing, your elaboration, your exposure to interference, how you search your memory store, how you reconstruct the event, and so forth. Given the multifaceted nature of memory, it should come as no surprise that there are many ways to improve memory. We discuss a variety of strategies in the Personal Application section.

Improving Everyday Memory

Key Learning Goals

▶ Discuss the importance of rehearsal, distributed practice, and interference in efforts to improve everyday memory.

▶ Discuss the value of deep processing, good organization, and mnemonic devices in efforts to improve everyday memory.

Mnemonic devices are methods used to increase the recall of information. They have a long history. One of the mnemonic devices covered in this Application—the method of loci—was described in Greece as early as 86–82 b.c.e. (Yates, 1966). Mnemonic devices were much more important in ancient times than they are today. In ancient Greece and Rome, for instance, paper and pencils were not readily available for people to write down things they needed to remember, so they had to depend heavily on mnemonic devices.

Are mnemonic devices the key to improving one's everyday memory? No. Mnemonic devices can clearly be helpful in some situations (Wilding & Valentine, 1996), but they are not a panacea. They can be difficult to use and difficult to apply to many everyday situations. Most books and training programs designed to improve memory probably overemphasize mnemonic techniques (Searleman & Herrmann, 1994). Although less exotic strategies such as increasing rehearsal, engaging in deeper processing, and organizing material are more crucial to everyday memory, we will discuss some popular mnemonics as we proceed through this Application.

Engage in Adequate Rehearsal

Practice makes perfect, or so you've heard. In reality, practice is not likely to guarantee perfection, but it usually leads to improved retention. Studies show that retention improves with increased rehearsal (Weaver, 2010). This improvement presumably occurs because rehearsal helps to transfer information into long-term memory. Although the benefits of practice are well known, people have a curious tendency to overestimate their knowledge of a topic and how well they will perform on a subsequent memory test of this knowledge (Koriat & Bjork, 2005). That's why it is a good idea to informally test yourself on information that you think you have mastered before confronting a real test.

In addition to checking your mastery, research suggests that testing actually enhances retention, a phenomenon dubbed the *testing effect* or *test-enhanced learning* (Pyc, Agarwal, & Roediger, 2014). Studies have shown that taking a test on material increases performance on a subsequent test even more than studying or rereading for an equal amount of time does. The testing effect has been seen across a wide range of different types of content, and the benefits grow as the retention interval gets longer (Pyc et al., 2014). The favourable effects of testing are enhanced if participants are provided feedback on their test performance (Kornell & Metcalfe, 2014). Studies have demonstrated that the laboratory findings on test-enhanced learning replicate in real-world educational settings (McDermott et al., 2014). Moreover, the testing effect is not limited to rote learning; it can enhance in-depth meaningful learning, as well (Karpicke & Blunt, 2011). Better yet, research suggests that testing improves not just the retention of information, but also the *application* of that information in new contexts (S. K. Carpenter, 2012). Unfortunately, given the recent nature of this discovery, relatively few students are aware of the value of testing in retention (Karpicke, 2012).

Why is testing so beneficial? The key appears to be that testing forces students to engage in effortful retrieval of information, which promotes future retention (Roediger et al., 2010). Indeed, even *unsuccessful* retrieval efforts can enhance retention (Kornell, Hays, & Bjork, 2009). In any event, self-testing appears to be an excellent memory tool.

One other point is worth mentioning. If you are memorizing some type of list, be aware of the serial-position effect, which is often observed when subjects are tested on their memory of lists (Murdock, 2001). The *serial-position effect* occurs when subjects show better recall for items at the beginning and end of a list than for items in the middle (see Figure 7.22). The reasons for the serial-position effect are complex and need not concern us, but its pragmatic implications are clear: If you need to learn a list, allocate extra practice trials to items in the middle of the list and check your memorization of those items very carefully.

Schedule Distributed Practice and Minimize Interference

Let's assume that you need to study nine hours for an exam. Should you cram all your studying into one nine-hour period (massed practice)? Or is it better to distribute your study among, say, three-hour periods on successive days (distributed practice)? The evidence indicates that retention tends to be greater after distributed practice than after massed practice (Kornell et al., 2010; Roher & Taylor, 2006). Moreover, a recent review of over 300 experiments (Cepeda et al., 2006) showed that the longer the retention interval between studying and testing, the greater the advantage for massed practice (see Figure 7.23). The same review concluded that the longer the retention interval, the longer the optimal "break" between practice trials. When an upcoming test is more than two days

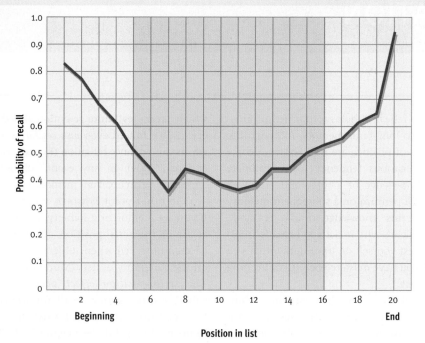

Figure 7.22
The serial-position effect. After learning a list of items to remember, people tend to recall more of the items from the beginning and the end of the list than from the middle, producing the characteristic U-shaped curve shown here. This phenomenon is called the *serial-position effect*.

Source: Adapted from Rundus, D. (1971). Analysis of rehearsal processes in free recall. *Journal of Experimental Psychology*, 89, 63–77. Copyright © 1971 by the American Psychological Association. Adapted by permission of the author. / © 2017 Cengage Learning

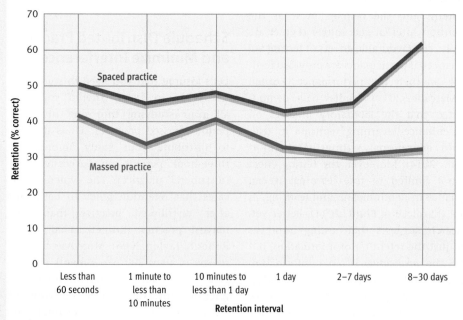

Figure 7.23
Effects of massed versus distributed practice on retention. In a review of more than 300 experiments on massed versus distributed practice, Cepeda et al. (2006) examined the importance of the retention interval. As you can see, spaced practice was superior to massed practice at all retention intervals, but the gap widened at longer intervals. These findings suggest that distributed practice is especially advantageous when you need or want to remember material over the long haul.

away, the optimal interval between practice periods appears to be around 24 hours. The superiority of distributed practice over massed practice suggests that cramming is an ill-advised approach to studying for exams (Marsh & Butler, 2013).

Because interference is a major cause of forgetting, you'll probably want to think about how you can minimize it. This issue is especially important for students, because memorizing information for one course can interfere with the retention of information for another course. It may help to allocate study for specific courses to separate days. Thorndyke and Hayes-Roth (1979) found that similar material produced less interference when it was learned on different days. Thus, the day before an exam in a course, you should study for that course only—if possible. If demands in other courses make that plan impossible, you should study the test material last.

Engage in Deep Processing and Organize Information

Research on levels of processing suggests that how *often* you go over material is less critical than the *depth* of processing that you engage in (Craik & Tulving, 1975). Thus, if you expect to remember what you read, you have to wrestle fully with its meaning (Einstein & McDaniel, 2004). Many students could probably benefit if they spent less time on rote repetition and devoted more effort to actually paying attention to and analyzing the meaning of their reading assignments. In particular, it is useful to make material *personally* meaningful. When you read your textbooks, try to relate information to your own life and experience. For example, when you read about classical conditioning, try to think of responses that you display that are attributable to classical conditioning.

Retention tends to be greater when information is well organized (Einstein & McDaniel, 2004). Gordon Bower (1970) has shown that hierarchical organization is particularly helpful when it is applicable. Thus, it may be a good idea to *outline* reading assignments for school. Consistent with this reasoning, there is some empirical evidence that outlining material from textbooks can enhance retention of the material (McDaniel, Waddill, & Shakesby, 1996).

Enrich Encoding with Mnemonic Devices

Many mnemonic devices—such as acrostics, acronyms, and narrative methods—are designed to make abstract material more meaningful. Other mnemonic devices depend on visual imagery. As you may recall, Allan Paivio (1986, 2007) believes that visual images create a second memory code and that two codes are better than one.

Acrostics and Acronyms *Acrostics* are phrases (or poems) in which the first letter of each word (or line) functions as a cue to help you recall information to be remembered (Herrmann, Raybeck, & Gruneberg, 2002). For instance, you may remember the order of musical notes with the saying "Every good boy does fine" (or "deserves favour"). A slight variation on acrostics is the *acronym*—a word formed out of the first letters of a series of words. Students memorizing the order of colours in the light spectrum often store the name "Roy G. Biv" to remember red, orange, yellow, green, blue, indigo, and violet. Notice that this acronym takes advantage of the principle of chunking.

Enrich Encoding with Visual Mnemonics

Memory can be enhanced by the use of visual imagery. As you may recall, Allan Paivio (1986) believes that visual images create a second memory code and that two codes are better than one for enhancing recall. Many popular mnemonic devices depend on visual imagery, including the link method, method of loci, and keyword method.

Link Method The *link method* involves forming a mental image of items to be remembered in a way that links them together. For instance, suppose you need to remember some items to pick up at the drugstore: a news magazine, shaving cream, film, and pens. To remember these items, you might visualize a public figure on the magazine cover shaving with a pen while being photographed. There is some evidence that the more bizarre you make your image, the more helpful it is likely to be (McDaniel & Einstein, 1986).

Method of Loci The *method of loci* involves taking an imaginary walk along a familiar path where images of items to be remembered are associated with certain locations. The first step is to commit to memory a series of loci, or places along a path. Usually these loci are specific locations in your home or neighbourhood. Then envision each thing you want to remember in one of these locations. Try to form distinctive, vivid images. When you need to remember the items, imagine yourself walking along the path. The various loci on your path should serve as cues for the retrieval of the images that you formed (see Figure 7.24). Evidence suggests that the method of loci can be effective in increasing retention (Gross et al., 2014; Moe & De Beni, 2004). Moreover, this method ensures that items are remembered in their *correct order* because the order is determined by the sequence of locations along the pathway.

Figure 7.24

The method of loci. In this example from Bower (1970), a person about to go shopping pairs items to remember with familiar places (loci) arranged in a natural sequence: (1) hot dogs/driveway; (2) cat food/garage interior; (3) tomatoes/front door; (4) bananas/coat closet shelf; (5) whiskey/kitchen sink. The shopper then uses imagery to associate the items on the shopping list with the loci, as shown in the drawing: (1) giant hot dog rolls down a driveway; (2) a cat noisily devours cat food in the garage; (3) ripe tomatoes are splattered on the front door; (4) bunches of bananas are hung from the closet shelf; (5) the contents of a bottle of whiskey gurgle down the kitchen sink. As the last panel shows, the shopper recalls the items by mentally touring the loci associated with them.

Source: From Bower, G.H. (1970). Analysis of a mnemonic device. *American Scientist*, 58 (Sept–Oct), 496–499. Copyright © 1970 by Scientific Research Society. Reprinted by permission.

Understanding the Fallibility of Eyewitness Accounts

A number of years ago, the Wilmington, Delaware, area was plagued by a series of armed robberies committed by a perpetrator who was dubbed the "gentleman bandit" by the press because he was an unusually polite and well-groomed thief. The local media published a sketch of the gentleman bandit and eventually an alert resident turned in a suspect who resembled the sketch. Much to everyone's surprise, the accused thief was a Catholic priest named Father Bernard Pagano—who vigorously denied the charges. Unfortunately for Father Pagano, his denials and alibis were unconvincing and he was charged with the crimes. At the trial, seven eyewitnesses confidently identified Father Pagano as the gentleman bandit. The prosecution was well on its way to a conviction when there was a stunning turn of events—another man, Ronald Clouser, confessed to the police that he was the gentleman bandit. The authorities dropped the charges against Father Pagano and the relieved priest was able to return to his normal existence (Rodgers, 1982).

This bizarre tale of mistaken identity—which sounds like it was lifted from a movie script—raises some interesting questions about memory. How could seven people "remember" seeing Father Pagano commit armed robberies that he had nothing to do with? How could they mistake him for Ronald Clouser, when the two really didn't look very similar (see the photos on the right)? How could they be so confident when they were so wrong? Perhaps you're thinking that this is just one case and it must be unrepresentative (which would be sound critical thinking). Well, yes, it *is* a rather extreme example of eyewitness fallibility, but researchers have compiled mountains of evidence that eyewitness testimony is not nearly as reliable or as accurate as widely assumed (Cutler & Penrod, 1995; Kassin et al., 2001; Wells & Olson, 2003; see Schacter et al., 2008,

for some methodological concerns). This finding is ironic in that people are most confident about their assertions when they can say, "I saw it with my own eyes." Television news shows like to use the title *Eyewitness News* to create the impression that they chronicle events with great clarity and accuracy. And our legal system accords special status to eyewitness testimony because it is considered much more dependable than hearsay or circumstantial evidence. Canadian psychologists such as Daniel Yarmey of the University of Guelph, Rod Lindsay of Queen's University, Mark Howe of Lancaster University, and Regina Schuller of York University have been important contributors to the literature on false memories and the accuracy and role of eyewitness testimony and to the literature on psychology and the law more generally (Howe, Gagnon, & Thouas, 2008; Lindsay et al., 2007; Lindsay, Allen, Chan, & Dahl, 2004; Schuller & Ogloff, 2001; Yarmey, 2003).

So, why are eyewitness accounts surprisingly inaccurate? Well, a host of factors and processes contribute to this inaccuracy. Let's briefly review some of the relevant processes that were introduced in the main body of the chapter; then we'll focus on two common errors in thinking that also contribute.

Can you think of any memory phenomena described in the chapter that seem likely to undermine eyewitness accuracy? You could point to the fact that *memory is a reconstructive process*, and eyewitness recall is likely to be distorted by the schemas that people have for various events. A second consideration is that *witnesses sometimes make source-monitoring errors* and get confused about where they saw a face. For example, one rape victim mixed up her assailant with a guest on a TV show that she was watching when she was attacked. Fortunately, the falsely accused suspect had an airtight alibi, as he could demonstrate that he was on live television when the rape occurred (Schacter, 1996). Perhaps the most pervasive factor is the misinformation effect (Loftus, 1993a). *Witnesses' recall of events is routinely distorted by information introduced after the event* by police officers, lawyers, news reports, and so forth. In addition to these factors, eyewitness inaccuracy is fuelled by the *hindsight bias* and *overconfidence effects*.

The Contribution of Hindsight Bias

The *hindsight bias* is the tendency to mould our interpretation of the past to fit how events actually turned out. When you know the outcome of an event, this knowledge slants your recall of how the event unfolded and what your thinking was at the time (Guilbault et al.,

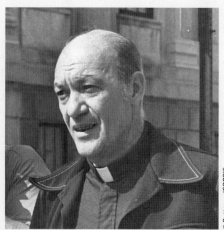

Although he doesn't look that much like the real "gentleman bandit," who is shown on the left, seven eyewitnesses identified Father Pagano (right) as the gentleman bandit, showing just how unreliable eyewitness accounts can be.

Although courts give special credence to eyewitness testimony, scientific evidence indicates that eyewitness accounts are less reliable than widely assumed.

2004). With the luxury of hindsight, there is a curious tendency to say, "I knew it all along" when explaining events that objectively would have been difficult to foresee. With regard to eyewitnesses, their recollections may often be distorted by knowing that a particular person has been arrested and accused of the crime in question. For example, Wells and Bradfield (1998) had simulated eyewitnesses select a perpetrator from a photo lineup. The eyewitnesses' confidence in their identifications tended to be quite modest, which made sense given that the actual perpetrator was not even in the lineup. But when some subjects were told, "Good, you identified the actual suspect," they became highly confident about their identifications, which obviously were incorrect.

In the last 15 years, a host of studies have replicated this effect (Steblay, Wells, & Douglass, 2014). When the authorities confirm people's lineup identifications, this confirmation alters their recollection of the crime scene. Their recall of how good their view was and how much attention they paid to the event increases dramatically, and their certainty about their identification grows, thanks to hindsight bias.

The Contribution of Overconfidence

Another flaw in thinking that contributes to inaccuracy in eyewitness accounts is people's tendency to be overconfident about the reliability of their memories. When tested for their memory of general information, people tend to overestimate their accuracy (Koriat & Bjork, 2005). In studies of eyewitness recall,

participants also tend to be overconfident about their recollections. Although jurors tend to be more convinced by eyewitnesses who appear confident, the assumption that confidence is an excellent indicator of accuracy is clearly wrong (Roediger, Wixted, & DeSoto, 2012). Research shows that there is only a modest correlation between eyewitness confidence and eyewitness accuracy (Shaw, McClure, & Dykstra, 2007). Hence, many convictions of innocent people have been attributed to the impact of testimony from highly confident but mistaken eyewitnesses (Loftus, 2013). In recent decades, the advent of DNA testing has led to the exoneration of hundreds of individuals who were wrongfully convicted of crimes. Faulty eyewitness testimony turned out to be a major factor in about three-quarters of those overturned convictions (Garrett, 2011).

Strategies to Reduce Overconfidence

Can you learn to make better judgments of the accuracy of your recall of everyday events? Yes, with effort you can get better at making accurate estimates of how likely you are to be correct in the recall of some fact or event. One reason that people tend to be overconfident is that if they can't think of any reasons that they might be wrong, they assume they must be right. Thus, overconfidence is fuelled by yet another common error in thinking—*the failure to seek disconfirming evidence*.

Thus, to make more accurate assessments of what you know and don't know, it helps to engage in a deliberate process of considering why you might be wrong. Here is an example. Based on your reading of Chapter 1, write down the schools of thought associated

with the following major theorists: William James, John B. Watson, and Carl Rogers. After you provide your answers, rate your confidence that the information you just provided is correct. Now, write three reasons that your answers might be wrong and three reasons that they might be correct. Most people will balk at this exercise, arguing that they cannot think of any reasons that they might be wrong, but after some resistance, they can come up with several. Such reasons might include "I was half asleep when I read that part of the chapter" or "I might be confusing Watson and James." Reasons that you think you're right could include "I distinctly recall discussing this with my friend" or "I really worked on those names in Chapter 1." After listing reasons that you might be right and reasons that you might be wrong, rate your confidence in your accuracy once again. Guess what? Most people are less confident after going through such an exercise than they were before (depending, of course, on the nature of the topic). See Table 7.1.

The new confidence ratings tend to be more realistic than the original ratings (Koriat, Lichtenstein, & Fischhoff, 1980). Why? Because this exercise forces you to think more deeply about your answers and to search your memory for related information. Most people stop searching their memory as soon as they generate an answer they believe to be correct. Thus, the process of considering reasons that you might be wrong about something—a process that people rarely engage in—is a useful critical thinking skill that can reduce overconfidence effects. Better assessment of what you know and don't know can be an important determinant of the quality of the decisions you make and the way you solve problems and reason from evidence.

Table 7.1

Critical Thinking Skills Discussed in This Application

SKILL	DESCRIPTION
Understanding the limitations	The critical thinker appreciates that memory is reconstructive and that even eyewitness accounts may be distorted or inaccurate.
Recognizing the bias in hindsight analysis	The critical thinker understands that knowing the outcome of events biases our recall and interpretation of the events.
Recognizing overconfidence in human cognition	The critical thinker understands that people are frequently overconfident about the accuracy of their projections for the future and their recollections of the past.
Understanding the need to seek disconfirming evidence	The critical thinker understands the value of thinking about how or why one might be wrong about something.

© Bill Fritch/Brand X/Corbis

ENCODING

- *Attention*, which entails a selective focus on certain input, enhances encoding.
- *Divided attention* undermines encoding and can have a negative effect on the performance of other tasks.
- *Levels-of-processing theory* proposes that deeper levels of processing result in more durable memory codes.
- *Elaboration*, which involves linking a stimulus to other information, can enrich encoding.
- According to *dual-coding theory*, visual imagery may facilitate memory by providing two memory codes rather than just one.
- Increasing the motivation to remember at the time of encoding can enhance memory.

STORAGE

- Information-processing theories propose people have three memory stores: *sensory memory, short-term memory (STM),* and *long-term memory (LTM).*
- Atkinson and Shiffrin posited that incoming information passes through two temporary storage buffers before being placed into long-term memory.

RETRIEVAL

- Recall is often guided by partial information, as demonstrated by the *tip-of-the-tongue phenomenon.*
- Reinstating the context of an event can often enhance retrieval efforts.
- Memories are sketchy reconstructions of the past that may be distorted.
- The *misinformation effect* occurs when recall of an event is changed by misleading post-event information.
- Even the simple act of retelling a story can introduce inaccuracies into memory.
- *Source monitoring* is the process of making inferences about the origins of memories.

Sensory memory

Wayne Weiten

- *Sensory memory* preserves information in its original form for a very brief time.
- Memory traces in the sensory store appear to decay in about one-quarter of a second.

Short-term memory

- *Short-term memory (STM)* can maintain unrehearsed information for about 10–20 seconds.
- STM has a limited capacity that has long been believed to be about seven items plus or minus two.
- However, a more recent estimate that the capacity of STM is four items plus or minus one is becoming increasingly influential.
- Baddeley proposed a more complex model of STM called *working memory.*
- *Working memory capacity (WMC)* refers to one's ability to hold and manipulate information in conscious attention.

Long-term memory

- *Long-term memory (LTM)* is an unlimited capacity store that can hold information indefinitely.
- Flashbulb memories suggest that LTM storage may be permanent, but the data are not convincing.
- Research has shown that the flashbulb memories are not as durable or accurate as claimed.

Dan Howell/Shutterstock.com

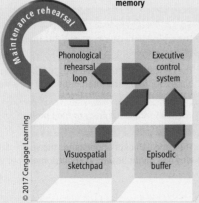

Working (short-term) memory

Maintenance rehearsal

Phonological rehearsal loop

Executive control system

Visuospatial sketchpad

Episodic buffer

LTM

© 2017 Cengage Learning

Organization in LTM

- People spontaneously organize information into categories for storage in memory.
- *A conceptual hierarchy* is a multilevel classification system based on common properties among items.
- A *schema* is an organized cluster of knowledge about a particular object or event.
- A *semantic network* consists of nodes representing concepts, joined together by pathways that link related concepts.

FORGETTING

Measuring forgetting

- People view forgetting as a deficiency, but it can be adaptive by making it easier to remember important information.

- Ebbinghaus's work suggested that most forgetting occurs very rapidly but subsequent research indicated that his *forgetting curve* was exceptionally steep.

- Retention can be assessed with a *recall* measure, a *recognition* measure, or a *relearning* measure.

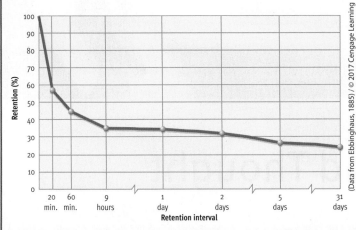

(Data from Ebbinghaus, 1885) / © 2017 Cengage Learning

Why we forget

- A great deal of forgetting, including pseudoforgetting, is due to *ineffective encoding*.

- *Decay theory* proposes that memory traces fade with time, but decay in long-term memory has proven hard to demonstrate.

- *Interference theory* asserts that people forget information because of competition from other material, which has proven easy to demonstrate.

- Forgetting is often due to *retrieval failure*, which can include repression.

The repressed memories controversy

- Recent years have seen a surge of reports of recovered memories of previously forgotten sexual abuse in childhood.

- Many clinicians accept these recovered memories, arguing that it is common for people to bury traumatic memories in their unconscious.

- Many memory researchers are skeptical of recovered memories because they have demonstrated that it is easy to create inaccurate memories in laboratory studies.

- Although it is clear that some therapists have created false memories in their patients, it seems likely that some cases of recovered memories are authentic.

- Memories recovered spontaneously appear more likely to be authentic than memories recovered in therapy.

PHYSIOLOGY OF MEMORY

Anatomy of memory

- In *retrograde amnesia*, a person loses memory for events prior to the amnesia.

- In *anterograde amnesia*, a person shows memory deficits for events subsequent to the onset of the amnesia.

- Studies of amnesia and other research suggest that the hippocampus and broader medial temporal lobe system play a major role in memory.

- These areas may be crucial to the *consolidation* of memories.

Neural circuitry of memory

- Thompson's research suggests that memory traces may consist of *localized neural circuits*.

- According to Kandel, memory traces reflect alterations in neurotransmitter release at specific synapses.

- *Neurogenesis* may contribute to the sculpting of neural circuits for memory.

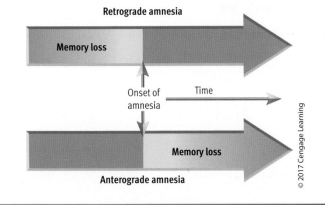

© 2017 Cengage Learning

PROPOSED MEMORY SYSTEMS

Declarative memory

Handles recall of factual information, such as names, dates, events, and ideas.

Nondeclarative memory

Handles recall of actions, skills, and operations, such as riding a bike or typing.

Semantic versus episodic memory

- *Semantic memory system* contains general knowledge that is not temporally dated.

- *Episodic memory system* handles temporally dated recollections of personal experiences.

Prospective versus retrospective memory

- *Prospective memory* involves remembering to perform actions in the future.

- *Retrospective memory* involves remembering events from the past or previously learned information.

APPLICATIONS

- Increased rehearsal and testing yourself on material both enhance retention.

- In memorizing lists, be wary of the serial-position effect.

- Distributed practice tends to be more efficient than massed practice.

- Deeper processing of material and organizing material both tend to result in greater retention.

- Meaningfulness can be enhanced through the use of mnemonic devices.

- Eyewitness memory is not nearly as reliable or as accurate as widely believed.

- Hindsight bias is the tendency to reshape one's interpretation of the past to fit with known outcomes.

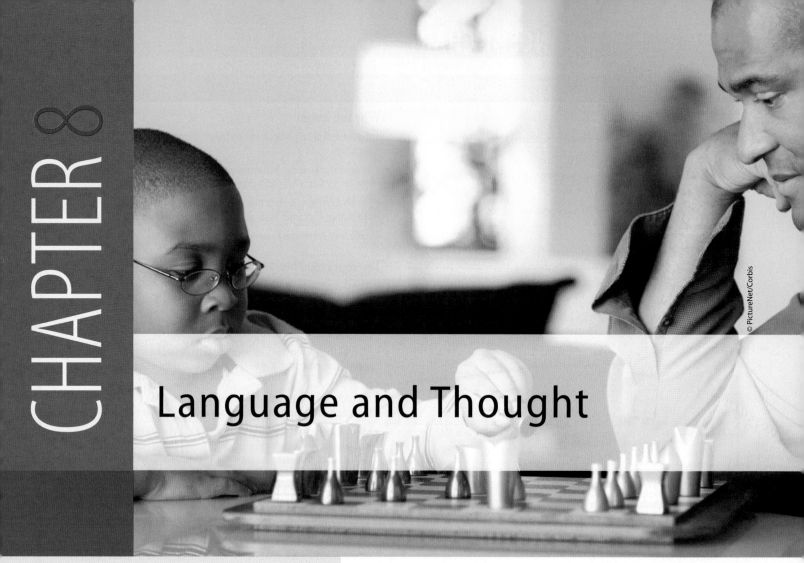

CHAPTER 8

Language and Thought

Themes in this Chapter

Empiricism   Cultural Heritage   Heredity & Environment   Experience

On October 17, 1968, Prime Minister Pierre Elliott Trudeau introduced legislation, the Official Languages Bill, that he believed reflected the reality of the Canadian experience and that he hoped would promote Canadian unity in the context of its diversity. He suggested that both French and English should be official languages of Canada. This was essential, he argued, because both language groups were "strong enough in numbers and in material and intellectual resources to resist the forces of assimilation . . . this underlying reality of our country has not been adequately reflected in many of our public institutions" (Library and Archives Canada, 2002). On becoming officially bilingual, Canada joined a small set of countries around the world such as Finland, Sweden, Belgium, South Africa, and Afghanistan that have more than one official language. The themes begun in the Official Languages Bill were continued in the later Canadian Charter of Rights and Freedoms (1982) and then in the Official Languages Act (1988). The implications of the bill were far-reaching—socially, culturally, economically, politically, and educationally. The opportunity to be educated in either or both of Canada's official languages is now well established.

There are advantages to be derived from bilingualism and immersion education in a second language. These include general educational and social benefits. In addition, recent research by developmental psychologist Ellen Bialystok and others suggests that there may be additional cognitive benefits that can even partially protect you against some of the cognitive deficits often found in the elderly. These are discussed later in this chapter.

We will look more closely at the potential cognitive benefits of bilingualism but before that we will consider the nature of language and language development in children in general. We will have to place the learning of two languages in the context of what we know about how children acquire language more generally.

Of course, bilingualism refers to more than just proficiency in English and French. Many students in Canada also have access to other heritage languages. After English and French, the languages most frequently spoken in Canada are Spanish, German, Italian, Hindi, Arabic, Chinese, Russian, and Hebrew. Over 6 million of us report speaking a language at home other than English or French (Statistics Canada, 2015).

We will also consider the nature of cognition itself, a task we began in Chapter 7. Cognition and language are closely linked, as we will discuss later in the chapter. *Cognition* **refers to the mental processes involved in acquiring knowledge.** In other words, cognition involves thinking. As we discussed in Chapter 1, the study of cognition has seen peaks

Pierre Elliott Trudeau, prime minister of Canada (1968–1979 and 1980–1984), was a champion of bilingualism.

and valleys in psychology. When psychology first emerged, it focused on the mind and the research method of choice was *introspection*. But the limitations of that method and the rise of behaviourism, with its focus on observables (have you ever seen a thought?), led to the demise of cognition as a serious scientific topic. It was not until the 1950s that the study of cognition came back, an era often referred to as the "cognitive revolution" (Baars, 1986). Renegade theorists such as Nobel Laureate Herbert Simon argued that behaviourists' exclusive focus on overt responses was doomed to yield an incomplete understanding of human functioning. Three major advances in one day, at a 1956 conference, ignited the cognitive revolution (Gardner, 1985). First, Herbert Simon and Allen Newell described the first computer program to successfully simulate human problem solving. Second, Noam Chomsky outlined a new model that changed the way psychologists studied language. Third, George Miller delivered a legendary discussion paper arguing that the capacity of short-term memory is seven (plus or minus two) items. Since then, cognitive science has grown into a dominant trend in psychology. We review some of this work in this chapter.

Besides memory, which we discussed in Chapter 7, cognitive psychologists investigate the complexities of language, inference, problem solving, decision making, and reasoning (e.g., Kruglanski & Orehek, 2007; Oppenheimer & Kelso, 2015).

Language: Turning Thoughts into Words

Language obviously plays a fundamental role in human behaviour (Joy, 2013). Indeed, if you were to ask people, "What characteristic most distinguishes humans from other living creatures?" a great many would reply, "Language." Spoken language and its accompanying gestures (Goldin-Meadow & Alibali, 2013) allows us to convey information, express ourselves, and bond with others. In this section, we'll discuss the nature, structure, and development of language and related topics, such as bilingualism and whether animals can learn language.

What Is Language?

A *language* consists of symbols that convey meaning, plus rules for combining those symbols, that can be used to generate an infinite variety of messages. Language systems include a number of critical properties.

First, language is *symbolic*. People use spoken sounds and written words to represent objects, actions, events, and ideas. Second, language is *semantic*, or meaningful. Third, language is *generative*. A limited number of symbols can be combined in an infinite variety of ways to *generate* an endless array of

novel messages. Every day you create and comprehend sentences that you have never spoken or heard before. Fourth, language is *structured*. Rules govern the arrangement of words into phrases and sentences; some arrangements are acceptable and some are not.

The Structure of Language

Human languages have a hierarchical structure (Ratner, Gleason, & Narasimhan, 1998). As Figure 8.1 shows, basic sounds are combined into units with meaning, which are combined into words. Words are combined into phrases, which are combined into sentences.

Phonemes

At the base of the language hierarchy are *phonemes*, the smallest speech units in a language that can be distinguished perceptually.

For all its rich vocabulary, the English language is composed of about 40 phonemes, corresponding roughly to the 26 letters of the alphabet plus several variations. A letter in the alphabet 'can represent more than one phoneme if it has more than one pronunciation, and some phonemes are represented by

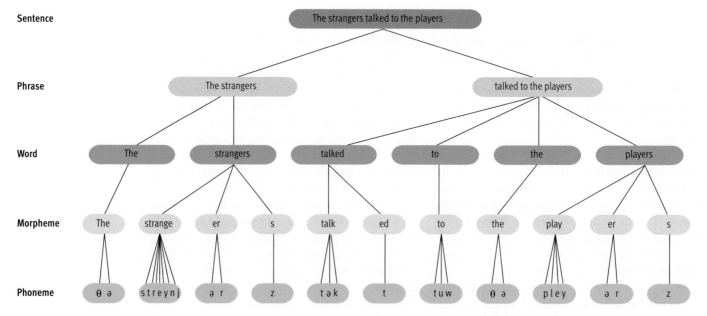

Figure 8.1

An analysis of a simple English sentence. As this example shows, verbal language has a hierarchical structure. At the base of the hierarchy are the phonemes, which are units of vocal sound that do not, in themselves, have meaning. The smallest units of meaning in a language are morphemes, which include not only root words but also such meaning-carrying units as the past-tense suffix *ed* and the plural *s*. Complex rules of syntax govern how the words constructed from morphemes may be combined into phrases, and phrases into meaningful statements, or sentences.

Source: A. Clarke-Stewart, S. Friedman, and J. Koch. 1985. *Child development: A topical approach* (p. 417). Copyright © 1985. Reproduced with permission from John Wiley & Sons, Inc.

combinations of letters, such as *ch* and *th*. Working with this handful of basic sounds, people can understand and generate all of the words in the English language—and invent new ones.

Morphemes and Semantics

Morphemes are the smallest units of meaning in a language. There are approximately 50 000 English morphemes, which include root words as well as prefixes and suffixes. Many words, such as *fire*, *guard*, and *friend*, consist of a single morpheme. Many others represent combinations of morphemes. For example, the word *unfriendly* consists of three morphemes: the root word *friend*, the prefix *un*, and the suffix *ly*. Each of the morphemes contributes to the meaning of the entire word. *Semantics* is the area of language concerned with understanding the meaning of words and word combinations. Learning about semantics entails learning about the infinite variety of objects and actions that words refer to. A word's meaning may consist of both its *denotation*, which is its dictionary definition, and its *connotation*, which includes its emotional overtones and secondary implications.

Syntax

Of course, most utterances consist of more than a single word. As we've already noted, people don't combine words randomly. *Syntax* is a system of rules that specify how words can be arranged into sentences. A simple rule of syntax is that a sentence must have both a *subject* and a *verb*. Thus, "The sound annoyed me" is a sentence. However, "The sound" is not a sentence because it lacks a verb. And virtually all English speakers know that an *article* (e.g., *the*) comes before the word it modifies. For example, you would never say "swimmer the" instead of "the swimmer." How children learn the complicated rules of syntax is one of the major puzzles investigated by psychologists interested in language. Like other aspects of language development, children's acquisition of syntax seems to progress at an amazingly rapid pace. Let's look at how this remarkable development unfolds.

Milestones in Language Development

Learning to use language requires learning a number of skills that become important at various points in a child's development (Siegler, 1998). We'll examine this developmental sequence by looking first at how children learn to pronounce words, then at their use of single words, and finally at their ability to combine words to form sentences (see Table 8.1).

Table 8.1
Overview of Typical Language Development

AGE	GENERAL CHARACTERISTICS
Months	
1–5	Reflexive communication: Vocalizes randomly, coos, laughs, cries, engages in vocal play, discriminates language from nonlanguage sounds
6–18	Babbling: Verbalizes in response to the speech of others; responses increasingly approximate human speech patterns
10–13	First words: Uses words, typically to refer to objects
12–18	One-word sentence stage: Vocabulary grows slowly; uses nouns primarily; overextensions begin
18–24	Vocabulary spurt: Fast mapping facilitates rapid acquisition of new words
Years	
2	Two-word sentence stage: Uses telegraphic speech; uses more pronouns and verbs
2.5	Three-word sentence stage: Modifies speech to take listener into account; overregularizations begin
3	Uses complete simple active sentence structure; uses sentences to tell stories that are understood by others; uses plurals
3.5	Expanded grammatical forms: Expresses concepts with words; uses four-word sentences
4	Uses five-word sentences
5	Well-developed and complex syntax: Uses more complex syntax; uses more complex forms to tell stories
6	Displays metalinguistic awareness

Note: Children often show individual differences in the exact ages at which they display the various developmental achievements outlined here.

Source: From Weiten. *Cengage Advantage Books: Psychology*, 9E. © 2013 South-Western, a part of Cengage, Inc. Reproduced by permission. www.cengage.com/permissions

Moving toward Producing Words

Three-month-old infants display a surprising language-related talent: They can distinguish phonemes from all of the world's languages, including phonemes that they do not hear in their environment. In contrast, adults cannot readily discriminate phonemes that are not used in their native language. Actually, neither can one-year-old children, as this curious ability gradually disappears between four months and 12 months of age (Kuhl et al., 2008; Werker & Tees, 1999). The exact mechanisms responsible for this transition are not understood, but it is clear that long before infants utter their first words, they are making remarkable progress in learning the sound structure of their native language (Mugitani et al., 2007). Progress toward recognizing whole words also occurs during the first year. Although they don't know what the words mean yet, by around eight months, infants begin to recognize and store common word forms (Swingley, 2008).

Janet Werker, a senior scientist at the University of British Columbia, has done pioneering work in the development of language in infants (Pena, Werker, & Dehaene-Lambertz, 2012; Sebastian-Galles, Albareda, & Werker, 2012; Werker et al., 2012). She argues that human infants are well prepared to learn language and that babies have perceptual biases that facilitate and guide the "acquisition of phonology" (Werker, 2003).

Werker suggests that there are *optimal periods* for the different subsystems involved in language acquisition but that they are not as rigidly absolute as is sometimes thought (Werker & Tees, 2005). Thus, while very young infants can discriminate even phonemes not inherent in their language context, this facility disappears without exposure. As they develop through the first year of life, the language acquisition systems of the infant become tuned to the speech properties of their native language. In her most recent work, Werker argues that the question regarding the existence of critical periods has been answered in the affirmative. A **critical period** refers to a limited time span in the development of an organism when it is optimal for certain capacities to emerge because the organism is especially responsive to certain experiences. The questions to be answered now concern the nature of the processes that open and close these important developmental windows (Werker & Hensch, 2015).

During the first six months of life, a baby's vocalizations are dominated by crying, cooing, and laughter, which have limited value as a means of communication. Soon, infants are *babbling*, producing a wide variety of sounds that correspond to phonemes and, eventually, many repetitive consonant–vowel combinations, such as "lalalalala." Babbling gradually

Photo by Christine Dietrich, Photo courtesy of Janet Werker

Janet Werker, Canada Research Chair in Psychology at the University of British Columbia, examines early processes involved in the acquisition of languages in infants. She was elected as a Fellow of the Royal Society of Canada in 2001.

Courtesy of Laura Petitto

Laura-Ann Petitto is a Gallaudet University psychologist who conducts research on various aspects of children's language acquisition.

becomes more complex and increasingly resembles the language spoken by parents and others in the child's environment (Hoff, 2005). Babbling lasts until around 18 months, continuing even after children utter their first words. According to Laura-Ann Petitto, babbling is considered to be one of the monumental milestones in language acquisition (Petitto et al., 2004).

Laura-Ann Petitto has done some important research on babbling. Some of these studies were conducted in Montreal with normal and deaf babies. Petitto found that the deaf babies exhibited "manual babbling"—babbling with their hands in a manner similar to the verbal babbling of hearing babies (Petitto & Marentette, 1991). She also found that the deaf babies' first "signed words" were continuous with their babbling—much like a baby who verbally babbles "bababa" and whose first word is "baby" (Vihman, 1985). This study on babbling is the focus of our Featured Study. Petitto also is well known for her work on the origins of language and on bilingualism (e.g., Jasinska & Petitto, 2013; Kovelman, Berens, & Petitto, 2013).

FEATURED STUDY

Babbling in the manual mode: Evidence for the ontogeny of language.

Description
In this study, Petitto and Marentette demonstrate that infants born without hearing go through the babbling stage just like hearing babies, except that they babble manually with their hands.

Investigators
Petitto, L. A., & Marentette, P. F. (1991). *Science, 251*(5000), 1493–1496.

Using Words

The first year of life is critical in the child's acquisition of language (Gervain & Mehler, 2010). At around 10 to 13 months of age, most children begin to utter sounds that correspond to words. Most infants' first words are similar in phonetic form and meaning—even in different languages (Waxman, 2002). The initial words resemble the syllables that infants most often babble spontaneously. For example, words such as *dada*, *mama*, and *papa* are names for parents in many languages because they consist of sounds that are easy to produce.

After children utter their first words, their vocabulary grows slowly for the next few months (Dapretto & Bjork, 2000). Toddlers typically can say between 3 and 50 words by 18 months. However, their *receptive vocabulary* is larger than their *productive vocabulary*. That is, they can comprehend more words spoken by others than they can actually produce to express themselves (Pan & Uccelli, 2009). Thus, toddlers can *understand* 50 words months before they can *say* 50 words. Toddlers' early words tend to refer most often to *objects* and secondarily to *social actions* (Camaioni, 2001). Children probably acquire nouns before verbs because the meanings of nouns, which often refer to distinct, concrete objects, tend to be easier to encode than the meanings of verbs, which often refer to more abstract relationships (Poulin-Dubois & Graham, 2007). However, this generalization may not apply to all languages (Bates, Devescovi, & Wulfeck et al., 2001).

Most youngsters' vocabularies soon begin to grow at a dizzying pace, as a *vocabulary spurt* often begins at around 18–24 months (Bates & Carnevale, 1993; Camaioni, 2001; see Figure 8.2). By Grade 1, the average child has a vocabulary of approximately 10 000 words, which builds to an astonishing 40 000 words by Grade 5 (Anglin, 1993; see Figure 8.3). In building these impressive vocabularies, some two-year-olds learn as many as 20 new words every week. *Fast mapping* appears to be one factor underlying this rapid growth of vocabulary (Carey, 2010; Gershkoff-Stowe & Hahn, 2007). **Fast mapping is the process by which children map a word onto an underlying concept after only one exposure.** Thus, children often add words like *tank*, *board*, and *tape* to their vocabularies after their first encounter with objects that illustrate these concepts. The vocabulary spurt may be attributable to children's improved articulation skills, improved understanding of syntax, underlying cognitive development, or some combination of these factors (MacWhinney, 1998).

Of course, these efforts to learn new words are not flawless. Toddlers often make errors, such as overextensions and underextensions (Harley, 2008). **An *overextension* occurs when a child incorrectly uses a word to describe a wider set of objects or actions than it is meant to.** For example, a child might use the word *ball* for anything round—oranges, apples, even the moon. Overextensions usually appear in children's speech between ages one and two-and-a-half. Specific overextensions typically last up to several months. Toddlers also tend to be guilty of **underextensions, which occur when a child incorrectly uses a word to describe a narrower set of objects or actions than it is meant to.** For example, a child might use the word *doll* to refer only to a single, favourite doll. Overextensions and underextensions show that toddlers are actively trying to learn the rules of language—albeit with mixed success.

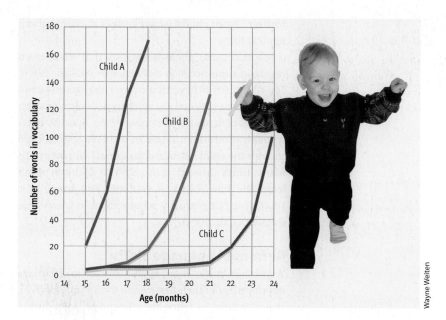

Figure 8.2

The vocabulary spurt. Children typically acquire their first 10–15 words very slowly, but they soon go through a vocabulary spurt—a period during which they rapidly acquire many new words. The vocabulary spurt usually begins at around 18–24 months, but children vary, as these graphs of three toddlers' vocabulary growth show.

Source: Adapted from Goldfield, B. A., and Resnick, J. S. (1990). Early lexical acquisition: Rate, content, and the vocabulary spurt. *Journal of Child Language*, 17, 171–183. Copyright © 1990 by Cambridge University Press. Adapted by permission.

Combining Words

Children typically begin to combine words into sentences near the end of their second year. Early sentences are characterized as *telegraphic* because they resemble telegrams. **Telegraphic speech consists mainly of content words; articles, prepositions, and other less critical words are omitted.** Thus, a child might say, "Give doll" rather than "Please give me the doll." Although not unique to the English language, telegraphic speech is not cross-culturally universal, as was once thought (de Villiers & de Villiers, 1999).

By the end of their third year, most children can express complex ideas such as the plural or the past tense. However, their efforts to learn the rules of language continue to generate revealing mistakes. *Overregularizations* occur when grammatical rules are incorrectly generalized to irregular cases where they do not apply. For example, children will say things like "The girl goed home" or "I hitted the ball." Typically, children initially use the correct noun, verb, or adjective forms, because they acquired them as new items. However, when they are learning general grammatical rules (e.g., for plurals), they extend the rules to nouns that are exceptions to the rule (e.g., "foots"). Overregularizations usually appear after children begin to learn grammatical rules. Thus, the progression goes from "feet" to "foots" and back

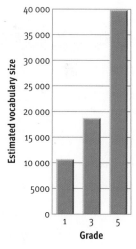

Figure 8.3

The growth of school children's vocabulary. Vocabulary growth is rapid during the early years of grade school. Youngsters' estimated vocabulary doubles about every two years between Grade 1 and Grade 5.

Source: Anglin, J.M. (1993). Vocabulary development: A morphological analysis. *Child Development*, 58, Serial 238. Copyright © 1993 The Society for Research in Child Development. Reprinted by permission.

to "feet" when children have further mastered grammatical rules.

Cross-cultural research suggests that these overregularizations occur in all languages (Slobin, 1985). Most theorists believe that overregularizations demonstrate that children are working actively to master the *rules* of language (Marcus, 1996). Specific overregularizations often linger in a child's speech even though the child has heard the correct constructions many times (Maslen et al., 2004). Children don't learn the fine points of grammar and usage in a single leap but gradually acquire them in small steps (Maslen et al., 2004).

Refining Language Skills

Youngsters make their largest strides in language development in their first four to five years. However, they continue to refine their language skills during their school-age years. They generate longer and more complicated sentences as they receive formal training in written language.

As their language skills develop, school-age children begin to appreciate ambiguities in language. They can, for instance, recognize two possible meanings in sentences such as "Visiting relatives can be bothersome." This interest in ambiguities indicates that they're developing *metalinguistic awareness*— the ability to reflect on the use of language. As metalinguistic awareness grows, children begin to "play" with language, coming up with puns and jokes. They begin to make more frequent and sophisticated use of metaphors, such as "We were packed in the room like sardines" (Gentner,1988). Between the ages of six and eight, most children begin to appreciate irony and sarcasm (Creusere, 1999).

concept check 8.1

Tracking Language Development

Check your understanding of how language skills progress in youngsters. Number the utterances below to indicate the developmental sequence in which they would probably occur. The answers can be found in Appendix A near the back of the book.

_____ **1.** "Doggie," while pointing to a cow.

_____ **2.** "The dogs runned away."

_____ **3.** "Doggie run."

_____ **4.** "The dogs ran away."

_____ **5.** "Doggie," while pointing to a dog.

_____ **6.** "Tommy thinks like his head is full of mashed potatoes."

Learning More than One Language: Bilingualism

Given the complexities involved in acquiring one language, you may be wondering about the ramifications of being asked to learn *two* languages (Gonzales & Lotto, 2013; Weisleder & Fernald, 2013). *Bilingualism* is the acquisition of two languages that use different speech sounds, vocabulary, and grammatical rules. Although not the norm in most of North America, bilingualism is quite common in Europe and many other regions, and nearly half of the world's population grows up bilingual (Hakuta, 1986; Snow, 1998). The learning of a second language is affected by many factors including the nature of one's attitude toward the learning situation and one's level of interest in the other groups' language (Lalonde & Gardner, 1984). Demand for French immersion continues to be very high in Canada (CBC News, 2013).

One assumption that some people have is that bilingualism hampers language development and has a negative impact on youngsters' educational progress. But does the empirical evidence support this assumption? Research on the topic of bilingualism is an extremely active area (Bialystok, 2015; Genesee, 2015). Let's take a look at some of the recent research on bilingualism.

Does Learning Two Languages in Childhood Slow Down Language Development?

If children are learning two languages simultaneously, does one language interfere with the other so that the acquisition of both is impeded? Some studies have found that bilingual children have smaller vocabularies in each of their languages than monolingual children have in their one language (Umbel et al., 1992). But when their two overlapping vocabularies are added, their total vocabulary is similar or slightly superior to that of children learning a single language (Oller & Pearson, 2002). Taken as a whole, the available evidence suggests that bilingual and monolingual children are largely similar in the course and rate of their language development (Costa & Sebastián-Gallés, 2014). There is little empirical support for the belief that bilingualism has serious negative effects on language development (Hoff, 2014).

Does Bilingualism Affect Cognitive Processes and Skills?

Does knowing two languages make thinking more difficult, or could bilingualism enhance thought processes (Bobb, Wodneicka, & Kroll, 2013)? While the evidence is somewhat mixed, depending on the variables measured and the exact nature of the subject populations that are compared, research suggests that bilingualism conveys some cognitive advantages (Greenberg et al., 2013) that at least argue for the need for additional research on the topic. On some types of tasks, bilinguals may have a slight disadvantage in terms of raw language-processing *speed* (Taylor & Taylor, 1990). When middle-class bilingual subjects who are fluent in both languages are studied, they tend to score somewhat *higher* than monolingual subjects on measures of cognitive flexibility, analytical reasoning, selective attention, and metalinguistic awareness (Bialystok, 1999; Campbell & Sais, 1995; Lambert, 1990).

reality check

Misconception

Bilingualism undermines cognitive development.

Reality

It is widely believed that bilingualism interferes with cognitive development. But when researchers control for social class in their comparisons, they do not find cognitive deficits in bilingual youngsters. Moreover, recent research suggests that bilingualism may be associated with unexpected cognitive benefits.

The issue of the potential cognitive benefits of bilingualism (e.g., Green & Abutalebi, 2013; Kroll & Bialystok, 2013; Morales et al., 2013) has been at the centre of Ellen Bialystok's recent research. Bialystok, of York University, has been examining the effects of bilingualism on children's cognition for many years. She suggests that there are some cognitive advantages to bilingualism for both children and adults. Her work has been guided by three hypotheses that have been supported by the results of research conducted in the past several years (Bialystok, 2007). First, since cognitive executive processes are necessary to deal successfully with the use of two languages, she suggests that bilingual children should develop control over executive processes earlier than monolingual children. They are related, in part, to our ability to control attention. Second, that as adults, the enhanced executive control characteristic of bilinguals should afford them advantages in cognitive tasks implicating executive processing. Finally, since executive processes are one of the first cognitive abilities to decline with age, bilinguals, because of their "continued reliance" on executive processes for dealing with their two languages, should show delayed decline relative to monolingual adults.

Bialystok (2001, 2007) has found that bilingualism is associated with higher levels of controlled processing on tasks that require control of attention. That is, bilingual children demonstrate greater facility at tasks where there is some type of misleading/distracting information and where response choice is involved. This makes sense, given the tasks that typically confront a bilingual individual. According to Kroll (2008; Kroll, Bobb, & Wodniecka, 2006), the evidence suggests that even when bilinguals are reading, listening, or speaking in one language, both languages remain active. She further suggests that bilinguals not only are proficient at two languages, but that they also develop the cognitive control ability to "juggle" the two languages relatively easily. According to Bialystok, some of the executive processes implicated in these differences between bilingual and monolingual children are those involving selective attention, attentional inhibition to distracting/misleading information, and switching among competing alternatives.

© iStockphoto.com/powerofforever

The utility of bilingual education programs has been a hotly debated issue across Canada. Critics argue that bilingualism has a negative effect on children's language and cognitive development, but there is relatively little empirical support for this assertion. Recent research suggests that bilingualism may have some cognitive benefits.

This research suggests that while bilingualism may not confer an advantage in all aspects of cognitive and linguistic processing, it is important to note that there are some documented advantages and few demonstrated disadvantages. There is evidence that the cognitive effects of bilingualism extend to social skills development, with bilinguals showing enhanced social skills (Fan, Liberman, Keysar, & Kinzler, 2016; Kinzler, 2016). In addition, research suggests that the cognitive effects of bilingual environments show up even before children themselves acquire language. Infants, "crib bilinguals," as young as seven months of age, show enhanced ability to control and switch attention if they are raised in a bilingual home environment (Bialystok, 2015).

Another consideration is derived from the results of some of Bialystok's more recent work on bilingualism and aging, conducted with a team of psychologists at York University, Dalhousie University, and the University of Toronto (Bialystok et al., 2004). Here, Bialystok and her colleagues found that the advantage conferred by bilingualism on controlled processing persists into adulthood and old age, suggesting that bilingualism may help attenuate age-related losses in certain aspects of cognition (Bialystok & Craik, 2010; Craik & Bialystok, 2008, 2010; Luk et al., 2013). For example, one influential study focused on people suffering from *dementia* (severe impairment of memory and cognitive functioning). It found that bilingual patients experienced the onset of dementia four years later, on average, than comparable monolingual patients (Bialystok, Craik, & Freedman, 2007). Bialystok notes that one of the objectives of her research was to determine if bilingualism "would provide a defense against the decline of these executive processes that occurs with

MCpl Dany Veillette, Rideau Hall, OSGG. © Her Majesty The Queen in Right of Canada represented by the Office of the Secretary to the Governor General, 2010. Reproduced with the permission of the OSGG, 2017.

Ellen Bialystok of York University, pictured with Governor General David Johnston, was awarded a 2010 Killam Prize for her work on the effects of bilingualism on cognitive processes and abilities, during a ceremony at Rideau Hall in Ottawa.

normal cognitive aging . . . the present results suggest that it does" (Bialystok et al., 2004, p. 301).

Can Animals Develop Language?

Can other species besides humans develop language? Scientists have taught some language-like skills to a number of species, including dolphins (Herman, Kuczaj, & Holder, 1993), sea lions (Schusterman & Gisiner, 1988), and an African grey parrot (Pepperberg, 1993, 2002), but their greatest success has come with the chimpanzee, an intelligent primate widely regarded as humans' closest cousin.

reality check

Misconception

Only humans can learn language.

Reality

It has long been assumed that language is unique to humans, but over the last 50 years researchers have helped quite a variety of animals to acquire some rudimentary language skills, including dolphins, sea lions, and a parrot, as well as apes and chimps. Admittedly, humans have a unique talent for language, but some other species are also capable of some language learning.

In early studies, researchers tried to teach chimps to speak (Hayes & Hayes, 1951). However, investigators quickly concluded that chimps simply didn't have the appropriate vocal apparatus to acquire human speech.

Subsequently, researchers tried training chimps to use a non-oral human language: American Sign Language (ASL). ASL is a complex language of hand gestures and facial expressions used by thousands of deaf people. The first effort of this sort with animals was begun by Allen and Beatrice Gardner (1967), who worked with a chimp named Washoe. The Gardners approached the task as if Washoe were a deaf child. They signed to her regularly, rewarded her imitations, and taught her complex signs by physically moving her hands through the required motions. In four years, Washoe acquired a sign vocabulary of roughly 160 words. She learned to combine these words into simple sentences, such as "Washoe sorry," "Gimme flower," and "More fruit."

Although these accomplishments were impressive, critics expressed doubts about whether Washoe and the other chimps that learned ASL had really acquired language skills. For example, Herbert Terrace

Key Learning Goals

▶ Describe the progress that has been made in teaching language to animals.

▶ Understand the connection between language and thought and the evolutionary significance of language.

(1986) argued that these chimps showed little evidence of mastering *rules* of language. According to Terrace, the chimps' sentences were the products of imitation and operant conditioning, rather than spontaneous generations based on linguistic rules.

In more recent years, Sue Savage-Rumbaugh and her colleagues have reported some striking advances with bonobo pygmy chimpanzees that have fuelled additional debate (Lyn & Savage-Rumbaugh, 2000; Savage-Rumbaugh, 1991; Savage-Rumbaugh, Rumbaugh, & Fields, 2006, 2009; Savage-Rumbaugh, Shanker, & Taylor, 1998). In this line of research, the bonobos have been trained to communicate with their caretakers by touching geometric symbols that represent words on a computer-monitored keyboard. Savage-Rumbaugh's star pupil has been a chimp named Kanzi, although many of his feats have been duplicated by his younger sister, Panbanisha. Kanzi has acquired hundreds of words and has used them in thousands of combinations. Many of these combinations were spontaneous and seemed to follow rules of language. For example, to specify whether he wanted to chase or be chased, Kanzi had to differentiate between symbol combinations in a way that appeared to involve the use of grammatical rules.

As the years went by, Kanzi's trainers noticed that he often seemed to understand the normal utterances that they exchanged with each other. Hence, they began to systematically evaluate his comprehension of spoken English. At age nine, they tested his understanding of 660 sentences that directed Kanzi to execute simple actions, such as "Put the collar in the water." To make sure that he really *understood* the sentences, they included many novel constructions in which the actions were not obvious given the objects involved, such as "Put the raisins in the shoe," or "Go get the balloon that's in the microwave." Kanzi correctly carried out 72 percent of the 660 requests. Moreover, he demonstrated remarkable understanding of sentence structure, as he could reliably distinguish the actions requested by "Pour the Coke in the lemonade," as opposed to "Pour the lemonade in the Coke."

How have the linguistics experts reacted to Kanzi's surprising progress in language development? Many remain skeptical. Wynne (2004) has raised questions about the scoring system used to determine whether Kanzi "understood" oral requests, arguing that it was extremely "generous." Wynne and other critics (Budiansky, 2004; Kako, 1999; Wallman, 1992) also question whether Kanzi's communications demonstrate all the basic properties of a language.

So, what can we conclude? Overall, it seems reasonable to assert that the ability to use language—in a very basic, primitive way—may not be entirely

© Mike Nichols

Kanzi, a pygmy chimpanzee, has learned to communicate with his caretakers in surprisingly sophisticated ways via computer-controlled symbol boards, thus raising some doubt about whether language is unique to humans.

unique to humans, as has been widely assumed. However, make no mistake, there is no comparison between human linguistic abilities and those of apes or other animals. As remarkable as the language studies with apes are, they should make us marvel even more at the fluency, flexibility, and complexity of human language. A normal human toddler quickly surpasses even the most successfully trained chimps. In mastering language, children outstrip chimps the way jet airplanes outrace horse-drawn buggies. Why are humans so well suited for learning language? According to some theorists, this talent for language is a product of evolution. Let's look at their thinking.

Language in an Evolutionary Context

All human societies depend on complex language systems. Even primitive cultures employ languages that are just as complicated as those used in modern societies. The universal nature of language suggests that it is an innate human characteristic. Consistent with this view, Steven Pinker argues that humans' special talent for language is a species-specific trait that is the product of natural selection (Pinker, 1994, 2004; Pinker & Jackendoff, 2005). As Pinker and Bloom (1992) point out, "There is an obvious advantage in being able to acquire information about the world second-hand ... one can avoid having to duplicate the possibly time-consuming and dangerous trial-and-error process that won that knowledge" (p. 460).

Courtesy of Sue Savage-Rumbaugh, Georgia State University Language Research Center

Sue Savage-Rumbaugh

"What Kanzi tells us is that humans are not the only species that can acquire language if exposed to it at an early age."

David Levenson/Getty Images

Steven Pinker

"If human language is unique in the modern animal kingdom, as it appears to be, the implications for a Darwinian account of its evolution would be as follows: none. A language instinct unique to modern humans poses no more of a paradox than a trunk unique to modern elephants."

Dunbar (1996) argues that language evolved as a device to build and maintain social coalitions in increasingly larger groups. Although the impetus for the evolution of language remains a matter of speculation and debate (Kirby, 2007), it does not take much imagination to envision how more effective communication among our ancient ancestors could have aided hunting, gathering, fighting, mating, and the avoidance of poisons, predators, and other dangers.

Although the adaptive value of language seems obvious, some scholars take issue with the assertion that human language is the product of evolution. For example, David Premack (1985) has expressed skepticism that small differences in language skill would influence reproductive fitness in primitive societies, where all one had to communicate about was the location of the closest mastodon herd. In an effort to refute this argument, Pinker and Bloom (1992) point out that very small adaptive disparities are sufficient to fuel evolutionary change. For example, they cite an estimate that a 1 percent difference in mortality rates among overlapping Neanderthal and human populations could have led to the extinction of Neanderthals in just 30 generations. They also note that a trait variation that produces on average just 1 percent more offspring than its alternative genetic expression would increase in prevalence from 0.1 percent to 99.9 percent of the population in 4000 generations. Four thousand generations may seem like an eternity, but in the context of evolution, it is a modest amount of time.

Whether or not evolution gets the credit, language acquisition in humans seems remarkably rapid. As you will see in the next section, this reality looms large in theories of language acquisition.

Theories of Language Acquisition

Since the 1950s, a great debate has raged about the key processes involved in language acquisition. As with arguments we have seen in other areas of psychology, this one centres on the *nature versus nurture* issue. The debate was stimulated by the influential behaviourist B. F. Skinner (1957), who argued that environmental factors govern language development. His provocative analysis brought a rejoinder from Noam Chomsky (1959), who emphasized biological determinism. Let's examine their views and subsequent theories that stake out a middle ground.

Behaviourist Theories

The behaviourist approach to language was first outlined by Skinner in his book *Verbal Behavior*

(1957). He argued that children learn language the same way they learn everything else: through imitation, reinforcement, and other established principles of conditioning. According to Skinner, vocalizations that are not reinforced gradually decline in frequency. The remaining vocalizations are shaped with reinforcers until they are correct. Behaviourists assert that by controlling reinforcement, parents encourage their children to learn the correct meaning and pronunciation of words (Staats & Staats, 1963). For example, as children grow older, parents may insist on closer and closer approximations of the word *water* before supplying the requested drink.

Behavioural theorists also use the principles of imitation and reinforcement to explain how children learn syntax. According to the behaviourists' view, children learn how to construct sentences by imitating the sentences of adults and older children. If children's imitative statements are understood, parents are able to answer their questions or respond to their requests, thus reinforcing their verbal behaviour.

Nativist Theories

Skinner's explanation of language acquisition soon inspired a critique and rival explanation from Noam Chomsky (1959, 1965). Chomsky pointed out that there are an infinite number of sentences in a language. It's therefore unreasonable to expect that children learn language by imitation. For example, in English, we often add *ed* to the end of a verb to construct past tense. Children routinely overregularize this rule, producing incorrect verbs such as *goed*, *eated*, and *thinked*. Mistakes such as these are inconsistent with Skinner's emphasis on imitation, because most adult speakers don't use ungrammatical words like *goed*. Children can't imitate things they don't hear. According to Chomsky, children learn *the rules of language*, not specific verbal responses, as Skinner proposed.

An alternative theory favoured by Chomsky and others is that humans have an inborn or "native" propensity to develop language (Chomsky, 1975, 1986, 2006). In this sense, *native* is a variation on the word *nature* as it's used in the nature versus nurture debate. *Nativist theory* proposes that humans are equipped with a *language acquisition* device (LAD)—an innate mechanism or process that facilitates the learning of language. According to this view, humans learn language for the same reason that birds learn to fly— because they're biologically equipped for it. The exact nature of the LAD has not been spelled out in nativist theories. It presumably consists of brain structures and neural wiring that leave humans well prepared

Noam Chomsky

"Even at low levels of intelligence, at pathological levels, we find a command of language that is totally unattainable by an ape."

Donna Coveney/MIT News Office

to discriminate among phonemes, to fast-map morphemes, to acquire rules of syntax, and so on.

Interactionist Theories

Like Skinner, Chomsky has his critics (Bohannon & Bonvillian, 2009). They ask: What exactly is a language acquisition device? How does the LAD work? What are the neural mechanisms involved? They argue that the LAD concept is terribly vague. Other critics question whether the rapidity of early language development is as exceptional as nativists assume. They assert that it isn't fair to compare the rapid progress of toddlers, who are immersed in their native language, against the struggles of older students, who may devote only 10–15 hours per week to their foreign language course.

The problems apparent in Skinner's and Chomsky's explanations of language development have led some researchers to outline interactionist theories of language acquisition. These theories (Bates, 1999; MacWhinney, 2001, 2004) assert that biology and experience both make important contributions to the development of language. Like the nativists, interactionists believe that the human organism is biologically well equipped for learning language. They also agree that much of this learning involves the acquisition of rules. However, like the behaviourists, they believe that social exchanges with parents and others play a critical role in moulding language skills (see Figure 8.4). Recent years have brought research

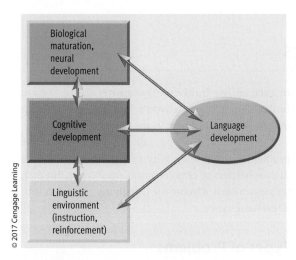

Figure 8.4

Interactionist theories of language acquisition. The interactionist view is that nature and nurture are both important to language acquisition. Maturation is thought to drive language development directly and to influence it indirectly by fostering cognitive development. Meanwhile, verbal exchanges with parents and others are also thought to play a critical role in moulding language skills. The complex bi-directional relationships depicted here shed some light on why there is room for extensive debate about the crucial factors in language acquisition.

that supports the assertion of both the nativists and the interactionists that humans are biologically prepared to learn language readily. A groundbreaking study using brain-imaging technology found that the human brain reacts differently to artificial syllables that are good and bad word candidates (Berent et al., 2014). This disparity is even seen in infants (G.mez et al., 2014). The findings suggest that the human brain is hardwired to readily recognize the sound patterns that make up human languages.

Culture, Language, and Thought

Another long-running controversy in the study of language concerns the relationships among culture, language, and thought (Fiedler, 2008). Obviously, people from different cultures generally speak different languages. But does your training in English lead you to think about certain things differently than someone who was raised to speak Chinese or French? In other words, does a cultural group's language determine their thoughts? Or does thought determine language?

Benjamin Lee Whorf (1956) has been the most prominent advocate of *linguistic relativity*, **the hypothesis that one's language determines the nature of one's thought.** Whorf speculated that different languages lead people to view the world differently. His classic example compared English and Inuit views of snow. He asserted that the English language has just one word for snow, whereas the Inuit language has many words that distinguish among falling snow, wet snow, and so on. Because of this language gap, Whorf argued that Inuit perceive snow differently than English-speaking people do. As another example, the Dani of the Indonesian province of Papua have just two words for colour (Heider, 1996)—*mili* for dark cool colours (e.g., black, green) and *mola* for warm and light colours (e.g., white, yellow). Accordingly, they should perceive colour differently than we do as we have many more colour words.

However, Whorf's conclusion about these perceptual differences was based on casual observation rather than systematic cross-cultural comparisons of perceptual processes. Moreover, critics subsequently noted that advocates of the linguistic relativity hypothesis had carelessly overestimated the number of Inuit words for snow, while conveniently ignoring the variety of English words that refer to snow, such as *slush* and *blizzard* (Martin, 1986; Pullum, 1991).

Whorf 's hypothesis has been the subject of considerable research and continues to generate debate (Chiu, Leung, & Kwan, 2007; Gleitman & Papafragou, 2005).

Does the language you speak determine how you think? Yes, said Benjamin Lee Whorf, who argued that the Inuit language, which has numerous words for snow, leads Inuit to perceive snow differently from English speakers. Whorf's hypothesis has been the subject of spirited debate.

Many studies have focused on cross-cultural comparisons of how people perceive colours because substantial variations exist among cultures in how colours are categorized with names. For example, some languages have a single colour name that includes both blue and green (Davies, 1998). If a language doesn't distinguish between blue and green, do people who speak that language think about colours differently than people in other cultures do?

Early efforts to answer this question suggested that the colour categories in a language have relatively little influence on how people perceive and think about colours (Berlin & Kay, 1969; Rosch, 1973). However, more recent studies have provided new evidence favouring the linguistic relativity hypothesis (Davidoff, 2001, 2004; Roberson et al., 2005). Studies of subjects who speak African languages that do not have a boundary between blue and green have found that language affects their colour perception. They have more trouble making quick discriminations between blue and green colours than English-speaking subjects do (Ozgen, 2004). Additional studies have found that a culture's colour categories shape subjects' similarity judgments and groupings of colours (Pilling & Davies, 2004; Roberson, Davies, & Davidoff, 2000). Other studies have found that language also has some impact on how people think about motion (Gennari et al., 2002); time (Boroditsky, 2001); and shapes (Roberson, Davidoff, & Shapiro, 2002).

So, what is the status of the linguistic relativity hypothesis? At present, the debate seems to centre on whether the new data are sufficient to support the original, "strong" version of the hypothesis (that a given language makes certain ways of thinking obligatory or impossible) or a "weaker" version of the hypothesis (that a language makes certain ways of thinking easier or more difficult). The current thinking seems to favour the weaker version of the linguistic relativity hypothesis (Kreiner, 2011).

Problem Solving: In Search of Solutions

Key Learning Goals

▶ Identify four common barriers to effective problem solving.

▶ Review general problem-solving strategies and heuristics, and discuss cultural variations in cognitive style.

Look at the two problems below. Can you solve them?

In the Thompson family, there are five brothers, and each brother has one sister. If you count Mrs. Thompson, how many females are there in the Thompson family?

Fifteen percent of the people in Halifax have unlisted telephone numbers. You select 200 names at random from the Halifax phone book. How many of these people can be expected to have unlisted phone numbers?

These problems, borrowed from Sternberg (1986, p. 214), are exceptionally simple, but many people fail to solve them. The answer to the first problem is *two:* The only females in the family are Mrs. Thompson and her one daughter, who is a sister

to each of her brothers. The answer to the second problem is *none*—you won't find any people with *unlisted* phone numbers in the phone book.

Why do many people fail to solve these simple problems? You'll learn why in a moment, when we discuss barriers to effective problem solving. But first, let's examine a scheme for classifying problems into a few basic types.

Types of Problems

Problem solving **refers to active efforts to discover what must be done to achieve a goal that is not readily attainable.** Obviously, if a goal is readily attainable, there isn't a problem. But in problem-solving situations, one must go beyond the information given to overcome obstacles and reach a goal. Jim Greeno (1978) has proposed that problems can be categorized into three basic classes:

1. *Problems of inducing structure* require people to discover the relationships among numbers, words, symbols, or ideas. The *series completion problems* and the *analogy problems* in Figure 8.5 are examples of problems of inducing structure.

2. *Problems of arrangement* require people to arrange the parts of a problem in a way that satisfies some criterion. The parts can usually be arranged in many ways, but only one or a few of the arrangements form a solution. The *string problem* and the *anagrams*

in Figure 8.5 fit in this category. Arrangement problems are often solved with a burst of insight. **Insight is the sudden discovery of the correct solution following incorrect attempts based primarily on trial and error** (Mayer, 1995).

3. *Problems of transformation* require people to carry out a sequence of transformations in order to reach a specific goal. The *hobbits and orcs problem* and the *water jar problem* in Figure 8.5 are examples of transformation problems. Transformation problems can be challenging. Even though you know exactly what the goal is, it's often not obvious how the goal can be achieved.

A. Analogy
What word completes the analogy?
Merchant : Sell : : Customer : _____
Lawyer : Client : : Doctor : _____

B. String problem
Two strings hang from the ceiling but are too far apart to allow a person to hold one and walk to the other. On the table are a book of matches, a screwdriver, and a few pieces of cotton. How could the strings be tied together?

C. Hobbits and orcs problem
Three hobbits and three orcs arrive at a river bank, and they all wish to cross to the other side. Fortunately, there is a boat, but unfortunately, the boat can hold only two creatures at one time. Also, there is another problem. Orcs are vicious creatures, and whenever there are more orcs than hobbits on one side of the river, the orcs will immediately attack the hobbits and eat them up. Consequently, you should be certain that you never leave more orcs than hobbits on either river bank. How should the problem be solved? It must be added that the orcs, though vicious, can be trusted to bring the boat back! (From Matlin, 1989, p. 319)

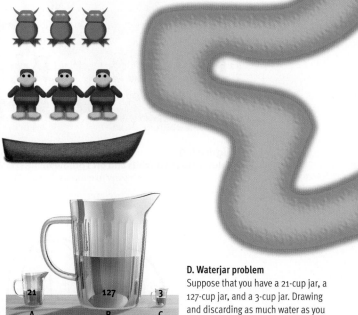

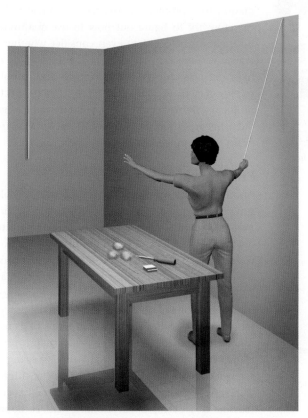

D. Waterjar problem
Suppose that you have a 21-cup jar, a 127-cup jar, and a 3-cup jar. Drawing and discarding as much water as you like, you need to measure out exactly 100 cups of water. How can this be done?

E. Anagram
Rearrange the letters in each row to make an English word.
RWAET
KEROJ

F. Series completion
What number or letter completes each series?
1 2 8 3 4 6 5 6 _____
A B M C D M _____

Photograph illustrating the string problem, with a person standing in a room reaching for a hanging string, with a table holding matches, a screwdriver, and cotton.

Figure 8.5
Six standard problems used in studies of problem solving. Try solving the problems and identifying which class each belongs to before reading further. The problems can be classified as follows. The *analogy problems* and *series completion problems* are problems of inducing structure. The solutions for the analogy problems are *Buy* and *Patient*. The solutions for the series completion problems are *4* and *E*. The *string problem* and the *anagram problems* are problems of arrangement. To solve the string problem, attach the screwdriver to one string and set it swinging as a pendulum. Hold the other string and catch the swinging screwdriver. Then you need only untie the screwdriver and tie the strings together. The solutions for the anagram problems are WATER and JOKER. The *hobbits and orcs problem* and the *water jar problem* are problems of transformation. The solutions for these problems are outlined in Figures 8.6 and 8.7.

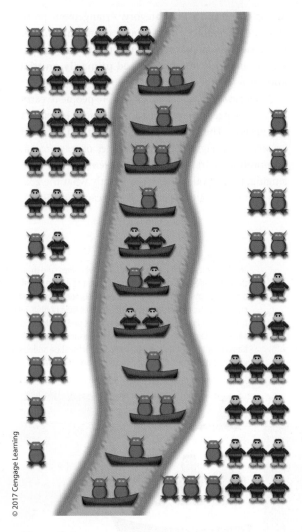

Figure 8.6
Solution to the hobbits and orcs problem. This problem is difficult because it is necessary to temporarily work *away* from the goal.

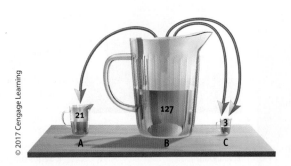

Figure 8.7
The method for solving the water jar problem. As explained in the text, the correct formula is B – A – 2C.

Greeno's list is not an exhaustive scheme for classifying problems, but it provides a useful system for understanding some of the variety seen in everyday problems.

Barriers to Effective Problem Solving

On the basis of their studies of problem solving, psychologists have identified a number of barriers that frequently impede subjects' efforts to arrive at solutions. Common obstacles to effective problem solving include a focus on irrelevant information, functional fixedness, mental set, and the imposition of unnecessary constraints.

Irrelevant Information

We began our discussion of problem solving with two simple problems that people routinely fail to solve (see the beginning of this section). The catch is that these problems contain *irrelevant information* that leads people astray. In the first problem, the number of brothers is irrelevant in determining the number of females in the Thompson family. In the second problem, subjects tend to focus on the figures of 15 percent and 200 names. But this numerical information is irrelevant, since all the names came out of the phone book.

Sternberg (1986) points out that people often incorrectly assume that all of the numerical information in a problem is necessary to solve it. They therefore try to figure out how to use quantitative information before they even consider whether it's relevant. Focusing on irrelevant information can have adverse effects on reasoning and problem solving (Gaeth & Shanteau, 2000). Hence, effective problem solving requires that you attempt to figure out what information is relevant and what is irrelevant before proceeding.

Functional Fixedness

Another common barrier to successful problem solving, identified by Gestalt psychologists, is *functional fixedness*—the tendency to perceive an item only in terms of its most common use. Functional fixedness has been seen in the difficulties that people have with the string problem in Figure 8.5 (Maier, 1931). Solving this problem requires finding a novel use for one of the objects: the screwdriver. Subjects tend to think of the screwdriver in terms of its usual functions—turning screws and perhaps prying things open. They have a hard time viewing the screwdriver as a weight. Their rigid way of thinking about the screwdriver illustrates functional fixedness (Bassok & Novick, 2012; Dominowski & Bourne, 1994). According to McCaffrey (2012; McCaffrey & Pearson, 2015), the root cause of functional fixedness is that people tend to overlook obscure, little-noticed features of problems. To combat functional fixedness, he has devised a strategy that helps people to discern the obscure features of a problem.

This strategy involves successively decomposing problems into their constituent parts. In an initial study, he found that training in this strategy led to enhanced problem solving.

Mental Set

Rigid thinking is also at work when a mental set interferes with effective problem solving. A *mental set* exists when people persist in using problem-solving strategies that have worked in the past. The effects of mental set were seen in a classic study by Gestalt psychologist Abraham Luchins (1942). He asked subjects to work a series of water jar problems, like the one introduced earlier. Six such problems are outlined in Figure 8.8, which shows the capacities of the three jars and the amounts of water to be measured out. Try solving these problems.

Were you able to develop a formula for solving these problems? The first four all require the same strategy, which was described in Figure 8.7. You have to fill jar B, draw off the amount that jar A holds once, and draw off the amount that jar C holds twice. Thus, the formula for your solution is B – A – 2C. Although there is an obvious and much simpler solution (A – C) for the fifth problem (see Figure 8.12 on page 295), Luchins found that most subjects stuck with the more cumbersome strategy that they had used in problems 1–4. Moreover, most subjects couldn't solve the sixth problem in the allotted time, because they kept trying to use their proven strategy, which does *not* work for this problem. The subjects' reliance on their "tried and true" strategy is an illustration of mental set in problem solving.

The compelling power of mental sets has even been demonstrated in chess experts working on chess problems (Bilalić, McLeod, & Gobet, 2010). Data on the chess players' eye movements indicated that the first solution that comes to mind focuses attention on information consistent with that solution and directs attention away from alternative strategies. Mental sets are not necessarily bad. They reflect sensible learning from past experience. In many situations, if you have an adequate solution, it may be inefficient to expend additional time and effort to search for an even better one. But, mental sets may explain why having expertise in an area sometimes backfires and hampers problem solving (Leighton & Sternberg, 2003).

Unnecessary Constraints

Effective problem solving requires specifying all the constraints governing a problem *without assuming any constraints that don't exist*. An example of a problem in which people place an unnecessary constraint on the solution is shown in Figure 8.9 (Adams, 1980). Without lifting your pencil from the paper, try to draw four straight lines that will cross through all nine dots. Most people will not draw lines outside the imaginary boundary that surrounds the dots. Notice that this constraint is not part of the problem statement. It's imposed only by the problem solver. Correct solutions, two of which are shown in Figure 8.13 on page 295, extend outside the imaginary boundary. People often make assumptions that impose unnecessary constraints on problem-solving efforts. A model and analysis of insight by James MacGregor of the University of Victoria and his colleagues (MacGregor, Ormerod, & Chronicle, 2001) suggest that failure in such problems results from both constraint and from some type of drive or dynamic that "steers activity into the constraint" (Ormerod et al., 2002, p. 798).

Approaches to Problem Solving

In their classic treatise on problem solving, Allen Newell and Herbert Simon (1972) use a spatial metaphor to describe the process of problem solving. They use the term *problem space* to refer to the set of possible pathways to a solution considered by the problem solver. Thus, they see problem solving as a search in space. The problem solver's task is to find a solution path among the potential pathways that could lead from the problem's initial state to its goal state. The problem space metaphor highlights the fact that people must choose from among a variety of conceivable pathways or strategies in attempting to solve problems (Hunt, 1994). In this section, we'll examine some general strategies.

© 2017 Cengage Learning

	Capacity of empty jars			Desired amount of water
Problem	A	B	C	
1	14	163	25	99
2	18	43	10	5
3	9	42	6	21
4	20	59	4	31
5	23	49	3	20
6	28	76	3	25

Figure 8.8
Additional water jar problems. Using jars A, B, and C, with the capacities indicated in each row, figure out how to measure out the desired amount of water specified on the far right. The solutions are shown in Figure 8.12 on page 295. (Based on Luchins, 1942)

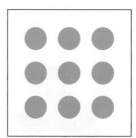

Figure 8.9
The nine-dot problem.
Without lifting your pencil from the paper, draw no more than four straight lines that will cross through all nine dots. For possible solutions, see Figure 8.13.

Source: Adams, J.L. (1980). *Conceptual blockbusting: A guide to better ideas.* New York: W.H. Freeman. Copyright © 1980 by James L. Adams. Reprinted by permission of W.H. Freeman & Co.

Figure 8.10
The matchstick problem.
Move two matches to form four equal squares. A solution can be found in Figure 8.14.

Source: Kendler, H.H. (1974). *Basic psychology.* Menlo Park, CA: Benjamin-Cummings. Copyright © 1974 The Benjamin-Cummings Publishing Co. Adapted by permission of Howard H. Kendler.

Using Algorithms and Heuristics

Trial and error is a common approach to solving problems. *Trial and error* involves trying possible solutions and discarding those that are in error until one works. Trial and error is often applied haphazardly, but people sometimes try to be systematic. An *algorithm* is a methodical, step-by-step procedure for trying all possible alternatives in searching for a solution to a problem. For instance, to solve the anagram IHCRA, you could write out all the possible arrangements of these letters until you eventually reached an answer (CHAIR). If an algorithm is available for a problem, it guarantees that one can eventually find a solution.

Algorithms can be effective when there are relatively few possible solutions to be tried out. However, algorithms do not exist for many problems, and they can become impractical when the problem space is large. Consider, for instance, the problem shown in Figure 8.10. The challenge is to move just two matches to create a pattern containing four equal squares. Sure, you could follow an algorithm in moving pairs of matches about. But you'd better allocate plenty of time to this effort, as there are over 60 000 possible rearrangements to check out (see Figure 8.14 on page 295 for the solution).

Because algorithms are inefficient, people often use shortcuts called *heuristics* in problem solving. A *heuristic* is a guiding principle or "rule of thumb" used in solving problems or making decisions. In solving problems, a heuristic allows you to discard some alternatives while pursuing selected alternatives that appear more likely to lead to a solution (Holyoak, 1995). Heuristics can be useful because they selectively narrow the problem space, but they don't guarantee success. Helpful heuristics in problem solving include forming subgoals, working backward, searching for analogies, and changing the representation of a problem.

Forming Subgoals

A useful strategy for many problems is to formulate *subgoals*, intermediate steps toward a solution. When you reach a subgoal, you've solved part of the problem. Some problems have fairly obvious subgoals, and research has shown that people take advantage of them. For instance, in analogy problems, the first subgoal usually is to figure out the possible relationship between the first two parts of the analogy. In a study by Simon and Reed (1976), subjects working on complex problems were given subgoals that weren't obvious. Providing subgoals helped the subjects solve the problems much more quickly.

The wisdom of formulating subgoals can be seen in the *tower of Hanoi problem,* depicted in Figure 8.11. The terminal goal for this problem is to move all three rings on peg A to peg C, while abiding by two restrictions: Only the top ring on a peg can be moved, and a larger ring must never be placed above a smaller ring. See whether you can solve the problem before continuing.

Dividing this problem into subgoals facilitates a solution (Kotovsky, Hayes, & Simon, 1985). If you think in terms of subgoals, your first task is to get ring 3 to the bottom of peg C. Breaking this task into sub-subgoals, subjects can figure out that they should move ring 1 to peg C, ring 2 to peg B, and ring 1 from peg C to peg B. These manoeuvres allow you to place ring 3 at the bottom of peg C, thus meeting your first subgoal. Your next subgoal—getting ring 2 over to peg C—can be accomplished in just two steps: Move ring 1 to peg A and ring 2 to peg C. It should then be obvious how to achieve your final subgoal—getting ring 1 over to peg C.

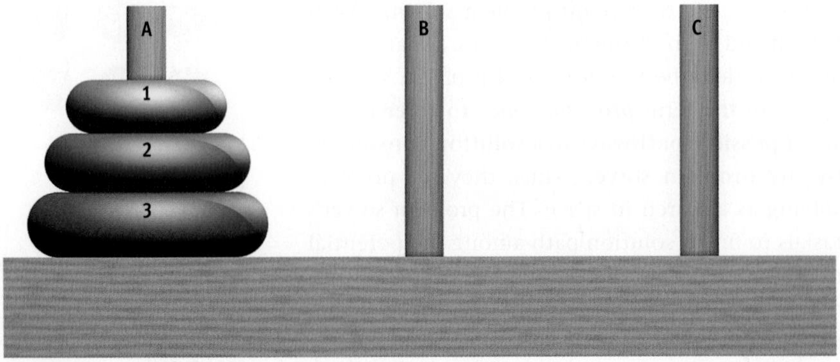

Searching for Analogies

Searching for analogies is another of the major heuristics for solving problems (Holyoak, 2012). We reason by analogy constantly (Sternberg, 2009), and these efforts to identify analogies can facilitate effective thinking (Gentner & Smith, 2013). If you can spot an analogy between problems, you may be able to use the solution to a previous problem to solve a current one. Of course, using this strategy depends on recognizing the similarity between two problems, which may itself be a challenging problem.

Analogies can be a powerful tool in efforts to solve problems. Unfortunately, people often are unable to recognize that two problems are similar and

Figure 8.11
The tower of Hanoi problem. Your mission is to move the rings from peg A to peg C. You can move only the top ring on a peg and can't place a larger ring above a smaller one. The solution is explained in the text.

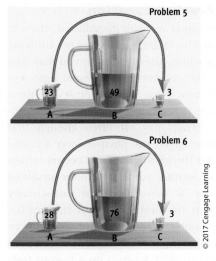

Figure 8.12
Solutions to the additional water jar problems. The solution for problems 1–4 is the same (B – A – 2C) as the solution shown in Figure 8.8. This method will work for problem 5, but there also is a simpler solution (A – C), which is the only solution for problem 6. Many subjects exhibit a mental set on these problems, as they fail to notice the simpler solution for problem 5.

Problem 5

Problem 6

© 2017 Cengage Learning

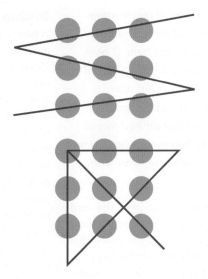

Figure 8.13
Two solutions to the nine-dot problem. The key to solving the problem is to recognize that nothing in the problem statement forbids going outside the imaginary boundary surrounding the dots.

Source: Adams, J.L. (1980). *Conceptual blockbusting: A guide to better ideas.* New York: W.H. Freeman. Copyright © 1980 by James L. Adams. Reprinted by permission of W.H. Freeman & Co.

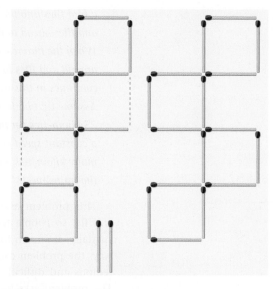

Figure 8.14
Solution to the matchstick problem. The key to solving this problem is to "open up" the figure, something that many subjects are reluctant to do because they impose unnecessary constraints on the problem.

Source: Kendler, H.H. (1974). *Basic psychology.* Menlo Park, CA: Benjamin-Cummings. Copyright © 1974 The Benjamin-Cummings Publishing Co. Adapted by permission of Howard H. Kendler.

that an analogy might lead to a solution (Kurtz & Lowenstein, 2007). One reason that people have difficulty recognizing analogies between problems is that they often focus on surface features of problems rather than their underlying structure (Bassok, 2003). Try to make use of analogies to solve the following two problems:

> *A teacher had 23 pupils in his class. All but seven of them went on a museum trip and thus were away for the day. How many students remained in class that day?*

> *Susan gets in her car in Edmonton and drives toward Lethbridge, averaging 100 kilometres per hour. Twenty minutes later, Ellen gets in her car in Lethbridge and starts driving toward Edmonton, averaging 120 kilometres per hour. Both women take the same route, which extends a total of 440 kilometres between the two cities. Which car is nearer to Edmonton when they meet?*

These problems, adapted from Sternberg (1986, pp. 213 and 215), resemble the ones that opened our discussion of problem solving. Each has an obvious solution that's hidden in irrelevant quantitative information. If you recognized this similarity, you probably solved the problems easily. If not, take

another look now that you know what the analogy is. Neither problem requires any calculation whatsoever. The answer to the first problem is *seven*. As for the second problem, when the two cars meet they're in the same place. Obviously, they have to be the same distance from Edmonton.

Changing the Representation of the Problem

Whether you solve a problem often hinges on how you envision it—your *representation of the problem*. Many problems can be represented in a variety of ways, such as verbally, mathematically, or spatially. You might represent a problem with a list, a table, an equation, a graph, a matrix of facts or numbers, a hierarchical tree diagram, or a sequential flow chart (Halpern, 2014). When you fail to make progress with your initial representation, changing your representation is often a good strategy (Novick & Bassok, 2005). As an illustration, see whether you can solve the *bird and train problem* (adapted from Bransford & Stein, 1993, p. 11):

> *Two train stations are 50 kilometres apart. At 1 p.m. on Sunday, a train pulls out from each of the stations and the trains start toward each other. Just as the trains pull out from the stations,*

a bird flies into the air in front of the first train and flies ahead to the front of the second train. When the bird reaches the second train, it turns around and flies toward the first train. The bird continues in this way until the trains meet. Assume that both trains travel at the speed of 25 kilometres per hour and that the bird flies at a constant speed of 100 kilometres per hour. How many kilometres will the bird have flown when the trains meet?

This problem asks about the *distance* the bird will fly, so people tend to represent the problem spatially, as shown in Figure 8.15. Represented this way, the problem can be solved, but the steps are tedious and difficult. But consider another angle. The problem asks how far the bird will fly in the time it takes the trains to meet. Since we know how fast the bird flies, all we really need to know is how much *time* it takes for the trains to meet. Changing the representation of the problem from a question of *distance* to a question of *time* makes for an easier solution, as follows: The train stations are 50 kilometres apart. Since the trains are travelling toward each other at the same speed, they will meet midway and each will have travelled 25 kilometres. The trains are moving at 25 kilometres per hour. Hence, the time it takes them to meet 25 kilometres from each station is one hour. Since the bird flies at 100 kilometres per hour, it will fly 100 kilometres in the hour it takes the trains to meet.

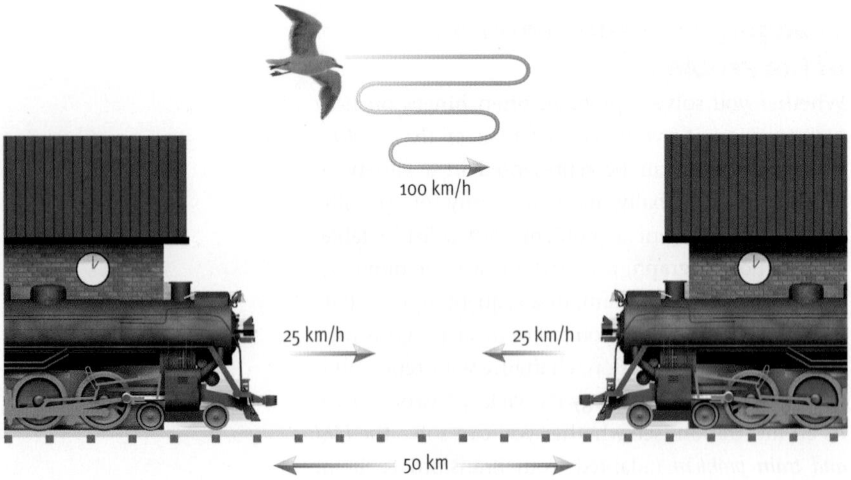

Figure 8.15
Representing the bird and train problem. The typical inclination is to envision this problem spatially, as shown here. However, as the text explains, this representation makes the problem much more difficult than it really is.

Source: From Weiten. *Cengage Advantage Books: Psychology,* 9E. © 2013 South-Western, a part of Cengage, Inc. Reproduced by permission. www.cengage.com/permissions

Taking a Break: Incubation

When a problem is resistant to solution, there is much to be said for taking a break and not thinking about it for a while. After the break, you may find that you see the problem in a different light and new solutions may spring to mind. Obviously, there is no guarantee that a break will facilitate problem solving. But breaks pay off often enough that researchers have given the phenomenon a name: *incubation.* An *incubation effect* occurs when new solutions surface for a previously unsolved problem after a period of not consciously thinking about the problem. Depending on the nature of the problem, incubation periods may be measured in minutes, hours, or days. The likelihood of an incubation effect depends on a host of task-related factors, but on the whole, incubation does tend to enhance problem solving (Dodds, Ward, & Smith, 2011; Sio & Ormerod, 2009). Research suggests that incubation effects can even occur during sleep (Cai et al., 2009; Stickgold & Walker, 2004). Some theorists believe that incubation effects occur because people continue to work on problems at an unconscious level after conscious effort has been suspended (Ellwood et al., 2009). However, other evidence suggests that a high level of mind wandering during the incubation break is associated with a greater likelihood of coming up with a new solution (Baird et al., 2012). Research on this and related topics such as cognitive insight will continue as we look for ways to ensure more accurate decisions (Konnis & Beeman, 2014).

Culture, Cognitive Style, and Problem Solving

Do the varied experiences of people from different cultures lead to cross-cultural variations in problem solving? Yes, at least to some degree. Researchers have found cultural differences in the cognitive style people exhibit in solving problems (Cole & Packer, 2011). Richard Nisbett and his colleagues (Nisbett, 2016; Nisbett et al., 2001; Nisbett & Miyamoto, 2005) argue that people from Eastern Asian cultures (such as China, Japan, and Korea) display a *holistic cognitive style* that focuses on context and relationships among elements, whereas people from Western cultures (North America and Europe) exhibit an *analytic cognitive style* that focuses on objects and their properties rather than context. To put it simply, Easterners see wholes where Westerners see parts.

concept **check** 8.2

In one test of this hypothesis, Masuda and Nisbett (2001) presented computer-animated scenes of fish and other underwater objects to Japanese and American participants and asked them to report what they had seen. The initial comments of American subjects typically referred to the focal fish, whereas the initial comments of Japanese subjects usually referred to background elements (see Figure 8.16). Furthermore, the Japanese participants made about 70 percent more statements about context or background and about twice as many statements about relationships between elements in the scenes. Based on these and many other findings, Nisbett et al. (2001) conclude that cultural differences in cognitive style are substantial and that "literally different cognitive processes are often invoked by East Asians and Westerners dealing with the same problem" (p. 305). These disparities in cognitive style seem to be rooted in variations in cultures' social orientation (Varnum et al., 2010). They appear to grow out of Western cultures' emphasis on the individual and independence, as opposed to Eastern cultures' emphasis on the group and interdependence.

Problems are not the only kind of cognitive challenge that people grapple with on a regular basis. Life also seems to constantly demand decisions.

Accordingly, it is critical that psychologists examine cognition as it relates to real-world challenges (Kingstone, Smilek, & Eastwook, 2008). As you might expect, cognitive psychologists have shown great interest in the process of decision making (Västfjäll & Slovic, 2013), which is our next subject.

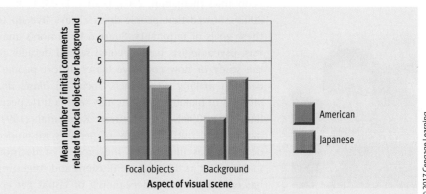

© 2017 Cengage Learning

Figure 8.16

Cultural disparities in cognitive style. In one of the studies conducted by Masuda and Nisbett (2001), the participants were asked to describe computer-animated visual scenes. As you can see, the initial comments made by American subjects referred more to focal objects in the scenes, whereas the initial comments made by Japanese subjects referred more to background elements in the scenes. These findings are consistent with the hypothesis that Easterners see wholes (a holistic cognitive style) where Westerners see parts (an analytic cognitive style). (Data from Masuda & Nisbett, 2001)

Decision Making: Choices and Chances

Key Learning Goals

▶ Articulate Simon's theory of bounded rationality, and discuss research on decisions about preferences.

▶ Understand the availability and representativeness heuristics and how they contribute to the tendency to ignore base rates and the conjunction fallacy.

▶ Describe the nature of fast and frugal heuristics, and discuss dual process theories of decision making.

The solution to the candle problem in Concept Check 8.2.

Jiaying Zhao is an assistant professor of psychology at the University of British Columbia. Her area of research focus is cognitive science. One of her research programs examines the impact of resource scarcity on cognitive functioning.

Decisions, decisions. Life is full of them. You decided to read this book today. Earlier today you decided when to get up, whether to eat breakfast, and if so, what to eat. Usually you make routine decisions like these with little effort. But on occasion you need to make important judgments and decisions that require more thought (Kahneman, 2011) and effort (Polman & Vohs, 2016). Big decisions—such as selecting a car, a home, or a job—tend to be difficult. The alternatives usually have a number of attributes that need to be weighed. For example, in choosing which university to attend, you may want to compare climate, the number of scholarships available, whether the city in which it is located has any professional sports teams, whether there are multiple program options for majoring in psychology, and so on. Scientists study decision making and rationality and the implicated processes and mechanisms (Hirsh et al., 2013) because they are so essential to our fundamental values, nature, and well-being (Stanovich, 2009; Stanovich, West, & Toplak, 2016). We know from this work that a variety of factors can affect the accuracy and efficiency of our decision making, including poverty, as was shown recently by University of British Columbia researcher Jiaying Zhao and her colleagues (Mani, Mullainathan, Shafir, & Zhao, 2013).

Decision making involves evaluating alternatives and making choices among them. Most people try to be systematic and rational in their decision making. But that rational approach can be shaped and derailed by a variety of factors (Beulow & Writh, 2017; Stern & West, 2016). For example, the work that earned Herbert Simon the 1978 Nobel Prize in Economics (Benjamin, 2003; Leahey, 2003; Pickren, 2003) showed that people don't always live up to these goals of rationality. Spurred by Simon's analysis, psychologists have devoted several decades to the study of how cognitive biases distort people's decision making. Researchers' focus on *biases and mistakes* in making decisions may seem a little peculiar, but as 2002 Noble Laureate Kahneman (1991) has pointed out, the study of people's misguided decisions has illuminated the process of decision making, just as the study of illusions and forgetting has enhanced our understanding of visual perception and memory, respectively.

Making Choices: Basic Strategies

Many decisions involve choices about *preferences*, which can be made using a variety of strategies (Goldstein & Hogarth, 1997). Barry Schwartz (2004) has argued that people in modern societies are overwhelmed by an overabundance of such choices about preferences. For example, Schwartz describes how a simple visit to a local supermarket can require a consumer to choose from 285 varieties of cookies, 61 types of suntan lotions, 150 varieties of lipstick, and 175 kinds of salad dressings.

reality check

Misconception

In making choices, people like to have lots of options; the more options the better.

Reality

Having choices is a good thing; people like to have a variety of options. But recent research on choice overload suggests that's true only up to a point. An overabundance of options can make decisions difficult and unpleasant, foster decision paralysis (an inability to decide), and lead to post-decision regret.

Although enormous freedom of choice sounds attractive, Schwartz argues that the overabundance of choices in modern life has unexpected costs. He feels that people routinely make errors even when choosing among a handful of alternatives and that errors become much more likely when decisions become more complex. And he explains how having more alternatives increases the potential for rumination and post-decision regret. Ultimately, he argues, the malaise associated with choice overload undermines individuals' happiness and contributes to depression.

Consistent with this analysis, quite a number of studies have suggested that when consumers have too many choices (for a specific product), they are more likely to leave a store empty-handed (Jessup et al., 2009; Park & Jang, 2013). Why? Studies show that when there are many choices available, people are more likely to struggle deciding which is the best option, and so defer their decision (White & Hoffrage, 2009). How many choices are too many? That depends on a host of factors, but it appears that people prefer more choices up to a point, and then further increases in options lead to decreased satisfaction with the situation (Reutskaja & Hogarth, 2009). That said, variations in how knowledgeable consumers feel about a specific product can influence the likelihood of choice overload.

In one recent study, participants who subjectively felt knowledgeable about specific products were less likely to buy when given many options (showing choice overload), but those who did not feel very knowledgeable tended to welcome additional options when the extra choices helped them to educate themselves about the product (Hadar & Sood, 2014). Thus, the prediction of when choice overload will occur is a complicated matter.

Another line of research has looked at whether decisions about preferences work out better when people engage in conscious deliberation or go with intuitive, unconscious feelings based on minimal deliberation. Ap Dijksterhuis and colleagues (Dijksterhuis & Nordgren, 2006; Dijksterhuis & van Olden, 2006) argue that, given the limited capacity of conscious thought, deliberate decisions should be superior to intuitive decisions when choices are simple, but intuitive, unconscious decisions should be superior when choices are complex. In a test of this hypothesis, they had a sample of people indicate how many facets they would evaluate in deciding to purchase 40 consumer products, such as shampoos, shoes, and cameras, yielding a decision complexity score for each product (Dijksterhuis et al., 2006). Subsequently, another group of participants picked a product they recently bought from this list, and were asked how much conscious thought they put into the decision and how satisfied they were with their choice. As predicted, deliberation promoted greater satisfaction when decisions were simple. However, just the opposite occurred for complex decisions. Dijksterhuis calls this phenomenon the deliberation-without-attention effect—when people are faced with complex choices, they tend to make better decisions if they don't devote careful attention to the matter. Dijksterhuis believes that deliberations are taking place, but outside conscious awareness. This assertion was bolstered by a recent replication of the deliberation-without-attention effect that incorporated neuroimaging (fMRI) of participants' brains while they engaged in conscious deliberation regarding a product choice

and while they worked on a distractor task thought to promote unconscious deliberation about the choice (Creswell, Bursley, & Satpute, 2013). The study found that the same brain regions that were activated by conscious deliberation about the decision remained active during the period of unconscious deliberation.

Taking Chances: Factors Weighed in Risky Decisions

Suppose you have the chance to play a dice game in which you might win some money. You must decide whether it would be to your advantage to play. You're going to roll a fair die. If the number 6 appears, you win $5. If one of the other five numbers appears, you win nothing. It costs you $1 every time you play. Should you participate?

This problem calls for a type of decision making that is somewhat different from making choices about preferences. In selecting alternatives that reflect preferences, people generally weigh known outcomes (apartment A will require a long commute to campus, car B will use less gas, and so forth). In contrast, *risky decision making* involves **making choices under conditions of uncertainty.** Uncertainty exists when people don't know what will happen. At best, they know the probability that a particular event will occur.

One way to decide whether to play the dice game would be to figure out the *expected value* of participation in the game. To do so, you would need to calculate the average amount of money you could expect to win or lose each time you play. The value of a win is $4 ($5 minus the $1 entry fee). The value of a loss is –$1. To calculate expected value, you also need to know the probability of a win or loss. Since a die has six faces, the probability of a win is one out of six, and the probability of a loss is five out of six. Thus, on five out of every six trials, you lose $1. On one out of six, you win $4. The game is beginning to sound unattractive, isn't it? We can figure out the precise expected value as follows:

$$\text{Expected value} = (1/6 \times 4) + (5/6 \times -1)$$
$$= 4/6 + (-5/6)$$
$$= -1/6$$

The expected value of this game is –1/6 of a dollar, which means that you lose an average of about 17 cents per turn. Now that you know the expected value, surely you won't agree to play. Or will you?

If we want to understand why people make the decisions they do, the concept of expected value is not enough. People frequently behave in ways that are inconsistent with expected value (Slovic, Lichtenstein,

Herbert Simon

"The capacity of the human mind for formulating and solving complex problems is very small compared with the size of the problems whose solution is required for objectively rational behavior in the real world…"

People often have to decide between alternative products, such as computers, cars, refrigerators, and so forth, that are not all that different. They often struggle with the abundant choices and delay making a decision. Extra deliberation does not necessarily lead to better decisions.

& Fischhoff, 1988). Anytime the expected value is negative, a gambler should expect to lose money. Yet a great many people gamble at racetracks and casinos and buy lottery tickets. Although they realize that the odds are against them, they continue to gamble.

To explain decisions that violate expected value, some theories replace the objective value of an outcome with its *subjective utility* (Fischhoff, 1988). Subjective utility represents what an outcome is personally worth to an individual. For example, buying a few lottery tickets may allow you to dream about becoming wealthy. Buying insurance may give you a sense of security. Subjective utilities like these vary from one person to another. If we know an individual's subjective utilities, we can better understand that person's risky decision making.

Another way to improve our understanding of risky decision making is to consider individuals' estimates of the *subjective probability* of events (Shafer & Tversky, 1988). If people don't know actual probabilities, they must rely on their personal estimates of probabilities. These estimates can have interesting effects on the perceived utility of various outcomes.

Heuristics in Judging Probabilities

- What are your chances of passing your next psychology test if you study for only three hours?
- How likely is a major downturn in the stock market during the upcoming year?
- What are the odds of your getting into graduate school in the field of your choice?

These questions ask you to make probability estimates. Amos Tversky and Daniel Kahneman (1974, 1982; Kahneman & Tversky, 2000) have conducted extensive research on the *heuristics*, or mental shortcuts, that people use in grappling with probabilities (Gigerenzer & Gaissmaier, 2011). This research on heuristics earned Kahneman the Nobel Prize in Economics in 2002 (unfortunately, his collaborator, Amos Tversky, died in 1996).

Availability is one such heuristic. The *availability heuristic* involves basing the estimated probability of an event on the ease with which relevant instances come to mind. For example, you may estimate the divorce rate by recalling the number of divorces among your friends' parents. Recalling specific instances of an event is a reasonable strategy to use in estimating the event's probability. However, if instances occur frequently but you have difficulty retrieving them from memory, your estimate will be biased. For instance, it's easier to think of words that begin with a certain letter than words that contain that letter at some other position. Hence, people

Amos Tversky

"People treat their own cases as if they were unique, rather than part of a huge lottery. You hear this silly argument that 'The odds don't apply to me.' Why should God, or whoever runs this lottery, give you special treatment?"

Daniel Kahneman

"The human mind suppresses uncertainty. We're not only convinced that we know more about our politics, our businesses, and our spouses than we really do, but also that what we don't know must be unimportant."

Daniel Kahneman

Daniel Kahneman was awarded the Noble Prize in Economics for his collaborative work with Amos Tversky on decision making. Kahneman is only the second non-economist to win this prize. The other was John Nash, profiled in Chapter 15, who was a mathematician.

should tend to respond that there are more words starting with the letter K than words having a K in the third position. To test this hypothesis, Tversky and Kahneman (1973) selected five consonants (K, L, N, R, V) that occur more frequently in the third position of a word than in the first. Subjects were asked whether each of the letters appears more often in the first or third position. Most of the subjects erroneously believed that all five letters were much more frequent in the first than in the third position, confirming the hypothesis.

Representativeness is another guide in estimating probabilities identified by Kahneman and Tversky (1982). The *representativeness heuristic* involves basing the estimated probability of an event on how similar it is to the typical prototype of that event. To illustrate, imagine that you flip a coin six times and keep track of how often the result is heads (H) or tails (T). Which of the following sequences is more likely?

1. T T T T T T
2. H T T H T H

People generally believe that the second sequence is more likely. After all, coin tossing is a random affair, and the second sequence looks much more representative of a random process than the first. In reality, the probability of each exact *sequence* is precisely the same ($1/2 \times 1/2 \times 1/2 \times 1/2 \times 1/2 \times 1/2 = 1/64$). Let's look at another phenomenon in which the representativeness heuristic plays a key role.

Stanford University News and Publication Service

Don Murray/Getty Images

AP Photo/Jonas Ekstromer/Pool

The Tendency to Ignore Base Rates

Steve is very shy and withdrawn, invariably helpful, but with little interest in people or in the world of reality. A meek and tidy soul, he has a need for order and structure and a passion for detail. Do you think Steve is a salesperson or a librarian? (Adapted from Tversky & Kahneman, 1974, p. 1124)

Using the *representativeness heuristic,* subjects tend to guess that Steve is a librarian because he resembles their prototype of a librarian (Tversky & Kahneman, 1982). In reality, this is not a very wise guess, because it *ignores the base rates* of librarians and salespeople in the population. Virtually everyone knows that salespeople outnumber librarians by a wide margin (roughly 75 to 1 in North America). This fact makes it much more likely that Steve is in sales. But in estimating probabilities, people often ignore information on base rates.

Although people do not *always* neglect base rate information, it is a persistent phenomenon (Birnbaum, 2004a; Koehler, 1996). Moreover, people are particularly bad about applying base rates to themselves. For instance, Weinstein (1984; Weinstein & Klein, 1995) has found that people underestimate the risks of their own health-impairing habits while viewing others' risks much more accurately. Thus, smokers are realistic in estimating the degree to which smoking increases someone else's risk of heart attack but underestimate the risk for themselves.

The Conjunction Fallacy

Imagine that you're going to meet a man who is an articulate, ambitious, power-hungry wheeler-dealer. Do you think it's more likely that he's a university professor or a university professor who's also a politician?

People tend to guess that the man is a "university professor who's also a politician" because the description fits with the typical prototype of politicians. But stop and think for a moment. The broader category of university professors completely includes the smaller subcategory of university professors who are politicians (see Figure 8.17). The probability of being in the subcategory cannot be higher than the probability of being in the broader category. It's a logical impossibility!

Tversky and Kahneman (1983) call this error the *conjunction fallacy.* The *conjunction fallacy* occurs when people estimate that the odds of two uncertain events happening together are greater than

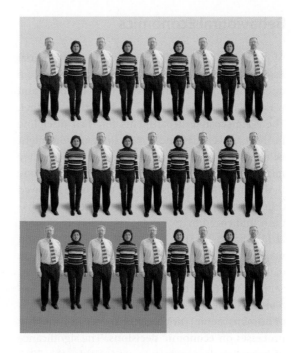

Figure 8.17
The conjunction fallacy.
People routinely fall victim to the conjunction fallacy, but as this diagram makes obvious, the probability of being in a subcategory (university professors who are also politicians) cannot be higher than the probability of being in the broader category (university professors). As this case illustrates, it often helps to represent a problem in a diagram.

Source: From WEITEN. *Psychology,* 6E. © 2004 South-Western, a part of Cengage, Inc. Reproduced by permission. www.cengage.com/permissions.

the odds of either event happening alone. The conjunction fallacy has been observed in a number of studies and has generally been attributed to the powerful influence of the representativeness heuristic (Epstein, Donovan, & Denes-Raj, 1999), although some doubts have been raised about this interpretation (Fisk, 2004).

concept check 8.3

Recognizing Heuristics and Fallacies in Decision Making

Check your understanding of heuristics in decision making by trying to identify the heuristics used in the following example. Each numbered element in the anecdote below illustrates a problem-solving heuristic. Write the relevant heuristic in the space on the left. You can find the answers in Appendix A.

_____ **1.** Marsha is introduced to another student at a campus party. Before she begins talking to the stranger, Marsha attempts to guess what major the other student is pursuing in her studies. The other woman seems quite conservative and a bit introverted. Marsha decides that she must be a biology major and that she certainly is not in the fine arts program. She has come to this decision based on the similarity of the other student to the way science majors are typically depicted on TV shows.

_____ **2.** When Marsha considers history as a major, she thinks to herself, "Gee, I know four history graduates who are still looking for work," and concludes that the probability of getting a job using a history degree is very low.

_____ **3.** Marsha recently attended a fundraiser for the homeless. At the fundraiser she met another woman she has seen before on campus. The other woman seems quite bright, and talks about her interest in social justice and describes how she has recently participated in a few protest marches. Marsha thinks the other woman may be either a librarian or a librarian who is also active in the feminist movement. Marsha decides on the latter. This is an example of which heuristic/fallacy?

Behavioural Economics

After reading the title for this section, "Behavioural Economics," you may have wondered why we are discussing economics in a psychology textbook and what the two disciplines have to do with each other. There are separate departments for each discipline in most universities and, while some of you might be taking introductory courses in each subject, they might seem quite distinct. You would not be alone in thinking this way. Historically, they have followed different paths. Recently, however, economics has been influenced by psychologists (Ariely & Norton, 2011; Thaler, 2015) working in the area of decision making, and in current economics textbooks you will see references to behavioural economics (e.g., Samuelson & Nordhaus, 2005). *Behavioural economics* is a field of study that examines the effects of humans' actual (not idealized) decision-making processes on economic decisions. The significance of behavioural economics is undeniable; the 2017 Nobel Prize for economics was awarded to Richard Thaler for his pioneering work on Behavioural Economics.

As we suggested earlier, most people try to be systematic and rational in their decision making. This is a model followed traditionally by much of the work in economics; the emphasis is on rationality. Work in the psychology of decision making has served to introduce evidence that this assumption of rationality in decision making has clear limits. The work that earned Herbert Simon the 1978 Nobel Prize (Simon, 1991) in Economics showed that people don't always live up to these goals of being systematic and rational. Before Simon's work, most traditional theories in economics assumed that people make rational choices to maximize their economic gains. Simon (1957) demonstrated that people have a limited ability to process and evaluate information on numerous facets of possible alternatives. Thus, Simon's *theory of bounded rationality* asserts that people tend to use simple strategies in decision making that focus on only a few facets of available options and often result in "irrational" decisions that are less than optimal.

Collaborative work by Kahneman and Tversky (Kahneman, 2003a, 2003b; Lewis, 2016; Sustein & Thaler, 2016) on the nature and prevalence of biases in decision making, some of which we have just reviewed, had a significant impact on economic theory. In fact, their paper entitled "Prospect Theory" (Kahneman & Tversky, 1979; Thaler, 2015), a model of decision making under uncertainty, is the most cited paper ever to appear in the major economics journal *Econimetrica* and it was the second most cited paper in all of economics between 1975 and 2000 (Wu, Zhang, & Gonzoles, 2004).

In their work, Kahneman and Tversky were able to document that humans in their decision making often departed from the "rationality" that dominated classical economic thought. They argued, for example, that how decision alternatives are *framed* dramatically affects our decisions. *Framing* refers to how decision issues are posed or how choices are structured. For instance, some oil companies charge gas station patrons more when they pay with a credit card. This fee clearly is a credit surcharge that results in a small financial loss. However, the oil companies never explicitly label it as a surcharge. Instead, they assert that they offer a discount for cash. Thus, they frame the decision as a choice between the normal price or an opportunity for a gain. They understand that it's easier for customers to forsake a gain than it is to absorb a loss. The concept of framing is further elaborated in the Personal Application on page 305.

Human thought is often biased (Rogerson et al., 2011)—biased by processes such as a belief in the law of small numbers (discussed in the Personal Application near the end of this chapter), and by a tendency to rely on heuristics such as availability and representativeness. Since the pioneering work of Kahneman and Tversky, a vast literature has grown up at the interface of psychology and economics (e.g., Ariely, 2008; Camerer, Loewenstein, & Rabin, 2004; De Cremer, Zeelenberg, & Murnighan, 2006; Frey & Stutzer, 2007; Lewis, 2008; McKenzie, 2010), painting a more realistic picture of decision making.

Evolutionary Analyses of Flaws in Human Decision Making

A central conclusion of the last three decades of research on decision making has been that human decision-making strategies are riddled with errors and biases that yield surprisingly irrational results (Goldstein & Hogarth, 1997; Risen & Gilovich, 2007; Shafir & LeBoeuf, 2002). Theorists have discovered that people have "mental limitations" and have concluded that people are not as bright and rational as they think they are. This broad conclusion has led some evolutionary psychologists to reconsider the work on human decision making. Their take on the matter is quite interesting.

First, they argue that traditional decision research has imposed an invalid and unrealistic standard of rationality, which assumes that people should be impeccable in applying the laws of deductive logic and statistical probability while objectively and precisely weighing multiple factors in arriving at decisions (Gigerenzer, 2000). Second, they argue that humans only *seem* irrational because cognitive psychologists have been asking the wrong questions and formulating problems in the wrong ways—ways that have nothing to do with the adaptive problems that the human mind has evolved to solve (Cosmides & Tooby, 1996).

According to Leda Cosmides and John Tooby (1994, 2015), the human mind consists of a large number of specialized cognitive mechanisms that have emerged over the course of evolution to solve specific adaptive problems, such as finding food, shelter, and mates and dealing with allies and enemies. Thus, human decision-making and problem-solving strategies have been tailored to handle real-world adaptive problems. Participants perform poorly in cognitive research, say Cosmides and Tooby, because it confronts them with contrived, artificial problems that do not involve natural categories and have no adaptive significance.

Thus, evolutionary theorists assert that many errors in human reasoning, such as neglect of base rates and the conjunction fallacy, should vanish if classic lab problems are reformulated in terms of raw frequencies rather than probabilities and base rates. Consistent with this analysis, evolutionary psychologists have shown that some errors in reasoning that are seen in lab studies disappear or are decreased when problems are presented in ways that resemble the type of input humans would have processed in ancestral times (Brase, Cosmides, & Tooby, 1998; Hertwig & Gigerenzer, 1999). So the debate continues (Shafir & LeBoeuf, 2002), but this evidence and other lines of research (Keys & Schwartz, 2007) are gradually reducing cognitive psychologists' tendency to characterize human reasoning as "irrational."

Thinking Fast and Thinking Slow: Two Systems of Thought

To further expand on the evolutionary point of view, Gerd Gigerenzer has argued that humans' reasoning largely depends on "fast and frugal heuristics" that are quite a bit simpler than the complicated mental processes studied in traditional cognitive research (Gigerenzer, 2000, 2004, 2008; Todd & Gigerenzer, 2000, 2007). According to Gigerenzer, organisms from toads to stockbrokers have to make fast decisions under demanding circumstances with limited information. In most instances, organisms (including humans) do not have the time, resources, or cognitive capacities to gather all of the relevant information, consider all of the possible options, calculate all of the probabilities and risks, and then make the statistically optimal

decision. Instead, they use quick-and-dirty heuristics that are less than perfect but that work well enough most of the time to be adaptive in the real world.

Gigerenzer and his colleagues have studied a variety of other quick, one-reason decision-making strategies and demonstrated that they can yield inferences that are just as accurate as much more elaborate and time-consuming strategies that carefully weigh many factors (Marewski, Gaissmaier, & Gigerenzerm, 2010). And they have demonstrated that people actually use these fast and frugal heuristics in a diverse array of situations (Gigerenzer & Todd, 1999; Rieskamp & Hoffrage, 1999).

Courtesy of Lena Cosmides

Courtesy of John Tooby

Leda Cosmides and John Tooby

"The problems our cognitive devices are designed to solve do not reflect the problems our modern life experiences lead us to see as normal. ... Instead, they are the ancient and seemingly esoteric problems that our hunter–gatherer ancestors encountered generation after generation over hominid evolution."

....

reality check

Misconception

Effective decision making requires careful analysis of the alternatives and thoughtful deliberation.

Reality

Research on fast and frugal heuristics and the deliberation-without-attention effect demonstrate that good decision making does not necessarily *require* systematic, thorough deliberation. Although many decisions call for careful reflection, it appears that intuition has been underrated. Quick, simple, intuitive strategies can also yield good decisions. The challenge is to know when to go with intuition and when to rely on deliberation.

How have traditional decision-making theorists responded to the challenge presented by Gigerenzer and other evolutionary theorists? They acknowledge that people often rely on fast and frugal heuristics, but they argue that this reality does not make decades of research on carefully reasoned approaches to decision making meaningless. Rather, they propose *dual-process theories*, positing that people depend on two very different modes or systems of thinking when making decisions (De Neys, 2006; Evans, 2007; Gilovich & Griffin, 2010; Kahneman, 2003, 2011, 2012; Stanovich & West, 2002). One system consists of quick, simple, effortless, automatic judgments, like Gigerenzer's fast and frugal heuristics, which traditional theorists prefer to characterize as "intuitive thinking." The second system consists of slower, more elaborate, effortful, controlled judgments, like those studied in traditional decision research.

Adapting terminology originally employed by Stanovich and West (2000), Nobel Laureate Daniel Kahneman (2011) has clearly articulated the differences between these two processes of thought. He refers to these two modes or systems of thought as *System 1* (thinking fast) and *System 2* (thinking slow).

Consistent with the research and theory just reviewed, System 1 is a more automatic mode of thinking in which we expend very little effort and over which we have no control. System 2 thinking is under our control and is more effortful. According to Kahneman, System 2 thinking is the thinking from which we derive our sense of choice, deliberation, concentration, and personal agency. System 1 is involved when we read words on a billboard, detect hostility in someone's voice, answer questions such as 2 + 2 +?, and so on (Kahneman, 2011). System 2 is invoked when we look for a person in a crowd at a Pearl Jam concert who is wearing a black polo shirt, when we fill out our income tax forms, or when we try to maintain a faster walking speed than is normal for us (Kahneman, 2011). Both systems are necessary, and while they are sometimes in conflict, they typically work to support each other. System 2 typically monitors and corrects the automatic System 1 as needed and takes over when complicated or important decisions loom. Thus, traditional theorists maintain that the "fast" operating System 1 and the "slower" reasoned, deliberate, rule-governed decision/thinking strategies of System 2 exist side by side and that both need to be studied to fully understand our thinking and decision making (House, 2016; Sherman, Gawronski, & Trope, 2014).

Putting It in Perspective: Themes 1, 5, 6, and 7

Four of our unifying themes have been especially prominent in this chapter. The first is the continuing question about the relative influences of heredity and environment. The controversy about how children acquire language skills replays the nature versus nurture debate. The behaviourist theory, that children learn language through imitation and reinforcement, emphasizes the importance of the environment. The nativist theory, that children come equipped with an innate language acquisition device, argues for the importance of biology. The debate is far from settled, but the accumulating evidence suggests that language development depends on both nature and nurture, as more recent interactionist theories have proposed.

The second pertinent theme is the empirical nature of psychology. For many decades, psychologists paid little attention to cognitive processes, because most of them assumed that thinking is too private to be studied scientifically. During the 1950s and 1960s, however, psychologists began to devise creative new ways to measure mental processes. These innovations fuelled the cognitive revolution that put the *psyche* (the mind) back in psychology. Thus, once again, we see how empirical methods are the lifeblood of the scientific enterprise.

Third, the study of cognitive processes shows how there are both similarities and differences across cultures in behaviour. The fourth theme is the subjective nature of human experience. We have seen that decision making is a highly subjective process. For example, probabilities weighed in decisions that are objectively identical can subjectively seem very different. The subjectivity of decision processes will continue to be prominent in the upcoming Personal Application, which discusses some more common pitfalls in reasoning about decisions.

Understanding Pitfalls in Reasoning about Decisions

Key Learning Goal

▶ Describe and distinguish between the gambler's fallacy, the law of small numbers, the confirmation bias, belief perseverance, the overconfidence effect, and the effects of framing.

Consider the following scenario:

Laura is in a casino, watching people play roulette. The 38 slots in the roulette wheel include 18 black numbers, 18 red numbers, and 2 green numbers. Hence, on any one spin, the probability of red or black is slightly less than 50–50 (0.474, to be exact). Although Laura hasn't been betting, she has been following the pattern of results in the game very carefully. The ball has landed in red seven times in a row. Laura concludes that black is long overdue and she jumps into the game, betting heavily on black.

Has Laura made a good bet? Do you agree with Laura's reasoning? Or do you think that Laura misunderstands the laws of probability? You'll find out soon, as we discuss how people reason their way to decisions— and how their reasoning can go awry.

The pioneering work of Amos Tversky and Daniel Kahneman (1974, 1982) led to an explosion of research on risky decision making. In their efforts to identify the heuristics that people use in decision making, investigators stumbled onto quite a few misconceptions, oversights, and biases (Kahneman & Klein 2009). It turns out that people deviate in predictable ways from optimal decision strategies—with surprising regularity (Dawes, 2001; Gilovich, Griffin, & Kahneman, 2002). Fortunately, however, some research suggests that increased awareness of common shortcomings in reasoning about decisions can lead to fewer errors in thinking and improved decision making (Milkman, Chugh, & Bazerman, 2009; Lilienfeld, Ammirati, & Landfield, 2009). With this goal in mind, let's look at some common pitfalls in decision making.

The Gambler's Fallacy

As you may have guessed by now, Laura's reasoning in our opening scenario is flawed. A great many people tend to believe that Laura has made a good bet (Stanovich, 2003; Tversky & Kahneman, 1982). However, they're wrong. Laura's behaviour illustrates the *gambler's fallacy*—the belief that the odds of a chance event increase if the event hasn't occurred recently. People believe that the laws of probability should yield fair results and that a random process must be self-correcting (Burns & Corpus, 2004). These aren't bad assumptions in the long run. However, they don't apply to individual, independent events.

The roulette wheel does not remember its recent results and make adjustments for them. Each spin of the wheel is an independent event. The probability of black on each spin remains at 0.474, even if red comes up 100 times in a row! The gambler's fallacy reflects the pervasive influence of the *representativeness heuristic*. In betting on black, Laura is predicting that future results will be more representative of a random process. This logic can be used to estimate the probability of black across a *string of spins*. But it doesn't apply to a *specific spin* of the roulette wheel.

The Law of Small Numbers

Envision a small urn filled with a mixture of red and green beads. You know that two-thirds of the beads are one colour and one-third are the other colour. However, you don't know whether red or green predominates. A blindfolded person reaches into the urn and comes up with three red beads and one green bead. These beads are put back into the urn and a second person scoops up 14 red beads and 10 green beads. Both samplings suggest that red beads outnumber green beads in the urn. But which sample provides better evidence? (Adapted from McKean, 1985, p. 25)

Many subjects report that the first sampling is more convincing because of the greater preponderance of red over green. What are the actual odds that each sampling accurately reflects the dominant colour in the urn? The odds for the first sampling are four to one. These aren't bad odds, but the odds that the second sampling is accurate are much higher—16 to 1. Why? Because the second sample is substantially larger than the first. The likelihood of misleading results is much greater in a small sample than in a large one. For example, in flipping a fair coin, the odds of getting all heads in a sample of five coin flips dwarfs the odds of getting all heads in a sample of 100 coin flips.

Most people appreciate the value of a large sample as an abstract principle, but they don't fully understand that results based on small samples are more variable and more likely to be a fluke (Well, Pollatsek, & Boyce, 1990). Hence, they frequently assume that results based on small samples are representative of the population (Poulton, 1994). Tversky and Kahneman (1971) call this the *belief in the law of small numbers*. This misplaced faith in small numbers explains why people are often willing to draw general conclusions based on a few individual cases.

Confirmation Bias and Belief Perseverance

Imagine a young physician examining a sick patient. The patient is complaining of a high fever and a sore throat. The physician must decide on a diagnosis from among a myriad of possible diseases. The physician thinks that it may be the flu. She asks the patient if he feels "achy all over." The answer is "yes." The physician asks if the symptoms began a few days ago. Again, the response is "yes." The physician concludes that the patient has the flu. (Adapted from Halpern, 1984, pp. 215–216)

Do you see any flaws in the physician's reasoning? Has she probed into the causes of the patient's malady effectively? No, she has asked about symptoms that would be consistent with her preliminary diagnosis, but she has not inquired about symptoms that could rule it out. Her questioning of the patient illustrates *confirmation bias*—the tendency to seek information that supports one's decisions and beliefs while ignoring disconfirming information (see Figure 8.18). This bias is common in medical diagnosis and other forms of decision making (Nickerson, 1998). There's nothing wrong with searching for confirming evidence to support one's decisions. However, people should also seek disconfirming evidence—which they often neglect to do.

Confirmation bias contributes to another, related problem called *belief perseverance*—the tendency to hang on to beliefs in the face of contradictory evidence (Gorman, 1989). It is difficult to dislodge an idea after having embraced it. To investigate this phenomenon, researchers have given subjects evidence to establish a belief (e.g., high-risk takers make better firefighters) and later exposed the subjects to information discrediting the idea. These studies have shown that the disconfirming

evidence tends to fall on deaf ears (Ross & Anderson, 1982). Thus, once people arrive at a decision, they are prone to accept supportive evidence at face value while subjecting contradictory evidence to tough, skeptical scrutiny.

The Effects of Framing

Another consideration in making decisions involving risks is the framing of questions (Tversky & Kahneman, 1988, 1991). *Framing* refers to how decision issues are posed or how choices are structured. People often allow a decision to be shaped by the language or context in which it's presented, rather than explore it from different perspectives. Consider the following scenario, which is adapted from Kahneman and Tversky (1984, p. 343):

> Imagine that a country is preparing for the outbreak of a dangerous disease, which is expected to kill 600 people. Two alternative programs to combat the disease have been proposed. Assume that the exact scientific estimates of the consequences of the programs are as follows:
> • If Program A is adopted, 200 people will be saved.

> • If Program B is adopted, there is a one-third probability that all 600 people will be saved and a two-thirds probability that no people will be saved.

Kahneman and Tversky found that 72 percent of their subjects chose the "sure thing" (Program A) over the "risky gamble" (Program B). However, they obtained different results when the alternatives were reframed as follows:

> • If Program C is adopted, 400 people will die.
> • If Program D is adopted, there is a one-third probability that nobody will die and a two-thirds probability that all 600 people will die.

Although framed differently, Programs A and B represent exactly the same probability situation as Programs C and D (see Figure 8.19).

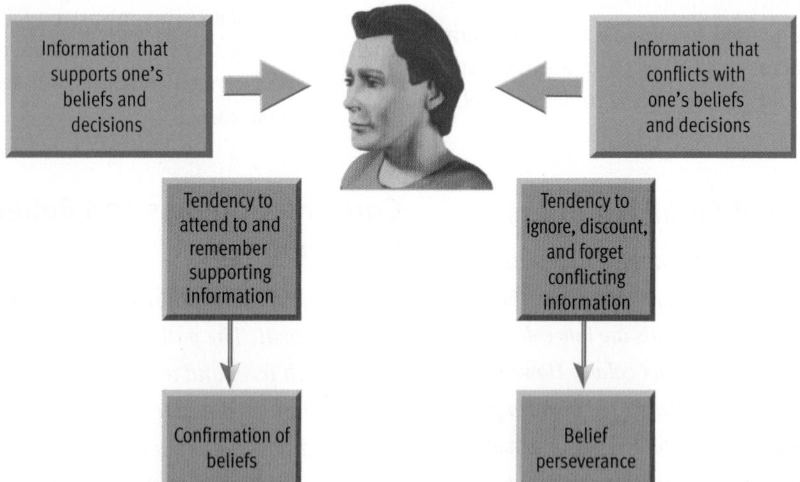

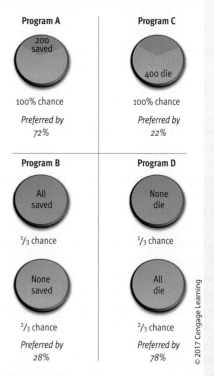

Figure 8.19
The framing of questions.
This chart shows that Programs A and C involve an identical probability situation, as do Programs B and D. When choices are framed in terms of possible gains, people prefer the safer plan. However, when choices are framed in terms of losses, people are more willing to take a gamble.

© 2017 Cengage Learning

Figure 8.18
Confirmation bias and belief perseverance. Confirmation bias exists when people seek out and react favourably to information that supports their beliefs. Belief perseverance is the tendency to cling to beliefs despite exposure to contradictory evidence.

In spite of this, 78 percent of the subjects chose Program D. Thus, subjects chose the sure thing when the decision was framed in terms of lives saved. They went with the risky gamble, however, when the decision was framed in terms of lives lost. Obviously, sound decision making should yield consistent decisions that are not altered dramatically by superficial changes in how options are presented, so framing effects once again highlight the foibles of human decision making.

Loss Aversion

Another interesting phenomenon is *loss aversion*—in general, losses loom larger than gains of equal size (Kahneman & Tversky, 1979; Novemsky & Kahneman, 2005). Thus, most people expect that the negative impact of losing $1000 will be greater than the positive impact of winning $1000. Loss aversion can influence decisions in many areas of life (Schinkler & Pfattheicher, 2017), including choices of consumer goods, investments, business negotiations, and approaches to health care (Camerer, 2005; Klapper, Ebling, & Temme, 2005).

The problem with loss aversion, as Daniel Gilbert and his colleagues have shown, is that people generally overestimate the intensity and duration of the negative emotions they will experience after all sorts of losses, ranging from losing a job or romantic partner to botching an interview or watching one's team lose in a big game (Gilbert, Driver-Linn, & Wilson, 2002; Kermer et al., 2006) (see Chapter 10). Interestingly, people overestimate the emotional impact of losses because they do not appreciate how good most of us are at rationalizing, discounting, and distorting negative events in our lives.

Shaping Thought with Language: "Only a Naïve Moron Would Believe That"

As explained in the chapter, the strong version of the *linguistic relativity hypothesis*—the idea that people's language determines how they think about things—has *not* been supported by research (Hunt & Agnoli, 1991). But research does show that carefully chosen words can exert subtle influence on people's feelings about various issues (Calvert, 1997; Johnson & Dowling-Guyer, 1996; Pohl, 2004; Weatherall, 1992). In everyday life, many people clearly recognize that language can tilt thought along certain lines. Used car dealers that sell "preowned cars" and airlines that outline precautions for "water landings" are manipulating language to influence thought. Indeed, bureaucrats, politicians, advertisers, and big business have refined the art of shaping thought by tinkering with language, and to a lesser degree the same techniques are used by many people in everyday interactions. Let's look at two of these techniques: semantic slanting and name-calling.

Semantic Slanting

Semantic slanting refers to deliberately choosing words to create specific emotional responses. For example, consider the crafty word choices made in the incendiary debate about abortion (Halpern, 1996). The anti-abortion movement recognized that it is better to be *for* something than to be *against* something and then decided to characterize its stance as "pro-life" rather than "anti-choice." Likewise, the faction that favoured abortion rights did not like the connotation of an "anti-life" or "pro-abortion" campaign, so they characterized their position as "pro-choice." The position advocated is exactly the same either way, but the label clearly influences how people respond. Thinking along similar lines,

some "pro-life" advocates have asserted that the best way to win the debate about abortion is to frequently use the words *kill* and *baby* in the same sentence (Kahane, 1992). Obviously, these are words that push people's buttons and trigger powerful emotional responses.

In his fascinating book *Doublespeak*, William Lutz (1989) describes an endless series of examples of how government, business, and advertisers manipulate language to bias people's thoughts and feelings. For example, in the language of the military, an invasion is a "pre-emptive counterattack," bombing the enemy is providing "air support," a retreat is a "backloading of augmentation personnel," civilians accidentally killed or wounded by military strikes are "collateral damage," and troops killed by their own troops are "friendly casualties." You can't really appreciate how absurd this process can become until you go shopping for "genuine imitation leather" or "real counterfeit diamonds."

In becoming sensitive to semantic slanting, notice how the people around you and those whom you see on television and read about in the newspapers refer to people from other racial and ethnic groups. You can probably determine a politician's attitudes toward immigration, for example, by considering the words the politician uses when speaking about people from other countries. Are the students on your campus who come from other countries referred to as "international students" or "foreign students?" The term "international" seems to convey a more positive image, with associations of being cosmopolitan and worldly. On the other hand, the term "foreign" suggests someone who is strange. Clearly, it pays to be careful when selecting the words you use in your own communication.

Name-Calling

Another way that word choice influences thinking is in the way people tend to label

Courtesy of Charles LeBlanc

Semantic slanting, which consists of carefully choosing words to create specific emotional reactions, has been used extensively by both sides in the debate about abortion.

Briefings on the status of military actions are renowned for their creative but unintelligible manipulation of language, which is often necessary to obscure the unpleasant realities of war.

implied threat that if you make an unpopular decision or arrive at a conclusion that is not favoured, a negative label will be applied to you. For example, someone might say, "Only a naïve moron would believe that" to influence your attitude on an issue. This strategy of *anticipatory name-calling* makes it difficult for you to declare that you favour the negatively valued belief because it means that you make yourself look like a "naïve moron." Anticipatory name-calling can also invoke positive group memberships, such as asserting that "all good Canadians will agree ..." or "people in the know think that ...." Anticipatory name-calling is a shrewd tactic that can be effective in shaping people's thinking. See Table 8.2.

and categorize others through the strategy of *name-calling*. People often attempt to neutralize or combat views they don't like by attributing such views to "radical feminists," "knee-jerk liberals," "right-wingers," "religious zealots," or "extremists." In everyday interactions, someone who inspires our wrath may be labelled as a "bitch," a "moron," or a "cheapskate." In these examples, the name-calling is not subtle and is easy to recognize. But name-calling can also be used with more cunning and finesse. Sometimes, there is an

Table 8.2

Critical Thinking Skills Discussed in This Application

SKILL	DESCRIPTION
Understanding the way language can influence thought	The critical thinker appreciates that when you want to influence how people think, you should choose your words carefully.
Recognizing semantic slanting	The critical thinker is vigilant about how people deliberately choose certain words to elicit specific emotional responses.
Recognizing name-calling and anticipatory name-calling	The critical thinker is on the lookout for name-calling and the implied threats used in anticipatory name-calling.

LANGUAGE

Language acquisition

- According to Skinner and other *behaviourists*, children acquire language through imitation, reinforcement, and other aspects of learning and experience.

- According to Chomsky and other *nativists*, humans are neurologically prewired to quickly acquire the rules of language.

- According to *interactionist* theories, an innate predisposition and a supportive environment both contribute to language development.

Bilingualism

- There is little empirical support for the belief that bilingualism slows language development.

- Bilinguals have a slight handicap in processing speed, but they have advantages in attention, working memory capacity, and reasoning.

Language and thought

- The *linguistic relativity hypothesis* asserts that one's language shapes the nature of one's thought processes.

- Empirical support for the linguistic relativity hypothesis has increased considerably in recent years.

Steven Kazlowski/Getty Images

PROBLEM SOLVING

Types of problems

- Greeno distinguished between problems of inducing structure, problems of arrangement, and problems of transformation.

Barriers to problem solving

- People are often distracted by irrelevant information.
- *Functional fixedness* is the tendency to perceive an item only in terms of its most common use.

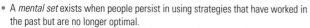

- A *mental set* exists when people persist in using strategies that have worked in the past but are no longer optimal.
- People often impose unnecessary constraints on their possible solutions.
- The gambler's fallacy is the belief that the odds of a chance event increase if the event hasn't occurred recently.
- People tend to inflate estimates of improbable events that garner heavy media coverage, because of the availability heuristic.
- Research shows that people overestimate the negative impact of losses.

Approaches to problem solving

- *Trial and error* is a common, albeit primitive, approach to problem solving.
- A *heuristic* is a rule of thumb or mental shortcut used in solving problems or making decisions.
- It is often useful to formulate intermediate subgoals.
- If you can spot an analogy between one problem and another, a solution may become apparent.
- When progress is stalled, changing the representation of a problem often helps.
- Research on *incubation effects* suggests that taking a break from a problem can sometimes enhance problem-solving efforts.

Culture and problem solving

- Cross-cultural disparities have been observed in problem-solving style.
- Research suggests that Eastern cultures exhibit a more holistic cognitive style, whereas Western cultures display a more analytical cognitive style.

DECISION MAKING

Basic strategies

- Simon's *theory of bounded rationality* asserts that people tend to use simple decision strategies that often yield seemingly irrational results because they can only juggle so much information at once.
- Schwartz argues that in modern societies, people suffer from choice overload, which leads to rumination, regret, and diminished well-being.
- Research suggests that intuitive, unconscious decisions often are more satisfying than those based on conscious deliberation.
- Risky decision making involves making choices under conditions of uncertainty.

Barry Austin Photography/Photodisc/Getty Images

Common heuristics and flaws

- The *availability heuristic* involves basing the estimated probability of an event on the ease with which relevant instances come to mind.

- The *representative heuristic* involves basing the estimated probability of an event on how similar it is to the typical prototype of that event.

- In estimating probabilities, people often ignore base rates because of the influence of the representativeness heuristic.

- The *conjunction fallacy* occurs when people estimate that the odds of two uncertain events happening together are greater than the odds of either event happening alone.

- Evolutionary psychologists argue that humans seem irrational because cognitive psychologists have been asking questions that have nothing to do with the adaptive problems the human mind has evolved to solve.

- According to Gigerenzer, people mostly depend on *fast and frugal heuristics* that are much simpler than the complicated inferential processes studied in traditional cognitive research.

- Dual-process theories assert that people depend on both quick, automatic, intuitive thinking and slower, effortful, controlled thinking.

CHAPTER 9

Intelligence and Psychological Testing

Themes in this Chapter

Sociohistorical
Context

Cultural
Heritage

Heredity &
Environment

As we suggested in Chapter 3, people seem to be continuously fascinated with the brain. The research and theory we discussed in that chapter revealed the many important functions that the brain serves and the abilities it affords us. Among these, of course—and this may be part of the reason for our fascination—is the notion of intelligence. Being smart or highly intelligent is often seen as a guarantee of success. If this is true, and we will evaluate the validity of this idea later in the chapter, then it makes sense that we should try to determine our absolute or relative level of intelligence. As we are growing up, it seems as if we are always trying to answer questions such as "Am I smart?" or "Who is the smartest kid in the class?" Of course, these questions raise additional questions such as "What is intelligence?" and "How would you know if you were intelligent?" The last question is a difficult one to answer and it often leads us to look for markers/tests of intelligence. But how can we assess someone's level of intelligence?

Thomas Edison, one of the greatest and most creative of American inventors, thought trivia was a way to assess intelligence and ability level and so he developed his own trivia intelligence test to give to prospective employees. But how do we know it is a valid test of intelligence? There was little scientific interest in Edison's test, but we do have one result that might help you decide about its status as a reliable and valid IQ test. On a visit to the United States in 1921, Albert Einstein took the test. His results were announced to the world by the *New York Times* in its headline: "Einstein Sees Boston: Fails on Edison Test" (*New York Times*, 1921). Einstein did not know, for example, the speed of sound. He did not think it was

Albert Einstein, one of history's great intellects, failed Thomas Edison's trivia test of intelligence.

important to remember such things since they are "readily available" in textbooks.

No matter how dismal his performance on Edison's test, when many of us think of highly intelligent people we often apply the label "genius" to someone like Albert Einstein. Einstein made critical contributions to our understanding of the nature of the universe, some of which we are only now, decades later, able to evaluate and confirm (Holz, 2011). Surely, any list of geniuses must also contain Marie Curie, who won two Nobel prizes in two different sciences. She is the only person to have ever achieved that (Nobel Lectures, 1967). Closer to home, some of us might point to Gerhard Herzberg, a Canadian who won Canada's first Nobel Prize in Chemistry in 1971. Canadians have won the Nobel Prize in Chemistry six times. Herzberg's main contributions were to the field of atomic and molecular spectroscopy (Stoicheff, 2002).

Variation in intelligence, especially assumed low intelligence, has had important personal consequences for many Canadians. Consider, for example, the story of Leilani Muir, who was sterilized in 1959 at the age of 14 in Alberta (Pringle, 1997). She had tested low on one IQ test and was considered a "mental defective." Before the operation, she was deceived and was told she was having surgery on her appendix. She was a resident of Alberta's Provincial Training School for Mental Defectives and was one of many who suffered a similar fate.

We'll begin by introducing some basic concepts in psychological testing. Then we'll explore the history of intelligence tests because they provided the model for subsequent psychological tests. Next we'll address practical questions about how intelligence tests work. And we'll explore some recent developments in the

Gerhard Herzberg (left) won the Nobel Prize in Chemistry in 1971. He worked at the University of Saskatchewan and the National Research Council. Marie Curie (right) won the Nobel Prize twice—in Physics in 1903 and for Chemistry in 1911.

study of intelligence. Along the way we will also discuss how racism has been implicated in the scientific debate about the nature of group differences in IQ and the primacy of genetics in explaining those group differences (Gould, 1996; Jensen, 1969). In the Personal Application, we'll discuss efforts to measure and understand another type of mental ability: creativity. In the Critical Thinking Application, we will critique some of the reasoning used in the vigorous debate about the roots of intelligence.

Key Concepts in Psychological Testing

A *psychological test* is a standardized measure of a sample of a person's behaviour. Psychological tests are measurement instruments. They're used to measure the *individual differences* that exist among people in such things as intelligence, aptitudes, interests, and aspects of personality.

Intelligence tests measure general mental ability. They're intended to assess intellectual potential rather than previous learning or accumulated knowledge. *Aptitude tests* are also designed to measure potential more than knowledge, but they break mental ability into separate components. Thus, *aptitude tests assess specific types of mental abilities.*

Like aptitude tests, *achievement tests* have a specific focus, but they're supposed to measure previous learning instead of potential. Thus, *achievement tests gauge a person's mastery and knowledge of various subjects* (such as reading, English, or history). Finally, *personality tests* measure various aspects of personality, including motives, interests, values, and attitudes. If you had to describe yourself in a few words, what words would you use? Are you introverted? Independent? Ambitious? Enterprising? Conventional? Assertive? Domineering? Words such as these refer to personality traits. These *traits* can be assessed systematically with personality tests.

Many psychologists prefer to call these tests personality *scales* because, unlike tests of mental abilities, the questions do not have right and wrong answers.

Most children become familiar with standardized psychological tests—intelligence, achievement, and aptitude tests—in school settings.

Mike Flippo/Shutterstock.com

We'll look at the various types of personality scales in Chapter 12.

Your responses to a psychological test represent a *sample* of your behaviour. The word *sample* should alert you to one of the key limitations of psychological tests: A particular behaviour sample may not be representative of your characteristic behaviour. Everyone has bad days. A stomachache, a fight with a friend, a problem with your car—all might affect your responses to a particular test on a particular day. Because of the limitations of the sampling process, test scores should always be interpreted *cautiously*.

Standardization and Norms

Both personality scales and tests of mental abilities are *standardized* measures of behaviour. **Standardization refers to the uniform procedures used in the administration and scoring of a test.** All participants get the same instructions, the same questions, and the same time limits so that their scores can be compared meaningfully.

The standardization of a test's scoring system includes the development of test norms. **Test norms provide information about where a score on a psychological test ranks in relation to other scores on that test.** The sample of people that the norms are based on is called a test's *standardization group*. Ideally, test norms are based on a large sample of people who were carefully selected to be representative of the broader population. For example, separate norms have been developed for Canadians and Americans on most intelligence tests. This might seem odd—aren't we very similar to those living to the south of us? Even though Canadian and U.S. societies are similar in many ways, there are also many important differences in culture, language, and educational systems that might be important considerations when evaluating an individual's performance on a test. Thus, for many tests, the most appropriate comparison group is other Canadians of similar age and status. Although intelligence tests have been standardized pretty carefully, the representativeness of standardization groups for other types of tests varies considerably from one test to another.

Key Learning Goals

▶ Identify the main categories of psychological tests and discuss what makes a test standardized.

▶ Describe test norms, percentile scores.

▶ Discuss the nature of reliability and how it is measured and identify the three types of validity.

Why are test norms needed? Because in psychological testing, everything is relative. Psychological tests tell you how you score *relative to other people*. They tell you, for instance, that you are average in creativity or slightly above average in clerical ability. These interpretations are derived from the test norms that help you understand what your test score means. Usually, test norms allow you to convert your "raw score" on a test into a *percentile*. A *percentile score* indicates the percentage of people who score at or below the score one has obtained.

Reliability

Any kind of measuring device, whether it's a tire gauge, a stopwatch, or a psychological test, should be reasonably consistent. That is, repeated measurements should yield reasonably similar results. Psychologists call this quality *reliability*. Consistency in measurement is essential to accuracy in measurement.

Reliability refers to the measurement consistency of a test (or of other kinds of measurement techniques). Like most other types of measuring devices, psychological tests are not perfectly reliable. A test's reliability can be estimated in several ways (Hempel, 2005). One widely used approach is to check *test–retest reliability*, which is estimated by comparing subjects' scores on two administrations of a test. If we wanted to check the test–retest reliability of a newly developed test of assertiveness, we would ask a group of participants to take the test on two occasions, probably a few weeks apart. The underlying assumption is that assertiveness is a fairly stable aspect of personality that won't change in a matter of a few weeks. Thus, changes in participants' scores across the two administrations of the test would presumably reflect inconsistency in measurement.

Reliability estimates require the computation of correlation coefficients, which we introduced in Chapter 2 (see Figure 9.1 for a brief recapitulation). A *correlation coefficient* is a numerical index of the degree of relationship between two variables. In estimating test–retest reliability, the two variables that must be correlated are the two sets of scores from the two administrations of the test. If people get fairly similar scores on the two administrations of our hypothetical assertiveness test, this consistency yields a substantial positive correlation. The magnitude of the correlation gives us a precise indication of the test's consistency. The closer the correlation comes to +1.00, the more reliable the test is.

Validity

Even if a test is quite reliable, we still need to be concerned about its validity. *Validity* refers to the ability of a test to measure what it was designed to measure. If we develop a new test of assertiveness, we have to provide some evidence that it really measures assertiveness. Increasingly, the term *validity* is also used to refer to the accuracy or usefulness of the *inferences* or *decisions* based on a test (Moss, 1994). This broader conception of validity highlights the fact that a specific test might be valid for one purpose, such as placing students in school, and invalid for another purpose, such as making employment decisions for a particular occupation. Validity can be estimated in several ways, depending on the nature and purpose of a test (Golden, Sawicki, & Franzen, 1990; Wasserman & Bracken, 2003). The most common and useful techniques for establishing validity are content, criterion-related, and construct validity.

Achievement tests and educational tests such as classroom exams should have adequate content validity. **Content validity** refers to the degree to which the content of a test is representative of the domain it's supposed to cover.

Criterion-related validity is estimated by correlating subjects' scores on a test with their scores on an independent criterion (another measure) of the trait assessed by the test. Psychological tests are often used to make predictions about specific aspects of individuals' behaviour. They are used to predict performance in university, job capability, and suitability for

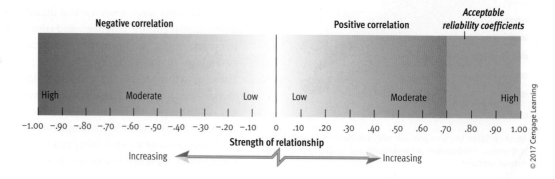

Figure 9.1
Correlation and reliability. As explained in Chapter 2, a positive correlation means that two variables co-vary in the *same* direction; a negative correlation means that two variables co-vary in *opposite* directions. The closer the correlation coefficient gets to either +1.00 or −1.00, the stronger the relationship. At a minimum, reliability estimates for psychological tests must be moderately high positive correlations. Most reliability coefficients fall between 0.70 and 0.95.

training programs, as just a few examples. Criterion-related validity is a central concern in such cases. For example, let's say you developed a test to measure aptitude for becoming an airplane pilot. You could check its validity by correlating subjects' scores on your aptitude test with subsequent ratings of their performance in their pilot training. The performance ratings would be the independent criterion of pilot aptitude. If your test has reasonable validity, there ought to be a reasonably strong positive correlation between the test and the criterion measure. Such a correlation would help validate your test's predictive ability.

Many psychological tests attempt to measure abstract personal qualities, such as creativity, intelligence, extraversion, or independence. No obvious criterion measures exist for these abstract qualities, which are called *hypothetical constructs*. In measuring abstract qualities, psychologists are concerned about *construct validity*—the extent to which there is evidence that a test measures a particular hypothetical construct.

The process of demonstrating construct validity can be complicated. It depends on starting with a clear idea of the hypothetical construct to be measured (Clark & Watson, 2003; Jackson, 1968), and it usually requires a series of studies that examine the correlations between the test and various measures *related* to the trait in question. A thorough demonstration of construct validity requires looking at the relationship between a test and many other measures (Han, 2000).

Ultimately, it's the overall pattern of correlations between the test being developed and tests assessing related concepts that provides convincing (or unconvincing) evidence of a test's construct validity.

concept **check** 9.1

Recognizing Basic Concepts in Testing

Check your understanding of basic concepts in psychological testing by answering the questions below. Select your responses from the following concepts. The answers are in Appendix A near the back of the book.

Test norms	Construct validity	
Test–retest reliability	Criterion-related validity	Content validity

1. At the request of the HiTechnoLand computer store chain, Professor Charlz develops a test to measure aptitude for selling computers. Two hundred applicants for sales jobs at HiTechnoLand stores are asked to take the test on two occasions, a few weeks apart. A correlation of +0.82 is found between applicants' scores on the two administrations of the test. Thus, the test appears to possess reasonable _____.

2. All 200 of these applicants are hired and put to work selling computers. After six months, Professor Charlz correlates the new workers' aptitude test scores with the dollar value of the computers that each sold during the first six months on the job. This correlation turns out to be –0.21. This finding suggests that the test may lack _____.

3. Back at the university, Professor Charlz is teaching a course in theories of personality. He decides to use the same midterm exam that he gave last year, even though the exam includes questions about theorists that he did not cover or assign reading on this year. There are reasons to doubt the _____ of Professor Charlz's midterm exam.

The Evolution of Intelligence Testing and Our Understanding of the Construct of Intelligence

Origins of Modern Intelligence Testing

The use of elaborate tests for selection purposes dates back to the Chinese imperial examinations that began over 1400 years ago. But the first modern psychological tests were invented only a little over a century ago and began with the work of a British scholar, Sir Francis Galton, in the later part of the 19th century (Galton, 1909). Galton studied family trees and found that success and eminence appeared consistently in some families over generations. For the most part, these families were much like Galton's: well-bred, upper-class families with access to superior schooling and social connections that pave the way to success. Yet Galton discounted the advantages of such an upbringing (Fancher, 2005). In his book *Hereditary*

Genius (1869), Galton concluded that success runs in families because great intelligence is passed from generation to generation through genetic inheritance.

To better demonstrate that intelligence is governed by heredity, Galton needed an objective measure of intelligence. His approach to this problem was guided by the theoretical views of his day and working from those ideas, he tried to assess innate mental ability by measuring simple sensory processes. His efforts at assessment met with little success. Research eventually showed that the sensory processes that he measured were largely unrelated to other criteria of mental ability that he was trying to predict, such as success in school or in professional life (Kaufman, 2000).

Nonetheless, his work was an important starting point. In pursuing this line of investigation, Galton

Key Learning Goals

▶ Summarize the contributions of Galton, Binet, Terman, and Wechsler to the evolution of intelligence testing.

▶ Describe what Spearman and Thurstone said about the structure of intelligence and its current status.

▶ Describe the ways in which the construct of intelligence has been broadened in recent formulations.

Table 9.1

Calculating the Intelligence Quotient

MEASURE	CHILD 1	CHILD 2	CHILD 3	CHILD 4
Mental age (MA)	6 years	6 years	9 years	12 years
Chronological age (CA)	6 years	9 years	12 years	9 years
$IQ = \dfrac{MA}{CA} \times 100$	$\dfrac{6}{6} \times 100 = 100$	$\dfrac{6}{9} \times 100 = 67$	$\dfrac{9}{12} \times 100 = 75$	$\dfrac{12}{9} \times 100 = 133$

© 2017 Cengage Learning

Bettmann/Contributor/Getty Images

Alfred Binet

"The intelligence of anyone is susceptible of development. With practice, enthusiasm, and especially with method one can succeed in increasing one's attention, memory, judgment, and in becoming literally more intelligent than one was before."

The Drs. Nicholas and Dorothy Cummings Center for the History of Psychology, The University of Akron.

David Wechsler

"The subtests [of the WAIS] are different measures of intelligence, not measures of different kinds of intelligence."

coined the phrase *nature versus nurture* to refer to the heredity–environment issue (Fancher, 2009). Along the way, he also invented the concepts of *correlation* and *percentile test scores* (Roberts et al., 2005). Although Galton's mental tests were a failure, his work created an interest in the measurement of mental ability, setting the stage for a subsequent breakthrough by Alfred Binet, a prominent French psychologist.

The key breakthrough came in 1904, when a commission on education in France asked Alfred Binet to devise a test to identify mentally subnormal children. The commission wanted to single out youngsters in need of special training. It also wanted to avoid complete reliance on teachers' evaluations, which might often be subjective and biased. In response to this need, Binet and a colleague, Theodore Simon, created the first useful test of general mental ability in 1905. Their scale was a success because it was inexpensive, easy to administer, objective, and capable of predicting children's performance in school fairly well (Siegler, 1992). Thanks to these qualities, its use spread across Europe and North America.

The Binet-Simon scale expressed a child's score in terms of "mental level" or "mental age." A *child's mental age* indicated that he or she displayed the mental ability typical of a child of that chronological (actual) age. Thus, a child with a mental age of six performed like the average six-year-old on the test. Binet realized that his scale was a somewhat crude initial effort at measuring mental ability. He revised it in 1908 and again in 1911. Unfortunately, his revising came to an abrupt end with his death in 1911. However, other psychologists continued to build on Binet's work.

In the United States, Lewis Terman and his colleagues at Stanford University soon went to work on a major expansion and revision of Binet's test. Their work led to the 1916 publication of the Stanford-Binet Intelligence Scale (Terman, 1916). This revision was quite loyal to Binet's original conceptions. However, it incorporated a new scoring scheme based on William Stern's "intelligence quotient" (Weiner, 2013b). An *intelligence quotient (IQ)* is a child's mental age divided by chronological age, multiplied by 100. IQ scores originally involved actual quotients, calculated as follows:

$$IQ = \frac{\text{Mental age}}{\text{Chronological age}} \times 100$$

The IQ ratio placed all children (regardless of age) on the same scale, which was centred at 100 if their mental age corresponded to their chronological age (see Table 9.1 for examples of IQ calculations).

Terman's technical and theoretical contributions to psychological testing were modest. Yet he made a strong case for the educational benefits of testing and became the key force behind American schools' widespread adoption of IQ tests. As a result of his efforts, the Stanford-Binet quickly became the world's foremost intelligence test and the standard of comparison for virtually all intelligence tests that followed. Today, it remains one of the world's most widely used psychological tests.

Further advances in intelligence testing came from the work of David Wechsler (1939), who published the first high-quality IQ test designed specifically for adults in 1939. His test, the Wechsler Adult Intelligence Scale (WAIS), introduced two major innovations. First, Wechsler made his test less dependent on subjects' verbal ability than the Stanford-Binet. He included many items that required nonverbal reasoning. To highlight the distinction between verbal and nonverbal ability, he formalized the computation of separate scores for verbal IQ, performance (nonverbal) IQ, and full-scale (total) IQ. Second, Wechsler discarded the intelligence quotient in favour of a new scoring scheme based on the normal distribution. This scoring system has since been adopted by most other IQ tests, including the Stanford-Binet. Although the term *intelligence quotient* lingers on in our vocabulary, scores on intelligence tests are no longer based on an actual quotient (Urbina, 2011).

The Debate about the Structure of Intelligence

The first half of the 20th century also witnessed a long-running debate about the structure of intellect. The debate was launched by Charles Spearman. He was a British psychologist who invented a complicated statistical procedure called *factor analysis*. In *factor analysis*, **correlations among many variables are analyzed to identify closely related clusters of variables.** If a number of variables correlate highly with one another, the assumption is that a single factor is influencing all of them. Factor analysis attempts to identify these hidden factors (Gorsuch, 1983).

Spearman (1904, 1927) used factor analysis to examine the correlations among tests of many specific mental abilities. He concluded that all cognitive abilities share an important core factor. He labelled this factor *g* for *general* mental ability. Spearman recognized that people also have "special" abilities (e.g., numerical reasoning or spatial ability). However, he thought that individuals' ability in these specific areas is largely determined by their general mental ability (see Figure 9.2).

A very different view of the structure of intellect was soon proposed by L. L. Thurstone. He was an American psychologist who developed the test that evolved into the *Scholastic Aptitude Test* (SAT; L. V. Jones, 2000). Using a somewhat different approach to factor analysis, Thurstone (1931, 1938, 1955) concluded that intelligence involves multiple abilities. Thurstone argued that Spearman and his followers placed far too much emphasis on *g*. In contrast, Thurstone carved intelligence into seven independent factors called *primary mental abilities:* word fluency, verbal comprehension, spatial ability, perceptual speed, numerical ability, inductive reasoning, and memory. Following in this tradition, J. P. Guilford (1959, 1985) extended this reasoning. Guilford's theory divided intelligence into 150 separate abilities and did away with *g* entirely (see Figure 9.3).

The debate about the structure of intelligence continued for many decades and in some respects the issue lingers in the background even today. Paradoxically, both views of the structure of intellect have remained influential. Armed with computers, modern researchers using enhanced approaches to factor analysis have shown again and again that batteries of cognitive tests are highly intercorrelated, as Spearman had suggested (Brody, 2005; Carroll, 1996; Gottfredson, 2009; Jensen, 1998). Today, researchers interested in the nature, determinants, and correlates of intelligence are still examining research evidence focused on understanding the structure of intelligence, often employing sophisticated technology only recently developed. Our Featured Study for this chapter is one example of this research. Conducted at Western University, it employed both traditional types of cognitive tests and models of brain functional intelligence.

FEATURED STUDY

Fractioning human intelligence.

Description

In this study the authors evaluate the hypothesis that human intelligence is composed of several types of intelligence, each of which is related to a distinct functional neural network.

Investigators

Hampshire, A., Highfield, R., Parkin, B., & Owen, A. M. (2012). *Neuron, 76*(6), 1225–1237.

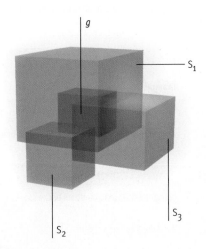

Figure 9.2
Spearman's *g*. In his analysis of the structure of intellect, Charles Spearman found that *specific* mental talents (S_1, S_2, S_3, and so on) were highly intercorrelated. Thus, he concluded that all cognitive abilities share a common core, which he labelled *g* for *general* mental ability.

Source: From Weiten. *Cengage Advantage Books: Psychology*, 9E. © 2013 South-Western, a part of Cengage, Inc. Reproduced by permission. www.cengage.com/permissions

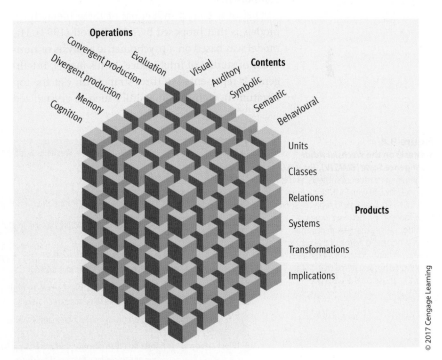

Figure 9.3
Guilford's model of mental abilities. In contrast to Spearman (see Figure 9.2), J. P. Guilford concluded that intelligence is made up of many separate abilities. According to his analysis, we may have as many as 150 distinct mental abilities that can be characterized in terms of the operations, contents, and products of intellectual activity.

© 2017 Cengage Learning

In the 1980s, the developers of IQ tests began moving in the opposite direction, from a focus on a single indicator of IQ to multiple indicators. Their motivation was to give clinicians, educators, and school systems more information (than a single, global score) that could better aid them in the diagnosis of learning disabilities and the evaluation of children's potential. New developments in intelligence research and theory captured by hierarchical models of intelligence proved useful. In hierarchical models of intelligence, intelligence is viewed as best represented as a series of layers or strata with general intelligence, *g*, at the top. As you move down the hierarchy, at each successive layer intelligence is subdivided into more specific abilities. For example, one model of intelligence proposed that *g* should be divided into *fluid intelligence* and *crystallized intelligence* (Carroll, 1993; Cattell, 1963; Horn, 1985; Stanovich, West, & Toplak, 2011, 2016). ***Fluid intelligence*** **involves reasoning ability, memory capacity, and speed of information processing.** ***Crystallized intelligence*** **involves ability to apply acquired knowledge and skills in problem solving.** Recent work in this area suggests that the prefrontal cortex is more involved in problem solving accessing fluid intelligence but less involved in tasks implicating crystallized intelligence (Nisbett et al., 2012). The initial distinction between fluid and crystallized intelligence led to further efforts to break *g* into basic components.

One of the most influential of these hierarchical models is that proposed by John Carroll (1993). His model was based on a psychometric analysis of hundreds of studies of intelligence. In his model, intelligence is represented in three strata, with *g* at the top (Stratum I), eight broad abilities such as crystallized and fluid intelligence (referred to as Gf and Gc) in the middle layer (Stratum II), and more specific abilities such as spelling at the bottom (Stratum III). Carroll's eight mid-level abilities include, in addition to crystallized and fluid intelligence, broad abilities such as visual perception and auditory perception, learning and memory, cognitive speediness, processing speed, and retrieval ability.

Contemporary IQ tests generally are based on a hierarchical model of intelligence, which subdivides *g* into a number of specific abilities. For example, the current version of the Stanford-Binet includes ten subtests, and the WAIS IV includes ten core and five supplemental subtests. The nature of the questions found on IQ tests varies somewhat from test to test. These variations depend on whether the test is intended for children or adults (or both) and whether the test is designed for individuals or groups. Overall, the questions are fairly diverse in format. The Wechsler scales, with their numerous subtests, provide a representative example of the kinds of items that appear on most IQ tests. The 4th edition of the WAIS scale was published in 2008. In addition to a full-scale IQ score, the test provides separate tests and scores for verbal comprehension, perceptual reasoning, processing speed, and working memory. Each of these four major scales is composed of specific core subtests. For example, the core subtests for verbal comprehension consist of vocabulary, information, and similarities and the subtests for working memory include digit span and arithmetic. As you can see in Figure 9.4, items in the Wechsler subtests require subjects to furnish information, recognize vocabulary, and demonstrate basic memory. Generally speaking, examinees are required to manipulate words, numbers, and images through abstract reasoning.

Figure 9.4
Subtests on the *Wechsler Adult Intelligence Scale (WAIS IV).* The WAIS IV contains a number of subtests, and is designed for use with individuals from ages 16 to 90. Scales yield separate scores for verbal comprehension, working memory, perceptual reasoning, and processing speed. Some of the subtests are shown here, along with examples of low-level (easy) test items that closely resemble those on the WAIS IV.

Wechsler Adult Intelligence Scale (WAIS IV)

Subtest	Description	Example
Information	Taps general range of information	On what continent is France?
Arithmetic	Tests arithmetic reasoning through verbal problems	How many hours will it take to drive 150 kilometres at 50 kilometres per hour?
Similarities	Asks in what way certain objects or concepts are similar; measures abstract thinking	How are a calculator and a typewriter alike?
Digit span	Tests attention and rote memory by orally presenting series of digits to be repeated forward or backward	Repeat the following numbers backward: 2 4 3 5 1 8 6
Vocabulary	Tests ability to define increasingly difficult words	What does audacity mean?
Block design	Tests ability to perceive and analyze patterns by presenting designs that must be copied with blocks	Assemble blocks to match this design: 

Broadening the Concept of Intelligence

As we have seen, interest in developing reliable and valid measures and a concern with the structural nature of intelligence has had a prominent place in the history of modern psychology. Many of these developments are based on psychometric analyses of intelligence scores—examining, for example, the correlations between scales designed to measure different aspects of intelligence. But these developments do not exhaust the ways in which our understanding of intelligence has evolved in the scientific literature on intelligence. In this section, we highlight some of the other additions to our understanding of the nature of intelligence.

Exploring Biological Correlates of Intelligence

Researchers have begun to explore the relations between variations in intelligence and variations in specific characteristics of the brain. The early studies in this area used various measures of head size as an indicator of brain size. These studies generally found positive but very small correlations (average = 0.15) between head size and IQ (Vernon et al., 2000). This result led researchers to speculate that head size is probably a very crude index of brain size. This line of research might have languished, but the invention of sophisticated brain-imaging technologies revived it. Since the 1990s, quite a few studies have examined the correlation between IQ scores and measures of overall brain volume based on MRI scans (see Chapter 3), yielding an average correlation of about 0.40 (Haier, 2011). Thus, it appears that larger brains are predictive of greater intelligence.

Other researchers have approached the neural bases of intelligence by analyzing the relations between IQ and measures of the amount of grey matter or white matter in individuals' brains. According to Luders et al. (2009), the amount of grey matter should reflect the density of neurons and their dendrites, which may be predictive of information-processing capacity. In contrast, the amount of white matter should reflect the quantity of axons in the brain and their degree of myelinization, which may be predictive of the efficiency of neuronal communication. The findings thus far suggest that higher intelligence scores are correlated with increased volume of both grey matter and white matter, with the association being a little stronger for grey matter (Luders et al., 2009; Narr et al., 2007; Taki et al., 2012).

One obvious implication of these findings, eagerly embraced by those who tout the influence of heredity on intelligence, is that genetic inheritance gives some people larger brains than others and that larger brain size promotes greater intelligence (Rushton, 2003). However, as always, we must be cautious about interpreting correlational data. As discussed in Chapter 3, research has demonstrated that an enriched environment can produce denser neural networks and heavier brains in laboratory rats (Rosenzweig & Bennett, 1996). Thus, it is also possible that causation runs in the opposite direction—that developing greater intelligence promotes larger brain size, much like weightlifting can promote larger muscles (Nisbett et al., 2012).

Research on the biological correlates of intelligence has turned up another interesting finding. IQ scores measured in childhood correlate with physical health and even longevity decades later (Deary & Batty, 2011; Wrulich et al., 2014). Quite a number of studies have arrived at the conclusion that smarter people tend to be healthier and live longer than others (see Figure 9.5). Why is higher IQ linked to increased longevity?

Researchers have offered a variety of explanations (Arden, Gottfredson, & Miller, 2009; Batterham, Christensen, & Mackinnon, 2009; Wrulich et al., 2013). One possibility is that good genes could

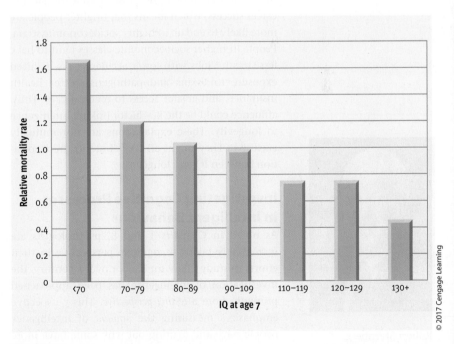

Figure 9.5
The relationship between childhood IQ and mortality. In a recent study, Leon et al. (2009) examined the association between IQ measured at age seven and mortality through the age of 57 in a sample of over 11 000 people in the United Kingdom. The data in the graph are age-adjusted relative morality rates in comparison to the reference group of people scoring near average (90–109) in intelligence. Thus, in comparison to the reference group, people who scored 70–79 were 22 percent more likely to die by age 57, and people who scored over 130 were less than half as likely to die by age 57. As you can see, there is a clear trend. As IQ scores go up, mortality rates decline.

Researchers are not sure why higher intelligence is associated with greater longevity. Several processes may be at work. All we know at this point is that extremely bright people, such as Jean Vanier, the Canadian philosopher, theologian, and humanitarian, have a better chance of living into their 80s and 90s than their less intelligent counterparts.

foster both higher intelligence and resilient health. A second possibility is that health self-care is a complicated lifelong mission, for which brighter people are better prepared. In other words, smarter people may be more likely to avoid health-impairing habits (such as smoking and overeating), to be proactive about health (such as exercising and taking vitamins), and to use medical care more effectively (such as knowing when to seek treatment). A third possibility is that intelligence fosters educational and career success, which means that brighter people are more likely to end up in higher socioeconomic strata. People in higher socioeconomic classes tend to have less-stressful jobs with lower accident risks, reduced exposure to toxins and pathogens, better health insurance, and greater access to medical care. Thus, affluence could be the key factor linking intelligence to longevity. These explanations are not mutually exclusive. They might all contribute to the association between IQ and longevity.

Investigating Cognitive Processes in Intelligent Behaviour

As noted in Chapters 1 and 8, psychologists are increasingly taking a cognitive perspective in their efforts to study many topics. For over a century, the investigation of intelligence has been approached primarily from a *testing perspective*. This perspective emphasizes measuring the *amount* of intelligence people have and figuring out why some have more than others. In contrast, the *cognitive perspective* focuses on how people *use* their intelligence.

Investigators interested in intelligence and scholars who have studied cognition have traditionally pursued separate lines of research that only rarely intersected. However, since the mid-1980s, Robert Sternberg

Robert Sternberg

"To understand intelligent behaviour, we need to move beyond the fairly restrictive tasks that have been used both in experimental laboratories and in psychometric tests of intelligence."

(1985, 1991, 2015, 2016) has spearheaded an effort to apply a cognitive perspective to the study of intelligence. His cognitive approach emphasizes the need to understand how people use their intelligence.

In recent versions of his triarchic theory of successful intelligence, Sternberg (1999, 2005b, 2012) asserts there are three aspects, or facets, of intelligence: analytical intelligence, creative intelligence, and practical intelligence (see Figure 9.6). *Analytical intelligence* involves abstract reasoning, evaluation, and judgment. It is the type of intelligence that is crucial to most schoolwork and that is assessed by conventional IQ tests. *Creative intelligence* involves the ability to generate new ideas and to be inventive in dealing with novel problems. *Practical intelligence* involves the ability to deal effectively with the kinds of problems people encounter in everyday life, such as on the job or at home. A big part of practical intelligence involves acquiring tacit knowledge—what one needs to know in a particular environment in order to work efficiently, but that is not explicitly taught and often is not even verbalized. According to Sternberg, successful intelligence consists of individuals' ability to harness their analytical, creative, and practical intelligence to achieve their life goals within their cultural context by taking advantage of their strengths and compensating for their weaknesses.

In a series of studies, Sternberg and his colleagues gathered data suggesting that (1) all three facets of intelligence can be measured reliably, (2) the three

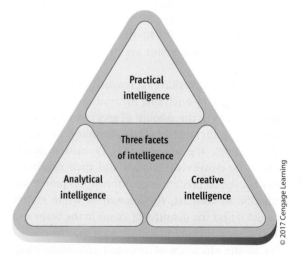

Figure 9.6
Sternberg's theory of intelligence. Sternberg's (2003a, 2005b) model of intelligence proposes that there are three aspects or types of intelligence: analytical intelligence, practical intelligence, and creative intelligence. According to Sternberg, traditional IQ tests focus almost exclusively on analytical intelligence. He believes that the prediction of real-world outcomes could be improved by broadening intelligence assessments to tap practical and creative intelligence.

facets of intelligence are relatively independent (uncorrelated), and (3) the assessment of all three aspects of intelligence can improve the prediction of intelligent behaviour in the real world (Henry, Sternberg, & Grigorenko, 2005; Sternberg, 2011). Some critics doubt that Sternberg's measures will facilitate better prediction of meaningful outcomes than done by traditional IQ tests (Gottfredson, 2003a), but that is an empirical question that should be resolved by future research. In any event, Sternberg certainly has been an articulate voice arguing for a broader, expanded concept of intelligence, which is a theme that has been echoed by others.

Multiple Intelligences

In recent years, a number of theorists besides Sternberg have concluded that the focus of traditional IQ tests is too narrow (Ceci, 1990; Greenspan & Driscoll, 1997). These theorists argue that to assess intelligence in a truly general sense, tests should sample from a wider range of tasks. The most prominent proponent of this view has been Howard Gardner (1983, 1993, 1998, 2004, 2006).

According to Gardner, IQ tests have generally emphasized verbal and mathematical skills to the exclusion of other important skills. He suggests the existence of a number of relatively autonomous *human intelligences*, which are listed in Figure 9.7. To build his list of separate intelligences, Gardner reviewed the evidence on cognitive capacities in normal individuals, people suffering from brain damage, and special populations, such as prodigies and savants. He concluded that humans exhibit eight intelligences: logical–mathematical, linguistic, musical, spatial, bodily–kinesthetic, interpersonal, intrapersonal, and naturalist. Gardner (1999) has also suggested the possibility that other intelligences may be identified, including that of an existential intelligence, which he describes as the "intelligence of big questions" (Gardner, 2003, p. 7). But to date, according to Gardner, the evidence is most supportive of the eight listed in Figure 9.7.

Gardner's books have been very popular and his theory clearly resonates with many people (Shearer, 2004). His ideas have had an impact on educators around the world (Kaufman, Kaufman,

Courtesy of Jay Gardner

Howard Gardner

"It is high time that the view of intelligence be widened to incorporate a range of human computational capacities. . . . But where is it written that intelligence needs to be determined on the basis of tests?"

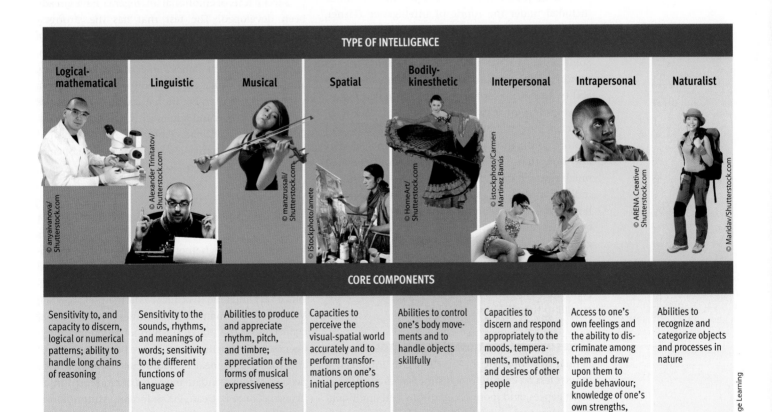

TYPE OF INTELLIGENCE

Logical-mathematical	Linguistic	Musical	Spatial	Bodily-kinesthetic	Interpersonal	Intrapersonal	Naturalist

CORE COMPONENTS

Sensitivity to, and capacity to discern, logical or numerical patterns; ability to handle long chains of reasoning	Sensitivity to the sounds, rhythms, and meanings of words; sensitivity to the different functions of language	Abilities to produce and appreciate rhythm, pitch, and timbre; appreciation of the forms of musical expressiveness	Capacities to perceive the visual-spatial world accurately and to perform transformations on one's initial perceptions	Abilities to control one's body movements and to handle objects skillfully	Capacities to discern and respond appropriately to the moods, temperaments, motivations, and desires of other people	Access to one's own feelings and the ability to discriminate among them and draw upon them to guide behaviour; knowledge of one's own strengths, weaknesses, desires, and intelligences	Abilities to recognize and categorize objects and processes in nature

Figure 9.7
Gardner's eight intelligences. Howard Gardner argues for an expanded view of intelligence. He asserts that humans display eight very different forms of intelligence, which he maintains are largely independent of one another.

© 2017 Cengage Learning

Recently retired Canadian Olympic women's hockey team member Hayley Wickenheiser is considered a prototypic example of someone with exceptional bodily–kinesthetic intelligence. She has won five Olympic medals—four gold and one silver. She is considered to have been Canada's best female hockey player.

& Plucker, 2013). He has done a superb job of synthesizing research from neuropsychology, developmental psychology, cognitive psychology, and other areas to arrive at fascinating speculations about the structure of human abilities. He has raised thought-provoking questions about what abilities should be included under the rubric of intelligence (Eisner, 2004). However, he has his critics (Hunt, 2001; Klein, 1997; Morgan, 1996; Waterhouse, 2006). Some argue that his use of the term *intelligence* is so broad, encompassing virtually any valued human ability, that it makes the term almost meaningless. These critics wonder whether there is any advantage to relabelling talents such as musical ability and motor coordination as forms of intelligence. Critics also note that Gardner's theory has not generated much research on the predictive value of measuring individual differences in the eight intelligences he has described. This research would require the development of tests to measure the eight intelligences, but Gardner is not particularly interested in the matter of assessment and he loathes conventional testing. This reality makes it difficult to predict where Gardner's theory will lead, as research is crucial to the evolution of a theory.

Measuring Emotional Intelligence

A final development in the theory of intelligence focuses less on cognition or distinct types of multiple intelligences, and more on emotions and emotional processing (e.g., Schutte & Maouff, 2013; Stein & Deonarine, 2015).

A variety of theorists have argued that the measurement of *emotional intelligence* can enhance the prediction of success at school, at work, and in interpersonal relationships (Mayer, Robert, & Barsade,

2008; Mayer, Salovey, & Caruso, 2008). The concept of emotional intelligence was originally developed by Peter Salovey and John Mayer (1990). Their concept languished in relative obscurity until Daniel Goleman (1995) wrote a compelling book entitled *Emotional Intelligence*, which made the best-seller lists. Since then, empirical research on the measurement of emotional intelligence has increased dramatically.

Emotional intelligence consists of the ability to perceive and express emotion, assimilate emotion in thought, understand and reason with emotion, and regulate emotion. Emotional intelligence includes four essential components (Salovey, Mayer, & Caruso, 2002). First, people need to be able to accurately perceive emotions in themselves and others and have the ability to express their own emotions effectively. Second, people need to be aware of how their emotions shape their thinking, decision making, and coping with stress. Third, people need to be able to understand and analyze their emotions, which may often be complex and contradictory. Fourth, people need to be able to regulate their emotions so that they can dampen negative emotions and make effective use of positive emotions.

Several tests of emotional intelligence have already been developed. The test that has the strongest empirical foundation is the *Multifactor Emotional Intelligence Scale* (MEIS) devised by Mayer, Caruso, and Salovey (1999). James Parker of Trent University, along with his colleague Reuven Bar-On, developed a youth version of an emotional intelligence measure to assess children and adolescents (Bar-On & Parker, 2000a). Parker, a Canada Research Chair in Emotion and Health, is an active researcher in the area of emotional intelligence (Bar-On & Parker, 2000b; Keefer, Wood, & Parker, 2009; Kristensen, Parker, et al., 2014; Parker et al., 2006).

The concept of emotional intelligence has not been without its critics (e.g., Murphy, 2006). Skeptics have questioned whether sophistication about emotion should be viewed as a form of intelligence and they have noted that definitions of emotional intelligence vary and tend to be fuzzy (Matthews et al., 2006; Murphy & Sideman, 2006b). Critics also assert that claims about the practical utility of emotional intelligence in the business world have been exaggerated, and that a great deal of additional research will be needed to fully validate measures of emotional intelligence (Conte & Dean, 2006; Jordan, Ashton-James, & Ashkanasy, 2006). In spite of these concerns, the concept of emotional intelligence has been accepted with great enthusiasm in the realm of business management, and hundreds of consultants provide a plethora of intervention programs to enhance leadership, teamwork, and productivity (Schmit, 2006).

Skeptics characterize these programs as little more than a fad in the business world, but many of these critics acknowledge that the concept may have some explanatory value if buttressed by more research (Hogan & Stokes, 2006; Murphy & Sideman, 2006a). Thus, the concept of emotional intelligence seems to have reached a crossroads. It will be interesting to see what unfolds over the next decade.

Basic Questions about Intelligence Testing

Misconceptions abound when it comes to intelligence tests. In this section, we will use a question-and-answer format to explain the basic principles underlying intelligence testing.

What Do Modern IQ Scores Mean?

As we've discussed, scores on intelligence tests once represented a ratio of mental age to chronological age. However, this system has given way to one based on the normal distribution and the standard deviation (see Chapter 2). The *normal distribution* **is a symmetric, bell-shaped curve that represents the pattern in which many characteristics are dispersed in the population.** When a trait is normally distributed, most cases fall near the centre of the distribution (an average score) and the number of cases gradually declines as one moves away from the centre in either direction (see Figure 9.8).

The normal distribution was first discovered by 18th-century astronomers. They found that their measurement errors were distributed in a predictable way that resembled a bell-shaped curve. Since then, research has shown that many human traits, ranging from height to running speed to spatial ability, also follow a normal distribution. Psychologists eventually recognized that intelligence scores also fall into a normal distribution. This insight permitted David Wechsler to devise a more sophisticated scoring system for his tests that has been adopted by

Key Learning Goals

► Explain the meaning of deviation IQ scores, and summarize evidence on the reliability and validity of IQ scores.

► Discuss how well IQ scores predict vocational success, and describe the use of IQ tests in non-Western cultures.

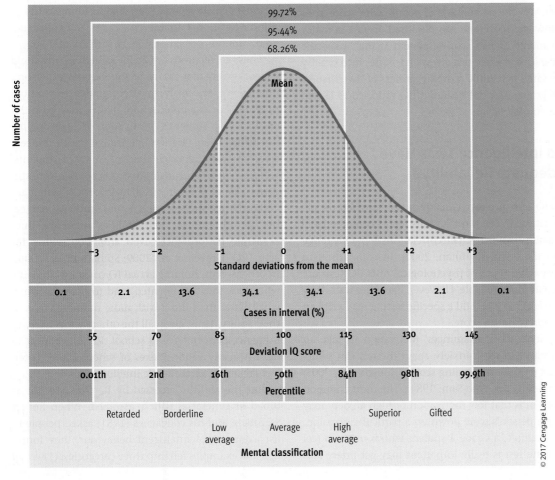

Figure 9.8
The normal distribution. Many characteristics are distributed in a pattern represented by this bell-shaped curve. The horizontal axis shows how far above or below the mean a score is (measured in plus or minus standard deviations). The vertical axis is used to graph the number of cases obtaining each score. In a normal distribution, the cases are distributed in a fixed pattern. For instance, 68.26 percent of the cases fall between 11 and −1 standard deviation. Modern IQ scores indicate where a person's measured intelligence falls in the normal distribution. On most IQ tests, the mean is set at an IQ of 100 and the standard deviation at 15. Any deviation IQ score can be converted into a percentile score. The mental classifications at the bottom of the figure are descriptive labels that roughly correspond to ranges of IQ scores.

© 2017 Cengage Learning

virtually all subsequent IQ tests. In this system, raw scores are translated into *deviation IQ scores* that locate subjects precisely within the normal distribution, using the standard deviation as the unit of measurement.

For most IQ tests, the mean of the distribution is set at 100 and the standard deviation (SD) is set at 15. These choices were made to provide continuity with the original IQ ratio (mental age to chronological age) that was centred at 100. In this system, which is depicted in Figure 9.8, a score of 115 means that a person scored exactly one SD (15 points) above the mean. A score of 85 means that a person scored one SD below the mean. A score of 100 means that a person showed average performance. You don't really need to know how to work with standard deviations to understand this system (but if you're interested, consult Appendix B near the back of the book). *The key point is that modern IQ scores indicate exactly where you fall in the normal distribution of intelligence.* Thus, a score of 120 does not indicate that you answered 120 questions correctly. Nor does it mean that you have 120 "units" of intelligence. A deviation IQ score places you at a specific point in the normal distribution of intelligence.

Deviation IQ scores can be converted into percentile scores (see Figure 9.8). A *percentile score* indicates the percentage of people who score at or below the score one has obtained. In fact, a major advantage of this scoring system is that a specific score on a specific test always translates into exactly the same percentile score, regardless of the person's age group. The old system of IQ ratio scores lacked this consistency.

Do Intelligence Tests Have Adequate Reliability?

Do IQ tests produce consistent results when people are retested? Yes. Most IQ tests report commendable reliability estimates. The correlations generally range into the 0.90s (Kaufman, 2000). In comparison to most other types of psychological tests, IQ tests are exceptionally reliable. However, like other tests, they *sample* behaviour, and a specific testing may yield an unrepresentative score.

Variations in examinees' motivation to take an IQ test or in their anxiety about the test can sometimes produce misleading scores (Hopko et al., 2005; Zimmerman & Woo-Sam, 1984). The most common problem is that low motivation or high anxiety may drag a person's score down on a particular occasion. For example, a Grade 4 student who is made to feel that the test is really important may get jittery and

be unable to concentrate. The same child might score much higher on a subsequent testing by another examiner who creates a more comfortable atmosphere. Although the reliability of IQ tests is excellent, caution is always in order in interpreting test scores.

Do Intelligence Tests Have Adequate Validity?

Do intelligence tests measure what they're supposed to measure? Yes, but this answer has to be qualified very carefully. IQ tests are valid measures of the kind of intelligence that's necessary to do well in academic work. But if the purpose is to assess intelligence in a broader sense, the validity of IQ tests is questionable.

As you may recall, intelligence tests were originally designed with a relatively limited purpose in mind: to predict school performance. This has continued to be the principal purpose of IQ testing. Efforts to document the validity of IQ tests have usually concentrated on their relationship to grades in school. Typically, positive correlations in the 0.40s and 0.50s are found between IQ scores and school grades (Kline, 1991). Moreover, a recent, huge study of over 70 000 children in England found an even stronger relationship between intelligence and educational achievement. Using composite measures of *g* and educational attainment, Deary and colleagues (2007) found correlations in the vicinity of 0.70.

These correlations are about as high as one could expect, given that many factors besides a person's intelligence are likely to affect grades and school progress. For example, school grades may be influenced by a student's motivation or personality, not to mention teachers' subjective biases. Indeed, a recent study reported that measures of students' *self-discipline* are surprisingly strong predictors of students' school performance (Duckworth & Seligman, 2005). Other studies suggest that students' subjective perceptions of their abilities influence their academic performance, even after controlling for actual IQ (Greven et al., 2009; Spinath et al., 2006). In other words, holding actual IQ constant, students who *think* they are talented tend to perform somewhat better than those with more negative views of their ability. Thus, given all the other factors likely to influence performance in school, IQ tests appear to be reasonably valid indexes of school-related intellectual ability, or academic intelligence.

But the abilities assessed by IQ tests are not as broad or general as widely assumed. When Robert Sternberg and his colleagues (1981) asked people to list examples of intelligent behaviour, they found that the examples fell into three categories: (1) *verbal* intelligence, (2) *practical intelligence*, and (3) *social intelligence* (see Figure 9.9). Thus, people generally recognize three basic components of intelligence. For the most part, IQ tests assess only the first of these three components. Although IQ tests are billed as measures of *general* mental ability, they actually focus somewhat narrowly on a specific type of intelligence: academic/verbal intelligence (Sternberg, 1998, 2003b).

Moreover, although the tests focus on *cognitive* abilities, Keith Stanovich (2009; Stanovich, West, & Toplak, 2016) argues that they do not predict rational thinking and effective decision making in the real world nearly as well as one might expect. He explains that this is not surprising because IQ tests do not assess the ability to think critically, weigh conflicting evidence, and engage in judicious reasoning.

reality check

Misconception

IQ tests measure mental ability in a truly general sense.

Reality

IQ tests are characterized as measures of *general* mental ability, and the public has come to believe that IQ tests measure mental ability in a truly broad sense. In reality, however, IQ tests have always focused only on the abstract reasoning and verbal fluency that are essential to academic success. The tests do not tap social competence, practical problem solving, creativity, mechanical ingenuity, or artistic talent.

reality check

Misconception

Intelligence is a fixed, unchangeable trait, as IQ scores rarely change over time.

Reality

Intelligence is a fairly stable trait, but it definitely is not fixed. IQ scores merely indicate people's relative standing on a specific test at a specific age. This relative standing could improve or decline depending on people's circumstances. Some people experience significant changes in measured intelligence.

Do Intelligence Tests Predict Vocational Success?

Vocational success is a vague, value-laden concept that's difficult to quantify. Nonetheless, researchers have attacked this question by examining correlations

LAYPERSONS' CONCEPTIONS OF INTELLIGENCE

Verbal intelligence	Practical intelligence	Social intelligence
Creative writer	Sees all aspects of a problem	Accepts others for what they are
Is verbally fluent	Sizes up situations well	Has social conscience
Is knowledgeable about a particular field	Makes good decisions	Thinks before speaking and doing
Reads with high comprehension	Poses problems in an optimal way	Is sensitive to other people's needs and desires

Photo by Marvin Joseph/The Washington Post via Getty Images
CP Photo/Larry MacDougal
© Biserka Livaja/Corbis

Figure 9.9

Robert Sternberg and his colleagues (1981) asked participants to list examples of behaviours characteristic of intelligence. The examples tended to sort into three groups that represent the three types of intelligence recognized by the average person: verbal intelligence, practical intelligence, and social intelligence. The three well-known individuals shown here are prototype examples of verbal intelligence (author/poet Maya Angelou), practical intelligence (scientist and broadcaster David Suzuki), and social intelligence (Craig Kielburger, founder of Free the Children).

Source: Adapted from Sternberg, R. J., Conway, B. E., Ketron, J. L., and Bernstein, M. (1981). People's conceptions of intelligence. *Journal of Personality and Social Psychology*, 41(1), 37–55. Copyright © 1981 by the American Psychological Association. Adapted with permission.

between IQ scores and specific indicators of vocational success, such as income, the prestige of subjects' occupations, or ratings of subjects' job performance. The data relating IQ to occupational attainment are pretty clear. *People who score high on IQ tests are more likely than those who score low to end up in high-status jobs* (Gottfredson, 2003b; Herrnstein & Murray, 1994; Schmidt & Hunter, 2004). Because IQ tests measure school ability fairly well and because school performance is important in reaching certain occupations, this link between IQ scores and job status makes sense. Of course, the correlation between IQ and occupational attainment is moderate. For example, in a meta-analysis of many studies of the issue, Strenze (2007) found a correlation of 0.37 between IQ and occupational status. That figure means that there are plenty of exceptions to the general trend. Some people probably outperform brighter colleagues through bulldog determination and hard work. The relationship between IQ and income appears to be somewhat weaker (Strenze, 2007; Zagorsky, 2007). These findings suggest that intelligence fosters vocational success, but the strength of the relationship is modest.

There is far more debate about whether IQ scores are effective predictors of performance within a

Courtesy of Dr. Keith Stanovich

Canada Research Chair in Education and University of Toronto Professor Keith Stanovich is a well-known researcher in psychology and education on the topics of reading and rationality.

particular occupation. On the one hand, research suggests that (a) there is a substantial correlation (about 0.50) between IQ scores and job performance, and (b) this correlation varies somewhat depending on the complexity of a job's requirements, but does not disappear even for low-level jobs (Kuncel & Hezlett, 2010; Ones, Viswesvaran, Dilchert, 2005). On the other hand, critics argue that the reported correlations have usually been corrected for statistical artifacts and that the raw, uncorrected correlations are lower (0.30s) (Outtz, 2002). They also note that even a correlation of 0.50 would provide only modest accuracy in prediction (accounting for about 25 percent of the variation in job performance). Concerns have also been raised that when IQ tests are used for job selection, they can have an adverse impact on employment opportunities for those in minority groups that tend to score somewhat lower (on average) on such tests (Murphy, 2002). In the final analysis, there is no question that intelligence is associated with vocational success. There is, however, room for argument about whether this association is strong enough to justify reliance on IQ testing in hiring employees

Are IQ Tests Widely Used in Other Cultures?

In other Western cultures with European roots, the answer to this question is "yes." In most non-Western cultures, the answer is "very little." IQ testing has a long history and continues to be a major enterprise in many Western countries, such as Britain, France, Norway, and Australia, as well as the United States and Canada (Irvine & Berry, 1988). However, efforts to export IQ tests to non-Western societies have met with mixed results. The tests have been well received in some non-Western cultures, such as Japan, where the Binet-Simon scales were introduced as early as 1908 (Iwawaki & Vernon, 1988), but they have been met with indifference or resistance in other cultures, such as China and India (Chan & Vernon, 1988; Sinha, 1983).

According to well-known cross-cultural researcher John Berry of Queen's University, the bottom line is that Western IQ tests do not translate well into the language and cognitive frameworks of many non-Western cultures (Berry, 1994; Sternberg, 2004). Berry (1984) asserts that this approach assumes that the cultural life of the two cultures differs only in language and that the cognitive abilities characteristic of the two cultures differs only in level. Using an intelligence test with a cultural group other than the one for which it was originally designed can be problematic. The entire process of test administration, with its emphasis on rapid information processing, decisive responding, and the notion that ability can be quantified, is foreign to some cultures. Moreover, different cultures have different conceptions of what intelligence is and value different mental skills (Niu & Brass, 2011; Sternberg, 2007, 2016).

Extremes of Intelligence

Key Learning Goals

▶ Describe the different levels of intellectual disability and what is known about the causes of intellectual disability.

▶ Discuss how children are typically selected for gifted programs and summarize what we know about their level of adjustment and evidence concerning whether or not they achieve eminence as adults.

What are the cutoff scores for extremes in intelligence that lead children to be designated as having intellectual disability or giftedness? On the low end, IQ scores roughly two standard deviations or more below the mean are regarded as subnormal. On the high end, children who score more than two or three standard deviations above the mean are regarded as gifted. However, designations of intellectual disability and giftedness should not be based exclusively on IQ test results. Let's look more closely at the concepts of intellectual disability and intellectual giftedness.

Intellectual Disability

The average IQ score is 100. Individuals who score well below average are referred to as having an intellectually disability. More formally, *intellectual disability* refers to general mental ability accompanied by deficiencies in adaptive skills, originating before age 18. Adaptive skills consist of everyday living skills in three broad domains. These domains are *conceptual skills* (e.g., managing money, writing a letter), *social skills* (e.g., making friends, coping with others' demands), and *practical skills* (e.g., preparing meals, using transportation, shopping) (AAIDD, 2013).

There are two noteworthy aspects to this definition. First, the IQ criterion of "well-below normal" is arbitrary. In the 1992 release of its classification manual, the AAMR (it is now known as the American Association on Intellectual and Developmental Disorders, or AAIDD) set a flexible cutoff line, which was an IQ score of 70 to 75 or below. This cutoff line could be drawn

TABLE 9.2

Categories of Intellectual Disability

CATEGORY OF INTELLECTUAL DISABILITY	IQ RANGE	EDUCATION POSSIBLE	LIFE ADAPTATION POSSIBLE
Mild	55–70	Typically, Grade 6 by late teens; special education helpful; some graduate high school	Can be self-supporting in nearly normal fashion if environment is stable and supportive; may need help with stress
Moderate	40–55	Grade 2–4 by late teens; special education necessary	Can be semi-independent in sheltered environment; needs help with even mild stress
Severe	25–40	Limited speech, toilet habits, and so forth, with systematic training	Can help contribute to self-support under total supervision
Profound	Below 25	Little or no speech; not toilet-trained; relatively unresponsive to training	Requires total care

Note: As explained in the text, diagnoses of intellectual disability should not be made on the basis of IQ scores alone.

elsewhere. Indeed, the AAMR made 70 the cutoff (with caveats) in its 2002 edition. These periodic changes in the scoring norms for IQ tests have had erratic effects on the percentage of children falling below the cutoffs (Flynn, 2000; Kanaya, Scullin, & Ceci, 2003). Five IQ points may not sound like much, but if the line is drawn exactly at 75 instead of 70, the number of people qualifying for special education programs doubles (King, Hodapp, & Dykens, 2005). Second, the requirement of deficits in adaptive, everyday living skills is included because experts feel that high stakes decisions should not be based on a single test score (Lichten & Simon, 2007). In fact, while previous versions of the *Diagnostic and Statistical Manual* of the American Psychiatric Association, one of the most important and frequently employed clinical manuals in the world, tended to classify disability in terms of IQ alone, the most recent version (i.e., the DSM-5) balances IQ and adaptive functioning in determining a classification. The DSM-5 (APA, 2013) also uses the term *intellectual disability* to replace the former term, *mental retardation*—a term that carries with it considerable negative baggage.

This requirement acknowledges that "school learning" is not the only important kind of learning. Unfortunately, the methods available for measuring everyday living skills have tended to be vague, imprecise, and subjective, although efforts to improve these assessments are under way (Detterman, Gabriel, & Ruthsatz, 2000; Lichten & Simon, 2007).

Levels of Intellectual Disability

Historically, estimates of the prevalence of intellectual disability have varied between 1 percent and 3 percent. Recent evidence suggests that the prevalence of intellectual disability probably is closer to the 1 percent end of this range (Ursano, Kartheiser, & Barnhill, 2008). Intellectual disability has traditionally been classified into four levels characterized as mild, moderate, severe, or profound. Table 9.2 lists the IQ range for each level and the typical behavioural and educational characteristics of individuals at each level.

The vast majority of people diagnosed with intellectual disability (85 percent) fall in the *mild* category (King et al., 2009). Ten percent fall within the *moderate* range and about 5 percent fall within the *severe* range. Thus, only about 15 percent of people diagnosed with intellectual disability exhibit the obvious mental deficiencies that most people envision when they think of intellectual disability. Many individuals with mild intellectual disability are not all that easily distinguished from the rest of the population. The mental deficiency of children in the mild disability category often is not noticed until they have been in school a few years. Outside of school, many are considered normal. Furthermore, as many as two-thirds of these children manage to shed the label of intellectual disability when they reach adulthood and leave the educational system (Popper et al., 2003). A significant portion of them become self-supporting and are integrated into the community. Some are even able to attend college and university (Getzel & Wehman, 2005).

Misconception

Most people who suffer from intellectual disability are severely disabled.

Reality

When people think about intellectual disability, their prototype for this condition is a severely disabled person who looks different and requires institutionalization. Working from this prototype, people assume that severe challenge is the most typical form of intellectual disability. In reality, it is the rarest form of intellectual disability. The vast majority (85 percent) of people with intellectual disability manifest mild disability.

Origins

Many organic conditions can cause intellectual disability (Szymanski & Wilska, 2003). For example, *Down syndrome* is a condition marked by distinctive physical characteristics (e.g., slanted eyes, stubby limbs, and thin hair) that is associated with mild to severe intellectual disability. Most children exhibiting this syndrome carry an extra chromosome. Children with such distinctive physical characteristics are sometimes the victims of bullying. Down syndrome occurs in about one in 800 births in Canada (Canadian Down Syndrome Society, 2009), and about the same in the United States (Sherman et al., 2007), and it is not restricted by gender or race. There is evidence, however, that the probability of Down syndrome increases with increasing age of the mother (Hook, 1982).

The FRM 1 gene contributes to the development of *fragile X syndrome (FXS)*, a common cause of hereditary intellectual disability (Clarke & Deb, 2012; Cornish, Sudhalter, & Turk, 2004). In FXS there is a mutation in the inherited gene. According to Kim Cornish (Cornish, Cole, et al., 2012; Cornish, Scerif, & Karmiloff-Smith, 2007), FXS is characterized by, among other things, an inhibitory control deficit. This deficit may lead to activation of neural connections irrelevant to the context or task facing the individual. *Phenylketonuria* is a metabolic disorder (due to an inherited enzyme deficiency) that can lead to intellectual disability if it is not caught and treated in infancy. In *hydrocephaly*, an excessive accumulation of cerebrospinal fluid in the skull destroys brain tissue and causes intellectual disability. Although about 1000 such organic syndromes are known to cause intellectual disability, with more being identified every year (Popper et al., 2003), diagnosticians are unable to pin down an organic cause for as many as 50 percent of cases (King et al., 2009).

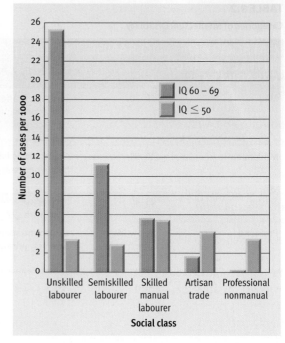

Figure 9.10
Social class and intellectual disability. This graph charts the prevalence of mild intellectual disability (IQ 60 to 69) and more severe forms of intellectual disability (IQ below 50) in relation to social class. Severe forms are distributed pretty evenly across the social classes, a finding that is consistent with the notion that they are the product of biological aberrations that are equally likely to strike anyone. In contrast, the prevalence of mild intellectual disability is greatly elevated in the lower social classes, a finding that meshes with the notion that mild intellectual disability is largely a product of unfavourable environmental factors. (Data from Popper and Steingard, 1994)

Source: From Weiten. *Cengage Advantage Books: Psychology,* 9E. © 2013 South-Western, a part of Cengage, Inc. Reproduced by permission. www.cengage.com/permissions

The cases of unknown origin tend to involve milder forms of intellectual disability. A number of theories have attempted to identify the factors that underlie intellectual disability in the absence of a known organic pathology (Hodapp, 1994). Some theorists believe that subtle, difficult-to-detect physiological defects contribute to many of these cases. However, others believe the majority of cases are caused by a variety of unfavourable environmental factors. Consistent with this hypothesis, the vast majority of children with mild disability come from the lower socioeconomic classes (see Figure 9.10), where a number of factors—such as greater marital instability and parental neglect, inadequate nutrition and medical care, and lower-quality schooling—may contribute to children's poor intellectual development (Popper et al., 2003).

Savants

Based on what we have learned so far, you might expect that someone who has below average IQ would not be expected to show any superior abilities or to show excellence in any intellectual or artistic domains. Consider then, the savant Kim Peek (Peek, 1996), who was the inspiration for Dustin Hoffman's character in the movie *Rain Man*. Kim walks with a "sidelong" gait, he is unable to manage the buttons on his clothes or to brush his teeth, or cope by himself with most of the ordinary demands of daily life (Treffert, 2010; Treffert & Christensen, 2006). He was born in 1951 with an enlarged head and with several brain abnormalities, including a malformed cerebellum, left hemisphere damage, and the complete absence of a corpus callosum (you will remember from Chapter 3 that this is the structure that connects the left and right brain). Given all of these issues, it might not surprise you to know that his tested IQ is below average. Kim was not diagnosed with autism, a disorder that is often linked to savants (we discuss autism in more detail in Chapter 15). Kim has shown evidence of amazing abilities. He memorized 9000 books and knows all the area codes and zip codes in the United States. He has memorized maps of most of the major cities in the United States and can provide "MapQuest-like travel directions with any major U.S. city or between any pair of them" (Treffert & Christensen, 2006, p. 50). He also has an appreciation of classical music. He cannot only identify and give biographical details about the composers of hundreds of compositions, but he can also enlighten on the "formal and tonal" aspects of the music. Other savants have shown equally amazing abilities in other domains including artistic pursuits (Sacks, 1990). One well-known savant, Daniel Tammet, has become a best-selling author (Tammet, 2007, 2009, 2013), and is able to recite the first 22 514 digits of *pi*. Tammet has also written on ways the rest of us can use his experiences to improve our own cognitive performance (Lehrer, 2009).

There is still much that we do not know about savant syndrome, its characteristics, and its causes (Treffert, 2010). At the very least, it should lead us to reconsider traditional notions of what intelligence is, for these conceptualizations do not help us explain individuals such as Kim Peek and Daniel Tammet.

Giftedness

Like intellectual disability, giftedness is widely misunderstood. This misunderstanding is a result, in part, of television and movies inaccurately portraying gifted children as social misfits and "nerds."

Identifying Gifted Children

Definitions of giftedness vary considerably (Kaufman & Sternberg, 2010), and some curious discrepancies exist between ideals and practice in how

Dustin Hoffman (pictured on the right beside Tom Cruise) won an Academy Award for his portrayal of a savant in the 1988 film *Rain Man*. His portrayal was based partly on real-life savant Kim Peek (pictured above). Sadly, Kim Peek died in 2009 of a heart attack (*New York Times*, 2009). It is interesting to note that the notoriety Kim gained after the release of *Rain Man* changed his life in positive ways, enabling him to break out of his self-imposed social isolation.

gifted children are identified. The experts consistently assert that giftedness should not be equated with high intelligence and they recommend that schools not rely too heavily on IQ tests to select gifted children (Robinson & Clinkenbeard, 1998; Sternberg, 2005; von Károlyi & Winner, 2005). In practice, however, efforts to identify gifted children focus almost exclusively on IQ scores and rarely consider qualities such as creativity, leadership, or special talent (Newman, 2010). Most school districts consider children who fall in the upper 2–3 percent of the IQ distribution to be gifted. Thus, the minimum IQ score for gifted programs usually falls somewhere around 130. The types of school programs and services available to gifted students vary enormously from one school district to the next (Olszewski-Kubilius, 2003).

Personal Qualities of the Gifted

Gifted children have long been stereotyped as weak, sickly, socially inept "bookworms" who are often emotionally troubled. The empirical evidence *largely* contradicts this view. The best evidence comes from a major longitudinal study of gifted children begun by Lewis Terman in 1921 (Terman, 1925; Terman & Oden, 1959). Other investigators have continued to study this group through the present (Cronbach, 1992; Holahan & Sears, 1995; Lippa, Martin, & Friedman, 2000). This project represents psychology's longest-running study.

Terman's original subject pool consisted of around 1500 youngsters who had an average IQ of 150.

Ellen Winner

"Moderately gifted children are very different from profoundly gifted children.... Most gifted children do not grow into eminent adults."

Young Sho made history when he became the youngest student at 21 to graduate from medical school at the University of Chicago in 2012. He began university at the age of 12. As a gifted child, he was reading by age two, writing at three, and composing music at five (*Chicago Tribune*, 2012). As amazing as this feat was, it is hard to say whether he will go on to achieve eminence, which typically requires a combination of exceptional intelligence, motivation, and creativity.

Judy Lupart, Canada Research Chair in Special Education at the University of Alberta, has done research on gifted education and the underrepresentation of female students in science. She has helped develop a mentoring program for girls in science and has won an award from the Women in Engineering Programs and Advocate Network for her work in this area.

reality check

Misconception

Gifted children tend to be frail, socially unskilled introverts with emotional problems.

Reality

This belief may have some validity for a small subset of gifted children who are profoundly talented. But when studies focus on high-IQ children as a whole, they find above-average physical, social, and emotional development. For the most part, the stereotype of gifted children as frail and introverted is an *inaccurate* one.

In comparison to subjects with normal IQ scores, Terman's gifted children were found to be above average in height, weight, strength, physical health, emotional adjustment, mental health, and social maturity. As a group, Terman's subjects continued to exhibit better-than-average physical health, emotional stability, and social satisfaction throughout their adult years. A variety of other studies have also found that samples of high-IQ children are either average or above average in social and emotional development (Robinson, 2010).

However, some other lines of research raise some questions about this conclusion (e.g., Winner, 1997, 1998). One line of research, which is discussed in more detail in the Personal Application, has focused on samples of people who have displayed truly exceptional creative achievement. Contrary to the findings of the Terman study, investigators have found elevated rates of mental illness in these samples (Andreasen, 2005; Ludwig, 1998).

Giftedness and Achievement in Life

Terman's gifted children grew up to be very successful by conventional standards. By midlife they had produced 92 books, 235 patents, and nearly 2200 scientific articles. Although Terman's gifted children accomplished a great deal, no one in the group achieved recognition for genius-level contributions. In retrospect, this finding may not be surprising. The concept of giftedness is applied to two very different groups. One consists of high-IQ children who are the cream of the crop in school. The other consists of eminent adults who make enduring contributions in their fields. According to Ellen Winner (2000), a sizable gap exists between these two groups. The accomplishments of the latter group involve a much higher level of giftedness.

Joseph Renzulli (1986, 1999, 2002) theorizes that this rarer form of giftedness depends on the intersection of three factors: high intelligence, high creativity, and high motivation (see Figure 9.11). He emphasizes that high intelligence alone does not usually foster genuine greatness. Thus, the vast majority of children selected for gifted school programs do not achieve eminence as adults or make genius-like contributions to society (Callahan, 2000; Richert, 1997; Winner, 2003).

Even in school itself, not all gifted children succeed. University of Alberta psychologist Judy Lupart and the University of Calgary's Michael Pyryt (1996) argue that specific subgroups of gifted children exist, including one they refer to as the "hidden gifted." These are gifted children who for a variety of reasons (e.g., learning disabled/gifted, cultural minority gifted, gifted females) may not be properly identified as gifted as they are underperforming academically. As a result, these hidden gifted students are not afforded the opportunities offered by educational programs designed to help gifted students meet their potential.

In sum, recent research has clearly demonstrated that quality training, monumental effort, and perseverance are crucial factors in greatness, but many experts on giftedness maintain that extraordinary achievement also requires rare, innate talent.

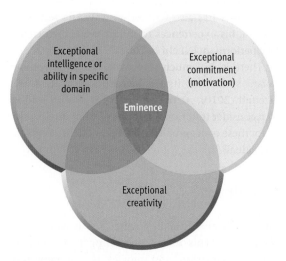

Figure 9.11

A three-ring conception of eminent giftedness. According to Renzulli (1986), high intelligence is only one of three requirements for achieving eminence. He proposes that a combination of exceptional ability, creativity, and motivation leads some people to make enduring contributions in their fields.

Source: From Renzulli, J. S. (1986). The three-ring conception of giftedness: A developmental model for creative productivity. In R. J. Sternberg and J. E. Davidson (Eds.) *Conceptions of giftedness* (pp. 53–92). New York: Cambridge University Press. Reprinted with the permission of Cambridge University Press.

Heredity and Environment as Determinants of Intelligence

Most early pioneers of intelligence testing maintained that intelligence is inherited (Mackintosh, 2011). Small wonder, then, that this view lingers in our society. Gradually, however, it has become clear that both heredity and environment influence intelligence (Davis, Arden, & Plomin, 2008; Tucker-Drob, Briley, & Harden, 2013). Does this mean that the nature versus nurture debate has been settled with respect to intelligence? Absolutely not. Theorists and researchers continue to argue vigorously about which is more important, in part because the issue has such far-reaching social and political implications.

Theorists who believe that intelligence is largely inherited downplay the value of special educational programs for underprivileged groups (Herrnstein & Murray, 1994; Kanazawa, 2006; Rushton & Jensen, 2005). They assert that a child's intelligence cannot be increased noticeably because genetic destiny cannot be altered. Other theorists take issue with this argument, pointing out that traits with a strong genetic component are not necessarily unchangeable (Flynn, 2007; Sternberg, Grigorenko, & Kidd, 2005). The people in this camp maintain that even more funds should be devoted to remedial education programs, improved schooling in lower-class neighbourhoods, and college financial aid for the underprivileged. Because the debate over the role of heredity in intelligence has direct relevance to important social issues and political decisions, we'll take a detailed look at this complex controversy.

Evidence for Hereditary Influence

Galton's observation that intelligence runs in families was quite accurate. However, *family studies* can determine only whether genetic influence on a trait is *plausible*, not whether it is certain (see Chapter 3). Family members share not just genes, but similar environments. If high intelligence (or low intelligence) appears in a family over several generations, this consistency could reflect the influence of either shared genes or shared environment. Because of this problem, researchers must turn to *twin studies* and *adoption studies* to obtain more definitive evidence on whether heredity affects intelligence.

Twin Studies

The best evidence regarding the role of genetic factors in intelligence comes from studies that compare identical and fraternal twins. The rationale for twin studies is that both identical and fraternal twins normally develop under similar environmental conditions. However, identical twins share more genetic kinship than fraternal twins. Hence, if pairs of identical twins are more similar in intelligence than pairs of fraternal twins, it's presumably because of their greater genetic similarity. (See Chapter 3 for a more detailed explanation of the logic underlying twin studies.)

What are the findings of twin studies regarding intelligence? The data from over 100 studies of intellectual similarity for various kinds of kinship relations and child-rearing arrangements are summarized in Figure 9.12. This figure plots the average correlation observed for various types of relationships. As you can see, the average correlation reported for identical twins (0.86) is very high, indicating that identical twins tend to be quite similar in intelligence. The average correlation for fraternal twins (0.60) is significantly lower. This correlation

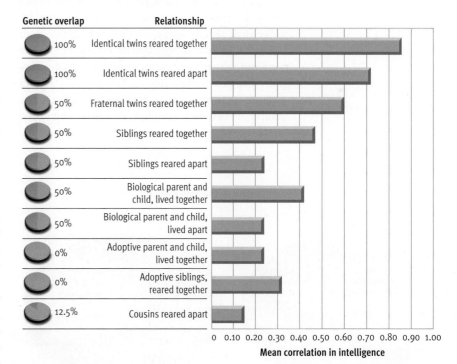

Figure 9.12

Studies of IQ similarity. The graph shows the mean correlations of IQ scores for people of various types of relationships, as obtained in studies of IQ similarity. Higher correlations indicate greater similarity. The results show that greater genetic similarity is associated with greater similarity in IQ, suggesting that intelligence is partly inherited (compare, for example, the correlations for identical and fraternal twins). However, the results also show that living together is associated with greater IQ similarity, suggesting that intelligence is partly governed by environment (compare, for example, the scores of siblings reared together and reared apart). (Data from McGue et al., 1993)

© 2017 Cengage Learning

indicates that fraternal twins also tend to be similar in intelligence, but noticeably less so than identical twins. These results support the notion that IQ is inherited to a considerable degree (Bouchard, 1998; Plomin & Spinath, 2004).

Of course, critics have tried to poke holes in this line of reasoning. They argue that identical twins are more alike in IQ because parents and others treat them more similarly than they treat fraternal twins. This environmental explanation of the findings has some merit. After all, identical twins are always the same sex, and gender influences how a child is raised. However, this explanation seems unlikely in light of the evidence on identical twins reared apart because of family breakups or adoption (Bouchard, 1997; Bouchard et al., 1990). *Although reared in different environments, these identical twins still display greater similarity in IQ (average correlation: 0.72) than fraternal twins reared together (average correlation: 0.60).* Moreover, the gap in IQ similarity between identical twins reared apart and fraternal twins reared together appears to widen in middle and late adulthood, suggesting paradoxically that the influence of heredity increases with age (Pedersen et al., 1992).

Adoption Studies

Research on adopted children also provides evidence about the effects of heredity (and of environment, as we shall see). If adopted children resemble their biological parents in intelligence even though they were not reared by these parents, this finding supports the genetic hypothesis. The relevant studies indicate that there is indeed more than chance similarity between adopted children and their biological parents (Plomin et al., 2008; refer again to Figure 9.12).

Heritability Estimates

Various experts have sifted through mountains of correlational evidence to estimate the *heritability* of intelligence. A *heritability ratio* is an estimate of the proportion of trait variability in a population that is determined by variations in genetic inheritance. Heritability can be estimated for any trait. For example, the heritability of height is estimated to be around 90 percent (Plomin, 2013). Heritability estimates for intelligence vary considerably (see Figure 9.13).

At the high end, a few theorists, such as Arthur Jensen (1980, 1998), maintain that the heritability of IQ ranges as high as 80 percent (Bouchard, 2004). That is, they believe that only about 20 percent of the variation in intelligence is attributable to environmental factors. Estimates at the low end of the spectrum suggest that the heritability of intelligence is around 40 percent (Plomin, 2003), which means 60 percent would be attributable to environmental factors. In recent years, the consensus estimates of the experts tend to hover around 50 percent (Petrill, 2005; Plomin & Spinath, 2004).

However, it's important to understand that heritability estimates have certain limitations (Grigorenko, 2000; Johnson et al., 2009). First, a heritability estimate is a group statistic based on studies of trait variability within a specific group. A heritability estimate cannot be applied meaningfully to individuals. In other words, even if the heritability of intelligence truly is 60 percent, this does not mean that each individual's intelligence is 60 percent inherited. Second, the heritability of a trait can fluctuate over the life span. For example, recent research has demonstrated that the heritability of intelligence increases with age. In other words, heritability estimates in young children start out relatively low, increase considerably by adolescence, and continue to escalate gradually through middle age (Briley & Tucker-Drob, 2013). Third, the heritability of a specific trait can vary from one group to another depending on a variety of factors (Mandelman & Grigorenko, 2011). For example, evidence suggests that the heritability of intelligence is notably lower in samples drawn from lower socioeconomic strata than it is in samples drawn from middle- and upper-class homes (Nisbett et al., 2012). It appears that heritability is suppressed by the negative environmental conditions associated with poverty.

Although the concept of heritability is not as simple as it first appears, it is absolutely clear that IQ is influenced by heredity. New approaches to analyzing

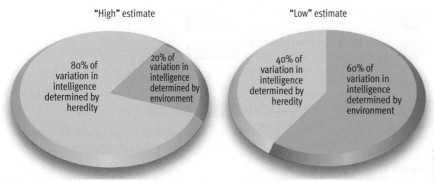

Heritability estimates for intelligence

"High" estimate   "Low" estimate

80% of variation in intelligence determined by heredity

20% of variation in intelligence determined by environment

40% of variation in intelligence determined by heredity

60% of variation in intelligence determined by environment

© 2017 Cengage Learning

Figure 9.13
The concept of heritability. A heritability ratio is an estimate of the portion of variation in a trait determined by heredity—with the remainder presumably determined by environment—as these pie charts illustrate. Typical heritability estimates for intelligence range between a high of 80 percent and a low of 40 percent, although some estimates have fallen outside this range. The consensus estimate tends to hover around 50 percent. Bear in mind that heritability ratios are *estimates* and have certain limitations that are discussed in the text.

molecular genetics data, which have permitted scientists to quantify heritability in entirely different ways, have yielded heritability estimates that converge nicely with the estimates based on decades of twin and adoptions studies (Davies et al., 2011; Plomin, Haworth, et al., 2013). That said, molecular genetics research that has attempted to identify the specific genes that shape intelligence has yielded disappointing findings (Deary, 2012). Candidate genes discovered thus far have been found to have miniscule effects on intelligence, accounting for only tiny portions (well under 1 percent each) of the variation in cognitive ability (Plomin, 2013). Moreover, many of the reported associations between genetic variants and intelligence have proven difficult to replicate in subsequent studies (Chabris et al., 2012). Although researchers remain hopeful, efforts to map out the specific genes that govern intelligence have a long way to go.

Evidence for Environmental Influence

Heredity unquestionably influences intelligence, but a great deal of evidence indicates that upbringing also affects mental ability. In this section, we'll examine various approaches to research that show how life experiences shape intelligence.

Adoption Studies

Research with adopted children provides useful evidence about the impact of experience as well as heredity (Nisbett et al., 2012). Many of the correlations in Figure 9.12 reflect the influence of the environment. For example, adopted children show some resemblance to their adoptive parents in IQ. This similarity is usually attributed to the fact that their adoptive parents shape their environment. Adoption studies also indicate that siblings reared together are more similar in IQ than siblings reared apart. This is true even for identical twins, who have the same genetic endowment. Moreover, entirely unrelated children who are raised in the same home also show a significant resemblance in IQ. All of these findings indicate that environment influences intelligence.

Environmental Deprivation and Enrichment

If environment affects intelligence, children who are raised in substandard circumstances should experience a gradual decline in IQ as they grow older (since other children will be progressing more rapidly). This *cumulative deprivation hypothesis* was tested decades ago. Researchers studied children consigned to understaffed orphanages and children raised in the poverty and isolation of the back hills of Appalachia (Sherman & Key, 1932; Stoddard, 1943). Generally, investigators *did* find that environmental deprivation led to the predicted erosion in IQ scores.

Conversely, children who are removed from a deprived environment and placed in circumstances more conducive to learning should benefit from their environmental enrichment. Their IQ scores should gradually increase. This hypothesis has been tested by studying children who have been moved from disadvantaged homes or institutional settings into middle- and upper-class adoptive homes (Scarr & Weinberg, 1977, 1983; Schiff & Lewontin, 1986). A recent meta-analysis of relevant studies found that adopted children scored notably higher on IQ tests than siblings or peers "left behind" in institutions or disadvantaged homes (van IJzendoorn & Juffer, 2005). These gains are sometimes reduced if children suffer from severe, lengthy deprivation prior to their adoptive placement. But the overall trends clearly show that improved environments lead to increased IQ scores for most adoptees (Grotevant & McDermott, 2014). These findings show that IQ scores are not unchangeable and that they are sensitive to environmental influences.

Generational Changes: The Flynn Effect

The most interesting, albeit perplexing, evidence showcasing the importance of the environment is the finding that performance on IQ tests has steadily increased over generations (Schleicher, 2013). This trend was not widely appreciated until recently because the tests are renormed periodically with new standardization groups, so that the mean IQ always remains at 100. However, in a study of the IQ tests used by the U.S. military, James Flynn noticed that the level of performance required to earn a score of 100 jumped upward every time the tests were renormed. Curious about this unexpected finding, he eventually gathered extensive data from 20 nations and demonstrated that IQ performance has been rising steadily all over the industrialized world since the 1930s (Flynn, 1987, 1994, 1998, 1999, 2003, 2007, 2012). Thus, the performance that today would earn you an average score of 100 would have earned you an IQ score of about 120 back in the 1930s (see Figure 9.14). Researchers who study intelligence are now scrambling to explain

Intelligence and Psychological Testing

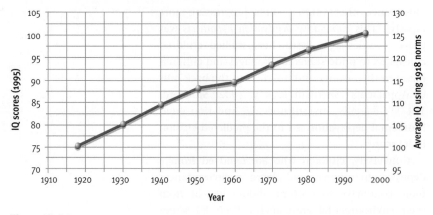

Figure 9.14
Generational increases in measured IQ. IQ tests are renormed periodically so that the mean score remains at 100. However, research by James Flynn has demonstrated that performance on IQ tests around the world has been increasing throughout most of the last century. This graph traces the estimated increases in IQ in the United States from 1918 to 1995. In relation to the axis on the right, the graph shows how average IQ would have increased if IQ tests had continued to use 1918 norms. In relation to the axis on the left, the graph shows how much lower the average IQ score would have been in earlier years if 1995 norms had been used. The causes of the "Flynn effect" are unknown, but they have to involve environmental factors.

Soucre: From Weiten. *Cengage Advantage Books: Psychology,* 9E. © 2013 South-Western, a part of Cengage, Inc. Reproduced by permission. www.cengage.com/permissions

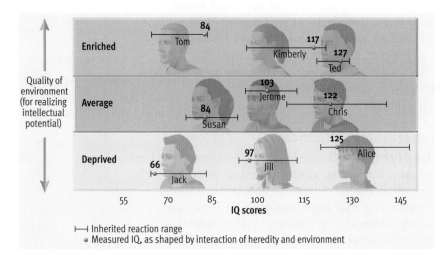

Figure 9.15
Reaction range. The concept of reaction range posits that heredity sets limits on one's intellectual potential (represented by the horizontal bars), while the quality of one's environment influences where one scores within this range (represented by the dots on the bars). People raised in enriched environments should score near the top of their reaction range, whereas people raised in poor-quality environments should score near the bottom of their range. Genetic limits on IQ can be inferred only indirectly, so theorists aren't sure whether reaction ranges are narrow (like Ted's) or wide (like Chris's). The concept of reaction range can explain how two people with similar genetic potential can be quite different in intelligence (compare Tom and Jack) and how two people reared in environments of similar quality can score quite differently (compare Alice and Jack).

(Dickens & Flynn, 2001; Neisser, 1998; Sternberg, Grigorenko, & Kidd, 2005).

At this point, the proposed explanations for the Flynn effect are conjectural, but it is worth reviewing some of them because they highlight the diversity of environmental factors that may shape IQ performance. Some theorists attribute generational gains in IQ test performance to reductions in the prevalence of severe malnutrition among children (Lynn, 2009). Others attribute the Flynn effect to increased access to schooling and more demanding curricula in schools over the course of the last century (Runnlund & Nilsson, 2009). W. M. Williams (1998) discusses the importance of a constellation of factors, including improved schools, smaller families, better-educated parents, and higher-quality parenting. All of these speculations have some plausibility and are not mutually exclusive (R. L. Williams, 2013). Thus, the causes of the Flynn effect remain under investigation.

The Interaction of Heredity and Environment

Clearly, heredity and environment both influence intelligence to a significant degree. And their effects involve intricate, dynamic, reciprocal interactions (Grigerenko, 2000; Johnson, 2010; Petrill, 2005). Genetic endowments influence the experiences that people are exposed to, and environments influence the degree to which genetic predispositions are realized. In fact, many theorists now assert that the question of whether heredity or environment is more important ought to take a back seat to the question of *how they interact* to govern IQ.

One influential model of this interaction was championed most prominently by Sandra Scarr (1991). The model posits that heredity may set certain limits on intelligence and that environmental factors determine where individuals fall within these limits (Bouchard, 1997; Weinberg, 1989). According to this idea, genetic makeup places an upper limit on a person's IQ that can't be exceeded even when environment is ideal. Heredity is also thought to place a lower limit on an individual's IQ, although extreme circumstances (e.g., being locked in an attic until age ten) could drag a person's IQ beneath this boundary. Theorists use the term *reaction range* to refer to these genetically determined limits on IQ (or other traits).

According to the reaction-range model, children reared in high-quality environments that promote the development of intelligence should score near the top of their potential IQ range (see Figure 9.15). Children reared under less ideal circumstances should

this trend, which has been dubbed the "Flynn effect." About the only thing they mostly agree on is that the Flynn effect has to be attributed to environmental factors, as the modern world's gene pool could not have changed overnight (in evolutionary terms, 70 years is more like a fraction of a second)

score lower in their reaction range. The concept of a reaction range can explain why high-IQ children sometimes come from poor environments. It can also explain why low-IQ children sometimes come from very good environments. Moreover, it can explain these apparent paradoxes without discounting the role that environment undeniably plays.

Scientists hope to achieve a more precise understanding of how heredity and environment interactively govern intelligence by identifying the specific genes that influence general mental ability. Advances in molecular genetics, including the mapping of the human genome, are allowing researchers to search for individual genes that are associated with measures of intelligence (Posthuma et al., 2005). However, these studies have yielded minimal progress thus far (Johnson, 2010; Plomin, Kennedy, & Craig, 2006).

Cultural Differences in IQ Scores

Although the full range of IQ scores is seen in all ethnic groups, the average IQ for many of the larger minority groups in the United States (such as African Americans, Native Americans, and Hispanics) is somewhat lower than the average for whites. The typical disparity is around 10 to 15 points, depending on the group tested and the IQ scale used (Hunt & Carlson, 2007; Nisbett, 2005). However, newer data suggest that the gap has shrunk in recent decades (Suzuki, Short, & Lee, 2011). There is relatively little argument about the existence of these group differences, variously referred to as racial, ethnic, or cultural differences in intelligence. The controversy concerns why the differences are found. A vigorous debate continues about whether cultural differences in intelligence are due to the influence of heredity or of environment.

Heritability as an Explanation

In 1969, Arthur Jensen sparked a heated war of words by arguing that cultural differences in IQ are largely due to heredity (Fox, 2012). The cornerstone for Jensen's argument was his analysis suggesting that the heritability of intelligence is about 80 percent. Essentially, he asserted (1) that intelligence is largely genetic in origin and (2) that, therefore, genetic factors are "strongly implicated" as the cause of ethnic differences in intelligence. Jensen's article triggered outrage, bitter criticism, and even death threats, as well as a flurry of research that shed additional light on the determinants of intelligence.

Twenty-five years later, Richard Herrnstein and Charles Murray (1994) reignited the same controversy with the publication of their widely discussed book *The Bell Curve*. They argued that ethnic differences in average intelligence are substantial, not easily reduced by educational programs for the disadvantaged, and at least partly genetic in origin. The implicit message throughout *The Bell Curve* was that disadvantaged groups cannot avoid their fate because it's their genetic destiny. And as recently as 2010, based on an extensive review of statistical evidence, J. Philippe Rushton and Arthur Jensen (2010) argued that genetic factors account for the bulk of the gap between races in average IQ.

As you might guess, these analyses and conclusions have elicited many lengthy and elaborate rebuttals. Critics argue that heritability explanations for ethnic differences in IQ have a variety of flaws and weaknesses (Brody, 2003; Horn, 2002; Nisbett, 2009; Sternberg, 2005a). For example, as noted earlier, the heritability of intelligence appears to be lower in the lower socioeconomic classes as opposed to higher socioeconomic classes (Tucker-Drob et al., 2011). Hence, there is doubt about the validity of applying heritability estimates based on the general population to cultural groups that are overrepresented in the lower socioeconomic classes.

Moreover, even if one accepts the assumption that the heritability of IQ is very high, it does not follow logically that differences in *group averages* must be due largely to heredity. Leon Kamin has presented a compelling analogy that highlights the logical fallacy in this reasoning (see Figure 9.16):

We fill a white sack and a black sack with a mixture of different genetic varieties of corn seed. We make certain that the proportions of each variety of seed are identical in each sack. We then plant the seed from the white sack in fertile Field A, while that from the black sack is planted in barren Field B. We will observe that within Field A, as within Field B, there is considerable variation in the height of individual corn plants. This variation will be due largely to genetic factors (seed differences). We will also observe, however, that the average height of plants in Field A is greater than that in Field B. That difference will be entirely due to environmental factors (the soil). The same is true of IQs: differences in the average IQ of various human populations could be entirely due to environmental

Sandra Scarr

"My research has been aimed at asking in what kind of environments genetic differences shine through and when do they remain hidden."

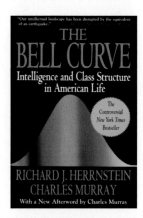

Arthur Jensen

"Despite more than half a century of repeated efforts by psychologists to improve the intelligence of children, particularly those in the lower quarter of the IQ distribution relative to those in the upper half of the distribution, strong evidence is still lacking as to whether or not it can be done."

In their 1994 bestseller, Herrnstein and Murray added fuel to the fire of the race–intelligence controversy.

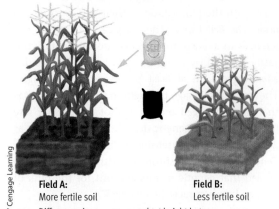

Individual variation in corn plant heights within each group (cause: genetic variation in the seeds)

Field A:
More fertile soil

Field B:
Less fertile soil

Differences in average corn plant height between groups (cause: the soils in which the plants were grown)

© 2017 Cengage Learning

Figure 9.16
Genetics and between-group differences on a trait.
Leon Kamin's analogy (see text) shows how between-group differences on a trait (the average height of corn plants) could be due to environment, even if the trait is largely inherited. The same reasoning presumably applies to ethnic-group differences in average intelligence.

differences, even if within each population all variation were due to genetic differences!
(Eysenck & Kamin, 1981, p. 97)

This analogy shows that even if *within-group differences* in IQ are highly heritable, *between-groups differences* in average IQ could still be caused *entirely* by environmental factors (Block, 2002). For decades, critics of Jensen's thesis have relied on this analogy rather than actual data to make the point that between-groups differences in IQ do not necessarily reflect genetic differences. They depended on the analogy because no relevant data were available. However, the recent discovery of the Flynn effect has provided compelling new data that are directly relevant (Dickens & Flynn, 2001; Flynn, 2003). Generational gains in IQ scores show that a between-group disparity in average IQ (in this case the gap is between generations rather than ethnic groups) can be environmental in origin, even though intelligence is highly heritable.

The available evidence certainly does not allow us to rule out the possibility that ethnic and cultural disparities in average intelligence are partly genetic. And the hypothesis should not be dismissed without study simply because many people find it offensive or distasteful. However, there are several alternative explanations for the culture gap in intelligence that seem more plausible. Let's look at them.

Socioeconomic Disadvantage as an Explanation

Many social scientists argue that minority students' IQ scores are depressed because these children tend to grow up in deprived environments that create a disadvantage—both in school and on IQ tests. There is no question that, on the average, whites and minorities tend to be raised in very different circumstances. Most minority groups have endured a long history of economic discrimination and are greatly overrepresented in the lower social classes. A lower-class upbringing tends to carry a number of disadvantages that work against the development of a youngster's full intellectual potential (Bigelow, 2006; Dupere et al., 2010; Evans, 2004; Noble, McCandliss, & Farah, 2007; Yoshikawa, Aber, & Beardslee, 2012). In comparison with children from the middle and upper classes, lower-class children tend to be exposed to fewer books, to have fewer learning supplies and less access to computers, to have less privacy for concentrated study, and to get less parental assistance in learning.

Socioeconomic disadvantages probably are a major factor in various minority groups' poor performance on IQ and other standardized tests, but some theorists maintain that other factors and processes are also at work. For example, Claude Steele (1992, 1997) has argued that derogatory stereotypes of stigmatized groups' intellectual capabilities create unique feelings of vulnerability in the educational arena. These feelings of *stereotype vulnerability* can undermine group members' performance on tests, as well as other measures of academic achievement. These feelings may also create *belonging uncertainty*, doubts in their mind about the quality of their social bonds and relationships in these situations (Walton & Cohen, 2007). All of these can contribute to poor performance in achievement situations (Steele, 2011).

Steele points out that demeaning stereotypes of stigmatized groups are widely disseminated, creating a subtle climate of prejudice, even in the absence of overt discrimination. He further notes that members of minority groups are keenly aware of any negative stereotypes that exist regarding their intellect. Hence, when a minority student does poorly on a test, he or she must confront a disturbing possibility: *that others will attribute the failure to racial inferiority.* Steele maintains that females face the same problem when they venture into academic domains where stereotypes suggest that they are inferior to males, such as mathematics, engineering, and the physical sciences. That is, *they worry about people blaming their failures on their gender.* According to Steele, minorities and women in male-dominated fields are in a no-win situation. When they do well and contradict stereotypes, people tend to view their success with suspicion, but when they do poorly, people readily view their failure as vindication of the stereotypes. Thus, stigmatized groups' apprehension about "confirming" people's negative stereotypes can contribute to academic underachievement. For example, standardized tests such as IQ tests may be especially anxiety-arousing for members of stigmatized groups because the importance attributed to the tests makes one's stereotype vulnerability particularly salient. This anxiety may impair students' test performance by temporarily disrupting their cognitive functioning.

Cultural Bias on IQ Tests as an Explanation

Some critics of IQ tests have argued that cultural differences in IQ scores are partly due to a cultural bias built into IQ tests. They argue that because IQ tests are constructed by white, middle-class psychologists, they naturally draw on experience and knowledge typical of white, middle-class lifestyles and use language and vocabulary that reflect the white, middle-class origins of their developers (Cohen, 2002; Helms, 1992, 2006; Hilliard, 1984). Fagan and Holland (2002, 2007) have collected data suggesting that the IQ gap between whites and blacks is due to cultural differences in knowledge due to disparities in *exposure to information.*

Most theorists acknowledge that IQ tests measure a combination of ability and knowledge (Ackerman & Beier, 2005; Cianciolo & Sternberg, 2004). Test developers try to tilt the balance toward the assessment of ability as much as possible, but factual knowledge clearly has an impact on IQ scores. According to Fagan and Holland (2002, 2007), cultural disparities in IQ reflect differences in *knowledge* rather than differences in *ability.*

Taken as a whole, the various alternative explanations for cultural and ethnic disparities in average IQ provide serious challenges to genetic explanations, which appear weak at best—and suspiciously racist at worst. Unfortunately, since the earliest days of IQ testing, some people have used IQ tests to further elitist goals. The current controversy about ethnic differences in IQ is just another replay of a record that has been heard before. For instance, beginning in 1913, Henry Goddard tested a great many immigrants to the United States at Ellis Island in New York. Goddard reported that the vast majority of Italian, Hungarian, and Jewish immigrants tested out as *feeble-minded* (Kamin, 1974). As you can see, claims about ethnic deficits in intelligence are nothing new—only the victims have changed.

The debate about ethnic differences in intelligence illustrates how IQ tests have often become entangled in thorny social conflicts. The controversy associated with intelligence tests has undermined somewhat their value. This is unfortunate, because it brings politics to the testing enterprise. Intelligence testing has many legitimate and valuable uses as we have discussed in this chapter.

Claude Steele

"I believe that in significant part the crisis in black Americans' education stems from the power of this vulnerability to undercut identification with schooling."

Intelligence and Psychological Testing

Putting It in Perspective: Themes 3, 5, and 6

As you probably noticed, three of our integrative themes surfaced in this chapter. Our discussions illustrated that cultural factors shape behaviour, that psychology evolves in a sociohistorical context, and that heredity and environment jointly influence behaviour.

Pervasive psychological testing is largely a Western phenomenon. The concept of general intelligence also has a special, Western flavour to it. Many non-Western cultures have very different ideas about the nature of intelligence. Within Western societies, the observed ethnic differences in average intelligence also illustrate the importance of cultural factors, as these disparities appear to be due in large part to cultural disadvantage and other culture-related considerations. Thus, we see once again that if we hope to achieve a sound understanding of behaviour, we need to appreciate the cultural contexts in which behaviour unfolds.

Human intelligence is shaped by a complex interaction of hereditary and environmental factors. We've drawn similar conclusions before in other chapters where we examined other aspects of behaviour. However, this chapter should have enhanced your appreciation of this idea in at least two ways. First, we examined more of the details of how scientists arrive at the conclusion that heredity and environment jointly shape behaviour. Second, we encountered dramatic illustrations of the immense importance attached to the nature-versus-nurture debate. For example, Arthur Jensen has been the target of savage criticism. After his controversial 1969 article, he was widely characterized as a racist. When he gave speeches, he was often greeted by protesters carrying signs, such as "Kill Jensen" and "Jensen Must Perish." J. Philippe Rushton has had similar experiences in Canada. As you can see, the debate about the inheritance of intelligence inspires passionate feelings in many people. In part, this is because the debate has far-reaching social and political implications, which brings us to another prominent theme in the chapter.

There may be no other area in psychology where the connections between psychology and society at large are so obvious. Prevailing social attitudes have always exerted some influence on testing practices and the interpretation of test results. In the first half of the 20th century, a strong current of racial and class prejudice was apparent in North America and Britain. This prejudice supported the idea that IQ tests measured innate ability and that "undesirable" groups scored poorly because of their genetic inferiority. Although these beliefs did not go unchallenged within psychology, their widespread acceptance in the field reflected the social values of the time. It's ironic that IQ tests have sometimes been associated with social prejudice. When used properly, intelligence tests provide relatively objective measures of mental ability that are less prone to bias than the subjective judgments of teachers or employers.

Today, psychological tests serve many diverse purposes. In the upcoming Personal Application, we focus on creativity tests and on the nature of creative thinking and creative people.

Understanding Creativity

Key Learning Goals

▶ Evaluate the role of insight and divergent thinking in creativity, and discuss creativity tests.

▶ Classify the associations between creativity and personality, intelligence, and mental illness.

Intelligence is not the only type of mental ability that psychologists have studied. They have devised tests to explore a variety of mental abilities. Among these, creativity is certainly one of the most interesting. People tend to view creativity as an essential trait for artists, musicians, and writers, but it is important in *many* walks of life (Simonton, 1984, 2012). In this Application, we'll discuss psychologists' efforts to measure and understand creativity.

The Nature of Creativity

Creativity involves the generation of ideas that are original, novel, and useful. Creative thinking is fresh, innovative, and inventive (Baas, Carsten, & Nijstad, 2008). But novelty by itself is not enough. In addition to being unusual, creative thinking must be adaptive. It must be appropriate to the situation and problem.

Does Creativity Occur in a Burst of Insight? It is widely believed that creativity usually involves sudden flashes of insight and great leaps of imagination. Robert Weisberg (1986) calls this belief the "Aha! myth." Undeniably, creative bursts of insight do occur (Feldman, 1988). However, the evidence suggests that major creative achievements generally are logical extensions of existing ideas, involving long, hard work and many small, faltering steps forward (Weisberg, 1993). Creative ideas do not come out of nowhere. Creative ideas come from a deep well of experience and training in a specific area, whether it's music, painting,

business, or science (Weisberg, 1999, 2006). As Snow (1986) puts it, "Creativity is not a light bulb in the mind, as most cartoons depict it. It is an accomplishment born of intensive study, long reflection, persistence, and interest" (p. 1033).

Does Creativity Depend on Divergent Thinking? According to many theorists, the key to creativity lies in *divergent thinking*—thinking "that goes off in different directions," as J. P. Guilford (1959) put it. In his model of mental abilities (see Figure 9.3 on page 317), Guilford distinguished between convergent thinking and divergent thinking. In *convergent thinking*, one tries to narrow down a list of alternatives to converge on a single correct answer. For example, when you take a multiple-choice exam, you try to eliminate incorrect options until you hit on the correct response. Most training in school encourages convergent thinking. In *divergent thinking*, one tries to expand the range of alternatives by generating many possible solutions. Imagine that you work for an advertising agency. To come up with as many slogans as possible for a client's product, you must use divergent thinking. Some of your slogans may be clear losers, and eventually you will have to engage in convergent thinking to pick the best, but coming up with the range of new possibilities depends on divergent thinking.

Thirty years of research on divergent thinking has yielded mixed results. As a whole, the evidence suggests that divergent thinking contributes to creativity (Runco, 2004), but it clearly does not represent the essence of creativity, as originally proposed (Brown, 1989; Plucker & Renzulli, 1999; Weisberg, 2006). In retrospect, it was probably unrealistic to expect creativity to depend on a single cognitive skill. According

to Sternberg (1988a), the cognitive processes that underlie creativity are multifaceted.

Measuring Creativity

Although its nature may be elusive, creativity clearly is important in today's world. Creative masterpieces in the arts and literature enrich human existence. Creative insights in the sciences illuminate people's understanding of the world. Creative inventions fuel technological progress. Thus, it is understandable that psychologists have been interested in measuring creativity with psychological tests.

How Do Psychological Tests Measure Creativity? A diverse array of psychological tests has been devised to measure individuals' creativity (Plucker & Makel, 2010). Usually, the items on creativity tests assess divergent thinking by giving respondents a specific starting point and then requiring them to generate as many possibilities as they can in a short period of time. Typical items on a creativity test might include the following: (1) List as many uses as you can for a newspaper. (2) Think of as many fluids that burn as you can. (3) Imagine that people no longer need sleep and think of as many consequences as you can. Subjects' scores on these tests depend on the *number* of alternatives they generate and on the *originality* and *usefulness* of the alternatives.

How Well Do Tests Predict Creative Productivity? In general, studies indicate that creativity tests are mediocre predictors of creative achievement in the real world (Hocevar & Bachelor, 1989; Plucker & Renzulli, 1999). Why? One reason is that these tests measure creativity in the abstract, as a *general trait*. However, the accumulation of

evidence suggests that *creativity is specific to particular domains* (Amabile, 1996; Feist, 2004; Kaufman & Baer, 2002, 2004). Despite some rare exceptions, creative people usually excel in a single field, in which they typically have considerable training and expertise (Policastro & Gardner, 1999). A remarkably innovative physicist might have no potential to be a creative poet or an inventive advertising executive. Measuring this person's creativity outside of physics may be meaningless. Thus, creativity tests may have limited value because they measure creativity out of context.

Even if better tests of creativity were devised, predicting creative achievement would probably still prove difficult. Why? Because creative achievement depends on many factors besides creativity (Cropley, 2000). Creative productivity over the course of an individual's career will depend on his or her motivation, personality, and intelligence, as well as situational factors, including training, mentoring, and good fortune (Amabile, 2001; Feldman, 1999; Simonton, 1999a, 2004; Simonton & Damian, 2013; Simonton & Flora, 2011).

Correlates of Creativity

What are creative people like? Are they brighter, or more open-minded, or less well adjusted than average? A great deal of research has been conducted on the correlates of creativity.

Is There a Creative Personality? There
is no single personality profile that accounts for creativity (Weisberg, 2006). However, investigators have found modest correlations between certain personality characteristics and creativity. Research suggests that highly creative people tend to be more independent, nonconforming, introverted, open to new experiences, self-confident, persistent, ambitious, dominant, and impulsive

Keystone/Getty Images

Gertrude Stein was an American expatriate who lived for 40 years in Paris, primarily at 27 Rue De Fleurus. She was an important feminist, and her experimental writings helped launch modernism (Daniel, 2009). Her prodigious creativity flowered when she left the United States to live abroad in Paris and become part of the intellectual life there. She also facilitated the creativity and careers of many other Paris artists, including Picasso, Matisse, Renoir, and Hemingway, at her famous Saturday night salons. Interestingly, she studied psychology at Harvard University and did research with William James. Her scientific publications appeared in important academic journals (e.g., Stein, 1898).

(Feist, 1998, 2010). At the core of this set of personality characteristics are the related traits of nonconformity and openness to new experiences. Creative people tend to think for themselves and are less easily influenced by the opinions of others than the average person is. The importance of openness to new experiences can be seen in a new line of research which suggests that living abroad enhances creativity.

Although living abroad has long been viewed as a rite of passage for creative artists and writers, no one thought to take an

empirical look at the impact of living abroad until recently. In a series of studies, Maddux and Galinsky (2009) found that the amount of time spent living abroad correlated positively with measures of creativity.

Interestingly, time spent in tourist travel abroad did *not* predict creativity. The contrasting effects of living and travelling abroad seem to depend on acculturation. Maddux and Galinsky found that the degree to which people adapted to foreign cultures was responsible for the association between living abroad and creativity. A subsequent study found that multicultural learning experiences appear to foster flexibility in thinking, which could enhance creativity (Maddux, Adam, & Galinsky, 2010).

Are Creativity and Intelligence Related? Are creative people exceptionally smart? Conceptually, creativity and intelligence represent different types of mental ability. Thus, it's not surprising that correlations between measures of creativity and measures of intelligence are generally weak (Sternberg & O'Hara, 1999). For example, a recent meta-analysis of many studies reported a correlation of only 0.17 (Kim, 2005). However, some findings suggest that the association between creativity and intelligence is somewhat stronger than that. When Silvia (2008) administered several intelligence scales and calculated estimates of *g* for subjects, this higher-order measure of intelligence correlated over 0.40 with creativity.

Is There a Connection between Creativity and Mental Illness? There
may be a connection between truly exceptional creativity and mental illness. We have always been fascinated by this connection (Sussman, 2007). The list of creative geniuses who have suffered from psychological disorders is endless (Prentky,

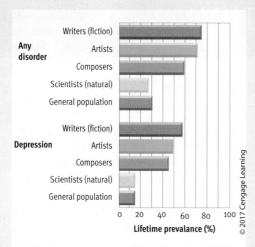

Figure 9.17
Estimated prevalence of psychological disorders among people who achieved creative eminence. Ludwig (1995) studied biographies of 1004 people who had clearly achieved eminence in one of 18 fields and tried to determine whether each person suffered from any specific mental disorders in their lifetimes. The data summarized here show the prevalence rates for depression and for a mental disorder of any kind for four fields where creativity is often the key to achieving eminence. As you can see, the estimated prevalence of mental illness was extremely elevated among eminent writers, artists, and composers (but not natural scientists) in comparison to the general population, with depression accounting for much of this elevation.

1989). Kafka, Hemingway, Rembrandt, van Gogh, Chopin, Tchaikovsky, Descartes, and Newton are but a few examples. Of course, a statistical association cannot be demonstrated by citing a handful of examples.

In this case, however, some statistical data are available. And these data *do* suggest a correlation between creative genius and maladjustment—in particular, mood disorders such as depression. When Nancy Andreasen studied 30 accomplished writers who had been invited as visiting faculty to the prestigious Iowa Writers' Workshop, she found that 80 percent of her sample had suffered a mood disorder at some point in their lives (Andreasen, 1987, 2005). In a similar study of 59 female writers from another writers' conference, Ludwig (1994) found that 56 percent had experienced depression. These figures are far above the base rate (roughly 15 percent) for mood disorders in the general population. Other studies have also found an association between creativity and mood disorders, as well as other kinds of psychological disorders (Nettle, 2001; Silvia & Kaufman, 2010). Perhaps the most ambitious examination of the issue has been

Arnold Ludwig's (1995) analyses of the biographies of 1004 people who achieved eminence in 18 fields. He found greatly elevated rates of depression and other disorders among eminent writers, artists, and composers (see Figure 9.17). Recent studies suggest that mental illness may be especially elevated among poets (Kaufman, 2001, 2005).

Thus, accumulating empirical data tentatively suggest that a correlation may exist between major creative achievement and vulnerability to mood disorders and other forms of psychopathology (Carson, 2011). According to Andreasen (1996, 2005), creativity and maladjustment probably are *not* causally related. Instead, she speculates that certain personality traits and cognitive styles may both foster creativity and predispose people to psychological disorders. Another, more mundane possibility is that creative individuals' elevated pathology may simply reflect all the difficulty and frustration they experience as they struggle to get their ideas or works accepted in artistic fields that enjoy relatively little public support (Csikszentmihalyi, 1994, 1999).

The Intelligence Debate, Appeals to Ignorance, and Reification

A *fallacy* is a mistake or error in the process of reasoning. Cognitive scientists who study how people think have developed long lists of common errors that people make in their reasoning processes. One of these fallacies has a curious name, which is the *appeal to ignorance*. It involves misusing the general lack of knowledge or information on an issue (a lack of knowledge is a kind of ignorance) to support an argument. This fallacy often surfaces in the debate about the relative influence of heredity and environment on intelligence. Before we tackle the more difficult issue of how this fallacy shows up in the debate about intelligence, let's start with a simpler example.

The Appeal to Ignorance

Do ghosts exist? This is probably not the kind of question you expected to find in your psychology textbook, but it can clarify the appeal to ignorance. Those who assert that ghosts *do* exist will often support their conclusion by arguing that no one can prove that ghosts *do not* exist; therefore, ghosts must exist. The lack of evidence or inability to show that ghosts do not exist is used to conclude the opposite. Conversely, those who assert that ghosts *do not* exist often rely on the same logic. They argue that no one can prove that ghosts exist; therefore, they must not exist. Can you see what is wrong with these appeals to ignorance? The lack of information on an issue cannot be used to support any conclusion—other than the conclusion that we are too ignorant to draw a conclusion.

One interesting aspect of the appeal to ignorance is that the same appeal can be used to support two conclusions that are diametrically opposed to each other. This paradox is a telltale clue that appeals to ignorance involve flawed reasoning. It is easy to see what is wrong with appeals to ignorance when the opposite arguments (ghosts exist—ghosts do not exist) are presented together and the lack of evidence on the issue under discussion is obvious. However, when the same fallacy surfaces in more complex debates and the appeal to ignorance is not as blatant, the strategy can be more difficult to recognize. Let's look at how the appeal to ignorance has been used in the debate about intelligence.

As you saw in the main body of the chapter, the debate about the relative contributions of nature and nurture to intelligence is one of psychology's longest-running controversies. This complex and multifaceted debate is exceptionally bitter and acrimonious because it has far-reaching sociopolitical repercussions. In this debate, one argument that has frequently been made is that we have little or no evidence that intelligence can be increased by environmental (educational) interventions; therefore, intelligence must be mostly inherited. In other words, the argument runs: No one has demonstrated that intelligence is largely shaped by environment, so it must be largely inherited. This argument was part of Jensen's (1969) landmark treatise that greatly intensified the debate about intelligence, and it was one of the arguments made by Herrnstein and Murray (1994) in their controversial book *The Bell Curve*.

The argument refers to the fact that educational enrichment programs such as Head Start, which have been designed to enhance the cognitive development of underprivileged children, generally have not produced substantial, long-term gains in IQ (Neisser et al., 1996). The programs produce other benefits, including enduring improvements in school achievement, but short-term gains in IQ scores typically have faded by the middle grades (Barnett, 2004). These findings may have some implications for government policy in the educational arena. However, the way in which they have been applied to the nature–nurture debate regarding intelligence has resulted in an appeal to ignorance. In its simplest form, the absence of evidence showing that environmental changes can increase intelligence is used to support the conclusion that intelligence is mostly determined by genetic inheritance. But the absence of evidence (ignorance) cannot be used to argue for or against a position.

By the way, if you have assimilated some of the critical thinking skills discussed in earlier chapters, you may be thinking, "Wait a minute. Aren't there alternative explanations for the failure of educational enrichment programs to increase IQ scores?" Yes, one could argue that the programs failed to yield improvements in IQ scores because they often were poorly executed, too brief, or underfunded (Ramey, 1999; Sigel, 2004). Moreover, Head Start programs were not really designed to increase IQ scores. They were designed to enhance deprived students' readiness for school (Schrag, Styfco, & Zigler, 2004). The inability of the enrichment programs to produce enduring increases in IQ does not necessarily imply that intelligence is unchangeable because it's largely a product of heredity.

You may also be wondering, "Aren't there contradictory data?" Once again, the answer is yes. Barnett (2004) argues that failures to

For the most part, educational enrichment programs for underprivileged children have not produced durable increases in participants' IQ scores. However, as the text explains, this finding does not provide logically sound support for the notion that intelligence is largely inherited.

find enduring gains in intelligence from Head Start programs can often be attributed to flaws and shortcomings in the research design of the studies. Furthermore, studies of some lesser-known educational enrichment programs attempted with smaller groups of children *have* yielded durable gains in IQ and other standardized test scores (Ramey & Ramey, 2004; Reynolds et al., 2001; Woodhead, 2004).

Reification

The dialogue on intelligence has also been marred by the tendency to engage in reification. *Reification* occurs when a hypothetical, abstract concept is given a name and then treated as though it were a concrete, tangible object. Some hypothetical constructs become so familiar and so taken for granted that we begin to think about them as if they were real. People often fall into this trap with the Freudian personality concepts of id, ego, and superego (see Chapter 12). They begin to think of the *ego*, for instance, as a genuine entity that can be strengthened or controlled, when the ego is really nothing more than a hypothetical abstraction.

The concept of intelligence has also been reified in many quarters. Like the ego, intelligence is nothing more than a useful abstraction—a hypothetical construct that is estimated, rather arbitrarily, by a collection of paper-and-pencil measures called IQ tests. Yet people routinely act as if intelligence is a tangible commodity, fighting vitriolic battles over whether it can be measured precisely, whether it can be changed, and whether it can ensure job success. This reification clearly contributes to the tendency for people to attribute excessive importance to the concept

Reification occurs when we think of hypothetical constructs as if they were real. Like intelligence, the concept of cyberspace has been subject to reification. The fact that cyberspace is merely an abstraction becomes readily apparent when artists are asked to "draw" cyberspace for conference posters or book covers.

of intelligence. It would be wise to remember that intelligence is no more real than the concept of "the environment" or "cyberspace."

Reification has also occurred in the debate about the *degree* to which intelligence is inherited. Arguments about the heritability coefficient for intelligence often imply that there is a single, true number lurking somewhere "out there," waiting to be discovered. In reality, heritability is a hypothetical construct that can be legitimately estimated in several ways that can lead to somewhat different results. Moreover, heritability ratios will vary from one population to the next, depending on the amount of genetic variability and the extent of environmental variability in the populations. No exactly accurate number that corresponds to "true heritability" awaits discovery (Hunt & Carlson, 2007; Sternberg et al., 2005). Thus, it is important to understand that hypothetical constructs have great heuristic value in the study of complex phenomena such as human thought and behaviour, but they do not actually exist in the world—at least not in the same way that a table or a person exists. See Table 9.3.

Table 9.3

Critical Thinking Skills Discussed in This Application

SKILL	DESCRIPTION
Recognizing and avoiding appeals to ignorance	The critical thinker understands that the lack of information on an issue cannot be used to support an argument.
Recognizing and avoiding reification	The critical thinker is vigilant about the tendency to treat hypothetical constructs as if they were concrete things.
Looking for alternative explanations for findings and events	In evaluating explanations, the critical thinker explores whether there are other explanations that could also account for the findings or events under scrutiny.
Looking for contradictory evidence	In evaluating the evidence presented on an issue, the critical thinker attempts to look for contradictory evidence that may have been left out of the debate.

MEASURING INTELLIGENCE

History of intelligence tests

- Modern intelligence testing was launched in 1905 by Binet, who devised a scale to measure a child's mental age.

- Terman revised the Binet scale to produce the Stanford-Binet in 1916, which introduced the *intelligence quotient (IQ)*.

- In 1939, Wechsler published an improved measure of intelligence for adults, which introduced the *deviation IQ score* based on the normal distribution.

Essentials of intelligence testing

- Modern deviation IQ scores indicate where people fall in the normal distribution for their age.

- Individuals' IQ scores can vary across testing occasions, but intelligence tests tend to have very high reliability.

- There is ample evidence that IQ tests are valid measures of academic/verbal intelligence, but they do not tap social or practical intelligence.

- IQ scores are correlated with occupational attainment, but doubts have been raised about how well they predict performance within a specific occupation.

- IQ tests are not widely used in most non-Western cultures.

BROADENING THE CONCEPT AND STUDY OF INTELLIGENCE

- Recent research has uncovered moderate positive correlations between IQ and overall brain volume and the volume of grey and white matter.

- Researchers have found that IQ measured in childhood correlates with longevity decades later.

- Sternberg's theory uses a cognitive perspective, which emphasizes the need to understand how people use their intelligence.

- According to Sternberg, the three facets of successful intelligence are analytical, creative, and practical intelligence.

- Gardner argues that the concept of intelligence should be expanded to encompass a diverse set of eight types of abilities, which are independent of one another.

EXTREMES OF INTELLIGENCE

Intellectual disability

- Intellectual disability refers to subaverage general mental ability (IQ <70) accompanied by deficits in adaptive skills, originating before age 18.

- Intellectual disability may be mild, moderate, severe, or profound. The vast majority (85%) of individuals have mild intellectual disability.

- Many organic conditions can cause intellectual disability, but a specific organic cause can be identified in only about 50% of cases.

- Cases of unknown origin tend to involve mild disability and are believed to be mainly caused by unfavourable environmental factors.

Giftedness

- In practice, efforts to identify gifted children focus almost exclusively on IQ scores, with a score of 130 as the typical minimum.

- For the most part, gifted children tend to be above average in social and emotional maturity.

- Although gifted children tend to be successful in life, very few go on to make genius-level contributions.

- The "drudge theory" proposes that extraordinary achievement depends on intensive training and monumental effort, but critics argue that innate talent is also crucial.

- *Savant* is a term that refers to individuals who typically have below average IQ but who nonetheless show remarkable ability in very specific areas.

HEREDITY AND ENVIRONMENT AS DETERMINANTS OF INTELLIGENCE

Evidence for hereditary influence

- *Twin studies* show that identical twins are more similar in intelligence than fraternal twins, suggesting that intelligence is at least partly inherited.

- Even more impressive, identical twins reared apart are more similar in intelligence than fraternal twins reared together.

- *Adoption studies* show that adopted children resemble their biological parents in intelligence.

- A *heritability ratio* is an estimate of the proportion of trait variability in a population that is determined by genetic variations.

- Estimates of the heritability of intelligence range from 40–80 percent, and mostly converge around 50 percent, but heritability ratios have limitations.

Evidence for environmental influence

- *Adoption studies* find that adopted children show some IQ resemblance to their foster parents and to their adoptive siblings.

- Studies of *environmental deprivation and enrichment* show that children's IQ scores change in response to altered circumstances.

- The *Flynn effect* refers to the finding that performance on IQ tests has steadily increased over generations.

The interaction of heredity and environment

- Evidence clearly shows that intelligence is shaped by both heredity and environment, and that these influences interact.

- The *reaction range model* posits that heredity sets limits to one's intelligence, and that environmental factors determine where people fall within these limits.

The debate about cultural differences in IQ scores

- Jensen and others have argued that cultural differences in IQ scores are largely due to heredity.

- Even if the heritability of IQ is high, group differences in IQ could be entirely environmental in origin.

- Many scientists believe that cultural differences in IQ are attributable to socioeconomic disadvantage.

APPLICATIONS

- Creativity does not usually involve sudden insight; creativity tests are mediocre predictors of creative productivity.

- The association between creativity and intelligence is weak; creative geniuses may exhibit heightened vulnerability to psychological disorders.

- The *appeal to ignorance* is the misuse of the general lack of knowledge on an issue to support an argument.

- *Reification* occurs when a hypothetical concept is given a name and then treated as though it were a concrete, tangible object.

CHAPTER 10

Motivation and Emotion

Themes in this Chapter

Theoretical
Diversity

Sociohistorical
Context

Multifactorial
Causation

Cultural
Heritage

Heredity &
Environment

Motivation and emotion are two important topics in psychology that are often discussed in the same chapter. While there are distinct literatures and theories in each of these areas, they are clearly linked. In the first part of the chapter, we discuss research and theory in the study of motivation. Motivation relates to the study of the processes involved in goal-directed behaviour. Our goal-directed behaviour, of course, is often associated with specific emotions. For example, think back to the goal you set for yourself on the first test in this course. You may have set a goal of getting an A on the first test and then studied hard to achieve it. Then think about your reaction when you found out your grade on that test. Your reaction would have been very different if you received an A than if you got a lower grade. Motivation and emotion, then, are often linked. Consider for a moment a different type of goal setting—setting a goal of winning an Olympic or Paralympic medal.

Chantal Petitclerc is one of Canada's finest athletes. Since losing the use of her legs in an accident at age 13, she has gone on to dominate women's wheelchair racing events. She holds many world, Commonwealth, and Paralympic records and has won multiple gold medals. She has received many honours, including Canadian Athlete of the Year and Paralympic Athlete of the Year. She became a Companion of the Order of Canada in 2009, she was inducted into the Canadian Sports Hall of Fame in 2010, and she was inducted into the Athletics Canada Hall of Fame in 2013. She was named the Chef de Mission for Canada's 2014 Commonwealth Team. In 2016, she was named to the Canadian Senate by Prime Minister Trudeau.

Most of us can only begin to imagine the dedication and motivation that bring an athlete such as Chantal Petitclerc to these levels. When asked what drives her, she states, "No matter what you do or what your dreams are, you always do it to achieve a goal and also to see what your limits are and eventually to see you have no limits" (interview with Chantal Petitclerc, 1996). Whatever their individual reasons, Olympic and Paralympic athletes must be highly motivated to continue to prepare for and compete in their chosen sports.

In this chapter, we will discuss the topic of motivation as it is broadly defined in psychology. This definition includes the motivations driving elite athletes as well as looking at a full range of topics from hunger motivation and eating to achievement motivation—the type of motivation that may have brought you to the study of psychology in the first place.

Adam Pretty/Getty Images

Paralympic wheelchair racer Chantal Petitclerc, who was recently appointed to the Canadian Senate, was just one of the highly motivated athletes who represented Canada in Beijing in 2008, winning five gold medals and setting three world records.

The other topic considered in this chapter is the study of emotion. The study of emotion has long been of interest to psychologists. Our lives are filled with emotions. Your reaction after obtaining your grade in the first test in this course would have been only one of many emotionally relevant experiences you had that day. In some cases, the explanation for our emotion is clear. You may be hurt, angry, or confused when you are excluded from the plans your friends have made for the weekend.

While the eliciting events and emotions experienced in this case seem quite obvious, it is not always so clear why we are feeling the way that we are or, indeed, what caused us to feel that way. In this chapter, we will discuss some of the theories and research examining our emotional experiences, including our reactions to being excluded by others. You may be surprised at what some of the research tells us about our emotions. Think back to the Featured Study in Chapter 2 in which males crossed high or low bridges spanning the Capilano River in British Columbia. Did you expect that their emotions could have been so easily manipulated by the experimenters? In the last part of this chapter, we will learn more about what factors affect our subjective feeling states.

Courtesy of Dr. Kimberley Amirault-Ryan

Dr. Kimberly Amirault

Psychologists often work with elite athletes to prepare them for competition. Dr. Kimberly Amirault has worked both with Olympic and professional athletes. She obtained her Ph.D. in psychology from the University of Calgary.

Motivational Theories and Concepts

Motives are the needs, wants, interests, and desires that propel people in certain directions, propel us to achieve important goals. In short, **motivation involves goal-directed behaviour.** As we will see later in this book, motivation to achieve relevant goals can be an important determinant of adjustment. There are a number of theoretical approaches to motivation. Let's look at some of these theories and the concepts they employ.

Drive Theories

Many theories view motivational forces in terms of *drives*. The drive concept appears in a diverse array of theories that otherwise have little in common, such as psychoanalytic (Freud, 1915) and behaviourist formulations (Hull, 1943). This approach to understanding motivation was explored most fully by Clark Hull in the 1940s and 1950s (Madsen, 1968).

Drive theories apply the concept of *homeostasis*, a state of physiological equilibrium or stability, to behaviour. A *drive* is an internal state of tension that motivates an organism to engage in activities that should reduce this tension. These unpleasant states of tension are viewed as disruptions of the preferred equilibrium. For example, when your body temperature rises or drops noticeably, automatic responses occur (see Figure 10.1). According to drive theories, when individuals experience a drive, they're motivated to pursue actions that will lead to *drive reduction*. During a long class you may begin to feel hungry. The hunger motive has usually been conceptualized as a drive system—if you go without food for a while, you begin to experience some discomfort. This internal tension (the drive) motivates you to obtain food. Eating reduces the drive and restores physiological equilibrium.

Drive theories have been very influential, and the drive concept continues to be widely used in modern psychology. *However, drive theories cannot explain all motivation* (Berridge, 2004). Homeostasis appears irrelevant to some human motives, such as a "thirst for knowledge." And think of all the times that you've eaten when you weren't the least bit hungry. Drive theories can't explain this behaviour very well.

Incentive Theories

Incentive theories propose that external stimuli regulate motivational states (Bolles, 1975; McClelland, 1975; Skinner, 1953). An *incentive* is an external goal that has the capacity to motivate behaviour. Ice cream, a juicy steak, a monetary prize, approval from friends, an A on an exam, and a promotion at work are all incentives. Some of these incentives may reduce drives, but others may not.

Drive and incentive models of motivation are often contrasted as *push-versus-pull* theories. Drive theories emphasize how *internal* states of tension *push* people in certain directions. Incentive theories emphasize how *external* stimuli *pull* people in certain directions. According to drive theories, the source of motivation lies *within* the organism. According to incentive theories, the source of motivation lies *outside* the organism, in the environment. This means that incentive models don't operate according to the principle of homeostasis, which hinges on internal changes in the organism. Thus, in comparison to drive theories, incentive theories emphasize environmental factors and downplay the biological bases of human motivation.

As you're painfully aware, people can't always obtain the goals they desire, such as good grades or choice promotions. *Expectancy-value models* of

Figure 10.1
Temperature regulation as an example of homeostasis. The regulation of body temperature provides a simple example of how organisms often seek to maintain homeostasis, or a state of physiological equilibrium. When your temperature moves out of an acceptable range, automatic bodily reactions (e.g., sweating or shivering) occur that help restore equilibrium. Of course, these automatic reactions may not be sufficient by themselves, so you may have to take other action (e.g., turning a furnace up or down) to bring your body temperature back into its comfort zone.

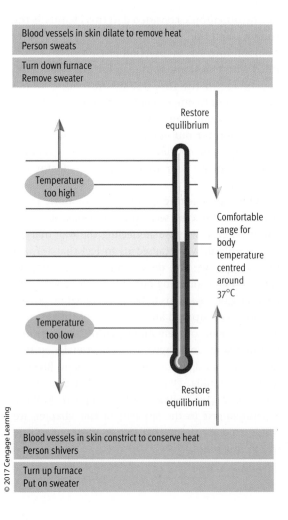

Blood vessels in skin dilate to remove heat
Person sweats

Turn down furnace
Remove sweater

Restore equilibrium

Temperature too high

Comfortable range for body temperature centred around 37°C

Temperature too low

Restore equilibrium

© 2017 Cengage Learning

Blood vessels in skin constrict to conserve heat
Person shivers

Turn up furnace
Put on sweater

motivation are incentive theories that take this reality into account (Atkinson & Birch, 1978). According to expectancy-value models, one's motivation to pursue a particular course of action will depend on two factors: (1) *expectancy* about one's chances of attaining the incentive and (2) the *value* of the desired incentive. Thus, your motivation to pursue a promotion at work will depend on your estimate of the likelihood that you can snare the promotion (expectancy) and on how appealing the promotion is to you (value). Expectancy-value models have proven to be useful in understanding a range of human behaviours and motivations (e.g., Westaby, 2006).

Evolutionary Theories

Psychologists who take an evolutionary perspective assert that human motives and those of other species are the products of evolution, just as anatomical characteristics are (Durrant & Ellis, 2003). They argue that natural selection favours behaviours that maximize reproductive success—that is, passing on genes to the next generation. Thus, they explain motives such as affiliation, achievement, dominance, aggression, and sex drive in terms of their adaptive value. If dominance is a crucial motive for a species, they say, it's because dominance provides a reproductive or survival advantage.

Evolutionary analyses of motivation are based on the premise that motives can best be understood in terms of the adaptive problems they solved for our hunter–gatherer ancestors (Tooby & Cosmides, 2005). For example, the need for dominance is thought to be greater in men than women because it could facilitate males' reproductive success in a variety of ways, including (1) females may prefer mating with dominant males, (2) dominant males may poach females from subordinate males, (3) dominant males may intimidate male rivals in competition for sexual access, and (4) dominant males may acquire more material resources, which may increase mating opportunities (Buss, 2014).

Consider, also, the affiliation motive, or need for belongingness. The adaptive benefits of affiliation for our ancestors probably included help with offspring, collaboration in hunting and gathering, mutual defence, opportunities for sexual interaction, and so forth (Griskevicius, Haselton, & Ackerman, 2015). Hence, humans developed a strong need to belong and a strong aversion to rejection (Neuberg & Schaller, 2015). David Buss (1995) points out that it is not by accident that achievement, power (dominance), and intimacy are among the most heavily studied motives because the satisfaction of each of these motives is likely to affect one's reproductive success.

Motivational theorists of all persuasions agree on one point: Humans display an enormous diversity of motives. These include a host of biological motives, such as hunger, thirst, and sex, and a variety of social motives, such as the needs for achievement, affiliation, autonomy, dominance, and order. Given the range and diversity of human motives, we can only examine a handful in depth. To a large degree, our choices reflect the motives psychologists have studied the most: hunger, sex, and achievement. After our discussion of these motivational systems, we will explore the elements of emotional experience and discuss various theories of emotion.

The Motivation of Hunger and Eating

Why do people eat? Because they're hungry. What makes them hungry? A lack of food. Any grade-school child can explain these basic facts. So hunger is a simple motivational system, right? Wrong! Hunger is deceptive. It only looks simple. Actually, it's a puzzling and complex motivational system. Despite extensive studies of hunger, scientists are still struggling to understand the factors that regulate eating behaviour. Let's examine a few of these factors.

Biological Factors in the Regulation of Hunger

You have probably had embarrassing occasions when your stomach growled loudly at an inopportune moment. Someone may have commented, "You must be starving!" Most people equate a rumbling stomach with hunger, and, in fact, the first scientific theories of hunger were based on this simple equation. In an elaborate 1912 study, Walter Cannon and A. L. Washburn verified what most people have noticed based on casual observation: There is an association between stomach contractions and the experience of hunger.

Based on this correlation, Cannon theorized that stomach contractions *cause* hunger. However, as we've seen before, correlation is no assurance of causation, and his theory was eventually discredited. Stomach contractions often accompany hunger, but they don't cause it. How do we know? Because later research showed that people continue to experience

Motivation and Emotion

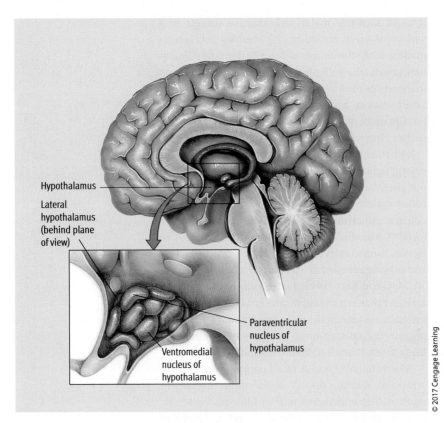

Hypothalamus

Lateral hypothalamus (behind plane of view)

Paraventricular nucleus of hypothalamus

Ventromedial nucleus of hypothalamus

© 2017 Cengage Learning

Figure 10.2

The hypothalamus. This small structure at the base of the forebrain plays a role in regulating a variety of human biological needs, including hunger. The detailed blowup shows that the hypothalamus is made up of a variety of discrete areas. Scientists used to believe that the lateral and ventromedial areas were the brain's on–off centres for eating. However, more recent research suggests that the paraventricular nucleus may be more crucial to the regulation of hunger and that thinking in terms of neural circuits rather than anatomical centres makes more sense.

Chris Ratcliffe/Bloomberg via Getty Images

Judith Rodin

"People's metabolic machinery is constituted in such a way that the fatter they are, the fatter they are primed to become."

and ventromedial areas of the hypothalamus are elements in the neural circuitry that regulates hunger. However, they are not the key elements, nor simple on–off centres (King, 2006; Meister, 2007). Today, scientists believe that two other areas of the hypothalamus—the *arcuate nucleus* and the *paraventricular nucleus*—play a larger role in the modulation of hunger (Scott, McDade, & Luckman, 2007). In recent years, the arcuate nucleus has been singled out as especially important (Moran & Sakai, 2013). This area in the hypothalamus appears to contain a group of neurons that are sensitive to incoming hunger signals and another group of neurons that respond to satiety signals.

Contemporary theories of hunger focus more on *neural circuits* that pass through areas of the hypothalamus rather than on *anatomical centres* in the brain. These circuits depend on a large variety of neurotransmitters and they appear to be much more complicated than anticipated. Evidence suggests that the neural circuits regulating hunger are massively and reciprocally interconnected with extensive parallel processing (Powley, 2009). This complex neural circuitry is sensitive to a diverse range of physiological processes.

Digestive and Hormonal Regulation

The digestive system includes a variety of mechanisms that influence hunger (Ritter, 2004). It turns out that Walter Cannon was not entirely wrong in hypothesizing that the stomach regulates hunger. After you have consumed food, the stomach can send a variety of signals to the brain that inhibit further eating (Woods & Stricker, 2008). For instance, the vagus nerve carries information about the stretching of the stomach walls that indicates when the stomach is full. Other nerves carry satiety messages that depend on how rich in nutrients the contents of the stomach are.

A variety of hormones circulating in the bloodstream appear to contribute to the regulation of hunger (Schwartz, 2012). For example, after the body goes

hunger even after their stomachs have been removed out of medical necessity (Wangensteen & Carlson, 1931). If hunger can occur without a stomach, then stomach contractions can't be the cause of hunger. This realization led to more elaborate theories of hunger that focus on a host of factors.

Brain Regulation

Research with lab animals eventually suggested that the experience of hunger is controlled in the brain—specifically, in the hypothalamus. As we have noted before, the *hypothalamus* is a tiny structure involved in the regulation of a variety of biological needs related to survival (see Figure 10.2). In the 1940s and 1950s, studies using brain lesioning techniques and electrical stimulation of the brain led to the conclusion that the *lateral hypothalamus (LH)* and the *ventromedial nucleus of the hypothalamus (VMH)* were the brain's on–off switches for the control of hunger (Stellar, 1954). However, over the course of several decades, a variety of empirical findings undermined the dual-centres model of hunger (Valenstein, 1973; Winn, 1995). The current thinking is that the lateral

Janson George/Shutterstock.com

The rat in front has had its ventromedial hypothalamus lesioned, resulting in a dramatic increase in weight.

without food for a while, the stomach secretes ghrelin, which causes stomach contractions and promotes hunger. In contrast, after food is consumed, the upper intestine releases a hormone called CCK that delivers satiety signals to the brain, thus reducing hunger.

Finally, evidence indicates that a hormone called leptin contributes to the long-term regulation of hunger, as well as the regulation of numerous other bodily functions (Ramsay & Woods, 2012). Leptin is produced by fat cells throughout the body and released into the bloodstream. Leptin circulates through the bloodstream and ultimately provides the hypothalamus with information about the body's fat stores (Dietrich & Horvath, 2012). When leptin levels are high, the propensity to feel hungry diminishes. When leptin levels are low, signals arriving in the brain promote increased hunger. Insulin, a hormone secreted by the pancreas, is also sensitive to fluctuations in the body's fat stores. The hormonal signals that influence hunger (the fluctuations of insulin, ghrelin, CCK, and leptin) all seem to converge in the hypothalamus, especially the arcuate and paraventricular nuclei (Moran & Sakai, 2013).

Environmental Factors in the Regulation of Hunger

Hunger clearly is a biological need, but eating is not regulated by biological factors alone (Hall, 2016). Studies show that social and environmental factors govern eating to a considerable extent. Three key environmental factors are (1) the availability of food, (2) learned preferences and habits, and (3) stress.

Food Availability and Related Cues

Most of the research on the physiological regulation of hunger has been based on the assumption that hunger operates as a drive system in which homeostatic mechanisms are at work. However, some theorists emphasize the incentive value of food and argue that humans and other animals are often motivated to eat not by the need to compensate for energy deficits but by the anticipated pleasure of eating (Finlayson, Dalton, & Blundell, 2012; Johnson, 2013). This perspective has been bolstered by evidence that the following variables exert significant influence over food consumption:

- *Palatability*. The better food tastes, the more of it people consume (de Castro, 2010). This principle is not limited to humans. The eating behaviour of rats and other animals is also influenced by palatability.
- *Quantity available*. A powerful determinant of the amount eaten is the amount available. People tend

to consume what's put in front of them. The more people are served, the more they eat (Rolls, 2012). This is often referred to as the *bin model* or *bin heuristic* (Geier, 2006). Individuals may focus on one unit of food as the appropriate amount rather than the quantity of food (Herman, Poliby, et al., 2015). In one study, young children requested almost twice as much cereal when it was served in a large bowl as opposed to a small one (Wansink, van Ittersum, & Payne, 2014). Similarly, diners at a buffet with large plates consumed 45 percent more (and wasted 135 percent more!) than diners given smaller plates (Wansink & van Ittersum, 2013). Unfortunately, in recent decades, the size of grocery store packages, restaurant portions, and dinnerware has increased steadily (Wansink, 2012). These bloated cues about what represents "normal" food consumption clearly fuel increased eating. Thus, the remarkably large and ever-expanding portions served in modern North American restaurants surely foster increased consumption (Geier, Rozin, & Doros, 2006).
- *Variety*. Humans and animals increase their consumption when a greater variety of foods is available (Raynor & Epstein, 2001; Temple et al., 2008). As you eat a specific food, its incentive value declines. This phenomenon is called *sensory-specific satiety* (Meillon et al., 2013). If only a few foods are available, the appeal of all of them can decline quickly. But if many foods are available, people can keep shifting to new foods and end up eating more overall. This principle explains why people are especially likely to overeat at buffets where many foods are available.
- *Presence of others*. On average, individuals eat 44 percent more when they eat with other people as opposed to eating alone. The more people present, the more people tend to eat (de Castro, 2010). When two people eat together, they tend to use each other as guides and eat similar amounts (Hermans et al., 2012). However, when women eat in the presence of an opposite-sex person they do not know well, they tend to reduce their intake (Young et al., 2009). When asked afterward, people seem oblivious to the fact that their eating is influenced by the presence of others (Vartanian, Herman, & Wansink, 2008).
- *Stress*. Stress has varied effects on eating, as some individuals eat less, but estimates suggest that roughly 40–50 percent of people increase their food consumption in times of stress (Sproesser, Schupp, & Renner, 2014). In many people, stress also appears to foster a shift toward less healthy food choices, such as loading up on sweets and fatty foods (Michels et al., 2012).

According to incentive models of hunger, the availability and palatability of food are key factors regulating hunger. An abundance of diverse foods tends to lead to increased eating.

Eating can also be triggered by exposure to environmental cues that have been associated with eating. You have no doubt had your hunger aroused by television commercials for delicious-looking food or by seductive odours coming from the kitchen. Consistent with this observation, studies by researchers such as Peter Herman and Janet Polivy of the University of Toronto and others have shown that hunger can be increased by exposure to pictures, written descriptions, and video depictions of attractive foods (Halford et al., 2004; Herman, Ostovich, & Polivy, 1999; Marcelino et al., 2001; Oakes & Slotterback, 2000). Studies have shown that exposure to soda and food advertisements incite hunger and lead to increased food intake (Harris, Bargh, & Brownell, 2009; Koordeman et al., 2010). Moreover, the foods consumed are not limited to those seen in the ads. And people tend to be unaware of how the ads influence their eating behaviour. Thus, it's clear that hunger and eating are governed in part by the incentive qualities of food.

It is also clear that eating is often a social action. Herman, Polivy, and their colleagues have considered the effects of cues and of the presence of others on one's intake of food (Coelho, Polivy, & Herman, 2008; Herman, Roth, & Polivy, 2003). They suggest that social cues based on the behaviour of others are some of the most important determinants of food intake. They have integrated a variety of ideas about the effects of the presence of others on our eating in developing their inhibitory norm model of social influence on eating. They suggest that the presence of others generally inhibits eating. But, under certain specific conditions, eating may increase. In essence, they suggest that our eating is influenced by extant social norms determined by the behaviour of the others around us at the time. Thus, while it's clear that hunger and eating are governed in part by the availability of food and the presence of a variety of

University of Toronto researchers Peter Herman and Janet Polivy are well known in the area of the psychology of eating. Their recent research has examined the effects of social cues on eating behaviour.

food-related cues, other social factors also play an important role. Given the continuing trend for adult Canadians to keep getting heavier (Statistics Canada, 2016), Herman and Polivy's view that more research is needed into the causes of overeating is very timely (Herman, van Strien, & Polivy, 2008).

Learned Preferences and Habits

Are you fond of eating calves' brains? How about eels or snakes? Could we interest you in a grasshopper? Probably not, but these are delicacies in some regions of the world. People in some countries like to eat maggots! You probably prefer chicken, apples, eggs, lettuce, potato chips, pizza, cornflakes, or ice cream. These preferences are acquired through learning. People from different cultures display very different patterns of food consumption (Rozin, 2007). If you doubt this fact, just visit a grocery store in an ethnic neighbourhood (not your own, of course).

Humans do have some innate taste preferences of a general sort. For example, a preference for sweet tastes is present at birth (Mennella & Beauchamp, 1996), and humans' preference for high-fat foods appears to be at least partly genetic in origin (Schiffman et al., 1998). Evidence also suggests that an unlearned preference for salt emerges at around four months of age in humans (Birch & Fisher, 1996). Nonetheless, learning wields a great deal of influence over what people prefer to eat (Rozin, 2007). Taste preferences are partly a function of learned associations formed through classical conditioning (Appleton, Gentry, & Shephard, 2006). For example, youngsters can be conditioned to prefer flavours paired with high caloric intake or other pleasant events. Of course, as we learned in Chapter 6, taste aversions can also be acquired through conditioning when foods are followed by nausea (Schafe & Bernstein, 1996).

To a large degree, food preferences are a matter of exposure (Cooke, 2007). People generally prefer familiar foods. But geographical, cultural, religious, and ethnic factors limit people's exposure to certain foods. Young children are more likely to taste an unfamiliar food if an adult tries it first. Repeated exposures to a new food usually lead to increased liking. However, as many parents have learned the hard way, forcing a child to eat a specific food can backfire (Benton, 2004).

Eating and Weight: The Roots of Obesity

As we've seen, hunger is regulated by a complex interaction of biological and psychological factors. The same kinds of complexities emerge when investigators explore the roots of *obesity*, the condition of being overweight. Most experts assess obesity in terms of body mass index (BMI)—weight (in kilograms) divided by height (in metres) squared (kg/m^2). This index of weight controls for variations in height. A BMI of 25.0–29.9 is typically regarded as overweight, and a BMI over 30 is generally considered obese. North American culture seems to be obsessed with slimness, but surveys show alarmingly high levels of Canadians classified as overweight and obese. Recent survey results obtained by Statistics Canada (2015) revealed that 20.2 percent of Canadians over the age of 18 were classified as obese based on reported height and weight. In the same survey, the result indicated that 40 percent of Canadian men and 27.5 percent of Canadian women over the age of 18 were classified as overweight. Combining the overweight and obese categories together, Statistics Canada estimated that 8.2 million men and 6.1 million women were susceptible to increased health risks based on their weight. Two Canadian provinces led the way in terms of lowest levels reported prevalence of obesity—Quebec and British Columbia. Provinces and territories with higher-than-average obesity levels included the Northwest Territories, Newfoundland and Labrador, New Brunswick, Nunavut, Prince Edward Island, Nova Scotia, Saskatchewan, and Manitoba.

Overweight adults have plenty of company from their children. Data has indicated that weight problems have tripled among children and adolescents (Ogden et al., 2012). A recent Canadian Senate report on Canadian obesity has referred to the problem as an "epidemic" (Campion-Smith, 2016). Moreover, the obesity epidemic has become a global problem, spreading from affluent countries to much of the world, including many relatively poor countries (Popkin, 2012).

Theorists have a plausible explanation for the dramatic increase in the prevalence of obesity (Blass, 2012; King, 2013). They point out that, over the course of history, most humans lived in environments characterized by fierce competition for limited, unreliable food resources. Thus, they evolved a propensity to consume more food than immediately necessary when the opportunity presented itself because food might not be available later. Excess calories were stored in the body (as fat) to prepare for future food shortages. However, in today's modern, industrialized societies, the vast majority of humans live in environments that provide an abundant, reliable supply of highly palatable food. In these environments, the evolved tendency to overeat when food is plentiful leads many people

The fact that culture influences food preferences is evident in these photos, in which you can see delicacies such as grilled bat (left) and crocodile soup (right).

down a path of chronic, excessive food consumption. Of course, because of variations in genetics, metabolism, and other factors, only some become overweight.

If obesity merely affected people's vanity, there would be little cause for concern. Unfortunately, obesity is a big health problem that elevates one's mortality risk. Obese individuals are more vulnerable than others to coronary disease, stroke, hypertension, diabetes, respiratory problems, gallbladder disease, arthritis, muscle and skeletal pain, sleep apnea, and some types of cancer (Corsica & Perri, 2013; Ogden, 2010). Moreover, recent evidence suggests that obesity may foster inflammatory and metabolic changes that contribute to the development of Alzheimer's disease (Letra, Santana, & Seica, 2014; Spielman, Little, & Klegeris, 2014). Figure 10.3 shows how the prevalence of diabetes, hypertension, coronary heart disease, and muscle and skeletal pain is elevated as BMI increases. Clearly, obesity are a significant health problem. Hence, scientists have devoted a great deal of attention to the causes of obesity. Let's look at some of the factors they have identified.

Genetic Predisposition

Research suggests that obesity is partly a matter of hereditary influence (Price, 2012). In an influential twin study, Stunkard and colleagues (1990) found that identical twins reared apart were far more similar in BMI than fraternal twins reared

Photo by Jonathan Bielaski/Used with permission from The University of Waterloo.

Christine Logel

Christine Logel is a social psychologist at Renison University College, University of Waterloo. Dr. Logel's research focuses on investigating basic social psychological concepts and how they might be applied to help solve social problems including some innovative work on obesity.

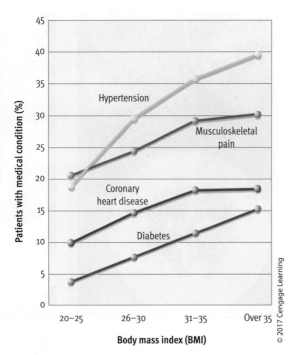

Figure 10.3
Weight and the prevalence of various diseases. This graph shows how obesity, as indexed by BMI, is related to the prevalence of four common types of illness. The prevalence of diabetes, heart disease, muscle pain, and hypertension all increase as BMI goes up. Clearly, obesity is a significant health risk. (Based on data in Brownell & Wadden, 2000)

together (see Figure 10.4). In another study of over 4000 twins, Allison and colleagues (1994) estimated that genetic factors account for 61 percent of the variation in weight among men and 73 percent among women. Thus, it appears that some people inherit a genetic vulnerability to obesity (Chung & Leibel, 2012).

Excessive Eating and Inadequate Exercise

The bottom line for overweight people is that they eat too much in relation to their level of exercise. In contemporary North America, the tendency to overeat and exercise too little is easy to understand (Henderson & Brownell, 2004). Tasty, high-calorie, high-fat foods and sugar-sweetened drinks are readily available nearly everywhere—not just in restaurants and grocery stores, but in shopping malls, airports, gas stations, schools, and workplaces. Today, North Americans spend almost one-half of their food dollars in restaurants, where they tend to eat more than they typically consume at home (Corsica & Perri, 2013). Unhealthy foods are heavily advertised, and these marketing efforts are very effective in getting people to increase their consumption of such foods (Horgen, Harris, & Brownell, 2012). The inability to control over eating has become so common that some theorists are coming around to the view that highly processed, high-fat, high-sugar foods may literally be addictive (Ahmed, 2012; Gearhardt & Corbin, 2012). Modern societies are thought to create a toxic, "obesogenic" environment for eating.

Unfortunately, the rise of this obesogenic environment has been paralleled by a significant decline in physical activity (Corsica & Perri, 2013). Modern conveniences, such as cars and elevators; changes in the world of work, such as the shift to more desk jobs; and increases in TV viewing and video-gaming have conspired to make our lifestyles more sedentary than ever before. The research results concerning Canadian children are particularly distressing. Recent figures from Statistics Canada (2015) reveal

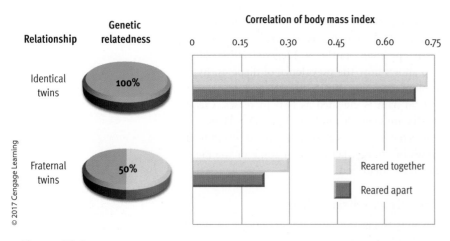

Figure 10.4
The heritability of weight. These data from a twin study by Stunkard et al. (1990) reveal that identical twins are much more similar in body mass index than fraternal twins, suggesting that genetic factors account for much of the variation among people in the propensity to become overweight. (Data from Stunkard et al., 1990)

Many theorists maintain that the increased prevalence of obesity is due to the fact that modern societies are characterized by obesogenic environments where tasty, tempting food is everywhere around us.

Lynne Sutherland/Alamy Stock Photo

that most school-aged children are not meeting the current Canadian physical activity guidelines. Especially vulnerable to inactivity are girls aged 12 to 17. Overall, Canadian kids are spending the majority of their waking hours (on average, two-thirds of their waking hours) being sedentary. Along with obesity, physical inactivity can lead to long-term health problems.

reality check

Misconception

Eating at night will lead to extra weight gain.

Reality

Changes in weight depend on one's caloric intake in relation to one's energy expenditure from physical activities and metabolic processes. *When* you consume your calories is irrelevant. It is the overall amount of caloric intake that is crucial.

The Concept of Set Point

People who lose weight on a diet have a rather strong tendency to gain back all the weight they lose, suggesting that homeostatic mechanisms defend against weight loss (Berthoud, 2012). It appears that a constellation of metabolic and neuroendocrine processes work to resist weight loss. For example, after significant weight loss, individuals' energy expenditure tends to decline (Goldsmith et al., 2010); that is, they burn calories more slowly, which gradually fosters weight gain. Even more important, reduced fat stores result in reduced levels of the hormone leptin. Low levels of leptin fuel increased hunger and blunt some of the satiety signals that normally keep a lid on eating, thus promoting increased food consumption (Kissilef et al., 2012). Obviously, these biological adaptations to weight loss eventually lead most people to regain the weight they have lost. Interestingly, the human body is also wired to resist weight gain. People who have to work to put weight on often have trouble keeping it on. The adaptive mechanisms that tend to maintain a fairly stable body weight suggest that everyone may have a set point for weight. *Set-point theory proposes that the body monitors fat-cell levels to keep them (and weight) fairly stable.* This set point is each individual's natural point of stability for weight. Originally viewed as a specific point of balance, it is now viewed as a narrow range of weight around that point (Pinel, Assanand, & Lehman, 2000). The set point concept raises a perplexing question: If the human body is wired to keep weight within a narrow range, why has obesity increased dramatically in recent decades? It turns out that the physiological processes that defend against weight loss are much stronger than those that defend against weight gain (Berthoud, 2012). Why? Probably because in ancestral environments where food resources were limited and unreliable, defending against weight loss would have been more adaptive for survival than defending against weight gain (Rosenbaum et al., 2010). Thus, another consideration promoting obesity is that the human body has been sculpted by evolution to defend against weight loss more effectively than against weight gain.

Dietary Restraint

Some investigators have proposed that variations in *dietary restraint* contribute to obesity (Polivy & Herman, 1995; Wardle et al., 2000). According to this theory, chronic dieters are *restrained eaters*—people who consciously work overtime to control their eating impulses and who feel guilty when they fail. To lose weight, restrained eaters go hungry much of the time, but they are constantly thinking about food. However, when their cognitive control is disrupted, they become *disinhibited* and eat to excess (Lowe, 2002). The crux of the problem is that restrained eaters assume, "Either I am on a diet, or I am out of control." A variety of events, such as drinking alcohol or experiencing emotional distress, can affect restrained eaters' control (Federoff, Polivy, & Herman, 2003; Kemp, Herman, Hollitt, Polivy, & Pritchard, 2016). But for many, the most common source of disinhibition is simply the perception that they have cheated on their diet. "I've already blown it," they think to themselves after perhaps just one high-calorie appetizer, "so I might as well enjoy as much as I want." They then proceed to consume a large meal or to go on an eating binge for the remainder of the day. Restrained eaters even tend to prepare for planned diets by overeating (Urbszat, Herman, & Polivy, 2002). Paradoxically, then, dietary restraint is thought to lead to frequent overeating and thus contribute to obesity.

Dietary restraint also contributes to the tendency to overeat just before beginning a diet, as shown in a study conducted by University of Toronto researchers (Urbzsat, Herman, & Polivy, 2002). Thus, it would appear that restrained eaters show a tendency to fall off the wagon before getting on—anticipation of food deprivation seems to act as another disinhibitor. Restrained eaters also seem to be particularly sensitive to the media's portrayal of idealized thin body types.

Understanding Factors in the Regulation of Hunger

Check your understanding of the effects of the various factors that influence hunger by indicating whether hunger would tend to increase or decrease in each of the situations described below. Indicate your choice by marking an I (increase), a D (decrease), or a ? (can't be determined without more information) next to each situation. You'll find the answers in Appendix A near the back of the book.

_____ **1.** The ventromedial nucleus of a rat's brain is destroyed by lesioning.

_____ **2.** Norman just ate, but his roommate just brought home his favourite food—a pizza that smells great.

_____ **3.** You're offered an exotic, strange-looking food from another culture and told that everyone in that culture loves it.

_____ **4.** You are participating in an experiment on the effects of leptin and have just been given an injection of leptin.

_____ **5.** Elton has been going crazy all day. It seems like everything's happening at once, and he feels totally stressed out. Finally, he's been able to break away for a few minutes so he can catch a bite to eat.

_____ **6.** You have been on a successful diet, but you just broke down and ate some appetizers at a party.

Sexual Motivation and Behaviour

How does sex resemble food? Sometimes it seems that people are obsessed with both. People joke and gossip about sex constantly. Magazines, novels, movies, and television shows are saturated with sexual activity and innuendo. The advertising industry uses sex to sell everything from mouthwash to designer jeans to automobiles. This intense interest in sex reflects the importance of sexual motivation.

Sex is clearly on people's minds. Children begin to experiment with sex as they enter their teens and this experimentation increases with age. Data collected as part of the Canadian Community Health Survey (2009/2010) reveals that 30 percent of Canadian teens ages 15–17 have engaged in sexual intercourse, and this frequency rises to almost 70 percent for those 18 and 19 (Roterman, 2012). The data also suggest that these rates have remained stable since the mid-1990s.

In this section, we will examine the physiology of the human sexual response, review evolutionary analyses of human sexual motivation, and analyze the roots of sexual orientation.

The Human Sexual Response

Assuming people are motivated to engage in sexual activity, exactly what happens to them physically? This may sound like a simple question, but scientists really knew very little about the physiology of the human sexual response before William Masters and

Virginia Johnson did groundbreaking research in the 1960s.

Their work yielded a detailed description of the human sexual response that eventually won them widespread acclaim. Masters and Johnson (1966, 1970) divided the sexual response cycle into four stages: excitement, plateau, orgasm, and resolution. Figure 10.5 shows how the intensity of sexual arousal changes as women and men progress through these stages.

During the excitement phase, the level of physical arousal usually escalates rapidly. In both genders, muscle tension, respiration rate, heart rate, and

William Masters and Virginia Johnson

"The conviction has grown that the most effective treatment of sexual incompatibility involves the technique of working with both members of the family unit."

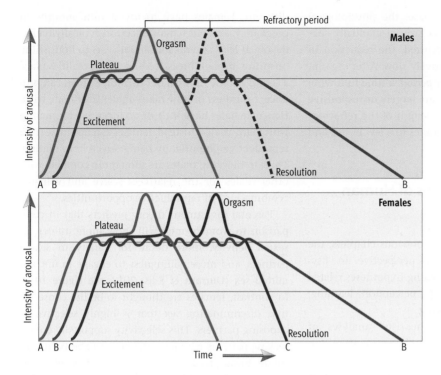

Figure 10.5

The human sexual response cycle. There are similarities and differences between men and women in patterns of sexual arousal. Pattern A, which culminates in orgasm and resolution, is the ideal sequence for both sexes but not something one can count on. Pattern B, which involves sexual arousal without orgasm followed by a slow resolution, is seen in both sexes but is more common among women (see Figure 10.6). Pattern C, which involves multiple orgasms, is seen almost exclusively in women, as men go through a refractory period before they are capable of another orgasm.

Source: Based on Masters, W. H., & Johnson, V. E. (1966). *Human sexual response.* Boston: Little Brown. Copyright © 1966 Little, Brown and Company.

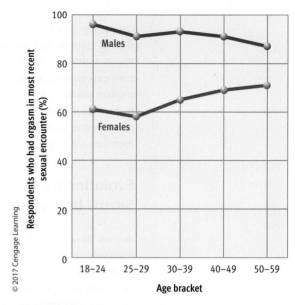

Figure 10.6

The gender gap in orgasm consistency. In their sexual interactions, men reach orgasm more reliably than women. When respondents are asked whether they always have an orgasm, the gender gap is huge. But the data shown here, which indicate whether people had an orgasm in their most recent sexual encounter, suggest that the gender gap is quite a bit smaller, although not insignificant. The data also indicate that the gender gap diminishes in older age groups. (Data from Herbenick et al., 2010)

blood pressure increase quickly. *Vasocongestion—engorgement of blood vessels*—produces penile erection and swollen testes in males. In females, vasocongestion leads to a swelling and hardening of the clitoris, expansion of the vaginal lips, and vaginal lubrication. During the plateau phase, physiological arousal usually continues to build, but at a much slower pace. When foreplay is lengthy, arousal tends to fluctuate in both genders.

Orgasm occurs when sexual arousal reaches its peak intensity and is discharged in a series of muscular contractions that pulsate through the pelvic area. The subjective experience of orgasm is very similar for men and women, but women are more likely than men to experience more than one orgasm in a brief time period (pattern C in Figure 10.5). That said, women are also more likely than men to engage in intercourse without experiencing an orgasm (Katz-Wise & Hyde, 2014). When respondents are asked whether they always have an orgasm with their partner, the gender gap in orgasmic consistency looks quite large. For example, among respondents ages 35–39, Laumann et al. (1994) found that

78 percent of men but only 28 percent of women reported always having an orgasm. However, a more recent, major survey of sexual behaviour approached the issue in a different way and found a smaller gender gap. Herbenick et al. (2010) asked respondents about many of the details of their most recent sexual interaction (what they did, how pleasurable it was, whether they had an orgasm, and so forth). As you can see in Figure 10.6, men were more likely to report having an orgasm, but the disparity was not nearly as huge as when respondents were asked about always having an orgasm.

Whether this gender gap reflects attitudes and sexual practices or physiological processes is open to debate. On the one hand, it's easy to argue that males' greater orgasmic consistency must be a product of evolution because it would have obvious adaptive significance for promoting men's reproductive fitness. On the other hand, gender differences in the socialization of guilt feelings about sex, as well as sexual scripts and practices that are less than optimal for women, could play a part (Katz-Wise & Hyde, 2014).

During the resolution phase, the physiological changes produced by sexual arousal gradually subside. If orgasm has not occurred, the reduction in sexual tension may be relatively slow. After orgasm, men experience a *refractory period*, a time following orgasm during which they are largely unresponsive to further stimulation. The length of the refractory period varies from a few minutes to a few hours, and increases with age.

Evolutionary Analyses of Human Sexual Behaviour

As you have already seen in previous chapters, the relatively new evolutionary perspective in psychology has generated intriguing hypotheses related to a host of topics, including perception, learning, language, and problem solving.

However, evolutionary theorists' analyses of sexual behaviour have drawn the most attention. Obviously, the task of explaining sexual behaviour is crucial to the evolutionary perspective, given its fundamental thesis that natural selection is fuelled by variations in reproductive success. The thinking in this area has been guided by Robert Trivers's (1972) *parental investment theory*, which maintains that a species' mating patterns depend on what each sex has to invest—in terms of time, energy, and survival risk—to produce and nurture offspring. According to Trivers, *the sex that makes the smaller investment will compete for mating opportunities with the sex that makes the larger investment, and the sex with the larger investment will tend to be more discriminating in selecting its partners.* Let's look at how this analysis applies to humans.

Like many mammalian species, human males are *required* to invest little in the production of offspring beyond the act of copulation, so their reproductive potential is maximized by mating with as many females as possible. The situation for females is quite different. Females have to invest nine months in pregnancy, and our female ancestors typically had to devote at least several additional years to nourishing offspring through breastfeeding. These realities place a ceiling on the number of offspring women can produce, regardless of how many males they mate with. Hence, females have little or no incentive for mating with many males. Instead, females can optimize their reproductive potential by being selective in mating. Thus, in humans, males are thought to compete with other males for the relatively scarce and valuable "commodity" of reproductive opportunities.

Parental investment theory predicts that in comparison to women, men will show more interest in sexual activity, more desire for variety in sexual partners, and more willingness to engage in uncommitted sex (Durrant & Ellis, 2013; see Figure 10.7). In contrast, females are thought to be the conservative, discriminating sex that is highly selective in choosing partners. This selectivity supposedly entails seeking partners who have the greatest ability to contribute toward feeding and caring for offspring. Why? Because in the world of our ancient ancestors, males' greater strength and agility would have been crucial assets in the never-ending struggle to find food and shelter and defend one's territory. A female who chose a mate who was lazy or unreliable or who had no hunting, fighting, building, farming, or other useful economic skills would have suffered a substantial disadvantage in her efforts to raise her children and pass on her genes.

Gender Differences in Patterns of Sexual Activity

Consistent with evolutionary theory, males generally show a greater interest in sex than females do. Men think about sex more often than women, initiate sex more often, and have more frequent and varied sexual fantasies (Baumeister, Catanese, & Vohs, 2001). Men are also much more likely to view and enjoy pornographic materials (Buss & Schmitt, 2011). Males masturbate quite a bit more than females and they are somewhat more likely to have extramarital affairs (Petersen & Hyde, 2011). When heterosexual couples are asked about their sex lives, male partners are more likely than their female counterparts to report that they would like to have sex more often. The findings of one study suggest that this disparity in sexual motivation only widens when people reach middle age (Lindau & Gavrilova, 2010). As you can see in Figure 10.8, in the 55–64 age bracket, 62 percent of men but only 38 percent of women report that they are still very interested in sex.

Men are also more motivated than women to pursue sex with a greater variety of partners (Buss &

Sex	Biological reality	Evolutionary significance	Behavioural outcomes
Males	Reproduction involves minimal investment of time, energy, and risk	Maximize reproductive success by seeking more sexual partners with high reproductive potential	More interest in uncommitted sex, greater number of sex partners over lifetime; look for youth and attractiveness in partners
Females	Reproduction involves substantial investment of time, energy, and risk	Maximize reproductive success by seeking partners willing to invest material resources in your offspring	Less interest in uncommitted sex, smaller number of sex partners over lifetime; look for income, status, and ambition in partners

© 2017 Cengage Learning

Figure 10.7
Parental investment theory and mating preferences. Parental investment theory suggests that basic differences between males and females in parental investment have great adaptive significance and lead to gender differences in mating propensities and preferences, as outlined here.

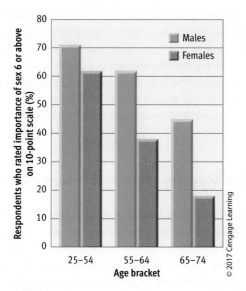

Figure 10.8

The gender gap in interest in sex. Lindau and Gavrilova (2010) summarized data from a nationally representative sample of over 3000 participants. In the survey, respondents were asked to rate how much thought and effort they put into the sexual aspect of their lives. The rating scale ranged from 0 (none) to 10 (very much). The graph shows the percentage of respondents who gave a rating of 6 or greater. As you can see, males generally expressed a greater interest in sex than females. The gender gap was modest, in the 25–54 age range, but widened considerably in older age groups.

Schmitt, 2011). For example, Buss and Schmitt (1993) found that college men indicated that they would ideally like to have 18 sex partners across their lives. College women, on the other hand, reported that they would prefer only five partners. Similar findings were observed in a follow-up study that examined desire for sexual variety in over 16 000 subjects from ten major regions of the world (Schmitt et al., 2003). Males expressed a desire for more partners than did females in all ten world regions. In most cases, the differences were substantial.

Clear gender disparities are also seen in regard to people's willingness to engage in casual or uncommitted sex. For example, in a compelling field study, Clark and Hatfield (1989) had average-looking men approach female (college-age) strangers and ask if they would go back to the man's apartment to have sex with him. None of the women agreed to this proposition. But when Clark and Hatfield had average-looking women approach males with the same proposition, 75 percent of the men eagerly agreed! Similar findings were seen in a more recent study that also looked at whether the person approached was in a relationship (Hald & Høgh-Olesen, 2010). Among those who were not in a relationship, 59 percent of the men and none of the women agreed to the invitation for casual sex. When the approached people

were in a relationship, acceptance of the proposition declined considerably in men, and the gender gap shrunk, with 18 percent of men and 4 percent of women agreeing to casual sex.

Gender Differences in Mate Preferences

Parental investment theory suggests some glaring disparities should exist between men and women in what they look for in a long-term mate (see Figure 10.7 again). The theory predicts that men should place more emphasis than women on such partner characteristics as youthfulness (which allows for more reproductive years) and attractiveness (which is assumed to be correlated with health and fertility). In contrast, parental investment theory predicts that women should place more emphasis than men on partner characteristics such as intelligence, ambition, education, income, and social status (which are associated with the ability to provide more material resources). If these evolutionary analyses of sexual motivation are on the mark, gender differences in mating preferences should be virtually universal and thus transcend culture.

To test this hypothesis, David Buss (1989) and 50 scientists from around the world surveyed more than 10 000 people from 37 cultures about what they looked for in a mate. As predicted by parental investment theory, they found that women placed a higher value than men on potential partners' status, ambition, and financial prospects (see Figure 10.9).

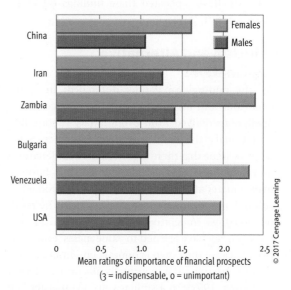

Figure 10.9

Gender and potential mates' financial prospects. Consistent with evolutionary theory, Buss (1989) found that females place more emphasis on potential partners' financial prospects than males do. Moreover, he found that this trend transcends culture. The specific results for 6 of the 37 cultures studies by Buss are shown here. (Data from Buss, 1989)

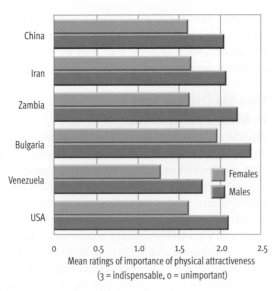

Figure 10.10
Gender and potential mates' physical attractiveness. Consistent with evolutionary theory, Buss (1989) found that all over the world, males place more emphasis on potential partners' good looks than females do. The specific results for 6 of the 37 cultures studies by Buss are shown here (Data from Buss, 1989).

Source: From Weiten. *Cengage Advantage Books: Psychology*, 9E. © 2013 South-Western, a part of Cengage, Inc. Reproduced by permission. www.cengage.com/permissions

These priorities were apparent in third-world cultures, socialist countries, and all varieties of economic systems. In contrast, men around the world consistently showed more interest than women in potential partners' youthfulness and physical attractiveness (see Figure 10.10). A number of studies, using diverse samples and a variety of research methods, have replicated these findings (Li et al., 2013; Schmitt, 2014).

Criticism and Alternative Explanations

So, the findings on gender differences in sexual behaviour and mating priorities mesh nicely with predictions derived from evolutionary theory. But, evolutionary theory has its share of critics. Some skeptics argue that there are alternative explanations for the findings. For example, women's emphasis on males' material resources could be a by-product of cultural and economic forces rather than the result of biological imperatives (Eagly & Wood, 1999). Women may have learned to value males' economic clout because their own economic potential has historically been limited in virtually all cultures (Kasser & Sharma, 1999). In a similar vein, Baumeister and Twenge (2002) argue that the gender disparity in sexual motivation may be largely attributable to extensive cultural processes that serve to suppress female sexuality. Recent research found some support for the idea that gender disparities in mating

preferences are influenced by culture (Zentner & Mitura, 2012). The study found that the size of the gender gap in mating preferences is smaller in nations that exhibit greater gender equality. To some extent, this finding undermines analyses that attribute the gender gap in mating preferences to how males' and females' brains have been wired by evolution.

The Mystery of Sexual Orientation

Sex must be a contentious topic, as the controversy swirling around evolutionary explanations of gender differences in sexuality is easily equalled by the controversy surrounding the determinants of *sexual orientation*. *Sexual orientation* refers to a person's preference for emotional and sexual relationships with individuals of the same sex, the other sex, or either sex. *Heterosexuals* seek emotional–sexual relationships with members of the other sex, *bisexuals* with members of either sex, and *homosexuals* with members of the same sex. In recent years, the terms *gay* and *straight* have become widely used to refer to homosexuals and heterosexuals, respectively. Although *gay* can refer to homosexuals of either sex, most homosexual women prefer to call themselves *lesbians*.

The controversy surrounding sexual orientation is particularly current in Canada. It was not so long ago (1965, in fact) that the Supreme Court of Canada upheld a lower court ruling that Everett Klippert be labelled a "dangerous offender" and imprisoned after he admitted to being gay and having sex with other males. He was finally released in 1971. In 1967, Pierre Elliott Trudeau, then the federal justice minister, proposed an amendment to the Criminal Code that would relax the laws against homosexuality. It was passed in 1969 and began the process of the decriminalization of homosexuality (Same-Sex Rights, 2005). In 2005, the Liberal government of Paul Martin tabled legislation that would make it legal for same-sex couples to marry. The legislation was passed on June 28, 2005, and became law on July 20, 2005. While hate crimes targeting individuals because of their sexual orientation have shown a recent decrease, it is disturbing that those who are the victims of sexual orientation hate crimes are more likely to experience physical injury than hate crimes based on other factors (Statistics Canada, 2017).

Figures from the Canadian census indicate that the number of same-sex couples increased by over 30 percent between 2001 and 2006, reflecting the new 2005 legislation (Statistics Canada, 2007b).

Singer Elton John married his partner of 11 years, David Furnish, after England's same-sex marriage law went into effect in December 2005. Furnish and John have two children.

The most recent figures (Statistics Canada, 2015c) counted 64 575 same-sex-couple families, 21 015 same-sex married families, and 43 560 same-sex common-law families. The number of same-sex-couple families is an increase of 42.4 percent from comparable figures in 2006. One high-profile same-sex marriage in England was that of a Canadian, David Furnish, who married singer Elton John after England's same-sex marriage law went into effect in December 2005 (Elton John, 2005).

Not everyone agrees on the factors affecting sexual orientation and, of course, not everyone supports this social trend. One index of this may be the higher rates of victimization reported by gays, lesbians, and bisexuals in Canada as compared to the rates reported by heterosexuals (Statistics Canada, 2008c).

People tend to view heterosexuality and homosexuality as an all-or-none distinction. However, in a large-scale survey of sexual behaviour, Alfred Kinsey (Rutherford, 2012) and his colleagues (1948, 1953) discovered that many people who define themselves as heterosexuals have had homosexual experiences—and vice versa. Thus, Kinsey and others have concluded that it is more accurate to view heterosexuality and homosexuality as endpoints on a continuum (Epstein, 2007; Haslam, 1997).

How common is homosexuality? Recent figures released by Statistics Canada based on a national survey (Statistics Canada, 2015) indicted that 1.7 percent of Canadians between the ages of 18 to 59 who answered the questions on sexual orientation considered themselves to be gay, and 1.3 percent considered themselves to be bisexual. But, no one knows for sure what the frequencies really are. Part of the problem is that this question is vastly more complex than it appears at first glance (Savin-Williams, 2006). Given that sexual orientation is best represented as a continuum, where do you draw the lines between heterosexuality, bisexuality, and homosexuality? And how do you handle the distinction between overt behaviour and latent desire?

Many surveys simply ask people whether they identify as heterosexual, homosexual, or bisexual, but one survey that dug deeper found that roughly three-quarters of those who acknowledged at least some same-sex attractions or behaviour did not self-identify as gay or bisexual (Chandra et al., 2011). So, self-identification and behaviour are two different things. Small wonder then that estimates of the portion of the population that is gay vary widely. In U.S. surveys, about 3.5 percent of people self-identify as gay or bisexual, whereas 8.2 percent acknowledge that they have engaged in sexual activity with a same-sex partner, and 11 percent acknowledge at least some attraction to people of the same sex (Gates, 2011, 2013).

Although Kinsey's continuum was proposed long ago, the conventional thinking on sexual orientation has been that the vast majority of people are either straight or gay. Hence, it has been widely assumed that most of those who report some same-sex attractions are exclusively homosexual—with bisexuals presumed to be infrequent exceptions who are often viewed skeptically as gays in denial about their homosexuality. In reality, recent, more fine-grained data from a variety of surveys suggest that among those who are not exclusively heterosexual (especially women), only a minority are exclusively homosexual (Diamond, 2014). These data suggest that bisexuality is much more common than previously appreciated, but Diamond points out that the term bisexuality suggests an equal attraction to both genders, whereas many of the people in this category are predominantly, but not exclusively, attracted to one sex or the other. She argues that it is probably more accurate to characterize these individuals as nonexclusive in their sexuality, as opposed to bisexual. Of course, the range of categories used in many of these surveys do not exhaust the range of possible gender identities, sometimes forcing individuals to indicate a category that they do not feel fully captures their identity. As you can see, the data on the demographics of sexual orientation are complicated.

Biological Theories

Over the years, many environmental theories have been floated to explain the origins of homosexuality, but when tested empirically, these theories have garnered remarkably little support. These findings suggest that biology plays a critical role. Despite indications that biology plays a greater role in homosexuality than environment, initial efforts to find a biological basis for homosexuality met with little success. We do know that there is evidence that gay males process some types of information differently than do heterosexual males and, according to neuroscientist Jennifer Steeves and her colleagues (Brewster, Mullin, Dobrin, & Steeves, 2010), differences in brain laterality may be implicated in this difference in processing. However, at this point, we do not know a great deal about the origin of these differences.

Thus, like environmental theorists, biological theorists were stymied for quite a while in their efforts to explain the roots of homosexuality. However, that picture changed in the 1990s when a pair of behavioural genetics studies reported findings suggesting that homosexuality has a hereditary basis. In the first study, conducted by Bailey and Pillard (1991), the subjects were gay men who had either a twin brother or an adopted brother. They found that 52 percent of the subjects' identical twins were gay, that 22 percent of their fraternal twins were gay, and that 11 percent of their adoptive brothers were gay. A companion study (Bailey et al., 1993) of lesbians yielded

Neuroscientist Jennifer Steeves has examined some of the ways in which gays and heterosexuals differ in terms of their processing of the coding of facial information.

Courtesy of Jennifer Steeves

© Amy Etra/Photoedit

Both biological and environmental factors appear to contribute to homosexuality, although its precise developmental roots remain obscure.

a similar pattern of results (see Figure 10.11). Given that identical twins share more genetic overlap than fraternal twins, who share more genes than unrelated adoptive siblings, these results suggest that there is a genetic predisposition to homosexuality (Hill, Dawood, & Puts, 2013). The heritability of sexual orientation appears to be similar in men and women (Rosario & Scrimshaw, 2014). Research also suggests that epigenetic processes that dampen or silence specific genes' effects may influence sexual orientation (Rice, Friberg, & Gavrilets, 2012; see Chapter 3 for an explanation of epigenetics).

Many theorists suspect that the roots of homosexuality may lie in the organizing effects of prenatal hormones on neurological development (Byne, 2007; James, 2005). Several lines of research suggest that hormonal secretions during critical periods of prenatal development may shape sexual development, organize the brain in a lasting manner, and influence subsequent sexual orientation (Berenbaum & Snyder, 1995). For example, researchers have found elevated rates of homosexuality among women exposed to unusually high androgen levels during prenatal development (because their mothers had an adrenal disorder or were given a synthetic hormone to reduce the risk of miscarriage) (Rosario & Scrimshaw, 2014). Several other independent lines of research suggest that atypical prenatal hormonal secretions may foster a predisposition to homosexuality (Mustanski, Kuper, & Greene, 2014).

However, much remains to be learned about the roots of homosexuality. One complication is that the pathways to homosexuality may be somewhat different for males than for females. Females' sexuality appears to be characterized by more *plasticity* than

Percentage of relations with gay sexual orientation

Relationship	Genetic relatedness
Identical twin	100%
Fraternal twin	50%
Adoptive sibling	0%

Males
Females

© 2017 Cengage Learning

Figure 10.11

Genetics and sexual orientation. If relatives who share more genetic relatedness show greater similarity on a trait than relatives who share less genetic overlap, this evidence suggests a genetic predisposition to the characteristic. Studies of both gay men and lesbians have found a higher prevalence of homosexuality among their identical twins than among their fraternal twins, who, in turn, are more likely to be homosexual than their adoptive siblings. These findings suggest that genetic factors influence sexual orientation. (Data from Bailey & Pillard, 1991; Bailey et al., 1993)

males' sexuality (Baumeister, 2000, 2004). In other words, women's sexual behaviour may be more easily shaped and modified by sociocultural factors. For example, although sexual orientation is assumed to be a stable characteristic, research shows that lesbian and bisexual women often change their sexual orientation over the course of their adult years (Diamond, 2003, 2013). And, in comparison to gay males, lesbians are less likely to trace their homosexuality back to their childhood and more likely to indicate that their attraction to the same sex emerged during adulthood (Diamond, 2013). These findings suggest that sexual orientation may be more fluid and malleable in women than in men.

The Need to Belong: Affiliation Motivation

How would you like to spend the rest of your life alone on a pleasant but deserted island? Most people would find this a terrible fate, as we seem to have a need to affiliate with others (Festinger, 1954; Schachter,1959). But we don't have to be left alone on an island to feel isolated. How would you feel if your friends went out to party on a Saturday night without inviting you? Why would being ostracized like this be so hurtful? Belonging to groups is important to our sense of self and well-being. In each of these examples, our fundamental need to belong and to be with others would be denied. Some animals such as bears and bald eagles don't mind going it alone, but humans are at heart social animals (Aronson, 2012), and social isolation can lead to significant psychological and physical illness (Cacioppo et al., 2015). We need meaningful contact with others. The *affiliation* motive is the need to associate with others and maintain social bonds. Affiliation encompasses one's needs for companionship, friendship, and love. In an overview of research on affiliation, Baumeister and Leary (1995) proposed the belongingness hypothesis, that "human beings have a pervasive need to form and maintain at least a minimum quantity of lasting, positive, and significant interpersonal relationships" (p. 497). They argue that we form important relationships readily and the we actively resist "dissolution" of these interpersonal bonds. They suggest that our need to belong has a strong evolutionary basis since bonds offer a host of survival and reproductive benefits. By joining together our ancestors could share food, provide better care for offspring, engage in more effective hunting or gathering, enhance their defence against predators, defuse risks, and provide more opportunities for mating.

Baumeister and Leary (1995) also describe evidence that the quality of people's personal happiness and well-being is determined in large part by the quality of their relationships and the belief that they belong. They also discuss the strong link between affiliation issues and negative emotions—how the threat of rejection triggers anxiety, jealousy, depression, and a host of other dysfunctional states.

Ostracism and the Fear of Rejection

Kip Williams (2001, 2007; Freedman, Williams, & Beer, 2016; Hales, Kassner, Williams, & Graziano, 2016) of Purdue University has been active in examining the nature and effects of ostracism. *Ostracism* involves being ignored and excluded by others in your social environment. It hurts and can lead to extreme reactions and is often linked to bullying. Consider the case of Amanda Todd, a British Columbia teen who committed suicide at age 15 after being the victim of cyberbullying and ostracism. Before she died, she posted a video on YouTube in which she expressed her reactions to having been ostracized. One of the more telling comments she made was by holding up a card stating, "I have nobody. I need someone."

Williams (2007) and others (Sleegers, Proulx, & Beest, 2017; Walton, Cohen, Cwir, & Spencer, 2011) have found that there are several reactions to being ostracized. It begins with pain, and then leads to behaviours designed to redress the situation—to gain back the feelings of belongingness and having a meaningful existence. When we do feel that we belong, that we are accepted by others, we are happier and our self-esteem increases (Leary, 1998). Ostracism not only affects our mood and behaviour—it even affects our brain, leading to increased activity

B.C. teen Amanda Todd committed suicide after being bullied and ostracized. In a YouTube video, she tells everyone that she needs to belong.

Key Learning Goals

▶ Describe affiliation motivation and its evolutionary roots.
▶ Define ostracism and discuss how it affects us.

....

When silence is not golden: Why acknowledgment matters even when being excluded.

Description
This study by Selma Rudert and colleagues examines factors associated with an ostracism experience that can reduce the negative effects of being excluded.

Investigators
Rudert, S. C., Hales, A. H., Greifeneder, R., & Williams, K. (2017). *Personality and Social Psychology Bulletin, 43*(5), 678–692.

in parts of the brain associated with feeling physical pain (Eisenberger, 2012, 2015), and showing activity patterns typically associated with unexpected outcomes (Zayas et al., 2009). The pain of ostracism is real.

While there has been a great deal of research concerning the negative effects of ostracism, less attention has been paid to how to ameliorate its effects. Our first Featured Study in this chapter presents one effort to examine factors that can "reduce the sting of ostracism" (Rudert et al., 2017, p. 678).

Achievement: In Search of Excellence

Key Learning Goals

▶ Describe the need for achievement and how it has been measured.

▶ Explain how the need for achievement and situational factors influence achievement strivings.

David McClelland

"People with a high need for achievement are not gamblers; they are challenged to win by personal effort, not by luck."

At the beginning of this chapter, we profiled one of Canada's Paralympians. Chantal Petitclerc has endured extraordinary hardships to achieve her goals. What motivates people to push themselves so hard? In all likelihood, it's a strong need for achievement. The *achievement motive* is the need to master difficult challenges, to outperform others, and to meet high standards of excellence. Above all else, the need for achievement involves the desire to excel, especially in competition with others.

David McClelland and his colleagues (McClelland, 1985; McClelland et al., 1953) have been studying the achievement motive for half a century. McClelland believes that achievement motivation is of the utmost importance. McClelland sees the need for achievement as the spark that ignites economic growth, scientific progress, inspirational leadership, and masterpieces in the creative arts. It's difficult to argue with his assertion about the immense importance of achievement motivation. Consider how much poorer our culture would be if people such as Charles Darwin, Nelson Mandela, Thomas Edison, Alexander Graham Bell, Pablo Picasso, Marie Curie, Abraham Lincoln, Mother Teresa, Martin Luther King, and David Suzuki hadn't had a fire burning in their hearts.

Individual Differences in the Need for Achievement

In May 2005, Steve Nash achieved what no Canadian before him had ever achieved: He was named the "Most Valuable Player" (MVP) in the National Basketball Association (NBA). Nash went on to win the award two years in a row. He was an undersized player (about 190 cm) in a sport often

dominated by much taller players. He struggled to find a college willing to offer him a scholarship so he could refine his skill. He is only the sixth guard in NBA history to be designated MVP. In his first game after achieving this honour, he led his team to a dramatic playoff win over his former team, the Dallas Mavericks, while the crowd chanted "M–V–P" (Smith, 2005). While he was clearly a talented player, other factors were needed to bring him to the top. High among these was his desire to achieve.

The need for achievement is a fairly stable aspect of personality. Hence, research in this area has focused mostly on individual differences in achievement motivation. Subjects' need for

Canadian basketball player Steve Nash, who finished his career with the Los Angeles Lakers, was named the NBA's MVP for both the 2004 and 2005 seasons. Early on, he was never considered to be a top player. He is known for his hard work and dedication to the game. But the contribution of his extremely high need for achievement should not be underestimated. He was known for having pushed himself in order to achieve his goals. In addition to his success on the court, Nash is also well known for his philanthropic work. He was named to the Order of Canada in 2007. Nash retired from professional basketball in 2015.

achievement and need for affiliation can be measured effectively with the *Thematic Apperception Test* (C. P. Smith, 1992; Spangler, 1992). The *Thematic Apperception Test* (TAT) is a *projective test*, one that requires subjects to respond to vague, ambiguous stimuli in ways that may reveal personal motives and traits (see Chapter 12). The stimulus materials for the TAT are pictures of people in ambiguous scenes open to interpretation. Examples include a man working at a desk and a woman seated in a chair staring off into space. Subjects are asked to write or tell stories about what's happening in the scenes and what the characters are feeling. The themes of these stories are then scored to measure the strength of various needs. Figure 10.12 shows examples of stories dominated by the themes of achievement and affiliation (the need for social bonds and belongingness).

The research on individual differences in achievement motivation has yielded interesting findings on the characteristics of people who score high in the need for achievement. They tend to work harder and more persistently on tasks than people low in the need for achievement (M. Brown, 1974) and they handle negative feedback about task performance more effectively than others (Fodor & Carver, 2000). They also are more future-oriented than others and more likely to delay gratification in order to pursue long-term goals (Mischel, 1961; Raynor & Entin, 1982).

Do people high in achievement need always tackle the biggest challenges available? Not necessarily. A curious finding has emerged in laboratory studies in which subjects were asked to choose the difficulty level of a task to work on. Participants high in the need for achievement tended to select tasks of intermediate difficulty (McClelland & Koestner, 1992). Research on the situational determinants of achievement behaviour has suggested a reason, as we will see in the next section.

reality **check**

Misconception

People with high achievement motivation are risk takers who prefer very challenging tasks.

Reality

People who score high in achievement motivation seem to need to experience success; many of them fear failure. Hence, they tend to select tasks that are moderately challenging and pursue goals that are reasonably realistic. They are not necessarily the most daring risk takers.

Affiliation arousal
George is an engineer who is working late. He is *worried that his wife will be annoyed* with him for neglecting her. She has been *objecting* that he cares more about his work than his wife and family. He seems *unable to satisfy* both his boss and his wife, but he *loves her* very much and will do his best to *finish up* fast and get home to her.

Achievement arousal
George is an engineer who *wants to win* a competition in which the man with the *most practicable drawing* will be awarded the contract to build a bridge. He is taking a moment to think *how happy he will be* if he wins. He has been *baffled by how to make such a long span strong*, but he remembers to *specify a new steel alloy* of great strength, submits his entry, but does not win, and is *very unhappy*.

Figure 10.12

Measuring motives with the *Thematic Apperception Test* (TAT). Subjects taking the TAT tell or write stories about what is happening in a scene, such as this one showing a man at work. The two stories shown here illustrate strong affiliation motivation (the need to associate with others and maintain social bonds) and strong achievement motivation. The italicized parts of the stories are thematic ideas that would be identified by a TAT scorer.

Source: Stories reprinted by permission of Dr. David McClelland.

Situational Determinants of Achievement Behaviour

Your achievement drive is not the only determinant of how hard you work. Situational factors can also influence achievement strivings. John Atkinson (1974, 1981, 1992) has elaborated extensively on McClelland's original theory of achievement motivation and has identified some important situational determinants of achievement behaviour. Atkinson theorizes that the tendency to pursue achievement in a particular situation depends on the following factors:

- The strength of one's *motivation to achieve success*. This is viewed as a stable aspect of personality.
- One's estimate of the *probability of success* for the task at hand. This varies from task to task.
- The *incentive value of success*. This depends on the tangible and intangible rewards for success on the specific task.

The last two variables are situational determinants of achievement behaviour (see Figure 10.13). That is, they vary from one situation to another. According to Atkinson, the pursuit of achievement increases as the probability and incentive value of success go up. Let's apply Atkinson's model to a simple example. According to his theory, your tendency to pursue a good grade in calculus should depend on your general motivation to achieve success, your estimate of the probability of getting a good grade in the class, and the value you place on getting a good grade in calculus. Thus, given a certain motivation to achieve success, you will pursue a good grade in calculus less

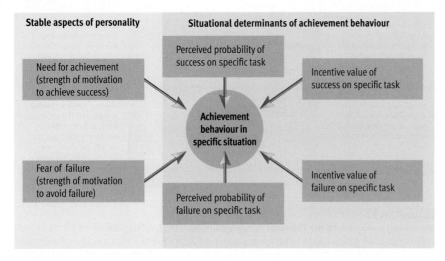

Figure 10.13
Determinants of achievement behaviour. According to John Atkinson, a person's pursuit of achievement in a particular situation depends on several factors. Some of these factors, such as need for achievement or fear of failure, are relatively stable motives that are part of the person's personality. Many other factors, such as the likelihood and value of success or failure, vary from one situation to another, depending on the circumstances.

vigorously if your professor gives impossible exams (thus lowering your expectancy of success) or if a good grade in calculus is not required for your major (lowering the incentive value of success).

The joint influence of these situational factors may explain why high achievers prefer tasks of intermediate difficulty. Atkinson notes that the probability of success and the incentive value of success on tasks are interdependent to some degree. As tasks get easier, success becomes less satisfying. As tasks get harder, success becomes more satisfying, but its likelihood obviously declines. When the probability

and incentive value of success are weighed together, moderately challenging tasks seem to offer the best overall value in terms of maximizing one's sense of accomplishment.

According to Atkinson, a person's fear of failure must also be considered to understand achievement behaviour (Atkinson & Birch, 1978). He maintains that people vary in their motivation to avoid failure. This motive is considered to be a stable aspect of personality. Together with situational factors such as the probability of failure and the negative value placed on failure, it influences achievement strivings. Figure 10.13 diagrams all of the factors in Atkinson's model that are thought to govern achievement behaviour.

Fear is one of the most fundamental emotions. Thus, the relationship between achievement behaviour and fear of failure illustrates how motivation and emotion are often intertwined (Zurbriggen & Sturman, 2002). On the one hand, emotion can cause motivation. For example, anger about your work schedule may motivate you to look for a new job. Jealousy of an ex-girlfriend may motivate you to ask out her roommate. On the other hand, motivation can cause emotion. For example, your motivation to win a photography contest may lead to great anxiety during the judging and either great joy if you win or great gloom if you don't. There may even be individual differences in the motivation to approach or avoid emotions (Maio & Esses, 2001). Thus, motivation and emotion are closely related, but that does not mean they're the same thing. We'll analyze the nature of emotion in the next section.

concept **check** 10.2

Understanding the Determinants of Achievement Behaviour

According to John Atkinson, one's pursuit of achievement in a particular situation depends on several factors. Check your understanding of these factors by identifying each of the following vignettes as an example of one of the following four determinants of achievement behaviour: (a) need for achievement, (b) perceived probability of success, (c) incentive value of success, (d) fear of failure. The answers can be found in Appendix A near the back of the book.

_____ **1.** Donna has just received a B in biology. Her reaction is typical of the way she responds to many situations involving achievement: "I didn't get an A, it's true, but at least I didn't flunk; that's what I was really worried about."

_____ **2.** Belinda is nervously awaiting the start of the finals of the 200-metre dash in the last

meet of her high school career. "I've gotta win this race! This is the most important race of my life!"

_____ **3.** Corey grins as he considers the easy time he's going to have this semester. "This class is supposed to be a snap. I hear the professor gives an A to nearly everyone."

_____ **4.** Diana's just as hard-charging as ever. She's received the highest grade on every test throughout the semester, yet she's still up all night studying for the final. "I know I've got an A in the bag, but I want to be the best student Dr. McClelland's ever had!"

The Elements of Emotional Experience

The most profound and important experiences in life are saturated with emotion. Think of the *joy* that people feel at weddings, the *grief* they feel at funerals, the *ecstasy* they feel when they fall in love. Emotions also colour everyday experiences. For instance, you might experience *anger* when a waiter treats you rudely, *dismay* when you learn that your car needs expensive repairs, and *happiness* when you see that you aced your economics exam. Clearly, emotions play an important role in people's lives.

Exactly what is an emotion? Everyone has plenty of personal experience with emotion, but it's an elusive concept to define (LeDoux, 1995). Emotion includes cognitive, physiological, and behavioural components, which are summarized in the following definition: *Emotion* involves (1) a subjective conscious experience (the cognitive component), accompanied by (2) bodily arousal (the physiological component), and (3) characteristic overt expressions (the behavioural component). That's a pretty complex definition. Let's take a closer look at each of these three components.

The Cognitive Component: Subjective Feelings

Emotions are pervasive in the human experience. It seems as if we constantly think about them by ourselves and discuss them with others. It should come as no surprise then that our language and words are filled with emotion. Hundreds of words in the English language refer to emotions (Averill, 1980). Analytical systems such as the ANEW program (Bradley & Lang, 1999) and the *Dictionary of Affect in Language* (DAL) (Whissell, 2008a), created by Laurentian University's Cynthia Whissell, have been developed to provide normative emotional ratings for the words we use. These systems allow researchers to examine a wide variety of features of human behaviour and experience (e.g., Whissell, 2006, 2008b).

Ironically, however, even given all this emotional content in our words, people often have difficulty describing their emotions to others (Zajonc, 1980). Emotion is a highly personal, subjective experience. In studying the cognitive component of emotions, psychologists generally rely on subjects' verbal reports of what they're experiencing. Their reports indicate that emotions are potentially intense internal feelings that sometimes seem to have a life of their own. People can't click their emotions on and off like a bedroom light. If it were as simple as that, you could choose to be happy whenever you wanted. As Joseph LeDoux puts it, "Emotions are things that happen to us rather than things we will to occur" (1996, p. 19). Actually, some degree of emotional control is possible (Thayer, 1996; Wadlinger & Isaacowitz, 2011), but emotions tend to involve automatic reactions that are difficult to regulate (Öhman & Wiens, 2003). In some cases, these emotional reactions may occur at an unconscious level of processing, outside of one's awareness (Winkielman & Berridge, 2004).

Cognition is important in several aspects of emotions, including control of our emotions (Koch et al., 2007) and our appraisal of important events that leads to emotions. People's cognitive appraisals of events in their lives are key determinants of the emotions they experience (Clore & Ortony, 2008; Ellsworth & Scherer, 2003; R. S. Lazarus, 1995). A specific event, such as giving a speech or singing in public (Sturm et al., 2008), may be highly threatening or embarrassing and thus anxiety-arousing for one person but a "ho-hum" routine matter for another. The conscious experience of emotion includes an *evaluative* aspect. People characterize their emotions as pleasant or unpleasant (Barrett et al., 2007; Neese & Ellsworth, 2009). Of course, individuals often experience "mixed emotions" that include both pleasant and unpleasant qualities (Cacioppo & Berntson, 1999). For example, an executive just given a promotion with challenging new responsibilities may experience both happiness and anxiety.

In recent years a curious finding has emerged regarding people's cognitive assessments of their emotions—we are not very good at anticipating our emotional responses to future setbacks and triumphs. Research on *affective forecasting*—efforts to predict one's emotional reactions to future events—demonstrates that people reliably mispredict their

Key Learning Goals

▶ Describe the cognitive and physiological components of emotion.

▶ Explain how emotions are reflected in facial expressions, and describe the facial feedback hypothesis.

▶ Review cross-cultural similarities and variations in emotional experience.

Emotions involve automatic reactions that can be difficult to control.

future feelings in response to good and bad events, such as getting a promotion at work, taking a long-awaited vacation, getting a poor grade in an important class, or being fired at work (Green et al., 2013; Hoerger et al., 2012a, 2012b; Wilson & Gilbert, 2003, 2005). People tend to be reasonably accurate in anticipating whether events will generate positive or negative emotions, but they often are way off in predicting the initial intensity and duration of their emotional reactions.

For example, Dunn, Wilson, and Gilbert (2003) asked college students to predict what their overall level of happiness would be if a campus housing lottery assigned them to a desirable or undesirable dormitory. The students expected that their dormitory assignments would have a pretty dramatic effect on their well-being. But when their happiness was assessed a year later after actually being assigned to the good or bad dorms, it was clear that their happiness was not affected by their dorm assignments. In a similar vein, research shows that young professors overestimate the unhappiness they will feel five years after being turned down for tenure, college students overestimate how despondent they will be after the breakup of a romantic relationship, and job applicants overestimate how distressed they will feel after being rejected for a job (Gilbert et al., 1998; Kushlev & Dunn, 2012).

Why are our predictions of our emotional reactions surprisingly inaccurate? A host of factors can contribute (Buechel, Zhang, & Moresedge, 2017; Schwartz & Sommers, 2013). One consideration is that most of us do not fully appreciate how effective people tend to be in rationalizing, discounting, and overlooking failures and mistakes. People exhibit a host of cognitive biases that help them to insulate themselves from the emotional fallout of life's difficulties. However, people do not factor this peculiar "talent" into the picture when making predictions about their emotional reactions to setbacks. In any event, as you can see, emotions are not only hard to regulate—they are also hard to predict.

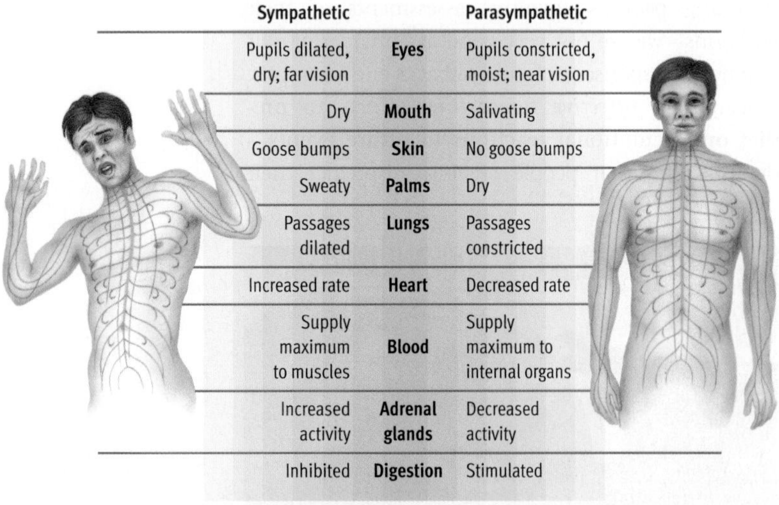

The Physiological Component: Diffuse and Multifaceted

Emotional processes are closely tied to physiological processes, but the interconnections are enormously complex. The biological bases of emotions are diffuse, involving many areas in the brain and many neurotransmitter systems, as well as the autonomic nervous system and the endocrine system.

Autonomic Arousal

Imagine your reaction as your car spins out of control on an icy highway. Your fear is accompanied by a variety of physiological changes. Your heart rate and breathing accelerate. Your blood pressure surges, and your pupils dilate. The hairs on your skin stand erect, giving you "goose bumps," and you start to perspire. Although the physical reactions may not always be as obvious as in this scenario, *emotions are accompanied by visceral arousal* (Larsen et al., 2008). Surely you've experienced a "knot in your stomach" or a "lump in your throat"—thanks to anxiety.

Much of the discernible physiological arousal associated with emotion occurs through the actions of the *autonomic nervous system* (Levinson, 2014), which regulates the activity of glands, smooth muscles, and blood vessels (see Figure 10.14). As you may recall from Chapter 3, the autonomic nervous system is responsible for the highly emotional *fight-or-flight response*, which is largely modulated by the release of adrenal *hormones* that radiate throughout the body. Hormonal changes clearly play a crucial role in emotional responses to stress and may contribute to many other emotions as well (Wirth & Gaffey, 2013).

One prominent part of emotional arousal is the *galvanic skin response (GSR)*, an increase in the electrical conductivity of the skin that occurs when sweat glands increase their activity. GSR is a convenient and sensitive index of autonomic arousal that has been used as a measure of emotion in many laboratory studies.

The connection between emotion and autonomic arousal provides the basis for the *polygraph*, or *lie detector*, a device that records autonomic

Sympathetic		Parasympathetic
Pupils dilated, dry; far vision	**Eyes**	Pupils constricted, moist; near vision
Dry	**Mouth**	Salivating
Goose bumps	**Skin**	No goose bumps
Sweaty	**Palms**	Dry
Passages dilated	**Lungs**	Passages constricted
Increased rate	**Heart**	Decreased rate
Supply maximum to muscles	**Blood**	Supply maximum to internal organs
Increased activity	**Adrenal glands**	Decreased activity
Inhibited	**Digestion**	Stimulated

© 2017 Cengage Learning

Figure 10.14
Emotion and autonomic arousal. The autonomic nervous system (ANS) is composed of the nerves that connect to the heart, blood vessels, smooth muscles, and glands (refer back to Figure 3.7 on page 82, for a more detailed view). The ANS is divided into the *sympathetic system*, which mobilizes bodily resources in response to stress, and the *parasympathetic system*, which conserves bodily resources. Emotions are frequently accompanied by sympathetic ANS activation, which leads to goose bumps, sweaty palms, and the other physical responses listed on the left side of the diagram.

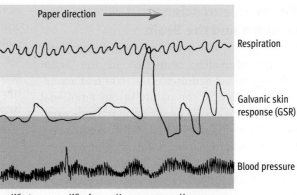

Paper direction ⟶

Respiration

Galvanic skin response (GSR)

Blood pressure

What department do you work in?

Who is your supervisor?

Have you ever taken money from the bank?

Have you ever falsified bank records?

Figure 10.15
Emotion and the polygraph. A lie detector measures the autonomic arousal that most people experience when they tell a lie. After using nonthreatening questions to establish a baseline, a polygraph examiner looks for signs of arousal (such as the sharp change in GSR shown here) on incriminating questions. Unfortunately, as your text explains, the polygraph is not a very dependable index of whether people are lying.

© 2017 Cengage Learning

fluctuations while a subject is questioned. Scientific research into physiological markers of deception has a long history (e.g., Bunn, 2007; Gamer et al., 2008; Verschuere et al., 2009; Verschuere, Prati, & De Houwer, 2009). The polygraph was invented in 1915 by psychologist William Marston—who also dreamed up the comic book superhero Wonder Woman (Knight, 2004). A polygraph can't actually detect lies. It's really an emotion detector. It monitors key indicators of autonomic arousal, typically heart rate, blood pressure, respiration rate, and GSR. The assumption is that when subjects lie, they experience emotion (presumably anxiety) that produces noticeable changes in these physiological indicators (see Figure 10.15). The polygraph examiner asks a subject a number of nonthreatening questions to establish the subject's baseline on these autonomic indicators. Then the examiner asks the critical questions (e.g., "Where were you on the night of the burglary?") and observes whether the subject's autonomic arousal changes.

reality check

Misconception

The lie detector is an accurate, reliable method for identifying dishonest responses.

Reality

The accuracy of the polygraph has long been exaggerated. For example, one influential study (Kleinmuntz & Szucko, 1984) found that lie detector tests would have led to incorrect verdicts for about one-third of the suspects who were proven innocent and about one-fourth of those who eventually confessed.

The polygraph has been controversial since its invention (Grubin & Madsen, 2005). Polygraph advocates claim that lie detector tests are about 85–90 percent accurate and that the validity of polygraph testing has been demonstrated in empirical studies, but these claims clearly are not supported by the evidence (Branaman & Gallagher, 2005; Fiedler, Schmid, & Stahl, 2002). Part of the problem is that people who are telling the truth may experience emotional arousal when they respond to incriminating questions. Thus, polygraph tests sometimes lead to accusations of lying against people who are innocent. Another problem is that some people can lie without experiencing anxiety or autonomic arousal. The crux of the problem, as Leonard Saxe (1994) notes, is that "there is no evidence of a unique physiological reaction to deceit" (p. 71). The polygraph *is* a potentially useful tool that can help police check out leads and alibis. However, polygraph results are not reliable enough to be submitted as evidence in Canadian criminal courtrooms. Some people believe that they are able to tell when someone is trying to deceive them. What does the evidence say about this claim? Are we accurate in detecting deception? Are individuals who are experienced in the law any better at spotting deception. See our second Featured Study for this chapter, conducted by researchers including scholars from Queen's University and McGill University.

FEATURED STUDY

"Intuitive" lie detection of children's deception by law enforcement officials and university students.

Description
This study examines the ability of police officers, customs officers, and university students to detect deception on the part of children.

Investigators
Leach, A-M., Talwar, V., Lee, K., Balan, N., & Lindsay, R. C. L. (2004). *Law and Human Behavior, 28*(6), 661–685.

Affective Neuroscience: Emotions and the Brain

The autonomic responses that accompany emotions are ultimately controlled in the brain. Psychologists and neuroscientists have had a long-standing interest in the nature of our emotional life and the role played by the brain in those experiences (Hortensius, Schutter, & Harmon-Jones, 2011). Work at the intersection of emotion and neuroscience reached a critical point in the mid-1990s, resulting in the identification of a new subdiscipline in psychology—the study of *affective neuroscience* (Davidson & Sutton, 1995). The focus of research in this area was the examination of the neurobiology of emotions. While much work remains to be done, considerable insight into the neurobiology of our emotions has been acquired over the past few years (Almada et al., 2013; Davidson, 2004; Panksepp, 2010). The hypothalamus, amygdala, and adjacent structures in the limbic system have long been viewed as the seat of emotions in the brain (MacLean, 1993). Let's consider some of what this work has told us about the brain and our emotions.

Evidence suggests that the amygdala plays a particularly central role in the acquisition of conditioned fears (Armony, 2013). According to Joseph LeDoux (2000), sensory inputs capable of eliciting emotions arrive in the thalamus, which simultaneously routes the information along two separate pathways: to the nearby amygdala and to areas in the cortex (see Figure 10.16). The amygdala processes the information very quickly. If it detects a threat, it almost instantly triggers activity in the hypothalamus, which leads to autonomic arousal and hormonal responses.

The processing in this pathway is extremely fast, so that emotions can be triggered even before the cortex has had a chance to really "think" about the input. LeDoux believes that this rapid-response pathway evolved because it is a highly adaptive warning system that can "be the difference between life and death." As LeDoux's theory would predict, evidence indicates that the amygdala can process emotion independent of cognitive awareness (Phelps, 2005). Consistent with the notion that the amygdala is the brain's fear centre, a recent study found that highly anxious children tend to have an enlarged amygdala, with increased connectivity to other brain regions (Qin et al., 2014). Although the amygdala clearly plays a role in fear, some theorists believe that it is merely a key part of a neural network that underlies the experience of fear. According to this view, various emotions depend on activity in neural networks that are broadly distributed across various regions of the brain, rather than that are discrete structures in the brain (Lindquist et al., 2012).

Joseph LeDoux

"In situations of danger, it is very useful to be able to respond quickly. The time saved by the amygdala in acting on the thalamic information, rather than waiting for the cortical input, may be the difference between life and death."

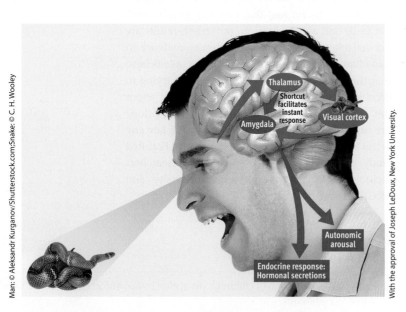

Figure 10.16
The amygdala and fear. Emotions are controlled by a constellation of interacting brain systems, but the amygdala appears to play a particularly crucial role. According to LeDoux (1996), sensory inputs that can trigger fear (such as seeing a snake while out walking) arrive in the thalamus and then are routed along a fast pathway (shown in red) directly to the amygdala and along a slow pathway (shown in blue) that allows the cortex time to think about the situation. Activity in the fast pathway also elicits the autonomic arousal and hormonal responses that are part of the physiological component of emotion. (Adapted from LeDoux, 1994)

The Behavioural Component: Nonverbal Expressiveness

At the behavioural level, people reveal their emotions through characteristic overt expressions such as smiles, frowns, furrowed brows, clenched fists, and slumped shoulders. In other words, *emotions are expressed in "body language," or nonverbal behaviour.*

Facial expressions reveal a variety of basic emotions (Lederman et al., 2007). In an extensive research project, Paul Ekman and Wallace Friesen asked subjects to identify what emotion a person was experiencing on the basis of facial cues in photographs. They have found that subjects are generally successful in identifying six fundamental emotions: happiness, sadness, anger, fear, surprise, and disgust (Ekman & Friesen, 1975, 1984). People can also identify a number of other emotions from facial expressions, such as contempt, embarrassment, shame, amusement, and sympathy, but less reliably than the basic six emotions (Keltner et al., 2003). Furthermore, the identification of emotions

Our emotions automatically express themselves nonverbally. Here, former U.S. President Barack Obama and his wife, former First Lady Michelle Obama, watched as the car carrying Queen Elizabeth and Prince Philip pulled up in front of the American ambassadorial residence in London, England, for a visit in May 2011. What do their faces tell you about the emotions they are experiencing at that moment?

Based on the facial-feedback hypothesis, researchers developed a novel treatment for depression involving the injection of Botox into the forehead to paralyze the facial muscles responsible for frowning. The assumption is that the feedback from constant frowning contributes to feelings of depression. A significant reduction in depressive symptoms was seen within six weeks, providing fascinating support for the facial-feedback hypothesis (Wollmer et al., 2012, 2014).

The facial expressions that go with various emotions may be largely innate (Eibl-Eibesfeldt, 1975; Izard, 1994). For the most part, people who have been blind since birth smile and frown much like everyone else, even though they've never seen a smile or frown (Galati, Scherer, & Ricci-Bitti, 1997). In an influential study, David Matsumoto and Bob Willingham (2009) carefully photographed the facial expressions of congenitally blind judo athletes in the Paralympic Games and sighted judo athletes in the Olympic Games. The photos for

from facial expressions tends to occur quickly and automatically (Tracy & Robins, 2008).

Some theorists believe that muscular feedback from one's own facial expressions contributes to one's conscious experience of emotions (Izard, 1990; Tomkins, 1991). Proponents of the *facial-feedback hypothesis* assert that facial muscles send signals to the brain and that these signals help the brain recognize the emotion that one is experiencing (see Figure 10.17). According to this view, smiles, frowns, and furrowed brows help create the subjective experience of various emotions. Consistent with this idea, studies show that if subjects are instructed to contract their facial muscles to mimic facial expressions associated with certain emotions, they tend to report that they actually experience these emotions to some degree (Dimberg & Soderkvist, 2011). The nature of the mechanisms producing this effect has been the subject of considerable research (Niedenthal, 2007; Niedenthal, Mermillod, Maringer, & Hess, in press; Zajonc, 1985; Zajonc et al., 1987).

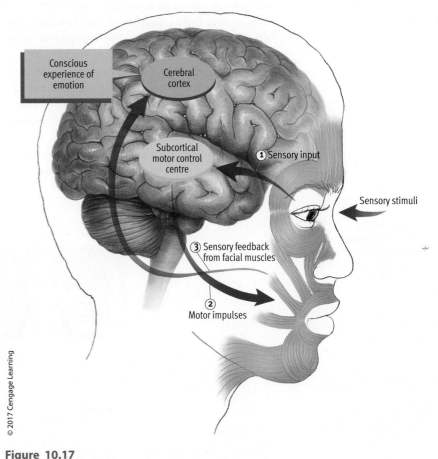

Figure 10.17
The facial-feedback hypothesis. According to the facial feedback hypothesis, inputs to subcortical centres automatically evoke facial expressions associated with certain emotions, and the facial muscles then feed signals to the cortex that help it to recognize the emotion that one is experiencing. According to this view, facial expressions help create the subjective experience of various emotions.

Photo by David E. Klutho /Sports Illustrated/Getty Images

Hockey player Sidney Crosby expressed his emotions clearly, hoisting the Stanley Cup over his head after winning game and series with the Pittsburgh Penguins versus the Nashville Predators in 2017.

comparison were taken just after the athletes had won or lost their crucial final matches (for gold, silver, or bronze medals). The analysis of thousands of photos of numerous athletes yielded clear results: the facial expressions of sighted and blind athletes were indistinguishable. These findings suggest that the facial expressions that go with emotions are wired into the human brain (Matsumoto & Hwang, 2011).

These findings strongly support the hypothesis that the facial expressions that go with emotions

are wired into the human brain. The long-held suspicion that facial expressions of emotion might be biologically built in has also led to extensive cross-cultural research on the dynamics of emotion. Let's look at what investigators have learned about culture and the elements of emotional experience.

Culture and the Elements of Emotion

Are emotions innate reactions that are universal across cultures? Or are they socially learned reactions that are culturally variable? The voluminous research on this lingering question has not yielded a simple answer. Investigators have found both remarkable similarities and dramatic differences between cultures in the experience of emotion.

Cross-Cultural Similarities in Emotional Experience

After demonstrating that Western subjects could discern specific emotions from facial expressions, Ekman and Friesen (1975) took their facial-cue photographs on the road to other societies to see whether nonverbal expressions of emotion transcend cultural boundaries. For example, they tested participants in Argentina, Spain, Japan, and other countries. They found considerable cross-cultural agreement in the identification of happiness, sadness, anger, fear, surprise, and disgust based on facial expressions (see Figure 10.18). They even took their photos to a remote area in New Guinea and

Figure 10.18
Cross-cultural comparisons of people's ability to recognize emotions from facial expressions. Ekman and Friesen (1975) found that people in highly disparate cultures showed fair agreement on the emotions portrayed in these photos. This consensus across cultures suggests that facial expressions of emotions may be universal and that they have a strong biological basis.

Source: Data from Ekman, R., and Friesen, W. V. (1975). *Unmasking the face.* Englewood Cliffs, NJ: Prentice-Hall. © 1975 by Paul Ekman.

	Fear	Disgust	Happiness	Anger
Country		**Agreement in judging photos (%)**		
United States	85	92	97	67
Brazil	67	97	95	90
Chile	68	92	95	94
Argentina	54	92	98	90
Japan	66	90	100	90
New Guinea	54	44	82	50

Paul Ekman, Ph.D./Paul Ekman Group, LLC

showed them to a group of natives (the Fore) who had had virtually no contact with Western culture. The people from this preliterate culture did a fair job of identifying the emotions portrayed in the pictures (see Figure 10.18), *leading to the conclusion that the facial expressions associated with basic emotions are universally recognized across cultures.* Cross-cultural similarities have also been found in the cognitive appraisals that lead to certain emotions (Matsumoto, Nezlek, & Koopmann, 2007). Likewise, researchers have found little cultural variance in the physiological arousal that accompanies emotional experience (Breugelmans et al., 2005). All that said, some theorists have questioned the assertion that facial expressions of emotion transcend culture. Nelson and Russell (2013) point out that there are some substantial variations across cultures in subjects' accuracy in identifying specific emotions. This line of research has also been criticized on the grounds that it has depended on a rather small set of artificial, highly posed, caricature-like photos that do not do justice to the variety of facial expressions that can accompany specific emotions (Barrett, 2011).

Cross-Cultural Differences in Emotional Experience

The cross-cultural similarities in emotional experience are impressive, but researchers have also found many cultural disparities in how people think about, experience, regulate, and express their emotions (Matsumoto, Yoo, Nakagawa, et al., 2008; Mesquita & Leu, 2007). For example, Japanese culture encourages the experience of *socially engaging emotions* (e.g., friendly feelings, sympathy, and guilt) more than North American culture, and Japanese participants report experiencing these types of emotion more (Kitayama, Mesquita, & Karasawa, 2006). In contrast, North American culture encourages *socially disengaging emotions* (e.g., pride and anger) more than Japanese culture, and North American subjects report experiencing these kinds of emotion more.

Fascinating variations have been observed in how cultures categorize emotions. Some basic categories of emotion that are universally understood in Western cultures appear to go unrecognized—or at least unnamed—in some non-Western cultures (Russell, 1991). For example, some cultures have no word that corresponds to *sadness*. Others lack words for *depression, anxiety,* or *remorse.*

Cultural disparities have also been found in regard to nonverbal expressions of emotion.

Canadian Olympic medalist Joannie Rochette did not hesitate to display her emotions over her mother's death during the 2010 Olympic Winter Games.

Display rules are norms that regulate the appropriate expression of emotions. They prescribe when, how, and to whom people can show various emotions. These norms vary from one culture to another (Ekman, 1992). The Ifaluk of Micronesia, for instance, severely restrict expressions of happiness because they believe that this emotion often leads people to neglect their duties. Japanese culture emphasizes the suppression of negative emotions in public. More so than in many other cultures, the Japanese are socialized to mask emotions such as anger, sadness, and disgust with stoic facial expressions or polite smiling. Thus, nonverbal expressions of emotions vary somewhat across cultures. Some of these cultural differences are evident in the ways that Canadian Olympic skater Joannie Rochette publicly displayed her grief (DiManno, 2011a) over her mother's death just days before her Olympic competition, compared to how many of the survivors of the 2011 tsunami in Japan were unable to publicly show their grief over relatives who were swept away by the tsunami (DiManno, 2011b).

Thus, nonverbal expressions of emotions vary somewhat across cultures because of culture-specific attitudes and display rules.

Theories of Emotion

Key Learning Goals

▶ Compare the James–Lange and Cannon–Bard theories of emotion.

▶ Explain the two-factor theory of emotion and evolutionary theories of emotion.

How do psychologists explain the experience of emotion? How do psychologists differentiate between types of emotions (e.g., Rempel & Burris, 2005)? A variety of theories and conflicting models exist. Some have been vigorously debated for over a century. As we describe these theories, you'll recognize a familiar bone of contention. Like so many other types of theories, theories of emotion differ in their emphasis on the innate biological basis of emotion versus the social, environmental basis.

James–Lange Theory

As we noted in Chapter 1, William James was a prominent early theorist who urged psychologists to explore the functions of consciousness. James (1884) developed a theory of emotion over 100 years ago that remains influential today. At about the same time, he and Carl Lange (1885) independently proposed that *the conscious experience of emotion results from one's perception of autonomic arousal*. Their theory stood common sense on its head. Everyday logic

suggests that when you stumble onto a rattlesnake in the woods, the conscious experience of fear leads to visceral arousal (the fight-or-flight response). The James–Lange theory of emotion asserts the opposite: that the perception of visceral arousal leads to the conscious experience of fear (see Figure 10.19). In other words, while you might assume that your pulse is racing because you're fearful, James and Lange argued that you're fearful because your pulse is racing.

The James–Lange theory emphasizes the physiological determinants of emotion. According to this view, *different patterns of autonomic activation lead to the experience of different emotions*. Hence, people supposedly distinguish emotions such as fear, joy, and anger on the basis of the exact configuration of physical reactions they experience.

Cannon–Bard Theory

Walter Cannon (1927) found the James–Lange theory unconvincing. Cannon pointed out that physiological arousal may occur without the

Figure 10.19
Theories of emotion.
Three influential theories of emotion are contrasted with one another and with the commonsense view. The James–Lange theory was the first to suggest that feelings of arousal cause emotion, rather than vice versa. Schachter (Schachter & Singer, 1962) built on this idea by adding a second factor—interpretation (appraisal and labelling) of arousal.

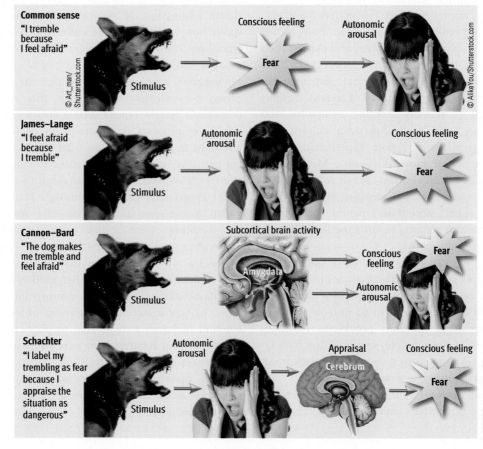

experience of emotion (if one exercises vigorously, for instance). He also argued that visceral changes are too slow to precede the conscious experience of emotion. Finally, he argued that people experiencing very different emotions, such as fear, joy, and anger, exhibit almost identical patterns of autonomic arousal.

Thus, Cannon espoused a different explanation of emotion. Later, Philip Bard (1934) elaborated on it. The resulting Cannon–Bard theory argues that emotion occurs when the thalamus sends signals *simultaneously* to the cortex (creating the conscious experience of emotion) and to the autonomic nervous system (creating visceral arousal). The Cannon–Bard model is compared to the James–Lange model in Figure 10.19. Cannon and Bard were off the mark a bit in pinpointing the thalamus as the neural centre for emotion. However, many modern theorists agree with the Cannon–Bard view that emotions originate in subcortical brain structures (LeDoux, 1996; Panksepp, 1991; Rolls, 1990) and with the assertion that people do not discern their emotions from different patterns of autonomic activation (Frijda, 1999; Wagner, 1989).

Schachter's Two-Factor Theory

In another influential analysis, Stanley Schachter asserted that people look at situational cues to differentiate among alternative emotions. According to Schachter (1964; Schachter & Singer, 1962, 1979), the experience of emotion depends on two factors: (1) autonomic arousal and (2) cognitive interpretation of that arousal. Schachter proposed that when you experience visceral arousal, you search your environment for an explanation (see Figure 10.19 again). If you're stuck in a traffic jam, you'll probably label your arousal as anger. If you're taking an important exam, you'll probably label it as anxiety. If you're celebrating your birthday, you'll probably label it as happiness.

You may recall that we used Schachter's theory in understanding the results of the Featured Study in Chapter 2 (see page 42). In that study, a classic test of the two-factor theory, Dutton and Aron (1974) arranged for young men crossing a footbridge in a park to encounter a young woman who asked them to stop briefly to fill out a questionnaire. The woman offered to explain the research at some future time and gave the men her phone number. Autonomic arousal was manipulated by enacting this scenario on two very different bridges. One was a long suspension bridge that swayed precariously 70 metres above a river. The other bridge

was a solid, safe structure above a small stream. The experimenters reasoned that the men crossing the frightening bridge would be experiencing emotional arousal and that some of them might attribute that arousal to the woman rather than to the bridge. If so, they might mislabel their emotion as lust rather than fear and infer that they were attracted to the woman. The dependent variable was how many of the men later called the woman to pursue a date. As predicted, more of the men who met the woman on the precarious bridge called her for a date. Thus, the findings supported the theory that people often infer emotion from their physiological arousal and label that emotion in accordance with their cognitive explanation for it.

Schachter agreed with the James–Lange view that emotion is inferred from arousal. However, he also agreed with the Cannon–Bard position that different emotions yield indistinguishable patterns of arousal. He reconciled these views by arguing that people look to external rather than internal cues to differentiate and label their specific emotions. In essence, Schachter suggested that people think along the following lines: "If I'm aroused and you're obnoxious, I must be angry."

Although the two-factor theory has received support, studies have revealed some limitations as well (Leventhal & Tomarken, 1986). Situations can't mould emotions in just any way at any time. And in searching to explain arousal, subjects don't limit themselves to the immediate situation (Sinclair et al., 1994). Thus, emotions are not as pliable as the two-factor theory initially suggested.

Stanley Schachter

"Cognitive factors play a major role in determining how a subject interprets his bodily feelings."

The Capilano suspension bridge, shown here, was used in the study by Dutton and Aron (1974) to manipulate autonomic arousal in a clever test of the two-factor theory of emotion.

Evolutionary Theories of Emotion

As the limitations of the two-factor theory were exposed, theorists began returning to ideas espoused by Charles Darwin over a century ago. Darwin (1872) believed that emotions developed because of their adaptive value. Fear, for instance, would help an organism avoid danger (Wise, 2011), and thus would aid in survival. Hence, Darwin viewed human emotions as a product of evolution. This premise serves as the foundation for several prominent theories of emotion developed independently by S. S. Tomkins (1980, 1991), Carroll Izard (1984, 1991), and Robert Plutchik (1984, 1993).

These *evolutionary theories* consider emotions to be largely innate reactions to certain stimuli. As such, emotions should be immediately recognizable under most conditions without much thought. After all, primitive animals that are incapable of complex thought seem to have little difficulty in recognizing their emotions. Evolutionary theorists believe that emotion evolved before thought. They assert that thought plays a relatively small role in emotion, although they admit that learning and cognition may have some influence on human emotions. Evolutionary theories generally assume that emotions originate in subcortical brain structures that evolved before the higher brain areas in the cortex associated with complex thought.

Evolutionary theories also assume that evolution has equipped humans with a small number of innate emotions with proven adaptive value. Hence, the principal question that many theories of emotion (e.g., Hutcherson & Gross, 2011), especially evolutionary theories, wrestle with is

What are the fundamental emotions? Table 10.1 summarizes the conclusions of the leading theorists in this area. As you can see, Tomkins, Izard, and Plutchik have not come up with identical lists, but there is considerable agreement. All three conclude that people exhibit eight to ten primary emotions. Moreover, five of these emotions appear on all three lists: fear, anger, joy, disgust, and surprise. The potential adaptive value of these basic emotions is key to the evolutionary argument. For example, consider *disgust*; what adaptive value do you think it might have (Tybur et al., 2013)? According to Australian researcher Megan Oaten and her colleagues (Oaten, Stevenson, & Case, 2009), disgust serves an important function as a disease-avoidance mechanism.

Like all animals, humans are faced daily with potential contact with a variety of pathogens, including viruses and bacteria. According to Oaten, we have developed a variety of behaviours that enable us to avoid many pathogens and one key to avoiding disease is the emotion we label *disgust*. The "revulsion" and "nausea" that frequently accompany our disgust elicits avoidance behaviour. One of us remembers just like it happened yesterday (even though it happened 40 years ago)—his disgust as a young boy at turning over a dead cat he found lying on the side of the road only to find it crawling with hundreds (it seemed like millions) of maggots. His disgust kicked in and he ran all the way home. In a careful and systematic review of studies conducted on the issue, Oaten concluded that the evidence supported the theory that disgust functions to enable us to avoid disease and infection.

Table 10.1

Primary Emotions

Evolutionary theories of emotion attempt to identify primary emotions. Three leading theorists—Silvan Tomkins, Carroll Izard, and Robert Plutchik—compiled different lists of primary emotions, but this chart shows great overlap among the basic emotions identified by these theorists. (Based on Mandler, 1984)

SILVAN TOMKINS	CARROLL IZARD	ROBERT PLUTCHIK
Fear	Fear	Fear
Anger	Anger	Anger
Enjoyment	Enjoyment	Enjoyment
Disgust	Disgust	Disgust
Interest	Interest	Interest
Surprise	Surprise	Surprise
Contempt	Contempt	
Shame	Shame	
	Sadness	Sadness
Distress		
	Guilt	
		Acceptance

© 2017 Cengage Learning

Understanding Theories of Emotion

Check your understanding of theories of emotion by matching the theories we discussed with the statements below. Let's borrow William James's classic example: Assume that you just stumbled upon a bear in the woods. The first statement expresses the common-sense explanation of your fear. Each of the remaining statements expresses the essence of a different theory; indicate which theory in the spaces provided. The answers are provided in Appendix A near the back of the book.

1. You tremble because you're afraid.

   Common sense
   _____

2. You're afraid because you're trembling.

   _____

3. You're afraid because situational cues (the bear) suggest that's why you're trembling.

   _____

4. You're afraid because the bear has elicited an innate primary emotion.

   _____

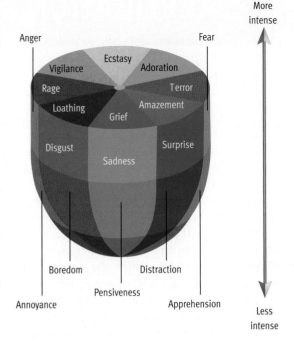

Figure 10.20

Emotional intensity in Plutchik's model. According to Plutchik, diversity in human emotion is a product of variations in emotional intensity, as well as blendings of primary emotions. Each vertical slice in the diagram is a primary emotion that can be subdivided into emotional expressions of varied intensity, ranging from most intense (top) to least intense (bottom).

Source: Based on art in Plutchik, R. (1980). A language for emotions. *Psychology Today*, 13 (9), 68–78. Psychology Today © Copyright 2014, www.Psychologytoday.com

This analysis confirms the potential adaptive value of what is considered to be one of the basic human emotions.

Of course, people experience more than just eight to ten emotions. How do evolutionary theories account for this variety? They propose that the many emotions that people experience are produced by (1) blends of primary emotions and (2) variations in intensity. For example, Robert Plutchik (1980, 1993) has devised an elegant model of how primary emotions such as fear and surprise may blend into secondary emotions such as awe. Plutchik's model also posits that various emotions, such as apprehension, fear, and terror, involve one primary emotion experienced at different levels of intensity (see Figure 10.20).

Putting It in Perspective: Themes 2, 3, 4, 5, and 6

Five of our organizing themes were particularly prominent in this chapter: the influence of cultural contexts, the dense connections between psychology and society at large, psychology's theoretical diversity, the interplay of heredity and environment, and the multiple causes of behaviour.

Our discussion of motivation and emotion demonstrated once again that there are both similarities and differences across cultures in behaviour. The neural, biochemical, genetic, and hormonal processes underlying hunger and eating, for instance, are universal. But cultural factors influence what people prefer to eat, how much they eat, and whether they worry about dieting. In a similar vein, researchers have found a great deal of cross-cultural congruence in the cognitive, physiological, and expressive elements of emotional experience, but they have also found cultural variations in how people think about and express their emotions. Thus, as we have seen in previous chapters, psychological processes are characterized by both cultural variance and invariance.

Our discussion of the controversies surrounding evolutionary theory and the determinants of sexual orientation show once again that psychology is not an ivory tower enterprise. It evolves in a sociohistorical context that helps to shape the debates in

Key Learning Goal

▶ Identify the five unifying themes highlighted in this chapter.

Exploring the Ingredients of Happiness

If you ask any of your friends about what leads to happiness, they will likely provide you with answers such as money, children, good health, or attractiveness. These assertions are all reasonable and widely believed hypotheses about the correlates of happiness, but they have not been supported by empirical research. Let's try another one related to the connection between money and happiness—it should be easier (Hune-Brown, 2013). Imagine that a woman you know has some extra money to spend. Do you think she would be happier spending it on herself or happier if she spent the money on someone else? The answer would surprise many of us: People seem to be happier spending money on others than on themselves, according to the results of a recent study conducted by Elizabeth Dunn at the University of British Columbia (Dunn, 2010; Dunn, Aknin, & Norton, 2008; Dunn, Gilbert, & Wilson, 2011).

This raises the question: How well do we understand our own emotional reactions to situations and events? Our emotional reactions are critical to our overall sense of well-being, and envisioning the future may affect our happiness (Quoidback, Wood, & Hansenne, 2009). Recent years have brought a surge of interest in the correlates of *subjective well-being*—individuals' personal perceptions of their overall happiness and life satisfaction (Busseri & Sadava, 2011; Deiner & Chan, 2011; Fischer & Van de Vliert, 2011; Gleibs et al., 2013).

The findings of these studies are quite interesting. Writers, social scientists, and the general public seem to believe that people around the world are predominantly dissatisfied and unhappy, yet empirical surveys consistently find that the vast majority of respondents—even those who are poor or disabled—characterize themselves as fairly happy (Diener & Diener, 1996; Myers & Diener, 1995).

When people are asked to rate their happiness, only a small minority place themselves below the neutral point on the various scales used (see Figure 10.21). When the average subjective well-being of entire nations is computed, based on almost 1000 surveys, the means cluster toward the positive end of the scale (Tov & Diener, 2007). That's not to say that everyone is equally happy. Researchers find substantial and thought-provoking disparities among people in subjective well-being and happiness (Kesebir & Diener, 2008), which we will analyze momentarily, but the overall picture seems rosier than anticipated. This is an encouraging finding, as subjective well-being tends to be relatively stable over the course of people's lives, and higher levels of happiness are predictive of better social relationships, greater career satisfaction, better physical health, and greater longevity (Lucas & Diener, 2015). Thus, one's subjective well-being can have important consequences.

Factors That Do Not Predict Happiness

Let us begin our discussion of individual differences in happiness by highlighting those things that turn out to be relatively unimportant determinants of subjective well-being. Quite a number of factors that you might expect to be influential appear to bear little or no relationship to general happiness.

Money There *is* a positive correlation between income and subjective feelings of

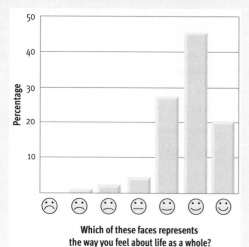

Figure 10.21

Measuring happiness with a nonverbal scale. Researchers have used a variety of methods to estimate the distribution of happiness. For example, in one study in the United States, respondents were asked to examine the seven facial expressions shown and select the one that "comes closest to expressing how you feel about your life as a whole." As you can see, the vast majority of participants chose happy faces. (Data adapted from Myers, 1992)

happiness, but in modern, affluent cultures the association is surprisingly weak (Diener & Seligman, 2004; Myers & Diener, 1995). For example, one study found a correlation of just 0.13 between income and happiness in the United States (Diener et al., 1993) and another investigation yielded an almost identical correlation of 0.12 (Johnson & Krueger, 2006). Admittedly, being very poor can make people unhappy. Yet it seems once people ascend above a certain level of income, additional wealth does not seem to foster greater happiness. One recent study in the United States estimated that once people exceed an income of around $75 000, little relationship is seen between wealth and subjective well-being (Kahneman & Deaton, 2010).

Research shows that happiness does not depend on people's positive and negative experiences as much as one would expect. Some people, presumably because of their personality, seem destined to be happy in spite of major setbacks, and others seem destined to cling to unhappiness even though their lives seem reasonably pleasant.

Why isn't money a better predictor of happiness? One reason is that there seems to be a disconnect between actual income and how people feel about their financial situation. Research (Johnson & Krueger, 2006) suggests that the correlation between actual wealth and people's subjective perceptions of whether they have enough money to meet their needs is surprisingly modest (around 0.30). Another problem is that pervasive advertising fuels escalating material desires that often outstrip what people can afford, causing dissatisfaction (Norris & Larsen, 2011). Thus, complaints about not having enough money are routine even among people who are very affluent by objective standards. Interestingly, there is some evidence that people who place an especially strong emphasis on materialistic goals tend to be somewhat less happy than others (Ahuvia & Izberk-Bilgin, 2013). Evidence also suggests that living in wealthy neighbourhoods

fuels increased materialism (Zhang, Howell, & Howell, 2014), providing yet another reason wealth does not necessarily foster happiness. Unfortunately, research suggests that levels of materialism in North America have been rising in recent decades to historically high levels (Twenge & Kasser, 2013).

Recent studies have provided some other interesting and unexpected insights about money and happiness. First, studies suggest that money spent purchasing experiences, such as concerts, travel, and outdoor activities, promotes more happiness than money spent purchasing material goods, such as clothes, jewellery, and appliances (Pchelin & Howell, 2014). Second, research indicates that across many cultures of varied wealth, people derive more happiness from money spent to help others than from money spent on themselves (Dunn, Aknin, & Norton, 2014).

Age Age and happiness are consistently found to be unrelated. For example, a study of over 7000 adults concluded that levels of happiness did not vary with age (Cooper et al., 2011). The key factors influencing subjective well-being may shift some as people grow older—work becomes less important, health more so. But people's average level of happiness tends to remain fairly stable over the life span.

Parenthood Children can be a tremendous source of joy and fulfillment, but they can also be a tremendous source of headaches and hassles. Compared to childless couples, parents worry more and experience more marital problems (Argyle, 1987). Apparently, the good and bad aspects of parenthood balance each other out, because the evidence indicates that people who have children are neither more nor less happy than people without children (Argyle, 2001).

Intelligence and Attractiveness
Intelligence and physical attractiveness are highly valued traits in modern society. Yet

researchers have not found an association between either characteristic and happiness (Diener, Kesebir, & Tov, 2009; Diener, Wolsic, & Fujita, 1995).

Moderately Good Predictors of Happiness

Research has identified three facets of life that appear to have a *moderate* association with subjective well-being: health, social activity, and religious belief.

Health Good physical health would seem to be an essential requirement for happiness, but people adapt to health problems. Research reveals that individuals who develop serious, disabling health conditions aren't as unhappy as one might guess (Myers, 1992; Riis et al., 2005). Furthermore, Freedman (1978) argues that good health does not, by itself, produce happiness, because people tend to take good health for granted. Considerations such as these may help to explain why researchers find only a moderate positive correlation (average = 0.32) between health status and subjective well-being (Argyle, 1999). While health may promote happiness to a moderate degree, happiness may also foster better health, as recent research has found a positive correlation between happiness and longevity (Veenhoven, 2008).

Social Activity Humans are social animals, and interpersonal relations do appear to contribute to people's happiness. Those who are satisfied with their social support and friendship networks and those who are socially active report somewhat higher levels of happiness than others do (Demir, Orthel, & Andelin, 2013; Lakey, 2013). One study found that at age 50, people with larger friendship networks reported greater psychological well-being than did those with fewer friends (Cable et al., 2013).

Religion The link between religiosity and subjective well-being is modest, but a number of large-scale surveys suggest that people with heartfelt religious convictions are more likely to be happy than people who characterize themselves as nonreligious (Argyle, 1999; Myers, 2008). Researchers aren't sure how religious faith fosters happiness, but Myers (1992) offers some interesting conjectures. Among other things, he discusses how religion can give people a sense of purpose and meaning in their lives; help them accept their setbacks gracefully; connect them to a caring, supportive community; and comfort them by putting their ultimate mortality into perspective.

Strong Predictors of Happiness

The list of factors that turn out to have fairly strong associations with happiness is surprisingly short. The key ingredients of happiness appear to involve relationship satisfaction, work, and genetics and personality.

Relationship Satisfaction Romantic relationships can be stressful, but people consistently rate being in love as one of the critical ingredients of happiness. Furthermore, although people complain a lot about their marriages, research consistently finds that married people tend to be happier than people who are single or divorced (Saphire-Bernstein & Taylor, 2013). This relationship holds around the world in widely different cultures (Diener et al., 2000). And among married people, level of marital satisfaction predicts personal well-being (Proulx, Helms, & Buehler, 2007). The research in this area has used marital status as a crude but easily measured marker of relationship satisfaction. In all likelihood, it is relationship satisfaction that fosters happiness. *Relationship satisfaction* probably has the same association with happiness in cohabiting heterosexual couples and gay couples. In support of this line of thinking, one study found that both married and cohabiting people were happier

than those who remained single (Musick & Bumpass, 2012).

Work Given the way people often complain about their jobs, one might not expect work to be a key source of happiness, but it is. Although less critical than love and marriage, job satisfaction has a substantial association with general happiness (Judge & Klinger, 2008; Warr, 1999). Studies also show that unemployment has strong negative effects on subjective well-being (Argyle, 1999; Lucas et al., 2004). It is difficult to sort out whether job satisfaction causes happiness or vice versa, but evidence suggests that causation flows both ways (Argyle, 1987, 2001).

Genetics and Personality The best predictor of individuals' future happiness is their past happiness (Pavot & Diener, 2013). Some people seem destined to be happy and others unhappy, regardless of their triumphs or setbacks. Actually, several lines of evidence suggest that happiness does not depend on external circumstances—buying a nice house, getting promoted—as much as on internal factors, such as one's outlook on life (Lykken & Tellegen, 1996; Lyubomirsky, Sheldon, & Schkade, 2005). With this reality in mind, researchers have investigated whether there might be a hereditary basis for variations in happiness. These studies suggest that people's genetic predispositions account for a very substantial portion of the variance in happiness—perhaps as much as 50 percent (Lyubomirsky, Sheldon, & Schkade, 2005; Stubbe et al., 2005).

How can one's genes influence one's happiness? Presumably, by shaping one's temperament and personality, which are known to be heritable (Weiss, Bates, & Luciano, 2008). Hence, researchers have begun to look for links between personality and subjective well-being, and they have found some interesting correlations. For example, *extraversion* (sometimes referred to as *positive emotionality*) is one of the better predictors of happiness. People who are outgoing, upbeat, and sociable tend to be happier than

others (Gale et al., 2013). Additional personality correlates of happiness include conscientiousness, agreeableness, self-esteem, and optimism (Lucas, 2008; Lyubomirsky, Tkach, & DiMatteo, 2006).

Conclusions about Subjective Well-Being

We must be cautious in drawing inferences about the causes of happiness, because the available data are correlational. Nonetheless, the empirical evidence suggests that many popular beliefs about the sources of happiness are unfounded. The data also demonstrate that happiness is shaped by a complex constellation of variables. In spite of this complexity, however, a number of worthwhile insights about the ingredients of happiness can be gleaned from the recent flurry of research.

First, research on happiness demonstrates that the determinants of subjective well-being are precisely that: subjective. *Objective realities are not as important as subjective feelings.* In other words, your health, your wealth, and your job are not as influential as how you *feel* about your health, wealth, and job (Schwarz & Strack, 1999).

Second, when it comes to happiness, everything is relative (Argyle, 1999; Hagerty, 2000). In other words, you evaluate what you have relative to what the people around you have. Generally, we compare ourselves with others who are similar to us. Thus, people who are wealthy assess what they have by comparing themselves with their wealthy friends and neighbours and their relative standing is crucial (Boyce, Brown, & Moore, 2010). This is one reason for the low correlation between wealth and happiness.

Third, *research on subjective well-being indicates that people often adapt to their circumstances.* This adaptation effect is one reason that increases in income don't necessarily bring increases in happiness. Thus, *hedonic adaptation* occurs when the mental scale that people use to judge the pleasantness–unpleasantness of their experiences shifts so that their neutral point (or baseline for comparison) changes. Unfortunately, when people's experiences improve, hedonic adaptation may *sometimes* put them on a *hedonic treadmill*—their neutral point moves upward, so that the improvements yield no real benefits (Kahneman, 1999). However, when people have to grapple with major setbacks, hedonic adaptation probably helps protect their mental and physical health. For example, some people who are sent to prison and some people who develop debilitating diseases are not as unhappy as one might assume, because they adapt to their changed situations and evaluate events from a new perspective (Frederick & Loewenstein, 1999).

That's not to say that hedonic adaptation in the face of life's difficulties is inevitable or complete, but that people adapt to setbacks much better than widely assumed (Lucas, 2007).

the field, and these debates often have far-reaching social and political ramifications for society at large. We ended the chapter with a discussion of various theories of emotion, which showed once again that psychology is characterized by great theoretical diversity.

Finally, we repeatedly saw that biological and environmental factors jointly govern behaviour. For example, we learned that eating behaviour, sexual desire, and the experience of emotion all depend on complicated interactions between biological and environmental determinants. Indeed, complicated interactions permeated the entire chapter, demonstrating that if we want to fully understand behaviour, we have to take multiple causes into account. In the upcoming Personal Application, we will continue our discussion of emotion, looking at recent research on the correlates of happiness. In the Critical Thinking Application that follows, we discuss how to carefully analyze the types of arguments that permeated this chapter.

Analyzing Arguments: Making Sense Out of Controversy

Key Learning Goal

▶ Identify the key elements in arguments, and recognize common fallacies in arguments.

Consider the following argument: "Dieting is harmful to your health because the tendency to be obese is largely inherited." What is your reaction to this reasoning? Do you find it convincing? We hope not, as this argument is seriously flawed. Can you see what's wrong? There is no relationship between the conclusion that "dieting is harmful to your health" and the reason given that "the tendency to be obese is largely inherited." The argument is initially seductive because you know from reading this chapter that obesity *is* largely inherited, so the reason provided represents a true statement. But the reason is unrelated to the conclusion advocated. This scenario may strike you as odd, but if you start listening carefully to discussions about controversial issues, you will probably notice that people often cite irrelevant considerations in support of their favoured conclusions.

This chapter was loaded with controversial issues that sincere, well-meaning people could argue about for weeks. Are gender differences in mating preferences a product of evolution or of modern economic realities? Is there a biological basis for homosexuality? Unfortunately, arguments about issues such as these typically are unproductive in terms of moving toward resolution or agreement because most people know little about the rules of argumentation. In this Application, we will explore what makes arguments sound or unsound in the hope of improving your ability to analyze and think critically about arguments.

The Anatomy of an Argument

In everyday usage, the word *argument* is used to refer to a dispute or disagreement between two or more people, but in the technical language of rhetoric, an *argument* consists of one or more premises that are used to provide support for a conclusion. *Premises* are the reasons that are presented to persuade someone that a conclusion is true or probably true. *Assumptions* are premises for which no proof or evidence is offered. Assumptions are often left unstated. For example, suppose that your doctor tells you that you should exercise regularly because regular exercise is good for your heart. In this simple argument, the conclusion is "You should exercise regularly." The premise that leads to this conclusion is the idea that "exercise is good for your heart." An unstated assumption is that everyone wants a healthy heart.

In the language of argument analysis, premises are said to support (or not support) conclusions. A conclusion may be supported by one reason or by many reasons. One way to visualize these possibilities is to draw an analogy between the reasons that support a conclusion and the legs that support a table (Halpern, 1996, 2003). As shown in Figure 10.22, a tabletop (conclusion) could be supported by one strong leg (a single strong reason) or many thin legs (lots of weaker reasons). Of course, the reasons provided for a conclusion may fail to support the conclusion. Returning to our table analogy, the tabletop might not be supported because the legs are too thin (very weak reasons) or because the legs are not attached (irrelevant reasons).

Arguments can get pretty complicated, as they usually have more parts than just reasons and conclusions. In addition, there often are *counterarguments*, which are reasons that take support away from a conclusion. And sometimes the most important part of an argument is a part that is not there—reasons that have been omitted, either deliberately or not, that would lead to a different conclusion if they were supplied. Given all of the complex variations that are possible in arguments, it is impossible to give you simple rules for judging arguments, but we can highlight some common fallacies and then provide some criteria that you can apply in thinking critically about arguments. See Table 10.2.

Common Fallacies

As noted in previous chapters, cognitive scientists have compiled lengthy lists of fallacies that people frequently display in their reasoning. These fallacies often show up in arguments. In this section, we will describe five common fallacies. To illustrate each one, we will assume the role of someone arguing that pornographic material on the Internet (cyberporn) should be banned or heavily regulated.

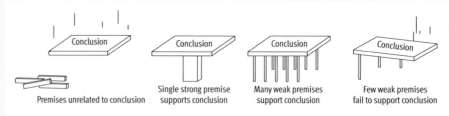

Figure 10.22
An analogy for understanding the strength of arguments. Halpern (1996) draws an analogy between the reasons that support a conclusion and the legs that support a table. She points out that a conclusion may be supported effectively by one strong premise or many weak premises. Of course, the reasons provided for a conclusion may also fail to provide adequate support.

Source: Republished with permission of Taylor & Francis, from *Thought and knowledge: An introduction to critical thinking*, Halpern, D. F. Copyright © 2003 Lawrence Erlbaum Associates.

Table 10.2

Critical Thinking Skills Discussed in This Application

SKILL	DESCRIPTION
Understanding the elements of an argument	The critical thinker understands that an argument consists of premises and assumptions that are used to support a conclusion.
Recognizing and avoiding common fallacies, such as irrelevant reasons, circular reasoning, slippery slope reasoning, weak analogies, and false dichotomies.	The critical thinker is vigilant about conclusions based on unrelated premises, conclusions that are rewordings of premises, superficial analogies, and contrived dichotomies.
Evaluating arguments systematically	The critical thinker carefully assesses the validity of the premises, assumptions, and conclusions in an argument, and considers counterarguments and missing elements.

Irrelevant Reasons Reasons cannot provide support for an argument unless they are relevant to the conclusion. Arguments that depend on irrelevant reasons—either intentionally or inadvertently—are quite common. You already saw one example at the beginning of this Application. The Latin term for this fallacy is *non sequitur*, which literally translates to *it doesn't follow*. In other words, the conclusion does not follow from the premise. For example, in the debate about Internet pornography, you might hear the following non sequitur: "We need to regulate cyberporn because research has shown that most date rapes go unreported."

Circular Reasoning In *circular reasoning* the premise and conclusion are simply restatements of each other. People vary their wording a little so it isn't obvious, but when you look closely, the conclusion is the premise. For example, in arguments about Internet pornography you might hear someone assert, "We need to control cyberporn because it currently is unregulated."

Slippery Slope The concept of *slippery slope* argumentation takes its name from the notion that if you are on a slippery slope and you don't dig in your heels, you will slide and slide until you reach the bottom. A slippery slope argument typically asserts that if you allow X to happen, things will spin out of control and far worse events will follow. The trick is that there is no inherent connection between X and the events that are predicted to follow. For example, in the debate about medical marijuana, opponents have argued, "If you legalize medical marijuana, the next thing you know, cocaine and heroin will be legal." In the debate about cyberporn, a slippery slope argument might go, "If we don't ban cyberporn, the next thing you know, grade-school children will be watching smut all day long in their school libraries."

Weak Analogies An *analogy* asserts that two concepts or events are similar in some way. Hence, you can draw conclusions about event B because of its similarity to event A. Analogies are useful in thinking about complex issues, but some analogies are weak or inappropriate because the similarity between A and B is superficial, minimal, or irrelevant to the issue at hand. For example, in the debate about Internet erotica, someone might argue, "Cyberporn is morally offensive, just like child molestation. We wouldn't tolerate child molestation, so we shouldn't permit cyberporn."

False Dichotomy A *false dichotomy* creates an either–or choice between two outcomes: the outcome advocated and some obviously horrible outcome that any sensible person would want to avoid. These outcomes are presented as the only two possibilities, when in reality there could be other outcomes, including ones that lie somewhere between the extremes depicted in the false dichotomy. In the debate about Internet pornography, someone might argue, "We can ban cyberporn, or we can hasten the moral decay of modern society."

Evaluating the Strength of Arguments

In everyday life, you may frequently need to assess the strength of arguments made by friends, family, co-workers, politicians, media pundits, and so forth. You may also want to evaluate your own arguments when you write papers or speeches for school or prepare presentations for your work. The following questions can help you make systematic evaluations of arguments (adapted from Halpern, 1996, 2003):

- What is the conclusion?
- What are the premises provided to support the conclusion? Are the premises valid?
- Does the conclusion follow from the premises? Are there any fallacies in the chain of reasoning?
- What assumptions have been made? Are they valid assumptions? Should they be stated explicitly?
- What are the counterarguments? Do they weaken the argument?
- Is there anything that has been omitted from the argument?

Motivation and Emotion

MOTIVATIONAL THEORIES AND CONCEPTS

- *Drive theories* emphasize how *internal* states of tension (due to disruptions of homeostasis) *push* organisms in certain directions.
- *Incentive theories* emphasize how *external goals pull* organisms in certain directions.
- Evolutionary theories assert that motives are a product of *natural selection* that have had adaptive value in terms of fostering reproductive fitness.
- Humans display an enormous diversity of *biological* and *social* motives.

MOTIVATION OF HUNGER

Biological factors regulating hunger

- Research originally suggested that the *lateral* and *ventromedial areas of the hypothalamus* were the brain's on–off switches for hunger, but the dual-centres model proved too simple.
- Today scientists think that *neural circuits* passing through the *arcuate* and *paraventricular* areas of the hypothalamus play a larger role in the regulation of hunger.
- In the digestive system, the stomach can send various types of satiety signals to the brain.
- Secretions of the hormone *ghrelin* cause stomach contractions and increased hunger.
- Secretions of the hormone *CCK* carry satiety signals from the intestine to the brain.
- The hormone *leptin* provides the hypothalamus with information about the body's fat stores.

Environmental factors regulating hunger

- Organisms consume more food when it is palatable, when more is available, and when there is greater variety.
- People tend to eat more in the presence of others and in response to food advertisements.
- Stressful events can increase food consumption in about 40–50 percent of people.
- Classical conditioning and observational learning shape what people prefer to eat.
- Food preferences are also governed by exposure, which is why there are huge cultural variations in eating habits.

The roots of obesity

- Surveys show surprisingly sharp increases in the incidence of obesity in recent decades.
  - Obesity is associated with an increased incidence of many health problems and elevated risk of mortality.
  - Some people inherit a genetic vulnerability to obesity.
  - Obesity is attributable to excessive eating and inadequate exercise.
  - Increased sleep deprivation in modern society probably fuels increased obesity.
  - The concept of a *set point* suggests that each individual has a natural range of stability for weight.

SEXUAL MOTIVATION

The human sexual response

- Masters and Johnson showed that the sexual response cycle consists of four stages: excitement, plateau, orgasm, and resolution.
- Intercourse leads to orgasm in women less consistently than in men, but women are much more likely to be multiorgasmic.

Evolutionary analyses

- According to *parental investment theory*, the gender that makes the smaller investment in offspring will compete for mating opportunities with the gender that makes the larger investment, which will be more discriminating in selecting partners.
- Human males are required to invest little in offspring, so their reproductive potential is maximized by mating with as many partners as possible.
- Human females have to invest months to years in carrying and nourishing offspring, so they maximize their reproductive potential by mating with males who are able to invest more resources in their offspring.

Sexual orientation

- People tend to view heterosexuality and homosexuality as an all-or-none distinction, but it is more accurate to view them as endpoints on a continuum.
- Environmental explanations of sexual orientation have not been supported by research.
- Biological explanations have fared better in recent years, as twin studies have shown that genetic factors influence sexual orientation.
- Research also suggests that idiosyncrasies in prenatal hormonal secretions can influence sexual orientation.
- Females' sexual orientation appears to be characterized by more *plasticity* than that of males.

SOCIAL MOTIVES

Achievement motivation

- David McClelland pioneered the use of the TAT to measure individual differences in need for achievement.
- People who score high in the need for achievement tend to work harder and more persistently than others and are more likely to delay gratification.
- However, people high in the need for achievement tend to choose challenges of intermediate difficulty.
- The pursuit of achievement goals tends to increase when the probability of success on a task and the incentive value of success are higher.
- Achievement pursuits may be influenced by fear of failure.

Affiliation motivation

- Humans have a fundamental need to belong, to affiliate with others.
- Our affiliation motivation has strong evolutionary roots, promoting survival and reproductive benefits.
- Ostracism involves being ignored and excluded by the group and is frequently a result of bullying.
- Ostracism leads to a reduction in self-esteem and increased negative mood.
- Ostracism can lead to increased neural activity in parts of the brain associated with physical pain.

Gender differences in sexual activity

- Males think about sex and initiate sex more often than females do.
- Males are more willing to engage in casual sex and tend to have more partners than females do.

Gender differences in mate preferences

- Males around the world place more emphasis than females do on potential partners' youthfulness and attractiveness.
- Females around the world place more emphasis than males do on partners' status, intelligence, and financial prospects.

APPLICATIONS

- Income, age, parenthood, intelligence, and attractiveness are largely uncorrelated with happiness.
- Physical health, good social relationships, and religious convictions have a modest association with happiness.
- Stronger predictors of happiness include love and marriage, work satisfaction, and personality and genetics.
- Subjective well-being is a relative concept, and people adapt to their circumstances.
- Arguments are often marred by fallacies, such as irrelevant reasons, weak analogies, circular reasoning, slippery slope scenarios, and false dichotomies.

EMOTION

Cognitive component

- The cognitive component of emotion consists of subjective feelings that are often intense and difficult to control.
- Cognitive appraisals of events influence the emotions people experience.
- Research on *affective forecasting* shows that people are surprisingly bad at predicting the intensity and duration of their emotional reactions to events.

Physiological component

- The physiological component of emotion is dominated by autonomic arousal.
- A *polygraph* detects emotional arousal, which is far from a perfect index of lying.
- According to Joseph LeDoux, the *amygdala* lies at the core of a complex set of neural circuits that process emotion, especially fear.

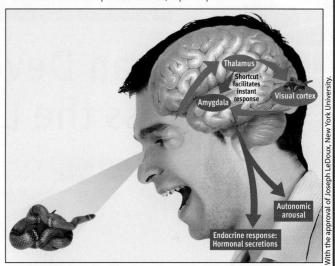

Man: © Aleksandr Kurganov/Shutterstock.com; Snake: © C. H. Wooley

With the approval of Joseph LeDoux, New York University.

Behavioural component

- At the behavioural level, emotions are revealed through body language.
- People can identify at least six emotions based on facial expressions.
- According to the *facial feedback hypothesis*, facial muscles send signals to the brain that aid in the recognition of emotions.

Cultural considerations

- Ekman and Friesen found cross-cultural agreement in the identification of emotions based on facial expressions.
- Cross-cultural similarities have also been found in the cognitive and physiological components of emotion.
- However, there are cultural disparities in how emotions are categorized and in public displays of emotions.

Theoretical views

- The *James–Lange theory* asserts that the conscious experience of emotion results from one's perception of autonomic arousal.
- The *Cannon–Bard theory* asserts that emotions originate in subcortical areas of the brain.
- According to the *two-factor theory*, people infer emotion from autonomic arousal and then label it in accordance with their cognitive explanation for the arousal.
- *Evolutionary theories of emotion* assert that emotions are innate reactions that do not depend on cognitive processes.

CHAPTER 11

Human Development across the Life Span

Themes in this Chapter

Theoretical Diversity

Sociohistorical Context

Multifactorial Causation

Cultural Heritage

Heredity & Environment

If you think about yourself now and compare yourself to how you looked and behaved ten years ago, and if you then add what has happened to you in the years in between, you would be able to generate a rather long list of the many ways in which you have changed and developed. But other things have remained the same. Your life provides an interesting illustration of the two themes that permeate the study of human development: *transition* and *continuity*. In investigating human development, psychologists study how people evolve through transitions over time. In looking at these transitions, developmental psychologists inevitably find continuity with the past.

As you grew older you undoubtedly were faced with new challenges. Some of the challenges you faced were likely quite difficult and you may have been able to talk about them with—and receive reassurance and support from—your parents or caregivers.

Their degree of involvement and parenting style affects many things, including your level of attachment. Attachment between a child and caregivers and its effects on later development are among the issues we will discuss in this chapter.

Cognitive and social–emotional development will also be a focus in this chapter. While children change dramatically in the way they think about themselves and the world, sometimes even very young children can show an amazing grasp of things. One of us had to pull his car over to the side of the road one day to catch his breath after his four-year-old son asked from the back seat, "Dad, what makes life possible?" Or consider another example, the definition recounted in a speech given in 1930 by famed Canadian artist Emily Carr when a young girl was asked about the process of creative art. When asked to describe how it's done, the young child responded, "I think, and then I draw a line round my think" (Carr, 1972, p. 8). Carr, herself a world-renowned artist, could not think of a better description of the creative process and she believed that children often grasp such things much more quickly and adequately than adults.

Even newborns and young infants have been found to show the most amazing abilities (e.g., Gopnik, 2001, 2009, 2016; Mize & Jones, 2012). Rather than being simply passive residents of their world, newborns and infants show evidence that very early they are on a journey of discovery and unfolding understanding concerning their world and those around them. On the other hand, young children frequently show misunderstanding of even simple logic. What do we know about the young child's developing sense of the social and physical general world around her or him? Research in psychology has taken us some distance toward understanding this developing theory of the world and how it works and specific characteristics of children at different ages.

Much of a child's development is the result of relatively predetermined physiological changes. We will discuss some of these in this chapter—standing, crawling, walking, and so on. The physical challenges and accomplishments facing the typical developing child are enormous. Although important, physical changes are only part of the story we focus on in this chapter. Children and their development are also affected by cultural forces, social class (Stephens, Markus, & Phillips, 2014), and social forces—forces that today may differ from those experienced by children in the past. The influence of external factors will be considered throughout this chapter.

It is not only children who are affected by changing social conditions. While it has been traditional for people like your parents to think of working to the age of 65 and then retiring, recently this idea has been challenged. Mandatory retirement at age 65 has been retired itself in most of Canada.

These types of social changes are also of interest to us in this chapter because the topic of development spans prenatal issues to adolescence, adulthood, and old age. As we see it, *development* is the sequence of age-related changes that occur as a person progresses from conception to death. It is a reasonably orderly, cumulative process that includes both the biological and behavioural changes that take place as people grow older. We'll divide the life span into four broad periods: (1) the prenatal period, between conception and birth, (2) childhood, (3) adolescence, and (4) adulthood. We'll examine aspects of development that are especially dynamic during each period. Let's begin by looking at events that occur before birth, during prenatal development.

Progress before Birth: Prenatal Development

The *prenatal period* extends from conception to birth, usually encompassing nine months of pregnancy. Significant development occurs before birth. In fact, development during the prenatal period is remarkably rapid. If you were an average-sized newborn and your physical growth had continued during the first year of your life at a prenatal pace, by your first birthday you would have weighed 90 kilograms!

Key Learning Goals

▶ Outline the major events of the three stages of prenatal development.

▶ Summarize the impact of environmental factors on prenatal development.

Fortunately, you didn't grow at that rate because in the final weeks before birth the frenzied pace of prenatal development tapers off dramatically.

In this section, we'll examine the usual course of prenatal development and discuss how environmental events can leave their mark on development even before birth exposes the newborn to the outside world.

The Course of Prenatal Development

The prenatal period is divided into three phases: (1) the germinal stage (the first two weeks), (2) the embryonic stage (two weeks to two months), and (3) the fetal stage (two months to birth). Some key developments in these phases are outlined here.

Germinal Stage

The *germinal stage* is the first phase of prenatal development, encompassing the first two weeks after conception. This brief stage begins when a zygote is created through fertilization. Within 36 hours, rapid cell division begins and the zygote becomes a microscopic mass of multiplying cells. This mass of cells slowly migrates along the mother's fallopian tube to the uterine cavity. On about the seventh day, the cell mass begins to implant itself in the uterine wall. This process takes about a week and is far from automatic. Many zygotes are rejected at this point. As many as one in five pregnancies end with the woman never being aware that conception has occurred (Simpson & Juaniaux, 2007).

During the implantation process, the placenta begins to form (Buster & Carson, 2002). The *placenta* is a structure that allows oxygen and nutrients to pass into the fetus from the mother's bloodstream, and bodily wastes to pass out to the mother. This critical exchange takes place across thin membranes that block the passage of blood cells, keeping the fetal and maternal bloodstreams separate.

Embryonic Stage

The *embryonic stage* is the second stage of prenatal development, lasting from two weeks until the end of the second month. During this stage, most of the vital organs and bodily systems begin to form in the developing organism, which is now called an *embryo*. Structures such as the heart, spine, and brain emerge gradually as cell division becomes more specialized. Although the embryo is typically only about 2.5 cm long at the end of this stage, it's already

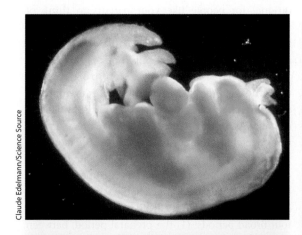

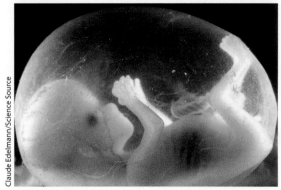

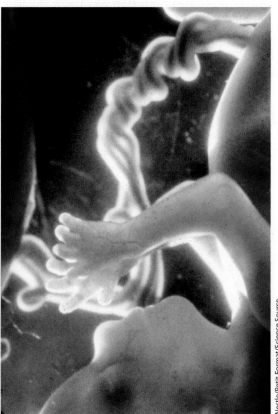

Prenatal development is remarkably rapid. (Top left) This 30-day-old embryo is just 6 mm in length. (Bottom left) At 14 weeks, the fetus is approximately 5 cm long. Note the well-developed fingers. The fetus can already move its legs, feet, hands, and head and displays a variety of basic reflexes. (Right) After four months of prenatal development, facial features are beginning to emerge.

beginning to look human. Arms, legs, hands, feet, fingers, toes, eyes, and ears are already discernible.

The embryonic stage is a period of great vulnerability because virtually all the basic physiological structures are being formed. If anything interferes with normal development during the embryonic phase, the effects can be devastating. Most miscarriages occur during this period (Simpson & Jauniaux, 2012). Most major structural birth defects also result from problems that occur during the embryonic stage (Niebyl & Simpson, 2012).

Fetal Stage

The *fetal stage* is the third stage of prenatal development, lasting from two months through birth. Some highlights of fetal development are summarized in Figure 11.1. The first two months of the fetal stage bring rapid bodily growth, as muscles and bones begin to form (Moore, Persaud, & Torchia, 2013). The developing organism, now called a *fetus*, becomes capable of physical movements as skeletal structures harden. Organs formed in the embryonic stage continue to grow and gradually begin to function. Sex organs start to develop during the third month.

During the final three months of the prenatal period, brain cells multiply at a brisk pace. A layer of fat is deposited under the skin to provide insulation, and the respiratory and digestive systems mature (Adolph & Bergen, 2011). All of these changes ready the fetus for life outside the cosy, supportive environment of its mother's womb. Sometime between 22 weeks and 26 weeks the fetus reaches the *age of viability*—the age at which a baby can survive in the event of a premature birth (Moore & Persaud, 2008).

Sometime between 23 weeks and 25 weeks, the fetus reaches the *threshold of viability*—the age at which a baby can survive in the event of a premature birth. At 23 weeks, the probability of survival is still slim (about 20 percent), but it climbs rapidly to around a 67 percent survival rate at 25 weeks (Seaton et al., 2013). Unfortunately, a great many of the premature infants born near the threshold of viability go on to experience a wide range of developmental problems (Cunningham et al., 2010).

Environmental Factors and Prenatal Development

Although the fetus develops in the protective buffer of the womb, events in the external environment can affect it indirectly through the mother. Because the developing organism and its mother are linked through the placenta, a mother's eating habits, drug use, and physical health, among other things, can affect prenatal development and have long-term health consequences (Hampton, 2004). *Teratogens are any external agents, such as drugs or viruses, that can harm an embryo or fetus.*

Maternal Drug Use

A major source of concern about fetal and infant well-being is the mother's consumption of drugs, including such widely used substances as tobacco and alcohol as well as prescription and recreational drugs. Unfortunately, most drugs consumed by a pregnant woman can pass through the membranes of the placenta.

Virtually all "recreational" drugs (see Chapter 5) can be harmful, with sedatives, narcotics, and cocaine being particularly dangerous. Babies of heroin users are born addicted to narcotics and have an increased

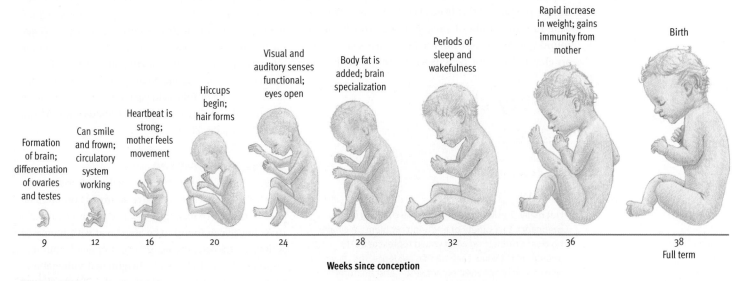

Figure 11.1
Overview of fetal development. This chart outlines some of the highlights of development during the fetal stage.

Human Development across the Life Span

risk of early death due to prematurity, birth defects, respiratory difficulties, and problems associated with their addiction (Finnegan & Kandall, 2005). Prenatal exposure to cocaine is associated with increased risk of birth complications (Sokol et al., 2007) and a variety of cognitive deficits that are apparent in childhood (Singer et al., 2002, 2004).

Problems can also be caused by a great variety of drugs prescribed for legitimate medical reasons, and even some over-the-counter drugs (Niebyl & Simpson, 2007). The impact of drugs on the embryo or fetus varies greatly depending on the drug, the dose, and the phase of prenatal development.

Alcohol consumption during pregnancy also carries risks (Lebel et al., 2010). It has long been clear that heavy drinking by a mother can be hazardous to a fetus (Popova et al., 2016; Reid et al., 2015). *Fetal alcohol syndrome disorder (FASD)* is a collection of congenital (inborn) problems associated with excessive alcohol use during pregnancy. According to figures released by Health Canada (2016), the estimates are that one in nine babies born in Canada each year are affected by FASD and that approximately 300 000 Canadians currently are living with its effects. Typical problems include microcephaly (a small head), heart defects, irritability, hyperactivity, and delayed mental and motor development (Dörrie et al., 2014). Fetal alcohol syndrome is the most common known cause of intellectual disability (Niccols, 2007), and it is related to an increased incidence of difficulties in school, depression, suicide, drug problems, and criminal behaviour in adolescence and adulthood (Kelly, Day, & Streissguth, 2000; Streissguth et al., 2004).

Furthermore, many children fall short of the criteria for fetal alcohol syndrome but still show serious impairments attributable to their mothers' drinking during pregnancy (Willford, Leech, & Day, 2006). A long-running study of pregnant women's drinking found that higher alcohol intake was associated with an elevated risk for deficits in IQ, motor skills, and

attention span, and with increased impulsive, antisocial, and delinquent behaviour (Streissguth, 2007). Clearly, even moderate drinking during pregnancy can have enduring and substantial negative effects.

Tobacco use during pregnancy is also hazardous to prenatal development (Centers for Disease Control, 2011). Smoking appears to increase a mother's risk for miscarriage, stillbirth, and prematurity, and newborns' risk for sudden infant death syndrome (Shea & Steiner, 2008). Prenatal exposure to tobacco is also associated with slower than average cognitive development, attention deficits, hyperactivity, and conduct problems, although it is difficult to tease out the causal relationships that may be at work (Button, Maughan, & McGuffin, 2007; Knopik, 2009).

Maternal Nutrition

Maternal nutrition is very important because the developing fetus needs a variety of essential nutrients. Severe maternal malnutrition increases the risk of birth complications and neurological deficits for the newborn (Coutts, 2000). The impact of moderate malnutrition is more difficult to gauge because it is often confounded with other risk factors associated with poverty, such as drug abuse and limited access to health care (Guerrini, Thomson, & Gurling, 2007).

Still, even when pregnant women have ample access to food, it is important for them to consume a balanced diet that includes essential vitamins and minerals (Monk, Georgieff, & Osterholm, 2013). Guidelines are available from Health Canada regarding eating habits designed to promote healthy maternal nutrition and for material weight gain during pregnancy (Health Canada, 2011). Too much or too little weight gain during gestation is associated with a variety of birth complications, and guidelines for maternal weight gain are based on pre-pregnancy body mass index. Health Canada suggestions include having expectant mothers follow *Canada's Food Guide* (available at http://www.hc-sc.gc.ca/fn-an/food-guide -aliment/index_e.html), having at least 150 g of cooked fish each week, taking multivitamins containing 0.4 mg of folic acid each day, and monitoring weight gain in light of Health Canada's guidelines (Health Canada, 2011).

Stress and Emotion

Recent studies suggest that maternal emotions in reaction to stressful events can have an impact on prenatal development. For example, elevated levels of prenatal stress have been found to be associated with increased stillbirths (Hogue et al., 2013), impaired immune response (Veru et al., 2014), heightened vulnerability to infectious disease (Nielsen et al., 2010), slowed motor development (Cao et al., 2014), below-average

....

reality check

Misconception

It is safe for pregnant women to engage in moderate social drinking.

Reality

Not really. Studies have linked social drinking during pregnancy to a variety of enduring problems. We have no clear evidence on what would represent a safe amount of drinking. Lacking that evidence, the only safe course of action is to completely abstain from alcohol during pregnancy.

cognitive development (Tarabulsy et al., 2014), and social deficits (Walder et al., 2014). Why is prenatal stress so harmful? Research suggests that prospective mothers' emotional reactions to stressful events can disrupt the delicate hormonal balance that fosters healthy prenatal development (Douglas, 2010).

Maternal Illness

The placenta screens out quite a number of infectious agents, but not all. Thus, many maternal illnesses can interfere with prenatal development. Diseases such as measles, rubella (German measles), syphilis, and chickenpox can be hazardous to the fetus (Bernstein, 2007); the nature of any damage depends, in part, on when the mother contracts the illness. The HIV virus that causes AIDS can also be transmitted by pregnant women to their offspring. The transmission of AIDS can occur prenatally through the placenta, during delivery, or through breastfeeding. Up through the mid-1990s, about 20–30 percent of HIV-positive pregnant women passed the virus on to their babies, but improved antiretroviral drugs (given to the mother) and more cautious obstetrical care have reduced this figure significantly (Cotter & Potter, 2006).

Environmental Toxins

Research also suggests that babies in the womb are exposed to a surprising variety of *environmental toxins* that can affect them (Houlihan et al., 2005). For example, prenatal exposure to air pollution has been linked to impairments in cognitive development at age five (Edwards et al., 2010) and increased obesity at age seven (Rundle et al., 2012). In a similar vein, exposure to the chemicals used in flame-retardant materials correlates with slower mental and physical development up through age six (Herbstman et al., 2010).

Fetal Origins of Adult Disease

Research on prenatal development has generally focused on its connection to the risk for birth defects and adverse outcomes that are apparent during early childhood. However, researchers have begun to explore the links between prenatal factors and adults' physical and mental health. Evidence suggests that events during prenatal development can "program" the fetal brain in ways that influence the person's vulnerability to various types of illness decades later (Barker, 2013; Skogen & Overland, 2012). For example, prenatal malnutrition has been linked to vulnerability to schizophrenia, which usually emerges in late adolescence or early adulthood (A. S. Brown, 2012a). Low birth weight, which is a marker for a variety of prenatal disruptions, has been found to be associated with an increased risk of heart disease many decades later in adulthood (Roseboom, de Rooij, & Painter, 2006). Studies have also linked aspects of prenatal development to adults' risk for depression and bipolar disorders (Bale et al., 2010; Talati et al., 2013), as well as obesity, diabetes, and some types of cancer (Calkins & Devaskar, 2011). These findings on the fetal origins of disease have provoked a dramatic reassessment of the factors that influence health and illness.

Science has a long way to go before it uncovers all of the factors that shape development before birth. Nonetheless, it's clear that critical developments unfold quickly during the prenatal period. In the next section, you'll learn that development continues at a fast pace during the early years of childhood. Of course, attention to maternal factors affecting the child's health continues long after birth. For example, maternal nutrition continues to affect the newborn during the breastfeeding period. Health Canada promotes breastfeeding (Health Canada, 2012) and recommends that exclusive breastfeeding be maintained up to six months, at which point the infant can be introduced to nutrient-rich, solid foods. It is recommended that breastfeeding continue up to at least two years (Health Canada, 2004). Canadian mothers seem to be following this advice; according to recent figures released by Statistics Canada, 89 percent of Canadian mothers breastfed their babies, an increase from previous years (Statistics Canada, 2015). While this figure is impressive, and it is higher than that of the United States, it still is below the rates of breastfeeding in other countries, such as Norway (95 percent) and Australia (92 percent).

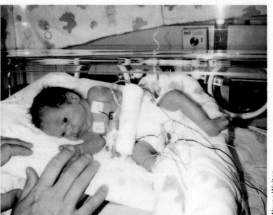

Premature births and infant deaths are much more common than most people realize. Shown here is Wayne Weiten's son, born prematurely in September 1992, receiving postnatal treatment in a hospital intensive care unit. Although prematurity is associated with a variety of developmental problems, T.J., like a great many premature infants, has matured into a robust, healthy young adult.

concept **check** 11.1

Understanding the Stages of Prenatal Development

Check your understanding of the stages of prenatal development by filling in the blanks in the chart below. The first column contains descriptions of a main event from each of the three stages. In the second column, write the name of the stage; in the third column, write the term used to refer to the developing organism during that stage; and in the fourth column, write the time span (in terms of weeks or months) covered by the stage. The answers are in Appendix A near the back of the book.

Event	Stage	Term for organism	Time span
1. Uterine implantation	_____	_____	_____
2. Muscle and bone begin to form	_____	_____	_____
3. Vital organs and body systems begin to form	_____	_____	_____

The Wondrous Years of Childhood

Key Learning Goals

▶ Understand the role of maturation and cultural variations in motor development.

▶ Describe Harlow's and Bowlby's views on attachment, and discuss research on patterns of attachment.

▶ Describe the basic tenets of Erikson's theory and his stages of childhood personality development.

▶ Describe Piaget's and Vygotsky's theories of cognitive development, and evaluate the notion that some cognitive abilities may be innate.

▶ Discuss Kohlberg's stages of moral development and criticism of his theory.

The study of infancy and early childhood has had a long history in psychology, a focus that has only increased since it has been found to influence development across the life span (Bornstein, 2014). A certain magic is associated with childhood. Young children have an extraordinary ability to captivate adults' attention, especially their parents'. Legions of parents apologize repeatedly to friends and strangers alike as they talk on and on about the cute things their kids do. Most wondrous of all are the rapid and momentous developmental changes of the childhood years. Helpless infants become curious toddlers almost overnight. Before parents can catch their breath, these toddlers show impressive problem-solving skills (Keen, 2011) and develop into school-children engaged in spirited play with young friends. Then, suddenly, they're insecure adolescents, worrying about dates, part-time jobs, cars, and university. The whirlwind transitions of childhood often seem miraculous.

Miraculous they are, but they should not be taken for granted. Developmental research not only allows us to map developmental trends and processes but also affords us the opportunity to provide supports for that development whenever possible.

While the transformations that occur in childhood *seem* magical, they actually reflect an orderly, predictable (Kagan, 2011), gradual progression. In this section you'll see what psychologists have learned about this progression. We'll examine various aspects of development that are especially dynamic during childhood. (Language development is omitted from this section because we covered it in Chapter 8.) Let's begin by looking at motor development.

Exploring the World: Motor Development

Motor development refers to the progression of muscular coordination required for physical activities. Basic motor skills include grasping and reaching for objects, manipulating objects, sitting up, crawling, walking, and running. Historically, a great deal of attention has been focused on walking, which is typically mastered around 12 months of age. One study of the transition to walking revealed that infants get an enormous amount of experience in short bursts of walking activity as they average 2368 steps and 17 falls per hour during free play (Adolph et al., 2012). Extrapolating from the hourly data suggests that infants may walk more than 14 000 steps per day, travelling the length of 46 football fields! Small wonder then that infants' walking improves rapidly.

Early motor development depends in part on physical growth, which is not only rapid during infancy but also more uneven than previously appreciated. Research has shown that in the first couple years of life, lengthy periods of no growth are punctuated by sudden bursts of growth. These growth spurts tend to be accompanied by restlessness, irritability, and increased sleep (Lampl & Johnson, 2011; Lampl, Veldhuis, & Johnson, 1992). Thus, parents who sometimes feel that their children are changing overnight may not be imagining it.

Early progress in motor skills has traditionally been attributed almost entirely to the process of maturation (Adolph & Berger, 2011). *Maturation* is development that reflects the gradual unfolding of one's genetic blueprint. It is a product of genetically programmed physical changes that come with age, rather than through experience and learning. However, research that has taken a closer look at the process of motor development suggests that infants are active agents, not passive organisms waiting for their brain and limbs to mature (Adolph & Berger, 2011; Thelen, 1995). According to this view, the driving force behind motor development is infants' ongoing exploration of their world and their need to master specific tasks (such as grasping a larger toy or looking out a window).

Understanding Developmental Norms

Parents often pay close attention to early motor development, comparing their child's progress with developmental norms. *Developmental norms* indicate the median age at which individuals display various behaviours and abilities. Developmental norms are useful benchmarks as long as parents don't expect their children to progress exactly at the pace specified in the norms. Some parents become unnecessarily alarmed when their children fall behind developmental norms, but variations from the typical age of accomplishment are entirely normal. What these parents overlook is that developmental norms are group *averages*. Variations from the average are entirely normal. This normal variation stands out in Figure 11.2, which indicates the age at which 25 percent, 50 percent, and 90 percent of youngsters can demonstrate various motor skills. As Figure 11.2 shows, a substantial portion of children often don't achieve a particular milestone until long after the average time cited in norms.

Cultural Variations and Their Significance

Cross-cultural research has highlighted the dynamic interplay between experience and maturation in motor development. Relatively rapid motor development has been observed in some cultures that provide special practice in basic motor skills (Adolph, Karasik, & Tamis-LeMonda, 2010). For example, the Kipsigis people of Kenya begin active efforts to train their infants to sit up, stand, and walk soon after birth. Thanks to this training, Kipsigis children achieve these developmental milestones (but not others) about a month earlier than babies in North America (Super, 1976). In contrast, relatively slow motor development has been found in some cultures that discourage motor exploration. For example, among the Aché, a nomadic people living in the rain forests of Paraguay, safety concerns dictate that children under three rarely venture more than a metre from their mothers, who carry them virtually everywhere. As a result of these constraints, Aché children are delayed in acquiring a variety of motor skills and typically begin walking about a year later than other children (Kaplan & Dove, 1987).

Cultural variations in the emergence of basic motor skills demonstrate that environmental factors can accelerate or slow down early motor development. Nonetheless, the similarities across cultures in the sequence and timing of early motor development outweigh the differences. This fact suggests that *early* motor development depends to

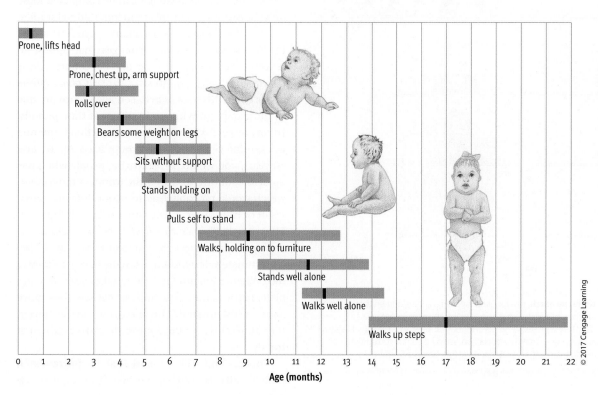

Figure 11.2
Landmarks in motor development. The left edge, interior mark, and right edge of each bar indicate the age at which 25 percent, 50 percent, and 90 percent of infants have mastered each motor skill shown. Developmental norms typically report only the median age of mastery (the interior mark), which can be misleading in light of the variability in age of mastery apparent in this chart.

Prone, lifts head
Prone, chest up, arm support
Rolls over
Bears some weight on legs
Sits without support
Stands holding on
Pulls self to stand
Walks, holding on to furniture
Stands well alone
Walks well alone
Walks up steps

0 1 2 3 4 5 6 7 8 9 10 11 12 13 14 15 16 17 18 19 20 21 22
Age (months)

© 2017 Cengage Learning

Tribes across the world use a variety of methods to foster rapid development of motor abilities in their children. The Kung San of the Kalahari, Botswana, teach their young to dance quite early, using poles to develop the kinesthetic sense of balance.

a considerable extent on maturation. *Later* motor development is another matter, however. As children in any culture grow older, they acquire more specialized motor skills, some of which may be unique to their culture.

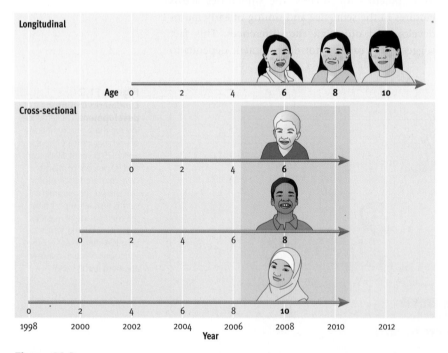

Figure 11.3

Longitudinal versus cross-sectional research. In a longitudinal study of development between ages six and ten, the same children would be observed at six, again at eight, and again at ten. In a cross-sectional study of the same age span, a group of six-year-olds, a group of eight-year-olds, and a group of ten-year-olds would be compared simultaneously. Note that data collection could be completed immediately in the cross-sectional study, whereas the longitudinal study would require four years to complete.

Source: From WEITEN. *Psychology*, 8E. © 2010 Wadsworth, a part of Cengage Learning, Inc. Reproduced by permission. www.cengage.com/permissions.

Easy and Difficult Babies: Differences in Temperament

Infants show considerable variability in temperament. *Temperament* refers to characteristic mood, activity level, and emotional reactivity. From the very beginning, some babies seem animated and cheerful while others seem sluggish and ornery. Infants show consistent differences in emotional tone, tempo of activity, and sensitivity to environmental stimuli very early in life (Martin & Fox, 2006).

Alexander Thomas and Stella Chess have conducted a major *longitudinal* study of the development of temperament (Thomas & Chess, 1977, 1989; Thomas, Chess, & Birch, 1970). In a *longitudinal design*, investigators observe one group of participants repeatedly over a period of time. This approach to the study of development is often contrasted with the cross-sectional approach (the logic of both approaches is diagrammed in Figure 11.3). In a *cross-sectional design*, investigators compare groups of participants of differing age at a single point in time. For example, in a cross-sectional study, an investigator tracing the growth of children's vocabulary might compare 50 six-year-olds, 50 eight-year-olds, and 50 ten-year-olds. In contrast, an investigator using the longitudinal method would assemble one group of 50 six-year-olds and measure their vocabulary at age six, again at age eight, and once more at age ten.

Each method has its advantages and disadvantages. Cross-sectional studies can be completed more quickly, easily, and cheaply than longitudinal studies, which often extend over many years. However, in cross-sectional studies, changes that appear to reflect development may really be cohort effects (Hartmann, Pelzel, & Abbott, 2011). *Cohort effects* occur when differences between age groups are due to the groups growing up in different time periods. For example, if you used the cross-sectional method to examine gender roles in groups aged 20, 40, and 60 years, you would be comparing people who grew up before, during, and after the women's movement, which would probably lead to major differences as a result of historical context rather than development. Thus, *longitudinal designs tend to be more sensitive to developmental changes* (Magnusson & Stattin, 1998). Unfortunately, longitudinal designs have weaknesses too. When a longitudinal study takes years to complete, participants often drop out because they move away or lose interest. The changing composition of the sample may produce misleading developmental trends.

Thomas and Chess found that "temperamental individuality is well established by the time the infant is two to three months old" (Thomas & Chess, 1977, p. 153). They identified three basic styles of temperament that were apparent in most of the children. About 40 percent of the youngsters were *easy children* who tended to be happy, regular in sleeping and eating, adaptable, and not readily upset. Another 15 percent were *slow-to-warm-up children* who tended to be less cheery, less regular in their sleeping and eating, and slower in adapting to change. These children were wary of new experiences, and their emotional reactivity was moderate. *Difficult children* constituted 10 percent of the group. They tended to be glum, erratic in sleeping and eating, resistant to change, and relatively irritable. The remaining 35 percent of the children showed mixtures of these three temperaments.

According to Chess and Thomas (1996), a child's temperament at three months was a fair predictor of the child's temperament at age ten. Infants categorized as "difficult" developed more emotional problems requiring counselling than other children did. Although basic changes in temperament were seen in some children, temperament was generally stable over time.

Individual differences in temperament appear to be influenced to a considerable degree by heredity (Rothbart & Bates, 2008). Although temperament tends to be fairly stable over time, theorists emphasize that it is *not* unchangeable (Thompson, Winer, & Goodvin, 2011). Interestingly, there appear to be some modest cultural differences in the prevalence of specific temperamental styles (Kagan, 2010). For example, an inhibited temperament is seen somewhat more frequently among Chinese children in comparison to North American children (Chen & Wang, 2010; Chen, Wang, & DeSouza, 2006). It is not clear whether this disparity is rooted in genetic differences, cultural practices, or both.

Early Emotional Development: Attachment

Infants are continually being presented with novel information about their social and nonsocial world. According to research by Canada Research Chair in Cognitive Development Valerie Kuhlmeier (Olmstead & Kuhlmeier, 2015; Robson & Kuhlmeier, 2016), very early on they are able to differentiate these two aspects of their world and to construe the actions of others in their social world as being goal-directed. The social world of babies is key to their development. What do we know about their developing emotional attachment to members of their social world, to some of those individuals with whom they share a special relationship? Do mothers and infants forge lasting emotional bonds in the

first few hours after birth? Do early emotional bonds affect later development? These are just some of the questions investigated by psychologists interested in attachment.

Attachment refers to the close, emotional bonds of affection that develop between infants and their caregivers. Researchers have shown a keen interest in how infant–mother attachments are formed early in life. While infants eventually form attachments to various significant others including fathers and grandparents, older siblings, and others (Cassidy, 2008), the first important attachment is usually with the mother, because in most cultures she is the principal caregiver, especially in the early years of life (Lamb & Lewis, 2011).

Contrary to popular belief, infants' attachment to their mothers is not instantaneous but by six to eight months of age, they show a preference for her and protest when separated from her (Lamb, Ketterlinus, & Fracasso, 1992). This is the first manifestation of *separation anxiety*—emotional distress seen in many infants when they are separated from people with whom they have formed an attachment. Separation anxiety, which may occur with fathers and other familiar caregivers as well as with mothers, typically peaks at around 14 to 18 months and then begins to decline.

reality check

Misconception

A strong attachment relationship depends on infant-mother bonding during the first few hours after birth.

Reality

Bonding immediately after birth can be a magical moment for mothers and probably should be encouraged for their sake. But there is no empirical evidence that this practice leads to healthier attachment relationships in the long run.

Theories of Attachment

Initially, behaviourists argued that this special attachment between infant and mother develops because mothers are associated with the powerful, reinforcing event of being fed. Thus, the mother becomes a conditioned reinforcer. Many mothers would likely argue that there is more to this attachment than simple reinforcement. This view was supported by Harry Harlow's famous studies of attachment in infant rhesus monkeys (Harlow, 1958, 1959).

Harlow removed monkeys from their mothers at birth and raised them in the laboratory with two types of artificial "substitute mothers." One type of artificial

Courtesy of Valerie Kuhlmeier

Valerie Kuhlmeier is a Canada Research Chair in Cognitive Development in the Department of Psychology at Queen's University. She does research on infants' cognitive abilities, social perception, and inferences about the mental states of other humans. You can learn more about her research by visiting her Infant Cognition Group website at http://www.infantcognitiongroup.com.

Photo by Nina Leen/The LIFE Picture Collection/Getty Images

Even if fed by a wire surrogate mother, Harlow's infant monkeys cuddled up with a terry cloth surrogate that provided contact comfort. When threatened by a frightening toy, the monkeys sought security from their terry cloth mothers.

Mary Salter Ainsworth

"Where familial security is lacking, the individual is handicapped by the lack of what might be called a secure base from which to work."

Courtesy of Dr. Erik Hesse

mother was made of terry cloth and could provide contact comfort. The other type of artificial mother was made of wire. Half of the monkeys were fed from a bottle attached to a wire mother and the other half were fed by a cloth mother. The young monkeys' attachment to their substitute mothers was tested by introducing a frightening stimulus, such as a strange toy. If reinforcement through feeding were the key to attachment, the frightened monkeys should have scampered off to the mother that had fed them. This was not the case. The young monkeys scrambled for their cloth mothers, even if they were *not* fed by them.

Harlow's work made a simple reinforcement explanation of attachment unrealistic for animals, let alone for more complex human beings. Attention then turned to an alternative explanation of attachment proposed by John Bowlby (1969, 1973, 1980). Bowlby was impressed by the importance of contact comfort to Harlow's monkeys and by the apparently unlearned nature of this preference. Influenced by evolutionary theories, Bowlby argued that there must be a biological basis for attachment. According to his view, infants are biologically programmed to emit behaviour (smiling, cooing, clinging, and so on) that triggers an affectionate, protective response from adults.

Bowlby also asserted that adults are programmed by evolutionary forces to be captivated by this behaviour and to respond with warmth, love, and protection. Obviously, these characteristics would be adaptive in terms of promoting children's survival. Attachment theory has had an evolutionary slant from its very beginning, long before evolutionary theory became influential in psychology. While John Bowlby (1969, 1973, 1980) analyzed attachment in terms of its *survival value* for infants, contemporary evolutionary theorists emphasize how attachment contributes to parents' and children's *reproductive fitness* (Belsky, Steinberg, & Draper, 1991; Chisholm, 1996; Simpson, 1999). For example, contemporary theorists point out that if parents expect to pass their genes on to future generations, they need to raise their offspring to reproductive age and help them develop the social maturity required for successful mating. Parent–child attachments make crucial contributions to these outcomes by fostering social and emotional development in children (Kobak, 1999).

Bowlby's theory has guided most of the research on attachment over the last several decades, including Mary Salter Ainsworth's influential work on patterns of attachment, which we discuss next.

Patterns of Attachment

Research by Ainsworth and her colleagues (Ainsworth, 1979; Ainsworth et al., 1978) suggests that attachment emerges out of a complex interplay between infant and mother. (You may recall that Mary Salter Ainsworth was one of the three women pioneers in Canadian psychology profiled in Chapter 1.) Ainsworth used a method called the *strange situation procedure*, in which infants are exposed to a series of eight separation and reunion episodes to assess the quality of their attachment. The three-minute episodes in this carefully orchestrated laboratory procedure involve events such as a stranger entering a room where an infant is playing with a parent nearby, followed by the parent leaving, returning, leaving, and returning again. The child's reactions (distress, comfort) to the parent's departures and returns are carefully monitored to gauge attachment quality.

Infant–mother attachments vary in quality. Ainsworth and her colleagues (1978) found that these attachments follow three patterns (see Figure 11.4). Fortunately, most infants develop a *secure attachment*. They play and explore comfortably with their mother present, become visibly upset when she leaves, and are quickly calmed by her return. However, some children display a pattern called *anxious-ambivalent attachment*. They appear anxious even when their mother is near

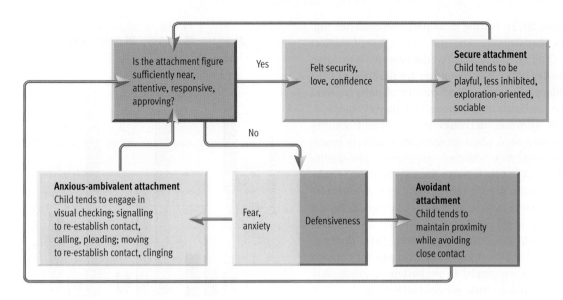

Figure 11.4
Overview of the attachment process. The unfolding of attachment depends on the interaction between a mother (or other caregiver) and an infant. Research by Mary Salter Ainsworth and others suggests that attachment relationships fall into three categories—secure, avoidant, and anxious-ambivalent—that depend on how sensitive and responsive caregivers are to their children's needs. The feedback loops shown in the diagram reflect the fact that babies are not passive bystanders in the attachment drama; their reactions to caregivers can affect the caregivers' behaviour.

Source: WEBER, ANN L.; HARVEY, JOHN H., PERSPECTIVES ON CLOSE RELATIONSHIPS, 1st Ed., © 1994. Reprinted by permission of Pearson Education, Inc., New York, New York.

and protest excessively when she leaves, but they are not particularly comforted when she returns. Children in the third category seek little contact with their mother and often are not distressed when she leaves, a condition labelled *avoidant attachment.* Years later, other researchers added a fourth category called *disorganized-disoriented* attachment (Main & Solomon, 1986, 1990). These children appear confused about whether they should approach or avoid their mother and are especially insecure (Lyons-Ruth & Jacobvitz, 2008).

Maternal behaviours appear to have considerable influence on the type of attachment that emerges between an infant and mother (Ainsworth et al., 1978; Posada et al., 2007). Sensitivity is particularly important (Posada et al., 2007; Thompson, 2013); mothers who are sensitive and responsive to their children's needs are more likely to promote secure attachments than mothers who are relatively insensitive or inconsistent in their responding (Easterbrooks, 2013). However, infants also have an important role to play as this process unfolds. They are active participants who influence the process with their crying, smiling, fussing, and babbling, and difficult infants slow the process of attachment (van IJzendoorn & Bakermans-Kranenburg, 2004). Thus, the type of attachment that emerges between an infant and mother may depend on the nature of the infant's temperament as well as the mother's sensitivity (Kagan & Fox, 2006).

Evidence suggests that the quality of the attachment relationship can have important consequences (Ein-Dor & Hirschberger, 2016; Yip, Ehrhardt, Black, & Walker, 2017), especially for children's subsequent development. The repercussions of attachment patterns in infancy appear to reach even into adulthood (Cassidy & Shaver, 1999; Mikulincer & Shaver, 2007; Sadikaj, Moskowitz, & Zuroff, 2011). In Chapter 13, we'll discuss thought-provoking evidence that infant attachment patterns set the tone for people's romantic relationships in adulthood, not to mention their gender roles, religious beliefs, and patterns of self-disclosure (Feeney, 2008; Kirkpatrick, 2005; Mikulincer & Shaver, 2007; Shaver & Mikulincer, 2009).

Infant–mother attachments vary in strength and quality and these variations in attachment relationships may have long-lasting repercussions. In this picture, Doug McCann's son Harry is seen interacting with his mother.

Day-Care and Attachment

Day-care is a common experience for many Canadian children, with almost one-half of Canadian parents reporting that they rely on some form of child care (Sinha, 2015). The impact of day-care on attachment has been the subject of some debate. The crucial question is whether frequent infant-mother separations might disrupt the attachment process

(Berlin, 2012). For the most part, the evidence suggests that day-care does not have a harmful effect on children's attachment relationships (Friedman & Boyle, 2008). When mothers are sensitive to their children, the amount and quality of day-care tend to be unrelated to attachment security (Thompson, 2008). However, decreases in attachment security have been seen when mothers are relatively insensitive and their children experience low-quality day-care (Vermeer & Bakermans-Kranenburg, 2008). Some studies suggest that infants with a "difficult" temperament may be particularly vulnerable to the potential negative effects of low-quality day-care (Burchinal, Lowe Vandell, & Belsky, 2014; Pluess & Belsky, 2010). So, there may be reasons for concern about children placed in understaffed, low-quality day-care who get little personal attention.

Culture and Attachment

Separation anxiety emerges in children at about six to eight months and peaks at about 14 to 18 months in cultures around the world (Grossmann & Grossmann, 1990). These findings, which have been replicated in quite a variety of non-Western cultures, suggest that attachment is a universal feature of human development. However, studies have found some modest cultural variations in the proportion of infants who fall into the three attachment categories described by Ainsworth. Working mostly with white, middle-class subjects in the United States, researchers have found that 67 percent of infants display a secure attachment, 21 percent an avoidant attachment, and 12 percent an anxious-ambivalent attachment (the fourth attachment pattern mentioned earlier is not included here because it has been tracked in only a minority of cross-cultural studies) (van IJzendoorn & Sagi-Schwartz, 2008). Studies in Japan and Germany have yielded somewhat different estimates of the prevalence of various types of attachment, as shown in Figure 11.5. That said, the differences are small and secure attachment appears to be the predominant type of attachment around the world.

Personality Development in Childhood

Many other aspects of development are especially dynamic during childhood. In this section we'll examine personality development. We will begin with a look at the work of Erik Erikson and introduce the concept of developmental stages.

How do individuals develop their unique constellations of personality traits over time? Many theories

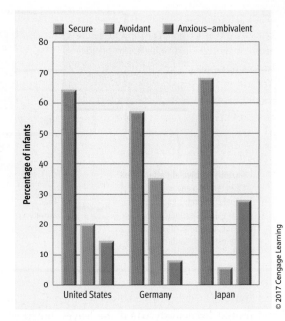

Figure 11.5
Cultural variations in attachment patterns. This graph shows the distribution of the three original attachment patterns found in specific studies in Germany, Japan, and the United States. As you can see, secure attachment is the most common pattern in all three societies, as it is around the world. However, there are some modest cultural differences in the prevalence of each pattern of attachment, which are probably attributable to cultural variations in child-rearing practices. (Data from van IJzendoorn & Krooneberg, 1988).

have addressed this question. The first major theory of personality development was put together by Sigmund Freud back around 1900. As we'll discuss in Chapter 12, he claimed that the basic foundation of an individual's personality is firmly laid down by age five. Half a century later, Erik Erikson (1963) proposed a sweeping revision of Freud's theory that has proven influential. Like Freud, Erikson concluded that events in early childhood leave a permanent stamp on adult personality. However, unlike Freud, Erikson theorized that personality continues to evolve over the entire life span.

Building on Freud's earlier work, Erikson devised a stage theory of personality development. As you'll see in reading this chapter, many theories describe development in terms of stages. A *stage* is a developmental period during which characteristic patterns of behaviour are exhibited and certain capacities become established. Stage theories assume that (1) individuals must progress through specified stages in a particular order because each stage builds on the previous stage, (2) progress through these stages is strongly related to age, and (3) development is marked by major discontinuities that usher in dramatic transitions in behaviour (see Figure 11.6).

Erikson's Stage Theory

Erikson partitioned the life span into eight stages, each of which brings a *psychosocial crisis* involving transitions in important social relationships. According to Erikson, personality is shaped by how individuals deal with these psychosocial crises. Each crisis involves a struggle between two opposing tendencies, such as trust versus mistrust or initiative versus guilt, both of which are experienced by the person. Erikson described the stages in terms of these antagonistic tendencies, which represent personality traits that people display in varying degrees over the remainder of their lives. Although the names for Erikson's stages suggest either–or outcomes, he viewed each stage as a tug of war that determined the subsequent *balance* between opposing polarities in personality. All eight stages in Erikson's theory are charted in Figure 11.7. We describe the first four childhood stages here and discuss the remaining stages in the upcoming sections on adolescence and adulthood.

Trust versus Mistrust. Erikson's first stage encompasses the first year of life, when an infant has to depend completely on adults to take care of its basic needs for such necessities as food, a warm blanket, and changed diapers. If an infant's basic biological needs are adequately met by his or her caregivers and sound attachments are formed, the child should develop an optimistic, trusting attitude toward the world. However, if the infant's basic needs are taken care of poorly, a more distrusting, pessimistic personality may result.

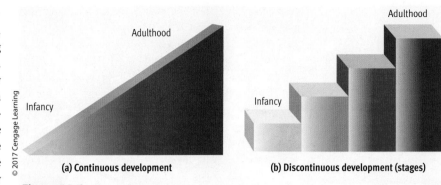

© 2017 Cengage Learning

(a) Continuous development

(b) Discontinuous development (stages)

Figure 11.6
Stage theories of development. Some theories view development as a relatively continuous process, albeit not as smooth and perfectly linear as depicted on the left. In contrast, stage theories assume that development is marked by major discontinuities (as shown on the right) that bring fundamental, qualitative changes in capabilities or characteristic behaviour.

Autonomy versus Shame and Doubt. Erikson's second stage unfolds during the second and third years of life, when parents begin toilet training and other efforts to regulate the child's behaviour. The child must begin to take some personal responsibility for feeding, dressing, and bathing. If all goes well, he or she acquires a sense of self-sufficiency. But, if parents are never satisfied with the child's efforts and there are constant parent–child conflicts, the child may develop a sense of personal shame and self-doubt.

Initiative versus Guilt. In Erikson's third stage, lasting roughly from ages three to six, children experiment and take initiatives that may sometimes conflict with their parents' rules. Overcontrolling

© Ted Streshinsky/CORBIS

Erik Erikson

"Human personality in principle develops according to steps predetermined in the growing person's readiness to be driven toward, to be aware of, and to interact with a widening social radius."

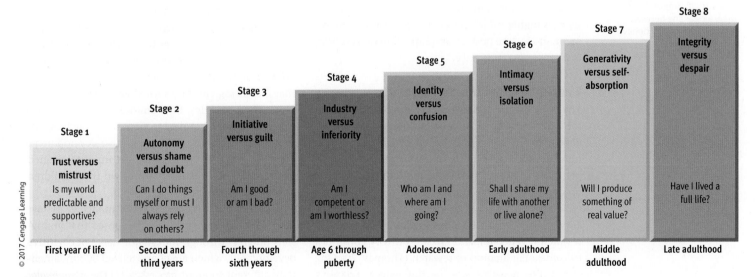

© 2017 Cengage Learning

Figure 11.7
Erikson's stage theory. Erikson's theory of personality development posits that people evolve through eight stages over the life span. Each stage is marked by a *psychosocial crisis* that involves confronting a fundamental question, such as "Who am I and where am I going?" The stages are described in terms of alternative traits that are potential outcomes from the crises. Development is enhanced when a crisis is resolved in favour of the healthier alternative (which is listed first for each stage).

According to Erik Erikson, school-age children face the challenge of learning how to function in social situations outside of their family, especially with peers and at school. If they succeed, they will develop a sense of competence; if they fail, they may feel inferior.

Jean Piaget

"It is virtually impossible to draw a clear line between innate and acquired behaviour patterns."

parents may begin to instill feelings of guilt, and self-esteem may suffer. Parents need to support their children's emerging independence while maintaining appropriate controls. In the ideal situation, children will retain their sense of initiative while learning to respect the rights and privileges of other family members.

Industry versus Inferiority. In the fourth stage (age six through puberty), the challenge of learning to function socially is extended beyond the family to the broader social realm of the neighbourhood and school. Children who are able to function effectively in this less nurturant social sphere where productivity is highly valued should learn to value achievement and to take pride in accomplishment, resulting in a sense of competence.

Evaluating Erikson's Theory

The strength of Erikson's theory is that it accounts for both continuity and transition in personality development. It accounts for transition by showing how new challenges in social relationships stimulate personality development throughout life. It accounts for continuity by drawing connections between early childhood experiences and aspects of adult personality. One measure of a theory's value is how much research it generates, and Erikson's theory continues to guide a fair amount of research (Thomas, 2005).

On the negative side of the ledger, Erikson's theory has depended heavily on illustrative case studies, which are open to varied interpretations (Thomas, 2005). Another weakness is that the theory

provides an "idealized" description of "typical" developmental patterns. Thus, it's not well suited for explaining the enormous personality differences that exist among people. Inadequate explanation of individual differences is a common problem with stage theories of development. This shortcoming surfaces again in the next section, where we'll examine Jean Piaget's stage theory of cognitive development.

The Growth of Thought: Cognitive Development

Cognitive development refers to transitions in youngsters' patterns of thinking, including reasoning, remembering, and problem solving. The investigation of cognitive development was dominated in most of the second half of the 20th century by the theory of Jean Piaget (Kessen, 1996) and there is no doubt that questions related to cognitive development continue to predominate in developmental psychology (e.g., Klahr & Chen, 2011). Much of our discussion of cognitive development is devoted to Piaget's theory and the research it generated, although we'll also delve into other approaches to cognitive development.

Overview of Piaget's Stage Theory

Jean Piaget (1929, 1952, 1970, 1983) was an interdisciplinary scholar whose own cognitive development was exceptionally rapid. In his early 20s, after he had earned a doctorate in natural science and published a novel, Piaget's interest turned to psychology. He met Theodore Simon, who had collaborated with Alfred Binet in devising the first useful intelligence tests (see Chapter 9). Working in Simon's Paris laboratory, Piaget administered intelligence tests to many children to develop better test norms. In doing this testing, Piaget became intrigued by the reasoning underlying the children's *wrong* answers. He decided that measuring children's intelligence was less interesting than studying how children *use* their intelligence. In 1921, he moved to Geneva, where he spent the rest of his life studying cognitive development. Many of his ideas were based on insights gleaned from careful observations of his own three children during their infancy.

Like Erikson's theory, Piaget's model is a *stage theory* of development. Piaget proposed that youngsters progress through four major stages of cognitive development, which are characterized by fundamentally different thought processes: (1) the *sensorimotor period* (birth to age two), (2) the *preoperational period* (ages two to seven), (3) the *concrete operational period* (ages 7 to 11), and (4) the *formal operational period*

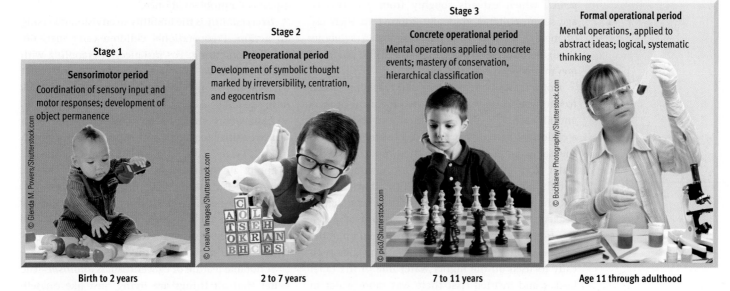

Stage 1	Stage 2	Stage 3	Stage 4
Sensorimotor period Coordination of sensory input and motor responses; development of object permanence	**Preoperational period** Development of symbolic thought marked by irreversibility, centration, and egocentrism	**Concrete operational period** Mental operations applied to concrete events; mastery of conservation, hierarchical classification	**Formal operational period** Mental operations, applied to abstract ideas; logical, systematic thinking
Birth to 2 years	2 to 7 years	7 to 11 years	Age 11 through adulthood

Figure 11.8

Piaget's stage theory. Piaget's theory of cognitive development identifies four stages marked by fundamentally different modes of thinking through which youngsters evolve. The approximate age norms and some key characteristics of thought at each stage are summarized here.

© 2017 Cengage Learning

(age 11 onward). Figure 11.8 provides an overview of each of these periods. Piaget regarded his age norms as approximations and acknowledged that transitional ages may vary, but he was convinced that all children progress through the stages of cognitive development in the same order.

Noting that children actively explore the world around them, Piaget asserted that interaction with the environment and maturation gradually alter the way children think. According to Piaget, children progress in their thinking through the complementary processes of assimilation and accommodation. *Assimilation* involves interpreting new experiences in terms of existing mental structures without changing them. In contrast, accommodation involves changing existing mental structures to explain new experiences. Accommodation and assimilation often occur interactively. For instance, a child who has learned to call four-legged pets "puppies" may apply this scheme the first time she encounters a cat (assimilation), but she will eventually discover that puppies and cats are different types of animals and make adjustments to her mental schemes (accommodation). With the companion processes of assimilation and accommodation in mind, let's turn now to the four stages in Piaget's theory.

Sensorimotor Period. One of Piaget's foremost contributions was to greatly enhance our understanding of mental development in the earliest

months of life. The first stage in his theory is the *sensorimotor period*, which lasts from birth to about age two. Piaget called this stage *sensorimotor* because infants are developing the ability to coordinate their sensory input with their motor actions.

The major development during the sensorimotor stage is the gradual appearance of symbolic thought. At the beginning of this stage, a child's behaviour is dominated by innate reflexes. But by the end of the stage, the child can use mental symbols to represent objects (e.g., a mental image of a favourite toy). The key to this transition is the acquisition of the concept of object permanence.

Object permanence develops when a child recognizes that objects continue to exist even when they are no longer visible. Although you surely take the permanence of objects for granted, infants aren't aware of this permanence at first. If you show a four-month-old an eye-catching toy and then cover the toy with a pillow, the child will not attempt to search for the toy. Piaget inferred from this observation that the child does not understand that the toy continues to exist under the pillow. The notion of object permanence does not dawn on children overnight. The first signs of this insight usually appear between four and eight months of age, when children will often pursue an object that is *partially* covered in their presence. Progress is gradual, and Piaget believed that children typically don't master the concept of object permanence until they're about 18 months old.

Human Development across the Life Span

Preoperational Period. During the *preoperational period*, which extends roughly from age two to age seven, children gradually improve in their use of mental images. Although progress in symbolic thought continues, Piaget emphasized the *shortcomings* in preoperational thought.

Consider a simple problem that Piaget presented to youngsters. He would take two identical beakers and fill each with the same amount of water. After a child had agreed that the two beakers contained the same amount of water, he would pour the water from one of the beakers into a much taller and thinner beaker (see Figure 11.9). He would then ask the child whether the two differently shaped beakers still contained the same amount of water. Confronted with a problem like this, children in the preoperational period generally said no. They typically focused on the higher water line in the taller beaker and insisted that there was more water in the slender beaker. They had not yet mastered the principle of conservation. *Conservation* is Piaget's term for the awareness that physical quantities remain constant in spite of changes in their shape or appearance.

Why are preoperational children unable to solve conservation problems? According to Piaget, their inability to understand conservation is due to some basic flaws in preoperational thinking. These flaws include centration, irreversibility, and egocentrism.

Centration is the tendency to focus on just one feature of a problem, neglecting other important aspects. When working on the conservation problem with water, preoperational children tend to concentrate on the height of the water while ignoring the width. They have difficulty focusing on several aspects of a problem at once.

Irreversibility is the inability to envision reversing an action. Preoperational children can't mentally "undo" something. For instance, in grappling with the conservation of water, they don't think about what would happen if the water was poured back from the tall beaker into the original beaker.

Egocentrism in thinking is characterized by a limited ability to share another person's viewpoint. Indeed, Piaget felt that preoperational children fail to appreciate that there are points of view other than their own. For instance, if you ask a preoperational girl whether her sister has a sister, she'll probably say no if they are the only two girls in the family. She's unable to view sisterhood from her sister's perspective (this also shows irreversibility).

A notable feature of egocentrism is *animism*—the belief that all things are living, just like oneself. Thus, youngsters attribute lifelike, human qualities to inanimate objects, asking questions such as "When does the ocean stop to rest?" or "Why does the wind get so mad?"

As you can see, Piaget emphasized the weaknesses apparent in preoperational thought. Indeed, that is why he called this stage *pre*operational. The ability to perform *operations*—internal transformations, manipulations, and reorganizations of mental structures—emerges in the next stage.

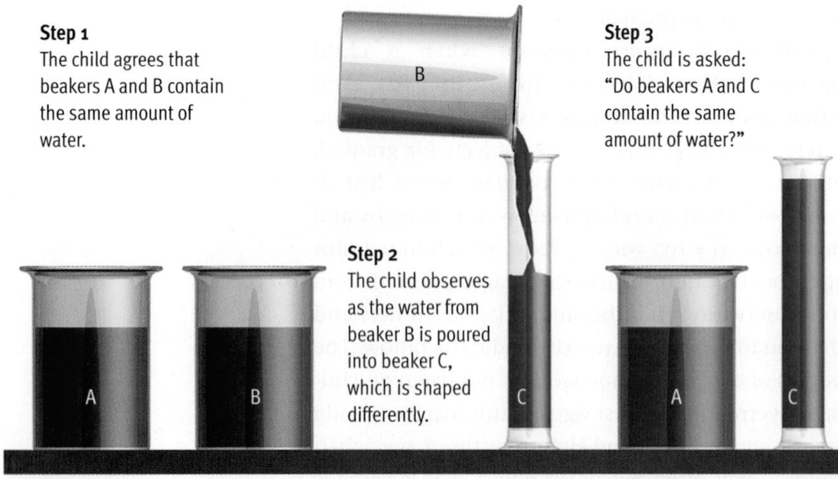

Concrete Operational Period. The development of mental operations marks the beginning of the *concrete operational period*, which usually lasts from about age 7 to age 11. Piaget called this stage *concrete operations* because children can perform operations only on images of tangible objects and actual events.

Among the operations that children master during this stage are reversibility and decentration. *Reversibility* permits a child to mentally undo an action. *Decentration* allows the child to focus on more than one feature of a problem simultaneously. The newfound ability to coordinate several aspects of a problem helps the child appreciate that there are several ways to look at things. This ability in turn leads to a *decline in egocentrism* and *gradual mastery of conservation* as it applies to liquid, mass, number, volume, area, and length (see Figure 11.10).

As children master concrete operations, they develop a variety of new problem-solving capacities. Let's examine another problem studied by Piaget. Give a preoperational child seven carnations and three daisies. Tell the child the names for the two types of flowers and ask the child to sort them into carnations and daisies. That should be no problem. Now ask the child whether there are more

Step 1
The child agrees that beakers A and B contain the same amount of water.

Step 2
The child observes as the water from beaker B is poured into beaker C, which is shaped differently.

Step 3
The child is asked: "Do beakers A and C contain the same amount of water?"

© 2017 Cengage Learning

Figure 11.9
Piaget's conservation task. After watching the transformation shown, a preoperational child will usually answer that the taller beaker contains more water. In contrast, the child in the concrete operational period tends to respond correctly, recognizing that the amount of water in beaker C remains the same as the amount in beaker A.

Typical age of mastery	Age 6–7		Age 7–8		Age 7–8		Age 8–9	
	Conservation of number		Conservation of mass		Conservation of length		Conservation of area	
Typical tasks used to measure conservation	Two equivalent rows of objects are shown to the child, who agrees that they have the same number of objects.	One row is lengthened, and the child is asked whether one row has more objects.	The child acknowledges that two clay balls have equal amounts of clay.	The experimenter changes the shape of one of the balls and asks the child whether they still contain equal amounts of clay.	The child agrees that two sticks aligned with each other are the same length.	After moving one stick to the left or right, the experimenter asks the child whether the sticks are of equal length.	Two identical sheets of cardboard have wooden blocks placed on them in identical positions; the child confirms that the same amount of space is left on each piece of cardboard.	The experimenter scatters the blocks on one piece of cardboard and again asks the child whether the two pieces have the same amount of unoccupied space.

Figure 11.10

The gradual mastery of conservation. Children master conservation during the concrete operational period, but their mastery is gradual. As outlined here, children usually master the conservation of number at age six or seven, but they may not understand the conservation of area until age eight or nine.

Source: From Weiten. *Cengage Advantage Books: Psychology*, 9E. © 2013 South-Western, a part of Cenfgage, Inc. Reproduced by permission. www.cengage.com/permissions

carnations or more daisies. Most children will correctly respond that there are more carnations. Now ask the child whether there are more carnations or more flowers. At this point, most preoperational children will stumble and respond incorrectly that there are more carnations than flowers. Generally, preoperational children can't handle *hierarchical classification* problems that require them to focus simultaneously on two levels of classification. However, the child who has advanced to the concrete operational stage is not as limited by centration and can work successfully with hierarchical classification problems.

Formal Operational Period. The final stage in Piaget's theory is the *formal operational period,* which typically begins around 11 years of age. In this stage, children begin to apply their operations to *abstract* concepts in addition to concrete objects. Indeed, during this stage, youngsters come to *enjoy* the heady contemplation of abstract concepts. Many adolescents spend hours mulling over hypothetical possibilities related to abstractions such as justice, love, and free will.

According to Piaget, youngsters graduate to relatively adult modes of thinking in the formal operations stage. He did *not* mean to suggest that no further cognitive development occurs once children reach this stage. However, he believed that after children achieve formal operations, further developments in

thinking are changes in *degree* rather than fundamental changes in the *nature* of thinking.

Adolescents in the formal operational period become more *systematic* in their problem-solving efforts. Children in earlier developmental stages tend to attack problems quickly, with a trial-and-error approach. In contrast, children who have achieved formal operations are more likely to think things through. They envision possible courses of action and try to use logic to reason out the likely consequences of each possible solution before they act. Thus, thought processes in the formal operational period can be characterized as abstract, systematic, logical, and reflective.

Evaluating Piaget's Theory

Jean Piaget made a landmark contribution to psychology's understanding of children in general and their cognitive development in particular (Beilin, 1992). Piaget's theory guided an enormous volume of productive research that continues through today (Feldman, 2013). This research has supported many of Piaget's central ideas (Flavell, 1996). In such a far-reaching theory, however, there are bound to be some weak spots. Here are some criticisms of Piaget's theory:

1. In many aspects, Piaget appears to have underestimated young children's cognitive development (Birney et al., 2005). For example, researchers have

Lev Vygotsky

Lev Vygotsky was a Russian developmental psychologist who highlighted, among other things, the contribution of the social context, culture, and social interaction to the cognitive development of children.

found evidence that children understand object permanence and are capable of some symbolic thought much earlier than Piaget thought (Birney & Sternberg, 2011). Similarly, some evidence suggests that preoperational children are not as egocentric as Piaget believed (Moll & Meltzoff, 2011).

2. Another problem is that children often simultaneously display patterns of thinking that are characteristic of several stages. This "mixing" of stages and the fact that the transitions between stages are gradual rather than abrupt call into question the value of organizing cognitive development in terms of stages (Bjorklund, 2012). Progress in children's thinking appears to occur in overlapping waves rather than distinct stages with clear boundaries.

3. Piaget believed that his theory described universal processes that should lead children everywhere to progress through uniform stages of thinking at roughly the same ages. Subsequent research has shown that the sequence of stages is largely invariant, but the timetable that children follow in passing through these stages varies considerably across cultures (Molitor & Hsu, 2011; Rogoff, 2003). Thus, Piaget underestimated the influence of cultural factors on cognitive development.

concept **check** 11.2

Recognizing Piaget's Stages

Check your understanding of Piaget's theory by indicating the stage of cognitive development illustrated by each of the examples below. For each scenario, fill in the letter for the appropriate stage in the space on the left. The answers are in Appendix A near the back of the book.

    A. Sensorimotor period
    B. Preoperational period
    C. Concrete operational period
    D. Formal operational period

_____**1.** Upon seeing a glass lying on its side, Sammy says, "Look, the glass is tired. It's taking a nap."

_____**2.** Maria is told that a farmer has nine cows and six horses. The teacher asks, "Does the farmer have more cows or more animals?" Maria answers, "More animals."

_____**3.** Alice is playing in the living room with a small red ball. The ball rolls under the sofa. She stares for a moment at the place where the ball vanished and then turns her attention to a toy truck sitting in front of her.

Vygotsky's Sociocultural Theory

In recent decades, as the limitations and weaknesses of Piaget's ideas have become more apparent, some developmental researchers have looked elsewhere for theoretical guidance. Ironically, the theory that has recently inspired the greatest interest—Lev Vygotsky's sociocultural theory—dates back to around the same time that Piaget began formulating his theory in the 1920s and 1930s. Vygotsky was a prominent Russian psychologist whose research ended prematurely in 1934 when he died of tuberculosis at the age of 37. Western scientists had little exposure to his ideas until the 1960s, and it was only in 1986 that a complete version of his principal book, *Thought and Language* (Vygotsky, 1934), was published in English. His theory has become and continues to be very influential (Clarà, 2017).

Vygotsky's and Piaget's perspectives on cognitive development have much in common, but they also differ in several important respects (Lourenco, 2012). First, in Piaget's theory, cognitive development is primarily fuelled by individual children's active exploration of the world around them. The child is viewed as the agent of change. In contrast, Vygotsky places enormous emphasis on how children's cognitive development is fuelled by social interactions with parents, teachers, and older children who can provide invaluable guidance. Second, Piaget viewed cognitive development as a universal process that should unfold in largely the same way across widely disparate cultures. Vygotsky, on the other hand, asserted that culture exerts great influence over how cognitive growth unfolds (Wertsch & Tulviste, 2005) so that cognitive development may not be universal as assumed in Piaget's theory. For Vygotsky, culture is a critical factor in how cognitive development unfolds. For example, the cognitive skills acquired in literate cultures that rely on schools for training will differ from those skills acquired in tribal societies with no formal schooling. Third, Piaget viewed children's gradual mastery of language as just another aspect of cognitive development, whereas Vygotsky argued that language acquisition plays a crucial, central role in fostering cognitive development (Kozulin, 2005). In fact, language and communication are seen to be crucial since cognitive development is affected by the information shared during cooperative activities with able partners.

According to Vygotsky, children acquire most of their culture's cognitive skills and problem-solving strategies through collaborative dialogues with more experienced members of their society. Vygotsky's emphasis on the primacy of language is reflected in his discussion of *private speech*. Preschool children talk aloud to themselves a lot as they go about their activities. Piaget viewed this speech as egocentric and insignificant. Vygotsky argued that children use this private speech to plan their strategies, regulate their actions, and accomplish their goals. As children grow older, this private speech is internalized and becomes the normal verbal dialogue that people have with themselves as they go about their business. Thus, language increasingly serves as the *foundation* for youngsters' cognitive processes.

He saw cognitive development as more like an *apprenticeship* than a journey of individual discovery. His emphasis on the social origins of cognitive development is apparent in his theoretical concepts, such as the *zone of proximal development* and *scaffolding*.

The zone of proximal development (ZPD) is the gap between what a learner can accomplish alone and what he or she can achieve with guidance from more skilled partners. The ZPD for a task is the area in which new cognitive growth is likely and the area that should be the focus of instructional efforts. These efforts are more likely to be helpful when an instructor practises scaffolding: Scaffolding facilitates learning (Plumert & Nichols-Whitehead, 1996). *Scaffolding* occurs when the assistance provided to a child is adjusted as learning progresses. Typically, less and less help is provided as a child's competence on a task increases.

Vygotsky's sociocultural theory is guiding a great deal of contemporary research on cognitive development (Feldman, 2003). This research has provided empirical support for many of Vygotsky's ideas (Rogoff, 1998; Winsler, 2003). Like Piaget's theory, Vygotsky's perspective promises to enrich our understanding of how children's thinking develops and matures (Veer, 2007). Vygotsky's theory continues to impact contemporary thinking about development and education (Allahayar & Nazari, 2012; Swain, Kinnear, & Steinman, 2011).

Are Some Cognitive Abilities Innate?

The frequent finding that Piaget underestimated infants' cognitive abilities has led to a rash of research suggesting that infants have a surprising grasp of many complex concepts. The new findings have been made possible by some innovative research methods that permit investigators to draw inferences about the abilities of very young children. Many studies have made use of the *habituation–dishabituation paradigm*. *Habituation* is a gradual reduction in the strength of a response when a stimulus event is presented repeatedly. If you show infants the same event over and over (e.g., an object dropping onto a platform), they habituate to it—their heart and respiration rates decline and they spend less time looking at the stimulus. *Dishabituation* occurs if a new stimulus

elicits an increase in the strength of a habituated response. Patterns of dishabituation can give researchers insights into what types of events infants can tell apart, which events surprise or interest them, and which events violate their expectations.

Working mostly with the habituation–dishabituation paradigm, researchers have discovered that infants understand basic properties of objects and some of the rules that govern them (Baillargeon, 2002, 2004). At three to four months of age, infants understand that objects are distinct entities with boundaries, that objects move in continuous paths, that one solid object cannot pass through another, that an object cannot pass through an opening that is smaller than the object, and that objects on slopes roll down rather than up (Baillargeon, 2008; Spelke & Newport, 1998). Infants also understand that liquids are different from objects. For example, five-month-old infants expect that liquids will change shape as they move and that they can be penetrated by solid objects (Hespos, Ferry, & Rips, 2009). In a similar vein, a recent study showed that six-month-old infants appear to understand that dried fruits derived from plants are more likely to be edible than dried fruits derived from artificial objects (Wertz & Wynn, 2014). In other words, they preferentially identify plants as sources of food at a surprisingly young age.

In this line of research, perhaps the most stunning discovery has been the finding that *infants seem to be able to add and subtract small numbers* (Lipton & Spelke, 2004; Wood & Spelke, 2005). If five-month-old infants are shown a sequence of events in which one object is added to another behind a screen, they expect to see two objects when the screen is removed, and they exhibit surprise when their expectation is violated (see Figure 11.11). According to research conducted by Yale University's Karen Wynn (Wynn, 2008; Yamaguchi, Kuhlmeier, Wynn, & VanMarel, 2009), this expectation suggests that they understand that $1 + 1 = 2$ (Wynn, 1992, 1996). Similar manipulations suggest that infants also understand that $2 - 1 = 1$, that $2 + 1 = 3$, and that $3 - 1 = 2$ (Hauser & Carey, 1998; Wynn, 1998). Wynn, has shown in her more recent work that nine-month-old infants even have some understanding that $5 + 5 = 10$ and that $10 - 5 = 5$ (McCrink & Wynn, 2004).

Again and again in recent years, research has shown that infants appear to understand surprisingly complex concepts that they have had virtually no opportunity to learn about. These findings have led some theorists to conclude that certain basic cognitive abilities are biologically built into humans' neural architecture (Spelke & Kinzler, 2007). The theorists who have reached this conclusion tend to fall into two camps: nativists and evolutionary

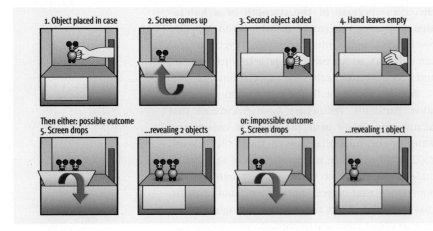

1. Object placed in case
2. Screen comes up
3. Second object added
4. Hand leaves empty

Then either: possible outcome
5. Screen drops
...revealing 2 objects

or: impossible outcome
5. Screen drops
...revealing 1 object

Figure 11.11
The procedure used to test infants' understanding of numbers. To see if five-month-old infants have some appreciation of addition and subtraction, Wynn (1992, 1996) showed them sequences of events like those depicted here. If children express surprise (primarily assessed by time spent looking) when the screen drops and they see only one object, this result suggests that they understand that 1 + 1 = 2. Wynn and others have found that infants seem to have some primitive grasp of simple addition and subtraction.

Source: Adapted from Wynn, K. (1992). Addition and subtraction by human infants. *Nature*, 358, 749–750. Copyright © 1992 Macmillan Magazines, Ltd. Reprinted with permission.

theorists. The *nativists* simply assert that humans are prewired to readily understand certain concepts without making any assumptions about *why* humans are prewired in these ways (Spelke, 1994; Spelke & Newport, 1998). Their principal interest is to sort out the complex matter of what is prewired and what isn't. *Evolutionary theorists* agree with the nativists that humans are prewired for certain cognitive abilities, but they are keenly interested in *why*. As you might expect, they maintain that this wiring is a product of natural selection, and they strive to understand its adaptive significance (Hauser & Carey, 1998; Wynn, 1998).

Critical Periods in Development

Some psychologists have argued that there are *critical or sensitive periods* for the development of some of our abilities and characteristics (Anderson, 2006; Blakemore & Mills, 2014; Lenneberg, 1967). Although the idea first surfaced many years ago and was made popular in the 1930s and 1940s by Konrad Lorenz in his formulation of animal imprinting (Lorenz, 1981), the issue of critical periods for development is still of concern today. A special issue of the journal *Developmental Psychobiology* edited by McMaster's Daphne Maurer (2005) was devoted to the topic. The idea is that there are age ranges or time periods that are optimal or essential for the development of particular abilities or characteristics. In our Chapter 3 Critical Thinking Application, "Building Better Brains" (page 106), we defined *critical period* as a *limited time span in the development of an organism when it is optimal for certain capacities to*

emerge because the organism is especially responsive to certain experiences. The term *critical period* is traditionally used to suggest that if the ability or knowledge is not acquired at that point, it will not be possible to acquire it later.

The term *sensitive period* suggests an optimal period for acquisition but one that does not obviate acquisition at a later point. For example, Clancy and Finlay (2001) have argued that there are sensitive periods for language learning in which the plasticity in the brain facilitates the learning of language. This does not mean, however, that language cannot be learned later. Similar arguments have been made for the acquisition of other abilities such as musical ability (Trainor, 2005). Some educational systems, for example, Maria Montessori's model of education (Lillard, 2005; Lillard & Else-Quest, 2006; Montessori, 1973), have incorporated the notion of sensitive periods as foundational (Toronto Montessori Institute, n.d.).

While there seems to be suggestive evidence for critical/sensitive periods in some areas, there is a great deal more to be done before we can generate a firm list of critical periods for human development (Johnson, 2005a). The same seems to be true for language processing (Thomas & Johnson, 2008; Werker & Tees, 2005). Researchers in the area even disagree on the terms to be used, some preferring the terms *sensitive* or *optimal period* (e.g., Werker & Tees, 2005) and some the term *critical period*. These are important issues with educational and clinical implications and the current view is that new technologies such as brain-imaging techniques will allow us greater insight in the future into the nature of critical or sensitive periods and the mechanisms that underlie them (Johnson, 2005b).

Theory of Mind. One of the most exciting and active areas of research over the past few years has been the work examining children's developing *theory of mind* (Legerstee, Haley, & Bornstein, 2013; Mar, Tackett, & Moore, 2010). Research on theory of mind examines the development of children's understanding about the mind and mental states, and how children conceive of another person's thought processes, knowledge, beliefs, and feelings (Flavell, 2004; Johnson, 2005b; Legerstee, 2005).

Imagine that you are witnessing the following scene. An experimenter shows a five-year-old child a candy box and asks her what she thinks it contains. She answers, "Candy." The child is then allowed to look inside the box and discovers that it really contains crayons. Then the experimenter asks the girl what another child who has *not* seen the contents of the box will think it contains. "Candy," she replies, showing her understanding of the planned deception. Now imagine the same experiment with a three-year-old. Events unfold in the same way until the experimenter asks what another child will think the candy box contains. The three-year-old typically will say, "Crayons," thinking that the other child will know what he knows about the hidden contents of the box. More perplexing yet, if questioned further, the three-year-old will probably insist that he originally thought and said that there were crayons in the candy box (Flavell, 1999). Why does the three-year-old respond in this way? What does this tell us about the child's theory of mind? According to classic research in this area, most children under the age of four do not yet appreciate that people can hold *false beliefs* that do not accurately reflect reality (Wellman, 2002). The *false belief method* (Symons, Kristin-Lee, & Collins, 2006) is just one of several research paradigms that researchers have used to explore children's developing ideas about the mind.

Children's understanding of the mind begins to turn a corner between ages three and four, so that four-year-olds typically begin to grasp the fact that people may hold false beliefs (Wellman & Gelman, 1998). While this does not happen overnight, after age four, youngsters' reasoning about mental states continues to improve. For example, four-year-olds are relatively poor at introspection; they struggle when asked to reconstruct their recent thoughts about something, but their capacity for introspection gradually increases over the next several years (Flavell, 1999). An understanding of the concept of false belief is often seen as the developmental achievement that marks the child's progression to a more mature theory of mind.

Researchers have mapped out some milestones in the development of children's understanding of mental states (Harris, 2006; Wellman, 2002). Around age two, children begin to distinguish between mental states and overt behaviour. The first mental states they understand are *desires* and *emotions*. By age three, children are talking about others' *beliefs* and *thoughts*, as well as their desires. It is not until about age four, however, that children consistently make the connection between mental states and behaviour. That is, they begin to understand how people's beliefs, thoughts, and desires motivate and direct their behaviour. Thus, they can appreciate that Harry *wants* to get a new watch, which would make him very *happy*, that he *believes* that it will be available at the mall, and that these mental states will *motivate* Harry to ask his dad to take him to the watch store. Of course, this developing theory of mind is essential if children are to competently enter their social world, where understanding others is critical.

The transition in cognitive sophistication appears to occur around the same age in a variety of cultures (Callaghan et al., 2005). After age four, youngsters' reasoning about mental states continues to improve. Children suffering from some childhood disorders show deficits in the development of theory mind. For example, children suffering from autistic spectrum disorder who are much older than four show deficits in their theory of mind. In fact, some have suggested that problems with their ability to develop a mature theory of mind—one that enables them to understand and appreciate the minds of others—may in part underlie the problems they experience in their disorder (Baron-Cohen, 1995; Frith, 2001). Baron-Cohen suggests that these children may suffer from *mind-blindness* or a lack of theory of mind, in which the processes that allow the normal development of a theory of mind in most children are impaired in children suffering from various forms of autism.

The Development of Moral Reasoning

In Europe, a woman was near death from cancer. One drug might save her, a form of radium that a druggist in the same town had recently discovered. The druggist was charging $2000, ten times what the drug cost him to make. The sick woman's husband, Heinz, went to everyone he knew to borrow the money, but he could get together only about half of what it cost. He told the druggist that his wife was dying and asked him to sell it cheaper or let him pay later. But the druggist said, "No." The husband got desperate and broke into the man's store to steal the drug for his wife. Should the husband have done that? Why? (Kohlberg, 1969, p. 379)

What's your answer to Heinz's dilemma? Would you have answered the same way three years ago? When you were in Grade 5? Can you guess what you might have said at age six?

By presenting similar dilemmas to subjects and studying their responses, Lawrence Kohlberg (1976, 1984; Colby & Kohlberg, 1987) devised a model of how moral reasoning develops. What is morality? That's a complicated question that philosophers have debated for centuries. For our purposes, it will suffice to say that *morality* involves the ability to discern right from wrong and to behave accordingly.

Lawrence Kohlberg

"Children are almost as likely to reject moral reasoning beneath their level as to fail to assimilate reasoning too far above their level."

Kohlberg's Stage Theory

Kohlberg's model is the most influential of a number of competing theories that attempt to explain how youngsters develop a sense of right and wrong. His work was derived from much earlier work by Jean Piaget (1932), who theorized that moral development is determined by cognitive development. By this he meant that the way individuals think out moral issues depends on their level of cognitive development. This assumption provided the springboard for Kohlberg's research.

Kohlberg's theory focuses on moral *reasoning* rather than overt *behaviour*. This point is best illustrated by describing Kohlberg's method of investigation. He presented his subjects with thorny moral questions such as Heinz's dilemma. He then asked them what the actor in the dilemma should do and, more important, why. It was the *why* that interested Kohlberg. He examined the nature and progression of subjects' moral reasoning.

The result of this work is the stage theory of moral reasoning outlined in Figure 11.12. Kohlberg found that individuals progress through a series of three levels of moral development, each of which can be broken into two sublevels, yielding a total of six stages. Each stage represents a different approach to thinking about right and wrong.

Younger children at the *preconventional level* think in terms of external authority. Acts are wrong because they are punished or right because they lead to positive consequences. Older children who have reached the *conventional level* of moral reasoning see rules as necessary for maintaining social order. They therefore accept these rules as their own. They "internalize" these rules not to avoid punishment but to be virtuous and win approval from others. Moral thinking at this stage is relatively inflexible. Rules are viewed as absolute guidelines that should be enforced rigidly.

During adolescence, some youngsters move on to the *postconventional level*, which involves working out a personal code of ethics. Acceptance of rules is less rigid, and moral thinking shows some flexibility. Subjects at the postconventional level allow for the possibility that someone might not comply with some of society's rules if they conflict with personal ethics. For example, subjects at this level might applaud a newspaper reporter who goes to jail rather than reveal a source of information who was promised anonymity.

Evaluating Kohlberg's Theory

How has Kohlberg's theory fared in research? The central ideas have received reasonable support. Studies have shown that youngsters generally do move through Kohlberg's stages of moral reasoning in the order he proposed (Walker, 1989). Furthermore, relations between age and level of moral reasoning are in the predicted directions (Rest, 1986; see Figure 11.13). Although these findings support Kohlberg's model, critics note that it is not unusual to find that a person shows signs of several adjacent levels of moral reasoning at a particular point in development (Krebs & Denton, 2005). As we noted in the critique of Piaget, this mixing of stages is a problem for virtually all stage theories. Evidence is also mounting that Kohlberg's theory reflects an individualistic ideology characteristic of modern Western nations that is much more culture specific than Kohlberg appreciated (Miller, 2006). Finally, a consensus is building that Kohlberg's theory has led to a constricted focus on reasoning about interpersonal conflicts, while ignoring many other important aspects of moral development (Walker, 2007). Contemporary theorists note that moral behaviour depends on many factors besides reasoning, including emotional reactions, variations in temperament, and cultural background (Haidt & Kesebir, 2010).

Figure 11.12
Kohlberg's stage theory.
Kohlberg's model posits three levels of moral reasoning, each of which can be divided into two stages. This chart summarizes some of the key facets in how individuals think about right and wrong at each stage.

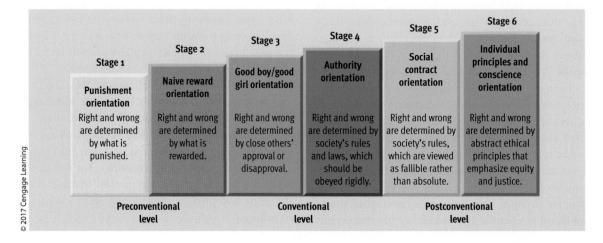

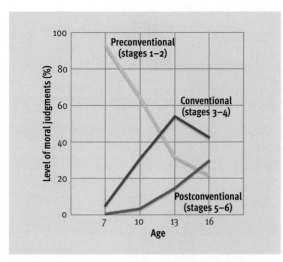

Figure 11.13

Age and moral reasoning. The percentages of different types of moral judgments made by subjects at various ages are graphed here (based on Kohlberg, 1963, 1969). As predicted, preconventional reasoning declines as children mature, conventional reasoning increases during middle childhood, and postconventional reasoning begins to emerge during adolescence. But at each age, children display a mixture of various levels of moral reasoning.

Source: Adapted from Kohlberg, L. J. (1963). The development of children's orientations toward a moral order. 1: Sequence in the development of moral thought. *Vita Humana*, 6, 11–33. Copyright © 2009, Karger Publishers.

concept **check** 11.3

Analyzing Moral Reasoning

Check your understanding of Kohlberg's theory of moral development by analyzing hypothetical responses to the following moral dilemma:

A biologist has conducted numerous studies demonstrating that simple organisms such as worms and paramecia can learn through conditioning. It occurs to her that perhaps she could condition fertilized human ova, to provide a dramatic demonstration that abortions destroy adaptable, living human organisms. This possibility appeals to her, as she is ardently opposed to abortion. However, there is no way to conduct the necessary research on human ova without sacrificing the lives of potential human beings. She desperately wants to conduct the research, but obviously, the sacrifice of human ova is fundamentally incompatible with her belief in the sanctity of human life. What should she do? Why? [Submitted by a student (age 13) to Professor Barbara Banas at Monroe Community College.]

In the spaces on the left of each numbered response, indicate the level of moral reasoning shown, choosing from the following: (a) preconventional level, (b) conventional level, or (c) postconventional level. The answers are in Appendix A near the back of the book.

_____ **1.** She should do the research. Although it's wrong to kill, there's a greater good that can be realized through the research.

_____ **2.** She shouldn't do the research because people will think that she's a hypocrite and condemn her.

_____ **3.** She should do the research because she may become rich and famous as a result.

The Transition of Adolescence

Adolescence is a transitional period between childhood and adulthood. Its age boundaries are not exact, but in our society, adolescence begins at around age 13 and ends at about age 22.

Although most societies have at least a brief period of adolescence, it is *not* universal across cultures (Larson & Wilson, 2004; Schlegel & Barry, 1991; Whiting, Burbank, & Ratner, 1986). In some cultures, young people move directly from childhood to adulthood. In our society, rapid technological progress has made lengthy education, and therefore prolonged economic dependence, the norm. Adolescence is a critical time for the development of important physical and psychological attributes, even a sense of identity (Meeus et al., 2010). Let's begin our discussion of adolescent development with its most visible aspect—the physical changes that transform the body of a child into that of an adult.

Physiological Changes

Recall for a moment your early high school days. Didn't it seem that your body grew so fast that your clothes just couldn't "keep up"? This phase of rapid growth in height and weight is called the *adolescent growth spurt*. Brought on by hormonal changes, it typically starts at about age 9–10 in girls and 10–12 in boys (Peper & Dahl, 2013). In addition to growing taller and heavier, children begin to develop the *secondary sex characteristics*—physical features that distinguish one sex from the other but that are not essential for reproduction—such as facial hair and broader shoulders in males, and breast growth and wider hips in females (Susman & Dorn, 2013; see Figure 11.14).

Soon, youngsters reach *puberty*—the stage during which sexual functions reach maturity, which marks the beginning of adolescence. It is during puberty that the **primary sex characteristics**—the structures necessary for reproduction—develop fully. In the male, these include the testes, penis, and related internal structures. Primary sex characteristics in the female include the ovaries, vagina, uterus, and other internal structures.

In females, puberty is typically signalled by *menarche*—the first occurrence of menstruation, which reflects the culmination of a series of hormonal changes. North American girls typically reach menarche at age 12–13, with further sexual maturation continuing until approximately age 16. North American boys typically experience *spermarche*—the

Key Learning Goals

▸ Review the physiological changes of puberty, and summarize research on neural development in adolescence.

▸ Discuss identity formation in adolescence and the stage of emerging adulthood.

Figure 11.14
Physical development at puberty. Hormonal changes during puberty lead not only to a growth spurt but also to the development of secondary sex characteristics. The pituitary gland sends signals to the adrenal glands and gonads (ovaries and testes), which secrete hormones responsible for various physical changes that differentiate males and females.

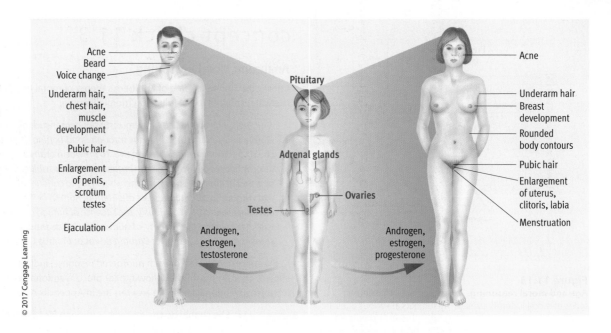

© 2017 Cengage Learning

first occurrence of ejaculation—at age 13–14, with further sexual maturation continuing until approximately age 18.

Interestingly, *generational* changes have occurred in the timing of puberty over the last 150 years. Today's adolescents begin puberty at a younger age, and complete it more rapidly, than their counterparts in earlier generations (Lee & Styne, 2013; Talma et al., 2013). This trend appears to be occurring in both genders. The reasons for this trend are the subject of debate. It seems likely that multiple factors have contributed (Bellis, Downing, & Ashton, 2006; Susman & Dorn, 2013). The most obvious potential causes are widespread improvements in nutrition and medical care, which would probably explain why the trend toward younger puberty has mostly been seen in modern, "developed" countries. Some theorists also believe that a variety of environmental pollutants serve as "endocrine disrupters" that hasten the onset of puberty (Lee & Styne, 2013).

The timing of puberty varies from one adolescent to the next. Generally, girls who mature early and boys who mature late seem to experience more subjective distress with the transition to adolescence (Susman, Dorn, & Schiefelbein, 2003). This experience of subjective stress may contribute to the elevated prevalence of psychological disorders seen in both groups, but especially females (Graber, 2013). However, in both males and females, early maturation is associated with greater use of tobacco, alcohol, and other drugs; more high-risk behaviour; greater aggression; and more trouble with the law (Lynne et al., 2007; Steinberg & Morris, 2001). Among females, early maturation is also correlated with a greater risk for eating problems (Klump, 2013). Thus, we might speculate that early maturation often thrusts both genders (but especially females) toward the adult world too soon.

Neural Development: The Teen Brain

If these physical changes were not enough, recent research has also suggested that there is a surprising amount of change going on in the adolescent's brain that may impact his or her behaviour and sense of self. Changes in the brain during the teen years have come under increased scientific scrutiny in the past few years (e.g., Tamnes et al., 2010; Vakorin et al., 2013; Whelan et al., 2012). Scientists used to think that brain growth

Kris Timken/Blend Images/Jupiter Images

The timing of sexual maturation can have important implications for adolescents. Youngsters who mature unusually early or unusually late often feel uneasy about this transition.

and change were primarily restricted to development in the womb and through the first 18 months of life. Some have referred to the teenage brain as a "work in progress" (Teen Brain, 2008).

In recent years, brain-imaging studies have shown that the volume of white matter in the brain grows throughout adolescence, while the volume of grey matter declines (Giedd & Rapoport, 2010). The growth of white matter suggests that *neurons are becoming more myelinated*, leading to enhanced connectivity in the brain, whereas the decrease in grey matter is thought to reflect synaptic pruning, which plays a key role in the formation of neural networks (Geier, 2013; see Chapter 3). Perhaps the most interesting discovery has been that increased myelinization and *synaptic pruning* are most pronounced in the prefrontal cortex (Sebastian, Burnett, & Blakemore, 2010) (see Figure 11.15). Thus, the *prefrontal cortex appears to be the last area of the brain to fully mature.* This maturation may not be complete until one's mid-20s. Much has been made of this finding because the prefrontal cortex has been characterized as an "executive control centre" that appears crucial to cognitive control and emotional regulation (Casey et al., 2005). Theorists have suggested that the immaturity of the prefrontal cortex may explain why risky behaviour (such as reckless driving, experimentation with drugs, dangerous stunts, unprotected sex, and so forth) peaks during adolescence and then declines in adulthood (Steinberg, 2008).

More recent research has suggested that the role of the prefrontal cortex in adolescent risk taking has been exaggerated, as other features of neural development also contribute (Casey & Caudle, 2013). Studies have demonstrated that adolescents exhibit heightened sensitivity to various types of rewards, such as the pleasures associated with tasty foods, financial payoffs, psychoactive drugs, and thrilling adventures (Galvan, 2013). This elevated sensitivity to reward is attributed to relatively early maturation of the subcortical dopamine circuits that mediate the experience of pleasure (Luna et al., 2013). Thus, the current thinking is that adolescent risk taking is fuelled by a mismatch in the maturation of subcortical reward centres in relation to the prefrontal areas underlying cognitive control (Mills et al., 2014). In other words, the brain's early-maturing reward system overpowers the late-maturing prefrontal cortex.

That said, other factors also contribute to risky behaviour during adolescence. Evidence suggests that teenagers are particularly sensitive to the social evaluations of others (Somerville, 2013). Adolescents spend a great deal of time with their peers. Hence, susceptibility to peer influence may also contribute to adolescent risk taking (Albert, Chein, & Steinberg, 2013).

One elegant lab study found that the presence of peers more than doubled the number of risks taken by teenagers in a video game involving in-the-moment decisions about crash risks (Gardner & Steinberg, 2005). In contrast, older adults' risk taking was not elevated by the presence of peers (see Figure 11.16).

Time of Turmoil?

Back around the turn of the last century, G. Stanley Hall (1904), one of psychology's great pioneers, proposed that the adolescent years are characterized by convulsive instability and disturbing inner turmoil. Hall attributed this turmoil to adolescents' erratic physical changes and resultant confusion about self-image. While there is continuity with other life stages (Mikami et al., 2010), there is no doubt that adolescence is a time of change and transition.

Statistics on adolescent depression and suicide would seem to support the idea that adolescence can be a time marked by turmoil and disturbance for some. We know that adolescence is a period of increased risk for a variety of problems (Frisco, Houle, & Martin, 2010; Rawana, Morgan, Ngyyen, & Craig, 2010). According to Constance Hammen at the University of California at Los Angeles, a prominent

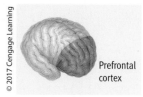

Figure 11.15
The prefrontal cortex.
Recent research suggests that neural development continues throughout adolescence. Moreover, the chief site for much of this development is the prefrontal cortex, which appears to be the last area of the brain to mature fully. This discovery may have fascinating implications for understanding the adolescent brain, as the prefrontal cortex appears to play a key role in emotional regulation and self-control.

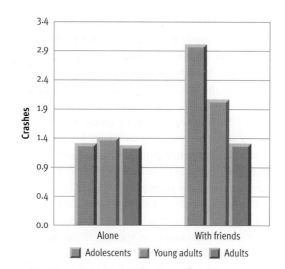

Figure 11.16
Peer influence on risk-taking. Gardner and Steinberg (2005) had adolescents, young adults, and adults play a video game involving simulated driving in which participants had to make quick decisions about crash risks. The dependent variable, which indexed subjects' risk-taking, was the number of crashes experienced. Some participants played the video game alone, whereas others played in the presence of peers. The data showed that the presence of peers increased risk-taking by young adults moderately and by adolescents considerably, but adults' risk-taking was unaffected. These findings suggest that susceptibility to peer influence may increase risky behaviour among adolescents and young adults.

Source: Republished with permission of SAGE Publications, from Risk taking in adolescence: New perspectives from brain and behavioral science, *Current Directions in Psychological Science*, L. Steinberg, Vol. 16, pp. 55–59, 2007, permission conveyed through Copyright Clearance Center, Inc.

researcher in depression, depression rates in adolescents can be as high as 20 percent. As we discuss in Chapter 15, depression is a risk factor for suicide.

In the United States, suicide is the third leading cause of death among adolescents (Goldston et al., 2008). It is the second leading cause of death for Canadians between the ages of 15 and 19 (Navaneelan, 2017). Suicide rates among teens have increased alarmingly over the past few decades. The Canadian Task Force on Preventive Health Care (2003) reported a fourfold increase in suicides for 15- to 19-year-old males and a threefold increase for females in that age group from 1960 to 1991; this was the greatest increase of any age group. It is important to note, however, that even with this increase, the rates for this age group, according to data from Statistics Canada (Langlois & Morrison, 2002), are lower than for older age groups. This highest rate of suicide in Canada is for those between the ages of 40 and 59 (Navaneelan, 2017). Attempted suicides are much higher for Canadian females than males, especially for adolescent girls.

Recent analyses of suicide rates have found that ethnic and racial groups differ both in suicide rates and their precipitants (Goldston et al., 2008). First Nations Canadians are especially vulnerable. The Canadian Task Force on Preventive Health Care (2003) reports that the suicide rates in this segment of Canadian society are twice the sex-specific rates and three times the age-specific rates reported for the general Canadian population. More recent data suggests the problem is even more serious, with suicide rates for First Nations youth reported to be seven times the rate of non-Aboriginal youth (Health Canada, 2013). The particularly high suicide rate among First Nations teens is of special concern and recently it has been getting much-needed publicity.

Canadian psychologists Michael Chandler and Christopher Lalonde have been conducting research in this area for many years (Chandler, 2000; Chandler & Lalonde, 2004, 2008; Lalonde, 2005, 2006, 2016). They suggest that the increased rate of suicide among First Nations Canadians is specific to certain contexts, rather than being true across that population. In some communities, the rate is as high as 800 times the national average, while in other communities, suicide is virtually unknown. Chandler and Lalonde believe that *cultural continuity factors* differentiate the settings where suicide rates are high, and argue that a sense of personal and cultural continuity is necessary, especially in times of change, to serve as a critical foundation for personal and cultural identity. While acknowledging the inevitability and importance of change, Chandler and Lalonde argue that a sense of personal continuity or personal persistence is fundamental to psychological health.

Chandler and Lalonde feel that two important sets of circumstances may combine to cause the high suicide levels among First Nations teens. One is the set of changes that most adolescents experience. The other arises "whenever one's culture, out of which the particulars of one's identity are necessarily composed, is also thrown into serious disarray. In either case, the grounds upon which a sense of self is ordinarily made to rest are cut away, life is made cheap, and the prospect of one's own death becomes a matter of indifference" (Chandler & Lalonde, 1998, p. 193). The Featured Study for this chapter links suicide rates of First Nations youth to contexts in which cultural continuity has or has not been emphasized.

FEATURED STUDY

Cultural continuity as a hedge against suicide in Canada's First Nations.

Description
This study by Chandler and Lalonde examines factors associated with cultural continuity for First Nations youth that can help reduce suicide rates in that population.

Investigators
Chandler, M., & Lalonde, C. (1998). *Transcultural Psychiatry, 35,* 191–219.

Returning to our original question, does the weight of evidence support the idea that adolescence is usually a period of turmoil and turbulence? Overall, recent consensus of the experts has been that adolescence is *not* an exceptionally difficult period (Offer, 1969, 2007; Petersen et al., 1993; Steinberg & Levine, 1997). Although turbulence and turmoil are not *universal* features of adolescence, challenging adaptations *do* have to be made during this period. In particular, most adolescents struggle to some extent in their effort to achieve a sound sense of identity.

The Search for Identity

Erik Erikson was especially interested in personality development during adolescence, which is the fifth of the eight major life stages he described. According to Erikson (1968), the premier challenge of adolescence is the struggle to form a clear sense of identity. This struggle involves working out a stable concept of oneself as a unique individual and embracing an ideology or system of values that provides a sense of direction. In Erikson's view, adolescents grapple with questions such as "Who am I, and where am I going in life?"

Recent research has focused on the consequences of identity confusion. Studies have found that

Christopher Lalonde from the University of Victoria has been recognized for his important work on culture, identity, and suicide in First Nations Communities in Canada.

Courtesy of Christopher Lalonde

identity confusion is associated with an increased risk for substance abuse, unprotected sexual activity, anxiety, low self-worth, and eating disorders (Schwartz et al., 2013).

Adolescents deal with identity formation in a variety of ways. Building on Erikson's insights, James Marcia (1966, 1980, 1994) proposed that the presence or absence of a sense of commitment (to life goals and values) and a sense of crisis (active questioning and exploration) can combine to produce four different *identity statuses* (see Figure 11.17). In order of increasing maturity, Marcia's four identity statuses begin with *identity diffusion*, a state of rudderless apathy, with no commitment to an ideology. *Identity foreclosure* is a premature commitment to visions, values, and roles—typically those prescribed by one's parents. Foreclosure is associated with conformity and not being very open to new experiences (Kroger, 2003). An *identity moratorium* involves delaying commitment for a while to experiment with alternative ideologies and careers. *Identity achievement* involves arriving at a sense of self and direction after some consideration of alternative possibilities.

Identity achievement is associated with higher self-esteem, conscientiousness, security, achievement motivation, and capacity for intimacy (Kroger, 2003; Kroger & Marcia, 2011). However, research suggests that people tend to reach identity achievement at later ages than originally envisioned by Marcia. In one large-scale study (Meeus et al., 2010), by late adolescence only 22–26 percent of the sample had reached identity achievement. Thus, the struggle for a sense of identity routinely extends into young adulthood. Indeed, some people continue to struggle with identity issues well into middle and even late adulthood (Newton & Stewart, 2012).

Emerging Adulthood as a New Developmental Stage

The finding that the search for identity routinely extends into adulthood is one of many considerations that have led Jeffrey Arnett to make the radical claim that we ought to recognize the existence of a new developmental stage in modern societies, which he has christened *emerging adulthood*. According to Arnett (2000, 2004, 2006), the years between age 18 and 25 (roughly) have become a distinct, new transitional stage of life. He attributes the rise of this new developmental period to a variety of demographic trends, such as more people delaying marriage and parenthood until their late 20s or early 30s, lengthier participation in higher education, increased barriers to financial independence, and so forth. "What is different today,"

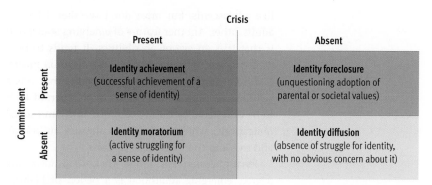

Figure 11.17

Marcia's four identity statuses. According to Canadian psychologist James Marcia (1980), the occurrence of identity crisis and exploration and the development of personal commitments can combine into four possible identity statuses, as shown in this diagram. The progressively darker shades of blue signify progressively more mature identity statuses.

Source: Adapted from Marcia, J. E. (1980). Identity in adolescence. In J. Adelson (Ed.), *Handbook of adolescent psychology* (pp. 159–210). New York: John Wiley. Copyright © 1980 by John Wiley. Reproduced with permission of John Wiley & Sons, Inc.

he says, "is that experiencing the period from the late teens through the mid-20s as a time of exploration and instability is now the norm" (Arnett, 2006, p. 4).

Arnett (2000, 2006, 2007) maintains that emerging adulthood is characterized by a number of prominent features. A central feature is the subjective feeling that one is in between adolescence and adulthood. When 18- to 25-year-olds are asked, "Do you feel like you have reached adulthood?" the modal response is "Yes and no" (see Figure 11.18). They don't feel

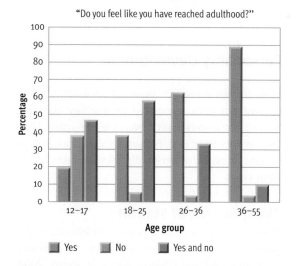

Figure 11.18

Emerging adulthood as a phase in between adolescence and adulthood. Arnett (2006) characterizes emerging adulthood as an "age of feeling in-between." This characterization comes from a study (2001) in which he asked participants of various ages "Do you feel like you have reached adulthood?" As you can see in the data shown here, the dominant response in the 18–25 age group was an ambivalent "Yes and no," but it shifted to predominantly "Yes" in the 26–35 age group.

Source: Arnett, J. J. (2006). Emerging adulthood: Understanding the new way of coming of age. In J. J. Arnett and J. L. Tanner (Eds.), *Emerging adults in America: Coming of age in the 21st century*. Washington, DC: American Psychological Association (p. 11). Reprinted with permission.

like adolescents, but most don't see themselves as adults either. Another feature of emerging adulthood is that it is an age of possibilities. It tends to be a time of great optimism about one's personal future. A third aspect of emerging adulthood is that it is a self-focused time of life. People in this period tend to be unfettered by duties, commitments, and social obligations, which gives them unusual autonomy and freedom to explore new options.

Finally, Arnett has found that, to a surprising degree, emerging adulthood is a period of identity formation. Although the search for identity has traditionally been viewed as an adolescent phenomenon, Arnett's research indicates that identity formation continues to be a crucial issue for most young adults. Arnett's provocative new theory has already inspired a good deal of research on the dynamics and developmental significance of emerging adulthood (Aquilino, 2006; Schwartz, 2016; Swanson, 2016). This research needs to determine whether emerging adulthood really represents a new stage of development or a historical curiosity associated with recent decades.

The Expanse of Adulthood

Key Learning Goals

▶ Discuss personality development in adulthood, and trace typical transitions in family relations during the adult years.

▶ Describe the physical changes associated with aging, and summarize information on Alzheimer's disease.

▶ Understand how memory and mental speed change in later adulthood.

▶ Discuss attitudes about death, the process of dying, and variations in how people cope with bereavement.

The concept of development was once associated almost exclusively with childhood and adolescence, but today it is widely appreciated that development is a lifelong journey.

Interestingly, patterns of development during the adult years are becoming increasingly diverse. The boundaries between young, middle, and late adulthood are becoming blurred as more and more people have children later than one is "supposed" to, retire earlier or later than one is "supposed" to (Statistics Canada, 2009), and so on. In the upcoming pages we'll look at some of the major developmental transitions in adult life. As we do, you should bear in mind that in adulthood there are many divergent pathways and timetables.

Personality Development

In recent years, research on adult personality development has been dominated by one key question: How stable is personality over the life span? We'll look at this issue and Erikson's view of adulthood in our discussion of personality development in the adult years.

The Question of Stability

After tracking subjects through adulthood, many researchers have been impressed by the amount of change observed (Helson, Jones, & Kwan, 2002; Whitbourne et al., 2002). Roger Gould (1975) studied two samples of men and women and concluded that "the evolution of a personality continues through the fifth decade of life." In contrast, many other researchers have been struck by the stability and durability they have found in personality. The general conclusion that emerged from several longitudinal studies using objective assessments of personality traits was that personality tends to be quite stable over periods of 20 to 40 years (Block, 1981; Caspi & Herbener, 1990; Costa & McCrae, 1994, 1997).

How can these contradictory conclusions be reconciled (Kogan, 1990)? It appears that *both* conclusions are accurate. They just reflect different ways of looking at the data (Bertrand, Graham, & Lachman, 2013). Recall from Chapter 9 that psychological test scores are *relative* measures. They show how one scores *relative to other people*. Raw scores are converted into *percentile scores* that indicate the precise degree to which one is above or below average on a particular trait. The data indicate that these percentile scores tend to be remarkably stable over lengthy spans of time. People's relative standing doesn't tend to change much (Allemand, Steiger, & Hill, 2013).

However, if we examine participants' raw scores on fundamental personality traits, we can see meaningful developmental trends. Although adults' mean raw scores on extraversion remain pretty stable, neuroticism scores tend to decline moderately with increasing age, while agreeableness, openness to experience, and conscientiousness tend to increase gradually (Soto et al., 2011; see Figure 11.19). Moreover, studies show that (1) there are variations among people in the extent to which they experience personality change, (2) the biggest changes in raw scores tend to occur between the ages of 20 and 40, (3) significant changes can even occur in old age, and (4) the typical developmental trends represent "positive" changes that move people toward great social maturity (Donnellan, Hill, & Roberts, 2015). In sum, it appears that personality in adulthood is characterized by both stability and change.

Erikson's View of Adulthood

Insofar as personality changes during the adult years, Erik Erikson's (1963) theory offers some clues

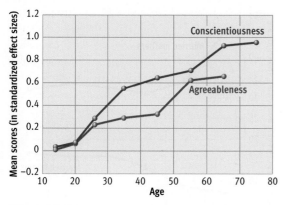

Figure 11.19

Examples of personality trends in the adult years.
According to Roberts and Mroczek (2008), when researchers examine participants' mean raw scores on personality measures, they find meaningful trends over the decades of adulthood. The trends for two specific traits—agreeableness and conscientiousness—are shown here as examples. Using subjects' test scores in adolescence as a baseline, you can see how measures of agreeableness and conscientiousness increase substantially over the decades.

Source: Republished with permission of SAGE Publications, from Personality trait change in adulthood, *Current Directions in Psychological Science*, B.W. Roberts & D. Mroczek, 17, pp. 31–35, 2008, permission conveyed through Copyright Clearance Center, Inc.

Figure 11.20

Median age at first marriage. The median age at which people in the United States marry for the first time has been creeping up for both males and females since the mid-1960s. This trend indicates that more people are postponing marriage. (Data from the U.S. Bureau of the Census)

Source: Zheng Wu. (1998). Recent trends in marriage. *Policy Options*, September 4. Reprinted by permission for the Institute for Research on Public Policy.

about the nature of changes people can expect. In his eight-stage model of development over the life span, Erikson divided adulthood into three stages. In the *early adulthood* stage, called *intimacy versus isolation*, the key concern is whether one can develop the capacity to share intimacy with others. Successful resolution of the challenges in this stage should promote empathy and openness. In *middle adulthood*, the psychosocial crisis pits *generativity versus self-absorption*. The key challenge is to acquire a genuine concern for the welfare of future generations, which results in providing unselfish guidance to younger people and concern with one's legacy.

During the *late adulthood* stage, called *integrity versus despair*, the challenge is to avoid the tendency to dwell on the mistakes of the past and on one's imminent death. People need to find meaning and satisfaction in their lives, rather than wallow in bitterness and resentment. Empirical research on the adult stages in Erikson's theory has been sparse, but generally supportive of the theory. For example, researchers have found that generativity increases between young adulthood and middle age, as Erikson's theory predicts (de St. Aubin, McAdams, & Kim, 2004; Stewart, Ostrove, & Helson, 2001).

Transitions in Family Life

Many of the important transitions in adulthood involve changes in family responsibilities and relationships. Everyone emerges from a family, and most

people go on to form their own families. However, the transitional period during which young adults are "between families" until they form a new family is being prolonged by more and more people. The percentage of young adults who are postponing marriage until their late 20s or early 30s has risen steadily (see Figure 11.20). This trend is probably the result of a number of factors. Chief among them are the availability of new career options for women, increased educational requirements in the world of work, and increased emphasis on personal autonomy. Nonetheless, more than 90 percent of adults eventually marry.

Adjusting to Marriage

Conjugal status is a term used by Statistics Canada when reporting the nature of a relationship between cohabiting couples. The most recent data available from Statistics Canada (Milan, 2013) indicates that most Canadian couples are still opting for marriage (80.1 percent of couples) as their preferred form of cohabitation, with about one-quarter living in a common-law relationships (19.9 percent). The percentage of common-law relationships has increased from 6.3 percent in 1981 to the current rate of about 20 percent. No matter the form of the relationship, committed new couples have adjustments to make. While not all married couples are happy—the divorce rate in Canada increased to 11.5 percent in 2011 from 5.1 percent in 1981 (Milan, 2013)—most new couples are pretty happy (Schramm et al., 2005). Still, 8–14 percent of newlyweds score in the distressed range on measures of marital satisfaction, with the most commonly reported problems being difficulties balancing work and marriage and financial concerns (Schramm et al., 2005). Optimism can help, but it depends on the nature of one's optimism. One recent study found that the *personality trait of optimism*, which involves a general tendency to expect good outcomes, fosters constructive problem solving and marital well-being (Neff & Geers, 2013). However, this study found that *relationship-specific optimism*, which involves idealistic expectations about marriage (my partner will always be affectionate, always communicate well, never intentionally hurt me, and so on), was associated with less constructive problem solving and steep declines in marital well-being during the first year of marriage. So, it may help to have realistic expectations about marriage.

You might guess that partners who cohabit prior to getting married would have an easier transition and greater marital success. However, until relatively recently, research demonstrated just the opposite. Studies found an association between premarital cohabitation and increased divorce rates (Teachman, 2003). Theorists speculated that people inclined to cohabit were less traditional, more individualistic, and had a weaker commitment to the institution of marriage. However, the findings on the effects of cohabitation have shifted (Liefbroer & Dourleijn, 2006). One reason may be that cohabitation prior to marriage has gradually become the norm rather than the exception (Cohan, 2013). In the 1970s, only about 10 percent of couples lived together before marriage, but that figure has risen to 66 percent (Manning, Brown, & Payne, 2014; Tach & Halpern-Meekin, 2009). A large-scale study in Australia that looked at trends over decades (from 1945 to 2000) found that cohabitants had higher rates of marital dissolution up through 1988, but then the trend started to gradually reverse itself, with cohabitants showing lower rates of divorce (Hewitt & de Vaus, 2009). In the United States, studies focusing on more recent marriages also failed to find cohabitation associated with marital instability (Manning & Cohen, 2012; Reinhold, 2010).

One major source of conflict in many new marriages is the negotiation of marital roles in relation to career commitments. More and more women are aspiring to demanding careers. However, research shows that husbands' careers continue to take priority over their wives' career ambitions (Cha, 2010). Moreover, many husbands maintain traditional role expectations about housework, child care, and decision making. Men's contribution to house-work/child care has increased noticeably since the 1960s.

Figure 11.21

Housework trends since the 1960s. As these data show, the gap between husbands and wives in hours devoted to housework/child care has narrowed in recent decades. Married fathers have doubled their contribution since the 1960s, but married mothers still allocate about twice as many hours to housework/child care. (Data from Bianchi et al., 2012).

But studies of couples with children indicate that wives are still doing about twice as much housework/child care as their husbands (Bianchi et al., 2012; see Figure 11.21). This is true even among highly paid and highly stressed female executives. Miller Burke and Attridge (2011a, 2011b) interviewed 106 successful men and women from the world of business who were mostly worth over a million dollars. Among the women, 44 percent reported they did most of the housework/child care, whereas only 4 percent of the men reported shouldering the bulk of housework/child care. All that said, husbands still put in more hours of paid work than wives on average, and most wives do not view their larger share of housework as unfair because most women don't expect a 50–50 split (Braun et al., 2008).

Adjusting to Parenthood

Although an increasing number of people are choosing to remain childless, the vast majority of married couples continue to have children, and they rate the birth experience and resulting parenthood as a highly positive experience (Demo, 1992). A survey of Canadian women who recently gave birth indicated that the majority of them found the experience itself to be "very positive" (Statistics Canada, 2007b). Nonetheless, the arrival of the first child represents a *major* transition (Senior, 2010), and can lead to negative emotions (Held & Rutherford, 2011), and the disruption of old routines can be extremely stressful (Carter, 1999). Dual roles for the mother also increase the level of stress and the tendency to experience marital dissatisfaction. More Canadian women than ever are returning to the workplace after having children (Statistics Canada, 2007d). A review of decades of research on parenthood and marital satisfaction found that (1) parents exhibit lower marital satisfaction than comparable non-parents, (2) mothers of infants report the steepest decline in marital satisfaction, and (3) the more children couples have, the lower their marital satisfaction tends to be (Twenge, Campbell, & Foster, 2003). Consistent with these trends, a recent longitudinal study found that the transition to parenthood was associated with a sudden deterioration in relationship quality (Doss et al., 2009). The decline in marital satisfaction tended to be small to medium in size. Ironically, the more satisfied couples were prior to birth of their first child, the more their marital satisfaction declined.

Although these findings are distressing, crisis during the transition to first parenthood is far from universal. One recent study found that average relationship satisfaction after the transition to parenthood showed the usual decline, but further analyses revealed that the average was dragged down by subgroups of parents who experienced steep decreases in satisfaction (Don & Mickelson, 2014). It turned out that relationship satisfaction held up pretty well for about one-half of the fathers and three-quarters of the mothers. So, as is often true, averages can be deceiving.

reality check

Misconception

Children are a key ingredient of marital bliss.

Reality

Children can be a source of great joy, but they also are a source of considerable stress. Although other factors are also at work, studies show that marital satisfaction generally declines after the arrival of children and often increases after grown children leave home.

As children grow up, parental influence over them tends to decline, and the early years of parenting—that once seemed so difficult—are often recalled with fondness. When youngsters reach adolescence and seek to establish their own identities, gradual realignments occur in parent–child relationships (Bornstein, Jager, & Steinberg, 2013). On the one hand, parent–adolescent relations generally are not as bitter or contentious as widely assumed (Laursen, Coy, & Collins, 1998). On the other hand, adolescents do spend less time in family activities

© Owen Franken/Corbis

Although children can be unparalleled sources of joy and satisfaction, the transition to parenthood can be extremely stressful, especially for mothers.

(Larson et al., 1996) and their closeness to their parents declines while conflicts become more frequent (Smetana, Campione-Barr, & Metzger, 2006). The conflicts tend to involve everyday matters (chores and appearance) more than substantive issues (sex and drugs) (Barber, 1994). When conflicts occur, they seem to have more adverse effects on the parents than the children (Steinberg & Steinberg, 1994). Ironically, although research has shown that adolescence is not as turbulent or difficult for youngsters as once believed, their parents *are* stressed out (Steinberg, 2001).

reality check

Misconception

Most people go through a midlife crisis around the age of 40.

Reality

Fabled though it may be, the midlife crisis does not appear to be a normal developmental transition. Research suggests that only a tiny minority of people (2–5 percent) go through a midlife crisis (Chiriboga, 1989; McCrae & Costa, 1990).

Aging and Physiological Changes

Our Canadian population is getting older. The life expectancies for Canadian women and men have increased in recent years. Lifestyle choices, genetics, and even personality seem to play a role in determining who will live past their mid-80s (Abraham, 2010; Friedman & Martin, 2011). It is projected that by 2031 the average life expectancy in Canada will be 81.9 for males and 86.0 for females (Statistics Canada, 2016). For the first time in 2004, the combined expectancy for both sexes surpassed 80 years,

Human Development across the Life Span

with women expected to live about five years longer than men (Statistics Canada, 2006b), but that gender gap continues to narrow (Statistics Canada, 2016). According to Canadian government estimates, by 2036 we can expect to have over 10 million seniors in Canada (Employment and Social Development Canada, 2014). The aging of the Canadian population has raised concerns with regard to health care, physical deterioration leading to loneliness (Ramage-Morin & Gilmour, 2013), how to test for capacity (Moye, Marson, & Edelstein, 2013), the quality and availability of retirement living, and the possibility that suicides among seniors may rise. Marnin Heisel, a suicide expert at Western University (Heisel et al., 2010), has found that the baby boomers who will swell our ranks of seniors tend to have higher suicide rates (Canadian Institutes of Health Research, 2009) compared to other generations at the same age (Rakobowchuk, 2011). The Calgary Centre for Suicide Prevention, for example, notes that in 2003, 172 Canadian seniors between the ages of 75 and 89 took their own lives. The number for this age group increased to 221 in 2007 (Rakobowchuk, 2011).

Canadians' end-of-life options dramatically changed with the passage in June 2016 of Bill C-14, legislation permitting doctor-assisted death in Canada in specified situations. The legislation permits Canadians to choose to die with the help of a doctor when facing a terminal illness where a natural death was "reasonably foreseeable." A poll of Canadians in 2014 revealed that 84 percent of Canadians were in favour of doctor-assisted death with certain conditions (CBC News, 2015). By December 2016, there had been 744 doctor-assisted deaths, an average of about four a day since June 17, 2016 (Slaughter, 2016).

Most Canadians remain relatively healthy as they age, but there are physical and psychological changes. With increasing age comes increasing attention to the physical changes associated with age. People obviously experience many physical changes as they progress through adulthood. In both sexes, hair tends to thin out and become grey, and many males confront receding hairlines and baldness. To the dismay of many, the proportion of body fat tends to increase with age, while the amount of muscle tissue decreases. Overall, weight tends to increase in most adults through the mid-50s, when a gradual decline may begin. These changes have little functional significance, but in our youth-oriented society, they often have an impact on self-concept, leading many people to view themselves as unattractive (Aldwin & Gilmer, 2004).

Curiously though, when elderly people are asked how old they feel, they mostly report feeling quite a bit younger than they actually are. For instance, in a study of people over the age of 70, on average the subjects reported that they felt 13 years younger than their chronological age (Kleinspehn-Ammerlahn, Kotter-Gruhn, & Smith, 2008). Obviously, there is some wishful thinking at work here, but it appears to be beneficial. Evidence suggests that feeling younger than one's real age is associated with better health and cognitive functioning and reduced mortality risk (Hsu, Chung, & Langer, 2010).

In the sensory domain, the key developmental changes occur in vision and hearing. The proportion of people with 20/20 visual acuity declines with age, while farsightedness and difficulty seeing in low illumination become more common (Schieber, 2006). Sensitivity to colour and contrast also decline (Fozard & Gordon-Salant, 2001). Hearing sensitivity begins declining gradually in early adulthood but usually isn't noticeable until after age 50. Hearing loss tends to be greater in men than in women, and for high-frequency sounds more than low-frequency sounds (Yost, 2000). Even mild hearing loss can undermine speech perception. Such loss puts an added burden on cognitive processing (Wingfield, Tun, & McCoy, 2005).

Age-related changes also occur in hormonal functioning during adulthood. Among women, these changes lead to *menopause*. This ending of menstrual periods, accompanied by a loss of fertility, typically occurs at around age 50 (Grady, 2006). Most women experience at least some unpleasant symptoms (e.g., hot flashes, headaches, night sweats, and mood changes), but the amount of discomfort varies considerably (Grady, 2006; Williams et al., 2007). Menopause is also accompanied by an elevated vulnerability to depression (Deecher et al., 2008). Not long ago, menopause was thought to be almost universally accompanied by severe emotional strain. However, it is now clear that most women experience relatively modest psychological distress (George, 2002; Walter, 2000).

Overall, the physiological changes brought on by aging tend to decrease functional capabilities, reduce biological resilience in the face of stress, and increase susceptibility to acute and chronic diseases (Freund, Nikitin, & Riediger, 2013). Hence, as you might guess, the proportion of people with chronic diseases climbs steadily with increased age (Ward, Schiller, & Goodman, 2014) (see Figure 11.22). That said, some people exhibit more "successful aging" than others do. Although people tend to assume that good health in old age depends primarily on physiological factors, such as good genes, quite a variety of *psychological factors* seem to have protective value in diminishing the deleterious effects of

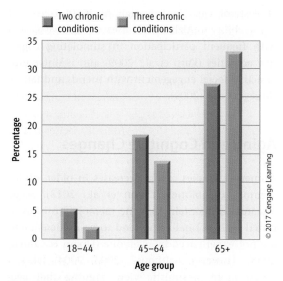

Figure 11.22
Age and chronic health conditions.
As people grow older, they do tend to experience more chronic health problems. This graph shows the percentage of people in three age brackets who wrestle with either two or three chronic health problems. (Data from Ward, Schiller, & Goodman, 2014)

aging. For example, in Chapter 9, we noted that higher *intelligence* is associated with greater health and longevity (Wrulich et al., 2014). In Chapter 12 we will discuss how health and longevity are associated with the personality traits of *optimism* (Carver & Scheier, 2014) and *conscientiousness* (Friedman et al., 2014). Research has also linked high *self-esteem* and the tendency to experience *positive emotions* to successful aging (Vondracek & Crouter, 2013). And, of course, healthy aging depends on *behavioural habits*, such as consuming a nutritious diet, getting adequate exercise, avoiding smoking and substance use, and being proactive about one's health by getting regular medical checkups and screenings (CDC, 2009). Thus, good health in old age may be as much about psychological processes as physiological processes.

Aging and Neural Changes

The amount of brain tissue and brain weight decline gradually in late adulthood, mostly after age 60 (Victoroff, 2005). These trends appear to reflect both a decrease in the number of active neurons in some areas of the brain and shrinkage of still-active neurons, with neuron loss perhaps being less important than once believed. Although this gradual loss of brain tissue sounds alarming, it is a normal part of the aging process. Its functional significance is the subject of some debate, but it doesn't appear to be a key factor in any of the age-related dementias.

Dementia is an abnormal condition marked by multiple cognitive deficits that include memory impairment.

Dementia can be caused by quite a variety of diseases, such as Alzheimer's disease, Parkinson's disease, Huntington's disease, and AIDS, to name just a few (Bourgeois, Seaman, & Servis, 2008). The prevalence of many of these diseases increases with age. Thus, dementia is seen in about 5–8 percent of people ages 65–70, and 15–20 percent of those ages 75–80 (Richards & Sweet, 2009). However, it is important to emphasize that dementia and "senility" are not part of the normal aging process.

Alzheimer's disease accounts for roughly 60–80 percent of all cases of dementia (Thies & Bleiler, 2013). The disease is accompanied by major structural deterioration in the brain. Alzheimer's patients exhibit profound and widespread loss of neurons and brain tissue, especially in the hippocampal region known to play a key role in memory (Braskie & Thompson, 2013). The hallmark early symptom is the forgetting of newly learned information after surprisingly brief periods of time. Impairments of working memory, attention, and executive function (planning, staying on task) are also quite common (Storandt, 2008). The course of the disease is one of progressive deterioration, typically over a period of 8–10 years, ending in death (Albert, 2008). Families of Alzheimer's patients experience enormous stress as they grapple with caregiving challenges and watch their loved ones slowly deteriorate (Thies & Bleiler, 2013).

The causes that launch this debilitating neural meltdown are not well understood. Genetic factors clearly contribute (Kauwe et al., 2013). Their exact role, though, remains unclear (Guerreiro, Gustafson, & Hardy, 2012). Recent evidence implicates chronic inflammation as a contributing factor (Obulesu & Jhansilakshmi, 2014). Some "protective" factors that diminish vulnerability to Alzheimer's disease have been identified. For example, risk is reduced among those who engage in regular exercise (Smith et al., 2013) and those with lower cardiovascular risk factors, such as absence of high blood pressure and no history of smoking or diabetes (Prince et al., 2014). Decreased vulnerability to Alzheimer's is also associated with frequent participation in stimulating cognitive activities (Landau et al., 2012) and maintenance of active social engagement with friends and family (James et al., 2011).

Studies continue to be conducted in attempts to document the range of memory deficits found in Alzheimer's patients. Research by Jill Rich and her colleagues (Rich et al., 2002), for example, has determined that language-based semantic judgments are especially impaired when a memory task is presented to patients with Alzheimer's in unstructured formats, as compared to relatively structured, supportive contexts. This suggests that Rich's sample of Alzheimer's patients were showing difficulties in the retrieval stage of memory. Results such as these emphasize the importance of supportive and structured environments for patients suffering from Alzheimer's. As the disease continues, many patients become restless and experience hallucinations, delusions, and paranoid thoughts. Eventually, victims become completely disoriented and are unable to care for themselves. There are some encouraging leads for treatments that might slow the progression of this horrific disease, but a cure does not appear to be on the horizon.

The causes that launch this debilitating neural meltdown are not well understood. Genetic factors clearly contribute (McQueen & Blacker, 2008), but their exact role remains unclear (Bertram & Tanzi, 2008). Recent evidence also implicates chronic inflammation as a contributing factor (Heneka et al., 2010). Some "protective" factors that diminish vulnerability to Alzheimer's disease have been identified (Hertzog et al., 2009). For example, risk is reduced among those who engage in regular exercise (Radak et al., 2010) and those with lower cardiovascular risk factors, such as high blood pressure and high cholesterol (Qui, Xu, & Fratiglioni, 2010). Decreased vulnerability to Alzheimer's disease is also associated with frequent participation in stimulating cognitive activities (Karp et al., 2009) and maintenance of active social engagement with friends and family (Krueger et al., 2009).

Aging and Cognitive Changes

Numerous studies report decreases in older adults' memory capabilities (Dixon et al., 2013). Some researchers maintain that the memory losses associated with normal aging tend to be moderate and are not experienced by everyone (Dixon & Cohen, 2003). However, Salthouse (2003, 2004) takes a much more pessimistic view, arguing that age-related decreases in memory are substantial in magnitude, that they begin in early adulthood, and that they affect everyone. One reason for these varied conclusions may be that a variety of memory types can be assessed (see Chapter 7), such as semantic, episodic, and procedural memory (Small et al., 2012). Episodic memory appears to be more vulnerable than semantic memory to age-related decline (Nyberg et al., 2012).

In the cognitive domain, aging seems to take its toll on speed first. Many studies indicate that speed in learning, solving problems, and processing information tends to decline with age (Salthouse, 1996, 2000). The evidence suggests that the erosion of processing speed may be a gradual, lengthy trend beginning in middle adulthood (see Figure 11.23). Although mental speed declines with age, problem-solving ability remains largely unimpaired if older people are given adequate time to compensate for their reduced speed.

A hot issue in recent years has been whether high levels of mental activity in late adulthood can delay the typical age-related declines in cognitive functioning. This possibility is sometimes referred to as the "use it or lose it" hypothesis. Several lines of evidence seem to provide support for this notion. For example, people who continue to work further into old age, especially people who remain in mentally demanding jobs, tend to show smaller decrements in cognitive abilities than their age-mates (Schooler, 2007). Other studies suggest that continuing to engage in intellectually challenging activities in late adulthood serves to buffer against cognitive declines (Nyberg et al., 2012). For example, one recent

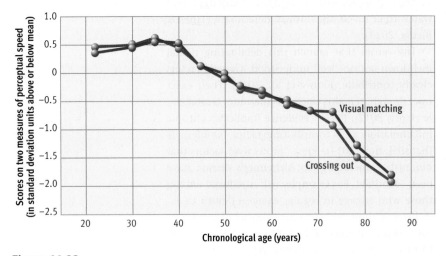

Figure 11.23

Age and mental speed. Many studies have found that mental speed decreases with age. The data shown here, from Salthouse (2000), are based on two perceptual speed tasks. The data points are means for large groups of subjects expressed in terms of how many standard deviations (see Appendix B) they are above or below the mean for all ages (which is set at 0). Similar age-related declines are seen on many tasks that depend on mental speed.

Source: Adapted from Salthouse, T. A. (2000). Aging and measures of processing speed. *Biological Psychology*, 54, 35–54. Reproduced by permission of Elsevier Science.

study of older individuals (average age = 72) found that three months of sustained engagement in learning new skills (quilting or digital photography) enhanced episodic memory (Park et al., 2014). Other studies suggest that bilingualism (Bialystok, 2017; Bialystok et al., 2016; Sullivan, Prescott, Goldberg, & Bialystok, 2016) serves to buffer against cognitive decline. You may recall that we discussed some of the positive consequences of being bilingual in Chapter 8.

With findings such as these in mind, some scientists have developed elaborate and challenging cognitive training programs for elderly people that are intended to slow their cognitive decline. Studies of these interventions have yielded some promising, albeit moderate, improvements in aspects of memory performance (Kanaan et al., 2014; Miller et al., 2013). That said, the evidence on memory training in the elderly is a mixed bag. It remains to be seen whether modest training effects can delay the onset or slow the progress of Alzheimer's disease.

Death and Dying

Life is indeed a journey, and death is the ultimate destination. Dealing with the deaths of close friends and loved ones is an increasingly frequent problem as people move through adulthood. Moreover, the final challenge of life is to confront one's own death.

Because death is a taboo topic in modern Western society, the most common strategy for dealing with it is *avoidance*. People often use euphemisms such as "passed away" to avoid even the word itself. Attitudes about death vary from culture to culture. Negativism and avoidance are not universal. For example, in Mexican culture, death is discussed frequently and is even celebrated on a national feast day, the Day of the Dead (DeSpelder & Strickland, 1983).

In some populations, fear of death has been found to increase from middle old age where it seems to plateau (Tange et al., 2016). Elderly adults are more likely to fear the period of uncertainty that comes before death than death itself. They worry about where they will live, who will take care of them, and how they will cope.

Pioneering research on the experience of dying was conducted by Elisabeth Kübler-Ross (1969, 1970) during the 1960s. Based on interviews with terminally ill patients, she concluded that people evolve through a series of five stages as they confront their own death: (1) denial, (2) anger, (3) bargaining (with God for more time), (4) depression, and (5) acceptance. Subsequent studies of dying patients have not all observed the same five emotions or the same progression of emotions she described (Corr, 1993; Friedman & James, 2008; Stroebe et al., 2017). But Kübler-Ross deserves credit for launching empirical research on death and dying. Her model is still used in discussions with the patient and his or her family members (Farley et al., 2015).

When a friend, spouse, or relative dies, individuals must cope with *bereavement*. Considerable variation exists among cultures in how people tend to deal with this highly stressful event. In North America and western European countries, the bereaved are typically encouraged to break their emotional ties with the deceased relatively quickly and to return to their regular routines. In Asian, African, and Hispanic cultures, the bereaved are encouraged to maintain emotional ties to their dead loved ones (Bonanno, 1998). For example, almost all Japanese homes have altars dedicated to family ancestors, and family members routinely talk to the deceased. Regardless of the particular form that mourning takes, all such rituals are designed to make death meaningful and to help the bereaved cope with the pain and disruption of death.

Studies of bereaved spouses suggest that grief reactions fall into five patterns (Bonanno, Wortman, & Neese, 2004). *Absent grief* or the *resilient pattern* is characterized by low levels of depression before and after the spouse's death. In *chronic grief*, low pre-loss depression is followed by sustained depression after the spouse's death. *Common grief* is characterized by a spike in depression shortly after the spouse's death and a decline in depression over time. In the *depressed-improved* pattern, high pre-loss depression is followed by a relatively quick and sustained decline in depression after the spouse's death. Chronic depression describes those who experience high levels of depression both before and long after spousal loss. Surprisingly, absent grief/resilience is the most common pattern, exhibited by roughly one-half of bereaved spouses. Many people believe that individuals who fail to engage in "grief work" will suffer long-term adjustment problems. However, this view has been contradicted by many studies (Bonanno et al., 2002; Wortman, Wolff, & Bonanno, 2004).

Hazel McCallion, at age 93, was Mississauga's longest serving mayor. She was first elected in 1978 and has been re-elected continuously ever since. Her most recent victory was in 2010. She retired from office in 2014.

Human Development across the Life Span

An Illustrated Overview of Human Development

Stage of development

Infancy
(birth–2)

Physical and sensorimotor development

Rapid brain growth; 75 percent of adult brain weight is attained by age 2.

Rapid improvement occurs in visual acuity; depth perception is clearly present by six months, perhaps earlier.

Ability to localize sounds is apparent at birth; ability to recognize parent's voice occurs within first week.

Landmarks in motor development: Infants sit without support around six months, walk around 12–14 months, run freely around two years.

© iStockphoto.com/Jose Manuel Gelphi Diaz

Major stage theories		Infancy	
	Piaget	Sensorimotor	
	Kohlberg	Premoral	
	Erikson	Trust vs. mistrust	Autonomy vs. shame
	Freud (see Chapter 12)	Oral	Anal

Cognitive development

Object permanence gradually develops.

Infant shows orienting response (pupils dilate, head turns) and attention to new stimulus, habituation (reduced orienting response) to repeated stimulus.

Babbling increasingly resembles spoken language.

First word is used around age one; vocabulary spurt begins around 18 months; frequent overextensions (words applied too broadly) occur.

Social and personality development

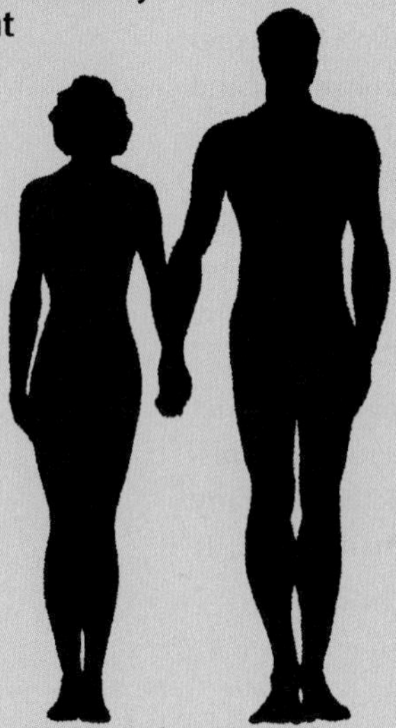

Temperamental individuality is established by two to three months; infants tend to be easy, difficult, or slow to warm up.

© Owen Franken/Corbis

Attachment to caregiver(s) is usually evident around six to eight months; secure attachment facilitates exploration.

"Stranger anxiety" often appears around six to eight months; separation anxiety peaks around 14 to 18 months.

Information compiled by Barbara Hansen Lemme, College of DuPage

Early childhood
(2–6)

Visual acuity reaches 20/20.

Connections among neurons continue to increase in density.

Bladder and bowel control is established.

Hand preference is usually solidified by three to four years; coordination improves; children learn to dress themselves.

© iStockphoto.com/Simone van den Berg

Middle childhood
(6–12)

Amos Morgan/Photodisc/Getty Images

In girls, growth spurt begins around age 11, bringing dramatic increases in height and weight.

Level of pituitary activity and sex hormones increases.

In girls, puberty begins around age 12; menstruation starts.

Girls' secondary sex characteristics (e.g., breast development and widening hips) begin to emerge.

Preoperational	Concrete operational
Preconventional	Conventional
Initiative vs. guilt	Industry vs. inferiority
Phallic	Latency

Thought is marked by egocentrism (limited ability to view world from another's perspective).

Thought is marked by centration (inability to focus on more than one aspect of a problem at a time) and irreversibility (inability to mentally undo an action).

Telegraphic speech (omitting nonessential words) appears at two to three years; syntax is well developed by age five; vocabulary increases dramatically.

Short-term memory capacity increases from two items at age two to five items around age six to seven; attention span improves.

Conservation (understanding that physical qualities can remain constant in spite of transformations in shape) is gradually mastered.

Child develops decentration (ability to focus on more than one feature of a problem at a time) and reversibility (ability to mentally undo an action).

Metalingustic awareness (ability to reflect on use of language) leads to play with language, use of puns, riddles, metaphors.

Long-term memory improves with increasing use of encoding strategies of rehearsal and organization.

Jupiter Images

Child realizes that gender does not change and begins to learn gender roles and form gender identity; social behaviour is influenced by observational learning, resulting in imitation.

Child progresses from parallel (side-by-side, noninteractive) play to cooperative play.

Social world is extended beyond family; first friendships are formed.

Banana Stock/Jupiter Images

Child experiences great increase in social skills, improved understanding of others' feelings; social world is dominated by same-sex peer relationships.

Role-taking skills emerge; fantasy is basis for thoughts about vocations and jobs.

Altruism tends to increase, aggression tends to decrease; aggression tends to become verbal rather than physical, hostile more than instrumental.

An Illustrated Overview of Human Development (*Continued*)

Adolescence
(12–20)

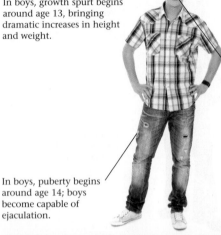

In boys, growth spurt begins around age 13, bringing dramatic increases in height and weight.

Level of pituitary activity and hormones increases.

Boys' secondary sex characteristics (e.g., voice change and growth of facial hair) begin to emerge.

In boys, puberty begins around age 14; boys become capable of ejaculation.

Edyta Pawlowska/Shutterstock.com

Young adulthood
(20–40)

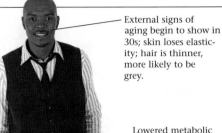

Reaction time and muscular strength peak in early to mid-20s.

External signs of aging begin to show in 30s; skin loses elasticity; hair is thinner, more likely to be grey.

Maximum functioning of all body systems, including senses, attained; slow decline begins in 20s.

Lowered metabolic rate contributes to increased body fat relative to muscle; gain in weight is common.

Sean Nel/Shutterstock.com

Formal operational

Postconventional (if attained)

Identity vs. confusion

Intimacy vs. isolation

Genital

Deductive reasoning improves; problem solving becomes more systematic, with alternative possibilities considered before solution is selected.

Thought becomes more abstract and reflective; individual develops ability to mentally manipulate abstract concepts as well as concrete objects.

Individual engages in idealistic contemplation of hypotheticals, "what could be."

Long-term memory continues to improve as elaboration is added to encoding strategies.

Intellectual abilities and speed of information processing are stable.

Greater emphasis is on application, rather than acquisition, of knowledge.

There is some evidence of a trend toward dialectical thought (ideas stimulate opposing ideas), leading to more contemplation of contradictions, pros and cons.

Person experiences increased interactions with opposite-sex peers; dating begins.

Attention is devoted to identity formation, questions such as "Who am I?" and "What do I want out of life?"

Realistic considerations about abilities and training requirements become more influential in thoughts about vocations and jobs.

Judith Haeusler/Taxi/Getty Images

Energies are focused on intimate relationships, learning to live with marriage partner, starting a family, managing a home.

Trial period is given for occupational choices, followed by stabilization of vocational commitment; emphasis is on self-reliance, becoming one's own person.

For many, close relationship develops with mentor (older person who serves as role model, adviser, and teacher).

Ryan McVay/Photodisc/Getty Images

Middle adulthood
(40–65)

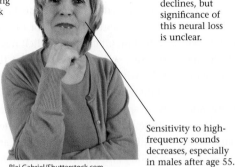

Changes occur in vision: increased farsightedness and difficulty recovering from glare; slower dark adaptation.

The amount of brain tissue declines, but significance of this neural loss is unclear.

In women, meno-pause occurs around age 50; in both sexes, sexual activity declines, although capacity for arousal changes only slightly.

Sensitivity to high-frequency sounds decreases, especially in males after age 55.

Blaj Gabriel/Shutterstock.com

Late adulthood
(65 and older)

Height decreases slightly because of changes in vertebral column; decline in weight also common.

Sensitivity of vision, hearing, and taste noticeably decreases.

Chronic diseases, especially heart disease, cancer, and stroke, increase.

Rate of aging is highly individualized.

Carme Balcells/Shutterstock.com

Generativity vs. self-absorption

There is some evidence for a trend toward improved judgment or "wisdom" based on accumulation of life experiences.

Effectiveness of retrieval from long-term memory begins slow decline, usually not noticeable until after age 55.

Individual experiences gradual decline in speed of learning, problem solving, and information processing.

In spite of decreased speed in cognitive processes, intellectual productivity and problem-solving skills usually remain stable.

Integrity vs. despair

Individual experiences gradual decline in cognitive speed and effectiveness of working memory.

Intellectual productivity depends on factors such as health and lifestyle; many people in 60s and 70s remain quite productive.

Decision making tends to become more cautious.

Fluid intelligence often declines, but crystallized intelligence remains stable or increases.

Midlife transition around age 40 leads to reflection, increased awareness of mortality and passage of time, but usually is not a personal crisis.

"Sandwich generation" is caught between needs of aging parents and children reaching adulthood.

Career development peaks; there is some tendency to shift energy from career concerns to family concerns.

Image Source/Jupiter Images

Steve Mason/Photodisc/Getty Imagess

Physical changes associated with aging require adjustments that affect life satisfaction.

Marital satisfaction often increases, but eventually death of spouse presents coping challenge.

Living arrangements are a significant determinant of satisfaction, as 60–90 percent of time is spent at home.

Putting It in Perspective: Themes 2, 3, 4, 5, and 6

Many of our seven integrative themes surfaced to some degree in our coverage of human development. We saw theoretical diversity in the discussions of attachment, cognitive development, and personality development. We saw that psychology evolves in a sociohistorical context, investigating complex, real-world issues. We encountered multifactorial causation of behaviour in the development of temperament and attachment, among other things. We saw cultural invariance and cultural diversity in our examination of attachment, motor development, cognitive development, and moral development.

But above all else, we saw how heredity and environment jointly mould behaviour. We've encountered the dual influence of heredity and environment before, but this theme is rich in complexity, and each chapter draws out different aspects and implications. Our discussion of development amplified the point that genetics and experience work *interactively* to shape behaviour. In the language of science, an interaction means that the effects of one variable depend on the effects of another. In other words, heredity and environment do not operate independently. Children with "difficult" temperaments will elicit different reactions from different parents, depending on the parents' personalities and expectations. Likewise, a particular pair of parents will affect children in different ways, depending on the inborn characteristics of the children. An interplay, or feedback loop, exists between biological and environmental factors. For instance, a temperamentally difficult child may elicit negative reactions from parents, which serve to make the child more difficult, which evokes more negative reactions. If this child develops into an ornery 11-year-old, which do we blame—genetics or experience? Clearly, this outcome is due to the reciprocal effects of both.

All aspects of development are shaped jointly by heredity and experience. We often estimate their relative weight or influence, as if we could cleanly divide behaviour into genetic and environmental components. Although we can't really carve up behaviour that neatly, such comparisons can be of great theoretical interest, as you'll see in our upcoming Personal Application, which discusses the nature and origins of gender differences in behaviour.

Understanding Gender Differences

Key Learning Goals

▶ Summarize evidence on gender differences in behaviour, and assess the significance of these differences.

▶ Explain how biological and environmental factors are thought to contribute to gender differences.

Are there genuine behavioural differences between the sexes (Hyde, 2013)? If so, why do these differences exist? How do they develop (Chaplin & Aldoo, 2013)? These are the complex and controversial questions that we'll explore in this Personal Application.

Before proceeding further, we need to clarify how some key terms are used, as terminology in this area of research has been evolving and remains a source of confusion. *Sex* usually refers to the biologically based categories of female and male. In contrast, *gender* usually refers to culturally constructed distinctions between femininity and masculinity. Individuals are born female or male. However, they become feminine or masculine through complex developmental processes that take years to unfold.

How Do the Sexes Differ in Behaviour?

Gender differences are actual disparities between the sexes in typical behaviour or average ability. Mountains of research, literally thousands of studies, exist on gender differences. What does this research show? Are the stereotypes of males and females accurate? Well, the findings are a mixed bag. The research indicates that genuine behavioural differences *do* exist between the sexes and that people's stereotypes are not entirely inaccurate (Eagly, 1995; Halpern, 2000). But the differences are fewer in number, smaller in size, and far more complex than stereotypes suggest (Hyde, 2014; Leaper, 2013).

Cognitive Abilities In the cognitive domain, it appears that there are three genuine—albeit very small—gender differences.

First, on the average, females tend to exhibit slightly better *verbal skills* than males (Leaper, 2013). For example, girls score higher in reading achievement around the world (Stoet & Geary, 2013). The size of females' advantage varies depending on the nature of the task, but the gender gaps generally are quite small (Halpern, 2012). Second, starting during high school, males show a slight advantage on tests of *mathematical ability*. When all students are compared, males' advantage is quite small. Indeed, it appears that the gender gap in math has disappeared in the general North American population (Hyde, 2014). Around the world, though, small to modest gender disparities are still seen in many countries, and these differences usually favour males (Else-Quest, Hyde, & Linn, 2010; Stoet & Geary, 2013). Also, at the high end of the ability distribution, a gender gap is still found in North America. About three to four times as many males as females manifest exceptional math skills (Wai, Putallaz, & Makel, 2012). Third, starting in the grade-school years, males tend to score higher than females on most measures of *visual-spatial ability* (Hines, 2013). Tasks requiring mental rotations in space and perception of movement in space tend to generate the biggest gender disparities (Halpern, 2012).

In regard to social behaviour, research findings support the existence of some additional gender differences. First, studies indicate that males tend to be much more *physically aggressive* than females (Archer, 2005; Card et al., 2008). This disparity shows up early in childhood. Its continuation into adulthood is supported by the fact that men account for a grossly disproportionate number of the violent crimes in our society (Kenrick, Trost, & Sundie, 2004). Contrary to popular belief, females and males seem pretty similar in their level of *verbal or relational aggression* (snide remarks and so forth), but this is the type of aggression females use most commonly, resulting in the "mean girls" stereotype (Leaper, 2013).

Second, there are gender differences in *nonverbal communication*. The evidence indicates that females are more sensitive than males to subtle nonverbal cues (Hampson, van Anders, & Mullin, 2006; Schmid et al., 2011) and that they pay more attention to interpersonal information (Hall & Mast, 2008). Third, males are more *sexually active* than females in a variety of ways. For example, males are more likely to engage in casual and premarital sex, masturbation, and the use of pornography (Petersen & Hyde, 2011).

Some Qualifications Although research has identified some genuine gender differences in behaviour, bear in mind that these are group differences that indicate nothing about individuals. Essentially, research results compare the "average man" with the "average woman." However, you are—and every individual is—unique. The average female and male are ultimately figments of our imagination. Furthermore, the genuine group differences noted are relatively small (Hyde, 2014). Figure 11.24 shows how scores on a trait, perhaps verbal ability, might be distributed for men and women. Although the group averages are detectably different, you can see the great variability within each group (sex) and the huge overlap between the two group distributions.

Biological Origins of Gender Differences

What accounts for the development of various gender differences? To what degree are they the product of learning or of biology? This question is yet another manifestation of the nature versus nurture issue. Investigations of the biological origins of gender differences have centred on the evolutionary bases of behaviour, hormones, and brain organization.

Evolutionary Explanations Evolutionary analyses usually begin by arguing that

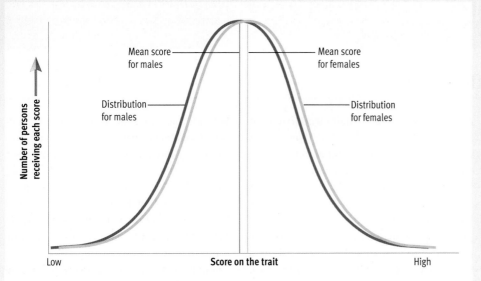

Figure 11.24

The nature of gender differences. Gender differences are group differences that indicate little about individuals because of the overlap between the groups. For a given trait, one sex may score higher on the average, but far more variation occurs within each sex than between the sexes.

Source: Adapted from Schaie, K. W. (1990). Intellectual development in adulthood. In J. E. Birren and K. W. Schaie (Eds.), *Handbook of the psychology of aging* (pp. 291–309). San Diego: Academic Press. Copyright © 1990 Elsevier Science (USA), reproduced with permission from the publisher.

gender differences in behaviour are largely the same across divergent cultures because cultural invariance suggests that biological factors are at work. Although research has turned up some fascinating exceptions, the better-documented gender differences in cognitive abilities, aggression, and sexual behaviour *are* found in virtually all cultures (Beller & Gafni, 1996; Kenrick et al., 2004). Evolutionary psychologists go on to argue that these universal gender differences reflect different natural selection pressures operating on males and females over the course of human history (Archer, 1996; Buss & Kenrick, 1998; Geary, 2007). For example, as we discussed in Chapter 10, males supposedly are more sexually active and permissive because they invest less than females in the process of procreation and can maximize their reproductive success by seeking many sexual partners (Buss, 1996; Schmitt, 2005; Webster, 2009).

The gender gap in aggression is also explained in terms of reproductive fitness. Because females are more selective about mating than males, males have to engage in more competition for sexual partners than females do. Greater aggressiveness is thought to be adaptive for males in this competition for sexual access because it should foster social dominance over other males and facilitate the acquisition of the material resources emphasized by females when they evaluate potential partners (Campbell, 2005; Cummins, 2005). Evolutionary theorists assert that gender differences in spatial ability reflect the division of labour in ancestral hunting-and-gathering societies in which males typically handled the hunting and females the gathering. Males' superiority on most spatial tasks has been attributed to the adaptive demands of hunting (Newcombe, 2007; Silverman & Choi, 2005; see Chapter 1).

Evolutionary analyses of gender differences are interesting, but controversial. On the one hand, it seems eminently plausible that evolutionary forces could have led to some divergence between males and females in typical behaviour. On the other hand, evolutionary hypotheses are highly speculative and difficult to test empirically (Eagly & Wood, 1999, 2013). The crucial problem for some critics is that evolutionary analyses are so "flexible" that they can be used to explain almost anything. For example, if the situation regarding spatial ability were reversed—if females scored higher than males—evolutionary theorists might attribute females' superiority to the adaptive demands of gathering food, weaving baskets,

and making clothes—and it would be difficult to prove otherwise (Cornell, 1997).

The Role of Hormones The potential role of prenatal hormones becomes apparent when something interferes with normal prenatal hormonal secretions. About half a dozen endocrine disorders can cause overproduction or underproduction of specific gonadal hormones during prenatal development. The general trend in this research is that females exposed prenatally to abnormally high levels of androgens exhibit more male-typical behaviour than other females do. Likewise, males exposed prenatally to abnormally low levels of androgens exhibit more female-typical behaviour than other males (Hines, 2004, 2013). These findings suggest that prenatal hormones contribute to the shaping of gender differences in humans. But the evidence is much stronger for females than for males, and it's always dangerous to draw conclusions about the general population based on small samples of people who have abnormal conditions (Basow, 1992; Jordan-Young, 2010).

Differences in Brain Organization Many theorists believe that gender differences in behaviour are rooted in male–female disparities in brain structure and organization (Cahill, 2006). For example, some theorists have tried to link gender differences to the specialization of the cerebral hemispheres in the brain (see Figure 11.25). As you may recall from Chapter 3, in most people, the left hemisphere is more actively involved in verbal processing, whereas the right hemisphere is more active in visual–spatial processing (Gazzaniga, Ivry, & Mangun, 2009). After these findings surfaced, theorists began to wonder whether this division of labour in the brain might be related to gender differences in verbal and spatial skills. Consequently, they began looking for sex-related disparities in brain organization.

Some thought-provoking findings *have* been reported. For instance, some studies have found that *males tend to exhibit more cerebral specialization than females* (Boles, 2005). Other studies suggest that *females tend to have a larger corpus callosum* (Gur & Gur, 2007), the band of fibres that connects the two hemispheres of the brain. Thus, some theorists

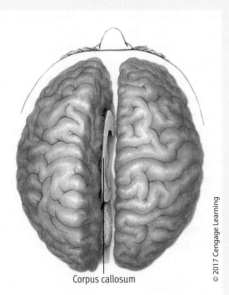

Figure 11.25
The cerebral hemispheres and the corpus callosum. In this drawing, the cerebral hemispheres have been "pulled apart" to reveal the corpus callosum, the band of fibres that connects the right and left halves of the brain. Research has shown that the right and left hemispheres are specialized to handle different types of cognitive tasks (see Chapter 3), leading some theorists to speculate that patterns of hemispheric specialization might contribute to gender differences in visual and spatial abilities.

Corpus callosum

© 2017 Cengage Learning

have concluded that differences between the genders in brain organization are responsible for gender differences in verbal and spatial ability (Clements et al., 2006; Hines, 2013).

This idea is intriguing, but psychologists have a long way to go before they can explain gender differences in terms of right brain/left brain specialization. Studies have not been consistent in finding that males have more specialized brain organization than females (Kaiser et al., 2009). In fact, a recent meta-analysis of 26 neuroimaging studies concluded that there was no gender disparity in language lateralization (Sommer et al., 2008). Also, serious doubts have been raised about the finding that females have a larger corpus callosum (Fine, 2010; Halpern et al., 2007). Moreover, even if these findings were replicated consistently, no one is really sure just how they would account for the observed gender differences in cognitive abilities (Fine, 2010).

In summary, researchers have made some intriguing progress in their efforts to document the biological roots of gender differences in behaviour. However, the idea that "anatomy is destiny" has proven difficult to demonstrate. Many theorists remain convinced that gender differences are largely shaped by experience. Let's examine their evidence.

Environmental Origins of Gender Differences

Socialization is the acquisition of the norms and behaviours expected of people in a particular society. In all cultures, the socialization process includes efforts to train children about gender roles. *Gender* roles are expectations about what is appropriate behaviour for each sex. Although gender roles are in a period of transition in modern Western society, there are still many disparities in how males and females are brought up. Investigators have identified three key processes involved in the development of gender roles: operant conditioning, observational learning, and self-socialization. First we'll examine these processes. Then we'll look at the principal sources of gender-role socialization: families, schools, and the media.

Operant Conditioning In part, gender roles are shaped by the power of reward and punishment—the key processes in operant conditioning (see Chapter 6). Parents, teachers, peers, and others often reinforce (usually with tacit approval) "gender-appropriate" behaviour and respond negatively to "gender-inappropriate" behaviour (Bussey & Bandura, 1999; Matlin, 2008). If you're a man, you might recall getting hurt as a young boy and being told that "big boys don't cry." If you succeeded in inhibiting your crying, you may have earned an approving smile or even something tangible like an ice cream cone. The reinforcement probably strengthened your tendency to "act like a man" and suppress emotional displays. If you're a woman, chances are your crying wasn't discouraged as gender-inappropriate. Studies suggest that fathers encourage and reward gender-appropriate behaviour in their youngsters more than mothers do and that boys experience more pressure to behave in gender-appropriate ways than girls do (Levy, Taylor, & Gelman, 1995).

Observational Learning *Observational learning* (see Chapter 6) by children can lead to the imitation of adults' gender-appropriate behaviour. Children imitate both males and females, but most children tend to imitate same-sex role models more than opposite-sex role models (Bussey & Bandura, 2004). Thus, imitation often leads young girls to play with dolls, dollhouses, and toy stoves. Young boys are more likely to tinker with toy trucks, miniature gas stations, or tool kits.

Self-Socialization Children themselves are active agents in their own gender-role socialization. Several *cognitive theories* of gender-role development emphasize self-socialization (Bem, 1985; Cross & Markus, 1993; Martin & Ruble, 2004). Self-socialization entails three steps. First, children learn to classify themselves as male or female and to recognize their sex as a permanent quality (around ages five to seven). Second, this self-categorization motivates them to value those characteristics and behaviours associated with their sex. Third, they strive to bring their behaviour in line with what is considered gender-appropriate in their culture. In other words, children get involved in their own socialization, working diligently

Gender-role socialization begins very early as parents provide their infants with "gender-appropriate" clothing, toys, and hairstyles.

Elisa Cincinelli/Brand X Pictures/Jupiter Images

to discover the rules that are supposed to govern their behaviour.

Sources of Gender-Role Socialization

There are three main sources of influence in gender-role socialization: families, schools, and the media. Of course, we are now in an era of transition in gender roles, so the generalizations that follow may say more about how you were socialized than about how children will be socialized in the future.

Families. A great deal of gender-role socialization takes place in the home (Berenbaum, Martin, & Ruble, 2008; Pomerantz, Ng, & Wang, 2004). Fathers engage in more "roughhousing" play with their sons than with their daughters, even in infancy (McBride-Chang & Jacklin, 1993). As children grow, boys and girls are encouraged to play with different types of toys (Freeman, 2007; Wood, Desmarais, & Gugula, 2002). Generally, boys have less leeway to play with "feminine" toys than girls do with "masculine" toys. When children are old enough to help with household chores, the assignments tend to depend on sex (Cunningham, 2001). For example, girls wash dishes and boys mow the lawn. And parents are more likely to explain scientific concepts to boys than to girls (Crowley et al., 2001).

Schools. Schools and teachers clearly contribute to the socialization of gender roles (Berenbaum et al., 2008). The books that children use in learning to read can influence their ideas about what is suitable behaviour for males and females (Diekman & Murnen, 2004). Traditionally, males have more likely been portrayed as clever, heroic, and adventurous in these books, while females have more likely been shown doing domestic chores. Preschool and grade-school teachers frequently reward sex-appropriate behaviour in their pupils (Fagot et al., 1985; Ruble & Martin, 1998). Interestingly, teachers tend to pay greater attention to males, helping them, praising them, and scolding them more than females (Sadker & Sadker, 1994). Schools may play a key role in the gender gap in outstanding math performance, as Hyde and Mertz (2009) note that girls traditionally have been much less likely than boys to be encouraged to enroll in advanced math, chemistry, and physics courses.

Media. Television and other mass media are another source of gender-role socialization (Bussey & Bandura, 2004). Although some improvement has been made in recent years, television shows have traditionally depicted men and women in highly stereotypic ways (Galambos, 2004; Signorielli, 2001). Women are often portrayed as submissive, passive, and emotional. Men are more likely to be portrayed as independent, assertive, and competent. Even commercials contribute to the socialization of gender roles (Furnham & Mak, 1999; Lippa, 2005). Recent research found an association between children's exposure to gender stereotyping in the media and their beliefs about gender roles (Oppliger, 2007).

Conclusion

As you can see, the findings on gender and behaviour are complex and confusing. Nonetheless, the evidence does permit one very general conclusion—a conclusion that you have seen before and will see again. Taken as a whole, the research in this area suggests that biological factors and environmental factors both contribute to gender differences in behaviour—as they do to all other aspects of development.

Are Fathers Essential to Children's Well-Being?

Key Learning Goal

▶ Clarify and critique the argument that fathers are essential for healthy development.

Are fathers essential for children to experience normal, healthy development? This question is currently the subject of heated debate. While much of this research has been conducted in the United States, it is an important issue for Canadians, too, given recent findings on the number of female-headed single-parent families in Canada. According to the 2001 Census, of the 8.4 million families in Canada, 15.7 percent were single-parent families, with 81 percent of those lone parents being female (Vanier Institute of the Family, 2005).

In recent years, a number of social scientists have mounted a thought-provoking argument that father absence is the chief factor underlying a host of modern social ills. For example, David Blankenhorn (1995) argues that "fatherlessness is the most harmful demographic trend of this generation. It is the leading cause of declining child well-being in our society" (p. 1). Expressing a similar view, David Popenoe (1996) maintains that "today's fatherlessness has led to social turmoil-damaged children, unhappy children, aimless children, children who strike back with pathological behaviour and violence" (p. 192).

The Basic Argument

What is the evidence for the proposition that fathers are essential to healthy development? Over the last 40 years, the proportion of children growing up without a father in the home has more than doubled. During the same time, we have seen dramatic increases in teenage pregnancy, juvenile delinquency, violent crime, drug abuse, eating disorders, teen suicide, and family dysfunction. Moreover, mountains of studies have demonstrated an association between father absence and an elevated risk for these problems.

Summarizing this evidence, Popenoe (1996) asserts that "fatherless children have a risk factor two to three times that of fathered children for a wide range of negative outcomes, including dropping out of high school, giving birth as a teenager, and becoming a juvenile delinquent" (p. 192), which leads him to infer that "fathers have a unique and irreplaceable role to play in child development" (p. 197). Working from this premise, Popenoe concludes, "If present trends continue, our society could be on the verge of committing social suicide" (p. 192). Echoing this dire conclusion, Blankenhorn (1995) comments that "to tolerate the trend of fatherlessness is to accept the inevitability of continued societal recession" (p. 222).

You might be thinking, "What's all the fuss about?" Surely, proclaiming the importance of fatherhood ought to be no more controversial than advocacy for motherhood or apple pie. But the assertion that a father is essential to a child's well-being has some interesting sociopolitical implications. It suggests that heterosexual marriage is the only appropriate context in which to raise children and that other family configurations are fundamentally deficient. Based on this line of reasoning, some people have argued for new laws that would make it more difficult to obtain a divorce and other policies and programs that would favour traditional families over families headed by single mothers, cohabiting parents, and gay and lesbian parents (Silverstein & Auerbach, 1999). Indeed, the belief that children need both a mother and a father has surfaced in some of the legal wrangling over same-sex marriage that has taken place in the United States. Thus, the question about the importance of fathers is creating a great deal of controversy, because it is really a question about alternatives to traditional family structure.

Evaluating the Argument

In light of the far-reaching implications of the view that fathers are essential to normal development, it makes sense to subject this view to critical scrutiny. How could you use critical thinking skills to evaluate this argument? At least three previously discussed ideas seem germane.

First, it is important to recognize that the position that fathers are essential for healthy development rests on a foundation of correlational evidence, and as we have seen repeatedly, *correlation is no assurance of causation*. Yes, there has been an increase in fatherlessness that has been paralleled by increases in teenage pregnancy, drug abuse, eating disorders, and other disturbing social problems. But think of all the other changes that have occurred over the last five decades, such as the decline of organized religion, the growth of mass media, dramatic shifts in sexual mores, and so forth. Increased fatherlessness has co-varied with a host of other cultural trends. Hence, it is highly speculative to infer that father absence is the chief cause of most modern social maladies.

Second, it always pays to think about whether there are specific, *alternative explanations* for findings that you might have doubts about. What other factors might account for the association between father absence and children's maladjustment? Think for a moment: What is the most frequent cause of father absence? Obviously, it is divorce. Divorces tend to be highly stressful events that disrupt children's entire lives. Although the evidence suggests that a majority of children seem to survive divorce

Are fathers crucial to children's well-being? This seemingly simple question has sparked heated debate.

Digital Vision/Getty Images

without lasting detrimental effects, it is clear that divorce elevates youngsters' risk for a wide range of negative developmental outcomes (Ehrenberg et al., 2014; Green et al., 2012). Given that father absence and divorce are inextricably intertwined, it is possible that the negative effects of divorce account for much of the association between father absence and social problems.

Are there any other alternative explanations for the correlation between fatherlessness and social maladies? Yes, critics point out that the prevalence of father absence co-varies with socioeconomic status. Father absence is much more common in low-income families (Anderson, Kohler, & Letiecq, 2002). Thus, the effects of father absence are entangled to some extent with the many powerful, malignant effects of poverty, which might account for much of the correlation between fatherlessness and negative outcomes (McLoyd, 1998).

A third possible strategy in thinking critically about the effects of father absence would be to ask *if there is contradictory evidence*. Once again, the answer is yes. Biblarz and Stacey (2010) reviewed studies comparing pairs of heterosexual parents against pairs of lesbian parents. If fathers are essential, the adjustment of children raised by heterosexual parents should be superior to that of children raised by lesbian parents. But the studies found negligible differences between these parental configurations.

A fourth strategy would be to look for some of the *fallacies in reasoning* introduced in Chapter 10 (irrelevant reasons, circular reasoning, slippery slope, weak analogies, and false dichotomy). A couple of the quotes from Popenoe and Blankenhorn were chosen to give you an opportunity to detect two of these fallacies in a new context. Take a look at the quotes once again and see whether you can spot the fallacies.

Popenoe's assertion that "if present trends continue, our society could be on the verge of social suicide" is an example of *slippery slope argumentation*, which involves predictions that if one allows X to happen, things will spin out of control and catastrophic events will follow. "Social suicide" is a little vague, but it sounds as if Popenoe is predicting that father absence will lead to the destruction of modern society. The other fallacy that you might have spotted was the *false dichotomy* apparent in Blankenhorn's assertion that "to tolerate the trend of fatherlessness is to accept the inevitability of continued societal recession." A false dichotomy creates an either–or choice between the position one wants to advocate (in this case, new social policies to reduce father absence) and some obviously horrible outcome that any sensible person would want to avoid (social decay), while ignoring other possible outcomes that might lie between these extremes.

In summary, we can find a number of flaws and weaknesses in the argument that fathers are *essential* to normal development. However, our critical evaluation of this argument *does not mean that fathers are unimportant*. Many types of evidence suggest that fathers generally make significant contributions to their children's development (McLanahan, Tach, & Schneider, 2013; Ramchandani et al., 2013). We could argue with merit that fathers typically provide a substantial advantage for children that fatherless children do not have. But there is a crucial distinction between arguing that fathers *promote* normal, healthy development and arguing that fathers are *necessary* for normal, healthy development. If fathers are *necessary*, children who grow up without them could not achieve the same level of well-being as those who have fathers, yet it is clear that a great many children from single-parent homes turn out just fine.

Fathers surely are important, and it seems likely that father absence *contributes* to a variety of social maladies. So, why do Blankenhorn (1995) and Popenoe (1996) argue for the much stronger conclusion—that fathers are *essential*? They appear to prefer the stronger conclusion because it raises much more serious questions about the viability of nontraditional family forms. Thus, they seem to want to advance a *political agenda* that champions traditional family values. They are certainly entitled to do so, but when research findings are used to advance a political agenda—whether conservative or liberal—a special caution alert should go off in your head. When a political agenda is at stake, it pays to scrutinize arguments with extra care, because research findings are more likely to be presented in a slanted fashion. The field of psychology deals with a host of complex questions that have profound implications for a wide range of social issues. The skills and habits of critical thinking can help you find your way through the maze of reasons and evidence that hold up the many sides of these complicated issues. See Table 11.1.

Table 11.1

Critical Thinking Skills Discussed in This Application

SKILL	DESCRIPTION
Understanding the limitations of correlational evidence	The critical thinker understands that a correlation between two variables does not demonstrate that there is a causal link between the variables.
Looking for alternative explanations for findings and events	In evaluating explanations, the critical thinker explores whether there are other explanations that could also account for the findings or events under scrutiny.
Recognizing and avoiding common fallacies, such as irrelevant reasons, circular reasoning, slippery slope reasoning, weak analogies, and false dichotomies	The critical thinker is vigilant about conclusions based on unrelated premises, conclusions that are rewordings of premises, unwarranted predictions that things will spin out of control, superficial analogies, and contrived dichotomies.

PRENATAL DEVELOPMENT

Stages

- During the *germinal stage*, a zygote becomes a mass of cells that implants in the uterine wall and the placenta begins to form.

- During the *embryonic stage*, most vital organs and bodily systems begin to form, making it a period of great vulnerability.

- During the *fetal stage*, organs continue to grow and gradually begin to function; the fetus reaches the *threshold of viability* around 23–25 weeks.

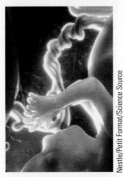

Nestle/Petit Format/Science Source

Environmental influences

- Maternal malnutrition during the prenatal period has been linked to birth complications and other problems, and maternal emotions can have an impact on prenatal development.

- Maternal use of illicit drugs can be dangerous to the unborn child. Even normal social drinking and routine tobacco use can be hazardous.

- Recent evidence suggests that prenatal development can "program" the fetal brain in ways that influence one's vulnerability to various types of illness decades later.

DEVELOPMENT IN CHILDHOOD

Motor development

- Physical growth is rapid and uneven during infancy, as there are sudden bursts of growth.

- Early progress in motor skills has traditionally been attributed to *maturation*, but recent research suggests that infants' exploration is also important.

- Researchers have found cultural variations in the pacing of motor development, which demonstrates the potential importance of learning.

Attachment

- *Attachment* refers to the close emotional bonds that develop between infants and caregivers.

- Harlow's studies of infant monkeys showed that reinforcement is not the key to attachment.

- Bowlby argued that attachment has a biological and evolutionary basis.

- Research by Ainsworth showed that infant-mother attachments fall into three categories: secure, anxious-ambivalent, and avoidant.

- Infants with a relatively secure attachment tend to become resilient, competent toddlers with high self-esteem.

- Cultural variations in child rearing influence the patterns of attachment seen in a society.

Personality development

- Erikson's theory proposes that individuals evolve through eight stages over the life span, with each stage marked by a specific *psychosocial crisis*.

- *Stage theories* assume that individuals progress through stages in a particular order, that progress is strongly related to age, and that new stages bring major changes.

- Erikson's four childhood stages are trust versus mistrust, autonomy versus shame and doubt, initiative versus guilt, and industry versus inferiority.

Cognitive development

- Piaget proposed that children evolve through four stages of cognitive development.

- The major achievement of the *sensorimotor period* (birth to age two) is the development of object permanence.

- Children's thought during the *preoperational period* (ages two to seven) is marked by centration, animism, irreversibility, and egocentrism.

- In the *concrete operational period* (ages 7–11), children develop the ability to perform operations on mental representations.

- In the *formal operational stage* (age 11 onward), thought becomes more systematic, abstract, and logical.

- Piaget may have underestimated some aspects of children's cognitive development, the mixing of stages, and the impact of culture.

- Vygotsky's sociocultural theory asserts that children's cognitive development is shaped by social interactions, language progress, and cultural factors.

- Researchers have found that infants understand complex concepts, such as addition, that they have had little opportunity to acquire through learning.

- These findings have led some theorists to conclude that some basic cognitive abilities are wired into humans' neural architecture.

Moral development

- Kohlberg's theory proposes that individuals progress through three levels of moral reasoning.

- *Preconventional reasoning* focuses on acts' consequences, *conventional reasoning* on the need to maintain social order, and *postconventional reasoning* on working out a personal code of ethics.

- Age-related progress in moral reasoning has been found in research, but there is a lot of overlap between stages.

DEVELOPMENT IN ADOLESCENCE

Physiological and neural development

- Brought on by hormonal changes, the *adolescent growth spurt* typically begins at about age 9–10 in girls and age 10–12 in boys.

- Puberty is the stage during which *primary sex characteristics* develop fully.

- Today's adolescents tend to begin puberty at an earlier age than previous generations, perhaps because of improvements in nutrition and medical care.

- Girls who reach puberty early and boys who mature relatively late have a greater risk for psychological and social difficulties.

- The *prefrontal cortex* appears to be the last area of the brain to fully mature, and this maturation is not complete until early adulthood.

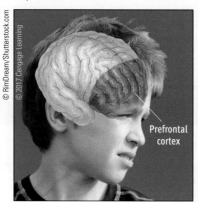

© RimDream/Shutterstock.com
© 2017 Cengage Learning

Prefrontal cortex

The search for identity

- According to Erikson, the main challenge of adolescence is the struggle for a sense of identity.

- Marcia asserted that adolescents deal with their identity crisis in four ways: *foreclosure, moratorium, identity diffusion,* and *identity achievement.*

- Arnett argued for the existence of a new developmental stage in modern societies, called *emerging adulthood.*

APPLICATIONS

- Genuine gender differences have been found in verbal ability, math ability, spatial ability, aggression, nonverbal communication, and sexual behaviour.

- However, many gender stereotypes are inaccurate, and most gender differences in behaviour are very small in magnitude.

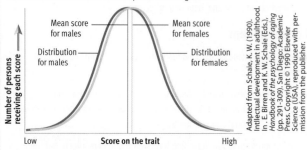

Mean score for males
Mean score for females
Distribution for males
Distribution for females

Number of persons receiving each score

Low   Score on the trait   High

Adapted from Schaie, K. W. (1990). Intellectual development in adulthood. In. E. Birren and K. W. Schaie (Eds.), *Handbook of the psychology of aging* (pp. 291–309). San Diego: Academic Press. Copyright © 1990 Elsevier Science (USA), reproduced with permission from the publisher.

- Evolutionary theorists attribute gender differences to natural selection based on different adaptive demands confronted by males and females.

- Evidence suggests that prenatal hormones contribute to gender differences, but the hypotheses on cerebral specialization have been highly speculative.

- Operant conditioning, observational learning, and self-socialization contribute to the development of gender differences.

- There are contradictory data and alternative explanations for the association between father absence and negative developmental outcomes.

DEVELOPMENT IN ADULTHOOD

Personality development

- During adulthood, personality is marked by both stability and change, as percentile scores remain stable but mean raw scores change in predictable ways.

- The adult years tend to bring gradual increases in agreeableness, openness to experience, and conscientiousness.

- According to Erikson, people evolve through three stages of development in the adult years: intimacy versus isolation, generativity versus self-absorption, and integrity versus despair.

Family transitions

- Optimism can ease the transition into marriage, but idealistic expectations about marriage are associated with steep declines in well-being.

- Premarital cohabitation used to be predictive of an increased likelihood of marital dissolution, but the situation seems to be changing.

- Adjusting to marriage is more likely to be difficult when spouses have different expectations about marital roles.

- Most parents are happy with their decision to have children, but the arrival of the first child represents a major transition, and the disruption of routines can be draining.

- Parent-adolescent relations are not as contentious as widely assumed, but conflicts do increase.

Physiological and neural changes

- In the sensory domain, vision and hearing acuity tend to decline, but glasses and hearing aids can compensate for these losses.

- Women's reactions to menopause vary, and menopause is not as stressful as widely believed.

- The proportion of people with chronic diseases climbs steadily with age, but some people exhibit more successful aging than others.

- Brain tissue and weight tend to decline after age 60, but this loss does not appear to be the key to age-related dementias.

- *Dementias* are seen in about 15–20 percent of people over age 75, but they are not part of the normal aging process.

- Alzheimer's patients exhibit profound loss of brain tissue and the accumulation of characteristic neural abnormalities.

Cognitive changes

- Many studies have found decreases in older adults' memory capabilities; there is debate about the severity of these memory losses.

- Speed in cognitive processing tends to begin a gradual decline during middle adulthood.

- Some studies suggest that high levels of mental activity in late adulthood can delay the typical age-related declines in cognitive functioning.

Death and dying

- Kübler-Ross concluded that people evolve through a series of five stages as they confront their death, but some subsequent studies did not find the same progression.

- Considerable variation exists among cultures in how people tend to deal with bereavement.

- Studies of bereaved spouses suggest that grief reactions fall into five patterns, with absent grief/resilience the most common pattern.

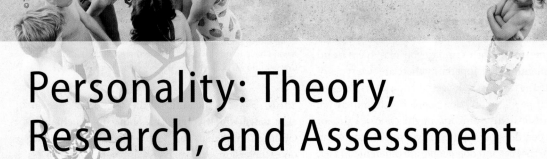

Personality: Theory, Research, and Assessment

Themes in this Chapter

Theoretical Diversity   Sociohistorical Context   Cultural Heritage

The scientific study of personality is one of the oldest topics in psychology. But interest in the nature of personality clearly exceeds the bounds of and predates the science of psychology. The ancient Greeks and Romans had their own view of character types and the causes of individual differences. In their theatre, actors used masks to signify different personalities and emotions (McDonald & Walton, 2007).

As you will see in the coming pages, there have been many conceptualizations of the nature of personality and how to assess it (Funder, 2016; Hampson, 2012; Mussel, 2013; Plouffe, Paunonen, & Saklofske, 2017; Turkheimer et al., 2014; van der Linden et al., 2017). While we will provide a more formal definition later, at this point it is sufficient to state that the study of personality focuses primarily on describing and understanding our individual differences. It seems as if everyone has a theory of what "types" of people there are in the world. For example, you may have heard friends mention that apparently there are two types of people in the world—cat lovers and dog lovers, referred to as "cat people" and "dog people." While there are many reasons why someone might choose a dog or cat as a pet, does personality play a role? Is there any evidence that cat and dog people are different? In fact, there is. Sam Gosling at the University of Texas does research on animal and human personality (Bensky, Gosling & Sinn, 2013; Fratkin et al., 2013) and he has researched personality differences between "dog people" and "cat people" (Gosling, Sandy, & Potter,

Sigmund Freud was a dog lover and he kept his dog with him in his office. In characterizing dogs and people, Freud stated that "dogs love their friends and bite their enemies, quite unlike people, who are incapable of pure love and always have to mix love and hate in their object-relations" (Masson, 1997, p. 3).

2010). Using a measure of the "Big Five" personality traits (which you'll learn about in this chapter), Gosling found that dog people tend to score higher on extraversion, agreeableness, and conscientiousness but lower on neuroticism and openness than do cat people. Perhaps these differences in pet lovers' personalities reflect differences in the pets themselves. As Bly (1988) quips, "Dogs come when they're called; cats take a message and get back to you later."

The pioneering personality theorist Sigmund Freud clearly was a dog person. Initially, he wanted a wolf as a pet, but when that proved impossible in Vienna, he turned to dogs. As an adult, he got his first dog and developed a life-long relationship with them. He kept a dog in his house and office both in Vienna and in England until the day he died. His preferred breed was a chow. While developing and practising psychoanalysis, the psychotherapy he conceived as a result of his clinical practice with hysterical patients in Vienna, he discovered that his chow Jo-Fi was able to assist in his therapy sessions. Jo-Fi sat with Freud when he was doing therapy and reportedly provided assessments of the stress level of his patients; Jo-Fi would lie close to Freud's couch if the patient was calm and across the room if the patient was tense. Jo-Fi also kept time; Jo-Fi would move to the door when the session was over, the 50-minute hour (Latham, 2011).

One of the reasons we psychologists are so interested in personality is that it is used as a way of predicting what someone will do—to predict their behaviour.

Personality testing is even part of the NASA selection and training program for astronauts (NASA, 2008). Astronaut candidates undergo a rigorous selection and training program lasting two years. In

Eight Canadian astronauts have been launched into space. The eight are Marc Garneu, Steve MacLean, Julie Payette, Dave Williams, Roberta Bondar, Chris Hadfield, Robert Thirsk, and Bjarni Tryggvanson. Pictured here is Chris Hadfield, who was appointed commander of the International Space Station in 2013.

addition to personality evaluation, there are physical, intellectual, academic, and citizenship criteria. So far, nine Canadians have flown in space—eight astronauts, and one civilian. One of the best-known Canadian astronauts is Chris Hadfield. In 1992, from an applicant field of 5330 Canadians, he was selected to be one of only four new Canadian astronauts. What type of personality should an aspiring astronaut have? A series of research studies have been conducted examining personality and other characteristics that should be considered when selecting astronaut candidates (Endler, 2004; McFadden, Helmreich, Rose, & Fogg, 1994; Musson, Sandal, & Helmreich, 2004; Sekiguchi, Umikura, Sone, & Kume, 1994; Suefeld, 2003; Suefeld & Steel, 2000). According to Bishop and Primeau (2002), for example, the desired or favourable characteristics of astronauts include high levels of task focus, positive interpersonal orientation and achievement motivation, and low levels of hostility, aggressiveness, and competitiveness.

In the pages that follow we'll devote most of our time to the influential personality theories of Freud, Skinner, Rogers, and several others. In addition we will consider biological, cultural, and other contemporary approaches to personality. In the Personal Application, we'll examine how psychological tests are used to measure aspects of personality. The Critical Thinking Application will explore how hindsight bias can taint people's analyses of personality.

The Nature of Personality

Personality is a complex hypothetical construct that has been defined in a variety of ways. Let's take a closer look at the concepts of personality and personality traits.

Defining Personality: Consistency and Distinctiveness

What does it mean to say that someone has an optimistic personality? This assertion indicates that the person has a fairly consistent tendency to behave in a cheerful, hopeful, enthusiastic way, looking at the bright side of things, across a wide variety of situations. Although no one is entirely consistent in behaviour, this quality of consistency across situations lies at the core of the concept of personality.

Distinctiveness is also central to the concept of personality. Personality is used to explain why not everyone acts the same way in similar situations. If you were stuck in an elevator with three people, each might react differently. One might crack jokes to relieve the tension. Another might make ominous predictions that "we'll never get out of here." The third might calmly think about how to escape. These varied reactions to the same situation occur because each person has a different personality. Each person has traits that are seen in other people, but each individual has his or her own distinctive *set* of personality traits.

In summary, the concept of personality is used to explain (1) the stability in a person's behaviour over time and across situations (consistency) and (2) the behavioural differences among people reacting to the same situation (distinctiveness). We can combine these ideas into the following definition: *Personality* **refers to an individual's unique constellation of** consistent behavioural traits. Let's look more closely at the concept of traits.

Personality Traits: Dispositions and Dimensions

Everyone makes remarks like "Jan is very conscientious." Or you might assert that "Bill is too timid to succeed in that job." These descriptive statements refer to personality traits. **A** *personality trait* **is a durable disposition to behave in a particular way in a variety of situations.** Adjectives such as *honest, dependable, moody, impulsive, suspicious, anxious, excitable, domineering,* and *friendly* describe dispositions that represent personality traits.

Most approaches to personality assume that some traits are more basic than others (Paunonen & Hong, 2015). According to this notion, a small number of fundamental traits determine other, more superficial traits. For example, a person's tendency to be impulsive, restless, irritable, boisterous, and impatient might all be derived from a more basic tendency to be excitable.

A number of psychologists have taken on the challenge of identifying the basic traits that form the core of personality (van der Linden et al., 2017). For example, Raymond Cattell (1950, 1966, 1990) used the statistical procedure of factor analysis (Cai, 2013) to reduce a huge list of personality traits compiled by Gordon Allport (1937) to just 16 basic dimensions of personality. As you may recall from Chapter 9, in *factor analysis*, **correlations among many variables are analyzed to identify closely related clusters of variables.** If the measurements of a number of variables (in this case, personality traits)

Key Learning Goals

▶ Clarify the meaning of personality and personality traits.

▶ Describe the five-factor model of personality and the relationship between the Big Five traits and life outcomes.

correlate highly with one another, the assumption is that a single factor is influencing all of them. Factor analysis is used to identify these hidden factors. In factor analyses of personality traits, these hidden factors are viewed as very basic, higher-order traits that determine less basic, more specific traits. Based on his factor analytic work, Cattell concluded that an individual's personality can be described completely by measuring just 16 traits.

The Five-Factor Model of Personality Traits

Based on factor analyses, Robert McCrae and Paul Costa (1987, 1997, 2008) maintain that most personality traits are derived from just five higher-order traits that have come to be known as the "Big Five" (see Figure 12.1):

- *Extraversion.* People who score high in extraversion are characterized as outgoing, sociable, upbeat, friendly, assertive, and gregarious. They also have a more positive outlook on life and are motivated to pursue social contact, intimacy, and interdependence (Wilt & Revelle, 2009).
- *Neuroticism.* People who score high in neuroticism tend to be anxious, hostile, self-conscious, insecure, and vulnerable. They also tend to exhibit more impulsiveness and emotional instability than others (Widiger, 2009).
- *Openness to experience.* Openness is associated with curiosity, flexibility, imaginativeness, intellectual pursuits, interests in new ideas, and unconventional attitudes. People who are high in openness also tend to be tolerant of ambiguity (McCrae & Sutin, 2009).

- *Agreeableness.* Those who score high in agreeableness tend to be sympathetic, trusting, cooperative, modest, and straightforward. Agreeableness is also correlated with empathy and helping behaviour (Graziano & Tobin, 2009).
- *Conscientiousness.* Conscientious people tend to be diligent, well-organized, punctual, and dependable. Conscientiousness is associated with strong self-discipline and the ability to regulate oneself effectively (Roberts et al., 2009).

Correlations have been found between the Big Five traits and quite a variety of important life outcomes. For instance, higher grades in college are associated with higher conscientiousness (McAbee & Oswald, 2013), perhaps because conscientious students work harder (Noftle & Robins, 2007). Several of the Big Five traits are associated with career success. Extraversion and conscientiousness are positive predictors of occupational attainment, whereas neuroticism is a negative predictor (Miller Burke & Attridge, 2011; Roberts, Caspi, & Moffitt, 2003). Agreeableness is negatively associated with income, especially among men (Judge, Livingston, & Hurst, 2012). The likelihood of divorce can also be predicted by personality traits because neuroticism elevates the probability of divorce, whereas agreeableness and conscientiousness reduce it (Roberts et al., 2007). Finally, and perhaps most important, several of the Big Five traits are related to health and mortality. Neuroticism is associated with an elevated prevalence of physical and mental disorders (Smith, Williams, & Segerstrom, 2015), whereas conscientiousness is correlated with the experience of less illness and with greater longevity (Friedman & Kern, 2014). Recent research suggests that openness to experience may also foster longevity (DeYoung, 2015).

Courtesy of Paul Trapnell

Paul Trapnell is a personality psychologist at the University of Winnipeg. He conducts research on, among other things, the Big Five personality traits.

Figure 12.1
The five-factor model of personality. Trait models attempt to analyze personality into its basic dimensions. In factor-analytic studies, the five traits shown here tend to emerge as higher-order factors that can account for other traits. McCrae and Costa (1985, 1987, 1997) maintain that personality can be described adequately by scores on the five traits identified here, which are widely referred to as the "Big Five."

Source: Kenrick, D. T., Griskevicius, V., Neuberg, S., & Schaller, M. (2010). Renovating the pyramid of needs: Contemporary extensions built upon ancient foundations. *Perspectives on Psychological Science, 5,* 292–314. Copyright © 2010, Association for Psychological Science. Reprinted with permission.

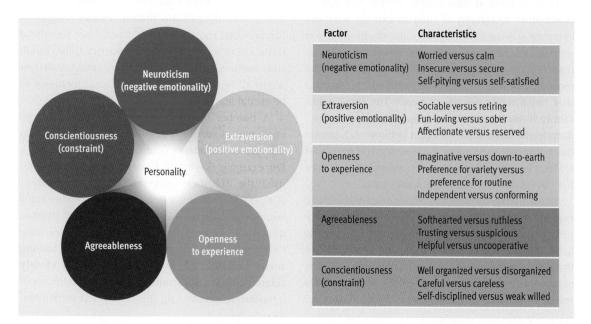

Factor	Characteristics
Neuroticism (negative emotionality)	Worried versus calm Insecure versus secure Self-pitying versus self-satisfied
Extraversion (positive emotionality)	Sociable versus retiring Fun-loving versus sober Affectionate versus reserved
Openness to experience	Imaginative versus down-to-earth Preference for variety versus preference for routine Independent versus conforming
Agreeableness	Softhearted versus ruthless Trusting versus suspicious Helpful versus uncooperative
Conscientiousness (constraint)	Well organized versus disorganized Careful versus careless Self-disciplined versus weak willed

Advocates of the five-factor model maintain that personality can be described adequately by measuring the basic traits they've identified. Their bold claim has been supported in many studies, and the Big Five model has become a dominant conception of personality structure in contemporary psychology (Habashi, Graziano, & Hoover, 2016; McCrae, Gaines, & Wellington, 2013). However, some theorists argue that only two or three traits are necessary to account for most of the variation seen in human personality, while others suggest that more than five traits are needed to describe personality adequately (Saucier & Srivastava, 2015). The debate about how many dimensions are necessary to describe personality and how traits affect behaviour (e.g., McCabe & Fleeson, 2016) is likely to continue.

Psychologists have approached the study of personality from a variety of perspectives. Traditionally, the study of personality has been dominated by "grand theories" that attempt to explain a great many facets of behaviour. These include the behavioural approach, humanistic approach, and others that we will review later in the chapter. In recent decades, however, the study of personality has shifted toward narrower research programs that examine specific issues related to personality. One example of this latter trend is research on the *Dark Triad* (e.g., Spurk, Keller, & Hirschi, 2016).

According to Delroy Paulhus at the University of British Columbia, the *Dark Triad* refers to a specific combination of three traits leading to negative, antisocial behavioural tendencies. The Dark Triad consists of three separate but intercorrelated traits—Machiavellianism, psychopathy, and narcissism (Paulhus & Williams, 2002). According to Paulhus, the three traits characterize someone who has a "socially malevolent character with behavioural tendencies toward self-promotion, emotional coldness, duplicity, and aggressiveness" (p. 557). *Psychopathy*

is a term we will explore in Chapter 15. Someone scoring high on psychopathy is someone we might refer to colloquially as a *psychopath*—someone who feels little empathy, who likes to control and hurt others, who is impulsive, and who often lives a parasitic lifestyle (Spurk, Keller, & Hirshchi, 2016). *Narcissism* refers to a tendency to focus almost exclusively on the self and one's self image, and to maintain an inflated view of the self and demand attention. Someone high in Machiavellianism is someone who enjoys, and is good at, manipulating others.

The traits forming the Dark Triad represent the dark side to human personality. Individuals displaying this personality type exhibit vengeful attitudes and show a tendency to engage in antisocial activities that harm others, such as exploiting others sexually in short-term relationships, showing no empathy for the suffering of their victims, and often enjoying the physical and emotional abuse they cause others (Adams et al., 2014; Baughman et al., 2014; Jones & Paulhus, 2017; Paulhus & Williams, 2002; Porter et al., 2014). Recently, Paulhus has added a fourth trait to the mix—*sadism*. The new term used by Paulhus to incorporate sadism is the *Dark Tetrad*. Sadism adds an additional type of negativity to the description of an evil personality: "The sadistic personality is unique among the Dark Tetrad in involving an appetite for cruelty—as opposed to callous indifference" (Paulhus, Curtis, & Jones, 2017, p. 89).

As you'll see throughout the rest of the chapter, the study of personality is an area in psychology that has a long history of "duelling theories." We'll divide these diverse personality theories into four broad groups that each share certain assumptions, emphases, and interests: (1) psychodynamic perspectives, (2) behavioural perspectives, (3) humanistic perspectives, and (4) biological perspectives. We'll begin our discussion of personality theories by examining the ideas of Sigmund Freud.

Psychodynamic Perspectives

Psychodynamic theories include all of the diverse theories descended from the work of Sigmund Freud, which focus on unconscious mental forces. Freud inspired many brilliant scholars to follow in his intellectual footsteps. Some of these followers simply refined and updated Freud's theory. Others veered off in new directions and established independent, albeit related, schools of thought. Today, the psychodynamic umbrella covers a large collection of loosely related theories that we can only sample from in this text. In this chapter, we'll examine the ideas of Sigmund Freud in some detail. Then we'll take a briefer look at the psychodynamic theories of Carl Jung and Alfred Adler.

Freud's Psychoanalytic Theory

Sigmund Freud was a physician specializing in neurology when he began his medical practice in Vienna toward the end of the 19th century. Like other neurologists in his era, he often treated people troubled by nervous problems, such as irrational fears, obsessions, and anxieties. Eventually he devoted himself to the treatment of mental disorders using an innovative procedure he had developed, which he called *psychoanalysis*. It required lengthy verbal interactions with patients, during which Freud probed deeply into their lives (see Chapter 16). Freud's (1901, 1924, 1940) *psychoanalytic theory* grew out of his decades of

Key Learning Goals

▶ Explain Freud's view of personality structure and the role of conflict and anxiety.

▶ Identify key defence mechanisms, and outline Freud's view of development.

▶ Summarize the psychodynamic theories proposed by Jung and Adler.

▶ Evaluate the strengths and weaknesses of the psychodynamic approach to personality.

Sigmund Freud
....

"No one who, like me, conjures up the most evil of those half-tamed demons that inhabit the human beast, and seeks to wrestle with them, can expect to come through the struggle unscathed."

interactions with his clients. Psychoanalytic theory attempts to explain personality by focusing on the influence of early childhood experiences, unconscious conflicts, and sexual urges.

Although Freud's theory gradually gained prominence, most of Freud's contemporaries were uncomfortable with his theory, for at least three reasons. First, in arguing that people's behaviour is governed by unconscious factors of which they are unaware, Freud made the disconcerting suggestion that individuals are not masters of their own minds. Second, in claiming that adult personalities are shaped by childhood experiences and other factors beyond one's control, he suggested that people are not masters of their own destinies. Third, by emphasizing the importance of how people cope with their sexual urges, he offended those who held the conservative, Victorian values of his time. Let's examine the ideas that generated so much controversy.

Structure of Personality

Freud divided personality structure into three components: the id, the ego, and the superego (see Figure 12.2). He saw a person's behaviour as the outcome of interactions among these three components.

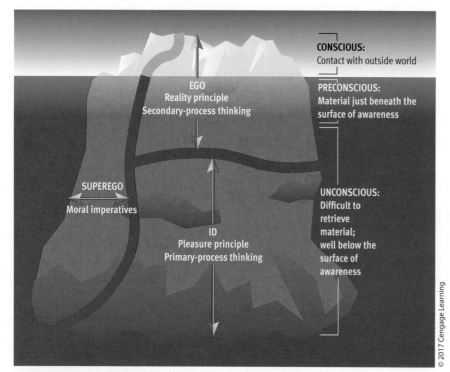

Figure 12.2
Freud's model of personality structure. Freud theorized that people have three levels of awareness: the conscious, the preconscious, and the unconscious. The enormous size of the unconscious is often dramatized by comparing it to the portion of an iceberg that lies beneath the water's surface. Freud also divided personality structure into three components—id, ego, and superego—which operate according to different principles and exhibit different modes of thinking. In Freud's model, the id is entirely unconscious, but the ego and superego operate at all three levels of awareness.

The *id* is the primitive, instinctive component of personality that operates according to the pleasure principle. Freud referred to the id as the reservoir of psychic energy. By this he meant that the id houses the raw biological urges (to eat, sleep, defecate, copulate, and so on) that energize human behaviour. The id operates according to the *pleasure principle*, which demands immediate gratification of its urges. The id engages in *primary-process thinking*, which is primitive, illogical, irrational, and fantasy-oriented.

The *ego* is the decision-making component of personality that operates according to the reality principle. The ego mediates between the id, with its forceful desires for immediate satisfaction, and the external social world, with its expectations and norms regarding suitable behaviour. The ego considers social realities—society's norms, etiquette, rules, and customs—in deciding how to behave. The ego is guided by the *reality principle*, which seeks to delay gratification of the id's urges until appropriate outlets and situations can be found. In short, to stay out of trouble, the ego often works to tame the unbridled desires of the id.

In the long run, the ego wants to maximize gratification, just as the id does. However, the ego engages in *secondary-process thinking*, which is relatively rational, realistic, and oriented toward problem solving. Thus, the ego strives to avoid negative consequences from society and its representatives (e.g., punishment by parents or teachers) by behaving "properly." It also attempts to achieve long-range goals that sometimes require putting off gratification.

While the ego concerns itself with practical realities, the *superego* is the moral component of personality that incorporates social standards about what represents right and wrong. Throughout their lives, but especially during childhood, people receive training about what constitutes good and bad behaviour. Many social norms regarding morality are eventually internalized. The superego emerges out of the ego at around three to five years of age. In some people, the superego can become irrationally demanding in its striving for moral perfection. Such people are plagued by excessive feelings of guilt. According to Freud, the id, ego, and superego are distributed differently across three levels of awareness, which we'll describe next.

Levels of Awareness

Perhaps Freud's most enduring insight was his recognition of how unconscious forces can influence behaviour. He inferred the existence of the unconscious from a variety of observations that he made with his patients. For example, he noticed that "slips of the tongue" often revealed a person's true feelings. He also realized that his patients' dreams often expressed hidden desires. Most important, through psychoanalysis, he often helped patients to discover feelings and conflicts of which they had previously been unaware.

Freud contrasted the unconscious with the conscious and preconscious, creating three levels of awareness. The *conscious* consists of whatever one is aware of at a particular point in time. For example, at this moment your conscious may include the train of thought in this text and a dim awareness in the back of your mind that your eyes are getting tired and you're beginning to get hungry. The *preconscious* contains material just beneath the surface of awareness that can easily be retrieved. Examples might include your middle name, what you had for supper last night, or an argument you had with a friend yesterday. The *unconscious* contains thoughts, memories, and desires that are well below the surface of conscious awareness but that nonetheless exert great influence on behaviour. Examples of material that might be found in your unconscious include a forgotten trauma from childhood, hidden feelings of hostility toward a parent, and repressed sexual desires.

Freud's conception of the mind is often compared to an iceberg that has most of its mass hidden beneath the water's surface (see Figure 12.2). He believed that the unconscious (the mass below the surface) is much larger than the conscious or preconscious. As you can see in Figure 12.2, he proposed that the ego and superego operate at all three levels of awareness. In contrast, the id is entirely unconscious, expressing its urges at a conscious level through the ego. Of course, the id's desires for immediate satisfaction often trigger internal conflicts with the ego and superego. These conflicts play a key role in Freud's theory.

Conflict and the Tyranny of Sex and Aggression

Freud assumed that behaviour is the outcome of an ongoing series of internal conflicts. He saw internal battles between the id, ego, and superego as routine. Why? Because the id wants to gratify its urges immediately, but the norms of civilized society frequently dictate otherwise. For example, your id might feel an urge to clobber a co-worker who constantly irritates you. However, society frowns on such behaviour, so your ego would try to hold this urge in check. Hence, you would find yourself in conflict. You may be experiencing conflict at this very moment. In Freudian terms, your id may be secretly urging you to abandon reading this chapter so that you can fix a snack and watch some videos on YouTube. Your ego may be weighing this appealing option against your society-induced need to excel in school.

Freud's psychoanalytic theory was based on decades of clinical work. He treated a great many patients in the consulting room pictured here. The room contains numerous artifacts from other cultures—and the original psychoanalytic couch.

Freud believed that people's lives are dominated by conflict. He asserted that individuals career from one conflict to another.

reality check

Misconception

People are generally aware of the factors that influence their behaviour.

Reality

Freud's insight from over a century ago, that people are often unaware of the unconscious factors that shape their behaviour, has proven prophetic. Decades of research on perception, cognition, and social behaviour have repeatedly demonstrated that unconscious goals, attitudes, and thoughts exert enormous influence over human behaviour (Bargh, Gollwitzer, & Oettingen, 2010; Dijksterhuis, 2010).

Freud believed that conflicts centring on sexual and aggressive impulses are especially likely to have far-reaching consequences. Why did he emphasize sex and aggression? Two reasons were prominent in his thinking. First, he thought that sex and aggression are subject to more complex and ambiguous social controls than other basic motives. The norms governing sexual and aggressive behaviour are subtle, and people often get inconsistent messages about what's appropriate. Thus, Freud believed that these two drives are the source of much confusion.

Second, he noted that the sexual and aggressive drives are thwarted more regularly than other basic biological urges. Think about it: If you get hungry or thirsty, you can simply head for a nearby vending machine or a drinking fountain. But if a department

Figure 12.3
Freud's model of personality dynamics. According to Freud, unconscious conflicts among the id, ego, and superego sometimes lead to anxiety. This discomfort may lead to the use of defence mechanisms, which may temporarily relieve anxiety.

store clerk infuriates you, you aren't likely to reach across the counter and slug him or her. Likewise, when you see a person who inspires lustful urges, you don't normally walk up and propose a tryst in a nearby broom closet. There's nothing comparable to vending machines or drinking fountains for the satisfaction of sexual and aggressive urges. Freud ascribed great importance to these needs because social norms dictate that they be routinely frustrated.

Anxiety and Defence Mechanisms

Most internal conflicts are trivial and are quickly resolved one way or the other. Occasionally, however, a conflict will linger for days, months, or even years, creating internal tension. More often than not, such prolonged and troublesome conflicts involve sexual and aggressive impulses that society wants to tame. These conflicts are often played out entirely in

the unconscious. Although you may not be aware of these unconscious battles, they can produce *anxiety* that slips to the surface of conscious awareness. The anxiety can be attributed to your ego worrying about (1) the id getting out of control and doing something terrible that leads to severe negative consequences or (2) the superego getting out of control and making you feel guilty about a real or imagined transgression.

The arousal of anxiety is a crucial event in Freud's theory of personality functioning (see Figure 12.3). Anxiety is distressing, so people try to rid themselves of this unpleasant emotion any way they can. This effort to ward off anxiety often involves the use of defence mechanisms. *Defence mechanisms* **are largely unconscious reactions that protect a person from unpleasant emotions such as anxiety and guilt (see Table 12.1).** Typically, they're mental manoeuvres that work through self-deception. Consider *rationalization,* which is creating false but plausible excuses to justify unacceptable behaviour. For example, after cheating someone in a business transaction, you might reduce your guilt by rationalizing that "everyone does it."

According to Delroy Paulhus from the University of British Columbia and his colleagues, repression is "the flagship in the psychoanalytic fleet of defense mechanisms" (Paulhus, Fridhandler, & Hayes, 1997); repression is the most basic and widely

Table 12.1

Defence Mechanisms, with Examples

DEFENCE MECHANISM	DEFINITION	EXAMPLE
Repression	Keeping distressing thoughts and feelings buried in the unconscious	A traumatized soldier has no recollection of the details of a close brush with death.
Projection	Attributing one's own thoughts, feelings, or motives to another	A woman who dislikes her boss thinks she likes her boss but feels that the boss doesn't like her.
Displacement	Diverting emotional feelings (usually anger) from their original source to a substitute target	After parental scolding, a young girl takes her anger out on her little brother.
Reaction formation	Behaving in a way that is exactly the opposite of one's true feelings	A parent who unconsciously resents a child spoils the child with outlandish gifts.
Regression	A reversion to immature patterns of behaviour	An adult has a temper tantrum when he doesn't get his way.
Rationalization	Creating false but plausible excuses to justify unacceptable behaviour	A student watches TV instead of studying, saying that "additional study wouldn't do any good anyway."
Identification	Bolstering self-esteem by forming an imaginary or real alliance with some person or group	An insecure young man joins a fraternity to boost his self-esteem.
Sublimation	Occurs when unconscious, unacceptable impulses are channelled into socially acceptable, perhaps even admirable, behaviours	A young man's longing for intimacy is channelled into his creative artwork.

Note: See Table 14.2 on page 529 for additional examples of defence mechanisms.

used defence mechanism. *Repression* is keeping distressing thoughts and feelings buried in the unconscious. People tend to repress desires that make them feel guilty, conflicts that make them anxious, and memories that are painful. Repression has been called "motivated forgetting." If you forget a dental appointment or the name of someone you don't like, repression may be at work.

Self-deception can also be seen in projection and displacement. *Projection* is attributing one's own thoughts, feelings, or motives to another. Usually, the thoughts one projects onto others are thoughts that would make one feel guilty. For example, if lusting for a co-worker makes you feel guilty, you might attribute any latent sexual tension between the two of you to the other person's desire to seduce you. *Displacement* is diverting emotional feelings (usually anger) from their original source to a substitute target. If your boss gives you a hard time at work and you come home and slam the door, kick the dog, and scream at your spouse, you're displacing your anger onto irrelevant targets. Unfortunately, social constraints often force people to hold back their anger, and they end up lashing out at the people they love most.

Other prominent defence mechanisms include reaction formation, regression, and identification. *Reaction formation* is behaving in a way that's exactly the opposite of one's true feelings. Guilt about sexual desires often leads to reaction formation. For example, Freud theorized that many males who ridicule homosexuals are defending against their own latent homosexual impulses. The telltale sign of reaction formation is the exaggerated quality of the opposite behaviour. *Regression* is a reversion to immature patterns of behaviour. When anxious about their self-worth, some adults respond with childish boasting and bragging (as opposed to subtle efforts to impress others). For example, a fired executive having difficulty finding a new job might start making ridiculous statements about his incomparable talents and achievements. Such bragging is regressive when it's marked by massive exaggerations that virtually anyone can see through. *Identification* is bolstering self-esteem by forming an imaginary or real alliance with some person or group. Youngsters often shore up precarious feelings of self-worth by identifying with rock stars, movie stars, or famous athletes. Adults may join exclusive country clubs or civic organizations as a means of identification.

Finally, Freud described the defence of *sublimation*, which occurs when unconscious, unacceptable impulses are channelled into socially acceptable, perhaps even admirable, behaviours. For example, intense aggressive impulses might be rechannelled by taking up boxing or football. Freud believed that many creative endeavours, such as painting, poetry, and sculpture, were sublimations of sexual urges. For instance, he argued that Leonardo da Vinci's painting of Madonna figures was a sublimation of his longing for intimacy with his mother (Freud, 1910). By definition, sublimation is regarded as a relatively healthy defence mechanism. Freud's work on defence mechanisms was important both to the development of psychoanalysis and its legacy since it is one aspect of his theory that endures and has contemporary currency (Erdelyi, 2001). Freud's daughter, Anna Freud, is well known for her contributions to the study of defence mechanisms (Freud, 1936) and as the founder of the child psychoanalytic movement (Flett, 2007).

Anna Freud, Sigmund Freud's youngest daughter, carried on and extended her father's work in psychoanalytic psychology. She made significant contributions to the development of child psychoanalysis and our understanding of defence mechanisms.

concept **check** 12.1

Identifying Defence Mechanisms

Check your understanding of defence mechanisms by identifying specific defences in the story below. Each example of a defence mechanism is underlined, with a number next to it. Write in the defence at work in each case in the numbered spaces after the story. The answers are in Appendix A near the back of the book.

My girlfriend recently broke up with me after we had dated seriously for several years. At first, I cried a great deal and <u>locked myself in my room, where I pouted endlessly.</u> (1.) I was sure that my former girlfriend felt as miserable as I did. <u>I told several friends that she was probably lonely and depressed.</u> (2.) Later, I decided that I hated her. <u>I was happy about the breakup and talked about how much I was going to enjoy my newfound freedom.</u> (3.) I went to parties and socialized a great deal and just forgot about her. <u>It's funny—at one point I couldn't even remember her phone number!</u> (4.) Then I started pining for her again. But eventually I began to look at the situation more objectively. I realized that she had many faults and that <u>we were bound to break up sooner or later, so I was better off without her.</u> (5.)

1. _____   4. _____

2. _____   5. _____

3. _____

Development: Psychosexual Stages

Freud believed that "the child is father to the man." In fact, he made the rather startling assertion that the basic foundation of an individual's personality has been laid down by the tender age of five. To shed light on these crucial early years, Freud formulated a stage theory of development. He emphasized how young children deal with their immature but powerful sexual urges (he used the term *sexual* in a general way to refer to many urges for physical pleasure). According to Freud, these sexual urges shift in focus as children progress from one stage of development to another. Indeed, the names for the stages (oral, anal, genital, and so on) are based on where children are focusing their erotic energy during that period. Thus, *psychosexual stages* **are developmental periods with a characteristic sexual focus that leave their mark on adult personality.**

Freud theorized that each psychosexual stage has its own unique developmental challenges or tasks (see Table 12.2). The way these challenges are handled supposedly shapes personality. The process of fixation plays an important role in this process. *Fixation* **is a failure to move forward from one stage to another as expected.** Essentially, the child's development stalls for a while. Fixation can be caused by excessive gratification of needs at a particular stage or by excessive frustration of those needs. Either way, fixations left over from childhood affect adult personality. Generally, fixation leads to an overemphasis on the psychosexual needs prominent during the fixated stage. Freud described a series of five psychosexual stages. Let's examine some of the highlights in this sequence.

Oral Stage. This stage encompasses the first year of life. During this period, the main source of erotic stimulation is the mouth (in biting, sucking, chewing, and so on). In Freud's view, the handling of the child's feeding experiences is crucial to subsequent development. He attributed considerable importance to the manner in which the child is weaned from the breast or the bottle. According to Freud, fixation at the oral stage could form the basis for obsessive eating or smoking later in life (among many other things).

Anal Stage. In their second year, children get their erotic pleasure from their bowel movements, through either the expulsion or retention of feces. The crucial event at this time is toilet training, which represents society's first systematic effort to regulate the child's biological urges. Severely punitive toilet training leads to a variety of possible outcomes. For example, excessive punishment might produce a latent feeling of hostility toward the "trainer," usually the mother. This hostility might generalize to women as a class. Another possibility is that heavy reliance on punitive measures could lead to an association between genital concerns and the anxiety that the punishment arouses. This genital anxiety derived from severe toilet training could evolve into anxiety about sexual activities later in life.

Phallic Stage. Around age four, the genitals become the focus for the child's erotic energy, largely through self-stimulation. During this pivotal stage, the Oedipal complex emerges. That is, little boys develop an erotically tinged preference for their mother. They also feel hostility toward their father, whom they view as a competitor for Mom's affection. Similarly, little girls develop a special attachment to their father. Around the same time, they learn that little boys have very different genitals, and supposedly they develop *penis envy*. According to Freud, young girls feel hostile toward their mother because they blame her for their anatomical "deficiency."

To summarize, in the *Oedipal complex*, children manifest erotically tinged desires for their

Table 12.2

Freud's Stages of Psychosexual Development

STAGE	APPROXIMATE AGES	EROTIC FOCUS	KEY TASKS AND EXPERIENCES
Oral	0–1	Mouth (sucking, biting)	Weaning (from breast or bottle)
Anal	2–3	Anus (expelling or retaining feces)	Toilet training
Phallic	4–5	Genitals (masturbating)	Identifying with adult role models; coping with Oedipal crisis
Latency	6–12	None (sexually repressed)	Expanding social contacts
Genital	Puberty onward	Genitals (being sexually intimate)	Establishing intimate relationships; contributing to society through working

© 2017 Cengage Learning

According to Freud, early childhood experiences such as toilet training (a parental attempt to regulate a child's biological urges) can influence an individual's personality, with consequences lasting throughout adulthood.

opposite-sex parent, accompanied by feelings of hostility toward their same-sex parent.** The name for this syndrome was taken from a tragic myth from ancient Greece. In this story, Oedipus was separated from his parents at birth. Not knowing the identity of his real parents, when he grew up he inadvertently killed his father and married his mother. The complex in girls is sometimes referred to as the *Electra complex* but this was not endorsed by Freud himself (Corsini, 1999).

According to Freud, the way parents and children deal with the sexual and aggressive conflicts inherent in the Oedipal complex is of paramount importance. The child has to resolve the Oedipal dilemma by purging the sexual longings for the opposite-sex parent and by crushing the hostility felt toward the same-sex parent. In Freud's view, healthy psychosexual development hinges on the resolution of the Oedipal conflict. Why? Because continued hostility toward the same-sex parent may prevent the child from identifying adequately with that parent. Freudian theory predicts that without such identification, sex typing, conscience, and many other aspects of the child's development won't progress as they should.

Latency and Genital Stages. From around age six through puberty, the child's sexuality is largely

suppressed—it becomes latent. Important events during this *latency* stage centre on expanding social contacts beyond the immediate family. With puberty, the child progresses into the genital stage. Sexual urges reappear and focus on the genitals once again. At this point, sexual energy is normally channelled toward peers of the other sex, rather than toward oneself, as in the phallic stage.

In arguing that the early years shape personality, Freud did not mean that personality development comes to an abrupt halt in middle childhood. However, he did believe that the foundation for adult personality has been solidly entrenched by this time. He maintained that future developments are rooted in early, formative experiences and that significant conflicts in later years are replays of crises from childhood.

In fact, Freud believed that unconscious sexual conflicts rooted in childhood experiences cause most personality disturbances. His steadfast belief in the psychosexual origins of psychological disorders eventually led to bitter theoretical disputes with two of his most brilliant colleagues: Carl Jung and Alfred Adler. Jung and Adler both argued that Freud overemphasized sexuality. Freud rejected their ideas, and the other two theorists felt compelled to go their own way, developing their own theories of personality.

Jung's Analytical Psychology

Carl Jung was an established young psychiatrist in Switzerland when he began to write to Freud in 1906. They exchanged 359 letters before their friendship and theoretical alliance were torn apart in 1913. Jung called his new approach *analytical psychology* to differentiate it from Freud's psychoanalytic theory. Like Freud, Jung (1921, 1933) emphasized the unconscious determinants of personality. However, he proposed that the unconscious consists of two layers. The first layer, called the *personal unconscious*, is essentially the same as Freud's version of the unconscious. The personal unconscious houses material that is not within one's conscious awareness because it has been repressed or forgotten. In addition, Jung theorized the existence of a deeper layer that he called the collective unconscious. The *collective unconscious* is a storehouse of latent memory traces inherited from people's ancestral past. According to Jung, each person shares the collective unconscious with the entire human race (see Figure 12.4).

Jung called these ancestral memories *archetypes*. They are not memories of actual, personal

Carl Jung

"I am not a Jungian . . . I do not want anybody to be a Jungian. I want people above all to be themselves."

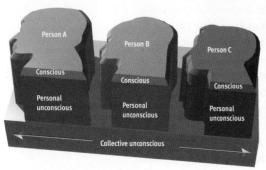

Mandalas from various cultures

Russia

Navajo Indians

From Weiten, Cengage Advantage Books: Psychology, 9E. © 2013 South-Western, a part of Cengage, Inc. Reproduced by permission. www.cengage.com/permissions

Tibet

© 2017 Cengage Learning

Figure 12.4
Jung's vision of the collective unconscious. Much like Freud, Jung theorized that each person has conscious and unconscious levels of awareness. However, he also proposed that the entire human race shares a collective unconscious, which exists in the deepest reaches of everyone's awareness. He saw the collective unconscious as a storehouse of hidden ancestral memories, called *archetypes*. Jung believed that important cultural symbols emerge from these universal archetypes. Thus, he argued that remarkable resemblances among symbols from disparate cultures (e.g., the mandalas shown here) are evidence of the existence of the collective unconscious. (Based on C. G. Jung Bild Und Wort, © Walter-Verlag AG, Olten, Switzerland, 1977)

experiences. Instead, *archetypes* are emotionally charged images and thought forms that have universal meaning. These archetypal images and ideas show up frequently in dreams and are often manifested in a culture's use of symbols in art, literature, and religion. According to Jung, symbols from very different cultures often show striking similarities because they emerge from archetypes that are shared by the entire human race. For instance, Jung found numerous cultures in which the *mandala*, or "magic circle," has served as a symbol of the unified wholeness of the self. Jung felt that an understanding of archetypal symbols helped him make sense of his patients' dreams. He thought that dreams contain important messages from the unconscious, and like Freud, depended extensively on dream analysis in his treatment of patients.

Adler's Individual Psychology

Alfred Adler

"The goal of the human soul is conquest, perfection, security, superiority."

Imagno/Hulton Archive/Getty Images

Growing up in Vienna, Alfred Adler was a sickly child who was overshadowed by an exceptionally successful older brother. Nonetheless, he went on to earn his medical degree and gradually became interested in psychiatry. He was a charter member of Freud's inner circle—the Vienna Psychoanalytic Society. However, he soon began to develop his own approach to personality, which he called *individual psychology*.

Like Jung, Adler (1917, 1927) argued that Freud had gone overboard in centring his theory on sexual conflicts. According to Adler, the foremost source of human motivation is a *striving for superiority*. Adler saw striving for superiority as a universal drive to adapt, improve oneself, and master life's challenges. He noted that young children understandably feel weak and helpless in comparison with more competent older children and adults. These early inferiority feelings supposedly motivate them to acquire new skills and develop new talents.

Adler asserted that everyone has to work to overcome some feelings of inferiority. He called this process compensation. *Compensation* involves efforts to overcome imagined or real inferiorities by developing one's abilities. Adler believed that compensation is entirely normal. However, in some people, inferiority feelings can become excessive, which can result in what is widely known today as an *inferiority complex*—exaggerated feelings of weakness and inadequacy. Adler thought that either parental pampering or parental neglect could cause an inferiority complex. Thus, he agreed with Freud on the importance of early childhood

Adler's theory has been used to analyze the tragic life of the legendary actress Marilyn Monroe (Ansbacher, 1970). During her childhood, Monroe suffered from parental neglect that left her with acute feelings of inferiority. Her inferiority feelings led her to overcompensate by flaunting her beauty, marrying celebrities (Joe DiMaggio and Arthur Miller), keeping film crews waiting for hours, and seeking the adoration of her fans.

© Bettman/CORBIS

experiences. However, he focused on different aspects of parent—child relations.

Adler maintained that some people engage in *overcompensation* in order to conceal, even from themselves, their feelings of inferiority. These people work to acquire status, power, and the trappings of success (fancy clothes, impressive cars) to cover up their underlying inferiority complex. Adler's theory stressed the social context of personality development (Carlson & Englar-Carlson, 2013). For instance, it was Adler who first focused attention on the possible importance of *birth order* as a factor governing personality. He noted that first-borns, second children, and later-born children enter varied home environments and are treated differently by parents and that these experiences are likely to affect their personality (Eckstein & Kaufman, 2012).

Evaluating Psychodynamic Perspectives

The psychodynamic approach has provided a number of far-reaching, truly "grand" theories of personality. These theories yielded some bold new insights when they were first presented. Although one might argue about exact details of interpretation, research has demonstrated that (1) unconscious forces can influence behaviour, (2) internal conflict often plays a key role in generating psychological distress, (3) early childhood experiences can have powerful influences on adult personality, and (4) people do use defence mechanisms to reduce their experience of unpleasant emotions (Bornstein, 2003; Porcerelli et al., 2010; Solms, 2004; Westen, Gabbard, & Ortigo, 2008).

In addition to being praised, psychodynamic formulations have also been criticized on several grounds, including the following (Eysenck, 1990b; Fine, 1990; Macmillan, 1991; Torrey, 1992):

1. *Poor testability*. Scientific investigations require testable hypotheses. Psychodynamic ideas have often been too vague and conjectural to permit a clear scientific test. For instance, how would you prove or disprove the assertion that the id is entirely unconscious?

2. *Inadequate evidence*. The empirical evidence on psychodynamic theories has often been characterized as "inadequate." Psychodynamic theories depend too heavily on clinical case studies in which it's much too easy for clinicians to see what they expect to see. Re-examinations of Freud's own clinical work suggest that he frequently distorted his patients' case histories to make them mesh with his theory (Esterson, 2001; Powell & Boer, 1995). Insofar as researchers have accumulated evidence on psychodynamic theories, the evidence has provided only modest support for many of the central hypotheses (Fisher & Greenberg, 1985, 1996; Westen & Gabbard, & Ortiga, 2008; Wolitzky, 2006).

3. *Sexism*. Many critics have argued that psychodynamic theories are characterized by a sexist bias against women. Freud believed that females' penis envy made them feel inferior to males. He also thought that females tended to develop weaker superegos and to be more prone to neurosis than males. The sex bias in modern psychodynamic theories has been reduced considerably. Nonetheless, the psychodynamic approach has generally provided a rather male-centred point of view (Lerman, 1986; Person, 1990). Many psychoanalytical theorists provided compelling critiques of Freud's sexist ideas. For example, prominent psychoanalyst Karen Horney (1926) criticized his phallocentric bias and argued that he "misrepresented" the female experience (Fancher & Rutherford, 2012). She also argued for the importance of culture in the development of personality. One of her most important criticisms of Freud's ideas had to do with the emphasis he placed in his theory on the central role played by infantile sexuality on personality development. Horney believed that the infant's need for a sense of security was a more important factor (Fancher & Rutherford, 2012).

4. *Unrepresentative samples*. Freud's theories were based on an exceptionally narrow sample of upper-class, neurotic, sexually repressed Viennese women. They were not even remotely representative of Western European culture, let alone other cultures.

It's easy to ridicule Freud for concepts such as penis envy, and it's easy to point to Freudian ideas that have turned out to be wrong. However, you have to remember that Freud, Jung, and Adler began to fashion their theories over a century ago. It's not entirely fair to compare these theories to other models that are only a decade or two old. That's like asking the Wright brothers to race a space shuttle. Freud and his colleagues deserve great credit for breaking new ground with their speculations about psychodynamics. In psychology as a whole, no other school of thought has been as influential, with the exception of behaviourism, which we turn to next.

© Bettmann/CORBIS

The brilliant psychoanalyst Karen Horney disagreed with Freud's views on female psychology and the importance of infantile sexuality. She also emphasized the role of culture in the development of personality.

Behavioural Perspectives

Key Learning Goals

▶ Understand Skinner's and Bandura's contributions to behavioural views of personality.

▶ Identify Mischel's principal thesis, and evaluate the behavioural approach to personality.

Behaviourism is a theoretical orientation based on the premise that scientific psychology should study only observable behaviour. As we saw in Chapter 1, behaviourism has been a major school of thought in psychology since 1913, when John B. Watson began campaigning for the behavioural point of view. Research in the behavioural tradition has focused largely on learning. For many decades behaviourists devoted relatively little attention to the study of personality. However, their interest in personality began to pick up after John Dollard and Neal Miller (1950) attempted to translate selected Freudian ideas into behavioural terminology. Dollard and Miller showed that behavioural concepts could provide enlightening insights about the complicated subject of personality.

In this section, we'll examine three behavioural views of personality, as we discuss the ideas of B. F. Skinner, Albert Bandura, and Walter Mischel. For the most part, you'll see that behaviourists explain personality the same way they explain everything else—in terms of learning.

Skinner's Ideas Applied to Personality

As we noted in Chapters 1 and 6, modern behaviourism's most prominent theorist has been B. F. Skinner, an American psychologist who lived from 1904 to 1990. Originally, Skinner had hoped to become a writer and he even sought out reviews of his work from famous authors, such as poet Robert Frost. Sadly for Skinner, he did not succeed as a writer. He then decided on a career in psychology (Skinner, 1980). After earning his doctorate in 1931, Skinner spent most of his career at Harvard University. There he achieved renown for his research on the principles of learning, which were mostly discovered through the study of rats and pigeons. Skinner's (1953, 1957) concepts of operant conditioning were never meant to be a theory of personality. However, his ideas have affected thinking in all areas of psychology and have been applied to the explanation of personality. Here we'll examine Skinner's views as they relate to personality structure and development.

Personality Structure: A View from the Outside

Skinner made no provision for internal personality structures similar to Freud's id, ego, and superego because such structures can't be observed. Following the tradition of Watson's radical behaviourism, Skinner showed little interest in what goes on "inside" people. He argued that it's useless to speculate about private, unobservable cognitive processes. Instead, he focused on how the external environment moulds overt behaviour. Indeed, he argued for a strong brand of determinism, asserting that behaviour is fully determined by environmental stimuli. He claimed that free will is but an illusion, saying, "There is no place in the scientific position for a self as a true originator or initiator of action" (Skinner, 1974, p. 225).

How can Skinner's theory explain the consistency that can be seen in individuals' behaviour? According to his view, people show some consistent patterns of behaviour because they have some stable response tendencies that they have acquired through experience. These response tendencies may change in the future, as a result of new experiences, but they're enduring enough to create a certain degree of consistency in a person's behaviour. Implicitly, then, Skinner viewed an individual's personality as a collection of response tendencies that are tied to various stimulus situations. A specific situation may be associated with a number of response tendencies that vary in strength, depending on past conditioning (see Figure 12.5).

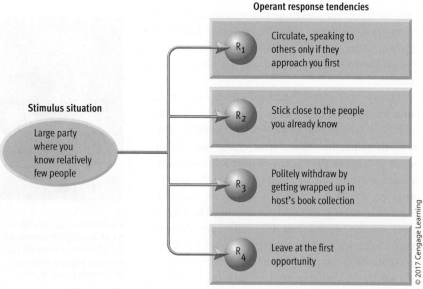

Operant response tendencies

Stimulus situation

Large party where you know relatively few people

R₁ Circulate, speaking to others only if they approach you first

R₂ Stick close to the people you already know

R₃ Politely withdraw by getting wrapped up in host's book collection

R₄ Leave at the first opportunity

© 2017 Cengage Learning

Figure 12.5
A behavioural view of personality. Staunch behaviourists devote little attention to the structure of personality because it is unobservable, but they implicitly view personality as an individual's collection of response tendencies. A possible hierarchy of response tendencies for a particular person in a specific stimulus situation (a large party) is shown here.

Personality Development as a Product of Conditioning

Skinner's theory accounts for personality development by explaining how various response tendencies are acquired through learning (Bolling, Terry, & Kohlenberg, 2006). He believed that most human responses are shaped by the type of conditioning that he described: operant conditioning. As we discussed in Chapter 6, Skinner maintained that environmental consequences—reinforcement, punishment, and extinction—determine people's patterns of responding. On the one hand, when responses are followed by favourable consequences (reinforcement), they are strengthened. For example, if your joking at a party pays off with favourable attention, your tendency to joke at parties will increase (see Figure 12.6). On the other hand, when responses lead to negative consequences (punishment), they are weakened. Thus, if your impulsive decisions always backfire, your tendency to be impulsive will decline.

Because response tendencies are constantly being strengthened or weakened by new experiences, Skinner's theory views personality development as a continuous, lifelong journey. Unlike Freud and many other theorists, Skinner saw no reason to break the developmental process into stages. Nor did he attribute special importance to early childhood experiences.

Skinner believed that conditioning in humans operates much the same as in the rats and pigeons

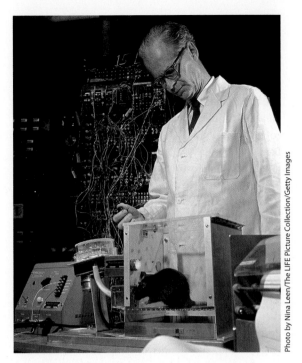

B. F. Skinner

"The practice of looking inside the organism for an explanation of behaviour has tended to obscure the variables which are immediately available for a scientific analysis. These variables lie outside the organism, in its environmental history. . . . The objection to inner states is not that they do not exist, but that they are not relevant."

that he studied in his laboratory. Hence, he assumed that conditioning strengthens and weakens response tendencies "mechanically"—that is, without the person's conscious participation. Thus, Skinner was able to explain consistencies in behaviour (personality) without being concerned about individuals' cognitive processes.

Skinner held to his radical position right to the end of his life. If anything, he stepped up his attacks on nonbehavioural theories once he knew that he was dying of terminal leukemia in 1990, giving his last speech on the topic eight days before he died (Flett, 2007). Skinner's ideas continue to be highly influential, but his mechanical, deterministic, noncognitive view of personality has not gone unchallenged by other behaviourists. In recent decades, several theorists have developed somewhat different behavioural models with a more cognitive emphasis.

Bandura's Social Cognitive Theory

Albert Bandura (2016a&b) is a modern theorist who has helped reshape the theoretical landscape of behaviourism. As you may recall, in Chapter 6, we highlighted some of Bandura's other contributions to learning theory, notably his groundbreaking

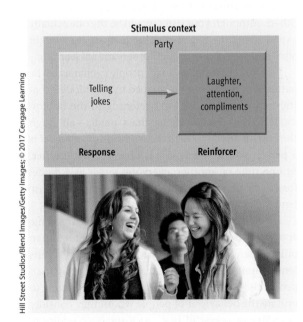

Figure 12.6

Personality development and operant conditioning.
According to Skinner, people's characteristic response tendencies are shaped by reinforcers and other consequences that follow behaviour. Thus, if your joking leads to attention and compliments, your tendency to be witty and humorous will be strengthened.

Albert Bandura

"Most human behaviour is learned by observation through modelling."

research with Waterloo University's Richard Walters on modelling and aggression.

Cognitive Processes and Reciprocal Determinism

Bandura is one of several theorists who have added a cognitive flavour to behaviourism since the 1960s. Bandura (1977), Walter Mischel (1973), and Julian Rotter (1982) take issue with Skinner's "pure" behaviourism. They point out that humans obviously are conscious, thinking, feeling beings. Moreover, these theorists argue that in neglecting cognitive processes, Skinner ignored the most distinctive and important feature of human behaviour. Bandura and like-minded theorists originally called their modified brand of behaviourism *social learning theory*. Today, Bandura refers to his model as *social cognitive theory*. Bandura's impact has been such that he is considered by many to be the greatest living psychologist, ranking just behind luminaries such as Piaget, Freud, and Skinner in terms of his overall historical influence (Haggbloom et al., 2002).

Bandura (1982, 1986) agrees with the fundamental thrust of behaviourism in that he believes that personality is largely shaped through learning. However, he contends that conditioning is not a mechanical process in which people are passive participants. Instead, he maintains that "people are self-organizing, proactive, self-reflecting, and self-regulating, not just reactive organisms shaped and shepherded by external events" (Bandura, 1999a, p. 154). Thus, people routinely attempt to influence their lives and their outcomes (Bandura, 2008). Bandura (2001a, 2006) also emphasizes the important role of forward-directed planning, noting that "people set goals for themselves, anticipate the likely consequences of prospective actions, and select and create courses of action likely to produce desired outcomes and avoid detrimental ones" (Bandura, 2001a, p. 7).

Comparing his theory to Skinner's highly deterministic view, Bandura advocates a position called *reciprocal determinism*. According to this notion, the environment does determine behaviour (as Skinner would argue). However, behaviour also determines the environment (in other words, people can act to alter their environment). Moreover, personal factors (cognitive structures such as beliefs and expectancies) determine and are determined by both behaviour and the environment (see Figure 12.7). Thus, *reciprocal determinism* **is the idea that internal mental events, external environmental events, and overt behaviour all influence one another.** According to Bandura, humans are neither masters of their own destiny nor hapless victims buffeted about by the environment. To some extent, people shape their environments.

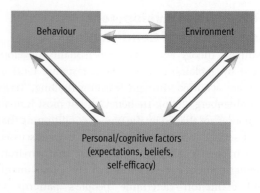

Figure 12.7
Bandura's reciprocal determinism. Bandura rejects Skinner's highly deterministic view that behaviour is governed by the environment and that freedom is an illusion. Bandura argues that internal mental events, external environmental contingencies, and overt behaviour all influence one another.

Source: From Weiten. *Cengage Advantage Books: Psychology*, 9E. © 2013 South-Western, a part of Cengage, Inc. Reproduced by permission. www.cengage.com/permissions

Observational Learning

Bandura's foremost theoretical contribution has been his description of observational learning, which we introduced in Chapter 6. *Observational learning* **occurs when an organism's responding is influenced by the observation of others, who are called models.** According to Bandura, both classical and operant conditioning can occur vicariously when one person observes another's conditioning. For example, watching your sister get cheated by someone giving her a bad cheque for her old stereo could strengthen your tendency to be suspicious of others. Although your sister would be the one actually experiencing the negative consequences, they might also influence you—through observational learning.

Bandura maintains that people's characteristic patterns of behaviour are shaped by the models that they're exposed to. He isn't referring to the fashion models who dominate the mass media—although they do qualify. In observational learning, **a *model* is a person whose behaviour is observed by another.** At one time or another, everyone serves as a model for others. Bandura's key point is that many response tendencies are the product of imitation.

As research has accumulated, it has become apparent that some models are more influential than others (Bandura, 1986). Both children and adults tend to imitate people they like or respect more than people they don't. People are also especially prone to imitate the behaviour of people whom they consider attractive or powerful (e.g., rock stars). In addition, imitation is more likely when people see similarity between models and themselves. Thus, children tend to imitate same-sex role models somewhat more than opposite-sex models. Finally, people are more likely to copy a model if they observe that the model's behaviour leads to positive outcomes.

Self-Efficacy

Bandura discusses how a variety of personal factors (aspects of personality) govern behaviour. In recent years, the factor he has emphasized most is self-efficacy (Bandura, 1990, 1993, 1995). *Self-efficacy refers to one's belief about one's ability to perform behaviours that should lead to expected outcomes.* When self-efficacy is high, individuals feel confident that they can execute the responses necessary to earn reinforcers. When self-efficacy is low, individuals worry that the necessary responses may be beyond their abilities. Perceptions of self-efficacy are subjective and specific to certain kinds of tasks. For instance, you might feel extremely confident about your ability to handle difficult social situations but doubtful about your ability to handle academic challenges.

Perceptions of self-efficacy can influence which challenges people tackle and how well they perform. Studies have found that feelings of greater self-efficacy are associated with greater success in giving up smoking (Schnoll et al., 2011), greater adherence to an exercise regimen (Ayotte, Margrett, & Hicks-Patrick, 2010), better outcomes in substance abuse treatment (Bandura, 1999b), more success in coping with medical rehabilitation (Waldrop et al., 2001), reduced disability from problems with chronic pain (Hadjistavropoulos et al., 2007), greater persistence and effort in academic pursuits (Zimmerman, 1995), higher levels of academic performance (Weiser & Riggio, 2010), reduced vulnerability to anxiety and depression in childhood (Muris, 2002), less jealousy in romantic relationships (Hu, Zhang, & Li, 2005), enhanced performance in athletic competition (Kane et al., 1996), greater receptiveness to technological training (Christoph, Schoenfeld, & Tansky, 1998), greater success in searching for a new job (Saks, 2006), higher work-related performance (Stajkovic & Luthans, 1998), reduced vulnerability to post-traumatic stress disorder in the face of severe stress (Hirschel & Schulenberg, 2009), and reduced strain from occupational stress (Grau, Salanova, & Peiro, 2001), among many other things.

Mischel and the Person–Situation Controversy

Walter Mischel was born in Vienna, not far from Freud's home. His family immigrated to the United States in 1939, when he was nine. After earning his doctorate in psychology, he spent many years on the faculty at Stanford, as a colleague of Bandura. He has since moved to Columbia University. Like Bandura, Mischel (1973, 1984, 2014, 2015) is an advocate of social learning theory. Mischel's chief contribution to personality theory has been to focus attention on the extent to which situational factors govern behaviour (Eigsti et al., 2006).

According to Mischel, people make responses that they think will lead to reinforcement in the situation at hand. For example, if you believe that hard work in your job will pay off by leading to raises and promotions, you'll probably be diligent and industrious. But if you think that hard work in your job is unlikely to be rewarded, you may behave in a lazy and irresponsible manner. Thus, Mischel's version of social learning theory predicts that people will often behave differently in different situations. Mischel (1968, 1973) reviewed decades of research and concluded that, indeed, people exhibit far less consistency across situations than had been widely assumed. For example, studies show that a person who is honest in one situation may be dishonest in another.

Mischel's provocative ideas struck at the heart of the concept of personality, which assumes that people are reasonably consistent in their behaviour. His theories sparked a robust debate about the relative importance of the *person* as opposed to the *situation* in determining behaviour. This debate has led to a growing recognition that *both* the person and the situation are important determinants of behaviour (Funder, 2001; Roberts & Pomerantz, 2004). As William Fleeson (2004) puts it, "The person–situation debate is coming to an end because both sides of the debate have turned out to be right" (p. 83). Fleeson reconciles the two opposing views by arguing that each prevails at a different level of analysis. When small chunks of behaviour are examined on a moment-to-moment basis, situational factors dominate and most individuals' behaviour tends to be highly variable. However, when larger chunks of typical behaviour over time are examined, people tend to be reasonably consistent and personality traits prove to be more influential.

Norman Endler of York University was a well-known advocate of an interactional approach to personality. Endler argued that personality traits interact with situational factors to produce behaviour (Endler & Magnusson, 1976). So, in order to accurately predict how someone will behave, you not only need to know something about that person's standing on relevant personality traits, but you also need information about the nature of the situational context he or she is facing. Neither factor alone will allow you to accurately predict an individual's behaviour.

Walter Mischel

"It seems remarkable how each of us generally manages to reconcile his seemingly diverse behaviour into one self-consistent whole."

Personality: Theory, Research, and Assessment

Evaluating Behavioural Perspectives

Behavioural theories are firmly rooted in extensive empirical research. Skinner's ideas have shed light on how environmental consequences and conditioning mould people's characteristic behaviour. Bandura's social cognitive theory has shown how learning from others can mould personality. Mischel deserves credit for increasing psychology's awareness of how situational factors shape behaviour.

Of course, each theoretical approach has its shortcomings, and the behavioural approach is no exception. The behaviourists used to be criticized because they neglected cognitive processes. The rise of social cognitive theory blunted this criticism. However, social cognitive theory undermines the foundation on which behaviourism was built—the idea that psychologists should study only observable behaviour. Thus, some critics complain that behavioural theories aren't very behavioural anymore. Other critics argue that behaviourists have indiscriminately

generalized from animal research to human behaviour (Burger, 2015). Humanistic theorists, whom we shall cover next, have been particularly vocal in criticizing behavioural views.

Humanistic Perspectives

Carl Rogers

"I have little sympathy with the rather prevalent concept that man is basically irrational, and that his impulses, if not controlled, will lead to destruction of others and self. Man's behaviour is exquisitely rational, moving with subtle and ordered complexity toward the goals his organism is endeavoring to achieve."

Humanistic theory emerged in the 1950s as something of a backlash against the behavioural and psychodynamic theories that we have just discussed (Cassel, 2000; DeCarvalho, 1991). The principal charge hurled at these two models was that they are dehumanizing. Freudian theory was criticized for its belief that behaviour is dominated by primitive, animalistic drives. Behaviourism was criticized for its preoccupation with animal research and for its mechanistic, fragmented view of personality. Critics argued that both schools of thought are too deterministic and that both fail to recognize the unique qualities of human behaviour.

Many of these critics blended into a loose alliance that came to be known as *humanism*, because of its exclusive focus on human behaviour. **Humanism is a theoretical orientation that emphasizes the unique qualities of humans, especially their freedom and their potential for personal growth.** Humanistic psychologists don't believe that animal research can reveal anything of any significance about the human condition. In contrast to most psychodynamic and behavioural theorists, humanistic theorists take an optimistic view of human nature. They assume that (1) people can rise above their primitive animal heritage and control their biological urges, and (2) people are largely conscious and rational beings who are not dominated by unconscious, irrational needs and conflicts.

Humanistic theorists also maintain that a person's subjective view of the world is more important than

objective reality (Wong, 2006). According to this notion, if you think that you're homely or bright or sociable, this belief will influence your behaviour more than the realities of how homely, bright, or sociable you actually are. Therefore, the humanists embrace the *phenomenological approach*, **which assumes that one has to appreciate individuals' personal, subjective experiences to truly understand their behaviour.**

Rogers's Person-Centred Theory

Carl Rogers (1951, 1961, 1980) was one of the founders of the human potential movement. This movement emphasizes self-realization through sensitivity training, encounter groups, and other exercises intended to foster personal growth. Rogers grew up in a religious, upper-middle-class home in the suburbs of Chicago. He was a bright student, but he had to rebel against his parents' wishes in order to pursue his graduate study in psychology. While he was working at the University of Chicago in the 1940s, Rogers devised a major new approach to psychotherapy. Like Freud, Rogers based his personality theory on his extensive therapeutic interactions with many clients. Because of its emphasis on a person's subjective point of view, Rogers's approach is called a *person-centred theory*.

The Self

Rogers viewed personality structure in terms of just one construct. He called this construct the *self*, although it's more widely known today as the *self-concept*. A *self-concept* is a collection of beliefs about one's own nature, unique qualities, and typical behaviour. Your self-concept is your own mental picture of yourself. It's a collection of self-perceptions. For example, a self-concept might include beliefs such as "I'm easygoing" or "I'm sly and crafty" or "I'm pretty" or "I'm hard-working." According to Rogers, individuals are aware of their self-concept. It's not buried in their unconscious.

Rogers stressed the subjective nature of the self-concept. Your self-concept may not be entirely consistent with your experiences. Most people tend to distort their experiences to some extent to promote a relatively favourable self-concept. For example, you may believe that you're quite bright, but your grade transcript might suggest otherwise. Rogers called the gap between self-concept and reality *incongruence*. *Incongruence* is the degree of disparity between one's self-concept and one's actual experience. In contrast, if a person's self-concept is reasonably accurate, it's said to be congruent with reality (see Figure 12.8). Everyone experiences some incongruence. The crucial issue is how much. As we'll see, Rogers maintained that too much incongruence undermines one's psychological well-being.

Development of the Self

In terms of personality development, Rogers was concerned with how childhood experiences promote congruence or incongruence between one's self-concept and one's experience. According to Rogers, people have a strong need for affection, love, and acceptance from others. Early in life, parents provide most of this affection. Rogers maintained that some parents make their affection *conditional*. That is, it depends on the child's behaving well and living up to expectations. When parental love seems conditional, children often block out of their self-concept those experiences that make them feel unworthy of love. They do so because they're worried about parental acceptance, which appears precarious.

At the other end of the spectrum, some parents make their affection *unconditional*. Their children have less need to block out unworthy experiences because they've been assured that they're worthy of affection, no matter what they do. Hence, Rogers believed that unconditional love from parents fosters congruence and that conditional love fosters incongruence. He further theorized that if individuals grow up believing that affection from others is highly conditional, they will go on to distort more and more of their experiences in order to feel worthy of acceptance from a wider and wider array of people (see Figure 12.9).

Anxiety and Defence

According to Rogers, experiences that threaten people's personal views of themselves are the principal cause of troublesome anxiety. The more inaccurate your self-concept, the more likely you are to have experiences that clash with your self-perceptions. Thus, people with highly incongruent self-concepts are especially likely to be plagued by recurrent anxiety (see Figure 12.9).

To ward off this anxiety, individuals often behave defensively in an effort to reinterpret their experience so that it appears consistent with their self-concept. Thus, they ignore, deny, and twist reality to protect and perpetuate their self-concept. Consider

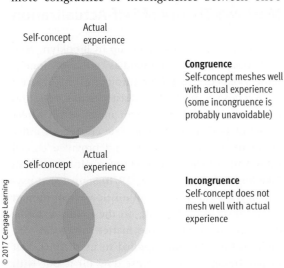

Figure 12.8
Rogers's view of personality structure. In Rogers's model, the self-concept is the only important structural construct. However, Rogers acknowledged that one's self-concept may not be consistent with the realities of one's actual experience—a condition called *incongruence*.

© 2017 Cengage Learning

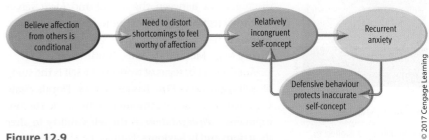

Figure 12.9
Rogers's view of personality development and dynamics. Rogers's theory of development posits that conditional love leads to a need to distort experiences, which fosters an incongruent self-concept. Incongruence makes one prone to recurrent anxiety, which triggers defensive behaviour, which fuels more incongruence.

© 2017 Cengage Learning

a young woman who, like most people, considers herself a "nice person." Let's suppose that in reality she is rather conceited and selfish. She gets feedback from both boyfriends and girlfriends that she is a "self-centred, snotty brat." How might she react in order to protect her self-concept? She might ignore or block out those occasions when she behaves selfishly. She might attribute her girlfriends' negative comments to their jealousy of her good looks. Perhaps she would blame her boyfriends' negative remarks on their disappointment because she won't get more serious with them. As you can see, people will sometimes go to great lengths to defend their self-concept.

Recent Directions in Research on the Self

Rogers's work emphasized the importance of the self and has influenced contemporary psychology in terms of its views of the centrality of the self for understanding personality (McCann & Sato, 2000), and the implications of incongruence in the self system for dysfunctional emotions (Higgins, 1987). For example, Tory Higgins of Columbia University has extended Rogers's ideas about self and congruence/incongruence in developing his influential theory of *self-discrepancy* (Higgins, 1987, 1999) and its implications for motivation and behaviour (Boldero, Higgins, & Hulbert, 2015; Calvallo, Zee, & Higgins, 2016). According to Higgins, discrepancy between the *actual self* (our beliefs about the kind of person we think we are) and two standards we hold for the self (the *ought self* and the *ideal self*) can lead to emotional discomfort and even psychopathology if the discrepancy is extreme enough.

The *ideal self* refers to our beliefs about the kind of person we wish to be (e.g., a top student)—our hopes, goals, and aspirations for ourselves. The *ought self* refers to our beliefs about the kind of person we have a duty or obligation to be (e.g., a faithful spouse). According to Higgins, discrepancy between the actual and ought selves leads to agitation and, in extreme cases, anxiety. And discrepancies between the actual and ideal selves lead to dejection and, in extreme cases, depression. Research has revealed impressive support for his theory (e.g., McCann & Sato, 2000).

Another major focus of work on the self is the study of self-regulation. Roy Baumeister of Florida State University is a major contributor to this work. He conceptualizes *self-regulation* as the self's ability to alter its actions and behaviours (Baumeister & Vohs, 2007). Self-regulation allows us to be flexible in reacting to the demands of and changes in the situations in which

we find ourselves (Boekaerts et al., 2000). When we self-regulate, we are adapting our behaviour to fit with important goals and standards we hold for ourselves (Carver & Scheier, 2000). For example, if attending law school is something that is important to you, then you may forgo some leisure activities in order to put extra time into studying for the LSATs.

There are several important theories of self-regulation and some have direct implications for the study of individual differences. In one of the most recent and influential of these theories, Higgins has extended his work on standards for the self in developing his theory of self-regulation and motivation and his conceptualizations of promotion and prevention focus (Higgins, 2016). He argues that there are individual differences in this regard and that some people are promotion focused while others are prevention focused. These two types of people orient themselves differently in pursuit of their goals (Halvorson & Higgins, 2013; Higgins, 2012). People with a promotion focus approach their personal goals with gain and advancement in mind; they focus on the rewards and benefits of their actions and are oriented toward experiencing positive outcomes. People who adopt a prevention focus are more oriented to playing it safe, doing what's necessary, and avoiding experiencing a negative outcome. Rather than playing to *win* rewards and benefits, they play *not to lose*—to avoid failure. Research has shown that these two orientations affect many facets of our behaviour, our thoughts, our feelings and mental health, and our actions (Higgins, 2012).

Maslow's Theory of Self-Actualization

Abraham Maslow, who grew up in Brooklyn, New York, described his childhood as "unhappy, lonely, [and] isolated." To follow through on his interest in psychology, he had to resist parental pressures to go into law. Maslow spent much of his career at Brandeis University, where he created an influential theory of motivation and provided crucial leadership for the fledgling humanistic movement. Like Rogers, Maslow (1968, 1970) argued that psychology should take an optimistic view of human nature instead of dwelling on the causes of disorders. "To oversimplify the matter somewhat," he said, "it's as if Freud supplied to us the sick half of psychology and we must now fill it out with the healthy half" (1968, p. 5). Maslow's key contributions were his analysis of how motives are organized hierarchically and his description of the healthy personality.

Abraham Maslow

"It is as if Freud supplied to us the sick half of psychology and we must now fill it out with the healthy half."

© Corbis

Hierarchy of Needs

Maslow proposed that human motives are organized into a *hierarchy of needs*—a systematic arrangement of needs, according to priority, in which basic needs must be met before less basic needs are aroused. This hierarchical arrangement is usually portrayed as a pyramid (see Figure 12.10). The needs toward the bottom of the pyramid, such as physiological or security needs, are the most basic. Higher levels in the pyramid consist of progressively less basic needs. When a person manages to satisfy a level of needs reasonably well (complete satisfaction is not necessary), *this satisfaction activates needs at the next level.*

Like Rogers, Maslow argued that humans have an innate drive toward personal growth—that is, evolution toward a higher state of being. Thus, he described the needs in the uppermost reaches of his hierarchy as *growth needs*. These include the needs for knowledge, understanding, order, and aesthetic beauty. Foremost among them is the need for *self-actualization*, which is the need to fulfill one's potential; it is the highest need in Maslow's motivational hierarchy. Maslow summarized this concept with a simple statement: "What a man can be, he must be." According to Maslow, people will be frustrated if they are unable to fully utilize their talents or pursue their true interests. For example, if you have great musical talent but must work as

an accountant, or if you have scholarly interests but must work as a salesclerk, your need for self-actualization will be thwarted.

The Healthy Personality

Because of his interest in self-actualization, Maslow set out to discover the nature of the healthy personality. He tried to identify people of exceptional mental health so that he could investigate their characteristics. In one case, he used psychological tests and interviews to sort out the healthiest 1 percent of a sizable population of college students. He also studied admired historical figures (e.g., Thomas Jefferson and William James) and personal acquaintances characterized by superior adjustment. Over a period of years, he accumulated his case histories and gradually sketched, in broad strokes, a picture of ideal psychological health. According to Maslow, *self-actualizing* persons are people with exceptionally healthy personalities, marked by continued personal growth. Maslow identified various traits characteristic of self-actualizing people. Many of these traits are listed in Table 12.3. In brief, Maslow found that self-actualizers are accurately tuned in to reality and that they're at peace with themselves. He found that they're open and spontaneous and that they retain a fresh appreciation of the world around them. Socially, they're sensitive to others' needs and

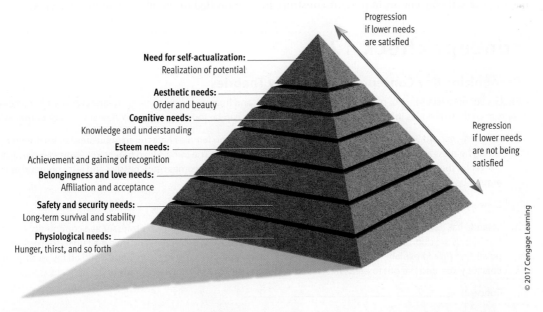

Figure 12.10
Maslow's hierarchy of needs. According to Maslow, human needs are arranged in a hierarchy, and people must satisfy their basic needs before they can satisfy higher needs. In the diagram, higher levels in the pyramid represent progressively less-basic needs. Individuals progress upward in the hierarchy when lower needs are satisfied reasonably well, but they may regress back to lower levels if basic needs are no longer satisfied.

Table 12.3

Maslow's View of the Healthy Personality

Humanistic theorists emphasize psychological health instead of maladjustment. Maslow's description of characteristics of self-actualizing people evokes a picture of the healthy personality.

CHARACTERISTICS OF SELF-ACTUALIZING PEOPLE

- Clear, efficient perception of reality and comfortable relations with it
- Spontaneity, simplicity, and naturalness
- Problem centring (having something outside themselves they "must" do as a mission)
- Detachment and need for privacy
- Autonomy, independence of culture and environment
- Continued freshness of appreciation

- Mystical and peak experiences
- Feelings of kinship and identification with the human race
- Strong friendships, but limited in number
- Democratic character structure
- Ethical discrimination between good and evil
- Philosophical, unhostile sense of humour
- Balance between polarities in personality

Source: Adapted from Potkay, C. R., and Allen, B. P. (1986). *Personality: Theory, research and applications.* Pacific Grove, CA: Brooks/Cole. Copyright © 1986 by C. R. Potkay and B. P. Allen. Adapted by permission of the authors / © 2017 Cengage Learning

enjoy rewarding interpersonal relations. However, they're not dependent on others for approval or uncomfortable with solitude. They thrive on their work, and they enjoy their sense of humour. Maslow also noted that they have "peak experiences" (profound emotional highs) more often than others. Finally, he found that they strike a nice balance between many polarities in personality. For instance, they can be both childlike and mature, both rational and intuitive, both conforming and rebellious.

Evaluating Humanistic Perspectives

The humanistic approach deserves credit for making the self-concept an important construct in psychology. The insight that a person's subjective views may be more important than objective reality has also proven compelling. One could argue that the humanists' optimistic, health-oriented approach laid the foundation for the emergence of the positive psychology movement that is increasingly influential today (Sheldon & Kasser, 2001; Taylor, 2001).

Of course, the balance sheet has a negative side, as well (Burger, 2015; Wong, 2006). Critics argue that (1) many aspects of humanistic theory are difficult to put to a scientific test, (2) humanists have been unrealistically optimistic in their assumptions about human nature and their descriptions of the healthy personality, and (3) more empirical research is needed to solidify the humanistic view.

concept check 12.2

Recognizing Key Concepts in Personality Theories

Check your understanding of psychodynamic, behavioural, and humanistic personality theories by identifying key concepts from these theories in the scenarios below. The answers can be found in Appendix A near the back of the book.

1. Thirteen-year-old Sarah watches a TV show in which the leading female character manipulates her boyfriend by acting helpless and purposely losing a tennis match against him. The female lead repeatedly expresses her slogan, "Never let them [men] know you can take care of yourself." Sarah becomes more passive and less competitive around boys her own age.

   Concept: _____

2. Yolanda has a secure, enjoyable, reasonably well-paid job as a tenured English professor at a community college. Her friends are dumbfounded when she announces that she's going to resign and give it all up to try writing a novel. She tries to explain, "I need a new challenge, a new mountain to climb. I've had this lid on my writing talents for years, and I've got to break free. It's something I have to try. I won't be happy until I do."

   Concept: _____

3. Vladimir, who is four years old, seems to be emotionally distant from and inattentive to his father. He complains whenever he's left with his dad. In contrast, he often cuddles up in bed with his mother and tries very hard to please her by behaving properly.

   Concept: _____

Biological Perspectives

Eysenck's Theory

Hans Eysenck was born in Germany but fled to London, England, during the era of Nazi rule. He went on to become one of Britain's most prominent psychologists. Eysenck (1967, 1982, 1990a) views personality structure as a hierarchy of traits, in which many superficial traits are derived from a smaller number of more basic traits, which are derived from a handful of fundamental higher-order traits, as shown in Figure 12.11. His studies suggest that all aspects of personality emerge from just three higher-order traits: extraversion, neuroticism, and psychoticism. You have already learned about the first two of these traits, which are key elements in the Big Five. Extraversion involves being sociable, assertive, active, and lively. Neuroticism involves being anxious, tense, moody, and low in self-esteem. Psychoticism involves being egocentric, impulsive, cold, and antisocial. Each of these traits is represented in the theory as a bipolar dimension, with the endpoints for each dimension as follows: extraversion–introversion, stability–neuroticism (instability), and psychoticism–self-control.

According to Eysenck, "Personality is determined to a large extent by a person's genes" (1967, p. 20). How is heredity linked to personality in Eysenck's model? In part, through conditioning concepts borrowed from behavioural theory. Eysenck theorizes that some people can be conditioned more readily than others because of differences in their physiological functioning. These variations in "conditionability" are assumed to influence the personality traits that people acquire through conditioning processes.

Eysenck has shown a special interest in explaining variations in extraversion–introversion, the trait dimension first described years earlier by Carl Jung. He has proposed that introverts tend to have higher levels of physiological arousal, or perhaps higher "arousability," which makes them more easily conditioned than extraverts. According to Eysenck, people who condition easily acquire more conditioned inhibitions than others. These inhibitions make them more bashful, tentative, and uneasy in social situations. This social discomfort leads them to turn inward. Hence, they become introverted.

Behavioural Genetics and Personality

Recent research in behavioural genetics has provided impressive support for the idea that genetic blueprints shape the contours of an individual's personality (South et al., 2015). For instance, in twin studies of the Big Five personality traits, identical twins were found to be much more similar than fraternal twins on all five traits (Zuckerman, 2013; see Figure 12.12). Especially telling is the finding that this is true even when the identical twins are reared in different homes. The latter finding argues against the possibility that environmental factors (rather than heredity) could be responsible for identical twins' greater personality resemblance. Overall, five decades of research on the determinants of the Big Five traits suggests that

Wikipedia Commons/Sybil Eysenck

Hans Eysenck

"Personality is determined to a large extent by a person's genes."

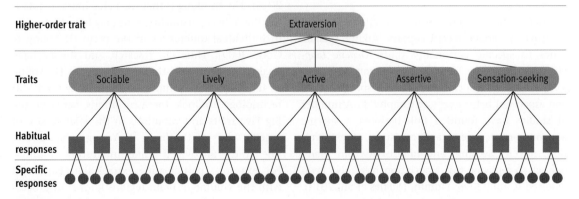

Figure 12.11

Eysenck's model of personality structure. Eysenck described personality structure as a hierarchy of traits. In this scheme, a few higher-order traits, such as extraversion, determine a host of lower-order traits, which determine a person's habitual responses.

Source: Eysenck, H. J. (1976). *The biological basis of personality*. Springfield, IL: Charles C. Thomas. Reprinted by permission of the publisher.

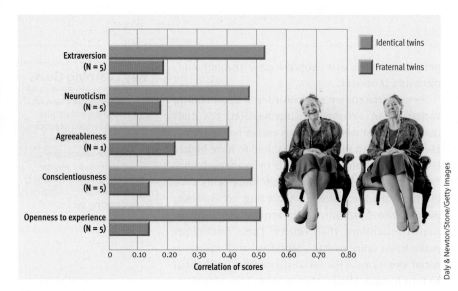

Figure 12.12
Twin studies of personality. Loehlin (1992) has summarized the results of twin studies that have examined the Big Five personality traits. The N under each trait indicates the number of twin studies that have examined that trait. The chart plots the average correlations obtained for identical and fraternal twins in these studies. As you can see, identical twins have shown greater resemblance in personality than fraternal twins have, suggesting that personality is partly inherited. (Based on data from Loehlin, 1992)

the heritability (see Chapter 9) of each trait is in the vicinity of 50 percent (South et al., 2013).

Research on the heritability of personality has inadvertently turned up a surprising finding: *shared family environment* appears to have remarkably little impact on personality. This unexpected finding has been observed quite consistently in behavioural genetics research (South et al., 2015). It is surprising in that social scientists have long assumed that the family environment shared by children growing up together led to some personality resemblance among them. This finding has led researchers to explore how children's subjective environments vary *within* families. But scientists continue to be perplexed by the minimal impact of shared family environment.

There has been some excitement—and controversy—about recent reports linking specific genes to specific personality traits. *Genetic mapping* techniques are beginning to permit investigators to look for associations between specific genes and aspects of behaviour (see Chapter 3). A number of studies have found a link between a specific dopamine-related gene and measures of extraversion, novelty seeking, and impulsivity, but many failures to replicate this association have also been reported (Canli, 2008; Plomin, DeFries et al., 2013). In a similar vein, a variety of studies have reported a link between a serotonin-related gene and measures

of neuroticism, but the results have been inconsistent (Canli, 2008; Plomin, DeFries et al., 2013). Both of these links could be genuine, but difficult to replicate consistently because the correlations are very weak (Munafò & Flint, 2011). Hence, subtle differences between studies in sampling or the specific personality tests used can lead to inconsistent findings (South et al., 2015). The ultimate problem, however, is probably that specific personality traits may be influenced by *hundreds, if not thousands,* of genes, each of which may have a very tiny effect that is difficult to detect (Krueger & Johnson, 2008; Munafò & Flint, 2011).

reality check

Misconception

Parents exert a great deal of influence over the personality of their offspring.

Reality

This seems like a logical supposition, but when behavioural genetics researchers have attempted to quantify the impact of shared family environment on personality, they have been stunned by its lack of influence. Other types of research in developmental psychology have suggested that parents have some influence over their children's personality (Maccoby, 2000), but this influence appears to be much more modest than widely assumed (Cohen, 1999; Harris, 1998).

The Neuroscience of Personality

In recent years neuroscientists have begun to explore the relationships between specific personality traits, behaviour, and aspects of brain structure and function (e.g., Amodio & Harmon-Jones, 2012; Read et al., 2010; Schmeichel, Crowell, & Harmon-Jones, 2016). The thinking is that the behavioural regularities that reflect personality traits may have their roots in individual differences in the brain (DeYoung & Gray, 2009). Thus far, research and theory have focused primarily on the Big Five traits (De Young et al., 2010). For example, a recent study used MRI technology to look for associations between the Big Five traits and variations in the relative size of specific areas of the brain (DeYoung et al., 2010). The study uncovered some interesting findings. For example, participants' extraversion correlated with the volume of brain regions known to process reward. Variations in neuroticism correlated with the volume of brain areas known to be activated by threat, punishment, and negative emotions. And the size of brain areas thought to regulate planning and voluntary control correlated with subjects' degree of conscientiousness. This line of research is brand new, but the promising initial results suggest that it may be fruitful to explore the neurological bases of personality traits.

The Evolutionary Approach to Personality

In the realm of biological perspectives on personality, the most recent development has been the emergence of evolutionary theory. Evolutionary theorists assert that personality has a biological basis because natural selection has favoured certain traits over the course of human history (Figueredo et al., 2005, 2009). Thus, evolutionary analyses focus on how various personality traits—and the ability to recognize these traits in others—may have contributed to reproductive fitness in ancestral human populations.

For example, David Buss (1991, 1995, 1997) argues that the Big Five personality traits stand out as important dimensions of personality across a variety of cultures because those traits have had significant adaptive implications. Buss points out that humans historically have depended heavily on groups, which afford protection from predators or enemies, opportunities for sharing food, and a diverse array of other benefits. In the context of these group interactions, people have had to make difficult but crucial judgments about the characteristics of others, asking such questions as: Who can I depend on when in need? Who will share their resources? According to Buss, the Big Five emerge as fundamental dimensions of personality because humans have evolved special sensitivity to variations in the ability to bond with others (extraversion), the willingness to cooperate and collaborate (agreeableness), the tendency to be reliable and ethical (conscientiousness), the capacity to be an innovative problem solver (openness to experience), and the ability to handle stress (low neuroticism). In a nutshell, Buss argues that the Big Five reflect the most salient features of others' adaptive behaviour over the course of evolutionary history.

Daniel Nettle (2006) takes this line of thinking one step further. He asserts that the traits themselves (as opposed to the ability to recognize them in others) are products of evolution that were adaptive in ancestral environments. For example, he discusses how extraversion could have promoted mating success,

how agreeableness could have fostered the effective building of coalitions, and so forth. Consistent with this analysis, a variety of personality traits are associated with variations in lifetime reproductive success (Berg et al., 2014; Buss & Penke, 2015).

One article informed by this view hypothesized that variations in extraversion may be shaped by variations in attractiveness and physical strength, two traits that could have influenced the reproductive value of extraversion in human ancestral environments (Lukaszewski & Roney, 2011). The authors assert that over the course of human history, the reproductive payoffs of extraverted behaviour probably were higher for men and women who exhibited greater physical attractiveness, and for men who exhibited greater physical strength. Hence, they theorize that, to some extent, individuals learn to adjust or calibrate their level of extraversion to reflect their levels of attractiveness and strength. Thus, they predict attractiveness should correlate positively with extraversion in both genders, and that strength should be predictive of extraversion in men. This is what they found in two studies. Thus, in addition to explaining why certain traits are important dimensions of personality, evolutionary analyses may be able to help explain the origins of individual variations on these dimensions.

Evaluating Biological Perspectives

Researchers have compiled convincing evidence that biological factors help shape personality, and findings on the meagre effects of shared family environment have launched intriguing new approaches to the investigation of personality development. Nonetheless, we must take note of some weaknesses in biological approaches to personality. Critics assert that too much emphasis has been placed on heritability estimates, which vary depending on sampling and statistical procedures (Funder, 2001). Critics also argue that efforts to carve behaviour into genetic and environmental components ultimately lead to artificial results. The effects of nature and nurture are twisted together in complicated interactions that can't be separated cleanly (Asbury & Plomin, 2014; Rutter, 2012). For example, a genetically influenced trait, such as a young child's surly, sour temperament, might evoke a particular style of parenting. In essence then, the child's genes have moulded his or her environment. Thus, genetic and environmental influences on personality are not entirely independent.

Courtesy of Dr. David Buss

David Buss

"In sum, the five factors of personality, in this account, represent important dimensions of the social terrain that humans were selected to attend to and act upon."

Four Views of Personality: An Illustrated Overview of Major Theories of Personality

THEORIST AND ORIENTATION	SOURCE OF DATA AND OBSERVATIONS	KEY ASSUMPTIONS

A PSYCHODYNAMIC VIEW

Sigmund Freud

© 2017 Cengage Learning

Case studies from clinical practice of psychoanalysis

© Peter Aprahamian/Corbis

Past events in childhood determine our adult personality.

Our behaviour is dominated by unconscious, irrational wishes, needs, and conflicts.

Personality development progresses through stages.

A BEHAVIOURAL VIEW

B. F. Skinner

© 2017 Cengage Learning

Laboratory experiments, primarily with animals

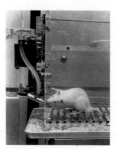

Courtesy of Professor Rick Stalling and Bradley University. Photo by Duane Zehr

Behaviour is determined by the environment, although this view was softened by Bandura's social cognitive theory.

Nurture (learning and experience) is more influential than nature (heredity and biological factors).

Situational factors exert great influence over behaviour.

A HUMANISTIC VIEW

Carl Rogers

© 2017 Cengage Learning

© Zigy Kaluzny/Stone/Getty Images

Case studies from clinical practice of client-centred therapy

People are free to chart their own courses of action; they are not hapless victims governed by the environment.

People are largely conscious, rational beings who are not driven by unconscious needs.

A person's subjective view of the world is more important than objective reality.

A BIOLOGICAL VIEW

Hans Eysenck

© 2017 Cengage Learning

Twin, family, and adoption studies of heritability; factor analysis studies of personality structure

Daly & Newton/Stone/Getty Images

Behaviour is largely determined by evolutionary adaptations, the wiring of the brain, and heredity.

Nature (heredity and biological factors) is more influential than nurture (learning and experience).

MODEL OF PERSONALITY STRUCTURE	VIEW OF PERSONALITY DEVELOPMENT	ROOTS OF DISORDER

Three interacting components (id, ego, super-ego) operating at three levels of consciousness

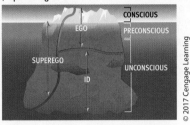

Emphasis on fixation or progress through psychosexual stages; experiences in early childhood (such as toilet training) can leave lasting mark on adult personality

Ruth Jenkinson/Dorling Kindersley/Getty Images

Unconscious fixations and unresolved conflicts from childhood, usually centring on sex and aggression

Collections of response tendencies tied to specific stimulus situations

Personality evolves gradually over the life span (not in stages); responses (such as extraverted joking) followed by reinforcement (such as appreciative laughter) become more frequent

Hill Street Studios/Blend Images/ Getty Images

Maladaptive behaviour due to faulty learning; the "symptom" is the problem, not a sign of under-lying disease

Self-concept, which may or may not mesh well with actual experience

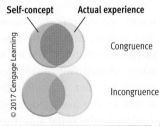

Children who receive unconditional love have less need to be defensive; they develop more accurate, congruent self-concept; conditional love fosters incongruence

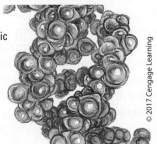

© Dereje/Shutterstock.com

Incongruence between self and actual experience (inaccurate self-concept); over-dependence on others for approval and sense of worth

Hierarchy of traits, with specific traits derived from more fundamental, general traits

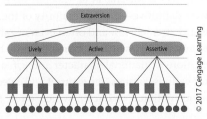

Emphasis on unfolding of genetic blueprint with maturation; inherited predispositions interact with learning experiences

© 2017 Cengage Learning

Genetic vulnera-bility activated in part by environ-mental factors

Understanding the Implications of Major Theories: Who Said This?

Check your understanding of the implications of the personality theories we've discussed by indicating which theorist is likely to have made the statements below. The answers are in Appendix A near the back of the book.

Choose from the following theorists:

Alfred Adler _____

Albert Bandura

Hans Eysenck _____

Sigmund Freud

Abraham Maslow _____

Walter Mischel

Quotes

1. "If you deliberately plan to be less than you are capable of being, then I warn you that you'll be deeply unhappy for the rest of your life."

2. "I feel that the major, most fundamental dimensions of personality are likely to be those on which [there is] strong genetic determination of individual differences."

3. "People are in general not candid over sexual matters . . . they wear a heavy overcoat woven of a tissue of lies, as though the weather were bad in the world of sexuality."

Culture and Personality

Key Learning Goal

▶ Clarify how researchers have found both cross-cultural similarities and disparities in personality.

Are there connections between culture and personality? In recent years, psychology's new interest in cultural factors has led to a renaissance of culture–personality research (e.g., Allik et al., 2010; Cheung et al., 2011; Church, 2010; Heine, Buchtel, & Norenzayan, 2008; Klimstra et al., 2011). This research has sought to determine whether Western personality constructs are relevant to other cultures and whether cultural differences can be seen in the prevalence of specific personality traits. As with cross-cultural research in other areas of psychology, these studies have found evidence of both continuity and variability across cultures.

For the most part, continuity has been apparent in cross-cultural comparisons of the trait structure of personality. When English-language personality scales have been translated and administered in other cultures, the predicted dimensions of personality have emerged from the factor analyses (Chui, Kim, & Wan, 2008; Paunonen & Ashton, 1998). For example, when scales that tap the Big Five personality traits have been administered and subjected to factor analysis in other cultures, the usual five traits have typically emerged (Katigbak et al., 2002; McCrae & Costa, 2008). Thus, research tentatively suggests that the basic dimensions of personality structure may be universal.

On the other hand, some cross-cultural variability is seen when researchers compare the average trait scores of samples from various cultural groups. For example, in a study comparing 51 cultures, McCrae and colleagues (2005) found that Brazilians scored relatively high in neuroticism, Australians in extraversion, Germans in openness to experience, Czechs in agreeableness, and Malaysians in conscientiousness, to give but a handful of examples. These findings should be viewed as very preliminary, as more data are needed from larger and more carefully selected samples. Nonetheless, the findings suggest that there may be genuine cultural differences on some personality traits. That said, the cultural disparities in average trait scores that were observed were quite modest in size.

The availability of the data from the McCrae et al. (2005b) study allowed Terracciano et al. (2005) to revisit the concept of *national character*—the idea that various cultures have widely recognized prototype personalities. Terracciano and his colleagues asked subjects from many cultures to describe the *typical* member of *their* culture on rating forms guided by the five-factor model. Generally, subjects displayed substantial agreement on these ratings of what was typical for their culture. The averaged ratings, which served as the measures of each culture's national character, were then correlated with the actual mean trait scores for various cultures compiled in the McCrae et al. (2005b) study. The results were definitive—the vast majority of the correlations were extremely low and often even negative. In other words, there was little or no relationship between perceptions of national character and actual trait scores for various cultures (see Figure 12.13). People's beliefs about national character, which often fuel cultural prejudices, turned out to be profoundly inaccurate stereotypes (McCrae & Terracciano, 2006).

Perhaps the most interesting recent work on culture and personality has been that of Hazel Markus and Shinobu Kitayama (Markus, 2016; Markus & Kitayama, 1991, 1994, 2003; Park, Uchida, & Kitayama, 2016), comparing American and Asian conceptions of the self. According to Markus and Kitayama, American parents teach their children to be self-reliant, to feel good about themselves, and to view themselves as special individuals. Children are encouraged to excel in competitive endeavours and to strive to stand out from the crowd. They are told that "the squeaky wheel gets the grease" and that "you have to stand up for yourself." Thus, Markus and Kitayama argue that American culture fosters an *independent* view of the self. American youngsters learn to define themselves in terms of their personal attributes, abilities, accomplishments, and possessions. Their unique strengths and achievements become the basis for their sense of self-worth. Hence, they are prone to emphasize their uniqueness.

Most North Americans take this individualistic mentality for granted. Indeed, Markus and Kitayama maintain that "most of what psychologists currently know about human nature is based on one particular view—the so-called Western view of the individual as an independent, self-contained, autonomous entity" (1991, p. 224). However, they marshal convincing evidence that this view is not universal. They argue that in Asian cultures such as Japan and China, socialization practices foster a more interdependent view of the self, which emphasizes the fundamental connectedness of people to each other (see Figure 12.14). In these cultures, parents teach their children that they can rely on family and friends, that they should be modest about their personal accomplishments so they don't diminish others' achievements, and that they should view themselves as part of a larger social matrix. Children are encouraged to fit in with others and to avoid standing out from the crowd. A popular adage in Japan reminds children that "the nail that stands out gets pounded down." Hence, Markus and Kitayama assert that Asian youngsters typically learn to define themselves in terms of the groups they belong to. Their harmonious relationships with others and their pride in group achievements become the basis for their sense of self-worth. Because their self-esteem does not hinge so much on personal strengths, they are less likely to emphasize their uniqueness. Consistent with this analysis, Markus and Kitayama report that Asian subjects tend to view themselves as more similar to their peers than American subjects do. Our Featured Study for this chapter addresses some of the issues central to Markus and Kitayama's work and that of others focused on culture and individual differences.

Photo and Campus Services, University of Michigan

Photo by Satoru Hirose. With permission of Shinobu Kitayama.

Hazel Markus and Shinobu Kitayama

"Most of what psychologists currently know about human nature is based on one particular view—the so-called Western view of the individual as an independent, self-contained, autonomous entity."

Figure 12.13

An example of inaccurate perceptions of national character. Terracciano et al. (2005) found that perceptions of national character (the prototype or typical personality for a particular culture) are largely inaccurate. The data shown here for one culture—Canadians—illustrates this inaccuracy. Mean scores on the Big Five traits for a sample of real individuals from Canada are graphed here in orange. Averaged perceptions of national character for Canadians are graphed in purple. The discrepancy between perception and reality is obvious. Terracciano et al. found similar disparities between views of national character and actual trait scores for a majority of the cultures they studied. (Adapted from McCrae & Terracciano, 2006)

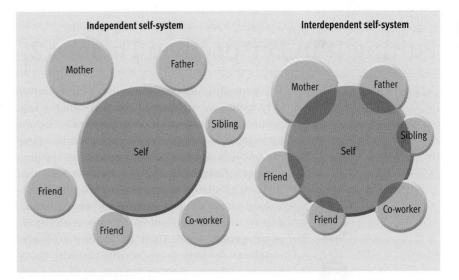

Figure 12.14

Culture and conceptions of self. According to Markus and Kitayama (1991), Western cultures foster an independent view of the self as a unique individual who is separate from others, as diagrammed on the left. In contrast, Asian cultures encourage an interdependent view of the self as part of an interconnected social matrix, as diagrammed on the right. The interdependent view leads people to define themselves in terms of their social relationships (e.g., as someone's daughter, employee, colleague, or neighbour).

Source: Adapted from Markus, H. R., & Kitayama, S. (1991). Culture and the self: Implications for cognition, emotion, and motivation. *Psychological Review, 98*(2), 224–253. Copyright © 1991 by the American Psychological Association. Adapted with permission.

Culture can shape personality. Children in Asian cultures, for example, grow up with a value system that allows them to view themselves as interconnected parts of larger social units. Hence, they tend to avoid positioning themselves so that they stand out from others.

Keren Su/Stone/Getty Images

FEATURED STUDY

Do collectivists know themselves better than individualists? Cross-cultural studies of the holier than thou phenomenon.

Description
This study by Balcetis and her colleagues examines the effects of culture on the accuracy of views that people have of themselves.

Investigators
Balcetis, E., Dunning, D., & Miller, R. L. (2008). *Journal of Personality and Social Psychology, 95,* 1252–1267.

Personality has often been studied in relation to the cultural syndromes of *individualism* versus collectivism, which represent different value systems and worldviews (Triandis & Suh, 2002). *Individualism* involves putting personal goals ahead of group goals and defining one's identity in terms of personal attributes rather than group memberships. In contrast, *collectivism* involves putting group goals ahead of personal goals and defining one's identity in terms of the groups one belongs to (e.g., one's family, tribe, work group, social class, caste, and so on).

These discrepant worldviews have a variety of implications for personality. For example, research has shown that individualism and collectivism foster cultural disparities in self-enhancement. *Self-enhancement* involves focusing on positive feedback from others, exaggerating one's strengths, and seeing oneself as above average. These tendencies tend to be pervasive in individualistic cultures, but far less common in collectivist cultures, where the norm is to be more sensitive to negative feedback and to reflect on one's shortcomings (Heine, 2003; Heine & Hamamura, 2007).

This observation is the springboard for the Featured Study for this chapter.

Putting It in Perspective: Themes 2, 3, and 5

The preceding discussion of culture and personality obviously highlighted the text's theme that people's behaviour is influenced by their cultural heritage. This chapter has also been ideally suited for embellishing two other unifying themes: psychology's theoretical diversity and the idea that psychology evolves in a sociohistorical context.

Few other areas of psychology are characterized by as much theoretical diversity as the study of personality, where there are literally dozens of insightful theories. Some of this diversity exists because different theories attempt to explain different facets of behaviour. However, much of this theoretical diversity reflects genuine disagreements on basic questions about personality. These disagreements are apparent on pages 460–461, which present an illustrated comparative overview of the ideas of Freud, Skinner, Rogers, and Eysenck, as representatives of the psychodynamic, behavioural, humanistic, and biological approaches to personality.

The study of personality also highlights the sociohistorical context in which psychology evolves. Personality theories have left many marks on modern culture; we can mention only a handful as illustrations. The theories of Freud, Adler, and Skinner have had an enormous impact on child-rearing practices. The ideas of Freud and Jung have found their way into literature (influencing the portrayal of fictional characters) and the visual arts. For example, Freud's theory helped inspire the surrealism movement's interest in the world of dreams.

Social learning theory has become embroiled in the public policy debate about whether media violence should be controlled because of its effects on viewers' aggressive behaviour. Maslow's hierarchy of needs and Skinner's affirmation of the value of positive reinforcement have influenced approaches to management in the world of business and industry.

Sociohistorical forces also leave their imprint on psychology. This chapter provided many examples of how personal experiences, prevailing attitudes, and historical events have contributed to the evolution of ideas in psychology. For example Freud's emphasis on sexuality was surely influenced by the Victorian climate of sexual repression that existed in his youth. Adler's views also reflected the social context in which he grew up. His interest in inferiority feelings and compensation appear to have sprung from his own sickly childhood and the difficulties he had to overcome. Likewise, it's reasonable to speculate that Jung's childhood loneliness and introversion may have sparked his interest in the introversion–extraversion dimension of personality. In a similar vein, we saw that both Rogers and Maslow had to resist parental pressures in order to pursue their career interests. Their emphasis on the need to achieve personal fulfillment may have originated in these experiences.

Understanding Personality Assessment

Everyone engages in efforts to size up his or her own personality as well as that of others. When you think to yourself that "Mary Ann is shrewd and poised," or when you remark to a friend that "Carlos is timid and submissive," you're making personality assessments. In a sense, then, personality assessment is an ongoing part of daily life. Given the popular interest in personality assessment, it's not surprising that psychologists have devised formal measures of personality.

Personality tests can be helpful in (1) making clinical diagnoses of psychological disorders, (2) vocational counselling, (3) personnel selection in business and industry, and (4) measuring specific personality traits for research purposes. Personality tests can be divided into two broad categories: *self-report inventories* and *projective tests*. In this Personal Application, we'll discuss some representative tests from both categories and discuss their strengths and weaknesses.

Self-Report Inventories

Self-report inventories are personality tests that ask individuals to answer a series of questions about their characteristic behaviour. The logic underlying this approach is simple: Who knows you better? Who has known you longer? Who has more access to your private feelings? Imperfect though they may be, self-ratings remain the gold standard for personality assessment (Paunonen & Hong, 2015). We'll look at two examples of self-report scales, the MMPI and the NEO Personality Inventory.

The MMPI The most widely used self-report inventory is the *Minnesota Multiphasic Personality Inventory* (MMPI) (Butcher, 2011). The MMPI was originally designed to aid clinicians in the diagnosis of psychological disorders. It measures ten personality traits that, when manifested to an extreme degree, are thought to be symptoms of disorders. Examples include traits such as paranoia, depression, and hysteria.

Are the MMPI clinical scales valid? That is, do they measure what they were designed to measure? Originally, it was assumed that the ten clinical subscales would provide direct indexes of specific types of disorders. In other words, a high score on the depression scale would be indicative of depression, a high score on the paranoia scale would be indicative of a paranoid disorder, and so forth. However, research revealed that the relationships between MMPI scores and various types of mental illness are much more complex than originally anticipated. People with most types of disorders show elevated scores on *several* MMPI subscales. This means that certain score *profiles* are indicative of specific disorders (see Figure 12.15). Thus, the interpretation of the MMPI is quite complicated, perhaps overly complicated according to some critics (Helmes, 2008). Nonetheless, the MMPI can be a helpful diagnostic tool for the clinician. The fact that the inventory has been translated into more than 115 languages is a testimonial to its usefulness (Adams & Culbertson, 2005).

The NEO Personality Inventory As we noted in the main body of the chapter, some theorists believe that only five trait dimensions are required to provide a full description of personality. This view has led to the creation of a relatively new test— the *NEO Personality Inventory*. Developed by Paul Costa and Robert McCrae (1985, 1992), the NEO inventory is designed to measure the Big Five traits: neuroticism, extraversion, openness to experience, agreeableness, and conscientiousness. The

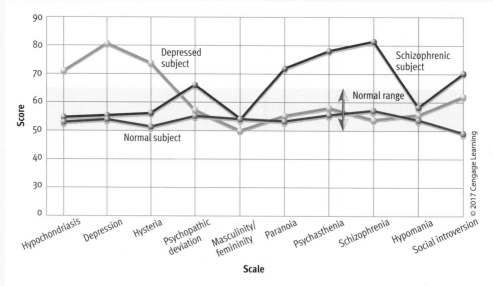

Figure 12.15

MMPI profiles. Scores on the ten clinical scales of the MMPI are often plotted as shown here to create a profile for a client. The normal range for scores on each subscale is 50 to 65. People with disorders frequently exhibit elevated scores on several clinical scales rather than just one.

NEO inventory is widely used in research and clinical work, and updated revisions of the scale have been released (Costa & McCrae, 2008; McCrae & Costa, 2004, 2007). An example of an NEO profile (averaged from many respondents) was shown in our discussion of culture and personality (see Figure 12.13 on page 463).

Strengths and Weaknesses of Self-Report Inventories To appreciate the strengths of self-report inventories, consider how else you might inquire about an individual's personality. For instance, if you want to know how assertive someone is, why not just ask the person? Why administer an elaborate 50-item personality inventory that measures assertiveness? The advantage of the personality inventory is that it can provide a more objective and more precise estimate of the person's assertiveness, one that is better grounded in extensive comparative data based on information provided by many other respondents.

Of course, self-report inventories are only as accurate as the information that respondents provide. They are susceptible to several sources of error (Ben-Porath, 2003; Kline, 1995; Paulhus, 1991), including the following:

1. *Deliberate deception.* Some self-report inventories include many questions whose purpose is easy to figure out. This problem makes it possible for some respondents to intentionally fake particular personality traits (Rees & Metcalfe, 2003). Some studies suggest that deliberate faking is a serious problem when personality scales are used to evaluate job applicants (Birkeland et al., 2006), but other studies suggest that the problem is not all that significant (Hogan & Chamoro-Premuzic, 2015).

2. *Social desirability bias.* Without realizing it, some people consistently respond to questions in ways that make them look good. The social desirability bias isn't a matter of deception so much as wishful thinking and it can distort test results to some degree (Paunonen & LeBel, 2012).

3. *Response sets.* A response set is a systematic tendency to respond to test items in a particular way that is unrelated to the content of the items. For instance, some people,

called *yea-sayers*, tend to agree with virtually every statement on a test. Other people, called *nay-sayers*, tend to disagree with nearly every statement.

Test developers have devised a number of strategies to reduce the impact of deliberate deception, social desirability bias, and response sets (Hough & Connelly, 2013; Paunonen & Hong, 2015). For instance, it's possible to insert a "lie scale" into a test to assess the likelihood that a respondent is engaging in deception. The best way to reduce the impact of social desirability bias is to identify items that are sensitive to this bias and drop them from the test. Problems with response sets can be reduced by systematically varying the way in which test items are worded. Although self-report inventories have some weaknesses, carefully constructed personality scales remain "an indispensable tool for applied psychologists" (Hogan, 2005, p. 331).

Projective Tests

Projective tests, which all take a rather indirect approach to the assessment of personality, are used extensively in clinical work. *Projective tests ask participants to respond to vague, ambiguous stimuli in ways that may reveal the subjects' needs, feelings, and personality traits.* The Rorschach test (Rorschach, 1921), for instance, consists of a series of ten inkblots. Respondents are asked to describe what they see in the blots. In the *Thematic Apperception Test* (TAT) (Murray, 1943), a series of pictures of simple scenes is presented to individuals who are asked to tell stories about what is happening in the scenes and what the characters are feeling. For instance, one TAT card shows a young boy contemplating a violin resting on a table in front of him (see Figure 12.16 for another example).

The Projective Hypothesis The "projective hypothesis" is that ambiguous materials can serve as a blank screen onto which people project their characteristic concerns, conflicts, and desires (Frank, 1939). Thus, a competitive person who is shown the TAT card of the boy at the table with the violin might concoct a story about how the boy is contemplating an

Figure 12.16
The Thematic Apperception Test (TAT). In taking the TAT, a respondent is asked to tell stories about scenes such as this one. The themes apparent in each story can be scored to provide insight about the respondent's personality.

Source: Reprinted by permission of the publishers from *THEMATIC APPERCEPTION TEST* by Henry A. Murray, Card 12F, Cambridge, Mass.: Harvard University Press, Copyright © 1943 by the President and Fellows of Harvard College, Copyright © renewed 1971 by Henry A. Murray.

upcoming musical competition at which he hopes to excel. The same card shown to a person high in impulsiveness might elicit a story about how the boy is planning to sneak out the door to go dirt-bike riding with friends.

The scoring and interpretation of projective tests is very complicated. Rorschach responses may be analyzed in terms of content, originality, the feature of the inkblot that determined the response, and the amount of the inkblot used, among other criteria. In fact, six different systems exist for scoring the Rorschach (Adams & Culbertson, 2005). TAT stories are examined in terms of heroes, needs, themes, and outcomes.

Strengths and Weaknesses of Projective Tests Proponents of projective tests assert that the tests have two unique strengths. First, they are not transparent to respondents. That is, the subject doesn't know how the test provides information to the tester. Hence, it may be difficult for people to engage in intentional deception (Weiner, 2013a). Second, the indirect approach used in these tests may make them especially sensitive to unconscious, latent features of personality.

Unfortunately, the scientific evidence on projective measures is unimpressive (Garb et al., 2005; Wood et al., 2010). In a thorough review of the relevant research, Lilienfeld, Wood, and Garb (2000) conclude that projective tests tend to be plagued by inconsistent scoring, low reliability, inadequate test norms, cultural bias, and poor validity estimates. They also assert that, contrary to advocates' claims, projective tests are susceptible to some types of intentional deception

(primarily, faking poor mental health). Based on their analysis, Lilienfeld and his colleagues argue that projective tests should be referred to as projective "techniques" or "instruments" rather than tests because "most of these techniques as used in daily clinical practice do not fulfill the traditional criteria for psychological tests" (p. 29). Another problem specific to the Rorschach is that all the inkblots have been posted on Wikipedia, along with common responses and their interpretation. Although psychologists have vigorously protested, the copyright for the test has expired, and the images are

in the public domain. Clinicians are concerned that this exposure of the inkblots could compromise the utility of the test (Hartmann & Hartmann, 2014; Schultz & Brabender, 2013).

In spite of these problems, projective tests, such as the Rorschach, continue to be used by many clinicians (Weiner & Meyer, 2009). Although the questionable scientific status of these techniques is a very real problem, their continued popularity suggests that they yield subjective information that many clinicians find useful (Meyer et al., 2013).

Hindsight in Everyday Analyses of Personality

Key Learning Goal

▶ Understand how hindsight bias affects everyday analyses and theoretical analyses of personality.

Consider the case of two close sisters who grew up together: Lorena and Christina. Lorena grew into a frugal adult who is careful about spending her money, shops only when there are sales, and saves every penny she can. In contrast, Christina became an extravagant spender who lives to shop and never saves any money. How do the sisters explain their striking personality differences? Lorena attributes her thrifty habits to the fact that her family was so poor when she was a child that she learned the value of being careful with money. Christina attributes her extravagant spending to the fact that her family was so poor that she learned to really enjoy any money that she might have. Now, it is possible that two sisters could react to essentially the same circumstances quite differently, but the more likely explanation is that both sisters have been influenced by the *hindsight bias*—the **tendency to mould one's interpretation of the past to fit how events actually turned out.** We saw how hindsight can distort memory in Chapter 7. Here, we will see how hindsight tends to make everyone feel as if they are personality experts and how it creates interpretive problems even for scientific theories of personality.

The Prevalence of Hindsight Bias

Hindsight bias is ubiquitous, which means that it occurs in many different settings, with all sorts of people. Most of the time, people are not aware of the way their explanations are skewed by the fact that the outcome is already known. The experimental literature on hindsight bias offers a rich array of findings on how the knowledge of an outcome biases the way people think about its causes (Hawkins & Hastie, 1990).

For example, when university students were told the results of hypothetical experiments, each group of students could "explain" why the studies turned out the way they did, even though different groups were given opposite results to explain (Slovic & Fischhoff, 1977). The students believed that the results of the studies were obvious when they were told what the experimenter found, but when they were given only the information that was available before the outcome was known, it was not obvious at all. This bias is also called the "I knew it all along" effect because that is the typical refrain of people when they have the luxury of hindsight. Indeed, after the fact, people often act as if events that would have been difficult to predict had in fact been virtually inevitable (Roese & Vohs, 2012). Looking back at the disintegration of the Soviet Union and the end of the Cold War, for instance, many people today act as though these events were bound to happen, but in reality these landmark events were predicted by almost no one.

Hindsight bias shows up in many contexts. For example, when a couple announces that they are splitting up, many people in their social circle will typically claim they "saw it coming." When a football team loses in a huge upset, you will hear many fans claim, "I knew they were overrated and vulnerable." When public officials make a difficult decision that leads to a disastrous outcome—such as the FBI's 1993 attack on the Branch Davidian compound in Waco, Texas—many of the pundits in the press are quick to criticize, often asserting that only incompetent fools could have failed to foresee the catastrophe. Interestingly, people are not much kinder to themselves when they make ill-fated decisions. When individuals make tough calls that lead to negative results—such as buying a car that turns out to be a lemon, or investing in a stock that plummets—they often say things like, "Why did I ignore the obvious warning signs?" or "How could I be such an idiot?"

Hindsight and Personality

Hindsight bias appears to be pervasive in everyday analyses of personality. Think about it: If you attempt to explain why you are so suspicious, why your mother is so domineering, or why your best friend is so insecure, the starting point in each case will be the personality outcome. It would probably be impossible to reconstruct the past without being swayed by your knowledge of these outcomes. Thus, hindsight makes everybody an expert on personality, as we can all come up with plausible explanations for the personality traits of people we know well. Perhaps this is why Judith Harris (1998) ignited a firestorm of protest when she wrote a widely read book arguing that parents have relatively little effect on their children's personalities beyond the genetic material that they supply.

In her book *The Nurture Assumption*, Harris summarizes behavioural genetics research and other evidence suggesting that family environment has surprisingly little impact on children's personality. As we discussed in the main body of the chapter, there is room for plenty of debate on this complex issue (Kagan, 1998; Tavris, 1998), but our chief interest here is that Harris made a cogent, compelling argument in her book, which attracted extensive coverage in the press—coverage that generated an avalanche of commentary from angry parents who argued that parents *do* matter. For example, *Newsweek* magazine received 350 letters, mostly from parents who provided examples of how they thought they influenced their children's personalities. However, parents' retrospective analyses of their children's personality development have to be treated with great skepticism, as they are likely to be distorted by hindsight bias (not to mention the selective recall frequently seen in anecdotal reports).

Unfortunately, hindsight bias is so prevalent it also presents a problem for scientific theories of personality. For example, the spectre of hindsight bias has been raised in many critiques of psychoanalytic theory (Torrey, 1992). Freudian theory was originally built mainly on a foundation of case studies of patients in therapy. Obviously, Freudian therapists who knew what their patients' adult personalities were like probably went looking for the types of childhood experiences hypothesized by Freud (oral fixations, punitive toilet training, Oedipal conflicts, and so forth) in their efforts to explain their patients' personalities. Another problem with hindsight bias is that once researchers know an outcome, more often than not they can fashion some plausible explanation for it.

Hindsight bias also presents thorny problems for evolutionary theorists, who generally work backward from known outcomes to reason out how adaptive pressures in humans' ancestral past may have led to those outcomes (Cornell, 1997). Consider, for instance, evolutionary theorists' assertion that the Big Five traits are found to be fundamental dimensions of personality around the world because those specific traits have had major adaptive implications over the course of human history (Buss, 1995; MacDonald, 1998). Their explanation makes sense, but what would have happened if some other traits had shown up in the Big Five? Would the evolutionary view have been weakened if dominance, or paranoia, or high sensation seeking had turned up in the Big Five? Probably not. With the luxury of hindsight, evolutionary theorists surely could have constructed plausible explanations for how these traits promoted reproductive success in the distant past. Thus,

Table 12.4

Critical Thinking Skill Discussed in This Application

SKILL	DESCRIPTION
Recognizing the bias in hindsight analysis	The critical thinker understands that knowing the outcome of events biases our recall and interpretation of the events.

hindsight bias is a fundamental feature of human cognition, and the scientific enterprise is not immune to this problem. See Table 12.4.

Other Implications of "20-20 Hindsight"

Our discussion of hindsight has focused on its implications for thinking about personality, but there is ample evidence that hindsight can bias thinking in all sorts of domains. For example, consider the practice of obtaining second opinions on medical diagnoses. The doctor providing the second opinion usually is aware of the first physician's diagnosis, which creates a hindsight bias (Arkes et al., 1981). Second opinions would probably be more valuable if the doctors rendering them were not aware of previous diagnoses. Hindsight bias frequently taints decision making in medicine, not to mention verdicts in malpractice cases (Arkes, 2013). Indeed, hindsight has the potential to distort legal decisions in many types of cases where jurors evaluate defendants' responsibility for known outcomes, such as a faulty braking system (Harley, 2007). For example, in trials involving allegations of negligence, jurors' natural

tendency to think "how could they have failed to foresee this problem?" may exaggerate the appearance of negligence. The ultimate problem with hindsight bias is that it tends to promote single-cause thinking and overconfidence when people analyze decisions that went awry (Roese & Vohs, 2012). In both medical and legal contexts these cognitive biases can have important consequences.

Hindsight bias is powerful. The next time you hear of an unfortunate outcome to a decision made by a public official, carefully examine the way news reporters describe the decision. You will probably find that they believe the disastrous outcome should have been obvious because they can clearly see what went wrong after the fact. Similarly, if you find yourself thinking, "Only a fool would have failed to anticipate this disaster" or "I would have foreseen this problem," take a deep breath and try to review the decision *using only information that was known at the time the decision was being made*. Sometimes good decisions based on the best available information can have terrible outcomes. Unfortunately, the clarity of "20-20 hindsight" makes it difficult for people to learn from their own and others' mistakes.

THE NATURE OF PERSONALITY

- A *personality trait* is a durable disposition to behave in a particular way across a variety of situations.

- According to the *five-factor model*, most aspects of personality are derived from five crucial traits: neuroticism, extraversion, openness to experience, agreeableness, and conscientiousness.

- The Big Five traits are predictive of important life outcomes, such as grades, occupational attainment, divorce, health, and mortality.

PSYCHODYNAMIC PERSPECTIVES

Freud's theory

- Freud's *psychoanalytic theory* grew out of his therapeutic work with clients and emphasized the importance of the unconscious.

- Freud divided personality structure into three components: the id, ego, and superego.

- The *id* is the instinctive component that follows the pleasure principle, the *ego* is the decision-making component that follows the reality principle, and the *superego* is the moral component.

- Freud described three levels of awareness: the *conscious* (current awareness), the *preconscious* (material just beneath the surface of awareness), and the *unconscious* (material well below the surface of awareness).

- Freud theorized that conflicts centring on sex and aggression are especially likely to lead to significant anxiety.

- According to Freud, anxiety and other unpleasant emotions are often warded off with *defence mechanisms*, which work through self-deception.

- Freud proposed that children evolve through five stages of psychosexual development: the oral, anal, phallic, latency, and genital stages.

- Certain experiences during these stages, such as handling of the *Oedipal complex*, can shape subsequent adult personality.

Jung's theory

- Jung's *analytical psychology* emphasized unconscious determinants of personality, but he divided the unconscious into the personal and collective unconscious.

- The *collective unconscious* is a storehouse of latent memory traces inherited from people's ancestral past.

- These memories consist of *archetypes*, which are emotionally charged thought forms that have universal meaning.

Adler's theory

- Adler's *individual psychology* emphasized how social forces shape personality development.

- Adler argued that *striving for superiority* is the foremost motivational force in people's lives.

- Adler attributed personality disturbances to excessive inferiority feelings that can pervert the normal process of striving for superiority and can result in *overcompensation*.

BEHAVIOURAL PERSPECTIVES

Skinner's theory

- Skinner's work on *operant conditioning* was not meant to be a theory of personality, but it has been applied to personality.

- Skinner's followers view personality as a collection of response tendencies that are tied to specific situations.

- Skinnerians view personality development as a lifelong process in which response tendencies are shaped by reinforcement.

Bandura's theory

- Bandura's *social cognitive theory* emphasizes how cognitive factors shape personality.

- According to Bandura, people's response tendencies are largely acquired through *observational learning*.

- Bandura stressed the role of *self-efficacy*—one's belief about one's ability to perform behaviours that should lead to expected outcomes.

Mischel's theory

- Mischel's brand of social learning theory emphasizes how people behave differently in different situations.

- His theory sparked debate about the relative importance of the person versus the situation in determining behaviour.

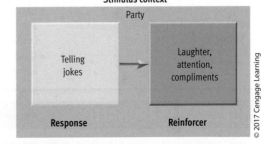

Defence Mechanism	Definition
Repression	Keeping distressing thoughts and feelings buried in the unconscious
Projection	Attributing one's own thoughts, feelings, or motives to another
Displacement	Diverting emotional feelings (usually anger) from their original source to a substitute target
Reaction formation	Behaving in a way that is exactly the opposite of one's true feelings
Regression	A reversion to immature patterns of behaviour
Rationalization	Creating false but plausible excuses to justify unacceptable behaviour
Identification	Bolstering self-esteem by forming an imaginary or real alliance with some person or group

HUMANISTIC PERSPECTIVES

Rogers's theory

- Rogers's *person-centred theory* focuses on the *self-concept*—a collection of subjective beliefs about one's nature.

- *Incongruence* is the degree of disparity between one's self-concept and one's actual experiences.

- According to Rogers, unconditional love during childhood fosters congruence, while conditional love fosters incongruence.

- Rogers asserted that people with highly incongruent self-concepts are prone to recurrent anxiety.

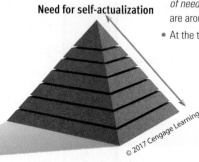

Need for self-actualization

© 2017 Cengage Learning

Maslow's theory

- Maslow proposed that human motives are organized into a *hierarchy of needs*, in which basic needs must be met before less basic needs are aroused.

- At the top of Maslow's hierarchy of needs is the need for *self-actualization*—the need to fulfill one's potential.

- Recently, theorists have proposed a major revision of Maslow's pyramid of needs in which the higher, growth needs are replaced by motives related to reproductive fitness.

- According to Maslow, *self-actualizing persons* are people with very healthy personalities, marked by continued personal growth.

BIOLOGICAL PERSPECTIVES

Eysenck's theory

- Eysenck viewed personality structure as a hierarchy of traits in which many superficial traits are derived from a handful of fundamental traits.

- According to Eysenck, personality is largely determined by genetic inheritance.

- Eysenck theorized that introversion and extraversion are shaped by inherited differences in ease of conditioning.

Behavioural genetics research

- Identical twins reared apart tend to be more similar in personality than fraternal twins reared together, which suggests that genetics shape personality.

- *Heritability estimates* for personality tend to hover around 50 percent.

- Behavioural genetics research revealed that *shared family environment* has surprisingly little impact on personality.

- Genetic mapping studies on personality yielded inconsistent, difficult to replicate findings.

The evolutionary approach

- According to Buss, the ability to recognize and judge other's status on the Big Five traits may have contributed to reproductive fitness.

- Nettle argues that the Big Five traits themselves (rather than the ability to recognize them) are products of evolution that were adaptive in ancestral times.

CULTURE AND PERSONALITY

- The basic trait structure of personality may be much the same across cultures because the Big Five traits usually emerge in cross-cultural studies.

- However, some cultural variability has been seen when researchers compare average trait scores for various cultural groups.

- Studies showed that perceptions of national character tend to be inaccurate stereotypes.

- Markus and Kitayama asserted that American culture fosters an *independent view* of the self, whereas Asian cultures foster an *interdependent view* of the self.

APPLICATIONS

- *Self-report inventories*, such as the MMPI and NEO, ask subjects to describe themselves.

- Self-report inventories are valuable assessment devices, but they are vulnerable to sources of error, including deception, the social desirability bias, and response sets.

- *Projective tests*, which depend on subjects' responses to ambiguous stimuli, have poor reliability and validity.

- *Hindsight bias* often leads people to assert that "I knew it all along" in discussing outcomes they did not actually predict.

CHAPTER 13

Social Behaviour

Themes in this Chapter

Empiricism

Cultural Heritage

Subjectivity

The Canadian Charter of Rights and Freedoms (1982) establishes equality before and under the law and equal protection and benefits of the law. It acts as a standard for the treatment of persons in Canada. This is of critical importance when considering racism, stereotyping, and prejudice, which exist at all levels within Canada. Consider the complaint brought against a Quebec firm early in the 21st century.

The Centre Maraîcher Eugène Guinois Jr. is located outside of Montreal and is one of Canada's largest commercial vegetable farms, comprising about 530 hectares. At the centre of the complaint were allegations made by four black farm workers that the working conditions at the farm included segregation, racism, and neglect. They alleged that there were two cafeterias—one for the whites and one for the black workers. The blacks' cafeteria was unheated and lacked running water, proper toilets, and refrigeration facilities (Patriquin, 2005). The black farm workers stated that they were the victims of verbal and physical abuse and racist graffiti. During harvest time, black farm workers were bussed in from Longueuil, and they were referred to as the "workers from Longueuil." One full-time black employee, Celissa Michel, reported that when he tried to heat his food in the whites' cafeteria, he was pushed out. Another black worker who tried to sit at the picnic tables near the cafeteria was told by the owner's wife that those tables were only for *Quebecers*. Michel commented on the experience, "It's frustrating and it hurts, but I had to stay there and just take it" (Patriquin, 2005, p. A9).

The circumstances considered by the Human Rights Tribunal in Quebec seemed more the stuff

Celissa Michel was one of the workers who brought a human rights complaint against a Quebec farm.

of fiction, or events that might have transpired in the southern United States in the early to middle part of the last century—not in Canada and surely not now. The presiding judge, Michèle Pauzé, felt compelled to contextualize her decision with the following: "The events you are going to read happened here, in Quebec, during the years 2000 and 2001" (Patriquin, 2005, p. A1). The courts awarded compensation to some of the victims in this case. Of course, it is not only black Canadians who find themselves the victims of prejudice, racism, and discrimination in Canada.

While it may not be consistent with Canadians' views of themselves or their country, stereotyping, prejudice, racism, and discrimination can be found here, as in other countries. According to the most recent data collected by Statistics Canada (2017), 1362 hate crimes were reported to police in 2015, with most targeting specific religious and ethnocultural groups. The data showed an increase of 61 percent from 2014 to 2015 in hate crimes that targeted the Muslim population of Canada. Overall, hate crimes based on religion constituted 35 percent of all hate crimes. Hate crimes based on sexual orientation (141) comprised 9 percent of all hate crimes. Violence and injury were most common in hate crimes targeting individuals because of their sexual orientation or those targeting Aboriginal Canadians (Leber, 2017). While we must keep in mind that the overall rate of reported hate crimes in Canada is relatively low, it is disturbing that race and ethnicity, religion, and sexual orientation emerge as the most common causes of reported hate crimes (Statistics Canada, 2017). Black Canadians are the most common target of racially oriented hate crimes. Hate crimes against Jewish populations and Muslim populations accounted for 13 percent and 12 percent, respectively, of all hate crimes in the country (Statistics Canada, 2017).

Racism is an important issue in Canada. Historically, we can see this in the marginalization of Asian immigrants. This was reflected in the treatment of the Chinese immigrants who helped build the Canadian Pacific Railway and the head tax that was levied on those emigrating from China (Shanahan, 2013). The Canadian government also instituted a program of internment and loss of rights and property of Japanese Canadians during World War II.

Aboriginal peoples have long been the targets of racism and stereotyping (Dokis, 2007), and the effects of the residential school policy are still being felt (CBC News, 2014). Hate crimes toward Aboriginal Canadians were most often directed toward males, and the victims tend to be younger than those of any other group targeted because of race or ethnicity

Courtesy of John Morstad

James Pon, an engineer and activist, emigrated with his mother to Canada in 1922 at the age of five to join his father who was already here. A head tax of $500 was charged for Chinese citizens who came to Canada. James Pon was invited in 2006 to come to Ottawa to receive the formal apology for the head tax from then-prime minister Stephen Harper on behalf of Canadians. Mr. Pon had worked for years to obtain the formal apology.

(Leber, 2017). Canada has a long history of systemic abuse of Aboriginal Canadians. For example, its residential school system, often referred to as a system of cultural genocide (Schwartz, 2015), operated from 1883 until 1996 and targeted up to 150 000 Aboriginal children. Over 6000 of these children are reported to have died as a result of the effects of the residential school experience. Aboriginal Canadians currently continue to be victimized at a rate proportionally much higher than the rate of criminal victimization for non-Aboriginal Canadians (Statistics Canada, 2016). The "historical trauma" faced by these citizens of Canada has had intergenerational negative effects on both physical and emotional health (Boska et al., 2015; Matheson et al., 2016; Reynaud, 2014).

How are we to make sense of stereotyping, prejudice, and discrimination (Lalonde, Jones, & Stroink, 2008)? What factors lead to such negative attitudes toward others? How do these attitudes affect our behaviour? Is there anything we can do to change such negative outcomes? These are just some of the issues we will be concerned with in this chapter, in which we examine social psychology. *Social psychology* is the branch of psychology concerned with the way individuals' thoughts, feelings, and behaviours are influenced by others. Our coverage of social psychology will focus on seven broad topics: person perception, attribution processes, interpersonal attraction, attitudes, conformity and obedience, behaviour in groups, and social neuroscience. The latter is the most recent research focus in social psychology. It deals with an examination of how structures and processes of the brain are associated with social phenomena such as prejudice and stereotyping.

Social psychologists study how people are affected by the actual, imagined, or implied presence of others (van Lange, 2013). Their interest is not limited to individuals' interactions with others, as people can engage in social behaviour even when they're alone. Social psychologists often study individual behaviour in a social context. This interest in understanding individual behaviour should be readily apparent in our first section, on person perception.

Saba Safdar of the University of Guelph conducts research in the area of cross-cultural psychology.

Person Perception: Forming Impressions of Others

Can you remember the first meeting of your introductory psychology class? What impression did your professor make on you that day? Did your instructor appear to be confident? Easygoing? Pompous? Open-minded? Cynical? Friendly? Were your first impressions supported or undermined by subsequent observations? Our perceptions and impressions of others are affected by a variety of factors including physical appearance, with the face being a particularly rich source (Jack & Schyns, 2017). Take a moment to look at the man pictured to the right. What do you think he is like? What does he do? What are his interests?

No matter whether you are correct or not, you probably found it easy to generate some idea of what he is like and what he is thinking (Wegner & Gray, 2016). We seem to be almost automatically drawn to

Our impressions of others are affected by physical appearance. What do you think this man is like?

trying to figure others out, to draw inferences and form an impression of them (Levordashka & Utz, 2017; Shimizu, Lee, & Uleman 2017). It might not surprise you to know that he currently works with computer software, developing software for video/film production. He just looks like a computer person, right? It might surprise you to know, however, that he was a musician and songwriter, and a pioneer in the use of computers in the Canadian music scene in the 1970s and 1980s. His acquaintances include Andy Warhol, Brian Ferry, Boy George, Robert Fripp, and British billionaire Richard Branson. He worked with well-known bands such as the Spoons, Joy Division, Roxy Music, and the Eurythmics, to name just a few. Does this additional information change what kind of person you think he is? We are often faced with the task of updating impressions we have formed of people as we get to know them better. Some of the information we obtain about people plays a special role in our impressions.

While we often gather many pieces of information about another person, our final impressions can often be dramatically affected by just one piece of information. In some of the classic research into impression formation, Solomon Asch (1946) demonstrated the importance that what he called *central traits* can have on the impressions we form of others. When you interact with people, you're constantly engaged in *person perception*, **the process of forming impressions of others.** People show considerable ingenuity in piecing together clues about others' characteristics. However, impressions are often inaccurate because of the many biases and fallacies that occur in person perception.

In this section, we consider some of the factors that influence, and often distort, people's perceptions of others.

Effects of Physical Appearance

"You shouldn't judge a book by its cover." "Beauty is only skin deep." People know better than to let physical attractiveness determine their perceptions of others' personal qualities. Or do they (Zebrowiz, 2017)? Studies have shown that judgments of others' personality are often swayed by their appearance, especially their physical attractiveness (Rohner & Rasmussen, 2012). One recent study by researchers at the University of British Columbia showed that good-looking people command more of our attention than less attractive individuals do (Lorenzo, Biesanz, & Human, 2010). While in many cases there are benefits to being perceived accurately (e.g., Human & Biesanz, 2013), perhaps if you are attractive you are willing to forgo some of this accuracy for research suggests that people tend to ascribe desirable personality characteristics to those who are good-looking. Attractive people tend to be seen as more sociable, friendly, poised, warm, and well adjusted than those who are less attractive (Macrae & Quadflieg, 2010; van Leeuwen, Matthijs, & Macrae, 2004). One recent study, focusing on the Big Five personality traits, found that attractive women were viewed as more agreeable, extraverted, conscientious, open to experience, and emotionally stable (lower in neuroticism) than less attractive women (Segal-Caspi, Roccas, & Sagiv, 2012). In reality, research findings suggest that little correlation exists between attractiveness and personality traits (Segal-Caspi et al., 2012).

Karen Dion of the University of Toronto (Dion, Berscheid, & Walster, 1972), in a study conducted with University of Toronto undergraduates, found that not only were the attractive targets ascribed all those positive characteristics, but they were also expected to have better lives, to be better spouses, and to be more successful in their chosen careers. In another study, Dion (1973) showed that linking the *beautiful* with the *good* starts early. In that study, three- to six-and-a-half-year-old children were shown pictures of attractive and unattractive kids, and were asked to make a series of judgments. As you can see in Table 13.1, the attractive kids were viewed more positively on a variety of dimensions. For example: Unattractive kids are scarier and hit you without a good reason, while attractive kids won't hit you back even if you hit them first.

You might guess that physical attractiveness would influence perceptions of competence less than

Table 13.1

Frequency of Assignment of Behavioural Descriptions to Attractive versus Unattractive Children

ATTRACTIVENESS OF CHILD CHOSEN		
Behavioural item	**Unattractive**	**Attractive**
Fights a lot	37	24
Hits without a good reason	42	19*
Says angry things	37	24
Scares you	42	18*
Might hurt you	40	21*
Very friendly to other children	16	45*
Helps children when they're hurt or sad	28	33
Doesn't like fighting or shouting	18	43*
Doesn't hit, even if someone else hits first	21	40*

*The items marked with an asterisk reflect significant differences.

Source: Adapted from Dion, K. (1973). Young children's stereotyping of facial attractiveness. *Journal of Personality and Social Psychology*, 9, 187. Copyright © 1972 by the American Psychological Association. Adapted with permission.

In general, people have a bias toward viewing good-looking men and women as bright, competent, and talented. However, people sometimes downplay the talent of successful women who happen to be attractive, attributing their success to their good looks instead of to their competence.

perceptions of personality, but the data suggest otherwise. A recent review of the relevant research found that people have a surprisingly strong tendency to view good-looking individuals as more competent than less attractive individuals (Langlois et al., 2000). This bias literally pays off for good-looking people, as they tend to secure better jobs and earn higher salaries than less attractive individuals (Collins & Zebrowitz, 1995; Engemann & Owyang, 2005; Senior et al., 2008).

Observers are also quick to draw inferences about people based on how they move, talk, and gesture—that is, their style of nonverbal expressiveness. Moreover, these inferences tend to be fairly accurate (Ambady & Rosenthal, 1993; Borkenau et al., 2004). For example, based on a mere ten seconds of videotape, participants can guess strangers' sexual orientation (heterosexual or homosexual) with decent accuracy (Ambady, Hallahan, & Conner, 1999). Based on similar "thin slices" of behaviour, observers can make accurate judgments of individuals' racial prejudice, social status, and intelligence (Ambady & Weisbuch, 2010). It is clear how these quick inferences might be adaptive if we are trying to assess a stranger's aggressiveness and fighting ability. There is evidence that research participants can relatively accurately infer the fighting ability and competitive success of professional MMA (mixed martial arts) fighters from looking at facial cues (Sell et al., 2009; Trebicky et al., 2013), especially for fighters in the heavyweight division.

Cognitive Schemas

Even though every individual is unique, people tend to categorize one another. Such labels reflect the use of cognitive schemas in person perception. As we discussed in Chapter 7, *schemas* are cognitive structures that guide information processing. Individuals use schemas to organize the world around them— including their social world. *Social schemas* are **organized clusters of ideas about categories of social events and people.** People have social schemas for events such as dates, picnics, committee meetings, and family reunions, as well as for certain categories of people, such as "dumb jocks," "social climbers," "frat rats," and "wimps" (see Figure 13.1). Individuals depend on social schemas because the schemas help them to efficiently process and store the wealth of information that they take in about others in their interactions. Hence, people routinely place one another in categories, and these categories influence the process of person perception (Fiske & Taylor, 2008).

We even have a schema for our self, referred to as a self-schema. Our *self-schema* is an **integrated set of memories, beliefs, and generalizations about one's behaviour in a given domain** (Kunda, 1999, p. 452) and self-schemas seem to operate the same way as any other type of schema. Self-schemas were

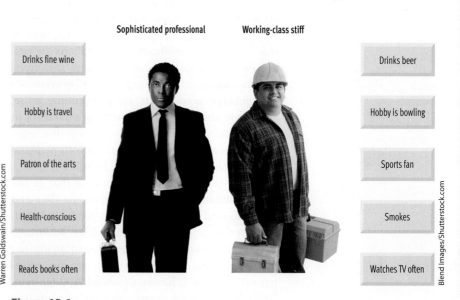

Figure 13.1

Examples of social schemas. Everyone has social schemas for various "types" of people, such as sophisticated professionals or working-class stiffs. Social schemas are clusters of beliefs that guide information processing.

first described and their effects assessed by Hazel Markus in 1977. She found that people with self-schemas in particular domains (e.g., a self-schema as athletic)—that is, people who are self-schematic for that domain—would show differences in how they processed and remembered information about themselves in that domain, affecting how efficiently they process information related to that domain, how easily they can make judgments about themselves in that domain, and how resistant they are to counter information about themselves in that domain (Kunda, 1999). Research has also found that your own self-schemas affects how you process information about others in terms of that domain (e.g., Markus et al., 1985). If you do not have a self-schema relevant to a particular domain, you are referred to as being *aschematic* in that domain (Markus et al., 1987).

Stereotypes

Some of the schemas that individuals apply to people are unique products of their personal experiences, while other schemas may be part of their shared cultural background (Bottom & Kong, 2012). *Stereotypes* are special types of schemas that fall into the latter category. **Stereotypes are widely held beliefs that people have certain characteristics because of their membership in a particular group.**

The most common stereotypes in our society are those based on sex, age, and membership in ethnic or occupational groups. People who subscribe to traditional *gender stereotypes* tend to assume that women are emotional, submissive, illogical, and passive, while men are unemotional, dominant, logical, and aggressive. *Age stereotypes* suggest that elderly people are slow, feeble, rigid, forgetful, and asexual. Notions that Germans are methodical, and Italians are passionate are examples of common *ethnic stereotypes*. *Occupational stereotypes* suggest that lawyers are manipulative, accountants are conforming, artists are moody, and so forth. We also show a tendency to associate skin colour and negativity such that negative actions are associated more often with perpetrators with darker skin (Alter et al., 2016).

Stereotyping is a cognitive process that is frequently automatic and that saves on the time and effort required to get a handle on people individually (Devine & Monteith, 1999; Fiske & Russell, 2010). Stereotypes save energy by simplifying our social world. But, just how accurate are our stereotypes (Dixon, 2017; Jussim, Crawford, & Rubinstein, 2015)? Some research suggests that this conservation of energy often comes at some cost in terms of accuracy (Stangor, 2009; Wang et al., 2014). Stereotypes frequently are broad overgeneralizations that ignore the diversity within social groups and foster inaccurate perceptions of people (Hilton & von Hippel, 1996). Obviously, not all males and lawyers behave alike. Most people who subscribe to stereotypes realize that not all members of a group are identical. For instance, they may admit that some men aren't competitive, and some lawyers aren't manipulative and mercenary. However, they may still tend to assume that males and lawyers are *more likely* than others to have these characteristics. Even if stereotypes mean only that people think in terms of slanted *probabilities,* their expectations may lead them to misperceive individuals with whom they interact. As we've noted in previous chapters, perception is subjective, and people often see what they expect to see.

Our perception of others is also subject to self-fulfilling prophecy; in effect, creating what we expect to see. This was clearly demonstrated in a classic study by Mark Zanna and his colleagues (Word, Zanna, & Cooper, 1974). The study was designed to show the operation of self-fulfilling prophecy. If you hold strong beliefs about the characteristics of another group, you may behave in such a way so as to bring about these characteristics. The research had two studies. In the first study, researchers had white undergraduate males interview either a black or white job applicant. The applicant was, in fact, an experimental accomplice or confederate. It was found that when the job applicant was black, the interviewers tended to sit farther away, end the interview more quickly, and make more speech errors (e.g., stuttering, stammering). Clearly, then, the white interviewers changed how they acted depending on the race of the interviewee. In interviewing a white accomplice, they adopted what was referred to as an *immediate* style (i.e., sitting closer, more eye contact), but when they interviewed a black accomplice they used a nonimmediate style (i.e., sitting farther away, making more speech errors, looking away).

In the second study, Word, Zanna, and Cooper attempted to find out how it would feel to have someone behave toward you in a nonimmediate style. In the study, white experimental accomplices interviewed other white students while adopting either the immediate or nonimmediate style. Students who had been interviewed in the nonimmediate style seemed more anxious and did not perform as well in the interview.

When we think about the effects of stereotypes, we often focus on the effects our stereotypes have on others and how self-fulfilling prophecy processes might serve to confirm those stereotypes. But, of course, our stereotypes also affect us; they influence our conceptualizations of our social environment.

But the influence of our stereotypes on us doesn't end there; they can also directly affect our own behaviour.

Subjectivity and Bias in Person Perception

Stereotypes and other schemas create biases in person perception that frequently lead to confirmation of people's expectations about others. According to University of Western Ontario social psychologist James Olson (Olson, Goffin, & Haynes, 2007), if someone's behaviour is ambiguous, people are likely to interpret what they see in a way that's consistent with their expectations (Olson, Roese, & Zanna, 1996). So, after dealing with a pushy female customer, a salesman who holds traditional gender stereotypes might characterize the woman as "emotional." In contrast, he might characterize a male who exhibits the same pushy behaviour as "aggressive."

People not only see what they expect to see, but also tend to overestimate how often they see it (Feidler, 2017). *Illusory correlation* occurs when people estimate that they have encountered more confirmations of an association between social traits than they have actually seen. People also tend to underestimate the number of disconfirmations that they have encountered, as illustrated by statements like "I've never met an honest lawyer."

Memory processes can contribute to confirmatory biases in person perception in a variety of ways. Often, individuals selectively recall facts that fit with their schemas and stereotypes (Fiske, 1998; Quinn, Macrae, & Bodenhausen, 2003). Evidence for such a tendency was found in a study by Cohen (1981). In this experiment, participants watched a videotape of a woman, described as either a waitress or a librarian, who engaged in a variety of activities, including listening to classical music, drinking beer, and watching TV. When asked to recall what the woman did during the filmed sequence, participants tended to remember activities consistent with their stereotypes of waitresses and librarians. For instance, subjects who thought the woman was a waitress tended to recall her drinking beer, while subjects who thought she was a librarian tended to recall her listening to classical music.

An Evolutionary Perspective on Bias in Person Perception

Why is the process of person perception riddled with bias? Evolutionary psychologists like Simon Fraser University's Dennis Krebs argue that some of the biases seen in social perception were adaptive in humans' ancestral environment (Krebs & Denton, 1997). For example, they argue that person perception is swayed by physical attractiveness because attractiveness was associated with reproductive potential in women and with health, vigour, and the accumulation of material resources in men.

What about the human tendency to automatically categorize others? Evolutionary theorists attribute this behaviour to our distant ancestors' need to quickly separate friend from foe. They assert that humans are programmed by evolution to immediately classify people as members of an *ingroup*—a group that one belongs to and identifies with, or as members of an *outgroup*—a group that one does not belong to or identify with. This crucial categorization is thought to structure subsequent perceptions. As Krebs and Denton (1997) put it, "It is as though the act of classifying others as ingroup or outgroup members activates two quite different brain circuits" (p. 27). Ingroup members tend to be viewed in a favourable light, whereas outgroup members tend to be viewed in terms of various negative stereotypes. According to Krebs and Denton, these negative stereotypes ("They are inferior; they are all alike; they will exploit us") move outgroups out of our domain of empathy, so we feel justified in not liking them or in discriminating against them, or even in some circumstances dehumanizing them (Haslan & Loughnan, 2014).

Evolutionary psychologists, then, ascribe much of the bias in person perception to cognitive mechanisms that have been shaped by natural selection.

Attribution Processes: Explaining Behaviour

It's Friday evening and you're sitting around at home feeling bored. You call a few friends to see whether they'd like to go out. They all say that they'd love to go, but they have other commitments and can't. Their commitments sound vague, and you feel that their reasons for not going out with you are rather flimsy. How do you explain these rejections? Do your friends really have commitments? Are they worn out by school and work? When they said that they'd love to go, were they being sincere? Or do they find you boring? Could they be right? Are you boring? These questions illustrate a process that people engage in

► Distinguish between internal and external attributions, and summarize Weiner's theory of attributions for success and failure.

► Identify some types of bias in patterns of attribution, including cultural variations.

University of Kansas

Fritz Heider

"Often the momentary situation which, at least in part, determines the behaviour of a person is disregarded and the behaviour is taken as a manifestation of personal characteristics."

routinely: the explanation of behaviour (Struthers, Dupuis, & Eaton, 2005). *Attributions* play a key role in these explanatory efforts. Hence, they have significant effects on social relations.

What are attributions? *Attributions* **are inferences that people draw about the causes of events, others' behaviour, and their own behaviour.** If you conclude that a friend turned down your invitation because she's overworked, you have made an attribution about the cause of her behaviour (and, implicitly, have rejected other possible explanations). If you conclude that you're stuck at home with nothing to do because you failed to plan ahead, you've made an attribution about the cause of an event (being stuck at home). If you conclude that you failed to plan ahead because you're a procrastinator, you've made an attribution about the cause of your own behaviour. People make attributions mainly because they have a strong need to understand their experiences. They want to make sense out of their own behaviour, others' actions, and the events in their lives. In this section, we'll take a look at some of the patterns seen when people make attributions.

Internal versus External Attributions

Fritz Heider (1958) was the first to describe how people make attributions. He asserted that people tend to locate the cause of behaviour either *within a person*, attributing it to personal factors, or *outside a person*, attributing it to environmental factors.

Elaborating on Heider's insight, various theorists have agreed that explanations of behaviour and events can be categorized as internal or external attributions (Jones & Davis, 1965; Kelley, 1967; Weiner, 1974).

Internal attributions **ascribe the causes of behaviour to personal dispositions, traits, abilities, and feelings.** *External attributions* **ascribe the causes of behaviour to situational demands and environmental constraints.** For example, if a friend's business fails, you might attribute it to his or her lack of business acumen (an internal, personal factor) or to negative trends in the nation's economic climate (an external, situational explanation). Parents who find out that their teenage son has just banged up the car may blame it on his carelessness (a personal disposition) or on slippery road conditions (a situational factor).

Internal and external attributions can have a tremendous impact on everyday interpersonal interactions. Blaming a friend's business failure on poor business acumen as opposed to a poor economy will have a great impact on how you view your friend. Likewise, if parents attribute their son's automobile accident to slippery road conditions, they're likely to deal with the event very differently than if they attribute it to his carelessness.

Attributions for Success and Failure

Some psychologists have sought to discover additional dimensions of attributional thinking besides the internal–external dimension. After studying the attributions that people make in explaining success and failure, Bernard Weiner (1980, 1986, 1994, 2004) concluded that people often focus on the *stability* of the causes underlying behaviour. According to Weiner, the stable–unstable dimension in attribution cuts across the internal–external dimension, creating four types of attributions for success and failure, as shown in Figure 13.2.

Let's apply Weiner's model to a concrete event. Imagine that you're contemplating why you failed to get a job that you wanted. You might attribute your setback to internal factors that are stable (lack of ability) or unstable (inadequate effort to put together an eye-catching résumé). Or you might attribute your setback to external factors that are stable (too much outstanding competition) or unstable (bad luck). If you got the job, your explanations for your success would fall into the same four categories: internal–stable (your excellent ability), internal–unstable (your hard work to assemble a superb résumé), external–stable (lack of top-flight competition), and external–unstable (good luck).

Weiner's model can be used to understand complex issues in the real world. For example, when people analyze the causes of poverty, their explanations tend to fit neatly into the cells of Weiner's model: internal-stable (laziness, lack of thrift);

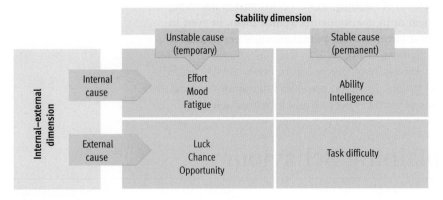

Figure 13.2

Weiner's model of attributions for success and failure. Weiner's model assumes that people's explanations for success and failure emphasize internal versus external causes and stable versus unstable causes. Examples of causal factors that fit into each of the four cells in Weiner's model are shown in the diagram.

Source: Weiner, B., Friese, I., Kukla, A., Reed, L., and Rosenbaum, R. M. (1972). Perceiving the causes of success and failure. In E. E. Jones, D. E. Kanouse, H. H. Kelley, R. E. Nisbett, S. Valins, and B. Weiner (Eds.), *Perceiving the causes of behaviour.* Morristown, NJ: General Learning Press. Used by permission of Bernard Weiner.

internal-unstable (financially draining illness); external-stable (discrimination, inadequate government programs for training); and external-unstable (bad luck, economic recession) (Weiner, Osborne, & Rudolph, 2011).

Bias in Attribution

Attributions are only inferences. Your attributions may not be the correct explanations for events. Paradoxical as it may seem, people often arrive at inaccurate explanations even when they contemplate the causes of *their own behaviour*. Attributions ultimately represent *guesswork* about the causes of events, and these guesses tend to be slanted in certain directions. Let's look at the principal biases seen in attribution.

The Fundamental Attribution Error and Actor–Observer Bias

Your view of your own behaviour can be quite different from the view of someone else observing you. When an actor and an observer draw inferences about the causes of the actor's behaviour, they often make different attributions. A common form of bias seen in observers is the *fundamental attribution error*, which refers to observers' bias in favour of internal attributions in explaining others' behaviour. Of course, in many instances, an internal attribution may not be an "error." However, observers have a curious tendency to overestimate the likelihood that an actor's behaviour reflects personal qualities rather than situational factors (Krull, 2001). Why? One reason is that situational pressures may not be readily apparent to an observer. In addition, it seems as if attributing others' behaviour to their dispositions is a relatively effortless, almost automatic process, whereas explaining people's behaviour in terms of situational factors requires more thought and effort (see Figure 13.3; Krull & Erickson, 1995). Another factor favouring internal attributions is that many people feel that few situations are so coercive that they negate all freedom of choice (Forsyth, 2004).

To illustrate the gap that often exists between actors' and observers' attributions, imagine that you're visiting your bank and you fly into a rage over a mistake made on your account. Observers who witness your rage are likely to make an internal attribution and infer that you are surly, temperamental, and quarrelsome. They may be right, but if asked, you'd probably attribute your rage to the frustrating situation. Perhaps you're normally a calm, easygoing person, but today you've been in line for 20 minutes, you just straightened out a similar error by the same bank last week, and you're being treated rudely

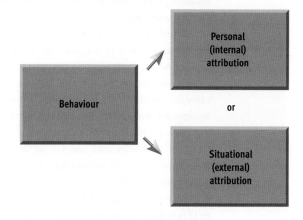

Traditional model of attribution

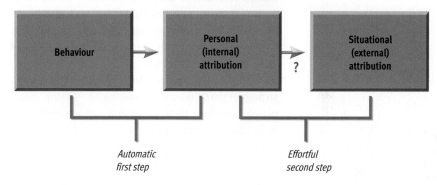

Alternative two-step model of attribution

Automatic first step   *Effortful second step*

Figure 13.3

An alternative view of the fundamental attribution error. According to Gilbert (1989) and others, the nature of attribution processes favours the *fundamental attribution error*. Traditional models of attribution assume that internal and external attributions are an either–or proposition requiring equal amounts of effort. In contrast, Gilbert posits that people tend to automatically make internal attributions with little effort, and then they *may* expend additional effort to adjust for the influence of situational factors, which can lead to an external attribution. Thus, external attributions for others' behaviour require more thought and effort, which makes them less frequent than personal attributions.

Source: Gilbert, D. T. (1989). Thinking lightly about others: Automatic components of the social inference precess. In J. S. Uleman & J. A. Bargh (Eds.), *Unintended thought limits of awareness, intention, and control.* New York: Guilford Press.

by the teller. Observers are often unaware of historical and situational considerations such as these, so they tend to make internal attributions for another's behaviour (Gilbert, 1998).

In contrast, the circumstances that have influenced an actor's behaviour tend to be more salient to the actor. Hence, actors are more likely than observers to locate the cause of their behaviour in the situation. In the *actor–observer bias*, actors favour external attributions for their behaviour, whereas observers are more likely to explain the same behaviour with internal attributions (Jones & Nisbett, 1971; Krueger, Ham, & Linford, 1996).

Self-Serving Bias and Defensive Attribution

The self-serving bias in attribution comes into play when people attempt to explain success and failure

(Mezulis et al., 2004). The *self-serving bias* is the tendency to attribute one's successes to personal factors and one's failures to situational factors. In explaining failure, the usual actor-observer biases are apparent. But in explaining success, the usual actor-observer differences are reversed to some degree: actors prefer internal attributions so they can take credit for their triumphs. Interestingly, this bias grows stronger as time passes after an event, so that people tend to take progressively more credit for their successes and less blame for their failures (Burger, 1986). The self-serving bias is intended to bolster self-esteem and subjective well-being, and the evidence suggests that it is at least partially successful in this regard (Sanjuan & Magallares, 2014).

The *defensive attribution* is the tendency to blame victims for their misfortunes, so that one feels less likely to be victimized in a similar way. The defensive attribution is relevant to situations in which you are attempting to explain calamities and setbacks that befall others. Here, an observer's tendency to make internal attributions becomes even stronger than normal. Blaming a victim helps people maintain their belief in a just world (Lerner & Goldberg, 1999), where they are unlikely to suffer a similar fate.

salamanderman/Shutterstock.com

A common example of defensive attribution is the tendency to blame the homeless for their plight.

Culture and Attributions

Do the patterns of attribution observed in subjects from Western societies transcend culture? Sometimes (e.g., De Freitas et al., 2017); but not always (Ojalehto, Medin, & Garcia, 2017; Robbins, Shepard, & Rochat, 2017). Some interesting cultural disparities have emerged in attribution processes.

......

concept **check** 13.1

Analyzing Attributions

Check your understanding of attribution processes by analyzing possible explanations for an athletic team's success. Imagine that the women's track team at your school has just won a provincial championship that qualifies it for the national tournament. Around the campus, you hear people attribute the team's success to a variety of factors. Examine the attributions shown below and place each of them in one of the cells of Weiner's model of attribution (just record the letter inside the cell). The answers are in Appendix A near the back of the book.

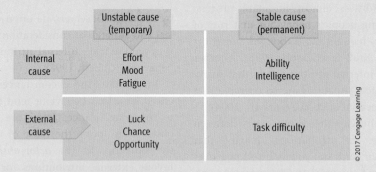

© 2017 Cengage Learning

	Unstable cause (temporary)	Stable cause (permanent)
Internal cause	Effort Mood Fatigue	Ability Intelligence
External cause	Luck Chance Opportunity	Task difficulty

a. "They won only because the best two athletes on Ottawa's team were out with injuries—talk about good fortune!"

b. "They won because they have some of the best talent in the country."

c. "Anybody could win in this province; the competition is far below average in comparison to the rest of the country."

d. "They won because they put in a great deal of last-minute effort and practice, and they were incredibly fired up for the regional tourney after last year's near miss."

Decades of research have shown that cultural differences in individualism versus collectivism influence attributional tendencies as well as many other aspects of social behaviour (Triandis, 1989, 2001; Triandis & Gelfand, 2012). *Individualism* involves putting personal goals ahead of group goals and defining one's identity in terms of personal attributes rather than group memberships. In contrast, *collectivism* involves putting group goals ahead of personal goals and defining one's identity in terms of the groups one belongs to (such as one's family, tribe, work group, social class, and caste). In comparison with individualistic cultures, collectivist cultures place a higher priority on shared values and resources, cooperation, mutual interdependence, and concern for how one's actions will affect other group members. Generally speaking, North American and Western European cultures tend to be individualistic, whereas Asian, African, and Latin American cultures tend to be collectivistic (Hofstede, 1980, 1983, 2001).

How does individualism versus collectivism relate to patterns of attribution? The evidence suggests that collectivist cultures may promote different attributional biases than individualistic cultures do. For example, although people from collectivist societies are not immune to the *fundamental attribution error*, they appear to be less susceptible to it than those from individualistic societies (Koenig & Dean, 2011). Research also suggests that self-serving bias may be particularly prevalent in individualistic, Western societies, where an emphasis on competition and high self-esteem motivates people to try to impress others, as well as themselves (Mezulis et al., 2004). Like the fundamental attribution error, the self-serving bias is seen in collectivist cultures, but not as frequently as in Western societies (Koenig & Dean, 2011).

Close Relationships: Liking and Loving

"I just don't know what she sees in him. She could do so much better for herself. I suppose he's a nice guy, but they're just not right for each other." You've probably heard similar remarks on many occasions. These comments illustrate people's interest in analyzing the dynamics of attraction. Research on attraction and relationships has revealed some key principles in understanding our close relationships with others (Finkel, Simpson, & Eastwick, 2017). We begin by considering the factors affecting interpersonal attraction. *Interpersonal attraction* refers to positive feelings toward another. Social

concept **check** 13.2

Recognizing Bias in Social Cognition

Check your understanding of bias in social cognition by identifying various types of errors that are common in person perception and attribution. Imagine that you're a non-voting student member of a committee that is hiring a new political science professor at your university. As you listen to the committee's discussion, you hear examples of (a) the illusory correlation effect, (b) stereotyping, (c) the fundamental attribution error, and (d) defensive attribution. Indicate which of these is at work in the excerpts from committee members' deliberations below. The answers are in Appendix A near the back of the book.

_____ 1. "I absolutely won't consider the fellow who arrived 30 minutes late for his interview. Anybody who can't make a job interview on time is either irresponsible or hopelessly disorganized. I don't care what he says about the airline messing up his reservations."

_____ 2. "You know, I was very, very impressed with the young female applicant, and I would love to hire her, but every time we add a young woman to the faculty in liberal arts, she gets pregnant within the first year." The committee chairperson, who has heard this line from this professor before replies, "You always say that, so I finally did a systematic check of what's happened in the past. Of the last 14 women hired in liberal arts, only one has become pregnant within a year."

_____ 3. "The first one I want to rule out is the guy who's been practising law for the last ten years. Although he has an excellent background in political science, I just don't trust lawyers. They're all ambitious, power-hungry, manipulative cutthroats. He'll be a divisive force in the department."

_____ 4. "I say we forget about the two candidates who lost their faculty slots in the massive financial crisis at Western Polytechnic last year. I know it sounds cruel, but they brought it on themselves with their fiscal irresponsibility over at Western. Thank goodness we'll never let anything like that happen around here. As far as I'm concerned, if these guys couldn't see that crisis coming, they must be pretty dense."

psychologists use this term broadly to encompass a variety of experiences, including liking, friendship, admiration, lust, and love. In this section, we'll analyze key factors that influence attraction and examine some theoretical perspectives on the mystery of love.

Key Factors in Attraction

Many factors influence who is attracted to whom. Here we'll discuss factors that promote the development of liking, friendship, and love. Although these are different types of attraction, the interpersonal dynamics at work in each are largely similar.

Physical Attractiveness

It is often said that "beauty is only skin deep." But the empirical evidence suggests that most people don't behave in a manner that is consistent with this saying. Research shows that the key determinant of romantic attraction for both genders is the physical attractiveness of the other person (Sprecher & Duck, 1994). Many studies have demonstrated the singular prominence of physical attractiveness in the initial stage of dating and have shown that it continues to influence the course of commitment as relationships evolve (Sprecher et al., 2015). In the realm of romance, being physically attractive appears to be more important for females' desirability (Regan, 2008). For example, in a study of college students (Speed & Gangestad, 1997), the correlation between romantic popularity (assessed by peer ratings) and physical attractiveness was higher for females (0.76) than for males (0.47).

Although people prefer physically attractive partners in romantic relationships, they may consider their own level of attractiveness in pursuing dates. The *matching hypothesis* proposes that **males and females of approximately equal physical attractiveness are likely to select each other as partners.** The matching hypothesis is supported by evidence that dating and married couples tend to be similar in level of physical attractiveness (Regan, 2008). There is some debate, however, about whether people match up by mutual choice. Some theorists believe that individuals mostly pursue highly attractive partners and that their matching is the result of social forces beyond their control, such as rejection by more attractive others (Taylor et al., 2011).

Similarity Effects

Is it true that "birds of a feather flock together," or do "opposites attract"? Research provides far more support for the former than the latter (Sprecher et al., 2015). One study found that people sit closer to others who are similar to them on simple physical traits, such as hair length, hair colour, and whether they wear glasses (Mackinnon, Jordan, & Wilson, 2011). Married and dating couples tend to be similar in age, race, religion, social class, education, intelligence, physical attractiveness, and attitudes (Kalmijn, 1998; Watson et al., 2004). The similarity principle operates in both friendships and romantic relationships regardless of sexual orientation (Fehr, 2008; Morry, 2009). The most obvious explanation for these correlations is that similarity causes attraction (Byrne, 1997), perhaps because we assume that similar others will like us (Montoya & Horton, 2012). However, research also suggests that attraction can foster similarity (Sprecher, 2014) because people who are close gradually modify their attitudes in ways that make them more congruent, a phenomenon called attitude alignment.

reality check

Misconception

In the realm of romance, opposites attract.

Reality

There is absolutely no empirical evidence to support this folklore. Research consistently shows that couples tend to be similar in intelligence, education, social status, ethnicity, physical attractiveness, and attitudes. Dissimilarity does not foster attraction.

Reciprocity Effects

In interpersonal attraction, *reciprocity* involves liking those who show that they like us. In general, research indicates that we tend to like those who show that they like us and that we tend to see others as liking us more if we like them. Thus, it appears that liking breeds liking, and loving promotes loving (Whitchurch, Wilson, & Gilbert, 2011). Reciprocating attraction generally entails providing friends and intimate partners with positive feedback that results in a self-enhancement effect—in other words, you help them feel good about themselves (Sedikides & Strube, 1997).

According to the matching hypothesis, males and females who are similar in physical attractiveness are likely to be drawn together. This type of matching may also influence the formation of friendships.

Perspectives on the Mystery of Love

Love has proven to be an elusive subject of study. It's difficult to define, difficult to measure, and frequently difficult to understand. Nonetheless, psychologists have begun to make some progress in their study of love (Reis & Aron, 2008). Let's look at their theories and research.

Passionate and Companionate Love

Two early pioneers in research on love were Elaine Hatfield (formerly Walster) and Ellen Berscheid (Berscheid, 1988, 2006, 2016; Berscheid & Walster, 1978; Hatfield & Rapson, 1993). They have proposed that romantic relationships are characterized by two kinds of love: passionate love and companionate love. *Passionate love* is a complete absorption in another that includes tender sexual feelings and the agony and ecstasy of intense emotion. *Companionate love* is warm, trusting, tolerant affection for another whose life is deeply intertwined with one's own. Passionate and companionate love can co-exist. They don't, however, necessarily go hand in hand. Initially, it was thought that passionate love peaks in intensity early in relationships and then declines significantly over time. However, more recent research suggests that in relationships that remain intact, the erosion of passionate love tends to be gradual and modest, with levels remaining fairly high in most couples (Fehr, 2015; O'Leary et al., 2012).

Research demonstrates that passionate love is a powerful motivational force that produces profound changes in people's thinking, emotion, and behaviour (Acevedo & Aron, 2014). Interestingly, brain-imaging research indicates that when people think about someone they are passionately in love with, these thoughts light up the dopamine circuits in the brain that are known to be activated by cocaine and other addictive drugs (Acevedo & Aron, 2014). Perhaps that explains why passionate love sometimes resembles an addiction.

Passionate and companionate love *may* co-exist, but they don't necessarily go hand in hand. Research suggests that, as a general rule, companionate love is more strongly related to relationship satisfaction than passionate love (Fehr, 2001). The distinction between passionate and companionate love has been further refined by Robert Sternberg (1988a, 2006). He subdivides companionate love into intimacy and commitment. *Intimacy* refers to warmth, closeness, and sharing in a relationship. *Commitment* is an intent to maintain a relationship in spite of the difficulties and costs that may arise.

Love as Attachment

In a groundbreaking analysis of love, Hazan and Shaver (1987) looked at similarities between adult love and attachment relationships in infancy. We noted in Chapter 11 that infant-caregiver bonding, or attachment, emerges in the first year of life. Early attachments vary in quality, and infants tend to fall into three groups (Ainsworth et al., 1978). Most infants develop a secure attachment. However, some are very anxious when separated from their caregiver, a syndrome called anxious-ambivalent attachment. A third group of infants, characterized by avoidant attachment, never bond very well with their caregiver.

According to Hazan and Shaver, romantic love is an attachment process, and people's intimate relationships in adulthood follow the same form as their attachments in infancy. In their theory, a person who had an anxious-ambivalent attachment in infancy will tend to have romantic relations marked by anxiety and ambivalence in adulthood. In other words, people relive their early bonding experiences with their parents in their romantic relationships in adulthood.

Hazan and Shaver's (1987) initial survey study provided striking support for their theory. They found that adults' love relationships could be sorted into groups that paralleled the three patterns of attachment seen in infants (see Figure 13.4). *Secure adults* found it relatively easy to get close to others and described their love relations as trusting. *Anxious-ambivalent* adults reported a preoccupation with love, accompanied by expectations of rejection, and they described their love relations as volatile and marked by jealousy. *Avoidant adults* found it difficult to get close to others and described their love relations as lacking intimacy and trust. Research eventually showed that attachment patterns are reasonably stable over time and that people's working models of attachment are carried forward from one relationship to the next (Simpson & Winterheld, 2012). These findings supported the notion that individuals' infant attachment experiences shape their intimate relations in adulthood.

Research on the correlates of adult attachment styles has grown exponentially since the mid-1990s. Consistent with the original theory, research has shown that securely attached individuals have more committed, satisfying, intimate, well-adjusted, and longer-lasting relationships than do people with

Elaine Hatfield

"Passionate love is like any other form of excitement. By its very nature, excitement involves a continuous interplay between elation and despair, thrills and terror."

Ellen Berscheid

"The emotion of romantic love seems to be distressingly fragile. As a 16th-century sage poignantly observed,' The history of a love affair is the drama of its fight against time.'"

Adult attachment style

Secure
I find it relatively easy to get close to others and am comfortable depending on them and having them depend on me. I don't often worry about being abandoned or about someone getting too close to me.

Avoidant
I am somewhat uncomfortable being close to others; I find it difficult to trust them, difficult to allow myself to depend on them. I am nervous when anyone gets too close, and often love partners want me to be more intimate than I feel comfortable being.

Anxious/ambivalent
I find that others are reluctant to get as close as I would like. I often worry that my partner doesn't really love me or won't want to stay with me. I want to merge completely with another person, and this desire sometimes scares people away.

© 2017 Cengage Learning

Figure 13.4
Attachment and romantic relationships. According to Hazan and Shaver (1987), people's romantic relationships in adulthood are similar in form to their attachment patterns in infancy, which fall into three categories. The three attachment styles seen in adult intimate relations are described here. (Based on Hazan & Shaver, 1986, 1987)

anxious-ambivalent or avoidant attachment styles (Pietromonaco & Beck, 2015). Moreover, studies have shown that people with different attachment styles are predisposed to think, feel, and behave differently

Marriages based on romantic love are the norm in Western cultures, whereas arranged marriages prevail in collectivist cultures.

Scotty Robson Photography/Getty Images

in their relationships (Mikulincer & Shaver, 2013). For example, people high in attachment anxiety tend to behave in awkward ways that undermine their dating success. Worried about the likelihood of rejection, they end up courting rejection by acting cold, wary, disengaged, and preoccupied with themselves (McClure & Lydon, 2014). When they do get involved in romantic relationships, people high in attachment anxiety tend to overreact emotionally to conflict with their partners. Their exaggerated expressions of hurt and vulnerability are designed to make their partners feel guilty, but these manipulative efforts end up having a negative impact on their relationship (Overall et al., 2014).

Culture and Close Relationships

Relatively little cross-cultural research has been conducted on the dynamics of close relationships. The limited evidence suggests both similarities and differences between cultures in romantic relationships (Hendrick & Hendrick, 2000; Schmitt, 2005). Psychologists such as the University of Toronto's Karen and Ken Dion suggest that cultures vary considerably in terms of how they understand and conceptualize love and relationships (Dion & Dion, 1996). They suggest that some of this variability is attributable to differences in societal and psychological differences in individualism and collectivism.

For the most part, similarities have been seen when research has focused on what people look for in prospective mates—such as mutual attraction, kindness, and intelligence (Fehr, 2013). Cultures vary, however, in their emphasis on love—especially passionate love—as a prerequisite for marriage. Passionate love as the basis for marriage is an 18th-century invention of individualistic Western culture (Stone, 1977). In contrast, marriages arranged by families and other go-betweens remain common in cultures high in collectivism, including India, Japan, China, and many Middle Eastern countries (Eastwick, 2013). In collectivist societies, people contemplating marriage tend to think in terms of "What will my parents and other people say?" rather than "What does my heart say?" Although romantic love is routinely seen in collectivist societies (Fehr, 2013), subjects from those societies are less likely than subjects from cultures high in individualism to report that romantic love is important for marriage (Fehr, 2015).

While mixed marriages are on the rise in Canada (Statistics Canada, 2016), sometimes the clash of cultural values can have tragic consequences. For example, Rajinder Singh Atwal of New Westminster, British Columbia, was convicted of second-degree murder in the July 2003 stabbing death of his 17-year-old-daughter, Amandeep, because she was in a relationship with Todd McIsaac, a boy of a different cultural group and religion. Atwal received an automatic life sentence, with no chance of parole for 16 years (Sikh Philosophy Network, 2005). While honour killings in Canada are limited, they do occur periodically. The Department of Justice estimates that there were a dozen such murders in Canada between 1999 and 2009 (Department of Justice, 2016).

The Internet and Close Relationships

In recent years, the Internet has dramatically expanded opportunities for people to meet and develop close relationships through social networking sites (Google+, Facebook), online dating services, email, and chat rooms. Critics are concerned that Internet relationships tend to be superficial. Research, however, suggests that virtual relationships can be just as intimate as face-to-face ones and are sometimes even closer (Bargh, McKenna, & Fitzsimons, 2002). Moreover, many virtual relationships evolve into face-to-face interactions (Boase & Wellman, 2006).

Facebook appears to fulfill two important motives: the need to belong and the need to engage in self-presentation or impression management (Nadkarni & Hofmann, 2012). Research on Facebook users suggests that people's profiles are reasonably accurate self-presentations (Wilson, Gosling, & Graham, 2012). Obviously, people try to portray themselves in a positive light, but so do people in offline interactions. Some theorists have expressed concern that as people spend more time in online interactions, they will spend less time with each other, resulting in loneliness and isolation (Turkle, 2011). Research suggests, paradoxically, that people's level of Facebook usage is correlated with both an increased sense of connection and disconnection (Sheldon, Abad, & Hinsch, 2011). On the one hand, feelings of loneliness appear to motivate greater dependence on Facebook as a coping strategy, but on the other hand, people who rely heavily on Facebook do forge rewarding connections with others. The benefits of Facebook are seen primarily in those who engage in active interaction with others (leaving wall posts, messaging friends), as opposed to those who passively view others' content and updates (Burke, Marlow, & Lento, 2010). That said, a recent study found that Facebook use was associated with temporary decreases in subjective well-being (Kross et al., 2013), perhaps because people feel envious of their friends' good news and impressive-looking self-presentations. Another study found that heavy use of Facebook sometimes caused conflicts between romantic partners (Clayton, Nagurney, & Smith, 2013).

The power of similarity effects provides the foundation for some of the Internet's most successful online dating sites. Prior to 2000, online dating sites were basically just an electronic variation on the personal ads that had been around for decades—with the addition of sophisticated search capabilities. But in 2000, eHarmony.com launched the first matching website. This site claims to use a "scientific approach" to matching people, based on compatibility. Members fill out lengthy questionnaires about their attitudes, values, interests, and so forth, and then matching algorithms are used to identify people who exhibit promising similarity. The commercial success of eHarmony.com has led many other online dating sites to add matching services. The architects of eHarmony claim that their services account for 5 percent of newlywed couples in the United States (Martin, 2011).

Online matching sites clearly have altered the landscape of dating and mating (Finkel et al., 2012). Online sites offer individuals access to vastly more dating candidates than they could ever meet in bars, churches, classes, and parties. The process of getting acquainted has become information-rich in unprecedented ways, as potential partners typically learn a great deal about each other before meeting face-to-face. Online matching sites claim they help people meet their "soul mates," and that their matching formulas lead to more successful romantic relationships than result from traditional dating. Is there any evidence to support these bold claims? For the most part, no (Sprecher et al., 2015). For business reasons, the competing matching sites have generally been unwilling to reveal the details of their matching algorithms and have chosen not to publish any internal research they may have conducted (Finkel et al., 2012). The notion that matching based on compatibility might foster romantic success is plausible, but with the exception of one recent study, there has been no published research. However, that single study, conducted with the cooperation of eHarmony, did yield surprisingly promising results (Cacioppo et al., 2013). Working with a sample of more than 19 000 respondents who married between 2005 and 2012, the researchers found that a marital

Social Behaviour

breakup had occurred in a lower portion of those who met online (5.96 percent) than those who met in traditional offline venues (7.67 percent). A single study does not settle the issue by any means, but the initial findings are encouraging.

An Evolutionary Perspective on Attraction

Evolutionary psychologists have a great deal to say about heterosexual attraction. For example, they assert that physical appearance is an influential determinant of attraction because certain aspects of good looks can be indicators of sound health, good genes, and high fertility, all of which can contribute to reproductive potential (Maner & Ackerman, 2013). Consistent with the evolutionary view, research has found that some standards of attractiveness are more consistent across cultures than previously believed (Sugiyama, 2005). For example, facial symmetry seems to be a key element of attractiveness in highly diverse cultures. Facial symmetry is thought to be valued because a variety of environmental insults and developmental abnormalities are associated with physical asymmetries, which can serve as markers of relatively poor genes or health (Fink et al., 2006). Another facet of appearance that may transcend culture is *women's waist-to-hip ratio* (Singh et al., 2010). Around the world, men seem to prefer women with a moderately low waist-to-hip ratio (in the vicinity of 0.70), which roughly corresponds to an "hourglass figure." This appears to be a meaningful correlate of females' reproductive potential (Gallup & Frederick, 2010), as it signals that a woman is healthy, young, and not pregnant.

The most thoroughly documented findings on the evolutionary bases of heterosexual attraction are those on gender differences in mating preferences, which appear to be consistent across highly varied cultures (Neuberg, Kenrick, & Schaller, 2010). In keeping with the notion that humans are programmed by evolution to behave in ways that enhance their reproductive fitness, evidence indicates that men generally are more interested than women in seeking youthfulness and physical attractiveness in their mates because these traits should be associated with greater reproductive potential. On the other hand, research shows that women place a greater premium on prospective mates' ambition, social status, and financial potential because these traits should be associated with the ability to invest material resources in children (Griskevicius, Haselton, & Ackerman, 2015; Kenrick, Neuberg, & White, 2013).

These findings have been questioned in some studies of speed dating, which found that dating prospects' physical attractiveness did not differentially predict males' and females' romantic interest (Asendorpf, Penke, & Back, 2011; Eastwick et al., 2011). However, critics have noted that the speed dating situation may evoke short-term mating strategies (Meltzer et al., 2014), and it has long been known that when women are asked about what they prefer in a short-term partner (for casual sex), they value physical attractiveness just as much as men do (Maner & Ackerman, 2013). Critics have also wondered whether the speed dating studies included enough variation in social status and attractiveness to provide a sensitive test of the impact of these variables (Li et al., 2013). A recent study that included more people at the low end of the spectrum in terms of attractiveness and social status (thus increasing the variation on these dimensions) yielded results consistent with evolutionary theory: men placed more emphasis on the attractiveness of dating prospects, whereas women emphasized social status more (Li et al., 2013). Moreover, another study that focused on couples in their first four years of marriage found that partners' physical attractiveness influenced the relationship satisfaction of husbands more than wives (Meltzer et al., 2014).

Evolutionary analyses also make some interesting predictions about how women's menstrual cycles may influence their mating preferences and tactics. When women are in mid-cycle approaching ovulation—that is, when they are most fertile—their preferences shift to favour men who exhibit masculine facial and bodily features, attractiveness, and dominance (Gangestad et al., 2007; Little, Jones, & Burriss, 2007). Women's mating strategies also change when their fertility is

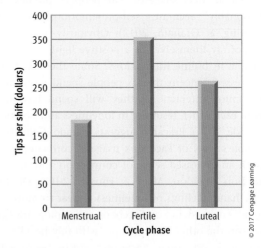

Figure 13.5

The menstrual cycle and strippers' earnings. Miller et al. (2007) found that strippers' tips were influenced by their menstrual cycle. As you can see in this graph, which shows the data for strippers who were not using hormonal contraception, the dancers' tips per shift were 58 percent higher when they were in their fertile period than when they were in their menstrual or luteal periods. (Based on Miller et al., 2007)

at its peak, as they tend to wear more provocative clothing and they are more flirtatious in the presence of attractive men (Cantu et al., 2014; Durante, Li, & Haselton, 2008). Interestingly, although ovulation is far from obvious in human females, strippers earn 58 percent more tip money per night when they are in their most fertile period (see Figure 13.5; Miller, Tybur, & Jordan, 2007). Researchers aren't sure whether male patrons are "detecting" the strippers' heightened fertility or whether the ovulating dancers come on to the customers more because they are more sexually motivated.

Attitudes: Making Social Judgments

Social psychology's interest in attitudes has a much longer history than its interest in attraction. Indeed, in its early days, social psychology was defined as the *study of attitudes*. In this section, we'll discuss the nature of attitudes, efforts to change attitudes through persuasion, and theories of attitude change.

What are attitudes? *Attitudes* **are positive or negative evaluations of objects of thought.** "Objects of thought" may include social issues (capital punishment or gun control, for example), groups (liberals, farmers), institutions (the Lutheran Church, the Supreme Court), consumer products (yogurt, computers), and people (the prime minister, your next-door neighbour).

Components and Dimensions of Attitudes

Attitudes can include up to three components (Briñol & Petty, 2012). The cognitive component of an attitude is made up of the beliefs people hold about the object of an attitude. The affective component consists of the emotional feelings stimulated by an object of thought. The behavioural component consists of predispositions to act in certain ways toward an attitude object. Figure 13.6 provides concrete examples of how someone's attitude about gun control might be divided into its components.

Attitudes also vary along several crucial dimensions. These include their *strength, accessibility,* and *ambivalence* (Howe & Krosnick, 2017; Maio, Olson, & Cheung, 2013). Definitions of attitude strength differ. However, strong attitudes are generally viewed as ones that are firmly held (resistant to change), that are durable over time, and that have a powerful impact on behaviour (Petty, Wheeler, & Tormala, 2013). The *accessibility* of an attitude refers to how often one thinks about it and how quickly it comes to mind. Highly accessible attitudes are quickly and readily available (Fabrigar, MacDonald, & Wegener, 2005). *Ambivalent attitudes* are conflicted evaluations that include both positive and negative feelings

about an object of thought. When ambivalence is high, an attitude tends to be more pliable in the face of persuasion (Fabrigar & Wegener, 2010).

How well do attitudes predict actual behaviour? Research on attitudes has yielded a surprising answer to this question. In the early 1930s, when prejudice against Asians was common in North America, Richard LaPiere journeyed across the United States with a Chinese couple. He was more than a little surprised when they weren't turned away from any of the restaurants they visited in their travels—184 restaurants in all. About six months after his trip, LaPiere surveyed the same restaurants and asked whether they would serve Chinese customers. Roughly half of the restaurants replied to the survey, and over 90 percent of them indicated that they would not seat Chinese patrons. Thus, LaPiere (1934) found that people who voice prejudicial attitudes may not

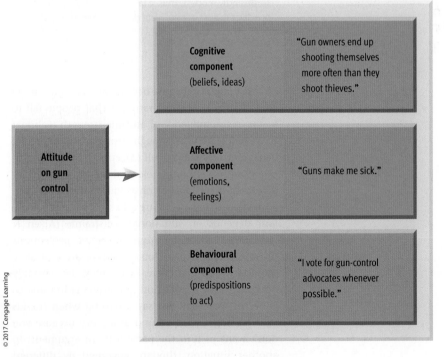

© 2017 Cengage Learning

Figure 13.6
The possible components of attitudes. Attitudes may include cognitive, affective, and behavioural components, as illustrated here for a hypothetical person's attitude about gun control.

behave in discriminatory ways. Since then, theorists have often asked: Why don't attitudes predict behaviour better?

Admittedly, LaPiere's study had a fundamental flaw that you may already have detected. The person who seated LaPiere and his Chinese friends may not have been the same person who responded to the mail survey sent later. The connection between attitudes and behaviour has been the focus of a great deal of research since LaPiere's study.

Studies have repeatedly shown that attitudes are mediocre predictors of people's behaviour (Ajzen & Fishbein, 2005). When Wallace and colleagues (2005) reviewed 797 attitude-behaviour studies, they found that the average correlation between attitudes and behaviour was 0.41. That correlation is high enough to conclude that attitudes are a meaningful predictor of actual behaviour, but they do not predict behaviour nearly as well as most people assume.

reality check

Misconception

People's attitudes are excellent predictors of their behaviour.

Reality

Decades of research have shown that attitudes are undependable predictors of behaviour. For a variety of reasons, the correlation between attitudes and behaviour is surprisingly modest. Thus, a favourable attitude about a specific product or candidate does not necessarily translate into a purchase or vote.

Why aren't attitude-behaviour relations more consistent? One consideration is that people fail to factor in the influence of attitude strength (Fabrigar & Wegener, 2010). Although strong attitudes predict behaviour reasonably well (Ajzen, 2012), many attitudes are not strongly held and are only weak predictors of behaviour. Inconsistent relations between attitudes and behaviour are also seen because behaviour depends on situational constraints (Ajzen & Fishbein, 2000, 2005). Your subjective perceptions of how people expect you to behave are especially important. For instance, you may be strongly opposed to the legalization of marijuana in Canada. However, you may not say anything when friends start passing a joint around at a party because you don't want to turn the party into an argument. In another situation, though, governed by different norms, such as a class discussion, you may speak out forcefully against marijuana legalization.

Implicit Attitudes: Looking Beneath the Surface

In recent years, theorists have begun to make a distinction between explicit and implicit attitudes (Blair, Dasgupta & Glasser, 2015; Carruthers, 2017; Kurdi & Banaji, 2017). *Explicit attitudes* are attitudes that we hold consciously and can readily describe. For the most part, these overt attitudes are what social psychologists have always studied until fairly recently. *Implicit attitudes* are covert attitudes that are expressed in subtle automatic responses over which we have little conscious control. It was only in the mid-1990s that social psychologists started digging beneath the surface to explore the meaning and importance of implicit attitudes. People can have implicit attitudes about virtually anything. But implicit attitudes were discovered in research on prejudice and their role in various types of prejudice continues to be the main focus of current inquiry.

Why are implicit attitudes a central issue in the study of prejudice? Because in modern societies most people have been taught that prejudicial attitudes are inappropriate and something to be ashamed of. Today, the vast majority of people reject racial prejudice, as well as prejudice against women, the elderly, gays, and those who are disabled or mentally ill. At the same time, however, people grow up in a culture where negative stereotypes about these groups are widely disseminated. Although most of us want to be unbiased, research has shown that these negative ideas can seep into our subconscious mind and contaminate our reactions to others. Thus, many people express explicit attitudes that condemn prejudice, but unknowingly harbour implicit attitudes that reflect subtle forms of prejudice (Devine & Sharp, 2009; Dovidio & Gaertner, 2008).

How are implicit attitudes measured? A number of techniques have been developed, but the most widely used is the *Implicit Association Test* (IAT) (Greenwald & Banaji, 1995; Greenwald, McGhee, & Schwartz, 1998). This computer-administered test measures how quickly people associate carefully chosen pairs of concepts. Let's consider how the IAT would be used to assess implicit prejudice against blacks. A series of words and pictures are presented onscreen and subjects are urged to respond to these stimuli as quickly and accurately as possible. In the first series of trials respondents are instructed to press a specific key with their left hand if the stimulus is a black person or a positive word and to press another key with their right hand if the stimulus is a white person or a negative word (see Figure 13.7). In the second series of trials, the instructions are changed and participants are told to press the left-hand key if the stimulus is a black person or a negative word and to press the right-hand key if the stimulus is a white person or positive word. The various types of stimuli are presented in quick succession and the computer records precise reaction times. Research shows that reaction times are quicker when liked faces are paired with positive words and disliked faces with negative words. So, if respondents have negative implicit attitudes about black people, the second series of trials will yield shorter average reaction times. And if this is so, the size of the difference between average reaction times in the two series provides an index of the strength of participants' implicit racism.

Since 1998, millions of people have responded to a Web-based version of the IAT (Nosek, Banaji, & Greenwald, 2002; Nosek, Greenwald, & Banaji, 2007). Although surveys of people's explicit attitudes suggest that prejudice has declined considerably, the IAT results show that over 80 percent of respondents, both young and old, show negative implicit attitudes about the elderly. And about three-quarters of white respondents exhibit implicit prejudice against blacks. The findings also indicate that implicit prejudice against gays, the disabled, and the obese is common.

Do IAT scores based on tiny differences in reaction times predict prejudicial behaviour in the real world? Yes, IAT scores are predictive of subtle but potentially important differences in behaviour (Greenwald et al., 2009; Greenwald, Banaji, & Nosek, 2015). For instance, white participants' degree of implicit racial prejudice predicts how far they choose to sit from a black partner whom they expect to work with on a task (Amodio & Devine, 2006). Higher implicit racism scores in white subjects are also associated with decreased smiling, reduced eye contact, and shorter speaking time in interracial interactions (Devos, 2008). Implicit prejudice also predicts discrimination in hiring, negative attitudes about immigration, and aggression in response to provocation (Fiske & Tablante, 2015). Beyond the realm of prejudice, implicit attitudes about math predict interest and performance in math, and implicit attitudes about political candidates predict voting behaviour (Blair et al., 2015).

Trying to Change Attitudes: Factors in Persuasion

The fact that attitudes aren't always good predictors of a person's behaviour doesn't stop others from trying to change those attitudes. Indeed, every day you're bombarded by efforts to alter your attitudes (Loken, 2006). Everyone from your parents to advertisers is trying to change your attitudes.

Figure 13.7
Measuring implicit attitudes. The IAT assesses implicit prejudice against blacks by tracking how quickly subjects respond to images of black and white people paired with positive or negative words. If participants are prejudiced against black people, they will react more quickly to the pairings in the condition on the right. The IAT has been used to measure implicit attitudes toward a variety of groups.

© 2017 Cengage Learning

"Doesn't it ever let up?" you wonder. When it comes to persuasion, the answer is "no." As Anthony Pratkanis and Elliot Aronson (2000) put it, we live in the "age of propaganda." Social psychologists have been very active in examining factors that affect whether persuasion attempts work or not (Petty & Brinol, 2008). Let's examine some of the factors that determine whether persuasion works.

The process of persuasion includes an examination of factors that affect persuasion (e.g., Chen et al., 2013), with research in the area emphasizing four basic elements: source, receiver, message, and channel (see Figure 13.8). **The *source* is the person who sends a communication, and the receiver is the person to whom the message is sent.** So, if you watch a political news conference on TV, the politician is the source, and you and millions of other viewers are the receivers. **The *message* is the information transmitted by the source, and the *channel* is the medium through which the message is sent.** Although the research on communication channels is interesting, we'll confine our discussion to source, message, and receiver variables, which are most applicable to persuasion.

Source Factors

Occasional exceptions to the general rule are seen, but persuasion tends to be more successful when the source has high *credibility* (Petty & Brinol, 2015). What gives a person credibility? Either expertise or trustworthiness. People try to convey their expertise by mentioning their degrees, their training, and their experience or by showing an impressive grasp of the issue at hand. Expertise is a plus, but *trustworthiness* can be even more important. Many people tend to

Figure 13.8
Overview of the persuasion process. The process of persuasion essentially boils down to *who* (the source) communicates *what* (the message) *by what means* (the channel) *to whom* (the receiver). Thus, there are four sets of variables that influence the process of persuasion: source, message, channel, and receiver factors. The diagram lists some of the more important factors in each category (including some that are not discussed in the text due to space limitations). (Adapted from Lippa, 1994)

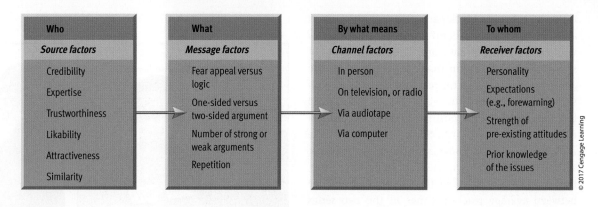

Who	**What**	**By what means**	**To whom**
Source factors	*Message factors*	*Channel factors*	*Receiver factors*
Credibility	Fear appeal versus logic	In person	Personality
Expertise	One-sided versus two-sided argument	On television, or radio	Expectations (e.g., forewarning)
Trustworthiness	Number of strong or weak arguments	Via audiotape	Strength of pre-existing attitudes
Likability	Repetition	Via computer	Prior knowledge of the issues
Attractiveness			
Similarity			

© 2017 Cengage Learning

accept messages from trustworthy sources with little scrutiny (Priester & Petty, 2003). Trustworthiness is undermined when a source appears to have something to gain. *Likability* also increases the effectiveness of a persuasive source (Neal et al., 2012). In addition, people respond better to sources who share similarity with them in ways that are relevant to the issue at hand (Petty & Brinol, 2015).

The importance of source variables can be seen in advertising. Many companies spend a fortune to obtain an ideal spokesperson. Right now one of the most sought-after spokespersons in Canada is Sidney Crosby. Crosby is billed as one of the superstars of the NHL and our Canadian Olympic Men's Hockey team.

Message Factors

If you were going to give a speech to a local community group advocating a reduction in taxes on corporations, you'd probably wrestle with a number of questions about how to structure your message. Should you look at both sides of the issue, or should you present just your side? Should you use all of the arguments at your disposal, or should you concentrate on the stronger arguments? Should you deliver a low-key, logical speech? Or should you try to strike fear into the hearts of your listeners? These questions are concerned with message factors in persuasion.

In general, two-sided arguments seem to be more effective than one-sided presentations (Petty & Wegener, 1998). Just mentioning that an issue has two sides can increase your credibility with an audience. Fear appeals appear to work—if the message is successful in arousing fear. Research reveals that many messages intended to induce fear fail to do so. Fear appeals are most likely to work when your listeners think the dire consequences you describe as exceedingly unpleasant are fairly probable if they don't take your advice and are avoidable if they do (Das, de Wit, & Stroebe, 2003).

Frequent repetition of a message also seems to be an effective strategy (Dechêne et al., 2010), probably because of the mere exposure effect first described by Robert Zajonc (Montoya et al., 2017). The mere exposure effect is the finding that repeated exposures to a stimulus promotes greater liking of the stimulus. In a groundbreaking study (Zajonc, 1968), participants were exposed to unfamiliar Turkish words 0, 1, 2, 5, 10, or 25 times. Subsequently, the subjects were asked to rate the degree to which they thought the words referred to something good or bad. The more subjects had been exposed to a specific word, the more favourably they rated it. Zajonc observed remarkably similar findings when participants rated

Claudio Bresciani/SCANPIX

Sidney Crosby, who plays for the Pittsburgh Penguins, is considered to be an NHL superstar and is highly sought after by advertisers. His very positive image is seen to be a real asset for their products.

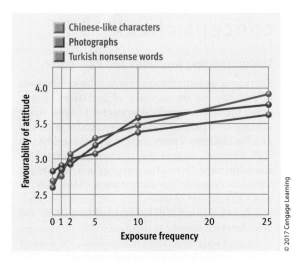

Figure 13.9

The mere exposure effect. In seminal research on the mere exposure effect, Robert Zajonc (1968) manipulated how often participants were exposed to various unfamiliar, neutral stimuli. As the data show here, he found that increased exposures led to increased liking. The mere exposure effect may shed light on why repetition is an effective strategy in persuasion.

the favourability of selected Chinese pictographs (the symbols used in Chinese writing) and when they rated the likability of people shown in yearbook photos (see Figure 13.9). The mere exposure effect has been replicated with many types of stimuli (Albarracin & Vargas, 2010).

reality check

Misconception

Familiarity breeds contempt: The more we are exposed to something, the less we like it.

Reality

People often comment that they are sick of an incessant commercial or overexposed celebrity, but a large body of research shows that repeated exposures to something, even neutral as opposed to favourable exposures, generally lead to increased liking.

Receiver Factors

What about the receiver of the persuasive message? Are some people easier to persuade than others? Undoubtedly, but researchers have not found any personality traits that are reliably associated with susceptibility to persuasion (Petty & Wegener, 1998). Other factors, such as the forewarning a receiver gets about a persuasive effort and the receiver's initial position on an issue, generally seem to be more influential than the receiver's personality.

An old saying suggests that "to be forewarned is to be forearmed." The value of *forewarning* applies to targets of persuasive efforts (Janssen, Fennis, & Pruyn, 2010; Wood & Quinn, 2003). When you shop for a new TV, you *expect* salespeople to work at persuading you, and to some extent this forewarning reduces the impact of their arguments. Considerations that stimulate counterarguing in the receiver tend to increase resistance to persuasion.

Furthermore, studies show that *stronger attitudes are more resistant to change* (Eagly & Chaiken, 1998; Miller & Peterson, 2004). Strong attitudes may be tougher to alter because they tend to be embedded in networks of beliefs and values that might also require change (Erber, Hodges, & Wilson, 1995). Finally, *resistance can promote resistance*. That is, when people successfully resist persuasive efforts to change specific attitudes, they often become more certain about those attitudes (Tormala & Petty, 2002, 2004).

Our review of source, message, and receiver variables has shown that attempting to change attitudes through persuasion involves a complex interplay of factors—and we haven't even looked beneath the surface yet. How do people acquire attitudes in the first place? What dynamic processes within people produce attitude change? We turn to these theoretical issues next.

Theories of Attitude Formation and Change

Many theories have been proposed to explain the mechanisms at work in attitude change (Kruglanski & Stroebe, 2005), whether or not it occurs in response to persuasion. We'll look at four theoretical perspectives: learning theory, dissonance theory, self-perception theory, and the elaboration likelihood model.

Learning Theory

We've seen repeatedly that *learning theory* can help explain a wide range of phenomena, from conditioned fears to the acquisition of sex roles to the development of personality traits. Now we can add attitude formation and change to our list. Attitudes may be learned from parents, peers, the media, cultural traditions, and other social influences (Banaji & Heiphetz, 2010).

The affective, or emotional, component in an attitude can be created through classical conditioning, just as other emotional responses can (Olson & Fazio, 2001, 2002; Walther & Langer, 2008). As we discussed in Chapter 6, *evaluative conditioning* consists of efforts to transfer the emotion attached to a UCS to a new CS (Kruglanski & Stroebe, 2005; Schimmack & Crites, 2005). Advertisers routinely try to take advantage of

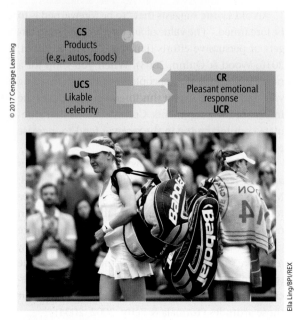

CS
Products
(e.g., autos, foods)

UCS
Likable
celebrity

CR
Pleasant emotional
response
UCR

© 2017 Cengage Learning

Ella Ling/BPI/REX

Figure 13.10

Classical conditioning of attitudes in advertising. Advertisers routinely pair their products with likable celebrities such as Canadian tennis star Eugenie Bouchard in the hope that their products will come to elicit pleasant emotional responses. See the Critical Thinking Application in Chapter 6 (page 224) for a more in-depth discussion of this practice.

classical conditioning by pairing their products with stimuli that elicit pleasant emotional responses, such as extremely attractive models, highly likable spokespersons, and cherished events, such as the Olympics (Grossman & Till, 1998; Till & Priluck, 2000). This conditioning process is diagrammed in Figure 13.10. It can occur without awareness and seems to be exceptionally resistant to extinction (Albarracin & Vargas, 2010).

Operant conditioning may come into play when you openly express an attitude, such as "I believe that husbands should do more housework." Some people may endorse your view, while others may jump down your throat. Agreement from other people generally functions as a reinforcer, strengthening your tendency to express a specific attitude (Bohner & Schwarz, 2001). Disagreement often functions as a form of punishment, which may gradually weaken your commitment to your viewpoint.

Another person's attitudes may rub off on you through *observational learning* (Banaji & Heiphetz, 2010; Oskamp, 1991). If you hear your uncle say, "Conservatives are nothing but puppets of big business," and your mother heartily agrees, your exposure to your uncle's attitude and your mother's reinforcement of your uncle may influence your attitude toward the Conservative Party. Studies show that parents and their children tend to have similar political attitudes (Sears, 1975) and that college students living in residence halls tend to show

Photo by Karen Zabulon © 1982; Courtesy of the New School for Social Research, by permission of Trudy Festinger

Leon Festinger

"Cognitive dissonance is a motivating state of affairs. Just as hunger impels a person to eat, so does dissonance impact a person to change his opinions or his behaviour."

some convergence in attitudes (Cullum & Harton, 2007). Observational learning presumably accounts for much of this similarity. The opinions of teachers, coaches, co-workers, talk-show hosts, rock stars, and so forth, are also likely to sway people's attitudes through observational learning.

Dissonance Theory

Leon Festinger's *dissonance theory* assumes that inconsistency among attitudes propels people in the direction of attitude change. Dissonance theory had a profound impact on the directions taken by researchers in social psychology (Aronson, 2010), and in other disciplines (e.g., Hinojosu et al., 2017; Nicholson et al., 2017). It burst into prominence in 1959 when Festinger and J. Merrill Carlsmith published a famous study of counterattitudinal behaviour. Let's look at their findings and at how dissonance theory explains them.

Festinger and Carlsmith (1959) had male college students come to a laboratory, where they worked on excruciatingly dull tasks such as turning pegs repeatedly. When a subject's hour was over, the experimenter confided that some participants' motivation was being manipulated by telling them that the task was interesting and enjoyable before they started it. Then, after a moment's hesitation, the experimenter asked if the subject could help him out of a jam. His usual helper was delayed and he needed someone to testify to the next "subject" (really an accomplice) that the experimental task was interesting. He offered to pay the subject if he would tell the person in the adjoining waiting room that the task was enjoyable and involving.

This entire scenario was enacted to coax participants into doing something that was inconsistent with their true feelings—that is, to engage in *counterattitudinal behaviour*. Some participants received a token payment of $1 for their effort, while others received a more substantial payment of $20 (an amount equivalent to about $164 today, in light of inflation). Later, a second experimenter inquired about the subjects' true feelings regarding the dull experimental task. Figure 13.11 summarizes the design of the Festinger and Carlsmith study.

Who do you think rated the task more favourably—the subjects who were paid $1 or those who were paid $20? Both common sense and learning theory would predict that the subjects who received the greater reward ($20) should come to like the task more. In reality, however, the subjects who were paid $1 exhibited more favourable attitude change—just as Festinger and Carlsmith had predicted. Why? Dissonance theory provides an explanation.

According to Festinger (1957), *cognitive dissonance* **exists when related cognitions are inconsistent—that is, when they contradict each other.** Cognitive dissonance is thought to create an unpleasant state of tension that motivates people to reduce their dissonance—usually by altering their cognitions. In the study by Festinger and Carlsmith, the subjects' contradictory cognitions were "The task is boring" and "I told someone the task was enjoyable." The subjects who were paid $20 for lying had an obvious reason for behaving inconsistently with their true attitudes, so these subjects experienced little dissonance. In contrast, the subjects paid $1 had no readily apparent justification for their lie and experienced high dissonance. To reduce it, they tended to persuade themselves that the task was

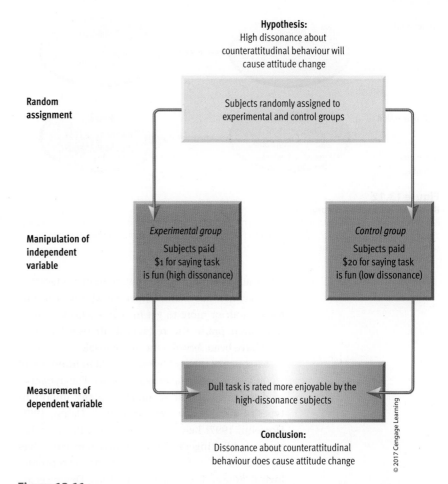

Figure 13.11

Design of the Festinger and Carlsmith (1959) study. The sequence of events in this landmark study of counterattitudinal behaviour and attitude change is outlined here. The diagram omits a third condition (no dissonance), in which subjects were not induced to lie. The results in the nondissonance condition were similar to those found in the low-dissonance condition.

more enjoyable than they had originally thought. Thus, dissonance theory sheds light on why people sometimes come to believe their own lies.

Cognitive dissonance is also at work when people turn attitudinal somersaults to justify efforts that haven't panned out, a syndrome called *effort justification*. Aronson and Mills (1959) studied effort justification by putting college women through a "severe initiation" before they could qualify to participate in what promised to be an interesting discussion of sexuality. In the initiation, the women had to read obscene passages out loud to a male experimenter. After all that, the highly touted discussion of sexuality turned out to be a boring, taped lecture on reproduction in lower animals. Subjects in the severe initiation condition experienced highly dissonant cognitions ("I went through a lot to get here" and "This discussion is terrible"). How did they reduce their dissonance? Apparently, by changing their attitude about the discussion, since they rated it more favourably than subjects in two control conditions.

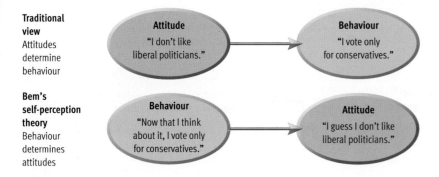

Traditional view
Attitudes determine behaviour

Bem's self-perception theory
Behaviour determines attitudes

Figure 13.12

Bem's self-perception theory. The traditional view is that attitudes determine behaviour. However, Bem stood conventional logic on its head when he proposed that behaviour often determines (or causes people to draw inferences about) their attitudes. Subsequent research on attribution has shown that sometimes people *do* infer their attitudes from their behaviour.

Effort justification may be at work in many facets of everyday life. For example, people who wait in line for an hour or more to get into an exclusive restaurant often praise the restaurant afterward even if they have been served a mediocre meal.

Dissonance theory has been tested in hundreds of studies with largely favourable results. The dynamics of dissonance appear to underlie many important types of attitude changes (Draycott & Dabbs, 1998; Hosseini, 1997; Keller & Block, 1999). Research has supported Festinger's claim that dissonance involves genuine psychological discomfort and even physiological arousal (Croyle & Cooper, 1983; Devine et al., 1999). Although it was developed 60 years ago, it still is of considerable theoretical and empirical interest today (Gawronski, 2012).

Dissonance theory is not without its critics. Daryl Bem (1967), for example, suggested that the effects typically attributed to dissonance were instead the result of what he referred to as *self-perception processes*. According to Bem's *self-perception theory*, people often *infer* their attitudes from their behaviour. Thus, Bem argued that in the study by Festinger and Carlsmith (1959), the subjects paid $1 probably thought to themselves, "A dollar isn't enough money to get me to lie, so I must have found the

task enjoyable." Bem originally believed that most findings explained by dissonance were really due to self-perception. However, studies eventually showed that self-perception is at work primarily when subjects do not have well-defined attitudes regarding the issue at hand (Olson & Roese, 1995). Although self-perception theory did not replace dissonance theory, Bem's work demonstrated that attitudes are sometimes inferred from one's own behaviour (Olson & Stone, 2005) (see Figure 13.12).

Elaboration Likelihood Model

The *elaboration likelihood model* of attitude change, originally proposed by Richard Petty and John Cacioppo (1986), asserts that there are two basic "routes" to persuasion (Petty, 2016; Petty, Barden, & Wheeler, 2009; Petty, Brinol, & Priester, 2009; Wagner & Petty, 2011). The *central route* is taken when people carefully ponder the content and logic of persuasive messages. The *peripheral route* is taken when persuasion depends on nonmessage factors, such as the attractiveness and credibility of the source, or on conditioned emotional responses (see Figure 13.13). For example, a politician who campaigns by delivering carefully researched speeches that thoughtfully analyze complex issues is following the central route to persuasion. In contrast, a politician who depends on marching bands, flag-waving, celebrity endorsements, and emotional slogans is following the peripheral route.

Both routes can lead to persuasion. However, according to the elaboration likelihood model, the durability of attitude change depends on the extent to which people elaborate on (think about) the contents of persuasive communications. Studies suggest that the central route to persuasion leads to more enduring attitude change than the peripheral route (Petty & Wegener, 1998). Research also suggests that attitudes changed through central processes predict behaviour better than attitudes changed through peripheral processes (Kruglanski & Stroebe, 2005; Petty & Briñol, 2010).

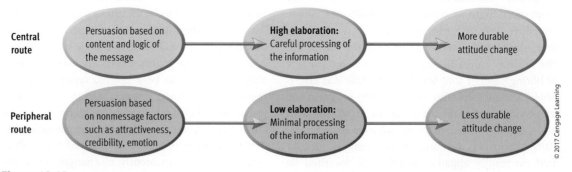

Figure 13.13

The elaboration likelihood model. According to the elaboration likelihood model (Petty & Cacioppo, 1986), the central route to persuasion leads to more elaboration of message content and more enduring attitude change than the peripheral route to persuasion.

Conformity and Obedience: Yielding to Others

Since the 1950s, social psychologists have shown an enduring fascination with the subject of social influence. Work in this area has yielded some of the most famous, influential, and controversial studies in the history of psychology. Let's look at some of this research.

Conformity

If you keep a well-manicured lawn and are a devoted fan of the band Rage Against the Machine, are you exhibiting conformity? According to social psychologists, it depends on whether your behaviour is the result of group pressure. *Conformity* **occurs when people yield to real or imagined social pressure.** For example, if you maintain a well-groomed lawn only to avoid complaints from your neighbours, you're yielding to social pressure. If you like Rage Against the Machine because you genuinely enjoy their music, that's *not* conformity. However, if you like Rage because doing so is "cool" and your friends would question your taste if you didn't, then you're conforming. That said, conformity lies in the eye of the beholder, as people have a curious tendency to see others as more conforming than themselves (Pronin, Berger, & Molouki, 2007). For example, when *your friends* buy the new iPhone, you may see their choices as mindless conformity, but when you buy the new iPhone, you may see your choice as a sensible decision based on the features you need. Thus, people tend to believe they are "alone in a crowd of sheep" because everyone else is so conforming.

In the 1950s, Solomon Asch (1951, 1955, 1956) devised a clever procedure that reduced ambiguity about whether subjects were conforming, allowing him to investigate the variables that govern conformity. Let's re-create one of Asch's (1955) classic experiments, which have become the most widely replicated studies in the history of social psychology (Markus, Kitayama, & Heiman, 1996). The subjects are male undergraduates recruited for a study of visual perception. A group of seven subjects is shown a large card with a vertical line on it and the subjects are then asked to indicate which of three lines on a second card matches the original "standard line" in length (see Figure 13.14). All seven subjects are given a turn at the task, and they announce their choice to the group. The subject in the sixth chair doesn't know it, but everyone else in the group is an accomplice of the experimenter, and they're about to make him wonder whether he has taken leave of his senses.

The accomplices give accurate responses on the first two trials. On the third trial, line 2 clearly is the correct response, but the first five "subjects" all say that line 3 matches the standard line. The genuine subject is bewildered and can't believe his ears. Over the course of the next 15 trials, the accomplices all give the same incorrect response on 11 of them. How does the real subject respond? The line judgments are easy and unambiguous. So, if the participant consistently agrees with the accomplices, he isn't making honest mistakes—he's conforming.

Averaging across all 50 participants, Asch (1955) found that the young men conformed on 37 percent of the trials. The subjects varied considerably in their tendency to conform, however. Of the 50 participants, 13 never caved in to the group, while 14 conformed on more than half of the trials. One could argue that the results show that people confronting a unanimous majority generally tend to *resist* the pressure to conform (Hodges & Geyer, 2006). However, given how clear and easy the line judgments were, most social scientists viewed the findings as a dramatic demonstration of humans' propensity to conform (Levine, 1999).

In subsequent studies, Asch (1956) found that *group size* and *group unanimity* are key determinants of conformity. To examine the impact of group size, Asch repeated his procedure with groups that included from 1 to 15 accomplices. Little conformity was seen when a subject was pitted against just one person, but conformity increased rapidly as group

Key Learning Goals

► Understand Asch's work on conformity and Milgram's research on obedience.

► Discuss cultural variations in conformity and obedience, and describe the Stanford Prison Simulation.

Courtesy of Solomon Asch

Solomon Asch

"That we have found the tendency to conformity in our society so strong that reasonably intelligent and well-meaning young people are willing to call white black is a matter of concern."

Figure 13.14

Stimuli used in Asch's conformity studies. In groups of seven, subjects were asked to match a standard line (top) with one of three other lines displayed on another card (bottom). The task was easy—until the six experiment accomplices started responding with obviously incorrect answers, creating a situation in which Asch evaluated the seventh subject's conformity.

Source: Adapted from Asch, S. (1955). Opinion and social pressure. *Scientific American, 193* (5), 31–35.

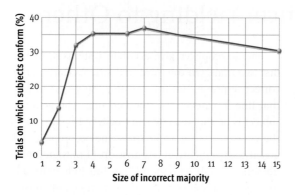

Figure 13.15

Conformity and group size. This graph shows the percentage of trials on which participants conformed as a function of group size in Asch's research. Asch found that conformity became more frequent as group size increased up to about four, and then conformity levelled off. (Data from Asch, 1955)

Source: Adapted from Asch, S. (1955). Opinion and social pressure. *Scientific American*, 193 (5), 31–35.

size went from two to four, and then levelled off (see Figure 13.15). Thus, Asch reasoned that as groups grow larger, conformity increases—up to a point, a conclusion that has been echoed by other researchers (Cialdini & Trost, 1998).

However, group size made little difference if just one accomplice "broke" with the others, wrecking their unanimous agreement. The presence of another dissenter lowered conformity to about one-quarter of its peak, even when the dissenter made *inaccurate* judgments that happened to conflict with the majority view. Apparently, the subjects just needed to hear someone else question the accuracy of the group's perplexing responses. The importance of unanimity in fostering conformity has been replicated in subsequent research (Hogg, 2010).

Why do people conform? Two key processes appear to contribute (Hogg, 2010). *Normative influence* operates when people conform to social norms for fear of negative social consequences. In other words, people often conform or comply because they are afraid of being criticized or rejected. People are also likely to conform when they are uncertain how to behave (Cialdini, 2008; Sherif, 1936). *Informational influence* operates when people look to others for guidance about how to behave in ambiguous situations. Thus, if you're at a nice restaurant and don't know which fork to use, you may watch others to see what they're doing. In situations like this, using others as a source of information about appropriate behaviour is a sensible strategy. Ultimately, informational influence is all about being right, whereas normative influence is all about being liked.

Obedience

Obedience is a form of compliance that occurs when people follow direct commands, usually from someone in a position of authority. To a surprising extent, when an authority figure says, "Jump!" many people simply ask, "How high?" For most people, willingness to obey someone in authority is the rule, not the exception.

Milgram's Studies

Stanley Milgram wanted to study this tendency to obey authority figures. Like many other people after World War II, he was troubled by how readily the citizens of Germany had followed the orders of dictator Adolf Hitler, even when the orders required morally repugnant actions, such as the slaughter of millions of Jews. Milgram, who had worked with Solomon Asch, set out to design a standard laboratory procedure for the study of obedience, much like Asch's procedure for studying conformity. The clever experiment that Milgram devised became one of the most famous and controversial studies in the annals of psychology (Benjamin & Simpson, 2009; Blass, 2009). It has been hailed as a "monumental contribution" to science and condemned as "dangerous, dehumanizing, and unethical research" (Ross, 1988).

Milgram's (1963) participants were a diverse collection of 40 men from the local community. They were told that they would be participating in a study concerned with the effects of punishment on learning. When they arrived at the lab, they drew slips of paper from a hat to get their assignments. The drawing was rigged so that the subject always became the "teacher" and an experimental accomplice became the "learner."

In the research, participants were induced to use shocks on learners in a learning experiment as feedback when the learners failed at a rigged task. While the learners were in fact confederates and the shocks were nonexistent, participants believed that they had delivered potentially harmful shocks to another person because they were told to do so by an authority figure, the experimenter. In the experiment, participants were induced to *increase* the shocks to what they believed would be dangerous levels as the learner continued to make mistakes in his task performance. Most participants went ahead and increased the shocks. Decades after the research was conducted, it still generates spirited debate (Berkowitz, 1999; Lutsky, 1995). Because of its importance, it's the Featured Study for this chapter.

FEATURED STUDY

Behavioural study of obedience.

Description
In this study Stanley Milgram examined the degree to which participants will obey directives from the experimenter to engage in behaviour that will harm another participant.

Investigators
Milgram, S. (1963). *Journal of Abnormal and Social Psychology, 67*(4), 371–378.

After his initial demonstration, Milgram (1974) tried about 20 variations on his experimental procedure, looking for factors that influence participants' obedience. In one variation, Milgram moved the study away from Yale's campus to see if the prestige of the university was contributing to the subjects' obedience. When the study was run in a seedy office building by the "Research Associates of Bridgeport," only a small decrease in obedience was observed (48 percent of the subjects gave all of the shocks). Even when the learner was in the same room with the subjects, 40 percent of the participants administered the full series of shocks. As a whole, Milgram was surprised at how high subjects' obedience remained as he changed various aspects of his experiment.

That said, there were some situational manipulations that reduced obedience appreciably. For example, if the authority figure was called away and the orders were given by an ordinary person (supposedly another participant), full obedience dropped to 20 percent. In another version of the study, Milgram borrowed a trick from Asch's conformity experiments and set up teams of three teachers that included two more accomplices. When they drew lots, the real subject was always selected to run the shock apparatus in consultation with the other two "teachers." When both accomplices accepted the experimenter's orders to continue shocking the learner, the pressure increased obedience a bit. However, if an accomplice defied the experimenter and supported the subject's objections, obedience declined dramatically (only 10 percent of the subjects gave all the shocks), just as conformity had dropped rapidly when dissent surfaced in Asch's conformity studies. These findings are interesting in that they provide further support for Milgram's thesis that situational factors exert great influence over behaviour. If the situational pressures favouring obedience are decreased, obedience declines, as one would expect.

The Ensuing Controversy

Milgram's study evoked a controversy that continues to the present. According to Murray Goddard of the University of New Brunswick (Goddard, 2009), some of the hesitation to accept Milgram's findings may have resulted from the fact that they were counter to human intuition. Other critics have argued that Milgram's results can't be generalized to apply to the real world (Baumrind, 1964; Orne & Holland, 1968). They maintain that the participants went along only because they knew it was an experiment and "everything must be okay." And some have argued that subjects who agree to participate in a scientific study *expect to obey* orders from an experimenter. Milgram (1964, 1968) replied by arguing that if subjects had thought, "everything must be okay," they wouldn't have experienced the enormous distress that they clearly showed.

As for the idea that research participants expect to follow an experimenter's commands, Milgram pointed out that so do real-world soldiers and bureaucrats who are accused of villainous acts performed in obedience to authority. "I reject Baumrind's argument that the observed obedience doesn't count because it occurred where it is appropriate," said Milgram (1964). "That is precisely why it *does* count." Overall, the evidence supports the generalizability of Milgram's results, which were consistently replicated for many years, in diverse settings, with a variety of subjects and procedural variations (Blass, 1999; Miller, 1986).

Critics also questioned the ethics of Milgram's procedure (Baumrind, 1964; Kelman, 1967). They noted that without prior consent, subjects were exposed to extensive deception that could undermine their trust in people and to severe stress that could leave emotional scars. Moreover, most participants also had to confront the disturbing fact that they caved in to the experimenter's commands to inflict harm on an innocent victim.

Milgram's defenders argued that the brief distress experienced by his subjects was a small price to pay for the insights that emerged from his obedience studies. Looking back, however, many psychologists seem to share the critics' concerns about the ethical implications of Milgram's work (Miller, 2004). His procedure is questionable by contemporary standards of research ethics, and no replications of his obedience study have been conducted in the United States from the mid-1970s (Blass, 1991) until recently (Elms, 2009), when Jerry Burger (2009) crafted a very cautious, *partial* replication that incorporated a variety of additional safeguards to protect the welfare of the participants.

INTERFOTO/Alamy Stock Photo

Stanley Milgram

"The essence of obedience is that a person comes to view himself as the instrument for carrying out another person's wishes, and he therefore no longer regards himself as responsible for his actions."

Burger (2009) wanted to see whether Milgram's findings would hold up 45 years later. After all, the world has changed in countless ways since Milgram's original research in the early 1960s. To accommodate modern ethical standards, Burger had to change some features of the Milgram procedure. Among other things, he screened participants with great care, excluding those who seemed likely to experience excessive stress, emphasized repeatedly that participants could withdraw from the study without penalty at any time, and provided instant debriefing after each participant completed the procedure. Most importantly, he enacted Milgram's scenario only up through the level of 150 volts. Burger chose 150 volts as the maximum because in Milgram's series of studies the vast majority of subjects who went past this point went on to administer all the levels of shock. So, the amount of obedience seen through this level would permit a good estimate of the percentage of participants who would exhibit full obedience. Interestingly, in spite of the extra precautions, Burger's study yielded obedience rates that were only slightly lower than those observed by Milgram 45 years earlier. Given Burger's repeated assurances that participants could withdraw from the study (which one would expect to reduce obedience), it seems likely that people today are just as prone to obedience as they were in the 1960s.

Cultural Variations in Conformity and Obedience

Are conformity and obedience unique to American or Western culture? By no means. Conformity and obedience experiments have been repeated in many countries including Canada, where they have yielded results roughly similar to those seen in the United States. Thus, the phenomena of conformity and obedience seem to transcend culture.

The replications of Milgram's obedience study have largely been limited to industrialized nations similar to the United States. Comparisons of the results of these studies must be made with caution because the composition of the samples and the experimental procedures have varied somewhat. But many of the studies have reported even higher obedience rates than those seen in Milgram's American samples. For example, obedience rates of over 80 percent have been reported for samples from Italy, Germany, Austria, Spain, and the Netherlands (P. B. Smith & Bond, 1994). So, the surprisingly high level of obedience observed by Milgram does not appear to be peculiar to the United States.

The Asch experiment has been repeated in a more diverse range of societies than the Milgram experiment. Like many other cultural differences in social behaviour, variations in conformity appear subject to cultural influences (Murray, Trudeau, & Schaller, 2011), including being related to the degree of *individualism versus collectivism* seen in a society. Various theorists have argued that collectivistic cultures, which emphasize respect for group norms, cooperation, and harmony, probably encourage more conformity than individualistic cultures (Schwartz, 1990) and have a more positive view of conformity (Kim & Markus, 1999). As Matsumoto (1994, p. 162) puts it, "To conform in American culture is to be weak or deficient somehow. But this is not true in other cultures. Many cultures foster more collective, group-oriented values, and concepts of conformity, obedience, and compliance enjoy much higher status." Consistent with this analysis, studies *have* found higher levels of conformity in collectivistic cultures than in individualistic cultures (Bond & Smith, 1996; Smith, 2001).

The Power of the Situation: The Stanford Prison Simulation

The research of Asch and Milgram provided dramatic demonstrations of the potent influence that situational factors can have on social behaviour. The power of the situation was underscored once again, about a decade after Milgram's obedience research, in a landmark study conducted by Philip Zimbardo, who was a high school classmate of Milgram's. Zimbardo and his colleagues designed the Stanford Prison Simulation to investigate why prisons tend to become abusive, degrading, violent environments (Haney, Banks, & Zimbardo, 1973; Zimbardo, Haney, & Banks, 1973).

The participants were college students recruited for a study of prison life through a newspaper ad. After 70 volunteers were given an extensive battery of tests and interviews, the researchers chose 24 students who appeared to be physically healthy and psychologically stable to be the subjects. A coin flip determined which of them would be "guards" and which would be "prisoners" in a simulated prison set up at Stanford University. The prisoners were "arrested" at their homes, handcuffed, and transported to a mock prison on the Stanford campus. Upon arrival, they were ordered to strip, sprayed with a delousing agent, given prison uniforms (smocks), assigned numbers as their identities, and locked up in iron-barred cells. The subjects assigned to be guards were given khaki uniforms, billy clubs, whistles, and reflective sunglasses. They were told that they could run their prison in whatever way they wanted, except that they were not allowed to use physical punishment.

What happened? In short order, confrontations occurred between the guards and prisoners, and the guards quickly devised a variety of sometimes cruel strategies to maintain total control over their prisoners. Meals, blankets, and bathroom privileges were selectively denied to some prisoners to achieve control. The prisoners were taunted, humiliated, and called demeaning names. Pointless, petty rules were strictly enforced. Difficult prisoners were punished with hard labour (doing push-ups and jumping jacks, cleaning toilets with their bare hands). And the guards creatively turned a 60 cm by 60 cm closet into a "hole" for solitary confinement of rebellious prisoners. Although there was some variation among the guards, collectively they became mean, malicious, and abusive in fulfilling their responsibilities. How did the prisoners react? A few of them showed signs of emotional disturbance and had to be released early, but they mostly became listless, apathetic, and demoralized. The study was designed to run for two weeks, but Zimbardo decided to end it prematurely after just six days because he was concerned about the rapidly escalating abuse and degradation of the prisoners. The subjects were debriefed, offered counselling, and sent home.

How did Zimbardo and his colleagues explain the stunning transformations of their subjects? First, they attributed the participants' behaviour to the enormous influence of social roles. *Social roles are widely shared expectations about how people* in certain positions are supposed to behave. We have role expectations for salespeople, waiters, ministers, medical patients, students, bus drivers, tourists, flight attendants, and, of course, prison guards and prisoners. The participants had a rough idea of what it meant to act like a guard or a prisoner, and they were gradually consumed by their roles (Haney & Zimbardo, 1998). Second, the researchers attributed their subjects' behaviour to the compelling power of situational factors. Before the study began, the tests and interviews showed no measurable differences in personality or character between those randomly assigned to be guards or prisoners. The stark differences in their behaviour had to be due to the radically different situations that they found themselves in. As a result, Zimbardo, like Milgram before him, concluded that situational pressures can lead normal, decent people to behave in sinister, repugnant ways.

Another parallel between Milgram's and Zimbardo's research is that both have proven controversial. Some critics argued that the Stanford Prison Simulation was more of an elaborate demonstration than an empirical study that collected precise data (Ribkoff, 2013). Other critics voiced concern that the guards were implicitly encouraged to be abusive, thus tainting the findings (Banuazizi & Movahedi, 1975; Haslam & Reicher, 2003). Still others questioned Zimbardo's explanation for the finding that people passively enact social roles dictated by situational factors (Reicher & Haslam, 2006; Turner, 2006).

Behaviour in Groups: Joining with Others

In most modern societies, groups are a part of our everyday lives. Individuals who join groups have their own individual goals and orientations and for the group to function effectively, individuals are often faced with decisions about how much to contribute to the group itself (Goldstone, Roberts, & Gureckis, 2008; Kameda, Tsukasaki, Hastie, & Berg, 2011). Given their ubiquitous nature, it is no surprise that social psychologists have devoted considerable resources to studying groups as well as individuals, but exactly what is a group? Are all of the divorced fathers living in Saskatoon a group? Are three strangers moving skyward in an elevator a group? What if the elevator gets stuck? How about four students from your psychology class who study together regularly? A jury deciding a trial? The Vancouver Canucks? The Canadian Parliament? Some of these collections of people are groups and others aren't. Let's examine the concept of a group to find out which of these collections qualify.

In social psychologists' eyes, a *group* consists of two or more individuals who interact and are interdependent. Historically, most groups have interacted on a face-to-face basis, but advances in telecommunications are rapidly changing that situation. In the era of the Internet, people can interact, become interdependent, and develop a group identity without ever meeting in person. Indeed, Hackman and Katz (2010) assert that the nature of groups is evolving because of advances in technology. They note that groups traditionally tended to be intact and stable with clear boundaries, whereas membership in modern groups is often continuously changing. Traditional groups usually had a designated leader, whereas modern groups often are self-managing, with shared leadership. Similarly, traditional groups tended to be created in a top-down fashion, whereas modern groups often coalesce on their own to explore shared interests. It will be interesting to see whether these shifts have an impact on how groups function.

Key Learning Goals

▶ Describe the bystander effect and social loafing.
▶ Explain group polarization and groupthink.

Behaviour Alone and in Groups: The Case of the Bystander Effect

Imagine that while waiting for the subway at the Yonge–Bloor station in downtown Toronto, you lose your balance and find yourself lying on the tracks with a train speeding toward you. Would you be better off if there were lots of people on the subway platform? It certainly makes sense since, after all, there's "safety in numbers." Logically, as group size increases, the probability of having a "good Samaritan" on the scene increases. Or does it? We've seen before that human behaviour isn't necessarily logical. When it comes to helping behaviour, many studies have uncovered an apparent paradox called the *bystander effect*: people are less likely to provide needed help when they are in groups than when they are alone.

Evidence that your probability of getting help declines as group size increases was first described by John Darley and Bibb Latané (1968), who were conducting research on the determinants of helping behaviour. Their research was motivated by an infamous incident in New York City in 1963 in which a young woman, Kitty Genovese, was murdered. It was reported in the newspapers that many people witnessed the murder but did nothing to help her, not even bothering to call the police while the assault was occurring (Kassin, 2017). Darley and Latané wanted to understand the inaction of the bystanders.

In the Darley and Latané (1968) study, students in individual cubicles connected by an intercom participated in discussion groups of three sizes. Early in the discussion, a student who was an experimental accomplice hesitantly mentioned that he was prone to seizures. Later in the discussion, the same accomplice faked a severe seizure and cried out for help. Although a majority of participants sought assistance for the student, the tendency to seek help *declined* with increasing group size.

Similar trends have been seen in many other experiments, in which subjects had opportunities to respond to apparent emergencies, including fires, asthma attacks, faintings, crashes, and flat tires, as well as less pressing needs to answer a door or to pick up objects dropped by a stranger (Fischer et al., 2011). Pooling the results of early research on the bystander effect, Latané and Nida (1981) estimated that participants who are alone provide help 75 percent of the time, whereas participants in the presence of others provide help only 53 percent of the time.

What accounts for the bystander effect? A number of factors may be at work, but the most important appears to be the *diffusion of responsibility* that occurs in a group situation. If you're by yourself when you encounter someone in need of help, the responsibility to provide help rests squarely on your shoulders. However, if other people are present, the responsibility is divided among you, and you may all say to yourselves, "Someone else will help." A reduced sense of responsibility may contribute to other aspects of behaviour in groups, as we'll see in the next section.

Group Productivity and Social Loafing

Have you ever driven through a road construction project—at a snail's pace, of course—and become irritated because so many workers seem to be just standing around? Maybe the irony of the posted sign "Your tax dollars at work" made you imagine that they were all dawdling. And then again, perhaps not. Individuals' productivity often *does* decline in larger groups (Karau & Williams, 1993). This fact is unfortunate, as many important tasks can be accomplished only in groups. Group productivity is crucial to committees, sports teams, firefighting crews, sororities, study groups, symphonies, and work teams of all kinds, from the morning crew in a little diner to the board of directors of a major company.

Two factors appear to contribute to reduced individual productivity in larger groups. One factor is *reduced efficiency* resulting from the *loss of coordination* among workers' efforts. As you put more people on a yearbook staff, for instance, you'll probably create more and more duplication of effort and increase how often group members end up working at cross-purposes.

The second factor contributing to low productivity in groups involves *effort* rather than efficiency. *Social loafing* is a reduction in effort by individuals when they work in groups as compared to when they work by themselves. To investigate social loafing, Latané and his colleagues (Latané, Williams, & Harkins, 1979) measured the sound output produced by subjects who were asked to cheer or clap as loud as they could. So that they couldn't see or hear other group members, the subjects were told that the study concerned the importance of sensory feedback and were asked to don blindfolds and put on headphones through which loud noise was played. This manoeuvre permitted a simple deception: Subjects were *led to believe* that they were either working alone or in a group of two or six, when in fact they were working alone and *individual* output was actually being measured.

When participants *thought* that they were working in larger groups, their individual output declined.

Since lack of coordination could not affect individual output, the subjects' decreased sound production had to be due to reduced effort. Latané and his colleagues also had the same subjects clap and shout in genuine groups of two and six and found an additional decrease in production that was attributed to loss of coordination. Figure 13.16 shows how social loafing and loss of coordination combined to reduce productivity as group size increased.

The social-loafing effect has been replicated in numerous studies in which subjects have worked on a variety of tasks, including cheering, pumping air, swimming in a relay race, solving mazes, evaluating editorials, and brainstorming for new ideas (Karau & Williams, 1995; Levine & Moreland, 1998). Social loafing and the bystander effect appear to share a common cause: diffusion of responsibility in groups (Comer, 1995; Latané, 1981). As group size increases, the responsibility for getting a job done is divided among more people, and many group members ease up because their individual contribution is less recognizable. Thus, social loafing occurs in situations where individuals can "hide in the crowd" (Karau & Williams, 1993).

Social loafing, however, is *not* inevitable. For example, social loafing is less likely when individuals' personal contributions to productivity are readily identifiable (Hoigaard & Ingvaldsen, 2006), and when group norms encourage productivity and personal involvement (Hoigaard, Säfvenbom, & Tonnessen, 2006). And social loafing is reduced when people work in smaller and more cohesive groups (Liden et al., 2004). Cultural factors may also influence the likelihood of social loafing. Studies with subjects from Japan, China, and Taiwan suggest that social loafing may be less prevalent in collectivistic cultures, which place a high priority on meeting group goals and contributing to one's ingroups (Karau & Williams, 1995; Smith, 2001).

Decision Making in Groups

Productivity is not the only issue that commonly concerns groups. When people join together in groups, they often have to make decisions about what the group will do and how it will use its resources. There is good evidence that decision making in groups may sometimes display or accentuate important biases when compared to individual decision making. These biases may be reflected in a variety of decision-making contexts, such as the common chore of making predictions regarding completion of one of the group's tasks. For example, research by Wilfrid Laurier University's Roger Buehler and his colleagues has shown that the tendency of individuals to make

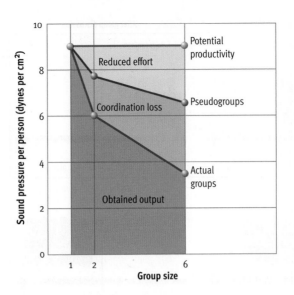

Figure 13.16
The effect of loss of coordination and social loafing on group productivity.
The amount of sound produced per person declined noticeably when people worked in actual groups of two or six (orange line). This decrease in productivity reflects both loss of coordination and social loafing. Sound per person also declined when subjects merely thought they were working in groups of two or six (purple line). This smaller decrease in productivity is due to social loafing.

Source: Adapted from Latané, B., Williams, K., and Harkins, S. (1979). Many hands make light the work: The causes and consequences of social loafing. *Journal of Personality and Social Psychology,* 37, 822–832. Copyright © 1979 by the American Psychological Association.

optimistic predictions regarding how long it will take to complete a task is accentuated as a result of group discussion (Buehler, Messervey, & Griffin, 2005).

Evaluating decision making is often more complicated than evaluating productivity. In many cases, the "right" decision may not be readily apparent. Who can say whether your study group ordered the right pizza or whether Parliament passed the right bills? Nonetheless, social psychologists have discovered some interesting tendencies in group decision making. We'll take a brief look at *group polarization* and *groupthink.*

Group Polarization

Who leans toward more cautious decisions: individuals or groups? Common sense suggests that groups will work out compromises that cancel out members' extreme views. Hence, the collective wisdom of the group should yield relatively conservative choices. Is common sense correct? To investigate this question, Stoner (1961) asked individual subjects to give their recommendations on tough decisions and then asked the same subjects to engage in group discussion to arrive at joint recommendations. When Stoner compared individuals' average recommendation against their group decision generated through discussion, he found that groups arrived at *riskier* decisions than individuals did. Stoner's finding was replicated in other studies (e.g., Pruitt, 1971), and the phenomenon acquired the name *risky shift.*

However, investigators eventually determined that groups can shift either way, toward risk or caution, depending on which way the group is leaning to begin with (Friedkin, 1999; Myers & Lamm, 1976). A shift toward a more extreme position, an effect called *polarization*, is often the result of group discussion (Tindale, Kameda, & Hinsz, 2003; van

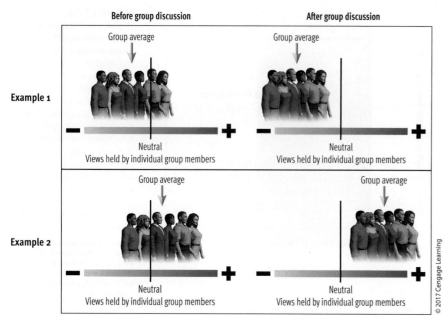

Before group discussion | After group discussion
Group average | Group average

Example 1

Neutral
Views held by individual group members

Neutral
Views held by individual group members

Group average | Group average

Example 2

Neutral
Views held by individual group members

Neutral
Views held by individual group members

© 2017 Cengage Learning

Figure 13.17
Group polarization. Two examples of group polarization are diagrammed here. In the first example (top), a group starts out mildly opposed to an idea, but after discussion, sentiment against the idea is stronger. In the second example (bottom), a group starts out with a favourable disposition toward an idea, and this disposition is strengthened by group discussion.

Swol, 2009). Thus, *group polarization* occurs when group discussion strengthens a group's dominant point of view and produces a shift toward a more extreme decision in that direction (see Figure 13.17). Group polarization does *not* involve widening the gap between factions in a group, as its name might suggest. In fact, group polarization can contribute to consensus in a group, as we'll see in our upcoming discussion of groupthink. Group polarization can occur in all sorts of groups. For example, recent studies have looked at how group polarization plays a role in the decision making of corporate boards (Zhu, 2013, 2014). It has been observed in online networks and may help partly explain the spread of extremism in groups (Brady et al., 2017; Cloninger & Leibo, 2017).

Why does group polarization occur? One reason is that group discussion often exposes group members to persuasive arguments that they had not thought about previously (Stasser, 1991). Another reason is that when people discover that their views are shared by others, they tend to express even stronger views because they want to be liked by their ingroups (Hogg, Turner, & Davidson, 1990).

Groupthink

In contrast to group polarization, which is a normal process in group dynamics, groupthink is more like a "disease" that can infect decision making in groups.

Groupthink occurs when members of a cohesive group emphasize concurrence at the expense of critical thinking in arriving at a decision. As you might imagine, groupthink doesn't produce very effective decision making. Indeed, groupthink can lead to major blunders that may look incomprehensible after the fact. Irving Janis (1972) first described groupthink in his effort to explain how former U.S. president John F. Kennedy and his advisors could have miscalculated so badly in deciding to invade Cuba at the Bay of Pigs in 1961. The attempted invasion failed miserably and, in retrospect, seemed remarkably ill-conceived.

Applying his many years of research and theory on group dynamics to the Bay of Pigs fiasco, Janis developed a model of groupthink that is summarized in Figure 13.18. When groups get caught up in groupthink, members suspend their critical judgment and the group starts censoring dissent as the pressure to conform increases. Soon, everyone begins to think alike. Moreover, some members serve as "mind guards" and try to shield the group from information that contradicts the group's view.

If the group's view is challenged from outside, victims of groupthink tend to think in simplistic "us versus them" terms. Members begin to overestimate the ingroup's unanimity, and they begin to view the outgroup as the enemy. Groupthink also promotes incomplete gathering of information. Like individuals, groups often display a confirmation bias, as they tend to seek and focus on information that supports their initial views (Schulz-Hardt et al., 2000).

Recent research has uncovered another factor that may contribute to groupthink—individual members often fail to share information that is unique to them (Postmes, Spears, & Cihangir, 2001). Sound decision making depends on group members combining their information effectively (Winquist & Larson, 1998). However, when groups discuss issues, they have an interesting tendency to focus mainly on the information that the members already share as opposed to encouraging offers of information unique to individual members (Stasser, Vaughn, & Stewart, 2000). Additional research is needed to determine why groups are mediocre at pooling members' information.

What causes groupthink? According to Janis, a key precondition is high group cohesiveness. *Group cohesiveness* refers to the strength of the liking relationships linking group members to each other and to the group itself. Members of cohesive groups are close-knit, are committed, have "team spirit," and are very loyal to the group (Swann et al., 2012). Cohesiveness itself isn't bad. It can facilitate group productivity (Mullen & Copper, 1994) and

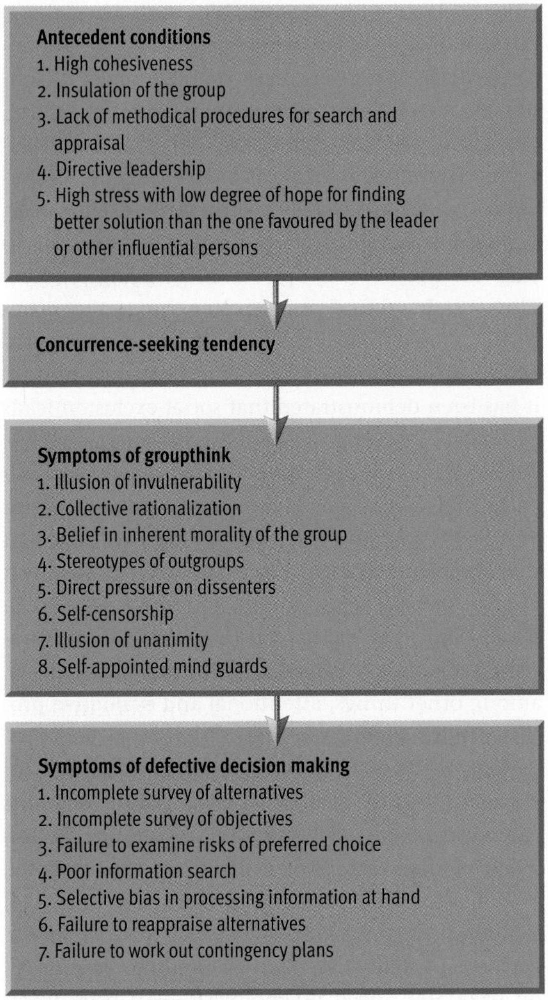

Antecedent conditions
1. High cohesiveness
2. Insulation of the group
3. Lack of methodical procedures for search and appraisal
4. Directive leadership
5. High stress with low degree of hope for finding better solution than the one favoured by the leader or other influential persons

Concurrence-seeking tendency

Symptoms of groupthink
1. Illusion of invulnerability
2. Collective rationalization
3. Belief in inherent morality of the group
4. Stereotypes of outgroups
5. Direct pressure on dissenters
6. Self-censorship
7. Illusion of unanimity
8. Self-appointed mind guards

Symptoms of defective decision making
1. Incomplete survey of alternatives
2. Incomplete survey of objectives
3. Failure to examine risks of preferred choice
4. Poor information search
5. Selective bias in processing information at hand
6. Failure to reappraise alternatives
7. Failure to work out contingency plans

Figure 13.18
Overview of Janis's model of groupthink. The antecedent conditions, symptoms, and resultant effects of groupthink postulated by Janis (1972) are outlined here. His model of groupthink has been very influential, but practical difficulties have limited research on the theory.

Source: From DECISION MAKING: A PSYCHOLOGICAL ANALYSIS OF CONFLICT, CHOICE, AND COMMITMENT by Irving L. Janis and Leon Mann. Copyright © 1977 by the Free Press. Reprinted with the permission of The Free Press, a division of Simon & Schuster, Inc. All rights reserved.

when the group's power structure is dominated by a strong, directive leader, and when the group is under stress to make a major decision (see Figure 13.18). Under these conditions, group discussions can easily lead to group polarization, strengthening the group's dominant view.

A relatively small number of experiments have been conducted to test Janis's theory, because the antecedent conditions thought to foster groupthink—such as high decision stress, strong group cohesiveness, and dominating leadership—are difficult to create effectively in laboratory settings (Aldag & Fuller, 1993). The evidence on groupthink consists mostly of retrospective case studies of major decision-making fiascos (Eaton, 2001). So, Janis's model of groupthink should probably be characterized as an innovative, sophisticated, intuitively appealing theory that needs to be subjected to much more empirical study (Esser, 1998).

concept **check** 13.4

Scrutinizing Common Sense

Check your understanding of the implications of research in social psychology by indicating whether the commonsense assertions listed below have been supported by empirical findings. Do the trends in research summarized in this chapter indicate that the following statements are true or false? The answers are in Appendix A near the back of the book.

_____ **1.** Generally, in forming their impressions of others, people don't judge a book by its cover.

_____ **2.** When it comes to attraction, birds of a feather flock together.

_____ **3.** In the realm of love, opposites attract.

_____ **4.** If you're the target of persuasion, to be forewarned is to be forearmed.

_____ **5.** When you need help, there's safety in numbers.

help groups achieve great things. But Janis maintains that the danger of groupthink is greater when groups are highly cohesive. Groupthink is also more likely when a group works in relative isolation,

Social Neuroscience

A Neuroscience Perspective on Social Psychology

As we suggested in Chapter 1, one of the most popular orientations in psychology today is that of neuroscience. This approach emphasizes research

examining the relationship of the brain, its structures and processes, to human social behaviour (Cacioppo & Berntson, 2005; Easton & Emery, 2005; Fiske & Taylor, 2017; Harmon-Jones & Winkielman, 2007; Kiat et al., 2017; Norman, Hawkley, Cole, Bernston, & Cacioppo, 2012). *Social neuroscience* is

Key Learning Goals

▶ Describe how the social neuroscience approach differs from the traditional approach in social psychology.

▶ Discuss examples of phenomena social neuroscientists have examined.

an approach to research and theory in social psychology that "integrates models of neuroscience and social psychology to study the mechanisms of social behaviour" (Amodio, 2008, p. 1). Its emergence as a distinct orientation is dated from a conference held in 2001 at the University of California, Los Angeles (Coleman, 2006), although its beginnings had roots much earlier (Cacioppo, 1994; Lieberman, 2010). Since that time it has rapidly gained in importance in the social psychological literature (Decety & Keenan, 2006; Lieberman, 2007, 2010; Willingham & Dunn, 2003). While psychologists in many areas of psychology have adopted a neuroscience approach in examining human behaviour for several years, social neuroscience differs from other areas of psychology in that it examines humans in their *social context*, not as isolated "units of analysis" (Cacioppo et al., 2007). Social neuroscientists employ the tools developed in neuroscience, primarily positron emission tomography (PET), functional magnetic resonance imaging (fMRI), event-related potentials (ERPs), the study of lesions, and transcranial magnetic stimulation (TMS) in examining the "mental mechanisms that create, frame, regulate, and respond to our experience of the social world" (Lieberman, 2010, p. 143). We discussed these neuroscience methods in detail in Chapter 3.

Topics in Social Neuroscience

The methods and theory of social neuroscience have been applied to a broad array of topics in social psychology, including understanding and controlling oneself, understanding others, and social psychological phenomena that occur at the interface of self and others (Jenkins & Mitchell, 2011; Lieberman, 2007). Some of the specific topics examined include theory of mind, cross-cultural differences in empathy, lying, aggression, attributions, social cognition, self and self-judgment, the social psychology of health and mental health, cognitive dissonance, and attitude change (Cacioppo et al., 2008; Chao et al., 2014; Eisenberger & Cole, 2012; Harmon-Jones et al., 2011; Libby, 2008; Lieberman et al., 2001; Mar, 2011; Mitchell, Macrae, & Banaji, 2004; Packer et al., 2011; Panasiti et al., 2014; Pfister et al., 2014; Rilling, & Sanfey, 2011; Schmitz, Kawahara-Baccus, & Johnson, 2004). Currently, Let's consider two examples of recent work to illustrate the social neuroscience approach.

In Chapter 10 (see page 363), we discussed the psychology of affiliation and the personal and psychological consequences of being socially rejected—that is, the effects of social ostracism (e.g., Knowles,

Gren, & Weidel, 2014; Pitts, Wilson, & Hugenberg, 2014; Schoel, Eck, & Greifeneder, 2014). Social neuroscientists, using a variety of neuroscience techniques, such as event-related brain potentials (ERPs), the facial electromyogram (EMG), the electroencephalogram (EEG), analysis of levels of cortisol and alphamylases (sAA), MRI, and fMRI examination of brain structures and processes, have begun to examine the neural implications of being rejected. This work has found, among other things, that ostracism is related to the inhibition of central stress pathways controlling the release of cortisol. In addition, it has been demonstrated that social exclusion leads to distinct changes in brain activity recorded by EEG, when previously ostracized experimental participants view disgusted as compared to neutral faces, and that social and physical pain rely on many of the same neurobiological substrates (Bass et al., 2014; Eisenberger, 2012; Kawamoto, Nittono, & Ura, 2013, 2014). Thus, the social pain that results from ostracism is real, it is personally significant, and it affects, among other things, attentional and evaluative processes in the brain.

One of the most researched topics in social neuroscience is the neuroscience of ethnic relations (Amodio, 2008, 2013; Amodio, Bartholow, & Ito, 2014; Fourie et al., 2014), including topics related to prejudice and stereotyping (Ratner et al., 2014; Ronquillo et al., 2007). As we will discuss in the Personal Application, "Understanding Prejudice," on page 509, social psychologists have been interested for some time in examining both explicit and implicit social judgments and evaluations. Explicit judgments and evaluations involve conscious and controlled thought, while implicit evaluation occurs automatically, without intention, and typically without the individual making the judgment even being aware of the process (Greenwald & Banaji, 1995). Among other things, explicit evaluations typically take more time to unfold than do implicit judgments.

William Cunningham,, a faculty member at the University of Toronto, and his colleagues, have examined a variety of social psychological topics from a social neuroscience perspective (e.g., Cunningham, 2016; Man, Ames, Todorov, Cunningham, & Kirkin, 2014). In one study they used the characteristics of implicit and explicit evaluations to explore the role of the amygdala in people's responses to white and black faces (Cunningham et al., 2004). Previous neuroscience research had often implicated the amygdala in fear responses (LaBar et al., 1998), and other social psychological research had shown that whites frequently show more negative evaluations of blacks than of whites. During the fMRI, white participants were presented with various stimuli, including neutral-expression black and white faces. The stimuli were presented briefly (30 milliseconds) or for a longer duration (525 milliseconds). Cunningham used the shorter presentation time to assess automatic responses to the stimuli, and the longer presentation times to assess controlled, conscious evaluations of the stimuli.

Cunningham expected that his white participants would show greater activation in the amygdala when presented with black faces, most notably under brief presentation times, when automatic responses were being assessed, and this is just what the result of his experiments revealed. In addition, Cunningham found that this heightened activation of the amygdala was especially true for participants that he had previously identified as being more racially biased. This and other similar research suggests that "implicit associations to a social group may result in automatic emotional response when encountering members of that group" (Cunningham et al., 2004, p. 811). Findings of greater amygdala response to black faces using fMRI methods is common in the literature (e.g., Lieberman et al., 2005; Ronquillo et al., 2007).

Other parallel research in the area has employed ERP techniques (e.g., Ito & Urland, 2003). At this point, it is unclear whether these effects reflect negative evaluations of black faces or are the result of greater "perceptual" expertise on the part of white participants for the faces of ingroup (i.e., white) members (Lieberman, 2010). Considerable research effort currently is being devoted to these and other questions in the neuropsychology of stereotypes and prejudice (e.g., Krendl et al., 2006).

While the social neuroscience approach has clear limitations (Amodio, 2008; Willingham & Dunn, 2003), we believe it will increasingly contribute to our understanding of human behaviour in a social context and that the range of the phenomena to which it is applied will continue to expand (Cunningham, Arbuckle, Jahn, Mower, & Abduljalil, 2010; Cunningham, Johnsen, & Waggoner, 2011). As neuroscientists continue to explore ways of integrating models of neuroscience with models of social psychology, we expect the literature to offer more, and more refined, explanations that contribute to our understanding of ourselves and others.

Putting It in Perspective: Themes 1, 5, and 7

Our discussion of social psychology has provided a final embellishment of three of our seven unifying themes. One of these is the value of psychology's commitment to empiricism—that is, its reliance on systematic observation through research to arrive at conclusions. The second theme that stands out is the importance of cultural factors in shaping behaviour, and the third is the extent to which people's experience of the world is highly subjective. Let's consider the virtues of empiricism first.

It's easy to question the need to do scientific research on social behaviour, because studies in social psychology often seem to verify common sense. While most people wouldn't presume to devise their own theory of colour vision, question the significance of REM sleep, or quibble about the principal causes of schizophrenia, everyone has beliefs about the nature of love, how to persuade others, and people's willingness to help in times of need. So, when studies demonstrate that credibility enhances persuasion, or that good looks facilitate attraction, it's tempting to conclude that social psychologists go to great lengths to document the obvious, and some critics say, "Why bother?"

You saw why in this chapter. Research in social psychology has repeatedly shown that the

predictions of logic and common sense are often wrong. Consider just a few examples. Even psychiatric experts failed to predict the remarkable obedience to authority uncovered in Milgram's research. The bystander effect in helping behaviour violates mathematical logic. Dissonance research has shown that after a severe initiation, the bigger the letdown, the more favourable people's feelings are. These principles defy common sense. Thus, research on social behaviour provides dramatic illustrations of why psychologists put their faith in empiricism.

Our coverage of social psychology also demonstrated once again that, cross-culturally, behaviour is characterized by both variance and invariance. Thus, we saw substantial cultural differences in patterns of attribution, the role of love in mating relationships, attitudes about conformity, the tendency to obey authority figures, and the likelihood of social loafing. Although basic social phenomena such as stereotyping, attraction, obedience, and conformity probably occur all over the world, cross-cultural studies of social behaviour show that research findings based on North American samples may not generalize precisely to other cultures.

Research in social psychology is also uniquely well suited for making the point that people's view of the world is highly personal and subjective. In this chapter, we saw how physical appearance can colour perception of a person's ability or personality, how social schemas can lead people to see what they expect to see in their interactions with others, how pressure to conform can make people begin to doubt their senses, and how groupthink can lead group members down a perilous path of shared illusions.

The subjectivity of social perception will surface once again in our Application features for this chapter. The Personal Application focuses on prejudice, a practical problem that social psychologists have shown great interest in, whereas the Critical Thinking Application examines aspects of social influence.

Understanding Prejudice

Prejudice is a major social problem. It can harm victims' self-concepts, suppress their potential, create enormous stress in their lives, cause depression and other mental health problems, and promote tension and strife between groups (Cox et al., 2012; Inzlicht & Kang, 2010). Far worse, racially based stereotypes can cause dangerous—and potentially horrific—split-second decisions in which people think they see a weapon that is not really there (Payne, 2006). In light of these problems, it is understandable that research on prejudice has grown dramatically in recent decades (Biernat & Danaher, 2013). The first step toward reducing prejudice is to understand its roots. Hence, in this Application, we'll strive to achieve a better understanding of why prejudice is so common.

In our modern society, prejudice often manifests in brief, everyday, apparently routine social interactions that subtly convey a particular group's perceived inferiority. These inconspicuous insults, which are sometimes unintentional, have been characterized as *microaggressions* (Sue, 2010). Examples include a white person providing friendlier service to a white customer than to a minority customer, or not sitting next to a minority person on a train or bus, or a man assuming a woman cannot do math, and so forth. Unfortunately, research indicates that these microaggressions can have substantial, cumulative effects on individuals' self-esteem and subjective well-being (Nadal et al., 2014; Ong et al., 2013).

Prejudice and discrimination are closely related, but not interchangeable concepts. *Prejudice* is a negative attitude held toward members of a group. Like other attitudes, prejudice can include three components

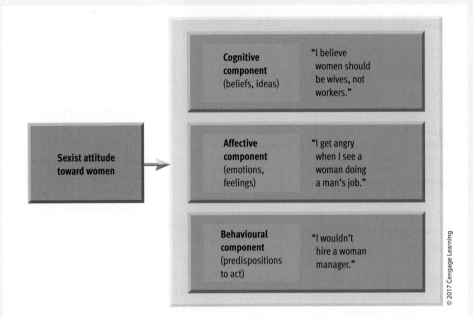

Figure 13.19

The three potential components of prejudice as an attitude. Attitudes can consist of up to three components. The tri-component model of attitudes, applied to prejudice against women, would view sexism as negative beliefs about women (cognitive component) that lead to a feeling of dislike (affective component), which in turn leads to a readiness to discriminate against women (behavioural component).

(see Figure 13.19): beliefs ("Indigenous males are mostly alcoholics"), emotions ("I despise"), and behavioural dispositions ("I wouldn't hire a woman"). Racial and ethnic prejudice receives the lion's share of publicity, but prejudice is not limited to ethnic groups. Women, gays, the aged, the disabled, the homeless, and the mentally ill are also targets of widespread prejudice (Fiske & Tablante, 2015). Thus, many people hold prejudicial attitudes toward one group or another, and many have been victims of prejudice.

Prejudice may lead to *discrimination*, which involves behaving differently, usually unfairly, toward the members of a group. Prejudice and discrimination tend to go hand in hand, but attitudes and behaviour do not necessarily correspond (see Figure 13.20). In our discussion, we'll concentrate primarily on the attitude of prejudice.

Stereotyping

There is no doubt that stereotypes play a large role in prejudice. That's not to say that stereotypes are inevitably negative. Although it's an overgeneralization, it's hardly insulting to assert that Canadians are polite, that Americans are ambitious, or that the Japanese are industrious. Unfortunately, many people do subscribe to derogatory stereotypes of various ethnic groups.

Although studies suggest that negative racial stereotypes have diminished over the last 50 years, they're not a thing of the past (Zarate, 2009). According to a variety of investigators, such as York University's Kerry Kawakami and her colleagues, modern racism has merely become more subtle (Dovidio, Gaertner, & Kawakami, 2010). Many people carefully avoid overt expressions of prejudicial attitudes but covertly continue to harbour negative views of racial minorities.

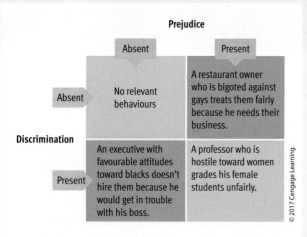

Figure 13.20
Relationship between prejudice and discrimination. As these examples show, prejudice can exist without discrimination and discrimination without prejudice. In the green cells, there is a disparity between attitude and behaviour.

Research indicates that stereotypes are so pervasive and insidious they are often activated automatically (Bodenhausen, Todd, & Richardson, 2009; Devine & Sharp, 2009; Pietraszewski, 2016), even in people who truly renounce prejudice. Thus, a man who rejects prejudice against homosexuals may still feel uncomfortable sitting next to a gay male on a bus, even though he regards his reaction as inappropriate.

Stereotypes persist because the *subjectivity* of person perception makes it likely that people will see what they expect to see when they actually come into contact with groups that they view with prejudice (Fiske & Russell, 2010). For example, Duncan (1976) had white subjects watch and evaluate interaction on a TV monitor that was supposedly live (actually it was a videotape) and varied the race of a person who gets into an argument and gives another person a slight shove. The shove was coded as "violent behaviour" by 73 percent of the subjects when the actor was black but by only 13 percent of the subjects when the actor was white. As we've noted before, people's perceptions are highly subjective. Because of stereotypes, even "violence" may lie in the eye of the beholder.

Biases in Attribution

Attribution processes can also help perpetuate stereotypes and prejudice. Research taking its cue from Weiner's (1980) model of attribution has shown that people often make *biased attributions for success and failure*. For example, men and women don't get equal credit for their successes (Swim & Sanna, 1996). Observers often discount a woman's success by attributing it to good luck, sheer effort, or the ease of the task (except on traditional feminine tasks). In comparison, a man's success is more likely to be attributed to his outstanding ability (see Figure 13.21). For example, one recent study found that when a man and woman collaborate on a stereotypically "male" task, both male and female observers downplay the woman's contribution (Heilman & Haynes, 2005). These biased patterns of attribution help sustain the stereotype that men are more competent than women.

Recall that the *fundamental attribution error* is a bias toward explaining events by pointing to the personal characteristics of the actors as causes (internal attributions). Research suggests that people are particularly likely to make this error when evaluating targets of prejudice (Hewstone, 1990). Thus, when people take note of ethnic neighbourhoods dominated by crime and poverty, the personal qualities of the residents are blamed for these problems, while other explanations emphasizing situational factors (job discrimination, poor police service, and so on) are downplayed or ignored. The old saying "They should be able to pull themselves up by their bootstraps" is a blanket dismissal of how situational factors may make it especially difficult for minorities to achieve upward mobility.

Forming and Preserving Prejudicial Attitudes

If prejudice is an attitude, where does it come from? Many prejudices appear to be handed down as a legacy from parents (Killen, Richardson, & Kelly, 2010). Research by McGill University's Frances Aboud shows that prejudicial attitudes can be found in children as young as ages four or five (Aboud & Amato, 2001). This transmission of prejudice across generations presumably depends to some extent on *observational learning*. For example, if a young boy hears his father ridicule homosexuals, the boy's exposure to his father's attitude is likely to affect his own attitude about gays. If the young boy then goes to school and makes disparaging remarks about gays that are reinforced by approval from peers, his prejudice will be strengthened through *operant conditioning*. Although parents clearly are important, as children grow older, their peer groups may become more influential than parents and other authority figures (Killen, Hitti, & Mulvey, 2015). Like parents, peers can foster either prejudice or egalitarian attitudes, depending on the views they endorse. Of course, prejudicial attitudes are not acquired only through direct experience. Stereotypic portrayals of various groups in the media can also foster prejudicial attitudes (Mutz & Goldman, 2010).

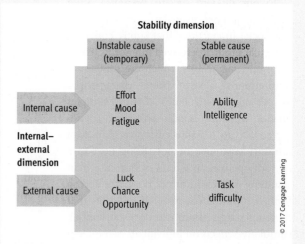

Figure 13.21
Bias in the attributions used to explain success and failure by men and women. Attributions about the two sexes often differ. For example, men's successes tend to be attributed to their ability and intelligence (blue cell), whereas women's successes tend to be attributed to hard work, good luck, or low task difficulty (green cells). These attributional biases help to perpetuate the belief that men are more competent than women.

Implicit Prejudice

Another characteristic of modern prejudice or racism that serves to make it intractable is that it has moved underground, often below the level of awareness of people harbouring the prejudice. We all make social inferences and judgments when we meet others. While some of these judgments are intentional, many of them are not. We make many spontaneous judgments and inferences about others without awareness, intention, or effort (Uleman, Saribay, & Gonzalez, 2007).

In some cases, people may not even be aware that they are carrying around this prejudice—this is often referred to as *implicit prejudice* (Dovidio, Kawakami, & Gaertner, 2002; Son Hing, Li, & Zanna, 2002). Implicit prejudice refers to negative associations to an outgroup that are activated automatically, without control or intention. If the racism is hidden, it may be even more difficult to change.

Competition between Groups

One of the oldest and simplest explanations for prejudice is that competition between groups can fuel animosity. If two groups compete for scarce resources, such as good jobs and affordable housing, one group's gain is the other's loss. *Realistic group conflict theory* asserts that intergroup hostility and prejudice are a natural outgrowth of fierce competition between groups.

A classic study at Robbers' Cave State Park in Oklahoma provided support for this theory many years ago (Sherif et al., 1961). The subjects were 11-year-old white boys attending a three-week summer camp at the park. They did not know that the camp counsellors were actually researchers (their parents knew). The boys were randomly assigned to one of two groups. During the first week, the boys got to know the other members of their own group through typical camp activities. They subsequently developed group identities. They called themselves the "Rattlers" and the "Eagles." In the second week, the Rattlers and Eagles were put into a series of competitive situations, such as a football game, a treasure hunt, and a tug of war, with trophies and other prizes at stake. As predicted by realistic

group conflict theory, hostile feelings quickly erupted between the two groups. Food fights broke out in the mess hall, cabins were ransacked, and group flags were burned.

If competition between groups of innocent children pursuing trivial prizes can foster hostility, you can imagine what is likely to happen when adults from very different backgrounds battle for genuinely important resources. Research by the University of Western Ontario's Vicky Esses and her colleagues has shown that conflict over scarce resources can fuel prejudice and discrimination (Esses, Jackson, & Bennett-AbuAyyash, 2010). Even the mere *perception* of competition can breed prejudice.

If competition can fuel prejudice, perhaps contact highlighting cooperation can help reduce it (Amir, 1969). This reasoning is behind one of the most successful educational approaches to reducing prejudice—Elliot Aronson's *jigsaw classroom* technique (Aronson, 2000, 2010; Aronson et al., 1977; Aronson & Bridgeman, 1979). In this approach to education, students are divided into small groups in the classroom. The lesson for the day is broken down into small components and each student in the group is assigned the responsibility to learn/research his or her component. Then, each student reports back to the group the results of his or her work. In this way, the only way the group can complete the assignment is for the group members to learn from each group member. Each student is necessary and all have equal status in terms of the group's task. "Just as in a jigsaw puzzle, each piece—each student's part—is essential for the completion and full understanding of the final product" (Jigsaw Classroom, 2011). The highly successful technique emphasizes, among other things, interaction, cooperation, and equal status for all. Students who participated in these classrooms did better in school, and the classrooms and schools became less subject to racial tensions. After overseeing years of research, Aronson commented, "Over the years, as we continued to implement the jigsaw technique, the findings remained the same . . . the schools that adopted this approach became more truly integrated" (Aronson, 2010, p. 206).

Dividing the World into Ingroups and Outgroups

As noted in the main body of the chapter, when people join together in groups, they sometimes divide the social world into "us versus them," or *ingroups versus outgroups* (Ambady & Adams, 2011; Lalonde & Gardner, 1989; Taylor & Moghaddam, 1994). This distinction has a profound impact on how we perceive, evaluate, and remember people (Dovidio & Gaertner, 2010). These social dichotomies can promote *ethnocentrism*—a tendency to view one's own group as superior to others and as the standard for judging the worth of foreign ways.

As you might anticipate, people tend to evaluate outgroup members less favourably than ingroup members (Krueger, 1996; Reynolds, Turner, & Haslam, 2000). One reason is that when people derogate an outgroup, they tend to feel superior as a result, and this feeling helps to affirm their self-worth (Fein & Spencer, 1997). The more strongly one identifies with an ingroup, the more one tends to note outgroup membership, and the more one tends to be prejudiced toward competing outgroups (Blascovich et al., 1997; Perreault & Bourhis, 1999). People also tend

Jacquie Vorauer is a social psychologist at the University of Manitoba. She conducts research on "metaperceptions," people's beliefs about how they are viewed by others. This includes examining how evaluative concerns affect people's interactions with outgroup members.

to think simplistically about outgroups. They tend to see diversity among the members of their ingroup but to overestimate the homogeneity of the outgroup (Boldry, Gaertner, & Quinn, 2007; Ostrom & Sedikides, 1992). At a simple, concrete level, the essence of this process is captured by the statement "They all look alike." The illusion of homogeneity in the outgroup makes it easier to sustain stereotypic beliefs about its members (Ryan, Park, & Judd, 1996).

Is it possible to reduce some of the negativity in intergroup relations through empathy? Research by Jacquie Vorauer and her colleagues at the University of Manitoba has examined the effects of outgroup members' empathy on minority group members' perceptions of the power and status of their own group. Empathy has often been suggested as a way of improving relations between groups. In an innovative study, Vorauer and Quesnel (2016) demonstrated that the targets of empathy may in fact come away with lowered evaluations of the power and status of their own group compared to situations in which the outgroup attempts to look at things from the minority group members' perspective (perspective-taking manipulations).

Remedial and Affirmative Action by the Disadvantaged

One issue that has surprisingly received only limited attention to date is analysis of factors that affect the tendency and ability of those disadvantaged by prejudice and discrimination to take affirmative actions that would benefit their group (Weiss & Lalonde, 2001). Under what conditions will the disadvantaged take action to redress their situation? What factors affect the tendency to engage in action?

Wilfrid Laurier University social psychologist Mindi Foster has examined the factors that affect the tendency of disadvantaged individuals to take action against discrimination and prejudice.

An important line of research initiated by Mindi Foster of Wilfrid Laurier University has begun to redress this situation. She has shown, among other things, that social identity bases of discrimination and how the discrimination is perceived have implications for the tendency of the disadvantaged to take affirmative action (Foster, 1999, 2001). For example, she has found that if the discrimination is believed to be global and pervasive that action is more likely, and that women whose social identity is based on social experiences (e.g., feeling unsafe or being paid less than men) are more likely to endorse collective action against discrimination than women whose social identity is based on stereotypes (e.g., women as nurturing and emotional; Foster, 1999).

In a more recent line of research, Foster (2009a, 2009b) has examined the effects of gender discrimination over time (Foster, 2013), and of perceiving that the discrimination you are experiencing is pervasive and not just an isolated, time-limited effect. She has convincingly demonstrated that the effects of such perceived pervasive discrimination on action and coping are dynamic over time and that "perceiving discrimination to be isolated appears to ultimately promote an acceptance of the status quo, but recognizing the pervasiveness of discrimination can have motivational qualities over time" (Foster, 2009a, p. 179). Recently, Foster (2014) has studied the potential of women's collective action as a way to ameliorate the effects of perceived discrimination. She has found, among other things, that women who perceive the discrimination as pervasive, benefit in terms of their well-being from taking actions such as informing the media about the discrimination.

We look forward to seeing additional findings in the future from this line of investigation. We can never know too much about how to fight back against discrimination and prejudice and the types of factors that facilitate or inhibit such action.

Our discussion has shown that many processes conspire to create and maintain personal prejudices against a diverse array of outgroups. Most of the factors at work reflect normal, routine processes in social behaviour. So, it is understandable that most people—whether privileged or underprivileged, minority members or majority members—probably harbour some prejudicial attitudes. Our analysis of the causes of prejudice may have permitted you to identify prejudices of your own or their sources. Perhaps it's wishful thinking on our part, but an enhanced awareness of your personal prejudices may help you become a little more tolerant of the endless diversity seen in human behaviour. If so, that alone would mean that our efforts in writing this book have been amply rewarded.

Whom Can You Trust? Analyzing Credibility and Social Influence Tactics

Key Learning Goal

▶ Identify useful criteria for evaluating credibility, and recognize standard social influence strategies.

You can run, but you can't hide. This statement aptly sums up the situation that exists when it comes to persuasion and social influence. There is no way to successfully evade the constant, pervasive, omnipresent efforts of others to shape your attitudes and behaviour. In this Application, we will discuss two topics that can enhance your resistance to manipulation. First, we will outline some ideas that can be useful in evaluating the credibility of a persuasive source. Second, we will describe some widely used social influence strategies that it pays to know about.

Evaluating Credibility

The salesperson at your local health food store swears that a specific herb combination improves memory and helps people stay healthy. A popular singer touts a psychic hotline, where the operators can "really help" with the important questions in life. Speakers at a "historical society" meeting claim that the Holocaust never happened. These are just a few real-life examples of how people are always attempting to persuade the public to believe something. In these examples, the "something" people are expected to believe runs counter to the conventional or scientific view, but who is to say who is right? After all, people are entitled to their own opinions, aren't they?

Yes, people *are* entitled to their own opinions, but that does not mean that all opinions are equally valid. Some opinions are just plain wrong, and others are highly dubious. Every person is not equally believable. In deciding what to believe, it is important to carefully examine the evidence presented and the logic of the argument that supports the conclusion (see the Critical Thinking Application

in Chapter 10, page 382). In deciding what to believe, you also need to decide *whom* to believe, a task that requires assessing the *credibility* of the source of the information. Let's look at some questions that can provide guidance in this decision-making process.

Does the source have a vested interest in the issue at hand? If the source is likely to benefit in some way from convincing you of something, you need to take a skeptical attitude. In the examples just mentioned, it is easy to see how the salesclerk and the popular singer will benefit if you buy the products they are selling, but what about the so-called historical society? How would members benefit by convincing large numbers of people that the Holocaust never happened? Like the salesclerk and the singer, they are also selling something—in this case, a particular view of history that they hope will influence future events in certain ways. Someone does *not* have to have a financial gain at stake to have a vested interest in an issue. Of course, the fact that these sources have a vested interest does not necessarily mean that the information they are providing is false or that their arguments are invalid. But a source's credibility needs to be evaluated with extra caution when the person or group has something to gain.

What are the source's credentials? Does the person have any special training, an advanced degree, or any other basis for claiming special knowledge about the topic? The usual training for a salesclerk or a singer does not include how to assess research results in medical journals or claims of psychic powers. The Holocaust deniers are more difficult to evaluate. Some of them have studied history and written books on the topic, but the books are mostly self-published and few of these "experts" hold positions at reputable universities where scholars are subject to peer evaluation. That's *not* to say that legitimate credentials ensure a source's credibility. A number of popular diets that are widely regarded by nutritional experts as worthless, if not hazardous (Drewnowski, 1995; Dwyer,

1995), were created and marketed by genuine physicians. Of course, these physicians have a *vested interest* in the diets, as they have made millions of dollars from them.

Is the information grossly inconsistent with the conventional view on the issue? Just being different from the mainstream view certainly does not make a conclusion wrong. But claims that vary radically from most other information on a subject should raise a red flag that leads to careful scrutiny. Bear in mind that charlatans and hucksters are often successful because they typically try to persuade people to believe things that they want to believe. Wouldn't it be great if we could effortlessly enhance our memory, foretell the future, eat all we want and still lose weight, and earn hundreds of dollars per hour working at home? And wouldn't it be nice if the Holocaust had never happened? It pays to be wary of wishful thinking.

What was the method of analysis used in reaching the conclusion? The purveyors of miracle cures and psychic advice inevitably rely on anecdotal evidence. But you have already learned about the perils and unreliability of anecdotal evidence (see Chapter 2). One method frequently used by charlatans is to undermine the credibility of conventional information by focusing on trivial inconsistencies. This is one of the many strategies used by the people who argue that the Holocaust never occurred. They question the credibility of thousands of historical documents, photographs, and artifacts, and the testimony of countless people, by highlighting small inconsistencies among historical records relating to trivial matters, such as the number of people transported to a concentration camp in a specific week, or the number of bodies that could be disposed of in a single day (Shermer, 1997). Some inconsistencies are exactly what one should expect based on piecing together multiple accounts from sources working with different portions of incomplete information. But the strategy of focusing on trivial inconsistencies is a standard method for raising doubts about credible information. For example, this strategy was employed brilliantly by the defence lawyers in the O. J. Simpson murder trial.

Recognizing Social Influence Strategies

It pays to understand social influence strategies because advertisers, salespeople, and fundraisers—not to mention our friends and neighbours—frequently rely on them to manipulate our behaviour. Let's look at four basic strategies: the foot-in-the-door technique, misuse of the reciprocity norm, the lowball technique, and feigned scarcity.

Door-to-door salespeople have long recognized the importance of gaining a *little* cooperation from sales targets (getting a "foot in the door") before hitting them with the real sales pitch. The *foot-in-the-door technique* involves getting people to agree to a small request to increase the chances that they will agree to a larger request later. This technique is widely used in all walks of life. For example, groups seeking donations often ask people to simply sign a petition first.

In an early study of the foot-in-the-door technique (Freedman & Fraser, 1966), the large request involved asking homemakers whether a team of six men doing consumer research could come into their home to classify *all* of their household products. Only 22 percent of the control subjects agreed to this outlandish request. However, when the same request was made three days after a small request (to answer a few questions about soap preferences), 53 percent of the participants agreed to the large request. Why does the foot-in-the-door technique work? According to Burger (1999), quite a variety of processes contribute to its effectiveness, including people's tendency to try to behave consistently (with their initial response) and

their reluctance to renege on their sense of commitment to the person who made the initial request.

Most of us have been socialized to believe in the *reciprocity norm*—the rule that we should pay back in kind what we receive from others. Robert Cialdini (2008) has written extensively about how the reciprocity norm is used in social influence efforts. For example, groups seeking donations routinely send address labels, key rings, and other small gifts with their pleas. Salespeople using the reciprocity principle distribute free samples to prospective customers. When they return a few days later, most of the customers feel obligated to buy some of their products. The reciprocity rule is meant to promote fair exchanges in social interactions. However, when people manipulate the reciprocity norm, they usually give something of minimal value in the hopes of getting far more in return (Howard, 1995). Many Internet scams involve manipulations of reciprocity (Muscanell, Guadago, & Murphy, 2014).

The lowball technique is even more deceptive. The name for this technique derives from a common practice in automobile sales, in which a customer is offered a terrific bargain on a car. The bargain price gets the customer to commit to buying the car. Soon after this commitment is made, however, the dealer starts revealing some hidden costs. Typically, the customer learns that options assumed to be included

in the original price are actually going to cost extra. Once they have committed to buying a car, most customers are unlikely to cancel the deal. Thus, the *lowball technique* involves getting someone to commit to an attractive proposition before its hidden costs are revealed.

Car dealers aren't the only ones who use this technique. For instance, a friend might ask whether you want to spend a week with him at his charming backwoods cabin. After you accept this seemingly generous proposition, he may add, "Of course there's some work for us to do. We need to repair the pier, paint the exterior, and. . . ." Lowballing is a surprisingly effective strategy (Cialdini & Griskevicius, 2010).

Many years ago, Jack Brehm (1966) demonstrated that telling people they can't have something only makes them want it more. This phenomenon helps explain why companies often try to create the impression that their products are in scarce supply. Scarcity threatens your freedom to choose a product, thus creating an increased desire for the scarce commodity. Advertisers frequently feign scarcity to drive up the demand for products. Thus, we constantly see ads that scream "limited supply available," "for a limited time only," "while they last," and "time is running out." Like genuine scarcity, feigned scarcity *can* enhance the desirability of a commodity (Cialdini & Griskevicius, 2010). See Table 13.2.

Table 13.2

Critical Thinking Skills Discussed in This Application

SKILL	DESCRIPTION
Judging the credibility of an information source	The critical thinker understands that credibility and bias are central to determining the quality of information and looks at factors such as vested interests, credentials, and appropriate expertise.
Recognizing social influence strategies	The critical thinker is aware of manipulative tactics such as the foot-in-the-door and lowball techniques, misuse of the reciprocity norm, and feigned scarcity.

PERSON PERCEPTION

- Judgments of others can be distorted by their physical appearance, as we tend to ascribe desirable personality characteristics and competence to those who are good looking.

- Perceptions of faces are especially influential and shape perceptions of competence, which can even affect voters' reactions to candidates.

- *Stereotypes* are widely held beliefs that others will have certain characteristics because of their membership in a particular group.

- Evolutionary theorists attribute the tendency to categorize people into *ingroups* and *outgroups* to our ancestors' need to quickly separate friend from foe.

ATTRIBUTION

Basic processes

- *Attributions* are inferences that people draw about the causes of events and behaviours.

- *Internal attributions* ascribe the causes of behaviour to personal traits, abilities, and feelings, whereas *external attributions* ascribe the causes of behaviour to situational demands and environmental factors.

- According to Weiner, attributions for success and failure can be analyzed along the stable-unstable and internal-external dimensions.

Biases

- The *fundamental attribution error* refers to observers' bias in favour of internal attributions in explaining others' behaviour.

- Actors favour external attributions in explaining their own behaviour, whereas observers favour internal attributions.

- The *self-serving* bias is the tendency to explain one's successes with internal attributions and one's failures with external attributions.

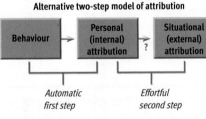

Traditional model of attribution

Behaviour → Personal (internal) attribution *or* Situational (external) attribution

Alternative two-step model of attribution

Behaviour → Personal (internal) attribution → ? → Situational (external) attribution

Automatic first step   *Effortful second step*

Gilbert, D.T. (1989). Thinking lightly about others: Automatic components of the social inference precess. In J.S. Uleman & J.A. Bargh (Eds.), *Unintended thought limits of awareness, intention, and control.* New York: Guilford Press.

Cultural influences

- Cultures vary in their emphasis on *individualism* (putting personal goals ahead of group goals) as opposed to *collectivism* (putting group goals ahead of personal goals), which influence attributional tendencies.

- People from collectivist cultures appear to be less prone to the fundamental attribution error and to the self-serving bias than are people from individualist cultures.

INTERPERSONAL ATTRACTION

Factors in attraction

- A key determinant of romantic attraction for both genders is the physical attractiveness of the other person.

- The *matching hypothesis* asserts that males and females of roughly equal physical attractiveness are likely to select each other as partners.

- Married and dating couples tend to be similar on many traits, probably because similarity causes attraction and attraction can foster similarity.

© Alamy Stock Photo

- Research on *reciprocity* shows that liking breeds liking and that loving breeds loving.

Perspectives on love

- Some theorists distinguish between *passionate love* and *companionate love*.

- Another approach views romantic love as an *attachment process* and argues that love relationships in adulthood mimic attachment patterns in infancy, which fall into three categories: secure, anxious-ambivalent, and avoidant.

- The traits people seek in prospective mates seem to transcend culture, but societies vary in their emphasis on romantic love as a prerequisite for marriage.

Scotty Robson Photography/Getty Images

Influences on attraction

- Although critics are concerned that Internet relationships are superficial and plagued by deception, they appear to be just as intimate and stable as relationships forged offline.

- The power of similarity effects provides the foundation for online matching sites.

- According to evolutionary psychologists, some aspects of good looks influence attraction because they are indicators of reproductive fitness.

- Men tend to be more interested than women in seeking youthfulness and attractiveness in mates, whereas women tend to emphasize potential mates' financial prospects.

ATTITUDES

STRUCTURE OF ATTITUDES

Components

- The *cognitive component* of an attitude is made up of the beliefs that people hold about the object of an attitude.
- The *affective component* of an attitude consists of the emotional feelings stimulated by an object of thought.
- The *behavioural component* of an attitude consists of predispositions to act in certain ways toward an attitudinal object.

Dimensions

- *Attitude strength* refers to how firmly attitudes are held.
- *Attitude accessibility* refers to how often and how quickly an attitude comes to mind.
- *Attitude ambivalence* refers to how conflicted one feels about an attitude.

Relations to behaviour

- Research demonstrates that attitudes are mediocre predictors of people's behaviour.
- *Explicit attitudes* are attitudes that we hold consciously and can readily describe, whereas *implicit attitudes* are covert attitudes that are expressed in subtle automatic responses. Implicit attitudes *can* influence behaviour.

TRYING TO CHANGE ATTITUDES

Source factors

- Persuasion tends to be more successful when a source has credibility, which may depend on expertise or trustworthiness.
- Likeability also tends to increase success in persuasion.

Message factors

- Two-sided arguments tend to be more effective than one-sided presentations.
- Fear appeals tend to work if they are successful in arousing fear.
- Repetition of a message can be effective, perhaps because of the mere exposure effect.

Receiver factors

- Persuasion is more difficult when the receiver is forewarned about the persuasive effort.
- Resistance is greater when strong attitudes are targeted.

THEORIES OF ATTITUDE CHANGE

Learning theory

- The affective component of an attitude can be shaped by classical conditioning.
- Attitudes can be strengthened by reinforcement or acquired through observational learning.

Dissonance theory

- According to Festinger, inconsistency between attitudes motivates attitude change.
- Dissonance theory can explain why people sometimes come to believe their own lies.

Elaboration likelihood model

- The *central route* to persuasion depends on the logic of one's message, whereas the *peripheral route* depends on nonmessage factors, such as emotions.
- Both routes can lead to effective persuasion, but the central route tends to produce more durable attitude change.

YIELDING TO OTHERS

Conformity

- Research by Asch showed that people have a surprisingly strong tendency to conform.
- Asch found that conformity becomes more likely as group size increases up to a size of seven.
- However, the presence of another dissenter in the group greatly reduces the conformity observed.
- Asch's findings have been replicated in many cultures, with even higher levels of conformity observed in collectivist cultures.

Obedience

- In Milgram's landmark study, adult men drawn from the community showed a remarkable tendency to follow orders to shock an innocent stranger, with 65 percent delivering the maximum shock.
- The generalizability of Milgram's findings has stood the test of time, but his work helped stimulate stricter ethical standards for research.
- Milgram's findings have been replicated in many modern nations, and even higher rates of obedience have been seen in many places.

The power of the situation

- The Stanford Prison Simulation demonstrated that social roles and other situational pressures can exert tremendous influence over social behaviour.
- Like Milgram, Zimbardo showed that situational forces can lead normal people to exhibit surprisingly callous, abusive behaviour.

BEHAVIOUR IN GROUPS

- The *bystander effect* refers to the fact that people are less likely to provide help when they are in groups than when they are alone because of the diffusion of responsibility.
- Productivity often declines in groups because of loss of coordination and *social loafing*, which refers to the reduced effort seen when people work in groups.
- *Group polarization* occurs when discussion leads a group to shift toward a more extreme decision in the direction it was already leaning.
- In *groupthink*, a cohesive group suspends critical thinking in a misguided effort to promote agreement.

APPLICATIONS

- Modern prejudice tends to be subtle and often is manifested in inconspicuous microaggressions.
- Negative racial stereotypes have diminished, but they still can fuel automatic, subtle racism.
- Attributional biases, such as the tendency to assume that others' behaviour reflects their disposition, can contribute to prejudice.
- Negative attitudes about groups are often acquired through observational learning and strengthened through operant conditioning.
- Realistic group conflict theory posits that competition between groups for scarce resources fosters prejudice.
- Outgroup derogation and ingroup favouritism both appear to contribute to discrimination.
- To resist manipulative efforts, be aware of social influence tactics, such as the foot-in-the-door technique, misuse of the reciprocity norm, the lowball technique, and feigned scarcity.

Stress, Coping, and Health

Themes in this Chapter

Multifactorial   Subjectivity of
Causation   Experience

Many circumstances can create stress. It comes in all sorts of packages: big and small, pretty and ugly, simple and complex. Sometimes stress is the result of everyday, relatively routine events, such as commuting, preparing for one of your many term tests, or receiving an unexpected bill in the mail. Sometimes the package bringing your stress might be extraordinary. We know that many new immigrants to Canada are particularly vulnerable to stress as they adapt to a new country, culture, and perhaps a new language (Islam, Khanlou, & Tamim, 2014; Miller et al., 2017; Robert & Gilkinson, 2012).

Or, consider how you might have reacted if you had been a passenger on the Canadian-based ecotourist ship *Explorer*. In November 2007, the ship was sailing in the waters off Antarctica when it hit a submerged object, rolled over, and began to sink, stranding the 154 passengers and crew in a very inhospitable and dangerous environment. Fortunately, there were enough lifeboats for all, and help did arrive in time to save everyone. In interviews with the media, passengers talked about their worries and the stress they felt as they floated in the frigid Antarctic waters for six hours until they were rescued. Of course, not all circumstances that cause stress are life threatening, even though at the time is seems as if they might be—just going to the dentist or studying for an exam can be extremely stressful for many people. Sometimes the effects of stress on us are immediate, as when your hands perspire before an important exam. Sometimes the effects are delayed, as in post-traumatic stress disorder. In this disorder the symptoms may not show up for months, or even years. According to clinical psychology researcher Geneviève Belleville and her colleagues (Belleville, Quellet, & Morin, 2017a, 1017b) at the Université Laval, many of the residents of Fort McMurray, Alberta, who experienced the devastating wildfires of 2016 are now showing significant post-traumatic stress symptoms.

Do you think your reactions to stress differ depending on whether it is a relatively routine event or something out of the ordinary? We will answer this and many other questions you might have about stress in this chapter. We'll discuss the nature of stress, how people cope with stress, and the potential effects of stress. Stress is more than just an academic topic—it's something we are all experts in, something with which we all have abundant experience, and something that can be difficult to handle and to treat (DeCicco, 2002). A Statistics Canada survey revealed that almost one-quarter of Canadian adults and children between 15 and 17 years of age say that they spend most of their days living under significant stress (Statistics Canada, 2014, 2017), with much of this stress coming from their work (Crompton, 2011). Daily stress was found to be the highest in the "core working ages" between 35 and 54 (Statistics Canada, 2015).

Colleges and universities are another source of stress. A recent survey revealed that Canadian college and university students are overwhelmed by their responsibilities. Results provided by the Ontario University and College Health Association (2016), for example, found that just over 89 percent of the students felt overwhelmed by all the things they had to do and that 59 percent believed that over the past 12 months their academics had been traumatic or very difficult to handle. But the stress due to academics begins long before university. A recent survey of over 100 000 students in Toronto revealed disturbing levels of worry and stress. In Grades 7 and 8, for example, 60 percent of students are stressed and worry, with 26 percent reporting they are stressed all the time. The percentage climbs even higher when high-school students are polled (Rushowy, 2013). There is no reason to assume that these numbers will be any different elsewhere.

Canadian universities and colleges have come to realize the importance of stress reduction for their students. Many now schedule *stress-buster* events to coincide with exam periods. A quick scan of university websites confirmed that this practice is common, including events such as free massages, dog walking or petting opportunities, guided meditation, professional advice on coping with stress, break dancing, carnival games, free video games, martial

When the ecotourist ship *Explorer* sank in the Antarctic, the 154 passengers and crew had to retreat to the lifeboats and wait six hours until help arrived. While there are often individual differences in what people find stressful, no doubt all of the passengers and crew were stressed as a result of this incident.

Michael Nolan/Robert Harding

arts training, and sports competitions. For example, MacEwan University in Edmonton has developed a PAWSS (Pets Assisting with Student Success) program in which students can book an individual or small group appointment for a close encounter with a certified wellness animal as a stress-buster (MacEwan University, 2017).

Our examination of the relationship between stress and physical illness will lead us into a broader discussion of the psychology of health. The way people in health professions think about physical illness has changed considerably in the past 30 years. The traditional view of physical illness as a purely biological phenomenon has given way to a biopsychosocial model of illness (Friedman & Adler, 2007; Suls, Luger, & Davidson, 2010). The *biopsychosocial model* holds that physical illness is caused by a complex interaction of biological, psychological, and sociocultural factors. This model does not suggest that biological factors are unimportant. It simply asserts that these factors operate in a psychosocial context that is also influential.

The growing recognition that psychological factors influence physical health eventually led to the emergence of a new specialty in psychology, called *health psychology* (Brannon, Feist, & Updegraff, 2018; Friedman, 2014). *Health psychology* is concerned with how psychosocial factors relate to the promotion and maintenance of health and with the

Laurence Gough/Shutterstock.com

Students attending university or college experience stress firsthand during exam periods.

causation, prevention, and treatment of illness. In the second half of this chapter, we'll explore this new domain of psychology. In the Personal Application, we'll focus on strategies for enhancing stress management, and in the Critical Thinking Application we'll discuss strategies for improving health-related decision making.

The Nature of Stress

The word *stress* has been used in different ways by different theorists. We'll define *stress* as any circumstances that threaten or are perceived to threaten one's well-being and that thereby tax one's coping abilities. The threat may be to immediate physical safety, long-range security, self-esteem, reputation, peace of mind, or many other things that one values. Stress is a complex concept, so let's explore it a little further.

Stress as an Everyday Event

The word *stress* tends to spark images of overwhelming, traumatic crises. People may think of tornadoes, hurricanes, floods, and earthquakes. Undeniably, major disasters such as the great flood of June 2013 in Alberta and the devastating wildfires in British Columbia in the summer of 2017 were extremely stressful events (Francey, 2013; Kaufman, 2013; *Managing Traumatic Stress*, 2005). Studies conducted

in the aftermath of natural disasters typically find elevated rates of psychological problems and physical illness in the communities affected by these disasters (Belleville, Quellet, & Morin, 2017a, 2017b; Stevens, Raphael, & Dobson, 2007; van Griensven et al., 2007; Weisler, Barbee, & Townsend, 2007).

However, these unusual events are only a small part of what constitutes stress. Many everyday events, such as waiting in line, having car trouble, shopping for gifts, misplacing your cell phone, and even commuting are stressful. In fact, concerns about the effects of commuting increase with our stress as the time we spend in our cars simply getting to work increases (Statistics Canada, 2013).

You might guess that minor stresses would produce minor effects, but that isn't necessarily true. Richard Lazarus and his colleagues developed a scale to measure everyday hassles. One of Lazarus's colleagues, Anita Delongis of the University of British Columbia (Delongis, 2014; Delongis et al., 2010; Lee-Flynn et al., 2011; Lehman et al., 2011), has

Key Learning Goals

▶ Evaluate the impact of minor stressors and people's appraisals of stress.

▶ Identify four major types of stress.

Anita Delongis is a health psychologist on faculty at the University of British Columbia. Her research focuses on stress, coping, and the role of social support.

Richard Lazarus

"We developed the Hassle Scale because we think scales that measure major events miss the point. The constant, minor irritants may be much more important than the large, landmark changes."

shown that routine hassles may have significant harmful effects on mental and physical health (Delongis, Folkman, & Lazarus, 1988). Stress adds up. Routine stresses at home, at school, and at work might be fairly benign individually, but collectively they could create great strain.

Appraisal: Stress Lies in the Eye of the Beholder

The experience of feeling stressed depends on what events one notices and how one chooses to appraise or interpret them (Folkman, 2011; Gomes, Faria, & Goncalves, 2013). Events that are stressful for one person may be routine for another (Steptoe, 2007). For example, many people find flying in an airplane somewhat stressful, but frequent fliers may not be bothered at all. Some people enjoy the excitement of going out on a date with someone new; others find the uncertainty terrifying.

In discussing appraisals of stress, Lazarus and Folkman (1984) distinguish between primary and secondary appraisal. *Primary appraisal* is an initial evaluation of whether an event is (1) irrelevant to you, (2) relevant but not threatening, or (3) stressful. When you view an event as stressful, you are likely to make a *secondary appraisal,* which is an evaluation of your coping resources and options for dealing with the stress. Thus, your primary appraisal would determine whether you saw an upcoming psychology exam as stressful. Your secondary appraisal would determine how stressful the exam appeared, in light of your assessment of your ability to deal with the event.

Often, people aren't very objective in their appraisals of potentially stressful events. A study of hospitalized patients awaiting surgery showed only a slight correlation between the objective seriousness of a person's upcoming surgery and the amount of fear experienced by the patients (Janis, 1958). Clearly, some people are more prone than others to feeling threatened by life's difficulties. A number of studies have shown that anxious, neurotic people report more stress than others (Cooper & Bright, 2001; Espejo et al., 2011), as do people who are relatively unhappy (Cacioppo et al., 2008). Thus, stress lies in the eye (actually, the mind) of the beholder.

Major Types of Stress

An enormous variety of events can be stressful for one person or another. To achieve a better understanding of stress, theorists have tried to analyze the nature of stressful events and divide them into subtypes. One sensible distinction involves differentiating between *acute stressors and chronic stressors* (Dougall & Baum, 2001; Stowell, 2008). *Acute stressors* are threatening events that have a relatively short duration and a clear endpoint. Examples would include having an encounter with a belligerent drunk, dealing with the challenge of a major exam, or having your home threatened by severe flooding. *Chronic stressors* are threatening events that have a relatively long duration and no readily apparent time limit. Examples would include persistent financial strains produced by huge credit card debts, ongoing pressures from a hostile boss at work, or the demands of caring for a sick family member over a period of years.

None of the proposed schemes for classifying stressful events has turned out to be altogether satisfactory. Classifying stressful events into nonintersecting categories is virtually impossible. Although this problem presents conceptual headaches for researchers, it need not prevent us from describing four major types of stress: frustration, conflict, change, and pressure. As you read about each of them, you'll surely recognize some familiar adversaries.

Frustration

As psychologists use the term, *frustration* is experienced whenever the pursuit of some goal is thwarted. In essence, you experience frustration when you want something and you can't have it. Everyone has to deal with frustration virtually every day. Traffic jams, difficult commutes, and annoying drivers, for instance, are a routine source of frustration that can elicit anger and aggression (Schaefer, 2005; Wener & Evans, 2011). Fortunately, most frustrations are brief and insignificant. You may be quite upset when you go to a repair shop to pick up your ailing laptop and find that it hasn't been fixed as promised. However, a week later, you'll probably have your computer back, and the frustration will be forgotten. Of course, some frustrations—such as failing to get a promotion at work or losing a boyfriend or girlfriend—can be sources of significant stress.

Internal Conflict

Like frustration, conflict is an unavoidable feature of everyday life. The perplexing question "Should I or shouldn't I?" comes up countless times in everyone's life. *Conflict* occurs when two or more incompatible motivations or behavioural impulses compete for expression. As discussed in Chapter 12, Sigmund Freud proposed over a century ago that internal conflicts generate considerable psychological distress.

Conflicts come in three types, which were originally described by Kurt Lewin (1935) and investigated extensively by Neal Miller (1944, 1959). These three basic types of conflict—approach–approach, avoidance–avoidance, and approach–avoidance—are diagrammed in Figure 14.1.

In an *approach–approach conflict*, a choice must be made between two attractive goals. The problem, of course, is that you can choose just one of the two goals. For example: You have a free afternoon, so should you play tennis or racquetball?

Among the three kinds of conflict, the approach–approach type tends to be the least stressful. People don't usually stagger out of restaurants exhausted by the stress of choosing which of several appealing entrées to eat. Approach–approach conflicts typically have a reasonably happy ending, whichever way you decide to go. Nonetheless, approach–approach conflicts over important issues may sometimes be troublesome. If you're torn between two appealing majors at university or two attractive boyfriends, you may find the decision-making process quite stressful, since whichever alternative is not chosen represents a loss of sorts.

In an *avoidance–avoidance conflict*, a choice must be made between two unattractive goals. Forced to choose between two repelling alternatives, you are, as they say, "caught between a rock and a hard place." For example, should you continue to collect unemployment cheques or should you take that degrading job at the car wash? Obviously, avoidance–avoidance conflicts are most unpleasant and highly stressful.

In an *approach–avoidance conflict*, a choice must be made about whether to pursue a single goal that has both attractive and unattractive aspects. For instance, imagine that you're offered a career promotion that will mean a large increase in pay, but you'll have to move to a city where you don't want to live. Approach–avoidance conflicts are common and can be quite stressful. Any time you have to take a risk to pursue some desirable outcome, you're likely to find yourself in an approach–avoidance conflict. Should

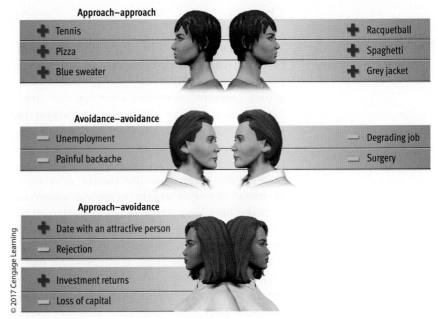

© 2017 Cengage Learning

Figure 14.1

Types of conflict. Psychologists have identified three basic types of conflict. In approach–approach and avoidance–avoidance conflicts, a person is torn between two goals. In an approach–avoidance conflict, there is only one goal under consideration, but it has both positive and negative aspects.

you risk rejection by asking out a person that you are attracted to? Should you risk your savings by investing in a new business that could fail? Approach–avoidance conflicts often produce *vacillation* (Miller, 1944). That is, you go back and forth, beset by indecision. You decide to go ahead, then you decide not to, and then you decide to go ahead again.

concept **check** 14.1

Identifying Types of Conflict

Check your understanding of the three basic types of conflict by identifying the type experienced in each of the following examples. The answers are in Appendix A near the back of the book.

Examples

_____ **1.** John can't decide whether to take a demeaning job in a car wash or to go on social assistance.

_____ **2.** Desirée wants to apply to a highly selective law school, but she hates to risk the possibility of rejection.

_____ **3.** Vanessa has been shopping for a new car and is torn between a nifty little sports car and a classy sedan, both of which she really likes.

Types of Conflict

a. approach–approach

b. avoidance–avoidance

c. approach–avoidance

Change

Thomas Holmes and Richard Rahe led the way in exploring the idea that life changes—including positive events, such as getting married or getting promoted—represent a key type of stress. *Life changes* are any substantial alterations in one's living circumstances that require readjustment. Based on their theory, Holmes and Rahe (1967) developed the Social Readjustment Rating Scale (SRRS) to measure life change as a form of stress. The scale assigns numerical values to 43 major life events. These values are supposed to reflect the magnitude of the readjustment required by each change (see Table 14.1). In using the scale, respondents are asked to indicate how often they experienced any of these 43 events during a certain time period (typically, the past year). The numbers associated with each checked event are then added. This total is an index of the amount of change-related stress the person has recently experienced.

The SRRS and similar scales based on it have been used in over 10 000 studies by researchers all over the world (Dohrenwend, 2006). Overall, these studies have shown that people with higher scores tend to be more vulnerable to many kinds of physical illness and to many types of psychological problems as well (Scully, Tosi, & Banning, 2000; Surtees & Wainwright, 2007). These results have attracted a great deal of attention. The SRRS has even been reprinted in many popular newspapers and magazines. The attendant publicity has led to the widespread conclusion that life change is inherently stressful.

Pressure

At one time or another, most people have remarked that they're "under pressure." What does this mean? Sometimes the pressure comes from a mismatch between what we have to or want to do and the time available. In one survey, over half of the Canadians surveyed said they did not have enough time to both work and spend adequate time with their families. In addition, the survey found that the number of people who were identified as being severely time-stressed had increased between 1992 and 1998 (Statistics Canada, 1999). This trend just seems to continue (Brooker & Hyman, 2010), and the more time pressure or time crunch we feel, the less we are able to get a good night's sleep (Statistics Canada, 2014).

Table 14.1

Social Readjustment Rating Scale

LIFE EVENT	MEAN VALUE
Death of a spouse	100
Divorce	73
Marital separation	65
Jail term	63
Death of a close family member	63
Personal injury or illness	53
Marriage	50
Fired at work	47
Marital reconciliation	45
Retirement	45
Change in health of family member	44
Pregnancy	40
Sex difficulties	39
Gain of a new family member	39
Business readjustment	39
Change in financial state	38
Death of a close friend	37
Change to a different line of work	36
Change in number of arguments with spouse	35
Mortgage or loan for major purchase (home, etc.)	31
Foreclosure of mortgage or loan	30
Change in responsibilities at work	29
Son or daughter leaving home	29
Trouble with in-laws	29
Outstanding personal achievement	28
Spouse begins or stops work	26
Begin or end school	26
Change in living conditions	25
Revision of personal habits	24
Trouble with boss	23
Change in work hours or conditions	20
Change in residence	20
Change in school	20
Change in recreation	19
Change in church activities	19
Change in social activities	18
Mortgage or loan for lesser purchase (car, TV, etc.)	17
Change in sleeping habits	16
Change in number of family get-togethers	15
Change in eating habits	15
Vacation	13
Christmas	12
Minor violations of the law	11

Source: Adapted from Holmes, T. H., & Rahe, R. (1967). The social readjustment rating scale. *Journal of Psychosomatic Research, 11,* 213–218. Copyright © 1967 by Elsevier Science Publishing Co. Reprinted by Permission.

Of course, time pressure is only one type of pressure we face in our daily lives. More generally, *pressure* involves expectations or demands that one behave in a certain way. You are under pressure to *perform* when you're expected to execute tasks and responsibilities quickly, efficiently, and successfully. Pressures to *conform* to others' expectations are also common in our lives. People in the business world are expected to dress in certain ways and college and university students are expected to show enthusiasm for similar activities and cultural and social trends.

Pressure from family relationships, peer relationships, and intimate relationships has been found to be related to a variety of psychological symptoms and problems (Weiten, 1988, 1998). In fact, pressure has turned out to be more strongly related to measures of mental health than the SRRS and other established measures of stress and researchers have investigated the link between these are other facets of stress and heart disease (e.g., Moksnes & Espnes, 2016).

reality check

Misconception

Stress is something that is imposed on individuals from outside forces.

Reality

It is hard to quantify, but a significant portion of people's stress is self-imposed. People routinely impose pressure on themselves by taking on extra work and new challenges. They court frustration by embracing unrealistic goals or engaging in self-defeating behaviour. And people create stress by making unrealistic appraisals of adverse events.

concept check 14.2

Recognizing Sources of Stress

Check your understanding of the major sources of stress by indicating which type or types of stress are at work in each of the examples below. Bear in mind that the four basic types of stress are not mutually exclusive. There's some potential for overlap, so a specific experience might include both change and pressure, for instance. The answers are in Appendix A.

Examples

_____ **1.** Marie is late for an appointment but is stuck in line at the bank.

_____ **2.** Tamika decides that she won't be satisfied unless she gets straight A's this year.

_____ **3.** José has just graduated from business school and has taken an exciting new job.

_____ **4.** Morris has just been fired from his job and needs to find another.

Types of stress

a. frustration
b. conflict
c. change
d. pressure

Responding to Stress

People's response to stress is complex and multidimensional (Segerstrom & O'Connor, 2012). You're driving home in heavy traffic and thinking about overdue papers, tuition increases, and parental pressures. Let's look at some of the reactions that were mentioned. When you groan in reaction to the traffic report, you're experiencing an *emotional response* to stress, in this case annoyance and anger. When your pulse quickens and your stomach knots up, you're exhibiting *physiological responses* to stress. When you shout insults at another driver, your verbal aggression is a *behavioural response* to the stress at hand. Thus, we can analyze a person's reactions to stress at three levels: (1) emotional responses, (2) physiological responses, and (3) behavioural responses. Figure 14.2 diagrams these three levels of response. It provides an overview of the stress process.

Emotional Responses

When people are under stress, they often react emotionally. Studies that have tracked stress and mood on a daily basis have found intimate relationships between the two (Affleck et al., 1994; van Eck, Nicolson, & Berkhof, 1998).

Emotions Commonly Elicited

No simple one-to-one connections have been found between certain types of stressful events and particular emotions. It may seem that our emotions go through phases during and after a stressful event. The emotional fallout can continue for a long time. Residents returning to Fort McMurray after the wildfire evacuation order was lifted had strong immediate emotional reactions that have persisted. They note that a year after the fire, even though they have rebuilt their homes and lives, "There is still pain. You still suffer" (Krugel, 2017).

Researchers *have* begun to uncover some strong links between *specific cognitive reactions to stress* (appraisals) and specific emotions (Smith & Lazarus, 1993). For example, self-blame tends to lead to guilt, helplessness to sadness, and so forth. Although many emotions can be evoked by stressful

Key Learning Goals

▶ Discuss the role of positive emotions in response to stress, and describe the effects of emotional arousal.

▶ Describe Selye's general adaptation syndrome and other physiological responses to stress.

▶ Evaluate the adaptive value of common coping strategies.

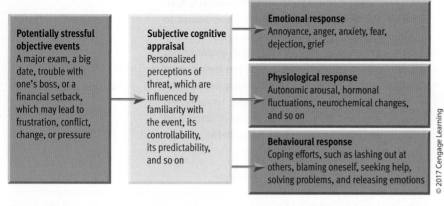

Potentially stressful objective events	Subjective cognitive appraisal	Emotional response

Potentially stressful objective events
A major exam, a big date, trouble with one's boss, or a financial setback, which may lead to frustration, conflict, change, or pressure

Subjective cognitive appraisal
Personalized perceptions of threat, which are influenced by familiarity with the event, its controllability, its predictability, and so on

Emotional response
Annoyance, anger, anxiety, fear, dejection, grief

Physiological response
Autonomic arousal, hormonal fluctuations, neurochemical changes, and so on

Behavioural response
Coping efforts, such as lashing out at others, blaming oneself, seeking help, solving problems, and releasing emotions

© 2017 Cengage Learning

Figure 14.2
Overview of the stress process. A potentially stressful event, such as a major exam, elicits a subjective appraisal of how threatening the event is. If the event is viewed with alarm, the stress may trigger emotional, physiological, and behavioural reactions, as people's response to stress is multidimensional.

events, some are certainly more likely than others. Common emotional responses to stress include (a) annoyance, anger, and rage, (b) apprehension, anxiety, and fear, and (c) dejection, sadness, and grief (Lazarus, 1993; Woolfolk & Richardson, 1978).

Although investigators have tended to focus heavily on the connection between stress and negative emotions, research shows that positive emotions also occur during periods of stress (Finan, Zautra, & Wershba, 2011; Folkman, 2008). Although this finding seems counterintuitive, researchers have found that people experience a diverse array

of pleasant emotions even while enduring dire circumstances. In the face of disasters, people are still able to feel gratitude for their own safety and that of their family, are able to take stock of what's left and count their blessings, and develop renewed appreciation and love for their family and close friends (Frederickson et al., 2003). One particularly interesting finding has been that a positive emotional style is associated with an enhanced immune response (Cohen & Pressman, 2006).

Positive emotions also appear to be protective against heart disease (Davidson, Mostofsky, & Whang, 2010). Indeed, evidence suggests that a positive emotional style may be associated with enhanced physical health in general (Moskowitz & Saslow, 2014). These effects probably contribute to the recently discovered association between the tendency to report positive emotions and longevity (Ong, 2010; Pressman & Cohen, 2012). Yes, people who experience a high level of positive emotions appear to live longer than others! One study exploring this association looked at photos of major league baseball players taken from the *Baseball Register* for 1952. The intensity of the players' smiles was used as a crude index of their tendency to experience positive emotions, which was then related to how long they lived. As you can see in Figure 14.3, greater smile intensity predicted greater longevity (Abel & Kruger, 2010). A more recent study looked at the use of positive words in the autobiographies of 88 well-known, deceased psychologists (Pressman & Cohen, 2012). Once again, the results suggest that a positive mentality was associated with greater longevity. Thus, it appears that the benefits of positive emotions may be more diverse and more far reaching than widely appreciated.

Effects of Emotional Arousal

Emotional responses are a natural and normal part of life. Even unpleasant emotions serve important purposes. Like physical pain, painful emotions can serve as warnings that one needs to take action. However, strong emotional arousal can also interfere with efforts to cope with stress. For example, there is evidence that high emotional arousal can interfere with attention and memory retrieval and can impair judgment and decision making (Janis, 1993; Lupien & Maheu, 2007; Mandler, 1993).

Although emotional arousal may hurt coping efforts, that isn't *necessarily* the case. The inverted-U hypothesis predicts that task performance should improve with increased emotional arousal—up to a

THE CANADIAN PRESS/Jonathan Hayward

In 2016, wildfires swept through the town of Fort McMurray, Alberta, forcing the evacuation of the residents and destroying thousands of homes and businesses. Returning residents had to deal with the trauma of losing all they owned. It will take considerable time to repair both the physical and the psychological damage caused by the fires.

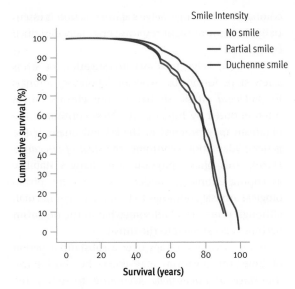

Figure 14.3
Percentage of Major League Baseball players surviving to a given age as a function of their smile intensity in photographs. Each curve represents the probability as predicted by a particular behaviour: no smile, partial smile, or full smile. Greater smile intensity predicted greater longevity (Abel & Kruger, 2010).

Source: Abel, E. L. & Kruger, M. L. (2010). Smile intensity in photographs predicts longevity. *Psychological Science*, February 26, 542–544. Copyright © 2010, Association for Psychological Science.

point, after which further increases in arousal become disruptive and performance deteriorates (Anderson, 1990; Mandler, 1993). This idea is referred to as the *inverted-U hypothesis* because when performance is plotted as a function of arousal, the resulting graphs approximate an upside-down U (see Figure 14.4). In

these graphs, the level of arousal at which performance peaks is characterized as the *optimal level of arousal* for a task.

This optimal level of arousal appears to depend in part on the complexity of the task at hand. The conventional wisdom is that *as a task becomes more complex, the optimal level of arousal (for peak performance) tends to decrease.* This relationship is depicted in Figure 14.4. As you can see, a fairly high level of arousal should be optimal on simple tasks (e.g., driving eight hours to help a friend in a crisis). However, performance should peak at a lower level of arousal on complex tasks (e.g., making a major decision in which you have to weigh many factors). Doubts have been raised about the validity of the inverted-U hypothesis (Hancock & Ganey, 2003). However, it does provide a plausible model of how emotional arousal could have either beneficial or disruptive effects on coping, depending on the nature of the stressful demands.

Physiological Responses

As we just discussed, stress frequently elicits strong emotional responses. Now we'll look at the important physiological changes that often accompany these responses.

The Fight-or-Flight Response

Walter Cannon (1932) was one of the first theorists to describe the fight-or-flight response. The *fight-or-flight response* is a physiological reaction to threat

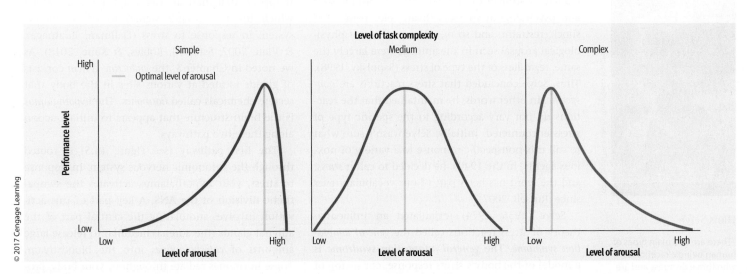

Figure 14.4
Emotional arousal and performance. Graphs of the relationship between emotional arousal and task performance tend to resemble an inverted U, as increased arousal is associated with improved performance up to a point, after which higher arousal leads to poorer performance. The optimal level of arousal for a task depends on the complexity of the task. On complex tasks, a relatively low level of arousal tends to be optimal. On simple tasks, however, performance may peak at a much higher level of arousal.

in which the autonomic nervous system mobilizes the organism for attacking (fight) or fleeing (flight) an enemy. As you may recall from Chapter 3, the *autonomic nervous system (ANS)* controls blood vessels, smooth muscles, and glands. The fight-or-flight response is mediated by the *sympathetic division* of the ANS (McCarty, 2007). In one experiment, Cannon studied the fight-or-flight response in cats by confronting them with dogs. Among other things, he noticed an immediate acceleration in their breathing and heart rate and a reduction in their digestive processes.

The physiological arousal associated with the fight-or-flight response is also seen in humans. In a sense, this automatic reaction is a "leftover" from humanity's evolutionary past. It's clearly an adaptive response in the animal kingdom, where the threat of predators often requires a swift response of fighting or fleeing. But in our modern world, the fight-or-flight response may be less adaptive for human functioning than it was thousands of generations ago (Nesse, Bhatnagar, & Young, 2007). Most human stresses can't be handled simply through fight or flight.

The General Adaptation Syndrome

The concept of stress was identified and named by Hans Selye (1936, 1956, 1982). Selye was born in Vienna, Austria, but came to Canada and began his professional career at McGill University in Montreal. He was also a professor and director of the Institute of Experimental Medicine and Surgery at the University of Montreal. Beginning in the 1930s, Selye exposed laboratory animals to a diverse array of both physical and psychological stressors (heat, cold, pain, mild shock, restraint, and so on). The patterns of physiological arousal seen in the animals were largely the same, regardless of the type of stress (Sapolsky, 1998). Thus, Selye concluded that stress reactions are *nonspecific*. In other words, he maintained that the reactions do not vary according to the specific type of stress encountered. Initially, Selye wasn't sure what to call this nonspecific response to a variety of noxious agents. In the 1940s, he decided to call it *stress*, and the word has been part of our vocabulary ever since (Russell, 2007).

Selye (1956, 1974) formulated an influential theory of stress reactions called the *general adaptation syndrome*. The *general adaptation syndrome* is a model of the body's stress response, consisting of three stages: alarm, resistance, and exhaustion. In the first stage of the general adaptation syndrome, an *alarm reaction* occurs when an organism first recognizes the existence of a threat. Physiological arousal occurs as the body musters its resources to

combat the challenge. Selye's alarm reaction is essentially the fight-or-flight response originally described by Cannon.

However, Selye took his investigation of stress a few steps further by exposing laboratory animals to *prolonged* stress, similar to the chronic stress often endured by humans. As stress continues, the organism may progress to the second phase of the general adaptation syndrome, the *stage of resistance.* During this phase, physiological changes stabilize as coping efforts get under way. Typically, physiological arousal continues to be higher than normal, although it may level off somewhat as the organism becomes accustomed to the threat.

If the stress continues over a substantial period of time, the organism may enter the third stage, the *stage of exhaustion.* According to Selye, the body's resources for fighting stress are limited. If the stress can't be overcome, the body's resources may be depleted. Eventually, he thought the organism would experience hormonal exhaustion, although we now know that the crux of the problem is that chronic overactivation of the stress response can have damaging physiological effects on a variety of organ systems (Sapolsky, 2007). These harmful physiological effects can lead to what Selye called "diseases of adaptation."

Brain–Body Pathways

Even in cases of moderate stress, you may notice that your heart has started beating faster, you've begun to breathe harder, and you're perspiring more than usual. How does all this (and much more) happen? It appears that there are two major pathways along which the brain sends signals to the endocrine system in response to stress (Dallman, Bhatnagar, & Viau, 2007; Sstowell, Robles, & Kane, 2013). As we noted in Chapter 3, the *endocrine system* consists of glands located at various sites in the body that secrete chemicals called *hormones*. The *hypothalamus* is the brain structure that appears to initiate action along these two pathways.

The first pathway (see Figure 14.5) is routed through the autonomic nervous system. In response to stress, your hypothalamus activates the sympathetic division of the ANS. A key part of this activation involves stimulating the central part of the adrenal glands (the adrenal medulla) to release large amounts of *catecholamines* into the bloodstream. These hormones radiate throughout your body, producing the physiological changes seen in the fight-or-flight response. The net result of catecholamine elevation is that your body is mobilized for action (Lundberg, 2007). Heart rate and blood flow increase, and more blood is pumped to your brain and

John Olson/Time Life Pictures/Getty Images

Hans Selye

"There are two main types of human beings: 'racehorses,' who thrive on stress and are only happy with a vigorous, fast-paced lifestyle, and 'turtles,' who in order to be happy require peace, quiet, and a generally tranquil environment."

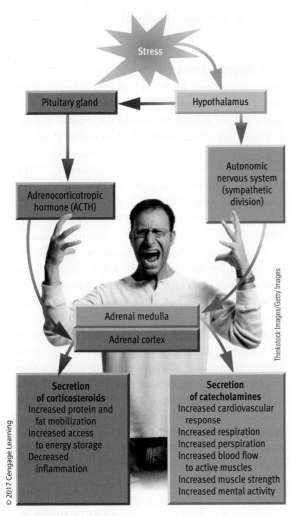

Figure 14.5

Brain–body pathways in stress. In times of stress, the brain sends signals along two pathways. The pathway through the autonomic nervous system controls the release of catecholamine hormones that help mobilize the body for action. The pathway through the pituitary gland and the endocrine system controls the release of corticosteroid hormones that increase energy and ward off tissue inflammation.

muscles. Respiration and oxygen consumption speed up, which facilitates alertness. Digestive processes are inhibited to conserve your energy. The pupils of your eyes dilate, increasing visual sensitivity.

The second pathway involves more direct communication between the brain and the endocrine system (see Figure 14.5). The hypothalamus sends signals to the so-called *master gland* of the endocrine system, the pituitary. In turn, the pituitary secretes a hormone (ACTH) (Anisman & Merali, 1999) that stimulates the outer part of the adrenal glands (the adrenal cortex) to release another important set of hormones—*corticosteroids*. These hormones stimulate the release of chemicals that help increase your energy and help inhibit tissue inflammation in case of injury (Miller, Chen, & Zhou, 2007; Munck, 2007).

An important new finding in research on stress and the brain is that stress can interfere with neurogenesis (Mahar et al., 2014; McEwen, 2009). As you may recall from Chapter 3, scientists have discovered that the adult brain is capable of *neurogenesis*—**the formation of new neurons**, primarily in key areas in the hippocampus. In Chapter 15 we will discuss evidence that suppressed neurogenesis may be a key cause of depression (Anacker, 2014). Thus, the capacity of stress to hinder neurogenesis may have important ramifications. This is currently the subject of intense research.

Behavioural Responses

Although people respond to stress at several levels, it's clear that *behaviour* is the crucial dimension of their reactions. Most behavioural responses to stress involve coping (Folkman, 2010). *Coping* **refers to active efforts to master, reduce, or tolerate the demands created by stress.** Notice that this definition is neutral as to whether coping efforts are healthful or maladaptive. The popular use of the term often implies that coping is inherently healthful. When people say that someone "coped with her problems," the implication is that she handled them effectively.

In reality, however, coping responses may be adaptive or maladaptive (Folkman & Moskowitz, 2004; Kleinke, 2007). For example, if you were flunking a history course at midterm, you might cope with this stress by (1) increasing your study efforts, (2) seeking help from a tutor, (3) blaming your professor, or (4) giving up on the class without really trying. Clearly, the first two of these coping responses would be more adaptive than the last two. In this section we'll focus most of our attention on styles of coping that tend to be less than ideal. We'll discuss more healthful coping strategies in the Personal Application on stress management.

Giving Up and Blaming Oneself

When confronted with stress, people sometimes simply give up and withdraw from the battle. Some people routinely respond to stress with fatalism and resignation, passively accepting setbacks that might be dealt with effectively. This syndrome is referred to as *learned helplessness* (Seligman, 1974, 1992). *Learned helplessness* **is passive behaviour produced by exposure to unavoidable aversive events.** Learned helplessness seems to occur when individuals come to believe that events are beyond their control. As you might guess, giving up is not a highly regarded method of coping. Consistent with this view, many

Albert Ellis

"People largely disturb themselves by thinking in a self-defeating, illogical, and unrealistic manner."

studies suggest that learned helplessness can contribute to depression (Isaacowitz & Seligman, 2007).

Although giving up is clearly less than optimal in many contexts, research suggests that when people struggle to pursue goals that turn out to be unattainable, it sometimes makes sense for them to cut their losses and disengage from the goal (Wrosch et al., 2012). Studies have shown that people who are better able to disengage from unattainable goals report better health and exhibit lower levels of a key stress hormone (Wrosch, 2011; Wrosch et al., 2007). Given the way people in our competitive culture tend to disparage the concept of "giving up," the authors note that it might be better to characterize this coping tactic as "goal adjustment."

Blaming oneself is another common response when people are confronted by stressful difficulties. The tendency to become highly self-critical in response to stress has been noted by a number of influential theorists. The late Albert Ellis (1973, 1987) called this phenomenon "catastrophic thinking." According to Ellis, catastrophic thinking causes, aggravates, and perpetuates emotional reactions to stress that are often problematic (see the Personal Application of this chapter). In a similar vein, Aaron Beck (1976, 1987) argues that negative self-talk can contribute to the development of depressive disorders (see Chapter 16). Although there is something to be said for recognizing one's weaknesses and taking responsibility for one's failures, Ellis and Beck agreed that excessive self-blame can be very unhealthy.

Striking Out at Others

People often respond to stressful events by striking out at others with aggressive behaviour. *Aggression is any behaviour that is intended to hurt someone, either physically or verbally.* Many years ago, a team of psychologists (Dollard et al., 1939) proposed the *frustration–aggression hypothesis,* which held that aggression is always caused by frustration. Decades of research have supported this idea of a causal link between frustration and aggression (Berkowitz, 1989). However, this research has also shown that there isn't an inevitable, one-to-one correspondence between frustration and aggression.

Freud theorized that behaving aggressively could get pent-up emotion out of one's system and thus be adaptive. He coined the term *catharsis* to refer to this release of emotional tension. The Freudian notion that it's a good idea to vent anger has become widely disseminated and accepted in modern society. However, experimental research generally has *not* supported the catharsis hypothesis. Indeed, *most studies find just the opposite: Behaving in an aggressive manner tends to fuel more*

anger and aggression (Bushman, 2002; Bushman & Huesmann, 2012).

Indulging Oneself

Stress sometimes leads to reduced impulse control, or *self-indulgence.* When troubled by stress, many people engage in unwise patterns of eating, drinking, spending money, and so forth. Thus, it's not surprising that studies have linked stress to increases in eating (O'Connor & Conner, 2011); smoking (Slopen et al., 2013); consumption of alcohol and drugs (Grunberg, Berger, & Hamilton, 2011); and gambling (Elman, Tschibelu, & Borsook, 2010). Gambling is not just a problem for adults. A study of gambling by Canadian adolescents conducted by members of McGill's International Centre for Youth Gambling found that stress related to negative life events was associated with youth problem gambling (Bergevin et al., 2006).

According to the Addictive Behaviours Laboratory at the University of Calgary (2014) and Statistics Canada (2010), gambling in Canada is a $13 billion a year industry. Problem gambling is increasingly becoming a concern in Canada. While problem gambling undoubtedly has many causes, including the increasing accessibility of legal gambling venues in Canada, it seems clear that one important contributing factor is life stress and how people cope with their stress.

Another example of self-indulgence as a coping strategy is stress-induced shopping. One recent study examined the relations among stress, materialism, and compulsive shopping in two Israeli samples, one of which was under intense stress due to daily rocket attacks (Ruvio, Somer, & Rindfleisch, 2014). The findings indicated that stress increases compulsive consumption and that this coping strategy is particularly common among those who are highly materialistic. The authors essentially conclude that *when the going gets tough, the materialistic go shopping.*

A relatively new manifestation of this coping strategy that has attracted much attention is the tendency to immerse oneself in the online world of the Internet. Kimberly Young (2009, 2013) has called this syndrome *Internet addiction.* Internet addiction typically involves one of three subtypes: excessive gaming; preoccupation with sexual content; or obsessive socializing (via Facebook, texting, and so forth; Weinstein et al., 2014). All three subtypes exhibit (1) excessive time online; (2) anger and depression when thwarted from being online; (3) an escalating need for better equipment and connections; and (4) adverse consequences, such as arguments and lying about Internet use, social isolation, and reductions in academic or work performance. Estimates of the prevalence of Internet addiction vary considerably from one country to another, but a recent meta-analysis of findings from 31 nations estimated that the average prevalence is around 6 percent of the population (Cheng & Li, 2014). The exact percentage is not as important as the recognition that the syndrome is *not* rare and that it is a global problem. Studies suggest that Internet addiction *is* fostered by high stress (Chen et al., 2014; Tang et al., 2014). Among other things, Internet addiction is associated with increased levels of anxiety, depression, and alcohol use (Ho et al., 2014). Although not all psychologists agree about whether excessive Internet use should be classified as an *addiction* (Hinic, 2011; Starcevic, 2013), it is clear that this coping strategy can be problematic (Muller et al., 2014).

Defensive Coping

Many people exhibit consistent styles of defensive coping in response to stress (Vaillant, 1994). In Chapter 12, we discussed how Sigmund Freud originally developed the concept of the *defence mechanism*. Although rooted in the psychoanalytic tradition, this concept has gained widespread acceptance from psychologists of most persuasions (Cramer, 2000). Building on Freud's initial insights, modern psychologists have broadened the scope of the concept and added to Freud's list of defence mechanisms.

Defence mechanisms are largely unconscious reactions that protect a person from unpleasant emotions, such as anxiety and guilt. Many specific defence mechanisms have been identified. For example, Laughlin (1979) lists 49 different defences. We described eight common defence mechanisms in our discussion of Freud's theory in Chapter 12: repression, projection, displacement, reaction formation, regression, rationalization, identification,

Rob Meinychukk/PhotoDisc/Getty Images

Experts disagree about whether excessive Internet use should be characterized as an addiction, but the inability to control online activity appears to be an increasingly common syndrome that illustrates the coping strategy of indulging oneself.

and sublimation (see Table 12.1 on page 442). Table 14.2 introduces another five defences that people use with some regularity.

The main purpose of defence mechanisms is to shield individuals from the unpleasant emotions so often elicited by stress (Cramer, 2008). They accomplish this purpose through *self-deception*, distorting reality so it doesn't appear so threatening. Defence mechanisms operate at varying levels of awareness, although they're largely unconscious (Cramer, 2001; Erdelyi, 2001).

Generally, defensive coping is less than optimal because avoidance and wishful thinking rarely solve personal problems (Grant et al., 2013; MacNeil

Table 14.2

Additional Defence Mechanisms

MECHANISM	DESCRIPTION	EXAMPLE
Denial of reality	Protecting oneself from unpleasant reality by refusing to perceive or face it	A smoker concludes that the evidence linking cigarette use to health problems is scientifically worthless.
Fantasy	Gratifying frustrated desires by imaginary achievements	A socially inept and inhibited young man imagines himself chosen by a group of women to provide them with sexual satisfaction.
Intellectualization (isolation)	Cutting off emotion from hurtful situations or separating incompatible attitudes so that they appear unrelated	A prisoner on death row awaiting execution resists appeal on his behalf and coldly insists that the letter of the law be followed.
Undoing	Atoning for or trying to magically dispel unacceptable desires or acts	A teenager who feels guilty about masturbation ritually touches door knobs a prescribed number of times following each occurrence of the act.
Overcompensation	Covering up felt weakness by emphasizing some desirable characteristics, or making up for frustration in one area by overgratification in another	A dangerously overweight woman goes on eating binges when she feels neglected by her husband.

Source: SARASON & SARASON, ABNORMAL PSYCHOLOGY, 5th Ed., © 1987. Reprinted by permission of Pearson Education, Inc., New York, New York.

Courtesy of Dr. Shelley Taylor

Shelley Taylor

"Rather than perceiving themselves, the world, and the future accurately, most people regard themselves, their circumstances, and the future as considerably more positive than is objectively likely. . . . These illusions are not merely characteristic of human thought; they appear actually to be adaptive, promoting rather than undermining good mental health."

et al., 2012). That said, there is some evidence that suggests that "positive illusions" can sometimes be adaptive for mental health (Taylor, 2011; Taylor & Brown, 1994). Some of the personal illusions people create through defensive coping can help them deal with life's difficulties. Roy Baumeister (1989) theorizes that it's all a matter of degree and that there is an "optimal margin of illusion." According to Baumeister, extreme distortions of reality are maladaptive, but small illusions can be beneficial.

Constructive Coping

Our discussion so far has focused on coping strategies that usually are less than ideal. Of course, people also exhibit many healthful strategies for dealing with stress. We'll use the term *constructive coping* to refer to relatively healthful efforts that people make to deal with stressful events. No strategy of coping can *guarantee* a successful outcome. Even the healthiest coping responses may turn out to be ineffective in some circumstances (Bonano & Burton, 2013). Thus, the concept of constructive coping is simply meant to connote a healthful, positive approach, without promising success.

What makes certain coping strategies constructive? Frankly, it's a grey area in which psychologists' opinions vary to some extent. Nonetheless, a consensus about the nature of constructive coping has emerged from the sizable literature on stress management. Key themes in this literature include the following:

1. Constructive coping involves confronting problems directly. It is task-relevant and action-oriented. It entails a conscious effort to rationally evaluate your options so that you can try to solve your problems.

2. Constructive coping is based on reasonably realistic appraisals of your stress and coping resources. A little self-deception may sometimes be adaptive, but excessive self-deception and highly unrealistic negative thinking are not.

3. Constructive coping involves learning to recognize, and in some cases regulate, potentially disruptive emotional reactions to stress.

These principles provide a rather general and abstract picture of constructive coping. We'll look at patterns of constructive coping in more detail in the Personal Application, which discusses various stress management strategies that people can use.

concept check 14.3

Identifying More Defence Mechanisms

In Chapter 12, you checked your understanding of several defence mechanisms by identifying instances of them in a story. In this chapter, you've learned about five additional defence mechanisms that are sometimes used as ways of coping with stress. Check your understanding of these defence mechanisms by identifying them in the story below. Each example of a defence mechanism is underlined, with a number next to it. Write the name of the defence mechanism exemplified in each case in the numbered spaces after the story. The answers are in Appendix A.

The guys at work have been trying to break it to me gently that they think my job's on the line because I've missed work too many days this year. I don't know how they came up with that idea; I've got nothing to worry about. (1.) Besides, every day I missed, I always did a lot of cleaning up and other chores around the house here. (2.) One of these days, the boss will finally recognize how really valuable I am to the company, and I'll be getting a big promotion. (3.) Anyway, since the guys have been dropping these hints about my not missing any more days, I've been trying really hard to make a good impression by saying "Hi" to everyone I see, especially the boss, and telling jokes. (4.) You know, it's really pretty interesting to observe how all these relationships unfold between guys who work together and the people who manage them. (5.)

1. _____   3. _____   5. _____

2. _____   4. _____

The Effects of Stress on Psychological Functioning

Key Learning Goals

- ► Describe burnout and identify its causes.

- ► Discuss post-traumatic stress disorder (PTSD) and describe its symptoms.

People struggle with many stresses every day. Most stresses come and go without leaving any enduring imprint. However, when stress is severe or when many stressful demands pile up, one's psychological functioning may be affected.

Research on the effects of stress has focused mainly on negative outcomes, so our coverage is slanted in

that direction. However, it's important to emphasize that stress is not inherently bad. You would probably suffocate from boredom if you lived a stress-free existence. Stress makes life challenging and interesting. Along the way, though, stress can be harrowing, sometimes leading to burnout, and to other problems including post-traumatic stress disorder.

Burnout

Burnout is an overused buzzword that means different things to different people. Nonetheless, a few researchers, including Acadia University's Michael Leiter, have described burnout in a systematic way that has facilitated scientific study of the syndrome (Maslach & Leiter, 1997, 2007). *Burnout* **involves physical and emotional exhaustion, cynicism, and a lowered sense of self-efficacy that can be brought on gradually by chronic work-related stress.** Exhaustion, which is central to burnout, includes chronic fatigue, weakness, and low energy. Cynicism is manifested in highly negative attitudes toward oneself, one's work, and life in general. Reduced self-efficacy involves declining feelings of competence at work, which give way to feelings of hopelessness and helplessness.

Burnout causes problems for both employers and employees. As you might expect, burnout is associated with increased absenteeism and reduced productivity at work, as well as increased vulnerability to a variety of health problems (Maslach & Leiter, 2000). Studies by Statistics Canada (2006, 2007) found that Canadians with high-stress jobs were much more likely to take disability days off work, to report lower work activity because of the stress, to report health-related work problems, and to experience stress-related depressive episodes.

What causes burnout? Factors in the workplace that appear to promote burnout include work overload, struggling with interpersonal conflicts at work, lack of control over work responsibilities and outcomes, and inadequate recognition for one's work (Leiter & Maslach, 2001; Maslach & Leiter, 2005; see Figure 14.6). According to Statistics Canada, 60 percent of highly stressed workers cite work as the main cause of their stress (Crompton, 2011). One study by Statistics Canada (2003) revealed a set of factors reported by Canadian workers that served as sources of workplace stress. One-third of respondents cited too many demands or work hours as the major source of stress. Other important sources of workplace stress include fear of job loss (13 percent), poor interpersonal relationships at work (15 percent), and risk of injury (13 percent). The latter source was most commonly reported by workers on rotating shifts (you may recall that we discussed some of the difficulties faced by shift workers in Chapter 5). Burnout is a potential problem in a wide variety of occupations (Adams et al., 2017; Adler et al. 2017; Kitchingman et al., 2017). Decades of research have shown that burnout is found all over the world in a wide variety of cultures (Schaufeli, Leiter, & Maslach, 2009). These high levels of stress have been linked to psychopathology,

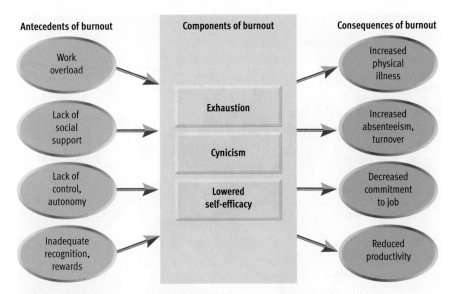

Figure 14.6

The antecedents, components, and consequences of burnout. Christina Maslach and Michael Leiter developed a systematic model of burnout that specifies the antecedents, components, and consequences of burnout. The antecedents on the left in the diagram are the stressful features of the work environment that cause burnout. The burnout syndrome itself consists of the three components shown in the centre of the diagram. Some of the unfortunate results of burnout are listed on the right. (Based on Leiter & Maslach, 2001)

Source: From Weiten. *Cengage Advantage Books: Psychology*, 9E. © 2013 South-Western, a part of Cengage, Inc. Reproduced by permission. www.cengage.com/permissions

and increased risk for memory loss, heart disease, arthritis, ulcers, asthma, and migraines (Crompton, 2011).

Post-Traumatic Stress Disorder

Extremely stressful, traumatic incidents can leave a lasting imprint on victims' psychological functioning. *Post-traumatic stress disorder (PTSD)* **involves enduring psychological disturbance attributed to the experience of a major traumatic event.** Researchers began to appreciate the frequency and severity of post-traumatic stress disorder after the Vietnam War ended in 1975 and a great many psychologically scarred veterans returned home. These veterans displayed a diverse array of psychological problems and symptoms that in many cases lingered much longer than expected (Schlenger et al., 1992). A series of eight suicides in the Canadian Armed Forces in just a few short months from November 2013 to early 2014 renewed concern for the effects of PTSD in the Canadian military (Tucker, 2014). Research findings released by Canada's Department of Veterans Affairs highlight the difficulties and range of problems faced by veterans when they retire from service (Van Til et al., 2013). These include a higher incidence of physical disorders such as chronic musculoskeletal disorders and obesity. In addition, recent research has found that almost 14 percent of members of

Research findings released by Canada's Department of Veterans Affairs highlight the difficulties and range of problems faced by veterans when they retire from service (Van Til et al., 2013). These include a higher incidence of physical disorders such as chronic musculoskeletal disorders and obesity, as well as psychological disorders such as PTSD.

the Canadian military who fought in Afghanistan now suffer from psychological disorders, the most common of which is PTSD (Daugherty, 2013). The Department of Veterans Affairs estimates that in general 10 percent of war-zone veterans will experience PTSD (Government of Canada, 2017).

Although highlighted in the context of American soldiers serving in the Vietnam War, post-traumatic stress disorder is increasingly associated with people in other front-line occupations, such as police officers, firefighters, ambulance attendants and paramedics, and even transit workers. Concerns have also been noted regarding the increasing rates of PTSD in Canada's law enforcement agencies, including municipal and provincial police and the RCMP. Accurate statistics can sometimes be difficult to find since, according to Cheryl Regehr of the University of Toronto, many law enforcement officers feel that there is still a stigma associated with acknowledging such problems (Mason, 2008; Regehr & Bober, 2005).

One of the difficulties facing mental health professionals working with first responders is the very limited research on this group. But events such as those we have just chronicled have motivated new research on the effects of the types of stress on the mental health of Canadian public safety personnel. In one of the first national surveys on workers exposed to potentially traumatic stress events, University of Regina psychologist Nicholas Carleton (Carleton et al., 2017) and his colleagues collected responses to online surveys from almost 6000 front-line workers from all across Canada, including firefighters, police, correctional workers, paramedics, RCMP officers, call centre operators, and dispatchers. The results were striking; almost half (44.5 percent) of the sample reported symptoms consistent with a serious mental illness, with some of the highest frequencies of positive screens for PTSD, depression, and anxiety disorders. This is cause for real concern because the symptom frequency "appears much higher than diagnostic rates for the general population" (Carleton et al., 2017, p. 9). Individuals in these occupations clearly put themselves at risk, both physically and psychologically.

PTSD and other serious stress reactions are not restricted solely to individuals who work in these types of occupations. It can happen to anyone who suffers trauma; it has been associated with other types of events including rape, assault, witnessing a death, and so on (Galea, Nandi, & Viahov, 2005). Unfortunately, traumatic events such as these appear to be much more common than widely assumed, and the effects can be just as dramatic. For example, in their preliminary research on the residents who were forced to evacuate from Fort McMurray because of the 2016 wildfires, Geneviève Belleville and her colleagues found that three months after the evacuation 60 percent of the respondents reported symptoms related to PTSD, and one in five reported elevated rates of depression, anxiety, panic disorder, trauma-related insomnia, and other illnesses (Belleville, Quellet, & Morin, 2017a, 2017b). The effects on participants and witnesses in dramatic events can be long-lasting.

The Effects of Stress on Physical Health

The effects of stress are not limited to mental health. Stress can also have an impact on one's physical health. For example, a recent report on the social determinants of health in Canada identified stress as one of the mediators of the link between poverty, poor living conditions, and health problems (Mikkonen &

Raphael, 2010). The authors of the report concluded that "continuous stress weakens the resistance to diseases and disrupts the functioning of the hormonal and metabolic systems" (p. 10).

The idea that stress can contribute to physical ailments is not entirely new. Evidence that stress can cause physical illness began to accumulate back in the 1930s. In this section, we'll look at the evidence on the apparent link between stress and physical illness, beginning with heart disease.

Personality, Hostility, and Heart Disease

In spite of declines, heart disease remains the leading cause of death in North America. *Coronary heart disease* involves a reduction in blood flow in the coronary arteries, which supply the heart with blood. This type of heart disease accounts for about 90 percent of heart-related deaths. Established risk factors for coronary disease include smoking, lack of exercise, high cholesterol levels, and high blood pressure (Bekkouche et al., 2011). According to recent statistics, one-quarter of Canadians between the ages of 20 and 79 suffer from high blood pressure, and almost 20 percent of those with hypertension were unaware that they suffered from it (Statistics Canada, 2016). While these risk factors have long been of interest, recently, attention has shifted to mounting evidence that *inflammation* plays a key role in the initiation and progression of coronary disease, as well as the acute complications that trigger heart attacks (Christodoulidis et al., 2014; Libby et al., 2014).

Research on the relationship between *psychological* factors and heart attacks began in the 1960s and 1970s, when a pair of cardiologists, Meyer Friedman and Ray Rosenman (1974), discovered an apparent connection between coronary risk and a syndrome they called the *Type A personality*, which involves self-imposed stress and intense reactions to stress. **The *Type A personality* includes three elements: (1) a strong competitive orientation, (2) impatience and time urgency, and (3) anger and hostility. Type A's are ambitious, hard-driving perfectionists who are exceedingly time-conscious. Often they are highly competitive, irritable workaholics who drive themselves with many deadlines. In contrast, the *Type B personality* is marked by relatively relaxed, patient, easygoing, amicable behaviour. Type B's are less hurried, less competitive, and less easily angered than Type A's.**

Decades of research uncovered a relatively modest correlation between Type A behaviour and increased coronary risk. More often than not, studies found a correlation between Type A personality and an elevated incidence of heart disease, but the findings were not as strong or as consistent as expected (Smith et al., 2012). However, in recent years, researchers have found a stronger link between personality and coronary risk by focusing on a specific component of the Type A personality: *anger and hostility* (Betensky, Contrada, & Glass, 2012; Smith, Williams, & Segerstrom, 2015). For example, in one study of almost 13 000 men and women who had no prior history of heart disease, investigators found an elevated incidence of heart attacks among participants who exhibited an angry temperament (Williams et al., 2000). Among participants with normal blood pressure, high-anger subjects experienced almost three times as many coronary events as low-anger subjects did (see Figure 14.7). The results of this study and many others suggest that hostility may be the crucial toxic element in the Type A syndrome.

Emotional Reactions, Depression, and Heart Disease

Recent studies suggest that people's emotions can also contribute to heart disease. One line of research has supported the hypothesis that transient mental stress and the resulting emotions people experience can tax the heart (Emery, Anderson, & Goodwin, 2013). Based on anecdotal evidence, cardiologists and laypersons have long voiced suspicions that strong emotional reactions might trigger heart attacks in individuals with coronary disease, but it was difficult to document this connection. However, advances in cardiac monitoring have facilitated investigation of the issue.

As suspected, laboratory experiments with cardiology patients have shown that brief periods of mental stress can trigger sudden symptoms of heart

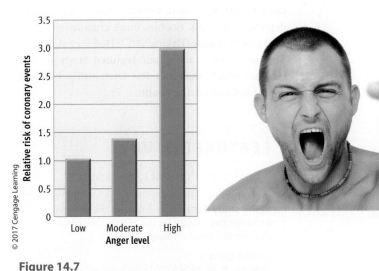

Figure 14.7

Anger and coronary risk. Working with a large sample of healthy men and women who were followed for a median of 4.5 years, Williams et al. (2000) found an association between anger and the likelihood of a coronary event. Among subjects who manifested normal blood pressure at the beginning of the study, a moderate anger level was associated with a 36 percent increase in coronary attacks and a high level of anger nearly tripled participants' risk for coronary disease (Based on data in Williams et al., 2000).

disease (Baker, Suchday, & Krantz, 2007). Overall, the evidence suggests that mental stress can elicit cardiac symptoms in about 30–70 percent of coronary patients (Emery et al., 2013). Outbursts of anger can be particularly dangerous. A recent meta-analysis of available evidence concluded that in the two hours immediately following an outburst of anger, there is nearly a fivefold jump in an individual's risk for a heart attack and a more than threefold increase in the risk for a stroke (Mostofsky, Penner, & Mittleman, 2014). These brief elevations in cardiovascular risk are transient, but in people who have frequent outbursts of anger, they can add up to significant increases in cardiovascular vulnerability.

Another line of research has implicated depression as a risk factor for heart disease (Glassman, Maj, & Sartorius, 2011). *Depressive disorders*, which are characterized by persistent feelings of sadness and despair, are a fairly common form of mental illness (see Chapter 15). In many studies, elevated rates of depression have been found among patients suffering from heart disease. Experts have tended to explain this correlation by asserting that being diagnosed with heart disease makes people depressed. However, recent evidence suggests that the causal relations may be just the opposite: *the emotional dysfunction of depression may cause heart disease* (Brunner et al., 2014; Gustad et al., 2014). For example, one study of almost 20 000 people who were initially free of heart disease reported striking results: Participants who suffered from depression were 2.7 times more likely to die of heart disease during the follow-up period than people who were not depressed (Surtees et al., 2008). Because the participants' depressive disorders preceded their heart attacks, it can't be argued that their heart disease caused their depression. Overall, studies suggest that depression roughly doubles one's chances of developing heart disease (Halaris, 2013; Herbst et al., 2007). This issue brings us to our Featured Study of this chapter, which examines the relationship between depression and cardiac health.

FEATURED STUDY

Is depression a risk factor for heart disease?

Description
In this study the authors examine the degree to which depression serves as a serious risk for developing heart disease.

Investigators
Penninx, B. W., et al. (2001). *Archives of General Psychiatry, 58*(3), 221–227.

Stress, Other Diseases, and Immune Functioning

The development of questionnaires to measure life stress has allowed researchers to look for correlations between stress and a variety of diseases. These researchers have uncovered many connections between stress and physical illness. For example, researchers have found an association between life stress and the course of rheumatoid arthritis (Davis et al., 2013). Other studies have connected stress to the development of diabetes (Nezu et al., 2013); herpes (Pedersen, Bovbjerg, & Zachariae, 2011); fibromyalgia (Malin & Littlejohn, 2013); and flare-ups of inflammatory bowel syndrome (Keefer, Taft, & Kiebles, 2013). Table 14.3 provides a longer list of health problems that have been linked to stress. Many of these stress-illness connections are based on tentative or inconsistent findings, but the sheer length and diversity of the list is remarkable. Why should stress

Table 14.3
Health Problems That May Be Linked to Stress

HEALTH PROBLEM	REPRESENTATIVE EVIDENCE
AIDS	Ironson et al. (1994)
Appendicitis	Creed (1989)
Asthma	Sriram & Silverman (1998)
Cancer	Holland & Lewis (1993)
Chronic back pain	Lampe et al. (1998)
Common cold	Cohen (2005)
Complications of pregnancy	Dunkel-Schetter et al. (2001)
Coronary heart disease	Orth-Gomer et al. (2000)
Diabetes	Riazi & Bradley (2000)
Epileptic seizures	Kelly & Schramke (2000)
Hemophilia	Buxton et al. (1981)
Herpes virus	Padgett & Sheridan (2000)
Hypertension	Pickering et al. (1996)
Hyperthyroidism	Yang, Liu, & Zang (2000)
Inflammatory bowel disease	Searle & Bennett (2001)
Migraine headaches	Ramadan (2000)
Multiple sclerosis	Mitsonis et al. (2006)
Periodontal disease	Marcenes & Sheiham (1992)
Rheumatoid arthritis	Huyser & Parker (1998)
Skin disorders	Arnold (2000)
Stroke	Harmsen et al. (1990)
Ulcers	Murison (2001)
Vaginal infections	Williams & Deffenbacher (1983)

increase the risk for so many kinds of illness? A partial answer may lie in the body's immune functioning.

The *immune response* is the body's defensive reaction to invasion by bacteria, viral agents, or other foreign substances. The immune response works to protect organisms from many forms of disease. A wealth of studies indicate that experimentally induced stress can impair immune functioning *in animals* (Ader, 2001; Kemeny, 2011). That is, stressors such as crowding, shock, food restriction, and restraint reduce various aspects of immune reactivity in laboratory animals (Prolo & Chiappelli, 2007).

Some studies have also related stress to suppressed immune activity *in humans* (Dhabhar, 2011; Kiecolt-Glaser, 2009). In one study, medical students provided researchers with blood samples so that their immune response could be assessed (Kiecolt-Glaser et al., 1984). They provided a baseline sample a month before final exams. They then contributed a high-stress sample on the first day of their finals. Reduced levels of immune activity were found during the extremely stressful finals week. Underscoring the practical significance of this immune suppression, studies have shown that when quarantined volunteers are exposed to respiratory viruses that cause the common cold, those who report high stress are more likely to be infected by the viruses (Marsland, Bachen, & Cohen, 2012).

Research in this area has mainly focused on the link between stress and immune suppression. However, recent studies have revealed other important connections between stress, immune function, and vulnerability to illness. Research suggests that exposure to long-term stress can sometimes promote chronic inflammation (Cohen et al., 2012; Gouin et al., 2012). Scientists have only begun to fully appreciate the potential ramifications of chronic inflammation. As we noted earlier, inflammation has recently been recognized as a factor in heart disease. But that's not all. Research has also demonstrated that chronic inflammation contributes to a diverse array of diseases, including arthritis, osteoporosis, respiratory diseases, diabetes, Alzheimer's disease, and some types of cancer (Gouin, Hantsoo, & Kiecolt-Glaser, 2011). Thus, chronic inflammation resulting from immune system dysregulation may be another key mechanism underlying the association between stress and a wide variety of diseases.

Sizing Up the Link between Stress and Illness

A wealth of evidence shows that stress is related to physical health, and converging lines of evidence suggest that stress contributes to the *causation* of illness (Cohen, Janicki-Deverts, & Miller, 2007; Pedersen, Bovbjerg, & Zachariae, 2011). But we have to put this intriguing finding into perspective. Virtually all of the relevant research is correlational, so it can't demonstrate *conclusively* that stress causes illness (T. W. Smith & Gallo, 2001). Subjects' elevated levels of stress and illness could both be due to a third variable, perhaps some aspect of personality (see Figure 14.8). For instance, some evidence suggests that neuroticism may make people overly prone to interpret events as stressful and overly prone to interpret unpleasant sensations as symptoms of illness, thus inflating the correlation between stress and illness (Espejo et al., 2011).

In spite of methodological problems favouring inflated correlations, the research in this area consistently indicates that the *strength* of the relationship between stress and health is *modest*. The correlations typically fall in the 0.20s and 0.30s (Schwarzer & Luszczynska, 2013). Clearly, stress is not an irresistible force that produces inevitable effects on health. Actually, this fact should come as no surprise, as stress is but one factor operating in a complex network of biopsychosocial determinants of health. Other key factors include one's genetic endowment, exposure to infectious agents and environmental toxins, nutrition, exercise, alcohol and drug use, smoking, use of medical care, and cooperation with medical advice. Furthermore, some people handle stress better than others, which is the matter we turn to next.

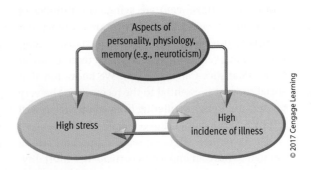

© 2017 Cengage Learning

Figure 14.8
The stress–illness correlation. One or more aspects of personality, physiology, or memory could play the role of a postulated third variable in the relationship between high stress and high incidence of illness. For example, neuroticism may lead some subjects to view more events as stressful and to remember more illness, thus inflating the apparent correlation between stress and illness.

Some people seem to be able to withstand the ravages of stress better than others (Epstein et al., 2013). Why? Because a number of *moderator variables* can lessen the impact of stress on physical and mental health. We'll look at three key moderator variables—social support, optimism, and conscientiousness—to shed light on individual differences in how well people tolerate stress.

Social Support

Friends may be good for your health and we want to be around others when we are stressed (Schachter, 1959; Townsend, Kim, & Mesquita, 2014). This conclusion emerges from studies on social support as a moderator of stress. **Social support refers to various types of aid and emotional sustenance provided by members of one's social networks.** Many studies have found positive correlations between high social support and greater immune functioning (Stowell, Robles, & Kane, 2013). In contrast, the opposite of social support—loneliness and social isolation—was found to predict reduced immune responding in one study of college students (Pressman et al., 2005). Meanwhile, studies have linked social isolation to poor health and increased mortality (Cacioppo & Cacioppo, 2014; Steptoe et al., 2013). In recent decades, a vast number of studies have found evidence that social support is favourably related to physical health (Gleason & Masumi, 2015; Uchino & Birmingham, 2011). The importance of social support and familiar, comfortable surroundings is especially true for those with long-term illnesses, disability, or those who are aging. The number of Canadians receiving care in their own homes has increased in recent years, with recent statistics indicating that over 2 million Canadians receive care at home (Statistics Canada, 2014). We know too that social support is essential to the recovery in the very young, and in those suffering from emotional as well as physical difficulties (Rueger et al., 2016).

The favourable effects of social support are strong enough to have an impact on participants' mortality! A recent meta-analysis of the results of 148 studies reported that solid social support increased people's odds of survival by roughly 50 percent (Holt-Lunstad, Smith, & Layton, 2010). The positive effects of important, supportive relationships extend to the effects of the quality of a marriage and health outcomes. A recent meta-analysis of research linking marital quality and health outcomes shows that positive marriages are associated with a range of positive health indicators, including a lowered risk of mortality (Robles, Slatcher, Trombello, & McGinn, 2014). Good marriages can be good for your health and your life expectancy!

While everyone needs relationships and the support of others (Festinger, 1954; Murray, 1938), some of us are particularly vulnerable to the effects of a lack of social support. Research suggests, for example, that people suffering from depression and low self-esteem are particularly sensitive to the absence of social support (e.g., Lakey & Orehek, 2011; Negron et al., 2013). Denise Marigold of the University of Waterloo has developed an important line of research examining the association between low self-esteem and social support (Marigold et al., 2014; Marigold, Holmes, & Ross, 2007, 2010). According to her work, the relation between self-esteem and relational social support is complex. While those with low self-esteem may need and want positive, social support from their relationship partners, because they doubt their own value, they may resist and/or distort positive, supportive feedback from their partners and may behave in ways that serve to alienate those partners (Marigold et al., 2007, 2010). Marigold suggests that providing positive, supportive feedback to a relationship partner with low self-esteem (LSE) may be difficult and that care must be taken when providing that support so that it will have the desired effect both for you and your partner. When faced with someone who seems to hold him- or herself in low regard, we often simply try to highlight the positive and reframe any negative experiences he or she may have had. According to Marigold, that strategy may not be the optimal one. As an alternative, her research (Marigold et al., 2014) suggests that "when [support] providers offer support that validates LSE's negative thoughts and feelings (and supports their self-verification and mood regulation goals), such interactions appear to be more successful" (p. 75).

In addition to individual differences in reactions to social support, recent research suggests that there are cultural disparities in the type of social support that people prefer. Studies have found that Asians are reluctant to seek support from others and that they assert that social support is not all that helpful to them (Kim et al., 2006; Taylor et al., 2004). In an effort to shed light on this puzzling observation, Shelley Taylor and colleagues (2007) discovered that Asians can benefit from social support, but they prefer a different kind of support than Americans. Taylor and her colleagues (2007) distinguish between

Denise Marigold is a social psychologist at Renison University College, University of Waterloo. Her research focuses on the cognitive processes involved in building and maintaining relationship well-being and individual differences in interpersonal behaviour.

Courtesy of Dr. Denise Marigold

explicit social support (overt emotional solace and instrumental aid from others) and *implicit social support* (the comfort that comes from knowing that one has access to close others who will be supportive). Research has shown that Americans generally prefer and pursue explicit social support. In contrast, Asians do not feel comfortable seeking explicit social support because they worry about the strain it will place on their friends and family (Kim, Sherman, & Taylor, 2008). But Asians do benefit from the implicit support that results when they spend time with close others (without discussing their problems) and when they remind themselves that they belong to valued social groups that would be supportive if needed.

Having connections with your community also seems to provide health benefits. One study (Shields, 2008) found that Canadians who perceive a strong sense of connection to their community were more likely to report having both good physical and mental health. Over two-thirds of those who felt they had a strong sense of community belonging reported good physical health and over 80 percent of those with a strong sense of community belonging reported good mental health. This study adds to the growing evidence that social relationships and bonds can be good for your health. The effect of some types of social support has also been found to be a function of culture, with individuals from cultures emphasizing community and interdependence benefiting more from emotional social support than those from cultures where independence is emphasized (Uchida et al., 2008).

Interestingly, a recent study suggests that even superficial social interactions with acquaintances and strangers—such as waiters, grocery store clerks, and people we see around our neighbourhood—can be beneficial. Sandstrom and Dunn (2014) asked participants about their recent interactions involving people with whom they had either strong ties or weak ties. As expected, greater interactions with strong ties correlated with greater subjective well-being, but surprisingly, so did greater interactions with weak ties.

Generally, researchers have assumed that our feelings of belongingness and social support are derived from our interactions with close friends and family, but the Sandstrom and Dunn (2014) study raises the possibility that weak ties can also contribute to our sense of support and well-being.

Optimism, Conscientiousness, and Hardiness

Optimism is a general tendency to expect good outcomes. Studies have found a correlation between optimism and relatively good physical health (Scheier, Carver, & Armstrong, 2012); more effective immune functioning (Segerstrom & Sephton, 2010); greater cardiovascular health (Hernandez et al., 2015); and increased longevity (Peterson et al., 1998). Why is optimism beneficial to health? Research suggests that optimists cope with stress in more adaptive ways than pessimists do (Carver, Scheier, & Segerstrom, 2010). Optimists are more likely to engage in action-oriented, problem-focused coping, and they are more likely to emphasize the positive in their appraisals of stressful events. Optimists also enjoy greater social support than pessimists, in part because they work harder on their relationships (Carver & Scheier, 2014). For the most part, research on optimism has been conducted in modern, industrialized societies. However, a recent study of representative samples from 142 countries yielded evidence that the link between optimism and health can be found around the world (Gallagher, Lopez, & Pressman, 2013).

Optimism is not the only personality trait that has been examined as a possible moderator of the relationship between stress and health. Research has shown that conscientiousness, one of the Big Five personality traits discussed in Chapter 12, is associated with good physical health and increased longevity (Friedman, 2011; Kern, Della Porta, & Friedman, 2014). Why does conscientiousness promote longevity? Several considerations appear to contribute (Shanahan et al., 2014). First, people who are high in conscientiousness are less likely than others to exhibit unhealthy habits, such as excessive drinking, drug abuse, dangerous driving, smoking, overeating, and risky sexual practices. Second, they tend to rely on constructive coping strategies and they are persistent in their efforts, so they may handle stressors better than others. Third, conscientiousness appears to promote better adherence to medical advice and more effective management of health problems. Fourth, conscientiousness is associated with higher educational attainment and job performance, which both foster career success and increased income, meaning that people high in conscientiousness tend to end up in the upper levels of socioeconomic status (SES). It may not be equitable, but a large body of research indicates that high SES confers a host of advantages that promote greater health and longevity. Age-adjusted mortality rates are two to three times higher among the poor than among the wealthy (Phelan, Link, & Tehranifar, 2010). These well-documented health disparities exist because wealthier people tend to endure lower levels of stress, benefit from better nutrition and more exercise, exhibit fewer unhealthy habits (see Figure 14.9), are exposed less to pollution and work

Stress, Coping, and Health

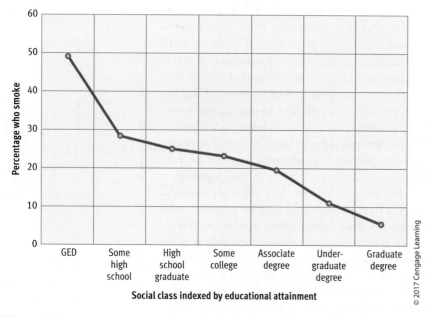

Figure 14.9

Social class and smoking. Higher SES is associated with a lower prevalence of most unhealthy habits, such as smoking, excessive drinking, and failing to exercise. In many cases, these associations are surprisingly strong, as you can see in this graph, which depicts the relationship between social class and the likelihood of smoking. Using educational attainment as an indicator of SES, it is clear that smoking drops precipitously as SES increases. That is not to say that the upper classes have no bad health habits, but on average, they do appear to make far fewer unhealthy choices than the lower classes. (Based on Dube et al., 2010)

in less toxic environments, and can afford easier access to higher-quality medical care (Ruiz, Prather, & Steffen, 2012).

Finally, some people tend to be able to withstand the demands of stress better than others; they are hardy. According to Lambert and Lambert (1999, p. 11), *hardiness* is a constellation of attitudes,

beliefs, and behavioural tendencies that consists of three components: commitment, control, and challenge. The concept was first detailed by Kobasa (1979), who examined the traits of a group of business executives who seemed to be able to resist the effects of stress. She referred to them as *hardy* types. She found that they were characterized by high levels of three traits all beginning with the letter C, control, challenge, and commitment. They tended to approach difficult tasks as *challenges*, they viewed their work as important and they were *committed* to it, and they saw themselves as in *control* of their time and efforts. As a prototypic example, consider human rights advocate Malala Yousafzai's reaction to a ban placed on girls attending school in parts of her native Pakistan. She publicly argued for this right despite the clear personal danger that this might cause her. Her promotion of this right put her on an assassination list, and she was shot three times—once in the head—while travelling on a school bus in Pakistan in 2012. Her hardiness was evident in her continued human rights advocacy after her recovery. In October 2014, at 17 years of age, she was awarded (along with co-recipient Kailash Satyarthi) the 2014 Nobel Peace Prize. She is the youngest person ever to receive this award. In April 2017, in a ceremony in Ottawa, Malala was made an Honorary Citizen of Canada. She is only the sixth person, as well as the youngest person, ever to be given this honour (Campion-Smith & Boutilier, 2017).

Stress Mindset

Could your attitudes and beliefs about stress and its effects influence your capacity to handle stress effectively? Recent research by Crum, Salovey, and Achor (2013) suggests that the answer is yes. They argue that most people assume stress is generally harmful. They label this attitude a *stress-is-debilitating mindset*. However, they note that some people view stress as an invigorating challenge and opportunity for growth. They call this attitude a *stress-is-enhancing mindset*. They assert that people's stress mindset is likely to shape their psychological experience of stressful events, as well as their behavioural reactions. Specifically, they hypothesize that a stress-is-enhancing mindset should be associated with intermediate arousal in response to stress and more effective coping strategies. Their initial data provided some support for this line of thinking. A great deal of additional research is needed, but one's stress mindset may turn out to be another factor moderating the impact of stressful events.

Malala Yousafzai was awarded the 2014 Nobel Peace Prize for her human rights advocacy for the right of all children to education. At 17, she is the youngest recipient of this award and is also the youngest person to have been made an Honorary Citizen of Canada.

Positive Effects of Stress

As we have discussed, most people seem to operate under the impression that the effects of stress are entirely negative, but this most certainly is not the case. Recent decades have brought increased interest in the positive aspects of the stress process, including favourable outcomes that follow in the wake of stress (Folkman & Moskowitz, 2000). To some extent, the new focus on the possible benefits of stress reflects a new emphasis on "positive psychology." As we noted in Chapter 1, the advocates of positive psychology argue for increased research on well-being, courage, perseverance, tolerance, and other human strengths and virtues (Seligman, 2003). One of these strengths is resilience in the face of stress; in fact, studies indicate that resilience is not as uncommon as widely assumed (Bonanno, Westphal, & Mancini, 2012).

Research on resilience suggests that stress can promote personal growth or self-improvement (Calhoun & Tedeschi, 2008, 2013). For example, studies of people grappling with major health problems show that the majority of respondents report they derived benefits from their adversity (Lechner, Tennen, & Affleck, 2009). Stressful events sometimes force people to develop new skills, re-evaluate priorities, learn new insights, and acquire new strengths. In other words, the adaptation process initiated by stress can lead to personal changes for the better. One study that measured participants' exposure to 37 major negative events found a curvilinear relationship between lifetime adversity and mental health (Seery, 2011). High levels of adversity predicted poor mental health, as expected, but people who had faced intermediate levels of adversity were healthier than those who experienced little adversity, suggesting that moderate amounts of stress can foster resilience. A follow-up study found a similar link between the amount of lifetime adversity and subjects' responses to laboratory stressors (Seery et al., 2013). Intermediate levels of adversity were predictive of the greatest resilience. Thus, having to grapple with a moderate amount of stress may build resilience in the face of future stress.

Health-Impairing Behaviour

On average, the life expectancy for Canadians is increasing. The life expectancy for women in 2017 is 83 years of age and for men it is 79, with the gender gap continuing to narrow (Statistics Canada, 2017). While most Canadians are living longer lives, some people seem determined to dig an early grave for themselves. They do precisely those things that are bad for their health. For example, some people drink heavily even though they know that they're damaging their liver. Others eat all the wrong foods even though they know that they're increasing their risk of a second heart attack. Behaviour that's downright self-destructive is surprisingly common. In this section, we'll discuss how health is affected by health-impairing lifestyles.

Smoking

The smoking of tobacco is widespread in our culture, but the percentage of people who smoke in North America has declined noticeably since the mid-1980s (see Figure 14.10). Nonetheless, according to Statistics Canada (2016), 21.4 percent of Canadians males and 14.8 percent of Canadian females continue to smoke.

According to the Surgeon General of the United States, smokers ingest more than 7000 chemicals in each puff on a cigarette (Associated Press, 2010). The chemicals rapidly spread throughout the body causing widespread cellular damage. It is the leading cause of premature death in North America (Curry, Mermelstein, & Sporer, 2009). The evidence clearly shows that smokers face a much greater risk of premature death than nonsmokers. For example, the average smoker has an estimated life expectancy *13–14 years shorter* than that of a similar nonsmoker (Schmitz & DeLaune, 2005).

Why are mortality rates higher for smokers? Smoking increases the likelihood of developing a surprisingly large range of diseases (Thun, Apicella,

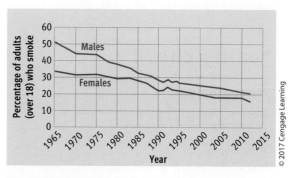

Figure 14.10
The prevalence of smoking. This graph shows how the percentage of adults who smoke has declined steadily since the mid-1960s. Although considerable progress has been made, smoking still accounts for a huge number of premature deaths in North America each year. (Based on data from the Centers for Disease Control and Prevention)

Key Learning Goals

▶ Evaluate the negative health impact of smoking, substance abuse, and lack of exercise.

▶ Clarify the relationship between behavioural factors and AIDS.

& Henley, 2000; Thun et al., 2013). Lung cancer and heart disease kill the largest number of smokers. However, smokers also have an elevated risk for oral, bladder, and kidney cancer, as well as cancers of the larynx, esophagus, and pancreas; for arteriosclerosis, hypertension, stroke, and other cardiovascular diseases; and for bronchitis, emphysema, and other pulmonary diseases. Most smokers know about the risks associated with tobacco use. Interestingly, though, they tend to underestimate the risks as applied to themselves (Ayanian & Cleary, 1999).

Lamentably, the dangers of smoking are not limited to smokers themselves. Family members and co-workers who spend a lot of time around smokers are exposed to *second-hand smoke* or *environmental tobacco smoke*. Second-hand smoke can increase their risk for a variety of illnesses, including lung cancer (Vineis, 2005) and heart disease (Ding et al., 2009). Young children may be particularly vulnerable to the effects of second-hand smoke (Homa et al., 2015).

Studies show that if people can give up smoking, their health risks decline reasonably quickly (Kenfield et al., 2008). Evidence suggests that most smokers would like to quit but are reluctant to give up a major source of pleasure. They also worry about craving cigarettes, gaining weight, becoming anxious and irritable, and feeling less able to cope with stress (Grunberg, Faraday, & Rahman, 2001).

Unfortunately, it's difficult to give up cigarettes. People who enroll in formal smoking cessation programs are only slightly more successful than people who try to quit on their own (Swan, Hudman, & Khroyan, 2003). Long-term success rates peak in the vicinity of only 25 percent. Many studies report even lower figures. Nonetheless, it *is* possible to quit smoking successfully. Interestingly, many people fail several times before they eventually succeed. Research suggests that the readiness to give up smoking builds gradually as people cycle through periods of abstinence and relapse (Prochaska et al., 2004).

....

reality check

Misconception

If you can't quit smoking the first time you try, you are unlikely to succeed in the future.

Reality

People attempting to give up smoking usually fail several times before eventually succeeding. Hence, if your first effort to quit smoking ends in failure, you should not give up hope—try again in a few weeks or a few months.

Studies show that if people can give up smoking, their health risks decline reasonably quickly (Samet, 1992; Williams et al., 2002). Unfortunately, it's difficult to give up cigarettes. Long-term success rates are in the vicinity of only 25 percent, and some studies report even lower figures.

Lack of Exercise

Considerable evidence links the lack of exercise and increases in sedentary activities, such as watching TV, to poor health and obesity (Statistics Canada, 2008d). Regular exercise reduces the risk of many health problems, including some types of cancer, obesity, high blood pressure, and several types of psychopathology (Colley et al., 2011), and is associated with increased longevity. Regular exercise also reduces the risks associated with diabetes. In 2008–2009, 2.4 million Canadians were living with diabetes (Park & Peters, 2014). For many of these conditions, exercise can be almost as effective as medications (Wang, 2013). The Public Health Agency of Canada recently adopted the World Health Organization recommendation of 150 minutes a week of moderate-to-vigorous physical activity in bouts of at least 10 minutes (MVPA) as the goal for Canadian adults. Recent data collected by Statistics Canada suggests that only 17 percent of men and 14 percent of women currently achieve this level of exercise (Colley et al., 2014). Unfortunately, physical fitness and activity levels appear to be declining in North America, especially for our children. The fitness levels of Canadian children and youth declined dramatically from 1981 to 2009, and among youth ages 15 to 19, when we should be most active, the proportion of Canadian youth whose waist circumference has increased enough to put them at a health risk has more than tripled (Statistics Canada, 2010c). This decline in fitness is accompanied by a sharp decline in the percentage of Canadian children who participate in regular, organized sports (Statistics Canada, 2008). Kids in Canada spend only 14 minutes on average after school engaged in physical activity (Picard, 2011). Rather than physical exercise, it seems as if Canadian children are spending increased amounts of time in sedentary activities in front of their TV, phone, and computer screen. Recent data collected by Statistics Canada indicates that the majority of younger children, especially those between the ages of three and four, are spending more than the recommended amount of time in sedentary activities in front of TV and computer screens (Statistics Canada, 2016). These activities put them at increased risk for obesity and have been found to be linked to deceased cognitive and social development. According to a recent report released by Active Healthy Kids Canada, Canadian kids are spending up to eight hours in front of the screen on a typical day (Active Healthy Kids Canada, 2014; Bielski, 2013). There are important reasons why we, as a society, should attempt to reverse these trends.

Why would exercise help people live longer? For one thing, an appropriate exercise program can enhance cardiovascular fitness and thereby reduce susceptibility to deadly cardiovascular problems (Brassington et al., 2012). Second, exercise can indirectly reduce one's risk for a variety of obesity-related health problems, such as diabetes and respiratory difficulties (Corsica & Perri, 2013). Third, recent studies suggest that exercise can help diminish chronic inflammation, which is thought to contribute to quite a variety of diseases (You et al., 2013). Fourth, exercise can serve as a buffer that reduces the potentially damaging physical effects of stress (Edenfield & Blumenthal, 2011). This buffering effect may occur because people high in fitness show less physiological reactivity to stress than do those who are less fit (Zschucke et al., 2015). Fifth, among the elderly, exercise is associated with a reduction in the brain shrinkage normally seen after age 60 (Gow et al., 2012) and a reduction in vulnerability to Alzheimer's disease (Radak et al., 2010).

Alcohol and Drug Use

Although there is some thought-provoking evidence that *moderate* drinking may offer some protection against cardiovascular disease (Brien et al., 2011; Ronksley et al., 2011), heavy consumption of alcohol clearly increases one's risk for a host of diseases (Johnson & Ait-Daoud, 2005). Recreational drug use is another common health-impairing habit. The risks associated with the use of various drugs were discussed in detail in Chapter 5. Unlike smoking, poor eating habits, and inactivity, drugs can kill directly and immediately when they are taken in an overdose or when they impair the user enough to cause an accident. In the long run, various recreational drugs may also elevate one's risk for infectious diseases; respiratory, pulmonary, and cardiovascular diseases; liver disease; gastrointestinal problems; cancer; neurological disorders; and pregnancy complications (see Chapter 5). Ironically, the greatest physical damage in the population as a whole is caused by alcohol, the one recreational drug that's legal.

Behaviour and AIDS

At present, some of the most problematic links between behaviour and health may be those related to AIDS. The first AIDS patients were reported in North America in 1981 (CBC News, 2011). In the years since those first patients were diagnosed, considerable progress had been made in terms of our understanding of AIDS. AIDS stands for ***acquired immune deficiency syndrome***, **a disorder in which the immune system is gradually weakened and eventually disabled by the human immunodeficiency virus (HIV).** Being infected with the HIV virus is *not* equivalent to having AIDS. AIDS is the final stage of the HIV infection process, typically manifested about ten years after the original infection (Carey & Vanable, 2003; Treisman, 1999). AIDS inflicts its harm indirectly by opening the door to other diseases because, with the onset of the syndrome, one is left virtually defenceless against a host of opportunistic infectious agents. The symptoms of AIDS vary widely, depending on the specific constellation of diseases that one develops (Cunningham & Selwyn, 2005).

In some parts of the world there has been a decrease in HIV and AIDS cases in the past few years. According to the Public Health Agency of Canada, there has been a general decrease in Canada in reported HIV and AIDS cases since reporting began in 1985. For AIDS cases, the 2012 number of reported cases showed an 18.1 percent decrease from 2011 and a 90.6 percent decrease since 1993. For cases of HIV, the number of reported cases in 2012 represented a 7.8 percent decrease from 2011, and it was the lowest number of cases since reporting began in 1985 (Public Health Agency of Canada, 2013). However, there was a slight increase in HIV cases in Canada from 2014 to 2015 (Statistics Canada, 2016). Unfortunately, the worldwide prevalence of this deadly disease continues to increase in other parts of the world at an alarming rate, with specific regions in Africa continuing to demonstrate disproportionately high overall rates of HIV infection (Kharsany & Karim, 2016).

HIV is transmitted through person-to-person contact involving the exchange of bodily fluids, primarily semen and blood. The two principal modes of transmission in North America have been sexual contact and the sharing of needles by intravenous (IV) drug users. In North America, sexual transmission has occurred primarily among gay and bisexual men, but heterosexual transmission has increased (Centers for Disease Control, 2011) in recent years. In 2012 in Canada, the largest risk exposure category, 50.3 percent of HIV cases, remains the category referred to as "men who have sex with men (MSM)" (Public Health Agency of Canada, 2013). This category of exposure is down from 80 percent of cases in 1985. In 2012, the MSM category is followed closely by exposure due to heterosexual contact, which represented 32.6 percent of reported cases.

The behavioural changes that minimize the risk of developing AIDS are fairly straightforward, although making the changes is often much easier said than done (Coates & Collins, 1998). In all groups, the more sexual partners that a person has, the higher the risk that the person will be exposed to the virus. So, people can reduce their risk by having sexual contacts with fewer partners and by using condoms to control the exchange of semen.

Research by Canadian psychologists has examined some of the factors contributing to the tendency not to use condoms and to engage in risky sexual behaviours. Carolyn Hafer of Brock University and her colleagues have found links between an individual's *belief in a just world*, a relatively stable dispositional characteristic (Choma, Hafer, Crosby, & Foster, 2012), and condom use (Hafer, Bogaert, & McMullen, 2001). Tara MacDonald of Queen's University has found links between the intention to engage in risky sexual behaviour and specific conditions of alcohol use, and between such intention and negative mood combined with low self-esteem (Hynie, MacDonald, & Marques, 2006; MacDonald, Fong, et al., 2000; MacDonald & Martineau, 2002).

Reactions to Illness

M. Robin DiMatteo

Courtesy of Dr. Robin DiMatteo

"A person will not carry out a health behaviour if significant barriers stand in the way, or if the steps interfere with favourite or necessary activities."

Adjusting to illness is difficult for most people, affecting them psychologically as well as physically (Helgeson & Zajdel, 2017). Research focused on helping patients and their families adjust, as well as research on how to motivate health behaviour change (Sheeran, Klein, & Rothman, 2017), is accelerating. What we do know is that some people respond to physical symptoms and illnesses by ignoring warning signs of developing diseases, while others engage in active coping efforts to conquer their diseases. Let's examine the decision to seek medical treatment, communication with health providers, and compliance with medical advice.

Deciding to Seek Treatment

Have you ever experienced nausea, diarrhea, stiffness, headaches, cramps, chest pains, or sinus problems? Of course you have; everyone experiences some of these problems periodically. However, whether someone views these sensations as *symptoms* is a matter of individual interpretation. When two people experience the same unpleasant sensations, one may shrug them off as a nuisance, while the other may rush to a physician (Martin & Leventhal, 2004). Studies suggest that people who are relatively high in anxiety and neuroticism tend to report more symptoms of illness than others do (Petrie & Pennebaker, 2004).

There are a couple of roadblocks to seeking treatment for medical problems. The first relates to the wait times for ER and specialist care in Canada. After seeing your family physician, you may be referred to a specialist. Unfortunately, waiting for a consultation with a specialist can add substantially to the overall wait time for medical care (Statistics Canada, 2010). Governments across Canada are committed to reducing these wait times (e.g., Ontario Ministry of Health, 2011). The second roadblock relates to how individuals appraise and react to health concerns. Variations in the perceived seriousness and disruptiveness of symptoms help explain some of the differences among people in their readiness to seek medical treatment (Cameron, Leventhal, & Leventhal, 1993). It has also been found that income level, gender, and whether you live in a city or rural area in Canada affect the frequency of seeing a physician. In Canada, city-dwelling women with higher incomes are more likely to visit a physician or a specialist (Statistics Canada, 2007g).

Perhaps the biggest problem in regard to treatment seeking is the tendency of many people to delay the pursuit of needed professional consultation. Delays can be critical because early diagnosis and quick intervention may facilitate more effective treatment of many health problems (Petrie & Pennebaker, 2004). Unfortunately, procrastination is the norm even when people are faced with a medical emergency, such as a heart attack (Martin & Leventhal, 2004). Why do people dawdle in the midst of a crisis? Robin DiMatteo (1991), a leading expert on patient behaviour, mentions a number of reasons, noting that people delay because they often (1) misinterpret and downplay the significance of their symptoms; (2) fret about looking silly if the problem turns out to be nothing; (3) worry about "bothering" their physician; (4) are reluctant to disrupt their plans (to go out to dinner, see a movie, and so forth); or (5) waste time on trivial matters (such as taking a shower, gathering personal items, or packing clothes) before going to a hospital emergency room.

Communicating with Health Providers

The quality of communication between patients and their health providers can influence individuals' health outcomes (Hall & Roter, 2011; Leung, 2016). A large portion of medical patients leave their doctors' offices not understanding what they have been told and what they are supposed to do (Johnson & Carlson, 2004). This situation is most unfortunate because good communication is a crucial requirement for sound medical decisions, informed choices about treatment, and appropriate follow-through by patients (Haskard et al., 2008).

There are many barriers to effective provider-patient communication (DiMatteo, 1997; Marteau & Weinman, 2004). Economic realities dictate that medical visits generally be quite brief, allowing little time for discussion. Many providers use too much medical jargon and overestimate their patients' understanding of technical terms. Patients who are upset and worried about their illness may simply forget to report some symptoms or to ask questions they meant to ask. Other patients are evasive about their real concerns because they fear a serious diagnosis. Many patients are reluctant to challenge doctors' authority and are too passive in their interactions with providers.

What can you do to improve your communication with health-care providers? The key is to not be a passive consumer of medical services (Berger, 2013). Arrive at a medical visit on time, with your questions and concerns prepared in advance. Try to be accurate and candid in replying to your doctor's questions. If you don't understand something the doctor says, don't be embarrassed about asking for clarification. And if you have doubts about the suitability or feasibility of your doctor's recommendations, don't be afraid to voice them.

Adhering to Medical Advice

Many patients fail to follow the instructions they receive from physicians and other health-care professionals. The evidence suggests that *nonadherence* to medical advice may occur 30 percent of the time when short-term treatments are prescribed for acute conditions and 50 percent of the time when long-term treatments are needed for chronic illness (Johnson & Carlson, 2004). Nonadherence takes many forms. Patients may fail to begin a treatment regimen, may stop the regimen early, may reduce or increase the levels of treatment that were prescribed,

Dana Hursey/Jupiterimages

Communication between health-care providers and patients tends to be far from optimal, for a variety of reasons.

or may be inconsistent and unreliable in following treatment procedures (Dunbar-Jacob & Schlenk, 2001). Nonadherence has been linked to increased sickness, treatment failures, and higher mortality (Dunbar-Jacob, Schlenk, & McCall, 2012). Moreover, nonadherence wastes expensive medical visits and medications and increases hospital admissions, leading to enormous economic costs. DiMatteo (2004b) speculates that in the United States alone, nonadherence may be a $300 billion a year drain on the health care system.

Why don't people comply with the advice they've sought from highly regarded health-care professionals? Physicians tend to attribute non-compliance to patients' personal characteristics, but research indicates that personality traits and demographic factors are surprisingly unrelated to adherence rates (DiMatteo, 2004b). The most commonly reported reason for poor adherence is simple forgetting (Dunbar-Jacob et al., 2012). One factor that *is* related to adherence is patients' *social support*. Adherence is improved when patients have family members, friends, or co-workers who remind them and help them comply with treatment requirements (DiMatteo, 2004a). Other considerations that influence the likelihood of adherence include the following (Hall & Roter, 2011; Johnson & Carlson, 2004):

1. Frequently, nonadherence occurs because the patient doesn't understand the instructions as given. Highly trained professionals often forget that what seems obvious and simple to them may be obscure and complicated to many of their patients.

2. Another key factor is how aversive or difficult the instructions are. If the prescribed regimen is unpleasant, adherence tends to decrease. And the more that following instructions interferes with routine behaviour, the less probable it is that the patient will cooperate successfully.

3. If a patient has a negative attitude toward a physician, the probability of noncompliance increases. When patients are unhappy with their interactions with the doctor, they're more likely to ignore the medical advice provided, no matter how important it may be.

Putting It in Perspective: Themes 4 and 7

Which of our themes were prominent in this chapter? As you probably noticed, our discussion of stress and health illustrated multifactorial causation and the subjectivity of experience. As we noted in Chapter 1, people tend to think simplistically, in terms of single causes. In recent years, the highly publicized research linking stress to health has led many people to point automatically to stress as an explanation for illness. In reality, stress has only a modest impact on physical health. Stress can increase the risk for illness, but health is governed by a dense network of factors. Important factors include inherited vulnerabilities, physiological reactivity, exposure to infectious agents, health-impairing habits, reactions to symptoms, treatment-seeking behaviour, compliance with medical advice, personality, and social support. In other words, stress is but one actor on a crowded stage. This should be apparent in Figure 14.11, which shows the multitude of biopsychosocial factors that jointly influence physical health. It illustrates multifactorial causation in all of its complexity.

The subjectivity of experience was demonstrated by the frequently repeated point that stress lies in the eye of the beholder. The same job promotion may be stressful for one person and invigorating for another. One person's pressure is another's challenge. When it comes to stress, objective reality is not nearly as important as subjective perceptions. More than anything else, the impact of stressful events seems to depend on how people view them. The critical importance of individual stress appraisals will continue to be apparent in the Personal Application on coping and stress management. Many stress management strategies depend on altering one's appraisals of events.

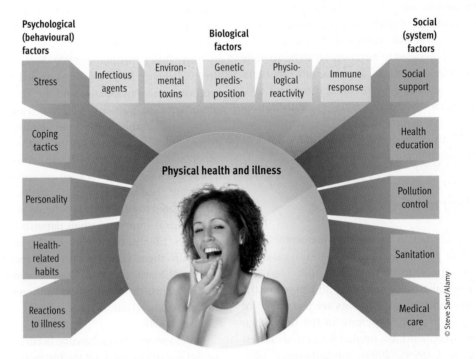

Figure 14.11

Biopsychosocial factors in health. Physical health can be influenced by a remarkably diverse set of variables, including biological, psychological, and social factors. The variety of factors that affect health provide an excellent example of multifactorial causation.

© 2017 Cengage Learning

Improving Coping and Stress Management

Courses and books on stress management have multiplied at a furious pace in the last couple of decades. They summarize experts' advice on how to cope with stress more effectively.

The key to managing stress does *not* lie in avoiding it. Stress is an inevitable element in the fabric of modern life. As Hans Selye noted, "Contrary to public opinion, we must not—and indeed cannot—avoid stress" (1973, p. 693). Thus, most stress management programs encourage people to confront stress rather than sidestep it. This requires training people to engage in action-oriented, rational, reality-based *constructive coping*. In this Application, we'll examine a variety of constructive coping tactics, beginning with Albert Ellis's ideas about changing one's appraisals of stressful events.

Reappraisal: Ellis's Rational Thinking

Albert Ellis (1913–2007) was a prominent theorist who believed that people can short-circuit their emotional reactions to stress by altering their appraisals of stressful events (Ellis, 1977, 1985, 1996, 2001). Ellis's insights about stress appraisal are the foundation for a widely used system of therapy that he devised. *Rational-emotive therapy* is an approach that focuses on altering clients' patterns of irrational thinking to reduce maladaptive emotions and behaviour.

Ellis maintained that *you feel the way you think*. He argued that problematic emotional reactions are caused by negative self-talk, which he called *catastrophic thinking*. *Catastrophic thinking* involves unrealistically negative appraisals of stress that

exaggerate the magnitude of one's problems. According to Ellis, people unwittingly believe that stressful events cause their emotional turmoil, but he maintains that emotional reactions to personal setbacks are actually caused by overly negative appraisals of stressful events (see Figure 14.12).

Ellis theorizes that unrealistic appraisals of stress are derived from irrational assumptions people hold. He maintains that if you scrutinize your catastrophic thinking, you'll find your reasoning is based on a logically indefensible premise, such as "I must have approval from everyone" or "I must perform well in all endeavours." These faulty assumptions, which people often hold unconsciously, generate catastrophic thinking and emotional turmoil. How can you reduce your unrealistic appraisals of

stress? Ellis asserts that you must learn (1) how to detect catastrophic thinking and (2) how to dispute the irrational assumptions that cause it.

Using Humour as a Stress Reducer

Empirical evidence showing that humour moderates the impact of stress has been accumulating over the last 25 years (M. H. Abel, 1998; Lefcourt, 2001, 2005), although Rod Martin at the University of Western Ontario has argued that the research to date has some inadequacies and that the area needs more theory-based, rigorous research (Martin, 2001, 2007). University of Waterloo psychologist Herbert Lefcourt and his colleagues (1995) argue that high-humour

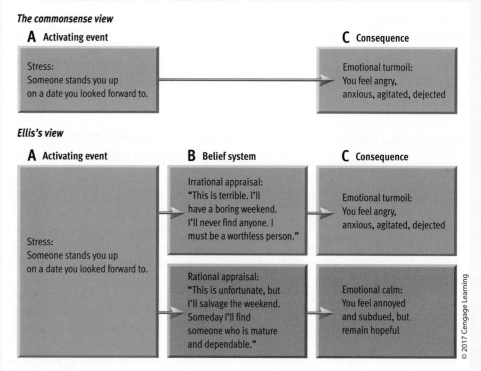

Figure 14.12

Albert Ellis's A–B–C model of emotional reactions. Although most people attribute their negative emotional reactions directly to negative events that they experience, Ellis argues that events themselves do not cause emotional distress—rather, distress is caused by the way people *think* about negative events. According to Ellis, the key to managing stress is to change one's appraisal of stressful events.

© 2017 Cengage Learning

Courtesy of Doug McCann

Animal assisted therapy (AAT) is currently a very popular intervention for both psychological and physical illnesses. It is used as a complement to traditional medical and psychological treatment. Pictured here are Doug McCann's dogs, Lucy Lui and Jackie Chan, two Shetland sheepdogs who have assisted with the recovery of patients suffering from cancer and from psychological disorders including anxiety and depression.

people may benefit from not taking themselves as seriously as low-humour people. As the authors put it, "If persons do not regard themselves too seriously and do not have an inflated sense of self-importance, then defeats, embarrassments, and even tragedies should have less pervasive emotional consequences for them" (p. 375).

Stress Reduction

One approach to stress reduction employs animals, often dogs, to help reduce stress and to aid in the recovery of both physical and psychological difficulties (Beetz, 2017; Beetz et al., 2012; Chandler, 2012). It has been reported that animal assisted therapy (AAT) can help patients reduce their levels of stress, lower blood pressure, assist some children with social difficulties feel more comfortable interacting with others, assist with cancer patient recovery and symptom reduction, lead to increased attentional focus, lower reports of fear and anxiety, and reduce depression and a sense of inadequacy,

among other effects (e.g., Beetz et al., 2012; Friedmann & Son, 2009; Marcus, 2012; Marcus, Blazek-O'Neill, & Kopar, 2014; Muela et al., 2017; White et al., 2015; Zilcha-Mano, Mikulincer, & Shaver, 2011, 2012). Research such as this has led the American Heart Association to endorse pets, especially dogs, as being of potential significance in reducing cardiovascular risk (Qyama & Serpeli, 2013).

While we might want to believe that getting a dog, or another pet, might be an easy and very effective way to ameliorate our problems, reduce our stress, and speed our recovery from serious psychological and physical illnesses, two caveats should be kept in mind. First, there have been some concerns about the robustness of the findings and the rigour of some of the work in this area, with suggested guidelines concerning how to improve the science (e.g., Crossman, 2017; Kazdin, 2017; McClune, Esposito, & Griffin, 2017; Serpell et al., 2017). Given the potential benefits to be derived from AAT, it is clear that more evidence is needed to clearly delineate the reality, nature, and parameters of those benefits. Second, even if the potential of AAT is established, we do not yet know what explains the effects—specifically, what psychological processes are involved (e.g., Beetz, 2017; Zicha, Mikulincer, & Shaver, 2011). As this approach grows in popularity, we can expect to see more scientific research on AAT.

Relaxing and Minimizing Physiological Vulnerability

Relaxation is a valuable stress-management technique that can soothe emotional turmoil and suppress problematic physiological arousal (McGuigan & Lehrer, 2007; Smith, 2007). The value of relaxation became apparent to Herbert Benson (1975) as a result of his research on meditation. Benson, a Harvard Medical School cardiologist, believes relaxation is the key to many of the beneficial effects of meditation. The components of a successful relaxation period according to Benson are described in Figure 14.13. But anything

that relaxes you—whether it's music, meditation, prayer, or a warm bath—can be helpful. Experts have also devised a variety of systematic relaxation procedures that can make relaxation efforts more effective. You may want to learn about techniques such as *progressive relaxation* (Jacobson, 1938); *autogenic training* (Schultz & Luthe, 1959); *mindfulness meditation* (Kabat-Zinn, 1995); and the *relaxation response* (Benson & Klipper, 1988).

As this chapter has made clear, the wear and tear of stress can be injurious to one's physical health. To combat this potential problem, it helps to keep your body in relatively sound shape. The potential benefits of regular exercise are substantial, including increased longevity (Gremeaux et al., 2012). Moreover, research has shown that you don't have to be a dedicated athlete to benefit from exercise because even a moderate amount of exercise reduces your risk of disease (Richardson et al., 2004; see Figure 14.14).

Embarking on an exercise program is difficult for many people. Exercise is time-consuming, and if you're out of shape, your initial attempts may be painful and discouraging. To avoid these problems, it's wise to (1) select an activity you find enjoyable, (2) increase your participation gradually, (3) exercise regularly without overdoing it, and (4) reinforce yourself for your efforts (Greenberg, 2002).

Good sleep habits can also help in the effort to minimize physiological vulnerability to stress. As we discussed in Chapter 5, sleep loss can undermine immune system responding (Motivala & Irwin, 2007) and fuel inflammatory responses (Patel et al., 2009). Evidence also suggests that poor sleep quality is associated with poor health (Grandner et al., 2012, 2014) and that sleep loss can elevate the risk of mortality (Magee et al., 2013). Thus, sound sleep patterns can contribute to stress management. The results of one study suggest that people need to get a sufficient amount of sleep and should strive for consistency in their patterns of sleeping (Barber et al., 2010).

1 Sit quietly in a comfortable position.

2 Close your eyes.

3 Deeply relax all your muscles, beginning at your feet and progressing up to your face. Keep them relaxed.

4 Breathe through your nose. Become aware of your breathing. As you breathe out, say the word "one" silently to yourself. For example, breathe in . . . out, "one"; in . . . out, "one"; and so forth. Breathe easily and naturally.

5 Continue for 10 to 20 minutes. You may open your eyes to check the time, but do not use an alarm. When you finish, sit quietly for several minutes, at first with your eyes closed and later with your eyes opened. Do not stand up for a few minutes.

6 Do not worry about whether you are successful in achieving a deep level of relaxation. Maintain a passive attitude and permit relaxation to occur at its own pace. When distracting thoughts occur, try to ignore them by not dwelling on them, and return to repeating "one." With practice, the response should come with little effort. Practise the technique once or twice daily but not within two hours after any meal, since digestive processes seem to interfere with the elicitation of the relaxation response.

Phil Date/Shutterstock.com

Figure 14.13

Benson's relaxation procedure. Herbert Benson's relaxation procedure is described here. According to Benson, his simple relaxation response can yield benefits similar to meditation. To experience these benefits, you should practise the procedure daily.

Source: Relaxation procedure [pp. 14–15] from *THE RELAXATION RESPONSE* by HERBERT BENSON, M.D. WITH MIRIAM Z. KLIPPER. Copyright © 1975 by William Morrow and Company, Inc. Reprinted by permission of HarperCollins Publishers.

Summary

In this Personal Application we have discussed various aspects of stress and how it negatively affects us. We end this section by summarizing our recommendations and adding in the top ten defences against the ravages of stress summarized by the Psychology Foundation of Canada (n.d.):

1. Aim to get seven to nine hours of sleep each night.

2. Prioritize so that you do not feel overwhelmed.

3. If you regularly commute long periods of time to work and back, try to reduce your stress levels on the road (e.g., listening to favourite CDs, carpooling).

4. Take care of your physical well-being.

5. Utilize all of your vacation time.

6. If you get sick, stay home.

7. Plan ahead.

8. Set firm boundaries between your work and your nonwork time.

9. Write down three things you are thankful for each day, even if you find it hard.

10. Create a strong support system.

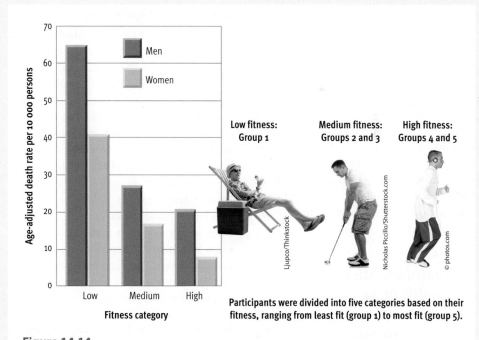

Low fitness: Group 1

Medium fitness: Groups 2 and 3

High fitness: Groups 4 and 5

Ljupco/Thinkstock

Nicholas Piccillo/Shutterstock.com

© photos.com

Participants were divided into five categories based on their fitness, ranging from least fit (group 1) to most fit (group 5).

Figure 14.14

Physical fitness and mortality. Blair and colleagues (1989) studied death rates among men and women who exhibited low, medium, or high fitness. As you can see, fitness was associated with lower mortality rates in both sexes.

Source: Adapted from Blair, S. N., Kohl, W. H., Paffenbarger, R. S., Clark, D. G., Cooper, K. H., & Gibbons, L. W. (1989). Physical fitness and all-cause mortality. *Journal of the American Medical Association, 262*, 2395–2401. Copyright © 1989 American Medical Association. Reprinted by permission.

Thinking Rationally about Health Statistics and Decisions

With so many conflicting claims about the best ways to prevent or treat diseases, how can anyone ever decide what to do? It seems that every day, a report in the media claims that yesterday's health news was wrong.

The inconsistency of health news is only part of the problem. We are also overwhelmed by health-related statistics. As mathematics pundit John Allen Paulos (1995, p. 133) puts it, "Health statistics may be bad for our mental health. Inundated by too many of them, we tend to ignore them completely, to accept them blithely, to disbelieve them close-mindedly, or simply to misinterpret their significance."

Making personal decisions about health-related issues may not be easy. Even medical personnel often struggle to make sense out of health statistics (Gigerenzer et al., 2007). Yet it's particularly important to try to think rationally and systematically about such issues. In this Application, we'll discuss a few insights that can help you think critically about statistics on health risks. Then we'll briefly outline a systematic approach to thinking through health decisions.

Evaluating Statistics on Health Risks

News reports seem to suggest that there are links between some type of physical illness and virtually everything people do, touch, and consume. For example, media have reported that coffee consumption is related to hypertension, that sleep loss is related to mortality, and that a high-fat diet is related to heart disease. It's enough to send even the most subdued person into a panic. Fortunately, your evaluation of data on health risks can become more sophisticated by considering the following.

Correlation Is No Assurance of Causation It is not easy to conduct experiments on health risks, so the vast majority of studies linking lifestyle and demographic factors to diseases are correlational studies. Hence, it pays to remember that there may not be a causal link between two variables that happen to be correlated. So, when you hear that a factor is related to some disease, try to dig a little deeper and find out why scientists think this factor is associated with the disease. The suspected causal factor may be something very different from what was measured.

Statistical Significance Is Not Equivalent to Practical Significance Reports on health statistics often emphasize that the investigators uncovered "statistically significant" findings. As explained in Chapter 2, statistically significant findings are findings that are not likely to be due to chance fluctuations. Statistical significance is a useful concept, but it can sometimes be misleading (Matthey, 1998). Medical studies are often based on rather large samples because they tend to yield more reliable conclusions than small samples. However, when a large sample is used, weak relationships and small differences between groups can turn out to be statistically significant, and these small differences may not have much practical importance.

Base Rates Should Be Considered in Evaluating Probabilities In evaluating whether a possible risk factor is associated with some disease, people often fail to consider the base rates of these events. If the base rate of a disease is relatively low, a small increase can sound quite large if it's reported as a percentage. For example, in the He et al. (1999) study, the prevalence of diabetes among subjects with the lowest sodium intake was 2.1 percent, compared to 3.8 percent for subjects with the highest sodium intake. Based on this small but statistically significant difference, one could say (the investigators did not) that high sodium intake was associated with an 81 percent increase ($[3.8 - 2.1] \div 2.1$) in the prevalence of diabetes. This would be technically accurate, but an exaggerated way of portraying the results. Base rates should also be considered when evaluating claims made about the value of medications and other medical treatments. If the base rate of a disease is low, a very modest decrease reported as a percentage can foster exaggerated perceptions of treatment benefits. For instance, Gigerenzer et al. (2007) describe an advertisement for Lipitor (a drug intended to lower cholesterol levels) that claimed that Lipitor reduced the risk of stroke by 48 percent. Although this was technically accurate, in absolute terms the protective benefits of Lipitor were actually rather modest. After four years, 1.5 percent of those taking Lipitor had a stroke versus 2.8 percent of those taking the placebo.

Thinking Systematically about Health Decisions

Health decisions are oriented toward the future, which means that there are always uncertainties. And they usually involve weighing potential risks and benefits. None of these variables is unique to health decisions—uncertainty, risks, and benefits play prominent roles in economic and political decisions as well as in personal decisions. Let's apply some basic principles of quantitative reasoning to a treatment decision involving whether to prescribe Ritalin for a boy who has been diagnosed with attention deficit disorder (ADD). Keep in mind that the general principles applied in this example can be used for a wide variety of decisions.

Seek Information to Reduce Uncertainty
Gather information and check it carefully for accuracy, completeness, and the presence or absence of conflicting information. For example, is the diagnosis of ADD correct? *Look for conflicting information* that does not fit with this diagnosis. For example, if the child can sit and read for a long period of time, maybe the problem is an undetected hearing loss that makes him appear to be hyperactive in some situations, or perhaps he is just a very active child who prefers physical activity to the sedentary. This is an important first step that is often omitted.

As you consider the additional information, begin *quantifying the degree of uncertainty* or its "flip side," your degree of confidence that the diagnosis is correct. A specific value is usually not possible, but a general approximation along a dimension ranging from "highly confident" to "not at all confident" is useful in helping you think about the next step. If you decide that you are not confident about the diagnosis, you may be trying to solve the wrong problem.

Make Risk–Benefit Assessments
What are the risks and benefits of Ritalin? How likely is this child to benefit from Ritalin, and just how much improvement can be expected? If the child is eight years old and unable to read and is miserable in school and at home, any treatment that could reduce his problems deserves serious consideration. As in the first step, the quantification is at an approximate level. A child who is two years behind in school and has no friends is, in a roughly quantifiable sense, worse off than one who is only six months behind in school and has at least one or two friends. How likely and how severe are the risks associated with Ritalin? If there is evidence that children do not grow as well when they are on Ritalin, for example, can they be taken off Ritalin over the summer months so they can catch up?

List Alternative Courses of Action
What are the alternatives to Ritalin? How well do they work? What are the risks associated with the alternatives, including the risk of falling further behind in school? *Consider the pros and cons of each alternative.* A special diet that sometimes works might be a good first step, along with the decision to start drug therapy if the child does not show improvement over some time period. What are the relative success rates for different types of treatment for children like the one being considered? To answer these questions, you will need to use probability estimates in your decision making.

As you can see from this example, many parts of the problem are quantified (confidence in the diagnosis, likelihood of improvement, probability of negative outcomes, and so forth). Precise probability values were not used because often the actual numbers are not known. Some of the values that are quantified reflect value judgments, others reflect likelihoods, and others assess the degree of uncertainty. The decision will have a different outcome depending on the particular child in question, the expected degree of success for alternative modes of treatment, and the associated risks for each. It is important to avoid the (understandable) tendency to give up and do nothing or to just do what the experts say to do, because every course of action has associated risks. It is also important to remember that doing nothing is also a decision, and it may not be the best one.

The decision-making process is not complete even after a decision is made. New decisions are needed as the future unfolds. When new information and new alternatives become available, the decision needs to be reviewed. Decision makers need to adopt deliberate strategies that require them to look for and seriously consider information that conflicts with any decision that was previously made, to avoid the tendency to notice and act only on information that confirms what you already believe to be true.

If you are thinking that the quantification of many unknowns in decision making is a lot of work, you are right. But, it is work worth doing. Whenever there are important decisions to be made about health, the ability to think with numbers will help you reach a better decision. And yes, that assertion is a virtual certainty. See Table 14.4.

Table 14.4

Critical Thinking Skills Discussed in This Application

SKILL	DESCRIPTION
Understanding the limitations of correlational evidence	The critical thinker understands that a correlation between two variables does not demonstrate that there is a causal link between the variables.
Understanding the limitations of statistical significance	The critical thinker understands that weak relationships can be statistically significant when large samples are used in research.
Utilizing base rates in making predictions and evaluating probabilities	The critical thinker appreciates that the initial proportion of some group or event needs to be considered in weighing probabilities.
Seeking information to reduce uncertainty	The critical thinker understands that gathering more information can often decrease uncertainty, and reduced uncertainty can facilitate better decisions.
Making risk–benefit assessments	The critical thinker is aware that most decisions have risks and benefits that need to be weighed carefully.
Generating and evaluating alternative courses of action	In problem solving and decision making, the critical thinker knows the value of generating as many alternatives as possible and assessing their advantages and disadvantages.

STRESS

- Stress is a common, everyday event, and even routine hassles can have harmful effects.

- People's *primary appraisals* of events determine what they find stressful.

- People's *secondary appraisals* assess their coping resources and influence the degree of stress experienced.

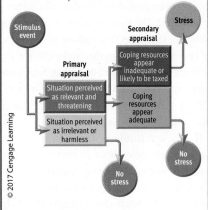

MAJOR TYPES OF STRESS

Frustration

- *Frustration* occurs when the pursuit of some goal is thwarted.

Conflict

- In an *approach–approach conflict*, a choice must be made between two attractive goals.

- In an *avoidance–avoidance conflict*, a choice must be made between two unattractive goals.

- In an *approach–avoidance conflict*, a choice must be made about whether to pursue a goal that has positive and negative aspects.

Change

- *Life changes* are alterations in living circumstances, including positive changes, that require adjustment.

- The Social Readjustment Rating Scale (SRRS) purports to measure change-related stress, but actually taps many types of stressful experiences.

- Many studies have shown that high scores on the SRRS are associated with increased vulnerability to physical illness and psychological problems.

Pressure

- People may be under *pressure* to perform well or to conform to others' expectations.

- Pressure is a predictor of psychological symptoms and heart disease.

STRESS RESPONSE

Emotional responses

- Many emotions can be evoked by stress, but anger-rage, anxiety-fear, and sadness-grief are especially common.

- Investigators tend to focus on negative emotions, but research shows that positive emotions also occur during periods of stress.

- Emotional arousal can interfere with coping efforts.

- The *inverted-U hypothesis* posits that as tasks become more complex, the optimal level of arousal decreases.

Physiological responses

- The *general adaptation syndrome* is Hans Selye's model of the body's response to stress, which can progress through three stages: alarm, resistance, and exhaustion.

- Prolonged stress can lead to what Selye called diseases of adaptation.

- Stress can cause the brain to send signals to the endocrine system along two pathways.

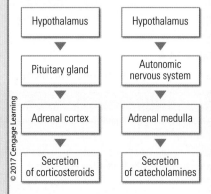

Behavioural responses

- Coping efforts intended to master or reduce stress can be healthy or unhealthy.

- *Giving up and blaming oneself* are less than optimal methods of coping with stress.

- Another unhealthy response is to strike out at others with acts of *aggression*.

- *Indulging oneself* is another common response to stress that tends to be less than optimal.

- *Defensive coping* protects against emotional distress, but it depends on self-deception and avoidance.

- However, small positive illusions about one's life can be adaptive for mental health.

- *Constructive coping* refers to relatively healthful efforts to handle the demands of stress.

STRESS EFFECTS

Effects on physical health

- Stress appears to contribute to many types of physical illness.

- The *Type A personality* has been identified as a contributing factor in coronary heart disease.

- Research suggests that *hostility* is the most toxic element of the Type A syndrome.

- Recent evidence suggests that strong emotional reactions can precipitate heart attacks.

- Research indicates that depression roughly doubles one's chances of developing heart disease.

- The association between stress and vulnerability to many diseases may reflect the negative impact of stress on immune function.

- The correlation between stress and illness is modest in strength because stress is only one of many factors that influence health.

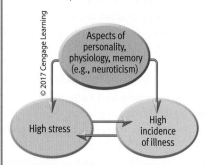

Variations in stress tolerance

- There are individual differences in how much stress people can tolerate without negative effects.

- Strong *social support* appears to buffer the impact of stress, and thus promote physical and psychological health.

- Asians prefer *implicit* social support, whereas Americans prefer *explicit* social support.

- Two personality traits, *optimism* and *conscientiousness*, appear to promote health.

- A *stress-is-enhancing mindset* may be associated with reduced stress arousal and more effective coping.

- Research on resilience suggests that stress can promote personal growth, self-improvement, and other benefits.

HEALTH-IMPAIRING BEHAVIOUR

Smoking

- Smokers have much higher mortality rates than nonsmokers because smoking elevates the risk for a wide range of diseases, including lung cancer and heart disease.

- When people quit smoking, their health risks decline fairly quickly.

- Long-term success rates for giving up smoking are only 25 percent or less.

Alcohol and drug use

- Moderate drinking may offer some protection against cardiovascular disease, but heavy consumption clearly increases one's risk for a host of diseases.

- Recreational drug use also elevates people's vulnerability to various types of illness.

Lack of exercise

- Research indicates that regular exercise is associated with increased longevity.

- Physical fitness can reduce vulnerability to deadly cardiovascular diseases, obesity-related problems, and chronic inflammation.

Behaviour and AIDS

- Behavioural patterns influence one's risk for AIDS, which is transmitted through person-to-person contact involving the exchange of bodily fluids, primarily semen and blood.

- In the world as a whole, sexual transmission has mostly taken place through heterosexual relations.

- Many young heterosexuals naïvely downplay their risk for HIV.

REACTIONS TO ILLNESS

The decision to seek treatment

- Whether people view physical sensations as symptoms of an illness depends on subjective interpretation.

- The biggest problem in regard to treatment seeking is the common tendency to delay the pursuit of needed treatment.

- People procrastinate because they worry about looking silly or bothering their physician or because they are reluctant to disrupt their plans.

Communicating with health providers

- A large portion of patients depart medical visits not understanding what they have been told.

- Barriers to effective provider–patient communication include short visits, overuse of medical jargon, and patients' reluctance to challenge physicians' authority.

- The key to improving communication is to be an active, not passive, consumer.

Dana Hursey/Jupiterimages

Adherence to medical advice

- Nonadherence to advice from health providers is very common.

- Nonadherence is often due to forgetting or the patient's failure to understand instructions.

- If a prescribed regimen is unpleasant or difficult to follow, compliance tends to decline.

- Noncompliance increases when patients have negative attitudes toward their health providers.

APPLICATIONS

- Ellis emphasized the importance of reappraising stressful events and rational thinking.

- Humour can dampen stress appraisals, increase positive emotions, and enhance social support.

- Relaxation, exercise, and good sleep habits can reduce vulnerability to the physical effects of stress.

- Evaluations of health risks can be enhanced by remembering that correlation is not an assurance of causation and that statistical significance is not equivalent to practical significance.

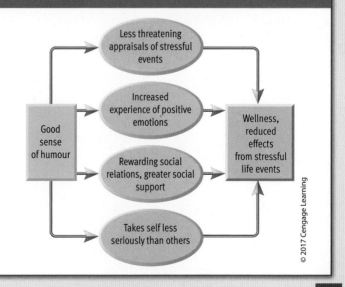

© 2017 Cengage Learning

Nick Dolding/Stone/Getty Images

CHAPTER 15

Psychological Disorders

Themes in this Chapter

Multifactorial Causation

Heredity & Environment

Sociohistorical Context

Cultural Heritage

The topic of psychological disorders draws many students to an introductory psychology course. Your interest in this topic may stem from your desire to understand the nature, prevalence, and cause of psychological disorders so that you can be better prepared to assist those in need. This is indeed a worthy aspiration and one that we are ourselves familiar with; it's one of the things that motivated us, too, in our early studies in psychology. You may also have been led to the topic because you are already too familiar with the costs that such disorders can exact on the afflicted and their families. We hope that this chapter on psychological disorders and Chapter 16, which deals with the treatment of psychological disorders, will contribute to your understanding of these important social and personal issues.

Given the rates of occurrence for the various disorders that we will discuss in this chapter, the chances are very good that you know someone, perhaps someone very close to you, who suffers from some type of psychological disturbance. There are a variety of statistics that give a clear indication of the scope of the problem. In any given year one in five Canadians experiences mental illness or problems. Nationwide, according to data released by the Mental Health Commission of Canada, almost 7 million Canadians are currently living with mental health problems and illness (Mental Health Commission, 2012). In a recent year, 17 000 Canadians were admitted to hospital for suicide and self-injury attempts (Picard, 2011). While the overall suicide rate has declined from 1979 to 2014, that decline was evident primarily for males. Women continue to show higher hospitalization rates for self-injury than males in Canada (Skinner et al., 2016). The use of antianxiety and antidepressant medications has increased significantly in recent decades (CAMH, 2011), and currently two of the top four medications prescribed in Canada for children and youth between the ages of 6 and 24 are for psychological conditions—attention deficit hyperactivity disorder (ADHD) and depression (Statistics Canada, 2015). It has been estimated that mental illness costs Canada at least $50 billion annually (Mental Health Commission, 2012) and will cost our economy more than $2.5 trillion over the next three decades. Of course, we are not alone in this situation. Japan, for example, has one of the highest suicide rates in the world—over double the rate in Canada (Fushimi, Sugawara, & Shimizu, 2005; Statistics Canada, 2010). Of course, beyond all of the statistics, views on etiology, and varieties of treatment, are the very human stories and the real suffering that result from psychological disorders.

One very notable story had its beginnings in the mid-1990s, and it has not yet been resolved for the people involved. By all accounts, Canadian Forces General Roméo Dallaire was at the apex of a long and distinguished career when he was given what all thought was a golden opportunity to put his considerable skills and experience to work for the good of others. As it turned out, however, he was being sent to do an impossible job—with inadequate resources and funding and virtually no support from his superiors.

Dallaire had been given the command of the United Nations Assistance Mission for Rwanda. Things were desperate in Rwanda at the time; genocide was being committed and in the end, approximately 800 000 Tutsis were slaughtered, many by machete, by their Hutu neighbours in Rwanda in just 100 days. As he has written in his book *Shake Hands with the Devil: The Failure of Humanity in Rwanda* (Dallaire, 2003), which was made into a feature film in 2007 and discussed in the award-winning documentary *Shake Hands with the Devil: The Journey of Roméo Dallaire,* Dallaire was restrained by the United Nations from intervening in the slaughter. In addition, he was unable to motivate anyone else in the international community to come to the Tutsis' aid. In fact, he believes he could have prevented the slaughter because of some advance information he had obtained. Dallaire had to stand by and do little but watch during the genocide.

The human toll included not only the murdered Tutsis and UN peacekeepers from Belgium, but also Dallaire himself. After his return to Canada, Dallaire

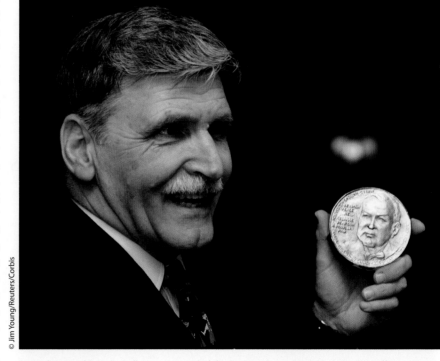

Retired General Roméo Dallaire was awarded the Pearson Peace Medal in 2005. He suffers from PTSD.

Courtesy of 11th Hour Films Inc., by permission of Don Copeman.

Percy Paul is a gifted mathematician, born in Saskatchewan. He has also suffered from bipolar disorder for several years. His condition has interfered with his personal life and his ability to solve some of the questions he has posed about the nature of the universe through his work on string theory.

began a descent into psychological disturbance and suicide attempts. The stress derived from what he saw, and his inability to do anything about it led to his diagnosis and treatment for post-traumatic stress disorder (PTSD). In 2013, Dallaire crashed his car on Parliament Hill. He explained that the accident resulted from a lack of sleep; he had been unable to sleep because he was still battling the memories of the Rwandan genocide nearly two decades later, and was troubled by the recent rash of suicides by Canadian veterans of the war in Afghanistan (Mas, 2013). Dallaire was appointed to the Canadian Senate in 2005 and retired in 2014.

Of course, you don't have to be a member of the military to suffer from a psychological disorder. Percy Paul was born in Patunack, a small Dene community in northern Saskatchewan. He started school early and very soon showed incredible promise in mathematics. He ended up studying at various universities, including Princeton. His real academic interest has been in the secrets of the universe (Chan, Paul, & Verlinde, 2000). Although his academic degrees are in math, his potential to make contributions to physics and the study of string theory has excited many academics in the field. String theory attempts to integrate Einstein's general theory of relativity and quantum mechanics in what might be the long-elusive, unified field theory, which many hope will end up to be the theory that explains everything in the universe (Greene, 1999, 2003). Paul was also recruited by the Canadian government to use his mathematical and computer skills to track down money laundering by terrorist groups.

Paul also suffers from bipolar disorder, in which his moods cycle from being very depressed and suicidal to the heights of mania. He finds the mania addictive, because when in this state, he has enormous energy and confidence in his ability and work. This disorder has disrupted both his personal and professional life, but Paul continues his studies in physics and on string theory at the University of Saskatchewan while battling the disorder's effects. Paul is profiled in the National Film Board's 2007 documentary *Flight from Darkness*. He is now a member of the world-famous Perimeter Institute for Theoretical Physics in Waterloo, Ontario (Perimeter Institute, 2017).

What is the basis for judging behaviour as normal versus abnormal? Are people who have psychological disorders dangerous? Are they violent? How common are such disorders? Can they be cured? Have mental disorders always been stigmatized? These are just a few of the questions that we will address in this chapter as we discuss psychological disorders and their complex causes.

Abnormal Behaviour: Myths, Realities, and Controversies

Key Learning Goals

▶ Evaluate the medical model of psychological disorders, and identify the key criteria of abnormality.

▶ Describe recent developments and issues related to the DSM-5 diagnostic system.

Misconceptions about abnormal behaviour are common, so we need to clear up some preliminary issues before we describe the various types of disorders. In this section, we will discuss (1) the medical model of abnormal behaviour, (2) the criteria of abnormal behaviour, (3) stereotypes regarding psychological disorders, (4) the classification of psychological disorders, and (5) how common such disorders are.

The Medical Model Applied to Abnormal Behaviour

The *medical model* proposes that it is useful to think of abnormal behaviour as a disease. This point of view is the basis for many of the terms used to refer to abnormal behaviour, including mental *illness*, psychological *disorder*, and psycho*pathology* (*pathology* refers to manifestations of disease). The medical model gradually became the dominant way of thinking about abnormal behaviour during the 18th and 19th centuries, and its influence remains strong today.

The medical model clearly represented progress over earlier models of abnormal behaviour. Prior to the 18th century, most conceptions of abnormal behaviour were based on superstition. People who behaved strangely were thought to be possessed by demons, to be witches in league with the devil, or to be victims of God's punishment. Their disorders were "treated" with chants, rituals, exorcisms, and such. If the people's behaviour was seen as threatening, they were candidates for chains, dungeons, torture, and death (see Figure 15.1).

The rise of the medical model brought improvements in the treatment of those who exhibited abnormal behaviour. As victims of an illness, they were viewed with more sympathy and less hatred and fear. Although living conditions in early asylums were typically deplorable, gradual progress was made toward more humane care of the mentally ill. It took time, but ineffectual approaches to treatment eventually gave way to scientific investigation of the causes and cures of psychological disorders.

In recent decades, some critics have suggested that the medical model may have outlived its usefulness (Deacon, 2013; Glasser, 2005; Rosemond, 2005). Some critics are troubled because medical diagnoses of abnormal behaviour pin potentially derogatory labels on people (Hinshaw, 2007). Being labelled as psychotic, schizophrenic, or mentally ill carries a social stigma that can be difficult to shake. Those characterized as mentally ill are viewed as erratic, dangerous, incompetent, and inferior (Corrigan & Larson, 2008). These stereotypes promote distancing, disdain, and rejection. This prejudice is a significant source of stress for people who suffer from mental illness (Rüsch et al., 2014). Perhaps even more important, the stigma associated with psychological disorders prevents many people from seeking the mental health care they need and could benefit from (Corrigan, Druss, & Perlick, 2014). Unfortunately, the stigma associated with psychological disorders appears to be deeply rooted. In recent decades, research has increasingly demonstrated that many psychological disorders are at least partly attributable to genetic and biological factors, making them appear more similar to physical illnesses, which carry far less stigma (Pescosolido, 2010). You would think that these trends would lead to a reduction in the stigma associated with mental illness, but research suggests that the stigmatization of mental disorders has remained stable or perhaps even increased (Hinshaw & Stier, 2008; Schnittker, 2008).

© Historical image collection by Bildagentur-online/Alamy Stock Photo

Figure 15.1
Historical conceptions of mental illness. In the Middle Ages, people who behaved strangely were sometimes thought to be in league with the devil. The top drawing depicts some of the cruel methods used to extract confessions from suspected witches and warlocks. Some psychological disorders were also thought to be caused by demonic possession. The bottom illustration depicts an exorcism.

Girolamo di Benvenuto, St. Catherine of Siena exorcising a possessed Woman, c. 1505. Denver art Museum Collection: Gift of the Samuel h. Kress Foundation, 1961.171. Photograph Courtesy Denver Art Museum.

Another line of criticism has been voiced by Thomas Szasz (1974, 1990). He asserts that "strictly speaking, disease or illness can affect only the body; hence there can be no mental illness. . . . Minds can be 'sick' only in the sense that jokes are 'sick' or economies are 'sick'" (1974, p. 267). He further argues that abnormal behaviour usually involves a deviation from social norms rather than an illness. He contends that such deviations are "problems in living" rather than medical problems. According to Szasz, the medical model's disease analogy converts moral and social questions about what is acceptable behaviour into medical questions.

The criticism of the medical model has some merit, and it is important to recognize the social roots

© David Lees/Corbis

Thomas Szasz

"Minds can be 'sick' only in the sense that jokes are 'sick' or economies are 'sick'."

and ramifications of the medical model. However, the bottom line is that the medical model continues to dominate thinking about psychological disorders. Medical concepts such as *diagnosis*, *etiology*, and *prognosis* have proven valuable in the treatment and study of abnormality. *Diagnosis* involves distinguishing one illness from another. *Etiology* refers to the apparent causation and developmental history of an illness. A *prognosis* is a forecast about the probable course of an illness. These medically based concepts have widely shared meanings that permit clinicians, researchers, and the public to communicate more effectively in their discussions about abnormal behaviour.

Criteria of Abnormal Behaviour

If your next-door neighbour scrubs his front porch twice every day and spends virtually all of his time cleaning and recleaning his house, is he normal? If your sister-in-law goes to one physician after another seeking treatment for ailments that appear to be imaginary, is she psychologically healthy? How are we to judge what's normal and what's abnormal? More important, who's to do the judging?

These are complex questions. In making diagnoses, clinicians rely on a variety of criteria, the foremost of which are the following:

1. *Deviance.* As Szasz has pointed out, people are often said to have a disorder because their behaviour deviates from what their society considers acceptable. What constitutes normality varies somewhat from one culture to another, but all cultures have such norms. When people violate these standards and expectations, they may be labelled mentally ill.

2. *Maladaptive behaviour.* In many cases, people are judged to have a psychological disorder because their everyday adaptive behaviour is impaired. This is the key criterion in the diagnosis of substance-use (drug) disorders. In and of itself, alcohol or drug use is not terribly unusual or deviant. However, when the use of cocaine, for instance, begins to interfere with a person's social or occupational functioning, a substance-use disorder exists. In such cases, it is the maladaptive quality of the behaviour that makes it disordered.

3. *Personal distress.* Frequently, the diagnosis of a psychological disorder is based on an individual's report of great personal distress. This is usually the criterion met by people who are troubled by depression or anxiety disorders. Depressed people, for instance, may or may not exhibit deviant or maladaptive behaviour. Such people are usually labelled as having a disorder when they describe their

This man clearly exhibits a certain type of deviance, but does that mean that he has a psychological disorder? The criteria of mental illness are more subjective and complicated than most people realize, and to some extent, judgments of mental health represent value judgments.

subjective pain and suffering to friends, relatives, and mental health professionals.

Although two or three criteria may apply in a particular case, people are often viewed as disordered when only one criterion is met. As you may have already noticed, diagnoses of psychological disorders involve *value judgments* about what represents normal or abnormal behaviour (Widiger & Sankis, 2000). The criteria of mental illness are not nearly as value-free as the criteria of physical illness. In evaluating physical diseases, people can usually agree that a malfunctioning heart or kidney is pathological, regardless of their personal values. However, judgments about mental illness reflect prevailing cultural values, social trends, and political forces, as well as scientific knowledge (Kutchins & Kirk, 1997; Mechanic, 1999).

Antonyms such as *normal* versus *abnormal* and *mental health* versus *mental illness* imply that people can be divided neatly into two distinct groups: those who are normal and those who are not. In reality, it is often difficult to draw a line that clearly separates normality from abnormality. On occasion, everybody acts in deviant ways, everyone displays some maladaptive behaviour, and everyone experiences personal distress. People are judged to have psychological disorders only when their behaviour becomes *extremely* deviant, maladaptive, or distressing. Thus, normality and abnormality exist on a continuum. It's a matter of degree, not an either–or proposition (see Figure 15.2).

Stereotypes of Psychological Disorders

We've seen that mental illnesses are not diseases in a strict sense and that judgments of mental health are not value-free. However, still other myths about abnormal behaviour need to be exposed as such. One important consideration is the negative effects that stigma can have on care seeking by those suffering from mental illness (Corrigan, Druss, & Perlick, 2014). Let's examine three stereotypes about psychological disorders that are largely inaccurate:

1. *Psychological disorders are incurable.* Admittedly, there are mentally ill people for whom treatment is largely a failure. However, they are greatly outnumbered by people who do get better, either spontaneously or through formal treatment (Lambert & Ogles, 2004). The vast majority of people who are diagnosed as mentally ill eventually improve and lead normal, productive lives. Even the most severe psychological disorders can be treated successfully.

2. *People with psychological disorders are often violent and dangerous.* Only a modest association has been found between mental illness and violence-prone tendencies (Monahan, 1997; Tardiff, 1999). This stereotype exists because incidents of violence involving the mentally ill tend to command media attention.

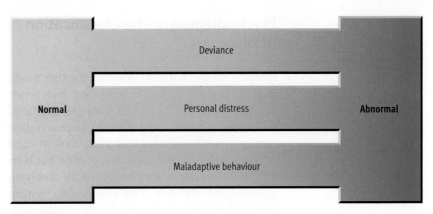

Figure 15.2
Normality and abnormality as a continuum. There isn't a sharp boundary between normal and abnormal behaviour. Behaviour is normal or abnormal in degree, depending on the extent to which one's behaviour is deviant, personally distressing, or maladaptive.

3. *People with psychological disorders behave in bizarre ways and are very different from normal people.* This is true only in a small minority of cases, usually involving relatively severe disorders. As noted earlier, the line between normal and abnormal behaviour can be difficult to draw. At first glance, people with psychological disorders usually are indistinguishable from those without disorders. A classic study by David Rosenhan (1973) showed that even mental health professionals may have difficulty distinguishing normality from abnormality. To study diagnostic accuracy, Rosenhan arranged for a number of normal people to seek admission to mental hospitals. These "pseudopatients" arrived at the hospitals complaining of one false symptom—hearing voices. Except for this single symptom, they acted as they normally would and gave accurate information when interviewed about their personal histories. *All* of the pseudopatients were admitted, and the average length of their hospitalization was 19 days!

David Rosenhan

"How many people, one wonders, are sane but not recognized as such in our psychiatric institutions?"

reality check

Misconception

People with psychological disorders are often violent and dangerous.

Reality

Only a modest association has been found between mental illness and violence-prone tendencies (Elbogen & Johnson, 2009; Freedman et al., 2007). This stereotype exists because incidents of violence involving the mentally ill tend to command media attention. However, the individuals involved in these incidents are not representative of the immense number of people who have struggled with psychological disorders.

reality check

Misconception

People with psychological disorders typically exhibit highly bizarre behaviour.

Reality

This is true only in a small minority of cases, usually involving relatively severe disorders. The vast majority of people with psychological disorders do not display strange behaviour. On the surface most are indistinguishable from those without disorders.

As you might imagine, Rosenhan's study evoked quite a controversy about our diagnostic system for mental illness. Let's take a look at how this diagnostic system has evolved.

Psychodiagnosis: The Classification of Disorders

Lumping all psychological disorders together would make it extremely difficult to understand them better. A sound taxonomy of mental disorders can facilitate empirical research and enhance communication among scientists and clinicians (First, 2008; Widiger & Crego, 2013). Thus, a great deal of effort has been invested in devising an elaborate system for classifying psychological disorders. This classification system, published by the American Psychiatric Association, is outlined in a book titled the *Diagnostic and Statistical Manual of Mental Disorders*. The fourth edition, titled DSM-IV, was used from 1994 until 2013, when the current fifth edition was released. The fifth edition is titled DSM-5 (instead of DSM-V) to facilitate incremental updates (such as DSM 5.1). The major diagnostic categories of disorder in the DSM-5 are listed in Figure 15.3. It is the product of more than a decade of research (Kupfer, Kuhl, & Regier, 2013). Clinical researchers collected extensive data; held numerous conferences; and engaged in heated debates about whether various syndromes should be added, eliminated, redefined, or renamed (Sachdev, 2013).

One major issue in the development of DSM-5 was whether to reduce the system's commitment to a *categorical* approach. In recent years, many critics of the DSM system have questioned the fundamental axiom that the diagnostic system is built on: the assumption that people can reliably be placed in discontinuous (nonoverlapping) diagnostic categories (Helzer et al., 2008). These critics note that there is enormous overlap among various disorders' symptoms, making the boundaries between diagnoses much fuzzier than would be ideal. Critics have also pointed out that people often qualify for more than one diagnosis (Lilienfeld & Landfield, 2008).

Because of problems such as these, some theorists argue that the traditional categorical approach to diagnosis should be replaced by a *dimensional approach*. A dimensional approach would describe disorders in terms of how people score on a limited number of continuous dimensions, such as the degree to which they exhibit anxiety, depression, agitation, anger, hypochondria, rumination, paranoia, and so forth (Kraemer, 2008; Widiger, Livesley, & Clark, 2009). The practical logistics of shifting to a dimensional approach to psychological disorders proved formidable and controversial (Blashfield et al., 2014). Experts would have had to agree about which dimensions to assess and how to measure them. Because of difficulties such as these, the authorities developing DSM-5 chose to retain primarily a categorical approach, although they supplemented the traditional system with dimensional approaches in some areas (Burke & Kraemer, 2014; Krueger & Markon, 2014).

Another area of concern related to the DSM has been its nearly exponential growth. The number of specific diagnoses in the DSM increased from 128 in the first edition to 541 in the current edition (Blashfield et al., 2014) (see Figure 15.4). Some of this growth was due to splitting existing disorders into narrower subtypes, but much of it was due to adding entirely new disorders. Some of the new disorders

1. Neurodevelopmental disorders
2. Schizophrenia spectrum and other psychotic disorders
3. Bipolar and related disorders
4. Depressive disorders
5. Anxiety disorders
6. Obsessive-compulsive and related disorders
7. Trauma- and stressor-related disorders
8. Dissociative disorders
9. Somatic symptom and related disorders
10. Feeding and eating disorders
11. Elimination disorders
12. Sleep-wake disorders
13. Sexual dysfunctions
14. Gender dysphoria
15. Disruptive, impulse-control, and conduct disorders
16. Substance-related and addictive disorders
17. Neurocognitive disorders
18. Personality disorders
19. Paraphilic disorders
20. Other mental disorders
21. Medication-induced movement disorders and other adverse effects of medication
22. Other conditions that may be the focus of clinical attention

Figure 15.3
Overview of the DSM-5 diagnostic classes. In this figure, we list the major categories of disorder listed in the DSM-5. Published by the American Psychiatric Association, the *Diagnostic and Statistical Manual of Mental Disorders* is the formal classification system used in the diagnosis of psychological disorders. (Based on American Psychiatric Association, DSM-5, 2013)

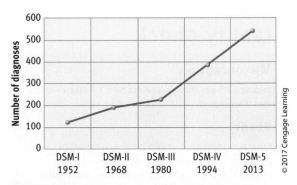

© 2017 Cengage Learning

Figure 15.4
Growth of the DSM diagnostic system. Published by the American Psychiatric Association, the *Diagnostic and Statistical Manual of Mental Disorders* has grown dramatically with each new edition. The number of specific diagnoses has more than quadrupled since the first edition was released. (Based on Blashfield et al., 2014)

encompass behavioural patterns that used to be regarded as mundane, everyday adjustment problems, rather than mental disorders. For example, DSM-5 includes diagnoses for caffeine intoxication (getting really buzzed from coffee), tobacco use disorder (inability to control smoking), disruptive mood dysregulation disorder (problems with recurrent temper tantrums in youngsters), binge-eating disorder (gluttonous overeating more than once a week for at least three months), and gambling disorder (inability to control gambling). Some of these syndromes can be serious problems for which people might want to seek treatment, but should they merit a formal designation as a mental illness? Some critics of the DSM argue that this approach "medicalizes" everyday problems and casts the stigma of pathology on normal self-control issues (Frances, 2013; Kirk et al., 2013). Critics also worry that turning everyday problems into mental disorders could trivialize the concept of mental illness.

Next, we briefly discuss two of the major diagnostic systems that serve as alternatives to the DSM. After reviewing these alternative systems, we will review some of the evidence regarding the prevalence of different disorders. Then we will be ready to start examining the specific types of psychological disorders. Obviously, in this chapter, we cannot cover all of the hundreds of specific diagnoses listed in DSM-5. However, we will introduce most of the major categories of disorders to give you an overview of the many forms abnormal behaviour takes. In discussing each set of disorders, we will begin with brief descriptions of the specific subtypes that fall in the category. If data are available, we will discuss the prevalence of the disorders in that category (i.e., how common the disorders are in the population). Then we will focus on the *etiology* of that set of disorders.

Alternative Diagnostic Systems

The DSM is not the only diagnostic system available for use in classifying mental illness. It is, however, the system that is most widely employed, especially in North America. Because of its significance, impact, and worldwide adoption, we will focus almost exclusively on its system of categorization. However, it is instructive to mention some of the major alternative systems, especially in light of the controversy the new edition of the DSM has engendered.

One major alternative to the DSM was developed by the World Health Organization (WHO), which is an agency of the United Nations. In fact,

the WHO developed one of the first significant classifications systems. Particularly significant was the 1969 WHO classification system that had a major impact on the development of the DSM. The most recent WHO system is the ICD-10 (WHO, 1992), or the *International Classification of Disease and Health Related Problems* (10th edition). Experts from all over the world participated in the development of the ICD-10 (including Canadians such as Dr Z. Lipowski from Toronto), with hospitals and universities in Montreal, London, and Edmonton serving as field trial reporting centres. You are more likely to encounter the ICD-10 in Europe than in North America. The 11th edition of the ICD is currently in development (Reigier, Kuhl, & Kupfer, 2013) and is scheduled to be released in 2018 (WHO, 2014).

In addition to the WHO, the National Institute of Mental Health (NIMH) in the United States has been working on the development of its own system of classification (Insel & Liegerman, 2013), the *Research Domain Criteria Project* (RDoC). According to the NIMH, this system is being developed primarily for research purposes and the system is to be based on *dimensions of observable behaviour and neurobiological* measures. In part, the intent is to base this system more directly on research findings and directions, applying what we know about basic psychological and neuropsychological processes to a consideration of psychopathology. According to NIMH, the "effort is to define basic dimensions of functioning (e.g., fear circuitry or working memory) to be studied across multiple units of analysis, from genes to neural circuits to behaviours, cutting across disorders as traditionally defined" (NIMH, n.d.). The project was initiated in 2009 and is still in its developmental stages. This system, once fully developed, should inform future research directions, affect research funding, and ultimately provide direction for future revisions of the DSM. The next few years may produce significant changes in the ways in which we classify and understand psychological disorders. For now, however, the dominant classification system is the DSM-5.

The Prevalence of Psychological Disorders

How common are psychological disorders? What percentage of the population is afflicted with mental illness? Is it 10 percent? Perhaps 25 percent? Could the figure range as high as 40 percent or 50 percent?

Such estimates fall in the domain of *epidemiology*—the study of the distribution of mental

Psychological Disorders

or physical disorders in a population. The 1980s and 1990s brought major advances in psychiatric epidemiology, as a host of large-scale investigations provided a huge, new database on the distribution of mental disorders (Wang et al., 2008). In epidemiology, *prevalence* **refers to the percentage of a population that exhibits a disorder during a specified time period.** In the case of mental disorders, the most interesting data are the estimates of *lifetime prevalence*, the percentage of people who endure a specific disorder at any time in their lives.

Studies published in the 1980s and early 1990s found psychological disorders in roughly *one-third* of the population (Regier & Kaelber, 1995; Robins, Locke, & Regier, 1991). Subsequent research suggested that about 44 percent of the adult population

will struggle with some sort of psychological disorder at some point in their lives (Kessler & Zhao, 1999; Regier & Burke, 2000). The most recent large-scale epidemiological study estimated the lifetime risk of a psychiatric disorder to be 51 percent (Kessler et al., 2005). Obviously, all these figures are *estimates* that depend to some extent on the sampling methods and assessment techniques used (Wakefield, 1999). The progressively higher estimates in recent years have begun to generate some controversy in the field. Some experts believe that recent estimates are implausibly high and that they may trivialize psychiatric diagnoses (Wakefield & Spitzer, 2002). The debate centres on where to draw the line between normal difficulties in functioning and full-fledged mental illness—that is, when symptoms qualify as a disease (Regier, Narrow, & Rae, 2004).

In any event, whether one goes with conservative or liberal estimates, the prevalence of psychological disorders is quite a bit higher than most people assume. Across all of North America, the most common types of psychological disorders are (1) substance (alcohol and drugs) use disorders, (2) anxiety disorders, and (3) depression.

Data from Statistics Canada (2015) gives us a snapshot of the prevalence and costs of psychological disorders in Canada. The data collected as part of a comprehensive survey of mental health and illness in Canada represents one of the best views that we have of mental health in Canada. Figure 15.5 presents the reported rates of selected disorders in Canada (Statistics Canada, 2015).

Overall, one in ten Canadians over 15 years of age reported symptoms consistent with one of the categories of disorder in the past year. One in three Canadians (about 9.1 million people) met the criteria at some point in their life. Approximately one-fifth (21.6 percent) of those surveyed met the diagnostic criteria for substance use disorder in their lifetime, and 12.6 percent (about 3.5 million people) met the diagnostic criteria for a mood disorder, with major depressive disorder being the most common. By the time Canadians reach 40 years of age, one half will have or have had a mental illness (CAMH, 2017). Most (68 percent) of the people who reported symptoms consistent with one of these disorders *did not* seek assistance.

More recent, smaller-scale studies confirm many of these findings. For example, in one study, several specific disorders were assessed, including major depression, bipolar disorder, generalized anxiety disorder, and abuse of or dependence on alcohol or cannabis and other drugs (Statistics Canada, 2013). The study revealed that over 10 percent of Canadians aged 15 and older reported symptoms

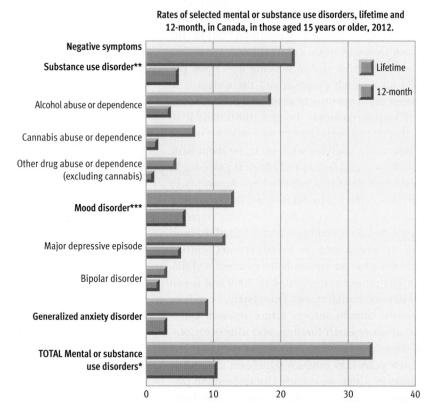

Rates of selected mental or substance use disorders, lifetime and 12-month, in Canada, in those aged 15 years or older, 2012.

* Mental or substance use disorders are comprised of: substance use disorders, mood disorders, and generalized anxiety disorder. However, these three disorders cannot be added to create this rate because these three categories are not mutually exclusive, meaning that people may have a profile consistent with one or more of these disorders.

** Substance use disorder includes alcohol abuse or dependence, cannabis abuse or dependence and other drug abuse or dependence.

*** Mood disorder includes depression (major depressive episode) and bipolar disorder.

Figure 15.5

Reported prevalence of psychological disorders in Canada. This figure presents the estimated percentage of people who have suffered from one of the selected sets of psychological disorders in the year preceding the survey and over the course of their lifetime. The estimates represent people surveyed with symptoms consistent with each type of disorder. The survey targeted Canadians 15 years and older.

Source: Caryn Pearson, Teresa Janz and Jennifer Ali, 2013. "Mental and substance use disorders in Canada," *Health at a Glance. September.* Ottawa: Statistics Canada, http://www.statcan.gc.ca/pub/82-624-x/2013001/article/11855-eng.htm.

over the past year consistent with one of the specific disorders, including mood disorders/depression (5.4 percent), generalized anxiety disorder (2.6 percent), alcohol abuse/dependence (1.3 percent), and cannabis abuse/dependence (1.3 percent). Seventeen percent of Canadians reported that they had the need for mental health care, with 33 percent of these reporting that their needs were either not met or only partially met.

In this chapter, we cannot discuss in detail all of the disorders listed in the DSM-5. Some of the disorders we have discussed in previous chapters (e.g., see Chapter 5 for a discussion of substance abuse). However, we will introduce you to many of the major categories of disorder to give you an overview of the many forms that psychological disorders can take.

In discussing each set of disorders, we will begin with brief descriptions of the specific syndromes or subtypes that fall into a category. Then we'll focus on the *etiology* of the disorders in that category. Although many paths can lead to specific disorders, some are more common than others. We'll highlight some of the common paths to enhance your understanding of the roots of abnormal behaviour.

Anxiety, Obsessive-Compulsive, and Post-Traumatic Stress Disorders

In the DSM-IV-TR anxiety, obsessive-compulsive disorders, and post-traumatic stress disorders were considered together, with the latter two constituting two subtypes of anxiety disorders. In the reorganized classification produced by the DSM-5, anxiety disorders, obsessive-compulsive disorders, and post-traumatic stress disorders are now separated into distinct categories (see Figure 15.3 on page 558). Accordingly, they are discussed separately in this section.

Anxiety Disorders

Anxiety disorders are a class of disorders marked by feelings of excessive apprehension and anxiety. The anxiety disorders include generalized anxiety disorder, specific phobias, panic disorder, agoraphobia, selective mutism, social anxiety disorder, and separation anxiety disorder.

Everyone experiences anxiety from time to time. It is a natural and common reaction to many of life's difficulties. For some people, however, anxiety becomes a chronic problem. These people experience high levels of anxiety with disturbing regularity. We will look at four principal types of anxiety disorders: generalized anxiety disorder, specific phobia, panic disorder, and agoraphobia. These disorders are not mutually exclusive, as many people who develop one anxiety syndrome often suffer from another at some point in their lives (Merikangas & Kalaydjian, 2009). Studies suggest that anxiety disorders are quite common. They occur in roughly 19 percent of the population (Dew, Bromet, & Switzer, 2000; Regier & Burke, 2000).

Generalized Anxiety Disorder

A *generalized anxiety disorder* is marked by a chronic, high level of anxiety that is not tied to any specific threat. This anxiety is sometimes called *free-floating anxiety* because it is nonspecific. People with this disorder worry constantly about yesterday's mistakes and tomorrow's problems (Newman et al., 2013). In particular, they worry about minor matters related to family, finances, work, and personal illness (Sanderson & Barlow, 1990). They hope that their worrying will help to ward off negative events (Beidel & Stipelman, 2007), but they nonetheless worry about how much they worry (Barlow et al., 2003). They often dread decisions and brood over them endlessly. Their anxiety is commonly accompanied by physical symptoms such as trembling, muscle tension, diarrhea, dizziness, faintness, sweating, and heart palpitations. Generalized anxiety disorder tends to have a gradual onset and is seen more frequently in females than males (Rowa & Antony, 2008).

Specific Phobias

In a specific phobic disorder, an individual's troublesome anxiety has a precise focus. A *specific phobia* involves a persistent and irrational fear of an object or situation that presents no realistic danger. The following case provides an example of a specific phobia:

> Hilda is 32 years of age and has a rather unusual fear. She is terrified of snow. She cannot go outside in the snow. She cannot even stand to see snow or hear about it on the weather report. Her phobia

severely constricts her day-to-day behaviour. Probing in therapy revealed that her phobia was caused by a traumatic experience at age 11. Playing at a ski lodge, she was buried briefly by a small avalanche of snow. She had no recollection of this experience until it was recovered in therapy. (Adapted from Laughlin, 1967, p. 227)

As Hilda's unusual snow phobia illustrates, people can develop phobic responses to virtually anything. For example, work by Cole and Wilkins (2013) has focused on *trypophobia*. People who suffer from trypophobia show an aversion to images of holes (Pipitone, Gallegos, & Walters, 2017). They have fear of visual stimuli that consists of configurations of holes that others would see as being innocuous. These stimuli include such things as soap bubbles, aerated chocolate, or a blue ringed octopus (pictured here). Cole and Wilkins (2013) suggest that its origins lie in part in the visual similarity of the configurations of holes to dangerous, often poisonous organisms.

While some phobias are rare, other types of phobias are relatively common, including acrophobia (fear of heights), claustrophobia (fear of small, enclosed places), brontophobia (fear of storms), hydrophobia (fear of water), and various animal and insect phobias (McCabe & Antony, 2008; see Figure 15.6). People troubled by phobias typically realize that their fears are irrational, but still are unable to calm themselves when confronted by a phobic object. Phobic fears appear to be quite common, as the lifetime prevalence of specific phobias is estimated to be around 10 percent; two-thirds of the victims are females (Sadock, Sadock, & Ruiz, 2015).

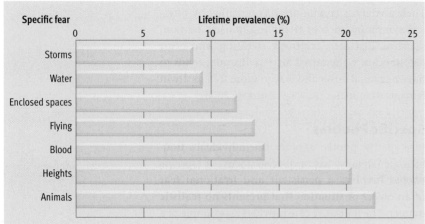

People who suffer from trypophobia may experience an aversive reaction when looking at a cluster of soap bubbles; the holes may elicit feelings of fear and uneasiness because such images share visual features with dangerous organisms.

© iStockphoto.com/MikaelEriksson

Panic Disorder

A *panic disorder* is characterized by recurrent attacks of overwhelming anxiety that usually occur suddenly and unexpectedly. These paralyzing attacks are accompanied by physical symptoms of anxiety and are sometimes misinterpreted as heart attacks. After a number of anxiety attacks, victims often become apprehensive and hypervigilant, wondering when their next panic attack will occur. About two-thirds of people who are diagnosed with panic disorder are female, and the onset of the disorder typically occurs during late adolescence or early adulthood (Schneier et al., 2014).

Agoraphobia

People with panic disorder often become increasingly concerned about exhibiting panic in public, to the point where they are afraid to leave home. This fear creates a condition called *agoraphobia*, **which is a fear of going out to public places** (its literal meaning is "fear of the marketplace or open places"). Because of this fear, some people become prisoners confined to their homes, although many will venture out if accompanied by a trusted companion (Hollander & Simeon, 2008). As its name suggests, agoraphobia was originally viewed as a phobic disorder. However, in DSM-III and DSM-IV, it was characterized as a common complication of panic disorder. In DSM-5, it is listed as a separate anxiety disorder that may or may not co-exist with panic disorder; as it turns out, it can co-exist with a variety of disorders (Asmundson, Taylor, & Smits, 2014). Like other disorders, agoraphobia can vary in severity, but it can be a very disabling condition.

Obsessive-Compulsive Disorder

In previous editions of the DSM, obsessive-compulsive disorder was considered to be a type of anxiety disorder. In the DSM-5, a new class of disorders was added, *obsessive-compulsive and related disorders*. This class of disorders includes such conditions as *body dysmporhic disorder*, in which an individual has a unrelenting preoccupation with what he or she perceives to be a physical flaw; *excoriation*, or skin-picking disorder; and *hoarding disorder*. According to the DSM-5 (APA, 2013), the disorders in this class are linked by an excessive preoccupation and/or repetitive behaviours. In this section we

Specific fear | **Lifetime prevalence (%)**

© 2017 Cengage Learning

Figure 15.6

Common phobic fears. This graph shows the lifetime prevalence of the most common types of phobic fears reported by participants in a study by Curtis et al. (1998). As you can see, a substantial number of people struggle with a variety of specific phobias. Bear in mind that only a portion of these people qualify for a diagnosis of phobic disorder, which is merited only if individuals' phobias seriously impair their everyday functioning.

briefly discuss obsessive-compulsive and hoarding disorders.

Obsessions are *thoughts* that repeatedly intrude on one's consciousness in a distressing way. Compulsions are *actions* that one feels forced to carry out. Thus, an *obsessive-compulsive disorder (OCD)* is marked by persistent, uncontrollable intrusions of unwanted thoughts (obsessions) and urges to engage in senseless rituals (compulsions). Canadian comedian and TV personality Howie Mandel suffers from OCD (Mandel, 2009). A veteran of TV, movies, and stand-up comedy, Mandel hosted a popular TV game show, *Deal or No Deal,* and when he greeted new contestants, rather than shaking hands, he would use a "knuckle bump" in which he would merely touch knuckles with them. It was his way of dealing with one of his obsessions, contamination and germs (mysophobia). While Mandel admits that he has had to shake hands once in a while, he wants to avoid what sometimes follows a handshaking episode. According to Mandel, "I have shaken hands and had a good evening, but I just don't want to trigger whatever I trigger. I would be in the bathroom for hours, and I'll scald [my hands] and I'll come out and then I can't think of anything else. I'll keep thinking I've got something to get off of my hands" (Hampson, 2007, p. R3). As Mandel explains it in his 2009 autobiography, *Here's the Deal: Don't Touch Me,* "it's not just that I'm scared of germs," he says. There's nothing wrong with shaking hands with someone and then washing your hands. But "there *is* something wrong with being totally consumed that you didn't get everything off your hand, that there's things crawling, so you wash it again, and you're so consumed that you wash it again, and you wash it again and you wash it again and you wash it again," Mandel says. "When you can't get past that, that's obsessive-compulsive disorder. It's not that you're afraid of germs, it's that you obsess about that thought and have to do things like hand washing to relieve the worry. I always have intrusive thoughts and rituals."

Mandel's obsession with germs is also the reason why he has shaved his head, he says. "For my germ phobia, it kind of helps me. It feels cleaner. . . ." (Mandel Uses Knuckle Knock, 2006). When he enters a hotel room, he typically orders 26 clean towels so that he can lay a path across the room to walk on. He also constructed a special *sterile house* on his property, a place where he can escape and be alone when he feels the need (Packer, 2007). He carries rubber gloves with him for times when he must touch things that cause him problems. Mandel is very forthcoming about his OCD and hopes that by publicizing his own issues, he will make it easier for others

Frederick M. Brown/Stringer/Getty Images

Well-known Canadian comedian and TV personality Howie Mandel is very public about his OCD. He is a spokesperson for the Anxiety Disorders Association of America's "Treat it, don't repeat it: Break free from OCD" ad campaign, which is designed to raise awareness about the nature and treatment of various anxiety disorders. Visit the association's website at http://www.adaa.org to learn more about OCD.

who suffer from similar concerns. It is interesting to see how he has made accommodations to his obsessions that allow him to continue successfully in his profession.

Obsessions sometimes centre on inflicting harm on others, personal failures, suicide, or sexual acts. People troubled by obsessions may feel that they have lost control of their mind and they may be plagued by uncertainty (Taffolo et al., 2013). Compulsions usually involve stereotyped rituals that temporarily relieve anxiety. Common examples include constant hand-washing, repetitive cleaning of things that are already clean, and endless rechecking of locks, faucets, and such (Pato, Eisen, & Phillips, 2003). Specific types of obsessions tend to be associated with specific types of compulsions. For example, obsessions about contamination tend to be paired with cleaning compulsions and obsessions about symmetry tend to be paired with ordering and arranging compulsions (Hollander & Simeon, 2008).

Many of us can be compulsive at times. Indeed, in samples of people without a mental disorder, many individuals report significant obsessions or compulsions (Clark et al., 2014). However, full-fledged obsessive-compulsive disorders occur in roughly 2–3 percent of the population (Zohar, Fostick, & Juven-Wetzler, 2009). OCD can be a particularly severe disorder and is often associated with serious social and occupational impairments (Dougherty, Wilhelm, & Jenike, 2014). OCD is unusual among anxiety-related problems in that it is seen in males and females in roughly equal numbers (Gallo et al., 2013).

While OCD is often seen as a unitary disorder, research by Laura Summerfeldt of Trent University, Ryerson University's Martin Antony, and their colleagues suggests that it may be a heterogeneous disorder (Antony, Purdon, & Summerfeldt, 2006; Summerfeldt, 2004; Summerfeldt et al., 1999). They factor-analyzed the symptom structure of 203 Canadians diagnosed with OCD and found that four factors seemed to underlie the symptoms: obsessions and checking, symmetry and order, cleanliness and washing, and hoarding. They conclude that "Our findings add to the growing body of evidence for the multidimensionality of OCD, but suggest that a comprehensive model of symptom structure has yet to be identified" (Summerfeldt et al., 1999, p. 309).

In the DSM-5 there are several new classes of disorders. Hoarding disorder is one of the new disorders introduced in this edition. The diagnostic criteria for this new disorder are presented in Table 15.1.

Individuals suffering from hoarding disorder, among other things, have difficulty discarding possessions no matter how worthless they are, tend to hang on to items to avoid the distress that throwing

Sheila Woody is a clinical psychologist in the Department of Psychology at the University of British Columbia. Her interests include compulsive hoarding, the treatment of obsessive-compulsive disorder, and culture and social anxiety.

Table 15.1

DSM-5 Diagnostic Criteria for Hoarding Disorder

A.	Persistent difficulty discarding or parting with possessions, regardless of their actual value.
B.	This difficulty is due to a perceived need to save the items and to distress associated with discarding them.
C.	The difficulty discarding possessions results in the accumulation of possessions that congest and clutter active living areas and substantially compromises their intended use. If living areas are uncluttered, it is only because of the interventions of third parties (i.e., family members, cleaners, authorities).
D.	The hoarding causes clinically significant distress or impairment in social, occupational, or other important areas of functioning (including maintaining a safe environment for self and others).
E.	The hoarding is not attributable to another medical condition (e.g., brain injury, cerebrovascular disease, Prader-Willi syndrome).
F.	The hoarding is not better explained by the symptoms of another mental disorder (e.g., obsessions in obsessive-compulsive disorder, decreased energy in major depressive disorder, delusions in schizophrenia or another psychotic disorder, cognitive deficits in major neurocognitive disorder, restricted interests in autism spectrum disorder).

Source: Reprinted with permission from the *Diagnostic and statistical manual of mental disorders,* Fifth Edition, (Copyright © 2013). American Psychiatric Association. All Rights Reserved.

Hoarding disorder is a new category of disorder added to the DSM-5. People who suffer from this disorder never throw anything away, convinced in most cases that they just might "need it later."

them away would engender, and hoard to the extent that their possessions disrupt normal living arrangements and interfere with their social and occupational activities (APA, 2013; Frost & Rasmussen, 2012; Frost, Steketee, & Tolin, 2012; Mataix-Cols et al., 2010; Pertusa et al., 2010). While we all tend to acquire things over the years that we get attached to and that have sentimental value that makes it hard to give or throw them away, people who suffer from hoarding disorder cannot discard such items. They collect and acquire things over the years and keep it all! Hoarding behaviour tends to increase with age, and the hoarder's family is often complicit in the disorder, by enabling the hoarding. According to Martin Antony, "It's referred to as accommodation—the tendency for family members to do things that ultimately make it easier for hoarders to continue hoarding" (Yelaja, 2012). Given its status as a disorder on its own in the newest edition of the DSM, there will likely be increasing research on its causes and treatment. Research and treatment initiatives such as that developed by Sheila Woody (Hsu, Woody, et al., 2012; Whittal, Woody, et al., 2010; Woody & Steketee, 2014), who heads the Hoarding Hub at the Centre for Collaborative Research on Hoarding at the University of British

Columbia, are attempting to better understand the etiology of compulsive hoarding and how best to treat it.

Post-Traumatic Stress Disorder (PTSD)

Post-traumatic stress disorder (PTSD) is part of a new class of disorders in the DSM-5, the *trauma- and stressor-related disorders*. All of these disorders are seen to follow an individual's exposure to some type of chronic or acute stressor. This class of disorder includes *reactive attachment disorder, disinhibited social engagement disorder, PTSD, acute stress disorder,* and *adjustment disorders.* In this section we focus on PTSD.

Although we began this chapter with a discussion of PTSD suffered by members of the military (Finkel, 2009; 2013; Kukutani, 2013; MacWhirter, 2013), PTSD is not restricted to this context. PTSD is often elicited by any of a variety of traumatic events (Riozoi & Harnell, 2013), including a rape or assault, a severe automobile accident, a natural disaster, or the witnessing of someone's death (Charuvastra & Cloitre, 2008; Koren, Arnon, & Klein, 1999; Neria, DiGrande, & Adams, 2011; Stein et al., 1997; Vernberg et al., 1996). In some instances, PTSD does not surface until many months or years after a person's exposure to severe stress (Holen, 2000) and is tied to memory for the events (Rubin, Bernsten, & Bohni, 2008; Rubin, Boals, & Berntsen, 2008). In 2005, the residents of New Orleans suffered one of the most devastating natural disasters the United States had ever experienced: Hurricane Katrina. Thousands of deaths and billions of dollars in property damage resulted from this hurricane. Mental health professionals were brought in to help with the effects of the disaster. They found that by seven months after the hurricane, almost one-half of the residents of New Orleans were estimated to be suffering from various mood and anxiety disorders, including a staggering 30 percent who were suffering from PTSD (Galea et al., 2007). It is difficult for the rest of us to imagine the continuing personal and economic cost of such a disaster.

Unfortunately, traumatic experiences appear to be much more common than widely assumed. Research suggests that 7–8 percent of people have suffered from PTSD at some point in their lives, with prevalence being higher among women (10 percent) than men (5 percent) (Flood, Davidson, & Beckham, 2008; Resick, Monson, & Rizvi, 2008). Currently, there is great concern about the number of military members returning from wars overseas who will develop PTSD (DeAngelis, 2008; Ramchand et al., 2010; Sundin et al., 2010). Common symptoms of PTSD include re-experiencing the traumatic event in the form of nightmares and flashbacks, emotional numbing, alienation, problems in social relationships, an increased sense of vulnerability, and elevated levels of arousal, anxiety, anger, and guilt (McClure-Tone & Pine, 2009).

Research suggests that a variety of factors are predictors of individuals' risk for PTSD (Keane, Marshall, & Taft, 2006; McNally, 2009; Norris et al., 2001). As you might expect, increased vulnerability is associated with greater personal injuries and losses, greater intensity of exposure to the traumatic event, and more exposure to the grotesque aftermath of the event. Often overlooked are the reactions of children to such disasters, including mental health concerns (Becker-Blease, Turner, & Finkelhor, 2010). In general, one key predictor of vulnerability that emerged in a recent review of the relevant research is the *intensity of one's reaction at the time of the traumatic event* (Ozer et al., 2003). Individuals who have especially intense emotional reactions during or immediately after the traumatic event go on to show elevated vulnerability to PTSD. Vulnerability seems to be greatest among people whose reactions are so intense that they report dissociative experiences (a sense that things are not real, that time is stretching out, that one is watching oneself in a movie).

The frequency and severity of post-traumatic symptoms usually decline gradually over time, but recovery tends to be gradual and in many cases, the symptoms never completely disappear. Many years after his experiences in Rwanda, General Roméo

THE CANADIAN PRESS/Ryan Remiorz

Natural disasters, such as the flooding shown here from Deux-Montagnes, Quebec, in 2017, result in enormous economic and personal devastation. The impact is both physical and psychological, and increased levels of PTSD are commonly found among the survivors.

Dallaire is still suffering the aftereffects of what he saw and heard about during his time in Rwanda.

Etiology of Anxiety and Anxiety-Related Disorders

Like most psychological disorders, anxiety disorders develop out of complicated interactions among a variety of biological and psychological factors.

Biological Factors

In studies that assess the impact of heredity on psychological disorders, investigators look at *concordance rates*. A *concordance rate* indicates the percentage of twin pairs or other pairs of relatives who exhibit the same disorder. If relatives who share more genetic similarity show higher concordance rates than relatives who share less genetic overlap, this finding supports the genetic hypothesis. The results of both *twin studies* (see Figure 15.7) and *family studies* (see Chapter 3 for discussions of both methods) suggest a moderate genetic predisposition to anxiety disorders (Fyer, 2009).

Recent evidence suggests that a link may exist between anxiety disorders and neurochemical activity in the brain. As you learned in Chapter 3, *neurotransmitters* are chemicals that carry signals from one neuron to another. Therapeutic drugs (such as Valium or Xanax) that reduce excessive anxiety appear to alter neurotransmitter activity at synapses that release a neurotransmitter called *GABA*. This finding and other lines of evidence suggest that disturbances in the neural circuits using GABA may play a role in some types of anxiety disorders (Rowa & Antony, 2008). Abnormalities in neural circuits using serotonin have been implicated in obsessive-compulsive disorders (Sadock et al., 2015).

Conditioning and Learning

Many anxiety responses may be *acquired through classical conditioning and maintained through operant conditioning* (see Chapter 6). Imagine, for example, a young child who is buried briefly in the snow by a small avalanche, and who now, as an adult, is afraid of snow. According to Mowrer (1947), an originally neutral stimulus (the snow) may be paired with a frightening event (the avalanche) so that it becomes a conditioned stimulus eliciting anxiety (see Figure 15.8(a)).

Once a fear is acquired through classical conditioning, the person may start avoiding the anxiety-producing stimulus. The avoidance response is negatively reinforced because it is followed by a reduction in anxiety. This process involves operant conditioning (see Figure 15.8(b)). Thus, separate conditioning processes may create and then sustain specific anxiety responses (Levis, 1989). Consistent with this view, studies find that a substantial portion of people suffering from phobias can identify a traumatic conditioning experience that probably contributed to their anxiety disorder (McCabe & Antony, 2008; Mineka & Zinbarg, 2006).

The tendency to develop phobias of certain types of objects and situations may be explained by Martin Seligman's (1971) concept of *preparedness*. He suggests that people are biologically prepared by their evolutionary history to acquire some fears much more easily than others. His theory would explain

(a) Classical conditioning: Acquisition of phobic fear

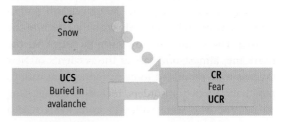

(b) Operant conditioning: Maintenance of phobic fear (negative reinforcement)

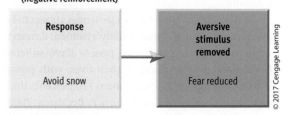

Figure 15.8
Conditioning as an explanation for phobias. (a) Many phobias appear to be acquired through classical conditioning when a neutral stimulus is paired with an anxiety-arousing stimulus. (b) Once acquired, a phobia may be maintained through operant conditioning. Avoidance of the phobic stimulus reduces anxiety, resulting in negative reinforcement.

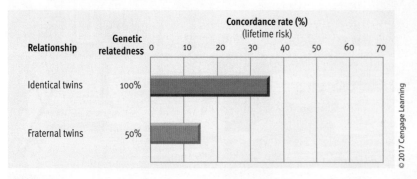

Figure 15.7
Twin studies of anxiety disorders. The concordance rate for anxiety disorders in identical twins is higher than that for fraternal twins, who share less genetic overlap. These results suggest that there is a genetic predisposition to anxiety disorders. (Data based on Noyes et al., 1987; Slater & Shields, 1969; Torgersen, 1979, 1983)

why people develop phobias of ancient sources of threat (e.g., snakes and spiders) much more readily than modern sources of threat (e.g., electrical outlets or hot irons). As we noted in Chapter 6, Arne Öhman and Susan Mineka (2001) have updated the notion of preparedness, which they call an *evolved module for fear learning*. They maintain that this evolved module is automatically activated by stimuli related to survival threats in evolutionary history and relatively resistant to intentional efforts to suppress the resulting fears. Consistent with this view, phobic stimuli associated with evolutionary threats tend to produce more rapid conditioning of fears and stronger fear responses (Mineka & Öhman, 2002).

Critics note a number of problems with conditioning models of phobias (Rachman, 1990). For instance, many people with phobias cannot recall or identify a traumatic conditioning experience that led to their phobia. Conversely, many people endure extremely traumatic experiences that should create a phobia but do not (Coelho & Purkis, 2009). Moreover, phobic fears can be acquired indirectly, by observing another's fear response to a specific stimulus or by absorbing fear-inducing information (imagine a parent harping on how dangerous lightning is) (Coelho & Purkis, 2009). Thus, the development of phobias may depend on synergistic interactions among a variety of learning processes.

Cognitive Factors

Cognitive theorists maintain that certain styles of thinking make some people particularly vulnerable to anxiety disorders (Craske & Waters, 2005). According to these theorists, some people are more likely to suffer from problems with anxiety because they tend to (a) misinterpret harmless situations as threatening, (b) focus excessive attention on perceived threats, and (c) selectively recall information that seems threatening (Beck, 1997; Beck & Haigh, 2014; Garner, Mogg, & Bradley, 2006; Hirsh, Mar, & Peterson, 2011; McNally, 1994, 1996). In one intriguing test of the cognitive view, anxious and nonanxious subjects were asked to read 32 sentences that could be interpreted in either a threatening or a nonthreatening manner (Eysenck et al., 1991). For instance, one such sentence was "The doctor examined little Emma's growth," which could mean that the doctor checked either her height or the growth of a tumour. As Figure 15.9 shows, the anxious participants interpreted the sentences in a threatening way more often than the nonanxious participants did. Thus, consistent with our theme that human experience is highly subjective, the cognitive view

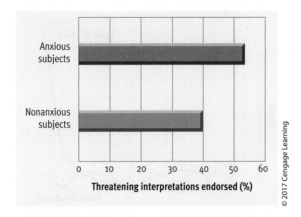

Figure 15.9
Cognitive factors in anxiety disorders. Eysenck and his colleagues (1991) compared how subjects with anxiety problems and nonanxious subjects tended to interpret sentences that could be viewed as threatening or nonthreatening. Consistent with cognitive models of anxiety disorders, anxious subjects were more likely to interpret the sentences in a threatening light.

holds that some people are prone to anxiety disorders because they see threat in every corner of their lives (Aikins & Craske, 2001; Riskind, 2005; Williams et al., 1997).

Stress

Obviously, cases of post-traumatic stress disorder are attributed to individuals' exposure to extremely stressful incidents. Research has also demonstrated that other types of anxiety disorders can be stress related (Beidel & Stipelman, 2007). For instance, Faravelli and Pallanti (1989) found that patients with panic disorder had experienced a dramatic increase in stress in the month prior to the onset of their disorder (see Figure 15.10). Other studies found that stress levels are predictive of the severity of OCD patients' symptoms (Lin et al., 2007; Morgado et al., 2013). Thus, there is reason to believe that high stress often helps to precipitate or to aggravate anxiety disorders.

Recently, there has been increased interest in the connections between childhood stress and psychopathology more generally. Until relatively recently, interest in the connection between stress and various disorders was largely limited to how adverse events in adolescence or adulthood might contribute to provoking the onset of certain disorders soon after the stress. However, in recent years, there has been a surge of research on how severe stress in early childhood may increase individuals' vulnerability to various disorders many years later. These studies have looked at many forms of early childhood trauma, such as physical abuse, sexual abuse, emotional neglect, parental death, childhood illness, and so forth. Two systematic reviews

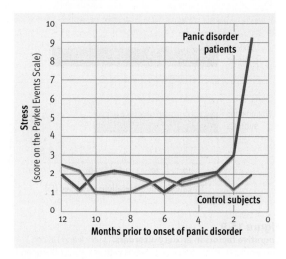

Figure 15.10

Stress and panic disorder. Faravelli and Pallanti (1989) assessed the amount of stress experienced during the 12 months before the onset of panic disorder in a group of 64 patients with this disorder and in a control group drawn from hospital employees and their friends. As you can see, there was a dramatic increase in stress in the month prior to the onset of the patients' panic disorders. These data suggest that stress may contribute to the development of panic disorders.

Source: Adapted from C. Faravelli & S. Pallanti (1989). Recent life events and panic disorder. *American Journal of Psychiatry, 146* (May): 622-626. Reprinted with permission from the American Journal of Psychiatry, (Copyright © 1989). American Psychiatric Association.

of this burgeoning research literature show that numerous studies have linked early-life stress to an increased prevalence of anxiety disorders, dissociative disorders, depressive disorders, bipolar disorders, schizophrenic disorders, personality disorders, and eating disorders (Carr et al., 2013; Martins et al., 2011). Admittedly, these studies have varied considerably in methodological quality. Many have relied on retrospective recollections of childhood trauma from patients and have not incorporated nonpatient comparison groups (Bendall et al., 2008). These are weak correlational methods that could inflate the apparent effects of childhood adversity and that do not permit conclusions about causality. So, more evidence is needed to establish causality, but the sheer number and consistency of the findings suggest that childhood trauma may have long-term ripple effects that heighten individuals' vulnerability to a broad range of psychological disorders. Why would this be so? The thinking is that adversity during childhood may alter critical features of developing brain structure and the reactivity of the HPA axis that regulates hormonal responses to stressors (Aust et al., 2014; Juruena, 2014).

Dissociative Disorders

Dissociative disorders are probably the most controversial set of disorders in the diagnostic system. They spark heated debate among normally subdued researchers and clinicians (Simeon & Loewenstein, 2009; Spiegel et al., 2013). *Dissociative disorders* are a class of disorders in which people lose contact with portions of their consciousness or memory, resulting in disruptions in their sense of identity. This category of disorders includes dissociative amnesia, dissociative identity disorder, and depersonalization/derealization disorder. In this section, we'll describe the first two: dissociative amnesia and dissociative identity disorder. Both of these appear to be relatively uncommon, although good data on the prevalence of these disorders are scarce (Kihlstrom, 2005).

Description

Dissociative amnesia is a sudden loss of memory for important personal information that is too extensive to be due to normal forgetting. Memory losses can occur for a single traumatic event (such as an automobile accident or home fire) or for an extended period of time surrounding the event. Cases of amnesia have been observed after people have experienced disasters, accidents, combat stress, physical abuse, and rape, among other things (Cardeña & Gleaves, 2007). In some cases, having forgotten their name, their family, where they live, and where they work, these people wander away from their home area. In spite of this wholesale forgetting, they remember matters unrelated to their identity, such as how to drive a car and how to do math.

The mystery writer Agatha Christie is reported to be one of the more celebrated examples of this disorder. She disappeared from her home on the night of December 3, 1926, and her abandoned car was found several kilometres away. A massive search was organized, and her disappearance was international news. She was located almost two weeks later in a different town, and was registered at a spa under a new name. When her husband came to identify her, she said, "Fancy, my brother has just arrived" (Burton, 2012). Her disappearance was attributed to the stress of the recent death of her mother and the extramarital affair carried out by her husband. She later resumed her storied writing career and never mentioned or explained the disappearance.

Dissociative identity disorder (DID) involves a disruption of identity marked by the experience of two or more largely complete, and usually very different, personalities. The name for this disorder used to be *multiple personality disorder*, which still enjoys informal usage. The name for the disorder was changed because the old name seemed to imply that different people inhabited the same body, whereas the modern view is that these individuals fail to integrate incongruent aspects of their personality into a normal, coherent whole (Cardeña et al., 2013). In dissociative identity disorder, the divergences in behaviour go far beyond those that people normally display in adapting to different roles in life. People with "multiple personalities" feel they have more than one identity. Each identity has his or her own name, memories, traits, physical mannerisms, and autonomy. Although it is relatively infrequent, this syndrome is often portrayed in novels, movies, and television shows. In popular media portrayals, the syndrome is often mistakenly called schizophrenia. As you will see later, schizophrenic disorders are entirely different.

In dissociative identity disorder, the various personalities generally report that they are unaware of each other, although objective measures of memory suggest otherwise (Huntjens et al., 2006). The alternate personalities commonly display traits that are quite foreign to the original personality. For instance, a shy, inhibited person might develop a flamboyant, extraverted alternate personality. Transitions between identities often occur suddenly. Dissociative identity disorder is seen more often in women than in men (Simeon & Loewenstein, 2009).

Starting in the 1970s, a dramatic increase was seen in the diagnosis of DID. Only 79 well-documented cases had accumulated up through 1970, but by the late-1990s, about 40 000 cases were estimated to have been reported (Lilienfeld & Lynn, 2003). Some theorists believe that the disorder used to be underdiagnosed (Maldonado & Spiegel, 2014). However, other theorists argue that a handful of clinicians have begun overdiagnosing the condition and that some clinicians unwittingly reinforce patients for progressively showing a seemingly exotic or exciting disorder (Boysen & VanBergen, 2013; Powell & Gee, 1999). Consistent with this view, a survey of all the psychiatrists in Switzerland found that 90 percent had never seen a case of DID, and six (of the 655 surveyed) accounted for two-thirds of the dissociative identity disorder diagnoses in Switzerland (Modestin, 1992).

Etiology of Dissociative Disorders

Dissociative amnesia is usually attributed to excessive stress. However, relatively little is known about why this extreme reaction to stress occurs in a tiny minority of people, but not in the vast majority who are subjected to similar stress.

The causes of dissociative identity disorder are particularly obscure. Some skeptical theorists (Lilienfeld et al., 1999; Lynn et al., 2012) believe that people with multiple identities come to believe, thanks in part to book and movie portrayals of dissociative identity disorder and reinforcement from their therapists, that independent entities within them are to blame for their peculiar behaviours, unpredictable moods, and ill-advised actions. Gradually, aided by subtle encouragement from their therapists and a tendency to fantasize, they come to attribute unique traits and memories to imaginary alternate personalities. Theorists who favour this line of thinking also note that recent research suggests that sleep disturbances can amplify dissociative symptoms (van der Kloet et al., 2012).

In spite of these concerns, many clinicians are convinced that dissociative identity disorder is an authentic disorder (Dorahy et al., 2014; van der Hart & Nijenhuis, 2009). They argue that there is no incentive for either patients or therapists to manufacture cases of multiple personalities, which are often greeted with skepticism and outright hostility. They maintain that most cases of dissociative identity disorder are rooted in severe emotional trauma that occurred during childhood (Maldonado & Spiegel, 2014). A substantial majority of people with dissociative identity disorder report a childhood history of rejection from parents and of physical and sexual abuse (van der Hart & Nijenhuis, 2009). However, this abuse typically has not been independently verified (Ross & Ness, 2010). In the final analysis, little is known about the causes of dissociative identity disorder, which remains a controversial diagnosis (Lilienfeld & Arkowitz, 2011).

Depressive and Bipolar Disorders

What do Kurt Cobain, Vincent van Gogh, Sting, Chris Cornell, Jean-Claude van Damme, Gwyneth Paltrow, Keanu Reeves, Ben Stiller, Axl Rose, Francis Ford Coppola, Marilyn Monroe, Margaret Trudeau, Winston Churchill, Leo Tolstoy, Jim Carrey, Margot Kidder, Sarah McLachlan, Percy Paul, and Canadian Olympic figure skater Elizabeth Manley have in common? Yes, they all achieved great prominence,

Soundgarden front man Chris Cornell and actor/karate champion Jean-Claude van Damme are two of the many celebrities who have made public their struggles with depression. Many celebrities hope to use their disclosure of mental illness to highlight the disorder and to fight the stigma associated with mental illness. Chris Cornell died in 2017.

Key Learning Goals

▶ Describe the symptoms of major depressive disorder and bipolar disorder and their relation to suicide.

▶ Understand how genetic, neural, hormonal, cognitive, social, and stress factors are related to the development of depressive and bipolar disorders.

albeit in different ways at different times. But, more pertinent to our interest, they all suffered from depression or bipolar disorder.

Although depression and bipolar disorders can be terribly debilitating (Munoz, Beardslee, & Leykin, 2012), people with these disorders may still achieve greatness, because such disorders tend to be *episodic*. In other words, mood disturbances often come and go, interspersed among periods of normality. These episodes of disturbance can vary greatly in length, but they typically last 3–12 months (Akiskal, 2000).

Of course, everybody has ups and downs in terms of mood. Life would be dull indeed if people's emotional tone were constant. Everyone experiences depression occasionally. Likewise, everyone has days that he or she sails through on an emotional high. Such emotional fluctuations are natural, but some people are subject to extreme and sustained distortions of mood. We know that prolonged episodes of mood disorders can interfere with an individual's personal and professional life. In one survey, 80 percent of Canadian workers who suffered from depression reported that it interfered with their ability to work (Statistics Canada, 2007h). Friends and family typically are quite concerned when they witness prolonged periods of sadness or depression in their loved ones. What are mood disorders and what do we know about their causes?

These disorders are a class of disorders marked by emotional disturbances of varied kinds that may spill over to disrupt physical, perceptual, social, and thought processes.

The DSM-5 has two separate classes of mood disorders. The first class is the *bipolar and related disorders*, which includes *bipolar I* and *bipolar II disorders*, and *cyclothymic disorder*. The second classification is the *depressive disorders*, which includes *major depressive disorder*, along with new categories of depressive disorder, including *disruptive mood dysregulation disorder*, *premenstrual dysphoric disorder*, and *persistent depressive disorder*. In this section we focus our discussion on major depressive disorder and bipolar disorder.

People with major depressive disorder experience emotional extremes at just one end of the mood continuum because they experience periodic bouts of depression. People with bipolar disorders generally experience emotional extremes at both ends of the mood continuum, going through periods of both *depression* and *mania* (excitement and elation) (see Figure 15.11). Actually, although the name for the disorder suggests that all bipolar individuals experience both depression and mania, a minority of people with bipolar disorder do not report episodes of depression (Johnson, Cuellar, & Peckham, 2014).

Major Depressive Disorder

The line between normal dejection and unhappiness and abnormal depression can be difficult to draw (Akiskal, 2009). Ultimately, it requires a subjective judgment. Crucial considerations in this judgment include the duration of the depression and its disruptive effects. When a depression significantly impairs everyday adaptive behaviour for more than a few weeks, there is reason for concern.

In *major depressive disorder,* people show persistent feelings of sadness and despair and a loss of interest in previous sources of pleasure. Negative emotions form the heart of the depressive syndrome, but many other symptoms may also appear. In addition to the negative mood, a central feature of depression is *anhedonia*—a diminished ability to experience pleasure. Depressed people lack the energy or motivation to tackle the tasks of living, to the point where they often have trouble getting out of bed (Craighead et al., 2008). Hence, they often give up activities that they used to find enjoyable. For example, a depressed person might quit going bowling or might give up a favourite hobby such as photography. Alterations in appetite and sleep patterns are common. People with depression often lack energy. They tend to move sluggishly and talk slowly. Anxiety, irritability, and brooding are commonly observed. Self-esteem tends to sink as the depressed person begins to feel worthless. Depression plunges people into feelings of hopelessness, dejection, and boundless guilt. To make matters worse, people who suffer from depression often exhibit other disorders as well. Co-existing anxiety disorders and substance-use disorders are particularly frequent (Boland & Keller, 2009).

The onset of depression can occur at any point in the life span. However, a substantial majority of cases emerge before age 40. Depression occurs in children and adolescents, as well as adults, although rates of depression are notably lower in children and somewhat lower in adolescents (Rohde et al., 2013). The vast majority of people who suffer from major depression experience more than one episode over the course of their lifetime (McInnis, Ribia, & Greden, 2014). The average number of depressive episodes is five to six. The average length of these episodes is about five to seven months (Keller et al., 2013). An earlier age of onset is associated with more recurrences, more severe symptoms, and a worse prognosis (Hammen & Keenan-Miller, 2013). Although depression tends to be episodic, some people suffer from chronic major depression that may persist for many years

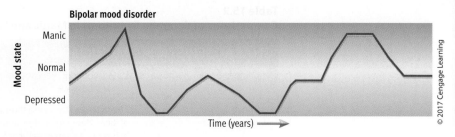

Figure 15.11

Episodic patterns in bipolar disorder. Time-limited episodes of emotional disturbance come and go unpredictably in mood disorders. People with depressive disorders suffer from bouts of depression only, whereas people with bipolar disorders experience both manic and depressive episodes. The time between episodes of disturbance varies greatly with the individual and the type of disorder.

(Klein & Allmann, 2014). Such chronic depression is associated with a particularly severe impairment of functioning. Depression is associated with an elevated risk for a variety of physical health problems and increases mortality by about 50 percent (Cuijpers et al., 2014).

How common are depressive disorders? Lifetime prevalence is estimated to be around 13–16 percent (Hammen & Keenan-Miller, 2013). At the low end, that estimate suggests that over 40 million people in North America have suffered or will suffer from depression! If this news isn't sufficiently depressing, there is new evidence that the prevalence of depression may be on the rise in recent birth cohorts (Twenge, 2015).

Research indicates that the prevalence of depression is about twice as high in women as it is in men (Gananca, Kahn, & Oquendo, 2014). The many possible explanations for this gender gap are the subject of considerable debate. The gap does not appear to be attributable to differences in genetic makeup (Franic et al., 2010). A portion of the disparity may be the result of women's elevated vulnerability to depression at certain points in their reproductive life cycle (Hilt & Nolen-Hoeksema, 2014). Obviously, only women have to worry about postpartum and postmenopausal depression. Susan Nolen-Hoeksema (2001) argues that women experience more depression than men because they are far more likely to be victims of sexual abuse and somewhat more likely to endure poverty, sexual harassment, and excessive pressure to be thin and attractive. In other words, she attributes a portion of the higher prevalence of depression among women to their experience of greater stress and adversity. Nolen-Hoeksema also believes that women have a greater tendency than men to ruminate about setbacks and problems. Evidence suggests that this tendency to dwell on one's difficulties elevates vulnerability to depression, as we will discuss momentarily.

Table 15.2

Comparisons of Common Symptoms in Manic and Depressive Episodes

CHARACTERISTICS	MANIC EPISODE	DEPRESSIVE EPISODE
Emotional	Elated, euphoric, very sociable, impatient at any hindrance	Gloomy, hopeless, socially withdrawn, irritable
Cognitive	Characterized by racing thoughts, flight of ideas, desire for action, and impulsive behaviour; talkative, self-confident; experiencing delusions of grandeur	Characterized by slowness of thought processes, obsessive worrying, inability to make decisions, negative self-image, self-blame, and delusions of guilt and disease
Motor	Hyperactive, tireless, requiring less sleep than usual, showing increased sex drive and fluctuating appetite	Less active, tired, experiencing difficulty in sleeping, showing decreased sex drive and decreased appetite

Source: Sarason & Sarason, *Abnormal Psychology,* 5th edition, © 1987, p. 283. Reprinted by permission of Pearson Education, Inc., Upper Saddle River, NJ.

Bipolar Disorder

Bipolar I disorder (formerly known as *manic-depressive disorder*) is characterized by the experience of one or more manic episodes as well as periods of depression. One manic episode is sufficient to qualify for this diagnosis. The symptoms seen in manic periods generally are the opposite of those seen in depression (see Table 15.2 for a comparison). In a manic episode, a person's mood becomes elevated to the point of euphoria. As was the case with Percy Paul, self-esteem often skyrockets as the

person bubbles over with optimism, energy, and extravagant plans. He or she becomes hyperactive and may go for days without sleep. The individual talks rapidly and shifts topics wildly, as his or her mind races at breakneck speed. Judgment is often impaired. Some people in manic periods gamble impulsively, spend money frantically, or become sexually reckless. Like depressive disorders, bipolar disorders vary considerably in severity. In *bipolar II disorder*, individuals suffer from episodes of major depression along with hypomania in which their change in mood and behaviour is less severe than

Singer/songwriters Serena Ryder and Nelly Furtado are two well-known Canadians who have struggled with mood disorders in spite of their considerable career success.

© Tom Cheney/The New Yorker Collection/The Cartoon Bank

"Those? Oh, just a few souvenirs from my bipolar-disorder days."

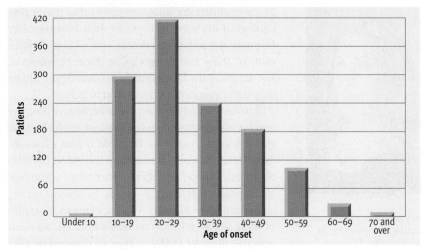

Figure 15.12

Age of onset for bipolar mood disorder. The onset of bipolar disorder typically occurs in adolescence or early adulthood. The data graphed here, which were combined from ten studies, show the distribution of age of onset for 1304 bipolar patients. As you can see, bipolar disorder emerges most frequently during the 20s decade.

Source: *Manic-depressive illness* by Goodwin & Jamison (1990) "Age of Onset for Bipolar Mood Disorder" p. 132. By permission of Oxford University Press, USA.

those seen in full mania. People are given a diagnosis of *cyclothymic disorder* when they exhibit chronic but relatively mild symptoms of bipolar disturbance.

You may be thinking that the euphoria in manic episodes sounds appealing. If so, you are not entirely wrong. In their milder forms, manic states can seem attractive. The increases in energy, self-esteem, and optimism can be deceptively seductive; Percy Paul even called his manic states *addictive*. Because of the increase in energy, many bipolar patients report temporary surges of productivity and creativity (Goodwin & Jamison, 2007).

Although manic episodes may have some positive aspects, these periods often have a paradoxical negative undercurrent of irritability and depression (Goodwin & Jamison, 2007). Moreover, mild manic episodes usually escalate to higher levels that become scary and disturbing. Impaired judgment leads many victims to do things that they greatly regret later, as you'll see in the following case history:

Robert, a dentist, awoke one morning with the idea that he was the most gifted dental surgeon in the area. He decided that he should try to provide services to as many people as possible, so that more people could benefit from his talents. So, he decided to remodel his two-chair dental office, installing 20 booths so that he could simultaneously attend to 20 patients. That same day, he drew up plans for this arrangement, telephoned a number of remodellers, and invited bids for the work. Later that day, impatient to get rolling on his remodelling, he rolled up his sleeves, got himself a sledgehammer, and began to knock down the walls in his office. Annoyed when that didn't go so well, he smashed his dental tools, washbasins, and X-ray equipment.

Later, Robert's wife became concerned about his behaviour and summoned two of her adult daughters for assistance. The daughters responded quickly, arriving at the family home with their husbands. In the ensuing discussion, Robert—after bragging about his sexual prowess—made advances toward his daughters. He had to be subdued by their husbands. (Adapted from Kleinmuntz, 1980, p. 309)

Although not rare, bipolar disorders are much less common than depressive disorders. Bipolar disorder affects about 1 percent of the North American population (Merikangas & Pato, 2009). Unlike depressive disorder, bipolar disorder is seen equally often in males and females (Rihmer & Angst, 2009). As Figure 15.12 shows, the onset of bipolar disorder is age-related (Carlson & Klein, 2014). The typical age of onset is in the late teens. The mood swings in bipolar disorder can be patterned in many ways. Manic episodes typically last about four months (Angst, 2009). Episodes of depression tend to run somewhat longer and most bipolar patients end up spending more time in depressed states than manic states (Bauer, 2008).

Diversity in Mood Disorders

In the preceding discussion, we presented the differences between the two main types of mood disorders: major depressive disorder and bipolar disorder.

Courtesy of Dr. Cindy-Lee Dennis

Cindy-Lee Dennis is a faculty member and researcher at the University of Toronto whose interests include postpartum depression and evaluation of interventions to directly improve maternal health, which indirectly enhances infant outcomes. She holds two research chairs, a Canada Research Chair in Perinatal Community Health at the University of Toronto and the Shirley Brown Chair in Women's Mental Health at the Centre for Addiction and Mental Health. Dr. Dennis is also a senior scientist at the Women's College Research Institute and is cross-appointed to the Department of Psychiatry in the University of Toronto's Faculty of Medicine.

Mood disorders are similar to most other major psychological disorders in terms of their heterogeneity in onset, presentation, etiology, and course. Within each of these two categories of disorder, however, the nature of the symptoms and course of the illness may differ somewhat from person to person.

The distinction between major depressive disorder and bipolar disorder does not exhaust the forms that mood disorders may take. The DSM system allows for "specifiers" that may accompany the mood disorder diagnosis. These specifiers contribute additional information that may be of use in understanding and treating the disorder. Two well-known examples of these subcategories of mood disorder are *seasonal affective disorder (SAD)*, a type of depression that follows a seasonal pattern, and *postpartum depression*, a type of depression that sometimes occurs after childbirth. In the former, the specifier relates to the seasonal pattern of the disorder and in the latter, the specifier relates to an onset of the disorder postpartum, within four weeks of childbirth.

For some individuals who experience either bipolar or major depressive disorder, their symptoms may show a regular relationship with the seasons of the year (Rosenthal et al., 1984), the most common form being winter depression (Lewy, 1993). As you might expect, this type of mood disorder has in general been found to be more common in countries such as Canada, where there is less sunlight in the winter months. How common is this type of depression in Canada? One Canadian study found that 11 percent of the surveyed individuals who had depression evidenced the SAD subtype (Levitt et al., 2000), with an overall estimated prevalence in the population of almost 3 percent of Canadians. The rates are even higher among the Inuit in the Canadian Arctic (Haggarty et al., 2002). There are suggestions that the onset of SAD is related to melatonin production and circadian rhythms (Goodwin & Jamison, 1990; Wirtz-Justice, 1998). One form of treatment for SAD is phototherapy, in which individuals suffering from SAD are exposed systematically to therapeutic light (Lee et al., 1997). According to Toru Sato (1997), the beneficial effects of phototherapy can be achieved with light exposure for a couple of hours a day with a minimum of side effects.

The symptoms of postpartum depression, which can include both depression and mania, occur at a time of life when most women expect to be happiest and most excited—after their children are born (Beck & Driscoll, 2006). Research on the prevalence of postpartum depression reveals a range of prevalence estimates but suggests that it occurs in about 10–20 percent of women who have given birth (Gaschler, 2008; Ross et al., 2005; Stewart et al., 2008).

Several variables affect the frequency of postpartum depression and its course (Dennis, 2014a, 2014b; Vigod, Tarasoff, Bryja, Dennis, et al., 2013), including where you live. For example, Cindy-Lee Dennis and her colleagues at the University of Toronto have found that women residing in urban settings have higher rates of postpartum depression than women in other settings. It has also been found that immigrant women in Canada appear to have an even higher rate of postpartum depression than do Canadian-born women. This higher risk for immigrant women may reflect increased stress related to their relocation, lack of social support, and unfamiliarity with the Canadian health-care system (Stewart et al., 2008). High-profile Canadian women such as Maureen McTeer and Margaret Trudeau, both wives of former Canadian prime ministers, have made their experiences with postpartum depression public (Galloway, 2006; McTeer, 2003) in an attempt to improve education about the disorder and increase funding for research into it.

No matter what the eliciting factors or onset characteristics of the depression are, it can be a debilitating disorder that negatively impacts an individual's personal and professional life, as we saw in the case of Percy Paul. As is too often the case, as it was for Paul, depression can be associated with suicide and suicide attempts. In the next section, we consider mood disorders and suicide.

Mood Disorders and Suicide

A tragic, heartbreaking problem associated with mood disorders is suicide. Official statistics underscore the nature and degree of this type of tragedy. According to the World Health Organization, more people around the world die from suicide than are killed in all of the armed conflicts that plague the world. It is one of the three leading causes of death of people between the ages of 15 and 34 (World Health Organization, 2007). In Canada, the overall suicide rate has remained fairly constant over the past 50 years. In 2013, there were 4054 reported suicides in Canada (Statistics Canada, 2017). It is the ninth leading cause of death in Canada overall, but for those between the ages of 15 and 34, it is the second leading cause of death, following accidents (Statistics Canada, 2012).

Suicide rates differ across various groupings, including gender, age, and rural/urban residence (Asarnow & Miranda, 2014). Suicidal thoughts and rates of suicide among most Aboriginal populations in Canada are higher than for non-Aboriginal groups (Statistics Canada, 2016). In Canada, there are also differences in the rates of immigrant and native-born Canadians, with the rate of suicide among immigrants averaging about half that of native-born Canadians (Malenfant, 2004). Official statistics may underestimate the scope of the problem. Many suicides are disguised as accidents, either by the suicidal person or by the survivors, who try to cover up afterward. Moreover, experts estimate that suicide attempts may outnumber completed suicides by a ratio of as much as 25 to 1 (Rothberg & Feinstein, 2014). Women attempt suicide three times more often than men, but men are more likely to actually kill themselves in an attempt, so they *complete* four times as many suicides as women (Rothberg & Feinstein, 2014).

With the luxury of hindsight, it is recognized that about 90 percent of the people who complete suicide suffer from some type of psychological disorder, although this disorder may not be readily apparent beforehand in some cases (Nock et al., 2014). As you might expect, suicide rates are highest for people with depressive and bipolar disorders. They account for about 50–60 percent of completed suicides (Nock et al., 2014). The likelihood of a suicide attempt increases as the severity of individuals' depression increases (MacLeod, 2013). Still, suicide is notoriously difficult to predict. Perhaps the best predictor is when one expresses a sense of hopelessness about the future, but even that can be difficult to gauge (MacLeod, 2013). Unfortunately, there is no foolproof way to prevent suicidal persons from taking their own lives, but we have compiled some useful tips in Figure 15.13.

Etiology of Depressive and Bipolar Disorders

Quite a bit is known about the etiology of depressive and bipolar disorders, although the puzzle hasn't been assembled completely. There appear to be a number of routes into these disorders, involving intricate interactions among psychological and biological factors.

Genetic Vulnerability

The evidence strongly suggests that genetic factors influence the likelihood of developing major depression (Lau et al., 2014) and bipolar disorder (Macritchie & Blackwood, 2013). *Twin studies* have found a huge disparity between identical and fraternal twins in concordance rates for mood disorders. The concordance rate for identical twins is much higher (see Figure 15.14). This evidence suggests that heredity can create a *predisposition* to mood

SUICIDE PREVENTION TIPS

1. *Take suicidal talk seriously.* When people talk about suicide in vague generalities, it's easy to dismiss it as "idle talk" and let it go. However, people who talk about suicide are a high-risk group and their veiled threats should not be ignored. The first step in suicide prevention is to directly ask such people if they're contemplating suicide.

2. *Provide empathy and social support.* It is important to show the suicidal person that you care. People often contemplate suicide because they see the world around them as indifferent and uncaring. Hence, you must demonstrate to the suicidal person that you are genuinely concerned. Suicide threats are often a last-ditch cry for help. It is therefore imperative that you offer to help.

3. *Identify and clarify the crucial problem.* The suicidal person is often terribly confused and feels lost in a sea of frustration and problems. It is a good idea to try to help sort through this confusion. Encourage the person to try to identify the crucial problem. Once it is isolated, the crucial problem may not seem quite so overwhelming.

4. *Do not promise to keep someone's suicidal ideation secret.* If you really feel like someone's life is in danger, don't agree to keep their suicidal plans secret to preserve your friendship.

5. *In an acute crisis, do not leave a suicidal person alone.* Stay with the person until additional help is available. Try to remove any guns, drugs, sharp objects, and so forth, that might provide an available means to commit suicide.

6. *Encourage professional consultation.* Most mental health professionals have some experience in dealing with suicidal crises. Many cities have suicide prevention centres with 24-hour hotlines. These centres are staffed with people who have been specially trained to deal with suicidal problems. It is important to try to get a suicidal person to seek professional assistance.

Figure 15.13

Preventing suicide. As Sudak notes, "It is not possible to prevent all suicides or to totally and absolutely protect a given patient from suicide. What is possible is to reduce the likelihood of suicide" (2005, p. 2449). So the advice summarized here may prove useful if you ever have to help someone through a suicidal crisis. (Based on American Association of Suicidology, 2007; American Foundation for Suicide Prevention, 2007; Fremouw, de Perczel, & Ellis, 1990; Rosenthal, 1988; Shneidman, Farberow, & Litman, 1994)

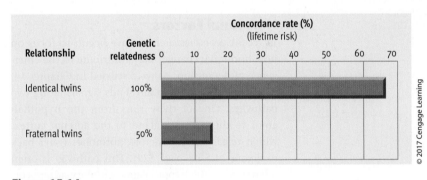

© 2017 Cengage Learning

Figure 15.14

Twin studies of mood disorders. The concordance rate for mood disorders in identical twins is much higher than that for fraternal twins, who share less genetic overlap. These results suggest that there must be a genetic predisposition to mood disorders (Data from Gershon, Berrettini, & Goldin, 1989).

dysfunction. Environmental factors probably determine whether this predisposition is converted into an actual disorder.

Neurochemical and Neuroanatomical Factors

Correlations have been found between mood disorders and abnormal levels of two neurotransmitters in the brain—norepinephrine and serotonin—although other neurotransmitter disturbances may also contribute (Thase, Hahn, & Berton, 2014).

The details remain elusive, but low levels of serotonin appear to be a crucial factor underlying most forms of depression.

Studies have also found some interesting correlations between mood disorders and a variety of structural abnormalities in the brain (Kempton et al., 2011). Perhaps the best-documented correlation is the association between depression and *reduced hippocampal volume*, especially in the dentate gyrus of the hippocampus (Treadway et al., 2015). A relatively new theory of the biological bases of depression may be able to account for this finding. The springboard for this theory is the discovery that the human brain continues to generate new neurons (neurogenesis) in adulthood, especially in the hippocampal formation, which was discussed in Chapter 3 (Kozorovitskiy & Gould, 2007, 2008). Recent evidence suggests that depression occurs when major life stress causes neurochemical reactions that suppress this neurogenesis, resulting in reduced hippocampal volume (Mahar et al., 2014). According to this view, the suppression of neurogenesis is the central cause of depression, and antidepressant drugs are successful because they promote neurogenesis (Boldrini et al., 2013). A great deal of additional research will be required to fully test this innovative model of the biological bases of depressive disorders.

Hormonal Factors

In recent years, researchers have begun to focus on how hormonal changes may contribute to the emergence of depression. As we discussed in Chapter 14, in times of stress, the brain sends signals along two pathways. One of these runs from the hypothalamus to the pituitary gland to the adrenal cortex, which releases corticosteroid hormones (refer back to Figure 14.5 on page 527). This pathway is often referred to as the hypothalamic-pituitary-adrenocortical (HPA) axis. Evidence suggests that overactivity along the HPA axis in response to stress can often play a role in the development of depression (Goodwin, 2009). Consistent with this hypothesis, a substantial portion of depressed patients show elevated levels of cortisol, a key stress hormone produced by HPA activity (Cleare & Rane, 2013). Some theorists believe that these hormonal changes eventually have an impact in the brain, where they may be the trigger for the suppression of neurogenesis that we just discussed (Duman, Polan, & Schatzberg, 2008).

Cognitive Factors

A variety of theories emphasize how cognitive factors contribute to depressive disorders (Clasen, Disner, & Beevers, 2013). For example, based largely on animal research, Seligman (1974) proposed that depression is caused by *learned helplessness*—passive "giving up" behaviour produced by exposure to unavoidable aversive events (such as uncontrollable shock in the lab). He originally considered learned helplessness to be a product of conditioning, but eventually revised his theory to give it a cognitive slant. The reformulated theory of learned helplessness asserts that the roots of depression lie in how people explain the setbacks and other negative events they experience (Abramson, Seligman, & Teasdale, 1978). According to Seligman (1990), people who exhibit a *pessimistic explanatory style* are especially vulnerable to depression. These people tend to attribute their setbacks to their personal flaws instead of to situational factors. Moreover, they tend to draw global, far-reaching conclusions about their personal inadequacies based on these setbacks.

In accord with this line of thinking, Susan Nolen-Hoeksema (1991, 2000) found that depressed people who *ruminate* about their depression remain depressed longer than those who try to distract themselves. People who respond to depression with rumination repetitively focus their attention on their feelings of depression. They think constantly about how sad, lethargic, and unmotivated they are. Excessive rumination tends to foster and amplify episodes of depression by increasing negative thinking, impairing problem solving, and undermining social support (Nolen-Hoeksema, Wisco, & Lyubomirsky, 2008). As we noted earlier, Nolen-Hoeksema believes women have a greater tendency to ruminate than men, and that this disparity may be a major reason depression is more prevalent in women.

In sum, cognitive models of depression maintain that negative thinking is what leads to depression in many people. The principal problem with cognitive theories is their difficulty in separating cause from effect. Does negative thinking cause depression? Or does depression cause negative thinking (see Figure 15.15)? Strong evidence favouring a causal role for negative thinking comes from a study by Alloy and colleagues (1999), who assessed explanatory style in first-year college students who were not depressed at the outset of the study, which followed students for 2.5 years. They found that a negative explanatory style predicted vulnerability to depression, with major depression emerging in 17 percent of students who exhibited negative thinking, but only 1 percent of those who did not. Our first Featured Study for Chapter 15 provides impressive evidence consistent with a causal link between negative thinking and vulnerability to depression.

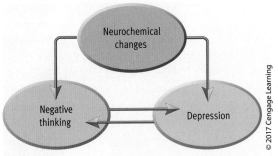

Figure 15.15
Interpreting the correlation between negative thinking and depression. Cognitive theories of depression assume that consistent patterns of negative thinking cause depression. Although these theories are highly plausible, depression could cause negative thoughts, or both could be caused by a third factor, such as neurochemical changes in the brain.

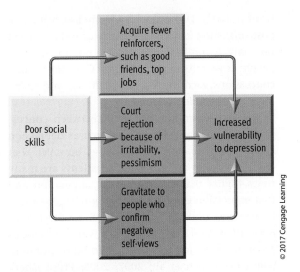

Figure 15.16
Interpersonal factors in depression. Behavioural theories about the etiology of depression emphasize how inadequate social skills may contribute to the development of the disorder through several mechanisms, as diagrammed here.

FEATURED STUDY

Depressogenic cognitive styles: Predictive validity, information processing and personality characteristics, and developmental origins.

Description
In this study the authors examine the degree to which cognitive style is predictive of depression.

Investigators
Alloy, L. B., et al. (1999). *Behaviour Research and Therapy, 37*(6), 503-531.

Interpersonal Roots

Behavioural approaches to understanding depression emphasize how inadequate social skills put people on the road to depressive disorders (see Figure 15.16; Coyne, 1999; Ingram, Scott, & Hamill, 2009). According to this notion, depression-prone people lack the social finesse needed to acquire many important kinds of reinforcers, such as good friends, top jobs, and desirable spouses. This paucity of reinforcers could understandably lead to negative emotions and depression. Consistent with this theory, research, such as that conducted at the University of Western Ontario by Ian Gotlib (Gotlib & Robinson, 1982) and others, has found associations between poor social skills and depression (Ingram, Scott, & Siegle, 1999; Joiner & Timmons, 2009).

Another interpersonal factor is that depressed people tend to be depressing (Joiner & Katz, 1999). Individuals suffering from depression often are irritable and pessimistic. They complain a lot and aren't particularly enjoyable companions. As a consequence, depressed people tend to court rejection from those around them (Joiner & Metalsky, 1995; Joiner & Timmons, 2009). Depressed people have fewer sources of social support than nondepressed people. Low social support can increase vulnerability to depression (Lakey & Cronin, 2008). Research suggests that lack of social support may make a larger contribution to depression in women than in men (Kendler, Myers, & Prescott, 2005).

Social rejection and lack of support may in turn aggravate and deepen a person's depression (Potthoff, Holahan, & Joiner, 1995). To compound these problems, evidence indicates that depressed people may gravitate to partners who view them unfavourably and hence reinforce their negative views of themselves (Joiner, 2002).

Sports Concussions and Depression

The topic of concussions in sports has received a great deal of attention in the past few years. While athletes in some sports were always at risk for head trauma, in years past they were often encouraged just to get back in the game. Recent high-profile concussions and deaths linked to these concussions have changed that attitude. For example, hockey star Sidney Crosby of the Pittsburgh Penguins suffered a concussion in the 2010–2011 NHL season and did not play for the last half of the season (Mirtle, 2011) or the beginning of the next season. NFL defensive back Andre Waters suffered severe head trauma and retired after 12 seasons playing football. After his retirement, Waters evidenced cognitive deficits as a result of his concussions, became depressed, and committed suicide at age 44 (Farrey, 2007). The forensic pathologist who examined Waters's brain stated that "the condition of Waters's brain tissue was what would be expected in an 85-year-old man"

(Farrey, 2007). Depression is a common feature of postconcussion syndrome. This is of clear concern not only to professional athletes but to ordinary people as well. As many as 30 000 Canadians suffer concussions each year (Ogilvie, 2011), and many more are likely not reported.

Research examining the links between concussions and mental health issues such as depression is still in its infancy. We do know, however, that depression rates in head trauma patients are many times higher than in the general population and that depression can be long-lasting (Deb, Lyons, & Koutzoukis, 1998; Jorge et al., 1993; Kreutzer, Seel, & Gourley, 2001). Research by Dr. Charles Tator in Toronto and by Jen-Kai Chen, Alain Ptito, and their colleagues (Chen et al., 2007, 2008; Ptito, Chen, & Johnstone, 2007) at the Montreal Neurological Institute is playing a key role in uncovering the nature of the connection between head trauma and depression. For example, in one study Chen and his colleagues (Chen et al., 2008) examined fMRI scans of a healthy control group and of athletes suffering from concussions with no depression, or with mild or moderate depression symptoms. The results of the brain scans showed that athletes who had suffered from concussions and depression, as compared to the other participants, showed "reduced activation in the dorsolateral prefrontal cortex and striatum and attenuated deactivation in medial frontal and temporal regions" (Chen et al., 2008, p. 81). The results also indicated that depression levels correlated with the level of neural response in areas typically associated with depression, along with grey matter loss in those areas. Tator and his colleagues (Manley et al., 2017) recently considered almost 4000 studies on the topic of concussions and sports, isolating a set of studies that met with strict scientific criteria. Their conclusions based on the subset of research that met their criteria led them to conclude that "there is evidence that some former athletes in contact, collision and combat sports suffer from depression and cognitive deficits later in life, and there is an association between these deficits and a history of multiple concussions" (p. 7).

Although more studies of this kind are necessary before definitive conclusions are possible, the authors did suggest that the depression experienced by some of these athletes could be the result of the head trauma they suffered. Research on this topic will continue as many pro athletes (including former CFL quarterback Matt Dunigan, who suffered a career-ending concussion) have decided to donate their brains to concussion research centres, such as the one run by Dr. Charles Tator and his colleagues. Tator is the project director of the Canadian Sports

THE CANADIAN PRESS/Larry MacDougal

Many pro athletes who have suffered concussions, such as CFL great Matt Dunigan, have agreed to donate their brains to research on the physical and mental health consequences of head trauma.

Concussion Project at the Krembil Neuroscience Centre, Toronto Western Hospital, which is conducting several research studies on concussion disorders, funded by the Ontario Brain Institute.

Precipitating Stress

Mood disorders sometimes appear mysteriously in people who are leading benign, nonstressful lives (Monroe & Harkness, 2005). For this reason, experts used to believe that stress had little influence on mood disorders. However, advances in the measurement of personal stress altered this picture. The evidence available today suggests the existence of a moderately strong link between stress and the onset of both major depression (Monroe, Slavich, & Georgiades, 2014) and bipolar disorder (Johnson et al., 2014). Of course, the vast majority of people who experience significant stress do not develop a mood disorder, so one's vulnerability to both stress and mood disorders must play a role (Bifulco, 2013). Unfortunately, vulnerability to depression seems to increase as people go through more recurrences of depressive episodes. Studies show that stress is less of a factor in triggering depression as episodes of depression accumulate over the years (Monroe et al., 2014).

Schizophrenia

Literally, *schizophrenia* means "split mind." However, when Eugen Bleuler coined the term in 1911, he was referring to the fragmentation of thought processes seen in the disorder—not to a "split personality." Unfortunately, writers in the popular media often assume that the split-mind notion, and thus schizophrenia, refers to the rare syndrome in which a person manifests two or more personalities. As you have already learned, this syndrome is actually called *dissociative identity disorder* or *multiple-personality disorder*. Schizophrenia is a much more common, and altogether different, type of disorder.

reality check

Misconception

Schizophrenia refers to the syndrome in which a person manifests two or more personalities.

Reality

Literally, *schizophrenia* means "split mind." However, when Eugen Bleuler coined the term in 1911, he was referring to the fragmentation of thought processes seen in schizophrenia—not to a "split personality." Unfortunately, writers in the popular media often erroneously equate the split-mind notion with split personality. As you have already learned, this syndrome is actually called *dissociative identity disorder* or *multiple-personality disorder*.

The DSM-5 includes schizophrenia in the schizophrenia spectrum and other psychotic disorders classification. In addition to schizophrenia, this category includes schizotypal disorder, delusional disorder, brief psychotic disorder, schizophreniform disorder, and schizoaffective disorder. One characteristic common to the disorders included in the schizophrenia spectrum disorders is a break from reality—a distortion of reality fuelled by symptoms such as delusions and hallucinations. In this section we will focus primarily on schizophrenia.

Schizophrenia is a disorder marked by delusions, hallucinations, disorganized speech, negative symptoms (e.g., diminished emotional expression), and deterioration of adaptive behaviour. Schizophrenia usually emerges during adolescence or early adulthood. About 75 percent of cases manifest by the age

of 30 (Perkins, Miller-Anderson, & Lieberman, 2006). Prevalence estimates suggest that about 1 percent of the population may suffer from schizophrenia (Sadock et al., 2015). That may not sound like much, but it means that in North America alone, several million people may be troubled by schizophrenic disturbances. Schizophrenia is an extremely costly illness for society because it is a severe, debilitating illness that tends to have an early onset and often requires lengthy hospital care (Samnaliev & Clark, 2008). Moreover, individuals suffering from schizophrenia show an increased risk for suicide and for premature mortality (early death) from natural causes (Nielsen et al., 2013).

While schizophrenia has a relatively low frequency compared to many of the other forms of psychopathology that we will discuss in this section, it does have a relatively high visibility both because of the severity of the illness and because of the way it has been portrayed in the media. An excellent example is the book *A Beautiful Mind* (Nasar, 1998) and director Ron Howard's (2002) film of the same name based on the book.

The book and film describe the life of mathematician John Nash, who suffered from paranoid schizophrenia. Nash is noteworthy, of course, because he won the 1994 Nobel Prize in Economics, and the Abel prize in Mathematics despite his illness. Nash was vocal in speaking out against the stigma associated

In the movie *A Beautiful Mind*, Nobel Prize-winning mathematician John Nash (right) is played by Russell Crowe (left). Nash passed away on May 23, 2015.

with mental illness and the factors that maintain them. It is also interesting to get a sense of how one comes to be nominated for a Nobel Prize (perhaps you have some aspirations in this regard). Creativity and innovative thinking appear to be the key, more important than the quantity of papers one produces. You might imagine that Nobel Prize winners have to publish hundreds of papers. Nash's formal publications number only 15 papers! Five of these are on game theory, for which he won his Nobel Prize, and ten are pure mathematics (Kuhn & Nasar, 2002).

General Symptoms

Many of the characteristics of schizophrenia are apparent in the following case history (adapted from Sheehan, 1982, pp. 104–105):

> Sylvia was first given a diagnosis of schizophrenia at age 15. She has been in and out of many types of psychiatric facilities since then. She has never been able to hold a job for any length of time. During severe flare-ups of her disorder, her personal hygiene deteriorates. She rarely washes, she wears clothes that neither fit nor match, she smears makeup on heavily but randomly, and she slops food all over herself. Sylvia occasionally hears voices talking to her. She tends to be argumentative, aggressive, and emotionally volatile. Over the years, she has been involved in innumerable fights with fellow patients, psychiatric staff members, and strangers. Her thoughts can be highly irrational, as is apparent from the following quote, which was recorded while she was a patient in a psychiatric facility called Creedmoor:
>
> "Mick Jagger wants to marry me. If I have Mick Jagger, I don't have to covet Geraldo Rivera. Mick Jagger is St. Nicholas and the Maharishi is Santa Claus. I want to form a gospel rock group called the Thorn Oil, but Geraldo wants me to be the music critic on Eyewitness News, so what can I do? Got to listen to my boyfriend. Teddy Kennedy cured me of my ugliness. I'm pregnant with the son of God. I'm going to marry David Berkowitz and get it over with. Creedmoor is the headquarters of the American Nazi Party. They're eating the patients here. Archie Bunker wants me to play his niece on his TV show. I work for Epic Records. I'm Joan of Arc. I'm Florence Nightingale. The door between the ward and the porch is the dividing line between New York and California. Divorce isn't a piece of paper, it's a feeling. Forget about Zip Codes. I need shock treatments. The body is run by electricity. My wiring is all faulty."

Sylvia's case clearly shows that schizophrenic thinking can be bizarre and that schizophrenia can be a severe and debilitating disorder. Although no single symptom is inevitably present, the following symptoms are commonly seen in schizophrenia (Lewis, Escalona, & Keith, 2009; Liddle, 2009).

Delusions and Irrational Thought

Disturbed, irrational thought processes are the central feature of schizophrenia (Heinrichs et al., 2013). Various kinds of delusions are common. **Delusions are false beliefs that are maintained even though they clearly are out of touch with reality.** For example, one patient's delusion that he is a tiger (with a deformed body) persisted for more than 15 years (Kulick, Pope, & Keck, 1990). More typically, affected persons believe that their private thoughts are being broadcast to other people, that thoughts are being injected into their minds against their will, or that their thoughts are being controlled by some external force (Maher, 2001). In *delusions of grandeur*, people maintain that they are famous or important. Sylvia expressed an endless array of grandiose delusions, such as thinking that Mick Jagger wanted to marry her, that she had dictated the *Hobbit* stories to J. R. R. Tolkien, and that she was going to win the Nobel Prize in Physiology or Medicine.

Another characteristic of schizophrenia is that the person's train of thought deteriorates. Thinking becomes chaotic rather than logical and linear. There is a "loosening of associations," as people shift topics in disjointed ways. The quotation from Sylvia illustrates this symptom dramatically.

Deterioration of Adaptive Behaviour

Schizophrenia usually involves a noticeable deterioration in the quality of the person's routine functioning in work, social relationships, and personal care (Harvey & Bowie, 2013). Friends will often make remarks such as "Hal just isn't himself anymore." This deterioration is readily apparent in Sylvia's inability to get along with others or to function in the work world. It's also apparent in her neglect of personal hygiene.

Hallucinations

A variety of perceptual distortions may occur with schizophrenia, the most common being auditory hallucinations. *Hallucinations* are sensory perceptions that occur in the absence of a real, external stimulus or are gross distortions of perceptual input. People with schizophrenia frequently report that they hear voices of nonexistent or absent people talking to them. Sylvia, for instance, said she heard messages from Paul McCartney. These voices often provide an insulting, running commentary on the person's behaviour ("You're an idiot for shaking his hand"). They may be argumentative ("You don't need a bath"), and they may issue commands ("Prepare your home for visitors from outer space").

Disturbed Emotions

Normal emotional tone can be disrupted in a variety of ways. Some victims show a flattening of emotions. In other words, they show little emotional responsiveness. Others show inappropriate emotional responses that don't jell with the situation or with what they are saying. People with schizophrenia can also become emotionally volatile. Because of this volatility, acts of aggression can be a problem with some schizophrenic patients (Serper, 2011).

Traditionally, four subtypes of schizophrenic disorders were recognized: paranoid, catatonic, disorganized, and undifferentiated schizophrenia (Minzenberg, Yoon, & Carter, 2008). As its name implies, *paranoid schizophrenia* was thought to be dominated by delusions of persecution, along with delusions of grandeur. *Catatonic schizophrenia* was marked by striking motor disturbances, ranging from the muscular rigidity seen in a withdrawn state called a catatonic stupor to random motor activity seen in a state of *catatonic excitement*. *Disorganized schizophrenia* was viewed as a particularly severe syndrome marked by frequent incoherence, obvious deterioration in adaptive behaviour, and virtually complete social withdrawal. People who were clearly schizophrenic but who could not be placed into any of the three previous categories were said to have *undifferentiated schizophrenia*, which involved idiosyncratic mixtures of schizophrenic symptoms.

However, in a radical departure from tradition, the DSM-5 discarded the four subtypes of schizophrenia. Why? For many years, researchers pointed out that there were not meaningful differences between the classic subtypes in etiology, prognosis, or response to treatment. The absence of such differences cast doubt on the value of distinguishing among the subtypes. Critics also noted that the catatonic and disorganized subtypes were rarely seen in contemporary clinical practice and that undifferentiated cases did not represent a subtype as much as

a hodgepodge of "leftovers." Finally, researchers had stopped focusing their studies on the specific subtypes of schizophrenia (Braff et al., 2013).

Another approach to understanding and describing schizophrenia is to distinguish between the *positive symptoms* and *negative symptoms* of the disorder (Stroup et al., 2014; see Figure 15.17). *Negative symptoms* involve behavioural deficits, such as flattened emotions, social withdrawal, apathy, impaired attention, poor grooming, lack of persistence at work or school, and poverty of speech. *Positive symptoms* involve behavioural excesses or peculiarities, such as hallucinations, delusions, incoherent thought, agitation, bizarre behaviour, and wild flights of ideas. Most patients exhibit both types of symptoms, but vary in the degree to which positive or negative symptoms dominate (Andreasen, 2009). A relative predominance of negative symptoms is associated with less effective social functioning (Robertson et al., 2014), and poorer overall treatment outcomes (Fervaha et al., 2014).

Etiology of Schizophrenia

You can probably identify, at least to some extent, with people who suffer from mood disorders and anxiety disorders. You can probably imagine events that could unfold that might leave you struggling with depression, grappling with anxiety, or worrying about your physical health. But what could account for Sylvia's thinking that she was Joan of Arc or that she had dictated the *Hobbit* stories to Tolkien? As mystifying as these delusions may seem, you'll see that the etiology of schizophrenic disorders is not all that different from the etiology of other psychological disorders. We'll begin our discussion by examining the matter of genetic vulnerability.

Genetic Vulnerability

Evidence is plentiful that hereditary factors play a role in the development of schizophrenic disorders (Bassett & Chow, 1999; Costain, McDonald-McGinn, & Bassett, 2013; Gur, Bassett, et al., 2017; Riley & Kendler, 2011). For instance, in twin studies, concordance rates average around 48 percent for identical twins, in comparison with about 17 percent for fraternal twins (Gottesman, 1991, 2001). Studies also indicate that a child born to two schizophrenic parents has about a 46 percent probability of developing a schizophrenic disorder (as compared with the probability in the general population of about 1 percent). These and other findings that show the genetic roots of schizophrenia are

Figure 15.17

Positive and negative symptoms in schizophrenia. Some theorists believe that schizophrenic disorders can be best understood by thinking in terms of two kinds of symptoms: positive symptoms (behavioural excesses) and negative symptoms (behavioural deficits). The percentages shown here, based on a sample of 111 schizophrenic patients studied by Andreasen (1987), provide an indication of how common each specific symptom is.

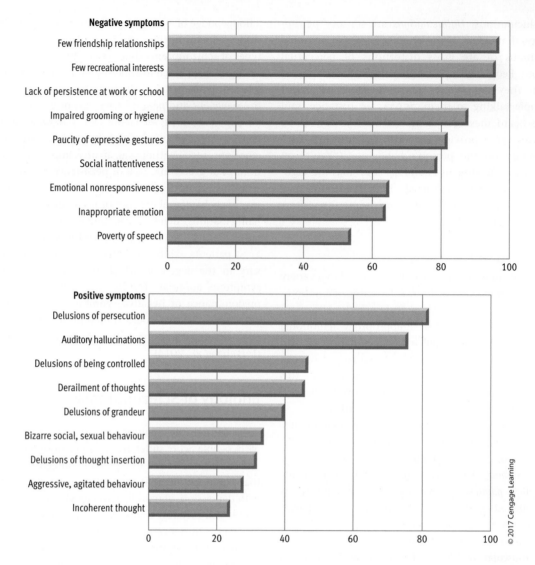

Dr. Anne Bassett holds the Canada Research Chair in Schizophrenia Genetics and Genomic Disorders in the Department of Psychiatry at the University of Toronto. Her research interests focus on the genetics of schizophrenia including 22q11.2 Deletion Syndrome (22q11.2DS).

summarized in Figure 15.18. Some theorists suspect that genetic factors may account for as much as 80 percent of the variability in susceptibility to schizophrenia (Pogue-Geile & Yokley, 2010). After years of inconsistent findings and difficulties in replicating results, genetic mapping studies are finally beginning to yield some promising insights regarding the specific combinations of genes and genetic mutations that increase individuals' risk for schizophrenia (Gelernter, 2015; Gershon & Alliey-Rodriguez, 2013; Hall et al., 2015).

Neurochemical Factors

Like depressive and bipolar disorders, schizophrenic disorders appear to be accompanied by changes in the activity of one or more neurotransmitters in the brain. The *dopamine hypothesis* asserts that excess dopamine activity is the neurochemical basis for schizophrenia (see Figure 15.19). This hypothesis makes sense because most of the drugs that are useful in the treatment of schizophrenia are known

to dampen dopamine activity in the brain (Stroup et al., 2014). Research suggests that increased dopamine *synthesis* and *release* in specific regions of the brain may be the crucial factor that triggers schizophrenic illness in vulnerable individuals (Howes et al., 2011; Winton-Brown et al., 2014). In recent years, the dopamine hypothesis has become more nuanced and complex. Researchers believe that dysregulation occurs in dopamine circuits and that the nature of this dysregulation may vary in different regions of the brain (Abi-Dargham & Grace, 2011).

Recent research has suggested that marijuana use *during adolescence* may help precipitate schizophrenia in young people who have a *genetic vulnerability* to the disorder (van Winkel & Kuepper, 2014). For example, a meta-analysis of 83 studies found that the onset of psychotic disorder tended to occur 2.7 years earlier in cannabis users than in non-users (Large et al., 2011). This unexpected finding has generated considerable debate about whether and how cannabis might contribute to the emergence of schizophrenia. Some critics suggest that schizophrenia could lead to cannabis use, rather than vice versa. In other words, emerging psychotic symptoms may prompt young people to turn to marijuana to self-medicate. However, carefully controlled studies have not supported the self-medication explanation (van Winkel & Kuepper, 2014). The evidence suggests a causal link between marijuana use and the emergence of schizophrenia, but the mechanism at work remains a mystery. Research suggests there may also be an association between methamphetamine use and the emergence of schizophrenia (Callaghan et al., 2012).

Structural Abnormalities in the Brain

Individuals with schizophrenia exhibit a variety of deficits in attention, perception, and information processing (Goldberg, David, & Gold, 2011). These cognitive deficits suggest that schizophrenic disorders may be caused by neurological defects. Brain-imaging studies have yielded intriguing findings that are consistent with this idea. The most reliable finding is that CT scans and MRI scans (see Chapter 3)

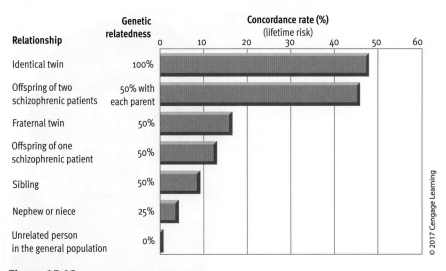

Figure 15.18
Genetic vulnerability to schizophrenic disorders. Relatives of schizophrenic patients have an elevated risk for schizophrenia. This risk is greater among closer relatives. Although environment also plays a role in the etiology of schizophrenia, the concordance rates shown here suggest that there must be a genetic vulnerability to the disorder. These concordance estimates are based on pooled data from 40 studies conducted between 1920 and 1987 (Data from Gottesman, 1991).

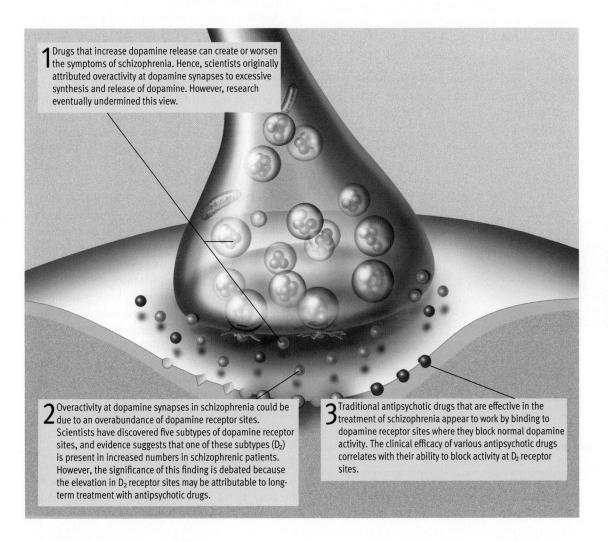

Figure 15.19
The dopamine hypothesis as an explanation for schizophrenia. Decades of research have implicated overactivity at dopamine synapses as a key cause of schizophrenic disorders. However, the evidence on the exact mechanisms underlying this overactivity, which is summarized in this graphic, is complex and open to debate. Recent hypotheses about the neurochemical bases of schizophrenia go beyond the simple assumption that dopamine activity is increased. For example, one theory posits that schizophrenia may be accompanied by decreased dopamine activity in one area of the brain (the prefrontal cortex) and increased activity or dysregulation in other areas of the brain (Egan & Hyde, 2000). Moreover, abnormalities in other neurotransmitter systems may also contribute to schizophrenia.

Source: From Weiten. *Cengage Advantage Books: Psychology,* 9E. © 2013 South-Western, a part of Cengage, Inc. Reproduced by permission. www.cengage.com/permissions

1 Drugs that increase dopamine release can create or worsen the symptoms of schizophrenia. Hence, scientists originally attributed overactivity at dopamine synapses to excessive synthesis and release of dopamine. However, research eventually undermined this view.

2 Overactivity at dopamine synapses in schizophrenia could be due to an overabundance of dopamine receptor sites. Scientists have discovered five subtypes of dopamine receptor sites, and evidence suggests that one of these subtypes (D_2) is present in increased numbers in schizophrenic patients. However, the significance of this finding is debated because the elevation in D_2 receptor sites may be attributable to long-term treatment with antipsychotic drugs.

3 Traditional antipsychotic drugs that are effective in the treatment of schizophrenia appear to work by binding to dopamine receptor sites where they block normal dopamine activity. The clinical efficacy of various antipsychotic drugs correlates with their ability to block activity at D_2 receptor sites.

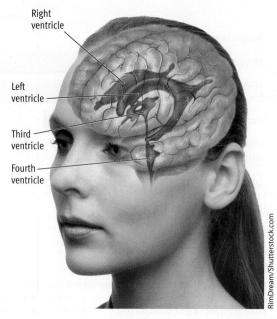

Right
ventricle

Left
ventricle

Third
ventricle

Fourth
ventricle

RimDream/Shutterstock.com

Figure 15.20

Schizophrenia and the ventricles of the brain. Cerebrospinal fluid (CSF) circulates around the brain and spinal cord. The hollow cavities in the brain filled with CSF are called *ventricles*. The four ventricles in the human brain are depicted here. Recent studies with CT scans and MRI scans suggest that there is an association between enlarged ventricles in the brain and the occurrence of schizophrenic disturbance.

© 2017 Cengage Learning

suggest an association between enlarged brain ventricles (the hollow, fluid-filled cavities in the brain depicted in Figure 15.20) and schizophrenic disturbance (Lawrie & Pantelis, 2011). Enlarged ventricles are assumed to reflect the degeneration of nearby

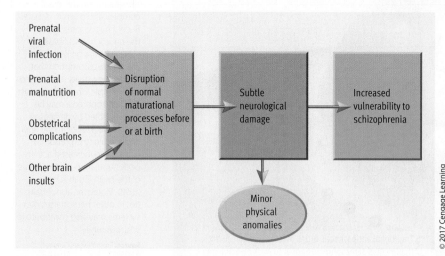

© 2017 Cengage Learning

Figure 15.21

The neurodevelopmental hypothesis of schizophrenia. Recent findings have suggested that insults to the brain sustained during prenatal development or at birth may disrupt crucial maturational processes in the brain, resulting in subtle neurological damage that gradually becomes apparent as youngsters develop. This neurological damage is believed to increase both vulnerability to schizophrenia and the incidence of minor physical anomalies (slight anatomical defects of the head, face, hands, and feet).

brain tissue. The significance of enlarged ventricles is hotly debated, however. This structural deterioration could be a consequence of schizophrenia, or it could be a contributing cause of the illness. Brain-imaging studies have also uncovered other structural abnormalities, including reductions in both grey matter and white matter in specific brain regions (Cannon et al., 2015; White et al., 2013).

The Neurodevelopmental Hypothesis

The *neurodevelopmental hypothesis* of schizophrenia asserts that schizophrenia is caused in part by various disruptions in the normal maturational processes of the brain before or at birth (Rapoport, Giedd, & Gogtay, 2012). According to this hypothesis, insults to the brain during sensitive phases of prenatal development or during birth can cause subtle neurological damage that elevates individuals' vulnerability to schizophrenia years later in adolescence and early adulthood (see Figure 15.21). What are the sources of these early insults to the brain? Thus far, research has focused on viral infection or malnutrition during prenatal development and on obstetrical complications during the birth process.

Quite a number of studies have found a link between exposure to influenza and other infections during prenatal development and an increased prevalence of schizophrenia (Brown & Derkits, 2010), with inflammation thought to be the critical process that disrupts neural maturation (Miller, Culpepper et al., 2013). Additionally, a study that investigated the possible impact of prenatal malnutrition found an elevated incidence of schizophrenia in a group of people who were prenatally exposed to a severe famine in 1944–1945, resulting from a Nazi blockade of food deliveries in the Netherlands during World War II (Susser et al., 1996). Other research has shown that schizophrenic patients are more likely than control subjects to have experienced obstetrical complications when they were born (McGrath & Murray, 2011). Finally, research suggests that minor physical anomalies (slight anatomical defects of the head, hands, feet, and face) that would be consistent with prenatal neurological damage are more common in people with schizophrenia than in others (Akabaliev, Sivkov, & Mantarkov, 2014). Collectively, these diverse studies argue for a relationship between early neurological trauma and a predisposition to schizophrenia (Rapoport et al., 2012).

Expressed Emotion

Studies of expressed emotion have primarily focused on how this element of family dynamics influences

concept **check** 15.1

Distinguishing Schizophrenic and Depression/Bipolar Disorder

Check your understanding of the nature of schizophrenic and depression/bipolar disorder by making preliminary diagnoses for the cases described below. Read each case summary and write your tentative diagnosis in the space provided. The answers are in Appendix A near the back of the book.

1. Max hasn't slept in four days. He's determined to write a great novel before his class reunion, which is a few months away. He expounds eloquently on his novel to anyone who will listen, talking at such a rapid pace that no one can get a word in edgewise. He feels like he's wired with energy and is supremely confident about the novel, even though he's written only 10 to 20 pages. Last week, he charged $8000 worth of new computer software, which is supposed to help him write his book.

Preliminary diagnosis: _____

2. Eduardo maintains that he invented the atomic bomb, even though he was born after its invention. He says he invented it to punish homosexuals, Nazis, and short people. It's short people that he's really afraid of. He's sure that all of the short people on TV are talking about him. He thinks that short people are conspiring to make him look like a Conservative. Eduardo frequently gets into arguments with people and is emotionally volatile. His grooming is poor, but he says it's okay because he's the defence minister.

Preliminary diagnosis: _____

3. Margaret has hardly gotten out of bed for weeks, although she's troubled by insomnia. She doesn't feel like eating and has absolutely no energy. She feels dejected, discouraged, spiritless, and apathetic. Friends stop by to try to cheer her up, but she tells them not to waste their time on "pond scum."

Preliminary diagnosis: _____

the *course* of schizophrenic illness, after the onset of the disorder (Leff & Vaughn, 1985). *Expressed emotion (EE)* is the degree to which a relative of a schizophrenic patient displays highly critical or emotionally overinvolved attitudes toward the patient. Audiotaped interviews of relatives' communication are carefully evaluated for critical comments, resentment toward the patient, and excessive emotional involvement (overprotective, overconcerned attitudes) (Hooley, 2004).

Studies show that a family's expressed emotion is a good predictor of the course of a schizophrenic patient's illness (Hooley, 2007). After release from a hospital, people with schizophrenia who return to a family high in expressed emotion show relapse rates about three times that of patients who return to a family low in expressed emotion (see Figure 15.22; Hooley, 2009). Part of the problem for patients returning to homes high in expressed emotion is that their families are probably more sources of stress than of social support (Cutting & Docherty, 2000).

Precipitating Stress

Most theories of schizophrenia assume that stress plays a key role in triggering schizophrenic disorders (Walker & Tessner, 2008). According to this notion,

various biological and psychological factors influence individuals' *vulnerability* to schizophrenia. High stress may then serve to precipitate a schizophrenic disorder in someone who is vulnerable (McGlashan & Hoffman, 2000). Research indicates that high stress can also trigger relapses in patients who have made progress toward recovery (Walker, Mittal, & Tessner, 2008). Patients who show strong emotional reactions to events seem to be particularly likely to have their symptoms exacerbated by stress (Docherty et al., 2009).

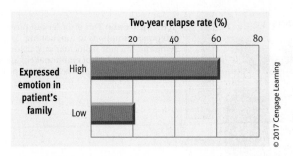

Figure 15.22
Expressed emotion and relapse rates in schizophrenia.
Schizophrenic patients who return to a home that is high in expressed emotion have higher relapse rates than those who return to a home low in expressed emotion. Thus, unhealthy family dynamics can influence the course of schizophrenia. (Data adapted from Leff & Vaughn, 1981)

An Illustrated Overview of Three Categories of Psychological Disorders

Diagnostic Category	Selected Subtypes	Prevalence/well-known victim

Anxiety disorders

Edvard Munch's *The Scream* expresses overwhelming feelings of anxiety.

Generalized anxiety disorder: Chronic, high level of anxiety not tied to any specific threat

Phobic disorder: Persistent, irrational fear of object or situation that presents no real danger

Panic disorder: Recurrent attacks of overwhelming anxiety that occur suddenly and unexpectedly

19% Prevalence

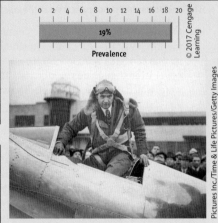

The famous industrialist Howard Hughes suffered from an anxiety disorder.

Mood disorders

Vincent van Gogh's *Portrait of Dr. Gachet* captures the profound dejection experienced in depressive disorders.

Major depressive disorder: Two or more major depressive episodes marked by feelings of sadness, worthlessness, despair

Bipolar disorder: One or more manic episodes marked by inflated self-esteem, grandiosity, and elevated mood and energy, usually accompanied by major depressive episodes

15% Prevalence

Musician Chris Cornell suffered from depression.

Schizophrenic disorders

The perceptual distortions seen in schizophrenia probably contributed to the bizarre imagery apparent in this portrait of a cat painted by Louis Wain.

Schizophrenia: This disorder can produce profound disruptions to functioning. Major symptoms include hallucinations, delusions, withdrawal and lack of emotional engagement, disorganized speech, and behavioural problems.

1% Prevalence

John Nash, the Nobel Prize-winning mathematician whose story was told in the film *A Beautiful Mind,* struggled with schizophrenia.

Etiology: Biological factors

Genetic vulnerability:
Twin studies and other evidence suggest a mild genetic predisposition to anxiety disorders.

Anxiety sensitivity:
Oversensitivity to physical symptoms of anxiety may lead to overreactions to feelings of anxiety, so anxiety breeds more anxiety.

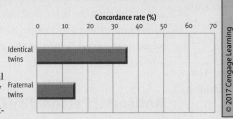

Concordance rate (%)

Neurochemical bases:
Disturbances in neural circuits releasing GABA may contribute to some disorders; abnormalities at serotonin synapses have been implicated in panic and obsessive-compulsive disorders.

Genetic vulnerability:
Twin studies and other evidence suggest a genetic predisposition to mood disorders.

Sleep disturbances:
Disruption of biological rhythms and sleep patterns may lead to neurochemical changes that contribute to mood disorders.

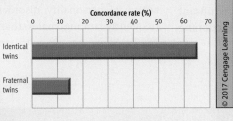

Concordance rate (%)

Neurochemical bases:
Disturbances in neural circuits releasing norepinephrine may contribute to some mood disorders; abnormalties at serotonin synapses have also been implicated as a factor in depression.

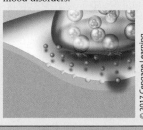

Genetic vulnerability:
Twin studies and other evidence suggest a genetic predispositon to schizophrenic disorders.

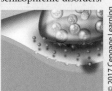

Concordance rate (%)

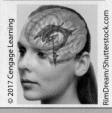

RimDream/Shutterstock.com

Neurochemical bases: Overactivity in neural circuits releasing dopamine is associated with schizophrenia; but abnormalities in other neurotransmitter systems may also contribute.

Structural abnormalities in brain:
Enlarged brain ventricles are associated with schizophrenia, but they may be an effect rather than a cause of the disorder.

Etiology: Psychological factors

Learning: Many anxiety responses may be acquired through classical conditioning or observational learning; phobic responses may be maintained by operant reinforcement.

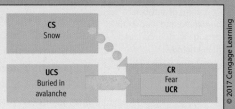

CS
Snow

UCS
Buried in avalanche

CR
Fear
UCR

Stress: High stress may help to precipitate the onset of anxiety disorders.

Cognition: People who misinterpret harmless situations as threatening and who focus excessive attention on perceived threats are more vulnerable to anxiety disorders.

Threatening interpretations endorsed (%)

Interpersonal roots:
Behavioural theories emphasize how inadequate social skills can result in a paucity of reinforcers and other effects that make people vulnerable to depression.

Stress: High stress can act as a precipitating factor that triggers depression or bipolar disorder.

Cognition: Negative thinking can contribute to the development of depression; rumination may extend and amplify depression.

Poor social skills → Acquire fewer reinforcers, such as good friends, top jobs / Court rejection because of irritability, pessimism / Gravitate to people who confirm negative self-views → Increased vulnerability to depression

Negative thinking ↔ Depression

Expressed emotion:
A family's expressed emotion is a good predictor of the course of a schizophrenic patient's illness.

Stress: High stress can precipitate schizophrenic disorder in people who are vulnerable to schizophrenia.

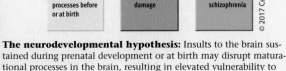

Two-year relapse rate (%)

Expressed emotion in patient's family — High / Low

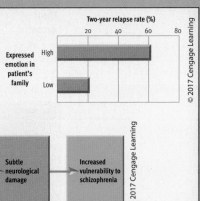

Disruption of normal maturational processes before or at birth → Subtle neurological damage → Increased vulnerability to schizophrenia

The neurodevelopmental hypothesis: Insults to the brain sustained during prenatal development or at birth may disrupt maturational processes in the brain, resulting in elevated vulnerability to schizophrenia.

© 2017 Cengage Learning

Psychological Disorders

Personality Disorders

Key Learning Goal

▶ Discuss the nature of personality disorders; the symptoms of antisocial, borderline, and narcissistic personality disorders; and their etiology.

Personality disorders are a class of disorders marked by extreme, inflexible personality traits that cause subjective distress or impaired social and occupational functioning. Personality disorders generally become recognizable during adolescence or early adulthood. One conservative estimate pegged the lifetime prevalence of personality disorders at around 12 percent (Caligor, Yeomans, & Levin, 2014).

The DSM-5 lists ten personality disorders. They are grouped into three related clusters: anxious/fearful, odd/eccentric, and dramatic/impulsive. These disorders are described briefly in Table 15.3. If you examine this table, you will find a diverse collection of maladaptive personality syndromes. You may also notice that some personality disorders essentially are milder versions of more severe disorders that we have already covered. For example, the schizoid and schizotypal personality disorders are milder cousins of schizophrenic disorders. Although personality disorders tend to be relatively mild disorders in comparison with anxiety, mood, and schizophrenic disorders, they often are associated with significant impairments of social and occupational functioning (Trull, Carpenter, & Widiger, 2013).

Antisocial, Borderline, and Narcissistic Personality Disorders

Given the sheer number of personality disorders, we can only provide brief descriptions of a few of the more interesting syndromes in this category. Hence, we will take a quick look at the antisocial, borderline, and narcissistic personality disorders.

Antisocial Personality Disorder

People with this disorder are *antisocial* in the sense that they choose to *reject widely accepted social norms* regarding moral principles. People with antisocial personalities chronically exploit others. The *antisocial personality disorder* is marked by impulsive, callous, manipulative, aggressive, and irresponsible behaviour. Since they haven't accepted the social norms they violate, people with antisocial personalities rarely feel guilty about their transgressions. Essentially, they lack an adequate conscience. The antisocial personality disorder occurs much more frequently among males than females (Torgersen, 2012). Some people with antisocial personalities

Table 15.3

Personality Disorders

CLUSTER	DISORDER	DESCRIPTION	% MALE/ % FEMALE
Anxious/ fearful	Avoidant personality disorder	Excessively sensitive to potential rejection, humiliation, or shame; socially withdrawn in spite of desire for acceptance from others	50/50
	Dependent personality disorder	Excessively lacking in self-reliance and self-esteem; passively allowing others to make all decisions; constantly subordinating own needs to others' needs	31/69
	Obsessive-compulsive personality disorder	Preoccupied with organization, rules, schedules, lists, trivial details; extremely conventional, serious, and formal; unable to express warm emotions	50/50
Odd/ eccentric	Schizoid personality disorder	Defective in capacity for forming social relationships; showing absence of warm, tender feelings for others	78/22
	Schizotypal personality disorder	Showing social deficits and oddities of thinking, perception, and communication that resemble schizophrenia	55/45
	Paranoid personality disorder	Showing pervasive and unwarranted suspiciousness and mistrust of people; overly sensitive; prone to jealousy	55/45
Dramatic/ impulsive	Histrionic personality disorder	Overly dramatic; tending to exaggerated expressions of emotion; egocentric, seeking attention	15/85
	Narcissistic personality disorder	Grandiosely self-important; preoccupied with success fantasies; expecting special treatment; lacking interpersonal empathy	70/30
	Borderline personality disorder	Unstable in self-image, mood, and interpersonal relationships; impulsive and unpredictable	38/62
	Antisocial personality disorder	Chronically violating the rights of others; failing to accept social norms, to form attachments to others, or to sustain consistent work behaviour; exploitive and reckless	82/18

Source: Estimated gender ratios from Millon (1981).

© 2017 Cengage Learning

keep their exploitive behaviour channelled within the boundaries of the law. Such people may even enjoy high status in our society (Babiak & Hare, 2006). In other words, the concept of the antisocial personality disorder can apply to cut-throat business executives and scheming politicians, as well as to con artists, drug dealers, and petty thieves. People with antisocial personalities exhibit quite a variety of maladaptive traits (Hare, 2006; Hare & Neumann, 2008). Among other things, they rarely experience genuine affection for others. Sexually, they are predatory and promiscuous. They can tolerate little frustration, and they pursue immediate gratification. These characteristics make them unreliable employees, unfaithful spouses, inattentive parents, and undependable friends. Many people with antisocial personalities have a checkered history of divorce, child abuse, and job instability.

Many people with antisocial personalities get involved in illegal activities (Porter & Porter, 2007). Moreover, according to University of British Columbia psychologist Robert Hare, antisocial personalities tend to begin their criminal careers at an early age, to commit offences at a relatively high rate, and to be versatile offenders who become involved in many types of criminal activity (Hare, 2006). Hare's work on *psychopathy* has become an important contribution to this field (e.g., Decety et al., 2014; Mokros, et al., 2013; Ogloff, 2006; Olver et al., 2013).

Robert Hare (Hare, 2016, 2017; Kristic, et al., 2017) is one of the world's leading experts on *psychopathy*, a term that is often used interchangeably with the term *antisocial personality disorder*. His influential book *Without Conscience: The Disturbing World of the Psychopaths Among Us* (Hare, 1999) is an important resource for scholars and laypersons alike (e.g., Neumann, Johansson, & Hare, 2013). Hare (1991) developed an important assessment device for psychopathy, the *Psychopathy Checklist–Revised* (PCL–R). For many, this measure is the "single, most important advancement to date toward what will hopefully become our ultimate understanding of psychopathy" (Wormith, 2000, p. 134). Research by a team of psychologists from Queen's University and the Mental Health Centre at Penetanguishene (Skilling et al., 2002) supports the validity of the PCL–R.

People with antisocial personalities exhibit quite a variety of maladaptive traits (Hare, 2006; Hare & Neumann, 2008; Patrick, 2007). Paul Bernardo, who was convicted for the 1991 murders of schoolgirls Leslie Mahaffy and Kristen French, has the classic features of someone with antisocial personality disorder. Bernardo kidnapped Mahaffy and French partially in order to dominate them sexually. He also confessed to 14 other rapes (Porter, 2015).

Our second Featured Study in this chapter, conducted by Hare and his colleagues (Krstic, Neumann, Roy, Robertson, Knight, & Hare, 2017), examines the role of psychopathy in sex offenders.

FEATURED STUDY

Using latent variable- and person-centered approaches to examine the role of psychopathic traits in sex offenders.

Description
In this study the authors examine the degree to which psychopathy is predictive of sex offenders.

Investigators
Krstic, S., et al. (2017). *Personality disorders: Theory, research, and treatment.* Advance online publication. http://dx.doi.org/10.1037/per0000249

Borderline Personality Disorder

The *borderline personality disorder* is marked by instability in social relationships, self-image, and emotional functioning. This disorder appears to be somewhat more common in females than males (Tomko et al., 2014). These individuals tend to have turbulent interpersonal relationships marked by fears of abandonment (Hooley, Cole, & Gironde, 2012). They often switch back and forth between idealizing people and devaluing them. They tend to be intense, with frequent anger issues and poor control of their emotions. They tend to be moody, shifting among panic, despair, and feelings of emptiness. They are prone to impulsive behaviour, such as reckless spending, drug use, or sexual behaviour. Individuals with borderline personality disorder often exhibit fragile, unstable self-concepts, as their goals, values, opinions, and career plans shift suddenly. Borderline personality disorder is also associated with an elevated risk for self-injurious behaviour, such as cutting or burning oneself and with an increased risk for suicide (Caligor et al., 2014). Recent research suggests that rather than being a completely unremitting condition, it may vary somewhat in response to specific features of situations (Conway, Hipwell, & Stepp, 2017).

Narcissistic Personality Disorder

People with narcissistic personality disorder exhibit the trait of narcissism to a very extreme degree. Hence, the *narcissistic personality disorder* is marked by a grandiose sense of self-importance, a sense of entitlement, and an excessive need for attention and admiration. This syndrome is more common in males (Trull et al., 2010). People with this disorder think they are unique and superior to others. They tend to be boastful and pretentious. Although they seem self-assured and confident, their self-esteem is actually quite fragile, leading them to fish for compliments and to be easily threatened by criticism. Their sense of entitlement manifests in arrogant expectations that they should merit special treatment and extra privileges. Their need for admiration is hard to fulfill. They routinely complain that others do not appreciate their accomplishments or give them the respect they deserve. Some critics have argued that the current diagnostic criteria for narcissistic personality disorder focus too much on the overt, grandiose presentation of the disorder and too little on its covert, vulnerable side (Levy, 2012; Skodol, Bender, & Morey, 2014).

Etiology of Personality Disorders

Like other disorders, the personality disorders all surely involve interactions between genetic predispositions and environmental factors, such as cognitive styles, coping patterns, and exposure to stress. As noted in Chapter 12, personality traits are shaped to a significant degree by heredity (South et al., 2013). Given that personality disorders consist of extreme manifestations of personality traits, it stands to reason that these disorders are also influenced by heredity, and the data from twin and family studies support this line of reasoning (Skodol et al., 2014). The environmental factors implicated in personality disorders vary considerably from one disorder to another, which makes sense given the diversity of the personality disorders. For example, contributing factors to antisocial personality disorder include dysfunctional family systems; erratic discipline; parental neglect; and parental modelling of exploitive, amoral behaviour (Farrington, 2006; Sutker & Allain, 2001). In contrast, borderline personality disorder has been attributed primarily to a history of early trauma, including physical and sexual abuse (Ball & Links, 2009; Widom, Czaja, & Paris, 2009). Different constellations of environmental factors have been implicated for each of the other eight personality disorders.

Neurodevelopmental Disorders

Key Learning Goal

▶ Describe the symptoms, prevalence, and etiology of autism spectrum disorder.

If you think back to your own early years or our discussions in Chapter 11 of development across the life span, it is clear that for most of us, childhood is a time of growth, curiosity, exploration, friendships, and gradual maturity. We play, we run, we make friends, and we explore our limits, and our physical and social environments. Sure, there are obstacles along the way—sometimes our parents don't understand us, sometimes we cry, fight, and throw tantrums, and sometimes we are confused and sad. But those problems seem mostly transient against the backdrop of all the other adventures we have. However, not all children have these experiences. For some, the sadness lasts longer and seems deeper; for some the confusion never clears up. Just like adults and teens, children suffer from psychological illness. According to the Canadian Mental Health Association (2011), roughly 20 percent of the children and youth in Canada will suffer from such illnesses. Many will go undiagnosed and untreated. In the province of Ontario alone, these statistics translate into more than 560 000 children and youths (Province of Ontario, 2010). Interest in infant and childhood disorders (Egger & Emde, 2011; Tronick & Beeghly, 2011) recently has become of increasing concern to professionals and laypersons alike.

Children suffer, much like adults, from too much stress, depression, PTSD, obsessive-compulsive disorder, and most of the other categories of disorders we have discussed so far in this chapter. In addition, however, there are a series of disorders that have traditionally been thought of as being specific to childhood and youth. Autism spectrum disorder (previously referred to as *autism*) is one of these. *Autism spectrum disorder* refers to a developmental disorder characterized by social and emotional deficits, along with repetitive and stereotypic behaviours, interests, and activities. Autism spectrum disorders are included in the *neurodevelopmental disorders* classification. This classification of disorders includes *intellectual disability, attention-deficit/ hyperactivity disorder, specific learning disorder, motor disorders,* and *tic disorders* (e.g., *Tourette's disorder*).

Autism spectrum disorder (ASD) is new to the DSM-5. Previous editions of the DSM listed four separate disorders, *autistic disorder (autism), Asperger's disorder, childhood disintegrative disorder,* and *pervasive developmental disorder not otherwise specified*. These four disorders were folded into one condition, ASD, which has different levels of severity (APA, 2013). The new classification of disorder is characterized by deficits in (a) social communication and interaction, and (b) restricted or repetitive behaviours, interests, and activities. One of the most controversial results of this change is the disappearance of Asperger's disorder as a diagnostic category. This could result in some individuals who would have previously been eligible for mental health services now being denied service because they do not meet the new ASD criteria (Wu et al., 2014). Autism has been the subject of considerable research since it was first identified by Kanner in 1943 (Volkmar & McPartland, 2014).

Autism Spectrum Disorder

Donald Gray Tripplett was the first person diagnosed with autism (Donovan & Zucker, 2010). He was the first subject of a series of case studies presented by Dr. Leo Kanner in a 1943 journal article (Kanner, 1943). Donald T (as he was referred to in the article) began life relatively normally but soon exhibited curious habits and obsessions. For example, he seemed to be obsessed with and developed a "mania" for spinning blocks and other objects, and when someone tried to interrupt his activities, he would throw a "tantrum." Soon thereafter, he exhibited an oddly detached orientation. He developed an "abstraction of the mind which made him perfectly oblivious, to everything about him . . . to get his attention almost requires one to break down a mental barrier between his inner consciousness and the outside world" (Kanner, 1943, p. 218). Kanner referred to this latter characteristic as *autistic aloneness*. Donald was exhibiting many of the symptoms that are classically associated with autism. Later work would extend Kanner's ideas on autism to consider autism as a *spectrum* of disorders including *Asperger's disorder* (Bernier & Gerdts, 2010).

While autism is relatively rare (Szatmari, 2000) compared to many other disorders such as depression or anxiety, it has been the subject of a great deal of publicity because of court cases in Canada dealing with the reluctance of some governments to fund its treatment (Parliament of Canada, 2006). While clearly multi-determined, genetic and neurobiological causes, among others, have been implicated in the disorder (Boucher, 2009; Cook, 2001; Tsai & Ghaziuddin, 1992).

Children suffering from autism were seen to exhibit three types of deficits—impairment in social interaction, impairment in communication, and repetitive, stereotyped behaviours/interests/activities (Bernier & Gerdts, 2010; Boucher, 2009; Oller & Oller, 2010; Zager, 1999). Children with autism show significant impairment in social interaction with others; this is the *autistic aloneness* Kanner (1973) referred to. In addition to these three sets of deficits, other problems including sensory difficulties have been identified (e.g., Pellicano, 2013).

The central feature of ASD is the child's lack of interest in other people. Children with autism act as though people in their environment are not different than nearby inanimate objects, such as toys, pillows, or chairs. They don't tend to make eye contact with others or need physical contact with their caregivers. They make no effort to connect with people and fail to bond with their parents or to develop normal peer relationships. Verbal communication can be greatly impaired, as about one-third of ASD children fail to develop speech (Wetherby & Prizant, 2005). Among those who do develop speech, their ability to initiate and sustain a conversation is limited, and their use of language tends to be marked by peculiarities, such as *echolalia*, which involves rote repetition of others' words. Autistic children's interests are restricted in that they tend to become preoccupied with objects or repetitive body movements (spinning, body rocking, playing with their hands, and so forth). They can also be extremely inflexible, and minor changes in their environment can trigger rages and tantrums. Some ASD children exhibit self-injurious behaviour, such as banging their heads, pulling their hair, or hitting themselves. About one-half of children with autism exhibit subnormal IQ scores (Volkmar et al., 2009).

Parents of autistic children typically become concerned about their child's development by about 15–18 months of age and usually seek professional consultation by about 24 months. The diagnosis of ASD is almost always made before affected children reach age three. More often than not, autism turns out to be a lifelong affliction, requiring extensive family and institutional support throughout adulthood. However, with early and effective intervention, around 15–20 percent of individuals with ASD are able to live independently in adulthood, and another 20–30 percent approach this level of functioning (Volkmar et al., 2009). Moreover, recent research suggests that a small minority experience a full recovery in adulthood (Fein et al., 2013).

Until relatively recently, the prevalence of autism was thought to be well under 1 percent (Newschaffer, 2007). Since the mid-1990s, however, there has been a dramatic (roughly fourfold) increase in the diagnosis of autism, with prevalence estimates approaching and even exceeding 1 percent (Brugha et al., 2011; Idring et al., 2014; Zahorodny et al., 2014). Most experts believe that this surge in ASD is largely due to greater awareness of the syndrome and the use of broader diagnostic criteria (Abbeduto et al., 2014). Contemporary prevalence estimates usually include related syndromes, such as *Asperger's disorder*, that are milder forms of the disease that

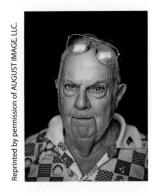

Donald Triplett, now 85, still lives in Forest, Mississippi, where he was born. He was the first person diagnosed with autism.

used to go uncounted, but are now included within the broadly defined DSM-5 version of autism *spectrum* disorder. Although these explanations make sense, scientists have not ruled out the possibility of a genuine increase in the prevalence of autism (Weintraub, 2011). Males account for about 80 percent of autism diagnoses, although curiously, females tend to exhibit more severe impairments (Ursano et al., 2008).

Etiology of ASD

Autism was originally blamed on cold, aloof parenting (Bettelheim, 1967), but that view was eventually discredited by research (Bhasin & Schendel, 2007). Given its appearance so early in life, most theorists today view autism as a disorder that originates in biological dysfunctions. Consistent with that viewpoint, twin studies and family studies have demonstrated that genetic factors make a major contribution to ASD (Abbeduto et al., 2014; Risch et al., 2014). Many theorists believe that autism must be attributable to some sort of brain abnormality, but until recently there was relatively little progress in pinpointing the nature of this abnormality. The most reliable finding has been that ASD is associated with generalized brain enlargement that is apparent by age two (Hazlett et al., 2011). Children with autism appear to have 67 percent more neurons in the prefrontal cortex than other children do (Courchesne et al., 2011). MRI studies suggest that this brain overgrowth begins sometime around the end of the first year, which, with the luxury of hindsight, is right around the time that autistic symptoms usually start to surface. However, a more recent study found evidence that this overgrowth may begin during prenatal development (Stoner et al., 2014). Theorists speculate that this overgrowth probably produces disruptions in neural circuits.

One hypothesis that has garnered a great deal of publicity is the idea that autism may be caused by the mercury used as a preservative in some childhood vaccines (Kirby, 2005). However, the 1998 study that first reported a link between vaccinations and autism has been *discredited as fraudulent* (Deer, 2011; Godlee, Smith, & Marcovitch, 2011). Moreover, independent efforts to replicate the purported association between vaccinations and ASD have consistently failed (Paul, 2009; Wing & Potter, 2009). Widespread belief in the apparently spurious relationship between autism and vaccinations may simply be due to the fact that children get scheduled vaccinations around the same age (12–15 months) that parents first start to realize their children are not developing normally (Doja & Roberts, 2006).

Finally, you may be interested in what happened to autism's first child (Donvan & Zucker, 2010), Donald Triplett. He continues to live (alone) in the house in which he was raised. Donald sticks to a few rooms of the house and follows his established routines. Surprisingly, and very mysteriously, he leaves town once a month and disappears. What does he do? Where does he go? Donald loves to travel. He travels all over the world by himself. This might seem quite surprising to you, that he would break free from his familiar surroundings to engage in this type of activity. But, of course, there are routines attached to his travel. For example, each trip lasts six days at most, and he tries to get photographs of scenes and buildings that he has already seen in pictures. He then places all the pictures in well-organized albums. He makes his own travel arrangements when travelling in the United States, and uses the same travel agent each time when he travels overseas.

Over the years, Donald has developed hobbies; he is an avid golfer and he loves to drive his Cadillac. He is comfortable living in the town of his birth. The small town he lives in protects and nurtures him, and his many friends warn strangers who come looking for Donald, "the celebrity," that "If what you are doing hurts Don, I know where to find you" (Donovan & Zucker, 2010).

Psychological Disorders and the Law

Key Learning Goal

▶ Discuss the nature of the insanity defence.

Hamilton, Ontario, psychologist Lori Triano-Antidormi (2013) and her husband, Tony, a social worker, are mental health professionals. They had had a great deal of exposure to the nature of mental illness in the course of their educational experiences, but they were unprepared for the horrific intrusion that mental illness would make into their personal lives in 1997. A neighbour, Lucia Piovesan, became convinced that Lori and Tony's son, Zachary, was the soul of her own deceased son, who was searching for some type of release. Piovesan tried to grant her son release by stabbing two-year-old Zachary to death in March 1997 (Could Zach's Death, 1999). When she was arrested, Piovesan was carrying a picture of her own son, Enrico, who had died six years before.

Zachary's parents had been concerned about Piovesan's obvious distress for some time but were unable to accomplish anything through the criminal justice system (Adams, Pitre, & Smith, 2001). Later at trial, Piovesan was found to be *not criminally responsible* for the murder because of mental illness (Davison et al., 2008). She suffered from paranoid schizophrenia and had been refusing to take her medication for some time before the murder.

What does it mean to be *not criminally responsible on account of mental disorder*? How is it judged? We entrust our protection to various levels of government in our society. Societies use laws to enforce their norms regarding appropriate behaviour. Tragically, those agencies of Canadian society given this trust failed Zachary and his parents. The law in our society has something to say about many issues related to psychological disorder and abnormal behaviour. In this section, we examine the role of the legal system with regard to psychological disorders.

Insanity

When many people refer to individuals suffering from a psychological disorder, they often use the term *insane* and refer to *insanity laws* or the *insanity defence*. In Canada, the proper term is not insanity. In Canadian law an individual can be judged "not criminally responsible on account of mental disorder." Neither it nor the older term, insanity, is a diagnosis. "Not criminally responsible on account of mental disorder" is an important legal concept, because criminal acts must be intentional. The law reasons that people who are "out of their mind" may not be able to appreciate the significance of what they're doing. This type of defence is used in criminal trials by defendants who admit that they committed the crime but claim that they lacked intent.

No simple relationship exists between specific diagnoses of mental disorders and court findings of insanity or not criminally responsible on account of mental disorder. Most people with diagnosed psychological disorders would *not* qualify as insane. The people most likely to qualify are those troubled by severe disturbances that display delusional behaviour. The courts apply various rules in making judgments about a defendant's mental state, depending on the jurisdiction (Simon & Shuman, 2008). According to one widely used rule, called the *M'Naghten rule,* insanity exists when a mental disorder makes a person unable to distinguish right from wrong. The M'Naghten rule originated in England when a delusional man attempted to kill the prime minister and shot one of the prime minister's assistants instead. This rule has served as the basis of insanity laws in many countries, including Canada. (As you can imagine, evaluating insanity as defined in the M'Naghten rule

can be difficult for judges and jurors, not to mention the psychologists and psychiatrists who are called into court as expert witnesses.) According to York University professor Regina Schuller (e.g., McKimmie, Masters, Schuller, et al., 2013; Schuller, Kazoleas, & Kawakami, 2013; Schuller & Vidmar, 2011) and Simon Fraser University's James Ogloff, the "growth in clinical psychology over the first half of the twentieth century resulted in an increased demand from the legal system for clinical evaluations and diagnoses of mental disorders" (Schuller & Ogloff, 2001, p. 6).

Over the years since the establishment of the M'Naghten rule, changes have been made to how psychological disorders are used in court. In Canada, the designation of being found not guilty by reason of insanity (NGRI) was changed in 1991 to "not criminally responsible on account of mental disorder" (NCRMD) (Ogloff & Whittemore, 2001). According to Simon Fraser University psychologists Jocelyn Lymburner and Ronald Roesch (1999), the use and success of this defence are rarer than most Canadians assume. They suggest that it is rarely successful, and typically is used only in cases of the most severely disordered defendants.

According to a team of scholars from Carleton University (Pozzulo, Bennell, & Forth, 2006), issues of fitness, insanity, and automatism are relevant to the two cornerstones of English–Canadian law—*actus reus* (a wrongful deed) and *mens rea* (criminal intent). Mental health professionals may play an important role at several stages of a trial. Defendants may be found *unfit to stand trial* if they are judged unable to conduct a defence at any point in the legal proceedings because of a psychological disorder such as schizophrenia. This may be due to their inability to understand the proceedings or possible consequences, or an inability to communicate with their lawyers. If fitness is restored, a defendant may stand trial.

If found fit to stand trial, psychological issues may arise in terms of the not criminally responsible defence. If it is found that the defendant was unable to appreciate the quality of the act and the fact that it was wrong, the defendant may be found not criminally responsible on account of mental disorder. If found NCRMD, the defendant may be absolutely discharged, given a conditional discharge, or ordered to a psychiatric facility (Pozzulo, Bennell, & Forth, 2006).

A final issue relevant to our discussion is that of *automatism*. Here the idea is that you should not be held responsible if you had no control over your behaviour. The conditions that have been recognized in Canadian courts include having sustained physical blows, carbon monoxide poisoning, sleepwalking, and others. In Chapter 5, we referred to the successful sleepwalking defence used in the

Courtesy of Regina Schuller

Psychologist Regina Schuller is an expert on the interface of psychology and Canadian law. Her research interests include cases involving violence against women.

1988 Ontario case of Ken Parks, who drove almost 40 kilometres and killed his mother-in-law. While a defendant may be sent to a psychiatric institution if he or she is judged NCRMD, a "successful (noninsane) automatism verdict means that the defendant is not guilty and is then released without conditions" (Pozzulo, Bennell, & Forth, 2006, p. 281).

Postscript: While alive, Zachary had a passion for music. After his death, his short life was honoured by the creation of a project designed to promote music to children: CDs of Zachary's favourite musician, the Canadian singer Raffi, were distributed to children's hospitals across Canada for children to enjoy (Famely, 2004).

Culture and Pathology

Key Learning Goal

▶ Discuss the nature of cultural differences in the prevalence and symptoms of psychological disorders.

The legal rules governing mental disorders and involuntary commitment obviously are culture-specific. And we noted earlier that judgments of normality and abnormality are influenced by cultural norms and values. Stigmas about mental illness and its effects on such things as willingness to admit to and seek treatment for mental illness also vary by culture (Fung et al., 2007; Gim, Atkinson, & Kim, 1991; Yang, 2007). For example, Asian North Americans seem particularly unwilling to take their concerns to therapists, with this level affected by factors such as the client's level of acculturation and the ethnicity of the therapist (Gim, Atkinson, & Whiteley, 1990). Asian Canadians have been found to have one of the lowest levels of accessing mental health services of all minority groups in Canada (Chen, Kazanjian, Wong, & Goldner, 2010). In light of these realities, would it be reasonable to infer that psychological disorders are culturally variable phenomena? Social scientists are sharply divided on the answer to this question. Some embrace a *relativistic view* of psychological disorders, whereas others subscribe to a *universalistic or pancultural view* (Tanaka-Matsumi, 2001). Theorists who embrace the *relativistic view* argue that the criteria of mental illness vary greatly across cultures and that there are no universal standards of normality and abnormality. According to the relativists, the DSM diagnostic system reflects an ethnocentric, Western, white, urban, middle- and upper-class cultural orientation that has limited relevance in other cultural contexts. In contrast, those who subscribe to the *pancultural view* argue that the criteria of mental illness are much the same around the world and that basic standards of normality and abnormality are universal across cultures. Theorists who accept the pancultural view of psychopathology typically maintain that Western diagnostic concepts have validity and utility in other cultural contexts.

The debate about culture and pathology basically boils down to two specific issues: (1) Are the psychological disorders seen in Western societies found throughout the world? (2) Are the symptom patterns of mental disorders invariant across cultures? Let's briefly examine the evidence on these questions and then reconsider the relativistic and pancultural views of psychological disorders.

Are Equivalent Disorders Found Around the World?

Most investigators agree that the principal categories of serious psychological disturbance—schizophrenia, depression, and bipolar illness—are identifiable in all cultures (Tsai et al., 2001). Most behaviours that are regarded as clearly abnormal in Western culture are also viewed as abnormal in other cultures. People who are delusional, hallucinatory, disoriented, or incoherent are thought to be disturbed in all societies, although there are cultural disparities in exactly what is considered delusional or hallucinatory.

Cultural variations are more apparent in the recognition of less severe forms of psychological disturbance (Mezzich, Lewis-Fernandez, & Ruiperez, 2003). Additional research is needed, but relatively mild types of pathology that do not disrupt behaviour in obvious ways appear to go unrecognized in many societies. Thus, syndromes such as generalized anxiety disorder, hypochondria, and narcissistic personality disorder, which are firmly established as diagnostic entities in the DSM, are viewed in some cultures as "run of the mill" difficulties and peculiarities rather than as full-fledged disorders.

Finally, researchers have discovered a small number of *culture-bound disorders* that further illustrate the diversity of abnormal behaviour around the world (Lewis-Fernandez, Buarnaccia, & Ruiz, 2009; Tseng, 2009). **Culture-bound disorders are abnormal syndromes found only in a few cultural groups.** For example, *koro*, an obsessive fear that one's penis will withdraw into one's abdomen, is seen only among Chinese males in Malaya and several other regions of southern Asia. *Windigo*, which involves an intense craving for human flesh and fear that one will turn into a cannibal, is seen only among Algonquin cultures, and *pibloktoq* is a type of Arctic hysteria associated with the Inuit. And until fairly recently, the eating disorder *anorexia nervosa*, discussed in this chapter's Personal Application, was largely seen only in affluent Western cultures (Russell, 2009).

The role of cultural context has been recognized in the various editions of the DSM over the years. For example, in the DSM-IV-TR, there was a distinct category of disorders included in the appendix— "culture-bound-disorders" that described specific disorders that seemed to occur only in specific cultures. These included *amok* (Malaysian), and *brain fag* (West African). The DSM-5 has benefited from the development of an updated Outline for Cultural Formulation and it also includes a new Cultural Formulation Interview assessment form to be used "to obtain information about the impact of a patient's culture on key aspects of care" (Black & Grant, 2013, p. 443). Sixteen questions are used to examine four domains: cultural definition of the problem; cultural perceptions of cause, context, and support; cultural factors affecting self-coping and past help seeking; and cultural factors affecting current help seeking.

Are Symptom Patterns Culturally Invariant?

Do the major types of psychological disorders manifest themselves in the same way around the world? It depends to some extent on the disorder. The more a disorder has a strong biological component, the more it tends to be expressed in similar ways across varied cultures (Marsella & Yamada, 2007). Thus, the constellations of symptoms associated with schizophrenia and bipolar illness are largely the same across widely disparate societies (Draguns, 1980, 1990). However, even in severe, heavily biological disorders, cultural variations in symptom patterns are also seen (Mezzich, Lewis-Fernandez, & Ruiperez, 2003). For example,

delusions are a common symptom of schizophrenia in all cultures, but the specific delusions that people report are tied to their cultural heritage (Brislin, 1993). In technologically advanced societies, schizophrenic patients report that thoughts are being inserted into their minds through transmissions from electric lines, satellites, or microwave ovens. Victims of schizophrenia in less technological societies experience the same phenomenon but blame sorcerers or demons. The influence of culture on symptom patterns is illustrated by recent reports of a new delusion in modern societies—patients are erroneously insisting that they are the stars of reality TV shows (DeAngelis, 2009).

Of the major disorders, symptom patterns are probably most variable for depression. For example, profound feelings of guilt and self-deprecation lie at the core of depression in Western cultures but are far less central to depression in many other societies. In non-Western cultures, depression tends to be expressed in terms of somatic symptoms, such as complaints of fatigue, headaches, and backaches, more than psychological symptoms, such as dejection and low self-esteem (Tsai et al., 2001; Young, 1997). These differences presumably occur because people learn to express symptoms of psychological distress in ways that are acceptable in their culture.

So, what can we conclude about the validity of the relativistic versus pancultural views of psychological disorders? Both views appear to have some merit. As we have seen in other areas of research, psychopathology is characterized by both cultural variance and invariance. Investigators have identified some universal standards of normality and abnormality and found considerable similarity across cultures in the syndromes that are regarded as pathological and in their patterns of symptoms. However, researchers have also discovered many cultural variations in the recognition, definition, and symptoms of various psychological disorders.

Putting It in Perspective: Themes 3, 4, 5, and 6

Our examination of abnormal behaviour and its roots has highlighted four of our organizing themes: multifactorial causation, the interplay of heredity and environment, the sociohistorical context in which psychology evolves, and the influence of culture on psychological phenomena.

We can safely say that every disorder described in this chapter has multiple causes. The development of mental disorders involves an interplay among a variety of psychological, biological, and social factors. We also saw that most psychological disorders

depend on an interaction of genetics and experience. This interaction shows up most clearly in the *stress-vulnerability models* for mood disorders and schizophrenic disorders (see Figure 15.23). *Vulnerability* to these disorders seems to depend primarily on heredity, whereas stress is largely a function of environment. According to stress-vulnerability theories, disorders emerge when high vulnerability intersects with high stress. A high biological vulnerability may not be converted into a disorder if a person's stress is low. Similarly, high stress may not lead to a disorder

Key Learning Goal

▶ Identify the four unifying themes highlighted in this chapter.

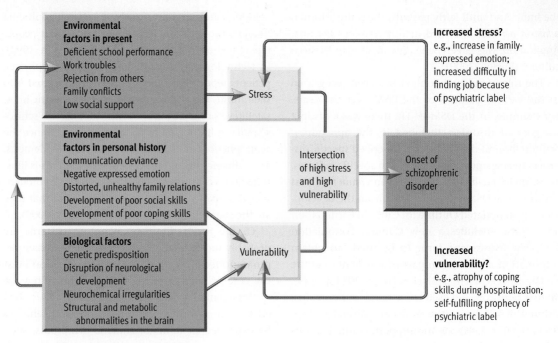

Figure 15.23
The stress-vulnerability model of schizophrenia. Multifactorial causation is readily apparent in current theories about the etiology of schizophrenic disorders. A variety of biological factors and personal history factors influence one's vulnerability to the disorder, which interacts with the amount of stress one experiences. Schizophrenic disorders appear to result from an intersection of high stress and high vulnerability.

Source: From Weiten. *Cengage Advantage Books: Psychology,* 9E. © 2013 South-Western, a part of Cengage, Inc. Reproduced by permission. www.cengage.com/permissions

if vulnerability is low. Thus, the impact of heredity depends on the environment, and the effect of environment depends on heredity.

This chapter also demonstrated that psychology evolves in a sociohistorical context. We saw that modern conceptions of normality and abnormality are largely shaped by empirical research, but social trends, economic necessities, and political realities also play a role. Finally, our discussion of psychological

disorders showed once again that psychological phenomena are shaped to some degree by cultural parameters. Although some standards of normality and abnormality transcend cultural boundaries, cultural norms influence many aspects of psychopathology. Indeed, the influence of culture will be apparent in our upcoming Personal Application on eating disorders. These disorders are largely a creation of modern, affluent, Western culture.

Understanding Eating Disorders

Key Learning Goals

▶ Identify the subtypes of eating disorders, and discuss their prevalence.

▶ Outline how genetic factors, personality, culture, family dynamics, and disturbed thinking contribute to eating disorders.

The psychological disorders that we discussed in the main body of the chapter have largely been recognized for centuries and most of them are found in one form or another in all cultures and societies. Eating disorders present a sharp contrast to this picture; they have been recognized only in recent decades and they have largely been confined to affluent, Westernized cultures (G.F.M. Russell, 1995; Szmukler & Patton, 1995). In spite of these fascinating differences, eating disorders have much in common with traditional forms of pathology.

Description

Although most people don't seem to take eating disorders as seriously as other types of psychological disorders, you will see that they are dangerous and debilitating (Thompson, Roehrig, & Kinder, 2007). No other psychological disorder is associated with a greater elevation in mortality (Striegel-Moore & Bulik, 2007). *Eating disorders* **are severe disturbances in eating behaviour characterized by preoccupation with weight and unhealthy efforts to control weight.** The DSM-5, includes the *feeding and eating disorders category*. This category includes *rumination disorder, avoidant/restrictive food intake disorder, anorexia nervosa, bulimia nervosa, binge-eating disorder,* and *other specified feeding or eating disorder.* In this section we focus on *anorexia nervosa* and *bulimia nervosa*, along with a discussion of *binge-eating disorder*.

Anorexia Nervosa

Anorexia nervosa **involves intense fear of gaining weight, disturbed body image, refusal to maintain normal weight, and dangerous measures to lose weight.** Two subtypes have been observed. In *restricting type anorexia nervosa*, people drastically reduce their intake of food, sometimes literally starving themselves. In *binge-eating/purging type anorexia nervosa*, individuals attempt to lose weight by forcing themselves to vomit after meals, by misusing laxatives and diuretics, and by engaging in excessive exercise.

Both types suffer from disturbed body image. No matter how frail and emaciated they become, they insist that they are too fat. Their morbid fear of obesity means that they are never satisfied with their weight. If they gain half a kilogram, they panic. The only thing that makes them happy is to lose more weight. The frequent result is a relentless decline in body weight. Because of their disturbed body image, people suffering from anorexia generally do *not* appreciate the maladaptive quality of their behaviour and rarely seek treatment on their own. They are typically coaxed or coerced into treatment by friends or family members who are alarmed by their appearance.

Anorexic patients frequently endure other psychological disorders, as well. More than half suffer from depressive disorders or anxiety disorders (Sadock et al., 2015). Anorexia nervosa eventually leads to a cascade of medical problems. These problems may include *amenorrhea* (a loss of menstrual cycles in women), gastrointestinal problems, low blood pressure, *osteoporosis* (a loss of bone density), and metabolic disturbances that can lead to cardiac arrest or circulatory collapse (Mitchell & Wonderlich, 2014). Anorexia is a debilitating illness that is associated with greatly elevated mortality rates (Franko et al., 2013).

Bulimia Nervosa

Bulimia nervosa **involves habitually engaging in out-of-control overeating followed by unhealthy compensatory efforts, such as self-induced vomiting, fasting, abuse of laxatives and diuretics,**

Eating disorders have become common and have been seen in many prominent women, such as Lindsay Lohan and Mary-Kate Olsen.

and excessive exercise. The eating binges are usually carried out in secret and are followed by intense guilt and concern about gaining weight. These feelings motivate ill-advised strategies to undo the effects of overeating. However, vomiting prevents the absorption of only about half of recently consumed food, and laxatives and diuretics have negligible impact on caloric intake, so people suffering from bulimia nervosa typically maintain a reasonably normal weight (Fairburn, Cooper, & Murphy, 2009). Medical problems associated with bulimia nervosa include cardiac arrhythmias, dental problems, metabolic deficiencies, and gastrointestinal problems (Mitchell & Wonderlich, 2014).

Obviously, bulimia nervosa shares many features with anorexia nervosa, such as a morbid fear of becoming obese, preoccupation with food, and rigid, maladaptive approaches to controlling weight that are grounded in naive all-or-none thinking. The close relationship between the disorders is demonstrated by the fact that many patients who initially develop one syndrome cross over to display the other syndrome (Tozzi et al., 2005). However, the two syndromes also differ in crucial ways. First and foremost, bulimia is a much less life-threatening condition. Second, although their appearance is usually more "normal" than that seen in anorexia, people with bulimia are much more likely to recognize that their eating behaviour is pathological and are more likely to cooperate with treatment (Guarda et al., 2007). Nonetheless, like anorexia, bulimia is associated with elevated mortality rates (Crow et al., 2009), but this elevated rate is only about one-third as great as that for anorexia nervosa (Arcelus et al., 2011).

Binge-Eating Disorder

A surprising number of people who exhibit disordered eating do not fit neatly into the anorexia or bulimia category. In the DSM-5 another eating disorder category was added to fill this gap. *Binge-eating disorder* involves distress-inducing eating binges that are not accompanied by the purging, fasting, and excessive exercise seen in bulimia. Obviously, this syndrome resembles bulimia, but it is a less severe disorder. Still, this disorder creates great distress, as

Kristin von Ranson is a clinical psychologist at the University of Calgary. Her research focuses on eating disorders, including questions related to etiology, classification, and assessment of eating problems in individuals of all ages. She is very interested in the debate over whether eating disorders are forms of addictions.

these people tend to be disgusted by their bodies and distraught about their overeating (von Ranson & Wallace, 2014). People with binge-eating disorder are frequently overweight. Their excessive eating is often triggered by stress (Gluck, 2006). Research suggests that this comparatively mild syndrome may be more common than anorexia or bulimia (Hudson et al., 2007).

Prevalence and Cultural Roots

Eating disorders are a product of modern, affluent Western culture, in which food is generally plentiful and the desirability of being thin is widely endorsed. Until recent decades, these disorders were not seen outside Western cultures (Hoek, 2002). However, advances in communication have exported Western culture to far-flung corners of the globe. Hence, eating disorders have started showing up in many non-Western societies, especially affluent Asian countries (Becker & Fay, 2006).

There are huge gender gaps in the likelihood of developing eating disorders. About 90–95 percent of individuals with anorexia nervosa and bulimia nervosa are female, and about 60 percent of those with binge-eating disorder are female (Devlin & Steinglass, 2014). The staggering gender disparities in the prevalence of the more serious eating disorders appear to be a result of cultural pressures rather than biological factors (Smolak & Murnen, 2001). Western standards of attractiveness emphasize slenderness more for females than for males, and women generally experience greater pressure to be physically attractive than men do (Strahan et al., 2008). Eating disorders mostly afflict young women. The typical age of onset for anorexia is 14–18; for bulimia it is 15–21 (see Figure 15.24).

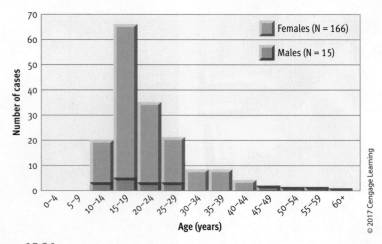

Figure 15.24

Age of onset for anorexia nervosa. Eating disorders tend to emerge during adolescence, as these data for anorexia nervosa show. This graph shows how age of onset was distributed in a sample of 166 female patients in Minnesota. As you can see, over half of the patients experienced the onset of their illness before the age of 20, with vulnerability clearly peaking between the ages of 15 and 19.

Source: Adapted from Lucas, A. R., Beard, C. M., O'Fallon, W. M., & Kurland, L. T. (1991). 50-year trends in the incidence of anorexia nervosa in Rochester, Minn.: A population-based study. *American Journal of Psychiatry, 148*, 917–922. Reprinted with permission from the *American Journal of Psychiatry* (Copyright © 1991). American Psychiatric Association.

How common are eating disorders in Western societies? Research suggests that among females, about 1 percent develop anorexia nervosa, roughly 1.5 percent develop bulimia nervosa, and about 3.5 percent exhibit binge-eating disorder (Hudson et al., 2007). In some respects, these figures may only scratch the surface of the problem (Keel et al., 2012). Evidence suggests that another 2–4 percent of people may struggle with serious eating problems that do not quite qualify for a formal diagnosis (Swanson et al., 2011). And community surveys suggest that there may be more undiagnosed eating disorders among men than generally appreciated (Field et al., 2014).

Etiology of Eating Disorders

Like other types of psychological disorders, eating disorders are caused by multiple determinants that work interactively. Let's take a brief look at some of the factors that contribute to the development of anorexia nervosa and bulimia nervosa.

Genetic Vulnerability. The stockpile of research findings is not as large as it is for many other types of psychopathology (such as anxiety, mood, and schizophrenic disorders), but some people may inherit a genetic vulnerability to eating disorders. There is convincing evidence for a hereditary component in both anorexia nervosa and bulimia nervosa, with genetics probably playing a stronger role in anorexia (Trace et al., 2013). A genetic predisposition also appears to contribute to binge-eating

disorder, but there are fewer studies of this newer diagnosis.

Personality Factors. Certain personality traits may increase vulnerability to eating disorders. There are innumerable exceptions, but victims of anorexia nervosa tend to be obsessive, rigid, and emotionally restrained, whereas victims of bulimia nervosa tend to be impulsive, overly sensitive, and low in self-esteem (Wonderlich, 2002). Recent research also suggests that perfectionism is a risk factor for anorexia (Keel et al., 2012).

Cultural Values. The contribution of cultural values to the increased prevalence of eating disorders can hardly be overestimated (Anderson-Fye & Becker, 2004; Stice, 2001; Striegel-Moore & Bulik, 2007). In Western society, young women are socialized to believe that they must be attractive, and to be attractive they must be as thin as the actresses and fashion models that dominate the media (Lavine, Sweeney, & Wagner, 1999). Thanks to this cultural milieu, many young women are dissatisfied with their weight because the societal ideals promoted by the media are unattainable for most of them (Thompson & Stice, 2001). Unfortunately, in a small portion of these women, the pressure to be thin, in combination with genetic vulnerability, family pathology, and other factors, leads to unhealthful efforts to control weight.

The Role of the Family. Quite a number of theorists stress how family dynamics can

contribute to the development of anorexia and bulimia in young women (Haworth-Hoeppner, 2000). The principal issue appears to be that some mothers contribute to eating disorders simply by endorsing society's message that "you can never be too thin" and by modelling unhealthy dieting behaviours of their own (Francis & Birch, 2005). In conjunction with media pressures, this role modelling leads many daughters to internalize the idea that the thinner you are, the more attractive you are. Of course, peers can also endorse beliefs and model behaviours that promote eating disorders (Keel et al., 2013). Another potentially family-related issue is that there is an association between childhood sexual and physical abuse and an elevated risk for eating disorders (Steiger, Bruce, & Israël, 2013).

Cognitive Factors. Many theorists emphasize the role of disturbed thinking in the etiology of eating disorders (Williamson et al., 2001). For example, anorexic patients' typical belief that they are fat when they actually are wasting away is a dramatic illustration of how thinking goes awry. Patients with eating disorders display rigid, all-or-none thinking and many maladaptive beliefs, such as "I must be thin to be accepted," "If I am not in complete control, I will lose all control," "If I gain one kilogram, I'll go on to gain an enormous amount of weight." Additional research is needed to determine whether distorted thinking is a *cause* or merely a *symptom* of eating disorders.

Working with Probabilities in Thinking about Mental Illness

As you read about the various types of psychological disorders, did you think to yourself that you or someone you know was being described? On the one hand, there is no reason to be alarmed. The tendency to see yourself and your friends in descriptions of pathology is a common one, sometimes called the *medical student's disease* because beginning medical students often erroneously believe that they or their friends have whatever diseases they are currently learning about. Consider the statistics in Figure 15.25, which outlines the lifetime prevalence of psychological disorders in

the United States. According to the figure, the likelihood of anyone having at least one DSM disorder is estimated to be about 44 percent.

This estimate strikes most people as surprisingly high. Why is this so? One reason is that when people think about psychological disorders they tend to think of severe disorders, such as bipolar disorder or schizophrenia, which are relatively infrequent, rather than "run of the mill" disturbances, such as anxiety and depressive disorders, which are much more common. When it comes to mental illness, people tend to think of patients in straitjackets or of obviously psychotic homeless people who do not reflect the broad and diverse population of people who suffer from psychological disorders. In other words, their *prototypes* or

"best examples" of mental illness consist of severe disorders that are infrequent, so they underestimate the prevalence of mental disorders. This distortion illustrates the influence of the ***representativeness heuristic, in which the estimated probability of an event is based on how similar the event is to the typical prototype of that event*** (see Chapter 8).

Do you still find it hard to believe that the overall prevalence of psychological disorders is about 44 percent? Another reason this number seems surprisingly high is that many people do not understand that the probability of having *at least one* disorder is much higher than the probability of having the most prevalent disorder by itself. For example, the probability of having a substance-use disorder, the single most common type of disorder, is approximately 24 percent, but the probability of having a substance-use disorder *or* an anxiety disorder *or* a mood disorder *or* a schizophrenic disorder jumps to 44 percent. These "or" relationships represent *cumulative probabilities*. See Table 15.4.

Yet another consideration that makes the prevalence figures seem high is that many people confuse different types of *prevalence rates*. The 44 percent estimate is for *lifetime prevalence*, which means it is the probability of having *any* disorder *at least once* at any time in one's lifetime. The lifetime prevalence rate is another example of "or" relationships. It is a value that takes into account the probability of having a psychological disorder in childhood *or* adolescence *or* adulthood *or* old age. *Point prevalence rates*, which estimate the percentage of people manifesting various disorders *at a particular point in time*, are much lower because many psychological disorders last only a few months to a few years.

What about "and" relationships—that is, relationships in which we want to know the probability of someone having condition A *and* condition B? For example, given

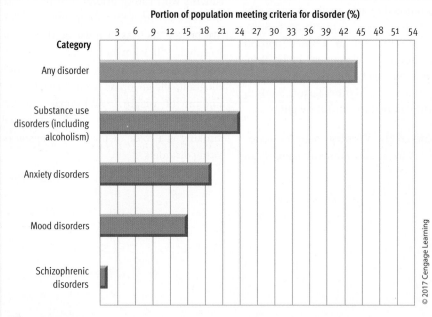

Figure 15.25
Lifetime prevalence of psychological disorders. The estimated percentage of people who have, at any time in their life, suffered from one of four types of psychological disorders or from a disorder of any kind (top bar) is shown here. Prevalence estimates vary somewhat from one study to the next, depending on the exact methods used in sampling and assessment. The estimates shown here are based on pooling data from Waves 1 and 2 of the *Epidemiological Catchment Area Studies* and the *National Comorbidity Study*, as summarized by Regier and Burke (2000) and Dew, Bromet, and Switzer (2000). These studies, which collectively evaluated over 28 000 subjects, provide the best data to date on the prevalence of mental illness in the United States.

Table 15.4

Critical Thinking Skills Discussed in This Application

SKILL	DESCRIPTION
Understanding the limitations of the representativeness heuristic	The critical thinker understands that focusing on prototypes can lead to inaccurate probability estimates.
Understanding cumulative probabilities	The critical thinker understands that the probability of at least one of several events occurring is additive, and increases with time and the number of events.
Understanding conjunctive probabilities	The critical thinker appreciates that the probability of two uncertain events happening together is less than the probability of either event happening alone.
Understanding the limitations of the availability heuristic	The critical thinker understands that the ease with which examples come to mind may not be an accurate guide to the probability of an event.

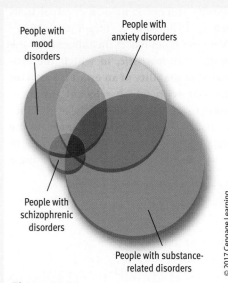

People with mood disorders

People with anxiety disorders

People with schizophrenic disorders

People with substance-related disorders

© 2017 Cengage Learning

Figure 15.26

Conjunctive probabilities. The probability of someone having all four disorders depicted here cannot be greater than the probability of the least common condition by itself, which is 1 percent for schizophrenia. The intersection of all four disorders (shown in black) has to be a subset of schizophrenic disorders and is probably well under 1 percent. Efforts to think about probabilities can sometimes be facilitated by creating diagrams that show the relationships and overlap among various events.

the lifetime prevalence estimates (from Figure 15.25) for each category of disorder, which are shown here in parentheses, what is the probability of someone having a substance-use disorder (24 percent prevalence) *and* an anxiety disorder (19 percent) *and* a mood disorder (15 percent) *and* a schizophrenic disorder (1 percent) during his or her lifetime? Such "and" relationships represent *conjunctive probabilities*. Stop and think: What must be true about the probability of having all four types of disorders? Will this probability be less than 24 percent, between 24 percent and 44 percent, or over 44 percent? You may be surprised to learn that this figure is probably well under 1 percent. You can't have all four disorders unless you have the least frequent disorder (schizophrenia), which has a prevalence of 1 percent, so the answer *must* be 1 percent or less. Moreover, of all of the people with schizophrenia, only a tiny subset of them are likely to have all three of the other disorders, so the answer is probably well under 1 percent (see Figure 15.26). If this type of question strikes you as contrived, think again. Epidemiologists have devoted an enormous amount of research to the estimation of *comorbidity*—the co-existence of two or more disorders—because it greatly complicates treatment issues.

These are two examples of using statistical probabilities as a critical thinking tool. Let's apply this type of thinking to another problem dealing with physical health. Here is a problem used in a study by Tversky and Kahneman (1983, p. 308) that many physicians got wrong:

A health survey was conducted in a sample of adult males in British Columbia, of all ages and occupations. Please give your best estimate of the following values:

What percentage of the men surveyed have had one or more heart attacks? ___

What percentage of the men surveyed both are over 55 years old and have had one or more heart attacks? ___

Fill in the blanks above with your best guesses. Of course, you probably have only a very general idea about the prevalence of heart attacks, but go ahead and fill in the blanks anyway.

The actual values are not as important in this example as the relative values are. Over 65 percent of the physicians who participated in the experiment by Tversky and Kahneman gave a higher percentage value for the second question than for the first. What is wrong with their answers? The second question is asking about the conjunctive probability of two events. Hopefully, you see why this figure *must* be less than the probability of either one of these events occurring alone. Of all of the men in the survey who had had a heart attack, only some of them are also over 55, so the second number must be smaller than the first. As we saw in Chapter 8, this

common error in thinking is called the *conjunction fallacy*. **The *conjunction fallacy* occurs when people estimate that the odds of two uncertain events happening together are greater than the odds of either event happening alone.**

Why did so many physicians get this problem wrong? They were vulnerable to the conjunction fallacy because they were influenced by the *representativeness heuristic*, or the power of prototypes. When physicians think "heart attack," they tend to envision a man over the age of 55. Hence, the second scenario fit so well with their prototype of a heart attack victim, they carelessly overestimated its probability.

Let's consider some additional examples of erroneous reasoning about probabilities involving how people think about psychological disorders. Toward the beginning of the chapter, we discussed the fact that many people tend to stereotypically assume that mentally ill people are likely to be violent. Other research suggests that people tend to wildly overestimate (37-fold in one study) how often the

Psychological Disorders

insanity defence is used in criminal trials (Silver, Cirincion, & Steadman., 1994). These examples reflect the influence of the *availability heuristic*, in which the estimated probability of an event is based on the ease with which relevant instances come to mind. Because of the availability heuristic, people tend to overestimate the probability of dramatic events that receive heavy media coverage, even when these events are rare, because examples of the events are easy to retrieve from memory. Violent acts by former psychiatric patients tend to get lots of attention in the press. And because of the *hindsight bias*, journalists tend to question why authorities couldn't foresee and prevent the violence (see the Critical Thinking Application for Chapter 12), so the mental illness angle tends to be emphasized. In a similar vein, press coverage is usually intense when a defendant in a murder trial mounts a not criminally responsible defence.

In sum, the various types of statistics that come up in thinking about psychological disorders demonstrate that we are constantly working with probabilities, even though we may not realize it. Critical thinking requires a good understanding of the laws of probability because there are very few certainties in life.

GENERAL CONCEPTS

The medical model

- The *medical model*, which assumes it is useful to view abnormal behaviour as a disease, led to more humane treatment for people who exhibit abnormal behaviour.
- However, mental illness carries a *stigma* that can be difficult to shake and creates difficulties for those who suffer from psychological disorders.
- The medical model has also been criticized on the grounds that it converts moral and social questions into medical questions.

Criteria of abnormality

- Judgments of abnormality are based on three criteria: deviance from social norms, maladaptive behaviour, and reports of personal distress.
- Judgments about mental illness reflect prevailing cultural values, social trends, and political forces, as well as scientific knowledge.
- Normality and abnormality exist on a continuum.

The diagnostic system

- The DSM-5, released in 2013, is the official psychodiagnostic classification system used in North America.
- The practical logistics of shifting to a *dimensional approach* to diagnosis proved controversial, so the DSM-5 retained a *categorical approach* to disorders.
- The number of diagnoses in the DSM increased from 128 in the first edition to 541 in the current edition.

ANXIETY DISORDERS, OCD, AND PTSD

Types

- *Generalized anxiety disorder* is marked by chronic high anxiety not tied to a specific threat.
- *Specific phobia* is marked by a persistent, irrational fear of an object or situation that is not dangerous.
- *Panic disorder* involves recurrent, sudden anxiety attacks that occur unexpectedly.
- *Agoraphobia* is a fear of going out to public places; it can co-exist with various disorders, but especially panic disorder.
- *Obsessive-compulsive disorder (OCD)* is marked by uncontrollable intrusions of unwanted thoughts and urges to engage in senseless rituals.
- *Post-traumatic stress disorder (PTSD)* involves enduring psychological disturbance attributable to the experience of a major traumatic event.

Etiology

- Twin studies suggest a *genetic predisposition* to anxiety disorders.
- Disturbances in the neural circuits using *GABA* and *serotonin* may play a role in some anxiety disorders.
- Many anxiety responses can be acquired through classical conditioning and maintained through operant conditioning.
- Cognitive theorists assert that the tendency to misinterpret harmless situations as threatening leads to anxiety disorders.
- Exposure to great stress can contribute to the emergence of some anxiety disorders.

DISSOCIATIVE DISORDERS

Types

- *Dissociative amnesia* is a sudden loss of memory for personal information that is too extensive to be due to normal forgetting.
- *Dissociative identity disorder (DID)* involves the co-existence of two or more largely complete and usually very different personalities.

Etiology

- Dissociative amnesia is usually attributed to extreme stress.
- Some theorists maintain that people with DID gradually come to believe that independent entities within them are to blame for their problems.
- Other theorists maintain that DID is rooted in severe emotional trauma that occurred during childhood.

DEPRESSIVE AND BIPOLAR DISORDERS

Types

- *Major depressive disorder* is marked by persistent feelings of sadness and despair, loss of interest in previous sources of pleasure, slowed thought processes, and self-blame.
- *Bipolar disorder* is marked by the experience of depressed and manic episodes, with the latter involving irrational euphoria, racing thoughts, impulsive behaviour, and increased energy.
- Both major depression and bipolar disorder are associated with substantial elevations in suicide rates.

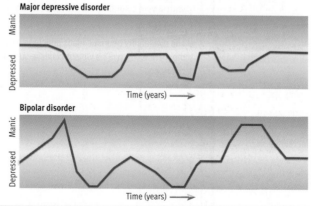

Etiology

- Twin studies suggest a *genetic predisposition* to depression and bipolar disorder.
- Disturbances in the neural circuits using *serotonin* and *norepinephrine* appear to contribute to depressive disorders.
- Researchers have found a correlation between depression and *reduced hippocampal volume*, which may reflect *suppressed neurogenesis* due to stress.
- Hormonal overactivity along the HPA axis in response to stress may play a role in depression.
- Cognitive theorists assert that people who exhibit a *pessimistic explanatory style* are especially vulnerable to depression.
- Behavioural theories emphasize how inadequate social skills increase vulnerability to depression.
- High stress is associated with increased vulnerability to both depression and bipolar disorder.

© 2017 Cengage Learning

SCHIZOPHRENIC DISORDERS

Symptoms

- Symptoms of schizophrenia include irrational thought, delusions, deterioration of adaptive behaviour, distorted perception, hallucinations, and disturbed emotion.

- The distinctions between schizophrenic subtypes (paranoid, catatonic, disorganized, and undifferentiated) were discarded in DSM-5.

- A newer approach to describing schizophrenia looks at the balance between the positive and negative symptoms of the disorder.

Etiology

- Twin studies and adoption studies suggest a *genetic vulnerability* to schizophrenia.

- Disturbances at *dopamine* synapses have been implicated as a possible cause of schizophrenia.

- Research uncovered an association between *enlarged brain ventricles* and schizophrenic disturbance.

- The *neurodevelopmental hypothesis* posits that vulnerability to schizophrenia is increased by disruptions of normal brain maturational processes during prenatal development or at birth.

- Schizophrenic patients from families high in *expressed emotion* have elevated relapse rates.

- High stress is associated with increased vulnerability to schizophrenic disorders.

CULTURE AND PATHOLOGY

- The *relativistic view* holds that the criteria of mental illness vary considerably across cultures.

- The *pancultural view* holds that the criteria of mental illness are much the same around the world.

- Research indicates that serious mental disorders are identifiable in all cultures, but there are cultural variations in the recognition of less severe forms of disturbance.

- Some cultural variations are seen in symptom patterns, but the symptoms associated with the more serious disorders are largely the same across different cultures.

NEURODEVELOPMENTAL DISORDERS

- *Autism spectrum disorder* is characterized by profound impairment of social communication and severely restricted interests and activities, apparent by age three.
- Autism tends to be a lifelong affliction requiring extensive family and institutional support.
- The recent increase in the diagnosis of autism is probably due to greater awareness of the syndrome and the use of broader diagnostic criteria.
- Genetic factors contribute to autistic disorders and brain overgrowth may play a role.
- Research has failed to find an association between vaccinations and the development of autism.

PSYCHOLOGY AND THE LAW

- Not criminally responsible on account of mental disorder (NCRMD) is a legal status indicating that a person cannot be held responsible for his or her actions because of mental illness. In many jurisdictions this is known as the "insanity defence."
- Although highly publicized and controversial, the NCRMD defence is not used frequently and is rarely successful.

APPLICATIONS

- The eating disorders include anorexia nervosa, bulimia nervosa, and binge-eating disorder.
- Anorexia and bulimia tend to develop in late adolescence, 90–95 percent of the victims are female.
- Due to the representativeness heuristic, people equate mental disorders with severe disorders, and hence underestimate the prevalence of mental disorders.
- The availability heuristic leads people to overestimate the likelihood that the mentally ill will be violent because such incidents receive heavy media coverage.

PERSONALITY DISORDERS

- *Personality disorders* are marked by extreme personality traits that cause subjective distress or impaired social and occupational functioning.
- *Antisocial personality disorder* is characterized by manipulative, impulsive, exploitive, aggressive behaviour.
- *Borderline personality disorder* is marked by instability in social relationships, self-concept, and emotional functioning.
- *Narcissistic personality disorder* involves a grandiose sense of self-importance, a sense of entitlement, and an excessive need for attention.

Treatment of Psychological Disorders

Themes in this Chapter

Theoretical
Diversity

Cultural
Heritage

What do you imagine when you hear the term *psychotherapy*? Unless you've had some personal exposure to therapy, your conception of it has likely been shaped by depictions you've seen on TV or in the movies. As you will see in this chapter, some of these images are to some degree accurate, but they don't exhaust the range of treatment contexts. Contemporary treatments of psychological disorders are varied and reflect a distinct set of theories about human functioning. We have touched on many of these theories in the preceding chapters.

Over the years, however, the history of treatment for psychological disorders also has had its controversial side. As ideas regarding the nature of psychological disorders have changed, so have approaches to treatment. Not all of these approaches have turned out to be positive. For example, if you were suffering from a psychological disorder in Canada in the 1960s, one therapist you might have been referred to was Dr. D. Ewen Cameron. He was the founder and director of the Allan Memorial Institute in Montreal and was a well-known and influential figure in the treatment of psychological disorders. During the late 1950s and early 1960s, Cameron was engaged in CIA-funded research allegedly designed to examine brainwashing and thought-control techniques. In Cameron's facility, patients were exposed to experimental techniques that included extended drug-induced periods of sleep (sometimes for weeks at a time), massive electroconvulsive (shock) therapy regimens, sensory deprivation, hours upon hours of tape-recorded messages, psychic driving, and LSD treatment. According to the patients themselves, most of this treatment was done without their knowledge or consent. Cameron's objective was to *depattern* the patients and to rid them of old behaviour patterns and replace them with new ones. Years later, many of the Canadian participants sued (Moore, 2007), and then–justice minister Kim Campbell finally agreed to establish a compensation fund in 1992.

The use of LSD in psychotherapy has other, more legitimate connections to Canada (Mills, 2010).

Reports of *d-lysergic acid diethylamide* (LSD) began appearing in the scientific literature in the 1940s, and its potential for psychiatric treatment was explored in a series of government-supported studies conducted by Dr. Humphrey Osmond and his colleagues at the Weyburn Mental Hospital in Saskatchewan in the 1950s and 1960s (Dyck, 2005, 2008). In addition to his work on the project, Dr. Osmond is notable for a couple of other things (Lattin, 2010). He coined the term *psychedelic* to describe the experience users have after taking mescaline, psilocybin, or LSD. He is also responsible for giving the famous writer Aldous Huxley his first experience with hallucinogens, immortalized by Huxley (1954) in his book *The Doors of Perception*. Despite some initial optimism, concern about methodological inadequacies and sociocultural concerns contributed to the end of the project. LSD was also used in treatment in the Social Therapy Unit at Ontario's maximum-security psychiatric institution, the Oak Ridge Division of the Penetanguishene Mental Health Centre. It was used as part of an innovative treatment program for psychopaths designed by Dr. Elliot Barker in the mid-1960s (Rice & Harris, 1993; Weisman, 1995). Ultimately, the program was considered a failure and some former patients sued, claiming coercion and lack of full consent. As we discussed in Chapter 2, ethical practices have changed over the years to maximize protection of the research participants (Koocher, 2007). Many of the current safeguards were not in place 50 years ago.

The last 50 years has seen significant advances in the development and scientific evaluation of treatments for psychological disorders. The range of treatment approaches is vast, ranging from those focusing on emotion, thought, and/or relationships, to those involving meditation, to biomedical treatments that rely on medication or physical treatments, some of which are designed to change specific aspects of the operation of the brain. This work is continually evolving, allowing clients and their therapists access to the most recent advances in psychology.

In this chapter, we'll take a down-to-earth look at *psychotherapy*, using the term in its broadest sense, to refer to all the diverse approaches used in the treatment of mental disorders and psychological problems. We'll start by discussing some general questions about the provision of treatment. After considering these issues, we'll examine the goals, techniques, and effectiveness of some of the more widely used approaches to therapy and discuss recent trends and issues in treatment. In the Personal Application, we'll look at practical questions related to finding and choosing a therapist and getting the most out of therapy. And in the Critical Thinking Application, we'll address problems involved in determining whether therapy actually helps.

McGill News/McGill University archives, PR019175

After Notman (VIEW-4867) © McCord Museum M2001.60.23 | Photograph | Allan Memorial Institute. Montreal, QC.

Dr. D. Ewen Cameron served as director of the Allan Memorial Institute when CIA-funded brainwashing research was conducted there in the late 1950s and early 1960s.

The Elements of the Treatment Process

Sigmund Freud is widely credited with launching modern psychotherapy and with calling into question the view that we are logical, rational beings (Breger, 2009). Ironically, the landmark case that inspired Freud involved a patient who actually was treated by one of his colleagues, Josef Breuer (Breger, 2009). Around 1880, Breuer began to treat a young woman referred to as Anna O (which was a pseudonym—her real name was Bertha Pappenheim). Anna exhibited a variety of physical maladies, including headaches, coughing, and a loss of feeling in and movement of her right arm. Much to his surprise, Breuer discovered that Anna's physical symptoms cleared up when he encouraged her to talk about emotionally charged experiences from her past.

When Breuer and Freud discussed the case, they speculated that talking things through had enabled Anna to drain off bottled-up emotions that had caused her symptoms. Breuer found the intense emotional exchange in this treatment not to his liking, so he didn't follow through on his discovery. However, Freud applied Breuer's insight to other patients, and his successes led him to develop a systematic treatment procedure, which he called *psychoanalysis*. Anna O called her treatment "the talking cure." However, as you'll see, psychotherapy isn't always curative, and many modern treatments place little emphasis on talking.

Freud's breakthrough ushered in a century of progress for psychotherapy. Psychoanalysis spawned many offspring, as Freud's followers developed their own systems of treatment. Since then, approaches to treatment have steadily grown more numerous, more diverse, and more effective. Today, people can choose from a bewildering array of therapies.

Treatments: How Many Types Are There?

In their efforts to help people, psychotherapists use many treatment methods (Tracey et al., 2014). These include discussion, advice, emotional support, persuasion, conditioning procedures, relaxation training, role-playing, drug therapy, biofeedback, and group therapy. No one knows exactly how many distinct types of psychotherapy there are. One expert (Kazdin, 1994) estimates that there may be over 400 approaches to treatment. Fortunately, we can impose some order on this chaos. As varied as therapists' procedures are, approaches to treatment can be classified into three major categories:

1. *Insight therapies.* Insight therapy is "talk therapy" in the tradition of Freud's psychoanalysis.

In insight therapies, clients engage in complex verbal interactions with their therapists. The goal in these discussions is to pursue increased insight regarding the nature of the client's difficulties and to sort through possible solutions.

2. *Behaviour therapies.* Behaviour therapies are based on the principles of learning, which were introduced in Chapter 6. Instead of emphasizing personal insights, behaviour therapists make direct efforts to alter problematic responses (phobias, for instance) and maladaptive habits (e.g., drug use). Behaviour therapists work on changing clients' overt behaviours. They use different procedures for different kinds of problems. Most of their procedures involve classical conditioning, operant conditioning, or observational learning.

3. *Biomedical therapies.* Biomedical approaches to therapy involve interventions into a person's biological functioning. The most widely used procedures are drug therapy and electroconvulsive (shock) therapy. In recent decades, drug therapy has become the dominant mode of treatment for psychological disorders. One large-scale study found that 57 percent of mental health patients were treated with medication only, up from 44 percent just nine years earlier (Olfson & Marcus, 2010). As the name *biomedical* therapies suggests, these treatments have traditionally been provided only by physicians with a medical degree (usually psychiatrists). This situation is changing, however, as psychologists have been campaigning for prescription privileges in Canada and the United States.

Clients: Who Seeks Therapy?

Our mental health seems to be on all of our minds these days. Perhaps it is because it seems as if we all know someone who is struggling. Or perhaps it is because mental health concerns have been highlighted by campaigns such as that initiated by Canadian Olympic gold medalist Clara Hughes, as she rode 11 000 kilometres across Canada in 2014 (Goodman, 2014). No matter what the source, our awareness of mental health concerns seems warranted. Canadians are as concerned about their mental health as they are about their physical health, and over 90 percent report that they make a conscious effort to take care of their mental health on a regular basis (Canadian Mental Health Association, 2005). When accessing mental health services, most Canadians believe their needs were met, but a sizable minority believe that they were only partially met or not met at all, with the greatest reported need

The case of Anna O, whose real name was Bertha Pappenheim, provided the inspiration for Sigmund Freud's invention of psychoanalysis.

Sigmund Freud

"The news that reaches your consciousness is incomplete and often not to be relied on."

Canadian Olympic champion Clara Hughes has devoted herself to raising awareness of mental health issues. She has been very public about her own struggles with depression and is the spokesperson for Bell Canada's Let's Talk program concerning mental health. She is one of the very few athletes to win Olympic medals in both the Winter and Summer Games.

THE CANADIAN PRESS/Fred Chartrand

coming from those who have mental health issues combined with high levels of stress and/or chronic physical conditions (Canadian Counselling and Psychotherapy Association, 2014).

People seeking mental health treatment represent the full range of human problems: anxiety, depression, unsatisfactory interpersonal relations, troublesome habits, poor self-control, low self-esteem, marital conflicts, self-doubt, a sense of emptiness, and feelings of personal stagnation. Among adults, the two most common presenting problems are depression and anxiety disorders (Olfson & Marcus, 2010).

People vary considerably in their willingness to seek psychotherapy. People often delay for many years before finally seeking treatment for their psychological problems (Wang, Berglund, et al., 2005). Research has shown that women are more likely than men to receive therapy and that there are cultural differences in people's willingness to pursue treatment. Treatment is also more likely when people have workplace medical insurance/benefits and when they have more education (Olfson & Marcus, 2010).

Unfortunately, it appears that many people who need therapy don't receive it (Kazdin & Rabbitt, 2013). People who could benefit from therapy do not seek it for a variety of reasons. Lack of health insurance and cost concerns appear to be major barriers to obtaining needed care for many people. Perhaps

the biggest roadblock is the stigma surrounding the receipt of mental health treatment (Corrigan, Druss, & Perlick, 2014). Unfortunately, many people equate seeking therapy with admitting personal weakness (Clement et al., 2015).

reality check

Misconception

Seeking psychotherapy is a sign of weakness; people should be able to deal with their problems.

Reality

This unfortunate, prejudicial belief prevents many people from seeking help that they need. Psychological disorders can be severe, debilitating maladies that require treatment. Recognizing that one needs help is more a sign of courage than weakness.

Therapists: Who Provides Professional Treatment?

People troubled by personal problems often solicit help from their friends, relatives, clergy, and primary care physicians. According to recent survey statistics, over one in six Canadians over 15 years of age reported experiencing a need for mental health services in the previous year (Sunderland & Findlay, 2015). Unfortunately, not all who need or want assistance are able to access professional services. The same survey found that over 1.5 million Canadians who perceived a mental health need reported that those needs were either unmet or only partially met. The rates for unmet needs were particularly high for individuals reporting anxiety or mood disorders.

Informal sources of assistance such as friends and family may provide excellent advice, but their counsel does not qualify as therapy. What types of professional help might Canadians access? Psychotherapy refers to *professional* treatment by someone with special training. However, a common source of confusion about psychotherapy is the variety of "helping professions" available to offer assistance (Murstein & Fontaine, 1993). Psychology and psychiatry are the principal professions involved in the provision of psychotherapy. However, therapy is increasingly provided by clinical social workers, psychiatric nurses, counsellors, and marriage and family therapists (see Table 16.1). Let's look at the various mental health professions.

Psychologists

Two types of psychologists may provide therapy. *Clinical psychologists* and *counselling psychologists* specialize in the diagnosis and treatment

Table 16.1
Types of Therapists

PROFESSION	DEGREE	EDUCATION BEYOND BACHELOR'S DEGREE	TYPICAL ROLES AND ACTIVITIES
Clinical psychologist	Ph.D. or Psy.D.	5–7 years	Psychological testing, diagnosis, treatment with insight or behaviour therapy
Counselling psychologist	Ph.D., Psy.D., or Ed.D.	5–7 years	Similar to clinical psychologist, but more focus on work, career, and adjustment problems
Psychiatrist	M.D.	8 years	Diagnosis and treatment, primarily with biomedical therapies, but also insight therapies
Clinical social worker	M.S.W., D.S.W.	2–5 years	Insight and behaviour therapy, often help inpatients with their return to the community
Psychiatric nurse	R.N., M.A., or Ph.D.	0–5 years	Inpatient care, insight and behaviour therapy
Counsellor	B.A. or M.A.	0–2 years	Vocational counselling, drug counselling, rehabilitation counseling
Marriage and family therapist	M.A. or Ph.D.	2–5 years	Marital/couples therapy, family therapy

© 2017 Cengage Learning

of psychological disorders and everyday behavioural problems. Clinical psychologists' training emphasizes the treatment of full-fledged disorders. Counselling psychologists' training is slanted toward the treatment of everyday adjustment problems. In practice, however, there is quite a bit of overlap between clinical and counselling psychologists in training, skills, and the clientele that they serve.

Traditionally, psychologists had to earn a doctoral degree (Ph.D., Psy.D., or Ed.D.) to practise. A doctorate in psychology requires about five to seven years of training beyond a bachelor's degree. More recently, some of the provinces and territories have changed their regulations, allowing that a psychologist may have either a Ph.D. or an M.A. (an M.A. degree typically takes two years). In some jurisdictions, those with Ph.D.s are referred to as *psychologists* and those with M.A.s as *psychological associates* (Hunsley & Johnson, 2000). A relatively new degree, a Psy.D., is offered in a limited number of graduate programs in Canada, including ones at Memorial University in Newfoundland and Labrador and the Université de Montréal, which offers programs both in clinical psychology and clinical neuropsychology. Psy.D. programs differ from Ph.D. programs in several ways, including a greater emphasis on the scientist–practitioner model in Ph.D. programs. For example, Memorial University's description of its Psy.D. program states that "the emphasis is on developing strong and knowledgeable professionals who understand and are educated consumers of research but may not necessarily produce original research as a primary part of their career path." The process of gaining admission to a graduate program in clinical psychology is highly competitive (about as difficult as getting into medical school). Psychologists receive most of their training in universities or independent professional schools. They then serve a one-year internship in a clinical setting, such as a hospital, often followed by one or two years of postdoctoral fellowship training. Currently, there are approximately 17 000 registered psychologists in Canada (CIHI, 2014).

In providing therapy, psychologists use either insight or behavioural approaches. In comparison to psychiatrists, they are more likely to use behavioural techniques and less likely to use psychoanalytic methods. Clinical and counselling psychologists do psychological testing as well as psychotherapy, and many also conduct research.

Psychiatrists

Psychiatrists are physicians who specialize in the diagnosis and treatment of psychological disorders. Many psychiatrists also treat everyday behavioural problems. However, in comparison to psychologists, psychiatrists devote more time to relatively severe disorders (schizophrenia, mood disorders) and less time to everyday marital, family, job, and school problems.

Psychiatrists have an M.D. degree. Their graduate training requires four years of course work in medical school and a four-year apprenticeship in a residency at a hospital. Their psychotherapy training occurs during their residency, since the required course work in medical school is essentially the same for everyone, whether they are going into surgery, pediatrics, or psychiatry.

In comparison with psychologists, psychiatrists are more likely to use psychoanalysis and less likely to use group therapies or behaviour therapies. That said, contemporary psychiatrists increasingly depend on medication as their principal mode of treatment (Olfson et al., 2014).

Other Mental Health Professionals

Several other mental health professions also provide psychotherapy services, and some of these professions are growing rapidly. In hospitals and other institutions, *clinical social workers* and *psychiatric nurses* often work as part of a treatment team with a psychologist or psychiatrist. Psychiatric nurses, who may have a bachelor's or master's degree in their field, play a large role in hospital inpatient treatment. Clinical social workers generally have a master's degree and typically work with patients and their families to ease the patient's integration back into the community. Although social workers and psychiatric nurses have traditionally worked in institutional settings, they increasingly provide a wide range of therapeutic services as independent practitioners.

Many kinds of *counsellors* also provide therapeutic services. Counsellors are usually found working in schools, colleges, and assorted human service agencies (youth centres, geriatric centres, family-planning centres, and so forth). Counsellors typically have a master's degree. They often specialize in particular types of problems, such as vocational counselling, marital counselling, rehabilitation counselling, and drug counselling.

Although there are clear differences among the helping professions in education and training, their roles in the treatment process overlap considerably. In this chapter, we will refer to psychologists or psychiatrists as needed, but otherwise we'll use the terms *clinician, therapist,* and *provider* to refer to mental health professionals of all kinds, regardless of their professional degrees.

Now that we have discussed the basic elements in psychotherapy, we can examine specific approaches to treatment in terms of their goals, procedures, and effectiveness. We'll begin with a few representative insight therapies.

Insight Therapies

Key Learning Goals

▶ Explain the logic of psychoanalysis and the techniques by which analysts probe the unconscious.

▶ Understand the role of therapeutic climate and therapeutic process in client-centred therapy.

▶ Explain how group therapy, couples therapy, and family therapy are generally conducted.

▶ Assess the efficacy of insight therapies and the role of common factors in therapy.

There are many schools of thought about how to do insight therapy. Therapists with various theoretical orientations use different methods to pursue different kinds of insights. However, what these varied approaches have in common is that *insight therapies* involve verbal interactions intended to enhance clients' self-knowledge and thus promote healthful changes in personality and behaviour.

Although there may be hundreds of insight therapies, the leading eight or ten approaches appear to account for the lion's share of treatment. In this section, we'll delve into psychoanalysis, related psychodynamic approaches, client-centred therapy, and positive psychology therapies. We'll also discuss how insight therapy can be done with groups as well as individuals.

Psychoanalysis

After the case of Anna O, Sigmund Freud worked as a psychotherapist for almost 50 years in Vienna. Through a painstaking process of trial and error, he developed innovative techniques for the treatment of psychological disorders and distress. His system of *psychoanalysis* came to dominate psychiatry for many decades (Luborsky, O'Reilly-Landry, & Arlow, 2011). Although the dominance of psychoanalysis has eroded in recent years, a diverse collection of psychoanalytic approaches to therapy continues to evolve and to remain influential today (Luborsky, O'Reilly-Landry, & Arlow, 2011; Maniacci et al., 2014; Safran & Kriss, 2014; Ursano & Carr, 2014).

Psychoanalysis is an insight therapy that emphasizes the recovery of unconscious conflicts, motives, and defences through techniques such as free association and transference. To appreciate the logic of psychoanalysis, we have to look at Freud's thinking about the roots of mental disorders. Freud mostly treated anxiety-dominated disturbances, such as phobic, panic, obsessive-compulsive, and conversion disorders, which were then called *neuroses*.

Freud believed that neurotic problems are caused by unconscious conflicts left over from early childhood. As explained in Chapter 12, he thought that these inner conflicts involve battles among the id, ego, and superego, usually over sexual and aggressive impulses. He theorized that people depend on defence mechanisms to avoid confronting these conflicts, which remain hidden in the depths of the unconscious (see Figure 16.1). However, he noted that defensive manoeuvres often lead to self-defeating behaviour. Furthermore, he asserted that defences tend to be only partially successful in alleviating anxiety, guilt, and other distressing emotions.

© 2017 Cengage Learning

Figure 16.1
Freud's view of the roots of disorders. According to Freud, unconscious conflicts among the id, ego, and superego sometimes lead to anxiety. This discomfort may lead to pathological reliance on defensive behaviour.

With this model in mind, let's take a look at the therapeutic procedures used in psychoanalysis.

Probing the Unconscious

Given Freud's assumptions, we can see that the logic of psychoanalysis is quite simple. The analyst attempts to probe the murky depths of the unconscious to discover the unresolved conflicts causing the client's neurotic behaviour. In a sense, the analyst functions as a "psychological detective." In this effort to explore the unconscious, the therapist relies on two techniques: free association and dream analysis.

In *free association,* clients spontaneously express their thoughts and feelings exactly as they occur, with as little censorship as possible. In free associating, clients expound on anything that comes to mind, regardless of how trivial, silly, or embarrassing it might be. Gradually, most clients begin to let everything pour out without conscious censorship. The analyst studies these free associations for clues about what is going on in the client's unconscious.

In *dream analysis,* the therapist interprets the symbolic meaning of the client's dreams. Freud saw dreams as the "royal road to the unconscious," the most direct means of access to patients' innermost conflicts, wishes, and impulses. Clients are encouraged and trained to remember their dreams, which they describe in therapy. The therapist then analyzes the symbolism in these dreams to interpret their meaning.

To better illustrate these matters, let's look at an actual case treated through psychoanalysis (adapted from Greenson, 1967, pp. 40–41). Mr. N was troubled by an unsatisfactory marriage. He claimed to love his wife, but he preferred sexual relations with prostitutes. Mr. N reported that his parents also endured lifelong marital difficulties. His childhood conflicts about their relationship appeared to be related to his

In psychoanalysis, the therapist encourages the client to reveal thoughts, feelings, dreams, and memories, which can then be interpreted in relation to the client's current problems.

problems. Both dream analysis and free association can be seen in the following description of a session in Mr. N's treatment:

> *Mr. N reported a fragment of a dream. All that he could remember is that he was waiting for a red traffic light to change when he felt that someone had bumped into him from behind. . . . The associations led to Mr. N's love of cars, especially sports cars. He loved the sensation, in particular, of whizzing by those fat, old expensive cars. . . . His father always hinted that he had been a great athlete, but he never substantiated it. . . . Mr. N doubted whether his father could really perform. His father would flirt with a waitress in a café or make sexual remarks about women passing by, but he seemed to be showing off. If he were really sexual, he wouldn't resort to that.*

As is characteristic of free association, Mr. N's train of thought meandered about with little direction. Nonetheless, clues about his unconscious conflicts are apparent. What did Mr. N's therapist extract from this session? The therapist saw sexual overtones in the dream fragment, where Mr. N was bumped from behind. The therapist also inferred that Mr. N had a competitive orientation toward his father, based on the free association about whizzing by fat, old expensive cars. As you can see, analysts must *interpret* their clients' dreams and free associations. This is a critical process throughout psychoanalysis.

Interpretation

Interpretation refers to the therapist's attempts to explain the inner significance of the client's thoughts, feelings, memories, and behaviours. Contrary to popular belief, analysts do not interpret everything, and they generally don't try to dazzle clients with startling revelations. Instead, analysts move forward inch by inch, offering interpretations that should be just out of the client's own reach. Mr. N's therapist eventually offered the following interpretations to his client:

> *I said to Mr. N near the end of the hour that I felt he was struggling with his feelings about his father's sexual life.*
>
> *He seemed to be saying that his father was sexually not a very potent man. . . . He also recalls that he once found a packet of condoms under his father's pillow when he was an adolescent and he thought, "My father must be going to prostitutes." I then intervened and pointed out that the condoms under his father's pillow seemed to indicate more obviously that his father*

Treatment of Psychological Disorders

© Bruce Ayres/Stone/Getty Images

used the condoms with his mother, who slept in the same bed. However, Mr. N wanted to believe his wish-fulfilling fantasy: Mother doesn't want sex with father and father is not very potent. The patient was silent and the hour ended.

As you may have already guessed, the therapist concluded that Mr. N's difficulties were rooted in an *Oedipal complex* (see Chapter 12). The man had unresolved sexual feelings toward his mother and hostile feelings about his father. These unconscious conflicts, rooted in Mr. N's childhood, were distorting his intimate relationships as an adult.

reality check

Misconception

If you enter into therapy, you will lie on a couch and talk about your past.

Reality

Only psychoanalytic therapists (and not all of them) expect their patients to lie on a couch and discuss the past. As you will see throughout this chapter, there are many approaches to treating psychological disorders, and in the vast majority of them clients do not reveal their feelings while reclining on a couch.

Resistance and Transference

How would you expect Mr. N to respond to the therapist's suggestion that he was in competition with his father for the sexual attention of his mother? Obviously, most clients would have great difficulty accepting such an interpretation. Freud fully expected clients to display some resistance to therapeutic efforts. **Resistance refers to largely unconscious defensive manoeuvres intended to hinder the progress of therapy.** Resistance is assumed to be an inevitable part of the psychoanalytic process (Samberg & Marcus, 2005). Why would clients try to resist the helping process? Because they don't want to face the painful, disturbing conflicts that they have buried in their unconscious. Although they have sought help, they are reluctant to confront their real problems. Analysts use a variety of strategies to deal with clients' resistance. Often, a key consideration is the handling of transference.

Transference occurs when clients start relating to their therapists in ways that mimic critical relationships in their lives. Thus, a client might start relating to a therapist as if the therapist were an overprotective mother, a rejecting brother, or a passive spouse.

© Roger Ressmeyer/CORBIS

Carl Rogers

"To my mind, empathy is in itself a healing agent."

In a sense, the client transfers conflicting feelings about important people onto the therapist (Høglend et al., 2011). Psychoanalysts often encourage transference so that clients can re-enact relations with crucial people in the context of therapy. These re-enactments can help bring repressed feelings and conflicts to the surface, allowing the client to work through the conflicts.

Undergoing psychoanalysis is not easy. It can be a slow, painful process of self-examination that routinely requires three to five years of hard work. It tends to be a lengthy process because patients need time to gradually work through their problems and genuinely accept unnerving revelations (Williams, 2005). Ultimately, if resistance and transference can be handled effectively, the therapist's interpretations should lead the client to profound insights. For instance, Mr. N eventually admitted, "The old boy is probably right, it does tickle me to imagine that my mother preferred me and I could beat out my father. Later, I wondered whether this had something to do with my own screwed-up sex life with my wife." According to Freud, once clients recognize the unconscious sources of conflicts, they can resolve these conflicts and discard their neurotic defences.

Modern Psychodynamic Therapies

Though still available, classical psychoanalysis as done by Freud is not widely practised anymore. Freud's psychoanalytic method was geared to a particular kind of clientele he was seeing in Vienna a century ago. As his followers fanned out across Europe and North America, many found it necessary to adapt psychoanalysis to different cultures, changing times, and new kinds of patients (Karasu, 2005). Thus, many variations on Freud's original approach to psychoanalysis have developed over the years. These descendants of psychoanalysis are collectively known as *psychodynamic approaches* to therapy.

As a result, today we have a rich diversity of psychodynamic approaches (Magnavita, 2008). Recent reviews of these treatments suggest that interpretation, resistance, and transference continue to play key roles in therapeutic effects (Høglend et al., 2008; Luborsky & Barrett, 2006). Other central features of modern psychodynamic therapies include (1) a focus on emotional experience, (2) exploration of efforts to avoid distressing thoughts and feelings, (3) identification of recurring patterns in patients' life experiences, (4) discussion of past experience, especially events in early childhood, (5) analysis of interpersonal relationships, (6) a focus on the therapeutic relationship itself, and (7) exploration of dreams and other aspects of fantasy life

(Shedler, 2010; see Figure 16.2). Recent research suggests that psychodynamic approaches can be helpful in the treatment of a diverse array of disorders (Barber et al., 2013; Josephs & Weinberger, 2013; Barber et al., 2013).

Client-Centred Therapy

You may have heard of people going into therapy to "find themselves" or to "get in touch with their real feelings." These now-popular phrases emerged out of the human potential movement, which was stimulated in part by the work of Carl Rogers (1951, 1986). Using a humanistic perspective, Rogers devised client-centred therapy (also known as *person-centred therapy*) in the 1940s and 1950s.

Client-centred therapy is an insight therapy that emphasizes providing a supportive emotional climate for clients, who play a major role in determining the pace and direction of their therapy. Rogers's theory about the principal causes of neurotic anxieties is quite different from the Freudian explanation. As discussed in Chapter 12, Rogers maintains that most personal distress is due to inconsistency, or "incongruence," between a person's self-concept and reality (see Figure 16.3). According to his theory, incongruence makes people feel threatened by realistic feedback about themselves from others. For example, if you inaccurately viewed yourself as a hard-working, dependable person, you would feel threatened by contradictory feedback from friends or co-workers. According to Rogers, anxiety about such feedback often leads to reliance on defence mechanisms, to distortions of reality, and to stifled personal growth. Excessive incongruence is thought to be rooted in clients' overdependence on others for approval and acceptance.

Given Rogers's theory, client-centred therapists seek insights that are quite different from the repressed conflicts that psychoanalysts go after. Client-centred therapists help clients to realize that they do not have to worry constantly about pleasing others and winning acceptance. They encourage

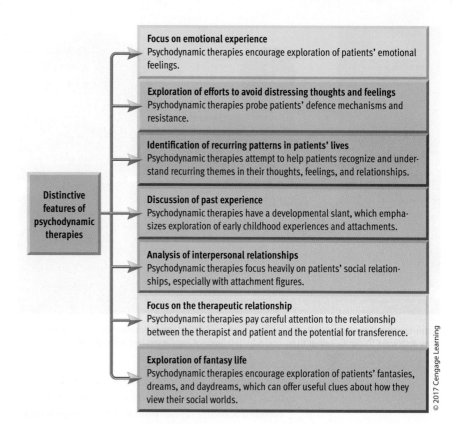

Figure 16.2
Core features of psychodynamic therapies. In an article on the efficacy of psychodynamic therapies, Jonathan Shedler (2010) outlined the distinctive aspects of modern psychodynamic techniques and processes. The seven features described here represent the core of contemporary psychodynamic treatment.

clients to respect their own feelings and values. They help people restructure their self-concept to correspond better to reality. Ultimately, they try to foster self-acceptance and personal growth.

Therapeutic Climate

According to Rogers, the *process* of therapy is not as important as the emotional *climate* in which the therapy takes place. He believes that it is critical for the therapist to provide a warm, supportive climate that creates a safe environment in which clients can confront their shortcomings without feeling threatened. The lack of threat should reduce clients' defensive tendencies and thus help them open up. To create

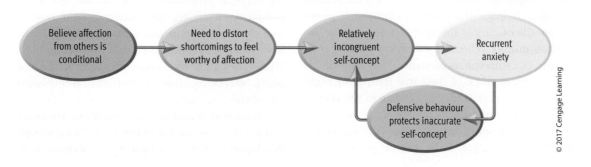

Figure 16.3
Rogers's view of the roots of disorders. Rogers's theory posits that anxiety and self-defeating behaviour are rooted in an incongruent self-concept that makes one prone to recurrent anxiety, which triggers defensive behaviour, which fuels more incongruence.

Client-centred therapists emphasize the importance of a supportive emotional climate in therapy. They also work to clarify, rather than interpret, the feelings expressed by their patients.

this supportive atmosphere, client-centred therapists must provide three conditions: (1) *genuineness* (honest communication), (2) *unconditional positive regard* (nonjudgmental acceptance of the client), and (3) *accurate empathy* (understanding of the client's point of view). Consistent with Rogers's view of the vital importance of therapeutic climate, research has found that measures of therapists' empathy and unconditional positive regard correlate with positive patient outcomes (Elliott et al., 2011; Farber & Doolin, 2011).

Rogers firmly believed that a supportive emotional climate is the critical force promoting healthy changes in therapy. However, some client-centred therapists, such as Laura Rice and Les Greenberg, have begun to place more emphasis on the therapeutic process (Rice & Greenberg, 1992).

Therapeutic Process

In client-centred therapy, the client and therapist work together as equals. The therapist provides relatively little guidance and keeps interpretation and advice to a minimum (Raskin, Rogers, & Witty, 2014). So, just what does the client-centred therapist do, besides creating a supportive climate? Primarily, the therapist provides feedback to help clients sort out their feelings. The therapist's key task is *clarification*. Client-centred therapists try to function like human mirrors, reflecting statements back to their clients, but with enhanced clarity. They help clients become more aware of their true feelings by highlighting themes that may be obscure in the clients' rambling discourse.

By working with clients to experience and clarify their feelings (Angus, 2012; Carryer & Greenberg,

2010), client-centred therapists hope to gradually build toward more far-reaching insights. In particular, they try to help clients better understand their interpersonal relationships and become more comfortable with their genuine selves. Obviously, these are ambitious goals.

Influential Canadian psychologist Les Greenberg (Greenberg, 2012) and his colleagues have developed *emotion-focused couples therapy* (Greenberg & Johnson, 1988; Johnson & Greenberg, 1995). One of the assumptions of *emotion-focused couples therapy* is that the relationship is not providing for the attachment needs of the relationship partners. In the process of therapy, the nature of the relationship issues and underlying emotions are first identified. The partners are then afforded an opportunity to identify and acknowledge their needs and are encouraged to express these needs and to arrive at solutions to the problems. Acknowledging and working with the underlying emotions are central to this approach. This type of emotion-focused therapy has its roots in earlier client-centred work by Carl Rogers and Fritz Perls and is considered important to any integrative approach to psychotherapy (L. S. Greenberg, 2002, 2008).

Client-centred therapy resembles psychoanalysis in that both seek to achieve a major reconstruction of a client's personality. We'll see more limited and specific goals in cognitive therapy, which we will discuss soon.

Therapies Inspired by Positive Psychology

The growth of the positive psychology movement has begun to inspire new approaches to insight therapy (Duckworth, Steen, & Seligman, 2005; Mongrain, 2013; Mongrain & Anselmo-Matthews, 2012; Peterson & Park, 2009; Seligman, 2016). As noted in Chapters 1 and 10, positive psychology uses theory and research to better understand the positive, adaptive, creative, and fulfilling aspects of human existence (Hefferon & Boniwell, 2011; Waterman, 2013). The advocates of positive psychology maintain that the field has historically focused far too heavily on pathology, weakness, and suffering (and how to heal these conditions) rather than health and resilience (Seligman, 2003; Seligman & Csikszentmihalyi, 2000). They argue for increased research on contentment, well-being, human strengths, and positive emotions.

This philosophical approach has led to new therapeutic interventions. For example, *well-being therapy*, developed by Giovanni Fava and colleagues (Fava,

1999; Ruini & Fava, 2004), seeks to enhance clients' self-acceptance, purpose in life, autonomy, and personal growth. It has been used successfully in the treatment of mood disorders and anxiety disorders (Fava et al., 2005).

Another new approach is *positive psychotherapy*, developed by Martin Seligman and colleagues (Rashid & Anjum, 2008; Seligman, 2016; Seligman, Rashid, & Parks, 2006). So far, positive psychotherapy has been used mainly in the treatment of depression. Positive psychotherapy attempts to get clients to recognize their strengths, appreciate their blessings, savour positive experiences, forgive those who have wronged them, and find meaning in their lives. Preliminary research suggests that positive psychotherapy can be an effective treatment for depression. For example, in one study, positive psychotherapy was compared to *treatment as usual* (whatever the therapist would normally do) and *treatment as usual with medication*. The data shown in Figure 16.4 compare mean depression scores at the end of the study for participants in these three conditions (Seligman, Rashid, & Parks, 2006). As you can see, the lowest depression scores were observed in the group that received positive psychotherapy. Developments in this area continue at an exciting pace.

Recent work by Canadian psychologist Myriam Mongrain has added to our knowledge concerning the efficacy of positive psychology based interventions (e.g., Mongrain et al., 2016; Sergeant & Mongrain, 2015). Mongrain and her colleague Leah Shapira, for example, examined the effectiveness of online interventions designed to increase either participants' self-compassion or optimism. The researchers were interested in the effects of these interventions on participants' depression and happiness scores. The interventions were deceptively simple in design. In the optimism intervention, for example, participants were asked to post online letters to themselves in which they wrote about visualizing "a future where current issues were resolved and gave themselves advice on how to get there" (Shapira & Mongrain, 2010, p. 378). Prior to the interventions, participants were assessed for their vulnerability to depression. Both the self-compassion and the optimism interventions were related to increases in happiness and decreases in depression scores, effects that were observed to last for several months. The results also suggested that individuals with particular types of vulnerabilities to depression might differentially benefit most from either the self-compassion or optimism interventions. Innovative interventions such as these, spurred by the positive psychology movement, are in their infancy, but the early findings seem promising and it will be interesting to see what the future holds.

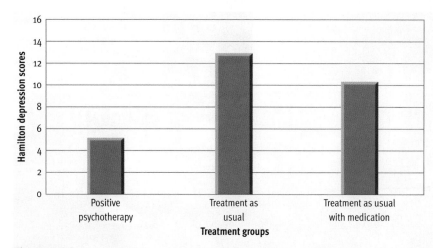

Figure 16.4

Positive psychotherapy for depression. In a study of the efficacy of positive psychotherapy, it was compared to treatment as usual (clinicians delivered whatever treatment they deemed appropriate) and to treatment as usual combined with antidepressant medication. At the end of 12 weeks of treatment, symptoms of depression were measured with the widely used *Hamilton Rating Scale for Depression*. The mean depression scores for each group are graphed here. As you can see, the positive psychotherapy group showed less depression than the other two treatment groups, suggesting that positive psychotherapy can be an effective intervention for depression.

Source: Adapted from Seligman, M. E. P., Rashid, T., & Parks, A. C. (2006). Positive psychotherapy. *American Psychologist, 61*, 774–788. Figure 2, p. 784. Copyright © 2006 by the American Psychological Association.

....

concept **check** 16.1

Understanding Therapists' Conceptions of Disorders

Check your understanding of the three approaches to insight therapy covered in the text by matching each approach with the appropriate explanation of the typical origins of clients' psychological disorders. The answers are in Appendix A near the back of the book.

Theorized Causes of Disorders

_____ **1.** Problems rooted in inadequate attention paid to one's strengths, blessings, and positive experiences.

_____ **2.** Problems rooted in unconscious conflicts left over from childhood

_____ **3.** Problems rooted in inaccurate self-concept and excessive concern about pleasing others

Therapy

a. Psychoanalysis

b. Client-centred therapy

c. Positive psychotherapy

Group Therapy

Many approaches to insight therapy can be conducted on either an individual or group basis. *Group*

Clinical psychologist Myriam Mongrain from York University is interested in the role played by individual differences as vulnerability factors for the onset of depressive episodes. Her recent work has addressed, among other things, some of the implications of positive psychology interventions for individuals suffering from depression.

Courtesy of Dr. Myriam Mongrain

Treatment of Psychological Disorders

Group treatments have proven particularly helpful when members share similar problems, such as alcoholism, overeating, or having been sexually abused as a child.

therapy is the simultaneous treatment of several clients in a group. Because of economic pressures in mental health care, the use of group therapy appears likely to grow in future years (Burlingame & Baldwin, 2011). Although group therapy can be conducted in a variety of ways, we can provide a general overview of the process (see Piper & Hernandez, 2013; Spitz, 2009).

A therapy group typically consists of four to twelve people, with six to eight participants regarded as ideal (Cox et al., 2008). The therapist usually screens the participants, excluding persons who seem likely to be disruptive. Some theorists maintain that judicious selection of participants is crucial to effective group treatment (Schachter, 2011). In group therapy, participants essentially function as therapists for one another (Stone, 2008). Group members describe their problems, trade viewpoints, share experiences, and discuss coping strategies. Most important, they provide acceptance and emotional support for one another. In this atmosphere, group members work at peeling away the social masks that cover their insecurities. As members come to value one another's opinions, they work hard to display healthy changes. In group treatment, the therapist's responsibilities include selecting participants, setting goals for the group, initiating and maintaining the therapeutic process, and preventing interactions among group members that might be psychologically harmful (Cox et al., 2008). The therapist often plays a relatively subtle role in group therapy, staying in the background and focusing mainly on promoting group cohesiveness.

Group therapies obviously save time and money, which can be critical in understaffed mental hospitals and other institutional settings (Cox et al., 2008). Therapists in private practice usually charge less for group than individual therapy, making therapy affordable for more people. However, group therapy is not just a less costly substitute for individual therapy (Knauss, 2005; Stone, 2008). Group therapy has unique strengths of its own, and certain kinds of problems are especially well suited to group treatment. Group treatments are being used successfully for an increasingly diverse collection of problems and disorders in contemporary clinical practice (Burlingame, Strauss, & Joyce, 2013).

Couples and Family Therapy

Like group therapy, marital and family therapy rose to prominence after World War II. As their names suggest, these interventions are defined in terms of who is being treated. *Couples or marital therapy* involves the treatment of both partners in a committed, intimate relationship, in which the main focus is on relationship issues. Couples therapy is not limited to married couples. It is frequently provided to cohabiting couples, including same-sex couples. *Family therapy* involves the treatment of a family unit as a whole, in which the main focus is on family dynamics and communication. Family therapy often emerges out of efforts to treat children or adolescents with individual therapy. A child's therapist, for instance, might come to the realization that treatment is likely to fail because the child returns to a home environment that contributes to the child's problems and so proposes a broader family intervention.

As with other forms of insight therapy, there are different schools of thought about how to conduct couples and family therapy (Goldenberg, Goldenberg, & Pelavin, 2011). Some of these diverse systems are extensions of influential approaches to individual therapy, including psychodynamic, humanistic, and behavioural treatments. Other approaches are based on innovative models of families as complex systems and are an explicit rejection of individual models of treatment. Although the various approaches to couples and family therapy differ in terminology and in their theoretical models of relationship and family dysfunction, they tend to share two common goals. First, they seek to understand the entrenched patterns of interaction that produce distress. In this endeavour, they view individuals as parts of a family ecosystem, and they assume that people behave as they do because of their role in the system (Lebow & Stroud, 2013). Second, they seek to help couples and families improve their communication and move toward healthier patterns of interaction.

How Effective Are Insight Therapies?

Whether insight therapies are conducted on a group or an individual basis, clients usually invest considerable time, effort, and money. Are these insight therapies worth the investment? Let's examine the evidence on their effectiveness.

Evaluating the effectiveness of any approach to psychotherapy is a complex matter (Comer & Kendall, 2013; Lilienfeld et al., 2014; Ogles, 2013). For one thing, psychological disorders sometimes clear up on their own, a phenomenon called spontaneous remission. If a client experiences a recovery after treatment, we can't automatically assume the recovery was due to the treatment (see the Critical Thinking Application at the end of this chapter). Evaluations of insight therapies are especially complicated given that various schools of thought pursue entirely different goals. Judgments of therapeutic outcome in insight therapy tend to be subjective, with little consensus about the best way to assess therapeutic progress. Moreover, people enter therapy with diverse problems of varied severity, which further complicates the evaluation process.

Despite these difficulties, thousands of outcome studies have been conducted to evaluate the effectiveness of insight therapy. These studies have examined a broad range of clinical problems and used a variety of methods to assess therapeutic outcomes, including looking at scores on psychological tests and ratings by family members, as well as therapists' and clients' ratings. These studies consistently indicate that insight therapy is superior to no treatment or to placebo treatment and that the effects of therapy are reasonably durable (Lambert, 2011, 2013). And when insight therapies are compared head-to-head against drug therapies, they usually show roughly equal efficacy (Arkowitz & Lilienfeld, 2007; Wampold, 2013). Studies generally find the greatest improvement early in treatment (roughly the first ten to twenty weekly sessions), with further gains gradually diminishing over time (Lambert, 2013), as the data from one study show in Figure 16.5. Of course, these broad generalizations mask considerable variability in outcome, but the general trends are encouraging.

How Do Insight Therapies Work?

Although there is considerable evidence that insight therapy tends to produce positive effects for a sizable majority of clients, vigorous debate continues about the mechanisms of action underlying these positive effects (Duncan & Reese, 2013). The advocates of various therapies tend to attribute the benefits of therapy to the particular methods used by each specific approach. In essence, they argue that different therapies achieve similar benefits through different processes. An alternative view espoused by many theorists is that the diverse approaches to therapy share certain common factors that account for much of the improvement experienced by clients (Wampold, 2001). Evidence supporting the common factors view has mounted in recent years (Lambert & Ogles, 2014; Sparks, Duncan, & Miller, 2008).

What are the common denominators that lie at the core of diverse approaches to therapy? The models proposed to answer this question vary considerably, but the most widely cited common factors include (1) the development of a therapeutic alliance with a professional helper; (2) the provision of emotional

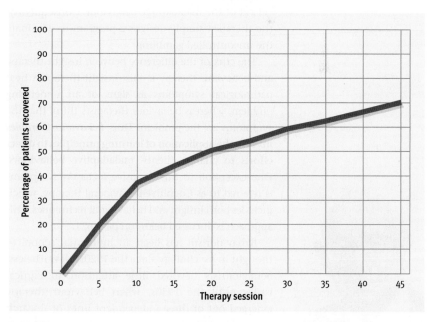

Figure 16.5

Recovery as a function of number of therapy sessions. Based on a national sample of over 6000 patients, Lambert, Hansen, and Finch (2001) mapped out the relationship between recovery and the duration of treatment. These data show that about half of the patients had experienced a clinically significant recovery after 20 weekly sessions of therapy. After 45 sessions of therapy, about 70 percent had recovered.

Source: Adapted from Lambert, M. J., Hansen, N. B., & Finch, A. E. (2001). Patient-focused research: Using patient outcome data to enhance treatment effects. *Journal of Consulting and Clinical Psychology, 69,* 159–172. Copyright © 2001 by the American Psychological Association.

Treatment of Psychological Disorders

support and empathy; (3) the cultivation of hope and positive expectations in the client; (4) the provision of a rationale for the client's problems and a plausible method for reducing them; and (5) the opportunity to express feelings, confront problems, and gain new insights (Laska, Gurman, & Wampold, 2014; Weinberger, 1995). How important are these factors in therapy? Some theorists argue that common factors account for virtually all the progress that clients make in therapy (Wampold, 2001). It seems more likely that the benefits of therapy represent the combined effects of common factors and specific procedures. One study attempted to quantify the influence of common factors in an analysis of 31 studies that focused on the treatment of depression. When the variance in patient outcomes was partitioned among various influences, the researchers estimated that 49 percent of this variance was attributable to common factors (Cuijpers et al., 2012). Admittedly, this is just one estimate based on one form of treatment for one specific disorder, so it does not provide a definitive answer regarding the importance of common factors. But it certainly suggests that common factors play a significant role in insight therapy.

Behaviour Therapies

Behaviour therapy is different from insight therapy (Spiegler & Guevremont, 2010) in that behaviour therapists make no attempt to help clients achieve grand insights about themselves. Why not? Because behaviour therapists believe that such insights aren't necessary to produce constructive change. For example, consider a client troubled by uncontrolled gambling. The behaviour therapist doesn't care whether this behaviour is rooted in unconscious conflicts or parental rejection. What the client needs is to get rid of the maladaptive behaviour. Consequently, the therapist simply designs a program to eliminate the uncontrolled gambling.

The crux of the difference between insight therapy and behaviour therapy is this: Insight therapists treat pathological symptoms as signs of an underlying problem, whereas behaviour therapists think that the symptoms are the problem. Thus, *behaviour therapies involve the application of learning principles to direct efforts to change clients' maladaptive behaviours.* One exception to this exclusive focus on symptoms is referred to as Cognitive-behavioural therapy, which includes both insight and behavioural techniques. This approach is discussed below on page 621.

Behaviourism has been an influential school of thought in psychology since the 1920s. Nevertheless, behaviourists devoted little attention to clinical issues until the 1950s, when behaviour therapy emerged out of three independent lines of research fostered by B. F. Skinner and his colleagues (Skinner, Solomon, & Lindsley, 1953) in the United States; by Hans Eysenck (1959) and his colleagues in Britain; and by Joseph Wolpe (1958) and his colleagues in South Africa (Wilson, 2011). Since then, there has been an explosion of interest in behavioural approaches to psychotherapy.

Behaviour therapies are based on certain assumptions (Stanley & Beidel, 2009). *First, it is assumed that behaviour is a product of learning.* No matter how self-defeating or pathological a client's behaviour might be, the behaviourist believes that it is the result of past learning and conditioning. *Second, it is assumed that what has been learned can be unlearned.* The same learning principles that explain how the maladaptive behaviour was acquired can be used to get rid of it. Thus, behaviour therapists attempt to change clients' behaviour by applying the principles of classical conditioning, operant conditioning, and observational learning.

Systematic Desensitization

Devised by Joseph Wolpe (1958), systematic desensitization revolutionized psychotherapy by giving therapists their first useful alternative to traditional "talk therapy" (Fishman, Rego, & Muller, 2011). *Systematic desensitization is a behaviour therapy used to reduce phobic clients' anxiety responses*

Joseph Wolpe

"Neurotic anxiety is nothing but a conditioned response."

Courtesy of Joseph Wolpe

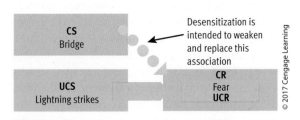

© 2017 Cengage Learning

Figure 16.6

The logic underlying systematic desensitization. Behaviourists argue that many phobic responses are acquired through classical conditioning, as in the example diagrammed here. Systematic desensitization targets the conditioned associations between phobic stimuli and fear responses.

through counterconditioning. The treatment assumes that most anxiety responses are acquired through classical conditioning (as we discussed in Chapter 15). According to this model, a harmless stimulus (e.g., a bridge) may be paired with a fear-arousing event (lightning striking the bridge), so that it becomes a conditioned stimulus eliciting anxiety. The goal of systematic desensitization is to weaken the association between the conditioned stimulus (the bridge) and the conditioned response of anxiety (see Figure 16.6). Systematic desensitization involves three steps.

First, the therapist helps the client build an anxiety hierarchy. The hierarchy is a list of anxiety-arousing stimuli related to the specific source of anxiety, such as flying, academic tests, or snakes. The client ranks the stimuli from the least anxiety-arousing to the most anxiety-arousing. This ordered list of stimuli is the *anxiety hierarchy*. An example of an anxiety hierarchy for one woman's fear of heights is shown in Figure 16.7.

The second step involves training the client in deep muscle relaxation. This second phase may begin during early sessions while the therapist and client are still constructing the anxiety hierarchy. Various therapists use different relaxation training procedures. Whatever procedures are used, the client must learn to engage in deep, thorough relaxation on command from the therapist.

In the third step, the client tries to work through the hierarchy, learning to remain relaxed while imagining

AN ANXIETY HIERARCHY FOR SYSTEMATIC DESENSITIZATION

Degree of fear

5	I'm standing on the balcony of the top floor of an apartment tower.
10	I'm standing on a stepladder in the kitchen to change a light bulb.
15	I'm walking on a ridge. The edge is hidden by shrubs and treetops.
20	I'm sitting on the slope of a mountain, looking out over the horizon.
25	I'm crossing a bridge 2 metres above a creek. The bridge consists of a 45-cm-wide board with a handrail on one side.
30	I'm riding a ski lift 2.5 metres above the ground.
35	I'm crossing a shallow, wide creek on a 45-cm-wide board, 1 metre above water level.
40	I'm climbing a ladder outside the house to reach a second-storey window.
45	I'm pulling myself up a 30-degree wet, slippery slope on a steel cable.
50	I'm scrambling up a rock, 2.5 metres high.
55	I'm walking 3 metres on a resilient, 45-cm-wide board, which spans a 2.5-metre-deep gulch.
60	I'm walking on a wide plateau, 60 cm from the edge of a cliff.
65	I'm skiing an intermediate hill. The snow is packed.
70	I'm walking over a railway trestle.
75	I'm walking on the side of an embankment. The path slopes to the outside.
80	I'm riding a chair lift 5 metres above the ground.
85	I'm walking up a long, steep slope.
90	I'm walking up (or down) a 15-degree slope on a 1-metre-wide trail. On one side of the trail the terrain drops down sharply; on the other side is a steep upward slope.
95	I'm walking on a 1-metre-wide ridge. The slopes on both sides are long and more than 25 degrees steep.
100	I'm walking on a 1-metre-wide ridge. The trail slopes on one side. The drop on either side of the trail is more than 25 degrees.

Figure 16.7

Example of an anxiety hierarchy. Systematic desensitization requires the construction of an anxiety hierarchy like the one shown here, which was developed for a woman who had a fear of heights but wanted to go hiking in the mountains.

Source: From Rudestam, K. E. (1980). *Methods of self-change: An ABC primer* (pp. 42–43). Belmont, CA: Wadsworth. Reprinted by permission of the author.

each stimulus. Starting with the least anxiety-arousing stimulus, the client imagines the situation as vividly as possible while relaxing. If the client experiences strong anxiety, he or she drops the imaginary scene and concentrates on relaxation. The client keeps repeating this process until he or she can imagine a scene with little or no anxiety. Once a particular scene is conquered, the client moves on to the next stimulus situation in the anxiety hierarchy. Gradually, over a number of therapy sessions, the client progresses through the hierarchy, unlearning troublesome anxiety responses. As clients conquer *imagined* phobic stimuli, they may be encouraged to confront the *real* stimuli.

David Taylor/Alamy Stock Photo

Systematic desensitization is a behavioural treatment for phobias. Early studies of the procedure's efficacy often used people who had snake phobias as research subjects because people with snake phobias were relatively easy to find. This research showed that systematic desensitization is generally an effective treatment.

The effectiveness of systematic desensitization in reducing phobic responses is well documented (Spiegler, 2016). However, interventions emphasizing real-life, direct exposures to anxiety-arousing situations have become behaviour therapists' treatment of choice for phobic and other anxiety disorders (Rachman, 2009). **In *exposure therapies*, clients are confronted with situations they fear so they learn that these situations are really harmless.** The exposures take place in a controlled setting and often involve a gradual progression from less-feared to more-feared stimuli. These real-life exposures to anxiety-arousing situations usually prove harmless, and individuals' anxiety responses decline. In recent decades, some therapists have resorted to highly realistic virtual-reality presentations of feared situations via computer-generated imagery (Meyerbröker & Emmelkamp, 2010; Reger et al., 2011). Exposure therapies are versatile in that they can be used with the full range of anxiety disorders, including obsessive-compulsive disorder, post-traumatic stress disorder, and panic disorder.

Aversion Therapy

Aversion therapy is far and away the most controversial of the behaviour therapies. It's not something that you would sign up for unless you were pretty desperate. Psychologists usually suggest it only as a treatment of last resort, after other interventions have failed. What's so terrible about aversion therapy? The client has to endure decidedly unpleasant stimuli, such as shocks or drug-induced nausea.

Aversion therapy is a behaviour therapy in which an aversive stimulus is paired with a stimulus that elicits an undesirable response. For example, alcoholics have had an *emetic drug* (one that causes nausea and vomiting) paired with their favourite drinks during therapy sessions (Landabaso et al., 1999). By pairing the drug with alcohol, the therapist hopes to create a conditioned aversion to alcohol (see Figure 16.8).

Aversion therapy takes advantage of the automatic nature of responses produced through classical conditioning. Admittedly, alcoholics treated with aversion therapy know that they won't be given an emetic outside of their therapy sessions. However, their reflex response to the stimulus of alcohol may be changed so that they respond to it with nausea and distaste (remember the "sauce béarnaise syndrome" described in Chapter 6). Obviously, this response should make it much easier to resist the urge to drink.

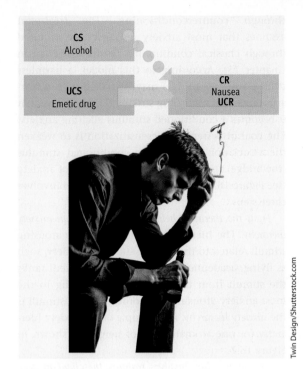

Figure 16.8
Aversion therapy. Aversion therapy uses classical conditioning to create an aversion to a stimulus that has elicited problematic behaviour. For example, in the treatment of drinking problems, alcohol may be paired with a nausea-inducing drug to create an aversion to drinking.

Source: From Weiten. Cengage *Advantage Books: Psychology*, 9E. © 2013 South-Western, a part of Cengage, Inc. Reproduced by permission. www.cengage.com/permissions

Aversion therapy is not a widely used technique, and when it is used, it is usually only one element in a larger treatment program. Troublesome behaviours treated successfully with aversion therapy have included drug and alcohol abuse, sexual deviance, gambling, shoplifting, stuttering, cigarette smoking, and overeating (Bordnick et al., 2004; Emmelkamp, 1994; Grossman & Ruiz, 2004; Maletzky, 2002).

Social Skills Training

Many psychological problems grow out of interpersonal difficulties. Behaviour therapists point out that people are not born with social finesse—they acquire social skills through learning. Unfortunately, some people have not learned how to be friendly, how to make conversation, how to express anger appropriately, and so forth. Social ineptitude can contribute to anxiety, feelings of inferiority, and various kinds of disorders. In light of these findings, therapists are increasingly using social skills training in efforts to improve clients' social abilities (Thase, 2012). This approach to therapy has yielded promising results in the treatment of social anxiety (Bogels & Voncken, 2008), autism (Otero et al., 2015), and schizophrenia (Mueser et al., 2013).

Social skills training is a behaviour therapy designed to improve interpersonal skills that emphasizes modelling, behavioural rehearsal, and shaping. This type of behaviour therapy can be conducted with individual clients or in groups. Social skills training depends on the principles of operant conditioning and observational learning. With *modelling*, the client is encouraged to watch socially skilled friends and colleagues in order to acquire appropriate responses (eye contact, active listening, and so on) through observation. In *behavioural rehearsal*, the client tries to practise social techniques in structured role-playing exercises. The therapist provides corrective feedback and uses approval to reinforce progress. Eventually, of course, clients try their newly acquired skills in real-world interactions. Usually, they are given specific homework assignments. *Shaping* is used in that clients are gradually asked to handle more complicated and delicate social situations. For example, a nonassertive client may begin by working on making requests of friends. Only much later will he or she be asked to tackle standing up to the boss at work.

Cognitive-Behavioural Therapies

In Chapter 15, we learned that cognitive factors play a key role in the development of many anxiety and mood disorders. Citing the importance of such findings, behaviour therapists in the 1970s started to focus more attention on their clients' cognitions (Beck & Weishaar, 2014). *Cognitive-behavioural treatments* use varied combinations of verbal interventions and behaviour modification techniques to help clients change maladaptive patterns of thinking. Some of these treatments, such as Albert Ellis's (Ellis, 1973; Kaufman, 2007) rational-emotive behaviour therapy and Aaron Beck's (1976) cognitive therapy, emerged out of an insight therapy tradition, whereas other treatments, such as the systems developed by Donald Meichenbaum (1977) and Michael Mahoney (1974), emerged from the behavioural tradition.

Here we will focus on Beck's cognitive therapy (Beck & Weishaar, 2014) as an example of a cognitive-behavioural treatment (see Chapter 14 for a discussion of some of Ellis's ideas). We also discuss one of the most recent additions to cognitive-behavioural treatments, *mindfulness-based cognitive therapy* (Segal, Williams, & Teasdale, 2002).

Cognitive therapy uses specific strategies to correct habitual thinking errors that underlie various types of disorders. Cognitive therapy was originally devised as a treatment for depression. However, in recent decades, cognitive therapy has been applied

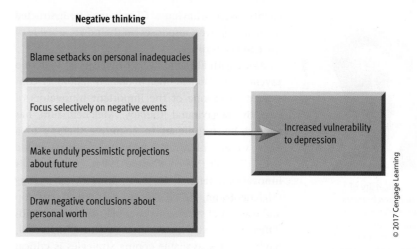

Negative thinking

Figure 16.9
Beck's view of the roots of disorders. Beck's theory initially focused on the causes of depression, although it was gradually broadened to explain other disorders. According to Beck, depression is caused by the types of negative thinking shown here.

fruitfully to an increasingly wide range of disorders (Hollon & Beck, 2013; Wright, Thase, & Beck, 2014). According to cognitive therapists, depression and other disorders are caused by "errors" in thinking (see Figure 16.9). For example, they assert that depression-prone people tend to (1) blame their setbacks on personal inadequacies, without considering circumstantial explanations; (2) focus selectively on negative events, while ignoring positive events; (3) make unduly pessimistic projections about the future; and (4) draw negative conclusions about their worth as a person, based on insignificant events. For instance, imagine you got a low grade on a minor quiz in a class. If you made the kinds of errors in thinking just described, you might blame the grade on your woeful stupidity, dismiss comments from a classmate that it was an unfair test, gloomily predict that you will surely flunk the course, and conclude you are not genuine college/university material.

The goal of cognitive therapy is to change clients' negative thoughts and maladaptive beliefs (Wright et al., 2014). To begin, clients are taught to detect their automatic negative thoughts—the self-defeating statements that people are prone to make when analyzing problems. Examples include "I'm just not smart enough," "No one really likes me," and "It's all my fault." Clients are then trained to subject these automatic thoughts to reality testing. The therapist helps them see how unrealistically negative the thoughts are.

Cognitive therapy uses a variety of behavioural techniques, such as modelling, systematic monitoring of one's behaviour, and behavioural rehearsal (Beck & Weishaar, 2014; Wright, Beck, & Thase, 2003). Cognitive therapists often give their clients "homework assignments" that focus on changing the

Aaron Beck

"Most people are barely aware of the automatic thoughts which precede unpleasant feelings or automatic inhibitions."

Courtesy of Donald Meichenbaum

Former University of Waterloo psychologist Donald Meichenbaum is well known for his role in the development of cognitive-behavioural therapy techniques.

Courtesy of Zindel Segal

Zindel Segal has been instrumental in the development of mindfulness-based cognitive therapy. This approach to cognitive therapy is based on mindfulness mediation and is directed at preventing relapse into depression. Segal is well known for his earlier research into and treatment of depression.

clients' overt behaviours. Clients may be instructed to engage in overt responses on their own, outside of the clinician's office.

Along with Ellis and Beck, University of Waterloo psychologist Donald Meichenbaum (2007) is considered to be one of the important innovators of cognitive-behavioural therapy. Meichenbaum has applied his techniques in cognitive therapy to a wide variety of issues, including post-traumatic stress disorder (Meichenbaum, 1994). In one of his innovations, referred to as *self-instructional training* (Meichenbaum, 1977), clients are taught to develop and use verbal statements that help them cope with difficult contexts. As we discussed in Chapter 14, having readily available coping strategies is critical in dealing with stress. Self-instructional training can help clients deal with current stressors and may serve to inoculate them against future stress.

One of the most recent developments in cognitive-behavioural treatment was pioneered by Zindel Segal and his colleagues (Segal, Williams, & Teasdale, 2002). Segal is director of the Cognitive Behaviour Therapy Unit at the Centre for Addiction and Mental Health in Toronto. This therapy integrates key ideas drawn from cognitive therapy and from mindfulness meditation (Felder, Segal, et al., 2017; Kabat-Zinn, 1995; Segal & Walsh, 2016). In this approach, traditional cognitive-behavioural techniques (e.g., those we just discussed) are combined with meditation-based techniques to heighten self-awareness of thoughts and emotions and to dysfunctional changes in the mind and body that can be targeted by cognitive-behavioural techniques (Evans & Segerstrom, 2011; Irving et al., 2015; Mrazek, Smallwood, & Schooler, 2012; Raedt et al., 2012).

Mindfulness emphasizes both attention regulation and an open, accepting approach to one's thoughts and experience (Chambers, Lo, & Allen, 2008; Frewen et al., 2008; Fruzetti & Erikson, 2010). In mindfulness, full attention is given to the present-moment experience and that experience is "employed equanimously, in that whatever arises is acknowledged and examined without judgment, elaboration, or reaction" (Chambers, Lo, & Allen, 2008, p. 322). In mindfulness meditation, thoughts are acknowledged and accepted, but not evaluated or reacted to. Mindfulness-based therapy was originally designed to prevent relapse in individuals who have previously but who do not currently suffer from depression (Crane et al., 2008; Williams, 2008). In therapy, individuals are taught to focus on troubling thoughts or emotions and to accept them without judging or elaborating on them. This allows the patient to observe and experience them without automatically reacting. According to Segal in a recent interview, this

"helps you to step back from automatic reactions built into emotions for evolutionary reasons" (McIlroy, 2008, A4). Enabling vulnerable individuals to extricate themselves from negative automatic thoughts is a goal of this technique. The mindfulness approach has since been applied to clients with currently active depression (Crane, 2008; Irving et al., 2015; Kenny & Williams, 2007) as well as having been extended to interventions with other disorders.

This approach to cognitive therapy has already been employed in a number of studies evaluating its effectiveness (Eberth & Sedlmeier, 2012; Holzel et al., 2011; Johansson, Bjuhr, & Ronnback, 2013). The results are impressive (Crane et al., 2008; Irving et al., 2015; Segal, Williams, & Teasdale, 2002), with studies finding that previously depressed individuals who received mindfulness training evidenced reduced rates of relapse (Teasdale et al., 2000) and show significantly decreased dysfunctional recollection of past events (Williams, Teasdale, Segal, & Soulsby, 2000). In other research, mindfulness and mindfulness-based cognitive-behavioural therapy (MBCT) has been found to be associated with less worry, with the generation of more specific future goals, with beliefs about self-efficacy for people with a history of suicidalilty, with distinct neural modes of self-reference, and even with affecting the structure of the brain (Barnhofer et al., 2010; Burg & Michalak, 2011; Crane et al., 2011; Evans & Segerstrom, 2011; Farb et al., 2007; Hölzel et al., 2011). It has also been demonstrated that mindfulness-based cognitive therapy can be delivered effectively in an online format (Dimidjian, Beck, et al., 2014; Felder, Segal, Beck, et al., 2017). Our Featured Study in this chapter, conducted at Wilfrid Laurier University, examines some of the mechanisms of change in mindfulness therapy.

FEATURED STUDY

Mindfulness and acceptance-based group therapy and traditional cognitive behavioural group therapy for social anxiety disorder: Mechanisms of change.

Description
In this study the authors highlight some of the processes responsible for change in mindfulness therapy.

Investigators
Kocovski, N. L., et al. (2015). *Behaviour Research and Therapy, 70*, 11–22.

Clinicians have also taken the approaches developed initially in the treatment of depression to the treatment of other disorders (e.g., Baer, Carmomdy,

& Hunsinger, 2012; Breslin, Zack, & McMain, 2002; Davis & Hayes, 2012; Garland, Gaylord, Boettiger, & Howard, 2010; Orsillo & Roemer, 2010). Orsillo and Roemer (2010), for example, have developed a mindfulness-based therapeutic approach to anxiety. They suggest that mindfulness practices are not only an important therapeutic tool, but that the skills people acquire will help them live the lives they want to live. These skills include (1) *increased awareness*—being able to notice where our attention is along with the ability to bring it back into focus, and expanding our awareness so that we will be able to capture the fullness of our experience; (2) *present moment*—being able to bring the mind back to the present moment whenever we begin to think of past difficulties and worries; (3) *self-compassion*—the ability to have compassion for yourself and your experiences; and (4) *accepting things as they are*—when we accept and respond to things as they are, we can avoid the dysfunctional reactivity that occurs when we contrast them to the way we want things to be.

Mindfulness-based practices are an exciting new tool that therapists can use in a variety of ways (e.g., Key et al., 2017) in treating their clients. No doubt work in this area will continue and this approach to cognitive therapy will see increasing use with individuals who have suffered from recurrent depression and other disorders.

How Effective Are Behaviour Therapies?

Behaviour therapists have historically placed more emphasis on the importance of measuring therapeutic outcomes than insight therapists have. Hence, there is ample evidence attesting to the effectiveness of behaviour therapy (Jacob & Pelham, 2005; Stanley & Beidel, 2009). Of course, behaviour therapies are not well suited to the treatment of some types of problems (vague feelings of discontent, for instance). Furthermore, it's misleading to make global statements about the effectiveness of behaviour therapies, because they include many types of procedures designed for very different purposes. For example, the value of systematic desensitization for phobias has no bearing on the value of aversion therapy for sexual deviance.

For our purposes, it is sufficient to note that there is favourable evidence on the efficacy of most of the widely used behavioural interventions (Zinbarg & Griffith, 2008). Cognitive-behavioural and cognitive therapies can make important contributions to the treatment of phobias, obsessive-compulsive disorders, sexual dysfunction, schizophrenia, drug-related problems, eating disorders, psychosomatic disorders, hyperactivity, autism, and intellectual disability (Craighead et al., 2013; Emmelkamp, 2013; Key et al., 2017; Wilson, 2011). Next we consider biomedical therapies. To some extent, the three major approaches to treatment have different strengths. Let's see where the strengths of the biomedical therapies lie.

concept **check** 16.2

Understanding Therapists' Goals

Check your understanding of therapists' goals by matching various therapies with the appropriate description. The answers are in Appendix A near the back of the book.

Principal Therapeutic Goals

_____ **1.** Elimination of maladaptive behaviours or symptoms

_____ **2.** Acceptance of genuine self, personal growth

_____ **3.** Recovery of unconscious conflicts, character reconstruction

_____ **4.** Detection and reduction of negative thinking

Therapy

a. Psychoanalysis

b. Client-centred therapy

c. Cognitive therapy

d. Behaviour therapy

concept **check** 16.3

Understanding the Types of Behaviour Therapy

Check your understanding of the varieties of behaviour therapy discussed in the text by matching the therapies with the appropriate description. Choose from the following: (a) systematic desensitization, (b) social skills training, and (c) aversion therapy. The answers are in Appendix A.

_____ **1.** Anxiety is reduced by conditioning the client to respond positively to stimuli that previously aroused anxiety.

_____ **2.** Unwanted behaviours are eliminated by conditioning the client to have an unpleasant response to stimuli that previously triggered the behaviour.

_____ **3.** Behavioural techniques are used to teach the client new behaviours aimed at enhancing the quality of their interactions with others.

Biomedical Therapies

Key Learning Goals

▶ Summarize the therapeutic actions and side effects of four categories of psychiatric drugs.

▶ Evaluate the overall efficacy of drug treatments, and discuss controversies surrounding pharmaceutical research.

▶ Describe electroconvulsive therapy, and assess its therapeutic effects and risks.

Biomedical therapies are physiological interventions intended to reduce symptoms associated with psychological disorders. These therapies assume that psychological disorders are caused, at least in part, by biological malfunctions. As we discussed in Chapter 15, this assumption clearly has merit for many disorders, especially the more severe ones.

Treatment with Drugs

Psychopharmacotherapy is the treatment of mental disorders with medication. We will refer to this kind of treatment more simply as *drug therapy*. The four main categories of therapeutic drugs for psychological problems are (1) antianxiety drugs, (2) antipsychotic drugs, (3) antidepressant drugs, and (4) mood-stabilizing drugs. As you can see in Figure 16.10, the rate at which psychiatrists prescribe these drugs has increased since the mid-1990s for all four of these drug classes (Olfson et al., 2014).

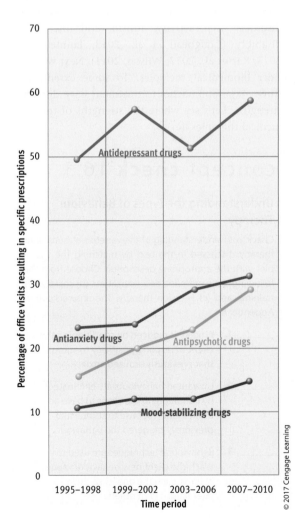

Figure 16.10
Increasing prescription of psychiatric drugs. Olfson et al. (2014) tracked prescription trends for psychiatric drugs over a period of 15 years. These data show the percentage of office visits to psychiatrists that resulted in prescriptions for various types of drugs. As you can see, reliance on all four categories of psychiatric drugs increased over this time period. (Based on data from Olfson et al., 2014)

Antianxiety Drugs

Most of us know someone who pops pills to relieve anxiety. The drugs involved in this common coping strategy are *antianxiety drugs*, which relieve tension, apprehension, and nervousness. The most popular of these drugs are Valium and Xanax. These are the trade names (the proprietary names that pharmaceutical companies use in marketing drugs) for diazepam and alprazolam, respectively.

Valium, Xanax, and other drugs in the *benzodiazepine* family are often called *tranquilizers*. These drugs exert their effects almost immediately, and they can be fairly effective in alleviating feelings of anxiety (Dubovsky, 2009). However, their effects are measured in hours, so their impact is relatively short-lived. Antianxiety drugs are routinely prescribed for people with anxiety disorders, but they are also given to millions of people who simply suffer from chronic nervous tension.

All of the drugs used to treat psychological problems have potentially troublesome side effects that show up in some patients but not others. The antianxiety drugs are no exception. The most common side effects of Valium and Xanax include drowsiness, depression, nausea, and confusion. These can present serious problems for some patients. These drugs also have potential for abuse, drug dependence, and overdose, although these risks have probably been exaggerated in the press (Martinez, Maragnell, & Martinez, 2008). Another drawback is that patients who have been on antianxiety drugs for a while often experience withdrawal symptoms when their drug treatment is stopped (Ferrando, Owen, & Levenson, 2014).

Antipsychotic Drugs

Antipsychotic drugs are used primarily in the treatment of schizophrenia. They are also given to people with severe mood disorders who become delusional. The trade names (with the generic names in parentheses) of some classic drugs in this category are Thorazine (chlorpromazine), Mellaril (thioridazine), and Haldol (haloperidol). *Antipsychotic drugs* are used to gradually reduce psychotic symptoms, including hyperactivity, mental confusion, hallucinations, and delusions. The traditional antipsychotics appear to decrease activity at dopamine synapses, although the exact relationship between their neurochemical effects and their clinical effects remains obscure (Miyamoto et al., 2008).

Studies suggest that antipsychotics reduce psychotic symptoms in about 70 percent of patients, albeit in varied degrees (Kane, Stroup, & Marder,

2009). When antipsychotic drugs are effective, they work their magic gradually, as shown in Figure 16.11. Patients usually begin to respond within one to three weeks, but considerable variability in responsiveness is seen (Emsley, Rabinowitz, & Medori, 2006). Further improvement may occur for several months. Many schizophrenic patients are placed on antipsychotics indefinitely, because these drugs can reduce the likelihood of a relapse into an active schizophrenic episode (van Kammen, Hurford, & Marder, 2009).

Antipsychotic drugs undeniably make a major contribution to the treatment of severe mental disorders, and psychiatrists' reliance on antipsychotic medications has increased dramatically in recent decades (Olfson et al., 2012). However, antipsychotic drugs present their share of problems. They have many unpleasant side effects (Ferrando et al., 2014). Drowsiness, constipation, and cottonmouth are common. Tremors, muscular rigidity, and impaired coordination can also occur. After being released from a hospital, many patients who have been placed on antipsychotics stop their drug regimen because of the side effects. Unfortunately, after patients stop taking antipsychotic medication, about 70 percent relapse within a year (van Kammen, Hurford, & Marder, 2009). One study found that even brief periods of partial noncompliance with one's drug regimen increased the risk of relapse (Subotnik et al., 2011). Another ten-year study showed that noncompliance was associated with increased mortality among schizophrenic patients (Cullen et al., 2013). In addition to their nuisance side effects, antipsychotics can cause a more severe and lasting problem called tardive dyskinesia, which is seen in about 15–25 percent of patients who receive long-term treatment with traditional antipsychotics (Stewart, Russakoff, & Stewart, 2014). *Tardive dyskinesia* **is a neurological disorder marked by involuntary writhing and tic-like movements of the mouth, tongue, face, hands, or feet.** Once this debilitating syndrome emerges, there is no cure, although spontaneous remission sometimes occurs after the discontinuation of antipsychotic medication.

Psychiatrists currently rely primarily on a newer class of antipsychotic agents called *second-generation antipsychotic drugs* (Marder, Hurford, & van Kammen, 2009). These drugs appear to be roughly similar to the first-generation antipsychotics in therapeutic effectiveness, but they offer several advantages (Meltzer & Bobo, 2009). For instance, they can help some treatment-resistant patients who do not respond to traditional antipsychotics, and they produce fewer unpleasant side effects and carry less risk for tardive dyskinesia. Of course, like all powerful drugs, they carry some risks: Second-generation antipsychotics appear to increase patients' vulnerability to diabetes and cardiovascular problems. In the hopes of reducing

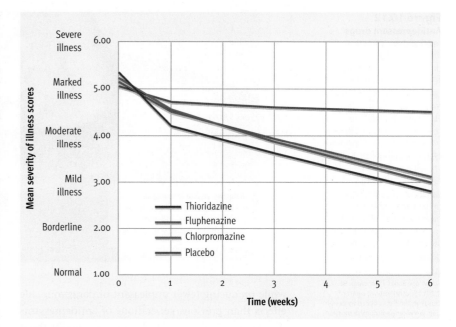

Figure 16.11

The time course of antipsychotic drug effects. Antipsychotic drugs reduce psychotic symptoms gradually, over a span of weeks, as graphed here. In contrast, patients given placebo medication show little improvement.

Source: Cole, J. O., Goldberg, S. C., & Davis, J. M. (1966). Drugs in the treatment of psychosis. In P. Solomon (Ed.), *Psychiatric drugs.* New York: Grune & Stratton. From data in the NIMH PSC Collective Study I. Reprinted by permission of J. M. Davis.

drug discontinuation by patients and associated high relapse rates, psychiatrists are experimenting with long-acting, injectable antipsychotic medications that only need to be administered on a monthly basis. However, the early research results on this new approach have not yielded the increases in efficacy clinicians hoped to see (Goff, 2014; McEvoy et al., 2014).

Antidepressant Drugs

As their name suggests, *antidepressant drugs* gradually elevate mood and help bring people out of depression. Reliance on antidepressants has increased dramatically in the last two decades, as antidepressants have become the most frequently prescribed class of medication in North America (Olfson & Marcus, 2009). Prior to 1987, there were two principal classes of antidepressants: *tricyclics* (e.g., Elavil) and *MAO inhibitors* (e.g., Nardil). These two sets of drugs affect neurochemical activity in different ways (see Figure 16.12) and tend to work with different patients. Overall, they are beneficial for about two-thirds of depressed patients (Gitlin, 2009). The tricyclics have fewer problems with side effects and complications than the MAO inhibitors (Potter et al., 2006).

Today, the most widely prescribed antidepressants are the *selective serotonin reuptake inhibitors* (SSRIs), which slow the reuptake process at serotonin synapses. The drugs in this class, which include Prozac (fluoxetine), Paxil (paroxetine), and Zoloft (sertraline), seem to yield rapid therapeutic gains in the treatment of depression (Boland & Keller, 2008),

Figure 16.12

Antidepressant drugs' mechanisms of action. The three types of antidepressant drugs all increase activity at serotonin synapses, which is probably the principal basis for their therapeutic effects. However, they increase serotonin activity in different ways, with different spillover effects (Marangell et al., 1999). Tricyclics and MAO inhibitors have effects at a much greater variety of synapses, which presumably explains why they have more side effects. The more recently developed SSRIs are much more specific in targeting serotonin synapses.

Source: From Weiten. *Cengage Advantage Books: Psychology*, 9E. © 2013 South-Western, a part of Cengage, Inc. Reproduced by permission. www.cengage.com/permissions

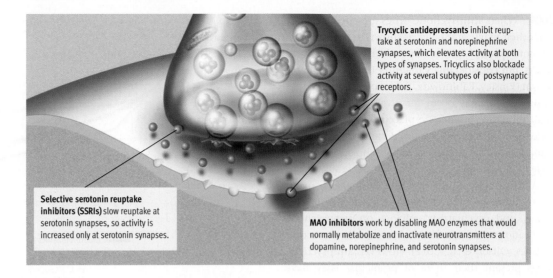

Trycyclic antidepressants inhibit reuptake at serotonin and norepinephrine synapses, which elevates activity at both types of synapses. Tricyclics also blockade activity at several subtypes of postsynaptic receptors.

Selective serotonin reuptake inhibitors (SSRIs) slow reuptake at serotonin synapses, so activity is increased only at serotonin synapses.

MAO inhibitors work by disabling MAO enzymes that would normally metabolize and inactivate neurotransmitters at dopamine, norepinephrine, and serotonin synapses.

while producing fewer unpleasant or dangerous side effects than previous generations of antidepressants (Sussman, 2009). However, there is some doubt about how effective the SSRIs (and other antidepressants) are in relieving episodes of depression among patients suffering from bipolar disorder (Pacchiarotti et al., 2013). Although the SSRIs present far fewer problems than earlier antidepressants, they are not without side effects. Adverse effects include nausea, dry mouth, drowsiness, sexual difficulties, weight gain, feeling emotionally numb, agitation, and increases in suicidal thinking (Read, Cartwright, & Gibson, 2014).

Like antipsychotic drugs, the various types of antidepressants exert their effects gradually over a period of weeks, but about 60 percent of patients' improvement tends to occur in the first two weeks (Gitlin, 2014). A research review that looked carefully at the severity of patients' depression when medication was initiated found that people with serious depression benefit the most from antidepressants, whereas antidepressants appear to provide a relatively modest benefit for patients with mild to moderate depression (Fournier et al. 2010).

A major concern in recent years has been evidence from a number of studies that SSRIs may increase the risk for suicide, especially in adolescents and young adults (Healy & Whitaker, 2003; Holden, 2004). The challenge of collecting definitive data on this issue is much more daunting than one might guess. The crux of the problem is that suicide rates are already elevated among people who exhibit the disorders for which SSRIs are prescribed (Berman, 2009). The research findings on this issue are complicated and contradictory. One influential meta-analysis concluded that antidepressants lead to a slight elevation in the risk of suicidal behaviour (Bridge et al., 2007). However, a more recent analysis of 41 antidepressant drug trials failed to find an increase in suicidal risk (Gibbons et al., 2012). Regulatory warnings from the

U.S. Food and Drug Administration (FDA) have led to a decline in the prescription of SSRIs in the United States among adolescents (Nemeroff et al., 2007). This trend has prompted concern that the well-intended warnings may have backfired and led to increases in suicide among untreated individuals (Dudley et al., 2008). A recent study yielded disturbing evidence that bolsters this concern. C. Y. Lu et al. (2014) found that in the second year after the FDA warnings, antidepressant use declined by 31 percent among adolescents and by 24 percent among young adults, while apparent suicide attempts via drug overdose (a method of suicide that was relatively easy to track in medical databases) increased by 22 percent among adolescents and by 34 percent among young adults. The association between reduced antidepressant use and increased suicide may not reflect a causal relationship, but the findings are worrisome. Clearly, the risks of putting young patients on antidepressants need to be weighed against the risks of not putting them on antidepressants. In the final analysis, this is a complex issue, but the one thing experts seem to agree on is that adolescents starting on SSRIs should be monitored closely by their families and physicians.

reality check

Misconception

Psychological disorders are largely chronic and incurable.

Reality

Admittedly, there are mentally ill people for whom treatment is a failure. However, they are greatly outnumbered by people who do get better, either spontaneously or through formal treatment. The majority of people who are diagnosed as mentally ill eventually improve and lead normal, productive lives. Even the most severe psychological disorders can be treated successfully.

626   CHAPTER 16   NEL

Mood Stabilizers

Mood stabilizers are drugs used to control mood swings in patients with bipolar mood disorders. For many years, lithium was the only effective drug in this category. Lithium has proven valuable in preventing *future* episodes of both mania and depression in patients with bipolar illness (Miklowitz, 2014; Post & Altshuler, 2009). Lithium can also be used in efforts to bring patients with bipolar illness out of *current* manic or depressive episodes (Keck & McElroy, 2006). However, antipsychotics and antidepressants are more frequently used for these purposes. On the negative side of the ledger, lithium does have some dangerous side effects if its use isn't managed skillfully (Jefferson & Greist, 2009). Lithium levels in the patient's blood must be monitored carefully, because high concentrations can be toxic and even fatal. Kidney and thyroid gland complications are the other major problems associated with lithium therapy.

In recent years, a number of alternatives to lithium have been developed. The most popular of these newer mood stabilizers is an anticonvulsant agent called *valproate*, which has become more widely used than lithium in the treatment of bipolar disorders (Thase & Denko, 2008). Valproate appears to be roughly as effective as lithium in efforts to treat current manic episodes and to prevent future affective disturbances, with fewer side effects (Muzina, Kemp, & Calabrese, 2008). In some cases, a combination of valproate and lithium may be used in treatment (Post & Altshuler, 2009).

Evaluating Drug Therapies

Drug therapies can produce clear therapeutic gains for many kinds of patients. What's especially impressive is that they can be effective with severe disorders that often defy therapeutic endeavours. Nonetheless, drug therapies are controversial. Critics have raised a number of issues (Bentall, 2009; Breggin, 2008; Healy, 2004; Kirsch, 2010; Spielmans & Kirsch, 2014; Whitaker, 2002). First, some critics argue that drug therapies are not as effective as advertised and that they often produce superficial, short-lived curative effects. For example, Valium does not really solve problems with anxiety; it merely provides temporary relief from an unpleasant symptom. Moreover, relapse rates are substantial when drug regimens are discontinued. Second, critics charge that many drugs are overprescribed and many patients overmedicated. According to these critics, a number of physicians routinely hand out prescriptions without giving adequate consideration to more complicated and difficult interventions. Consistent with this line of criticism, a study of office visits to psychiatrists found that they increasingly prescribe two and even three medications to patients, even though relatively little is known about the interactive effects of psychiatric drugs (Mojtabai & Olfson, 2010). Moreover, the growing reliance on medication has undermined the provision of insight and behavioural interventions. Although the empirical evidence on the value of insight and behavioural therapies has never been greater, the medicalization of psychological disorders has led to a decline in the use of psychosocial interventions that may be just as effective and safer than drug therapies (Gaudiano & Miller, 2013). Third, some critics charge that the damaging side effects of therapeutic drugs are underestimated by psychiatrists and that these side effects are often worse than the illnesses the drugs are supposed to cure. Some critics also have argued that psychiatric drugs may be helpful in the short term but that they disrupt neurotransmitter systems in ways that actually *increase* patients' vulnerability to psychological disorders in the long-term picture (Andrews et al., 2011).

Critics maintain that the negative effects of psychiatric drugs are not fully appreciated because the pharmaceutical industry has managed to gain undue influence over the research enterprise as it relates to drug testing (Angell, 2004; Healy, 2004; Insel, 2010). Today, most researchers who investigate the benefits and risks of medications and write treatment guidelines have lucrative financial arrangements with the pharmaceutical industry (Bentall, 2009; Cosgrove & Krimsky, 2012). Their studies are funded by drug companies, and they often receive substantial consulting fees. Unfortunately, these financial ties appear to undermine the objectivity required in scientific research because studies funded by drug companies are far less likely to report unfavourable results than are nonprofit-funded studies (Bekelman, Li, & Gross, 2003; Perlis et al., 2005). Industry-financed drug trials also tend to be too brief to detect the long-term risks associated with new drugs (Vandenbroucke & Psaty, 2008). Additionally, positive findings on drugs are almost always published, whereas when unfavourable results emerge, the data are often withheld from publication (Spielmans & Kirsch, 2014; Turner et al., 2008). Also, research designs are often slanted in a variety of ways to exaggerate the positive effects and minimize the negative effects of the drugs under scrutiny (Carpenter, 2002; Chopra, 2003; Spielmans & Kirsch, 2014). The conflicts of interest that appear to be pervasive in contemporary drug research raise grave concerns that require attention from researchers, universities, and government agencies.

Electroconvulsive Therapy (ECT)

In the 1930s, a Hungarian psychiatrist named Ladislas von Meduna speculated that epilepsy and schizophrenia could not coexist in the same body. On the basis of this observation, which turned out to be inaccurate, von Meduna theorized that it might be useful to induce epileptic-like seizures in schizophrenic patients. Initially, a drug was used to trigger these seizures. However, by 1938 a pair of Italian psychiatrists (Cerletti & Bini, 1938) demonstrated that it was safer to elicit the seizures with electric shock. Thus, modern electroconvulsive therapy was born.

Electroconvulsive therapy (ECT) **is a biomedical treatment in which electric shock is used to produce a cortical seizure accompanied by convulsions.** In ECT, electrodes are attached to the skull over the temporal lobes of the brain. A light anesthesia is induced, and the patient is given a variety of drugs to minimize the likelihood of complications. An electric current is then applied either to the right side or to both sides of the brain for about a second. Unilateral shock delivered to the right hemisphere is the preferred method of treatment today (Sackeim et al., 2009). The current triggers a brief (about 30 seconds) convulsive seizure. The patient normally awakens in an hour or two and manifests some confusion, disorientation, and nausea, which usually clear up in a matter of hours. People typically receive between 6 and 20 treatments over a period of a month or so (Fink, 2009).

The clinical use of ECT peaked in the 1940s and 1950s, before effective drug therapies were widely available. ECT has long been controversial, and its use did decline in the 1960s and 1970s. Only about 8 percent of psychiatrists administer ECT (Hermann et al., 1998), but it cannot be considered a rare form of treatment. Some critics argue that ECT is overused because it's a lucrative procedure that boosts psychiatrists' income while consuming relatively little of their time in comparison to insight therapy (Frank, 1990). Conversely, some ECT advocates argue that ECT is underutilized because the public harbours many misconceptions about its effects and risks (McDonald et al., 2004). ECT is used in the treatment of a variety of disorders. In recent decades, however, it has primarily been recommended for the treatment of depression.

Controversy about ECT has been fuelled by patients' reports that the treatment is painful, dehumanizing, and terrifying. Substantial improvements in the administration of ECT have made it less disagreeable than it once was (Bernstein et al., 1998). Nonetheless, some patients continue to report that they find the treatment extremely aversive (Johnstone, 1999). Two personal reports by Canadians, one on each side of the controversy, are interesting places to begin your consideration of the use of ECT. One, written by Wendy Funk (1998), addresses concerns

This patient is being prepared for electroconvulsive therapy (ECT). In ECT, an electric shock is used to elicit a brief cortical seizure. The shock is delivered through electrodes attached to the patient's skull.

Will & Deni McIntyre/Getty Images

she has over her treatment. The other, by Canadian psychologist Norman Endler (1982), is based on his own ECT treatment and is supportive of its use.

Effectiveness of ECT

The evidence of the therapeutic efficacy of ECT is open to varied interpretations. Proponents maintain that it is a remarkably effective treatment for major depression (Fink, 2014; Prudic, 2009). Moreover, they note that many patients who do not benefit from antidepressant medication improve in response to ECT (Nobler & Sackeim, 2006). However, opponents argue that the available studies are flawed and inconclusive and that ECT is probably no more effective than a placebo (Rose et al., 2003). Overall, there does seem to be enough favourable evidence to justify conservative use of ECT in treating severe mood disorders in patients who have not responded to medication (Kellner et al., 2012). ECT patients who recover from their depression and do not relapse report great improvements in the quality of their lives (McCall et al., 2013). Unfortunately, relapse rates after ECT are distressingly high. A review of 32 studies found that the risk of relapse into depression was 38 percent after six months and 51 percent after one year (Jelovac,

Kolshus, & McLoughlin, 2013). However, these high relapse rates may occur because ECT is largely reserved for patients who have severe, chronic depression that has not responded to drug treatment (Fekadu et al., 2009). In other words, if ECT is only used for the toughest cases, high relapse rates are to be expected.

New Brain Stimulation Techniques

Given the side effects and risks associated with ECT and drug treatments, scientists are always on the lookout for new methods of treating psychological disorders that might exhibit greater efficacy or fewer complications. Some innovative, new approaches to treatment involving stimulation of the brain are being explored with promising results, although they remain highly experimental at this time.

One new approach is transcranial magnetic stimulation, which was discussed in Chapter 3 as a method for studying brain function. *Transcranial magnetic stimulation (TMS)* is a new technique that permits scientists to temporarily enhance or depress activity in a specific area of the brain. In TMS, a magnetic coil mounted on a small paddle is held over specific areas of the head to increase or decrease activity in discrete regions of the cortex (Nahas et al., 2007). Neuroscientists are experimenting with TMS mostly as a treatment for depression, either by itself or combined with medications (Brunoni et al., 2013). So far, treatments delivered to the right and left prefrontal cortex show promise in reducing depressive symptoms (Janicak et al., 2010; Mantovani et al., 2012; O'Reardon et al., 2007). TMS generally is well tolerated, no anesthetic is required, and it seems to have minimal side effects. But a great deal of additional research will be necessary before the therapeutic value of TMS can be determined.

The other new approach to treatment is deep brain stimulation. In *deep brain stimulation (DBS)*, a thin electrode is surgically implanted in the brain and connected to an implanted pulse generator so that various electrical currents can be delivered to brain tissue adjacent to the electrode (George, 2003; see Figure 16.13). DBS has proven to be valuable in the treatment of the motor disturbances associated with Parkinson's disease, tardive dyskinesia, and some seizure disorders (Halpern et al., 2007; Oswal et al., 2016; Tinkhauser et al., 2017). Researchers are currently exploring whether DBS may have value in the treatment of depression or obsessive-compulsive disorder (Denys et al., 2010; Sartorius et al., 2010). Obviously, this highly

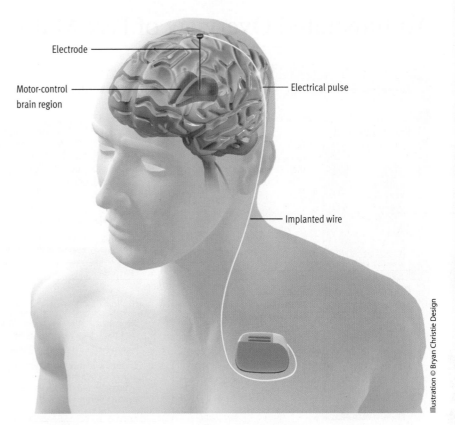

Illustration © Bryan Christie Design

Figure 16.13
Deep brain stimulation. Deep brain stimulation requires a surgical procedure in which a thin electrode (about the width of a human hair) is inserted into deep areas of the brain. The electrode is connected to a pulse generator implanted under the skin of the chest. The placement of the electrode and the type of current generated depend on what condition is being treated. The electrode shown here was implanted in a motor area of the brain to treat the tremors associated with Parkinson's disease. Researchers are experimenting with other electrode placements in efforts to treat depression and obsessive-compulsive disorder.

invasive procedure requiring brain surgery will never be a frontline therapy for mental disorders, but scientists hope that it may be valuable for highly treatment-resistant patients who do not benefit from conventional therapies (Kuehn, 2007).

concept **check** 16.4

Understanding Biomedical Therapies

Check your understanding of biomedical therapies by matching each treatment with its chief use. The answers are in Appendix A near the back of the book.

Treatment

_____ **1.** Antianxiety drugs

_____ **2.** Antipsychotic drugs

_____ **3.** Antidepressant drugs

_____ **4.** Mood stabilizers

_____ **5.** Electroconvulsive therapy (ECT)

Chief Purpose

a. To reduce psychotic symptoms

b. To bring a major depression to an end

c. To suppress tension, nervousness, and apprehension

d. To prevent future episodes of mania or depression in bipolar disorders

An Illustrated Overview of Five Major Approaches to Treatment

Therapy/founder

Roots of Disorders

Psychoanalysis

Developed by Sigmund Freud in Vienna, from the 1890s through the 1930s

National Library of Medicine

Intrapsychic conflict (among id, ego, and superego) → Anxiety → Reliance on defence mechanisms

© 2017 Cengage Learning

Unconscious conflicts resulting from fixations in earlier development cause anxiety, which leads to defensive behaviour. The repressed conflicts typically centre on sex and aggression.

Client-centred therapy

Created by Carl Rogers at the University of Chicago during the 1940s and 1950s

© Roger Ressmeyer/CORBIS

Believe affection from others is conditional → Need to distort shortcomings to feel worthy of affection → Relatively incongruent self-concept → Recurrent anxiety

Defensive behaviour protects inaccurate self-concept

© 2017 Cengage Learning

Overdependence on acceptance from others fosters incongruence, which leads to anxiety and defensive behaviour and thwarts personal growth.

Cognitive therapy

Devised by Aaron Beck at the University of Pennsylvania in the 1960s and 1970s

Courtesy of Dr. Aaron T. Beck

Negative thinking

Blame setbacks on personal inadequacies

Focus selectively on negative events

Make unduly pessimistic projections about future

Draw negative conclusions about personal worth

→ Increased vulnerability to depression

© 2017 Cengage Learning

Pervasive negative thinking about events related to self fosters anxiety and depression.

Behaviour therapy

Launched primarily by South African Joseph Wolpe's description of systematic desensitization in 1958

Courtesy of Joseph Wolpe

© 2017 Cengage Learning

CS Bridge

UCS Lightning strikes

CR Fear **UCR**

Maladaptive patterns of behaviour are acquired through learning. For example, many phobias are thought to be created through classical conditioning and maintained by operant conditioning.

Biomedical therapy

Many researchers contributed; key breakthroughs in drug treatment made around 1950 by John Cade in Australia, Henri Laborit in France, and Jean Delay and Pierre Deniker, also in France

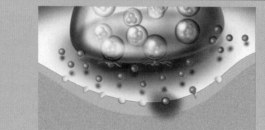

Most disorders are attributed to genetic predisposition and physiological malfunctions, such as abnormal neurotransmitter activity. For example, schizophrenia appears to be associated with overactivity at dopamine synapses.

Source: From Weiten. *Cengage Advantage Books: Psychology*, 9E. © 2013 South-Western, a part of Cengage, Inc. Reproduced by permission. www.cengage.com/permissions

Therapeutic Goals

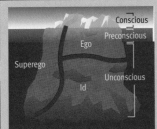

Insights regarding unconscious conflicts and motives; resolution of conflicts; personality reconstruction

© 2017 Cengage Learning

Increased congruence between self-concept and experience; acceptance of genuine self; self-determination and personal growth

© 2017 Cengage Learning

Reduction of negative thinking; substitution of more realistic thinking

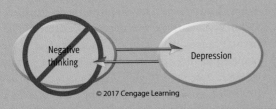

© 2017 Cengage Learning

Elimination of maladaptive symptoms; acquisition of more adaptive responses

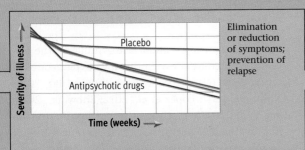

© 2017 Cengage Learning

Elimination or reduction of symptoms; prevention of relapse

Therapeutic Techniques

Free association, dream analysis, interpretation, transference

© Bruce Ayres/Stone/Getty Images

Genuineness, empathy, unconditional positive regard, clarification, reflecting back to client

© Zigy Kaluzny/Stone/Getty Images

Thought stopping, recording of automatic thoughts, refuting of negative thinking, homework assignments

Rachel Epstein/PhotoEdit

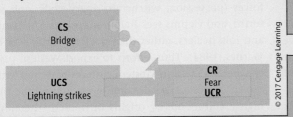

Classical and operant conditioning, systematic desensitization, aversive conditioning, social skills training, reinforcement, shaping, punishment, extinction, biofeedback

David Taylor/Alamy Stock Photo

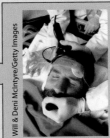

Antianxiety, antidepressant, and antipsychotic drugs; lithium; electroconvulsive therapy

Will & Deni McIntyre/Getty Images

Source: Cole, J. O., Goldberg, S. C., and Davis, J. M. (1966). Drugs in the treatment of psychosis. In P. Solomon (Ed.), *Psychiatric drugs*. New York: Grune & Stratton. From data in the NIMH PSC Collective Study I. Reprinted by permission of J.M. Davis.

Current Trends and Issues in Treatment

Key Learning Goals

▶ Analyze the barriers that lead to underutilization of mental health services by ethnic minorities and possible solutions.

▶ Discuss efforts to expand the delivery of clinical services through technology and the merits of blending approaches to therapy.

As we saw in our discussion of insight, behavioural, and drug therapy, recent decades have brought many changes in the world of mental health care (Gaudiano, 2013; Greenfield et al., 2013; Nordal, 2010; Rotheram-Borus et al., 2012). In this section, we'll discuss three trends that are not tied to a particular mode of treatment. Specifically, we'll look at efforts to respond more effectively to increasing cultural diversity, initiatives to increase the availability of psychotherapy through the use of technology, and the trend toward blending various approaches to therapy.

Blending Approaches to Treatment

In this chapter, we have reviewed many approaches to treatment. While some research is intended to compare the effectiveness of competing orientations or to determine what therapy works best with what specific client type (e.g., Colman et al., 2011; Elkin et al., 1989; Fournier et al., 2008), other clinicians work with the assumption that there is no rule that a client must be treated with just one approach (e.g., Paris, 2013). Often, a clinician will use several techniques in working with a client (e.g., Hunt et al., 2007). For example, a depressed person (Craighead & Dunlop, 2014) might receive cognitive therapy (an insight therapy), social skills training (a behaviour therapy), and antidepressant medication, or a combination (Blier et al., 2010; Thase, 2011) of medications (a biomedical therapy). Multiple approaches are particularly likely when a treatment team provides therapy. Studies suggest that combining approaches to treatment has merit (Glass, 2004; Riba & Miller, 2003; Szigethy & Friedman, 2009).

The value of multiple approaches to treatment may explain why a significant trend seems to have crept into the field of psychotherapy: a movement away from strong loyalty to individual schools of thought and a corresponding move toward integrating various approaches to therapy (Norcross & Goldfried, 1992; D. A. Smith, 1999). Most clinicians used to depend exclusively on one system of therapy while rejecting the utility of all others. This era of fragmentation may be drawing to a close. One recent survey of psychologists' theoretical orientations found that 36 percent of respondents describe themselves as *eclectic* in approach (Norcross, Hedges, & Castle, 2002).

Eclecticism in the practice of therapy involves drawing ideas from two or more systems of therapy instead of committing to just one system. Therapists can be eclectic in a number of ways (Feixas & Botella, 2004; Goin, 2005; Norcross & Beutler, 2011). Two common approaches are theoretical integration and technical eclecticism. In *theoretical integration,* two or more systems of therapy are combined or blended to take advantage of the strengths of each. Paul Wachtel's (1977, 1991) efforts to blend psychodynamic and behavioural therapies are a prominent example. *Technical eclecticism* involves borrowing ideas, insights, and techniques from a variety of sources while tailoring one's intervention strategy to the unique needs of each client. Advocates of technical eclecticism, such as Arnold Lazarus (1989, 1992, 1995), maintain that therapists should ask themselves, "What is the best approach for this specific client, problem, and situation?" and then adjust their strategy accordingly.

Increasing Multicultural Sensitivity in Treatment

Modern psychotherapy emerged during the second half of the 19th century in Europe and North America, spawned in part by a cultural milieu that viewed the self as an independent, reflective, rational being, capable of self-improvement (Cushman, 1992). Psychological disorders were assumed to have natural causes like physical diseases and to be amenable to medical treatments derived from scientific research. But the individualized, medicalized institution of modern psychotherapy reflects Western cultural values that are far from universal (Sue & Sue, 1999). In many nonindustrialized societies, psychological disorders are attributed to supernatural forces (possession, witchcraft, angry gods, and so forth), and victims seek help from priests, shamans, and folk healers, rather than doctors (Wittkower & Warnes, 1984). Thus, efforts to export Western psychotherapies to non-Western cultures have met with mixed success. Indeed, some even argue that the highly culture-bound origins of modern therapies have raised questions about their applicability to ethnic minorities *within* Western culture (Miranda et al., 2005).

Research on how cultural factors influence the process and outcome of psychotherapy has burgeoned in recent years (Carr & West, 2013; Camas-Diaz, 2011; Kirmayer, 2007; Lopez et al., 2012; Snowden, 2012; Sue et al., 2012), motivated in part by the need to improve mental health services for ethnic minority groups (Lee & Ramirez, 2000; Worthington, Soth-McNett, & Moreno, 2007). The data are ambiguous for a couple of ethnic groups, but studies suggest that North American minority groups generally underutilize therapeutic services (Bender et al., 2007; Folsom et al., 2007; Sue et al., 2009). Why? A variety of barriers appear to contribute to this problem, including the following (Snowden & Yamada, 2005; U.S. Department of Health and Human Services, 1999; Zane et al., 2004):

1. *Cultural barriers.* In times of psychological distress, some cultural groups are reluctant to turn to formal, professional sources of assistance. Given their socialization, they prefer to rely on informal assistance from family members, the clergy, respected elders, herbalists, acupuncturists, and so forth, who share their cultural heritage. Many members of minority groups have a history of frustrating interactions with bureaucracies and are distrustful of large, intimidating, foreign institutions, such as hospitals and community mental health centres (Pierce, 1992). We know, for example, that Asian Canadians, especially Chinese Canadians, are much less likely to access mental health services (Chen, Kazanjian, Wong, & Goldner, 2010; Tiwari & Wang, 2008). These groups are much more likely to shelter those family members who suffer from mental illness and to use family resources instead (Li & Browne, 2000; Naidoo, 1992; Peters, 1988). When they do see a professional, Asian Canadians are more likely to emphasize and report somatic or physical symptoms than emotional symptoms. Once again, this may be because of stigmas against admitting *psychological* illness in these communities (Lee, Lei, & Sue, 2001; Ryder et al., 2008). If you can make the illness *physical*, that is much more acceptable. In many cases, those suffering from psychological disorders are hidden from view because of these stigmas.

2. *Language barriers.* Effective communication is crucial to the provision of psychotherapy, yet most hospitals and mental health agencies are not adequately staffed with therapists who speak the languages used by minority groups in their service areas. The resulting communication problems make it awkward and difficult for many minority group members to explain their problems and to obtain the type of help that they need.

3. *Institutional barriers.* When all is said and done, Stanley Sue and Nolan Zane (1987) argue that the "single most important explanation for the problems in service delivery involves the inability of therapists to provide culturally responsive forms of treatment" (p. 37). The vast majority of therapists have been trained almost exclusively in the treatment of white, middle-class clients and are not familiar with the cultural backgrounds and unique characteristics of various ethnic groups. This culture gap often leads to misunderstandings, ill-advised treatment strategies, and reduced rapport. Unfortunately, there is a grievous shortage of ethnic therapists to meet the needs of various ethnic groups (Mays & Albee, 1992).

Issues concerning diversity are of clear relevance to the Canadian context. Canada is a true multicultural society in which diversity is highlighted and championed. In fact, according to recent statistics, just over 20 percent of the population of Canada was born outside Canada (Statistics Canada, 2016).

To treat their clients appropriately and effectively, clinicians need to be sensitive to diverse cultural conventions and sensitivities. This may be especially important with First Nations peoples. We saw in previous chapters that the suicide rate in some Aboriginal communities is extremely high, and these high suicide rates are accompanied by high rates of psychological disorders (Ames, Rawana, Gentile, & Morgan, 2013). Research examining therapeutic intervention with Aboriginal populations has become an important priority (e.g., Pomerville & Burrage, 2016). In a study of First Nations, Métis, and Inuit peoples of Canada, McGill University's Laurence Kirmayer and his colleagues found elevated levels of many disorders and problems, including substance abuse, depression, violence, and suicide (Kirmayer, Brass, & Tait, 2000). The authors note that Indigenous healing practices, often called *pan-Amerindian* healing movements, are increasingly visible and popular in Aboriginal treatment centres. They also note that therapy settings that fail to take into account Indigenous experience are not effective: "In most urban areas, mental health services have not adapted well to the needs of Aboriginal clients and this is reflected in low rates of use" (Kirmayer, Brass, & Tait, 2000, p. 612).

The special needs of our First Nations peoples were acknowledged in the 2012 mental health strategy announced by the Canadian government (see http://strategy.mentalhealthcommission.ca/pdf/strategy-images-en.pdf). This was Canada's first comprehensive, national mental health strategy paper and it explicitly acknowledged both the needs of Aboriginal peoples and the fact that resources should be targeted to that population. One of the six main priority goals of the strategy is to work with First Nations, Inuit, and Métis to address their mental health needs, acknowledging their distinct circumstances, rights, and cultures. In addition, in order to highlight First Nations issues, the Canadian Psychological Association has established an Aboriginal Psychology section (see http://www

Treatment of Psychological Disorders

.cpa.ca/aboutcpa/cpasections/aboriginalpsychology/) that is mandated to acknowledge the historical and political issues that impact Aboriginal mental health and advocate for culturally appropriate research and clinical practice for Aboriginal peoples across Canada.

What else can be done to improve mental health services for minority groups? Researchers in this area have offered a variety of suggestions (Hong, Garcia, & Soriano, 2000; Miranda et al., 2005; Pedersen, 1994; Yamamoto et al., 1993). Discussions of possible solutions usually begin with the need to recruit and train more ethnic minority therapists. Studies show that ethnic minorities are more likely to go to mental health facilities that are staffed by a higher proportion of people who share their ethnic background (Snowden & Hu, 1996; Sue, Zane, & Young, 1994). Individual therapists have been urged to work harder at building a vigorous *therapeutic alliance* (a strong supportive bond) with their ethnic minority clients. A strong therapeutic alliance is associated with better therapeutic outcomes regardless of ethnicity, but some studies suggest that it is especially crucial for minority clients (Bender et al., 2007; Comas-Diaz, 2006). Psychological and physical interventions can be designed to incorporate traditional practices. For example, in the case of Canada's Aboriginal peoples, interventions can draw upon practices such as the Medicine Wheel, Healing Circles, and the Sweat Lodge (Fiske, 2008; Robbins & Dewar, 2011; University of Ottawa, 2009; Waldram, 2008). A recent review of research that has examined the effects of culturally adapted interventions found evidence that this tailoring process often yields positive effects, although the evidence was mixed (Huey et al., 2014).

Finally, most authorities urge further investigation of how contemporary approaches to therapy such as CBT can be modified and tailored to be more compatible with specific cultural groups' attitudes, values, norms, and traditions (Hwang, 2006).

According to the University of Calgary's Meyen Hertzsprung and Keith Dobson, past president of the Canadian Psychological Association, while there are a host of arguments for incorporating diversity issues into clinical psychology training in Canada, the process has been slow and difficult. In a survey examining the extent of diversity training in clinical programs in Canada, Hertzsprung and Dobson (2000) conclude that while clear progress has been made, much more needs to be done in this area: "Indeed, there is a need for further *indigenous* research on diversity issues in Canada, which has a unique history, population composition, and cultural base" (p. 190).

Courtesy of Dr. Keith Dobson

Keith Dobson is a clinical psychologist at the University of Calgary. His interests include cognitive models of depression, CBT, and stigma in psychopathology.

Using Technology to Expand the Delivery of Clinical Services

Although the problem is especially acute among ethnic minorities and in some locales, such as northern Canada and many Canadian First Nations communities (Kielland & Simeone, 2014), inadequate availability of mental health care is a broad problem that reaches into every corner of our society. In an influential article, Alan Kazdin and Stacey Blase (2011) argue that there just are not enough clinicians and treatment facilities available to meet our mental health needs. This shortage of clinicians is particularly serious in small towns, rural areas, and the remote north. Moreover, Kazdin and Blase note that the traditional model of one-on-one therapy imposes constraints on the availability of treatment. To address these problems, clinicians are increasingly attempting to harness technology to expand the delivery of mental health services and to reduce the costs of therapy.

These efforts to use technology to create new platforms for the delivery of therapeutic services have taken many forms. One of the simpler approaches is to deliver both individual and group therapy over the phone. For example, this method has been used in the treatment of elderly clients with anxiety problems (Brenes, Ingram, & Danhauer, 2012) and others suffering from loneliness and depression (Davis, Guyker, & Persky, 2012). Another relatively simple innovation has been to use videoconferencing technology to provide both individual and group therapy. A review of research on this approach to treatment concluded that clinical outcomes are about the same as in face-to-face therapy and that clients tend to report high satisfaction (Backhaus et al., 2012).

Interventions delivered via the Internet hold promise for reaching larger swaths of people who might otherwise go untreated. For example, software programs have been created for the treatment of substance abuse (Campbell et al., 2014); generalized anxiety disorder (Amir & Taylor, 2012); obsessive-compulsive disorder (Andersson et al., 2011); and phobic disorders (Opriş et al., 2012). Most of these treatments involve online, interactive, multimedia adaptations of cognitive-behavioural therapies. The computerized treatments typically consist of a series of modules that educate individuals about the nature and causes of their disorder and cognitive strategies for ameliorating their problems, along with practice exercises and homework assignments. In most cases, the interventions include limited access to an actual therapist through the Internet, but some programs are fully automated, with no therapist contact. Studies of computerized therapies suggest they can be effective for many types of disorders, but more research and higher-quality research are needed before solid conclusions can be drawn regarding their value (Kiluk et al., 2011). Thus, it appears likely that the future will see increased efforts to improve access to treatment through innovations in technology.

Institutional Treatment in Transition

Traditionally, much of the treatment of mental illness has been carried out in institutional settings, primarily in mental hospitals. In the United States, a national network of state-funded mental hospitals started to emerge in the 1840s through the efforts of Dorothea Dix and other reformers (see Figure 16.14). Prior to these reforms, the mentally ill who were poor were housed in jails and poorhouses or were left to wander the countryside. Dorothea Dix also played an important role in the treatment of those suffering from psychological disorders in Canada (Goldman, 1990).

Sable Island, a remote island 300 kilometres offshore from Halifax, once was a place where some Nova Scotians sent their relatives—often without their consent—who suffered from psychological disorders. Dorothea Dix often spent her summers in Halifax, where she heard about what were referred to at the time as the "banished lunatics," so she set sail for Sable Island to see things for herself (Goldman, 1990). At the time, Nova Scotia was the only Canadian province without a major psychiatric hospital. Dix advocated for a psychiatric hospital before the Nova Scotia legislature and even selected the Sable Island site. It opened on December 26, 1857.

Dix was not a woman to leave things unattended to—after noticing the inadequate life-saving resources available on Sable Island to rescue the victims of shipwrecks, she also raised money and purchased lifeboats for the island. Dix was also credited with helping to establish the psychiatric hospital in St. John's, Newfoundland, employing there, as elsewhere, her formidable skills in persuasion and fundraising.

Today, mental hospitals continue to play an important role in the delivery of mental health services. However, since World War II, institutional care for mental illness has undergone a series of major transitions—and the dust hasn't settled yet. Let's look at how institutional care has evolved in recent decades.

Disenchantment with Mental Hospitals

By the 1950s, it had become apparent that public mental hospitals were not fulfilling their goals very well (Mechanic, 1980; Menninger, 2005). Experts began to realize that hospitalization often *contributed* to the development of pathology instead of curing it.

What were the causes of these unexpected negative effects? Part of the problem was that the facilities were usually underfunded (Hogan & Morrison, 2008), which meant that the facilities were overcrowded and understaffed. Hospital personnel were undertrained and overworked, making them hard-pressed to deliver minimal custodial care. Despite gallant efforts at treatment, the demoralizing conditions made most public mental hospitals decidedly nontherapeutic (Scull, 1990). These problems were aggravated by the fact that mental hospitals served large geographic regions, resulting in the fact that many patients were uprooted from their communities and isolated from their social support networks.

Disenchantment with the public mental hospital system inspired the *community mental health movement* that emerged in the 1960s (Duckworth & Borus, 1999; Huey, Ford, et al., 2009). The community mental health movement emphasizes (1) local,

Figure 16.14

Dorothea Dix and the advent of mental hospitals in North America. During the 19th century, Dorothea Dix (inset) campaigned tirelessly to obtain funds for building mental hospitals in the United States and in some parts of Canada. Many of these hospitals were extremely large facilities. Although public mental hospitals improved the care of the mentally ill, they had a variety of shortcomings, which eventually prompted the deinstitutionalization movement.

Source: Inset: Detail of painting in Harrisburg State Hospital, photo by Ken Smith/LLR Collection

community-based care, (2) reduced dependence on hospitalization, and (3) the prevention of psychological disorders. Thus, in the 1960s much of the responsibility for the treatment of psychological disorders was turned over to community mental health centres, which supplement mental hospitals with decentralized and more accessible services.

Deinstitutionalization

Mental hospitals continue to care for many people troubled by chronic mental illness, but their role in patient care has diminished. Since the 1960s, a policy of deinstitutionalization has been followed in Canada, the United States, and most other Western countries (Fakhoury & Priebe, 2002). *Deinstitutionalization* refers to transferring the treatment of mental illness from inpatient institutions to community-based facilities that emphasize outpatient care. This shift in responsibility was made possible by two developments: (1) the emergence of effective drug therapies for severe disorders and (2) the deployment of community mental health centres to coordinate local care (Goff & Gudeman, 1999).

The exodus of patients from mental hospitals has been dramatic. In the United States, the average inpatient population in state and county mental hospitals dropped from a peak of nearly 550 000 in the mid-1950s to around 70 000 in the late 1990s (see Figure 16.15). Similar trends have been observed in Canada. In their analysis of 40 years of deinstitutionalization in Canada, Patricia Sealy and Paul Whitehead of the University of Western Ontario note that deinstitutionalization is not just an event that took place in the 1960s—it has been continuous for the past four decades (Sealy & Whitehead, 2004). The number of beds in psychiatric hospitals per 100 000 population fell from four to one between 1964 and 1981, with Alberta and Quebec leading in the closings (Sealy & Whitehead, 2004).

These trends, however, do not mean that hospitalization for mental illness has become a thing of the past. A great many people are still hospitalized, but there's been a shift toward placing them in local general hospitals for brief periods instead of distant psychiatric hospitals for long periods (Hogan & Morrison, 2008). When people are admitted to psychiatric hospitals or specialized units, they tend to stay for shorter periods of time. In Canada, the length of stay in psychiatric hospitals and in psychiatric units in general hospitals has decreased dramatically since 1985. In keeping with the philosophy of deinstitutionalization, these local facilities try to get patients stabilized and back into the community as swiftly as possible.

How has deinstitutionalization worked out? It gets mixed reviews. On the positive side, many people have benefited by avoiding or shortening disruptive and unnecessary hospitalization. Ample evidence suggests that alternatives to hospitalization can be both as effective as and less costly than inpatient care (Hamden et al., 2011; Kunitch, 2013; Reinharz, Lesage, & Contandriopoulos, 2000). Moreover, follow-up studies of discharged patients reveal that a substantial majority prefer the greater freedom provided by community-based treatment (Leff, 2006).

Nonetheless, some unanticipated problems have arisen (Novelk, 2010). Many patients suffering from chronic psychological disorders had nowhere to go when they were released. They had no families, friends, or homes to return to. Many had no work skills and were poorly prepared to live on their own. These people were supposed to be absorbed by "halfway houses," sheltered workshops, and other types of intermediate care facilities. Unfortunately, many communities were never able to fund and build the planned facilities (Hogan & Morrison, 2008; Lamb, 1998). Thus, deinstitutionalization left two major problems in its wake: a "revolving door" population of people who flow in and out of psychiatric facilities, and a sizable population of homeless mentally ill people.

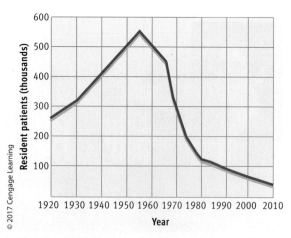

Figure 16.15

Declining inpatient population at state and county mental hospitals. The inpatient population in public mental hospitals has declined dramatically since the late 1950s, as a result of deinstitutionalization and the development of effective antipsychotic medication.

© 2017 Cengage Learning

Mental Illness, the Revolving Door, and Homelessness

Most of the people caught in the mental health system's revolving door suffer from chronic, severe disorders (usually schizophrenia) that often require hospitalization (Machado, Leonidas, & Santos, 2012). They respond to drug therapies in the hospital; however, after they're stabilized through drug therapy, they no longer qualify for expensive hospital treatment according to the new standards mandated by deinstitutionalization. Thus, they're sent back out the door, into communities that often aren't prepared to provide adequate outpatient care. Because they lack appropriate care and support, their condition deteriorates, and they soon require readmission to a hospital, where the cycle begins once again (Botha et al., 2010). Overall, around the world, about one in seven psychiatric inpatients is readmitted within 30 days (Vigod et al., 2015), with 40–50 percent of patients rehospitalized within a year of their release (Bridge & Barbe, 2004). Readmission rates are particularly high among patients who have a concurrent substance abuse problem (Frick et al., 2013).

Deinstitutionalization has been blamed for contributing to the growing population of homeless people. According to the Canadian Mental Health Association (2017), those suffering from mental illness are "disproportionately" influenced by homelessness. They tend to have less contact with their family and friends and have more trouble finding and keeping jobs. Homelessness has many causes, but inadequately treated mental illness appears to be a key factor that increases individuals' vulnerability to homelessness. Studies have consistently found elevated rates of mental illness among the homeless. Taken as a whole, the evidence suggests that roughly one-third of homeless people suffer from severe mental illness (schizophrenic and mood disorders), that another one-third or more are struggling with alcohol and drug problems, that many qualify for multiple diagnoses, and that the prevalence of mental illness among the homeless may be increasing (Bassuk et al., 1998; Hodgson, Shelton, & Bree, 2015; North et al., 2004; Viron et al., 2014). In essence, homeless shelters have become a de facto element of the mental health care system (Callicutt, 2006). So too, by the way, have our jails and prisons because the homeless mentally ill are frequently incarcerated, leading to an epidemic of psychological disorders in the prison system (Baillargeon et al., 2009). Indeed, the revolving door for some mentally ill individuals refers to their frequently being reincarcerated.

Ultimately, it's clear that our society is not providing adequate care for a sizable segment of the mentally ill population (Appelbaum, 2002; Gittelman, 2005; Torrey, 2014). That's not a new development. Inadequate care for mental illness has always been the norm. Societies always struggle with the problem of what to do with the mentally ill and how to pay for their care (Duckworth & Borus, 1999). Ours is not different. Unfortunately, in recent years, the situation has deteriorated rather than improved. Although overall health care spending has been increasing steadily in recent years, funding for mental health care has diminished dramatically (Geller, 2009). Today, most U.S. states have a shortage of psychiatric beds, resulting in waiting lists for admission, overcrowding, and increasingly brief hospitalizations (Geller, 2009). Lamentably, the situation has deteriorated to the point where the *Journal of the American Medical Association* recently published an opinion piece that advocated for a partial rollback of deinstitutionalization. In arguing for the return of the abandoned mental asylums, the authors assert that "the choice is between the prison-homelessness-acute hospitalization-prison cycle or long-term psychiatric institutionalization" (Sisti, Segal, & Emanuel, 2015, p. 244).

Putting It in Perspective: Themes 2 and 5

In our discussion of psychotherapy, one of our unifying themes—the value of theoretical diversity—was particularly prominent, and one other theme—the importance of culture—surfaced briefly. Let's discuss the latter theme first. The approaches to treatment described in this chapter are products of modern, white, middle-class, Western culture. Some of these therapies have proven useful in some other cultures, but many have turned out to be irrelevant or counterproductive when used with different cultural groups, including ethnic minorities in Western society. Thus, we have seen once again that cultural factors influence psychological processes and that Western psychology cannot assume that its theories and practices have universal applicability.

As for theoretical diversity, its value can be illustrated with a rhetorical question: Can you imagine what the state of modern psychotherapy would be if

Key Learning Goal

▶ Identify the two unifying themes highlighted in this chapter.

everyone in psychology and psychiatry had simply accepted Freud's theories about the nature and treatment of psychological disorders? If not for theoretical diversity, psychotherapy might still be in the dark ages. Psychoanalysis can be a useful method of therapy, but it would be a tragic state of affairs if it were the *only* treatment available. Multitudes of people have benefited from alternative approaches to treatment that emerged out of tensions between psychoanalytic theory and other theoretical perspectives. People have diverse problems, rooted in varied origins, that call for the pursuit of different therapeutic goals. Thus, it's fortunate that people can choose from a diverse array of approaches to treatment. The graphic overview on pages 630–631 summarizes and compares the approaches that we've discussed in this chapter. This illustrated overview shows that each of the major approaches to treatment has its own vision of the nature of human discontent and the ideal remedy.

Of course, diversity can be confusing. The range and variety of available treatments in modern psychotherapy leave many people puzzled about their options. So, in our Personal Application, we'll sort through the practical issues involved in selecting a therapist.

Looking for a Therapist

Key Learning Goal

▶ Identify the key issues in selecting the right therapist.

The task of finding an appropriate therapist is complex. Should you see a psychologist or a psychiatrist? Should you opt for individual therapy or group therapy? Should you see a client-centred therapist or a behaviour therapist? The unfortunate part of this situation is that people seeking psychotherapy often feel overwhelmed by personal problems. The last thing they need is to be confronted by yet another complex problem.

Nonetheless, the importance of finding a good therapist cannot be overestimated. Treatment can sometimes have harmful rather than helpful effects. We have already discussed how drug therapies and ECT can sometimes be damaging, but problems are not limited to these interventions. Talking about your problems with a therapist may sound pretty harmless, but studies indicate that insight therapies can also backfire (Lambert & Ogles, 2004; Lilienfeld, 2007). Although a great many talented therapists are available, psychotherapy, like any other profession, has incompetent practitioners as well. Therefore, you should shop for a skilled therapist, just as you would for a good lawyer or a good mechanic.

In this Application, we'll go over some information that should be helpful if you ever have to look for a therapist for yourself or for a friend or family member (based on Beutler, Bongar, & Shurkin, 1998; Bruckner-Gordon, Gangi, & Wallman, 1988; Ehrenberg & Ehrenberg, 1994; Pittman, 1994).

Where Do You Find Therapeutic Services?

Psychotherapy can be found in a variety of settings. Contrary to general belief, most therapists are not in private practice. Many work in institutional settings such as community mental health centres, hospitals, and

Table 16.2

Principal Sources of Therapeutic Services

SOURCE	COMMENTS
Private practitioners	Self-employed therapists are listed in the Yellow Pages under their professional category, such as psychologists or psychiatrists. Private practitioners tend to be relatively expensive, but they also tend to be highly experienced therapists.
Community mental health centres	Community mental health centres have salaried psychologists, psychiatrists, and social workers on staff. The centres provide a variety of services and often have staff available on weekends and at night to deal with emergencies.
Hospitals	Several kinds of hospitals provide therapeutic services. There are both public and private mental hospitals that specialize in the care of people with psychological disorders. Many general hospitals have a psychiatric ward, and those that do not usually have psychiatrists and psychologists on staff and on call. Although hospitals tend to concentrate on inpatient treatment, many provide outpatient therapy as well.
Human service agencies	Various social service agencies employ therapists to provide short-term counselling. Depending on your community, you may find agencies that deal with family problems, juvenile problems, drug problems, and so forth.
Schools and workplaces	Most high schools, colleges, and universities have counselling centres where students can get help with personal problems. Similarly, some large businesses offer in-house counselling to their employees.

© 2017 Cengage Learning

human service agencies. The principal sources of therapeutic services are described in Table 16.2. The exact configuration of therapeutic services available will vary from one community to another. To find out what your community has to offer, it is a good idea to consult your friends, your local phone book, or your local community mental health centre.

Is the Therapist's Profession or Sex Important?

Psychotherapists may be trained in psychology, psychiatry, social work, counselling, psychiatric nursing, or marriage and family therapy. Researchers have *not* found any reliable association between therapists' professional background and therapeutic efficacy (Beutler et al., 2004), probably because many talented therapists can be found in all of these professions. Thus, the kind of degree that a therapist holds doesn't need to be a crucial consideration in your

selection process. At the present time, it is true that psychiatrists are the only type of therapist who can prescribe drugs. However, other types of therapists can refer you to a psychiatrist if they think that drug therapy would be helpful.

Whether a therapist's sex is important depends on your attitude (Nadelson, Notman, & McCarthy, 2005). If *you* feel that the therapist's sex is important, then for you it is. The therapeutic relationship must be characterized by trust and rapport. Feeling uncomfortable with a therapist of one sex or the other could inhibit the therapeutic process. Hence, you should feel free to look for a male or female therapist if you prefer to do so. This point is probably most relevant to female clients whose troubles may be related to the extensive sexism in our society (A. G. Kaplan, 1985). It is entirely reasonable for women to seek a therapist with a feminist perspective if that would make them feel more comfortable.

Is Treatment Always Expensive?

Although it is not always low-priced (Picard, 2013), psychotherapy does not have to be prohibitively expensive. Private practitioners tend to be the most expensive, charging between $75 and $200 per (50-minute) hour. These fees may seem high, but they are in line with those of similar professionals, such as dentists and lawyers. Community mental health centres and social service agencies are usually supported by tax dollars. Provincial health-care programs often cover the services of a psychiatrist, but the services of psychologists in private practice are not universally covered.

Is the Therapist's Theoretical Approach Important?

Logically, you might expect that the diverse approaches to therapy vary in effectiveness. For the most part, this is *not* what researchers find, however. After reviewing many studies of therapeutic efficacy, Jerome Frank (1961) and Lester Luborsky and his colleagues (Luborsky, Singer, & Luborsky, 1975) both quote the dodo bird who has just judged a race in *Alice in Wonderland*: "*Everybody* has won, and *all* must have prizes." Improvement rates for various theoretical orientations are fairly similar according to most studies (Lambert, Bergin, & Garfield, 2004; Luborsky et al., 2002; Wampold, 2001; see Figure 16.16).

However, these findings are a little misleading, as the estimates of overall effectiveness have been averaged across many types of patients and many types of problems. Most experts seem to think that *for certain types of problems, some approaches to therapy are more effective than others* (Beutler, 2002; Crits-Christoph, 1997; Norcross, 1995). For example, Martin Seligman (1995) asserts that panic disorders respond best to cognitive therapy, that specific phobias are most amenable to treatment with systematic desensitization, and that obsessive-compulsive disorders are best treated with behaviour therapy or medication. So, for a specific type of problem, a therapist's theoretical approach *may* make a difference.

It is also important to point out that the finding that different approaches to therapy are roughly equal in overall efficacy does not mean that all *therapists* are created equal.

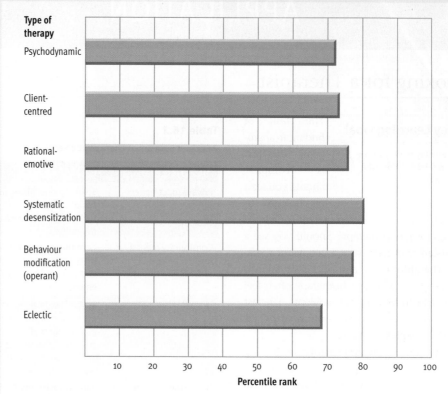

Figure 16.16

Estimates of the effectiveness of various approaches to psychotherapy. Smith and Glass (1977) reviewed nearly 400 studies in which clients who were treated with a specific type of therapy were compared with a control group made up of individuals with similar problems who went untreated. The bars indicate the percentile rank (on outcome measures) attained by the average client treated with each type of therapy when compared to control subjects. The higher the percentile, the more effective the therapy was. As you can see, the various approaches were fairly similar in their overall effectiveness.

Source: Adapted from Smith, M. L., & Glass, G. V. (1977). Meta-analysis of psychotherapy outcome series. *American Psychologist, 32,* 752–760. Copyright © 1977 by the American Psychological Association. Adapted by permission of the author.

Some therapists unquestionably are more effective than others. However, these variations in effectiveness appear to depend on individual therapists' personal skills rather than on their theoretical orientation (Beutler et al., 2004). Good, bad, and mediocre therapists are found within each school of thought. Indeed, the tremendous variation among individual therapists, in skills, may be one of the main reasons why it is hard to find efficacy differences between theoretical approaches to therapy (Staines, 2008).

The key point is that effective therapy requires skill and creativity. Arnold Lazarus, who devised multimodal therapy, emphasizes that therapists "straddle the fence between science and art." Therapy is scientific in that interventions are based on extensive theory and empirical research (Forsyth & Strong, 1986). Ultimately, though, each client is a unique human being, and the therapist has to creatively fashion a treatment program that will help that individual (Goodheart, 2006).

What Should You Look for in a Prospective Therapist?

Some clients are timid about asking prospective therapists questions about their training, approach, fees, and so forth. However, these are reasonable questions, and the vast majority of therapists will be most accommodating in providing answers. Usually, you can ask your preliminary questions over the phone. If things seem promising, you may decide to make an appointment for an interview (for which you will probably have to pay). In this interview, the therapist will gather more information to determine the likelihood of helping you, given his or her training and approach to treatment. At the same time,

Therapy is both a science and an art. It is scientific in that practitioners are guided in their work by a huge body of empirical research. It is an art in that therapists often have to be creative in adapting their treatment procedures to individual patients and their idiosyncrasies.

Tetra Images/Getty Images

Otherwise, it will be difficult to establish the needed rapport.

Given the very real possibility that poor progress may be due to resistance, you should not be too quick to leave therapy when dissatisfied. However, it *is* possible that your therapist isn't sufficiently skilled or that the two of you are incompatible. So, after careful and deliberate consideration, you should feel free to terminate your therapy.

What Should You Expect from Therapy?

It is important to have realistic expectations about therapy, or you may be unnecessarily disappointed. Some people expect miracles. They expect to turn their lives around quickly with little effort. Others expect their therapist to run their lives for them. These are unrealistic expectations.

Therapy is usually a slow process. Your problems are not likely to melt away quickly. Moreover, therapy is hard work, and your therapist is only a facilitator. Ultimately, *you* have to confront the challenge of changing your behaviour, your feelings, or your personality. This process may not be pleasant. You may have to face up to some painful truths about yourself. As Ehrenberg and Ehrenberg (1986) point out, "Psychotherapy takes time, effort, and courage."

you should be making a similar judgment about whether you believe the therapist can help you with your problems.

What should you look for? First, you should look for personal warmth and sincere concern. Try to judge whether you will be able to talk to this person in a candid, nondefensive way. Second, look for empathy and understanding. Is the person capable of appreciating your point of view? Third, look for self-confidence. Self-assured therapists will communicate a sense of competence without trying to intimidate you with jargon or boasting needlessly about what they can do for you. When all is said and done, you should *like* your therapist.

Treatment of Psychological Disorders

From Crisis to Wellness—But Was It the Therapy?

It often happens this way. Problems seem to go from bad to worse—the trigger could be severe pressures at work, an acrimonious fight with your spouse, or a child's unruly behaviour spiralling out of control. At some point, you recognize that it might be prudent to seek professional assistance from a therapist, but where do you turn?

If you are like most people, you will probably hesitate before actively seeking professional help. People hesitate because therapy carries a stigma, because the task of finding a therapist is daunting, and because they hope that their psychological problems will clear up on their own—which *does* happen with some regularity. When people finally decide to pursue mental health care, it is often because they feel like they have reached rock bottom in terms of their functioning and they have no choice. Motivated by their crisis, they enter into treatment, looking for a ray of hope. Will therapy help them to feel better?

It may surprise you to learn that the answer *generally* would be "yes," even if professional treatment itself were utterly worthless and totally ineffectual. There are two major reasons that people entering therapy are likely to get better, regardless of whether their treatment is effective. You can probably guess one of these reasons, which has been mentioned repeatedly in the chapter: the power of the *placebo*. **Placebo effects** occur when people's expectations lead them to experience some change even though they receive a fake treatment (like being given a sugar pill instead of a real drug). Clients generally enter therapy with expectations that it will have positive effects, and as we have emphasized throughout this text, *people have a remarkable tendency to see what they expect to see*. Because of this factor, studies of the efficacy of medical

Placebo effects and regression toward the mean are two prominent factors that make it difficult to evaluate the efficacy of various approaches to therapy.

drugs always include a placebo condition in which subjects are given fake medication (see Chapter 2). Researchers are often quite surprised by just how much the placebo subjects improve (Fisher & Greenberg, 1997; Walsh et al., 2002). Placebo effects can be very powerful and should be taken into consideration whenever efforts are made to evaluate the efficacy of some approach to treatment.

The other factor at work is the main focus in this Application. It is an interesting statistical phenomenon that we have not discussed previously: *regression toward the mean*. *Regression toward the mean* occurs when people who score extremely high or low on some trait are measured a second time and their new scores fall closer to the mean (average). Regression effects work in both directions: On the second measurement, high scorers tend to fall back toward the mean and low scorers tend to creep upward toward the mean. For example, let's say we wanted to evaluate the effectiveness of a one-day coaching program intended to improve performance on a new high school math test.

We reason that coaching is most likely to help students who have performed poorly on the test, so we recruit a sample of participants who have previously scored in the bottom 20 percent on the test. Thanks to regression toward the mean, most of these students will score higher if they take that test a second time, so our coaching program may *look* effective even if it has no value.

By the way, if we set out to see whether our coaching program could increase the performance of high scorers, regression effects would be working *against* us. If we recruited a sample of students who had scored in the upper 20 percent on the math test, there would be a tendency for their scores to move downward when tested a second time, which could cancel out most or all of the beneficial effects of the coaching program. The processes underlying regression toward the mean are complex matters of probability, but they can be approximated by a simple principle: If you are near the bottom, there's almost nowhere to go but up, and if you are near the top, there's almost nowhere to go but down.

What does all of this have to do with the effects of professional treatment for psychological problems and disorders? Well, chance variations in the ups and downs of life occur for all of us. But recall that most people enter psychotherapy during a time of severe crisis, when they are at a really low point in their lives. If you measure the mental health of a group of people entering therapy, they will mostly get relatively low scores. If you measure their mental health again a few months later, chances are that most of them will score higher—with or without therapy—because of regression toward the mean. This is not a matter of idle speculation. Studies of untreated subjects demonstrate that poor scores on measures of mental health regress toward the mean when participants are assessed a second time (Flett, Vredenburg, & Krames, 1995; L. M. Hsu, 1995).

Does the fact that most people will get better even without therapy mean that there is no sound evidence that psychotherapy works? No, regression effects, along with placebo effects, do create major headaches for researchers evaluating the efficacy of various therapies, but these problems *can* be circumvented. Control groups, random assignment, placebo conditions, and statistical adjustments can be used to control for regression and placebo effects, as well as for other threats to validity. As discussed in the main body of the chapter, researchers have accumulated rigorous evidence that most approaches to therapy have demonstrated efficacy. However, our discussion of placebo and regression effects shows you some of the factors that make this type of research far more complicated and challenging than might be anticipated. See Table 16.3.

Recognizing how regression toward the mean can occur in a variety of contexts is an important critical thinking skill, so let's look at some additional examples. Think about an outstanding young pro baseball player who has a fabulous first season and is named "Rookie of the Year." What sort of performance would you predict for this athlete for the next year? Before you make your prediction, think about regression toward the mean. Statistically speaking, our Rookie of the Year is likely to perform well above average the next year, but not as well as he did in his first

year. If you are a sports fan, you may recognize this pattern as the "sophomore slump." Many sports columnists have written about the sophomore slump, which they typically blame on the athlete's personality or motivation ("He got lazy," "He got cocky," "The money and fame went to his head," and so forth). A simple appeal to regression toward the mean could explain this sort of outcome, with no need to denigrate the personality or motivation of the athlete. Of course, sometimes the Rookie of the Year performs even better during his second year. Thus, our baseball example can be used to emphasize an important point: Regression toward the mean is not an inevitability. It is a statistical tendency that predicts what will happen far more often than not, but it is merely a matter of probability—which means it is a much more reliable principle when applied to groups (say, the top ten rookies in a specific year) rather than to individuals.

Let's return to the world of therapy for one last thought about the significance of both regression and placebo effects. Over the years, a host of quacks, charlatans, con artists, herbalists, and faith healers have marketed and sold an endless array of worthless treatments for both psychological problems and physical maladies. In many instances, people who have been treated with these phony therapies have expressed satisfaction or even praise and gratitude. For instance, you may have heard someone sincerely rave about some herbal remedy or psychic advice that you were pretty sure was really worthless. If so, you were probably puzzled by their glowing testimonials. Well, you now have two highly plausible explanations for why people can honestly believe that they have derived great benefit from harebrained,

bogus treatments: placebo effects and regression effects. The people who provide testimonials for worthless treatments may have experienced *genuine* improvements in their conditions, but those improvements were probably the results of placebo effects and regression toward the mean. Placebo and regression effects add to the many reasons that you should always be skeptical about anecdotal evidence. And they help explain why charlatans can be so successful and why unsound, ineffective treatments can have sincere proponents.

Tony Freeman/PhotoEdit

In North American society, we are frequently exposed to claims of programs that will improve our wellness. Rigorous and systematic scientific research is the only way to verify these claims.

Table 16.3

Critical Thinking Skills Discussed in This Application

SKILL	DESCRIPTION
Recognizing situations in which placebo effects might occur	The critical thinker understands that if people have expectations that a treatment will produce a certain effect, they may experience that effect even if the treatment was fake or ineffectual.
Recognizing situations in which regression toward the mean may occur	The critical thinker understands that when people are selected for their extremely high or low scores on some trait, their subsequent scores will probably fall closer to the mean.
Recognizing the limitations of anecdotal evidence	The critical thinker is wary of anecdotal evidence, which consists of personal stories used to support one's assertions. Anecdotal evidence tends to be unrepresentative, inaccurate, and unreliable.

ELEMENTS OF TREATMENT

Treatment approaches

Insight therapies involve verbal interactions intended to enhance clients' self-knowledge and thus promote healthful changes.

Behaviour therapies involve the application of the principles of learning and conditioning to direct efforts to change clients' maladaptive behaviours.

Biomedical therapies are physiological interventions intended to reduce symptoms associated with psychological disorders.

INSIGHT THERAPIES

Psychoanalysis

- Freud believed that neuroses are caused by *unconscious conflicts* regarding sex and aggression left over from childhood.

- In psychoanalysis, *dream analysis* and *free association* are used to explore the unconscious.

- When an analyst's interpretations touch on sensitive issues, *resistance* can be expected.

- The *transference* relationship can be used to overcome resistance and promote insight.

- Classical psychoanalysis is not widely practiced today, but a diverse array of psychodynamic therapies remain in use.

Client-centred therapy

- According to Rogers, neurotic anxieties are due to *incongruence* between one's self-concept and reality.

- Rogers maintained that the *process* of therapy is not as crucial as the therapeutic *climate*.

- To create a healthy climate, therapists must be genuine and provide unconditional positive regard and empathy.

- The key process at work in client-centred therapy is the *clarification* of clients' feelings.

Group therapy

- Most insight therapies can be conducted on a group basis, which involves the simultaneous treatment of several or more clients.

- In group therapy, participants essentially function as therapists for one another as they share experiences, coping strategies, and support.

- Group therapists usually play a subtle role, staying in the background and working to promote group cohesiveness and supportive interactions.

Couples and family therapy

- *Couples*, or *marital, therapy* involves the treatment of both partners in a committed, intimate relationship, focusing on relationship issues.

- *Family therapy* involves the treatment of a family unit as a whole, focusing on family dynamics and communication.

- Marital and family therapists seek to understand the entrenched patterns of interaction that produce distress for their clients.

BEHAVIOUR THERAPIES

General principles

- Behaviourists assume that even pathological behaviour is a product of learning and that what has been learned can be unlearned.

- In behaviour therapy, different procedures are used for different types of clinical problems.

Systematic desensitization and exposure therapies

- Wolpe's *systematic desensitization*, a treatment for phobias, involves the construction of an anxiety hierarchy, relaxation training, and movement through the hierarchy pairing relaxation with each phobic stimulus.

- In *exposure therapies*, clients are confronted with situations they fear so they learn that these situations are really harmless.

- Exposure therapy can be conducted with virtual reality presentations.

Social skills training

- Many psychological problems grow out of interpersonal difficulties attributable to deficits in social skills.

- *Social skills training* is designed to improve clients' interpersonal interactions through modelling, behavioural rehearsal, and shaping.

Cognitive-behavioural treatments

- Cognitive-behavioural treatments combine verbal interventions and behaviour modification techniques to help clients change maladaptive patterns of thinking.

- *Cognitive therapy* was devised by Aaron Beck as a treatment for depression, but is now used for a variety of disorders.

- Beck asserts that most disorders are caused by irrational, rigid, negative thinking.

Evaluating behaviour therapies

- There has been extensive research on the effectiveness of various behaviour therapies.

- Favourable evidence exists for the efficacy of most of the widely used behavioural interventions.

Evaluating insight therapies

- Evaluating the effectiveness of any approach to treatment is extremely complicated and subjective.

- Hundreds of outcome studies collectively suggest that insight therapy is superior to placebo treatment and that the beneficial effects of therapy are reasonably durable.

- Many theorists believe that common factors account for much of the improvement seen in insight therapies.

Clients

- Clients bring a wide variety of problems to therapy and do not necessarily have a disorder.

- The likelihood of receiving treatment is greater among women, whites, those who are well-educated, and those who have insurance.

- People vary in their willingness to seek therapy, and many who need therapy don't receive it.

Therapists

- *Clinical* and *counselling psychologists* specialize in the diagnosis and treatment of mental disorders and everyday problems.

- *Psychiatrists* are physicians who specialize in the diagnosis and treatment of mental disorders.

- *Psychiatric social workers, psychiatric nurses, counsellors,* and *marriage and family therapists* also provide psychotherapy services.

Phase4Photography/Shutterstock.com

BIOMEDICAL THERAPIES

Drug treatments

- *Antianxiety drugs*, which are used to relieve nervousness, are effective in the short term.

- *Antipsychotic drugs* can gradually reduce psychotic symptoms, but they have many unpleasant side effects.

- *Antidepressant drugs* can gradually relieve episodes of depression, but even the newer SSRIs are not free of side effects.

- *Mood stabilizers*, such as lithium, can help to prevent future episodes of both mania and depression in bipolar patients.

- Drug therapies can lead to impressive positive effects, but critics worry that drugs produce short-lived gains, are overprescribed, and more dangerous than widely appreciated.

- Critics also argue that conflicts of interest are a pervasive problem in research on new medications, leading to overestimates of drugs' efficacy and underestimates of their negative side effects.

ECT

- In *electroconvulsive therapy (ECT)*, electric shock is used to produce a cortical seizure and convulsions, which are believed to be beneficial in the treatment of depression.

- Proponents of ECT maintain that it is a very effective treatment, but critics have raised doubts, and its use has declined.

- Memory losses are a short-term side effect of ECT, but there is debate about whether ECT carries significant long-term risks.

CURRENT ISSUES IN TREATMENT

- The culture-bound origins of Western therapies have raised doubts about their applicability to other cultures and even to ethnic groups in Western societies.

- Ethnic minorities underutilize mental health services because of cultural distrust, language difficulties, and institutional barriers.

- Clinicians are increasingly attempting to harness technology to expand the delivery of mental health services and to reduce the costs of therapy.

- Combinations of insight, behavioural, and biomedical therapies are often used fruitfully in treatment.

INSTITUTIONAL TREATMENT IN TRANSITION

- Disenchantment with traditional mental hospitals led to the *community mental health movement*, which advocates local, community-based care and prevention of mental disorders.

- *Deinstitutionalization* refers to the transfer of mental health care from inpatient institutions to community-based outpatient facilities.

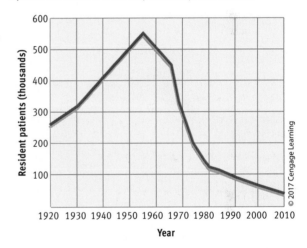

© 2017 Cengage Learning

- Deinstitutionalization has worked for some patients, but it has contributed to the *revolving door problem*.

- Deinstitutionalization has also contributed to the growth of homelessness and the increased incidence of mental illness among the homeless.

- It is clear that our society is not providing adequate care for a sizable segment of the mentally ill population, and the situation is only getting worse.

APPLICATIONS

- Therapists' personal skills are more important than their professional degree.

- Various theoretical approaches to therapy appear to be roughly similar in overall effectiveness.

- However, for certain types of problems, some approaches are probably more effective than others.

- Regression toward the mean and placebo effects can help explain why people often are deceived by phony, ineffectual treatments.

The answers to the Concept Checks for each chapter are provided here on a chapter-by-chapter basis.

Chapter 1

Concept Check 1.1

1. c. John B. Watson (1930, p. 103), dismissing the importance of genetic inheritance while arguing that traits are shaped entirely by experience.

2. a. Wilhelm Wundt (1874/1904, p. v), campaigning for a new, independent science of psychology.

3. b. William James (1890), commenting negatively on the structuralists' efforts to break consciousness into its elements and his view of consciousness as a continuously flowing stream.

Concept Check 1.2

1. b. B. F. Skinner (1971, p. 17), explaining why he believed that freedom is an illusion.

2. a. Sigmund Freud (1905, pp. 77–78), arguing that it is possible to probe into the unconscious depths of the mind.

3. c. Carl Rogers (1961, p. 27), commenting on others' assertion that he had an overly optimistic (Pollyannaish) view of human potential and discussing humans' basic drive toward personal growth.

Concept Check 1.3

a. 2. Psychology is theoretically diverse.

b. 6. Heredity and environment jointly influence behaviour.

c. 4. Behaviour is determined by multiple causes.

d. 7. Our experience of the world is highly subjective.

Chapter 2

Concept Check 2.1

1. IV: Film violence (present versus absent)

   DV: Heart rate and blood pressure (there are two DVs)

2. IV: Courtesy training (training versus no training)

   DV: Number of customer complaints

3. IV: Stimulus complexity (high versus low) and stimulus contrast (high versus low) (there are two IVs)

   DV: Length of time spent staring at the stimuli

4. IV: Group size (large versus small)

   DV: Conformity

Concept Check 2.2

1. d. Survey. You would distribute a survey to obtain information on subjects' social class, education, and attitudes about nuclear disarmament.

2. c. Case study. Using a case study approach, you could interview people with anxiety disorders, interview their parents, and examine their school records to look for similarities in childhood experiences. As a second choice, you might have people with anxiety disorders fill out a survey about their childhood experiences.

3. b. Naturalistic observation. To answer this question properly, you would want to observe baboons in their natural environment, without interference.

4. a. Experiment. To demonstrate a causal relationship, you would have to conduct an experiment. You would manipulate the presence or absence of food-related cues in controlled circumstances where subjects had an opportunity to eat some food, and monitor the amount eaten.

Concept Check 2.3

1. b. and e. The other three conclusions all equate correlation with causation.

2. a. Negative. As age increases, more people tend to have visual problems and acuity tends to decrease.

   b. Positive. Studies show that highly educated people tend to earn higher incomes and that people with less education tend to earn lower incomes.

   c. Negative. As shyness increases, the size of one's friendship network should decrease. However, research suggests that this inverse association may be weaker than widely believed.

Chapter 3

Concept Check 3.1

1. d. dendrite
2. f. myelin
3. b. neuron
4. e. axon
5. a. glia
6. g. terminal button
7. h. synapse

Concept Check 3.2

1. d. serotonin
2. b. and d. serotonin and norepinephrine
3. e. endorphins
4. c. dopamine
5. a. acetylcholine

Concept Check 3.3

1. Left hemisphere damage, probably to Wernicke's area
2. Deficit in dopamine synthesis in an area of the midbrain
3. Degeneration of myelin sheaths surrounding axons
4. Disturbance in dopamine activity, possibly associated with enlarged ventricles in the brain

Note: Neuropsychological assessment is not as simple as this introductory exercise may suggest. There are many possible causes of most disorders, and we have discussed only a handful of leading causes for each.

Concept Check 3.4

1. closer relatives; more distant relatives

2. identical twins; fraternal twins

3. biological parents; adoptive parents

4. genetic overlap or closeness; trait similarity

Chapter 4

Concept Check 4.1

Dimension	Rods	Cones
Physical shape	Elongated	Stubby
Number in the retina	125 million	6.4 million
Area of the retina in which they are dominant receptor	Periphery	Centre/fovea
Critical to colour vision	No	Yes
Critical to peripheral vision	Yes	No
Sensitivity to dim light	Strong	Weak

Concept Check 4.2

✓ 1. Interposition. Some of the columns cut off parts of the statues behind

✓ 2. Height in plane. The back of the corridor is higher on the horizontal plane than the front of the corridor is.

✓ 3. Texture gradient. The squares on the floor become denser and less distinct with increasing distance.

✓ 4. Relative size. The statues and columns in the distance are smaller than those in the foreground.

✓ 5. Light and shadow. Light shining in from the windows on the right contrasts with shadow elsewhere.

✓ 6. Linear perspective. The lines of the corridor converge in the distance.

Concept Check 4.3

Dimension	Vision	Hearing
1. Stimulus	Light waves	Sound waves
2. Elements of stimulus and related perceptions	Wavelength/hue Amplitude/brightness Purity/saturation	Frequency/pitch Amplitude/loudness Purity/timbre
3. Receptors	Rods and cones	Hair cells
4. Location of receptors	Retina	Basilar membrane
5. Main location of processing in brain	Occipital lobe/visual cortex	Temporal lobe/auditory cortex
6. Spatial aspect of perception	Depth perception	Auditory localization

Concept Check 4.4

Dimension	Taste	Smell	Touch
1. Stimulus	Soluble chemicals in saliva	Volatile chemicals in air	Mechanical, thermal, and chemical energy due to external contact
2. Receptors	Clusters of taste cells	Olfactory cilia (hairlike structures)	Many (at least 6) types
3. Location of receptors	Taste buds on tongue	Upper area of nasal passages	Skin
4. Basic elements of perception	Sweet, sour, salty, bitter	No satisfactory classification scheme	Pressure, hot, cold, of pain

Chapter 5

Concept Check 5.1

Characteristic	REM sleep	NREM sleep
1. Type of EEG activity	"Wide awake" brain waves, mostly beta	Varied, lots of delta waves
2. Eye movements	Rapid, lateral	Slow or absent
3. Dreaming	Frequent, vivid	Less frequent
4. Depth (difficulty in awakening)	Varied, generally difficult to awaken	Varied, generally easier to awaken
5. Percentage of total sleep (in adults)	About 20%	About 80%
6. Increases or decreases (as a percentage of sleep) during childhood	Percentage decreases	Percentage increases
7. Timing in sleep cycle (dominates early or late)	Dominates late in cycle	Dominates early in cycle

Concept Check 5.2

1. Beta. Video games require alert information processing, which is associated with beta waves.

2. Alpha. Meditation involves relaxation, which is associated with alpha waves, and studies show increased alpha in meditators.

3. Theta. In stage 1 sleep, theta waves tend to be prevalent.

4. Delta. Sleepwalking usually occurs in deep NREM sleep, which is dominated by delta activity.

5. Beta. Nightmares are dreams, so you're probably in REM sleep, which paradoxically produces "wide awake" beta waves.

Chapter 6

Concept Check 6.1

1. CS: Fire in fireplace
   UCS: Pain from burn   CR/UCR: Fear
2. CS: Brake lights in rain
   UCS: Car accident   CR/UCR: Tensing up
3. CS: Sight of cat
   UCS: Cat dander   CR/UCR: Wheezing

Concept Check 6.2

1. FR. Each sale is a response and every third response earns reinforcement.
2. VI. A varied amount of time elapses before the response of doing yard work can earn reinforcement.
3. VR. Reinforcement occurs after a varied number of unreinforced casts (time is irrelevant; the more casts Martha makes, the more reinforcers she will receive).
4. CR. The designated response (reading a book) is reinforced (with a gold star) every time.
5. FI. A fixed time interval (three years) has to elapse before Skip can earn a salary increase (the reinforcer).

Concept Check 6.3

1. Punishment.
2. Positive reinforcement.
3. Negative reinforcement (for Audrey); the dog is positively reinforced for its whining.
4. Negative reinforcement.
5. Extinction. When Sharma's co-workers start to ignore her complaints, they are trying to extinguish the behaviour (which had been positively reinforced when it won sympathy).

Concept Check 6.4

1. Classical conditioning. Midori's blue windbreaker is a CS eliciting excitement in her dog.
2. Operant conditioning. Playing new songs leads to negative consequences (punishment), which weaken the tendency to play new songs. Playing old songs leads to positive reinforcement, which gradually strengthens the tendency to play old songs.
3. Classical conditioning. The song was paired with the passion of new love so that it became a CS eliciting emotional, romantic feelings.
4. Both. Ralph's workplace is paired with criticism so that his workplace becomes a CS eliciting anxiety. Calling in sick is operant behaviour that is strengthened through negative reinforcement because it reduces anxiety.

Chapter 7

Concept Check 7.1

Feature	Sensory memory	Short-term memory	Long-term memory
Main encoding format	Copy of input	Largely phonemic	Largely semantic
Storage capacity	Limited	Small (7 ± 2 chunks)	No known limit
Storage duration	About 1/4 second	Up to ± 20 seconds	Minutes to years

Concept Check 7.2

1. Ineffective encoding due to lack of attention
2. Retrieval failure due to motivated forgetting
3. Proactive interference (previous learning of Joe Cocker's name interferes with new learning)
4. Retroactive interference (new learning of sociology interferes with older learning of history)

Concept Check 7.3

1. a. declarative memory
2. e. long-term memory
3. j. sensory memory
4. d. implicit memory
5. b. episodic memory
6. f. procedural memory
7. i. semantic memory
8. g. prospective memory
9. k. short-term memory

Chapter 8

Concept Check 8.1

1. 1. One-word utterance in which the word is overextended to refer to a similar object.
2. 4. Words are combined into a sentence, but the rule for past tense is overregularized.
3. 3. Telegraphic sentence.
4. 5. Words are combined into a sentence, and past tense is used correctly.
5. 2. One-word utterance without overextension.
6. 6. "Longer" sentence with metaphor.

Concept Check 8.2

1. functional fixedness
2. forming subgoals
3. insight
4. searching for analogies
5. arrangement problem

Concept Check 8.3

1. Representativeness heuristic
2. Availability heuristic
3. Conjunction fallacy

Chapter 9

Concept Check 9.1

1. Test–retest reliability

2. Criterion-related validity

3. Content validity

Concept Check 9.2

1. H. Given that the identical twins were reared apart, their greater similarity in comparison to fraternals reared together can be due only to heredity. This comparison is probably the most important piece of evidence supporting the genetic determination of IQ.

2. E. We tend to associate identical twins with evidence supporting heredity, but in this comparison, genetic similarity is held constant since both sets of twins are identical. The only logical explanation for the greater similarity in identicals reared together is the effect of their being reared together (environment).

3. E. This comparison is similar to the previous one. Genetic similarity is held constant and a shared environment produces greater similarity than being reared apart.

4. B. This is nothing more than a quantification of Galton's original observation that intelligence runs in families. Since families share both genes and environment, either or both could be responsible for the observed correlation.

5. B. The similarity of adopted children to their biological parents can be due only to shared genes, and the similarity of adopted children to their adoptive parents can only be due to shared environment, so these correlations show the influence of both heredity and environment.

Chapter 10

Concept Check 10.1

1. I. Early studies indicated that lesioning the ventromedial nucleus of the hypothalamus leads to overeating (although it is an oversimplification to characterize the VMH as the brain's "stop-eating" centre).

2. I or ?. Food cues generally trigger hunger and eating, but reactions vary among individuals.

3. D. Food preferences are mostly learned, and we tend to like what we are accustomed to eating. Most people will not be eager to eat a strange-looking food.

4. D. When leptin levels are increased, hunger tends to decrease.

5. I. Reactions vary, but stress generally tends to increased eating.

6. I. Research on dietary restraint suggests that when people feel that they have cheated on their diet, they tend to become disinhibited and eat to excess.

Concept Check 10.2

1. d. fear of failure

2. c. incentive value of success

3. b. perceived probability of success

4. a. need for achievement

Concept Check 10.3

1. James–Lange theory

2. Schachter's two-factor theory

3. and 4. Evolutionary theories

Chapter 11

Concept Check 11.1

	Event	Stage	Organism	Time span
1.	Uterine implantation	Germinal	Zygote	0–2 weeks
2.	Muscle and bone begin to form	Fetal	Fetus	2 months to birth
3.	Vital organs and body systems begin to form	Embryonic	Embryo	2 weeks to 2 months

Concept Check 11.2

1. B. Animism is characteristic of the preoperational period.

2. C. Mastery of hierarchical classification occurs during the concrete operational period.

3. A. Lack of object permanence is characteristic of the sensorimotor period.

Concept Check 11.3

1. c. Commitment to personal ethics is characteristic of postconventional reasoning.

2. b. Concern about approval of others is characteristic of conventional reasoning.

3. a. Emphasis on positive or negative consequences is characteristic of preconventional reasoning.

Chapter 12

Concept Check 12.1

1. Regression

2. Projection

3. Reaction formation

4. Repression

5. Rationalization

Concept Check 12.2

1. Bandura's observational learning. Sarah imitates a role model from television.

2. Maslow's need for self-actualization. Yolanda is striving to realize her fullest potential.

3. Freud's Oedipal complex. Vladimir shows preference for his opposite-sex parent and emotional distance from his same-sex parent.

Concept Check 12.3

1. Maslow (1970, p. 36), commenting on the need for self-actualization.

2. Eysenck (1977, pp. 407–408), commenting on the biological roots of personality.

3. Freud (in Malcolm, 1981), commenting on the repression of sexuality.

Chapter 13

Concept Check 13.1

	Unstable	Stable
Internal	d	b
External	a	c

Concept Check 13.2

1. c. Fundamental attribution error (assuming that arriving late reflects personal qualities)

2. a. Illusory correlation effect (overestimating how often one has seen confirmations of the assertion that young female professors get pregnant soon after being hired)

3. b. Stereotyping (assuming that all lawyers have these negative traits)

4. d. Defensive attribution (derogating the victims of misfortune to minimize the apparent likelihood of a similar mishap)

Concept Check 13.3

1. *Target:* Cognitive component of attitudes (beliefs about program for regulating nursing homes)

   Persuasion: Message factor (advice to use one-sided instead of two-sided arguments)

2. *Target:* Affective component of attitudes (feelings about candidate)

   Persuasion: Source factor (advice on smiling more and appearing sincere and compassionate)

3. *Target:* Behavioural component of attitudes (making contributions)

   Persuasion: Receiver factor (considering audience's initial position regarding the candidate)

Concept Check 13.4

1. False 2. True 3. False 4. True 5. False

Chapter 14

Concept Check 14.1

1. b. a choice between two unattractive options

2. c. weighing the positive and negative aspects of a single goal

3. a. a choice between two attractive options

Concept Check 14.2

1. a. frustration due to delay

2. d. pressure to perform

3. c. change associated with leaving school and taking a new job

4. a. frustration due to loss of job

   c. change in life circumstances

   d. pressure to perform (in quickly obtaining new job)

Concept Check 14.3

1. denial of reality
2. undoing
3. fantasy
4. overcompensation
5. intellectualization

Chapter 15

Concept Check 15.1

1. Bipolar disorder, manic episode (key symptoms: extravagant plans, hyperactivity, reckless spending)

2. Schizophrenia (key symptoms: delusions of persecution and grandeur, along with deterioration of adaptive behaviour)

3. Major depression (key symptoms: feelings of despair, low self-esteem, lack of energy)

Chapter 16

Concept Check 16.1

1. c   2. a   3. b

Concept Check 16.2

1. d   2. b   3. a   4. c

Concept Check 16.3

1. a. systematic desensitization

2. c. aversion therapy

3. b. social skills training

Concept Check 16.4

1. c   2. a   3. b   4. d   5. b

Empiricism depends on observation; precise observation depends on measurement; and measurement requires numbers. Thus, scientists routinely analyze numerical data to arrive at their conclusions. Over 3000 empirical studies are cited in this text, and all but a few of the simplest ones required a statistical analysis. *Statistics* is the use of mathematics to organize, summarize, and interpret numerical data. We discussed statistics briefly in Chapter 2, but in this appendix we take a closer look.

To illustrate statistics in action, imagine a group of students who want to test a hypothesis that has generated quite an argument in their psychology class. The hypothesis is that university students who watch a great deal of television aren't as bright as those who watch TV infrequently. For the fun of it, the class decides to conduct a correlational study of itself, collecting survey and psychological test data. All of the classmates agree to respond to a short survey on their TV viewing habits.

Because everyone at that school has had to take the *Scholastic Aptitude Test* (SAT), the class decides to use scores on the SAT verbal subtest as an index of how bright students are. The SAT is one of a set of tests that high school students in the United States take before applying to college or university. Universities frequently use test scores like these, along with the students' high school grades and other relevant information, when considering admitting students to university. In this class, all of the students agree to allow the records office at the university to furnish their SAT scores to the professor, who replaces each student's name with a subject number (to protect students' right to privacy). Let's see how they could use

statistics to analyze the data collected in their pilot study (a small, preliminary investigation).

Graphing Data 1c

After collecting the data, the next step is to organize the data to get a quick overview of our numerical results. Let's assume that there are 20 students in the class, and when they estimate how many hours they spend per day watching TV, the results are as follows:

3	2	0	3	1
3	4	0	5	1
2	3	4	5	2
4	5	3	4	6

One of the simpler things that they can do to organize data is to create a *frequency distribution*—an orderly arrangement of scores indicating the frequency of each score or group of scores. **Figure B.1(a)** shows a frequency distribution for the data on TV viewing. The column on the left lists the possible scores (estimated hours of TV viewing) in order, and the column on the right lists the number of subjects or participants with each score. Graphs can provide an even better overview of the data. One approach is to portray the data in a *histogram*, which is a bar graph that presents data from a frequency distribution. Such a histogram, summarizing our TV viewing data, is presented in **Figure B.1(b)**.

Another widely used method of portraying data graphically is the *frequency polygon*—a line figure used to present data from a frequency distribution. **Figures B.1(c)** and **B.1(d)** show how the TV viewing data can be converted from a histogram to

FIGURE B.1

Graphing data. (a) The raw data are tallied into a frequency distribution. (b) The same data are portrayed in a bar graph called a *histogram*. (c) A frequency polygon is plotted over the histogram. (d) The resultant frequency polygon is shown by itself.

Score	Tallies	Frequency
6	I	1
5	III	3
4	IIII	4
3	THI	5
2	III	3
1	II	2
0	II	2

(a) Frequency distribution

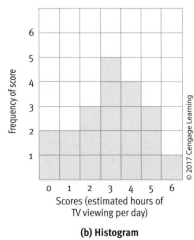

(b) Histogram

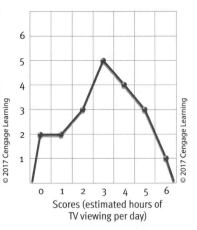

(c) Conversion of histogram into frequency polygon

(d) Frequency polygon

a frequency polygon. In both the bar graph and the line figure, the horizontal axis lists the possible scores and the vertical axis is used to indicate the frequency of each score. This use of the axes is nearly universal for frequency polygons, although sometimes it is reversed in histograms (the vertical axis lists possible scores, so the bars become horizontal).

The graphs improve on the jumbled collection of scores that they started with, but *descriptive statistics*, which are used to organize and summarize data, provide some additional advantages. Let's see what the three measures of central tendency tell us about the data.

Measuring Central Tendency

In examining a set of data, it's routine to ask, "What is a typical score in the distribution?" For instance, in this case, we might compare the average amount of TV watching in the sample to national estimates, to determine whether the subjects appear to be representative of the population. The three measures of central tendency—the median, the mean, and the mode—give us indications regarding the typical score in a data set. As explained in Chapter 2, the *median* is the score that falls in the centre of a distribution, the mean is the arithmetic average of the scores, and the mode is the score that occurs most frequently.

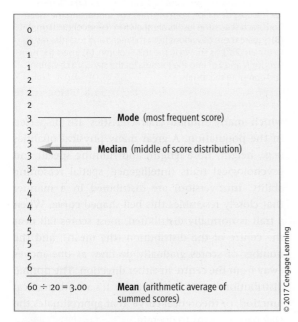

FIGURE B.2

Measures of central tendency. Although the mean, median, and mode sometimes yield different results, they usually converge, as in the case of the TV viewing data.

All three measures of central tendency are calculated for the TV viewing data in **Figure B.2**. As you can see, in this set of data, the mean, median, and mode all turn out to be the same score, which is 3. Although our example in Chapter 2 emphasized that the mean, median, and mode can yield different estimates of central tendency, the correspondence among them seen in the TV viewing data is quite common.

Lack of agreement usually occurs when a few extreme scores pull the mean away from the centre of the distribution. When a distribution is symmetric, the measures of central tendency fall together, but this is not true in skewed or unbalanced distributions.

In a *negatively skewed distribution*, most scores pile up at the high end of the scale (*negative skew* refers to the direction in which the curve's "tail" points). In a *positively skewed distribution*, scores pile up at the low end of the scale. In both types of skewed distributions, a few extreme scores at one end pull the mean, and to a lesser degree the median, away from the mode. In these situations, the mean may be misleading and the median usually provides the best index of central tendency.

In any case, the measures of central tendency for the TV viewing data are reassuring, since they all agree and they fall reasonably close to national estimates regarding how much young adults watch TV (Nielsen Media Research, 1998). Given the small size of the student group, this agreement with national norms doesn't *prove* that the sample is representative of the population, but at least there's no obvious reason to believe that it is unrepresentative.

Measuring Variability

Of course, the subjects in the sample did not report identical TV viewing habits. Virtually all data sets are characterized by some variability. *Variability* refers to how much the scores tend to vary or depart from the mean score. For example, the distribution of golf scores for a mediocre, erratic golfer would be characterized by high variability, while scores for an equally mediocre but consistent golfer would show less variability.

The *standard deviation* is an index of the amount of variability in a set of data. It reflects the dispersion of scores in a distribution. This principle is portrayed graphically in **Figure B.3**, where the two distributions of golf scores have the same mean but the upper one has less variability because the scores are "bunched up" in the centre (for the consistent golfer). The distribution in **Figure B.3(b)** is characterized by more variability, as the erratic golfer's scores are more spread out. This distribution will yield a

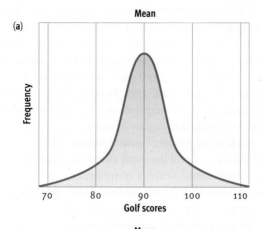

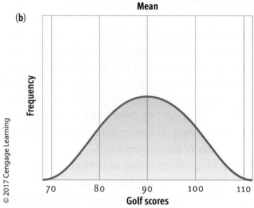

FIGURE B.3

The standard deviation and dispersion of data. Although both of these distributions of golf scores have the same mean, their standard deviations will be different. In **(a)** the scores are bunched together and there is less variability than in **(b)**, yielding a lower standard deviation for the data in distribution **(a)**.

TV viewing score (X)	Deviation from mean (d)	Deviation squared (d^2)
0	−3	9
0	−3	9
1	−2	4
1	−2	4
2	−1	1
2	−1	1
2	−1	1
3	0	0
3	0	0
3	0	0
3	0	0
3	0	0
4	+1	1
4	+1	1
4	+1	1
4	+1	1
5	+2	4
5	+2	4
5	+2	4
6	+3	9

$N = 20$

$\Sigma X = 60$ $\Sigma d^2 = 54$

$$\text{Mean} = \frac{\Sigma X}{N} = \frac{60}{20} = 3.0$$

$$\text{Standard deviation} = \sqrt{\frac{\Sigma d^2}{N}} = \sqrt{\frac{54}{20}}$$

$$= \sqrt{2.70} = 1.64$$

FIGURE B.4

Steps in calculating the standard deviation. (1) Add the scores (ΣX) and divide by the number of scores (N) to calculate the mean (which comes out to 3.0 in this case). **(2)** Calculate each score's deviation from the mean by subtracting the mean from each score (the results are shown in the second column). **(3)** Square these deviations from the mean and total the results to obtain (Σd^2), as shown in the third column. **(4)** Insert the numbers for N and Σd^2 into the formula for the standard deviation and compute the results.

higher standard deviation than the distribution in **Figure B.3(a)**.

The formula for calculating the standard deviation is shown in **Figure B.4**, where d stands for each score's deviation from the mean and Σ stands for summation. A step-by-step application of this formula to our TV viewing data, shown in Figure B.4, reveals that the standard deviation for our TV viewing data is 1.64. The standard deviation has a variety of uses. One of these uses will surface in the next section, where we discuss the normal distribution.

The Normal Distribution

The hypothesis in the study was that brighter students watch less TV than relatively dull students. To test this hypothesis, the students decided to correlate TV viewing with SAT scores. But to make effective use of the SAT data, they need to understand what SAT scores mean, which brings us to the normal distribution.

The *normal distribution* is a symmetrical, bell-shaped curve that represents the pattern in which many human characteristics are dispersed in the population. A great many physical qualities (e.g., height, nose length, and running speed) and psychological traits (intelligence, spatial reasoning ability, introversion) are distributed in a manner that closely resembles this bell-shaped curve. When a trait is normally distributed, most scores fall near the centre of the distribution (the mean), and the number of scores gradually declines as one moves away from the centre in either direction. The normal distribution is *not* a law of nature. It's a mathematical function, or theoretical curve, that approximates the way nature seems to operate.

The normal distribution is the bedrock of the scoring system for most psychological tests, including the SAT. As we discuss in Chapter 9, psychological tests are *relative measures*; they assess how people score on a trait in comparison to other people. The normal distribution gives us a precise way to measure how people stack up in comparison to each other.

Although you may not have realized it, you probably have taken many tests in which the scoring system is based on the normal distribution, such as IQ tests. On the SAT, for instance, raw scores (the number of items correct on each subtest) are converted into standard scores that indicate where a student falls in the normal distribution for the trait measured. In this conversion, the mean is set arbitrarily at 500 and the standard deviation at 100, as shown in **Figure B.5**. Therefore, a score of 400 on the SAT verbal subtest means that the student scored one standard deviation below the mean, while an SAT score of 600 indicates that the student scored one standard deviation above the mean. Thus, SAT scores tell us how many standard deviations above or below the mean a specific student's score was. This system also provides the metric for IQ scales and many other types of psychological tests (see Chapter 9).

Test scores that place examinees in the normal distribution can always be converted to percentile scores, which are a little easier to interpret. A **percentile score** indicates the percentage of people who score at or below a particular score. For example, if you score at the 60th percentile on an IQ test, 60 percent of the people who take the test score the same or below you, while the remaining 40 percent score above you. There are tables available that permit us

to convert any standard deviation placement in a normal distribution into a precise percentile score.

Of course, not all distributions are normal. Some distributions are skewed in one direction or the other. As an example, consider what would happen if a classroom exam was much too easy or much too hard. If the test was too easy, scores would be bunched up at the high end of the scale. If the test was too hard, scores would be bunched up at the low end.

Measuring Correlation

To determine whether TV viewing is related to SAT scores, the students have to compute a **correlation coefficient**—a numerical index of the degree of relationship between two variables. As discussed in Chapter 2, a *positive* correlation means that two variables—say X and Y—co-vary in the *same* direction. This means that high scores on variable X are associated with high scores on variable Y and that low scores on X are associated with low scores on Y.

A *negative* correlation indicates that two variables co-vary in the *opposite* direction. This means that people who score high on variable X tend to score low on variable Y, whereas those who score low on X tend to score high on Y. In their study, the psychology students hypothesized that as TV viewing increases, SAT scores will decrease, so they should expect a negative correlation between TV viewing and SAT scores.

The *magnitude* of a correlation coefficient indicates the *strength* of the association between two variables. This coefficient can vary between 0 and ± 1.00. The coefficient is usually represented by the letter r (e.g., $r = 0.45$). A coefficient near 0 tells us that there is no relationship between two variables. A coefficient of $+1.00$ or -1.00 indicates that there is a perfect, one-to-one correspondence between two variables. A perfect correlation is found only rarely when working with real data. The closer the coefficient is to either -1.00 or $+1.00$, the stronger the relationship is.

The direction and strength of correlations can be illustrated graphically in scatter diagrams (see **Figure B.6**). A *scatter diagram* is a graph in which paired X and Y scores for each subject are plotted as single points. Figure B.6 shows scatter diagrams for positive correlations in the upper half and for negative correlations in the bottom half. A perfect positive correlation and a perfect negative correlation are shown on the far left. When a correlation is perfect, the data points in the scatter diagram fall exactly in a straight line. However, positive and negative correlations yield lines slanted in the opposite direction because the lines map out

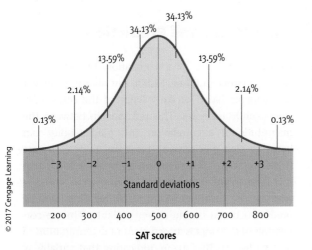

© 2017 Cengage Learning

FIGURE B.5

The normal distribution and SAT scores. The normal distribution is the basis for the scoring system on many standardized tests. For example, on the SAT, the mean is set at 500 and the standard deviation at 100. Hence, an SAT score tells you how many standard deviations above or below the mean a student scored. For example, a score of 700 means that person scored 2 standard deviations above the mean.

Statistical Methods

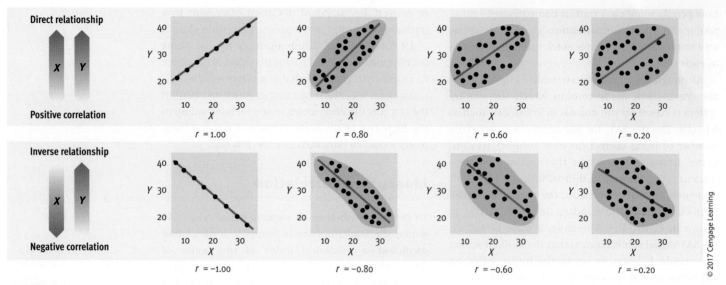

Direct relationship

X   Y

Positive correlation

$r = 1.00$ $r = 0.80$ $r = 0.60$ $r = 0.20$

Inverse relationship

X   Y

Negative correlation

$r = -1.00$ $r = -0.80$ $r = -0.60$ $r = -0.20$

© 2017 Cengage Learning

FIGURE B.6

Scatter diagrams of positive and negative correlations. Scatter diagrams plot paired X and Y scores as single points. Score plots slanted in the opposite direction result from positive (top row) as opposed to negative (bottom row) correlations. Moving across both rows (to the right), you can see that progressively weaker correlations result in more and more scattered plots of data points.

opposite types of associations. Moving to the right in Figure B.6, you can see what happens when the magnitude of a correlation decreases. The data points scatter farther and farther from the straight line that would represent a perfect relationship.

What about the data relating TV viewing to SAT scores? **Figure B.7** shows a scatter diagram of these data. Having just learned about scatter diagrams, perhaps you can estimate the magnitude of the correlation between TV viewing and SAT scores. The scatter diagram of our data looks a lot like the one shown in the bottom right corner of Figure B.6, suggesting that the correlation will be in the vicinity of –0.20.

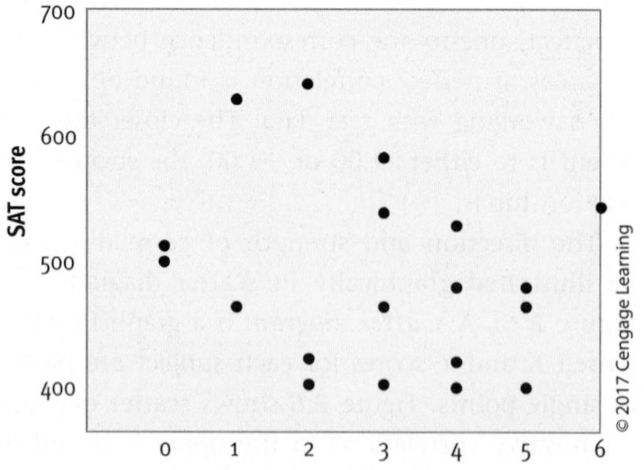

The formula for computing the most widely used measure of correlation—the Pearson product–moment correlation—is shown in **Figure B.8**, along with the calculations for the data on TV viewing and SAT scores. The data yield a correlation of $r = -0.24$. This coefficient of correlation reveals that there is a weak inverse association between TV viewing and performance on the SAT. Among the sample of participants, as TV viewing increases, SAT scores decrease, but the trend isn't very strong. We can get a better idea of how strong this correlation is by examining its predictive power.

Correlation and Prediction

As the magnitude of a correlation increases (gets closer to either –1.00 or +1.00), our ability to predict one variable based on knowledge of the other variable steadily increases. This relationship between the magnitude of a correlation and predictability can be quantified precisely. All we have to do is square the correlation coefficient (multiply it by itself) and this gives us **the *coefficient of determination*,** the percentage of variation in one variable that can be predicted based on the other variable. Thus, a correlation of 0.70 yields a coefficient of determination of 0.49 ($0.70 \times 0.70 = 0.49$), indicating that variable X can account for 49 percent of the variation in variable Y. **Figure B.9** shows how the coefficient of determination goes up as the magnitude of a correlation increases.

Unfortunately, a correlation of 0.24 doesn't give us much predictive power. The students can account for only a little over 6 percent of the variation in

FIGURE B.7

Scatter diagram of the correlation between TV viewing and SAT scores. The hypothetical data relating TV viewing to SAT scores are plotted in this scatter diagram. Compare it to the scatter diagrams shown in Figure B.6 and see whether you can estimate the correlation between TV viewing and SAT scores in the students' data (see the text for the answer).

© 2017 Cengage Learning

variable Y. So, if they tried to predict individuals' SAT scores based on how much TV those individuals watched, their predictions wouldn't be very accurate. Although a low correlation doesn't have much practical, predictive utility, it may still have theoretical value. Just knowing that there is a relationship between two variables can be theoretically interesting. However, we haven't yet addressed the question of whether the observed correlation is strong enough to support the hypothesis that there is a relationship between TV viewing and SAT scores. To make this judgment, we have to turn to *inferential statistics* and the process of hypothesis testing.

Hypothesis Testing

Inferential statistics go beyond the mere description of data. ***Inferential statistics*** are used to interpret data and draw conclusions. They permit researchers to decide whether their data support their hypotheses.

In Chapter 2, we showed how inferential statistics can be used to evaluate the results of an experiment; the same process can be applied to correlational data. In the study of TV viewing, the students hypothesized that they would find an inverse relationship between the amount of TV watched and SAT scores. Sure enough, that's what they found. However, a critical question remains: Is this observed correlation large enough to support the hypothesis, or might a correlation of this size have occurred by chance?

We have to ask a similar question nearly every time we conduct a study. Why? Because we are working with only a sample. In research, we observe a limited *sample* (in this case, 20 participants) to draw

Subject number	TV viewing score (X)	X^2	SAT score (Y)	Y^2	XY
1	0	0	500	250 000	0
2	0	0	515	265 225	0
3	1	1	450	202 500	450
4	1	1	650	422 500	650
5	2	4	400	160 000	800
6	2	4	675	455 625	1350
7	2	4	425	180 625	850
8	3	9	400	160 000	1200
9	3	9	450	202 500	1350
10	3	9	500	250 000	1500
11	3	9	550	302 500	1650
12	3	9	600	360 000	1800
13	4	16	400	160 000	1600
14	4	16	425	180 625	1700
15	4	16	475	225 625	1900
16	4	16	525	275 625	2100
17	5	25	400	160 000	2000
18	5	25	450	202 500	2250
19	5	25	475	225 625	2375
20	6	36	550	302 500	3300
$N = 20$	$\Sigma X = 60$	$\Sigma X^2 = 234$	$\Sigma Y = 9815$	$\Sigma Y^2 = 4\,943\,975$	$\Sigma XY = 28\,825$

Formula for Pearson product-moment correlation coefficient

$$r = \frac{N\,\Sigma XY - (\Sigma X)(\Sigma Y)}{\sqrt{[(N)\,\Sigma X^2 - (\Sigma X)^2][(N)\,\Sigma Y^2 - (\Sigma Y)^2]}}$$

$$= \frac{(20)(28\,825) - (60)(9815)}{\sqrt{[(20)(234) - (60)^2][(20)(4\,943\,975) - (9815)^2]}}$$

$$= \frac{-12\,400}{\sqrt{[1080][2\,545\,275]}}$$

$$= -0.237$$

© 2017 Cengage Learning

FIGURE B.8

Computing a correlation coefficient. The calculations required to compute the Pearson product–moment coefficient of correlation are shown here. The formula looks intimidating, but it's just a matter of filling in the figures taken from the sums of the columns shown above the formula.

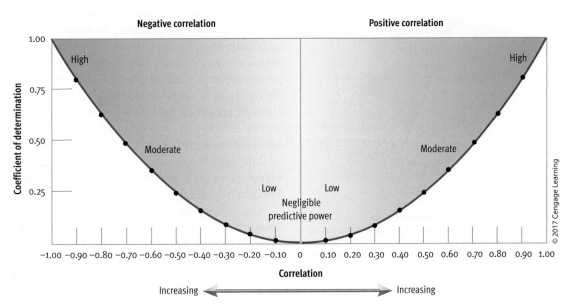

FIGURE B.9

Correlation and the coefficient of determination. The coefficient of determination is an index of a correlation's predictive power. As you can see, whether positive or negative, stronger correlations yield greater predictive power.

© 2017 Cengage Learning

Statistical Methods

conclusions about a much larger *population* (students in general). In any study, there's always a possibility that if we drew a different sample from the population, the results might be different. Perhaps our results are unique to our sample and not generalizable to the larger population. If we were able to collect data on the entire population, we would not have to wrestle with this problem, but our dependence on a sample necessitates the use of inferential statistics to precisely evaluate the likelihood that our results are due to chance factors in sampling. Thus, inferential statistics are the key to making the inferential leap from the sample to the population (see **Figure B.10**).

Although it may seem backward, in hypothesis testing, we formally test the *null hypothesis*. As applied to correlational data, **the *null hypothesis* is the assumption that there is no true relationship between the variables observed.** In the students' study, the null hypothesis is that there is no genuine association between TV viewing and SAT scores. They want to determine whether their results will permit them to *reject* the null hypothesis and thus conclude that their *research hypothesis* (that there *is* a relationship between the variables) has been supported.

In such cases, why do researchers directly test the null hypothesis instead of the research hypothesis? Because our probability calculations depend on assumptions tied to the null hypothesis. Specifically, we compute the probability of obtaining the results that we have observed if the null hypothesis is indeed true. The calculation of this probability hinges on a number of factors. A key factor is the amount of variability in the data, which is why the standard deviation is an important statistic.

Statistical Significance

When we reject the null hypothesis, we conclude that we have found *statistically significant* results. *Statistical significance* is said to exist when the probability that the observed findings are due to chance is very low, usually fewer than five chances in 100. This means that if the null hypothesis is correct and we conduct our study 100 times, drawing a new sample from the population each time, we will get results such as those observed only five times out of 100. If our calculations allow us to reject the null hypothesis, we conclude that our results support our research hypothesis. Thus, statistically significant results typically are findings that *support* a research hypothesis.

The requirement that there be fewer than five chances in 100 that research results are due to chance is the *minimum* requirement for statistical significance. When this requirement is met, we say the results are significant at the 0.05 level. If researchers calculate that there is less than one chance in 100 that their results are due to chance factors in sampling, the results are significant at the 0.01 level. If there is less than a one in 1000 chance that findings are attributable to sampling error, the results are significant at the 0.001 level. Thus, there are several *levels* of significance that you may see cited in scientific articles.

Because we are dealing only in matters of probability, there is always the possibility that our decision to accept or reject the null hypothesis is wrong. The various significance levels indicate the probability of erroneously rejecting the null hypothesis (and inaccurately accepting the research hypothesis). At the 0.05 level of significance, there are five chances in 100 that we have made a mistake when we conclude that our results support our hypothesis, and at the 0.01 level of significance, the chance of an erroneous conclusion is one in 100. Although researchers hold the probability of this type of error quite low, the probability is never zero. This is one of the reasons that competently executed studies of the same question can yield contradictory findings. The differences may be due to chance variations in sampling that can't be prevented.

What do we find when we evaluate the data linking TV viewing to students' SAT scores? The calculations indicate that, given the sample size and the variability in the data, the probability of obtaining a correlation of −0.24 by chance is greater than 20 percent. That's not a high probability, but it's *not* low

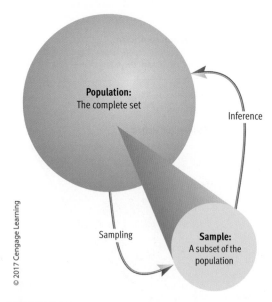

© 2017 Cengage Learning

FIGURE B.10

The relationship between the population and the sample. In research, we are usually interested in a broad population, but we can observe only a small sample from the population. After making observations of our sample, we draw inferences about the population, based on the sample. This inferential process works well as long as the sample is reasonably representative of the population.

enough to reject the null hypothesis. Thus, the findings are not strong enough to allow us to conclude that the students have supported their hypothesis.

Statistics and Empiricism

In summary, conclusions based on empirical research are a matter of probability, and there's always a possibility that the conclusions are wrong. However, two major strengths of the empirical approach are its precision and its intolerance of error. Scientists can give you precise estimates of the likelihood that their conclusions are wrong, and because they're intolerant of error, they hold this probability extremely low. It's their reliance on statistics that allows them to accomplish these goals.

AAIDD. (2013). Definition of intellectual disability. Retrieved from http://aaidd.org/intellectual-disability/definition#.VICbaihy9j4.

Abbeduto, L., Ozonoff, S., Thurman, A. J., McDuffie, A., & Schweitzer, J. (2014). Neurodevelopmental disorders. In R. E. Hales, S. C. Yudofsky, & L. W. Roberts (Eds.), *The American Psychiatric Publishing textbook of psychiatry* (6th ed.). Washington, DC: American Psychiatric Publishing.

Abbott, A. (2004). Striking back. *Nature, 429*, 338–339. Retrieved February 11, 2008, from http://www.nature.com/nature/journal/v429/n6990/full/429338a.html.

Abel, E. L., & Kruger, M. L. (2010). Smile intensity in photographs predicts longevity. *Psychological Science, 21*(4), 542–544.

Abel, M. H. (1998). Interaction of humor and gender in moderating relationships between stress and outcomes. *Journal of Psychology, 132*, 267–276.

Abi-Dargham, A., & Grace, A. (2011). Dopamine and schizophrenia. In D. R. Weinberger & P. Harrison (Eds.), *Schizophrenia* (3rd ed.). Malden, MA: Wiley-Blackwell.

Aboud, F. E., & Amato, M. (2001). Developmental and socialization influences on intergroup bias. In R. Brown & S. L. Gaertner (Eds.), *Blackwell handbook of social psychology: Intergroup processes*. Malden, MA: Blackwell.

Abraham, A., Thybusch, K., Pieritz, K., & Hermann, C. (2014). Gender differences in creative thinking: Behavioral and fMRI findings. *Brain Imaging and Behavior, 8*(1), 39–51. doi:org/10.1007/s11682-013-9241-4.

Abraham, C. (2002). *Possessing genius: The true account of the bizarre odyssey of Einstein's brain*. New York, NY: St. Martin's Press.

Abraham, C. (2010, July 2). An age-old puzzle solved: Who will live to be 100. *Toronto Star*, p. A1.

Abraham, W. C. (2006). Memory maintenance. *Current Directions in Psychological Science, 15*(1), 5–8.

Abramov, I., Gordon, J., Feldman, O., & Chavarga, A. (2012). Sex and vision II: Color appearance of monochromatic lights. *Biology of Sex Differences, 3*(1), 21.

Abrams, R. L., Klinger, M. R., & Greenwald, A. G. (2002). Subliminal words activate semantic categories (not automated motor responses). *Psychonomic Bulletin & Review, 9*(1), 100–106.

Abramson, L. Y., Seligman, M. E. P., & Teasdale, J. (1978). Learned helplessness in humans: Critique and reformulation. *Journal of Abnormal Psychology, 87*, 32–48.

Accardi, M., Cleere, C., Lynn, S. J., & Kirsch, I. (2013). Placebo versus "standard" hypnosis rationale: Attitudes, expectancies, hypnotic responses, and experiences. *American Journal of Clinical Hypnosis, 56*, 103–114. doi: 10.1080/00029157.2013.769087.

Acevedo, B. P., & Aron, A. P. (2014). Romantic love, pair-bonding, and the dopaminergic reward system. In M. Mikulincer & P. R. Shaver (Eds.), *Mechanisms of social connection: From brain to group*. Washington, DC: American Psychological Association.

Achermann, P., & Borbely, A. A. (2011). Sleep homeostasis and models of sleep regulation. In M. H. Kryger, T. Roth, & W. C. Dement (Eds.), *Principles and practice of sleep medicine* (5th ed.). Saint Louis, MO: Elsevier Saunders.

Ackerman, P. L., & Beier, M. E. (2005). Knowledge and intelligence. In O. Wilhelm & R. W. Engle (Eds.), *Handbook of understanding and measuring intelligence*. Thousand Oaks, CA: SAGE.

Ackerman, S. (2015). Canada frees Omar Khadr, once Guantanamo Bay's youngest immate. *The Guardian*, May 7, 2015. Retrieved from https://www.theguardian.com/world/2015/may/07/canada-free-bail-omar-khadr-guantanamo-bay-youngest.

Active Healthy Kids Canada. (2014). The 2014 Active Healthy Kids Canada report card on physical activity for children and youth. Retrieved from http://www.activehealthykids.ca/ReportCard/2014Report Card.aspx.

Adam, T. C., & Epel, E. (2007). Stress, eating and the reward system. *Physiology and Behavior, 91*, 449–458.

Adams, C. J., Hough, H., Proecshold-Bell, R. J., Yao, J., & Kolkin, M. (2017). Clergy burnout: A comparison study with other helping professions. *Pastoral Psychology, 66*, 145–175.

Adams, H. M., Luevano, V. X., & Jonason, P. K. (2014). Risky business: Willingness to be caught in an extra-pair relationship, relationship experience, and the Dark Triad. *Personality and Individual Differences, 66*, 204–207.

Adams, J. L. (1980). *Conceptual blockbusting*. San Francisco, CA: W. H. Freeman.

Adams, R. L., & Culbertson, J. L. (2005). Personality assessment: Adults and children. In B. J. Sadock & V. A. Sadock (Eds.), *Kaplan & Sadock's comprehensive textbook of psychiatry*. Philadelphia, PA: Lippincott Williams & Wilkins.

Adams, S. J., Pitre, N. L., & Smith, A. (2001). Criminal harassment by patients with mental disorders. *Canadian Journal of Psychiatry, 46*, 173–176.

Addictive Behaviours Laboratory. (2014). *Gambling in Canada*. University of Calgary. Retrieved from http://www.addiction.ucalgary.ca/.

Addis, D. R., Wong, A. T., & Schacter, D. L. (2007). Remembering the past and imagining the future: Common and distinct neural substrates during event construction and elaboration. *Neuropsychologia, 45*, 1363–1377.

Ader, R. (2001). Psychoneuroimmunology. *Current Directions in Psychological Science, 10*(3), 94–98.

Adler, A. (1917). *Study of organ inferiority and its psychical compensation*. New York, NY: Nervous and Mental Diseases Publishing Co.

Adler, A. (1927). *Practice and theory of individual psychology*. New York, NY: Harcourt, Brace & World.

Adler, A. B., Adrian, A. L., Hemphill, M. S., Scaro, N. H., & Sipos, M. L. (2017). Professional stress and burnout in U.S. military medical personnel deployed to Afghanistan. *Military Medicine, 183*, 1169–1176.

Adler, L. L. (Ed.). (1993). *International handbook on gender roles*. Westport, CT: Greenwood.

Adolph, K. E., & Berger, S. E. (2011). Physical and motor development. In M. H. Bornstein & M. E. Lamb (Eds.), *Developmental science: An advanced textbook* (pp. 109–198). New York, NY: Psychology Press.

Adolph, K. E., Cole, W. G., Komati, M., Garciaguirre, J. S., Badaly, D., Lingeman, J. M., . . . Sotsky, R. B. (2012). How do you learn to walk? Thousands of steps and dozens of falls per day. *Psychological Science, 23*, 1387–1394. doi:10.1177/0956797612446346.

Adolph, K. E., Karasik, L. B., & Tamis-LeMonda, C. S. (2010). Using social information to guide action: Infants' locomotion over slippery slopes. *Neural Networks, 23*, 1033–1042.

Affleck, G., Tennen, H., Urrows, S., & Higgins, P. (1994). Person and contextual features of daily stress reactivity: Individual differences in relations of undesirable daily events with mood disturbance and chronic pain intensity. *Journal of Personality and Social Psychology, 66*, 329–340.

Agid, O., Siu, C. O., Potkin, S. G., Kapur, S., Watsky, E., Vanderburg, D., . . . Remington, G. (2013). Meta-regression analysis of placebo response in antipsychotic rials, 1970–2010. *The American Journal of Psychiatry, 170*, 1335–1344.

Ahmed, S. H. (2012). Is sugar as addictive as cocaine. In K. D. Brownell, & M. S. Gold (Eds.), *Food and addiction: A comprehensive handbook*. New York, NY: Oxford University Press.

Ahuvia, A., & Izberk-Bilgin, E. (2013). Well-being in consumer societies. In S. A. David, I. Boniwell, & A. Conley Ayers (Eds.), *The Oxford handbook of happiness*. New York, NY: Oxford University Press.

Aikins, D. E., & Craske, M. G. (2001). Cognitive theories of generalized anxiety disorder. *Psychiatric Clinics of North America, 24*(1), 57–74.

Ainslie, G. (2007). Foresight has to pay off in the present moment. *Behavioral and Brain Sciences, 30*, 313–314.

Ainsworth, M. D. S. (1979). Attachment as related to mother–infant interaction. In J. S. Rosenblatt, R. A. Hinde, C. Beer, & M. Busnel (Eds.), *Advances in the study of behavior* (Vol. 9). New York, NY: Academic Press.

Ainsworth, M. D. S., Blehar, M. C., Waters, E., & Wall, S. (1978). *Patterns of attachment: A psychological study of the strange situation*. Hillsdale, NJ: Erlbaum.

Ajzen, I. (2012). Attitudes and persuasion. In K. Deaux & M. Snyder (Eds.), *Oxford handbook of personality and social psychology*. New York, NY: Oxford University Press.

Ajzen, I., & Fishbein, M. (2000). Attitudes and the attitude-behavior relation: Reasoned and automatic processes. In W. Stroebe & M. Hewstone (Eds.), *European review of social psychology* (Vol. 11). Chichester, UK: Wiley.

Ajzen, I., & Fishbein, M. (2005). The influence of attitudes on behavior. In D. Albarracin, B. T. Johnson, & M. P. Zanna (Eds.), *The handbook of attitudes*. Mahwah, NJ: Erlbaum.

Akabaliév, V. H., Sivkov, S. T., & Mantarkov, M. Y. (2014). Minor physical anomalies in schizophrenia and bipolar I disorder and the neurodevelopmental continuum of psychosis. *Bipolar Disorders, 16*, 633–641. doi:10.1111/bdi.12211.

Akerstedt, T., Hume, K., Minors, D., & Waterhouse, J. (1997). Good sleep—its timing and physiological sleep characteristics. *Journal of Sleep Research, 6*, 221–229.

Akerstedt, T., & Kecklund, G. (2012). Sleep, work, and occupational stress. In C. M. Morin, & C. A. Espie (Eds.), *Oxford handbook of sleep and sleep disorders*. New York, NY: Oxford University Press.

Akins, C. K., & Panicker, S. (2012). Ethics and regulation of research with nonhuman animals. In H. Cooper, P. M. Camic, D. L. Long, A. T. Panter, D. Rindskopf, & K. J. Sher (Eds.), *APA handbook of research methods in psychology: Vol. 1. Foundations, planning, measures, and psychometrics*. Washington, DC: American Psychological Association.

Akiskal, H. S. (2000). Mood disorders: Clinical features. In B. J. Sadock & V. A. Sadock (Eds.), *Kaplan and Sadock's comprehensive textbook of psychiatry* (7th ed., Vol. 1, pp. 1338–1376). Philadelphia, PA: Lippincott, Williams & Wilkins.

Akiskal, H. S. (2009). Mood disorders: Clinical features. In B. J. Sadock, V. A. Sadock, & P. Ruiz (Eds.), *Kaplan & Sadock's comprehensive textbook of psychiatry* (9th ed., pp. 1693–1733). Philadelphia, PA: Lippincott, Williams & Wilkins.

Albarracin, D., & Vargas, P. (2010). Attitudes and persuasion: From biology to social responses to persuasive intent. In S. T. Fiske, D. T. Gilbert, G. Lindzey, & S. T. Fiske (Eds.), *Handbook of social psychology* (5th ed., Vol. 1, pp. 353–393). Hoboken, NJ: Wiley.

Albert, D., Chein, J., & Steinberg, L. (2013). The teenage brain: Peer influences on adolescent decision making. *Current Decisions in Psychological Science, 22*, 114–120. doi:10.1177/0963721412471347.

Albert, M. A. (2008). Neuropsychology of the development of Alzheimer's disease. In F. I. M. Craik & T. A. Salthouse (Eds.), *Handbook of aging and cognition* (2nd ed., pp. 97–132). New York, NY: Psychology Press.

Albouy, G., King, B. R., Maquet, P., & Doyon, J. (2013). Hippocampus and striatum: Dynamics and interaction during acquisition and sleep-related motor sequence memory consolidation. *Hippocampus, 23*(11), 985–1004. doi:org/10.1002/hipo.22183.

Aldag, R. J., & Fuller, S. R. (1993). Beyond fiasco: A reappraisal of the groupthink phenomenon and a new model of group decision processes. *Psychological Bulletin, 113*, 533–552.

Aldington, S., Harwood, M., Cox, B., Weatherall, M., Beckert, L., Hansell, A., . . . Cannabis and Respiratory Disease Research Group. (2008). Cannabis use and risk of lung cancer: A case-control study. *European Respiratory Journal, 31*, 280–286.

Aldwin, C. M., & Gilmer, D. F. (2004). Health, illness, and optimal aging: Biological and psychosocial perspectives. Thousand Oaks, CA: SAGE.

Alexander, C. N., Robinson, P., Orme-Johnson, D. W., Schneider, R. H., & Walton, K. G. (1994). The effects of transcendental meditation compared with other methods of relaxation and meditation in reducing risk factors, morbidity, and mortality. *Homeostasis in Health and Disease, 35*, 243–263.

Allahyar, & Nazari, A. (2012). Potentiality of Vygotsky's sociocultural theory in exploring the role of teacher perceptions, expectations, and interaction strategies. *Journal of Working Papers in Language Pedagogy, 6*, 79–92.

Allan, R. W. (1998). Operant–respondent interactions. In W. O'Donohue (Ed.), *Learning and behavior therapy*. Boston, MA: Allyn & Bacon.

Allemand, M., Steiger, A. E., & Hill, P. L. (2013). Stability of personality traits in adulthood: Mechanisms and implications. *GeroPsych: The Journal of Gerontology and Geriatric Psychiatry, 26*, 5–13. doi:10.1024/1662-9647/a000080.

Allik, J., et al. (2010). How people see others is different from how people see themselves: A replicable pattern across cultures. *Journal of Personality and Social Psychology, 99*, 870–882.

Allison, D. B., Heshka, S., Neale, M. C., Lykken, D. T., & Heymsfield, S. B. (1994). A genetic analysis of relative weight among 4,020 twin pairs, with an emphasis on sex effects. *Health Psychology, 13*, 362–365.

Alloy, L. B., Abramson, L. Y., Whitehouse, W. G., Hogan, M. E., Tashman, N. A., Steinberg, D. L., et al. (1999). Depressogenic cognitive styles: Predictive validity, information processing and personality characteristics, and developmental origins. *Behaviour Research and Therapy, 37*(6), 503–531.

Allport, G. W. (1937). *Personality: A psychological interpretation*. New York, NY: Holt.

Almada, L. F., Pereira, A., Jr., Carrara-Augustenborg, C. (2013). What affective neuroscience means for science of consciousness. *Mens Sana Monograph, 11*, 253–273.

Alter, A. L., Stern, C., Granot, Y., & Balcetis, E. (2016). The "bad is black" effect: Why people believe evildoers have darker skin than do-gooders. *Personality and Social Psychology Bulletin, 42*, 1653–1655.

Altman, I. (1990). Centripetal and centrifugal trends in psychology. In L. Brickman & H. Ellis (Eds.), *Preparing psychologists for the 21st century: Proceedings of the National Conference on Graduate Education in Psychology*. Hillsdale, NJ: Erlbaum.

Alvarez, P., & Squire, L. (1994). Memory consolidation and the medial temporal lobe: A simple network model. *Proceedings of the National Academy of Sciences, USA, 91*, 7041–7045.

Amabile, T. M. (1996). *Creativity in context*. Boulder, CO: Westview.

Amabile, T. M. (2001). Beyond talent: John Irving and the passionate craft of creativity. *American Psychologist, 56*, 333–336.

Ambady, D. J. & Adams, R. B. (2011). Us versus them. In A. B. Todorov, S. T. Fiske, & D. A. Prentice (Eds.). *Social neuroscience: Toward understanding the underpinnings of the social mind* (211–245). New York, NY: Oxford University Press.

Ambady, N., Hallahan, M., & Conner, B. (1999). Accuracy of judgments of sexual orientation from thin slices of behavior. *Journal of Personality and Social Psychology, 77*(3), 538–547.

Ambady, N., & Rosenthal, R. (1993). Half a minute: Predicting teacher evaluations from thin slices of nonverbal behavior and physical attractiveness. *Journal of Personality and Social Psychology, 64*(3), 431–441.

Ambady, N., & Weisbuch, M. (2010). Nonverbal behavior. In S. T. Fiske, D. T. Gilbert, & G. Lindzey (Eds.), *Handbook of social psychology* (5th ed., Vol. 1) (pp. 353–393). Hoboken, NJ: Wiley.

Amedi, A., Floel, A., Knecht, S., Zohary, E., & Cohen, L. G. (2004). Transcranial magnetic stimulation of the occipital pole interferes with verbal processing in blind subjects. *Nature Neuroscience, 7*, 1266–1270.

American Association of Suicidology. (2007). Understanding and helping the suicidal individual. Retrieved April 12, 2007, from http://www.suicidology.org/associations/1045/files/Understanding.pdf.

American Foundation for Suicide Prevention. (2007). When you fear someone may take their own life. Retrieved April 12, 2007, from http://www.afsp.org/index.cfm?page_id=F2F25092-7E90-9BD4-C4658F1D2B5D19A0.

American Psychiatric Association. (2013a). *Diagnostic and statistical manual of mental disorders* (5th ed.). Arlington, VA: American Psychiatric Publishing.

American Psychiatric Association. (2013b). Highlights of changes from DSM-IV-TR to DSM-5. Retrieved from http://www.dsm5.org/Documents/changes%20from%20dsm-iv-tr%20to%20dsm-5.pdf.

American Psychological Association. (1984). *Behavioral research with animals*. Washington, DC: Author.

American Psychological Association. (2006). Evidence-based practice in psychology. *American Psychologist, 61*, 271–285.

American Psychological Association. (2010). *Melzack and Stanovich win Grawemeyer awards*. Retrieved from http://www.apa.org/science/about/psa/2010/01/grawemeyer.aspx.

American Psychological Association. (2012). Daniel L. Schacter: Award for distinguished scientific contributions. *American Psychologist, 67*, 601–603.

American Psychological Association. (2013). Elizabeth Loftus: Gold Medal award for life achievement in the science of psychology. *American Psychologist, July/August*, 331–333.

American Psychological Association. (2015). A reproducibility crisis? The headlines were hard to miss: Psychology, they proclaim, is in crisis. Retrieved from http://www.apa.org/monitor/2015/10/share-reproducibility.aspx.

American Psychological Association. (2016). Gold medal award for life achievement in the Science of psychology: Richard E. Nisbett. *American Psychologist, 71*, 363–365.

American Psychological Association. (2016a). *Position on ethics and interrogation*. Retrieved from http://www.apa.org/ethics/programs/position/index.aspx.

American Psychological Association. (2016b). Timeline of APA policies and actions related to detainee welfare and professional ethics in the context of interrogation and national security. Retrieved from http://www.apa.org/news/press/statements/interrogations.aspx.

Ames, M., Rawana, J. S., Gentile, P., & Morgan, A. S. (2013). The protective role of optimism and self-esteem on depressive symptom pathways among Canadian Aboriginal youth. *Journal of Youth and Adolescence*. doi: 10.1007/s10964-013-0016-4.

Amir, N., & Taylor, C. T. (2012). Combining computerized home-based treatments for generalized anxiety disorder: An attention modification program and cognitive behavioral therapy. *Behavior Therapy, 43*, 546–559. doi:10.1016/j.beth.2010.12.008.

Amir, Y. (1969). Contact hypothesis in ethnic relations. *Psychological Bulletin, 71*, 319–342.

Amodio, D. M. (2008). The social neuroscience of intergroup relations. *European Review of Social Psychology, 19*, 1–54.

Amodio, D. M. (2013). The social neuroscience of prejudice: Then, now, and what's to come. In C. Stangor and C. Crandall (Eds.), *Stereotyping and prejudice* (pp. 1–28). New York, NY: Psychology Press.

Amodio, D. M., & Devine, P. G. (2006). Stereotyping and evaluation in implicit race bias: Evidence for independent constructs and unique effects on behavior. *Journal of Personality and Social Psychology, 91*(4), 652–661.

Amodio, D. M., Bartholow, B. D., & Ito, T. A. (2014). Tracking the dynamics of the social brain: ERP approaches for social cognitive & affective neuroscience. *Social Cognitive & Affective Neuroscience, 9*, 385–393.

Amodio, D. M., & Harmon-Jones, E. (2012). Neuroscience approaches to social and personality psychology. In M. Snyder & K. Deaux (Eds.), *Handbook of social and personality psychology* (pp. 11–67). New York, NY: Oxford University Press.

Amodio, D. M., & Ratner, K. G. (2013). The neuroscience of social cognition. In D. Carlston (Ed.), *The Oxford handbook of social cognition* (pp. 234–276). New York, NY: Oxford University Press.

Anacker, C. (2014). Adult hippocampal neurogenesis in depression: Behavioral implications and regulation by the stress system. In C. M. Pariante & M. D. Lapiz-Bluhm (Eds.), *Behavioral neurobiology of stress-related disorders*. New York, NY: Springer-Verlag Publishing.

Anderson, C. (2006, June 19). *Critical periods in development*. Paper presented at the annual meeting of the XVth Biannual International Conference on Infant Studies, Westin Miyako, Kyoto, Japan.

Anderson, C. A., Shibuya, A., Ihori, N., Swing, E. L., Bushman, B. J., Sakamoto, A., . . . Saleem, M. (2010). Violent video game effects on aggression, empathy, and prosocial behavior in Eastern and Western countries: A meta-analytic review. *Psychological Bulletin, 136*, 151–173. doi:10.1037/a0018251.

Anderson, K. J. (1990). Arousal and the inverted-U hypothesis: A critique of Neiss's "reconceptualizing arousal." *Psychological Bulletin, 107*, 96–100.

Anderson, M. C., & Neely, J. H. (1996). Interference and inhibition in memory retrieval. In E. L. Bjork & R. A. Bjork (Eds.), *Memory*. San Diego, CA: Academic Press.

Anderson-Fye, E. P., & Becker, A. E. (2004). Sociocultural aspects of eating disorders and obesity. In J. K. Thompson (Ed.), *Handbook of eating disorders and obesity*. New York, NY: Wiley.

Andersson, E., Ljótsson, B., Hedman, E., Kaldo, V., Paxling, B., Andersson, G., . . . Rück, C. (2011). Internet-based cognitive behavior therapy for obsessive compulsive disorder: A pilot study. *BMC Psychiatry, 11*(125), 1–10. doi:10.1186/1471-244X-11-125.

Andreasen, N. C. (1987). The diagnosis of schizophrenia. *Schizophrenia Bulletin, 13*(1), 9–22.

Andreasen, N. C. (1996). Creativity and mental illness: A conceptual and historical overview. In J. J. Schildkraut & A. Otero (Eds.), *Depression and the spiritual in modern art: Homage to Miro*. New York, NY: Wiley.

Andreasen, N. C. (2005). *The creating brain: The neuroscience of genius*. New York, NY: Dana Press.

Andreasen, N. C. (2009). Schizophrenia: A conceptual history. In M. C. Gelder, N. C. Andreasen, J. J. Lopez-Ibor, Jr., & J. R. Geddes (Eds.), *New Oxford textbook of psychiatry* (2nd ed., Vol. 1). New York, NY: Oxford University Press.

Andrews, P. W., Kornstein, S. G., Halberstadt, L. J., Gardner, C. O., & Neale, M. C. (2011). Blue again: Perturbational effects of antidepressants suggest monoaminergic homeostasis in major depression. *Frontiers in Psychology, 2*(159), 1–24. doi:10.3389/fpsyg.2011.00159.

Angell, M. (2004). *The truth about the drug companies: How they deceive us and what to do about it*. New York, NY: Random House.

Anglin, J. M. (1993). Vocabulary development: A morphological analysis. *Monographs of the Society for Research in Child Development, 58*.

Angst, J. (2009). Course and prognosis of mood disorders. In M. C. Gelder, N. C. Andreasen, J. J. López-Ibor, Jr., & J. R. Geddes (Eds.), *New Oxford textbook of psychiatry* (2nd ed., Vol. 1). New York, NY: Oxford University Press.

Angus, L. (2012). Toward an integrative understanding of narrative and emotion processes in emotion-focused therapy of depression: Implications for theory, research, and practice. *Psychology Research, 30*, 1–14.

Anisman, H, & Merali, Z. (1999). Understanding stress: Characteristics and caveats. *Alcohol Research and Health, 23*, 241–249.

Annese, J., Schenker-Ahmed, N. M., Bartsch, H., Maechler, P., Sheh, C., Thomas, N., . . . Corkin, S. (2014). Postmortem examination of patient HM's brain based on histological sectioning and digital 3D reconstruction. *Nature Communications, 5*, 3122. doi:10.1038/ncomms4122.

Ansbacher, H. (1970, February). Alfred Adler, individual psychology. *Psychology Today, 66*, 42–44.

Antony, M. M., & McCabe, R. E. (2003). Anxiety disorders: Social and specific phobias. In A. Tasman, J. Kay, & J. A. Lieberman (Eds.), *Psychiatry*. New York, NY: Wiley.

Antony, M. M., Purdon, C., & Summerfeldt, L. J. (Eds.). (2006). *Psychological treatment of OCD: Fundamentals and beyond*. Washington, DC: American Psychological Association Press.

Appelbaum, P. S. (2002). Responses to the presidential debate: The systematic defunding of psychiatric care: A crisis at our doorstep. *American Journal of Psychiatry, 159*, 1638–1640.

Appleton, K. M., Gentry, R. C., & Shepherd, R. (2006). Evidence of a role for conditioning in the development of liking for flavors in humans in everyday life. *Physiology & Behavior, 87*, 478–486.

Apuzzo, J., Fink. S., & Risen, J. (2016). How U.S. torture left a legacy of damaged minds. *New York Times*. Retrieved from https://www.nytimes.com/2016/10/09/world/cia-torture-guantanamo-bay.html.

Aquilino, W. S. (2006). Family relationships and support systems in emerging adulthood. In J. J. Arnett & J. L. Tanner (Eds.), *Emerging adults in America: Coming of age in the 21st century*. Washington, DC: American Psychological Association.

Arcelus, J., Mitchell, A. J., Wales, J., & Nielsen, S. (2011). Mortality rates in patients with anorexia nervosa and other eating disorders: A meta-analysis of 36 studies. *Archives of General Psychiatry, 68*, 724–731. doi:10.1001/archgenpsychiatry.2011.74.

Arcelus, J., Whight, D., Langham, C., Baggott, J., McGrain, L., Meadows, L., & Meyer, C. (2009). A case series evaluation of the modified version of interpersonal psychotherapy (IPT) for the treatment of bulimic eating disorders: A pilot study. *European Eating Disorders Review, 17*(4), 260–268. doi:10.1002/(ISSN)1099-096810.1002/erv.v17:410.1002/erv.932.

Archer, J. (1996). Sex differences in social behavior: Are the social role and evolutionary explanations compatible? *American Psychologist, 51*, 909–917.

Archer, J. (2005). Are women or men the more aggressive sex? In S. Fein, G. R. Goethals, & M. J. Sansdtrom (Eds.), *Gender and aggression: Interdisciplinary perspectives*. Mahwah, NJ: Erlbaum.

Arden, R., Bensky, M. K., & Adams, M. J. (2016). A review of cognitive abilities in dogs, 1911 through 2016. *Current Directions in Psychological Science, 25*, 307–312.

Arden, R., Gottfredson, L. S., & Miller, G. (2009). Does a fitness factor contribute to the association between intelligence and health outcomes? Evidence from medical abnormality counts among 3654 U.S. veterans. *Intelligence, 37*(6), 581–591.

Arendt, J. (2009). Managing jet lag: Some of the problems and possible new solutions. *Sleep Medicine Reviews, 13*(4), 249–256.

Arendt, J. (2010). Shift work: Coping with the biological clock. *Occupational Medicine, 60*(1), 10–20.

Arendt, J., & Skene, D. J. (2005). Melatonin as a chronobiotic. *Sleep Medicine Review, 9*(1), 25–39.

Argyle, M. (1987). *The psychology of happiness*. London, UK: Metheun.

Argyle, M. (1999). Causes and correlates of happiness. In D. Kahneman, E. Diener & N. Schwarz (Eds.), *Well-being: The foundations of hedonic psychology*. New York, NY: Russell Sage Foundation.

Argyle, M. (2001). *The psychology of happiness*. New York, NY: Routledge.

Ariely, D. (2008). *Predictably irrational*. New York, NY: HarperCollins.

Ariely, D., & Norton, M. I. (2010). From thinking too little to thinking too much: A continuum of decision making. *Wiley Interdisciplinary Reviews: Cognitive Science, 2*(1), 39–46.

Arkes, H. R. (2013). The consequences of the hindsight bias in medical decision making. *Current Directions in Psychological Science, 22*, 356–360. doi:10.1177/0963721413489988.

Arkes, H. R. (2016). A levels of processing interpretation of dual-system theories of judgment and decision making. *Theory and Research, 26*, 459–475.

Arkes, H. R., Wortmann, R. L., Saville, P. D., & Harkness, A. R. (1981). Hindsight bias among physicians weighing the likelihood of diagnoses. *Journal of Applied Psychology, 66*, 252–254.

Arkowitz, H., & Lilienfeld, S. O. (2007). The best-medicine? How drugs stack up against talk therapy for the treatment of depression. *Scientific American Mind, 18*(5), 80–83.

Armbruster, B. B. (2000). Taking notes from lectures. In R. F. Flippo & D. C. Caverly (Eds.), *Handbook of college reading and study strategy research*. Mahwah, NJ: Erlbaum.

Armony, J. L. (2013). Current emotion research in behavioral neuroscience: The role(s) of the amygdala. *Emotion Review, 5*(1), 104–115. doi:10.1177/1754073912457208.

Arnett, J. J. (2000). Emerging adulthood: A theory of development from the late teens through the twenties. *American Psychologist, 55*, 469–480.

Arnett, J. J. (2004). *Emerging adulthood: The winding road from the late teens through the twenties*. New York, NY: Oxford University Press.

Arnett, J. J. (2006). Emerging adulthood: Understanding the new way of coming of age. In J. J. Arnett & J. L. Tanner (Eds.), *Emerging adults in America: Coming of age in the 21st century* (p. 11). Washington, DC: American Psychological Association.

Arnett, J. J. (2007). Suffering, selfish, slackers? Myths and reality about emerging adults. *Journal of Youth and Adolescence, 36*, 23–29.

Arnett, J. J. (2008). The neglected 95%: Why American psychology needs to become less American. *American Psychologist, 63*(7), 602–614.

Arnold, D. H. Williams, J. D., Phipps, N. E., & Goodale, M. A. (2016). Sharpening vision by adapting to flicker. *Proceedings of the National Academy of Sciences, 113*(44),12556–12561.

Arnold, L. M. (2000). Psychocutaneous disorders. In B. J. Sadock & V. A. Sadock (Eds.), *Kaplan and Sadock's comprehensive textbook of psychiatry* (7th ed., pp. 1818–1827). Philadelphia, PA: Lippincott, Williams & Wilkins.

Aronson, E. (2000). *Nobody left to hate: Teaching compassion after Columbine*. New York, NY: W. H. Freeman.

Aronson, E. (2010). *Not by chance alone: My life as a social psychologist*. New York, NY: Basic Books.

Aronson, E. (2012). *The social animal*. New York, NY: Guilford Press.

Aronson, E., Blaney, N. T., Stephan, C., Rosenfield, R., & Sikes, J. (1977). Interdependence in the classroom: A field study. *Journal of Educational Psychology, 69*, 121–128.

Aronson, E., & Bridgeman, D. (1979). Jigsaw groups and the desegregated classroom: In pursuit of common goals. *Personality and Social Psychology Bulletin, 5*, 438–446.

Aronson, E., & Mills, J. (1959). The effect of severity of initiation on liking for a group. *Journal of Abnormal and Social Psychology, 59*, 177–181.

Asarnow, J. R., & Miranda, J. (2014). Improving care for depression and suicide risk in adolescents: Innovative strategies for bringing treatments to community settings. *Annual Review of Clinical Psychology, 10*, 275–303.

Asbridge, M., Hayden, J. A., & Cartwright, J. L. (2012). Acute cannabis consumption and motor vehicle collision risk: Systematic review of observational studies and meta-analysis. *British Medical Journal, 344*, e536. doi:10.1136/bmj.e536.

Asbury, K., & Plomin, R. (2014). *G is for genes: The impact of genetics on education and achievement*. Malden, MA: Wiley-Blackwell.

Asch, S. (1946). Forming impressions on personality. *Journal of Abnormal and Social Psychology, 41*, 258–290.

Asch, S. (1951). Effects of group pressure upon the modification and distortion of judgments. In H. Guetzkow (Ed.), *Groups, leadership and men: Research in human relations* (pp. 177–190). Oxford, UK: Carnegie Press.

Asch, S. E. (1955). Opinions and social pressures. *Scientific American, 193*(5), 31–35.

Asch, S. E. (1956). Studies of independence and conformity: A minority of one against a unanimous majority. *Psychological Monographs, 70*(9, Whole No. 416).

Asendorpf, J. B., Penke, L., & Back, M. D. (2011). From dating to mating and relating: Predictors of initial and long-term outcomes of speed-dating in a community sample. *European Journal of Personality, 25*, 16–30. doi:10.1002/per.768.

Aserinsky, E., & Kleitman, N. (1953). Regularly occurring periods of eye mobility and concomitant phenomena during sleep. *Science, 118*, 273–274.

Asmundson, G. G., Taylor, S., & Smits, J. J. (2014). Panic disorder and agoraphobia: An overview and commentary on DSM-5 changes. *Depression and Anxiety, 31*(6), 480–486. doi:10.1002/da.22277.

Asmundson, G. J. G., & Katz, J. (2009). Understanding the co-occurrence of anxiety disorders and chronic pain: State of the art. *Depression and Anxiety, 26*, 889–901.

Assaad, J. M., Pihl, R. O., Seguin, J., Nagin, D., Vitaro, F., & Tremblay, R. (2006). Heart rate response to alcohol and intoxicated aggressive behavior. *Alcoholism: Clinical and Experimental Research, 30*, 774–792.

Assefi, S. L., & Garry, M. (2003). Absolut® memory distortions: Alcohol placebos influence the misinformation effect. *Psychological Science, 14*(1), 77–80.

Assefi, S., & Garry, M. (2003). Thinking yourself tipsy. *Psychological Science, 14*, 77–80.

Associate Press. (2010). Surgeon General: 1 Cigarette could kill you. Associated Press, December 9, 2010. Retrieved May 2, 2011, from http://www.foxnews.com/health/2010/12/09/surgeon-general-cigarette-puff-kill/.

Astuti, R., & Bloch, M. (2010). Why a theory of human nature cannot be based on the distinction between universality and variability: Lessons from anthropology. *Behavioral and Brain Sciences, 33*, 83–84.

Atkinson, J. W. (1974). The mainsprings of achievement- oriented activity. In J. W. Atkinson & J. O. Raynor (Eds.), *Motivation and achievement*. New York, NY: Wiley.

Atkinson, J. W. (1981). Studying personality in the context of an advanced motivational psychology. *American Psychologist, 36*, 117–128.

Atkinson, J. W. (1992). Motivational determinants of thematic apperception. In C. P. Smith (Ed.), *Motivation and personality: Handbook of thematic content analysis*. New York, NY: Cambridge University Press.

Atkinson, J. W., & Birch, D. (1978). *Introduction to motivation*. New York, NY: Van Nostrand.

Atkinson, R. C., & Shiffrin, R. M. (1968). Human memory: A proposed system and its control processes. In K. W. Spence & J. T. Spence (Eds.), *The psychology of learning and motivation* (Vol. 2). New York, NY: Academic Press.

Atkinson, R. C., & Shiffrin, R. M. (1971). The control of short-term memory. *Scientific American, 225*, 82–90.

AUCC. (2010). *Trends in Higher Education, Volume 1: Enrolment*. Retrieved from https://www.univcan.ca/wp-content/uploads/2015/11/trends-vol1-enrolment-june-2011.pdf.

Augedal, A. W., Hansen, K. S., Kronhaug, C. R., Harvey, A. G., & Pallesen, S. (2013). Randomized controlled trials of psychological and pharmacological treatments for nightmares: A meta-analysis. *Sleep Medicine Reviews, 17*, 143–152.

Aust, S., Stasch, J., Jentschke, S., Härtwig, E. A., Koelsch, S., Heuser, I., & Bajbouj, M. (2014). Differential effects of early life stress on hippocampus and amygdala volume as a function of emotional abilities. *Hippocampus, 24*, 1094–1101. doi:10.1002/hipo.22293.

Averill, J. A. (1980). A constructivist view of emotion. In R. Plutchik & H. Kellerman (Eds.), *Emotion: Theory, research, and experience (Vol. 1): Theories of emotion.* New York, NY: Academic Press.

Axel, R. (1995, April). The molecular logic of smell. *Scientific American, 273*, 154–159.

Ayanian, J. Z., & Cleary, P. D. (1999). Perceived risks of heart disease and cancer among cigarette smokers. *JAMA, 281*, 1019–1021.

Ayotte, B. J., Margrett, J. A., & Hicks-Patrick, J. (2010). Physical activity in middle-aged and young-old adults: The roles of self-efficacy, barriers, outcome expectancies, self-regulatory behaviors and social support. *Journal of Health Psychology, 15*(2), 173–185. doi:10.1177/1359105309342283.

Azevedo, F. C., Carvalho, L. B., Grinberg, L. T., Farfel, J. M., Ferretti, R. L., Leite, R. P., . . . Herculano-Houzel, S. (2009). Equal numbers of neuronal and nonneuronal cells make the human brain an isometrically scaled-up primate brain. *The Journal of Comparative Neurology, 513*, 532–541. doi:10.1002/cne.21974.

Baars, B. J. (1986). *The cognitive revolution in psychology.* New York, NY: Guilford.

Baas, M., Carsten, D. D., & Nijstad, B. (2008). A meta-analysis of 25 years of mood creativity research: Hedonic tone, activation, or regulatory focus. *Psychological Bulletin, 134*, 779–806.

Babiak, P., & Hare, R. D. (2006). *Snakes in suits: When psychopaths go to work.* New York, NY: Regan Books/Harper Collins Publishers.

Backhaus, A., Agha, Z., Maglione, M. L., Repp, A., Ross, B., Zuest, D., . . . Thorp, S. R. (2012). Videoconferencing psychotherapy: A systematic review. *Psychological Services, 9*(2), 111–131. doi:10.1037/a0027924.

Baddeley, A. (2012). Working memory: Theories, models, and controversies. *Annual Review of Psychology, 63*, 1–29.

Baddeley, A. D. (1986). *Working memory.* New York, NY: Oxford University Press.

Baddeley, A. D. (1989). The uses of working memory. In P. R. Soloman, G. R. Goethals, C. M. Kelley, & B. R. Stephens (Eds.), *Memory: Interdisciplinary approaches.* New York, NY: Springer-Verlag.

Baddeley, A. D. (1992). Working memory. *Science, 255*, 556–559.

Baddeley, A. D. (2001). Is working memory still working? *American Psychologist, 56*, 851–864.

Baddeley, A. D. (2003). Working memory: Looking back and looking forward. *Nature Reviews Neuroscience, 4*, 829–839.

Baddeley, A. D., & Hitch, G. (1974). Working memory. In G. H. Bower (Ed.), *The psychology of learning and motivation (Vol. 8).* New York, NY: Academic Press.

Baddeley, J. L., Pennebaker, J. W., & Beevers, C. G. (2013). Everyday social behavior during a major depressive episode. *Social Psychology and Personality Science, 4*(4), 445–452. doi:10.1177/1948550612461654.

Bae, G. Y., & Flombaum, J. I. (2013). Two items remembered as precisely as one: How integral features can improve working memory. *Psychological Science, 24*(10), 2038–2047.

Baer, R. A., Carmody, J., & Hunsinger, M. (2012). Weekly change in mindfulness and perceived stress in a mindfulness-based stress reduction program. *Journal of Clinical Psychology, 68*(7), 755–765.

Bahrick, H. P. (2000). Long-term maintenance of knowledge. In E. Tulving & F. I. M. Craik (Eds.), *The Oxford handbook of memory* (pp. 347–362). New York, NY: Oxford University Press.

Bailey, C. H., & Kandel, E. R. (2009). Synaptic and cellular basis of learning. In G. G. Berntson & J. T. Cacioppo (Eds.), *Handbook of neuroscience for the behavioral sciences* (Vol. 1, pp. 528–551). Hoboken, NJ: Wiley.

Bailey, J. M., & Pillard, R. C. (1991). A genetic study of male homosexual orientation. *Archives of General Psychology, 48*, 1089–1097.

Bailey, J. M., Pillard, R. C., Neale, M. C. I., & Agyei, Y. (1993). Heritable factors influence sexual orientation in women. *Archives of General Psychiatry, 50*, 217–223.

Baillargeon, J., Binswanger, I. A., Penn, J. V., Williams, B. A., & Murray, O. J. (2009). Psychiatric disorders and repeat incarcerations: The revolving prison door. *The American Journal of Psychiatry, 166*(1), 103–109.

Baillargeon, R. (2002). The acquisition of physical knowledge in infancy: A summary in eight lessons. In U. Goswami (Ed.), *Blackwell handbook of childhood cognitive development.* Malden, MA: Blackwell.

Baillargeon, R. (2004). Infants' physical world. *Current Directions in Psychological Science, 13*(3), 89–94.

Baillargeon, R. (2008). Innate ideas revisited: For a principle of persistence in infants' physical reasoning. *Perspectives on Psychological Science, 3*(1), 2–13.

Bains, J. S., & Oliet, S. H. R. (2007). Glia: They make your memories stick! *Trends in Neuroscience, 30*, 417–424.

Baird, A. D., Scheffer, I. E., & Wilson, S. J. (2011). Mirror neuron system involvement in empathy: A critical look at the evidence. *Social Neuroscience, 6*, 327–335. doi:10.1080/174709 19.2010.547085.

Baird, B., Smallwood, J., Mrazek, M. D., Kam, J. Y., Franklin, M. S., & Schooler, J. W. (2012). Inspired by distraction: Mind wandering facilitates creative incubation. *Psychological Science, 23*, 1117–1122. doi:10.1177/0956797612446024.

Bakan, P. (1971, August). The eyes have it. *Psychology Today*, pp. 64–69.

Baker, C. I. (2013). Visual processing in the primate brain. In R. J. Nelson, S. J. Y. Mizumori, & I. B. Weiner (Eds.), *Handbook of psychology: Vol. 3. Behavioral neuroscience* (2nd ed.). New York, NY: Wiley.

Baker, G. J., Suchday, S., & Krantz, D. S. (2007). Heart disease/attack. In G. Fink (Ed.), *Encyclopedia of stress.* San Diego, CA: Elsevier.

Balas, R., & Sweklej, J. (2013). Changing prejudice with evaluative conditioning. *Polish Psychological Bulletin, 44*, 379–383. doi:10.2478/ppb-2013-0041.

Balcetis, E., & Dunning, D. (2010). Wishful seeing: More desired objects are seen as closer. *Psychological Science, 21*(1), 147–152.

Baldwin, E. (1993). The case for animal research in psychology. *Journal of Social Issues, 49*(1), 121–131.

Baldwin, W. (2000). Information no one else knows: The value of self-report. In A. A. Stone, J. S. Turkkan, C. A. Bachrach, J. B. Jobe, H. S. Kurtzman, & V. Cain (Eds.), *The science of self-report: Implications for research and practice.* Mahwah, NJ: Erlbaum.

Bale, T. L., Baram, T. Z., Brown, A. S., Goldstein, J. M., Insel, T. R., McCarthy, M. M., et al. (2010). Early life programming and neurodevelopmental disorders. *Biological Psychiatry, 68*(4), 314–319.

Ball, J. S., & Links, P. S. (2009). Borderline personality disorder and childhood trauma: Evidence for a causal relationship. *Current Psychiatry Reports, 11*(1), 63–68. doi:10.1007/s11920-009-0010-4.

Balsam, P. D. (1988). Selection, representation, and equivalence of controlling stimuli. In R. C. Atkinson, R. J. Herrnstein, G. Lindzey, & R. D. Luce (Eds.), *Stevens' handbook of experimental psychology.* New York, NY: Wiley.

Balter, M. (2010). Did working memory spark creative culture? *Science, 328*(5975), 160–163. doi:10.1126/science.328.5975.160.

Bamidis, P., Vivas, A., Styliadis, C., Frantzidis, C., Klados, M., Schlee, W., . . . Papageorgiou, S. (2014). A review of physical and cognitive interventions in aging. *Neuroscience and Biobehavioral* Reviews, 44, 206–220. doi:10.1016/j.neubiorev.2014.03.019.

Banaji, M. R., & Heiphetz, L. (2010). Attitudes. In S. T. Fiske, D. T. Gilbert, & G. Lindzey (Eds.), *Handbook of social psychology* (Vol. 1, 5th ed., pp. 353–393). Hoboken, NJ: Wiley.

Bandura, A. (1965). Influence of model's reinforcement contingencies on the acquisition of imitated responses. *Journal of Personality and Social Psychology, 1*, 589–595.

Bandura, A. (1977). *Social learning theory.* Englewood Cliffs, NJ: Prentice-Hall.

Bandura, A. (1986). *Social foundations of thought and action: A social-cognitive theory.* Englewood Cliffs, NJ: Prentice-Hall.

Bandura, A. (1990). Perceived self-efficacy in the exercise of personal agency. *Journal of Applied Sport Psychology, 2*(2), 128–163.

Bandura, A. (1993). Perceived self-efficacy in cognitive development and functioning. *Educational Psychologist, 28*(2), 117–148.

Bandura, A. (1995). Exercise of personal and collective efficacy in changing societies. In A. Bandura (Ed.), *Self-efficacy in changing societies.* New York, NY: Cambridge University Press.

Bandura, A. (1999). Social cognitive theory of personality. In L. A. Pervin & O. P. John (Eds.), *Handbook of personality: Theory and research.* New York, NY: Guilford Press.

Bandura, A. (2006). Toward a psychology of human agency. *Perspectives on Psychological Science, 1*, 164–180.

Bandura, A. (2012). Social cognitive theory. In P. A. Van Lange, A. W. Kruglanski, & E. T. Higgins (Eds.), *Handbook of theories of social psychology* (Vol. 1). Los Angeles, CA: SAGE.

Bandura, A., Ross, D., & Ross, S. A. (1961). Transmission of aggression through imitation of aggressive models. *Journal of Abnormal and Social Psychology, 63*, 575–582.

Bandura, A., Ross, D., & Ross, S. A. (1963). Imitation of film-mediated aggressive models. *Journal of Abnormal and Social Psychology, 66*, 3–11.

Bandura, A., & Walters, R. H. (1959). *Adolescent aggression: A study of the influence of child-training practices and family interrelationships.* New York, NY: The Ronald Press Company.

Bandura, A., & Walters, R. H. (1963). *Social learning and personality development.* New York, NY: Holt, Rinehart & Winston, Inc.

Banks, S., & Dinges, D. F. (2011). Chronic sleep deprivation. In M. H. Kryger, T. Roth, & W. C. Dement (Eds.), *Principles and practice of sleep medicine* (5th ed.). Saint Louis, MO: Elsevier Saunders.

Banks, S. J., Feindel, W., Milner, B., & Jones-Gotman M. (2016). Cognitive function fifty-six years after surgical treatment of temporal lobe epilepsy: A case study. *Epilepsy & Behavior Case Reports, 2*, 31–36.

Banks, W. P., & Krajicek, D. (1991). Perception. *Annual Review of Psychology, 42*, 305–331.

Banuazizi, A., & Movahedi, S. (1975). Interpersonal dynamics in a simulated prison: A methodological analysis. *American Psychologist, 30*, 152–160.

Banyard, V. L., & Williams, L. M. (1999). Memories for child sexual abuse and mental health functioning: Findings on a sample of women and implications for future research. In L. M. Williams & V. L. Banyard (Eds.), *Trauma & memory.* Thousand Oaks, CA: SAGE.

Barabasz, A. F., & Barabasz, M. (2015). The new APA definition of hypnosis: Spontaneous hypnosis MIA. *American Journal of Clinical Hypnosis, 57*, 459–463.

Barba, G. D., Parlato, V., Jobert, A., Samson, Y., & Pappata, S. (1998). Cortical networks implicated in semantic and episodic memory: Common or unique. *Cortex, 34*, 547–561.

Barber, B. K. (1994). Cultural, family, and personal contexts of parent–adolescent conflict. *Journal of Marriage and the Family, 56*, 375–386.

Barber, J. P., Muran, C., McCarthy, K. S., & Keefe, J. R. (2013). Research on dynamic therapies. In M. J. Lambert (Ed.). *Bergin and Garfield's handbook of psychotherapy and behavior change* (6th ed.). New York, NY: Wiley.

Barber, L., Munz, D., Bagsby, P., & Powell, E. (2010). Sleep consistency and sufficiency: Are both necessary for less psychological strain? *Stress & Health: Journal of the International Society for the Investigation of Stress, 26*(3), 186–193.

Barber, T. X. (1979). Suggested ("hypnotic") behavior: The trance paradigm versus an alternative paradigm. In E. Fromm & R. E. Shor (Eds.), *Hypnosis: Developments in research and new perspectives*. New York, NY: Aldine.

Bard, P. (1934). On emotional experience after decortication with some remarks on theoretical views. *Psychological Review, 41*, 309–329.

Bargh, J. A., Gollwitzer, P. M., & Oettingen, G. (2010). Motivation. In S. T. Fiske, D. T. Gilbert, & G. Lindzey (Eds.), *Handbook of social psychology* (5th ed., Vol. 1, pp. 268–316). New York, NY: Wiley.

Bargh, J. A., McKenna, K. Y. A., & Fitzsimons, G. M. (2002). Can you see the real me? Activation and expression of the "true self" on the Internet. *Journal of Social Issues, 58*, 33–48.

Bargh, J. A., & Morsella, E. (2008). The unconscious mind. *Perspectives on Psychological Science, 3*, 73–79.

Barker, D. J. P. (2013). The developmental origins of chronic disease. In N. S. Landale, S. M. McHale, & A. Booth (Eds.), *Families and child health: National Symposium on family issues* (Vol. 3). New York, NY: Spring Science + Business Media. doi:10.1007/978-1-4614-6194-4_1.

Barlow, D. H., Pincus, D. B., Heinrichs, N., & Choate, M. L. (2003). Anxiety disorders. In G. Stricker & T. A. Widiger (Eds.), *Handbook of psychology (Vol. 8): Clinical psychology*. New York, NY: Wiley.

Barnes, S., Brown, K. W., Krusemark, E., Campbell, W. K., & Rogge, R. D. (2007). The role of mindfulness in romantic relationship satisfaction and responses to relationship stress. *Journal of Marital and Family Therapy, 33*(4), 482–500.

Barnes, V. A., Treiber, F., & Davis, H. (2001). The impact of Transcendental Meditation on cardiovascular function at rest and during acute stress in adolescents with high normal blood pressure. *Journal of Psychosomatic Research, 51*, 597–605.

Barnett, S. W. (2004). Does Head Start have lasting cognitive effects? The myth of fade-out. In E. Zigler & S. J. Styfco (Eds.), *The Head Start debates*. Baltimore, MD: Paul H. Brooks Publishing.

Barnhofer, T., Chittka, T., Nightingale, H., Visser, C., & Crane C. (2010). State effects of two forms of meditation on prefrontal EEG asymmetry in previously depressed individuals. *Mindfulness, 1*, 21–27.

Barnier, A. J., Cox, R. E., & McConkey, K. M. (2014). The province of "highs": The high hypnotizable person in the science of hypnosis and in psychological science. *Psychology of Consciousness: Theory, Research, and Practice, 1*, 168–183. doi:10.1037/cns0000018.

Bar-On, R., & Parker, J. D. A. (2000a). *Bar-On Emotional Quotient Inventory (Youth Version): Technical manual*. Toronto, ON: Multi-Health Systems.

Bar-On, R., & Parker, J. D. A. (2000b). *Handbook of emotional intelligence: Theory, development, assessment, and application at home, school, and in the workplace*. San Francisco, CA: Jossey-Bass.

Baron-Cohen, S. (1995). *Mindblindness: An essay on autism and theory of mind*. Cambridge, MA: MIT Press/Bradford Books.

Barraza, J., McCullough, M., & Zak, P. J. (2011). Oxytocin infusion increases charitable donations. *Hormones and Behavior, 60*, 148–151.

Barrett, D. (2011). Answers in your dreams. *Scientific American Mind, 22*(5), 26–32.

Barrett, L. F., Lindquist, K. A., & Gendron, M. (2007). Language as context for the perception of emotion. *Trends in Cognitive Science, 11*, 327–332.

Barrios-Miller, N. L., & Siefferman, L. (2013). Evidence that fathers, but not mothers, respond to mate and offspring coloration by favouring high-quality offspring. *Animal Behaviour, 85*(6), 1377–1383. doi:10.1016/j.anbehav.2013.03.029.

Bartlett, F. C. (1932). *Remembering: A study in experimental and social psychology*. New York, NY: Macmillan.

Bartlett, T. (2014). The search for psychology's lost boy. Retrieved from http://www.chronicle.com/interactives/littlealbert.

Bartol, C., & Bartol, A. M. (2015). *Introduction to forensic psychology: Research and applications*. Thousand Oaks, CA: SAGE.

Bartoshuk, L. M. (1993a). Genetic and pathological taste variation: What can we learn from animal models and human disease? In D. Chadwick, J. Marsh, & J. Goode (Eds.), *The molecular basis of smell and taste transduction*. New York, NY: Wiley.

Bartoshuk, L. M. (1993b). The biological basis of food perception and acceptance. *Food Quality and Preference, 4*, 21–32.

Bartoshuk, L. M., Duffy, V. B., & Miller, I. J. (1994). PTC/PROP taste: Anatomy, psychophysics, and sex effects. *Physiology & Behavior, 56*, 1165–1171.

Basbaum, A. I., & Jessell, T. M. (2000). The perception of pain. In E. R. Kandel, J. H. Schwartz, & T. M. Jessell (Eds.), *Principles of neural science*. New York, NY: McGraw-Hill.

Basow, S. A. (1992). *Gender: Stereotypes and roles*. Pacific Grove, CA: Brooks/Cole.

Bass, E. C., Stednitz, S. J., Simonson, K., Shen, T., & Gahtan, E. (2014). Physiological stress reactivity and empathy following social exclusion: A test of the defensive emotional analgesia hypothesis. *Social Neuroscience, 5*, 504–513.

Bassett, A. S., & Chow, E. W. C. (1999). 22q11 Deletion syndrome: A genetic subtype of schizophrenia. *Biological Psychiatry, 46*, 882–891.

Bassok, M. (2003). Analogical transfer in problem solving. In J. E. Davidson & R. J. Sternberg (Eds.), *The psychology of problem solving*. New York, NY: Cambridge University Press.

Bassok, M., & Novick, L. R. (2012). Problem solving. In K. J. Holyoak & G. Morrison (Eds.), *Oxford handbook of thinking and reasoning*. New York, NY: Oxford University Press.

Basson, M. D., Bartoshuk, L. M., Dichello, S. Z., Panzini, L., Weiffenbach, J. M., & Duffy, V. B. (2005). Association between 6-n-propylthiouracil (PROP) bitterness and colonic neoplasms. *Digestive Diseases Sciences, 50*, 483–489.

Bassuk, E. L., Buckner, J. C., Perloff, J. N., & Bassuk, S. S. (1998). Prevalence of mental health and substance use disorders among homeless and low-income housed mothers. *American Journal of Psychiatry, 155*, 1561–1564.

Bates, E. (1999). Plasticity, localization, and language development. In S. H. Broman & J. M. Fletcher (Eds.), *The changing nervous system: Neurobehavioral consequences of early brain disorders* (pp. 214–247). New York, NY: Oxford University Press.

Bates, E., & Carnevale, G. F. (1993). New directions in research on language development. *Developmental Review, 13*, 436–470.

Bates, E., Devescovi, A., & Wulfeck, B. (2001). Psycholinguistics: A cross-language perspective. *Annual Review of Psychology, 52*, 369–396.

Bates, M. S., Edwards, W. T., & Anderson, K. O. (1993). Ethnocultural influences on variation in chronic pain perception. *Pain, 52*(1), 101–112.

Bateson, P. (2011). Ethical debates about animal suffering and the use of animals in research. *Journal of Consciousness Studies, 18*(9–10), 186–208.

Batterham, P. J., Christensen, H., & Mackinnon, A. J. (2009). Fluid intelligence is independently associated with all-cause mortality over 17 years in an elderly community sample: An investigation of potential mechanisms. *Intelligence, 37*(6), 551–560.

Bauer, M. S. (2008). Mood disorders: Bipolar (manic-depressive) disorders. In A. J. Kay, J. A. Lieberman, M. B. First, & M. Maj (Eds.), *Psychiatry* (3rd ed.). New York, NY: Wiley-Blackwell.

Baughman, H. M., Jonason, P. K., Veselka, L., & Vernon, P. A. (2014). Four shades of sexual fantasies linked to the Dark Triad. *Personality and Individual Differences, 67*, 47–51.

Baumard, N., & Sperber, D. (2010). Weird people, yes, but also weird experiments. *Behavioral and Brain Sciences, 33*, 84–85.

Baumeister, R. F. (1989). The optimal margin of illusion. *Journal of Social and Clinical Psychology, 8*, 176–189.

Baumeister, R. F. (2000). Gender differences in erotic plasticity: The female sex drive as socially flexible and responsive. *Psychological Bulletin, 126*, 347–374.

Baumeister, R. F. (2004). Gender and erotic plasticity: Sociocultural influences on the sex drive. *Sexual and Relationship Therapy, 19*, 133–139.

Baumeister, R. F., Bratslavsky, E., Finkenauer, C., & Vohs, K. D. (2001a). Bad is stronger than good. *Review of General Psychology, 5*, 323–370.

Baumeister, R. F., Catanese, K. R., & Vohs, K. D. (2001). Is there a gender difference in strength of sex drive? Theoretical views, conceptual distinctions, and a review of relevent evidence. *Personality and Social Psychology Review, 5*(3), 242–273. doi:10.1207/S15327957PSPR0503_5.

Baumeister, R. F., & Leary, M. R. (1995). The need to belong: Desire for interpersonal attachments as a fundamental human motivation. *Psychological Bulletin, 117*, 497–529.

Baumeister, R. F., Masicampo, E. J., & Vohs, K. D. (2011). Do conscious thoughts cause behavior? *Annual Review of Psychology, 62*, 331–361.

Baumeister, R. F., & Twenge, J. M. (2002). Cultural suppression of female sexuality. *Review of General Psychology, 6*, 166–203.

Baumeister, R. F., & Vohs, K. D. (2001). Narcissism as addiction to esteem. *Psychological Inquiry, 12*(4), 206–210.

Baumeister, R. F., & Vohs, K. D. (2007). Self-regulation, ego depletion, and motivation. *Social and Personality Psychology Compass, 1*, 1–14.

Baumrind, D. (1964). Some thoughts on the ethics of reading Milgram's "Behavioral study of obedience." *American Psychologist, 19*, 421–423.

Baumrind, D. (1985). Research using intentional deception: Ethical issues revisited. *American Psychologist, 40*, 165–174.

Baylis, G. C., & Driver, J. (1995). One-sided edge assignment in vision: 1. Figure-ground segmentation and attention to objects. *Current Directions in Psychological Science, 4*, 140–146.

Beahrs, J. O. (1983). Co-consciousness: A common denominator in hypnosis, multiple personality and normalcy. *American Journal of Clinical Hypnosis, 26*(2), 100–113.

Beck, A. T. (1976). *Cognitive therapy and the emotional disorders*. New York, NY: International Universities Press.

Beck, A. T. (1987). Cognitive therapy. In J. K. Zeig (Ed.), *The evolution of psychotherapy*. New York, NY: Brunner/Mazel.

Beck, A. T. (1997). Cognitive therapy: Reflections. In J. K. Zeig (Ed.), *The evolution of psychotherapy: The third conference*. New York, NY: Brunner/Mazel.

Beck, A. T., & Haigh, E. A. P. (2014). Advances in cognitive theory and therapy: The generic cognitive model. *Annual Review of Clinical Psychology, 10*, 1–24.

Beck, A. T., & Weishaar, M. E. (2014). Cognitive therapy. In D. Wedding & R. J. Corsini (Eds.), *Current psychotherapies* (10th ed., 231–264). Belmont, CA: Brooks/Cole.

Beck, C. T., & Driscoll, J. W. (2006). *Postpartum mood and anxiety disorders: A clinician's guide*. Sudbury, MA: Jones and Bartlett Publishers.

Beck, H. P., Levinson, S., & Irons, G. (2009). Finding Little Albert: A journey to John B. Watson's infant laboratory. *American Psychologist, 64*(7), 605–614.

Beck, H. P., Levinson, S., & Irons, G. (2010). The evidence supports Douglas Merritte as Little Albert. *American Psychologist, 65*, 301–303.

Becker, A. E., & Fay, K. (2006). Sociocultural issues and eating disorders. In S. Wonderlich, J. Mitchell, M. de Zwaan, & H. Steiger (Eds.), *Annual review of eating disorders*. Oxon, UK: Radcliffe.

Becker, A. L. (2009, November 29). Science of memory: Researchers to study pieces of unique brain. *The Hartford Courant*. Retrieved from http://www.courant.com.

Becker, S., & Wojtowicz, J. M. (2007). A model of hip-pocampal neurogenesis in memory and mood disorders. *Trends in Cognitive Sciences, 11*(2), 70–76.

Becker-Blease, K. A., Turner, H. A., & Finkelhor, D. (2010). Disasters, victimization, and children's mental health. *Child Development, 81*, 1040–1052.

Beer, J. S., Shimamura, A. P., & Knight, R. T. (2004). Frontal lobe contributions to executive control of cognitive and social behavior. In M. S. Gazzaniga (Ed.), *The cognitive neurosciences*. Cambridge, MA: MIT Press.

Beetz, A., Uvnas-Moberg, K., Julius, H., & Kotschal, K. (2012). Psychosocial and psychophysiological effects of human-animal interactions: The possible role of oxytocin. *Frontiers of Psychology, 3*, 234–356.

Beetz, A. M. (2017). Theories and possible processes of action in animal assisted interventions. *Applied Developmental Science, 21*, 139–149.

Beidel, D. C., & Stipelman, B. (2007). Anxiety disorders. In M. Hersen, S. M. Turner, & D. C. Beidel (Eds.), *Adult psychopathology and diagnosis*. New York, NY: Wiley.

Beilin, H. (1992). Piaget's enduring contribution to developmental psychology. *Developmental Psychology, 28*, 191–204.

Bekelman, J. E., Li, Y., & Gross, C. P. (2003). Scope and impact of financial conflicts of interest in biomedical research. *Journal of the American Medical Association, 289*, 454–465.

Bekkouche, N. S., Holmes, S., Whittaker, K. S., & Krantz, D. S. (2011). Stress and the heart: Psychosocial stress and coronary heart disease. In R. J. Contrada & A. Baum (Eds.), *The handbook of stress science: Biology, psychology, and health* (pp. 111–121). New York, NY: Springer Publishing.

Beller, M., & Gafni, N. (1996). The 1991 international assessment of educational progress in mathematics and sciences: The gender differences perspective. *Journal of Educational Psychology, 88*, 365–377.

Belleville, G., Ouellet, M.-C., & Morin, C. M. (2017a). Post-traumatic stress among evacuees from the 2016 Fort McMurray wildfires. Poster presented at the 7th meeting of the Canadian Association for Cognitive and Behavioural Therapies, Ottawa, Canada.

Belleville, G., Ouellet, M.-C., & Morin, C. M. (2017b). Trauma-related insomnia among evacuees from the 2016 Fort McMurray wildfires. Poster presented at the 8th Conference of the Canadian Sleep Society, Calgary, Canada.

Belli, R. F., Winkielman, P., Read, J. D., Schwarz, N., & Lynn, S. J. (1998). Recalling more childhood events leads to judgments of poorer memory: Implications for the recovered/false memory debate. *Psychonomic Bulletin & Review, 5*, 318–323.

Bellis, M. A., Downing, J., & Ashton, J. R. (2006). Adults at 12? Trends in puberty and their public health consequences. *Journal of Epidemiology and Community Health, 60*, 910–911.

Belsky, J., Steinberg, L., & Draper, P. (1991). Childhood experience, interpersonal development, and reproductive strategy: An evolutionary theory of socialization. *Child Development, 62*, 647–670.

Bem, D. J. (1967). Self-perception: An alternative interpretation of cognitive dissonance phenomena. *Psychological Review, 74*, 183–200.

Bem, S. L. (1985). Androgyny and gender schema theory: A conceptual and empirical integration. In T. B. Sonderegger (Ed.), *Nebraska symposium on motivation, 1984: Psychology and gender* (Vol. 32). Lincoln, NE: University of Nebraska Press.

Benarroch, E. E. (2013). Adult neurogenesis in the dentate gyrus: General concepts and potential implications. *Neurology, 81*, 1443–1452. doi:10.1212/WNL.0b013e3182a9a156.

Bendall, S., Jackson, H. J., Hulbert, C. A., & McGorry, P. D. (2008). Childhood trauma and psychotic disorders: A systematic, critical review of the evidence. *Schizophrenia Bulletin, 34*, 568–579. doi:10.1093/schbul/sbm121.

Bender, D. S., Skodol, A. E., Dyck, I. Markowitz, J. C., Shea, M. T., Yen, . . . Grilo, C. M. (2007). Ethnicity and mental health treatment utilization by patients with personality disorders. *Journal of Consulting and Clinical Psychology, 75*, 992–999.

Benedetti, F. (2008). *Placebo effects: Understanding the mechanisms in health and disease*. New York, NY: Oxford University Press.

Benedetti, F. (2009). *Placebo effects: Understanding the mechanisms in health and disease*. New York, NY: Oxford University Press.

Benedetti, F. (2013). Placebo and the new physiology of the doctor-patient relationship. *Physiological Reviews, 93*(3), 1207–1246. doi:10.1152/physrev.00043.2012.

Benjafield, J. G. (2008). George Kelly: Cognitive psychologist, humanistic psychologist, or something else entirely? *History of Psychology, 11*, 239–262.

Benjamin, L. T., Jr. (2000). The psychology laboratory at the turn of the 20th century. *American Psychologist, 55*, 318–321.

Benjamin, L. T., Jr. (2003). Behavioral Science and the Nobel Prize. *American Psychologist, 58*, 731–741.

Benjamin, L. T., Jr. (2014). *A brief history of modern psychology* (2nd ed.). New York, NY: Wiley.

Benjamin, L. T., Jr., & Baker, D. B. (2004). *From seance to science: A history of the profession of psychology in America*. Belmont, CA: Wadsworth.

Benjamin, L. T., Jr., & Simpson, J. A. (2009). The power of the situation: The impact of Milgram's obedience studies on personality and social psychology. *American Psychologist, 64*, 12–19. doi:10.1037/a0014077.

Bennett, A. J. (2012). Animal research: The bigger picture and why we need psychologists to speak out. *Psychological Science Agenda, 26*(4). doi:10.1037/e553492012-010.

Ben-Porath, Y. S. (2013). Self-report inventories: Assessing personality and psychopathology. In J. R. Graham, J. A. Naglieri, & I. B. Weiner (Eds.), *Handbook of psychology: Vol. 10. Assessment psychology* (2nd ed.). Hoboken, NJ: Wiley.

Bensky, M., Gosling, S., & Sinn, D. (2013). The world from a dog's point of view: A review and synthesis of dog cognition Research. *Advances in the Study of Behavior, 45*, 209–245.

Benson, H. (1975). *The relaxation response*. New York, NY: Morrow.

Benson, H., & Klipper, M. Z. (1988). *The relaxation response*. New York, NY: Avon.

Bentall, R. P. (2009). *Doctoring the mind: Is our current treatment of mental illness really any good?* New York, NY: New York University Press.

Benton, D. (2004). Role of parents in the determination of the food preferences of children and the development of obesity. *International Journal of Obesity, 28*, 858–869.

Berenbaum, S. A., Martin, C. L., & Ruble, D. N. (2008). Gender development. In W. Damon & R. M. Lerner (Eds.), *Child and adolescent development: An advanced course* (pp. 647–681). New York, NY: Wiley.

Berenbaum, S. A., & Snyder, E. (1995). Early hormonal influences on childhood sex-typed activity and playmate preferences: Implications for the development of sexual orientation. *Developmental Psychology, 31*, 31–42.

Berent, I., Pan, H., Zhao, X., Epstein, J., Bennett, M. L., Deshpande, V., . . . Stern, E. (2014). Language universals engage Broca's area. *PloS One, 9*(4), e95155. doi:10.1371/journal. pone.009515.

Berg, V., Lummaa, V., Lahdenperä, M., Rotkirch, A., & Jokela, M. (2014). Personality and long-term reproductive success measured by the number of grandchildren. *Evolution and Human Behavior, 35*, 533–539. doi:10.1016/j.evolhumbehav.2014.07.006.

Berger, Z. (2013). *Talking to your doctor: A patient's guide to communication in the exam room and beyond*. Lanham, MD: Rowman & Littlefield Publishers.

Bergevin, T., Gupta, R., Derevensky, J., & Kaufman, F. (2006). Adolescent gambling: Understanding the role of stress and coping. *Journal of Gambling Studies, 22*, 195–208.

Berkowitz, L. (1989). Frustration-aggression hypothesis: Examination and reformulation. *Psychological Bulletin, 106*, 59–73.

Berkowitz, L. (1999). Evil is more than banal: Situationism and concept of evil. *Personality and Social Psychology Review, 3*, 246–253.

Berlin, B., & Kay, P. (1969). *Basic color terms: Their universality and evolution*. Berkeley, CA: University of California Press.

Berlin, L. J. (2012). Leveraging attachment research to revision infant/toddler care for poor families. In S. L. Odom, P. E. Pungello, & N. Gardner-Neblett (Eds.), *Infants, toddlers, and families in poverty: Research implications for early child care*. New York, NY: Guilford Press.

Berman, A. L. (2009). Depression and suicide. In I. H. Gotlib & C. L. Hammen (Eds.), *Handbook of depression* (2nd ed.). New York, NY: Guilford Press.

Bernier, R., & Gerdts, J. (2010). *Autism spectrum disorders*. Santa Barbara, CA: ABC-CLIO.

Bernstein, H. (2007). Maternal and perinatal infection-viral. In S. G. Gabbe, J. R. Niebyl, & J. L. Simpson (Eds.) *Obstetrics: Normal and problem pregnancies* (5th ed., pp. 1203–1232). Philadelphia, PA: Elsevier.

Bernstein, H. J., Beale, M. D., Burns, C., & Kellner, C. H. (1998). Patient attitudes about ECT after treatment. *Psychiatric Annuals*, 524–527.

Berridge, K. C. (2004). Motivation concepts in behavioral neuroscience. *Physiology and Behavior, 81*(2), 179–209.

Berry, J. W. (1984). Towards a universal psychology of cognitive competence. In P. S. Fry (Ed.), *Changing conceptions of intelligence and intellectual functioning* (pp. 35–61). Amsterdam: Elsevier Science Publishers.

Berry, J. W. (1994). Cross-cultural variations in intelligence. In R. J. Sternberg (Ed.), *Encyclopedia of human intelligence*. New York, NY: Macmillan.

Berry, J. W., Poortinga, Y., Segall, M., & Dasen, P. (1992). *Cross-cultural psychology*. New York, NY: Cambridge University Press.

Berscheid, E. (1988). Some comments on love's anatomy: Or, whatever happened to old-fashioned lust. In R. J. Sternberg & M. L. Barnes (Eds.), *The psychology of love*. New Haven, CT: Yale University Press.

Berscheid, E. (2006). Searching for the meaning of "love." In R. J. Sternberg & K. Weis (Eds.), *The new psychology of love*. New Haven, CT: Yale University Press.

Berscheid, E. (2016). The next one. In R. Sternberg, S. Fiske, D. J. Foss (Eds.), *Scientists making a difference* (pp. 379–382). New York, NY: Cambridge University Press.

Berscheid, E., & Walster, E. (1978). *Interpersonal attraction*. Reading, MA: Addison-Wesley.

Berthoud, H. (2012). Central regulation of hunger, satiety, and body weight. In K. D. Brownell, & M. S. Gold (Eds.), *Food and addiction: A comprehensive handbook*. New York, NY: Oxford University Press.

Bertram, L., & Tanzi, R. E. (2008). Thirty years of Alzheimer's disease genetics: The implications of systematic meta-analyses. *Nature Reviews Neuroscience, 9*(10), 768–778.

Bertrand, R. M., & Lachman, M. E. (2003). Personality development in adulthood and old age. In R. M. Lerner, M. A. Easterbrooks, & J. Mistry (Eds.), *Handbook of psychology, Vol. 6: Developmental psychology*. New York, NY: Wiley.

Besner, D., Risko, E. F., Stolz, J. A., White, D., Reynolds, M., O'Malley, S., & Robidoux, S. (2016). Varieties of attention: Their roles in visual word identification. *Current Directions in Psychological Science, 25*, 162–168.

Betensky, J. D., Contrada, R. J., & Glass, D. C. (2012). Psychosocial factors in cardiovascular disease: Emotional states, conditions, and attributes. In A. Baum, T. A. Revenson, & J. Singer (Eds.), *Handbook of health psychology* (2nd ed.). New York, NY: Psychology Press.

Bettelheim, B. (1967). *The empty fortress*. New York, NY: Free Press.

Beutler, L. E. (2002). The dodo bird is extinct. *Clinical Psychology: Science & Practice, 9*(1), 30–34.

Beutler, L. E., Bongar, B., & Shurkin, J. N. (1998). *Am I crazy, or is it my shrink?* New York, NY: Oxford University Press.

Beutler, L. E., Malik, M., Alimohamed, S., Harwood, T. M., Talebi, H., Noble, S., & Wong, E. (2004). Therapist variables. In M. J. Lambert (Ed.), *Bergin and Garfield's handbook of psychotherapy and behavior change*. New York, NY: Wiley.

Bhanpuri, N. H., Okamura, A. M., & Bastian, A. J. (2013). Predictive modeling by the cerebellum improves proprioception. *The Journal of Neuroscience, 33*, 14301–14306. doi:10.1523/JNEUROSCI.0784-13.2013.

Bhasin, T., & Schendel, D. (2007). Sociodemographic risk factors for autism in a U.S. metropolitan area. *Journal of Autism and Developmental Disorders, 37*, 667–677.

Bhatt, G., Tonks, R. G., & Berry, J. W. (2013). Culture in the history of psychology in Canada. *Canadian Psychology, 54*, 115–123.

Bi, G. Q., & Poo, M. -M. (2001). Synaptic modification by correlated activity: Hebb's postulate revisited. *Annual Review of Neuroscience, 24*, 139–166.

Bialystok, E. (1999). Cognitive complexity and attentional control in the bilingual mind. *Child Development, 70*, 636–644.

Bialystok, E. (2001). *Bilingualism in development: Language, literacy and cognition*. Cambridge, UK: Cambridge University Press.

Bialystok, E. (2007). Cognitive effects of bilingualism: How linguistic experience leads to cognitive change. *International Journal of Bilingual Education and Bilingualism, 10*, 210–223.

Bialystok, E. (2015). Bilingualism and the development of executive function: The role of attention. *Child Development Perspectives, 9*, 115–121.

Bialystok, E. (2017). The bilingual adaptation: How minds accommodate experience. *Psychological Bulletin, 143*, 233–262.

Bialystok, E., Abutalebi, J., Bak T. H., Burke, D. M., & Kroll, J. F. (2016). Aging in two languages: Implications for public health. *Ageing Research Reviews, 27*, 56–60.

Bialystok, E., & Craik, F. I. M. (2010). Cognitive and linguistic processing in the bilingual mind. *Current Directions in Psychological Science, 19*(1), 19–23.

Bialystok, E., Craik, F. I. M., & Freedman, M. (2007). Bilingualism as a protection against the onset of symptoms of dementia. *Neuropsychologia, 45*(2), 459–464.

Bialystok, E., Craik, F. I. M., Klein, R., & Viswanathan, M. (2004). Bilingualism, aging, and cognitive control: Evidence from the Simon task. *Cognition and Aging, 19*, 290–303.

Bianchi, M. T., Williams, K. L., McKinney, S., & Ellenbogen, J. M. (2013). The subjective-objective mismatch in sleep perception among those with insomnia and sleep apnea. *Journal of Sleep Research, 22*, 557–568. doi:10.1111/jsr.12046.

Bianchi, S. M., Sayer, L. C., Milkie, M. A., & Robinson, J. P. (2012). Housework: Who did, does or will do it, and how much does it matter? *Social Forces, 91*, 55–63. doi:10.1093/sf/sos120.

Biblarz, T. J., & Stacey, J. (2010). How does the gender of parents matter? *Journal of Marriage and Family, 72*(1), 3–22.

Biederman, I., Hilton, H. J., & Hummel, J. E. (1991). Pattern goodness and pattern recognition. In G. R. Lockhead & J. R. Pomerantz (Eds.), *The perception of structure*. Washington, DC: American Psychological Association.

Bielski, Z. (2013). How much screen time is too much. *The Globe and Mail*, Friday, August 23, p. L3.

Biermann, T., Estel, D., Sperling, W., Bleich, S., Kornhuber, J., & Reulbach, U. (2005). Influence of lunar phases on suicide: The end of a myth? A population-based study. *Chronobiology International, 22*, 1137–1143.

Biernat, & Danaher, K. (2013). Prejudice. In H. Tennen, J. Suls, & I. B. Weiner (Eds.), *Handbook of psychology: Vol. 5. Personality and social psychology* (2nd ed.). New York, NY: Wiley.

Bifulco, A. (2013). Psychosocial models and issues in major depression. In Power (Ed.), *The Wiley-Blackwell handbook of mood disorders* (2nd ed.). Malden, MA: Wiley-Blackwell.

Bigelow, B. J. (2006). There's an elephant in the room: The impact of early poverty and neglect on intelligence and common learning disorders in children, adolescents, and their parents. *Developmental Disabilities Bulletin, 34*(1–2), 177–215.

Bilali, M., McLeod, P., & Gobet, F. (2010). The mechanism of the Einstellung (set) effect: A pervasive source of cognitive bias. *Current Directions in Psychological Science, 19*(2), 111–115. doi:10.1177/0963721410363571.

Bilanovic, A., Irvine, J., Kovacs, A. H., Hill, A., Cameron, D., & Katz, J. (2013). Uncovering phantom shocks in cardiac patients with an implantable cardioverter defibrillator. *Pacing and Clinical Electrophysiology, 36*(6), 673–683.

Birch, L. L., & Fisher, J. A. (1996). The role of experience in the development of children's eating behavior. In E. D. Capaldi (Ed.), *Why we eat what we eat: The psychology of eating* (pp. 113–143). Washington, DC: American Psychological Association.

Birkeland, S. A., Manson, T. M., Kisamore, J. L., Brannick, M. T., & Smith, M. A. (2006). A meta-analytic investigation of job applicant faking on personality measures. *International Journal of Selection and Assessment, 14*, 317–335.

Birnbaum, M. H. (2004a). Base rates in Bayesian inference. In F. P. Rudiger (Ed.), *Cognitive illusions*. New York, NY: Psychology Press.

Birney, D. P., Citron-Pousty, J. H., Lutz, D. J., & Sternberg, R. J. (2005). The development of cognitive and intellectual abilities. In M. H. Bornstein & M. E. Lamb (Eds.), *Developmental science: An advanced textbook*. Mahwah, NJ: Erlbaum.

Birney, D. P., & Sternberg, R. J. (2011). The development of cognitive abilities. In M. H. Bornstein & M. E. Lamb (Eds.), *Developmental science: An advanced textbook* (pp. 353–388). New York, NY: Psychology Press.

Bishop, S. I., & Primeau, I. (2002). Through the long night: Stress and group dynamics in Antarctica. International Astronautical Congress (IAC) of the International Astronautical Federation (IAF), International Academy of Astronautics (IAA), and the International Institute of Space Law (HSL), Human Factors for Long Duration Spaceflight, World Space Congress. Houston, Texas, October, 2002.

Bjork, R. A. (1992). Interference and forgetting. In L. R. Squire (Ed.), *Encyclopedia of learning and memory*. New York, NY: Macmillan.

Bjorklund, D. F. (2012). *Children's thinking: Cognitive development and individual differences* (5th ed.). Belmont, CA: Wadsworth.

Black, D. W., & Grant, J. (2013). *DSM-5 guidebook: The essential companion to the diagnostic and statistical manual of mental disorders* (5th ed.). Arlington, VA: American Psychiatric Association Publishing.

Blagrove, M. (1992). Dreams as a reflection of our waking concerns and abilities: A critique of the problem-solving paradigm in dream research. *Dreaming, 2*, 205–220.

Blagrove, M. (1996). Problems with the cognitive psychological modeling of dreaming. *Journal of Mind and Behavior, 17*, 99–134.

Blair, I. V., Dasgupta, N., & Glaser, J. (2015). Implicit attitudes. In M. Mikulincer, P. R. Shaver, E. Borgida, & J. A. Bargh (Eds.), *APA handbook of personality and social psychology: Vol. 1. Attitudes and social cognition*. Washington, DC: American Psychological Association.

Blair, S. N., Kohl, H. W., Paffenbarger, R. S., Clark, D. G., Cooper, K. H., & Gibbons, L. W. (1989). Physical fitness and all-cause mortality: A prospective study of healthy men and women. *Journal of the American Medical Association, 262*, 2395–2401.

Blakemore, S-J., Mills, K. L. (2014). Is adolescence a sensitive period for sociocultural processing? *Annual Review of Psychology, 65*, 187–207.

Blankenhorn, D. (1995). *Fatherless America: Confronting our most urgent social problem*. New York, NY: Basic Books.

Blascovich, J., Wyer, N. A., Swart, L. A., & Kibler, J. L. (1997). Racisim and racial categorization. *Journal of Personality and Social Psychology, 72*, 1364–1372.

Blashfield, R. K., Keeley, J. W., Flanagan, E. H., & Miles, S. R. (2014). The cycle of classification: DSM-I through DSM-5. *Annual Review of Clinical Psychology, 10*, 25–51.

Blass, E. M. (2012). Phylogenic and ontogenetic contributions to today's obesity quagmire. In K. D. Brownell, & M. S. Gold (Eds.), *Food and addiction: A comprehensive handbook*. New York, NY: Oxford University Press.

Blass, E. M. (2012). Phylogenic and ontogenetic contributions to today's obesity quagmire. In K. D. Brownell, & M. S. Gold (Eds.), *Food and addiction: A comprehensive handbook*. New York, NY: Oxford University Press.

Blass, T. (1999). The Milgram Paradigm after 35 years: Some things we now know about obedience to authority. *Journal of Applied Social Psychology, 29*, 955–978.

Blass, T. (2009). From New Haven to Santa Clara: A historical perspective on the Milgram obedience experiments. *American Psychologist, 64*(1), 37–45. doi:10.1037/a0014434.

Blier, P., Ward, H. E., Trembly, P., Laberge, L., Herbert, C., & Bergeron, R. (2010). Combination of antidepressant medications from treatment initiation for major depressive disorder: A double-blind randomized study. *American Journal of Psychiatry, 167*(3), 281–288.

Bliwise, D. L. (2005). Normal aging. In M. H. Kryger, T. Roth, & W. C. Dement (Eds.), *Principles and practice of sleep medicine*. Philadelphia, PA: Elsevier Saunders.

Bliwise, D. L. (2011). Normal aging. In M. H. Kryger, T. Roth, & W. C. Dement (Eds.), *Principles and practice of sleep medicine* (5th ed.). Saint Louis, MO: Elsevier Saunders.

Block, J. (1981). Some enduring and consequential structures of personality. In A. I. Rabins, J. Aronoff, A. Barclay, & R. Zucker (Eds.), *Further explorations in personality*. New York, NY: Wiley.

Block, J. R., & Yuker, H. E. (1992). *Can you believe your eyes?: Over 250 illusions and other visual oddities*. New York, NY: Brunner/Mazel.

Block, N. (2002). How heritability misleads us about race. In Fish (Ed.), *Race and intelligence: Separating science from myth*. Mahwah: NJ: Earlbaum.

Boak, A., Hamilton, H. H., Adlaf, E. F., & Mann, R. E. (2015). Drug use among Ontario Students. CAMH Research Document Series No. 41. Retrieved from https://www.camh.ca/en/research/news_and_publications/ontario-student-drug-use-and-health-survey/Documents/2015%20OSDUHS%20Documents/2015OSDUHS_Detailed_DrugUseReport.pdf.

Boase, J., & Wellman, B. (2006). Personal relationships: On and off the Internet. In A. L. Vangelisti & D. Perlman (Eds.), *The Cambridge handbook of personal relationships*. New York, NY: Cambridge University Press.

Bobb, S. C., Wodniecka, Z., & Kroll, J. F. (2013). What bilinguals tell us about cognitive control: Overview to the special issue. *Journal of Cognitive Psychology, 25*(5), 493–496.

Bodenhausen, G. V., Todd, A. R., & Richeson, J. A. (2009). Controlling prejudice and stereotyping: Antecedents, mechanisms, and contexts. In T. D. Nelson (Ed.), *Handbook of prejudice, stereotyping, and discrimination* (pp. 1–22). New York, NY: Psychology Press.

Boecker, H., Sprenger, T., Spilker, M. E., Henriksen, G., Koppenhoefer, M., & Wagner, K. J., et al. (2008). The runner's high: Opioidergic mechanisms in the human brain. *Cerebral Cortex, 18*(11), 2523–2531.

Boekaerts, M., Pintrich, P. R., & Zeidner, M. (2000). *Handbook of self-regulation*. San Diego, CA: Academic Press.

Bögels, S. M., & Voncken, M. (2008). Social skills training versus cognitive therapy for social anxiety disorder characterized by fear of blushing, trembling, or sweating. *International Journal of Cognitive Therapy, 1*(2), 138–150.

Bohacek, J., Gapp, K., Saab, B. J., & Mansuy, I. M. (2013). Transgenerational epigenetic effects on brain functions. *Biological Psychiatry, 73*, 313–320. doi:10.1016/j.biopsych.2012.08.019.

Bohannon, J. N., III, & Bonvillian, J. D. (2009). Theoretical approaches to language acquisition. In J. B. Gleason & N. B. Ratner (Eds.), *The development of language*. Boston, MA: Pearson.

Bohner, G., & Schwarz, N. (2001). Attitudes, persuasion, and behavior. In A. Tesser & N. Schwarz (Eds.), *Blackwell handbook of social psychology: Intraindividual processes*. Malden, MA: Blackwell.

Boland, R. J., & Keller, M. B. (2008). Antidepressants. In A. Tasman, J. Kay, J. A. Lieberman, M. B. First, & M. Maj (Eds.), *Psychiatry* (3rd ed.). New York, NY: Wiley-Blackwell.

Boland, R. J., & Keller, M. B. (2009). Course and outcome of depression. In I. H. Gotlib & C. L. Hammen (Eds.), *Handbook of depression* (2nd ed., pp. 23–43). New York, NY: Guilford Press.

Boldero, J., Higgins, E. T., & Hulbert, C. A. (2015). Self-regulation and narcissistic grandiosity and vulnerability: Common and discriminant relations. *Personality and Individual Differences, 76*, 171–176.

Boldrini, M., Santiago, A. N., Hen, R., Dwork, A. J., Rosoklija, G. B., Tamir, H., . . . Mann, J. J. (2013). Hippocampal granule neuron number and denate gyrus volume in antidepressant-treated and untreated major depression. *Neuropsychopharmacology, 38*, 1068–1077. doi:10.1038/npp.2013.5.

Boldry, J. G., Gaertner, L., & Quinn, J. (2007). Measuring the measures: A meta-analytic investigation of the measures of outgroup homogeneity. *Group Processes & Intergroup Relations, 10*, 157–178.

Boles, D. B. (2005). A large-sample study of sex differences in functional cerebral lateralization. *Journal of Clinical and Experimental Neuropsychology, 27*(6), 759–768.

Bolles, R. C. (1975). *Theory of motivation*. New York, NY: Harper & Row.

Bolling, M. Y., Terry, C. M., & Kohlenberg, R. J. (2006). Behavioral theories. In J. C. Thomas & D. L. Segal (Eds.), *Comprehensive handbook of personality and psychopathology*. New York, NY: Wiley.

Boly, M., Faymonville, M.-E., Vogt, B. A., Maquet, P., & Laureys, S. (2007). Hypnotic regulation of consciousness and the pain neuromatrix. In G. A. Jamieson (Ed.), *Hypnosis and conscious states: The cognitive neuroscience perspective*. New York, NY: Oxford University Press.

Bonanno, G. A. (1998). The concept or "working through" loss: A critical evaluation of the cultural, historical, and empirical evidence. In A. Maercker, M. Schuetzwohl, & Z. Solomon (Eds.), *Posttraumatic stress disorder: Vulnerability and resilience in the lifespan*. Gottingen, Germany: Hogrefe and Huber.

Bonanno, G. A., & Burton, C. L. (2013). Regulatory flexibility: An individual differences perspective on coping and emotion regulation. *Perspectives on Psychological Science, 8*, 591–612. doi:10.1177/1745691613504116.

Bonanno, G. A., Wortman, C. B., Lehman, D. R., Tweed, R. G., Harrig, M., Sonnega, J., . . . Nesse, R. M. (2002). Resilience to loss and chronic grief: A prospective study from preloss to 18-months postloss. *Journal of Personality and Social Psychology, 83*, 1150–1164.

Bonanno, G. A., Wortman, C. B., & Nesse, R. M. (2004). Prospective patterns of resilience and maladjustment during widowhood. *Psychology and Aging, 19*, 260–271. doi:10.1037/0882-7974.19.2.260.

Bonanno, G., Westphal, M., & Mancini, A. D. (2012). Loss, trauma, and resilience in adulthood. In B. Hayslip, Jr., & G. C. Smith (Eds.), *Annual review of gerontology and geriatrics: Vol. 32. Emerging perspectives on resilience in adulthood and later life*. New York, NY: Springer Publishing Co.

Bond, R., & Smith, P. B. (1996). Culture and conformity: A meta-analysis of studies using Asch's line judgment task. *Psychological Bulletin, 119*, 111–137.

Bonnet, M. H. (2005). Acute sleep deprivation. In M. H. Kryger, T. Roth, & W. C. Dement (Eds.), *Principles and practice of sleep medicine*. Philadelphia, PA: Elsevier Saunders.

Boot, W. R., Simons, D. J., Stothart, C., & Stutts, C. (2013). The pervasive problems with placebos in psychology: Why active control groups are not sufficient to rule out placebo effects. *Perspective on Psychological Science, 8*(4), 445–454. doi:10.1177/1745691613491271.

Bootzin, R. R., Manber, R., Loewy, D. H., Kuo, T. F., & Franzen, P. L. (2001). Sleep disorders. In P. B. Sutker & H. E. Adams (Eds.), *Comprehensive handbook of psychopathology*. New York, NY: Kluwer Academic/Plenum.

Bordens, K. S., & Abbott, B. B. (2002). *Research design and methods: A process approach* (5th ed.). New York, NY: McGraw-Hill.

Bordnick, P. S., Elkins, R. L., Orr, T. E., Walters, P., & Thyer, B. A. (2004). Evaluating the relative effectiveness of three aversion therapies designed to reduce craving among cocaine abusers. *Behavioral Interventions, 19*(1), 1–24.

Borgida, E., & Nisbett, R. E. (1977). The differential impact of abstract vs. concrete information on decisions. *Journal of Applied Social Psychology, 7*, 258–271.

Boring, E. G. (1966). A note on the origin of the word psychology. *Journal of the History of the Behavioral Sciences, 2*, 167.

Borkenau, P., Mauer, N., Riemann, R., Spinath, F. M., & Angleitner, A. (2004). Thin slices of behavior as cues of personality and intelligence. *Journal of Personality and Social Psychology, 86*(4), 599–614.

Bornstein, M. H. (2014). Infancy. *Annual Review of Psychology, 65*, 121–158.

Bornstein, M. H., Jager, J., & Steinberg, L. D. (2013). Adolescents, parents, friends/peers: A relationships model. In R. M. Lerner, M. A. Easterbrooks, J. Mistry, & I. B. Weiner (Eds.), *Handbook of psychology: Vol. 6. Developmental psychology*. New York, NY: Wiley.

Bornstein, R. F. (2003). Psychodynamic models of personality. In T. Millon & M. J. Lerner (Eds.), *Handbook of psychology (Vol. 5): Personality and social psychology*. New York, NY: Wiley.

Boroditsky, L. (2001). Does language shape thought? Mandarin and English speakers' conceptions of time. *Cognitive Psychology, 43*(1), 1–22.

Boska, P., Joober, R., & Kirmayer, L. J. (2015). Mental wellness in Canada's aboriginal communities: Striving toward reconciliation. *Journal of Psychiatry and Neuroscience, 40*, 363–365.

Botha, U. A., Koen, L., Joska, J. A., Parker, J. S., Horn, N., Hering, L. M., & Oosthuizen, P. P. (2010). The revolving door phenomenon in psychiatry: Comparing low-frequency and high-frequency users of psychiatric inpatient services in a developing country. *Social Psychiatry and Psychiatric Epidemiology, 45*, 461–468. doi:10.1007/s00127-009-0085-6.

Bottom, W. P., & Kong, D. T. (2012). The casual cruelty of our prejudices: On Walter Lippmann's theory of stereotype and its obliteration in psychology and social science. *Journal of the History of the Behavioural Sciences, 48*, 363–394.

Bottoms, H. C., Eslick, A. N., & Marsh, E. J. (2010). Memory and the Moses illusion: Failures to detect contradictions with stored knowledge yield negative memorial consequences. *Memory, 18*(6), 670–678. doi:org/10.1080/09658211.2010.501558.

Bouchard, T. J., Jr. (1997). IQ similarity in twins reared apart: Findings and responses to critics. In R. J. Sternberg, & E. L. Grigorenko (Eds.), *Intelligence, heredity, and environment*. New York, NY: Cambridge University Press.

Bouchard, T. J., Jr. (1998). Genetic and environmental influences on adult intelligence and special mental abilities. *Human Biology, 70*, 257–279.

Bouchard, T. J., Jr. (2004). Genetic influence on human psychological traits: A survey. *Current Directions in Psychological Science, 13*(4), 148–151.

Bouchard, T. J., Jr., Lykken, D. T., McGue, M., Segal, N. L., & Tellegen, A. (1990). Sources of human psychological differences: The Minnesota study of twins reared apart. *Science, 250*, 223–228.

Boucher, J. (2009). *The autistic spectrum: Characterisitcs, causes, and practical issues*. Los Angeles, CA: SAGE.

Bourgeois, J. A., Seaman, J. S., & Servis, M. E. (2003). Delirium, dementia, and amnestic disorders. In R. E. Hales & S. C. Yudofsky (Eds.), *Textbook of clinical psychiatry*. Washington, DC: American Psychiatric Publishing.

Bourgeois, J. A., Seamen, J. S., & Servis, M. E. (2008). Delirium, dementia, and amnestic and other cognitive disorders. In R. E. Hales, S. C. Yudofsky, & G. O. Gabbard (Eds.), *The American Psychiatric Publishing textbook of psychiatry*, (5th ed., pp. 30–35). Washington, DC: American Psychiatric Publishing.

Bousfield, W. A. (1953). The occurrence of clustering in the recall of randomly arranged associates. *Journal of General Psychology, 49*, 229–240.

Bouton, M. E., & Todd, T. P. (2014). A fundamental role for context in instrumental learning and extinction. *Behavioural Processes, 104*, 13–19. doi:10.1016/j.beproc.2014.02.012.

Bouton, M. E., Todd, T. P., Vubric, D., & Winterbauer, N. E. (2011). Renewal after the extinction of free operant behavior. *Learning and Behavior, 39*, 57–67.

Bouton, M. E., & Woods, A. M. (2009). Extinction: Behavioral mechanisms and their implications. In J. H. Byrne (Ed.), *Concise learning and memory: The editor's selection*. San Diego, CA: Elsevier.

Bowd, A. D., & Shapiro, K. J. (1993). The case against laboratory animal research in psychology. *Journal of Social Issues, 49*(1), 133–142.

Bower, G. H. (1970). Organizational factors in memory. *Cognitive Psychology, 1*, 18–46.

Bower, G. H. (2000). A brief history of memory research. In E. Tulving & F. I. M. Craik (Eds.), *The Oxford handbook of memory* (pp. 3–32). New York, NY: Oxford University Press.

Bower, G. H., Clark, M. C., Lesgold, A. M., & Winzenz, D. (1969). Hierarchical retrieval schemes in recall of categorized word lists. *Journal of Verbal Learning and Verbal Behavior, 8*, 323–343.

Bower, G. H., & Springston, F. (1970). Pauses as recoding points in letter series. *Journal of Experimental Psychology, 83*, 421–430.

Bowlby, J. (1969). *Attachment and loss (Vol. 1): Attachment*. New York, NY: Basic Books.

Bowlby, J. (1973). *Attachment and loss (Vol. 2): Separation, anxiety and anger*. New York, NY: Basic Books.

Bowlby, J. (1980). *Attachment and loss (Vol. 3): Sadness and depression*. New York, NY: Basic Books.

Boyce, C. J., Brown, G. D. A., & Moore, S. C. (2010). Money and happiness: Rank of income, not income, affects life satisfaction. *Psychological Science, 21*, 471–475.

Boyce, J. (2016). *Victimization of aboriginal people in Canada, 2014*. Statistics Canada. Retrieved from https://www.statcan.gc.ca/pub/85-002-x/2016001/article/14631-eng.htm.

Boysen, G. A., & VanBergen, A. (2013). A review of published research on adult dissociative identity disorder: 2000– 2010. *Journal of Nervous and Mental Disease, 201*(1), 5–11. doi:10.1097/NMD.0b013e31827aaf81.

Bradely, M., & Lang, P. J. (1999). *Affective Norms for English World (ANEW): Instruction manual and affective ratings*. Technical report C-I, The Center for Research in Psychophysiology, University of Florida.

Bradshaw, J. (2013). Students reaching for ADHD drugs to deal with academic stress. *The Globe and Mail*, Friday, October 13. Retrieved from http://www.theglobeandmail.com/news/national/education/drugs-as-study-aid-a-growing-trend-on-campuses/article14945567/.

Bradshaw, J. L. (1989). *Hemispheric specialization and psychological function*. New York, NY: Wiley.

Brady, W. J., Wills, J. A., Jost, J. T., Tucker, J. A., & Van Bavel, J. (2017). Emotion shapes the diffusion of moralized content in social networks. *PNAS Proceedings of the National Academy of Sciences of the United States of America, 114*, 7313–7318.

Braff, D. L., Ryan, J., Rissling, A. J., & Carpenter, W. T. (2013). Lack of use in the literature from the last 20 years supports dropping traditional schizophrenia subtypes from DSM-5 and ICD-11. *Schizophrenia Bulletin, 39*, 751–753. doi:10.1093/schbul/sbt068.

Braginsky, D. D. (1985). Psychology: Handmaiden to society. In S. Koch & D. E. Leary (Eds.), *A century of psychology as science.* New York, NY: McGraw-Hill.

Branaman, T. F., & Gallagher, S. N. (2005). Polygraph testing in sex offender treatment: A review of limitations. *American Journal of Forensic Psychology, 23*(1), 45–64.

Brannon, L., Feist, J., & Updegraff, J. A. (2018). *Health psychology: An introduction to behavior and health* (9th ed.). New York, NY: Wadsworth Publishing Company.

Bransford, J. D., & Stein, B. S. (1993). *The IDEAL problem solver.* New York, NY: W. H. Freeman.

Branswell, H., & Hall, J. (2007, November 23). No time but the present. *Toronto Star*, A6.

Brase, G. L., Cosmides, L., & Tooby, J. (1998). Individuation, counting, and statistical inference: The role of frequency and whole-object representations in judgment under certainty. *Journal of Experimental Psychology: General, 127*, 3–21.

Braskie, M. N., & Thompson, P. M. (2013). Understanding cognitive deficits in Alzheimer's disease based on neuroimaging findings. *Trends in Cognitive Sciences, 17*, 510–516. doi:10.1016/j.tics.2013.08.007.

Brassington, G. S., Hekler, E. B., Cohen, Z., & King, A. C. (2012). Health-enhancing physical activity. In A. Baum, T. A. Revenson, & J. Singer (Eds.), *Handbook of health psychology* (2nd ed.). New York, NY: Psychology Press.

Braun, M., Lewin-Epstein, N., Stier, H., & Baumgärtner, M. K. (2008). Perceived equity in the gendered division of household labor. *Journal of Marriage and Family, 70*(5), 1145–1156.

Bravo, M. (2010). Context effects in perception. In E. B. Goldstein (Ed.), *Encyclopedia of perception.* Thousand Oaks, CA: SAGE.

Breger, L. (2009). *A dream of undying fame: How Freud betrayed his mentor and invented psychoanalysis.* New York, NY: Basic Books.

Breggin, P. R. (2008). *Medication madness: A psychiatrist exposes the dangers of mood-altering medications.* New York, NY: St. Martin's Press.

Brehm, J. W. (1966). *A theory of psychological reactance.* New York, NY: Academic Press.

Breland, K., & Breland, M. (1961). The misbehavior of organisms. *American Psychologist, 16*, 681–684.

Breland, K., & Breland, M. (1966). *Animal behavior.* New York, NY: Macmillan.

Bremner, A. J., Doherty, M. J., Caparaos, S., de Fockert, J., Linnell, K. J., et al. (2016). Effects of culture and the urban environment on the development of the Ebbinghaus illusion. *Child Development, 87*, 962–981.

Brenes, G. A., Ingram, C. W., & Danhauer, S. C. (2012). Telephone-delivered psychotherapy for late-life anxiety. *Psychological Services, 9*(2), 219–220. doi:10.1037/a0025950.

Breslau, N., Kilbey, M., & Andreski, P. (1991). Nicotine dependence, major depression, and anxiety in young adults. *Archives of General Psychiatry, 48*, 1069–1074.

Breslau, N., Kilbey, M. M., & Andreski, P. (1993). Nicotine dependence and major depression: New evidence from a prospective investigation. *Archives of General Psychiatry, 50*, 31–35.

Breslin, F. C., Zack, M., & McMain, S. (2002). An information-processing analysis of mindfulness: Implications for relapse prevention in the treatment of substance abuse. *Clinical Psychology: Science and Practice, 9*, 275–299.

Breslin, P. A. S. (2010). Taste, genetics of. In E. B. Goldstein (Ed.), *Encyclopedia of perception.* Thousand Oaks, CA: SAGE.

Breugelmans, S. M., Poortinga, Y. H., Ambadar, Z., Setiadi, B., Vaca, J. B., Widiyanto, P., et al. (2005).

Body sensations associated with emotions in Raramuri Indians, rural Javanese, and three student samples. *Emotion, 5*, 166–174.

Brewer, C. L. (1991). Perspectives on John B. Watson. In G. A. Kimble, M. Wertheimer, & C. White (Eds.), *Portraits of pioneers in psychology.* Hillside, NJ: Erlbaum.

Brewer, W. F. (2000). Bartlett, functionalism, and modern schema theories. *Journal of Mind and Behavior, 21*, 37–44.

Brewer, W. F., & Treyens, J. C. (1981). Role of schemata in memory for places. *Cognitive Psychology, 13*, 207–230.

Brewin, C. R. (2003). *Posttraumatic stress disorder: Malady or myth.* New Haven, CT: Yale University Press.

Brewin, C. R. (2007). Autobiographical memory for trauma: Update on four controversies. *Memory, 15*, 227–248.

Brewin, C. R. (2012). A theoretical framework for understanding recovered memory experiences. In R. F. Belli (Ed.), *True and false recovered memories: Toward a reconciliation of the debate.* New York, NY: Springer.

Brewster, P. W. H. , Mullin, C. R. , Dobrin, R. A., & Steeves, J. K. E. (2010). Sex differences in face processing are mediated by handedness and sexual orientation. *Laterality: Asymmetries of Body, Brain and Cognition, 13*, 51–70.

Bridge, J. A., & Barbe, R. P. (2004). Reducing hospital readmission in depression and schizophrenia: Current evidence. *Current Opinion in Psychiatry, 17*, 505–511.

Bridge, J. A., Iyengar, S., Salary, C. B., Barbe, R. P., Birmaher, B., Pincus, H. A., . . . Brent, D. A. (2007). Clinical response and risk for reported suicidal ideation and suicide attempts in pediatric antidepressant treatment: A meta-analysis of randomized controlled trials. *JAMA, 297*, 1683–1969.

Brien, S. E., Ronksley, P. E., Turner, B. J., Mukamal, K. J., & Ghali, W. A. (2011). Effect of alcohol consumption on biological markers associated with risk of coronary heart disease: Systematic review and meta-analysis of interventional studies. *British Medical Journal, 342*(7795), 480.

Briere, J., & Conte, J. R. (1993). Self-reported amnesia for abuse in adults molested as children. *Journal of Traumatic Stress, 6*(1), 21–31.

Briley, D. A., & Tucker-Drob, E. M. (2013). Explaining the increasing heritability of cognitive ability across development: A meta-analysis of longitudinal twin and adoption studies. *Psychological Science, 24*, 1704–1713. doi:10.1177/0956797613478618.

Briñol, P., & Petty, R. E. (2012). A history of attitudes and persuasion research. In A. W. Kruglanski & W. Stroebe (Eds.), *Handbook of the history of social psychology.* New York, NY: Psychology Press.

Briscoe, R. & Schwenkler, J. (2015). Conscious vision in action. *Cognitive Science, 39*, 1435–1465.

Brislin, R. (1993). *Understanding culture's influence on behavior.* Fort Worth: Harcourt Brace College Publishers.

Brislin, R. (2000). *Understanding culture's influence on behavior.* Belmont, CA: Wadsworth.

Broadbent, D. E. (1958). *Perception and communication.* New York, NY: Pergamon Press.

Brock, A. (2013). Introduction to the special issue on the history of psychology in Canada. *Canadian Psychology, 54*, 87–93.

Brock, A. C. (2006). Rediscovering the history of psychology: Interview with Kurt Danziger. *History of Psychology, 9*, 1–16.

Bröder, A. (1998). Deception can be acceptable. *American Psychologist, 53*, 805–806.

Brody, N. (2003). Jensen's genetic interpretation of racial differences in intelligence: Critical evaluation. In H. Nyborg (Ed.), *The scientific study of general intelligence: Tribute to Arthur R. Jensen.* Oxford, UK: Pergamon.

Brody, N. (2005). To g or not to g—that is the question. In O. Wilhelm & R. W. Engle (Eds.), *Handbook of understanding and measuring intelligence.* Thousand Oaks, CA: SAGE.

Brooker, A-S., & Hyman, I. (2010). Time use. Canadian Index of Well-being. Retrieved June 30, 2011, from http://www.ciw.ca/en/TheCanadianIndexOfWellbeing/DomainsOfWellbeing/TimeUse.aspx.

Broughton, R. (1994). Important underemphasized aspects of sleep onset. In R. D. Ogilvie & J. R. Harsh (Eds.), *Sleep onset: Normal and abnormal processes.* Washington, DC: American Psychological Association.

Broughton, R., Billings, R., Cartwright, R., Doucette, D., Edmeads, J., Edwardh, M., et al. (1994). Homicidal somnambulism: A case report. *Sleep, 17*, 253–264.

Brown, A. D., Kouri, N., & Hirst, W. (2012). Memory's malleability: its role in shaping collective memory and social identity. *Frontiers of Psychology, 3*, 257–268.

Brown, A. S. (2012a). Epidemiological studies of exposure to prenatal infection and risk of schizophrenia and autism. *Developmental Neurobiology, 72*, 1272–1276. doi:10.1002/dneu.22024.

Brown, A. S. (2012b). *The tip of the tongue state.* New York, NY: Psychology Press.

Brown, A. S., & Derkits, E. J. (2010). Prenatal infection and schizophrenia: A review of epidemiologic and translational studies. *American Journal of Psychiatry, 167*(3), 261–280.

Brown, M. (1974). Some determinants of persistence and initiation of achievement-related activities. In J. W. Atkinson & J. O. Raynor (Eds.), *Motivation and achievement.* Washington, DC: Halsted.

Brown, M. R., DeSouza, J. F., Goltz, H. C., Ford, K., Menon, R. S., Goodale, M. A., et al. (2004). Comparison of memory- and visually-guided saccades using event-related fMRI. *Journal of Neurophysiology, 91*, 873–889.

Brown, R. D., Goldstein, E., & Bjorklund, D. F. (2000). The history and zeitgeist of the repressed–false-memory debate: Scientific and sociological perspectives on suggestibility and childhood memory. In D. F. Bjorklund (Ed.), *False-memory creation in children and adults* (pp. 1–30). Mahwah, NJ: Erlbaum.

Brown, R., & Kulik, J. (1977). Flashbulb memories. *Cognition, 5*, 73–79.

Brown, R., & McNeill, D. (1966). The "tip-of-the-tongue" phenomenon. *Journal of Verbal Learning and Verbal Behavior, 5*(4), 325–337.

Brown, R. T. (1989). Creativity: What are we to measure? In J. A. Glover, R. R. Ronning, & C. R. Reynolds (Eds.), *Handbook of creativity.* New York, NY: Plenum.

Brown, S. C., & Craik, F. I. M. (2000). Encoding and retrieval of information. In E. Tulving & F. I. M. Craik (Eds.), *The Oxford handbook of memory* (pp. 93–108). New York, NY: Oxford University Press.

Brownell, H. H., & Gardner, H. (1981). Hemisphere specialization: Definitions not incantations. *Behavioral and Brain Sciences, 4*, 64–65.

Brownell, K. D., & Wadden, T. A. (2000). Obesity. In B. J. Sadock & V. A. Sadock (Eds.), *Kaplan and Sadock's comprehensive textbook of psychiatry* (7th ed., Vol. 2, pp. 1787–1796). Philadelphia, PA: Lippincott, Williams & Wilkins.

Bruckner-Gordon, F., Gangi, B. K., & Wallman, G. U. (1988). *Making therapy work: Your guide to choosing, using, and ending therapy.* New York, NY: Harper & Row.

Bruder, C. E., Piotrowski, A., Gijsbers, A. A., Andersson, R., Erickson, S., Diaz de Ståhl, T., . . . Dumanski, J. P. (2008). Phenotypically concordant and discordant monozygotic twins display different DNA copy-number-variation profiles. *American Journal of Human Genetics, 82*(3), 763–771. doi:10.1016/j.ajhg.2007.12.011.

Bruer, J. T. (2002). Avoiding the pediatricians error: How neuroscientists can help educators (and themselves). *Nature Neuroscience, 5*, 1031–1033.

Brugha, T. S., McManus, S., Bankart, J., Scott, F., Purdon, S., Smith, J., . . . Meltzer, H. (2011). Epidemiology of autism spectrum disorders in adults in the community in England. *Archives of General Psychiatry, 68*(5), 459–466. doi:10.1001/archgenpsychiatry.2011.38.

Brunner, E. J., Shipley, M. J., Britton, A. R., Stansfeld, S. A., Heuschmann, P. U., Rudd, A. G., . . . & Kivimaki, M. (2014). Depressive disorder, coronary heart disease, and stroke: Dose-response and reverse causation effects in the Whitehall II cohort study. *Preventive Cardiology, 21,* 340–346. doi:10.1177/2047487314520785.

Brunoni, A. R., Veliengo, L., Baccaro, A., et al. (2013). The sertraline vs electrical current therapy for treating depression clinical study: Results from a factorial, randomized, controlled trial. *Journal of the American Medical Association Psychiatry, 70*(4), 383–391.

Bryck, R. L., & Fisher, P. A. (2012). Training the brain: Practical applications of neural plasticity from the intersection of cognitive neuroscience, developmental psychology, and prevention science. *American Psychologist, 67*(2), 87–100.

Buccino, G., & Riggio, L. (2006). The role of the mirror neuron system in motor learning. *Kinesiology, 38*(1), 5–15.

Buck, L. B. (2000). Smell and taste: The chemical senses. In E. R. Kandel, J. H. Schwartz, & T. M. Jessell (Eds.), *Principles of neural science.* New York, NY: McGraw-Hill.

Buck, L. B. (2004). Olfactory receptors and coding in mammals. *Nutrition Reviews, 62,* S184–S188.

Buck, L. B., & Bargmann, C. I. (2013). Smell and taste: The chemical senses. In E. R. Kandel, J. H. Schwartz, T. M. Jessell, S. A. Siegelbaum, & A. J. Hudspeth (Eds.), *Principles of neural science* (5th ed.). New York, NY: McGraw-Hill.

Buckingham, G., & Goodale, M. A. (2013). When the brain gets it really wrong. *Brain and Behavioral Sciences, 36,* 208–209.

Buckley, K. W. (1982). The selling of a psychologist: John Broadus Watson and the application of behavioral techniques to advertising. *Journal of the History of Behavioral Sciences, 18*(3), 207–221.

Buckley, K. W. (1994). Misbehaviorism: The case of John B. Watson's dismissal from Johns Hopkins University. In J. T. Todd & E. K. Morris (Eds.), *Modern perspectives on John B. Watson and classical behaviorism.* Westport, CT: Greenwood.

Budiansky, S. (2004). Human and animal intelligence: The gap is a chasm. *Cerebrum, 6*(2), 85–95.

Budney, A. J., Vandrey, R. L., & Fearer, S. (2011). Cannabis. In P. Ruiz, & E. C. Strain (Eds.), *Lowinson and Ruiz's substance abuse: A comprehensive textbook* (5th ed.). Philadelphia, PA: Wolters Kluwer Lippincott Williams & Wilkins.

Buechel, E. C., Zhang, J., & Morewedge, C. K. (2017). Impact bias or underestimation? Outcome specifications predict the direction of affective forecasting errors. *Journal of Experimental Psychology: General, 146,* 746–751.

Buehler, R., Messervey, D., & Griffin, D. (2005). Collaborative planning and prediction: Does group discussion affect optimistic biases in time estimation? *Organizational Behavior and Human Decision Processes, 97,* 47–63.

Buelow, M. T., & Wirth, J. H. (2017). Decisions in the face of known risks: Ostracism increases risky decision-making. *Journal of Experimental Social Psychology, 69,* 210–217.

Bufe, B., Breslin, P. A. S., Kuhn, C., Reed, D. R., Tharp, C. D., Slack, J. P., et al. (2005). The molecular basis of individual differences in phenylthiocarbamide and propylthiouracil bitterness perception. *Current Biology, 15,* 322–327.

Bühler, C., & Allen, M. (1972). *Introduction to humanistic psychology.* Pacific Grove, CA: Brooks/Cole.

Bull, D. L. (1999). A verified case of recovered memories of sexual abuse. *American Journal of Psychotherapy, 53,* 221–224.

Bunn, G. C. (2007). Spectacular science: The lie detector's ambivalent powers. *History of Psychology, 10,* 156–178.

Burchinal, M. R., Lowe Vandell, D., & Belsky, J. (2014). Is the prediction of adolescent outcomes from early child care moderated by later maternal sensitivity? Results from the NICHD Study of Early Child Care and Youth Development. *Developmental Psychology, 50,* 542–553. doi:10.1037/a0033709.

Burg, J., & Michalak, J. (2011). The healthy quality of mindful breathing: Associations with rumination and depression. *Cognitive Therapy and Research, 35,* 179–185.

Burger, J. M. (1986). Temporal effects on attributions: Actor and observer differences. *Social Cognition, 4,* 377–387.

Burger, J. M. (1999). The foot-in-the-door compliance procedure: A multiple process analysis review. *Personality and Social Psychology Review, 3,* 303–325.

Burger, J. M. (2009). Replicating Milgram: Would people still obey today? *American Psychologist, 64*(1), 1–11.

Burger, J. M. (2015). *Personality* (9th ed.). San Francisco, CA: Cengage Learning.

Burgess, A. (2007). On the contribution of neurophysiology to hypnosis research: Current state and future directions. In G. A. Jamieson (Ed.), *Hypnosis and conscious states: The cognitive neuroscience perspective.* New York, NY: Oxford University Press.

Burke, J. D., & Kraemer, H. C. (2014). DSM-5 as a framework for psychiatric diagnosis. In R. E. Hales, S. C. Yudofsky, L. W. Roberts, R. E. Hales, S. C. Yudofsky, & L. W. Roberts (Eds.), *The American Psychiatric Publishing textbook of psychiatry* (6th ed.). Washington, DC: American Psychiatric Publishing.

Burke, M., Marlow, C., & Lento, T. (2010). Social network activity and social well-being. *Postgraduate Medical Journal, 85,* 455–459.

Burlingame, G. M., & Baldwin, S. (2011). Group therapy. In J. C. Norcross, G. R. Vandenbos, & D. K. Freedheim (Eds.), *History of psychotherapy: Continuity and change* (2nd ed.). Washington, DC: American Psychological Association.

Burlingame, G. M., Strauss, B., & Joyce, A. S. (2013). Change mechanisms and effectiveness of small group treatments. In M. J. Lambert (Ed.). *Bergin and Garfield's handbook of psychotherapy and behavior change* (6th ed.). New York, NY: Wiley.

Burns, B. D., & Corpus, B. (2004). Randomness and inductions from streaks: "Gambler's fallacy" versus "hot hand." *Psychonomic Bulletin & Review, 11*(1), 179–184.

Burns, J. K. (2013). Pathways from cannabis to psychosis: A review of the evidence. *Frontiers in Psychiatry, 4,* 128. doi:10.3389/fpsyt.2013.00128.

Burton, N. (2012). Dissociative fugue: The mystery of Agatha Christie. *Hide and Seek, Psychology Today.* Retrieved from http://www.psychologytoday.com/blog/hide-and-seek/201203/dissociative-fugue-the-mystery-agatha-christie.

Bushman, B. J. (2002). Does venting anger feed or extinguish the flame? Catharsis, rumination, distraction, anger, and aggressive responding. *Personality and Social Psychology Bulletin, 28,* 724–731.

Bushman, B. J., & Anderson, C. A. (2001). Media violence and the American public: Scientific facts versus media misinformation. *American Psychologist, 56,* 477–489.

Bushman, B. J., & Anderson, C. A. (2009). Comfortably numb: Desensitizing effects of violent media on helping others. *Psychological Science, 20*(3), 273–277.

Bushman, B. J., & Huesmann, L. R. (2012). Effects of violent media on aggression. In D. G. Singer, & J. L. Singer (Eds.), *Handbook of children and the media* (2nd ed.). Thousand Oaks, CA: SAGE.

Bushman, B. J., & Huesmann, L. R. (2014). Twenty-five years of research on violence in digital games and aggression revisited: A reply to Elson and Ferguson (2013). *European Psychologist, 19,* 47–55. doi:10.1027/1016-9040/a000164.

Buss, D. M. (1985). Human mate selection. *American Scientist, 73,* 47–51.

Buss, D. M. (1989). Sex differences in human mate preferences: Evolutionary hypotheses tested in 37 cultures. *Behavioral and Brain Sciences, 12,* 1–49.

Buss, D. M. (1991). Evolutionary personality psychology. *Annual Review of Psychology, 42,* 459–491.

Buss, D. M. (1995). Evolutionary psychology: A new paradigm for psychological science. *Psychological Inquiry, 6,* 1–30.

Buss, D. M. (1996). The evolutionary psychology of human social strategies. In E. T. Higgins & A. W. Kruglanski (Eds.), *Social psychology: Handbook of basic principles.* New York, NY: Guilford.

Buss, D. M. (1997). Evolutionary foundation of personality. In R. Hogan, J. Johnson, & S. Briggs (Eds.), *Handbook of personality psychology.* San Diego, CA: Academic Press.

Buss, D. M. (2009). The great struggles of life: Darwin and the emergence of evolutionary psychology. *American Psychologist, 64*(2), 140–148.

Buss, D. M. (2012). *Evolutionary psychology: The new science of the mind* (5th ed.). Boston, MA: Pearson.

Buss, D. M., & Kenrick, D. T. (1998). Evolutionary social psychology. In D. T. Gilbert, S. T. Fiske, & G. Lindzey (Eds.), *The handbook of social psychology.* New York, NY: McGraw-Hill.

Buss, D. M., & Penke, L. (2015). Evolutionary personality psychology. In M. Mikulincer, P. R. Shaver, M. L. Cooper, & R. J. Larsen (Eds.), *APA handbook of personality and social psychology: Vol. 4. Personality processes and individual differences.* Washington, DC: American Psychological Association.

Buss, D. M., & Schmitt, D. P. (1993). Sexual strategies theory: A evolutionary perspective on mating. *Psychological Review, 100,* 204–232.

Buss, D. M., & Schmitt, D. P. (2011). Evolutionary psychology and feminism. *Sex Roles, 64,* 768–787. doi:10.1007/s11199-011-9987-3.

Busseri, M. A., & Sadava, S. W. (2011). A review of the tripartite structure of well-being: Implications for conceptualization, operationalization, analysis, and synthesis. *Personality and Social Psychology Review, 15*(3), 290–314.

Bussey, K., & Bandura, A. (1999). Social cognitive theory of gender development and differentiation. *Psychological Review, 106,* 676–713.

Bussey, K., & Bandura, A. (2004). Social cognitive theory of gender development and functioning. In A. H. Eagly, A. E. Beall, & R. J. Sternberg (Eds.), *The psychology of gender.* New York, NY: Guilford.

Bustamante, J., Uengoer, M., & Lachnit, H. (2016). Reminder cues modulate the renewal effect in human predictive learning. *Frontiers of Psychology, 7,* 1968–1975.

Buster, J. E., & Carson, S. A. (2002). Endocrinology and diagnosis of pregnancy. In S. G. Gabbe, J. R. Niebyl, & J. L. Simpson (Eds.), *Obstetrics: Normal and problem pregnancies.* New York, NY: Churchill Livingstone.

Butcher, J. N. (2011). *A beginner's guide to the MMPI-2* (3rd ed.). Washington, DC: American Psychological Association.

Button, T. M. M., Maughan, B., & McGuffin, P. (2007). The relationship of maternal smoking to psychological problems in the offspring. *Early Human Development, 83,* 727–732.

Buxton, M. N., Arkey, Y., Lagos, J., Deposito, F., Lowenthal, F., & Simring, S. (1981). Stress and platelet aggregation in hemophiliac children and their family members. *Research Communications in Psychology, Psychiatry and Behavior, 6*(1), 21–48.

Buysse, D. J. (2011). Clinical pharmacology of other drugs used as hypnotics. In M. H. Kryger, T. Roth, & W. C. Dement (Eds.), *Principles and practice of sleep medicine* (5th ed.). Saint Louis, MO: Elsevier Saunders.

Buzan, D. S. (2004, March 12). I was not a lab rat. *The Guardian.* Retrieved from http://www.guardian.co.uk/education/2004/mar/12/highereducation.uk.

Byne, W. (2007). Biology and sexual minority status. In I. H. Meyer & M. E. Northridge (Eds.). *The health of sexual minorities: Public health perspectives on lesbian, gay, bisexual, and transgender populations.* New York, NY: Springer Science & Business Media.

Byrne, D. (1997). An overview (and underview) of research and theory within the attraction paradigm. *Journal of Social and Personal Relationships, 14,* 417–431.

Byrne, J. H. (2008). Postsynaptic potentials and synaptic integration. In L. Squire, D. Berg, F. Bloom, S. Du Lac, A. Ghosh, & N. Spitzer (Eds.), *Fundamental neuroscience* (3rd ed., pp. 227–246). San Diego, CA: Elsevier.

Cable, N., Bartley, M., Chandola, T., & Sacker, A. (2013). Friends are equally important to men and women, but family matters more for men's well-being. *Journal of Epidemiology And Community Health, 67*(2), 166–171. doi:10.1136/jech-2012-201113.

Cacioppo, J. T. (1994). Social neuroscience; Automatic, neuroendocrine, and immune responses to stress. *Psychophysiology, 31,* 113–128.

Cacioppo, J. T., Amaral, D. G., Blanchard, J. J., Cameron, J. L., Sue, C. C., Crews, D., et al. (2007). Social neuroscience: Progress and implications for mental health. *Perspectives on Psychological Science, 2,* 99–123.

Cacioppo, J. T., & Berntson, G. G. (1999). The affect system: Architecture and operating characteristics. *Current Directions in Psychological Science, 8,* 133–137.

Cacioppo, J. T., & Berntson, G. G. (2005). *Social neuroscience.* New York, NY: Psychology Press.

Cacioppo, J. T., Berntson, G. G., & Nusbaum, H. C. (2008). Neuroimaging as a new tool in the toolbox of psychological science. *Current Directions in Psychological Science, 17,* 62–67.

Cacioppo, J. T., & Cacioppo, S. (2014). Social relationships and health: The toxic effects of perceived social isolation. *Social and Personality Psychology Compass, 8,* 58–72. doi:10.1111/spc3.12087.

Cacioppo, J. T., Cacioppo, S., Capitanio, J. T., & Cole, S. W. (2015). The neuroendrocrinology of social isolation. *Annual Review of Psychology, 66,* 733–767.

Cacioppo, J. T., Cacioppo, S., Gonzaga, G. C., Ogburn, E. L., & VanderWeele, T. J. (2013). Marital satisfaction and break-ups differ across online and offline meeting venues. *PNAS Proceedings of the National Academy of Sciences of the United States of America, 110,* 10135–10140. doi:10.1073/pnas.1222447110.

Cacioppo, J. T., Hawkley, L. C., Kalil, A., Hughes, M. E., Waite, L., & Thisted, R. A. (2008). Happiness and the invisible threads of social connection: The Chicago health, aging, and social relations study. In M. Eid & R. J. Larsen (Eds.), *The science of subjective well-being.* New York, NY: Guilford Press.

Cade, R., & Gates, J. (2017). Gamers and video game culture: An introduction for counselors. *The Family Journal: Counseling and Therapy for Couples and Families, 25,* 70–75.

Cahill, L. (2006). Why sex matters for neuroscience. *Nature Reviews Neuroscience, 7,* 477–484.

Cahn, B. R., & Polich, J. (2006). Meditation states and traits: EEG, ERP, and neuroimaging studies. *Psychological Bulletin, 132,* 180–211.

Cai, D. J., Mednick, S. A., Harrison, E. M., Kanady, J. C., & Mednick, S. C. (2009). REM, not incubation, improves creativity by priming associative networks. *Proceedings of the National Academy of Sciences of the United States of America, 106*(25), 10130–10134.

Cai, L. (2013). Factor analysis of tests and items. In K. F. Geisinger, B. A. Bracken, J. F. Carlson, J. C. Hansen, N. R. Kuncel, S. P. Reise, & M. C. Rodriguez (Eds.), *APA handbook of testing and assessment in psychology: Vol. 1. Test theory and testing and assessment in industrial and organizational psychology.* Washington, DC: American Psychological Association. doi:10.1037/14047-005.

Cain, W. S. (1988). Olfaction. In R. C. Atkinson, R. J. Herrnstein, G. Lindzey, & R. D. Luce (Eds.), *Stevens' handbook of experimental psychology: Perception and motivation* (Vol. 1). New York, NY: Wiley.

Calhoun, L. G., & Tedeschi, R. G. (2008). The paradox of struggling with trauma: Guidelines for practice and directions for research. In S. Joseph & P. A. Linley (Eds.), *Trauma, recovery, and growth: Positive psychological perspectives on posttraumatic stress.* Hoboken, NJ: Wiley.

Calhoun, L. G., & Tedeschi, R. G. (2013). *Posttraumatic growth in clinical practice.* New York, NY: Routledge/Taylor & Francis Group.

Caligor, E., Yeomans, F., & Levin, Z. (2014). Feeding and eating disorders. In J. L. Cutler (Ed.), *Psychiatry* (3rd ed.). New York, NY: Oxford University Press.

Calkins, K., & Devaskar, S. U. (2011). Fetal origins of adult disease. *Current Problems in Pediatric and Adolescent Health Care, 41,* 158–176. doi:10.1016/j.cppeds.2011.01.001.

Callaghan, R. C., Allebeck, P., & Sidorchuk, A. (2013). Marijuana use and risk of lung cancer: A 40-year cohort study. *Cancer Causes & Control, 24,* 1811–1820.

Callaghan, R. C., Cunningham, J. K., Allebeck, P., Arenovich, T., Sajeev, G., Remington, G., . . . Kish, S. J. (2012). Methamphetamine use and schizophrenia: a population-based cohort study in California. *American Journal of Psychiatry, 169,* 389–396.

Callaghan, T., Rochat, P., Lillard, A., Claux, M., Odden, H., Itakura, S., et al. (2005). Synchrony in the onset of mental-state reasoning: Evidence from five cultures. *Psychological Science, 16*(5), 378–384.

Callahan, C. M. (2000). Intelligence and giftedness. In R. J. Sternberg (Ed.), *Handbook of intelligence* (pp. 159–175). New York, NY: Cambridge University Press.

Callicutt, J. W. (2006). Homeless shelters: An uneasy component of the de facto mental health system. In J. Rosenberg & S. Rosenberg (Eds.), *Community mental health: Challenges for the 21st century.* New York, NY: Routledge.

Callwood, J. (1990). *Sleepwalker.* Toronto, ON: Lester & Orpen Dennys.

Calvallo, J. V., Zee, K. S., & Higgins, E. T. (2016). Giving the help that is needed: How regulatory mode influences social support. *Personality and Social Psychology Bulletin, 42,* 1111–1128.

Calvert, C. (1997). Hate speech and its harms: A communication theory perspective. *Journal of Communication, 47,* 4–19.

Camaioni, L. (2001). Early language. In G. Bremner & A. Fogel (Eds.), *Blackwell handbook of infant development.* Malden, MA: Blackwell.

Camas-Diaz, L. (2011). *Multicultural care: A clinician's guide to cultural competence* (Psychologists in Independent Practice) (Psychologists in Independent Practice Books). Washington DC: American Psychological Association.

Camerer, C. (2005). Three cheers—psychological, theoretical, empirical—for loss aversion. *Journal of Marketing Research, 42*(2), 129–133.

Camerer, C. F., Loewenstein, G., & Rabin, M. (Eds.). (2004). *Advances in behavioral economics.* Princeton, NJ: Russell Sage Foundation.

Cameron, L., Leventhal, E. A., & Leventhal, H. (1993). Symptom representations and affect as determinants of care seeking in a community-dwelling, adult sample population. *Health Psychology, 12,* 171–179.

CAMH. (2011a). Addiction and mental health indicators among Ontario adults. Retrieved from http://www.camh.ca/en/research/news_and_publications/CAMH%20Monitor/CM2011_eReport_Final.pdf.

CAMH. (2011b). Drinking, cannabis use and psychological distress increase, CAMH survey finds. Retrieved June 20, 2011, from http://www.camh.net/News_events/News_releases_and_media_advisories_and_backgrounders/CAMH_monitor_2011.html.

Cami, J., & Farre, M. (2003). Mechanisms of disease: Drug addiction. *New England Journal of Medicine, 349,* 975–986.

Camos, V. (2015). Storing verbal information in working memory. *Current Directions in Psychology, 24,* 440–445.

Campbell, A. (2005). Aggression. In D. M. Buss (Ed.), *The handbook of evolutionary psychology.* New York, NY: Wiley.

Campbell, A. C., Nunes, E. V., Matthews, A. G., Stitzer, M., Miele, G. M., Polsky, D., . . . Ghitza, U. E. (2014). Internet-delivered treatment for substance abuse: A multisite randomized controlled trial. *The American Journal of Psychiatry, 171,* 683–690. doi:10.1176/appi.ajp.2014.13081055.

Campbell, R., & Sais, E. (1995). Accelerated metalinguistic (phonological) awareness in bilingual children. *British Journal of Developmental Psychology, 13,* 61–68.

Campion-Smith, B., & Boutillier, A. (2017). Malala Yousafzai has become an honorary Canadian citizen. *The Toronto Star,* April 12, 2017. Retrieved from https://www.thestar.com/news/canada/2017/04/12/malala-yousafzai-to-receive-canadian-citizenship-delayed-by-parliament-hill-shooting-in-2014.html.

Canadian Centre on Substance Abuse. (2016). Ecstasy or Molly (MDMA). Retrieved from http://www.ccsa.ca/Resource%20Library/CCSA-Canadian-Drug-Summary-MDMA-2016-en.pdf.

Canadian Community Health Survey. (2009/2010). Retrieved from http://www.statcan.gc.ca/pub/82-003-x/2012001/article/11632/summary-sommaire-eng.htm.

Canadian Counselling and Psychotherapy Association. (2014). The urgent need for counselling services. Retrieved from https://www.ccpa-accp.ca/wp-content/uploads/2015/11/IssuePaper-TheUrgentNeedforCounsellingServices.pdf.

Canadian Down Syndrome Society. (2009). What is Down syndrome? Retrieved from http://www.cdss.ca/information/general-information/what-is-down-syndrome.html.

Canadian Institute for Health Information. (2014). Psychologists. Retrieved from http://www.cihi.ca/cihi-ext-portal/internet/en/document/.../hpdb_psych.

Canadian Institutes of Health Research. (2009). When I'm 65. Retrieved May 29, 2011, from http://www.cihr-irsc.gc.ca/e/39468.html.

Canadian Medical Association. (2015a). Harms associated with opioids and other psychoactive prescription drugs. Retrieved from http://policybase.cma.ca/dbtw-wpd/Policypdf/PD15-06.pdf.

Canadian Mental Health Association. (2005). Physical and mental health equally important to Canadians. Retrieved July 3, 2005, from http://www.cmha.ca/bins/content_page.asp?cid=6-20-21-386.

Canadian Mental Health Association. (2017). *Homelessness.* Retrieved from http://www.cmha.ca/public-policy/subject/homelessness/.

Canadian Paediatric Society. (2017). *Screen time and young children: Promoting Health and development in a digital world.* Retrieved from http://www.cps.ca/en/documents/position/screen-time-and-young-children.

Canadian Press. (2013). Canadians no longer the biggest web addict, report shows. March 4, 2013. Retrieved from http://www.cbc.ca/news/technology/canadians-no-longer-the-biggest-web-addict-report-shows-1.1412059.

Canadian Psychological Association. (2016). *Annual Report 2015–2016.* Retrieved from http://www.cpa.ca/docs/File/Governance/2016/2016AnnualreportFINAL_ENG_260516.pdf.

Canadian Psychological Association. (2016). *Code of ethics for Psychologists* (3rd ed.). Retrieved from http://www.cpa.ca/cpasite/UserFiles/Documents/Canadian%20Code%20of%20Ethics%20for%20Psycho.pdf.

Canadian Task Force on Preventive Health Care. (2003). Prevention of suicide. Retrieved June 19, 2005, from http://www.canadiancrc.com/Can_Preventive_Care_suicide.htm.

Canli, T. (2008). Toward a "molecular psychology" of personality. In O. P. John, R. W. Robbins, & L. A. Pervin (Eds.), *Handbook of personality: Theory and research* (Vol. 3, pp. 311–327). New York, NY: Guilford Press.

Cannon, T. D., Chung, Y., He, G., Sun, D., Jacobson, A., van Erp, T. G., . . . Heinssen, R. (2015). Progressive reduction in cortical thickness as psychosis develops: A multisite longitudinal neuroimaging study of youth at elevated clinical risk. *Biological Psychiatry, 77*(2), 147–157. doi:10.1016/j.biopsych.2014.05.023.

Cannon, W. B. (1927). The James–Lange theory of emotions: A critical examination and an alternative theory. *American Journal of Psychology, 39,* 106–124.

Cannon, W. B. (1932). *The wisdom of the body*. New York, NY: Norton.

Cantu, S. M., Simpson, J. A., Griskevicius, V., Weisberg, Y. J., Durante, K. M., & Beal, D. J. (2014). Fertile and selectively flirty: Women's behavior toward men changes across the ovulatory cycle. *Psychological Science, 25,* 431–438. doi:10.1177/0956797613508413.

Cao, M. T., Guilleminault, C., & Kushida, C. A. (2011). Clinical features and evaluation of obstructive sleep apnea and upper airway resistance syndrome. In M. H. Kryger, T. Roth, & W. C. Dement (Eds.), *Principles and practice of sleep medicine* (5th ed.). Saint Louis, MO: Elsevier Saunders.

Cao, X., Laplante, D. P., Brunet, A., Ciampi, A., & King, S. (2014). Prenatal maternal stress affects motor function in 5 1/2-year-old children: Project ice storm. *Developmental Psychobiology, 56,* 117–125. doi:10.1002/dev.21085.

Card, N. A., Stucky, B. D., Sawalani, G. M., & Little, T. D. (2008). Direct and indirect aggression during childhood and adolescence: A meta-analytic review of gender differences, intercorrelations, and relations to maladjustment. *Child Development, 79,* 1185–1229.

Cardeña, E., Butler, L. D., Reijman, S., & Spiegel, D. (2013). Disorders of extreme stress. In T. A. Widiger, G. Stricker, I. B. Weiner, G. Stricker, T. A. Widiger, & I. B. Weiner (Eds.), *Handbook of psychology: Vol. 8. Clinical psychology* (2nd ed.). New York, NY: Wiley.

Cardeña, E., & Gleaves, D. H. (2007). Dissociative disorders. In M. Hersen, S. M. Turner, & D. C. Beidel (Eds.), *Adult psychopathology and diagnosis*. New York, NY: Wiley.

Cardoso, C., Ellenbogen, M. A., & Linnen, A. (2012). Acute intranasal oxytocin improves positive self-perceptions of personality. *Psychopharmacology, 220,* 741–749. doi:10.1007/s00213-011-2527-6.

Carew, T. J., Hawkins, R. D., Abrams, T. W., & Kandel, E. R. (1984). A test of Hebb's postulate at identified synapses which mediate classical conditioning in Aplysia. *Journal of Neuroscience, 4*(5), 1217–12245.

Carey, B. (2009, December 21). Building a search engine of the brain, slice by slice. *The New York Times.* Retrieved from http://www.newyorktimes.com.

Carey, B. (2016). Suzanne Corkin, who helped pinpoint nature of memory, dies at 79. *The New York Times,* May 27, 2016. Retrieved from https://www.nytimes.com/2016/05/28/science/suzanne-corkin-who-helped-pinpoint-nature-of-memory-dies-at-79.html.

Carey, M. P., & Vanable, P. A. (2003). AIDS/HIV. In A. M. Nezu, C. M. Nezu, & P. A. Geller (Eds.), *Handbook of psychology (Vol. 9): Health psychology*. New York, NY: John Wiley.

Carey, S. (2010). Beyond fast mapping. *Language Learning and Development, 6*(3), 184–205.

Carleton, R. N., et al. (2017). Mental disorder symptoms among public safety personnel in Canada. *The Canadian Journal of Psychiatry* (epub ahead of publication). Retrieved from journals.sagepub.com/doi/full/10.1177/0706743717723825.

Carlson, G. A., & Klein, D. N. (2014). How to understand divergent views on bipolar disorder in youth. *Annual Review of Clinical Psychology, 10,* 529–551.

Carlson, J. D., & Englar-Carlson, M. (2013). Adlerian therapy. In J. Frew, & M. D. Spiegler (Eds.), *Contemporary psychotherapies for a diverse world* (1st rev. ed.). New York, NY: Routledge/Taylor & Francis Group.

Carnagey, N. L., Anderson, C. A., & Bushman, B. J. (2007). The effect of video game violence on physiological desensitization. *Journal of Experimental Social Psychology, 43,* 489–496.

Carpenter, S. K. (2012). Testing enhances the transfer of learning. *Current Directions in Psychological Science, 21,* 279–283. doi:10.1177/0963721412452728.

Carpenter, W. T. (2002). From clinical trial to prescription. *Archives of General Psychology, 59,* 282–285.

Carr, E. (1972). *Fresh Seeing: Two addresses by Emily Carr.* Toronto, ON: Clarke, Irwin & Co.

Carr, E. R., & West, L. M. (2013). Inside the therapy room: A case study for training African American men from a multicultural/feminist perspective. *Journal of Psychotherapy Integration, 23,* 120–133.

Carroll, J. B. (1993). *Human cognitive abilities: A survey of factor-analytic studies*. Cambridge, UK: Cambridge University Press.

Carroll, J. B. (1996). A three-stratum theory of intelligence: Spearman's contribution. In I. Dennis & P. Tapsfield (Eds.), *Human abilities: Their nature and measurement*. Mahwah, NJ: Erlbaum.

Carroll, M. E., & Overmier, J. B. (2001). *Animal research and human health*. Washington, DC: American Psychological Association.

Carruthers, P. (2017). Implicit versus explicit attitudes: Differing manifestations of the same representational structures? *Review of Philosophical Psychology*. Retrieved from https://pdfs.semanticscholar.org/cca6/ad122214e65c05fb9876d431d77cee0c885e.pdf?_ga=2.198535279.1920229095.1511712989-58904333.1511712989.

Carryer, J. R., & Greenberg, L. S. (2010). Optimal levels of emotional arousal in experiential therapy of depression. *Journal of Consulting and Clinical Psychology, 78,* 190–199.

Carskadon, M. A., & Dement, W. C. (1994). Normal human sleep: An overview. In M. Kryger, T. Roth, and W. Dement (Eds.), *Principles and practice of sleep medicine* (pp. 3–15). Philadelphia, PA: WB Saunders.

Carskadon, M. A., & Dement, W. C. (2005). Normal human sleep: An overview. In M. H. Kryger, T. Roth, & W. C. Dement (Eds.), *Principles and practice of sleep medicine*. Philadelphia, PA: Elsevier Saunders.

Carskadon, M. A., & Rechtschaffen, A. (2005). Monitoring and staging human sleep. In M. H. Kryger, T. Roth, & W. C. Dement (Eds.), *Principles and practice of sleep medicine*. Philadelphia, PA: Elsevier Saunders.

Carson, S. H. (2011). Creativity and psychopathology: A shared vulnerability model. *Canadian Journal of Psychiatry, 56,* 144–153.

Carter, B. (1999). Becoming parents: The family with young children. In B. Carter & M. McGoldrick (Eds.), *The expanded family life cycle: Individual, family, and social perspectives* (3rd ed., pp. 249–273). Boston, MA: Allyn & Bacon.

Carter, R. (1998). *Mapping the mind*. Berkeley, CA: University of California Press.

Carter, S. (2014). Oxytocin pathways and the evolution of human behaviour. *Annual Review of Psychology, 65,* 1–23.

Cartwright, R. D. (1977). *Night life: Explorations in dreaming*. Englewood Cliffs, NJ: Prentice-Hall.

Cartwright, R. D. (1991). Dreams that work: The relation of dream incorporation to adaptation to stressful events. *Dreaming, 1,* 3–9.

Cartwright, R. D. (2004). The role of sleep in changing our minds: A psychologist's discussion of papers on memory reactivation and consolidation in sleep. *Learning & Memory, 11,* 660–663.

Cartwright, R. D. (2006). Sleepwalking. In T. Lee-Chiong (Ed.), *Sleep: A comprehensive handbook*. Hoboken, NJ: Wiley-Liss.

Cartwright, R. D., & Lamberg, L. (1992). *Crisis dreaming*. New York, NY: HarperCollins.

Carver, C. S., & Scheier, M. F. (2000). On the structure of behavioral self-regulation. In M. Boekaerts, P. R. Pintrich, & M. Zeidner (Eds.), *Handbook of self-regulation* (pp. 42–80). San Diego, CA: Academic Press.

Carver, C. S., & Scheier, M. F. (2014). Dispositional optimism. *Trends in Cognitive Sciences, 18,* 293–299. doi:10.1016/j.tics.2014.02.003.

Carver, C. S., Scheier, M. F., & Segerstrom, S. C. (2010). Optimism. *Clinical Psychology Review, 30*(7), 879–889.

Casanova, C., Merabet, L., Desautels, A., & Minville, K. (2001). Higher-order motion processing in the pulvinar. *Progress in Brain Research, 134,* 71–82.

Casey, B. J., & Caudle, K. (2013). The teenage brain: Self control. *Current Directions in Psychological Science, 22,* 82–87. doi:10.1177/0963721413480170.

Casey, B. J., Tottenham, N., Listen, C., & Durston, S. (2005). Imaging the developing brain: What have we learned about cognitive development? *Trends in Cognitive Sciences, 9*(3), 104–110. doi:10.1016/j.tics.2005.01.011.

Caspi, A., & Herbener, E. S. (1990). Continuity and change: Assortative marriage and the consistency of personality in adulthood. *Journal of Personality and Social Psychology, 58*(2), 250–258.

Cassel, R. N. (2000). Third force psychology and person-centered theory: From ego-status to ego-ideal. *Psychology: A Journal of Human Behavior, 37*(3), 44–48.

Cassidy, J. (2008). The nature of the child's ties. In J. Cassidy & P. R. Shaver (Eds.), *Handbook of attachment: Theory, research, and clinical applications* (2nd ed., pp. 3–22). New York, NY: Guilford Press.

Cassidy, J., & Shaver, P. R. (1999). *Handbook of attachment: Theory, research, and clinical application*. New York, NY: Guilford Press.

Catania, A. C. (1992). Reinforcement. In L. R. Squire (Ed.), *Encyclopedia of learning and memory*. New York, NY: Macmillan.

Cattell, R. B. (1950). *Personality: A systematic, theoretical and factual study*. New York, NY: McGraw-Hill.

Cattell, R. B. (1963). Theory of fluid and crystallized intelligence: A critical experiment. *Journal of Educational Psychology, 54,* 1–22.

Cattell, R. B. (1966). *The scientific analysis of personality*. Chicago: Aldine.

Cattell, R. B. (1990). Advances in Cattellian personality theory. In L. A. Pervin (Ed.), *Handbook of personality: Theory and research*. New York, NY: Guilford.

Cautin, R. L., Freedheim, D. K., & DeLeon, P. H. (2013). Psychology as a profession. In D. K. Freedheim, & I. B. Weiner (Eds.), *Handbook of psychology: Vol. 1. History of psychology* (2nd ed., pp. 32–54). New York, NY: Wiley.

Caverly, D. C., Orlando, V. P., & Mullen, J. L. (2000). Textbook study reading. In R. F. Flippo & D. C. Caverly (Eds.), *Handbook of college reading and study strategy research*. Mahwah, NJ: Erlbaum.

CBC News. (2007). One in three Alberta teen boys watch porn online. Retrieved from http://www.cbc.ca/news/canada/edmonton/one-in-three-alberta-teen-boys-watch-porn-online-study-1.662941.

CBC News. (2011). HIV/AIDS anniversary. Retrieved from http://www.cbc.ca/news/thenational/hiv-aids-anniversary-1.1755354.

CBC News. (2013). Canadians no longer the biggest web addict, report shows. Retrieved from http://www.cbc.ca/news/technology/canadians-no-longer-the-biggest-web-addict-report-shows-1.1412059.

CBC News. (2013). Cory Monteith's overdose detailed in coroner's report. Retrieved from http://www.cbc.ca/m/touch/arts/story/1.1876597.

CBC News. (2013). French immersion programs face high demand, challenges. Retrieved from http://www.cbc.ca/news/canada/french-immersion-programs-face-high-demand-challenges-1.1295618.

CBC News. (2014). *Distracted driving laws across Canada*. Retrieved from http://www.cbc.ca/news/canada/distracted-driving-laws-across-canada-1.2576880.

CBC News. (2014a). Philip Seymour Hoffman dead at 46. Retrieved from http://www.cbc.ca/news/arts/philip-seymour-hoffman-dead-at-46-1.2520522.

CBC News. (2014b). Posttraumatic stress disorder: Is the Canadian military dealing with the issue. Retrieved from http://www.cbc.ca/m/touch/news/story/1.2635328.

CBC News. (2015). Sleep disorders will affect 40% of Canadians, pose serious health risks. Retrieved from http://www.cbc.ca/news/canada/british-columbia/sleep-disorder-ubc-1.3294306.

CBC News. (2015). Timeline: Assisted suicide in Canada. Retrieved from http://www.cbc.ca/news/health/timeline-assisted-suicide-in-canada-1.2946485.

CBC News. (2016). Canada's Olympic women's eight team hopes extra sleep coverts to Olympic gold. Retrieved from ww.cbc.ca/news/canada/calgary/rio-olympics-womens-eight-rowing-sleep-study-1.3714220.

Ceci, S. J. (1990). *On intelligence … more or less: A bio-ecological treatise on intellectual development*. Englewood Cliffs, NJ: Prentice-Hall.

Centers for Disease Control and Prevention. (2009). Climate change and public health. Retrieved from http://www.cdc.gov/ClimateChange/policy.htm.

Centers for Disease Control and Prevention. (2011a). Diagnoses of HIV infection and AIDS in the United States and dependent areas, 2009. *HIV Surveillance Report, 21*. Retrieved from http://www.cdc.gov/hiv/surveillance/resources/reports/2009report/.

Centers for Disease Control and Prevention. (2011b). Tobacco use and pregnancy. Retrieved May 24, 2011, from http://www.cdc.gov/reproductivehealth/tobaccousepregnancy/.

Centre for Addiction and Mental Health. (2015). Drug use among Ontario students. Retrieved from http://www.camh.ca/en/research/news_and_publications/ontario-student-drug-use-and-health-survey/Pages/default.aspx.

Centre for Addition and Mental Health. (2017). *Mental illness and Addictions: Facts and statistics*. Retrieved from http://www.camh.ca/en/hospital/about_camh/newsroom/for_reporters/Pages/addictionmentalhealthstatistics.aspx.

Cepeda, N. J., Pashler, H., Vul, E., Wixted, J. T., & Rohrer, D. (2006). Distributed practice in verbal recall tasks: A review and quantitative synthesis. *Psychological Bulletin, 132*, 354–380.

Cerletti, U., & Bini, L. (1938). Un nuevo metodo di shock-terapie "L'elettro-shock." *Bull. Acad. Med. Roma, 64*, 136–138.

Cha, Y. (2010). Reinforcing separate spheres: The effect of spousal overwork on men's and women's employment in dual-earner households. *American Sociological Review, 75*(2), 303–329.

Chabris, C. F., Hebert, B. M., Benjamin, D. J., Beauchamp, J., Cesarini, D., van der Loos, M., . . . Laibson, D. (2012). Most reported genetic associations with general intelligence are probably false positives. *Psychological Science, 23*, 1314–1323. doi:10.1177/0956797611435528.

Chabris, C., & Simons, D. (2010). *The invisible gorilla*. New York, NY: Crown Publishers.

Chambers, R., Lo, B. C. Y., & Allen, N. B. (2008). The impact of mindfulness training on attentional control, cognitive style, and affect. *Cognitive Therapy and Research, 32*, 303–322.

Chan, C. S., Paul, P. L., & Verlinde, H. (2000). A note on warped string compactification. *Nuclear Physics Bulletin, 581*, 156–164.

Chan, J. W. C., & Vernon, P. E. (1988). Individual differences among the peoples of China. In S. H. Irvine & J. W. Berry (Eds.), *Human abilities in cultural context*. New York, NY: Cambridge University Press.

Chance, P. (1999). Thorndike's puzzle boxes and the origins of the experimental analysis of behavior. *Journal of the Experimental Analysis of Behavior, 72*, 433–440.

Chance, P. (2001, September/October). The brain goes to school: Why neuroscience research is going to the head of the class. *Psychology Today*, p. 72.

Chandler, C. K. (2012). *Animal assisted therapy in counseling (2nd Ed.)*. New York, NY: Routledge.

Chandler, M. J. (2000). Surviving time: The persistence of identity in this culture and that. *Culture and Psychology, 6*, 209–231.

Chandler, M. J., & Lalonde, C. (1998). Cultural continuity as a hedge against suicide in Canada's First Nations. *Transcultural Psychiatry, 35*, 191–219.

Chandler, M. J., & Lalonde, C. E. (2004). Culture, selves, and time: Theories of personal persistence in native and non-native youth. In C. Lightfoot, C. Lalonde, & M. Chandler (Eds.), *Changing conceptions of psychological life* (pp. 207–229). Mahwah, NJ: Erlbaum.

Chandler, M. J., & Lalonde, C. E. (2008). Cultural continuity as a protective factor against suicide in First Nations youth. *Horizons, 9*(4), 13–24.

Chandra, A., Copen, C. E., & Mosher, W. D. (2011). Sexual behavior, sexual attraction, and sexual identity in the United States: Data from the 20062008 National Survey of Family Growth. *National Health Statistics Reports, 3*, 1–36.

Chaplin, T., & Aldoo, A. (2013). Gender differences in emotion expression in children: A meta-analytic review. *Psychological Bulletin, 179*, 735–765.

Chapman, C. D., Nilsson, E. K., Nilsson, V. C., Cedernaes, J., Rangtell, F. H., Vogel, H., . . . Benedict, C. (2013). Acute sleep deprivation increases food purchasing in men. *Obesity, 21*, E555–E560. doi:10.1002/oby.20579.

Chapman, C. S., & Goodale, M. A. (2010). Obstacle avoidance during online corrections. *Journal of Vision, 10*(11), 1–14.

Chapman, D. A., & Lickel, B. (2016). Climate change and disasters: How framing affects justifications for giving or withholding aid to disaster victims. *Social Psychology and Personality Science, 7*, 13–20.

Charuvastra, A., & Cloitre, M. (2008). Social bonds and posttraumatic stress disorder. *Annual Review of Psychology, 59*, 301–328.

Chase, W. G., & Simon, H. A. (1973). Perception in chess. *Cognitive Psychology, 4*, 55–81.

Chen J. K., Johnston, K. M, Petrides, M., & Ptito, A. (2008). Neural substrates of symptoms of depression following concussion in male athletes with persisting post-concussion symptoms. *Archives of General Psychiatry, 65*(1), 81–89.

Chen, A. W., Kazanjian, A., Wong, H., & Goldner, E. M. (2010). Mental health service use by Chinese immigrants with severe and persistent mental illness, *Canadian Journal of Psychiatry, 55*, 35–42.

Chen, F. S., Minson, J. A., Schone, M., & Heinrichs, M. (2013). In the eye of the beholder: Eye contact increases resistance to persuasion. *Psychological Science, 24*, 254–261.

Chen, J. K., Johnston, K. M., Collie, A., McCrory, P., & Ptito, A. (2007). A validation of the Post Concussion Symptom Scale in the assessment of complex concussion using cognitive testing and fMRI. *Journal of Neurology, Neurosurgery and Psychiatry, 78*(11), 1231–1238.

Chen, M. C., Yu, H., Huang, Z., & Lu, J. (2013). Rapid eye movement sleep behavior disorder. *Current Opinion in Neurobiology, 23*, 793–798.

Chen, Q., & Yan, Z. (2013). New on driving performance: A review. *International Journal of Cyber Behavior, Psychology and Learning, 3*(3), 46–61. doi:10.4018/ijcbpl.2013070104.

Chen, S., Gau, S. F., Pikhart, H., Peasey, A., Chen, S., & Tsai, M. (2014). Work stress and subsequent risk of Internet addiction among information technology engineers in Taiwan. *Cyberpsychology, Behavior, and Social Networking, 17*, 542–550. doi:10.1089/cyber.2013.0686.

Chen, X., & Wang, L. (2010). China. In M. H. Bornstein (Ed.), *Handbook of cultural developmental science* (pp. 429–440). New York, NY: Psychology Press.

Chen, X., Wang, L., & DeSouza, A. (2006). Temperament and socio-emotional functioning in Chinese and North American children. In X. Chen, D. French, & B. Schneider (Eds.), *Peer relationships in cultural context* (pp. 123–147). New York, NY: Cambridge University Press.

Cheng, C., & Li, A. Y. -I. (2014). Internet addiction prevalence and quality of (real) life: A meta-analysis of 31 nations across seven world regions. *Cyberpsychology, Behavior, and Social Networking, 17*, 755–760. doi:10.1089/cyber.2014.0317.

Chess, S., & Thomas, A. (1996). *Temperament: Theory and practice*. New York, NY: Brunner/Mazel.

Cheung, F., van de Vijver, F. J. R., & Leonge, F. T. L. (2011). Toward a new approach to the study of personality in culture. *American Psychologist, 66*(7), 593–603.

Chiao J. Y., & Cheon, B. K. (2010). The weirdest brains in the world. *Behavioral and Brain Science, 33*, 88–90.

Chicago Tribune. (2012). College freshman at age 9, medical degree at 21. June 3, 2012. Retrieved from http://articles.chicagotribune.com/2012-06-03/news/ct-met-boy-wonder-20120603_1_yano-medical-degree-medical-team.

Chief Public Health Officer of Canada. (2015). *Alcohol consumption in Canada*. Retrieved from http://healthycanadians.gc.ca/publications/department-ministere/state-public-health-alcohol-2015-etat-sante-publique-alcool/alt/state-phac-alcohol-2015-etat-aspc-alcool-eng.pdf.

Chiriboga, D. A. (1989). Mental health at the midpoint: Crisis, challenge, or relief? In S. Hunter & M. Sundel (Eds.), *Sage sourcebooks for the human services series, Vol. 7. Midlife myths: Issues, findings, and practice implications* (pp. 116–144). Thousand Oaks, CA: SAGE.

Chisholm, J. S. (1996). The evolutionary ecology of attachment organization. *Human Nature, 7*, 1–38.

Chiu, C., Kim, Y., & Wan, W. W. N. (2008). Personality: Cross-cultural perspectives. In G. J. Boyles, G. Matthews, & D. H. Saklofske (Eds.), *The Sage handbook of personality theory and assessment: Personality theories and models* (Vol. 1, pp. 124–144). Los Angles, CA: SAGE.

Chiu, C. Y., Leung, A. K. Y., & Kwan, L. (2007). Language, cognition, and culture: Beyond the Whorfian hypothesis. In S. Kitayama & D. Cohen (Eds.), *Handbook of cultural psychology* (pp. 668–690). New York, NY: Guilford.

Cholewiak, R. W., & Cholewiak, S. A. (2010). Pain: Physiological mechanisms. In E. B. Goldstein (Ed.), *Encyclopedia of perception*. Thousand Oaks, CA: SAGE.

Choma, B., Hafer, C. L., Crosby, F. J., & Foster, M. D. (2012). Perceptions of personal sex discrimination: The role of belief in a just world and situational ambiguity. *Journal of Social Psychology, 152*, 568–585.

Chomsky, N. (1957). *Syntactic structures*. The Hague: Mouton.

Chomsky, N. (1959). A review of B. F. Skinner's "Verbal Behavior." *Language, 35*, 26–58.

Chomsky, N. (1965). *Aspects of theory of syntax*. Cambridge, MA: MIT Press.

Chomsky, N. (1975). *Reflections on language*. New York, NY: Pantheon.

Chomsky, N. (1986). *Knowledge of language: Its nature, origins, and use*. New York, NY: Praeger.

Chomsky, N. (2006). *Language and mind* (3rd ed.). New York, NY: Cambridge University Press.

Chopra, S. S. (2003). Industry funding of clinical trials: Benefit of bias? *Journal of the American Medical Association, 290*, 113–114.

Christensen, C. C. (2005). Preferences for descriptors of hypnosis: A brief communication. *International Journal of Clinical and Experimental Hypnosis, 53*, 281–289.

Christmas, B. (2010, May 28). Memory lapses: Why you might need a helping hand. *The Globe and Mail*, B14.

Christodoulidis, G., Vittorio, T. J., Fudim, M., Lerakis, S., & Kosmas, C. E. (2014). Inflammation in coronary artery disease. *Cardiology Review, 22*, 279–288.

Christoph, R. T., Schoenfeld, G. A., & Tansky, J. W. (1998). Overcoming barriers to training utilizing technology: The influence of self-efficacy factors on multimedia-based training receptiveness. *Human Resource Development Quarterly, 9*, 25–38.

Chrobak, Q. M., & Zaragoza, M. S. (2013). The misinformation effect: Past research and recent advances. In A. M. Ridley, F. Gabbert, & D. J. La Rooy (Eds.), *Suggestibility in legal contexts: Psychological research and forensic implications*. Malden, MA: Wiley-Blackwell.

Chu, J. A., Frey, L. M., Ganzel, B. L., & Matthews, J. A. (1999). Memories of childhood abuse: Dissociation, amnesia, and corroboration. *American Journal of Psychiatry, 156*, 749–755.

Chudler, E. H. (2007). The power of the full moon. Running on empty? In S. Della Sala (Ed.), *Tall tales about the mind & brain: Separating fact from fiction* (pp. 401–410). New York, NY: Oxford University Press.

Chun, M. M., & Wolfe, J. M. (2001). Visual attention. In E. B. Goldstein (Ed.), *Blackwell handbook of perception*. Malden, MA: Blackwell.

Chung, W. K., & Leibel, R. L. (2012). Genetics of body weight regulation. In K. D. Brownell, & M. S. Gold (Eds.), *Food and addiction: A comprehensive handbook*. New York, NY: Oxford University Press.

Church, A. (2010). Current perspectives in the study of personality across cultures. *Perspectives on Psychological Science, 5*(4), 441–449.

Cialdini, R. B. (2001). *Influence: Science and practice.* Boston, MA: Allyn & Bacon.

Cialdini, R. B. (2007). *Influence: Science and practice.* New York, NY: HarperCollins.

Cialdini, R. B. (2008). *Influence: Science and practice* (5th ed.). Boston, MA: Allyn & Bacon.

Cialdini, R. B., & Griskevicius, V. (2010). Social influence. In R. F. Baumeister & E. J. Finkel (Eds.), *Advanced social psychology: The state of the science* (pp. 385–417). New York, NY: Oxford University Press.

Cialdini, R. B., & Trost, M. R. (1998). Social influence: Social norms, conformity, and compliance. In D. T. Gilbert, S. T. Fiske, & G. Lindzey (Eds.), *The handbook of social psychology.* New York, NY: McGraw-Hill.

Cianciolo, A. T., & Sternberg, R. J. (2004). *Intelligence: A brief history.* Malden, MA: Blackwell.

Cicero, T. J., Inciardi, J. A., & Munoz, A. (2005). Trends in abuse of Oxycontin and other opioid analgesics in the United States. *Journal of Pain, 6*(10), 662–672.

Clancy, B., & Finlay, B. (2001). Neural correlates of early language learning. In E. Bates & M. Tomasello (Eds.), *Language development: The essential readings.* Malden, MA: Blackwell.

Clarà, M. (2017). How instruction influences conceptual development: Vygotsky's theory revisited. *Educational Psychologist, 52*, 50–62.

Clark, D. A., Abramowitz, J., Alcolado, G. M., Alonso, P., Belloch, A., Bouvard, M., . . . Wong, W. (2014). Part 3. A question of perspective: The association between intrusive thoughts and obsessionality in 11 countries. *Journal of Obsessive-Compulsive and Related Disorders, 3*(3), 292–299. doi:10.1016/j.jocrd.2013.12.006.

Clark, L. A., & Watson, D. (2003). Constructing validity: Basic issues in objective scale development. In A. E. Kazdin (Ed.), *Methodological issues & strategies in clinical research* (pp. 207–231). Washington, DC: American Psychological Association.

Clark, R. D., & Hatfield, E. (1989). Gender differences in receptivity to sexual offers. *Journal of Psychology & Human Sexuality, 2*(1), 39–55.

Clarke, D. M., & Deb, S. (2012). Syndromes causing intellectual disability. In M. G. Gelder, N. S. Andreasen, J. J. Lopez, & J. R. Geddes (Eds.), *New Oxford handbook of psychiatry* (2nd ed., Vol. 2, pp. 1838–1853). New York, NY: Oxford University Press.

Clasen, P. C., Disner, S. G., & Beevers, C. G. (2013). Cognition and depression: Mechanisms associated with the onset and maintenance of emotional disorder. In M. D. Robinson, E. Watkins, & E. Harmon-Jones (Eds.), *Handbook of cognition and emotion.* New York, NY: Guilford Press.

Clausen, J., & Levy, N. (2015). *Handbook of neuroethics.* New York, NY: Springer.

Clayton, R. B., Nagurney, A., & Smith, J. R. (2013). Cheating, breakup, and divorce: Is Facebook use to blame? *Cyberpsychology, Behavior, and Social Networking, 16*, 717–720. doi:10.1089/cyber.2012.0424.

Cleare, A. J., & Rane, L. J. (2013). Biological models of unipolar depression. In M. Power (Ed.), *The Wiley-Blackwell handbook of mood disorders* (2nd ed.). Malden, MA: Wiley-Blackwell.

Cleary, A. M., & Claxton, A. B. (2015). The tip-of-the-tongue heuristic: How tip-of-the-tongue states confer perceptibility on inaccessible words. *Journal of Experimental Psychology: Learning, Memory, and Cognition, 41*, 1533–1539.

Clement, S., Schauman, O., Graham, T., Maggioni, F., Evans-Lacko, S., Bezborodovs, N., . . . Thornicroft, G. (2015). What is the impact of mental health–related stigma on help-seeking? A systematic review of quantitative and qualitative studies. *Psychological Medicine, 45*(1), 11–27. doi:10.1017/S0033291714000129.

Clements, A. M., Rimrodt, S. L., Abel, J. R., Blankner, J. G., Mostofsky, S. H., Pekar, J. J., et al. (2006). Sex differences in cerebral laterality of language and visuospatial processing. *Brain and Language, 98*(2), 150–158.

Cloninger, S. C., & Leibo, J. (2017). *Understanding angry groups.* Santa Barbara, CA: Praeger.

Clore, G. L., & Ortony, A. (2008). Appraisal theories: How cognition shapes affect into emotion. In M. Lewis, J. M. Haviland-Jones, & L. F. Barrett, *Handbook of emotions* (3rd ed.). New York, NY: Guilford Press.

Clow, A. (2001). The physiology of stress. In F. Jones & J. Bright (Eds.), *Stress: Myth, theory, and research.* Harlow, UK: Pearson.

Coates, T. J., & Collins, C. (1998). Preventing HIV infection. *Scientific American, 279*(1), 96–97.

Coelho, C., & Purkis, H. (2009). The origins of specific phobias: Influential theories and current perspectives. *Review of General Psychology, 13*(4), 335–348.

Coelho, J. S., Polivy, J., & Herman, C. P. (2008). Effects of food-cue exposure on dieting-related goals: A limitation to counteractive control theory. *Appetite, 51*, 357–359.

Cohan, C. L. (2013). The cohabitation conundrum. In M. A. Fine & F. D. Fincham (Eds.), *Handbook of family theories: A content-based approach.* New York, NY: Routledge/Taylor & Francis Group.

Cohen, C. E. (1981). Person categories and social perception: Testing some boundaries of the processing effects of prior knowledge. *Journal of Personality and Social Psychology, 40*, 441–452.

Cohen, D. B. (1999). *Stranger in the nest: Do parents really shape their child's personality, intelligence, or character?* New York, NY: Wiley.

Cohen, M. N. (2002). An anthropologist looks at "race" and IQ testing. In J. M. Fish (Ed.), *Race and intelligence: Separating science from myth* (pp. 201–224). Mahwah, NJ: Erlbaum.

Cohen, S. (2005). Pittsburgh common cold studies: Psychosocial predictors of susceptibility to respiratory infectious illness. *International Journal of Behavioral Medicine, 12*(3), 123–131.

Cohen, S., Janicki-Deverts, D., & Miller, G. E. (2007). Psychological stress and disease. *JAMA, 298*, 1685–1687.

Cohen, S., Janicki-Deverts, D., Doyle, W. J., Miller, G. E., Frank, E., Rabin, B. S., & Turner, R. B. (2012). Chronic stress, glucocorticoid receptor resistance, inflammation, and disease risk. *PNAS Proceedings of the National Academy of Sciences in the United States of America, 109*, 5995–5999. doi:10.1073/pnas.1118355109.

Cohen, S., & Pressman, S. D. (2006). Positive affect and health. *Current Directions in Psychological Science, 15*(3), 122–125.

Colagiuri, B., & Boakes, R. A. (2010). Perceived treatment, feedback, and placebo effects in double-blind RCTs: An experimental analsis. *Psychopharmacology, 208*, 433–441.

Colangelo, J. J. (2009). Case study: The recovered memory controversy: A representative case study. *Journal of Child Sexual Abuse: Research, Treatment, & Program Innovations For Victims, Survivors, & Offenders, 18*, 103–121. doi:10.1080/10538710802584601.

Colby, A., & Kohlberg, L. (1987). *The measurement of moral judgment* (Vols. 1–2). New York, NY: Cambridge University Press.

Cole, G. G., & Wilkins, A. J. (2013). Fear of holes. *Psychological Science, 24*(10), 1980–1985.

Cole, M., & Packer, M. (2011). Culture and cognition. In K. D. Keith (Ed.), *Cross-cultural psychology: Contemporary themes and perspectives.* Malden, MA: Wiley-Blackwell.

Cole, S., Balcetis, E., & Zhang, S. (2013). Visual perception and regulatory conflict: Motivation and physiology influence distance perception. *Journal of Experimental Psychology: General, 142*, 18–22.

Colley, R. C., Didier, G., Garriguet, I., Cora, L., Craig, C. L., Clarke, J., & Tremblay, M. S. (2014). *Physical activity of Canadian children and youth: Accelerometer results from the 2007 to 2009 Canadian Health Measures Survey.* Statistics Canada. Retrieved from https://www.statcan.gc.ca/pub/82-003-x/2011001/article/11397-eng.

Colley, R. C., Garriguet, D., Janssen, I., Craig, C. L., Clarke, J., & Tremblay, M. S. (2011). Physical activity of Canadian adults: Accelerometer results from the 2007 to 2009 Canadian Health Measures Survey. *Health Reports, 22*(1), 7–14.

Collins, A. M., & Loftus, E. F. (1975). A spreading activation theory of semantic processing. *Psychological Review, 82*, 407–428.

Collins, M. A., & Zebrowitz, L. A. (1995). The contributions of appearance to occupational outcomes in civilian and military settings. *Journal of Applied Social Psychology, 25*, 129–163.

Collop, N. A. (2006). Polysomnography. In T. Lee-Chiong (Ed.), *Sleep: A comprehensive handbook.* Hoboken, NJ: Wiley-Liss.

Colman, I., Zeng, Y., Ataullahajan, A., Senthilselvan, A., & Patten, S. (2011). The association between antidepressant uses and depression eight years later: A national cohort study. *Journal of Psychiatric Research, 45*, 1042–1048.

Colwill, R. M. (1993). An associative analysis of instrumental learning. *Current Directions in Psychological Science, 2*(4), 111–116.

Comas-Diaz, L. (2006). Cultural variation in the therapeutic relationship. In C. D. Goodheart, A. E. Kazdin, & R. J. Sternberg (Eds.), *Evidence-based psychotherapy: Where practice and research meet.* Washington, DC: American Psychological Association.

Comer, D. R. (1995). A model of social loafing in real work groups. *Human Relations, 48*, 647–667.

Comer, J. S., & Kendall, P. C. (2013). Methodology, design, and evaluation in psychotherapy research. In M. J. Lambert (Ed.). *Bergin and Garfield's handbook of psychotherapy and behavior change* (6th ed.). New York, NY: Wiley.

Cona, G., & Treccani, B. (2016). Is cognitive control automatic? New insights from transcranial magnetic stimulation. *Psychonomic Bulletin and Review, 23*, 77–89.

Cong, L., Ran, F. A., Cox, D., Lin, S., Barretto, R., Habib, N., . . . Zhang, F. (2013). Multiplex genome engineering using CRISPR/Cas systems. *Science, 339*, 819–823.

Connor, C. E., Pasupathy, A., Brincat, S., & Yamane, Y. (2009). Neural transformation of object information by ventral pathway visual cortex. In M. S. Gazzaniga (Ed.), *The cognitive neurosciences.* Cambridge, MA: MIT Press.

Conte, J. M., & Dean, M. A. (2006). Can emotional intelligence be measured? In K. R. Murphy (Ed.), *A critique of emotional intelligence: What are the problems and how can they be fixed?* (pp. 59–78). Mahwah, NJ: Erlbaum.

Conway, C. C., Hipwell, A. E., & Stepp, S. D. (2017). Seven-year course of borderline personality disorder features: Borderline pathology is as unstable as depression during adolescence. *Clinical Psychology Science, 5*, 742–749.

Conway, M. A., & Williams, H. L. (2008). Autobiographical memory. In G. Cohen & M. A. Conway (Eds.), *Memory in the Real World* (3rd ed., 21–90). London, UK: Psychology Press.

Cook, E. H., Jr. (2001). Genetics of autism. *Child and Adolescent Psychiatric Clinics of North America, 10*, 333–350.

Cooke, L. (2007). The importance of exposure for healthy eating in childhood: A review. *Journal of Human Nutrition and Dietetics, 20*, 294–301.

Coolidge, F. L., & Wynn, T. (2009). *The rise of homo sapiens: The evolution of modern thinking.* Malden, MA: Wiley-Blackwell. doi:10.1002/9781444308297.

Cooper, C., Bebbington, P., King, M., Jenkins, R., Farrell, M., Brugha, T., . . . Livingston, G. (2011). Happiness across age groups: Results from the 2007 National Psychiatric Morbidity Survey. *International Journal of Geriatric Psychiatry, 26*, 608–614. doi:10.1002/gps.2570.

Cooper, J. (2013). On fraud, deceit and ethics. *Journal of Experimental Social Psychology, 49*, 314.

Cooper, L., & Bright, J. (2001). Individual differences in reactions to stress. In F. Jones & J. Bright (Eds.), *Stress: Myth, theory and research*. Harlow, UK: Pearson Education.

Corballis, M. C. (1991). *The lopsided ape*. New York, NY: Oxford University Press.

Corballis, M. C. (2007). The dual-brain myth. In S. Della Sala (Ed.), *Tall tales about the mind & brain: Separating fact from fiction* (pp. 291–313). New York, NY: Oxford University Press.

Corballis, P. M. (2003). Visuospatial processing and the right-hemisphere interpreter. *Brain & Cognition, 53*(2), 171–176.

Coren, S. (1992). *The left-hander syndrome: The causes and consequences of left-handedness*. New York, NY: Free Press.

Coren, S. (1996). Accidental death and the shift to Daylight Savings Time. *Perceptual and Motor Skills, 83*, 921–922.

Coren, S., & Girgus, J. S. (1978). *Seeing is deceiving: The psychology of visual illusions*. Hillsdale, NJ: Erlbaum.

Corkin, S. (1984). Lasting consequences of bilateral medial temporal lobectomy: Clinical course and experimental findings in H. M. *Seminars in Neurology, 4*, 249–259.

Corkin, S. (2013). *Permanent present tense: The unforgettable life of the amnesic patient H.M.* New York, NY: Penguin Books Limited.

Cornell, D. G. (1997). Post hoc explanation is not prediction. *American Psychologist, 52*, 1380.

Cornish, K., Cale, V., Longhi, E., Karmiloff-Smith, A., & Scerif, G. (2012). Does attention constrain developmental trajectories in Fragile X Syndrome? A 3-year prospective longitudinal study. *American Journal on Intellectual and Developmental Disabilities, 117*, 103–120.

Cornish, K., Scerif, G., & Karmiloff-Smith, A. (2007). Tracing syndrome specific trajectories of attention across the lifespan. *Cortex, 43*, 672–685.

Cornish, K., Sudhalter, V., & Turk, J. (2004). Attention and language in Fragile X. *Mental Retardation and Developmental Disabilities Research Reviews, 10*, 11–16.

Cornwell, J. F. M., & Higgins, E. T. (2016). Eager feelings and vigilant reasons: Regulatory focus differences in judging moral wrongs. *Journal of Experimental Psychology: General, 145*, 338–345.

Corr, C. A. (1993). Coping with dying: Lessons that we should and should not learn from the work of Elisabeth Kubler-Ross. *Death Studies, 17*, 69–83.

Corrigan, P. W., Druss, B. G., & Perlick, D. A. (2014). The impact of mental illness stigma on seeking and participating in mental health care. *Psychological Science in the Public Interest, 15*(2), 37–70. doi:10.1177/1529100614531398.

Corrigan, P. W., & Larson, J. E. (2008). Stigma. In K. T. Mueser & D. V. Jeste (Eds.), *Clinical handbook of schizophrenia* (pp. 533–540). New York, NY: Guilford Press.

Corsica, J. A., & Perri, M. G. (2013). Understanding and managing obesity. In A. M. Nezu, C. M. Nezu, P. A. Geller, & I. B. Weiner (Eds.), *Handbook of psychology: Vol. 9. Health psychology* (2nd ed.). Hoboken, NJ: Wiley.

Corsini, R. J. (1999). *The dictionary of psychology*. Philadelphia, PA: Brunner/Mazel.

Cosgrove, L., & Krimsky, S. (2012). A comparison of DSM-IV and DSM-5 panel members' financial associations with industry: a pernicious problem persists. *PLoS Medicine, 9*(3), e1001190. doi:10.1371/journal. pmed.1001190.

Cosmides, L., & Tooby, J. (1989). Evolutionary psychology and the generation of culture. Part II. Case study: A computational theory of social exchange. *Ethology and Sociobiology, 10*, 51–97.

Cosmides, L., & Tooby, J. (1994). Beyond intuition and instinct blindness: Toward an evolutionarily rigorous cognitive science. *Cognition, 50*, 41–77.

Cosmides, L., & Tooby, J. (1996). Are humans good intuitive statisticians after all? Rethinking some conclusions from the literature on judgment under uncertainty. *Cognition, 58*, 1–73.

Cosmides, L., & Tooby, J. (2013). Evolutionary psychology: New perspectives on Cognition and motivation. *Annual Review of Psychology, 64*, 201–229.

Costa, A., & Sebastián-Gallés, N. (2014). How does the bilingual experience sculpt the brain? *Nature Reviews Neuroscience, 15*, 336–345. doi:10.1038/nrn3709.

Costa, P. T., Jr., & McCrae, R. R. (1985). *NEO Personality Inventory*. Odessa, FL: Psychological Assessment Resources.

Costa, P. T., Jr., & McCrae, R. R. (1992). *Revised NEO Personality Inventory: NEO PI and NEO Five-Factor Inventory* (professional manual). Odessa, FL: Psychological Assessment Resources.

Costa, P. T., Jr., & McCrae, R. R. (1994). Set like plaster? Evidence for the stability of adult personality. In T. F. Heatherton & J. L. Weinberger (Eds.), *Can personality change?* Washington, DC: American Psychological Association.

Costa, P. T., Jr., & McCrae, R. R. (1997). Longitudinal stability of adult personality. In R. Hogan, J. Johnson, & S. Briggs (Eds.), *Handbook of personality psychology*. San Diego, CA: Academic Press.

Costa, P. T., Jr., & McCrae, R. R. (2008). The revised NEO Personality Inventory (NEO-PR-R). In G. J. Boyle, G. Matthews, & D. H. Saklofske (Eds.), *The Sage handbook of personality theory and assessment: Personality measurement and testing* (Vol. 2, pp. 179–198). Los Angeles, CA: SAGE.

Costain, G., McDonald-McGinn, D. M., & Bassett, A. S. (2013). Prenatal genetic testing with chromosomal microarray analysis identifies major risk variants for schizophrenia and other later-onset disorders. *American Journal of Psychiatry, 170*(2), 1498–1507.

Cotter, A., & Potter, J. E. (2006). Mother to child transmission. In J. Beal, J. J. Orrick, & K. Alfonso (Eds.), *HIV/AIDS: Primary care guide* (pp. 503–515). Norwalk, CT: Crown House.

Could Zach's death have been prevented? (1999, September 14). *CBC News*. Retrieved July 31, 2008, from http://www.cbc.ca/news/story/1999/09/14/anti990914.html.

Courchesne, E., Mouton, P. R., Calhoun, M. E., Semendeferi, K., Ahrens-Barbeau, C., Hallet, M. J., . . . Pierce, K. (2011). Neuron number and size in prefrontal cortex of children with autism. *JAMA, 306*, 2001–2010. doi:10.1001/jama.2011.1638.

Courtney, S. M. (2004). Attention and cognitive control as emergent properties of information representation in working memory. *Cognitive, Affective, and Behavioral Neuroscience, 4*, 501–516.

Coutts, A. (2000). Nutrition and the life cycle. 1: Maternal nutrition and pregnancy. *British Journal of Nursing, 9*, 1133–1138.

Cowan, N. (1988). Evolving conceptions of memory storage, selective attention, and their mutual constraints within the human information-processing system. *Psychological Bulletin, 104*, 163–191.

Cowan, N. (2005). *Working memory capacity*. New York, NY: Psychology Press.

Cowan, N. (2010). The magical mystery four: How is working memory capacity limited, and why? *Current Directions in Psychological Science, 19*(1), 51–57.

Cowart, B. J. (2005). Taste, our body's gustatory gate-keeper. *Cerebrum, 7*(2), 7–22.

Cowart, B. J., & Rawson, N. E. (2001). Olfaction. In E. B. Goldstein (Ed.), *Blackwell handbook of perception*. Malden, MA: Blackwell.

Cox, D., Meyers, E., & Sinha, P. (2004). Contextually evoked object-specific responses in human visual cortex. *Science, 304*, 115–117.

Cox, R. E., & Bryant, R. A. (2008). Advances in hypnosis research: Methods, designs and contributions of intrinsic and instrumental hypnosis. In M. R. Nash & A. J. Barnier (Eds.), *The Oxford Handbook of Hypnosis: Theory, research and practice* (pp. 311–336). New York, NY: Oxford University Press.

Cox, W. T. L., Abramson, L. Y., Devine, P. G., & Hollon, S. D. (2012). Stereotypes, prejudice, and depression: The integrated perspective.

Perspective on Psychological Science, 7, 427–449. doi:10.1177/1745691612455204.

Coyne, J. C. (1999). Thinking interactionally about depression: A radical restatement. In T. E. Joiner & J. C. Coyne (Eds.), *Interpersonal processes in depression* (pp. 369–392). Washington, DC: American Psychological Association.

Craig, J. C., & Rollman, G. B. (1999). Somesthesis. *Annual Review of Psychology, 50*, 305–331.

Craighead, W. E., Craighead, L. W., Ritschel, L. A., & Zagoloff, A. (2013). Behavior therapy and cognitive-behavioral therapy. In G. Stricker & T. A. Widiger (Eds.), *Handbook of psychology: Vol. 8. Clinical psychology* (2nd ed.). New York, NY: Wiley.

Craighead, W. E., & Dunlop, B. W. (2014). Combination psychotherapy and antidepressant medication treatment for depression: For whom, when, and how. *Annual Review of Psychology, 65*, 267–300.

Craighead, W. E., Ritschel, L. A., Arnarson, E. O., & Gillespie, C. F. (2008). Major depressive disorder. In W. E. Craighead, D. J. Miklowitz, & L. W. Craighead (Eds.), *Psychopathology: History, diagnosis, and empirical foundations*. New York, NY: Wiley.

Craik, F. I. M. (2001). Effects of dividing attention on encoding and retrieval processes. In H. L. Roediger III, J. S. Nairne, I. Neath, & A. M. Surprenant (Eds.), *The nature of remembering: Essays in honor of Robert G. Crowder* (pp. 55–68). Washington, DC: American Psychological Association.

. . .

Craik, F. I. M. (2002). Levels of processing: Past, present … and future? *Memory, 10*(5–6), 305–318.

Craik, F. I. M., & Bialystok, E. (2008). Lifespan cognitive development: The roles of representation and control. In F. I. M. Craik & T. Salthouse (Eds.), *The handbook of aging* (3rd ed., pp. 557–601). New York, NY: Psychology Press.

Craik, F. I. M., & Bialystok, E. (2010). Bilingualism and aging: Costs and benefits. In L. Bäckman & L. Nyberg (Eds.), *Memory, aging and the brain: A Festschrift in honour of Lars-Göran Nilsson* (pp. 115–131). New York, NY: Psychology Press.

Craik, F. I. M., & Lockhart, R. S. (1972). Levels of processing: A framework for memory research. *Journal of Verbal Learning and Verbal Behavior, 11*, 671–684.

Craik, F. I. M., & Tulving, E. (1975). Depth of processing and the retention of words in episodic memory. *Journal of Experimental Psychology: General, 104*, 268–294.

Cramer, P. (2000). Defense mechanisms in psychology today: Further processes for adaptation. *American Psychologist, 55*(6), 637–646.

Cramer, P. (2001). The unconscious status of defense mechanisms. *American Psychologist, 56*, 762–763.

Cramer, P. (2008). Seven pillars of defense mechanism theory. *Social and Personality Psychology Compass, 2*(5), 1963–1981. doi:org/10.1111/j.1751-9004.2008.00135.x.

Crane, C., Barnhofer, T., Duggan, D. S., Hepburn, S., Fennell, M. V., & Williams, J. M. G. (2008). Mindfulness-based cognitive therapy and discrepancy in recovered depressed patients with a history of depression and suicidality. *Cognitive Therapy and Research, 32*, 123–137.

Crane, C., et al. (2011). Suicidal imagery in a previously depressed community sample. *Clinical Psychology & Psychotherapy, 10*, 741–753.

Crane, R. (2008). *Mindfulness-based cognitive therapy*. London, UK: Routledge.

Craske, M. G., & Waters, A. M. (2005). Panic disorders, phobias, and generalized anxiety disorder. *Annual Review of Clinical Psychology, 1*, 197–225.

Crawford, J. D., Medendorp, W. P., & Marotta, J. J. (2004). Spatial transformations for eye–hand coordination. *Journal of Neurophysiology, 92*, 10–19.

Creed, F. (1989). Appendectomy. In G. W. Brown & T. O. Harris (Eds.), *Life events and illness*. New York, NY: Guilford.

Creswell, J. D., Bursley, J. K., & Satpute, A. B. (2013). Neural reactivation links unconscious thought to decision-making performance. *Social Cognitive and Affective Neuroscience, 8*, 863–869. doi:10.1093/scan/nst004.

Creusere, M. A. (1999). Theories of adults' understanding and use of irony and sarcasm: Applications to and evidence from research with children. *Developmental Review, 19*, 213–262.

Crits-Christoph, P. (1997). Limitations of the dodo bird verdict and the role of clinical trials in psychotherapy research: Comment on Wampold et al. *Psychological Bulletin, 122*, 216–220.

Crompton, A. (2011). What's stressing the stressed? Main sources of stress among workers. *Statistics Canada*. Retrieved from http://www.statcan.gc.ca/pub/11-008 -x/2011002/article/11562-eng.htm.

Cronbach, L. J. (1992). *Acceleration among the Terman males: Correlates in midlife and after*. Paper presented at the Symposium in Honor of Julian Stanley, San Francisco, CA.

Cropley, A. J. (2000). Defining and measuring creativity: Are creativity tests worth using? *Roeper Review, 23*, 72–79.

Cross, S. E., & Markus, H. R. (1993). Gender in thought, belief, and action: A cognitive approach. In A. E. Beall & R. J. Sternberg (Eds.), *The psychology of gender*. New York, NY: Guilford.

Crossman, M. K. (2017). Effects of interactions with animals on human psychological distress. *Journal of Clinical Psychology, 73*, 761–784.

Crow, S. J., Peterson, C. B., Swanson, S. A., Raymond, N. C., Specker, S., Eckert, E. D., & Mitchell, J. E. (2009). Increased mortality in bulimia nervosa and other eating disorders. *American Journal of Psychiatry, 166*(12), 1342–1346.

Crowder, R. G., & Greene, R. L. (2000). Serial learning: Cognition and behavior. In E. Tulving & F. I. M. Craik (Eds.), *The Oxford handbook of memory* (pp. 125–136). New York, NY: Oxford University Press.

Crowe, K. (2012). 31% of Canadian kids are overweight or obese. *CBC News*. Retrieved from http://www.cbc.ca/news/health/31-of-canadian-kids-are-overweight-or-obese-1.1154456.

Crowley, K., Callanan, M. A., Tenenbaum, H. R., & Allen, E. (2001). Parents explain more often to boys than to girls during shared scientific thinking. *Psychological Science, 12*, 258–261.

Croyle, R. T., & Cooper, J. (1983). Dissonance arousal: Physiological evidence. *Journal of Personality and Social Psychology, 45*, 782–791.

Crum, A. J., Salovey, P., & Achor, S. (2013). Rethinking stress: The role of mindsets in determining stress response. *Journal of Personality and Social Psychology, 104*, 716–733. doi:10.1037/a0031201.

Csikszentmihalyi, M. (1993). *The evolving self: A psychology for the third millennium*. New York, NY: HarperCollins.

Csikszentmihalyi, M. (1994). Creativity. In R. J. Sternberg (Ed.), *Encyclopedia of human intelligence*. New York, NY: Macmillan.

Csikszentmihalyi, M. (1999). Implications of a systems perspective for the study of creativity. In R. J. Sternberg (Ed.), *Handbook of creativity*. New York, NY: Cambridge University Press.

Csikszentmihalyi, M. (2000). The contribution of flow to positive psychology. In J. E. Gillham (Ed.), *The science of optimism and hope: Research essays in honor of Martin E. P. Seligman*. Philadelphia, PA: Templeton Foundation Press.

Cuijpers, P., Driessen, E., Hollon, S. D., van Oppen, P., Barth, J., & Andersson, G. (2012). The efficacy of non-directive supportive therapy for adult depression: A meta-analysis. *Clinical Psychology Review, 32*(4), 280–291. doi:10.1016/j.cpr.2012.01.003.

Cuijpers, P., Van Straten, A., Andersson, G., & van Oppen, P. (2008). Psychotherapy for depression in adults: A meta-analysis of comparative outcome studies. *Journal of Consulting and Clinical Psychology, 76*, 909–922.

Cuijpers, P., Vogelzangs, N., Twisk, J., Kleiboer, A., Li, J., & Penninx, B. W. (2014). Comprehensive meta-analysis of excess mortality in depression in the general community versus patients with specific illnesses. *The American Journal of Psychiatry, 171*, 453–462. doi:10.1176/appi.ajp.2013.13030325.

Cullen, B. A., McGinty, E. E., Zhang, Y., dosReis, S. C., Steinwachs, D. M., Guallar, E., & Daumit, G. L. (2013). Guideline-concordant antipsychotic use and mortality in schizophrenia. *Schizophrenia Bulletin, 39*, 1159–1168. doi:10.1093/schbul/sbs097.

Cullum, J., & Harton, H. C. (2007). Cultural evolution: Interpersonal influence, issue importance, and the development of shared attitudes in college residence halls. *Personality and Social Psychology Bulletin, 33*, 1327–1339.

Cummins, D. (2005). Dominance, status, and social hierarchies. In D. M. Buss (Ed.), *The handbook of evolutionary psychology*. New York, NY: Wiley.

Cunningham, C. O., & Selwyn, P. A. (2005). HIV-related medical complications and treatment. In J. H. Lowinson, P. Ruiz, R. B. Millman, & J. G. Langrod (Eds.), *Substance abuse: A comprehensive textbook*. Philadelphia, PA: Lippincott, Williams & Williams.

Cunningham, F., Leveno, K., Bloom, S., Hauth, J., Rouse, D., & Spong, C. (2010). *Williams obstetrics* (23rd ed.). New York, NY: McGraw-Hill.

Cunningham, W. A., Arbuckle, N. L., Jahn, A., Mowrer, S. M., & Abduljalil, A. M. (2010). Aspects of neuroticism and the amygdala: Chronic tuning from motivational styles. *Neuropsychologia, 48*(12), 3399–3404.

Cunningham, W. A., Johnsen, I. R., & Waggoner, A. S. (2011). Orbitofrontal cortex provides cross-modal valuation of self-generated stimuli. *Social Cognitive and Affective Neuroscience.*

Cunningham, W. A., Johnson, M. K., Raye, C. L., Gatenby, C., Gore, J. C., & Banaji, M. R. (2004). Separable neural components in the processing of black and white faces. *Psychological Science, 15*, 806–813.

Cunningham, W. A., Van Bavel, J. J., & Johnsen, I. R. (2008). Affective flexibility: Evaluative processing goals shape amygdala activity. *Psychological Science, 19*(2), 152–160. doi:10.1111/j.1467-9280.2008.02061.x.

Curci, A., Lanciano, T., Soleti, E., & Rimé, B. (2013). Negative emotional experiences arouse rumination and affect working memory capacity. *Emotion, 13*, 867–880. doi:10.1037/a0032492.

Curran, P. J., & Bauer, D. J. (2011). The disaggregation of within-person and between-person effects in longitudinal models of change. *Annual Review of Psychology, 62*, 583–619.

Curry, S. J., Mermelstein, R. J., & Sporer, A. K. (2009). Therapy for specific problems: Youth tobacco cessation. *Annual Review of Psychology, 60*, 229–255.

Curtis, G. C., Magee, W. J., Eaton, W. W., Wittchen, H., & Kessler, R. C. (1998). Specific fears and phobias: Epidemiology and classification. *British Journal of Psychiatry, 173*, 212–217. doi:10.1192/bjp.173.3.212.

Cushman, P. (1992). Psychotherapy to 1992: A historically situated interpretation. In D. K. Freedheim (Ed.), *History of psychotherapy: A century of change*. Washington, DC: American Psychological Association.

Cutler, B. L., & Penrod, S. D. (1995). *Mistaken identification: The eyewitness, psychology, and the law*. New York, NY: Cambridge University Press.

Cutting, L. P., & Docherty, N. M. (2000). Schizophrenia outpatients' perceptions of their parents: Is expressed emotion a factor? *Journal of Abnormal Psychology, 109*, 266–272.

Cynkar, A. (2007). The changing composition of psychology. *American Psychological Association Monitor, 38*, 7.

Cyranoski, D. (2016). CRISPR gene-editing tested in a person for the first time. *Nature News*, November 15, 2016. Retrieved from http://www.nature.com/news/crispr-gene-editing-tested-in-a-person-for-the-first-time-1.20988.

Cytowic, R. E. (2002). *Synesthesia: A union of the senses* (2nd ed.). Cambidge, MA: MIT press.

Dager, A. D., Anderson, B. M., Rosen, R., Khadka, S., Sawyer, B., Jiantonio-Kelly, R. E., . . . Pearson, G. D. (2014). Functional magnetic resonance imaging (fMRI) response to alcohol pictures predicts subsequent transition to heavy drinking in college students. *Addiction, 109*, 585–595. doi:10.1111/add.12437.

Dai, H., & Micheyl, C. (2012). Separating the contributions of primary and unwanted cues in psychophysical studies. *Psychological Review, 119*, 770–788.

Daiek, D. B., & Anter, N. M. (2004). *Critical reading for college and beyond*. New York, NY: McGraw-Hill.

Dallaire, R. A. (2003). *Shake hands with the devil: The failure of humanity in Rwanda*. Toronto, ON: Random House.

Dallman, M. F., Bhatnagar, S., & Viau, V. (2007). Hypothalamic-pituitary-adrenal axis. In G. Fink (Ed.), *Encyclopedia of stress*. San Diego, CA: Elsevier.

Daly, M., & Wilson, M. (1985). Child abuse and other risks of not living with both parents. *Ethology and Sociobiology, 6*, 197–210.

D'Andrade, R. G. (1961). Anthropological studies of dreams. In F. Hsu (Ed.), *Psychological anthropology: Approaches to culture and personality*. Homewood, IL: Dorsey Press.

Daniel, L. (2009). *Gertrude Stein*. London, UK: Reakiton Books.

Danks, D., & Rose, D. (2010). Diversity in representations: Uniformity in learning. *Behavioral and Brain Sciences, 33*, 90–91.

Danziger, K. (1990). *Constructing the subject: Historical origins of psychological research*. Cambridge, UK: Cambridge University Press.

Dapretto, M., & Bjork, E. (2000). The development of word retrieval abilities in the second year and its relation to early vocabulary growth. *Child Development, 71*, 635–648.

Dark crystal. (2005). CBC: The fifth estate. Retrieved April 1, 2008, from http://www.cbc.ca/fifth/darkcrystal.facts.html.

Darley, J. M., & Latané, B. (1968). Bystander intervention in emergencies: Diffusion of responsibility. *Journal of Personality and Social Psychology, 8*, 377–383.

Darwin, C. (1859). *The origin of species*. London, UK: Murray.

Darwin, C. (1872). *The expression of emotions in man and animals*. New York, NY: Philosophical Library.

Das, E. H. H. J., de Wit, J. B. F., & Stroebe, W. (2003). Fear appeals motivate acceptance of action recommendations: Evidence for a positive bias in the processing of persuasive messages. *Personality and Social Psychology Bulletin, 29*(5), 650–664.

Daughtery, A. (2013). Veterans plagued by mental disorders. *The Globe and Mail*, Wednesday, July 3, L6.

Davidoff, J. (2001). Language and perceptual categorization. *Trends in Cognitive Sciences, 5*, 382–387.

Davidoff, J. (2004). Coloured thinking. *Psychologist, 17*, 570–572.

Davidson, J. E. (2003). Insights about insightful problem solving. In J. E. Davidson & R. J. Sternberg (Eds.), *The psychology of problem solving*. New York, NY: Cambridge University Press.

Davidson, K. W., Mostofsky, E., & Whang, W. (2010). Don't worry, be happy: Positive affect and reduced 10-year incident coronary heart disease: The Canadian Nova Scotia Health Survey. *European Heart Journal, 31*, 1065–1070.

Davidson, R. J. (2004). Well-being and affective style: Neural substrates and biobehavioural correlates. *Philosophical Transactions of the Royal Society of London, 359*, 1359–1411.

Davidson, R. J., & Kaszniak, A. W. (2015). Conceptual and methodological issues in Research on mindfulness and meditation. *American Psychologist, 70*, 581–592.

Davidson, R. J., & Sutton, S. K. (1995). Affective neuroscience: The emergence of a discipline. *Current Biology, 5*, 217–224.

Davies, G., Tenesa, A., Payton, A., Yang, J., Harris, S. E., Liewald, D., . . . Deary, I. J. (2011). Genome-wide association studies establish that human intelligence is highly heritable and polygenic. *Molecular Psychiatry, 16*, 996–1005. doi:10.1038/mp.2011.85.

Davies, I. R. L. (1998). A study of colour in three languages: A test of linguistic relativity hypothesis. *British Journal of Psychology, 89,* 433–452.

Davis, A., & Bremner, G. (2006). The experimental method in psychology. In G. M. Breakwell, S. Hammond, C. Fife-Schaw, & J. A. Smith (Eds.), *Research methods in psychology* (3rd ed.). London, UK: SAGE.

Davis, A. S., & Dean, R. S. (2005). Lateralization of cerebral functions and hemispheric specialization: Linking behavior, structure, and neuroimaging. In R. C. D'Amato, E. Fletcher-Janzen, & C. R. Reynolds (Eds.), *Handbook of school neuropsychology* (pp. 120–141). Hoboken, NJ: Wiley.

Davis, D., & Hayes, J. A. (2012). What are the benefits of mindfulness. *American Psychological Association Monitor, 43*(7), 1–11.

Davis, M., Guyker, W., & Persky, I. (2012). Uniting veterans across distance through a telephone-based reminiscence group therapy intervention. *Psychological Services, 9*(2), 206–208. doi:10.1037/a0026117.

Davis, M. C., Burke, H. M., Zautra, A. J., & Stark, S. (2013). Arthritis and musculoskeletal conditions. In A. M. Nezu, C. M. Nezu, P. A. Geller, & I. B. Weiner (Eds.), *Handbook of psychology: Vol. 9. Health psychology* (2nd ed.). New York, NY: Wiley.

Davis, M. C., Zautra, A. J., Younger, J., Motivala, S. J., Attrep, J., & Irwin, M. R. (2008). Chronic stress and regulation of cellular markers of inflammation in rheumatoid arthritis: Implications for fatigue. *Brain, Behavior, and Immunity, 22*(1), 24–32.

Davison, G. C., Blankstein, K. R., Flett, G. L., & Neale, J. M. (2008). *Abnormal psychology* (3rd Cdn. ed.). Mississauga, ON: Wiley.

Dawes, R. M. (2001). *Everyday irrationality: How pseudoscientists, lunatics, and the rest of us systematically fail to think rationally.* Boulder, CO: Westview Press.

Deacon, B. J. (2013). The biomedical model of mental disorder: A critical analysis of its validity, utility, and effects on psychotherapy research. *Clinical Psychology Review, 33,* 846–861. doi:10.1016/j.cpr.2012.09.007.

DeAngelis, T. (2008). PTSD treatments grow in evidence, effectiveness. *Monitor on Psychology, 39,* 40–43.

DeAngelis, T. (2009). A new kind of delusion? *Monitor on Psychology, 40*(6). Retrieved from http://www.apa.org/monitor/2009/06/delusion.aspx.

DeAngelis, T. (2012). Was "Little Albert" ill during the famed conditioning study? *Monitor on Psychology, 43*(3), 12.

Deary, I. J. (2012). Intelligence. *Annual Review of Psychology, 63,* 453–482.

Deary, I. J., & Batty, G. D. (2011). Intelligence as a predictor of health, illness; and death. In R. J. Sternberg, & S. B. Kaufman (Eds.), *Cambridge handbook of intelligence.* New York, NY: Cambridge University Press.

Deary, I. J., Strand, S., Smith, P., & Fernandes, C. (2007). Intelligence and educational achievement. *Intelligence, 35,* 13–21.

Deb, S., Lyons, I., & Koutzoukis, C. (1998). Neuropsychiatric sequelae one year after a minor head injury. *Journal of Neurology, Neurosurgery, and Psychiatry, 65,* 899–902.

DeCarvalho, R. J. (1991). *The founders of humanistic psychology.* New York, NY: Praeger.

de Castro, J. M. (2010). The control of food intake of free-living humans: Putting the pieces back together. *Physiology & Behavior, 100*(5), 446–453.

Decety, J., & Keenan, J. P. (Eds.). (2006). Social neuroscience: A new journal. *Social Neuroscience, 1,* 1–4.

Decety, J., Skelly, L., Yoder, K. J., Keihl, K. A. (2014). Neural processing of dynamic facial expressions in psychopaths. *Social Neuroscience, 9*(1), 36–49.

Dechêne, A., Stahl, C., Hansen, J., & Wänke, M. (2010). The truth about the truth: A meta-analytic review of the truth effect. *Personality and Social Psychology Review, 14*(2), 238–257.

DeCicco, T. L. (2002). *Skills for coping with stress and anxiety: A handbook for patients.* Toronto, ON: James Publishing.

De Cremer, D., Zeelenberg, M., & Murnighan, J. K. (2006). *Social psychology and economics.* Mahwah, NJ: Erlbaum.

Deecher, D., Andree, T. H., Sloan, D., & Schechter, L. E. (2008). From menarche to menopause: Exploring the underlying biology of depression in women experiencing hormonal changes. *Psychoneuroendocrinology, 33*(1), 3–17.

Deer, B. (2011). How the case against the MMR vaccine was fixed. *British Medical Journal, 342,* 77–82.

Deese, J. (1959). On the prediction of occurrence of particular verbal intrusions in immediate recall. *Journal of Experimental Psychology, 58,* 17–22.

DeFreitas, J., Sarkissian, H., Newman, G. E., Grossmann, I., De Brigard, F., et al. (2017). Consistent belief in a good self in misanthropes and three interdependent cultures. *Cognitive Science* [Epub ahead of print]. Retrieved from https://www.ncbi.nlm.nih.gov/pubmed/28585702.

De Houwer, J. (2011). Evaluative conditioning: A review of functional knowledge and mental process theories. In T. R. Schachtman, & S. Reilly (Eds.), *Associative learning and condition theory: Human and non-human applications.* New York, NY: Oxford University Press.

Deiner, E., & Chan, M. Y. (2011). Happy people live longer: Subjective well-being contributes to health and longevity. *Applied Psychology: Health and Well-Being, 3,* 1–43.

Deitmer, J. W., & Rose, C. R. (2009). Ion changes and signaling in perisynaptic glia. *Brain Research Reviews, 63*(1–2), 113–129.

Delis, D. C., & Lucas, J. A. (1996). Memory. In B. S. Fogel, R. B. Schiffer, & S. M. Rao (Eds.), *Neuropsychiatry.* Baltimore, MD: Williams & Wilkins.

De Koninck, J. (1997). Sleep, the common denominator for psychological adaptation. *Canadian Psychology, 38,* 191–195.

De Koninck, J. (2000). Waking experiences and dreaming. In M. H. Kryger, T. Roth, & W. C. Dement (Eds.), *Principles and practice of sleep medicine.* Philadelphia, PA: Saunders.

De Koninck, J. (2012). Dreams and dreaming. In C. Moring & C. Epsie (Eds.), *Handbook of sleep and sleep disorders* (pp. 150–171). Oxford, UK: Oxford University Press.

DeLongis, A. (2014). Daily Hassles Scale. In A. C. Michalos (Ed.), *Encyclopedia of Life and Well-Being Research* (pp. 22–45). Dordrecht, Netherlands: Springer Publishing.

DeLongis, A., Folkman, S., & Lazarus, R. S. (1988). The impact of daily stress on health and mood: Psychological and social resources as mediators. *Journal of Personality and Social Psychology, 54,* 486–495.

DeLongis, A., Holtzman, S, Puterman, E., & Lam, M. (2010). Dyadic coping: Support from the spouse in times of stress. In J. Davila & K. Sullivan (Eds.), *Social support processes in intimate relationships* (pp. 151–174). New York, NY: Oxford Press.

Dement, W. C. (1999). *The promise of sleep.* New York, NY: Delacorte Press.

Dement, W. C. (2003). Knocking on Kleitman's door: The view from 50 years later. *Sleep Medicine Reviews, 7*(4), 289–292.

Dement, W. C. (2005). History of sleep psychology. In M. H. Kryger, T. Roth, & W. C. Dement (Eds.), *Principles and practice of sleep medicine.* Philadelphia, PA: Elsevier Saunders.

Dement, W. C., & Vaughan, C. (1999). *The promise of sleep.* New York, NY: Delacorte Press.

Dement, W. C., & Wolpert, E. (1958). The relation of eye movements, bodily motility, and external stimuli to dream content. *Journal of Experimental Psychology, 53,* 543–553.

Demers, P. A., Wong, I., & McLeod, C. (2010). The prevalence of shift work in Canada. Retrieved from http://www.iwh.on.ca/shift-work-symposium/demers.

Demir, M., Orthel, H., & Andelin, A. K. (2013). Friendship and happiness. In S. A. David, I. Boniwell, &

A. Conley Ayers (Eds.), *The Oxford handbook of happiness.* New York, NY: Oxford University Press.

Demo, D. H. (1992). Parent–child relations: Assessing recent changes. *Journal of Marriage and the Family, 54,* 104–117.

Dempster, E. L., Pidsley, R., Schalkwyk, L. C., Owens, S., Georgiades, A., Kane, F., . . . Mill, J. (2011). Disease-associated epigenetic changes in monozygotic twins discordant for schizophrenia and bipolar disorder. *Human Molecular Genetics.* doi:10.1093/hmg/ddr416.

De Neys, W. (2006). Dual processing in reasoning: Two systems but one reasoner. *Psychological Science, 17,* 428–433.

Denis, D., & Poerio, G. L. (2017). Terror and bliss? Commonalities and distinctions between sleep paralysis, lucid dreaming, and their associations with waking life experiences. *Sleep Research, 26,* 38–47.

Dennis, C-L. (2014a). The process of developing and implementing a telephone-based peer support program for postpartum depression: Results from a randomized controlled trial. *Trials, 15,* 131.

Dennis, C-L. (2014b). Psychosocial interventions for the treatment of perinatal depression. *Best Practice & Research Clinical Obstetrics & Gynecology.* 28, 97–111.

Denys, D., Mantione, M., Figee, M., van den Munckhof, P., Koerselman, F., Westenberg, H., et al. (2010). Deep brain stimulation of the nucleus accumbens for treatment-refractory obsessive-compulsive disorder. *Archives of General Psychiatry, 67*(10), 1061–1068.

Department of Justice, Government of Canada. (2016a). *Preliminary examination of so called "honour killings" in Canada.* Retrieved from http://www.justice.gc.ca/eng/rp-pr/cj-jp/fv-vf/hk-ch/index.html.

Department of Justice, Government of Canada. (2016b). The criminal law and managing children's behaviour. Retrieved from http://www.justice.gc.ca/eng/rp-pr/cj-jp/fv-vf/mcb-cce/index.html.

DePrince, A. P., Brown, L. S., Cheit, R. E., Freyd, J. J., Gold, S. N., Pezdek, K., & Quina, K. (2012). Motivated forgetting and misremembering: Perspectives from betrayal trauma theory. In R. F. Belli (Ed.), *True and false recovered memories: Toward a reconciliation of the debate.* New York, NY: Springer.

Deregowski, J. B. (2015). Illusions within an illusion. *Perception, 44,* 1416–1421.

Desmurget, M., Song, Z., Mottolese, C., & Sirigu, A. (2013). Re-establishing the merits of electrical brain stimulation. *Trends in Cognitive Sciences, 17,* 442– 449. doi:10.1016/j.tics.2013.07.002.

DeSpelder, L. A., & Strickland, A. L. (1983). *The last dance: Encountering death and dying.* Palo Alto, CA: Mayfield.

de St. Aubin, E., McAdams, D. P., & Kim, T. (2004). *The generative society: Caring for future generations.* Washington, DC: American Psychological Association.

Detterman, L. T., Gabriel, L. T., & Ruthsatz, J. M. (2000). Intelligence and mental retardation. In R. J. Sternberg (Ed.), *Handbook of intelligence* (pp. 141–158). New York, NY: Cambridge University Press.

de Villiers, J. G., & de Villiers, P. A. (1999). Language development. In M. H. Bornstein & M. E. Lamb (Eds.), *Developmental psychology: An advanced textbook* (pp. 313–373). Mahwah, NJ: Erlbaum.

De Villiers, P. (1977). Choice in concurrent schedules and a quantitative formulation of the law of effect. In W. K. Honig & J. E. R. Staddon (Eds.), *Handbook of operant behavior.* Englewood Cliffs, NJ: Prentice-Hall.

Devine, P. G., & Monteith, M. J. (1999). Automaticity and control in stereotyping. In S. Chaiken & Y. Trope (Eds.), *Dual-process theories in social psychology.* New York, NY: Guilford.

Devine, P. G., & Sharp, L. B. (2009). Automaticity and control in stereotyping and prejudice. In T. D. Nelson (Ed.), *Handbook of prejudice, stereotyping, and discrimination* (pp. 1–22). New York, NY: Psychology Press.

Devine, P. G., Tauer, J. M., Barron, K. E., Elliot, A. J., & Vance, K. M. (1999). Moving beyond attitude change in the study of dissonance-related processes.

In E. Harmon-Jones & J. Mills (Eds.), *Cognitive dissonance: Progress on a pivotal theory in social psychology*. Washington, DC: American Psychological Association.

Devitt A. L., & Addis, D. R. (2016). Bidirectional interactions between memory and imagination. In K. Michaelian, S. B. Klein, & K. K. Szpunar (Eds.), *Seeing the future: Theoretical perspectives on future-oriented mental time travel* (pp. 93–115). New York, NY: Oxford University Press.

Devlin, M. J., & Steinglass, J. E. (2014). Feeding and eating disorders. In J. L. Cutler (Ed.), *Psychiatry* (3rd ed.). New York, NY: Oxford University Press.

Devonis, D. (2012). Timothy Leary's mid-career shift: Clean break or inflection point. *Journal of the History of the Behavioural Sciences, 48*(1), 16–39.

Devos, T. (2008). Implicit attitudes 101: Theoretical and empirical insights. In W. D. Crano, & R. Prislin (Eds.), *Attitudes and attitude change* (pp. 61–84). New York, NY: Psychology Press.

Dew, M. A., Bromet, E. J., & Switzer, G. E. (2000). Epidemiology. In M. Hersen & A. S. Bellack (Eds.), *Psychopathology in adulthood*. Boston, MA: Allyn & Bacon.

De Waal, F. (2001). *The ape and the sushi master: Cultural reflections of a primatologist*. New York, NY: Basic Books.

Dewald, J. F., Meijer, A. M., Oort, F. J., Kerkhof, G. A., & Bogels, S. M. (2010). The influence of sleep quality, sleep duration and sleepiness on school performance in children and adolescents: A meta-analytic review. *Sleep Medicine Reviews, 14*, 179–189. doi:10.1016/j.smrv.2009.10.004.

De Wit, J. B. F., Das, E., & Vet, R. (2008). What works best: Objective statistics or a personal testimonial? An assessment of the persuasive effects of different types of message evidence on risk perception. *Health Psychology, 27*, 110–115.

Dewsbury, D. A. (2009). Charles Darwin and psychology at the Bicentennial and Sesquicentennial. *American Psychologist, 64*, 67–74.

DeYoung, C. G. (2015). Openness/ intellect: A dimension of personality reflecting. In M. Mikulincer, P. R. Shaver, M. L. Cooper & R. J. Larsen (Eds.), *APA handbook of personality and social psychology: Vol. 4. Personality processes and individual differences*. Washington, DC: American Psychological Association.

DeYoung, C. G., & Gray, J. R. (2009). Personality neuroscience: Explaining individual differences in affect, behaviour and cognition. In P. J. Corr & G. Matthews (Eds.), *The Cambridge handbook of personality psychology* (pp. 323–346). New York, NY: Cambridge University Press.

DeYoung, C. G., Hirsch, J. B., Shane, M. S., Papademetris, X., Rajeevan, N., & Gray, J. R. (2010). Testing predictions from personality neuroscience: Brain structure and the big five. *Psychological Science, 21*(6), 820–828.

Dhabhar, F. S. (2011). Effects of stress on immune function: Implications for immunoprotection and immunopathology. In R. J. Contrada & A. Baum (Eds.), *Handbook of stress science: Biology, psychology, and health*. New York, NY: Springer Publishing Company.

Diamond, L. M. (2003). Was it a phase? Young women's relinquishment of lesbian/bisexual identities over a 5-year period. *Journal of Personality and Social Psychology, 84*, 352–364.

Diamond, L. M. (2013). Concepts of female sexual orientation. In C. J. Patterson, & A. R. D'Augelli (Eds.), *Handbook of psychology and sexual orientation*. New York, NY: Oxford University Press.

Diamond, L. M. (2014). Gender and same-sex sexuality. In D. L. Tolman, L. M. Diamond, J. A. Bauermeister, W. H. George, J. G. Pfaus, & L. M. Ward (Eds.), *APA handbook of sexuality and psychology: Vol. 1. Person-based approaches*. Washington, DC: American Psychological Association.

Diamond, M. C., Scheibel, A. B., Murphy, Jr., G. M., & Harvey, T. (1985). On the brain of a scientist Albert Einstein. *Experimental Neurology 88*, 198–204.

Di Chiara, G. (1999). Drug addiction as a dopamine-dependent associative learning disorder. *European Journal of Pharmacology, 375*, 13–30.

DiCicco-Bloom, E., & Falluel-Morel, A. (2009). Neural development & neurogenesis. In B. J. Sadock, V. A. Sadock, & P. Ruiz (Eds.), *Kaplan & Sadock's comprehensive textbook of psychiatry* (9th ed., Vol. 1, pp. 42–64). Philadelphia, PA: Lippincott, Williams & Wilkins.

Dick, D. M., & Rose, R. J. (2002). Behavior genetics: What's new? What's next? *Current Directions in Psychological Science, 11*(2), 70–74.

Dickens, W. T., & Flynn, J. R. (2001). Heritability estimates versus large environmental effects: The IQ paradox resolved. *Psychological Review, 108*, 346–369.

Diekman, A. B., & Murnen, S. K. (2004). Learning to be little women and little men: The inequitable gender equality of nonsexist children's literature. *Sex Roles, 50*, 373–385.

Diener, E., & Diener, C. (1996). Most people are happy. *Psyhological Science, 7*, 181–185.

Diener, E., Kesebir, P., & Tov, W. (2009). Happiness. In M. Leary & R. H. Hoyle (Eds.), *Handbook of individual differences in social behavior* (pp. 147–160). New York, NY: Guilford Press.

Diener, E., Sandvik, E., Seidlitz, L., & Diener, M. (1993). The relationship between income and subjective well-being. Relative or absolute? *Social Indicators Research, 28*, 195–223.

Diener, E., & Seligman, M. E. P. (2004). Beyond money: Toward an economy of well-being. *Psychological Science in the Public Interest, 5*(1), 1–31.

Diener, E., Wolsic, B., & Fujita, F. (1995). Physical attractiveness and subjective well-being. *Journal of Personality and Social Psychology, 69*, 120–129.

Dietrich, M. O., & Horvath T. L. (2012). Neuroendocrine regulation of energy balance. In K. D. Brownell, & M. S. Gold (Eds.), *Food and addiction: A comprehensive handbook*. New York, NY: Oxford University Press.

Dijksterhuis, A. (2010). Automaticity and the unconscious. In S. T. Fiske, D. T. Gilbert, & G. Lindzey (Eds.), *Handbook of social psychology* (5th ed., Vol. 1, pp. 228–267). New York, NY: Wiley.

Dijksterhuis, A., Bos, M. W., Nordgren, L. F., & van Baaren, R. B. (2006). On making the right choice: The deliberation-without-attention effect. *Science, 311*, 1005–1007.

Dijksterhuis, A., & Nordgren, L. F. (2006). A theory of unconscious thought. *Perspectives on Psychological Science, 1*, 95–109.

Dijksterhuis, A., & van Olden, Z. (2006). On the benefits of thinking unconsciously: Unconscious thought can increase post-choice satisfaction. *Journal of Experimental Social Psychology, 42*, 627–631.

Dillbeck, M. C., & Orme-Johnson, D. W. (1987). Physiological differences between transcendental meditation and rest. *American Psychologist, 42*, 879–881.

Di Lorenzo, P. M., & Rosen, A. M. (2010). Taste. In E. B. Goldstein (Ed.), *Encyclopedia of perception*. Thousand Oaks, CA: SAGE.

Di Lorenzo, P. M., & Youngentob, S. L. (2003). Olfaction and taste. In M. Gallagher & R. J. Nelson (Eds.), *Handbook of psychology (Vol. 3): Biological psychology*. New York, NY: Wiley.

Di Lorenzo, P. M., & Youngentob, S. L. (2013). Taste and olfaction. In R. J. Nelson, S. J. Y. Mizumori, & I. B. Weiner (Eds.), *Handbook of psychology: Vol. 3. Behavioral neuroscience* (2nd ed.). New York, NY: Wiley.

DiManno, R. (2011a, February 22). Rochette turned personal tragedy into a nation's triumph, *Toronto Star*. Retrieved May 2, 2011, from http://www.thestar.com/sports/olympics/article/943249—dimanno-rochette-turned-personal-tragedy-into-a-nation-s-triumph.

DiManno, R. (2011b, March 20). No escape valve for so much grief, *Toronto Star*. Retrieved May 2, 2011, from http://www.thestar.com/news/world/article/957069—dimanno-no-escape-valve-for-so-much-grief.

DiMatteo, M. R. (1991). *The psychology of health, illness, and medical care: An individual perspective*. Pacific Grove, CA: Brooks/Cole.

DiMatteo, M. R. (1997). Health behaviors and care decisions: An overview of professional-patient communication. In D. S. Gochman (Ed.), *Handbook of health behavior research II: Provider determinants*. New York, NY: Plenum.

DiMatteo, M. R. (2004a). Social support and patient adherence to medical treatment: A meta analysis. *Health Psychology, 23*, 207–218.

DiMatteo, M. R. (2004b). Variations in patients' adherence to medical recommendations: A quantitative review of 50 years of research. *Medical Care, 42*, 200–209.

Dimberg, U., & Söderkvist, S. (2011). The voluntary facial action technique: A method to test the facial feedback hypothesis. *Journal of Nonverbal Behavior, 35*(1), 17–33. doi:10.1007/s10919-010-0098-6.

Dimidjian, S., Beck, A., Felder, J. N., Boggs, J., Gallop, R., & Segal, Z. V. (2014). Web-based mindfulness-based cognitive therapy of reducing residual depressive symptoms: An open trial and quasi-experimental comparison to propensity score matched controls. *Behavior Research and Therapy, 63*, 83–89.

Dimidjian, S., & Segal, Z. V. (2015). Prospects for a clinical science of mindfulness-based intervention. *American Psychologist, 70*, 593–620.

Dinehart, M. E., Hayes, J. E., Bartoshuk, L. M., Lanier, S. L., & Duffy, V. B. (2006). Bitter taste markers explain variability in vegetable sweetness, bitterness, and intake. *Physiology & Behavior, 87*, 304–313.

Ding, D., Fung, J. W., Zhang, Q., Yip, G. W., Chang, C., & Yu, C. (2009). Effect of household passive smoking exposure on the risk of ischaemic heart disease in never-smoke female patients in Hong Kong. *Tobacco Control: An International Journal, 18*, 354–357. doi:10.1136/tc.2008.026112.

Dinges, D. F. (1993). Napping. In M. A. Carskadon (Ed.), *Encyclopedia of sleep and dreaming*. New York, NY: Macmillan.

Dinsmoor, J. A. (1998). Punishment. In W. O'Donohue (Ed.), *Learning and behavior therapy*. Boston, MA: Allyn & Bacon.

Dion, K. (1973). Young children's stereotyping of facial attractiveness. *Developmental Psychology, 9*, 183–188.

Dion, K. K., Berscheid, E., & Walster, E. (1972). What is beautiful is good. *Journal of Personality and Social Psychology, 24*, 285–290.

Dion, K. K., & Dion, K. L. (1996). Cultural perspectives on romantic love. *Personal Relationships, 3*, 5–17.

Dismukes, R. K. (2012). Prospective memory in workplace and everyday situations. *Current Directions in Psychological Science, 21*, 215–220. doi:10.1177/0963721412447621.

Dittrich, L. (2010). The brain that changed everything. *Esquire*, November, 112–119.

Dittrich, L. (2016). *Patient H.M.: A story of memory, madness and family secrets*. New York, NY: Random House.

Dixon, J. (2017). "Thinking ill of others without sufficient warrant?": Transcending the accuracy-inaccuracy dualism in prejudice and stereotyping research. *British Journal of Social Psychology, 56*, 4–27.

Dixon, R. A., & Cohen, A. (2003). Cognitive development in adulthood. In R. M. Lerner, M. A. Easterbrooks, & J. Mistry (Eds.), *Handbook of psychology (Vol. 6): Developmental psychology*. New York, NY: Wiley.

Dixon, R. A., McFall, G. P., Whitehead, B. P., & Dolcos, S. (2013). Cognitive development in adulthood and aging. In R. M. Lerner, M. A. Easterbrooks, J. Mistry, & I. B. Weiner (Eds.), *Handbook of psychology: Vol. 6. Developmental psychology*. New York, NY: Wiley.

Dobson, K. (2016). Clinical psychology in Canada: Challenges and opportunities. *Canadian Psychology, 57*, 211–219.

Docherty, N. M., St-Hilaire, A., Aakre, J. M., & Seghers, J. P. (2009). Life events and high-trait reactivity together predict psychotic symptom increases in schizophrenia. *Schizophrenia Bulletin, 35*(3), 638–645.

Dodds, R. A., Ward, T. B., & Smith, S. M. (2011). A review of experimental literature on incubation in problem solving and creativity. In M. A. Runco (Ed.),

Creativity research handbook (Vol. 3). Cresskill, NJ: Hampton.

Dohrenwend, B. P. (2006). Inventorying stressful life events as risk factors for psychopathology: Toward resolution of the problem of intracategory variability. *Psychological Bulletin, 132,* 477–495.

Doja, A., & Roberts, W. (2006). Immunizations and autism: A review of the literature. *Canadian Journal of Neurological Sciences, 33,* 341–346.

Dokis, D. (2007). Racism against First Nations People and First Nations humour as a coping mechanism. *Totem: The University of Western Ontario Journal of Anthropology, 15.* Retrieved from http://ir.lib.uwo.ca/totem/vol15/iss1/8/.

Dollard, J., Doob, L. W., Miller, E., Mowrer, O. H., & Sears, R. R. (1939). *Frustration and aggression.* New Haven, CT: Yale University Press.

Dollard, J., & Miller, N. E. (1950). *Personality and psychotherapy: An analysis in terms of learning, thinking and culture.* New York, NY: McGraw-Hill.

Domhoff, G. W. (2001). A new neurocognitive theory of dreams. *Dreaming, 11,* 13–33.

Domhoff, G. W. (2005a). The content of dreams: Methodological and theoretical implications. In M. H. Kryger, T. Roth, & W. C. Dement (Eds.), *Principles and practice of sleep medicine.* Philadelphia, PA: Elsevier Saunders.

Domhoff, G. W. (2005b). Refocusing the neurocognitive approach to dreams: A critique of the Hobson versus Solms debate. *Dreaming, 15*(1), 3–20.

Dominowski, R. L., & Bourne, L. E., Jr. (1994). History of research on thinking and problem solving. In R. J. Sternberg (Ed.), *Thinking and problem solving.* San Diego, CA: Academic Press.

Domjan, M., & Purdy, J. E. (1995). Animal research in psychology: More than meets the eye of the general psychology student. *American Psychologist, 50,* 496–503.

Dömötör, Z., Ruíz-Barquín, R., & Szabo, A. (2016). Superstitious behavior in sport: A literature review. *Scandinavian Journal of Psychology, 57,* 368–382.

Don, B. P., & Mickelson, K. D. (2014). Relationship satisfaction trajectories across the transition to parenthood among low-risk parents. *Journal of Marriage and Family, 76,* 677–692. doi:10.1111/jomf.12111.

Donaldson, Z. R., & Young, L. J. (2008). Oxytocin, vasopressin, and the neurogenetics of sociality. *Science, 322*(5903), 900–904.

Donderi, D. C. (2006). Visual complexity: A review. *Psychological Bulletin, 132,* 73–97.

Donnellan, M. B., Hill, P. L., & Roberts, B. W. (2015). Personality development across the life span: Current findings and future directions. In M. Mikulincer, P. R. Shaver, M. L. Cooper, & J. Larsen (Eds.), *APA handbook of personality and social psychology: Vol. 4. Personality processes and individual differences.* Washington, DC: American Psychological Association.

Dorahy, M. J., Brand, B. L., s ar, V., Krüger, C., Stavropoulos, P., Martínez-Taboas, A., . . . Middleton, W. (2014). Dissociative identity disorder: An empirical overview. *Australian and New Zealand Journal of Psychiatry, 48,* 402–417. doi:10.1177/0004867414527523.

Doron, K. W., Bassett, D. S., & Gazzaniga, M. S. (2012). Dynamic network structure of interhemispheric coordination. *PNAS Proceedings of the National Academy of Sciences of the United States of America, 109,* 18661–18668. doi:10.1073/pnas.1216402109.

Dörrie, N., Focker, M., Freunscht, I., & Hebebrand, J. (2014). Fetal alcohol spectrum disorders. *European Child & Adolescent Psychiatry, 23,* 863–875. doi:10.1007/s00787-014-0571-6.

Doss, B. D., Rhoades, G. K., Stanley, S. M., & Markman, H. J. (2009). The effect of the transition to parenthood on relationship quality: An 8-year prospective study. *Journal of Personality and Social Psychology, 96*(3), 601–619.

Doty, R. L. (1991). Olfactory system. In T. V. Getchell, R. L. Doty, L. M. Bartoshuk, & J. B. Snow, Jr. (Eds.), *Smell and taste in health and disease.* New York, NY: Raven.

Doty, R. L. (2010a). Olfaction. In E. B. Goldstein (Ed.), *Encyclopedia of perception.* Thousand Oaks, CA: Sage.

Doty, R. L. (2010b). *The great pheromone myth.* New York, NY: Hopkins Fulfillment Service.

Doty, R. L. (2010c). The pheromone myth: Sniffing out the truth. *New Scientist, 2479.* Retrieved March 2, 2011, from http://www.newscientist.com/article/mg20527491.100-the-pheromone-myth-sniffing-out-the-truth.html.

Dougall, A. L., & Baum, A. (2001). Stress, health, and illness. In A. Baum, T. A. Revenson & J. E. Singer (Eds.), *Handbook of health psychology* (pp. 321–338). Mahwah, NJ: Erlbaum.

Dougherty, D. D., Wilhelm, S., & Jenike, M. A. (2014). Obsessive-compulsive and related disorders. In R. E. Hales, S. C. Yudofsky, & L. W. Roberts (Eds.), *The American Psychiatric Publishing textbook of psychiatry* (6th ed.). Washington, DC: American Psychiatric Publishing.

Douglas, A. J. (2010). Baby on board: Do responses to stress in the maternal brain mediate adverse pregnancy outcome? *Frontiers in Neuroendocrinology, 31*(3), 359–376.

Dovern, A., Fink, G. R., Fromme, A. C. B., Wohlschager, A. M., Weiss, P. H., & Riedl, V. (2012). Intrinsic network connectivity reflets consistency of sythesthetic experiences. *Journal of Neuroscience, 32,* 7614–7621.

Dovidio, J. F., & Gaertner, S. L. (2008). New directions in aversive racism research: Persistence and pervasiveness. In C. Willis-Esqueda (Ed.), *Motivational aspects of prejudice and racism* (pp. 43–67). New York, NY: Springer Science & Business Media. doi:10.1007/978-0-387-73233-6_3.

Dovidio, J. F., & Gaertner, S. L. (2010). Intergroup bias. In S. T. Fiske, D. T. Gilbert, & G. Lindzey (Eds.), *Handbook of social psychology* (5th ed., Vol. 1, pp. 353–393). Hoboken, NJ: Wiley.

Dovidio, J. F., Gaertner, S. L., & Kawakami, K. (2010). Racism. In J. F. Dovidio, M. Hewstone, P. Glick, & V. M. Esses (Eds.), *The Sage handbook of prejudice, stereotyping, and discrimination.* Los Angeles, CA: SAGE.

Dovidio, J. F., Kawakami, K., & Gaertner, S. L. (2002). Implicit and explicit prejudice and interracial interaction. *Journal of Personality and Social Psychology, 82,* 62–82.

Dow, L. E., Fisher, J., O'Rourke, K. P., Muley, A., Kastenhuer, E. R., Livshits, G., . . . Lowe, S. W. (2015). Inducible in vivo genome editing with CRISPR-Cas9. *Nature Bitechnology, 33,* 390–394.

Dowling, K. W. (2005). The effect of lunar phases on domestic violence incident rates. *The Forensic Examiner, 14*(4), 13–18.

Downey, C. A., & Chang, E. C. (2014). Positive psychology: Current knowledge, multicultural considerations, and the future of the movement. In F. L. Leong, L. Comas-Díaz, G. C. Nagayama Hall, V. C. McLoyd, & J. E. Trimble (Eds.), *APA handbook of multicultural psychology: Vol. 2. Applications and training.* Washington, DC: American Psychological Association. doi:10.1037/14187-008.

Draganski, B., Gaser, C., Busch, V., Schuierer, G., Bogdahn, U., & May, A. (2004). Changes in grey matter induced by training. *Nature, 427,* 311–312.

Draguns, J. G. (1980). Psychological disorders of clinical severity. In H. C. Triandis & J. Draguns (Eds.), *Handbook of cross-cultural psychology* (Vol. 6). Boston, MA: Allyn & Bacon.

Draguns, J. G. (1990). Applications of cross-cultural psychology in the field of mental health. In R. Brislin (Ed.), *Applied cross-cultural psychology.* Newbury Park, CA: Sage.

Drake, C. L., & Wright, Jr., K. P. (2011). Shift work, shift-work disorder, and jet lag. In M. H. Kryger, T. Roth, & W. C. Dement (Eds.), *Principles and practice of sleep medicine* (5th ed.). Saint Louis, MO: Elsevier Saunders.

Dranovsky, A., & Hen, R. (2006). Hippocampal neurogenesis: Regulation by stress and antidepressants. *Biological Psychiatry, 59,* 1136–1143.

Drew, L. J., Fusi, S., & Hen, R. (2013). Adult neurogenesis in the mammalian hippocampus: Why the dentate gyrus? *Learning & Memory, 20,* 710–729. doi:10.1101/lm.026542.112.

Drew, T., Vo, M. L-H., & Wolfe, J. M. (2013). The invisible gorilla strikes again: Sustained inattentional blindness in expert observers. *Psychological Science, 24*(9), 1848–1853.

Drewnowski, A. (1995). Standards for the treatment of obesity. In K. D. Brownell, & C. G. Fairburn (Eds.), *Eating disorders and obesity: A comprehensive handbook.* New York, NY: Guilford.

Drews, F. A., Pasupathi, M., & Strayer, D. L. (2008). Passenger and cell phone conversations in simulated driving. *Journal of Experimental Psychology: Applied, 14*(4), 392–400.

Drews, F. A., Yazdani, H., Godfrey, C. N., Cooper, J. M., & Strayer, D. L. (2009). Text messaging during simulated driving. *Human Factors, 51*(5), 762–770.

Dubno, J. R. (2010). Aging and hearing. In E. B. Goldstein (Ed.), *Encyclopedia of perception.* Thousand Oaks, CA: SAGE.

Dubovsky, S. L. (2009). Benzodiazepine receptor agonists and antagonists. In B. J. Sadock, V. A. Sadock, & P. Ruiz (Eds.), *Kaplan & Sadock's comprehensive textbook of psychiatry* (pp. 3044–3055). Philadelphia, PA: Lippincott Williams & Wilkins.

Duckworth, A. L., & Seligman, M. E. P. (2005). Self-discipline outdoes IQ in predicting academic performance of adolescents. *Psychological Science, 16,* 939–944.

Duckworth, A. L., Steen, T. A., & Seligman, M. E. P. (2005). Positive psychology in clinical practice. *Annual Review of Clinical Psychology, 1*(1), 629–651.

Duckworth, K., & Borus, J. F. (1999). Population-based psychiatry in the public sector and managed care. In A. M. Nicholi (Ed.), *The Harvard guide to psychiatry.* Cambridge, MA: Harvard University Press.

Dudai, Y. (2004). The neurobiology of consolidation, or, how stable is the engram? *Annual Review of Psychology, 55,* 51–86.

Dudley, M., Hadzi-Pavlovic, D., Andrews, D., & Perich, T. (2008). New-generation antidepressants, suicide and depressed adolescents: How should clinicians respond to changing evidence? *Australian and New Zealand Journal of Psychiatry, 42*(6), 456–466.

Duffy, J. F., Willson, H. J., Wang, W., & Czeisler, C. A. (2009). Healthy older adults better tolerate sleep deprivation than young adults. *Journal of the American Geriatrics Society, 57*(7), 1245–1251.

Duffy, V. B. (2004). Associations between oral sensation, dietary behaviors and risk of cardiovascular disease (CVD). *Appetite, 43*(1), 5–9.

Duffy, V. B., Lucchina, L. A., & Bartoshuk, L. M. (2004). Genetic variation in taste: Potential biomarker for cardiovascular disease risk? In J. Prescott & B. J. Tepper (Eds.), *Genetic variations in taste sensitivity: Measurement, significance and implications* (pp. 195–228). New York, NY: Dekker.

Duffy, V. B., Peterson, J. M., & Bartoshuk, L. M. (2004). Associations between taste genetics, oral sensations and alcohol intake. *Physiology & Behavior, 82,* 435–445.

Duke, A. A., Bègue, L., Bell, R., & Eisenlohr-Moul, T. (2013). Revisiting the serotonin–aggression relation in humans: A meta-analysis. *Psychological Bulletin, 139,* 1148–1172. doi:10.1037/a0031544.

Dum, R. P., & Strick, P. L. (2009). Basal ganglia and cerebellar circuits with the cerebral cortex. In M. S. Gazzanigia (Ed.), *The cognitive neuro-sciences* (4th ed., pp. 553–564). Cambridge, MA: MIT Press.

Duman, R. S., Polan, H. J., & Schatzberg, A. (2008). Neurobiologic foundations of mood disorders. In A. Tasman, J. Kay, J. A. Lieberman, M. B. First, & M. Maj (Eds.), *Psychiatry* (3rd ed.). New York, NY: Wiley-Blackwell.

Dunbar, R. (1996). *Grooming, gossip, and the evolution of language.* Cambridge, MA: Harvard University Press.

Dunbar-Jacob, J., & Schlenk, E. (2001). Patient adherence to treatment regimen. In A. Baum, T. A. Revenson,

& J. E. Singer (Eds.), *Handbook of health psychology* (pp. 571–580). Mahwah, NJ: Erlbaum.

Dunbar-Jacob, J., Schlenk, E., & McCall, M. (2012). Patient adherence to treatment regimen. In A. Baum, T. A. Revenson, & J. Singer (Eds.), *Handbook of health psychology* (2nd ed.). New York, NY: Psychology Press.

Dunbar-Jacob, J., Schlenk, E., & McCall, M. (2012). Patient adherence to treatment regimen. In A. Baum, T. A. Revenson, & J. Singer (Eds.), *Handbook of health psychology* (2nd ed.). New York, NY: Psychology Press.

Duncan, B. L. (1976). Differential social perception and attribution of intergroup violence: Testing the lower limits of stereotyping of blacks. *Journal of Personality and Social Psychology, 34,* 590–598.

Duncan, B. L., & Reese, R. J. (2013). Empirically supported treatments, evidence-based treatments, and evidence-based practice. In G. Stricker & T. A. Widiger (Eds.), *Handbook of psychology: Vol. 8. Clinical psychology* (2nd ed.). New York, NY: Wiley.

Dunkel-Schetter, C., Gurung, R. A. R., Lobel, M., & Wadhwa, P. D. (2001). Stress processes in pregnancy and birth: Psychological, biological, and sociocultural influences. In A. Baum, T. A. Revenson, & J. E. Singer (Eds.), *Handbook of health psychology* (pp. 495–518). Mahwah, NJ: Erlbaum.

Dunlosky, J., Rawson, K. A., Marsh, E. J., Nathan, M. J., & Willingham, D. T. (2013). Improving students' learning with effective learning techniques: Promising directions from cognitive and educational psychology. *Psychological Science in the Public Interest, 14*(1), 4–58. doi:10.1177/1529100612453266.

Dunn, E. W. (2010). In the pursuit of happiness. *International Society for Research on Emotion, 26,* 4–5.

Dunn, E. W., Aknin, L. B., & Norton, M. I. (2008). Spending money on others promotes happiness. *Science, 319,* 1687–1688.

Dunn, E. W., Aknin, L. B., & Norton, M. I. (2014). Prosocial spending and happiness: Using money to benefit others pays off. *Current Directions in Psychological Science, 23*(1), 41–47. doi:10.1177/0963721413512503.

Dunn, E. W., Buchtel, E. E., & Aknin, L. B. (2011). Consensus at the heart of division: Commentary on Norton & Ariely (2011). *Perspectives on Psychological Science, 6,* 13–14.

Dunn, E. W., Wilson, T. D., & Gilbert, D. T. (2003). Location, location, location: The misprediction of satisfaction in housing lotteries. *Personality and Social Psychology Bulletin, 29*(11), 1421–1432.

Dupere, V., Leventhal, T., Crosnoe, R., & Dion, E. (2010). Understanding the positive role of neighborhood socioeconomic advantage in achievement: The contribution of the home, child care, and school environments. *Developmental Psychology, 46,* 1227–1244. doi:10.1037/a0020211.

Durante, K. M., Li, N. P., & Haselton, M. G. (2008). Changes in women's choice of dress across the ovulatory cycle: Naturalistic and laboratory task-based evidence. *Personality and Social Psychology Bulletin, 34,* 1451–1460.

Durrant, J., & Ensom, R. (2012). Physical punishment of children: Lessons from 20 years of research. *Canadian Medical Association Journal,* 1373–1377. doi:10.1503/cmaj.101314.

Durrant, R., & Ellis, B. J. (2003). Evolutionary psychology. In M. Gallagher & R. J. Nelson (Eds.), *Handbook of psychology (Vol. 3): Biological psychology.* New York, NY: Wiley.

Durrant, R., & Ellis, B. J. (2013). Evolutionary psychology. In R. J. Nelson, S. Y. Mizumori, & I. B. Weiner (Eds.), *Handbook of psychology: Vol. 3. Behavioral neuroscience* (2nd ed.). New York, NY: Wiley.

Dutton, D. G., & Aron, A. P. (1974). Some evidence for heightened sexual attraction under conditions of high anxiety. *Journal of Personality and Social Psychology, 30,* 510–517.

Dwyer, J. (1995). Popular diets. In K. D. Brownell & C. G. Fairburn (Eds.), *Eating disorders and obesity.* New York, NY: Guilford.

Dyck, E. (2005). Flashback: Psychiatric experimentation with LSD in historical perspective. *Canadian Journal of Law and Psychiatry, 50,* 381–388.

Dyck, E. (2008). *Psychedelic psychiatry: LSD from clinic to campus.* Baltimore, MD: Johns Hopkins University Press.

Eagle, M. N. (2013). The implications of conceptual critiques and empirical research on unconscious processes for psychoanalytic theory. *Psychoanalytic Review, 100,* 881–917. doi:10.1521/prev.2013.100.6.881.

Eagly, A. H. (1995). The science and politics of comparing women and men. *American Psychologist, 50,* 145–158.

Eagly, A. H., & Chaiken, S. (1998). Attitude structure and function. In D. T. Gilbert, S. T. Fiske, & G. Lindzey (Eds.), *The handbook of social psychology.* New York, NY: McGraw-Hill.

Eagly, A. H., Eaton, A., Rose, S. M., Riger, S., & McHugh, M. C. (2012). Feminism and psychology. *American Psychologist, 67,* 211–230.

Eagly, A. H., & Wood, W. (1999). The origins of sex differences in human behavior: Evolved dispositions versus social roles. *American Psychologist, 54,* 408–423.

Eagly, A. H., & Wood, W. (2013). The nature-nurture debates: 25 years of challenges in understanding the psychology of gender. *Perspectives on Psychological Science, 8,* 340–357. doi:10.1177/1745691613484767.

Easterbrooks, M. A., Bartlett, J. D., Beeghly, M., & Thompson, R. A. (2013). Social and emotional development in infancy. In R. M. Lerner, M. A. Easterbrooks, J. Mistry, & I. B. Weiner (Eds.), *Handbook of psychology: Vol. 6. Developmental psychology.* New York, NY: Wiley.

Easterlin, B. L., & Cardeña, E. (1999). Cognitive and emotional differences between short- and long-term Vipassana meditators. *Imagination, Cognition and Personality, 18*(1), 68–81.

Easton, A., & Emery, N. J. (Eds.). (2005). *The cognitive neuroscience of social behaviour.* New York, NY: Psychology Press.

Eastwick, P. W. (2013). Cultural influences on attraction. In J. A. Simpson & L. Campbell (Eds.), *Oxford handbook of close relationships.* New York, NY: Oxford University Press.

Eastwick, P. W., Eagly, A. H., Finkel, E. J., & Johnson, S. E. (2011). Implicit and explicit preferences for physical attractiveness in a romantic partner: A double dissociation in predictive validity. *Journal of Personality and Social Psychology, 101,* 993–1011. doi:10.1037/a0024061.

Eastwood, J. (2013). Children advised against taking melatonin. *Toronto Globe and Mail,* July 10, 2013, L6.

Eaton, J. (2001). Management communication: The threat of groupthink. *Corporate Communications, 6,* 183–192.

Ebbinghaus, H. (1885/1964). *Memory: A contribution to experimental psychology* (H. A. Ruger & E. R. Bussenius, Trans.). New York, NY: Dover (Original work published 1885).

Ebel-Lam, A. P., MacDonald, T. K., Zanna, M. P., & Fong, G. T. (2009). An experimental investigation of the interactive effects of alcohol and sexual arousal on intentions to have unprotected sex. *Basic and Applied Social Psychology, 31,* 226–233.

Eberth, J., & Sedlmeier, P. (2012). The effects of mindfulness meditation: A meta-analysis. *Mindfulness, 3,* 174–189.

Ebrahim, I. O., Shapiro, C. M., Williams, A. J., & Fenwick, P. B. (2013). Alcohol and sleep I: Effects on normal sleep. *Alcoholism: Clinical and Experimental Research, 37,* 539–549. doi:10.1111/acer.12006.

Eckstein, D., & Kaufman, J. A. (2012). The role of birth order in personality: An enduring intellectual legacy of Alfred Adler. *The Journal of Individual Psychology, 68*(1), 60–61.

Economist,The. (2015). How America's psychologists ended up endorsing torture. *The Economist,* July 28, 2015. Retrieved from https://www.economist.com/blogs/democracyinamerica/2015/07/terror-torture-and-psychology.

Edenfield, T. M., & Blumenthal, J. A. (2011). Exercise and stress reduction. In R. J. Contrada & A. Baum (Eds.), *Handbook of stress science: Biology, psychology, and health.* New York, NY: Spring Publishing Company.

Edwards, S., Jedrychowski, W., Butscher, M., Camann, D., Kieltyka, A., Mroz, E., et al. (2010). Prenatal exposure to airborne polycyclic aromatic hydrocarbons and children's intelligence at 5 years of age in a prospective cohort study in Poland. *Environmental Health Perspectives, 118*(9), 1326–1331.

Egan, J. P. (1975). *Signal detection theory and ROC-analysis.* New York, NY: Academic Press.

Egan, M. F., & Hyde, T. M. (2000). Schizophrenia: Neurobiology. In B. J. Sadock & V. A. Sadock (Eds.), *Kaplan and Sadock's comprehensive textbook of psychiatry* (7th ed., Vol. 1, pp. 1129–1146). Philadelphia, PA: Lippincott, Williams & Wilkins.

Egger, H. L., & Emde, R. N. (2011). Developmentally sensitive diagnostic criteria for mental health disorders in early childhood: The DSM-IV, the RDC-PA, and the CD-3R. *American Psychologist, 66,* 95–106.

Ehde, D. M., Dillworth, T. M., & Turner, J. A. (2014). Cognitive-behavioral therapy for individuals with chronic pain. *American Psychologist, 69,* 153–166.

Ehrenberg, M., Regev, R., Lazinski, M., Behrman, L. J., & Zimmerman, J. (2014). Adjustment to divorce for children. In L. Grossman & S. Walfish (Eds.), *Translating psychological research into practice.* New York, NY: Spring Publishing Co.

Ehrenberg, O., & Ehrenberg, M. (1986). *The psychotherapy maze.* Northvale, NJ: Aronson.

Ehrenberg, O., & Ehrenberg, M. (1994). *The psychotherapy maze: A consumer's guide to getting in and out of therapy.* Northvale, NJ: Jason Aronson.

Eibl-Eibesfeldt, I. (1975). *Ethology: The biology of behavior.* New York, NY: Holt, Rinehart, & Winston.

Eichenbaum, H. (2013). Memory systems. In R. J. Nelson, S. Y. Mizumori, & I. B. Weiner (Eds.), *Handbook of psychology: Vol. 3. Behavioral neuroscience* (2nd ed.). New York, NY: Wiley.

Eigsti, I., Zayas, V., Mischel, W., Shoda, Y., Ayduk, O., Dadlani, M. B., et al. (2006). Predictive cognitive control from preschool to late adolescence and young adulthood. *Psychological Science, 17,* 478–484.

Ein-Dor, T., & Hirschberger, G. (2016). Rethinking theory: From a theory of relationships to a theory of individual and group survival. *Current Directions in Psychological Science, 25,* 223–227.

Einstein, G. O., & McDaniel, M. A. (2004). *Memory fitness: A guide for successful aging.* New Haven, CT: Yale University Press.

Eippert, F., Bingel, U., Schoell, E. D., Yacubian, J., Klinger, R., Lorenz, J., & Büchel, C. (2009). Activation of the opioidergic descending pain control system underlies placebo analgesia. *Neuron, 63*(4), 533–543.

Eisenberger, N. I. (2012). The pain of social disconnection: Examining the shared neural underpinnings of physical and social pain. *Nature Reviews Neuroscience,13,* 421–434.

Eisenberger, N. I. (2015). Social pain and the brain: Controversies, questions, and where to go from here. *Annual Review of Psychology, 66,* 601–629.

Eisenberger, N. I., & Cole, S. W. (2012). Social neuroscience and heath: Neurophysiological mechanisms linking social ties with physical health. *Nature Reviews Neuroscience, 15,* 669–674.

Eisner, E. W. (2004). Multiple intelligences. *Teachers College Record, 106*(1), 31–39.

Ekman, P. (1992). Facial expressions of emotion: New findings, new questions. *Psychological Science, 3,* 34–38.

Ekman, P., & Friesen, W. V. (1975). *Unmasking the face.* Englewood Cliffs, NJ: Prentice-Hall.

Ekman, P., & Friesen, W. V. (1984). *Unmasking the face.* Palo Alto: Consulting Psychologists Press.

Elbogen, E. B., & Johnson, S. C. (2009). The intricate link between violence and mental disorder: Results from the national epidemiologic survey on alcohol and related conditions. *Archives of General Psychiatry, 66*(2), 152–161. doi:10.1001/archgenpsychiatry.2008.537.

Elkin, J., Shea, M., Watkins, J., et al. (1989). National Institutes of Mental Health treatment of depression collaborative research program: General effectiveness of treatments. *Archive of General Psychiatry, 46*, 971–982.

Elliot, A. J., & Maier, M. A. (2012). Color-in-context theory. In P. Devine & A. Plant (Eds.), *Advances in experimental social psychology*. San Diego, CA: Academic Press.

Elliot, A. J., & Maier, M. A. (2013). Color psychology: Effects of perceiving color on psychological functioning in Humans. *Annual Review of Psychology, 65,* 95–120.

Elliot, A. J., & Maier, M. A. (2014). Color psychology: Effects of perceiving color on psychological functions in humans. *Annual Review of Psychology, 65,* 95–120.

Elliot, A. J., Maier, M. A., Moller, A. C., Friedman, R., & Meinhardt, J. (2007). Color and psychological functioning: The effect of red on performance attainment. *Journal of Experimental Psychology: General, 136*(1), 154–168.

Elliot, A. J., Maier, M. A., Moller, A. C., Friedman, R., & Meinhardt, J. (2007). Color and psychological functioning: The effect of red on performance attainment. *Journal of Experimental Psychology: General, 136*(1), 154–168. doi:10.1037/0096-3445.136.1.154.

Elliot, A. J., & Niesta, D. (2008). Romantic red: Red enhances men's attraction to women. *Journal of Personality and Social Psychology, 95*(5), 1150–1164. doi:10.1037/0022-3514.95.5.1150.

Elliot, A. J., Tracy, J. L., Pazda, A. D., & Beall, A. T. (2013). Red enhances women's attractiveness to me: First evidence suggesting universality. *Journal of Experimental Social Psychology, 49*, 165–168.

Elliott, R., Bohart, A. C., Watson, J. C., & Greenberg, L. S. (2011). Empathy. *Psychotherapy, 48*(1), 43–49.

Ellis, A. (1973). *Humanistic psychotherapy: The rational-emotive approach*. New York, NY: Julian Press.

Ellis, A. (1977). *Reason and emotion in psychotherapy*. Seacaucus, NJ: Lyle Stuart.

Ellis, A. (1985). *How to live with and without anger*. New York, NY: Citadel Press.

Ellis, A. (1987). The evolution of rational-emotive therapy (RET) and cognitive behavior therapy (CBT). In J. K. Zeig (Ed.), *The evolution of psychotherapy*. New York, NY: Brunner/Mazel.

Ellis, A. (1996). How I learned to help clients feel better and get better. *Psychotherapy, 33,* 149–151.

Ellis, A. (2001). *Feeling better, getting better: Profound self-help therapy for your emotions*. Atascadero, CA: Impact Publishers.

Ellsworth, P. C., & Scherer, K. R. (2003). Appraisal processes in emotion. In R. J. Davidson, K. R. Scherer, & H. H. Goldsmith (Ed.), *Handbook of affective sciences*. New York, NY: Oxford University Press.

Ellwood, S., Pallier, G., Snyder, A., & Gallate, J. (2009). The incubation effect: Hatching a solution? *Creativity Research Journal, 21*(1), 6–14.

Elman, I., Tschibelu, E., & Borsook, D. (2010). Psychosocial stress and its relationship to gambling urges in individuals with pathological gambling. *The American Journal on Addictions, 19*, 332–339.

Elms, A. C. (2009). Obedience lite. *American Psychologist, 64*(1), 32–36. doi:10.1037/a0014473.

Else-Quest, N. M., Hyde, J., & Linn, M. C. (2010). Cross-national patterns of gender differences in mathematics: A meta-analysis. *Psychological Bulletin, 136*(1), 103–127.

Emavardhana, T., & Tori, C. D. (1997). Changes in self-concept, ego defense mechanisms, and religiosity following seven-day Vipassana meditation retreats. *Journal for the Scientific Study of Religion, 36*, 194–206.

Emery, C. F., Anderson, D. R., & Goodwin, C. L. (2013). Coronary heart disease and hypertension. In A. M. Nezu, C. M. Nezu, P. A. Geller, & I. B. Weiner (Eds.), *Handbook of psychology: Vol. 9. Health psychology* (2nd ed.). New York, NY: Wiley.

Emmelkamp, P. M. (2013). Behavior therapy with adults. In M. J. Lambert (Ed.). *Bergin and Garfield's handbook of psychotherapy and behavior change* (6th ed.). New York, NY: Wiley.

Emmelkamp, P. M. G. (1994). Behavior therapy with adults. In A. E. Bergin & S. L. Garfield (Eds.), *Handbook of psychotherapy and behavior change* (4th ed.). New York, NY: Wiley.

Employment and Social Development Canada. (2014). *Canadians in context—aging population*. Retrieved from http://www4.hrsdc.gc.ca/.3ndic.1t.4r@-eng.jsp?iid=33.

Emsley, R., Rabinowitz, J., & Medori, R. (2006). Time course for antipsychotic treatment response in first-episode schizophrenia. *American Journal of Psychiatry, 163*, 743–745.

Endler, N. S. (1982). *Holiday of darkness: A psychologist's personal journey out of his depression*. New York, NY: Wiley.

Endler, N. S. (2004). The joint effects of person and situation factors on stress in spaceflight. *Aviation, Space, and Environmental Medicine, 75*, C22–C27.

Endler, N. S., & Magnusson, D. (1976). Toward an interactional psychology of personality. *Psychological Bulletin, 83*, 956–979.

Engbert, R., & Kliegl, R. (2003). Microsaccades uncover the orientation of covert attention. *Vision Research, 43,* 1035–1045.

Engemann, K. M., & Owyang, M. T. (2005, April). So much for that merit raise: The link between wages and appearance. *The Regional Economist*, pp. 10–11.

Engle, R. W. (2001). What is working memory capacity? In H. L. Roediger, III, J. S. Nairne, I. Neath, & A. M. Surprenant (Eds.), *The nature of remembering: Essays in honor of Robert G. Crowder*. Washington, DC: American Psychological Association.

Engle, R. W., & Zentall, T. R. (2016). Editor's introduction: Special issue on cognition in dogs. *Current Directions in Psychological Science, 25*, 199.

Epstein, D. H., Phillips, K. A., & Preston, K. L. (2011). Opioids. In P. Ruiz, & E. C. Strain (Eds.), *Lowinson and Ruiz's substance abuse: A comprehensive textbook* (5th ed.). Philadelphia, PA: Lippincott Williams & Wilkins.

Epstein, L., & Mardon, S. (2007). *The Harvard medical school guide to a good night's sleep*. New York, NY: McGraw-Hill.

Epstein, R. (2007). Smooth thinking about sexuality: "Gay" and "straight" are misleading terms. *Scientific American Mind, 18*(5), 14.

Epstein, S., Donovan, S., & Denes-Raj, V. (1999). The missing link in the paradox of the Linda conjunction problem: Beyond knowing and thinking of the conjunction rule, the intrinsic appeal of heuristic processing. *Personality and Social Psychology Bulletin, 25*, 204–214.

Era, V, Candidi, M., & Aglioti, S. M. (2015). Subliminal presentation of emotionally negative vs positive primes increases the perceived beauty of target stimuli. *Experimental Brain Research, 233*, 3271–3281.

Erber, M. W., Hodges, S. D., & Wilson, T. D. (1995). Attitude strength, attitude stability, and the effects of analyzing reasons. In R. E. Petty & J. A. Krosnick (Eds.), *Attitude strength: Antecedents and consequences*. Mahwah, NJ: Erlbaum.

Erdelyi, M. H. (2001). Defense processes can be conscious or unconscious. *American Psychologist, 56*, 761–762.

Erickson, R. P., DiLorenzo, P. M., & Woodbury, M. A. (1994). Classification of taste responses in brain stem: Membership in fuzzy sets. *Journal of Neurophysiology, 71*, 2139–2150.

Erikson, E. (1963). *Childhood and society*. New York, NY: Norton.

Erikson, E. (1968). *Identity: Youth and crisis*. New York, NY: Norton.

Espejo, E., Ferriter, C., Hazel, N., Keenan-Miller, D., Hoffman, L., & Hammen, C. (2011). Predictors of subjective ratings of stressor severity: The effects of current mood and neuroticism. *Stress & Health: Journal of the International Society for the Investigation of Stress, 27*(1), 23–33.

Esser, J. K. (1998). Alive and well after twenty-five years: A review of groupthink research. *Organizational Behavior & Human Decision Processes, 73*, 116–141.

Esses, V. M., Jackson, L. M., & Bennett-AbuAyyash, C. (2010). Intergroup competition. In J. F. Dovidio, M. Hewstone, P. Glick, & V. M. Esses (Eds.), *The Sage handbook of prejudice, stereotyping, and discrimination*. Los Angeles, CA: SAGE.

Esterson, A. (2001). The mythologizing of psychoanalytic history: Deception and self-deception in Freud's accounts of the seduction theory episode. *History of Psychiatry, 7*, 329–352.

Estes, W. K. (1999). Models of human memory: A 30-year retrospective. In C. Izawa (Ed.), *On human memory: Evolution, progress, and reflections on the 30th anniversary of the Atkinson-Shiffrin model*. Mahwah, NJ: Erlbaum.

Evans, D. R., & Segerstrom, S. C. (2011). Why do mindful people worry less? *Cognitive Therapy and Research, 35*, 505–510.

Evans, G. W. (2004). The environment of childhood poverty. *American Psychologist, 59*(2), 77–92.

Evans, J. T. (2007). *Hypothetical thinking: Dual processes in reasoning and judgment*. New York, NY: Psychology Press.

Evans, R. I. (1980). *The making of social psychology: Discussions with creative contributors*. New York, NY: Gardner Press, Inc.

Evans, R. I. (1989). *Albert Bandura: The man and his ideas—a dialogue*. New York, NY: Praeger.

Everitt, B. J., & Robbins, T. W. (2016). Drug addiction: Updating actions to habits to compulsions Ten years on. *Annual Review of Psychology, 67*, 23–50.

Eysenck, H. J. (1959). Learning theory and behaviour therapy. *Journal of Mental Science, 195*, 61–75.

Eysenck, H. J. (1967). *The biological basis of personality*. Springfield, IL: Charles C. Thomas.

Eysenck, H. J. (1982). *Personality, genetics and behavior: Selected papers*. New York, NY: Praeger.

Eysenck, H. J. (1990a). Biological dimensions of personality. In L. A. Pervin (Ed.), *Handbook of personality: Theory and research*. New York, NY: Guilford.

Eysenck, H. J. (1990b). *Decline and fall of the Freudian empire*. Washington, DC: Scott-Townsend.

Eysenck, H. J., & Kamin, L. (1981). *The intelligence controversy*. New York, NY: Wiley.

Eysenck, M. W., Mogg, K., May, J., Richards, A., & Mathews, A. (1991). Bias in interpretation of ambiguous sentences related to threat in anxiety. *Journal of Abnormal Psychology, 100*, 144–150.

Fabrigar, L. R., & Wegener, D. T. (2010). Attitude structure. In R. F. Baumeister & E. J. Finkel (Eds.), *Advanced social psychology: The state of the science* (pp. 177–216). New York, NY: Oxford University Press.

Fabrigar, L. R., MacDonald, T. K., & Wegener, D. T. (2005). The structure of attitudes. In D. Albarracin, B. T. Johnson, & M. P. Zanna (Eds.), *The handbook of attitudes*. Mahwah, NJ: Erlbaum.

Fagan, J. F., & Holland, C. R. (2002). Equal opportunity and racial differences in IQ. *Intelligence, 30*, 361–387.

Fagan, J. F., & Holland, C. R. (2007). Racial equality in intelligence: Predictions from a theory of intelligence as processing. *Intelligence, 35*, 319–334.

Fagot, B. I., Hagan, R., Leinbach, M. D., & Kronsberg, S. (1985). Differential reactions to assertive and communicative acts of toddler boys and girls. *Child Development, 56*, 1499–1505.

Fairburn, C. G., Cooper, Z., & Murphy, R. (2009). Bulimia nervosa. In M. C. Gelder, N. C. Andreasen, J. J. López-Ibor, Jr., & J. R. Geddes (Eds.). *New Oxford textbook of psychiatry* (2nd ed., Vol. 1). New York, NY: Oxford University Press.

Fakhoury, W., & Priebe, S. (2002). The process of deinstitutionalization: An international overview. *Current Opinion in Psychiatry, 15*(2), 187–192.

Falk, D. (2009). New information about Albert Einstein's brain. *Frontiers Evolutionary Neuroscience, 1*, 3.

Falls, W. A. (1998). Extinction: A review of therapy and the evidence suggesting that memories are not erased with nonreinforcement. In W. O'Donohue (Ed.), *Learning and behavior therapy*. Boston, MA: Allyn & Bacon.

Falzon, L., Davidson, K. W., & Bruns, D. (2010). Evidence searching for evidence-based psychology practice. *Professional Psychological Research and Practice, 41*, 550–557.

Famely, P. (2004). The gift of music. (2004, June). *Hospital News*. Retrieved July 31, 2008, from http://hospitalnews/com/modules/magazines.

Fan, S. P., Liberman, Z., Keysar, B., & Kinzler, D. D. (2015). The exposure advantage: Early exposure to multilingual environment promotes effective communication. *Psychological Science, 26*, 1090–1097.

Fancher, R. E. (2005). Galton: "Hereditary talent and character." *General Psychologist, 40*(2), 13–14.

Fancher, R. E. (2009). Scientific cousins: The relationship between Charles Darwin and Francis Galton. *American Psychologist, 64*(2), 84–92.

Fancher, R., & Rutherford, A. (2012). *Pioneers of psychology: A history*. New York, NY: W.W. Norton.

Faraday, A. (1974). *The dream game*. New York, NY: Harper & Row.

Faravelli, C., & Pallanti, S. (1989). Recent life events and panic disorders. *American Journal of Psychiatry, 146*, 622–626.

Farb, N. A. S., Segal, Z. V., Mayberg, H., et al. (2007). Attending to the present: Mindfulness meditation reveals distinct neural modes of self-reference. *Social Cognitive and Affective Neuroscience, 2*(4), 313–322.

Farber, B. A., & Doolin, E. M. (2011). Positive regard and affirmation. In J. C. Norcross (Ed.), *Psychotherapy relationships that work: Evidence-based responsiveness* (2nd ed.). New York, NY: Oxford University Press. doi:10.1093/acprof: oso/9780199737208.003.0008.

Farley, K. J., Fennessey, G. J., & Jones, D. (2015). Communicating in intensive care. In R. Iedema, D. Piper, & Manidis (Eds.), *Communicating quality and safety in health care* (pp. 77–92). New York, NY: Cambridge University Press.

Farrey, T. (2007). Pathologist says Waters' brain tissue had deteriorated. ESPN. Retrieved from http://sports .espn.go.com/nfl/news/story?id=2734941.

Farrington, D. P. (2006). Family background and psychopathy. In C. J. Patrick, & C. J. Patrick (Eds.), *Handbook of psychopathy* (pp. 229–250). New York, NY: Guilford Press.

Fava, G. A., Ruini, C., Rafanelli, C., Finos, L., Salmaso, L., Mangelli, L., et al. (2005). Well-being therapy of generalized anxiety disorder. *Psychotherapy and Psychosomatics, 74*(1), 26–30.

Fazio, L. K., Barber, S. J., Rajaram, S., Ornstein, P. A., & Marsh, E. J. (2013). Creating illusions of knowledge: Learning errors that contradict prior knowledge. *Journal of Experimental Psychology: General, 142*(1), 1–5. doi:10.1037/a0028649.

Federoff, I., Polivy, J., & Herman, C. P. (2003). The specificity of restrained versus unrestrained eaters' responses to food cues: General desire to eat, or craving for the cued food. *Appetite, 41*(1), 7–13.

Feeney, J. A. (2008). Adult romantic attachment: Developments in the study of couple relationships. In J. Cassidy & P. R. Shaver (Eds.), *Handbook of attachment: Theory, research, and clinical applications* (2nd ed., pp. 456–481). New York, NY: Guilford Press.

Fehr, B. (2008). Friendship formation. In S. Sprecher, A. Wenzel, & J. Harvey (Eds.), *Handbook of relationship initiation* (pp. 235–247). New York, NY: Psychology Press.

Fehr, B. (2013). The social psychology of love. In J. A. Simpson & L. Campbell (Eds.), *Oxford handbook of close relationships*. New York, NY: Oxford University Press.

Fehr, B. (2015). Love: Conceptualization and experience. In M. Mikulincer, P. R. Shaver, J. A. Simpson, & J. F. Dovidio (Eds.), *APA handbook of personality and social psychology Vol. 3: Interpersonal relations*. Washington, DC: American Psychological Association.

Feidler, K. (2017). What constitutes strong psychological science? The (neglected) role of diagnosticitiy and a priori theorizing. *Perspectives on psychological Science, 12*, 46–71.

Fein, D., Barton, M., Eigsti, I., Kelley, E., Naigles, L., Schultz, R. T., & . . . Tyson, K. (2013). Optimal outcome in individuals with a history of autism. *Journal of Child Psychology and Psychiatry, 54*(2), 195–205. doi:10.1111/jcpp.12037.

Fein, S., & Spencer, S. J. (1997). Prejudice as self-image maintenance: Affirming the self through derogating others. *Journal of Personality and Social Psychology, 73*, 31–44.

Feist, G. J. (1998). A meta-analysis of personality in scientific and artistic creativity. *Personality and Social Psychology Review, 2*, 290–309.

Feist, G. J. (2004). The evolved fluid specificity of human creativity talent. In R. J. Sternberg, E. L. Grigorenko, & J. L. Singer (Eds.), *Creativity: From potential to realization*. Washington, DC: American Psychological Association.

Feist, G. J. (2010). The function of personality in creativity: The nature and nurture of the creative personality. In J. C. Kaufman & R. J. Sternberg (Eds.), *The Cambridge handbook of creativity* (pp. 113–130). New York, NY: Cambridge University Press.

Feixas, G., & Botella, L. (2004). Psychotherapy integration: Reflections and contributions from a constructivist epistemology. *Journal of Psychotherapy Integration, 14*(2), 192–222.

Fekadu, A., Wooderson, S. C., Markopoulo, K., Donaldson, C., Papadopoulos, A., & Cleare, A. J. (2009). What happens to patients with treatment-resistant depression? A systematic review of medium to long term outcome studies. *Journal of Affective Disorders, 116*(1–2), 4–11. doi:10.1016/j.jad.2008.10.014.

Felder, J. N., & Segal, Z. V. , Beck, A., Sherwood, N., & Goodman, S. H. (2017). An open trial of web-based mindfulness-based cognitive therapy for perinatal women at risk for depressive relapse. *Cognitive and Behavioral Practice, 24*, 26–37.

Feldman, D. H. (1988). Creativity: Dreams, insights, and transformations. In R. J. Sternberg (Ed.), *The nature of creativity: Contemporary psychological perspectives*. Cambridge, UK: Cambridge University Press.

Feldman, D. H. (1999). The development of creativity. In R. J. Sternberg (Ed.), *Handbook of creativity*. New York, NY: Cambridge University Press.

Feldman, D. H. (2003). Cognitive development in childhood. In R. M. Lerner, M. A. Easterbrooks, & J. Mistry (Eds.), *Handbook of psychology (Vol. 6): Developmental psychology*. New York, NY: Wiley.

Feldman, D. H. (2013). Cognitive development in childhood: A contemporary perspective. In R. M. Lerner, M. A. Easterbrooks, J. Mistry, & I. B. Weiner (Eds.), *Handbook of psychology: Vol. 6. Developmental psychology*. New York, NY: Wiley.

Feng, J., Spence, I., & Pratt, J. (2007). Playing an action-video game reduces gender differences in spatial cognition. *Psychological Science, 18*(10), 850–855.

Fenwick, P. (1987). Meditation and the EEG. In M. A. West (Ed.), *The psychology of meditation*. Oxford: Clarendon Press.

Ferguson, C. J. (2013). Violent video games and the Supreme Court: Lessons for the scientific community in the wake of Brown v. Entertainment Merchants Association. *American Psychologist, 68*, 57–74. doi:10.1037/a0030597.

Ferguson, C. J., & Savage, J. (2012). Have recent studies addressed methodological issues raised by five decades of television violence research? A critical review. *Aggression and Violent Behavior, 17*, 129–139. doi:10.1016/j.avb .2011.11.001.

Fernald, A. (2010). Getting beyond the "convenience sample" in research on early cognitive development. *Behavioral and Brain Sciences, 33*, 91–92.

Ferrando, S. J., Owen, J. A., & Levenson, J. L. (2014). Psychopharmacology. In R. E. Hales, S. C. Yudofsky, & L. W. Roberts (Eds.), *The American Psychiatric Publishing textbook of psychiatry* (6th ed.). Washington, DC: American Psychiatric Publishing.

Ferster, C. S., & Skinner, B. F. (1957). *Schedules of reinforcement*. New York, NY: Appleton-Century-Crofts.

Fervaha, G., Foussias, G., Agid, O., & Remington, G. (2014). Impact of primary negative symptoms on functional outcomes in schizophrenia. *European Psychiatry, 29*, 449–455. doi:10.1016/j.eurpsy.2014.01.007.

Festinger, L. (1954). A theory of social comparison processes. *Human Relations, 7*, 117–140.

Festinger, L. (1957). *A theory of cognitive dissonance*. Stanford, CA: Stanford University Press.

Festinger, L., & Carlsmith, J. M. (1959). Cognitive consequences of forced compliance. *Journal of Abnormal and Social Psychology, 58*, 203–210.

Ficca, G., Axelsson, J., Mollicone, D. J., Muto, V., & Vitiello, M. V. (2010). Naps, cognition and performance. *Sleep Medicine Reviews, 14*(4), 249–258. doi:10.1016/j.smrv.2009.09.005.

Fiedler, K. (2008). Language: A toolbox for sharing and influencing social reality. *Perspectives on Psychological Science, 3*, 38–47.

Field, A. E., Sonneville, K. R., Crosby, R. D., Swanson, S. A., Eddy, K. T., Camargo, C. A., . . . Micali, N. (2014). Prospective associations of concerns about physique and the development of obesity, binge drinking, and drug use among adolescent boys and young adult men. *JAMA Pediatrics, 168*(1), 34–39. doi:10.1001/jamapediatrics.2013.2915.

Field, A. P., & Purkis, H. M. (2012). Associating learning and phobias. In M. Haselgrove, & L. Hogarth (Eds.), *Clinical applications of learning theory*. New York, NY: Psychology Press.

Fiedler, K., Schmid, J., & Stahl, T. (2002). What is the current truth about polygraph lie detection? *Basic & Applied Social Psychology, 24*, 313–324.

Fiedler, K., & Schwarz, N. (2016). Questionable research practices revisited. *Social Psychology and Personality Science, 7*, 45–52.

Fields, R. (2011, May 1). The hidden brain. *Scientific American: Mind, 22*(2), 52–59.

Fields, R. D. (2014). Myelin: More than insulation. *Science, 344*, 264–266.

Fife, R. (2017). Ottawa pays out $10.5 million to Khadr amid potential legal battle. *The Toronto Globe and Mail*, July 6, 2017. Retrieved from https://www.google.ca/search?q=Fife,+R.++(2017).++Ottawa+pays+out+%2410.5 +million+to+Khadr+amid+potential+legal+battle. ++The+Toronto+Globe+and+Mail,+Thursday+July+6, +2017&ie=utf-8&oe=utf-8&gws_rd=cr&dcr=0&ei=tWfSW buhOcaK0wLzhpe4CA.

Figueredo, A. J., Gladden, P., Vásquez, G., Wolf, P. S. A., & Jones, D. N. (2009). Evolutionary theories of personality. In P. J. Corr & G. Matthews (Eds.), *Cambridge handbook of personality psychology* (pp. 265–274). New York, NY: Cambridge University Press.

Figueredo, A. J., Sefcek, J. A., Vasquez, G., Brumbach, B. H., King, J. E., & Jacobs, W. J. (2005). Evolutionary personality psychology. In D. M. Buss (Ed.), *The handbook of evolutionary psychology*. New York, NY: Wiley.

Finan, P. H., Zautra, A. J., & Wershba, R. (2011). The dynamics of emotion in adaptation to stress. In R. J. Contrada & A. Baum (Eds.), *The handbook of stress science: Biology, psychology, and health* (pp. 111–121). New York, NY: Springer.

Fine, C. (2010). From scanner to sound bite: Issues in interpreting and reporting sex differences in the brain. *Current Directions in Psychological Science, 19*(5), 280–283.

Fine, R. (1990). *The history of psychoanalysis*. New York, NY: Continuum.

Fink, B., Neave, N., Manning, J. T., & Grammer, K. (2006). Facial symmetry and judgments of attractiveness, health and personality. *Personality and Individual Differences, 41*, 1253–1262.

Fink, M. (2014). What was learned: Studies by the consortium for research in ECT (CORE) 1997–2011. *Acta*

Psychiatrica Scandinavica, 129(6), 417–426. doi:10.1111/acps.12251.

Fink, M. F. (2009). Non-pharmacological somatic treatments: Electroconvulsive therapy. In M. C. Gelder, N. C. Andreasen, J. J. López-Ibor, Jr., & J. R. Geddes (Eds.), *New Oxford textbook of psychiatry* (2nd ed., Vol. 1). New York, NY: Oxford University Press.

Finkel, D. (2009). *Thank you for your service.* New York, NY: Macmillan.

Finkel, D. (2013). The Return: The traumatized veterans of Iraz and Afghanistan. *The New Yorker,* September 9, 2013. Retrieved from http://www.newyorker.com/magazine/2013/09/09/the-return-9.

Finkel, E. J., Eastwick, P. W., Karney, B. R., Reis, H. T., & Sprecher, S. (2012). Online dating: A critical analysis from the perspective of psychological science. *Psychological Science in the Public Interest, 13,* 3–66. doi:10.1177/1529100612436522.

Finkel, E. J., Eastwick, P. W., & Reis, H. T. (2015). Best research practices in psychology: Illustrating epistemological and pragmatic considerations with the case of relationship science. *Journal of Personality and Social Psychology, 108,* 275–297.

Finkel, E. J., Simpson, J. A., & Eastwik, P. W. (2017). The psychology of close relationships: Fourteen core principles. *Annual Review of Psychology, 68,* 383–411.

Finlayson, G., Dalton, M., & Blundell, J. E. (2012). Liking versus wanting food in human appetite: Relation to craving. In K. D. Brownell, & M. S. Gold (Eds.), *Food and addiction: A comprehensive handbook.* New York, NY: Oxford University Press.

Finnegan, L. P., & Kandall, S. R. (2005). Neonatal abstinence syndromes. In J. Aranda & S. J. Jaffe (Eds.), *Neonatal and pediatric pharmacology: Therapeutic principles in practice* (3rd ed., pp. 23–47). Philadelphia, PA: Lippincott Williams & Wilkins.

First, M. B. (2008). Psychiatric classification. In A. Tasman, J. Kay, J. A. Lieberman, M. B. First, & M. Maj (Eds.), *Psychiatry* (3rd ed.). New York, NY: Wiley-Blackwell.

Fischer, P., Krueger, J. I., Greitemeyer, T., Vogrincic, C., Kastenmuller, A., Frey, D., . . . Kainbacher, M. (2011). The bystander-effect. A meta-analytic review on bystander intervention in dangerous and non-dangerous emergencies. *Psychological Bulletin, 137,* 517–537. doi:10.1037/a0023304.

Fischer, R., & Van de Vleirt, E. (2011). Does climate undermine subjective well-being? A 58-nation study. *Personality and Social Psychology Bulletin, 37,* 1031–1041.

Fischhoff, B. (1988). Judgment and decision making. In R. J. Sternberg & E. E. Smith (Eds.), *The psychology of human thought.* Cambridge, UK: Cambridge University Press.

Fisher, S., & Greenberg, R. P. (1985). *The scientific credibility of Freud's theories and therapy.* New York, NY: Columbia University Press.

Fisher, S., & Greenberg, R. P. (1996). *Freud scientifically reappraised: Testing the theories and therapy.* New York, NY: Wiley.

Fisher, S., & Greenberg, R. P. (1997). The curse of the placebo: Fanciful pursuit of a pure biological therapy. In S. Fisher & R. P. Greenberg (Eds.), *From placebo to panacea: Putting psychiatric drugs to the test.* New York, NY: Wiley.

Fishman, D. B., Rego, S. A., & Muller, K. L. (2011). Behavioral theories of psychotherapy. In J. C. Norcross, G. R. VandenBos, & D. K. Freedheim, (Eds.), *History of psychotherapy: Continuity and change* (2nd ed.). Washington, DC: American Psychological Association. doi:10.1037/12353-004.

Fisk, J. E. (2004). Conjunction fallacy. In F. P. Rudiger (Ed.), *Cognitive illusions.* New York, NY: Psychology Press.

Fiske, S. T. (1998). Stereotyping, prejudice, and discrimination. In D. T. Gilbert, S. T. Fiske, & G. Lindzey (Eds.), *The handbook of social psychology.* New York, NY: McGraw-Hill.

Fiske, S. T., & Russell, A. M. (2010). Cognitive processes. In J. F. Dovidio, M. Hewstone, P. Glick, & V. M. Esses (Eds.), *The Sage handbook of prejudice, stereotyping, and discrimination.* Los Angeles, CA: Sage.

Fiske, S. T., & Tablante, C. B. (2015). Stereotyping: Process and content. In M. Mikulincer, P. R. Shaver, E. Borgida, & J. A. Bargh (Eds.), *APA handbook of personality and social psychology Vol. 1: Attitudes and social cognition.* Washington, DC: American Psychological Association.

Fiske, S. T., & Taylor, S. E. (2008). *Social cognition: From brains to culture.* New York, NY: McGraw-Hill.

Fiske, S. T., & Taylor, S. E. (2017). *Social cognition: From brains to culture.* New York, NY: SAGE.

Fitzgerald, P. B. (2009). Repetitive transcranial magnetic stimulation treatment for depression: Lots of promise but still lots of questions. *Brain Stimulation, 2*(4), 185–187.

Fitzgerald, R. J., & Price, H. L. (2015). Eyewitness identification across the lifespan. *Psychological Bulletin, 141,* 1228–1265.

Flausino, N. H., Da Silva Prado, J. M., De Queiroz, S. S., Tufik, S., & De Mello, M. T. (2012). Physical exercise performed before bedtime improves the sleep pattern of healthy young good sleepers. *Psychophysiology, 49*(2), 186–192. doi:10.1111/j.1469-8986.2011.01300.x.

Flavell, J. H. (1996). Piaget's legacy. *Psychological Science, 7,* 200–203.

Flavell, J. H. (1999). Cognitive development: Children's knowledge about the mind. *Annual Review of Psychology, 50,* 21–45.

Flavell, J. H. (2004). Theory-of-mind development: Retrospect and prospect. *Merrill-Palmer Quarterly, 50,* 274–290.

Fleeson, W. (2004). Moving personality beyond the person–situation debate: The challenge and the opportunity of within-person variability. *Current Directions in Psychological Science, 13*(2), 83–87.

Flett, G. L. (2007). *Personality theory and research.* Toronto, ON: Wiley.

Flett, G. L., Vredenburg, K., & Krames, L. (1995). The stability of depressive symptoms in college students: An empirical demonstration of regression to the mean. *Journal of Psychopathology & Behavioral Assessment, 17,* 403–415.

Flood, A. M., Davidson, J. R. T., & Beckham, J. C. (2008). Anxiety disorders: Traumatic stress disorders. In A. Tasman, J. Kay, J. A. Lieberman, M. B. First, & M. Maj (Eds.), *Psychiatry* (3rd ed.). New York, NY: Wiley-Blackwell.

Flor, H. (2014). Psychological pain interventions and neurophysiology: Implications for a mechanism based approach. *American Psychologist, 69*(2), 178–187.

Florentine, M., & Heinz, M. (2010). Audition: Loudness. In E. B. Goldstein (Ed.), *Encyclopedia of perception.* Thousand Oaks, CA: SAGE.

Flynn, J. R. (1987). Massive IQ gains in 14 nations: What IQ tests really measure. *Psychological Bulletin, 101,* 171–191.

Flynn, J. R. (1994). IQ gains over time. In R. J. Sternberg (Ed.), *The encyclopedia of human intelligence.* New York, NY: Macmillan.

Flynn, J. R. (1998). IQ gains over time: Toward finding the causes. In U. Neisser (Ed.), *The rising curve: Long-term gains in IQ and related measures.* Washington, DC: American Psychological Association.

Flynn, J. R. (1999). Searching for justice: The discovery of IQ gains over time. *American Psychologist, 54,* 5–20.

Flynn, J. R. (2000). The hidden history of IQ and special education: Can the problems be solved? *Psychology, Public Policy, & Law, 6*(1), 191–198.

Flynn, J. R. (2003). Movies about intelligence: The limitations of g. *Current Directions in Psychological Science, 12*(3), 95–99.

Flynn, J. R. (2007). *What is intelligence? Beyond the Flynn effect.* New York, NY: Cambridge University Press.

Flynn, J. R. (2012). *Are we getting smarter? Rising IQ in the twenty-first century.* Cambridge, UK: Cambridge University Press.

Flynn, M. G., McFarlin, B. K., & Markofski, M. M. (2007). The anti-inflammatory actions of exercise training. *American Journal of Lifestyle Medicine, 1,* 220–235.

Fodor, E. M., & Carver, R. A. (2000). Achievement and power motives, performance feedback, and creativity. *Journal of Research in Personality, 34,* 380–396.

Foley, R. T., Whitwell, R. L., & Goodale, M. A. (2015). The two-visual systems hypothesis and the perspective features of visual experience. *Consciousness and Cognition, 35,* 225–233.

Folkman, S. (2008). The case for positive emotions in the stress process. *Anxiety, Stress and Coping: An International Journal, 21*(1), 3–14.

Folkman, S. (2010). *The Oxford handbook of stress, health, and coping* (pp. 78–91). New York, NY: Oxford University Press.

Folkman, S. (2011). Stress, health, and coping: Synthesis, commentary, and future directions. In S. Folkman (Ed.), *Oxford handbook of stress, health, and coping.* New York, NY: Oxford University Press.

Folkman, S., & Moskowitz, J. T. (2000). Positive affect and the other side of coping. *American Psychologist, 55,* 647–654.

Folkman, S., & Moskowitz, J. T. (2004). Coping: Pitfalls and promise. *Annual Review of Psychology, 55,* 745–774.

Follette, W. C., & Davis, D. (2009). Clinical practice and the issue of repressed memories: Avoiding an ice patch on the slippery slope. In W. O'Donohue & S. R. Graybar (Eds.), *Handbook of contemporary psychotherapy: Toward an improved understanding of effective psychotherapy* (pp. 47–73). Thousand Oaks, CA: Sage.

Folsom, D. P., Gilmer, T., Barrio, C., Moore, D. J., Bucardo, J., Lindamer, L. A., et al. (2007). A longitudinal study of the use of mental health services by persons with serious mental illness: Do Spanish-speaking Latinos differ from English-speaking Latinos and Caucasians? *American Journal Psychiatry, 164,* 1173–1180.

Forsyth, D. R. (2004). Inferences about actions performed in constraining contexts: Correspondence bias or correspondent inference? *Current Psychology: Developmental, Learning, Personality, Social, 23*(1), 41–51.

Forsyth, D. R., & Strong, S. R. (1986). The scientific study of counseling and psychotherapy: A unificationist view. *American Psychologist, 41,* 113–119.

Foster, M. (2001). The motivational quality of global attributions in hypothetical and experienced situations of gender discrimination. *Psychology of Women Quarterly, 25,* 242–253.

Foster, M. (2013). Everyday confrontation of discrimination: The well-being costs and benefits to women over time. *International Journal of Psychological Studies, 5,* 135–154.

Foster, M. (2014). The relationship between collective action and well-being and its moderators: Pervasiveness of discrimination and dimensions of action. *Sex Roles, 70,* 165–182.

Foster, M. D. (1999). Acting out against discrimination: The effects of different social identities. *Sex Roles, 40,* 167–186.

Foster, M. D. (2009a). Perceiving pervasive discrimination over time: Implications for coping. *Psychology of Women Quarterly, 33,* 172–182.

Foster, M. D. (2009b). The dynamic nature of coping with gender discrimination: Appraisals, strategies, and well-being over time. *Sex Roles, 60,* 694–707.

Foster, R. G. (2004). Are we trying to banish biological time? *Cerebrum, 6,* 7–26.

Foulkes, D. (1985). *Dreaming: A cognitive-psychological analysis.* Hillsdale, NJ: Erlbaum.

Foulkes, D. (1996). Dream research: 1953–1993. *Sleep, 19,* 609–624.

Fourie, M. M., Thomas, K. G. F., Amodio, D. M., Warton, C. M. R., & Meintjes, E. M. (2014). Neural correlates of experienced moral emotion: An fMRI investigation of emotion in response to prejudice feedback. *Social Neuroscience, 9,* 203–218.

Fournier, J. C., et al. (2008). Prediction of response to medication & cognitive therapy in the treatment of moderate to severe depression. *Journal of Consulting & Clinical Psychology, 77,* 775–778.

Fournier, J. C., DeRubeis, R. J., Hollon, S. D., Dimidjian, S., Amsterdam, J. D., Shelton, R. C., & Fawcett, J. (2010). Antidepressant drug effects and depression severity: A patient-level meta-analysis. *JAMA, 303*(1), 47–53.

Fowers, B. J., & Davidov, B. J. (2006). The virtue of multiculturalism: Personal transformation, character, and openness to the other. *American Psychologist, 61,* 581–594.

Fox, K. C., Spreng, R. M., Ellamil, M., Andrews-Hanna, J. R., & Christoff, K. (2015). The wandering brain: Meta-analysis of functional neuroimaging studies of mind-wandering and related spontaneous processes. *Neuroimage, 111,* 611–621.

Fox, M. (2012). Arthur R. Jensen dies at 89: Set off debate about I.Q. *The New York Times,* November 1, 2012. Retrieved from http://www.nytimes.com/2012/11/02/science/arthur-r-jensen-who-set-off-debate-on-iq-dies.html?pagewanted=all&_r=0.

Fox, M. J. (2002). *Lucky man: A memoir.* New York, NY: Hyperion.

Fozard, J. L., & Gordon-Salant, S. (2001). Changes in vision and hearing with aging. In J. E. Birren & K. W. Schaie (Eds.), *Handbook of the psychology of aging* (5th ed., pp. 240–265). San Diego, CA: Academic Press.

Frances, A. (2013). *Saving normal: An insider's revolt against out-of-control psychiatric diagnosis, DSM-5, Big Pharma, and the medicalization of ordinary life.* New York, NY: Morrow.

Frances, A. (2013a). *Saving normal: An insider's revolt against out-of-control psychiatric diagnosis, DSM-5, big pharma, and the medicalization of ordinary life.* New York, NY: HarperCollins.

Frances, A. (2013b). *Essentials of psychiatric diagnosis: Responding to the challenge of DSM-5.* New York, NY: Guilford Press.

Francis, L. A., & Birch, L. L. (2005). Maternal influences on daughters' restrained eating behavior. *Health Psychology, 24,* 548–554.

Franco, A., Malhotra, H., & Simonovits, G. (2016). Underreporting in psychology experiments: Evidence from a Study registry. *Social Psychology and Personality Science, 7,* 8–12.

Franić, S., Middeldorp, C. M., Dolan, C. V., Ligthart, L., & Boomsma, D. I. (2010). Childhood and adolescent anxiety and depression: beyond heritability. *Journal of the American Academy of Child & Adolescent Psychiatry, 49,* 820–829.

Frank, J. D. (1961). *Persuasion and healing.* Baltimore, MD: Johns Hopkins University Press.

Frank, L. K. (1939). Projective methods for the study of personality. *Journal of Psychology, 8,* 343–389.

Frank, L. R. (1990). Electroshock: Death, brain damage, memory loss, and brainwashing. *The Journal of Mind and Behavior, 11*(3/4), 489–512.

Frank, M. G. (2006). The function of sleep. In T. Lee-Chiong (Ed.), *Sleep: A comprehensive handbook.* Hoboken, NJ: Wiley-Liss.

Frankland, P. W., & Bontempi, B. (2005). The organization of recent and remote memories. *Nature Reviews Neuroscience, 6*(2), 119–130.

Franko, D. L., Keshaviah, A., Eddy, K. T., Krishna, M., Davis, M. C., Keel, P. K., & Herzog, D. B. (2013). A longitudinal investigation of mortality in anorexia nervosa and bulimia nervosa. *The American Journal of Psychiatry, 170,* 917–925. doi:10.1176/appi.ajp.2013.12070868.

Fratkin, J. L., Sinn, D. L., Patall, E. A., & Gosling, S. D. (2013). Personality consistency in dogs: A meta-analysis. *PLOS ONE, 8,* e54907.

Frederick, S., & Loewenstein, G. (1999). Hedonic adaptation. In D. Kahneman, E. Diener, & N. Schwarz (Eds.), *Well-being: The foundations of hedonic psychology.* New York, NY: Russell Sage Foundation.

Fredrickson, B. L. (2002). Positive emotions. In C. R. Snyder & S. J. Lopez (Eds.), *Handbook of positive psychology* (pp. 120–134). New York, NY: Oxford University Press.

Fredrickson, B. L., Tugade, M. M., Waugh, C. E., & Larkin, G. R. (2003). What good are positive emotions in crises? A prospective study of resilience and emotions following the terrorist attacks on the United States on September 11, 2001. *Journal of Personality and Social Psychology, 84,* 365–376.

Freedman, G., Williams, K., & Beer, J. S. (2016). Softening the blow of social exclusion: The Responsive theory of social exclusion. *Frontiers in Psychology, 7,* 1570.

Freedman, J. L. (1978). *Happy people.* New York, NY: Harcourt Brace Jovanovich.

Freedman, J. L., & Fraser, S. C. (1966). Compliance without pressure: The foot-in-the-door technique. *Journal of Personality and Social Psychology, 4,* 195–202.

Freedman, R., Ross, R., Michels, R., Appelbaum, P., Siever, L., Binder, R., et al. (2007). Psychiatrists, mental illness, and violence. *American Journal of Psychiatry, 164*(9), 1315–1317. doi:10.1176/appi.ajp.2007.07061013.

Freeman, N. K. (2007). Preschoolers' perceptions of gender appropriate toys and their parents' beliefs about genderized behaviors: Miscommunication, mixed messages, or hidden truths? *Early Childhood Education Journal, 34*(5), 357–366.

Fremouw, W. J., de Perczel, M., & Ellis, T. E. (1990). *Suicide risk: Assessment and response guidelines.* Elmsford, NY: Pergamon.

Frenda, S. J., Nichols, R. M., & Loftus, E. F. (2011). Current issues and advances in misinformation research. *Current Directions in Psychological Science, 20*(1), 20–23. doi:10.1177/0963721410396620.

Freud, A. (1936). *The ego and the mechanisms of defense.* London, UK: Hogarth Press and Institute of Psycho-Analysis.

Freud, S. (1900/1953). The interpretation of dreams. In J. Strachey (Ed.), *The standard edition of the complete psychological works of Sigmund Freud* (Vols. 4 and 5). London, UK: Hogarth.

Freud, S. (1901/1960). The psychopathology of everyday life. In J. Strachey (Ed.), *The standard edition of the complete psychological works of Sigmund Freud* (Vol. 6). London, UK: Hogarth.

Freud, S. (1910/1957). *Leonardo da Vinci: A study in psychosexuality* (Vol. 11). London, England: Hogarth Press. (original work published 1910)

Freud, S. (1915/1959). Instincts and their vicissitudes. In E. Jones (Ed.), *The collected papers of Sigmund Freud* (Vol. 4). New York, NY: Basic Books.

Freud, S. (1933/1964). *New introductory lectures on psychoanalysis.* In J. Strachey (Ed.), *The standard edition of the complete psychological works of Sigmund Freud* (Vol. 22). London, UK: Hogarth.

Freud, S. (1940). An outline of psychoanalysis. *International Journal of Psychoanalysis, 21,* 27–84.

Freund, A. M., Nikitin, J., & Riediger, M. (2013). Successful aging. In R. M. Lerner, M. A. Easterbrooks, J. Mistry, & I. B. Weiner (Eds.), *Handbook of psychology: Vol. 6. Developmental psychology.* New York, NY: Wiley.

Frewen, P. A., Evans, E. M., Maraj, N., Dozois, D. J. A., & Partridge, K. (2008). Letting go: Mindfulness and negative automatic thinking. *Cognitive Therapy and Research, 32,* 758–774.

Frey, B. S., & Stutzer, A. (2002). What can economists learn from happiness research? *Journal of Economic Literature, 40,* 402–435.

Freyd, J. J. (1996). *Betrayal trauma: The logic of forgetting childhood abuse.* Cambridge, MA: Harvard University Press.

Freyd, J. J. (2001). Memory and dimensions of trauma: Terror may be "all-too-well remembered" and betrayal buried. In J. R. Conte (Ed.), *Critical issues in child sexual abuse: Historical, legal, and psychological perspectives.* Thousand Oaks, CA: Sage.

Freyd, J. J., DePrince, A. P., & Gleaves, D. H. (2007). The state of betrayal trauma theory: Reply to McNally—Conceptual issues and future directions. *Memory, 15,* 295–311.

Frick, U., Frick, H., Langguth, B., Landgrebe, M., Hübner-Liebermann, B., & Hajak, G. (2013). The revolving door phenomenon revisited: Time to readmission in 17,415 patients with 37,697 hospitalisations at a German psychiatric hospital. *Plos ONE, 8*(10). Article ID e75612.

Fried, A. L. (2012). Ethics in psychological research: Guidelines and regulations. In H. Cooper, P. M. Camic, D. L. Long, A. T. Panter, D. Rindskopf, & K. J. Sher (Eds.), *APA handbook of research methods in psychology: Vol. 1. Foundations, planning, measures, and psychometrics.* Washington, DC: American Psychological Association.

Friedkin, N. E. (1999). Choice shift and group polarization. *American Sociological Review, 64,* 856–875.

Friedman, H. S. (2011). Personality, disease, and self-healing. In H. S. Friedman (Ed.), *Oxford handbook of health psychology.* New York, NY: Oxford University Press.

Friedman, H. S., & Adler, N. E. (2007). The history and background of health psychology. In H. S. Friedman & R. C. Silver (Eds.), *Foundations of health psychology.* New York, NY: Oxford University Press.

Friedman, H. S., & Kern, M. L. (2014). Personality, well-being, and health. *Annual Review of Psychology, 65,* 719–742. doi:10.1146/annurev-psych-010213-115123.

Friedman, H. S., Kern, M. L., Hampson, S. E., & Duckworth, A. L. (2014). A new life-span approach to conscientiousness and health: Combining the pieces of the causal puzzle. *Developmental Psychology, 50,* 1377–1389. doi:10.1037/a0030373.

Friedman, H. S., & Martin, L. R. (2011). *The longevity project: Surprising discoveries for health and long life from the landmark eight-decade study.* New York, NY: Hudson Street Press.

Friedman, M., & Rosenman, R. F. (1974). *Type A behavior and your heart.* New York, NY: Knopf.

Friedman, R., & James, J. W. (2008). The myth of the sages of dying, death and grief. *Skeptic, 14,* 37–41.

Friedman, S. L., & Boyle, D. E. (2008). Attachment in U.S. children experiencing nonmaternal care in the early 1990s. *Attachment & Human Development, 10,* 225–261. doi:10.1080/14616730802113570.

Friedmann, E., & Son, H. (2009). The human-companion animal bond: How humans benefit. *Veterinary Clinic North American Small Animal Practice, 39,* 293–326.

Frijda, N. H. (1999). Emotions and hedonic experience. In D. Kahneman, E. Diener, & N. Schwarz (Eds.), *Well-being: The foundations of hedonic psychology.* New York, NY: Russell Sage Foundation.

Frisco, M. L., Houle, J. N., & Martin, M. A. (2010).The image in the mirror and the number on the scale: Weight perceptions, and adolescent depressive symptoms. *Journal of Health and Social Behavior, 51*(2), 215–228.

Friston, K. J. (2003). Characterizing functional asymmetries with brain mapping. In K. Hugdahl & R. J. Davidson (Eds.), *The asymmetrical brain* (pp. 161–186). Cambridge, MA: MIT Press.

Frith, U. (2001). Mind blindness and the brain in autism. *Neuron, 32,* 969–979.

Fromm, E. (1979). The nature of hypnosis and other altered states of consciousness: An ego-psychological theory. In E. Fromm & R. E. Shor (Eds.), *Hypnosis: Developments in research and new perspectives.* New York, NY: Aldine.

Fromm, E. (1992). An ego-psychological theory of hypnosis. In E. Fromm & M. R. Nash (Eds.), *Contemporary hypnosis research.* New York, NY: Guilford.

Frost, R. O., & Rasmussen, J. L. (2012). Phenomenolgy and characteristics of compulsive hoarding. In G. Steketee (Ed.), *The Oxford handbook of obsessive-compulsive and spectrum disorders* (pp. 71–88). New York, NY: Oxford University Press.

Frost, R. O., Steketee, G., & Tolin, D. F. (2012). Diagnosis and assessment of hoarding disorder. *Annual Review of Clinical Psychology, 8,* 219–242.

Fruzzetti, A. E., & Erikson, K. R. (2010). Mindfulness and acceptance interventions in cognitive behavioural therapy. In K. S. Dobson (Ed.), *Handbook of cognitive-behavioural therapies* (3rd ed., pp. 347–372). New York, NY: Guilford Press.

Fuller, P. M., & Lu, J. (2009). Hypothalamic regulation of sleep. In R. Stickgold & M. P. Walker (Eds.), *The Neuroscience of Sleep* (pp. 91–98). San Diego, CA: Academic Press.

Funder, D. C. (2001). Personality. *Annual Review of Psychology, 52,* 197–221.

Funder, D. C. (2014). Best practices. Society for Personality and Social Psychology. Retrieved from http://www.spsp.org/publications/best-practices.

Funder, D. C. (2016). Taking situations seriously: The situation construal model and the Riverside Situational Q-sort. *Current Directions in Psychological Science, 25,* 203–208.

Fung, K. M. T., Hector, W. H. T., Corrigan, P. W., Lam, C. S., & Cheng, W-M. (2007). Measuring self-stigma of mental-illness in China and its implications for recovery. *International Journal of Social Psychiatry, 53,* 408–418.

Funk, W. (1998). *What difference does it make? The journey of a soul survivor.* Cranbrook, BC: Wild Flower Publisher.

Furnham, A., & Mak, T. (1999). Sex-role stereotyping in television commercials: A review and comparison of fourteen studies done on five continents over 25 years. *Sex Roles, 41,* 413–437.

Fushimi, M., Sugawara, J., & Shimizu, T. (2005). Suicide patterns and characteristics in Akita, Japan. *Psychiatry and Clinical Neurosciences, 59*(3), 296–302.

Fyer, A. J. (2009). Anxiety disorders: Genetics. In B. J. Sadock, V. A. Sadock, & P. Ruiz (Eds.), *Kaplan & Sadock's comprehensive textbook of psychiatry* (9th ed., pp. 1898–1905). Philadelphia, PA: Lippincott Williams & Wilkins.

Gachter, S. (2010). (Dis)advantages of student subjects: What is your research question. *Behavioral and Brain Sciences, 33,* 31–43.

Gackenbach, J. I., & Sheikh, A. (Eds.). (1991). *Dream images: A call to mental arms.* New York, NY: Baywood.

Gaeth, G. J., & Shanteau, J. (2000). Reducing the influence of irrelevant information on experienced decision makers. In T. Connolly, H. R. Arkes, & K. R. Hammond (Eds.), *Judgment and decision making: An interdisciplinary reader* (2nd ed., pp. 305–323). New York, NY: Cambridge University Press.

Gage, F. H. (2002). Neurogenesis in the adult brain. *Journal of Neuroscience, 22,* 612–613.

Galambos, N. L. (2004). Gender and gender role development in adolescence. In R. M. Lerner & L. Steinberg (Eds.), *Handbook of adolescent psychology.* New York, NY: Wiley.

Galati, D., Scherer, K. R., & Ricci-Bitti, P. E. (1997). Voluntary facial expression of emotion: Comparing congenitally blind with normally sighted encoders. *Journal of Personality and Social Psychology, 73,* 1363–1379.

Gale, C. R., Booth, T., Mõttus, R., Kuh, D., & Deary, I. J. (2013). Neuroticism and extraversion in youth predict mental well-being and life satisfaction 40 years later. *Journal of Research in Personality, 47,* 687–697. doi:10.1016/j.jrp.2013.06.005.

Galea, S., Brewin, C. R., Gruber, M., Jones, R. T., King, D. W., King, L. A., et al. (2007). *Archives of General Psychiatry, 64,* 1427–1434.

Galea, S., Nandi, A., & Viahov D. (2005). The epidemiology of post-traumatic stress disorder after disasters. *Epidemiologic Reviews, 27,* 78–91.

Gallagher, M. W., Lopez, S. J., & Pressman, S. D. (2013). Optimism is universal: Exploring the presence and benefits of optimism in a representative sample of the world. *Journal of Personality, 81,* 429–440. doi:10.1111/jopy.12026.

Gallant, N., & Hadjistavropoulous, T. (2017). Experiencing pain in the presence of others: A structured laboratory investigation of older adults. *Journal of Pain, 18,* 456–467.

Gallese, V., Fadiga, L., Fogassi, L., & Rizzolatti, G. (1996). Action recognition in the premotor cortex. *Brain, 119,* 593–609.

Gallo, D., & Lampinen, J. M. (2016). Three pillars of false memory prevention: Orientation, evaluation, and corroboration. In J. Dunlosky & S. K. Tauber (Eds.), *The Oxford handbook of metamemory* (pp. 378–404). New York, NY: Oxford University Press.

Gallo, D. A., & Wheeler, M. E. (2013). Episodic memory. In D. Reisberg (Ed.), *Oxford handbook of cognitive psychology.* New York, NY: Oxford University Press.

Gallo, K. P., Thompson-Hollands, J., Pincus, D. B., & Barlow, D. H. (2013). Anxiety disorders. In T. A. Widiger, G. Stricker, I. B. Weiner, G. Stricker, T. A. Widiger, & I. B. Weiner (Eds.), *Handbook of psychology: Vol. 8. Clinical psychology* (2nd ed.). New York, NY: Wiley.

Galloway, G. (2006, May 6). Margaret Trudeau's dark place of despair. *The Globe and Mail,* A4.

Gallup, G. G., Jr., & Frederick, D. A. (2010). The science of sex appeal: An evolutionary perspective. *Review of General Psychology, 14*(3), 240–250.

Galton, F. (1869). *Hereditary genius: An inquiry into its laws and consequences.* New York, NY: Appleton.

Galton, F. (1909). *Memories of my life.* New York, NY: E. P. Dutton and Company.

Galvan, A. (2013). The teenage brain: Sensitivity to rewards. *Current Directions in Psychological Science, 22,* 88–93. doi:10.1177/0963721413480859.

Gamer, M., Verschuere, B., Crombez, G., & Vossel, G. (2008). Combining physiological measures in the detection of concealed information. *Physiology and Behavior, 95,* 333–340.

Gananca, L., Kahn, D. A., & Oquendo, M. A. (2014). Mood disorders. In J. L. Cutler (Ed.), *Psychiatry* (3rd ed.). New York, NY: Oxford University Press.

Gangestad, S. W., Garver-Apgar, J. (2007). Changes in women's mate preferences across the ovulatory cycle. *Journal of Personality and Social Psychology, 92,* 151–163.

Garb, H. N., Wood, J. M., Lilienfeld, S. O., & Nezworski, M. T. (2005). Roots of the Rorschach controversy. *Clinical Psychology Review, 25*(1), 97–118. doi:10.1016/j.cpr.2004.09.002.

Garcia, J. (1989). Food for Tolman: Cognition and cathexis in concert. In T. Archer & L. G. Nilsson (Eds.), *Aversion, avoidance, and anxiety: Perspectives on aversively motivated behavior.* Hillsdale, NJ: Erlbaum.

Garcia, J., Clarke, J. C., & Hankins, W. G. (1973). Natural responses to scheduled rewards. In P. P. G. Bateson & P. Klopfer (Eds.), *Perspectives in ethology.* New York, NY: Plenum.

Garcia, J., & Koelling, R. A. (1966). Learning with prolonged delay of reinforcement. *Psychonomic Science, 5,* 121–122.

Garcia, J., & Rusiniak, K. W. (1980). What the nose learns from the mouth. In D. Muller-Schwarze & R. M. Silverstein (Eds.), *Chemical signals.* New York, NY: Plenum.

Garcia-Rill, E. (2009). Reticular activating system. In R. Stickgold & M. P. Walker (Eds.), *The neuroscience of sleep* (pp. 133–139). San Diego, CA: Academic Press.

Gardner, B. T., & Gardner, R. A. (1967). Teaching sign language to a chimpanzee: II. Demonstrations. *Psychonomic Bulletin, 1*(2), 36.

Gardner, E. P., & Kandel, E. R. (2000). Touch. In E. R. Kandel, J. H. Schwartz, & T. M. Jessell (Eds.), *Principles of neural science.* New York, NY: McGraw-Hill.

Gardner, H. (1983). *Frames of mind: The theory of multiple intelligences.* New York, NY: Basic Books.

Gardner, H. (1985). *The mind's new science: A history of the cognitive revolution.* New York, NY: Basic Books.

Gardner, H. (1993). *Multiple intelligences: The theory in practice.* New York, NY: Basic Books.

Gardner, H. (1998). A multiplicity of intelligences. *Scientific American Presents Exploring Intelligence, 9,* 18–23.

Gardner, H. (1999). *Intelligence reframed: Multiple intelligences for the 21st century.* New York, NY: Basic Books.

Gardner, H. (2003). Three distinct meanings of intelligence. In R. Sternberg, J. Lautrey, & T. I. Lubart (Eds.), *Models of intelligence: International perspectives* (pp. 43–54). Washington, DC: American Psychological Association.

Gardner, H. (2004). Audiences for the theory of multiple intelligences. *Teachers College Record, 106*(1), 212–220.

Gardner, H. (2006). *Multiple intelligences: New horizons.* New York, NY: Basic Books.

Gardner, M., & Steinberg, L. (2005). Peer influence on risk-taking, risk preference, and risky decision-making in adolescence and adulthood: An experimental study. *Developmental Psychology, 41,* 625–635.

Garland, E. L., Farb, N. A., Goldin, P. R., Fredrickson, B. L. (2015). Mindfulness broadens awareness and builds eudaimonic meaning: A process model of mindful positive emotion regulation. *Psychological Inquiry, 26,* 293–314.

Garland, E. L., Gaylord, S. A., Boettiger, C. A., & Howard, M. O. (2010). Mindfulness training modifies cognitive, affective, and physiological mechanisms implicated in alcohol dependence: Results of a randomized controlled pilot trial. *Journal of Psychoactive Drugs, 42*(2), 213–235.

Garner, M., Mogg, K., & Bradley, B. P. (2006). Orienting and maintenance of gaze to facial expressions in social anxiety. *Journal of Abnormal Psychology, 115,* 760–770.

Garrett, B. L. (2011). *Convicting the innocent.* Cambridge, MA: Harvard University Press.

Gaschler, K. (2008). Misery in motherhood. *Scientific American Mind, 19,* 66–73.

Gatchel, R. J., & Maddrey, A. M. (2004). The biopsychosocial perspective of pain. In J. M. Raczynski & L. C. Leviton (Eds.), *Handbook of clinical health psychology (Vol. 2): Disorders of behavior and health.* Washington, DC: American Psychological Association.

Gates, G. J. (2011). *How many people are lesbian, gay, bisexual and transgender?* Los Angeles, CA: The Williams Institute, UCLA School of Law.

Gates, G. J. (2013). Demographic perspectives on sexual orientation. In J. Patterson, & A. R. D'Augelli (Eds.), *Handbook of psychology and sexual orientation.* New York, NY: Oxford University Press.

Gaudiano, B. A. (2013). Psychotherapy's image problem. *The New York Times,* September 29. Retrieved from http://www.nytimes.com/2013/09/30/opinion/psychotherapys-image-problem.html?_r=0.

Gaudiano, B. A., & Miller, I. W. (2013). The evidence-based practice of psychotherapy: Facing the challenges that lie ahead. *Clinical Psychology Review, 33,* 813–824. doi:10.1016/j.cpr.2013.04.004.

Gawronski, B. (2012). Back to the future of dissonance theory: Cognitive consistency as a core motive. *Social Cognition, 30,* 652–668.

Gazzaniga, M. S. (1970). *The bisected brain.* New York, NY: Appleton-Century-Crofts.

Gazzaniga, M. S. (2005). Forty-five years of split-brain research and still going strong. *Nature Reviews Neuroscience, 6,* 653–659.

Gazzaniga, M. S. (2008). Spheres of influence. *Scientific American Mind, 19*(2), 32–39.

Gazzaniga, M. S., Bogen, J. E., & Sperry, R. W. (1965). Observations on visual perception after disconnection of the cerebral hemispheres in man. *Brain, 88,* 221–236.

Gazzaniga, M. S., Ivry, R. B., & Mangum, G. R. (2009). *Cognitive neuroscience: The biology of the mind* (3rd ed.). New York, NY: Norton.

Gearhardt, A. N., & Corbin, W. R. (2012). Food addiction and diagnostic criteria for dependence. In K. C. Brownell, & M. S. Gold (Eds.), *Food and addiction: A comprehensive handbook.* New York, NY: Oxford University Press.

Geary, D. C. (2007). An evolutionary perspective on sex difference in mathematics and the sciences. In S. J. Ceci & W. M. Williams (Eds.), *Why aren't more women in science?* (pp. 173–188). Washington, DC: American Psychological Association.

Gegenfurtner, K. (2010). Color perception: Physiological. In E. B. Goldstein (Ed.), *Encyclopedia of perception.* Thousand Oaks, CA: Sage.

Gehrman, P., Findley, J., & Perlis, M. (2012). Insomnia I: Etiology and conceptualization. In C. M. Morin, & C.

A. Espie (Eds.), *Oxford handbook of sleep and sleep disorders*. New York, NY: Oxford University Press.

Geier, A. B., Rozin, P., & Doros, G. (2006). Unit bias: A new heuristic that helps explain the effect of portion size on food intake. *Psychological Science, 17*, 521–526.

Geier, C. F. (2013). Adolescent cognitive control and reward processing: Implications for risk taking and substance use. *Hormones and Behavior, 64*, 333–342. doi:10.1016/j. yhbeh.2013.02.008.

Gelernter, J. (2015). Genetics of complex traits in psychiatry. *Biological Psychiatry, 77*(1), 36–42. doi:10.1016/j.biopsych.2014.08.005.

Geller, J. L. (2009). The role of the hospital in the care of the mentally ill. In B. J. Sadock, V. A. Sadock, & P. Ruiz (Eds.), *Kaplan & Sadock's comprehensive textbook of psychiatry* (9th ed., pp. 4299–4314). Philadelphia, PA: Lippincott Williams & Wilkins.

Genesee, F. (2015), Myths about early childhood bilingualism. *Canadian Psychology, 56*, 6–15.

Geng, L., Liu, L., Xu, J., Zhou, K., & Fang, Y. (2013). Can evaluative conditioning change implicit attitudes towards recycling? *Social Behavior and Personality, 41*, 947–956.

Gennari, S. P., Sloman, S. A., Malt, B. C., & Fitch, W. T. (2002). Motion events in language and cognition. *Cognition, 83*(1), 49–79.

Gentile, D. A., & Bushman, B. J. (2012). Reassessing media violence effects using a risk and resilience approach to understanding aggression. *Psychology of Popular Media Culture, 1*, 138–151. doi:10.1037/a0028481.

Gentner, D. (1988). Metaphor as structure mapping: The relational shift. *Child Development, 59*, 47–59.

Gentner, D., & Smith, L. A. (2013). Analogical learning and reasoning. In D. Reisberg (Ed.), *Oxford handbook of cognitive psychology*. New York, NY: Oxford University Press.

George, M. S. (2003, September). Stimulating the brain. *Scientific American, 289*(3), 66–93.

George, M. S., Bohning, D. E., Lorberbaum, J. P., Nahas, Z., Anderson, B., Borckardt, J. J., et al. (2007). Overview of transcranial magnetic stimulation: History, mechanisms, physics, and safety. In M. S. George & R. H. Belmaker (Eds.), *Transcranial magnetic stimulation in clinical psychiatry*. Washington, DC: American Psychiatric Publishing.

George, S. A. (2002). The menopause experience: A woman's perspective. *Journal of Obstetric, Gynecologic, and Neonatal Nursing, 31*, 71–85.

Geraerts E. (2012). Cognitive underpinnings of recovered memories of childhood abuse. In R. F. Belli (Ed.), *True and false recovered memories: Toward a reconciliation of the debate*. New York, NY: Springer.

Gershkoff-Stowe, L., & Hahn, E. R. (2007). Fast mapping skills in the developing lexicon. *Journal of Speech, Language, and Hearing Research, 50*, 682–696.

Gershoff, E. T. (2002). Parental corporal punishment and associated child behaviors and experiences: A meta-analytic and theoretical review. *Psychological Bulletin, 128*, 539–579.

Gershoff, E. T. (2013). Spanking and child development: We know enough now to stop hitting our children. *Child Development Perspectives, 7*, 133–137. doi:10.1111/cdep.12038.

Gershoff, E. T., Lansford, J. E., Sexton, H. R., Davis-Kean, P., & Sameroff, A. J. (2012). Longitudinal links between spanking and children's externalizing behaviors in a national sample of white, black, Hispanic, and Asian American families. *Child Development, 83*, 838–843. doi:10.1111/j.1467-8624.2011.01732.x.

Gershon, E. S., & Alliey-Rodriguez, N. (2013). New ethical issues for genetic counseling in common mental disorders. *The American Journal of Psychiatry, 170*, 968–976. doi:10.1176/appi.ajp.2013.12121558.

Gershon, E. S., Berrettini, W. H., & Goldin, L. R. (1989). Mood disorders: Genetic aspects. In H. I. Kaplan & B. J. Sadock (Eds.), *Comprehensive textbook of psychiatry/V*. Baltimore, MD: Williams & Wilkins.

Gervain, J., & Mehler, J. (2010). Speech perception and language acqusition in the first year of life. *Annual Review of Psychology, 61*, 191–218.

Getzel, E. E., & Wehman, P. (2005). *Going to college: Expanding opportunities with disabilities*. Baltimore, MD: Brookes.

Ghassemzadeh, H., Posner, M. I., & Rothbart, M. K. (2013). Contributions of Hebb and Vygotsky to an integrated science of mind. *Journal of the History of the Neurosciences, 22*, 292–306.

Gibbons, D. E., & Lynn, S. J. (2010). Hypnotic inductions: A primer. In S. J. Lynn, J. W. Rhue, & I. Kirsch (Eds.), *Handbook of Clinical Hypnosis* (2nd ed., pp. 267–292). Washington, DC: American Psychological Association.

Gibbons, R. D., Brown, C. H., Hur, K., Davis, J. M., & Mann, J. J. (2012). Suicidal thoughts and behavior with antidepressant treatment: Reanalysis of the randomized placebo-controlled studies of fluoxetine and venlafaxine. *Archives of General Psychiatry, 69*(6), 580–587. doi:10.1001/archgenpsychiatry.2011.2048.

Gibson, B., & Zielaskowski, K. (2013). Subliminal priming of winning images prompts increased betting in slot machine play. *Journal of Applied Psychology, 43*, 122–145.

Gibson, C., Folley, B. S., & Park, S. (2009). Enhanced divergent thinking and creativity in musicians: A behavioral and near-infrared spectroscopy study. *Brain and Cognition, 69*(1), 162–169.

Giedd, J. N., Blumenthal, J., Jeffries, N. O., Castellanos, F. X., Liu, H., Zijdenbos, A., et al. (1999). Brain development during childhood and adolescence: A longitudinal MRI study. *Nature Neuroscience, 2*, 861–863.

Gigerenzer, G. (2000). *Adaptive thinking: Rationality in the real world*. New York, NY: Oxford University Press.

Gigerenzer, G. (2004). Fast and frugal heuristics: The tools of bounded rationality. In D. J. Koehler & N. Harvey (Eds.), *Blackwell handbook of judgment and decision making*. Malden, MA: Blackwell.

Gigerenzer, G. (2008). Why heuristics work. *Perspective on Psychological Science, 3*(1), 20–29.

Gigerenzer, G., & Gaissmaier, W. (2011). Heuristic decision making. *Annual Review of Psychology, 62*, 451–482.

Gigerenzer, G., & Todd, P. M. (1999). Fast and frugal heuristics: The adaptive toolbox. In G. Gigerenzer, P. M. Todd, & ABC Research Group (Eds.), *Simple heuristics that make us smart* (pp. 3–36). New York, NY: Oxford University Press.

Gigerenzer, G., Gaissmaier, W., Kurz-Milcke, E., Schwartz, L. M., & Woloshin, S. (2007). Helping doctors and patients make sense of health statistics. *Psychological Science in the Public Interest, 8*(2), 53–96. doi:10.1111/j.1539-6053.2008.00033.x.

Gilbert, D. T. (1989). Thinking lightly about others: Automatic components of the social inference process. In J. S. Uleman & J. A. Bargh (Eds.), *Unintended thought: Limits of awareness, intention, and control*. New York, NY: Guilford Press.

Gilbert, D. T. (1998). Speeding with Ned: A personal view of the correspondence bias. In J. M. Darley & J. Cooper (Ed.), *Attribution and social interaction: The legacy of Edward E. Jones*. Washington, DC: American Psychological Association.

Gilbert, D. T., Driver-Linn, E., & Wilson, T. D. (2002). The trouble with Vronsky: Impact bias in the forecasting of future affective states. In L. F. Barrett & P. Salovey (Eds.), *The wisdom in feeling: Psychological processes in emotional intelligence* (pp. 114–143). New York, NY: Guilford Press.

Gilbert, D., King, G., Pettigrew, S., & Wilson, T. D. (2016). Comment on estimating the reproducibility of psychological science. *Science, 351*, 1037.

Gilgen, A. R. (1982). *American psychology since World War II: A profile of the discipline*. Westport, CT: Greenwood Press.

Gillen-O'Neel, C., Huynh, V. W., & Fuligni, A. J. (2013). To study or sleep? The academic costs of extra studying at the expense of sleep. *Child Development, 84*, 133–142.

Gilmour, H. (2015). Chronic pain, activity restriction and flourishing mental health. Health Reports: Statistics Canada. Retrieved from http://www.statcan.gc.ca/pub/82-003-x/2015001/article/14130-eng.pdf.

Gilovich, T. D., & Griffin, D. W. (2010). Judgment and decision making. In S. T. Fiske, D. T. Gilbert, & G. Lindzey (Eds.), *Handbook of social psychology*, (5th ed., Vol. 1, pp. 542–588). Hoboken, NJ: Wiley.

Gilovich, T. D., Griffin, D., & Kahneman, D. (2002). *Heuristics and biases: The psychology of intuitive judgment*. New York, NY: Cambridge University Press.

Gim, R. H., Atkinson, D. R., & Kim, S. J. (1991). Asian-American acculturation, counselor ethnicity, and cultural sensitivity, and ratings of counselors. *Journal of Counseling Psychology, 38*, 37–62.

Gim, R. H., Atkinson, D. R., & Whitelhy, S. (1990). Asian-American acculturation, severity of concerns, and willingness to see a counselor. *Journal of Counseling Psychology, 37*, 281–283.

Gimmig, D., Huguet, P., Caverni, J., & Cury, F. (2006). Choking under pressure and working memory capacity: When performance pressure reduces fluid intelligence. *Psychonomic Bulletin & Review, 13*(6), 1005–1010.

Gitlin, M. J. (2009). Pharmacotherapy and other somatic treatments for depression. In I. H. Gotlib & C. L. Hammen (Eds.), *Handbook of depression* (pp. 554–585). New York, NY: Guilford Press.

Gitlin, M. J. (2014). Pharmacotherapy and other somatic treatments for depression. In I. H. Gotlib & C. L. Hammen, (Eds.), *Handbook of depression* (3rd ed.). New York, NY: Guilford Press.

Gittelman, M. (2005). The neglected disaster. *International Journal of Mental Health, 34*(2), 9–21.

Gladding, R. (2013). *Use your mind to change your brain: How to overcome self-defeating thoughts and actions*. Retrieved from http://www.psychologytoday.com/blog/use-your-mind-change-your-brain.

Gladstone, J., & Cooper, J. E. (2010). Migraine in Canada … we can and should do better. *Canadian Journal of Neurological Science, 37*, 553–534.

Gläscher, J., Adolphs, R., Damasio, H., Bechara, A., Rudrauf, D., Calamia, M., . . . Tranel, D. (2012). Lesion mapping of cognitive control and value-based decision making in the prefrontal cortex. *PNAS Proceedings of The National Academy of Sciences of the United States of America, 109*, 14681–14686. doi:10.1073/pnas.1206608109.

Glass, R. M. (2004). Treatment of adolescents with major depression: Contributions of a major trial. *JAMA, 292*, 861–863.

Glasser, W. (2005). Warning: Psychiatry can be hazardous to your mental health. In R. H. Wright & N. A. Cummings (Eds.), *Destructive trends in mental health: The well-intentioned path to harm*. New York, NY: Routledge.

Glassman, A., Maj, M., & Sartorius, N. (2011). *Depression and heart disease*. Hoboken, NJ: Wiley.

Gleason, M. E. J., & Masumi, I. (2015). Social support. In M. Mikulincer, P. R. Shaver, E. Borgida, & I. A. Bargh (Eds.), *APA handbook of personality and social psychology: Vol. 3. Interpersonal relations*. Washington, DC: American Psychological Association.

Gleibs, I. H., Morton, T. A., Rabinovich, A., Haslam, S., & Helliwel, J. F. (2013). Unpacking the hedonic paradox: A dynamic analysis of the relationships between financial capital, social capital, and life satisfaction. *British Journal of Social Psychology, 52*, 25–43.

Gleitman, L., & Papafragou. (2005). Language and thought. In K. J. Holyoak & R. G. Morrison (Eds.), *The Cambridge handbook of thinking and reasoning*. New York, NY: Cambridge University Press.

Gluck, M. A., & Myers, C. E. (1997). Psychobiological models of hippocampal function in learning and memory. *Annual Review of Psychology, 48*, 481–514.

Gluck, M. E. (2006). Stress response and binge eating disorder. *Appetite, 46*(1), 26–30.

Goddard, M. J. (2009). The impact of human intuition in psychology. *Review of General Psychology, 13*, 167–174.

Godlee, F., Smith, J., & Marcovitch, H. (2011). Wakefield's article linking MMR vacine and autism was fraudulent. *British Medical Journal, 342*, 64–66.

Goff, D. C. (2014). Maintenance treatment with long-acting injectable antipsychotics: Comparing old with new. *JAMA, 311*, 1973–1974.

Goff, D. C., & Gudeman, J. E. (1999). The person with chronic mental illness. In A. M. Nicholi (Ed.), *The Harvard guide to psychiatry*. Cambridge, MA: Harvard University Press.

Goin, M. K. (2005). A current perspective on the psychotherapies. *Psychiatric Services, 56*(3), 255–257.

Goldberg, M. E., & Hudspeth, A. J. (2000). The vestibular system. In E. R. Kandel, J. H. Schwartz, & T. M. Jessell (Eds.), *Principles of neural science*. New York, NY: McGraw-Hill.

Goldberg, T. E., David, A., & Gold, J. M. (2011). Neurocognitive impairments in schizophrenia: Their character and their role in symptom formation. In D. R. Weinberger & P. Harrison (Eds.), *Schizophrenia* (3rd ed.). Malden, MA: Wiley-Blackwell.

Golden, C. J., Sawicki, R. F., & Franzen, M. D. (1990). Test construction. In G. Goldstein & M. Hersen (Eds.), *Handbook of psychological assessment*. New York, NY: Pergamon Press.

Goldenberg, H. (1983). *Contemporary clinical psychology*. Pacific Grove, CA: Brooks/Cole.

Goldenberg, I., Goldenberg, H., & Pelavin, E. G. (2011). Family therapy. In R. J. Corsini & D. Wedding (Eds.), *Current psychotherapies* (9th ed.). Belmont, CA: Brooks/Cole.

Goldin-Meadow, S., & Alibali, M. W. (2011). Gesture's role in speaking, learning, and creating language. *Annual Review of Psychology, 64*, 257–283.

Goldman, D. L. (1990). Dorothea Dix and her two missions of mercy in Nova Scotia. *Canadian Journal of Psychiatry, 35*, 139–142.

Goldsmith, R., Joanisse, D. R., Gallagher, D., Pavlovich, K., Shamoon, C., Leibel, R. L., & Rosenbaum, M. (2010). Effects of experimental weight perturbation on skeletal muscle work efficiency, fuel utilization, and biochemistry in human subjects. *American Journal of Physiology-Regulatory, Integrative and Comparative Physiology, 298*, R79–R88.

Goldstein, E., & Farmer, K. (Eds.) (1993). *True stories of false memories*. Boca Raton, FL: Sir Publishing.

Goldstein, E. B. (2001). Pictorial perception and art. In E. B. Goldstein (Ed.), *Blackwell handbook of perception*. Malden, MA: Blackwell.

Goldstein, E. B. (2010). Constancy. In E. B. Goldstein (Ed.), *Encyclopedia of perception*. Thousand Oaks, CA: Sage.

Goldstein, W. M., & Hogarth, R. M. (1997). Judgement and decision research: Some historical context. In W. M. Goldstein, & R. M. Hogarth (Eds.), *Research on judgement and decision making*. New York, NY: Cambridge University Press.

Goldston, D. B., Molock, S. D., Whitbeck, L. B., Murakami, J. L., Zayas, L. H., & Hall, G. C. (2008). Cultural considerations in adolescent suicide prevention and psychosocial treatment. *American Psychologist, 63*, 14–31.

Goldstone, R. L., Roberts, M. E., & Gureckis, T. M. (2008). Emergent processes in group behaviour. *Current Directions in Psychological Science, 17*, 10–17.

Goleman, D. (1995). *Emotional intelligence*. New York, NY: Bantam Books.

Gomes, A. R., Faria, S., & Goncalves, A. M. (2013). Cognitive appraisal as a mediator in the relationship between stress and burnout. *Work & Stress, 27*, 351–367. doi:10.1080/02678373.2013.840341.

Gómez, D. M., Berent, I., Benavides-Varela, S., Bion, R. H., Cattarossi, L., Nespor, M., & Mehler, J. (2014). Language universals at birth. *PNAS Proceedings of the National Academy of Sciences of the United States of America, 111*, 5837–5841. doi:10.1073/pnas.1318261111.

Gonzales, K., & Lotto, A. J. (2013). A *bafri*, un *pafri*: Bilinguals pseudoword identifications support language specific phonetic systems. *Psychological Science, 24*(11), 2135–2142.

Goodale, M. A. (2010, August 4). Transforming vision into action. *Vision Research*, epub ahead of print.

Goodale, M. A. (2013). Separate visual systems for perception and action: A framework for understanding cortical visual impairment. *Developmental Medicine and Child Neurology, 55*, 9–12.

Goodale, M. A. (2014). How (and why) the visual control of action differs from visual perception. *Proceedings of the Royal Society: Proceedings B, 281*:20140337 10.1098/rspb.2014.0337.

Goodale, M. A., & Humphrey, G. K. (1988). The objects of action and perception. *Cognition, 67*, 181–207.

Goodale, M. A., & Humphrey, G. K. (2001). Separate visual systems for action and perception. In E. B. Goldstein (Ed.), *Blackwell handbook of perception* (pp. 309–343). Oxford, UK: Blackwell.

Goodale, M. A., & Milner, A. D. (1992). Separate visual pathways for perception and action. *Trends in Neuroscience, 15*, 20–25.

Goodale, M. A., & Milner, A. D. (2004). *Sight unseen: An exploration of conscious and unconscious vision*. Oxford, UK: Oxford University Press.

Goodale, M. A., & Westwood, D. A. (2004). An evolving view of duplex vision: Separate but interacting cortical pathways for perception and action. *Current Opinion in Neurobiology, 14*, 203–211.

Goodall, J. (1986). Social rejection, exclusion, and shunning among the Gombe chimpanzees. *Ethology & Sociobiology, 7*, 227–236.

Goodall, J. (1990). *Through a window: My thirty years with the chimpanzees of Gombe*. Boston, MA: Houghton, Mifflin.

Goodheart, C. D. (2006). Evidence, endeavor, and expertise in psychology practice. In C. D. Goodheart, A. E. Kazdin, & R. J. Sternberg (Eds.), *Evidence-based psychotherapy: Where practice and research meet* (pp. 37–62). Washington, DC: American Psychological Association.

Goodman, G. S., Quas, J. A., & Ogle, C. M. (2009). Child maltreatment and memory. *Annual Review of Psychology, 61*, 325–351.

Goodman, L-A. (2014). Olympian ends cross-Canada mental health ride on Parliament Hill. *The Globe and Mail*, Tuesday, July 1. Retrieved from http://www.theglobeandmail.com/news/national/olympian-ends-cross-canada-mental-health-ride-on-parliament-hill/article19407185/.

Goodwin, C. J. (1991). Misportraying Pavlov's apparatus. *American Journal of Psychology, 104*(1), 135–141.

Goodwin, F. K., & Jamison, K. R. (1990). *Manic-depressive illness*. New York, NY: Oxford University Press.

Goodwin, F. K., & Jamison, K. R. (2007). *Manic-depressive illness: Bipolar disorders and recurrent depression*. New York, NY: Oxford University Press.

Goodwin, G. (2009). Neurobiological aetiology of mood disorders. In M. C. Gelder, N. C. Andreasen, J. J. Lopez-Ibor, Jr., & J. R. Geddes (Eds.), *New Oxford textbook of psychiatry* (2nd ed., Vol. 1). New York, NY: Oxford University Press.

Gopnik, A. (2001). *The scientist in the crib: What early learning tells us about the mind*. New York, NY: William Morris and Company.

Gopnik, A. (2009). *The philosophical baby: What children's minds tell us about truth, love, and the meaning of life*. New York, NY: Farrar, Straus, and Giroux.

Gopnik, A. (2016). *The Gardner and the Carpenter: What the new science of child development tells us about the relationship between parents and children*. New York, NY: Farrar, Straus, and Giroux.

Gopnik, A., Meltzoff, A. N., & Kuhl, P. K. (1999). *The scientist in the crib: Minds, brains, and how children learn*. New York, NY: Morrow.

Gordon, J., & Abramov, I. (2001). Color vision. In E. B. Goldstein (Ed.), *Blackwell handbook of perception*. Malden, MA: Blackwell.

Gore, A. (2008). Neuroendocrine systems. In L. Squire, D. Berg, F. Bloom, S. Du Lac, A. Ghosh, & N. Spitzer (Eds.), *Fundamental neuroscience* (3rd ed., pp. 905–930). San Diego, CA: Elsevier.

Gorman, J. (2013). Scientists trace memories of things that never happened. *The New York Times*, July 25. Retrieved from http://www.nytimes.com/2013/07/26/science/false-memory-planted-in-a-mouse-brain-study-shows.html?_r=0.

Gorman, M. E. (1989). Error, falsification and scientific inference: An experimental investigation. *Quarterly Journal of Experimental Psychology, 41*(2–A), 385–412.

Gorski, R. A. (2000). Sexual differentiation of the nervous system. In E. R. Kandel, J. H. Schwartz, & T. M. Jessell (Eds.), *Principles of neural science*. New York, NY: McGraw-Hill.

Gorsuch, R. L. (1983). *Factor analysis*. Hillsdale, NJ: Erlbaum.

Gosling, S. D., Sandy, C. J., & Potter, J. (2010). Personalities of self-identified "dog people" and "cat people." *Anthrozoös, 23*(3), 213–222.

Goswami, U. (2006). Neuroscience and education: From research to practice? *Nature Reviews Neuroscience, 7*(5), 2–7.

Gotlib, I. H., & Robinson, L. A. (1982). Responses to depressed individuals: Discrepancies between self-reports and observer-rated behavior. *Journal of Abnormal Psychology, 91*, 231–240.

Gottesman, I. I. (1991). *Schizophrenia genesis: The origins of madness*. New York, NY: W. H. Freeman.

Gottesman, I. I. (2001). Psychopathology through a life span–genetic prism. *American Psychologist, 56*, 867–878.

Gottesman, I. I., & Hanson, D. R. (2005). Human development: Biological and genetic processes. *Annual Review of Psychology, 56*, 263–286.

Gottfredson, L. S. (2003a). Dissecting practical intelligence theory: Its claims and evidence. *Intelligence, 31*, 343–397.

Gottfredson, L. S. (2003b). *G*, jobs and life. In H. Nyborg (Ed.), *The scientific study of general intelligence: Tribute to Arthur R. Jensen*. Oxford, UK: Pergamon.

Gottfredson, L. S. (2009). Logical fallacies used to dismiss the evidence on intelligence testing. In R. P. Phelps (Ed.), *Correcting fallacies about educational and psychological testing* (pp. 11–65). Washington, DC: American Psychological Association.

Gouin, J., Hantsoo, L. V., & Keicolt-Glaser, J. K. (2011). Stress, negative emotions, and inflammation. In J. T. Cacioppo & J. Decety (Eds.), *Oxford handbook of social neuroscience*. New York, NY: Oxford University Press.

Gould, E. (2004). Stress, deprivation, and adult neurogenesis. In M. S. Gazzaniga (Ed.), *The cognitive neurosciences* (pp. 139–148). Cambridge, MA: MIT Press.

Gould, R. L. (1975, February). Adult life stages: Growth toward self-tolerance. *Psychology Today*, pp. 74–78.

Gould, S. J. (1996). *The mismeasure of man*. New York, NY: W.W. Norton.

Government of Canada. (2016). *About prescription drug use*. Retrieved from https://www.canada.ca/en/health-canada/services/substance-abuse/prescription-drug-abuse/about-prescription-drug-abuse.html.

Government of Canada. (2017). Post-traumatic stress disorder (PTSD) and war-related stress. Retrieved from http://www.veterans.gc.ca/eng/services/health/mental-health/publications/ptsd-warstress.

Gow, A. J., Bastin, M. E., Munoz Maniega, S., Valdes Hernandez, M. C., Morris, Z., Murray, C., . . . Wardlaw, J. M. (2012). Neuroprotective lifestyles and the aging brain: Activity, atrophy, and white matter integrity. *Neurology, 23*, 1802–1808. doi:10.1212/WNL.0b013e3182703fd2.

Graber, J. A. (2013). Pubertal timing and the development of psychopathology in adolescence and beyond. *Hormones and Behavior, 64*, 262–269. doi:10.1016/j.yhbeh.2013.04.003.

Gradisar, M., Gardner, G., & Dohnt, H. (2011). Recent worldwide sleep patterns and problems during adolescence: A review and meta-analysis of age, region, and sleep. *Sleep Medicine, 12*, 110–118.

Grady, D. (2006). Management of menopausal symptoms. *New England Journal of Medicine, 355*, 2338–2347.

Graf, P., & Gallie, K. A. (1992). A transfer-appropriate processing account for memory and amnesia. In L. R. Squire & N. Butters (Eds.), *Neuropsychology of memory* (2nd ed.). New York, NY: Guilford.

Graham, D. (2008). Desperate for sleep. *Toronto Star*, January 29.

Granberg, G., & Holmberg, S. (1991). Self-reported turnout and voter validation. *American Journal of Political Science, 35*, 448–459.

Grandner, M. A., Chakravorty, S., Perlis, M. L., Oliver, L., & Gurubhagavatula, I. (2014). Habitual sleep duration associated with self-reported and objectively determined cardiometabolic risk factors. *Sleep Medicine, 15*, 42–50. doi:10.1016/j.sleep.2013.09.012.

Grandner, M. A., Hale, L., Moore, M., & Patel, N. P. (2010). Mortality associated with short sleep duration: The evidence, the possible mechanisms, and the future. *Sleep Medicine Reviews, 14*(3), 191–203.

Grandner, M. A., Jackson, N. J., Pak, V. M., & Gehrman, P. R. (2012). Sleep disturbance is associated with cardiovascular and metabolic disorders. *Journal of Sleep Research, 21*, 427–433. doi:10.1111/j.1365-2869.2011.00990.x.

Granger, L. (2006). *Psychology*. The Canadian Encyclopedia. Retrieved from http://www .thecanadianencyclopedia.ca/en/article/psychology/.

Granic, I., Lobel, A., & Engels, R. C. M. E. (2014). The benefits of playing video games. *American Psychologist, 69*, 66–78. doi:10.1037/a0034857.

Grant, D. A., Bieling, P. J., Segal, Z. V., & Cochrane, M. M. (2013). Cognitive models and issues. In M. Power (Ed.), *The Wiley-Blackwell handbook of mood disorders* (2nd ed.). Malden, MA: Wiley-Blackwell.

Grant, J. A., Courtemanche, J., Duerden, E. G., Duncan, G. H., & Rainville, P. (2010). Cortical thickness and pain sensitivity in zen meditators. *Emotion, 10*(1), 43–53.

Grant, J. A., & Rainville, P. (2009). Pain sensitivity and analgesic effects of mindful states in Zen meditators: A cross-sectional study. *Psychosomatic Medicine, 71*(1), 106–114.

Grau, R., Salanova, M., & Peiro, J. M. (2001). Moderator effects of self-efficacy on occupational stress. *Psychology in Spain, 5*(1), 63–74.

Gray, C., & Della Sala, S. (2007). The Mozart effect: It's time to face the music! In S. Della Sala (Ed.), *Tall tales about the mind & brain: Separating fact from fiction* (pp. 148–157). New York, NY: Oxford University Press.

Gray, K., & Wegner, D. M. (2008). The sting of intentional pain. *Psychological Science, 19*(12), 1260–1262.

Graziano, W. G., & Tobin, R. M. (2009). Agreeableness. In M. R. Leary & R. H. Hoyle (Eds.), *Handbook of individual differences in social behavior* (pp. 46–61). New York, NY: Guilford Press.

GRE: General test overview. (2008). Educational Testing Service. Retrieved January 20, 2008, from http://www .ets.org/portal/site/ets/menuitem.1488512ecfd5b8849a77 b13bc3921509/?vgnextoid=e1b42d3631df4010VgnVCM 10000022f95190RCRD&vgnextchannel=5416e3b5f64f40 10VgnVCM10000022f95190RCRD.

Green, C. D. (2004). The hiring of James Mark Baldwin and James Gibson Hume at the University of Toronto in 1889. *History of Psychology, 7*, 130–153.

Green, C. D. (2009). Darwinian theory, functionalism, and the first American psychological revolution. *American Psychologist, 64*(2), 75–83.

Green, C. D., & Groff, P. R. (2003). *Early psychological thought: Ancient accounts of mind and soul*. Westport, CT: Praeger.

Green, D. W., & Abutalebi, J. (2013). Language control in bilinguals: The adaptive control hypothesis. *Journal of Cognitive Psychology, 2*(5), 515–530.

Green, J. D., Davis, J. L., Luchies, L. B., Coy, A. E., Van Tongeren, D. R., Reid, C. A., & Finkel, E. J. (2013). Victims versus perpetrators: Affective and empathic forecasting regarding transgressions in romantic relationships. *Journal of Experimental Social Psychology, 49*, 329–333.

Green, J. P. (1999). Hypnosis, context effects, and recall of early autobiographical memories. *International Journal of Clinical & Experimental Hypnosis, 47*, 284–300.

Green, J. P., Laurence, J., & Lynn, S. J. (2014). Hypnosis and psychotherapy: From Mesmer to mindfulness. *Psychology of Consciousness: Theory, Research, and Practice, 1*, 199–212. doi:10.1037/cns0000015.

Greenberg, A., Bellena, B., & Bialystok, E. (2013). Perspective taking ability in bilingual children: Extending advantages in executive control to spatial reasoning. *Cognitive Development, 28*, 41–50.

Greenberg, J. S. (2002). *Comprehensive stress management: Health and human performance*. New York, NY: McGraw-Hill.

Greenberg, L. S. (2002). Integrating an emotion-focused approach to treatment into psychotherapy integration. *Journal of Psychotherapy Integration, 12*, 111–125.

Greenberg, L. S. (2008). Emotion and cognition in psychotherapy: The transforming power of affect. *Canadian Psychology, 49*, 49–59.

Greenberg, L. S. (2012). Emotions, the great captains of our lives: Their role in the process of change in psychotherapy. *American Psychologist, 67*, 697–707.

Greenberg, L. S., & Johnson, S. M. (1988). *Emotion focussed couples therapy*. New York, NY: Guilford Press.

Greene, B. (1999). *The elegant universe: Superstrings, hidden dimensions, and the quest for the ultimate theory*. London, UK: Jonathan Cape.

Greene, B. (2003). A theory of everything. *PBS Online*. Retrieved July 29, 2008, from http://www.pbs.org/wgbh/ nova/elegant/everything/html.

Greenfield, R. (2006). *Timothy Leary*. London, UK: Harcourt Press.

Greeno, J. G. (1978). Nature of problem-solving abilities. In W. K. Estes (Ed.), *Handbook of learning and cognitive processes* (Vol. 5). Hillsdale, NJ: Erlbaum.

Greenough, W. T. (1975). Experiential modification of the developing brain. *American Scientist, 63*, 37–46.

Greenough, W. T., & Volkmar, F. R. (1973). Pattern of dendritic branching in occipital cortex of rats reared in complex environments. *Experimental Neurology, 40*, 491–504.

Greenson, R. R. (1967). *The technique and practice of psychoanalysis* (Vol. 1). New York, NY: International Universities Press.

Greenspan, S., & Driscoll, J. (1997). The role of intelligence in a broad model of personal competence. In D. P. Flanagan, J. L. Genshaft, & P. L. Harrison (Eds.), *Contemporary intellectual assessment: Theories, tests, and issues*. New York, NY: Guilford.

Greenwald, A. G., & Banaji, M. R. (1995). Implicit social cognition: Attitudes, self-esteem, and stereotypes. *Psychological Review, 102*(1), 4–27.

Greenwald, A. G., Banaji, M. R., & Nosek, B. A. (2015). Statistically small effects of the Implicit Association Test can have societally large effects. *Journal of Personality and Social Psychology, 108*, 533–561.

Greenwald, A. G., McGhee, D. E., & Schwartz, J. K. (1998). Measuring individual differences in implicit cognition: The Implicit Association Test. *Journal of Personality and Social Psychology, 74*(6), 1464–1480.

Greenwald, A. G., Poehlman, T., Uhlmann, E., & Banaji, M. R. (2009). Understanding and using the Implicit Association Test: III. Meta-analysis of predictive validity. *Journal of Personality and Social Psychology, 97*(1), 17–41. doi:10.1037/a0015575.

Gregersen, P. K., Kowalsky, E., Lee, A., Baron-Cohen, S., Fisher, S. E., Asher, J. E. et al (2013). Absolute pitch exhibits phenotypic and genetic overlap with synesthesia. *Human Molecular Genetics, 22*(10), 2097–2104.

Gregory, R. L. (1973). *Eye and brain*. New York, NY: McGraw-Hill.

Gregory, R. L. (1978). *Eye and brain* (2nd ed.). New York, NY: McGraw-Hill.

Greiner, E., Ryan, M., Mithani, Z., & Junquera, P. (2013). Cannabis use and psychosis: Current perspectives. *Addictive Disorders & Their Treatment, 12*, 136–139. doi:10.1097/ADT.0b013e3182624271.

Greitemeyer, T. (2014). Intense acts of violence during video game play make daily life aggression appear innocuous: A new mechanism of why violent video games increase aggression. *Journal of Experimental Social Psychology, 50*, 52–56. doi:10.1016/j.jesp.2013.09.004.

Gremeaux, V., Gayda, M., Lepers, R., Sosner, P., Juneau, M., & Nigam, A. (2012). Exercise and longevity. *Maturitas, 73*, 312–317. doi:10.1016/ j.maturitas.2012.09.012.

Greven, C. U., Harlaar, N., Kovas, Y., Chamorro-Premuzic, T., & Plomin, R. (2009). More than just IQ: School achievement is predicted by self-perceived abilities—but for genetic rather than environmental reasons. *Psychological Science, 20*(6), 753–762.

Grigorenko, E. L. (2000). Heritability and intelligence. In R. J. Sternberg (Ed.), *Handbook of intelligence* (pp. 53–91). New York, NY: Cambridge University Press.

Grinspoon, L., Bakalar, J. B., & Russo, E. (2005). Marihuana: Clinical aspects. In J. H. Lowinson, P. Ruiz, R. B. Millman, & J. G. Langrod (Eds.), *Substance abuse: A comprehensive textbook*. Philadelphia, PA: Lippincott Williams & Wilkins.

Griskevicius, V., Haselton, M. G., & Ackerman, J. M. (2015). Evolution and close relationships. In M. Mikulincer, P. R. Shaver, J. A. Simpson, & J. F. Dovidio (Eds.), *APA handbook of personality and social psychology Vol. 3: Interpersonal relations*. Washington, DC: American Psychological Association.

Gross, A. L., Brandt, J., Bandeen-Roche, K., Carlson, M. C., Stuart, E. A., Marsiske, M., & Rebok, G. W. (2014). Do older adults use the method of loci? Results from the active study. *Experimental Aging Research, 40*, 140–163. doi:10.1080/0361073X.2014.882204.

Gross, C. (2012). Disgrace: On Marc Hauser. *The Nation*, January 2012, 9–16.

Gross, C. (2016). Scientific misconduct. *Annual Review of Psychology, 67*, 693–711.

Gross, C. G. (2000). Neurogenesis in the adult brain: Death of a dogma. *Nature Reviews Neuroscience, 1*, 67–73.

Grossman, J. B., & Ruiz, P. (2004). Shall we make a leap-of-faith to disulfiram (Antabuse)? *Addictive Disorders & Their Treatment, 3*(3), 129–132.

Grossman, P. (2004). Mindfulness-based stress reduction and health benefits: A meta-analysis. *Journal of Psychosomatic Research, 57*, 35–43.

Grossman, R. P., & Till, B. D. (1998). The persistence of classically conditioned brand attitudes. *Journal of Advertising, 27*, 23–31.

Grossmann, K. E., & Grossmann, K. (1990). The wider concept of attachment in cross-cultural research. *Human Development, 33*, 31–47.

Grotevant, H. D., & McDermott, J. M. (2014). Adoption: Biological and social processes linked to adaptation. *Annual Review of Psychology, 65*, 235–265. doi:10.1146/annurev-psych-010213-115020.

Gruberger, M., Ben-Simon, E., Levkovitz, Y.,Zangen, A. & Hendler, T. (2011). Towards a neuroscience of mind-wandering. *Human Neuroscience, 5*, 56–67.

Grubin, D., & Madsen, L. (2005). Lie detection and the polygraph: A historical review. *Journal of Forensic Psychiatry & Psychology, 16*, 357–369.

Grunberg, N. E., Berger, S. S., & Hamilton, K. R. (2011). Stress and drug use. In R. J. Contrada & A. Baum (Eds.), *The handbook of stress science: Biology, psychology, and health* (pp. 111–121). New York, NY: Springer Publishing.

Grunberg, N. E., Faraday, M. M., & Rahman, M. A. (2001). The psychobiology of nicotine self-administration. In A. Baum, T. A. Revenson, & J. E. Singer (Eds.), *Handbook of health psychology* (pp. 249–262). Mahwah, NJ: Erlbaum.

Grundgeiger, T., Bayen, U. J., & Horn, S. S. (2014). Effects of sleep deprivation on prospective memory. *Memory, 22*, 679–686. doi:10.1080/09658211.2013.812220.

Guarda, A. S., Pinto, A. M., Coughlin, J. W., Hussain, S., Haug, N. A., & Heinberg, L. J. (2007). Perceived coercion and change in perceived need for admission in patients hospitalized for eating disorders. *American Journal of Psychiatry, 164*, 108–114.

Gudjonsson, G. H. (2001). Recovered memories: Effects upon the family and community. In G. M. Davies & T. Dalgleish (Eds.), *Recovered memories: Seeking the middle ground.* Chichester, England: Wiley.

Guenther, K. (1988). Mood and memory. In G. M. Davies & D. M. Thomson (Eds.), *Memory in context: Context in memory.* New York, NY: Wiley.

Guerreiro, R. J., Gustafson, D. R., & Hardy, J. (2012). The genetic architecture of Alzheimer's disease: Beyond APP, PSENs and APOE. *Neurobiology of Aging, 33*, 437–456. doi:10.1016/j.neurobiolaging.2010.03.025.

Guerrini, I., Thomson, A. D., & Gurling, H. D. (2007). The importance of alcohol misuse, malnutrition, and genetic susceptibility on brain growth and plasticity. *Neuroscience & Biobehavioral Reviews, 31*, 212–220.

Guilbault, R. L., Bryant, F. B., Brockway, J. H., & Posavac, E. J. (2004). A meta-analysis of research on hindsight bias. *Basic & Applied Social Psychology, 26*(2–3), 103–117.

Guilford, J. P. (1959). Three faces of intellect. *American Psychologist, 14*, 469–479.

Guilford, J. P. (1985). The structure-of-intellect model. In B. B. Wolman (Ed.), *Handbook of intelligence: Theories, measurements and applications.* New York, NY: Wiley.

Guilleminault, C., & Cao, M. T. (2011). Narcolepsy: Diagnosis and management. In M. H. Kryger, T. Roth, & W. C. Dement (Eds.), *Principles and practice of sleep medicine* (5th ed.). Saint Louis, MO: Elsevier Saunders.

Gul, P., Korosteliove, A., Caplan, L., Ball, L. C., Bazar, J. L., Rodkey, E. N., . . . Rutherfor, A. (2013). Reconstructing the experiences of first generation women in Canadian psychology. *Canadian Psychology, 54*, 94–104.

Gunn, D. V., Warm, J. S., Dember, W. N., & Temple, J. N. (2000). Subjective organization and the visibility of illusory contours. *American Journal of Psychology, 113*, 553–568.

Gunn, S. R., & Gunn, W. S. (2006). Are we in the dark about sleepwalking's dangers? In C. A. Read (Ed.), *Cerebrum: Emerging ideas in brain sciences* (pp. 1–12). New York, NY: Dana Press.

Gur, R. C., & Gur, R. E. (2007). Neural substrates for sex differences in cognition. In S. J. Ceci & W. M. Williams (Eds.), *Why aren't more women in science?* (pp. 189–198). Washington, DC: American Psychological Association.

Gur, R. E., Bassett, A. S., McDonald-McGinn, D. M., Bearden, C. E., Chow, E., et al. (2017). A neurogenetic model for the study of schizophrenia spectrum disorders: The international 22q11.2 deletion syndrome brain behavior consortium. *Molecular Psychiatry* (edpub ahead of print). Retrieved from https://www.ncbi.nlm.nih.gov/pubmed/28761081.

Gustad, L. T., Laugsand, L. E., Janszky, I., Dalen, H., & Bjerkeset, O. (2014). Symptoms of anxiety and depression and risk of heart failure: The HUNT study. *European Journal of Heart Failure, 16*, 861–870. doi:10.1002/ejhf.133.

Habashhi, M. M., Graziano, W. G., & Hoover, A. E. (2016). Searching for the prosocial personality: A big five approach to linking personality and prosocial behavior. *Personality and Social Psychology Bulletin, 42*, 1177–1192.

Hackett, T. A., & Kaas, J. H. (2009). Audition. In G. G. Berntson & J. T. Cacioppo (Eds.), *Handbook of neuroscience for the behavioral sciences.* New York, NY: Wiley.

Hackman, J. R., & Katz, N. (2010). Attitudes. In S. T. Fiske, D. T. Gilbert, & G. Lindzey (Eds.), *Handbook of social psychology* (5th ed., Vol. 1, pp. 353–393). Hoboken, NJ: Wiley.

Hackney, C. M. (2010). Auditory processing: Peripheral. In E. B. Goldstein (Ed.), *Encyclopedia of perception.* Thousand Oaks, CA: Sage.

Hadar, L., & Sood, S. (2014). When knowledge is demotivating: Subjective knowledge and choice overload. *Psychological Science, 25*, 1739–1747. doi:10.1177/0956797614539165.

Hadjistavropoulos, H., Dash, H., Hadjistavropoulos, T., & Sullivan, T. (2007). Recurrent pain among university students: Contributions of self-efficacy and perfectionism to the pain experience. *Personality and Individual Differences, 42*, 1081–1091.

Hadjistavropoulous, T. (2016). Recognizing pain in dementia. In L. Garcia-Larrea & P. Jackson (Eds.), *Pain and conscious brain* (pp. 167–181). Philadelphia, PA: Walters Kluwer Health.

Hafer, C., Bogaert, A. F., & McMullen, S.-L. (2001). Belief in a just world and condom use in a sample of gay and bisexual men. *Journal of Applied Social Psychology, 31*, 1892–1910.

Hagerty, M. R. (2000). Social comparisons of income in one's community: Evidence from national surveys of income and happiness. *Journal of Personality and Social Psychology, 78*, 764–771.

Haggarty, J. M., Cernovask, Z., Husni, M., Minor, K., Kermeen, P., & Merskey, H. (2002). Seasonal affective disorder in an Arctic community. *Acta Psychiatrica Scandinavica, 105*, 378–384.

Haggbloom, S. J., Warnick, R., Warnick, J. E., Jones, V. K., Yarbrough, G. L., Russell, T. M., et al. (2002). The 100 most eminent psychologists of the 20th century. *Review of General Psychology, 6*, 139–152.

Haidt, J., & Kesebir, S. (2010). Morality. In S. T. Fiske, D. T. Gilbert, & G. Lindzey (Eds.), *Handbook of social psychology* (Vol. 2, 5th ed.). Hoboken NJ: Wiley.

Haier, R. J. (2009). Neuro-intelligence, neuro-metrics and the next phase of brain imaging studies. *Intelligence, 37*(2), 121–123.

Hajcak, G. (2016). *The clinical neuroscience of mistakes.* American Psychological Association. Retrieved from http://www.apa.org/science/about/psa/2016/02/clinical-neuroscience.aspx.

Hakuta, K. (1986). *Mirror of language.* New York, NY: Basic Books.

Halaris, A. (2013). Inflammation, heart disease, and depression. *Current Psychiatry Reports, 15*, 400. doi:10.1007/s11920-013-0400-5.

Halassa, M. M., & Haydon, P. G. (2010). Integrated brain circuits: astrocytic networks modulate neuronal activity and behavior. *Annual Review of Physiology, 72*, 335–355.

Hald, G. M., & Høgh-Olesen, H. (2010). Receptivity to sexual invitations from strangers of the opposite gender. *Evolution and Human Behavior, 31*, 453–458. doi:10.1016/j.evolhumbehav.2010.07.004.

Hales, A. H., Kassner, M. P., Williams, K. D., & Graziano, W. G. (2016). *Personality and Social Psychology Bulletin, 42*, 782–797.

Halford, J. C. G., Gillespie, J., Brown, V., Pontin, E. E., & Dovey, T. M. (2004). Effect of television advertisements for foods on food consumption in children. *Appetite, 42*(2), 221–225.

Hall, C. I. (2014). The evolution of the revolution: The successful establishment of multicultural psychology. In F. L. Leong, L. Comas-Díaz, G. C. Nagayama Hall, V. C. McLoyd, & J. E. Trimble (Eds.), *APA handbook of multicultural psychology: Vol. 1. Theory and research.* Washington, DC: American Psychological Association. doi:10.1037/14189-001.

Hall, C. S. (1966). *The meaning of dreams.* New York, NY: McGraw-Hill.

Hall, C. S. (1979). The meaning of dreams. In D. Goleman & R. J. Davidson (Eds.), *Consciousness: Brain, states of awareness, and mysticism.* New York, NY: Harper & Row.

Hall, G. S. (1904). *Adolescence.* New York, NY: Appleton.

Hall, J., Trent, S., Thomas, K. L., O'Donovan, M. C., & Owen, M. J. (2015). Genetic risk for schizophrenia: Convergence on synaptic pathways involved in plasticity. *Biological Psychiatry, 77*(1), 52–58. doi:10.1016/j.biopsych.2014.07.011.

Hall, J. A., & Mast, M. S. (2008). Are women always more interpersonally sensitive than men? Impact of goals and content domain. *Personality and Social Psychology Bulletin, 34*, 144–155.

Hall, J. A., & Roter, D. L. (2011). Physician-patient communication. In H. S. Friedman (Ed.), *Oxford handbook of health psychology.* New York, NY: Oxford University Press.

Hall, M., Halliday, T., & Open University. (1998). *Behaviour and evolution.* Berlin: Springer, in association with the Open University.

Hall, P. A. (2016). Executive control processes in high-calorie food consumption. *Current Directions in Psychological Science, 25*, 91–98.

Hall, W. D., & Degenhardt, J. (2009). Cannabis-related disorders. In B. J. Sadock, V. A. Sadock, & P. Ruiz (Eds.), *Kaplan & Sadock's comprehensive textbook of psychiatry* (9th ed.). Philadelphia, PA: Lippincott Williams & Wilkins.

Halpern, C., Hurtig, H., Jaggi, J., Grossman, M., Won, M., & Baltuch, G. (2007). Deep brain stimulation in neurologic disorders. *Parkinsonism & Related Disorders, 13*(1), 1–16.

Halpern, D. F. (1984). *Thought and knowledge: An introduction to critical thinking.* Hillsdale, NJ: Erlbaum.

Halpern, D. F. (1996). *Thought and knowledge: An introduction to critical thinking.* Mahwah, NJ: Erlbaum.

Halpern, D. F. (1997). Sex differences in intelligence: Implications for education. *American Psychologist, 52*, 1091–1102.

Halpern, D. F. (1998). Teaching critical thinking for transfer across domains: Dispositions, skills, structure training, and metacognitive monitoring. *American Psychologist, 53*, 449–455.

Halpern, D. F. (2000). *Sex differences in cognitive abilities.* Mahwah, NJ: Erlbaum.

Halpern, D. F. (2003). *Thought and knowledge: An introduction to critical thinking.* Mahwah, NJ: Erlbaum.

Halpern, D. F. (2007). The nature and nurture of critical thinking. In R. J. Sternberg, H. L. Roediger III, & D. F. Halpern (Eds.), *Critical thinking in psychology* (pp. 1–14). New York, NY: Cambridge University Press.

Halpern, D. F. (2012). *Sex differences in cognitive abilities* (4th ed.). New York, NY: Psychology Press.

Halpern, D. F. (2014). *Thought and knowledge: An introduction to critical thinking* (5th ed.). New York, NY: Psychology Press.

Halvorson, H. G., & Higgins, E. T. (2013). *Focus: Use different ways of seeing the world for success and influence.* New York, NY: Hudson Street Press.

Hamami, A., Serbun, S. J., & Guthess, A. H. (2011). Self-referencing enhances memory specificity with age. *Psychology of Aging, 26*, 636–646.

Hambrick, D. Z., & Meinz, E. J. (2013). Working memory capacity and musical skill. In T. Packiam Alloway, & R. G. Alloway (Eds.), *Working memory: The connected intelligence.* New York, NY: Psychology Press.

Hamden, A., Newton, R., McCauley-Elsom, K., & Cross, W. (2011). Is deinstitutionalization working in our community? *International Journal of Mental Health Nursing, 20*(4), 274–283. doi:10.1111/j.1447-0349.2010.00726.x.

Hamill, R., Wilson T. D., & Nisbett, R. E. (1980). Insensitivity to sample bias: Generalizing from atypical cases. *Journal of Personality and Social Psychology, 39*, 578–589.

Hamilton, D. L., Chen, J. M., Ko, D. M., Winczewski, L, Banerji, I., & Thurston, J. A. (2015). Sowing the seeds of stereotypes: Spontaneous inferences about groups. *Journal of Personality and Social Psychology, 109*, 569–588.

Hammen, C., & Keenan-Miller, D. (2013). Mood disorders. In T. A. Widiger, G. Stricker, I. B. Weiner, G. Stricker, T. A. Widiger, & I. B. Weiner (Eds.), *Handbook of psychology: Vol. 8. Clinical psychology* (2nd ed.). New York, NY: Wiley.

Hampson, E., van Anders, S. M., & Mullin, L. I. (2006). A female advantage in the recognition of emotional facial expressions: Test of an evolutionary hypothesis. *Evolution and Human Behavior, 27,* 401–416.

Hampson, S. (2007, January 27). Howie Mandel: Luxuriating in the moment. *The Globe and Mail,* R3.

Hampson, S. E. (2012). Personality processes: Mechanisms by which personality "gets outside the skin." *Annual Review of Psychology, 63,* 319–339.

Hampton, T. (2004). Fetal environment may be profound long-term consequences for health. *Journal of the American Medical Association, 292,* 1285–1286.

Han, K. F. G. C. (2000). Construct validity. In A. E. Kazdin (Ed.), *Encyclopedia of psychology* (pp. 281–283). Washington, DC: American Psychological Association.

Hancock, P. A., & Ganey, H. C. N. (2003). From the inverted-U to the extended-U: The evolution of a law of psychology. *Journal of Human Performance in Extreme Environments, 7*(1), 5–14.

Hanczakowski, M., Zawadzka, K., & Coote, L. (2014). Context reinstatement in recognition: Memory and beyond. *Journal of Memory and Language, 72,* 85–97. doi:10.1016/j.jml.2014.01.001.

Haney, C., Banks, W. C., & Zimbardo, P. G. (1973). Interpersonal dynamics in a simulated prison. *International Journal of Criminology and Penology, 1,* 69–97.

Haney, C., & Zimbardo, P. G. (1998). The past and future of U.S. prison policy: Twenty-five years after the Stanford Prison Experiment. *American Psychologist, 53,* 709–727.

Hanna-Pladdy, B., & MacKay, A. (2011). The relation between instrumental musical activity and cognitive aging. *Neuropsychology, 25,* 378–386. doi:10.1037/a0021895.

Hanson, K., Winward, J., Schweinsburg, A., Medina, K., Brown, S., & Tapert, S. (2010). Longitudinal study of cognition among adolescent marijuana users over three weeks of abstinence. *Addictive Behaviors, 35*(11), 970–976.

Hardt, O., Einarsson, E. Ö., & Nader, K. (2010). A bridge over troubled water: Reconsolidation as a link between cognitive and neuroscientific memory research traditions. *Annual Review of Psychology, 61,* 141–167. doi:10.1146/annurev. psych.093008.100455.

Hardt, O., Nader, K., & Nadel, L. (2013). Decay happens: The role of active forgetting in memory. *Trends in Cognitive Sciences, 17,* 111–120. doi:10.1016/j.tics.2013.01.001.

Hare, B. (2017). Survival of the friendliest: *Homo Sapiens* evolved via selection for prosociality. *Annual Review of Psychology, 68,* 155–186.

Hare, R. D. (1991a). *The Hare psychopathy checklist—revised.* Toronto, ON: Multihealth Systems.

Hare, R. D. (1991b). *Without conscience: The disturbing world of the psychopaths among us.* New York, NY: Guilford Press.

Hare, R. D. (2006). Psychopathy: A clinical and forensic overview. *Psychiatric Clinics of North America, 29,* 709–724. doi:10.1016/j.psc.2006.04.007.

Hare, R. D. (2016). Psychopathy, the PCL-R, and criminal justice: Some new findings and current issues. *Canadian Psychology, 57,* 21–34.

Hare, R. D., & Neumann, C. S. (2008). Psychopathy as a clinical and empirical construct. *Annual Review of Clinical Psychology, 4,* 217–246. doi:10.1146/annurev. clinpsy.3.022806.091452.

Harley, E. M. (2007). Hindsight bias in legal decision making. *Social Cognition, 25,* 48–63.

Harley, T. A. (2008). *The psychology of language: From data to theory.* New York, NY: Psychology Press.

Harlow, H. F. (1958). The nature of love. *American Psychologist, 13,* 673–685.

Harlow, H. F. (1959). Love in infant monkeys. *Scientific American, 200*(6), 68–74.

Harmon-Jones, E., & Harmon-Jones C. (2007). Cognitive dissonance theory after 50 years of development. *Zeitschrift fur Sozialpsychologie, 38*(1), 7–16.

Harmon-Jones, E., Harmon-Jones, C., Amodio, D., & Gable, P. A. (2011). Attitudes toward emotions. *Journal of Personality and Social Psychology, 101,* 1332–1350.

Harmon-Jones, E., & Winkielman, P. (2007). A brief overview of social neuroscience. In E. Harmon-Jones & P. Winkielman (Eds.), *Social Neuroscience: Integrating Biological and Psychological Explanations of Social Behavior* (pp. 3–11). New York, NY: Guilford Publications.

Harmsen, P., Rosengren, A., Tsipogianni, A., & Wilhelmsen, L. (1990). Risk factors for stroke in middle-aged men in Goteborg, Sweden. *Stroke, 21,* 23–29.

Harrington, A., & Dunne, J. D. (2015). When mindfulness is therapy: Ethical qualms Historical perspectives. *American Psychologist, 70,* 621–631.

Harrington, M. E., & Mistlberger, R. E. (2000). Anatomy and physiology of the mammalian circadian system. In M. H. Kryger, T. Roth, & W. C. Dement (Eds.), *Principles and practice of sleep medicine.* Philadelphia, PA: Saunders.

Harris, J. E. (1984). Remembering to do things: A forgotten topic. In J. E. Harris & P. E. Morris (Eds.), *Everyday memory, actions, and absent-mindedness.* New York, NY: Academic Press.

Harris, J. L., Bargh, J. A., & Brownell, K. D. (2009). Priming effects of television food advertising on eating behavior. *Health Psychology, 28*(4), 404–413.

Harris, J. R. (1998). *The nurture assumption: Why children turn out the way they do.* New York, NY: Free Press.

Harris, P. L. (2006). Social cognition. In D. Kuhn, R. S. Siegler, W. Damon, & R. L. Lerner (Eds.), *Handbook of child psychology: Cognition, perception, and language* (6th ed., Vol. 2, pp. 811–858). Hoboken, NJ: Wiley.

Harte, J. L., Eifert, G. H., & Smith, R. (1995). The effects of running and meditation on beta-endorphin, corticotropin-releasing hormone and cortisol in plasma, and on mood. *Biological Psychology, 40*(3), 251–265.

Hartmann, D. P., Pelzel, K. E., & Abbott, C. B. (2011). Design, measurement, and analysis in developmental research. In M. H. Bornstein & M. E. Lamb (Eds.), *Developmental science: An advanced textbook* (pp. 109–198). New York, NY: Psychology Press.

Hartmann, E., & Hartmann, T. (2014). The impact of exposure to Internet-based information about the Rorschach and the MMPI–2 on psychiatric outpatients' ability to simulate mentally healthy test performance. *Journal of Personality Assessment, 96,* 432–444. doi:10.1080/0022 3891.2014.882342.

Harvard Magazine. (2012). Marc Hauser "engaged in research misconduct." *Harvard Magazine.* Retrieved from http://harvardmagazine.com/2012/09/hauser-research-misconduct-reported.

Harvey, P. D., & Bowie, C. R. (2013). Schizophrenia spectrum disorders. In T. A. Widiger, G. Stricker, I. B. Weiner, G. Stricker, T. A. Widiger, & I. B. Weiner (Eds.), *Handbook of psychology: Vol. 8. Clinical psychology* (2nd ed.). New York, NY: Wiley.

Haskard, K. B., Williams, S. L., DiMatteo, M., Rosenthal, R., White, M., & Goldstein, M. G. (2008). Physician and patient communication training in primary care: Effects on participation and satisfaction. *Health Psychology, 27*(5), 513–522. doi:10.1037/0278-6133.27.5.513.

Haslam, N. (1997). Evidence that male sexual orientation is a matter of degree. *Journal of Personality and Social Psychology, 73,* 862–870.

Haslam, N., & Loughnan, S. (2014). Dehumanization and infrahumanization. *Annual Review of Psychology, 65,* 399–423.

Haslam, S. A., & Reicher, S. (2003). Beyond Stanford: Questioning a role-based explanation of tyranny. *Dialogue, 18,* 22–25.

Hastorf, A., & Cantril, H. (1954). They saw a game: A case study. *Journal of Abnormal and Social Psychology, 49,* 129–134.

Hatfield, E., & Rapson, R. L. (1993). *Love, sex, and intimacy: Their psychology, biology, and history.* New York, NY: HarperCollins.

Hauser, M., & Carey, S. (1998). Building a cognitive creature from a set of primitives: Evolutionary and developmental insights. In D. D. Cummins & C. Allen (Eds.),

The evolution of mind. New York, NY: Oxford University Press.

Hawkins, R. D., Lalevic, N., Clark, G. A., & Kandel, E. R. (1989). Classical conditioning of the aplysia siphon-withdrawl reflex exhibits response specificitiy. *Proceedings of the National Academy of Science, 86,* 7620–7624.

Hawkins, S. A., & Hastie, R. (1990). Hindsight: Biased judgments of past events after the outcomes are known. *Psychological Bulletin, 107,* 311–327.

Haworth-Hoeppner, S. (2000). The critical shapes of body image: The role of culture and family in the production of eating disorders. *Journal of Marriage and the Family, 62,* 212–227.

Hayati, A. M., & Shariatifar, S. (2009). Mapping strategies. *Journal of College Reading and Learning, 39,* 53–67.

Hayes, K. J., & Hayes, C. (1951). The intellectual development of a home-raised chimpanzee. *Proceedings of the American Philosophical Society, 95,* 105–109.

Hazan, C., & Shaver, P. (1986). *Parental caregiving style questionnaire.* Unpublished questionnaire.

Hazan, C., & Shaver, P. (1987). Romantic love conceptualized as an attachment process. *Journal of Personality and Social Psychology, 52,* 511–524.

Hazlett, H. C., Poe, M. D., Gerig, G., Styner, M., Chappell, C., Smith, R. G., & . . . Piven, J. (2011). Early brain overgrowth in autism associated with an increase in cortical surface area before age 2 years. *Archives of General Psychiatry, 68*(5), 467–476. doi:10.1001/archgenpsychiatry.2011.39.

He, J., Ogden, L. G., Vupputuri, S., Bazzano, L. A., Loria, C., & Whelton, P. K. (1999). Dietary sodium intake and subsequent risk of cardiovascular disease in overweight adults. *JAMA, 282,* 2027–2034.

Health Canada. (2004). *Exclusive breastfeeding duration—2004 Health Canada recommendation.* Retrieved from http://www.hc-sc.gc.ca/hpfb-dgpsa/onpp-bppn/exclusive_breastfeeding_duration_e.html.

Health Canada. (2010a). *Drug and alcohol use statistics.* Retrieved February 11, 2011, from http://www.hc-sc.ca/hc-ps/drugs-drogues/stat/index-eng.php.

Health Canada. (2010b). *Personal stereo systems and the risk of hearing loss.* Retrieved from https://www.canada.ca/en/health-canada/services/healthy-living/your-health/lifestyles/personal-stereo-systems-risk-hearing-loss.html.

Health Canada. (2013). *First nations and Inuit Health.* Retrieved from http://www.hc-sc.gc.ca/fniah-spnia/index-eng.php.

Health Canada. (2014). *Canadian alcohol and drug monitoring survey.* Retrieved from https://www.canada.ca/en/health-canada/services/health-concerns/drug-prevention-treatment/drug-alcohol-use-statistics/canadian-alcohol-drug-use-monitoring-survey-summary-results-2012.html.

Health Canada. (2016). Fetal alcohol spectrum disorder. Retrieved from https://www.canada.ca/en/health-canada/services/healthy-living/your-health/diseases/fetal-alcohol-spectrum-disorder.html.

Healy, D. (2004). *Let them eat Prozac: The unhealthy relationship between the pharmaceutical industry and depression.* New York, NY: NYU Press.

Healy, D., & Whitaker, C. (2003). Antidepressants and suicide: Risk-benefit conundrums. *Journal of Psychiatry & Neuroscience, 28*(5), 28.

Hebb, D. O. (1949). *The organization of behavior: A neuropsycholgical theory.* New York, NY: Wiley.

Hebb, D. O. (2002). *The organization of behavior: A neuropsychological theory.* Mahwah, NJ: Erlbaum.

Hecht, L. N., Cosman, J. D., & Vecera, S. P. (2016). Enhanced spatial resolution on figures versus grounds. *Attention, Perception, & Psychophysics, 78,* 1444–1452.

Hefferon, K., & Boniwell, I. (2011). *Positive psychology: Theory, research and applications.* New York, NY: McGraw-Hill.

Heider, F. (1958). *The psychology of interpersonal relations.* New York, NY: Wiley.

Heider, K. G. (1996). *Grand Valley Dani: Peaceful warriors.* Fort Worth, TX: Holt, Rinehart & Winston.

Heilman, M. E., & Haynes, M. C. (2005). No credit where credit is due: Attributional rationalization of women's success in male-female teams. *Journal of Applied Psychology, 90*, 905–916.

Heine, S. J. (2003). Making sense of East Asian self-enhancement. *Journal of Cross-Cultural Psychology, 34*(5), 596–602.

Heine, S. J. (2015). *Cultural psychology* (3rd ed.). Toronto, ON: McGraw-Hill.

Heine, S. J., & Buchtel, E. E. (2009). Personality: The universal and culturally specific. *Annual Review of Psychology, 60*, 369–394.

Heine, S. J., Buchtel, E. E., & Norenzayan, A. (2008). What do cross-national comparisons of personality traits tell us? The case of consci-entiousness. *Psychological Science, 19*, 309–313. doi:10.1111/j.1467-9280.2008.02085.x.

Heine, S. J., & Hamamura, T. (2007). In search of East Asian self-enhancement. *Personality and Social Psychology Review, 11*(1), 1–24.

Heinrichs, R. W., Miles, A. A., Ammari, N., & Muharib, E. (2013). Cognition as a central illness feature in schizo-phrenia. In P. D. Harvey (Ed.), *Cognitive impairment in schizophrenia: Characteristics, assessment and treatment.* New York, NY: Cambridge University Press. doi:10.1017/CBO9781139003872.002.

Heisel, M. J., Duberstein, P. R., Lyness, J. M., & Feldman, M. D. (2010). Screening for suicide ide-ation among older primary care patients. *Journal of the American Board of Family Medicine, 23*, 260–269.

Held, L., & Rutherford, A. (2011). Can't a mother sing the blues? Postpartum depression and the construction of motherhood in late 20th-century America. *History of Psychology, 15*(2), 107–123.

Helgeson, V. S., & Zajdel, M. (2017). Adjusting to chronic health conditions. *Annual Review of Psychology, 68*, 545–571.

Helmes, E. (2008). Modern applications of the MMPI/MMPI-2 in assessment. In G. J. Boyle, G. Matthews, & D. H. Saklofske (Eds.), *The Sage handbook of personality theory and assessment: Personality measurement and testing* (Vol. 2, pp. 589–607). Los Angeles, CA: Sage.

Helms, J. E. (1992). Why is there no study of cultural equivalence in standard cognitive ability testing? *American Psychologist, 47*, 1083–1101.

Helms, J. E. (2006). Fairness is not validity or cultural bias in racial-group assessment: A quantitative perspec-tive. *American Psychologist, 61*, 845–859.

Helson, R., Jones, C., & Kwan, V. S. Y. (2002). Personality change over 40 years of adulthood: Hierarchical linear modeling analyses of two longitu-dinal studies. *Journal of Personality & Social Psychology, 83*, 752–766.

Helzer, J. E., Wittchen, H.-U., Krueger, R. F., & Kraemer, H. C. (2008). Dimensional options for DSM-V: The way forward. In J. E. Helzer, H. C. Kraemer, R. F. Krueger, H.-U, Wittchen, P. J. Sirovatka, et al. (Eds.), *Dimensional approaches in diagnostic classification: Refining the research agenda for DSM-V* (pp. 115–127). Washington, DC: American Psychiatric Association.

Hempel, S. (2005). Reliability. In J. Miles & P. Gilbert (Eds.), *A handbook of research methods for clinical and health psychology* (pp. 193–204). New York, NY: Oxford University Press.

Henderson, K. E., & Brownell, K. D. (2004). The toxic environment and obesity: Contribution and cure. In J. K. Thompson (Ed.), *Handbook of eating disorders and obesity.* New York, NY: Wiley.

Hendrick, S. S., & Hendrick, C. (2000). Romantic love. In S. S. Hendrick & C. Hendrick (Eds.), *Close relationships.* Thousand Oaks, CA: Sage.

Heneka, M. T., O'Banion, M., Terwel, D., & Kummer, M. (2010). Neuroinflammatory processes in Alzheimer's disease. *Journal of Neural Transmission, 117*(8), 919–947.

Henrich, J., Heine, S. J., & Norenzayan, A. (2010). The weirdest people in the world. *Behavioral and Brain Sciences, 33*, 61–83.

Henry, P. J., Sternberg, R. J., & Grigorenko, E. L. (2005). Capturing successful intelligence through measures of analytic, creative, and practical skills. In O. Wilhelm & R. W. Engle (Eds.), *Handbook of understanding and measuring intelligence.* Thousand Oaks, CA: Sage.

Herbenick, D., Reece, M., Schick, V., Sanders, S. A., Dodge, B., & Fortenberry, J. (2010). An event-level anal-ysis of the sexual characteristics and composition among adults ages 18 to 59: Results from a national probability sample in the United States. *Journal of Sexual Medicine, 7*(Suppl. 5), 346–361.

Herbst, S., Pietrzak, R. H., Wagner, J., White, W. B., & Petry, N. M. (2007). Lifetime major depression is associ-ated with coronary heart disease in older adults: Results from the national epidemiologic survey on alcohol and related conditions. *Psychosomatic Medicine, 69*, 729–734.

Herbstman, J., Sjodin, A., Kurzon, M., Lederman, S., Jones, R., Rauh, V., et al. (2010). Prenatal exposure to PBDEs and neurodevelopment. *Environmental Health Perspectives, 118*(5), 712–719.

Herman, C. P., Ostovich, J. M., & Polivy, J. (1999). Effects of attentional focus on subjective hunger ratings. *Appetite, 33*, 181–193.

Herman, C. P., Polivy, J., Pliner, P., & Vartanian, L. R. (2015). Mechanisms underlying the portion-size effect. *Physiology and Behavior, 144*, 129–136.

Herman, C. P., Roth, D., & Polivy, J. (2003). Effects of the presence of others on food intake: A normative inter-pretation. *Psychological Bulletin, 129*, 873–886.

Herman, C. P., van Strien, T., & Polivy, J. (2008). Undereating or eliminating overeating? *American Psychologist, 63*, 202–203.

Herman, L. M., Kuczaj, S. A., & Holder, M. D. (1993). Responses to anomalous gestural sequences by a language-trained dolphin: Evidence for processing of semantic relations and syntactic information. *Journal of Experimental Psychology: General, 122*, 184–194.

Hermann, R. C., Ettner, S. L., Dorwart, R. A., Hoover, C. W., & Yeung, E. (1998). Characteristics of psychia-trists who perform ECT. *American Journal of Psychiatry, 155*, 889–894.

Hermans, H. J. M., & Kempen, H. J. G. (1998). Moving cultures: The perilous problems of cultural dichoto-mies in a globalizing society. *American Psychologist, 53*, 1111–1120.

Hermans, R. C., Lichtwarck-Aschoff, A., Bevelander, K. E., Herman, C. P., Larsen, J. K., & Engels, R. C. (2012). Mimicry of food intake: the dynamic interplay between eating companions. *PloS One, 7*(2), e31027. doi:10.1371/journal.pone.0031027.

Hernandez, R., Kershaw, K. N., Siddique, J., Boehm, J. K., Kubzansky, L. D., Diez-Roux, A., . . . Lloyd-Jones, D. M. (2015). Optimism and cardiovascular health: Multi-Ethnic Study of Atherosclerosis (MESA). *Health Behavior and Policy Review, 2*, 62–73. doi:10.14485/HBPR.2.1.6.

Hernandez-Avila, C. A., & Kranzler, H. R. (2011). Alcohol use disorders. In P. Ruiz, & E. C. Strain (Eds.), *Lowinson and Ruiz's substance abuse: A comprehensive textbook* (5th ed.). Philadelphia, PA: Wolters Kluwer Lippincott Williams & Wilkins.

Herrmann, D., Raybeck, D., & Gruneberg, M. (2002). *Improving memory and study skills: Advances in theory and practice.* Ashland, OH: Hogrefe & Huber.

Herrnstein, R. J., & Murray, C. (1994). *The bell curve: Intelligence and class structure in American life.* New York, NY: Free Press.

Hertwig, R., & Gigerenzer, G. (1999). The "conjunction fallacy" revisited: How intelligent inferences look like reasoning errors. *Journal of Behavioral Decision Making, 12*, 275–306.

Hertzog, C., Kramer, A. F., Wilson, R. S., Lindenberger, U. (2009). Enrichment effects on adult cognitive devel-opment: Can the functional capacity of older adults be preserved and enhanced? *Psychological Science in the Public Interest, 9*(1), 1–65.

Hertzsprung, E. A. M., & Dobson, K. S. (2000). Diversity training: Conceptual issues and practices for Canadian clinical psychology programs. *Canadian Psychology, 41*, 184–191.

Hervé, P., Zago, L., Petit, L., Mazoyer, B., & Tzourio-Mazoyer, N. (2013). Revisiting human hemispheric specialization with neuroimaging. *Trends in Cognitive Sciences, 17*(2), 69–80. doi:10.1016/j.tics.2012.12.004.

Hespos, S. J., Ferry, A. L., & Rips, L. J. (2009). Five-month-old infants have different expectations for solids and liquids. *Psychological Science, 20*(5), 603–611.

Hettich, P. I. (1998). *Learning skills for college and career.* Pacific Grove, CA: Brooks/Cole.

Hewitt, B., & de Vaus, D. (2009). Change in the associa-tion between premarital cohabitation and separation, Australia 1945–2000. *Journal of Marriage and Family, 71*(2), 353–361.

Hewstone, M. (1990). The "ultimate attribution error"? A review of the literature on intergroup causal attribution. *European Journal of Social Psychology, 20*, 311–335.

Heyman, R. E., Lorber, M. F., Eddy, J. M., & West, T. V. (2014). Behavioral observation and coding. In H. T. Reis & C. M. Judd (Eds.), *Handbook of research methods in social and personality psychology* (2nd ed.). New York, NY: Cambridge University Press.

Higgins, E. T. (1987). Self-discrepancy theory. *Psychological Review, 94*, 319–340.

Higgins, E. T. (1999). Why do self-discrepancies have specific relations to emotions? The second-generation question of Tangney, Niedenthal, Covert, and Barlow (1998). *Journal of Personality and Social Psychology, 77*, 1313–1317.

Higgins, E. T. (2004). Making a theory useful: Lessons handed down. *Personality and Social Psychology Review, 8*(2), 138–145.

Higgins, E. T. (2012). Regulatory focus theory. In Van Lange, P., Kruglanski, A. W., & Higgins, E. T. (Eds.), *Handbook of theories of social psychology* (Vol. 1, pp. 483–504). Thousand Oaks, CA: Sage. 126, 347–354.

Higgins, E. T. (2016). Promotion and prevention moti-vations. In R. J. Sternberg, S. T. Fiske, & D. J. Foss (Eds.), *Scientists making a difference: One hundred eminent behav-ioral and brain scientists talk about their most important con-tributions.* Cambridge, MA: Cambridge University Press.

Higgs, J. (2006). *I have America surrounded: The life of Timothy Leary.* London, UK: Friday Books.

Hilgard, E. R. (1986). *Divided consciousness: Multiple con-trols in human thought and action.* New York, NY: Wiley.

Hilgard, E. R. (1987). *Psychology in America: A historical survey.* San Diego, CA: Harcourt Brace Jovanovich.

Hilgard, E. R. (1992). Dissociation and theories of hyp-nosis. In E. Fromm & M. R. Nash (Eds.), *Contemporary hypnosis research.* New York, NY: Guilford.

Hill, A. K., Dawood, K, & Puts, D. A. (2013). Biological foundations of sexual orientation. In C. J. Patterson, & A. R. D'Augelli (Eds.), *Handbook of psychology and sexual orientation.* New York, NY: Oxford University Press.

Hilliard, A. G., III. (1984). IQ testing as the emperor's new clothes: A critique of Jensen's *Bias in Mental Testing.* In C. R. Reynolds & R. T. Brown (Eds.), *Perspectives on bias in mental testing.* New York, NY: Plenum.

Hilt, L. M., & Nolen-Hoeksema, S. (2014). Gender dif-ferences in depression. In I. H. Gotlib & C. L. Hammen (Eds.), *Handbook of depression* (3rd ed.). New York, NY: Guilford Press.

Hilton, J. L., & von Hippel, W. (1996). Stereotypes. *Annual Review of Psychology, 47*, 237–271.

Hines, M. (2004). Androgen, estrogen, and gender: Contributions of the early hormone environment to gender-related behavior. In A. H. Eagly, A. E. Beall, & R. J. Sternberg (Eds.), *The psychology of gender.* New York, NY: Guilford.

Hines, M. (2013). Sex and sex differences. In P. D. Zelazo (Ed.), *Oxford handbook of developmental psychology: Vol. 1. Body and mind.* New York, NY: Oxford University Press.

Hingson, R., & Sleet, D. A. (2006). Modifying alcohol use to reduce motor vehicle injury. In A. C. Gielen, D. A. Sleet, & R. J. DiClemente (Eds.), *Injury and violence* prevention: Behavioral science theories, methods, and applications. San Francisco, CA: Jossey-Bass.

Hinic, D. (2011). Problems with "Internet addiction" diagnosis and classification. *Psychiatria Danubina, 23,* 145–151.

Hinojosa, A. S., Gardner, W. L., Walker, H. J., Cogliser, C., & Gullifor, D. (2017). A review of cognitive dissonance theory in management research: Opportunities for further development. *Journal of Management, 43,* 170–199.

Hinshaw, S. P. (2007). *The mark of shame: Stigma of mental illness and an agenda for change.* New York, NY: Oxford University Press.

Hinshaw, S. P., & Stier, A. (2008). Stigma as related to mental disorders. *Annual Review of Clinical Psychology, 4,* 367–393.

Hinton, G. (2003). The ups and downs of Hebb synapses. *Canadian Psychology, 44,* 21–26.

Hinvest, N. S., Brosnan, M. J., Rogers, R. D., & Hodgson, T. L. (2014). fMRI evidence for procedural invariance underlying gambling preference reversals. *Journal of Neuroscience, Psychology, and Economics, 7*(1), 48–63. doi:10.1037/npe0000007.

Hirschel, M. J., & Schulenberg, S. E. (2009). Hurricane Katrina's impact on the Mississippi Gulf Coast: General self-efficacy's relationship to PTSD prevalence and severity. *Psychological Services, 6*(4), 293–303.

Hirsh, I. J., & Watson, C. S. (1996). Auditory psychophysics and perception. *Annual Review of Psychology, 47,* 461–484.

Hirsh, J. B., Mar, R. A., & Peterson, J. B. (2011). Psychological entropy: A framework for understanding uncertainty-related anxiety. *Psychological Review, 119*(2), 304–320.

Hirst, W., & Echterhoff, G. (2012). Remembering in conversations: The social sharing and reshaping of memories. *Annual Review of Psychology, 63,* 55–79.

Hirst, W., & Phelps, E. A. (2016). Flashbulb memories. *Current Directions in Psychological Science, 25,* 36–41.

Hirst, W., Phelps, E. A., Buckner, R. L., Budson, A. E., Cuc, A., Gabrieli, J. E., et al. (2009). Long-term memory for the terrorist attack of September 11: Flashbulb memories, event memories, and the factors that influence their retention. *Journal of Experimental Psychology: General, 138*(2), 161–176.

Hirstein, W. *(2010). The misidentification syndromes as mindreading disorders. Cognitive Neuropsychiatry, 15*(1), 233–260.

Ho, R. C., Zhang, M. W. B., Tsang, T. Y., Toh, A. H., Pan, F., Lu, Y., . . . Mak, K. (2014). The association between Internet addiction and psychiatric comorbidity: A meta-analysis. *BMC Psychiatry, 14,* 183.

Hobson, J. A. (1988). *The dreaming brain.* New York, NY: Basic Books.

Hobson, J. A. (1989). *Sleep.* New York, NY: Scientific American Library.

Hobson, J. A. (2002). *Dreaming: An introduction to the science of sleep.* New York, NY: Oxford University Press.

Hobson, J. A. (2007). Current understanding of cellular models of REM expression. In D. Barrett & P. McNamara (Eds.), *The new science of dreaming.* Westport, CT: Praeger.

Hobson, J. A., & McCarley, R. W. (1977). The brain as a dream state generator: An activation-synthesis hypothesis of the dream process. *American Journal of Psychiatry, 134,* 1335–1348.

Hobson, J. A., Pace-Schott, E. F., & Stickgold, R. (2000). Dreaming and the brain: Toward a cognitive neuroscience of conscious states. *Behavioral and Brain Sciences, 23,* 793–842; 904–1018; 1083–1121.

Hocevar, D., & Bachelor, P. (1989). A taxonomy and critique of measurements used in the study of creativity. In J. A. Glover, R. R. Ronning, & C. R. Reynolds (Eds.), *Handbook of creativity.* New York, NY: Plenum.

Hochberg, J. (1988). Visual perception. In R. C. Atkinson, R. J. Herrnstein, G. Lindzey, & R. D. Luce (Eds.), *Stevens' handbook of experimental psychology* (2nd ed., Vol. 1). New York, NY: Wiley.

Hodapp, R. M. (1994). Cultural-familial mental retardation. In R. J. Sternberg (Ed.), *Encyclopedia of human intelligence.* New York, NY: Macmillan.

Hodges, B. H., & Geyer, A. (2006). A nonconformist account of the Asch experiments: Values, pragmatics, and moral dilemmas. *Personality and Social Psychology Review, 10*(1), 2–19.

Hodgkin, A. L., & Huxley, A. F. (1952). Currents carried by sodium and potassium ions through the membrane of the giant axon of Loligo. *Journal of Physiology, 116,* 449–472.

Hodgson, K. J., Shelton, K. H., & Bree, M. M. (2015). Psychopathology among young homeless people: Longitudinal mental health outcomes for different subgroups. *British Journal of Clinical* Psychology. Advance online publication. doi:10.1111/bjc.12075.

Hoek, H. W. (2002). Distribution of eating disorders. In C. G. Fairburn & K. D. Brownell (Eds.), *Eating disorders and obesity: A comprehensive handbook.* New York, NY: Guilford Press.

Hoerger, M., Chapman, B. P., Epstein, R. M., & Duberstein, P. R. (2012a). Emotional intelligence: A theoretical framework for individual differences in affective forecasting. *Emotion, 12,* 716–725.

Hoerger, M., Quirk, S. W., Chapman, B. P., & Duberstein, P. R. (2012b). Affective forecasting and self-rated symptoms of depression, anxiety, and hypomania: Evidence for a dysphoric forecasting bias. *Cognition & Emotion, 26,* 1098–1106.

Hofbauer, R. K., Rainville, P., Duncan, G. H., & Bushnell, M. C. (2001). Cortical representation of the sensory dimension of pain. *Journal of Neurophysiology, 86,* 402–411.

Hoff, E. (2005). *Language development.* Belmont, CA: Wadsworth.

Hoff, E. (2014). *Language development* (5th ed.). Belmont, CA: Wadsworth.

Hoff, T. L. (1992). Psychology in Canada one hundred years ago: James Mark Baldwin at the University of Toronto. *Canadian Psychology, 33,* 683–694.

Hoffman, D. D. (2016). The interface theory of perception. *Current Directions in Psychological Science, 25,* 157–161.

Hoffman, D. H., et al. (2015). *Report to the special committee of the board of directors of the American Psychological Association: Independent review relation to APA ethics guidelines, national security interrogations, and torture.* Retrieved from https://www.apa.org/independent-review/APA-FINAL-Report-7.2.15.pdf.

Hoffman, E. M., Linda, M. Z., Crowston, J. G., & Weinreb, R. N. (2007). Optic disk size and glaucoma. *Survey of Ophthalmology, 52,* 32–49.

Hofstede, G. (1980). *Culture's consequences: International differences in work-related values.* Beverly Hills, CA: Sage.

Hofstede, G. (1983). Dimensions of national cultures in fifty countries and three regions. In J. Deregowski, S. Dziurawiec, & R. Annis (Eds.), *Explications in cross-cultural psychology.* Lisse: Swets and Zeitlinger.

Hofstede, G. (2001). *Culture's consequences: Comparing values, behaviors, institutions, and organizations across nations.* Thousand Oaks, CA: Sage.

Hogan, M. F., & Morrison, A. K. (2008). Organization and economics of mental health treatment. In A. Tasman, J. Kay, J. A. Lieberman, M. B. First, & M. Maj (Eds.), *Psychiatry* (3rd ed.). New York, NY: Wiley-Blackwell.

Hogan, R. (2005). In defense of personality measurement: New wine for old whiners. *Human Performance, 18,* 331–341.

Hogan, R., & Chamorro-Premuzic, T. (2015). Personality and career success. In M. Mikulincer, P. R. Shaver, M. L. Cooper, & R. J. Larsen (Eds.), *APA handbook of personality and social psychology, Volume 4: Personality processes and individual differences.*

Hogan, R., & Stokes, L. W. (2006). Business susceptibility to consulting fads: The case of emotional intelligence. In K. R. Murphy (Ed.), *A critique of emotional*

intelligence: What are the problems and how can they be fixed? (pp. 263–280). Mahwah, NJ: Erlbaum.

Hogg, M. A. (2010). Influence and leadership. In S. T. Fiske, D. T. Gilbert, & G. Lindzey (Eds.), *Handbook of social psychology* (5th ed., Vol. 1, pp. 353–393). Hoboken, NJ: Wiley.

Hogg, M. A., Turner, J. C., & Davidson, B. (1990). Polarized norms and social frames of reference: A test of the self-categorization theory of group polarization. *Basic and Applied Social Psychology, 11,* 77–100.

Høglend, P., Bøgwald, K.-P., Amlo, S., Marble, A., Ulberg, R., Sjaastad, M. C., . . . Johansson, P. (2008). Transference interpretations in dynamic psychotherapy: Do they really yield sustained effects? *American Journal of Psychiatry, 165,* 763–771.

Høglend, P., Hersoug, A. G., Bøgwald, K., Amlo, S., Marble, A., Sørbye, Ø., . . . Crits-Christoph, P. (2011). Effects of transference work in the context of therapeutic alliance and quality of object relations. *Journal of Consulting and Clinical Psychology, 79,* 697–706. doi:10.1037/a0024863.

Hogue, C. J. R., Parker, C. B., Willinger, J. R., Temple, C. M., Bann, R. M., Silver, D. J., . . . Goldenberg, R. L. (2013). A population-based case-control study of stillbirth: The relationship of significant life events to the racial disparity for African American. *American Journal of Epidemiology, 177,* 755–767. doi:10.1093/aje/kws381.

Hoigaard, R., & Ingvaldsen, R. P. (2006). Social loafing in interactive groups: The effects of identifiability on effort and individual performance in floorball. *Athletic Insight: Online Journal of Sport Psychology, 8*(2), 1–12.

Hoigaard, R., Säfvenbom, R., & Tonnessen, F. E. (2006). The relationship between group cohesion, group norms, and perceived social loafing in soccer teams. *Small Group Research, 37,* 217–232.

Holahan, C., & Sears, R. (1995). *The gifted group in later maturity.* Stanford, CA: Stanford University Press.

Holden, C. (2004). FDA weighs suicide risk in children on antidepressants. *Science, 303,* 745.

Holden, G. W., Williamson, P. A., & Holland, G. W. O. (2014). Eavesdropping on the family: A pilot investigation of corporal punishment in the home. *Journal of Family Psychology, 28,* 401–406. doi:10.1037/a0036370.

Holen, A. (2000). Posttraumatic stress disorder, delayed. In G. Fink (Ed.), *Encyclopedia of stress* (Vol. 3, pp. 179–180). San Diego, CA: Academic Press.

Holland, A. C., & Kensinger, E. A. (2010). Emotion and autobiographical memory. *Physical Life Review, 7,* 88–131.

Holland, J. C., & Lewis, S. (1993). Emotions and cancer: What do we really know? In D. Goleman & J. Gurin (Eds.), *Mind/body medicine: How to use your mind for better health.* Yonkers, NY: Consumer Reports Books.

Hollander, E., & Simeon, D. (2008). Anxiety disorders. In R. E. Hales, S. C. Yudofsky, & G. O. Gabbard (Eds.), *The American Psychiatric Publishing textbook of psychiatry.* Washington, DC: American Psychiatric Publishing.

Hollands, C. (1989). Trivial and questionable research on animals. In G. Langley (Ed.), *Animal experimentation: The consensus changes.* New York, NY: Chapman & Hall.

Hollands, G. J., Prestwich, A., & Marteau, T. M. (2011). Using aversive images to enhance healthy food choices and implicit attitudes: An experimental test of evaluative conditioning. *Health Psychology, 30,* 195–203. doi:10.1037/a0022261.

Hollis, K. L. (1997). Contemporary research on Pavlovian conditioning: A "new" functional analysis. *American Psychologist, 52,* 956–965.

Hollon, S. D., & Beck, A. T. (2013). Cognitive and cognitive-behavioral therapies. In M. J. Lambert (Ed.). *Bergin and Garfield's handbook of psychotherapy and behavior change* (6th ed.). New York, NY: Wiley.

Holmes, D. S. (1987). The influence of meditation versus rest on physiological arousal: A second examination. In M. A. West (Ed.), *The psychology of meditation.* Oxford: Clarendon Press.

Holmes, D. S. (1990). The evidence for repression: An examination of sixty years of research. In J. Singer (Ed.),

Repression and dissociation: Implications for personality, theory, psychopathology, and health. Chicago, IL: University of Chicago Press.

Holmes, T. H., & Rahe, R. H. (1967). The Social Readjustment Rating Scale. *Journal of Psychosomatic Research, 11,* 213–218.

Holtgraves, T. (2004). Social desirability and self-reports: Testing models of socially desirable responding. *Personality and Social Psychology Bulletin, 30,* 161–172.

Holt-Lunstad, J., Smith, T. B., & Layton, J. B. (2010). Social relationships and mortality risk: A meta-analytic review. *PLoS Medicine, 7*(7), 1–20.

Holyoak, K. J. (1995). Problem solving. In E. E. Smith & D. N. Osherson (Eds.), *Thinking* (2nd ed., pp. 267–295). Cambridge, MA: MIT Press.

Holyoak, K. J. (2012). Analogy and relational reasoning. In K. J. Holyoak, & G. Morrison (Eds.), *Oxford handbook of thinking and reasoning.* New York, NY: Oxford University Press.

Hölzel, B., Carmody, J., Vangel, M., Congleton, C., Yerramsetti, S. M., Gard, T., & Lazar, S. (2011). Mindfulness practice leads to increases in regional brain gray matter density. *Psychiatry Research: Neuroimaging, 191*(1), 36–42.

Homa, D., Neff, L. J., King, B. A., Caraballo, R. S., Bunnell, R. E., Babb, S. S., . . . Centers for Disease Control and Prevention (CDC). (2015). Vital signs: Disparities in nonsmokers' exposure to secondhand smoke—United States, 1999–2012. *MMWR Morbidity and Mortality Weekly Report, 64*(4), 103–108.

Hong, G. K., Garcia, M., & Soriano, M. (2000). Responding to the challenge: Preparing mental health professionals for the new millennium. In I. Cuellar & F. A. Paniagua (Eds.), *Handbook of multicultural mental health: Assessment and treatment of diverse populations.* San Diego, CA: Academic Press.

Honig, W. K., & Alsop, B. (1992). Operant behavior. In L. R. Squire (Ed.), *Encyclopedia of learning and memory.* New York, NY: Macmillan.

Hook, E. B. (1982). The epidemiology of Down syndrome. In S. M. Pueschel (Ed.), *Advances in biomedicine and the behavioral sciences* (pp. 11–88). Cambridge, MA: Ware Press.

Hooley, J. M. (2004). Do psychiatric patients do better clinically if they live with certain kinds of families? *Current Directions in Psychological Science, 13*(5), 202–205.

Hooley, J. M. (2007). Expressed emotion and relapse of psychopathology. *Annual Review of Clinical Psychology, 3,* 329–352.

Hooley, J. M. (2009). Schizophrenia: Interpersonal functioning. In P. H. Blaney & T. Millon (Eds.), *Oxford textbook of psychopathology* (2nd ed., pp. 333–360). New York, NY: Oxford University Press.

Hooley, J. M., Cole, S. H., & Gironde, S. (2012). Borderline personality disorder. In T. A. Widiger, & T. A. Widiger (Eds.), *The Oxford handbook of personality disorders.* New York, NY: Oxford University Press. doi:10.1093/oxfordhb/9780199735013.013.0020.

Hooper, J., & Teresi, D. (1986). *The 3-pound universe: The brain.* New York, NY: Laurel.

Hopko, D. R., Crittendon, J. A., Grant, E., & Wilson, S. A. (2005). The impact of anxiety on performance IQ. *Anxiety, Stress, & Coping: An International Journal, 18*(1), 17–35.

Horgen, K. B., Harris, J. L., & Brownell, K. D. (2012). Food marketing: Targeting young people in a toxic environment. In D. G. Singer, & J. L. Singer (Eds.), *Handbook of children and the media* (2nd ed.). Thousand Oaks, CA: Sage.

Hori, M., Numata, K., & Nakajima, S. (2014), Is superstitious behavior more easily acquired by negative reinforcement schedules than positive reinforcement schedules? Examinations of the polarity and the duration of a consequence. *Japanese Journal of Psychology, 84,* 625–631.

Horn, J. L. (1985). Remodeling old models of intelligence. In B. B. Wolman (Ed.), *Handbook of intelligence.* New York, NY: Wiley.

Horn, J. L. (2002). Selections of evidence, misleading assumptions, and oversimplifications: The political message of *The Bell Curve.* In J. M. Fish (Ed.), *Race and intelligence: Separating science from myth* (pp. 297–326). Mahwah, NJ: Erlbaum.

Horn, J. P., & Swanson, L. W. (2013). The autonomic motor system and the hypothalamus. In E. R. Kandel, J. H. Schwartz, T. M. Jessell, S. A. Siegelbaum, & A. J. Hudspeth (Eds.), *Principles of neural science* (5th ed.). New York, NY: McGraw-Hill.

Horney, K. (1926). The flight from womanhood. *International Journal of Psychoanalysis, 7,* 324–329.

Horowitz, F. D. (1992). John B. Watson's legacy: Learning and environment. *Developmental Psychology, 28,* 360–367.

Hortensius, R., Schutter, D. J. L. G., & Harmon-Jones, E. (2011). When anger leads to aggression: Induction of relative left frontal cortical activity with transcranial direct current stimulation increases the anger–aggression relationship. *Social Cognitive Affective Neuroscience, 7,* 342–347.

Hosseini, H. (1997). Cognitive dissonance as a means of explaining economics of irrationality and uncertainty. *Journal of Socio-Economics, 26,* 181–189.

Hothersall, D. (1995). *History of psychology.* New York, NY: McGraw-Hill.

Houben, K., Schoenmakers, T. M., & Wiers, R. W. (2010). I didn't feel like drinking but I don't know why: The effects of evaluative conditioning on alcohol-related attitudes, craving and behavior. *Addictive Behaviors, 35,* 1161–1163. doi:10.1016/j.addbeh.2010.08.012.

Hough, L. M., & Connelly, B. S. (2013). Personality measurement and use in industrial and organizational psychology. In K. F. Geisinger, B. A. Bracken, J. F. Carlson, J. C. Hansen, N. R. Kuncel, S. P. Reise, & M. C. Rodriguez (Eds.), *APA handbook of testing and assessment in psychology: Vol. 1. Test theory and testing and assessment in industrial and organizational psychology.* Washington, DC: American Psychological Association. doi:10.1037/14047-028.

Houlihan, J., Kropp, T., Wiles, R., Gray, S., & Campbell, C. (2005). *Body burden: The pollution in newborns.* Washington, DC: Environmental Working Group.

House, E. R. (2016). The role of values and evaluation in thinking. *American Journal of Evaluation, 37,* 104–113.

Houston, J. (2008). Inuit myth and legend. *The Canadian Encyclopedia.* Retrieved March 14, 2008, from http://www.thecanadianencyclopedia.com/index.

Howard, D. J. (1995). "Chaining" the use of influence strategies for producing compliance behavior. *Journal of Social Behavior and Personality, 10,* 169–185.

Howe, L. C., & Krosnick, J. A. (2017). Attitude strength. *Annual Review of Psychology, 68,* 327–351.

Howe, M. L., Gagnon, N., & Thouas, L. (2008). Development of false memories in bilingual children and adults. *Journal of Memory and Language, 58,* 669–681.

Howes, O. D., Bose, S. K., Turkheimer, F., Valli, I., Egerton, A., Valmaggia, L. R., . . . McGuire, P. (2011). Dopamine synthesis capacity before onset of psychosis: A prospective [18F]-DOPA PET imaging study. *The American Journal of Psychiatry, 168*(12), 1311–1317.

Hsu, L. M. (1995). Regression toward the mean associated with measurement error and the identification of improvement and deterioration in psychotherapy. *Journal of Consulting and Clinical Psychology, 63*(1), 141–144. doi:org/10.1037/0022-006X.63.1.141.

Hsu, L. M., Chung, J., & Langer, E. J. (2010). The influence of age-related cues on health and longevity. *Perspectives on Psychological Science, 5,* 632–648. doi:10.1177/1745691610388762.

Hsu, L., Woody, S. R., Lee, H.-J., Peng, Y., Zhou, X., & Ryder, A. G. (2012). Social anxiety among East Asians in North America: East Asian socialization or the challenge of acculturation? *Cultural Diversity & Ethnic Minority Psychology, 18,* 181–191.

Hu, Y., Zhang, R., & Li, W. (2005). Relationships among jealousy, self-esteem and self-efficacy. *Chinese Journal of Clinical Psychology, 13,* 165–166, 172.

Hua, J. Y., & Smith, S. J. (2004). Neural activity and the dynamics of central nervous system development. *Nature Neuroscience, 7,* 327–332.

Hubel, D. H., & Wiesel, T. N. (1962). Receptive fields, binocular interaction and functional architecture in the cat's visual cortex. *Journal of Physiology, 160,* 106–154.

Hubel, D. H., & Wiesel, T. N. (1963). Receptive fields of cells in striate cortex of very young visually inexperienced kittens. *Journal of Neurophysiology, 26,* 994–1002.

Hubel, D. H., & Wiesel, T. N. (1979). Brain mechanisms of vision. In Scientific American (Eds.), *The brain.* San Franciso, CA: W. H. Freeman.

Huber, R., & Tononi, G. (2009). Sleep and waking across the lifespan. In G. G. Berntson & J. T. Cacioppo (Eds.), *Handbook of neuroscience for the behavioral sciences* (Vol. 1, pp. 461–481). New York, NY: Wiley.

Hudson, J. I., Hiripi, E., Pope Jr., Harrison, G., & Kessler, R. C. (2007). The prevalence and correlates of eating disorders in the national comorbidity survey replication. *Biological Psychiatry, 61,* 348–358.

Hudson, W. (1960). Pictorial depth perception in subcultural groups in Africa. *Journal of Social Psychology, 52,* 183–208.

Hudson, W. (1967). The study of the problem of pictorial perception among unacculturated groups. *International Journal of Psychology, 2,* 89–107.

Huey, E. D., Krueger, F., & Grafman, J. (2006). Representations in the human prefrontal cortex. *Current Directions in Psychological Science, 15,* 167–171.

Huey, L. Y., Cole, S., Cole, R. F., Daniels, A. S., & Katzelnick, D. J. (2009). Health care reform. In B. J. Sadock, V. A. Sadock, & P. Ruiz (Eds.), *Kaplan & Sadock's comprehensive textbook of psychiatry* (pp. 4282–4298). Philadelphia, PA: Lippincott Williams & Wilkins.

Huey, S. J., Tilley, J. L., Jones, E. O., & Smith, C. A. (2014). The contribution of cultural competence to evidence-based care for ethnically diverse populations. *Annual Review of Clinical Psychology, 10,* 305–338. doi:10.1146/annurev-clinpsy-032813-153729.

Hughes, J., Smith, T. W., Kosterlitz, H. W., Fothergill, L. A., Morgan, B. A., & Morris, H. R. (1975). Identification of two related pentapeptides from the brain with the potent opiate agonist activity. *Nature, 258,* 577–579.

Huguet, A., McGrath, P., Stinson, J., Tougas, M. E., & Doucette, S. (2014). Efficacy of psychological treatment for headaches: An overview of systematic reviews and analysis of potential modifiers of treatment efficacy. *Clinical Journal of Pain, 30,* 353–369.

Hull, C. L. (1943). *Principles of behavior.* New York, NY: Appleton.

Human, L. J., & Biesanz, J. C. (2013). Targeting the good target: An integrative review of the characteristics and consequences of being accurately perceived. *Personality and Social Psychology Review, 17,* 248–272.

Hune-Brown, N. (2013). Money might buy you happiness, if you spend it right. *The Globe and Mail,* Saturday, May 18, 2013. Retrieved from http://www.theglobeandmail.com/life/money-might-buy-you-happiness-if-you-spend-it-right/article12005553/?page=all.

Hung, S. P., & Mantyh, P. W. (2001). Molecular basis of pain control. *National Review of Neuroscience, 2,* 83–91.

Hunsley, J., & Johnston, C. (2000). The role of empirically supported treatments in evidence-based psychological practice: A Canadian perspective. *Clinical Psychology: Science and Practice, 7,* 269–272.

Hunt, E. (1994). Problem solving. In R. J. Sternberg (Ed.), *Thinking and problem solving.* San Diego, CA: Academic Press.

Hunt, E. (2001). Multiple views of multiple intelligence [Review of the book *Intelligence reframed: Multiple intelligence in the 21st century*]. *Contemporary Psychology, 46,* 5–7.

Hunt, E., & Agnoli, F. (1991). The Whorfian hypothesis: A cognitive psychology perspective. *Psychological Review, 98,* 377–389.

Hunt, E., & Carlson, J. (2007). Considerations relating to the study of group differences in intelligence. *Perspectives on Psychological Science, 2*(2), 194–213. doi:10.1111/j.1745-6916.2007.00037.x.

Hunt, H. (1989). *The multiplicity of dreams: Memory, imagination and consciousness.* New Haven, CT: Yale University Press.

Hunt, M., Schloss, H., Mooat, S., Poulous, S., & Weiland, J. (2007). Emotional processing versus cognitive restructuring in response to a depressing life event. *Cognitive Therapy and Research, 31*, 833–851.

Huntjens, R. C., Peters, M. L., Woertman, L., Bovenschen, L. M., Martin, R. C., & Postma, A. (2006). Inter-identity amnesia in dissociative identity disorder: A simulated memory impairment? *Psychological Medicine, 36*, 857–863. doi:10.1017/S0033291706007100.

Hurst, M. (2014). Who gets any sleep these days? Sleep patterns of Canadians. Statistics Canada. Retrieved from https://www.statcan.gc.ca/pub/11-008-x/2008001/article/10553-eng.htm.

Hurvich, L. M. (1981). *Color vision.* Sunderland, MA: Sinnauer Associates.

Huston, A. C., Donnerstein, E., Fairchild, H., Feshbach, N. D., Katz, P. A., & Murray, J. P. (1992). *Big world, small screen: The role of television in American society.* Lincoln: University of Nebraska Press.

Huston, A. C., & Wright, J. C. (1982). Effects of communications media on children. In C. B. Kopp & J. B. Krakow (Eds.), *The child: Development in a social context.* Reading, MA: Addison-Wesley.

Hutcherson, C. A., & Gross, J. J. (2011). The moral emotions: A social-functionalist account of anger, disgust, and contempt. *Journal of Personality and Social Psychology, 100*, 719–737.

Huttenlocher, P. R. (1994). Synaptogenesis in human cerebral cortex. In G. Dawson & K. W. Fischer (Eds.), *Human behavior and the developing brain.* New York, NY: Guilford.

Huttenlocher, P. R. (2002). *Neural plasticity: The effects of environment on the development of the cerebral cortex.* Cambridge, MA: Harvard University Press.

Huxley, A. (1954). *The doors of perception.* London, UK: Chatto and Windus.

Huyser, B., & Parker, J. C. (1998). Stress and rheumatoid arthritis: An integrative review. *Arthritis Care and Research, 11*, 135–145.

Hyde, J. S. (2013). Gender-similarities and differences. *Annual Review of Psychology, 65*, 373–398.

Hyde, J. S. (2014). Gender similarities and differences. *Annual Review of Psychology, 65*, 373–398. doi:10.1146/annurev-psych-010213-115057.

Hyde, J. S., & Mertz, J. E. (2009). Gender, culture, and mathematics performance. *Proceedings of the National Academy of Sciences of the United States of America, 106*(22), 8801–8807.

Hyman, I. E., Jr., & Kleinknecht, E. E. (1999). False childhood memories: Research, theory, and applications. In L. M. Williams & V. L. Banyard (Eds.), *Trauma & memory.* Thousand Oaks, CA: Sage.

Hyman, I. E., Jr., Husband, T. H., & Billings, J. F. (1995). False memories of childhood experiences. *Applied Cognitive Psychology, 9*, 181–197.

Hyman, I., Adolph, K. E., Baddeley, A., Brewer, W. F., Ceci, S. J., Cutting, J., & Winograd, E. (2012). Remembering the father of cognitive psychology: Ulric Neisser (1928–2012). *Observer, 25.* Retrieved from https://www.psychologicalscience.org/observer/remembering-the-father-of-cognitive-psychology.

Hynie, M., MacDonald, T. K., & Marques, S. (2006). Self-conscious emotions and self-regulation in the promotion of condom use. *Personality and Social Psychology Bulletin, 32*(8), 1072–1084.

Iacoboni, M. (2009). Imitation, empathy, and mirror neurons. *Annual Review of Psychology, 60*, 653–670.

Iacoboni, M. (2012). The human mirror neuron system and its role in imitation and empathy. In F. M. de Waal, & P. F. Ferrari (Eds.), *The primate mind: Built to connect with other minds* (pp. 32–47). Cambridge, MA: Harvard University Press.

Iacoboni, M., & Dapretto, M. (2006). The mirror neuron system and the consequences of its dysfunction. *Nature Reviews Neuroscience, 7*, 942–951.

Idring, S., Lundberg, M., Sturm, H., Dalman, C., Gumpert, C., Rai, D., . . . Magnusson, C. (2014). Changes in prevalence of autism spectrum disorders in 2001–2011: Findings from the Stockholm youth cohort. *Journal of Autism and Developmental Disorders.* Advance online publication. doi:10.1007/s10803-014-2336-y.

Illes, J., & Sahakian, B. J. (2011). *The Oxford handbook of neuroethics.* New York, NY: Oxford University Press.

Infante, J. R., Torres-Avisbal, M., Pinel, P., Vallejo, J. A., Peran, F., Gonzalez, F., et al. (2001). Catecholamine levels in practitioners of the transcendental meditation technique. *Physiology & Behavior, 72*(1–2), 141–146.

Ingram, R. E., Scott, W. D., & Hamill, S. (2009). Depression: Social and cognitive aspects. In P. H. Blaney & Millon (Eds.), *Oxford textbook of psychopathology* (2nd ed., pp. 230–252). New York, NY: Oxford University Press.

Ingram, R. E., Scott, W., & Siegle, G. (1999). Depression: Social and cognitive aspects. In T. Millon, P. H. Blaney, & R. D. Davis (Eds.), *Oxford textbook of psychopathology* (pp. 203–226). New York, NY: Oxford University Press.

Insel, T. R. (2010). Psychiatrists' relationships with pharmaceutical companies: Part of the problem or part of the solution? *JAMA, 303*(12), 1192–1193. doi:10.1001/jama.2010.317.

Insel, T. R., & Lieberman, J. A. (2013). *DSM-5 and RDoC: Shared interests.* Retrieved from http://www.nimh.nih.gov/news/science-news/2013/dsm-5-and-rdoc-shared-interests.shtml.

Inzlicht, M., & Kang, S. K. (2010). Stereotype threat spillover: How coping with threats to social identity affects aggression, eating, decision making, and attention. *Journal of Personality and Social Psychology, 99*(3), 467–481. doi:10.1037/a0018951.

Iredale, S. K., Nevill, C. H., & Lutz, C. K. (2010). The influence of observer presence on baboon (*Papio spp.*) and rhesus macaque (*Macaca mulatta*) behavior. *Applied Animal Behaviour Science, 122*(1), 53–57.

Ireland, N. (2016). *The year of the fentanyl crisis: How we got here.* CBC News. Retrieved from http://www.cbc.ca/news/health/fentanyl-carfentanil-opioid-crisis-spreading-across-canada-1.3909986.

Ironson, G., Klimas, N. G., Antoni, M., Friedman, A., Simoneau, J., LaPerriere, A., et al. (1994). Distress, denial, and low adherence to behavioral interventions predict faster disease progression in gay men infected with human immunodeficiency virus. *International Journal of Behavioral Medicine, 1*, 90–98.

Irvine, S. H., & Berry, J. W. (1988). *Human abilities in cultural context.* New York, NY: Cambridge University Press.

Irving, J. A., Farb, N. A. S., & Segal, Z. V. (2015). Mindfulness-based cognitive therapy for depression. In K. Brown, Creswell, J. D., & Ryan, R. (Eds.), *Handbook of mindfulness: Theory, research, and practice* (pp. 54–89). New York, NY: Guilford Press.

Isaacowitz, D. M., & Seligman, M. E. P. (2007). Learned helplessness. In G. Fink (Ed.), *Encyclopedia of stress.* San Diego, CA: Elsevier.

Islam, F., Khanlou, N., & Tamim, H. (2014). South Asian populations in Canada: Migration and mental health. *BMC Psychiatry, 14*, 154–165.

Israel, S., Hart, E., & Winter, E. (2013). Oxytocin decreases accuracy in the perception of social deception. *Psychological Science, 25*, 293–295. doi:10.1177/0956797613500794.

Ito, T. A., & Urland, G. R. (2003). Race and gender on the brain: Electrocortical measures of attention to the race and gender of multiply categorizable individuals. *Journal of Personality and Social Psychology, 85*, 616–626.

Iwawaki, S., & Vernon, P. E. (1988). Japanese abilities and achievements. In S. H. Irvine & J. W. Berry (Eds.), *Human abilities in cultural context.* New York, NY: Cambridge University Press.

Izard, C. E. (1984). Emotion-cognition relationships and human development. In C. E. Izard, J. Kagan, & R. B. Zajonc (Eds.), *Emotions, cognition and behavior.* Cambridge, UK: Cambridge University Press.

Izard, C. E. (1990). Facial expressions and the regulation of emotions. *Journal of Personality and Social Psychology, 58*, 487–498.

Izard, C. E. (1991). *The psychology of emotions.* New York, NY: Plenum.

Izard, C. E. (1994). Innate and universal facial expressions: Evidence from developmental and cross-cultural research. *Psychological Bulletin, 115*, 288–299.

Jack, R. E., & Schyns, P. G. (2017). Toward a social physics of face communication. *Annual Review of Psychology, 68*, 269–297.

Jackson, D. N. (1968). Content and style in personality assessment. *Psychological Bulletin, 55*, 243–252.

Jackson, M. (2007). The problem of pain. *University of Toronto Magazine, 34*, 23–27.

Jacob, R. G., & Pelham, W. (2005). Behavior therapy. In B. J. Sadock & V. A. Sadock (Eds.), *Kaplan and Sadock's comprehensive textbook of psychiatry* (pp. 2498–2547). Philadelphia, PA: Lippincott, Williams & Wilkins.

Jacobson, E. (1938). *Progressive relaxation.* Chicago, IL: University of Chicago Press.

Jacoby, L. L. (1988). Memory observed and memory unobserved. In U. Neisser & E. Winograd (Eds.), *Remembering reconsidered: Ecological and traditional approaches to the study of memory.* Cambridge, UK: Cambridge University Press.

Jacoby, L. L., Hessels, S., & Bopp, K. (2001). Proactive and retroactive effects in memory performance: Dissociating recollection and accessibility bias. In H. L. Roediger, J. S. Nairne, I. Neath, & A. M. Surprenant (Eds.), *The nature of remembering: Essays in honor of Robert G. Crowder* (pp. 35–54). Washington, DC: American Psychological Association.

Jakubovski, E., et al. (2016). Systematic review and meta-analysis: Dose-response relationship of selective serotonin reuptake inhibitors in major depressive disorder. *American Journal of Psychiatry, 173*, 174–183.

James, B. D., Wilson, R. S., Barnes, L. L., & Bennett, D. A. (2011). Late-life social activity and cognitive decline in old age. *Journal of International Neuropsychological Society, 17*, 998–1005. doi:10.1017/S1355617711000531.

James, C. E., Oechslin, M. S., Van De Ville, D., Hauert, C., Descloux, C., & Lazeyras, F. (2014). Musical training intensity yields opposite effects on grey matter density in cognitive versus sensorimotor networks. *Brain Structure & Function, 219*, 353–366. doi:10.1007/s00429-013-0504-z.

James, K. H., Humphrey, G. K., & Goodale, M. A. (2001). Manipulating and recognizing virtual objects: Where the action is. *Canadian Journal of Experimental Psychology/Revue canadienne de psychologie expérimentale, 55*(2), 111–120.

James, W. (1884). What is emotion? *Mind, 19*, 188–205.

James, W. (1890). *The principles of psychology.* New York, NY: Holt.

James, W. (1902). *The varieties of religious experience.* New York, NY: Modern Library.

James, W. H. (2005). Biological and psychosocial determinants of male and female human sexual orientation. *Journal of Biosocial Science, 37*, 555–567.

Janicak, P. G., Nahas, Z., Lisanby, S. H., Solvason, H., Sampson, S. M., McDonald, W. M., et al. (2010). Durability of clinical benefit with transcranial magnetic stimulation (TMS) in the treatment of pharmacoresistant major depression: Assessment of relapse during a 6-month, multisite, open-label study. *Brain Stimulation, 3*(4), 187–199.

Janis, I. L. (1958). *Psychological stress.* New York, NY: Wiley.

Janis, I. L. (1972). *Victims of groupthink.* Boston, MA: Houghton Mifflin.

Janis, I. L. (1993). Decision making under stress. In L. Goldberger & S. Breznitz (Eds.), *Handbook of stress: Theoretical and clinical aspects* (2nd ed.). New York, NY: Free Press.

Janssen, L., Fennis, B. M., & Pruyn, A. H. (2010). Forewarned is forearmed: Conserving self-control strength to resist social influence. *Journal of Experimental Social Psychology, 46*(6), 911–921. doi:10.1016/j.jesp.2010.06.008.

Jasinska, K., & Petitto, L. A. (2013). How age of bilingual exposure can change the neural systems for language in the developing brain: A functional near infrared spectroscopy investigation of syntactic processing in monolingual and bilingual children. *Developmental Neuroscience, 6,* 87–101.

Jefferson, J. W., & Greist, J. H. (2009). Lithium. In B. J. Sadock, V. A. Sadock, & P. Ruiz (Eds.), *Kaplan & Sadock's comprehensive textbook of psychiatry* (pp. 3132–3144). Philadelphia, PA: Lippincott, Williams & Wilkins.

Jellinger, K. A. (2013). Organic bases of late-life depression: A critical update. *Journal of Neural Transmission, 120,* 1109–1125. doi:10.1007/s00702-012-0945-1.

Jelovac, A., Kolshus, E., & McLoughlin, D. M. (2013). Relapse following successful electroconvulsive therapy for major depression: A meta-analysis. *Neuropsychopharmacology, 38,* 2467–2474. doi:10.1038/npp.2013.149.

Jenkins, A. C., & Mitchell, J. P. (2011). How has cognitive neuroscience contributed to social psychological theory? In A. B. Todorov, S. T. Fiske, & D. A. Prentice (Eds.). (2011). *Social neuroscience: Toward understanding the underpinnings of the social mind* (pp. 2–26). New York, NY: Oxford University Press.

Jennings, B. K. (2015). *In defense of scientism: An insider's view of science.* New York, NY: Random House.

Jensen, A. R. (1969). How much can we boost IQ and scholastic achievement? *Harvard Educational Review, 39,* 1–23.

Jensen, A. R. (1980). *Bias in mental testing.* New York, NY: Free Press.

Jensen, A. R. (1998). *The g factor: The science of mental ability.* Westport, CT: Praeger.

Jensen, A. R. (2000). Testing: The dilemma of group differences. *Psychology, Public Policy, and Law, 6,* 121–127.

Jensen, J. S. (2016). Stability and variability in perceptual cognition and visual noticing. Retrieved from http://hdl.handle.net/2142/72959.

Jensen, K. B., et al. (2012). Nonconscious activation of placebo and noncebo pain responses. *Proceedings of the National Academy of Sciences, USA, 109,* 15959–15964.

Jensen, M. P., & Patterson, D. R. (2014). Hypnotic approaches for chronic pain management: Clinical implications of recent research findings. *American Psychologist, 69*(2), 167–177. doi:10.1037/a0035644.

Jensen, M. P., & Turk, D. C. (2014). Contributions of psychology to the understanding and treatment of people with chronic pain: Why it matters to all psychologists. *American Psychologist, 69*(2), 100–118.

Jensen, M. S., Yao, R., Whitney, N., & Street, D. J. (2011). Change blindness and inattentional blindness. *WIREs Cognitive Science.* doi: 10.1002/wcs.130.

Jessberger, S., Aimone, J. B., & Gage, F. H. (2009). Neurogenesis. In J. H. Byrne (Ed.), *Concise learning and memory: The editor's selection.* San Diego, CA: Elsevier.

Jessup, R. K., Veinott, E. S., Todd, P. M., & Busemeyer, J. R. (2009). Leaving the store empty-handed: Testing explanations for the too-much-choice effect using decision field theory. *Psychology & Marketing, 26*(3), 299–320.

Jha, A. J. (2013). Being in the now. *Scientific American Mind, 24*(1), 26–33.

Ji, R. R., Berta, T., & Nedergaard, M. (2013). Glia and pain: Is chronic pain a gliopathy? *Pain, 154,* S10–S28. doi:10.1016/j.pain.2013.06.022.

Jigsaw Classroom. (2011). Overview of the technique. Retrieved July 16, 2011, from http://www.jigsaw.org/overview.htm.

Joffe, R. T. (2009). Neuropsychiatric aspects of multiple sclerosis and other demyelinating disorders. In B. J.

Sadock, V. A. Sadock, & P. Ruiz (Eds.), *Kaplan & Sadock's comprehensive textbook of psychiatry* (9th ed., Vol. 1, pp. 248–272). Philadelphia, PA: Lippincott, Williams & Wilkins.

Johansson, B., Bjuhr, H., & Ronnback, L. (2013). Evaluation of an advanced mindfulness program following a mindfulness-based stress reduction program for participants suffering from mental fatigue after acquired brain injury. *Mindfulness,* doi:10.1007/s12671-013-0249-z.

John, U., Rumpf, H., Bischof, G., Hapke, U., Hanke, M., & Meyer, C. (2013). Excess mortality of alcohol-dependent individuals after 14 years and mortality predictors based on treatment participation and severity of alcohol dependence. *Alcoholism: Clinical and Experimental Research, 37*(1), 156–163. doi:10.1111/j.1530-0277.2012.01863.x.

Johnson, A. W. (2003). Procedural memory and skill acquisition. In A. F. Healy & R. W. Proctor (Eds.), *Handbook of psychology: Vol. 4. Experimental psychology.* New York, NY: Wiley.

Johnson, A. W. (2013). Procedural memory and skill acquisition. In A. F. Healy, R. W. Proctor, & I. B. Weiner (Eds.), *Handbook of psychology: Vol. 4. Experimental psychology* (2nd ed.). New York, NY: Wiley.

Johnson, B. A., & Ait-Daoud, N. (2005). Alcohol: Clinical aspects. In J. H. Lowinson, P. Ruiz, R. B. Millman, & J. G. Langrod (Eds.), *Substance abuse: A comprehensive textbook.* Philadelphia, PA: Lippincott, Williams & Wilkins.

Johnson, B. T., & Eagly, A. H. (2014). Meta-analysis of research in social psychology and personality psychology. In H. T. Reis & C. M. Judd (Eds.), *Handbook of research methods in social and personality psychology* (2nd ed.). New York, NY: Cambridge University Press.

Johnson, J. (2013). Vulnerable subjects? The case of non-human animals in experimentation. *Journal of Bioethical Inquiry, 10*(4), 497–504. doi:10.1007/s11673-013-9473-4.

Johnson, M. E., & Dowling-Guyer, S. (1996). Effects of inclusive vs. exclusive language on evaluations of the counselor. *Sex Roles, 34,* 407–418.

Johnson, M. H. (2005a). Sensitive periods in functional brain development: Problems and prospects. *Developmental Psychobiology, 46,* 287–292.

Johnson, M. H. (2005b). *Developmental cognitive neuroscience* (2nd ed.). Malden, MA: Blackwell.

Johnson, M. K. (1996). Fact, fantasy, and public policy. In D. J. Herrmann, C. McEvoy, C. Hertzog, P. Hertel, & M. K. Johnson (Eds.), *Basic and applied memory research: Theory in context* (Vol. 1). Mahwah, NJ: Erlbaum.

Johnson, M. K. (2006). Memory and reality. *American Psychologist, 61,* 760–771.

Johnson, M. K., Raye, C. L., Mitchell, K. J., & Ankudowich, E. (2012). The cognitive neuroscience of the true and false memories. In R. F. Belli (Ed.), *True and false recovered memories: Toward a reconciliation of the debate.* New York, NY: Springer.

Johnson, S. B., & Carlson, D. N. (2004). Medical regimen adherence: Concepts assessment, and interventions. In J. M. Raczynski & L. C. Leviton (Eds.), *Handbook of clinical health psychology: Vol 2. Disorders of behavior and health.* Washington, DC: American Psychological Association.

Johnson, S. L., Cuellar, A. K., & Peckham, A. D. (2014). Risk factors for bipolar disorder. In I. H. Gotlib & C. L. Hammen (Eds.), *Handbook of depression* (3rd ed.). New York, NY: Guilford Press.

Johnson, S. M., & Greenberg, L. S. (1995). The emotion focussed approach to problems of adult attachment. In N. S. Jacobson & A. S. Gurman (Eds.), *Clinical handbook of couples therapy* (pp. 124–144). New York, NY: Guilford.

Johnson, W. (2010). Understanding the genetics of intelligence: Can height help? Can corn oil? *Current Directions in Psychological Science, 19*(3), 177–182.

Johnson, W., & Krueger, R. F. (2006). How money buys happiness: Genetic and environmental processes linking finances and life satisfaction. *Journal of Personality and Social Psychology, 90,* 680–691.

Johnson, W., Turkheimer, E., Gottesman, I. I., & Bouchard, T. R. (2009). Beyond heritability: Twin studies in behavioral research. *Current Directions in Psychological Science, 18*(4), 217–220. doi:10.1111/j.1467-8721.2009.01639.x.

Johnston, J. C., & McClelland, J. L. (1974). Perception of letters in words: Seek not and ye shall find. *Science, 184,* 1192–1194.

Johnstone, L. (1999). Adverse psychological effects of ECT. *Journal of Mental Health (UK), 8,* 69–85.

Joiner, T. E. (2002). Depression in its interpersonal context. In I. H. Gotlib & C. L. Hammen (Eds.), *Handbook of depression.* New York, NY: Guilford.

Joiner, T. E., & Katz, J. (1999). Contagion of depressive symptoms and mood: Meta-analytic review and explanations from cognitive, behavioral, and interpersonal viewpoints. *Clinical Psychology: Science and Practice, 6,* 149–164.

Joiner, T. E., Jr., & Metalsky, G. I. (1995). A prospective test of an integrative interpersonal theory of depression: A naturalistic study of college students. *Journal of Personality and Social Psychology, 69,* 778–788.

Joiner, T. E., Jr., & Timmons, K. A. (2009). Depression in its interpersonal context. In I. H. Gotlib & C. L. Hammen (Eds.), *Handbook of depression* (2nd ed., pp. 322–339). New York, NY: Guilford Press.

Jones, D. N., & Paulhus, D. L. (2017). Duplicity among the Dark Triad: Three faces of deceit. *Journal of Personality and Social Psychology, 113,* 392–412.

Jones, E. E., & Davis, K. E. (1965). From acts to dispositions: The attribution process in person perception. In L. Berkowitz (Ed.), *Advances in experimental social psychology* (Vol. 2). New York, NY: Academic Press.

Jones, E. E., & Nisbett, R. E. (1971). The actor and the observer: Divergent perceptions of the causes of behavior. In E. E. Jones, D. E. Kanouse, H. H. Kelley, R. E. Nisbett, S. Valins, & B. Weiner (Eds.), *Attribution: Perceiving the causes of behavior.* Morristown, NJ: General Learning Press.

Jones, L. V. (2000). Thurstone, L. L. In A. E. Kazdin (Ed.), *Encyclopedia of psychology* (pp. 83–84). Washington, DC: American Psychological Association.

Jones, S. G., & Benca, R. M. (2013). Sleep and biological rhythms. In R. J. Nelson, S. Y. Mizumori, & I. B. Weiner (Eds.), *Handbook of psychology: Vol. 3. Behavioral neuroscience* (2nd ed., pp. 365–394). New York, NY: Wiley.

Jonker, T. R., Seli, P., & MacLeod, C. M. (2015). Retrieval-induced forgetting and context. *Current Directions in Psychological Science, 24,* 273–278.

Jordan, B. (1983). *Birth in four cultures.* Quebec: Eden Press.

Jordan, P. J., Ashton-James, C. E., & Ashkanasy, N. M. (2006). Evaluating the claims: Emotional intelligence in the workplace. In K. R. Murphy (Ed.), *A critique of emotional intelligence: What are the problems and how can they be fixed?* (pp. 189–210). Mahwah, NJ: Erlbaum.

Jordan-Young, R. M. (2010). *Brainstorm: The flaws in the science of sex differences.* Cambridge, MA: Harvard University Press.

Jorge, R. E., Robinson, R. G., Arndt, S. V., Starkstein, S. E., Forrester, A. W., & Geisler F. (1993). Depression following traumatic brain injury: A 1 year longitudinal study. *Journal of Affective Disorders, 27*(4), 233–243.

Josephs, L., & Weinberger, J. (2013). Psychodynamic psychotherapy. In G. Stricker & T. A. Widiger (Eds.), *Handbook of psychology: Vol. 8. Clinical psychology* (2nd ed.). New York, NY: Wiley.

Josse, G., & Tzourio-Mazoyer, N. (2004). Hemispheric specialization for language. *Brain Research Reviews, 44,* 1–12.

Judge, T. A., & Klinger, R. (2008). Job satisfaction: Subjective well-being at work. In M. Eid & R. J. Larsen (Eds.), *The science of subjective well-being* (pp. 393–413). New York, NY: Guilford.

Judge, T. A., Livingston, B. A., & Hurst, C. (2012). Do nice guys—and gals—really finish last? The joint effects of sex and agreeableness on income. *Journal of Personality* and *Social Psychology, 102*, 390–407. doi:10.1037/a0026021.

Julien, R. M., Advokat, C. D., & Comaty, J. E. (2008). *A primer of drug action: A comprehensive guide to the actions, uses, and side effects of psychoactive drugs.* New York, NY: Worth.

Jung, C. G. (1921/1960). *Psychological types.* In H. Read, M. Fordham, & G. Adler (Eds.), *Collected works of C. G. Jung* (Vol. 6). Princeton, NJ: Princeton University Press.

Jung, C. G. (1933). *Modern man in search of a soul.* New York, NY: Harcourt, Brace & World.

Juruena, M. F. (2014). Early-life stress and HPA axis trigger recurrent adulthood depression. *Epilepsy & Behavior, 38*, 148–159. doi:10.1016/j.yebeh.2013.10.020.

Jusczyk, P. W., & Klein, R. M. (1980). *The nature of thought: Essays in honour of D. O. Hebb.* Hillsdale, NJ: Erlbaum.

Jussim, L., Crawford, J. T., & Rubinstein, R. S. (2015). *Current Directions in Psychological Science, 24*, 490–497.

Kaas, J. H. (2000). The reorganization of sensory and motor maps after injury in adult mammals. In M. S. Gazzaniga (Ed.), *The new cognitive neurosciences.* Cambridge, MA: The MIT Press.

Kaas, J. H., O'Brien, B. M. J., & Hackett, T. A. (2013). Auditory processing in primate brains. In R. J. Nelson, S. J. Y. Mizumori, & I. B. Weiner (Eds.), *Handbook of psychology: Vol. 3. Behavioral neuroscience* (2nd ed.). New York, NY: Wiley.

Kabat-Zinn, J. (1995). *Mindfulness meditation.* New York, NY: Simon & Shuster.

Kagan, J. (1998, November/ December). A parent's influence is peerless. *Harvard Education Letter.*

Kagan, J. (2010). Emotions and temperament. In M. H. Bornstein (Ed.), *Handbook of cultural developmental science* (pp. 175–194). New York, NY: Psychology Press.

Kagan, J. (2011). Three lessons learned. *Psychological Science, 6*, 107–113.

Kagan, J., & Fox, A. (2006). Biology, culture, and temperamental biases. In N. Eisenberg, W. Damon, & R. M. Lerner (Eds.), *Handbook of child psychology: Social, emotional, and personality development* (pp. 167–225). Hoboken, NJ: Wiley.

Kahane, H. (1992). *Logic and contemporary rhetoric: The use of reason in everyday life.* Belmont, CA: Wadsworth.

Kahn, D. (2007). Metacognition, recognition, and reflection while dreaming. In D. Barrett & P. McNamara (Eds.), *The new science of dreaming.* Westport, CT: Praeger.

Kahneman, D. (1991). Judgment and decision making: A personal view. *Psychological Science, 2*, 142–145.

Kahneman, D. (1999). Objective happiness. In D. Kahneman, E. Diener, & N. Schwarz (Eds.), *Well-being: The foundations of hedonic psychology.* New York, NY: Russell Sage Foundation.

Kahneman, D. (2003a). A perspective on judgment and choice: Mapping bounded rationality. *American Psychologist, 58*, 697–720.

Kahneman, D. (2003b). Experiences of collaborative research. *American Psychologist, 58*, 723–730.

Kahneman, D. (2003c). Maps of bounded rationality: Psychology for behavioral economics. *The American Economic Review, 93*, 1449–1475.

Kahneman, D. (2011). *Thinking fast and slow.* Toronto, ON: Random House Canada.

Kahneman, D. (2012). Of 2 minds: How fast and slow thinking shape perception and choice. *Scientific American.* Retrieved from http://www.scientificamerican.com/article/kahneman-excerpt-thinking-fast-and-slow/.

Kahneman, D., & Deaton, A. (2010). High income improves evaluation of life but not emotional well-being. *Proceedings of the National Academy of Sciences of the United States of America, 107*(38), 16489–16493.

Kahneman, D., & Klein, G. (2009). Conditions for intuitive expertise: A failure to disagree. *American Psychologist, 64*, 516–526.

Kahneman, D., & Tversky, A. (1979). Prospect theory: An analysis of decision under risk. *Econometrica, 47*, 263–292.

Kahneman, D., & Tversky, A. (1982). Subjective probability: A judgment of representativeness. In D. Kahneman, P. Slovic, & A. Tversky (Eds.), *Judgment under uncertainty: Heuristics and biases.* Cambridge, UK: Cambridge University Press.

Kahneman, D., & Tversky, A. (1984). Choices, values, and frames. *American Psychologist, 39*, 341–350.

Kahneman, D., & Tversky, A. (2000). *Choices, values, and frames.* New York, NY: Cambridge University Press.

Kaiser, A., Haller, S., Schmitz, S., & Nitsch, C. (2009). On sex/gender related similarities and differences in fMRI language research. *Brain Research Reviews, 61*(2), 49–59.

Kakizaki, M., Kuriyama, S., Nakaya, N., Sone, T., Nagai, M., Sugawara, Y., . . . Tsuji, I. (2013). Long sleep duration and cause-specific mortality according to physical function and self-rated health: The Oshaki Cohort Study. *Journal of Sleep Research, 22*, 209–216. doi:10.1111/j.1365-2869.2012.01053.x.

Kako, E. (1999). Elements of syntax in the systems of three language-trained animals. *Animal Learning and Behavior, 27*, 1–14.

Kalkstein, D. A., Kleiman, T., Wakslak, C. J., Liberman, N., & Trope, Y. (2016). Social learning across psychological distance. *Journal of Personality and Social Psychology, 110*, 1–19.

Kameda, T., Tsukasaki, T., Hastie, R., & Berg, N. (2011). Democracy under uncertainty: The wisdom of crowds and the free-rider problem in group decision-making. *Psychological Review, 118*, 76–96.

Kamin, L. J. (1974). *The science and politics of IQ.* Hillsdale, NJ: Erlbaum.

Kanaan, S. F., McDowd, J. M., Colgrove, Y., Burns, J. M., Gajewski, B., & Pohl, P. S. (2014). Feasibility and efficacy of intensive cognitive training in early-stage Alzheimer's disease. *American Journal of Alzheimer's Disease and Other Dementias, 29*, 150– 158. doi:10.1177/1533317513506775.

Kanaya, T., Scullin, M. H., & Ceci, S. J. (2003). The Flynn effect and U. S. policies: The impact of rising IQ scores on American society via mental retardation diagnoses. *American Psychologist, 58*(10), 778–790.

Kanazawa, S. (2006). Mind the gap … in intelligence: Reexamining the relationship between inequality and health. *British Journal of Health Psychology, 11*, 623–642.

Kandel, E. (2000a). The molecular biology of memory storage: A dialog between genes and synapses. Retrieved from http://www.nobelprize.org/nobel_prizes/medicine/laureates/2000/kandel-lecture.html.

Kandel, E. (2000b). Eric Kandel's speech at the Nobel Banquet, December 10, 2000. Retrieved from http://www.nobelprize.org/nobel_prizes/medicine/laureates/2000/kandel-speech.html.

Kandel, E. (2006). *In search of memory: The emergence of a new science of mind.* New York, NY: Norton Books.

Kandel, E. (2008). Mapping memory in the brain. HHMI Holiday Lectures on Science. Retrieved from http://media.hhmi.org/hl/08Lect1.html.

Kandel, E. R. (2001). The molecular biology of memory storage: A dialogue between genes and synapses. *Science, 294*, 1030–1038.

Kandel, E. R., & Jessell, T. M. (1991). Touch. In E. R. Kandel, J. H. Schwartz, & T. M. Jessell (Eds.), *Principles of neural science* (3rd ed.). New York, NY: Elsevier.

Kandel, E. R., & Siegelbaum, S. A. (2013). Signaling at the nerve-muscle synapse: Directly gated transmission. In E. R. Kandel, J. H. Schwartz, T. M. Jessell, S. A. Siegelbaum, & A. J. Hudspeth (Eds.), *Principles of neural science* (5th ed.). New York, NY: McGraw-Hill.

Kane, J. M., Stroup, T. S., & Marder, S. R. (2009). Schizophrenia: Pharmacological treatment. In B. J. Sadock, V. A. Sadock, & P. Ruiz (Eds.), *Kaplan & Sadock's comprehensive textbook of psychiatry* (pp. 1547–1555). Philadelphia, PA: Lippincott Williams & Wilkins.

Kane, T. D., Marks, M. A., Zaccaro, S. J., & Blair, V. (1996). Self-efficacy, personal goals, and wrestlers' self-regulation. *Journal of Sport & Exercise Psychology, 18*, 36–48.

Kanner, L. (1943). Autistic disturbances of affective contact. *Nervous Child, 2*, 217–250.

Kanner, L. (1973). *Childhood psychosis: Initial studies and new insights.* New York, NY: Wiley.

Kanwisher, N., & Yovel, G. (2009). Face perception. In G. G. Berntson & J. T. Cacioppo (Eds.), *Handbook of neuroscience for the behavioral sciences.* New York, NY: Wiley.

Kaplan, A. G. (1985). Female or male therapists for women patients: New formulations. *Psychiatry, 48*, 111–121.

Kaplan, H., & Dove, H. (1987). Infant development among the Ache of Eastern Paraguay. *Developmental Psychology, 23*, 190–198.

Kaplan, K. A., Itoi, A., & Dement, W. C. (2007). Awareness of sleepiness and ability to predict sleep onset: Can drivers avoid falling asleep at the wheel? *Sleep Medicine, 9*(1), 71–79.

Karasu, T. B. (2005). Psychoanalysis and psychoanalytic psychotherapy. In B. J. Sadock & V. A. Sadock (Eds.), *Kaplan and Sadock's comprehensive textbook of psychiatry* (pp. 2472–2497). Philadelphia, PA: Lippincott, Williams & Wilkins.

Karau, S. J., & Williams, K. D. (1993). Social loafing: A meta-analytic review and theoretical integration. *Journal of Personality and Social Psychology, 65*, 681–706.

Karau, S. J., & Williams, K. D. (1995). Social loafing: Research findings, implications, and future directions. *Current Directions in Psychological Science, 4*, 134–140.

Karlson, P., & Luscher, M. (1959). "Pheromones": A new term for a class of biologically active substances. *Nature, 183*, 55–56.

Karp, A., Andel, R., Parker, M. G., Wang, H., Winblad, B., & Fratiglioni, L. (2009). Mentally stimulating activities at work during midlife and dementia risk after age 75: Follow-up study from the Kungsholmen Project. *American Journal of Geriatric Psychiatry, 17*(3), 227–236.

Karpicke, J. D. (2012). Retrieval-based learning: Active retrieval promotes meaningful learning. *Current Directions in Psychological Science, 21*, 157–163. doi:10.1177/0963721412443552.

Karpicke, J. D., & Blunt, J. R. (2011). Retrieval practice produces more learning than elaborate studying with concept mapping. *Science, 331*, 772– 775. doi:10.1126/science.1199327.

Karremans, J. C., Schellenkens, M. J. P., & Kappen, F. (2017). Bridging the sciences of mindfulness and romantic relationships: A theoretical model and research agenda. *Personality and Social Psychology Review, 21*, 29–49.

Kassam, K. S., Gilbert, D. T., Swencionis, J. K., & Wilson, T. D. (2009). Misconceptions of memory. *Psychological Science, 20*(5), pp. 551–552.

Kasser, T., & Sharma, Y. S. (1999). Reproductive freedom, educational equality, and females' preference for resource-aquisition characteristics in mates. *Psychological Science, 10*, 374–377.

Kassin, S. M. (2012). Why confessions trump innocence. *American Psychologist, 67*, 431–445.

Kassin, S. M. (2017). The killing of Kitty Genovese: What else does this case tell us? *Perspectives on Psychological Science, 12*, 374–381.

Kassin, S. M., Tubb, V. A., Hosch, H. M., & Memon, A. (2001). On the "general acceptance" of eyewitness testimony research: A new survey of the experts. *American Psychologist, 56*, 405–416.

Katigbak, M. S., Church, A. T., Guanzon-Lapena, M. A., Carlota, A. J., & del Pilar, G. H. (2002). Are indigenous personality dimensions culture specific? Philippine inventories and the five-factor model. *Journal of Personality and Social Psychology, 82*, 89–101.

Katz, J., & Fashler, S. (2015). Phantom limbs. In J. D. Wright (Ed.), *International encyclopedia of social and behavioral sciences* (2nd ed.). Oxford, UK: Elsevier.

Katz, J., & Seltzer, Z. (2009). The transition from acute to chronic post surgical pain: Risk factors and protective factors. *Expert Review of Neurotherapeutics, 9*(5), 723–744.

Katz, J., Buis, T. L., & Cohen, B. (2008). Locked out and still knocking: Predictors of excessive demands for postoperative intravenous patient-controlled analgesia. *Canadian Journal of Anesthesia, 55,* 88–99.

Katz, J., Rosenbloom, B. N., & Fashler, S. (2015). Chronic pain, psychopathology, and DSM-5 somatic symptom disorder. *The Canadian Psychiatric Association Journal, 60,* 160–167.

Katz-Wise, S. L., & Hyde, J. S. (2014). Sexuality and gender: The interplay. In D. L. Tolman, L. M. Diamond, J. A. Bauermeister, W. H. George, J. G. Pfaus, & L. M. Ward (Eds.), *APA handbook of sexuality and psychology: Vol. 1. Person-based approaches.* Washington, DC: American Psychological Association.

Kaufman, A. S. (2000). Tests of intelligence. In R. J. Sternberg (Ed.), *Handbook of intelligence* (pp. 445–476). New York, NY: Cambridge University Press.

Kaufman, B. (2013). Calgary refugee camp opens for Alberta residents displaced by June floods. *Calgary Sun,* Tuesday, October 15, 2013. Retrieved from http://www.calgarysun.com/2013/10/15/calgary-refugee-camp-opens-for-alberta-residents-displaced-by-june-floods.

Kaufman, J. C. (2001). The Sylvia Plath effect: Mental illness in eminent creative writers. *Journal of Creative Behavior, 35*(1), 37–50.

Kaufman, J. C. (2005). The door that leads into madness: Eastern European poets and mental illness. *Creativity Research Journal, 17*(1), 99–103.

Kaufman, J. C., & Baer, J. (2002). Could Steven Spielberg manage the Yankees? Creative thinking in different domains. *Korean Journal of Thinking & Problem Solving, 12*(2), 5–14.

Kaufman, J. C., & Baer, J. (2004). Hawking's haiku, Madonna's math: Why it is hard to be creative in every room of the house. In R. J. Sternberg, E. L. Grigorenko, & J. L. Singer (Eds.), *Creativity: From potential to realization.* Washington, DC: American Psychological Association.

Kaufman, J. C., Kaufman, S. B., & Plucker, J. A. (2013). Contemporary theories of intelligence. In D. Reisberg (Ed.), *Oxford handbook of cognitive psychology.* New York, NY: Oxford University Press.

Kaufman, L., Vassiliades, V., Noble, R., Alexander, R., Kaufman, J., & Edlund, S. (2007). Perceptual distance and the moon illusion. *Spatial Vision, 20,* 155–175. doi:10.1163/156856807779369698.

Kaufman, M. T. (2007). Albert Ellis, 93, influential psychotherapist, dies. *The New York Times,* July 25. Retrieved from http://www.nytimes.com/2007/07/25/nyregion/25ellis.html?pagewanted=all.

Kaufman, S. B., & Sternberg, R. J. (2010). Conceptions of giftedness. In S. I. Pfeiffer (Ed.), *Handbook of giftedness in children: Psychoeducational theory, research, and best practices.* New York, NY: Springer.

Kauwe, J. S. K., Ridge, P. G., Foster, N. L., Cannon-Albright, L. A. (2013). Strong evidence for a genetic contribution to late-onset Alzheimer's disease mortality: A population-based study. *PLoS ONE, 8,* e77087.

Kawamoto, T., Nittono, H., & Ura, M. (2013). Cognitive, affective, and motivational changes during ostracism: An ERP, EMG, and EEG study using a computerized cyberball task. *Neuroscience Journal,* Article ID 304674, 11 pages, http://dx.doi.org/10.1155/2013/304674.

Kazdin, A. E. (1982). History of behavior modification. In A. S. Bellack, M. Hersen, & A. E. Kazdin (Eds.), *International handbook of behavior modification and behavior therapy.* New York, NY: Plenum.

Kazdin, A. E. (1994). Methodology, design, and evaluation in psychotherapy research. In A. E. Bergin & S. L. Garfield (Eds.), *Handbook of psychotherapy and behavior change* (4th ed.). New York, NY: Wiley.

Kazdin, A. E. (2001). *Behavior modification in applied settings* (6th ed.). Belmont, CA: Wadsworth.

Kazdin, A. E. (2011). Evidence-based treatment research: Advances, limitations, and next steps. *American Psychologist, 66,* 685–695.

Kazdin, A. E. (2017). Strategies to improve the evidence base of animal-assisted interventions. *Applied Developmental Science, 21,* 150–164.

Kazdin, A. E. (2017). Strategies to improve the evidence base of animal-assisted interventions. *Applied Developmental Science, 21,* 150–164.

Kazdin, A., & Benjet, C. (2003). Spanking children: Evidence and issues. *Current Directions in Psychological Science, 12*(3), 99–103.

Kazdin, A. E., & Blase, S. L. (2011). Rebooting psychotherapy research and practice to reduce the burden of mental illness. *Perspectives on Psychological Science, 6*(1), 21–37. doi:10.1177/1745691610393527.

Kazdin, A. E., & Rabbitt, S. M. (2013). Novel models for delivering mental health services and reducing the burdens of mental illness. *Clinical Psychological Science, 1*(2), 170–191. doi:10.1177/2167702612463566.

Keane, T. M., Marshall, A. D., & Taft, C. T. (2006). Posttraumatic stress disorder: Etiology, epidemiology, and treatment outcome. *Annual Review of Clinical Psychology, 2,* 161–197.

Keck, P. E., Jr., & McElroy, S. L. (2006). Lithium and mood stabilizers. In D. J. Stein, D. J. Kupfer, & A. F. Schatzberg (Eds.), *Textbook of mood disorders* (pp. 281–290). Washington, DC: American Psychiatric Publishing.

Keefer, K., Wood, L. M., & Parker, J. D. A. (2009, June). *Assessing emotional intelligence in children and adolescents: Congruence between self-report and parent ratings.* Paper presented at the annual meeting of the Canadian Psychological Association, Montreal, Quebec.

Keefer, L., Taft, T. H., & Kiebles, J. L. (2013). Gastrointestinal diseases. In A. M. Nezu, C. M. Nezu, P. A. Geller, & I. B. Weiner (Eds.), *Handbook of psychology: Vol. 9. Health psychology* (2nd ed.). New York, NY: Wiley.

Keel, P. K., Brown, T. A., Holland, L. A., & Bodell, L. P. (2012). Empirical classification of eating disorders. *Annual Review of Clinical Psychology, 8,* 381–404. doi:10.1146/annurev-clinpsy-032511-143111.

Keel, P. K., Forney, K. J., Brown, T. A., & Heatherton, T. F. (2013). Influence of college peers on disordered eating in women and men at 10-year follow-up. *Journal of Abnormal Psychology, 122,* 105–110. doi:10.1037/a0030081.

Keen, R. (2011). The development of problem solving in young children: A critical cognitive skill. *Annual Review of Psychology, 62,* 1–21.

Kefalov, V. J. (2010). Visual receptors and transduction. In E. B. Goldstein (Ed.), *Encyclopedia of perception.* Thousand Oaks, CA: Sage.

Keller, M. B., Boland, R., Leon, A., Solomon, D., Endicott, J., & Li, C. (2013). Clinical course and outcome of unipolar major depression. In M. B. Keller, W. H. Coryell, J. Endicott, J. D. Maser, & P. J. Schettler (Eds.), *Clinical guide to depression and bipolar disorder: Findings from the Collaborative Depression Study.* Washington, DC: American Psychiatric Press.

Keller, P. A., & Block, L. G. (1999). The effect of affect-based dissonance versus cognition-based dissonance on motivated reasoning and health-related persuasion. *Journal of Experimental Psychology: Applied, 5,* 302–313.

Kelley, H. H. (1950). The warm–cold variable in first impressions of persons. *Journal of Personality, 18,* 431–439.

Kelley, H. H. (1967). Attributional theory in social psychology. *Nebraska Symposium on Motivation, 15,* 192–241.

Kellner, C. H., Greenberg, R. M., Murrough, J. W., Bryson, E. O., Briggs, M. C., & Pasculli, R. M. (2012). ECT in treatment-resistant depression. *The American Journal of Psychiatry, 169,* 1238–1244. doi:10.1176/appi.ajp.2012.12050648.

Kelly, G. A. (1955). *The psychology of personal constructs* (Vols. 1 & 2). New York, NY: Norton.

Kelly, J. P. (1991). The sense of balance. In E. R. Kandel, J. H. Schwartz, & T. M. Jessell (Eds.), *Principles of neural science* (3rd ed.). New York, NY: Elsevier.

Kelly, K. M., & Schramke, C. J. (2000). Epilepsy. In G. Fink (Ed.), *Encyclopedia of stress* (pp. 66–70). San Diego, CA: Academic Press.

Kelly, S. J., Day, N., & Streissguth, A. P. (2000). Effects of prenatal alcohol exposure on social behavior in humans and other species. *Neurotoxicology & Teratology, 22,* 143–149.

Kelman, H. C. (1967). Human use of human subjects: The problem of deception in social psychological experiments. *Psychological Bulletin, 67,* 1–11.

Kelman, H. C. (1982). Ethical issues in different social science methods. In T. L. Beauchamp, R. R. Faden, R. J. Wallace, Jr., & L. Walters (Eds.), *Ethical issues in social science research.* Baltimore, MD: Johns Hopkins University Press.

Keltner, D., Ekman, P., Gonzaga, G. C., & Beer, J. (2003). Facial expression of emotion. In R. J. Davidson, K. R. Scherer, & H. H. Goldsmith (Eds.), *Handbook of affective sciences.* New York, NY: Oxford University Press.

Kemeny, M. E. (2011). Psychoneuroimmunology. In H. S. Friedman (Ed.), *Oxford handbook of health psychology.* New York, NY: Oxford University Press.

Kemps, E., Herman, C. P., Holitt S., Polivy, J., Prichard, I., et al. (2016). Contextual cues exposure effects on food intake in restrained eaters. *Physiology and Behavior, 167,* 71–75.

Kempton, M. J., Salvador, Z., Munafò, M. R., Geddes, J. R., Simmons, A., Frangou, S., & Williams, S. R. (2011). Structural neuroimaging studies in major depressive disorder: Meta-analysis and comparison with bipolar disorder. *Archives of General Psychiatry, 68,* 675–690. doi:10.1001/archgenpsychiatry.2011.60.

Kendler, K. S. (2005a). "A gene for …?": The nature of gene action in psychiatric disorders. *American Journal of Psychiatry, 162,* 1243–1252.

Kendzerska, T., Mollayeva, T., Gershon, A. S., Leung, R. S., Hawker, G., & Tomlinson, G. (2014). Untreated obstructive sleep apnea and the risk of serious long-term adverse outcomes: A systematic review. *Sleep Medicine Reviews, 18,* 49–59. doi:10.1016/j.smrv.2013.01.003.

Kenfield, S. A., Stampfer, M. J., Rosner, B. A., & Colditz, G. A. (2008). Smoking and smoking cessation in relation to mortality in women. *JAMA, 299,* 2037–2047.

Kennedy, T. E., Hawkins, R. D., & Kandel, E. R. (1992). Molecular interrelationships between short- and long-term memory. In L. R. Squire & N. Butters (Eds.), *Neuropsychology of memory* (2nd ed.). New York, NY: Wiley.

Kenny, M. A., & Williams, J. M. G. (2007). Treatment-resistant depressed patients show a good response to mindfulness-based cognitive therapy. *Behaviour Research and Therapy, 45,* 616–625.

Kenrick, D. T., & Gutierres, S. E. (1980). Contrast effects and judgments of physical attractiveness: When beauty becomes a social problem. *Journal of Personality and Social Psychology, 38,* 131–140.

Kenrick, D. T., Neuberg, S. L., & White, A. E. (2013). Relationships from an evolutionary life history perspective. In J. A. Simpson & L. Campbell (Eds.), *Oxford handbook of close relationships.* New York, NY: Oxford University Press.

Kenrick, D. T., Trost, M. R., & Sundie, J. M. (2004). Sex roles as adaptations: An evolutionary perspective on gender differences and similarities. In A. H. Eagly, A. E. Beall, & R. J. Sternberg (Eds.), *The psychology of gender.* New York, NY: Guilford.

Kermer, D. A., Driver-Linn, E., Wilson, T. D., & Gilbert, D. T. (2006). Loss aversion is an affective forecasting error. *Psychological Science, 17,* 649–653.

Kern, M. L., Della Porta, S. S., & Friedman, H. S. (2014). Lifelong pathways to longevity: Personality, relationships, flourishing, and health. *Journal of Personality, 82,* 472–484. doi:10.1111/jopy.12062.

Kesebir, P., & Diener, E. (2008). In pursuit of happiness: Empirical answers to philosophical questions. *Perspectives on Psychological Science, 3,* 117–125,

Kessen, W. (1996). American psychology just before Piaget. *Psychological Science, 7,* 196–199.

Kessler, R. C., & Zhao, S. (1999). The prevalence of mental illness. In A. V. Horvitz & T. L. Scheid (Eds.), *A handbook for the study of mental health: Social contexts, theories, and systems.* New York, NY: Cambridge University Press.

Kessler, R. C., Berglund, P., Demler, O., Jin, R., Merikangas, K. R., & Walters, E. E. (2005). Lifetime prevalence and age-of-onset distributions of DSM-IV disorders in the national comorbidity survey replication. *Archives of General Psychiatry, 62,* 593–602.

Ketelaar, T. (2015). Evolutionary theories. In B. Gawronski & G. Bodenhausen (Eds.), *Theory and explanation in social psychology* (pp. 224–241). New York, NY: Guilford Press.

Key, B. L., Rowa, K., Bieling, P., McCabe, R., & Pawluck, E. J. (2017). Mindfulness-based cognitive therapy as an augmentation treatment for obsessive-compulsive disorder. *Clinical Psychology and Psychotherapy* (Epub ahead of publication).

Keys, D. J., & Schwartz, B. (2007). "Leaky" rationality: How research on behavioral decision making challenges normative standards of rationality. *Perspectives on Psychological Science, 2*(2), 162–180.

Keysers, C., & Perrett, D. I. (2004). Demystifying social cognition: A Hebbian perspective. *Trends in Cognitive Science, 8,* 501–507.

Kharsany, A. B., & Karim, Q. A. (2016). HIV infection and AIDS in sub-Saharan Africa: Current challenges and opportunities. *Open AIDS Journal, 8,* 34–48.

Kiat, J. E., Straley, E., & Cheadle, J. E. (2017). Why won't they it with me? An exploratory investigation of stereotyped cues, social exclusion, and the P3b. *Social Neuroscience, 12,* 612–625.

Kiecolt-Glaser, J. K. (2009). Psychoneuroimmunology: Psychology's gateway to biomedical future. *Perspective on Psychological Science, 4,* 367–369. doi:10.1111/j.1745-6924.2009.01139.x.

Kiecolt-Glaser, J. K., Garner, W., Speicher, C., Penn, G. M., Holliday, J., & Glaser, R. (1984). Psychosocial modifiers of immunocompetence in medical students. *Psychosomatic Medicine, 46*(1), 7–14.

Kielland, N., & Simeone, T. (2014). *Current issues in mental health in Canada: The mental health of First Nations and Inuit communities.* Library of Parliament Research Publications. Retrieved from https://lop.parl.ca/content/lop/ResearchPublications/2014-02-e.pdf.

Kihlstrom, J. F. (2004). An unbalanced balancing act: Blocked, recovered, and false memories in the laboratory and clinic. *Clinical Psychology: Science & Practice, 11*(1), 34–41.

Kihlstrom, J. F. (2005). Dissociative disorders. *Annual Review of Clinical Psychology, 1,* 227–253.

Kihlstrom, J. F., Barnhardt, T. M., & Tataryn, D. J. (1992). Implicit perception. In R. F. Bornstein & T. S. Pittman (Eds.), *Perception without awareness: Cognitive, clinical, and social perspectives.* New York, NY: Guilford.

Killeen, P. R. (1981). Learning as causal inference. In M. L. Commons & J. A. Nevin (Eds.), *Quantitative analyses of behavior (Vol. 1): Discriminative properties of reinforcement schedules.* Cambridge, MA: Ballinger.

Killen, M., Hitti, A., & Mulvey, K. L. (2015). Social development and intergroup relations. In M. Mikulincer, P. R. Shaver, J. F. Dovidio, & J. A. Simpson (Eds.), *APA handbook of personality and social psychology: Vol. 2. Group processes* (pp. 177– 201).

Killen, M., Richardson, C. B., & Kelly, M. C. (2010). Developmental perspectives. In J. F. Dovidio, M. Hewstone, P. Glick, & V. M. Esses (Eds.), *The Sage handbook of prejudice, stereotyping, and discrimination.* Los Angeles, CA: Sage.

Kiluk, B. D., Sugarman, D. E., Nich, C., Gibbons, C. J., Martino, S., Rounsaville, B. J., & Carroll, K. M. (2011). A methodological analysis of randomized clinical trials of computer-assisted therapies for psychiatric disorders: Toward improved standards for an emerging field. *The American Journal of Psychiatry, 168,* 790–799. doi:10.1176/appi.ajp.2011.10101443.

Kim, H., & Markus, H. R. (1999). Deviance or uniqueness, harmony or conformity? A cultural analysis. *Journal of Personality and Social Psychology, 77,* 785–800.

Kim, H. S., Sherman, D. K., Ko, D., & Taylor, S. E. (2006). Pursuit of comfort and pursuit of harmony: Culture, relationships, and social support seeking. *Personality and Social Psychology Bulletin, 32*(12), 1595–1607.

Kim, H. S., Sherman, D. K., & Taylor, S. E. (2008). Culture and social support. *American Psychologist, 63*(6), 518–526.

Kim, K. H. (2005). Can only intelligent people be creative? *Journal of Secondary Gifted Education, 16,* 57–66.

Kimura, D. (1973). The asymmetry of the human brain. *Scientific American, 228,* 70–78.

King, B. H., Hodapp, R. M., & Dykens, E. M. (2005). Mental retardation. In B. J. Sadock & V. A. Sadock (Eds.), *Kaplan & Sadock's comprehensive textbook of psychiatry* (pp. 3076–3106). Philadelphia, PA: Lippincott, Williams & Wilkins.

King, B. H., Toth, K. E., Hodapp, R. M., & Dykens, E. M. (2009). Intellectual disability. In B. J. Sadock, V. A. Sadock, & P. Ruiz (Eds.), *Kaplan & Sadock's comprehensive textbook of psychiatry* (Vol. 2). Philadelphia, PA: Lippincott, Williams & Wilkins.

King, B. M. (2006). The rise, fall, and resurrection of the ventromedial hypothalamus in the regulation of feeding behavior and body weight. *Physiology & Behavior, 87,* 221–244.

King, B. M. (2013). The modern obesity epidemic, ancestral hunter-gatherers, and the sensory/reward control of food intake. *American Psychologist, 68*(2), 88–96. doi:10.1037/a0030684.

King, D. B., Woody, W. D., & Viney, W. (2013). *A history of psychology: Ideas and context.* New York, NY: Pearson.

Kingstone, A., Smilek, D., & Eastwood, J. D. (2008). Cognitive ethology: A new approach for studying human cognition. *British Journal of Psychology, 99,* 317–340.

Kinsbourne, M. (1997). What qualifies a representation for a role in consciousness? In J. D. Cohen & J. W. Schooler (Eds.), *Scientific approaches to consciousness.* Mahwah, NJ: Erlbaum.

Kinsey, A. C., Pomeroy, W. B., & Martin, C. E. (1948). *Sexual behavior in the human male.* Philadelphia, PA: Saunders.

Kinsey, A. C., Pomeroy, W. B., Martin, C. E., & Gebhard, P. H. (1953). *Sexual behavior in the human female.* Philadelphia, PA: Saunders.

Kinzler, K. (2016). The superior social skills of bilinguals. *The New York Times,* March 11, 2016. Retrieved from https://www.nytimes.com/2016/03/13/opinion/sunday/the-superior-social-skills-of-bilinguals.html.

Kirby, D. (2005). *Evidence of harm: Mercury in vaccines and the autism epidemic: A medical controversy.* New York, NY: St. Martin's Press.

Kirby, S. (2007). The evolution of language. In R. I. M. Dunbar & L. Barrett (Eds.), *Oxford handbook of evolutionary psychology.* New York, NY: Oxford University Press.

Kirk, S. A., Gomory, T., & Cohen, D. (2013). *Mad science: Psychiatric coercion, diagnosis, and drugs.* New Brunswick, NJ: Transaction Publishers.

Kirkpatrick, L. A. (2005). *Attachment, evolution, and the psychology of religion.* New York, NY: Guilford.

Kirmayer, L. J. (2007). Psychotherapy and the cultural concept of the person. *Transcultural Psychiatry, 44,* 232–257.

Kirmayer, L. J., Brass, G. M., & Tait, C. L. (2000). The mental health of aboriginal peoples: Transformations of identity and community. *Canadian Journal of Psychiatry, 45,* 607–612.

Kirov, G., & Owen, M. J. (2009). Genetics of schizophrenia. In B. J. Sadock, V. A. Sadock, & P. Ruiz (Eds.), *Kaplan & Sadock's comprehensive textbook of psychiatry* (9th ed., Vol. 1, pp. 1462–1472). Philadelphia, PA: Lippincott, Williams & Wilkins.

Kirsch, I. (1997). Response expectancy theory and application: A decennial review. *Applied and Preventive Psychology, 6,* 69–79.

Kirsch, I. (2010). *The emperor's new drugs: Exploding the antidepressant myth.* New York, NY: Basic Books.

Kirsch, I., Mazzoni, G., & Montgomery, G. H. (2007). Remembrance of hypnosis past. *American Journal of Clinical Hypnosis, 49,* 171–178.

Kirschenbaum, H., & Joudan, A. (2005). The current status of Carl Rogers and the person-centered approach. *Psychotherapy: Theory, Research, Practice, Training, 42,* 37–51.

Kis, A., Kemerle, K., Hernadi, A., & Topal, J. (2013). Oxytocin and social pretreatment have similar effects on processing of negative emotion faces in healthy adult males. *Frontiers in Psychology: Cognition, 4,* 1–9.

Kissileff, H. R., Thornton, J. C., Torres, M. I., Pavlovich, K., Mayer, L. S., Kalari, V., . . . Rosenbaum, M. (2012). Leptin reverses declines in satiation in weight-reduced obese humans. *The American Journal of Clinical Nutrition, 95,* 309–317.

Kitayama, S., Mesquita, B., & Karasawa, M. (2006). Cultural affordances and emotional experience: Socially engaging and disengaging emotions in Japan and the United States. *Journal of Personality and Social Psychology, 91,* 890–903.

Kitchingman, T. A., Wilson, C. J., Caputi, P., Wilson, I., & Woodward, A. (2017). Telephone crisis support workers' psychological distress and impairment: A systematic review. *The Journal of Crisis Intervention and Suicide Prevention. 36,* 407–415.

Kitner, C. (2002). Neurogenesis in embryos and adult neural stem cells. *Journal of Neuroscience, 22,* 639–643.

Kittler, P. G., & Sucher, K. P. (2008). *Food and culture.* Belmont, CA: Wadsworth.

Klahr, D., & Chen, Z. (2011). Finding one's place in transfer space. *Child Development Perspectives.* Retrieved May 30, 2011, from http://onlinelibrary.wiley.com/doi/10.1111/j.1750-8606.2011.00171.x/full.

Klapper, D., Ebling, C., & Temme, J. (2005). Another look at loss aversion in brand choice data: Can we characterize the loss-averse consumer? *International Journal of Research in Marketing, 22,* 239–254.

Klein, D. N., & Allmann, A. E. (2014). Course of depression: Persistence and recurrence. In I. H. Gotlib & C. L. Hammen (Eds.), *Handbook of depression* (3rd ed.). New York, NY: Guilford Press.

Klein, P. D. (1997). Multiplying the problems of intelligence by eight: A critique of Gardner's theory. *Canadian Journal of Education, 22,* 377–394.

Klein, R. M. (1999). The Hebb legacy. *Canadian Journal of Behavioural Science, 53,* 1–20.

Klein, W. M. P., Geaghan, T. R., & MacDonald, T. K. (2007). Unplanned sexual activity as a consequence of alcohol use: A prospective study of risk perceptions and alcohol use among college freshmen. *Journal of American College Health, 56,* 317–323.

Kleinke, C. L. (2007). What does it mean to cope? In A. Monat, R. S. Lazarus, & G. Reevy (Eds.), *The Praeger handbook on stress and coping.* Westport, CT: Praeger.

Kleinmuntz, B. (1980). *Essentials of abnormal psychology.* San Francisco, CA: Harper & Row.

Kleinmuntz, B., & Szucko, J. J. (1984). Lie detection in ancient and modern times: A call for contemporary scientific study. *American Psychologist, 39*(7), 766–776.

Kleinspehn-Ammerlahn, A., Kotter-Grühn, D., & Smith, J. (2008). Self-perceptions of aging: Do subjective age and satisfaction with aging change during old age? *The Journals of Gerontology: Series B: Psychological Sciences and Social Sciences, 63B*(6), 377–385.

Klerman, E. B., & Dijk, D. J. (2008). Age-related reduction in the maximal capacity for sleep-implications for insomnia. *Current Biology, 18,* 1118–1123.

Klimsta, T. A., Crocetti, E., Hale III, W. W., Fermani, A., & Meeus, W. H. J. (2011). Big Five personality dimensions in Italian and Dutch adolescents: A cross-cultural comparison of mean-levels, sex differences, and associations with internalizing symptoms. *Journal of Research in Personality, 45,* 285–296.

Kline, P. (1991). *Intelligence: The psychometric view.* New York, NY: Routledge, Chapman, & Hall.

Kline, P. (1995). A critical review of the measurement of personality and intelligence. In D. H. Saklofske & M. Zeidner (Eds.), *International handbook of personality and intelligence.* New York, NY: Plenum.

Kling, R. N., McLeod, C. B., & Koehoorn, M. (2010). Sleep problems and workplace injuries in Canada. *Sleep, 33*, 611–618.

Klosch, G., & Kraft, U. (2005). Sweet dreams are made of this. *Scientific American Mind, 16*(2), 38–45.

Klump, K. L. (2013). Puberty as a critical risk period for eating disorders: A review of human and animal behaviors. *Hormones and Behavior, 64*, 399–410. doi:10.1016/j.yhbeh.2013.02.019.

Knapp, C. M., & Kornetsky, C. (2009). Neural basis of pleasure and reward. In G. G. Berntson & J. T. Cacioppo (Eds.), *Handbook of neuroscience for the behavioral sciences* (Vol. 1, pp. 781–806). New York, NY: Wiley.

Knauss, W. (2005). Group psychotherapy. In G. O. Gabbard, J. S. Beck, & J. Holmes (Eds.), *Oxford textbook of psychotherapy*. New York, NY: Oxford University Press.

Knecht, S., Drager, B., Floel, A., Lohmann, H., Breitenstein, C., Henningsen, H., & Ringelstein, B. (2001). Behavioural relevance of atypical language lateralization in healthy subjects. *Brain, 124*, 1657–1665.

Knight, J. (2004). The truth about lying. *Nature, 428*, 692–694.

Knopik, V. S. (2009). Maternal smoking during pregnancy and child outcomes: Real or spurious effect? *Developmental Neuropsychology, 34*(1), 1–36.

Knowles, M., Green, A., & Weidel, A. (2014). Social rejection biases estimates of interpersonal distance. *Social Psychological and Personality Science, 5*, 158–167.

Knutson, K. L. (2012). Does inadequate sleep play a role in vulnerability to obesity? *American Journal of Human Biology, 24*, 361–371.

Kobak, R. (1999). The emotional dynamics of disruptions in attachment relationships: Implications for theory, research, and clinical intervention. In J. Cassidy & P. R. Shaver (Eds.), *Handbook of attachment*. New York, NY: Guilford.

Kobasa, S. C. (1979). Stressful life events, personality, and health: An inquiry into hardiness. *Journal of Personality and Social Psychology, 37*, 1–11.

Koch, C., Massimini, M., Boly, M., & Tononi, G. (2015). The neural correlates of consciousness: Progress and problems. *Nature Neuroscience, 17*, 307–321.

Koch, C., & Tsuchiya, N. (2006). Attention and consciousness: Two distinct brain processes. *Trends in Cognitive Science, 11*, 16–22.

Koch, K., Pauly, K., Kellerman, T., Sieferth, N. Y., et al. (2007). Gender differences in the cognitive control of emotions: An fMRI study. *Neuropsychologica, 45*, 2744–2754.

Koehl, M., & Abrous, D. N. (2011). A new chapter in the field of memory: Adult hippocampal neurogenesis. *European Journal of Neuroscience, 33*, 1101–1114. doi:10.1111/j.1460-9568.2011.07609.x.

Koehler, J. J. (1996). The base rate fallacy reconsidered: Descriptive, normative, and methodological challenges. *Behavioral Brain Sciences, 19*, 1–53.

Koenig, A. M., & Dean, K. K. (2011). Cross-cultural differences and similarities in attribution. In K. D. Keith (Ed.), *Cross-cultural psychology: Contemporary themes and perspectives*. Malden, MA: Wiley-Blackwell.

Kofink, D., Boks, M. M., Timmers, H. M., & Kas, M. J. (2013). Epigenetic dynamics in psychiatric disorders: Environmental programming of neurodevelopmental processes. *Neuroscience and Biobehavioral Reviews, 37*, 831–845. doi:10.1016/j.neubiorev.2013.03.020.

Kogan, N. (1990). Personality and aging. In J. E. Birren & K. W. Schaie (Eds.), *Handbook of the psychology of aging*. San Diego, CA: Academic Press.

Kohl, J. V., Atzmueller, M., Fink, B., & Grammer, K. (2003). Human pheromones: Integrating neuroendocrinology and ethology. *Neuroendocrinology Letters, 22*, 309–321.

Kohlberg, L. (1963). The development of children's orientations toward a moral order: I. Sequence in the development of moral thought. *Vita Humana, 6*, 11–33.

Kohlberg, L. (1969). Stage and sequence: The cognitive-developmental approach to socialization. In D. A.

Goslin (Ed.), *Handbook of socialization theory and research*. Chicago: Rand McNally.

Kohlberg, L. (1976). Moral stages and moralization: Cognitive-developmental approach. In T. Lickona (Ed.), *Moral development and behavior: Theory, research and social issues*. New York, NY: Holt, Rinehart & Winston.

Kohlberg, L. (1984). *Essays on moral development (Vol. 2): The psychology of moral development*. San Francisco, CA: Harper & Row.

Kohman, R. A., & Rhodes, J. S. (2013). Neurogenesis, inflammation and behavior. *Brain, Behavior, and Immunity, 27*, 22–32. doi:10.1016/j.bbi.2012.09.003.

Kolb, B., & Gibb, B. (2007). Brain plasticity and recovery from early cortical injury. *Developmental Psychobiology, 49*, 107–118.

Kolb, B., Gibb, R., & Robinson, T. E. (2003). Brain plasticity and behavior. *Current Directions in Psychological Science, 12*, 1–5.

Kolb, B., & Whishaw, I. Q. (1998). Brain plasticity and behavior. *Annual Review of Psychology, 49*, 43–64.

Konnis, J., & Beeman, M. (2014). The cognitive neuroscience of insight. *Annual Review of Psychology, 65*, 32–56.

Koob, G. F. (2012). Neuroanatomy of addiction. In K. D. Brownell & M. S. Gold (Eds.), *Food and addiction: A comprehensive handbook*. New York, NY: Oxford University Press.

Koob, G. F., & Le Moal, M. (2006). *Neurobiology of addiction*. San Diego, CA: Academic Press.

Koob, G. F., Everitt, B. J., & Robbins, T. W. (2008). Reward, motivation, and addiction. In L. Squire, D. Berg, F. Bloom, S. Du Lac, A. Ghosh, N. Spitzer (Eds.), *Fundamental neuroscience* (3rd ed., pp. 87–111). San Diego, CA: Elsevier.

Koocher, G. P. (2007). Twenty-first-century ethical challenges for psychology. *American Psychologist, 62*, 375–384.

Koordeman, R., Anschutz, D. J., van Baaren, R. B., & Engels, R. E. (2010). Exposure to soda commercials affects sugar-sweetened soda consumption in young women. An observational experimental study. *Appetite, 54*, 619–622.

Koppel, J., & Rubin, D. C. (2016). Recent advances in understanding the reminiscence bump: The importance of cues in guiding recall from autobiographical memory. *Current Directions in Psychological Science, 25*, 135–140.

Koren, D., Arnon, I., & Klein, E. (1999). Acute stress response and posttraumatic stress disorder in traffic accident victims: A one-year prospective, follow-up study. *American Journal of Psychiatry, 156*, 367–373.

Koriat, A., & Bjork, R. A. (2005). Illusions of competence in monitoring one's knowledge during study. *Journal of Experimental Psychology: Learning, Memory, and Cognition, 31*(2), 187–194.

Koriat, A., Goldsmith, M., & Pansky, A. (2000). Toward a psychology of memory accuracy. *Annual Review of Psychology, 51*, 481–537.

Koriat, A., Lichtenstein, S., & Fischhoff, B. (1980). Reasons for confidence. *Journal of Experimental Psychology, 6*, 107–118.

Kornell, N., & Metcalfe, J. (2014). The effects of memory retrieval, errors and feedback on learning. In V. A. Benassi, C. E. Overson, & C. M. Hakala (Eds.), *Applying science of learning in education: Infusing psychological science into the curriculum*. Washington, DC: Society for the Teaching of Psychology.

Kornell, N., Castel, A. D., Eich, T. S., & Bjork, R. A. (2010). Spacing as the friend of both memory and induction in young and older adults. *Psychology and Aging, 25*(2), 498–503.

Kornell, N., Hays, M., & Bjork, R. A. (2009). Unsuccessful retrieval attempts enhance subsequent learning. *Journal of Experimental Psychology: Learning, Memory, and Cognition, 35*(4), 989–998.

Kosfeld, M., Heinrichs, M., Zak, P. J., Fischbacher, U., & Fehr, E. (2005). Oxytocin increases trust in humans. *Nature, 435*(7042), 673–676.

Kostreva, M., McNelis, E., & Clemens, E. (2002). Using a circadian rhythms model to evaluate shift schedules. *Ergonomics, 45*, 739–763.

Kotovsky, K., Hayes, J. R., & Simon, H. A. (1985). Why are some problems hard? Evidence from Tower of Hanoi. *Cognitive Psychology, 17*, 248–294.

Kovelman, I., Berens, M., & Petitto, L. A. (2013). Learning to read in two languages: Should bilingual children learn reading in two languages at the same time or in sequence? Evidence of a bilingual reading advantage in children in bilingual schools from monolingual English-only homes. *Bilingual Research Journal, 11*(2), 203–223.

Kowalski, P., & Taylor, A. K. (2009). The effect of refuting misconceptions in the introductory psychology class. *Teaching of Psychology, 36*(3), 153–159. doi:10.1080/00986280902959986.

Kozorovitskiy, Y., & Gould, E. (2007). Adult neurogenesis and regeneration in the brain. In Y. Sern (Ed.), *Cognitive reserve: Theory and applications*. Philadelphia, PA: Taylor and Francis.

Kozorovitskiy, Y., & Gould, E. (2008). Adult neurogenesis in the hippocampus. In C. A. Nelson, & M. Luciana (Eds.), *Handbook of developmental cognitive neuroscience* (2nd ed., pp. 51–61). Cambridge, MA: MIT Press.

Kozulin, A. (2005). The concept of activity in Soviet psychology: Vygotsky, his disciples and critics. In H. Daniels (Ed.), *An introduction to Vygotsky*. New York, NY: Routledge.

Kracke, W. (1991). Myths in dreams, thought in images: An Amazonian contribution to the psychoanalytic theory of primary process. In B. Tedlock (Ed.), *Dreaming: Anthropological and psychological interpretations*. Santa Fe, NM: School of American Research Press.

Kraemer, H. C. (2008). DSM categories and dimensions in clinical and research contexts. In J. E. Helzer, H. C. Kraemer, R. F. Krueger, H.-U. Wittchen, P. J. Sirovatka, et al. (Eds.), *Dimensional approaches in diagnostic classification: Refining the research agenda for DSM-V* (pp. 5–17). Washington, DC: American Psychiatric Association.

Kraha, A., & Boals, A. (2014). Why so negative? Positive flashbulb memories for a personal event. *Memory, 22*, 442–449. doi:10.1080/09658211.2013.798121.

Krahe, B. (2013). Violent video games and aggression. In K. E. Dill (Ed.), *Oxford handbook of media psychology*. New York, NY: Oxford University Press.

Krahe, B., Moller, I., Huesmann, L. R., Kirwil, L., Felber, J., & Berger, A. (2011). Desensitization to media violence: Links with habitual media violence exposure, aggressive cognitions, and aggressive behavior. *Journal of Personality and Social Psychology, 100*, 630–646. doi:10.1037/a0021711.

Krakauer, D., & Dallenbach, K. M. (1937). Gustatory adaptation to sweet, sour, and bitter. *American Journal of Psychology, 49*, 469–475.

Kramer, A. F., & Erickson, K. I. (2007). Capitalizing on cortical plasticity: Influence of physical activity on cognition and brain function. *Trends in Cognitive Sciences, 11*, 342–348.

Krebs, D. L., & Denton, K. (1997). Social illusions and self-deception: The evolution of biases in person perception. In J. A. Simpson & D. T. Kenrick (Eds.), *Evolutionary social psychology*. Mahwah, NJ: Erlbaum.

Krebs, D. L., & Denton, K. (2005). Toward a more pragmatic approach to morality: A critical evaluation of Kohlerg's model. *Psychological Review, 112*, 629–649.

Kreiner, D. (2011). Linguistic relativity is alive and well. *PsychCritiques, 56*, 32–47.

Kremen, W. S., Jacobsen, K. C., Xian, H., Eisen, S. A., Eaves, L. J., Tsuang, M. T., & Lyons, M. J. (2007). Genetics of verbal working memory processes: A twin study of middle-aged men. *Neuropsychology, 21*(5), 569–580.

Krendl, A. C., Macrae, C. N., Kelley, W. M., Fugelsang, J. A., & Hetherington, T. F. (2006). The good, the bad, and the ugly: An fMRI investigation of the functional anatomical correlates of stigma. *Social Neuroscience, 1*, 5–15.

Kreutzer, J. S., Seel, R. T., & Gourley, E. (2001). The prevalence and symptom rates of depression after traumatic brain injury: A comprehensive examination. *Brain Injury, 15*(7), 563–576.

Kriegsfeld, L. J., & Nelson, R. J. (2009). Biological rhythms. In G. G. Berntson & J. T. Cacioppo (Eds.), *Handbook of neuroscience for the behavioral sciences* (Vol. 1, pp. 56–81). New York, NY: Wiley.

Kripke, D. F., Langer, R. D., & Kline, L. E. (2012). Hypnotics' association with mortality or cancer: A matched cohort study. *British Medical Journal Open, 2*, e000850. doi:10.1136/bjmopen-2012-000850.

Kristensen, H. A., Parker, J. D. A., Taylor, R. M., Keefer, K. V., Kloosterman, P. H., & Summerfeldt, L. J. (2014). The relationship between trait emotional intelligence and ADHD symptoms in adolescents and young adults. *Personality and Individual Differences, 65*, 36–41.

Kroger, J. (2003). Identity development during adolescence. In G. R. Adams & M. D. Berzonsky (Eds.), *Blackwell handbook of adolescence*. Malden, MA: Blackwell.

Kroger, J., & Marcia, J. E. (2011). The identify statuses: Origins, meanings, and interpretations. In S. J. Schwartz, K. Luyckx, & V. L. Vignoles (Eds.), *Handbook of identity theory and research* (Vols. 1 & 2). New York, NY: Springer Science + Business Media.

Kroll, J. (2008). Juggling two languages in one mind. *APA Online Psychological Science Agenda, 22*. Retrieved January 24, 2008, from http://www.apa.org/science/psa/kroll_prnt.html.

Kroll, J. F., & Bialystok, E. (2013). Understanding the consequences of bilingualism for language processing and cognition. *Journal of Cognitive Psychology, 25*(5), 497–514.

Kroll, J., Bobb, S., & Wodniecka, Z. (2006). Language selectivity is the exception, not the rule: Arguments against a fixed locus of language selection in bilingual speech. *Bilingualism: Language and Cognition, 9*, 119–135.

Krosnick, J. A. (1999). Survey research. *Annual Review Psychology, 50*, 537–567.

Krosnick, J. A. Lavrakas, P. J., & Kim, N. (2014). Survey research. In H. T. Reis & C. M. Judd (Eds.), *Handbook of research methods in social and personality psychology* (2nd ed.). New York, NY: Cambridge University Press.

Krosnick, J. A., & Fabrigar, L. R. (1998). *Designing good questionnaires: Insights from psychology*. New York, NY: Oxford University Press.

Kross, E., Verduyn, P., Demiralp, E., Park, J., Lee, D. S., Lin, N., . . . Ybarra. (2013). Facebook use predicts declines in subjective well-being in young adults. *PLoS ONE, 8*, e69841.

Krstic, S., Neumann, C. S., Roy, S., Robertson, C. A., Knight, R. A., & Hare, R. D. (2017). Using latent variable- and person-centered approaches to examine the role of psychopathic traits in sex offenders. *Personality Disorders* (Epub ahead of print). Retrieved from https://www.ncbi.nlm.nih.gov/pubmed/28406657.

Krueger, J. (1996). Personal beliefs and cultural stereotypes about racial characteristics. *Journal of Personality and Social Psychology, 71*, 536–548.

Krueger, J., Ham, J. J., & Linford, K. M. (1996). Perceptions of behavioral consistency: Are people aware of the actor-observer effect? *Psychological Science, 7*, 259–264.

Krueger, K. R., Wilson, R. S., Kamenetsky, J. M., Barnes, L. L., Bienias, J. L., & Bennett, D. A. (2009). Social engagement and cognitive function in old age. *Experimental Aging Research, 35*(1), 45–60.

Krueger, R. F., & Johnson, W. (2008). Behavioral genetics and personality: A new look at the integration of nature and nurture. In O. P. John, R. W. Robbins, & L. A. Pervin (Eds.), *Handbook of personality: Theory and research* (Vol. 3, pp. 287–310). New York, NY: Guilford Press.

Krueger, R. F., & Markon, K. E. (2014). The role of the DSM-5 personality trait model in moving toward a quantitative and empirically based approach to classifying personality and psychopathology. *Annual Review of Clinical Psychology, 10*, 477–501. doi:10.1146/annurevclinpsy-032813-153732.

Krugel, L. (2017). A roller-coaster of emotions for Fort McMurray man who lost his home, won lottery. The

Canadian Press, April 28, 2017. Retrieved from http://www.cbc.ca/news/canada/edmonton/fort-mcmurray-man-loses-home-wins-lottery-wildfire-anniversary-1.4090443.

Kruglanski, A. W., & Orehek, E. (2007). Partitioning the domain of social inference: Dual mode and systems. *Annual Review of Psychology, 58*, 241–316.

Kruglanski, A. W., & Stroebe, W. (2005). The influence of beliefs and goals on attitudes: Issues of structure, function, and dynamics. In D. Albarracin, B. T. Johnson, & M. P. Zanna (Eds.), *The handbook of attitudes*. Mahwah, NJ: Erlbaum.

Krull, D. S. (2001). On partitioning the fundamental attribution error: Dispositionalism and the correspondence bias. In G. B. Moskowitz (Ed.), *Cognitive social psychology: The Princeton Symposium on the legacy and future of social cognition*. Mahwah, NJ: Erlbaum.

Krull, D. S., & Erickson, D. J. (1995). Inferential hopscotch: How people draw social inferences from behavior. *Current Directions in Psychological Science, 4*, 35–38.

Kryger, M. H. (1993). Snoring. In M. A. Carskadon (Ed.), *Encyclopedia of sleep and dreaming*. New York, NY: Macmillan.

Kübler-Ross, E. (1969). *On death and dying*. New York, NY: Macmillan.

Kübler-Ross, E. (1970). The dying patient's point of view. In O. G. Brim, Jr., H. E. Freeman, S. Levine, & N. A. Scotch (Eds.), *The dying patient*. New York, NY: Sage.

Kucharczyk, E. R., Morgan, K., & Hall, A. P. (2012). The occupational impact of sleep quality and insomnia symptoms. *Sleep Medicine Reviews, 16*, 547–559. doi:10.1016/j.smrv.2012.01.005.

Kuehn, B. M. (2007). Scientists probe deep brain stimulation: Some promise for brain injury, psychiatric illness. *Journal of the American Medical Association, 298*, 2249–2251.

Kuhl, P. K., Conboy, B. T., Coffey-Corina, S., Padden, D., Rivera-Gaxiola, M., & Nelson, T. (2008). Phonetic learning as a pathway to language: New data and native language magnet theory expanded (NLM-e). *Philosophical Transactions of the Royal Society of London, B, 363*, 979–1000.

Kuhlmann, B. D., & Bayen, U. J. (2016). Metacognitive aspects of source monitoring. In J. Dunlosky & S. K, Tauber (Eds.), *The Oxford handbook of metamemory* (pp. 149–168). New York, NY: Oxford University Press.

Kuhn, H. W., & Nasar, S. (2002). *The essential John Nash*. Princeton, NJ: Princeton University Press.

Kukutani M. (2013). Battles without end. *The New York Times*, September 30, 2013. Retrieved from http://www.nytimes.com/2013/10/01/books/thank-you-for-your-service-by-david-finkel.html?_r=0.

Kulick, A. R., Pope, H. G., & Keck, P. E. (1990). Lycanthropy and self-identification. *Journal of Nervous & Mental Disease, 178*(2), 134–137.

Kuncel, N. R., & Hezlett, S. A. (2010). Fact and fiction in cognitive ability testing for admissions and hiring decisions. *Current Directions in Psychological Science, 19*, 339–345. doi:10.1177/0963721410389459.

Kunda, Z. (1999). *Social cognition: Making sense of people*. Cambridge, MA: The MIT Press.

Kung, S., & Mrazek, D. A. (2005). Psychiatric emergency department visits on full-moon nights. *Psychiatric Services, 56*, 221–222.

Kunitoh, N. (2013). From hospital to the community: The influence of deinstitutionalization on discharged long-stay psychiatric patients. *Psychiatry and Clinical Neurosciences, 67*, 384–396. doi:10.1111/pcn.12071.

Kuo, M-F., Paulus, W., & Nitsche, M. A. (2014). Therapeutic effects of non-invasive brain stimulation with direct currents (tDCS) in neuropsychiatric diseases. *Neuroimage, 85*, 948–960.

Kupfer, D. J., Kuhl, E. A., & Regier, D. A. (2013). DSM-5: The future arrived. *JAMA, 309*, 1691–1692.

Kurdi, B., & Banaji, M. R. (2017). Repeated evaluative pairings and evaluative statements: How effectively do they shift attitudes. *Journal of Experimental Psychology: General, 146*, 194–213.

Kurtz, K. J., & Loewenstein, J. (2007). Converging on a new role for analogy in problem solving and retrieval: When two problems are better than one. *Memory & Cognition, 35*, 334–342.

Kushlev, K., & Dunn, E. W. (2012). Affective forecasting: Knowing how we will feel in the future. In S. Vazire, & T. D. Wilson (Eds.), *Handbook of self-knowledge*. New York, NY: Guilford Press.

Kutchins, H., & Kirk, S. A. (1997). *Making us crazy: DSM—The psychiatric Bible and the creation of mental disorders*. New York, NY: The Free Press.

Kwan, D., Craver, C. F., Green, L., Myerson, J., Boyer, P., & Rosenbaum, R. S. (2012). Future decision-making without episodic mental time travel. *Hippocampus, 22*, 1215–1219.

la Cour, L. T., Stone, B. W., Hopkins, W., Menzel, C., & Fragaszy, D. M. (2014). What limits tool use in nonhuman primates? Insights from tufted capuchin monkeys (*Sapajus spp.*) and chimpanzees (Pan troglodytes) aligning three-dimensional objects to a surface. *Animal Cognition, 17*(1), 113–125. doi:10.1007/s10071-013-0643-x.

LaBar, K. S., Gatenby, J. C., Gore, J. C., Le Doux, J. E., & Phelps, E. A. (1998). Human amygdala activation during conditioned fear acquisition and extinction: A mixed-trial fMRI study. *Neuron, 20*, 937–945.

Laberge, S. (2009). *Lucid dreaming: A concise guide to awakening in your dreams and in your life*. New York, NY: Random House.

Laborda, M. A., McConnell, B. L., & Miller, R. R. (2011). Behavioral techniques to reduce relapse after exposure therapy: Applications of studies of experimental extinction. In T. R. Schachtman, & S. Reilly (Eds.), *Associative learning and condition theory: Human and non-human applications*. New York, NY: Oxford University Press.

Laceulle, O. M., Ormel, J., Aggen, S. H., Neale, M., & Kendler, K. S. (2013). Genetic and environmental influences on the longitudinal structure of neuroticism: A trait-state approach. *Psychological Science, 24*(9), 1780–1790.

Lachman, S. J. (1996). Processes in perception: Psychological transformations of highly structured stimulus material. *Perceptual and Motor Skills, 83*, 411–418.

Lachter, J., Forster, K. I., & Ruthruff, E. (2004). Forty-five years after Broadbent (1958): Still no identification without attention. *Psychological Review, 111*, 880–913.

Lader, M. H. (2002). Managing dependence and withdrawal with newer hypnotic medications in the treatment of insomnia. *Journal of Clinical Psychiatry, 4*(Suppl. 1), 33–37.

LaFee, S. (2009, November 30). H. M. recollected. *Sign On San Diego*. Retrieved December 3, 2009, from http://www.signonsandiego.com/news/2009/nov/30/hm-recollected-famous-amnesic-launches-bold-new-br/.

Lagopoulos, J., Xu, J., Rasmussen, I., Vik, A., Malhi, G., Eliassen, C. F., et al. (2009). Increased theta and alpha EEG activity during nondirective meditation. *The Journal of Alternative and Complementary Medicine, 15*(11), 1187–1192.

Lago-Rodriguez, A., Lopez-Alonso, V., & Fernandez-del-Olmo, M. (2013). Mirror neuron system and observational learning: Behavioral and neurophysiological evidence. *Behavior and Brain Research, 248*, 104–113.

Laird, J. D., & Lacasse, K. (2014). Bodily influences on emotional feelings: Accumulating evidence and extensions of William James's theory of emotion. *Emotion Review, 6*(1), 27– 34. doi:10.1177/1754073913494899.

Lakein, A. (1996). *How to get control of your time and your life*. New York, NY: New American Library.

Lakey, B. (2013). Perceived social support and happiness: The role of personality and relational processes. In S. A. David, I. Boniwell, & A. Conley Ayers (Eds.), *The Oxford handbook of happiness*. New York, NY: Oxford University Press.

Lakey, B., & Cronin, A. (2008). Low social support and major depression: Research, theory and methodological issues. In K. S. Dobson & D. A. Dozois (Eds.), *Risk factors in depression* (pp. 385–408). San Diego, CA: Academic Press.

Lakey, B., & Orehek, E. (2011). Relational regulation theory: A new approach to explain the link between perceived social support and mental health. *Psychological Review, 118*(3), 482–495.

Lalonde, C. E. (2005). *Creating an index of healthy Aboriginal communities. Developing a healthy communities index: A collection of papers* (pp. 21–27). Report prepared for the Canadian Population Health Initiative, Canadian Institute for Health Information.

Lalonde, C. E. (2006). Identity formation and cultural resilience in Aboriginal communities. In Flynn, R. J., Dudding, P., & Barber, J. (Eds.), *Promoting resilience in child welfare* (pp. 52–71). Ottawa: University of Ottawa Press.

Lalonde, C. E. (2016). Some days a printer cable makes me cry: Reflections on suicide—First Nations communities and beyond. *Visions: BC's Mental Health and Addictions Journal, 11*, 23–15.

Lalonde, R. N., & Gardner, R. C. (1984). Investigating a causal model of second language acquisition: Where does personality fit in? *Canadian Journal of Behavioural Science, 16*, 224–237.

Lalonde, R. N., & Gardner, R. C. (1989). An intergroup perspective on stereotype organization and processing. *British Journal of Social Psychology, 28*, 289–303.

Lalonde, R. N., Jones, J. M., & Stroink, M. L. (2008). Racial identity, racial attitudes, and race socialization among black Canadian parents. *Canadian Journal of Behavioural Science, 40*, 129–139.

Lamb, H. R. (1998). Deinstitutionalization at the beginning of the new millenium. *Harvard Review of Psychiatry, 6*, 1–10.

Lamb, M. E., & Lewis, C. (2011). The role of parent–child relationships in child development. In M. H. Bornstein & M. E. Lamb (Eds.), *Developmental science: An advanced textbook* (pp. 469–518). New York, NY: Psychology Press.

Lamb, M. E., Ketterlinus, R. D., & Fracasso, M. P. (1992). Parent–child relationships. In M. H. Bornstein & M. E. Lamb (Eds.), *Developmental psychology: An advanced textbook* (3rd ed.). Hillsdale, NJ: Erlbaum.

Lambert, C. D., Jr., & Lambert, V. A. (1999). Psychological hardiness: State of the science. *Holistic Nursing Practitioners, 1*(3), 11–19.

Lambert, M. J. (2011). Psychotherapy research and its achievements. In J. C. Norcross, G. R. Vandenbos, & D. K. Freedheim (Eds.), *History of psychotherapy: Continuity and change* (2nd ed.). Washington, DC: American Psychological Association.

Lambert, M. J. (2013). The efficacy and effectiveness of psychotherapy. In M. J. Lambert (Ed.). *Bergin and Garfield's handbook of psychotherapy and behavior change* (6th ed.). New York, NY: Wiley.

Lambert, M. J., & Ogles, B. M. (2004). The efficacy and effectiveness of psychotherapy. In M. J. Lambert (Ed.), *Bergin and Garfield's handbook of psychotherapy and behavior change*. New York, NY: Wiley.

Lambert, M. J., & Ogles, B. M. (2014). Common factors: Post hoc explanation or empirically based therapy approach? *Psychotherapy, 51*, 500–504. doi:10.1037/a0036580.

Lambert, M. J., Bergin, A. E., & Garfield, S. L. (2004). Introduction and historical overview. In M. J. Lambert (Ed.), *Bergin and Garfield's handbook of psychotherapy and behavior change*. New York, NY: Wiley.

Lambert, M. J., Hansen, N. B., & Finch, A. E. (2001). Patient-focused research: Using patient outcome data to enhance treatment effects. *Journal of Consulting and Clinical Psychology, 69*, 159–172.

Lambert, W. E. (1990). Persistent issues in bilingualism. In B. Harley, P. Allen, J. Cummins, & M. Swain (Eds.), *The development of second language proficiency*. Cambridge, UK: Cambridge University Press.

Lampe, A., Soellner, W., Krismer, M., Rumpold, G., Kantner-Rumplmair, W., Ogon, M., & Rathner, G. (1998). The impact of stressful life events on exacerbation of chronic low-back pain. *Journal of Psychosomatic Research, 44*, 555–563.

Lampinen, J. M., Neuschatz, J. S., & Payne, D. G. (1999). Source attributions and false memories: A test of the demand characteristics account. *Psychonomic Bulletin & Review, 6*, 130–135.

Lampl, M., & Johnson, M. L. (2011). Infant growth in length follows prolonged sleep and increased naps. *Sleep: Journal of Sleep and Sleep Disorders Research, 34*, 641–650.

Lampl, M., Veldhuis, J. D., & Johnson, M. L. (1992). Saltation and stasis: A model of human growth. *Science, 258*, 801–803.

Landabaso, M. A., Iraurgi, I., Sanz, J., Calle, R., Ruiz de Apodaka, J., Jimenez-Lerma, J. M., & Gutierrez-Fraile, M. (1999). Naltrexone in the treatment of alcoholism. Two-year follow up results. *European Journal of Psychiatry, 13*, 97–105.

Landau, S. M., Marks, S. M., Mormino, E. C., Rabinovici, G. D., Oh, H., O'Neil, J. P., . . . Jagust, W. J. (2012). Association of lifetime cognitive engagement and low 13-amyloid deposition. *Archive of Neurology, 69*, 623–629. doi:10.1001/archneurol.2011.2748.

Lane, A., Luminet, O., Rimé, B., Gross, J. J., de Timary, P., & Mikolajczak, M. (2013). Oxytocin increases willingness to socially share one's emotions. *International Journal of Psychology, 48*, 676–681. doi:10.1080/00207594.2012.677540.

Laney, C., & Loftus, E. F. (2005). Traumatic memories are not necessarily accurate memories. *Canadian Journal of Psychiatry, 50*, 823–828.

Lange, C. (1885). One leuds beveegelser. In K. Dunlap (Ed.), *The emotions*. Baltimore, MD: Williams & Wilkins.

Langlois, J. H., Kalakanis, L., Rubenstein, A. J., Larson, A., Hallam, M., & Smoot, M. (2000). Maxims or myths of beauty? A meta-analytic and theoretical review. *Psychological Bulletin, 126*, 390–423.

Lango, A. H., Estrada, K., Lettre, G., Berndt, S. I., Weedon, M. N., & Rivadeneira, F., et al. (2010). Hundreds of variants clustered in genomic loci and biological pathways affect human height. *Nature, 467*, 832–838.

LaPiere, R. T. (1934). Attitude and actions. *Social Forces, 13*, 230–237.

Large, M., Sharma, S., Compton, M. T., Slade, T., & Nielssen, O. (2011). Cannabis use and earlier onset of psychosis: A systematic meta-analysis. *Archives of General Psychiatry, 68*, 555–561. doi:10.1001/archgenpsychia try.201.5.

Larsen, J. T., Berntson, G. G., Poehlmann, K. M., Ito, T. A., & Cacioppo, J. T. (2008). The psychophysiology of emotion. In M. Lewis, J. M. Haviland-Jones, & L. F. Barrett (Eds.), *Handbook of emotions* (3rd ed., pp. 180–195). New York, NY: Guilford Press.

Larson, R., & Wilson, S. (2004). Adolescence across place and time: Globalization and the changing pathways to adulthood. In R. M. Lerner & L. Steinberg (Eds.), *Handbook of adolescent psychology*. New York, NY: Wiley.

Larson, R., Richards, M., Moneta, G., Holmbeck, G., & Duckett, E. (1996). Changes in adolescents' daily interactions with their families from ages 10 to 18: Disengagement and transformation. *Developmental Psychology, 32*, 744–754.

Laska, K. M., Gurman, A. S., & Wampold, B. E. (2014). Expanding the lens of evidence-based practice in psychotherapy: A common factors perspective. *Psychotherapy, 51*, 467–481. doi:10.1037/a0034332.

Laska, M., Seibt, A., & Weber, A. (2000). "Microsmatic" primates revisited: Olfactory sensitivity in the squirrel monkey. *Chemical Senses, 25*, 47–53.

Lassonde, M., & Quimet, C. (2010). The split-brain. *Cognitive Science, 1*, 191–201.

Latané, B. (1981). The psychology of social impact. *American Psychologist, 36*, 343–356.

Latané, B., & Nida, S. A. (1981). Ten years of research on group size and helping. *Psychological Bulletin, 89*, 308–324.

Latané, B., Williams, K., & Harkins, S. (1979). Many hands make light the work: The causes and consequences of social loafing. *Journal of Personality and Social Psychology, 37*, 822–832.

Latham, T. (2011). Dogs, man's best therapist. *Psychology Today*. Retrieved from http://www.psychologytoday.com/blog/therapy-matters/201104/dogs-man-s-best-therapist.

Lattal, K. A. (1992). B. F. Skinner and psychology [Introduction to the Special Issue]. *American Psychologist, 27*, 1269–1272.

Lattin, D. (2010). *The Harvard psychedelic club*. New York, NY: Harper Collins Publishers.

Lau, J. Y., Lester, K. J., Hodgson, K., & Eley, T. C. (2014). The genetics of mood disorders. In I. H. Gotlib & C. L. Hammen (Eds.), *Handbook of depression* (3rd ed.). New York, NY: Guilford Press.

Laughlin, H. (1967). *The neuroses*. Washington, DC: Butterworth.

Laughlin, H. (1979). *The ego and its defenses*. New York, NY: Jason Aronson.

Laumann, E. O., Gagnon, J. H., Michael, R. T., & Michaels, S. (1994). *The social organization of sexuality: Sexual practices in the United States*. Chicago, IL: University of Chicago Press.

Laursen, B., Coy, K. C., & Collins, W. A. (1998). Reconsidering changes in parent–child conflict across adolescence: A meta-analysis. *Child Development, 69*, 817–832.

Lavine, H., Sweeney, D., & Wagner, S. H. (1999). Depicting women as sex objects in television advertising: Effects on body dissatisfaction. *Personality and Social Psychology Bulletin, 25*, 1049–1058.

Lawrie, S. M., & Pantelis, C. (2011). Structural brain imaging in schizophrenia and related populations. In C. R. Weinberger & P. Harrison (Eds.), *Schizophrenia* (3rd ed.). Malden, MA: Wiley-Blackwell.

Lazarus, A. A. (1989). Multimodal therapy. In R. J. Corsini & D. Wedding (Eds.), *Current psychotherapies*. Itasca, IL: F. E. Peacock.

Lazarus, A. A. (1992). Multimodal therapy: Technical eclecticism with minimal integration. In J. C. Norcross & M. R. Goldfried (Eds.), *Handbook of psychotherapy integration*. New York, NY: Basic Books.

Lazarus, A. A. (1995). Different types of eclecticism and integration: Let's be aware of the dangers. *Journal of Psychotherapy Integration, 5*, 27–39.

Lazarus, R. S. (1993). Why we should think of stress as a subset of emotion. In L. Goldberger & S. Breznitz (Eds.), *Handbook of stress: Theoretical and clinical aspects* (2nd ed.). New York, NY: Free Press.

Lazarus, R. S. (1995). Vexing research problems inherent in cognitive-mediational theories of emotion—and some solutions. *Psychological Inquiry, 6*, 183–196.

Lazarus, R. S., & Folkman, S. (1984). *Stress, appraisal, and coping*. New York, NY: Springer.

Leaper, C. (2013). Gender development during childhood. In P. D. Zelazo (Ed.), *Oxford handbook of developmental psychology: Vol. 2. Self and other*. New York, NY: Oxford University Press. doi:10.1093/oxfordhb/9789199958474.013.0014.

Leary, D. E. (2003). A profound and radical change: How William James inspired the reshaping of American psychology. In R. J. Sternberg (Ed.), *The anatomy of impact: What makes the great works of psychology great* (pp. 19–42). Washington, DC: American Psychological Association.

Leary, T. (1957). *Interpersonal diagnosis of personality*. New York, NY: Ronald Press.

Lebel, C., et al. (2010). Brain microstructure is related to math ability in children with fetal alcohol spectrum disorder. *Alcoholism: Clinical and Experimental Research, 34*, 354–363.

Leber, B. (2017). *Police-reported hate crimes in Canada, 2015*. Juristat, Statistics Canada. Retrieved from https://www.statcan.gc.ca/pub/85-002-x/2017001/article/14832-eng.htm.

Lebow, J. L., & Stroud, C. B. (2013). Family therapy. In G. Stricker & T. A. Widiger (Eds.), *Handbook of psychology: Vol. 8. Clinical psychology* (2nd ed.). New York, NY: Wiley.

Lechner, S. C., Tennen, H., & Afileck, G. (2009). Benefit-finding and growth. In S. J. Lopez & C. R. Snyder (Eds.), *Oxford handbook of positive psychology* (2nd ed.). New York, NY: Oxford University Press.

Lederman, S. J., Klatzky, R. L., Abramowicz, A., Salsman, K., Kitada, R., & Hamilton, C. (2007). Haptic recognition of static and dynamic expressions of emotions in the live face. *Psychological Science, 18*, 158–164.

LeDoux, J. E. (1994). Emotion, memory and the brain. *Scientific American, 270*, 50–57.

LeDoux, J. E. (1995). Emotion: Clues from the brain. *Annual Review of Psychology, 46*, 209–235.

LeDoux, J. E. (1996). *The emotional brain.* New York, NY: Simon & Schuster.

LeDoux, J. E. (2000). Emotion circuits in the brain. *Annual Review of Neuroscience, 23*, 155–184.

LeDoux, J. E., & Damasio, A. R. (2013). Emotions and feelings. In E. R. Kandel, J. H. Schwartz, T. M. Jessell, S. A. Siegelbaum, & A. J. Hudspeth (Eds.), *Principles of neural science* (5th ed., pp. 1079–1093). New York, NY: McGraw-Hill.

Ledoux, S. F. (2012). Behaviorism at 100. *American Scientist, 100*, 60–65.

Lee, J. D., McNeely, J., & Gourevitch, M. N. (2011). Medical complications of drug use/dependence. In P. Ruiz, & E. C. Strain (Eds.), *Lowinson and Ruiz's substance abuse: A comprehensive textbook* (5th ed.). Philadelphia, PA: Wolters Kluwer Lippincott Williams & Wilkins.

Lee, J. E., Lee, C. H., Lee, S. J., Ryu, Y., Lee, W. H., Yoon, I. Y., . . . Kim, J. W. (2013). Mortality of patients with obstructive sleep apnea in Korea. *Journal of Clinical Sleep Medicine, 9*, 997–1002.

Lee, J., Lei, A., & Sue, S. (2001). The current state of mental health research of Asian Americans. *Journal of Human Behavior in the Social Environment. 3*, 159–178.

Lee, R. M., & Ramirez, M. (2000). The history, current status, and future of multicultural psychotherapy. In I. Cuellar & F. A. Paniagua (Eds.), *Handbook of multicultural mental health: Assessment and treatment of diverse populations.* San Diego, CA: Academic Press.

Lee, S. J., Grogan-Kaylor, A., & Berger, L. M. (2014). Parental spanking of 1-year old children and subsequent child protective services involvement. *Child Abuse & Neglect, 38*, 875–883. doi:10.1016/j.chiabu.2014.01.018.

Lee, Y., & Styne, D. (2013). Influences on the onset and tempo of puberty in human beings and implications for adolescent psychological development. *Hormones and Behavior, 64*, 250–261. doi:10.1016/j.yhbeh.2013.03.014.

Lee-Chiong, T., & Sateia, M. (2006). Pharmacologic therapy of insomnia. In T. Lee-Chiong (Ed.), *Sleep: A comprehensive handbook.* Hoboken, NJ: Wiley-Liss.

Lee-Flynn, S., Pomaki, G., DeLongis, A., Biesanz, J., & Puterman, E. (2011, February). The role of self-concept clarity in the stress process. *Personality & Social Psychology Bulletin, 37*, 255–268.

Leeper, R. W. (1935). A study of a neglected portion of the field of learning: The development of sensory organization. *Journal of Genetic Psychology, 46*, 41–75.

Lefcourt, H. M. (2001). The humor solution. In C. R. Snyder (Ed.), *Coping with stress: Effective people and processes* (pp. 68–92). New York, NY: Oxford University Press.

Lefcourt, H. M. (2005). Humor. In C. R. Snyder & S. J. Lopez (Eds.), *Handbook of positive psychology.* New York, NY: Oxford University Press.

Lefcourt, H. M., Davidson, K., Shepherd, R., Phillips, M., Prkachin, K., & Mills, D. (1995). Perspective-taking humor: Accounting for stress moderation. *Journal of Social and Clinical Psychology, 14*, 373–391.

Leff, J. (2006). Whose life is it anyway? Quality of life for long-stay patients discharged from psychiatric hospitals. In H. Katschnig, H. Freeman, & N. Sartorius (Eds.), *Quality of life in mental disorders.* New York, NY: Wiley.

Leff, J. P., & Vaughn, C. E. (1981). The role of maintenance therapy and relatives' expressed emotion in relapse of schizophrenia: A two-year follow-up. *The British Journal of Psychiatry, 139*, 102–104. doi:org/10.1192/bjp.139.2.102.

Leff, J. P., & Vaughn, C. E. (1985). *Expressed emotion in families.* New York, NY: Guilford Press.

Legault, E., & Laurence, J.-R. (2007). Recovered memories of childhood sexual abuse: Social worker, psychologist, and psychiatrist reports of beliefs, practices, and cases. *Australian Journal of Clinical & Experimental Hypnosis, 35*, 111–133.

Legerstee, M. (2005). *Infants' sense of people: Precursors to a theory of mind.* Cambridge, UK: Cambridge University Press.

Legerstee, M., Haley. D., & Bornstein, M. (Eds.). (2013). *The developing infant mind: Integrating biology and experience.* New York, NY: Guilford Press.

Lehman, A. J., Pratt, D., DeLongis, A., Collins, J. B., Shojania, K., Koehler, B., Offer, R., & Esdaile, J. M. (2011). Do spouses know how much fatigue, pain, and physical limitation their partners with rheumatoid arthritis experience? Implications for social support. *Arthritis Care & Research, 1*, 120–127.

Lehman, D. R., Chiu, C., & Schaller, M. (2004). Psychology and culture. *Annual Review of Psychology, 55*, 689–714.

Lehman, M, & Malmberg, K. J. (2013). A buffer model of encoding and temporal correlations in retrieval. *Psychological Review, 120*(1), 155–189.

Lehrer, J. (2009). Think better: Tips from a savant. *Scientific American*, April/May/June, 2009, 61–63.

Leibovic, K. N. (1990). Vertebrate photoreceptors. In K. N. Leibovic (Ed.), *Science of vision.* New York, NY: Springer-Verlag.

Leighton, J. P., & Sternberg, R. J. (2003). Reasoning and problem solving. In A. F. Healy & R. W. Proctor (Eds.), *Handbook of psychology (Vol. 4): Experimental psychology.* New York, NY: Wiley.

Leiter, M. P., & Maslach, C. (2001). Burnout and health. In A. Baum, T. A. Revenson, & J. E. Singer (Eds.), *Handbook of health psychology* (pp. 415–426). Mahwah, NJ: Erlbaum.

Lenneberg, E. H. (1967). *Biological foundations of language.* New York, NY: Wiley.

Leon, D. A., Lawlor, D. A., Clark, H. H., Batty, G. D., & Macintyre, S. S. (2009). The association of childhood intelligence with mortality risk from adolescence to middle age: Findings from the Aberdeen Children of the 1950s cohort study. *Intelligence, 37*(6), 520–528.

Lepine, R., Barrouillet, P., & Camos, V. (2005). What makes working memory spans so predictive of high-level cognition? *Psychonomic Bulletin & Review, 12*(1), 165–170.

Lerman, H. (1986). *A mote in Freud's eye: From psychoanalysis to the psychology of women.* New York, NY: Springer.

Lerner, M. J., & Goldberg, J. H. (1999). When do decent people blame victims? The differing effects of the explicit/rational and implicit/experiential cognitive systems. In S. Chaiken & Y. Trope (Eds.), *Dual-process theories in social psychology.* New York, NY: Guilford.

Lesher, G. W. (1995). Illusory contours: Toward a neurally based perceptual theory. *Psychonomic Bulletin & Review, 2*, 279–321.

Letra, L., Santana, I., & Seiça, R. (2014). Obesity as a risk factor for Alzheimer's disease: The role of adipocytokines. *Metabolic Brain Disease, 29*, 563–568. doi:10.1007/s11011-014-9501-z.

Leuner, B., & Gould, E. (2010). Structural plasticity and hippocampal function. *Annual Review of Psychology, 61*, 111–140.

Leuner, B., Gould, E., & Shors, T. J. (2006). Is there a link between adult neurogenesis and learning? *Hippocampus, 16*, 216–224.

Leung, W. (2016). The six most common patient faux pas, according to doctors. *The Globe and Mail.* Thursday, July 21, 2016. Retrieved from https://beta.theglobeandmail.com/life/health-and-fitness/health/how-to-be-a-better-patient-according-to-doctors-health/article31055879/?ref=http://www.theglobeandmail.com.

Leventhal, H., & Tomarken, A. J. (1986). Emotion: Today's problems. *Annual Review of Psychology, 37*, 565–610.

Levin, D., & Baker, L. (2015). Change blindness and inattentional blindness. In J. M. Fawcett, E. F. Risko, & A. Kingstone (Eds.), *The handbook of attention* (199–231). Boston, MA: MIT Press.

Levine, J. M. (1999). Solomon Asch's legacy for group research. *Personality and Social Psychology Review, 3*, 358–364.

Levine, J. M., & Moreland, R. L. (1998). Small groups. In D. T. Gilbert, S. T. Fiske, & G. Lindzey (Eds.), *The handbook of social psychology.* New York, NY: McGraw-Hill.

Levinson, R. (2014). The autonomic nervous system and emotion. *Emotion Review, 6*, 100–112.

Levinthal, C. F. (2014). *Drugs, behavior, and modern society* (8th ed.). Boston, MA: Pearson.

Levis, D. J. (1989). The case for a return to a two-factor theory of avoidance: The failure of non-fear interpretations. In S. B. Klein & R. R. Bowrer (Eds.), *Contemporary learning theories: Pavlovian conditioning and the status of traditional learning theory.* Hillsdale NJ: Erlbaum.

Levitt, J. B. (2010). Receptive fields. In E. B. Goldstein (Ed.), *Encyclopedia of perception.* Thousand Oaks, CA: Sage.

Levordashka, A., & Utz, S. (2017). Spontaneous trait inferences on social media. *Social Psychology and Personality Science, 8*, 93–101.

Levy, G. D., Taylor, M. G., & Gelman, S. A. (1995). Traditional and evaluative aspects of flexibility in gender roles, social conventions, moral rules, and physical laws. *Child Development, 66*, 515–531.

Levy, J., Trevarthen, C., & Sperry, R. W. (1972). Perception of bilateral chimeric figures following hemispheric disconnection. *Brain, 95*, 61–78.

Levy, K. N. (2012). Subtypes, dimensions, levels, and mental states in narcissism and narcissistic personality disorder. *Journal of Clinical Psychology, 68*, 886–897. doi:10.1002/jclp.21893.

Lewin, K. (1935). *A dynamic theory of personality.* New York, NY: McGraw-Hill.

Lewis, A. (Ed.). (2008). *The Cambridge handbook of psychology and economic behaviour.* Cambridge, UK: Cambridge University Press.

Lewis, M. (2016). *The undoing project.* New York, NY: W.W. Norton.

Lewis, S., Escalona, P. R., & Keith, S. J. (2009). Phenomenology of schizophrenia. In B. J. Sadock, V. A. Sadock, & P. Ruiz (Eds.), *Kaplan & Sadock's comprehensive textbook of psychiatry* (9th ed., pp. 1433–1450). Philadelphia, PA: Lippincott, Williams & Wilkins.

Lewis-Fernandez, R., Guarnaccia, P. J., & Ruiz, P. (2009). Culture-bound syndromes. In B. J. Sadock, V. A. Sadock, & P. Ruiz (Eds.), *Kaplan & Sadock's comprehensive textbook of psychiatry* (9th ed.). Philadelphia, PA: Lippincott, Williams & Wilkins.

Lewy, A. J. (1993). Seasonal mood disorders. In D. L. Dunner (Ed.), *Current psychiatric therapy* (pp. 212–234). Philadelphia, PA: Saunders Publishing Co.

Li, C., & Hoffstein, V. (2011). Snoring. In M. H. Kryger, T. Roth, & W. C. Dement (Eds.), *Principles and practice of sleep medicine* (5th ed.). Saint Louis, MO: Elsevier Saunders.

Li, H. Z., & Browne, A. J. (2000). Defining mental illness and accessing mental health services: Perspectives of Asian Canadians. *Canadian Journal of Community Mental Health, 19*, 143–154.

Li, N. P., Yong, J. C., Tov, W., Sng, O., Fletcher, G. O., Valentine, K. A., . . . Balliet, D. (2013). Mate preferences do predict attraction and choices in the early stages of mate selection. *Journal of Personality and Social Psychology, 105*, 757–776. doi:10.1037/a0033777.

Libby, L. K. (2008). A neural signature of the current self. *Social Cognitive and Affective Neuroscience, 3*, 192–194.

Libby, P., Tabas, I., Fredman, G., & Fisher, E. A. (2014). Inflammation and its resolution as determinants of acute coronary syndromes. *Circulation Research, 114*, 1867–1879. doi:10.1161/CIRCRESAHA.114.302699.

Liberal Party of Canada. (2017). Marijuana. Retrieved from https://www.liberal.ca/realchange/marijuana/.

Library and Archives Canada. (2001). Statement on the introduction of the Official Languages Bill, October 17, 1968. Retrieved May 11, 2005, from http://www.collectionscanada.ca/primeministers/h4-4066-e.html.

Lichstein, K. L., Taylor, D. J., McCrae, C. S., & Ruiter, M. E. (2011). Insomnia: Epidemiology and risk factors. In M. H. Kryger, T. Roth, & W. C. Dement (Eds.), *Principles and practice of sleep medicine* (5th ed.). Saint Louis, MO: Elsevier Saunders.

Lichten, W., & Simon, E. W. (2007). Defining mental retardation: A matter of life or death. *Intellectual and Developmental Disabilities, 45,* 335–346.

Lichtner, V., et al. (2016). The assessment an management of pain in patients with dementia in hospital settings: A multi-case exploratory study from a decision making perspective. *BMC Health Services Research, 16,* 427.

Liddle, P. F. (2009). Descriptive clinical features of schizophrenia. In M. C. Gelder, N. C. Andreasen, J. J. López-Ibor, Jr., & J. R. Geddes (Eds.). *New Oxford textbook of psychiatry* (2nd ed., Vol. 1). New York, NY: Oxford University Press.

Liden, R. C., Wayne, S. J., Jaworski, R. A., & Bennett, N. (2004). Social loafing: A field investigation. *Journal of Management, 30,* 285–304.

Lieberman, J. A., Stoup, T. S., McEvoy, J. P., Swartz, M. S., Rosenheck, R. A., & Perkins, D. O., et al. (2005). Effectiveness of antipsychotic drugs in patients with chronic schizophrenia. *New England Journal of Medicine, 353,* 1209–1223.

Lieberman, M. D. (2007). Social cognitive neuroscience: A review of core processes. *Annual Review of Psychology, 58,* 259–289.

Lieberman, M. D. (2010). Social cognitive neuroscience. In S. Fiske, D. T. Gilbert, & G. Lindzey (Eds.), *Handbook of social psychology* (5th ed., pp. 143–193). New York, NY: Wiley.

Lieberman, M. D., Ochsner, K. N., Gilbert, D. T., & Schacter, D. (2001). Do amnesics exhibit cognitive dissonance reduction? The role of explicit memory and attention in attitude change. *Psychological Science, 12,* 135–140.

Liebert, R. M., & Sprafkin, J. (1988). *The early window: Effects of television on children and youth.* Oxford, England: Pergamon Press.

Liefbroer, A. C., & Dourleijn, E. (2006). Unmarried cohabitation and union stability: Testing the role of diffusion using data from 16 European countries. *Demography, 43,* 203–221.

Lien, M.-C., Ruthruff, E., & Johnston, J. C. (2006). Attentional limitations in doing two tasks at once. *Current Directions in Psychological Science, 15,* 89–93.

Lilienfeld, S., & Arkowitz, H. (2011, September/October). Can People Have Multiple Personalities? *Scientific American Mind,* 64–65.

Lilienfeld, S. O. (2007). Cognitive neuroscience and depression: Legitimate versus illegitimate reductionism and five challenges. *Cognitive Therapy and Research, 31,* 263–272.

Lilienfeld, S. O. (2007). Psychological treatments that cause harm. *Perspectives on Psychological Science, 2,* 53–70.

Lilienfeld, S. O., Ammirati, R., & Landfield, K. (2009). Giving debiasing away: Can psychological research on correcting cognitive errors promote human welfare? *Perspectives on Psychological Science, 4*(4), 390–398. doi:10.1111/j.1745-6924.2009.01144.x.

Lilienfeld, S. O., & Arkowitz, H. (2009, February/March). Lunacy and the full moon: Does a full moon really trigger strange behavior? *Scientific American Mind,* 64–65.

Lilienfeld, S. O., & Landfield, K. (2008). Issues in diagnosis: Categorical vs. dimensional. In W. E. Craighead, D. J. Miklowitz, & L. W. Craighead (Eds.), *Psychopathology: History, diagnosis, and empirical foundations.* New York, NY: Wiley.

Lilienfeld, S. O., & Lynn, S. J. (2003). Dissociative identity disorder: Multiple personalities, multiple controversies. In S. O. Lilienfeld, S. J. Lynn, & J. M. Lohr (Eds.), *Science and pseudoscience in clinical psychology.* New York, NY: Guilford Press.

Lilienfeld, S. O., Lynn, S. J., Kirsch, I., Chaves, J. F., Sarbin, T. R., Ganaway, G. K., & Powell, R. A. (1999). Dissociative identity disorder and the sociocognitive

model: Recalling the lessons of the past. *Psychological Bulletin, 125,* 507–523.

Lilienfeld, S. O., Lynn, S. J., Ruscio, J., & Beyerstein, B. L. (2010). *50 Great myths of popular psychology: Shattering widespread misconceptions about human behavior.* Malden, MA: Wiley-Blackwell.

Lilienfeld, S. O., Ritschel, L. A., Lynn, S. J., Cautin, R. L., & Latzman, R. D. (2014). Why ineffective psychotherapies appear to work: A taxonomy of causes of spurious therapeutic effectiveness. *Perspectives on Psychological Science, 9,* 355–387. doi:10.1177/1745691614535216.

Lilienfeld, S. O., Wood, J. M., & Garb, H. N. (2000). The scientific status of projective tests. *Psychological Science in the Public Interest, 1*(2), 27–66.

Lillard, A. (2005). *Montessori: The science behind the genius.* Oxford, UK: Oxford University Press.

Lillard, A., & Else-Quest, N. (2006). The early years: Evalating Montessori education. *Science, 313,* 1893–1894.

Lim, M. M., & Young, L. J. (2006). Neuropepridergic regulation of affiliative behavior and social bonding in animals. *Hormones and Behavior, 50*(4), 506–517.

Lin, H., Katsovich, L., Ghebremichael, M., Findley, D. B., Grantz, H., Lombroso, P. J., . . . Leckman, J. F. (2007). Psychosocial stress predicts future symptom severities in children and adolescents with Tourette syndrome and/or obsessive-compulsive disorder. *Journal of Child Psychology and Psychiatry, 48*(2), 157–166. doi:10.1111/j.1469-7610.2006.01687.x.

Lindau, S., & Gavrilova, N. (2010). Sex, health, and years of sexually active life gained due to good health: Evidence from two U.S. population based cross sectional surveys of ageing. *British Medical Journal, 340,* c810.

Lindgren, H. C. (1969). *The psychology of college success: A dynamic approach.* New York, NY: Wiley.

Lindquist, K. A., Wager, T. D., Kober, H., Bliss-Moreau, E., & Barrett, L. F. (2012). The brain basis of emotion: A meta-analytic review. *Behavioral and Brain Sciences, 35*(3), 121–143. doi:10.1017/S0140525X11000446.

Lindsay, D. S., & Read, J. D. (1994). Psychotherapy and memories of childhood sexual abuse: A cognitive perspective. *Applied Cognitive Psychology, 8,* 281–338.

Lindsay, P. H., & Norman, D. A. (1977). *Human information processing.* New York, NY: Academic Press.

Lindsay, R. C. L., Ross, D. F., Read, J. D., & Toglia, M. (Eds.). (2007). *Handbook of eyewitness psychology: Memory for people* (Vol. 2). Philadelphia, PA: Erlbaum (Taylor & Francis Group, LLC).

Lindsay, S. D., Allen, B. P., Chan, J. C. K., & Dahl, L. C. (2004). Eyewitness suggestibility and source similarity: Intrusions of details from one event into memory reports of another event. *Journal of Memory & Language, 50*(1), 96–111.

Lippa, R. A. (1994). *Introduction to social psychology.* Pacific Grove, CA: Brooks/Cole.

Lippa, R. A. (2005). *Gender, nature, and nurture.* Mahwah, NJ: Erlbaum.

Lippa, R. A., Martin, L. R., & Friedman, H. S. (2000). Gender-related individual differences and mortality in the Terman longitudinal study: Is masculinity hazardous to your health? *Personality and Social Psychology Bulletin, 26,* 1560–1570.

Lipton, J. S., & Spelke, E. S. (2004). Discrimination of large and small numerosities by human infants. *Infancy, 5,* 271–290.

Lisberger, S. G., & Thach, W. T. (2013). The cerebellum. In E. R. Kandel, J. H. Schwartz, T. M. Jessell, S. A. Siegelbaum, & A. J. Hudspeth (Eds.), *Principles of neural science* (5th ed.). New York, NY: McGraw-Hill.

Lissek, S., Rabin, S., Heller, R. E., Lukenbaugh, D., Geraci, M., Pine, D. S., & Grillon, C. (2010). Overgeneralization of conditioned fear as a pathogenic marker of panic disorder. *American Journal of Psychiatry, 167*(1), 47–55.

Little, A. C., Jones, B. C., & Burriss, R. P. (2007). Preferences for masculinity in male bodies change across the menstrual cycle. *Hormones and Behavior, 51,* 633–639.

Livingstone, A. (2013). Thank them for what they have done to us all. *Toronto Star,* Thursday July 18, 2013, A1.

Lizarraga, M. L. S., & Ganuza, J. M. G. (2003). Improvement of mental rotation in girls and boys. *Sex Roles, 40,* 277–286.

Lockhart, R. S. (1992). Measurement of memory. In L. R. Squire (Ed.), *Encyclopedia of learning and memory.* New York, NY: Macmillan.

Lockhart, R. S. (2000). Methods of memory research. In E. Tulving & F. I. M. Craik (Eds.), *The Oxford handbook of memory* (pp. 45–58). New York, NY: Oxford University Press.

Lockhart, R. S., & Craik, F. I. (1990). Levels of processing: A retrospective commentary on a framework for memory research. *Canadian Journal of Psychology, 44*(1), 87–112.

Loehlin, J. C. (1992). *Genes and environment in personality development.* Newbury Park, CA: Sage.

Loftus, E. F. (1979). *Eyewitness testimony.* Cambridge, MA: Harvard University Press.

Loftus, E. F. (1992). When a lie becomes memory's truth: Memory distortion after exposure to misinformation. *Current Directions in Psychological Science, 1,* 121–123.

Loftus, E. F. (1993a). Psychologist in the eyewitness world. *American Psychologist, 48,* 550–552.

Loftus, E. F. (1994). The repressed memory controversy. *American Psychologist, 49,* 443–445.

Loftus, E. F. (1997, September). Creating false memories. *Scientific American,* 71–75.

Loftus, E. F. (1998). Remembering dangerously. In R. A. Baker (Ed.), *Child sexual abuse and false memory syndrome.* Amherst, NY: Prometheus Books.

Loftus, E. F. (2000). Remembering what never happened. In E. Tulving (Ed.), *Memory, consciousness, and the brain: The Tallinn conference* (pp. 106–118). Philadelphia, PA: Psychology Press.

Loftus, E. F. (2003). Make believe memories. *American Psychologist, 58,* 864–873.

Loftus, E. F. (2005). Memories of things unseen. *Current Directions in Psychology, 13,* 145–147.

Loftus, E. F. (2005). Planting misinformation in the human mind: A 30-year investigation of the malleability of memory. *Learning & Memory, 12,* 361–366.

Loftus, E. F. (2013). 25 Years of eyewitness science . . . finally pays off. *Perspectives on Psychological Science, 8,* 556–557. doi:10.1177/1745691613500995.

Loftus, E. F. (2013). Eyewitness testimony in the Lockerbie bombing case. *Memory, 21,* 584–590.

Loftus, E. F., & Cahill, L. (2007). Memory distortion: From misinformation to rich false memory. In J. S. Nairne (Ed.), *The foundations of remembering: Essays in honor of Henry L. Roediger III.* New York, NY: Psychology Press.

Loftus, E. F., & Davis, D. (2006). Recovered memories. *Annual Review of Clinical Psychology, 2,* 469–498.

Loftus, E. F., & Palmer, J. C. (1974). Reconstruction of automobile destruction: An example of the interaction between language and memory. *Journal of Verbal Learning and Verbal Behavior, 13,* 585–589.

Loftus, E. F., Garry, M., & Feldman, J. (1998). Forgetting sexual trauma: What does it mean when 38% forget? In R. A. Baker (Ed.), *Child sexual abuse and false memory syndrome.* Amherst, NY: Prometheus Books.

Logie, R. H. (2011). The functional organization and capacity limits of working memory. *Current Directions in Psychological Science, 20,* 240–245. doi:10.1177/0963721411415340.

Logopoulos, J., et al. (2009). Increased theta and alpha EEG activity during nondirective meditation. *Journal of Alternative and Complementary Medicine, 15*(11), 1187–1192.

Logue, A. W. (1991). *The psychology of eating and drinking* (2nd ed.). New York, NY: W. H. Freeman.

Lohmann, R. I. (2007). Dreams and ethnography. In D. Barrett & P. McNamara (Eds.), *The new science of dreaming.* Westport, CT: Praeger.

Loken, B. (2006). Consumer psychology: Categorization, inferences, affect, and persuasion. *Annual Review of Psychology, 57,* 435–485.

Long, Z., Medlock, C., Dzemidzic, M., Shin, Y., Goddard, A. W., & Dydak, U. (2013). Decreased GABA levels in anterior cingulate cortex/medial prefrontal cortex in panic disorder. *Progress in Neuro-Psychopharmacology & Biological Psychiatry, 44*, 131–135. doi:10.1016/j.pnpbp.2013.01.020.

Longman, D. G., & Atkinson, R. H. (2002). *College learning and study skills*. Belmont, CA: Wadsworth.

Lopez, R., Jaussent, I., Scholz, S., Bayard, S., Montplaisir, J., & Dauvilliers, Y. (2013). Functional impact in adult sleepwalkers: A case-control study. *SLEEP, 36*, 345–351.

López, S. R., Barrio, C., Kopelowicz, A., & Vega, W. A. (2012). From documenting to eliminating disparities in mental health care for Latinos. *American Psychologist, 67*, 511–523. doi:10.1037/a0029737.

Lopez-Caneda, E., Rodriguez Holguin, S., Corral, M., Doallo, S., & Cadaveira, F. (2014). Evolution of the binge drinking pattern in college students: Neurophysiological correlates. *Alcohol, 48*, 407–418. doi:10.1016/j.alcohol.2014.01.009.

Lorenz, K. (1981). *Foundations of ethology*. New York, NY: Springer-Verlag.

Lorenzo, G. L., Biesanz, J. C., & Human, L. J. (2010). What is beautiful is good and more accurately understood: Physical attractiveness and accuracy in first impressions of personality. *Psychological Science, 21*(12), 1777–1782. doi:10.1177/0956797610388048.

Lothane, Z. (2006). Freud's legacy—is it still with us? *Psychoanalytic Psychology, 23*(2), 285–301.

Lourenco, O. (2012). Piaget and Vygotsky: Many resemblances, and a crucial difference. *New Ideas in Psychology, 30*, 281–295.

Lowden, A., Akerstedt, T., & Wibom, R. (2004). Suppression of sleepiness and melatonin by bright light exposure during breaks in night work. *Journal of Sleep Research, 12*(1), 37–43.

Lowe, M. R. (2002). Dietary restraint and overeating. In C. G. Fairburn & K. D. Brownell (Eds.), *Eating disorders and obesity: A comprehensive handbook* (pp. 88–92). New York, NY: Guilford.

Lu, C. Y., Zhang, F., Lakoma, M. D., Madden, J. M., Rusinak, D., Penfold, R. B., . . . Soumerai, S. B. (2014). Changes in antidepressant use by young people and suicidal behavior after FDA warnings and media coverage: quasi-experimental study. *British Medical Journal, 348*, g3596. doi:10.1136/bmj.g3596.

Luber, B., & Lisanby, S. H. (2014). Ehancement of human cognitive performance using transcranial magnetic stimulation (TMS). *Neuroimage, 85*, 961–970.

Luborsky, E. B., O'Reilly-Landry, M., & Arlow, J. A. (2011). Psychoanalysis. In R. J. Corsini & D. Wedding (Eds.), *Current psychotherapies* (9th ed.). Belmont, CA: Brooks/Cole.

Luborsky, L., & Barrett, M. S. (2006). The history and empirical status of key psychoanalytic concepts. *Annual Review Clinical Psychology, 2*, 1–19.

Luborsky, L., Rosenthal, R., Diguer, L., Andrusyna, T. P., Berman, J. S., Levitt, J. T., et al. (2002). The dodo bird verdict is alive and well—mostly. *Clinical Psychology: Science & Practice, 9*, 2–12.

Luborsky, L., Singer, B., & Luborsky, K. (1975). Comparative studies of psychotherapies: Is it true that everyone has won and all must have prizes? *Archives of General Psychiatry, 32*, 995–1008.

Lucas, R. E. (2007). Adaptation and the set-point model of subjective well-being: Does happiness change after major life events? *Current Directions in Psychological Science, 16*, 75–79.

Lucas, R. E. (2008). Personality and subjective well-being. In M. Eid & R. J. Larsen (Eds.), *The science of subjective well-being* (pp. 171–194). New York, NY: Guilford.

Lucas, R. E., Clark, A. E., Georgellis, Y., & Diener, E. (2004). Unemployment alters the set point for life satisfaction. *Psychological Science, 15*(1), 8–13.

Lucas, R. E., & Diener, E. (2015). Personality and subjective well-being: Current issues and controversies. In M. Mikulincer, P. R. Shaver, M. L. Cooper, & R. J. Larsen (Eds.), *APA handbook of personality and social psychology: Vol. 4. Personality processes and individual differences*. Washington, DC: American Psychological Association.

Luchins, A. S. (1942). Mechanization in problem solving. *Psychological Monographs, 54*(6, Whole No. 248).

Lucid dreaming. (2005). University of Montreal, Hôpital du Sacré-Cœur de Montréal, Centre de recherche. Retrieved March 11, 2005, from http://www.crhsc .umontreal.ca/dreams.ld.htm.

Luders, E., Narr, K. L., Thompson, P. M., & Toga, A. W. (2009). Neuroanatomical correlates of intelligence. *Intelligence, 37*(2), 156–163.

Luders, E., Toga, A. W., Lepore, N., & Gaser, C. (2009). The underlying anatomical correlates of long-term meditation: Larger hippocampal and frontal volumes of gray matter. *Neuroimage, 45*(3), 672–678.

Ludwig, A. M. (1994). Mental illness and creative activity in female writers. *American Journal of Psychiatry, 151*, 1650–1656.

Ludwig, A. M. (1995). *The price of greatness: Resolving the creativity and madness controversy*. New York, NY: Guilford.

Ludwig, A. M. (1998). Method and madness in the arts and sciences. *Creativity Research Journal, 11*, 93–101.

Lugaresi, E., Cirignotta, F., Montagna, P., & Sforza, E. (1994). Snoring: Pathogenic, clinical, and therapeutic aspects. In M. H. Kryger, T. Roth, & W. C. Dement (Eds.), *Principles and practice of sleep medicine* (2nd ed.). Philadelphia, PA: Saunders.

Luh, C. W. (1922). The conditions of retention. *Psychological Monographs, 31*.

Luk, G., & Bialystok, E. (2013). Bilingualism is not a categorical variable: Interaction between language proficiency and usage. *Journal of Cognitive Psychology, 25*(5), 605–621.

Lukaszewski, A. W., & Roney, J. R. (2011). The origins of extraversion: Joint effects of facultative calibration and genetic polymorphism. *Personality and Social Psychology Bulletin, 37*, 409–421. doi:10.1177/0146167210397209.

Luna, B., Paulsen, D. J., Padmanabhan, A., & Geier, C. (2013). The teenage brain: Cognitive control and motivation. *Current Directions in Psychological Science, 22*, 94–100. doi:10.1177/0963721413478416.

Lunau, K. (2013). Inside a comatose mind. *Maclean's*, October 13, 2013. Retrieved from http://www.macleans .ca/society/technology/beyond-words/.

Lundberg, U. (2007). Catecholamines. In G. Fink (Ed.), *Encyclopedia of stress*. San Diego, CA: Elsevier.

Lupart, J. L., & Pyryt, M. C. (1996). Hidden gifted students: Underachiever prevalence and profile. *Journal for the Education of the Gifted, 20*, 36–53.

Lupien, S. J., & Maheu, F. S. (2007). Memory and stress. In G. Fink (Ed.), *Encyclopedia of stress*. San Diego, CA: Elsevier.

Luppi, P., Clément, O., & Fort, P. (2013). Paradoxical (REM) sleep genesis by the brainstem is under hypothalamic control. *Current Opinion in Neurobiology, 23*, 786–792. doi:10.1016/j.conb.2013.02.006.

Lustig, C., Berman, M. G., Nee, D., Lewis, R. L., Sledge Moore, K., & Jonides, J. (2009). Psychological and neural mechanisms of short-term memory. In G. G. Berntson & J. T. Cacioppo (Eds.), *Handbook of neuroscience for the behavioral sciences* (Vol 1, pp. 567–585). Hoboken, NJ: Wiley.

Lutsky, N. (1995). When is "obedience" obedience? Conceptual and historical commentary. *Journal of Social Issues, 51*, 55–65.

Lutz, A., Dunne, J. D., & Davidson, R. J. (2007). Meditation and the neuroscience of consciousness: An introduction. In P. D. Zelazo, M. Moscovitch, & E. Thompson (Eds.), *The Cambridge handbook of consciousness* (pp. 499–551). New York, NY: Cambridge University Press.

Lutz, A., Jha, A. P., Dunne, J. D., & Sarpon, C. D. (2015). Investigating the phenomenological matrix of mindfulness-related practices from a neurocognitive perspective. *American Psychologist, 70*, 632–658.

Lutz, W. (1989). *Doublespeak*. New York, NY: Harper Perennial.

Lykken, D. T., & Tellegen, A. (1996). Happiness is a stochastic phenomenon. *Psychological Science, 7*, 186–189.

Lymburner, J. A., & Roesch, R. (1999). The insanity defense: Five years of research (1993–1997). *International Journal of Law and Psychiatry, 22*, 213–240.

Lyn, H., & Savage-Rumbaugh, E. S. (2000). Observational word learning in two bonobos (*Pan paniscus*): Ostensive and nonostensive contexts. *Language & Communication, 20*, 255–273.

Lynch, G., & Gall, C. M. (2006). Ampakines and the threefold path to cognitive enhancement. *Trends in Neurosciences, 29*, 554–562.

Lynch, M. A. (2004). Long-term potentiation and memory. *Psychological Review, 84*, 87–136.

Lynn, R. (2009). What has caused the Flynn effect? Secular increases in the development quotients of infants. *Intelligence, 37*(1), 16–24. doi:10.1016/j. intell.2008.07.00.

Lynn, S. J., Kirsch, I., Barabasz, A., Cardeña, E., & Patterson, D. (2000). Hypnosis as an empirically supported clinical intervention: The state of the evidence and a look to the future. *International Journal of Clinical & Experimental Hypnosis, 48*, 239–259.

Lynn, S. J., Kirsch, I., & Hallquist, M. N. (2008). Social cognitive theories of hypnosis. In M. R. Nash & A. J. Barnier (Eds.), *Oxford handbook of hypnosis: Theory, research and practice* (pp. 111–140). New York, NY: Oxford University Press.

Lynn, S. J., Kirsch, I., Knox, J., Fassler, O., & Lilienfeld, S. O. (2007). Hypnotic regulation of consciousness and the pain neuromatrix. In G. A. Jamieson (Ed.), *Hypnosis and conscious states: The cognitive neuroscience perspective* (pp. 145–166). New York, NY: Oxford University Press.

Lynn, S. J., Lilienfeld, S. O., Merckelbach, H., Giesbrecht, T., & van der Kloet, D. (2012). Dissociation and dissociative disorders: Challenging conventional wisdom. *Current Directions in Psychological Science, 21*(1), 48–53. doi:10.1177/0963721411429457.

Lynn, S. J., Lock, T., Loftus, E. F., Krackow, E., & Lilienfeld, S. O. (2003). The remembrance of things past: Problematic memory recovery techniques in psychotherapy. In S. O. Lilienfeld, S. J. Lynn, & J. M. Lohr (Eds.), *Science and pseudoscience in clinical psychology*. New York, NY: Guilford.

Lynn, S. J., & Nash, M. (1994). Truth in memory: Ramifications for psychotherapy and hypnotherapy. *Journal of Clinical Hypnosis, 36*, 194–208.

Lynne, S. D., Graber, J. A., Nichols, T. R., & Brooks-Gunn, J., & Botwin, G. J. (2007). Links between pubertal timing, peer influences, and externalizing behaviors among urban students followed through middle school. *Journal of Adolescent Health, 40*(2), 313–342.

Lyons-Ruth, K., & Jacobvitz, D. (2008). Attachment disorganization: Genetic factors, parenting contexts, and developmental transformation from infancy to adulthood. In J. Cassidy & P. R. Shaver (Eds.), *Handbook of attachment: Theory, research, and clinical applications* (2nd ed., pp. 666–697). New York, NY: Guilford Press.

Lyubomirsky, S., Sheldon, K. M., & Schkade, D. (2005). Pursuing happiness: The architecture of sustainable change. *Review of General Psychology, 9*, 111–131.

Lyubomirsky, S., Tkach, C., & DiMatteo, R. M. (2006). What are the differences between happiness and self-esteem? *Social Indicators Research, 78*, 363–404.

Maccoby, E. E. (2000). Parenting and its effects on children: On reading and misreading behavior genetics. *Annual Review of Psychology, 51*, 1–27.

MacCoun, R. J. (1998). Biases in the interpretation and use of research results. *Annual Review Psychology, 49*, 259–287.

MacDonald, F. (2016). Two more classic psychology studies just failed the reproducibility test: The scientific method in action. Retrieved from https://www.sciencealert .com/two-more-classic-psychology-studies-just-failed-the -reproducibility-test.

MacDonald, G., Zanna, M. P., & Holmes, J. G. (2000). An experimental test of the role of alcohol in relationship conflict. *Journal of Experimental Social Psychology, 36,* 182–193.

MacDonald, K. (1998). Evolution, culture, and the five-factor model. *Journal of Cross-Cultural Psychology, 29,* 119–149.

MacDonald, M. C. (2016). Speak, act, remember: The language-production basis of serial order and maintenance in verbal memory. *Current Directions in Psychological Science, 25,* 47–53.

MacDonald, T. K., & Hynie, M. (2008). Ambivalence and unprotected sex: Failing to predict sexual activity is associated with decreased condom use. *Journal of Applied Social Psychology, 38,* 1092–1107.

MacDonald, T. K., & Martineau, A. M. (2002). Self-esteem, mood, and intentions to use condoms: When does low self-esteem lead to risky health behaviors? *Journal of Experimental Social Psychology, 38,* 299–306.

MacDonald, T. K., Fong, G. T., Zanna, M. P., & Martineau, A. M. (2000). Alcohol myopia and condom use: Can alcohol intoxication be associated with more prudent behavior? *Journal of Personality and Social Psychology, 78,* 605–619.

MacEwan University. (2017). *Pets assisting with student success (PASS).* Retrieved from http://www.macewan.ca/wcm/MacEwanEvents/PAWSS_SEP2017.

MacGregor, J. N., Ormerod, T. C., & Chronicle, E. P. (2001). Information processing and insight: A process model of performance on the nine-dot and related problems. *Journal of Experimental Psychology: Learning, Memory and Cognition, 27,* 176–201.

Machado, S., Arias-Carrión, O., Castillo, A. O., Lattari, E., Silva, A. C., & Nardi, A. E. (2013). Hemispheric specialization and regulation of motor behavior on a perspective of cognitive neuroscience. *Salud Mental, 3,* 513–520.

Machado, V., Leonidas, C., Santos, M. A., & Souza, J. (2012). Psychiatric readmission: An integrative review of the literature. *International Nursing Review, 59,* 447–457. doi:10.1111/j.1466-7657.2012.01011.x.

Mack, A. (2003). Inattentional blindness: Looking without seeing. *Current Directions in Psychological Science, 12*(5), 180–184.

MacKenzie, M. J., Nicklas, E., Waldfogel, J., & Brooks-Gunn, J. (2013). Spanking and child development across the first decade of life. *Pediatrics, 132,* e1118–e1125. doi:10.1542/peds.2013-1227.

Mackey, A. P., Whitaker, K. J., & Bunge, S. A. (2012). Experience-dependent plasticity in white matter microstructure: reasoning training alters structural connectivity. *Frontiers in Neuroanatomy, 6*(32). doi:10.3389/fnana.2012.00032.

Mackinnon, S. P., Jordan, C. H., & Wilson, A. E. (2011). Birds of a feather sit together: Physical similarity predicts seating choice. *Personality and Social Psychology Bulletin, 37,* 879– 892. doi:10.1177/0146167211402094.

Mackintosh, N. J. (2011). History of theories and measurement of intelligence. In R. J. Sternberg, & S. B. Kaufman (Eds.), *Cambridge handbook of intelligence.* New York, NY: Cambridge University Press.

MacLean, P. D. (1954). Studies on limbic system ("visceral brain") and their bearing on psychosomatic problems. In E. D. Wittkower & R. A. Cleghorn (Eds.), *Recent developments in psychosomatic medicine.* Philadelphia, PA: Lippincott.

MacLean, P. D. (1993). Cerebral evolution of emotion. In M. Lewis & J. M. Haviland (Eds.), *Handbook of emotions.* New York, NY: Guilford.

MacLeod, A. K. (2013). Suicide and attempted suicide. In M. Power (Ed.), *The Wiley-Blackwell handbook of mood disorders* (2nd ed.). Malden, MA: Wiley-Blackwell.

MacMillan, H. L., Boyle, M. H., Wong, M. Y. Y., Duku, E. K., Fleming, J. E., & Walsh, C. A. (1999). Slapping and spanking in childhood and its association with lifetime prevalence of psychiatric disorders in a general population sample. *Canadian Medical Association Journal, 161,* 805–809.

MacMillan, H. L., Fleming, J. E., Trocme, N., Boyle, M. H., Wong, M., Racine, Y. A., et al. (1997). Prevalence of child physical and sexual abuse in the community: Results from the Ontario health supplement. *Journal of the American Medical Association, 278,* 131–135.

Macmillan, M. (1991). *Freud evaluated: The completed arc.* Amsterdam: North-Holland.

MacNeil, L., Espostio-Smythers, C., Mahlenbeck, R., & Weismoore, J. (2012). The effects of avoidance coping and coping self-efficacy on eating disorder attitudes and behaviors: A stress-diathesis model. *Eating Behaviors, 13,* 293–296. doi:10.1016/j.eatbeh.2012.06.005.

Macrae, C. N., & Quadflieg, S. (2010). Perceiving people. In S. T. Fiske, D. T. Gilbert, & G. Lindzey (Eds.), *Handbook of social psychology* (5th ed., Vol. 1, pp. 353–393). Hoboken, NJ: Wiley.

Macritchie, K., & Blackwood, D. (2013). Neurobiological theories of bipolar disorder. In M. Power (Ed.), *The Wiley-Blackwell handbook of mood disorders* (2nd ed.). Malden, MA: Wiley-Blackwell.

MacWhinney, B. (1998). Models of the emergence of language. *Annual Review of Psychology, 49,* 199–227.

MacWhinney, B. (2001). Emergentist approaches to language. In J. Bybee & P. Hooper (Eds.), *Frequency and the emergence of linguistic structure.* Amsterdam: John Benjamins Publishing.

MacWhinney, B. (2004). A multiple process solution to the logical problem of language acquisition. *Journal of Child Language, 31,* 883–914.

MacWhirter, J. (2013). *A soldier's tale: A Newfoundland soldier in Afghanistan.* St. John's, Newfoundland: DRC Publishing Company.

Maddux, W. W., Adam, H., & Galinsky, A. D. (2010). When in Rome … Learn why the Romans do what they do: How multicultural learning experiences facilitate creativity. *Personality and Social Psychology Bulletin, 36*(6), 731–741.

Maddux, W. W., & Galinsky, A. D. (2009). Cultural borders and mental barriers: The relationship between living abroad and creativity. *Journal of Personality and Social Psychology, 96*(5), 1047–1061.

Madsen, K. B. (1968). *Theories of motivation.* Copenhagen: Munksgaard.

Magee, C. A., Holliday, E. G., Attia, J., Kritharides, L., & Banks, E. (2013). Investigation of the relationship between sleep duration, all-cause mortality, and preexisting disease. *Sleep Medicine, 14,* 591–596. doi:10.1016/j.sleep.2013.02.002.

Magnavita, J. J. (2008). Psychoanalytic psychotherapy. In J. L. Lebow (Ed.), *Twenty-first century psychotherapies: Contemporary approaches to theory and practice.* New York, NY: Wiley.

Magnusson, D., & Stattin, H. (1998). Person-context interaction theories. In W. Damon (Ed.), *Handbook of child psychology (Vol. 1): Theoretical models of human development.* New York, NY: Wiley.

Maguire, W., Weisstein, N., & Klymenko, V. (1990). From visual structure to perceptual function. In K. N. Leibovic (Ed.), *Science of vision.* New York, NY: Springer-Verlag.

Maguire, W., Weisstein, N., & Klymenko, V. (1990). From visual structure to perceptual function. In K. N. Leibovic (Ed.), *Science of vision.* New York, NY: Springer-Verlag.

Mahar, I., Bambico, F. R., Mechawar, N., & Nobrega, J. N. (2014). Stress, serotonin, and hippocampal neurogenesis in relation to depression and antidepressant effects. *Neuroscience and Biobehavioral Reviews, 38,* 173–192. doi:10.1016/j.neubiorev.2013.11.009.

Maher, B. A. (2001). Delusions. In P. B. Sutker & H. E. Adams (Eds.), *Comprehensive handbook of psychopathology* (3rd ed., pp. 309–370). New York, NY: Kluwer Academic/Plenum Publishers.

Mahoney, M. J. (1974). *Cognition and behavior modification.* Cambridge, MA: Ballinger.

Mahowald, M. W., & Schenck, C. H. (2005). Insights from studying human sleep disorders. *Nature, 437,* 1279–1285.

Maier, N. R. F. (1931). Reasoning and learning. *Psychological Review, 38,* 332–346.

Main, M., & Solomon, J. (1986). Discovery of a new, insecure–disorganized/disoriented attachment pattern. In T. B. Brazelton & M. W. Yogman (Eds.), *Affective development in infancy.* Norwood, NJ: Ablex.

Main, M., & Solomon, J. (1990). Procedures for identifying infants as disorganized/disoriented during the Ainsworth strange situation. In M. T. Greenberg, D. Ciccehetti, & E. M. Cummings (Eds.), *Attachment in the preschool years: Theory, research, and intervention.* Chicago, IL: University of Chicago Press.

Maio, G. R., & Esses, V. M. (2001). The need for affect: Individual differences in the motivation to approach or avoid emotions. *Journal of Personality, 69,* 883–919.

Maio, G. R., Olson, J. M., & Cheung, I. (2013). Attitudes in social behavior. In H. Tennen, J. Suls, & I. B. Weiner (Eds.), *Handbook of psychology: Vol. 5. Personality and social psychology* (2nd ed.). New York, NY: Wiley.

Maldonado, J. R., & Spiegel, D. (2014). Dissociative disorders. In R. E. Hales, S. C. Yudofsky, & L. W. Roberts (Eds.), *The American Psychiatric Publishing textbook of psychiatry* (6th ed.). Washington, DC: American Psychiatric Publishing.

Malenfant, E. C. (2004). Suicide in Canada's immigrant population. *Statistics Canada: Health Reports, 15,* 9–17.

Maletzky, B. M. (2002). The paraphilias: Research and treatment. In P. E. Nathan & J. M. Gorman (Eds.), *A guide to treatments that work.* London, UK: Oxford University Press.

Malin, A. (2012). Psychologists at Guantanamo Bay: Can their ethical violations be justified? *Journal of Ethics in Mental Health, 7,* 1–5.

Malin, K., & Littlejohn, G. O. (2013). Stress modulates key psychological processes and characteristic symptoms in females with fibromyalgia. *Clinical Experimental Rheumatology, 31,* S64–S71.

Man, V., Ames, D. L., Todorov, A., & Cunningham, W. A. (2016). Amygdala tuning toward self and other. *Journal of Experimental Psychology: General, 145,* 419–433.

Managing traumatic stress: After the hurricanes. (2005). American Psychological Association Help Centre. Retrieved July 23, 2008, from http://apahelpcenter.org/articles/article.php?id=107.

Mandel uses knuckle knock to overcome OCD. (2006). *NBC10 News.* Retrieved July 23, 2008, from http://www.nbc10.com/entertainment/9081482/detail.html.

Mandel, H. (2009). *Here's the deal: Don't touch me.* New York, NY: Bantam Books.

Mandelman, S. D., & Grigorenko, E. L. (2011). Intelligence: Genes, environments, and their interactions. In R. J. Sternberg, & S. B. Kaufman (Eds.), *Cambridge handbook of intelligence.* New York, NY: Cambridge University Press.

Mandler, G. (1984). *Mind and body.* New York, NY: Norton.

Mandler, G. (1989). Memory: Conscious and unconscious. In P. R. Soloman, G. R. Goethals, C. M. Kelley, & B. R. Stephens (Eds.), *Memory: Interdisciplinary approaches.* New York, NY: Springer-Verlag.

Mandler, G. (1993). Thought, memory, and learning: Effects of emotional stress. In L. Goldberger & S. Breznitz (Eds.), *Handbook of stress: Theoretical and clinical aspects* (2nd ed.). New York, NY: Free Press.

Mandler, G. (2002). Origins of the cognitive revolution. *Journal of the History of the Behavioral Sciences, 38,* 339–353.

Manenti, R. R., Tettamanti, M. M., Cotelli, M. M., Miniussi, C. C., & Cappa, S. F. (2010). The neural bases of word encoding and retrieval: A fMRI-guided transcranial magnetic stimulation study. *Brain Topography, 22*(4), 318–332.

Maner, J. K., & Ackerman, J. M. (2013). Love is a battlefield: Romantic attraction, intrasexual competition, and conflict between the sexes. In J. A. Simpson & L. Campbell (Eds.), *Oxford handbook of close relationships.* New York, NY: Oxford University Press.

Mani, A., Mullainathan, S., Shafir, E., & Zhao, J. (2013). Poverty impedes cognitive function. *Science, 30*, 976–980.

Maniacci, M. P., Sackett-Maniacci, L., & Mosak, H. M. (2014). Adlerian psychotherapy. In D. Wedding & R. J. Corsini (Eds.), *Current psychotherapies* (10th ed., 62–94). Belmont, CA: Brooks/Cole.

Manley, G. T., et al. (2017). A systematic review of potential long-term effects of sport-related concussion. *British Journal of Sports Medicine.* Published Online First April 28, 2017.

Manna, A., Raffone, A., Perrucci, M., Nardo, D., Ferretti, A., Tartaro, A., et al. (2010). Neural correlates of focused attention and cognitive monitoring in meditation. *Brain Research Bulletin, 82*(1–2), 46–56.

Manning, W. D., & Cohen, J. A. (2012). Premarital cohabitation and marital dissolution: An examination of recent marriages. *Journal of Marriage and Family, 74*, 377–387. doi:10.1111/j.1741-3737.2012.00960.x.

Manning, W. D., Brown, S. L., & Payne, K. K. (2014). Two decades of stability and change in age at first union formation. *Journal of Marriage and Family, 76*, 247–260. doi:10.1111/jomf.12090.

Mansnerus, L. (1996). Timothy Leary, pied piper of psychedilic 60's dies at 75. Obituary, *New York Times.* Retrieved February 10, 2011, from http://www.nytimes .com/learning/general/onthisday/dday/1022.html.

Mantovani, A., Pavlicova, M., Avery, D., et al. (2012). Long-term efficacy of repeated daily prefrontal transcranial magnetic stimulation (TMS) in treatment resistant depression. *Depression and Anxiety, 29*(10), 883–890.

Manuck, S. B., & McCaggery, J. M. (2014). Gene-environment interaction. *Annual Review of Psychology, 65*, 41–70.

Mar, R. A. (2011). The neural bases of social cognition and story comprehension. *Annual Review of Psychology, 62*, 103–134.

Mar, R. A., Tackett, J. L., & Moore, C. (2010). Exposure to media and theory-of-mind development in preschoolers. *Cognitive Development, 25*, 69–78.

Marangell, L. B., Silver, J. M., & Yudofsky, S. C. (1999). Psychopharmocology and electroconvulsive therapy. In R. E. Hales, S. C. Yudofsky, & J. A. Talbott (Eds.), *American Psychiatric Press textbook of psychiatry.* Washington, DC: American Psychiatric Press.

Marcelino, A. S., Adam, A. S., Couronne, T., Koester, E. P., & Sieffermann, J. M. (2001). Internal and external determinants of eating initiation in humans. *Appetite, 36*, 9–14.

Marcenes, W. G., & Sheiham, A. (1992). The relationship between work stress and oral health status. *Social Science and Medicine, 35*, 1511.

Marcia, J. E. (1966). Development and validation of ego identity status. *Journal of Personality and Social Psychology, 3*, 551–558.

Marcia, J. E. (1980). Identity in adolescence. In J. Adelson (Ed.), *Handbook of adolescent psychology.* New York, NY: Wiley.

Marcia, J. E. (1994). The empirical study of ego identity. In H. A. Bosma, T. L. G. Graafsma, H. D. Grotevant, & D. J. de Levita (Eds.), *Identity and development: An interdisciplinary approach.* Thousand Oaks, CA: Sage.

Marcus, D. A., Blazek-O'Neill, B., & Kopar, J. L. (2014). Symptom reduction identified after offering animal-assisted activity at a cancer infusion center. *American Journal of Hospice and Palliative Care, 31*, 420–421.

Marcus, G. F. (1996). Why do children say "breaked"? *Current Directions in Psychological Science, 5*, 81–85.

Marder, S. R., Hurford, I. M., & van Kammen, D. P. (2009). Second-generation antipsychotics. In B. J. Sadock, V. A. Sadock, & P. Ruiz (Eds.), *Kaplan & Sadock's comprehensive textbook of psychiatry* (pp. 3206–3240). Philadelphia, PA: Lippincott Williams & Wilkins.

Marewski, J. N., Gaissmaier, W., & Gigerenzer, G. (2010). Good judgments do not require complex cognition. *Cognitive Processing, 11*(2), 103–121.

Marigold, D. C., Cavallo, J. V., Holmes, J. G., & Wood, J. V. (2014). You can't always give what you want: The challenge of providing social support to low self-esteem individuals. *Journal of Personality and Social Psychology, 107*, 56–80.

Marigold, D. C., Holmes, J. G., & Ross, M. (2007). More than words: Reframing compliments from romantic partners fosters security in low self-esteem individuals. *Journal of Personality and Social Psychology, 92*, 212–248.

Marigold, D. C., Holmes, J. G., & Ross, M. (2010). Fostering relationship resilience: An intervention for low self-esteem individuals. *Journal of Experimental Social Psychology, 46*, 624–630.

Markowitsch, H. J. (2000). Neuroanatomy of memory. In E. Tulving & F. I. M. Craik (Eds.), *The Oxford handbook of memory* (pp. 465–484). New York, NY: Oxford University Press.

Marks, G. A. (2006). The neurobiology of sleep. In T. Lee-Chiong (Ed.), *Sleep: A comprehensive handbook.* Hoboken, NJ: Wiley-Liss.

Marks, L. E. (2014). Synesthesia: A teeming multiplicity. In E. Cardeña, S. J. Lynn, & S. C. Krippner (Eds.), *Varieties of anomalous experience: Examining the scientific evidence* (pp. 79–108). Washington, DC: American Psychological Association.

Markus, H. R. (2016). What moves people to action? Culture and motivation. *Current Opinion in Psychology, 8*, 161–166.

Markus, H. R., & Kitayama, S. (1991). Culture and the self: Implications for cognition, emotion, and motivation. *Psychological Review, 98*, 224–253.

Markus, H. R., & Kitayama, S. (1994). The cultural construction of self and emotion: Implications for social behavior. In S. Kitayama & H. R. Markus (Eds.), *Emotions and culture: Empirical studies of mutual influence.* Washington, DC: American Psychological Association.

Markus, H. R., & Kitayama, S. (2003). Culture, self, and the reality of the social. *Psychological Inquiry, 14*(3–4), 277–283.

Markus, H., Hamill, R., & Sentis, K. P. (1987). Thinking fat: Self-schemas for body weight and the processing of weight relevant information. *Journal of Applied Social Psychology, 17*, 50–71.

Markus, H., Smith, J., & Moreland, R. (1985). Role of the self-concept in perception of others. *Journal of Personality and Social Psychology, 49*, 1494–1512.

Markus, H. R., Kitayama, S., & Heiman, R. J. (1996). Culture and "basic" psychological principles. In E. T. Higgins, & A. W. Kruglanski (Eds.), *Social psychology: Handbook of basic principles.* New York, NY: Guilford.

Marschark, M. (1992). Coding processes: Imagery. In L. R. Squire (Ed.), *Encyclopedia of learning and memory.* New York, NY: Macmillan.

Marsella, A. J., & Yamada, A. M. (2007). Culture and psychopathology: Foundations, issues, and directions. In S. Kitayama & D. Cohen (Eds.), *Handbook of cultural psychology.* New York, NY: Guilford.

Marsh, E. J. (2007). Retelling is not the same as recalling: Implications for memory. *Current Directions in Psychological Science, 16*(1), 16–20.

Marsh, E. J., & Tversky, B. (2004). Spinning the stories of our lives. *Applied Cognitive Psychology, 18*, 491–503.

Marsh, J. M., & Butler, A. C. (2013). Memory in educational settings, In D. Reisberg (Ed.), *Oxford handbook of cognitive psychology.* New York, NY: Oxford University Press.

Marsh, L., & Margolis, R. L. (2009). Neuropsychiatric aspects of movement disorders. In B. J. Sadock, V. A. Sadock, & P. Ruiz, *Kaplan & Sadock's comprehensive textbook of psychiatry* (9th ed., pp. 481–493). Philadelphia, PA: Lippincott Williams & Wilkins.

Marsland, A. L., Bachen, E. A., & Cohen, S. (2012). Stress, immunity, and susceptibility to upper respiratory infectious disease. In A. Baum, T. A. Revenson, & J. Singer (Eds.), *Handbook of health psychology.* New York, NY: Psychology Press.

Marteau, T. M., & Weinman, J. (2004). Communicating about health threats and treatments. In S. Sutton, A. Baum, & M. Johnston (Eds.), *The Sage handbook of health psychology.* Thousand Oaks, CA: Sage.

Martin, C. L., & Ruble, D. (2004). Children's search for gender cues: Cognitive perspectives on gender development. *Current Directions in Psychological Science, 13*(2), 67–70.

Martin, J. N., & Fox, N. A. (2006). Temperament. In K. McCartney & D. Phillips (Eds.), *Blackwell handbook of early childhood development* (pp. 126–146). Malden, MA: Blackwell.

Martin, L. (1986). "Eskimo words for snow": A case study in the genesis and decay of an anthropological example. *American Psychologist, 88*, 418–423.

Martin, R. A. (2001). Humor, laughter, and physical health: Methodological issues and research findings. *Psychological Bulletin, 127*, 504–519.

Martin, R., & Leventhal, H. (2004). Symptom perception and health care– seeking behavior. In J. M. Raczynski & L. C. Leviton (Eds.), *Handbook of clinical health psychology: Vol. 2. Disorders of behavior and health.* Washington, DC: American Psychological Association.

Martin, R. A. (2007). *The psychology of humor: An integrative approach.* Burlington, MA: Elsevier Academic Press.

Martin, S. (2011). The behavioral scientist behind eHarmony said today's web technology offers rich possibilities for researchers. *Monitor on Psychology, 42*, 69.

Martinez, M., Marangell, L. B., & Martinez, J. M. (2008). Psychopharmacology. In R. E. Hales, S. C. Yudofsky, & G. O. Gabbard (Eds.), *The American Psychiatric Publishing textbook of psychiatry* (pp. 1053–1132). Washington, DC: American Psychiatric Publishing.

Martinez-Conde, S. (2006). Fixational eye movements in normal and pathological vision. *Progress in Brain Research, 154*, 151–176.

Martinez-Conde, S., & Macknik, S. L. (2007). Windows on the mind. *Scientific American, 297*, 56–62.

Martinez-Conde, S., & Macknik, S. L. (2011). Shifting focus. *Scientific American Mind, 22*(5), 48–55.

Martins, C. S., de Carvalho Tofoli, S. M., Von Werne Baes, C., & Juruena, M. (2011). Analysis of the occurrence of early life stress in adult psychiatric patients: A systematic review. *Psychology & Neuroscience, 4*(2), 219–227. doi:10.3922/j.psns.2011.2.007.

Mas, S. (2013). Senator Romeo Dallaire in car crash on Parliament Hill. *CBC News.* Retrieved from http://www .cbc.ca/news/politics/senator-roméo-dallaire-in-car-crash -on-parliament-hill-1.2449420.

Maslach, C., & Leiter, M. P. (1997). *The truth about burnout.* San Francisco, CA: Jossey-Bass.

Maslach, C., & Leiter, M. P. (2000). Burnout. In G. Fink (Ed.), *Encyclopedia of stress* (Vol. 1, pp. 358–362). San Diego, CA: Academic Press.

Maslach, C., & Leiter, M. P. (2005). Stress and burnout: The critical research. In C. L. Cooper (Ed.), *Handbook of stress medicine and health.* Boca Raton, FL: CRC Press.

Maslach, C., & Leiter, M. P. (2007). Burnout. In G. Fink (Ed.), *Encyclopedia of stress.* San Diego, CA: Elsevier.

Maslen, R. J. C., Theakston, A. L., Lieven, E. V. M., & Tomasello, M. (2004). A dense corpus study of past tense and plural overregularization in English. *Journal of Speech, Language, & Hearing Research, 47*, 1319–1333.

Maslow, A. H. (1954). *Motivation and personality.* New York, NY: Harper & Row.

Maslow, A. H. (1968). *Toward a psychology of being.* New York, NY: Van Nostrand.

Maslow, A. H. (1970). *Motivation and personality.* New York, NY: Harper & Row.

Mason, G. (2008, May 31). When do we cry? *The Globe and Mail,* F1, F4, F5.

Massaro, D. W., & Loftus, G. R. (1996). Sensory and perceptual storage: Data and theory. In E. L. Bjork & R. A. Bjork (Eds.), *Memory.* San Diego, CA: Academic Press.

Masson, J. M. (1997). *Dogs never lie about love.* New York, NY: Crown Publishers, Ind.

Master, S. L., Eisenberger, N. I., Taylor, S. E., Naliboff, B. D., Shirinyan, D., & Lieberman, M. D. (2009). A picture's worth: Partner photographs reduce experimentally induced pain. *Psychological Science, 20*(11), 1316–1318.

Masters, W. H., & Johnson, V. E. (1966). *Human sexual response*. Boston, MA: Little, Brown.

Masters, W. H., & Johnson, V. E. (1970). *Human sexual inadequacy*. Boston, MA: Little, Brown.

Masuda, T. (2010). Cultural effects on visual perception. In E. B. Goldstein (Ed.), *Encyclopedia of perception*. Thousand Oaks, CA: Sage.

Masuda, T., & Nisbett, R. E. (2001). Attending holistically versus analytically: Comparing the context sensitivity of Japanese and Americans. *Journal of Personality and Social Psychology, 81*, 922–934.

Mataix-Cols, D., Frost, R. O., Pertusa, A., Clark, L. A., Saxena, S., Leckman, J. F., Stein, D. J., Matsunaga, H., & Wilhelm, S. (2010). Hoarding disorder: a new diagnosis for DSM-5? *Depression and Anxiety, 23*, 44–56.

Matheson, K., Bombay, A., Haslam, S. A., & Anisman, H. (2016). Indigenous identity transformations: The pivotal role of student-to-student abuse in Indian Residential schools. *Transcultural Psychiatry, 53*, 551–573.

Matheson, S. L., Green, M. J., Loo, C., & Carr, V. J. (2010). Quality assessment and comparison of evidence for E.C.T. and repetitive transcranial magnetic stimulation for schizophrenia. *Schizophrenia Research, 118*, 201–210.

Matlin, M. W. (2008). *The psychology of women*. Belmont, CA: Wadsworth.

Matsumoto, D. (1994). *People: Psychology from a cultural perspective*. Pacific Grove, CA: Brooks/Cole.

Matsumoto, D. (2003). Cross-cultural research. In S. F. Davis (Ed.), *Handbook of research methods in experimental psychology*. Malden, MA: Blackwell.

Matsumoto, D., & Hwang, H. S. (2011). Culture, emotion, and expression. In K. D. Keith (Ed.), *Cross-cultural psychology: Contemporary themes and perspectives*. Malden, MA: Wiley-Blackwell.

Matsumoto, D., Nezlek, J. B., & Koopmann, B. (2007). Evidence for universality in phenomenological emotion response system coherence. *Emotion, 7*, 57–67.

Matsumoto, D., & Willingham, B. (2009). Spontaneous facial expressions of emotion of congenitally and non-congenitally blind individuals. *Journal of Personality and Social Psychology, 96*(1), 1–10.

Matsumoto, D., Yoo, S. H., Nakagawa, S., & 37 Members of the Multinational Study of Cultural Display Rules. (2008). Culture, emotion regulation, and adjustment. *Journal of Personality and Social Psychology, 94*, 925–937.

Matthews, G., Emo, A. K., Roberts, R. D., & Zeidner, M. (2006). What is this thing called emotional intelligence? In K. R. Murphy (Ed.), *A critique of emotional intelligence: What are the problems and how can they be fixed?* (pp. 3–36). Mahwah, NJ: Erlbaum.

Matthey, S. (1998). P<.05—But is it clinically *significant*?: Practical examples for clinicians. *Behaviour Change, 15*, 140–146.

Matute, H., & Miller, R. R. (1998). Detecting causal relations. In W. O'Donohue (Ed.), *Learning and behavior therapy*. Boston, Allyn & Bacon.

Maugh, T. H., II. (2008, December 9). Henry M. dies at 82: Victim of brain surgery accident offered doctors key insights into memory. *Los Angeles Times*. Retrieved from http://www.latimes.com/news/science/la-me-molaison9-2008dec09,0,2820409.story.

Maurer, D. (2005). Introduction to the special issue on critical periods reexamined: Evidence from human sensory development. *Developmental Psychobiology, 46*, 162.

Maxwell, S. E., Lau, M. Y., & Howard, G. S. (2015). Is psychology suffering from a replication crisis? *American Psychologist, 70*, 478–498.

May, C. P., Hasher, L., & Foong, N. (2005). Implicit memory, age, and time of day. *Psychological Science, 16*, 96–100.

Mayer, J. (1955). Regulation of energy intake and the body weight: The glucostatic theory and the lipostatic hypothesis. *Annals of the New York Academy of Science, 63*, 15–43.

Mayer, J., Roberts, R., & Barsade, S. G. (2008). Human abilities: Emotional intelligence. *Annual Review of Psychology, 59*, 507–536.

Mayer, J. D., Caruso, D. R., & Salovey, P. (1999). Emotional intelligence meets traditional standards for an intelligence. *Intelligence, 27*, 267–298.

Mayer, J. D., Salovey, P., & Caruso, D. R. (2008). Emotional intelligence: New ability or eclectic traits. *American Psychologist*, 503–517.

Mayes, A. (1992). Brain damage and memory disorders. In M. M. Gruneberg, & P. E. Morris (Eds.), *Aspects of memory (Vol.1): The practical aspects* (2nd ed., pp. 86–123). Florence, KY: Taylor & Frances/Routledge.

Mayes, A. R. & Roberts, N. (2001). Theories of episodic memory. *Philosophical Transactions of the Royal Society of London, 356*, 1395–1408.

Maylor, E. A. (1998). Changes in event-based prospective memory across adulthood. *Aging, Neuropsychology, and Cognition, 5*, 107–128.

Mays, V. M., & Albee, G. W. (1992). Psychotherapy and ethnic minorities. In D. K. Freedheim (Ed.), *History of psychotherapy: A century of change*. Washington, DC: American Psychological Association.

Mays, V. M., Rubin, J., Sabourin, M., & Walker, L. (1996). Moving toward a global psychology: Changing theories and practice to meet the needs of a changing world. *American Psychologist, 51*, 485–487.

Mazzoni, G., Heap, M., & Scoboria, A. (2010). Hypnosis and memory: Theory, laboratory research, and applications. In S. Lynn, J. W. Rhue, & I. Kirsch (Eds.), *Handbook of clinical hypnosis* (2nd ed.) (pp. 709–741). Washington, DC: American Psychological Association.

Mazzoni, G., Laurence, J., & Heap, M. (2014). Hypnosis and memory: Two hundred years of adventures and still going! *Psychology of Consciousness: Theory, Research, and Practice, 1*, 153–167. doi:10.1037/cns0000016.

Mazzoni, G., Venneri, A., McGeown, W. J., & Kirsch, I. (2013). Neuroimaging resolution of the altered state hypothesis. *Cortex: A Journal Devoted to the Study of the Nervous System and Behavior, 49*, 400–410. doi:10.1016/j.cortex.2012.08.005.

McAbee, S. T., & Oswald, F. L. (2013). The criterion-related validity of personality measures for predicting GPA: A meta-analytic validity competition. *Psychological Assessment, 25*, 532–544. doi:10.1037/a0031748.

McBride-Chang, C., & Jacklin, C. N. (1993). Early play arousal, sex-typed play, and activity level as precursors to later rough-and-tumble play. *Early Education & Development, 4*, 99–108.

McBurney, D. H. (1996). *How to think like a psychologist: Critical thinking in psychology*. Upper Saddle River, NJ: Prentice-Hall.

McBurney, D. H. (2010). Evolutionary approach: Perceptual adaptations. In E. B. Goldstein (Ed.), *Encyclopedia of perception*. Thousand Oaks, CA: Sage.

McCabe, C., Rolls, E. T., & Bilderbeck, A., & McGlone, F. (2008). Cognitive influences on the affective representation of touch and the sight of touch in the human brain. *Social Cognitive and Affective Neuroscience, 3*, 97–108.

McCabe, K. O., & Fleeson, W. (2016). Are traits useful? Explaining trait manifestations as tools in the pursuit of goals. *Journal of Personality and Social Psychology, 110*, 287–301.

McCabe, R. E., & Antony, M. M. (2008). Anxiety disorders: Social and specific phobias. In A. Tasman, J. Kay, J. A. Lieberman, M. B. First, & M. Maj (Eds.), *Psychiatry* (3rd ed.). New York, NY: Wiley-Blackwell.

McCaffrey, T. (2012). Innovation relies on the obscure: A key to overcoming the classic problem of functional fixedness. *Psychological Science, 23*, 215– 218. doi:10.1177/0956797611429580.

McCaffrey, T., & Pearson, J. (2015). Find innovation where you least expect it. *Harvard Business Review*, December 2015. Retrieved from https://hbr.org/2015/12/find-innovation-where-you-least-expect-it.

McCall, W. V., Reboussin, D., Prudic, J., Haskett, R. F., Isenberg, K., Olfson, L., . . . Sackeim, H. A. (2013). Poor health-related quality of life prior to ECT in depressed patients normalizes with sustained remission after ECT. *Journal of Affective Disorders, 147*(1–3), 107–111. doi:10.1016/j.jad.2012.10.018.

McCann, D., & Sato, T. (2000). Personality, cognition and the self. *European Journal of Personality, 14*, 449–462.

McCarley, R. W. (1994). Dreams and the biology of sleep. In M. H. Kryger, T. Roth, & W. C. Dement (Eds.), *Principles and practice of sleep medicine* (2nd ed.). Philadelphia, PA: Saunders.

McCarty, R. (2007). Fight-or-flight response. In G. Fink (Ed.), *Encyclopedia of stress*. San Diego, CA: Elsevier.

McCauley, M. E., Eskes, G., & Moscovitch, M. (1996). The effect of imagery on explicit and implicit tests of memory in young and old people: A double dissociation. *Canadian Journal of Experimental Psychology, 50*, 34–41.

McClelland, D. C. (1975). *Power: The inner experience*. New York, NY: Irvington.

McClelland, D. C. (1985). How motives, skills and values determine what people do. *American Psychologist, 40*, 812–825.

McClelland, D. C., & Koestner, R. (1992). The achievement motive. In C. P. Smith (Ed.), *Motivation and personality: Handbook of thematic content analysis*. New York, NY: Cambridge University Press.

McClelland, D. C., Atkinson, J. W., Clark, R. A., & Lowell, E. L. (1953). *The achievement motive*. New York, NY: Appleton-Century-Crofts.

McClelland, J. L. (1992). Parallel-distributed processing models of memory. In L. R. Squire (Ed.), *Encyclopedia of learning and memory*. New York, NY: Macmillan.

McClelland, J. L. (2000). Connectionist models of memory. In E. Tulving & F. I. M. Craik (Eds.), *The Oxford handbook of memory* (pp. 583–596). New York, NY: Oxford University Press.

McClelland, J. L., & Rogers, T. T. (2003). The parallel distributed processing approach to semantic cognition. *Nature Reviews Neuroscience, 4*, 310–322.

McClelland, J. L., & Rumelhart, D. E. (1985). Distributed memory and the representation of general and specific information. *Journal of Experimental Psychology: General, 114*, 159–188.

McClune, S., Espjosito, L., & Griffin, J. A. (2017). Introduction to a thematic series on animal-assisted interventions in special populations. *Applied Developmental Science, 21*, 136–138.

McClure, M. J., & Lydon, J. E. (2014). Anxiety doesn't become you: How attachment anxiety compromises relational opportunities. *Journal of Personality and Social Psychology, 106*, 89–111. doi:10.1037/aa34532.

McClure-Tone, E. B., & Pine, D. S. (2009). Clinical features of the anxiety disorders. In B. J. Sadock, V. A. Sadock, & P. Ruiz (Eds.), *Kaplan & Sadock's comprehensive textbook of psychiatry* (9th ed., pp. 1844–1855). Philadelphia, PA: Lippincott, Williams & Wilkins.

McConkey, K. M. (1992). The effects of hypnotic procedures on remembering: The experimental findings and their implications for forensic hypnosis. In E. Fromm & M. R. Nash (Eds.), *Contemporary hypnosis research*. New York, NY: Guilford.

McConnell, J. V. (1962). Memory transfer through cannibalism in planarians. *Journal of Neuropsychiatry, 3*(Suppl. 1), 542–548.

McConnell, J. V., Cutler, R. L., & McNeil, E. B. (1958). Subliminal stimulation: An overview. *American Psychologist, 13*, 229–242.

McCracken, L. M., Vowles, K. E. (2014). Acceptance and commitment therapy and mindfulness for chronic pain: Model, process, and progress. *American Psychologist, 69*(2), 178–187.

McCrae, R. R., & Costa, P. T., Jr. (1985). Updating Norman's "adequate taxonomy": Intelligence and personality dimensions in natural language and in questionnaires. *Journal of Personality and Social Psychology, 49*, 710–721.

McCrae, R. R., & Costa, P. T., Jr. (1987). Validation of the five-factor model of personality across instruments and observers. *Journal of Personality and Social Psychology, 52*, 81–90.

McCrae, R. R., & Costa, P. T., Jr. (1990). *Personality in adulthood.* New York, NY: Guilford Press.

McCrae, R. R., & Costa, P. T., Jr. (1997). Personality trait structure as a human universal. *American Psychologist, 52,* 509–516.

McCrae, R. R., & Costa, P. T., Jr. (2004). A contemplated revision of the NEO five-factor inventory. *Personality and Individual Differences, 36,* 587–596.

McCrae, R. R., & Costa, P. T., Jr. (2007). Brief versions of the NEO-PI-3. *Journal of Individual Differences, 28,* 116–128.

McCrae, R. R., & Costa, P. T., Jr. (2008). The five-factor theory of personality. In O. P. John, R. W. Robbins, & L. A. Pervin (Eds.), *Handbook of personality: Theory and research* (Vol. 3, pp. 159–181). New York, NY: Guilford Press.

McCrae, R. R., Gaines, J. F., & Wellington, M. A. (2013).The five-factor model in fact and fiction. In H. Tennen, J. Suls, & I. B. Weiner (Eds.), *Handbook of psychology:Vol. 5. Personality and social psychology* (2nd ed.). New York, NY: Wiley.

McCrae, R. R., & Sutin, A. R. (2009). Openness to experience. In M. R. Leary & R. H. Hoyle (Eds.), *Handbook of individual differences in social behavior* (pp. 257–273). New York, NY: Guilford Press.

McCrae, R. R., & Terracciano, A. (2006). National character and personality. *Current Directions in Psychological Science, 15,* 156–161.

McCrae, R. R., Terracciano, A., & 78 Members of the Personality Profiles of Cultures Project. (2005b). Universal features of personality traits from the observer's perspective: Data from 50 cultures. *Journal of Personality and Social Psychology, 88,* 547–561.

McCrae, R. R., & Terracciano, A., & Personality Profiles of Cultures Project. (2005). Personality profiles of cultures: Aggregate personality traits. *Journal of Personality and Social Psychology, 89,* 407–425.

McCrink, K., & Wynn, K. (2004). Large-number addition and subtraction by 9-month old infants. *Psychological Science, 15,* 776–81.

McDaniel, M. A., & Einstein, G. O. (1986). Bizarre imagery as an effective memory aid: The importance of distinctiveness. *Journal of Experimental Psychology: Learning, Memory & Cognition, 12,* 54–65.

McDaniel, M. A., Waddill, P. J., & Shakesby, P. S. (1996). Study strategies, interest, and learning from text: The application of material appropriate processing. In D. J. Herrmann, C. McEvoy, C. Hertzog, P. Hertel, & M. K. Johnson (Eds.), *Basic and applied memory research: Theory in context* (Vol. 1). Mahwah, NJ: Erlbaum.

McDermott, K. B. (2007). Inducing false memories through associated lists: A window onto everyday false memories? In J. S. Nairne (Ed.), *The foundations of remembering: Essays in honor of Henry L. Roediger III.* New York, NY: Psychology Press.

McDermott, K. B., Agarwal, P. K., D'Antonio, L., Roediger, H. I., & McDaniel, M. A. (2014). Both multiple-choice and short-answer quizzes enhance later exam performance in middle and high school classes. *Journal of Experimental Psychology: Applied, 20*(1), 3–21. doi:10.1037/ xap0000004.

McDevitt, M. A., & Williams, B. A. (2001). Effects of signaled versus unsignaled delay of reinforcement on choice. *Journal of the Experimental Analysis of Behavior, 75,* 165–182. doi:10.1901/jeab.2001.75-165.

McDonald, C., & Murphy, K. C. (2003). The new genetics of schizophrenia. *Psychiatric Clinics of North America, 26*(1), 41–63.

McDonald, J., & Walton, R. (2007). *The Cambridge companion for Greek and Roman theatre.* Cambridge, UK: Cambridge University Press.

McDonald, R. V., & Siegel, S. (2004). Intra-administration associations and withdrawal symptoms: Morphine-elicited morphine withdrawal. *Experimental and Clinical Psychopharmacology, 12,* 3–11.

McDonald, W. M., Thompson, T. R., McCall W. V., & Zormuski, C. F. (2004). Electroconvulsive therapy. In A. F. Schatzberg & C. B. Nemeroff (Eds.), *Textbook of psychopharmacology.* Washington, DC: American Psychiatric Publishing.

McEvoy, J. P., Byerly, M., Hamer, R. M., Dominik, R., Swartz, M. S., Rosenheck, R. A., . . . Stroup, T. S. (2014). Effectiveness of paliperidone palmitate vs haloperidol decanoate for maintenance treatment of schizophrenia: A randomized clinical trial. *JAMA, 311,* 1978–1986. doi:10.1001/jama.2014.4310.

McEwen, B. S. (2009). Stress and coping. In G. G. Berntson & J. T. Cacioppo (Eds.), *Handbook of neuroscience for the behavioral sciences* (Vol. 2, pp. 1220–1235). Hoboken, NJ: Wiley.

McFadden, T. J., Helmreich, R. I., Rose, R. M., & Fogg, L. F. (1994). Predicting astronauts' effectiveness: A multivariate approach. *Aviation, Space, and Environmental Medicine, 65,* 904–909.

McGeoch, J. A., & McDonald, W. T. (1931). Meaningful relation and retroactive inhibition. *American Journal of Psychology, 43,* 579–588.

McGinty, D., & Szymusiak, R. (2011). Neural control of sleep in mammals. In M. H. Kryger, T. Roth, & W. C. Dement (Eds.), *Principles and practice of sleep medicine* (5th ed., pp. 76–91). St. Louis, MO: Elsevier Saunders.

McGlashan, T. H., & Hoffman, R. E. (2000). Schizophrenia: Psychodynamic to neurodynamic theories. In B. J. Sadock & V. A. Sadock (Eds.), *Kaplan and Sadock's comprehensive textbook of psychiatry* (7th ed., Vol. 1, pp. 1159–1168). Philadelphia, PA: Lippincott, Williams & Wilkins.

McGrath, J. J., & Murray, R. M. (2011). Environmental risk factors for schizophrenia. In D. R. Weinberger & P. Harrison (Eds.), *Schizophrenia* (3rd ed.). Malden, MA: Wiley-Blackwell.

McGrath, P. J. (1999). Clinical psychology issues in migraine headaches. *Canadian Journal of Neurological Science, 26,* 33–36.

McGue, M., Bouchard, T. J., Jr., Iacono, W. G., & Lykken, D. T. (1993). Behavioral genetics of cognitive ability: A life-span perspective. In R. Plomin & G. E. McClearn (Eds.), *Nature, nurture and psychology.* Washington, DC: American Psychological Association.

McGugin, R. W., Gatenby, J. C., Gore, J. C., & Gauthier, I. (2012). High-resolution imaging of expertise reveals reliable object selectivity in the fusiform face area related to perceptual performance. *Proceedings of the National Academy of Sciences, 109*(42), 17063–17068. doi:10.1073/pnas.1116333109.

McGuigan, F. J., & Lehrer, P. M. (2007). Progressive relaxation: Origins, principles, and clinical applications. In P. M. Lehrer, R. L. Woolfolk, & W. E. Sime (Eds.), *Principles and practice of stress management.* New York, NY: Guilford Press.

McHugh, L., Barnes-Holmes, Y., & Barnes-Holmes, D. (2004). Perspective-taking as relational responding: A developmental profile. *The Psychological Record, 54,* 115–144.

McIlroy, A. (2008, August 15). Meditating through mental illness. *The Globe and Mail,* A1, A4.

McInnis, M. G., Ribia, M., & Greden, J. F. (2014). Anxiety disorders. In R. E. Hales, S. C. Yudofsky, & L. W. Roberts (Eds.), *The American Psychiatric Publishing textbook of psychiatry* (6th ed.). Washington, DC: American Psychiatric Publishing.

McKean, K. (1985, June). Decisions, decisions. *Discover,* 22–31.

McKeefry, D. J., Burton, M. P., & Morland, A. B. (2010). The contribution of human cortical area V3A to the perception of chromatic motion: A transcranial magnetic stimulation study. *European Journal of Neuroscience, 31*(3), 575–584.

McKelvie, P., & Low, J. (2002). Listening to Mozart does not improve children's spatial ability: Final curtains for the Mozart effect. *British Journal of Development Psychology, 20,* 241–258.

McKenzie, R. B. (2010). Predictability rational? In search of defenses for rational behavior of economics. Heidelberg, Germany: Springer-Verlag.

McKiernan, A., & Fleming, K. (2017). *Canadian youth perceptions on cannabis.* Ottawa, ON: Canadian Centre on Substance Abuse.

McKimmie, B. M., Masters, J. M., Masser, B. M., Schuller, R. A., & Terry, D. J. (2013). Stereotypical and counterstereotypical defendants: Who is he and what was the case against her? *Psychology, Public Policy, and Law, 13,* 33–45.

McLanahan, S., Tach, L., & Schneider, D. (2013). The causal effects of father absence. *Annual Review of Sociology, 39,* 399–427.

McLay, R. N., Daylo, A. A., & Hammer, P. S. (2006). No effect of lunar cycle on psychiatric admissions or emergency evaluations. *Military Medicine, 171,* 1239–1242.

McLellan, A. T., Lewis, D. C., O'Brien, C. P., & Kleber, H. D. (2000). Drug dependence, a chronic mental illness: Implications for treatment, insurance, and outcome evaluation. *Journal of the American Medical Association, 284,* 1689–1695.

McLoyd, V. C. (1998). Socioeconomic disadvantage and child development. *American Psychologist, 53,* 185–204.

McNally, R. J. (1994). Cognitive bias in panic disorder. *Current Directions in Psychological Science, 3,* 129–132.

McNally, R. J. (1996). *Panic disorder: A critical analysis.* New York, NY: Guilford.

McNally, R. J. (2003). *Remembering trauma.* Cambridge, MA: Belknap Press/Harvard University Press.

McNally, R. J. (2007). Betrayal trauma theory: A critical appraisal. *Memory, 15,* 280–294.

McNally, R. J. (2009). Posttraumatic stress disorder. In P. H. Blaney & T. Millon (Eds.), *Oxford textbook of psychopathology* (2nd ed., pp. 176–197). New York, NY: Oxford University Press.

McNally, R. J., & Geraerts, E. (2009). A new solution to the recovered memory debate. *Perspectives on Psychological Science, 4*(2), 126–134. doi:10.1111/j.1745-6924.2009.01112.x.

McNamara, T. P. (2013). Semantic memory and priming. In A. F. Healy, R. W. Proctor, & I. B. Weiner (Eds.), *Handbook of psychology: Vol. 4. Experimental psychology* (2nd ed.). New York, NY: Wiley.

McQueen, M. B., & Blacker, D. (2008). Genetics of Alzheimer's disease. In J. W. Smoller, B. R. Sheidley, & M. T. Tsuang (Eds.), *Psychiatric genetics: Applications in clinical practice* (pp. 177–193). Arlington, VA: American Psychiatric Publishing.

McTeer, M. (2003). *In my own name.* Toronto, ON: Vintage Books.

McVay, J. C., & Kane, M. J. (2010). Does mind wandering reflect executive function or executive failure? Comment on Smallwood and Schooler (2006) and Watkins (2008). *Psychological Bulletin, 136,* 188–197.

Mechanic, D. (1980). *Mental health and social policy.* Englewood Cliffs, NJ: Prentice-Hall.

Mechanic, D. (1999). Mental health and mental illness. In A. V. Horvitz & T. L. Scheid (Eds.), *A handbook for the study of mental health: Social contexts, theories, and systems.* New York, NY: Cambridge University Press.

Mednick, S. C., & Drummond, S. P. A. (2009). Napping. In R. Stickgold & M. P. Walker (Eds.), *The neuroscience of sleep* (pp. 254–262). San Diego, CA: Academic Press.

Mednick, S. C., Cali, D. J., Kanady, J., & Drummond, S. A. (2008). Comparing the benefits of caffeine, naps and placebo on verbal, motor and perceptual memory. *Behavioural Brain Research, 193*(1), 79–86.

Meeus, W., van de Schoot, R., Keijsers, L., Schwartz, S. J., & Branje, S. (2010). On the progression and stability of adolescent identity formation: A five-wave longitudinal study in early-to-middle and middle-to-late adolescence. *Child Development, 81,* 1565–1581.

Meichenbaum, D. (1977). *Cognitive-behavior modification.* New York, NY: Plenum Press.

Meichenbaum, D. (1994). *Clinical handbook/practical therapist manual for assessing and treating adults with post-traumatic stress disorder (PTSD).* Waterloo, ON: Institute Press.

Meichenbaum, D. (2007). Cognitive–behavioral therapy with Donald Meichenbaum. *Systems of Psychotherapy Video Series.* Washington, DC: American Psychological Association.

Meillon, S., Thomas, A., Havermans, R., Pénicaud, L., & Brondel, L. (2013). Sensory-specific satiety for a food is unaffected by the ad libitum intake of other foods during a meal. Is SSS subject to dishabituation? *Appetite, 63*, 112–118. doi:10.1016/j.appet.2012.12.004.

Meister, B. (2007). Neurotransmitters in key neurons of the hypothalamus that regulate feeding behavior and body weight. *Physiology & Behavior, 92*, 263–271.

Meister, M., & Tessier-Lavigne, M. (2013). Low-level visual processing: The retina. In E. R. Kandel, J. H. Schwartz, T. M. Jessell, S. A. Siegelbaum, & A. J. Hudspeth (Eds.), *Principles of neural science* (5th ed.). New York, NY: McGraw-Hill.

Meltzer, A. L., McNulty, J. K., Jackson, G. L., & Karney, B. R. (2014). Sex differences in the implications of partner physical attractiveness for the trajectory of marital satisfaction. *Journal of Personality and Social Psychology, 106*, 418–428. doi:10.1037/a0034424.

Meltzer, H. Y., & Bobo, W. V. (2009). Antipsychotic and anticholinergic drugs. In M. C. Gelder, N. C. Andreasen, J. J. López-Ibor, Jr., & J. R. Geddes (Eds.), *New Oxford textbook of psychiatry* (2nd ed., Vol. 1). New York, NY: Oxford University Press.

Melzack, R. (1975). The McGill pain questionnaire: Major properties and scoring methods. *Pain, 1*, 277–299.

Melzack, R. (2001). Pain and the neuromatrix in the brain. *Journal of Dental Education, 65*, 1378–1382.

Melzack, R., & Katz, J. (2004). The gate control theory: Reaching for the brain. In T. Hadjistavropoulos & K. D. Craig (Eds.), *Pain: Psychological perspectives* (pp. 13–34). Mahwah, NJ: Erlbaum.

Melzack, R., & Wall, P. D. (1965). Pain mechanisms: A new theory. *Science, 150*, 971–979.

Melzack, R., & Wall, P. D. (1982). *The challenge of pain.* New York, NY: Basic Books.

Men, W., Falk, D., Sun, T., Chen, W., Li, J., Yin, D., . . . Fan, M. (2013). The corpus callosum of Albert Einstein's brain: Another clue to his high intelligence? *Brain, 24*, 1–8. doi:10.1093/brain/awt252.

Mendelson, W. (2011). Hypnotic medications: Mechanisms of action and pharmacologic effects. In M. H. Kryger, T. Roth, & W. C. Dement (Eds.), *Principles and practice of sleep medicine* (5th ed.). Saint Louis, MO: Elsevier Saunders.

Mennella, J. A., & Beauchamp, G. K. (1996). The early development of human flavor preferences. In E. D. Capaldi (Ed.), *Why we eat what we eat: The psychology of eating* (pp. 83–112). Washington, DC: American Psychological Association.

Menninger, W. W. (2005). Role of the psychiatric hospital in the treatment of mental illness. In B. J. Sadock & V. A. Sadock (Eds.), *Kaplan & Sadock's comprehensive textbook of psychiatry*. Philadelphia, PA: Lippincott Williams & Wilkins.

Mental Health Commission of Canada. (2012). *Changing directions changing lives: A mental health strategy for Canada.* Retrieved from http://strategy .mentalhealthcommission.ca/pdf/strategy -images-en.pdf.

Merikangas, K. R., & Kalaydjian, A. E. (2009). Epidemiology of anxiety disorders. In B. J. Sadock, V. A. Sadock, & P. Ruiz (Eds.), *Kaplan & Sadock's comprehensive textbook of psychiatry* (9th ed., pp. 1856–1863). Philadelphia, PA: Lippincott, Williams & Wilkins.

Merikangas, K. R., & Pato, M. (2009). Recent developments in the epidemiology of bipolar disorder in adults and children: Magnitude, correlates, and future directions. *Clinical Psychology: Science and Practice, 16*(2), 121–133.

Merikle, P. M. (2000). Subliminal perception. In A. E. Kazdin (Ed.), *Encyclopedia of psychology* (pp. 497–499). New York, NY: Oxford University Press.

Merolla, J. L., Burnett, G., Pyle, K. V., Ahmadi, S., & Zak, P. J. (2013). Oxytocin and the biological basis for interpersonal and political trust. *Political Behavior, 35*, 753–776. doi:10.1007/s11109-012-9219-8.

Mesquita, B., & Leu, J. (2007). The cultural psychology of emotion. In S. Kitayama & D. Cohen (Eds.), *Handbook of cultural psychology* (pp. 734–759). New York, NY: Guilford Press.

Mesulam, M. (2013). Cholinergic circuitry of the human nucleus basalis and its fate in Alzheimer's disease. *The Journal of Comparative Neurology, 521*, 4124–4144. doi:10.1002/cne.23415.

Meyer, D. E., & Schvaneveldt, R. W. (1976). Meaning, memory structure, and mental processes. *Science, 192*, 27–33.

Meyer, G. J., Hsiao, W., Viglione, D. J., Mihura, J. L., & Abraham, L. M. (2013). Rorschach scores in applied clinical practice: A survey of perceived validity by experienced clinicians. *Journal of Personality Assessment, 95*, 351–365. doi:10.1080/00223891.2013.770399.

Meyer, R. E. (1996). The disease called addiction: Emerging evidence in a 200-year debate. *The Lancet, 347*, 162–166.

Meyer, R. G. (1992). *Practical clinical hypnosis: Techniques and applications.* New York, NY: Lexington Books.

Meyerbröker, K., & Emmelkamp, P. G. (2010). Virtual reality exposure therapy in anxiety disorders: A systematic review of process-and-outcome studies. *Depression and Anxiety, 27*(10), 933–944. doi:10.1002/da.20734.

Mezulis, A. H., Abramson, L. Y., Hyde, J. S., & Hankin, B. L. (2004). Is there a universal positivity bias in attributions? A meta-analytic review of individual, developmental and cultural differences in the self-serving attributional bias. *Psychological Bulletin, 130*, 711–747.

Mezzich, J. E., Lewis-Fernandez, R., & Ruiperez, M. A. (2003). The cultural framework of psychiatric disorders. In A. Tasman, J. Kay, & J. A. Lieberman (Eds.), *Psychiatry*. New York, NY: Wiley.

Michaelian, K. (2016). *Mental time travel.* Cambridge, MA: MIT Press.

Michels, N., Sioen, I., Braet, C., Eiben, G., Hebestreit, A., Huybrechts, I., . . . De Henauw, S. (2012). Stress, emotional eating behaviour and dietary patterns in children. *Appetite, 59*, 762–769. doi:10.1016/j.appet .2012.08.010.

Mikami, A. Y., Szwedo, D. E., Allen, J. P., Meredyth, A. E., & Hare, A. L. (2010). Adolescent peer relationships and behavior problems predict young adults' communication on social networking websites. *Developmental Psychology, 46*, 46–56.

Mikkonen, J., & Raphael, D. (2010). *Social determinants of health: The Canadian facts.* Toronto, ON: York University School of Health Policy and Management.

Miklowitz, D. J. (2014). Pharmacotherapy and psychosocial treatments. In I. H. Gotlib & C. L. Hammen, (Eds.), *Handbook of depression* (3rd ed.). New York, NY: Guilford Press.

Mikulincer, M., & Shaver, P. R. (2007). *Attachment in adulthood: Structure, dynamics, and change.* New York, NY: Guilford Press.

Mikulincer, M., & Shaver, P. R. (2013). The role of attachment security in adolescent and adult close relationships. In J. A. Simpson & L Campbell (Eds.), *Oxford handbook of close relationships*. New York, NY: Oxford University Press.

Milan, A. (2013). Marital Status. Statistics Canada. Retrieved from http://www.statcan.gc.ca/pub/91 -209-x/2013001/article/11788-eng.pdf.

Milgram, S. (1963). Behavioral study of obedience. *Journal of Abnormal and Social Psychology, 67*, 371–378.

Milgram, S. (1964). Issues in the study of obedience. *American Psychologist, 19*, 848–852.

Milgram, S. (1968). Reply to the critics. *International Journal of Psychiatry, 6*, 294–295.

Milgram, S. (1974). *Obedience to authority.* New York, NY: Harper & Row.

Milkman, K. L., Chugh, D., & Bazerman, M. H. (2009). How can decision making be improved? *Perspectives on Psychological Science, 4*(4), 379–383.

Millecamps, M., Seminowicz, D. A., Bushnell, M. C., & Coderre, T. J. (2013). The biopsychology of pain. In R. J. Nelson, S. Y. Mizumori, & I. B. Weiner (Eds.), *Handbook of psychology: Vol. 3. Behavioral neuroscience* (2nd ed., pp. 240–271). New York, NY: Wiley.

Miller, A., Hess, J. M., & Bybee, D. (2017). Understanding the mental health consequences of family separation for refugees: Implications for policy and practice. *American Journal of Orthopsychiatry, 87*, 567–574.

Miller, A. G. (1986). *The obedience experiments: A case study of controversy in social science.* New York, NY: Praeger.

Miller, A. G. (2004). What can the Milgram obedience experiments tell us about the Holocaust?: Generalizing from the social psychology laboratory. In A. G. Miller (Ed.), *The social psychology of good and evil* (pp. 193–239). New York, NY: Guilford Press.

Miller, B. J., Culpepper, N., Rapaport, M. H., & Buckley, P. (2013). Prenatal inflammation and neurodevelopment in schizophrenia: A review of human studies. *Progress in Neuro-Psychopharmacology & Biological Psychiatry, 42*, 92–100.

Miller, E., & Wallis, J. (2008). The prefrontal cortex and executive brain functions. In L. Squire, D. Berg, F. Bloom, S. Du Lac, A. Ghosh, & N. Spitzer (Eds.), *Fundamental neuroscience* (3rd ed., pp. 1199–1222). San Diego, CA: Elsevier.

Miller, G. (2005). Neuroscience: Reflecting on another's mind. *Science, 308*, 945–947.

Miller, G. (2009). The Brain Collector. *Science, 324*(5935), 1634–1636.

Miller, G., Tybur, J. M., & Jordan, B. D. (2007). Ovulatory cycle effects on tip earnings by lap dancers: Economic evidence for human estrus? *Evolution and Human Behavior, 28*, 375–381.

Miller, G. A. (1956). The magical number seven, plus or minus two: Some limits on our capacity for processing information. *Psychological Review, 63*, 81–97.

Miller, G. A. (2003). The cognitive revolution: A historical perspective. *Trends in Cognitive Sciences, 7*(3), 141–144.

Miller, G. A., Galanter, E., & Pribram, K. H. (1960). *Plans and the structure of behavior.* New York, NY: Holt, Rinehart & Winston.

Miller, G. E., Chen, E., & Zhou, E. S. (2007). If it goes up, must it come down? Chronic stress and the hypothalamic-pituitary-adrenocortical axis in humans. *Psychological Bulletin, 133*, 25–45.

Miller, I. J., & Reedy, F. E. Jr. (1990). Variations in human taste-bud density and taste intensity perception. *Physiological Behavior, 47*, 1213–1219.

Miller, J. G. (2006). Insights into moral development from cultural psychology. In M. Killen & J. G. Smetana (Eds.), *Handbook of moral development*. Mahwah, NJ: Erlbaum.

Miller, J. M., & Peterson, D. A. M. (2004). Theoretical and empirical implications of attitude strength. *Journal of Politics, 66*, 847–867.

Miller, N. E. (1944). Experimental studies of conflict. In J. M. Hunt (Ed.), *Personality and the behavior disorders* (Vol. 1). New York, NY: Ronald.

Miller, N. E. (1959). Liberalization of basic S-R concepts: Extension to conflict behavior, motivation, and social learning. In S. Koch (Ed.), *Psychology: A study of a science* (Vol. 2). New York, NY: McGraw-Hill.

Miller, R. R., & Grace, R. C. (2003). Conditioning and learning. In A. F. Healy & R. W. Proctor (Eds.), *Handbook of psychology (Vol. 4): Experimental psychology*. New York, NY: Wiley.

Miller, R. R., & Grace, R. C. (2013). Conditioning and learning. In A. F. Healy, R. W. Proctor, & I. B. Weiner (Eds.), *Handbook of psychology: Vol. 4. Experimental psychology* (2nd ed.). New York, NY: Wiley.

Miller Burke, J., & Attridge, M. (2011a). Pathways to career and leadership success: Part 1—A psychosocial profile of $100k professionals. *Journal of Workplace Behavioral Health, 26*(3), 175–206.

Miller Burke, J., & Attridge, M. (2011b). Pathways to career and leadership success: Part 2—Striking gender similarities among $100k professionals. *Journal of Workplace Behavioral Health, 26*(3), 207–239.

Milligan, E. D., & Watkins, L. R. (2009). Pathological and protective roles of glia in chronic pain. *Nature Reviews Neuroscience, 10*(1), 23–36.

Millon, T. (1981). *Disorders of personality: DSM-III, Axis II.* New York, NY: Wiley.

Mills, J. A. (2010). Hallucinogens as hard science: The adrenochrome hypothesis for the biogenesis of schizophrenia. *History of Psychology, 13*, 178–195.

Mills, K. L., Goddings, A., Clasen, L. S., Giedd, J. N., & Blakemore, S. (2014). The developmental mismatch in structural brain maturation during adolescence. *Developmental Neuroscience, 36*, 147–160. doi:10.1159/000362328.

Millstone, E. (1989). Methods and practices of animal experimentation. In G. Langley (Ed.), *Animal experimentation: The consensus changes.* New York, NY: Chapman & Hall.

Milner, A. D., & Goodale, M. A. (2013). Does grasping in patient D. F. depend on vision? *Trends in Cognitive Science, 16*, 256–257.

Milner, B. (1977). Memory mechanisms. *Canadian Medical Association Journal, 116*, 1374–1376.

Milner, B., & Klein, D. (2016). Loss of recent memory after bilateral lesions: Memory and memories-looking back and looking-forward. *Journal of Neurology and Neurosurgical Psychiatry, 87*, 230.

Milner, B., Corkin, S., & Teuber, H. (1968). Further analysis of the hippocampal amnesic syndrome: 14-year follow-up study of H. M. *Neuropsychologia, 6*, 215–234.

Milner, P. (2003). A brief history of the Hebbian learning rule. *Canadian Psychology, 44*, 5–9.

Miltenberger, R. G. (2012). *Behavior modification: Principles and procedures.* Belmont, CA: Cengage Learning.

Mineka, S., & Öhman, A. (2002). Phobias and preparedness: The selective, automatic and encapsulated nature of fear. *Biological Psychiatry, 52*, 927–937.

Mineka, S., & Zinbarg, R. (2006). A contemporary learning theory perspective on the etiology of anxiety disorders: It's not what you thought it was. *American Psychologist, 61*, 10–26.

Minkel, J. D., & Dinges, D. F. (2009). Circadian rhythms in sleepiness, alertness, and performance. In R. Stickgold & M. P. Walker (Eds.), *The neuroscience of sleep* (pp. 183–190). San Diego, CA: Academic Press.

Minzenberg, M. J., Yoon, J. H., & Carter, C. S. (2008). Schizophrenia. In R. E. Hales, S. C. Yudofsky, & G. O. Gabbard (Eds.), *The American Psychiatric Publishing textbook of psychiatry* (5th ed., pp. 407–456). Washington, DC: American Psychiatric Publishing.

Miranda, J., Bernal, G., Lau, A., Kohn, L., Hwang, W., & LaFromboise, T. (2005). State of the science on psychosocial interventions for ethnic minorities. *Annual Review of Clinical Psychology, 1*, 113–142.

Mirtle, J. (2011, April 29). Crosby suffers concussion setback. *Globe and Mail.* Retrieved from http://www.theglobeandmail.com/sports/hockey/globe-on-hockey/crosby-suffers-setback/article2004362/.

Mischel, W. (1961). Delay of gratification, need for achievement, and acquiescence in another culture. *Journal of Abnormal and Social Psychology, 62*, 543–552.

Mischel, W. (1968). *Personality and assessment.* New York, NY: Wiley.

Mischel, W. (1973). Toward a cognitive social learning conceptualization of personality. *Psychological Review, 80*, 252–283.

Mischel, W. (1984). Convergences and challenges in the search for consistency. *American Psychologist, 39*, 351–364.

Mischel, W. (2014), The master of self-control. *The Psychologist, 27*, 942–944.

Mischel, W. (2015). A social learning view of sex differences in behavior. In V. Burr (Ed.), *Gender and Psychology* (Vol. 1, pp. 108–129). New York, NY: Routledge/Taylor & Francis Group.

Mitchell, D. B. (2006). Nonconscious priming after 17 years. *Psychological Science, 17*(11), 925–929.

Mitchell, D. B., & Brown, A. S. (1988). Persistent repetition priming in picture naming and its dissociation from recognition memory. *Journal of Experimental Psychology: Learning, Memory, and Cognition, 14*, 213–222.

Mitchell, J. E., & Wonderlich, S. A. (2014). Feeding and eating disorders. In R. E. Hales, S. C. Yudofsky, & L. W. Roberts (Eds.), *The American Psychiatric Publishing textbook of psychiatry* (6th ed.). Washington, DC: American Psychiatric Publishing.

Mitchell, J. P., Macrae, C. N., & Banaji, M. R. (2004). Encoding-specific effects of social cognition on the neural correlates of subsequent memory. *Journal of Neuroscience, 26*, 4912–4917.

Mitsonis, C., Zervas, I., Potagas, K., Mandellos, D., Koutsis, G., & Sfagos, K. (2006). The role of stress in multiple sclerosis: Three case reports and review of the literature. *Psychiatriki, 17*, 325–342.

Mittner, M., Hawkins, G. E., Boekel, W., & Forstmann, B. U. (2016). A neural model of mind wandering. *Trends in Cognitive Science, 20*, 570–578.

Miyamoto, S., Merrill, D. B., Lieberman, J. A., Fleischacker, W. W., & Marder, S. R. (2008). Antipsychotic drugs. In A. Tasman, J. Kay, J. A. Lieberman, M. B. First, & M. Maj (Eds.), *Psychiatry* (3rd ed.). New York, NY: Wiley-Blackwell.

Mize, K. D., & Jones, N. A. (2012). Infant physiological and behavioral responses to loss of maternal attention to a social rival. *International Journal of Psychophysiology, 83*, 16–23.

Modestin, J. (1992). Multiple personality disorder in Switzerland. *American Journal of Psychiatry, 149*, 88–92.

Moe, A., & De Beni, R. (2004). Studying passages with the loci method: Are subject-generated more effective than experimenter-supplied loci pathways? *Journal of Mental Imagery, 28*(3–4), 75–86.

Mojtabai, R., & Olfson, M. (2010). National trends in psychotropic medication polypharmacy in office-based psychiatry. *Archives of General Psychiatry, 67*(1), 26–36.

Mokros, A., Habermeyer, E., Neumann, C. S., Schilling, F., Hare, R. D., & Eher, R. (2013). Assessment of psychopathy in Austria: Psychometric properties of the Psychopathy Checklist-Revised. *European Journal of Psychological Assessment.* doi: 10.1027/1015-5759/a000177.

Moksnes, U. K., & Espnes, G. A. (2016). Stress: Concepts, models, and measures. In M. E. Alvarenga & D. Byrne (Eds.), *Handbook of psychocardiology* (Vol. 1, pp. 143–162). New York, NY: Springer-Verlag.

Molitor, A., & Hsu, H. (2011). Child development across cultures. In K. D. Keith (Ed.), *Cross-cultural psychology: Contemporary themes and perspectives.* Malden, MA: Wiley-Blackwell.

Moll, H., & Meltzoff, A. N. (2011). How does it look? Level 2 perspective-taking at 36 months of age. *Child Development, 82*(2), 661–673. doi:org/10.1111/j.1467-8624.2010.01571.x.

Molton, I. R., & Terrill, A. L. (2014). Overview of persistent pain in older adults. *American Psychologist, 69*(2), 197–207.

Monahan, J. (1997). Major mental disorders and violence to others. In D. M. Stoff, J. Breiling, & J. D. Maser (Eds.), *Handbook of antisocial behavior.* New York, NY: Wiley.

Mongrain, M., & Anselmo-Matthews, T. (2012). Do positive psychology exercises work? A replication of Seligman et al. (2005). *Journal of Clinical Psychology, 68*(4), 382–389.

Mongrain, M., Komeylian, Z., & Barnhart, R. (2016). Happiness vs. mindfulness exercises for individuals vulnerable to depression. *The Journal of Positive Psychology, 11*, 366–377.

Monk, C., Georgieff, M. K., & Osterholm, E. A. (2013). Research review: Maternal prenatal distress and poor nutrition: Mutually influencing risk factors affecting infant neurocognitive development. *Journal of Child Psychology and Psychiatry, 54*, 115–130. doi:10.1111/jcpp.12000.

Monk, T. H. (2000). Shift work. In M. H. Kryger, T. Roth, & W. C. Dement (Eds.), *Principles and practice of sleep medicine.* Philadelphia, PA: Saunders.

Monk, T. H. (2005a). Aging human circadian rhythms: Conventional wisdom may not always be right. *Journal of Biological Rhythms, 20*(4), 366–374.

Monk, T. H. (2005b). Shift work: Basic principles. In M. H. Kryger, T. Roth, & W. C. Dement (Eds.). *Principles and practice of sleep medicine.* Philadelphia, PA: Elsevier Saunders.

Monk, T. H. (2006). Jet lag. In T. Lee-Chiong (Ed.), *Sleep: A comprehensive handbook.* Hoboken, NJ: Wiley-Liss.

Monroe, S. M., & Harkness, K. L. (2005). Life stress, the "kindling" hypothesis, and the recurrence of depression: Considerations from a life stress perspective. *Psychological Review, 112*, 417–445. doi:10.1037/0033-295X.112.2.417.

Monroe, S. M., Slavich, G. M., & Georgiades, K. (2014). The social environment and depression: The roles of life stress. In I. H. Gotlib & C. L. Hammen (Eds.), *Handbook of depression* (3rd ed.). New York, NY: Guilford Press.

Montessori, M. (1973). *The discovery of the child.* New York, NY: Random House, Inc.

Montoya, R., & Horton, R. S. (2012). The reciprocity of liking effect. In M. A. Paludi (Ed.), *The psychology of love.* Santa Barbara, CA: Praeger/ABC-CLIO.

Montoya, R. M., Horton, R. S., Vevea, J. L., Citowicz, M,. & Lauber, E. A. (2017). Re-examination of the mere exposure effect: The influence of repeated exposure on recognition, familiarity, and liking. *Psychological Bulletin, 143*, 459–498.

Mook, D. G. (1983). In defense of external invalidity. *American Psychologist, 38*, 379–387.

Moore, A., & Malinowski, P. (2009). Meditation, mindfulness and cognitive flexibility. *Conscious Cognition, 18*, 176–186.

Moore, B. C. J. (2010). Audition. In E. B. Goldstein (Ed.), *Encyclopedia of perception.* Thousand Oaks, CA: Sage.

Moore, D. (2007, January 8). Brainwashed "guinea pig" seeks more damages. *Toronto Star*, A4.

Moore, K. L., & Persaud, T. V. N. (2008). *Before we are born* (7th ed.). Philadelphia, PA: Saunders.

Moore, K. L., Persaud, T. V. N., & Torchia, M. G. (2013). *Before we are born: Essentials of embryology and birth defects* (8th ed., 233–276). Philadelphia, PA: Elsevier.

Moore, R. Y. (2006). Biological rythms and sleep. In T. Lee-Chiong (Ed.), *Sleep: A comprehensive handbook.* Hoboken, NJ: Wiley-Liss.

Morales, J., Gomez-Ariza, C. J., & Bajo, M. T. (2013). Dual mechanisms of cognitive control in bilinguals and monolinguals. *Journal of Cognitive Psychology, 25*(5), 531–546.

Moran, T. H., & Sakai R. R. (2013). Food and fluid intake. In R. J. Nelson, S. Y. Mizumori, & I. B. Weiner (Eds.), *Handbook of psychology: Vol. 3. Behavioral neuroscience* (2nd ed.). New York, NY: Wiley.

Moreno, S., Bialystok, E., Barac, R., Schellenberg, E. G., Cepeda, N. J., & Chau, T. (2011). Short-term music training enhances verbal intelligence and executive function. *Psychological Science, 22*, 1425–1433. doi:10.1177/0956797611416999.

Morgado, P., Freitas, D., Bessa, J. M., Sousa, N., & Cerqueira, J. J. (2013). Perceived stress in obsessive-compulsive disorder is related with obsessive but not compulsive symptoms. *Frontiers In Psychiatry, 4*, Article ID 21.

Morgan, H. (1996). An analysis of Gardner's theory of multiple intelligence. *Roeper Review, 18*, 263–269.

Morgan, K. (2012). The epidemiology of sleep. In C. M. Morin, & C. A. Espie (Eds.), *Oxford handbook of sleep and sleep disorders.* New York, NY: Oxford University Press.

Morin, C. M. (2011). Psychological and behavioral treatments for insomnia I: Approaches and efficacy. In M. H. Kryger, T. Roth, & W. C. Dement (Eds.), *Principles and practice of sleep medicine* (5th ed.). Saint Louis, MO: Elsevier Saunders.

Morrison, A. R. (2003). The brain on night shift. *Cerebrum, 5*(3), 23–36.

Morry, M. M. (2009). Similarity principle of attraction. In H. T. Reis & S. Sprecher (Eds.), *Encyclopedia of human relationships* (pp. 1500–1504), Los Angeles, CA: Sage.

Moruzzi, G. (1964). Reticular influences on the EEG. *Electroencephalography and Clinical Neurophysiology, 16,* 2–17.

Mosby, I. (2013). Adminstering colonial science: Nutrition research and human biochemical experimentation in aboriginal communities and residential schools, 1942–1952. *Social History, 46*(91), 111–134.

Moscovitch, M., Cabza, R., Wonocur, G., & Nadel, L. (2016). Episodic memory and beyond: The hippocampus and neocortex in transformation. *Annual Review of Psychology, 67,* 105–134.

Moskowitz, J. T., & Saslow, L. R. (2014). Health and psychology: The importance of positive affect. In M. M. Tugade, M. N. Shiota, & L. D. Kirby (Eds.), *Handbook of positive emotions.* New York, NY: Guilford Press.

Moss, P. (1994). Validity. In R. J. Sternberg (Ed.), *Encyclopedia of human intelligence.* New York, NY: Macmillan.

Mostofsky, E., Penner, E. A., Mittleman, M. A. (2014). Outbursts of anger as trigger of acute cardiovascular events: A systematic review and meta-analysis. *European Heart Journal, 35,* 1404–1410. doi:10.1093/eurheartj/ ehu033.

Motivala, S. J., & Irwin, M. R. (2007). Sleep and immunity: Cytokine pathways linking sleep and health outcomes. *Current Directions in Psychological Science, 16,* 21–25.

Motivala, S. J., & Irwin, M. R. (2007). Sleep and immunity: Cytokine pathways linking sleep and health outcomes. *Current Directions in Psychological Science, 16,* 21–25.

Mowrer, O. H. (1947). On the dual nature of learning: A reinterpretation of "conditioning" and "problem-solving." *Harvard Educational Review, 17,* 102–150.

Moye, J., Marson, D. C., & Edelstein, B. (2013). Assessment of capacity in an aging society. *American Psychologist, 68,* 158–171.

Mrazek, M. D., Smallwood, J., & Schooler, J. W. (2012). Mindfulness and mind-wandering: Finding convergence through opposing constructs. *Emotion, 12,* 442–448.

Muchnik, C., Amir, N., Shabtai, E., & Kaplan-Neeman, R. (2012). Preferred listening levels of personal listening devices in young teenagers: Self reports and physical measurements. *International Journal of Audiology, 51*(4), 287–293. doi:10.3109/14992027.2011.631590.

Muela, A., Nekane, B., Amiano, N., Caldentey, M. A., & Aliri, J. (2017). Animal-assisted psychotherapy for young people with behavioural problems in residential care. *Clinical Psychology and Psychotherapy, 32,* 75–90.

Mueser, K. T., Deavers, F., Penn, D. L., & Cassisi, J. E. (2013). Psychosocial treatments for schizophrenia. *Annual Review of Clinical Psychology, 9,* 465–497. doi:10.1146/annurev-clinpsy-050212-185620.

Mugitani, R., Fais, L., Kajikawa, S., Werker,J, & Amano, S. (2007). Age-related changes in sensitivity to native phonotactics in Japanese infants. *Journal of the Acoustic Society of America, 122,* 1332–1334.

Mukamel, M. R., & Fried, I. (2012). Human intercranial recordings and cognitive neuroscience. *Annual Review of Psychology, 65,* 511–537.

Mullen, B., & Copper, C. (1994). The relation between group cohesiveness and performance: An integration. *Psychological Bulletin, 115,* 210–227.

Muller, K. W., Glaesmer, H., Brahler, D., Woelfling, K., & Beutel, M. E. (2014). Prevalence of Internet addiction in the general population: Results from a German population-based survey. *Behaviour & Information Technology, 33,* 757–766. doi:10.1080/0144929X.2013.810778.

Mulligan, N. W. (1998). The role of attention during encoding in implicit and explicit memory. *Journal of Experimental Psychology: Learning, Memory, & Cognition, 24,* 27–47.

Mulligan, N. W., & Besken, M. (2013). Implicit memory, In D. Reisberg (Ed.), *Oxford handbook of cognitive psychology.* New York, NY: Oxford University Press.

Munafò, M. R., & Flint, J. (2011). Dissecting the genetic architecture of human personality. *Trends in Cognitive Sciences, 15,* 395–400.

Munck, A. (2007). Corticosteroids and stress. In G. Fink (Ed.), *Encyclopedia of stress.* San Diego, CA: Elsevier.

Munoz, R. F., Beardslee, W. R., & Leykin, Y. (2012). Major depression can be prevented. *American Psychologist, 67,* 285–295.

Murdock, B. (2001). Analysis of the serial position curve. In H. L. Roediger III, J. S. Nairne, I. Neath, & A. M. Surprenant (Eds.), *The nature of remembering: Essays in honor of Robert G. Crowder* (pp. 151–170). Washington, DC: American Psychological Association.

Muris, P. (2002). Relationships between self-efficacy and symptoms of anxiety disorders and depression in a normal adolescent sample. *Personality and Individual Differences, 32,* 337–348.

Murison, R. (2001). Is there a role for psychology in ulcer disease? *Integrative Physiological and Behavioral Science, 36*(1), 75–83.

Murphy, K. R., & Sideman, L. (2006a). The fadification of emotional intelligence. In K. R. Murphy (Ed.), *A critique of emotional intelligence: What are the problems and how can they be fixed?* (pp. 283–300). Mahwah, NJ: Erlbaum.

Murphy, K. R., & Sideman, L. (2006b). The two EIs. In K. R. Murphy (Ed.), *A critique of emotional intelligence: What are the problems and how can they be fixed?* (pp. 37–58). Mahwah, NJ: Erlbaum.

Murphy, K. R. (2002). Can conflicting perspectives on the role of *g* in personnel selection be resolved? *Human Performance, 15,* 173–186.

Murphy, K. R. (2006). *A critique of emotional intelligence: What are the problems and how can they be fixed?* Mahwah, NJ: Erlbaum and Associates.

Murray, B. (2003). The seven sins of memory. *APA Monitor, 34,* 28.

Murray, D., Trudeau, R., & Schaller, M. (2011). On the origins of cultural differences in conformity: Four tests of the pathogen prevalence hypothesis. *Personality and Social Psychology Bulletin, 37,* 318–329.

Murray, E. A. (2007, November). The amygdala, reward and emotion. *Trends in Cognitive Sciences, 11,* 489–497.

Murray, H. A. (1938). *Explorations in personality.* New York, NY: Oxford University Press.

Murray, H. A. (1943). *Thematic Apperception Test—manual.* Cambridge, MA: Harvard University Press.

Murstein, B. I., & Fontaine, P. A. (1993). The public's knowledge about psychologists and other mental health professionals. *American Psychologist, 48,* 839–845.

Muscanell, N. L., Guadagno, R. E., & Murphy, S. (2014). Weapons of influence misused: A social influence analysis of why people fall pretty to Internet scams. *Social and Personality Psychology Compass, 8,* 388–396. doi:10.1111/spc3.12115.

Musick, K., & Bumpass, L. (2012). Reexamining the case for marriage: Union formation and changes in wellbeing. *Journal of Marriage and Family, 74*(1), 1–18.

Mussell, P. (2013). Intellect: A theoretical framework for personality traits related to intellectual achievements. *Journal of Personality and Social Psychology, 104,* 885–906.

Musson, D. M., Sandal, G. M., & Helmreich, R. L. (2004). Personality characteristics and trait clusters in final stage astronaut selection. *Aviation, Space, and Environmental Medicine, 75,* 342–349.

Mustanski, B. S., Kuper, L., & Greene, G. J. (2014). Development of sexual orientation and identity. In D. L. Tolman, L. M. Diamond, J. A. Bauermeister, W. H. George, J. G. Pfaus, & L. M. Ward (Eds.), *APA handbook of sexuality and psychology: Vol. 1. Person-based approaches.* Washington, DC: American Psychological Association.

Mutz, D. C., & Goldman, S. K. (2010). Mass media. In J. F. Dovidio, M. Hewstone, P. Glick, & V. M. Esses (Eds.), *The Sage handbook of prejudice, stereotyping, and discrimination.* Los Angeles, CA: Sage.

Muzina, D. J., Kemp, D. E., & Calabrese, J. R. (2008). Mood stabilizers. In A. Tasman, J. Kay, J. A. Lieberman, M. B. First, & M. Maj (Eds.), *Psychiatry* (3rd ed.). New York, NY: Wiley-Blackwell.

Myers, D. G. (1992). *The pursuit of happiness: Who is happy—and why.* New York, NY: Morrow.

Myers, D. G. (2008). Religion and human flourishing. In M. Eid & R. J. Larsen (Eds.), *The science of subjective well-being* (pp. 323–346). New York, NY: Guilford.

Myers, D. G., & Diener, E. (1995). Who is happy? *Psychological Science, 6,* 10–19.

Myers, D. G., & Lamm, H. (1976). The group polarization phenomenon. *Psychological Bulletin, 83,* 602–627.

Naci, L., & Owen, A. M. (2013). Making every word count for vegetative patients. *JAMA Neurology, 80*(4), 345–52.

Nadal, K. L., Wong, Y., Sriken, J., Griffin, K., & Fujii-Doe, W. (2014). Racial microaggressions and Asian Americans: An exploratory study on within-group differences and mental health. *Asian American Journal of Psychology,* np. doi:10.1037/a0038058.

Nadelson, C. C., Notman, M. T., & McCarthy, M. K. (2005). Gender issues in psychotherapy. In G. O. Gabbard, J. S. Beck, & J. Holmes (Eds.), *Oxford textbook of psychotherapy.* New York, NY: Oxford University Press.

Nadkarni, A., & Hofmann, S. G. (2012). Why do people use Facebook? *Personality and Individual Differences, 52,* 243–249. doi:10.1016/j.paid.2011.11.007.

Nahas, Z., Kozel, F. A., Molnar, C., Ramsey, D., Holt, R., Ricci, R., et al. (2007). Methods of administering transcranial magnetic stimulation. In M. S. George & R. H. Belmaker (Eds.), *Transcranial magnetic stimulation in clinical psychiatry* (pp. 39–58). Washington, DC: American Psychiatric Publishing.

Naidoo, J. C. (1992). The mental health of visible ethnic minorities in Canada. *Psychology and Developing Societies, 4,* 165–187.

Nairne, J. S. (2003). Sensory and working memory. In A. F. Healy & R. W. Proctor (Eds.), *Handbook of psychology (Vol. 4): Experimental psychology.* New York, NY: Wiley.

Nairne, J. S., & Neath, I. (2013). Sensory and working memory. In A. F. Healy, R. W. Proctor, & I. B. Weiner (Eds.), *Handbook of psychology: Vol. 4. Experimental psychology* (2nd ed.). New York, NY: Wiley.

Nairne, J. S., Pandeirada, J. N. S., & Thompson, S. R. (2008). Adaptive memory: The comparative value of survival processing. *Psychological Science, 19,* 176–180.

Narr, K. L., Woods, R. P., Thompson, P. M., Szeszko, P., Robinson, D., Dimtcheva, T., et al. (2007). Relationships between IQ and regional cortical gray matter thickness in healthy adults. *Cerebral Cortex, 17*(9), 2163–2171.

NASA. (2008). *Astronaut Candidate Program.* Retrieved June 3, 2011, from http://astronauts.nasa.gov/content/ broch00.htm.

Nasar, S. (1998). *A beautiful mind: A biography of John Forbes Nash, Jr., winner of the Nobel Prize in Economics.* New York, NY: Simon & Schuster.

Nash, M. R. (2001, July). The truth and hype of hypnosis. *Scientific American, 285,* 36–43.

Nathan, P. E. (2009). Clinical psychology: A national perspective on origins, contemporary practice, and future prospects. In S. Carta (Ed.), *Encyclopedia of life support systems: Psychology.* Paris, France: Eolss Publishers, Developed under the Auspices of the UNESCO.

National Institute of Mental Health. (n.d.). *Research domain criteria.* Retrieved from http://www.nimh.nih .gov/research-priorities/rdoc/index.shtml.

National Institute on Alcohol Abuse and Alcoholism. (2013). *Alcohol facts and statistics.* Retrieved from http://www.niaaa.nih.gov/alcohol-health/ overview-alcohol-consumption/alcohol-facts-and-statistics.

National Sleep Foundation. (2010). *Sleep in America poll: Summary of findings.* Retrieved from http://www .sleepfoundation.org/sites/default/ files/nsaw/NSF%20 Sleep%20in%20 %20America%20Poll%20-%20 Summary%20of%20Findings %20.pdf.

Navaneelan, T. (2017). Suicide rates: An overview. Statistics Canada. Retrieved from http://www.google.ca/search? q=tanya+navaneelan+suicide+rates+an+overview&ie=utf -8&oe=utf-8&gws_rd=cr&dcr=0&ei=3A3qWbKtLevajwSTv rCAAg.

Neal, T. M. S., Guadagno, R. E., Eno, C. A., & Brodsky, S. L. (2012). Warmth and competence on the witness stand: Implications for the credibility of male and female expert witnesses. *Journal of the American Academy of Psychiatry and the Law, 40,* 488–497.

Nedergaard, M., & Verkhratsky, A. (2012). Artifact versus reality: How astrocytes contribute to synaptic events. *Glia, 60,* 1013–1023. doi:10.1002/glia.22288.

Neese, R. M., & Ellsworth, P. (2009). Evolution, emotions, and emotional disorders. *American Psychologist, 64,* 129–139.

Neff, L. A., & Geers, A. L. (2013). Optimistic expectations in early marriage: A resource or vulnerability for adaptive relationship function? *Journal of Personality and Social Psychology, 105,* 38–60. doi:10.1037/a0032600.

Negron, R., Martin, A., Balbierz, A., & Howell, E. A. (2013). Social support during the postpartum period: Mothers' views on needs, expectations, and mobilization of support. *Maternal and Children's Health, 17*(4), 616–623.

Neisser, U. (1967). *Cognitive psychology.* New York, NY: Appleton-Century-Crofts.

Neisser, U. (1998). Introduction: Rising test scores and what they mean. In U. Neisser (Ed.), *The rising curve: Long-term gains in IQ and related measures.* Washington, DC: American Psychological Association.

Neisser, U., Boodoo, G., Bouchard, T. J., Jr., Boykin, A. W., Brody, N., Ceci, S. J., et al. (1996). Intelligence: Knowns and unknowns. *American Psychologist, 51,* 77–101.

Nelson, N. L., & Russell, J. A. (2013). Universality revisited. *Emotion Review, 5*(1), 8–15. doi:10.1177/1754073912457227.

Nemeroff, C. B., Kalali, A., Keller, M. B., Charney, D. S., Lenderts, S. E., Cascade, E. F., et al. (2007). Impact of publicity concerning pediatric suicidality data on physician practice patterns in the United States. *Archives of General Psychiatry, 64,* 466–472.

Neria, Y., DiGande, L., & Adams, B. G. (2011). Posttraumatic stress disorder following the September 11, 2001, terrorist attacks. *American Psychologist, 66,* 429–446.

Nestler, E. J. (2014). Epigenetic mechanisms of drug addiction. *Neuropharmacology, 76*(Part B), 259–268. doi:10.1016/j.neuropharm.2013.04.004.

Nestler, E. J., & Malenka, R. C. (2004). The addicted brain. *Scientific American, 290*(3), 78–85.

Nettle, D. (2001). *Strong imagination, madness, creativity, and human nature.* New York, NY: Oxford University Press.

Nettle, D. (2006). The evolution of personality variation in humans and other animals. *American Psychologist, 61,* 622–631.

Neuberg, S. L., & Schaller, M. (2015). Evolutionary social cognition. In M. Mikulincer, P. R. Shaver, E. Borgida, & J. A. Bargh (Eds.), *APA handbook of personality and social psychology Vol. 1: Attitudes and social cognition.* Washington, DC: American Psychological Association.

Neuberg, S. L., Kenrick, D. T., & Schaller, M. (2010). Evolutionary social psychology. In S. T. Fiske, D. T. Gilbert, & G. Lindzey (Eds.), *Handbook of social psychology* (5th ed., Vol. 2, pp. 761–796). Hoboken, NJ: Wiley.

Neugroschl, J. A., Kolevzon, A., Samuels, S. C., & Marin, D. B. (2005). Dementia. In B. J. Sadock & V. A. Sadock (Eds.), *Kaplan & Sadock's comprehensive textbook of psychiatry* (pp. 1068–1092). Philadelphia, PA: Lippincott, Williams & Wilkins.

Neumann, C. S., Johansson, P. J., & Hare, R. D. (2013). The Psychopathy Checklist-Revised (PCL-R), low anxiety, and fearlessness: A structural equation modeling analysis. *Personality Disorders: Theory Research, and Treatment, 4*(2), 129–137.

Neuschatz, J. S., Lampinen, J. M., Preston, E. L., Hawkins, E. R., & Toglia, M. P. (2002). The effect of memory schemata on memory and the phenomenological experience of naturalistic situations. *Applied Cognitive Psychology, 16,* 687–708.

Neuschatz, J. S., Lampinen, J. M., Toglia, M. P., Payne, D. G., & Cisneros, E. P. (2007). False memory research: History, theory, and applied implications. In M. P. Toglia, J. D. Read, D. F. Ross, & R. C. L. Lindsay (Eds.), *Handbook*

of eyewitness psychology: Volume 1. Memory for events. Mahwah, NJ: Erlbaum.

New York Times. (1921). Einstein sees Boston: Fails on Edison Test. Retrieved June 20, 2011, from http://query.nytimes.com/gst/abstract.html?res=F60D15FE345B1B7A93CAA8178ED85F458285F9.

New York Times. (2009). Kim Peek, inspiration for "Rain Man" dies at 58, Obituary. Retrieved June 20, 2011, from http://www.nytimes.com/2009/12/27/us/27peek.html.

Newcombe, N. S. (2007). Taking science seriously: Straight thinking about spatial sex differences. In S. J. Ceci & W. M. Williams (Eds.), *Why aren't more women in science?* (pp. 69–78). Washington, DC: American Psychological Association.

Newell, A., & Simon, H. A. (1972). *Human problem solving.* Englewood Cliffs, NJ: Prentice-Hall.

Newman, G. E., Keil, F. C., Kuhlmeier, V. A., & Wynn, K. (2010). Early understandings of the link between agents and order. *Proceedings of the National Academy of Sciences, 107,* 17140–17145.

Newman, M. G., Leira, S. J., Erickso, T. M., Przeworski, A., & Constonguay, L. G. (2013). Worry and generalized anxiety disorder: A review and theoretical synthesis of evidence on nature, etiology mechanisms, and treatment. *Annual Review of Clinical Psychology, 9,* 275–297.

Newschaffer, C. J., Croen, L. A., Daniels, J., Giarelli, E., Grether, J. K., Levy, S. E., . . . Windham, G. C. (2007). The epidemiology of autism spectrum disorders. *Annual Review of Public Health, 28,* 235–258.

Newton, N. J., & Stewart, A. J. (2012). Personality development in adulthood. In S. K. Whitbourne & M. J. Sliwinski (Eds.), *Wiley-Blackwell handbook of adulthood and aging.* Malden, MA: Wiley-Blackwell.

Nezu, A. M., Raggio, G., Evans, A. N., & Nezu, C. M. (2013). Diabetes mellitus. In A. M. Nezu, C. M. Nezu, P. A. Geller, & I. B. Weiner (Eds.), *Handbook of psychology: Vol. 9. Health psychology* (2nd ed.). New York, NY: Wiley.

Nguyen, N. D., Tucker, M. A., Stickgold, R., & Wamsley, E. J. (2013). Overnight sleep enhances hippocampus-dependent aspects of spatial memory. *Sleep: Journal of Sleep and Sleep Disorders Research, 36,* 1051–1057.

Nguyen, T. A., Heffner, J. L., Lin, S. W., & Anthenelli, R. M. (2011). Genetic factors in the risk for substance use disorders. In P. Ruiz, & E. C. Strain (Eds.), *Lowinson and Ruiz's substance abuse: A comprehensive textbook* (5th ed.). Philadelphia, PA: Lippincott Williams & Wilkins.

Niccols, A. (2007). Fetal alcohol syndrome and the developing socio-emotional brain. *Brain and Cognition, 65,* 135–142.

Nicholson, S. B., & Lutz, D. J. (2017). The importance of cognitive dissonance in treating victims of intimate partner violence. *Journal of Aggression, Maltreatment & Trauma, 26,* 475–492.

Nickerson, R. S. (1998). Confirmation bias: A ubiquitous phenomenon in many guises. *Review of General Psychology, 2,* 175–220.

Niebyl, J. R., & Simpson, J. L. (2007). Drugs and environmental agents in pregnancy and lactation: Embryology, teratology, epidemiology. In S. G. Gabbe, J. R. Niebyl, & J. L. Simpson (Eds.) *Obstetrics: Normal and problem pregnancies* (5th ed., pp. 184–214). Philadelphia, PA: Elsevier.

Niebyl, J. R., & Simpson, J. L. (2012). Drug and environmental agents in pregnancy and lactation: Embryology, teratology, epidemiology. In S. G. Gabbe, J. R. Niebyl, J. L. Simpson, M. B. Landon, H. L. Galan, E. R. M. Jauniaux, & D. A. Driscoll (Eds.), *Obstetrics: Normal and problem pregnancies* (6th ed.). Philadelphia, PA: Elsevier.

Niedenthal, P. M. (2007). Embodied emotion. *Science, 316,* 1002–1004.

Niedenthal, P. M., Mermillod, M., Maringer, M. & Hess, U. (in press). The Simulation of Smiles (SIMS) Model: Embodied simulation and the meaning of facial expression. Target article for *Behavioral and Brain Sciences.*

Niedźwieńska, A., & Barzykowski, K. (2012). The age prospective memory paradox within the same sample in

time-based and event-based tasks. *Aging, Neuropsychology, and Cognition, 19*(1–2), 58–83.

Nielsen Media Research. (1998). *Report on television: 1998.* New York, NY: Author.

Nielsen, J. A., Zielinski, B. A., Ferguson, M. A., Lainhart, J. E., & Anderson, J. S. (2013). An evaluation of the left-brain vs. right-brain hypothesis with resting state functional connectivity magnetic resonance imaging. *PloS One, 8,* e71275.

Nielsen, N. M., Hansen, A. V., Simonsen, J., & Hviid, A. (2010). Prenatal stress and risk of infectious diseases in offspring. *American Journal of Epidemiology, 173,* 990–997. doi:10.1093/aje/kwq492.

Nielsen, T. (2011). Ultradian, circadian, and sleep-dependent features of dreaming. In M. H. Kryger, T. Roth, & W. C. Dement (Eds.), *Principles and practice of sleep medicine* (5th ed.). Saint Louis, MO: Elsevier Saunders.

Nielsen, T. A., & Stenstrom, P. (2005). What are the memory sources of dreaming? *Nature, 437,* 1286–1289.

Nielsen, T. A., & Zadra, A. (2000). Dreaming disorders. In M. H. Kryger, T. Roth, & W. C. Dement (Eds.), *Principles and practice of sleep medicine.* Philadelphia, PA: Saunders.

Nielsen, T. A., & Zadra, A., et al. (2003). Typical dreams of Canadian university students. *Dreaming, 13,* 211–235.

Nielsen, T., & Levin, R. (2009). Theories and correlates of nightmares. In R. Stickgold & M. P. Walker (Eds.), *The neuroscience of sleep* (pp. 323–329). San Diego, CA: Academic Press.

Nikelly, A. G. (1994). Alcoholism: Social as well as psycho-medical problem—The missing "big picture." *Journal of Alcohol & Drug Education, 39,* 1–12.

Nir, Y., & Tononi, G. (2010). Dreaming and the brain: From phenomenology to neurophysiology. *Trends in Cognitive Sciences, 14*(2), 88–100.

Nisbett, R. (2016). Gold medal award for life achievement in the science of psychology. *American Psychologist, 71,* 363–365.

Nisbett, R. E. (2005). Heredity, environment, and race differences in IQ: A commentary on Rushton and Jensen. *Psychology, Public Policy, and the Law, 11,* 302–310.

Nisbett, R. E. (2009). *Intelligence and how to get it: Why schools and cultures count.* New York, NY: Norton.

Nisbett, R. E. (Ed.). (1993). *Rules for reasoning.* Hillsdale, NJ: Erlbaum.

Nisbett, R. E., & Miyamoto, Y. (2005). The influence of culture: Holistic versus analytic perception. *Trends in Cognitive Sciences, 9,* 467–473.

Nisbett, R. E., & Wilson, T. D. (1977). The halo effect: Evidence for unconscious alteration of judgments. *Journal of Personality and Social Psychology, 35*(4), 250–256.

Nisbett, R. E., Aronson, J., Blair, C., Dickens, W., Flynn, J., Halpern, D. F., & Turkheimer, E. (2012). Intelligence: New findings and theoretical developments. *American Psychologist, 67,* 130–159.

Nisbett, R. E., Peng, K., Choi, I., & Norenzayan, A. (2001). Culture and systems of thought: Holistic versus analytic cognition. *Psychological Review, 108,* 291–310.

Nist, S. L., & Holschuh, J. L. (2000). Comprehension strategies at the college level. In R. F. Flippo & D. C. Caverly (Eds.), *Handbook of college reading and study strategy research.* Mahwah, NJ: Erlbaum.

Nithianantharajah, J., & Hannan, A. J. (2006). Enriched environments, experience-dependent plasticity and disorders of the nervous system. *Nature Reviews Neuroscience, 7,* 697–709.

Niu, W., & Brass, J. (2011). Intelligence in worldwide perspective. In R. J. Sternberg, & S. B. Kaufman (Eds.), *Cambridge handbook of intelligence.* New York, NY: Cambridge University Press.

Nobel Lectures. (1967). Marie Curie—facts. Retrieved from http://www.nobelprize.org/nobel_prizes/chemistry/laureates/1911/marie-curie-facts.html.

Noble, K. G., McCandliss, B. D., & Farah, M. J. (2007). Socioeconomic gradients predict individual differences in neurocognitive abilities. *Developmental Science, 10,* 464–480.

Nobler, M. S., & Sackeim, H. A. (2006). Electroconvulsive therapy and transcranial magnetic stimulation. In D. J. Stein, D. J. Kupfer, & A. F. Schatzberg (Eds.), *Textbook of mood disorders.* Washington, DC: American Psychiatric Publishing.

Nock, M. K., Millner, A. J., Deming, C. A., & Glenn, C. R. (2014). Depression and suicide. In I. H. Gotlib & C. L. Hammen (Eds.), *Handbook of depression* (3rd ed.). New York, NY: Guilford Press.

Noftle, E. E., & Robins, R. W. (2007). Personality predictors of academic outcomes: Big Five correlates of GPA and SAT scores. *Journal of Personality and Social Psychology, 93,* 116–130.

Nolen-Hoeksema, S. (1991). Responses to depression and their effects on the duration of depressive episodes. *Journal of Abnormal Psychology, 100,* 569–582.

Nolen-Hoeksema, S. (2000). The role of rumination in depressive disorders and mixed anxiety/depressive symptoms. *Journal of Abnormal Psychology, 109,* 504–511.

Nolen-Hoeksema, S. (2001). Gender differences in depression. *Current Directions in Psychological Science, 10,* 173–176.

Nolen-Hoeksema, S., Wisco, B. E., & Lyubomirsky, S. (2008). Rethinking rumination. *Perspectives on Psychological Science, 3*(5), 400–424.

Norcross, J. C. (1995). Dispelling the dodo bird verdict and the exclusivity myth in psychotherapy. *Psychotherapy, 32,* 500–504.

Norcross, J. C., Hedges, M., & Castle, P. H. (2002). Psychologists conducting psychotherapy in 2001: A study of the Division 29 membership. *Psychotherapy: Theory, Research, Practice, Training, 39,* 97–102.

Nordal, K. C. (2010). Where has all the psychotherapy gone. *Monitor on Psychology, 41*(10), 17.

Norenzayan, A., & Heine, S. J. (2005). Psychological universals: What are they and how can we know? *Psychological Bulletin, 131,* 763–784.

Norman, G. J., Hawkley, L. C., Cole, S. W., Bernston, G. G., & Cacioppo, J. T. (2012). Social neuroscience: The social brain, oxytocin, and health. *Social Neuroscience, 7,* 18–29.

Norman, T. R. (2009). Melatonin: Hormone of the night. *Acta Neuropsychiatrica, 21*(5), 263–265.

Norris, F. H., with Byrne, C. M., Diaz, E., & Kaniasty, K. (2001). *Risk factors for adverse outcomes in natural and human-caused disasters: A review of the empirical literature.* Retrieved November 21, 2001, from U.S. Department of Veterans Affairs National Center for PTSD Website: http://www.ncptsd.org/facts/disasters/fs_riskfactors.html.

Norris, I. J., & Larsen, J. T. (2011). Wanting more than you have and its consequences for well-being. *Journal of Happiness Studies, 12,* 877–885. doi:10.1007/s10902-010-9232-8.

North, C. S., Eyrich, K. M., Pollio, D. E., & Spitznagel, E. L. (2004). Are rates of psychiatric disorders in the homeless population changing? *American Journal of Public Health, 94*(1), 103–108.

Norton, C. (2005). Animal experiments: A cardinal sin? *The Psychologist, 18*(2), 69.

Nosek, B. A., Banaji, M., & Greenwald, A. G. (2002). Harvesting implicit group attitudes and beliefs from a demonstration web site. *Group Dynamics: Theory, Research, and Practice, 6*(1), 101–115.

Nosek, B. A., Greenwald, A. G., & Banaji, M. R. (2007). The *Implicit Association Test* at age 7: A methodological and conceptual review. In J. A. Bargh (Ed.), *Social Psychology and the unconscious: The automaticity of higher mental processes* (pp. 265–292). London, UK: Psychology Press.

Novemsky, N., & Kahneman, D. (2005). The boundaries of loss aversion. *Journal of Marketing Research, 42,* 119–128.

Novick, L. R., & Bassok, M. (2005). Problem solving. In K. J. Holyoak & R. G. Morrison (Eds.), *The Cambridge handbook of thinking and reasoning.* New York, NY: Cambridge University Press.

Noyes, R., Clarkson, C., Crowe, R. R., Yates, W. R., & McChesney, C. M. (1987). A family study of generalized anxiety disorder. *American Journal of Psychiatry, 144,* 1019–1024.

Nunio, M., & Yashikawa, S. (2016). Deep processing makes stimuli more preferable over long durations. *Journal of Cognitive Psychology, 28,* 756–763.

Nurnberger, J. I., & Zimmerman, J. (1970). Applied analysis of human behavior: An alternative to conventional motivational inferences and unconscious determination in therapeutic programming. *Behavior Therapy, 1,* 59–69.

Nutt, D., King, L. A., Saulsbury, W., & Blakemores, C. (2007). Development of a rational scale to assess the harm of drugs of potential misuse. *Lancet, 369,* 1047–1053.

Nyberg, L., Lovden, M., Riklund, K., Lindenberger, U., & Backman, L. (2012). Memory aging and brain maintenance. *Trends in Cognitive Science, 16,* 292–305. doi:10.1016/j. tics.2012.04.005.

Oakes, M. E., & Slotterback, C. S. (2000). Self-reported measures of appetite in relation to verbal cues about many foods. *Current Psychology: Developmental, Learning, Personality, Social, 19,* 137–142.

Oaten, M., Stevenson, R. J., & Case, T. I. (2009). Disgust as a disease-avoidance mechanism. *Psychological Bulletin, 135,* 303–321.

Oberauer, K, & Lewandowsky, S. (2014). Further evidence against decay in working memory. *Journal of Memory and Language, 73,* 15–30. doi:10.1016/j.jml.2014.02.003.

Obulesu, M., & Jhansilakshmi, M. (2014). Neuroinflammation in Alzheimer's disease: An understanding of physiology and pathology. *International Journal of Neuroscience, 124,* 227–235. doi:10.3109/00207454.2013.831852.

O'Connor, D. B., & Conner, M. (2011). Effects of stress on eating behavior. In R. J. Contrada & A. Baum (Eds.), *The handbook of stress science: Biology, psychology, and health* (pp. 111–121). New York, NY: Springer.

Oechslin, M. S., Descloux, C., Croquelois, A., Chanal, J., Van De Ville, D., Lazeyras, F., & James, C. E. (2013). Hippocampal volume predicts fluid intelligence in musically trained people. *Hippocampus, 23*(7), 552–558. doi:10.1002/hipo.22120.

Oehlberg, K., & Mineka, S. (2011). Fear conditioning and attention to threat: An integrative approach to understanding the etiology of anxiety disorders. In T. R. Schachtman, & S. Reilly (Eds.), *Associative learning and condition theory: Human and nonhuman applications.* New York, NY: Oxford University Press.

Offer, D. (1969). *The psychological world of the teenager: A study of normal adolescent boys.* New York, NY: Basic books.

Ogden, C. L., Lamb, M. M., Kit, B. K., & Wright, J. D. (2012). Weight and diet among children and adolescents in the United States. In K. D. Brownell, & M. S. Gold (Eds.), *Food and addiction: A comprehensive handbook.* New York, NY: Oxford University Press.

Ogden, J. (2010). *The psychology of eating: From healthy to disordered behavior.* Malden, MA: Wiley-Blackwell.

Ogilvie, M. (2011, April 8). Why a blow to the head is a big deal, *Toronto Star.* Retrieved November 16, 2011, from http://www.healthzone.ca/health/newsfeatures/article/971546-why-a-blow-to-the-head-is-a-big-deal.

Ogles, B. M. (2013). Measuring change in psychotherapy research. In M. J. Lambert (Ed.). *Bergin and Garfield's handbook of psychotherapy and behavior change* (6th ed.). New York, NY: Wiley.

Ogloff, J. R. (2006). Psychopathy/antisocial personality conundrum. *Australian and New Zealand Journal of Psychiatry, 40*(6–7), 519–528.

Ogloff, J. R. P., & Whittemore, K. E. (2001). Fitness to stand trial and criminal responsibility in Canada. In R. A. Schuller & J. R. P. Ogloff (Eds.), *Introduction to psychology and law: Canadian perspectives* (pp. 283–313). Toronto, ON: University of Toronto Press.

Ohayon, M. M., Carskadon, M. A., Guilleminault, C., & Vitiello, M. V. (2004). Meta-analysis of quantitative sleep parameters from childhood to old age in

healthy individuals: Developing normative sleep values across the human lifespan. *Sleep: Journal of Sleep & Sleep Disorders Research, 27,* 1255–1273.

Ohayon, M. M., Mahowald, M. W., Dauvilliers, Y., Krystal, A. D., & Leger, D. (2012). Prevalence and comorbidity of nocturnal wandering in the US adult general population. *Neurology, 78,* 1583–1589.

Öhman, A., & Mineka, S. (2001). Fears, phobia, and preparedness: Toward an evolved module of fear and fear learning. *Psychological Review, 108,* 483–522.

Öhman, A., & Mineka, S. (2001). Fears, phobias, and preparedness: Toward an evolved module of fear and fear learning. *Psychological Review, 108,* 483–522.

Öhman, A., & Wiens, S. (2003). On the automaticity of autonomic responses in emotion: An evolutionary perspective. In R. J. Davidson, K. R. Scherer, & H. H. Goldsmith (Eds.), *Handbook of affective sciences.* New York, NY: Oxford University Press.

Ojalehto, B. I., Medin, D. J., & Garcia, S. G. (2017). Grounding principles for inferring kinds: Two cultural perspectives. *Cognitive Psychology, 95,* 50–78.

Oken, B. S. (2008). Placebo effects: Clinical aspects and neurobiology. *Brain: A Journal of Neurology,131*(11), 2812–2823. doi:10.1093/brain/awn116.

Olabarria, M., Noristani, H. N., Verkhratsky, A., & Rodríguez, J. J. (2010). Concomitant astroglial atrophy and astrogliosis in a triple transgenic animal model of Alzheimer's disease. *Glia, 58,* 831–838.

Olds, J. (1956). Pleasure centers in the brain. *Scientific American, 193,* 105–116.

Olds, J., & Milner, P. (1954). Positive reinforcement produced by electrical stimulation of the septal area and other regions of the rat brain. *Journal of Comparative and Physiological Psychology, 47,* 419–427.

Olds, M. E., & Fobes, J. L. (1981). The central basis of motivation: Intracranial self-stimulation studies. *Annual Review of Psychology, 32,* 523–574.

O'Leary, K. D., Acevedo, B. P., Aron, A., Huddy, L., & Mashek, D. (2012). Is long-term love more than a rare phenomenon? If so, what are its correlates? *Social Psychological and Personality Science, 3,* 241–249.

O'Leary, K. D., Kent, R. N., & Kanowitz, J. (1975). Shaping data collection congruent with experimental hypotheses. *Journal of Applied Behavior Analysis, 8,* 43–51.

Olfson, M., Blanco, C., Liu, S.-M., Wang, S., & Correll, C. U. (2012). National trends in the office-based treatment of children, adolescents, and adults with antipsychotics. *JAMA Psychiatry, 69*(12), 1247–1256.

Olfson, M., Kroenke, K., Wang, S., & Blanco, C. (2014). Trends in office-based mental health care provided by psychiatrists and primary care physicians. *Journal of Clinical Psychiatry, 75,* 247–253. doi:10.4088/JCP.13m08834.

Olfson, M., & Marcus, S. C. (2009). National patterns in antidepressant medication treatment. *Archives of General Psychiatry, 66*(8), 848–856.

Olfson, M., & Marcus, S. C. (2010). National trends in outpatient psychotherapy. *The American Journal of Psychiatry, 167*(12), 1456–1463.

Oliveria, M. (2013). Canadians watch 30 hours of TV but for many web dominates free time. *The Toronto Star,* Friday, April 26. Retrieved from ttp://www.thestar.com/life/technology/2013/04/26/canadians_watch_30_hours _of_tv_but_for_many_web_dominates_free_time.html.

Oller, K., & Pearson, B. Z. (2002). Assessing the effects of bilingualism. In D. K. D. Oller & R. E. Eilers (Eds.), *Language and literacy in bilingual children.* Clevedon, UK: Multilingual Matters.

Oller, K., & Pearson, B. Z. (2002). Assessing the effects of bilingualism. In D. K. D. Oller & R. E. Eilers (Eds.), *Language and literacy in bilingual children.* Clevedon, UK: Multilingual Matters.

Olmstead, M. C., & Kuhlmeier, V. A. (2015). *Comparative cognition.* Cambridge, UK: Cambridge University Press.

Olson, E. J., & Park, J. G. (2006). Snoring. In T. Lee-Chiong (Ed.), *Sleep: A comprehensive handbook.* Hoboken, NJ: Wiley-Liss.

Olson, J. M., & Roese, N. J. (1995). The perceived funniness of humorous stimuli. *Personality and Social Psychology Bulletin, 21*, 908–913.

Olson, J. M., & Stone, J. (2005). The influence of behavior on attitudes. In D. Albarracin, B. T. Johnson, & M. P. Zanna (Eds.), *The handbook of attitudes.* Mahwah, NJ: Erlbaum.

Olson, J. M., Roese, N. J., & Zanna, M. P. (1996). Expectancies. In E. T. Higgins & A. W. Kruglanski (Eds.), *Social psychology: Handbook of basic principles.* New York, NY: Guilford Press.

Olson, M. A., & Fazio, R. H. (2001). Implicit attitude formation through classical conditioning. *Psychological Science, 12*, 413–417.

Olson, M. A., & Fazio, R. H. (2002). Implicit acquisition and manifestation of classically conditioned attitudes. *Social Cognition, 20*(2), 89–104.

Olszewski-Kubilius, P. (2003). Gifted education programs and procedures. In W. M. Reynolds & G. E. Miller (Eds.), *Handbook of psychology (Vol. 7): Educational psychology.* New York, NY: Wiley.

Olver, M. E., Neumann, C. S., Wong, S. C. P., & Hare, R. D. (2013). The structural and predictive properties of the Psychopathy Checklist–Revised in Canadian Aboriginal and Non-Aboriginal offenders. *Psychological Assessment, 25*(1), 167–179.

O'Neil, P. (2011). The evolution of research ethics in Canada: Current developments. *Canadian Psychology, 5*(3)2, 180–184.

Ones, D. S., Viswesvaran, C., & Dilchert, S. (2005). Cognitive ability in selection decisions. In O. Wilhelm & R. W. Engle (Eds.), *Handbook of understanding and measuring intelligence.* Thousand Oaks, CA: Sage.

Ong, A. D. (2010). Pathways linking positive emotion and health in later life. *Current Directions in Psychological Science, 19*(6), 358–362. doi:10.1177/0963721410388805.

Ong, A. D., Burrow, A. L., Fuller-Rowell, T. E., Ja, N. M., & Sue, D. W. (2013). Racial microaggressions and daily well-being among Asian Americans. *Journal of Counseling Psychology, 60*, 188–199. doi:10.1037/a0031736.

Ono, H., & Wade, N. J. (2005). Depth and motion in historical descriptions of motion parallax. *Perception, 34*, 1263–1273.

Ontario Ministry of Health. (2011). *Ontario wait times.* Retrieved June 30, 2011, from http://www.health.gov.on.ca/en/public/programs/waittimes/surgery/default.aspx.

Ontario University and College Health Association. (2016). *National College Health Assessment (NCHA).* Retrieved from http://oucha.ca/ncha.php.

Open Science Collaboration. (2015). Estimating the reproducibility of psychological science. *Science, 349*, 943–959.

Oppenheim, G. M., & Dell, G. S. (2010). Motor movement matters: The flexible abstractness of inner speech. *Memory and Cognition, 38*(8), 1147–1160.

Oppenheimer, D. M., & Kelso, E. (2015). Information processing as a paradigm for decision making. *Annual Review of Psychology, 66*, 277–294.

Oppliger, P. A. (2007). Effects of gender stereotyping on socialization. In R. W. Preiss, B. M. Gayle, N. Burrell, M. Allen, & J. Bryant (Eds.), *Mass media effects research: Advances through meta-analysis* (pp. 192–214). Mahwah, NJ: Erlbaum.

Opriş, D., Pintea, S., García-Palacios, A., Botella, C., Szamosközi, S., & David, D. (2012). Virtual reality exposure therapy in anxiety disorders: A quantitative meta-analysis. *Depression and Anxiety, 29*(2), 85–93. doi:10.1002/da.20910.

O'Reardon, J. P., Solvason, H. B., Janicak, P. G., Sampson, S., Isenberg, K. E., Nahas, Z., et al. (2007). Efficacy and safety of transcranial magnetic stimulation in the acute treatment of major depression: A multisite randomized controlled trial. *Biological Psychiatry, 62*, 1208–1216.

Ormerod, T. C., MacGregor, J. N., & Chronicle, E. P. (2002). Dynamics and constraints in insight problem solving. *Journal of Experimental Psychology: Learning, Memory and Cognition, 28*, 791–799.

Orne, M. T. (1951). The mechanisms of hypnotic age regression: An experimental study. *Journal of Abnormal and Social Psychology, 46*, 213–225.

Orne, M. T., & Holland, C. C. (1968). On the ecological validity of laboratory deceptions. *International Journal of Psychiatry, 6*, 282–293.

Ornstein, R. E. (1997). *The right mind: Making sense of the hemispheres.* San Diego, CA: Harcourt.

Orsillo, S. M., & Roemer, L. (2010). *The mindful way through anxiety: Break free from chronic worry and reclaim your life.* New York, NY: The Guilford Press.

Orth-Gomer, K., Wamala, S. P., Horsten, M., Schenck-Gustafsson, K., Schneiderman, N., & Mittleman, M. A. (2000). Marital stress worsens prognosis in women with coronary heart disease: The Stockholm female coronary risk study. *Journal of the American Medical Association, 284*, 3008–3014.

Ortmann, A., & Hertwig, R. (1997). Is deception acceptable? *American Psychologist, 52*, 746–747.

Oskamp, S. (1991). *Attitudes and opinions.* Englewood Cliffs, NJ: Prentice-Hall.

Ost, J. (2013). Recovered memories and suggestibility for entire events. In A. M. Ridley, F. Gabbert, & D. J. La Rooy (Eds.), *Suggestibility in legal contexts: Psychological research and forensic implications.* Wiley-Blackwell.

Ostrom, T. M., & Sedikides, C. (1992). Outgroup homogeneity effects in natural and minimal groups. *Psychological Bulletin, 112*, 536–552.

Oswal, A., Beudel, M., Zrinzo, L., Limousin, P., Hariz, M. et al. (2016). Deep brain stimulation modulates synchrony within spatially and spectrally distance resting state networks in Parkinson's disease. *Brain: A Journal of Neurology, 139*, 1482–1496.

Otero, T. L., Schatz, R. B., Merrill, A. C., & Bellini, S. (2015). Social skills training for youth with autism spectrum disorders: A follow-up. *Child and Adolescent Psychiatric Clinics of North America, 24*(1), 99–115.

Outtz, J. L. (2002). The role of cognitive ability tests in employment selection. *Human Performance, 15*, 161–171.

Overall, N. C., Girme, Y. U., Lemay, Jr., E. P., & Hammond, M. D. (2014). Attachment anxiety and reactions to relationship threat: The benefits and costs of inducing guilt in romantic partners. *Journal of Personality and Social Psychology, 106*, 235–256.

Owen, A. (2013). Detecting consciousness: A unique role for neuroimaging. *Annual Review of Psychology, 64*, 109–133.

Owen, A. (2017). *Into the gray zone.* New York, NY: Simon and Schuster.

Owen, A. M., Coleman, M. R., Boly, M., Davis, M. H., Laureys, S., & Pickard, J. D. (2006). Detecting awareness in the vegetative state. *Science, 313*, 1402–1406.

Oyama, M. A., & Serpell, J. A. (2013). General commentary: Rethinking the role of animals in human well-being. *Frontiers of Psychology, 4*, 374–375.

Oyserman, D., & Lee, S. W. S. (2008). Does culture influence what and how we think? *Psychological Bulletin, 101*, 67–99.

Ozer, E. J., Best, S. R., Lipsey, T. L., & Weiss, D. S. (2003). Predictors of posttraumatic stress disorder and symptoms in adults: A meta-analysis. *Psychological Bulletin, 129*, 52–73.

Ozgen, E. (2004). Language, learning, and color perception. *Current Directions in Psychological Science, 13*(3), 95–98.

Pacchiarotti, I., Bond, D. J., Baldessarini, R. J., Nolen, W. A., Grunze, H., Licht, R. W., . . . Vieta, E. (2013). The International Society for Bipolar Disorders (ISBD) task force report on antidepressant use in bipolar disorders. *The American Journal of Psychiatry, 170*, 1249–1262.

Pace-Schott, E. F. (2009). Sleep architecture. In R. Stickgold & M. P. Walker (Eds.), *The neuroscience of sleep* (pp. 11–17). San Diego, CA: Academic Press.

Pace-Schott, E. F. (2011). The neurobiology of dreaming. In M. H. Kryger, T. Roth, & W. C. Dement (Eds.), *Principles and practice of sleep medicine* (5th ed.). Saint Louis, MO: Elsevier Saunders.

Pace-Schott, E. F., Hobson, J. A., & Stickgold, R. (2008). Sleep, dreaming, and wakefulness. In L. Squire, D. Berg, F. Bloom, S. Du Lac, A. Ghosh, & N. Spitzer (Eds.), *Fundamental neuroscience* (3rd ed., pp. 959–986). San Diego, CA: Academic Press.

Pace-Schott, E. F., Nave, G., Morgan, A., & Spencer, R. M. C. (2012). Sleep-dependent modulation of affectively guided decision-making. *Journal of Sleep Research, 21*, 30–39.

Packer, D. J., Kesek, A., & Cunningham, W. A. (2011). Self-regulation and evaluative processing. In A. B. Todorov, S. T., Fiske, & D. A. Prentice, (Eds.), *Social neuroscience: Toward understanding the underpinnings of the social mind* (pp. 232–267). New York, NY: Oxford University Press.

Packer, L. E. (2007). Tourette syndrome "plus." Retrieved July 31, 2007, from http://www.tourettesyndrome.net/index.htm.

Paczynski, R. P., & Gold, M. S. (2011). Cocaine and crack. In P. Ruiz, & E. C. Strain (Eds.), *Lowinson and Ruiz's substance abuse: A comprehensive textbook* (5th ed., pp. 191–213). Philadelphia, PA: Lippincott Williams & Wilkins.

Padgett, D. A., & Sheridan, J. F. (2000). Herpes viruses. In G. Fink (Ed.), *Encyclopedia of stress* (pp. 357–363). San Diego, CA: Academic Press.

Page, M. G., Stinson, J., Campbell, F., Isaac, L., & Katz, J. (2013). Identification of pain-related psychological risk factors for the development and maintenance of pediatric chronic postsurgical pain. *Journal of Pain Research, 6*, 167–178.

Paivio, A. (1969). Mental imagery in associative learning and memory. *Psychological Review, 76*, 241–263.

Paivio, A. (1986). *Mental representations: A dual coding approach.* New York, NY: Oxford University Press.

Paivio, A. (2007). *Mind and its evolution: A dual coding theoretical approach.* Mahwah, NJ: Erlbaum.

Paivio, A., Khan, M., & Begg, I. (2000). Concreteness of relational effects on recall of adjective-noun pairs. *Canadian Journal of Experimental Psychology, 54*(3), 149–160.

Paivio, A., Smythe, P. E., & Yuille, J. C. (1968). Imagery versus meaningfulness of nouns in paired-associate learning. *Canadian Journal of Psychology, 22*, 427–441.

Palermo, T. M., Valrie, C. R., & Karlson, C. M. (2014). Family and parent influences on pediatric chronic pain: A developmental perspective. *American Psychologist, 69*(2), 145–152.

Palm, G., Knoblauch, A., Hauser, F., & Schuz, A. (2014). Cell assemblies in the cerebral cortex. *Biological Cybernetics, 108*, 559–572.

Palmer, S. E. (2003). Visual perception of objects. In A. F. Healy & R. W. Proctor (Eds.), *Handbook of psychology (Vol. 4): Experimental psychology.* New York, NY: Wiley.

Pan, B. A., & Uccelli, P. (2009). Semantic development: Learning the meaning of words. In J. B. Gleason & N. B. Ratner (Eds.), *The development of language.* Boston, MA: Pearson.

Panasiti, M. S., Pavone, E. F., Mancini, A., Merla, A., Grisoni, L., & Salvatore, M. A. (2014). The motor cost of telling lies: Electrocortical signatures of personality foundations of spontaneous deception. *Social Neuroscience*, DOI:10.1080/17470919.2014.934394.

Panel on Research Ethics. (2015). TCPS 2—The latest edition of the *Tri-Council Policy Statement: Ethical Conduct for research involving humans.* Retrieved from http://www.ethics.gc.ca/eng/policy-politique/initiatives/tcps2-eptc2/Default/.

Panel on Research Ethics. (2016). Navigating the ethics of human research. Retrieved from http://www.ethics.gc.ca/eng/index/.

Panksepp, J. (1991). Affective neuroscience: A conceptual framework for the neurobiological study of emotions. In K. T. Strongman (Ed.), *International review of studies on emotion.* Chichester, England: Wiley.

Pansu, P., Lima, L., & Fointiat, V. (2014). When saying no leads to compliance: The door-in-the-face technique for changing attitudes and behaviors towards smoking at work. *European Review of Applied Psychology, 64*, 19–27.

Parakh, P., & Basu, D. (2013). Cannabis and psychosis: Have we found the missing links? *Asian Journal of Psychiatry, 6*, 281–287. doi:10.1016/j.ajp.2013.03.012.

Paris, J. (2013). How the history of psychotherapy interferes with integration. *Journal of Psychotherapy Integration, 23*, 99–107.

Park, D. C., Lodi-Smith, J., Drew, L., Haber, S., Hebrank, A., Bischof, G. N., & Aamodt, W. (2014). The impact of sustained engagement of cognitive function in older adults: The synapse project. *Psychological Science, 25*, 103–112. doi:10.1177/0956797613499592.

Park, J., & Jang, S. (2013). Confused by too many choices? Choice overload in tourism. *Tourism Management, 35*, 1–12. doi:10.1016/j.tourman.2012.05.004.

Park, J., & Peters, P. A. (2014). Mortality from diabetes mellitus, 2004 to 2008: A multiple cause of death analysis. *Statistics Canada Health Reports, 25*, 12–16.

Parker, E. S., Cahill, L., & McGaugh, J. L. (2006). A case of unusual autobiographical remembering. *Neurocase, 12*, 35–49.

Parker, J. D. A., Hogan, M. J., Eastabrook, J. M., Oke, A., & Wood, L. M. (2006). Emotional intelligence and student retention: Predicting the successful transition from high school to university. *Personality and Individual Differences, 41*, 1329–1336.

Parliament of Canada. (2006). Childhood autism in Canada: Some issues relating to behavioural intervention. Retrieved from https://lop.parl.ca/content/lop/researchpublications/prb0593-e.htm.

Partinen, M., & Hublin, C. (2011). Epidemiology of sleep disorders. In M. H. Kryger, T. Roth, & W. C. Dement (Eds.), *Principles and practice of sleep medicine* (5th ed.). Saint Louis, MO: Elsevier Saunders.

Pascual-Leone, A. (2009). Characterizing and modulating neuroplasticity of the adult human brain. In M. S. Gazzangia (Ed.), *The cognitive neurosciences* (4th ed., pp. 141–152). Cambridge, MA: MIT Press.

Pashler, H., & Carrier, M. (1996). Stuctures, processes, and the flow of information. In E. L. Bjork & R. A. Bjork (Eds.), *Memory*. San Diego, CA: Academic Press.

Pashler, H., Johnston, J. C., & Ruthruff, E. (2001). Attention and performance. *Annual Review of Psychology, 52*, 629–651.

Passer, K. M., & Warnock, J. K. *(1991). Pimozide in the treatment of Capgras' syndrome. A case report. Psychosomatics, 32*(4), 446–448.

Patel, S. R., Malhotra, A., Gottlieb, D. J., White, P., & Hu, F. B. (2006). Correlates of long sleep deprivation. *Sleep: Journal of Sleep and Sleep Disorders Research, 29*, 881–889.

Patel, S. R., Zhu, X., Storfer-Isser, A., Mehra, R., Jenny, N. S., Tracy, R., & Redline, S. (2009). Sleep duration and biomarkers of inflammation. *Sleep: Journal of Sleep and Sleep Disorders Research, 32*(2), 200–204.

Patihis, L., Ho, L. Y, Tingen, I. W., Lilienfeld, S. O., & Loftus, E. F. (2013). Are the "memory wars" over? A scientist-practitioner gap in beliefs about repressed memory. *Psychological Science, 25*(2), 519–530.

Patihis, L., Ho, L. Y., Tingen, I. W., Lilienfeld, S. O., & Loftus, E. F. (2014). Are the "memory wars" over? A scientist-practitioner gap in beliefs about repressed memory. *Psychological Science, 25*, 519–530.

Pato, M. T., Eisen, J. L., & Phillips, K. A. (2003). Obsessive-compulsive disorder. In A Tasman, J. Kay, & J. A. Lieberman (Eds.), *Psychiatry*. New York, NY: Wiley.

Patrick, C. J. (Ed.). (2007). *Handbook of psychopathy*. New York, NY: Guilford Press.

Patriquin, M. (2005, April 30). Quebec farm segregated black workers. *The Globe and Mail*, A1, A2.

Patston, L. M., Kirk, I. J., Rolfe, M. S., Corballis, M. C., & Tippett, L. J. (2007). The unusual symmetry of musicians: Musicians have equilateral interhemispheric transfer for visual information. *Neuropsychologia, 45*(9), 2059–2065.

Pattanashetty, R., Sathiamma, S., Talakkad, S., Nityananda, P., Trichur, R., & Kutty, B. M. (2010). Practitioners of vipassana meditation exhibit enhanced slow wave sleep and REM sleep states across different age groups. *Sleep and Biological Rhythms, 8*(1), 34–41.

Paul, R. (2009). Parents ask: Am I risking autism if I vaccinate my children? *Journal of Autism and Developmental Disorders, 39*(6), 962–963.

Paulhus, D. L. (1991). Measurement and control of response bias. In J. P. Robinson, P. Shaver, & L. S. Wrightsman (Eds.), *Measures of personality and social psychological attitudes*. San Diego, CA: Academic Press.

Paulhus, D. L., Curtis, S. R., & Jones, D. N. (2017). Aggression as a trait: the Dark Tetrad alternative. *Current Opinions in Psychology, 19*, 88–92.

Paulhus, D. L., Fridhandler, B., & Hayes, S. (1997). Psychological defense: Contemporary theory and research. In R. Hogan, J. Johnson, & S. Briggs (Eds.), *Handbook of personality psychology*. San Diego, CA: Academic Press.

Paulhus, D. L., & Williams, K. M. (2002). The dark triad of personality: Narcissism, Machiavellianism, and psychopathy. *Journal of Research in Personality, 36*, 556–563.

Paulhus, D. L., & Williams, K. M. (2002). The dark triad of personality: Narcissism, Machiavellianism, and psychopathy. *Journal of Research in Personality, 36*, 556–563.

Paulos, J. A. (1995). *A mathematician reads the newspaper*. New York, NY: Doubleday.

Paunonen, S. V., & Ashton, M. C. (1998). The structured assessment of personality across cultures. *Journal of Cross-Cultural Psychology, 29*, 150–170.

Paunonen, S. V., & Hong, R. Y. (2015). On the properties of personality traits. In M. Mikulincer, P. R. Shaver, M. L. Cooper, & R. J. Larsen (Eds.), *APA handbook of personality and social psychology: Vol. 4. Personality processes and individual differences*. Washington, DC: American Psychological Association.

Paunonen, S. V., & LeBel, E. P. (2012). Socially desirable responding and its elusive effects on the validity of personality assessments. *Journal of Personality and Social Psychology, 103*(1), 158–175. doi:10.1037/a0028165.

Pavlov, I. P. (1906). The scientific investigation of psychical faculties or processes in the higher animals. *Science, 24*, 613–619.

Pavlov, I. P. (1927). *Conditioned reflexes* (G. V. Anrep, Trans.). London, UK: Oxford University Press.

Pavot, W, & Diener, E. (2013). Happiness experienced: The science of subjective well-being. In S. A. David, I. Boniwell, & A. Conley Ayers (Eds.), *The Oxford handbook of happiness*. New York, NY: Oxford University Press.

Payne, B. K. (2006). Weapon bias: Split-second decisions and unintended stereotyping. *Current Directions in Psychological Science, 15*, 287–291. doi:10.1111/j.1467-8721.2006.00454.x.

Payne, D. G., & Blackwell, J. M. (1998). Truth in memory: Caveat emptor. In S. J. Lynn & K. M. McConkey (Eds.), *Truth in memory*. New York, NY: Guilford.

Payne, J. D., Tucker, M. A., Ellenbogen, J. M., Wamsley, E. J., Walker, M. P., Schacter, D. L., & Stickgold, R. (2012). Memory for semantically related and unrelated declarative information: The benefit of sleep, the cost of wake. *PLoS ONE, 7*, e33079. doi:10.1371/journal.pone.0033079.

Pazzaglia, M. (2015). Body and odors: Not just molecules after all. *Current Directions in Psychological Science, 24*, 329–333.

Pchelin, P., & Howell, R. T. (2014). The hidden cost of value-seeking: People do not accurately forecast the economic benefits of experiential purchases. *The Journal of Positive Psychology, 9*, 322–334. doi:10.1080/17439760.2014.898316.

Pearce, T. (2012). Spanking your child: Does it help or hurt? *The Globe and Mail*, February 2, 2012. Retrieved from http://www.oacas.org/news/12/feb/02spank.pdf.

Pearn, J., & Gardner-Thorpe, C. (2002). Jules Cotard (1840–1889): His life and the unique syndrome that bears his name. *Neurology, 58*, 1400–1403.

Pedersen, A. F., Bovbjerg, D. H., & Zachariae, R. (2011). Stress and susceptibility to infectious disease. In R. J. Contrada & A. Baum (Eds.), *The handbook of stress science: Biology, psychology, and health* (pp. 111–121). New York, NY: Springer.

Pedersen, N. L., McClearn, G. E., Plomin, R., & Nesselroade, J. R. (1992). Effects of early rearing environment on twin similarity in the last half of the life span. *British Journal of Developmental Psychology, 10*(3), 255–267.

Pedersen, P. (1994). A culture-centered approach to counseling. In W. J. Lonner & R. Malpass (Eds.), *Psychology and culture*. Boston, MA: Allyn & Bacon.

Peek, F. (1996). *The real Rain Man*. Salt Lake City, UT: Harkness Publishing Consultants.

Peele, S. (1989). *Diseasing of America: Addiction treatment out of control*. Lexington, MA: Lexington Books.

Peele, S. (2000). What addiction is and is not: The impact of mistaken notions of addiction. *Addiction Research, 8*, 599–607.

Peigneux, P., Urbain, C., & Schmitz, R. (2012). Sleep and the brain. In C. M. Morin, & C. A. Espie (Eds.), *Oxford handbook of sleep and sleep disorders*. New York, NY: Oxford University Press.

Pelley, L. (2016). Solving the sleep problem: We all need it, but we are not getting enough. *The Toronto Star*, June 6, 2016. Retrieved from https://www.thestar.com/life/health_wellness/2016/06/06/solving-the-sleep-problem-we-all-need-it-but-were-not-getting-enough.html.

Pellicano, E. (2013). Sensory symptoms in autism: A blooming, buzzing, confusion. *Child Development Perspectives, 7*, 143–148.

Pena, M., Werker, J. F., & Dehaene-Lambertz, G. (2012). Earlier speech exposure does not accelerate speech acquisition. *Journal of Neuroscience, 32*, 11159–11163.

Penfield, W., & Perot, P. (1963). The brain's record of auditory and visual experience. *Brain, 86*, 595–696.

Peng, J. H., Tao, Z. Z., & Huang, Z. W. (2007). Risk of damage in hearing from personal listening devices in young adults. *Journal of Otolaryngology, 36*(3), 181–185.

Peper, J. S., & Dahl, R. E. (2013). The teenage brain: Surging hormones—Brain-behavior interactions during puberty. *Current Directions in Psychological Science, 22*, 134–139. doi:10.1177/0963721412473755.

Pepperberg, I. M. (1993). Cognition and communication in an African Grey parrot (*Psittacus erithacus*): Studies on a nonhuman, nonprimate, nonmammalian subject. In H. L. Roitblat, L. H. Herman, & P. E. Nachtigall (Eds.), *Language and communication: Comparative perspectives*. Hillsdale, NJ: Erlbaum.

Pepperberg, I. M. (2002). Cognitive and communicative abilities of grey parrots. *Current Directions in Psychological Science, 11*(3), 83–87.

Perimeter Institute. (2017). *Driven by curiosity: Percy Paul on the power of exploration*. Retrieved from https://insidetheperimeter.ca/driven-by-curiosity-percy-paul-on-the-power-of-exploration/.

Perkins, D. O., Miller-Anderson, L., & Lieberman, J. A. (2006). Natural history and predictors of clinical course. In J. A. Lieberman, T. S. Stroup, & D. O. Perkins (Eds.), *Textbook of schizophrenia* (pp. 289–302). Washington, DC: American Psychiatric Publishing.

Perlis, R. H., Perlis, C. S., Wu, Y., Hwang, C., Joseph, M., & Nierenberg, A. A. (2005). Industry sponsorship and financial conflict of interest in the reporting of clinical trials in psychiatry. *American Journal of Psychiatry, 162*, 1957–1960.

Perone, M., Galizio, M., & Baron, A. (1988). The relevance of animal-based principles in the laboratory study of human operant conditioning. In G. Davey & C. Cullen (Eds.), *Human operant conditioning and behavior modification*. New York, NY: Wiley.

Perreault, S., & Bourhis, R. Y. (1999). Ethnocentrism, social identification, and discrimination. *Personality and Social Psychology Bulletin, 25*, 92–103.

Perry, D. G., Kusel, S. J., & Perry, L. C. (1988). Victims of peer aggression. *Developmental Psychology, 24,* 807–814.

Perry, W., & Braff, D. L. (1994). Information-processing deficits and thought disorder in schizophrenia. *American Journal of Psychiatry, 151,* 363–367.

Person, E. S. (1990). The influence of values in psycho-analysis: The case of female psychology. In C. Zanardi (Ed.), *Essential papers in psychoanalysis.* New York, NY: New York University Press.

Pert, C. B., & Snyder, S. H. (1973). Opiate receptor: Demonstration in the nervous tissue. *Science, 179,* 1011–1014.

Pertusa, A., Frost, R. O., Fullana, M. A., Samuels, J., Steketee, G., Tolin, D., Saxena, S., Leckman, J. F., & Mataix-Cols, D. (2010). Refining the diagnostic bound-aries of compulsive hoarding: A critical review. *Clinical Psychology Review, 11,* 23–45.

Perugini, E. M., Kirsch, I., Allen, S. T., Coldwell, E., Meredith, J. M., Montgomery, G. H., & Sheehan, J. (1998). Surreptitious observation of response to hypnotically suggested hallucinations: A test of the compliance hypothesis. *International Journal of Clinical & Experimental Hypnosis, 46,* 191–203.

Pescosolido, B. A., Martin, J. K., Long, J., Medina, T. R., Phelan, J. C., & Link, B. G. (2010). "A disease like any other"? A decade of change in public reactions to schizophrenia, depression, and alcohol dependence. *American Journal of Psychiatry, 167*(11), 1321–1330. doi:10.1176/appi.ajp.2010.09121743.

Peterhans, E., & Von Der Heydt, R. (1991). Elements of form perception in monkey prestriate cortex. In A. Gorea, Y. Fregnac, Z. Kapoula, & J. Findlay (Eds.), *Representations of vision—Trends and tacit assumptions in vision research.* Cambridge, MA: Cambridge University Press.

Peters, R. (1988, February). The interagency mental health council's committee on multiculturalism and mental health: Progress update. Vancouver: Greater Vancouver Mental Health Services Society.

Petersen, A. C., Compas, B. E., Brooks-Gunn, J., Stemmler, M., Ey, S., & Grant, K. E. (1993). Depression in adolescence. *American Psychologist, 48,* 155–168.

Petersen, J. L., & Hyde, J. S. (2011). Gender differences in sexual attitudes and behaviors: A review of meta-ana-lytic results and large datasets. *Journal of Sex Research, 48,* 149–165. doi:10.1080/00224499.2011.551851.

Peterson, C. (2000). The future of optimism. *American Psychologist, 55*(1), 44–55.

Peterson, C., & Park, N. (2009). Positive psychology. In B. J. Sadock, V. A. Sadock, & P. Ruiz (Eds.), *Kaplan & Sadock's comprehensive textbook of psychiatry* (pp. 2939–2951). Philadelphia, PA: Lippincott Williams & Wilkins.

Peterson, L. R., & Peterson, M. J. (1959). Short-term retention of individual verbal items. *Journal of Experimental Psychology, 58,* 193–198.

Petit, D., Pennestri, M. H., Paquet, J., Desautels, A., Zadra, A., Vitaro, F., Tremblay, R. E., Boivin, M., & Monplaisir, J. (2015). Childhood sleepwalking and night terrors: A longitudinal study of prevalence and familial aggregation. *Journal of the American Medical Association: Pediatrics, 227,* 653–658.

Petitto, L. A., & Marentette, P. (1991). Babbling in the manual mode: Evidence for the ontogeny of language. *Science, 251*(5000), 1493–1496.

Petitto, L. A., Holowka, S., Sergio, L. E., Levy, B., & Ostry, D. J. (2004). Baby hands that move to the rhythm of language: Hearing babies acquiring sign languages babble silently on the hands. *Cognition, 93,* 43–73.

Petrie, K. J., & Pennebaker, J. W. (2004). Health-related cognitions. In S. Sutton, A. Baum, & M. Johnston (Eds.), *The Sage handbook of health psychology.* Thousand Oaks, CA: Sage.

Petrill, S. A. (2005). Behavioral genetics and intelligence. In O. Wilhelm & R. W. Engle (Eds.), *Handbook of under-standing and measuring intelligence.* Thousand Oaks, CA: Sage.

Petty, R. (2016). Two routes to persuasion. In R. Sternberg, S. Fiske, D. J. Foss (Eds.), *Scientists making a difference* (pp. 373–376). New York, NY: Cambridge University Press.

Petty, R. E., Barden, J., & Wheeler, S. C. (2009). The elaboration likelihood model persuasion: Developing health promotions for sustained behavioral change. In R. J. DiClemente, R. A. Crosby & M. C. Kegler (Eds.), *Emerging theories in health promotion practice and research* (2nd ed., pp. 185–214). San Francisco, CA: Jossey-Bass.

Petty, R. E., & Briñol, P. (2008). Persuasion: From single to multiple to metacognitive processes. *Perspectives on Psychological Science, 3,* 137–147.

Petty, R. E., & Briñol, P. (2010). Attitude change. In R. F. Baumeister & E. J. Finkel (Eds.), *Advanced social psy-chology: The state of the science* (pp. 217–259). New York, NY: Oxford University Press.

Petty, R. E., & Briñol, P. (2015). Processes of social influ-ence through attitude change. In M. Mikulincer, P. R. Shaver, E. Borgida, & J. A. Bargh (Eds.), *APA handbook of per-sonality and social psychology Vol. 1: Attitudes and social cogni-tion.* Washington, DC: American Psychological Association.

Petty, R. E., Briñol, P., & Priester, J. R. (2009). Mass media attitude change: Implications of the Elaboration Likelihood Model of persuasion. In J. Bryant & M. B. Oliver (Eds.), *Media effects: Advances in theory and research* (3rd ed., pp. 125–164). New York, NY: Routledge.

Petty, R. E., & Cacioppo, J. T. (1986). *Communication and persuasion: Central and peripheral routes to attitude change.* New York, NY: Springer-Verlag.

Petty, R. E., & Wegener, D. T. (1998). Attitude change: Multiple roles for persuasion variables. In D. T. Gilbert, S. T. Fiske, & G. Lindzey (Eds.), *The handbook of social psy-chology.* New York, NY: McGraw-Hill.

Petty, R. E., Wheeler, S. C., & Tormala, Z. L. (2013). Persuasion and attitude change. In H. Tennen, J. Suls, & I. B. Weiner (Eds.), *Handbook of psychology: Vol. 5. Personality and social psychology* (2nd ed.). New York, NY: Wiley.

Pfau, M., Kenski, H. C., Nitz, M., & Sorenson, J. (1990). Efficacy of inoculation strategies in promoting resistance to political attack messages: Application to direct mail. *Communication Monographs, 57,* 25–43.

Phelan, J. C., Link, B. G., & Tehranifar, P. (2010). Social conditions as fundamental causes of health inequalities: Theory, evidence, and policy implica-tions. *Journal of Health and Social Behavior, 51,* S28–S40. doi:10.1177/0022146510383498.

Phelps, E. A. (2005). The interaction of emotion and cognition: The relation between the human amygdala and cognitive awareness. In R. R. Hassin, J. S. Uleman, & J. A. Bargh (Eds.), *The new unconcious: Oxford series in social cognition and social neuroscience* (pp. 61–76). New York, NY: Oxford University Press.

Phelps, E. A. (2006). Emotion and cognition: Insights from studies of the human amygdala. *Annual Review of Psychology, 57,* 27–53.

Philip, P., Sagaspe, P., & Taillard, J. (2011). Drowsy driving. In M. H. Kryger, T. Roth, & W. C. Dement (Eds.), *Principles and practice of sleep medicine* (5th ed.). Saint Louis, MO: Phillips Elsevier Saunders.

Phillips, B. A., & Kryger, M. H. (2011). Management of obstructive sleep apnea-hypopnea syndrome. In M. H. Kryger, T. Roth, & W. C. Dement (Eds.), *Principles and practice of sleep medicine* (5th ed.). Saint Louis, MO: Elsevier Saunders.

Phillips, W. L. (2011). Cross-cultural differences in visual perception of color, illusions, depth, and pic-tures. In K. D. Keith (Ed.), *Cross-cultural psychology: Contemporary themes and perspectives.* Malden, MA: Wiley-Blackwell.

Piaget, J. (1929). *The child's conception of the world.* New York, NY: Harcourt, Brace.

Piaget, J. (1932). *The moral judgment of the child.* Glencoe, IL: Free Press.

Piaget, J. (1952). *The origins of intelligence in children.* New York, NY: International Universities Press.

Piaget, J. (1954). *The construction of reality in the child.* New York, NY: Basic Books.

Piaget, J. (1970). *Genetic epistemology.* New York, NY: W.W. Norton & Company.

Piaget, J. (1983). Piaget's theory. In P. H. Mussen (Ed.), *Handbook of child psychology* (Vol. 1). New York, NY: Wiley.

Picard, A. (2011, April 26). After-school exercise: A mere 14 minutes. *The Globe and Mail,* L5.

Picard, A. (2011, June 9). 17,500 Canadians hospitalized for suicide attempts and self-injury last year. *The Globe and Mail,* L6.

Picard, A. (2013). Exposing Canada's ugly mental-health secret. *The Globe and Mail,* Sunday, October 13. Retrieved from http://www.theglobeandmail.com/life/health-and-fitness/health/exposing-canadas-ugly-mental-health-secret/article14828590/.

Pickering, G. J., Jain, A. K., & Bezawada, R. (2013). Super-tasting gastronomes? Taste phenotype character-ization of foodies and wine experts. *Food Quality and Preference, 28,* 85–91.

Pickering, T. G., Devereux, R. B., James, G. D., Gerin, W., Landsbergis, P., Schnall, P. L., & Schwartz, J. E. (1996). Environmental influences on blood pressure and the role of job strain. *Journal of Hypertension, 14,* S179–S185.

Pickles, J. O. (1988). *An introduction to the physiology of hearing* (2nd ed.). London, UK: Academic Press.

Pickren, W. E. (2003). An elusive honor: Psychology, behavior, and the Nobel Prize. *American Psychologist, 58,* 721–722.

Pickren, W., & Rutherford, A. (2010). *A history of modern psychology in context.* Toronto, ON: University of Toronto Press.

Pierce, C. M. (1992). Contemporary psychiatry: Racial perspectives on the past and future. In A. Kales, C. M. Pierce, & M. Greenblatt (Eds.), *The mosaic of contemporary psychiatry in perspective.* New York, NY: Springer-Verlag.

Pierce, R. C., & Kumaresan, V. (2006). The mesolimbic dopamine system: The final common pathway for the reinforcing effect of drugs of abuse? *Neuroscience Biobehavioral Reviews, 30,* 215–238.

Pietraszewski, D. (2016). Priming race: Does the mind inhibit categorization by race at encoding or recall. *Social Psychological and Personality Science, 7,* 85–91.

Pietromonaco, P. R., & Beck, L. A. (2015). Attachment processes in adult romantic relationships. In M. Mikulincer, P. R. Shaver, J. A. Simpson, & J. F. Dovidio (Eds.), *APA hand-book of personality and social psychology Vol. 3: Interpersonal relations.* Washington, DC: American Psychological Association.

Pietschnig, J., Voracek, M., & Formann, A. K. (2010). Mozart effect–Shmozart effect: A meta-analysis. *Intelligence, 38*(3), 314–323.

Pihl, R. O., Assaad, J. M., & Hoaken, P. N. S. (2003). The alcohol–aggression relationship and differential sen-sitivity to alcohol. *Aggressive Behavior, 29,* 302–315.

Pilling, M., & Davies, I. R. L. (2004). Linguistic rela-tivism and colour cognition. *British Journal of Psychology, 95,* 429–455.

Pinel, J. P. J., Assanand, S., & Lehman, D. R. (2000). Hunger, eating, and ill health. *American Psychologist, 55,* 1105–1116.

Pinker, S. (1994). *Language is to us as flying is to geese.* New York, NY: Morrow.

Pinker, S. (2004). Language as an adaptation to the cognitive niche. In D. T. Kenrick & C. L. Luce (Eds.), *The functional mind: Readings in evolutionary psychology.* Essex, England: Pearson Education Limited.

Pinker, S. (2005). So how does the mind work? *Mind and Language, 20*(1), 1–24.

Pinker, S., & Bloom, P. (1992). Natural language and natural selection. In J. H. Barkow, L. Cosmides, & J. Tooby (Eds.), *The adapted mind: Evolutionary psychology and the generation of culture.* New York, NY: Oxford University Press.

Pinker, S., & Jackendoff, R. (2005). The faculty of lan-guage: What's special about it? *Cognition, 95,* 201–236.

Piomelli, D. (2004). The endogenous cannabinoid system and the treatment of marijuana dependence. *Neuropharmacology, 47,* 359–367.

Piper, W. E., & Hernandez, C. A. (2013). Group psychotherapies. In G. Stricker & T. A. Widiger (Eds.), *Handbook of psychology: Vol. 8. Clinical psychology* (2nd ed.). New York, NY: Wiley.

Pipitone, R. N., Gallegos, B., & Walters, D. (2017). Physiological responses to trypophobic images and further scale validity of the trypophobia questionnaire. *Personality and Individual Differences, 108,* 66–68.

Pitcher, B. J., Harcourt, R. G., & Charrier, I. (2012). Individual identity encoding and environmental constraints in vocal recognition of pups by Australian sea lion mothers. *Animal Behaviour, 83,* 681–690.

Pittman, F., III. (1994, January/February). A buyer's guide to psychotherapy. *Psychology Today,* 50–53, 74–81.

Pitts, S., Wilson, J., & Hugenberg, K. (2014). When one is ostracized, others loom: Social rejection makes other people appear closer. *Social Psychological and Personality Science, 5,* 550–557.

Pizzagalli, D., Shackman, A. J., & Davidson, R. J. (2003). The functional neuroimaging of human emotion: Asymmetric contributions of cortical and subcortical circuitry. In K. Hugdahl & R. J. Davidson (Eds.), *The asymmetrical brain.* Cambridge, MA: MIT Press.

Plomin, R. (1993). Nature and nurture: Perspective and prospective. In R. Plomin & G. E. McClearn (Eds.), *Nature, nurture and psychology.* Washington, DC: American Psychological Association.

Plomin, R. (2003). General cognitive ability. In R. Plomin & J. C. DeFries (Eds.), *Behavioral genetics in the postgenomic era.* Washinton, DC: American Psychological Association.

Plomin, R. (2004). Genetics and developmental psychology. *Merrill-Palmer Quarterly, 50,* 341–352.

Plomin, R. (2013). Child development and molecular genetics: 14 years later. *Child Development, 84,* 104–120. doi:10.1111/j.1467-8624.2012.01757.x.

Plomin, R., DeFries, J. C., Knopik,V. S., & Neiderhiser, J. M. (2013). *Behavioral genetics* (6th ed.). New York, NY: Worth Publishers.

Plomin, R., DeFries, J. C., McClearn, G. E., & McGuffin, P. (2008). *Behavioral genetics.* New York, NY: Worth.

Plomin, R., Haworth, C. A., Meaburn, E. L., Price, T. S., & Davis, O. P. (2013). Common DNA markers can account for more than half of the genetic influence on cognitive abilities. *Psychological Science, 24,* 562–568. doi:10.1177/0956797612457952.

Plomin, R., Kennedy, J. K. J., & Craig, I. W. (2006). The quest for quantitative, trait loci associated with intelligence. *Intelligence, 34,* 513–526.

Plomin, R., & Spinath, F. M. (2004). Intelligence: Genetics, genes, and genomics. *Journal of Personality & Social Psychology, 86,* 112–129.

Plouffe, R. A., Paunonen, S. V., & Saklofske, D. (2017). Item properties and the convergent validity of personality assessment: A peer rating study. *Personality and Individual Differences, 111,* 95–105.

Plucker, J. A., & Makel, M. C. (2010). Assessment of creativity. In J. C. Kaufman & R. J. Sternberg (Eds.), *The Cambridge handbook of creativity* (pp. 48–73). New York, NY: Cambridge University Press.

Plucker, J. A., & Renzulli, J. S. (1999). Psychometric approaches to the study of human creativity. In R. J. Sternberg (Ed.), *Handbook of creativity.* New York, NY: Cambridge University Press.

Pluess, M., & Belsky, J. (2010). Differential susceptibility to parenting and quality child care. *Developmental Psychology, 46,* 379–390. doi:10.1037/a0015203.

Plumert, J. M., & Nichols-Whitehead, P. (1996). Parental scaffolding of young children's spatial communication. *Developmental Psychology, 32,* 523–532.

Plutchik, R. (1980, February). A language for the emotions. *Psychology Today,* pp. 68–78.

Plutchik, R. (1984). Emotions: A general psychoevolutionary theory. In K. R. Scherer & P. Ekman (Eds.), *Approaches to emotion.* Hillsdale, NJ: Erlbaum.

Plutchik, R. (1993). Emotions and their vicissitudes: Emotions and psychopathology. In M. Lewis & J. M. Haviland (Eds.), *Handbook of emotions.* New York, NY: Guilford.

Pogue-Geile, M. F., & Yokley, J. L. (2010). Current research on the genetic contributors to schizophrenia. *Current Directions in Psychological Science, 19*(4), 214–219.

Pohl, R. F. (2004). Effects of labeling. In F. P. Rudiger (Ed.), *Cognitive illusions.* New York, NY: Psychology Press.

Poldrack, R. A., & Wagner, A. D. (2008). The interface between neuroscience and psychological science. *Current Directions between Neuroscience and Psychological Science, 17,* 61–63.

Policastro, E., & Gardner, H. (1999). From case studies to robust generalizations: An approach to the study of creativity. In R. J. Sternberg (Ed.), *Handbook of creativity.* New York, NY: Cambridge University Press.

Polivy, J., & Herman, C. P. (1995). Dieting and its relation to eating disorders. In K. D. Brownell & C. G. Fairburn (Eds.), *Eating disorders and obesity: A comprehensive handbook.* New York, NY: Guilford.

Polman, E. & Vohs, K. D. (2016). Decision fatigue: Choosing for others, and self-construal. *Social Psychology and Personality Science, 7,* 471–478.

Pomerantz, E. M., Ng, F. F. Y., & Wang, Q. (2004). Gender socialization: A parent-child model. In A. H. Eagly, A. E. Beall, & R. J. Sternberg (Eds.), *The psychology of gender.* New York, NY: Guilford.

Pomerville, A., Burrage, R. L., & Gone, J. P. (2016). Empirical findings from psychotherapy research with indigenous populations: A systematic review. *Journal of Consulting and Clinical Psychology, 84,* 1023–1038.

Pool, E., Brosch, T., Delplanque, S., & Sander, D. (2016). Attentional bias for positive emotional stimuli: A meta-analytic investigation. *Psychological Bulletin, 142,* 79–106.

Pope, H. G., Jr., & Hudson, J. I. (1998). Can memories of childhood sexual abuse be repressed? In R. A. Baker (Ed.), *Child sexual abuse and false memory syndrome.* Amherst, NY: Prometheus Books.

Popenoe, D. (1996). *Life without father.* New York, NY: Pressler Books.

Popkin, B. M. (2012). The changing face of global diet and nutrition. In K. D. Brownell, & M. S. Gold (Eds.), *Food and addiction: A comprehensive handbook.* New York, NY: Oxford University Press.

Popova, S., Lange, S., Sheild, K., Mihic, A., Chudley, A. E., Mukherjee, R., Bekmuradov, D., & Rehm, J. (2016). Co-morbidity of fetal alcohol spectrum disorder: A systematic literature review and meta-analysis. *The Lancet, 387,* 978–987.

Popper, C. W., & Steingard, R. J. (1994). Disorders usually first diagnosed in infancy, childhood, or adolescence. In R. E. Hales, S. C. Yudofsky, & J. A. Talbott (Eds.), *The American Psychiatric Press textbook of psychiatry.* Washington, DC: American Psychiatric Press.

Popper, C. W., Gammon, G. D., West, S. A., & Bailey, C. E. (2003). Disorders usually first diagnosed in infancy, childhood, and adolescence. In Robert E. Hales & Stuart C. Yudofsky (Eds.), *Textbook of clinical psychiatry.* Washington, DC: American Psychiatric Publishing.

Porcerelli, J. H., Cogan, R., Kamoo, R., & Miller, K. (2010). Convergent validity of the Defense Mechanisms Manual and the Defensive Functioning Scale. *Journal of Personality Assessment, 92*(5), 432–438.

Porter, C. (2015). Paul Bernardo has applied for a day parole in the Toronto area. *The Toronto Star,* Friday, July 3, 2015. Retrieved from https://www.thestar.com/news/crime/2015/07/03/paul-bernardo-has-applied-for-day-parole-in-toronto-area.html.

Porter, J., Craven, B., Khan, R. M., Chang, S., Kang, I., Judkewitz, B., Volpe, J., et al. (2007). Mechanisms of scent-tracking in humans. *Nature Neuroscience, 10*(1), 27–29.

Porter, S., & Porter, S. (2007). Psychopathy and Violent Crime. In H. Hervé, J. C. Yuille, H. Hervé, & J. C. Yuille (Eds.), *The Psychopath: Theory, Research, and Practice.* Mahwah, NJ: Lawrence Erlbaum Associates Publishers.

Porter, S., Bhanwer, A., Woodworth, M., & Black, P. J. (2014). Soldiers of misfortune: An examination of the dark triad and the experience of schadenfreude. *Personality and Individual Differences, 67,* 64–68.

Posada, G., Kaloustian, G., Richmond, K., & Moreno, A. J. (2007). Maternal secure base support and preschoolers' secure base behavior in natural environments. *Attachment & Human Development, 9,* 393–411.

Posner, M. I., & Rothbart, M. K. (2004). Hebb's neural networks support the integration of psychological science. *Canadian Psychology, 45,* 265–278.

Post, R. M. & Altshuler, L. L. (2009). Mood disorders: Treatment of bipolar disorders. In B. J. Sadock, V. A. Sadock, & P. Ruiz (Eds.), *Kaplan & Sadock's comprehensive textbook of psychiatry* (pp. 1743–1812). Philadelphia, PA: Lippincott, Williams & Wilkins.

Posten, A-C., Ockenfels, A., & Mussweiler, T. (2014). How activating cognitive content shapes trust: A subliminal priming study. *Journal of Economic Psychology, 41,* 12–19.

Posthuma, D., Luciano, M., de Geus, E. J. C., Wright, M. J., Slagboom, P. E., Montgomery, G. W., et al. (2005). A genome-wide scan for intelligence identifies quantitative trait loci on 2q and 6p. *American Journal of Human Genetics, 77,* 318–326.

Postle, B. R. (2016). How does the brain keep information "in mind"? *Current Directions in Psychological Science, 25,* 151–156.

Postman, L. (1985). Human learning and memory. In G. A. Kimble & K. Schlesinger (Eds.), *Topics in the history of psychology.* Hillsdale, NJ: Erlbaum.

Postmes, T., Spears, R., & Cihangir, S. (2001). Quality of decision making and group norms. *Journal of Personality and Social Psychology, 80,* 918–930.

Potter, W. Z., Padich, R. A., Rudorfer, M. V., & Krishnan, K. R. R. (2006). Tricyclics, tetracyclics, and monoamine oxidase inhibitors. In D. J. Stein, D. J. Kupfer, & A. F. Schatzberg (Eds.), *Textbook of mood disorders* (pp. 251–262). Washington, DC: American Psychiatric Publishing.

Potthoff, J. G., Holahan, C. J., & Joiner, T. E., Jr. (1995). Reassurance-seeking, stress generation, and depressive symptoms: An integrative model. *Journal of Personality and Social Psychology, 68,* 664–670.

Poulin-Dubois, D., & Graham, S. A. (2007). Cognitive processes in early word learning. In E. Hoff & M. Shatz (Eds.), *Blackwell handbook of language development* (pp. 191–212). Malden, MA: Blackwell.

Poulton, E. C. (1994). *Behavioral decision theory: A new approach.* Cambridge, England: Cambridge University Press.

Powell, R. A. (2010). Little Albert still missing. *American Psychologist, 65,* 299–300.

Powell, R. A., & Boer, D. P. (1995). Did Freud misinterpret reported memories of sexual abuse as fantasies? *Psychological Reports, 77,* 563–570.

Powell, R. A., Digdon, N., Harris, B., & Smithson, C. (2014). Correcting the record on Watson, Rayner, and Little Albert: Albert Barger as "psychology's lost boy." *American Psychologist, 69,* 600–611.

Powell, R. A., & Gee, T. L. (1999). The effects of hypnosis on dissociative identity disorder: A reexamination of the evidence. *Canadian Journal of Psychiatry, 44,* 914–916.

Powell, R. A., Honey, P. L., & Symbaluk, D. G. (2017). *Introduction to learning and behavior* (5th ed.). Boston, MA: Cengage Learning.

Powley, T. L. (2008). Central control of autonomic functions: Organization of the autonomic nervous system. In L. Squire, D. Berg, F. Bloom, S. Du Lac, A. Ghosh, & N. Spitzer (Eds.), *Fundamental neuroscience* (3rd ed., pp. 809–828). San Diego, CA: Elsevier.

Powley, T. L. (2009). Hunger. In G. G. Berntson & J. T. Cacioppo (Eds.), *Handbook of neuroscience for the behavioral sciences,* (Vol. 2, pp. 659–679). Hoboken, NJ: Wiley.

Pozzulo, J., Bennell, C., & Forth, A. (2006). *Forensic psychology.* Toronto, ON: Pearson Education Inc.

Pratkanis, A. R., & Aronson, E. (2000). *Age of propaganda: The everyday use and abuse of persuasion.* New York, NY: Freeman.

Prebble, S. C., Addis, D. R., & Tippett, L. J. (2013). Autobiographical memory and sense of self. *Psychological Bulletin, 139,* 815–849.

Premack, D. (1985). "Gavagai!" or the future history of the animal language controversy. *Cognition, 19,* 207–296.

Prentky, R. A. (1989). Creativity and psychopathology: Gamboling at the seat of madness. In J. A. Glover, R. R. Ronning, & C. R. Reynolds (Eds.), *Handbook of creativity.* New York, NY: Plenum.

Pressman, S. D., & Cohen, S. (2005). Does positive affect influence health? *Psychological Bulletin, 131,* 925–971.

Pressman, S. D., & Cohen, S. (2012). Positive emotion word use and longevity in famous deceased psychologists. *Health Psychology, 31,* 297–305. doi:10.1037/a0025339.

PrevNet. (2017). *Age trends in the prevalence of bullying.* Retrieved from http://www.prevnet.ca/research/fact-sheets/age-trends-in-the-prevalence-of-bullying.

Price, M. (2008). Div. 55's drive for RxP: The American Society for the Advancement of Pharmacotherapy pushes for prescriptive authority. *Monitor on Psychology, 39*(2).

Price, R. A. (2012). Genetics and common human obesity. In J. J. Nurnberger, & W. H. Berrettini (Eds.), *Principles of psychiatric genetics.* New York, NY: Cambridge University Press. doi:10.1017/CBO9781139025997.022.

Priester, J. R., & Petty, R. E. (2003). The influence of spokesperson trustworthiness on message elaboration, attitude strength, and advertising. *Journal of Consumer Psychology, 13,* 408–421.

Prince, M., Albanese, E., Guerchet, M., & Prina, M. (2014). *World Alzheimer report 2014 dementia and risk reduction: An analysis of protective and modifiable factors.* London, UK: Alzheimer's Disease International.

Pringle, H. (1997). Alberta barren. *Saturday Night,* June 1997, pp. 30–74.

Prochaska, J. O., Velicer, W. F., Prochaska, J. M., & Johnson, J. L. (2004). Size, consistency, and stability of stage effects for smoking cessation. *Addictive Behaviors, 29,* 207–213.

Proffitt, D. R., & Caudek, C. (2003). Depth perception and the perception of events. In A. F. Healy & R. W. Proctor (Eds.), *Handbook of psychology, Vol. 4: Experimental psychology.* New York, NY: Wiley.

Prolo, P., & Chiappelli, F. (2007). Immune suppression. In G. Fink (Ed.), *Encyclopedia of stress.* San Diego, CA: Elsevier.

Pronin, E., Berger, J., & Molouki, S. (2007). Alone in a crowd of sheep: Asymmetric perceptions of conformity and their roots in an introspection illusion. *Journal of Personality and Social Psychology, 92,* 585–595. doi:10.1037/0022-3514.92.4.585.

Pronin, E., Wegner, D. M., McCarthy, K., & Rodriguez, S. (2006). Everyday magical powers: The role of apparent mental causation in the overestimation of personal influence. *Journal of Personality and Social Psychology, 91,* 218–231.

Proulx, C. M., Helms, H. M., & Buehler, C. (2007). Marital quality and personal well-being: A meta-analysis. *Journal of Marriage and Family, 69*(3), 576–593.

Province of Ontario. (2010). *Children's Mental Health Ontario.* Retrieved June 2, 2011, from http://www.kidsmentalhealth.ca/documents/res_cmho_final_prebudget_submission_2010_final.pdf.

Prudic, J. (2009). Electroconvulsive therapy. In B. J. Sadock, V. A. Sadock, & P. Ruiz (Eds.), *Kaplan & Sadock's comprehensive textbook of psychiatry* (pp. 3285–3300). Philadelphia, PA: Lippincott Williams & Wilkins.

Pruitt, D. G. (1971). Choice shifts in group discussion: An introductory review. *Journal of Personality and Social Psychology, 20,* 339–360.

Psychology Foundation of Canada. (n.d.). The struggle to juggle stress management: Stategies for you and your family. Retrieved May 20, 2011, from http://www.psychologyfoundation.org.

Ptito, A., Chen, J. K., & Johnstone, K. M. (2007). Contributions of functional magnetic resonance imaging (fMRI) to sport concussion evaluation. *NeuroRehabilitation, 22*(3), 217–227.

Public Health Agency of Canada. (2013). HIV/AIDS surveillance in Canada. Retrieved from http://www.phac-aspc.gc.ca/aids-sida/publication/index-eng.php.

Public Health Toronto. (2006). Early child development family abuse prevention project actions to prevent physical punishment of children.

Pullum, G. K. (1991). *The Great Eskimo vocabulary hoax.* Chicago: University of Chicago Press.

Punch, J. L., Elfenbein, J. L, & James, R. R. (2011). Targeting hearing health messages for users of personal listening devices. *American Journal of Audiology, 20,* 69–82.

Purves, D. (2009). Vision. In G. G. Berntson & J. T. Cacioppo (Eds.), *Handbook of neuroscience for the behavioral sciences.* New York, NY: Wiley.

Pyc, M. A., Agarwal, P. K., & Roediger, H. I. (2014). Test-enhanced learning. In V. A. Benassi, C. E. Overson, & C. M. Hakala (Eds.), *Applying science of learning in education: Infusing psychological science into the curriculum.* Washington, DC: Society for the Teaching of Psychology.

Qin, S., Young, C. B., Duan, X., Chen, T., Supekar, K., & Menon, V. (2014). Amygdala subregional structure and intrinsic functional connectivity predicts individual differences in anxiety during early childhood. *Biological Psychiatry, 75,* 892–900. doi:10.1016/j.biopsych.2013.10.006.

Qui, C., Xu, W., & Fratiglioni, L. (2010). Vascular and psychosocial factors in Alzheimer's disease: Epidemiological evidence toward intervention. *Journal of Alzheimer's Disease, 20,* 689–697.

Quinn, K. A., Macrae, C. N., & Bodenhausen, G. V. (2003). Stereotyping and impression formation: How categorical thinking shapes person perception. In M. A. Hogg & J. Cooper (Eds.), *The Sage handbook of social psychology.* Thousand Oaks, CA: Sage.

Quoidbach, J., Wood, A. M., & Hansenne, M. (2009). Back to the future: The effect of daily practice of mental time travel into the future on happiness and anxiety. *Journal of Positive Psychology, 4,* 349–355.

Rachman, S. J. (1990). *Fear and courage.* New York, NY: W. H. Freeman.

Rachman, S. J. (2009). Psychological treatment of anxiety: The evolution of behavior therapy and cognitive behavior therapy. *Annual Review of Clinical Psychology, 5,* 97–119.

Radak, Z., Hart, N., Sarga, L., Koltai, E., Atalay, M., Ohno, H., & Boldogh, I. (2010). Exercise plays a preventive role against Alzheimer's disease. *Journal of Alzheimer's Disease, 20*(3), 777–783.

Rafal, R. (2001). Virtual neurology. *Nature Neuroscience, 4,* 862–864.

Rains, G. D. (2002). *Principles of human neuropsychology.* New York, NY: McGraw-Hill.

Rakic, P., Bourgeois, J. P., & Goldman-Rakic, P. S. (1994). Synaptic development of the cerebral cortex: Implications for learning, memory, and mental illness. *Progress in brain research, 102,* 227–243.

Rakobowchuk, P. (2011, March 22). Senior suicides expected to rise as boomers age. *Toronto Star,* E9.

Rama, A. N., Cho, S. C., & Kushida, C. A. (2006). Normal human sleep. In T. Lee-Chiong (Ed.), *Sleep: A comprehensive handbook.* Hoboken, NJ: Wiley-Liss.

Ramachandran, V. S., & Oberman, L. M. (2006). Broken mirrors: A theory of autism. *Scientific American, 295,* 62–69.

Ramadan, N. M. (2000). Migraine. In G. Fink (Ed.), *Encyclopedia of stress* (pp. 757–770). San Diego, CA: Academic Press.

Ramage-Morin, P. L., & Gilmour, H. (2013). Urinary incontinence and loneliness in Canadian seniors. *Heath Reports, Statistics Canada Catalogue no. 82-003-X.* Retrieved from http://www.statcan.gc.ca/pub/82-003-x/2013010/article/11872-eng.htm.

Ramage-Morin, P. L., & Gilmour, H. (2014). *Prevalence of migraine in the Canadian household population.* Statistics Canada. Retrieved from http://www.statcan.gc.ca/pub/82-003-x/2014006/article/14033-eng.htm.

Ramchand, R., Schell, T. L., Karney, B. R., Osilla, K., Burns, R. M., & Caldarone, L. (2010). Disparate prevalence estimates of PTSD among service members who served in Iraq and Afghanistan: Possible explanations. *Journal of Traumatic Stress, 23*(1), 59–68.

Ramchandani, P. G., Domoney, J., Sethna, V., Psychogiou, L., Vlachos, H., & Murray, L. (2013). Do early father-infant interactions predict the onset of externalizing behaviours in young children? Findings from a longitudinal cohort study. *Journal of Child Psychology and Psychiatry, 54,* 56–64.

Ramey, C. T., & Ramey, S. L. (2004). Early learning and school readiness: Can early intervention make a difference? *Merrill-Palmer Quarterly, 50,* 471–491.

Ramey, S. L. (1999). Head Start and preschool education: Toward continued improvement. *American Psychologist, 54,* 344–346.

Ramsay, D. S., & Woods, S. C. (2012). Food intake and metabolism. In K. D. Brownell, & M. S. Gold (Eds.), *Food and addiction: A comprehensive handbook.* New York, NY: Oxford University Press.

Rapoport, J. L., Giedd, J. N., & Gogtay, N. (2012). Neurodevelopmental model of schizophrenia: Update 2012. *Molecular Psychiatry, 17,* 1228–1238. doi:10.1038/mp.2012.23.

Rascmany, M., Conway, M. A., & Demeter, G. (2010). Consolidation of episodic memories during sleep: Long-term effects of retrieval practice. *Psychological Science, 21,* 80–85.

Rashid, T., & Anjum, A. (2008). Positive psychotherapy for young adults and children. In J. Z. Abela & B. L. Hankin (Eds.), *Handbook of depression in children and adolescents* (pp. 250–287). New York, NY: Guilford Press.

Raskin, N. J., Rogers, C. R., & Witty, M. C. (2014). Client-centered therapy. In D. Wedding & R. J. Corsini (Eds.), *Current psychotherapies* (10th ed., 95–150). Belmont, CA: Brooks/Cole.

Ratner, K. G., Dotsch, R., Wigboldus, D., van Knippenberg, A., & Amodio, D. M. (2014). Visualizing minimal ingroup and outgroup faces: Implications for impressions, attitudes, and behavior. *Journal of Personality and Social Psychology, 106,* 897–911.

Ratner, N. B., Gleason, J. B., & Narasimhan, B. (1998). An introduction to psycholinguistics: What do language users know? In J. B. Gleason & N. B. Ratner (Eds.), *Psycholinguistics* (2nd ed., pp. 1–40). Fort Worth, TX: Harcourt College Publishers.

Rauscher, F. H., Shaw, G. L., & Ky, K. N. (1993). Music and spatial task performance. *Nature, 365,* 611.

Rauscher, F. H., Shaw, G. L., & Ky, K. N. (1995). Listening to Mozart enhances spatial-temporal reasoning: Towards a neurophysiological basis. *Neuroscience Letters, 185,* 44–47.

Rawal, S., Hayes, J. E., Wallace, M. R., Bartoshuk, L. M., & Duffy, V. B. (2013). Do polymorphisms in the TAS1R1 gene associate with broader differences in human taste intensity? *Chemical Senses,* doi: 10.1093/chemse/bjt040.

Rawana, J. S., Morgan, A. S., Nguyen, H., & Craig, S. G. (2010). The relation between eating- and weight-related disturbances and depression in adolescence: A review. *Clinical Child Family Psychological Review, 13,* 213–230.

Raynor, H. A., & Epstein, L. H. (2001). Dietary variety, energy regulation, and obesity. *Psychological Bulletin, 127,* 325–341.

Raynor, J. O., & Entin, E. E. (1982). Future orientation and achievement motivation. In J. O. Raynor & E. E. Entin (Eds.), *Motivation, career striving, and aging.* New York, NY: Hemisphere.

Razavi, A. H., Matwin, S., Amini, R., De Koninck, J. (2014). Dream sentiment analysis using second order soft co-occurrences and time course representations. *Journal of Intelligent Information Systems, 42,* 393–413.

Read, J., Cartwright, C., & Gibson, K. (2014). Adverse emotional and interpersonal effects reported by 1829 New

Zealanders while taking antidepressants. *Psychiatry Research, 216*(1), 67–73. doi:10.1016/j.psychres.2014.01.042.

Read, S. J., Monroe, B. M., Brownstein, A. L., Yang, Y., Chopra, G., & Miller, L. C. (2010). A neural network model of the structure and dynamics of human personality. *Psychological Review, 117*, 61–92.

Rebok, G. W., Ball, K., Guey, L. T., Jones, R. N., Kim, H., King, J. W., . . . Willis, S. L. (2014). Ten-year effects of the advanced cognitive training for independent and vital elderly cognitive training trial on cognition and everyday functioning in older adults. *Journal of the American Geriatrics Society, 62*(1), 16–24. doi:10.1111/jgs.12607.

Recht, L. D., Lew, R. A., & Schwartz, W. J. (1995). Baseball teams beaten by jet lag. *Nature, 377*, 583.

Rechtschaffen, A. (1994). Sleep onset: Conceptual issues. In R. D. Ogilvie & J. R. Harsh (Eds.), *Sleep onset: Normal and abnormal processes*. Washington, DC: American Psychological Association.

Reder, L. M., Park, H., & Keiffaber, P. D. (2009). Memory systems do not divide on consciousness: Reinterpreting memory in terms of activation and binding. *Psychological Bulletin, 135*, 23–49.

Redline, S. (2011). Genetics of obstructive sleep apnea. In M. H. Kryger, T. Roth, & W. C. Dement (Eds.), *Principles and practice of sleep medicine* (5th ed.). Saint Louis, MO: Elsevier Saunders.

Rees, C. J., & Metcalfe, B. (2003). The faking of personality questionnaire results: Who's kidding whom? *Journal of Managerial Psychology, 18*(2), 156–165.

Reese, H. W. (2010). Regarding Little Albert. *American Psychologist, 65*, 300–301.

Refinetti, R. (2006). *Circadian physiology*. Boca Raton, FL: Taylor & Francis.

Regan, P. C. (2008). *The mating game: A primer on love, sex, and marriage* (2nd ed.). Thousand Oaks, CA: Sage.

Regehr, C., & Bober, T. (2005). *In the line of fire: Trauma in the emergency services*. New York, NY: Oxford University Press.

Reger, G. M., Holloway, K. M., Candy, C., Rothbaum, B. O., Difede, J., Rizzo, A. A., & Gahm, G. A. (2011). Effectiveness of virtual reality exposure therapy for active duty soldiers in a military mental health clinic. *Journal of Traumatic Stress, 24*(1), 93–96. doi:10.1002/jts.20574.

Regier, D. A., & Burke, J. D. (2000). Epidemiology. In B. J. Sadock & V. A. Sadock (Eds.), *Kaplan and Sadock's comprehensive textbook of psychiatry*. Philadelphia, PA: Lippincott Williams & Wilkins.

Regier, D. A., & Kaelber, C. T. (1995). The Epidemiologic Catchment Area (ECA) program: Studying the prevalence and incidence of psychopathology. In M. T. Tsuang, M. Tohen, & G. E. P. Zahner (Eds.), *Textbook in psychiatric epidemiology*. New York, NY: Wiley.

Regier, D. A., Narrow, W. E., & Rae, D. S. (2004). For DSM-V, It's the "disorder threshold," stupid. *Archives of General Psychiatry, 61*, 1051.

Rehm, J., Gmel, G., Probst, C., & Shield, K. D. (2015). Lifetime-risk of alcohol-attributable mortality based on different levels of alcohol consumption in seven European countries: Implications for low-risk drinking guidelines. Toronto, ON: Centre for Addiction and Mental Health.

Reicher, S. D., & Haslam, S. A. (2006). Rethinking the psychology tyranny: The BBC prison study. *British Journal of Social Psychology, 45*, 1–40.

Reichert, T. (2003). The prevalence of sexual imagery in ads targeted to young adults. *Journal of Consumer Affairs, 37*, 403–412.

Reichert, T., & Lambiase, J. (2003). How to get "kissably close": Examining how advertisers appeal to consumers' sexual needs and desires. *Sexuality & Culture: An Interdisciplinary Quarterly, 7*(3), 120–136.

Reid, N., Dawe, S., Shelton, D., Harnett, P., Warner, J., Armstrong, E., Le Gros, K., & Callaghan, F. (2015). Systematic review of fetal alcohol spectrum disorder interventions across the life span. *Alcoholism: Clinical and Experimental Research, 39*, 2283–2295.

Reid, R. C., & Usrey, W. M. (2008). Vision. In L. Squire, D. Berg, F. Bloom, S. du Lac, A. Ghosh, & N. Spitzer (Eds.), *Fundamental neuroscience*. San Diego, CA: Elsevier.

Reigier, D. A., Kuhl, E., & Kupfer, D. J. (2013). The DSM-5: Classification and criteria changes. *World Psychiatry, 12*, 92–98.

Reinharz, D., Lesage, A. D., & Contandriopoulos, A. P. (2000). Cost-effectiveness analysis of psychiatric deinstitutionalization. *Canadian Journal of Psychiatry, 45*, 533–538.

Reinhold, S. (2010). Reassessing the link between premarital cohabitation and marital instability. *Demography, 47*, 719–733. doi:10.1353/dem.0.0122.

Reis, H. T., & Aron, A. (2008). Love: What is it, why does it matter, and how does it operate? *Perspectives on Psychological Science, 3*, 80–86.

Reisner, A. D. (1998). Repressed memories: True and false. In R. A. Baker (Ed.), *Child sexual abuse and false memory syndrome*. Amherst, NY: Prometheus Books.

Rempel, J. K., & Burris, C. T. (2005). Let me count the ways: An integrative theory of love and hate. *Personal Relationships, 12*, 297–313.

Renzulli, J. S. (1986). The three-ring conception of giftedness: A developmental model for creative productivity. In R. J. Sternberg & J. E. Davidson (Eds.), *Conceptions of giftedness*. Cambridge, UK: Cambridge University Press.

Renzulli, J. S. (1999). What is this thing called giftedness, and how do we develop it? A twenty-five year perspective. *Journal for the Education of the Gifted, 23*, 3–54.

Renzulli, J. S. (2002). Emerging conceptions of giftedness: Building a bridge to the new century. *Exceptionality, 10*, 67–75.

Repetto, M., & Gold, M. S. (2005). Cocaine and crack: Neurobiology. In J. H. Lowinson, P. Ruiz, R. B. Millman, & J. G. Langrod (Eds.), *Substance abuse: A comprehensive textbook*. Philadelphia, PA: Lippincott/Williams & Wilkins.

Repovš, G., & Baddeley, A. (2006). The multi-component model of working memory: Explorations in experimental cognitive psychology. *Neuroscience, 139*, 5–21.

Rescorla, R. A. (1978). Some implications of a cognitive perspective on Pavlovian conditioning. In S. H. Hulse, H. Fowler, & W. K. Honig (Eds.), *Cognitive processes in animal behavior*. Hillsdale, NJ: Erlbaum.

Rescorla, R. A. (1980). *Pavlovian second-order conditioning*. Hillsdale, NJ: Erlbaum.

Rescorla, R. A., & Wagner, A. R. (1972). A theory of Pavlovian conditioning: Variations in the effectiveness of reinforcement and nonreinforcement. In A. H. Black & W. F. Prokasky (Eds.), *Classical conditioning: II. Current research and theory*. New York, NY: Appleton-Century-Crofts.

Resick, P. A., Monson, C. M., & Rizvi, S. L. (2008). Posttraumatic stress disorder. In W. E. Craighead, D. J. Miklowitz, & L. W. Craighead (Eds.), *Psychopathology: History, diagnosis, and empirical foundations*. New York, NY: Wiley.

Resnick, R. A. (2002). Change detection. *Annual Review of Psychology, 53*, 247–277.

Rest, J. R. (1986). *Moral development: Advances in research and theory*. New York, NY: Praeger.

Reuter-Lorenz, P. A., & Miller, A. C. (1998). The cognitive neuroscience of human laterality: Lessons from the bisected brain. *Current Directions in Psychological Science, 7*, 15–20.

Reutskaja, E., & Hogarth, R. M. (2009). Satisfaction in choice as a function of the number of alternatives: When "goods satiate." *Psychology & Marketing, 26*(3), 197–203.

Reynaud, A-M. (2014). Dealing with difficult emotions: Anger at the Truth and reconciliation commission of Canada. *Anthropologica: Waterloo, 56*, 369–382.

Reynolds, A. J., Temple, J. T., Robertson, D. L., & Mann, E. A. (2001). Long-term effects of an early childhood intervention on educational achievement and juvenile arrest: A 15-year follow-up of low-income children in public schools. *Journal of the American Medical Association, 285*, 2339–2346.

Reynolds, K. J., Turner, J. C., & Haslam, S. A. (2000). When are we better than them and they worse than us?

A closer look at social discrimination in positive and negative domains. *Journal of Personality and Social Psychology, 78*, 64–80.

Rhodes, G. (2013). Face recognition. In D. Reisberg (Ed.), *The Oxford handbook of cognitive psychology*. New York, NY: Oxford University Press.

Riazi, A., & Bradley, C. (2000). Diabetes, Type I. In G. Fink (Ed.), *Encyclopedia of stress* (pp. 688–693). San Diego, CA: Academic Press.

Riba, M. B., & Miller, R. R. (2003). Combined therapies: Psychotherapy and pharmacotherapy. In A. Tasman, J. Kay, & J. A. Lieberman (Eds.), *Psychiatry*. New York, NY: Wiley.

Ribkoff, F. (2013). Unheeded post-traumatic unpredictability: Philip G. Zimbardo's Stanford Prison Experiment as absurdist performance. *Liminalities: A Journal of Performance Studies, 9*, np. Retrieved from http:// liminalities.net/9-1/unheeded.pdf.

Rice, L. N., & Greenberg, L. S. (1992). Humanistic approaches to psychotherapy. In D. K. Freedheim (Ed.), *History of psychotherapy: A century of change*. Washington, DC: American Psychological Association.

Rice, M., & Harris, G. T. (1993). Ontario's maximum security hospital at Penetanguishene. *International Journal of Law and Psychiatry, 16*, 195–215.

Rice, W. R., Friberg, U., & Gavrilets, S. (2012). Homosexuality as a consequence of epigenetically canalized sexual development. *The Quarterly Review of Biology, 87*, 343–368.

Rich, J. B., Park, N. W., Dopkins, S., & Brandt, J. (2002). What do Alzheimer's disease patients know about animals? It depends on task structure and presentation format. *Journal of the International Neuropsychological Society, 8*, 83–94.

Richards, S. S., & Sweet, R. A. (2009). Dementia. In B. J. Sadock, V. A. Sadock, & P. Ruiz (Eds.), *Kaplan & Sadock's comprehensive textbook of psychiatry* (9th ed., Vol. 1, pp. 1167–1197). Philadelphia, PA: Lippincott Williams & Wilkins.

Richardson, C. R., Kriska, A. M., Lantz, P. M., & Hayword, R. A. (2004). Physical activity and mortality across cardiovascular disease risk groups. *Medicine and Science in Sports and Exercise, 36*, 1923–1929.

Richardson, G. S. (1993). Circadian rhythms. In M. A. Carskadon (Ed.), *Encyclopedia of sleep and dreaming*. New York, NY: Macmillan.

Richert, E. S. (1997). Excellence with equity in identification and programming. In N. Colangelo, & G. A. Davis (Eds.), *Handbook of gifted education*. Boston, MA: Allyn & Bacon.

Rieskamp, J., & Hoffrage, U. (1999). When do people use simple heuristics and how can we tell? In G. Gigerenzer, P. Todd, & the ABC Research Group (Eds.), *Simple heuristics that make us smart* (pp. 25–47). Oxford: Oxford University Press.

Riggio, H. R., & Halpern, D. F. (2006). Understanding human thought: Educating students as critical thinkers. In W. Buskist & S. F. Davis (Eds.), *Handbook of the teaching of psychology* (pp. 78–84). Malden, MA: Blackwell.

Rihmer, Z., & Angst, J. (2009). Mood disorders: Epidemiology. In B. J. Sadock, V. A. Sadock, & P. Ruiz (Eds.), *Kaplan & Sadock's comprehensive textbook of psychiatry* (9th ed., pp. 1645–1652). Philadelphia, PA: Lippincott, Williams & Wilkins.

Riis, J., Loewenstein, G., Baron, J., Jepson, C., Fagerlin, A., & Ubel, P. A. (2005). Ignorance of hedonic adaptation to hemodialysis: A study using ecological momentary assessment. *Journal of Experimental Psychology: General, 134*(1), 3–9.

Riley, B., & Kendler, K. S. (2011). Classical genetic studies of schizophrenia. In D. R. Weinberger & P. Harrison (Eds.), *Schizophrenia* (3rd ed.). Malden, MA: Wiley-Blackwell.

Rilling, J. K., & Sanfey, A. G. (2011). The neuroscience of social decision-making. *Annual Review of Psychology, 62*, 23–48.

Rilling, M. (1996). The mystery of the vanished citations: James McConnell's forgotten 1960s quest for planarian learning, a biochemical engram, and celebrity. *American Psychologist, 51,* 589–598.

Risch, N., Hoffmann, T. J., Anderson, M., Croen, L. A., Grether, J. K., & Windham, G. C. (2014). Familial recurrence of autism spectrum disorder: Evaluating genetic and environmental contributions. *The American Journal of Psychiatry, 171,* 1206–1213. doi:10.1176/appi.ajp.2014.13101359.

Risen, J. (2015). American psychological association bolstered C.I.A. torture program, report says. *The New York Times,* April 30, 2015. Retrieved from https://www.nytimes.com/2015/05/01/us/report-says-american-psychological-association-collaborated-on-torture-justification.html.

Risen, J. (2015). Outside psychologists shielded U.S. torture program, report finds. *The New York Times,* July 10, 2015. Retrieved from https://www.nytimes.com/2015/07/11/us/psychologists-shielded-us-torture-program-report-finds.html.

Risen, J. L. (2016). Believing what we do not believe: Acquiescence to superstitious beliefs and other powerful intuitions. *Psychological Review, 123,* 182–207.

Risen, J., & Gilovich, T. (2007). Informal logical fallacies. In R. J. Sternberg, H. L. Roediger III, & D. F. Halpern (Eds.), *Critical thinking in psychology.* New York, NY: Cambridge University Press.

Riskind, J. H. (2005). Cognitive mechanisms in generalized anxiety disorder: A second generation of theoretical perspectives. *Cognitive Therapy & Research, 29*(1), 1–5.

Rissman, J., & Wagner, A. D. (2012). Distributed representations in memory: Insights from functional brain imaging. *Annual Review of Psychology, 63,* 101–128.

Ritter, R. C. (2004). Gastrointestinal mechanisms of satiation for food. *Physiology & Behavior, 81,* 249–273.

Rizzolatti, G., & Craighero, L. (2004). The mirror-neuron system. *Annual Review of Neuroscience, 27,* 169–192.

Rizzolatti, G., & Sinigaglia, C. (2008). *Mirrors in the brain—How our minds share actions and emotions.* Oxford, UK: Oxford University Press.

Rizzolatti, G., Fabbri-Destro, M., & Cattaneo, L. (2009). Mirror neurons and their clinical relevance. *Nature Clinical Practice and Neurology, 5,* 24–34.

Rizzolatti, G., Fadiga, L., Gallese, V., & Fogassi, L. (1996). Premotor cortex and the recognition of motor actions. *Cognitive Brain Research, 3,* 131–141.

Robbins, E., Shepard, J., & Rochat, P. (2017). Variations in judgments of intentional action and moral evaluation across eight cultures. *Cognition, 164,* 22–30.

Robbins, J. A., & Dewar, J. (2011). Traditional indigenous approaches to healing and the modern welfare of traditional knowledge, spirituality, and lands: A critical reflection on practices and policies taken from the Canadian Indigenous example. *The International Indigenous Policy Journal, 2.* Retrieved from http://ir.lib.uwo.ca/ipij/vol2/iss4/2.

Roberson, D., Davidoff, J., Davies, I. R. L., & Shapiro, L. R. (2005). Color categories: Evidence for the cultural relativity hypothesis. *Cognitive Psychology, 50,* 378–411.

Roberson, D., Davidoff, J., & Shapiro, L. (2002). Squaring the circle: The cultural relativity of good shape. *Journal of Cognition & Culture, 2*(1), 29–51.

Roberson, D., Davies, I., & Davidoff, J. (2000). Color categories are not universal: Replications and new evidence from a stone-age culture. *Journal of Experimental Psychology: General, 129,* 369–398.

Robert, A-M., & Gilkinson, T. (2012). Mental health and well-being of recent immigrants in Canada: Evidence from the longitudinal survey of immigrants to Canada. Citizenship and Immigration Canada. Retrieved from http://www.cic.gc.ca/english/resources/research/mental-health.asp.

Roberts, B. W., & Pomerantz, E. M. (2004). On traits, situations, and their integration: A developmental perspective. *Personality and Social Psychology Review, 8,* 402–416.

Roberts, B. W., Caspi, A., & Moffitt, T. (2003). Work experiences and personality development in young

adulthood. *Journal of Personality and Social Psychology, 84,* 582–593.

Roberts, B. W., Jackson, J. J., Fayard, J. V., Edmonds, G., & Meints, J. (2009). Conscientiousness. In M. R. Leary & R. H. Hoyle (Eds.), *Handbook of individual differences in social behavior* (pp. 257–273). New York, NY: Guilford Press.

Roberts, B. W., Kuncel, N. R., Shiner, R., Caspi, A., & Goldberg, L. R. (2007). The power of personality: The comparative validity of personality traits, socioeconomic status, and cognitive ability for predicting important life outcomes. *Perspectives on Psychological Science, 2,* 313–345.

Roberts, B. W., Walton, K. E., & Bogg, T. (2005). Conscientiousness and health across the life course. *Review of General Psychology, 9*(2), 156–168.

Roberts, B. W., Wood, D., & Caspi, A. (2008). The development of personality traits in adulthood. In O. P. John, R. W. Robins, & L. A. Pervin (Eds.), *Handbook of personality: Theory and research* (3rd ed., pp. 375–398). New York, NY: Guilford Press.

Roberts, M. C., Brown, K. J., & Smith-Boydston, J. M. (2003). The scientific process and publishing research. In M. C. Roberts & S. S. Ilardi (Eds.), *Handbook of research methods in clinical psychology* (pp. 31–51). London, UK: Blackwell.

Roberts, W., & Macpherson, K. (2016). Of dogs and men. *Current Directions in Psychological Science, 25,* 38–45.

Robertson, B. R., Prestia, D., Twamley, E. W., Patterson, T. L., Bowie, C. R., & Harvey, P. D. (2014). Social competence versus negative symptoms as predictors of real world social functioning in schizophrenia. *Schizophrenia Research, 160*(1–3), 136–141. doi:10.1016/j.schres.2014.10.037.

Robins, L. N., Locke, B. Z., & Regier, D. A. (1991). An overview of psychiatric disorders in America. In L. N. Robins & D. A. Regier (Eds.), *Psychiatric disorders in America: The epidemiologic catchment area study.* New York, NY: Free Press.

Robinson, A., & Clinkenbeard, P. R. (1998). Giftedness: An exceptionality examined. *Annual Review of Psychology, 49,* 117–139.

Robinson, N. M. (2010). The social world of gifted children and youth. In S. I. Pfeiffer (Ed.), *Handbook of giftedness in children: Psychoeducational theory, research, and best practices.* New York, NY: Springer.

Robles, T. F., Slatcher, R. B., Trombello, J. M., & McGinn, M. M. (2014). *Psychological Bulletin, 140,* 140–187.

Robson, S. J., & Kuhlmeier, V. A. (2016). Infants' understanding of object-directed action: An interdisciplinary synthesis. *Frontiers in Psychology, 7,* 1–14.

Rock, I. (1986). The description and analysis of object and event perception. In K. R. Boff, L. Kaufman, & J. P. Thomas (Eds.), *Handbook of perception and human performance* (Vol. 2). New York, NY: Wiley.

Rodgers, J. E. (1982). The malleable memory of eyewitnesses. *Science Digest, 3,* 32–35.

Rodrigues, A. C., Loureiro, M. A., & Caramelli, P. (2010). Musical training, neuroplasticity and cognition. *Dementia & Neuropsychologia, 4,* 277–286.

Roediger, H. L., III. (1980). Memory metaphors in cognitive psychology. *Memory & Cognition, 8,* 231–246.

Roediger, H. L., III. (1990). Implicit memory: Retention without remembering. *American Psychologist, 45,* 1043–1056.

Roediger, H. L., III. (2000). Why retrieval is the key process in understanding human memory. In E. Tulving (Ed.), *Memory, consciousness, and the brain: The Tallinn conference* (pp. 52–75). Philadelphia, PA: Psychology Press.

Roediger, H. L., III, Agarwal, P. K., Kang, S. K., & Marsh, E. J. (2010). Benefits of testing memory: Best practices and boundary conditions. In G. M. Davies & D. B. Wright, (Eds.), *Current issues in applied memory research* (pp. 13–49). New York, NY: Psychology Press.

Roediger, H. L., III, Gallo, D. A., & Geraci, L. (2002). Processing approaches to cognition: The impetus from the levels-of-processing framework. *Memory, 10,* 319–332.

Roediger, H. L., III, & McDermott, K. B. (1995). Creating false memories: Remembering words not presented in lists. *Journal of Experimental Psychology: Learning, Memory, and Cognition, 21,* 803–814.

Roediger, H. L., III, & McDermott, K. B. (2000). Tricks of memory. *Current Directions in Psychological Science, 9,* 123–127.

Roediger, H. I., III, Weinstein, Y., & Agarwal, P. K. (2010). Forgetting: Preliminary considerations. In S. Della Sala (Ed.), *Forgetting.* New York, NY: Psychology Press.

Roediger, H. I., III, Wixted, J. H., & DeSoto, K. A. (2012). The curious complexity between confidence and accuracy in reports from memory. In L. Nadel, & W. P. Sinnott-Armstrong (Eds.), *Memory and law.* New York, NY: Oxford University Press.

Roese, N. J., & Vohs, K. D. (2012). Hindsight bias. *Perspectives on Psychological Science, 7,* 411–426. doi:10.1177/1745691612454303.

Roffwarg, H. P., Muzio, J. N., & Dement, W. C. (1966). Ontogenetic development of the human sleep–dream cycle. *Science, 152,* 604–619.

Rogers, C. R. (1951). *Client-centered therapy: Its current practice, implications, and theory.* Boston, MA: Houghton Mifflin.

Rogers, C. R. (1961). *On becoming a person: A therapist's view of psychotherapy.* Boston, MA: Houghton Mifflin.

Rogers, C. R. (1980). *A way of being.* Boston, MA: Houghton Mifflin.

Rogers, C. R. (1986). Client-centered therapy. In I. L. Kutash & A. Wolf (Eds.), *Psychotherapist's casebook.* San Francisco, CA: Jossey-Bass.

Rogers, N. L., & Dinges, D. F. (2002). Shiftwork, circadian disruption, and consequences. *Primary Psychiatry, 9*(8), 50.

Rogers, T. B., Kuiper, N. A., & Kirker, W. S. (1977). Self-reference and the encoding of personal information. *Journal of Personality and Social Psychology, 35,* 677–688.

Rogerson J. D., Gottlieb, M. C., Handelsman, M. M., Knapp, S., & Younggren, J. (2011). Nonrational processes in ethical decision making. *American Psychologist, 66,* 614–623.

Rogoff, B. (1998). Cognition as a collaborative process. In D. Kuhn & R. S. Siegler (Eds.), *Handbook of child psychology (Vol. 2): Cognition perception, and language.* New York, NY: Wiley.

Rogoff, B. (2003). *The cultural nature of human development.* New York, NY: Oxford University Press.

Rohde, P., Lewinsohn, P. M., Klein, D. N., Seeley, J. R., & Gau, J. M. (2013). Key characteristics of major depressive disorder occurring in childhood, adolescence, emerging adulthood, and adulthood. *Clinical Psychological Science, 1*(1), 41–53. doi:10.1177/2167702612457599.

Rohner, J. C., & Rasmussen, A. (2012). Recognition bias and the physical attractiveness stereotype. *Scandinavian Journal of Psychology, 53*(3), 239–246.

Rohrer, D., & Taylor, K. (2006). The effects of overlearning and distributed practice on the retention of mathematics knowledge. *Applied Cognitive Psychology, 20,* 1209–1224.

Rollman, G. B. (1992). Cognitive effects in pain and pain judgements. In D. Algom (Ed.), *Psychophysical approaches to cognition.* Amsterdam: North Holland.

Rolls, B. J. (2012). The impact of portion size and energy density on eating. In K. D. Brownell, & M. S. Gold (Eds.), *Food and addiction: A comprehensive handbook.* New York, NY: Oxford University Press.

Rolls, E. T. (1990). A theory of emotion, and its application to understanding the neural basis of emotion. *Cognitive and Emotion, 4,* 161–190.

Ronksley, P. E., Brien, S. E., Turner, B. J., Mukamal, K. J., & Ghali, W. A. (2011). Association of alcohol consumption with selected cardiovascular disease outcomes: a systematic review and meta-analysis. *British Medical Journal, 342*(7795), 479.

Ronquillo, J., Denson, T. F., Lickel, B., Zhong-Lin, L., Nandy, A., & Maddox, D. B. (2007). The effect of skin tone on race-related amygdala activity: An fMRI investigation. *Social Cognitive Affective Neuroscience, 2*, 39–44.

Roofeh, D., Tumuluru, D., Shilpakar, S., & Nimgaonkar, V. L. (2013). Genetics of schizophrenia. Where has the heritability gone? *International Journal of Mental Health, 42*(1), 5–22. doi:10.2753/IMH0020-7411420101.

Rorschach, H. (1921). *Psychodiagnostik*. Berne: Birchen.

Rosario, M., & Schrimshaw, E. W. (2014). Theories and etiologies of sexual orientation. In D. L. Tolman, L. M. Diamond, J. A. Bauermeister, W. H. George, J. G. Pfaus, & L. M. Ward (Eds.), *APA handbook of sexuality and psychology: Vol. 1. Person-based approaches*. Washington, DC: American Psychological Association.

Rosch, E. H. (1973). Natural categories. *Cognitive Psychology, 4*, 328–350.

Rose, A. (2012). Animal tales: Observations of the emotions in american experimental psychology, 1890–1940. *Journal of the History of the Behavioral Sciences*. (Online Early View, Wiley-Blackwell Journals, August 28, 2012).

Rose, D., Wykes, T., Leese, M., Bindman, J., & Fleischmann, P. (2003). Patient's perspectives on electroconvulsive therapy: Systematic review. *British Medical Journal, 326*, 1363–1365.

Roseboom, T., de Rooij, S., & Painter, R. (2006). The Dutch famine and its long-term consequences for adult health. *Early Human Development, 82*, 485–491.

Rosemond, J. K. (2005). The diseasing of America's children: The politics of diagnosis. In R. H. Wright & N. A. Cummings (Eds.), *Destructive trends in mental health: The well-intentioned path to harm*. New York, NY: Routledge.

Rosenbaum, M., Kissileff, H. R., Mayer, L. S., Hirsch, J., & Leibel, R. L. (2010). Energy intake in weight-reduced humans. *Brain Research, 1350*, 95–102. doi:10.1016/j.brainres.2010.05.062.

Rosenbaum, R. S., Murphy, K. J., & Rich, J. B. (2011). The Amnesias. *Wiley Interdisciplinary Reviews: Cognitive Science, 3*, 47–63.

Rosenbaum, S., Kohler, S., Schacter, D. L., Mosovitch, M., Westmacott, R., Black, S. E., Gao, F., & Tulving, E. (2005). The case of K.C.: Contributions of a memory-impaired person to memory theory. *Neuropsychologia, 43*, 989–1021.

Rosenbaum, W., Linares, D., & Nishida, S. (2015). Sensory adaptation for timing perception. *Proceedings of Biological Science, 282*, 1805–1826.

Rosenblum, K. (2009). Conditioned taste aversion and taste learning: Molecular mechanisms. In J. H. Byrne (Ed.), *Concise learning and memory: The editor's selection*. San Diego, CA: Elsevier.

Rosenhan, D. L. (1973). On being sane in insane places. *Science, 179*, 250–258.

Rosenthal, H. (1988). *Not with my life I don't: Preventing suicide and that of others*. Muncie, IN: Accelerated Development.

Rosenthal, L. (2006). Physiologic processes during sleep. In T. Lee-Chiong (Ed.), *Sleep: A comprehensive handbook*. Hoboken, NJ: Wiley-Liss.

Rosenthal, N. E., Sack, D. A., Gillin, J. C., Lewy, A. J., Goodwin, F. K., Davenport, Y., et al. (1984). Seasonal affective disorder: A description of the syndrome and preliminary findings with light therapy. *Archives of General Psychiatry, 41*(1), 72–80.

Rosenthal, R. (1976). *Experimenter effects in behavioral research*. New York, NY: Halsted.

Rosenthal, R. (1994). Interpersonal expectancy effects: A 30-year perspective. *Current Directions in Psychological Science, 3*, 176–179.

Rosenthal, R. (2002). Experimenter and clinical effects in scientific inquiry and clinical practice. *Prevention & Treatment, 5*(38), 7–23.

Rosenthal, R., & Fode, K. L. (1963). Three experiments in experimenter bias. *Psychological Reports, 12*, 491–511.

Rosenzweig, M. R., & Bennett, E. L. (1996). Psychobiology of plasticity: Effects of training and experience on brain and behavior. *Behavioural Brain Research, 78*(5), 57–65.

Rosenzweig, M. R., Krech, D., & Bennett, E. L. (1961). Heredity, environment, brain biochemistry, and learning. In *Current trends in psychological theory*. Pittsburgh, PA: University of Pittsburgh Press.

Rosenzweig, M., Krech, D., Bennett, E. L., & Diamond, M. (1962). Effects of environmental complexity and training on brain chemistry and anatomy: A replication and extension. *Journal of Comparative and Physiological Psychology, 55*, 429–437.

Rosler, F. (2005). From single-channel recordings to brain-mapping devices: The impact of electroencephalography on experimental psychology. *History of Psychology, 8*, 95–117.

Ross, C. A., & Ness, L. (2010). Symptom patterns in dissociative identity disorder patients and the general population. *Journal of Trauma & Dissociation, 11*, 458–468. doi:10.1080/15299732.2010.495939.

Ross, H., & Plug, C. (2002). *The mystery of the moon illusion: Exploring the size perception*. New York, NY: Oxford.

Ross, L. D. (1988). The obedience experiments: A case study of controversy. *Contemporary Psychology, 33*, 101–104.

Ross, L. D., & Anderson, C. A. (1982). Shortcomings in the attribution process: On the origins and maintenance of erroneous social assessments. In D. Kahneman, P. Slovic, & A. Tversky (Eds.), *Judgement under uncertainty: Heuristics and biases*. Cambridge, UK: Cambridge University Press.

Ross, L. E., Dennis, C.-L., Robertson-Blackmore, E., Stewart, D. E. (2005). *Postpartum depression: A guide for front-line health and social service providers*. Toronto, ON: Centre for Addiction & Mental Health.

Ross, L., & Nisbett, R. E. (1991). *The person and the situation: Perspectives of social psychology*. New York, NY: McGraw-Hill.

Rosso, I. M., Weiner, M. R., Crowley, J., Silveri, M. M., Rauch, S. L., & Jensen, J. E. (2014). Insula and anterior cingulate GABA levels in posttraumatic stress disorder: Preliminary findings using magnetic resonance spectroscopy. *Depression and Anxiety, 31*(2), 115–123. doi:10.1002/da.22155.

Rotermann, M. (2012). Sexual behaviour and condom use of 15- to 24-year-olds in 2003 and 2009/2010. *Health Reports, 23*(1), 1–5.

Rothbart, M. K., & Bates, J. E. (2008). Temperament. In W. Damon & R. M. Lerner (Eds.), *Child and adolescent development: An advanced course* (pp. 54–65). New York, NY: Wiley.

Rothberg, B., & Feinstein, R. E. (2014). Suicide. In J. L. Cutler (Ed.), *Psychiatry* (3rd ed.). New York, NY: Oxford University Press.

Rotheram-Borus, M. J., & Swendeman, D., & Chorpita, B. F. (2012). *American Psychologist, 67*, 463–476.

Rotter, J. B. (1982). *The development and application of social learning theory*. New York, NY: Praeger.

Rouiller, E. M. (1997). Functional organization of the auditory pathways. In G. Ehret & R. Romand (Eds.), *The central auditory system*. Oxford, England: Oxford University Press.

Rounder, J. N., & Morey, R. D. (2009). The nature of thresholds. *Psychological Review, 116*, 655–660.

Routh, D. K. (2013). Clinical psychology. In D. K. Freedheim, & I. B. Weiner (Eds.), *Handbook of psychology Vol. 1: History of psychology* (2nd ed., pp. 377–387). New York, NY: Wiley.

Rouw, R., & Scholte, H. S. (2016). Personality and cognitive profiles of general synesthetic train. *Neuropsychologica, 88*, 35–48.

Rowa, K., & Antony, M. M. (2008). Generalized anxiety disorders. In W. D. Craighead, D. J. Miklowitz, & L. W. Craighead (Eds.), *Psychopathology: History, diagnosis, and empirical foundations*. New York, NY: Wiley.

Roy, M., Piche, M., Chen, J., Peretz, I., & Rainville, P. (2009). Cerebral and spinal modulation of pain by emotions. *Proceedings of the National Academy of Sciences of the United States of America, 106*(49), 20900–20905.

Rozin, P. (1990). The importance of social factors in understanding the acquisition of food habits. In E. D. Capaldi & T. L. Powley (Eds.), *Taste, experience, and feeding*. Washington, DC: American Psychological Association.

Rozin, P. (2007). Food and eating. In S. Kitayama & D. Cohen (Eds.), *Handbook of cultural psychology* (pp. 391–416). New York, NY: Guilford.

Rubin, D. C., Bernsten, D., & Bohni, M. K. (2008). A memory-based model of posttraumatic stress disorder: Evaluating basic assumptions underlying PTSD diagnosis. *Psychological Review, 115*, 985–1011.

Rubin, D. C., Boals, A., & Berntsen, D. (2008). Memory in posttraumatic stress disorder: Properties of voluntary and involuntary, traumatic and non-traumatic autobiographical memories in people with and without PTSD symptoms. *Journal of Experimental Psychology: General, 137*, 591–614.

Ruble, D. N., & Martin, C. L. (1998). Gender development. In W. Damon (Ed.), *Handbook of child psychology (Vol. 3): Social, emotional, and personality development*. New York, NY: Wiley.

Rudert, S. C., Hales, A. H., Greifeneder, R., & Williams, K. (2017). When silence is not golden: Why acknowledgment matters even when being excluded. *Personality and Social Psychology Bulletin, 43*(5), 678–692.

Rueger, S. Y., Malecki, C. K., Pyun, Y., Aycock, C., & Coyle, S. (2016). A meta-analytic review of the association between perceived social support and depression in childhood and adolescence. *Psychological Bulletin, 142*, 1017–1067.

Ruini, C., & Fava, G. A. (2004). Clinical application of well-being therapy. In P. A. Linley & S. Joseph (Eds.), *Positive psychology in practice*. Hoboken, NJ: Wiley.

Ruiz, J. M., Prather, C. C., & Steffen, P. (2012). Socioeconomic status and health. In A. Baum, T. A. Revenson, & J. Singer (Eds.), *Handbook of health psychology* (2nd ed.). New York, NY: Psychology Press.

Ruiz, P., & Strain, E. C. (2011). *Lowinson and Ruiz's substance abuse: A comprehensive textbook* (5th ed.). Philadelphia, PA: Lippincott Williams & Wilkins.

Rummel, J., & Boywitt, C. D. (2014). Controlling the stream of thought: Working memory capacity predicts adjustment of mind-wandering to situational demands. *Psychonomic Bulletin & Review, 21*, 1309–1315. doi:10.3758/s13423-013-0580-3.

Runco, M. A. (2004). Divergent thinking, creativity, and giftedness. In R. J. Sternberg (Ed.), *Definitions and conceptions of giftedness* (pp. 47–62). Thousand Oaks, CA: Corwin Press.

Rundle, A., Hoepner, A., Hassoun, S., Oberfield, G., Freyer, D., Holmes, M., . . . Whyatt, R. (2012). Association of childhood obesity with maternal exposure to ambient air polycyclic aromatic hydrocarbons during pregnancy. *American Journal of Epidemiology, 175*, 1163–1172. doi:10.1093/aje/kwr455.

Rüsch, N., Corrigan, P. W., Heekeren, K., Theodoridou, A., Dvorsky, D., Metzler, S., . . . Rössler, W. (2014). Well-being among persons at risk of psychosis: The role of self-labeling, shame, and stigma stress. *Psychiatric Services, 65*, 483–489. doi:10.1176/appi.ps.201300169.

Ruscio, J. (2002). *Clear thinking with psychology: Separating sense from nonsense*. Belmont, CA: Wadsworth.

Rushowy, K. (2013). Students feel stress, anxiety about future. *The Toronto Star*, Wednesday, February 13, A1.

Rushton, J. P. (2003). Race differences in g and the "Jensen effect." In H. Nyborg (Ed.), *The scientific study of general intelligence: Tribute to Arthur R. Jensen*. Oxford, UK: Pergamon.

Rushton, J. P., & Jensen, A. R. (2005). Thirty years of research on race differences in cognitive ability. *Psychology, Public Policy, and Law, 11*, 235–294.

Rushton, J. P., & Jensen, A. R. (2010). Editorial. The rise and fall of the Flynn Effect as a reason to expect a narrowing of the Black–White IQ gap. *Intelligence, 38*, 213–219.

Russell, G. F. M. (1995). Anorexia nervosa through time. In G. Szmukler, C. Dare, & J. Treasure (Eds.), *Handbook of eating disorders: Theory, treatment, and research*. New York, NY: Wiley.

Russell, G. F. M. (2009). Anorexia nervosa. In M. C. Gelder, N. C. Andreasen, J. J. López-Ibor, Jr., & J. R. Geddes (Eds.). *New Oxford textbook of psychiatry* (2nd ed., Vol. 1). New York, NY: Oxford University Press.

Russell, J. A. (1991). Culture and the categorization of emotions. *Psychological Bulletin, 110*, 426–450.

Russell, J. A. (2007). Stress milestones. *Stress: The International Journal on the Biology of Stress, 10*(1), 1–2.

Rutherford, A. (2000). Radical behaviorism and psychology's public: B. F. Skinner in the popular press, 1934–1990. *History of Psychology, 3*, 371–395.

Rutherford, A. (2005a). B. F. Skinner. *Dictionary of modern American philosophers*. Bristol, England: Thoemmes Press.

Rutherford, A. (2005b). *Beyond the box*. Toronto, ON: University of Toronto Press.

Rutherford, A. (2012). Problems of sex and the problem with nature: A commentary on "Beyond Kinsey." *History of Psychology, 15*, 228–223.

Rutherford, W. (1886). A new theory of hearing. *Journal of Anatomy and Physiology, 21*, 166–168.

Rutter, M. (2006). *Genes and behavior: Nature—nurture interplay explained*. Maiden, MA: Blackwell.

Rutter, M. (2007). Gene-environment interdependence. *Developmental Science, 10*(1), 12–18.

Rutter, M. (2012). Gene-environment interdependence. *European Journal of Developmental Psychology, 9*, 391–412. doi:10.1080/17405629.2012.661174.

Rutter, M., & Silberg, J. (2002). Gene–environment interplay relation to emotional and behavioral disturbance. *Annual Review of Psychology, 53*, 463–490.

Ruvio, A., Somer, E., & Rindfleisch, A. (2014). When bad gets worse: The amplifying effect of materialism on traumatic stress and maladaptive consumption. *Journal of the Academy of Marketing Science, 42*, 90–101.

Ryan, C. S., Park, B., & Judd, C. M. (1996). Assessing stereotype accuracy: Implications for understanding the stereotyping process. In C. N. Macrae, C. Stangor, & M. Hewstone (Eds.), *Stereotypes and stereotyping*. New York, NY: Guilford.

Ryckeley, R. (2005, May). Don't send in the clowns. *The Citizen*.

Ryder, A. G., et al (2008). The cultural shaping of depression: Somatic symptoms in China, psychological symptoms in North America? *Journal of Abnormal Psychology, 117*, 300–313.

Ryder, R. D. (2006). Speciesism in the laboratory. In P. Singer (Ed.), *In defense of animals: The second wave*. Malden, MA: Blackwell.

Sachdev, P. S. (2013). Is DSM-5 defensible? *Australian and New Zealand Journal of Psychiatry, 47*(1), 10–11. doi:10.1177/0004867412468164.

Sack, A. T., & Linden, D. E. J. (2003). Combining transcranial magnetic stimulation and functional imaging in cognitive brain research: Possibilities and limitations. *Brain Research Reviews, 43*(1), 41–56.

Sackeim, H. A., Dillingham, E. M., Prudic, J., Cooper, T., McCall, W. V., Rosenquist, P., et al. (2009). Effect of concomitant pharmacotherapy on electroconvulsive therapy outcomes: Short-term efficacy and adverse effects. *Archives of General Psychiatry, 66*(7), 729–737.

Sacks, O. W. (1990). *The man who mistook his wife for a hat and other clinical tales*. New York. Perennial Library.

Sadikaj, G., Moskowitz, D. S., & Zuroff, D. C. (2011). Attachment-related affective dynamics: Differential reactivity to others' interpersonal behavior. *Journal of Personality and Social Psychology, 100*, 905–917.

Sadker, M., & Sadker, D. (1994). *Failing at fairness: How America's schools cheat girls*. New York, NY: Scribners.

Sadock, B. J., Sadock, V. A., & Ruiz, P. (2015). *Kaplan and Sadock's synopsis of psychiatry: Behavioral sciences/clinical psychiatry* (11th ed.). Philadelphia, PA: Wolters Kluwer.

Safran, J. D., & Kriss, A. (2014). Psychoanalytic psychotherapies. In D. Wedding & R. J. Corsini (Eds.), *Current psychotherapies* (10th ed., 19–61). Belmont, CA: Brooks/Cole.

Saks, A. M. (2006). Multiple predictions and criteria of job search success. *Journal of Vocational Behavior, 68*, 400–415.

Sakurai, T. (2013). Orexin deficiency and narcolepsy. *Current Opinion in Neurobiology, 23*, 760–766. doi:10.1016/j.conb.2013.04.007.

Salmon, P., Sephton, S., Weissbecker, I., Hoover, K., Ulmer, C., & Studts, J. L. (2004). Mindfulness mediation in clinical practice. *Cognitive and Behavioral Practice, 11*, 434–446.

Salovey, P., & Mayer, J. D. (1990). Emotional intelligence. *Imagination, Cognition, and Personality, 9*, 185–211.

Salovey, P., Mayer, J. D., & Caruso, D. (2002). The positive psychology of emotional intelligence. In C. R. Synder & J. Lopez (Eds.), *Handbook of positive psychology*. New York, NY: Oxford University Press.

Salthouse, T. A. (1996). The processing-speed theory of adult age differences in cognition. *Psychological Review, 103*, 403–428.

Salthouse, T. A. (2000). Aging and measures of processing speed. *Biological Psychology, 54*, 35–54.

Salthouse, T. A. (2003). Memory aging from 18–80. *Alzheimer Disease & Associated Disorders, 17*(3), 162–167.

Salthouse, T. A. (2004). What and when of cognitive aging. *Current Directions in Psychological Science, 13*(4), 140–144.

Salthouse, T. A., & Mandell, A. R. (2013). Do age-related increases in tip-of-the-tongue experiences signify episodic memory impairments? *Psychological Science, 24*, 2489–2497. doi:10.1177/0956797613495881.

Samberg, E., & Marcus, E. R. (2005). Process, resistance, and interpretation. In E. S. Person, A. M. Cooper, & G. O. Gabbard (Eds.), *Textbook of psychoanalysis*. Washington, DC: American Psychiatric Publishing.

Same-sex rights Canada timeline. (2005). *CBC News Indepth*. Retrieved May 10, 2005, from http://www.cbc .ca/news/background/samesexrights/timeline.

Samet, J. M. (1992). The health benefits of smoking cessation. *Medical Clinics of North America, 76*, 399–414.

Samnaliev, M., & Clark, R. E. (2008). The economics of schizophrenia. In K. T. Mueser & D. V. Jeste (Eds.), *Clinical handbook of schizophrenia* (pp. 25–34). New York, NY: Guilford Press.

Samuelson, P. A., & Nordhaus, W. D. (2005). *Economics* (18th ed.). Boston, MA: McGraw-Hill.

Sanbonmatsu, D. M., Strayer, D. L., Medeiros-Ward, N., & Watson, J. M. (2013). Who multi-tasks and why? Multi-tasking ability, perceived multi-tasking ability, impulsivity, and sensation seeking. *PloS One, 8*, e54402. doi:10.1371/journal.pone.0054402.

Sanchez-Armass, O. (2015). A defining moment: Commentary on the revised APA division 30 definition of hypnosis. *The American Journal of Clinical Hypnosis, 57*, 45–47.

Sanders, M. H., & Givelber, R. J. (2006). Overview of obstructive sleep apnea in adults. In T. Lee-Chiong (Ed.), *Sleep: A comprehensive handbook*. Hoboken, NJ: Wiley-Liss.

Sanderson, W. C., & Barlow, D. H. (1990). A description of patients diagnosed with DSM-III-R generalized anxiety disorder. *Journal of Nervous and Mental Disease, 178*, 588–591.

Sandrini, M., & Manenti, R. (2009). Transcranial magnetic stimulation as a tool for cognitive studies. *Giornale Italiano di Psicologia, 36*(2), 347–372.

Sandstrom, G. M., & Dunn, E. W. (2014). Social interactions and well-being: The surprising power of weak ties. *Personality and Social Psychology Bulletin, 40*, 910–922. doi:10.1177/0146167214529799.

Sanjuan, P., & Magallares, A. (2014). Coping strategies as mediating variables between self-serving attributional bias and subjective well-being. *Journal of Happiness Studies, 15*, 443–453. doi:10.1007/s10902-013-9430-2.

Saper, C. B. (2000). Brain stem, reflexive behavior, and the cranial nerves. In E. R. Kandel, J. H. Schwartz, & T. M. Jessell (Eds.), *Principles of neural science* (pp. 873–888). New York, NY: McGraw-Hill.

Saphire-Bernstein, S., & Taylor, S. E. (2013). Close relationships and happiness. In S. A. David, I. Boniwell, & A. Conley Ayers (Eds.), *The Oxford handbook of happiness*. New York, NY: Oxford University Press.

Sapolsky, R. M. (1998). *Why zebras don't get ulcers*. New York, NY: W.H. Freeman and Company.

Sapolsky, R. M. (2007). Stress, stress-related disease, and emotion regulation. In J. J. Gross (Ed.), *Handbook of emotion regulation*. New York, NY: Guilford Press.

Sartorius, A., Kiening, K. L., Kirsch, P., von Gall, C. C., Haberkorn, U., Unterberg, A. W., et al. (2010). Remission of major depression under deep brain stimulation of the lateral habenula in a therapy-refractory patient. *Biological Psychiatry, 67*(2), e9–e11.

Satel, S., & Lilienfeld, S. O. (2013). *Brainwashed: The seductive appeal of mindless neuroscience*. New York, NY: Basic Books.

Sato, T. (1997). Seasonal affective disorder and phototherapy: A critical review. *Professional Psychology: Research and Practice, 28*, 164–169.

Saucier, G., & Srivastava S. (2015). What makes a good structural model of personality? Evaluating the big five and alternatives. In M. Mikulincer, P. R. Shaver, M. L. Cooper, & R. J. Larsen (Eds.), *APA handbook of personality and social psychology: Vol. 4. Personality processes and individual differences*. Washington, DC: American Psychological Association.

Savage, L. C. (2013). The sleep crisis. *Maclean's*, 48–53.

Savage-Rumbaugh, E. S. (1991). Language learning in the bonobo: How and why they learn. In N. A. Krasnegor, D. M. Rumbaugh, & R. L. Schiefelbusch/M. Studdert-Kennedy (Eds.), *Biological and behavioral determinants of language development*. Hillsdale, NJ: Erlbaum.

Savage-Rumbaugh, S., Rumbaugh, D. M., & Fields, W. M. (2006). Language as a window on rationality. In S. Hurley & M. Nudds (Eds.), *Rational animals?* (pp. 513–552). New York, NY: Oxford University Press.

Savage-Rumbaugh, S., Rumbaugh, D. M., & Fields, W. M. (2009). Empirical Kanzi: The ape language controversy revisited. *Skeptic, 15*(1), 25–33.

Savage-Rumbaugh, S., Shanker, S. G., & Taylor, T. J. (1998). *Apes, language, and the human mind*. New York, NY: Oxford University Press.

Savin-Williams, R. C. (2006). Who's gay? Does it matter? *Current Directions in Psychological Science, 15*, 40–44.

Saxe, L. (1994). Detection of deception: Polygraph and integrity tests. *Current Directions in Psychological Science, 3*, 69–73.

Scarr, S. (1991). *Theoretical issues in investigating intellectual plasticity*. S. E. Brauth, W. S. Hall, & R. Dooling (Eds.), *Plasticity of development*. Cambridge, MA: MIT Press.

Scarr, S., & Weinberg, R. A. (1977). Intellectual similarities within families of both adopted and biological children. *Intelligence, 32*, 170–190.

Scarr, S., & Weinberg, R. A. (1983). The Minnesota adoption studies: Genetic differences and malleability. *Child Development, 54*, 260–267.

Schachter, R. (2011). Using the group in cognitive group therapy. *Group, 35*(2), 135–149.

Schachter, S. (1959). *The psychology of affiliation*. Stanford, CA: Stanford University Press.

Schachter, S. (1964). The interaction of cognitive and physiological determinants of emotional state. In L. Berkowitz (Ed.), *Advances in experimental social psychology* (Vol. 1). New York, NY: Academic Press.

Schachter, S., & Singer, J. E. (1962). Cognitive, social and physiological determinants of emotional state. *Psychological Review, 69*, 379–399.

Schachter, S., & Singer, J. E. (1979). Comments on the Maslach and Marshall–Zimbardo experiments. *Journal of Personality and Social Psychology, 37*, 989–995.

Schachtman, T. R., Walker, J., & Fowler, S. (2011). Effects of conditioning in advertising. In T. R.

Schachtman, & S. Reilly (Eds.), *Associative learning and condition theory: Human and non-human applications.* New York, NY: Oxford University Press.

Schacter, D. (2001). *The seven sins of memory: How the mind forgets and remembers.* Boston, MA: Houghton Mifflin Company.

Schacter, D. I., Addis, D. R., & Szpunar, K. K. (2017). Escaping the past: Contributions of the hippocampus to future thinking and imagination. In M. C. Duff & D. Hannula (Eds.), *The hippocampus from cells to systems: Structure, connectivity, and functional contributions to memory and flexible cognition.* New York, NY: Springer.

Schacter, D. L. (1987). Implicit memory: History and current status. *Journal of Experimental Psychology: Learning, Memory and Cognition, 14,* 501–518.

Schacter, D. L. (1989). On the relation between memory and consciousness: Dissociable interactions and conscious experience. In H. L. Roediger, III, & F. I. M. Craik (Eds.), *Varieties of memory and consciousness.* Hillsdale, NJ: Erlbaum.

Schacter, D. L. (1992). Understanding implicit memory: A cognitive neuroscience approach. *American Psychologist, 47,* 559–569.

Schacter, D. L. (1994). Priming and multiple memory systems: Perceptual mechanisms of implicit memory. In D. L. Schacter & E. Tulving (Eds.), *Memory systems.* Cambridge, MA: MIT Press.

Schacter, D. L. (1996). *Searching for memory: The brain, the mind, and the past.* New York, NY: Basic Books.

Schacter, D. L. (1999). The seven sins of memory: Insights from psychology and cognitive neuroscience. *American Psychologist, 54,* 182–203.

Schacter, D. L. (2001). The seven sins of memory: How the mind forgets and remembers. Boston, MA: Houghton Mifflin.

Schacter, D. L. (2016). Memory: Beyond remembering. In R. J. Sternberg, S. T. Fiske, & D. J. Foss (Eds.), *Scientists making a difference: One hundred eminent behavioral and brain scientists talk about their most important contributions.* Cambridge, MA: Cambridge University Press.

Schacter, D. L., & Addis, D. R. (2007a). The cognitive neuroscience of constructive memory: Remembering the past and imagining the future. *Philosophical Transactions of the Royal Society (B), 362,* 773–786.

Schacter, D. L., & Addis, D. R. (2007b). On the constructive episodic simulation of past and future events. *Behavioral and Brain Sciences, 30,* 331–332.

Schacter, D. L., & Addis, D. R. (2007c). The ghosts of past and future. *Nature, 445,* 27.

Schacter, D. L., & Dodson, C. S. (2001). Misattribution, false recognition and the sins of memory. *Philosophical Transactions of the Royal Society of London, 356,* 1385–1393.

Schacter, D. L., & Loftus, E. F. (2013). Memory and law: What can cognitive neuroscience contribute? *Nature Neuroscience, 16,* 119–123. doi:10.1038/nn.3294.

Schacter, D. L., Chiu, C. Y. P., & Ochsner, K. N. (1993). Implicit memory: A selective review. *Annual Review of Neuroscience, 16,* 159–182.

Schacter, D. L., Dawes, R., Jacoby, L. L., Kahneman, D., Lempert, R., Roediger, H. L., & Rosenthal, R. (2008). Policy forum: Studying eyewitness investigations in the field. *Law and Human Behavior, 21,* 3–5.

Schacter, D. L., Gaesser, B., & Addis, D. R. (2013). Remembering the past and imagining the future in the elderly. *Gerontoloty, 59,* 143–151.

Schacter, D. L., Wagner, A. D., & Buckner, R. L. (2000). Memory systems of 1999. In E. Tulving & F. I. M. Craik (Eds.), *Oxford handbook of memory.* New York, NY: Oxford University Press.

Schaefer, A. (2005). Commuting takes its toll. *Scientific American Mind, 16*(3), 14–15.

Schaeffer, N. C. (2000). Asking questions about threatening topics: A selective overview. In A. A. Stone, J. S. Turkkan, C. A. Bachrach, J. B. Jobe, H. S. Kurtzman, & V. Cain (Eds.), *The science of self-report: Implications for research and practice.* Mahwah, NJ: Erlbaum.

Schafe, G. E., & Bernstein, I. E. (1996). Taste aversion learning. In E. D. Capaldi (Ed.), *Why we eat what we eat: The psychology of eating* (pp. 31–52). Washington, DC: American Psychological Association.

Schaffhausen, J. (2007). The day his world stood still. *Brain Connection.* Retrieved February 28, 2007, from http://www.brainconnection.com/topics/?main=fa/hm-memory.

Schaufeli, W. B., Leiter, M. P., & Maslach, C. (2009). Burnout: 35 years of research and practice. *The Career Development International, 14*(3), 204–220.

Scheef, L., Jankowski, J., Daamen, M., et al. (2012). An fMRI study on the acute effects of exercise on pain processing in trained athletes. *Pain, 153*(8), 1702–1714.

Scheier, M. F., Carver, C. S., & Armstrong, G. H. (2012). Behavioral self-regulation, health, and illness. In A. Baum, T. A. Revenson, & J. Singer (Eds.), *Handbook of health psychology* (2nd ed.). New York, NY: Psychology Press.

Schellenberg, E. (2006). Long-term positive associations between music lessons and IQ. *Journal of Educational Psychology, 98*(2), 457–468.

Schellenberg, E. G. (2011). Examining the association between music lessons and intelligence. *British Journal of Psychology, 102,* 283–302. doi:10.1111/j.2044-8295.2010.02000.x.

Schieber, F. (2006). Vision and aging. In J. E. Birren & K. W. Schaie (Eds.), *Handbook of the psychology of aging.* San Diego, CA: Academic Press.

Schiff, M., & Lewontin, R. (1986). *Education and class: The irrelevance of IQ genetic studies.* Oxford: Clarendon Press.

Schiffman, S. S., Graham, B. G., Sattely-Miller, E. A., & Warwick, Z. S. (1998). Orosensory perception of dietary fat. *Current Directions in Psychological Science, 7,* 137–143.

Schilbach, L., Eickhoff, S. B., Mojzisch, A., & Vogeley, K. (2008). What's in a smile? Neural correlates of facial embodiment in social interaction. *Social Neuroscience, 3*(1), 37–50.

Schimmack, U., & Crites, S. L. (2005). The structure of affect. In D. Albarracin, B. T. Johnson, & M. P. Zanna (Eds.), *The handbook of attitudes.* Mahwah, NJ: Erlbaum.

Schindler, S., & Pfattheicher, S. (2017). The frame of the game: Loss-framing increases dishonest behavior. *Journal of Experimental Social Psychology, 69,* 172–177.

Schirillo, J. A. (2010). Gestalt approach. In E. B. Goldstein (Ed.), *Encyclopedia of perception.* Thousand Oaks, CA: Sage.

Schlegel, A., & Barry, H., III. (1991). *Adolescence: An anthropological inquiry.* New York, NY: Free Press.

Schleicher, A. (2013). Making sense of rising IQ scores. *Science, 339,* 394–395.

Schlenger, W. E., Kulka, R. A., Fairbank, J. A., Hough, R. L., Jordan, B. K., Marmar, C. R., & Weiss, D. S. (1992). The prevalence of post-traumatic stress disorder in the Vietnam generation: A multimethod, multisource assessment of psychiatric disorder. *Journal of Traumatic Stress, 5*(3), 333–363.

Schmeichel, B. J., Crowell, A., & Harmon-Jones, E. (2016). Exercising self-control increased relative left frontal cortical activation. *Social Cognitive and Affective Neuroscience, 11,* 282–288.

Schmid, P. C., Mast, M. S., Bombari, D., & Mast, F. W. (2011). Gender effects in information processing on a nonverbal decoding task. *Sex Roles, 65,* 102–107. doi:10.1007/s11199-011-9979-3.

Schmidt, F. L. (2013). Meta-analysis. In J. A. Schinka, W. F. Velicer, & I. B. Weiner (Eds.), *Handbook of psychology: Vol. 2. Research methods in psychology* (2nd ed.). Hoboken, NJ: Wiley.

Schmidt, F. L., & Hunter, J. (2004). General mental ability in the world of work: Occupational attainment and job performance. *Journal of Personality and Social Psychology, 86,* 162–173.

Schmidt, H. D., Vassoler, F. M., & Pierce, R. C. (2011). Neurobiological factors of drug dependence and addiction. In P. Ruiz, & E. C. Strain (Eds.), *Lowinson and Ruiz's substance abuse: A comprehensive textbook* (5th ed., pp. 55–78). Philadelphia, PA: Lippincott Williams & Wilkins.

Schmit, D. T. (2010). The mesmerists inquire about "oriental mind powers": West meets east in the search for the universal trance. *Journal of the History of the Behavioral Sciences, 46*(1), 1–26.

Schmit, M. J. (2006). EI in the business world. In K. R. Murphy (Ed.), *A critique of emotional intelligence: What are the problems and how can they be fixed?* (pp. 211–234). Mahwah, NJ: Erlbaum.

Schmitt, D. P. (2005). Fundamentals of human mating strategies. In D. M. Buss (Ed.), *The handbook of evolutionary psychology.* New York, NY: Wiley.

Schmitt, D. P. (2014). Evaluating evidence of mate preference adaptations: How do we really know what Homo sapiens sapiens really want? In V. A. Weekes-Shackelford, & T. K. Shackelford (Eds.), *Evolutionary perspectives on human sexual psychology and behavior.* New York, NY: Springer Science + Business Media. doi:10.1007/978-1-4939-0314-6.

Schmitt, D. P., & 118 members of the International Sexuality Description Project. (2003). Universal sex differences in the desire for sexual variety: Tests from 52 nations, 6 continents, and 13 islands. *Journal of Personality and Social Psychology, 85,* 85–104.

Schmitz, J. M., & DeLaune, K. A. (2005). Nicotine. In J. H. Lowinson, P. Ruiz, R. B. Millman, & J. G. Langrod (Eds.), *Substance abuse: A comprehensive textbook.* Philadelphia, PA: Lippincott, Williams & Williams.

Schmitz, T. W., Kawahara-Baccus, T. N., & Johnson, S. C. (2004). Metacognitive evaluation, self-relevance, and the right prefrontal cortex. *Neuroimage, 22,* 941–947.

Schmolck, H., Buffalo, E. A., & Squire, L. R. (2000). Memory distortions develop over time: Recollections of the O. J. Simpson trial verdict after 15 and 32 months. *Psychological Science, 11,* 39–45.

Schneier, F. R., Vidair, H. B., Vogel, L. R., & Muskin, P. R. (2014). Anxiety, obsessive-compulsive, and stress disorders. In J. L. Cutler (Ed.), *Psychiatry* (3rd ed.). New York, NY: Oxford University Press.

Schnittker, J. (2008). An uncertain revolution: Why the rise of a genetic model of mental illness has not increased tolerance. *Social Science & Medicine, 67*(9), 1370–1381.

Schnoll, R. A., Cappella. J., Lerman, C., Pinto, A., Patterson, F., Wileyto , E. P., Bigman, C., & Leone, F. (2011). A novel recruitment message to increase enrollment into a smoking cessation treatment program: Preliminary results from a randomized trial. *Health Communication, 26*(8), 735–742.

Schoel, C., Eck, J., & Greifeneder, R. (2014). A matter of vertical position: Consequence of ostracism differ for those above versus below its perpetrators. *Social Psychological and Personality Science, 5,* 149–157.

Schooler, C. (2007). Use it—and keep it, longer, probably: A reply to Salthouse. *Perspectives on Psychological Science, 2,* 24–29.

Schooler, J. W. (1999). Seeking the core: The issues and evidence surrounding recovered accounts of sexual trauma. In L. M. Williams & V. L. Banyard (Eds.), *Trauma & memory.* Thousand Oaks, CA: Sage.

Schrag, R. D. A., Styfco, S. J., & Zigler, E. (2004). Familiar concept, new name: Social competence. In E. Zigler & S. J. Styfco (Eds.), *The Head Start debate.* Baltimore, MD: Paul H. Brookes Publishing.

Schramm, D. G., Marshall, J. P., Harris, V. W., & Lee, T. R. (2005). After "I do": The newlywed transition. *Marriage and Family Review, 38,* 45–67.

Schredl, M. (2009). Nightmares. In R. Stickgold & M. P. Walker (Eds.), *The neuroscience of sleep* (pp. 140–145). San Diego, CA: Academic Press.

Schredl, M. (2010). Nightmare frequency and nightmare topics in a representative German sample. *European Archives of Psychiatry and Clinical Neuroscience, 260,* 565–570.

Schreiner, A. M., & Dunn, M. E. (2012). Residual effects of cannabis use on neurocognitive performance after prolonged abstinence: A meta-analysis. *Experimental and Clinical Psychopharmacology, 20,* 420–429. doi:10.1037/a0029117.

Schuller, R. A., & Ogloff, J. R. P. (2001). Psychology and law. In R. A. Schuller & J. R. P. Ogloff (Eds.), *Introduction to psychology and law: Canadian perspectives* (pp. 3–28). Toronto, ON: University of Toronto Press.

Schuller, R. A., & Vidmar, N. (2011). The Canadian criminal jury. *Chicago-Kent Law Review, 86,* 497–515.

Schuller, R., Kazoleas, V., & Kawakami, K. (2009). The impact of prejudice screening procedures on racial bias in the courtroom. *Law and Human Behavior, 33,* 320–238.

Schultz, D. S., & Brabender, V. M. (2013). More challenges since Wikipedia: The effects of exposure to Internet information about the Rorschach on selected Comprehensive System variables. *Journal of Personality Assessment, 95*(2), 149–158. doi:10.1080/00223891.2012.725438.

Schultz, J. H., & Luthe, W. (1959). *Autogenic training.* New York, NY: Grune & Stratton.

Schulz-Hardt, S., Frey, D., Luethgens, C., & Moscovici, S. (2000). Biased information search in group decision making. *Journal of Personality & Social Psychology, 78,* 655–669.

Schuman, H., & Kalton, G. (1985). Survey methods. In G. Lindzey & E. Aronson (Eds.), *Handbook of social psychology* (3rd ed.). New York, NY: Random House.

Schure, M. B., Christopher, J., & Christopher, S. (2008). Mind-body medicine and the art of self-care: Teaching mindfulness to counseling students through yoga, meditation, and qigong. *Journal of Counseling & Development, 86,* 47–56.

Schusterman, R. J., & Gisiner, R. (1988). Artificial language comprehension in dolphins and sea lions: The essential cognitive skills. *Psychological Record, 38,* 311–348.

Schutte, N. S., & Malouff, J. M. (2013). Adaptive emotional functioning: A comprehensive model of emotional intelligence. In C. Mohiyeddini, M. Eysenck, & S. Bauer (Eds.), *Handbook of psychology of emotions* (Vol. 1, pp. 459–488). Hauppauge, NY: Nova Science Publishers.

Schwabe, L., Nader, K., & Pruessner, C. (2014). Reconsolidation of human memory: Brain mechanisms and clinical relevance. *Biological Psychiatry, 76,* 274–280. doi:10.1016/j.biopsych.2014.03.008.

Schwartz, B. (2004). *The paradox of choice: Why more is less.* New York, NY: Ecco.

Schwartz, B. L., & Metcalfe, J. (2014). Tip-of-the-tongue (TOT) states: Mechanisms and metacognitive control. In B. L. Schwartz, & A. S. Brown (Eds.), *Tip-of-the-tongue states and related phenomena.* New York, NY: Cambridge University Press.

Schwartz, B., & Cleary, A. M. (2016). Tip-of-the-tongue states, déjà vu experiences, and other odd metacognitive experiences. In J. Dunlosky & S.K. Tauber (Eds.), *The Oxford handbook of metamemory* (pp. 95–108). New York, NY: Oxford University Press.

Schwartz, B., & Robbins, S. J. (1995). *Psychology of learning and behavior* (4th ed.). New York, NY: Norton.

Schwartz, B., & Sommers, R. (2013). Affective forecasting and well-being. In D. Reisberg (Ed.), *The Oxford handbook of cognitive psychology.* New York, NY: Oxford University Press. doi:10.1093/oxfordhb/9780195376746.013.0044.

Schwartz, D. (2015). *Omar Khadr tells his Guantanamo story in new documentary.* CBC News. Retrieved from http://www.cbc.ca/news/canada/omar-khadr-tells-his-guantanamo-story-in-new-documentary-1.3089953.

Schwartz, D. (2015). *Truth and reconciliation commission: By the numbers.* Retrieved from http://www.cbc.ca/news/indigenous/truth-and-reconciliation-commission-by-the-numbers-1.3096185.

Schwartz, G. J. (2012). Peripheral regulation of hunger and satiety. In D. Brownell, & M. S. Gold (Eds.), *Food and addiction: A comprehensive handbook.* New York, NY: Oxford University Press.

Schwartz, S. (2016). Turning point for a turning point: Advancing emerging adulthood theory and research. *Emerging Adulthood, 4,* 307–317.

Schwartz, S. H. (1990). Individualism–collectivism: Critique and proposed refinements. *Journal of Cross-Cultural Psychology, 21,* 139–157.

Schwartz, S. J., Donnellan, M. B., Ravert, R. D., Luyckx, K., & Zamboanga, B. L. (2013). Identity development, personality, and wellbeing in adolescence and emerging adulthood: Theory, research, and recent advances. In R. M. Lerner, M. A. Easterbrooks, J. Mistry, & I. B. Weiner (Eds.), *Handbook of psychology: Vol. 6. Developmental psychology.* New York, NY: Wiley.

Schwarz, A. (2008, September 23). 12 athletes leaving brains to concussion study. *New York Times.* Retrieved December 15, 2010, from http://www.nytimes.com/2008/09/24/sports/football/24concussions.html.

Schwarz, N., & Strack, F. (1999). Reports of subjective well-being: Judgmental processes and their methodological implications. In D. Kahneman, E. Diener, & N. Schwarz (Eds.), *Well-being: The foundations of hedonic psychology.* New York, NY: Russell Sage Foundation.

Schwarzer, R., & Luszczynska, A. (2013). Stressful life events. In A. M. Nezu, C. M. Nezu, P. A. Geller, & I. B. Weiner (Eds.), *Handbook of psychology: Vol. 9. Health psychology* (2nd ed.). New York, NY: Wiley.

Schweizer, T., et al. (2013). From the thalamus with love: A rare window into the locus of emotional synesthesia. *Neurology, 81,* 509–510.

Scoboria, A., Mazzoni, G., Kirsch, I., & Milling, L. S. (2002). Immediate and persisting effects of misleading questions and hypnosis on memory reports. *Journal of Experimental Psychology: Applied, 8*(1), 26–32.

Scott, K. (2008). Chemical senses: Taste and olfaction. In L. Squire, D. Berg, F. Bloom, S. du Lac, A. Ghosh, & N. Spitzer (Eds.), *Fundamental neuroscience.* San Diego, CA: Elsevier.

Scott, V., McDade, D. M., & Luckman, S. M. (2007). Rapid changes in the sensitivity of arcuate nucleus neurons to central ghrelin in relation to feeding status. *Physiology & Behavior, 90,* 180–185.

Scoville, W. B., & Milner, B. (1957). Loss of recent memory after bilateral hippocampal lesions. *Journal of Neurology, Neurosurgery & Psychiatry, 20,* 11–21.

Scull, A. (1990). Deinstitutionalization: Cycles of despair. *The Journal of Mind and Behavior, 11*(3/4), 301–312.

Scully, J. A., Tosi, H., & Banning, K. (2000). Life event checklists: Revisiting the social readjustment rating scale after 30 years. *Educational & Psychological Measurement, 60,* 864–876.

Sealy, P., & Whitehead, P. C. (2004). Forty years of deinstitutionalization of psychiatric services in Canada: An empirical assessment. *Canadian Journal of Psychiatry, 49,* 249–257.

Searle, A., & Bennett, P. (2001). Psychological factors and inflammatory bowel disease: A review of a decade of literature. *Psychology, Health and Medicine, 6,* 121–135.

Searleman, A., & Herrmann, D. (1994). *Memory from a broader perspective.* New York, NY: McGraw-Hill.

Sears, D. O. (1975). Political socialization. In F. I. Greenstein & N. W. Polsby (Eds.), *Handbook of political science* (Vol. 2). Reading, MA: Addison-Wesley.

Seaton, S. E., King, S., Manktelow, B. N., Draper, E. S., & Field, D. J. (2013). Babies born at the threshold of viability: Changes in survival and workload over 20 years. *Archive of Disease of Childhood: Fetal and Neonatal Edition, 98,* F15–F20. doi:10.1136/fetalneonatal-2011-301572.

Sebastian, C., Burnett, S., & Blakemore, S. (2010). The neuroscience of social cognition in teenagers: Implications for inclusion in society. In C. L. Cooper, J. Field, U. Goswami, R. Jenkins, & B. J. Sahakian (Eds.), *Mental capital and wellbeing.* Hoboken, NJ: Wiley-Blackwell.

Sebastian-Galles, A. B., Wiekum, W., & Werker, J. F. (2012). A bilingual advantage in visual language discrimination in infancy. *Psychological Science, 23*(9), 994–999.

Sedikides, C., & Strube, M. J. (1997). Self-evaluation: To thine own self be good, to thine own self be sure, to thine own self be true, and to thine own self be better. In M. P. Zanna (Ed.), *Advances in experimental social psychology.* New York, NY: Academic Press.

Seery, M. D. (2011). Resilience: A silver lining to experiencing adverse life events? *Current Directions in Psychological Science, 20,* 390–394. doi: 10.1177/0963721411424740.

Seery, M. D., Leo, R. J., Lupien, S. P., Kondrak, C. L., & Almonte, J. L. (2013). An upside to adversity? Moderate cumulative lifetime adversity is associated with resilient responses in the face of controlled stressors. *Psychological Science, 24,* 1181–1189.

Segal, Z., Williams, J. M. G., & Teasdale, J. D. (2007). *Mindfulness-based cognitive therapy for depression.* New York, NY: Guilford Press.

Segal, Z., Williams, J. M. G., & Teasdale, J. D. (Eds.) (2002). *Mindfulness-based cognitive therapy for depression.* New York, NY: Guilford Press.

Segal, Z. V., & Walsh, K. M. (2016). Mindfulness-based cognitive therapy for residual depressive symptoms and relapse prophylaxis. *Current Opinion in Psychiatry, 29,* 7–12.

Segal-Caspi, L., Roccas, S., & Sagiv, L. (2012). Don't judge a book by its cover, revisited: Perceived and reported traits and values of attractive women. *Psychological Science, 23,* 1112–1116. doi:10.1177/0956797612446349.

Segall, M. H., Campbell, D. T., Herskovits, M. J. (1966). *The influence of culture on visual perception.* Indianapolis, IN: Bobbs-Merrill.

Segall, M. H., Dasen, P. R., Berry, J. W., & Poortinga, Y. H. (1990). *Human behavior in global perspective: An introduction to cross-cultural psychology.* New York, NY: Pergamon Press.

Segerstrom, S. C., & O'Connnor, D. B. (2012). Stress, health, and illness: Four challenges for the future. *Psychology and Health, 27,* 128–140. doi:10.1080/08870446.2012.659516.

Segerstrom, S. C., & Sephton, S. E. (2010). Optimistic expectancies and cell-mediated immunity: The role of positive affect. *Psychological Science, 21*(3), 448–455. doi:10.1177/0956797610362061.

Sejnowski, T. J. (2003). The once and future Hebb synapse. *Canadian Psychology, 44,* 17–20.

Sejnowski, T. J., & Tesauro, G. (1989). The Hebb rule for synaptic plasticity: Algorithms and implementation. In J. O. Byrne & W. O. Berry (Eds.), *Neural models of Plasticity* (pp. 94–124). New York, NY: Academic Press.

Sekiguchi, C., Umikura, S., Sone, K., & Kume, M. (1994). Psychological evaluation of Japanese astronaut applicants. *Aviation, Space, and Environmental Medicine, 65,* 920–924.

Self, D. W. (1997). Neurobiological adaptations to drug use. *Hospital Practice, April,* 5–9.

Seli, P., Risko, E. F., Smilek, D., & Schacter, D. L. (2016). Mind-wandering with and without intention. *Trends in Cognitive Science, 20,* 605–617.

Seligman, M. (2016). How Positive psychology happened and where it is going. In R. Sternberg, S. Fiske, D. J. Foss (Eds.), *Scientists making a difference* (pp. 478–480).New York, NY: Cambridge University Press.

Seligman, M. E. P. (1971). Phobias and preparedness. *Behavior Therapy, 2,* 307–321.

Seligman, M. E. P. (1974). Depression and learned helplessness. In R. J. Friedman & M. M. Katz (Eds.), *The psychology of depression: Contemporary theory and research.* New York, NY: Wiley.

Seligman, M. E. P. (1990). *Learned optimism.* New York, NY: Pocket Books.

Seligman, M. E. P. (1992). *Helplessness: On depression, development, and death.* New York, NY: Freeman.

Seligman, M. E. P. (1995). The effectiveness of psychotherapy. *American Psychologist, 50,* 965–974.

Seligman, M. E. P. (2003). The past and future of positive psychology. In C. L. M. Keyes & J. Haidt (Eds.), *Flourishing: Positive psychology and the life well-lived.* Washington, DC: American Psychological Association.

Seligman, M. E. P., & Csikszentmihalyi, M. (2000). Positive psychology: An introduction. *American Psychologist, 55,* 5–14.

Seligman, M. E. P., & Hager, J. L. (1972, August). Biological boundaries of learning (The sauce béarnaise syndrome). *Psychology Today,* 59–61, 84–87.

Seligman, M. E. P., Parks, A. C., & Steen, T. (2006). A balanced psychology and a full life: In F. Huppert, B. Keverne, & N. Baylis (Eds.), *The science of well-being* (pp. 275–282). Oxford: Oxford University Press.

Seligman, M. E. P., Rashid, T., & Parks, A. C. (2006). Positive psychotherapy. *American Psychologist, 61*, 774–788.

Sell, A., Cosmides, L., Tooby, J., Sznycer, D., von Rueden, C., & Gurven, M. (2009). Human adaptations for the visual assessment of strength and fighting ability from the body and face. *Proceedings of the Royal Society B: Biological Sciences, 276*, 575–584.

Selye, H. (1936). A syndrome produced by diverse noc-uous agents. *Nature, 138*, 32.

Selye, H. (1956). *The stress of life.* New York, NY: McGraw-Hill.

Selye, H. (1973). The evolution of the stress concept. *American Scientist, 61*(6), 672–699.

Selye, H. (1974). *Stress without distress.* New York, NY: Lippincott.

Selye, H. (1982). History and present status of the stress concept. In L. Goldberger & S. Breznitz (Eds.), *Handbook of stress: Theoretical and clinical aspects.* New York, NY: Free Press.

Senior, C., Thomson, K., Badger, J., & Butler, M. J. R. (2008). Interviewing strategies in the face of beauty: A psychophysiological investigation into the job negotia-tion process. *Annals of the New York Academy of Sciences, 1118*, 142–162.

Senior, J. (2010, July 4). All joy and no fun. *New York Magazine.* Retrieved July 9, 2010, from http://nymag.com/print/?/news/features67024/.

Sergeant, S., & Mongrain, M. (2015). Distressed users report a better response to online positive psychology interventions than nondistressed users. *Canadian Psychology, 56*, 322–331.

Serpell, J., McCune, S., Gee, N., & Griffin, J. (2017). Current challenges to research on animal-assisted inter-ventions. *Applied Developmental Science, 21*, 223–233.

Serper, M. R. (2011). Aggression in schizophrenia. *Schizophrenia Bulletin, 37*(Suppl 5), 897–898. doi:10.1093/schbul/sbr090.

Shackelford, T. K., & Liddle, J. R. (2014). Understanding the mind from an evolutionary perspec-tive: An overview of evolutionary psychology. *WIREs Cognitive Science, 5*, 247–260.

Shadish, W. R., & Cook, T. D. (2009). The renaissance of field experimentation in evaluating interventions. *Annual Review of Psychology, 60*, 607–609.

Shafer, G., & Tversky, A. (1988). Languages and designs for probability judgement. In D. E. Bell, H. Raiffa, & A. Tversky (Eds.), *Decision making: Descriptive, normative, and prescriptive interactions.* New York, NY: Cambridge University Press.

Shafir, E., & LeBoeuf, R. A. (2004). Context and conflict in multi-attribute choice. In D. J. Koehler & N. Harvey (Eds), *Blackwell handbook of judgment and decision making.* Malden, MA: Blackwell.

Shamay-Tsoory, S. G., Abu-Akel, A., Palgi, S., Sulieman, R., Fischer-Shofty, M., Levkovitz, Y., & Decety, J. (2013). Giving peace a chance: Oxytocin increases empathy to pain in the context of the Israeli–Palestinian conflict. *Psychoneuroendocrinology, 38*, 3139–3144. doi:10.1016/j.psyneuen.2013.09.015.

Shanahan, M. J., Hill, P. L., Roberts, B. W., Eccles, J., & Friedman, H. S. (2014). Conscientiousness, health, and aging: The life course of personality model. *Developmental Psychology, 50*, 1407–1425. doi:10.1037/a0031130.

Shanahan, N. (2013). James Pon: He led the call for Chinese head-tax redress. *The Globe and Mail,* Wednesday, April 17, S8.

Shanks, D. R. (2010). Learning: From association to cog-nition. *Annual Review of Psychology, 61*, 273–301.

Shapira, L. B., & Mongrain, M. (2010, September). The benefits of self-compassion and optimism exercises for individuals vulnerable to depression. *Journal of Positive Psychology, 5*, 377–389.

Shapiro, D. H., Jr. (1984). Overview: Clinical and physiological comparison of meditation with other self-control strategies. In D. H. Shapiro, Jr., & R. N. Walsh (Eds.), *Meditation: Classic and contemporary perspectives.* New York, NY: Aldine.

Shapiro, J. R., & Neuberg, S. L. (2007). From stereotype threat to stereotype threats: Implications of a multi-threat framework for causes, moderators, mediators, consequences, and interventions. *Personality & Social Psychology Review, 11*, 107–130.

Shapiro, M. (2015). A limited positioning system for memory. *Hippocampus, 25*, 690–696.

Shatz, C. J. (1992, September). The developing brain. *Scientific American,* 60–67.

Shaver, P. R., & Mikulincer, M. (2009). Attachment styles. In M. R. Leary & R. H. Hoyle (Eds.), *Handbook of individual differences in social behavior* (pp. 62–81). New York, NY: Guilford Press.

Shaw, J. S. I., McClure, K. A., & Dykstra, J. A. (2007). Eyewitness confidence from the witnessed event through trial. In M. P. Toglia, J. D. Read, D. F. Ross, & R. C. L. Lindsay (Eds.), *Handbook of eyewitness psychology: Volume 1. Memory for events.* Mahwah, NJ: Erlbaum.

Shea, A. K., & Steiner, M. (2008). Cigarette smoking during pregnancy. *Nicotine & Tobacco Research, 10*, 267–278.

Shearer, B. (2004). Multiple intelligences theory after 20 years. *Teachers College Record, 106*(1), 2–16.

Shedler, J. (2010). The efficacy of psychodynamic psychotherapy. *American Psychologist, 65*(2), 98–109. doi:10.1037/a0018378.

Sheehan, S. (1982). *Is there no place on earth for me?* Boston, MA: Houghton Mifflin.

Sheehana , K. J., Van Reetb, J., & M. Bloomb, C. M. (2012). Measuring preschoolers' superstitious tendencies. *Behavioural rocesses, 91*(2), 172–176.

Sheeran, P., Klein, W. M. P., & Rothman, A. J. (2017). Health behavior change: Moving from observation to intervention. *Annual Review of Psychology, 68*, 573–600.

Sheldon, K. M., & Kasser, T. (2001). Goals, congru-ence, and positive well-being: New empirical support for humanistic theories. *Journal of Humanistic Psychology, 41*(1), 30–50.

Sheldon, K. M., Abad, N., & Hinsch, C. (2011). A two-process view of Facebook use and relatedness need-satisfaction: Disconnection drive use, and connection rewards it. *Journal of Personality and Social Psychology, 100*, 766–775. doi:10.1037/a0022407.

Shenton, M. E., & Kubicki, M. (2009). Structural brain imaging in schizophrenia. In B. J. Sadock, V. A. Sadock, & P. Ruiz (Eds.), *Kaplan & Sadock's comprehensive textbook of psychiatry* (9th ed., Vol. 1, pp. 1494–1506). Philadelphia, PA: Lippincott, Williams & Wilkins.

Shepard, R. N. (1990). *Mind sights.* New York, NY: W. H. Freeman.

Shephard, M. (2008). *Guantanamo's child: The untold story of Omar Khadr.* Mississauga, ON: John Wiley & Sons Canada.

Shepherd, G. M. (2004). The human sense of smell: Are we better than we think? *PLoS Biology, 2*(5), 0572–0575.

Sherif, M. (1936). *The psychology of social norms.* Oxford, England: Harper.

Sherif, M., Harvey, O., White, B., Hood, W., & Sherif, C. (1961). *Intergroup conflict and cooperation: The Robber's Cave experiment.* Norman: University of Oklahoma, Institute of Group Behavior.

Sherman, M., & Key, C. B. (1932). The intelligence of isolated mountain children. *Child Development, 3*, 279–290.

Sherman, S. L., Allen, E. G., Bean, L. H., & Freeman, S. B. (2007). Epidemiology of Down Syndrome. *Mental Retardation and Developmental Disabilities Research Reviews, 13*, 221–227.

Sherman, S. M. (2009). Thalamocortical relations. In G. G. Bernston & J. T. Cacioppo (Eds.), *Handbook of neurosci-ence for the behavioral sciences* (Vol. 1, pp. 201–223). New York, NY: Wiley, Inc.

Sherman, S., Gawronski, B., & Trope, Y. (Eds). (2014). *Dual process theories of the mind.* New York, NY: Guilford Press.

Shermer, M. (1997). *Why people believe weird things: Pseudoscience, superstition, and other confusions of our time.* New York, NY: W. H. Freeman.

Sherry, D. F. (1992). Evolution and learning. In L. R. Squire (Ed.), *Encyclopedia of learning and memory.* New York, NY: Macmillan.

Shettleworth, S. J. (1998). *Cognition, evolution, and behavior.* New York, NY: Oxford University Press.

Shield, K. D., Rylett, M., Gmel, G., Kehoe-Chan, T. A., & Rehm, J. (2013). Global alcohol exposure estimates by country, territory, and region for 2005—A contribution to the comparative risk assessment for the 2010 global burden of disease study. *Addiction, 108*, 912–922.

Shields, M. (2008). Community belonging and self-perceived health. Statistics Canada: Health Reports, 19. Retrieved July 23, 2008, from http://www.statcan.ca/english/freepub/82-003-XIE/2008002/article/10552-en.pdf.

Shields, M., & Tremblay, M. S. (2008). Sedentary Behaviour and obesity. Statistics Canada, Retrieved May 2, 2011, from http://www.statcan.gc.ca/pub/82-003-x/2008002/article/10599-eng.pdf.

Shiffrin, R. M. (1988). Attention. In R. C. Atkinson, R. J. Herrnstein, G. Lindzey, & R. D. Luce (Eds.), *Stevens' handbook of experimental psychology* (Vol. 2). New York, NY: Wiley.

Shimizu, Y., Lee, H., & Uleman, J. S. (2017). Culture as automatic processes for making meaning: Spontaneous trait inferences. *Journal of Experimental Social Psychology, 69*, 79–85.

Shlisky, J. D., Hartman, T. J., Kris-Etherton, P. M., Rogers, C. J., Sharkey, N. A., & Nickols-Richardson, S. M. (2012). Partial sleep deprivation and energy bal-ance in adults: An emerging issue for consideration by dietetics practitioners. *Journal of the Academy of Nutrition and Dietetics, 112*, 1785–1797.

Shneidman, E. S., Farberow, N. L., & Litman, R. E. (1994). *The psychology of suicide: A clinician's guide to evaluation and treatment.* Northvale, NJ: J. Aronson.

Shobe, K. K., & Schooler, J. W. (2001). Discovering fact and fiction: Case-based analyses of authentic and fabri-cated discovered memories of abuse. In G. M. Davies & T. Dalgleish (Eds.), *Recovered memories: Seeking the middle ground.* Chichester, England: Wiley.

Shrager, Y., & Squire, L. R. (2009). Medial temporal lobe function and human memory. In M. S. Gazzaniga (Eds.), *The cognitive neurosciences* (4th ed., pp. 675–690). Cambridge, MA: MIT Press.

Siebert, A. (1995). *Student success: How to succeed in college and still have time for your friends.* Fort Worth: Harcourt Brace Jovanovich.

Siebner, H. R., Hartwigsen, G., Kassuba, T., & Rothwell, J. C. (2009). How does transcranial magnetic stimulation modify neuronal activity in the brain? Implications for studies of cognition. *Cortex: A Journal Devoted to the Study of the Nervous System and Behavior, 45*(9), 1035–1042.

Siegel, J. M. (2005). REM sleep. In M. H. Kryger, T. Roth, & W. C. Dement (Eds.). *Principles and practice of sleep medicine.* Philadelphia, PA: Elsevier Saunders.

Siegel, J. M. (2009). Sleep viewed as a state of adaptive inactivity. *Nature Reviews Neuroscience, 10*(10), 747–753.

Siegel, J. M. (2011). REM sleep. In M. H. Kryger, T. Roth, & W. C. Dement (Eds.), *Principles and practice of sleep medicine* (5th ed.). Saint Louis, MO: Elsevier Saunders.

Siegel, S. (1976). Morphine analgesic tolerance: Its situ-ational specificity supports a Pavlovian conditioning model. *Science, 193*, 323–325.

Siegel, S. (2001). Pavlovian conditioning and drug over-dose: When tolerance fails. *Addiction Research & Theory, 9*, 503–513.

Siegel, S. (2002). The ghost in the addict: Drug antici-pation and drug addiction. *Proceedings of the Royal Society of Canada*: http://www.rsc.ca/files/publications/

transactions/2002/siegel.pdfrsc.ca/files/publications/transactions/2002/siegel.pdf.

Siegel, S. (2005). Drug tolerance, drug addiction, and drug anticipation. *Current Directions in Psychological Science, 14,* 296–300.

Siegel, S. (2016). The heroin overdose mystery. *Current Directions in Psychological Science, 25,* 375–379.

Siegel, S., Baptista, M. A. S., Kim, J. A., McDonald, R. V., & Weise-Kelly, L. (2000). Pavlovian psychopharmacology: The associative basis of tolerance. *Experimental and Clinical Psychopharmacology, 8,* 276–293.

Siegel, S., & Ramos, B. C. (2002). Applying laboratory research: Drug anticipation and the treatment of drug addiction. *Experimental and Clinical Psychopharmacology, 10,* 162–183.

Siegler, R. S. (1992). The other Alfred Binet. *Developmental Psychology, 28,* 179–190.

Siegler, R. S. (1998). *Children's thinking.* Upper Saddle River, NJ: Prentice-Hall.

Sigel, I. E. (2004). Head Start-Revisiting a historical psychoeducational intervention: A revisionist of perspective. In E. Zigler & S. J. Styfco (Eds.), *The Head Start debate.* Baltimore, MD: Paul H. Brookes Publishing.

Signorielli, N. (2001). Television's gender role images and contribution to stereotyping: Past present future. In D. G. Singer & J. L. Singer (Eds.), *Handbook of children and the media.* Thousand Oaks, CA: Sage.

Sikh Philosophy Network. (2005, June 22). Father's parole eligibility set at 16 years in murder of daughter. Retrieved October 24, 2008, from http://www.sikhism.us/interfaith-dialogues/4441-father-get-parole-16-years-murdering.html.

Silvanto, J., & Cattaneo, Z. (2010). Transcranial magnetic stimulation reveals the content of visual short-term memory in the visual cortex. *Neuroimage, 50*(4), 1683–1689.

Silver, E., Cirincione, C., & Steadman, H. J. (1994). Demythologizing inaccurate perceptions of the insanity defense. *Law and Human Behavior, 18*(1), 63–70. doi:10.1007/BF01499144.

Silverman, I., & Choi, J. (2005). Locating places. In D. M. Buss (Ed.), *The handbook of evolutionary psychology.* New York, NY: Wiley.

Silverman, I., & Eals, M. (1992). Sex differences in spatial ability: Evolutionary theory and data. In J. Barkow, L. Cosmides, & J. Tooby (Eds.), *The adapted mind.* New York, NY: Oxford University Press.

Silverman, I., & Phillips, K. (1998). The evolutionary psychology of spatial sex differences. In C. Crawford & D. L. Krebs (Eds.), *Handbook of evolutionary psychology: Ideas, issues, and applications.* Mahwah, NJ: Erlbaum.

Silverman, I., Choi, J., Mackewn, A., Fisher, M., Moro, J., & Olshansky, E. (2000). Evolved mechanisms underlying wayfinding: Further studies on the hunter–gatherer theory of spatial sex differences. *Evolution and Human Behavior, 21,* 201–213.

Silverstein, L. B., & Auerbach, C. F. (1999). Deconstructing the essential father. *American Psychologist, 54, 397–407.

Silvia, P. J. (2008). Another look at creativity and intelligence: Exploring higher-order models and probable confounds. *Personality and Individual Differences, 44,* 1012–1021.

Silvia, P. J., & Kaufman, J. C. (2010). Creativity and mental illness. In J. C. Kaufman & R. J. Sternberg (Eds.), *The Cambridge handbook of creativity* (pp. 381–394). New York, NY: Cambridge University Press.

Simard, D. (2014). La controverse de l'attirance sexuelle par les phéromones chez l'être humain. *Sexology, 23,* 23–28.

Simeon, D., & Loewenstein, R. J. (2009). Dissociative disorders. In B. J. Sadock, V. A. Sadock, & P. Ruiz (Eds.), *Kaplan & Sadock's comprehensive textbook of psychiatry* (9th ed., pp. 1965–2026). Philadelphia, PA: Lippincott Williams & Wilkins.

Simner, J., Mayo, N., & Spiller, M-J. (2009). A foundation for savantism? Visuo-spatial synaesthetes present with cognitive benefits. *Cortex, 45,* 1246–1260.

Simon, H. A. (1957). *Models of man.* New York, NY: Wiley.

Simon, H. A. (1974). How big is a chunk? *Science, 183,* 482–488.

Simon, H. A. (1991). *Models of my life.* New York, NY: Basic Books.

Simon, H. A., & Reed, S. K. (1976). Modeling strategy shifts in a problem-solving task. *Cognitive Psychology, 8,* 86–97.

Simon, R. I., & Shuman, D. W. (2008). Psychiatry and the law. In R. E. Hales, S. C. Yudofsky, & G. O. Gabbard (Eds.), *The American Psychiatric Publishing textbook of psychiatry* (5th ed. pp. 1555–1600). Washington, DC: American Psychiatric Publishing.

Simons, D. J., & Chabris, C. F. (1999). Gorillas in our midst: Sustained inattentional blindness for dynamic events. *Perception, 28,* 1059–1074.

Simons, D. J., & Chabris, C. F. (2011). What people believe about how memory works: A representative survey of the US population. *PloS One, 6*(8), e22757. doi:10.1371/journal.pone.0022757.

Simonton, D. K. (1984). *Genius, creativity, and leadership.* Cambridge, MA; Harvard University Press.

Simonton, D. K. (1999a). Creativity and genius. In L. A. Pervin & O. John (Eds.), *Handbook of personality theory and research.* New York, NY: Guilford.

Simonton, D. K. (2004). *Creativity in science: Chance, logic, genius, and Zeitgeist.* New York, NY: Cambridge University Press.

Simonton, D. K. (2012). The science of genius. *Scientific American Mind, 23*(5), 34–41.

Simonton, D. K., & Damian, R. I. (2013). Creativity. In D. Reisberg (Ed.), *Oxford handbook of cognitive psychology.* New York, NY: Oxford University Press.

Simonton, D. K., & Flora, C. (2011, Winter). Spark of genius [Introduction, *Genius* Special Issue]. *Discover Magazine,* 2–3.

Simpson, J. A. (1999). Attachment theory in modern evolutionary perspective. In J. Cassidy & P. R. Shaver (Eds.), *Handbook of attachment: Theory, research, and clinical applications.* New York, NY: Guilford.

Simpson, J. A., & Winterheld, H. A. (2012). Person-by-situation perspectives on close relationships. In K. Deaux & M. Snyder (Eds.), *Oxford handbook of personality and social psychology.* New York, NY: Oxford University Press.

Simpson, J. L., & Jauniaux, E. (2007). Pregnancy loss. In S. G. Gabbe, J. R. Niebyl & J. L. Simpson (Eds.) *Obstetrics: Normal and problem pregnancies* (5th ed., pp. 628–649). Philadelphia, PA: Elsevier.

Simpson, J. L., & Jauniaux, E. (2012). Pregnancy loss. In S. G. Gabbe, J. R. Niebyl, J. L. Simpson, M. B. Landon, H. L. Galan, E. R. M. Jauniaux, D. A. Driscoll (Eds.), *Obstetrics: Normal and problem pregnancies* (6th ed.). Philadelphia, PA: Elsevier.

Sims, C. R., Jacobs, R. A., & Knill, D. C. (2012). An ideal observer analysis of visual working memory. *Psychological Review, 119,* 807–830.

Sinclair, D. (1981). *Mechanisms of cutaneous stimulation.* Oxford, England: Oxford University Press.

Sinclair, R. C., Hoffman, C., Mark, M. M., Martin, L. L., & Pickering, T. L. (1994). Construct accessibility and the misattribution of arousal: Schachter and Singer revisited. *Psychological Science, 5,* 15–19.

Singer, L. T., Arendt, R., Minnes, S., Farkas, K., Salvator, A., Kirchner, H. L., & Kliegman, R. (2002). Cognitive and motor outcomes of cocaine-exposed infants. *Journal of the American Medical Association, 287,* 1952–1960.

Singer, L. T., Minnes, S., Short, E., Arendt, R., Farkas, K., Lewis, B., et al. (2004). Cognitive outcomes of pre-school children with prenatal cocaine exposure. *Journal of the American Medical Association, 291,* 2448–2456.

Singer, W. (2007). Large-scale temporal coordination of cortical activity as a prerequisite for conscious experience. In M. Velmans & S. Schneider (Eds.), *The Blackwell companion to consciousness.* Malden, MA: Blackwell.

Singh, B. P., Hummel, T., Gerber, J. C., & Landis, B. N., & Iannilli, E. (2015). Cerebral processing of umami: A Pilot study on the effects of familiarity. *Brain Research, 1614,* 67–74.

Singh, D., Dixson, B. J., Jessop, T. S., Morgan, B. B., & Dixson, A. F. (2010). Cross-cultural consensus for waist-hip ratio and women's attractiveness. *Evolution and Human Behavior, 31,* 176–181. doi:10.1016/j.evolhumbehav.2009.09.001.

Sinha, D. (1983). Human assessment in the Indian context. In S. H. Irvine & J. W. Berry (Eds.), *Human assessment and cultural factors.* New York, NY: Plenum.

Sinha, M. (2014). Child Care in Canada. Statistics Canada. Retrieved from http://www.statcan.gc.ca/pub/89-652-x/89-652-x2014005-eng.pdf.

Sinigaglia, C., & Rizzolatti, G. (2015). The space of mirrors. In P. F. Ferarri & G. Rizzolatti (Eds.), *New frontiers in mirror neurons research* (pp. 331–347). New York, NY: Oxford University Press.

Sio, U., & Ormerod, T. C. (2009). Does incubation enhance problem solving? A meta-analytic review. *Psychological Bulletin, 135*(1), 94–120.

Sio, U. N., Monaghen, P., & Ormerod, T. (2013). Sleep on it, but only if it is difficult: Effects of sleep on problem solving. *Memory & Cognition, 41,* 159–166.

Sisti, D. A., Segal, A. G., & Emanuel, E. J. (2015). Improving long-term psychiatric care: Bring back the asylum. *JAMA, 313*(3), 243–244. doi:10.1001/jama.2014.16088.

Sivertsen, B., Lallukka, T., Salo, P., Pallesen, S., Hysing, M., Krokstad, S., & Overland, S. (2014). Insomnia as a risk factor for ill health: Results from the large population-based prospective HUNT study in Norway. *Journal of Sleep Research, 23,* 124–132.

Skilling, T. A., Harris, G. T., Rice, M. E., & Quinsey, V. L. (2002). Identifying persistently antisocial offenders using the Hare Psychopathy Checklist and the DSM antisocial personality disorder criteria. *Psychological Assessment, 14,* 27–38.

Skinner, A. E. G. (2001). Recovered memories of abuse: Effects on the individual. In G. M. Davies, & T. Dalgleish (Eds.), *Recovered memories: Seeking the middle ground.* Chichester, England: Wiley.

Skinner, B. F. (1938). *The behavior of organisms.* New York, NY: Appleton-Century-Crofts.

Skinner, B. F. (1945, October). Baby in a box: The mechanical baby-tender. *Ladies' Home Journal,* pp. 30–31, 135–136, 138.

Skinner, B. F. (1948a/2005). *Walden Two.* Indianapolis, IN: Hackett Publishing Company Inc.

Skinner, B. F. (1948b), "Superstition" in the pigeon. *Journal of Experimental Psychology, 38,* 168–173.

Skinner, B. F. (1953). *Science and human behavior.* New York, NY: Macmillan.

Skinner, B. F. (1957). *Verbal behavior.* New York, NY: Appleton-Century-Crofts.

Skinner, B. F. (1969). *Contingencies of reinforcement.* New York, NY: Appleton-Century-Crofts.

Skinner, B. F. (1971). *Beyond freedom and dignity.* New York, NY: Knopf.

Skinner, B. F. (1974). *About behaviorism.* New York, NY: Knopf.

Skinner, B. F. (1980). *Notebooks* (edited by R. Epstein). Englewood Cliffs, NJ: Prentice-Hall.

Skinner, B. F. (1984). Selection by consequences. *Behavioral and Brain Sciences, 7*(4), 477–510.

Skinner, B. F., Solomon, H. C., & Lindsley, O. R. (1953). *Studies in behavior therapy: Status report I.* Waltham, MA: Unpublished report, Metropolitan State Hospital.

Skinner, R, McFaull, S., Draca, J., Frechette, M., Kaur, J., Pearson, C., & Thompson, W. (2016). Suicide and self-inflicted injury hospitalization in Canada (1979 to 2014/5). *Health Promotion and Chronic Disease Prevention in Canada: Research, Policy, and Practice, 36,* 243–251.

Skodol, A. E., Bender, D. S., & Morey, L. C. (2014). Narcissistic personality disorder in DSM-5. *Personality

Disorders: Theory, Research, and Treatment, 5, 422–427. doi:10.1037/per0000023.

Skogen, J. C., & Overland, S. (2012). The fetal origins of adult disease: A narrative review of the epidemiological literature. *Journal of the Royal Society of Medicine, 3,* 59. doi:10.1258/shorts.2012.012048.

Slamecka, N. J. (1985). Ebbinghaus: Some associations. *Journal of Experimental Psychology: Learning, Memory and Cognition, 11,* 414–435.

Slater, E., & Shields, J. (1969). Genetical aspects of anxiety. In L. H. Lader (Ed.), *Studies of anxiety.* Ashford, England: Headley Brothers.

Slaughter, G. (2016). *At least 744 assisted-deaths in Canada since law passed.* CTV News. Retrieved from http://www.ctvnews.ca/health/at-least-744-assisted-deaths-in-canada-since-law-passed-ctv-news-analysis-1.3220382.

Sleegers, W. W. A., Proulx, T., & van Beest, I. (2017). The social pain of cyberball: Decreased pupillary reactivity to exclusion cues. *Journal of Experimental Social Psychology, 69,* 187–200.

Sletten, T. L., & Arendt, J. (2012). Circadian rhythm disorders III: Jet lag. In C. M. Morin, & C. A. Espie (Eds.), *Oxford handbook of sleep and sleep disorders.* New York, NY: Oxford University Press.

Slobin, D. I. (1985). *A cross-linguistic study of language acquisition.* Hillsdale, NJ: Erlbaum.

Sloman, S. A., Hayman, C. G, Ohta, N., Law, J., & Tulving, E. (1988). Forgetting in primed fragment completion. *Journal of Experimental Psychology: Learning, Memory, and Cognition, 14,* 223–239.

Slopen, N., Kontos, E. Z., Ryff, C. D., Ayanian, J. Z., Albert, M. A., & Williams, D. R. (2013). Psychosocial stress and cigarette smoking persistence, cessation, and relapse over 9–10 years: A prospective study of middle-aged adults in the United States. *Cancer Causes & Control, 24,* 1849–1863.

Slovic, P., & Fischhoff, B. (1977). On the psychology of experimental surprises. *Journal of Experimental Psychology: Human Perception and Performance, 3,* 544–551.

Slovic, P., Lichtenstein, S., & Fischhoff, B. (1988). Decision making. In R. C. Atkinson, R. J. Herrnstein, G. Lindzey, & R. D. Luce (Eds.), *Stevens' handbook of experimental psychology* (Vol. 2). New York, NY: Wiley.

Small, B. J., Rawson, K. S., Eisel, S., & McEvoy, C. L. (2012). Memory and aging. In S. K. Whitbourne & M. J. Sliwinski (Eds.), *Wiley-Blackwell handbook of adulthood and aging.* Malden, MA: Wiley-Blackwell.

Small, S. A., & Heeger, D. J. (2013). Functional imaging of cognition. In E. R. Kandel, J. H. Schwartz, T. M. Jessell, S. A. Siegelbaum, & A. J. Hudspeth (Eds.), *Principles of neural science* (5th ed.). New York, NY: McGraw-Hill.

Smallwood, J., & Schooler, J. W. (2006). The restless mind. *Psychological Bulletin, 132,* 946–958.

Smallwood, J., & Schooler, J. W. (2013). The science of mind wandering: Empirically navigating the stream of consciousness. *Annual Review of Psychology, 66,* 487–518.

Smedley, S. R., & Eisner, T. (1996). Sodium: A male moth's gift to its offspring. *Proceedings of the National Academy of Sciences, 93,* 809–813.

Smetana, J. G., Campione, B. N., & Metzger, A. (2006). Adolescent development in interpersonal and societal contexts. *Annual Review of Psychology, 57,* 255–284.

Smith, B. W., Epstein, E. M., Ortiz, J. A., Christopher, P. J., & Tooley, E. M. (2013). The foundations of resilience: What are the critical resources for bouncing back from stress? In S. Prince-Embury & D. H. Saklofske (Eds.), *Resilience in children, adolescents, and adults: Translating research into practice.* New York, NY: Spring Science + Business Media.

Smith, B. W., Epstein, E. M., Ortiz, J. A., Christopher, P. J., & Tooley, E. M. (2013). The foundations of resilience: What are the critical resources for bouncing back from stress? In S. Prince-Embury & D. H. Saklofske (Eds.), *Resilience in children, adolescents, and adults: Translating research into practice.* New York, NY: Spring Science + Business Media.

Smith, C. (1996). Sleep states, memory processes and synaptic plasticity. *Behavioural Brain Research, 78,* 49–56.

Smith, C. (2003). The REM sleep window and memory processing. In Maquet, P., Smith, C., & Stickgold, R. (Eds.), *Sleep and brain plasticity* (pp. 116–133). Oxford, UK: Oxford University Press.

Smith, C. A., & Lazarus, R. S. (1993). Appraisal components, core relational themes, and the emotions. *Cognition and Emotion, 7,* 233–269.

Smith, C. P. (1992). Reliability issues. In C. P. Smith (Ed.), *Motivation and personality: Handbook of thematic content analysis.* New York, NY: Cambridge University Press.

Smith, D. (2005, May 10). Hot Nash burns Mavs. *Toronto Star,* E1, E4.

Smith, D. A. (1999). The end of theoretical orientations? *Applied & Preventative Psychology, 8,* 269–280.

Smith, G. T., Spillane, N. S., & Annus, A. M. (2006). Implications of an emerging integration of universal and culturally specific psychologies. *Perspectives on Psychological Science, 1,* 211–233.

Smith, J. C. (2007). The psychology of relaxation. In P. M. Lehrer, R. L. Woolfolk, & W. E. Sime (Eds.), *Principles and practice of stress management.* New York, NY: Guilford Press.

Smith, J. D., Boomer, J., Zakrzewski, A. C., Roeder, J. L., Church, B. A., & Ashby, F. G. (2014). Deferred feedback sharply dissociates implicit and explicit category learning. *Psychological Science, 25,* 447–457.

Smith, M. L., & Glass, G. V. (1977). Meta-analysis of psychotherapy outcome studies. *American Psychologist, 32,* 752–760.

Smith, M. R., Fogg, L. F., & Eastman, C. I. (2009). A compromise circadian phase position for permanent night work improves mood, fatigue, and performance. *Sleep: Journal of Sleep and Sleep Disorders Research, 32*(11), 1481–1489.

Smith, P. B. (2001). Cross-cultural studies of social influence. In D. Matsumoto (Ed.), *The handbook of culture and psychology.* New York, NY: Oxford University Press.

Smith, P. B., & Bond, M. H. (1994). *Social psychology across cultures: Analysis and perspectives.* Boston, MA: Allyn & Bacon.

Smith, R. E. (2016). Prospective memory: A framework for research on metaintentions. In J. Dunlosky & S.K. Tauber (Eds.), *The Oxford handbook of metamemory* (pp. 217–244). New York, NY: Oxford University Press.

Smith, S. M., Brown, H. O., Toman, J. E. P., & Goodman, L. S. (1947). The lack of cerebral effects of d-tubocuarine. *Anesthesiology, 8*(1), 1–14.

Smith, T. W., & Gallo, L. C. (2001). Personality traits as risk factors for physical illness. In A. Baum, T. A. Revenson, & J. E. Singer (Eds.), *Handbook of health psychology* (pp. 139–174). Mahwah, NJ: Erlbaum.

Smith, T. W., Gallo, L. C., Shivpuri, S., & Brewer, A. L. (2012). Personality and health: Current issues and emerging perspectives. In A. Baum, T. A. Revenson, & J. Singer (Eds.), *Handbook of health psychology* (2nd ed.). New York, NY: Psychology Press.

Smith, T. W., Williams, P. G., Segerstrom, S. C. (2015). Personality and physical health. In M. Mikulincer, P. R. Shaver, M. L. Cooper, & R. J. Larsen (Eds.), *APA handbook of personality and social psychology: Vol. 4. Personality processes and individual differences.* Washington, DC: American Psychological Association.

Smith, W. P., Compton, W. C., & West, W. B. (1995). Meditation as an adjunct to a happiness enhancement program. *Journal of Clinical Psychology, 51,* 269–273.

Smolak, L., & Murnen, S. K. (2001). Gender and eating problems. In R. H. Striegel-Moore & L. Smolak (Eds.), *Eating disorders: Innovative directions in research and practice* (pp. 91–110). Washington, DC: American Psychological Association.

Smolensky, P. (1995). On the proper treatment of connectionism. In C. Macdonald & G. Macdonald (Eds.), *Connectionism: Debates on psychological explanation.* Cambridge, USA: Blackwell.

Snedecor, S. M., Pomerleau, C. S., Mehringer, A. M., Ninowski, R., & Pomerleau, O. F. (2006). Differences in smoking-related variables based on phenylthiocabamide "taster" status. *Addictive Behaviors, 31,* 2309–2312.

Snow, C. E. (1998). Bilingualism and second language acquisition. In J. B. Gleason & N. B. Ratner (Eds.), *Psycholinguistics.* Fort Worth, TX: Harcourt College Publishers.

Snow, R. E. (1986). Individual differences in the design of educational programs. *American Psychologist, 41,* 1029–1039.

Snowden, L. R. (2012). Health and mental health policies' role in better understanding and closing African American–White American disparities in treatment access and quality of care. *American Psychologist, 67,* 524–531. doi:10.1037/a0030054.

Snowden, L. R., & Hu, T. W. (1996). Outpatient service use in minority-serving mental health programs. *Administration and Policy in Mental Health, 24,* 149–159.

Snowden, L. R., & Yamada, A. (2005). Cultural differences in access to care. *Annual Review of Clinical Psychology, 1,* 143–166.

So, K. T., & Orme-Johnson, D. W. (2001). Three randomized experiments on the longitudinal effects of the Transcendental Meditation technique on cognition. *Intelligence, 29,* 419–440.

Society for Neuroscience. (2008). *Brain briefings: Mirror neurons.* Retrieved June 20, 2011, from http://www.sfn.org/index.aspx?pagename=brainBriefings_MirrorNeurons.

Soldatos, C. R., Allaert, F. A., Ohta, T., & Dikeos, D. G. (2005). How do individuals sleep around the world? Results from a single-day survey in ten countries. *Sleep Medicine, 6,* 5–13.

Solinas, M., Justinova, Z., Goldberg, S. R., & Tanda, G. (2006). Anandamide administration alone and after inhibition of fatty acid amide hydrolase (FAAH) increases dopamine levels in the nucleus accumbens shell in rats. *Journal of Neurochemistry, 98,* 408–419.

Solinas, M., Panlilio, L. V., Antoniou, K., Pappas, L. A., & Goldberg, S. R. (2003). The cannabinoid CB1 antagonist N-piperidinyl-5-(4-chlorophenyl)-1-(2,4-dichlorophenyl)-4-methylpyrazole-3-carboxamide (SR-141716A) differentially alters the reinforcing effects of heroin under continuous reinforcement, fixed ratio, and progressive ratio schedules of drug self-administration in rats. *Journal of Pharmacology and Experimental Therapeutics, 306,* 93–102.

Solms, M. (2004). Freud returns. *Scientific American, 290*(5), 83–88.

Solowij, N., Stephens, R. S., Roffman, R. A., Babor, T., Kadden, R., Miller, M., et al. (2002). Cognitive functioning of long-term heavy cannabis users seeking treatment. *Journal of the American Medical Association, 287,* 1123–1131.

Solso, R. L. (1994). *Cognition and the visual arts.* Cambridge, MA: MIT Press.

Somerville, L. H. (2013). The teenage brain: Sensitivity to social evaluation. *Current Directions in Psychological Science, 22,* 121–127. doi:10.1177/0963721413476512.

Sommer, I. E., Aleman, A., Somers, M., Boks, M. P., & Kahn, R. S. (2008). Sex differences in handedness, asymmetry of the planum temporale and functional language lateralization. *Brain Research, 1206,* 76–88.

Son Hing, L. S., Li, W., & Zanna, M. P. (2002). Inducing hypocrisy to reduce prejudicial responses among aversive racists. *Journal of Experimental Social Psychology, 38*(1), 71–78.

Song, S., Sjostrom, P. J., Reigl, M., Nelson, S., & Chklovskii, D. B. (2005). Highly nonrandom features of synaptic connectivity in local cortical circuits. *PLoS Biol, 3*(3), 1–13.

Sotiriou, P. E. (2002). *Integrating college study skills: Reasoning in reading, listening, and writing.* Belmont, CA: Wadsworth.

Soto, C. J., John, O. P., Gosling, S. D., & Potter, J. (2011). Age differences in personality traits from 10 to 65: Big five domains and facets in a large cross-sectional sample. *Journal of Personality and Social Psychology, 100,* 330–348. doi:10.1037/a0021717.

Sousa, D. A. (2000). *How the brain learns: A classroom teacher's guide.* Thousand Oaks, CA: Corwin Press.

South, S. C., Reichborn-Kjennerud, T., Eaton, N. R., & Krueger, R. F. (2013). Genetics of personality.

In H. Tennen, J. Suls, & I. B. Weiner (Eds.), *Handbook of psychology: Vol. 5. Personality and social psychology* (2nd ed.). New York, NY: Wiley.

Spangler, W. D. (1992). Validity of questionnaire and TAT measures of need for achievement: Two meta-analyses. *Psychological Bulletin, 112,* 140–154.

Spanos, N. P. (1986). Hypnotic behavior: A social-psychological interpretation of amnesia, analgesia, and "trance logic." *Behavioral & Brain Sciences, 9*(3), 449–467.

Spanos, N. P. (1994). Multiple identity enactments and multiple personality disorder: A sociocognitive perspective. *Psychological Bulletin, 116,* 143–165.

Spanos, N. P., & Coe, W. C. (1992). A social-psychological approach to hypnosis. In E. Fromm & M. R. Nash (Eds.), *Contemporary hypnosis research.* New York, NY: Guilford.

Sparing, R., Hesse, M. D., & Fink, G. R. (2010). Neuronavigation for transcranial magnetic stimulation (TMS): Where we are and where we are going. *Cortex: A Journal Devoted to the Study of the Nervous System and Behavior, 46*(1), 118–120.

Sparks, J. A., Duncan, B. L., & Miller, R. D. (2008). Common factors in psychotherapy. In J. L. Lebow (Ed.), *Twenty-first century psychotherapies: Contemporary approaches to theory and practice.* New York, NY: Wiley.

Spear, J. H. (2007). Prominent schools or other active specialties? A fresh look at some trends in psychology. *Review of General Psychology, 11*(4), 363–380.

Spearman, C. (1904). "General intelligence" objectively determined and measured. *American Journal of Psychology, 15,* 201–293.

Spearman, C. (1927). *The abilities of man, their nature and measurement.* London, UK: Macmillan.

Speed, A., & Gangestad, S. W. (1997). Romantic popularity and mate preferences: A peer-nomination study. *Personality and Social Psychology Bulletin, 23,* 928–936.

Spelke, E. S. (1994). Initial knowledge: Six suggestions. *Cognition, 50,* 431–455.

Spelke, E. S., & Kinzler, K. D. (2007). Core knowledge. *Developmental Science, 10*(1), 89–96.

Spelke, E. S., & Newport, E. L. (1998). Nativism, empiricism, and the development of knowledge. In W. Damon (Ed.), *Handbook of child psychology (Vol. 1): Theoretical models of human development.* New York, NY: Wiley.

Spence, I., Wong, P., Rusan, M., & Rastegar, N. (2006). How color enhances visual memory for natural scenes. *Psychological Science, 14*(1), 1–6.

Sperling, G. (1960). The information available in brief visual presentations. *Psychological Monographs, 74*(11, Whole No. 498).

Sperry, R. W. (1982). Some effects of disconnecting the cerebral hemispheres. *Science, 217,* 1223–1226, 1250.

Spiegel, D. (1995). Hypnosis, dissociation, and trauma: Hidden and overt observers. In J. L. Singer (Ed.), *Repression and dissociation: Implications for personality theory, psychopathology, and health.* Chicago: University of Chicago Press.

Spiegel, D. (2003a). Hypnosis and traumatic dissociation: Therapeutic opportunities. *Journal of Trauma & Dissociation, 4*(3), 73–90.

Spiegel, D. (2003b). Negative and positive visual hypnotic hallucinations: Attending inside and out. *International Journal of Clinical & Experimental Hypnosis, 51*(2), 130–146.

Spiegel, D., Cutcomb, S., Ren, C., & Pribram, K. (1985). Hypnotic hallucination alters evoked potentials. *Journal of Abnormal Psychology, 94,* 249–255.

Spiegel, D., Lewis-Fernandez, R., Lanius, R., Vermetten, E., Simeon, D., & Friedman, M. (2013). Dissociative disorder in DSM-5. *Annual Review of Clinical Psychology, 9,* 299–326.

Spiegler, M. D. (2016). *Contemporary behavior therapy* (6th ed.). Belmont, CA: Wadsworth.

Spiegler, M. D., & Guevremont, D. C. (2010). *Contemporary behavior therapy* (5th ed.). Belmont, CA: Wadsworth.

Spielman, L. J., Little, J. P., & Klegeris, A. (2014). Inflammation and insulin/ igf-1 resistance as the possible link between obesity and neurodegeneration. *Journal of Neuroimmunology, 273*(1–2), 8–21. doi:10.1016/j.jneuroim.2014.06.004.

Spielmans, G. I., & Kirsch, I. (2014). Drug approval and drug effectiveness. *Annual Review of Clinical Psychology, 10,* 741–766. doi:10.1146/annurev-clinpsy-050212-185533.

Spinath, B., Spinath, F. M., Harlaar, N., & Plomin, R. (2006). Predicting school achievement from general cognitive ability, self-perceived ability, and intrinsic value. *Intelligence, 34*(4), 363–374.

Spitz, H. I. (2009). Group psychotherapy. In B. J. Sadock, V. A. Sadock, & P. Ruiz (Eds.), *Kaplan & Sadock's comprehensive textbook of psychiatry* (pp. 2832–2856). Philadelphia, PA: Lippincott Williams & Wilkins.

Sprecher, S. (2014). Effects of actual (manipulated) and perceived similarity on liking in get-acquainted interactions: The role of communication. *Communication Monographs, 81,* 4–27. doi:10.1080/03637751.2013.839884.

Sprecher, S., & Duck, S. (1994). Sweet talk: The importance of perceived communication for romantic and friendship attraction experienced during a get-acquainted date. *Personality and Social Psychology Bulletin, 20,* 391–400.

Sprecher, S., Felmlee, D., Metts, S., & Cupach, W. (2015). Relationship initiation and development. In M. Mikulincer, P. R. Shaver, J. A. Simpson, & J. F. Dovidio (Eds.), *APA handbook of personality and social psychology Vol. 3: Interpersonal relations.* Washington, DC: American Psychological Association.

Sprenger, C., Eippert, F., Finsterbusch, J., Bingel, U., Rose, M., & Buchel, C. (2012). Attention modulates spinal cord responses to pain. *Current Biology, 22*(11), 1019–1022. doi:10.1016/j.cub.2012.04.006.

Sprenger, M. (2001). *Becoming a "wiz" at brain-based teaching: From translation to application.* Thousand Oaks, CA: Corwin Press.

Springer, S. P., & Deutsch, G. (1998). *Left brain, right brain.* New York, NY: W. H. Freeman.

Sproesser, G., Schupp, H. T., & Renner, B. (2014). The bright side of stress-induced eating: Eating more when stressed but less when pleased. *Psychological Science, 25*(1), 58–65. doi:10.1177/0956797613494849.

SPSP Board of Directors. (2016). The state of our science. Retrieved from http://spsp.org/news-center/blog/the-state-of-our-science-executive-board-perspectives.

Spurk, D., Keller, A. C., & Hirschi, A. (2016). Do bad guys get ahead or fall behind? Relationships of the Dark Triad of personality with objective and subjective career success. *Social Psychological and Personality Science, 7,* 113–121.

Squire, L. R. (1987). *Memory and brain.* New York, NY: Oxford University Press.

Squire, L. R. (1994). Declarative and nondeclarative memory: Multiple brain systems supporting learning and memory. In D. L. Schacter & E. Tulving (Eds.), *Memory systems.* Cambridge, MA: MIT Press.

Squire, L. R. (2004). Memory systems of the brain: A brief history and current perspective. *Neurobiology of Learning & Memory, 82*(3), 171–177.

Squire, L. R. (2009). Memory and brain systems: 1969–2009. *The Journal of Neuroscience, 29*(41), 12711–12716.

Squire, L. R., & Wixted, J. T. (2011). The cognitive neuroscience of human memory since H.M. *Annual Review of Neuroscience, 34,* 259–288.

Squire, L. R., Knowlton, B., & Musen, G. (1993). The structure and organization of memory. *Annual Review of Psychology, 44,* 453–495.

Sriram, T. G., & Silverman, J. J. (1998). The effects of stress on the respiratory system. In J. R. Hubbard & E. A. Workman (Eds.), *Handbook of stress medicine: An organ system approach.* New York, NY: CRC Press.

St. Jacques, P. L., & Schacter, D. L. (2013). Modifying memory: Selectively enhancing and updating personal memories for a museum tour by reactivating them. *Psychological Science, 24,* 537–543. doi:10.1177/0956797612457377.

Staats, A. W., & Staats, C. K. (1963). *Complex human behavior.* New York, NY: Holt, Rinehart & Winston.

Staddon, J. E. R., & Simmelhag, V. L. (1971). The "superstition" experiment: A reexamination of its implications for the principles of adaptive behavior. *Psychological Review, 78,* 3–43.

Stahre, M., Roeber, J., Kanny, D., Brewer, R. D., & Zhang, X. (2014). Contribution of excessive alcohol consumption to deaths and years of potential life lost in the United States. *Preventing Chronic Disease, 11,* 130293. doi:10.5888/pcd11.130293.

Staines, G. L. (2008). The relative efficacy of psychotherapy: Reassessing the methods-based paradigm. *Review of General Psychology, 12*(4), 330–343.

Stajkovic, A. D., & Luthans, F. (1998). Self-efficacy and work-related performance: A meta-analysis. *Psychological Bulletin, 124,* 240–261.

Staley, J. K., & Krystal, J. H. (2009). Radiotracer imaging and positron emission topography and single photon emission computer topography. In B. J. Sadock, V. A. Sadock, & P. Ruiz (Eds.), *Kaplan & Sadock's comprehensive textbook of psychiatry* (9th ed., Vol. 1, pp. 42–64). Philadelphia, PA: Lippincott, Williams & Wilkins.

Stalling, R. B. (1992). Mood and pain: The influence of positive and negative affect on reported body aches. *Journal of Social Behavior and Personality, 7*(2), 323–334.

Stanley, M. A., & Beidel, D. C. (2009). Behavior therapy. In B. J. Sadock, V. A. Sadock, & P. Ruiz (Eds.), *Kaplan & Sadock's comprehensive textbook of psychiatry* (pp. 2781–2803). Philadelphia, PA: Lippincott Williams & Wilkins.

Stanovich, K. E. (2003). The fundamental computational biases of human cognition: Heuristics that (sometimes) impair decision making and problem solving. In J. E. Davidson & R. J. Sternberg (Eds.), *The psychology of problem solving.* New York, NY: Cambridge University Press.

Stanovich, K. E. (2004). *How to think straight about psychology.* Boston, MA: Allyn & Bacon.

Stanovich, K. E. (2009). *Decision making and rationality in the modern world.* New York, NY: Oxford University Press.

Stanovich, K. E. (2009). *What intelligence tests miss: The psychology of rational thought.* New Haven, CT: Yale University Press.

Stanovich, K. E., & West, O. F. (2000). Individual differences in reasoning: Implications for the rationality debate. *Behavioural and Brain Sciences, 23,* 645–665.

Stanovich, K. E., West, R. F., & Toplak, M. (2016). *The rationality quotient: Toward a test of rational thinking.* Cambridge, MA: MIT press.

Stanovich, K. E., West, R. F., & Toplak, M. E. (2011). Intelligence and rationality. In R. J. Sternberg & S. B. Kaufman (Eds.), *Cambridge handbook of intelligence* (pp. 312–356). New York, NY: Cambridge University Press.

Starcevic, V. (2013). Is Internet addiction a useful concept? *Australian and New Zealand Journal of Psychiatry, 47,* 16–19. doi:10.1177/0004867412461693.

Stasser, G. (1991). Pooling of unshared information during group discussion. In S. Worchel, W. Wood, & J. Simpson (Eds.), *Group process and productivity.* Beverly Hills, CA: Sage.

Stasser, G., Vaughan, S. I., & Stewart, D. D. (2000). Pooling unshared information: The benefits of knowing how access to information is distributed among group members. *Organizational Behavior and Human Decision Processes, 82,* 102–116.

Statistics Canada. (1999). General social survey: Time use. *The Daily,* November 9, 1999. Retrieved June 21, 2005, from http://www.statcan.ca/Daily/English/991109/d991109a.htm.

Statistics Canada. (2001). *Disability among working-age adults (aged 15–64).* Retrieved February 12, 2008, from http://www.statcan.ca/english/freepub/89-577-XIEE/workage.htm.

Statistics Canada. (2003). Sources of workplace stress. *The Daily,* June 25, 2003. Retrieved June 21, 2005, from http://www.statcan.ca/Daily/English/030625/d030625c.htm.

Statistics Canada. (2006a). Trends in weight change among Canadian adults. *The Daily,* November 6, 2006.

Retrieved June 11, 2006, from http://www.statcan.ca/english/research/82-618-MIE/82-618-MIE2006005.htm.

Statistics Canada. (2006b). Deaths. *The Daily,* December 20, 2006. Retrieved March 1, 2007, from http://www.statcan.ca/Daily/English/061220/d061220b.htm.

Statistics Canada. (2006c). Health reports: Job satisfaction, stress, and depression. *The Daily,* October 17, 2006. Retrieved October 17, 2006, from http://www.statcan.gc.ca/Daily/English/061017/d061017a.htm.

Statistics Canada. (2007a). Physically active Canadians. *The Daily,* August 22, 2007. Retrieved August 22, 2007, from http://www.statcan.ca/Daily/English/070822/d070822b.htm.

Statistics Canada. (2007b). 2006 Census: Families, marital status, households and dwelling characteristics. *The Daily,* September 12, 2007. Retrieved December 9, 2007, from http://www.statcan.ca/Daily/English/070912/d070912a.htm.

Statistics Canada. (2007c). Maternity experiences survey. *The Daily,* November 27, 2007. Retrieved November 28, 2007, from http://www.statcan.ca/Daily/English/071127/d071127d.htm.

Statistics Canada. (2007d). Returning to work after childbirth. *The Daily,* December 19, 2007. Retrieved February 1, 2008, from http://www.statcan.ca/Daily/English/071219/d071219e.htm.

Statistics Canada. (2007e). Delayed transitions of young adults. *The Daily,* September 18, 2007. Retrieved September 18, 2007, from http://www.statcan.ca/Daily/English/070918/d070918b.htm.

Statistics Canada. (2007f). Work stress and job performance. *The Daily,* December 19, 2007. Retrieved January 2, 2008, from http://www.statcan.ca/Daily/English/071219/d071219d.htm.

Statistics Canada. (2007g). Going to see the doctor. *The Daily,* February 21, 2007. Retrieved Feburary 21, 2007, from http://www.statcan.ca/Daily/English/0702.

Statistics Canada. (2007h). Depression and work impairment. *The Daily,* January 12, 2007. Retrieved January 16, 2007, from http://www.statcan.ca/Daily/English/070112/d070112a.htm.

Statistics Canada. (2008). Sexual orientation and violence. *The Daily,* February 28, 2008. Retrieved June 20, 2011, from http://www.statcan.gc.ca/daily-quotidien/080228/dq080228c-eng.htm.

Statistics Canada. (2008a). Sleep patterns of Canadians. *The Daily,* April 22, 2008. Retrieved June 30, 2011, from http://www.statcan.gc.ca/daily-quotidien/080422/dq080422b-eng.htm.

Statistics Canada. (2008a). Study: Female offenders. *The Daily,* January 24, 2008. Retrieved January 30, 2008, from http://www.statcan.ca/Daily/English/080124/d080124a.htm.

Statistics Canada. (2008b). University enrolment. *The Daily,* February 7, 2008. Retrieved February 8, 2008, from http://www.statcan.ca/Daily/English/080207/d080207a.htm.

Statistics Canada. (2008c). Sexual orientation and victimization. *The Daily,* February 28, 2008. Retrieved February 28, 2008, from http://www.statcan.ca/Daily/English/080228/d080228c.htm.

Statistics Canada. (2008d). Sedentary behaviour and obesity. *The Daily,* June 18, 2008. Retrieved June 23, 2008, from http://www.statcan.ca/Daily/English/080618/d080618b.htm.

Statistics Canada. (2008e). Organized sports participation among children. *The Daily,* June 3, 2008. Retrieved June 8, 2008, from http://www.statcan.ca/Daily/English/080603/d080603a.htm.

Statistics Canada. (2008f). *Hate crime in Canada: Findings.* Retrieved August 24, 2008, from http://www.statcan.ca/english/research/ 85F0033MIE2008017/findings.

Statistics Canada. (2009). The Internet in our daily lives. Retrieved July 10, 2011, from http://www.statcan.gc.ca/pub/56f0004m/2006013/s1-eng.htm.

Statistics Canada. (2010). Gambling. *The Daily,* August 27, 2010. Retrieved June 30, 2011, from http://www.statcan.gc.ca/daily-quotidien/100827/dq100827b-eng.htm.

Statistics Canada. (2010). Suicide rate by sex and by age group. Retrieved June 1, 2011, from http://www40.statcan.ca/l01/cst01/hlth66a-eng.htmShimizu.

Statistics Canada. (2010a). Blood pressure in adults. *The Daily,* February 17, 2010. Retrieved February 17, 2010, from http://www.statcan.gc.ca/daily-quotidien/100217/dq100217b-eng.htm.

Statistics Canada. (2010a). General social survey: Victimization. *The Daily,* September 28, 2010. Retrieved September 30, 2010, from http://www.statcan.gc.ca/daily-quotien/100928/dq100928a-eng.htm.

Statistics Canada. (2010a). Police-reported hate crime. *The Daily,* June 14, 2010. Retreived July 10, 2011, from http://www.statcan.gc.ca/daily-quotidien/100614/dq100614b-eng.htm.

Statistics Canada. (2010b). A portrait of couples in mixed unions. *Canadian Social Trends,* no. 89. Retrieved July 15, 2011, from http://www.statcan.gc.ca/pub/11-008-x/2010001/article/11143-eng.htm.

Statistics Canada. (2010b). Deaths. *The Daily,* February 23, 2010. Retrieved Februray 23, 2010, from http://www.statcan.gc.ca/daily-quotidien/100223/dq100223a-eng.htm.

Statistics Canada. (2010b). Survey methods and practices. *The Daily,* September 27, 2010. Retrieved September 30, 2010, from http://www.statcan.gc.ca/daily-quotien/100927/dq100927e-eng.htm.

Statistics Canada. (2010c). Canadian internet use survey. *The Daily,* May 10, 2010. Retrieved May 15, 2010, from http://www.statcan.gc.ca/daily-quotidien/100510/dq100510a-eng.htm.

Statistics Canada. (2010c). Canadian measures survey. *The Daily,* January 13, 2010. Retrieved January 14, 2010, from http://www.statcan.gc.ca/daily-quotidien/100113/dq100113a-eng.htm.

Statistics Canada. (2011). 2011 National Household survey: Portrait of Canada's labour force. *The Daily,* Wednesday, June 26. Retrieved from http://www.statcan.gc.ca/daily-quotidien/130626/dq130626b-eng.htm.

Statistics Canada. (2011). Adult obesity in Canada and the United States. Retrieved February 1, 2011, from http://www.statcan.gc.ca/pub/82-625-x/2011001/article/11411-eng.htm.

Statistics Canada. (2011). Adult obesity prevalence in Canada and the United States. Retrieved June 20, 2011, from http://www.statcan.gc.ca/pub/82-625-x/2011001/article/11411-eng.htm.

Statistics Canada. (2011). *Immigration and ethnocultural diversity in Canada: National Household survey, 2011.* Retrieved from http://www12.statcan.gc.ca/nhs-enm/2011/as-sa/99-010-x/99-010-x2011001-eng.cfm.

Statistics Canada. (2011). *Immigration and ethnocultural diversity in Canada.* Retrieved from http://www12.statcan.gc.ca/nhs-enm/2011/as-sa/99-010-x/99-010-x2011001-eng.cfm.

Statistics Canada. (2011). *Immigration and ethnocultural diversity in Canada.* Retrieved from http://www12.statcan.gc.ca/nhs-enm/2011/as-sa/99-010-x/99-010-x2011001-eng.cfm.

Statistics Canada. (2011). Retirement, health and employment among older Canadians. *The Daily,* January 31, 2011. Retrieved Feburary 5, 2011, from http://www.statcan.gc.ca/daily-quotidien/110131/dq110131c-eng.htm.

Statistics Canada. (2012). Suicide rates, an overview, 1950 to 2009. *The Daily, Wednesday,* July 25, 2012. Retrieved from http://www.statcan.gc.ca/daily-quotidien/120725/dq120725a-eng.htm.

Statistics Canada. (2013). *Anxiety disorders.* Retrieved from http://www.statcan.gc.ca/pub/82-619-m/2012004/sections/sectionb-eng.htm.

Statistics Canada. (2013). Canadian community health survey: Mental health, 2012. *The Daily,* September 18, 2013. Retrieved from http://www.statcan.gc.ca/daily-quotidien/130918/dq130918a-eng.htm.

Statistics Canada. (2013a). Deaths, 2010 and 2011. *The Daily,* Wednesday, September 25, 2013. Retrieved from http://www.statcan.gc.ca/daily-quotidien/130925/dq130925a-eng.htm.

Statistics Canada. (2013b). Perceived life stress. http://www.statcan.gc.ca/pub/82-229-x/2009001/status/pls-eng.htm.

Statistics Canada. (2014). Police-reported hate crimes, 2012. *The Daily,* Thursday, June 26, 2014. Retrieved from http://www.statcan.gc.ca/daily-quotidien/140626/dq140626b-eng.htm.

Statistics Canada. (2014). Who gets any sleep these days? Sleep patterns of Canadians. Retrieved from http://www.statcan.gc.ca/pub/11-008-x/2008001/article/10553-eng.htm.

Statistics Canada. (2014a). Receiving care at home. *The Daily, Friday, June 13, 2014.* Retrieved from http://www.statcan.gc.ca/pub/89-652-x/89-652-x2014002-eng.htm.

Statistics Canada. (2014b). Prevalence of migraine in the Canadian household population. *The Daily,* Wednesday, June 18. Retrieved from http://www5.statcan.gc.ca/olc-cel/olc.action?objId=82-003-X201400614033&objType=47&lang=en&limit=0.

Statistics Canada. (2014c). Causes of death, 2010 and 2011. *The Daily,* January 28, 2014. Retrieved from http://www.statcan.gc.ca/daily-quotidien/140128/dq140128b-eng.htm.

Statistics Canada. (2015). Aboriginal statistics at a glance. Retrieved from http://www.statcan.gc.ca/pub/89-645-x/89-645-x2015001-eng.htm.

Statistics Canada. (2015). Homicide in Canada, 2014. *The Daily,* November 25, 2015. Retrieved from https://www.statcan.gc.ca/daily-quotidien/151125/dq151125a-eng.htm.

Statistics Canada. (2015). *Linguistic characteristics of Canadians.* Retrieved from http://www12.statcan.gc.ca/census-recensement/2011/as-sa/98-314-x/98-314-x2011001-eng.cfm.

Statistics Canada. (2015). *Perceived life stress, 2014.* Retrieved from http://www.statcan.gc.ca/pub/82-625-x/2015001/article/14188-eng.htm.

Statistics Canada. (2015). *Prescription medication use by Canadians aged 6 to 79.* Retrieved from https://www.statcan.gc.ca/pub/82-003-x/2014006/article/14032-eng.htm.

Statistics Canada. (2015). *Rates of selected mental or substance use disorders, lifetime and 12 month, Canada, household population 15 and older.* Retrieved from http://www.statcan.gc.ca/pub/82-624-x/2013001/article/tbl/tbl-eng.htm.

Statistics Canada. (2015a). Same-sex couples and sexual orientation ... by the numbers. Retrieved from https://www.statcan.gc.ca/eng/dai/smr08/2015/smr08_203_2015.

Statistics Canada. (2015b). Obesity among children and adolescents, 1978, 2004, and 2009-2013. Retrieved from http://www.statcan.gc.ca/daily-quotidien/150826/dq150826a-eng.htm.

Statistics Canada. (2015c). Overweight and obese adults (self-reported), 2014. Retrieved from http://www.statcan.gc.ca/pub/82-625-x/2015001/article/14185-eng.htm.

Statistics Canada. (2015d). Directly measured physical activity of children and youth, 2012 and 2013. Retrieved from http://www.statcan.gc.ca/pub/82-625-x/2015001/article/14136-eng.htm.

Statistics Canada. (2015e). Portrait of families and living arrangements in Canada. Retrieved from http://www.statcan.gc.ca/pub/82-625-x/2015001/article/14136-eng.htm.

Statistics Canada. (2016). Aboriginal people's survey 2012: Lifetime suicidal thoughts among First Nations living off reserve, Métis and Inuit, aged 26 to 59. Retrieved from http://www.statcan.gc.ca/pub/89-653-x/89-653-x2016008-eng.htm.

Statistics Canada. (2016). Canadian health measures survey: Household and physical measures data, 2014 and 2015. Retrieved from http://www.statcan.gc.ca/daily-quotidien/161013/dq161013c-eng.htm.

Statistics Canada. (2016). *Health reports: Physical activity and sedentary behaviour of Canadian children aged three to five.* Retrieved from http://www.statcan.gc.ca/daily-quotidien/160921/dq160921b-eng.htm.

Statistics Canada. (2016). *HIV in Canada: Surveillance summary tables, 2014–2015.* Retrieved from health/services/publications/diseases-conditions/

hiv-in-canada-surveillance-summary-tables-2014-2015
.html.

Statistics Canada. (2016). *Immigration and ethnocultural diversity in Canada.* Retrieved from http://www12.statcan .gc.ca/nhs-enm/2011/as-sa/99-010-x/99-010-x2011001 -eng.cfm.

Statistics Canada. (2016). Police-reported data on hate crime and cybercrime. Retrieved from http://www.statcan .gc.ca/daily-quotidien/160412/dq160412b-eng.htm.

Statistics Canada. (2016). Smokers, by sex, provinces, and territories. Retrieved from http://www.statcan.gc.ca/ tables-tableaux/sum-som/l01/cst01/health74b-eng.htm.

Statistics Canada. (2016). *Study: Difficulty accessing health care services in Canada 2003 to 2013.* Retrieved from http://www.statcan.gc.ca/pub/82-624-x/2016001/ article/14683-eng.pdf.

Statistics Canada. (2016). Victimization of Aboriginal people in Canada, 2014. Retrieved from http://www.statcan .gc.ca/pub/85-002-x/2016001/article/14631-eng.htm.

Statistics Canada. (2016a). *Heavy drinking.* Retrieved from http://www.statcan.gc.ca/pub/82-229-x/2009001/ deter/hdx-eng.htm.

Statistics Canada. (2016b). Impaired driving in Canada, 2015. *The Daily,* December 14, 2016. Retrieved from https://www.statcan.gc.ca/daily-quotidien/161214/ dq161214b-eng.htm.

Statistics Canada. (2017). Police-reported hate crimes, 2015. Retrieved from https://www.statcan.gc.ca/pub/85 -002-x/2017001/article/14832-eng.htm.

Statistics Canada. (2017). Police-reported hate crimes, 2015. Retrieved from https://www.statcan.gc.ca/pub/85 -002-x/2017001/article/14832-eng.htm.

Statistics Canada. (2017). Study: Women in Canada: The girl child. *The Daily, February 22, 2017.* Retrieved from http://www.statcan.gc.ca/daily-quotidien/170222/ dq170222b-eng.htm.

Statistics Canada. (2017a). *Health at a Glance.* Retrieved from http://www.statcan.gc.ca/pub/82-624-x/2012001/ article/11696-eng.htm.

Statistics Canada. (2017b). *Life expectancy.* Retrieved from https://www.statcan.gc.ca/eng/help/bb/info/life.

Steblay, N. K., Wells, G. L., & Douglass, A. B. (2014). The eyewitness post identification feedback effect 15 years later: Theoretical and policy implications. *Psychology, Public Policy, and Law, 20*(1), 1–18. doi:10.1037/law0000001.

Steele, C. (2011). Pursuing effective integrated education. *Journal of Social Issues, 67*(3), 431–434.

Steele, C. M. (1992, April). Race and the schooling of black Americans. *The Atlantic Monthly,* pp. 68–78.

Steele, C. M. (1997). A threat in the air: How stereotypes shape intellectual identity and performance. *American Psychologist, 52,* 613–629.

Steele, K. M. (2003). Do rats show a Mozart effect? *Music Perception, 21,* 251–265.

Steiger, H., Bruce, K. R., & Israël, M. (2013). Eating disorders: Anorexia nervosa, bulimia nervosa, and binge eating disorder. In G. Stricker, T. A. Widiger, & I. B. Weiner (Eds.), *Handbook of psychology: Vol. 8. Clinical psychology* (2nd ed.). New York, NY: Wiley.

Stein, B. E., & Meredith, M. A. (1993). *Vision, touch, and audition: Making sense of it all.* Cambridge, MA: MIT Press.

Stein, B. E., Wallace, M. T., & Stanford, T. R. (2000). Brain mechanisms for synthesizing information from different sensory modalities. In E. B. Goldstein (Ed.), *Blackwell handbook of perception.* Malden, MA: Blackwell.

Stein, B. E., Wallace, M. T., & Stanford, T. R. (2000). Merging sensory signals in the brain: The development of multisensory integration in the superior colliculus. In M. S. Gazzaniga (Ed.), *The new cognitive neurosciences.* Cambridge, MA: The MIT Press.

Stein, G. (1898). Cultivated motor automatism: A study of character in its relation to attention. *The Psychological Review, 5,* 305, 295–306.

Stein, M. B., Walker, J. R., Hazen, A. L., & Forde, D. R. (1997). Full and partial posttraumatic stress disorder: Findings from a community survey. *American Journal of Psychiatry, 154,* 1114–1119.

Stein, S., & Deonarine, J. M. (2015). Current concepts in the assessment of emotional intelligence. In S. Goldstein, D. Princiotta, & J. A. Naglieri (Eds.), *Handbook of intelligence: Evolutionary theory, historical perspectives, and current concepts* (pp. 381–402). New York, NY: Springer.

Steinberg, L. (2001). We know some things: Adolescent–parent relationships in retrospect and prospect. *Journal of Research on Adolescence, 11,* 1–20.

Steinberg, L. (2008). A social neuroscience perspective on adolescent risk-taking. *Developmental Review, 28*(1), 78–106. doi:10.1016/j.dr.2007.08.002.

Steinberg, L., & Levine, A. (1997). *You and your adolescent: A parents' guide for ages 10 to 20.* New York, NY: Harper Perennial.

Steinberg, L., & Morris, A. S. (2001). Adolescent development. *Annual Review of Psychology, 52,* 83–110.

Steinberg, L., & Steinberg, W. (1994). *Crossing paths: How your child's adolescence triggers your own crisis.* New York, NY: Simon & Schuster.

Stellar, E. (1954). The physiology of motivation. *Psychological Review, 61,* 5–22.

Stem cell basics. (2007). *Stem cell information.* National Institutes of Health Resource for Stem Cell Research. Retrieved Feburary 11, 2008, from http://stemcells.nih .gov./info/basics.

Stephens, N. M., Markus, H. R., & Phillips. L. T. (2014). Social class culture cycles: How three gateway contexts shape selves and fuel inequality. *Annual Review of Psychology, 65,* 1–16.

Stephens, R. S. (1999). Cannabis and hallucinogens. In B. S. McCrady & E. E. Epstein (Eds.), *Addictions: A comprehensive guidebook.* New York, NY: Oxford University Press.

Steptoe, A. (2007). Stress effects: Overview. In G. Fink (Ed.), *Encyclopedia of stress.* San Diego, CA: Elsevier.

Steptoe, A., Shankar, A., Demakakos, P., & Wardle, J. (2013). Social isolation, loneliness, and all-cause mortality in older men and women. *PNAS Proceedings of the National Academy of Sciences of the United States of America, 110,* 5797–5801.

Steriade, M. (2005). Brain electrical activity and sensory processing during waking and sleep states. In M. H. Kryger, T. Roth, & W. C. Dement (Eds.). *Principles and practice of sleep medicine.* Philadelphia, PA: Elsevier Saunders.

Stern, C., & West, T. V. (2016). Ideological differences in anchoring and adjustment during social inferences. *Personality and Social Psychology Bulletin, 42,* 1466–1480.

Sternberg, R. J. (1985). *Beyond IQ: A triarchic theory of human intelligence.* New York, NY: Cambridge University Press.

Sternberg, R. J. (1986). *Intelligence applied: Understanding and increasing your intellectual skills.* New York, NY: Harcourt Brace Jovanovich.

Sternberg, R. J. (1988a). A three-facet model of creativity. In R. J. Sternberg (Ed.), *The nature of creativity: Contemporary psychological perspectives.* Cambridge, England: Cambridge University Press.

Sternberg, R. J. (1988b). *The triarchic mind: A new theory of human intelligence.* New York, NY: Viking.

Sternberg, R. J. (1991). Theory-based testing of intellectual abilities: Rationale for the triarchic abilities test. In H. A. H. Rowe (Ed.), *Intelligence: Reconceptualization and measurement.* Hillsdale, NJ: Erlbaum.

Sternberg, R. J. (1999). The theory of successful intelligence. *Review of General Psychology, 3,* 292–316.

Sternberg, R. J. (2003a). Construct validity of the theory of successful intelligence. In R. J. Sternberg, J. Lautrey, & T. I. Lubart (Eds.), *Models of intelligence: International perspectives.* Washington, DC: American Psychological Association.

Sternberg, R. J. (2003b). My house is a very, very, very fine house—But it is not the only house. In H. Nyborg (Ed.), *The scientific study of general intelligence: Tribute to Arthur R. Jensen.* Oxford, UK: Pergamon.

Sternberg, R. J. (2004). Culture and Intelligence. *American Psychologist, 59,* 325–338.

Sternberg, R. J. (2005a). There are no public policy implications: A reply to Rushton and Jensen. *Psychology, Public Policy, and the Law, 11,* 295–301.

Sternberg, R. J. (2005b). The triarchic theory of successful intelligence. In D. P. Flanagan & P. L. Harrison (Eds.), *Contemporary intellectual assessment: Theories, tests and issues* (pp. 103–119). New York, NY: Guillford Press.

Sternberg, R. J. (2006). A duplex theory of love. In R. J. Sternberg & K. Weis (Eds.), *The new psychology of love.* New Haven, CT: Yale University Press.

Sternberg, R. J. (2007). Intelligence and culture. In S. Kitayama & D. Cohen (Eds.), *Handbook of cultural psychology* (pp. 547–568). New York, NY: Guilford.

Sternberg, R. J. (2009). Component processes in analogical reasoning. In J. C. Kaufman & E. L. Grigorenko (Eds.), *The essential Sternberg: Essays on intelligence, psychology, and education* (pp. 145–179). New York, NY: Springer.

Sternberg, R. J. (2011). The flaw of overall rankings. *Inside Higher Education,* January 24, 2011. Retrieved February 28, 2011 from http://www.insidehighered.com/ views/2011/01/24/sternberg.

Sternberg, R. J. (2012). The triarchic theory of successful intelligence. In D. P. Flanagan, & P. L. Harrison (Eds.), *Contemporary intellectual assessment: Theories, tests, and issues* (3rd ed.). New York, NY: Guilford Press.

Sternberg, R. J. (2015). Still searching for the Zipperump-a-Zoo: A reflection after 40 years. *Child Development Perspectives, 9*(2), 106–110.

Sternberg, R. J. (2016). Groundhog day: Is the field of human intelligence caught in a time warp? A comment on Kovacs and Conway. *Psychological Inquiry, 27,* 236–240.

Sternberg, R. J., Conway, B. E., Ketron, J. L., & Bernstein, M. (1981). People's conceptions of intelligence. *Journal of Personality and Social Psychology, 41,* 37–55.

Sternberg, R. J., Grigorenko, E. L., & Kidd, K. K. (2005). Intelligence, race, and genetics. *American Psychologist, 60,* 45–69.

Sternberg, R. J., & O'Hara, L. A. (1999). Creativity and intelligence. In R. J. Sternberg (Ed.), *Handbook of creativity.* New York, NY: Cambridge University Press.

Sternberg, R. J., & Williams, W. M. (1997). Does the Graduate Record Exam predict meaningful success in the graduate training of psychologists?: A case study. *American Psychologist, 52,* 630–641.

Sterniczuk, R. Theou, O., Rusak, B., & Rockwood, K. (2013). Sleep disturbance is associated with incident dementia and mortality. *Current Alzheimer Research, 10,* 767–775.

Stevens, G., Raphael, B., & Dobson, M. (2007). Effects of public disasters and mass violence. In G. Fink (Ed.), *Encyclopedia of stress.* San Diego, CA: Elsevier.

Stevenson, S. (2014). *Sleep smarter: 21 proven tips to sleep your way to a better body, better health and bigger success.* Florissant, MO: Model House Publishing.

Stewart, A. J., Ostrove, J. M., & Helson, R. (2001). Middle aging in women: Patterns of personality change from the 30s to the 50s. *Journal of Adult Development, 8*(1), 23–37.

Stewart, D. E., Gagnon, A., Saucier, J.-F., Wahoush, O., & Dougherty, G. (2008). Postpartum depression symptoms in newcomers. *Canadian Journal of Psychiatry, 53,* 121–124.

Stewart, J. A., Russakoff, M., & Stewart, J. W. (2014). Pharmacotherapy, ECT, and TMS. In J. L. Cutler, (Ed.), *Psychiatry* (3rd ed.). New York, NY: Oxford University Press.

Stewart-Williams, S. (2004). The placebo puzzle: Putting the pieces together. *Health Psychology, 23,* 198–206.

Stice, E. (2001). Risk factors for eating pathology: Recent advances and future directions. In R. H. Striegel-Moore & L. Smolak (Eds.), *Eating disorders: Innovative directions in research and practice* (pp. 51–74). Washington, DC: American Psychological Association.

Stickgold, R. (2013). Parsing the role of sleep in memory processing. *Current Opinion in Neurobiology, 23,* 847–853. doi:10.1016/j.conb.2013.04.002.

Stickgold, R., & Walker, M. P. (2004). To sleep, perchance to gain creative insight. *Trends in Cognitive Sciences, 8*(5), 191–192.

Stickgold, R., & Wamsley, E. J. (2011). Why we dream. In M. H. Kryger, T. Roth, & W. C. Dement (Eds.), *Principles and practice of sleep medicine* (5th ed.). Saint Louis, MO: Elsevier Saunders.

Stockman, A. (2010). Color mixing. In E. B. Goldstein (Ed.), *Encyclopedia of perception*. Thousand Oaks, CA: Sage.

Stoddard, G. (1943). *The meaning of intelligence*. New York, NY: Macmillan.

Stoet, G., & Geary, D. C. (2013). Sex differences in mathematics and reading achievement are inversely related: Within- and across-nation assessment of 10 years of PISA data. *PLoS ONE, 8,* e57988. doi:10.1371/journal.pone.0057988.

Stoicheff, B. (2002). *Gerhard Herzberg: An illustrious life in science*. Ottawa, ON: NRC Press, McGill–Queens Press.

Stone, L. (1977). *The family, sex and marriage in England 1500–1800*. New York, NY: Harper & Row.

Stone, W. N. (2008). Group psychotherapy. In A. Tasman, J. Kay, J. A. Lieberman, M. B. First, & M. Maj (Eds.), *Psychiatry* (3rd ed.). New York, NY: Wiley-Blackwell.

Stoner, J. A. F. (1961). *A comparison of individual and group decisions involving risk*. Unpublished master's thesis, Massachusetts Institute of Technology.

Stoner, R., Chow, M. L., Boyle, M. P., Sunkin, S. M., Mouton, P. R., Roy, S., . . . Courchesne, E. (2014). Patches of disorganization in the neocortex of children with autism. *The New England Journal of Medicine, 370,* 1209–1219. doi:10.1056/NEJMoa1307491.

Stoohs, R. A., Blum, H. C., Haselhorst, M., Duchna, H. W., Guilleminault, C., & Dement, W. C. (1998). Normative data on snoring: A comparison between younger and older adults. *European Respiratory Journal, 11,* 451–457.

Storandt, M. (2008). Cognitive deficits in the early stages of Alzheimer's disease. *Current Directions in Psychological Science, 4,* 198–202.

Storm, B. C. (2011). The benefit of forgetting in thinking and remembering. *Current Directions in Psychological Science, 20,* 291–295. doi:10.1177/0963721411418469.

Stowell, J. R. (2008). Stress and stressors. In S. F. Davis & W. Buskist (Eds.), *21st century psychology: A reference handbook*. Thousand Oaks, CA: Sage.

Stowell, J. R., Robles, T. F., & Kane, H. S. (2013). Psychoneuroimmunology: Mechanisms, individuals differences, and interventions. In A. M. Nezu, C. M. Nezu, P. A. Geller, & I. B. Weiner (Eds.), *Handbook of psychology: Vol. 9. Health psychology* (2nd ed.). New York, NY: Wiley.

Strahan, E. J., Lafrance, A., Wilson, A. E., Ethier, N., Spencer, S. J., & Zanna, M. P. (2008). Victoria's dirty secret: How sociocultural norms influence adolescent girls and women. *Personality and Social Psychology Bulletin, 34*(2), 288–301.

Strange, D., Clifasefi, S., & Garry, M. (2007). False memories. In M. Garry & H. Hayne (Eds.), *Do justice and let the sky fall: Elizabeth F. Lotus and her contributions to science, law, and academic freedom*. Mahwah, NJ: Erlbaum.

Stranges, S., Tigbe, W., Gomez-Olive, F. X., Thorogood, M., & Kandala, N. (2012). Sleep problems: An emerging global epidemic? Findings from the INDEPTH WHO-SAGE study among more than 40,000 older adults from 8 countries across Africa and Asia. *SLEEP, 35,* 1173–1181.

Straus, M. A., & Stewart, J. H. (1999). Corporal punishment by American parents: National data on prevalence, chronicity, severity, and duration, in relation to child family characteristics. *Clinical Child & Family Psychology Review, 2*(2), 55–70.

Straus, M. A., Douglas, E. M., & Medeiros, R. A. (2014). *The primordial violence: Spanking children, psychological development, violence, and crime*. New York, NY: Routledge/Taylor & Francis Group.

Strayer, D. L., Drews, F. A., & Crouch, D. J. (2006). A comparison of the cell phone driver and the drunk driver. *Human Factors, 48,* 381–391.

Streissguth, A. P. (2007). Offspring effects of prenatal alcohol exposure from birth to 25 years: The Seattle prospective longitudinal study. *Journal of Clinical Psychology in Medical Settings, 14,* 81–101.

Streissguth, A. P., Bookstein, F. L., Barr, H. M., Sampson, P. D., O'Malley, K., & Young, J. K. (2004). Risk factors for adverse life outcomes in fetal alcohol syndrome and fetal alcohol effects. *Journal of Developmental & Behavioral Pediatrics, 25,* 228–238.

Strenze, T. (2007). Intelligence and socioeconomic success: A meta-analytic review of longitudinal research. *Intelligence, 35,* 401–426.

Strick, M., van Baaren, R. B., Holland, R. W., & van Knippenberg, A. (2009). Humor in advertisements enhances product liking by mere association. *Journal of Experimental Psychology: Applied, 15,* 35–45.

Striegel-Moore, R. H., & Bulik, C. M. (2007). Risk factors for eating disorders. *American Psychologist, 62,* 181–198.

Strobe, M., Schut, H., & Boener, K. (2017). Cautioning health-care professionals: Bereaved persons are misguided through the stages of grief. *Omega: Journal of Death and Dying, 74,* 455–483.

Stroup, T. S., Lawrence, R. E., Abbas, A. I., Miller, B. R., Perkins, D. O., & Lieberman, J. A. (2014). Schizophrenia spectrum and other psychotic disorders. In R. E. Hales, S. C. Yudofsky, & L. W. Roberts (Eds.), *The American Psychiatric Publishing textbook of psychiatry* (6th ed., pp. 273–310). Washington, DC: American Psychiatric Publishing.

Struthers, C. W., Dupuis, R., & Eaton, J. (2005). Promoting forgiveness among co-workers following a workplace transgression: The effects of social motivation training. *Canadian Journal of Behavioural Sciences* (Special Issue on Creating a Healthy Workplace) 37(4), 299–308.

Stubbe, J. H., Posthuma, D., Boomsma, D. I., & de Geus, E. J. C. (2005). Heritability of life satisfaction in adults: A twin study. *Psychological Medicine, 35,* 1581–1588.

Stumbrys, T., & Daniel, M. (2010). An exploratory study of creative problem solving in lucid dreams: Preliminary findings and methodological considerations. *International Journal of Dream Research, 3,* 121–129.

Stunkard, A. J., Harris, J. R., Pederson, N. L., & McClearn, G. E. (1990). The body-mass index of twins who have been reared apart. *New England Journal of Medicine, 322,* 1483–1487.

Sturm, V. E., Ascher, E. A., Miller, B. L., & Levenson, R. W. (2008). Diminished self-conscious emotional responding in frontotemporal lobar degeneration patients. *Emotion, 8,* 861–869.

Subotnik, K. L., Nuechterlein, K. H., Ventura, J., Gitlin, M. J., Marder, S., Mintz, J., . . . Singh, I. R. (2011). Risperidone nonadherence and return of positive symptoms in the early course of schizophrenia. *American Journal of Psychiatry, 168*(3), 286–292.

Sudak, H. S. (2005). Suicide. In B. J. Sadock & V. A. Sadock (Eds.), *Kaplan & Sadock's comprehensive textbook of psychiatry*. Philadelphia, PA: Lippincott, WIlliams & Wilkins.

Suddendorf, T., & Corballis, M. C. (2007). The evolution of foresight: What is mental time travel, and is it unique to humans? *Behavioral and Brain Sciences, 30,* 299–313.

Sue, D. W. (2010). Microaggressions, marginality, and oppression: An introduction. In D. W. Sue (Ed.), *Microaggressions and marginality: Manifestation, dynamics, and impact*. Hoboken, NJ: Wiley.

Sue, D. W., & Sue, D. (1999). *Counseling the culturally different: Theory and practice*. New York, NY: Wiley.

Sue, S. (2003). In defense of cultural competency in psychotherapy and treatment. *American Psychologist, 58,* 964–970.

Sue, S., & Zane, N. (1987). The role of culture and cultural techniques in psychotherapy: A critique and reformulation. *American Psychologist, 42,* 37–45.

Sue, S., Cheng, J. Y., Saad, C. S., & Chu, J. P. (2012). Asian American mental health: A call to action. *American Psychologist, 67,* 532–544. doi:10.1037/a0028900.

Sue, S., Zane, N., Hall, G., & Berger, L. K. (2009). The case for cultural competency in psychotherapeutic interventions. *Annual Review of Psychology, 60,* 525–548.

Sue, S., Zane, N., & Young, K. (1994). Research on psychotherapy with culturally diverse populations. In A. E. Bergin & S. L. Garfield (Eds.), *Handbook of psychotherapy and behavior change* (4th ed.). New York, NY: Wiley.

Suedfeld, P. (2003). Canadian space psychology: The future may be almost here. *Canadian Psychology, 44,* 85–92.

Suedfeld, P. (2016). On the road from WEIRD to STEM, psychology hits a bump. *Canadian Psychology, 57,* 60–64.

Suedfeld, P., & Steel, G. D. (2000). The environmental psychology of capsule inhabitants. *Annual Review of Psychology, 51,* 227–253.

Sugita, Y. (2009). Innate face processing. *Current Opinion in Neurobiology, 19*(1), 39–44. doi:10.1016/j.conb.2009.03.001.

Sugiyama, L. S. (2005). Physical attractiveness in adaptionist perspective. In D. M. Buss (Ed.), *The handbook of evolutionary psychology*. New York, NY: Wiley.

Sullivan, M. D., Prescott, Y., Goldberg, D., & Bialystok, E. (2016). Executive control processes in verbal and nonverbal working memory: The role of aging and bilingualism. *Linguistic Approaches to Bilingualism, 6,* 147–170.

Suls, J. M., Luger, T., & Martin, R. (2010). The biopsychosocial model and the use of theory in health psychology. In J. M. Suls, K. W. Davidson, & R. M. Kaplan (Eds.), *Handbook of health psychology and behavioral medicine* (pp. 15–27). New York, NY: Guilford Press.

Summerfeldt, L. J. (2004). Understanding and treating incompleteness in obsessive-compulsive disorder. *Journal of Clinical Psychology, 60,* 1155–1168.

Summerfeldt, L. J., Richter, M. A., Antony, M. M., & Swinson, R. P. (1999). Symptom structure in obsessive-compulsive disorder: A confirmatory factor-analytic study. *Behaviour Research and Therapy, 37,* 297–311.

Sunderland, A., & Findlay, L. C. (2015). *Perceived need for mental health care in Canada: Results from the 2012 Canadian community health survey—Mental health*. Retrieved from http://www.statcan.gc.ca/pub/82-003-x/2013009/article/11863-eng.htm.

Sundin, J. J., Fear, N. T., Iversen, A. A., Rona, R. J., & Wessely, S. S. (2010). PTSD after deployment to Iraq: Conflicting rates, conflicting claims. *Psychological Medicine: A Journal of Research in Psychiatry and the Allied Sciences, 40*(3), 367–382.

Super, C. M. (1976). Environmental effects on motor development: A case of African infant precocity. *Developmental Medicine and Child Neurology, 18,* 561–567.

Supreme Court upholds spanking law. (2004, January 30). *CBC News*. Retrieved March 13, 2008, from http://www.cbc.ca/news/story/2004/01/30/spanking040130.htm.

Surtees, P., & Wainwright, N. (2007). Life events and health. In G. Fink (Ed.), *Encyclopedia of stress*. San Diego, CA: Elsevier.

Surtees, P., Wainwright, N., Luben, R., Wareham, N., Bingham, S., & Khaw, K. (2008). Depression and ischemic heart disease mortality: Evidence from the EPIC-Norfolk United Kingdom Prospective Cohort Study. *American Journal of Psychiatry, 165*(4), 515–523.

Susman, E. J., & Dorn, L. D. (2013). Puberty: Its role in development. In R. M. Lerner, M. A. Easterbrooks, J. Mistry, & I. B. Weiner (Eds.), *Handbook of psychology: Vol. 6. Developmental psychology*. New York, NY: Wiley.

Susman, E. J., Dorn, L. D., & Schiefelbein, V. L. (2003). Puberty, sexuality, and health. In R. M. Lerner, M. A. Easterbrooks, & J. Mistry (Eds.), *Handbook of psychology (Vol. 6): Developmental psychology*. New York, NY: Wiley.

Susser, E. B., Neugebauer, R., Hoek, H. W., Brown, A. S., Lin, S., Labovitz, D., & Gorman, J. M. (1996). Schizophrenia after prenatal famine: Further evidence. *Archives of General Psychiatry, 53,* 25–31.

Sussman, A. (2007). Mental Illness and creativity: A neurological view of the "Tortured Artist." *Stanford Journal of Neuroscience, 1,* 21–24.

Sussman, N. (2009). Selective serotonin reuptake inhibitors. In B. J. Sadock, V. A. Sadock, & P. Ruiz (Eds.), *Kaplan & Sadock's comprehensive textbook of psychiatry* (pp. 3190–3205). Philadelphia, PA: Lippincott Williams & Wilkins.

Sustein, C., & Thaler, R. (2016). The two friends who changed how we think about how we think. *The New Yorker*, December 7, 2016. Retrieved from https://www.newyorker.com/books/page-turner/the-two-friends-who-changed-how-we-think-about-how-we-think.

Sutker, P. B., & Allain, A. J. (2001). Antisocial personality disorder. In P. B. Sutker, H. E. Adams, P. B. Sutker, & H. E. Adams (Eds.), *Comprehensive handbook of psychopathology* (3rd ed.). New York, NY: Kluwer Academic/Plenum.

Suzuki, L. A., Short, E. L., & Lee, C. S. (2011). Racial and ethnic group differences in intelligence in the United States. In R. J. Sternberg, & S. B. Kaufman (Eds.), *Cambridge handbook of intelligence*. New York, NY: Cambridge University Press.

Swain, M., Kinnear, P., & Steinman, L. (2011). *Sociocultural theory in second language education: An introduction through narratives*. Bristol, UK: Multilingual Matters.

Swan, G. E., Hudmon, K. S., & Khroyan, T. V. (2003). Tobacco dependence. In A. M. Nezu, C. M. Nezu, & P. A. Geller (Eds.), *Handbook of psychology: Vol. 9. Health Psychology*. New York, NY: Wiley.

Swann, W. B., Jolanda, J., Gomez, A., Whitehouse, H., & Bastian, B. (2012). When group membership gets personal. *Psychological Review, 119*, 441–456.

Swanson, J. A. (2016). Trends in literature about emerging adulthood: Review of empirical studies. *Emerging Adulthood, 4*, 391–402.

Swanson, S. A., Crow, S. J., Le Grange, D., Swendsen, J., & Merikangas, K. R. (2011). Prevalence and correlates of eating disorders in adolescents: Results from the national comorbidity survey replication adolescent supplement. *Archives of General Psychiatry, 68*, 714–723.

Sweatt, J. D. (2009). Long-term potentiation: A candidate cellular mechanism for information storage in the CNS. In J. H. Byrne (Ed.), *Concise learning and memory: The editor's selection*. San Diego, CA: Elsevier.

Swim, J. K., & Sanna, L. J. (1996). He's skilled, she's lucky: A meta-analysis of observers' attributions for women's and men's successes and failures. *Personality and Social Psychology Bulletin, 22*, 507–519.

Swingley, D. (2008). The roots of the early vocabulary in infants' learning from speech. *Current Directions in Psychological Science, 17*(5), 308–312.

Symons, C. S., & Johnson, B. T. (1997). The self-reference effect in memory: A meta-analysis. *Psychological Bulletin, 121*, 371–394.

Symons, D. K., Kristin-Lee, M., F., & Collins, T. B. (2006). A longitudinal study of belief and desire state discourse during mother–child play and later false belief understanding. *Social Development, 15*, 676–691.

Szalma, J. L., & Hancock, P. A. (2013). A signal improvement to signal detection analysis: Fuzzy SDT on the ROCs. *Journal of Experimental Psychology: Human Perception and Performance, 39*, 1714–1762.

Szasz, T. (1974). *The myth of mental illness*. New York, NY: Harper & Row.

Szasz, T. (1990). Law and psychiatry: The problems that will not go away. *The Journal of Mind and Behavior, 11*(3/4), 557–564.

Szatmari, P. (2000). The classification of autism, Asperger's syndrome, and pervasive developmental disorder. *Canadian Journal of Psychiatry, 45*, 731–738.

Szigethy, E. M., & Friedman, E. S. (2009). Combined psychotherapy and pharmacology. In B. J. Sadock, V. A. Sadock, & P. Ruiz (Eds.), *Kaplan & Sadock's comprehensive textbook of psychiatry* (pp. 2923–2931). Philadelphia, PA: Lippincott Williams & Wilkins.

Szmukler, G. I., & Patton, G. (1995). Sociocultural models of eating disorders. In G. Szmukler, C. Dare, & J. Treasure (Eds.), *Handbook of eating disorders: Theory, treatment, and research*. New York, NY: Wiley.

Szpunar, K. K., & McDermott, K. B. (2009). Episodic memory: An evolving concept. In J. H. Byrne (Ed.), *Concise learning and memory: The editor's selection*. San Diego, CA: Elsevier.

Szymanski, L. S., & Wilska, M. (2003). Childhood disorders: Mental retardation. In A. Tasman, J. Kay, & J. A. Lieberman (Eds.), *Psychiatry*. New York, NY: Wiley.

Szymusiak, R. (2009). Thermoregulation during sleep and sleep deprivation. In R. Stickgold & M. P. Walker (Eds.), *The neuroscience of sleep* (pp. 218–222). San Diego, CA: Academic Press.

Tach, L., & Halpern-Meekin, S. (2009). How does premarital cohabitation affect trajectories of marital quality? *Journal of Marriage and Family, 71*(2), 298–317.

Tait, D. M., & Carroll, J. (2010). Color deficiency. In E. B. Goldstein (Ed.), *Encyclopedia of perception*. Thousand Oaks, CA: Sage.

Takarangi, M. T., Polaschek, D. L., Garry, M., & Loftus, E. F. (2008). Psychological science, victim advocates, and the problem of recovered memories. *International Review of Victimology, 15*(2), 147–163.

Taki, Y., Hashizume, H., Sassa, Y., Takeuchi, H., Asano, M., Asano, K., . . . Kawashima, R. (2012). Correlation among body height, intelligence, and brain gray matter volume in healthy children. *Neuroimage, 59*, 1023–1027. doi:10.1016/j.neuroimage.2011.08.092.

Talarico, J. M., & Rubin, D. C. (2003). Confidence, not consistency, characterizes flashbulb memories. *Psychological Science, 14*, 455–461.

Talarico, J. M., & Rubin, D. C. (2007). Flashbulb memories are special after all; in phenomenology, not accuracy. *Applied Cognitive Psychology, 21*, 557–578.

Talarico, J. M., & Rubin, D. C. (2009). Flashbulb memories result from ordinary memory processes and extraordinary event characteristics. In O. Luminet & A. Curci (Eds.), *Flashbulb memories: New issues and new perspectives* (pp. 79–97). New York, NY: Psychology Press.

Talati, A., Bao, Y., Kaufman, J., Shen, L., Schaefer, C. A., & Brown, A. S. (2013). Maternal smoking during pregnancy and bipolar disorder in offspring. *American Journal of Psychiatry, 170*, 1178–1185.

Talma, H., Schonbeck, Y., van Dommelen, P., Bakker, B., van Buuren, S., & Hirasang, R. A. (2013). Trends in menarcheal age between 1955 and 2009 in the Netherlands. *PLoS ONE, 8*, e60056. doi:10.1371/journal.pone.0060056.

Tamakoshi, A., Ohno, Y., & JACC Study Group. (2004). Self-reported sleep duration as a predictor of all-cause mortality: Results from JACC study, Japan. *Sleep: A Journal of Sleep and Sleep Disorders Research, 27*, 51–54.

Tamburri, R. (2012). *Heavy drinking a problem at most Canadian campuses: Report*. Retrieved from http://www.universityaffairs.ca/news/news-article/heavy-drinking-a-problem-at-most-canadian-campuses-report/.

Tammet, D. (2007). *Born on a blue day: Inside the extraordinary mind of an autistic savant*. New York, NY: Free Press.

Tammet, D. (2009). *Embracing the wide sky: A tour across the horizons of the mind*. New York, NY: Free Press.

Tammet, D. (2013). *Thinking in numbers*. New York, NY: Little, Brown.

Tamnes, C. K., Ostby, Y., Walhovd, K. B., Westlye, L. T., Due-Tonnessen, P., & Fjell, A. M. (2010). Neuroanatomical correlates of executive functions in children and adolescents: A magnetic resonance imaging (MRI) study of cortical thickness. *Neuropsychologia, 48*, 2496–2508.

Tanaka, J., Weiskopf, D., & Williams, O. (2001). The role of color in high-level vision. *Trends in Cognitive Sciences, 5*, 211–215.

Tanaka-Matsumi, J. (2001). Abnormal psychology and culture. In D. Matsumoto (Ed.), *The handbook of culture & psychology*. New York, NY: Oxford University Press.

Tang, J., Yu, Y., Du, Y., Ma, Y., Zhang, D., & Wang, J. (2014). Prevalence of Internet addiction and its association with stressful life events and psychological symptoms among adolescent Internet users. *Addictive Behaviors, 39*, 744–747. doi:10.1016/j.add-beh.2013.12.010.

Tang, Y-Y., Holzel, B. K., & Posner, M. I. (2015). The neuroscience of mindfulness meditation. *Nature Neuroscience Reviews, 16*, 213–225.

Tange, C., Nishita, Y., Tomida, M., Ostuka, R., Fujiko, A., et al. (2016). Longitudinal study of attitudes toward death among middle-aged and elderly Japanese. *Japanese Journal of Developmental Psychology, 27*, 232–242.

Tapia, J. C., & Lichtman, J. W. (2008). Synapse elimination. In L. Squire, D. Berg, F. Bloom, S. Du Lac, A. Ghosh, & N. Spitzer (Eds.), *Fundamental neuroscience* (3rd ed., pp. 469–490). San Diego, CA: Elsevier.

Tarabulsy, G. M., Pearson, J., Vaillancourt-Morel, M., Bussieres, Madigan, S., Lemelin, J., . . . Royer, F. (2014). Meta-analytic findings of the relation between maternal prenatal stress and anxiety and child cognitive outcome. *Journal of Developmental and Behavioral Pediatrics, 35*, 38–43.

Tardiff, K. (1999). Violence. In R. E. Hales, S. C. Yudofsky, & J. A. Talbott (Eds.), *American Psychiatric Press textbook of psychiatry*. Washington, DC: American Psychiatric Press.

Tart, C. T. (1988). From spontaneous event to lucidity: A review of attempts to consciously control nocturnal dreaming. In J. Gackenbach & S. LaBerge (Eds.), *Conscious mind, sleeping brain: Perspectives on lucid dreaming*. New York, NY: Plenum.

Tavris, C. (1998, September 13). Peer pressure (Review of *The Nurture Assumption*). *The New York Times Book Review, 103*, p. 14.

Taylor, D. M., & Moghaddam, F. M. (1994). *Theories of intergroup relations: International, social psychological perspectives*. New York, NY: Praeger Publications.

Taylor, D. M., Lydon, J. E., Bougie, E., & Johannsen, K. (2004). "Street kids": Towards an understanding of their motivational context. *Canadian Journal of Behavioural Science, 36*, 1–16.

Taylor, E. (1999). An intellectual renaissance of humanistic psychology. *Journal of Humanistic Psychology, 39*, 7–25.

Taylor, E. (2001). Positive psychology and humanistic psychology: A reply to Seligman. *Journal of Humanistic Psychology, 41*(1), 13–29.

Taylor, G. (2016). *The Chief Public Health Officer's report on the state of public health in Canada, 2015: Alcohol consumption in Canada*. Retrieved from https://www.canada.ca/en/public-health/services/publications/chief-public-health-officer-reports-state-public-health-canada/2015-alcohol-consumption-canada.html.

Taylor, I., & Taylor, M. M. (1990). *Psycholinguistics: Learning and using language*. Englewood Cliffs, NJ: Prentice-Hall.

Taylor, L. S., Fiore, A. T., Mendelsohn, G. A., & Cheshire, C. (2011). "Out of my league": A real-world test of the matching hypothesis. *Personality and Social Psychology Bulletin, 37*, 942–954. doi:10.1177/0146167211409947.

Taylor, S. E. (2011). *Health psychology* (8th ed.). New York, NY: McGraw Hill.

Taylor, S. E. (2011). Positive illusions: How ordinary people become extraordinary. In M. Gernsbacher, R. W. Pew, L. M. Hough, & J. R. Pomerantz (Eds.), *Psychology and the real world: Essays illustrating fundamental contributions to society*. New York, NY: Worth Publishers.

Taylor, S. E., & Brown, J. D. (1994). Positive illusions and well-being revisited: Separating fact from fiction. *Psychological Bulletin, 116*, 21–27.

Taylor, S. E., Welch, W. T., Kim, H. S., & Sherman, D. K. (2007). Cultural differences in the impact of social support on psychological and biological stress responses. *Psychological Science, 18*(9), 831–837. doi:10.1111/j.1467-9280.2007.01987.x.

Teachman, J. (2003). Premarital sex, premarital cohabitation and the risk of subsequent marital dissolution among women. *Journal of Marriage and Family, 65*(2), 444–455.

Teasdale, J. D., Segal, Z. V., Williams, J. M. G., Ridgeway, V., Soulsby, J. M., & Lau, M. A. (2000). The prevention of relapse/recurrence of major depression by mindfulness-based cognitive therapy. *Journal of Consulting and Clinical Psychology, 68*, 615–623.

Teen brain: A work in progress. (2008). National Institute of Mental Health. Retrieved June 23, 2008, from http:// www.nimh.nih.gov/health/publications/teenage-brain -a-work-in-progress.shtml.

Tees, R. (2003). A book review of Donald O. Hebb's (1949) *The Organization of behavior: A neuropsychological theory, Canadian Psychology, 44*(1), 74–76.

Temple, J. L., Giacomelli, A. M., Roemmich, J. N., & Epstein, L. H. (2008). Dietary variety impairs habituation in children. *Health Psychology, 27*, S10–S19.

Terman, L. M. (1916). *The measurement of intelligence.* Boston, MA: Houghton Mifflin.

Terman, L. M. (1925). *Genetic studies of genius (Vol.1): Mental and physical traits of a thousand gifted children.* Stanford, CA: Stanford University Press.

Terman, L. M., & Oden, M. H. (1959). *Genetic studies of genius (Vol. 5): The gifted group at mid-life.* Stanford, CA: Stanford University Press.

Terr, L. (1994). *Unchained memories.* New York, NY: Basic Books.

Terracciano, A., Abdel-Khalak, A. M., Adam, N., Adamovova, L., Ahn, C. K., Ahn, H. N., . . . McCrae, R. R. (2005). National character does not reflect mean personality trait levels in 49 cultures. *Science, 310*, 96–100.

Terrace, H. S. (1986). *Nim: A chimpanzee who learned sign language.* New York, NY: Columbia University Press.

Testa, K. (1996). Church to pay $1 million in false-memory case. *San Jose Mercury News*, 8A.

Teuber, M. (1974). Sources of ambiguity in the prints of Maurits C. Escher. *Scientific American, 231*, 90–104.

Thaler, R. (2015). *Misbehaving.* New York, NY: W.W. Norton.

Thames, A. D., Arbid, N., & Sayegh, P. (2014). Cannabis use and neurocognitive functioning in a non-clinical sample of users. *Addictive Behaviors, 39*, 994–999. doi:10.1016/j.addbeh.2014.01.019.

Thase, M. E. (2011). Antidepressant combinations: Widely used, but far from empirically validated. *Canadian Journal of Psychiatry, 56*, 317–323.

Thase, M. E. (2012). Social skills training for depression and comparative efficacy research: A 30-year retrospective. *Behavior Modification, 36*, 545–557. doi:10.1177/0145445512445610.

Thase, M. E., & Denko, T. (2008). Pharmacotherapy of mood disorders. *Annual Review of Clinical Psychology, 4*, 53–91.

Thase, M. E., Hahn, C., & Berton, O. (2014). Neurobiological aspects of depression. In I. H. Gotlib & C. L. Hammen (Eds.), *Handbook of depression* (3rd ed.). New York, NY: Guilford Press.

Thatcher, P. V. (2008). University students and the "all-nighter": Correlates and patterns of students' engagement in a single night of total sleep deprivation. *Behavioral Sleep Medicine, 6*, 16–31.

Thayer, A., & Lynn, S. J. (2006). Guided imagery and recovered memory therapy: Considerations and cautions. *Journal of Forensic Psychology Practice, 6*, 63–73.

Thayer, R. E. (1996). *The origin of everyday moods.* New York, NY: Oxford University Press.

Theeuwes, J., Belopolsky, A., & Olivers, C. N. L. (2009). Interactions between working memory, attention, and eye movements. *Acta Psychologica, 132*, 106–114.

Thelen, E. (1995). Motor development: A new synthesis. *American Psychologist, 50*, 79–95.

Thies, W., & Bleiler, L. (2013). 2013 Alzheimer's disease facts and figures. *Alzheimer's and Dementia, 9*, 208– 245. doi:10.1016/j.jalz.2013.02.003.

Thomas, A., & Chess, S. (1977). *Temperament and development.* New York, NY: Brunner/Mazel.

Thomas, A., & Chess, S. (1989). Temperament and personality. In G. A. Kohnstamm, J. E. Bates, & M. K. Rothbart (Eds.), *Temperament in childhood.* New York, NY: Wiley.

Thomas, A., Chess, S., & Birch, H. G. (1970). The origin of personality. *Scientific American, 223*(2), 102–109.

Thomas, D. R. (1992). Discrimination and generalization. In L. R. Squire (Ed.), *Encyclopedia of learning and memory.* New York, NY: Macmillan.

Thomas, M. S. C., & Johnson, M. H. (2008). New advances in understanding sensitive periods in brain development. *Current Directions in Psychological Science, 17*, 1–5.

Thomas, R. M. (2005). *Comparing theories of child development.* Belmont, CA: Wadsworth.

Thompson, J. K., & Stice, E. (2001). Thin-ideal internalization: Mounting evidence for a new risk factor for body-image disturbance and eating pathology. *Current Directions in Psychological Science, 10*(5), 181–183.

Thompson, J. K., Roehrig, M., & Kinder, B. N. (2007). Eating disorders. In M. Hersen, S. M. Turner, & D. C. Beidel (Eds.), *Adult psychopathology and diagnosis.* New York, NY: Wiley.

Thompson, R. A. (2008). Early attachment and later development: Familiar questions, new answers. In J. Cassidy & P. R. Shaver (Eds.), *Handbook of attachment: Theory, research, and clinical applications* (2nd ed., pp. 348–365). New York, NY: Guilford Press.

Thompson, R. A. (2008). Measure twice, cut once: Attachment theory and the NICHD Study of Early Child Care and Youth Development. *Attachment & Human Development, 10*, 287–297. doi:10.1080/14616730802113604.

Thompson, R. A., & Nelson, C. A. (2001). Developmental science and the media: Early brain development. *American Psychologist, 56*, 5–15.

Thompson, R. A., Winer, A. C., & Goodwin, R. (2011). The individual child: Temperament, emotion, self, and personality. In M. H. Bornstein & M. E. Lamb (Eds.), *Developmental science: An advanced textbook* (pp. 427–468). New York, NY: Psychology Press.

Thompson, R. F. (1989). A model system approach to memory. In P. R. Solomon, G. R. Goethals, C. M. Kelley, & B. R. Stephens (Eds.), *Memory: Interdisciplinary approaches.* New York, NY: Springer-Verlag.

Thompson, R. F. (1992). Memory. *Current Opinion in Neurobiology, 2*, 203–208.

Thompson, R. F., & Zola, S. M. (2003). In D. K. Freedheim (Ed.), *Handbook of psychology* (Vol. 2). New York, NY: Wiley.

Thompson, W. F., Schellenberg, E. G., & Husain, G. (2001). Arousal, mood and the Mozart effect. *Psychological Science, 12*, 248–251.

Thorndike, E. L. (1913). *Educational psychology: The psychology of learning* (Vol. 2). New York, NY: Teachers College.

Thorndyke, P. W., & Hayes-Roth, B. (1979). The use of schemata in the acquisition and transfer of knowledge. *Cognitive Psychology, 11*, 83–106.

Thornhill, R. (1976). Sexual selection and nuptial feeding behavior in *Bittacus apicalis* (Insecta: Mecoptera). *American Naturalist, 110*, 529–548.

Thornton, B., & Moore, S. (1993). Physical attractiveness contrast effect: Implications for self-esteem and evaluations of the social self. *Personality and Social Psychology Bulletin, 19*, 474–480.

Thorpy, M., & Yager, J. (2001). *Sleeping well: The sourcebook for sleep and sleep disorders.* New York, NY: Checkmark Books.

Thun, M. J., Apicella, L. F., & Henley, S. J. (2000). Smoking vs. other risk factors as the cause of smoking-attributable deaths: Confounding in the courtroom. *JAMA, 284*, 706–712.

Thun, M. J., Carter, B. D., Freskanich, D., Freedman, N. D., Prentice, R., Lopez, A. D., . . . Gapstur, S. M. (2013). 50-year trends in smoking-related mortality in the United States. *The New England Journal of Medicine, 368*, 351–364. doi:10.1056/NEJMsa1211127.

Thurstone, L. L. (1931a). The measurement of social attitudes. *Journal of Abnormal and Social Psychology, 26*, 249–269.

Thurstone, L. L. (1931b). Multiple factor analysis. *Psychological Review, 38*, 406–427.

Thurstone, L. L. (1938). *Primary mental abilities* (Psychometric Monographs No. 1). Chicago: University of Chicago Press.

Thurstone, L. L. (1955). *The differential growth of mental abilities* (Psychometric Laboratory Rep. No. 14). Chapel Hill: University of North Carolina.

Till, B. D., & Priluck, R. L. (2000). Stimulus generalization in classical conditioning: An initial investigation and extension. *Psychology and Marketing, 17*, 55–72.

Tindale, R. S., Kameda, T., & Hinsz, V. B. (2003). Group decision making. In M. A. Hogg & J. Cooper (Eds.), *The Sage handbook of social psychology.* Thousand Oaks, CA: Sage.

Tinkhauser, G., Pogosyan, A., Little, S., Beudel, M., Herz, D. M., et al. (2017). The modulatory effect of adaptive deep brain stimulation on beta bursts in Parkinson's disease. *Brain: A Journal of Neurology, 140*, 1953–1067.

Tinti, C., Schmidt, S., Testa, S., & Levine, L. J. (2014). Distinct processes shape flashbulb and event memories. *Memory & Cognition, 42*, 539–551. doi:10.3758/ s13421-013-0383-9.

Titsworth, B. S., & Kiewra, K. A. (2004). Spoken organizational lecture cues and student notetaking as facilitators of student learning. *Contemporary Educational Psychology, 29*, 447–461.

Tiwari, S. K., & Wang, J. L. (2008). Ethnic differences in mental health service use among White, Chinese, South Asian, and South East Asian populations living in Canada. *Social Psychiatry and Psychiatric Epidemiology, 43*, 866–871.

Tjepkema, M. (2005). Insomnia. Statistics Canada. Retrieved from https://www.statcan.gc.ca/pub/82 -003-x/2005001/article/8707-eng.pdf.

Todd, J. T., & Morris, E. K. (1992). Case histories in the great power of steady misrepresentation. *American Psychologist, 47*, 1441–1453.

Todd, J. T., & Morris, E. K. (Eds.). (1994). *Modern perspectives on John B. Watson and classical behaviorism.* Westport, CT: Greenwood Press.

Todd, M. (2003). Characteristics associated with superstitious behavior in track and field athletes: Are there NCAA divisional differences? *Journal of Sport Behavior, 26*, 168–178.

Todd, P. M., & Gigerenzer, G. (2000). Precis of simple heuristics that make us smart. *Behavioral & Brain Sciences, 23*, 727–780.

Todd, P. M., & Gigerenzer, G. (2007). Environments that make us smart: Ecological rationality. *Current Directions in Psychological Science, 16*, 167–171.

Todes, D. P. (1997). From the machine to the ghost within: Pavlov's transition from digestive physiology to conditional reflexes. *American Psychologist, 52*, 947–955.

Tolman, E. C. (1922). A new formula for behaviorism. *Psychological Review, 29*, 44–53.

Tolman, E. C. (1932). *Purposive behavior in animals and men.* New York, NY: Appleton-Century-Crofts.

Tolman, E. C. (1938). The determiners of behavior at a choice point. *Psychological Review, 45*, 1–41.

Tolman, E. C., & Honzik, C. H. (1930). Introduction and removal of reward, and maze performance in rats. *University of California Publications in Psychology, 4*, 257–275.

Tomkins, S. S. (1980). Affect as amplification: Some modifications in theory. In R. Plutchik & H. Kellerman (Eds.), *Emotion: Theory, research and experience* (Vol. 1). New York, NY: Academic Press.

Tomkins, S. S. (1991). *Affect, imagery, consciousness: 3. Anger and fear.* New York, NY: Springer-Verlag.

Tomko, R. L., Trull, T. J., Wood, P. K., & Sher, K. J. (2014). Characteristics of borderline personality disorder in a community sample: Comorbidity, treatment utilization, and general functioning. *Journal of Personality Disorders, 28*, 734–750. doi:10.1521/pedi_2012_26_093.

Tong, F., & Pratte, M. S. (2012). Decoding patterns of human brain activity. *Annual Review of Psychology, 63*, 483–509.

Tooby, J., & Cosmides, L. (2015). The theoretical foundations of evolutionary psychology. In D. M. Buss (Ed.), *The Handbook of evolutionary psychology* (Volume 1, 2nd ed., pp. 3–87). Hoboken, NJ: John Wiley & Sons.

Torgersen, S. (1979). The nature and origin of common phobic fears. *British Journal of Psychiatry, 119,* 343–351.

Torgersen, S. (1983). Genetic factors in anxiety disorders. *Archives of General Psychiatry, 40,* 1085–1089.

Torgersen, S. (2012). Epidemiology. In T. A. Widiger (Ed.), *The Oxford handbook of personality disorders.* New York, NY: Oxford University Press.

Tormala, Z. L., & Petty, R. E. (2002). What doesn't kill me makes me stronger: The effects of resisting persuasion on attitude certainty. *Journal of Personality and Social Psychology, 83,* 1298–1313.

Tormala, Z. L., & Petty, R. E. (2004). Resistance to persuasion and attitude certainty: The moderating role of elaboration. *Personality and Social Psychology Bulletin, 30,* 1446–1457.

Toronto Montessori Institute. (n.d.). *Montessori Education.* Retrieved June 22, 2008, from http://www.tmi.edu/motion.asp?menuid=4687&lgid=1&siteid=100344.

Torrey, E. F. (1992). *Freudian fraud: The malignant effect of Freud's theory on American thought and culture.* New York, NY: Harper Perennial.

Torrey, E. F. (2014). *American psychosis: How the federal government destroyed the mental illness treatment system.* New York, NY: Oxford University Press.

Tourangeau, R. (2004). Survey research and societal change. *Annual Review of Psychology, 55,* 775–801.

Tov, W., & Diener, E. (2007). Culture and subjective well-being. In S. Kitayama & D. Cohen (Eds.), *Handbook of cultural psychology* (pp. 691–713). New York, NY: Guilford.

Townsend, S., Kim, H., & Mesquita, B. (2014). Are you feeling what I'm feeling? Emotional similarity buffers stress. *Social Psychological and Personality Science, 5*(5), 526–533.

Tozzi, F., Thornton, L. M., Klump, K. L., Fichter, M. M., Halmi, K. A., Kaplan, A. S., et al. (2005). Symptom fluctuation in eating disorders: Correlates of diagnostic crossover. *American Journal of Psychiatry, 162,* 732–740.

Trace, S. E., Baker, J. H., Peñas-Lledó, E., & Bulik, C. M. (2013). The genetics of eating disorders. *Annual review of clinical psychology, 9,* 589–620. doi:10.1146/annurev-clinpsy-050212-185546.

Tracey, T. J. G., Wampold, B. E., Lichtenberg, J. W., & Goodyear, R. K. (2014). Expertise in psychotherapy: An elusive goal? *American Psychologist, 69,* 218–229.

Tracy, J. L., & Robins, R. W. (2008). The automaticity of emotion recognition. *Emotion, 8,* 81–95.

Trainor, L. J. (2005). Are there critical periods for musical development? *Developmental Psychobiology, 46,* 262–278.

Travis, F. (2001). Autonomic and EEG patterns distinguish transcending from other experiences during Transcendental Meditation practice. *International Journal of Psychophysiology, 42,* 1–9.

Treadway, M. T., Waskom, M. L., Dillon, D. G., Holmes, A. J., Park, M. M., Chakravarty, M. M., . . . Pizzagalli, D. A. (2015). Illness progression, recent stress, and morphometry of hippocampal subfields and medial prefrontal cortex in major depression. *Biological Psychiatry, 77*(3), 285–294. doi:10.1016/j.biopsych.2014.06.018.

Trebicky, V., Havlicek, J., Roberts, S. C., Little, A. C., & Kleisner, K. (2013). Perceived aggressiveness predicts fighting performance in mixed-martial-arts fighters. *Psychological Science, 24*(9), 1664–1672.

Treffert, D. A. (2010). *Islands of genius: The bountiful mind of the autistic, acquired and sudden savant.* London, UK: Kinglsey, Inc.

Treffert, D. A., & Christensen, D. D. (2006, June/July). Inside the mind of a savant. *Scientific American,* 50–55.

Treisman, A. (2009). Attention: Theoretical and psychological perspectives. In M. S. Gazzaniga (Ed.), *The cognitive neurosciences* (4th ed., pp. 189–204). Cambridge, MA: MIT Press.

Treisman, G. J. (1999). AIDS education for psychiatrists. *Primary Psychiatry, 6*(5), 71–73.

Triandis, H. C. (1989). Self and social behavior in differing cultural contexts. *Psychological Review, 96,* 269–289.

Triandis, H. C. (2001). Individualism and collectivism: Past, present, and future. In D. Matsumoto (Ed.), *The handbook of culture and psychology.* New York, NY: Oxford University Press.

Triandis, H. C., & Gelfand, M. J. (2012). A theory of individualism and collectivism. In P. A. M. Van Lange, A. W. Kruglanski, & E. T. Higgins (Eds.), *Handbook of theories of social psychology* (Vol. 2). Thousand Oaks, CA: Sage.

Triandis, H. C., & Suh, E. M. (2002). Cultural influences on personality. *Annual Review of Psychology, 53,* 133–160.

Triano-Antidormi, L. (2013). Stigmatizing the mentally ill does not make society any safer. *Toronto Star,* Wednesday, July 3, 2013.

Trivers, R. L. (1972). Parental investment and sexual selection. In B. Campbell (Ed.), *Sexual selection and the descent of man.* Chicago: Aldine.

Tronick, E, & Beeghly, M. (2011). Infants' meaning-making and the development of mental health problems. *American Psychologist, 66,* 107–119.

Trull, T. J., Carpenter, R. W., & Widiger, T. A. (2013). Personality disorders. In T. A. Widiger, G. Stricker, I. B. Weiner, G. Stricker, T. A. Widiger, & I. B. Weiner (Eds.), *Handbook of psychology: Vol. 8. Clinical psychology* (2nd ed.). New York, NY: Wiley.

Trull, T. J., Jahng, S., Tomko, R. L., Wood, P. K., & Sher, K. J. (2010). Revised NESARC personality disorder diagnoses: Gender, prevalence, and comorbidity with substance dependence disorders. *Journal of Personality Disorders, 24,* 412–426. doi:10.1521/pedi.2010.24.4.412.

Tsai, J. L., Butcher, J. N., Muñoz, R. F., & Vitousek, K. (2001). Culture, ethnicity, and psychopathology. In P. B. Sutker & H. E. Adams (Eds.), *Comprehensive handbook of psychopathology.* New York, NY: Kluwer Academic/Plenum.

Tsai, L. Y. & Ghaziuddin, M. (1992). Biomedical research in autism. In D. E. Berkell (Ed.), *Autism: Identification, education, and treatment* (pp. 53–74). Hillsdale, NJ: Erlbaum.

Tsankova, N., Renthal, W., Kumar, A., & Nestler, E. J. (2007). Epigenetic regulation in psychiatric disorders. *Nature Reviews Neuroscience, 8*(5), 355–367.

Tseng, W. S. (2009). Culture-related specific psychiatric syndromes. In M. C. Gelder, N. C. Andreasen, J. J. López-Ibor, Jr., & J. R. Geddes (Eds.). *New Oxford textbook of psychiatry* (2nd ed., Vol. 1). New York, NY: Oxford University Press.

Tucker, A. M., Dinges, D. F., & Van Dongen, H. P. A. (2007). Trait interindividual differences in the sleep physiology of healthy young adults. *Journal of Sleep Research, 16,* 170–180.

Tucker, E. (2014). Timeline: Recent soldier suicides in Canada's military. *Global News,* January 20, 2014.

Tucker-Drob, E. M., Briley, D. A., & Harden, K. P. (2013). Genetic and environmental influences on cognition across development and context. *Current Directions in Psychological Science, 22,* 349–355. doi:10.1177/0963721413485087.

Tucker-Drob, E. M., Rhemtulla, M., Harden, K. P., Turkheimer, E., & Fask, D. (2011). Emergence of a gene x socioeconomic status interaction on infant mental ability between 10 months and 2 years. *Psychological Science, 22*(1), 125–133. doi:10.1177/0956797610392926.

Tuckey, M. R., & Brewer, N. (2003). The influence of schemas, stimulus ambiguity, and interview schedule on eyewitness memory over time. *Journal of Experimental Psychology: Applied, 9,* 101–118.

Tulving, E. (1972). Episodic and semantic memory. In E. Tulving & W. Donaldson (Eds.), *Organization of memory* (pp. 381–403). New York, NY: Academic Press.

Tulving, E. (1986). What kind of a hypothesis is the distinction between episodic and semantic memory? *Journal of Experimental Psychology: Learning, Memory and Cognition, 12,* 307–311.

Tulving, E. (2001). Episodic memory and common sense: How far apart? *Philosophical Transactions of the Royal Society of London, 356,* 1505–1515.

Tulving, E. (2001). Origin of autonoesis in episodic memory. In H. L. Roediger III, J. S. Nairne, I. Neath, & A. M. Surprenant (Eds.), *The nature of remembering: Essays in honor of Robert G. Crowder* (pp. 17–34). Washington, DC: American Psychological Association.

Tulving, E. (2002). Episodic memory: From mind to brain. *Annual Review of Psychology, 53,* 1–25.

Tulving, E. (2005). Episodic memory and autonoesis: Uniquely human? In H. S. Terrance & J. Metcalfe (Eds.), *The missing link in cognition: Origins of self-reflective consciousness* (pp. 3–36). Oxford, UK: Oxford University Press.

Tulving, E., & Pearlstone, Z. (1966). Availability and accessibility of information in memory for words. *Journal of Verbal Learning and Verbal Behavior, 5,* 381–391.

Tulving, E., & Schacter, D. L. (1990). Priming and human memory systems. *Science, 247,* 301–306.

Tulving, E., Schacter, D. L., & Stark, H. A. (*1982*). Priming effects in word-fragment completion are independent of recognition memory. *Journal of Experimental Psychology: Learning, Memory and Cognition, 8,* 336–342.

Tulving, E., & Szpunar, K. K. (2009). Episodic memory. *Scholarpedia, 4,* 3332.

Tulving, E., & Thomson, D. M. (1973). Encoding specificity and retrieval processes in episodic memory. *Psychological Review, 80,* 352–373.

Tunnell, K. D. (2005). The Oxycontin epidemic and crime panic in rural Kentucky. *Contemporary Drug Problems, 32,* 225–258.

Turcotte, M. (2011). *Women and education: A Gender-based statistical report.* Statistics Canada. Retrieved from http://www.statcan.gc.ca/pub/89-503-x/2010001/article/11542-eng.htm.

Turk, D. C. (1994). Perspectives on chronic pain: The role of psychological factors. *Current Directions in Psychological Science, 3,* 45–48.

Turk, D. C., & Okifuji, A. (2003). Pain management. In A. M. Nezu, C. M. Nezu, & P. A. Geller (Eds.), *Handbook of psychology (Vol. 9): Health psychology.* New York, NY: Wiley.

Turkheimer, E., Pettersson, E., & Horn, E. E. (2014). Genetics of personality. *Annual Reviews of Psychology, 65,* 515–540.

Turkle, S. (2011). *Alone together: Why we expect more from technology and less from each other.* New York, NY: Basic Books.

Turner, E. H., Matthews, A. M., Linardos, E., Tell, R. A., & Rosenthal, R. (2008). Selective publication of antidepressant trials and its influence on apparent efficacy. *New England Journal of Medicine, 358,* 252–260.

Turner, J. C. (2006). Tyranny, freedom and social structure: Escaping our theoretical prisons. *British Journal of Social Psychology, 25,* 41–46.

Tversky, A., & Kahneman, D. (1971). Belief in the law of small numbers. *Psychological Bulletin, 76,* 105–110.

Tversky, A., & Kahneman, D. (1973). Availability: A heuristic for judging frequency and probability. *Cognitive Psychology, 5,* 207–232.

Tversky, A., & Kahneman, D. (1974). Judgments under uncertainty: Heuristics and biases. *Science, 185,* 1124–1131.

Tversky, A., & Kahneman, D. (1982). Judgment under uncertainty: Heuristics and biases. In D. Kahneman, P. Slovic, & A. Tversky (Eds.), *Judgment under uncertainty: Heuristics and biases.* New York, NY: Cambridge University Press.

Tversky, A., & Kahneman, D. (1983). Extensional versus intuitive reasoning: The conjunction fallacy in probability judgment. *Psychological Review, 90,* 283–315.

Tversky, A., & Kahneman, D. (1988). Rational choice and the framing of decisions. In D. E. Bell, H. Raiffa, & A. Tversky (Eds.), *Decision making: Descriptive, normative, and prescriptive interactions.* New York, NY: Cambridge University Press.

Tversky, A., & Kahneman, D. (1991). Loss aversion in riskless choice: A reference-dependent model. *Quarterly Journal of Economics, 106,* 1039–1061.

Twenge, J. M. (2015). Time period and birth cohort differences in depressive symptoms in the U.S., 1982–2013. *Social Indicators Research, 121*, 437–454. doi:10.1007/s11205-014-0647-1.

Twenge, J. M., & Kasser, T. (2013). Generational changes in materialism and work centrality, 1976–2007: Associations with temporal changes in societal insecurity and materialistic role modeling. *Personality and Social Psychology Bulletin, 39*, 883–897. doi:10.1177/0146167213484586.

Twenge, J. M., Campbell, W. K., & Foster, C. A. (2003). Parenthood and marital satisfaction: A metaanalytic review. *Journal of Marriage and the Family, 65*, 574–583.

Tybur, J. M., Lieberman, D., Kurzban, R., & DeSicoli, P. (2013). Disgust: Evolved function and structure. *Psychological Review, 120*, 65–84.

Uchino, B. N., & Birmingham, W. (2011). Stress and support processes. In R. J. Contrada & A. Baum (Eds.), *The handbook of stress science: Biology, psychology, and health* (pp. 111–121). New York, NY: Springer Publishing.

Uchino, B. N., Uno, D., & Holt-Lunstad, J. (1999). Social support, physiological processes, and health. *Current Directions in Psychological Science, 8*, 145–148.

Uleman, J. S., Saribay, S. A., & Gonzalez, C. M. (2007). Spontaneous inferences, implicit impressions, and implicit theories. *Annual Review of Psychology, 59*, 329–360.

Umbel, V. M., Pearson, B. Z., Fernandez, S. C., & Oller, D. K. (1992). Measuring bilingual children's receptive vocabularies. *Child Development, 63*, 1012–1020.

Underwood, B. J. (1961). Ten years of massed practice on distributed practice. *Psychological Review, 68*, 229–247.

Ungerleider, L. G., & Mishkin, N. (1982). Two cortical systems. In D. J. Ingle, M. A. Goodale, & R. J. W. Mansfield (Eds.), *Analysis of visual behavior* (pp. 549–586). Cambridge MA: MIT Press.

University of Ottawa. (2009). *Aboriginal medicine and healing practices.* Retrieved from http://www.med.uottawa.ca/sim/data/Aboriginal_Medicine_e.htm.

Unsworth, N., Fukuda, K., Awh, E., & Vogel, E. K. (2014). Working memory and fluid intelligence: Capacity, attention control, and secondary memory retrieval. *Cognitive Psychology, 71*, 1–26. doi:10.1016/j.cogpsych.2014.01.003.

Unsworth, N., Heitz, R. P., Schrock, J. C., & Engle, R. W. (2005). An automated version of the operation span task. *Behavior Research Methods, 37*, 498–505.

Urbina, S. (2011). Tests of intelligence. In R. J. Sternberg, & S. B. Kaufman (Eds.), *Cambridge handbook of intelligence.* New York, NY: Cambridge University Press.

Urbszat, D., & Herman, C. P., & Polivy, J. (2002). Eat. Drink, and be merry for tomorrow we diet: Effects of anticipated deprivation on food intake in restrained and unrestrained eaters. *Journal of Abnormal Psychology, 111*, 396–401.

Urcelay, G. P., & Miller, R. R. (2014). The functions of contexts in associative learning. *Behavioural Processes, 104*, 2–12. doi:10.1016/j.beproc.2014.02.008.

Ursano, A. M., Kartheiser, P. H., & Barnhill, L. J. (2008). Disorders usually first diagnosed in infancy, childhood, or adolescence. In R. E. Hales, S. C. Yudofsky, & G. O. Gabbard (Eds.), *The American Psychiatric Publishing textbook of psychiatry* (5th ed., pp. 861–920). Washington, DC: American Psychiatric Publishing.

Ursano, R. J., & Carr, R. B. (2014). Psychodynamic psychotherapy. In R. E. Hales, S. C. Yudofsky, & L. W. Roberts (Eds.), *The American Psychiatric Publishing textbook of psychiatry* (6th ed.). Washington, DC: American Psychiatric Publishing.

Ursano, R. J., Sonnenberg, S. M., & Lazar, S. G. (2008). Psychodynamic psychotherapy. In R. E. Hales, S. C. Yudofsky, & G. O. Gabbard (Eds.), *The American Psychiatric Publishing textbook of psychiatry* (pp. 1171–1190). Washington, DC: American Psychiatric Publishing.

U.S. Department of Health and Human Services. (1999). *Mental health: A report of the Surgeon General.* Washington, DC: U.S. Government Printing Office.

Vaillant, G. E. (1994). Ego mechanisms of defense and personality psychopathology. *Journal of Abnormal Psychology, 103*, 44–50.

Vakorin, V., McIntosh, A. R., Bratislav, M., Krakovska, O., Poulsen, C., Martinu, K., & Paus, T. (2013). Exploring age-related changes in dynamical non-stationarity in electroencephalographic signals during early adolescence. *PLoS ONE, 8*(3), e57217.

Valenstein, E. S. (1973). *Brain control.* New York, NY: Wiley.

Valentine, J. C. (2012). Meta-analysis. In H. Cooper, P. M. Camic, D. L. Long, A. T. Panter, D. Rindskopf, & K. J. Sher (Eds.), *APA handbook of research methods in psychology: Vol. 3. Data analysis and research publication.* Washington, DC: American Psychological Association.

Valli, K., & Revonsuo, A. (2009). Sleep: Dreaming data and theories. In W. P. Banks (Ed.), *Encyclopedia of consciousness* (pp. 341–356). San Diego, CA: Academic Press.

Valsiner, J. (2012). Introduction: Culture in psychology: A renewed encounter of inquisitive minds. In Valsiner, J. (Ed.). *Oxford handbook of culture and psychology.* New York, NY: Oxford University Press.

Van Blerkom, D. L. (2012). *College study skills: Becoming a strategic learner.* Belmont, CA: Wadsworth.

Van de Castle, R. L. (1994). *Our dreaming mind.* New York, NY: Ballantine Books.

Vandenbroucke, A. R. E., Sligte, I. G., Barrett, A. B., Seth, A. K., Fahrenfort, J. J., & Lamme, V. A. F. (2014). Accurate metacognition for visual sensory memory representations. *Psychological Science, 25*(4), 861–73.

Vandenbroucke, J. P., & Psaty, B. M. (2008). Benefits and risks of drug treatments: How to combine the best evidence on benefits with the best data about adverse effects. *JAMA, 300*(20), 2417–2419.

Van den Eynde, F., Claudino, A. M., Mogg, A., Horrell, L., Stahl, D., Ribeiro, W., et al. (2010). Repetitive transcranial magnetic stimulation reduces cue-induced food craving in bulimic disorders. *Biological Psychiatry, 67*(8), 793–795.

van der Gaag, C., Minderaa, R. B., & Keysers, C. (2007). Facial expressions: What the mirror neuron system can and cannot tell us. *Social Neuroscience, 2*, 179–222.

van der Hart, O., & Nijenhuis, E. R. S. (2009). Dissociative disorders. In P. H. Blaney & T. Millon (Eds.), *Oxford textbook of psychopathology* (2nd ed., pp. 452–481). New York, NY: Oxford University Press.

van der Kloet, D., Merckelbach, H., Giesbrecht, T., & Lynn, S. J. (2012). Fragmented sleep, fragmented mind: The role of sleep in dissociative symptoms. *Perspectives on Psychological Science, 7*(2), 159–175. doi:10.1177/1745691612437597.

Van Der Linden, D., Pekaar, K. A., Bakker, A. B., Schermer, J. A., Vernon, P. A., Dunkel, C. S., & Petrides, K. V. (2017). Overlap between the general factor of personality and emotional intelligence: A meta-analysis. *Psychological Bulletin, 143*, 36–52.

Van Dongen, H. P. A., & Dinges, D. F. (2005). Circadian rhythms in sleepiness, alertness, and performance. In M. H. Kryger, T. Roth, & W. C. Dement (Eds.), *Principles and practice of sleep medicine.* Philadelphia, PA: Elsevier Saunders.

van Eck, M., Nicolson, N. A., & Berkhof, J. (1998). Effects of stressful daily events on mood states: Relationship to global perceived stress. *Journal of Personality and Social Psychology, 75*, 1572–1585.

Van Gog, T., Paas, F., Marcus, N., Ayres, P., & Sweller, J. (2009). The mirror neuron system and observational learning: Implications for the effectiveness of dynamic visualizations. *Educational Psychology Review, 21*, 21–30.

van Griensven, F., Chakkraband, M. L. S., Thienkrua, W., Pengjuntr, W., Cardozo, B. L., & Tantipiwatanaskul, P. et al. (2007). Mental health problems among adults in tsunami-affected areas in Southern Thailand. *Journal of the American Medical Association, 296*, 537–548.

Vanier Institute of the Family. (2005). *Family Facts.* Retrieved June 20, 2005, from http://www.vifamily.ca/library/facts/facts/html.

Vanier Institute of the Family. (2013). Sleep patterns in Canada. Retrieved from http://vanierinstitute.ca/resources/fact-sheets/.

van IJzendoorn, M. H., & Bakermans-Kranenburg, M. J. (2004). Maternal sensitivity and infant temperament in the formation of attachment. In G. Bremner & A. Slater (Eds.), *Theories of infant development* (pp. 233–257). Malden, MA: Blackwell.

van IJzendoorn, M. H., & Juffer, F. (2005). Adoption is a successful natural intervention enhancing adopted children's IQ and school performance. *Current Directions in Psychological Science, 14*, 326–330.

van IJzendoorn, M. H., & Sagi-Schwartz, A. (2008). Cross-cultural patterns of attachment: Universal and contextual dimensions. In J. Cassidy & P. R. Shaver (Eds.), *Handbook of attachment: Theory, research, and clinical applications* (2nd ed., pp. 3–22). New York, NY: Guilford Press.

van Kammen, D. P., Hurford, I., & Marder, S. R. (2009). First-generation antipsychotics. In B. J. Sadock, V. A. Sadock, & P. Ruiz (Eds.), *Kaplan & Sadock's comprehensive textbook of psychiatry* (pp. 3105–3126). Philadelphia, PA: Lippincott Williams & Wilkins.

Van Lange, P. A. M. (2013). What we should expect from theories in social psychology: Truth, abstraction, progress, and applicability as standards (TAPAS). *Personality and Social Psychology Review, 17*, 40–55.

van Leeuwen, M. L., & Macrae, C. N. (2004). Is beautiful always good? Implicit benefits of facial attractiveness. *Social Cognition, 22*, 637–649.

Varnum, M. W., Grossmann, I., Kitayama, S., & Nisbett, R. E. (2010). The origin of cultural differences in cognition: The social orientation hypothesis. *Current Directions in Psychological Science, 19*(1), 9–13.

Van Swol, L. M. (2009). Extreme members and group polarization. *Social Influence, 4*(3), 185–199. doi:10.1080/15534510802584368.

Van Til, L., Macintosh, S., Thompson, J. M., et al. (2013). Synthesis of life after service studies. *Veterans Affairs Canada, Research Directorate Synthesis Report*, July 3. Retrieved from http://www.veterans.gc.ca/pdf/about-us/research-directorate/2013-life-after-service-studies.pdf.

van Winkel, R., & Kuepper, R. (2014). Epidemiological, neurobiological, and genetic clues to the mechanisms linking cannabis use to risk for nonaffective psychosis. *Annual Review of Clinical Psychology, 107*, 67–791. doi:10.1146/annurev-clinpsy-032813-153631.

Vartanian, L. R., Herman, C., & Wansink, B. (2008). Are we aware of the external factors that influence our food intake? *Health Psychology, 27*(5), 533–538.

Västfjäll, D., & Slovic, P. (2013). Cognition and emotion in judgment and decision making. In M. D. Robinson, E. R. Watkins, & E. Harmon-Jones (Eds.), *Handbook of cognition and emotion* (pp. 252–271). New York, NY: Guilford Press.

Veenhoven, R. (2008). Healthy happiness: Effects of happiness on physical health and the consequences for preventive health care. *Journal of Happiness Studies, 9*(3), 449–469.

Veer, R. van der. (2007). *Lev Vygotsky.* London, UK: Continuum Books.

Vermeer, H. J., & Bakermans-Kranenburg, M. J. (2008). Attachment to mother and nonmaternal care: Bridging the gap. *Attachment & Human Development, 10*, 263–273. doi:10.1080/14616730802113588.

Vernberg, E. M., La Greca, A. M., Silverman, W. K., & Prinstein, M. J. (1996). Prediction of posttraumatic stress symptoms in children after Hurricane Andrew. *Journal of Abnormal Psychology, 105*, 237–248.

Vernon, P. A., Wickett, J. C., Bazana, P. G., & Stelmack, R. M. (2000). The neuropsychology and psychophysiology of human intelligence. In R. J. Sternberg (Ed.), *Handbook of intelligence* (pp. 245–266). Cambridge, MA: Cambridge University Press.

Verschuere, B., Crombez, G., Degrootte, T. & Rosseel, Y. (2009). Detecting concealed information with reaction times: Validity and comparison with the polygraph. *Applied Cognitive Psychology, 23*, 1–11.

Veru, F., Laplante, D. P., Luhesi, G., & King, S. (2014). Prenatal maternal stress exposure and immune function in the offspring. *Stress: The International Journal on the Biology of Stress, 17*, 133–148. doi:10.3109/10253890.2013.876404.

Verweij, I. M., Onuki, Y., Van Someren, E. J., & Van der Werf, Y. (2016). Sleep to the beat: A nap favours consolidation of timing. *Behavioral Neuroscience, 130*, 298–304.

Victoroff, J. (2005). Central nervous system changes with normal aging. In B. J. Sadock & V. A. Sadock (Eds.), *Kaplan & Sadock's comprehensive textbook of psychiatry.* Philadelphia, PA: Lippincott Williams & Wilkins.

Vidal, J., & Chamizo, V. D. (2009). Taste-aversion conditioning, but not immunosuppression conditioning, occurs under partial water deprivation. *The Journal of General Psychology, 36*, 71–89.

Vierck, C. (1978). Somatosensory system. In R. B. Masterston (Ed.), *Handbook of sensory neurobiology.* New York, NY: Plenum.

Vigod, S. N., Kurdyak, P. A., Seitz, D., Herrmann, N., Fung, K., Lin, E., . . . Gruneir, A. (2015). READMIT: A clinical risk index to predict 30-day readmission after discharge from acute psychiatric units. *Journal of Psychiatric Research, 61*, 205–213. doi:10.1016/j.jpsychires.2014.12.003.

Vigod, S., Tarasoff, L., Bryja, B., Dennis, C-L., Yudin, M., & Ross, L. (2013). Relation between place of residence and postpartum depression. *Canadian Medical Association Journal, 185*, 1129–1135.

Vihman, M. M. (1985). Language differentiation by the bilingual infant. *Journal of Child Language, 12*, 297–324.

Vineis, P. (2005). Environmental tobacco smoke and risk of respiratory cancer and chronic obstructive pulmonary disease in former smokers and never smokers in the EPIC prospective study. *BMJ: British Medical Journal, 330*(7486), 277–280.

Viron, M., Bello, I., Freudenreich, O., & Shtasel, D. (2014). Characteristics of homeless adults with serious mental illness served by a state mental health transitional shelter. *Community Mental Health Journal, 50*, 560–565. doi:10.1007/s10597-013-9607-5.

Vitiello, M. V. (2009). Recent advances in understanding sleep and sleep disturbances in older adults: Growing older does not mean sleeping poorly. *Current Directions in Psychological Science, 18*(6), 316–320.

Vlassova, A., & Pearson, J. (2013). Look before you leap: Sensory memory improves decision making. *Psychological Science, 24*, 1635–1643.

Vogel, I., Brug, J., Hosli, E. J., van der Ploeg, C. P. B., & Raat, H. (2008). MP3 players and hearing loss: Adolescents' perceptions of loud music and hearing conservation. *Journal of Pediatrics, 152*(3), 400–404.

Volkmar, F. R., & McPartland, J. C. (2014). From Kanner to DSM-5: Autism as an evolving diagnostic concept. *Annual Review of Clinical Psychology, 10*, 193–212.

Volkmar, F. R., Klin, A., Schultz, R. T., & State, M. W. (2009). Pervasive developmental disorders. In B. J. Sadock, A. Sadock, & P. Ruiz (Eds.), *Kaplan & Sadock's comprehensive textbook of psychiatry* (9th ed., pp. 3540–3559). Philadelphia, PA: Lippincott Williams & Wilkins.

Volkow, N. D., Fowler, J. S., & Wang, G. J. (2004). The addicted human brain viewed in the light of imaging studies: Brain circuits and treatment strategies. *Neuropharmacology, 47*, 3–13.

von Ranson, K., & Wallace, L. (2014). Eating disorders. In E. J. Mash, R. A. Barkley (Eds.), *Child psychopathology* (3rd ed., pp. 801–847). New York, NY: Guildford Press.

Vondracek, F. W., & Crouter, A. C. (2013). Health and human development. In R. M. Lerner, M. A. East-erbrooks, J. Mistry, & I. B. Weiner (Eds.), *Handbook of psychology: Vol. 6. Developmental psychology.* New York, NY: Wiley.

von Helmholtz, H. (1852). On the theory of compound colors. *Philosophical Magazine, 4*, 519–534.

von Helmholtz, H. (1863). *On the sensations of tone as a physiological basis for the theory of music* (A. J. Ellis, Trans.). New York, NY: Dover.

Von Hofsten, C., & Rosander, K. (2015). On the development of the mirror neuron system. In P. F. Ferari & G. Rizzolatti (Eds.), *New frontiers in mirror neuron research.* New York, NY: Oxford University Press.

von Károlyi, C., & Winner, E. (2005). Extreme giftedness. In R. J. Sternberg & J. E. Davidson (Eds.), *Conceptions of giftedness.* New York, NY: Cambridge University Press.

Vorauer, J. D., & Quesnel, M. (2016). Don't bring me down: Divergent effects of being the target of empathy versus perspective taking on minority group members' perceptions of their group's social standing. *Group Processes and Intergroup Relations, 19*, 94–104.

Vorauer, J. D., & Quesnel, M. (in press a). Ideology and voice: Salient multiculturalism enhances minority group members' persuasiveness in intergroup interaction. *Social Psychological and Personality Science.*

Vorauer, J. D., & Quesnel, M. (in press b). Salient multiculturalism enhances minority group members' feelings of power. *Personality and Social Psychology Bulletin.*

Voss, U. (2011). Lucid dreams unlock clues about consciousness. *Scientific American Mind*, November 2011, 33–35.

Voss, U., Holzmann, R., Tuin, I., & Hobson, A. (2009). Lucid dreaming: A state of consciousness with features of both waking and non-lucid dreaming. *Sleep, 32*, 1191–1200.

Votta-Bleeker, L., Tiessen, M., & Murdoch, M. (2016). A snapshot of Canada's psychology graduates: Initial analysis of the 2015 Psychology Graduates Survey. *Canadian Psychology/Psychologie canadienne, 57*(3), 172–180.

Voyer, D., Bowes, A., & Soraggi, M. (2009). Response procedure and laterality effects in emotion recognition: Implications for models of dichotic listening. *Neuropsychologia, 47*, 23–29.

Voyer, D., Nolan, C., & Voyer, S. (2000). The relation between experience and spatial performance in men and women. *Sex Roles, 43*, 891–915.

Vriend, J. L., Davidson, F. D., Corkum, P. V., Rusack, B., & Chambers, C. T. (2013). Manipulating sleep duration alters emotional functioning and cognitive performance in children. *Journal of Pediatric Psychology, 38*, 1058–1069.

Vriend, J. L., Davidson, F., Rusak, B., & Corkum, P. (2015). Emotional and cognitive impact of sleep restriction. *Sleep Medicine Clinics, 10*, 107–115.

Vyas, M. V., Garg, A. X., Iansavichus, A. V., Costella, J., Donner, A., Laugsand, L. E., . . . Hackam, D. G. (2012). Shift work and vascular events: Systematic review and meta-analysis. *British Medical Journal, 345*, e4800. doi:10.1136/bmj.e4800.

Vygotsky, L. S. (1934/1962). *Thought and language.* E. Hanfmann, & G. Vakar (Trans). Cambridge, MA: MIT Press.

Waage, S., Moen, B., Pallesen, S., Eriksen, H. R., Ursin, H., Åkerstedt, T., & Bjorvatn, B. (2009). Shift work disorder among oil rig workers in the North Sea. *Sleep: Journal of Sleep and Sleep Disorders Research, 32*(4), 558–565.

Wachtel, P. L. (1977). *Psychoanalysis and behavior therapy: Toward an integration.* New York, NY: Basic Books.

Wachtel, P. L. (1991). From eclectism to synthesis: Toward a more seamless psychotherapeutic integration. *Journal of Psychotherapy Integration, 1*, 43–54.

Wadlinger, H. A., & Isaacowitz, D. M. (2011). Fixing our focus: Training attention to regulate emotion. *Personality and Social Psychology Review, 15*, 75–102.

Wager, T. D., Hernandez, L., & Lindquist, M. A. (2009). Essentials of functional neuroimaging. In G. G. Bernston & J. T. Cacioppo (Eds.), *Handbook of neuroscience for the behavioral sciences* (Vol. 1, pp. 152–197). New York, NY: Wiley.

Wager, T. D., Scott, D. J, & Zubieta, J. K. (2007). Placebo effects on human mu-opiod ativity during pain. *Proceedings of the National Academy of Sciences, 104*, 11056–11061.

Wagner, B. C., & Petty, R. E. (2011). The elaboration likelihood model of persuasion: Thoughtful and non-thoughtful social influence. In D. Chadee (Ed.), *Theories in social psychology* (pp. 96–116). Oxford: Blackwell.

Wagner, H. (1989). The physiological differentiation of emotions. In H. Wagner & A. Manstead (Eds.), *Handbook of social psychophysiology.* New York, NY: Wiley.

Wagstaff, G. F., David, D., Kirsch, I., & Lynn, S. J. (2010). The cognitive-behavioral model of hypnotherapy. In S. J. Lynn, J. W. Rhue, & I. Kirsch (Eds.), *Handbook of clinical hypnosis* (2nd ed., pp. 179–208). Washington, DC: American Psychological Association.

Wai, J., Cacchio, M., Putallaz, M., & Makel, M. C. (2010). Sex differences in the right tail of cognitive abilities: A 30-year examination. *Intelligence, 38*(4), 412–423.

Wakefield, J. C. (1999). The measurement of mental disorder. In A. V. Horvitz & T. L. Scheid (Eds.), *A handbook for the study of mental health: Social contexts, theories, and systems.* New York, NY: Cambridge University Press.

Wakefield, J. C., & Spitzer, R. L. (2002). Lowered estimates—But of what? *Archives of General Psychiatry, 59*(2), 129–130.

Wald, G. (1964). The receptors of human color vision. *Science, 145*, 1007–1017.

Walder, D. J., Laplante, D. P., Sousa-Pires, A., Veru, F., Brunet, A., & King, S. (2014). Prenatal maternal stress predicts autism traits in 6 1/2 year-old children: Project ice storm. *Psychiatry Research, 219*, 353–360. doi:10.1016/j.psychres.2014.04.034.

Waldram, J. B. (Ed.). (2008). *Aboriginal healing in Canada: Studies in therapeutic meaning and practice.* Ottawa, ON: Aboriginal Healing Foundation.

Waldrop, D., Lightsey, O. R., Ethington, C. A., Woemmel, C. A., & Coke, A. L. (2001). Self-efficacy, optimism, health competence, and recovery from orthopedic surgery. *Journal of Counseling Psychology, 48*, 233–238.

Walker, E., & Tessner, K. (2008). Schizophrenia. *Perspectives on Psychological Science, 3*, 30–37.

Walker, E., Mittal, V., & Tessner, K. (2008). Stress and the hypothalamic pituitary adrenal axis in the developmental course of schizophrenia. *Annual Review of Clinical Psychology, 4*, 189–216.

Walker, L. J. (1989). A longitudinal study of moral reasoning. *Child Development, 60*, 157–166.

Walker, L. J. (2007). Progress and prospects in the psychology of moral development. In G. W. Ladd (Ed.), *Appraising the human developmental sciences: Essays in honor of Merrill-Palmer Quarterly* (pp. 226–237). Detroit: Wayne State University Press.

Walker, M. P. (2012). The role of sleep in neurocognitive functioning. In C. M. Morin, & C. A. Espie (Eds.), *Oxford handbook of sleep and sleep disorders.* New York, NY: Oxford University Press.

Walker, M. P., Brakefield, T., Morgan, A., Hobson, J. A., & Stickgold, R. (2002). Practice with sleep makes perfect: Sleep dependent motor skill learning. *Neuron, 35*, 205–211.

Walker, M. P., & Stickgold, R. (2004). Sleep-dependent learning and memory consolidation. *Neuron, 44*, 121–133.

Walker, M. P., & Stickgold, R. (2006). Sleep, memory, and plasticity. *Annual Review of Psychology, 57*, 139–166.

Wallace, B., & Fisher, L. E. (1999). *Consciousness and behavior.* Boston, MA: Allyn & Bacon.

Wallace, D. S., Paulson, R. M., Lord, C. G., & Bond, C. F. Jr. (2005). Which behaviors do attitudes predict? Meta-analyzing the effects of social pressure and perceived difficulty. *Review of General Psychology, 9*, 214–227.

Wallman, J. (1992). *Aping language.* Cambridge, England: Cambridge University Press.

Wallner, B., & Machatschke, I. H. (2009). The evolution of violence in men: The function of central cholesterol and serotonin. *Progress in Neuro-Psychopharmacology & Biological Psychiatry, 33*(3), 391–397.

Walsh, B. T., Seidman, S. N., Sysko, R., & Gould, M. (2002). Placebo response studies of major depression: Variable, substantial and growing. *JAMA, 287*, 1840–1847.

Walsh, J. K., & Roth, T. (2011). Pharmacological treatment of insomnia: Benzodiazepine receptor agonists. In M. H. Kryger, T. Roth, & W. C. Dement (Eds.), *Principles and practice of sleep medicine* (5th ed.). Saint Louis, MO: Elsevier Saunders.

Walsh, J. K., Dement, W. C., & Dinges, D. F. (2011). Sleep medicine, public policy, and public health. In M. H. Kryger, T. Roth, & W. C. Dement (Eds.), *Principles and practice of sleep medicine* (5th ed.). Saint Louis, MO: Elsevier Saunders.

Walsh, R., & Shapiro, S. L. (2006). The meeting of meditative disciplines and Western psychology: A mutually enriching dialogue. *American Psychologist, 61*, 227–239.

Walter, C. A. (2000). The psychological meaning of menopause: Women's experiences. *Journal of Women and Aging, 12*(3–4), 117–131.

Walther, E., & Langer, T. (2008). Attitude formation and change through association: An evaluative conditioning account. In W. D. Crano, & R. Prislin (Eds.), *Attitudes and attitude change* (pp. 61–84). New York, NY: Psychology Press.

Walther, E., Nagengast, B., & Trasselli, C. (2005). Evaluative conditioning in social psychology: Facts and speculations. *Cognition and Emotion, 19*(2), 175–196.

Walton, G. M., & Cohen, G. L. (2007). A question of belonging: Race, social fit, and achievement. *Journal of Personality and Social Psychology, 92*, 82–96.

Walton, G. M., Cohen, G. L., Cwir, D., & Spencer, S. J. (2011). Mere belonging: The power of social connections. *Journal of Personality and Social Psychology, 102*, 513–532.

Walton, K. G., Fields, J. Z., Levitsky, D. K., Harris, D. A., Pugh, N. D., & Schneider, R. H. (2004). Lowering cortisol and CVD risk in postmenopausal women: A pilot study using Transcendental Meditation program. In R. Yehuda, & B. McEwen (Eds.), *Biobehavioral stress response: Protective and damaging effects* (pp. 211–215). New York, NY: Annals of the New York Academy of Sciences.

Wammes, J. D., et al. (2016a). Mind wandering during lectures I: Changes in rates across an entire semester. *Scholarship of Teaching and Learning in Psychology, 2*(1), 13–32.

Wammes, J. D., et al. (2016b). Mind wandering during lectures II: Relation to academic performance. *Scholarship of Teaching and Learning in Psychology, 2*(1), 33–48.

Wampold, B. E. (2001). *The great psychotherapy debate.* Mahwah, NJ: Erlbaum.

Wampold, B. E. (2013). The good, the bad, and the ugly: A 50-year perspective on the outcome problem. *Psychotherapy, 50*(1), 16–24. doi:10.1037/a0030570.

Wampold, B. E., Imel, Z. E., & Minami, T. (2007). The story of placebo effects in medicine: Evidence in context. *Journal of Clinical Psychology, 63*(4), 379–390.

Wampold, B. E., Minami, T., Tierney, S. C., Baskin, T. W., & Bhati, K. S. (2005). The placebo is powerful: Estimating placebo effects in medicine and psychotherapy from randomized clinical trials. *Journal of Clinical Psychology, 61*(7), 835–854.

Wamsley, E. J., & Stickgold, R. (2009). Incorporation of waking events into dreams. In R. Stickgold & M. P. Walker (Eds.), *The neuroscience of sleep* (pp. 330 –336). London, UK: Academic Press.

Wang, C., Ku, G., Tai, K., & Galinsky, A. (2014). Stupid doctors and smart construction workers: Perspective taking reduces stereotyping of both negative and positive targets. *Social Psychological and Personality Science, 5*, 430–436.

Wang, P. S., Berglund, P., Olfson, M., Pincus, H. A., Wells, K. B., & Kessler, R. C. (2005). Failure and delay in initial treatment contact after first onset of mental disorders in the National Comorbidity Survey Replication. *Archives of General Psychiatry, 62*, 603–613.

Wang, P. S., Tohen, M., Bromet, E. J., Angst, J., & Kessler, R. C. (2008). Psychiatric epidemiology. In A. Tasman, J. Kay, J. A. Lieberman, M. B. First, & M. Maj (Eds.), *Psychiatry* (3rd ed.). New York, NY: Wiley-Blackwell.

Wang, S. (2006). Mindfulness meditation: Its personal and professional impact on psychotherapists. Doctoral Thesis, Capella Universiti.

Wang, S. S. (2013). Exercise as good as medications. *The Globe and Mail,* Friday October 4, L6.

Wangensteen, O. H., & Carlson, A. J. (1931). Hunger sensation after total gastrectomy. *Proceedings of the Society for Experimental Biology, 28*, 545–547.

Wansink, B. (2012). Specific environmental drivers of eating. In K. D. Brownell, & M. S. Gold (Eds.), *Food and addiction: A comprehensive handbook.* New York, NY: Oxford University Press.

Wansink, B., & Chandon, P. (2014). Slim by design: Redirecting the accidental drivers of mindless overeating. *Journal of Consumer Psychology, 24*, 413–431. doi:10.1016/j.jcps.2014.03.006.

Wansink, B., & van Ittersum, K. (2013). Portion size me: Plate-size induced consumption norms and win-win solutions for reducing food intake and waste. *Journal of Experimental Psychology: Applied, 19*(4), 320–332. doi:10.1037/a0035053.

Warburton, W. (2014). Apples, oranges, and the burden of proof— Putting media violence findings into context: A comment on Elson and Ferguson (2013). *European Psychologist, 19*, 60–67. doi:10.1027/1016-9040/a000166.

Ward, B. W., Schiller, J. S., & Goodman, R. A. (2014). Multiple chronic conditions among U.S. adults: A 2012 update. *Preventing Chronic Disease, 11*, 130389. doi:10.5888/pcd11.130389.

Ward, J. (2013). Synesthesia. *Annual Review of Psychology, 64*, 49–75.

Wardle, J., Steptoe, A., Oliver, G., & Lipsey, Z. (2000). Stress, dietary restraint and food intake. *Journal of Psychosomatic Research, 48*, 195–202.

Warr, P. (1999). Well-being and the workplace. In D. Kahneman, E. Diener, & N. Schwarz (Eds.), *Well-being: The foundations of hedonic psychology.* New York, NY: Russell Sage Foundation.

Warrington, E. K., & Weiskrantz, L. (1970). Amnesic syndrome: Consolidation or retrieval? *Nature, 228*, 629–630.

Washburn, M. F. (1908). *The animal mind.* New York, NY: Macmillan.

Wasserman, J. D., & Bracken, B. A. (2003). Psychometric characteristics of assessment procedures. In J. R. Graham & J. A. Naglieri (Eds.), *Handbook of psychology (Vol. 10): Assessment psychology.* New York, NY: Wiley.

Waterhouse, L. (2006). Multiple intelligences, the Mozart effect, and emotional intelligence: A critical review. *Educational Psychologist, 41*, 207–225.

Waterman, A. S. (2013). The humanistic psychology-positive psychology divide: Contrasts in philosophical foundations. *American Psychologist, 68*, 124–133.

Watson, D. L., & Tharp, R. G. (2014). *Self-directed behavior: Self-modification for personal adjustment.* Belmont, CA: Cengage Learning.

Watson, D., Klohen, E. C., Casillas, A., Nus Simms, E., Haig, J., & Berry, D. S. (2004). Match makers and deal breakers: Analyses of assortative mating in newlywed couples. *Journal of Personality, 72*, 1029–1068.

Watson, J. B. (1913). Psychology as the behaviorist views it. *Psychological Review, 20*, 158–177.

Watson, J. B. (1919). *Psychology from the standpoint of a behaviorist.* Philadelphia, PA: Lippincott.

Watson, J. B. (1924). *Behaviorism.* New York, NY: Norton.

Watson, J. B., & Rayner, R. (1920). Conditioned emotional reactions. *Journal of Experimental Psychology, 3*, 1–14.

Waugh, N. C., & Norman, D. A. (1965). Primary memory. *Psychological Review, 72*, 89–104.

Waxman, S. R. (2002). Early word-learning and conceptual development: Everything had a name and each name gave birth to a new thought. In U. Goswami (Ed.), *Blackwell handbook of childhood cognitive development* (pp. 102–126). Malden, MA: Blackwell.

Weatherall, A. (1992). Gender and languages: Research in progress. *Feminism & Psychology, 2*, 177–181.

Weaver, D. R., & Reppert, S. M. (2008). Circadian timekeeping. In L. Squire, D. Berg, F. Bloom, S. Du Lac, A. Ghosh, & N. Spitzer (Eds.), *Fundamental neuroscience* (3rd ed., pp. 931–958). San Diego, CA: Academic Press.

Weaver, J. (2010). Why some memories stick. *Nature,* published online.

Weaver, T. E., & George, C. F. P. (2011). Cognition and performance in patients with obstructive sleep apnea. In M. H. Kryger, T. Roth, & W. C. Dement (Eds.), *Principles and practice of sleep medicine* (5th ed.). Saint Louis, MO: Elsevier Saunders.

Webb, W. B. (1992b). *Sleep: The gentle tyrant.* Bolton, MA: Anker.

Webb, W. B., & Dinges, D. F. (1989). Cultural perspectives on napping and the siesta. In D. F. Dinges & R. J. Broughton (Eds.), *Sleep and alertness: Chronobiological, behavioral, and medical aspects of napping.* New York, NY: Raven.

Weber, R. (2013). Hungry aboriginal kids, adults, were subject of experiments: paper. *Maclean's Magazine,* July 7, 2013.

Webster, G. D. (2009). Parental investment theory. In H. T. Reis & S. Sprecher (Eds.), *Encyclopedia of human relationships* (Vol. 3, pp. 1194–1197). Los Angeles, CA: Sage.

Webster, M. (2010). Color perception. In E. B. Goldstein (Ed.), *Encyclopedia of perception.* Thousand Oaks, CA: Sage.

Wechsler, D. (1939). *The measurement of adult intelligence.* Baltimore, MD: Williams & Wilkins.

Wechsler, D. (1949). *Wechsler intelligence scale for children.* New York, NY: Psychological Corporation.

Wechsler, D. (1955). *Manual, Wechsler adult intelligence scale.* New York, NY: Psychological Corporation.

Wechsler, D. (1967). Manual for the Wechsler preschool and primary scale of intelligence. New York, NY: Psychological Corporation.

Wechsler, D. (1981). *Manual for the Wechsler adult intelligence scale—revised.* New York, NY: Psychological Corporation.

Wechsler, D. (1991). *WISC-III manual.* San Antonio: Psychological Corporation.

Wechsler, D. (2003). *Wechsler Intelligence Scale for Children–Fourth Edition (WISC IV).* San Antonio, TX: Psychological Corporation.

Wechsler, H., Lee, J. E., Kuo, M, Seibring, M., Nelson, T. F., & Lee, H. (2002). Trends in college binge drinking during a period of increased prevention efforts: Findings from 4 Harvard School of Public Health College Alcohol Study surveys: 1993– 2001. *Journal of American College Health, 50*, 203–217.

Wegner, D. M. (1997). Why the mind wanders. In J. D. Cohen & J. W. Schooler (Eds.), *Scientific approaches to consciousness.* Mahwah, NJ: Erlbaum.

Wegner, D., & Gray, K. (2016). *The mind club: Who thinks, what feels, and why it matters.* New York, NY: Viking Press.

Weich, S., Pearce, H. L., Croft, P., Singh, S., Crome, I., Bashford, J., & Fisher, M. (2014). Effect of anxiolytic and hypnotic drug prescriptions on mortality hazards: Retrospective cohort study. *British Medical Journal, 348*, g1996. doi:10.1136/bmj.g1996.

Weinberg, R. A. (1989). Intelligence and IQ: Landmark issues and great debates. *American Psychologist, 44*, 98–104.

Weinberger, J. (1995). Common factors aren't so common: The common factors dilemma. *Clinical Psychology: Science and Practice, 2*(1), 45–69. doi:10.1111/j.1468-2850.1995.tb00024.x.

Weiner, B. (1980). *Human motivation.* New York, NY: Holt, Rinehart & Winston.

Weiner, B. (1994). Integrating social and personal theories of achievement striving. *Review of Educational Research, 64*, 557–573.

Weiner, B. (Ed.). (1974). *Achievement motivation and attribution theory.* Morristown, NJ: General Learning Press.

Weiner, B., Osborne, D., & Rudolph, U. (2011). An attributional analysis of reactions to poverty: The political ideology of the giver and the perceived morality of the receiver. *Personality and Social Psychology Review, 15,* 199–213. doi:10.1177/1088868310387615.

Weiner, I. B. (2013a). Applying Rorschach assessment. In G. P. Koocher, J. C. Norcross, & B. A. Greene (Eds.), *Psychologists' desk reference* (3rd ed.). New York, NY: Oxford University Press.

Weiner, I. B. (2013b). Assessment psychology. In D. K. Freedheim, & I. B. Weiner (Eds.), *Handbook of psychology: Vol. 1. History of psychology* (2nd ed.). New York, NY: Wiley.

Weiner, I. B., & Meyer, G. J. (2009). Personality assessment with the Rorschach Inkblot Method. In I. N. Butcher (Ed.), *Oxford handbook of personality assessment.* New York, NY: Oxford University Press.

Weiner, M. F. (2014). Neurocognitive disorders. In R. E. Hales, S. C. Yudofsky, & L. W. Roberts (Eds.), *The American Psychiatric Publishing textbook of psychiatry* (6th ed., pp. 815–850). Washington, DC: American Psychiatric Publishing.

Weinstein, N. D. (1984). Why it won't happen to me: Perceptions of risk factors and susceptibility. *Health Psychology, 3,* 431–458.

Weinstein, N. D., & Klein, W. M. (1995). Resistance of personal risk perceptions to debiasing interventions. *Health Psychology, 14,* 132–140.

Weinsten, A., Curtiss, F., Rosenberg, I. P., & Dannon, P. (2014). Internet addiction disorder: Overview and controversies. In K. P. Rosenberg & J. Curtiss Feder (Eds.), *Behavioral addictions: Criteria, evidence, and treatment.* San Diego, CA: Elsevier Academic Press.

Weintraub, K. (2011). Autism counts. *Nature, 479*(7371), 22–24.

Weisberg, R. W. (1986). *Creativity: Genius and other myths.* New York, NY: W. H. Freeman.

Weisberg, R. W. (1993). *Creativity: Beyond the myth of genius.* New York, NY: W. H. Freeman.

Weisberg, R. W. (1999). Creativity and knowledge: A challenge to theories. In R. J. Sternberg (Ed.), *Handbook of creativity.* New York, NY: Cambridge University Press.

Weisberg, R. W. (2006). *Creativity: Understanding innovation in problem solving, science, invention, and the arts.* New York, NY: Wiley.

Weise-Kelly, L., & Siegel, S. (2001). Self-administration cues as signals: Drug self-administration and tolerance. *Journal of Experimental Psychology: Animal Behavior Processes, 27,* 125–136.

Weiser, D. A., & Riggio, H. R. (2010). Family background and academic achievement: Does self-efficacy mediate outcomes? *Social Psychology of Education, 13*(3), 367–383.

Weisleder, A., & Fernald, A. (2013). Talking to children matters: Early language experience strengthens processing and builds vocabulary. *Psychological Science,* doi: 10.1177/0956797613488145.

Weisler, R. H., Barbee, J. G., & Townsend, M. H. (2007). Mental health and recovery in the Gulf Coast after Hurricanes Katrina and Rita. *Journal of the American Medical Association, 296,* 585–588.

Weisman, O., Zagoory-Sharon, O., & Feldman, R. (2014). Oxytocin administration, salivary testosterone, and father-infant social behavior. *Progress in Neuro-Psychopharmacology & Biological Psychiatry, 49,* 47–52. doi:10.1016/j.pnpbp.2013.11.006.

Weisman, R. (1995). Reflections on the Oak Ridge experiment with mentally disordered offenders, 1965–1968. *International Journal of Law and Psychiatry, 18,* 265–290.

Weiss, A., Bates, T. C., & Luciano, M. (2008). Happiness is a personal(ity) thing. *Psychological Science, 19,* 205–210.

Weiss, D., & Lalonde, R. N. (2001). Responses of female undergraduates to sexual harassment by male professors or teaching assistants. *Canadian Journal of Behavioural Science, 33,* 148–163.

Weiten, W. (1988). Pressure as a form of stress and its relationship to psychological symptomatology. *Journal of Social and Clinical Psychology, 6*(1) 127–139.

Weiten, W. (1998). Pressure, major life events, and psychological symptoms. *Journal of Social Behavior and Personality, 13,* 51–68.

Weiten, W., & Wight, R. D. (1992). Portraits of a discipline: An examination of introductory psychology textbooks in America. In A. E. Puente, J. R. Matthews, & C. L. Brewer (Eds.), *Teaching psychology in America: A history.* Washington, DC: American Psychological Association.

Well, A. D., Pollatsek, A., & Boyce, S. J. (1990). Understanding the effects of sample size on the variability of the mean. *Organizational Behavior and Human Decision Processes, 47,* 289–312.

Wellman, H. M. (2002). Understanding the psychological world: Developing a theory of mind. In U. Goswami (Ed.), *Blackwell handbook of childhood cognitive development* (pp. 166–187). Malden, MA: Blackwell.

Wellman, H. M., & Gelman, S. A. (1998). Knowledge acquisition in foundational domians. In W. Damon (Ed.), *Handbook of child psychology (Vol. 2): Cognition, perception, and language.* New York, NY: Wiley.

Wells, G. L., & Bradfield, A. L. (1998). "Good, you identified the suspect": Feedback to eyewitnesses distorts their reports of the witnessing experience. *Journal of Applied Psychology, 83,* 360–376.

Wells, G. L., & Olson, E. A. (2003). Eyewitness testimony. *Annual Review of Psychology, 54,* 277–295.

Wells, H. G. (1895/1995). *The time machine.* New York, NY: Dover Publications.

Wells, J. (2016). Is video gaming bad for you? The science for and against. *The Telegraph,* June 9, 2016. Retrieved from http://www.telegraph.co.uk/men/thinking-man/is-video-gaming-bad-for-you-the-science-for-and-against/.

Wener, R. E., & Evans, G. W. (2011). Comparing stress of car and train commuters. *Transportation Research Part F: Traffic Psychology and Behavior, 14,* 111–116. doi:10.1016/j.trf.2010.11.008.

Werker J., & Tees, R. C. (2005). Speech perception as a window for understanding the plasticity and commitment in language systems of the brain. *Developmental Psychobiology, 46,* 233–251.

Werker, J. F. (2003). Baby steps to learning language. *Journal of Pediatrics, 143* (Supplement), 62–69.

Werker, J. F., & Hensch, T. K. (2015). Critical periods in speech perception: New Directions. *Annual Review of Psychology, 66,* 173–196.

Werker, J. F., & Tees, R. C. (1999). Experiential influences on infant speech processing: toward a new synthesis. In J. T. Spence (Ed.), J. M. Darley & D. J. Foss (Associate Editors), *Annual review of psychology, 50* (pp. 509–535). Palo Alto, CA: Annual Reviews.

Werker, J. F., Yeung, H. H., & Yoshida, K. (2012). How do infants become experts at native speech perception? *Current Directions in Psychological Science, 21*(4), 221–226.

Wertheimer, M. [Max]. (1912). Exper-imentelle studien über das sehen von bewegung. *Zeitschrift für Psychologie, 60,* 312–378.

Wertheimer, M. [Michael]. (2012). *A brief history of psychology.* New York, NY: Psychology Press.

Wertsch, J. V., & Tulviste, P. (2005). L. S. Vygotsky and contemporary developmental psychology. In H. Daniels (Ed.), *An introduction to Vygotsky.* New York, NY: Routledge.

Wertz, A. E., & Wynn, K. (2014). Selective social learning of plant edibility in 6- and 18-month-old infants. *Psychological Science, 25,* 874–882. doi:10 .1177/0956797613516145.

Wertz, F. J. (1998). The role of the humanistic movement in the history of psychology. *Journal of Humanistic Psychology, 38,* 42–70.

Westaby, J. D. (2006). Identifying specific factors underlying attitudes toward change: Using multiple methods to compare expectancy-value theory to reasons theory. *Journal of Applied Social Psychology, 32,* 1083–1106.

Westen, D. Gabbard, G. O., & Ortigo, K. M. (2008). Psychoanalytic approaches to personality. In O. P. John, R. W. Robins, & L. A. Pervin (Eds.), *Handbook of personality psychology: Theory and research* (3rd ed.; pp. 61–113). New York, NY: Guilford Press.

Wetherby, A. M., & Prizant, B. M. (2005). Enhancing language and communication development in autism spectrum disorders: Assessment and intervention guidelines. In D. Zager (Ed.), *Autism spectrum disorders: Identification, education, and treatment* (3rd ed., pp. 327–365). Hillside, NJ: Lawrence Erlbaum Associates.

Whelan, R., Conrod, P. J., Poline, J. B., Lourdusamy, A., Banaschewski, T., Barker, G., et al. (2012). Adolescent impulsivity phenotypes characterized by distinct brain networks. *Nature Neuroscience,15,* 920–925.

Whissell, C. (2006). Emotion in the sounds of pets' names. *Perceptual and Motor Skills, 102,* 121–124.

Whissell, C. (2008a). A comparison of two lists providing emotional norms for English words (ANEW and the DAL). *Psychological Reports, 102,* 597–600.

Whissell, C. (2008b). Emotional fluctuations in Bob Dylan's lyrics measured by the Dictionary of Affect accompany events and phases in his life. *Psychological Reports, 102,* 469–483.

Whitaker, R. (2002). *Mad in America: Bad science, bad medicine, and the enduring mistreatment of the mentally ill.* New York, NY: Perseus Publishing.

Whitbourne, S. K., Sneed, J. R., & Skultety, K. M. (2002). Identity processes in adulthood: Theoretical and methodological challenges. *Identity, 2,* 29–45.

Whitchurch, E. R., Wilson, T. D., & Gilbert, D. T. (2011). "He loves me, he loves me not . . .": Uncertainty can increase romantic attraction. *Psychological Science, 22,* 172–175.

White, C. M., & Hoffrage, U. (2009). Testing the tyranny of too much choice against the allure of more choice. *Psychology & Marketing, 26*(3), 280–298.

White, J. H., Quinn, M., Garland, S., Dirkse, D., Wiebe, P., Hermann, M., & Carlson, L. E. (2015). Animal-assisted therapy and counseling support for women with breast cancer. *Integrative Cancer Therapies, 14,* 460–467.

White, T., Ehrlich, S., Ho, B., Manoach, D. S., Caprihan, A., Schulz, S. C., . . . Magnotta, V. A. (2013). Spatial characteristics of white matter abnormalties in schizophrenia. *Schizophrenia Bulletin, 39,* 1077–1086.

Whitfield, C. L. (1995). *Memory and abuse: Remembering and healing the effects of trauma.* Deerfield Beach, FL: Health Communications.

Whiting, J. W. M., Burbank, V. K., & Ratner, M. S. (1986). The duration of maidenhood. In J. B. Lancaster & B. A. Hamburg (Eds.), *School age pregnancy and parenthood.* Hawthorne, NY: Aldine de Gruyter.

Whittal, M. L., Woody, S. R., McLean, P. D., Rachman, S. J., & Robichaud, M. (2010). Treatment of obsessions: A randomized controlled trial. *Behaviour Research and Therapy, 48,* 295–303.

Whitwell, R. L., Milner, D., Cavina-Pratesi, C., Byrne, C. M., & Goodale, M. A. (2013). DF's visual brain in action: The role of tactile cues. *Neuropsychologica, 55,* 41–50.

Whorf, B. L. (1956). Science and linguistics. In J. B. Carroll (Ed.), *Language, thought and reality: Selected writings of Benjamin Lee Whorf.* Cambridge, MA: MIT Press.

Wickens, T. D. (1999). Measuring the time course of retention. In C. Izawa (Ed.), *On human memory: Evolution, progress, and reflections on the 30th anniversary of the Atkinson–Shiffrin model.* Mahwah, NJ: Erlbaum.

Widiger, T. A. (2009). Neuroticism. In M. R. Leary & R. H. Hoyle (Eds.), *Handbook of individual differences in social behavior* (pp. 129–146). New York, NY: Guilford Press.

Widiger, T. A., & Crego, C. (2013). Diagnosis and classification. In T. A. Widiger, G. Stricker, I. B. Weiner, G. Stricker, T. A. Widiger, & I. B. Weiner (Eds.), *Handbook of psychology: Vol. 8. Clinical psychology* (2nd ed.). New York, NY: Wiley.

Widiger, T. A., & Sankis, L. M. (2000). Adult psychopathology: Issues and controversies. *Annual Review of Psychology, 51,* 377–404.

Widiger, T. A., Livesley, W., & Clark, L. (2009). An integrative dimensional classification of personality disorder. *Psychological Assessment, 21*(3), 243–255.

Widom, C. S., Czaja, S. J., & Paris, J. (2009). A prospective investigation of borderline personality disorder in abused and neglected children followed up into adulthood. *Journal of Personality Disorders, 23*(5), 433–446.

Wiesel, T. N., & Hubel, D. H. (1963). Single-cell responses in striate cortex of kittens deprived of vision in one eye. *Journal of Neurophysiology, 26*, 1003–1017.

Wiesel, T. N., & Hubel, D. H. (1965). Extent of recovery from the effects of visual deprivation in kittens. *Journal of Neurophysiology, 28*, 1060–1072.

Wiggs, C. L., Weisberg, J., & Martin, A. (1999). Neural correlates of semantic and episodic memory retreival. *Neuropsychologia, 37*, 103–118.

Wikelgren, I. (1999). Nature helps mold able minds. *Science, 283*, 1832–1834.

Wilde, E. A., Kim, H. F., Schulz, P. E., & Yudofsky, S. C. (2014). Neurocognitive disorders. In R. E. Hales, S. C. Yudofsky, & L. W. Roberts (Eds.), *The American Psychiatric Publishing textbook of psychiatry* (6th ed.). Washington, DC: American Psychiatric Publishing.

Wilding, J., & Valentine, E. (1996). Memory expertise. In D. J. Herrmann, C. McEvoy, C. Hertzog, P. Hertel, & M. K. Johnson (Eds.), *Basic and applied memory research: Theory in context* (Vol. 1). Mahwah, NJ: Erlbaum.

Willford, J. A., Leech, S. L., & Day, N. L. (2006). Moderate prenatal alcohol exposure and cognitive status of children at age 10. *Alcoholism: Clinical and Experimental Research, 30*, 1051–1059.

Williams, B. A. (1988). Reinforcement, choice, and response strength. In R. C. Atkinson, R. J. Herrnstein, G. Lindzey, & R. D. Luce (Eds.), *Stevens' handbook of experimental psychology*. New York, NY: Wiley.

Williams, B. A. (1994). Conditioned reinforcement: Neglected or outmoded explanatory construct? *Psychonomic Bulletin & Review, 1*, 457–475.

Williams, J. E., Paton, C. C., Siegler, I. C., Eigenbrodt, M. L., Neito, F. J., & Tyroler, H. A. (2000). Anger proneness predicts coronary heart disease risk. *Circulation, 101*, 2034–2039.

Williams, J. M. G., Teasdale, J. D., Segal, Z. V., & Soulsby, J. (2000). Mindfulness-based cognitive therapy reduced over general autobiographical memory in formerly depressed patients. *Journal of Abnormal Psychology, 109*, 150–155.

Williams, J. M. G., Teasdale, J., Kabat-Zinn, J., & Segal, Z. V. (2007). *The mindful way through depression: Freeing yourself from chronic unhappiness*. Oxford, UK: Oxford University Press.

Williams, J. M. G., Watts, F. N., MacLeod, C., & Mathews, A. (1997). *Cognitive psychology and emotional disorders*. Chichester, England: Wiley.

Williams, K. D. (2001). *Ostracism: The power of silence*. New York, NY: Guilford Press.

Williams, K. D. (2007). Ostracism. *Annual Review of Psychology, 58*, 425–52.

Williams, L. M. (1994). Recall of childhood trauma: A prospective study of women's memories of child sexual abuse. *Journal of Consulting and Clinical Psychology, 62*, 1167–1176.

Williams, N. A., & Deffenbacher, J. L. (1983). Life stress and chronic yeast infections. *Journal of Human Stress, 9*(1), 26–31.

Williams, P. (2005). What is psychoanalysis? What is a psychoanalyst? In E. S. Person, A. M. Cooper, & G. O. Gabbard (Eds.), *Textbook of psychoanalysis*. Washington, DC: American Psychiatric Publishing.

Williams, R. L. (2013). Overview of the Flynn effect. *Intelligence, 41*, 753– 764. doi:10.1016/j.intell.2013 .04.010.

Williams, R. L., & Eggert, A. (2002). Notetaking predictors of test performance. *Teaching of Psychology, 29*(3), 234–237.

Williams, W. M. (1998). Are we raising smarter children today? School-and-home-related influences on IQ. In U. Neisser (Ed.), *The rising curve: Longterm gains in IQ and related measures*. Washington, DC: American Psychological Association.

Williams, W. M., & Ceci, S. J. (1997). Are Americans becoming more or less alike?: Trends in race, class, and ability differences in intelligence. *American Psychologist, 52*, 1226–1235.

Williamson, D. A., Zucker, N. L., Martin, C. K., & Smeets, M. A. M. (2001). Etiology and management of eating disorders. In P. B. Sutker & H. E. Adams (Eds.), *Comprehensive handbook of psychopathology*. New York, NY: Kluwer Academic/Plenum.

Willingham, D. T., & Dunn, E. W. (2003). What neuroimaging and brain localization can do, cannot do, and should not do for social psychology. *Journal of Personality and Social Psychology, 85*, 1–10.

Wilson, G. T. (2011). Behavior therapy. In R. J. Corsini & D. Wedding (Eds.), *Current psychotherapies* (9th ed.). Belmont, CA: Brooks/Cole.

Wilson, R. E., Gosling, S. D., & Graham, L. T. (2012). A review of Facebook research in the social sciences. *Perspectives on Psychological Science, 7*, 203–220. doi:10.1177/1745691612442904.

Wilson, T. D., & Gilbert, D. T. (2003). Affective forecasting. In M. P. Zanna (Eds.), *Advances in experimental social psychology*, Vol. 35 (pp. 345–411). San Diego, CA: Academic Press.

Wilson, T. D., & Gilbert, D. T. (2005). Affective forecasting: Knowing what to want. *Current Directions in Psychological Science, 14*, 131–134.

Wilt, J., & Revelle, W. (2009). Extraversion. In M. R. Leary & R. H. Hoyle (Eds.), *Handbook of individual differences in social behavior* (pp. 257–273). New York, NY: Guilford Press.

Windholz, G. (1997). Ivan P. Pavlov: An overview of his life and psychological work. *American Psychologist, 52*, 941–946.

Wing, L., & Potter, D. (2009). The epidemiology of autism spectrum disorders: Is the prevalence rising? In S. Goldstein, J. A. Naglieri, & S. Ozonoff (Eds.), *Assessment of autism spectrum disorders* (pp. 18–54). New York, NY: Guilford Press.

Wingfield, A., Tun, P. A., & McCoy, S. L. (2005). Hearing loss in older adulthood: What it is and how it interacts with cognitive performance. *Current Directions in Psychological Science, 14*, 144–148.

Winkielman, P., & Berridge, K. C. (2004). Unconscious emotion. *Current Directions in Psychological Science, 13*(3), 120–123.

Winn, P. (1995). The lateral hypothalmus and motivated behavior: An old syndrome reassessed and a new perspective gained. *Current Directions in Psychological Science, 4*, 182–187.

Winner, E. (1997). Exceptionally high intelligence and schooling. *American Psychologist, 52*, 1070–1081.

Winner, E. (1998). Uncommon talents: Gifted children, prodigies and savants. *Scientific American Presents Exploring Intelligence, 9*, 32–37.

Winner, E. (2000). The origins and ends of giftedness. *American Psychologist, 55*, 159–169.

Winner, E. (2003). Creativity and talent. In M. H. Bornstein & L. Davidson (Eds.), *Well-being: Positive development across the life course*. Mahwah, NJ: Erlbaum.

Winograd, T. (1975). Frame representations and the declarative-procedural controversy. In D. Bobrow & A. Collins (Eds.), *Representation and understanding: Studies in cognitive science*. New York, NY: Academic Press.

Winquist, J. R., & Larson, J. R., Jr. (1998). Information pooling: When it impacts group decision making. *Journal of Personality and Social Psychology, 74*, 371–377.

Winsler, A. (2003). Introduction to special issue: Vygotskian perspectives in early childhood education. *Early Education & Development, 14*(3), 253–269.

Winton-Brown, T. T., Fusar-Poli, P., Ungless, M. A., & Howes, O. D. (2014). Dopaminergic basis of salience dysregulation in psychosis. *Trends in Neurosciences, 37*(2), 85–94. doi:10.1016/j.tins.2013.11.003.

Wirth, M. M., & Gaffey, A. E. (2013). Hormones and emotion: Stress and beyond. In M. D. Robinson, E. Watkins, & E. Harmon-Jones (Eds.), *Handbook of cognition and emotion*. New York, NY: Guilford Press.

Wirtz-Justice, A. (1998). Beginning to see the light. *Archives of General Psychiatry, 55*, 861–862.

Wise, J. (2011). *Extreme fear: The science of your mind in danger*. New York, NY: Palgrave Macmillan.

Wise, R. A. (2013). Dual roles of dopamine in food and drug seeking: The drive-reward paradox. *Biological Psychiatry, 73*, 819–826. doi:10.1016/j.biopsych.2012.09.001.

Witelson, S. F., Kigar, D. L., & Harvey, T. (1999). The exceptional brain of Albert Einstein. *The Lancet, 353*, 2149–2153.

Witthoft, N., & Winawer, J. (2013). Learning, memory, and synesthesia. *Psychological Science, 24*(3), 258–265.

Wittkower, E. D., & Warnes, H. (1984). Cultural aspects of psychotherapy. In J. E. Mezzich & C. E. Berganza (Eds.), *Culture and psychopathology*. New York, NY: Columbia University Press.

Wolfe, D. A., Jaffe, P. G., & Crooks, C. (2006). *Adolescent risk behaviours: Why teens experiment and strategies to keep them safe*. New Haven, CT: Yale University Press.

Wolford, G., Miller, M. B., & Gazzaniga, M. S. (2004). Split decisions. In M. S. Gazzaniga (Ed.), *The cognitive neurosciences*. Cambridge, MA: MIT Press.

Wolitzky, D. L. (2006). Psychodynamic theories. In J. C. Thomas, & D. L. Segal (Eds.), *Comprehensive handbook of personality and psychopathology*. New York, NY: Wiley.

Wollmer, M. A., de Boer, C., Kalak, Beck, J., Götz, T., Schmidt, T., . . . Kruger, T. H. (2012). Facing depression with botulinum toxin: A randomized controlled trial. *Journal of Psychiatric Research, 46*, 574–581. doi:10.1016/ j.jpsychires.2012.01.027.

Wollmer, M. A., Kalak, N., Jung, S., de Boer, C., Magid, M., Reichenberg, J. S., . . . Kruger, T. C. (2014). Agitation predicts response of depression to botulinum toxin treatment in a randomized controlled trial. *Frontiers in Psychiatry, 5*, 36. doi:10.3389/fpsyt.2014.00036.

Wolpe, J. (1958). *Psychotherapy by reciprocal inhibition*. Stanford, CA: Stanford University Press.

Wonderlich, S. A. (2002). Personality and eating disorders. In C. G. Fairburn & K. D. Brownell (Eds.), *Eating disorders and obesity: A comprehensive handbook*. New York, NY: Guilford Press.

Wong, L. A. (2006). *Essential study skills*. Boston, MA: Houghton Mifflin.

Wong, W. (2009). Retracing the steps of Willhelm Wundt: Explorations in the disciplinary frontiers of psychology and in *Völkerpsychologie*. *Journal of the History of Psychology, 12*, 229–265.

Wood, D. K., & Goodale, M. A. (2010). Selection of wrist posture in conditions of motor ambiguity. *Experimental Brain Research, 208*, 607–620.

Wood, E., Desmarais, S., & Gugula, S. (2002). The impact of parenting experience on gender stereotyped toy play of children. *Sex Roles, 47*(1–2), 39–49.

Wood, J. M., Lilienfeld, S. O., Nezworski, M. T., Garb, H. N., Allen, J. H., & Wildermuth, J. L. (2010). Validity of Rorschach Inkblot scores for discriminating psychopaths from nonpsychopaths in forensic populations: A meta-analysis. *Psychological Assessment, 22*, 336–349. doi:10.1037/a0018998.

Wood, J. N., & Spelke, E. S. (2005). Chronometric studies of numerical cognition in five-month-old infants. *Cognition, 97*, 23–39.

Wood, N. L., & Cowan, N. (1995). The cocktail party phenomenon revisited: Attention and memory in the classic selective listening procedure of Cherry (1953). *Journal of Experimental Psychology: Learning, Memory, & Cognition, 21*, 255–260.

Wood, W., & Quinn, J. M. (2003). Forewarned and forearmed? Two meta-analytic syntheses of forewarnings of influence appeals. *Psychological Bulletin, 129*, 119–138.

Woodhead, M. (2004). "Children's rights and children's development: Rethinking the paradigm" in Children's Rights Centre, *Ghent Papers on Children's Rights*. Ghent: University of Ghent.

Woods, S. C., & Stricker, E. M. (2008). Food intake and metabolism. In L. Squire, D. Berg, F. Bloom, S. du Lac, A. Ghosh, & N. Spitzer (Eds.), *Fundamental neuroscience* (3rd ed.). San Diego, CA: Academic Press.

Woody, E. Z., & Sadler, P. (2008). In M. R. Nash & A. J. Barnier (Eds.). *Oxford handbook of hypnosis: Theory, research and practice* (pp. 81–110). New York, NY: Oxford University Press.

Woody, S. R., & Steketee, G. (2014). Compulsive hoarding. In J. Smits (Ed.), *Cognitive behavioral therapy: A complete reference guide Part 2: Specific disorders* (p. 1087–1108). New York, NY: Wiley.

Woolfolk, R. L., & Richardson, F. C. (1978). *Stress, sanity and survival.* New York, NY: Sovereign/Monarch.

Woollett, K., & Maguire, E. A. (2011). Acquiring "the knowledge" of London's layout drives structural brain changes. *Current Biology, 21,* 2109– 2114. doi:10.1016/j.cub.2001.11.018.

Word, D. H., Zanna, M. P., & Cooper, J. (1974). The nonverbal mediation of self-fulfilling prophesies in interracial interaction. *Journal of Experimental Social Psychology, 10,* 109–120.

World Health Organization. (1992). *The ICD-10 Classification of mental and behavioural disorders* (10th ed.). Retrieved from http://www.who.int/classifications/icd/en/bluebook.pdf.

World Health Organization. (2007). *Suicide: Country reports and charts.* Retrieved August 31, 2008, from http://www.who.int/mental_health/prevention/suicide/country_reports/en/index.html.

World Health Organization. (2014). Health behaviour in school-aged children (HBSC). Retrieved from http://www.hbsc.org/.

World Health Organization. (2014). *ICD-11 at WHO.* Retrieved from http://www.who.int/classifications/icd/revision/en/.

Wormith, S. (2000). Without conscience: The disturbing world of the psychopaths among us. (Review). *Canadian Psychology, 41,* 134–137.

Worthen, J. B., & Wade, C. E. (1999). Direction of travel and visiting team athletic performance: Support for a circadian dysrhythmia hypothesis. *Journal of Sport Behavior, 22,* 279–287.

Worthington, R. L., Soth-McNett, A. M., & Moreno, M. V. (2007). Multicultural counseling competencies research: A 20-year content analysis. *Journal of Counseling Psychology, 54,* 351–361.

Wortman, C. B., Wolff, K., & Bonanno, G. A. (2004). Loss of an intimate partner through death. In D. J. Mashek & A. Aron (Eds.), *Handbook of closeness and intimacy.* Mahwah, NJ: Erlbaum.

Wright, J. H., Beck, A. T., & Thase, M. E. (2003). Cognitive therapy. In R. E. Hales & S. C. Yudofsky (Eds.), *Textbook of clinical psychiatry.* Washington, DC: American Psychiatric Publishing.

Wright, J. H., Thase, M. E., & Beck, A. T. (2014). Cognitive-behavior therapy. In R. E. Hales, S. C. Yudofsky, & L. W. Roberts (Eds.), *The American Psychiatric Publishing textbook of psychiatry* (6th ed.). Washington, DC: American Psychiatric Publishing.

Wright, M. J. (1992). Women groundbreakers in Canadian psychology: World War II and its aftermath. *Canadian Psychology, 33,* 675–685.

Wright, M. J., & Myers, C. R. (1982). *History of academic psychology in Canada.* Toronto, ON: C. J. Hogrefe, Inc.

Wrosch, C. B. (2011). Self-regulation of unattainable goals and pathways to quality of life. In S. Folkman (Ed.), *Oxford handbook of stress, health, and coping.* New York, NY: Oxford University Press.

Wrosch, C. B., Miller, G. E., Scheier, M. F., & de Pontet, S. B. (2007). Giving up on unattainable goals: Benefits for health? *Personality and Social Psychology Bulletin, 33,* 251–265.

Wrosch, C. B., Scheier, M. F., Miller, G. E., & Carver, C. S. (2012). When meaning is threatened: The importance of goal adjustment for psychological and physical health. In P. T. P. Wong (Ed.), *Human quest for meaning: Theories, research, and applications* (2nd ed.). New York, NY: Routledge/Taylor & Francis Group.

Wrulich, M., Brunner, M., Stadler, G., Schalke, D., Keller, U., & Martin, R. (2014). Forty years on:

Childhood intelligence predicts health in middle adulthood. *Health Psychology, 33,* 292–296. doi:10.1037/a0030727.

Wrulich, M., Brunner, M., Stadler, G., Schalke, D., Keller, U., Chmiel, M., & Martin, R. (2013). Childhood intelligence and adult health: The mediating roles of education and socioeconomic status. *Intelligence, 41,* 490–500. doi:10.1016/j.intell.2013.06.015.

Wu, G., Zhang, J., & Gonzalez, R. (2004). Decision under risk. In D. Koehler & N. Harvey (Eds.), *The Blackwell handbook of judgment and decision making* (pp. 399–423). Oxford: Oxford University Press.

Wu, J. Q., Boettcher, H., Durand, V. M., & Barlow, D. H. (2014). *A guide to the American Psychiatric Association's diagnostic and statistical manual 2013 (DSM-5).* Toronto, ON: Nelson Publishing.

Wu, Q., Chang, C-F., Xi, S., Huang, I-W., Lui, A., et al. (2015). A critical role of temporoparietal junction in the integration of top-down and bottom-up attentional control. *Human Brain Mapping, 36,* 4317–4333.

Wundt, W. (1874/1904). *Principles of physiological psychology.* Leipzig: Engelmann.

Wynn, K. (1992). Addition and subtraction by human infants. *Nature, 358,* 749–750.

Wynn, K. (1996). Infants' individuation and enumeration of sequential actions. *Psychological Science, 7,* 164–169.

Wynn, K. (1998). An evolved capacity for number. In D. D. Cummins & C. Allen (Eds.), *The evolution of mind.* New York, NY: Oxford University Press.

Wynn, K. (2008). Some innate foundations of social and moral cognition. In P. Carruthers, S. Laurence, & S. Stich (Eds.), *The innate mind: Foundations and the future.* Oxford: Oxford University Press.

Wynne, C. D. L. (2004). *Do animals think?* Princeton, NJ: Princeton University Press.

Yabe, Y., Dave, H., & Goodale, M. (2017). Temporal distortion in the perception of actions and events. *Cognition, 158,* 1–9.

Yamaguchi, M., Kuhlmeier, V., Wynn, K. & van Marle, K. (2009). Continuity in social cognition from infancy to childhood. *Developmental Science, 12,* 746–752.

Yamamoto, J., Silva, J. A., Justice, L. R., Chang, C. Y., & Leong, G. B. (1993). Cross-cultural psychotherapy. In A. C. Gaw (Ed.), *Culture, ethnicity, and mental illness.* Washington, DC: American Psychiatric Press.

Yang, H., Liu, T., & Zang, D. (2000). A study of stressful life events before the onset of hypothyroidism. *Chinese Mental Health Journal, 14,* 201–202.

Yang, L. H. (2007). Application of mental illness stigma theory to Chinese societies: Synthesis and new directions. *Singapore Medical Journal, 48,* 977–991.

Yarmey, A. D. (2003). Eyewitness identification: Guidelines and recommendations for identification procedures in the United States and in Canada. *Canadian Psychology, 44*(3), 181–189.

Yates, F. A. (1966). *The art of memory.* London, UK: Routledge & Kegan Paul.

Yelaja, P. (2012). Hoarder habit may be enabled by families. *CBC News.* Retrieved from http://www.cbc.ca/news/canada/hoarder-habit-may-be-enabled-by-families-1.1162577.

Yeomans, M. R., Tepper, B. J., Rietzschel, J., & Prescott, J. (2007). Human hedonic responses to sweetness: Role of taste genetics and anatomy. *Physiology & Behavior, 91,* 264–273.

Yerkes, R. M., & Morgulis, S. (1909). The method of Pavlov in animal psychology. *Psychological Bulletin, 6,* 257–273.

Yeshurun, U., & Sobel, N. (2010). An odor is not worth a thousand words: From multidimensional odors to unidimensional odor objects. *Annual Review of Psychology, 61,* 219–241.

Yim, H., Dennis, S. J., & Sloutsky, V. M. (2013). The development of episodic memory: Items, contexts, and relations. *Psychological Science, 4*(11), 2163–2172.

Yip, J., Ehrhardt, K., Black, H., & Walker, D. O. (2017). Attachment at work: A review and directions for future research. *Journal of Organizational Behavior,* Version of record online: 8 June 2017, doi: 10.1002/job.2204.

Yoon, J., Witthoft, N., Winawer, J., Frank, M. C., Everett, D. L., et al. (2014). Cultural differences in perceptual reorganization in the US and Piraha adults. *PLoS One, 9,* e110225. doi:10.1371/journal.pone.0110225.

Yoshikawa, H., Aber, J. L., & Beardslee, W. R. (2012). The effects of poverty on the mental, emotional, and behavioral health of children and youth: Implications for prevention. *American Psychologist, 67,* 272–284. doi:10.1037/a0028015.

Yost, W. A. (2000). *Fundamentals of hearing: An introduction.* San Diego, CA: Academic Press.

Yost, W. A. (2010). Audition: Pitch perception. In E. B. Goldstein (Ed.), *Encyclopedia of perception.* Thousand Oaks, CA: Sage.

Yost, W. A. (2013). Audition. In A. F. Healy, R. W. Proctor, & I. B. Weiner (Eds.), *Handbook of psychology: Vol. 4. Experimental psychology* (2nd ed.). New York, NY: Wiley.

You, T., Arsenis, N. C., Disanzo, B. L., & LaMonte, M. J. (2013). Effects of exercising training on chronic inflammation in obesity: Current evidence and potential mechanisms. *Sports Medicine, 43,* 243–256. doi:10.1007/s40279-13-0023-3.

Young, D. M. (1997). Depression. In W. S. Tseng & J. Streltzer (Eds.), *Culture and psychopathology: A guide to clinical assessment.* New York, NY: Brunner/Mazel.

Young, G. B., Owen, A. M., Estraneo, A., Moretta, P., & Trojano, L. (2013). Predictors of recovery of responsiveness in prolonged anozi vegetative state. *Neurology, 81,* 1274–1275.

Young, K. S. (2009). Internet addiction: Diagnosis and treatment considerations. *Journal of Contemporary Psychotherapy, 39*(4), 241–246. doi:10.1007/s10879-009-9120-x.

Young, K. S. (2013). Treatment outcomes using CBT-IA with Internet-addicted patients. *Journal of Behavioral Addictions, 2,* 209–215. doi:10.1556/JBA.2.2013.4.3.

Young, M. E., Mizzau, M., Mai, N. T., Sirisegaram, A., & Wilson, M. (2009). Food for thought: What you eat depends on your sex and eating companions. *Appetite, 53*(2), 268–271.

Young, T. B. (2004). Epidemiology of daytime sleepiness: Definitions, symptomatology, and prevalence. *Journal of Clinical Psychiatry, 65*(Suppl. 16), 12–16.

Zadra, A., & Domhoff, G. W. (2011). Dream content: Quantitative findings. In M. H. Kryger, T. Roth, & W. C. Dement (Eds.), *Principles and practice of sleep medicine* (5th ed.). Saint Louis, MO: Elsevier Saunders.

Zadra, A., & Pilon, M. (2012). Parasomnias II: Sleep terrors and somnambulism. In C. M. Morin, & C. A. Espie (Eds.), *Oxford handbook of sleep and sleep disorders.* New York, NY: Oxford University Press.

Zager, D. B. (Ed.). (1999). *Autism.* Hillsdale, NJ: Erlbaum.

Zagorsky, J. L. (2007). Do you have to be smart to be rich? The impact of IQ on wealth, income and financial distress. *Intelligence, 35,* 489–501.

Zahorodny, W., Shenouda, J., Howell, S., Rosato, N. S., Peng, B., & Mehta, U. (2014). Increasing autism prevalence in metropolitan New Jersey. *Autism, 18*(2), 117–126. doi:10.1177/1362361312463977.

Zajonc, R. B. (1968). Attitudinal effects of mere exposure. *Journal of Personality and Social Psychology, 9,* 1–29.

Zajonc, R. B. (1980). Feeling and thinking: Preferences need no inferences. *American Psychologist, 35,* 151–175.

Zajonc, R. B. (1985). Emotion and facial efference: A theory reclaimed. *Science, 228,* 15–20.

Zajonc, R. B., Adelmann, P. K., Murphy, S. T, & Niedenthal, P. M. (1987). Convergence in the physical appearance of spouses. *Motivation and Emotion, 11,* 335–346.

Zak, P. J. (2012). *The moral molecule: Vampire economics and the new science of good and evil.* Hialeah, FL: Dutton Press.

Zaki, J., & Ochsner, K. (2012). The neuroscience of empathy: Progress, pitfalls and promise. *Nature Neuroscience, 15,* 675–680.

Zane, N., Hall, G. C. N., Sue, S., Young, K., & Nunez, J. (2004). Research on psychotherapy with culturally diverse populations. In M. J. Lambert (Ed.), *Bergin and Garfield's handbook of psychotherapy and behavior change.* New York, NY: Wiley.

Zaragoza, M. S., Belli, R. F., & Payment, K. E. (2007). Misinformation effects and the suggestibility of eyewitness memory. In M. Garry & H. Hayne (Eds.), *Do justice and let the sky fall: Elizabeth F. Lotus and her contributions to science, law, and academic freedom.* Mahwah, NJ: Erlbaum.

Zárate, M. A. (2009). Racism in the 21st century. In T. D. Nelson (Ed.), *Handbook of prejudice, stereotyping, and discrimination* (pp. 1–22). New York, NY: Psychology Press.

Zatzick, D. F., & Dimsdale, J. E. (1990). Cultural variations in response to painful stimuli. *Psychosomatic Medicine, 52*(5), 544–557.

Zayas, V., Shoda, Y., Mischel, W., Osterhout, L., & Takahashi, M. (2009). Neural responses to partner rejection cues. *Psychological Science, 20*(7), 813–821.

Zebrowitz, L. A. (2017). First impressions from faces. *Current Directions in Psychological Science, 26,* 237–242.

Zechmeister, E. B., & Nyberg, S. E. (1982). *Human memory: An introduction to research and theory.* Pacific Grove, CA: Brooks/Cole.

Zeidan, F., et al. (2015). Mindfulness meditation-based pain relief employs different neural mechanisms than placebo and sham mindfulness meditation-induced analgesia. *Journal of Neuroscience, 18,* 15307–15325.

Zeidan, F., Gordon, N. S., Merchant, J., & Goolkasian, P. (2010). The effects of brief mindfulness meditation training on experimentally induced pain. *Journal of Pain, 11*(3), 199–209.

Zeiler, M. (1977). Schedules of reinforcement: The controlling variables. In W. K. Honig & J. E. R. Staddon (Eds.), *Handbook of operant behavior.* Englewood Cliffs, NJ: Prentice-Hall.

Zentner, M., & Mitura, K. (2012). Stepping out of the caveman's shadow: Nations' gender gap predicts degree of sex differentiation in mate preferences. *Psychological Science, 23,* 1176–1185. doi:10.1177/0956797612441004.

Zepelin, H., Siegel, J. M., & Tobler, I. (2005). Mammalian sleep. In M. H. Kryger, T. Roth, & W. C. Dement (Eds.), *Principles and practice of sleep medicine.* Philadelphia, PA: Elsevier Saunders.

Zhang, J. W., Howell, R. T., & Howell, C. J. (2014). Living in wealthy neighborhoods increases material desires and maladaptive consumption. *Journal of Consumer Culture, 0,* 1–20. doi:10.1177/1469540514521085.

Zhu, D. H. (2013). Group polarization on corporate boards: Theory and evidence on board decisions about acquisition premiums. *Strategic Management Journal, 34,* 800–822. doi:10.1002/smj.2039.

Zhu, D. H. (2014). Group polarization in board decisions about CEO compensation. *Organization Science, 25,* 552–571. doi:10.1287/orsc.2013.0848.

Zilcha-Mano, S., Mikulincer, M., & Shaver, P. R. (2011). Pet in the therapy room: An attachment perspective on animal-assisted therapy. *Attachment and Human Development, 13,* 541–561.

Zilcha-Mano, S., Mikulincer, M., & Shaver, P. R. (2012). Pets as safe havens and secure bases: The moderating role of pet attachment orientations. *Journal of Research in Personality, 46,* 571–580.

Zillmer, E. A., Spiers, M. V., & Culbertson, W. C. (2008). *Principles of neuropsychology.* Belmont, CA: Wadsworth.

Zimbardo, P. G. (2004, May 9). Power turns good soldiers into "bad apples." *Boston Globe.* Retrieved from http://www.boston.com/news/globe/editorial_opinion/oped/articles/2004/05/09.

Zimbardo, P. G., Haney, C., & Banks, W. C. (1973, April 8). The mind is a formidable jailer: A Pirandellian prison. *New York Times Magazine,* Section 6, p. 36.

Zimmerman, B. J. (1995). Self-efficacy and educational development. In A. Bandura (Ed.), *Self-efficacy in changing societies.* New York, NY: Cambridge University Press.

Zimmerman, I. L., & Woo-Sam, J. M. (1984). Intellectual assessment of children. In G. Goldstein & M. Hersen (Eds.), *Handbook of psychological assessment.* New York, NY: Pergamon Press.

Zinbarg, R. E., & Griffith, J. W. (2008). Behavior Therapy. In J. L. Lebow (Ed.), *Twenty-first century psychotherapies: Contemporary approaches to theory and practice.* New York, NY: Wiley.

Zink, N., & Pietrowsky, R. (2015). Theories of dreaming and lucid dreaming: An integrative review towards sleep, dreaming and consciousness. *International Journal of Dream Research, 8,* 35–53.

Zohar, J., Fostick, L., & Juven-Wetzler, E. (2009). Obsessive-compulsive disorder. In M. C. Gelder, N. C. Andreasen, J. J. López-Ibor, Jr., & J. R. Geddes (Eds.). *New Oxford textbook of psychiatry* (2nd ed., Vol. 1). New York, NY: Oxford University Press.

Zola, S. M., & Squire, L. R. (2000). The medial temporal lobe and the hippocampus. In E. Tulving & F. I. M. Craik (Eds.), *The Oxford handbook of memory* (pp. 485–500). New York, NY: Oxford University Press.

Zorumski, C. F., Isenberg, K. E., & Mennerick, S. (2009). Cellular and synaptic electrophysiology. In B. J. Sadock, V. A. Sadock, & P. Ruiz (Eds.), *Kaplan & Sadock's comprehensive textbook of psychiatry* (9th ed., Vol. 1, pp. 129–146). Philadelphia, PA: Lippincott, Williams & Wilkins.

Zrenner, E., Abramov, I., Akita, M., Cowey, A., Livingstone, M., & Valberg, A. (1990). Color perception: Retina to cortex. In L. Spillman & J. S. Werner (Eds.), *Visual perception: The neurophysiological foundations.* San Diego, CA: Academic Press.

Zschucke, E., Renneberg, B., Dimeo, F., Wustenberg, T., & Strohle, A. (2015). The stress-buffering effect of acute exercise: Evidence for HPA axis negative feedback. *Psychoneuroendocrinology, 51,* 414–425. doi:10.1016/j.psyneuen.2014.10.019.

Zuckerman, M. (2013). Biological bases of personality. In H. Tennen, J. Suls, & I. B. Weiner (Eds.), *Handbook of psychology: Vol. 5. Personality and social psychology* (2nd ed.). New York, NY: Wiley.

Zurbriggen, E. L., & Sturman, T. S. (2002). Linking motives and emotions: A test of McClelland's hypothesis. *Personality & Social Psychology Bulletin, 28,* 521–535.

Zwanzger, P., Fallgatter, A. J., Zavorotnyy, M. M., & Padberg, F. F. (2009). Anxiolytic effects of transcranial magnetic stimulation—An alternative treatment option in anxiety disorders? *Journal of Neural Transmission, 116*(6), 767–775.

NAME INDEX

A

AAIDD, 326
Aakre, J. M., 585
Aamodt, W., 421
Abad, N., 487
Abbas, A. I., 581, 582
Abbeduto, L., 591, 592
Abbott, A., 91
Abbott, B. B., 51
Abbott, C. B., 394
Abdel-Khalak, A. M., 462, 463f
Abduljalil, A. M., 389, 507
Abel, E. L., 524, 525f
Abel, J. R., 429
Abel, M. H., 545
Aber, J. L., 336
Abi-Dargham, A., 582
Aboud, F. E., 510
Abraham, A., 85
Abraham, C., 67, 263, 417
Abraham, L. M., 468
Abramov, I., 121, 123
Abramowicz, A., 370
Abramowitz, J., 564
Abrams, R. L., 113
Abrams, T. W., 76
Abramson, L. Y., 482, 483, 509, 576, 577
Abrous, D. N., 91, 263
Abu-Akel, A., 96, 474
Abutalebi, J., 285, 421
Accardi, M., 176
Acevedo, B. P., 485
Achermann, P., 165
Achor, S., 538
Ackerman, J. M., 349, 488
Ackerman, P. L., 337
Ackerman, S., 57f
Active Healthy Kids Canada, 541
Adam, A. S., 352
Adam, H., 340
Adam, N., 462, 463f
Adam, T. C., 79
Adamovova, L., 462, 463f
Adams, B. G., 565
Adams, C. J., 531
Adams, Douglas, 239
Adams, H. M., 439
Adams, J. L., 293
Adams, J. L., 293f, 295f
Adams, M. J., 58
Adams, R. B., 511
Adams, R. L., 466, 467
Adams, S. J., 593
Addictive Behaviours Laboratory at the University of Calgary, 528
Addis, D. R., 85, 85f, 239, 268
Adelmann, P. K., 371
Ader, R., 535
Adlaf, E. F., 180

Adler, A., 8, 445, 446f, 447
Adler, A. B., 531
Adler, L. L., 29
Adler, N. E., 519
Adolph, K. E., 13, 389, 392, 393
Adolphs, R., 90
Adrian, A. L., 531
Advokat, C. D., 184
Affleck, G., 523
Afileck, G., 539
Agarwal, P. K., 256, 271
Aggen, S. H., 99
Agha, Z., 634
Agid, O., 54, 581
Aglioti, S. M., 113
Agnoli, F., 308
Agyei, Y., 362, 362f
Ahmadi, S., 96
Ahmed, S. H., 354
Ahn, C. K., 462, 463f
Ahn, H. N., 462, 463f
Ahrens-Barbeau, C., 592
Ahuvia, A., 379
Aikins, D. E., 567
Aimone, J. B., 263
Ainslie, G., 239
Ainsworth, M. D. S., 12f, 396, 397, 397f, 398, 485
Ait-Daoud, N., 541
Ajzen, I., 490
Akabaliev, V. H., 584
Akerstedt, T., 158, 159
Akins, C. K., 58
Akiskal, H. S., 570, 571
Akita, M., 123
Aknin, L. B., 378, 379
Albanese, E., 419
Albarracin, D., 493, 494
Albee, G. W., 633
Albers, Josef, 150, 151f
Albert, D., 411
Albert, M. A., 419, 528
Albouy, G., 88
Alcolado, G. M., 564
Aldag, R. J., 505
Aldington, S., 186
Aldoo, A., 427
Aldwin, C. M., 418
Aleman, A., 429
Alexander, C. N., 177
Alexander, R., 132
Ali, Muhammad, 78f, 199f
Alibali, M. W., 280
Alimohamed, S., 639, 640
Allaert, F. A., 164
Allahyar, N., 405
Allain, A. J., 590
Allan, R. W., 198
Allebeck, P., 186, 583
Allemand, M., 414
Allen, B. P., 253, 259, 274, 456t

Allen, E., 430
Allen, E. G., 328
Allen, J. H., 468
Allen, J. P., 411
Allen, M., 9
Allen, N. B., 177, 622
Allen, S. T., 176
Alliey-Rodriguez, N., 582
Allik, J., 462
Allison, D. B., 354
Allmann, A. E., 571
Alloy, L. B., 576, 577
Allport, G. W., 437
Almada, L. F., 370
Almonte, J. L., 539
Alonso, P., 564
Alpert, Richard, 181
Alsop, B., 212–213
Alter, A. L., 478
Altman, I., 23
Altshuler, L. L., 627
Alvarez, P., 264
Amabile, T. M., 340
Amano, S., 282
Amaral, D. G., 506
Amato, M., 510
Ambadar, Z., 373
Ambady, D. J., 511
Ambady, N., 477
Amedi, A., 91
American Association of Suicidology, 575t
American Foundation for Suicide Prevention, 575t
American Psychiatric Association, 558
American Psychological Association, 21f, 22f, 34, 57, 58, 59, 63, 143, 204, 261, 327, 562, 564, 590
Ames, Adelbert, 131
Ames, D. L., 506
Ames, M., 633
Amini, R., 158
Amir, N., 134, 634
Amir, Y., 511
Amirault, Kimberly, 347f
Amlo, S., 612
Ammari, N., 580
Ammirati, R., 305
Amodio, D., 506
Amodio, D. M., 15, 458, 491, 506, 507
Amsterdam, J. D., 79, 626
Anacker, C., 527
Andel, R., 420
Andelin, A. K., 379
Anderson, B., 85
Anderson, B. M., 85
Anderson, C., 406
Anderson, C. A., 225, 226, 306

Anderson, D. R., 533, 534
Anderson, J. S., 105, 579
Anderson, K. J., 525
Anderson, K. O., 143
Anderson, M., 592
Anderson, M. C., 256
Anderson-Fye, E. P., 599
Andersson, E., 634
Andersson, G., 53, 618, 634
Andersson, R., 97
Andreasen, N. C., 330, 341, 581, 582f
Andree, T. H., 418
Andreski, P., 51
Andrews, D., 626
Andrews, P. W., 627
Andrews-Hanna, J. R., 156
Andrusyna, T. P., 640
Angell, M., 627
Angelou, Maya, 325f
Angleitner, A., 477
Anglin, J. M., 283f
Angst, J., 560, 573
Angus, L., 614
Anisman, H., 475, 527
Anjum, A., 615
Ankudowich, E., 253
Annese, J., 264, 264f
Annus, A. M., 15
Ansbacher, H., 446f
Anschutz, D. J., 352
Anselmo-Matthews, T., 18, 614
Anter, N. M., 27
Anthenelli, R. M., 190
Antoni, M., 534t
Antoniou, K., 184
Antony, M. M., 198, 561, 562, 564, 566
Apicella, L. F., 540
Appelbaum, P., 557
Appelbaum, P. S., 637
Appleton, K. M., 352
Apuzzo, J., 57
Arbid, N., 186
Arbuckle, N. L., 389, 507
Arcelus, J., 43, 598
Archer, J., 427, 428
Arden, R., 58, 319
Arendt, J., 158, 159, 160
Arendt, R., 390
Arenovich, T., 583
Argyle, M., 379, 380
Ariely, D., 302
Aristotle, 3, 244
Arkes, H. R., 242, 470
Arkey, Y., 534t
Arkowitz, H., 63f, 569, 617
Arlow, J. A., 8, 610
Armbruster, B. B., 27
Armony, J. L., 370
Armstrong, E., 390

Armstrong, G. H., 96, 537
Arnarson, E. O., 571
Arndt, S. V., 578
Arnett, J. J., 54, 413–414, 413f
Arnold, D. H., 114
Arnold, L. M., 534t
Arnon, I., 565
Aron, A., 485
Aron, A. P., 42, 375, 485
Aronson, E., 363, 491, 494, 495, 511
Aronson, J., 318, 319, 332, 333
Arsenis, N. C., 541
Asano, K., 319
Asano, M., 319
Asarnow, J. R., 574
Asbridge, M., 187
Asbury, K., 100, 459
Asch, S., 126, 476, 497, 497f, 498, 498f, 499, 500
Ascher, E. A., 367
Asendorpf, J. B., 488
Aserinsky, E., 161
Ashby, F. G., 266
Asher, J. E., 111
Ashkanasy, N. M., 322
Ashton, J. R., 410
Ashton, M. C., 462
Ashton-James, C. E., 322
Asmundson, G. G., 562
Asmundson, G. J. G., 143
Assaad, J. M., 187
Assanand, S., 355
Assefi, S. L., 54, 183
Associated Press, 539
Astuti, R., 54
Atalay, M., 420, 541
Ataullahajan, A., 632
Atkinson, D. R., 594
Atkinson, J. W., 349, 364, 365–366, 366, 366f
Atkinson, R. C., 244, 244f
Atkinson, R. H., 27
Atkinson, R. C., 135f
Atkinson, R. L., 135f
Attia, J., 546
Attridge, M., 416, 438
Atwal, Rajinder Singh, 487
Atzmueller, M., 141
AUCC, 11
Auerbach, C. F., 431
Augedal, A. W., 170
Aust, S., 568
Averill, J. A., 367
Avery, D., 629
Awh, E., 248
Axel, R., 140
Axelsson, J., 188
Ayanian, J. Z., 528, 540
Ayduk, O., 451
Ayotte, B. J., 451
Ayres, P., 227
Azevedo, F. C., 68, 69

B

Baars, B. J., 279
Baas, M., 339
Babb, S. S., 540
Babiak, P., 589
Babor, T., 186, 186f
Baccaro, A., 629
Bachelor, P., 339
Bachen, E. A., 535
Back, M. D., 488
Backhaus, A., 634
Backman, L., 420
Badaly, D., 392
Baddeley, A., 13, 247
Baddeley, A. D., 245, 247, 247f
Baddeley, J. L., 42
Badger, J., 477
Bae, G. Y., 247
Baer, J., 340
Baer, R. A., 622–623
Baggott, J., 43
Bagsby, P., 546
Bahrick, H. P., 254
Bailey, C. E., 327, 328
Bailey, C. H., 262
Bailey, J. M., 362, 362f
Baillargeon, J., 637
Baillargeon, R., 405
Bains, J. S., 68
Baird, A. D., 90
Baird, B., 296
Bajbouj, M., 568
Bajo, M. T., 285
Bak T. H., 421
Bakalar, J. B., 186
Bakan, P., 104
Baker, C. I., 116, 118
Baker, D. B., 13
Baker, G. J., 534
Baker, J. H., 599
Baker, L., 125
Bakermans-Kranenburg, M. J., 397, 398
Bakker, A. B., 436, 437
Bakker, B., 410
Balan, N., 369
Balas, R., 199
Balbierz, A., 536
Balcetis, E., 130, 464, 478
Baldessarini, R. J., 626
Baldwin, E., 58
Baldwin, James Mark, 11
Baldwin, S., 616
Baldwin, W., 55
Bale, T. L., 391
Ball, J. S., 590
Ball, K., 107
Ball, L. C., 11
Balliet, D., 360, 488
Balsam, P. D., 202
Balter, M., 248
Baltuch, G., 429, 629
Bambico, F. R., 527, 576
Bamidis, P., 107

Banaji, M., 491
Banaji, M. R., 490, 491, 493, 494, 506, 507
Banaji, Mahzarin, 55f
Banaschewski, T., 410
Bandeen-Roche, K., 273
Bandura, A., 223–224, 223f, 225, 228, 429, 430, 449–451, 449f, 450f, 452
Banerji, I., 33
Bankart, J., 591
Banks, E., 546
Banks, S., 165, 188
Banks, S. J., 12
Banks, W. C., 500
Banks, W. P., 126
Bann, R. M., 390
Banning, K., 522
Banuazizi, A., 501
Banyard, V. L., 258
Bao, Y., 391
Baptista, M. A. S., 200
Barabasz, A., 174
Barabasz, A. F., 174
Barabasz, M., 174
Barac, R., 107
Baram, T. Z., 391
Barba, G. D., 268
Barbe, R. P., 626, 637
Barbee, J. G., 519
Barber, B. K., 417
Barber, J. P., 613
Barber, L., 546
Barber, S. J., 253
Barber, Theodore, 175, 175f
Bard, P., 375
Barden, J., 496
Barger, Albert, 204
Bargh, J. A., 156, 352, 487
Bargmann, C. I., 140
Barker, D. J. P., 391
Barker, Elliot, 606
Barker, G., 410
Barlow, D. H., 561, 564, 591
Barnes, L. L., 419, 420
Barnes, S., 177
Barnes, V. A., 177
Barnes-Holmes, D., 258
Barnes-Holmes, Y., 258
Barnett, S. W., 342
Barnhardt, T. M., 113
Barnhart, R., 615
Barnhill, L. J., 327
Barnhofer, T., 622
Barnier, A. J., 175
Baron, A., 215
Baron, J., 379
Bar-On, R., 322
Baron-Cohen, S., 111, 407
Barr, H. M., 390
Barraza, J., 96
Barrett, A. B., 245
Barrett, D., 373
Barrett, L. F., 367, 370
Barrett, M. S., 612

Barretto, R., 100
Barrio, C., 632, 633
Barrios-Miller, N. L., 43
Barron, K. E., 496
Barrouillet, P., 248
Barry, H., III., 409
Barsade, S. G., 322
Barth, J., 618
Bartholow, B. D., 506
Bartlett, F. C., 252
Bartlett, J. D., 397
Bartlett, T., 204
Bartley, M., 379
Bartol, A. M., 81, 82
Bartol, C., 81, 82
Barton, M., 591
Bartoshuk, L. M., 138, 138f, 139f, 140
Bartsch, H., 264
Barzykowski, K., 269
Basbaum, A. I., 144
Bashford, J., 168
Baskin, T. W., 55
Basow, S. A., 428
Bass, E. C., 506
Bassett, A. S., 581, 582
Bassett, D. S., 94
Bassok, M., 292, 295
Basson, M. D., 140
Bassuk, E. L., 637
Bassuk, S. S., 637
Bastian, A. J., 86
Bastin, M. E., 541
Basu, D., 186
Bates, E., 283, 289
Bates, J. E., 395
Bates, M. S., 143
Bates, T. C., 380
Bateson, P., 58
Batterham, P. J., 319
Batty, G. D., 319
Bauer, D. J., 41
Bauer, M. S., 573
Baughman, H. M., 439
Baum, A., 520
Baumard, N., 54
Baumeister, R. F., 156, 358, 360, 363, 454, 530
Baumgartner, M. K., 416
Baumrind, D., 57, 499
Bayard, S., 169, 170
Bayen, U. J., 253, 269
Baylis, G. C., 127
Bazana, P. G., 319
Bazar, J. L., 11
Bazerman, M. H., 305
Bazzano, L. A., 548
Beahrs, J. O., 176
Beal, D. J., 489
Beale, M. D., 628
Beall, A. T., 35, 35f, 61f
Bean, L. H., 328
Beard, C. M., 598f
Bearden, C. E., 581
Beardslee, W. R., 336, 570

Beauchamp, G. K., 352
Beauchamp, J., 333
Bebbington, P., 379
Bechara, A., 90
Beck, A., 622
Beck, A. T., 528, 567, 621, 630
Beck, C. T., 574
Beck, H. P., 204
Beck, L. A., 486
Becker, A. E., 598, 599
Becker, A. L., 264
Becker, S., 263
Becker-Blease, K. A., 565
Beckert, L., 186
Beckham, J. C., 565
Beeghly, M., 397, 590
Beeman, M., 296
Beer, J., 370
Beer, J. S., 90, 363
Beetz, A., 546
Beetz, A. M., 546
Beevers, C. G., 42, 576
Begg, I., 243
Begue, L., 79
Behrman, L. J., 432
Beidel, D. C., 561, 567, 618, 623
Beier, M. E., 337
Beilin, H., 403
Bekelman, J. E., 627
Bekkouche, N. S., 533
Bekmuradov, D., 390
Bell, R., 79
Bellena, B., 285
Beller, M., 428
Belleville, G., 518, 519, 532
Belli, R. F., 252–253, 259
Bellini, Gentile & Giovanni, 148, 148f
Bellini, S., 620
Bellis, M. A., 410
Bello, I., 637
Belloch, A., 564
Belopolsky, A., 247
Belsky, J., 396, 398
Bem, D. J., 429, 496
Benarroch, E. E., 91
Benavides-Varela, S., 289
Benca, R. M., 86
Bendall, S., 568
Bender, D. S., 590, 633, 634
Benedetti, F., 54, 55, 143
Benedict, C., 167
Benjafield, J. G., 13
Benjamin, D. J., 333
Benjamin, L. T., Jr., 4, 13, 298, 452, 498–499
Benjet, C., 219
Bennell, C., 593, 594
Bennett, A. J., 58
Bennett, D. A., 419, 420
Bennett, E. L., 106f, 319
Bennett, M. L., 289
Bennett, N., 503
Bennett, P., 534t
Bennett-AbuAyyash, C., 511

Ben-Porath, Y. S., 467
Ben-Simon, E., 156
Bensky, M., 436
Bensky, M. K., 58
Benson, H., 546, 547f
Bentall, R. P., 627
Benton, D., 352
Berenbaum, S. A., 362, 430
Berens, M., 282
Berent, I., 289
Berg, N., 501
Berg, V., 459
Berger, A., 226
Berger, J., 497
Berger, L. K., 24, 633
Berger, L. M., 220
Berger, S. E., 389, 392, 393
Berger, S. S., 528
Berger, Z., 543
Bergeron, R., 632
Bergevin, T., 528
Bergin, A. E., 640
Berglund, P., 560, 608
Bergman, Ingmar, 171
Berkhof, J., 523
Berkowitz, L., 498–499, 528
Berlin, B., 290
Berlin, L. J., 398
Berman, A. L., 626
Berman, J. S., 640
Berman, M. G., 246
Bernal, G., 632, 634
Bernardo, Paul, 589
Berndt, S. I., 100
Bernier, R., 591
Bernstein, H., 391
Bernstein, H. J., 628
Bernstein, I. E., 352
Bernstein, M., 324
Bernsten, D., 432
Bernston, G. G., 505
Berntsen, D., 565
Berntson, G. G., 367, 505
Berrettini, W. H., 575f
Berridge, K. C., 348, 367
Berry, D. S., 484
Berry, J. W., 11, 129, 133, 326
Berscheid, E., 476, 485
Berta, T., 69
Berthoud, H., 355
Berton, O., 575
Bertram, L., 420
Bertrand, R. M., 414
berts, M. C., 37
Besken, M., 267
Besner, D., 156
Bessa, J. M., 567
Best, S. R., 565
Betensky, J. D., 533
Bettelheim, B., 592
Beudel, M., 629
Beutel, M. E., 529
Beutler, L. E., 639, 640
Bevelander, K. E., 351
Beyerstein, B. L., 2, 2f

Bezawada, R., 139
Bezborodovs, N., 608
Bhanpuri, N. H., 86
Bhanwer, A., 439
Bhasin, T., 592
Bhati, K. S., 55
Bhatnagar, S., 526
Bhatt, G., 11
Bi, G. Q., 263
Bialystok, E., 107, 279, 284, 285, 285–286, 286, 286f, 421
Bianchi, M. T., 167
Bianchi, S. M., 416, 416f
Biblarz, T. J., 432
Biederman, I., 127
Bieling, P., 623
Bieling, P. J., 529
Bielski, Z., 178, 541
Bienias, J. L., 420
Biermann, T., 63f
Biernat, M., 509
Biesanz, J., 519
Biesanz, J. C., 476
Bifulco, A., 578
Bigelow, B. J., 336
Bigman, C., 451
Bilalić, M., 293
Bilanovic, A., 143
Bilderbeck, A., 141
Billings, J. F., 259
Billings, R., 155
Bilodeau, A., 200f, 267f
Binder, R., 557
Bindman, J., 628
Binet, Alfred, 316, 316f, 400
Bingel, U., 144
Bingham, S., 534
Bini, L., 628
Binswanger, I. A., 637
Bion, R. H., 289
Birch, D., 349, 366
Birch, H. G., 394
Birch, L. L., 352, 599
Birkeland, S. A., 467
Birmaher, B., 626
Birmingham, W., 536
Birnbaum, M. H., 301
Birney, D. P., 403, 404
Bischof, G., 186
Bischof, G. N., 421
Bishop, S. I., 437
Bjerkeset, O., 534
Bjork, E., 90, 282
Bjork, R. A., 256
Bjork, R. A., 271, 275
Bjorklund, D. F., 259, 404
Bjorvatn, B., 159
Bjuhr, H., 622
Black, D. W., 595
Black, H., 397
Black, P. J., 439
Black, S. E., 239, 268
Blacker, D., 420
Blackwell, J. M., 248
Blackwood, D., 575

Blagrove, M., 173
Blair, C., 318, 319, 332, 333
Blair, I. V., 490, 491
Blair, S. N., 547f
Blair, V., 451
Blakemore, S., 411
Blakemore, S-J., 406
Blakemores, C., 185
Blanchard, J. J., 506
Blanco, C., 609, 624, 624f, 625
Blaney, N. T., 511
Blankenhorn, D., 431, 432
Blankner, J. G., 429
Blankstein, K. R., 593
Blascovich, J., 511
Blase, Stacey, 634
Blashfield, R. K., 558, 558f
Blass, E. M., 353
Blass, T., 498–499, 499
Blazek-O'Neill, B., 546
Blehar, M. C., 396, 397, 485
Bleich, S., 63f
Bleiler, L., 419
Bleuler, Eugen, 579
Blier, P., 632
Bliss-Moreau, E., 370
Bliwise, D. L., 159, 162
Bloch, M., 54
Block, J., 414
Block, J. R., 125f
Block, L. G., 496
Block, N., 336
Bloom, P., 287, 288
Bloomb, C. M., 214
Blum, H. C., 188
Blumenthal, J. A., 541
Blundell, J. E., 351
Blunt, J. R., 271
Boak, A., 180
Boakes, R. A., 55
Boals, A., 248, 565
Boase, J., 487
Bobb, S., 285
Bobb, S. C., 284
Bober, T., 532
Bobo, W. V., 625
Bodell, L. P., 599
Bodenhausen, G. V., 479, 510
Boecker, H., 79
Boehm, J. K., 537
Boekaerts, M., 454
Boekel, W., 156
Boener, K., 421
Boer, D. P., 447
Boettcher, H., 591
Boettiger, C. A., 623
Bogdahn, U., 91
Bogels, S. M., 166
Bögels, S. M., 620
Bogen, J. E., 14, 92, 93
Bogg, T., 316
Boggs, J., 622
Bøgwald, K., 612
Bøgwald, K.-P., 612

Eastabrook, J. M., 268, 322
Easterbrooks, M. A., 397
Easterlin, B. L., 177
Eastman, C. I., 160
Easton, A., 505
Eastwick, P. W., 34, 486, 487, 488
Eastwik, P. W., 483
Eastwood, J., 159
Eastwood, J. D., 297
Eaton, A., 6
Eaton, J., 480, 505
Eaton, N. R., 458, 590
Eaton, W. W., 562f
Eaves, L. J., 247
Ebbinghaus, H., 254, 254f
Ebel-Lam, A. P., 186
Eberth, J., 622
Ebling, C., 307
Ebrahim, I. O., 189
Eccles, J., 537
Echterhoff, G., 239
Eck, J., 506
Eckert, E. D., 598
Eckstein, D., 447
The Economist, 57
Eddy, J. M., 42
Eddy, K. T., 597, 599
Edelstein, B., 418
Edenfield, T. M., 541
Edison, Thomas, 253, 312, 312f
Edlund, S., 132
Edmeads, J., 155
Edmonds, G., 438
Edwardh, M., 155
Edwards, S., 391
Edwards, W. T., 143
Egan, J. P., 113
Egan, M. F., 583f
Egerton, A., 582
Egger, H. L., 590
Eggert, A., 27, 540
Ehde, D. M., 142
Eher, R., 589
Ehrenberg, M., 432, 639, 641
Ehrenberg, O., 639, 641
Ehrhardt, K., 397
Ehrlich, S., 584
Eiben, G., 351
Eibl-Eibesfeldt, I., 371
Eich, T. S., 271
Eichenbaum, H., 88, 265, 267
Eickhoff, S. B., 227
Eifert, G. H., 79
Eigenbrodt, M. L., 533, 533f
Eigsti, I., 451, 591
Einarsson, E. O., 265
Ein-Dor, T., 397
Einstein, Albert, 67, 68, 94, 312, 312f, 554
Einstein, G. O., 272, 273
Eippert, F., 144
Eisel, S., 420
Eisen, J. L., 563
Eisen, S. A., 247

Eisenberger, N. I., 143, 506
Eisenlohr-Moul, T., 79
Eisner, E. W., 322
Eisner, T., 103
Ekman, P., 370, 370–371, 373
Ekman, R., 370, 372, 372f
Elbogen, E. B., 557
Eley, T. C., 575
Elfenbein, J. L., 134
Eliassen, C. F., 84
Elkin, J., 632
Elkins, R. L., 620
Ellamil, M., 156
Ellenbogen, J. M., 166, 167
Ellenbogen, M. A., 96
Elliot, A. J., 34, 35, 35f, 37, 37f, 60, 61f, 496
Elliot, Andrew, 34–35, 37, 60
Elliott, R., 614
Ellis, A., 528, 545, 621
Ellis, B. J., 102, 349, 358
Ellis, T. E., 575t
Ellsworth, P., 367
Ellsworth, P. C., 367
Ellwood, S., 296
Elman, I., 528
Elms, A. C., 499
Else-Quest, N., 406
Else-Quest, N. M., 427
Emanuel, E. J., 637
Emavardhana, T., 177
Emde, R. N., 590
Emery, C. F., 533, 534
Emery, N. J., 505
Emmelkamp, P. G., 620
Emmelkamp, P. M., 623
Emmelkamp, P. M. G., 620
Emo, A. K., 322
Employment Social Development Canada, 418
Emsley, R., 625
Endicott, J., 571
Endler, N. S., 437, 451, 628
Engbert, R., 116
Engels, R. C., 351
Engels, R. C. M. E., 226
Engels, R. E., 352
Engemann, K. M., 477
Englar-Carlson, M., 447
Engle, R. W., 58, 247
Eno, C. A., 492
Ensom, R., 219, 220
Entin, E. E., 365
Epel, E., 79
Eppinger, B., 227
Epstein, D. H., 187
Epstein, E. M., 419
Epstein, J., 289
Epstein, L., 188
Epstein, L. H., 351
Epstein, R., 361
Epstein, R. M., 368
Epstein, S., 301
Era, V., 113
Erber, M. W., 493

Erdelyi, M. H., 443, 529
Erickso, T. M., 561
Erickson, D. J., 481
Erickson, K. I., 91
Erickson, R. P., 138
Erickson, S., 97
Eriksen, H. R., 159
Erikson, E., 398, 399–400, 399f, 412, 414–415
Erikson, K. R., 622
Escalona, P. R., 580
Escher, M. C., 149
Esdaile, J. M., 519
Eskes, G., 243
Eslick, A. N., 253
Espejo, E., 520, 535
Espjosito, L., 546
Espnes, G. A., 523
Esposito, Phil, 195
Espostio-Smythers, C., 529–530
Esser, J. K., 505
Esses, V. M., 366, 511
Estel, D., 63f
Esterson, A., 447
Estes, W. K., 244
Estrada, K., 100
Estraneo, A., 68
Ethier, N., 598
Ethington, C. A., 451
Ettner, S. L., 628
Evans, A. N., 534
Evans, D. R., 622
Evans, E. M., 622
Evans, G. W., 336
Evans, J. T., 303
Evans, R. I., 223, 225
Evans-Lacko, S., 608
Everett, D. L., 132
Everitt, B. J., 89, 183
Ey, S., 412
Eyrich, K. M., 637
Eysenck, H. J., 336, 447, 457, 457f, 460–461, 618
Eysenck, M. W., 567, 567f

F

Fabbri-Destro, M., 227
Fabrigar, L. R., 55, 489, 490
Fadiga, L., 89, 227
Fagan, J. F., 337
Fagerlin, A., 379
Fagot, B. I., 430
Fahrenfort, J. J., 245
Fairbank, J. A., 531
Fairburn, C. G., 598
Fairchild, H., 225
Fais, L., 282
Fakhoury, W., 636
Falk, D., 67, 94
Fallgatter, A. J., 85
Falls, W. A., 214
Falluel-Morel, A., 91
Falzon, L., 63
Famely, P., 594
Fan, M., 94

Fan, S. P., 286
Fancher, R., 43, 447
Fancher, R. E., 315, 316
Fang, Y., 199
Faraday, A., 189
Faraday, M. M., 540
Farah, M. J., 336, 628
Faravelli, C., 567, 568f
Farb, N. A., 176
Farb, N. A. S., 622
Farber, B. A., 614
Farberow, N. L., 575t
Faria, S., 520
Farkas, K., 390
Farley, K. J., 421
Farmer, K., 259
Farre, M., 184
Farrell, M., 379
Farrey, T., 577–578
Farrington, D. P., 590
Fashler, S., 142, 143
Fask, D., 335
Fassler, O., 175, 410
Fava, G. A., 614–615, 615
Fawcett, J., 79, 626
Fay, K., 598
Fayard, J. V., 438
Faymonville, M.-E., 175
Fazio, L. K., 253
Fazio, R. H., 234, 493
Fear, N. T., 565
Fearer, S., 186
Fechner, Gustav, 111, 112, 112f, 113
Federoff, I., 355
Feeney, J. A., 397
Fehr, B., 484, 485, 486
Fehr, E., 96
Feidler, K., 479
Fein, D., 591
Fein, S., 511
Feindel, W., 12
Feinstein, R. E., 575
Feist, G. J., 340
Feist, J., 519
Feixas, G., 632
Fekadu, A., 629
Felber, J., 226
Felder, J. N., 622
Feldman, D. H., 339, 340, 403, 405
Feldman, J., 259
Feldman, M. D., 418
Feldman, O., 121
Feldman, R., 96
Fellini, Federico, 171
Felmlee, D., 484, 487
Feng, J., 25
Fennell, M. V., 622
Fennessey, G. J., 421
Fennis, B. M., 493
Fenwick, P., 177
Fenwick, P. B., 189
Ferenczi, Sandor, 8f

Pluess, M., 398
Plug, C., 132
Plumert, J. M., 405
Plutchik, R., 376, 376t, 377, 377f
Poe, M. D., 592
Poehlman, T., 491
Poerio, G. L., 172
Pogosyan, A., 629
Pogue-Geile, M. F., 582
Pohl, P. S., 421
Pohl, R. F., 308
Polan, H. J., 576
Polaschek, D. L., 259
Poldrack, R. A., 67
Policastro, E., 340
Polich, J., 177
Poline, J. B., 410
Polivy, J., 351, 352, 352f, 355
Pollatsek, A., 305
Pollio, D. E., 637
Polman, E., 298
Polsky, D., 634
Pomaki, G., 519
Pomerantz, E. M., 430, 451
Pomerleau, C. S., 140
Pomerleau, O. F., 140
Pomerville, A., 633
Pon, James, 475f
Pontin, E. E., 352
Poo, M.-M., 263
Pool, E., 53
Poortinga, Y., 129
Poortinga, Y. H., 133, 373
Pope, H. G., 580
Pope, H. G., Jr., 259
Pope Jr., 598, 599
Popenoe, D., 431, 432
Popkin, B. M., 353
Popova, S., 390
Popper, C. W., 327, 328
Porcerelli, J. H., 447
Porter, C., 589
Porter, J., 141
Porter, S., 439, 589
Posada, G., 397
Posavac, E. J., 274–275
Posner, M. I., 14, 15, 76, 177
Post, R. M., 627
Posten, A-C., 113
Posthuma, D., 335, 380
Postle, B. R., 157
Postma, A., 569
Postman, L., 254
Postmes, T., 504
Potagas, K., 534t
Potkay, C. R., 456t
Potkin, S. G., 54
Potter, D., 592
Potter, J., 414, 436
Potter, J. E., 391
Potter, W. Z., 625
Potthoff, J. G., 577
Poulin-Dubois, D., 283
Poulous, S., 632
Poulsen, C., 410

Poulton, E. C., 305
Powell, E., 546
Powell, R. A., 204, 214, 447, 569
Powley, T. L., 81, 350
Pozzulo, J., 593, 594
Prather, C. C., 538
Pratkanis, Anthony, 491
Pratt, D., 519
Pratt, J., 25
Pratte, M. S., 83
Prebble, S. C., 239
Premack, David, 288
Prentice, R., 540
Prentky, R. A., 340–341
Prescott, J., 139
Prescott, Y., 421
Pressman, S. D., 524, 536, 537
Prestia, D., 581
Preston, E. L., 250
Preston, K. L., 187
Prestwich, A., 199
Pribram, K., 175
Pribram, K. H., 247
Price, H. L., 53
Price, Jill, 268, 268f
Price, R. A., 353
Price, T. S., 333
Prichard, I., 355
Priebe, S., 636
Priester, J. R., 492, 496
Priluck, R. L., 199, 234, 494
Primeau, I., 437
Prina, M., 419
Prince, M., 419
Pringle, H., 312
Prinstein, M. J., 565
Prizant, B. M., 591
Prkachin, K., 545
Probst, C., 178
Prochaska, J. M., 540
Prochaska, J. O., 540
Proecshold-Bell, R. J., 531
Proffitt, D. R., 129
Prolo, P., 535
Pronin, E., 214, 497
Proulx, C. M., 380
Proulx, T., 363
Province of Ontario, 590
Prudic, J., 628
Pruessner, C., 265
Pruitt, D. G., 503
Pruyn, A. H., 493
Przeworski, A., 561
Psaty, B. M., 627
Psychogiou, L., 432
Ptito, A., 578
Public Health Agency of
    Canada, 541
Public Health Toronto, 219
Pugh, N. D., 177
Pullum, G. K., 289
Punch, J. L., 134
Purdon, C., 564
Purdon, S., 591

Purdy, J. E., 58
Purkis, H., 567
Purkis, H. M., 196, 198
Purves, D., 123
Putallaz, M., 427
Puterman, E., 519
Puts, D. A., 362
Pyc, M. A., 271
Pyle, K. V., 96
Pyryt, Michael, 330

Q

Qin, S., 271, 370
Quadflieg, S., 476
Quas, J. A., 258
Quesnel, M., 512
Qui, C., 420
Quimet, C., 92, 94
Quina, K., 258
Quinn, J., 512
Quinn, J. M., 493
Quinn, K. A., 479
Quinn, M., 546
Quinsey, V. L., 589
Quoidbach, J., 239, 378

R

Raat, H., 134
Rabbitt, S. M., 608
Rabin, B. S., 535
Rabin, M., 302
Rabin, S., 203
Rabinovich, A., 378
Rabinovici, G. D., 419
Rabinowitz, J., 625
Rachman, S. J., 564, 567, 620
Racine, Y. A., 241f, 258, 259f
Radak, Z., 420, 541
Rae, D. S., 560
Rafal, R., 85
Rafanelli, C., 615
Raffi, 594
Raffone, A., 177, 416
Raggio, G., 534
Rahe, R., 522f
Rahe, Richard, 522
Rahman, M. A., 540
Rai, D., 591
Rains, G. D., 91
Rainville, P., 143, 176, 177, 178
Rajaram, S., 253
Rajeevan, N., 458
Rakic, P., 107
Rakobowchuk, P., 418
Rama, A. N., 162, 227
Ramadan, N. M., 534t
Ramage-Morin, P. L., 142, 418
Ramchand, R., 565
Ramchandani, P. G., 432
Ramey, C. T., 343
Ramey, S. L., 342, 343
Ramirez, M., 632
Ramos, B. C., 185, 200
Ramsay, D. S., 351

Ramsey, D., 629
Ran, F. A., 100
Rane, L. J., 576
Rangtell, F. H., 167
Rapaport, M. H., 421, 584
Raphael, B., 519
Raphael, D., 532
Rapoport, J. L., 411, 584
Rapson, R. L., 485
Rascmany, M., 265
Rashid, T., 18, 615, 615f
Raskin, N. J., 614
Rasmussen, A., 476
Rasmussen, I., 84
Rasmussen, J. L., 564
Rastegar, N., 121
Rathner, G., 534t
Ratner, K. G., 15, 506
Ratner, M. S., 409
Ratner, N. B., 280
Rauch, S. L., 79
Rauh, V., 391
Rauscher, F. H., 107
Ravert, R. D., 413
Rawal, S., 138
Rawana, J. S., 411, 633
Rawson, K. A., 27
Rawson, K. S., 420
Rawson, N. E., 141
Raybeck, D., 273
Raye, C. L., 253, 506, 507
Raymond, N. C., 598
Rayner, R., 203
Rayner, Rosalie, 203f
Raynor, H. A., 351
Raynor, J. O., 365
Razavi, A. H., 158
Read, J., 626
Read, J. D., 259, 274
Read, S. J., 458
Rebok, G. W., 107, 273
Reboussin, D., 628
Recht, L. D., 159, 159f
Rechtschaffen, A., 160
Reder, L. M., 266
Redline, S., 167, 169, 546
Reece, M., 357, 357f
Reed, D. R., 139
Reed, L., 480f
Reed, S. K., 294
Reedy, F. E. Jr., 139
Rees, C. J., 467
Reese, H. W., 204
Reese, R. J., 617
Refinetti, R., 158
Regan, P. C., 484
Regehr, C., 532
Reger, G. M., 620
Regev, R., 432
Regier, D. A., 558, 560, 561, 600f
Rego, S. A., 618
Rehm, J., 178, 390
Reichborn-Kjennerud, T., 458,
    590
Reicher, S., 501

Rozin, P., 138, 351, 352
Rubenstein, A. J., 477
Rubin, D. C., 248, 268, 432, 565
Rubin, J., 15
Rubinstein, R. S., 478
Ruble, D., 429
Ruble, D. N., 430
Ruble, D. N., 430, 565
Ruck, C., 634
Rudd, A. G., 534
Rudert, S. C., 364
Rudestam, K. E., 619f
Rudolph, U., 481
Rudorfer, M. V., 625
Rudrauf, D., 90
Ruini, C., 615
Ruiperez, M. A., 594, 595
Ruiter, M. E., 168f
Ruiz, J. M., 538
Ruiz, P., 180, 562, 566, 579, 594, 597, 620
Ruiz de Apodaka, J., 620
Ruiz-Barquin, R., 213, 214
Rumbaugh, D. M., 287
Rumelhart, D. E., 251
Rummel, J., 247
Rumpf, H., 186
Rumpold, G., 534t
Runco, M. A., 339
Rundle, A., 391
Rundus, D., 272f
Rusack, B., 165
Rusak, B., 164, 165
Rusak, Benjamin, 164
Rusan, M., 121
Rüsch, N., 555
Ruscio, J., 62
Ruscio, J., 2, 2f
Rushton, J. P., 319, 331, 335, 338
Rusinak, D., 626
Rusiniak, K. W., 206
Russakoff, M., 625
Russell, A. M., 478, 510
Russell, G. F. M., 595, 597
Russell, J. A., 373, 526
Russell, T. M., 450
Russo, E., 186
Rutherfor, A., 11
Rutherford, A., 3, 6, 9, 43, 196–197, 208, 361, 416, 447
Rutherford, W., 136
Ruthruff, E., 240, 241
Ruthsatz, J. M., 327
Rutter, M., 24, 100, 459
Ruvio, A., 528
Ryan, C. S., 512
Ryan, J., 581
Ryan, M., 186
Ryckeley, R., 195
Ryder, A. G., 564, 633
Ryder, R. D., 58
Ryder, Serena, 572
Ryff, C. D., 528
Rylett, M., 178
Ryu, Y., 169

S

Saab, B. J., 101
Saad, C. S., 632
Sabourin, M., 15
Sachdev, P. S., 558, 628
Sack, A. T., 85
Sack, D. A., 574
Sackeim, H. A., 628
Sacker, A., 379
Sackett-Maniacci, L., 610
Sacks, O. W., 329
Sadava, S. W., 378
Sadikaj, G., 397
Sadker, D., 430
Sadker, M., 430
Sadler, P., 176
Sadock, B. J., 562, 566, 579, 597
Sadock, V. A., 562, 566, 579, 597
Safdar, Saba, 475f
Safran, J. D., 610
Safvenbom, R., 503
Sagaspe, P., 165
Sagi-Schwartz, A., 398
Sagiv, L., 476
Sahakian, B. J., 15
Sais, E., 285
Sajeev, G., 583
Sakai R. R., 350, 351
Sakamoto, A., 225
Saklofske, D., 436
Saks, A. M., 451
Salanova, M., 451
Salary, C. B., 626
Saleem, M., 225
Salmaso, L., 615
Salmon, P., 177
Salo, P., 167
Salovey, P., 322, 538
Salsman, K., 370
Salthouse, T. A., 251, 420, 420f
Salvador, Z., 576
Salvator, A., 390
Salvatore, M. A., 506
Samberg, E., 612
Sameroff, A. J., 219
Same-Sex Rights, 360
Samet, J. M., 540
Samnaliev, M., 579
Sampson, P. D., 390
Sampson, S., 629
Sampson, S. M., 629
Samson, Y., 268
Samuels, J., 564
Samuels, S. C., 78
Samuelson, P. A., 302
Sanbonmatsu, D. M., 241
Sanchez-Armass, O., 174
Sandal, G. M., 437
Sander, D., 53
Sanders, M. H., 169
Sanders, S. A., 357, 357f
Sanderson, W. C., 561
Sandrini, M., 85
Sandstrom, G. M., 537

Sandvik, E., 378
Sandy, C. J., 436
Sanfey, A. G., 506
Sanjuan, P., 482
Sankis, L. M., 556
Sanna, L. J., 510
Santana, I., 353
Santiago, A. N., 576
Santos, M. A., 94, 637
Sanz, J., 620
Saper, C. B., 86
Saphire-Bernstein, S., 380
Sapolsky, R. M., 526
Sarbin, T. R., 569
Sarga, L., 420, 541
Saribay, S. A., 511
Sarkissian, H., 482
Sarpon, C. D., 176
Sartorius, A., 629
Sartorius, N., 534
Saslow, L. R., 524
Sassa, Y., 319
Sateia, M., 168
Satel, S., 190
Sathiamma, S., 177
Sato, T., 454, 574
Satpute, A. B., 299
Sattely-Miller, E. A., 352
Satyarthi, Kailash, 538
Saucier, G., 439
Saucier, J.-F., 574
Saucier, S., 171t
Saulsbury, W., 185
Savage, J., 226
Savage, L. C., 155
Savage-Rumbaugh, E. S., 287
Savage-Rumbaugh, S., 287, 287f
Saville, P. D., 470
Savin-Williams, R. C., 361
Sawalani, G. M., 427
Sawicki, R. F., 314
Sawyer, B., 85
Saxe, Leonard, 369
Saxena, S., 564
Sayegh, P., 186
Sayer, L. C., 416, 416f
Scaro, N. H., 531
Scarr, S., 333
Scarr, Sandra, 334, 335f
Scerif, G., 328
Schachter, R., 616
Schachter, S., 38, 39, 39f, 40f, 363, 375, 375f, 536
Schachtman, T. R., 234, 235
Schacter, D., 506
Schacter, D. I., 85
Schacter, D. L., 63, 85, 85f, 156, 166, 239, 248, 252, 254, 261, 265, 266, 268, 274
Schaefer, A., 520
Schaefer, C. A., 391
Schaeffer, N. C., 55
Schafe, G. E., 352
Schaffhausen, J., 263
Schaie, K. W., 428f

Schalke, D., 319, 419
Schalkwyk, L. C., 101
Schaller, M., 15, 349, 438f, 488, 500
Schatz, R. B., 620
Schatzberg, A., 576
Schaufeli, W. B., 531
Schauman, O., 608
Schechter, L. E., 418
Scheef, L., 79
Scheffer, I. E., 90
Scheibel, A. B., 68
Scheier, M. F., 96, 419, 454, 528, 537
Schell, T. L., 565
Schellenberg, E., 107
Schellenberg, E. G., 107
Schellenkens, M. J. P., 176
Schenck, C. H., 168, 170
Schenck- Gustafsson, K., 534t
Schendel, D., 592
Schenker-Ahmed, N. M., 264
Scherer, K. R., 367, 371
Schermer, J. A., 436, 437
Schick, V., 357, 357f
Schieber, F., 418
Schiefelbein, V. L., 96, 410
Schiff, M., 333
Schiffman, S. S., 352
Schilbach, L., 227
Schiller, J. S., 418, 419f
Schilling, F., 589
Schimmack, U., 493
Schindler, S., 307
Schirillo, J. A., 126
Schkade, D., 380
Schlee, W., 107
Schlegel, A., 409
Schleicher, A., 333
Schlenger, W. E., 531
Schlenk, E., 543
Schloss, H., 632
Schmeichel, B. J., 458
Schmid, J., 369
Schmid, P. C., 427
Schmidt, F. L., 53, 325
Schmidt, H. D., 78, 89, 184
Schmidt, S., 248
Schmidt, T., 371
Schmit, D. T., 174
Schmit, M. J., 322
Schmitt, D. P., 358, 358–359, 359, 360, 428, 486
Schmitz, J. M., 539
Schmitz, R., 160
Schmitz, S., 429
Schmitz, T. W., 506
Schmolck, H., 248
Schnall, P. L., 534t
Schneider, D., 432
Schneider, R. H., 177
Schneiderman, N., 534t
Schneier, F. R., 562
Schnittker, J., 555
Schnoll, R. A., 451

White, W. B., 534
Whitehead, B. P., 420
Whitehead, Paul, 636
Whitehouse, W. G., 576, 577
Whitelhy, S., 594
Whitfield, C. L., 258
Whiting, J. W. M., 409
Whitney, N., 125
Whittaker, K. S., 533
Whittal, M. L., 564
Whittemore, K. E., 593
Whitwell, R. L., 120
Whorf, B. L., 289, 290f
Whyatt, R., 391
Whyte, Robert, 4
Wibom, R., 159
Wickenheiser, Hayley, 322f
Wickens, T. D., 245
Wickett, J. C., 319
Widiger, T. A., 438, 556, 558, 588
Widiyanto, P., 373
Widom, C. S., 590
Wiebe, P., 546
Wiekum, W., 282
Wiens, S., 367
Wiers, R. W., 199
Wiesel, T. N., 89, 125
Wiesel, Torsten, 14, 106, 119, 119f
Wigboldus, D., 506
Wiggs, C. L., 268
Wight, R. D., 5
Wikelgren, I., 15
Wilde, E. A., 83, 84
Wildermuth, J. L., 468
Wilding, J., 271
Wiles, R., 391
Wileyto, E. P., 451
Wilhelm, S., 564
Wilhelmsen, L., 534t
Wilkins, A. J., 562
Willford, J. A., 390
Williams, A. J., 189
Williams, B. A., 214, 637
Williams, D. R., 528
Williams, Dave, 436f
Williams, H. L., 268
Williams, J. D., 114
Williams, J. E., 533, 533f
Williams, J. M. G., 177, 418, 567, 621, 622
Williams, K., 363, 364, 502–503, 503f
Williams, K. D., 363, 502, 503
Williams, K. L., 167
Williams, K. M., 439
Williams, Kip, 363
Williams, L. M., 258, 259
Williams, N. A., 534t
Williams, O., 121
Williams, P., 612
Williams, P. G., 438, 533
Williams, R. L., 27, 334, 540
Williams, S. L., 543
Williams, S. R., 576

Williams, Serena, 195, 195f
Williams, W. M., 51, 215, 334
Williamson, D. A., 599
Williamson, P. A., 220
Willinger, J. R., 390
Willingham, Bob, 371
Willingham, D. T., 27, 506, 507
Willis, S. L., 107
Wills, J. A., 504
Willson, H. J., 163
Wilska, M., 328
Wilson, A. E., 484
Wilson, A. E., 598
Wilson, C. J., 531
Wilson, G. T., 618, 623
Wilson, I., 531
Wilson, J., 506
Wilson, M., 18, 351
Wilson, R. E., 487
Wilson, R. S., 419, 420
Wilson, S., 409
Wilson, S. A., 324
Wilson, S. J., 90
Wilson, T. D., 55, 261, 307, 368, 378, 484, 493
Wilson T. D., 62
Wilt, J., 438
Winawer, J., 111, 132
Winblad, B., 420
Winczewski, L., 33
Windham, G. C., 591, 592
Windholz, G., 197
Winer, A. C., 395
Wing, L., 592
Wingfield, A., 418
Winkielman, P., 259, 367, 505
Winn, P., 350
Winner, E., 329, 330, 330f
Winograd, E., 13
Winograd, T., 267
Winquist, J. R., 504
Winsler, A., 405
Winter, E., 96
Winterbauer, N., 202
Winterbauer, N. E., 212
Winterheld, H. A., 485
Winton-Brown, T. T., 582
Winward, J., 186
Winzenz, D., 249f
Wirth, M. M., 368
Wirtz-Justice, A., 574
Wisco, B. E., 576
Wise, J., 376
Wise, R. A., 78
Witelson, S. F., 67
Wittchen, H., 562f
Wittchen, H.-U., 558
Wittgenstein, Ludwig, 111
Witthoft, N., 111, 132
Wittkower, E. D., 632
Witty, M. C., 614
Wixted, J. H., 275
Wixted, J. T., 43, 271, 272f
Wodniecka, Z., 284, 285

Woelfling, K., 529
Woemmel, C. A., 451
Woertman, L., 569
Wohlschager, A. M., 111
Wojtowicz, J. M., 263
Wolf, P. S. A., 459
Wolfe, D. A., 141
Wolfe, J. M., 125
Wolff, K., 421
Wolford, G., 92
Wolitzky, D. L., 447
Wollmer, M. A., 371
Woloshin, S., 548
Wolpe, J., 618, 630
Wolpert, E., 172
Wolsic, B., 379
Won, M., 429, 629
Wonderlich, S. A., 597, 598, 599
Wong, A. T., 85
Wong, Alana, 85f
Wong, E., 639, 640
Wong, H., 594, 633
Wong, I., 159
Wong, L. A., 452, 456
Wong, M., 241f, 258, 259f
Wong, M. Y. Y., 219
Wong, P., 121
Wong, S. C. P., 589
Wong, W., 4, 564
Wong, Y., 509
Wonocur, G., 268
Wood, A. M., 239, 378
Wood, D. K., 121
Wood, E., 430
Wood, J. M., 468
Wood, J. N., 405
Wood, J. V., 536
Wood, L. M., 268, 322
Wood, N. L., 241
Wood, P. K., 589
Wood, W., 360, 428, 493
Woodbury, M. A., 138
Wooderson, S. C., 629
Woodhead, M., 343
Woods, A. M., 202
Woods, R. P., 319
Woods, S. C., 350, 351
Woodward, A., 531
Woodworth, M., 439
Woody, E. Z., 176
Woody, S. R., 564
Woody, Sheila, 564
Woody, W. D., 7
Woolfolk, R. L., 524
Woollett, K., 91
Woo-Sam, J. M., 324
Word, D. H., 478
World Health Organization, 182, 559, 574
Wormith, S., 589
Worthen, J. B., 159
Worthington, R. L., 632
Wortman, C. B., 421
Wortmann, R. L., 470

Wright, J. C., 225
Wright, J. D., 353
Wright, J. H., 621
Wright, K. P., Jr., 159
Wright, M. J., 11, 12f, 335
Wrosch, C. B., 528
Wrulich, M., 319, 419
Wu, G., 302
Wu, J. Q., 591
Wu, Q., 126
Wu, Y., 627
Wulfeck, B., 283
Wundt, W., 4, 4f, 5f, 111
Wustenberg, T., 541
Wyer, N. A., 511
Wykes, T., 628
Wynn, K., 329, 405, 406, 406f
Wynn, T., 248
Wynne, C. D. L., 287

X

Xi, S., 126
Xian, H., 247
Xu, J., 84, 199
Xu, W., 420

Y

Yabe, Y., 120
Yacubian, J., 144
Yager, J., 188
Yamada, A., 633
Yamada, A. M., 595
Yamaguchi, M., 405
Yamamoto, J., 634
Yamane, Y., 119
Yan, Z., 241
Yang, H., 534t
Yang, J., 333
Yang, L. H., 594
Yang, Y., 458
Yao, J., 531
Yao, R., 125
Yarbrough, G. L., 450
Yarmey, A. D., 274
Yarmey, Daniel, 274
Yashikawa, S., 242
Yates, F. A., 271
Yates, W. R., 566f
Yazdani, H., 241
Ybarra, 487
Yelaja, P., 564
Yen, Grilo, C. M., 633, 634
Yeomans, F., 588, 589
Yeomans, M. R., 139
Yerkes, R. M., 197f
Yerramsetti, S. M., 178, 622
Yeshurun, U., 140
Yeung, E., 628
Yeung, H. H., 282
Yim, H., 267
Yin, D., 94
Yip, G. W., 540
Yip, J., 397

Yoder, K. J., 589
Yokley, J. L., 582
Yong, J. C., 360, 488
Yoo, S. H., 373
Yoon, I. Y., 169
Yoon, J., 132
Yoon, J. H., 581
Yoshida, K., 282
Yoshikawa, H., 336
Yost, W. A., 137, 418
You, T., 541
Young, C. B., 271, 370
Young, D. M., 595
Young, G. B., 68
Young, J. K., 390
Young, K., 633, 634
Young, Kimberly, 528
Young, L. J., 96
Young, M. E., 351
Young, T. B., 163
Youngentob, S. L., 139, 140
Younggren, J., 302
Yousafzai, Malala, 538
Yovel, G., 119
Yu, C., 540
Yu, Y., 529
Yudin, M., 574
Yudofsky, S. C., 83, 84, 626f
Yuille, J. C., 243
Yuker, H. E., 125f

Z

Zaccaro, S. J., 451
Zachariae, R., 534, 535
Zack, M., 623
Zadra, A., 169, 170, 171
Zadra, A. L., 171t
Zager, D. B., 591
Zago, L., 94, 105
Zagoloff, A., 623
Zagoory-Sharon, O., 96
Zagorsky, J. L., 325
Zahorodny, W., 591
Zajdel, M., 542
Zajonc, R. B., 367, 371, 492–493, 493f
Zak, P. J., 96
Zaki, J., 15
Zakrzewski, A. C., 266
Zamboanga, B. L., 413
Zane, N., 24, 633, 634
Zang, D., 534t
Zangen, A., 156
Zanna, M. P., 186, 187, 478, 479, 511, 542, 598
Zaragoza, M. S., 252–253, 253
Zarate, M. A., 509
Zatzick, D. F., 143
Zautra, A. J., 524, 534
Zavorotnyy, M. M., 85
Zawadzka, K., 251

Zayas, L. H., 412
Zayas, V., 451
Zebrowitz, L. A., 476, 477
Zechmeister, E. B., 26
Zee, K. S., 454
Zeelenberg, M., 302
Zeidan, F., 177
Zeidner, M., 322, 454
Zeiler, M., 215
Zeng, Y., 632
Zentall, T. R., 58
Zentner, M., 360
Zepelin, H., 165
Zervas, I., 534t
Zhang, D., 529
Zhang, F., 100, 626
Zhang, J., 302, 368
Zhang, J. W., 379
Zhang, M. W. B., 529
Zhang, Q., 540
Zhang, R., 451
Zhang, S., 130
Zhang, X., 186, 191f
Zhang, Y., 625
Zhao, J., 298, 298f
Zhao, S., 560
Zhao, X., 289
Zheng Wu, 415f
Zhong-Lin, L., 506, 507
Zhou, E. S., 527

Zhou, K., 199
Zhou, X., 564
Zhu, D. H., 504
Zhu, X., 167, 546
Zielaskowski, K., 113
Zielinski, B. A., 105, 579
Zigler, E., 342
Zilcha-Mano, S., 546
Zillmer, E. A., 80, 91
Zimbardo, P. G., 452, 500, 501
Zimmerman, B. J., 451
Zimmerman, I. L., 324
Zimmerman, J., 432
Zinbarg, R., 566
Zinbarg, R. E., 623
Zink, N., 172
Zohar, J., 564
Zohary, E., 91
Zola, S. M., 14, 264
Zormuski, C. F., 70, 628
Zrenner, E., 123
Zrinzo, L., 629
Zschucke, E., 541
Zubieta, J. K., 55
Zucker, N. L., 599
Zuckerman, M., 457
Zuest, D., 634
Zurbriggen, E. L., 366
Zuroff, D. C., 397
Zwanzger, P., 85

child development, 392–409
  aggression, 234–235
  attachment, 395–398
  cognitive development, 400–407
  critical periods, 106–107
  cultural variations, 393–394
  developmental norms, 393
  enriched environments, 106–107
  Erikson's Stage theory, 399–400
  fatherlessness, 431–432
  language acquisition, 282–284
  media violence, 234–235
  moral reasoning, 407–409
  motor development, 392–394
  overview of, 422–423f
  personality development, 398–400
  television watching, 234–235
  temperament, 394–395
childhood disintegrative disorder, 590
children
  aggression, 224–227, 226f
  exercise, 354–355
  giftedness, identifying, 329
  IQ and mortality, 319f
  night terrors, 169
  nightmares, 170
  obesity, 353
  well-being and fathers, 431–432
child's mental age, 316, 316t
A Christmas Carol (Dickens), 239
chromosomes, 96–97, 97f
chronic grief, 421
chronic pain. See pain
chronic stressors, 520
chronological age, 316, 316t
chunking, 246–247
circadian rhythms, 158–160, 158f
circular reasoning, 383
clarification, 614
classical conditioning, 196–207,
    197f, 228–229f
  acquisition, 201, 202f
  in advertising, 199–200, 200f, 234, 494f
  anxiety disorders, 566–567, 566f
  apparatus, 197f
  basic processes, 198f, 201–202, 213t
  becoming more aware of, 235
  biological effects, 205–207
  in business negotiations, 234
  cognition, 205
  compensatory CRs, 200
  conditioned reflex, 198
  conditioned response, 198, 198f, 200
  conditioned stimulus, 197f, 198, 198f,
    200, 205–206
  defined, 196
  eliciting, 198, 200
  evaluative conditioning, 199–200
  in everyday life, 198–201
  evolutionary effects, 205–207
  extinction, 201–202, 202f
  fear, 199f
  higher-order conditioning, 204, 204f
  vs. operant conditioning, 213t
  in politics, 234–235, 235f
  predictive value, 205
  procedures, 197–198
  psychic reflexes, 196–197
  signal relations, 205
  spontaneous recovery, 202, 202f
  stimulus discrimination, 204
  stimulus generalization, 202–205
  taste preferences and, 352

terminology, 197–198
  trials, 198
  unconditioned response, 197, 198f
  unconditioned stimulus, 197, 197f,
    198f, 204f, 205–206
client-centred therapy, 11, 452–454,
    613–614, 614f, 640f
clinical psychologists, 608–609, 609t
clinical psychology, 12–13, 20–21, 22f
clinical services, delivery of, 634–635
clinical social workers, 609t, 610
close relationships, 483
  cultural differences, 486–487
  Internet and, 487–488
closure, 127, 127f
clustering, 249
cocaine, 181, 185, 390
cochlea, 135, 136f
cocktail party phenomenon, 240–241
Code of Ethics for Psychologists, 58t
coefficient of determination, A-10,
    A-11f
cognition, 10f, 14f
  aging and, 420–421
  bilingualism, 279, 284–286
  classical conditioning and, 205
  defined, 13–15
  emotional experience and, 367–368
  gender differences, 427
  intelligence and, 320–321
cognitive abilities, 325
cognitive components, 28
cognitive development, 400–407
  critical periods, 406–407
  innate abilities, 405–406
  Piaget's stage theory, 400–404
  Vygotsky's sociocultural theory,
    404–405
cognitive dissonance, 495
cognitive interpretation of
    arousal, 375
cognitive maps, 220–221
cognitive performance, and
    cannabis, 186f
cognitive perspective, 13, 320
cognitive processes, 104–105, 450
cognitive psychology, 21f
cognitive schemas, 477–478
cognitive styles, 105, 296–297, 297f
cognitive theory, behaviourism
    and, 220
cognitive therapy, 621–622
cognitive-behavioural therapy (CBT),
    177, 621–623
cohabitation, 416
cohesiveness, 504–505
cohort effects, 394
collective unconscious, 445, 446f
collectivism, 464, 483, 500
collectivist cultures, 486f–487
colour circle, 122, 123f
colour mixing, 121f
colour perception, 290
colour vision, 121–124
  opponent process theory, 122–123
  stimulus for, 121–122
  theories of, 123–124, 124f
  trichromatic theory of, 122
colourblindness, 122
colours, emotions and behaviour, 33,
    34–37, 37f
commitment, 485
common grief, 421

communication, 491
community mental health
    movement, 635–636
comorbidity, 601
companionate love, 485
comparitors, 150
compensation, 446
compensatory CRs, 200
complementary colours, 122, 123f
complex thought, 89–90
computations, 45
conceptual hierarchy, 249
conceptual skills, 326
conclusions, 382
concordance rate, 566, 566f
concrete operational period, 401f,
    402–403, 403f
concussions, 577–578
conditional affection, 453
conditional stimuli, 184
conditioned fear and anxiety, 198–199
conditioned reflex, 198
conditioned reinforcers, 210
conditioned response, 198, 198f, 200
conditioned stimulus, 197f, 198,
    198f, 200, 205–206
conditioned taste aversion, 205–206,
    206f
conditioning, 196, 205–207, 221–222.
    See also classical conditioning;
    operant conditioning
conditioning/learning, anxiety
    disorders and, 566–567
cones, 116f, 117, 123, 123f
confirmation bias, 305–306,
    306f, 479
conflict, 441–442, 521, 521f
conformity, 497–498, 497f, 498f,
    500, 523
confounding of variables, 40
conjugal status, 415
conjunction fallacy, 301, 301f, 601
conjunctive probabilities, 601, 601f
connectionist networks, 250–251
connotation, 281
conscientiousness, 419, 438, 438f,
    537–538
conscious, 441
consciousness
  attention and, 156
  brain activity, 157, 157f
  brain and, 157
  defined, 156
  EEG patterns, 157, 157t
  electroencephalograph (EEG), 157,
    157t, 160–161, 161f
  Freud's model, 440–441, 440f
  meditation, 176–178
  nature of, 156–157
conservation, 402, 402f
consolidation of memories, 88, 161,
    166, 264–265
constraints, 293
construct validity, 315
constructive coping, 530, 545
content validity, 314
context cues, 200, 251–252
context effects, 128–129, 128f
contingencies, 222, 232–233
continuity, 127, 127f, 387
continuous reinforcement, 214
contradictory evidence, 432
contrast effects, 150–151, 151f

control, variations in, 156
control group, 38–39, 40f
conventional level, 408, 408f
convergent thinking, 339
coordination, loss of, 502, 503f
coping, 527
cornea, 114, 115f
coronary heart disease, 533, 533f
corporal punishment. See physical
    punishment
corpus callosum, 87f, 89, 89f, 92,
    428, 429f
correct rejections, 113
correlation, A-9–A-11, A-10f, 50f, 314f
  causation and, 51–52, 51f
  Galton and, 316
  in health risks, 548
  positive and negative, 47, 50
  prediction and, 50–51
  strength of, 50
correlation coefficient, A-9, A-11f,
    47, 50f, 314
correlational analyses, 47
corticosteroids, 527
counselling psychologists, 608–609
counselling psychology, 20, 22f, 609t
counsellors, 609t, 610
counterarguments, 382
counterattitudinal behaviour, 495
counterconditioning, 619
couples therapy, 616–617
crack cocaine, 181
creative intelligence, 320, 320f
creativity, 339–341
  correlates of, 340–341
  defined, 339
  dreams and, 170–171
  intelligence and, 340
  measurement, 339–340
  mental illness, 340–341, 341f
  nature of, 339
  psychological testing, 339–340
  sleep and, 166
credentials, 513
credibility, 491, 513–514
criminal responsibility, 593–594
CRISPR, 100
criterion-related validity, 314–315
critical periods, 106, 282, 406–407
critical thinking skills, 28–29, 29t
cross-sectional design, 394, 394f
crystal meth, 181
crystallized intelligence, 318
CT (computerized tomography) scan,
    83, 83f
cues, 251
cultural continuity factors, 412
cultural differences
  attachment, 398, 398f
  attributions, 482–483
  bereavement, 421
  child development, 393–394
  close relationships, 486–487
  conformity, 500
  dreams, 172
  emotional experience, 372–373, 372f
  intelligence quotient, 335–337
  intelligence testing, 326
  language acquisition, 284, 290
  motor development, 393–394, 394f
  obedience, 500
  psychological disorders, 594–595
  romantic relationships, 486–487

cultural diversity, 478
cultural genocide, 475
culture, 15
  defined, 24
  dreams and, 172
  language, 289–290
  personality and, 462–464, 463f
  problem solving, 296–297
  sleep, 164
  taste preferences, 139f
culture-bound disorders, 594
cumulative deprivation hypothesis, 333
cumulative probabilities, 600
cumulative recorder, 209, 210f
cyberbullying, 2
cyberspace, 343
cyclothymic disorder, 570, 573

D

Dani people, 289
Dark Tetrad, 439
Dark Triad, 439
data analysis, 36–37
data collection, 36, 36t
Day of the Dead, 421
day residue, 172
day-care, 397–398
Daylight Saving Time, 159
deactivation, 73
deaf, manual babbling, 282
death and dying, 421
decay, 245
decay theory, 256
decentration, 402
deception, 57, 467
decibels (dB), 134
decision making, 298–304, 503–505
  base rates, ignoring, 301
  basic strategies, 298–299
  behavioural economics, 302
  belief perseverance, 305–306
  confirmation bias, 305–306
  conjunction fallacy, 301
  evolutionary analyses, 302–303
  fast vs. slow, 303–304
  framing, 306–307
  gambler's fallacy, 305
  heuristics, 300
  law of small numbers, 305
  loss aversion, 307
  risky, 299–300, 305
declarative memory, 266–267, 266f
deep brain stimulation, 629f
deep muscle relaxation, 619
deep processing, 242f, 272–273
Deese-Roediger-McDermott (DRM) paradigm, 260
default mode network, 156
defence mechanisms, 442–443, 442f, 442t, 529–530, 529t
defensive attribution, 481–482, 482f
defensive coping, 529–530
degradation, 73
deinstitutionalization, 636, 636f, 637
deliberate decisions, 299
deliberation-without-attention effect, 299
delta waves, 157
delusions, 580
delusions of grandeur, 580
dementia, 286, 419

dendrites, 69f, 70
denial, 421
denial of reality, 529t
denotation, 281
dentate gyrus, 263
Department of Veterans Affairs, 531–532
depattern, 606
dependent variables, 38, 40f, 41
depolarization, 74
depressed-improved pattern, 421
depression. See depressive disorders
depressive disorders, 569–578
  bipolar disorder, 572–573
  cognitive factors, 576
  diversity in, 573–574
  etiology of, 575–578
  fetal origins of, 391
  genetic vulnerability, 575
  hormonal factors, 576
  interpersonal factors, 577f
  interpersonal roots, 577
  major depressive disorder, 571
  negative thinking and, 576–577, 577f
  neuroanatomical factors, 575–576
  neurochemical factors, 575–576
  positive psychotherapy, 615f
  precipitating stress, 578
  prevalence of, 571
  sports concussions, 577–578
  stress and, 533–534
  suicide, 574–575
  symptoms, 572t
depressive episode, 572t
depth cues, 130f, 148
depth perception, 129–130
description, 33–34
descriptive statistics, A-7, 46–47, 50–53
descriptive/correlational research methods, 42–45
desensitization, 226
despair, 415
detectability, 113
development
  adolescence, 409–414
  adulthood, 414–421
  childhood, 392–409
  continuity, 387
  defined, 387
  overview of, 422–425f
  prenatal, 387–391
  transition, 387
developmental norms, 393
Developmental Psychobiology, 406
developmental psychology, 21f
deviance, 556–557, 556f
deviation IQ scores, 324
Dexedrine, 78
diabetes, 391, 534, 540
diabetes, sleep and, 167
diagnosis, 556, 558f
Diagnostic and Statistical Manual (DSM-5), 327, 558–559, 558f, 564, 564t, 565, 579, 588
dichromats, 122
Dictionary of Affect in Language (DAL), 367
dietary restraint, 355
different cognitive processes, 266
difficult children, 395
diffusion of responsibility, 502
direct observation, 36t

disciplinary procedures, 218
disconfirming evidence, 275
discrimination, 212–213, 474–475, 509, 510f
discriminative stimulus, 213
discussion, in journal articles, 61
disease, and stress, 534–535
disgust, 370–371, 376, 376t, 377f
dishabituation, 405
disinhibited social engagement disorder, 565
disinhibition, 175, 355
disorganized schizophrenia, 581
disorganized-disoriented attachment, 397
displacement, 442t, 443
display rules, 373
disruptive mood dysregulation disorder, 570
dissociation, 176
dissociative amnesia, 568, 569
dissociative disorders, 568–569
dissociative identity disorder, 569, 579
dissonance theory, 494–496, 495f
distal stimuli, 127, 128f
distance perception, 129–130
distinctiveness, 437
distracted driving, 241
distributed practice, 271–272, 272f
divergent thinking, 339
diversity, 15
divided consciousness, 176
DNA, 97f, 100
doctor-assisted death, 418
door-in-the face technique, 150, 150f
The Doors of Perception (Huxley), 606
dopamine, 78, 78f, 183f, 184
dopamine circuits, 184
dopamine hypothesis, 77t, 582, 583f
dorsal stream, 119–120, 119f, 121
double-blind procedure, 56
Doublespeak (Lutz), 308
doubt, 399
Down syndrome, 328
dream analysis, 611
dream interpretation, 259
dream symbolism, 189
dreams, 170–173
  activation- synthesis model, 173
  activation-synthesis model, 173f
  cognitive, problem-solving view, 173, 173f
  common questions, 189
  common themes, 171t
  contents of, 171
  cultural differences, 172
  culture and, 172
  day residue, 172
  interpretation, 189
  latent content, 173
  links with waking life, 171–172
  manifest content, 173
  problem-solving view, 173, 173f
  theories of, 172–173, 173f
  wish fulfillment, 173f
drive reduction, 348
drive theories, 348
drives, 348
drug therapy, 624–627
  antianxiety drugs, 624
  antidepressant drugs, 625–626
  antipsychotic drugs, 624–625

evaluation of, 627
  increase in, 624f
  mood stabilizers, 627
drug tolerance, 183, 200
drug use
  addiction, 183
  alcohol, 178, 179t, 180, 180t, 182, 182f, 183t, 185, 186, 187, 189
  altering consciousness, 178–187
  cannabinoid receptors, 184
  cannabis, 178, 180t, 182, 183t, 184, 186, 186f
  cocaine, 181, 185
  conditioning and drug effects, 200–201
  dependence, 183t, 184–185
  direct effects, 185–186
  ecstasy (MDMA), 182
  effects of, 178–182
  endocannabinoids, 184
  factors influencing, 182–183
  hallucinations, 181
  hallucinogens, 175, 180t, 181, 183t
  health and, 185–187, 541
  health risks, 183t
  indirect effects, 186–187
  LSD, 181
  maternal, 389–390
  mechanisms of, 183–184
  narcotics, 180–181, 180t, 183t, 185
  opiates, 180–181
  overdose potential, 183t
  overdoses, 185
  overview of, 179t
  physical dependence, 184–185
  prevalence of, 178, 180
  psychoactive drugs, 178, 180, 180t, 183t
  psychological dependence, 185
  sedatives, 168, 169, 180t, 181, 183t, 185, 186
  stimulants, 169, 180t, 181, 183f, 183t, 185
  tolerance, 183, 183t
DSM-5. *See Diagnostic and Statistical Manual*
dual-centres model of hunger, 350
dual-coding theory, 243
dual-process theories, 303

E

eardrum, 134, 136f
early adulthood stage, 415
early selection, 241, 241f
ears, 134–135, 136f
easy children, 395
eating, excessive, 354–355
eating disorders, 597–599
  anorexia nervosa, 597
  binge-eating disorder, 598
  bulimia nervosa, 597–598
  cognitive factors, 599
  cultural roots of, 598–599
  cultural values, 599
  description, 597
  etiology of, 599
  family, role of, 599
  genetic vulnerability, 599
  personality factors, 599
  prevalence of, 598–599
echolalia, 591
eclecticism, 632, 640f

ganglion cells, 116f, 117, 123
gate-control theory, 143, 144
gender, 427
gender differences
  aggression, 427, 428
  biological origins, 427–429
  brain organization, 428–429
  cognitive abilities, 427
  eating disorders, 598
  environmental origins, 429–430
  evolutionary analyses, 427–428
  gender-role socialization, 430
  hormones, 428
  mate preferences, 359–360
  mathematical ability, 427
  nature of, 428f
  observational learning, 429
  self-socialization, 429–430
  in sexual activity, 358–359
  sexual activity, 427
  sexual motivation/behaviour,
    357–359, 359f
  spatial skills, 25, 28–29
  taste, 140
  therapists, 639
  verbal skills, 427
  visual-spatial ability, 427
gender discrimination, 512
gender roles, 429
gender stereotypes, 478
gender-role socialization, 429f, 430
general adaptation syndrome, 526
general mental ability (g), 317,
  317f, 318
General Social Survey (GSS), 44
generalizability, 41
generalization, 212–213
generalization gradients, 203, 203f
generalized anxiety disorders, 561
generational changes, 410
generativity, 415
genes, 96–97
genetic mapping, 100, 458
genetic material, 97f
genetic relatedness, 98f
genetics, 96–97. See also heredity
genital stage, 444t, 445
genotypes, 97
genuineness, 614
geometric illusions, 131f
germinal stage, 388
Gestalt principles of perception,
  126–129, 127f
Gestalt psychology, 126, 149
ghrelin, 351
giftedness, 329–330, 330f
glial cells, 68–69
goal-directed behaviour, 347
gonadotropin hormones, 96
gonads, 96
graded potentials, 74, 75
gradual mastery of conservation,
  402, 403f
Graduate Record Exam (GRE), 51
grapheme-colour synesthesia, 111
graphic organizers, 27
graphing data, A-6–A-7, A-6f
group cohesiveness, 504–505
group polarization, 503–504, 504f
group size, 497, 498f
group therapy, 615–616, 616f
group unanimity, 497

groups
  behaviour and, 501–505
  bystander effect, 502
  competition between, 511
  decision making, 503–505
  defined, 501
  productivity, 502–503
  social loafing, 502–503
groupthink, 504–505, 505f
grubs, 139f
Guantanamo Bay detainees, 57, 57f
*Guidelines for Human Pluripotent Stem
  Cell Research* (*Updated Guidelines*,
  2010), 91
guilt, 399–400
gustatory system, 138–140, 146–147f

H

habituation, 405
habituation–dishabituation
  paradigm, 405
hair cells, 135
Haldol (haloperidol), 624
hallucinations, 175, 180t, 181, 183t,
  580–581
halo effect, 55
Hamilton Rating Scale for Depression,
  615f
hammer, 135, 136f
happiness, 363, 368, 370–371,
  378–381, 378f
hardiness, 537–538
Harry Potter and the Prisoner of Azkaban
  (Rowling), 239
hashish, 182
hate crimes, 360, 474–475
Head Start programs, 342
Healing Circles, 634
health
  alcohol and drug use, 541
  biopsychosocial factors, 544f
  decision making, 548–549
  drug use and, 185–187
  exercise, 540–541
  happiness and, 379
  health-impairing behaviour, 539–542
  illness, reactions to, 542–544
  intelligence and, 319–320, 320f
  meditation and, 177–178
  obesity, 353, 354f
  personality and, 438
  risks, evaluation of, 548–549
  sleep and, 167
  smoking, 539–540
  statistics, 548–549
  stress and, 532–535, 534t
Health Canada, 178, 390
health care providers, communication with, 543
health psychology, 21f, 519
health statistics, 548–549
healthy personality, 455–456, 456t
hearing, split-brain research, 92–93
heart disease, 533–534, 533f
Hebb Synapse, 76
Hebbian learning rule, 76, 263
hedonic adaptation, 380
hedonic treadmill, 381
height in plane, 129, 130f, 148f
hemispheric specialization, 92,
  93–94, 104f, 428–429

Hereditary Genius (Galton), 315
heredity, 24
  behaviour and, 96–101
  environment and, 100–101
  happiness and, 380
  intelligence, 331–336
  obesity, 354f
  research methods, 97–100
  sexual orientation, 362, 362f
Here's the Deal (Mandel), 563
heritability ratio, 332–333, 332f
herpes, 534
hertz (Hz), 134
heterosexuals, 360, 361
heuristics, 294, 300
hierarchical classification, 403
hierarchy of needs, 455, 455f
higher-order conditioning, 204, 204f
high-frequency tones, 134
highway hypnosis, 176
hindbrain, 80f, 86, 87f
hindsight bias, 274–275, 469–470
hippocampal region, 264–265
hippocampal volume, 576
hippocampus, 87f, 88, 263, 263f, 264
histogram, A-6–A-7, A-6f
hits, 113
hoarding disorder, 562, 564–565,
  564f, 564t
hobbits and orcs problem, 291,
  291f, 292f
holistic cognitive style, 296
homelessness, 637
homeostasis, 348, 348f, 355
homosexuality, 360, 361, 362–363.
  See also sexual orientation
hormones, 95–96, 350–351, 368, 428,
  526–527, 576
hostility, 533
housework trends, 416, 416f
human behaviour, 9
human development. *See*
  development
Human Genome Project, 100
human hearing capacities, 134
human immunodeficiency virus
  (HIV), 541
human intelligences, 321
Human Rights Tribunal, 474
humanism, 9–11, 10f, 452–456
humour, 545–546
hunger/eating, 349–355
  biological factors, 349–351
  brain regulation, 350, 350f
  digestive and hormonal regulation,
    350–351
  environmental factors, 351–352
  food availability/cues, 351–352
  learned preferences/habits, 352
  obesity, 352–355
Huntington's disease, 419
Hurricane Katrina, 565
hydrocephaly, 328
hyperpolarization, 74
hypertension, 167, 533
hyperthymestic syndrome, 268, 268f
hypnic jerks, 160
hypnosis, 174–176
  altered state of consciousness, 176
  amnesia, 175
  anesthesia, 175
  defined, 174

disinhibition, 175
dissociation, 176
hallucinations, 175
highway, 176
hypnotic induction, 174–175
memory and, 252
misconceptions, 174f
posthypnotic suggestions, 175
recovered memories and, 259
sensory distortions, 175
susceptibility to, 174–175
theories of, 175–176
hypnotic induction, 174–175
hypnotic trance, 175
hypothalamic-pituitary-adrenocortical
  (HPA) axis, 576
hypothalamus, 87f, 88, 95, 96f, 164,
  350, 350f, 526
hypothesis, 34–35, 40f
hypothesis testing, A-11–A-12
hypothetical constructs, 315

I

"I have a friend who" syndrome, 63
id, 343, 440f
ideal self, 454
identical (monozygotic) twins,
  98–99, 99f, 331–332, 353–354,
  354f, 362, 362f, 440, 458f, 581
identification, 442t, 443
identity, search for, 412–413
identity achievement, 413, 413f
identity diffusion, 413, 413f
identity foreclosure, 413, 413f
identity formation, 413
identity moratorium, 413, 413f
identity statuses, 413, 413f
ignorance, appeals to, 342–343
illness, 519
  health care providers, communication
    with, 543
  medical advice, adhering to, 543–544
  reactions to, 542–544
  treatments, 542
illusory correlation, 479
imagery, 243
imaging (fMRI). *See* functional
  magnetic resonance imaging (fMRI)
immediate style, 478
immune functioning, 534–535
immune response, 535
Implicit Association Test (IAT), 55f,
  490–491, 491f
implicit attitudes, 490–491
implicit measures, 55f
implicit memory, 262, 265–266
implicit prejudice, 511
implicit social support, 537
implied threat, 309
impressions of others
  cognitive schemas, 477–478
  formation of, 475–479
  physical appearance, 476–477
  stereotypes, 478–479
  subjectivity and bias, 479
In Search of Memory (Kandel), 262
inattentional blindness, 125
incentive theories, 348–349
incentive value of success,
  365–366, 366f
incentives, 348

incongruence, 453, 453f
incubation, 296
incubation effect, 296
independent memory systems, 266–267, 266f
independent variables, 38, 40f, 41, 41f
independent view of the self, 463
individual differences, 313
individual psychology, 446–447
individualism, 464, 483, 500
individualistic cultures, 486–487
inducing structure, 291
industrial and organizational psychology, 20, 22f
industry, 400
infant development. *See* child development
infant–mother attachments, 396–397, 397f
infants
  babbling, 282
  deaf, 282
  language acquisition, 282
  sleep and, 162
  understanding of numbers, 405, 406f
inferential statistics, A-11, 52–53
inferiority, 400
inferiority complex, 446, 446f
inflammation, 533
inflammatory bowel syndrome, 534
information organization, 272–273
information processing, 117, 119–120
informational influence, 498
information-processing theories, 244
infrared spectrum, 114
ingroups, 479, 511–512
inhibitory postsynaptic potentials, 74, 79
initiative, 399–400
innate abilities, 405–406
innate taste preferences, 352
inner ear, 135, 136f
insanity defence, 593–594
insight, 291
insight therapies, 607, 610–618
  client-centred therapy, 613–614, 614f
  couples therapy, 616–617
  effectiveness of, 617
  family therapy, 616–617
  group therapy, 615–616, 616f
  mechanisms of, 617–618
  positive psychology, 614–615, 615f
  psychoanalysis, 610–613
  recovery as a function of number of sessions, 617f
insomnia, 167–169, 168f, 188–189
instinctive drift, 221–222
institutional treatment, 635–636
instrumental learning, 207
insular cortex, 138
insulin, 351
integrity, 415
intellectual disabilities, 326–329, 327t
  Down syndrome, 328
  fragile X syndrome, 328
  levels of, 327
  origins of, 328
  phenylketonuria, 328
  savants, 328–329
  social class, 328f

intellectual disability, 590
intellectualization, 529t
intelligence
  adoption studies, 332, 333
  biological correlates, 319–320
  brain and, 319–320
  cognitive processes, 320–321
  creativity and, 340
  debate over, 342–343
  emotional, 322–323
  environment and, 333–335, 334f, 336f
  extremes of, 326–330
  Flynn effect, 333–334
  giftedness, 329–330
  happiness and, 379
  health and, 319–320, 320f
  heredity, 331–333, 335–336
  hydrocephaly, 328
  intellectual disabilities, 326–329
  interaction of heredity and environment, 334–335
  longevity and, 319–320, 419
  multiple, 321–322
  nature versus nurture, 316, 331
  nonverbal, 316
  practical, 320, 320f, 325, 325f
  social, 325, 325f
  socioeconomic differences, 336–337
  structure of, 316–318
  twin studies, 99f, 331–332
  verbal, 316, 324–325, 325f
intelligence quotient (IQ), 335–337
  calculating, 316t
  cultural bias, 337
  defined, 316
  family studies, 331f
  normal distribution, 323–324, 323f
intelligence testing
  Binet-Simon scale, 316, 326
  cultural bias, 337
  cultural differences, 326
  defined, 313
  family studies, 331f
  intelligence quotient (IQ), 323–324
  origins of, 315–316
  racial differences, 326
  reliability, 324
  Spearman's g, 317, 317f, 318
  types of, 313
  validity, 324–325
  vocational success and, 325–326
interactionist theories, 289, 289f
interdependent view of the self, 463, 464f
interference, 245
interference theory, 256–257, 256f
intermediate processing, 242f
intermittent reinforcement, 214
intermittent schedules of reinforcement, 214
internal attributions, 480
internal conflict, 521
International Classification of Disease and Health Related Problems (ICD-10), 559
International Classification of Sleep Disorders: Diagnostic and Coding Manual, 167
Internet, close relationships and, 487–488
Internet addiction, 528–529
interpersonal attraction, 483

interpersonal intelligence, 321, 321f
interpersonal psychotherapy (IPT), 43–44
interposition, 129, 130f, 148f
interpretation, 611–612
intersubjectivity, 227
interval schedules, 215, 215f
interviews, 36t
intimacy, 415, 485
intrapersonal intelligence, 321, 321f
intrapsychic conflict, 442f
introduction, in journal articles, 61
introspection, 5, 196, 279
intuitive decisions, 299
Inuit language, 289, 290f
inverted-U hypothesis, 525, 525f
involuntary commitment, 594
ions, 70
IQ. *See* intelligence quotient (IQ)
iris, 116
irrational thoughts, 580
irrelevant information, 292
irrelevant reasons, 383
irreversibility, 402
isolation, 415

J

James-Lange theory, 374, 374f
jet lag, 159f
jigsaw classroom technique, 511
joint custody, 62
journal articles, 60–61
Journal of Experimental Social Psychology, 37, 61
Journal of the American Medical Association, 637
journals, 37, 60
joy, 376, 376t
Jung's analytical psychology
  archetypes, 445–446
  collective unconscious, 445, 446f
  personal unconscious, 445
just noticeable difference (JND), 112
just world theory, 482, 542

K

kinesthetic system, 144, 145
knowledge representation/ organization, 248–251
Kohlberg's Stage theory, 408, 408f

L

language
  acquisition, 288–289
  animals and, 286–287
  bilingualism, 279, 279f, 284–286, 285f
  brain and, 93
  comprehension of, 92
  culture and, 289–290
  defined, 280
  development of, 281–284, 281t
  evolutionary context of, 287–288
  linguistic relativity, 289–290
  morphemes, 280f, 281
  natural selection and, 287
  phonemes, 280–281, 280f
  semantics, 281
  structure of, 280–281, 280f
  syntax, 281

language acquisition
  animals and, 286–287
  babbling, 282
  behaviourist, 288
  bilingualism, 284–285
  cultural differences, 284, 289–290
  interactionist theories, 289f
  manual babbling, 282
  metalinguistic awareness, 284
  optimal periods, 282
  overextensions, 283
  overregularizations, 283f
  telegraphic speech, 283f
  theories of, 288–289
  underextensions, 283
  vocabulary, 283, 283f
language acquisition device (LAD), 288–289
language development, 284
language processing, 92, 92f
lasting effects, 107
late adulthood stage, 415
late selection, 241, 241f
latency stage, 444t, 445
latent content of dreams, 173
latent learning, 220–221, 221f
lateral geniculate nucleus (LGN), 118, 118f, 123
lateral hypothalamus (LH), 350, 350f
law of effect, 207–208, 208f
law of Pragnanz, 127
law of small numbers, 305
leading questions, 259
learned helplessness, 527–528, 576
learned preferences/habits, 352
learning
  classical conditioning, 196–207, 228–229f
  defined, 195
  evaluative conditioning, 199–200
  evolutionary perspectives, 222
  introduction to, 195–196
  observational, 223–227
  observational learning, 223f, 224f, 228–229f
  operant conditioning, 207–222, 228–229f
  overview of, 228–229f
learning theory, 493–494
lectures, 27
left hemisphere, 94
lens, 114, 115f
leptin, 351, 355
lesioning, 83
levels-of-processing theory, 241–242, 242f
lie detector, 368–369, 369f
life changes, 522
lifetime prevalence, 559–560, 600–601, 600f
light, 115f
light and shadow, 129, 130f
light as stimulus, 114
light exposure, 159
likability, 492
limbic system, 88–90
linear perspective, 129, 130f, 148, 148f
linguistic intelligence, 321, 321f
linguistic relativity, 289–290
linguistic relativity hypothesis, 308
link method, 273
lithium, 627

Necker cube, 128, 128f
need for affiliation, 38–39, 39f
negative correlation, A-10f, 47, 50, 50f
negative reinforcement, 216–218, 216f, 218f
negative symptoms, 581, 582f
negative thinking, 576–577, 577f
negatively skewed distribution, A-7
NEO Personality Inventory, 466–467
nervous system. *See also* central nervous system
  anatomy of, 68–79
  glial cells, 68–69
  neurons, 69–76
  neurotransmitters, 77–78
  organization of, 80–82, 80f
neural circuits, 262–263, 350
neural development, 106–107, 106f, 410–411
neural impulse, 71f
neural reorganization, 91
neurodevelopmental hypothesis, 584, 590–592
neuroethics, 15
neurogenesis, 91, 106, 263, 527
neuromatrix theory of pain, 144
neurons, 69–76
  action potential, 71–72
  activity of, 74–76
  defined, 68
  graded potentials, 74
  resting potential, 70–71
  structure of, 69f
  synaptic transmission, 72–73
neuroscience, 13–15, 14f
  personality and, 458–459
  social, 505–507
neuroses, 610
neuroticism, 438, 438f
neurotransmitters, 566
  behaviour and, 77–78
  defined, 72–73, 75
  drug use and, 183, 183f
  vs. hormones, 95
  overview of, 77t
neutral stimulus (NS), 196, 198f, 199, 204f
New York Times, 312
Newsweek, 104
nicotine, 188
night shift workers, 159–160
night terrors, 169
nightmares, 170
nine-dot problem, 293f, 295f
Nobel Peace Prize, 538
Nobel Prize, 76, 92, 119, 123, 196, 262, 298, 302, 312
nodes, 251
nominal fallacy, 191
non sequitur, 383
nonadherence to medical advice, 543–544
nonbenzodiazepine sedatives, 168, 169
nondeclarative memory, 266–267, 266f, 267f
nonimmediate style, 478
non-REM (NREM) sleep, 161–162
nonsense syllables, 254, 254f, 255f
nontasters, 138–139
nonverbal behaviour, 477
nonverbal communication, 427
nonverbal expressiveness, 370–372, 371f

norepinephrine, 77t, 78, 183f, 184
normal distribution, A-8–A-9, A-9f, 47, 47f, 323–324, 323f
normality, 557f
normative influence, 498
norms, 313–314
not criminally responsible on account of mental disorder (NCRMD), 593
not guilty by reason of insanity (NGRI), 593
nucleus accumbens, 184
null hypothesis, A-12
The Nurture Assumption (Harris), 469
nutrition, maternal, 390, 391

O

obedience, 498–500
obesity
  defined, 353
  dietary restraint, 355
  excessive eating, 354–355
  fetal origins of, 391
  genetic predisposition, 353–354
  health and, 353, 354f
  heritability, 354f
  inadequate exercise, 354–355
  roots of, 352–355
  set-point theory, 355
  sleep and, 167
obesogenic environment, 354, 354f
object permanence, 401
objects, perception of, 124–126
observational learning, 223, 223f, 224f, 429
  attitudes and, 494
  basic processes, 224
  brain and, 227
  media violence, 224–227
  overview of, 228–229f
  personality and, 450–451
  prejudice and, 510
obsessive-compulsive disorders, 562–565
occipital lobe, 89, 90f
occupational stereotypes, 478
Oedipal complex, 444–445, 612
Official Languages Bill, 279
olfactory system, 140–141, 141f, 146–147f
On the Origin of Species (Darwin), 101
one-sided presentations, 492
online dating sites, 487–488
open monitoring, 177
openness to experience, 438, 438f
operant chamber, 209
operant conditioning, 196, 207–222
  acquisition, 211–212
  anxiety disorders, 566–567
  attitudes and, 494
  basic processes, 211–213, 213t
  biological effects on, 221–222
  vs. classical conditioning, 213t
  cognitive maps, 220–221
  cognitive processes, 220–221
  defined, 207
  discrimination, 212–213
  evolutionary effects on, 221–222
  extinction, 212
  gender differences, 429
  generalization, 212–213
  latent learning, 220–221

  overview of, 228–229f
  personality and, 449, 449f
  positive vs. negative reinforcement, 216–218
  prejudice and, 510
  procedures, 209–210
  punishment, 218–220
  reinforcement, 209, 209f, 213–214
  schedule of reinforcement, 214–216
  shaping, 211–212
  Skinner box, 208–209
  stimulus control, 212–213
  superstitious behaviour, 213–214
  terminology, 209–210
  Thorndike's law of effect, 207–208
operant responding, 211f
operational definition, 35
opiates, 180–181
opioids, 79
opponent process theory, 122–123, 123f, 124f
optic chiasm, 118, 118f
optic disk, 116–117, 116f
optic nerve, 117, 118f
optimal level of arousal for peak performance, 525–526, 525f
optimal period, 406
optimal periods, 282
optimism, 419, 537–538
optimism intervention, 615
oral stage, 444, 444t
organic amnesia, 263
organisms, 102
The Organization of Behavior (Hebb), 76
orgasm, 357
ossicles, 135
osteoporosis, 597
ostracism, 363–364
ought self, 454
outgroups, 479, 511–512
oval window, 135
overcompensation, 447, 529t
overconfidence effects, 275
overdoses, 185
overeating, 233f
overextension, 283
overextrapolations, 107
overregularizations, 283f
oxycodone, 180–181
oxytocin, 95–96

p

pain, 142–144, 142f, 177–178
pain tolerance, 177–178
palatability, 351, 352f
pan-Amerindian, 633
pancultural view, 594
panic disorder, 203, 562, 568f
papillae, 139f
parallel distributed processing, 250–251
Paralympic athletes, 347
paranoid schizophrenia, 581
parasympathetic division, 81–82
parathyroid glands, 96f
paraventricular nucleus, 350, 350f
parental favouritism, 43
parental investment theory, 358, 358f, 359
parenthood, 379, 416–417
parietal lobe, 89–90, 90f
parietal region, 67

Parkinson's disease, 78, 78f, 86, 170, 419
partial reinforcement, 214
partial sleep deprivation, 165
participants, 36
passionate love, 485, 486
pathology, 554–555
pathways of pain, 142f
patterns, perception of, 124–126
Pavlovian conditioning, 196. *See also* classical conditioning
PAWSS (Pets Assisting with Student Success) program, 519
Paxil (paroxetine), 79, 625
PDP models. *See* parallel distributed processing
Pearson product-moment correlation, A-10
Penetanguishene Mental Health Centre, 606
percentile scores, A-9, 47, 314, 324, 414
percentile test scores, 316
perception. *See* sensation and perception
perception of flavour, 140
perceptual asymmetries, 94, 105f
perceptual constancy, 130
perceptual hypothesis, 127–129
perceptual set, 124
perfectionism, 599
performance, 224
peripheral nervous system, 80–82, 80f
peripheral route, 496
persistence, 261
persistent depressive disorder, 570
person perception, 475–479
  cognitive schemas, 477–478
  evolutionary analyses, 479
  physical appearance, 476–477
  stereotypes, 478–479
  subjectivity and bias, 479
personal distress, 556f
personal unconscious, 445
personality, 21f
  Bandura's social cognitive theory, 449–451
  behavioural genetics, 457–458
  behavioural theories, 448–452, 448f
  Big Five personality traits, 436, 438–439, 438f, 457, 459, 462, 463f, 466–467
  biological theories, 457–459
  creativity and, 340
  culture and, 462–464, 463f
  defined, 437
  development of and conditioning, 449
  development theories, 399f
  evolutionary approach, 459
  Eysenck's theory, 457
  Freud's psychoanalytic theory, 439–445
  happiness and, 380
  health and, 438
  healthy, 455–456, 456t
  hindsight bias, 469–470
  humanistic perspectives, 452–456
  introduction to, 436–437
  Jung's analytical psychology, 445–446
  Maslow's theory of self-actualization, 454–456
  narcissism, 439
  nature of, 437–439
  neuroscience, 458–459

personality, 21f (Continue)
  operant conditioning and, 449, 449f
  overview of, 460–461f
  person-situation controversy, 451
  psychodynamic theories, 439–447
  Rogers' person-centred theory,
    452–454
  Skinner's personality development
    theory, 448–449
  stress and, 533
  structure of, 440, 440f, 448, 457f
  traits, 437–438
  trends, 415f
  twin studies, 99f, 457–458, 458f
personality assessments, 466–468
personality development, 398–400,
  414–415
personality disorders
  antisocial personality disorder,
    588–589
  borderline personality disorder, 589
  classification of, 588t
  etiology of, 590
  narcissistic personality disorder
    (NPD), 589–590
personality dynamics model, 442f
personality structure, Eysenck's
  model of, 457, 457f
personality tests, 313
personality trait of optimism, 416,
  419
personality traits, 437–438
person-centred therapy, 11, 452–454,
  613–614, 614f, 640f
person-situation controversy, 451
persuasion, 491–493, 492f
pervasive developmental disorder
  not otherwise specified, 590
pessimistic explanatory style, 576
PET (positron emission tomography)
  scans, 84, 85f, 177, 506
phallic stage, 444–445, 444t
phantom-limb pain, 144
phenomenological approach, 452
phenotypes, 97
phenylketonuria, 328
pheromones, 141
phi phenomenon, 126
philosophy, 3, 4
phobias, 3, 196, 198–199, 206–207,
  207f, 561–562, 562f, 619, 619f, 623
phonemes, 280–281, 280f
phonemic encoding, 242, 242f, 256
phonological loop, 247, 247f
physical appearance, 475, 476–477,
  476t, 477f
  attractiveness, 151, 151f, 359f, 379,
    476t, 477f, 483–484
  nonverbal expressiveness, 477
physical characteristics, 102, 103f
physical dependence, 184–185
physical fitness, 547f
physical punishment
  aggression, 219, 219f, 220f
  side effects of, 219–220
physiological responses to stress,
  525–527
physiological/neural recording, 36t
physiology, 3
Piaget's Stage theory, 400–404, 401f
pictorial depth cues, 129, 130f, 148
pineal gland, 96f, 158
pinna, 134, 136f

pituitary gland, 87f, 95, 96f
place theory, 136–137
placebo effects, 54–55, 55f, 143,
  183, 642
placenta, 388
Plato, 3, 244
pleasure centres, 88, 88f
pleasure principle, 440
Poggendorff illusion, 131f
point prevalence rates, 600
pointillism, 148–149
polarization, 503–504, 504f
political agenda, 432
politics, 234–235, 235f
polling, 54f
polygenic traits, 97
polygraph, 368–369, 369f
pons, 86, 87f, 164
Ponzo illusion, 131, 131f, 132f
populations, A-12f, 53, 54f, 102
pornography, 358
positive correlation, 47, 50, 50f
positive emotionality, 380
positive emotions, 419, 524
positive individual traits, 18
positive institutions and
  communities, 18
positive psychology, 18–19, 539,
  614–615, 615f
positive reinforcement, 216–218, 216f
positive subjective experiences, 18
positive symptoms, 581, 582f
positively skewed distribution, A-7
Possessing Genius (Abraham), 67
postconcussion syndrome, 578
postconventional level, 408, 408f
posthypnotic suggestions, 175
postpartum depression, 574
postsynaptic neuron, 72
postsynaptic potential, 78
post-traumatic stress disorder, 518,
  531–532, 532f, 554, 565–566
practical intelligence, 320, 320f,
  325, 325f
practical skills, 326
preconscious, 440f, 441
preconventional level, 408, 408f
prediction, A-10–A-11, 34, 50–51
predictive value, 205
predisposition, 575
preferences, 298
prefrontal cortex, 90, 90f, 411, 411f,
  629
prejudice, 474–475, 506, 508–512,
  509f, 510f, 555
premature birth, 389, 391f
premenstrual dysphoric disorder, 570
premises, 382, 382f
prenatal development, 387–391,
  389f, 390f
  embryonic stage, 388–389
  environmental factors, 389–391
  environmental toxins, 391
  fetal origins of adult disease, 391
  fetal stage, 389
  germinal stage, 388
  maternal drug use, 389–390
  maternal illness, 391
  maternal nutrition, 390
  nutrition, 391
  stress and emotion, 390–391
prenatal period, 387–388
preoperational period, 401f, 402

preparedness, 206–207, 207f, 566
present moment, 623
pressure, 141–142, 522–523
presynaptic membrane, 73
presynaptic neuron, 72
prevalence, 559–560
prevalence rates, 600
PREVNet, 2
primary appraisal, 520
primary auditory cortex, 89
primary colours, 122
primary emotions, 376, 376t, 377, 377f
primary mental abilities, 317
primary motor cortex, 89, 90f, 91f
primary reinforcers, 210
primary sex characteristics, 409
primary somatosensory cortex, 89,
  90f
primary tastes, 138, 139f
primary visual cortex, 90f, 118, 118f,
  119f
primary-process thinking, 440
Principles of Psychology (James), 5
private speech, 404–405
proactive interference, 257, 257f
probabilities, 300
probability of success, 365–366, 366f
problem solving, 290–297
  approaches to, 293–296
  arrangement, 291
  barriers to, 292–293
  cognitive, 296–297
  culture and, 296–297
  incubation, 296
  inducing structure, 291
  representation, 295–296
  transformation, 291
  types of problems, 290–292
  unnecessary constraints, 293
  working backward, 294
problem space, 293
problem-solving view of dreams,
  173, 173f
procedural memory, 266–267, 266f,
  267f, 420
processing, levels of, 241–242
productive vocabulary, 283
productivity, 502–503, 503f
prognosis, 556
program design, 232–233
program execution, 233
progressive relaxation, 546
projection, 442t, 443
projective hypothesis, 467
projective tests, 365, 467–468
PROP (propylthiouracil), 138
"Prospect Theory" (Kahneman &
  Tversky), 302
prospective memory, 268–269, 269f
proximal stimuli, 127, 128f
proximity, 127, 127f
Prozac (fluoxetine), 79, 625
pseudoforgetting, 255–256
psilocybin, 181
psychedelic, 606
psychiatric nurses, 609t, 610
psychiatrists, 609, 609t
psychiatry, 20–21
psychic reflexes, 196–197, 198
psychoactive drugs, 178, 180,
  180t, 183t
psychoanalysis, 7, 9, 10f, 14f, 439,
  441, 607, 610–613, 611f

psychoanalytic theory, 7, 439–445
  anxiety and defence mechanisms,
    442–443, 442t
  awareness, levels of, 440–441
  conflict, 441–442
  hindsight bias, 469–470
  personality, structure of, 440
  psychosexual stages, 444–445, 444t
  sex and aggression, 441–442
psychodiagnosis, 558–559
psychodynamic theories, 439–447,
  613f
psychodynamic therapies, 612–613,
  640f
psychological associates, 609
psychological dependence, 185
psychological disorders. See also
  mental illness; treatment of psychological disorders
  abnormal behaviour, 554–561
  alternative diagnosis systems, 559
  anxiety disorders, 561–562
  anxiety disorders, etiology of, 566–568
  bipolar disorder, 572–573
  classification of, 558–559, 558f
  culture and pathology, 594–595
  depressive disorders, 569–578
  dissociative disorders, 568–569
  eating disorders, 597–599
  introduction to, 553–554
  legal aspects, 592–594
  lifetime prevalence, 600–601, 600f
  neurodevelopmental hypothesis,
    590–592
  obsessive-compulsive disorders,
    562–565
  overview of, 586–587f
  personality disorders, 588–590
  post-traumatic stress disorder, 518,
    531–532, 532f, 565–566
  prevalence of, 553, 559–561, 560f
  root of, Beck's view, 621f
  root of, Freud's view, 610f
  root of, Rogers's view, 613f
  schizophrenia, 579–585
  stereotypes, 557
psychological functioning and stress,
  530–532
psychological research, 60–61
psychological testing, 313–314
  creativity, 339–340
  defined, 313
  intelligence. see intelligence testing
  mental ability tests, 313
  norms, 313–314
  reliability, 314, 314f
  standardization, 313–314
  types of, 313
  validity, 314–315
psychological tests, 36t
psychologists, 20t, 59, 608–609
psychology
  Adler's individual psychology,
    446–447
  behaviourism, 6–7, 8–9
  Canadian, 11–12
  cognition and neuroscience, 13–15
  culture and diversity, 15
  current state of, 19–22
  defined, 3, 19
  diversity in, 15
  evolutionary, 15, 18
  functionalism, 4–6

history of, 3–19, 16–17f
humanism, 9–11
important figures in, 8f
misconceptions, 2t
nature versus nurture, 6–7
positive, 18–19
professional specialties, 20–22, 22f
professionalization, 12–13
research areas, 19, 21f
research laboratories, 5f
structuralism, 4–6
structuralism vs. functionalism, 4–6
themes of, 22–23
theories of, 10f, 14f, 23
unconscious, 7–8
variety of topics, 2–3
women in, 6, 11–12, 12f
work settings and activities, 20t
Psychology's Feminist Voices, 6
psychometrics, 21f
psychopathy, 439, 589
Psychopathy Checklist–Revised
(PCL–R), 589
psychopharmacotherapy, 624
psychophysics, 111–114
psychosexual stages, 444–445, 444t
psychosocial crisis, 399
psychotherapy
client-centred therapy, 11, 452–454,
613–614, 614f, 640f
effectiveness of various approaches, 640f
misconceptions, 606
therapeutic alliance, 634
use of LSD in, 606
PsycINFO, 60–61, 61f
PTC (phenythiocarbamide), 138
puberty, 409, 410f
Public Health Agency of Canada,
219, 541
punishment, 218–220, 218f, 233
pupil, 115f, 116
purity, 114, 134
push-versus-pull theories, 348

Q

questionnaires, 36t, 55

R

racial differences, intelligence
testing, 326
racism, 474
Rain Man, 329, 329f
random assignment, 40, 40f
rapid eye movements. See REM sleep
ratio schedules, 214
rational-emotive therapy, 545, 545f,
640f
rationality, 302
rationalization, 442, 442t
reaction formation, 442t, 443
reaction range, 334–335, 334f
reactive attachment disorder, 565
reactivity, 43
reading ahead, 27
reading methods, 26–27
realistic group conflict theory, 511
reality principle, 440
recall measure, 255, 255f
receiver factors, 492f, 493
receptive fields, 117, 124f, 141, 142f
receptive vocabulary, 282–283

receptors, 73
reciprocal determinism, 450, 450f
reciprocity, 484
reciprocity norm, 234, 514
recognition measure, 255, 255f
reconsolidation, 265
reconstructions, 252
recovered memories, 259–260
recreational drug use. See drug use
references, in journal articles, 61
reflex pathways, 266
refractory period, 358
regression, 442t, 443
regression toward the mean, 642–643
rehearsal, 245, 271
reification, 343
reinforcement, 209, 209f, 213–214,
216–218, 222, 232, 233
reinforcement contingencies, 209
reinforcement schedules. See
schedule of reinforcement
reinforcers, 232, 232f
rejection, fear of, 363–364
relational aggression, 427
relationship satisfaction, 380
relationships, close, 483
relationship-specific optimism, 416
relative measures, A-8, 47
relative size, 129, 130f, 148f
relativistic view, 594
relativity, 150–151
relaxation response, 546
relaxation training, 546, 547f
relearning measure, 255
release, 73
reliability, 314, 314f, 324
religion, and meditation, 176–177
religion, happiness and, 379–380
REM sleep, 161, 161f, 162, 162f,
165–166, 188, 189
REM sleep behaviour disorder
(RED), 170
remedial action, 512
remember to remember, 269
"Remembering to Do Things"
(Harris), 268
renewal effect, 202, 212
repetition of messages, 492
replication, 34, 53
representation of the problem,
295–296
representative sample, 53, 54f
representativeness heuristic, 300–
301, 305, 600, 601
repressed memories, 258–260
repression, 257–260, 442t, 443
reproduction, 224
reproductive fitness, 396
research
data collection, 36
descriptive/correlational research
methods, 42–45
ethics in, 56–59
evaluation of, 53–56
experimental, 38–42
publication of, 37
scientific approach to behaviour, 33–38
scientific method, 34–38
statistics and, 45–53
Research Domain Criteria Project
(RDoC), 559
research hypothesis, A-12
research laboratories, 5f

research methods
basic elements of experiments, 40f
brain and, 83–85
control group, 38–39, 40f
deception in, 57
defined, 38
dependent variables, 38, 40f, 41
descriptive/correlational research
methods, 42–45
ethics in, 56–59
experiment design, 40–41
experimental, 38–42
experimental group, 38–39, 40f
extraneous variables, 39–40
hereditary influence, 97–100
independent variables, 38, 40f, 41, 41f
in journal articles, 61
overview of, 48–49f
selection of, 36
resilient pattern, 421
resistance, 612
resistance to change, 493
resistance to extinction, 212
response patterns, 215f
response sets, 55, 467
response strength, 232–233
response–outcome (R–O)
associations, 212
response–outcome relations, 222
The Restaurant at the End of the Universe
(Adams), 239
resting potential, 70–71, 75
restrained eaters, 355
restricting type anorexia nervosa, 597
results, in journal articles, 61
retention, 224, 242f, 243f, 254–255,
255f, 272f
retention interval, 254
reticular formation, 80f, 86, 87f, 164
retina, 114, 116–117, 116f, 118f
retinal disparity, 129
retrieval cues, 251
retrieval failure, 257
retrieval of memory, 240, 251–253
retroactive interference, 257, 257f
retrograde amnesia, 263, 263f
retrospective memory, 268–269, 269f
reuptake, 73
reversibility, 402
reversible figures, 124, 128f, 149
review articles, 60
reward pathway, 184, 184f
Rey Auditory Verbal Learning Test,
186f
Rez Sisters (Highway), 172
right hemisphere, 94
risk-benefit assessments, 549
risk-taking, 411f
risky decision making, 299–300, 305
risky shift, 503
Ritalin, 78
RNA transfer, 262
rods, 116f, 117
Rogers' client-centred theory, 11,
452–454, 453f, 613–614, 614f, 640f
role-playing, hypnosis as, 175–176
romantic relationships, cultural
differences, 486–487
Rorschach test, 467
rules of language, 283, 284, 287, 288
rumination, 576
rumination disorder, 597
runner's high, 79f

S

Sable Island, 635
saccades, 116
sadism, 439
sadness, 370–371, 377f
same-sex marriage, 360–361, 361f
sample, A-12f, 53, 54f, 313, 447
sampling bias, 53–54, 54f, 63
saturation, 114, 115f
Saturday Night Live, 155
"sauce béarnaise syndrome," 205,
206f
savants, 328–329
scaffolding, 405
scales, personality, 313
scatter diagram, A-9–A-10, A-10f
Schachter's experiment on anxiety
and affiliation, 38–40, 40f, 56
Schachter's two-factor theory, 42,
374f, 375, 375f
schedule of reinforcement,
214–216, 215f
schemas, 249–250, 252f, 274,
477–478
schizophrenia, 579–585
adaptive behaviour, deterioration of,
580
brain, structural abnormalities,
583–584, 584f
delusions/irrational thought, 580
disturbed emotions, 581
emotion, expressed, 584–585
etiology of, 581–585
expressed emotions, 584–585, 585f
family studies, 98, 98f
fetal origins of, 391
genetic vulnerability, 581–582, 583f
hallucinations, 580–581
heredity and environment, 100
neurochemical factors, 582–583
neurodevelopmental hypothesis, 584,
584f
overview of, 586–587f
precipitating stress, 585
stress-vulnerability model of, 596f
symptoms, 580–581
twin studies, 581
vulnerability to, 100
Scholastic Aptitude Test (SAT), 317
schools, and gender-role
socialization, 430
scientific method, 6
advantages of, 37–38
goals of, 33–34
steps in, 34–37, 35f
scientific theory, 34. *See also* theory
screen time, 224
seasonal affective disorder (SAD),
574
secondary appraisal, 520
secondary reinforcers, 210
secondary sex characteristics, 409
secondary-process thinking, 440
second-generation antipsychotic
drugs, 625
second-hand smoke, 540
secure adults, 485, 486f
secure attachment, 396, 397f,
398, 485
sedatives, 168, 169, 180t, 181, 183t,
185, 186
selection pressures, 102

SUBJECT INDEX

stimulants, 169, 180t, 181, 183f, 183t, 185
stimuli, 112
stimulus, 112
stimulus contiguity, 201
stimulus control, 212–213
stimulus discrimination, 204, 213, 213t
stimulus generalization, 202–205, 213, 213t
stirrup, 135, 136f
storage, 240, 244–251
strange situation procedure, 396
stream of consciousness, 5, 156
strength, 489
stress
  aggression and, 528
  anxiety disorders and, 567–568
  appraisal of, 520
  behavioural responses, 527–530
  biopsychosocial model, 519
  brain-body pathways, 526–527
  brain-body pathways in stress, 527f
  change, 522
  colleges and universities, 518–519
  conscientiousness, 537–538
  constructive coping, 530
  defensive coping, 529–530
  defined, 519
  depressive disorders and, 578
  eating and, 351
  emotional responses, 523–525
  as everyday event, 519–520
  frustration, 520
  general adaptation syndrome, 526
  hardiness, 537–538
  health and, 532–535, 534t
  humour and, 545–546
  illness and, 532–535, 535f
  internal conflict, 521
  introduction to, 518–519
  learned helplessness, 527–528
  management of, 545–547
  mindset, 538
  moderating the impact of, 536–539
  moderator variables, 536–539
  natural disasters, 519
  nature of, 519–520
  optimism, 537–538
  panic disorder and, 568f
  physiological responses, 525–527
  physiological vulnerability, minimizing, 546
  positive effects of, 539
  prenatal development, 390–391
  pressure, 522–523
  process of, 524f
  psychological functioning and, 530–532
  reappraisal, 545
  responses to, 523–530
  schizophrenia and, 585
  self-indulgence, 528–529
  social support, 536–537
  types of, 520–523
  workplace, 518
stress reduction, 546
stress-buster events, 518–519
stress-is-debilitating mindset, 538
stress-is-enhancing mindset, 538
stress-vulnerability model of schizophrenia, 596f
striking out at others, 528
string problem, 291, 291f

striving for superiority, 446
structural encoding, 242, 242f
structuralism, 4–6
study, design of, 36, 40–41
study habits, 26
subgoals, 294
subjective contours, 126, 126f
subjective feelings, 367–368
subjective probability, 300
subjective utility, 300
subjective well-being, 378, 380
subjectivity, 24–25, 29, 479, 510
subjectivity of experience, 24–25, 29, 183
subjects, 36
sublimation, 442t, 443
subliminal perception, 113–114
substance abuse. See drug use
subtractive colour mixing, 121–122, 121f
success, 365–366, 366f
  attributions for, 480–481, 510, 510f
suggestibility, 261
suicide, 412, 418
  prevention, 575f
  rates of, 574–575
  SSRIs and, 626
Sunday Afternoon on the Island of La Grande Jatte (Seurat), 149, 149f
superego, 343, 440, 440f
superior colliculus, 118f, 119
superstitious behaviours, 195, 195f, 213–214
supertasters, 139–140
suprachiasmatic nucleus (SCN), 158
Supreme Court of Canada, 219, 360
surprise, 370–371, 376, 376t, 377f
Surrealists, 149
surveys, 44–45
survival advantages, 102f
survival value, 396
Sweat Lodge, 634
Sylvian fissure, 67
symbolism, 280
sympathetic division, 81, 526
symptoms, 542
synapses, 69f, 72, 73f, 75, 183
synaptic clefts, 72
synaptic pruning, 75f, 76, 107, 411
synaptic transmission, 75
synaptic vesicles, 73
synesthesia, 111
syntax, 281, 288
synthesis, 72–73
System 2 thought, 303–304
System I thought, 303–304
systematic desensitization, 618–620, 618f, 619f, 640f

T

tactile system, 141–144, 146–147f
tardive dyskinesia, 625
target behaviours, 231
taste, 138–140, 139f
taste aversion, 205–206, 206f
taste buds, 138, 139f
taste preferences, 352
taste-touch synesthesia, 111
technical eclecticism, 632
technical journals, 60
technology, and delivery of clinical services, 634–635

telegraphic speech, 283f
television watching, 234–235. See also media violence
temperament, 394–395
temperature regulation, 348, 348f
temporal lobe, 89, 90f
temporal summation, 74
teratogens, 390
terminals, 69f, 70
test norms, 313
test-enhanced learning, 271
testing effect, 271
testing perspective, 320
test-retest reliability, 314
test-taking strategies, 26
texting, 241
texture gradients, 129, 130f
thalamus, 86–88, 87f, 118f, 164
Thematic Apperception Test (TAT), 365, 365f, 467, 467f
theoretical integration, 632
theory, 23, 34
theory of bounded rationality, 302
theory of mind, 406–407
therapeutic alliance, 634
therapeutic climate, 613–614
therapeutic process, 614
therapeutic services, 639–641, 639t
therapists, 608–610, 609t, 639–641
theta waves, 157, 177
thinking, modes of, 104
third variable problem, 51–52
Thorazine (chlorpromazine), 624
Thorndike's law of effect, 207–208, 208f
Thought and Language (Vygotsky), 404
thought-control techniques, 606
threshold of viability, 390
thresholds, 112, 135f
thymus, 96f
thyroid gland, 96f
tic disorders, 590
timbre, 134
The Time Machine (Wells), 239
"time stress," 162
time travel, 239
Timeline (Crichton), 239
tip-of-the-tongue phenomenon, 251, 257
tobacco use, 390
tolerance. See drug tolerance
tongue, 139f
top-down processing, 126, 126f
torture, 57
touch, 141–144, 146–147f
Tourette's disorder, 590
tower of Hanoi problem, 294, 294f
toxins, 391
traits, 313
tranquilizers, 624
transcendental meditation (TM), 176, 177
transcontextual skills, 28
transcranial magnetic stimulation (TMS), 85, 85f, 506, 629
transference, 612
transformation, 291
transience, 261
transition, 387
treatment as usual, 615
treatment as usual with medication, 615

treatment of psychological disorders
  behaviour therapies, 607, 618–623
  biomedical therapies, 607, 624–629
  blending approaches, 632
  clients, 607–608
  costs of, 640
  cultural barriers, 633
  current trends in, 632–635
  delivery of clinical services, technology and, 634–635
  insight therapies, 607, 610–618
  institutional barriers, 633
  institutional treatment, 635–636
  introduction to, 606
  language barriers, 633
  multicultural sensitivity, 632–634
  overview of, 630–631f
  therapists, 608–610, 609t
  types of, 607
trial and error, 294
trials, 198
triarchic theory of successful intelligence, 320–321, 320f
trichromatic theory of colour vision, 122, 124f
Tri-Council (Canada), 59
tricyclics, 625, 626f
trust, 399
trustworthiness, 491–492
trypophobia, 562
Tuskegee Syphilis Study, 57
twin studies, 98–99, 99f, 331–332, 354f, 362f, 457–458, 458f, 566, 566f, 575, 575f, 581
two-factor theory, 374f, 375, 375f
two-sided arguments, 492
Type A personality, 533
Type B personality, 533
Typical Dreams Questionnaire, 171

U

ultraviolet spectrum, 114
umami, 138
uncommitted sex, 358, 359
unconditional affection, 453
unconditional positive regard, 614
unconditional stimulus, 184
unconditioned response, 197, 198f
unconditioned stimulus, 197, 197f, 198f, 204f, 205–206
unconscious, 7–8, 156, 440f, 441, 611
underextensions, 283
understanding, 34
undifferentiated schizophrenia, 581
undoing, 529t
unfit to stand trial, 593
United Nations Assistance Mission for Rwanda, 553
universalistic view, 594
unnecessary constraints, 293
Upside-down T illusion, 131f
U.S. Food and Drug Administration (FDA), 626

V

validity, 314–315, 324–325
Valium, 624
valproate, 627
value judgments, 556f
variability, A-7–A-8, 46–47, 46f
variable-interval schedule, 215, 215f

variable-ratio schedule, 214, 215f, 216
variables, 34, 38, 40f, 41, 41f
variety of foods, 351
vasocongestion, 357
ventral stream, 119, 119f, 121
ventricles, 82f, 584f
ventromedial nucleus of the hypothalamus (VMH), 350, 350f
verbal aggression, 427
Verbal Behavior (Skinner), 288
verbal intelligence, 324–325, 325f
verbal skills, 427
verbal stimuli, 94
vested interest, 513
vestibular system, 144–145
vibration of air molecules, 134
vibration of movable bones, 134
victimization of Aboriginal people, 44, 44f
video games, 226
Vienna Psychoanalytic Society, 446
Vietnam War, 531
violence. *See also* media violence
    Aboriginal people and, 44, 44f
    on television, 234–235
visceral arousal, 368, 374
vision
    critical periods, 106
    split-brain research, 92–93, 93f, 94f
vision for action, 120
vision for perception, 120

visual acuity, 117
visual agnosia, 120
visual cortex, 118f, 119–120
visual field, 92–93, 94f
visual illusions, 130–133
visual imagery, 243, 243f
visual mnemonics, 273
visual pathways to the brain, 118–119, 118f
visual perception, 151f
visual receptors, 117
visual system, 114–124
    action and, 120–121
    brain and, 118–120
    colour. *see* colour vision
    colour vision, 121–124
    cultural differences, 129
    depth and distance, 129–130
    eyes, 114–116
    feature analysis, 125–126
    forms/patterns/objects, 124–126
    Gestalt principles of perception, 126–129
    light, 114
    overview of, 146–147f
    perception and, 120–121
    perceptual constancy, 130
    retina, 116–117
    visual illusions, 130–133
visual-spatial ability, 25, 28–29, 427
visual-spatial tests, 94
visuospatial sketchpad, 247, 247f

vocabulary growth, 283f
vocabulary spurt, 283, 283f
vocational success, 325–326
Vygotsky's sociocultural theory, 404–405

W

waist-to-hip ratio, 488
waking cycle, 160–170
water jar problem, 291, 291f, 292f, 293, 293f, 295f
Waterfall (Escher), 149, 149f
wavelength, 114, 115f, 134
waves in a fluid, 134
weak analogies, 383
Weber fraction, 112
Weber's law, 112
Wechsler Adult Intelligence Scale (WAIS IV), 316, 318, 318f
Weiner's model of attributions, 480, 480f
well-being therapy, 614–615
Wernicke's area, 92, 92f
what pathways, 119–120, 119f–120f, 121
where pathways, 119–120, 119f, 121
wildfires, 524, 524f, 532
wish fulfillment, 172–173, 173f
within-group differences, 336, 336f
within-subjects design, 41
Without Conscience (Hare), 589

women. *See also* gender differences
    depressive disorders, 574
    eating disorders, 597–599
    taste and, 140
    waist-to-hip ratio, 488
words, 282–284
word-taste synesthesia, 111
work, 380
working backward, 294
working memory, 247–248, 247f
working memory capacity, 247–248
World Health Organization (WHO), 559, 574
World War II, 13

X

Xanax, 624

Y

yea-sayers, 467
yoga, 176

Z

Zen Buddhism, 177
Zollner illusion, 131f
Zoloft (sertraline), 625
zone of proximal development (ZPD), 405
zygotes, 388